Drug Abuse Handbook

Editor-in-Chief
Steven B. Karch, M.D.
Assistant Medical Examiner
City and County of San Francisco
San Francisco, California

CRC Press
Boca Raton   Boston   London   New York   Washington, D.C.

Acquiring Editor: *Paul Petralia*
Project Editor: *Susan Fox*
Cover Design: *Denise Craig*
Prepress: *Carlos Esser, Kevin Luong*

Library of Congress Cataloging-in-Publication Data

Catalog record is available from the Library of Congress.

PREFACE

Anyone who takes the time to read more than a few pages of this Handbook will encounter quite a few surprises, some good and some bad. The good news is that during the last decade, a tremendous amount has been learned about abused drugs. The bad news is that progress has not been equally rapid on all fronts. Molecular biologists and neurochemists who, perhaps not coincidentally receive the lion's share of federal funding, have made breathtaking advances. They are tantalizingly close to characterizing the basic mechanisms of addiction. Progress has been somewhat less dramatic on other fronts.

Testing workers for drugs has become a huge, competitive business. Market forces have ensured that the necessary research was done. Regulated urine drug testing is now a reliable and reasonably well-understood process. Yet, desperately needed studies to test the efficacy (as opposed to the accuracy) of workplace drug testing programs are not on the horizon, and we still do not know with any certainty whether the enormous amount of money being spent really has an effect on worker absenteeism, accident rates, and productivity.

In areas where government and industry share common interests, there has been impressive progress. Researchers interested in impairment testing have received sufficient funding to finally place this discipline on firm scientific footing. But practical workplace applications for impairment testing are hampered by the paucity of data relating blood, hair, sweat, and saliva drug concentrations with other workplace performance measures.

The use of alternate testing matrices poses a daunting challenge. Until very recently, alternate approaches to workplace testing were not permitted. There was little government interest, and no potential market in sight. With no money to be made, industry leaders saw no reason to invest in new technologies. Now it appears that pressure from private industry has altered government perceptions, and changes may be imminent. But a great deal of science remains to be done. In particular, basic pharamcokinetic research is needed to describe the disposition of abused drugs in alternate specimens. Without such data, the utility of alternate specimens is limited, and reliable interpretation of test results is nearly impossible.

Farther away from university and government laboratories, at the bedside and at the autopsy table, the picture is not quite so rosy. SAMSHSA supported the development of LAAM, the long acting methadone substitute, and funding has gone into improving metha-done maintenance programs. But methadone clinics are not ivory towers, and controlled studies with non-compliant patients are fiendishly difficult. Politicians intent on being "tough on drugs" have created a regulatory climate where control of treatment has largely been taken away from physicians, and political considerations outweigh reasoned scientific judgment. The recent suggestion by National Drug Control Policy Director Barry McCaffrey that physicians be allowed to prescribe methadone, may mark an important shift in the way our leaders address these problems.

Even so, research into the medical management of drug users is not exactly a priority issue. One might suppose that given the very sophisticated techniques now available for therapeutic drug monitoring, the kinetics of abused drugs would be well characterized. There are several reasons why they have not. Discounting the fact that such projects have little commercial appeal, and seem not to be a priority for our government (even though most of the important research has been done at the federally funded Addiction Research Center), the greatest handicaps are ethical and political. Drug abusers take drugs in quantities that no Institutional Review Board would ever approve and that doctors would refuse to administer. Whether or not the body metabolizes 50 mg of cocaine given intravenously the same way it manages 250 mg is, for the moment, at least, anyone's guess. However, the results of recent studies from the Addiction Research Center suggest that chronic oral dosing with cocaine may allow researchers to simulate the high doses used on the street.

Cocaine and heroin abuse claim the lives of more than 15,000 Americans every year, but no pathologist sits on the advisory board that passes on drug research grants, and there is no federal funding for pathology or for pathologists interested in drug abuse. The sorry state of the DAWN report (Drug Abuse Warning Network) offers a hint of the importance our government accords to the investigation of drug-related deaths; results for 1995 were finally released in May of 1997! Three-year-old epidemiologic data may be of some interest to historians, but it certainly is of little value to clinicians.

At least the epidemiologic studies get funded. Lack of federal support means that a great many promising leads are being passed up. There is mounting evidence that chronic drug abuse produces identifiable morphologic changes in the heart, brain, lungs, and liver. But there are no federal funds to support the studies needed to translate these preliminary observations into useful diagnostic tools.

Toxicologists studying postmortem materials have done no better than the pathologists. Technologic innovations in workplace testing and therapeutic drug monitoring now allow the routine measurement of nanogram quantities of drugs in tissue obtained at autopsy, but the interpretation of these measurements is not a straightforward process. Even though postmortem drug concentrations are frequently debated in court, research on the interpretation of postmortem drug levels consists of little more than a handful of case reports, published by a few dedicated researchers. During the last decade, more than 50,000 Americans have died using cocaine, but postmortem tissue levels have only been reported in a handful of cases.

Even if the tissue levels were better characterized, tolerance occurs. It is impossible to speak of "lethal" and "non-lethal" cocaine and morphine concentrations because tolerant users may be unaffected by levels that would be lethal in naive drug users. But, poorly informed physicians and attorneys continue to ignore these subtleties, just as they continue to ignore the wealth of scientific knowledge that has been accumulated on the effects of alcohol, both in the living and the dead. The same legal arguments are debated again and again, even though the science has been very well worked out.

Important research remains to be done, yet we have already learned a great deal. Unfortunately, that knowledge is not being shared effectively, not with the rest of the medical community, not with the courts, and certainly not with drug policy makers. If we can do a better job of educating, then sometime in the not too distant future, we may be able to obtain the support for the work that we know needs to be done. I hope this book helps in that process.

THE EDITOR

Dr Karch received his bachelors degree from Brown University, did graduate work in cell biology and biophysics at Stanford, and attended Tulane Medical School. He studied neuropathology at the Barnard Baron Institue in London, and cardiac pathology at Stanford. During the 1970s, he was a Medical Advisor for Bechtel in Southeast Asia. He is an Assistant Medical Examiner in San Francisco, where he consults on cases of drug-related death. His textbook, *The Pathology of Drug Abuse*, is used around the world, and is generally considered the standard reference on the subject. He and his wife, Donna, live in Berkeley, California.

Photo courtesy of Brandon White, Berkeley, California

CONTRIBUTORS

Wilmo Andollo
Quality Assurance Officer
Dade County Medical Examiner
    Department
Toxicology Laboratory
Miami, Florida

John Baenziger, M.D.
Director, Chemical Pathology
Department of Pathology and Laboratory
    Medicine
Indiana University School of Medicine
Indianapolis, Indiana

Joanna Banbery
The Leeds Addiction Unit
Leeds, U.K.

Michael H. Baumann
Clincial Pharmacology Section
Intramural Research Program
National Institute on Drug Abuse
National Institutes of Health
Baltimore, Maryland

Michael D. Bell, M.D
Associate Medical Examiner
Dade County Medical Examiner Office
Miami, Florida

Neal L. Benowitz, M.D.
Professor of Medicine
Chief, Division of Clinical Pharmacology
    and Experimental Therapeutics
University of California
San Francisco, California

John W. Boja
Department of Pharmacology
Northeastern Ohio Universities
College of Medicine
Rootstown, Ohio

Joseph P. Bono, MA
Supervisory Chemist
Drug Enforcement Administration
Special Testing and Research Laboratory
McLean, Virginia

Edward B. Bunker
National Institute on Drug Abuse
Intramural Research Program
Addiction Research Center
Baltimore, Maryland

Allen P. Burke, M.D.
Department of Cardiovascular Pathology
Armed Forces Institute of Pathology
Washington, D.C.

Donna M. Bush, Ph.D., D-ABFT
Drug Testing Team Leader
Division of Workplace Programs
Center for Substance Abuse Prevention
Substance Abuse and Mental Health
    Services Administration
Washington, D.C.

J.C. Callaway, Ph.D.
Department of Pharmaceutical Chemistry
University of Kuopio
Kuopio, Finland

Yale H. Caplan, Ph.D.
National Scientific Services
Baltimore, Maryland

Don H. Catlin, M.D.
Department of Molecular and Medical
    Pharmacology
Department of Medicine
UCLA School of Medicine
University of California
Los Angeles, California

Edward J. Cone, Ph.D.
Intramural Research Program
National Institute on Drug Abuse
National Institutes of Health
Baltimore, Maryland

Dennis J. Crouch
Center for Human Toxicology
University of Utah
Salt Lake City, Utah

Ross C. Cuneo
Department of Endocrinolonology
Diabetes & Metabolic Medicine
United and Medical and Dental School of
    Guy's and St. Thomas' Hospitals
London, U.K.

Alan E. Davis
Director of Toxicology
Lab*One*, Inc
Kansas City, Kansas

Björn Ekblom
Department of Physiology and
    Pharmacology
Karolinska Institute
Stockholm, Sweden

Reginald V. Fant
National Institute on Drug Abuse
Intramural Research Program
Addiction Research Center
Baltimore, Maryland

Andrew Farb, M.D.
Department of Cardiovascular Pathology
Armed Forces Institute of Pathology
Washington, D.C.

Douglas Fraser
The Leeds Addiction Unit
Leeds, U.K.

Bruce A. Goldberger, Ph.D.
Director of Toxicology and Assistant
    Professor
University of Florida College of Medicine
Gainesville, Florida

Alastair W.M. Hay
University of Leeds
Research School of Medicine
Leeds, U.K.

Wm. Lee Hearn, Ph.D.
Director of Toxicology
Metro Dade County Medical Examiner
    Department
Miami, Florida

Stephen J. Heishman, Ph.D.
Clinical Pharmacology Branch
Division of Intramural Research
National Institute on Drug Abuse
Baltimore, Maryland

Anders Helander
Department of Clinical Neuroscience
Karolinska Institute
St. Görans Hospital
Stockholm, Sweden

Bradford R. Hepler, Ph.D.
Toxicology Laboratory
Wayne County Medical Examiner
Detroit, Michigan

Marilyn A. Huestis, Ph.D.
Laboratory of Chemistry and Drug
    Metabolism
Addiction Research Center
National Institute on Drug Abuse
Baltimore, Maryland

Daniel S. Isenschmid, Ph.D.
Toxicology Laboratory
Wayne County Medical Examiner
Detroit, Michigan

Amanda J. Jenkins, Ph.D
Intramural Research Program
National Institute on Drug Abuse
National Institutes of Health
Baltimore, Maryland

Alan Wayne Jones
Department of Forensic Toxicology
University Hospital
Linköping, Sweden

Graham R. Jones
Office of the Chief Medical Examiner
Edmonton, Alberta, Canada

Steven B. Karch, M.D.
Assistant Medical Examiner
City and County of San Francisco
San Francisco, California

Thomas H. Kelly
Department of Behavioral Science
College of Medicine
University of Kentucky
Lexington, Kentucky

Frank D. Kolodgie, Ph.D.
Department of Cardiovascular Pathology
Armed Forces Institute of Pathology
Washington, D.C.

Barry Logan
Washington State Toxicology Laboratory
Department of Laboratory Medicine
University of Washington
Seattle, Washington

Christopher S. Martin
Western Psychiatric Institute and Clinic
Department of Psychiatry
University of Pittsburgh School of Medicine
Pittsburgh, Pennsylvania

Deborah C. Mash
Departments of Neurology and Molecular
    and Cellular Pharmacology
University of Miami School of Medicine
Miami, Florida

D.J. McKenna, Ph.D.
Heffter Research Institute
Sante Fe, New Mexico

William M. Meil
Department of Pharmacology
Northeastern Ohio Universities
College of Medicine
Rootstown, Ohio

Stephen M. Mohaupt, MD
USC Institute of Psychiatry, Law, and the
    Behavioral Sciences
Los Angeles, California

Florabel G. Mullick, M.D.
Department of Cardiovascular Pathology
Armed Forces Institute of Pathology
Washington, D.C.

Jagat Narula, M.D., Ph.D.
Harvard Medical School
and Northeastern University
Boston, Massachusetts

Kent R. Olson, MD
Clinical Professor of Medicine, Pediatrics,
    and Pharmacy
UCSF
Medical Director
California Poison Control System
San Francisco General Hospital
San Francisco, California

Michael Peat, Ph.D.
Executive Vice President, Toxicology
LabOne, Inc
Kansas City, Kansas

Wallace B. Pickworth
National Institute on Drug Abuse
Intramural Research Program
Addiction Research Center
Baltimore, Maryland

Derrick J. Pounder
Department of Forensic Medicine
University of Dundee
Scotland, U.K.

Kenzie L. Preston, Ph.D.
Intramural Research Program
National Institute on Drug Abuse
Johns Hopkins University School of
    Medicine
Baltimore, Maryland

Duncan Raistrick
The Leeds Addiction Unit
Leeds, U.K.

Brett Roth, MD
Postdoctoral Fellow
Division of Clinical Pharmacology and
    Toxicology
University of California
San Francisco, California

Richard B. Rothman
Clinical Psychopharmacology Section
Intramural Research Program
National Institute on Drug Abuse
National Institutes of Health
Baltimore, Maryland

Steven St. Clair, M.D., M.P.H.
Executive Director
American Association of Medical Review
    Officers
Durham, North Carolina

Wilhelm Schänzer
German Sports University of Cologne
Institute of Biochemistry
Cologne, Germany

Jordi Segura
Institut Municipal d' Investigació Mèdica,
    IMIM
Departament de Farmacologia i Toxicologia
Barcelona, Spain

David W. Self
Division of Molecular Psychiatry
Yale University School of Medicine and
    Connecticut Mental Health Center
New Haven, Connecticut

Theodore F. Shults
Quadrangle Research
Research Triangle Park
Durham, North Carolina

Donna R. Smith, Ph.D.
Senior Vice President, Planning &
    Implementation
Substance Abuse Management, Inc.
Boca Raton, Florida

Peter Sönksen
Professor
Department of Endocrinolonology
Diabetes & Metabolic Medicine
United and Medical and Dental School of
    Guy's and St. Thomas' Hospitals
London, U.K.

Julie K. Staley, Ph.D.
Department of Neurology
University of Miami School of Medicine
Miami, Florida

Richard C. Taylor
Clinical Pharmacology Branch
Division of Intramural Research
National Institute on Drug Abuse
Baltimore, Maryland

Rafael de la Torre, PharmD
Department of Pharmacology and
    Toxicology
Institute Municipal d'Investigació Mèdico
Barcelona, Spain

Renu Virmani, M.D.
Department of Cardiovascular Pathology
Armed Forces Institute of Pathology
Washington, D.C.

Jennifer D. Wallace
Department of Endocrinolonology
Diabetes & Metabolic Medicine
United and Medical and Dental School of
    Guy's and St. Thomas' Hospitals
London, U.K.

H. Chip Walls
University of Miami
Department of Pathology
Forensic Toxicology Laboratory
Miami, Florida

J. Michael Walsh, Ph.D.
The Walsh Group, P.A.
Bethesda, Maryland

Sharon L. Walsh, Ph.D.
Johns Hopkins University School of
    Medicine
Baltimore, Maryland

Charles V. Wetli, MD
Suffolk Country Medical Examiner
Happauge, New York

Ruth E. Winecker, Ph.D.
Deputy Chief Toxicologist
Office of the Chief Medical Examiner
Chapel Hill, North Carolina

Kim Wolff
National Addiction Centre
Institute of Psychiatry
University of London
London, England

Shoshana Zevin, MD
Postdoctoral Fellow
Division of Clinical Pharmacology and
    Toxicology
University of California
San Francisco, California

DEDICATION

For RBT

ACKNOWLEDGMENTS

All of the section editors deserve a special note of thanks. Orchestrating 80 contributors is no easy task, and the work was particularly hard for some. My special thanks to Lee Hearn and Yale Caplan. Each of their chapters could have been separate books, and the effort they expended shows. Thanks also to the management at CRC Press (including Paul Petralia) for having the vision to undertake the project in the first place, and to Susan Fox for putting it all together. Sara Morabito gave valuable help with the manuscripts, and Bill Keach remains the world's greatest fact checker. I hope CRC is satisfied with the result. Hardwin Meade and Roger Wincle continue to make their own unique contributions. And my wife, Donna, who continues to be supportive.

TABLE OF CONTENTS

CHAPTER 1

CRIMINALISTICS—INTRODUCTION TO CONTROLLED SUBSTANCES

JOSEPH P. BONO, MA

SUPERVISORY CHEMIST, DRUG ENFORCEMENT ADMINISTRATION, SPECIAL TESTING AND
RESEARCH LABORATORY, MCLEAN, VIRGINIA

TABLE OF CONTENTS

1.1 DEFINITION AND SCHEDULING OF CONTROLLED SUBSTANCES

A "controlled substance" is a drug or substance of which the use, sale, or distribution is regulated by the federal government or a state government entity. These controlled substances are listed specifically or by classification on the federal level in the Controlled Substances Act (CSA) or in Part 1308 of the Code of Federal Regulations. The purpose of the CSA is to minimize the quantity of useable substances available to those who are likely to abuse them. At the same time, the CSA provides for the legitimate medical, scientific, and industrial needs of these substances in the U.S.

1.2 SCHEDULING OF CONTROLLED SUBSTANCES

Eight factors are considered when determining whether or not to schedule a drug as a controlled substance:

1. Actual or relative potential for abuse.
2. Scientific evidence of pharmacological effect.
3. State of current scientific knowledge.
4. History of current pattern of abuse.
5. Scope, duration, and significance of abuse.
6. Risk to the public health.
7. Psychic or physiological dependence liability.
8. Immediate precursor.

The definition of potential for abuse is based upon an individual taking a drug of his own volition in sufficient amounts to cause a health hazard to himself or to others in the community. Data is then collected to evaluate three factors: (1) actual abuse of the drug; (2) the clandestine manufacture of the drug; (3) trafficking and diversion of the drug or its precursors from legitimate channels into clandestine operations. Pre-clinical abuse liability studies are then conducted on animals to evaluate physiological responses to the drug. At this point, clinical abuse liability studies can be conducted with human subjects, which evaluate preference studies and epidemiology.

Accumulating scientific evidence of a drug's pharmacological effects involves examining the scientific data concerning whether the drug elicits a stimulant, depressant, narcotic, or hallucinogenic response. A determination can then be made as to how closely the pharmacology of the drug resembles that of other drugs that are already controlled.

Evidence is also accumulated about the scientific data on the physical and chemical properties of the drug. This can include determining which salts and isomers are possible and which are available. There is also a concern for the ease of detection and identification using analytical chemistry. Since many controlled substances have the potential for clandestine synthesis, there is a requirement for evaluating precursors, possible synthetic routes, and theoretical yields in these syntheses. At this phase of the evaluation, medical uses are also evaluated.

The next three factors—(1) history and patterns of abuse; (2) scope, duration, and significance of abuse; and (3) risks to public health—all involve sociological and medical considerations. The results of these studies focus on data collection and population studies. Psychic and physiological dependence liability studies must be satisfied for a substance to be placed into Schedules II through V. This specific finding is not necessary to place a drug into Schedule I. A practical problem here is that it is not always easy to prove a development of dependence.

The last factor is one that can involve the forensic analyst. Under the law, an "immediate precursor" is defined as a substance that is an immediate chemical intermediary used or likely to be used in the manufacture of a specific controlled substance. Defining synthetic pathways in the clandestine production of illicit controlled substances requires knowledge possessed by the experienced analyst.

A controlled substance will be classified and named in one of five schedules. Schedule I includes drugs or other substances that have a high potential for abuse, no currently accepted use in the treatment of medical conditions, and little, if any, accepted safety criteria under the supervision of a medical professional. Use of these substances will almost always lead to abuse and dependence. Some of the more commonly encountered Schedule I controlled substances are heroin, marijuana, lysergic acid diethylamide (LSD), 3,4-methylenedioxy-amphetamine (MDA), and psilocybin mushrooms.

Progressesing from Schedule II to schedule V, abuse potential decreases. Schedule II controlled substances also include drugs or other substances that have a high potential for abuse, but also have some currently accepted, but severely restricted, medical uses. Abuse of Schedule II substances may lead to dependence which can be both physical and/or psychological. Because Schedule II controlled substances do have some recognized medical uses, they are usually available to health professionals in the form of legitimate pharmaceutical preparations. Cocaine hydrochloride is still used as a topical anesthetic in some surgical procedures. Methamphetamine, up until a few years ago, was used in the form of Desoxyn to treat hyperactivity in children. Raw opium is included in Schedule II. Amobarbital and secobarbital, which are used as central nervous system depressants are included, as is phencyclidine (PCP) which was used as a tranquilizer in veterinary pharmaceutical practices. In humans, PCP acts as a hallucinogen. Though many of the substances seized under Schedule II were not prepared by legitimate pharmaceutical entities, cocaine hydrochloride and methamphetamine are two examples of Schedule II drugs which, when confiscated as white to off-white powder or granules in plastic or glassine packets, have almost always been prepared on the illicit market for distribution. As one progresses from Schedules III through V, most legitimate pharmaceutical preparations will be encountered.

1.3 CONTROLLED SUBSTANCE ANALOGUE ENFORCEMENT ACT OF 1986

In recent years, the phenomenon of controlled substance analogues and homologues has presented a most serious challenge to the control of drug trafficking and successful prosecution of clandestine laboratory operators. These homologues and analogues are synthesized drugs that are chemically and pharmacologically similar to substances that are listed in the Controlled Substances Act, but which themselves are not specifically controlled by name. (The term "designer drug" is sometimes used to describe these substances.) The concept of synthesizing controlled substances analogues in an attempt to circumvent existing drug law was first noticed in the late 1960s. At about this time there were seizures of clandestine laboratories engaged in the production of analogues of controlled phenethylamines. In the 1970s variants of methaqualone and phencyclidine were being seized in clandestine laboratories. By the 1980s, Congress decided that the time had come to deal with this problem with a federal law enforcement initiative. The Controlled Substance Analogue Enforcement Act of 1986 amends the Comprehensive Drug Abuse Prevention and Control Act of 1970 by including the following section:

> Section 203. A controlled substance analogue shall to the extent intended for human consumption, be treated, for the purposes of this title and title III as a controlled substance in schedule I.

The 99th Congress went on to define the meaning of the term "controlled substance analogue" as a substance:

> (i) the chemical structure of which is substantially similar to the chemical structure of a controlled substance in schedule I or II;

> (ii) which has a stimulant, depressant, or hallucinogenic effect on the central nervous system that is substantially similar to or greater than the stimulant, depressant, or hallucinogenic effect on the central nervous system of a controlled substance in schedule I or II; or

(iii) with respect to a particular person, which person represents or intends to have a stimulant, depressant, or hallucinogenic effect on the central nervous system of a controlled substance in schedule I or II."

The Act goes on to exclude:

(i) a controlled substance

(ii) any substance for which there is an approved new drug application

(iii) with respect to a particular person any substance, if an exemption is in effect for investigational use, for that person, under section 505...to the extent conduct with respect to such substance is pursuant to such exemption; or

(iv) any substance to the extent not intended for human consumption before such an exemption takes effect with respect to that substance.

Treatment of exhibits falling under the purview of the federal court system is described in Public Law 91-513 or Part 1308 of the Code of Federal Regulations. Questions relating to controlled substance analogues and homologues can usually be answered by reference to the Controlled Substances Analogue and Enforcement Act of 1986.

1.4 CONTROLLED SUBSTANCES

1.4.1 HERION

Whenever one thinks about drugs of abuse and addiction, heroin is one of the most recognized drugs. Heroin is a synthetic drug, produced from the morphine contained in the sap of the opium poppy. The abuse of this particular controlled substance has been known for many years. The correct chemical nomenclature for heroin is O^3, O^6 -diacetylmorphine. Heroin is synthesized from morphine in a relatively simple process. The first synthesis of diacetylmorphine reported in the literature was in 1875 by two English chemists, G.H. Beckett and C.P. Alder Wright. [1] In 1898 in Eberfield, Germany, the Farbenfarbriken vorm Friedrich Bayer and Company produced the drug commercially. An employee of the company, H. Dresser, named the morphine product "Heroin".[2] There is no definitive documentation as to where the name "heroin" originated. However, it probably had its origin in the "heroic remedies" class of drugs of the day.

Heroin was used in place of codeine and morphine for patients suffering from lung diseases such as tuberculosis. Additonally, the Bayer Company advertised heroin as a cure for morphine addiction. The analgesic properties of the drug were very effective. However, the addictive properties were quite devastating. In 1924, Congress amended the Narcotic Drug Import and Export Act to prohibit the importation of opium for the manufacture of heroin. However, stockpiles were still available and could be legally prescribed by physicians. The 1925 International Opium Convention imposed drug controls that began to limit the supply of heroin from Europe. Shortly thereafter, the clandestine manufacture of heroin was reported in China. The supplies of opium in the Far East provided a ready source of morphine—the starting material for the synthesis. The medical use of heroin in the U.S. was not banned until July 19, 1956 with the passage of Public Law 728, which required all inventories to be surrendered to the federal government by November 19, 1956.

In the past 50 or so years, the source countries for opium used in clandestine heroin production have increased dramatically. Political and ecomomic instability in many areas of the world account for much of the increased production of heroin. The opium that is used to produce the heroin that enters the U.S. today has four principal sources. Geographically all of these regions are characterized by a temperate climate with appropriate rainfall and proper soil conditions. However, there are differences in the quality of opium, the morphine content, and the number of harvests from each of these areas. Labor costs are minimal and the profit margins are extremely high for those in the upper echelons of heroin distribution networks.

1.4.1.1 Heroin Sources by Region

The "Golden Triangle" areas of Burma, China, and Laos are the three major source countries in this part of the world for the production of illicit opium. Of these three countries, 60 to 80% of the total world supply of heorin comes from Burma. Heroin destined for the U.S. transits a number of countries including Thailand, Hong Kong, Japan, Korea, the Philippines, Singapore, and Taiwan. Southeast Asian heroin is usually shipped to the U.S. in significant quantities by bulk cargo carriers. The techniques for hiding the heroin in the cargo are quite ingenious. The shipment of Southeast Asian (SEA) Heroin in relatively small quantities is also commonplace. Criminal organizations in Nigeria have been deeply involved in the small quanitity smuggling of SEA heroin into the U.S. The "body carry" technique and ingestion are two of the better known methods of concealment by the Nigerians. SEA heroin is high quality and recognized by its white crystalline appearance. Though the cutting agents are numerous, caffeine and acetaminophen appear quite frequently.

Southwest Asia—Turkey, Iraq, Iran, Afghanistan, Pakistan, India, Lebanon, and the Newly Independent States of the former Soviet Union (NIS) are recognized as source countries in this part of the world. Trafficking of Southwest Asian heroin has been on the decline in the U.S. since the end of 1994. Southwest Asian heroin usage is more predominant in Europe than in the U.S. The Southwest Asian heroin that does arrive in the U.S. is normally transhipped through Europe, Africa, and the NIS. The political and economic conditions of the NIS and topography of the land make these countries ideal as transit countries for heroin smuggling. The rugged mountainous terrain and the absence of significant enforcement efforts enable traffickers to proceed unabated. Most Southwest Asian heroin trafficking groups in the originating countries, the transitting countries, and the U.S. are highly cohesive ethnic groups. These groups rely less on the bulk shipment and more on smaller quantity commercial cargo smuggling techniques. Southwest Asian heroin is characterized by its off-white to tan powdery appearance as compared to the white SEA heroin. The purity of Southwest Asian heroin is only slightly lower than that of SEA heroin. The cutting agents are many. Phenobarbital, caffeine, acetaminophen, and calcium carbonate appear quite frequently.

Central America—Mexico and Guatemala are the primary source countries for heroin in Central America. Mexico's long border with the U.S. provides easy access for smuggling and distribution networks. Smuggling is usually small scale and often involves illegal immigrants and migrant workers crossing into the U.S. Heroin distribution in the U.S. is primarily the work of Mexican immigrants from the States of Durango, Michoacan, Nuevo Leon, and Sinaloa. Concealment in motor vehicles, public transportation, external body carries, and commercial package express are common. This heroin usually ranges from a dark brown powder to a black tar. The most commonly encountered adulterants are amorphous (formless and indeterminate) materials and sugars. The dark color of Mexican heroin is attributed to processing by-products. The purity of Mexican heroin varies greatly from seizure to seizure.

South America—Heroin production in this part of the world is a relatively new phenomenon. Cultivation of opium has been documented along the Andean mountain range within Colombia in the areas of Cauca, Huila, Tolima, and Santaner. There have been a number of morphine base and heroin processing facilities seized in Colombia in the past few years. Smuggling of South American heroin into the U.S. increased dramatically in 1994 and 1995. The primary method of smuggling has been by Colombian couriers aboard commercial airliners using false-sided briefcases and luggage, hollowed out shoes, or by ingestion. Miami and New York are the primary ports of entry into the U.S. One advantage which the traffickers from South America have is the importation networks that are already in place for the distribution of cocaine into the U.S. Transhipment of this heroin through other South American countries and the Caribbean is also a common practice. South American heroin has many of the same physical characteristics of Southwest Asian heroin. However, the purity of South American heroin is higher with fewer adulterants than Southwest Asian heroin. Cocaine in small quantities is oftentimes encountered in South American heroin exhibits. In such cases, it is not always clear whether the cocaine is present as a contaminant introduced due to common packaging locations of cocaine and heroin, or whether it has been added as an adulterant.

1.4.1.2 Isolation of Morphine and Heroin Production

There are some very specific methods for producing heroin. However, all involve the same four steps: (1) The opium poppy (*Papaver Somniferum L.*) is cultivated; (2) the poppy head is scored and the opium latex is collected; (3) the morphine is the isolated from the latex; and (4) the morphine is treated with an acetylating agent. Isolation of the morphine in Step 3 is accomplished using a rendition of one of the following five methods:

1. **The Thiboumery and Mohr Process (TMP)**—This is the most well known of the reported methods for isolating morphine followed by the acetylation to heroin. Dried opium latex is dissolved in three times its weight of hot water. The solution is filtered hot which removes undissolved botanical substances. These undissolved botanicals are washed with hot water and filtered. This is done to ensure a maximized yield of morphine in the final product. The filtrate is reduced to half its volume by boiling off the water. The laboratory operator then adds to the filtrate a boiling solution of calcium hydroxide which forms the water soluble calcium morphinate. The precipitates, which include the insoluble alkaloids from the opium, and the insoluble materials from this step are filtered. These insolubles are then washed three more times with water and filtered. The resulting filtrate, which contains calcium morphinate still in solution, is then evaporated to a weight of approximately twice the weight of the original weight of the opium and then filtered. This results in a concentrated calcium morphinate solution which is heated to a boil. Ammonium chloride is then added to reduce the pH below 9.85. When this solution cools, morphine base precipitates and is collected by filtration. The morphine base is dissolved in a minimum volume of warm hydrochloric acid. When this solution cools the morphine hydrochloride precipitates. The precipitated morphine hydrochloride is then isolated by filtration.

2. **The Robertson and Gregory Process (RGP)**—This method is similar to the Thiboumery and Mohr Process. The laboratory operator washes the opium with five to ten times its weight of cold water. The solution is then evaporated to a syrup which is then re-extracted with cold water and filtered. The filtrate is evaporated until the specific gravity of the solution is 1.075. The solution is boiled and calcium chloride is added. Cold water is added to the calcium morphinate solution which is then filtered. The solution is concentrated and the calcium morphinate then precipitates out of solution as the liquid evaporates. The calcium morphinate is then redissolved in water and filtered. To the filtrate is added ammonia which allows the

morphine base to precipitate. This morphine base can then be further treated to produce the pharmaceutical quality morphine.

The Thiboumery and Mohr Process and the Robertson and Gregory Process are used by commercial suppliers for the initial isolation of morphine from opium. In clandestine laboratories, the same methodologies and rudimentary steps are followed. However, since the operators are using "bucket chemistry", there are modifications to hasten and shortcut the processes.

Three other methods can then be utilized to convert the relatively crude morphine base through purification processes to high quality morphine base or morphine hydrochloride crystals. Modifications of these purifications are used by clandestine laboratory operators.

3. **The Barbier Purification**—The morphine base is dissolved in 80°C water. Tartaric acid is added until the solution becomes acidic to methyl orange. As the solution cools, morphine bitartrate precipitates, is filtered, washed with cold water, and dried. The morphine bitartrate is then dissolved in hot water and ammonia is added to pH 6. This results in a solution of morphine monotartrate. The laboratory operator then adds activated carbon black, sodium bisulfite, sodium acetate, and ammonium oxalate. This process results in a decolorization of the morphine. When this decolorization process is complete, ammonia is added to the solution which results in white crystals of morphine base. These purified morphine base crystals are then filtered and dried. This high quality morphine base is converted to morphine hydrochloride by adding 30% ethanolic HCl to a warm solution of morphine in ethanol. The morphine hydrochloride crystallizes from solution as the solution cools.

4. **The Schwyzer Purification**—The acetone insoluble morphine base (from either the TMB or RGP) is washed in with acetone. The morphine base is then re-crystallized from hot ethyl alcohol.

5. **The Heumann Purification**—The laboratory operator washes the morphine base (from either the TMB or RGP) with trichloroethylene, followed by a cold 40% ethanol wash. This is subsequently followed by an aqueous acetone wash.

The quality of the clandestine product is usually evaluated by the color and texture of the morphine from one of these processes. If the clandestine laboratory operator is producing morphine as his end product, with the intention of selling the morphine for conversion by a second laboratory, the morphine will usually be very pure. However, if he continues with the acetylation of the morphine to heroin, the "intermediate" morphine will frequently be relatively impure.

Heroin can be produced synthetically, but requires a 10-step process and extensive expertise in synthetic organic chemistry. The total synthesis of morphine has been reported by Gates and Tschudi in 1952 and by Elad and Ginsburg in 1954.[3,4] A more recent synthesis was reported by Rice in 1980.[5] All of these methods require considerable forensic expertise and result in low yield. There are also methods reported in the literature for converting codeine to morphine using an O-demethylation. The morphine can then be acetylated to heroin. One of these procedures is referred to as "homebake" and was described in the literature by Rapoport et al.[6] This particular procedure has been reported only in New Zealand and Australia.

Acetylation of Morphine to Diacetylmorphine (Heroin)—This process involves placing dried morphine into a reaction vessel and adding excess acetic anhydride (Figure 1.4.1.2). Sometimes a co-solvent is also used. The mixture is heated to boiling and stirred for varying periods of time ranging from 30 min up to 3 or 4 h. The vessel and contents are cooled and diluted in cold water. A sodium carbonate solution is then added until precipitation of the

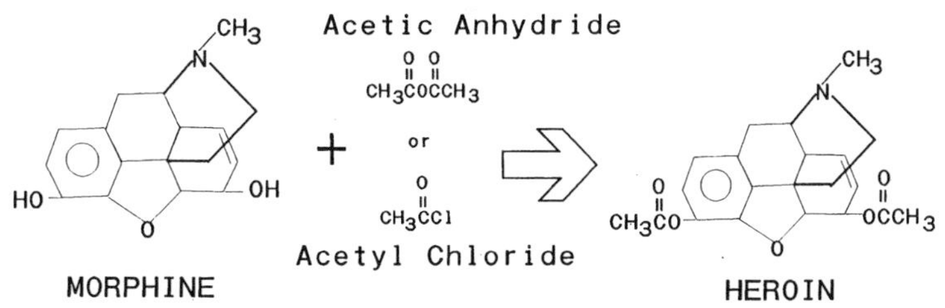

Figure 1.4.1.2 Clandestine laboratory synthesis of heroin

heroin base is complete and settles to the bottom of the reaction vessel. The heroin base is then either filtered and dried, or undergoes further processing to enhance the purity or to convert the base to heroin hydrochloride.

Processing By-Products and Degradation Products in Heroin—Pharmaceutical grade heroin has a purity of greater than 99.5%. Impurities include morphine, the O-3- and O-6-monoacetylmorphines, and other alkaloidal impurities and processing by-products. The impurities found in clandestinely produced heroin include but are certainly not limited to: the monoacetylmorphines, morphine, codeine, acetylcodeine, papaverine, noscapine, thebaine, meconine, thebaol, acetylthebaol, norlaudanosine, reticuline, and codamine. These impurities (from both quantitative and qualitative perspectives) are retained as the result of anomalies in processing methodologies.

REFERENCES

1. Anon. Heroin, *J. Chem. Soc. London,* 28: 315-318, 1875.
2. Anon. Heroin, *Arch. Gesam. Physilogie,* 72: 487, 1898.
3. Gates, M. and Tschudi, G., The synthesis of morphine, *J. Am. Chem. Soc.,* 74: 1109-1110, 1952.
4. Elad, E. and Ginsburg, D., The synthesis of morphine, *J. Am. Chem. Soc.,* 76: 312-313, 1954.
5. Rice, K.C., Synthetic opium alkaloids and derivatives. A short total synthesis of (+-)-dihydrothebainone, (+-)-dihydrocodinone, and (+-)-nordihydrocodinone as an approach to the practical synthesis of morphine, codeine, and congeners, *J. Org. Chem.,* 45: 3135-3137, 1980.
6. Rapoport, H. and Bonner, R.M., Delta-7-desoxymorphine, *J. Am. Chem. Soc.,* 73:5485, 1951.

1.4.2 COCAINE

The social implications of cocaine abuse in the U.S. have been the subject of extensive media coverage during much of the 1980s and most of the 1990s. As a result, the general public has acquired some of the terminology associated with the cocaine usage. "Smoking crack" and "snorting coke" are terms that have become well understood in the American culture from elementary school through adulthood. However, there are facts associated with this drug which are not well understood by the general public. There are documented historical aspects associated with coca and cocaine abuse which go back 500 years. Recognizing some of these historical aspects enables the public to place today's problem in perspective. Cocaine addiction has been with society for well over 100 years.

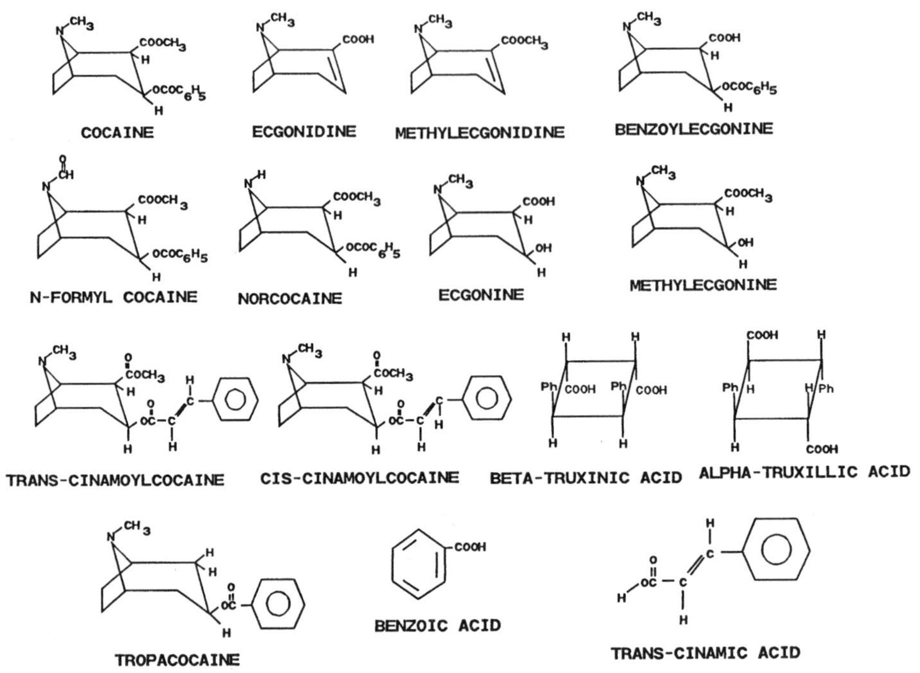

Figure 1.4.2.1

There are four areas of interest this section will address: (1) Where does cocaine come from? (2) How is cocaine isolated from the coca plant? (3) What does one take into the body from cocaine purchased on the street? (4) How does the chemist analyzing the drug identify and distinguish between the different forms of cocaine?

Cocaine is a Schedule II controlled substance. The wording in Title 21, Part 1308.12(b)(4) of the Code of Federal Regulations states:

> Coca leaves (9040) and any salt, compound, derivative or preparation of coca leaves (including cocaine (9041) and ecgonine (9180) and their salts, isomers, derivatives and salts of isomers and derivatives), and any salt, compound, derivative, or preparation thereof which is chemically equivalent or identical with any of these substances, except that the substances shall not include decocanized coca leaves, or extractions of coca leaves, do not contain cocaine or ecgonine.

It is significant that the term "coca leaves" is the focal point of that part of the regulation controlling cocaine. The significance of this fact will become more apparent as this discussion progresses.

1.4.2.1 Sources of Cocaine

Cocaine is just one of the alkaloidal substances present in the coca leaf. Other molecules, some of them psychoactive (norcocaine being the most preominent) are shown in Figure 1.4.2.1 Cocaine is extracted from the leaves of the coca plant. The primary of source of cocaine imported into the U.S. is South America, but the coca plant also grows in the Far East in Ceylon, Java, and India. The plant is cultivated in South America on the eastern slopes of the Andes in Peru, and Bolivia. There are four varieties of coca plants — *Erythroxylon coca* var. *coca* (ECVC), *Erythroxylon coca* var. *ipadu*, *Erythroxylum novogranatense* var. *novogranatense*, and

Erythroxylum novogranatense var. *truxillense*.[1-3] ECVC is the variety that has been used for the manufacture of illicit cocaine. While cultivated in many countries of South America, Peru and Bolivia are the world's leading producers of the coca plant. Cocaine is present in the coca leaves from these countries at dry weight concentrations of from 0.1 to 1%. The average concentration of cocaine in the leaf is 0.7%. The coca shrub has a life expectancy of 50 years and can be harvested three or four times a year.

The method of isolating cocaine from the coca leaf does not require a high degree of technical expertise or experience. It requires no formal education or expensive scientific equipment or chemicals. In most instances the methodology is passed from one generation to the next.

1.4.2.2 Historical Considerations

Prior to the 1880s, the physiological properties of cocaine and the coca leaf were not readily distinguishable in the literature. During that year, H.H. Rusby and W.G. Mortimer made the distinction between the physiological properties of "isolated" cocaine and the coca leaf. Mortimer wrote,

> ...the properties of cocaine, remarkable as they are, lie in an altogether different direction from those of coca.[1]

In 1884, two significant papers appeared in the literature. Sigmund Freud published the first of his five papers on the medicinal properties of cocaine.[2] A few months later, Karl Koller discovered the use of cocaine as local anesthetic.[2A] In 1886, Sir Arthur Conan Doyle, an eye specialist who had studied at Vienna General Hospital, where Freud and Koller made their discoveries, made reference to Sherlock Holmes' use of cocaine in *The Sign of Four*.[3] During the same year in Atlanta, Georgia, John Pemberton introduced to this country, caught up in the frenzy of alcohol prohibition, a beverage consisting of coca leaf extracts, African kola nuts, and a sweet carbonated syrup. The product was named "Coca-Cola".[4] Pemberton received his inspiration from Angelo Mariani, a Corsican pharmacist working in Paris, who had been selling a coca leaf-Bordeaux wine tincture since the early 1860s. Mariani's product was the most popular tonic of its time, and was used by celebrities, poets, popes, and presidents.[5] Patterns of coca consumption changed dramatically as society entered the 20th century. In the 19th century, cocaine was only available in the form of a botanical product or a botanical product in solution. When chemical houses, such as Merck, began to produce significant quantites of refined cocaine, episodes of toxicity became much more frequent, the views of the medical profession changed, and physicians lost much of their enthusiasm for the drug.

Until 1923, the primary source of cocaine was from the coca leaf. In that year, Richard Willstatter was able to synthesize a mixture of d-cocaine, l-cocaine, d-pseudococaine, and l-pseudococaine. This multi-step synthesis requires a high degree of technical expertise in organic chemistry and results in low yields.[6] These financial and technical factors make the extraction of cocaine from the coca leaf the method by which most, if not all, of the cocaine is isolated for distribution on both the licit and illicit markets.

1.4.2.3 Isolation and Purification

The extraction and isolation of cocaine from the coca leaf is not difficult. There is more than one way to do it. South American producers improvise depending on the availability of chemicals. All of the known production techniques involve three primary steps: (1) extraction of crude coca paste from the coca leaf; (2) purification of coca paste to cocaine base; and (3) conversion of cocaine base to cocaine hydrochloride. The paste and base laboratories in South America are deeply entrenched and widespread with thousands of operations, whereas the conversion laboratories are more sophisticated and centralized. They border on semi-industrial pilot-plant type laboratories involving a knowledge of chemistry and engineering.

The primary isolation method used until recently is a Solvent Extraction Technique. The essential methodology involves macerating a quantity of coca leaves with lime water, and then adding kerosene with stirring. After a while the kerosene is separated from the aqueous layer. A dilute sulfuric acid solution is added to the kerosene with stirring. This time the kerosene is separated from the aqueous layer and set aside. It is common to save the kerosene for another extraction of the leaves. The aqueous layer is retained and neutralized with limestone or some other alkaline substance. The material that precipitates after the addition of limestone is crude coca paste containing anywhere from 30 to 80% cocaine, with the remainder of the cocaine matrix composed primarily of other alkaloids, hydrolysis products, and basic inorganic salts used in the processing. This solid material is isolated by filtration for purification of the cocaine.

The coca paste is then dissolved in dilute sulfuric acid, and dilute potassium permanganate solution is added to oxidize the impurities. This solution is then filtered, and ammonium hydroxide is added to the filtrate to precipitate cocaine base. This "cocaine" is not ready for shipment to the U.S. The cocaine will first be converted to hydrochloride for easier packaging, handling, and shipment.

A second method of isolating cocaine from the leaf which is more predominant today is the Acid Extraction Technique. In this method, the cocaine leaves are placed directly in the maceration pit with enough sulfuric acid to cover the leaves. The pit is a hole dug into the ground and lined with heavy duty plastic. The leaves are macerated by workers who stomp in the sulfuric acid/coca leaf pit. This stomping leaches the cocaine base from the leaf and forms an aqueous solution of cocaine sulfate. This stomping can continue for a matter of hours to ensure maximum recovery of the cocaine.

After stomping is complete, the coca solution is poured through a course filter to remove the insolubles including the plant material. More sulfuric acid is added to the leaves and a second or even third extraction of the remaining cocaine will take place. Maximized recovery of cocaine is important to the laboratory operators. After the extractions and filterings are completed, an excess basic lime or carbonate solution is added to the acidic solution with stirring and neutralizing the excess acid and cocaine sulfate. A very crude coca paste forms. The addition of the base is monitored until the solution is basic to an ethanolic solution of phenolphthalein. The coca paste is then back-extracted with a small volume of kerosene. The solution sets until a separation of the layers occurs. The kerosene is then back-extracted this time with a dilute solution of sulfuric acid. Then, an inorganic base is added to precipitate the coca paste. This coca paste is essentially the same as that generated by the solvent extraction method. The advantage to this Acid Extraction Technique is that a minimal volume of organic solvent is required. And while it is more labor intensive, the cost of labor in Bolivia, the major producing country of coca paste, is very low when compared to the financial return.

The resultant cocaine base, produced by either technique, is dissolved in acetone, ether, or a mixture of both. A dilute solution of hydrochloric acid in acetone is then prepared. The two solutions are mixed and a precipitate of cocaine hydrochloride forms almost immediately and is allowed to settle to the bottom of the reaction vessel (usually an inexpensive bucket). The slurry will then be poured through clean bed sheets filtering the cocaine hydrochloride from the solvent. The sheets are then wrung dry to eliminate excess acetone, and the high quality cocaine hydrochloride is dried in microwave ovens, under heat lamps, or in the sunlight. It is then a simple matter to package the cocaine hydrochloride for shipment. One of the more common packaging forms encountered in laboratories analyzing seizures of illicit cocaine is the "one kilo brick". This is a brick-shaped package of cocaine wrapped in tape or plastic, sometimes labeled with a logo, with the contents weighing near 1 kg. Once the cocaine hydrochloride arrives in the U.S., drug wholesalers may add mannitol or inositol as diluents, or procaine, benzocaine, lidocaine, or tetracaine as adulterants. This cocaine can then be sold on the underground market in the U.S. either in bulk or by repackaging into smaller containers.

1.4.2.4 Conversion to "Crack"

"Crack" is the term used on the street and even in some courtrooms to describe the form of cocaine base which has been converted from the cocaine hydrochloride and can be smoked in a pipe. This procedure of conversion from the acid to the base is usually carried out in the U.S. Cocaine base usually appears in the form of a rock-like material, and is sometimes sold in plastic packets, glass vials, or other suitable packaging. Cocaine hydrochloride is normally ingested by inhalation through a tube or straw, or by injection. Cocaine base is ingested by smoking in an improvised glass pipe. Ingestion in this manner results in the cocaine entering the blood stream through the lungs and rushes to the brain very quickly.

Cocaine hydrochloride is converted to cocaine base in one of two ways. The first method involves dissolving the cocaine hydrochloride in water and adding sodium bicarbonate or household ammonia. The water is then boiled for a short period until all of the precipitated cocaine base melts to an oil, and ice is added to the reaction vessel. This vessel will usually be a metal cooking pan or a deep glass bowl. As the water cools, chunks of cocaine base oil will solidify at the bottom of the cooking vessel. After all the cocaine base has formed, the water can be cooled and then poured off leaving the solid cocaine base which is easily removed from the collection vessel. The cocaine base can be cut with a knife or broken into "rocks" which can then be dried either under a heat lamp or in a microwave oven. It is not unusual when analyzing cocaine base produced from this method to identify sodium bicarbonate mixed with the rock-like material. This cocaine base sometimes has a high moisture content due to incomplete drying.

A second method of producing cocaine base from cocaine hydrochloride involves dissolving the salt (usually cocaine hydrochloride) in water. Sodium bicarbonate or household ammonia is added to the water and mixed well. Diethyl ether is then added to the solution and stirred. The mixture then separates into two layers with the ether layer on top of the aqueous layer. The ether is decanted leaving the water behind. The ether is then allowed to evaporate and high quality cocaine base remains. If any of the adulterants mentioned previously (excluding sugars, which are diluents) are mixed with the cocaine hydrochloride prior to conversion, then they will also be converted to the base and will be a part of the rock-like material that results from this process. The term "free base" is used to describe this form of cocaine. Cocaine base in this form is also smoked in a glass pipe. However, residual (and sometimes substantial) amounts of ether remaining in these samples from the extraction process make ignition in a glass pipe very dangerous.

1.4.2.5 Other Coca Alkaloids

In the process of examining cocaine samples in the laboratory, it is not uncommon to identify other alkaloids and manufacturing by-products with the cocaine. These other alkaloids are carried over from the coca leaf in the extraction of the cocaine. Many manufacturing by-products result from the hydrolysis of the parent alkaloids (benzoylecgonine from cocaine, or truxillic acid from truxilline). As a forensic chemist, it is important to recognize the sources of these alkaloids as one progresses through an analytical scheme.

The major alkaloidal "impurities" present in the coca leaf which are carried over in the cocaine extraction are the cis- and trans-cinnamoylcocaines and the truxillines. There are 11 isomeric truxillic and truxinic acids resulting from the hydrolysis of truxilline. Another naturally occurring minor alkaloid from the coca leaf is tropacocaine. The concentration of tropacocaine will rarely, if ever, exceed 1% of the cocaine concentration and is well below the concentrations of the cis- and trans-cinnamoylcocaines and the truxillines. Two other alkaloids from the coca leaf which have been identified are cuscohygrine and hygrine. These two products are not found in cocaine, just in the leaf.

The second class of substances found in the analysis of cocaine samples is the result of degradation or hydrolysis. Ecgonine, benzoylecgonine, and methylecgonine found in cocaine samples will be the result of the hydrolysis of cocaine. It is important to recognize that some of these manufacturing by-products, such as ecgonine, can be detected by gas chromatography only if they are derivatized prior to injection. Methyl ecgonidine is a by-product of the hydrolysis of cocaine and is often times identified in the laboratory by gas chromatography/ mass spectrometry. This artifact can also result from the thermal degradation of cocaine or the truxillines in the injection port of the GC. Benzoic acid is the other product identified when this decomposition occurs.

There are at least two substances that result directly from the permanganate oxidation of cocaine. N-formyl cocaine results from oxidation of the N-methyl group of cocaine to an N-formyl group. Norcocaine is a hydrolysis product resulting from a Schiff's base intermediate during the permanganate oxidation. There is also evidence that norcocaine can result from the N-demethylation of cocaine, a consequence of the peroxides in diethyl ether.

1.4.2.6 Cocaine Adulterants

The primary adulterants identified in cocaine samples are procaine and benzocaine. Lidocaine is also found with less regularity. These adulterants are found in both the cocaine base and cocaine hydrochloride submissions. The primary diluents are mannitol and inositol. Many other sugars have been found, but not nearly to the same extent. Cocaine hydrochloride concentrations will usually range from 20 to 99%. The moisture content of cocaine hydrochloride is usually minimal. Cocaine base concentrations will usually range from 30 to 99%. There will usually be some moisture in cocaine base ("crack") submissions from the water/sodium bicarbonate or water/ammonia methods. The concentration of cocaine base ("free base") from the ether/sodium bicarbonate or ether/ammonia methods will usually be higher and free of water.

The methods for identifying cocaine in the laboratory include but are not limited to: infrared spectrophotometry (IR), nuclear magnetic resonance spectroscopy (NMR), mass spectrometry (MS), and gas chromatography (GC). IR and NMR will enable the analyst to distinguish between cocaine hydrochloride and cocaine base. However, it is not possible to identify the form in which the cocaine is present utilizing this instrumentation.

CONCLUSION

The user of either cocaine base or cocaine hydrochloride not only ingests the cocaine, but also other alkaloids from the coca plant, processing by-products, organic and inorganic reagents used in processing, diluents, and adulterants. There is no realistic way in which a cocaine user can ensure the quality of the cocaine purchases on the street, and "innocent" recreational drug use may provide more danger than the user would knowingly risk.

REFERENCES

1. Rusby, H.H., Bliss, A.R., and Ballard, C.W., *The Properties and Uses of Drugs,* Blakiston's Son & Co., Philadephia, 1930, 125, 386, 407.
2. Byck, R., Ed., *Cocaine Papers by Sigmond Freud,* Stonehill, New York, 1975.

2A. Becker, H.K., 261, 276, 283-6.

3. Musto, D., A study in cocaine: Sherlock Holmes and Sigmund Freud, *JAMA,* 204: 125, 1968.

4. Brecher, E. and the Editors of Consumer Reports, *Licit and Illicit Drugs,* Little, Brown and Co., Boston, 1972, 33-6, 270.

5. Mariani, A., Ed., Album Mariani, Les Figures Contemporaines. Contemporary Celebrities from the Album Mariani, etc., various publishers for Mariani & Co., 13 Vols., 1891-1913.

6. Willstatter, R., Wolfes, O., and Mader, H., Synthese des Naturlichen Cocains, *Justus Liebigs's Annalen Der Chimie,* 434: 111-139, 1923.

7. Casale, J.F. and Klein, RFX, Illicit cocaine production, *Forensic Sci Rev ,* 5: 96-107, 1993.

1.4.3 MARIJUANA

1.4.3.1 History and Terminology

Marijuana is a Schedule I controlled substance. In botanical terms, "marijuana" is defined as *Cannabis sativa L.* Legally, marijuana is defined as all parts of the plant, *Canabis sativa L.* (and any of its varieties) whether growing or not, the seeds thereof, the resin extracted from any part of the plant, and every compound, manufacture, salt, derivative, mixture, or preparation of such plant; its seeds and resins. Such terms do not include the mature stalk of the plants, fibers produced from such plants, oils or cakes made from the pressed seeds of such plants, any other compound, manufacture, salt derivative, mixture or preparation of such mature stalks (except the resin extracted therefrom), fiber, oil or cake, pressed seed, or the sterilized seed which is incapable of germination.[1] Pharmaceutical preparations that contained the resinous extracts of cannabis were available on the commercial market from the 1900s to 1937. These products were prescribed for their analgesic and sedative effects. In 1937 the Food and Drug Administration declared these products to be of little medical utility and they were removed from the market in 1937. Cannabis, in the forms of the plant material, hashish, and hashish oil, is the most abused illicit drug in the world.

Cannabis is cultivated in many areas of the world. Commerical *Cannabis sativa L.* is referred to as "hemp". The plant is cultivated for cloth and rope from its fiber. A valuable drying oil used in art and a substitute for linseed oil is available from the seeds. Bird seed mixtures are also found to contain sterilized marijuana seeds. In the early days of the U.S., hemp was grown in the New England colonies. Its cultivation spread south into Pennsylvania and Virginia. From there it spread south and west most notably into Kentucky and Missouri. Its abundance in the early days of the country is still evident by the fact that it still grows wild in many fields and along many roadways. The plant is now indigenous to many areas, and adapts easily to most soil and moderate climatic conditions.

Marijuana is classifed as a hallucinogenic substance. The primary active constituents in the plant are cannabinol, cannabidiol, and the tetrahydrocannabinols, illustrated in Figure 1.4.3.1. The tetrahydrocannabinols (THCs) are the active components responsible for the hallucinogenic properties of marijuana. The THC of most interest is the $\Delta^{9\text{-}}$ tetrahydrocannabinol. The other THCs of interest in marijuana are the Δ^{1} cis- and trans- tetrahydrocannabinols, the Δ^{6} cis- and trans- tetrahydrocannabinols, and the $\Delta^{3\text{-}}$ and $\Delta^{4\text{-}}$ tetrahydrocannibinols. The concentrations varies dramatically from geographic area to geographic area, from field to field, and from sample to sample. This concentration range varies from less than 1% to as high as 30%. In recent hash oil exhibits, the highest official reported concentration of Δ^{9}-THC is 43%.[2] Five other terms associated with marijuana are

> **Hashish:** Resinous material removed from cannabis. Hashish is usually found in the form of a brown to black cake of resinous material. The material is ingested by smoking in pipes or by consuming in food.

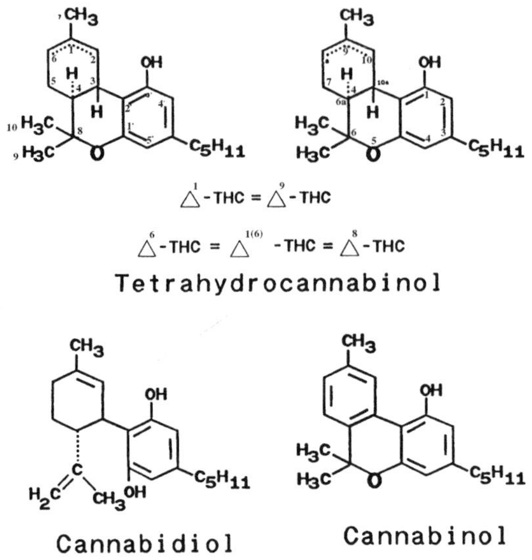

Figure 1.4.3.1 The primatry active constituents in marijuana.

Hashish oil: Extract of the marijuana plant which has been heated to remove the extracting solvents. The material exists as a colorless to brown or black oil or tar-like substance.

Sinsemilla: The flowering tops of the unfertilized female cannabis plant. (There are no seeds on such a plant.) Sensemilla is usually considered a "gourmet" marijuana because of its appearance and relatively high concentrations of the THCs.

Thai sticks: Marijuana leaves tied around stems or narrow diameter bamboo splints. Thai sticks are considered a high quality product by the drug culture. The THC concentrations of the marijuana leaves on Thai sticks are higher than domestic marijuana. Unlike hashish and sinsemilla, seeds, and small pieces of stalks and stems are found in Thai sticks.

Brick or **Kilo:** Marijuana compressed into a brick-shaped package with leaves, stems, stalk, and seeds. The pressed marijauna is usually tightly wrapped in paper and tape. This is the form of marijuana encountered in most large scale seizures. These large scale seizure packages weigh approximately 1000 g (1 kg). This is the packaging form of choiced for clandestine operators because of the ease of handling, packaging, shipping, and distribution.

1.4.3.2 Laboratory Analysis

The specificity of a marijuana analysis is still a widely discussed topic among those in the forensic and legal communities. In the course of the past 25 years, the concensus of opinion concerning the analysis of marijuana has remained fairly consistent. In those situations where plant material is encountered, the marijuana is first examined using a stereomicroscope. The presence of the bear claw cystolithic hairs and other histological features are noted using a compound microscope. The plant material is then examined chemically using Duquenois–Levine reagent in a modified Duenois Levine testing sequence. These two tests are considered to be conclusive within the realm of existing scientific certainty in establishing the presence of marijauana.[3–5]

The Modified Duquenois–Levine test is conducted using Duquenois reagent, concentrated hydrochloric acid, and chloroform. The Duquenois reagent is prepared by dissolving 2 g of vanillin and 0.3 ml of acetaldehyde in 100 ml of ethanol. Small amounts (25 to 60 mg is usually sufficient) of suspected marijuana leaf is placed in a test tube and approximately 2 ml of Duquenois reagent is added. After 1 min, approximately 1 ml of concentrated hydrochloric acid is added. Small bubbles rise from the leaves in the liquid. These are carbon dioxide bubbles produced by the reaction of the hydrochloric acid with the calcium carbonate at the base of the cystolithic hair of the marijuana. A blue to blue-purple color forms very quickly in the solution. Approximately 1 ml of chloroform is then added to the Duquenois reagent/ hydrochloric acid mixture. Because chloroform is not miscible with water, and because it is heavier than water, two liquid layers are visible in the tube—the Duquenois reagent/hydrochloric acid layer is on top, and the chloroform layer is on the bottom. After mixing with a vortex stirrer and on settling, the two layers are again clearly distinguishable. However, the chloroform layer has changed from clear to the blue to blue-purple color of the Duquenois reagent/hydrochloric acid mixture.

One variation in this testing process involve pouring off the Duquenois reagent sitting in the tube with the leaves before adding the hydrochloric acid. The remainder of the test is conducted using only the liquid. Another variation involves conducting the test in a porcelain spot plate. This works, although some analysts find the color change a bit more difficult to detect. A third variation involves extracting the cannabis resin with ether or some other solvent, separating the solvent from the leaves, allowing the solvent to evaporate, and conducting the Modified Duquenois–Levine test on the extract.

Marquis reagent is prepared by mixing 1 ml of formaldehyde solution with 9 ml of sulfuric acid. The test is done by placing a small amount of sample (1 to 5 mg) into the depression of a spot plate, adding one or two drops of reagent, and observing the color produced. This color will usually be indicative of the class of compounds, and the first color is usually the most important. A weak reponse may fade, and samples containing sugar will char on standing because of the sulfuric acid. Marquis reagent produces the following results:

1. Purple with opiates (heroin, codeine).
2. Orange turning to brown with amphetamine and methamphetamine.
3. Black with a dark purple halo with 3,4-methylenedioxyamphetamine (MDA) and 3,4- methylenedioxymethamphetamine (MDMA).
4. Pink with aspirin.
5. Yellow with diphenhydramine.

A thin-layer chromatographic (TLC) analysis, which detects a systematic pattern of colored bands, can then be employed as an additional test.[6,7] Though it is not required, some analysts will run a gas chromatograph/mass spectrometrometer (GC/MS) analysis to identify the cannabinoids in the sample.

The solvent insoluble residue of hashish should be examined with the compound microscope. Cystolythic hairs, resin glands, and surface debris should be present. However, if most of the residue is composed of green leaf fragments, the material is pulverized marijuana or imitation hashish.

1.4.4 PEYOTE

Peyote is a cactus plant which grows in rocky soil in the wild. Historical records document use of the plant by Indians in northern Mexico from as far back as pre-Christian times, when it was used by the Chichimaec tribe in religious rites. The plant grows as small cylindrical-like

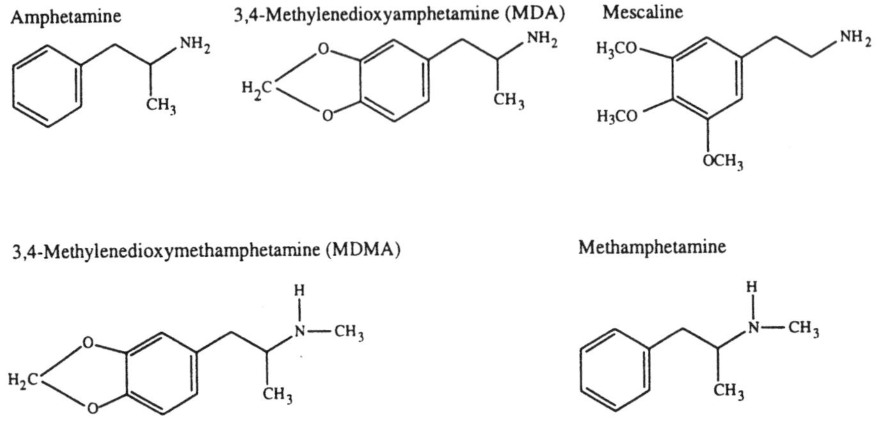

Amphetamine

3,4-Methylenedioxyamphetamine (MDA)

Mescaline

3,4-Methylenedioxymethamphetamine (MDMA)

Methamphetamine

Figure 1.4.4 Chemical structure of mescaline.

"buttons". The buttons were used to relieve fatigue and hunger, and to treat victims of disease. The peyote buttons were used in group settings to achieve a trance state in tribal dances.[8]

It was used by native Americans in ritualistic ceremonies. In the U.S., peyote was cited in 1891 by James Mooney of the Bureau of American Ethology. [9] Mooney talked about the use of peyote by the Kiowa Indians, the Comanche Indians, and the Mescalero Apache Indians, all in the southern part of the country. In 1918, he came to the aid of the Indians by incorporating the "Native American Church" in Oklahoma to ensure their rights in the use of peyote in religious ceremonies. Although several bills have been introduced over the years, the U.S. Congress has never passed a law prohibiting the Indians' religious use of peyote. Both mescaline and peyote are listed as Schedule I controlled substances in the Comprehensive Drug Abuse Prevention and Control Act of 1970.

The principal alkaloid of peyote responsible for its hallucinogenic response is mescaline, a derivative of ß-phenethylamine. Chemically, mescaline is 3,4,5-trimethoxyphenethylamine. As illustrated in Figure 1.4.4, its strucutre is similar to the amphetamine group in general. Mescaline was first isolated from the peyote plant in 1894 by the German chemist A. Heffter.[10] The first complete synthesis of mescaline was in 1919 by E. Späth.[11] The extent of abuse of illicit mescaline has not been accurately determined. The use of peyote buttons became popular in the 1950's and again in the period from 1967 to 1970. These two periods showed a dramatic increase in experimentation with hallucinogens in general.

1.4.5 PSILOCYBIN MUSHROOMS

The naturally occuring indoles responsible for the hallucinogen properties in some species of mushrooms are psilocybin (Figure 1.4.5) and psilocin. [12] The use of hallucinogenic mushrooms dates back to the 16th century occuring during the coronation of Montezuma in 1502.[8] In 1953, R. G. Wassen and V.P. Wasson were credited with the rediscovery of the ritual of the Indian cultures of Mexico and Central America. [13] They were able to obtain samples of these mushrooms. The identification of the mushrooms as the species *Psilocybe* is credited to the French mycologist, Roger Heim. [14]

Albert Hofmann (the discoverer of lysergic acid diethlamine) and his colleagues at Sandoz laboratories in Switzerland are credited with the isolation and identification of psilocybin (phosphorylated 4-hydroxydimethyltryptamine) and psilocin (4-hydroxydimethyltryptamine).[15]

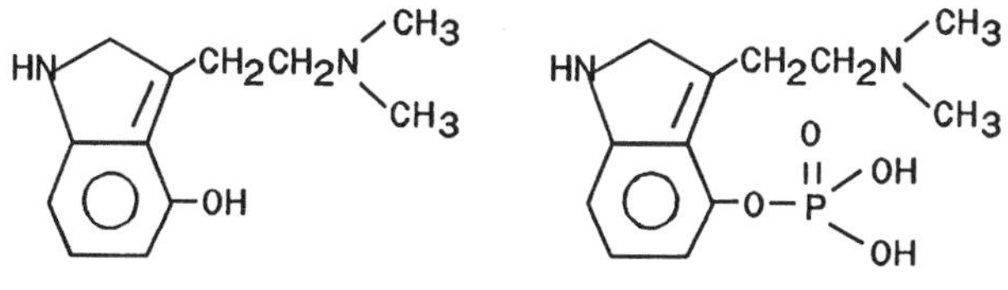

Figure 1.4.5 Chemical structure of psilocin and psilocybin.

Psilocybin was the major component in the mushrooms, and psilocin was found to be a minor component. However, psilocybin is very unstable and is readily metabolized to psilocin in the body. This phonomenon of phosphate cleavage from the psilocybin to form the psilocin occurs quite easily in the forensic science laboratory. This can be a concern in ensuring the specifity of identification.

The availability of the mushroom has existed worldwide wherever proper climactic conditions exist — that means plentiful rainfall. In the U.S., psilcoybib mushrooms are reported to be plentiful in Florida, Hawaii,[16] the Pacific Northwest, and Northern California.[17] Mushrooms that are analyzed in the forensic science laboratory confirm the fact that the mushrooms spoil easily. The time factor between harvesting the mushrooms and the analysis proves to be the greatest detriment to successfully identifying the psilocybin or pscilocyn. Storage prior to shipment is best accomplished by drying the mushrooms. Entrepreneurs reportedly resort to storage of mushrooms in honey to preserve the psychedelic properties.[18]

Progressing through the analytical scheme of separating and isolating the psilocybin and psilocin from the mushroom matrix, cleavage of the phosphate occurs quite easily. Prior to beginning the analysis, drying the mushrooms in a desicator with phosphorous pentoxide ensures a dry starting material. In many instances, the clean-up procedure involves an extraction process carried out through a series of chloroform washes from a basic extract and resolution of the components by TLC. The spots or, more probably, streaks are then scaped from the plate, separated by a back-extraction, and then analyzed by IR. Direct analysis by GC is very difficult because both psilocybin and psilocin are highly polar and not suitable for direct GC analysis. Derivatization followed by GC/MS is an option except in those instances where the mushrooms have been preserved in sugar.[19] With the development and availability of HPLC, the identification and quatitation of psilocybin and psilocyn in mushrooms are becoming more feasible for many forensic science laboratories. [20]

REFERENCES

1. Section 102 (15), Public Law 91-513
2. ElSohly, M.A. and Ross, S.A., *Quarterly Report Potency Monitoring Project, Report #53, January 1, 1995 - March 31, 1995.*
3. Nakamura, G.R., Forensic aspects of cystolithic hairs of cannabis and other plants, *J. Assn. Offic. Analyt. Chem.,* 52: 5-16, 1969.
4. Thornton, J.I. and Nakamura, G.R., The identification of marijuana, *J. Forensic Sci. Soc.,* 24: 461-519, 1979.
5. Hughes, R.B. and Warner, V.J., A study of false positives in the chemical identification of marijuana, *J. Forensic Sci.,* 23: 304-310, 1978.
6. Hauber, D.J., Marijuana analysis with recording of botanical features present with and without the environmental pollutants of the Duquenois-Levine test, *J. Forensic Sci.,* 37:1656 -1661, 1992.

7. Hughes, R.B. and Kessler, R.R., Increased safety and specificity in the thin-layer chromatographic identification of marijuana," *J. Forensic Sci.*, 24: 842-846, 1979.

8. Report Series, National Clearinghouse for Drug Abuse Information, *Mescaline*, Series 15, No. 1, May 1973.

9. Mooney, J., The mesacal plant and ceremony, *Therapeutic Gazette,* 12: 7-11, 1896.

10. Heffter, A., Ein beitrag zur pharmakologishen Kenntniss der Cacteen, *Archiv. F. Exp Pathol. U. Pharmakol.*, 34, 65-86, 1894.

11. Spath, E., Uber die Anhalonium-Alkaloide, Anhalin und Mescalin, Monatshefte furh Chemie and verwandte Teile anderer Wissenschaften, 40, 1929, 1919.

12. Hofman, A., Heim, R., Brack, A., and Kobel, H., Psilocybin, ein psychotroper Wirkstoff aus dem mexikanishen rauschpitz Psilocybe mexicana Heim, *Experiencia*, 14:107-109, 1958.

13. Wasson, V.P. and Wasson, R.G., *Mushrooms, Russia, and History.* Pantheon Books, New York, 1957.

14. Heim, R., Genest, K., Hughes, D.W., and Belec, G., Botanical and chemical characterisation of a forensic mushroom specimen of the genus psilocybe, *Forensic Sci. Soc. J.*, 6: 192-201, 1966.

15. Hofmann, A., Chemical aspects of psilocybin, the psychotropic principle from the Mexican fungus, *Psilocybe mexicana Heim*, in Bradley, P.B., Deniker, P., and Radouco-Thomas, C., Eds. *Neuropsychopharmacology.* Elsevier, Amsterdam, 1959, pp. 446-448.

16. Pollock, S.H., A novel experience with Panaeolus: a case study from Hawaii, *J. Psychedelic Drugs*, 6: 85-90. 1974.

17. Weil, H., Mushroom hunting in Oregon, *J. Psychedelic Drugs*, 7: 89-102, 1975.

18. Pollock, S.H., Psilocybian Mycetismus With Special Reference to Panaeolus, *J. Psychedelic Drugs*, 8(1), 50.

19. Repke, D.B., Leslie, D.T., Mandell, D.M., and Kish, N.G., GLC-mass spectral analysis of psilocin and psilocybin, *J. Psychedelic Drugs*, 66: 743-744, 1977.

20. Thomas, B.M., Analysis of psilocybin and psilocin in mushroom extracts by reversed-phase high performance liquid chromatography, *J. Forensic Sci.*, 25: 779-785, 1980.

1.4.6 LYSERGIC ACID DIETHYLAMIDE (LSD)

LSD is an hallucinogenic substance produced from lysergic acid, a substance derived from the ergot fungus (*Clavica purpurea*) which grows on rye. It can also be derived from lysergic acid amide which is found in morning glory seeds.[1] LSD is also refered to as LSD-25 because it was the twenty-fifth in a series of compounds produced by Dr. Albert Hofmann in Basel, Switzerland. Hoffman was interested in the chemistry of ergot compounds, especially their effect on circulation. He was trying to produce compounds that might improve circulation without exhibiting the other toxic effects associated with ergot poisoning. One of the products he produced was Methergine™, which is still in use today. When LSD-25 was first tested on animals, in 1938, the results were disappointing. Five years later, in 1943, Hoffman decided to reevaluate LSD-25. The hallucinogenic experience that ensued when he accidentally ingested some of the compound led to the start of experimentation with "psychedelic" drugs.

LSD is the most potent hallucinogenic substance known to man. Dosages of LSD are measured in micrograms (one microgram equals one-one millionth of a gram). By comparison, dosage units of cocaine and heroin are measured in milligrams (one milligram equals one-one thousanth of a gram). LSD is available in the form of very small tablets ("microdots"), thin squares of gelatin ("window panes"), or impregnated on blotter paper ("blotter acid"). The most popular of these forms in the 1990s is blotter paper perforated into 1/4 inch squares. This paper is usually brightly colored with psychedelic designs or line drawing. There have been recent reports of LSD impregnated on sugar cubes.[2] These LSD-laced sugar cubes were commonplace in the 1970s. The precursor to LSD, Lysergic Acid, is a Schedule III controlled substance. LSD is classified as a Schedule I controlled substance. The synthetic route utilized for the clandestine manufacture of LSD is shown in Figure 1.4.6.

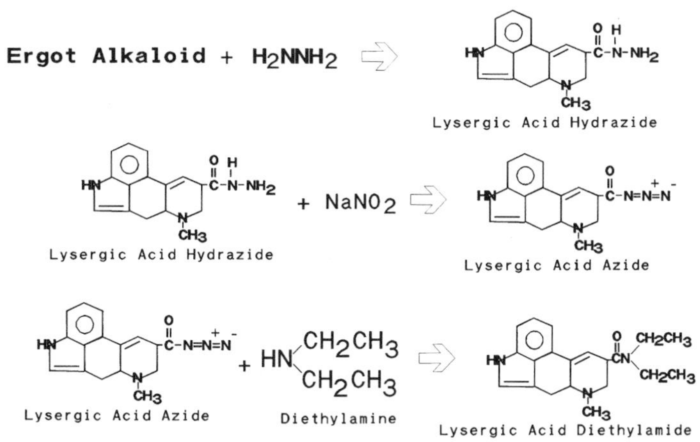

Figure 1.4.6 Synthetic route utilized for the clandestine manufacture of LSD.

1.4.7 PHENCYCLIDINE (PCP)

The chemical nomenclature of phencyclidine is phenylcyclohexylpiperidine. The term "PCP" is used most often used when referring to this drug. The acronym PCP has two origins that are consistent. In the 1960s phencyclidine was trafficked as a peace pill ("**Pea**Ce**P**ill"). **P**henyl**C**yclohexyl**P**iperidine can also account for the PCP acronym.

PCP was first synthesized in 1926.[3] It was developed as a human anesthetic in 1957, and found use in veterinary medicine as a powerful tranquilizer. In 1965 human use was discontinued because, as the anesthetic wore off confusional states and freightening hallucinations were common. Strangely, these side effects were viewed as desirable by those inclined to experiment with drugs. Today even the use of phencyclidine as a primate anesthetic has been all but discontinued. In 1978, the commercial manufacture of phencyclidine ceased and the drug was transferred from Schedule III to Schedule II of the Controlled Substances Act. Small amounts of PCP are manufactured for research purposes and as a drug standard.

The manufacture of PCP in clandestine laboratories is simple and inexpensive. Figure 1.4.7 shows three of the synthetic routes utilized for its illegal production. The first clandestinely produced PCP appeared in 1967 shortly after Parke Davis withdrew phencyclidine as a pharmaceutical.[4] The clandestine laboratory production of PCP requires neither formal knowledge of chemistry nor a large inventory of laboratory equipment. The precursor chemicals produce phencyclidine when combined correctly using what is termed "bucket chemistry". The opportunities for a contaminated product from a clandestine PCP are greatly enhanced because of the recognized simplicity of the chemical reactions in the production processes. The final product is often contaminated with starting materials, reaction intermediates, and by-products.[5] Clandestine laboratory operators have been known to modify the manufacturing processes to obtain chemically related analogues capable of producing similar physiological responses. The most commonly encountered analogues are N-ethyl-1-phenylcyclohexylamine (PCE), 1-(1-phenylcyclohexyl)- pyrrolidine (PCPy), and 1-[1-(2-thienyl-cyclohexyl)]-piperidine (TCP).

In the 1960s, PCP was distributed as a white to off-white powder or crystalline material and ingested orally. In recent years, PCP has been encountered as the base and dissolved in diethyl ether. The liquid is then placed into small bottles which are recognized to hold

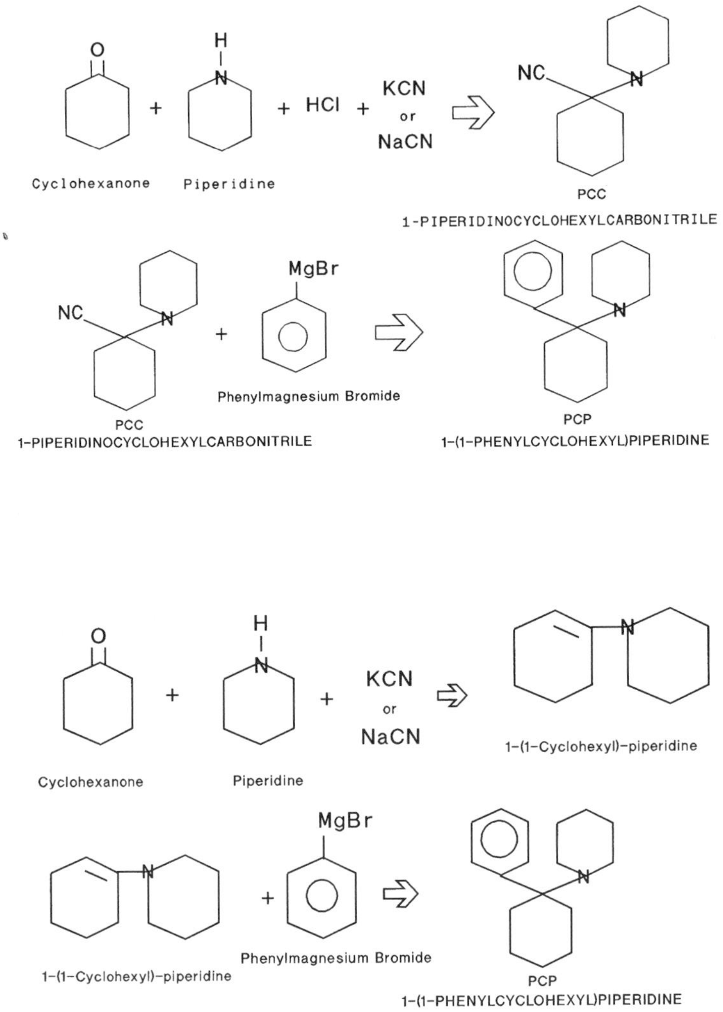

Figure 1.4.7 Synthetic routes utilized for illegal production of PCP.

commercial vanilla extract. This ether solution is then sprayed on leaves such as parsley and smoked. PCP is commonly encountered on long thin dark cigarettes ("Sherms") which have been dipped in the PCP/ether solution.

1.4.8 FENTANYL

Fentanyl [the technical nomeclature is N-(1-phenethyl-4-piperidyl)propionanilide] is a synthetic narcotic analgesic approximately 50 to 100 times as potent as morphine.[6] The drug had its origin in Belgium as a synthetic product of Janssen Pharmaceutica.[7] In the 1960s in Europe and in the 1970s in the U.S., it was introduced for use as an anesthesia and for the relief of post-operative pain. Almost 70% of all surgical procedures in the U.S. use fentanyl for one of these purposes.[8]

Joseph P. Bono

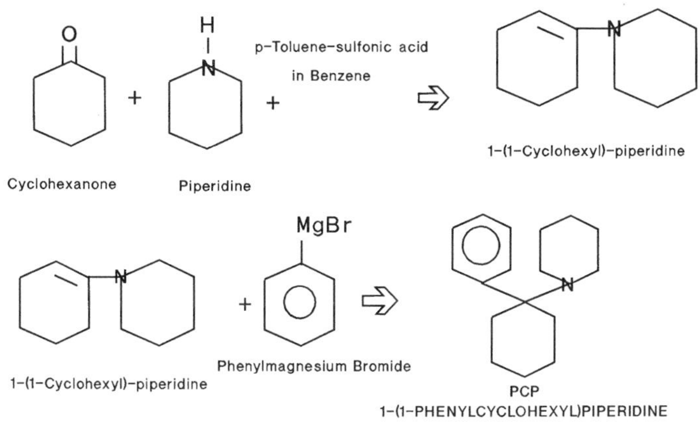

Figure 1.4.7 (continued) Synthetic routes utilized for illegal production of PCP.

Fentanyl has been called "synthetic heroin". This is a misnomer. Victims of fentanyl overdoses were often heroin abusers with "tracks" and the typical paraphenalia. The fentanyls as a class of drugs are highly potent synthetic narcotic analgesics with all the properties of opiates and opinoids.[9] However, the fentanyl molecule does not resemble heroin. Fentanyl is strictly a synthetic product while the morphine used in heroin production is derived from the opium poppy.

Beginning in the late 1970s with -methylfentanyl,[10] nine homologues and one analogue (excluding enantiomers) of fentanyl appeared in the illicit marketplace.[11] The degrees of potency vary among the fentanyl homologues and analogues. The potencies of the fentanyl derviatives are much higher than those of the parent compound. But the high potencies cited above explain why even dilute exhibits result in the deaths of users who believe they are dealing with heroin. Another name used by addicts when referring to Fentanyl and its derivatives is "China White". This term was first used to described substances seized and later identified as alpha-methylfentanyl in 1981.[12]

There are many fentanyl homologues and analogues . Because of the size and complexity of fentanyl derivatives, the interpretation of IR, MS, and NMR spectral data prove very valuable in elucidating specific structural information required for the identification of the material.[13]

Several synthetic routes are possible. As shown in Figure 1.4.8.1a and 1.4.8.1 b, one of the methods requires that fentanyl precursor, N-(1-phenetyl)-4-piperidinlyl) analyine, be produced first . Alternatively, fentanyl can be produced by reacting phenethylamine and methylacrylate to produce the phenethylamine diester (see Figure 1.4.8.2)

1.4.9 PHENETHYLAMINES

The class of compounds with the largest number of individual compounds on the illicit drug market is the **Phenethylamines**. This class of compounds consists of a series of compounds having a phenethylamine skeleton. Phenethylamines are easily modified chemically by adding or changing substituents at various positions on the molecule. Phenethylamines fall into one of two categories in terms of physiological effects — these compounds are either stimulants or

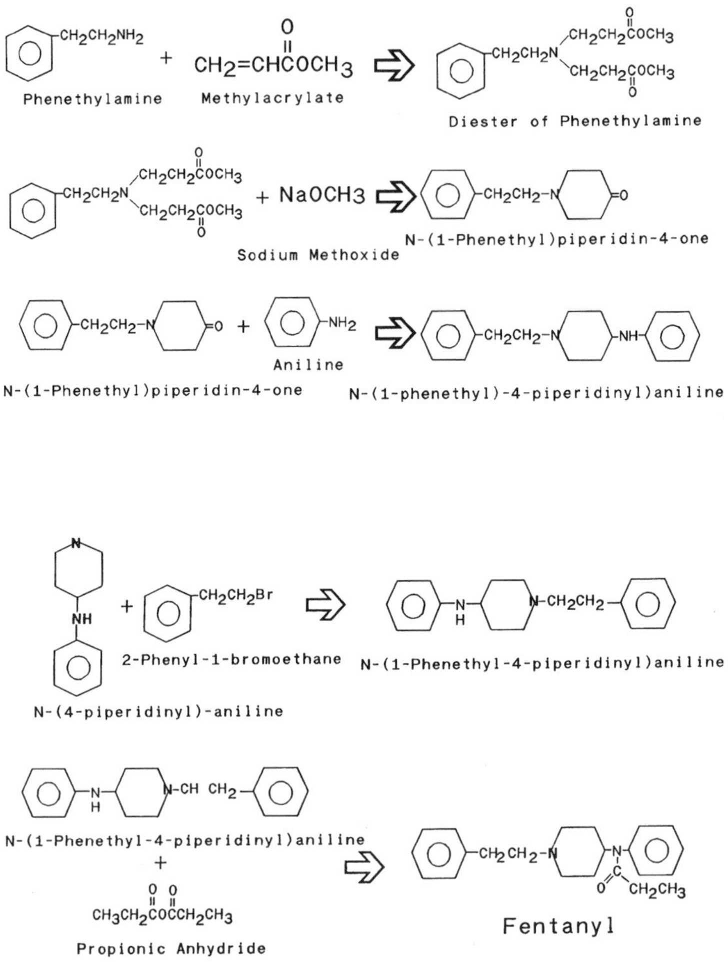

Figure 1.4.8.1 (a) Clandestine laboratory synthesis of fentanyl precursor. (b) Clandestine laboratory synthesis of fentanyl.

hallucinogens. Phenethylamines are suitable for clandestine laboratory production. The parent compound in the phenethylamine series is amphetamine, a central nervous system stimulant (CNS). With this molecule, the modifications begin by adding a methyl group to the nitrogen on the side chain. The resulting structure is the most popular clandestinely produced controlled substance in the U.S. in 1995 — methamphetamine (Figure 1.4.9).

Like amphetamine, methamphetamine is also a CNS stimulant. It is easily produced in clandestine laboratories using two basic synthetic routes. The traditional route used by "meth cooks" began with phenyl-2-propanone; however, when bulk sales were limited by law, most clandestine chemists began using ephedrine as a precursor (Figure 1.4.9.2), although, as illustrated in Figure 1.4.9.2, some now synthesize their own supply of phenyl-2-propanone, and still other routes are possible (Figure 1.4.9.3). New legislation has now limited bulk

Joseph P. Bono

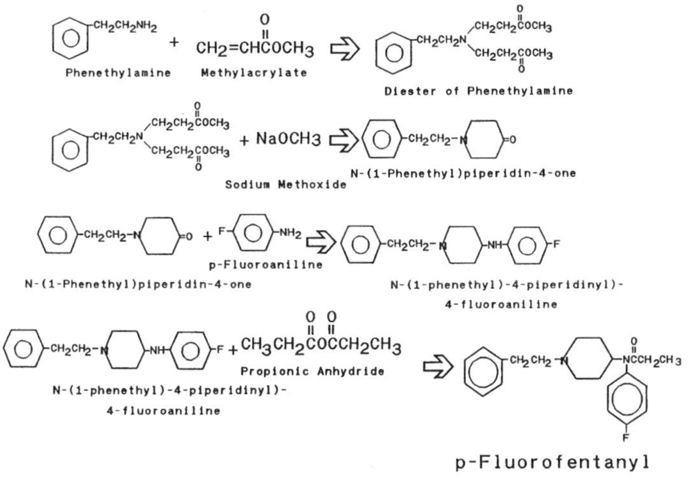

Figure 1.4.8.2 Clandestine laboratory synthesis of p-fluorofentanyl.

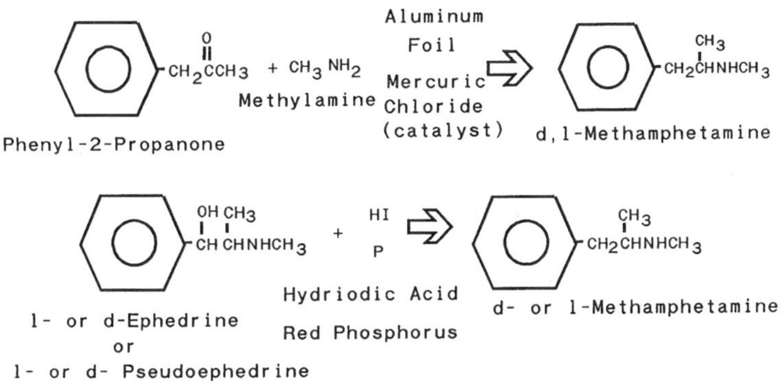

Figure 1.4.9 Clandestine laboratory synthesis of methamphetamine.

purchases of ephedrine in the U.S., though not in neigboring countries. And the chemical structure is such that further molecular synthetic modifications are easily accomplished resulting in a number of homologues and analogues. Few of the synthetic modifications of phenethylamines by clandestine laboratory "chemists" are novel. Most have been documented either in the scientific literature or in underground scientific literature. And the Internet now provides answers to anyone tenacious enough to search for a simple method to synthesize any analogue or homologue of a phenethylamine.

The parent compound of a second set of phenethylamine homologues and analogues (Figure 1.4.9.4) is 3,4-methylenedioxyamphetamine (MDA). This compound was first reported in the literature in 1910.[14] In the mid-1980s, the N-methyl analogue of MDA came into

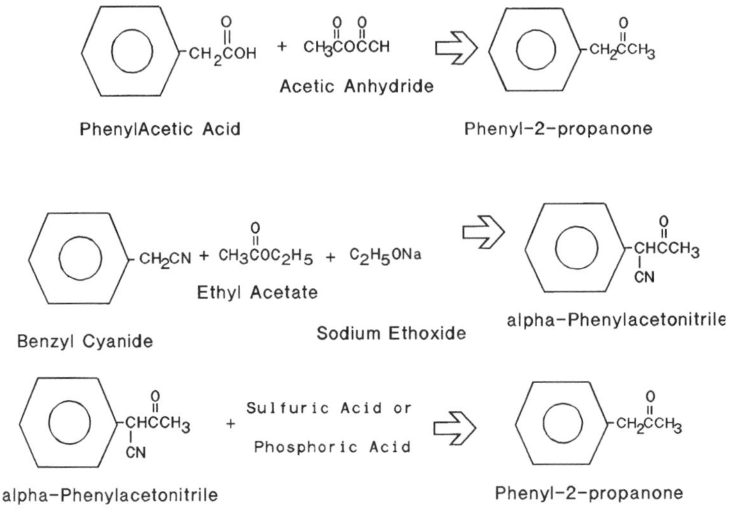

Figure 1.4.9.2 Clandestine laboratory synthesis of phenyl-2-propanone (p-2-p).

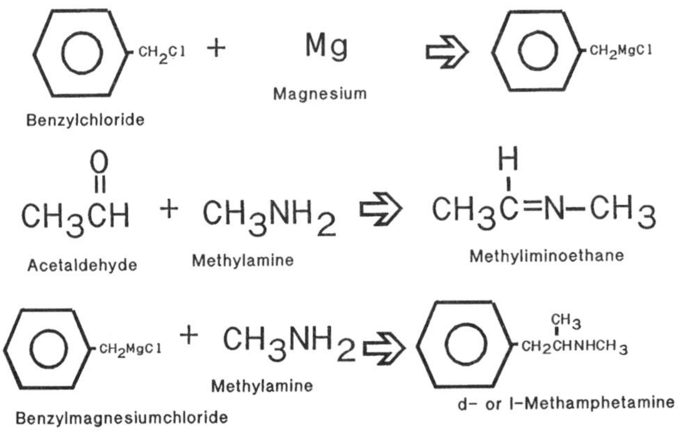

Figure 1.4.9.3 Clandestine laboratory synthesis of methamphetamine.

vogue and was known then and is still referred to as "Ecstasy". The synthesis of 3,4-methylenedioxymethamphetamine (MDMA) follows the same synthetic protocols as the less complicated phenethylamines. The clandestine laboratory operator or research chemist selectively adds one N-methy group, an N,N-dimethyl group, an N-ethyl group, an N-propyl, an N-isopropyl group, and so on. In 1985 the N-hydroxy MDA derivative was reported.[15] This

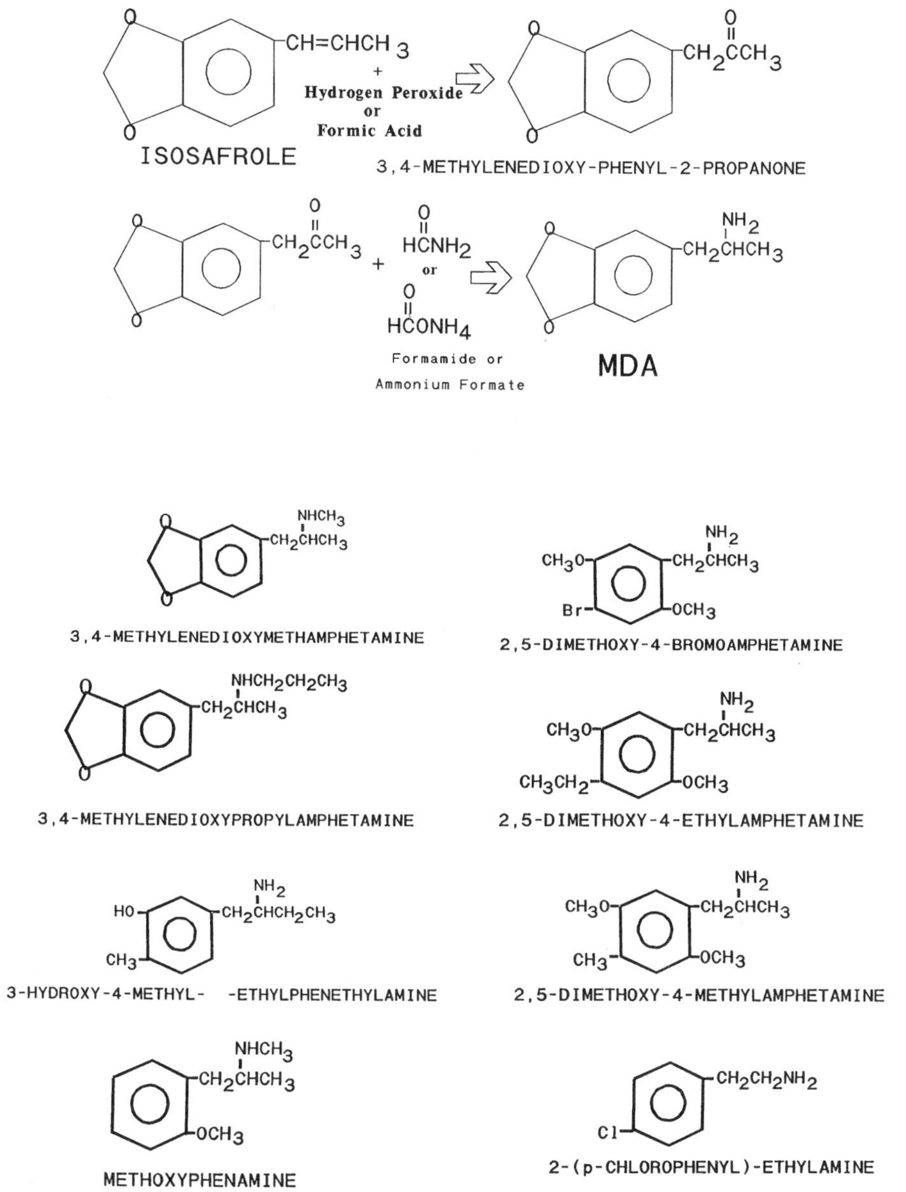

ISOSAFROLE

3,4-METHYLENEDIOXY-PHENYL-2-PROPANONE

Formamide or
Ammonium Formate

MDA

3,4-METHYLENEDIOXYMETHAMPHETAMINE

2,5-DIMETHOXY-4-BROMOAMPHETAMINE

3,4-METHYLENEDIOXYPROPYLAMPHETAMINE

2,5-DIMETHOXY-4-ETHYLAMPHETAMINE

3-HYDROXY-4-METHYL- -ETHYLPHENETHYLAMINE

2,5-DIMETHOXY-4-METHYLAMPHETAMINE

METHOXYPHENAMINE

2-(p-CHLOROPHENYL)-ETHYLAMINE

Figure 1.4.9.4 Clandestine laboratory synthesis of 3,4-methylenedioxyamphetamine (MDA).

was significant because here the modification involved the addition of a hydroxyl group as opposed to an alkyl substitution on the nitrogen. Clandestine laboratory synthesis of MDA and MDMA are shown in Figures 1.4.9.4 and 1.4.9.5

The identification of the phenethylamines in the laboratory requires great care because of the chemical and molecular similarities of the exhibits. IR combined with MS and NMR

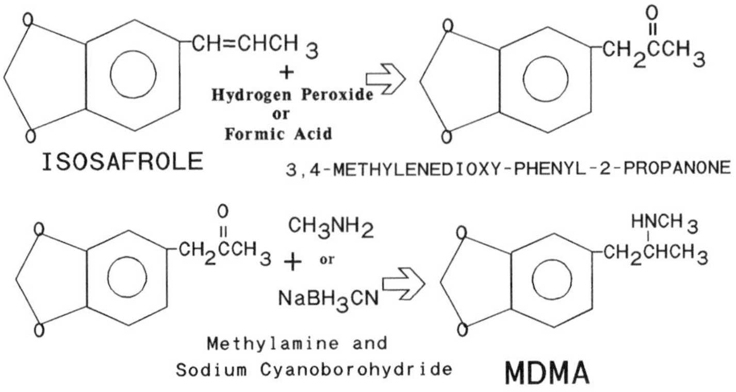

Figure 1.4.9.5 Clandestine laboratory synthesis of 3,4-methylenedioxymethamphetamine (MDMA)

spectrometry provide the most specificity in the identifications of phenethylamines in the forensic science laboratory.[15, 16] From a legal perspective, the laboratory identification of the phenethylamine is Part 1 in the forensic process. If prosecution is an option and the phenethylamine in question is not specified as a controlled substance under Public Law 91-513[17] or Part 1308 of the Code of Federal Regulations, another legal option is available.

In 1986, the U.S. Congress realized that the legal system was at a standstill in attempting to prosecute clandestine laboratory operators involved in molecular modification of phenethylamines and other homologues and analogues of controlled substances. The attempted closing of this loophole was the passage of the Controlled Substances Analogue and Enforcement Act of 1986.[18]

1.4.10 METHCATHINONE (CAT)

Methcathinone is a structural analogue of methamphetamine and cathinone Figure 1.4.10.1 and 1.4.10.2). It is potent and it, along with the parent compound, are easily manufactured. They are sold in the U.S. under the name CAT. It is distributed as a white to off-white chunky powdered material and is sold in the hydrochloride salt form. Outside of the U.S., methcathinone is known as ephedrone and is a significant drug of abuse in Russia and some of the Baltic States.[19]

Methcathinone was permanently placed in Schedule I of the Controlled Substances Act in October 1993. Prior to its scheduling, two federal cases were effectly prosecuted in Ann Arbor and Marquette, Michigan, utilizing the analogue provision of the Controlled Substances Analogue and Enforcment Act of 1986.

1.4.11 CATHA EDULIS (KHAT)

Khat consists of the young leaves and tender shoots of the Catha Edulis plant that is chewed for its stimulant properties.[20] *Catha edulis*, a species of the plant family Celastraceae, grows in eastern Africa and southern Arabia. Its effects are similar to the effects of amphetamine. The active ingredients in Khat are cathinone [(-)-a-aminopropiophenone] , a Schedule I controlled substance which is quite unstable, and cathine [(+)-norpseudoephedrine] a Schedule IV

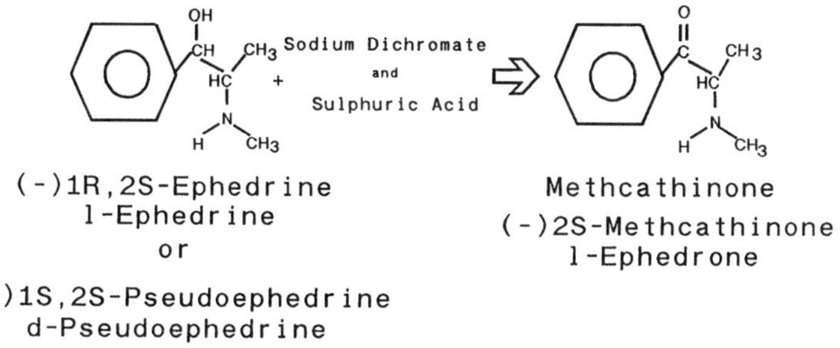

Figure 1.4.10.1 Clandestine laboratory synthesis of methcathinone.

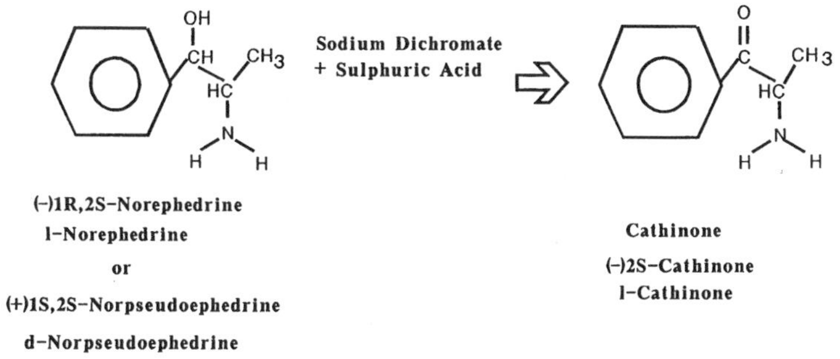

Figure 1.4.10.2 Clandestine laboratory synthesis of cathinone.

controlled substance. The identification of cathinone in the laboratory presents problems because of time and storage requirements to minimize degradation.[21] Some of the decomposition or transformation products of Catha edulis are norpseudoephedrine, norephedrine, 3,6-dimethyl-2,5- diphenylpyrazine, and 1-phenyl-1,2-propanedione.[22]

REFERENCES

1. *Drugs of Abuse*, U.S. Department of Justice, Drug Enforcement Administration, 1989, p. 49.
2. Kilmer, S.D., The isolation and identification of lysergic acid diethylamide (LSD) from sugar cubes and a liquid substrate, *J. Forensic Sci.*, 39: 860-862, 1994.
3. Feldman, H.W., Agar, M.H., and Beschner, G.M., Eds., *Angel Dust, An Ethanographic Study of PCP Users*, 1979, p.8.
4. Henderson, G.L., Designer drugs: Past history and future prospects, *J. Forensic Sci.*, 33: 569-575, 1988.

5. Angelos, S.A., Raney, J.K., Skoronski, G.T., and Wagenhofer, R.J., The Identification of Unreacted Precursors, Impurities, and By-Products in Clandestinely Produced Phencyclidine Preparations, *J. Forensic Sci.,* 35: 1297-1302, 1990.
6. Smialek, J.E., Levine, B., Chin, L., Wu, S.C., and Jenkins, A.J., A fentanyl epidemic in Maryland 1992, *J. Forensic Sci.,* 3:159-164, 1994.
7. Janssen, P.A.J., U.S. Patent 316400, 1965.
8. Henderson, G.L., The fentanyls, *American Association for Clinical Chemistry in-Service Training and Continuing Education,* 12(2), 5-17, Aug. 1990.
9. Henderson, *Designer,* p. 570.
10. Riley, R.N. and Bagley, J.R., *J. Med. Chem.,* 22:1167-1171.
11. Cooper, D., Jacob, M., and Allen, A., Identification of Fentanyl Derivatives, *J. Forensic Sci.,* 31: 511-528, 1986.
12. Kram, T.C., Cooper, D.A., and Allen, Behind the identification of China White," *Analytical Chem,* 53:1379-1386, 1981.
13. Cooper, *Identification,* p. 513.
14. Mannich, C. and Jacobsohn, W., Hydroxyphenylalkylamines and Dihydroxyphenylalkylamines, *Berichte,* 43:189-197, 1910.
15. Dal Cason, T.A., The characterization of some 3,4-methylenedioxyphenyl- isopropylamine (MDA) analogues, *J. Forensic Sci.,* 34:928-961, 1989.
16. Bost, R.O., 3,4-methylenedioxymethamphetamine (MDMA) and other amphetamine derivatives, *J. Forensic Sci.,* 33:576-587, 1988.
17. Comprehensive drug abuse prevention and control act of 1970, Public Law 91-513, 91st Congress, 27 Oct. 1970.
18. Controlled substance analogue and enforcement act of 1986, Public Law 99-570, Title I, Subtitle E, 99th Congress, 27 Oct. 1986.
19. Zhingel, K.Y., Dovensky, W., Crossman, A., and Allen, A., Ephedrone: 2- methylamino-1-phenylpropan-1-one (jell), *J. Forensic Sci.,* 36: 915-920, 1991.
20. Cath edulis (khat): Some Introductory Remarks," *Bulletin on Narcotics,* 32:1-3, 1980.
21. Lee, M.M., The identification of cathinone in khat (Catha edulis): A time study, *J. Forensic Sci.,* 40:116-121, 1995.
22. Szendrei, K., The chemistry of khat, *Bull. Narcotics,* 32, 5-34, 1980.

1.4.12 ANABOLIC STEROIDS

1.4.12.1 Regulatory History

In recent years anabolic steroid abuse has become a significant problem in the U.S. There are two physiological responses associated with anabolic steroids: **androgenic activity** induces the development of male secondary sex characteristics; **anabolic activity** promotes the growth of various tissues including muscle and blood cells. The male sex hormone testosterone is the prototype anabolic steroid. Individuals abuse these drugs in an attempt to improve athletic performance or body appearance. The more common agents are shown in Figure 1.4.12.1.

Black market availability of anabolic steroids has provided athletes and bodybuilders with a readily available supply of these drugs. Both human and veterinary steroid preparations are found in the steroid black market. Anabolic steroid preparations are formulated as tablets, capsules, and oil- and water-based injectable preparations. There is also a thriving black market for preparations that are either counterfeits of legitimate steroid preparations, or are simply bogus.

Control of Steroids

In 1990, the U.S. Congress passed the Anabolic Steroid Control Act. This act placed anabolic steroids, along with their salts, esters, and isomers, as a class of drugs, into Schedule III of the

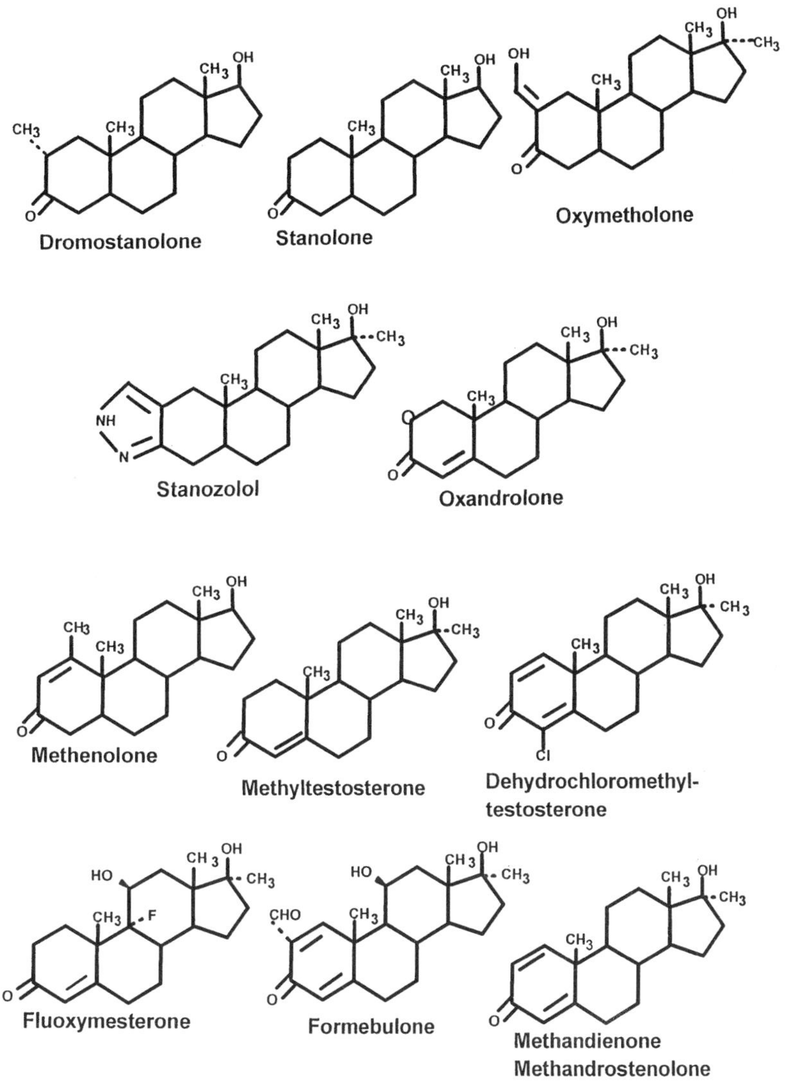

Figure 1.4.12.1 Common agents.

Federal Controlled Substances Act (CSA). This law provided 27 names of steroids that were specifically defined under the CSA as anabolic steroids. This list, which is provided in the *Federal Code of Regulations* is reproduced below.

1. Boldenone
2. Chlorotestosterone
3. Clostebol
4. Dehydrochlormethyltestosterone
5. Dihydrotestosterone
6. Drostanolone
7. Ethylestrenol
8. Fluoxymesterone
9. Formebolone
10. Mesterolone
11. Methandienone
12. Methandranone
13. Methandriol
14. Methandrostenolone
15. Methenolone
16. Methyltestosterone
17. Mibolerone
18. Nandrolone

19 Norethandrolone	23. Stanolone
20. Oxandrolone	24. Stanozolol
21. Oxymesterone	25. Testolactone
22. Oxymetholone	26. Testosterone

27. Trenbolone

Unfortunately, the list contains three sets of duplicate names (chlorotestosterone and Clostebol; dihydrotestosterone and stanolone; and methandrostenolone and methandienone) as well as one name (methandranone) for a drug that did not exist. So, the actual number of different steroids specifically defined under the law as anabolic steroids is 23, not 27. Realizing that the list of 23 substances would not be all inclusive, Congress went on to define within the law the term "anabolic steroid" to mean "any drug or hormonal substance, chemically or pharmacologically related to testosterone (other than estrogens, progestins, and corticosteroids) and that promote muscle growth".

The scheduling of anabolic steroids has necessitated forensic laboratories to analyze exhibits containing steroids. In those cases involving the detection of one or more of the 23 steroids specifically defined as anabolic steroids under the law, questions of legality are not likely to arise. However, when a steroid is identified that is not specifically defined under the law, it becomes necessary to further examine the substance to determine if it qualifies as an anabolic steroid under the definition of such a substance under the CSA. The forensic chemist must positively identify the steroid and convey to the pharmacologist the entire structure of the steroid. It then becomes the responsibility of the pharmacologist to determine the pharmacological activity, including effects on muscle growth, of the identified steroid.

1.4.12.2 Structure Activity Relationship

The pharmacology of the identified steroid may be evaluated in at least two ways. The first, and most important way, is to examine the scientific, medical, and patent literature for data on the pharmacological effects of the steroid. Over the years, numerous steroids have been examined in animal and/or human studies for anabolic/androgenic activity. It is possible that the identified steroid will be among that group of steroids. The second method is to evaluate possible pharmacological activity using **structure-activity relationships**. Such analysis is based on the assumption of a relationship between the structure of the steroid and its pharmacological effects. Small alterations of chemical structure may either enhance, diminish, eliminate, or have no effect on the pharmacological activity of the steroid. The structure-activity relationships of androgens and anabolic steroids have been reviewed extensively.[1,2]

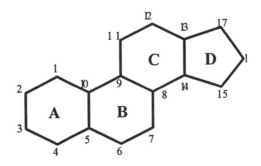

Figure 1.4.12.2 Cyclopentanoperhydrophenanthrene.

Extensive studies of the structure-activity relationships of anabolic/androgenic steroids have demonstrated that the following structural attributes are necessary for maximal androgenic and anabolic effects: rings A and B must be in the *trans* configuration;[3] hydroxy function at C17 must be in the ß conformational state;[5,6] and high electron density must be present in the area of C_2 and C_3.[7] The presence of a keto or hydroxl group at position 3 in the A-ring usually enhances androgenic and anabolic activity, but it is not absolutely necessary for these effects.[7] A few examples of structural alterations that enhance anabolic activity include: removal of the C-19 methyl group;[8] methyl groups at the 2a and 7a positions;[9,10] a flourine at the 9a position; or a chlorine at the 4a position.[10,11] To make it easier to visualize where these modifications are made in the ring structure, a numbered steroid skeletal ring structure, namely the cyclopentanoperhydrophenanthrene ring, is shown in Figure 1.4.12.2.

It is essential to understand that structure-activity analysis can only predict whether or not a steroid is likely to produce androgenic/anabolic effects. It then becomes necessary to examine the steroid in the laboratory to determine whether the prediction is, in fact, true. It is also important to note that numerous studies performed over the years and designed to separate androgenic activity from anabolic activity have failed to obtain such a separation of pharmacological effect. That is, steroids found to possess androgenic activity also have anabolic activity and vice versa. An examination of the scientific and medical literature reveals that there are, indeed, additional steroids that are not specifically listed in the law but which do, based upon available data, probably produce androgenic/anabolic effects. A listing of some of these steroids is provided below.

Androisoaxazole	Mestanolone
Bolandiol	Methyltrienolone
Bolasterone	Norbolethone
Bolenol	Norclostebol
Flurazebol	Oxabolone Cypionate
Mebolazine	Quinbolone
Mesabolone	Stenbolone

1.4.12.3 Forensic Analysis

For the forensic chemist, when a steroid is tentatively identified, an additional problem arises, namely obtaining an analytical standard. Many products found in the illicit U.S. market are commercially available only outside of the U.S. Locating and making contact with a foreign distributor is one problem. Requesting and then receiving a legitimate standard is another problem. The expense incurred in obtaining these standards can be quite high. Once the standard has been received, authentication then enters the analytical process. If a primary standard is unavailable, an optimized analytical process presents a real problem. Fortunately, most steroids received by forensic science laboratories are labeled directly or have labeled packaging. So a manufacturer can be identified, and there is a starting point for the chemist in confirming the material as a particular steroid.

There are no known color tests, crystal tests, or TLC methods which are specific to anabolic steroids. Screening can be accomplished by GLC or HPLC. GLC sometimes presents a problem because of thermal decomposition in the injection port thereby resulting in several peaks. The steroid will not always be the largest peak. On-column injection will usually solve this problem. However, oil-base steroids rapidly foul or degrade GC columns. Samples in oils can be extracted with methanol/water 9:1 prior to injection onto a GC. Retention times for some anabolic steroids are quite long and nearly triple or quadruple that of heroin. Recognizing that several anabolic steroids are readily oxidized in polar, protic solvents vs. halogenated hydrocarbons, screening and analysis must be accomplished as soon as possible after isolation and dilution.

GC/MS does provide definitive spectra; however, different MS systems may provide differences in the spectra for the same steroid. These differences can be traced to the quality of the MS source and the injection liner, thermal decomposition products, and induced hydration reactions related to high source temperatures set by the MS. C^{13}NMR is the most rigorous identification technique. The limitation here is the need for pure samples and high sample concentrations. Identification by infrared alone can result in problems due to polymorphism. This can be minimized by ensuring that the sample and standard are recrystallized from the same solvent.

Ideally, all anabolic steroids should be identified using two analytical methodologies which yield the same conclusions. The collection of a library of analytical data on different anabolic steroids is essential for the subsequent identification of steroids sent to the laboratory. An ability to interpret mass spectral data will be important in making an identification in so far as determining a molecular formula. Interpreting NMR data will be important in determining how substitutents are attached to the parent steroid ring structure.

It should be noted that selected steroids, such as testosterone, nandrolone, methenolone, boldenone, methandriol, and trenbolone, will often be encountered by the laboratory, not as the parent drug, but instead as an ester. The type of ester will be dependent upon the particular steroid. For example, nandrolone is primarily found as a decanoate, laurate, or phenpropionate ester. Testosterone, although it is found as a parent drug, is actually most commonly encountered as the propionate, enanthate, cypionate, decanoate, isocaproate, or undecanoate esters. Less commonly encountered testosterone esters include the acetate, valerate, and undecylenate esters. Methenolone is almost always found in either the acetate or enanthate esterified form.

Upon reaching the forensic science laboratory, steroid preparations will be handled differently depending on the way each preparation is formulated. Tablets can be handled by finely grinding and extracting with chloroform or methanol. Aqueous suspensions can be handled by dilution/solution with methanol for HPLC screening or by extraction with chloroform for GC screening. Oils require a more specialized extraction which is outlined below:

1. 1 ml of oil is mixed with 10 mls of methanol/water 9:1 and the mixture is allowed to sit overnight at 0°C.
2. Methanol water mixture is removed by evaporating to dryness under a stream of nitrogen at 60°C.
3. The resulting solid is subjected directly to an IR analysis or taken up in an appropriate solvent for MS or NMR analysis.
4. Exhibits containing mixtures of anabolic steroids require semi-prep scale HPLC for rigorous isolation and identification.
5. Isocratic or gradient HPLC is recommended for quantitation of anabolic steroids.

What steroids have been the most predominate in the United States in the past few years? From January 1990 to October 1994, the following steroids or their esters have been identified by DEA laboratories.

This list provides an objective evaluation of what this chemist has encountered in the not too distant past. The data on these particular steroids should form the basis of a reference collection for comparison with future submissions.

Steroids or esters of a steroid	Numbers of Cases	Exhibits
Testosterone	260	882
Nandrolone	140	244
Methenolone	99	189
Methandrostenolone	76	158
Oxymetholone	67	103
Stanozolol	61	115
Fluoxymesterone	54	7
Methyltestosterone	48	75
Boldenone	24	28
Mesterolone	21	22
Oxandrolone	16	21
Trenbolone	13	20
Methandriol	10	8
Drostanolone	6	7
Mibolerone	4	7
Stanolone	2	2
Testolactone	1	1

ACKNOWLEDGMENT

The author wishes to acknowledge the assistance of Dr. James Tolliver, Pharmacologist, of the DEA Office of Diversion Control, for collaborating in the preparation of this manuscript.

REFERENCES

1. Counsell, R.E. and Klimstra, P.D., Androgens and anabolic agents, in *Medicinal Chemistry* 3rd ed., Burger, A., Ed., Wiley-Interscience, New York, 1970, 923.
2. Vida, J.A., *Androgens and Anabolic Agents: Chemistry and Pharmacology*, Academic Press, United Kingdom, 1969.
3. Huggins, C., Jensen, E.V., and Cleveland, A.S., Chemical structure of steroids in relation to promotion of growth of the vagina and uterus of the hypophysectomized rat, *J. Exp. Med.*, 100, 225-246, 1954.
4. Gabbard, R.B. and Segaloff, A., Facile preparation of 17 beta-hydroxy-5 beta-androstan-3- one and its 17 alpha-methyl derivative, *J. Organic Chem.*, 27, 655, 1962.
5. Kochakian, C.D. Recent progress in hormonal research, 1, 177, 1948.
6. Kochakian, C.D., *Am. J. Physiol.*, 160, 53, 1950.
7. Bowers, A., Cross, A.D., Edwards, J.A., Carpio, H., Calzada, M.C., and Denot, E., *J. Med. Chem.*, 6, 156, 1963.
8. Hershberger L.G., Shipley, E.G., and Meyer, R.K., *Proc. Soc. Experiment. Biol. Med.*, 83, 175. 1953.
9. Counsell, R.E., Kimstra, P.D., and Colton, F.B., Anabolic agents, derivatives of 5 alpha-androst-1-ene, *J. Organic Chem.*, 27, 248, 1962.
10. Sala G. and Baldratti, G., Proc. Soc. Experiment. Biol. Med., 95, 22, 1957.
11. Backle, R.M., *Brit. Med. J.*, 1, 1378, 1959.

1.5 LEGITIMATE PHARMACEUTICAL PREPARATIONS

The Controlled Substances Act (CSA) of 1970 created a closed system for the production and distribution of legitimately manufactured controlled substances. The CSA includes contingencies to regulate the domestic commerce, importation, and exportation of these pharmaceutical preparations. Even with all of the controls that are in place, legitimate pharmaceuticals intended to help those in need are diverted onto the illegitimate market. Most of the diversion of these pharmaceuticals occurs at the retail rather than the wholesale level.

The analysis of pharmaceutical preparations in the forensic science laboratory is one of the most straightforward types of analysis. These samples are usually recognizable by their labels which usually include the manufacturers' logo and name. There are some samples that even have the name of the product inscribed on the tablet or capsule. In those instances where the manufacturer's logo is not recognized, the *Physician's Desk Reference* (PDR) is a readily available source of information which includes photographs and descriptions of the product along with information of the formulation. Another source of this information is the *Logo Index for Tablets and Capsules.*[1] This particular text lists data including inscriptions on most known products including generics. After the tablet or capsule has been tentatively identified in a reference text, it is the responsibility of the forensic chemist to conduct a series of analyses to verify the presence of a controlled substance. This verification process will usually consist of many of the same analytical processes utilized in the analysis and evaluation of any controlled substance.

1.5.1 BENZODIAZEPINES

The benzodiazepines form one of the largest classes of abused pharmaceuticals. These products are sedative/hypnotics, tranquilizers, and anti-anxiety drugs and they produce a calming effect and are often prescribed as tranquilizers. The drugs in this class are numerous and are included under Schedule IV control because while they do have a potential for abuse, there are recognized medical benefits that are both physiological and psychological. The most frequently diverted and abused benzodiazepines are alprazolam (Xanax®) and diazepam (Valium®). Other frequently abused benzodiazepines are lorazepam (Activan®), triazolam (Halcion®), chlordiazepoxide (Librium®), flurazepam (Dalmane®), and temazepam (Restoril®). Another phenomenon that has been noted for several years is the abuse of legitimate pharmaceuticals in conjunction with illicit controlled substances. Clonazepam (Klonipin®) is just such a product. It is an anxiety reducer that is used in combination with methadone and heroin.

There has been a recent influx of flunitrazepam (Rohypnol®) into the Gulf Coast and other areas of the U.S. This product is a benzodiazepine manufactured principally in Colombia, Mexico, and Switzerland. It is also manufactured in lesser amounts in Argentina, Brazil, Peru, Uruguay, and Venezuela. It is neither manufactured nor marketed legally in the U.S. This is a powerful drug reported to be 7 to 10 times more potent than diazepam.

1.5.2 OTHER CENTRAL NERVOUS SYSTEM DEPRESSANTS

The oldest of the synthetic sleep inducing drugs dates back to 1862. Chloral hydrate is marketed as a soft gelatinous capsule under the name Noctec® , and controlled under Schedule V. Its popularity declined after the introduction of barbiturates. Barbiturates are the drugs prescribed most frequently to induce sedation. Roughly 15 derivatives of barbituric acid are currently in use to calm nervous conditions. In larger doses they are used to induce sleep.

The actions of barbiturates fall into four categories. Some of the ultrashort acting barbiturates are hexobarbital (Sombulex®), methohexital (Brevital®), thiamylal (Surital®), and thio-

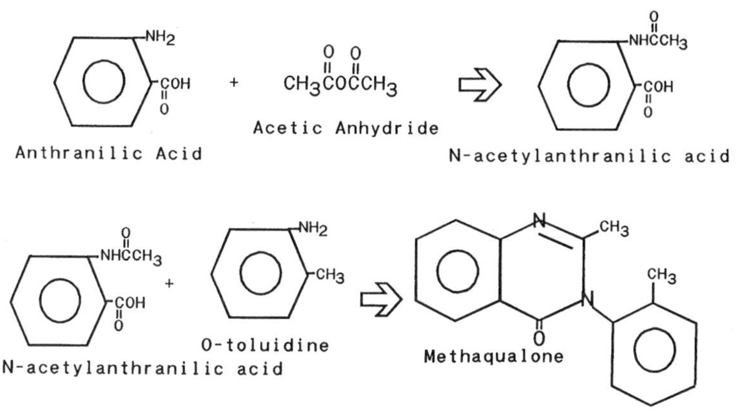

Figure 1.5.2 Clandestine laboratory synthesis of methaqualone.

pental (Pentothal®). Short-acting and intermediate-acting barbiturates include pentobarbital (Nembutal®), secobarbital (Seconal®), and amobarbital (Amytal®). These three drugs have been among the most abused barbituric acid derivatives. Also included in these categories but not as abused are butabarbital (Butisol®), talbutal (Lotusate®), and aprobarbital (Alurate®). The last category is the long-acting barbiturates. These drugs are used medicinally as sedatives, hypnotics, and anticonvulsants. The group includes phenobarbital (Luminal®), mephobarbital or methylphenobarbital (Mebaral®), and metharbital (Gemonil®).

Three other CNS depressants that have been marketed as legitimate pharmaceutical preparations and have a history of abuse include glutethimide (Doriden®), methaqualone (Quaalude®, Parest®, Mequin®, Optimil®, Somnafac®, Sopor®, and Mandrax®), and meprobamate (Miltown®, Equanil®, and SK-Bamate®). The route for the clandestine synthesis of methaqualone is shown in Figure 1.5.2.

1.5.3 NARCOTIC ANALGESICS

When one thinks of opium-like compounds, morphine and heroin immediately come to mind. However, there is another subset of this class of compounds which includes pharmaceutical preparations used to relieve pain and are purchased legitimately or illegitimately from a pharmacy with a prescription. Frequently used pharmaceutical opiates include oxycodone (Percodan®), hydromorphone (Dilaudid®), hydrocodone (Tussionex® and Vicodin®), pentazocine (Talwin®), and codeine combinations such as Tylenol® with Codeine and Empirin® with Codeine. All of these compounds are addictive.

Along with Tylenol® with Codeine and Empirin® with Codeine, which are Schedule III controlled substances, codeine is also available in combination with another controlled substance (butalbital) and sold under the trade name of Fiorinal® with Codeine. It is available with acetaminophen in Phenaphen®. Codeine is available in liquid preparations under the manufacturers' names Cosanyl®, Robitussin A-C®, Cheracol®, Cerose®, and Pediacof®. Because of the amounts of codeine in these preparations, they are controlled under Schedule V. There are also pharmaceutical codeine tablets which contain no drug other than codeine and are controlled under Schedule II.

While the compounds listed above are considered opiates, there is another class of compounds also classified as narcotic, but with synthetic origins. Meperidine (Demerol®) is one of the most widely used analgesics for the relief of pain. Methadone (Amidone® and Dolophine®) is another of these synthetic narcotics. It was synthesized during World War II by German scientists because of a morphine shortage. Although it is chemically unlike morphine or heroin, it produces many of the same effects and is often used to treat narcotic addictions.

Dextropropoxyphene is one of those drugs which falls into one of two controlled substance schedules. When marketed in dosage form under the trade names Darvon®, Darvocet®, Dolene®, or Propacet®, dextropropoxyphene is a Schedule IV controlled substance. However, when marketed in bulk non-dosage forms, dextropropoxyphene is a Schedule II controlled substance. The significance here is that the penalties for possession of a Schedule II controlled substance are usually much greater than for possession of a Schedule IV controlled substance.

1.5.4 CENTRAL NERVOUS SYSTEM STIMULANTS

Amphetamine (Benzedrine® and Biphetamine®), dextroamphetamine (Dexedrine^R), and methamphetamine (Desoxyn®) are three of the best known CNS stimulants and were prescribed for many years to treat narcolepsy. At one time, these drugs were sold over the counter without a prescription. For many years these drugs were sold as appetite suppressants. Their availability in the form of prescription drugs has all but been eliminated except under the close scrutiny of a physician. However, the clandestine laboratory production of methamphetamine in the forms of a powder or granular material has been one of the major problems facing law enforcement personnel in the past 20 or so years in the U.S.

Phenmetrazine (Preludin®) and methylphenidate (Ritalin®) are two other CNS stimulants which have patterns of abuse similar to the amphetamine and methamphetamine products. In recent years, a number of pharmaceutical products have appeared on the market as appetite suppressants and as replacements for the amphetamines. These anorectic drugs include benzphetamine (Didrex®), chlorphentermine (Pre-Sate®), clortermine (Voranil®), diethylpropion (Tenuate® and Tepanil®), fenfluramine (Pondimin®), mazindol (Sanorex® and Mazanor®), phendimetrazine (Plegine®, Bacarate®, Melifat®, Statobex®, and Tanorex®), and phentermine (Ionamin® , Fastin®, and Adipex-P®).

1.5.5 IDENTIFYING GENERIC PRODUCTS

There are a number of generic products on the market which are legitimate pharmaceutical preparations. These products will usually contain the active ingredient of the brand name product, but at the same time have a different formulation in the way of diluents and binders. These products are cataloged in various publications. When these products are encountered in the forensic science laboratory, the analyst will usually make a preliminary identification using one of the many publications listing the tablet or capsule's description and the code number that appears in the face of the product. This "preliminary" identification affords a starting point in the analytical process. The analyst will then proceed using the standard chemical techniques and instrumental methods to make an independent identification.

REFERENCE

1. Franzosa, E.S. and Harper W.W., *The Logo Index for Tablets and Capsules,* 3rd ed., GPO, 1995, 392-2401.

1.6 UNIQUE IDENTIFY FACTORS

1.6.1 PACKAGING LOGOS

There are unique factors associated with controlled substance examinations which involve packaging. Heroin and cocaine are usually imported into the U.S. clandestinely packaged. Sometimes this packaging takes the form of legitimate household or commercial products which have been hollowed out or have natural crevices into which drugs can be stored for shipment. These kinds of packages will usually be transported via commercial carriers to distributors who will reclaim the drugs and repackage them for street distribution. Sometimes drugs are shipped via human beings who store packages in body cavities, or swallow small packages in order to clear customs checks at points of entry. In these cases, it is not unusual for the packaging to break while in the body of the person transporting the drug. This usually results in severe injury or death.

Another common way of transporting controlled substances is to package the controlled substance in brick-size, 1 kg, packages for shipment to the U.S. This is often the case with shipments of heroin, cocaine, and marijuana, and the packages are usually wrapped in paper or tape. Sometimes a logo, serving as a type of trademark for the illicit distributor, will be affixed. Logos can take the form of any number of designs . They are applied using a stamping or printing device. Some commonly encountered designs include, but are not limited to, animals, symbols from Greek mythology, replications of brand name product logos, replications of the names of polictical figures, cartoon characters, and numbers.

When a number of these logos are encountered, examinations can be conducted to determined whether two logos have a common source. If the examiner determines that two logos are the same, and were produced using the same printing or stamping device, then the two packages must have originated from the same source. This kind of information is especially useful in tracking distribution networks.

Glassine envelopes measuring approximately 1 in. × 2 in. are commonly used to distribute heroin "on the street" directly to the primary user. More often than not, these glassine envelopes have rubber stamped images affixed. These rubber stamped images take many forms. Cartoon characters or words with social implications are common. The examiner can determine whether these rubber stamped images have a commonality of source and use this information to track distribution patterns of heroin within a geographical area.

1.6.2 TABLET MARKINGS AND CAPSULE IMPRINTS

Counterfeit tablets and capsules, which closely resemble tablets and capsules of legitimate pharmaceutical companies, are readily available on the clandestine market. They generally contain controlled substances that have been formulated in such a way as to mimic legitimate pharmaceutical preparations.[1] They are designed to be sold either on the clandestine or the legitimate market. These counterfeits sometimes are expertly prepared and closely resemble the pharmaceutical products that they are designed to represent. At other times, they are poorly made, inadequate representations of the products they are purported to represent.

The examiner in these types of cases will evaluate the suspected tablets or capsules by examining both the class and individual characteristics of the products. Legitimate products are usually prepared with few significant flaws on tablet or capsule surfaces. The lettering or numbering will be symmetrical in every way. The tablet surfaces will have minimal chips or gouges and will usually be symmetrical. The homogeneity of the tablet will be of the highest quality. Counterfeits will usually have tableting flaws. These flaws can take the forms of imperfect lettering or numbering, rough surfaces, or inconsistencies in the tablet formulation. This can result in different hardening characteristics of the tablet. Legitimate capsules will be highly symmetrical. The lettering or numbering will usually line up on both halves of the capsule.[2,3]

In recent years, methamphetamine and amphetamine tablets and capsules, crafted to mimic Dexedrine® and Benzedrine®, have been encountered with some frequency. These two products were distributed and used quite extensively on the legitimate market up until the 1970s. And while they are are still available commercially with a prescription, they have been controlled under Schedule II since 1972 and their legal distribution and useage in the medical community has become fairly limited. Counterfeit barbiturate, methaqualone, and benzodiazepine tablets, sometimes from documented clandestine source laboratories from 20 years ago, have been encountered in recent seizures. Counterfeit Quaalude®, Mandrax®, and Valium® tablets are examples of legitimate trademark products that have been the favorites of clandestine laboratory operators. The "look-alike" market was especially lucrative in the 1970s and 1980s and became a $50,000,000 a year industry.[4,5]

A unique problem, encountered with regularity up until 1975, involved the refilling of capsules. Legitimate capsules were diverted from legitimate manufacturing sources. The capsules were then emptied of their contents and refilled with some innocuous material, such as starch or baking soda, and sold. The original filling usually containing a controlled substance was then diverted for sale on the illicit market. These capsules can usually be identified by imperfections in their surface characteristics. There may be small indentations on the gelatinous surface of the capsule and fingerprints indicating excessive handling. The seal holding both halves of the capsule together will not be tight. And there will usually be traces of powder around the seal of the capsule. Refilling capsules by hand or by improvised mechanical devices is not easy and usually results in these visible powder residues. A more common problem today is the refilling of over-the-counter capsules with heroin for distribution at the retail level.

A similar problem that is encountered with some frequency in the forensic science laboratory is the pre-packaged syringe from a hospital which is labeled and supposed to contain an analgesic such as meperidine. Patients complains they are receiving no relief from the injection they have been given. The syringes are then sent to the laboratory for analysis. Not infrequently, they are found to contain water, substituted for the active drug by an addicted doctor or nurse.

Legitimate tablets and capsules from reputable manufacturers are formulated with specific diluents, binders, and lubricants. Stearic acid and palmitic acid are examples of materials frequently used to hold the tablets together. Using microscopy and microchemical techniques, an examiner can determine whether a tablet or capsule is legitimate by examining the chemical composition. By evaluating the diluents, binders, lubricants, and active chemical components both qualitatively and quantitatively, the examiner can determine whether the tablet or capsule is legitimate or a counterfeit. Counterfeits take three forms—sometimes a counterfeit will actually contain the controlled substance which the legitimate product would contain; it will contain another controlled substance which has been substituted for the labeled product; at other times, it may contain only fillers, binders, and some non-controlled medicinal product.

The most commonly counterfeited tablets are diazepam tablets which look very much like legitimate commercially prepared Valium® tablets. Counterfeit Mandrax® and Quaalude®, which were produced legitimately in the 1980s and contained methaqualone or diazepam, are still available on the illicit market in the 1990s. Counterfeit anabolic steroid tablets are the newest illicit products to hit the market. They are usually manufactured to look like products manufactured in Europe. Sometimes they actually contain an anabolic steroid (which may or may not be the product as labeled), and sometimes they contain innocuous materials such as cooking oils which look very much like injectable steroids.

Joseph P. Bono

Clandestinely manufactured controlled substances are often-times encountered. These products are usually in the form of tablets that are prepared using punch presses. These presses usually consist of tableting dies into which powder is placed and high pressure applied forming a molded tablet. When tablets from different seizures are examined, the class and individual characteristics can be compared to determine source commonality. Since many of these clandestine punch presses have more than one set of dies, successful matches become more problematic. There are salient differences in the individual characteristics of tablets from the same punch press operation where different sets of tableting dies are configured on multi-punch machines to simultaneously produce tablets. The examiner must demonstrate skill and patience in determining which set of dies from a punch press was responsible for a particular set of tablets. The punch presses dies will always have surface imperfections which are transferred to the tablets and can be used to determine source commonality. In recent years, these clandestine tabletting operations have been involved in the production of 3,4-methylenedioxymethamphetamine (MDMA) and 3,4-methylenedioxyethamphetamine (MDEA) tablets.

1.6.3 BLOTTER PAPER LSD

LSD has been available for years in the forms of small tablets (microdots), small gelatinous squares, clear plastic-like squares (window panes), powders or crystals, liquid, or in capsules. The most commonly encountered form of LSD available today is impregnated blotter paper. This LSD medium is prepared by dissolving the clandestinely produced LSD powder in an alcohol solution, and then spraying or soaking the paper with the solution. The alcohol solution used most frequently is EverClear®, a commercial ethyl alcohol product available in liquor stores. This LSD-impregnated paper is referred to as "blotter acid". It is usually distributed on sheets of paper perforated into 1/4 in. × 1/4 in. squares. These sheets of paper range in size to hold from 1 square up to 1000 squares. These sheets of blotter paper can be plain white or single colored with no design imprints. More often than not, there will be a brightly colored design on the paper. The design can be simple such as a black and white circle, or it can be extremely intricate. One such design was brightly colored and with a detailed depiction of the crucifixion of Jesus Christ. The design can cover each and every individual square of a 1000-perforated square sheet of paper, or one design can cover the entire sheet of blotter paper where each 1/4 in. × 1/4 in. perforation square makes up 1/1000 of the total design.

By examining the intricate designs on LSD blotter paper from different seizures, it is possible to determine whether there is a common source. Depending on the printing process and the quality of the image, the examiner may be able to characterize an exhibit as having originated from the image transfer process and a specific printing device. This ability to determine source commonality is most valuable in determining the origins of LSD exhibits seized from different parts of the world.

The processes described above are most valuable in linking seizures to a particular source. Investigators who are skillful and fortunate enough to seize printing or tableting devices even without the actual controlled substances can have their efforts rewarded by terminating a controlled substance production operation. A qualified scientific examiner has the opportunity to use these devices as standards and to search reference collections of tablets, capsules, LSD blotter paper designs, or heroin or cocaine packaging logos to determine possible associations to past seizures. When this happens, the opportunity to eliminate another source of illicit drug distribution becomes a possibility.

REFERENCES

1. Franzosa, E.S., Solid dosage forms: 1975-1983, *J. Forensic Sci.,* 30:1194-1205, 1985.
2. Eisenberg, W.V. and Tillson, A.H., Identification of counterfeit drugs, particularly barbiturates and amphetamines by microscopic, chemical, and instrumental techniques, *J. Forensic Sci.,* 11 529-551, 1966.
3. Tillson, A.H. and Johnson, D.W., Identification of drug and capsule evidence as to source, *J. Forensic Sci.,* 19: 873-883, 1974.
4. Crockett, J. and Franzosa, E., Illicit solid dosage forms: Drug trafficking in the United States, presented at the 6th Interpol Forensic Sciences Symposium in 1980.
5. Crockett, J. and Sapienza, F., Illicit solid dosage forms: Drug trafficking in the United States, presented at the 10th Interpol Forensic Sciences Symposium in 1983.

1.7 ANALYZING DRUGS IN THE FORENSIC SCIENCE LABORATORY

1.7.1 SCREENING TESTS

No other topic related to the identification of controlled substances causes as much controversy as testing specificity. Forensic science laboratories conduct two different categories of tests. Tests in the first category are called "screening tests". They include a series of tests used to make a preliminary determination of whether a particular drug or class of drugs is present. It must be emphasized that screening tests are not used to positively identify any drug. At best, screening tests can only be used to determine the possibility that members of a particular class of drug may be present. Some say that screening tests can result in "false positives", meaning that either the test indicates the possible presence of a controlled substance when none is present or that the test indicates the possible presence of one controlled substance when a different controlled substance is present. That should not be a problem, so long as it is understood that screening tests have very little if any specificity, and that a false positive test will only lead to more testing, not a false conclusion. The identification of any drug by a chemical analysis is a systematic process involving a progression from less specific methods to more specific methods. The most specific methods involve instrumental analyses. Properly trained scientists should know when a false positive is possible, and how to take steps to narrow the focus of the testing. The more tests used, the fewer the chances for error.

False negative screening tests also occur. Very weak or diluted samples containing controlled substances may yield a negative screening test. An example of this situation would be a 1% heroin sample cut with a brown powder. Testing this sample with Marquis Reagent, which contains sulfuric acid and formaldehyde, may result in a charring of the brown powder and subsequent masking of the bleeding purple color characteristic of an opium alkaloid. Weak or old reagents may also yield false negatives. Examiner fallibility or inexperience in discerning colors may also result in false negatives. The possibility of a false negative leads many examiners to conduct a series of screening tests or, when warranted, to progress directly to more narrowly focused screening tests.

Specificity is the key to the forensic identification of controlled substances. There is no one method that will work as a specific test for any and all exhibits at any and all times. The choice of which specific method one utilizes must be determined by the type of controlled substance, the concentration of the controlled substance in the sample, the nature of the diluents and adulterants, the available instrumentation, and the experience of the examiner. There is an ongoing debate as to whether one can achieve this scientific certainty by combining a series of non-specific tests. This will be discussed later in this section.

1.7.1.1 Physical Characteristics

Occassionaly an experienced forensic analyst can just look at an exhibit in a drug case and determine the probable nature of the substance. However, "probable natures" are not enough for an identification, and most examiners will usually conduct more than one test before reporting the presence of a controlled substance. The morphology of botanical substances such as marijuana and the peyote cactus are familiar enough to many laboratory analysts. Marijuana is one of those controlled substances which is examined with such frequency in the laboratory that a preliminary identification is probable based on the morphology of the botanical substance, gross physical appearance, texture, and odor. However, even after a microscopic examination of the cystolithic hairs using a micrcoscope, the modified Duquenois–Levine test is usually run to corroborate the identification. The peyote cactus with its button-like appearance is also unique. In a like manner, the identification of the opium poppy requires a confirmation of the morphine; and the identification of the pysilocibin mushroom requires an identification of the psilocybin or the psilocin.

The physical characteristics of these four agronomic substances might enable an expert witness with a background in plant taxonomy and botany to make an identification based solely on these characteristics. The forensic analyst relies on the physical characteristics and corroborating chemical examinations to identify these materials as controlled substances.

1.7.1.2 Color Tests

The color test is usually the first chemical examination examiners conduct after a package suspected of containing controlled substances is opened and weighed. Small amounts of the unknown material are placed in depressions in a porcelain spot plate or a disposable plastic or glass spot plate. Chemical reagents are then added to the depressions and the results noted: color changes, the way in which the color changes take place (flashing or bleeding), the rate at which the color changes take place, and the intensity of the final colors. The most common color reagents are the Marquis reagent for opium alkaloids, amphetamines, and phenethylamines such as MDA or MDMA; cobalt thyocyanate reagent for cocaine and phencyclidine (PCP); Dille-Koppanyi reagent for barbiturates; Duquenois reagent for marijuana; and Ehrlich's reagent for LSD. A more complete listing of these tests is available in the literature.[1] Many of these tests are multi-step and multi-component.

These color tests are designed as a starting place for the examiner in deciding how to proceed as the pyramid of focus narrows in forming a conclusion. Adulterants and diluents can also cause color changes and are sometimes said to be responsible for "false positives." The resulting color changes are not really false. They simply reflect the presence of a substance which is not the primary focus of the analytical scheme. Problems of "false negatives" and "false positives" are usually recognized very early in the analytical scheme, and they are resolved logically and rationally.

1.7.1.3 Thin Layer Chromatography

Thin-layer chromatography (TLC) is a separation technique. The method utilizes a glass plate which is usually coated evenly with a thin layer adsorbant. The most commonly used adsorbant is silica gel. A small amount of the sample is put into solution with a chemical solvent. A capillary pipet is then used to place a small amount of the liquid onto the TLC plate approximately 2 cm from the bottom of the plate. A second capillary pipet containing a small amount of a known controlled substance in solution is used to place a second spot on the plate usually next to, but not overlapping, the first spot.

The plate is then placed into a tank containing a solvent system which rises about 1 cm from the bottom of the tank. Through capillary action, the solvent will migrate up the plate, and the components of the unknown will usually separate as the solvent migrates. The separated components can usually be visualized using longwave or shortwave ultraviolet light, a chemical spray, or some combination of both. The distance each sample migrates is then divided by the distance the solvent in the tank migrates up the plate (know as the Rf value). The result is then compared to published values that have been established for pure samples of the abused drugs. If one of the components of the unknown migrates the same distance up the plate as the known, the examiner has another piece of corroborating information. If the unknown does not contain a component that migrates the same distance as the known, there are many explanations. Perhaps the known and unknown are not the same. Perhaps there is a component in the unknown solution which is binding the chemical of interest to the silica gel. The explanations for matches are numerous. The explanations for non-matches are just as numerous.

The literature is replete with values for drug/solvent migration ratios. However, these values can be affected by many factors, including the storage conditions of the TLC plates and solvent temperature. It is not uncommon for the Rf values in the laboratory to differ from those in the literature. The importance of a TLC analysis lies in its ability to separate components in a mixture. A match is another piece of corroborating information. A non-match can usually be explained.

Using TLC to identify marijuana, hashish, or hash oil is a much more complicated process than using it to identify other controlled substances.[2] The TLC analysis of cannabis exhibits results in a series of bands on the thin-layer plate. Depending on the solvent system, the number of bands can range from at least three to at least six bands.[3] Each band will have a specific color and lie at a specified place on the plate corresponding to the known cannabinoids in a standard marijuana, hashish, or THC sample.[4] The key point here is that this type of identification involves a specific chromatographic pattern as opposed to one spot where a known is compared directly with an unknown. Even with the increased specificity of a TLC analysis in the examination of cannabis or a cannabis derivative, a modified Duquenois–Levine test is suggested.

1.7.2 CONFIRMATORY CHEMICAL TESTS

1.7.2.1 Microcrystal Identifications

Microcrystal tests are conducted using a polarized light microscope and chemical reagents. These microscopic examinations are not screening tests. The analyst will usually place a small amount of the sample on a microscope slide and add a chemical reagent and note the formation of a specific crystal formation. These crystals are formed from specified reagents. There should be very little subjectivity in evaluating a microcrystal test.[5] Either the crystal forms or it does not form. If the appropriate crystal forms in the presence of the reagent, the drug is present. If the crystal does not form and the drug is present, the problem is usually one in which the drug concentration is too dilute, or the reagent has outlived its shelf life.

One disadvantage of microcrystal tests is the absence of a hard copy of what the analyst sees. Unless a photograph is taken of the crystal formation, the examiner cannot present for review documentation of what he saw under the microscope. Microcystal tests are an excellent way of evaluating the relative concentration of a drug in a sample to determine the kind of extraction technique for separation and further confirmation.

1.7.2.2 Gas Chromatography

Gas chromatography (GC) has been a standard operating procedure in forensic science laboratories for the past three decades. In this technique, a gaseous mobile phase is passed through a column containing a liquid coated, stationary solid, support phase. The most common form of GC uses a capillary column of a very fine diameter for separating the component of a mixture. The sample is usually put into solution using an organic solvent such as methanol. The liquid is then introduced into the injection port of the gas chromatograph using a fine needle syringe capable of delivering microliter quantities of the solution. The amount injected depends on the concentration of the sample. One microliter (one-one hundreth of a milliliter) of 1 mg of solute per l ml of solvent is a typical injection amount. The sample is vaporized in the heated injection port, and with the aid of a carrier gas travels through the long capillary column where the different components are separated. There are many different kinds of capillary columns with different internal coatings, lengths (which can vary from one foot up to tens of meters), and diameters (measured in micrometers). This separation is determined by the polarity and molecular size of each component. Each component exits the column onto a detector. A flame ionization detector (FID) is the most common detector used in most laboratories. Other types of less frequently encountered detectors include the nitrogen phosphorous detector and the electron capture detector.

As each component elutes from the column through the FID, a signal is generated which results in a "peak" on a recording device. The recorder is used to document the resulting data. This recorder is usually a part of a data station that not only generates a representation of the chromatogram on a monitor, but also controls instrument parameters and ensures the consistancy of the analysis. The peaks of interest are evaluated by their retention times (RT's) and by the areas under the peaks. The retention time data can be used either as confirmation of the probable identity of the substance generating the peak, or the data can be evaluated as screening information to determine the possible presence of a controlled substance . This RT data is compared to the retention time of a known standard injected onto the same column in the same instrument at the same temperature and rate flow conditions. The RTs of the known and the unknown should be almost the same within a very narrow window. The area under the peak can be used to quantitatively determine the relative concentration of the substance.

There are some disadvantages of GC. Retention times are not absolute and usually fall within a narrow window. Other compounds may fall within this same RT window. One way to overcome this problem is to analyze the same sample using a second capillary column with a different internal coating and to note its retention time as compared to the known standard. The values should be the same within a narrow RT window. A second disadvantage of GC is that some samples degrade in the injection liner at high temperatures and must be evaluated by using a derivatizing agent. This derivatizing agent is added to the drug and forms a molecular complex. The molecule complex remains intact as it passes from the injection port, through the column, and onto the detector.

GC by itself is a very powerful tool for the forensic analyst. Its most useful application today remains one in which it is interfaced with a mass spectrometer (mass selective detector) which serves as a detector and separate instrumental identification method unto itself. Gas chromatography/mass spectrometry will be discussed later in this section.

1.7.2.3 High Performance Liquid Chromatography (HPLC)

This chromatographic technique is also a separation technique, but with a bit more selectivity than GC. In HPLC, the mobile phase is a liquid and the stationary phase is a solid support or a liquid-coated solid support. In GC, a carrier gas is used to carry the sample through the chromatography column. In HPLC, a high pressure pump is used to carry the solvent containing the compound of interest through the column. Separation results from selective interactions between the stationary phase and the liquid mobile phase.[6] Unlike GC, the mobile phase plays a major role in the separation. HPLC can be used for the direct analysis of a wide spectrum of compounds and is not dependent on solute volatility or polarity. The operator need not worry about chemical changes in the molecule which can occur in GC due to thermal degradation.

HPLC chromatograms are evaluated based on retention time and area under the peak of interest. Retention time is not an absolute value, but a time within a narrowly defined window. The five basic parts of the liquid chromatograph include the solvent reservoir, the pump, the sample injection system, the column, and the detector. A recorder is used to document the resulting data. This recorder is usually a part of a data station which controls instrument parameters and ensures the consistancy of the analysis. The most common detectors are the ultraviolet/visible detector (UV/VIS), the florescence detector, the electrochemical detector, the refractive index detector, and the mass spectrometer. The UV/VIS detector is the most widely used device, and it is dependent on the solute's ability to absorb ultraviolet or visible light. The variable wavelength detector allows the analyst to select any wavelength in the ultraviolet or visible range. The diode array or rapid scan detector is also used which allows a rapid scan of the entire UV spectrum to identify the components eluting from the column.

Because the components elute from the UV detector in solution, they do not undergo degradation or destruction. This one very useful characteristic of HPLC affords the analyst the option of collecting fractions of the eluent for further analysis. This is not possible in GC because the eluent is destroyed by the FID.

1.7.2.4 Capillary Electrophoresis (CE)

Capillary electrophoresis is a technique that separates components on the basis of charge-to-mass ratios under the influence of an electrical field. It uses high voltage for fast separations and high efficiencies. Osmotic flow is the main driving force in CE, especially at higher pH values, and results primarily from the interaction of positive ions in solution with the silanol groups on the capillary in the presence of an applied field. Narrow bore capillary columns of uncoated fused silica are used for heat dissipation during the separation process. The detector is normally an ultraviolet detector.

Micellar electrokinetic capillary chromatography (MECC) is a form of CE which allows for the separation of cations, neutral solutes, and anions.

CE has several advantages over HPLC and GC. The method can be used with ionic and neutral solutes which present problems in GC. There is a higher efficiency, resolving power, and speed of analysis compared to HPLC. From a cost perspective, CE requires much less solvent than HPLC, and the CE capillary column is much less expensive than the HPLC or GC capillary columns. Two disadvantages of CE are the limited sensitivity for UV detection (30 to 100 times less than that of HPLC); and fraction collection is troublesome because of mechnical problems and small sample size. This technique uses a micelle as a run buffer additive to give separations that are both electrophoretic and chromatographic.

One of the advantages of MECC is the ability to separate racemic mixtures of compounds into the d- and l-isomers. This is an ability that is extremely valuable when identifying compounds where one isomer is controlled (dextropropoxyphene) and the other isomer is not controlled (levopropoxyphene). This is usually accomplished by adding cyclodextrins to the run buffer.

1.7.2.5 Infrared Spectrophotometry (IR)

Infrared spectrophotometry is one of the most specific instrumental methods for the identification of a controlled substance. A pure drug as a thin film on a KBr salt plate, or as crystals mounted in a KBr matrix are placed into the sample compartment of the infrared spectrophotometer. A source of electromagnetic radiation in the form of light from a Nernst glower passes light through the sample. The instrument, through a mechanical means, splits the beam into a reference beam and an incident beam. The reference beam passes unobstructed through a monochrometer to a photometer; the incident beam passes through the mounted sample through the same monochrometer to the photometer. The reference beam passes 100%

unobstructed to the photometer. The incident beam passing through the sample has some of its enegy absorbed by the sample. This energy is absorbed at differenct wave lengths across the infrared spectrum from 4000 cm-1 down to 250 cm-1. The amount of relative absorption and where on this spectrum the absorption takes place is dependent upon the molecular structure and, more specifically, the functional groups of the drug. Different functional groups and molecular interactions brought on by symmetrical and assymetrical molecular stretching vibrations and in-plane and out-of-plane bending vibrations result in a number of peaks and valleys on the IR chart. The resultant spectrum is usually formed on an x/y coordinate axes. The wavelength (μ) or wave number (cm^{-1}) where the absorption occurs is depicted on the x-axis, and a measure of the amount of light absorbed by the sample, but usually referenced by transmittance units from 0 to 100%, is depicted on the y-axis

The infrared spectrum of a suspected drug results in a specific pattern that can be used to positively determine the identity of the substance. For most controlled substances, the resulting spectrum consists of 20 to 70 peaks. These peaks form a pattern that is unique to the chemical structure of the drug. This pattern can then be compared with a reference IR spectrum of a primary drug standard. If the analyst determines that the two spectra match within the limits of scientific certainty, an identification is possible. It is rarely, if ever, possible to overlay the reference spectra with the spectra of the unknown and have a "perfect match". The analyst is looking for a match in the patterns. Any shifts in peak intensity or wave number must be evaluated in conjunction with the pattern. Small shifts of 1 or 2 cm^{-1} and minor intensity variations of individual peaks are expected. However, major variations must be evaluated on a case by case basis. Some authors refer to IR as a "fingerprint" identification method. This implies an ability to overlay two spectra and obtain a perfect match in every way. This degree of perfection is rarely, if ever, possible.

Another factor that must be considered is that when two spectra are being compared peak-by-peak as opposed to pattern-by-pattern, they ideally should be from the same instrument and collected at about the same time. Comparing a literature reference spectrum with an unknown for a pattern match is acceptable. Comparing the same literature reference spectrum wave number by wave number, absolute transmittance value by absolute transmittance value will probably result in minor differences.

IR does have limitations. In order to obtain an acceptable spectrum, the sample must be very clean and dry. For forensic exhibits, this usually means that most samples must go through extraction processes to remove impurities. In the past, sample size was a problem. However, because of advances in Fourier transform IR technology and the interfacing of an IR spectro-photometer with a microscope, evaluting microgram quantities of a sample results in excellent spectra which are conclusive for the identification of a controlled substance. IR has very definite limitations in its ability to quantitate controlled substances, and differentiating some isomers of controlled substances can pose problems.

1.7.2.6 Gas Chromatography/Mass Spectroscopy (GC/MS)

Gas chromatography/mass spectrometry is by far the most popular method of identifying controlled substances in the forensic science laboratory. In this method, a gas chromatograph is interfaced with a mass selective detector (MSD). The sample undergoing an examination is placed into solution with a solvent such as methanol. A very small injection volume of 1 or 2 μl is injected into the GC injection port. It then travels through the column where the different components of the sample are separated. The separated components can then be directed into the ionization chamber of MSD where they are bombarded by an electron beam. In electron impact gas chromatography/mass spectrometry (EI MS), high energy electrons impact the separated component molecules. The resulting spectrum of each component is typically complex with a large number of mass fragments. These fragments are represented as peaks of varying intensity that provide the basis for comparison with a primary reference standard. The components are then ionized and positively charged. This ionization also results in a fission, or fragmentation process. The molecular fragments traverse into a magnetic field where they are separated according to their masses. In this magnetic field, larger mass fragments are less affected by the magnetic field, and smaller fragments are more affected and undergo a deflection. Upon exiting the magnetic field, these fragments impact a detector losing the charge generated by the beam of electrons impacting the sample. The result of this fragmentation process is a pattern unique for the substance that is being analyzed.

The resulting mass spectrum consists of an x/y coordinate axis. The numerical value on the x-axis represents the mass number determined by the number of neutrons and protons in the nucleus. It is usually the molecular weight of a specific fragment. The largest magnitude peak on the x-axis will often be the **molecular ion** and will represent the molecular weight of the unfragmented compound. There will usually be a very small peak to the right of the molecular ion which represents the molecular weight plus 1. The y-axis represents the relative abundance of each peak comprising the mass spectrum. The tallest peak on the y-axis is the **base peak** and represents that part of the molecule which is the most stable and undergoes the least amount of fragmentation. The base peak is assigned a relative abundance value of 100. The other peaks in the resulting spectrum are assigned relative values along the y-axis.

The numerical values on the x- and y-axis are calculated and assigned by the data station which is interfaced with the mass spectrometer. The accuracy of these numbers is predicated on the fact that the instrument has been properly tuned. This tuning process can be compared to checking the channel tuning on a television set. This might be accomplished by opening a television guide to determine what programs are scheduled at a particular hour. The television is then turned on and the program for each channel checked. If the programs cited in the televison magazine appear on corresponding channels at the proper times, the television has been proven to be properly tuned. The tuning of a mass analyzer presents an analagous situation.

The tuning process of a mass analyzer involves a procedure in which a chemical of a known molecular weight and fragmentation pattern is analyzed and the resulting data evaluated. This process includes verifying instrument parameters and the resulting spectrum. If the response of the tuning process falls within specified limits, the mass spectrometer is deemed operationally reliable, and the resulting data can be considered reliable. One such chemical used to tune mass spectrometers is perflurotributylamine (PFTBA).

Fragmentation patterns of controlled substances are typically unique. Once a fragmentation pattern has been obtained, the forensic analyst should be able to explain the major peaks of the spectrum and relate them to the molecular structure. If properly evaluated, mass spectral data can usually be used to form a conclusion as to the identity of a controlled substance.

GC/MS has many advantages in the analysis of controlled substances. The sample being analyzed need not be pure. Multi-component samples are separated and each soluble organic component can be individually identified. The analyst must be aware of isomeric compounds that have very similar chemical structures and similar fragmentation patterns. These kinds of situations can usually be handled by noting the GC retention time data to discriminate between similar compounds. Possible coelution of compounds from the capillary GC column and thermal degradation as noted in the gas chromatography section of this chapter should also be recognized. GC/MS does not allow the forensic analyst to directly identify the salt form of the drug. This task can be accomplished by considering the solubility properties of the drug being analyzed. In using this knowledge and performing extractions prior to injection onto the GC column, the salt form can be determined indirectly.

When all methods of instrumental analysis of controlled substances are considered, GC/MS is recognized in most instances as one of the efficient analytical techniques. If the analyst is cognizant of maintaining instrument reliability standards and the guidelines of mass spectral interpretation, GC/MS affords one of the highest degrees of specificity in the identification of controlled substances.

1.7.2.7 Nuclear Magnetic Resonance (NMR) Spectroscopy

Nuclear magnetic resonance spectroscopy is one of the most powerful instrumental techniques available to the forensic chemist. In those laboratories fortunate enough to have NMR technology, extensive capabilities exist. Data interpretation of NMR sprectra requires a high degree of expertise. This instrumental technique allows the analyst to detect paramagnetic atoms. (^{1}H, ^{2}H, ^{13}C, ^{15}N, ^{17}O, ^{31}P, ^{11}B, and ^{19}F are examples.) Most forensic applications of NMR focus on ^{1}H and ^{13}C. The resonant fequency of hydrogen (^{1}H) in the current high field magnets ranges from 200 to 750 mHz. This instrument generates a high magnetic field more than capable of damaging encrypted data on the back of a credit card. The NMR is a very expensive instrument requiring a high degree of specialized expertise to maintain and interpret the resulting data. The NMR is the one instrument which affords the analyst the ability to determine both the molecular structure and the three-dimensional orientation of some individual atoms of the molecule. This means that structural isomers can be determined directly. However, the extent of this kind of information is usually required only by research scientists in those instances where no other information is available from other instrumental methods, or where no primary analytical standard is available to confirm the presence of a controlled substance.

The major component of the NMR spectrometer is a high field super conducting magnet. The sample is dissolved in a deuterated solvent and then transferred to a long cylindrical glass tube usually measuring 5 mm in diameter. The tube is placed into the NMR probe located near the center of the magnetic field. In proton NMR, the magnetic field causes the hydrogen atoms on the molecule to orient in a particular direction. In order to obtain high-resolution spectra, the field produced by the magnet must be homogenous over the entire area of the sample in the probe. The resonance frequencies for all protons in a molecule may be different. These frequencies are dependent upon the molecular environment of the nucleus. This correlation between resonance frequencies and molecular environment enables the analyst to make judgements regarding the structure of the drug that he is analyzing.

The NMR spectrum is traced on a two-dimensional x/y coordinate axes. By evaluating an NMR proton spectrum, an analyst can determine an important factor that facilitates the identification of the compound — the area under each peak indicates the number of nuclei that are undergoing a transition and the number of protons that are present.

There are other types of examinations that are possible with high field NMR. A carbon-13 (^{13}C) evaluation enables an analyst to determine the number of carbons and their relative positioning in the molecule. ^{13}C is an isotope of the more abundant ^{12}C. About 1% of naturally occuring carbon is ^{13}C. There are two additional NMR " 2D experiments" which are very valuable to the forensic analyst. Correlation spectroscopy (COSY) measures proton to proton (^{1}H - ^{1}H) interactions; and nuclear overhauser effect spectroscopy (NOESY) measures the interaction of protons which are close to one another, but not necessarily on adjoining atoms. Carbon 13, COSY, and NOESY spectra are all much more difficult to interpret and require specialized knowledge.

In the forensic analysis of controlled substances, most molecules are comprised of carbon and hydrogen. Proton NMR provided a unique spectral pattern which can be used to identify a controlled substance. This pattern also enables the analyst to distinguish between the basic and a salt form of the drug. NMR cannot distinguish halogenated salt forms. For instance, it cannot distinguish between heroin hydrochloride and heroin hydrobromide. But it can distinguish between a heroin salt and heroin base.

REFERENCES

1. Johns, S.H., Wist, A.A., and Najam, A.R., Spot tests: A color chart reference for forensic chemists, *J. Forensic Sci.*, 24: 631-649.
2. Hughes, R.B. and Kessler, R.R., Increased safety and specificity in the yhin-layer chromatographic identification of marijuana, *J. Forensic Sci.*, 24: 842-846.
3. Baggi, T.R., 3-methylbenzthiazolinone-2-hydrazone (MBTH) as a new visualization reagent in the detection of cannabinoids on thin-layer chromatography, *J. Forensic Sci.*, 25: 691-694.
4. Parker, K.D., Wright, J, A., Halpern, A.F., and Hine, C.H., Preliminary report on the separation and quantitative detemination of cannabis constituents present in plant material and when added to urine by thin-layer and gas chromatography, *Bull. Narc.*, 20: 9-14.
5. Fulton, C.C., *Modern Microcrystal Tests for Drugs*, John Wiley & Sons, New York, 1969.
6. Lurie, I. S. and Witmer, *J.D.*, *High Performance Liquid Chromatography*, Marcel Decker, New York, 1983.

1.7.3 CONTROLLED SUBSTANCES EXAMINATIONS

Every examination made by a forensic chemist has a potential legal ramification or consequence. Forensic chemists must be prepared to depart from the familiar natural science setting of the laboratory and to enter the confrontational setting of the courtroom and be able to communicate with a prosecuting attorney, a defense attorney, a judge, 12 jurors, and on occasion, the press. The forensic chemist must be able to explain the significance of complicated analytical procedures to individuals with little or no scientific training. If the forensic analyst is to have any credibility on the witness stand, he must be able to describe what he has done in terminology understood by those individuals with whom he is communicating.

1.7.3.1 Identifying and Quantitating Controlled Substances

Whenever a controlled substance is identified, the possibility exists that an individual could be imprisoned or suffer some other legal consequence as a result. There is, therefore, an absolute, uncompromised requirement for certainty in the identification of controlled substances. Prior to 1960, the results of microscopic crystal tests, color screening tests, and TLC were considered definitive. From the 1960s through the mid-1970s, ultraviolet spectrophotometry and GC gained acceptance. It is interesting in 1997 to look back 20 years and contemplate the absolute faith placed in a retention time on a gas chromatogram, or upon the ultraviolet absorption maxima in acidic or basic solutions. In some instances these numerical values were measured with a ruler!

From 1975 through 1985 there were major advances in IR and MS. During those years "specificity", as we understand the term today, was, for the first time, actually attainable in most cases. As the technology continually evolved, with increased Fourier transform peak resolution in IR and NMR, and multi-component separations improved with capillary column gas chromatography, specificity also increased.

In the mid-1980s the advent of "designer drugs" (properly referred to as "controlled substance analogues") resurected the problem of specificity. In attempts at circumventing existing controlled substance laws, clandestine laboratory chemists began to alter chemical structures of controlled drugs by increasingly sophisticated syntheses. By replacing a methyl group with an ethyl group, or by using a five-membered ring instead of a six-membered ring in a synthesis, these clandestine laboratory chemists developed what at the time were non-controlled analogues. The Controlled Substance Analogue and Enforcement Act of 1986 was passed by Congress, largely as a response to this problem. This particular piece of legislation also reinforced the responsibility of the chemist to accurately discriminate between controlled substances and endless lists of possible analogues.

Joseph P. Bono

A direct consequence of the new law's passage was the development of analytical procedures in Fourier Transform Infrared Spectrophotometry (FTIR), Fourier Transform Nuclear Magnetic Resonance Spectroscopy (FTNMR), Gas Chromatography/Fourier Transform Infrared Spectroscopy (GC/FTIR), and CE. These instrumental methods have made their way into the forensic science laboratory and now provide the increased specificity required by the courts.

Controlled substances sold on the street are usually mixed with adulterants and diluents in a crude and mostly unspecified manner. In some laboratories, the analysts are required to identify and quantitate both the controlled substance and the adulterant drugs and diluent materials. Color tests, thin layer chromatography, and microcrystal tests of the pre-1960s vintage are still used for screening. These testing procedures were valid then and are still valid today, but today additional instrumental techniques are utilized to make the absolute identification and quantitation.

After the analysis has been completed, it must be documented. The final report must be clear, concise, and accurate, with all conclusions substantiated by analytical data. The data may be in the form of notations on paper in the analyst's writing, or on chromatograms, spectra, or other instrumental printouts. Dates must be checked, and the documented description of the exhibit(s) must be consistent with the actual exhibit. Each time a report is signed, the analyst places his reputation and credibility before the scrutiny of the court and his peers. Discovering a "mistake" after the report has been submitted to the courts is not good.

Cocaine can exist as either the hydrochloride (HCl) salt or as the base. Pursuant to federal law, there are sentencing guidelines based on the identification of cocaine as either the base or as the salt form (usually HCl). Cocaine can be adulterated with benzocaine, procaine, lidocaine, or any combination of these non-controlled drugs, and further diluted with mannitol, lactose, or other processing sugars. A variety of instrumental techniques can be used to distinguish cocaine HCl from cocaine base. FTIR spectrophotometry is commonly available and used in many laboratories. The IR spectra of cocaine HCl and cocaine base are quite different and easily distinguished. The IR spectrum of a cocaine HCl sample mixed with an adulterant presents a problem. The same sample analyzed by GC/FTIR presents the chemist with a total response chromatogram showing all peaks in a mixture. The resulting IR spectrum and mass spectrum are identifiable. However, in this technique, cocaine HCl and cocaine base cannot be distinguished. At this point, NMR can provide a solution to distinguishing the two forms of cocaine and identifying the adulterants.

The solubility properties of controlled substances can be used to separate different forms of controlled substances. For instance, cocaine base is soluble in diethyl ether, cocaine HCl is insoluble. Therefore, if an analyst is analyzing a material which is believed to be cocaine in a questionable form, he can try placing the material into solution with diethyl ether, separate the ether from the insolubles, evaporate the diethyl ether, and analyze the resulting powder by GC/MS. The resulting cocaine spectrum would indicate the presence of cocaine base because cocaine HCl would not have gone into solution.

Methamphetamine is produced in clandestine laboratories from the reaction of ephedrine with hydriodic acid and red phosphorus, or from the reaction of phenyl-2-propanone (P-2-P) with methylamine. Methamphetamine samples submitted to the forensic science laboratory usually contain precursors from the synthesis, by-products for side reactions, and adulterants such as nicotinamide which has been added by the clandestine laboratory operator. As is true of the mass spectrum of some other phenethylamines, the mass spectrum of methamphetamine may not provide enough specificity for positive identification. The most accurate way to identify many phenethylamines is with IR. However, NMR is at least as specific as FTIR, and it also allows for an identification in the presence of diluents. Unfortunately, NMR is not available in many laboratories. Nicotinamide is one of the more commonly encountered adulterants with methamphetamine and can easily be distinguished from isonicotinamide by NMR spectroscopy.

The IR spectrum of methamphetamine hydrochloride in a potassium chloride salt matrix is very specific, and GC/FTIR is excellent at separating the components of a methamphetamine sample. However, this method requires great care in selecting the optimized temperature and flow parameters, and column selection.

GC/MS is the method most often used for identifying heroin. The mass spectrum of heroin is very specific. Heroin is relatively simple to separate, and identification of the degradation products and the by-products of the heroin synthesis, from morphine and acetic anhydride, is relatively straightforward. Because morphine is derived from opium, many of the by-products from the opium processing are carried over to the final heroin product. Acetylcodeine and acetylmorphine are clearly identified from the corresponding mass spectra. The GC/FTIR also provides excellent spectra for making identifications of heroin, its by-products, degradation products, and precursors. The chloroform insoluble diluents from heroin samples can also be identified in a potassium bromide matrix by FTIR. These materials will usually consist of sugars such as mannitol and inositol. When the heroin has been isolated from diluents and adulterants, FTIR and NMR can be utilized to confirm the salt form of the heroin.

Phencyclidine, more properly identified as phenylcyclohexylpiperidine (PCP), is usually submitted to the laboratory as an exhibit of PCP base in diethly ether, a powder, or sprayed or coated on marijuana. The analysis of PCP is relatively direct by GC/MS. The resulting mass spectrum is specific. The GC/FTIR spectrum of PCP is not as specific when one compares this spectrum with that of PCP analogues and precursors such as phenylcyclohexyl carbonitrile (PCC) and phenylcyohexyl pyrrolidine (PCPy). FTIR spectrophotometry of the solid in a potassium bromide matrix is very specific. A word of caution is in order for anyone handling PCP. PCP is a substance that is believed to be easily absorbed through the skin of the analyst. Minimum handling is recommended.

1.7.3.2 Identifying Adulterants and Diluents

The terms adulterants and diluents are sometimes used in the context of illicitly distributed controlled substances. Adulterants are chemicals added to illicit drugs which, in and of themselves, can affect some sort of a physiological response. This response can range from very mild to quite severe. Diluents are chemicals added to controlled substances which are used more as fillers than to elicit a physiological response. They can be added to affect the color and composition for the sake of satisfying the user. Adulterants and diluents are usually added to the controlled substance mixture by those involved in illicit distribution. There is a third class of materials that is found in controlled substance mixtures. This class includes by-products. These by-products can be processing by-products, or they can exist as naturally occurring by-products found in botanical substances such as the coca leaf or the opium poppy.

Most "street" exhibits of heroin and cocaine contain adulterants and diluents. Samples taken from large scale, brick size, kilogram seizures will be relatively pure. Except for some by-products from the opium poppy and the coca leave, there will be little in the way of foreign materials. Adulterants are encountered, in increasing proportions, as the heroin and cocaine progress down the distribution chain from the main supplier to the dealers to the users.

Adulterants commonly encountered in heroin include quinine, procaine, acetaminophen, caffeine, diphenhydramine, aspirin, phenobarbital, and lidocaine. Adulterants commonly encountered in cocaine include procaine, benzocaine, and lidocaine. Diluents found in heroin include different kinds of starches. It is not uncommon to find in heroin substances such as calcium carbonate which had been added during the morphine extraction processes. Diluents found in both cocaine and heroin include lactose, mannitol, sucrose, and dextrose.

The identification of adulterants and diluents may or may not be a requirement as a part of the identification scheme in the forensic science laboratory. In most instances, the requirements of the judicial system will be limited to the identification of the controlled substance. This will usually be accomplished by separating the sample into its component parts, and then identifying all or some of these components. In the case of a heroin exhibit, cut with quinine and mannitol, a capillary GC/MS examination might result in a chromatogram and corresponding spectra with an acetylcodeine peak, an acetylmorphine peak, a morphine peak, a quinine peak, and a heroin peak. The first two peaks are most probably processing by-products; the morphine is from the opium poppy; the heroin is the main peak of interest, and the quinine has probably been added as an adulterant. There is no need to separate the components by extractions to make the identifications. However, if the analyst is desirous of conducting an IR examination or a NMR examination to identify the heroin, an extraction of the heroin from a 3 N hydrochloric acid medium using chloroform is an option. Depending upon whether the heroin exists as a salt (heroin hydrochloride) or as heroin base, a set of serial extractions can be conducted to isolate the heroin from the quinine and the other substances. The identification of cocaine in a mixture follows the same procedures. Depending upon the type of analysis, the cocaine may or may not need to be chemically separated from the adulterants for an identification.

The simplest way to identify diluents in controlled substance mixtures is by microscopic identification. Common diluents along with the sugars/carbohydrates/starches described above include sodium chloride, calcium carbonate, and various types of amorphous materials. Because of their optical properties, these materials lend themselves well to a microscopic identification. Chemical separations are fairly easy because these materials are usually insoluble in solvents such as diethyl ether or hexane, and slightly soluble in solvents such as methanol. Most organic materials are soluble in methanol or some other polar solvent. The sugars/carbohydrates/starches can be further identified using IR following the separation if only one sugar is present. If not, HPLC can be used to identify the sugars.

Even if the identification of all adulterants, diluents, and by-products are not required in the final report generated by the analyst, such information can prove useful in evaluating trends and possible distribution patterns.

1.7.3.3 Quantitating Controlled Substances

A number of different methods can be used to quantitate controlled substances. Capillary column GC or HPLC are probably the two most utilized instrumental methods to accomplish this task. The choice of which instrumental method to use depends upon the chemical properties of the substance in question. GC works well with those compounds that are not highly polar, are relatively stable at high temperatures, and are soluble in organic solvents such as methanol or chloroform. Even if these conditions exist, GC can still be used if a derivatizing agent is used.

If GC is used, the most common analytical method for quantitation involves the use of an internal standard, providing a consistent concentration of a known chemical in solution. In order to avoid the obvious problem of choosing an internal standard which might be present in the sample as an adulterant or diluent, the internal standard can be a straight chain hydrocarbon (tetracosane, eicosane, or dodecane) which is added in equal amounts to both the sample being analyzed and the calibration samples. The internal standard method is especially advantageous because the expected flame ionization detector response for the internal standard to the drug can be checked for each and every injection. The critical factor for each injection is the ratio of the detector response of the internal standard to the calibration solution of known concentration. This is especially critical if the sample size of the injection is off target by a minuscule amount. The absolute integration values for the known peak and the internal standard peaks may vary. However, the ratio will not be affected. If the detector is responding properly to the internal standard in solution, it is also responding properly for the substance being quantitated.

Controlled substances can also be quantitated using what is referred to as the external standard method. In this method, calibration standards of known concentrations are prepared. Injections are then made into the GC injection port, and a calibration table is established. The accuracy of this method is quite good, provided that the injection amounts used in establishing the calibration table are exactly the same from injection to injection. Even small variations of less than 10% volume, when dealing with a 1 μl injection, can lead to less than optimized results. This problem can be overcome by making multiple injections and checking the consistency of the detector response and the injection volume. The ability to be consistent can be developed by an analyst with a good eye. The ability to read the sample size on the microsyringe is, for some, as much an art as a scientific technique. Automatic injectors are now available on many gas chromatographs which approach consistency from one injection to the next. However, this method will work only when there is a verfiable linear response of the detector within a specified concentration range.

In both the internal and external standard methods, there must be a linear response of the detector to the solutions of different concentrations. This is determined by injecting solutions of known concentrations and establishing a calibration table. With most instrument data stations, this is relatively simple. The instrument will then calculate the response ratio of internal standard to drug for the solution of unknown concentration and compare this to the response ratios of internal standard to drug for the solutions of known concentrations in the calibration table. This ratio can then be used to calculate the concentration of the drug that is being analyzed.

HPLC can be useful for quantitating controlled substances in solution. This instrumental method also measures the response of different compounds at different ultraviolet/visible absorption bands. These responses are then compared to calibration table values. Internal standards can be used in the same way they are used in GC quantitations. The limitations and comparisons of HPLC and GC are discussed elsewhere.

Ultraviolet/visible spectrophotometry (UV/VIS) is a technique that has been in use for many years. UV/VIS uses one of the basic tenets of physics — Beer's Law. Absorption of monochromatic light is proportional to the concentration of a sample in solution. The concentration of an exhibit in solution can be determined by comparison with calibration tables. This type of analysis is dependent upon the solubility properties of the substance being quantitated in acid, basic, and organic solutions. The UV/VIS method is accurate and reliable only when the compound of interest is pure with no interfering substances. GC and HPLC are used more often because of the added reliability check provided by the internal standard methodology.

NMR spectrometry can also be used for the quantitation of controlled substances. The quantitative analytical techniques in NMR are more complicated than those discussed above and require a specialized instrumental expertise.

All of the methods discussed above are reliable and accurate when properly and conscientiously conducted. There is one very important difference which applies to any quantitative method when compared to an identification method. With proper methods, an analyst can make an identification of a controlled substance with scientific certainty. The quantitation of a controlled substance will usually result in values falling within a narrowly defined "window" of from one-tenth to one or two absolute percent. The reported value will usually be an average value.

1.7.3.4 Reference Standards

The first step in ensuring the accuracy of the identification of any controlled substance should be a collection of authenticated reference standards. Reference standards for the forensic science examinations should be 98+% pure. They can be purchased from a reputable manufacturer or distributer, synthesized by an organic chemist within the laboratory, or purified from a bulk secondary standard by using an appropriate methodology. "Reference Standards" that have been authenticated are available from the United States Pharmacopeia (USP) and National Formulary (NF). Samples obtained from any other source should be authenticated using the appropriate methodology. This authentication process will involve a two step process of first positively identifying the proposed reference standard and then determining the purity of this standard.

At a minimum, the identification of a reference standard should be conducted using IR and MS. The resulting spectra are then compared with reference spectra in the literature. The chemist should be able to evaluate data from both of these instruments and be able to explain the major peaks using, respectively, a functional group analysis or a molecular fragmentation analysis. If no literature spectra are available, a more sophisticated structural analysis such as NMR spectroscopy will be necessary to verify the chemical structure. Additional methods that can be used to supplement, but not replace, IR, MS, and NMR, include optical crystallography, X-ray crystallography, and a melting point analysis.

The next step in the process is to quantitate the reference standard against a "primary standard". A primary standard is a sample that has been subjected to the authentication process and meets the criteria of a positive identification and 98%+ purity. The quantitation methods of choice are GC or HPLC. With either method, the concentrations of the injections of both the prmary standard and the authentication sample must be within the linear range of the detector. The method should utilize an internal standard. The results of all injections should have a relative standard deviation of less than 3%.[1]

If a primary standard is not available, a purity determination can be accomplished by a peak area percent determination using capillary GC with a flame ionization detector and HPLC using a photo-array ultraviolet detector. A third instrumental method using a differential scanning calorimeter (DSC) should also be considered. In a peak area percent analysis, the area percent of the standard compound is determined vs. any impurities that are present in the batch. A blank injection of the solvent is done prior to the standard injection to detect peaks common to both the solvent and the authentication standard. The GC solution is checked for insolubles. If these insolubles are present, they can be isolated and identified by IR. Of course, if there are insolubles, the sample is no longer considered an authentication standard until it is purified and the foreign material is removed.

HPLC can also be used in a peak area percent analysis. For basic drugs, the analyst would use a gradient mobile phase using methanol and an acidic aqueous phosphate buffer. For neutral and acidic drugs, he would use a gradient with methanol and an acidic aqueous phosphate buffer containing sodium dodecyl sulfate. For anabolic steroids, he would use a methanol/water gradient mobile phase. As is the case with GC, with HPLC a blank injection of the solvent always precedes the injection of the authentication standard. Three wavelengths, 210 nm, 228 nm, and 240 nm, are monitored for most drugs. For anabolic steroids, the analyst should monitor 210 nm, 240 nm, and 280 nm. If the resulting UV spectra of all pertinent peaks are similar, the integration of the peaks with the most sensitive wavelengths are used for the calculation of purity.

DSC is a method of adding heat to a preweighed sample and monitoring temperature and heat flow as the sample goes through its melting point.[2] If decomposition does not occur during the melt, the peak shown on the thermogram can be used to determine melting point and the molar concentration of any melt soluble impurities present. With this data, the analyst can determine the purity of the authentication standard. One drawback of DSC is that structurally dissimilar impurities such as sugars in a supposed heroin "standard" are not always detected by this method. This is because the impurity does not go into solution in the melting main component. With almost all authentication standards, most impurities will be structurally similar to the drug of interest. The dissimilar compounds should have been removed prior to the DSC analysis or detected by GC or HPLC.

REFERENCES

1. *CRC Handbook of Tables for Probability and Statistics*, CRC Press, 2nd ed., 1968, p.5.
2. McNaughton, J.L. and Mortimer, C.T., Differential scanning calorimetry, *IRS; Physical Cemistry Series*, 2, 1975, vol. 10.

1.8 COMPARATIVE ANALYSIS

1.8.1 DETERMINING COMMONALITY OF SOURCE

Two different kinds of controlled substance analyses are routinely conducted in the forensic science laboratory. The first is the "identification". The goal is self-evident — to identify a controlled substance by name. The second, less common, type of analysis is the "comparative analysis". Its purpose is to determine a commonality of source. A comparative analysis will include a comprehensive examination of the sample's chemical and physical characteristics, with the goal of demonstrating, with a high degree of certainty, a common origin for two or more samples.[1]

Sometime it is possible to determine when two items of evidence have a common origin just by physically fitting them together. This applies to exhibits such as a screwdriver and a broken blade, two large paint chips that have broken apart, or a piece of paper torn in two or more pieces. In the forensic examination of illicit drugs, it is possible to state with a high degree of certainty that two exhibits of a white powder share a common source. The wording in stating such a conclusion is critical. Words must be carefully selected so as to convey the conclusion clearly and concisely, without overstepping the scientific certainty that exists. The following quote, about two samples of cocaine, is from the transcript of drug trial held in 1991. It illustrates the apropriate language to be used on such occassions.

> After a review of all analytical data, it can be stated with a high level of scientific certainty and beyond a reasonable doubt that a close chemical relationship exists between [the two samples] strongly suggesting that they were derived from the same manufacturing process...and that they were probably derived from the same batch.[2]

Before undertaking a detailed examination of two samples, a broad overview is desirable. The color and granularity of the exhibits should be examined, and then the components of the sample identifyed and quantitated. If all of the data from one exhibit compare favorably with all of the data from the second exhibit, the analyst can proceed to a second set of procedures to evaluate the processing by-products and trace materials in the exhibits. It is important to realize that in order to successfully evaluate two exhibits to determine commonality of source, each exhibit must be analyzed in the same way using the same methodology, instruments, and chemicals and solvents from the same containers.

Controlled substances such as cocaine and heroin are the simplest to compare because they are derived from botanical substances (the coca leaf and the opium poppy, respectively).[3,4] Many naturally occurring by-products from the plants are carried through the processing stages of the drugs, and these can be used to confirm the existence of a common source.

1.8.2   COMPARING HEROIN EXHIBITS

Capillary column gas chromatography (ccGC) and HPLC are the two methods most often utilized in comparing two or more heroin exhibits to determine whether they came from the same source. HPLC can be utilized in the first part of the analytical scheme because the components being evaluated usually are present in substantial amounts. The major components including heroin, acetylmorphine, acetylcodeine, morphine, codeine, noscapine, papaverine, thebaine, and most diluents can be identified and quantitated. A high degree of resolving power is not required at this point in the analytical scheme. If the HPLC analysis demonstrates that the samples being compared are similar, the analyst proceeds to the second part of the analytical scheme.

In the second part of this scheme to evaluate the trace components of the exhibits, ccGC is usually the method of choice, both because of its resolving power and because of its ability to detect minute quantities of the component of interest. The second step of the isolation process involves multiple extractions and derivatizations to isolate the acidic and neutral compounds for analysis and evaluation. This process isolates the precursors, solvents, and respective contaminants, by-products, intermediates, and degradation products. It is desireable to remove the heroin from the sample during the extraction processes in order to keep most of the trace components at the same level of chromatographic attenuation. Once the heroin has been identified and quantitated, only then are the other elements analyzed. If after these two processes the analyst sees no chromatographic differences in the samples being evaluated, a conclusion can be formulated. The number of compents from this second part of the process can number from 100 to 300. If all of these components are present in both exhibits at similar relative levels, a conclusion regarding commonality of source is warranted.

1.8.3   COMPARING COCAINE EXHIBITS

The process is different for cocaine comparisons. For one thing, the cocaine need not be removed from the sample. Four different ccGC examinations can be conducted which evaluate and compare the by-products and impurities down to trace levels by:

1. Flame ionization gas chromatography (GC-FID) to evaluate cocaine hydrolysis products, manufacturing impurities, and naturally occurring alkaloids;[5]
2. GC-FID to determine trimethoxy-substituted alkaloids as well as other minor naturally occurring tropanes;[6]
3. Electron capture gas chromatography (GC-ECD) to determine the hydroxycocaines and N-nor related compounds;[4] and
4. GC-ECD to determine the 10 intact truxillines.[7]

These four gas chromatographic methods provide an in-depth evalutation of trace level components and allow the precise comparison of two different cocaine exhibits. The number of components evaluated range in the hundreds. This data provides the analyst with an abundance of analytical points to form a conclusion regarding commonality of source.

Extraction of the impurities and by-products can be accomplished using a derivatizing reagent.[8,9] Heptafluorobutyric anhydride (HFBA) is often used for this purpose. The GC-FID and GC-ECD analyses that follow will result in organic profiles of the many compounds from the cocaine and heroin samples being analyzed. A further MS analysis may serve to identify the chemical composition of many of the components of each exhibit. Many of the resulting peaks represent compounds formed during the manufacturing process; others will be oxidation or hydrolysis products of known compounds; and other peaks will have a degree of uncertainty regarding their exact chemical structure. However, what will be known is that these peaks are present in both exhibits being compared using the ccGC methods and represent cocaine and heroin manufacturing impurities or by-products.

REFERENCES

1. Perillo, B.A., Klein, R.F.X., and Franzosa, E.S., Recent advances by the U.S. drug enforcement administration in drug signature and comparative analysis, *Forensic Sci. Int.,* 69: 1-6, 1994.
2. Moore, J.M., Meyers, R.P., and Jiminez, M.D., The anatomy of a cocaine comparison case: a prosecutorial and chemistry perspective, *J. Forensic Sci.,* 38: 1305-1325, 1993.
3. Moore, J.M. and Cooper, D.A., The application of capillary gas chromatography-electron capture detection in the comparative analyses of illicit cocaine samples, *J. Forensic Sci.,* 38: 1286-1304, 1993.
4. Moore, J.M. and Casale, J.F., In-depth chromatographic analyses of illicit cocaine and its precursor, coca leaves, *J. Chromatography,* 674: 165-205, 1994.
5. Casale, J.F. and Waggoner, R.W., A chromatographic impurity signature profile analysis for cocaine using capillary gas chromatography, *J. Forensic Sci.,* 36: 1321-1330, 1991.
6. Casale, J.F. and Moore, J.M., 3', 4', 5'-Trimethoxy-substituted analogues of cocaine, cis-/ trans-cinnamoylcocaine and tropacocaine: Characterization and quantitation of new alkaloids in coca leaf, coca paste and refined illicit cocaine, *J. Forensic Sci.,* 39: 462-472, 1994.
7. Moore, J.M., Cooper, D.A., L:urie, I.S., Kram, T.C., Carr, S., Harper, C., and Yeh, J., Capillary gas chromatographic-electron capture detection of coca leaf related imputities of illicit cocaine: 2,4-diphenylcyclobutane-1,3-dicarboxylic acids, 1,4-diphenylcyclobutane-2,3-dicarboxylic acids and their alkaloidal precursors, the truxillines, *J. Chromatography,* 410: 297-318, 1987.
8. Moore, J.M., Allen, A.C., and Cooper, D.A., Determination of manufacturing impurities in heroin by capillary gas chromatography with electron capture detection after derivatization with heptafluorobutyric acid, *Analt. Chem.,* 56: 642-646, 1984.
9. Moore, J.M., The application of chemical derivatization in forensic drug chemistry for gas and high performance liquid chromatographic methods of analysis, *Forensic Sci. Rev.,* 2: 79-124, 1990.

1.9 CLANDESTINE LABORATORIES

There are two kinds of clandestine laboratories. The first is the **operational** clandestine laboratory. This laboratory, usually operating in secrecy, is engaged in the production of controlled substances, precursors to controlled substances, or controlled substance homologues or analogues. The second is the **non-operational** clandestine laboratory. This usually is a storage facility that is under investigation because of information obtained from precursor and essential chemical monitoring.[1]

For the forensic scientist involved in the seizure of a clandestine laboratory, the task of evaluating the possibilities and probabilities begins prior to arrival at the laboratory site. The individual tasked with securing the laboratory for the purpose of collecting evidence must, for his own protection, be trained and certified competent in dealing with the safety and technical considerations of clandestine laboratory seizures. Forensic chemists may be asked to provide assistance in preparing search warrants based on available information, as when investigators know that certain chemicals and pieces of analytical equipment such as gas cylinders, and glassware such as large triple neck round bottom flasks have been purchased. This sort of information is critical in determining what kind of synthesis is taking place. The forensic scientist will also provide technical advice regarding the importance of specific safety considerations and offer suggestions on handling situations such as on-going reactions.

After the clandestine laboratory site has been secured by the appropriate law enforcement authorities, the forensic scientist may enter the site to evaluate the environment and decide on the most appropriate actions. The investigator's most important function is to minimize any health risk to enforcement personel. This may involve ventilating the environment by opening doors, windows, and using a fan; securing open containers, turning off gases and water; and removing obstacles on the floor which may prove hazardous to anyone entering the site. The investigator may also decide on whether chemcial reactions in progress should be stopped or allowed to proceed. After all of these and other decisions are made and the site is secure, the forensic analyst will begin to sample, package, and mark evidence containers. This process will usually proceed slowly and methodically to ensure accuracy and completeness.

Once the clandestine laboratory has been seized and the evidence collected, the forensic analyst will proceed to the laboratory to complete the administrative processes of ensuring accountability and security. When the time approaches for the analytical procedures to commence, the person tasked with this process will attempt to identify as many of the samples as deemed necessary for the required judicial action. This may mean identifying any and all exhibits that were seized, or it may mean that only those exhibits required to form a conclusion as to an identification of the final product are necessary. The extent of the analysis can be more of a legal question than a scientific question. The forensic scientist should be able to provide the basics of the reaction mechanisms. This information will be based on the chemicals at the site and those identified in the reaction mixtures. He should also be able to provide a theoretical yield of the final product based on the amounts of the chemical precursors.

After the work in the laboratory has been completed, the forensic scientist has the responsibility of assisting the legal authorities in understanding what was happening in the clandestine laboratory — what was being synthesized, how was it being synthesized, and what environmental ramifications existed due to the disposing of waste solvents and other chemicals found in the soil or plumbing. The forensic analyst must recognize his responsibilities as an expert witness and provide factual information in as much detail as necessary. However, this task carries with it the responsibility of avoiding unsubstantiated speculation.

Evaluating a clandestine laboratory, from the time of notification until the time of testimony in the courtroom, requires an open-minded and analytical approach. As information is gathered and data collection proceeds, the analyst may be involved in an ever evolving decision-making process. This will probably require him to change his strategies as more information becomes available. Conclusions should be reserved until all the necessary exhibits have been collected and analyzed, the clandestine laboratory operator has been debriefed, the analytical data has been evaluated, and, if necessary, consultations with colleagues have been completed. In the courtroom, the forensic analyst will preserve his status as a credible expert witness by basing his testimony on factual data and possibilities that are within the realm of scientific probability.

1.9.1 SAFETY CONCERNS

A hazard evaluation is an absolute requirement prior to entering a clandestine laboratory. This should involve an evaluation of the physical and environmental hazards that may be present. This evaluation is usually the result of questioning other law enforcement personnel familiar with the laboratory, or the laboratory operator. Great care should be exercised in evaluating and acting on information from the laboratory operator. The forensic analyst should determine the minimum level of safety equipment required for entry into the laboratory. If there is knowledge regarding the type of drug being synthesized in the clandestine laboratory and the processing methodology, the forensic scientist will have some idea as to the types of chemicals that may be encountered. If records are available regarding the purchasing activity of the clandestine laboratory operator, the quantities of the chemicals facing the investigators will be available.

All this information should be documented and used to decide the safest and most prudent manner in which to enter the clandestine laboratory. Other concerns that must be considered are the weather conditions, and entry and egress options. Extremes in either heat or cold can affect the way the safety and sampling equipment will function. These conditions will also effect how long the forensic chemist can be expected to work in the appropriate clothing. Egress options from a clandestine laboratory must be determined before entry. In the event of a fire or explosion, those individuals processing the clandestine laboratory must know how to exit the dangerous environment. As a part of the planning scenario for processing the clandestine laboratory, the appropriate authority should make the nearest medical facility aware of the fact that if an investigator is injured, medical attention will be sought. The medical facility may have some requirement for treating a chemical injury. This should be determined beforehand and a protocol to meet these requirements should be established.

The most important responsibility of the forensic analyst involved in a clandestine laboratory investigation and seizure is safety. Safety must be considered from a number of perspectives. The forensic scientist must be concerned with the safety and well-being of anyone entering the suspected clandestine laboratory. His training and experience will have prepared him to recognize many of the obvious dangers of the chemical hazards and physical hazards at the site. This awareness is not stagnant. There will usually be a condition that requires an immediate adjustment and reevaluation. He must be constantly aware of the possible hazards when the combination of two minimally unsafe conditions result in fatalities. This results from a failure to recognize that while each condition is dangerous in its own right, combining the dangers is a recipe for disaster if certain precautions are not followed.

For instance, if the odor of ether is detected in an enclosed dark room, a possible first step might be to turn on the lights. However, any short circuit in the light switch resulting in a spark could cause the ether vapors in combination with the oxygen in the air to explode. The correct action would be to obtain an outside lighting equipment to determine the source of the ether vapors, rectify the conditions resulting in the ether vapors, ventilate the room, check the light switch and wiring, and then turn on the lights. This situation is one in which a chemical hazard in combination with a physical hazard could combine and result in serious injury or death.

Before entering the clandestine laboratory, the forensic analyst must take precautions to ensure eye, lung, and skin protection. This will usually mean proper clothing including head gear, boots, outerwear and gloves; safety glasses and/or a face shield; and the appropriate air purification and breathing apparatus. Consideration should also be given to use of air monitoring devices which can detect concentrations of combustible gases or vapors in the atmosphere, oxygen deficiencies, and gas concentrations to lower explosive limits. There are also devices available in the form of glass tubes filled with specific detection granules which allow for the reasonable determination of airborne chemical hazards in the atmosphere. When these devices are used properly, the forensic scientist entering the clandestine laboratory maximizes his chances for protecting the safety of the seizure team, including himself.

Even after the atmosphere has been sampled and ventilation has progressed, once inside the clandestine laboratory, the forensic chemist should be aware of the many possibilities posing a threat. The potential chemical dangers include an explosion potential, flammable and combustible chemicals, corrosive chemicals, oxidizers, poisons, compressed gases, irritants, and booby traps. Physical hazards include but are certainly not limited to broken glass, bare electrical wiring, slippery floors, and loud noises. These chemical and physical hazards can be accentuated by a reduction in dexterity because of safety equipment and clothing, a narrow field of vision due to a breathing apparatus, diminished communications, physical and mental stress, heat or cold stress, a confined work space environment, and a prolonged period of time spent processing the clandestine laboratory.

After the laboratory processing has been completed, the forensic scientist should be a part of the team which reduces the level of environmental contamination to a controllable level. This will usually involve prior planning for the proper disposal of hazardous chemicals and protective clothing by a waste disposal authority. There should be a standard operating procedure for the decontamination of anyone who entered the clandestine laboratory. This should include provisions for an emergency shower and an eyewash station, first aid kits, and decontamination procedures for injured workers.

One of the most important factors anyone processing a clandestine laboratory must remember is the following — no matter how much protective clothing is available, no matter how much pre-planning is done, no matter how careful a person might be in collecting chemicals and assessing danger, if that person fails to recognize his limitations in knowledge or physical ability, a disaster is waiting to happen. The greatest danger facing anyone who processes a clandestine laboratory is a false sense of security.

1.9.2 COMMONLY ENCOUNTERED CHEMICALS IN THE CLANDESTINE LABORATORY

The following tabulation of data is intended as an overview of those chemicals most frequently encountered as precursors in clandestine laboratory settings. A **precursor** is a chemical that becomes a part of the controlled substance either as the basis of the molecular skeleton or as a substituent of the molecular skeleton. This list is not all inclusive. Modifications to typical synthetic routes on the parts of ingenious organic chemists are typical and cannot always be predicted.

1.9.3 TABLES OF CONTROLLED SUBSTANCES

1.9.3.1 Generalized List by Category of Physiological Effects and Medical Uses of Controlled Substances

Precursor	Controlled substance
Acetic anhydride	Heroin
	Methaqualone
	Phenyl-2-Propanone (P2P)
Acetonitrile	Amphetamine
N-Acetylanthranilic acid	Methaqualone
	Mecloqualone
Acetylacetone	Methaqualone
4-Allyl-1,2-methylenedioxybenzene	3,4-Methylenedioxyamphetamine (MDA)
Ammoniun formate	Amphetamine
	MDA
Amphetamine	alpha-Methyl fentanyl
Aniline	alpha-Methyl fentanyl
Anthranilic acid	Methaqualone
Benzaldehyde	Amphetamine
	P-2-P

Benzene	Amphetamine
	P-2-P
Benzyl cyanide	Methamphetamine
Bromobenzene	N-Ethyl-1-phenylcyclohexylamine (PCE)
	Phencyclidine (PCP)
	1-Phenylcyclohexylpyrrolidine (PCPy)
	P-2-P
1-Bromo-2,5-dimethoxybenzene	4-Bromo-2,5-dimethoxyamphetamine (DOB)
Bromohydroquinone	DOB
5-Bromoisatin	Lysergic Acid
ortho-Bromophenol	4-Bromo-2,5-dimethoxyphenethylamine (Nexus)
Bromosafrole	3,4-Methylenedioxyethylamphetamine (MDEA)
	3,4-Methylenedioxymethamphetamine (MDMA)
2-Bromothiophene	1-[1-(2-Thienyl)cyclohexyl]piperidine (TCP)
Chloroacetic acid	P-2-P
Chloroacetone	P-2-P
1-Chloro2,5-dimethoxybenzene	Nexus
2-Chloro-N,N-dimethylpropylamine	Methadone
2-Chloroethylbenzene	Fentanyl
alpha-Chloroethylmethyl ether	P-2-P
Chlorohydroquinone	DOB
Chlorosafrole	MDEA
	MDMA
ortho-Cresol	4-Methyl-2,5-dimethoxyamphetamine (STP)
Diethylamine	Diethyltryptamine
	Lysergic Acid Diethylamide (LSD)
Ephedrine	Methamphetamine
	Methcathinone
Ergonovine	LSD
Ergotamine	LSD
Ethylamine	Ethylamphetamine
	3,4-Methylenedioxyethylamphetamine (MDEA)
N-Ethylephedrine	N-Ethyl-N-methylamphetamine
N-Ethylpseudoephedrine	N-Ethyl-N-methylamphetamine
orth-Ethylphenol	4-Ethyl-2,5-dimethoxyamphetamine
Formamide	Amphetamine
	MDA
Isosafrole	4-Methylenedioxyamphetamine (MDA)
	3,4-Methylenedioxymethamphetamine (MDMA)
	MDEA
Lysergic acid	LSD
Methylamine	Methamphetamine
	MDMA

3,4-Methylenedioxyphenyl- 2-propanon	MDA MDMA MDEA
N-Methyephedrine	N,N-Dimethylamphetamine
N-Methylpseudoephedrine	N,N-Dimethylamphetamine
Nitroethane	P-2-P Amphetamine MDA
1,2-Methylenedioxy-4- propenylbenzene	MDEA
N-Methylephedrine	P-2-P
N-Methylformamide	Methamphetamine
N-Methylformanilide	STP
2-Methyl-4-[3H]-quinazolinone	Methaqualone
Methyl-3,4,5-trimethoxybenzoate	Mescaline
Norpseudoephedrine	4-Methylaminorex
Phenethylamine	Fentanyl para-Fluoro fentanyl 2-Methyl fentanyl
N-(1-Phenethyl)-Piperidin-4-one	Fentanyl para-Fluoro fentanyl
N-(1-Phenethyl-4-piperidinyl)-aniline	Fentanyl
Phenylacetic Acid	P-2-P
Phenylacetonitrile	P-2-P
Phenylacetyl Chloride	P-2-P
D-Phenylalanine	Amphetamine Methamphetamine
2-Phenyl-1-bromoethane	Fentanyl
1-Phenyl-2-bromopropane	alpha-Methyl fentanyl
Phenylmagnesium Bromid	PCP PCPy P-2-P
Phenylpropanolamine	Amphetamine 4-Methylaminorex
Phenyl-2-propanone (P-2-P)	Amphetamine Methamphetamine
Piperidin	Phencyclidine (PCP)
N-(4-Piperidinyl)aniline	Fentanyl alpha-Methyl fentanyl
Piperonal	MDA MDMA MDEA
Piperonylacetone	N-Hydroxy MDA
Propionic Anhydride1	Fentanyl analogues

Clandestine Laboratories

Propiophenone	Methamphetamine
Pyrrolidine	PCPy
Pseudoephedrine	Methamphetamine
Safrole	MDA
	MDMA
	3,4-Methylenedioxy P-2-P
3,4,5-Trimethoxybenzaldehyde	Mescaline
	3,4,5-Trimethoxyamphetamine

Table 1.9.3.1   Controlled Substances

Below is a categorized listing of the most commonly encountered controlled substnaces.

Drug	CSA Schedules	Trade or other names	Medical uses
Narcotics			
Heroin	I	Diacetylmorphine, Horse, Smack	None in U.S., analgesic, antitussive
Morphine	II	Duramorph, MS-Contin, Roxanol, Oramorph SR	Analgesic
Codeine	II, III, IV	Tylenol w/Codeine, Empirin w/Codeine, Robitussin A-C, Fiorinal w/Codeine, APAP w/Codeine	Analgesic, antitussive
Hydrocodone	II, III	Tussionex, Vicodin, Dycodan, Lorcet	Analgesic, antitussive
Hydromorphone	II	Dilaudid	Analgesic
Oxycodone	II	Percodan, Percocet, Tylox, Roxicet, Roxidone	Analgesic
Methadone and LAAM	I, II	Dolophine, Levo-alpha-acetylmethadol, Levomethadyl acetate	Alalgesic, treatment of dependence
Fentanyl and analogues	I, II	Innovar, Sublimaze, Alfenta, Sufenta, Duragesic	Analgesic, adjunct to anesthesia, anesthetic
Other narcotics	II, III, IV, V	Percocan, Percocet, Tylox, Opium, Darvon, Talwin[2], Buprenorphine, Meperidine (Pethidine)	Analgesic, antidiarrheal
Depressants			
Chloral hydrate	IV	Noctec, Somnos, Felsules	Hypnotic
Barbiturates	II, III, IV	Amytal, Fiorinal, Membutal, Seconal, Tuinal, Penobarbital, Pentobarbital	Sedative hypnotic, veterinary euthanasia agent

Drug	CSA Schedules	Trade or other names	Medical uses
Benzodiazepines	IV	Ativan, Dalmane, Diazepam, Librium, Xanax, Serax, Valium, Tranxene, Verstran, Versed, Halcion, Paxipam, Restoril	Antianxiety, sedative, anticonvulsant, hypnotic
Glutethimide	II	Doriden	Sedative, hypnotic
Other depressants	I, II, III, IV	Equanil, Miltown, Noludar, Placidyl, Valmid, Methaqualone	Antianxiety, sedative, hypnotic
Stimulants			
Cocaine[1]	II	Coke, Flake, Snow, Crack	Local anesthetic
Amphetamine/ methamphetamine	II	Biphetamine, Desoxyn, Dexedrine, Obetrol, Ice	Attention deficit disorder, narcolepsy, weight control
Methylphenidate	II	Ritalin	Attention deficit disorder
Other stimulants	I, II, III, IV	Adipex, Didrex, Ionamin, Melfiat, Plegine, Captagon, Sanorex, Tenuate, Tepanil, Prelu-2, Preludin	Weight control
Cannabis			
Marijuana	I	Pot, Acapulco Gold, Grass, Reefer, Sinsemilla, Thai Sticks	None
Tetrahydro- cannabinol	I, II	THC, Marinol	Antinauseant
Hashish and hashish oil	I	Hash, Hash Oil	None
Hallucinogens			
LSD	I	Acid, Blotter Acid, Microdots	None
Mescaline and peyote	I	Mescal, Buttons, Cactus	None
Phenethylamines	I	2,5-DMA, STP, MDA, MDMA, Ecstacy, DOM, DOB	None
Phencyclidine and analogues	I, II	PCP, PCE, PCPy, TCP, Hog, Loveboat, Angel Dust	None
Other hallucinogens	I	Bufotenine, Ibogaine, DMT, DET, Psilcybin, Psylocin	None
Anabolic steroids			
Testosterone	III	Depo-testosterone,	Hypogonadism

Drug	CSA Schedules	Trade or other names	Medical uses
		Delatestryl (Cypionate, Enanthate)	
Nandrolone	III	Nandrolone, Durabolin, Deca-Durabolin, Deca	Anemia, breast cancer
Oxymetholone	III	Anadrol-50	Anemia

[1]Designated a narcotic under the CSA.

[2]Not designated a narcotic under the CSA.

REFERENCE

1. Frank, R.S., The clandestine laboratory situation in the United States, *J. Forensic Sci.*, 28: 18-31, 1993.

1.9.3.2 Listing of Controlled Substances by Schedule Number

Listed below are those substances specifically controlled under the Controlled Substances Act as of January 26, 1996. This list does not inlcude all controlled steroids or controlled substance analogues. These are classes of compounds that are controlled based on chemical and pharmacological criteria which have been discussed earlier in this chapter.

Table 1.9.3.2   Controlled Substances by Schedule Number

Drug name	CSA sch.	Synonyms
1-(1-Phenylcyclohexyl)pyrrolidine	I	PCPy, PHP, rolicyclidine
1-(2-Phenylethyl)-4-phenyl-4-acetoxypiperidine	I	PEPAP, synthetic heroin
1-Methyl-4-phenyl-4-propionoxypiperdine	I	MPPP, synthetic heroin
1-[1-(2-Thienyl)cyclohexyl]piperidine	I	TCP, tenocyclidine
1-[1-(2-Thienyl)cyclohexyl]pyrrolidine	I	TCPy
2,5-Dimethoxy-4-ethylamphetamine	I	DOET
2,5-Dimethoxyamphetamine	I	DMA, 2,5-DMA
3,4,5-Trimethoxyamphetamine	I	TMA
3,4-Methylenedioxy-N-ethylamphetamine	I	N-ethyl MDA, MDE, MDEA
3,4-Methylenedioxyamphetamine	I	MDA, Love Drug
3,4-Methylenedioxymethamphetamine	I	MDMA, Ecstasy, XTC
3-Methylfentanyl	I	China White, fentanyl
3-Methylthiofentanyl	I	China White, fentanyl
4-Bromo-2,5-dimethoxyamphetamine	I	DOB, 4-bromo-DMA
4-Bromo-2,5-dimethoxyphenethylamine	I	Nexus, 2-CB, has been sold as Ecstasy, i.e., MDMA
4-Methoxyamphetamine	I	PMA
4-Methyl-2,5-dimethoxyamphetamine	I	DOM, STP
4-Methylaminorex (cis isomer)	I	U4Euh, McN-422
5-Methoxy-3,4-methylenedioxyamphetamineq	I	MMDA

Drug name	CSA sch.	Synonyms
Acetorphine	I	
Acetyl-alpha-methylfentanyl	I	
Acetyldihydrocodeine	I	Acetylcodone
Acetylmethadol	I	Methadyl acetate
Allylprodine	I	
Alpha-Ethyltryptamine	I	ET, Trip
Alpha-Methylfentanyl	I	China White, fentanyl
Alpha-Methylthiofentanyl	I	China White, fentanyl
Alphacetylmethadol except levo-alphacetylmethadol	I	
Alphameprodine	I	
Alphameprodine	I	
Alphamethadol	I	
Aminoex	I	Has been sold as methamphetamine
Benzethidine	I	
Benzylmorphine	I	
Beta-Hydroxy-3-methylfentanyl	I	China White, fentanyl
Beta-Hydroxyfentanly	I	China White, fentanyl
Betacetylmethadol	I	
Betameprodine	I	
Betamethadol	I	
Betaprodine	I	
Bufotenine	I	MAPPINE, N,N-dimethylserotonin
Cathinone	I	Constituent of "khat" plant
Clonitazene	I	
Codeine methylbromide	I	
Codeine-N-oxide	I	
Cyprenorphine	I	
Desomorphine	I	
Dextromoramide	I	Palfium, Jetrium, Narcolo
Diampromide	I	
Diethylthiambutene	I	
Diethyltryptamine	I	DET
Difenoxin	I	LYSPAFEN
Dihydromorphine	I	
Dimenoxadol	I	
Dimepheptanol	I	
Dimethylthiambutene	I	
Dimethyltryptamine	I	DMT
Dioxaphetyl butyrate	I	
Dipipanone	I	Dipipan, phenylpiperone HCL, Diconal, Wellconal
Drotebanol	I	Metebanyl, oxymethebanol
Ethylmethylthiambutene	I	

Drug name	CSA sch.	Synonyms
Etonitazene	I	
Etorphine (except HCL)	I	
Etoxeridine	I	
Fenethylline ethyltheophylline amphetamine	I	Captagon, amfetyline
Furethidine	I	
Heroin	I	Diacetylmorphine, diamorphine
Hydromorphinol	I	
Hydroxpethidine	I	
Ibogaine	I	Constituent of "Tabernanthe iboga" plant
Ketobemidone	I	Cliradon
Levomoramide	I	
Levophenacylmorphan	I	
Lysergic adic deithylamide	I	LSD, Lysergide
Marinuana	I	Cannabis, Marijuana
Mecloqualone	I	Nubarene
Mescaline	I	Constituent of "Peyote" cacti
Methaqualone	I	Quaalude, Parest, Somnafac, Opitimil, Mandrax
Methcathinone	I	N-Methylcathinone, "cat"
Methyldesorphine	I	
Methyldihydromorphine	I	
Morpheridine	I	
Morphine methylbromide	I	
Morphine methylsulfonate	I	
Morphine methylsulfonate	I	
Morphine-N-oxide	I	
Myrophine	I	
N,N-Dimethylamphetamine	I	
N-Ethyl-1-phenylcyclohexylamine	I	PCE
N-Ethyl-3-piperidyl benzilate	I	JB 323
N-Ethylamphetamine	I	NEA
N-Hydroxy-3,4-methylenedioxyamphetamine	I	N-hydroxy MDA
N-Methyl-3-piperidyl benzilate	I	JB336
Nicocodeine	I	
Nicomorphine	I	Vilan
Noracymethadol	I	
Norlevorphanol	I	
Normethadone	I	Phenyldimazone
Normorphine	I	
Norpipanone	I	
Para-fluorofentanyl	I	China White, fentanyl

Drug name	CSA sch.	Synonyms
Parahexyl	I	Synhexyl
Peyote	I	Cactus which contains mescaline
Phenadoxone	I	
Phenampromide	I	
Phenomorphan	I	
Phenoperidine	I	Oparidine, Lealgin
Pholcodine	I	Copholco, Adaphol, Codisol, Lantuss, Pholcolin
Piritramide	I	Piridolan
Proheptazine	I	
Properidine	I	
Propiram	I	Algaril
Psilocybin	I	Constituent of "Magic Mushrooms"
Psilocyn	I	Psilocin, constituent of "Magic Mushrooms"
Racemoramide	I	
Tetrahydrocannabinols	I	THC, Delta-8 THC, Delta-9 THC, and others
Thebacon	I	Acetylhydrocodone, Acedicon, Thebacetyl
Thiofentanyl	I	China White, fentanyl
Tilidine	I	Tilidate, Valoron, Kitadol, Lak, Tilsa
Trimeperidine	I	Promedolum
1-Phenyleyelohexylamine	II	Prcusor of PCP
1-Piperidinoeyelohexanecarbonitrile	II	PCC, precursor of PCP
Alfentanil	II	Alfenta
Alphaprodine	II	Nisentil
Amobarbital	II	Amytal, Tuinal
Amphetamine	II	Dexedrine, Biphatamine
Anilerdine	II	Leritine
Benzoylecgonine	II	Cocaine metabolite
Bezitramide	II	Burgodin
Carfentanil	II	Wildnil
Coca Leaves	II	
Cocaine	II	Methyl benzoylecgoni, Crack
Codeine	II	Morphine methyl ester, methyl morphine
Dextropropoxyphene, bulk (non-dosage forms)	II	Propoxyphene
Dihydrocodeine	II	Didrate, Parzone
Diphenoxylate	II	
Diprenorphine	II	M50-50

Drug name	CSA sch.	Synonyms
Dronabinol in sesame oil in soft gelatine capsule	II	Marinol, synthetic THC in sesame oil/soft gelatine
Ecgonine	II	Cocaine precursor, in coca leaves
Ethylmorphine	II	Dionin
Etorphine HCL	II	M 99
Fentanyl	II	Innovar, Sublimazw, Duragesic
Glutethimide	II	Doriden, Dorimide
Hydrocodone	II	Hycodan, dihydrocodeinone
Hydromorphone	II	Dilaudid, dihydromorphinone
Isomethadone	II	Isoamidone
Levo-alphacetylmethadol	II	LAAM, long acting methadone, levomathadyl acetate
Levomethorphan	II	
Levorphanol	II	Levo-Dromoran
Meperidine	II	Demerol, Mepergan, pethidine
Meperidine intermediate-A	II	Meperidine precursor
Meperidine intermediate-B	II	Meperdine precursor
Meperidine intermediate-C	II	Meperidine precursor
Metazocine	II	
Methadone	II	Dolophine, Methadose, Amidone
Methadone intermediate	II	Methadone precursor
Methamphetamine	II	Desoxyn, D-desoxyephedrine, ICE, Crank, Speed
Methylphenidate	II	Ritalin
Metopon	II	
Moramide-intermediate	II	
Morphine	II	MS Contin, Roxanol, Duramorph, RMS, MSIR
Nabilone	II	Cesamet
Opium extracts	II	
Opium fluid extract	II	
Opium poppy	II	Papaver somniferum
Opium tincture	II	Laudanum
Opium, granulated	II	Granualted opium
Opium, Powdered	II	Powdered opium
Opium, raw	II	Raw opium, gum opium
Oxycodone	II	Percodan, Percocet, Tylox, Roxicodone, Roxicet
Oxymorphone	II	Numorphan
Pentabarbital	II	Nembutal
Phenazocine	II	Narphen, Prinadol
Phencyclidine	II	PCP, Sernylan

Drug name	CSA sch.	Synonyms
Phenmetrazine	II	Preludin
Phenylacetone	II	P2P, phenyl-2-propanone benzyl methyl ketone
Piminodine	II	
Poppy straw	II	Opium poppy capsules, poppy heads
Poppy straw concentrate	II	Concentrate of poppy straw, CPS
Racemethorphan	II	
Racemorphan	II	Dromoran
Secobarbital	II	Seconel, Tuinal
Sufentanil	II	Sufenta
Thebaine	II	Precursor of many narcotics
Amobarbital and noncontrolled active ingredients	III	Amobarbital/ephedrine capsules
Amobarbital suppository dosage form	III	
Anabolic steroids	III	"Body Building" drugs
Aprobarbital	III	Alurate
Barbituric acid derivative	III	Barbiturates not specifically listed
Benzphetamine	III	Didrex, Inapetyl
Boldenone	III	Equipoise, Parenebol, Vebonol, dehydrotestosterone
Butabarbital	III	Butisol, Butibel
Butalbital	III	Fiorinal, Butalbital with aspirin
Chlorhexadol	III	Mechloral, Mecoral, Medodorm, Chloralodol
Chlorotestosterone (same as clostebol)	III	If 4-chlorotestosterone then clostebol
Chlorphentermine	III	Pre-Sate, Lucofen, Apsedon, Desopimon
Clortermine	III	Voranil
Clostebol	III	Alfa-Trofodermin, Clostene, 4-chlorotestosterone
Codeine and isoquinoline alkaloid 90 mg/du	III	Codeine with papaverine or noscapine
Codeine combination product 90 mg/du	III	Empriin, Fiorinal, Tylenol, ASA or APAP w/codeine
Dehydrochlormethyltestotsterone	III	Oral-Turinabol
Dihydrocodeine combination product 90 mg/du	III	Synalgos-DC, Compal
Dihydrotestosterone (same as stanolone)	III	See stanolone
Drostanolone	III	Drolban, Masterid, Permastril
Ethylestrenol	III	Maxibolin, Orabolin, Durabolin O, Duraboral
Ethylmorphine comgination product 15 mg/du	III	
Fluoxymesterone	III	Anadroid-F, Halotestin, Ora-Testryl
Formebolone (incorrect spelling in law)	III	Eaiclene, Hubernol

Drug name	CSA sch.	Synonyms
Hydrocodone and isoquinoline alkaloid 15 mg/du	III	Dihydrocodeinone+papaverine or noscapine
Hydrocodone combination product 15 mg/du	III	Tussionex, Tussend, Lortab, Vicodin, Anexsia and many more
Lysergic acid	III	LSD prcursor
Lysergic acid amide	III	LSD prcursor
Mesteroline	III	Proviron
Methandienone (see Methandrostenolone)	III	
Methandranone	III	?Incorrect spelling of methandienone?
Methandriol	III	Sinasex, Stenediol, Troformone
Methandrostenolone	III	Dianabol, Methabolina, Nerobol, Parbolin
Methenolone	III	Primobolan, Primobolan Depot, Primobolan S
Methyltestosterone	III	Android, Oreton, Testred, Virilon
Methyprylon	III	Noludar
Mibolerone	III	Cheque
Morphine comgination product/ 50 mg/100 ml or gm	III	
Nalorphine	III	Nalline
Nandrolonoe	III	Deca-Durabolin, Durabolin, Durabolin-50
Norethandrolone	III	Nilavar, Solevar
Opium combination product 25 mg/du	III	Paegoric, other combination products
Oxandrolone	III	Anavar, Lonavar, Provitar, Vasorome
Oxymesterone	III	Anamidol, Balnimax, Oranabol, Oranabol 10
Oxymetholone	III	Anadrol-50, Adroyd, Anapolon, Anasteron, Pardroyd
Pentobarbital and noncontrolled active ingredients	III	FP-3
Pentobarbital suppositry dosage form	III	WANS
Phendimetrazine	III	Plegine, Prelu-2, Bontril, Melfiat, Statobex
Secobarbital and noncontrolled active ingredients	III	Various
Secobarbital suppository dosage form	III	Various
Stanolone	III	Anabolex, Andractim, Pesomax, Dihydrotestosterone
Stanozolol	III	Winstrol, Winstrol-V
Stimulant compunds previously excepted	III	Mediatric
Sulfondiethylmethane	III	
Sulfonethylmethane	III	

Drug name	CSA sch.	Synonyms
Sulfonmethnae	III	
Talbutal	III	Lotusate
Testalactone	III	Teslac
Testosterone Dalatestryl	III	Android-T, Adrolan, Depotest,
Thiamylal	III	Surital
Thiopental	III	Pentothal
Tiletamine and zolazepam combination product	III	Telazol
Trnbolone	III	Finaplix-S, Finajet, Parabolan
Vinbarbital	III	Delvinal, Vinbarbitone
Alprazolam	IV	Xanax
Barbital	IV	Veronal, Plexaonla, Barbitone
Bromazepam	IV	Lexotan, Lexatin, Lexotanil
Camazepam	IV	Albego, Limpidon, Paxor
Cathine	IV	Constituent of "Khat" plat
Chloral betaine	IV	Beta Chlor
Chloral hydrate	IV	Noctac
Chlordiazepoxide	IV	Librium, Libritabs, Lombitrol, SK-Lygen
Clobazam	IV	Urbadan, Urbanyl
Clonazepam	IV	Klonopin, Clonopin
Clorazepate	IV	Tranxane
Clotiazepam	IV	Trecalmo, Rizo
Cloxazolam	IV	Enadal, Sepazon, Tolestan
Delorazepam	IV	
Dextropropoxyphene Dosage Forms	IV	Darvon, Propoxyphene, Darvocet, Dolene, Propacet
Diazepam	IV	Valium, Valrelease
Diethylpropion	IV	Tenuate, Tepanil
Difenoxin 1 mg/25 ug ATS04/du	IV	Motofen
Estazolam	IV	ProSom, Domnamid, Eurdin, Nuctalon
Ethchlorvynol	IV	Placidyl
Ethinamate	IV	Valmid, Valamin
Ethyl loflazepate	IV	
Fencamfamin	IV	Reactivan
Fenfluramine	IV	Pondimin, Ponderal
Fenproporex	IV	Gacilin, Solvolip
Fludiazepam	IV	
Flunitrazepam	IV	Rohypnol, Narcozep, Darkene, Roipnol
Flurazepam	IV	Dalmane

Drug name	CSA sch.	Synonyms
Halazepam	IV	Pexipam
Haloxazolam	IV	
Ketazolam	IV	Anxon, Loftran, Solatran, Contamex
Lorpazolam	IV	
Lorazepam	IV	Ativan
Lormetazepam	IV	Noctamid
Mazindol	IV	Sanorex, Mazanor
Mebutamate	IV	Capla
Medazepam	IV	Nobrium
Mefenorex	IV	Aneorexic, Amaxate, Doracil, Pondinil
Meprobamate	IV	Miltown, Equanil, Deprol, Equagesic, Meprospan
Methohexital	IV	Brevital
Methylphenobarbital (mephobarbital)	IV	Mebaral, Mephobarbital
Midazolam	IV	Versed
Nimetazepam	IV	Erimin
Nitrazepam	IV	Mogadon
Nordiazepam	IV	Nordazepam, Demadar, Madar
Oxazepam	IV	Serax, Serenid-D
Oxazolam	IV	Erenal, Convertal
Paraldehyde	IV	Paral
Pemoline	IV	Cylert
Pentazocine	IV	Talwin, Talwin NX, Talacen, Talwin Compound
Petrichloral	IV	Pentaerythritol, Chloral, Periclor
Phenobarbital	IV	Luminal, Donnatal, Bellergal-S
Phentermine	IV	Ionamin, Fastin, Adipex-P, Obe-NIX, Zantryl
Pinazepam	IV	Domar
Pipradrol	IV	Detaril, Stimolag Fortis
Prazepam	IV	Centrax
Quazepam	IV	Doral, Dormalin
SPA	IV	1-Dimethylamino-1,2diphenylethane, lefetamine
Temazepam	IV	Restoril
Tetrazepam	IV	
Triazolam	IV	Halcion
Zolpidem	IV	Ambien
Buprenorphine	V	Buprenex, Temgesic
Codeine preparations — 200 mg/100 ml or 100 gm	V	Cosanyl, Robitussin A-C, Cheracol, Cerose, Pediacof

Drug name	CSA sch.	Synonyms
Difenoxin preparations — 0.5 mg/25 ug ATS04/du	V	Motofen
Dihydrocodeine preparations — 10 mg/200 ml or 100 gm	V	Cophene-S, various others
Diphenoxylate preparations — 2.5 mg/25 ug ATS04	V	Lomotil, Logen
Ethylmorphine preparations — 100 mg/100 ml or 100 gm	V	
Opium preparations — 100 mg/100 ml or 100 gm	V	Parepectolin, Kapectolin PG, Kaolin Pectin P.G.
Pyrovalerone	V	Centroton, Thymergix

The author gratefully acknowledges the assistance of Dr. Judy Lawrence, Pharmacologist, DEA office of Diversion Control, for profiding the information utilized in compiling this listing of controlled substances.

CHAPTER 2

PATHOLOGY OF DRUG ABUSE

EDITED BY CHARLES V. WETLI, M.D.

SUFFOLK COUNTY MEDICAL EXAMINER, HAPPAUGE, NEW YORK

TABLE OF CONTENTS

0-8493-2637-0/98/$0.00+$.50
© 1998 by CRC Press LLC

In a very broad sense, the pathology of drug abuse is determined by the particular drug abused, how it is used and administered, its toxic effects, and the behavioral modifications it causes. To be comprehensive, therefore, one would include physical injuries from drunk driving and hallucinogenic drugs, a variety of communicable diseases such as viral hepatitis and AIDS from needle sharing, and indirect complications of addiction (homicide, prostitution, child abuse and neglect, etc.). However, this section will devote itself to the pathological changes resulting from the pharmacologic effects of various drugs that are abused, and from the ways that these drugs are administered. In short, what one would likely encounter at the autopsy table.

A large volume of literature on drug abuse and its pathology has amassed over the past three or four decades, much of which has been recently collected into excellent comprehensive treatises.[1,2] Instead of repeating these accomplishments, this chapter will focus on issues of pathology not adequately covered in other references, and concentrate on emerging concepts and newly discovered phenomena. Accordingly, emphasis is placed on death scene investigation, evaluation of the drug abuse victim (living or deceased), and cardiovascular pathology. In many instances the authors have relied on their own academic and investigative experiences to provide a practical approach to evaluating these drug abuse victims.

Much of what is known about the pathology of drug abuse has been derived from thorough and carefully performed autopsies. It should therefore be expected that much of this section deals with the autopsy and is therefore of particular interest to the pathologist. However, far from this being an academic exercise, it is hoped that the reader will discern applications to clinical situations. This, in fact, has been accomplished over the years as clinicians have better appreciated the pathophysiology of diseases resulting from drug abuse. What is lacking currently, however, is the proper toxicologic evaluation of the drug abuse victim at the time of admission to a hospital. Except for ethanol, reliance is too often made on a urine drug screen. Blood specimens for toxicologic testing, if obtained at all, are too often

Charles V. Wetli

quantitatively insufficient or qualitatively inadequate due to lack of proper preservation. Should death occur, for whatever reason, days or weeks later, it is often impossible to adequately evaluate the victim toxicologically. In many instances (e.g., delayed deaths from cocaine-induced psychosis), this leads to deleterious speculation about who may be responsible for the death (e.g., police action or inaction) and forms the nidus of lawsuits. Conversely, adequate analysis at the beginning may readily eliminate much needless speculation, and absolve or implicate culpability on the part of others.

Although such evaluations are ideal, the goal is not likely in the immediate future with an environment of cost containment and a medical focus that best describes a patient as a problem of "here and now". This leaves little consideration for events or questions which may arise in the future regarding adequacy of patient care, or subsequent questions posed by future investigators, including medical examiners, police, and attorneys.[3]

REFERENCES

1. Karch, S.B., The Pathology of Drug Abuse, 2nd ed., CRC Press, Boca Raton, FL, 1996.
2. Lowinson, J.H., Ruiz, P., Millman, R.B., and Lancrod J.G., Eds., *Substance Abuse — A Comprehensive Textbook*, Williams & Wilkins, Baltimore, Maryland, 1992.
3. Wetli, C.V., Forensic issues, in *The Textbook of Penetrating Trauma*, Ivatury, R.R. and Cayten, C.G., Eds., Williams & Wilkins, Media, PA, 1996, chapt. 85.

2.1 PRELIMINARY OBSERVATIONS

2.1.1 INVESTIGATING THE SCENE OF DEATH

Paramount to any investigation, evaluation, or inquiry is the knowledge of terminal events and pre-terminal characteristics of the victim. In most hospital deaths, this is readily provided by the medical record. In the world of forensic pathology, such history is often lacking, and reliance must be placed on an open mind with a conscious realization that drug abuse may have had a significant contribution to a person's death regardless of initial impressions. Infectious diseases such as hepatitis or endocarditis may be the result of intravenous drug abuse; cocaine may trigger convulsions or precipitate hypertensive crises and myocardial ischemia; CNS depressants may lead to positional asphyxia, etc.

There must also be an awareness that people with natural disease may, intentionally or not, abuse drugs which may exacerbate their underlying disease process and significantly contribute to their death. Drugs create pathological states, with or without death, by their immediate pharmacologic effects, the way in which the drug is taken, by the cumulative effects of chronic abuse, and by interaction with pre-existing pathologic conditions.[1,2] Therefore, what once could have been discussed as a complication of hypertension (e.g., spontaneous aortic dissection) must now be evaluated as a possible effect of acute and chronic cocaine abuse.[3,4]

As noted previously, every death scene must be aproached with a conscious effort to evaluate the role of drugs and alcohol regardless of the apparent cause or manner of death. The scene investigator must therefore be ever cognizant of two possibilities: (1) because a person has a disease does not necessarily mean it is the cause of death; and (2) the scene of a drug overdose is frequently cleaned before investigators are even called. Consequently, it is important to evaluate all medication containers at the death scene, noting the identity of the drug and its purpose, the instructions for usage, and the number of pills remaining. Such a preliminary inventory (followed later by a more complete inventory and drug confirmation) often leads to a suspicion for drug overdose. However, since others may well have previously

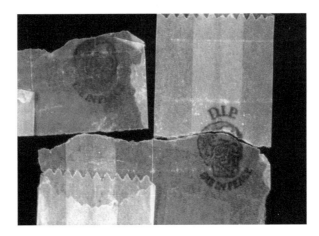

Figure 2.1.2.1 Packets of drugs.

tampered with the scene, a search should be made for containers that may be concealed such as in waste baskets, beneath the bed, in a purse, etc.

All medication and medication containers should be confiscated for a more complete inventory and possible toxicologic evaluation.[2] Likewise, all drug paraphernalia must be removed from the premises. Recognizing such paraphernalia requires that the investigator be aware of what illicit drugs prevail in a particular community and how they are used. Thus, a small spoon attached to the cap of a small vial, a gold- plated razor with a mirror, and a soda can with holes punched in the sides are all paraphernalia of cocaine abuse. Packets of drugs (often with a crude logo) (Figure 2.1.2.1) and used syringes are particularly important because these items may be the only way to determine the type of drug being abused, its purity, and its excipients. This is especially true for "designer drugs" which may be many thousand times more potent than heroin and therefore difficult to detect on routine toxicologic analysis of biological specimens.

Besides actual drug containers and paraphernalia, observation should be made which might reflect orientation toward a drug subculture: certain tattoos, evidence of gang affiliation (clothes, hair style, etc.), magazines, posters of drug-oriented music groups, etc. Periodicals and books of right-to-die organizations such as the Hemlock Society and its members should suggest the possibility of suicide or assisted suicide. This literature provides specific instructions about using drugs and plastic bags to commit suicide, and gives suggestions about avoiding (or cooperating) with a medical examiner's investigation.[5,6]

Following scrutiny of the environment, attention should turn to the victim. The exact position of the body when it was found[2] is of particular importance to establish the possibility of postural or positional asphyxia.[7] This is a situation where a person collapses in a position such that the airway (nose, mouth) is partially or completely obstructed. Because of the anesthetic effect of the drugs (with or without alcohol), the victim does not move to create an unobstructed airway, and death results from mechanical asphyxia. If the airway obstruction is partial, it may take some hours for death to actually occur from respiratory acidosis and carbon dioxide retention. During this time, the drugs and alcohol continue to be metabolized and eliminated in urine, sweat, or breath. Toxicologic analysis will then reveal a low level of drugs and, if the likelihood of positional asphyxia cannot be established, the cause of death may be a conundrum. At the scene of death it is important to interview the person who first discovered the body and ask specific questions to ascertain whether the airway could have been obstructed.

Examination of the victim at the scene should include a careful inspection of the hands and mouth for drug residue or pills, palpation for hyperthermia (or, better, a direct measurement with a plastic indicator strip or rectal thermometer) which could suggest death from a stimulant drug, tattoos which could suggest a drug culture, and fine parallel scars of the wrists or neck suggestive of a prior suicide attempt. A nearby plastic bag, particularly in the death of an elderly person with a chronic disease, suggests a death from the combination of asphyxia and drug overdose to terminate prolonged suffering (a method advocated by right-to-die organizations).

A fairly common mistake of some scene investigators is failure to turn the body over (which may reveal previously hidden drugs or drug paraphernalia), and failure to adequately examine the clothing. Pockets must be turned out or cut open, and underwear searched because they may contain packets or residue of drugs. Two death scenes have sufficient characteristics to suggest specific syndromes of cocaine abuse: cocaine-induced excited delirium and the cocaine body packer.

2.1.1.1 Excited Delirium

Excited delirium is a medical emergency with a psychiatric presentation.[8] The etiology may be infectious or pharmacologic and today it is most often seen with the abuse of cocaine or amphetamines. A similar syndrome of acute exhaustive mania may be seen wth psychiatric patients or schizophrenics who have been treated with neuroleptic medication. Clinical and neuropharmacologic studies have linked the neuroleptic malignant syndrome and drug-induced excited delirium to disturbances of dopamine release and transport in the striatum of the central nervous system.[9]

The syndrome is characterized by bizarre and violent behavior, hyperthermia, and tremendous, unexpected, strength. It usually takes several people to restrain the victim who is otherwise likely to injure themselves or others. Shortly after being restrained, the victim suddenly collapses and dies, often in police custody. If CPR is successful, there is still a potential for death in a few days from myoglobinuric nephrosis secondary to massive rhabdomyolysis.[10,11] The violence is often associated with extensive property damage, inappropriate disrobing, and varying injuries incurred from smashing glass or the struggle with law enforcement personnel. The injuries may, of themselves, be lethal and hence require careful evaluation and documentation. With cocaine-induced excited delirium, blood and brain concentrations of cocaine are typically quite low whereas concentrations of benzoylecognine are relatively high.[12,13]

The "typical" scenario is most often that of a male who has been in a violent struggle, who may be naked and with usually minor injuries sustained in a struggle with police. The most common injuries are those involving the ankles or wrists from fighting against handcuffs or hobble restraints. Scalp and neck injuries may also be seen, and require careful evaluation to exclude a traumatic death. Body temperatures of 104°F or more are common, and there is usually evidence of extensive property damage, especially smashed glass.

2.1.1.2 Body Packers

Body packers are individuals who swallow packets of drugs in one country and transport them to another, and subsequently retrieve the packets by the use of laxatives.[14] Occasionally, larger packets may be inserted in the vagina or rectum. The most popular drug smuggled by this method into the U.S. in the past two decades has been cocaine. More recently, a number of heroin body packers have been reported.[15] The amount smuggled may total nearly a kilogram of the drug. Death may occur from a pharmacologic overdose if a drug packet breaks or leaks, or if water should cross a semipermeable membrane (e.g., a condom used as a drug packet) and allow the drug to dialyze into the gastrointestinal lumen to be absorbed rapidly into the blood. Intestinal obstruction is another potentially fatal complication.

Cocaine body packers may collapse or have fatal grand mal seizures aboard an airplane or in the airport, or may be found dead in a hotel room. Evidence in the hotel room death scene usually consists of passports, foreign currency or airplane tickets indicating recent arrival from a drug supplying country (e.g., Colombia), hyperthermia (high body temperature, wet towels, or other evidence suggesting attempts at cooling), seizure activity (usually bite marks of the lower lip or tongue), presence of laxatives or enemas and, sometimes, drug packets hidden in a closet or suitcase. Heroin body packers do not have evidence of hyperthermia or of seizure activity, but often have a massive amount of white frothy pulmonary edema fluid about the nose and mouth. Also, the bodies of heroin body packers are more likely to be dumped alongside a roadway, and accomplices may have attempted to remove the packets via a crude post-mortem laparotomy.[15]

The drug packets have been fashioned from balloons, condoms, and other materials. Most commonly, however, the drug is compressed into a cylinder about 1/2 in. in diameter and 1 in. long, wrapped in plastic and heat sealed, and wrapped again in several layers of latex (e.g., fingers of latex gloves). The ends are tied and sometimes the packet is dipped in wax. The drug packets are visible radiographically, and they may be accentuated by a halo of radiolucency as gas seeps between the layers of wrapping material.[16]

2.1.2 GENERAL AUTOPSY CONSIDERATIONS

External examination in cases of oral drug abuse (i.e., pills or liquid medications) is generally not rewarding unless actual medication or medication residue is observed in the mouth or on the hands. However, as noted earlier, multiple parallel scars on the wrists or neck suggest prior suicide attempts and a subsequent suicidal drug overdose. Bite marks (contusions and lacerations) of the tongue and lower lip should be specifically sought because these frequently accompany terminal convulsions which may be the result of cocaine or tricyclic antidepressant toxicity.

The prevalence of cocaine requires careful inspection of the nasal septum (preferably with a nasal speculum) to detect inflammation, necrosis, or perforation (Figure 2.1.2.2 a and b) from the chronic nasal insufflation (snorting) of cocaine hydrochloride. Also, it should be noted that crystals of cocaine may occasionally be observed in the nasal hairs or attached to the bristles of a mustache.

Stigmata of intravenous drug abuse are, naturally, the identification of fresh, recent, and old injection sites (Figure 2.1.2.3). Sometimes these may not be evident if the user makes a conscious attempt to conceal such marks by using very small gauge needles, rotating injection sites, and by injecting in areas normally concealed even by warm weather clothing. This is especially likely to occur among those in the health professions or in occupations where inspections are frequent (e.g., police, military personnel). These abusers may inject into the ankle or foot, beneath a watch band, in the axillary region or even directly through the abdominal wall and into the peritoneal cavity. If the suspicion is high, "blind" incisions into these areas as well as more likely areas (e.g., antecubital fossae) may reveal extravasated blood in the subcutaneous tissue and around a vein, which is typical for a fresh or recent injection (Figure 2.1.2.4). Mostly, however, fresh and recent injection sites appear as small subcutaneous ecchymoses surrounding a cutaneous puncture. With cocaine, the needle puncture may be surrounded by a clear halo which in turn is surrounded by an extensive ecchymosis; recent injection sites appear as poorly demarcated ecchymoses. Intravenous cocaine users may have little or no perivenous scarring even after years of intravenous injections.[4]

Repeated intravenous injections of narcotics generally leave characteristic hyperpigmented or hypopigmented zones of perivenous scarring commonly referred to as "tracks". These arise because narcotic addicts frequently mix heroin with oral medication containing starch or talc fillers.[1] These act like myriads of microscopic splinters to elicit inflammatory (particularly granulomatous) reactions which eventually form scar tissue. This process, plus venous thrombosis, may eventually occlude the vein. Externally, these tracks appear as irregular subcutaneous "ropes" that follow the veins of the hands and forearms.

Charles V. Wetli

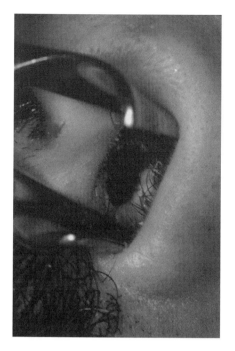
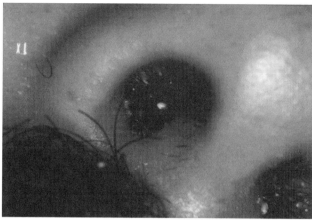

Figure 2.1.2.2 Inspection of the nasal septum.

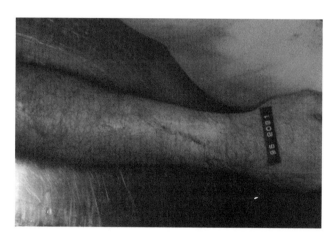

Figure 2.1.2.3 Stigmata of intravenous drug abuse are the identification of injection sites.

Round atrophic scars clustered predominantly on the arms and legs are frequently seen in intravenous drug abusers,[4] particularly cocaine abusers. These may represent healed abscesses or healed ischemic ulcers due to the vasoconstrictive effect of cocaine (which is also directly toxic to capillary endothelium). More rarely encountered are dramatic instances of necrotizing fasciitis (Figure 2.1.2.5) whch may involve an entire extremity and be accompanied by a severe lymphedema, multiple surrounding ovoid scars, and cellulitis. In extreme cases, auto-amputation of the extremity may occur. The etiology of the fasciitis and the lymphedema is unknown.

Internally, some drugs (e.g., alcohol, ethchlorvynol) may impart a characteristic odor, and some medications contain dyes that may impart a red, green, or blue discoloration to the

Figure 2.1.2.4 "Blind" incision reveals extravasated blood in the subcutaneous tissue and around a vein. This is typical for a fresh or recent injection.

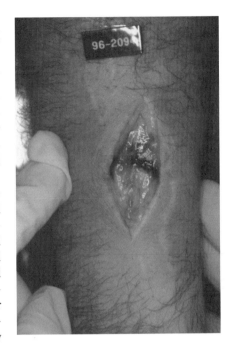

gastrointestinal tract. *In situ* changes typical of intravenous narcotic abuse include hepatosplenomegaly, enlargement of lymph nodes about the celiac axis and/or porta hepatis, and fecal impaction (from the pharmacologic property of opiates that inhibits intestinal motility).

Toxicologic analysis requires specimens to be obtained for drug screening, confirmation, and quantitation as well as tissue distribution and evaluation of drug metabolites. Thus, samples for alcohol determination should be obtained from peripheral blood (e.g., femoral vein), vitreous fluid, and central blood (e.g., aorta or pulmonary trunk); brain alcohol determinations are often useful as well. Urine is ideal for qualitative drug screening. Drugs such as tricyclic antidepressants and propoxyphene are best evaluated by analyzing liver for concentrations of the parent drug and its major metabolites.

This is also important for drugs that give spuriously elevated levels in postmortem blood because of leaching from tissue (tricyclic antidepressants and digitalis are particularly well known to leach from tissues and cause spurious increases in postmortem blood samples). Other drugs, such as cocaine, not only readily hydrolyze in the postmortem state but may leach from tissues as well, rendering interpretation of postmortem drug concentrations in blood even more difficult. For cocaine, the brain is the best substance for toxicologic analysis. For routine toxicologic evaluation, samples from the following sites are recommended: peripheral (femoral) blood, blood from aorta and pulmonary trunk, vitreous fluid, bile, liver, brain, and gastric content. In addition, one sample of blood should be centrifuged for postmortem serum (preserved by freezing) and one preserved with sodium fluoride and refrigerated for long term storage. Injection sites, the contents of the entire small intestine, hair, and other samples should be obtained as the case dictates.

Figure 2.1.2.5 Necrotizing fasciitis.

Charles V. Wetli

REFERENCES

1. Wetli, C.V., *Illicit Drug Abuse in Pathology of Environmental and Occupational Disease*, Craighead, J.D., Ed., Mosby-Year Book, Inc., St. Louis, Chapt. 15. pp 259-268, 1995.
2. Wetli, C.V., Investigation of drug-related deaths — An overview, *Am. J. Forensic Med. Path.*, 5:111-120, 1984.
3. Mittleman, R.E. and Wetli, C.V., Cocaine and apparent "natural death", *J. Forensic Sci.*, 32:11-19, 1987.
4. Mittleman, R.E. and Wetli, C.V., The pathology of cocaine abuse, *Adv. Pathol. Lab. Med.*, 4:37-73, 1991.
5. Humphry, D., *Final Exit*, The Hemlock Society, Eugene, Oregon, 1991.
6. Haddix. T.L., Harruff, R.C., Reay, D.T., and Haglund, W.D., Asphyxial suicides, *Am. J. Forensic Pathol.*, 17: 308-311, 1996.
7. Bell, M.D., Rao, V.J., Wetli, C.V., and Rodriguez, R.N., Positional asphyxiation in adults — A series of 30 cases from the Dade and Broward County Florida Medical Examiner Offices from 1982 to 1990, *Am. J. Forensic Med. Pathol.*, 13(2):101-107, 1992.
8. Wetli, C.V., and Fishbain, D.A., Cocaine-induced psychosis and sudden death in recreational cocaine users, *J. Forensic Sci.*, 30:873-880, 1985.
9. Wetli, C.V., Mash, D., and Karch, S.B., Cocaine-associated agitated delirium and the neuroleptic malignant syndrome, *Am. J. Emerg. Med.*, 14:425-428, 1996.
10. Mittleman, R.E., Rhabdomyolysis associated with cocaine and ethanol abuse, *Am. Soc. Clin. Pathol.*, 37:95-104, 1995
11. Roth, D., Alarcon, F.J., Fernandez, J.A. et al., Acute rhabdomyolysis associated with cocaine intoxication, *New Eng. J. Med.*, 319:673-677, 1988
12. Raval, M.P. and Wetli, C.V., Sudden death from cocaine induced excited delirium: An analysis of 45 cases (abstract), *Am. J. Clinical Path.*, 104(3):329, 1995.
13. Ruttenber, A.J., Lawler-Hernandez, J., Yin, M., et al., Fatal excited delirium following cocaine use: Epidemiologic findings provide new evidence for mechanism of cocaine toxicity, *J. Forensic Sci.*, in press.
14. Wetli, C.V. and Mittleman, R.E., The body packer syndrome — toxicity following ingestion of illicit drugs packaged for transportation, *J. Forensic Sci.*, 26:492-500, 1981
15. Wetli, C.V., Rao, A., and Rao, V.J., Fatal heroin body packing, *Am. J. Forensic Med. Pathol.*, in press.
16. Beerman, R., Nunez, D., and Wetli, C.V., Radiographic evaluation of the cocaine smuggler, *Gastrointestinal Radiol.*, 11:3512-354, 1986

2.2 DISEASES OF THE HEART

2.2.1 TECHNIQUES FOR EXAMINATION OF THE HEART*

RENU VIRMANI, M.D., ALLEN P. BURKE, M.D., AND ANDREW FARB, M.D.

DEPARTMENT OF CARDIOVASCULAR PATHOLOGY,
ARMED FORCES INSTITUTE OF PATHOLOGY, WASHINGTON, D.C.

This chapter is written with the forensic pathologist in mind as often he has to autopsy a large number of cases in a single day and therefore does not have the luxury of time. It is of utmost importance that the heart be examined carefully and methodically in order to obtain maximal information to establish the cause of death. The most common method of examination of the heart has been the opening of each of the four chambers according to the direction of the flow of blood.[1,2]

Briefly, the right atrium is opened from the inferior vena cave to the tip of the atrial appendage; the right ventricle is opened along its lateral border through the tricuspid valve and annulus to the apex of the right ventricle with extension to the pulmonary outflow tract close to the ventricular septum. The left atrium is opened by cutting across the roof of the atrium between the left and right pulmonary veins; and the left ventricle is opened laterally between the anterior and posterior papillary muscles to the apex and then cut along the anterior wall adjacent to the ventricular septum through the aortic outflow tract. The classic method is a logical approach for congenital heart disease, in which preservation of the landmarks is useful. However, it is not optimal for evaluation of myocardial infarction, acute or healed, and for infiltrative diseases and cardiomyopathies, because it does not readily allow for the assessment of ventricular cavity diameter and ventricular septal thickness. This chapter is especially directed towards the practice of forensic pathology, and outlines optimal methods for sectioning the heart in ischemic heart disease, valvular heart disease, and cardiomyopathy.

2.2.1.1 Removal of the Heart

The examination of the adult heart begins after the anterior chest plate has been removed. A longitudinal cut through the anterior aspect of the pericardial sac is made. The amount of pericardial fluid is measured, and its character is noted. The surface of the visceral as well as parietal pericardium is also examined for exudates, adhesions, tumor nodules, or other lesions. A short longitudinal incision 2 cm above the pulmonary valve will enable a check for thromboemboli in the main pulmonary trunk *in situ*. The heart is removed by cutting the inferior vena cava just above the diaphragm and lifting the heart by the apex, reflecting it anteriorly and cephalad to facilitate exposure of the pulmonary veins at their pericardial reflection. After it is confirmed that the pulmonary veins enter normally into the left atrium, the pulmonary veins are cut. The aorta and the pulmonary trunk, the last remaining connec-

---

* Reproduced in part and modified from Virmani R., Ursell, P.C., and Fenoglio, J.J. Jr., Examination of the heart, *Human Pathology*, 18:432,1987, and Virmani. R., Ursell, P.C., and Fenoglio, J.J. Jr., Examination of the heart, in *Cardiovascular Pathology*, Virmani, R., Atkinson, J.B., and Fenoglio, J.J. Jr., Eds., W.B. Saunders, Philadelphia 1991, pp 1-20.

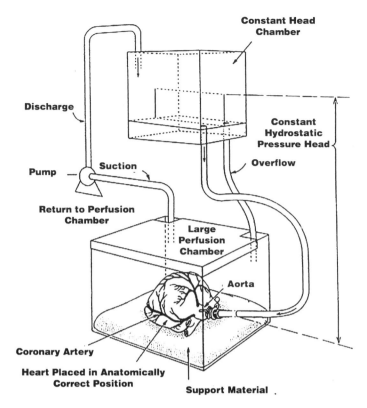

Figure 2.2.1.1 Diagram showing the method used for perfusion fixation of the heart. The constant head chamber is placed 135 cm above the perfusion chamber, and is connected via polyethylene tubing to the ascending aorta through the Lucite plug. The excess formaldehyde is suctioned back into the constant head chamber via a pump. Both chambers are covered in order to reduce formalin vapors. (Courtesy J. Frederick Cornhill, D. Phil.)

tions, are cut transversely 2 cm above the semilunar valves. Following removal of the heart from the pericardial cavity and before weighing the specimen, postmortem blood clots should be removed manually and gently by flushing the heart with water from the left and right atria.

2.2.1.2 Examination of Coronary Arteries

The ideal method of examining the coronary arterial tree requires injecting the coronary arteries with a barium-gelatin mixture and studying the vessels in radiographs.[3,4] This method is tedious and time consuming, and most medical examiners are not provided with a large staff who have knowledge of basic anatomic landmarks. It is therefore recommended that, instead of barium-gelatin coronary injections, the heart be perfusion fixed with 10% buffered formaldehyde retrograde from the ascending aorta at 100 mm Hg pressure (Figure 2.2.1.1) for at least 1 h.

A specially constructed Lucite plug or a rubber stopper with a central tubing is inserted into the aorta, taking care that the Lucite/rubber plug does not touch the aortic valve. The Lucite plug is attached to tubing that is connected to the perfusion chamber.[5] The latter is placed 135 cm above the specimen, and this provides gravity perfusion pressure that is equivalent to 100 mm Hg. As a result, the coronary arteries are fixed in a distended state that approximates the dimensions observed in living patients. Myocardial fixation is also affected, but cardiac chambers are not fixed in a distended state.

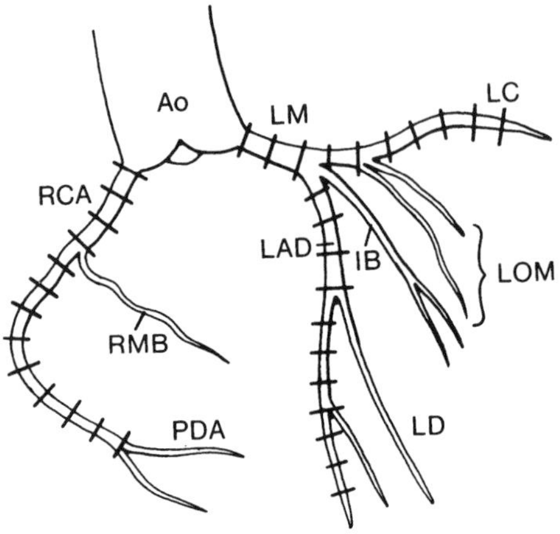

Figure 2.2.1.2A Diagram of the right and left epicardial coronary arteries as they arise from the aorta. The four major arteries that must be described in detail are right (RCA), left main (LM), left anterior descending coronary (LAD), and the left circumflex (LC) coronary arteries. Not uncommonly severe coronary (>75% cross-sectional area luminal narrowing) artery disease may effect the smaller branches (IB = intermediate or also called ramus branch, LD = left diagonal, LOM= left obtuse marginal, PDA = posterior descending artery, and RMB = right marginal branch).

This method is fairly simple, does not require sophisticated equipment in order to achieve good fixation, and the heart can be cut immediately after perfusion fixation. If perfusion fixation is impractical, the heart should be fixed for 24 h in 10% formaldehyde (10 parts of formaldehyde to 1 part of specimen) before cutting. Radiography of the heart is recommended in order to determine the extent of coronary and valvular calcification but is not essential; if coronary arteries are heavily calcified, they need to be decalcified prior to cutting at 3 to 4 mm intervals.

The vessels that must be examined in all hearts include the four major epicardial coronary arteries: the left main, the left anterior descending, the left circumflex, and the right coronary arteries. However, it is not unusual to see severe luminal narrowing in smaller branches of the main coronary arteries; left diagonals, left obtuse marginal, ramus (intermediate) branch, and the posterior descending coronary arteries (Figure 2.2.1.2A).

Following fixation and/or decalcification, the coronary arteries are cut transversely at 3 to 4 mm intervals with a sharp scalpel blade by a gentle sawing motion (not by firm pressure) to confirm sites of narrowing and to evaluate the pathologic process (e.g., atherosclerotic plaques, thrombi, dissections) directly. If the coronary arteries are heavily calcified, it is desirable to remove the coronary arteries intact. Following dissection of the vessel from the epicardial surface, each coronary artery is carefully trimmed of excess fat and the intact arterial tree is placed in a container of formic acid for slow decalcification over 12 to 18 h.

Decalcification of isolated segments of vessel may be sufficient for cases in which the coronary arteries are only focally calcified. The areas of maximal narrowing are noted by specifying the degrees of reduction of the cross-sectional area of the lumen (e.g., 0 to 25%, 26 to 50%, 51 to 75%, 76 to 90%, 91 to 99%, and 100%). Most cardiologists agree that, in the absence of other cardiac disease, significant or severe coronary artery narrowing is that exceeding a 75% cross-sectional luminal narrowing. Particular attention should be paid to the left main coronary artery because disease in this vessel is very important clinically but frequently overlooked at autopsy.[6]

Cross-sections from areas of maximal narrowing from each of the four major epicardial coronary arteries or their branches are selected for histologic examination. Sections of all coronary arteries containing thrombi are taken to aid in determining the type of underlying plaque morphology, i.e., plaque rupture or plaque erosion (ulceration). The site of maximal narrowing must be specified, i.e., proximal, middle, or distal coronary involvement. This is of great medicolegal importance in cases where the patient may have been inadequately examined in the physicians office or emergency room or in the hospital following chest pain. It is the location of the severe narrowing which determines if the patient is operable or not; presence of distal disease signifies non-operability.

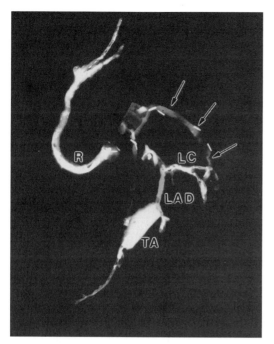

Figure 2.2.1.3 Radiograph of epicardial coronary arteries and saphenous vein bypass graft (arrows) to left circumflex (LC) removed at autopsy. Note focal calcification of the native arteries and absence of calcification of the vein graft. A portion of the left anterior coronary artery is surrounded by myocardium (bridged or tunneled coronary artery). Arteries are decalcified prior to sectioning and embedding in paraffin. (From Virmani, R., Ursell, P.C., and Fenoglio, J.J., Examination of the heart, in Virmani, R., Atkinson, J.B., and Fenoglio, J.J., Eds., *Cardiovascular Pathology*, W.B. Saunders, Philadelphia, 1991, pp 1-20. With permission.)

2.2.1.3 Examination of Bypass Grafts

When removing the heart at autopsy, care must be taken to avoid injury to the saphenous vein bypass grafts. A longer segment of the ascending aorta is left in continuity with the heart to enable examination of vein grafts from aortic orifice to distal anastomosis. Twists, as well as excessive tautness between aorta and distal anastomosis, are noted.[7] As in the native coronary arteries, the full extent of the saphenous vein grafts is best visualized by barium-gelatin mixture followed by radiography. It is best to inject all the vein grafts simultaneously and to obtain radiographs before injection of the coronary arteries. This enables more detailed study of the native coronary arteries distal to the graft as well as at the coronary graft anastomosis.

Measurements of lumen diameters may be made from the radiographs. In those cases in which the internal mammary artery is anastomosed to the coronary system, the internal mammary artery is injected from where it has been severed during removal of the heart. The native coronary arteries are injected, fixed, and radiographed to evaluate the extent of disease in the remainder of the coronary arterial tree. If, as mentioned previously, it is not feasible to inject the heart with a barium-gelatin mixture, then the heart may be perfusion fixed with formaldehyde from the aortic stump taking care that the graft orifices are below the Lucite plug and the internal mammary artery should be ligated near the site of severance from the chest wall.

The grafts and native arteries may then be removed from the heart, radiographed, and cut at 3- to 4-mm intervals to determine the extent of luminal narrowing, the presence or absence of thrombi, and/or the extent of atherosclerosis in vein grafts and coronary arteries.[8-11] In cases where it is not possible to perfusion fix the heart, the heart may be immersion fixed in 10% buffered formaldehyde overnight and dissection of the grafts and native vessels is carried out the next morning. Prior to cutting the arteries and the grafts, it is useful to radiograph and decalcify them when necessary (Figure 2.2.1.3).

When there are no lesions grossly identifiable, random sections of the entire length of the grafts should be taken. Anastomotic sites are sectioned in different ways depending on whether the connection is end to end or end to side (Figure 2.2.1.4). When reporting the findings in the heart, it is important to mention each graft separately; including the location of the aortic orifice, whether it is involved by atherosclerotic ulcerated lesion or not, and if present mention

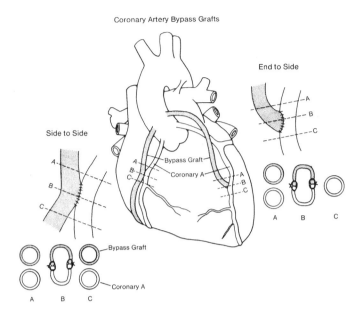

Figure 2.2.1.4 Diagram illustrating coronary artery bypass grafts that have end-to-side and side-to-side anastomoses in two separate grafts (shaded area) to left anterior descending and right coronary arteries, respectively. The figure illustrates the method used for sectioning of anastomotic site with end-to-side and side-to-side anastomoses to demonstrate if any of the three mechanisms for obstruction in the anastomotic site are present (i.e., compression or loss of arterial lumen, which may occur if the majority of the arterial wall has been used for anastomosis; thrombosis at the site of anastomosis; and dissection of the native coronary–artery at the site of anastomosis) and if the coronary artery has severe narrowing at the site of anastomosis due to severe atherosclerotic change. (Modified from Bulkley, B.H. and Hutchins, G.M., Pathology of coronary artery bypass graft surgery, *Arch. Patrol.,* 102:273, 1978. From Virmani, R., Ursell, P.C., and Fenoglio, J.J., Examination of the heart, in Virmani, R., Atkinson, J.B., and Fenoglio, J.J., Eds., *Cardiovascular Pathology,* W.B. Saunders, Philadelphia, 1991, pp 1-20. With permission.)

if atheroemboli could have embolized and may be the source of the infarct noted in the heart. Describe the course of the graft and which native coronary vessel to which it is distally anastomosed. Give the size of the native vessel, i.e., less than or greater than 1 mm diameter; vessels less than 1 mm in diameter usually do not carry enough blood to meet the demands of the myocardium. Also, determine if there is severe distal disease present in the grafted vessel.

2.2.1.4. Examination of the Myocardium in Ischemic Heart Disease

In the presence or absence of acute or healed myocardial infarction, the myocardium is best examined by slicing the ventricles in a manner similar to a loaf of bread. To evaluate the specimen, a series of short-axis cuts are made through the ventricles from apex to base (Figure 2.2.1.5A). This method is best accomplished using a long, sharp knife on the intact fixed specimen following examination of the coronary arteries. With the anterior aspect of the heart downward (against the cutting board), the cuts are made parallel to the posterior atrioventricular sulcus at 1- to 1.5-cm intervals from the apex of the heart to a point approximately 2 cm caudal to the sulcus or up to the mid-portion of the papillary muscles of the left ventricle.

The result is a series of cross-sections through the ventricles, including papillary muscles with the atrioventricular valve apparatus left intact in the remainder of the specimen. The location and extent of the infarct is noted. Locations may be stated using terms relating to the

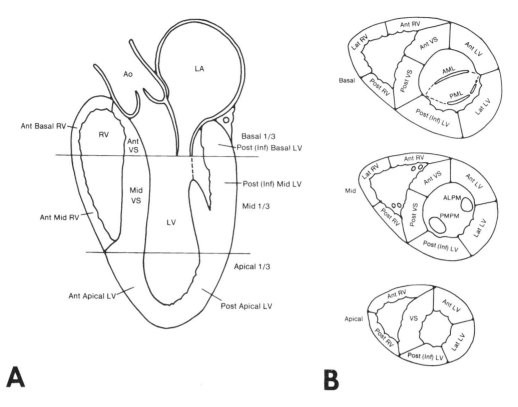

Figure 2.2.1.5 The location and extent of myocardial infarction must be indicated by the size, that is, how much of the base to apex is infarcted: basal one third, and/or middle one third, and/or apical one third or more than one third from base to apex. The diagram in (A) shows a long axis view of the heart with regional nomenclature. (B) The location of the myocardial infarction in the left ventricle must also indicate the wall in which the infarction occurred: anterior, posterior, lateral, septal, or any combination of these. This diagram illustrates a short-axis view through the basal, middle, and apical portions of the right and left ventricles. (Ao = aorta; Ant = anterior; ALPM = anterolateral papillary muscle; AML = anterior mitral leaflet; Inf = inferior; LA = left atrium; LV = left ventricle; Mid = middle; PML = posterior mitral leaflet; PMPM = posteromedial papillary muscle; Post = posterior; RV = right ventricle; VS = ventricular septum) (Modified from Edwards, W.D., Tajik, A.J., and Seward, J.B., Standardized nomenclature and anatomic basis for regional tomographic analysis of the heart, *Mayo Clin. Proc.,* 56:479, 1981. From Virmani, R., Ursell, P.C., and Fenoglio, J.J., Examination of the heart, in Virmani, R., Atkinson, J.B., and Fenoglio, J.J., Eds., *Cardiovascular Pathology,* W.B. Saunders, Philadelphia, 1991, pp 1-20. With permission.)

standard anatomic terms of reference (e.g., anteroseptal, posterolateral). The extent of infarction may be described in terms of circumference of the ventricle involved[12–14] and longitudinal portion of the ventricle involved (e.g., basal third, middle third, apical third) (Figure 2.2.1.5 A and B).

The distribution within the wall is also described (e.g., transmural or subendocardial; transmural when the infarct extends from the endocardium to the epicardium, and subendocardial when <50% of the left ventricular wall is infarcted). The gross pathologic appearance of the myocardium serves as a relatively good index as to the age of the infarct but must be confirmed by histologic examination. Even if infarction cannot be identified grossly, it is important to section the myocardium in the distribution of the severely diseased coronary arteries more extensively.

2.2.1.5 Examination of the Heart in Cardiomyopathy

The short-axis sectioning (bread loafing) method described above serves well for the examination of the cardiomyopathic heart. Cardiac hypertrophy and dilation may be demonstrated quite effectively by this method. If the left ventricular cavity measures >4 cm, excluding the papillary muscles, it is considered that the patient was in congestive heart failure prior to death even if there is no history to corroborate the autopsy findings. Left ventricular hypertrophy is said to be present if the LV wall measures >1.5 cm. On the other hand, if the left ventricular wall measures <1.5 cm but the heart weight is increased and the left ventricular cavity is enlarged, then there will be microscopic appreciation of myocyte hypertrophy.

Histologic examination of the myocardium is critical to determining the cause of the cardiomyopathy. Thus, in addition to sections of tissue with obvious gross pathology, samples of the walls of all four cardiac chambers, the septum, and papillary muscles should be taken. In the past, the right ventricle has been relatively ignored, but because of the greater awareness of right ventricular infarction and right ventricular dysplasia/cardiomyopathy, it should be a routine to examine the right ventricle carefully. For establishing the diagnosis of right ventricular cardiomyopathy, the most helpful single observation to make is one of fibrosis or scarring in the right ventricular wall with intermingling of fat; these lesions are most often seen in the inflow region of the right ventricle on the posterior wall or in the anterior wall of the right ventricular outflow tract. These lesions can be commonly appreciated grossly if a careful examination of the heart is carried out.

The heart also may be cut in four chamber view by cutting the heart from the apex to base, along the acute margin of the right ventricle and the obtuse margin of the left ventricle and continuing the plane of section through the atria (Figure 2.2.1.6). This four chamber view is best for evaluating the atrial and ventricular chamber size. In cases of hypertrophic cardiomyopathy, the heart should be cut in the long axis view of the left ventricular outflow tract. The plane of dissection of the aortic valve leaflet is through the right coronary and the posterior non-coronary leaflets, the anterior and the posterior mitral leaflets, the posterior and the anterior left atrial wall, ventricular septum, posterolateral wall of LV and the anterior right ventricular wall (Figure 2.2.1.7). Sections to determine the presence of fibromuscular disarray are taken in the transverse plane, usually from the septal location with the largest dimension.

2.2.1.6 Examination of the Heart Valves

In the case of valvular heart disease, the valves are best studied intact. The atrial and ventricular aspect of the atrioventricular valves and the ventricular and arterial aspects of the semilunar valves are examined (Figure 2.2.1.8). Thus, the tricuspid valve is exposed by a lateral incision through the right atrium from the superior vena cave to 2 cm above the valve annulus. Similarly, the mitral valve may be studied following opening of the left atrium via an incision extending from one of the left pulmonary veins to one of the right pulmonary veins and another incision continuing through the atrium laterally to a point 2 cm above the annulus. If a valve abnormality requires closer inspection, the atria, including the interatrial septum, may be removed 1 to 2 cm above the atrioventricular valves (Figure 2.2.1.8A). The ventricular aspects of the atrioventricular valves may be viewed following removal of the serial slices of ventricle as described previously.

The semilunar valves are best studied after removal of the aorta (Figure 2.2.1.8C) and the main pulmonary artery at a point just above the coronary ostia or valve annulus. In selected cases, the valvular pathology may be best visualized using a four-chamber cut[15-17] in the plane including both the acute and obtuse margins of the heart (Figure 2.2.1.6). The aortic valve may be demonstrated by a left ventricular long-axis cut passing from the apex through the outflow tract, ventricular septum, anterior mitral valve leaflet, and aortic valve (Figure 2.2.1.7).

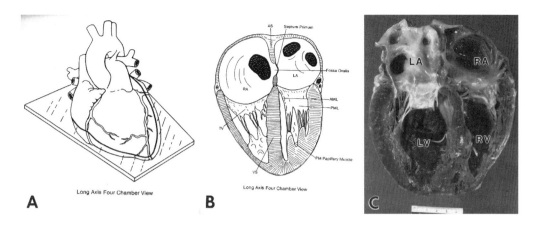

Figure 2.2.1.6 (A) Diagram of the heart demonstrating the ultrasonic tomographic plane used for obtaining the long axis view of the heart. This four-chamber view is best used for evaluating the atrial and ventricular dimensions, intracavitary masses, ventricular and atrial septal defects, atrioventricular valve abnormalities, ventricular aneurysms, and the drainage of pulmonary veins. (B) Diagram demonstrating the four chamber view of the heart. This method involves sectioning the heart from apex to base, along the acute margin of the right ventricle and the obtuse margin of the left ventricle and continuing the plane of sectioning through the atria. The bisected specimen that is photographed should match the ante mortem cardiac image. (C) Tomographic analysis of a heart from a 17-year-old boy who developed progressive heart failure over the course of 8 months, showing four-chamber view with biventricular hypertrophy, four-chamber dilatation, and apical right and left ventricular thrombus. (RA = right atrium; LA = left atrium; VS = ventricular septum; TV = tricuspid valve; AML = anterior mitral leaflet; PML = posterior mitral leaflet) (Modified from Tajik, A.L., Seward, I., Hager, D.J., Muir, D.D., and Lie, J.T., Two dimensional real-time ultrasonic imaging of the heart and great vessels: Technique, image orientation, structure notification and validation, *Mayo Clin. Proc.,* 53:271, 1978. From Virmani, R., Ursell, P.C., and Fenoglio, J.J., Examination of the heart, in Virmani, R., Atkinson, J.B., and Fenoglio, J.J., Eds., *Cardiovascular Pathology,* W.B. Saunders, Philadelphia, 1991, pp 1-20. With permission.)

Measurement of the circumference of annuli, especially in valvular stenosis, is on the whole not very useful. In ectasia of the aorta, it is indeed a must to measure the aortic annulus as the valve will be normal in appearance but the annulus will be dilated. Examination of the heart valves should document the type and severity of the valvular disease and its effect on the cardiac chambers and this includes microscopic evaluation.

In cases in which histology of a valve may be helpful, the leaflets are sectioned together with a portion of the adjacent chambers and/or vessel walls. For example, the posterior leaflet of the mitral valve is sectioned including a portion of the left atrium and left ventricular free wall, while the anterior leaflet includes ventricular septum and non-coronary cusp of the aortic valve. In cases of rheumatic heart disease, sections of the atrial appendages are submitted for histologic examination because the incidence of Aschoff's nodules is highest in these structures.

2.2.1.7 Prosthetic Heart Valves

The objectives for examinations of valve implants include determination of (1) the type of implant (bioprosthesis or mechanical valve) and its size and position regarding annulus and chamber; (2) adequacy of movement of the valve apparatus; (3) presence of thrombi, vegetations, and paravalvular abscesses or leaks; and (4) evidence of valve degeneration.[15] In particular, paravalvular abscesses may not be visible without careful inspection of the native annulus

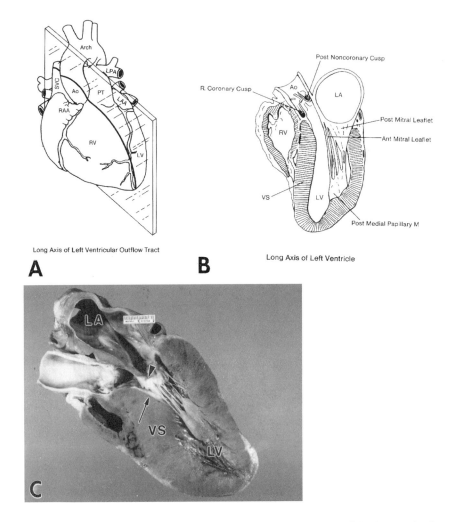

Figure 2.2.1.7 (A) Diagram of the heart demonstrating the ultrasonic plane of the long axis view of the left ventricular outflow tract. The normal anatomic relationship of septal-aortic and mitral-aortic continuity are best shown by this plane of dissection. This method is used for aortic root pathology, including valvular, supravalvular, and intravalvular obstructions, left ventricular chamber size, posterior wall abnormalities, ventricular septal defects, mitral valve disease, and left atrial size. (B) Anatomic landmarks seen with a long-axis view of the left ventricle. The plane of dissection of aortic valve leaflets is through the right coronary and posterior non-coronary leaflets. (C) Left ventricular long-axis section in hypertrophic cardiomyopathy, showing asymmetric septal hypertrophy with a discrete left ventricular outflow tract plaque (arrow) and a thickened anterior mitral leaflet (arrow head). (Ao = aorta; LA = left atrium; LPA = left pulmonary artery; LV = left ventricle; RAA = right atrial appendage; RV = right ventricle; SVC = superior vena cave; VS = ventricular septum) (Modified from Tajik, A.J., Seward, J.B., Hager, D.J., Muir, D.D., and Lie, J.T., Two-dimensional real- time ultrasonic imaging of the heart and great vessels: Technique, image orientation, structure identification and validation, *Mayo Clin. Proc.,* 53:271, 1978. From Virmani, R., Ursell, P.C., and Fenoglio, J.J., Examination of the heart, in Virmani, R., Atkinson, J.B., and Fenoglio, J.J., Eds., *Cardiovascular Pathology,* W.B. Saunders, Philadelphia, 1991, pp 1-20. With permission.)

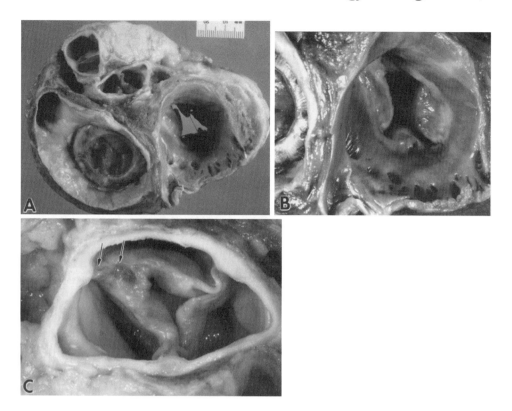

Figure 2.2.1.8 (A) The appearance of the atrioventricular valves after removal of both the atria. The mitral valve has been replaced with a bioprosthetic porcine valve which shows a tear in the muscular leaflet close to the ring (arrow head). (B) The right atrium has been removed close to the tricuspid valve. Note the valve margins are thickened and the commissure between the posterior and the septal leaflet is fused secondary to chronic rheumatic valvulitis. (C) The aortic valve is examined on removal of the aorta close to sinotubular junction. There is diffuse thickening of the valve, which is more marked at the free margins with one of the three commissures fused (arrow). These changes are consistent with chronic rheumatic valvulitis. (AV = aortic valve; MV = mitral valve; PV = pulmonary valve; TV = tricuspid valve). (From Virmani, R., Ursell, P.C., and Fenoglio, J.J., Examination of the heart, in Virmani, R., Atkinson, J.B., and Fenoglio, J.J., Eds., *Cardiovascular Pathology*, W.B. Saunders, Philadelphia, 1991, pp 1-20. With permission.)

following removal of the implant. Demonstration of any pathology may be enhanced using short-axis cuts through the atrioventricular junction.

2.2.1.8 Examination of the Aorta

Because atherosclerosis is the most common lesion affecting the aorta, the aorta should be opened longitudinally along its posterior or dorsal aspect from the ascending aorta through the bifurcation and into both common iliac arteries. The extent of disease and the types of lesions may then be described. While this method enables inspection of the complete intimal surface, it may not be optimal for certain types of pathology, such as aortic aneurysms, which may best be demonstrated by cross-sectional slices 1 to 1.5 cm apart in the perfusion-fixed, distended specimen (Figure 2.2.1.9). Aortic dissections may be examined by a longitudinal cut (long-axis cut) with the aorta cut into anterior and posterior halves (Figure 2.2.1.10) or by transverse cut at 1- to 1.5-cm intervals after the aorta has been allowed to fix for 24 hours in a distended state or free floating in anatomic position in formaldehyde.

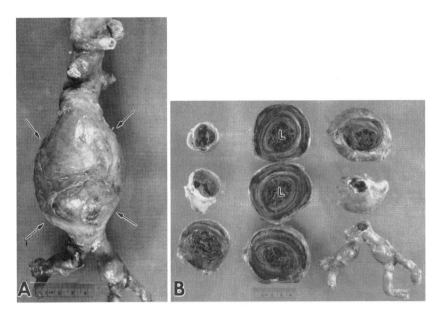

Figure 2.2.1.9 (A) External view of the abdominal aorta with an infrarenal aneurysm (arrows). Note the size, which is best expressed as the largest diameter. In this case, it is 7 cm. (B) Same aneurysm cut transversely at 1.0 to 1.5 cm apart. Note the extent of luminal (L) narrowing secondary to an organizing thrombus. (From Virmani, R., Ursell, P.C., and Fenoglio, J.J., Examination of the heart, in Virmani, R., Atkinson, J.B., and Fenoglio, J.J., Eds., *Cardiovascular Pathology*, W.B. Saunders, Philadelphia, 1991, pp 1-20. With permission.)

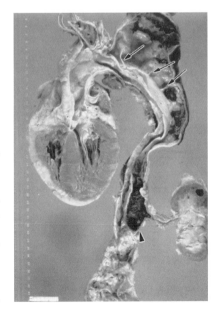

Figure 2.2.1.10 The heart has been cut in the long-axis plane, exposing the right and left ventricles and the aortic root and valve. In this plane, the anterior wall of the aorta has been removed. Note the dissecting aneurysm that starts just distal to the subclavian artery and extends along the greater curvature of the aorta to just below the left renal artery (arrowhead). Within the false lumen there are fibrous strands (arrows) connecting the outer media and adventitia to the inner media and intima. Note also the organizing thrombus within a fusiform aneurysm distal to the subclavian and within the abdominal aorta of the false lumen. (From Virmani, R., Ursell, P.C., and Fenoglio, J.J., Examination of the heart, in Virmani, R., Atkinson, J.B., and Fenoglio, J.J., Eds., *Cardiovascular Pathology*, W.B. Saunders, Philadelphia, 1991, pp 1-20. With permission.)

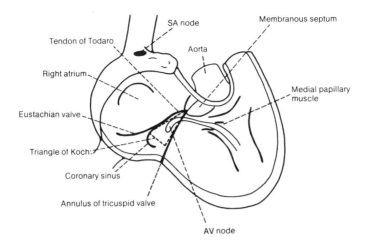

Figure 2.2.1.11 Diagram of location of the atrioventricular (AV) and sinoatrial (SA) nodes along with the landmarks that help in locating their positions during sectioning of the heart. (Modified from Davies, M.J., Anderson, R.H., and Becker, A.E., *The Conduction System of the Heart*, Butterworth & Co, London, 1983. From Virmani, R., Ursell, P.C., and Fenoglio, J.J., Examination of the heart, in Virmani, R., Atkinson, J.B., and Fenoglio, J.J., Eds., *Cardiovascular Pathology*, W.B. Saunders, Philadelphia, 1991, pp 1-20. With permission.)

2.2.1.9 EXAMINATION OF THE CONDUCTION SYSTEM

For cases in which conduction disturbances were suspected clinically, histologic examination of the cardiac conduction tissues is often rewarding in terms of documenting a structural basis for the problem. Many pathologists are intimidated by the prospect of doing conduction system studies because the pertinent tissue cannot be visualized grossly. Yet, with practice and careful attention to anatomic landmarks, this part of the examination of the heart is really not so difficult.[18,19]

In most humans, the sinus node is a spindle-shaped structure located in the sulcus terminalis on the lateral aspect of the superior vena cava and the right atrium (Figure 2.2.1.11). In some patients, it is a horseshoe-shaped structure wrapped across the superior aspect of this cavoatrial junction. Histologically, the sinus node consists of relatively small-diameter, haphazardly oriented atrial muscle cells admixed with connective tissue, collagen, and elastic fibers (Figure 2.2.1.12). Often, the artery to the sinus node can be identified in or around the nodal tissue. Because the sinus node is not visible grossly, the entire block of tissue from the suspected area should be taken and serially sectioned, either in the plane perpendicular to the sulcus terminalis (parallel to the long axis of the superior vena cave) or in the plane containing the sulcus (perpendicular to the vessel). In small infants, serial sectioning of the entire cavoatrial junction is preferred.

There are no anatomically distinct muscle tracts for conduction through the atria. The impulse is collected in the atrioventricular node, which is located within the triangle of Koch in the floor of the right atrium. In the heart dissected in the traditional manner along the lines of blood flow, this region is delineated by the following landmarks: the tricuspid valve annulus inferiorly, the coronary sinus posteriorly, and the continuation of the valve guarding the coronary sinus (tendon of Todaro) superiorly (Figure 2.2.1.11). The atrioventricular node lies within Koch's triangle (Figure 2.2.1.11), and the apex of the triangle anteriorly denotes the point at which the common bundle of His penetrates the fibrous annulus to reach the left

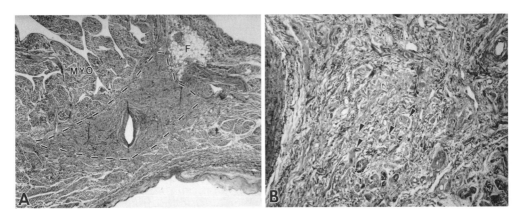

Figure 2.2.1.12 (A) The sinus node (outlined) lies in the subepicardium. The superficial layer is surrounded by epicardial fat (F), and the deeper layers anastomose with the surrounding atrial myocardium (MYO). (Movat, x 25) (From Virmani, R., Ursell, P.C., and Fenoglio, J.J., Examination of the heart, in Virmani, R., Atkinson, J.B., and Fenoglio, J.J., Eds., *Cardiovascular Pathology,* W.B. Saunders, Philadelphia, 1991, pp 1-20. With permission.) (B) High power view of the SA node showing fibrous tissue, elastin fibers, and small SA node haphazardly arranged fibers.

ventricle. After penetrating the fibrous annulus at the crest of the ventricular septum, the bundle of His divides into left and right bundle branches.

Thus, the tissue excised for study of the conduction system must include this area completely. From the opened right atrioventricular aspect (with the aortic outflow tract adjacent to the cutting surface) the block to be excised reaches from the anterior margin of the coronary sinus to the medial papillary muscle of the right ventricle, including 1 cm of atrium and ventricle on both sides of the valve. Alternatively, from the left ventricle outflow tract, the block can be cut perpendicular to the aortic valve from the margin of attachment of the anterior leaflet of the mitral valve to the left edge of the membranous septum.

The block should include the noncoronary cusp of the aortic valve and the crest of the ventricular septum (Figure 2.2.1.13). In either case, the block of tissue removed should be divided in the plane perpendicular to the annulus, from posterior to anterior; the block to be sectioned should be marked with India ink so its orientation can be maintained throughout the embedding process. For infant hearts, the entire block of tissue should be step-sectioned with every fifth 10-mm thick section stained with Movat stain initially. In the adult heart, the entire tissue should be step-sectioned and every 25th or 50th section stained with Movat stain. Practically, the block of tissue is usually divided into five segments and one or two sections are cut from each segment.

The atrioventricular node, bundle, and bundle branches are histologically easily identifiable. The atrioventricular node consists of a network of muscle fibers which are smaller than the atrial and ventricular fibers. The cytoplasm is pale in comparison to the ventricular myocardium but striations and intercalated disk are present. The nuclei are oval in longitudinal sections. The conduction tissue is markedly cellular due to the presence of a large number of endothelial cells and there is a greater amount of elastic tissue than in the surrounding myocardium. As the node extends to penetrate the fibrous body and become bundle of His, the fibers are less plexiform and more longitudinally oriented (Figure 2.2.1.14).

2.2.1.10 Evaluating Cardiac Hypertrophy

One of the most important decisions while examining the heart is to determine if the heart is normal or abnormal. The heart may not show any anatomic structural abnormality except that

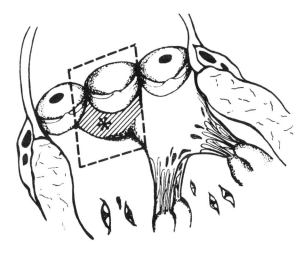

Figure 2.2.1.13 Diagram of landmarks for excising the major conduction from the left outflow tract. The membranous septum is marked by an asterisk. (From Virmani, R., Ursell, P.C., and Fenoglio, J.J., Examination of the heart, in Virmani, R., Atkinson, J.B., and Fenoglio, J.J., Eds., *Cardiovascular Pathology*, W.B. Saunders, Philadelphia, 1991, pp 1-20. With permission.)

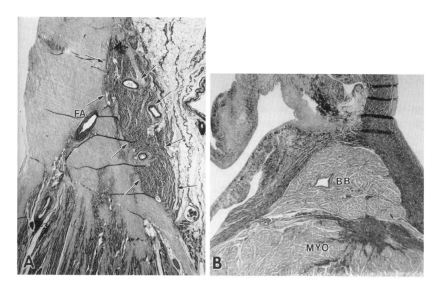

Figure 2.2.1.14 (A) The atrioventricular node (arrows) is shown nested against the fibrous annulus (FA). (From Virmani, R., Ursell, P.C., and Fenoglio, J.J., Examination of the heart, in Virmani, R., Atkinson, J.B., and Fenoglio, J.J., Eds., *Cardiovascular Pathology*, W.B. Saunders, Philadelphia, 1991, pp 1-20. With permission.) (B) The bundle of His branching portion. Note the location underneath the fibrous body (FB) and above the septal myocardium (MYO). (Movat stain x25.)

it is hypertrophied. Because cardiac hypertrophy may be a cause of death if severe, and physiologic in cases of chronic conditioning, the criteria for increased heart weight are important. We usually utilize the tables published from the Mayo Clinic giving the 95% confidence intervals for the height and weight of male and female individuals from birth to 99 years.[20,21] We recommend that at least four sections of the left ventricle be examined from the four walls of the heart and one section of the posterior wall of the right ventricle; sections should be taken from the mid-ventricular slice. In the elderly we also like to take one section each from both the atria, as amyloidosis and drug reactions may be limited to the atria.

2.2.1.11 Conclusions

This brief description of the examination of the heart is no substitute for the practice of examination and cutting open the heart oneself. In practice, not all methods may be applicable in each laboratory, for each individual, or in all situations. The description is more geared to the forensic pathologist and the examination of the adult heart with intent to making the method easy yet thorough; for a careful examination of the heart is worth the time and effort.

REFERENCES

1. Layman, T.E. and Edwards, J.E., A method for dissection of the heart and major pulmonary vessels, *Arch. Pathol.*, 82:314, 1966.
2. Ludwig, J. and Titus, J.L., Heart and vascular system, in Ludwig, J., Ed., *Current Method of Autopsy Practice*, WB Saunders, Philadelphia, 1979.
3. Hales, M.R. and Carrington, C.B., A pigment gelatin mass for vascular injection, *Yale J. Biol. Med.*, 43;257, 1971.
4. Hutchins, G.M., Buckley, B.H., Ridolfi, R.L., et al., Correlation of coronary arteriograms and left ventriculograms with postmortem studies, *Circulation*, 56:32, 1977.
5. Glagov, S., Eckner, F.A.O., and Ler, M., Controlled pressure fixation approaches for hearts, *Arch. Patrol.*, 76:640, 1963.
6. Isner, J.M., Kishel, J., Kent, K.M. et al., Accuracy of angiographic determination of the left main coronary arterial narrowing: Angiographic-histologic correlative analysis in 28 patients, *Circulation*, 63:1056, 1981.
7. Roberts, W.C., Lachman, A.S., and Virmani, R., Twisting of an aortic-coronary bypass conduit: A complication of coronary surgery, *J. Thorac. Cardiovasc. Surg.*, 75:722, 1978.
8. Atkinson, J.B., Forman, M.B., Perry, J.M., Virmani, R., Correlation of saphenous vein bypass graft angiography with histologic changes at autopsy, *Am. J. Cardiol.*, 55:952, 1985.
9. Atkinson, J.B., Forman, M.B., Vaughn, W.K. et al., Morphologic changes in long-term saphenous bypass grafts, *Chest*, 88:341, 1985.
10. Buckley, B.H. and Hutchins, C.M., Accelerated "atherosclerosis": A morphologic study of 97 saphenous vein coronary artery bypass grafts, *Circulation*, 55:163, 1977.
11. Buckley, B.H. and Hutchins, G.M., Pathology of coronary artery bypass graft surgery, *Arch. Pathol.*, 102:273, 1978.
12. Virmani, R. and Roberts, W.C., Quantification of coronary arterial narrowing and of left ventricular myocardial scarring in healed myocardial infarction with chronic, eventually fatal, congestive heart failure, *Am. J. Med.*, 68:831, 1980.
13. Hackel, B.D. and Ratliff, N.J. Jr., A technique to estimate the quantity of infarcted myocardium post mortem, *Am. J. Pathol.*, 61:242, 1974.
14. Lichtig, C., Glagov, S., Feldman, S., and Wissler, R.W., Myocardial ischemia coronary artery atherosclerosis: A comprehensive approach to postmortem studies, *Med. Clin. North Am.*, 57:79, 1973.
15. Roberts, W.C., Technique of opening the heart at autopsy, in Hurst, J.W., Logue, R.B., Schlant, R.C., and Wenger, N.K., Eds., *The Heart*, 5th ed., McGraw-Hill, New York, 1982.
16. Edwards, W.D., Anatomic basis for tomographic analysis of the heart at autopsy, in Weller, B.F., Ed., *Cardiology Clinics: Cardiac Morphology*, Vol 2, No 4. WB Saunders, Philadelphia, 1984.
17. Tajik, A.J., Seward, J.B., Hagler, D.J. et al., Two dimensional real-time ultrasonic imaging of the heart and great vessels: Techniques, image orientation, structure identification and validation, *Mayo Clin. Pro.*, 53:271, 1978.

18. Davies, M.J., Anderson, R.H., and Becker, A.E., *The Conduction System of the Heart,* Butterworth & Co, London, 1983.
19. Anderson, R.H., Ho, S.Y., Smith, A., et al., Studies of the cardiac conduction tissue in the pediatric age group, *Diagn. Histopathol.,* 4:3 1981.
20. Scholz, D.G., Kitzman, D.W., Hagen, P.T., Ilstrup, D.M., and Edwards, W.D., Age-related changes in normal human hearts during the first 10 decades of life. Part I (Growth): A quantitative anatomic study of 200 specimens from subjects from birth to 19 years old, *Mayo Clin. Proc.,* 63:126, 1988.
21. Kitzman, D.W., Scholz, D.G., Hagen, P.T., Ilstrup, D.M., and Edwards, W.D., Age-related changes in normal human hearts during the first 10 decades of life. Part II (Maturity): A quantitative anatomic study of 765 specimens from subjects 20-99 years old, *Mayo Clin. Proc.,* 63:137,1988.
22. Virmani, R., Ursell, P.C., and Fenoglio, J.J., Examination of the heart, in *Cardiovascular Pathology,* Virmani, R., Atkinson, J.B., and Fenoglio, J.J., Eds., W.B. Saunders, Philadelphia, 1991, pp 1-20.

2.2.2 MYOCARDIAL ALTERATIONS IN DRUG ABUSERS

STEVEN B. KARCH, M.D.

ASSISTANT MEDICAL EXAMINER, CITY AND COUNTY OF SAN FRANCISCO, CALIFORNIA

The frequency of heart disease in drug abusers is not known with any certainty, and is difficult even to estimate. The observed frequency of any particular cardiac lesion depends on the pattern of drug abuse within the population being studied. Before the HIV era, in areas where heroin was the favored drug, the incidence of heart disease in drug users appeared to be not significantly different from that seen in controls.[1] In Siegel and Helpern's classic paper on the "Diagnosis of Death from Intravenous Narcotism", heart disease was not even mentioned,[2] nor were any significant cardiac abnormalities noted in Wetli's study of 100 consecutively autopsied narcotic abusers.[3] Thirty years ago, when Louria analyzed the discharge diagnosis of addicts admitted to Bellevue Hospital's general medicine service, the incidence of endocarditis was under 10% and no other cardiac disorders were noted.[4] By contrast, pathologists in Scandinavia, where amphetamine abuse is common, often report finding contraction band necrosis, fibrosis, and inflammatory infiltrates.[5]

2.2.2.1 Epidemology Considerations

The probability of finding myocardial alterations depends not only on the type of drug being abused, but also on the way it is abused. In areas where the injection of pills meant for oral use is still a fairly common practice, granulomatous lung disease and pulmonary hypertension are frequently observed.[6–8] When pills are injected, the abnormalities are due to excipients injected along with the drug, not the drug itself.

Another confounding factor is the increasing number of violence-related drug deaths. Evidence for direct opiate or stimulant mediated cardiac damage may be detected, but the frequency of incidental cardiac lesions in addicts dying of trauma has never been tabulated, nor, for that matter, have there been any recent (post HIV) studies analyzing the type of frequency of lesions seen in the hearts of non-drug using trauma victims.

Earlier studies of heart disease in drug users must be interpreted with a great deal of caution, particularly those where the diagnosis was not confirmed with toxicologic testing.

Dressler and Roberts, for example, analyzed 168 drug-related deaths and reported that the incidence of cardiac abnormalities in drug abusers was nearly 100%![9] However, toxicologic findings were not known for the individual patients, and all of the cases had been referred to a tertiary center for diagnosis. The availability of comprehensive toxicologic screening has been something of a mixed blessing because polypharmacy is now more often detected. In San Francsico, more than half of the drug related deaths are due to drugs taken in combination, often stimulants and narcotics. Attempts at correlating specific drugs with certain types of lesions are futile when more than one drug is present. Even when just one drug is detected, the possibility of past multi-drug use is not ruled out.

Nonetheless, certain generalizations are possible. The hearts of stimulant abusers, whether of cocaine or methamphetamine, often manifest changes consistent with the known effects of prolonged catecholamine excess. The hearts of heroin abusers generally do not show evidence of catecholamine excess, but they may frequently manifest HIV related changes. Hearts from both stimulant and opiate abusers may also demonstrate modest degrees of ventricular hypertrophy, either as a consequence of catecholamine effect, or as a result of pulmonary hypertension, or both, or via mechanisms that remain to be characterized. There is, for example, some evidence for the activiation of early expression genes.[10] In this section, the myocardial alterations associated with the different patterns of drug abuse will be illustrated and categorized.

2.2.2.2 Myocardial Hypertrophy

Stimulant abusers are prone to modest degrees of myocardial hypertrophy, and there is some evidence that opiate abusers may also share this tendency. Increased left ventricular mass is an independent risk factor for sudden cardiac death.[11,12] As ventricular mass increases, coronary artery reserve declines,[13] and myocardial contractility becomes impaired.[14] Increased mass makes ventricular arrhythmias, and sudden death, more likely,[15] even in the absence of relative myocardial ischemia provoked by the decline in coronary artery reserve.[16] This combination of effects may well explain many cases of cocaine-related sudden death.

The mechanism by which stimulant abuse causes myocyte hypertrophy is not known. In general, stimuli associated with myocardial hypertrophy activate G-proteins, and either adenyl cyclase or phospholipase C. When one of the latter is activated, genes needed to make the proteins necessary for cell growth are also activated.[17] After myocardial infarction, there is activation of early expression genes such as *c-fos, c jun,* and *c-myc.* Whether the same process also occurs in cocaine and methamphetamine users is not known, but *c-fos* activation has been observed in the aortas of cocaine-treated rabbits.[10] In laboratory experiments, rats and rabbits chronically treated with cocaine have larger left ventricles than controls.[10,18–20] They also have increased collagen content, higher levels of atrial naturetic hormone, and increased expression of the low ATPase myosin isoform V3,[21] In clinical studies, hypertrophy has been confirmed by comparing electrocardiograms of age-sex matched controls to those of asymptomatic cocaine users in rehabilitation, and with symptomatic cocaine users with chest pain.[22,23] Echocardiographic studies have yielded conflicting results. Studies of asymptomatic users in rehabilitation have found significant increases in left ventricular mass and posterior wall thickness,[24,25] although others have failed to confirm this finding.[26,27]

Autopsy evidence has shown that the increase in heart size is modest,[28] but quite real.[28-31] When heart weights of asymptomatic cocaine using trauma fatalities were compared with drug-free trauma victims, the hearts of the cocaine users were found to be 10% heavier than those of controls, even though the heart weights of both groups fell within ranges generally considered to be normal.[28] A related study compared the heart weights of individuals dying of drug toxicity (either cocaine, methamphetamine, or heroin) with heart weights of drug-free trauma victims. Heart weights for the drug users were significantly greater than those observed in the controls.[32]

Steven B. Karch

Changes in heart weight that amount to less than 10% are likely to go unrecognized at autopsy. Even if wall thickness is fastidiously measured, which is not always the case, the increase would most likely go undetected. Yet it is important that the increase be detected because it very likely is the cause of death, and may well be the only abnormality detected at autopsy.

Such small changes go unnoticed because several different systems for determining normal heart weight are in use. Some pathologists still believe that arbitrary cutoffs can be used: 380 or 400 grams for men and 350 grams for women. Others determine normality by using a formula: heart weights less than 0.4% of the body weight (0.45% for women) are considered normal.[32] Hearts weighing more than those percentages are considered enlarged. Neither of these approaches has proven accurate or reliable. A normalized weight nomogram is the most accurate tool for detecting modest degrees of enlargement. The Mayo Clinic nomogram relates heart weight to body weight (see Appendix III for nomogram). It is based on measurements made in hundreds of autopsies of individuals found to be free of heart disease.[33] If a heart weighs significantly more than predicted by the nomogram, it is abnormal, even if the heart weighs less than the 400 grams.

Similar weight increases are to be expected in methamphetamine-related deaths, though methamphetamine toxicity has not received nearly the attention devoted to cocaine.[31] Surprisingly, there is evidence that similar increases in heart size are to be seen in heroin abusers. The results of several, as yet unpublished, preliminary studies, indicate that increases comparable to those produced by cocaine may occur.[31,34] Hypertrophy in stimulant abusers is thought to be catecholamine related. There is, however, no satisfactory explanation for the changes in the opiate abusers. The injection practices of heroin users can, of course, lead to pulmonary granulomas and pulmonary hypertension, but preliminary data suggest that the observed increases are not related to that mechanism.

2.2.2.3 Myocardial Disease in Stimulant Abusers

Clinical reports of dilated cardiomyopathy, where neither biopsies nor arteriograms are obtained, are impossible to interpret, and the real diagnosis must remain in question.[35-39] But even in the absence of florid heart failure, certain types of morphologic alterations are frequently seen in the hearts of individuals dying from stimulant abuse. Most of the observed changes appear to be catecholamine mediated[40-42]. Chronic catecholamine toxicity is a well-recognized entity in animals and humans. Norepinephrine "myocarditis" was first described over 40 years ago.[43,44] The histologic changes associated with norepinephrine treatment are indistinguishable from those seen in patients and animals with pheochromocytoma.[45] Contraction band necrosis is the earliest recognizable lesion in both situations.[46-49]

Several features distinguish catecholamine necrosis from ischemic necrosis. The most obvious is the distribution of the lesions. In ischemic injury, all cells supplied by a given vessel are affected, leading to homogeneous zones of necrosis. In catecholamine injury, individual necrotic myocytes are found interspersed between normal cells, and the pattern of injury appears unrelated to the blood supply.[49]

The arrangement of the myofilaments also helps distinguish the two processes. In ischemia, myofilaments remain in register. In cases of catehcolamine-toxicity, the filaments are disrupted. After 12 or more hours have elapsed, a mononuclear infiltrate, predominantly lymphocytic, may be seen. Necrotic myocytes are eventually reabsorbed, and replaced by non-conducting fibrous tissue. After repeat bouts of necrosis, the myocardium becomes increasingly fibrotic. Fibrosis of this type alters ventricular function and, more importantly, may lead to abnormal impulse propagation[40,50] (see Figures 2.2.2.1 and 2.2.2.2).

Biopsy findings in a group of cocaine users with recent onset of chest pain and congestive failure showed changes very similar to those described above, with microfocal interstitial

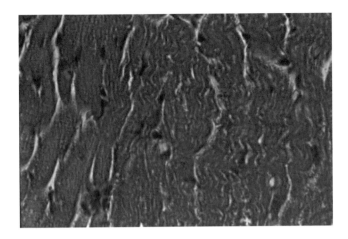

Figure 2.2.2.1. Contraction band necrosis in a 32-year-old cocaine abuser with arrhythmic sudden death. The dark cross banded lesions are a marker for intracytasolic calicum overload secondary to catecholamine excess. Cells with these lesions may or may not be viable. If severe, the cells are replaced by fibrous tissue with abnormal conduction properties.

Figure 2.2.2.2 Patchy myocardial fibrosis in a 28-year-old cocaine abuser who died in a motor vechicle accident. Fibrosis is confined to focal areas, not corresponding to blood supply. This pattern is typically seen in cases of catecholamine excess, not just in instances of cocaine toxicity. The presence of such microfocal fibrosis may be an underlying cause of arrhythmic sudden death.

fibrosis evident in all cases.[41] Lymphocytic infiltrates were seen in only two of the cases, and eosinophils were not seen at all. Identical changes have been described in chronic amphetamine abusers.[51] Because contraction band necrosis is a prominent feature of all myocardial biopsies, regardless of the underlying cause, the presence of these lesions in biopsy material is difficult, but not impossible, to assess.[52] The presence of nuclear pyknosis in damaged cells may be one way to distinguish preexisting contraction band lesions from those produced by the biopsy process itself. In some cases, Z-band remnants have been identified with electron microscopy. This particular finding is classically associated with dilated congestive cardiomyopathy and is not generally associated with the type of necrosis resulting from catecholamine toxicity.

Nonetheless, it has been documented in patients with amphetamine toxicity,[51] where its presence probably signifies only that necrosis was very severe .

The first reports of contraction band-like lesions and cellular infiltrates in the heart of a cocaine users were published in the 1920s![53] However, more than half a century elapsed before another paper, describing similar findings, was published in 1986.[54] A biopsy of one of the cocaine users described in that report disclosed eosinophilic infiltrates. Others have observed both lymphocytic and eosinophilic interstitial infiltrates.[46,47,55–58]

More often than not, when mononuclear infiltrates are present, there is no associated myocyte necrosis.[47] According to generally accepted criteria, myocarditis cannot be diagnosed without necrosis.[59] In the only study ever to directly address the issue, immunologic and histologic findings were tabulated in 15 HIV negative, intravenous drug abusers.[58] Five cases demonstrated active myocarditis, and five others had borderline myocarditis. Antimyocardial antibodies were positive in 4 of the 15 cases, including patients with active, borderline, and absent myocarditis, and toxicology studies did not implicate any particular drug of abuse. Thus, intravenous drug abuse appears to be an independent risk factor for myocarditis, a factor which should be taken into consideration when evaluating possible cases of HIV-associated myocarditis.

The presence of eosinophilic infiltrates suggests that what is being described is not myocarditis at all, but rather a hypersensitivity phenomenon. Hypersensitivity myocarditis is distinguished from toxic myocarditis by the fact that its occurrence is not dose-related. Lesions are all of the same age, hemorrhages are rare, and there is no myocyte necrosis. The list of drugs causing hypersensitivity myocarditis is increasing.[60] Eosinophilic myocarditis is a very rare disorder. When it is diagnosed, it is often an incidental finding or a surprise finding at autopsy or in biopsy specimens obtained to evaluate chest pain, heart failure, or arrhythmia.

Clinical manifestations of this disorder are so nonspecific that the diagnosis is rarely suspected during life.[61] None of the cocaine users with eosinophilic infiltrates have had signs of extra cardiac involvement such as polyarteritis nodosa or eosinophilic leukemia. These patients do not match the picture classically associated with acute necrotizing myocarditis,[62] nor do they resemble patients with eosinophilic coronary arteritis (Churg- Strauss syndrome, also called allergic granulomatosis angiitis), although one case of cocaine-associated Churg-Strauss has been reported.[63]

A heterogeneous group of agents can cause toxic myocarditis, and since cocaine can be adulterated with a very long list of agents, implicating cocaine as the cause of eosinophilic myocarditis is difficult. A review paper published in 1988 listed sugars (lactose, sucrose, and manitol) as the most common cocaine adulterants, followed by stimulant drugs (caffeine, amphetamines) and local anesthetic agents as the most common agents found mixed with cocaine samples.[64] Eosinophilic infiltrates in the myocardium could be in response to any of these agents, alone or in combination. Furthermore, most adult drug abusers are polydrug abusers, which further enlarges the list of possible offenders.

2.2.2.4 Myocardial Disease in Opiate Abusers

Lesions in the hearts of opiate abusers appear to be much less common than in stimulant abusers. Myocardial heroin uptake is substantial, with measured concentrations nearly as high as those in blood.[65] But when judged by clinical or autopsy findings, the effects of high myocardial opiate levels appear to be negligible. Autopsy studies of heroin abusers done during the 1960s and early 1970s did not even mention heart disease.[2,3] Clinical studies from that same time were equally unrevealing. Among addicts admitted to Bellevue Hospital's general medicine service, the incidence of endocarditis was under 10% and no other cardiac disorders were noted.[66]

While no general pattern of myocardial diseases is associated with opiate abuse, an assortment of drug abuse-related disorders may occasionally be encountered. Myocardial fibrosis is not uncommon, but its presence probably is just a consequence of concomitant stimulant abuse. Perivascular fibrosis, when it occurs, usually signals previous bouts of healed endocarditis. Larger zones of fibrosis are the results of ischemia and healed infarction. But unlike cocaine users, who appear to be prone to accelerated coronary artery disease,[28,67] there is no evidence that coronary artery disease is any more common among heroin abusers than it is in the general population. Intravenous drug abusers are prone to pulmonary hypertension as a consequence of granuloma formation in the pulmonary bed,[68] and the occasional talc granuloma may even be seen in the myocardium.[69]

2.2.2.5 Myocardial Disease Associated with HIV Infection

In some areas of the U.S. more than one half of all intravenous drug abusers carry the HIV virus. Given that endocarditis is the only cardiac disorder unequivocally associated with intravenous opiate abuse, it is highly probable that any myocardial lesion encountered in the heart of an intravenous heroin abuser is there as a result of either concomitant stimulant abuse, HIV infection, or an opportunistic infection related to HIV infection. In most cases, cardiac manifestations of HIV infection are clinically silent and not discovered during life.[70,71]

Pericardial effusion is the cardiac lesion most commonly seen in AIDS patients. One third of the patients dying of AIDS have effusions, with or without pericarditis,[71,72] and the probability is that the effusion will not have been symptomatic during life. Ventricular hypertrophy is even more common than pleural and pericardial effusions,[71] with evidence of ventricular thickening in nearly half the HIV victims autopsied. Right ventricular hypertrophy is not particularly surprising in drug abusers who are likely to have both angiothrombotic lung disease from their drug abuse, and AIDS-related fibrotic interstitial lung disease. However, left ventricular hypertrophy was reported in 40% of one series,[71] and the mechanism remains unexplained.

The incidence of mononuclear infiltrates, without or without evidence of myocarditis, has been placed at 10% in two different series.[71,72] The incidence of opportunistic infection, especially disseminated cryptococcosis and CMV infections, is also high, and usually unsuspected during life. Soft tissue sarcoma is the most common malignant neoplasm of the heart, pericardium, and great vessels and may embolize to the lungs or peripheral arteries. Except in HIV infected patients, these tumors are relatively rare. Angiosarcoma is the most common cardiac sarcoma, and the most aggressive of these tumors. It usually arises in the right atrium. Kaposi's sarcoma of the heart has been found in patients with AIDS and in immunosuppressed organ transplant recipients.[73]

REFERENCES

1. Kringsholm, B. and Christoffersen, P., Lung and heart pathology in fatal drug addiction. A consecutive autopsy study, *Forensic Sci. Int.,* 1987;34:39-51.
2. Siegel, H., Helpern, M., and Ehrenreich, T., The diagnosis of death from intravenous narcotism, with emphasis on the pathologic aspects, 1966;11(1):1-16.
3. Wetli, C., Davis, J., and Blackbourne, B., Narcotic addiction in Dade County , Florida — an analysis of 100 consecutive autopsies, *Arch. Pathol. Lab. Med.,* 1972;93:330-343.
4. Louria, D., The major medical complications of heroin addicition, *Ann. Int. Med.,* 1967;67:1-22.
5. Rajs, J. and Falconer, B., Cardiac lesions in intravenous drug addicts, *Forensic Sci. Int.,* 1979;13:193-209.

6. Bainborough A, Jericho K. Cor pulmonale secondary to talc granulomata in the lungs of a drug addict. *Can Med Assn J* 1970;103:1297-1298.
7. Arnett E, Battle W, Russo J, et al. Intravenous injection of talc-containing drugs intended for oral use — a cause of pulmonary granulomatous and pulmonary hypertension. *Am J Med* 1976;60:711-718.
8. Riddick L. Disseminated granulomatosis through a patent foramen ovale in an intravenous drug user with pulmonary hypertension. *Am J Forensic Med Pathol* 1987;8(4):326- 333.
9. Dressler F, Roberts W. Modes of death and types of cardiac diseases in opiate addicts: analysis of 168 necropsy cases. *Am J Cardiol* 1989;64:909-920.
10. Sutliff R, Cai G, Gurdal H, et al. Cardiovascular hypertrophy and increased vascular contractile responsiveness following repeated cocaine administration in rabbits. *Life Sciences* 1996;58:675-82.
11. Levy D, Anderson K, Savage D, et. al. Echocardiographiclly detected left ventriicular hypertrophy: prevalance and risk factors: the Framingham Heart Study. *Ann Intern Med* 1988;108:7-13.
12. Levy D, Garrison R, Savage D, et al. Prognostic implications of echocardiographically determined left ventricular mass in the Framingham Heart Study. *N Engl J Med* 1990;322;1561-1566
13. Strauer B. Ventricular functions and coronary hemodynamics in hypertensive heart disease. *Am J Cardiol* 1979;44:999-1006.
14. de Simone G, Devereux R, Roman M, et. al. Assessment of left ventricular function by the midwall fractional shortening/end-systolic stress relation in human hypertension. *J Am Coll Cardiol* 1994;23:1444-1451.
15. Messerli F. Hypertension, left ventricular hypertrophy, ventricular ectopy, and sudden death. *Am J Hypertension* 1993;6:335-336.
16. Schmieder R, Martus P, Klingbeil A. Reversal of left ventricular hypertrophy in essential hypertension. A meta-analysis of randomized double-blind studies. *JAMA* 1996;275:1507-1513.
17. Francis G, Carlyle W. Hypothetical pathways of cardiac myocyte hypertrophy: response to myocardial injury. *Euro Heart J* 1993;14(Suppl J):49-56.
18. Besse S, Assayag P, Latour C, et.al. Effects of cocaine on messenger RNA levels of rat myocardium. *FASEB J* 1994;8(4):A311.
19. Besse S, Assayag P, Latour C, et al. Myocardial effects of acute and chronic cocaine treatment. *Circulation* 1994;90(4, Part 2):I-580.
20. Tseng Y, Rockhold R, Hoskins B, Ho I. Cardiovascular toxicities of nandrolone and cocaine in spontaneously hypertensive rats. *Fund Appl Toxicol* 1994;22:113-121.
21. Morris G, Fiore P, Hamlin R, et al. Effects of long-term administration and exercise on cardiac metabolism and isomyosin expression. *Can J Physiol Pharmacol* 1994;72:1-5.
22. Chakko S, Sepulveda S, Kessler K, et al. Frequency and type of electrocardiographic abnormalities in cocaine abusers (electrocardiogram in cocaine abuse). *Am J Cardiol* 1994;74:710-713.
23. Nademanee K, Taylor R, Bailey W, et al. Mechanisms of cocaine-induced sudden death and cardiac arrhythmias. *Circulation* 1994;90(4, Pt 2):I-455.
24. Brickner E, Willard J, Eichorn E, et al. Left ventricular hypertrophy associated with chronic cocaine abuse. *Circulation* 1991;84(3):1130-1135.
25. Om A, Ellahham S, Vetrovec G, et al. Left ventricular hypertrophy in normotensive cocaine users. *Am Heart J* 1993;5(1):1441-1443.
26. Hoegerman G, Lewis C, Flack J, et al. Lack of association of recreational cocaine and alcohol use with left ventricular mass in young adults - the coronary artery risk development in young adults (CARDIA) study. *J Am Coll Cardiol* 1995;25(4):895-900.
27. Eisenberg M, Jue J, Mendelson J, et.al. Left ventricular morphologic features and function in non-hospitalized cocaine users: a quantitative two dimensional echocardiographic study. *Am Heart J* 1995;129:941-946.
28. Karch S, Green G, Young S. Myocardial hypertrophy and coronary artery disease in male cocaine users. *J Forensic Sci* 1995; 40(4):591-596.

29. Escabedo L, Ruttenber A, Anda R, et al. Coronary artery disease, left ventricular hypertrophy, and the risk of cocaine overdose death. *Coronary Art Dis* 1992;3:853-857.

30. Wetli C, Raval M. Update on agitated delirium. Read at the American Academy of Forensic Science Annual Meedting, February 15, 1995, Seattle.

31. Karch S. *J. Forensic Sci*, In press

32. Ludwig J. *Current Methods of Autopsy Practice*. 2nd Ed., Philadelphia: WB Saunders Company,1979.

33. Kitzman D, Scholz D, et al. Age-related changes in normal human hearts during the first 10 decades of life. Part II (Maturity): a quantitative anatomic study of 765 specimens from subjectes 20 to 99 years old. *Mayo Clin Proc* 1988;63:137-146.

34. Virmani R. Cardiac lesions in opiate abusers; read at the Annual meeting of the AAFS, Nashville. 1996.

35. Wiener R, Lockhart J, Schwartz R. Dilated cardiomyopathy and cocaine aubse: report of two cases. *Am J Med* 1986;81:699-701.

36. Chokshi S, Moore R, Pandian N, Isner J. Reversible cardiomyopathy associated with cocaine intoxication. *Ann Intern Med* 1989;111:1039-1040.

37. Duell P. Chronic cocaine abuse and dilated cardiomyopathy. *Am J Med* 1987;83:601.

38. Wolfson Ha. Chronic cocaine abuse associated with dilated cardiomyopathy. *Am J Emerg Med* 1990.

39. Mendelson M, Chandler J. Postpartum cardiomyopathy associated with maternal cocaine abuse. *Am J Cardiol* 1992;70:1092-1094.

40. Karch S, Billingham M. The pathology and etiology of cocaine-induced heart disease. *Arch Pathol Lab Med* 1988;112:225-230.

41. Peng S, French W, Pelikan P. Direct cocaine cardiotoxicity demonstrated by endomyocardial biopsy. *Arch Pathol Lab Med* 1989;113:842-845.

42. Henzlova MJ, Smith SH, Prchal VM, Helmcke FR. Apparent 5eversibility of cocaine- induced congestive cardiomyopathy. *Am Heart J* 1991;122(2):577-579.

43. Szakacs J, Dimmette R, Cowart E. Pathologic implications of the catecholamines epinephrine and norepinephrine. *US Armed Forces Med J* 1959;10:908-925.

44. Szakacs J, Cannon A. l-Norepinephrine myocarditis. *Am J Clin Pathol* 1958;30:425-434.

45. Rosenbaum J, Billingham M, Ginsburg R, et al. Cardiomyopathy in a rat model of pheochromocytoma: morphological and functional alterations. *J Pharmacol Exp Ther* 1987;241:354-360.

46. Simpson R, Edwards W. Pathogenesis of cocaine-induced ischemic heart disease. *Arch Patho Lab Med* 1986;110:479.

47. Tazelaar H, Karch S, Billingham M, Stephens B. Cocaine and the heart. *Hum Pathol* 1987;18:195-199.

48. Gardin J, Wong N, Alker K, et al. Acute cocaine administration induces ventricular regional wall motion and ultrastructural abnormalities in an anesthetized rabbit model. *Am Heart J* 1994;128:1117-29.

49. Karch S, Billingham ME. Myocardial Contraction Bands Revisited. *Hum Pathol* 1986;17:9-13.

50. Weber K, Sun Y, Tyagi S, Cleutjens J. Collagen network of the myocardium: function, structural remodeling and regulatory mechanisms. *J Mol Cell Cardiol* 1994;26:279-292.

51. Smith H, Roche A, Jagusch M, Herdson P. Cardiomyopathy associated with amphetamine administration. *Am Heart J* 1976;91:792-797.

52. Adomian G, Laks M, Billingham M. The incidence and significance of contraction bands in endomyocardial biopsies from normal human hearts. *Am Heart J* 1978;95:348-351.

53. Bravetta E, Invernizzi G. Il Cocainismo. Osservazione cliniche. Richerche sp´rimentali e anatomo-pathologiche. *Note Riv Psichiatr* 1922;10:543-552.

54. Isner J, Estes N, Thompson P, et al. Acute cardiac events temporally related to cocaine abuse. *N Engl J Med* 1986;315:1438-1443.

55. Anderson D, Virmani R, Macher A. Cardiac pathology and cardiovascular cause of death in patients dying with the Acquired Immunodeficiency Syndrome (AIDS). The Third International Conference on AIDS, 1987.

56. Virmani R, Rabinowitz M, Smialek J, Smyth D. Cardiovascular effects cocaine: an autopsy study of 40 patients. *Am Heart J* 1988;115(5):1068-1076.

57. Talebzadeh V, Chevrolet J, Chatelain P, et al. Myocardite à éosinophiles et hypertension pulmonaire chez une toxicomane. *Ann Pathol* 1990;10(1):40-46.

58. Turnicky R, Goodin J, Smialek J, et.al. Incidental myocarditis with intravenous drug abuse. The pathology, immunopathology, and potential implications for human immunodeficiency virus-associated myocarditis. *Hum Pathol* 1992;23:138-143.

59. Aretz H, Billingham M, Edwards W, et al. Myocarditis: a histopathologic definition and classification. *Am J Cardiovas Path* 1986;1(1):3-14.

60. Billingham M. Drug-induced cardiotoxicity: the morphologic aspect. *Heart Vessels* 1985;1(Suppl 1):386-394.

61. Taliercio C, Olney V, Lie J. Myocarditis related to drug hypersensitivity. *Mayo Clin Proc* 1985;60:463-468.

62. Herzog C, Snover D, Staley N. Acute necrotising eosinophilic myocarditis. *Brit Heart J* 1984;52:343-348.

63. Orriols R, Munox X, Ferrer J, et al. Cocaine-induced Churg-Strauss vasculitis. *Euro Resp J* 1996; 9:175-177.

64. Shannon M. Clinical toxicity of cocaine adulterants. *Ann Emerg Med* 1988;17(11):1243-1247.

65. Kintz P, Mangin P, Lugnier A, Chaumont A. Toxicological data after heroin overdose. *Hum Toxicol* 1989;8:487-489.

66. Louria D. The major medical complications of heroin addicition. *Ann Int Med* 1967;67:1- 22.

67. Kolodgie FD, Virmani R, Cornhill JF, Herderick EE, Smialek J. Increase in Atherosclerosis and Adventitial Mast Cells in Cocaine Abusers - An Alternative Mechanism of Cocaine-Associated Coronary Vasospasm and Thrombosis. *J Am Coll Cardiol* 1991;17(7):1553-1560.

68. Robertson C, Reynolds R, WIlson J. Pulmonary hypertension and foreign body granulomas in intravenous drug abusers: documentation by cardiac catheterisation and lung biopsy. *Am J Med* 1976;61:657-664.

69. Riddick L. Disseminated granulomatosis through a patent foramen ovale in an intravenous drug user with pulmonary hypertension. *Am J Forensic Med Pathol* 1987;8(4):326- 333.

70. Fong I, Howard R, A E, et al. Cardiac involvement in human immunodeficiency virus- infected patients. *J Acquired Immune Deficiency Syndromes* 1993;6:380-385.

71. Rosales-Guzman I, Rosales L, Zghaib A. [The autopsy findings in 51 cases of AIDS with cardiovascular damage]. *Archivos del Instituto de Cardiologia de Mexico* 1994;64:485- 490.

72. Lewis W. AIDS: cardiac findings from 115 autopsies. *Prog Cardiovasc DIs* 1989;32:207- 251.

73. Raaf H, Raaf J. Sarcomas related to the heart and vasculature. *Seminars Surg Onc* 1994;10:374-82.

2.2.3 ENDOCARDITIS

MICHAEL D. BELL, M.D.

ASSOCIATE MEDICAL EXAMINER, DADE COUNTY MEDICAL EXAMINER OFFICE, MIAMI, FLORIDA

Bacterial endocarditis is a well-established complication of intravenous drug abuse, regardless of the class of drug injected. The infecting microbe may be found on a contaminated needle, among the addict's normal skin flora, or in a pre-existing cellulitis or phlebitis. The bacteria (or fungi rarely) gain access into the bloodstream via the needle track.

2.2.3.1 Incidence and Clinical Profile

Although intravenous drug abuse is a recognized risk factor for infectious endocarditis, this complication is *not* a frequent complication among intravenous drug users. The incidence of

Table 1.   Uncommon Pathogens in Endocarditis of Intravenous Drug Abusers[11]

Group B Streptococcus *(Streptococcus agalactiae)* [12]
Staphylococcus epidermidis
Gram negative bacteria (Pseudomonas, Serreatia, etc.)
Corynebacterium
Haemophilus sp.
Eikenella corrodens
Erysipelothrix
Kingella kingae
Anaerobic bacteria (Bacteroides, Veillonella, etc.)
Fungi (Candida)

infective endocarditis in intravenous drug abusers is estimated at 1.5-2.0 cases per 1000 intravenous drug abusers admitted to the hospital.[1] Intravenous drug abusers with infective endocarditis are more likely to be young men (ave. age = 29 years, M:F = 3:1) compared with non-addicts with endocarditis (ave. age = 50, M:F = 2:1).[2] The frequency of underlying heart disease in intravenous drug abusers with endocarditis is 26% compared with 60% of non-addicts with endocarditis. In a cohort of 85 intravenous drug abusers, echocardiography failed to detect any valvular vegetation consistent with endocarditis.[3] Eight intravenous drug abusers had thickened or redundant leaflets (with or without prolapse) of the mitral, aortic, or tricuspid valve. Focally thickened leaflets of the mitral and tricuspid valves have been reported in other series of asymptomatic intravenous drug abusers who were examined by echocardiography.[4] These subtle morphologic abnormalities may be the stratum upon which endocarditis builds. Most researchers agree that endothelial injury or damage initiates fibrin, platelet, and bacterial deposition that produce endocarditis.

In Dressler and Robert's series of 80 autopsied intravenous drug abusers with infective endocarditis, the tricuspid valve was involved in half of the victims compared with 15% of victims dying of acute endocarditis that did not use intravenous drugs.[5] However, IV drug abusers can and often have left-sided valve involvement. The aortic and mitral valves are involved in 35% and 30% of intravenous drug abusers with infective endocarditis. The majority (82%) of acute endocarditis in intravenous drug abusers is caused by *Staphycoccus aureus* compared with streptococcal species that commonly cause endocarditis in victims not injecting intravenous drugs.[6] A minority (18%) of *S. aureus* isolates are methacillin resistant. Other bacteria co-infect 9% of intravenous drug abusers with *S. aureus* endocarditis. *Streptococcus viridans* causes right-sided endocarditis in 11% of intravenous drug abusers. Candida endocarditis is usually superimposed on a previous episode of bacterial endocarditis and has a more indolent clinical course. Unusual pathogens causing endocarditis in intravenous drug abusers are summarized in Table 1.

2.2.3.2 Postmortem Appearance

Grossly, infective endocarditis is characterized by friable, white, or tan vegetations found on the valve leaflets along the closure lines. The vegetations may be single or, more often, multiple. The mean vegetation size in intravenous drug abusers with acute right-sided bacterial endocarditis was 1.5 to 0.7 cm. in one clinical series.[6] The size, color, and appearance of the vegetations can, however, vary. Streptococcal vegetation grow more slowly than staphylococcal vegetations, but may get much larger. Fungal vegetations are usually larger than bacterial vegetations. The vegetations are usually on the atrial side of the atrioventricular valves and on the ventricular side of the aortic or pulmonic valves. Suppurative bacteria such as Staphylococ-

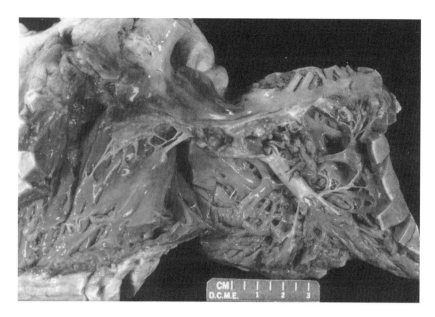

Figure 2.2.3.1 Large necrotizing vegetations on the tricuspid valve of this 31-year-old addict who commonly injected drugs subcutaneously, "skin popping". Blood cultures were positive for *Streptococcus hominus*.

cus may cause valve perforation and acute insufficiency. The infection may extend into the adjacent myocardium producing necrotic fistulas, aneurysms, or ring abscesses (usually aortic valve involved). Further extension can produce pericarditis, which is present in 4 to 27% cases of left-sided infective endocarditis.[7] Chordae tendinae involvement can produce rupture and valvular insufficiency. Vegetations of the tricuspid and pulmonic valves can embolize to the lungs producing suppurative abscesses (Figures 2.2.3.1 and 2.2.3.2). Perforation, indentation, or aneurysm of the valve cusp or chordae tendinae is presumptive evidence of healed endocarditis.

Microscopically, acute bacterial endocarditis is characterized by masses of fibrin, platelets, and polymorphonuclear leukocytes surrounding bacterial colonies on the valve surface. Bacteria are less frequent after antibiotic treatment and may not be demonstrable by gram stain, even if present.[8] Later, organization with capillary proliferation, a mixed cellular infiltrate, and granulation tissue dominate the microscopic appearance. The lesions eventually (if the person survives) heal with fibrosis and re-endothelialize. Calcification may be present in the healed lesions.

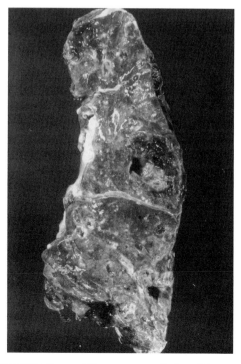

Figure 2.2.3.2 The lung from the victim in Figure 2.2.3.1 has multiple suppurative abscesses and extensive dark red consolidation.

Table 2.   Comparison of Right- and Left-Sided Endocarditis

Right-sided	Left-sided
1. Intravenous drug abusers most common	Congenital heart disease most common
2. Staphyloccous aureus most common	Streptococcus viridans most common
3. Occassionaly due to polymicrobial involvement	Polymicrobial involvement rare
4. 10% of all cases	90% of all cases
5. Good prognosis	Poor prognosis
6. Immediate valve replacement usually not required	Usually requires immediate valve replacement

2.2.3.3 Clinical Diagnosis

The clinical diagnosis of acute infectious endocarditis includes the acute onset of fever, chills, and heart murmur. Right-sided valve murmurs (as in intravenous drug abusers) may be less audible than left-sided valve murmurs because the reduced chamber pressures of the right heart produce less turbulence and less noise. Signs of early tricuspid insufficiency may be minimal with only an atrial or ventricular gallop and no murmur. Later, a systolic regurgitant murmur (that is louder with inspiration) appears. Large v waves in the neck veins and a pulsating liver are signs of severe tricuspid regurgitation.[9] Confirmation of the diagnosis includes isolation of the causative organism from 2 or more blood cultures and identification of a valvular vegetation by two-dimensional echocardiography. Chest pain and dyspnea with chest radiographic abnormalities (multiple segmental infiltrates with lower lobe predilection) suggest septic pulmonary emboli from a right-sided valvular vegetation. Systemic embolization can occur in right-sided endocarditis from septic pulmonary vein thrombi, left-sided valvular involvement, or paradoxical embolization through a patent foramen ovale. Table 2 compares the clinical features of right- and left-sided endocarditis.[10] Mortality in intravenous drug abusers with acute right-sided endocarditis varies from 4 to 14%.[6]

REFERENCES

1. Weinstein L, Brusch JL. Endocarditis in intravenous drug abusers. In: Weinstein L, Brusch JL (Eds.) *Infective Endocarditis*, Oxford University Press, New York, NY, 1996, pp. 194-209.
2. Reisberg BE. Infective endocarditis in the narcotic addict. *Prog Cardiovasc Dis* 22: 193- 204, 1979.
3. Willoughby SB, Vlahov D, Herskowitz A. Frequency of left ventricular dysfunction and other echocardiographic abnormalities in human immunodeficiency virus seronegative intravenous drug abusers. *Am J Cardiol* 71: 446-447, 1993.
4. Pons-Llado G, Carreras F, Borras X, et. al. Findings on Doppler echocardiography in asymptomatic intravenous heroin users. *Am J Cardiol* 69: 238-241, 1992.
5. Dressler F, Roberts W. Infective endocarditis in opiate addicts: analysis of 80 cases studied at autopsy. *Am J Cardiol* 63: 1240-1257, 1989.
6. Hecht SR, Berger M. Right-sided endocarditis in intravenous drug users: prognostic features in 102 episodes. *Ann Int Med* 117: 560-566, 1992.
7. Buchbinder NA, Roberts WC. Left-sided valvular active infective endocarditis: a study of forty-five patients. *Am J Med* 53: 20-35, 1972.
8. McFarland MM. Pathology of infective endocarditis. Chapter 4 In: Kaye D (Ed.) *Infective Endocarditis*, 2nd edition, Raven Press, New York, 1992, pp. 57-83.

Michael D. Bell

9. Cannon NJ, Cobbs CG. Infective endocarditis in drug addicts. Chapter 8 In: Kaye D (Ed.) *Infective Endocarditis,* University Park Press, Baltimore, 1976, pp. 111-127.

10. Chan P, Ogilby JD, Segal B. Tricuspid valve endocarditis. *Am Heart J* 117: 1140-1146, 1989.

11. Sande MA, Lee BL, Mills J, Chambers III HF. Endocarditis in intravenous drug users. Chapter 19 In: Kaye D (Ed.) *Infective Endocarditis,* 2nd edition, Raven Press, New York, 1992, pp. 345-359.

12. Watanakunakorn C, Habte-Gabr, E. Group B streptococcal endocarditis of tricuspid valve. *Chest* 100: 569-571, 1991.

2.2.4 VASCULAR EFFECTS OF SUBSTANCE ABUSE*

FRANK D. KOLODGIE, PH.D., ALLEN BURKE, M.D., JAGAT NARULA, M.D., PH.D., FLORABEL G. MULLICK, M.D., AND RENU VIRMANI, M.D.

ARMED FORCES INSTITUTE OF PATHOLOGY, HARVARD MEDICAL SCHOOL, BOSTON AND NORTHEASTERN UNIVERSITY, BOSTON, MASSACHUSETTS

Statistics provided by the Drug Abuse Warning Network (DAWN) over the past two decades have documented an increasing prevalence in substance abuse as manifested by emergency room and Medical Examiner data (i.e., drug mentions). For example, the Office of the Chief Medical Examiner (OCME) has reported a marked increase in the number of drug abuse deaths in Maryland from 1986 to 1993, with drug deaths increasing sharply from 119 cases in 1986 to 356 in 1993, a 199% increase over seven years.[1] Narcotic drugs, specifically heroin, have played a major role in the rising number of drug abuse deaths.[1] Not surprisingly, cardiovascular complications have accompanied this increase. However, characterizing the effects of drugs of abuse on the vasculature is difficult because not all abused drugs result in anatomic changes. Direct human studies are scarcely available, and the studies that exist are performed under limited, controlled conditions which do not replicate the usage picture or conditions of the drug abuser. The drugs may have multiple effects depending on the dose, route of administration, impurities, underlying risk factors for cardiovascular disease, and concomitant use of other drugs such as ethanol and caffeine. In this section, the underlying pathogenic mechanisms associated with substance abuse leading to vascular complications (Table 2.2.4) is discussed..

Vasoconstriction at the epicardial or microvascular level may result in ischemia of almost any organ, but the vessel often fails to show any morphologic change. Drugs may also lead to formation of intravascular thrombi resulting in organ infarcts. A common complication of drug-abuse may be cutaneous or cerebral manifestations of vasculitis. In some instances, acute hemodynamic worsening of hypertension may also lead to dissection of the aorta and rupture of arterial aneurysms resulting in intracranial hemorrhage.

There are several morphologic manifestations of drug-induced vascular disease. Vasoconstriction in itself is rarely identifiable by histologic methods, although contraction band necrosis of smooth muscle cells has rarely been reported in cases of clinically documented vasoconstriction. Chronic vasoconstriction may result in medial hypertrophy. Luminal thrombosis may be secondary to endothelial damage, underlying atherosclerosis, or effects of drugs on the clotting cascade. Atherosclerosis, which is a complex process involving lipid metabolism, endothelial dysfunction, immune activation, and thrombosis may be accelerated in persons

---

* The opinions and assertions contained herein are the private views of the authors and are not to be construed as official or reflecting the views of the Army, Navy, Air Force, or Department of Defense.

Table 2.2.4 Pathologic Vascular Manifestations of Substance Abuse

Drugs	Vasospasm	Thrombosis	Hypersensitivity vasculitis	Necrotozing (toxic) arteritis	Fibrointimal proliferation	Accelerated atherosclerosis	Veno-Occlusive disease
Recreational							
Cocaine	X	X	X	X	X	X	—
Heroin	—	—	X	—	—	—	X
Amphetamine/ and methamphetamine	X	X	—	X	X	—	—
Nicotine	X	X	X	—	—	X	—
Glue sniffing/ solvents	X	—	—	—	—	—	—
Prescription							
Tricyclic antidepressants and phenothiazines	X	—	—	—	—	—	—
Ergot alkaloids	X	X	—	—	X	—	—
Ephedrine/ pseudoephedrine	X	—	X	X	—	—	—
Non-prescription							
Phenylpropanolamine/ and anorexiants	X	—	—	X	—	—	—
L-Tryptophan	X	—	—	X	X	—	—

Frank D. Kolodgie et al.

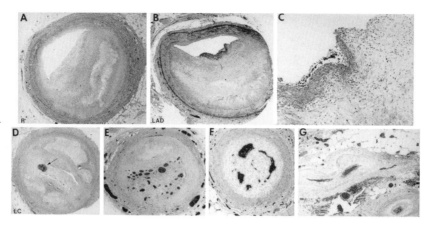

Figure 2.2.4.1 Cocaine-induced coronary atherosclerosis. The right (A) and the left anterior descending (LAD, B) coronary arteries are severely narrowed by atheroscletrotic plaque. The LAD (B) shows a superficial luminal thrombus (plaque erosion) consisting of fibrin and few inflammatory cells. The left circumflex (D,E, F) shows organized thrombus totally occluding the lumen. In (D), the recannalized channel is occluded by a thrombus (arrow). (G) Epicardial small branches of coronary arteries show severe intimal proliferation probably secondary to an organizing thrombus. The patient was a 30-year-old male known cocaine abuser.

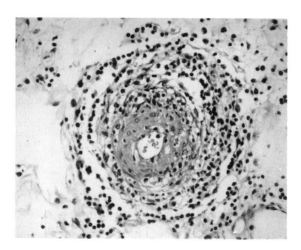

Figure 2.2.4.2 Small cell (hypersensitivity) vasculitis. There is a predominantly lymphoid infiltrated surrounding an arteriole, with focal neutrophilic karyorrhexis within the arterial wall. The patient had a cutaneous rash (palpable purpura) following exposure to diazepam, to which she was sensitized.

exposed to drugs (Figure 2.2.4.1). Fibrointimal proliferation (increased numbers of intimal smooth muscle cells either via migration from the media or intimal proliferation) may be secondary to toxic endothelial damage. Inflammatory vascular diseases (vasculitis) have been described as a drug-related effect. The two major types of drug-induced vasculitis occur either via antigen-antibody complex deposition, usually in arterioles and venules (small vessel or hypersensitivity vasculitis, Figure 2.2.4.2), or via direct toxic damage (toxic vasculitis, Figure 2.2.4.3), generally involving muscular arteries. Both types of vasculitis are characterized by

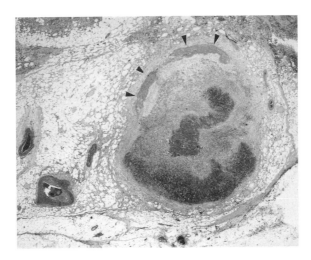

Figure 2.2.4.3. Toxic arteritis (polyarteritis). There is segmental destruction of the media with aneurysm formation. Residual intact media is present (arrowheads). The patient was a 24-year-old amphetamine addict who expired from mesenteric arteritis and peritoneal hemorrhage.

fibrinoid necrosis of vascular walls, especially toxic vasculitis with occlusion by luminal thrombosis and/or fibrointimal proliferation and vessel rupture.

2.2.4.1 Cocaine

Of all the known drugs of abuse associated with vascular toxicity, cocaine abuse is the most common. The recent increase in cocaine abuse has predominantly occurred due to the availability of cocaine base, known on the streets as crack, which produces an instant euphoria when smoked. The mechanisms of cocaine-induced vascular toxicity are complex. Acute administration of cocaine (whether in the base or hydrochloride form) causes an increase in heart rate and blood pressure. Myocardial oxygen consumption increases from systemic catecholamine release and increased alpha-adrenergic effects due to a blockade of norepinephrine reuptake.[2-4] Cocaine also acts as a local anesthetic by inhibiting sodium influx into cells, and this is most likely responsible for the vasodilatory action of the drug. The anesthetic effects of cocaine are expected at higher doses while the sympathomimetic actions are more likely to be prevalent at lower concentrations. Cocaine is detected in the circulation immediately after its consumption with a plasma half-life of approximately 1 hour. However, the half-life for euphoria is less than 1 hour which may lead to the repetitive use of cocaine.

The blood cocaine levels required to produce the euphoric effects is approximately 10^{-7} to 10^{-5} mol/L; median plasma levels following intravenous cocaine use in cocaine related deaths is reported to be approximately 6×10^{-7} mol/L to 3×10^{-4} mol/L.[5-7] "Binge users" of cocaine are known to use high doses for extended periods, oftentimes up to 200 hours.[8] Plasma concentrations during a "binge" have not been documented although it is thought that the effects of cocaine on the cardiovascular system are especially significant during bingeing. Following absorption, cocaine is cleared from the circulation, primarily hydrolyzed to benzoylecgonine and metabolized to ecgonine methyl ester (by plasma cholinesterases). At least in cerebral vessels, cocaine metabolites appear to be biologically active and may partially contribute to cocaine's toxic effects.[9] Furthermore, because of individual variability in plasma cholinesterase activity, cocaine abusers with low enzyme levels may be predisposed to the cardiotoxic effects of the drug. In humans, cocaine is rapidly metabolized, and less than 1% is excreted in urine; the major fraction of an administered dose of cocaine is recovered in urine predominantly as ecgonine methyl ester and benzoylecgonine.[10,11]

2.2.4.1.1 Vasospasticity and Microvascular Resistance

Coronary spasm has been repeatedly proposed as a mechanism of the unexplained sudden cardiac death in young cocaine abusers.[12] Clinical studies with intranasal cocaine administration in patients undergoing coronary arteriography for the evaluation of chest pain have demonstrated a moderate reduction in luminal caliber and microvascular resistance.[13] Although cocaine-induced vasospasm has not been demonstrated clinically, ergonovine-induced coronary spasm has been reported to occur at the site of severe coronary lesions in young cocaine abusers.[14] Animal experiments have confirmed that cocaine results in only a minimal diffuse diminution in coronary artery caliber.[15] Such non-critical reduction in luminal diameter is presumably clinically insignificant. It therefore seems likely that acceleration of atherosclerotic lesions must form a substrate for the hypersensitive vasoconstrictive response of a vessel to cocaine consumption. In support of this, cocaine-induced vasoconstriction has been shown to be enhanced at sites of significant fixed stenosis.[16]

Alternatively, coronary vasospasm in cocaine abusers may be associated with an increase in adventitial mast cells. A significantly higher prevalence of adventitial mast cells in victims of cocaine-associated sudden cardiac death have been reported when compared to individuals without a history of substance abuse.[17] Similarly, increased adventitial mast cells have been demonstrated at autopsy in patients who had clinically documented vasospastic angina in the absence of severe atherosclerotic coronary disease.[18] Mast cells are a rich source of histamine, which is often used as a provocative test to induce spasm in patients with suspected variant angina.[19,20] Furthermore, other mast cell products such as prostaglandin D2 and leukotrienes C4 and D4 are also modulators of vascular smooth muscle tone; prostaglandin D2-induced vasoconstriction is 5- to 10-fold more potent than norepinephrine.[21]

2.2.4.1.2 Thrombosis

Multiple studies have reported angiographic evidence of coronary thrombosis in young cocaine abusers, predominantly associated with minor atherosclerotic irregularities of coronary arteries. On the other hand, the autopsy data from the young patients with cocaine abuse-associated acute coronary thrombosis leading to sudden cardiac death have demonstrated that approximately 40% of patients suffer from severe atherosclerotic lesions of one or more major coronary arteries.[22,23] The average age of the cocaine abusers in these reports was approximately 30 years. However, the decreased prevalence of angiographically determined atherosclerotic disease in cocaine abusers may result from angiographic underestimation of the atherosclerotic lesions due to the relatively diffuse nature of the disease.[24-26] The thrombi isolated from these autopsy examinations have been demonstrated to be rich in platelets[17,22,23] and are characteristically not associated with rupture of the underlying plaques (Figure 2.2.4.4).

The mechanism of cocaine-induced thrombosis is not clear. Reports of the direct effects of cocaine on platelet function *in vitro* have been inconclusive and contradictory: cocaine either stimulates or inhibits aggregation.[27-31] However, it is thought that cocaine-induced platelet activation may occur *in vivo* due to indirect effects of the drug. Evidence in support of this hypothesis comes from studies in which platelet activation assessed *ex vivo* by P-selectin expression was increased in long-term habitual cocaine abusers and in dogs treated with cocaine.[32,33] Alternatively, coronary spasm may also explain the increased prevalence of thrombosis associated with cocaine abuse.

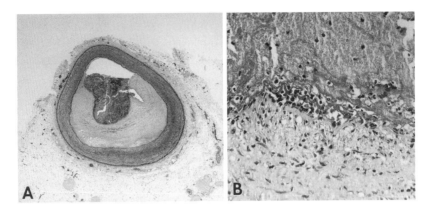

Figure 2.2.4.4 Cocaine-induced coronary thrombosis. (A) There is moderate (50%) luminal narrowing by atherosclerotic plaque composed of fibrointimal thickening consisting of smooth muscle cells in a proteoglycan-collagen matrix. (B) A higher magnification demonstrating a platelet thrombus overlying a plaque rich in smooth muscle cells and proteoglycans (plaque erosion).

2.2.4.1.3 Accelerated Atherosclerosis

Recent post-mortem studies in patients have emphasized that accelerated atherosclerosis may be an important etiologic factor in cocaine-induced acute coronary syndromes.[17,22-24] Kolodgie et al.[35] conducted a retrospective analysis of aortic sudanophilic lesions in asymptomatic young (median age, 25 years) cocaine abusers. After controlling for known risk factors of atherosclerosis, cocaine abuse was the only significant predictor of the extent of sudanophilia, suggesting that cocaine abuse was an independent risk factor for lipid infiltration in the vessel wall.[35] Accelerated atherosclerosis attributed to cocaine has been demonstrated experimentally in hypercholesterolemia-induced atherosclerosis in rabbits.[36] Also, cocaine abusers with coronary thrombosis have an increase in inflammatory cell infiltrate in severely narrowed atherosclerotic coronary arteries (Figure 2.2.4.1). Various mechanisms such as cocaine-related increase in plasma lipids, direct and indirect increase in endothelial permeability, higher prevalence of mast cells and other inflammatory cells in plaques may contribute to the lesions as discussed below.

2.2.4.1.4 Endothelial Dysfunction

As described above, atherosclerotic lesions occur prematurely and are likely to be more severe in cocaine abusers. Furthermore, these lesions develop regardless of the presence of conventional risk factors. Cocaine-induced endothelial cell dysfunction may be one of the predisposing factors, but whether this involves a direct and/or indirect action of the drug is unknown. Cocaine has been shown to disrupt the balance of endothelial prostacyclin and thromboxane production, which may be related to the increased tendency toward thrombosis and vasospasm observed in some cocaine abusers.[37,38] *In vitro* cell culture studies have demonstrated that cocaine increases the permeability function of endothelial cell monolayers as a possible mechanism of accelerated atherosclerosis.[36] Cocaine-treated endothelial cell monolayers demonstrated an increased permeability to horseradish peroxidase without affecting cell viability. Furthermore, cocaine-induced release of intracellular calcium stores may result in dysregulation of cytoskeletal integrity.[39] It has also been suggested that cocaine may suppress endothelial cell growth,[39] cause focal loss of endothelial cell integrity, or produce areas of extensive endothelial cell sloughing.[40,41]

As discussed earlier, the sympathomimetic effects of cocaine are associated with a transient but marked increase in blood pressure and some degree of vasoconstriction. These transient hemodynamic aberrations may cause endothelial injury. Indeed, cholesterol-fed rabbits typi-

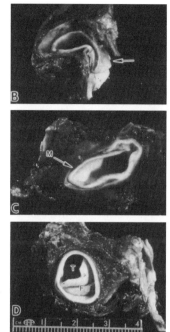

Figure 2.2.4.5 Cocaine-induced aortic dissection. (A) Multiple cross-sections through the aorta from the ascending aorta to the descending thoracic segment demonstrate dissection beginning at the aortic arch. (B) A cross-section through the descending thoracic aorta demonstrates the rupture site (arrow) of the false lumen. This rupture resulted in hemothorax and the death of the patient, who was a 24-year-old habitual cocaine abuser. (C) The dissection plane within the media (M) is clearly evident in this cross section that demonstrates the intimal tear. (D) The true (T) and false (F) lumens can be distinguished readily in this cross-section demonstrating the medial flap.

cally develop atherosclerotic lesions in the thoracic aorta at sites of increased endothelial cell turnover.

Cocaine-related endothelial dysfunction may be associated with impairment of endothelium-dependent vasorelaxation. Forearm blood flow during acetylcholine infusion in long-term cocaine abusers was significantly lower when compared with subjects without a prior history of drug abuse.[42] Whether attenuation of endothelial-dependent vasodilatory mechanisms by cocaine results from lethal injury to the endothelium, insensitivity of smooth muscle cells to nitric oxide, or inhibition of enzymatic pathways responsible for nitric oxide synthesis remains to be determined.

2.2.4.1.5 Hemodynamic Alterations

Hypertension related vascular complications have been commonly reported with sympathomimetic drugs such as cocaine. Sympathomimetic actions secondary to acute or chronic cocaine abuse are well documented and may result from peripheral inhibition of neuronal reuptake of monoamines and increased epinephrine release from the adrenal medulla as well as central activation of the sympathetic nervous system. The transient increase in blood pressure, at least after acute cocaine abuse, has been associated with aortic dissection (Figure 2.2.4.5), rupture of aortic aneurysms, and hemorrhagic strokes in patients with preexisting hypertension.[43-45] Recently, intracranial hemorrhage has also been shown to be associated with cocaine abuse.[46-49] Of the 17 non-traumatic cases of intracranial hemorrhage analyzed at autopsy, 10 were associated with cocaine: seven cases had intracerebral hemorrhage while three had ruptured berry aneurysms.[49] No pathologic evidence of vasculopathy was present in these patients.

2.2.4.1.6 Vasculitis

Cocaine-vasculitis has rarely been observed. Occasional cases of hypersensitivity vasculitis, similar to development of an Arthus reaction in experimental animals,[50-56] have been observed. Vasculitis characteristically results in fibrinoid necrosis of arteriolar and venular walls associated with disintegrating polymorphonuclear cells and histochemical localization of immunoglobulins and complement.[57,58] The lesions may eventually evolve into loose granulomas consisting of pallisading lymphocytes admixed with eosinophils and macrophages and, seldom, giant cells.[57,58] The most common site of vascular involvement in humans is skin; kidneys are involved in one-half and liver in a third.[58]

Cocaine is also reported to induce systemic necrotizing arteritis of predominantly medium and small-sized cerebral arterial vessels frequently at branch points.[54,59] Affected areas characteristically have marked necrotic lesions with neutrophilic infiltration and various stages of healing. No giant cells or granulomas are seen, and the vascular adventitia is not involved. The mechanism of drug-induced necrotizing vasculitis has not been established and could be either immunological or directly toxic.

2.2.4.1.7 Synergy with Other Drugs

It is estimated that half the individuals consume alcohol during cocaine bingeing, and this promotes hepatic transformation of cocaine to cocaethylene.[60-67] Cocaethylene has a substantially longer half-life and therefore its persistent systemic presence may increase the likelihood of cocaine cardiotoxicity. Cocaethylene has more potent sodium channel blocking activity compared to cocaine and its proarrhythmic effects may also be related to sudden death in the setting of ischemic myocardium.[69]

Another common drug that may be abused with cocaine is morphine. Morphine is a known secretogogue of mast cells that have been shown to be present in strikingly higher numbers in cocaine-associated atherosclerotic lesions. Mast cells are believed to play an important role in cocaine-related vasospastic manifestations.[70]

Similarly, synergistic interactions have been demonstrated for cocaine and cigarette smoking. Both agents are known to increase the metabolic demands on the heart but may also reduce oxygen supply. Moliteno et al.[71] have reported the influence of intranasal cocaine and cigarette smoking, alone and together, on myocardial oxygen demand and coronary artery dimensions in 42 subjects with and without atherosclerosis. Although none of the patients developed chest pain or ischemic electrocardiographic changes after cocaine use or cigarette smoking, oxygen demand increased by approximately 10% after either cigarette smoking or cocaine use, and by 50% after their simultaneous consumption. While the diameter of the normal coronary artery decreased by 6 to 7% with the use of either or both substances, reduction in the luminal diameter of the diseased artery segments for cigarette smoking, cocaine use, and both substances was 5%, 10%, and 20%, respectively.

2.2.4.2 Methamphetamine

The vascular effects of amphetamines have considerable similarity with sympathomimetic amines (ephedrine, phenylpropanolamine) and cocaine, which is alike structurally. Methamphetamine is abused orally, intravenously, or smoked in a crystal form ("ice"). Methamphetamine is metabolized to amphetamine, independent of the route of administration. Acute toxicity to amphetamine may manifest as rhabdomyolysis, disseminated intravascular coagulation, pulmonary edema, vascular spasm, and acute myocardial infarction. The ring substituted amphetamines 3,4-methylenedioxymethyl-amphetamine (MDMA, "ecstasy") and

3,4-methylenedioxyethylamphetamine (MDEA, "eve") have emerged as popular recreational drugs of abuse over the last decade.[72] Pharmacological studies indicate that these substances produce a mixture of central stimulant and psychedelic effects, many of which appear to be mediated by brain monoamines, particularly serotonin and dopamine.[73]

Chronic use of amphetamines may result in systemic and coronary artery vasospasm that results in an increased cardiac workload, impaired myocardial blood supply, and congestive failure, similar to end-stage hypertension. Sudden cardiac death may also occur. A few reports describe acute myocardial infarction associated with amphetamine abuse.[74] Potential explanations include coronary vasospasm, excessive catecholamine discharge resulting in ischemic myocardial necrosis, and catecholamine-mediated platelet aggregation with subsequent thrombus formation. The syndrome closely resembles acute myocardial infarction by cocaine abuse. As with cocaine toxicity, a deleterious effect of associated treatment with beta-blockers in the setting of myocardial infarction has also been observed.[71,75] Acute renal failure due to accelerated hypertension following the ingestion of 3,4-methylenedioxymethamphetamine ("ecstasy") has been reported.[76]

A necrotizing vasculitis resembling polyarteritis nodosa (Figure 2.2.4.3) has been reported in young abusers of methamphetamine, which may affect cerebral or visceral arteries. Histologically, there is fibrinoid necrosis of the media and intima of muscular arteries, with a neutrophilic eosinophilic, lymphocytic, and histiocytic infiltrate. Lesions at various stages may be seen with fresh thrombi in early lesions, florid intimal proliferation with marked luminal narrowing in subacute lesions, and destruction of the elastic lamina with replacement by collagen and luminal obliteration in later lesions. The cerebral effects of amphetamines are similar to those of other sympathomimetic amines (ephedrine and phenylpropranolamine).

2.2.4.3 Heroin

Heroin (diacetylmorphine) is a synthetic morphine derivative which, after administration, is hydrolytically deacetylated to 6-acetyl-morphine and excreted in the urine. Heroin has been associated with cerebral arteritis[77] and visceral polyarteritis.[78] Heroin may also have a direct toxic effect on the terminal hepatic veins,[79] the acute lesion being described as an inflammatory infiltrate of neutrophils and mononuclear cells in sinusoidal lumina and terminal veins which progresses to fibrosis of the central veins. Heroin is also associated with glomerular injury which may result in malignant hypertension. This heroin-associated nephropathy seen in African-American intravenous drug addicts has given way in the 1990s to HIV-associated nephropathy as a result of shared needles.[80]

2.2.4.4 Nicotine

Nicotine is well known to simulate the release of catecholamines, resulting in vasoconstriction and other vascular effects of catecholamine release.[81,82] In addition, there may be direct toxicity of nicotine to vascular endothelial cells *in-vitro*,[83] and an inhibition of apoptosis, which may contribute to an increase in smooth muscle cells within atherosclerotic plaques, possibly by monoclonal proliferation.[84] Nicotine has been found to be chemotactic for human neutrophils but not monocytes,[85] and in contrast to most other chemoattractants for neutrophils, does affect degranulation or superoxide production. Thus, nicotine may promote inflammation which may indirectly contribute to some of the associated vasculopathies. Nicotine transdermal patches used to help nicotine addiction have been associated with a leucocytoclastic vasculitis.[86,87]

2.2.4.5 Solvents ("Glue Sniffing")

Inhalation abuse of volatile solvents, previously known generically as "glue sniffing", is typically pursued by adolescents.[88] Glue sniffing has been associated with myocardial infarction, presumably secondary to coronary spasm as no fixed coronary lesions were identified by angiography.[89] The mechanism of sudden death in solvent sniffers is believed to be related to enhanced cardiac sensitivity to endogenous catecholamines.[90]

2.2.4.6 Vasculopathies Associated with Legitimate Medications

The sympathomimetic effects of tricyclic antidepressants are well documented, and overdose with these tricyclic amines is a major source of morbidity and mortality.[91] The most common cardiovascular effect of tricyclic amines is orthostatic hypotension, which is particularly serious in the elderly because it may lead to falls resulting in serious physical injuries. Severe orthostatic hypotension is more likely to develop in depressed patients with left ventricular impairment and/or in patients taking other drugs such as diuretics or vasodilators.[92] With chronic therapeutic administration, tricyclic antidepressants and phenothiazines have been associated with myocardial ischemia and infarction in the absence of fixed coronary lesions.[93]

2.2.4.6.1 Ergot Alkaloids

The ergot alkaloids are characterized by a nucleus of lysergic acid with the addition of side chains which divide the group into amino acids and amine alkaloids. Ergotamine, an example of an amino acid alkaloid, and methysergide, an example of an amine alkaloid, are both currently used in the prophylaxis and treatment of migraine headaches. The scleroticum of the fungus *Claviceps purpurea* is especially rich in ergot alkaloid, and was responsible for outbreaks of epidemic ergotism (St. Anthony's fire) following the mass ingestion of improperly stored rye in wet seasons. Ergot alkaloids have been used in large doses as an abortafacient.[94]

The toxic effects of ergot alkaloids include acute poisoning resulting in vasospasm and gangrene (usually as a complication of the induction of abortion), and acute idiosyncratic vasospasm secondary to a small dose of the drug. In this country, by far the most common form of ergot alkaloid toxicity is secondary to chronic ingestion of ergotamine, although outbreaks of St. Anthony's fire are still occasionally documented in developing countries.[94,95] Of recent incidence, bromocriptine mesylate, when used for the suppression of lactation in the puerperium, has been reported to cause generalized or focal vasospasm affecting the cardiac and/or cerebral blood vessels.[95]

The most common clinical manifestations of ergot alkaloid vasospasm are upper and lower extremity ischemia, which may result in claudication and ischemic ulcers of gangrene.[96] Other vasospastic sequelae of methylsergide or ergotamine toxicity include transient ischemic attacks, stroke (Figure 2.2.4.6), cardiac angina, and intestinal angina. Angiographic studies reveal narrowed vessels, which may show gradual smooth narrowing or irregular outlines with focal stenosis.[96,97] Laboratory studies are generally normal. A history will reveal chronic ingestion of ergotamine or methysergide, usually for migraine headaches, often by self-medication or doses exceeding the therapeutic recommendations. Symptoms often remit following cessation or lowering of medication dosage.

Pathologically, there are few vascular changes in acute cases of ergot poisoning, although contraction bands and medial necrosis may be noted within arterial walls. Chronic forms of ergotamine toxicity may have normal histologic findings[98] or changes consistent with chronic vasoconstriction, including medial hypertrophy, intimal proliferation, intimal hyalinization, and luminal thrombosis.

The mechanism(s) of ergot alkaloid toxicity are not yet completely clear. Physiologic doses result in vasoconstriction of painfully dilated cranial arteries, generally by the interaction of ergot with alpha-adrenergic receptors (alpha-adrenergic blockade) and serotonin antagonism.[99] Toxic vasoconstriciton may occur secondarily to a direct effect of ergot on the arterial media, exacerbated by a direct toxic effect on the capillary endothelium. High levels of

Figure 2.2.4.6 Ergotomine-induced fibrointimal proliferation. The carotid artery demonstrates marked narrowing by minimally cellular fibrointimal proliferation. The patient was a 45-year-old woman with chronic ergotamine toxicity who expired from a cerebrovascular accident. Elastic van Gieson stain.

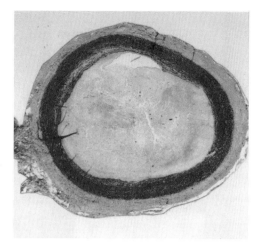

platelet-derived growth factor have been detected in an individual with chronic ergotism, suggesting that growth factors are released as a result of chronic endothelial damage.[98]

2.2.4.6.2 Ephedrine and Pseudoephedrine

Ephedrine and pseudoephedrine are sympathomimetic amines that may cause hypertension and tachyarrhythmias due to beta-adrenergic stimulation. Toxic effects may result from overdose, drug interactions (e.g., serotonin reuptake inhibitors), or diseases that increase sensitivity to sympathomimetic agents.[100] Reported adverse events range in severity from tremor and headache to death and include reports of stroke, myocardial infarction, chest pain, seizures, insomnia, nausea and vomiting, fatigue, and dizziness.[101,102] Ephedrine is the preferred vasoconstrictor for the treatment of hypotension after epidural and spinal anesthesia in obstetrics because it preserves uterine perfusion better than pure alpha-adrenergic agonists. Although during pregnancy the vasoconstrictor response to ephedrine is diminished, its stimulatory effect on nitric oxide synthase may release nitric oxide.[103]

The incidence of patients developing cerebral hemorrhage, presumably by the development of toxic vasculitis, is rare.[104] Reported cases of cerebral hemorrhage secondary to ephedrine are fewer than those complicating the use of phenylpropanolamine and amphetamines.[104-107] Clinical management of ephedrine overdose is mostly supportive and requires establishing respiration, initiating emesis, administering activated charcoal and a cathartic, and monitoring the patient's blood pressure, ECG, fluid intake, and urinary output.[108]

2.2.4.6.3 Phenylpropanolamine

Phenylpropanolamine is a synthetic sympathomimetic amine that is found in cold medications and diet pills. Although the vascular effects of phenylpropanolamine were previously considered minor, relative to ephedrine and amphetamine, increasing reports of toxicity in patients taking larger doses of this drug, especially in diet pills, have led to a reappraisal of the potential toxicity of the drug.

Cerebral hemorrhage has been reported in phenylpropanolamine toxicity after a dose of 50 mg or more.[106] In some commonly used anorexiants, including methamphetamine and phenylpropanolamine, an association with stroke has been reported.[108,109] Angiography in individuals with phenylpropanolamine toxicity has demonstrated vascular beading that has been ascribed to both vasospasm and to vasculitis.[106,110] In occasional instances in which histologic examination was performed, a necrotizing vasculitis has been identified.[105,106] It is unknown what proportion of phenylpropanolamine-, amphetamine-, and ephedrine-induced cerebral hemorrhages are due to vasculitis, and what proportion are due to vasospam related to catecholamine release.[106]

2.2.4.6.4 L-Tryptophan

The eosinophilia-myalgia syndrome associated with the ingestion of L-tryptophan was first recognized in late 1989.[111] Similar pathologic manifestations of eosinophilic myalgia syndrome share many features with the toxic oil syndrome caused by ingestion of adulterated rapeseed oil in Spain.[112] Although available over the counter in the U.S., L-tryptophan is dispensed only by prescription in Germany. Epidemiologic studies strongly suggest that the offending toxin is a contaminant used in the preparation of tryptophan, and not tryptophan itself.[113] Putative offending agents from suspected lots of L-tryptophan include 1,1'-ethylidenebis(tryptophan) and 3-phenylamino-1,2-propanediol, an aniline derivative. Most symptomatic patients are those that chronically ingest large doses of tryptophan (500 mg to several grams a day), although a dose-related toxic effect was not observed in an epidemiological study of German patients.[111] Vascular effects include pulmonary hypertension resulting from obstruction of pulmonary vessels.[112] Intermittent coronary spasm resulting in episodes of myocardial damage has also been reported.[115] Fibrointimal proliferation of small coronary arteries has also been described in patients with eosinophilia myalgia syndrome associated with L-tryptophan.[116]

Because L-tryptophan is metabolized to a number of compounds, including kynurenine, quinolate, serotonin, 5-hydroxyindoacetic acid, and homovanillic acid, a potential vasospastic role of one or more of these compounds has been investigated. A recent study did not find a link between any of these compounds and coronary vasospasm, but implicated increased levels of eosinophil granule major basic protein.[115]

REFERENCES

1. Li L, Smialek JE. Observations on drug abuse deaths in the state of Maryland. *J Forensic Sci* 1996;41:106-9.
2. Muscholl E. Effect of cocaine and related drugs on the uptake of noradrenaline by heart and spleen. *Br J Pharmacol* 1961;62:352.
3. Fuder H, Bath F, Wiebelt H, Muscholl E. Autoinhibition of noradrenaline release from the rat heart as a function of the biophase concentration. Effects of exogenous alpha-adrenoceptor agonists, cocaine, and perfusion rate. *Naunyn Schmiedebergs Arch Pharmacol* 1984;325:25-33.
4. Perper JA, Van Thiel DH. Cardiovascular complications of cocaine abuse. *Recent Dev Alcohol* 1992;10:343-61.
5. Van Dyke C, Barash PG, Jatlow P, Byck R. Cocaine: plasma concentrations after intranasal application in man. *Science* 1976;191:859-61.
6. Poklis A, Maginn D, Barr JL. Tissue disposition of cocaine in man: a report of five fatal poisonings. *Forensic Sci Int* 1987;33:83-8.
7. Poklis A, Mackell MA, Graham M. Disposition of cocaine in fatal poisoning in man. *J Anal Toxicol* 1985;9:227-9.
8. Gawin FH. Cocaine addiction: psychology and neurophysiology [published erratum appears in Science 1991 Aug 2;253(5019):494]. *Science* 1991;251:1580-6.
9. Madden JA, Powers RH. Effect of cocaine and cocaine metabolites on cerebral arteries in vitro. *Life Sci* 1990;47:1109-14.
10. Ambre J. The urinary excretion of cocaine and metabolites in humans: a kinetic analysis of published data. *J Anal Toxicol* 1985;9:241-5.
11. Jeffcoat AR, Perez-Reyes M, Hill JM, Sadler BM, Cook CE. Cocaine disposition in humans after intravenous injection, nasal insufflation (snorting), or smoking. *Drug Metab Dispos* 1989;17:153-9.
12. Minor RL, Jr., Scott BD, Brown DD, Winniford MD. Cocaine-induced myocardial infarction in patients with normal coronary arteries [see comments]. *Ann Intern Med* 1991;115:797-806.
13. Lange RA, Cigarroa RG, Yancy CW, Jr., Willard JE, Popma JJ, Sills MN, McBride W, Kim AS, Hillis LD. Cocaine-induced coronary-artery vasoconstriction [see comments]. *N Engl J Med* 1989;321:1557-62.
14. Smith HWd, Liberman HA, Brody SL, Battey LL, Donohue BC, Morris DC. Acute myocardial infarction temporally related to cocaine use. Clinical, angiographic, and pathophysiologic observations. *Ann Intern Med* 1987;107:13-8.

15. Hale SL, Alker KJ, Rezkalla S, Figures G, Kloner RA. Adverse effects of cocaine on cardiovascular dynamics, myocardial blood flow, and coronary artery diameter in an experimental model. *Am Heart J* 1989;118:927-33.

16. Flores ED, Lange RA, Cigarroa RG, Hillis LD. Effect of cocaine on coronary artery dimensions in atherosclerotic coronary artery disease: enhanced vasoconstriction at sites of significant stenoses. *J Am Coll Cardiol* 1990;16:74-9.

17. Kolodgie FD, Virmani R, Cornhill JF, Herderick EE, Smialek J. Increase in atherosclerosis and adventitial mast cells in cocaine abusers: an alternative mechanism of cocaine-associated coronary vasospasm and thrombosis. *J Am Coll Cardiol* 1991;17:1553-60.

18. Forman MB, Oates JA, Robertson D, Robertson RM, Roberts LJd, Virmani R. Increased adventitial mast cells in a patient with coronary spasm. *N Engl J Med* 1985;313:1138-41.

19. Kaski JC, Crea F, Meran D, Rodriguez L, Araujo L, Chierchia S, Davies G, Maseri A. Local coronary supersensitivity to diverse vasoconstrictive stimuli in patients with variant angina. *Circulation* 1986;74:1255-65.

20. Ginsburg R, Bristow MR, Kantrowitz N, Baim DS, Harrison DC. Histamine provocation of clinical coronary artery spasm: implications concerning pathogenesis of variant angina pectoris. *Am Heart J* 1981;102:819-22.

21. Burke JA, Levi R, Guo ZG, Corey EJ. Leukotrienes C4, D4 and E4: effects on human and guinea-pig cardiac preparations in vitro. *J Pharmacol Exp Ther* 1982;221:235-41.

22. Mittleman RE, Wetli CV. Cocaine and sudden "natural" death. *J Forensic Sci* 1987;32:11-9.

23. Dressler FA, Malekzadeh S, Roberts WC. Quantitative analysis of amounts of coronary arterial narrowing in cocaine addicts. *Am J Cardiol* 1990;65:303-8.

24. Sheikh KH, Harrison JK, Harding MB, Himmelstein SI, Kisslo KB, Davidson CJ, Bashore TM. Detection of angiographically silent coronary atherosclerosis by intracoronary ultrasonography. *Am Heart J* 1991;121:1803-7.

25. Tobis JM, Mallery J, Mahon D, Lehmann K, Zalesky P, Griffith J, Gessert J, Moriuchi M, McRae M, Dwyer ML, et al. Intravascular ultrasound imaging of human coronary arteries in vivo. Analysis of tissue characterizations with comparison to in vitro histological specimens. *Circulation* 1991;83:913-26.

26. McPherson DD, Hiratzka LF, Lamberth WC, Brandt B, Hunt M, Kieso RA, Marcus ML, Kerber RE. Delineation of the extent of coronary atherosclerosis by high-frequency epicardial echocardiography. *N Engl J Med* 1987;316:304-9.

27. Heesch CM, Negus BH, Steiner M, Snyder RW, II, McIntire DD, Grayburn PA, Ashcraft J, Hernandez JA, Eichhorn EJ. Effects of in vivo cocaine administration on human platelet aggregation. *Am J Cardiol* 1996;78:237-9.

28. Kugelmass AD, Oda A, Monahan K, Cabral C, Ware JA. Activation of human platelets by cocaine. *Circulation* 1993;88:876-83.

29. Jennings LK, White MM, Sauer CM, Mauer AM, Robertson JT. Cocaine-induced platelet defects. *Stroke* 1993;24:1352-9.

30. Rezkalla SH, Mazza JJ, Kloner RA, Tillema V, Chang SH. Effects of cocaine on human platelets in healthy subjects. *Am J Cardiol* 1993;72:243-6.

31. Togna G, Tempesta E, Togna AR, Dolci N, Cebo B, Caprino L. Platelet responsiveness and biosynthesis of thromboxane and prostacyclin in response to in vitro cocaine treatment. *Haemostasis* 1985;15:100-7.

32. Kugelmass AD, Shannon RP, Yeo EL, Ware JA. Intravenous cocaine induces platelet activation in the conscious dog. *Circulation* 1995;91:1336-40.

33. Rinder HM, Ault KA, Jatlow PI, Kosten TR, Smith BR. Platelet alpha-granule release in cocaine users. *Circulation* 1994;90:1162-7.

34. Fogo A, Superdock KR, Atkinson JB. Severe arteriosclerosis in the kidney of a cocaine addict. *Am J Kidney Dis* 1992;20:513-5.

35. Kolodgie FD, Virmani R, Cornhill JF, Herderick EE, Malcom GT, Mergner WJ. Cocaine: an independent risk factor for aortic sudanophilia. A preliminary report. *Atherosclerosis* 1992;97:53-62.

36. Kolodgie FD, Wilson PS, Cornhill JF, Herderick EE, Mergner WJ, Virmani R. Increased prevalence of aortic fatty streaks in cholesterol-fed rabbits administered intravenous cocaine: the role of vascular endothelium. *Toxicol Pathol* 1993;21:425-35.
37. Eichhorn EJ, Demian SE, Alvarez LG, Willard JE, Molina S, Bartula LL, Prince MD, Inman LR, Grayburn PA, Myers SI. Cocaine-induced alterations in prostaglandin production in rabbit aorta. *J Am Coll Cardiol* 1992;19:696-703.
38. Cejtin HE, Parsons MT, Wilson L, Jr. Cocaine use and its effect on umbilical artery prostacyclin production. *Prostaglandins* 1990;40:249-57.
39. Welder AA, Grammas P, Fugate RD, Rohrer P, Melchert RB. A primary culture system of rat heart-derived endothelial cells for evaluating cocaine-induced vascular injury. *Toxicol Methods* 1993;3:109-18.
40. Gilloteaux J, Dalbec JP. Transplacental cardiotoxicity of cocaine: atrial damage following treatment in early pregnancy. *Scanning Microsc* 1991;5:519-29; discussion 29-31.
41. Jones LF, Tackett RL. Chronic cocaine treatment enhances the responsiveness of the left anterior descending coronary artery and the femoral artery to vasoactive substances. *J Pharmacol Exp Ther* 1990;255:1366-70.
42. Havranek EP, Nademanee K, Grayburn PA, Eichhorn EJ. Endothelium-dependent vasorelaxation is impaired in cocaine arteriopathy. *J Am Coll Cardiol* 1996;28:1168-74.
43. Gadaleta D, Hall MH, Nelson RL. Cocaine-induced acute aortic dissection. *Chest* 1989;96:1203-5.
44. Cohle SD, Lie JT. Dissection of the aorta and coronary arteries associated with acute cocaine intoxication. *Arch Pathol Lab Med* 1992;116:1239-41.
45. McDermott JC, Schuster MR, Crummy AB, Acher CW. Crack and aortic dissection. *Wis Med J* 1993;92:453-5.
46. Aggarwal SK, Williams V, Levine SR, Cassin BJ, Garcia JH. Cocaine-associated intracranial hemorrhage: absence of vasculitis in 14 cases. *Neurology* 1996;46:1741-3.
47. Nalls G, Disher A, Daryabagi J, Zant Z, Eisenman J. Subcortical cerebral hemorrhages associated with cocaine abuse: CT and MR findings. *J Comput Assist Tomogr* 1989;13:1-5.
48. Green RM, Kelly KM, Gabrielsen T, Levine SR, Vanderzant C. Multiple intracerebral hemorrhages after smoking "crack" cocaine. *Stroke* 1990;21:957-62.
49. Nolte KB, Brass LM, Fletterick CF. Intracranial hemorrhage associated with cocaine abuse: a prospective autopsy study. *Neurology* 1996;46:1291-6.
50. Merkel PA, Koroshetz WJ, Irizarry MC, Cudkowicz ME. Cocaine-associated cerebral vasculitis. *Semin Arthritis Rheum* 1995;25:172-83.
51. Gradon JD, Wityk R. Diagnosis of probable cocaine-induced cerebral vasculitis by magnetic resonance angiography. *South Med J* 1995;88:1264-6.
52. Giang DW. Central nervous system vasculitis secondary to infections, toxins, and neoplasms. *Semin Neurol* 1994;14:313-9.
53. Morrow PL, McQuillen JB. Cerebral vasculitis associated with cocaine abuse. *J Forensic Sci* 1993;38:732-8.
54. Fredericks RK, Lefkowitz DS, Challa VR, Troost BT. Cerebral vasculitis associated with cocaine abuse. *Stroke* 1991;22:1437-9.
55. Kaye BR, Fainstat M. Cerebral vasculitis associated with cocaine abuse. *Jama* 1987;258:2104-6.
56. Cerebral vasculitis associated with cocaine abuse or subarachnoid hemorrhage? [letter]. *JAMA* 1988;259:1648-9.
57. Krendel DA, Ditter SM, Frankel MR, Ross WK. Biopsy-proven cerebral vasculitis associated with cocaine abuse. *Neurology* 1990;40:1092-4.
58. Enriquez R, Palacios FO, Gonzalez CM, Amoros FA, Cabezuelo JB, Hernandez F. Skin vasculitis, hypokalemia and acute renal failure in rhabdomyolysis associated with cocaine [letter]. *Nephron* 1991;59:336-7.
59. Daras M, Tuchman AJ, Koppel BS, Samkoff LM, Weitzner I, Marc J. Neurovascular complications of cocaine. *Acta Neurol Scand* 1994;90:124-9.
60. Barinaga M. Miami vice metabolite [news]. *Science* 1990;250:758.

61. Hearn WL, Flynn DD, Hime GW, Rose S, Cofino JC, Mantero-Atienza E, Wetli CV, Mash DC. Cocaethylene: a unique cocaine metabolite displays high affinity for the dopamine transporter. *J Neurochem* 1991;56:698-701.

62. Jatlow P, Hearn WL, Elsworth JD, Roth RH, Bradberry CW, Taylor JR. Cocaethylene inhibits uptake of dopamine and can reach high plasma concentrations following combined cocaine and ethanol use. *NIDA Res Monogr* 1991;105:572-3.

63. Hearn WL, Rose S, Wagner J, Ciarleglio A, Mash DC. Cocaethylene is more potent than cocaine in mediating lethality. *Pharmacol Biochem Behav* 1991;39:531-3.

64. Perez-Reyes M, Jeffcoat AR. Ethanol/cocaine interaction: cocaine and cocaethylene plasma concentrations and their relationship to subjective and cardiovascular effects. *Life Sci* 1992;51:553- 63.

65. Perez-Reyes M. Subjective and cardiovascular effects of cocaethylene in humans. *Psychopharmacology* (Berl) 1993;113:144-7.

66. Covert RF, Schreiber MD, Tebbett IR, Torgerson LJ. Hemodynamic and cerebral blood flow effects of cocaine, cocaethylene and benzoylecgonine in conscious and anesthetized fetal lambs. *J Pharmacol Exp Ther* 1994;270:118-26.

67. Wilson LD, Henning RJ, Suttheimer C, Lavins E, Balraj E, Earl S. Cocaethylene causes dose-dependent reductions in cardiac function in anesthetized dogs. *J Cardiovasc Pharmacol* 1995;26:965-73.

68. Randall T. Cocaine, alcohol mix in body to form even longer lasting, more lethal drug [news]. *JAMA* 1992;267:1043-4.

69. Xu YQ, Crumb WJ, Jr., Clarkson CW. Cocaethylene, a metabolite of cocaine and ethanol, is a potent blocker of cardiac sodium channels. *J Pharmacol Exp Ther* 1994;271:319-25.

70. Klein LM, Lavker RM, Matis WL, Murphy GF. Degranulation of human mast cells induces an endothelial antigen central to leukocyte adhesion. *Proc Natl Acad Sci USA* 1989;86:8972-6.

71. Moliterno DJ, Willard JE, Lange RA, Negus BH, Boehrer JD, Glamann DB, Landau C, Rossen JD, Winniford MD, Hillis LD. Coronary-artery vasoconstriction induced by cocaine, cigarette smoking, or both. *N Engl J Med* 1994;330:454-9.

72. Milroy CM, Clark JC, Forrest AR. Pathology of deaths associated with "ecstasy" and "eve" misuse. *J Clin Pathol* 1996;49:149-53.

73. Steele TD, McCann UD, Ricaurte GA. 3,4-Methylenedioxymethamphetamine (MDMA, "Ecstasy"): pharmacology and toxicology in animals and humans. *Addiction* 1994;89:539-51.

74. Bashour TT. Acute myocardial infarction resulting from amphetamine abuse: a spasm- thrombus interplay? *Am Heart J* 1994;128:1237-9.

75. Ragland AS, Ismail Y, Arsura EL. Myocardial infarction after amphetamine use. *Am Heart J* 1993;125:247-9.

76. Woodrow G, Harnden P, Turney JH. Acute renal failure due to accelerated hypertension following ingestion of 3,4-methylenedioxymethamphetamine ('ecstasy'). *Nephrol Dial Transplant* 1995;10:399-400.

77. King J, Richards M, Tress B. Cerebral arteritis associated with heroin abuse. *Med J Aust* 1978;2:444-5.

78. Citron BP, Halpern M, McCarron M, Lundberg GD, McCormick R, Pincus IJ, Tatter D, Haverback BJ. Necrotizing angiitis associated with drug abuse. *N Engl J Med* 1970;283:1003-11.

79. de Araujo MS, Gerard F, Chossegros P, Porto LC, Barlet P, Grimaud JA. Vascular hepatotoxicity related to heroin addiction. *Virchows Arch A Pathol Anat Histopathol* 1990;417:497-503.

80. Bakir AA, Dunea G. Drugs of abuse and renal disease. *Curr Opin Nephrol Hypertens* 1996;5:122-6.

81. Murphy DA, O'Blenes S, Nassar BA, Armour JA. Effects of acutely raising intracranial pressure on cardiac sympathetic efferent neuron function. *Cardiovasc Res* 1995;30:716-24.

82. Grassi G, Seravalle G, Calhoun DA, Bolla GB, Giannattasio C, Marabini M, Del Bo A, Mancia G. Mechanisms responsible for sympathetic activation by cigarette smoking in humans. *Circulation* 1994;90:248-53.

83. Pitillo R, Cigarette smoking and endothelial injury: A review. *Tobacco Smoking and Atherosclerosis*. 1989, New York: Plenum Press.

84. Wright SC, Zhong J, Zheng H, Larrick JW. Nicotine inhibition of apoptosis suggests a role in tumor promotion. *Faseb J* 1993;7:1045-51.

85. Totti Nd, McCusker KT, Campbell EJ, Griffin GL, Senior RM. Nicotine is chemotactic for neutrophils and enhances neutrophil responsiveness to chemotactic peptides. *Science* 1984;223:169-71.

86. Lagrue G, Verra F, Lebargy F. Nicotine patches and vascular risks [letter; comment]. *Lancet* 1993;342:564.

87. Van der Klauw MM, Van Hillo B, Van den Berg WH, Bolsius EP, Sutorius FF, Stricker BH. Vasculitis attributed to the nicotine patch (Nicotinell). *Br J Dermatol* 1996;134:361-4.

88. Steffee CH, Davis GJ, Nicol KK. A whiff of death: fatal volatile solvent inhalation abuse. *South Med J* 1996;89:879-84.

89. Cunningham SR, Dalzell GW, McGirr P, Khan MM. Myocardial infarction and primary ventricular fibrillation after glue sniffing. *Br Med J* (Clin Res Ed) 1987;294:739-40.

90. McLeod AA, Marjot R, Monaghan MJ, Hugh-Jones P, Jackson G, Timmis AD, Smyth P, Monaghan M, Walker L, Daly K, McLeod AA, Jewitt DE. Chronic cardiac toxicity after inhalation of 1,1,1-trichloroethane Milrinone in heart failure. Acute effects on left ventricular systolic function and myocardial metabolism. *Br Med J* (Clin Res Ed) 1987;294:727-9.

91. Warrington SJ, Padgham C, Lader M. The cardiovascular effects of antidepressants. *Psychol Med Monogr* Suppl 1989;16:i-iii, 1-40.

92. Glassman AH, Preud'homme XA. Review of the cardiovascular effects of heterocyclic antidepressants. *J Clin Psychiatry* 1993;54 Suppl:16-22.

93. Chamsi-Pasha H, Barnes PC. Myocardial infarction: a complication of amitriptyline overdose. *Postgrad Med J* 1988;64:968-70.

94. Magee R. Saint Anthony's fire revisited. Vascular problems associated with migraine medication. *Med J Aust* 1991;154:145-9.

95. Weaver R, Phillips M, Vacek JL. St. Anthony's fire: a medieval disease in modern times: case history. *Angiology* 1989;40:929-32.

96. Iffy L, McArdle JJ, Ganesh V, Hopp L. Bromocriptine related atypical vascular accidents postpartum identified through medicolegal reviews. *Med Law* 1996;15:127-34.

97. McKiernan TL, Bock K, Leya F, Grassman E, Lewis B, Johnson SA, Scanlon PJ. Ergot induced peripheral vascular insufficiency, non-interventional treatment. *Cathet Cardiovasc Diagn* 1994;31:211-4.

98. Raroque HG, Jr., Tesfa G, Purdy P. Postpartum cerebral angiopathy. Is there a role for sympathomimetic drugs? *Stroke* 1993;24:2108-10.

99. Pietrogrande F, Caenazzo A, Dazzi F, Polato G, Girolami A. A role for platelet-derived growth factor in drug-induced chronic ergotism? A case report. *Angiology* 1995;46:633-6.

100. Oliver JW, Abney LK, Strickland JR, Linnabary RD. Vasoconstriction in bovine vasculature induced by the tall fescue alkaloid lysergamide. *J Anim Sci* 1993;71:2708-13.

101. Skop BP, Finkelstein JA, Mareth TR, Magoon MR, Brown TM. The serotonin syndrome associated with paroxetine, an over-the-counter cold remedy, and vascular disease [see comments]. *Am J Emerg Med* 1994;12:642-4.

102. Wiener I, Tilkian AG, Palazzolo M. Coronary artery spasm and myocardial infarction in a patient with normal coronary arteries: temporal relationship to pseudoephedrine ingestion. *Cathet Cardiovasc Diagn* 1990;20:51-3.

103. Adverse events associated with ephedrine-containing products—Texas, December 1993- September 1995. *MMWR Morb Mortal Wkly Rep* 1996;45:689-93.

104. Li P, Tong C, Eisenach JC. Pregnancy and ephedrine increase the release of nitric oxide in ovine uterine arteries. *Anesth Analg* 1996;82:288-93.

105. Wooten MR, Khangure MS, Murphy MJ. Intracerebral hemorrhage and vasculitis related to ephedrine abuse. *Ann Neurol* 1983;13:337-40.

106. Glick R, Hoying J, Cerullo L, Perlman S. Phenylpropanolamine: an over-the-counter drug causing central nervous system vasculitis and intracerebral hemorrhage. Case report and review. *Neurosurgery* 1987;20:969-74.

107. Forman HP, Levin S, Stewart B, Patel M, Feinstein S. Cerebral vasculitis and hemorrhage in an adolescent taking diet pills containing phenylpropanolamine: case report and review of literature. *Pediatrics* 1989;83:737-41.
108. Nadeau SE. Intracerebral hemorrhage and vasculitis related to ephedrine abuse [letter]. *Ann Neurol* 1984;15:114-5.
109. Sawyer DR, Conner CS, Rumack BH. Managing acute toxicity from nonprescription stimulants. *Clin Pharm* 1982;1:529-33.
110. Kokkinos J, Levine SR. Possible association of ischemic stroke with phentermine. *Stroke* 1993;24:310-3.
111. Fallis RJ, Fisher M. Cerebral vasculitis and hemorrhage associated with phenylpropanolamine. *Neurology* 1985;35:405-7.
112. Mayeno AN, Gleich GJ. The eosinophilia-myalgia syndrome: lessons from Germany [editorial; comment]. *Mayo Clin Proc* 1994;69:702-4.
113. Tabuenca JM. Toxic-allergic syndrome caused by ingestion of rapeseed oil denatured with aniline. *Lancet* 1981;2:567-8.
114. Carr L, Ruther E, Berg PA, Lehnert H. Eosinophilia-myalgia syndrome in Germany: an epidemiologic review [see comments]. *Mayo Clin Proc* 1994;69:620-5.
115. Campagna AC, Blanc PD, Criswell LA, Clarke D, Sack KE, Gold WM, Golden JA. Pulmonary manifestations of the eosinophilia-myalgia syndrome associated with tryptophan ingestion. *Chest* 1992;101:1274-81.
116. Hertzman PA, Maddoux GL, Sternberg EM, Heyes MP, Mefford IN, Kephart GM, Gleich GJ. Repeated coronary artery spasm in a young woman with the eosinophilia-myalgia syndrome. *JAMA* 1992;267:2932-4.
117. Hayashi T, James TN. Immunohistochemical analysis of lymphocytes in postmortem study of the heart from fatal cases of the eosinophilia myalgia syndrome and of the toxic oil syndrome. *Am Heart J* 1994;127:1298-308.

2.3 LUNG DISEASE

MICHAEL D. BELL, M.D.

ASSOCIATE MEDICAL EXAMINER, DADE COUNTY MEDICAL EXAMINER OFFICE, MIAMI, FLORIDA

2.3.1 PATHOLOGY ENCOUNTERED IN "CRACK" SMOKERS

Bailey et al.[1] examined the lungs of dead cocaine abusers and found the most common pulmonary findings were pulmonary congestion (88%), edema (77%), and acute/chronic alveolar hemorrhage (71%). These findings have been also reported by Murray et al.[2,3] found hemosiderin-laden macrophages in 35% (7/20) of the victims of cocaine intoxication and opined that occult alveolar hemorrhage occurs more frequently in cocaine users than is clinically recognized. They also noted pulmonary artery medial hypertrophy in 20% (4/20) of these cocaine abusers who had no histologic evidence of foreign material embolization. The cause of the alveolar hemorrhage was thought to be ischemic damage to the capillary endothelium from constriction of the pulmonary vascular bed after cocaine inhalation, or as a direct toxic effect of cocaine on the capillary endothelium. Neither hypothesis is proven. Hemosiderin-laden macrophages may be seen in bronchoalveolar lavage fluid or in bronchoscopy biopsy specimens. One cocaine abuser who presented with diffuse alveolar hemorrhage had no vasculitis. Electron microscopy did not demonstrate any disruption in the alveolar or capillary basement membranes.[3] Pulmonary hemorrhage has not only been associated with alkaloidal

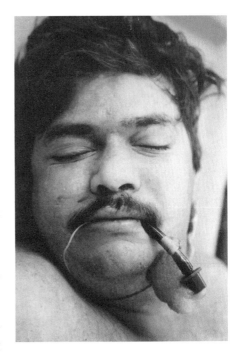

Figure 2.3.1 Abundant blood-tinged foam escapes from the end of the endotrachial tube in this drug abuser with pulmonary edema.

"crack" cocaine smoking, but also with intravenous and nasal routes[4] of administration. Pulmonary congestion in fatal cocaine intoxication is usually caused by the slow cessation of cardiac function associated with brain stem hypoxia during seizures or direct cocaine toxicity.

Fatal and non-fatal pulmonary edema (Figure 2.3.1) has been reported in cocaine smokers without obvious cardiac or central nervous system disease.[5-8] Some of these patients had resolution of the pulmonary edema without specific treatment and chest radiographs have shown normal cardiac silhouettes. No reports have shown any hemodynamic data from these patients with pulmonary edema. One patient underwent bronchoalveolar lavage and had an elevated protein level (4x normal) suggesting that the edema was due to altered alveolar capillary permeability.[7] Bronchial biopsy usually revealed no histologic abnormalities[7] or only "mild interstitial inflammatory changes".[8]

Pneumonitis, as defined by widening of the alveolar septae with a polymorphous infiltrate (lymphocytes, neutrophils, macrophages, eosinophils) or fibrosis, was seen in one fourth of the victims studied by Bailey et al.[1] Patel et al.[9] describe a patient with broncholitis obliterans and organizing pneumonia (BOOP) associated with regular free-base use in the weeks prior to the onset of clinical symptoms (non-productive cough, fever, dyspnea). An open lung biopsy demonstrated patchy bronchocentric interstitial and intra-alveolar chronic inflammation (lymphocytes, macrophages, and few polymorphonuclear leukocytes and eosinphils) with granulation tissue and collagen occupying bronchioles and adjacent alveolar ducts. The blood vessels were normal. A hypersensitivity reaction to cocaine or an adulterant was the presumed cause. This mechanism also presumably causes "crack lung", a clinical syndrome with chest pain, hemoptysis, and diffuse alveolar infiltrates associated with smoking "crack" cocaine.[10,11] Finally, 11% of the cocaine fatalities had polarizable material, usually talc, within the lungs. Most of these victims were, not unexpectedly, intravenous drug abusers.

Cocaine users who smoked cocaine free base or "crack" may forcefully blow smoke into another user's mouth to augment the drug's effect. Smokers also prolong the Valsalva maneuver to avoid expiring the precious cocaine smoke. The resulting increased intra-alveolar pressure ruptures the alveolar walls, allowing air to dissect along the perivascular tissues into the mediastinum and surrounding cavities. These mechanisms have produced various forms of barotrauma including pneumothorax, pneumo-mediastinum,[12-14] pneumopericardium,[15] pneumoperitoneum,[16] and subcutaneous emphysema. In the few cases,[17] where the duration of cocaine use prior to clinical symptoms was accurately known, patients freebased cocaine for 8 to 12 hours and snorted cocaine for 1 to 2 hours. The clinical course of cocaine-associated barotrauma is generally non-fatal. This barotrauma is not specific for cocaine smokers and has been described in marijuana smokers.[18]

Smoking cocaine can cause acute severe exacerbation of asthma in chronic asthmatics.[19,20] Insufflation of cocaine hydrochloride has also been associated with near-fatal status asthmaticus.[21] Blackened sputum and pulmonary cytologic specimens with excessive carbonaceous material

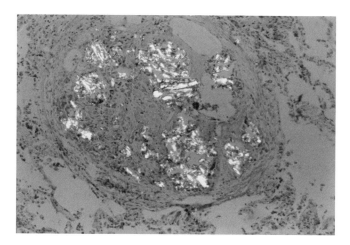

Figure 2.3.2 Abundant birefrigent material lies within this pulmonary artery thrombus from an intravenous drug abuser (Hematoxylin and eosin, polarized light, 80x).

have been associated with crack cocaine use.[22] This is most likely from inhalation of nonvolatilized impurities when crack and its tarry residue are smoked: As crack is smoked, a dark, tarry residue forms on the inside of the pipe's bowl and barrel. Many smokers consider this residue to be concentrated cocaine and they scrape it free, reheat it, and vigorously inhale it.

The long-term pulmonary effects and pathology of smoking cocaine are unknown. Pulmonary function studies are confounded by the fact that cocaine smokers also smoke tobacco and marijuana in addition to cocaine. Cocaine smokers have a reduced diffusing capacity of carbon monoxide, but no spirometric abnormalities have been demonstrated.[23]

2.3.2 ALTERATIONS ASSOCIATED WITH INTRAVENOUS DRUG ABUSE

Intravenous drug abusers may crush oral medications and make them soluble for intravenous injection. Methadone[24] and propoxyphene[25] are examples of oral drugs that are abused in this fashion. The filler material in the pills contains insoluble particles that cause thrombosis, granulomatous inflammation, and fibrosis in the lungs. The granulomas have numerous multinucleated giant cells and birefrigent foreign material (Figure 2.3.2). In addition to their morphology, the foreign particles can be identified by selected-area electron diffraction and energy dispersive x-ray analysis. The functional consequence of these lesions is often pulmonary hypertension with its accompanying complications, including sudden death. The granulomatous and fibrotic reaction can be in the interstitium, presumably due to particle migration through the arterial walls. Large fibrotic pulmonary masses have been described with huge particle counts and occasional giant cells. The fibrotic masses are usually bilateral, asymmetric, and confined to the middle and upper lung fields. These are similar to the progressive massive fibrosis seen in complicated pneumoconiosis.[27-29]

Pulmonary hypertension from pulmonary artery thromboses has been reported from repeated intravenous injection of "blue velvet", a mixture of paregoric and tripelennamine (Pyribenzamine) tablets.[30,31] Methylphenidate (Ritalin) tablets contain talc (magnesium silicate) and cornstarch, which can cause pulmonary hypertension and sudden death, often within 6 to 7 months of using the drugs. (Note that Ritalin tablets may be used as a stimulant to counteract the sedative effects of methadone maintenance in addicts). While cornstarch can cause foreign body granulomas, the reaction is generally milder and less frequent than the granulomatous inflammation caused by talc,[32] which is irritating to tissues and may cause

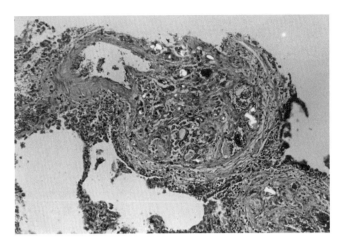

Figure 2.3.3 Angiomatoid lesion with birefrigent talc in an intravenous drug abuser (Hematoxylin and eosin, polarized light, 80x).

thrombosis with occlusion of pulmonary arterioles and capillaries, and a granulomatous inflammation with parenchymal fibrosis.[26] The end result is a restrictive lung disease with impaired oxygen transfer across the alveolar- capillary membrane and pulmonary hypertension. The pulmonary arteries may have multiple intravascular and perivascular foreign body granulomas filled with birefrigent talc. The pulmonary arteries may also have medial hypertrophy, fibrointimal hyperplasia, and angiomatoid lesions[32] (Figure 2.3.3).

Pulmonary emphysema has been described in a subgroup of intravenous drug abusers who inject methylphenidate (Ritalin-SA). These patients present with dyspnea at an average age of 36 years. All have moderate to severe airflow obstruction with hyperinflation on chest radiography. The bullae are often seen in the lower lobes and the disease may mimic the emphysema seen in alpha-1- antitrypsin deficiency. Morphologically, there is panacinar emphysema with no interstitial fibrosis and variable degrees of pulmonary talc granulomatosis.

2.3.3 ASPIRATION PNEUMONIA

Alcoholism is a common predisposing condition for aspiration pneumonia. Aspiration of orogastric material (bacteria, acid, food) can also occur in victims rendered unconscious by drugs directly (narcotics) or indirectly by drug-induced seizures (cocaine). The posterior segments of the upper lobes or superior segments of the left lower lobe are involved when the victim is recumbent during aspiration. The basal lung segments are affected when the victim is upright and the anterior segment of the middle lobe is involved when the victim is prone or inclined forward. Gastric acid can produce bronchiolitis, hemorrhagic edema, and diffuse alveolar damage. Fluid contaminated with *Streptococcus pneumoniae* or *Klebsiella pneumoniae* characteristically produce a subpleural pneumonia with hemorrhagic edema.[36] Aspiration pneumonia often has a mixture of both aerobic and anaerobic bacteria. Striated muscle and vegetable fibers can be seen microscopically within the bronchioles and alveoli. Necrotizing bacteria may produce lung abscesses. Septic thromboemboli from tricuspid valve endocarditis can also produce multiple lung abscesses and pneumonia in the intravenous drug abuser (Figures 2.3.4 and 2.3.5).

Michael D. Bell

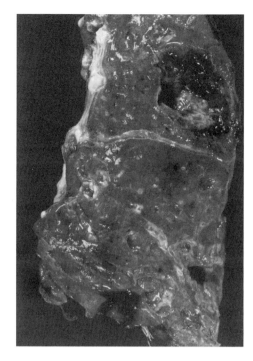

Figure 2.3.4 This sectioned lung has multiple abscess cavities. The victim was a 31-year-old cocaine "skin popper".

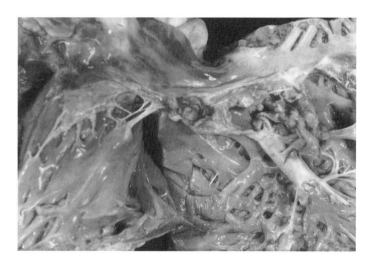

Figure 2.3.5 The victim in Figure 2.3.4 had acute bacterial endocarditis of the tricuspid valve with septic thromboemboli.

REFERENCES

1. Bailey ME, Fraire AE, Greenberg SD, Barnard J, Cagle PT. Pulmonary histopathology in cocaine abusers. *Hum Pathol* 25: 203-207, 1994.
2. Murray RJ, Smialek JE, Golle M, Albin RJ. Pulmonary artery medial hypertrophy in cocaine users without foreign particle microembolization. *Chest* 96: 1050-1053, 1989.
3. Murray RJ, Albin RJ Mergner W, Criner GJ. Diffuse alveolar hemorrhage temporally related to cocaine smoking. *Chest* 93: 427-429, 1988.
4. Walek JW, Masson RG, Siddiqui M. Pulmonary hemorrhage in a cocaine abuser[letter]. *Chest* 96: 222, 1989.
5. Allred RJ, Ewer S. Fatal pulmonary edema following intravenous "freebase" cocaine use. *Ann Emerg Med* 10: 441-442, 1981.
6. Efferen L, Palat D, Meisner J. Nonfatal pulmonary edema following cocaine smoking. *NY State J Med* 89: 415-416, 1989.
7. Cucco RA, Yoo OH, Cregler L, Chang JC. Nonfatal pulmonary edema after "freebase" cocaine smoking. *Am Rev Respir Dis* 136: 179-181, 1987.
8. Hoffman CK, Goodman PC. Pulmonary edema in cocaine smokers. *Radiology* 172: 463- 465, 1989.
9. Patel RC, Dutta D, Schonfeld SA. Freebase cocaine use associated with bronchiolitis obliterans organizing pneumonia. *Ann Int Med* 107: 186-187, 1987.
10. Forrester JM, Steele AW, Waldron JA, Parsons PE. Crack lung: An acute pulmonary syndrome with a spectrum of clinical and histopathologic findings. *Am Rev Respir Dis* 142: 462-467, 1990.
11. Kissner DG, Lawrence WD, Selis JE, Flint A. Crack lung: Pulmonary disease caused by cocaine abuse. *Am Rev Respir Dis* 136: 1250-1252, 1987.
12. Shesser R, Davis C, Edelstein S. Pneumomediastinum and pneumothorax after inhaling alkaloidal cocaine. *Ann Emerg Med* 10: 213-215, 1981.
13. Aroesty DJ, Stanley RB, Crockett DM. Pneumomediastinum and cervical emphysema from the inhalation of "freebase" cocaine: Report of three cases. *Otolaryngol Head Neck Surg* 94: 372-374, 1986.
14. Bush MN, Rubenstein R, Hoffman I, Bruno MS. Spontaneous pneumomediastinum as a consequence of cocaine use. *NY State J Med* 84: 618-619, 1984.
15. Adrouny A, Magnusson P. Pneumopericardium from cocaine inhalation[letter]. *NEJM* 313: 48-49, 1985.
16. Andreone P, L'Heureux P, Strate RG. An unusual case of massive nonsurgical pneumoperitoneum: Case report. *J Trauma* 29: 1286-1288, 1989
17. Shesser R, Davis C, Edelstein S. Pneumomediastinum and pneumothorax after inhaling alkaloidal cocaine. *Ann Emerg Med* 10: 213-215, 1981.
18. Birrer RB, Calderon J. Pneumothorax, pneumomediastinum, and pneumopericardium following Valsalva maneuver during marijuana smoking. *NY State J Med* 84: 619-620, 1984.
19. Rubin RB, Neugarten J. Cocaine-associated asthma. *Am J Med* 88: 438-439, 1990.
20. Rebhun J. Association of asthma and freebase smoking. *Ann Allergy* 60: 339-342, 1988.
21. Averbach M, Casey KK, Frank E. Near fatal status asthmaticus induced by nasal insufflation of cocaine. *South Med J* 89: 340-341, 1996.
22. Greenebaum E, Copeland A, Grewal R. Blackened bronchoalveolar lavage fluid in crack smokers: a preliminary study. *Am J Clin Path* 100: 481-487, 1993.
23. Itkonen J, Schnoll S, Glassroth J. Pulmonary dysfunction in "freebase" cocaine users. *Arch Intern Med* 144: 2195-2197, 1984.
24. Lamb D, Roberts G. Starch and talc emboli in drug addicts' lungs. *J Clin Path* 25: 876- 881, 1972.
25. Butz WC. Pulmonary arteriole foreign body granulomata associated with angiomatoids resulting from the intravenous injection of oral medications, e.g. Propoxyphene hydrochloride (Darvon). *J Forensic Sci* 14: 317-326, 1969.

Michael D. Bell

26. Puro HE, Wolf PJ, Skirgaudas J, Vazquez J. Experimental Puro HE, Wolf PJ, Skirgaudas J, Vazquez J. Experimental production of human "Blue Velvet" and "Red Devil" lesions. *JAMA* 197:1100-1102, 1966.
27. Crouch E, Churg A. Progressive massive fibrosis of the lung secondary to intravenous injection of talc. A pathologic and mineralogic analysis. *Am J Clin Path* 80:520-526, 1983.
28. Pare JAP, Fraser RG, Hogg JC, Howlett JG, Murphy SB. Pulmonary 'mainline' granulomatosis: Talcosis of intravenous methadone abuse. *Medicine* 58: 229-239, 1979.
29. Sieniewicz DJ, Nidecker AC. Conglomerate pulmonary disease: A form of talcosis in intravenous methadone abusers. *Am J Roent* 135: 697-702, 1980.
30. Wendt VE, Puro HE, Shapiro J, Mathews W, Wolf PL. Angiothrombotic pulmonary hypertension in addicts. *JAMA* 188: 755-757, 1964.
31. Szwed JJ. Pulmonary angiothrombosis caused by "blue velvet" addiction. *Ann Intern Med* 73: 771-774, 1970.
32. Hahn HH, Schweid AI, Beaty HN. Complications of injecting dissolved methylphenidate tablets. *Arch Int Med* 123: 656-659, 1969.
33. Lewman LV. Fatal pulmonary hypertension from intravenous injection of methylphenidate (Ritalin) tablets. *Hum Pathol* 3: 67-70, 1972.
34. Hopkins GB, Taylor DG. Pulmonary talc granulomatosis. Amer *Rev Resp Dis* 101: 101- 104, 1970.
34a. Sherman CB, Hudson LD, Pierson DJ. Severe precocious emphysema in intravenous methylphenidate (Ritalin) abusers. *Chest* 92: 1085-1087, 1987.
35. Wright JL. Consequences of aspiration and bronchial obstruction. Chapter 31, In: Thurlbeck WM, Churg AM. *Pathology of the Lung*, 2nd Edition, Thieme Medical Publ. Inc., New York, 1995, pp. 1111-1127.

2.4 DISORDERS OF THE CENTRAL NERVOUS SYSTEM

2.4.1 ALCOHOL RELATED DISORDERS

Marchiafava-Bignami[1-3] disease is a demyelinating disorder affecting the corpus callosum and was first described in malnourished Italian men drinking cheap red wine. It has since been described in other countries and as occuring with other alcoholic beverages. Grossly, there is a discolored or partially cystic demyelinated region in the genu and body of the corpus callosum with sparing of the thin fibers along the dorsal and[4] ventral surfaces of the corpus callosum. The optic chiasm and anterior commissures may also be involved. The lesion is bilateral and symmetric with sparing of the gray matter. Microscopically, there is demyelination sparing of the axon cylinders. The number of oligodendrocytes is reduced. Lipid-laden macrophages are often abundant.

Central pontine myelinolysis (CPM) is a demyelinating disorder of the central basis pontis that was first described in malnourished alcoholics by Adams.[4] Patients with CPM have a sudden change in mental status, flaccid quadriparesis with hyperreflexia, pseudobulbar palsy, and an extensor plantar response unless coma obscures these signs. CPM is associated with the rapid correction or overcorrection of hyponatremia[5] and the symptoms appear a few days (ave.=6 days) after overcorrection with a serum sodium rise of at least 20 mmol/L. Grossly, victims have a discolored, finely granular demyelinated zone in the central basis pontis with sparing of the tegmentum, ventral pons, and corticospinal tracts (Figure 2.4.1).[6] Extrapontine myelinolysis has become more recognized.[7] The demyelinated area varies from a few millimeters to the entire basis pontis and may be triangular, diamond, or butterfly-shaped. Microscopically, there is demyelination with relative preservation of axon cylinders and neurons. Axonal spheroids are commonly observed. Acute lesions contain lipid-laden macrophages, but no

136 / Drug Abuse Handbook

Figure 2.4.1 Discolored granular zone of myelinolysis in the central pons of this 28-year-old alcoholic who was treating aggressively for hyponatremia.

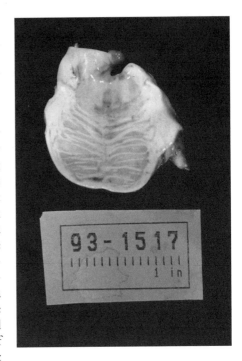

93-1517

other inflammatory cells. Oligodendrocytes are reduced or absent and reactive astrocytes are present.

Cerebellar degeneration of alcoholics is clinically manifested by truncal instability, lower extremity ataxia, and wide-based gait, symptoms appearing gradually over months or years.[3] The pathogenesis is still unknown and may be due to the direct toxic effect of alcohol or to thiamine deficiency, or from rapid correction or overcorrection of hyponatremia similar to central pontine myelinolysis. Grossly, the folia of the rostral vermis and anterosuperior cerebellar hemispheres are atrophic and shrunken with widened interfolial sulci. This is best demonstrated by a sagittal section through the vermis rather than the usual coronal sectioning. Microscopically, the folial crests are more severely affected than the depths of the interfolial sulci in contrast to anoxic-ischemic injury. There is Purkinje cell loss, patchy granular cell loss, molecular layer atrophy, and gliosis with Bregmann glial proliferation.

Acute alcohol intoxication can cause death due to central cardiopulmonary paralysis.[3] While blood ethanol concentrations over 450 to 500 mg/dL are usually considered lethal, there is considerable variability due to tolerance. Children are considered more susceptible to the lethal effects than are adults. Cerebral edema may be present or the neuropathologic examination may be normal. Delirium tremens or withdrawal seizures are not associated with any specific neuropathologic abnormalities.[8]

Chronic alcohol use may be associated with cerebral atrophy, although this is a disputed effect of alcoholism.[3] The cerebral atrophy involves the upper dorsolateral frontal lobes and may extend inferiorly to the inferior frontal gyri and posteriorly to the superior parietal lobule.[1] There is mild ventricular enlargement. Microscopic changes are not specific. The cerebral atrophy may be associated with a dementia that is potentially reversible at its early stages.[9]

Fetal alcohol syndrome is a constellation of birth defects found in children of alcohol-abusing mothers. It is the most common cause of birth defect associated with mental retardation. Other clinical manifestations include irritability, seizures, hypotonia, and cerebellar dysfunction. The neuropathologic findings are non-specific and include microcephaly, compensatory hydrocephalus, neuroglial heterotopia of the ventricles or leptomeninges, and atrophy or hypoplasia of the cerebellum or centrum semiovale.[3,10]

Thiamine deficiency is responsible for the clinical manifestations (gaze paralysis, ataxia, nystagmus, and mental confusion) of Wernicke's encephalopathy and Korsakoff psychosis (retrograde amnesia, impaired short-term memory) seen in alcoholics.[3] The morphologic features (seen in 1.7 to 2.7% of consecutive autopsies)[11] include petechiae and pink discoloration of the mammillary bodies (Figure 2.4.2), hypothalamus, periventricular region of the thalamus, periaqueductal grey matter, and beneath the floor of the fourth ventricle.[1] The lesions are bilateral and symmetric when present. These gross features are seen in only 50% of acute cases,[12] therefore microscopic examination is essential. The lesions vary with the stage and severity of the deficiency. Acute lesions consist of dilated, congested capillaries with perivascular ball and ring hemorrhages and ischemic neuronal changes (Figure 2.4.3). Chronic lesions

Michael D. Bell

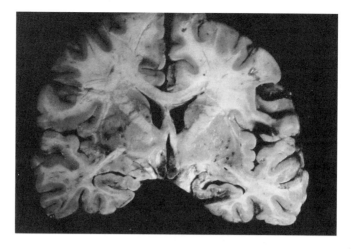

Figure 2.4.2 Coronal section of cerebrum demonstrates the mammillary body hemorrhage in Wernicke-Korsakoff syndrome.

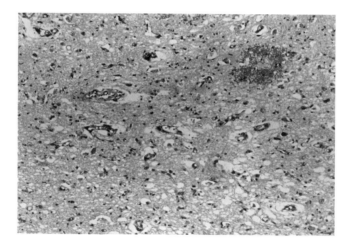

Figure 2.4.3 Ball hemorrhage, capillary proliferation, and gliosis are present in this alcoholic with Wernicke encephalopathy (Hematoxylin and eosin, 20x).

have vascular endothelial cell swelling and proliferation and gliosis. Affected blood vessels may have irregular or bead-like swellings.

2.4.2 COMMONLY ABUSED DRUGS

2.4.2.1 Excited Delirium

Excited delirium is a drug-induced delirium or psychosis accompanied by agitation and hyperthermia, and often ending with respiratory arrest and sudden death. Cocaine is the drug most often implicated in this syndrome,[13] but amphetamines have also been implicated in some cases. The syndrome is not due to any contaminants that may accompany the cocaine sample.

The pathogenesis of cocaine-induced excited delirium is unknown. One hypothesis is that cocaine initially elevates brain dopamine levels causing the delirium. This cocaine-induced

Table 2.4.2.1   Comparison Between Neuroleptic Malignant Syndrome and Cocaine-Induced Agitated Delirium

Symptom	NMS	Cocaine delirium
Hyperthermia	++	++
Delirium	++	++
Agitation	+	++
Akinesia/rigidity	++	±

++ = present in almost all cases; + = present in many cases; ± = may occur late during syndrome[16]

brain dopamine elevation has been demonstrated in animals.[14] The syndrome is thought to be similar to the neuroleptic malignant syndrome (NMS) in Parkinson disease patients withdrawn from levodopa, a dopaminergic drug. Patients experience hyperthermia, autonomic instability, and delirium (see Table 2.4.2.1). NMS is characterized by diffuse muscular rigidity, but this is not seen in cocaine-induce excited delirium. One author has suggested that akinesia of the respiratory muscles may be the fatal mechanism of sudden death in these victims.[16]The neurochemical alterations underlying the cocaine-related syndrome have recently been characterized and are described in Chapter 6.

There are no specific gross or microscopic findings in victims dying of cocaine-induced agitated delirium. A postmortem core body temperature (if taken soon after death) will be elevated. A thorough postmortem examination is essential to rule out other causes of sudden death. Cocaine and its metabolites must be present in toxicology specimens. Victims dying of agitated delirium have postmortem blood cocaine concentrations (average = 0.6 mg/L with range of 0.14 to 0.92 mg/L) that are 10 times lower than those concentrations in cocaine overdose victims.[17]

Agitated delirium may occur following cocaine ingestion by all routes of administration (snorting, smoking, injection), except chewing coca leaves. The majority of victims are men. Soon after cocaine ingestion, the person becomes paranoid, delirious, and aggressive. The victim is often seen running, yelling, breaking glass and overturning furniture, disrobing, and hiding. Witnesses report that the person has unexpected strength. The victim often becomes calm and quiet before having a cardiopulmonary arrest, often during police custody or medical transport.

This disorder is frequently accompanied by sudden death. Restraint procedures that could compromise respiration should be avoided. The restrained person should be closely observed, especially after the agitation subsides.[18]

2.4.2.2 Cerebral Hemorrhage

Drug-induced cerebrovascular disease or stroke is any non-traumatic intracerebral hemorrhage (including subarachnoid hemorrhage) or cerebral infarction that results directly or indirectly from drug ingestion. An accurate clinical history and/or positive toxicologic testing corroborates the recent drug ingestion. Forty-seven percent of patients who are under 35 years old and present with an acute stroke have drug use as a predisposing condition.[19] Clinically, a patient with cerebrovascular disease presents with sudden loss of function, neurologic deficit, and involvement of the corresponding vascular supply. If the blood vessel is occluded, ischemia and infarction occur. If the vessel is damaged, hemorrhage results.

Cocaine is frequently associated with intracerebral hemorrhage.[20-23] Other stimulant drugs including amphetamine,[19,24] phenylpropanolamine,[25] phencyclidine,[25] pseudoephedrine,[25] and methylphenidate[19,25] have been associated with intracranial hemorrhage.

Michael D. Bell

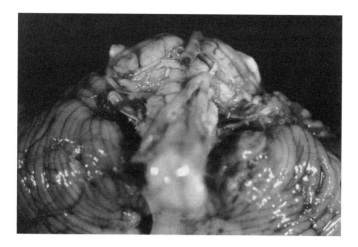

Figure 2.4.4 There is an occlusive thrombus in the basilar artery of this 28-year-old cocaine addict.

Cocaine blocks the uptake of catecholamines at adrenergic nerve endings, thus potentiating sympathetic responses and causing a dose dependent elevation of arterial pressure and heart rate in humans[26] and dogs.[27] Amphetamines can also produce transient hypertension and tachycardia. Intracerebral hemorrhage is postulated to occur from a sudden marked elevation in systemic blood pressure in susceptible persons with pre-existing vascular malformations such as arteriovenous malformations, berry aneurysms, or Charcot- Bouchard microaneurysms in hypertensive individuals. Another postulated mechanism of intraparenchymal hemorrhage in cocaine users is acute increased cerebral blood flow into an area of ischemia produced by prior cocaine-induced vasoconstriction.[28] Interestingly, intrauterine exposure to cocaine does not influence the prevalence or severity of intraventricular hemorrhage in the preterm infant.[29]

Cocaine can cause cerebral infarction by arterial thrombosis, arterial embolism, arterial spasm, and circulatory compromise with secondary cerebral hypoperfusion. In the latter case, cocaine can cause acute myocardial infarction or ventricular arrhythmia resulting in hypotension and secondary cerebral hypoperfusion.

The middle cerebral artery is most commonly affected with resulting sudden paraplegia.[30] The anterior cerebral, posterior cerebral, and basilar/vertebral arteries can also be affected causing a variety of clinical signs and symptoms (Figures 2.4.4 and 2.4.5). Most victims develop symptoms suddenly within 3 hours of cocaine ingestion. Other victims wake up with the neurologic deficit after heavy drug use the previous evening.

The most common sites of cocaine-induced intracerebral hemorrhage are the cerebral hemispheres (57%) followed by the putamen (18%), and subarachnoid and intraventricular sites (Figure 2.4.6 and 2.4.7). Cocaine-induced subarachnoid hemorrhage is usually due to rupture of a pre-existing arteriovenous malformation or berry aneurysm of the cerebral arteries[30] (Figure 2.4.8). In a recent retrospective study from San Diego, 21% of victims dying from ruptured berry aneurysms had cocaine or methamphetamine (or both) in their postmortem blood.[31] This was higher than the 5% incidence of cocaine or methamphetamine intoxication in all adult autopsies from the same jurisdiction. If no vascular malformation is found to explain the subarachnoid hemorrhage in a drug addict, one must consider a traumatic cause for the subarachnoid hemorrhage (such as extracranial veretebral artery laceration)[32] before ascribing it to cocaine or another stimulant. Intraparenchymal hemorrhage due to cocaine use can occur in sites typical of patients with hypertension-related intracerebral hemorrhage. The blood vessels, when examined, are usually normal grossly and microscopically.[33] Charcot-Bouchard microaneurysms, typically seen in hypertensive cerebral hemorrhage,[34] are not seen in drug-induced intracerebral hemorrhage.

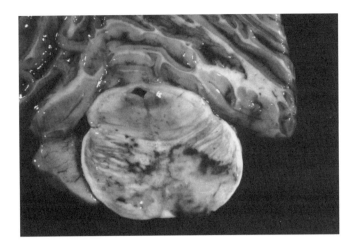

Figure 2.4.5 There is an irregular zone of infarction in the basis pontis of the victim in Figure 2.4.4. He was found comatose at home.

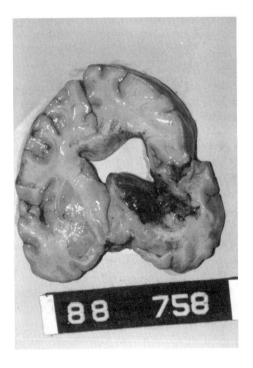

Figure 2.4.6 This 35-year-old woman developed an acute intracerebral hematoma after cocaine use.

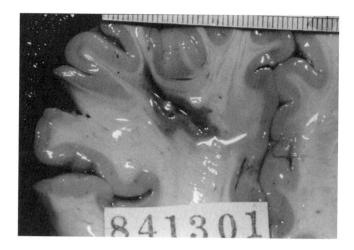

Figure 2.4.7 This brown slit-like cavity in the frontal white matter is all that remains of a previous cocaine-induced intracerebral hemorrhage.

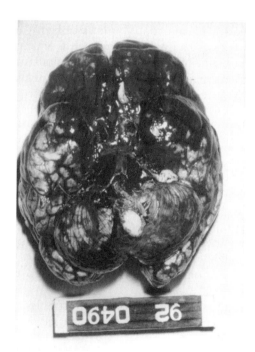

Figure 2.4.8 Subarachnoid hemorrhage in cocaine abusers is often due to a berry aneurysm that ruptures from the sudden blood pressure elevation caused by cocaine.

Patients are usually in their third to fifth decades of life with both men and women affected. Intracerebral hemorrhage occurs after snorting, smoking, or injecting cocaine. The time between drug use and symptom onset is usually within 3 hours, but can range from immediate to 12 hours. Most patients present with acute headache or are comatose. Confusion is a less frequent presenting symptom. There is a 36% mortality rate in patients who present to the emergency room with acute stroke strongly linked to recent drug use.[19]

2.4.2.3 Vasculitis

Cerebral vasculitis has been associated with cocaine and amphetamine use. The association between cerebral vasculitis and cocaine use is tenuous and only supported by a few (eight) case reports, some of which have only angiographic evidence ("beading" or segmental arterial narrowing) of vasculitis with no histologic confirmation (Table 2.4.2). The remaining case reports have histologic evidence of vasculitis but no angiographic narrowing or other abnormalities.[37-40] Half of the victims presented with encephalopathy and coma without intracranial hemorrhage or infarction. The other half presented with intracerebral hemorrhage or cerebral infarction. Transient ischemic attacks (TIA) with multifocal segmental arterial stenoses on angiography have been reported in chronic cocaine users. All these patients were young (mean age = 28 years with age range = 22 to 36) with multiple routes of drug administration used (nasal insufflation, smoking, intravenous injection). Histologic examination demonstrated acute and chronic small vessel inflammation. Four cases had lymphocytic infiltration in the cerebral blood vessels. Two cases had polymorphonuclear leukocyte infiltration in the small arteries and venules of the brain. No giant cells or granulomas were seen in any case. The pathogenesis of cocaine-associated cerebral vasculitis remains unknown. Metamphetamine and structurally related drugs have reportedly caused necrotizing cerebral vasculitis.

2.4.2.4 Seizures

Drug-induced seizures are seizures that occur after the ingestion of a drug and are not caused by other pathologic processes (intracranial hemorrhage, blunt head trauma). The drug ingestion should be corroborated by an accurate clinical history or positive toxicology testing.

Cocaine has been reported to lower the threshold for seizures and commonly causes seizures.[42] Also cocaine was the most common drug of abuse detected in one series of patients with seizure activity as the primary admitting diagnosis.[43] In this series, cocaine was more likely to cause brief, self-limiting seizures compared to the other drugs of abuse (amphetamine, methamphetamine, phencyclidine, sedative-hyponotic withdrawal). Seizure initiation depends not only on binding with serotonin transporter sites but also brain muscarinic and sigma binding sites.[44]

There are no specific gross or microscopic neuropathologic findings in fatal cocaine-induced seizure victims. Tongue contusions are non-specific findings in patients who die of terminal seizures (Figure 2.4.9).

Cocaine-induced seizures are a common neurologic complication (2.3 to 8.4% of cocaine victims present with seizures to the emergency room)[45] and affects both men and women.[46] The average age is 27 years with a range of 17 to 42 years. Seizures occur after snorting, smoking, or injecting cocaine. The seizures are usually generalized, tonic- clonic, isolated, and self-limiting. They usually last less than 5 minutes and can occur with first-time and chronic cocaine users. The interval between cocaine ingestion and seizure onset varies from minutes to 12 hours. In one emergency room study, 1 of 137 patients (8%) with cocaine intoxication presented with seizures as their chief problem and none died.[45]

Table 2.4.2.2 Reported Cases of Cocaine-Associated Vasculitis

Report	Age/Sex	Route	Clinical syndrome	Angiogram	Time Interval	Pathology	Outcome
Kaye, 1987	22 M	Nasal	Cerebral infarct	Beading, occlusion, narrowing	Unknown	None	Improvement with steroids
Klonoff, 1989	29 F	Smoke	ICH	Beading, narrowing	Unknown	None	Stabilized after hematoma removed
Krendel, 1990	36 M	Smoke	Weakness, dysarthria, confusion	Occlusion, narrowing	3.5 weeks	Acute vasculitis, small cortical vessels, cortical infarct with multinucleated giant cells	Improvement with steroids
Krendell, 1990	31 F	Smoke, IV	Coma, cerebral edema	Normal	42 days	Lymphocytic infiltration, small vessels and larger vessels normal, no granulomas, multiple cystic, necrotic and gliotic areas in white matter with multinucleated giant cells	Death
Fredericks, 1991	32 M	Nasal, IV	Confusion, ataxia	Normal	13 days	Lymphocytic infiltration, small vessels and endothelial swelling	Improvement with steroids
Morrow, 1993	25 F	Nasal	Seizure, coma	Not done	5 days	Lymphocytic infiltration in small vessels of cortex and brainstem, small infarcts, cerebral edema with diffuse encephalomalacia	Death
Merkel, 1995	32 M	Nasal	ICH	Normal	2 days	Non-necrotizing leukocytoclastic vasculitis, neutrophils and mononuclear cells in venules	Improvement without steroids
Merkel, 1995	20 M	Nasal	ICH	Narrowing	<6 months	Neutrophil infiltration and fibrinoid degeneration in small arterioles and veins	Partial recovery

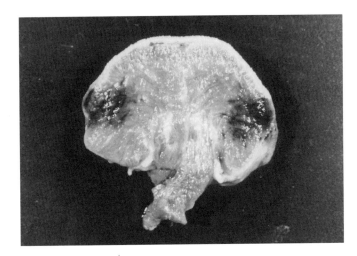

Figure 2.4.9 This cross-section of tongue demonstrates the contusions that may be seen in drug-induced seizures.

2.4.2.5 Parkinsonism

Parkinson's syndrome has been reported in addicts who receive the synthetic meperidine analog contaminated with MPTP (1-methyl-4-phenyl-1,2,3,6-tetrahydropyridine). MPTP is produced during the careless synthesis of MPPP (1-methyl-4-phenyl-4-propionoxypiperidene) often in clandestine laboratories. Neurotoxic symptoms include resting tremor, rigidity, bradykinesia, and other signs and symptoms of Parkinsonism. Neuropathologic examination has demonstrated substantia nigra degeneration confined to the zona compacta. There is astrocytosis, focal gliosis, and extraneuronal melanin pigment.[47] MPPP contaminated with MPTP has been reported to produce Parkinson's syndrome within days of injecting this drug mixture.[48] MPTP-induced Parkinson's syndrome can also result from snorting the drug.[49] The severe rigidity that results from MPTP-induced Parkinonism has been implicated in the asphyxiation death of one victim who was unable to move his head from a suffocating posture.[50] Postmortem neuropathologic examination also revealed severe neuronal loss in his substantia nigra.

2.4.2.6 Anoxic Ischemic Encephalopathy

Drugs of abuse commonly produce anoxic-ischemic encephalopathy.[51-53] This can occur from insufficient oxygen reaching the blood from the lungs, insufficient oxygen carriage, or inadequate cerebral blood perfusion. This is a common mechanism in drug abusers who have a delayed death after drug intoxication.

The morphology of anoxic-ischemic encephalopathy is variable with preferentially affected areas in the brain. In the gray matter, the watershed zones are commonly affected with laminar necrosis involving lamina zones III, V, VI. The h1 segment (Sommer's sector) and endplate in the hippocampus is commonly involved. Other vulnerable sites include the Purkinje cells of the cerebellum and the caudate and putamen. The brain is often swollen and soft with a pale or dusky gray matter. Laminar necrosis may be apparent if sufficient time has elapsed between the time of anoxia and death. Microscopic changes are not recognizable until 6 to 8 hours after the anoxic-ischemic insult. The affected neurons become shrunken with eosinophilic cytoplasm and nuclear pyknosis, and gradually disappear. There is also non- specific capillary proliferation with endothelial swelling, spongiform change, and gliosis in the affected neuropil.

Michael D. Bell

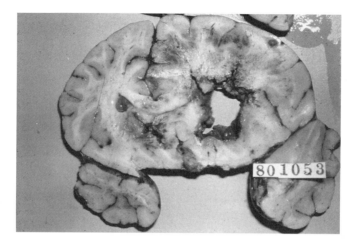

Figure 2.4.10 Coronal section of brain with multiple necrotic abscesses in an intravenous drug abuser.

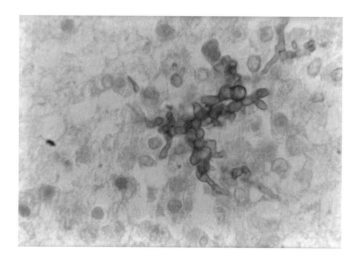

Figure 2.4.11 Within the necrotic cerebral cavities on the patient in this figure are branching, septated fungi (Gomori methanamine silver, 80x).

2.4.2.7 Drug-Associated Central Nervous System Infections

Primary fungal cerebritis due to Rhizopus has been reported in cocaine,[54] heroin,[55-59] and amphetamine[60] users with no other systemic foci identified at autopsy. The victims are usually men in their 3rd or 4th decades of life and present with hemiplegia, facial weakness, and headache. The brain lesions are usually multiple with frequent bilateral involvement of the basal ganglia. The phycomycoses are angiotrophic fungi that commonly occlude and invade the cerebral blood vessels causing hemorrhagic infarcts. Fungal cerebritis or meningitis have been reported in intravenous drug abusers (Figures 2.4.10 and 2.4.11) with HIV infection. In addition to fungal cerebritis, HIV-infected intravenous drug abusers can develop a large variety of central nervous infections and neoplasms (Table 2.4.2.3) and thus fulfill the criterion for AIDS. Intravenous drug abusers may develop multifocal brain abscesses or cerebritis from embolic vegetations arising from valvular endocarditis.[61] Nasal insufflation of drugs can also cause frontal sinusitis and overlying frontal lobe abscess.[62]

Table 2.4.2.3   Central Nervous System Infections in Intravenous Drug Abusers with AIDS

HIV encephalitis

Progressive multifocal leukoencephalopathy

Cytomegalovirus ventriculitis and cerebritis

Toxoplasma cerebritis

Cryptococcal meningitis and cerebritis

Histoplasma cerebritis

Nocardia cerebritis

Mycobacterium infections (including tuberculosis, avian-intracellulare)

Fungal meningitis and cerebritis (Candida, Aspergillus, Rhizopus)

Cysticercosis

Entameba histolytica

Acanthameba castellani

REFERENCES

1. Courville CB. *Effects of Alcohol on the Nervous System of Man*. San Lucas Press, Los Angeles, CA, 1966.
2. Bohrod MG. Primary degeneration of the corpus callosum (Marchiafava's disease). *Arch Neurol Psychiat* 47:465-473, 1942.
3. Schocet Jr SS. Exogenous toxic-metabolic diseases including vitamin deficiency. In: Davis RL, Robertson DM (Eds.), *Textbook of Neuropathology*, Willams & Wilkins, Baltimore, 1985, pp. 372-402.
4. Adams RD, Victor M, Mancall EL. Central pontine myelinolysis: a hitherto undescribed disease occurring in alcoholics and malnourished patients. *Arch Neurol Psychiat* 81: 154-172, 1959.
5. Norenberg MD, Leslie KO, Robertson AS. Association between rise in serum sodium and central pontine myelinolysis. *Ann Neurol* 11: 128-135, 1982.
6. Norenberg MD, Gregorios JB. Central nervous system manifestations of systemic disease. In: Davis RL, Robertson DM (Eds.), *Textbook of Neuropathology*, Willams & Wilkins, Baltimore, 1985, pp. 422-423.
7. Laureno R, Karp BI. Myelinolysis after correction of hyponatremia. *Ann Int Med* 126: 57-62, 1997.
8. Powers JM, Haroupian DS. "Central Nervous System" In: Damjanov I, Linder J (Eds.) *Anderson's Pathology*. 10th Ed., Mosby-Year Book, St. Louis, 1996, p.2791.
9. Tomlinson BE. "Aging and the Dementias" In Adams JH, Duchen LW (Eds.) *Greenfield's Neuropathology*. 5th Ed., Oxford University Press, New York, 1992.
10. Claren SK. Recognition of fetal alcohol syndrome. *JAMA* 245: 2436-2439, 1981.
11. Cravioto H, Korein J, Silberman J. Wernicke's encephalopathy: a clinical and pathological study of 28 autopsied cases. Arch Neurol 4:510-519,1961.
12. Harper, C. Wernicke's encephalopathy: a more common disease than realized. A neuropathological study of 51 cases. J Neurol Neurosurg Psychiatr 42:226-231,1979.
13. Campbell BG. Cocaine abuse with hyperthermia, seizures and fatal complications. *Med J Austal* 149: 387-389, 1988.
14. Pettit HO, Pan H, Parsons LH. Justice, Jr., JB. Extracellular concentrations of cocaine and dopamine are enhanced during chronic cocaine administration. *J Neurochem* 55:798-804, 1990.
15. Karoum F, Suddath RL, Wyatt RJ. Chronic cocaine and rat brain catecholamines: Long term reduction in hypothalamic and frontal cortex dopamine metabolism. *Eur J Pharm* 186:1-8, 1990.

16. Kosten TR, Kleber HD. Rapid death during cocaine abuse: a variant of the neuroleptic malignant syndrome? *Am J Drug Alcohol Abuse* 14:335-346, 1988.

17. Wetli CV, Fishbain DA. Cocaine-induced psychosis and sudden death in recreational cocaine users. *J Forensic Sci* 30: 873-880, 1985.

18. Davis, GD. Cocaine-induced excited delirium. *Forensic Pathology Check Sample*, No. FP 96-9. Chicago, Ill: American Society of Clinical Pathologists, 1996.

19. Kaku DA, Lowenstein DH. Emergence of recreational drug abuse as a major risk factor for stroke in young adults. *Ann Int Med* 113: 821-827, 1990.

20. Levine SR, Brust JCM, Futrell N, Ho, KL, Blake D, Millikan CH, et. al. Cerebrovascular complications of the use of the "crack" form of alkaloidal cocaine. *NEJM* 323: 699-704, 1990.

21. Mody CK, Miller BL, McIntyre HB, Cobb SK, Goldberg MA. Neurologic complications of cocaine abuse. *Neurology* 38: 1189-1193, 1988.

22. Mangiardi JR, Daras M, Geller ME, Weitzner I, Tuchman AJ. Cocaine-related intracranial hemorrhage. Report of nine cases and review. *Acta Neurol Scand* 77: 177-180, 1988.

23. Aggarwal SK. Cocaine-associated intracranial hemorrhage: absence of vasculitis in 14 cases. *Neurology* 46: 1741-1743, 1996.

24. Harrington H, Heller HA, Dawson D, Caplan L, Rumbaugh C. Intracerebral hemorrhage and oral amphetamine. *Arch Neurol* 40: 503-507, 1983.

25. Sloan MA, Kittner SJ, Rigamonti D, Price TR. Occurrence of stroke associated with use/abuse of drugs. *Neurology* 41: 1358-1364, 1991.

26. Fischman MW, Schuster CR, Resnekov L, Shick JFE, Krasnegar NA, Fennell W, Freedman DX. Cardiovascular and subjective effects of intravenous cocaine administration in humans. *Arch Gen Psych* 33: 983-989, 1976.

27. Wilkerson RD. Cardiovascular effects of cocaine in conscious dogs: Importance of fully functional autonomic and central nervous systems. *J Pharmacol Exp Ther* 246: 466-471, 1988.

28. Caplan L. Intracerebral hemorrhage revisited. *Neurology* 38: 624-627, 1988.

29. McLenan DA, Ajayi OA, Rydman RJ, Pildes RS. Evaluation of the relationship between cocaine and intraventricular hemorrhage. *J Nat Med Assoc* 86: 281-287, 1994.

30. Daras M, Tuchman AJ, Koppel BS, Samkoff LM, Weitzner I, Marc J. Neurovascular complications of cocaine. *Acta Neurol Scand* 90: 124-129, 1994.

31. Davis GG, Swalwell CI. The incidence of acute cocaine or methamphetamine intoxication in deaths due to ruptured cerebral (berry) aneurysms. *J Forensic Sci* 41: 626-628, 1996.

32. Contostavlos DL. Massive subarachnoid hemorrhage due to laceration of the vertebral artery associated with fracture of the transverse process of the atlas. *J Forensic Sci* 16: 40-56, 1971.

33. Nolte KB, Gelman BB. Intracerebral hemorrhage associated with cocaine abuse. *Arch Pathol Lab Med* 113: 812-813, 1989.

34. Fisher CM. Pathological observations in hypertensive cerebral hemorrhage. *J Neuropathol Exp Neurol* 30: 536-550, 1971.

35. Kaye BR, Fainstat M. Cerebral vasculitis associated with cocaine abuse. *JAMA* 258: 2104-2106, 1987.

36. Klonoff DC, Andrews BT, Obana WG. Stroke associated with cocaine use. *Arch Neurol* 46: 989-993, 1989.

37. Krendel DA, Ditter SM, Frankel MR, Ross WK. Biopsy-proven cerebral vasculitis associated with cocaine abuse. *Neurology* 40: 1092-1094, 1990.

38. Morrow PL, McQuillen JB. Cerebral vasculitis associated with cocaine abuse. *J Forensic Sci* 38: 732-738, 1993.

39. Fredericks RK, Lefkowitz DS, Challa VR, et. al. Cerebral vasculitis associated with cocaine abuse. *Stroke* 22: 1437-1439, 1991.

40. Merkel PA, Koroshetz WJ, Irizarry MC, Cudkowicz ME. Cocaine-associated cerebral vasculitis. *Sem Arthritis Rheum* 25: 172-183, 1995.

41. Moore PM, Peterson PL. Nonhemorrhagic cerebrovascular complications of cocaine abuse. *Neurology* 39: 302, 1989 (Suppl. 1; abstract).

42. Pascual-Leone A, Dhuna A, Altafullah I, Anderson DC. Cocaine-induced seizures. *Neurology* 40: 404-407, 1990.

43. Olson KR, Kearney TE, Dyer JE, Benowitz NL, Blanc PD. Seizures associated with poisoning and drug overdose. *Am J Emerg Med* 12: 392-395, 1994.

44. Ritz MC, George FR. Cocaine-induced seizures and lethality appear to be associated with distinct central nervous system binding sites. *J Pharm Exp Ther* 264: 1333-1343, 1993.

45. Derlet RW, Albertson TE. Emergency department presentation of cocaine intoxication. *Ann Emerg Med* 18: 182-186, 1989.

46. Lowenstein DH, Massa SM, Rowbotham MC, Collins SD, McKinney HE, Simon RP. Acute neurologic and psychiatric complications associated with cocaine abuse. *Am J Med* 83: 841-846, 1987.

47. Davis G, Williams A, Markey S et al. Chronic parkinsonism secondary to intravenous injection of meperedine analogs. *Psych Res* 1: 249-254, 1979.

48. Langston J, Ballard P, Tetrud J, Irwin I. Chronic parkinsonism in humans due to a product of meperidine-analog synthesis. *Science* 219: 979-980, 1983.

49. Wright JM, Wall RA, Perry TL, Paty DW. Chronic parkinsonism secondary to intranasal administration of a product of meperidine-analog synthesis. *NEJM* 310: 325, 1984 [Letter].

50. Kaplan J, Karluk D. Suffocation due to drug-induced parkinsonism[Abstract]. *National Association of Medical Examiner Meeting*, Traverse City, MI, Sept. 1996.

51. Brierley J. The neuropathology of brain hypoxia. *Scientific Foundations of Neurology*, M. Critchley (Ed.). Philadelphia, F.A. Davis Company, 1972.

52. Adams J, Brierley J, Connor R, Treip CS. The effects of systemic hypotension upon the human brain: clinical and neuropathological observations in 11 cases. *Brain* 89: 235-268, 1966.

53. Norenberg MD, Gregorios JB. Central nervous system manifestations of systemic disease. Chapter 10 In: Davis RL, Robertson DM (Eds.), *Textbook of Neuropathology*, Williams & Wilkins, Baltimore MD, 1985, pp. 403-414.

54. Wetli CV, Weiss SD, Cleary TJ, Gyori El. Fungal cerebritis from intravenous drug abuse. *J Forensic Sci* 29: 260-268, 1984.

55. Hameroff S, Eckholdt J, Linderburg R. Cerebral phycomycosis in a heroin addict. *Neurology* 20: 261-265, 1970.

56. Kasantikul V, Shuangshoti S, Taecholarn C. Primary phycomycosis of the brain in heroin addicts. *Surg Neurol* 28: 468-472, 1987.

57. Masucci EF, Fabara JA, Saini N, Kurtzke JF. Cerebral mucomycosis (phycomycosis) in a heroin addict. *Arch Neurol* 39: 304-306, 1982.

58. Adelman L, Aronson S. The neuropathologic complications of narcotics addiction. *Bull NY Acad Med* 45: 225-234, 1969.

59. Pierce, Jr. PF, Solomon SL, Kaufman L, Garagusi VF, Parker RH, Ajello L. Zygomycetes brain abscesses in narcotic addicts with serological diagnosis. *JAMA* 248: 2881-2882, 1982.

60. Micozzi MS, Wetli CV. Intravenous amphetamine abuse, primary mucomycosis, and acquired immunodeficiency. *J Forensic Sci* 30: 504-510, 1985.

61. Ziment I. Nervous system complications in bacterial endocarditis. *Am J Med* 47: 593-607, 1969.

62. Rao AN. Brain abscess: a complication of cocaine inhalation. *NY State J Med* 10: 548-550, 1988.

2.5 MISCELLANEOUS COMPLICATIONS

Charles V. Wetli, M.D.

Suffolk County Medical Examiner, Happauge, New York

The most frequently encountered renal abnormality among drug abusers seen today is myoglobinuric nephrosis secondary to cocaine-induced rhabdomyolysis. These are frequently seen in victims of drug-induced excited delirium accompanied by hyperpyrexia and intense muscular activity.[1] Survival for several days reveals, at autopsy, massive necrosis of skeletal muscle which is easily identified because of its distinctive yellow (instead of dark brown) coloration.[2] These deaths are invariably marked by pronounced elevations in serum creatine kinase, profound hypotension, and disseminated intravascular coagulation. Abuse of stimulant drugs has also been associated with renal artery thrombosis and infarction, and renal vasculitis.[1] Maternal cocaine abuse has been associated with a plethora of fetal anomalies, most notably urogenital abnormalities such as hydronephrosis and atresia of the distal ureters.[1]

Heroin addicts may develop the nephrotic syndrome secondary to bacterial endocarditis, renal amyloidosis, or heroin-associated nephropathy (HAN). The latter is characterized by focal segmental (occasionally global) glomerulosclerosis.[1] The etiology is probably immunologic, but there is also evidence favoring an ischemic glomerulopathy.[3]

Liver damage from drug abuse is often related to direct drug toxicity, allergic or idiosyncratic reactions, or various forms of hepatitis.[4] Alcohol-induced fatty change, alcoholic hepatitis and cirrhosis are well-known entities which may exacerbate the effects of other drugs of abuse taken concomitantly. Hepatic damage from cocaine has been induced in laboratory animals[5] but does not appear to occur in humans.[1,6] Intravenous heroin addiction has been associated with a sometimes intense lymphoid infiltrate (occasionally with germinal centers) of the portal zones,[7] often referred to as "triaditis". This appears to be independent of viral hepatitis and may represent an immunologic phenomenon. These infiltrates are, however, not invariable with intravenous drug abusers and may be seen in apparently normal people (but usually to a lesser degree). Another nonspecific but fairly typical finding in heroin addicts is mild to moderate hepatosplenomegaly, sometimes associated with enlarged lymph nodes of the porta hepatis or celiac axis, and lymphoid hyperplasia of the spleen.[7]

The pathology of drug abuse will continue to evolve as people continue to abuse drugs over the years. The long term cardiovascular damage from chronic cocaine abuse is coming into focus, and other organ damage (e.g., of the central nervous system) may become apparent in the years to come. Drugs are constantly being rediscovered and wax and wane in recreational popularity; other drugs appear which are new. All have, or will have, the potential for severe morbidity and death through behavioral modification, acute toxicity and overdose, and long term functional and structural damage to the body. Unfortunately, it takes years and many fatalities before the pathology of newly abused drugs becomes evident.

REFERENCES

1. Pardo, V., Wetli, C.V., Strauss, J. and Bourgoignis, E.: *Renal Complications of Drug Abuse and Human Immunodeficiency Virus, in Renal Pathology,* 2nd edition, Tischer, C.C. and Brenner, B.M. (eds), J.B. Lippincott, Philadelphia 1994, pp 390-418.
2. Mittleman, R.E.: Rhabdomyolysis Associated with Cocaine and Ethanol Abuse. *Am Soc Clin Path Check Sample FP* 95-6 37(6): 93-104, 1995.
3. DiPaolo, M., Fineschi, V. & DiPaolo, N.: Danno Renale in Eroinomani: Studio Istopatologico in Soggetti Deceduti Per Overdose RIV IE Med Leg 16:453-473, 1994.
4. Lee, W.M.: Drug-Induced Hepatotoxicity. *New Eng J Med.* 333:1118-1127, 1995
5. Powell, C.J., Charles, S.J. & Mullervy, J.: Cocaine Hepatotoxicity: A Study on the Pathogenesis of Periportal Necrosis. *Int. J. Exp, Pathol.* 75:415-424, 1994
6. Mittleman, R.E. and Wetli, C.V.: The Pathology of Cocaine Abuse, *Adv Pathol and Lab Med* 4:37-73, 1991
7. Wetli, C.V.; Davis, J.H.; and Blackbourne, B.D.; Narcotic Addiction in Dade County, Florida: An Analysis of 100 Consecutive Autopsies, *Arch Path* 93:330-343, 1972.

CHAPTER 3

PHARMACOKINETICS: DRUG ABSORPTION, DISTRIBUTION, AND ELIMINATION

Amanda J. Jenkins, Ph.D. and Edward J. Cone, Ph.D.

Intramural Research Program, National Institute on Drug Abuse, National Institutes of Health, Baltimore, Maryland

TABLE OF CONTENTS

Amanda J. Jenkins and Edward J. Cone

Pharmacokinetics is defined as the study of the quantitative relationship between administered doses of a drug and the observed plasma/blood or tissue concentrations.[1] The pharmacokinetic model is a mathematical description of this relationship. Models provide estimates of certain parameters, such as elimination half-life, which provide information about basic drug properties. The models may be used to predict concentration vs. time profiles for different dosing patterns.

The field of pharmacokinetics is concerned with drug absorption, distribution, biotransformation, and excretion or elimination. These processes, in addition to the dose, determine the concentration of drug at the effector or active site and, therefore, the intensity and duration of drug effect. The practice of pharmacokinetics has been used in clinical medicine for many years in order to optimize the efficacy of medications administered to treat disease. Through a consideration of pharmacokinetics, physicians are able to determine the drug of choice, dose, route and frequency of administration and duration of therapy, in order to achieve a specific therapeutic objective. In the same manner, study of the pharmacokinetics of abused drugs aids investigators in addiction medicine, forensic toxicology, and clinical pharmacology in understanding why particular drugs are abused, factors that affect their potential for abuse, how their use can be detected and monitored over time, and also provide a rational, scientific basis for treatment therapies.

3.1 BASIC CONCEPTS AND MODELS

3.1.1 TRANSFER ACROSS BIOLOGICAL MEMBRANES

The processes of absorption, distribution, biotransformation, and elimination of a particular substance involve the transfer or movement of a drug across biological membranes. Therefore, it is important to understand those properties of cell membranes and the intrinsic properties of drugs which affect movement. Although drugs may gain entry into the body by passage through a single layer of cells, such as the intestinal epithelium, or through multiple layers of cells, such as the skin, the blood cell membrane is a common barrier to all drug entry and therefore is the most appropriate membrane for general discussion of cellular membrane structure. The cellular blood membrane consists of a phospholipid bilayer of 7 to 9 nm thickness with hydrocarbon chains oriented inward and polar head groups oriented outward. Interspersed between the lipid bilayer are proteins, which may span the entire width of the membrane permitting the formation of aqueous pores.[2] These proteins act as receptors in chemical and electrical signaling pathways and also as specific targets for drug actions.[3] The lipids in the cell membrane may move laterally, confering fluidity at physiological temperatures and relative impermeability to highly polar molecules. The fluidity of plasma membranes is largely determined by the relative abundance of unsaturated fatty acids. Between cell membranes are pores which may permit bulk flow of substances. This is considered to be the main mechanism by which drugs cross the capillary endothelial membranes, except in the central nervous system which possesses tight junctions that limit intercellular diffusion.[3]

Physicochemical properties of a drug also affect its movement across cell membranes. These include its molecular size and shape, solubility, degree of ionization, and relative lipid solubility of its ionized and nonionized forms. Another factor to consider is the extent of protein binding to plasma and tissue components. Although such binding is reversible and usually rapid, only the free unbound form is considered capable of passing through biological membranes.

Drugs cross cell membranes through passive and active or specialized processes. Passive movement across biological membranes is the dominant process in the absorption and distribution of drugs. In passive transfer, hydrophobic molecules cross the cell membrane by simple diffusion along a concentration gradient. In this process there is no expenditure of cellular energy. The magnitude of drug transfer in this manner is dependent on the magnitude of the concentration gradient across the membrane and the lipid:water partition coefficient. Once steady state has been reached, the concentration of free (unbound) drug will be the same on both sides of the membrane. The exception to this situation is if the drug is capable of ionization under physiological conditions. In this case, concentrations on either side of the cell membrane will be influenced by pH differences across the membrane. Small hydrophilic molecules are thought to cross cell membranes through the aqueous pores.[4] Generally, only unionized forms of a drug cross biological membranes due to their relatively high lipid solubility. The movement of ionized forms is dependent on the pKa of the drug and the pH gradient. The partitioning of weak acids and bases across pH gradients may be predicted by the Henderson-Hasselbalch equation. For example, an orally ingested weakly acidic drug may be largely unionized in the acidic environs of the stomach but ionized to some degree at the neutral pH of the plasma. The pH gradient and difference in the proportions of ionized/nonionized forms of the drug promote the diffusion of the weak acid through the lipid barrier of the stomach into the plasma.

Water moves across cell membranes either by the simple diffusion described above or as the result of osmotic differences across membranes. In the latter case, when water moves in bulk through aqueous pores in cellular membranes due to osmotic forces, any molecule that is small enough to pass through the pores will also be transferred. This movement of solutes is called filtration. Cell membranes throughout the body possess pores of different sizes; for example, the pores in the kidney glomerulus are typically 70 nm, but the channels in most cells are < 4 nm.[2]

The movement of some compounds across membranes cannot be explained by simple diffusion or filtration. These are usually high molecular weight or very lipid soluble substances. Therefore, specialized processes have been postulated to account for the movement. Active processes typically involve the expenditure of cellular energy to move molecules across biological membranes. Characteristics of active transport include selectivity, competitive inhibition, saturability, and movement across an electrochemical or concentration gradient. The drug complexes with a macromolecular carrier on one side of the membrane, traverses the membrane and is released on the other side. The carrier then returns to the original surface. Active transport processes are important in the elimination of xenobiotics. They are involved in the movement of drugs in hepatocytes, renal tubular cells and neuronal membranes. For example, the liver has four known active transport systems, two for organic acids, one for organic bases, and one for neutral organic compounds.[2] A different specialized transport process is termed facilitated diffusion. This transport is similar to the carrier mediated transport described above except that no active processes are involved. The drug is not moved against an electrochemical or concentration gradient and there is no expenditure of energy. A biochemical example of such transport is the movement of glucose from the gastrointestinal tract through the intestinal epithelium.

3.1.1.1 Absorption

In order for a drug to exert its pharmacological effect, it must first gain entry into the body, be absorbed into the bloodstream and transported or distributed to its site of action. This is true except in the case of drugs that exert their effect locally or at the absorption site. The absorption site, or port of entry, is determined by the route of drug administration.

Routes of administration are either enteral or parenteral. The former term denotes all routes pertaining to the alimentary canal. Therefore, sublingual, oral, and rectal are enteral routes of administration. All other routes, such as intravenous, intramuscular, subcutaneous, dermal, vaginal, and intraperitoneal, are parenteral routes.

Absorption describes the rate and extent to which a drug leaves its site of administration and enters the general circulation. Factors which, therefore, affect absorption include: the physicochemical properties of the drug which determine transfer across cell membranes as described earlier; formulation or physical state of the drug; site of absorption; concentration of drug; circulation at absorption site; and area of absorbing surface.

3.1.1.1.1 Gastrointestinal

Absorption of drug may occur at any point along the tract including the mouth, stomach, intestine, and rectum. Because the majority of drugs are absorbed by passive diffusion, the nonionized, lipid soluble form of the drug is favored for rapid action. Therefore, according to the Henderson-Hasselbalch equation, the absorption of weak acids should be favored in the stomach and the absorption of weak bases in the alkaline environment of the small intestine. However, other factors such as relative surface area will influence absorption. The stomach is lined by a relatively thick mucus-covered membrane to facilitate its primary function of digestion. In comparison, the epithelium of the small intestine is thin, with villi and microvilli providing a large surface area to facilitate its primary function of absorption of nutrients. Therefore, any factor that increases gastric emptying will tend to increase the rate of drug absorption, regardless of the ionization state of the drug.

The G.I. tract possesses carrier mediated transport systems for the transfer of nutrients and electrolytes across the gastric wall. These systems may also carry drugs and other xenobiotics into the organism. For example, lead is absorbed by the calcium transporter.[5] Absorption also depends on the physical characteristics of a drug. For example, a highly lipid soluble drug will not dissolve in the stomach. In addition, solid dosage forms will have little contact with gastric mucosa and the drug will not be absorbed until the solid is dissolved. Further, the particle size affects absorption, since dissolution rate is proportional to particle size.[6] Compounds that increase intestinal permeability or increase the residence time in the intestine by altering intestinal motility will thereby increase absorption of other drugs through that segment of the alimentary canal.

Once a drug has been absorbed through the G.I. tract, the amount of the compound that reaches the systemic circulation depends on several factors. The drug may be biotransformed by the G.I. cells or removed by the liver through which it must pass. This loss of drug before gaining access to the systemic circulation is known as the first pass effect.

Although oral ingestion is the most common route of G.I. absorption, drugs may be administered sublingually. Despite the small surface area for absorption, certain drugs which are nonionic and highly lipid soluble are effectively absorbed by this route. The drugs nitroglycerin and buprenorphine are administered by this route. The blood supply in the mouth drains into the superior vena cava and because of this anatomic characteristic, drugs are protected from first pass metabolism by the liver.

Although an uncommon route by which abused drugs are self-administered, rectal administration is used in medical practice when vomiting or other circumstances preclude oral administration. Approximately 50% of the drug that is absorbed will bypass the liver.[3] The disadvantage of this route for drug absorption is that the process is often incomplete and irregular and some drugs irritate the mucosal lining of the rectum.

3.1.1.1.2 Pulmonary

Gases, volatile liquids, and aerosols may be absorbed through the lungs. Access to the circulation by this route is rapid because of the large surface area of the lungs and extensive capillary network in close association with the alveoli. In the case of absorption of gases and volatilizable liquids, the ionization state and lipid solubility of the substance are less important than in G.I. absorption. This is because diffusion through cell membranes is not the rate limiting step in the absorption process. The reasons include low volatility of ionized molecules, the extensive capillary network in close association with the alveoli resulting in a short distance for diffusion, and the rapid removal of absorbed substances by the blood. Some substances may not reach the lungs due to being deposited and absorbed in the mucosal lining of the nose.

Drugs may be atomized or volatilized and inhaled as droplets or particulates in air, a common example being the smoking of drugs. The advantages of this route include rapid transport into the blood, avoidance of first pass hepatic metabolism, and avoidance of the medical problems associated with other routes of illicit drug administration. Disadvantages include local irritant effect on the tissues of the nasopharynx and absorption of particluate matter in the nasopharynx and bronchial tree. For a drug to be effectively absorbed it should reach the alveoli. However, absorption of particulate matter is governed by particulate size and water solubility. Particles with diameters >5 μm are usually deposited in the nasopharyngeal region;[2] particles in the 2 to 5 μm range are deposited in the tracheobronchiolar region and particles 1 μm and smaller reach the alveolar sacs.

3.1.1.1.3 Dermal

The skin is impermeable to most chemicals. For a drug to be absorbed it must pass first through the epidermal layers or specialized tissue such as hair follicles or sweat and sebaceous glands. Absorption through the outer layer of skin, the stratum corneum, is the rate limiting step in the dermal absorption of drugs. This outer layer consists of densely packed keratinized cells and is commonly referred to as the "dead" layer of skin because the cells comprising this layer are without nuclei. Drug substances may be absorbed by simple diffusion through this layer. The lower layers of the epidermis, and the dermis, consist of porous nonselective cells which pose little barrier to absorption by passive diffusion. Once a chemical reaches this level, it is then rapidly absorbed into the systemic circulation because of the extensive network of venous and lymphatic capillaries located in the dermis. Drug absorption through the skin depends on the characteristics of the drug and on the condition of the skin. Since the stratum corneum is the main barrier to absorption, damage to this area by sloughing of cells due to abrasion or burning enhances absorption, as does any mechanism which increases cutaneous blood flow. Hydration of the stratum corneum also increases its permeability and therefore enhances absorption of chemicals.

3.1.1.1.4 Parenteral Injection

Drugs are often absorbed through the G.I. tract, lungs, and skin but many illicit drugs have historically been self-administered by injection. These routes typically include intravenous, intramuscular, and subcutaneous administration. The intravenous route of administration introduces the drug directly into the venous bloodstream, thereby eliminating the process of absorption altogether. Substances that are locally irritating may be administered intravenously since the blood vessel walls are relatively insensitive. This route permits the rapid introduction of drug to the systemic circulation and allows high concentrations to be quickly achieved. Intravenous administration may result in unfavorable physiological responses because once introduced, the drug cannot be removed. This route of administration is dependent on maintaining patent veins and can result in extensive scar tissue formation due to chronic drug administration. Insoluble particulate matter deposited in the blood vessels is another medical problem associated with the intravenous route.

Intramuscular and subcutaneous administration involves absorption from the injection site into the circulation by passive diffusion. The rate of absorption is limited by the size of the capillary bed at the injection site and by the solubility of the drug in the interstitial fluid.[3] If blood flow is increased at the administration site, absorption will be increased.

3.1.1.2 Distribution

After entering circulation, drugs are distributed throughout the body. The extent of distribution is dependent on the physicochemical properties of the drug and physiological factors. Drugs cross cell membranes throughout the body by passive diffusion or specialized transport processes. Small water soluble molecules and ions cross cell membranes through aqueous pores whereas lipid soluble substances diffuse through the membrane lipid bilayer. The rate of distribution of a drug is dependent on blood flow and the rate of diffusion across cell mebranes of various tissues and organs. The affinity of a substance for certain tissues also affects the rate of distribution.

Because only unbound drug (the free fraction) is in equilibrium throughout the body, disposition is affected by binding to or dissolving in cellular constituents. While circulating in blood, drugs may be reversibly bound to several plasma proteins. For example, basic compounds often bind to a1-acid glycoprotein; acidic compounds bind to albumin. The extent of plasma protein binding varies among drugs, nicotine is 5% bound whereas the barbiturate, secobarbital, is 50% bound, and the benzodiazepine, diazepam is 96% bound.[7] The fraction of drug that is bound is governed by the drug concentration, its affinity for binding sites, and the number of binding sites. At low drug concentrations, the fraction bound is a function of the number of binding sites and the dissociation constant, a measure of binding affinity. When drug concentrations exceed the dissociation constant, concentration also governs the amount of protein binding. Therefore, published protein binding fractions for drugs only apply over a certain concentration range, usually the therapeutic concentration. Plasma protein binding limits the amount of drug entering tissues. Because plasma protein binding of drugs is relatively non-selective, drugs and endogenous substances compete for binding sites, and drug displacement from binding sites by another substance can contribute to toxicity by increasing the free fraction.

3.1.1.2.1 Binding to Tissue Constituents

In addition to binding to plasma proteins, drugs may bind to tissue constituents. The liver and kidney have a large capacity to act as storage depots for drugs. The mechanisms responsible for transfer of many drugs from the blood appear to be active transport processes.[2] Ligandin, a cytoplasmic liver protein, has a high affinity for many organic acids while metallothionein binds metals in the kidney and liver.

Lipid soluble drugs are stored in neutral fat by dissolution. Since the fat content of an obese individual may be 50% body weight, it follows that large amounts of drug can be stored in this tissue. Once stored in fat, the concentration of drug is lowered throughout the body, in the blood and also in target organs. Any activity, such as dieting or starvation, which serves to mobilize fat, could potentially increase blood concentrations and hence contribute to an increase in the risk of drug toxicity.

Drugs may also be stored in bone. Drugs diffuse from the extracellular fluid through the hydration shell of the hydroxyapatite crystals of the bone mineral. Lead, fluoride, and other compounds may be deposited and stored in bone. Deposition may not necessarily be detrimental. For example, lead is not toxic to bone tissue. However, chronic fluoride deposition results in the condition known as skeletal fluorosis. Generally, storage of compounds in bone is a reversible process. Toxicants may be released from the bone by ion exchange at the crystal surface or by dissolution of the bone during osteoclastic activity. If osteolytic activity is increased, the hydroxyapatite lattice is mobilized resulting in an increase in blood concentrations of any stored xenobiotics.

3.1.1.2.2 Blood Brain Barrier

The blood-brain barrier is often viewed as an impenetrable barrier to xenobiotics. However, this is not true and a more realistic representation is as a site that is less permeable to ionized substances and high molecular weight compounds than other membranes. Many toxicants do not enter the brain because the capillary endothelial cells are joined by tight junctions with few pores between cells; the capillaries of the central nervous system are surrounded by glial processes; and the interstitial fluid of the CNS has a low protein concentration. The first two anatomical processes limit the entry of small- to medium-sized water soluble molecules, whereas the entry of lipid soluble compounds is limited by the low protein content which restricts paracellular transport. It is interesting to note that the permeability of the brain to toxicants varies from area to area. For example, the cortex, area postrema, and pineal body are more permeable than other regions.[2] This may be due to differences in blood supply or the nature of the barrier itself. Entrance of drugs into the brain is governed by the same factors that determine transfer across membranes in other parts of the body. Only the unbound fraction is available for transfer and lipid solubility and the degree of ionization dictate the rate of entry of drugs into the brain. It should be noted that the blood-brain barrier is not fully developed at birth. In animal studies, morphine has been found to be 3 to 10 times more toxic to newborns than adults.[8]

3.1.1.2.3 Pregnancy

During pregnancy, drugs may also be distributed from the mother to the fetus by simple diffusion across the placenta. The placenta comprises several cell layers between the maternal and fetal circulations. The number of layers varies between species and state of gestation. The same factors govern placental drug transfer as movement by passive diffusion across other membranes. The placenta plays an additional role in preventing transfer of xenobiotics to the fetus by possessing biotransformation capabilities.

3.1.2 BIOTRANSFORMATION

Lipophilicity, a desirable drug characteristic for absorption and distribution across biological membranes, is a hindrance to elimination. To prevent accumulation of xenobiotics, the body chemically alters lipophilic compounds to more water soluble products. The sum of all the processes that convert lipophilic substances to more hydrophilic metabolites is termed biotransformation. These biochemical processes are usually enzymatic and are commonly divided into Phase I and Phase II reactions.[9] Phase I reactions generally expose or introduce a polar group to the parent drug, thereby increasing its water solubility. These reactions are oxidative or hydrolytic in nature and include *N*- and *O*-dealkylation, aliphatic and aromatic hydroxylation, *N*- and *S*-oxidation, and deamination. These reactions usually result in loss of pharmacological activity, although there are numerous examples of enhanced activity. Indeed, formation of a Phase I product is desirable in the case of administration of prodrugs.

Phase II reactions are conjugation reactions and involve covalent bonding of functional groups with endogenous compounds. Highly water soluble conjugates are formed by combination of the drug or metabolite with glucuronic acid, sulfate, glutathione, amino acids, or acetate. Again, these products are generally pharmacologically inactive or less active than the parent compound. An exception is the metabolite, morphine-6-glucuronide. In this case, glucuronidation at the 6-position increases the affinity of morphine for binding at the mu receptor and results in equivalent or enhanced pharmacological activity.[10]

The enzymes that catalyze the biotransformation of drugs are found mainly in the liver. This is not surprising considering the primary function of the liver is to handle compounds absorbed from the G.I. tract. In addition, the liver receives all the blood perfusing the splanchnic area. Therefore, this organ has developed a high capacity to remove substances from blood, and store, transform, and/or release substances into the general circulation. In its primary role of biotransformation, the liver acts as a homogenous unit, with all parenchymal cells or hepatocytes exhibiting enzymatic activity. In tissues involved in extrahepatic biotransformation processes, typically only one or two cell types are used. Many organs have demonstrated activity towards foreign compounds but the major extrahepatic tissues are those involved in the absorption or excretion of chemicals. These include the kidney, lung, intestine, skin, and testes. The main cells containing biotransformation enzymes in these organs are the proximal tubular cells, clara cells, mucosa lining cells, epithelial cells, and seminiferous tubules, respectively.

3.1.2.1 Phase I Enzymes

Phase I enzymes are located primarily in the endoplasmic reticulum of cells. These enzymes are membrane bound within a lipoprotein matrix and are referred to as microsomal enzymes. This is in reference to the subcellular fraction isolated by differential centrifugation of a liver homogenate. The two most important enzyme systems involved in Phase I biotransformation reactions are the cytochrome P-450 system and the mixed function amine oxidase. With the advances in recombinant DNA technology, eight major mammalian gene families of hepatic and extrahepatic cytochrome P-450 have been identified.[2] A comprehensive discussion of the cytochrome P-450 system is beyond the scope of this chapter and the reader is referred to a number of reviews.[11-13] Briefly, this system is comprised of two coupled enzymes: NADPH-cytochrome P-450 reductase and a heme containing enzyme, cytochrome P-450. This complex is associated with another cytochrome, cytochrome b_5 with a reductase enzyme. In reactions catalyzed by cytochrome P-450, the substrate combines with the oxidized form of cytochrome P-450 ($Fe3+$) to form a complex. This complex accepts an electron from NADPH which reduces the iron in the cytochrome P-450 heme moiety to $Fe2+$. This reduced substrate-cytochrome P450 complex then combines with molecular oxygen which in turn accepts another electron from NADPH. In some cases, the second electron is provided by NADH via cytochrome b_5. Both electrons are transferred to molecular oxygen, resulting in a highly reactive and unstable species. One atom of the unstable oxygen molecule is transferred to the substrate and the other is reduced to water. The substrate then dissociates as a result, regenerating the oxidized form of cytochrome P-450.

3.1.2.2 Phase II Enzymes

Many of the Phase II enzymes are located in the cytosol or supernatant fraction after differential centrifugation of a liver homogenate. These reactions are biosynthetic and therefore require energy. This is accomplished by transforming the substrate or cofactors to high energy intermediates. One of the major Phase II reactions is glucuronidation. The resultant glucuronides are eliminated in the bile or urine. The enzyme, uridine diphosphate (UDP) glucuronosyltransferase is located in the endoplasmic reticulum. This enzyme catalyzes the reaction between UDP-glucuronic acid and the functional group of the substrate. The location of this enzyme means that it has direct access to the products of Phase I enzymatic reactions. Another important conjugation reaction in humans is sulfation of hydroxyl groups. The sulfotransferases are a group of soluble enzymes, classified as aryl, hydroxysteroid, estrone, and bile salt sulfotransferases. Their primary function is the transfer of inorganic sulfate to the hydroxyl moiety of phenol or aliphatic alcohols.

Another important family of enzymes is the glutathione -S-transferases which are located in both the cytoplasm and endoplasmic reticulum of cells. The activity of the cytosolic transferase is 5 to 40 times greater than the endoplasmic enzyme. These transferase enzymes catalyze the reaction between the sulfhydryl group of the tripeptide glutathione with substances containing electrophilic carbon atoms. The glutathione conjugates are cleaved to cysteine derivatives, primarily in the kidney. These derivatives are then acetylated resulting in mercapturic acid conjugates which are excreted in the urine.

Many factors affect the rate at which a drug is biotransformed. One of the important factors is obviously the concentration of the drug at the site of action of biotransforming enzymes. Physicochemical properties of the drug, such as lipophilicity, are important, in addition to dose and route of administration. Certain physiological, pharmacological, and environmental factors may also affect the rate of biotransformation of a compound. Numerous variables affect biotransformation including sex, age, genetic polymorphisms, time of day or circadian rhythms, nutritional status, enzyme induction or inhibition, hepatic injury, and disease states.

3.1.3 ELIMINATION

Drugs are excreted or eliminated from the body as parent compounds or metabolites. The organs involved in excretion, with the exception of the lungs, eliminate water soluble compounds more readily than lipophilic substances. The lungs are important for the elimination of anaesthetic gases and vapors. The processes of biotransformation generally produce more polar compounds for excretion. The most important excretory organ is the kidney. Substances in the feces are mainly unabsorbed drugs administered orally or compounds excreted into the bile and not reabsorbed. Drugs may also be excreted in breast milk[14] and even though the amounts are small, they represent an important pathway because the recipient of any drugs by this route is the nursing infant.

For a comprehensive discussion of renal excretion of drugs, the reader is referred to Weiner and Mudge.[15] Excretion of drugs and their metabolites involves three processes, namely, glomerular filtration, passive tubular reabsorption, and active tubular secretion. The amount of a drug that enters the tubular lumen of the kidney is dependent on the glomerular filtration rate and the fraction of drug that is plasma protein bound. In the proximal renal tubular organic anions and cations are added to the filtrate by active transport processes. Glucuronide drug metabolites are secreted in this way by the carrier mediated system for naturally occurring organic acids. In the proximal and distal tubules of the kidney, the nonionized forms of weak acids and bases are passively reabsorbed. The necessary concentration gradient is created by the reabsorption of water with sodium. The passive reabsorption of ionized forms is pH dependent because the tubular cells are less permeable to these moieties. Therefore, in the treatment of drug poisoning, the excretion of some drugs can be increased by alkalinization or acidification of the urine.

Under normal physiological conditions, excretion of drugs in the sweat, saliva, and by the lacrimal glands is quantitatively insignificant. Elimination by these routes is dependent on pH and diffusion of the unionized lipid soluble form of the drug through the epithelial cells of the glands. Drugs excreted in saliva enter the mouth and may be reabsorbed and swallowed. Drugs have also been detected in hair and skin, and although quantitatively unimportant, these routes may be useful in drug detection and therefore have forensic significance.

3.1.4 PHARMACOKINETIC PARAMETERS

Pharmacokinetics assumes that a relationship exists between the concentration of drug in an accessible site, such as the blood, and the pharmacological or toxic response. The concentration of drug in the systemic circulation is related to the concentration of drug at the site of action. Pharmacokinetics attempts to quantify the relationship between dose and drug disposition and provide the framework, through modeling, to interpret measured concentrations in biological fluids.[3] Several pharmacokinetic parameters are utilized to explain various pharmacokinetic processes. It is often changes in these parameters, through disease, genetic abnormalities, or drug interactions, which necessitate modifications of dosage regimens for therapeutic agents. The most important parameters are clearance, the ability of the body to eliminate drug, volume of distribution, a measure of the apparent volume of the body available to occupy the drug, bioavailability, the proportion of drug absorbed into the systemic circulation, and half-life, a measure of the rate of drug elimination from the blood. These concepts are discussed below.

3.1.4.1 Clearance

Clearance is defined as the proportionality factor that relates the rate of drug elimination to the blood or plasma drug concentration:[16]

$$\text{Clearance} = \text{Rate of elimination/Concentration}$$

In the above equation, the concentration term refers to drug concentration at steady state. The units of clearance are volume per unit time and, therefore, this parameter measures the volume of biological fluid, such as blood, that would have to have drug removed to account for drug elimination. Therefore, clearance is not a measure of the amount of drug removed.

The concept of clearance is useful in pharmacokinetics because clearance is usually constant over a wide range of concentrations, providing that elimination processes are not saturated. Saturation of biotransformation and excretory processes may occur in overdose and toxicokinetic effects should be considered. If a constant fraction of drug is eliminated per unit time, the elimination follows first order kinetics. However, if a constant amount of drug is eliminated per unit time, the elimination is described by zero order kinetics. Some drugs, for example, ethanol, exhibit zero order kinetics at "normal" or non-intoxicating concentrations. However, for any drug that exhibits first order kinetics at therapeutic or non-toxic concentrations, once the mechanisms for elimination become saturated, the kinetics become zero order and clearance becomes variable.[3]

Clearance may also be viewed as the loss of drug from an organ of elimination such as the liver or kidney. This approach enables evaluation of the effects of a variety of physiological factors such as changes in blood flow, plasma protein binding, and enzyme activity. Therefore, total systemic clearance is determined by adding the clearance (CL) values for each elimination organ or tissue:

$$CL_{systemic} = CL_{renal} + CL_{hepatic} + CL_{lung} + CL_{other}$$

Clearance from an individual organ is a product of blood flow and the extraction ratio. The extraction ratio is derived from the concentration of drug in the blood entering the organ and the concentration of drug in the blood leaving the organ. If the extraction ratio is zero, no drug is removed. If it is 1, then all the drug entering the organ is removed from the blood. Therefore, the clearance of an organ may be determined from the following equation:

$$CL_{organ} = Q(C_A - C_V/C_A) = Q \times E$$

where

Q = blood flow

C_A = arterial drug concentration

C_V = venous drug concentration

E = extraction ratio

3.1.4.2 Volume of Distribution

The plasma drug concentration reached after distribution is complete is a result of the dose and the extent of uptake by tissues. The extent of distribution can be described by relating the amount of drug in the body to the concentration. This parameter is known as the volume of distribution. This volume does not indicate a defined physiological dimension but the volume of fluid required to contain all the drug in the body at the same concentration as in the plasma or blood. Therefore, it is often called the apparent volume of distribution (V) and is determined at steady state when distribution equilibrium has been reached between drug in plasma and tissues.

$$V = \text{Amount in body/ Plasma drug concentration}$$

The volume of distribution depends on the pKa of the drug, the degree of plasma protein and tissue binding, and the lipophilicity of the drug. As would be expected, drugs that distribute widely throughout the body have large volumes of distribution. In the equation above, the body is considered one homogeneous unit and therefore exhibits a one compartment model. In this model, drug administration occurs in the central compartment, and distribution is instantaneous throughout the body. For most drugs, the simple one compartment model does not describe the time course of drug in the body adequately and drug distribution and elimination is more completely described in multiple exponential terms using multicompartmental models. In these models, the volume of distribution, Varea, is calculated as the ratio of clearance to the rate of decline of the concentration during the elimination phase:

$$V_{area} = CL/k$$

where k= rate constant.

3.1.4.3 Bioavailability

The bioavailability of a drug refers to the fraction of the dose that reaches the systemic circulation. This parameter is dependent on the rate and extent of absorption at the site of drug adminsitration. Obviously, it follows that drugs administered intravenously do not undergo absorption, but immediately gain access to the systemic circulation and are considered 100% bioavailable. In the case of oral administration, if the hepatic extraction ratio is known, it is possible to predict the maximum bioavailability of drug by this route assuming first order processes, according to the following equation:[3]

$$F_{max} = 1-E = 1-(CL_{hepatic}/Q_{hepatic})$$

The bioavailability of a drug by various routes, may also be determined by comparing the area under the curve (AUC) obtained from the plasma concentration vs. time curve after intravenous and other routes of administration:[9]

$$\text{Bioavailability} = AUC_{oral}/AUC_{IV}$$

Amanda J. Jenkins and Edward J. Cone

3.1.4.4 Half-Life

The half-life is the time it takes for the plasma drug concentration to decrease by 50%. Half-life is usually determined from the log-terminal phase of the elimination curve. However, it is important to remember that this parameter is a derived term and is dependent on the clearance and volume of distribution of the drug. Therefore, as CL and V change with disease, drug interactions, and age, so a change in the half-life should be expected. The half-life is typically calculated from the following equation:

$$t_{1/2} = 0.693/k$$

where

$t_{1/2}$ = half life

k = elimination rate constant

Because k = CL/V, the inter-relationship between these parameters is clearly evident.

3.1.5 DOSAGE REGIMENS

Pharmacokinetic principles, in addition to clinical factors such as the state of the patient, are utilized in determining dosage regimens. Factors that relate to the safety and efficacy of the drug such as activity-toxicity relationships (therapeutic window and side effects), and pharmaceutical factors, such as dosage form and route of administration, must be considered.[16]
    The goal of a therapeutic regimen is to achieve therapeutic concentrations of a drug continuously or intermittently. The latter is useful if tolerance to the drug develops, or if the therapeutic effects of the drug persist and increase in intensity even with rapid drug disappearance. Adjustments to the dosage regimen are made to maintain therapeutically effective drug concentrations and minimize undesirable effects. Optimization of drug therapy is typically determined empirically; that is changing the dose based on response of the individual. However, there is often better correlation between blood or plasma concentration or amount of drug in the body than the dose administered. Therefore, pharmacokinetic data is useful in the design of dosage regimens. In theory, data following a single dose may be used to estimate plasma concentrations following any dosing design.
    For drugs whose effects are difficult to measure, or whose therapeutic index is low, a target level or steady state plasma concentration is desirable. A dose is computed to achieve this level, drug concentrations are measured, and the dose is adjusted accordingly. In order to apply this strategy, the therapeutic range should be determined. For many drugs the lower limit of this range appears to be the concentration that produces 50% maximal response. The upper limit is determined by drug toxicity and is commonly determined by the concentration at which 5 to 10% of patients experience a toxic effect.[3] The target concentration is then chosen at the middle of the therapeutic range.

3.1.5.1 Loading Doses

The loading dose is one or a series of doses that are administered at the beginning of therapy. The objective is to reach the target concentration rapidly. The loading dose can be estimated with the following formula:

$$\text{Loading Dose} = \text{Target Cp} \times \text{Vss/F}$$

where

Cp = Concentration in plasma

V ss= Volume of Distribution at steady state

F = Fractional bioavailability of the dose

A loading dose is desirable if the time to achieve steady state is long compared to the need for the condition being treated. One disadvantage of a loading dose is the acute exposure to high concentrations of the drug which may result in toxic effects in sensitive individuals.

3.1.5.2 Dosing Rate

In the majority of clinical situations, drugs are administered as a series of repeated doses or as a continuous infusion in order to maintain a steady state concentration. Therefore, a maintenance dose must be calculated such that the rate of input is equal to the rate of drug loss. This may be determined using the following formula:

$$\text{Dosing Rate} = \text{Target} \times \text{CL}/\text{F}$$

where

CL= Clearance

F= Fractional bioavailability of the dose

It is obvious from the above that in order to design an appropriate dosage regimen, several pharmacokinetic factors, including CL, F, Vss, and half-life, must be known in addition to an understanding of the principles of absorption and distribution of the drug in question. The clinician must also be aware of variations in these factors in a particular patient. One should note that even "normal" individuals exhibit variations in these parameters. For example, one standard deviation on clearance values may be 50%. These unpredicted variations in pharmacokinetic parameters may result in a wide range of drug concentrations. This is unacceptable in most cases especially for those drugs with a low therapeutic index. Therefore, Cp should be measured and estimates of CL, F, and Vss calculated directly.

3.1.6 THERAPEUTIC DRUG MONITORING

Blood or plasma drug concentrations at steady state are typically measured to refine estimates of CL/F for the individual. Updated estimates are then used to adjust maintenance doses to reach the desired target concentration. Drug concentrations can be misleading if the relevant pharmacokinetics (and toxicokinetics, see below) are not considered. In addition, individual variability in drug response, due to multiple drug use, disease, genetic differences, and tolerance must be considered. Pharmacokinetic characteristics of drugs may differ with development and age. Therefore, drug effects may vary considerably between infants, children, and adults. For example, water constitutes 80% of the weight of a newborn whereas in adults it constitutes approximately 60%. These differences effect distribution of drugs throughout the body.

3.1.6.1 Plasma

Measurement of drug concentrations in plasma is the cornerstone of therapeutic drug monitoring (TDM), but it is not without pitfalls. In many instances, clinical response does not correlate with plasma drug concentrations. Other considerations may be as follows.

3.1.6.1.1 Time Delays

It often takes time for a response to reflect a given plasma concentration due to the individual kinetics of the drug. Until this equilibrium is reached, correlation between response and concentration is difficult and may lead to misinterpretation of the clinical picture. Delay may be due to lack of equilibration between plasma and target organ as the drug distributes throughout the body. In addition, delay may be because the response measured is an indirect measure of drug effect, e.g., a change in blood pressure is an indirect measure of either change in peripheral resisitance or cardiac output or both.

3.1.6.1.2 Active Metabolites

Poor correlation may be found between response and plasma concentration of parent drug if active metabolites are present and not measured. Formation of active metabolites may be a function of the route of drug administration because oral ingestion generally produces an initial surge of metabolites due to the first pass effect of the liver compared with drugs administered intravenously.

3.1.6.1.3 Exposure Duration

Some drugs exhibit unusual concentration/response relationships which minimizes the utility of TDM. In these cases, clinical response correlates more with duration of dosing than the actual dose or resultant plasma concentrations.

3.1.6.1.4 Tolerance

The effectiveness of a drug may diminish with continual use. Tolerance denotes a decreased pharmacological responsiveness to a drug. This is demonstrated by several drugs of abuse including ethanol and heroin. The degree of tolerance varies but is never complete. For example, tolerance to the effects of morphine quickly develops, but the user is not totally unresponsive to the pharmacological effects. To compensate for the development of tolerance, the dose is increased. Tolerance may develop slowly, such as in the case of tolerance to the CNS effects of ethanol, or can occur acutely (tachyphylaxis) as in the case of nicotine. In these cases, a correlation may be found between plasma drug concentration and the intensity of response at a given moment, but the relationship is not consistent and varies with time.[16]

3.1.6.2 Saliva

In recent years, saliva has been utilized for TDM. The advantage is that collection is noninvasive and painless and so it has been used as a specimen of choice in pediatric TDM. Due to the low protein content of saliva, it is considered to represent the unbound or free fraction of drug in plasma. Since this is the fraction considered available for transfer across membranes and therefore responsible for pharmacological activity, its usefulness is easy to understand. Saliva collection methods are known to influence drug concentrations but if these are compensated for and a standardized procedure utilized, correlation between plasma and saliva drug concentrations may be demonstrated for several drugs (e.g., phenytoin). Inconsistent results have been found for some drugs such as phenobarbital, so additional studies are needed to clearly define the limitations of testing saliva for TDM.

3.2. PHARMACOKINETIC MODELING

3.2.1 COMPARTMENTAL MODELING

The pharmacokinetic profile of a drug is described by the processes of absorption, distribution, metabolism, and excretion. The disposition of a drug in the body may be further delineated by mathematical modelling. These models are based on the concept that the body may be viewed as a series of compartments in which the drug is distributed. If the compartmental concept is considered literally, then each tissue and organ becomes an individual compartment. However, in pharmacokinetic modelling, several organs or tissues exhibit similar characteristics in drug deposition and are often considered the same compartment. The pharmacokinetic profiles of many drugs may be explained using one or two compartment models, but more complex models exist and, with the advances in computer software, the ability to describe drug disposition has increased. The use of models does not mean that the drug distributes into distinct physiological compartments, but that these mathematical models adequately describe the fate of the drug in the human body.

3.2.1.1 One Compartment Models

In the one compartment model the entire body is considered as one unit (Figure 3.2.1.1A) The drug is administered into the compartment and distributed throughout the compartment (the body) instantaneously.[17] Similarly, the drug is eliminated directly from the one compartment at a rate measured by k_{el}, the elimination rate constant. The time course of the drug, as measured in the readily accessible blood or plasma, is typically graphed as a log concentration vs. time profile. Figure 3.2.1.1B shows the log plasma concentration vs. time plot for a drug that distributes according to a one compartment model. The dotted line demonstrates the time course after intravenous administration and the solid line demonstrates the time course after oral administration. Since intravenous administration does not have an absorption phase, the time course of drug in the plasma is linear. For oral administration, the drug concentration on the blood is slower to reach a peak due to absorptive processes of the G.I. tract.

3.2.1.2 Two Compartment Models

Figure 3.2.2.1C illustrates the concept of the two compartment model. In this model, drug is administered into the central compartment and then there is a time lag due to slower distribution into other tissues and organs. These other organs are represented by the peripheral compartment(s). More complex models may be developed if distribution to other organs occurs at different rates which can be mathematically differentiated. In the two compartment model, equilibirum is reached between the central and peripheral compartments and this marks the end of the distribution phase. The beginning of the distribution phase may be observed graphically by an initial rapid decline after peaking in the drug concentration in the central compartment (represented by the plasma/blood) as shown in Figure 3.2.1.1D. Rate constants may be estimated for drug movement between the central and peripheral compartments, but drug elimination from the body is assumed to occur from the central compartment.[17] As mentioned previously, more complex models may be developed including models in which the number of compartments into which the drug distributes is not assumed in the initial modelling.

3.2.1.3 Elimination Kinetics

The concept of zero or first order kinetics may be utilized to describe any rate process in pharmacokinetics. Therefore, if we are discussing drug absorption, a drug exhibits zero order kinetics if a constant amount of drug is absorbed regardless of dose.[9] Conversely, a drug exhibits first order absorption kinetics if the amount absorbed is dependent on dose, i.e., is a fraction of the dose. Similarly, when considering drug excretion, ethanol exhibits zero order elimination kinetics because a constant amount of drug is excreted per unit time regardless of the drug concentration (unless processes become saturated). Most drugs exhibit first order elimination kinetics in which a constant fraction of drug is eliminated per unit time.

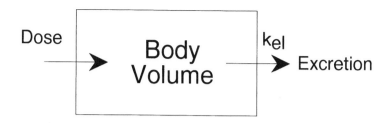

1-Compartment Model

(A)

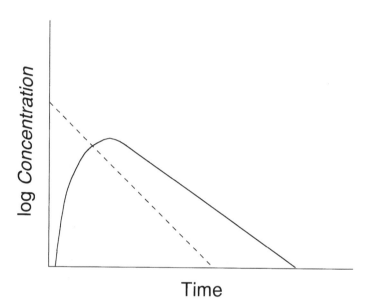

(B)

3.2.1.1. (A) Schematic representation of a one compartment model. (B) Log plasma concentration vs. time curve after intravenous (---) and oral (-) administration. Adapted from Hagan, R. L., Basic Pharmacokinetics. In-Service Training and Continuing Education AACC/TDM, American Association for Clinical Chemistry, Inc., Washington, D.C. 17(9):231-247 (1996).

Zero order elimination kinetics are described by the following equation:[17]

$$C = C_0 - kt$$

where

C = drug concentration at time, t

C_0 = the concentration at time zero or the initial concentration

k = the elimination rate constant

A plot of this equation is linear with a slope, -k, and a y-intercept, C_0. The elimination half-life may be calculated from this equation for a drug which exhibits zero order elimination. When $t = t1/2$, then $C = 1/2\ C_0$, the initial or peak concentration. This results in the following equation:

$$t1/2 = 1/2\ C_0/k$$

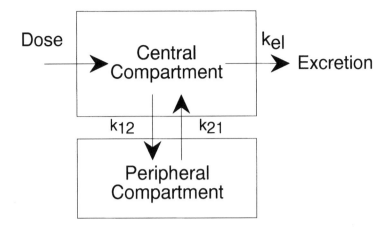

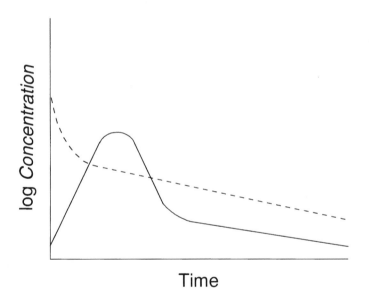

(C)

(D)

Figure 3.2.1.1 (C) Schematic representation of a two compartment model. (D) Log plasma concentration vs. time curve after intravenous(---) and oral (-) administration. Adapted from Hagan, R. L., Basic Pharmacokinetics. In-Service Training and Continuing Education AACC/TDM, American Association for Clinical Chemistry, Inc., Washington, D.C. 17(9):231-247 (1996).

This equation has a concentration term, C_0, indicating that the half-life is variable and dependent on drug concentration. Changes in pharmacokinetic parameters that occur as a function of dose or drug concentration are referred to as non-linear pharmacokinetic processes. Non-linearity is usually due to saturation of protein binding, hepatic metabolism, or active renal transport of the drug.[3]

First order elimination kinetics are described by the equation:[17]

$$C = C_0 e^{-kt}$$

Amanda J. Jenkins and Edward J. Cone

Taking the natural logarithm of this equation and plotting it semilogarithmically results in a linear graph with a slope of -k, and a y-intercept of ln C_0. Again, to determine the half-life, $1/2$ C_0 is substituted into the equation to give:

$$1/2C_0 = C_0 e^{-kt1/2}$$

Taking natural logs and solving for $t1/2$:

$$t1/2 = 0.693/k$$

It is important to note that the elimination half-life is a derived term, and any process that changes k will change the half-life of the drug. Factors that may affect pharmacokinetic parameters are discussed elsewhere, but in this example may include disease states, changes in urinary pH, changes in plasma protein binding, and coadministration of other drugs.

3.2.2 PHYSIOLOGICAL MODELS

An alternate method of building a pharmacokinetic profile of a drug in the body is to utilize anatomic and physiological information. Such a model does not make assumptions about body compartments or first order processes for drug absorption and elimination.[16] The first step in such modelling is to decide whether drug distribution into a particular tissue is perfusion rate or membrane transport limited.[2] These decisions are based on the physicochemical character- istics of the drug and physiological conditions in addition to reference to any experimental data. In order to write a mass balance equation, blood flow, Q, and the volume, V, of the organ or tissue of interest is needed and may be obtained frrom the literature. The other parameters, venous drug concentration, C_v, and the partition coefficient, R, are determined experimen- tally.[2] A simple mass balance equation may be written as:[2]

$$V_t \times dC_t/dt = Q_t \times [C_v - C_t/R_t]$$

where t = tissue.

Mass balance equations may be constructed for each organ or tissue considered and algebraic equations added to account for growth, changes in tissue weight ratios, and other physiological parameters.The advantage of this modelling over the more traditional compart- mental method is provision of a time course of drug distribution to any organ or tissue, and this model allows estimation of the effects of changing physiological parameters on tissue concentrations. Disadvantages include the need for complex mathematical equations and the lack of data on the physiological parameters necessary to construct the differential equations.[2]

3.3 PHARMACOKINETIC-PHARMACODYNAMIC CORRELATIONS

Pharmacodynamics (PD) may be defined as the quantitative relationship between the measured plasma or tissue concentration of the active moiety and the magnitude of the observed pharmacological effect(s).[1] The study of pharmacokinetics (PK) has been defined previously. A PK/PD model is a mathematical description of the relationship. Knowledge of the model and model parameter estimates permits prediction of concentration vs. time and effect vs. time profiles for different dosing regimens.[1] Different drugs are characterized by different PK and PD models and by differences in model parameters such as volume of distribution and receptor affinity. Understanding the PK/PD model permits comparison of the pharmacological prop- erties for different drugs. For a specific compound, there may be significant variation in model parameters between individuals. PK/PD modeling allows assessment of the contribution of the variability in model parameters to the overall variability in drug response.[1]

In order to fully understand the significance of PK/PD modeling, it is important to note that the observed effect vs. time profile for a particular individual is determined by several factors. These include: (1) drug input-dose, rate and route of administration; (2) intrinsic PK drug properties; and (3) intrinsic PD drug properties. Modeling allows estimation of PK/PD parameters. Further, PK/PD modeling provides dose response curves for the onset, magnitude, and duration of effects which can be utilized to optimize dose and dosing regimens. Models have been described for reversible and irreversible drug effects and for a range of drug classes including analgesics, benzodiazepines, and anticonvulsants. For a more detailed explanation of PK/PD modeling and correlations and description of computer applications, the reader is referred elsewhere.[1]

3.4 TOXICOKINETICS

Toxicokinetics is the study of drug disposition in overdose. The biochemical processes that constitute the science of pharmacokinetics may be altered when drugs are administered in high concentrations. G.I. absorption may be altered in overdose due to delayed gastric emptying, changes in intestinal motility and therapy with activated charcoal.[2] Drugs such as morphine, ethanol, and barbiturates delay gastric emptying and as a consequence slow drug movement into the small intestine. In addition, morphine decreases intestinal motility, resulting in increased transit time through the intestine and increased absorption. Little is known about changes in drug distribution throughout the body after overdose. Several mechanisms may be at work in overdose to cause changes in drug disposition. For example, the bioavailability of a drug with a high first pass metabolism may be increased when the hepatic metabolizing enzymes become saturated. In a similar manner, the concentration of free drug in the plasma may be increased when protien binding becomes saturated. This may result in significant toxicity for those drugs that are highly plasma protein bound. Also, changes in peripheral blood flow due to the cardiac effects of some drugs may result in prolonged drug distribution and higher blood drug concentrations.

Drug metabolism may be altered in overdose when those enzymes responsible for metabolism become saturated. In this event, clearance is decreased, half-life is prolonged, and therefore high drug concentrations exist for a longer time. If multiple drugs are co-ingested, competitive inhibition of metabolism may occur. In addition, if hepatic blood flow is decreased, due to impaired liver function or cardiovascular drug effects, biotransformation of xenobiotics may be decreased.

Renal excretion may or may not be altered in drug overdose. Alteration of renal drug clearance may be utilized therapeutically to enhance drug elimination. Urinary pH is adjusted to increase the clearance of acidic and basic drugs. For example, administration of sodium bicarbonate will raise the urine pH above 7.5, concentrating the ionized form in the renal tubule and, therefore, enhancing elimination of salicylate. Conversely, acidification of the urine may be utilized to enhance renal excretion of basic drugs. However, with some drugs, such as phencyclidine, there is controversy about the role of urinary acidification in enhanced excretion and whether this procedure improves clinical outcome. Acidification is contraindicated with myoglobinuria and may also increase the risk of metabolic complications.[18]

3.5 FACTORS AFFECTING PHARMACOKINETIC PARAMETERS

Toxicokinetics is utilized to describe the changes in pharmacokinetic processes as a result of drug overdose. Other factors may contribute to changes in pharmacokinetic parameters when non-toxic doses are therapeutically or illicitly administered. Besides species differences in the variability in drug response, which will not be discussed here, other factors that contribute to changes in parameters include drug formulation and route of administration, gender differences, age, weight or body composition, disease, genetic abnormalities, and drug interactions.

3.5.1 GENETIC FACTORS

When a distinguishable difference between individuals is under genetic control, it is known as genetic polymorphism. Some drug responses have been found to be genetically determined. For example, the activity of the liver enzyme N-acetyltransferase differs between individuals such that the population may be divided into slow and fast acetylators. Approximately 60% of the U.S. population are slow acetylators and may show toxicity unless doses of drugs requiring acetylation for metabolism are reduced. Other inherited variations in pharmacokinetics include deficiency of one or more hepatic cytochrome -P450 isozymes or plasma cholinesterase.[2]

3.5.2 SEX DIFFERENCES

Examples of sex differences in drug pharmacokinetics have also been identified. These differences may be due to variations in body composition, hepatic metabolism, renal elimination, protein binding, or absorption. Differences in weight may influence muscle mass, organ blood flow, body water spaces, and hence affect the pharmacokinetic parameters of many drugs. In addition, women tend to have a higher percentage of body fat than men, which will effect the volume of distribution of lipophilic drugs. The clinical significance of differences in body composition is unclear but there are some important examples: women have a lower volume of distribution (V) of ethanol[19] and a higher V for diazepam than men.

A number of studies have examined the effect of gender on hepatic metabolism and drug elimination. Greenblatt et al.[20] found that young women have a significantly higher CL for diazepam than young men. In contrast, clearances of oxazepam[21] and chlordiazepoxide[22] are higher in men than in women and no sex difference has been observed in the metabolism of nitrazepam or lorazepam.[19] Differences can be explained by differences in metabolic pathways because oxazepam is metabolized primarily through conjugation, nitrazepam is metabolized by reduction of the nitro group, and most of the other benzodiazepines are metaboilzed by various cytochrome P-450 isozymes. It has been found that the isozyme cytochrome3A4, responsible for the metabolism of many drugs, is approximately 1.4 times more active in women than men. The isozymes P2D6 and P2C19 display genetic polymorphism that is not influenced by gender. The isozyme P1A2 may be influnced by sex although the data is inconclusive. The work of Relling et al.[23] suggests that the activity of this isozyme is lower in women than men. As mentioned above, gender differences have been demonstrated in the elimination of drugs that are metabolized solely by conjugation. The male:female clearance ratio for oxazepam is approximately 1.5:1.

When considering renal elimination, the glomerular filtration rate (GFR) is on average higher in men than women[19] but this may be a weight rather than a gender effect as GFR is directly proportional to weight. The effects of gender on tubular secretion and reabsorption have not been well characterized. The influence of gender on plasma protein binding appears to be minimal. Albumin levels are not altered by sex in contrast to the protein a1-acid glycoprotein which is reduced by estrogen.[24] Other plasma constituents whose levels are influenced by gender include cortico-steroid binding globulin and various lipoproteins.[25] Gender differences in the binding of diazepam and chlordiazepoxide have been demonstrated.

Some studies have suggested that gender influences gastric emptying rate and intestinal transit time.[26] Women empty solids from the stomach more slowly than men and the activity of the stomach enzyme, alcohol dehydrogenase, may be much lower in women. The G.I. tract also contains large concentrations of the isozyme cytochrome P3A4, so gender differences in the activity of this enzyme could effect the bioavailability of certain drugs. Gender differences observed after intramuscular drug administration may be due to differences in blood flow or incorrect injection into fat in women. Drug absorption in the lung may differ according to gender. Knight et al.[27] found significantly less deposition of an aerosolized drug in women than men, which the authors attributed to differences in breathing characteristics.

It should be noted that female specific issues may have significant effects on drug distribution and metabolism. For example, pregnancy may increase the elimination of certain drugs, reducing their efficacy. In addition, oral contraceptive use can affect the metabolism of drugs. The effects of menopause, menstruation, and hormone replacement on the pharmacokinetics of drugs are largely unknown.

3.5.3 AGE

Changes in the rate but not the extent of drug absorption are usually observed with age.[16] Factors that affect drug absorption, such as gastric pH and emptying, intestinal motility, and blood flow, change with age. Gastric acid secretion does not approach adult levels until the age of three and gastric emptying and peristalsis is slow during the first few months of life. Because skeletal muscle mass is limited, muscle contractions, which aid blood flow, are minimal, and therefore, will limit the distribution of intramuscularly administered drug. Higher gastric pH, delayed gastric emptying, and decreased intestinal motility and blood flow are observed in the elderly.

3.5.4 DRUG AND DISEASE INTERACTIONS

The pharmacokinetics of several drugs have been shown to be influenced by concurrent disease processes.[16] The clearance of many drugs decreases in those individuals with chronic hepatic disease such as cirrhosis. In contrast, in acute reversible liver conditions, such as acute viral hepatitis, the clearance of some drugs is decreased or the half-life increased and for others, no change is detected. The volumes of distribution of some drugs are unaltered in hepatic disease while an increase is observed for other drugs, especially those bound to albumin in individuals with cirrhosis. This phenomenon is due to the decreased synthesis of albumin and other proteins. The influence of liver disease on drug absorption is unclear. It is probable though that the oral bioavailability of drugs highly extracted from the liver is increased in cirrhosis. The reasons are decreased first pass hepatic metabolism and the development of portal bypass in which blood enters the superior vena cava directly via esophageal varices.

Renal diseases such as uremia may result in decreased renal clearance of certain drugs.[16] Gastrointestinal diseases, such as Crohn's disease, result in increased plasma protein binding of several drugs due to increased levels of binding proteins. Further, respiratory diseases such as cystic fibrosis increase the renal clearance of some drugs.

Patients commonly receive two or more drugs concurrently and most individuals who abuse drugs are poly-drug users. Multiple drug use may result in drug interactions. This occurs when the pharmacokinetics or pharmacodynamics of one drug is altered by another. This concept is important to consider because interaction may result in decreased therapeutic efficacy or an increased risk of toxicity. The degree of drug interaction depends on the relative concentrations and therefore dose and time.[16] Changes in absorption rate, competition for binding sites on plasma proteins, oral bioavailability, volume of distribution, and hepatic and renal clearance have been demonstrated for therapeutic drugs. Few studies have systematically documented pharmacokinetic interactions between illicit drugs.

Amanda J. Jenkins and Edward J. Cone

REFERENCES

1. *Handbook of Pharmacokinetic/Pharmacodynamic Correlation.* H. Derendorf and G. Hochhaus eds. CRC Press Inc. Boca Raton, FL, 1995.
2. *Casarett and Doull's Toxicology The Basic Science of Poisons.* M.O. Amdur, J. Doull and C.D. Klaassen, eds. Pergamon Press, Inc., Elmsford, NY, 1991.
3. *Goodman & Gilman's The Pharmacological Basis of Therapeutics,* J.G. Hardman and L.E. Limbird, eds.-in -chief. McCraw-Hill Companies, Inc., NY, NY, 1996.
4. Benz, R., Janko, K., and Langer, P.: Pore formation by the matrix protein (porin) to *Escherichia coli* in planar bilayer membranes. *Ann. N.Y. Acad. Sci.* 358:13-24, 1980.
5. Sobel, A.E., Gawron, O., and Kramer, B.: Influence of vitamin D in experimental lead poisoning. *Proc. Soc. Exp. Biol. Med.* 38: 433-435, 1938.
6. Bates, T.R., and Gibaldi, M.: Gastrointestinal absorption of drugs. In Swarbuck, J. ed.: *Current concepts in the pharmaceutical sciences: biopharmaceutics.* Lea & Febiger, Philadelphia, PA, 1970.
7. R. C. Baselt, and R.H. Cravey. *Disposition of Toxic Drugs and Chemicals in Man.* Chemical Toxicology Institute, Foster City, CA, 1995.
8. Kupferberg, H.J., and Way, E.L.: Pharmacologic basis for the increased sensitivity of the newborn rat to morphine. *J. Pharmacol. Exp. Ther.* 141: 105-112,1963.
9. *Principles of Drug Action The Basis of Pharmacology.* W.B. Pratt and P. Taylor eds. Churchill Livingstone Inc., New York, NY, 1990.
10. *Sulfation of Drugs and Related Compounds,* Mulder, G.J., ed. CRC Press, Inc., Boca Raton, FL, 1981.
11. *Hepatic cytochrome P-450 monooxygenase system.* Schenkman, J.B. and Kupfer, D., eds. Pergamon Press, Oxford, England, 1982.
12. Gonzalez, F.J.: The molecular biology of cytochrome P450s. *Pharmacol. Rev.* 40: 243, 1988.
13. Conney, A.H.: Induction of microsomal cytochrome P-450 enzymes. *Life Sci.* 39:2493, 1986.
14. Stowe, C.M., and Plaa, G.L.: Extrarenal excretion of drugs and chemicals, *Annu. Rev. Pharmacol.* 8:337-356, 1968.
15. Weiner, I.M., and Mudge, G.H.: Renal tubular mechanisms for excretion of organic acids and bases. *Am. J. Med.* 36:743-762, 1964.
16. *Clinical Pharmacokinetics Concepts and Applications,* Rowland, M. and Tozer, T.N., Lea & Febiger, Philadelphia, PA, 1989.
17. Hagan, R.L. : Basic Pharmacokinetics. In-Service Training and Continuing Education AACC/ TDM, American Association for Clinical Chemistry, Inc., Washington, D.C. 17 (9): 231-247 (1996).
18. Ellenhorn, M.J., and Barceloux, D.G.: *Medical toxicology, diagnosis and treatment of human poisoning.* New York: Elsevier (1988).
19. Harris, R.Z., Benet, L.Z., and Schwartz, J.B.: Gender effects in pharmacokinetics and pharmacodynamics. *Drugs* 50 (2): 222-239 (1995).
20. Greenblatt, D.J., Allen, M.D., Harmatz, J.S.: Diazepam disposition determinants. *Clin. Pharmacol. Ther.* 27:301-312 (1980).
21. Greenblatt, D.J., Divoll, M., and Harmatz, J.S.: Oxazepam kinetics: effects of age and sex. *J. Pharmacol. Exp. Ther.* 215:86-91 (1980).
22. Greenblatt, D.J., Divoll, M., and Abernathy, D.R.: Age and gender effects on chlordiazepoxide kinetics: relation to antipyrine disposition. *Pharmacology* 38: 327-334 (1989).
23. Relling, M.V., Lin, J.S., and Ayers, G.D.: Racial and gender differences in N-acetyltransferase, xanthine oxidase, and CYP1A2 activities. *Clin. Pharmacol. Ther.* 52: 643-658 (1992).
24. Routledge, P.A., Stargel, W.W., and Kitchell, B.B.: Sex-related differences in the plasma protein binding of lignocaine and diazepam. *Br. J. Clin. Pharmacol.* 11:245-250 (1981).
25. Wilson, K.: Sex-related differences in drug disposition in man. *Clin. Pharmacokinet.* 9: 189-202 (1984).

26. Yonkers, K.A., Kando, J.C., and Cole, J.O.: Gender differences in pharmacokinetics and pharmacodynamics of psychotropic medication. *Am. J. Pyschiatry* 149:587-595 (1992).
27. Knight, V., Yu, C.P., and Gilbert, B.E.: Estimating the dosage of ribavirin aerosol according to age and other variables. *J. Infect. Dis.* 158: 443-447 (1988).

3.6 PHARMACOKINETICS OF SPECIFIC DRUGS

3.6.1 AMPHETAMINE

The term amphetamines refers to the group of stimulants that includes amphetamine, meth-amphetamine, methylenedioxyamphetamine, and methylenedioxymethamphetamine. These low molecular weight basic drugs are sympathomimetic phenethylamine derivatives possessing central and peripheral stimulant activity. Amphetamines suppress appetite and produce CNS and cardiovascular stimulation. These effects are mediated by increasing synaptic concentrations of norepinephrine and dopamine either by stimulating neurotransmitter release or inhibiting uptake. Clinical uses of amphetamine and methamphetamine include chronic administration for the treatment of narcolepsy in adults and attention deficit hyperactivity disorder in children.[1]

These drugs are abused for their stimulant effect. The effects are usually longer lasting than those of cocaine and may prevent fatigue. The latter factor has led to their study in athletes and in military field situations. It is postulated that the disturbances in perception and psychotic behavior, which may occur at high doses, may be due to dopamine release from dopaminergic neurons and also serotonin release from tryptaminergic neurons located in the mesolimbic area of the brain.

Amphetamine and methamphetamine occur as structural isomers and stereoisomers. Structural isomers are compounds with the same empirical formula but a different atomic arrangement, e.g., methamphetamine and phentermine. Stereoisomers differ in the three-dimensional arrangement of the atoms attached to at least one asymmetric carbon and are nonsuperimposable mirror images. Therefore, amphetamine and methamphetamine occur as both d- and l-isomeric forms. The two isomers together form a racemic mixture. The d-amphetamine form has significant stimulant activity, and possesses approximately 3 to 4 times the central activity of the l-form. It is also important to note that the d- and l-enantiomers may not only have different pharmacological activity but also varying pharmacokinetic characteristics.

When indicated for therapeutic use, 5 to 60 mg or 5 to 20 mg of amphetamine or methamphetamine, respectively, are administered orally. An oral dose of amphetamine typically results in a peak plasma concentration of 110 ng/mL.[2] When abused, ampetamines may be self-administered by the oral, intravenous, or smoked route. The latter route of administration is common for methamphetamine. With heavy use, addicts may ingest up to 2000 mg per day.

3.6.1.1 Absorption

Limited data is available on the G.I. absorption of amphetamine in humans. Beckett et al.[3] reported serum concentrations of amphetamine in two healthy volunteers after a 15 mg oral dose of the d-isomer. Peak serum concentrations of 48 and 40 ng/mL were achieved at 1.25 h when the volunteers' urine was acidified. Slightly higher serum concentrations were observed (52 and 47 ng/mL) if the urine pH conditions were not controlled. Rowland[4] observed a peak blood concentration of 35 ng/mL, 2 h after a 10 mg oral dose of d-amphetamine to a healthy 66 kg adult. The half-life for the d-isomer was 11 to 13 h compared with a 39% longer half life for the l-isomer. If the urine was acidified, excretion was enhanced and the half-lives of both

Amanda J. Jenkins and Edward J. Cone

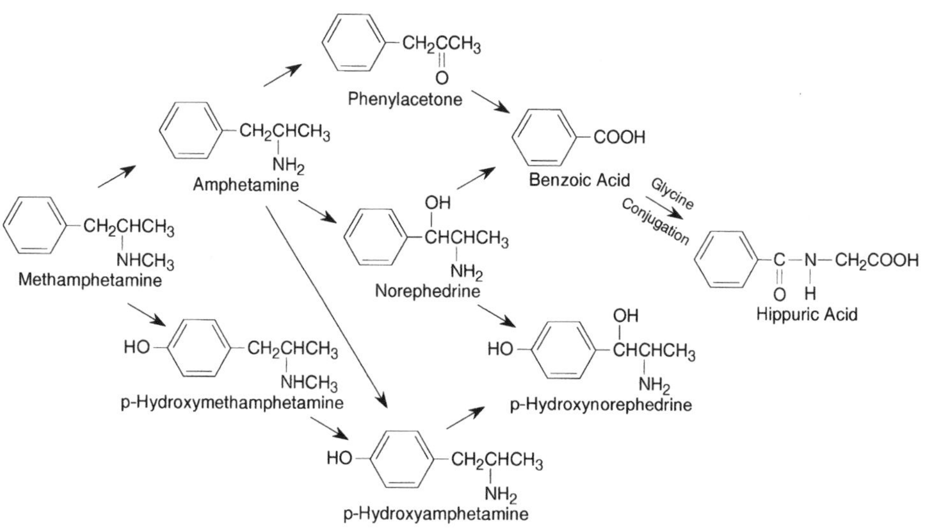

3.6.2.2A. Metabolic pathway of amphetamine and methamphetamine.

isomers were reduced to approximately 7 h.[5] Amphetamine demonstrates a linear one compartment open model over the dose range 20 to 200 mg.

3.6.1.2 Distribution

The plasma protein binding of amphetamine in humans is approximately 16 to 20% and is similar in drug dependent and naive subjects.[6] Research by Rowland[4] and Franksson and Anggard[6] indicated that there was a difference in the volume of distribution between non-users (3.5 to 4.6 L/kg) and drug dependent individuals (6.1 L/kg). It has been suggested that the larger Vd observed in drug dependent subjects may be due to a higher tissue affinity for amphetamine in these individuals. Evidence to support this suggestion is found in studies with amphetamine dependent animals in which higher tissue concentrations of amphetamine were found.[7]

3.6.1.3 Metabolism and Excretion

Amphetamine is metabolized by deamination, oxidation, and hydroxylation. Figure 3.6.2.2A illustrates the metabolic scheme for amphetamine. Deamination produces the inactive metabolite, phenylacetone, which is further oxidized to benzoic acid and then excreted in urine as hippuric acid and glucuronide conjugates. In addition, amphetamine is also converted to norephedrine by oxidation and then this metabolite and the parent compound are p-hydroxylated. Several metabolites, including norephedrine, its hydroxy metabolite, and hydroxyamphetamine, are pharmacologically active. The excretion of amphetamine depends on urinary pH. In healthy men who were administered 5 mg of isotopically labeled d,l-amphetamine, approximately 90% of the dose was excreted in the urine within 3 to 4 days.[8] Approximately 70% of the dose was excreted in the 24-h urine with 30% as unchanged drug. This was increased to 74% under acidic conditions and reduced to 1% in alkaline urine. Under normal conditions, <1% is excreted as phenylacetone, 16 to 28% as hippuric acid, 4% as benzoylglucuronide, 2% as norephedrine, <0.5% as p-hydroxynorephedrine, and 2 to 4% as p-hydroxyamphetamine.[9] l-Amphetamine is not as extensively metabolized as the d-isomer. When volunteers were orally administered 5 to 15 mg of d- or l-amphetamine, the mean excretion of unchanged d-amphetamine was 33% of the dose and that of the l-isomer was 49% of the dose.[2]

The metabolism of amphetamine has been studied in those presenting with amphetamine pyschosis. In the presence of acidified urine, the renal elimination of amphetamine increased significantly. The intensity of the psychosis was found to correlate with the amount of basic polar metabolites excreted in the urine, such as norephedrine and p-hydroxyamphetamine, and not with the plasma amphetamine concentration. This suggests that these metabolites may play an important role in the development of paranoid pyschosis in chronic amphetamine users.[6]

3.6.2 METHAMPHETAMINE

d-Methamphetamine, the N-methyl derivative of amphetamine, was first synthesized in 1919. Methamphetamine is available in the d- and l-forms. The d-form has reportedly greater central stimulant activity than the l-isomer, which has greater peripheral sympathomimetic activity. The d-form is the commonly abused form while the l-isomer is typically found in non-prescription inhalers as a decongestant.

Although initially available as an injectable solution for the treatment of obesity, d-methamphetamine hydrochloride is currently available as conventional and prolonged release tablets. Illicit methamphetamine is synthesized from the precursors phenylacetone and N-methylformamide (dl mixture) or alternatively from ephedrine by red phosphorus/acid reduction.

3.6.2.1 Absorption

Doses of 5 to 10 mg methamphetamine typically result in blood concentrations between 20 to 60 ng/mL. In one study,[10] six healthy adults were orally administered a single dose of 0.125 mg/kg methamphetamine. Peak plasma concentrations were achieved at 3.6 h with a mean concentration of 20 ng/mL. In a second study, Lebish et al.[11] observed a peak blood concentration of 30 ng/mL, 1 h after a single oral dose of 10 mg methamphetamine to one subject.

3.6.2.2 Metabolism and Excretion

In humans, both the d- and l-forms undergo hydroxylation and N-demethylation to their respective p-hydroxymethamphetamine and amphetamine metabolites. Amphetamine is the major active metabolite of methamphetamine. Under normal conditions, up to 43% of a d-methamphetamine dose is excreted unchanged in the urine in the first 24 hours and 4 to 7% will be present as amphetamine. In acidic urine, up to 76% is present as parent drug[10] compared with 2% under alkaline conditions. Approximately 15% of the dose was present as p-hydroxymethamphetamine and the remaining minor metabolites were similar to those found after amphetamine administration. Urine concentrations of methamphetamine are typically 0.5 to 4 mg/L after an oral dose of 10 mg. However, methamphetamine and amphetamine urine concentrations vary widely among abusers. Lebish et al.[11] reported urine methamphetamine concentrations of 24 to 333 mg/L and amphetamine concentrations of 1 to 90 mg/L in the urine of methamphetamine abusers.

l-Methamphetamine is biotransformed in a similar manner to the d-isomer but at a slower rate. Following a 13.7 mg oral dose, the 24 h urine contained an average of 34% of the dose as l-methamphetamine and 1.7% of the dose as l-amphetamine.[3]

d-Methamphetamine is commonly self-administered by the smoked route. Both the freebase and hydrochloride salt of methamphetaime are volatile and > 90% of parent drug can be recovered intact when heated to temperatures of 300°C. When cigarettes containing tobacco mixed with methamphetamine were pyrolyzed, amphetamine, phenylacetone, dimethylamphetamine, and N-cyanomethyl methamphetamine were the major resulting products.[12] Cook[13]

Amanda J. Jenkins and Edward J. Cone

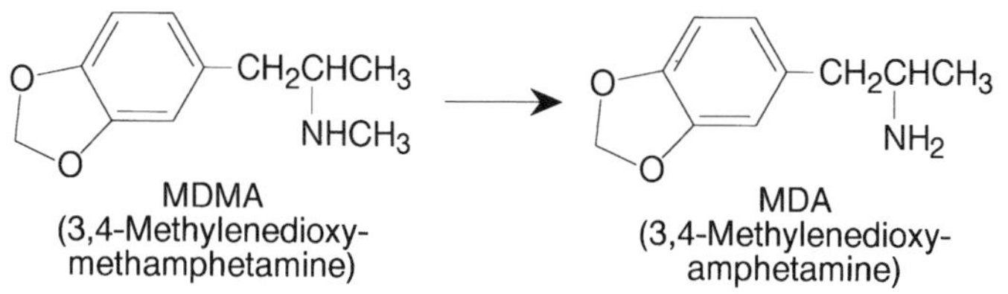

3.7.2.2B. Structures of MDA and MDMA.

conducted a study in which six volunteers were administered 30 mg d-methamphetamine from a pipe that was heated to approximately 300°C. Blood samples and physiological and subjective measures were collected after drug administration. Plasma methamphetamine concentrations rose rapidly after the start of smoking. However, concentrations plateaued (40 to 44 ng/mL) after 1 h with a slight increase in concentration over the next 1h. Thereafter, concentrations in plasma declined slowly, reaching the same concentration at 8 h on the downward side of the curve as reached at 30 min on the upward side. The authors used a noncompartmental model to determine an average elimination half-life of 11.7 h with a range of 8 to 17 h. These authors also administered methamphetamine (0.250 mg/kg) orally and the resulting plasma data were fit to a one compartment model with first order elimination and a lag time. A maximum plasma concentration of 35 to 38 ng/mL was achieved at 3.1 h with a terminal elimination half-life of 10 h. Although the plasma concentration time curves for smoked and oral methamphetamine appeared similar, the subjective effects were markedly different, with a greater "high" being reported after smoked methamphetamine. This indicates that it may be the rate of change of plasma drug concentrations that is a significant factor in determining subjective effects.

3.6.3 3,4-METHYLENEDIOXYAMPHETAMINE

3,4-Methylenedioxyamphetamine (MDA) is a potent pyschotropic amphetamine derivative first synthesized in 1910 (Figure 3.6.2.2B). It has no accepted medical use but is self-administered orally or intravenously in doses of 50 to 250 mg for illicit use.[10] Blood concentrations following normal use have not been reported and, to date, there are no reported clinical studies delineating the pharmacokinetic or pharmacodynamic characteristics of this drug. Blood concentrations in humans have been reported following overdose. The average blood concentration in 12 fatal cases was 9.3 mg/L (range 1.8 to 26).[10] The metabolism of MDA in humans has not been studied, but in other animals MDA is metabolized by O-dealkylation, deamination, and conjugation.[14]

3.6.4 3,4-METHYLENEDIOXYMETHAMPHETAMINE

3,4-Methylenedioxymethamphetamine (MDMA) is a ring substituted derivative of methamphetamine (Figure 3.6.2.2B) that has widespread use as a recreational drug. Self-administration is typically by the oral route in doses of 100 to 150 mg. Helmlin et al.[15] reported a mean peak plasma MDMA concentration of 300 ng/mL at 2.3 h after an oral dose of 1.5 mg/kg to adult subjects.

MDMA is metabolized to MDA with 65% of the dose excreted as parent drug within 3 days. Both MDMA and MDA are hydroxylated to mono- and di-hydroxy derivatives and subsequently conjugated before elimination. The plasma half-life has been reported to be 7.6 h.[10]

REFERENCES

1. *Physicians Desk Reference 1995.* Medical Economics Data, a division of Medical Economics Company, Inc, Montvale, NJ.
2. Baylor, M.R., and Crouch, D.J.: Sympathomimetic Amines:Pharmacology, Toxicology, and Analysis. In-Service Training and Continuing Education AACC/TDM, American Association for Clinical Chemistry, Inc., Washington, D.C. 14 (5): 101-111 (1993).
3. Beckett, A.H., and Rowland, M.: Urinary excretion kinetics of amphetamine in man. *J. Pharm. Pharmacol.* 17: 628-639 (1965).
4. Rowland, M.: Amphetamine blood and urine levels in man. *J. Pharm. Sci.* 58: 508-509 (1969).
5. Matin, S.B., Wan, S.H., and Knight, J.B.: Quantitative determination of enantiomeric compounds. *Biomed. Mass Spec.* 4: 118-121 (1977).
6. Franksson, G, and Anggard, E.: The plasma protein binding of amphetamine, catecholamines and related compounds. *Acta Pharmacol. Toxicol.* 28: 209-214 (1970).
7. Ellison, T., Siegel., M, Silverman, A.G., Okun, R.: Comparative metabolism of d,l H3-amphetamine hydrochloride in tolerant and non tolerant cats. *Proceed. Western Pharmacol. Soc.* 11:75-77 (1968).
8. Dring, L.G., Smith R.L., and Williams, R.T.: The metabolic fate of amphetamine in man and other species. *Biochem. J.* 116: 425-435 (1970).
9. Sever, P.S., Caldwell, J., Dring, L.G., and Williams R.T.: The metabolism of amphetamine in dependent subjects. *Eur. J. Clin. Pharm.* 6: 177-180 (1973).
10. *Disposition of Toxic Drugs and Chemicals in Man* 4th ed. Baselt, R.C., and Cravey, R.H. Chemical Toxicology Institute, Foster City, CA (1995).
11. LeBish, P., Finkle, B.S., and Brackett, J.W., Jr.: Deterrmination of amphetamine, methamphetamine, and related amines in blood and urine by gas chromatography by hydrogen-flame ionization detector. *Clin. Chem.* 16: 195-200 (1970).
12. Sekine, H., and Nakahara, Y. : Abuse of smoking methamphetamine mixed with tobacco: I. Inhalation efficiency and pyrolysis products of methamphetamine. *J. Forens. Sci.* 32 (5): 1271-1280 (1987).
13. Cook, C.E.: Pyrolytic characteristics, pharmacokinetics, and bioavailability of smoked heroin, cocaine, phencyclidine and methamphetamine *NIDA Research Monograph* 99: 6-23. DHHS Pub. No. 1990.
14. Midha, K.K., McGilveray, I.J., Bhatnager, S.P., and Cooper, J.K.: GLC identification and determination of 3,4-methylenedioxyamphetamine in vivo in dog and monkey. *Drug Met. Disp.* 6: 623-630 (1978).
15. Helmlin, H.J., Bracher, K., Salamone, S.J., and Brenneisen, R.: Analysis of 3,4-methylenedioxy-methamphetamine (MDMA) and its metabolites in human plasma and urine. Society of Forensic Toxicologists, Inc., Phoenix, AZ, October 1993 [Abstract].

3.6.5 BARBITURATES

Barbituric acid, 2,4,6-trioxohexahydropyrimidine, was first synthesized in 1864.[1] In 1903 it was marketed for use as an anti-anxiety and sedative hypnotic medication. Barbituric acid is without CNS depressant activity but by substituting an aryl or alkyl group on C-5, anxiolytic and sedative properties may be conferred. Substitution of sulfur on C-2 produces the thiobarbituates which have characteristically greater lipophilicity. Generally, structural changes that increase lipophilicity result in decreased duration of action, decreased latency to onset of action, increased biotransformation, and increased hypnotic potency.[2] Although the use of barbiturates as sedative-hypnotic agents has largely been replaced by the benzodiazepines, the barbiturates maintain an important role as anticonvulsant and anesthetic drugs.

Amanda J. Jenkins and Edward J. Cone

3.6.5.1 Pharmacology

As a class of drugs, barbiturates exert hypnotic, sedative, anxiolytic, anticonvulsant, and anesthetic properties. The clinical use of these drugs is based on their shared properties and also unique properties of individual drugs within this class.[1] As CNS depressants, barbiturates exert effects on excitatory and inhibitory synaptic neurotransmission. Barbiturates are known to decrease excitatory amino acid release and post-synaptic response in experimental animals by blocking the excitatory glutamate response. This may be due to a direct effect on the glutamate sensitive channel, or an indirect effect on calcium channels.[1] The ultra short acting barbiturates used for anaesthesia, such as thiopental, depress excitatory neuronal transmission to a greater extent than the anticonvulsant barbiturates.[3]

Barbiturates also exert an effect on gamma-aminobutyric acid neurotransmission. Barbiturates, such as pentobarbital, enhance the binding of GABA to $GABA_A$ receptors. This effect occurs both in the CNS and the spinal cord. The enhanced action of GABA depresses both normal physiological processes, such as post-synaptic potential evocation, and pathophysiological processes such as seizures.[1] Barbiturates also enlarge GABA-induced chloride currents by extending the time for chloride channel opening.[3] It is important to note that some barbiturates such as 5-(1,3-dimethylbutyl)-5-ethyl barbituric acid (DMBB), promote convulsions by directly depolarizing the neuronal membrane and increasing transmitter release.

3.6.5.2 Absorption

When utilized as sedative-hypnotics, barbiturates are administered orally. They are rapidly and completely absorbed by this route with nearly 100% bioavailability and an onset of action ranging from 10 to 60 min.[3] Sodium salts are more rapidly absorbed than free acids. Intramuscular injections of sodium salts should be made deep into the muscle to prevent pain and tissue damage. Some barbiturates are also administered rectally; barbiturates utilized for the induction and maintenance of anaesthesia (thiopental) or for treating status epilepticus (phenobarbital) are administered intravenously.

Pentobarbital is a short acting barbiturate available for oral, intramuscular, rectal, and intravenous administration. After a single oral dose of 100 mg, peak serum concentrations of 1.2 to 3.1 mg/L were achieved at 0.5 to 2.0 h.[4] These concentrations diminished slowly to an average of 0.3 mg/L at 48 h. When administered intravenously, in a 5 min continuous infusion of 50 mg, plasma concentrations averaged 1.18 mg/L (N=5) at 0.08 h, declining to 0.54 mg/L after 1 h and reaching 0.27 mg/L after 24 h.[5] Repeated intravenous doses of pentobarbital, typically 100 to 200 mg every 30 to 60 min, are administered to reduce intracranial pressure and decrease cerebral oxygen demand in patients with severe head trauma or anoxic brain damage.[6] Doses are adjusted to maintain plasma concentrations between 25 to 40 mg/L.

Amobarbital is a barbituric acid derivative of intermediate duration of action. It is administered orally in doses of 15 to 200 mg as a sedative-hypnotic and in ampules of 65 to 500 mg for intravenous and intramuscular injection for the seizure control.[6] Following a single oral dose of 120 mg, peak serum concentrations averaged 1.8 mg/L after 2 h.[7] After an oral dose of 600 mg distributed over a 3-h period, the peak blood concentration was achieved after 30 min, averaging 8.7 mg/L, with a decline to 4.1 mg/L by 18 h.[6]

Phenobarbital is utilized as a daytime sedative and anticonvulsant. It also induces several cytochrome P-450 isozymes. Compared to other barbiturates, phenobarbital has a low oil/water partition coefficent which results in slow distribution into the brain. It is available for oral, intravenous, or intramuscular administration. Doses for epileptic patients range from 60 to 200 mg per day. After a single oral dose of 30 mg, peak serum concentrations averaged 0.7

mg/L (N=3). Repeated doses over a period of 7 days resulted in an average peak concentration of 8.1 mg/L.[6] Chronic administration of 200 mg per day as anticonvulsant medication resulted in an average blood concentration of 29 mg /L (range= 16-48 mg/L).[9]

3.6.5.3 Distribution

Barbiturates are generally widely distributed throughout the body. The highly lipophilic barbiturates, especially those used to induce anaesthesia, undergo redistribution when administered intravenously. Barbiturates enter less vascular tissues over time, such as muscle and adipose tissue, and this redistribution decreases concentrations in the blood and brain. With drugs such as thiopental, this redistribution results in patients waking up within 5 to 15 minutes after injection of a anaesthetic dose.

Pentobarbital is 65% plasma protein bound with a volume of distribution of 0.5 to 1.0L/kg.[6] After intravenous administration, estimates of the plasma half-life have averaged between 20 to 30 h. Amobarbital is similar to pentobarbital in the degree of plasma protein binding (59%) with a slightly larger volume of distribution (0.9 to 1.4 L/kg). The plasma half-life, however, is dose dependent, with a range of 15 to 40 h.[6] Phenobarbital is approximately 50% plasma protein bound with a volume of distribution of 0.5 to 0.6 L/kg. The plasma half-life averages 4 days with a range of 2 to 6 days.

3.6.5.4 Metabolism and Elimination

Generally, barbiturates are metabolized by oxidation and conjugation in the liver prior to renal excretion. The oxidation of substituents at the C5 position is the most important factor in terminating pharmacological activity.[2] Oxidation of barbiturates results in the formation of alcohols, phenols, ketones, or carboxylic acids with subsequent conjuation with glucuronic acid. Other metabolic transformations include N-hydroxylation, desulfuration of thiobarbiturates to oxybarbiturates, opening of the barbituric acid ring, and N-dealkylation of N-alkylbarbiturates to active metabolites, e.g., mephobarbital to phenobarbital.[2]

Pentobarbital is biotransformed by oxidation of the penultimate carbon of the methyl butyl side-chain to produce a mixture of alcohols, and by N-hydroxylation. The alcoholic metabolites of pentobarbital are pharmacologically inactive. Approximately 86% of a radioactive dose is excreted in the urine in 6 days, about 1% as unchanged drug and up to 73% as the l- and d-diastereoisomers of 3'-hydroxypentobarbital in a 5.4:1 ratio, and up to 15% as N-hydroxypentobarbital.[8] None of these metabolites are eliminated as conjugates.

Amobarbital is extensively metabolized to polar metabolites in a process that is saturable and best described by zero order kinetics at therapeutic doses.[10] Two major metabolites are produced by hydroxylation and N-glycosylation. 3'-Hydroxyamobarbital possesses pharmacological activity. Approximately 92% of a single dose is excreted in the urine with 5% excreted in the feces over a 6-day period. Approximately 2% is excreted unchanged in the urine, 30 to 40% is excreted as free 3'-hydroxyamobarbital, 29% as N-glycosylamobarbital, and 5% as the minor metabolite, 3'-carboxyamobarbital.

Phenobarbital is primarily metabolized via N-glycosylation and by oxidation to form p-hydroxyphenobarbital followed by conjugation with glucuronic acid (Figure 3.6.5). A dihydrohydroxy metabolite has been identified in minor amounts, thought to arise from an epoxide intermediate.[11] Approximately 80% of a single labeled dose is excreted in the urine within 16 days. Unchanged drug accounts for 25 to 33% of the dose, N-glucosyl-phenobarbital for 24 to 30%, and free or conjugated p-hydroxyphenobarbital for 18 to 19%.[12] When administered chronically, approximately 25% of the dose is excreted unchanged in the 24 hour urine with 8% free and 9% conjugated p-hydroxyphenobarbital.

Amanda J. Jenkins and Edward J. Cone

3.6.5. Metabolic pathway of phenobarbital.

REFERENCES

1. Smith, M.C., and Riskin, B. J.: The clinical use of barbiturates in neurological disorders. *Drugs* 42 (3): 365-378 (1991).
2. *Goodman & Gilman's The Pharmacological Basis of Therapeutics*, J.G. Hardman and L.E. Limbird, eds.-in -chief. McCraw-Hill Companies, Inc., NY, NY, 1996.
3. MacDonald, R.L., and Barker, J.L.: Anticonvulsant and anesthetic barbiturates: different postsynaptic action in cultured mammalian neurons. *Neurology* 29: 432-477 (1979).
4. Sun, S., and Chun, A.H.C.: Determination of pentobarbital in serum by electron capture GLC. *J. Pharm. Sci.* 66: 477-480 (1977).
5. Smith, R.B., Dittert, L.W., Griffen, W.O., Jr., and Doluisio, J.T.: Pharmacokinetics of pento-barbital after intravenous and oral administration. *J. Pharm. Biopharm.* 1: 5-16 (1973).
6. Baselt, R. C., and Cravey, R., H.. Disposition of Toxic Drugs and Chemicals in Man. Chemical Toxicology Institute, Foster City, CA, (1995).
7. Tang, B.K., Inaba, T., Endrenyi, L. and Kalow, W.: Amobarbital-a probe of hepatic drug oxidation on man. *Clin. Pharmacol. Ther.* 20: 439-444 (1976).
8. Tang, B.K., Inaba, T., and Kalow, W.: N-hydroxylation of pentobarbital in man. *Drug Met. Disp.* 5:71-74 (1977).
9. Plaa, G.L., and Hine, C.H.: Hydantoin and barbiturate blood levels observed in epileptics. *Arch. Int. Pharm. Ther.* 128: 375-383 (1960).
10. Garrett, E.R., Bres, J., Schnelle, K., and Rolf, L.L., Jr.: Pharmacokinetics of saturably metabo-lized amobarbital. *J. Pharm. Biopharm.* 2:43-103 (1974).
11. Harvey, D.L., Glazener, L., and Stratton, L.: Detection of a 5-(3,4-dihydroxy-1,5-cyclohexadien-1-yl)-metabolite of phenobarbital and mephobarbital in rat, guinea pig and human. *Res. Comm. Chem. Path. Pharm.* 3:557-565 (1972).
12. Tang, B.K., and Kalow, W., and Grey, A.A.: Metabolic fate of phenobarbital in man. *Drug Met. Disp.* 7:315-318 (1979).

3.6.8 BENZODIAZEPINES

The benzodiazepines are among the most commonly encountered prescribed drugs in forensic analysis. It has been estimated that between 10 and 20% of the adult population in the western world has ingested these drugs within any year.[1] They are prescribed for the treatment of anxiety or panic disorder, and as a sleeping aid, anticonvulsant, or muscle relaxant. Abuse of this family of drugs is observed primarily in two forms: persistent therapeutic use, i.e., use longer than generally recommended; and illicit use, in which the drug is self-administered without physician approval or supervision. The former type of abuse is common and typically involves use at low doses compared to the rarely encountered illicit use which may involve high doses and clear indications of acute intoxication and impairment.[2]

3.6.8.1 Pharmacology

Benzodiazepines exert central depressant effects on spinal reflexes, in part mediated by the brainstem reticular system.[3] For example, chlordiazepoxide depresses the duration of electrical after discharge in the limbic system. Most benzodiazepines elevate the seizure threshold and therefore may be used as anticonvulsant medications. Diazepam, clonazepam, and clorazepate may be prescribed for this therapeutic purpose.

Benzodiazepines potentiate the inhibitory effects of gamma-aminobutyric acid (GABA) and neurophysiological studies have identified specific benzodiazepine binding sites in the cerebellum, cerebral cortex, and limbic system.[4] These sites are located in a complex protein macromolecule that includes $GABA_A$ receptors and a chloride channel. Binding of benzodiazepines is modulated by both GABA and chloride. Several benzodiazepine antagonists, such as flumazenil, and inverse agonists (compounds with opposite physiological effects to benzodiazepines), such as ethyl-ß-carboline-3-carboxylate, competitively inhibit the binding of benzodiazepines.

Benzodiazepines are used as hynoptics as they have the ability to increase total sleep time. They demonstrate minimal cardiovascular effects, but do have the ability to increase heart rate and decrease cardiac output. Most CNS depressants, including the benzodiazepines, exhibit the ability to relax skeletal muscles.

3.6.8.2 Absorption

The benzodiazepines are comprised of a large family of lipophilic acids (diazepam pKa = 3.4) with high octanol/water coefficients. They demonstrate a wide range of absorption rates when orally administered. Diazepam is absorbed rapidly, with peak concentrations occurring in 1 hour in adults and as rapidly as 15 to 30 min in children. Following a single oral dose of 10 mg, peak blood diazepam concentrations averaged 148 ng/mL at 1 h, declining to 37 ng/mL by 24 h.[5] Bioavailability is dependent on drug formulation and route of administration, with approximately 100% bioavailability of diazepam when administered orally as tablets or in suspension, decreasing to 50 to 60% when administered intramuscularly or as suppositories. The rapid rate of absorption may be explained in part by the lipophilicity of diazepam. In contrast, less lipophilic benzodiazepines, such as lorazepam, exhibit slower rates of absorption, with an average time to peak blood concentration of 2 h. Prazepam and clorazepate act as prodrugs and are decarboxylated in the stomach to nordiazepam. Consequently, absorption is slowed and a delay occurs to the onset of action of these drugs.

3.6.8.3 Distribution

The benzodiazepines exhibit a two compartment pharmacokinetic model.[6] Central compartment distribution is rapid and a slower distribution occurs into less perfused tissues, such as adipose. One compartment pharmacokinetic models have been described for some benzodiazepines, such as lorazepam.[5] It is obvious that the more lipophilic benzodiazepines distribute more rapidly than less lipophilic drugs. Therefore, after a single dose, diazepam, a highly lipophilic drug, will have a shorter duration of action than lorazepam because it will be rapidly redistributed throughout the body. This may not be easily understood when considering the

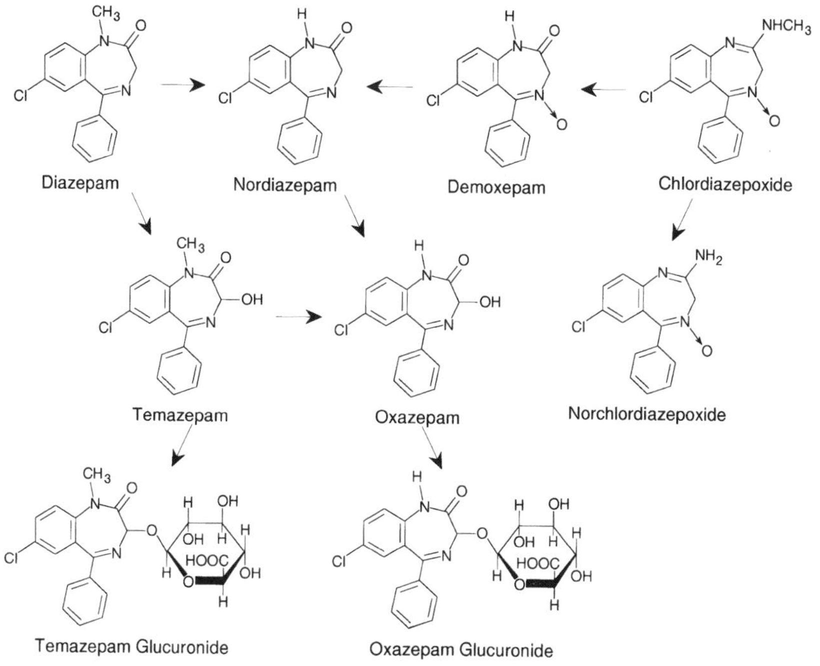

3.6.8 Metabolic pathway of the benzodiazepines.

half-life because diazepam has a longer half-life (approximately 30 h) than lorazepam (12 to 15 h). Therefore, a long elimination half-life does not necessarily imply long duration of action after a single dose.

The majority of benzodiazepines are highly bound to plasma proteins (85 to 95%) with apparent volumes of distribution ranging from 1 to 3 L/kg^3 due to rapid removal from plasma to brain, lungs, and adipose tissue.

3.6.8.4 Metabolism and Elimination

The benzodiazepines are extensively metabolized producing multiple metabolites, many of which share common pathways (Figure 3.6.8). Metabolic processes include hydroxylation, demethylation, and glucuronidation.

Diazepam undergoes N-demethylation to an active metabolite, nordiazepam. Both of these compounds are then hydroxylated to temazepam and oxazepam, respectively. These metabolites are also active, but are usually rapidly excreted and do not accumulate in plasma. Only small amounts of diazepam and nordiazepam are detected in urine, with 33% of a dose excreted as oxazepam glucuronide and another 20% excreted as various conjugates.[5] Oxazepam, the 3-hydroxy metabolite of nordiazepam, is rapidly conjugated with glucuronic acid to form an inactive metabolite. This conjugate accounts for 61% of an oral dose in the 48-h urine. Trace amounts of free drug are detected in the urine and other hydroxylation products account for less than 5% of a dose.[7] Lorazepam is also rapidly conjugated, forming the inactive product, lorazepam glucuronide. This conjugate is not rapidly excreted but may achieve plasma concentrations exceeding the parent drug, with an elimination half life of approximately 16 hours.[5] Approximately 75% of a dose is eliminated in the urine as the conjugate over 5 days. Minor metabolites, such as ring hydroxylation products and quinazoline derivatives, constitute another 14% of the dose. Trace amounts of free drug are found in urine.

Chlordiazepoxide is metabolized to four active metabolites. The drug is N-demethylated to norchlordiazepoxide, then deaminated to form demoxepam. These metabolites demonstrate pharmacological activity similar to the parent drug. Demoxepam is reduced to form nordiazepam, which accumulates in plasma with multiple dosing. Nordiazepam is then hydroxylated to produce oxazepam. Less than 1% of the dose is excreted unchanged in the urine with approximately 6% excreted as demoxepam and the rest as glucuronide conjugates.[8] Temazepam undergoes N-demethylation to form the active metabolite, oxazepam. Both parent and metabolite are subsequently conjugated. An average of 82% of a dose is excreted in urine and 12% in the feces.[5]

Alprazolam, a triazolobenzodiazepine, is also extensively metabolized by oxidation and conjugation. Metabolites include a-hydroxyalprazolam, 4-hydroxyalprazolam, and a,4-dihydroxyalprazolam. The first two metabolites possess approximately 66% and 19% of the pharmacological activity of the parent, respectively. 3-Hydroxy-5-methyltriazolyl, an analogue of chlorobenzophenone, is also formed. Approximately 94% of a dose is excreted within 72 h with 80% excreted in the urine.[9] Flunitrazepam, the N-methyl-2'-fluoro analogue of nitrazepam, undergoes biotransformation via N-demethylation, 3-hydroxylation, and glucuronidation. In addition, the nitro group is reduced to an amine and is subsequently acetylated. Approximately 84% of a labelled dose is excreted in the urine over one week, and 11% is excreted in the feces.[5] Less than 0.5% is excreted unchanged. Norflunitrazepam and 7-aminoflunitrazepam may be detected in plasma for 1 day after a single dose of 2 mg. Triazolam is extensively metabolized by hydroxylation and subsequent conjugation. The major metabolite, 1-hydroxymethyltriazolam, possesses pharmacological activity. Only trace amounts of unchanged drug are excreted in the urine, with approximately 80% of a dose appearing in the urine in 72 h, mainly as glucuronide conjugates.

REFERENCES

1. Balter, M.B., Manheimer, D.I., Mellinger, G.D., and Uhlenhuth, E.H.: A cross-national comparison of anti-anxiety/sedative drug use. *Curr. Med. Res. Opin.* 8 (Supp 4) :5-20 (1984).
2. Busto, U., Bendayan, R., and Sellers, E.M.: Clinical pharmacokinetics of non-opiate abused drugs. *Clin. Pharmacokinet.* 16: 1-26 (1989).
3. *Goodman & Gilman's The Pharmacological Basis of Therapeutics,* J.G. Hardman and L.E. Limbird, eds.-in -chief. McCraw-Hill Companies, Inc., NY, NY. 1996.
4. Potokar, J., and Nutt, D.J.: Anxiolytic potential of benzodiazepines receptor partial agonists. *CNS Drugs.* 1:305-315 (1994).
5. Baselt, R. C., and Cravey, R., H. Disposition of Toxic Drugs and Chemicals in Man. Chemical Toxicology Institute, Foster City, CA, 1995.
6. Bailey,L., Ward., M., and Musa, M.N.: Clinical pharmacokinetics of benzodiazepines. *J. Clin. Pharmacol.* 34: 804-811 (1994).
7. Knowles, J.A., and Ruelius, H.W.: Absorption and excretion of 7-chloro-1,3-dihydro-3-hydroxy-5-phenyl-2H- 1,4-benzodiazepin-2-one (oxazepam) in humans. *Arz. Forsch.* 22: 687-692 (1972).
8. Schwartz, M.A.: Pathways of metabolism of benzodiazepines. In *The Benzodiazepines,* Garattini,S., Mussini, E., and Randall, L.O., eds. Raven Press, New York, p 53-74 (1973).
9. Dawson, G.W., Jue, S.G., and Brogden, R.N.: Alprazolam. A review of its pharmacodynamic properties and efficacy in the treatment of anxiety and depression. *Drugs* 27:132-147 (1984).

3.6.9 COCAINE

Cocaine is a naturally occurring alkaloid obtained from the plant *Erythroxylon coca* L. This plant grows in the Andes region of South America, ideally at elevations between 1,500 to 5,000 ft.[1]

Amanda J. Jenkins and Edward J. Cone

A second closely related species has been identified , *Erythroxylon novogranatense* H., and each species has one variety known as *E. coca var. ipadu* Plowman and *E. coca novogranatense* var. *truxilllense*, respectively. Cocaine may also be chemically synthesized with cold aqueous succinaldehyde and cold aqueous methylamine, methylamine hydrochloride, and the potassium salt of acetone-dicarboxylic acid monomethyl ester.[2]

Cocaine is used medically by otorhinolaryngologists and plastic surgeons as an epinephrine cocaine mixture. Solutions for topical application are typically less than 4% cocaine hydrochloride. In the U.S. cocaine is a scheduled drug under the federal Controlled Substances Act of 1970. Refined cocaine, in the form of the base or hydrochloride salt, is self-administered by many routes, including snorting, smoking, genital application, and by injection.

3.6.9.1 Pharmacology

Cocaine inhibits the presynaptic reuptake of the neurotransmitters norepinehrine, serotonin, and dopamine at synaptic junctions. This results in increased concentrations in the synaptic cleft. Since norepinephrine acts within the sympathetic nervous system, increased sympathetic stimulation is produced. Physiological effects of this stimulation include tachycardia, vasoconstriction, mydriasis, and hyperthermia.[3] Central nervous system stimulation results in increased alertness, diminished appetite, and increased energy. The euphoria or psychological stimulation produced by cocaine is thought to be related to the inhibition of serotonin and dopamine re-uptake. Cocaine also acts as a local anesthetic due to its ability to block sodium channels in neuronal cells.[3]

3.6.9.2 Absorption

Cocaine is rapidly absorbed from mucous membranes and the pulmonary vasculature. However, differences in the rate of appearance of cocaine in blood is dependent on the route of administration. Coca leaves were chewed by native South Americans over 3,000 years ago. Recent studies of the oral route of administration found that chewing powdered coca leaves containing between 17 and 48 mg of cocaine produced peak plasma concentrations of 11 to 149 ng/mL (N=6) at 0.4 to 2 h after administration.[4] In another study, healthy male volunteers were administered cocaine hydrochloride (2 mg/kg) in gelatin capsules. Peak plasma concentrations of 104 to 424 ng/mL were achieved at 50 to 90 min. One of the most common routes of self-administration of cocaine in North America is the intranasal route. Wilkinson et al.[5] found that peak plasma concentrations of cocaine were reached 35 to 90 min after "snorting" but another study using equivalent doses found that peak plasma concentrations were achieved between 120 and 160 min.[6] Intravenous administration of 32-mg cocaine hydrochloride resulted in an average peak plasma concentration of 308 ng/mL at 5 min.[6] Cocaine may also be self-administered by the smoked route in the form of cocaine base, commonly called "crack" or by a process known as "free-basing" in which powdered cocaine hydrochloride is converted to its base form. In a study in which 6 subjects smoked 50 mg of cocaine, the average peak plasma cocaine concentration of 203 ng/mL was achieved at 5 min.[7] The bioavailability of cocaine after smoking depends on several factors including the temperature of volatilization and losses of drug in main and sidestream smoke.

Perez-Reyes et al.[8] estimated that only 32% of a dose of cocaine base in a pipe is inhaled by the smoker. Cone[9] compared the pharmacokinetics and pharmacodynamics of cocaine by the intravenous, intranasal, and smoked routes of administration in the same subjects. Venous plasma cocaine concentrations peaked within 5 min by the intravenous and smoked routes. Estimated peak cocaine concentrations ranged from 98 to 349 ng/mL and 154 to 345 ng/mL after intravenous administration of 25-mg cocaine hydrochloride and 42-mg cocaine base by the smoked route, respectively. After dosing by the intranasal route (32-mg cocaine hydrochloride) estimated peak plasma cocaine concentrations ranged from 40 to 88 ng/mL

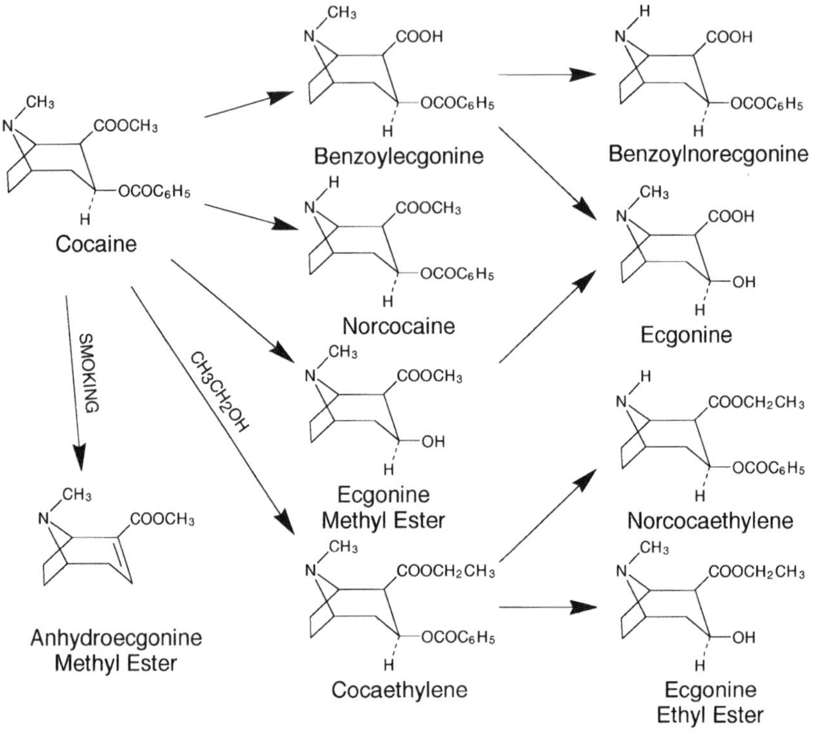

3.6.9 Metabolic pathway of cocaine.

after 0.39 to 0.85 h.[9] In this study, the average bioavailability of cocaine was 70.1% by the smoked route, and 93.7% by the intranasal route.

3.6.9.3 Distribution

After an intravenous dose of radiolabelled cocaine to rats, the highest concentrations were found in the brain, spleen, kidney, and lung after 15 min, with the lowest concentrations in the blood, heart and muscle.[10] Plasma protein binding in humans is approximately 91% at low concentrations.[10] Cocaine binds to the plasma protein, albumin, and also to $\alpha 1$-acid glycoprotein. The steady state volume of distribution is large (1.6 to 2.7 L/kg), reflecting extensive extravascular distribution.[11]

A two-compartment open linear model has been described for the pharmacokinetic profile of cocaine after intravenous administration.[12] The distribution phase after cocaine administration is rapid and the elimination half-life estimated as 31 to 82 min.[12] Cone[9] fitted data to a two-compartment model with bolus input and first order elimination for the intravenous and smoked routes. For the intranasal route, data were fitted to a 2-compartment model with first order absorption and first order elimination. The average elimination half-life ($t_1/2\beta$) was 244 min after intravenous administration, 272 min after smoked administration, and 299 min after intranasal administration.

3.6.9.4 Metabolism

In humans, the principle route of metabolism of cocaine is by hydrolysis of the ester linkages. Plasma and liver cholinesterases produce the inactive metabolite, ecgonine methyl ester (EME) (Figure 3.6.9). The second major metabolite, benzoylecgonine (BE), is formed spontaneously at physiological pH. N-demethylation of benzoylecgonine produces benzoylnorecgonine.

Amanda J. Jenkins and Edward J. Cone

Further metabolism of EME and BE produces ecgonine. Further hydrolysis of cocaine and BE produce minor metabolites, meta- and para- hydroxy- cocaine and -BE. The proportion produced and activity of these metabolites have yet to be completely described.

Cocaine may be N-demethylated by the cytochrome P-450 system to produce an active metabolite, norcocaine. Further breakdown produces N-hydroxynorcocaine and norcocaine nitroxide. Further metabolism produces a highly reactive free radical which is thought to be responsible for the hepatotoxicity observed in cocaine users.[1]

When cocaine is coadministered with ethanol, cocaethylene is formed in the liver by transesterification. This lipophilic compound crosses the blood-brain barrier and is known to contribute to the psychological effects produced by cocaine.[1] When cocaine is smoked, a pyrolysis product, anhydroecgonine methyl ester (AEME), is formed. Therefore, the presence of this compound indicates exposure to smoked cocaine. The pharmacological and toxicological properties of this compound have not been studied.

3.6.9.5 Elimination

Approximately 85 to 90% of a cocaine dose is recovered in the 24-h urine.[13] Unchanged drug accounts for 1 to 9% of the dose depending on urine pH, BE, 35 to 54%, and EME, 32 to 49%. In one study, excretion data was obtained from subjects administered a bolus intravenous injection of cocaine followed by an intravenous infusion, supplying total doses of 253, 444, and 700 mg cocaine.[14] Elimination half-lives averaged 0.8 h, 4.5 h, and 3.1 h, for cocaine, BE, and EME, respectively. After intranasal application of 1.5 mg/kg, urine cocaine concentrations averaged 6.7 mg/L during the first hour, and BE concentrations peaked between 4 to 8 hours at 35 mg/L.[11] Oral ingestion of 25 mg cocaine by a single individual resulted in a peak urine BE concentration of 7.9 mg/L in the 6- to 12-h collection period, with a decline to 0.4 mg/L by 48 h.[15] The minor metabolites, including the p- and m-hydroxy metabolites, and also the pyrolysis product, AEME, have been detected in urine after cocaine administration.[16,17]

REFERENCES

1. Karch, S.: *The Pathology of Drug Abuse.* CRC Press, Boca Raton, FL,1993.
2. Saferstein, R.: *Forensic Science Handbook* Vol. II. Prentice Hall Englewood Cliffs, NJ, 1988.
3. Warner, E. A.: Cocaine Abuse. *Ann. Int. Med.* 119(3): 226-235 (1993).
4. Holmstedt, B., Lindgren, J., Rivier, L., and Plowman, T.: Cocaine in blood of coca chewers. *J. Ethnopharm.* 1: 69-78 (1979).
5. Wilkinson, P., Van Dyke, C., Jatlow, P., Barash, P., and Byck, R.: Intranasal and oral cocaine kinetics. *Clin. Pharmacol. Ther.* 27: 386-394 (1980).
6. Javaid, J.I., Musa, M.N., Fischman, M., Schuster, C.R., and Davis, J.M.: Kinetics of cocaine in humans after intravenous and intranasal administration. *Biopharm. Drug Disp.* 4: 9-18 (1983).
7. Jeffcoat, A.R., Perez-Reyes, and Hill, J.M.: Cocaine disposition in humans after intravenous injection, nasal insufflation (snorting), or smoking. *Drug Met. Disp.* 17:153-159 (1989).
8. Perez-Reyes, M., DiGuiseppi, S., Ondrusek, G., Jeffcoat, A.R., and Cook, C.E.: Free base cocaine smoking. *Clin. Pharmacol. Ther.* 32: 459-465 (1982).
9. Cone, E.J.: Pharmacokinetics and pharmacodynamics of cocaine. *J. Anal. Toxicol.* 19: 459-478 (1995).
10. Busto, U., Bendayan, R., and Sellers, E.M.: Clinical pharmacokinetics of non-opiate abused drugs. *Clin. Pharmacokin.* 16 :1-26 (1989).
11. *Disposition of Toxic Drugs and Chemicals in Man* 4th ed. Baselt, R.C., and Cravey, R.H. Chemical Toxicology Institute, Foster City, CA (1995).
12. Chow, M.J., Ambre, J.J., Ruo, T.I., Atkinson, A.J., and Bowsher, D.J.: Kinetics of cocaine distribution, elimination and chronotropic effects. *Clin. Pharmacol. Ther.* 38:318-324 (1985).

13. Jatlow, P.:Cocaine:Analysis, pharmacokinetics and disposition. *Yale J. Biol. Med.* 61: 105-113 (1988).

14. Ambre, J., Ruo,T.I.,Nelson, J., and Belknap, S.: Urinary excretion of cocaine, benzoylecgonine, and ecgonine methyl ester in humans. *J. Anal. Toxicol.* 12:301-306 (1988).

15. Baselt, R., and Chang, R.: Urinary excretion of cocaine and benzoylecgonine following oral ingestion in a single subject. *J. Anal. Toxicol.* 11:81-82 (1987).

16. Jacob, P.III, Lewis, E.R., Elias-Baker, B.A., and Jones, R.: A pyrolysis product, anhydroecgonine methyl ester (methylecgonidine) is in the urine of cocaine smokers. *J. Anal. Toxicol.* 14: 353-357 (1990).

17. Zhang, J.Y., and Foltz, R.L.: Cocaine metabolism in man: identification of four previously unreported cocaine metabolites in human urine. *J. Anal. Toxicol.* 14: 201-205 (1990).

3.6.10 LYSERGIC ACID DIETHYLAMIDE

Lysergic Acid Diethylamide (LSD) is an indolealkylamine discovered by Albert Hoffman of Sandoz Laboratories in 1943.[1] It may be synthesized from lysergic acid and diethylamine. Lysergic acid, a naturally occurring ergot alkaloid, is present in grain parasitized by the fungus *Claviceps purpurea*. A closely related alkaloid, lysergic acid amide, is present in morning glory seeds and the Hawaiian baby wood rose.[1] In the 1950s, LSD was used as an aid in the treatment of alcoholism, opioid addiction, pyschoneurosis, and sexual disorders, but currently it is classified under Schedule I of the federal Controlled Substances Act with no accepted medical use in the U.S. It is available illicitly as a powder, tablet, or gelatin capsule, or impregnated in sugar cubes, gelatin squares, blotter paper, or postage stamps.

3.6.10.1 Pharmacology

LSD is a potent centrally acting drug. The d-isomer is pharmacologically active while the l-isomer is apparently inactive.[1] Neuropharmacological studies have shown that LSD exerts a selective inhibitory effect on the brain's raphe system by causing a cessation of the spontaneous firing of serotonin containing neurons of the dorsal and median raphe nuclei. In this way, LSD acts as an indirect serotonin antagonist. However, inhibition of raphe firing is not sufficient to explain the psychotomimetic effects of LSD because the compound lisuride is a more potent inhibitor of the raphe system yet does not demonstrate hallucinogenic potential in humans. Therefore, other post-synaptic mechanisms such as action on glutamate or serotonin receptors, may be involved.[2] Also, there is evidence that LSD indirectly exerts effects on the cytoskeleton by reducing the amount of serotonin released by the raphe system.[3] LSD produces sympathomimetic, parasympathomimetic and neuromuscular effects which include mydriasis, lacrimation, tachycardia, and tremor.

3.6.10.2 Absorption

LSD may be self administered orally, nasally, or by parenteral ingestion; however, the oral route is the most common. Doses of 50 to 300 ug are ingested, with a minimum effective dose of 20 to 25 ug. Absorption is rapid and complete regardless of the route of administration. However, food in the stomach slows absorption when ingested. Effects are observed within 5 to 10 min, with psychosis evident after 15 to 20 min. Peak effects have been reported 30 to 90 min after dosing; effects decline after 4 to 6 h.[4] The duration of effects may be 8 to 12 h.

Pharmacokinetic studies in humans are limited with much of the data dating from the 1960s. Following intravenous administration of 2 ug/kg, a peak plasma LSD concentration of 5 ng/mL was observed after 1 h.[1] At 8 h, the plasma concentration had declined to 1 ng/mL.[1]

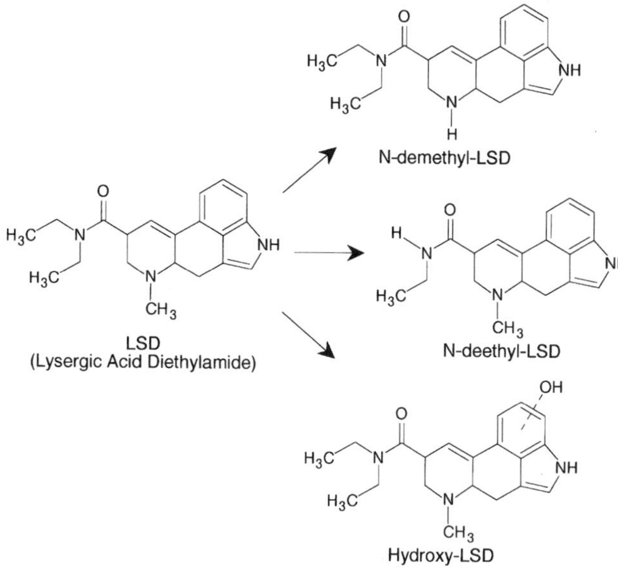

3.6.10 Metabolic pathway of LSD.

3.6.10.3 Distribution

Plasma protein binding of LSD is >80%. As the drug penetrates the CNS, it is concentrated in the visual brain areas, and the limbic and reticular activating systems, correlating with perceived effects. LSD is also found in the liver, spleen and lungs.[4] The volume of distribution is reported to be low at 0.28 L/kg.[1] Wagner et al.[5] described a two compartment open model for LSD with an elimination half life of 3 h.

3.6.10.4 Metabolism and Excretion

The metabolism and elimination of LSD in humans has received limited study. Animal studies demonstrated extensive biotransformation via N-demethylation, N-deethylation, and hydroxylation to inactive metabolites (Figure 3.6.10).[6] In humans, demethylation and aromatic hydroxylation occur to produce N-desmethyl-LSD and 13- and 14-hydroxy-LSD. Hydroxylated metabolites undergo glucuronidation to form water soluble conjugates. Excretion into the bile accounts for approximately 80% of a dose.[4] Concentrations of unchanged drug ranged from 1 to 55 ng/mL in the 24-h urine after ingestion of 200 to 400 ug LSD in humans.[7] LSD or its metabolites were detectable for 34 to 120 h following a 300 ug oral dose in 7 human subjects.[8] The clearance of LSD in humans is unknown.

REFERENCES

1. *Disposition of Toxic Drugs and Chemicals in Man* 4th ed. Baselt, R.C., and Cravey, R.H. Chemical Toxicology Institute, Foster City, CA (1995).
2. Goldberger, B. A. : Lysergic Acid Diethylamide. In-Service Training and Continuing Education AACC/TDM, American Association for Clinical Chemistry, Inc., Washington, D.C. 14 (6): 99-100 (1993).
3. Van Woerkom, A.E.: The major hallucinogens and the central cytoskeleton: an association beyond coincidence? Towards sub-cellular mechanisms in schizophrenia. *Medical Hypotheses* 31:7-15 (1990).

4. Leikin, J.B., Karantz, A.J., Zell-Kanter, M., Barkin, R.L., and Hryhorczuk, D.O.: Clinical features and management of intoxication due to hallucinogenic drugs. *Med. Toxicol. Adverse Drug Exp.* 4 (5): 324-350 (1989).
5. Wagner, J.G., Aghajanian, G.K., and Bing, O.H.L.: Correlation of performance test scores with "tissue concentration" of lysergic acid diethylamide in human subjects. *Clin. Pharmacol. Ther.* 9: 635-638 (1968).
6. Axelrod, J., Brady, R.O., Witkop, B., and Evarts, E.V.: Metabolism of lysergic acid diethylamide. *Nature* 178: 143-144 (1956).
7. Taunton-Rigby, A., Sher, S.E., and Kelley, P.R.: Lysergic acid diethylamide: radioimmunoassay. *Science* 181: 165-166 (1973).
8. Peel, H.W., and Boynton, A.L.: Analysis of LSD in urine using radioimmunoassay- excretion and storage effects. *Can. Soc. For. Sci. J.* 13: 23-28 (1980).

3.6.11 MARIJUANA

The term "marijuana" refers to all parts of the plant *Cannabis sativa* L., whether growing or not: the seeds; resin extracted from any part of such plant; and every compound, salt, derivative or mixture, but does not include the mature stalks, fiber produced from the stalks, or oil or cake prepared from the seeds.[1] *Cannabis sativa* L. is an annual plant that grows in all parts of the world to a height of 16 to 18 ft. Commercially, it is cultivated for hemp production, with the bulk of the plant consisting of stalks with very little foliage, except at the apex. In contrast, the wild plant and those cultivated illegally possess numerous branches as the psychoactive ingredient is concentrated in the leaves and flowering tops. There may be significant differences in the gross appearance of marijuana plants due to climatic and soil conditions, the closeness of other plants during growth, and the origin of the seed. Although the principal marijuana plant is considered to be the *sativa* variety, there are purported to be two other *Cannabis* species, namely, *indica* and *ruderalis*. The latter is not native to the West but is found in the former Soviet Union and surrounding regions.

Over 400 compounds have been identified in *Cannabis sativa* L. with at least 60 identified as substituted monoterpenoids known as cannabinoids. The major pyschoactive constituent of marijuana is Δ-9-tetrahydrocannabinol, commonly referred to as THC. Different parts of the plant contain varying concentrations of THC, with leaves containing <1% to 10% THC by weight, and hashish, a resin prepared from the flowering tops, containing approximately 15% THC. THC may be synthesized using citral and olivetol in boron trifluoride and methylene chloride.[1]

3.6.11.1 Pharmacology

Marijuana is typically self-administered orally or by smoking in doses of 5 to 20 mg.[2] It may produce a variety of pharmacological effects including sedation, euphoria, hallucinations, and temporal distortion. In addition, THC possesses activity at benzodiazepine and opioid receptors and has effects on prostaglandin synthesis and DNA, RNA and protein metabolism.[3] Due to the numerous pharmacological effects demonstrated by THC, a non-specific mechanism of action was considered likely. However, in the late 1980s a specific cannabinoid receptor was identified in the brains of rats.[4] More recently an endogenous cannabinoid ligand was identified.[5] This compound, arachidonylethanolamide, or anandamide, an arachidonic acid derivative, mimicked THC in binding and pharmacodynamic activity studies.

3.6.11.2 Absorption

Marijuana is commonly self-administered by the smoked route by rolling dried marijuana leaves in tobacco paper and smoking as a cigarette. Smoking results in rapid drug delivery from the lungs to the brain. However, loss of drug occurs during the smoking process due to pyrolysis

Amanda J. Jenkins and Edward J. Cone

and side stream smoke. In an *in vitro* study in which loss due to side stream smoke was minimized, Davis et al.[6] reported a 30% loss of THC due to pyrolysis. Sidestream THC losses of 40 to 50% have been reported. Once THC reaches the lungs, it is rapidly absorbed with peak plasma THC concentrations of 100 to 200 ng/mL occurring after 3 to 8 min.[7] Huestis et al.[8] demonstrated that THC is present in blood after the first puff from a marijuana cigarette. Mean +/- SD THC concentrations of 7.0 +/- 8.1 ng/mL and 18.1 +/- 12.0 ng/mL were observed after the first inhalation of low or high dose marijuana cigarettes (1.75%, 3.55%), respectively. These authors also demonstrated that peak concentrations occurred at 9 min after the first puff. Lemberger et al.[9] and Huestis et al.[8] demonstrated that physiological and subjective measures of drug effect occurred simultaneously with the rise in blood THC concentrations.

After oral administration, THC is also well absorbed, being 90 to 95% complete. However, the oral route results in lower peak plasma concentrations at a later time. Perez-Reyes et al.[10] reported a mean peak plasma THC concentration of 6 ng/mL after ingestion of 20 mg. Wall and Perez-Reyes[11] noted that peak plasma THC concentrations occurred 30 min after intravenous administration of 4 to 5 mg, with a mean concentration (N=7) of 62 ng/mL. The bioavailability of THC following smoking was reported to be 18 to 50%. This wide range reflects the large inter- and intra-subject variability that occurs in smoking dynamics. The amount of drug delivered may be varied by altering the number, duration, and spacing of puffs, the length of time the inhalation is held, and the inhalation volume or depth of puff. In addition, minimizing losses due to side and mainstream smoke and optimizing the temperature for drug volatilization will increase the amount of drug available for delivery to the lungs. One facet of smoking which cannot be controlled by the smoker is drug deposition on non- or poorly absorbing surfaces within the body. This is usually a function of drug particle or vapor size. Drug may be deposited in the nasopharyngeal region or the upper bronchial tree. This reduces the amount of drug reaching the lung alveoli where rapid absorption into the blood and subsequent transport to the brain occurs.

Ohlsson et al.[12] compared the bioavailability of THC after intravenous, smoked, and oral administration. Eleven healthy subjects were administered 5 mg intravenously, 19 mg smoked, and 20 mg orally. Plasma concentrations rose rapidly after intravenous administration, reaching 161 to 316 ng/mL at 3 min and declining rapidly thereafter. Peak plasma concentrations also occurred at 3 min after smoking, with lower concentrations of THC ranging from 33 to 118 ng/mL. The plasma concentration time curve after smoking was similar to that obtained after intravenous administration but at lower concentrations. In contrast, low THC concentrations were found after oral administration, with much higher inter subject variability. The authors determined the bioavailability of THC to be 8 to 24% after smoking compared with 4 to 12% after oral ingestion.

3.6.11.3 Distribution

THC is 97 to 99% plasma protein bound with little present in red blood cells. Due its lipophilicity, THC is rapidly distributed into tissues. Highly perfused organs, such as the brain, accumulate THC rapidly after administration, whereas THC distributes more slowly into poorly perfused tissues such as fat. Harvey et al.[13] reported maximum THC concentrations in the brains of mice 30 min after a single intravenous dose. The distribution of THC into various tissues and organs such as brain, liver, heart, kidney, salivary glands, breast milk, fat, and lung, is reflected in the large volume of distribution (4 to 14 L/kg).[2] Following an intravenous dose of THC, Hunt and Jones[14] proposed a four compartment model to describe four tissue composites into which THC distributes. These investigators reported average half-lives of 1 min, 4 min, 1 h, and 19 h to describe these compartments. These authors determined that a "pseudoequilibrium" is achieved between plasma and tissues 6 h after an intravenous dose. Thereafter, THC is slowly eliminated as THC diffuses from tissue to the blood. The terminal

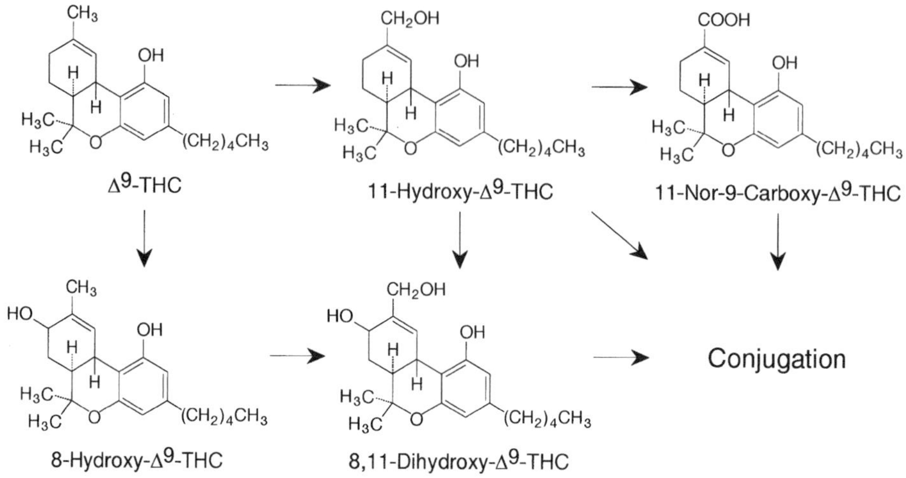

3.7.11 Metabolic pathway of delta-9-THC.

elimination half-life is approximately 1 day but has been reported to be 3 to 13 days in frequent users.[2]

3.6.11.4 Metabolism and Excretion

Metabolism is the major route of elimination of THC from the body as little is excreted unchanged. In humans, over 20 metabolites have been identified in urine and feces.[15] Metabolism in humans involves allylic oxidation, epoxidation, aliphatic oxidation, decarboxylation and conjugation. The two monohydroxy metabolites (Figure 3.6.11) 11-hydroxy (OH)-THC and 8-beta-hydroxy THC are active, with the former exhibiting similar activity and disposition to THC, while the latter is less potent. Plasma concentrations of 11-OH-THC are typically <10% of the THC concentration after marijuana smoking. Two additional hydroxy compounds have been identified, namely, 8-alpha-hydroxy-THC and 8,11-dihydroxy-THC and are believed to be devoid of THC-like activity. Further oxidation of 11-OH-THC produces the inactive metabolite, 11-nor-9-carboxy-THC, or THC-COOH. This metabolite may be conjugated with glucuronic acid and is excreted in substantial amounts in the urine.

The average plasma clearance is 600 to 980 mL/min with a blood clearance of 1.0 to 1.6 L/min. which is close to hepatic blood flow. This indicates that the rate of metabolism of THC is dependent on hepatic blood flow.

Approximately 70% of a dose of THC is excreted in the urine (30%) and feces (40%) within 72 h.[2] Because a significant amount of the metabolites are excreted in the feces, enterohepatic recirculation of THC metabolites may occur. This would also contribute to the slow elimination and hence long plasma half-life of THC. Unchanged THC is present in low amounts in the urine and 11-OH-THC accounts for only 2% of a dose. The remainder of the urinary metabolites consist of conjugates of THC-COOH and unidentified acidic products. Following a single 10-mg dose of THC by the smoked route, urinary THC-COOH concentrations peaked within 16 h of smoking, at levels of 6 to 129 ng/mL (N=10).[16] Passive exposure to marijuana smoke may also produce detectable urinary metabolite concentrations. Cone et al.[17] exposed 5 volunteers to the smoke of 16 marijuana cigarettes (2.8%THC content) for 1 h each day for 6 consecutive days. After the first session, THC-COOH concentrations in urine ranged from 0 to 39 ng/mL. A maximum THC-COOH concentration of 87 ng/mL was detected in 1 subject on Day 4 of the study.

Amanda J. Jenkins and Edward J. Cone

REFERENCES

1. Saferstein R.: *Forensic Science Handbook* Vol. II. Prentice Hall Englewood Cliffs, NJ, 1988.
2. *Disposition of Toxic Drugs and Chemicals in Man* 4th ed. Baselt, R.C., and Cravey, R.H. Chemical Toxicology Institute, Foster City, CA (1995).
3. Huestis, M.A. : Pharmacology and Toxicology of Marijuana. In-Service Training and Continuing Education AACC/TDM, American Association for Clinical Chemistry, Inc., Washington, D.C. 14 (6): 129-142 (1993).
4. Devane, W.A., Dysarz F.A., Johnson, M.R., Melvin, L.S., and Howlett, A.C.: Determination and Characterization of a cannabinoid receptor in rat brain. *Mol. Pharmacol.* 34:605-613 (1988).
5. Devane, W.A., Hanus, L., And Breuer, A.: Isolation and structure of a brain constituent that binds to the cannabinoid receptor. *Science* 258: 1946-1949 (1992).
6. Davis, K.H., McDaniel, I.A., Cadwell, L.W., and Moody, P.L.: Some smoking characteristics of marijuana cigarettes. In: Agurell, S., Dewey, W.L., and Willette, R.E., eds. *Cannabinoids, Chemical, Pharmacologic, and Therapeutic Aspects.* New York:Academic Press, 1984 p97-109.
7. Hollister, L.E., Gillespie, H.K., Ohlsson, A., Lindgren, J.E., Wahlen, A., and Agurell, S.: Do plasma concentrations of delta-9-THC reflect the degree of intoxication? *J. Clin. Pharmacol.* 21:171s-177s (1981).
8. Huestis, M.A., Sampson, A.H., Holicky, B.J., Henningfield, J.E., and Cone, E.J.: Characterization of the absorption phase of marijuana smoking. *Clin. Pharmacol. Ther.* 52 (1): 31-41 (1992).
9. Lemberger, L, Silberstein, S.D., Axelrod, J., and Kopin, I.J.: Marijuana: Studies on the disposition and metabolism of delta-9-tetrahydrocannabinol in man. *Science* 170: 1320-1322 (1970).
10. Perez-Reyes, M, Owens, S.M., and DiGuiseppi,S.: The clinical pharmacology and dynamics of marijuana cigarette smoking. *J. Clin. Pharmacol.* 21: 201-7S (1981).
11. Wall, M.E., and Perez-Reyes, M.: The metabolism of delta-9-tetrahydrocannabinol and related cannabinoids in man. *J. Clin. Pharmacol.* 21: 178s-189s (1981).
12. Ohlsson, A., Lindgren, J.E., Wahlen, A., Agurell, S., Hollister, L.E, and Gillespie, H.K: Plasma delta-9-tetrahydrocannabinol concentrations and clinical effects after oral and intravenous administration and smoking. *Clin. Pharmacol. Ther.* 28: 409-416 (1980).
13. Harvey, D.J.: Chemistry, metabolism and pharmacokinetics of cannabinoids. In *Marijuana in Science and Medicine,* Nahas, G., ed., Raven Press, New York, p 38-108, (1984).
14. Hunt, C.A., and Jones, R.T.: Tolerance and disposition of tetrahydrocannabinol in man. *J. Pharmacol. Exp. Ther.* 215: 35-44 (1980).
15. Widman, M., Halldin, M.M., and Agurell, S.: Metabolism of delta-1-tetrahydrocannabinol in man. In *Pharmacokinetics and Pharmacodynamics of Psychoactive Drugs* ., Barnett, G., and Chiang, C.N., eds. Biomedical Publications, Foster City, CA. p 415-426 (1985).
16. McBurney, L.J., Bobbie, B.A., and Sepp, L.A.: GC/MS and EMIT analyses for delta-9-tetrahydrocannabinol metabolites in plasma and urine of human subjects. *J. Anal. Toxicol.* 10:56-64 (1986).
17. Cone, E.J., Johnson, R.E., and Darwin, W.E.: Passive inhalation of marijuana smoke: urinalysis and room air levels of delta-9-tetrahydrocannabinol. *J. Anal. Toxicol.* 11: 89-96 (1987).

3.6.12 OPIOIDS

The term "opioids" refers to natural, semisynthetic, and synthetic alkaloid derivatives either prepared from opium or synthesized possessing morphine-like activity. This group includes natural compounds (usually denoted "opiates") such as morphine and codeine; and synthetic and semisynthetic compounds such as oxycodone, buprenorphine, fentanyl, methadone, and tramadol. The pharmacological effects and pharmacokinetic parameters of opioid drugs share many characteristics and will be illustrated with the prototypic drug in this class, morphine.

Morphine is a naturally occurring opioid obtained from opium. Opium is itself obtained from the milky exudate from incisions made in the unripe seed capsule of the poppy plant, *Papaver somniferum*. Opium contains 10 to 17% morphine.

Morphine is the recommended and most widely used potent opioid analgesic for chronic pain[1] and therefore a relatively large volume of pharmacokinetic data exists describing clinical studies. The effects of route of administration,[2] renal dysfunction,[3] and anaesthetic technique[4] on morphine pharmacokinetics have been described in addition to its use as an anaesthetic for major abdominal surgery, for sedation and analgesia in premature neonates, for control of pain in children following cardiac surgery,[5] and for the relief of labour pain.[6]

3.6.12.1 Morphine

3.6.12.1.1 Pharmacology

Morphine and other opioids produce their pharmacological effects by binding to opioid receptors located throughout the body. At least four distinct opioid receptor classes have been described within the CNS in addition to several subtypes. Members of each class of opioid receptor have been cloned by cDNA and the predicted amino acid sequences described. Receptor binding studies have elucidated distinct selectivity profiles for four receptor types, namely, μ (mu), κ (kappa), σ (sigma), and δ (delta), whereas functional studies have revealed unique pharmacological profiles.[7] Morphine and other opioids produce analgesia primarily through interaction with mu receptors. In addition, binding with μ-receptors produces respiratory depression, miosis, reduced gastrointestinal activity, and euphoria. Drugs that bind selectively to kappa receptors also produce analgesia but act principally in the spinal cord and result in less intense miosis or respiratory depression compared with mu agonists.[7] Kappa agonists produce spinal analgesia, sedation, and miosis whereas sigma agonists produce dysphoric psychomimetic effects. The effects produced by binding to delta opioid receptors are unclear. The enkephalins are the endogenous ligands for these receptors. Binding to this receptor type also produces spinal and supraspinal analgesia. The highest concentrations of opioid receptors are found in the limbic system, thalamus, hypothalamus, striatum, mid brain, and spinal cord.[8] Morphine possesses greater agonist activity at mu rather than kappa receptors, some activity at delta receptors, and minimal activity at sigma receptors.

At least three mechanisms have been proposed to account for opioid-induced analgesia. Opioid receptors on the terminals of primary afferent nerves mediate inhibition of the release of neurotransmitters. Morphine also exerts postsynaptic inhibitory actions on interneurons and on the output neurons of the spinothalmic tract that transports nociceptive information to higher centers in the brain.[7] Morphine causes constriction of the pupil by an excitatory action on the parasympathetic nerve innervating the pupil. Morphine also causes respiratory depression, due to a direct effect on the respiratory centers of the brainstem by reducing the responsiveness to carbon dioxide. Opioids depress the pontine and medullary centers involved in regulating the rhythmicity of breathing.[7] Nausea and vomiting caused by morphine and other opioids is due to direct stimulation of the chemoreceptor trigger zone in the medulla oblongata.

3.6.12.1.2 Absorption

Morphine may be administered orally, by subcutaneous or intramuscular injection, or by intravenous or epidural dosing or continuous infusion. The oral bioavailability of morphine is low due to extensive first pass hepatic metabolism. After epidural administration, morphine is completely absorbed with 7% of the dose reaching the cerebrospinal fluid and spinal cord.[9] Peak concentrations of morphine in plasma were achieved approximately 30 min after a single dose. After continuous epidural infusion of 0.75 mg/h, plasma concentrations of 5 ng/mL were consistently measured.[9]

Amanda J. Jenkins and Edward J. Cone

Intermittent intravenous administration of morphine may result in wide variations in morphine concentrations. For example, variations of 200 ng/mL may be observed after the administration of 5 mg every 4 h (peak concentrations of approximately 200 ng/mL within minutes of administration declining to less than 20 ng/mL by 1 h).[9] However, if morphine is infused at a rate of 1.5 mg/h, then plasma concentrations are maintained at approximately 20 ng/mL after 1 h of accumulation. Assuming pain relief is achieved when plasma morphine concentrations are in the range 15 to 50 ng/mL, effective pain relief would be achieved by continuous intravenous infusion rather than intermittent intravenous dosing in the scenarios outlined above. These actions of morphine are explained by the pharmacokinetic characteristics such as a small central compartment volume, a large volume of distribution, and a rapid clearance.

A single intravenous dose of 0.125 mg/kg of morphine to adults resulted in a peak serum concentration at 0.5 min of 440 ng/mL, declining to 20 ng/mL by 2 h.[10] Intramuscular injection of the same dose resulted in an average peak serum concentration of 70 ng/mL, 10 to 20 min after administration, declining to 20 ng/mL after 4 h. Epidural administration of a single dose of 0.1 mg/kg of morphine to surgical patients produced an average peak serum concentration of 80 ng/mL after 10 min, declining to approximately 10 ng/mL after 4 h (N=9).[11] The oral bioavailability of morphine is approximately 38% with a reported range of 15 to 64%.[12] Oral doses of 20 to 30 mg of morphine administered to adult terminally ill cancer patients maintained morphine serum concentrations above 20 ng/mL for 4 to 6 h.[13]

3.6.12.1.3 Distribution

The volume of distribution of morphine ranges from 2 to 5 L/kg in humans.[12] Plasma protein binding of morphine in healthy humans ranges from 12 to 35% and appears to be independent of concentration over approximately a 1000-fold range although a slight decrease (24 to 20% bound) was observed when the concentration was increased from therapeutic by 60-fold.[14] Morphine is bound mainly to albumin with approximately 5% bound to γ-globulin and 5% to α1-acid glycoprotein. The blood/plasma concentration ratio for morphine in healthy humans averages 1.02.[12] This ratio was found to be consistent in the concentration range 35-140 nM.[14] The plasma half-life averaged 1.8 h and 2.9 h in female and male surgical patients, respectively.[15] Aitkenhead et al.[10] found no increase in half-life in patients with renal failure but it is doubled in cirrhotic patients.[16]

Morphine is relatively hydrophilic and therefore distributes slowly into tissues and does not persist. In the adult, small amounts cross the blood-brain barrier, with more lipophilic opioids such as heroin and methadone crossing rapidly.[7] Morphine administered epidurally or directly into the spinal canal is effective in producing prolonged analgesia. However, there is rostral spread of the drug in the spinal fluid which may result in respiratory depression and other adverse effects later.

3.6.12.1.4 Metabolism and Excretion

The major pathway for the metabolism of morphine is by conjugation with glucuronic acid (Figure 3.6.12.1). The free phenolic hydroxyl group undergoes glucuronidation to produce morphine-3-glucuronide, a highly water soluble inactive metabolite. The metabolite, morphine-6-glucuronide is pharmacologically active and when administered systemically was found to be twice as potent as morphine. However, when administered intrathecally or intracerebroventricularly to rodents, morphine 6-glucuronide was approximately 100-fold more potent than the parent compound. Higher blood concentrations of this metabolite are measured in patients undergoing chronic oral dosing, suggesting a significant role in producing analgesia in such individuals.

3.6.12.1. Metabolic pathway of heroin and morphine.

Approximately 5% of a dose of morphine is *N*-demethylated to normorphine. This metabolite is also pharmacologically active, although its relative potency is less than morphine and due to the low concentrations typically measured after morphine administration, may not contribute significantly to the overall pharmacological effects.

Metabolism occurs primarily in the liver with 90% of a dose excreted in the urine and 10% in the feces. There is extensive enterohepatic circulation of both conjugated and unconjugated morphine. Approximately 87% of a dose of morphine is excreted in the 72-h urine, 75% as morphine-3-glucuronide, 10% as free morphine, and the remainder as morphine-6-glucuronide, morphine-3-sulfate, normorphine, and conjugates. The clearance of morphine was found to vary between 1.2 to 1.9 L/min/70kg in several human studies.[14]

3.6.12.2 Heroin

Heroin, or 3,6-diacetylmorphine, was first synthesized from morphine by C.R. Wright in 1874. The Bayer Company of Germany subsequently marketed the drug as an analgesic in 1898. Currently in the U.S. heroin has no accepted medical use and is placed in Schedule I of the federal Controlled Substances Act of 1970.

Heroin is typically self-administered by intramuscular or intravenous injection and also by nasal insufflation ("snorting") or smoking. Peak heroin concentrations in blood are achieved within 1 to 5 min after intravenous and smoked administration[17] and within 5 min after intranasal and intramuscular administration.[18] In a study in which the method of smoked heroin delivery was optimized to reduce loses due to pyrolysis and sidestream smoke, Jenkins et al.[17] reported similar pharmacokinetic profiles for the smoked and intravenous routes. Mean elimination half-lives for two subjects across three doses of heroin were 3.3 minnd 3.6 min, after smoked and intravenous administration, respectively. The mean residence time of heroin was less than 10 min after all doses by both routes. Cone et al.[18] reported that the pharmaco-

Amanda J. Jenkins and Edward J. Cone

kinetic profile of intranasal heroin was equivalent to that for the intramuscular route. Mean elimination half-lives (hours plus or minus SD) were determined to be 0.09 ± 0.05, 0.07 ± 0.02, and 0.13 ± 0.07, following intranasal administration of 6 mg and 12 mg, and intramuscular administration of 6 mg of heroin, respectively. The relative potency of intranasal heroin was estimated to be approximately one-half that of intramuscular administration.

It is known from *in vitro* studies that heroin is rapidly deacetylated to an active metabolite, 6-acetylmorphine, which is then hydrolyzed to morphine (Figure 3.6.12.1). Spontaneous hydrolysis to 6-acetylmorphine may occur under various conditions. Heroin is susceptible to base catalyzed hydrolysis but will also hydrolyze in the presence of protic compounds such as ethanol, methanol, and aqueous media.

The addition of two acetyl-ester groups to the morphine molecule produces a more lipophilic compound. Because heroin exhibits little affinity to opiate receptors in the mammalian brain, it has been postulated that it acts as a prodrug, to facilitate the entry of the active, but less lipophilic, compounds 6-acetylmorphine and morphine.

Following intravenous infusion of 70 mg of heroin to human volunteers, 45% of the dose was recovered in urine after 40 h. Over 38% was recovered as conjugated morphine, approximately 4% as free morphine, 1% as 6-acetylmorphine and 0.1% as heroin.[12] Urinary elimination half-lives of 0.6, 4.4, and 7.9 hours were reported for 6-acetylmorphine, morphine, and conjugated morphine, respectively, after administration of 6 mg of heroin by the intramuscular route.[19]

3.6.12.3 Methadone

Methadone is a synthetic opioid, clinically available in the U.S. since 1947.[12] It exists in the dextro- and levo-rotatory forms with the levo-isoform possessing approximately 8 to 50 times more pharmacological activity.[20] Methadone acts on the central nervous and cardiovascular systems producing respiratory and circulatory depression. Methadone also produces miosis and increases the tone of smooth muscle in the lower gastrintestinal tract while decreasing the amplitude of contractions. It is used clinically for the treatment of severe pain and in maintenance programs for morphine and heroin addicts.[12]

Methadone is typically administered orally, with peak blood concentrations occurring after 4 h. Inturrisi and Verebely[21] reported a peak plasma concentration of 75 ng/mL at 4 h after a single 15-mg oral dose. Concentrations declined slowly, with a half-life of 15 h, reaching 30 ng/mL by 24 h. A single 10-mg intravenous dose of methadone resulted in initial plasma concentrations of 500 ng/mL declining to 50 ng/mL after 1 to 2 h.[22] Peak plasma concentrations (mean = 830 ng/mL) after 4 h were also observed with chronic oral administration of 100 to 200 mg/day.[21] Concentrations of methadone reach a maximum in brain tissue approximately 1 to 2 h after an oral dose.[20] Methadone is highly plasma protein bound (87%) with 70% bound to albumin.[20] Methadone distributes rapidly to tissues, especially the lungs, liver, kidneys, and spleen. The volume of distribution is 4-5 L/kg.[12]

Methadone is metabolized in the liver by *N*-demethylation to produce unstable metabolites which undergo cyclization to form the metabolites, 2-ethylidene-1,5-dimethyl-3,3-diphenylpyrrolidine (EDDP) and 2-ethyl-5-methyl-3,3-diphenylpyrroline (EMDP) (Figure 3.6.12.3). These metabolites and the parent drug undergo para-hydroxylation with subsequent conjugation with glucuronic acid. All three are excreted in the bile and are the major excretory products measured in the urine after methadone administration. Minor metabolites, methadol, and normethadol exhibit pharmacological activity similar to methadone but are produced in low concentrations.

Large individual variations in the urine excretion of methadone are observed depending on urine volume and pH, the dose and rate of metabolism. Acidifciation of the urine may increase the urinary output of methadone from 5 to 22%.[20] Typically, following a 5-mg oral dose,

3.6.12.3. Metabolic pathway of methadone.

methadone and EDDP account for 5% of the dose in the 24-h urine. In those individuals on maintenance therapy, methadone may account for 5 to 50% of the dose in the 24-h urine and EDDP may account for 3 to 25% of the dose.

REFERENCES

1. Hoskin, P.J., and Hanks, G.W: Morphine: pharmacokinetics and clinical practice. *Br. J. Cancer* 62: 705-707 (1990).
2. Davis, T., Miser, A.W., Loprinzi, C.L., Kaur, J.S., Burnham, N.L., Dose, A.M., and Ames, M.M.: Comparative morphine pharmacokinetics following sublingual, intramuscular, and oral administration in patients with cancer. *The Hopsice J.* 9 (1): 85-90 (1993).
3. Davies, G., Kingswood, C., and Street, M.: Pharmacokinetics of opioids in renal dysfunction. *Clin. Pharmacokinet.* 31 (6): 410-422 (1996).
4. Shelly, M.P., Taylor, B.L., Quinn, K.G., and Park, G.R.: The influence of anaesthetic technique on metabolism of oral morphine. *Anaesthesia* 43: 733-737 (1988).
5. Dagan, O., Klein, J., Bohn, D., Barker, G., and Koren., G.: Morphine pharmacokinetics in children following cardiac surgery: effects of disease and inotropic support. *J. Cardiothorac. Vas. Anesth.* 7 (4): 396-398 (1993).
6. Gerdin, E., Salmonson, T., Lindberg, B., and Rane, A.: Maternal kinetics of morphine during labour. *J. Perinat. Med.* 18: 479-487 (1990).
7. *Goodman & Gilman's The Pharmacological Basis of Therapeutics,* J.G. Hardman and L.E. Limbird, eds.-in -chief. McCraw-Hill Companies, Inc., NY, NY, 1996.
8. Leikin, J.B., Krantz, A.J., Zell-Kanter, M., Barkin, R.L., and Hryhorczuk, D.O.: Clinical features and management of intoxication due to hallucinogenic drugs. *Med. Toxicol. Adverse Drug Exp.* 4 (5): 324-350 (1989).
9. Warner, A., and Denson, D.D. : New approaches to pain control: The team approach. In-Service Training and Continuing Education AACC/TDM, American Association for Clinical Chemistry, Inc., Washington, D.C. 11(5): 5-19 (1989).
10. Aitkenhead, A.R., Vater, M., Achola, K., et al. Pharmacokinetics of single dose i.v. morphine in normal volunteers and patients with end-stage renal failure. *Brit. J. Anaesth.* 56:813-818 (1984).
11. Drost, R.H., Ionescu, T.I., van Rossum, J.M., and Maes, R.A.: Pharmacokinetics of morphine after epidural administration in man. *Arz. Forsch.* 36: 1096-1100 (1996).
12. *Disposition of Toxic Drugs and Chemicals in Man* 4th ed. Baselt, R.C., and Cravey, R.H. Chemical Toxicology Institute, Foster City, CA (1995).

Amanda J. Jenkins and Edward J. Cone

13. Sawe, J., Dahlstrom, B., Paalzow, L., and Rane, A.: Morphine kinetics in cancer patients. *Clin. Pharmacol. Ther.* 30: 629-635 (1981).

14. Milne, R.W., Nation, R.L., and Somogyi, A.A: The disposition of morphine and its 3- and 6-glucuronide metabolites in humans and animals, and the importance of the metabolites to the pharmacological effects of morphine. *Drug Metab. Rev.* 28 (3): 345-472 (1996).

15. Rigg, J.R.A., Browne, R.A., and Daavis, C.: Variation in the disposition of morphine after I.M. administration in surgical patients. *Brit. J. Anaesth.* 50: 1125-1130 (1978).

16. Mazoit, J.X., Sandouk, P., Zetlauoi, P., and Scherrmann, J.M.: Pharmacokinetics of unchanged morphine in normal and cirrhotic patients. *Anesth. Anal.* 66: 293-298 (1987).

17. Jenkins, A.J., Keenan, R.M., Henningfield, J.E., and Cone, E.J.: Pharmacokinetics and pharmacodynamics of smoked heroin. *J. Anal. Toxicol.* 18: 317-330 (1994).

18. Cone, E.J., Holicky, B.A., Grant, T.M., Darwin, W.D., and Goldberger, B.A.: Pharmacokinetics and pharmacodynamics of intranasal "snorted" heroin. *J. Anal. Toxicol.* 17: 327-337 (1993).

19. Cone, E.J., Welch, P., Mitchell, J.M., and Paul, B.P.: Forensic drug testing for opiates: I. *J. Anal. Toxicol.* 15: 1-7 (1991).

20. Chamberlain, R.T. : Methadone. In-Service Training and Continuing Education AACC/ TDM, American Association for Clinical Chemistry, Inc., Washington, D.C.10 (9): 5-17 (1989).

21. Inturrisi, C, and Verebely, K.: Disposition of methadone in man after a single oral dose. *Clin. Pharmacol. Ther.* 13: 923-930 (1972).

22. Inturrisi, C., Colburn, W.A.,and Kaiko, R.F.: Pharmacokinetics and pharmacodynamics of methadone in patients with chronic pain. *Clin. Pharmacol. Ther.* 41: 392-401 (1987).

3.6.13 PHENCYCLIDINE

Phencyclidine, PCP, or 1-(1-phenylcyclohexyl) piperidine is an arylcyclohexamine with structural similarities to ketamine. It is a lipophilic weak base with a pKa of 8.5. Phencyclidine was originally synthesized and marketed under the trade name Sernyl®, by Parke-Davis for use as an intravenously administered anaesthetic agent in humans. Distribution began in 1963 but was discontinued in 1965 due to a high incidence (10 to 20%) of post-operative delirium and psychoses. However, its use continued as a veterinary tranquilizer for large animals until 1978, when all manufacture was prohibited and PCP was placed in Schedule II of the federal Controlled Substances Act (1970).

Illicit use of PCP as a hallucinogenic agent was first reported in San Francisco in 1967.[1] It was first abused in oral form but then gained popularity in the smoked form as this mode of drug delivery allowed better control over dose. Because illicit synthesis is relatively easy and inexpensive, abuse became widespread in the 1970s and early 1980s. Today, use of PCP tends to be highly regionalized and located in certain areas of the U.S., notably, the Washington D.C./Baltimore corridor, New York City, and Los Angeles.[2]

3.6.13.1 Pharmacology

Phencyclidine binds with high affinity to sites located in the cortex and limbic structures of the brain. Binding results in blockade of N-methyl-D-aspartic acid (NMDA)- type glutamate receptors. The actions of glutamate and aspartate at the NMDA receptor allow movement of cations across the cell membrane. PCP exerts its action by binding to the glutamate receptor, thus preventing the flux of cations.[3] PCP is also known to exert effects on catecholamines, serotonin, gamma-hydroxy butyric acid, and acetylcholine neurotransmitter release, but its role is incompletely defined. Due to its action on several systems, the physiological and behavioral effects of PCP are varied and depend on not only the dose, but the route of administration and user's previous experience.

3.6.13.2 Absorption

Phencyclidine is typically self-administered by the oral, intravenous, or smoked routes. After oral administration to healthy human volunteers, the bioavailability was found to vary between 50 to 90%.[4] In this study, peak plasma concentrations were achieved after 1.5 h and appeared to correlate with the time to reach maximum pharmacological effects. However, because there have been no comprehensive clinical controlled studies of phencyclidine, a correlation between PCP blood concentrations and pharmacological effects has not been definitively documented. Maximum serum PCP concentrations ranged between 2.7 and 2.9 ng/mL after 1 mg PCP administered orally.[4]

PCP is commonly self-administered by the smoked route. Liquid PCP is soaked in parsley flakes and rolled as a cigarette; powdered PCP is sprinkled over a marijuana joint or the end of a tobacco cigarette is dipped in liquid PCP and then smoked. Cook et al.[5] studied the pharmacokinetic properties of PCP deposited on parsley cigarettes. Upon smoking, PCP is partially volatilized to 1-phenylcyclohexene (PC). These investigators found that $69 \pm 5\%$ of the PCP available in the cigarette was inhaled, 39% as PCP and 30% as PC.[5] The pharmacological and toxicological properties of PC have not been established. Peak plasma concentrations of PCP were reached within 5 to 20 min. In 80% of the subjects, a second peak was observed in plasma PCP concentrations, occurring 1 to 3 h after the end of smoking. This may have been due to trapping of PCP in the mouth, where it could be released and absorbed by the G.I. tract or, alternatively, it could be due to absorption by the lung and bronchial tissue with slower release into the systemic circulation.[6] Long-term users of PCP report feeling the effects of the drug within 2 to 5 min of smoking, with a peak effect after 15 to 30 min and residual effects for 4 to 6 h.[7]

3.6.13.3 Distribution

Plasma protein binding of PCP in healthy individuals remains relatively constant between 60 to 70% over the concentration range of 0.007 to 5000 ng/mL.[5] PCP binding to serum albumin accounts for only 24% of the binding[6] which suggests binding to another protein may occur to a significant extent. When studied *in vitro*, α_1-Acid glycoprotein was also found to bind phencyclidine.[6] The volume of distribution has been shown to be large, between 5.3 to 7.5 L/kg,[8] providing evidence of extensive distribution to extravascular tissues.

Wall et al.[9] administered 1.3 ug/kg of 3H-PCP intravenously to human volunteers and collected blood samples for 72 h. Data from this study suggested a two compartment pharmacokinetic model with a plasma half life for PCP of 7 to 16 h. Domino et al.[10] further analyzed the data from Wall et al. and developed a more complex three compartment PK model. The reported half-lives for each compartment were 5.5 min, 4.6 h, and 22 h. The specific tissues and organs represented by the multicompartment model were not identified. Half-lives of greater than 3 days have been reported in cases of PCP overdose.[11]

3.6.13.4 Metabolism and Excretion

PCP is metabolized by the liver through oxidative hydroxylation. Unchanged PCP, two monohydroxylated, and one dihydroxylated metabolite have been identified in urine after oral and intravenous administration.[12] The monohydroxlyated metabolites have been identiifed as 4-phenyl-4-(1-piperidinyl)-cyclohexanol (PPC) and 1-(1-phenylcyclohexyl)-4-hydroxypiperidine (PCHP). These metabolites are pharmacologically inactive in humans and PPC is present in both cis- and trans-isomeric forms. The cis/trans ratio was found to be 1:1.4 in human urine.[5] The dihydroxylated metabolite was identified as 4-(4-hydroxypiperidino)-4-phenylcyclohexanol (HPPC). These metabolites are present in urine as glucuronide conjugates in addition to their unconjugated forms.[8]

Amanda J. Jenkins and Edward J. Cone

Approximately 30 to 50% of a labeled intravenous dose is excreted over a 72-h period in urine as unchanged drug (19.4%) and 80.6% as polar metabolites, mainly 4-phenyl-4-(1-piperidinyl) cyclohexanol.[5] Only 2% of a dose is excreted in feces.[10] After 10 days, an average of 77% of an intravenous dose is found in the feces and urine.[9] Green et al.[12] reported urine PCP concentrations between 40 to 3400 ng/mL in ambulatory users.

Urine pH is an important determinant of renal elimination of PCP. In a study in which urine pH was uncontrolled (6.0 to 7.5), the average total clearance of PCP was 22.8 ± 4.8 L/h after intravenous administration.[4] In the same study, renal clearance was 1.98 ± 0.48 L/h. When the urine was made alkaline, the renal clearance of PCP was found to decrease to 0.3 ± 0.18 L/h. If the urine was acidified (pH 6.1) in the same subjects, renal clearance increased to 2.4 ± 0.78 L/h.[13] Aronow et al.[14] determined that if the urine pH was decreased to < 5.0, renal clearance increases significantly to 8.04 ± 1.56 L/h. There is disagreement about the utility of urine acidification in the treatment of PCP overdose, even though excretion may be increased by as much as 100-fold.[15] It should be noted that acidification may increase the risk of metabolic complications.[16]

REFERENCES

1. Nicholl, A. M. :The non therapeutic use of pyschoactive drugs. *N. Eng. J. Med.* 308:925-933 (1983).
2. Epidemiologic trends in drug abuse, data from the Drug Abuse Early Warning Network, Vol. 11. Rockville, MD: Dept. Health and Human Services, National Institute on Drug Abuse, June (1994).
3. Stone, J. A. : Phencyclidine. In-Service Training and Continuing Education AACC/TDM, American Association for Clinical Chemistry, Inc., Washington, D.C. 17 (8): 199-202 (1996).
4. Cook, C.E., Brine, D.R., Jeffcoat, A.R., Hill, J.M., and Wall, M.E.: Phencyclidine disposition after intravenous and oral doses. *Clin. Pharmacol. Ther.* 31: 625-634 (1982).
5. Cook, C.E., Brine, D.R., Quin, G.D., Perez-Reyes, M., and DiGuiseppi, S.R.: Phencyclidine and phenylcyclohexene disposition after smoking phencyclidine. *Clin. Pharmacol. Ther.* 31: 635-641 (1982).
6. Busto, U., Bendayan, R., and Sellers, E.M.: Clinical pharmacokinetics of non-opiate abused drugs. *Clin. Pharmacokin.* 16 :1-26 (1989).
7. Perry, D.C. : PCP revisited. *Clin. Toxicol.* 9: 339-348 (1976).
8. *Disposition of Toxic Drugs and Chemicals in Man* 4th ed. Baselt, R.C., and Cravey, R.H. Chemical Toxicology Institute, Foster City, CA (1995).
9. Wall, M.E., Brine, D.R., Jeffcoat, R.A., and Cook, C.E.: Phencyclidine metabolism and disposition in man following a 100 ug intravenous dose. *Res. Commun. Substance Abuse* 2:161-172 (1981).
10. Domino, S.E., Domino, L.E., and Domino, E.F.: Comparison of two and three compartment models of phencyclidine in man. *Subst. Alcohol Actions Misuse* 2: 205-211 (1982).
11. Done, A.K., Aronow, R., and Miceli, J.N.: The pharmacokinetics of phencyclidine in overdosage and its treatment. National Institute on Drug Abuse, Rockville, MD, *Res. Monograph* 21:210-217 (1978).
12. Green, D.E., Chao, F.C., Loeffler, K.O., and Lemon, R.: Phencyclidine blood levels by probability based matching GC/MS. *Proc. West. Pharm. Soc.* 19: 355-361 (1976).
13. Perez-Reyes, M., DiGuiseppi, S., Brine, D.R., Smith, H., and Cook, C.E.: Urine pH and phencyclidine excretion. *Clin. Pharmacol. Ther.* 32: 635-641 (1982).
14. Aronow, R., Miceli, J.N., and Done, A.K.: Clinical observations during phencyclidine intoxication and treatment based on ion-trapping. National Institute on Drug Abuse, Rockville, MD., *Res. Monograph Ser.* 21: 218-228 (1978).
15. Milhorn, H.T.: Diagnosis and management of phencyclidine intoxication. *Am. Fam. Physic.* 43: 1293-1301 (1991).
16. Ellenhorn, M.J., and Barceloux, D.G.: *Medical Toxicology, Diagnosis and Treatment of Human Poisoning.* New York: Elsevier, :764-777 (1988).

CHAPTER 4
PHARMACODYNAMICS

Edited by Stephen J. Heishman, Ph.D.

Clinical Pharmacology Branch, Division of Intramural Research, National Institute on Drug Abuse, National Institutes of Health, Baltimore, Maryland

Department of Psychiatry and Behavioral Sciences, Johns Hopkins University School of Medicine, Baltimore, Maryland

TABLE OF CONTENTS

Stephen J. Heishman

4.1 EFFECTS OF ABUSED DRUGS ON HUMAN PERFORMANCE: LABORATORY ASSESSMENT

4.1.1 EFFECTS OF DRUGS ON PERFORMANCE

The experimental investigation of the effects of psychoactive drugs on human performance has enjoyed a long history. Some of the earliest university laboratories in departments of psychology and physiology were dedicated to the study of caffeine, nicotine, and other drugs.[1,2] Advances in technology and methodology have resulted in a comprehensive body of research, and for most drugs of abuse, we have a general idea of their effects on performance. For example, it is well known that psychomotor stimulants, such as *d*-amphetamine, increase one's ability to sustain attention over prolonged periods of time when performing monotonous tasks.[3,4] However, numerous inconsistencies exist in the literature concerning the effects of certain drugs on various aspects of human performance, and few studies take into account nonpharmacological variables that, in addition to the drug dose, ultimately determine behavioral effects of psychoactive drugs.[5,6]

The purpose of this chapter is to provide an overview of the effects of abused drugs on human performance as assessed in the laboratory. This will not be an exhaustive review of the literature. Rather, I take as my starting point several general overviews[7-9] and drug-specific reviews[3,4,6,10-16] and update these findings with recent studies. The classes of drugs included in this review are: (1) psychomotor stimulants, including *d*-amphetamine and cocaine; (2) nicotine and tobacco; (3) sedative-hypnotics, focusing on benzodiazepines as the prototypical sedative-hypnotic in use today (effects of ethanol are discussed elsewhere in this volume); (4) opioid analgesics and anesthetics; and (5) marijuana. Within each drug category, results will be organized into sensory, motor, attentional, and cognitive abilities. Such a classification scheme allows a focus on behavior compared with, for example, a classification based on specific performance tests.

Because of the widespread use of psychoactive drugs throughout society, employers have become increasingly concerned about drugs in the workplace and the potential for impaired job performance or onsite drug-related accidents. Following the summary of drug effects on performance, applications of the methodology and knowledge of human performance testing in the laboratory setting to that of the workplace will be discussed. Specifically, several weaknesses and strengths of laboratory research methodology as it applies to performance

Stephen J. Heishman

assessment in the workplace will be presented. The chapter concludes with a discussion of some gaps in the research literature and recommendations for future research.

4.1.1.1 Psychomotor Stimulants: Cocaine and d-Amphetamine

The psychomotor stimulants, cocaine and *d*-amphetamine, will be considered together because they share a similar psychopharmacological profile.[17,18] Low to moderate doses of both drugs given acutely to nontolerant, nonanxious subjects produce increases in positive mood (euphoria), energy, and alertness. Experienced cocaine users were unable to distinguish between intravenous (IV) cocaine and *d*-amphetamine,[19] and cross-tolerance between cocaine and *d*-amphetamine with respect to their anorectic effect has been demonstrated.[20] Additionally, the toxic psychosis observed after days or weeks of continued use of both psychostimulants is very similar. The fully developed toxic syndrome, characterized by vivid auditory and visual hallucinations, paranoid delusions, and disordered thinking, is often indistinguishable from paranoid schizophrenia.[18] Derlet et al.[21] reported that the most prominent presenting symptoms seen in 127 cases of amphetamine toxicity were agitation, suicidal ideation, hallucinations, delusions, confusion, and chest pain. Once drug use ceases, symptoms usually resolve within one week.

Research studies on human performance have typically involved the administration of cocaine and *d*-amphetamine in single doses that do not produce toxic psychosis. In the studies reviewed, d-amphetamine was administered orally (PO). Given that the performance effects of *d*-amphetamine have been studied for more than 60 years and its widespread use during the Second World War,[22] it is not surprising that much is known about *d*-amphetamine's effects on vigilance and attention. However, the effect of psychostimulants on higher-order cognitive processes has not been widely studied.

4.1.1.1.1 Sensory Abilities

A frequently used measure of central nervous system (CNS) functioning is critical flicker frequency (CFF) threshold. The task requires subjects to view a light stimulus and to note the point (frequency) at which the steady light begins to flicker (or vice versa), as the experimenter changes the frequency of the light. An increase in CFF threshold indicates increased cortical and behavioral arousal, whereas a decrease suggests lowered CNS arousal.[23] *d*-Amphetamine reliably increases CFF threshold.[8,23] In the only study, to my knowledge, intranasal cocaine (100 mg) had no effect on CFF threshold.[24]

4.1.1.1.2 Motor Abilities

Finger tapping is considered to be a measure of relatively pure motor activity. One study found that *d*-amphetamine (10 mg) produced a 5% increase in tapping rate,[25] whereas three other studies reported no effect.[26-28] The circular lights test is a measure of gross motor coordination in which subjects extinguish lights by pressing buttons that are arranged in a 72-cm diameter circle on a wall-mounted panel. The test is typically performed for 1 min. *d*-Amphetamine (25 mg) increased response rate on the circular lights test in one study,[29] but another study reported no effect of 20 mg *d*-amphetamine.[30] The effect of cocaine on finger tapping and circular lights performance has not been examined.

4.1.1.1.3 Attentional Abilities

Attention is a broad psychological category encompassing behaviors such as searching, scanning, and detecting visual and auditory stimuli for brief or long periods of time.[31,32] In nearly all performance tests assessing attention, responding is measured in some temporal form, such as reaction or response time, time off target, or response rate. If appropriate, response accuracy is also reported. Because of differential drug effects, it can be helpful to distinguish between focused, selective, divided, and sustained attention.[6]

Focused attention involves attending to one task for a brief period of time, usually about 5 min or less. In this regard, d-amphetamine[7] and cocaine[24] have been shown to improve performance in auditory and visual reaction time tests, although other studies have reported no effect of d-amphetamine. A brief, frequently used test of psychomotor skills and attention is the digit symbol substitution test (DSST), which originated as a paper and pencil subtest of the Wechsler Adult Intelligence Scale and now exists in a computerized version.[33] The DSST requires subjects to draw the symbol or type the pattern associated with each numeral 1 through 9. The number of attempted and correct symbols or patterns during the 90-second test is recorded. In general, d-amphetamine[7] and cocaine[34,35] enhanced performance on the DSST, although Foltin et al.[36] reported that cocaine decreased the number of attempted trials.

The effect of d-amphetamine and cocaine on divided attention has not been widely investigated; one study reported small increases in accuracy on a divided attention test after administration of d-amphetamine.[37] Several studies have shown that d-amphetamine reliably enhanced performance in tests of visual and auditory vigilance.[7,38] The time of effect in these studies was 1 to 4 h after drug administration, suggesting that d-amphetamine improved performance by preventing the vigilance decrement that typically occurs in tests of sustained attention.

4.1.1.1.4 Cognitive Abilities

Psychostimulants have produced inconsistent effects on tests of cognition. Several studies have investigated the effect of cocaine on a test of repeated acquisition and performance of response sequences. In the acquisition component, subjects attempt to learn by trial and error a predetermined sequence of 10 numbers within 20 trials. Subjects learn a new sequence each time they performed the test. In the performance component, the response sequence remains constant throughout the experiment, and thus subjects repeat an already learned sequence. Two studies have reported no effect of either intranasal (IN) or IV cocaine on the test.[34,36] However, Higgins et al.[39] reported that cocaine (96 mg, IN) decreased response rate during the acquisition phase and increased response accuracy during the performance component. In a similar serial acquisition procedure, cocaine has been shown to have no effect.[40,41]

Cocaine[24] and d-amphetamine[7] had no effect on simple arithmetic skills. With respect to memory, most studies have also indicated no effect of d-amphetamine on immediate recall of lists of numbers.[7] However, Soetens et al.[42] reported that d-amphetamine (10 mg) administered PO before learning and intramuscularly (IM) after learning enhanced recall of a word list for up to 3 days.

4.1.1.1.5 Summary

The performance effects of d-amphetamine have been studied to a greater extent than those of cocaine; however, because of their similar pharmacology, both drugs generally produce comparable effects. Psychostimulants in low to moderate doses typically produce behavioral and cortical arousal, and thus d-amphetamine reliably increases CFF threshold and has been shown in some studies to increase finger tapping rate and gross motor coordination. A relatively large body of literature indicates that d-amphetamine and cocaine enhance attentional abilities, including brief tests requiring focused attention and vigilance tasks requiring sustained attention. The majority of studies have shown that cocaine and d-amphetamine have no effect on learning, memory, and other cognitive processes, such as solving arithmetic problems.

Stephen J. Heishman

4.1.1.2 Nicotine and Tobacco

The vast majority of people who use nicotine (either cigarettes or smokeless tobacco products) use the drug on a daily basis and are considered to be addicted to or dependent on nicotine. In contrast, a minority of people who use the other psychoactive drugs considered in this chapter for nonmedical purposes develop a drug dependence. Daily smokers accumulate plasma levels of nicotine that increase during the day, decline overnight, but never reach zero. This poses a unique problem when conducting behavioral studies with smokers. When improvements in performance are observed after nicotine is given to smokers who have been tobacco abstinent overnight (a common design strategy), it is impossible to determine whether such improvements represent a true enhancement of performance or the alleviation of withdrawal-induced performance deficits. The latter explanation would simply represent a reversal to the person's normal smoking behavioral baseline, not a true enhancement above baseline performance. Unlike other drugs of abuse that are typically tested in nondependent, nontolerant subjects, this issue must always be considered when interpreting the effects of nicotine on smokers' performance.

Two recent papers have thoroughly reviewed the literature on the effects of nicotine and cigarette smoking on human performance.[6,15] In general, both reviews concluded that nicotine does not universally enhance performance and cognition and that any nicotine-induced performance improvements are small in magnitude. Heishman et al.[6] suggested that the limited performance-enhancing effects of nicotine are not likely to be an important factor in the initiation of cigarette smoking by adolescents (the modal age for starting tobacco use is between 11 and 15; beginning after high school is rare[43]). However, once an individual is dependent on nicotine, data suggest that nicotine deprivation maintains smoking, at least in part, because nicotine can reverse withdrawal-induced performance decrements.[6]

Because the majority of studies in this area are methodologically deficient, only studies that used placebo control conditions and single- or double-blind drug administration procedures are included in this section. Additionally, because of the problem of interpreting nicotine-induced changes in smokers' performance as discussed above, a distinction will be made between studies that administered nicotine to subjects under conditions of nicotine deprivation and no deprivation. Studies involving no nicotine deprivation include nondeprived smokers and nonsmokers.

4.1.1.2.1 Sensory Abilities

Sherwood et al.[44] administered nicotine polacrilex gum (0 and 2 mg) three times at 1-h intervals to smokers who were overnight deprived and measured CFF after each administration. CFF threshold was increased over predose baseline after the first 2-mg dose, but no further increase after the second and third doses were observed. Thus, the initial dose appeared to reverse a deprivation-induced deficit, and subsequent doses maintained normal functioning. Baseline CFF was not measured before subjects were tobacco abstinent. No effect of nicotine on CFF was reported following administration of nicotine polacrilex or subcutaneous (SC) nicotine injections to 24-h abstinent smokers, nonabstinent smokers, and nonsmokers.[45-48] The lack of effect of nicotine in the absence of nicotine deprivation is consistent with the data of Sherwood et al.,[44] further suggesting that nicotine reverses withdrawal-induced deficits, but does not produce true enhancement of CFF threshold.

4.1.1.2.2 Motor Abilities

Perkins et al.[49] administered placebo and nicotine nasal spray (15 µg/kg) to smokers who were tobacco deprived for at least 12 h. Nicotine reliably increased finger tapping rate in all subjects, and produced a nonsignificant trend toward improved hand steadiness. In a subsequent study, Perkins et al.[50] reported that nicotine (5, 10, and 20 µg/kg) increased finger tapping rate, but impaired hand steadiness and hand tremor in nonsmokers and overnight tobacco abstinent smokers. Finger tapping rate was also increased by nicotine in nonsmokers who were administered nicotine nasal solution or spray[49,51] or SC nicotine injections.[46] In contrast, Foulds et al.[48] found that nicotine injections (0.3 and 0.6 mg, SC) had no effect on finger tapping rate in nonsmokers, and only 0.3 mg nicotine produced a slight tapping rate increase in 24-h abstinent smokers.

4.1.1.2.3 Attentional Abilities

Numerous studies investigating focused attention have used reaction time tests. Nicotine polacrilex gum (2 mg) produced faster motor reaction time, but did not affect recognition reaction time in overnight deprived smokers,[44] nonabstinent smokers,[45] and a group of nonabstinent smokers and nonsmokers.[47] Le Houezec et al.[52] found that SC nicotine (0.8 mg) increased the number of fast reaction times, but did not affect task accuracy. However, Hindmarch et al.[45] reported no effect of 2-mg polacrilex on reaction time in nonsmokers.

Selective attention can be defined as the ability to attend to a target stimulus while simultaneously ignoring irrelevant or distracting stimuli. In 12-h tobacco deprived smokers, nicotine polacrilex (2 and 4 mg) reversed deprivation-induced impairments in letter searching to pre-deprivation baseline[53] and had no effect on Stroop and letter cancellation tests.[54] The Stroop test compares the time required for subjects to name the ink color of color words that are incongruent (e.g., the word red printed in blue ink) vs. the ink color of neutral stimuli, such as non-color words or colored squares. Typically, the incongruent task takes more time than the neutral stimulus task because the tendency to read the color word interferes with naming its ink color; the difference in time between the two tasks is considered a measure of selective attention or distractibility.[55] In two studies comparing abstinent smokers and nonsmokers on the Stroop test, nicotine nasal spray (5, 10, and 20 µg/kg) improved response time, but impaired accuracy with regard to the Stroop conflict,[50] whereas nicotine injections (0.3 and 0.6 mg, SC) had no effect.[48] Using the Stroop test with nonsmokers, Wesnes and Revell[56] found no effect of 1.5-mg nicotine tablets, whereas Provost and Woodward[57] reported faster response time after 2-mg nicotine polacrilex. Heishman et al.[58] found no effect of polacrilex (2 and 4 mg) on letter searching response time or accuracy in nonsmokers.

Using a divided attention test that required subjects to perform simultaneously a central tracking task and respond to peripheral visual stimuli, Sherwood et al.[44] found that 2-mg polacrilex decreased tracking errors, but had no effect on reaction time to the peripheral lights in overnight deprived smokers. There were fewer tracking errors after the third nicotine dose compared to the first dose, and placebo responding was unchanged, suggesting a true enhancement of performance. In the same divided attention test, nicotine decreased errors on the tracking task in nonabstinent smokers[45,47] but had no effect in nonsmokers.[45]

The rapid visual information processing (RVIP) test has been used in numerous studies investigating the effects of smoking and nicotine on sustained attention. This test requires subjects to press a button when they detect three consecutive even or odd digits in a series of single digits presented on a video monitor at 600-ms intervals. In tobacco-deprived smokers, RVIP accuracy was improved after subjects smoked cigarettes,[59] were administered nicotine polacrilex,[54,60] or received SC injections of nicotine.[48] However, in smokers who were abstinent for 2 h, polacrilex (4 mg) had no effect on RVIP performance.[61] Wesnes et al.[62] reported that the decline in signal detection during an 80-min vigilance test was less after active nicotine tablets compared with placebo in 12-h deprived smokers. Testing nonsmokers, three studies reported that nicotine had no effect on the RVIP test compared to placebo conditions,[46,63,64] whereas Foulds et al.[48] reported faster reaction time after nicotine injections (0.3 and 0.6 mg,

SC). Nonsmokers were also administered nicotine tablets in the Wesnes et al.[62] study, and no difference between abstinent smokers and nonsmokers was observed, suggesting that nicotine functioned to reverse deprivation-induced deficits in the 12-h abstinent smokers.

4.1.1.2.4 Cognitive Abilities

Testing a verbal rote learning paradigm in overnight-deprived smokers, Andersson and Post[65] reported that after the first cigarette, anticipatory responding was improved in the placebo compared to the nicotine condition, but after the second cigarette, there was no difference between conditions. Another study reported that, after learning a word-pair list, smoking a cigarette reduced errors when subjects were tested one week later.[66]

The effects of nicotine and smoking on memory have been widely investigated. In two studies conducted with 10-h abstinent smokers,[67,68] most subjects recalled a greater number of words after nicotine tablets or cigarettes; however, some subjects' recall improved after placebo tablets or denicotinized cigarettes, and some showed no difference between conditions. More recent studies with 12- to 24-h abstinent smokers found that nicotine nasal spray[50] and SC nicotine injections[48] improved recognition memory. In a study with minimally tobacco deprived (1 h) smokers, three experiments found no effect of smoking after word list presentation on delayed intentional word recall, but one experiment found improved free recall when subjects smoked before list presentation.[69] Krebs et al.[70] reported that subjects' recall of prose passages was better after smoking a 0.7-mg nicotine cigarette compared to 0.1- or 1.5-mg nicotine cigarettes, suggesting that optimal arousal was produced by the medium, compared with the high, nicotine-containing cigarette. Reaction time on the Sternberg memory test, which measures scanning and retrieval from short-term memory, was faster after smoking[44] and administration of nicotine polacrilex[71] compared to placebo conditions; however, Foulds et al.[48] reported no effect of SC nicotine on the Sternberg memory test in 24-h abstinent smokers and nonsmokers.

In contrast to these positive effects of nicotine on memory, three studies[53,60,72] reported no effect of nicotine on tests of immediate and delayed recall in nicotine-deprived smokers, and Houston et al.[73] reported that immediate and delayed recall was impaired after smoking a nicotine cigarette compared to a nicotine-free cigarette. In studies of nondeprived smokers or nonsmokers, two reported that nicotine improved some aspects of memory in Alzheimer patients,[46,74] two found enhanced reaction time on the Sternberg memory test,[47,71] three reported no effect of nicotine on tests of immediate and delayed recall,[45,46,58] and one found that nicotine polacrilex impaired immediate and delayed recall and recognition memory.[75] Foulds et al.[48] reported that SC nicotine enhanced response time but decreased accuracy in a digit recall test in nonsmokers.

Several studies have examined the effect of nicotine on other cognitive abilities. Snyder and Henningfield[53] reported that polacrilex (2 and 4 mg) enhanced response time but had no effect on accuracy in an arithmetic test and had no effect on either speed or accuracy in a test of logical reasoning in 12-h abstinent smokers. However, Foulds et al.[48] reported that nicotine injections (0.3 and 0.6 mg, SC) improved response time on the logical reasoning test in 24-h deprived smokers. Three studies conducted with nonsmokers reported no effect of nicotine on several cognitive tests, including the ability to generate correct answers to word and number problems[75] and logical reasoning and mental arithmetic.[48,58]

4.1.1.2.5 Summary

Results of studies conducted with nicotine-deprived smokers are difficult to interpret. Without pre-deprivation baseline data, which few studies report, it is difficult to conclude whether nicotine reversed deprivation-induced deficits or enhanced performance beyond that observed in the nonabstinent state. In general, however, nicotine and smoking at least reversed deprivation-induced deficits in certain abilities in abstinent smokers, but such beneficial effects have not been observed consistently across a range of performance measures. For example, about half of the studies that measured sustained attention and memory reported a positive effect of nicotine; however, the effects were limited to some subjects or one aspect of test performance.

The strongest conclusions concerning the effects of nicotine and smoking on human performance can be drawn from studies conducted with nondeprived smokers and nonsmokers. These studies indicated that nicotine enhanced finger tapping rate and motor responding in tests of focused and divided attention. On the basis of more limited evidence, nicotine produced faster motor responses in the Sternberg memory test, enhanced recognition memory, and reversed the vigilance decrement in a sustained attention test. However, no studies reported true enhancement of sensory abilities, hand steadiness, selective attention, learning, and other cognitive abilities.

4.1.1.3 Sedative-Hypnotics: Benzodiazepines

Since their advent in the 1960s, benzodiazepines have been prescribed widely as anxiolytic and sedative-hypnotic medications, essentially replacing barbiturates because of their greater safety margin. Compared with barbiturates, an acute benzodiazepine overdose is much less likely to produce fatal respiratory depression.[18] There are currently over a dozen benzodiazepines available for medical use; all produce sedation with varying potency. Benzodiazepines with longer duration of action, such as diazepam and lorazepam, are typically prescribed for the treatment of anxiety disorders, whereas those with shorter duration of action, such as triazolam, are used as hypnotics for insomnia. A concern with benzodiazepines being used at night to induce sleep has been the potential for sedation and impaired performance the next day. A review of 52 studies[76] indicated that all benzodiazepine hypnotics, at high enough doses, produced next-day performance impairment. The degree of impairment was dose-related, suggesting that the lowest effective hypnotic dose should be prescribed.

As with all drugs that produce changes in mood, benzodiazepines have the potential to be abused,[77,78] and methodologies have been developed to test the abuse liability of benzodiazepines and related drugs in the laboratory.[79] The pattern of benzodiazepine abuse varies from occasional episodes of intoxication to daily, compulsive use of large doses. Tolerance and physical dependence develop with continued use, such that individuals taking therapeutic doses of benzodiazepines for several months typically experience withdrawal symptoms even if the dose is gradually tapered.[18] The benzodiazepine withdrawal syndrome includes insomnia, restlessness, dizziness, nausea, headache, inability to concentrate, and fatigue. Although unpleasant, benzodiazepine withdrawal is not life-threatening, unlike withdrawal from barbiturates.

The effects of benzodiazepines have been studied extensively with respect to human performance and cognition. Because of their sedative effects, not surprisingly, benzodiazepines generally impair all aspects of performance.[7,80] However, some decrements, such as the well-studied anterograde amnesia, have been shown to be independent of general sedation.[12] Benzodiazepines will be considered as the prototypic sedative-hypnotic drug, recognizing that other CNS depressant drugs, such as barbiturates and ethanol, produce somewhat distinct performance impairment profiles. In the studies reviewed, benzodiazepines were administered PO.

4.1.1.3.1 Sensory Abilities

Consistent with their depressant and sedative effects, benzodiazepines administered acutely typically decrease CFF threshold.[80,81] Specifically, significant decreases have been reported for 1-mg alprazolam, 10-mg diazepam, and 15-mg quazepam;[82] 4- to 11-mg midazolam;[83] 7.5- to 50-mg oxazepam;[84] 1- and 2-mg lorazepam;[85] and 0.5-mg triazolam and 1-mg flunitrazepam.[81]

Stephen J. Heishman

As is evident, this effect on CFF threshold was observed at therapeutic doses of each drug, and when multiple doses were tested, the effect was dose-related. However, there are reports of acute, therapeutic doses of diazepam (5 mg)[86] and lorazepam (1 and 2 mg)[86,87] having no effect on CFF threshold. One study investigating numerous benzodiazepines[81] reported next-day impairment after acute doses of triazolam (0.5 mg) and lormetazepam (1 to 2 mg). No studies were found that examined the effect of chronic benzodiazepine administration on CFF threshold.

Blom et al.[82] recorded horizontal saccadic eye movements as subjects viewed the successive illumination of red light stimuli. They reported that alprazolam, diazepam, and quazepam reduced peak saccadic velocity; alprazolam produced the greatest degree of impairment. Maximal reductions occurred 1 to 4 h after dosing, and effects had not returned to placebo levels at 8 h. Rettig et al.[88] reported that 1 mg lormetazepam and 15 mg midazolam given the night before increased imbalance of the ocular muscles as measured by the Maddox Wing test. This muscular imbalance produces strabismus, which is the inability of both eyes to converge directly on a visual stimulus. Such ocular impairment could be the basis of a wide range of benzodiazepine-induced performance deficits.

4.1.1.3.2 Motor Abilities

Numerous studies have reported that various benzodiazepines decrease finger tapping rate.[80,83,85,89] Kunsman et al.[80] noted that finger tapping rate was generally less sensitive to the effects of benzodiazepines than more complex tasks, such as reaction time and tracking. However, the studies reporting decreases in tapping rate used doses that were in the therapeutic range; thus simple motor skills can be impaired at clinically relevant doses.

A large number of studies have shown that benzodiazepines impair gross motor coordination, as measured by the ability to balance on one leg and the circular lights test. Alprazolam (0.5 to 2 mg),[90] lorazepam (1 and 4 mg),[91] and triazolam (0.25 to 0.75)[92-94] impaired balance or circular lights performance in a dose-related manner. In a population of sedative abusers, acute administration of 40 or 80 mg diazepam and 1 or 2 mg triazolam impaired circular lights performance, and diazepam, but not triazolam, impaired performance the next day.[95] Bondet al.[89] reported that 1-mg alprazolam increased body sway as measured in an automated ataxiameter.

In contrast to these reports of benzodiazepine-induced motor impairment, Kumar et al.[96] found that chronic administration of 1-mg lorazepam and 0.5-mg alprazolam for 5 days had no effect on fine motor coordination as assessed using a standard pegboard test. Additionally, Tobler et al.[97] reported that performance on a typing test was not impaired the day after an acute dose of 7.5-mg midazolam.

4.1.1.3.3 Attentional Abilities

The effects of benzodiazepines on reaction time tests and the DSST have been investigated in many studies, the majority of which reported impairment of attentional abilities necessary to perform such tests successfully. Because these tests typically are of short duration (less than 5 min), focused attention is primarily required, although other abilities are also involved. Numerous studies have reported that simple or choice reaction time to visual stimuli was increased (slowed) by acute, therapeutic doses of various benzodiazepines, including adinazolam,[98] alprazolam,[90] diazepam and flunitrazepam,[99] lorazepam,[91,100] oxazepam,[84] temazepam,[80] and triazolam.[92] Linnoila et al.[101,102] reported that diazepam, alprazolam, and adinazolam impaired reaction time and accuracy in a word recognition test. Flurazepam (30 mg, but not 15 mg) produced next-day impairment of simple and choice visual reaction time, whereas 15-mg midazolam had no residual effect.[103] In contrast, diazepam (5 mg) and lorazepam (1 mg) had no effect on an auditory reaction time test.[86] It is possible that, compared with visual tests, auditory reaction time tests are less sensitive to the impairing effects of benzodiazepines; however, such a conclusion is premature based on only one study.

Like reaction time tests, nearly all studies have reported that acute administration of benzodiazepines impair performance on the DSST. Lorazepam (1 to 9 mg),[86,91,100,104-106] triazolam (0.25 to 0.75 mg),[92,94,105,107-109] alprazolam (0.5 to 4 mg),[90,104] temazepam (15 to 60 mg),[80,107] diazepam (5 to 10 mg),[104,110] and estazolam (1 to 4 mg)[109] have been shown to impair response speed and/or accuracy on the DSST in a dose-related manner. However, Kelly et al.[111] reported that diazepam (5 or 10 mg) had no effect on DSST performance. It is unlikely that low doses of diazepam accounted for the lack of effect, as suggested by Kelly et al.,[111] because numerous studies have reported DSST impairment after 10-mg diazepam.[7] In a test similar to the DSST, symbol copying, Saano et al.[86] reported no effect of diazepam (5 mg) and lorazepam (1 mg).

Another test requiring focused attention is digit or letter cancellation, in which subjects mark through a certain numeral in a page of random numbers or a certain letter in a page of text or random letters. The typical duration of cancellation tests is 1-2 minutes. Two recent studies reported that diazepam (10 or 15 mg)[112] and lorazepam (1 and 2 mg)[85] impaired digit cancellation performance. Interestingly, Brown et al.[112] found that impaired focused attention was not correlated with the ability to encode associative information. These studies confirm numerous previous studies that reported benzodiazepine-induced decrements in cancellation tests.[7]

Brief tests of tracking abilities can also be considered tests of focused attention. In such tests, subjects attempt to maintain a moving target within a certain area of the video monitor or a cursor within a moving target. Tracking performance is uniformly impaired by benzodiazepines at doses similar to those reported above for reaction time and DSST impairment.[80,101,102] One study investigating the effects of multiple doses of three benzodiazepines reported that lorazepam produced the greatest degree of tracking impairment, followed by alprazolam and then diazepam.[104] Because the manipulandum used to control the moving target in some studies was a steering wheel, tracking tests have occasionally been considered laboratory tests of driving ability. In studies of on-road driving, Volkerts et al.[113] reported that driving was impaired the morning after dosing with oxazepam (50 mg) and slightly impaired after lormetazepam (1 mg). Brookhuis et al.[114] found that next-day driving was significantly impaired after flurazepam (30 mg) and less impaired after lormetazepam (2 mg). Diazepam (15 mg) impaired performance on a clinical test for drunkenness, which comprised 13 tests assessing motor, vestibular, mental, and behavioral functioning.[115]

Compared with focused attention, fewer studies have examined the effects of benzodiazepines on selective attention. Performance on the Stroop test was impaired by lorazepam.[80] Acute administration of triazolam and lorazepam produced dose-dependent decrements in response rate and accuracy in a simultaneous matching-to-sample task, which required subjects to determine which of two comparison visual stimuli was identical to the sample stimulus.[105,116] The drug effects differed as a function of task difficulty, such that the benzodiazepine-induced impairment was reduced when discriminability of the non-matching stimulus was increased.

Benzodiazepines have been shown to impair divided attention.[80] Kerr et al.[84] reported that oxazepam (7.5 to 50 mg) impaired performance on a test that required subjects to divide their attention between a central tracking task and responding to light stimuli in the peripheral visual field. Using a similar test of divided attention, Moskowitz et al.[103] found that 30-mg flurazepam and 15-mg midazolam impaired performance the day after drug administration.

Consistent with the other types of attention, benzodiazepines impair performance in tests of sustained attention or vigilance.[14,101,103] There is no evidence that benzodiazepines exacerbate the vigilance decrement normally observed during prolonged, tedious tests. The impairment caused by benzodiazepines in tests of sustained attention is not secondary to sedation, but rather a direct effect on perceptual sensitivity, resulting in decreased hits and increased response time in detecting stimulus targets.

4.1.1.3.4 Cognitive Abilities

The most widely studied aspect of cognition with respect to benzodiazepines is memory.[12,117] One of the most reliable effects of benzodiazepines is to impair recall of information presented after drug administration (anterograde amnesia). In contrast, information presented before administration of benzodiazepines is not affected. The memory decrement produced by benzodiazepines is a function of task difficulty, such that little or no impairment is observed for immediate recall of a few items, whereas more complex or delayed memory tests reveal profound impairment.[12] The benzodiazepine antagonist, flumazenil, has been used to block the sedative effects of benzodiazepines, but the amnestic effect was not affected, suggesting that benzodiazepine-induced amnesia is independent of sedation.[83,118] It has also been demonstrated that some benzodiazepines selectively impaired explicit memory (e.g., recall of a word list), but left other aspects of memory intact.[117] In this way, benzodiazepines have been used as pharmacological tools to identify distinct memory processes.

Roy-Byrne et al.[119] reported that diazepam (10 mg) impaired attentional processes during auditory presentation of a word list and immediate recognition of words that had been presented twice; however, naming examples of a category, such as vegetables (semantic memory) and self-evaluation of memory performance (meta-cognition) were not affected. Triazolam (0.25 to 0.5 mg) impaired free recall of a word list, but had no effect on implicit (memory without awareness ofthe source of information) or semantic memory.[120,121] Linnoila et al.[101] reported that adinazolam (15 or 30 mg) impaired attention during list presentation, but had no effect on delayed (1 min) free recall of words. Using a battery of tests that assessed numerous memory functions, Bishop et al.[85] reported that lorazepam (1 and 2 mg) impaired explicit (free recall), semantic, and implicit memory, but had no effect on working memory (manipulation of information for less than 30 seconds) and procedural memory (knowledge required for skills reflected as improved performance with practice). Such selective drug effects on memory and similarly selective clinical amnestic syndromes resulting from brain injury or disease[117] have allowed a greater understanding of cognitive functioning and the processes subserving learning and memory.

A large number of studies have investigated the effect of acute benzodiazepine administration on either immediate or delayed recall or recognition of word lists, numbers, or pictures in healthy volunteers. Impaired memory has been reported for adinazolam (20 to 30 mg),[98] alprazolam (0.5 to 2 mg),[90,102,122] diazepam (5 to 15 mg),[112,123] estazolam (1 to 4 mg),[109] lorazepam (1 to 4 mg),[91,124] temazepam (15 to 60 mg),[107] and triazolam (0.25 to 0.75 mg).[92-94,107,109,125] Testing subjects with histories of sedative abuse, Roache and Griffiths[95,100] reported that immediate and delayed recall and recognition of digits and symbols were impaired by diazepam (40 or 80 mg), lorazepam (1.5 to 9 mg), and triazolam (1 or 2 mg). After 5 days of dosing healthy subjects with either alprazolam (0.5 mg) or lorazepam (1 mg), anterograde amnesia was observed for word lists.[96] Hindmarch et al.[81] examined the effects of several benzodiazepines on the Sternberg memory test, which measures scanning and retrieval from short-term memory. They reported that acute administration of flunitrazepam (1 mg), lormetazepam (1 to 2 mg), and triazolam (0.5 mg) significantly slowed response time on the test and that performance remained impaired the next day with lormetazepam and triazolam. However, Kelly et al.[111] reported no effect of diazepam (5 and 10 mg) on the Sternberg test.

The effect of a number of benzodiazepines has been investigated on the repeated acquisition and performance of response sequences task, which comprises separate acquisition (learning) and performance components.[126] This task thus allows independent assessment of drug effects on acquisition of new information and performance of already learned information.

In general, doses of benzodiazepines that increased errors in the acquisition component did not impair the performance component, although high doses decreased response rate and increased errors in both components. Impairment of acquisition of the response sequence has been reported following acute administration of alprazolam (1 to 3 mg),[126] diazepam (5 to 30 mg),[11,126,127] estazolam (1 to 4 mg),[109] lorazepam (2.8 to 5.6 mg),[106] temazepam (15 to 60 mg),[107] and triazolam (0.375 to 0.75 mg).[107-109,126,127] In these studies, only the highest doses impaired the performance component of the task. In one of the few studies to examine the chronic effects of benzodiazepines on cognitive processes, Bickel et al.[128] administered diazepam (80 mg daily) for 3 days to sedative abusers and found increased errors and decreased response rate in the acquisition component on Day 1 that decreased on Days 2 and 3, suggesting the development of tolerance. In the performance component, response rate was decreased on Day 1; the magnitude of effect decreased over days. Performance error rate was relatively unaffected.

Few studies have examined the effects of benzodiazepines on other cognitive abilities. Rusted et al.[123] reported that 5- and 10-mg diazepam impaired performance on a logical reasoning test, but had no effect on a mental rotation task. Judd et al.[129] found that 30-mg flurazepam, but not 15-mg midazolam, impaired arithmetic (addition) abilities the day after drug administration. In contrast, flurazepam had no effect on reading comprehension.

4.1.1.3.5 Summary

When administered acutely to nontolerant, healthy volunteers, therapeutic doses of benzodiazepines produce sedation, which typically impairs most aspects of performance in a dose-dependent manner. In patients taking benzodiazepines medically and in individuals who abuse benzodiazepines recreationally, both of whom have developed tolerance, it is necessary to increase the dose of benzodiazepine to observe impaired performance. Benzodiazepines have been shown to decrease CFF threshold, a direct indication of CNS depression, and to impair ocular performance. Motor abilities are impaired by benzodiazepines, including fine (finger tapping) and gross (balance, circular lights, and body sway) motor coordination. Numerous studies have documented that benzodiazepines impair tests requiring focused, selective, divided, and sustained attention. One of the most well-studied cognitive effects of benzodiazepines is their ability to produce anterograde amnesia, memory loss for information presented after drug administration. It has been demonstrated that these memory deficits are not secondary to benzodiazepine-induced sedation and that explicit memory (free recall of presented stimuli) functions are typically impaired, whereas other memory processes can remain unaffected. Benzodiazepines have also been shown to impair the acquisition (learning) of new information.

4.1.1.4 Opioid Analgesics and Anesthetics

The class of drugs referred to as opioids consists of a wide range of naturally occurring derivatives from the opium poppy, *Papaver somniferum*, such as morphine and codeine; semisynthetic derivatives from opium, such as heroin and hydromorphone; and completely synthetic opioids, such as meperidine and fentanyl. The primary pharmacological effect of all opioids is analgesia; a common side effect is sedation. At high doses, respiratory depression occurs, which is the usual cause of death from acute opioid overdose. The full range of clinical pain can be effectively treated with various opioids, and fentanyl and related synthetic congeners (sufentanil, alfentanil) are generally used clinically as anesthetics, but are also used for postoperative analgesia.

Opioids can be classified according to their pharmacological actions into those that function like morphine, producing their agonist effects primarily through the mu opioid receiver and those that produce mixed effects, such as agonist-antagonists or partial agonists.[130] Mixed agonist-antagonists function as agonists at one type of opioid receptor (e.g., delta or kappa) and as an antagonist at other (e.g., mu) receptors. Partial agonists produce only limited effects at a given receptor. Morphine-like opioids are used clinically for moderate to severe pain, whereas agonist-antagonists and partial agonists produce less analgesia and are thus useful in the treatment of mild pain.

Previous reviews have concluded that opioids produce minimal impairment of human performance even at high doses.[130,131] However, a recent review by Zacny[16] challenges this benign notion. In healthy, nontolerant research subjects, opioids impair psychomotor performance to a greater extent than cognitive abilities. Typically, opioids slow responses in tests requiring speed, but do not impair test accuracy. In contrast, individuals who have developed tolerance to opioids, such as chronic pain patients[132] or methadone-maintained persons,[131] generally show little or no behavioral impairment after administration of their maintenance dose. The time required for tolerance to develop to any performance-impairing effects of methadone has been estimated at 3 to 4 weeks in methadone-maintained patients.[131] The studies reviewed here report the performance effects of opioids in nontolerant research volunteers, unless otherwise indicated.

4.1.1.4.1 Sensory Abilities

Studies investigating the effects of morphine, meperidine, buprenorphine, and nalbuphine on CFF threshold have, in general, found impaired functioning, consistent with the CNS depressant effect of opioids.[16] Veselis et al.[133] targeted fentanyl plasma concentrations of 1.0, 1.5, and 2.5 ng/ml using continuous IV infusion and found that CFF threshold was decreased at 1.5 ng/ml, whereas other performance measures were only affected at concentrations greater than 2.5 ng/ml. In contrast, pentazocine (30 mg) had no effect on CFF threshold;[134] however, other studies using higher doses of pentazocine have reported decreased CFF threshold.[16]

Zacny and colleagues have examined the effects of several opioids on the Maddox Wing test, a measure of ocular muscle imbalance indicating divergence of the eyes. Administration of morphine (2.5 to 10 mg, IV),[135] butorphanol (0.5 to 2.0 µg, IV),[136] dezocine (2.5 to 10 mg, IV),[137] and pentazocine (30 mg, IM)[134] impaired performance on the Maddox Wing test in a dose-related manner. In contrast, fentanyl (25 to 100 µg, IV)[138] and meperidine (0.25 to 1.0 mg, IV)[139] were found to have no effect on Maddox Wing performance. Additionally, fentanyl (50 µg, IV)[140] and an IV combination of fentanyl (50 µg) plus propofol (35 mg),[141] an IV anesthetic, had no effect on the Maddox Wing test. Thus, many opioids have been shown to decrease CFF threshold, a measure of overall CNS arousal, whereas some, but not all, opioids impaired ocular muscle balance.

4.1.1.4.2 Motor Abilities

Compared with other measures of performance, few studies have investigated the effects of opioids on pure motor abilities, such as finger tapping and coordination.[16] Kerr et al.[142] used individually tailored steady-state infusions to target several plasma concentrations of morphine (20, 40, and 80 ng/ml). They found that only the high dose of morphine impaired finger tapping and the ability to maintain low constant levels of isometric force, which required precise motor control. Finger tapping rate was also decreased in a group of cancer patients who had received an increase of greater than 30% in their dose of opioid (morphine, hydromorphone, oxycodone, or codeine) compared to a group of patients who did not receive a dosage increase.[143] In contrast, pentazocine (30 mg) had no effect on finger tapping.[134] Slightly over half the studies investigating the effect of opioids on body sway, a measure of gross motor coordination, reported impairment.[16]

4.1.1.4.3 Attentional Abilities

A relatively large number of studies have investigated the effects of opioids on tests requiring focused attention. Morphine (2.5 to 10 mg, IV)[135] and propofol (70 mg, IV)[140] impaired an auditory simple reaction time test, and fentanyl (1 to 2.5 ng/ml, IV)[133] impaired a visual choice reaction time test. Jenkins et al.[144] reported that IV (3 to 20 mg) and smoked (2.6 to 10.5 mg) heroin impaired performance on a simple visual reaction time task. However, three studies reported no effect of butorphanol (0.5 to 2.0 mg, IV),[136] fentanyl (25 to 100 µg, IV),[138] and meperidine (0.25 to 1.0 mg, IV)[139] on an auditory simple reaction time test. It may be that visual reaction time tests are more sensitive than auditory tests to the effects of opioids, which would be consistent with opioid-induced impairment on the Maddox Wing test, discussed in the preceding section.

Numerous studies have reported that performance on the DSST was impaired by various opioids, including morphine (2.5 to 10 mg),[135] fentanyl (1 to 2.5 ng/ml),[133] pentazocine (30 mg),[134] butorphanol (0.5 to 2 mg),[136] dezocine (2.5 to 10 mg),[137] propofol (22 to 70 mg),[140,145] and the combination of fentanyl (50 µg) plus propofol (35 mg).[141] In contrast, meperidine was found to have no effect on the DSST.[139] Because the DSST is a timed test, it would appear that opioids slow speeded responses in a fairly consistent manner in opioid-naive subjects. However, in opioid abusers or opioid-dependent persons, Preston and colleagues have reported no effect on DSST performance of several opioids, including morphine (7.5 to 30 mg, IM),[146] hydromorphone (0.125 to 3 mg, IM),[147] buprenorphine (0.5 to 8 mg, IM),[148] pentazocine (7.5 to 120 mg, IM),[149] butorphanol (0.375 to 1.5 mg, IV),[150] and nalbuphine (3 to 24 mg, IM).[151]

Many of these same studies have also reported opioid-induced impairment of a 1-min tracking test in which subjects tracked a randomly moving target on a video monitor with a mouse-controlled cursor. This task measures visual-motor coordination and focused attentional abilities. Fentanyl (25 to 100 µg, IV),[138,140] meperidine (0.25 to 1.0 mg, IV),[139] butorphanol (0.5 to 2 mg, IV),[136] dezocine (2.5 to 10 mg, IV),[137] and propofol (0.08 to 0.32 mg/kg, IV) alone[145] and in combination with fentanyl (50 µg, IV).[141] Morphine (2.5 to 10 mg, IV) had no effect on the same tracking task.[135] In one of the few studies to investigate the effects of opioids on divided attention, pentazocine (30 mg, IM) was shown to impair the choice reaction time component, but had no effect on the tracking component of a divided attention test.[134] Fentanyl (100 µg, IV) slowed reaction time and movement time in a driving simulator.[152] Some studies with morphine have documented impaired sustained attention; however, the few studies that have been conducted with other opioids found no effect on a variety of vigilance tasks.[16]

4.1.1.4.4 Cognitive Abilities

A relatively large number of studies have examined the effects of opioids on memory and other cognitive functions; a minority of these studies have reported impairment.[16] Kerr et al.[142] found that steady-state levels of morphine (20 to 80 ng/ml, IV) slowed reading time of prose passages. When asked questions about the passage immediately after reading, subjects' recall was not impaired, but delayed questioning revealed impaired comprehension. Fentanyl (1 to 2.5 ng/ml, IV) was shown to impair a range of memorial abilities, including auditory-verbal recall of common words, picture recall, and digit recall.[133] In a group of cancer patients whose opioid (morphine, hydromorphone, oxycodone, or codeine) dose was increased by at least 30%, decreases were observed in an arithmetic test, backward digit span, and a test of visual memory.[143] Propofol (0.08 to 0.32 mg/kg, IV) impaired delayed, but not immediate, recall of a word list only at the highest dose level.[145] In another study, propofol (70 mg, IV), but not fentanyl (50 µg, IV) impaired immediate free recall of words.[140] Zacny et al.[136] reported that butorphanol (0.5 to 2 mg, IV) had no effect on a test of logical reasoning, which is consistent

Stephen J. Heishman

with other studies finding little impairment of opioids on cognitive abilities other than memory.[16]

4.1.1.4.5 Summary

Administration of acute, therapeutic doses of opioids to nontolerant research subjects produces effects typical of CNS depressant drugs, including decreased CFF threshold. Some, but not all, opioids produce ocular muscle imbalance as assessed in the Maddox Wing test. Finger tapping and gross motor coordination were found to be impaired in some, but not all, studies. A relatively large number of studies have reported that opioids produce decrements in brief tests requiring focused attention and fine motor coordination, such visual reaction time, DSST, and visual-motor tracking. Very few studies have examined that effects of opioids on selective, divided, and sustained attention. The effects of opioids on cognitive functioning are mixed, with the majority of studies indicating no impairment, but some well-designed studies showing decrements in memory. When administered to opioid-tolerant individuals, such as opioid abusers or chronic pain patients, opioids typically produce little or no performance impairment.

4.1.1.5 Marijuana

Marijuana consists of the dried and crushed leaves and stems of the plant *Cannabis sativa*, which grows worldwide. In the U.S., marijuana is typically rolled in cigarettes (joints) and smoked, although in various parts of the world, other preparations of the cannabis plant are eaten or fumes from the ignited plant material are inhaled. The acute effects of smoked marijuana and δ^9-tetrahydrocannabinol (THC), the primary psychoactive constituent of marijuana, have been investigated in numerous studies over the past several decades.[10,11] One of the most reliable behavioral effects of acute marijuana is impairment of memory processes; less consistent impairment has been reported for motor and attentional tests. Documenting the effects of chronic marijuana use has been somewhat elusive, with early studies reporting no impairment of cognitive functioning;[153] however, more recent studies have shown chronic marijuana users to be impaired in perceptual-motor abilities,[154] selective attention,[155] mathematical and verbal skills,[156] and learning and memory.[156,157]

Unless otherwise noted, the studies reviewed here examined the acute effects of marijuana and were conducted with experienced marijuana users who smoked standard marijuana cigarettes provided by the National Institute on Drug Abuse (NIDA). These marijuana cigarettes resemble in size an unfiltered tobacco cigarette, weigh 700 to 900 mg, and are assayed by NIDA to determine the percentage of THC by weight. Doses are typically manipulated by using cigarettes that differ in THC content or by varying the number of puffs administered to subjects (5 to 8 puffs are equivalent to one cigarette). Placebo cigarettes have had active THC removed chemically from the plant material, but when burned, smell identical to an active marijuana cigarette.

Over the years, an intriguing research question with important practical implications has been whether marijuana impairs performance beyond the period of acute intoxication, which typically lasts 2 to 6 h after smoking one or two cigarettes. Recently, studies have documented performance decrements 12 to 24 h after smoking marijuana.[158] One series of studies reported that 24 h after smoking a single marijuana cigarette (2.2% THC), experienced aircraft pilots were impaired attempting to land a plane in a flight simulator;[159,160] however, a third study failed to replicate this next-day effect.[161] In another series of studies, a comprehensive battery of tests revealed that only time estimation[162] and memory[163] were impaired 9 to 17 h after smoking two marijuana cigarettes (2.1 to 2.9% THC), leading the authors to conclude that evidence for next-day performance effects of marijuana was weak. Yet another series of studies found next-day impairment on tests of memory and mental arithmetic after smoking two or four marijuana cigarettes (2.6% THC) over a 4-h period,[164] but not after smoking one marijuana cigarette.[164,165] Thus, residual impairment appears to be a dose-related phenomenon, with effects more likely to be observed at higher marijuana doses.

Another controversial issue has been the amotivational syndrome supposedly caused by heavy, chronic marijuana use. This syndrome has been characterized by feelings of lethargy and apathy and an absence of goal-directed behavior.[166,167] However, studies conducted in countries where segments of the population use marijuana heavily[168-170] and laboratory-based studies in the U.S.[171,172] have not found empirical support for an amotivational syndrome. Foltin and colleagues[173-175] have conducted several inpatient studies lasting 15 to 18 days with subjects reporting weekly marijuana use. Subjects were required to perform low-probability tasks such as the DSST, word-sorting, and vigilance to gain access to more highly desired (high-probability) work and recreational activities. On days that subjects smoked active marijuana, the amount of time spent on low-probability tasks increased, which is inconsistent with an amotivational syndrome. Additionally, the effect of marijuana on time spent on low- vs. high-probability activities differed for work and recreational activities, indicating that the behavioral effects of marijuana are context-dependent and not readily predicted by a simplistic amotivational hypothesis.[10]

4.1.1.5.1 Sensory Abilities

In one of the few studies to investigate the effects of marijuana on CFF threshold, Block et al.[176] reported that one marijuana cigarette (2.6% THC) decreased CFF threshold compared to placebo. Although more a perceptual process than a sensory ability, a commonly reported effect of marijuana is to increase the subjective passage of time relative to clock time. This typically results in subjects either overestimating an experimenter-generated time interval[162] or underproducing a subject-generated interval.[177] However, Heishman et al.[178] recently found that marijuana (3.6% THC; 4, 8, or 16 puffs) had no effect on either time estimation or production.

4.1.1.5.2 Motor Abilities

In their review, Chait and Pierri[11] indicated that marijuana produced moderate impairment of balance (increased body sway) and hand steadiness. Consistent with this motor impairment, one marijuana cigarette (1.5% THC) was found to decrease postural balance as subjects attempted to maintain balance while standing on a platform that moved at random intervals.[179] Cone et al.[180] found that two marijuana cigarettes (2.8% THC) impaired performance on the circular lights task; however, Heishman et al.[181] reported no effect of marijuana (1.3 and 2.7% THC, 2 cigarettes) on circular lights performance. The time taken to sort a deck of playing cards was increased after smoking one marijuana cigarette (2.9% THC).[162] In contrast, several studies have shown that marijuana did not influence finger tapping rate.[11]

4.1.1.5.3 Attentional Abilities

A relatively large number of studies have investigated the effects of marijuana on focused attention, including reaction time tests and the DSST. Marijuana (1.8 and 3.6% THC) was shown to slow responding on a simple, visual reaction time task;[182] however, others have not found marijuana to impair simple reaction time performance.[11,36,178] In contrast, marijuana has been shown to impair complex or choice reaction time tasks in a consistent manner.[11,176]

In general, marijuana also impaired performance on the DSST. In concentrations ranging from 1.8 to 3.6% THC, marijuana has been shown to decrease the number of attempted responses (speed) and/or decrease the number of correct responses (accuracy) on the DSST.[177,178,181-185] Oral THC (10 and 20 mg) also impaired DSST performance.[186] However, other studies have reported no effect of marijuana (1.3 to 3.6% THC) on the DSST.[36,162,187] The reasons for a lack of effect in these latter studies is unclear given that doses of marijuana were comparable and, in one study,[187] task presentation was identical to those studies reporting impairment. Marijuana (1.2% THC) also impaired selective attention as evidenced by slower responding and greater interference scores in the Stroop color naming test.[188]

Divided attention has generally been shown to be impaired by marijuana. Many divided attention tests consist of a central or primary task and a secondary or peripheral task. Several studies have shown that marijuana impaired detection accuracy and/or stimulus reaction time in one or both test components.[177,184,189-191] Kelly et al.[192] used a complex, 5-min divided attention test, in which an arithmetic task (addition and subtraction of three-digit numbers) was presented in the center of the video monitor and three other stimulus detection tasks were presented in the corners of the monitor. Performance was impaired in a dose-related manner after smoking one marijuana cigarette (2.0 or 3.5% THC). This finding illustrates that marijuana readily disrupts performance in complex tasks requiring continuous monitoring and the ability to shift attention rapidly between various stimuli. These same abilities are required when operating a motor vehicle. Not surprisingly, laboratory tests that model various components of driving[193] and standardized tests used by law enforcement officials to determine whether a person can safely drive[194] have been shown to be impaired by marijuana. A comprehensive test of on-road driving found that marijuana moderately increased lateral movement of the vehicle within the driving lane on a highway.[195]

Marijuana also impairs sustained attention. In a 30-min vigilance task, hashish users exhibited more false alarms than non-using control subjects.[196] This finding is consistent with the observation that the impairing effects of marijuana on sustained attention are most evident in tests that last 30 to 60 min; tests with durations of 10 min are not adversely affected by marijuana.[11]

4.1.1.5.4 Cognitive Abilities

Marijuana has been shown to impair learning in the repeated acquisition and performance of response sequences task. Increased errors in the acquisition phase were reported after smoked marijuana (2.0 and 3.5% THC)[183] and oral THC (10 and 20 mg).[186] However, other studies have found no effect of smoked marijuana on this test.[36,40] Block et al.[176] reported that one marijuana cigarette (2.6% THC) impaired paired-associative learning.

As stated previously, one of the most reliable effects of marijuana is the impairment of memory processes. Numerous studies have found that smoked marijuana decreased the number of words or digits recalled and/or increased the number of intrusion errors in either immediate or delayed tests of free recall after presentation of information to be remembered.[162,164,176,178,184,185,188,192] Using an extensive battery of cognitive tests, Block et al.[176] reported that marijuana (2.6% THC) slowed response time for producing word associations, slowed reading of prose, and impaired tests of reading comprehension, verbal expression, and mathematics. Heishman et al.[164] also found that simple addition and subtraction skills were impaired by smoking one, two, or four marijuana cigarettes (2.6% THC). Finally, Kelly et al.[192] reported that marijuana (2.0 and 3.5% THC) slowed response time in a spatial orientation test requiring subjects to determine whether number and letters were displayed normally or as a mirror image when they were rotated between 90 and 270 degrees.

4.1.1.5.5 Summary

Laboratory studies in which subjects smoked marijuana have documented that marijuana impaired sensory-perceptual abilities by reducing CFF threshold and by increasing the subjective passage of time relative to clock time. Marijuana impaired gross motor coordination as measured by body sway and postural balance. However, inconsistent findings have been reported for fine motor control; hand steadiness was impaired, whereas several studies have shown no effect of marijuana on finger tapping. Marijuana has been shown to impair complex, but not simple, reaction time tests. A majority of studies have found that marijuana disrupted performance on the DSST. Complex divided attention tests, including driving a vehicle, were readily impaired by marijuana, as were tests requiring sustained attention for more than 30 min. Numerous studies have documented that smoked marijuana and oral THC impaired learning, memory, and other cognitive processes.

4.1.2. APPLICATION OF LABORATORY TESTING TO APPLIED SETTINGS

Effects on human performance are only one aspect of a drug's complete effect profile, which also includes changes in subjective states (e.g., feelings, mood), physiological and biochemical parameters (e.g., heart rate, blood pressure, immune functioning), and other behaviors (e.g., socializing, sleeping patterns). A complete knowledge of the behavioral and physiological mechanisms underlying a drug's effect is central to an understanding of drug abuse and dependence. Behavioral pharmacologists have known for many decades that a drug's actions are fully manifested only when an organism is interacting with its environment, which involves antecedent stimuli and consequences for all behaviors.[197,198] This theoretical notion is particularly relevant when attempting to assess drug-induced performance changes in workplace settings, in part, because of the important consequences that employment holds for most people.

Because of the widespread use of psychoactive drugs throughout society, employers have become increasingly concerned about drugs in the workplace and the potential for impaired job performance and onsite drug-related accidents. In this section, applications of the methodology and knowledge of human performance testing in the controlled laboratory setting to that of the workplace are discussed. Specifically, three weaknesses and three strengths of current laboratory research methodology, as it applies to performance assessment in the workplace, are presented.

4.1.2.1 Weaknesses in Laboratory Research Methods

4.1.2.1.1 Lack of a Useful Performance Assessment Battery

The first, and probably most critical, problem in the application of laboratory research methods to the workplace is that standardized performance assessment batteries that are valid, reliable, sensitive, practical to implement, and generalize to the demands of the workplace are rare. These five testing concepts can be applied to all measurement instruments and, if satisfied, provide the basis for a useful assessment tool. Thus, they can be referred to collectively as the "criteria for usefulness" of any performance test. In the broadest sense, validity refers to whether the test is measuring what it is intended to measure. A test is reliable if it produces consistent results over time. Thus, an unimpaired person should score about the same during repeated practice trials of a reliable test. A useful test must be sensitive enough to detect a drug effect, if one is present, and show varying degrees of an effect, such as a dose-response function. On the other hand, a test that is too sensitive, yielding an effect when an insignificant amount of drug has been ingested, will be useless in meaningfully predicting impairment. A practical test should be easily administered, of relatively short duration, involve simple instructions, and require minimal practice for optimal performance. Finally, the results of a useful laboratory test should generalize (i.e., demonstrate criterion validity) to the performance demands of the particular workplace. Thus, the issue of matching the performance test with the components of the actual work requirement is a central concern. It should be noted that for laboratory testing purposes, as described in the previous sections of this chapter, the criterion of generalization is not necessarily important; however, the other four criteria of usefulness remain essential.

Stephen J. Heishman

Some performance tests may meet some, but not all, of these criteria for usefulness. For example, the Performance Assessment Battery (PAB) developed by researchers at Walter Reed Army Institute for Research (see Kelly et al. this volume) consists of several tasks measuring various cognitive abilities, such as memory, arithmetic, logical reasoning, and spatial skills. The PAB has been shown to be valid, reliable, and sensitive to the manipulations of a variety of psychoactive drugs, including short- and long-lasting effects of acute drug administration and drug withdrawal effects.[53,164,199,200] However, some of the PAB tasks require considerable practice to achieve optimal, consistent performance, which would limit its implementation in the workplace. Further, whether the skills and abilities measured by the various PAB tasks generalize in any meaningful way to those of the workplace remains to be determined. This issue of the generalization of abilities assessed through laboratory tasks to performance in the workplace is difficult to resolve and is itself a problem facing researchers in this area.

4.1.2.1.2 Generalization of Laboratory Performance to Workplace Performance

The problem of generalization of performance from laboratory tasks to workplace duties will always be a critical issue and will have to be resolved for each attempt to match performance tests to specific job requirements. The most appropriate match will be reached through a two-step decisional process. First, the nature of the performance required at the worksite must be determined. Obviously, this will differ from job to job, and many aspects of human performance are involved in any job (e.g., memory); however, the most salient or critical elements for successful completion of the workplace duties should be determined. For example, although typists use numerous skills, motor dexterity is one critical aspect of their job performance. Second, a performance task that meets the other criteria for usefulness should be chosen that measures the critical aspect of performance. To continue with our example, a test measuring motor skills, such as finger tapping or hand steadiness, might be an appropriate match for assessing the motor abilities required for typing.

4.1.2.1.3 Focus on Profound Performance Impairment

A third weakness of laboratory performance assessment as it applies to performance in the workplace is that the majority of studies have focused on profound drug-induced impairment following acute drug administration. Such studies have contributed greatly to our understanding of the pharmacological and behavioral mechanisms underlying drug-induced performance impairment. However, it is likely that most performance impairment observed in the workplace will be subtle in nature, the result of next-day (hangover) effects or drug deprivation (withdrawal). Although some studies have documented cognitive performance impairment on the day after drug intake[76,158] and during nicotine withdrawal,[53,200] the subtle effects of drugs are only beginning to be fully appreciated.[201] Investigation of such subtle drug effects using sensitive performance tests would be an extremely fruitful research endeavor.

4.1.2.2 Strengths of Laboratory Research Methods

4.1.2.2.1 Criteria for Usefulness of a Performance Test

As described earlier, the testing issues of validity, reliability, sensitivity, practicality, and generalizability constitute the criteria for a useful measure of human performance. Testing of an assessment battery of performance tasks in the laboratory can provide information concerning these testing issues. In fact, the controlled conditions of the laboratory offer an ideal setting for these issues to be initially determined. However, it would also be critically important for these criteria for usefulness to be reassessed when the performance battery was implemented in the workplace.

Although few performance measures have undergone such rigorous laboratory testing, the methodology exists for assessing the validity, reliability, and sensitivity of a performance task.[202-204] The issue of whether a task is practical to implement can also be examined in the laboratory. The number of trials needed to achieve asymptotic performance and the ease with which the task's instructions are understood can be measured readily. The generalizability, or criterion validity, of a laboratory performance task to the demands of the workplace may be more difficult to assess; however, it is feasible. An objective criterion measure of the workplace job would first be determined (e.g., words typed per minute). This real-world criterion would then be tested with the other battery of performance tasks under drug and no-drug conditions. Performance on the criterion measure would be correlated with performance on the laboratory tasks. Those laboratory tasks showing the highest degree of correlation would have been validated by a real-world criterion measure of performance and would be presumed to have the greatest generalizability to performance on the job.

Thus, assessment of the criteria for usefulness of measures of human performance can be conducted in controlled laboratory settings. In general, however, such assessment has not been the focus of typical laboratory psychopharmacological performance research. The criteria of practicality and generalizability, especially, have not received much attention. The main reason is that most laboratory research is concerned with basic mechanisms, and applied research issues, such as these criteria for usefulness, have not been viewed as particularly relevant to an understanding of basic, underlying mechanisms of the effects of drugs. However, such research is feasible and needed if a solid, scientific basis for performance testing in the workplace is to be developed.

4.1.2.2.2 Temporal and Interactive Effects of Drugs

The primary strength of laboratory studies is that variables can be carefully manipulated and monitored in a controlled environment. As a result, the time course of a drug's effects and complex drug interactions can be precisely investigated. By charting the complete time course of a drug's effect in the laboratory, the time to maximal effect and the point at which effects have dissipated (i.e., are no longer measurable) can be determined. It is also possible to measure long-lasting drug effects by testing several hours or days after drug administration. By simultaneously taking blood samples, the important relationship between plasma concentrations of the drug and performance impairment can be determined. All of this information is potentially important for onsite testing purposes. The lack of any drug-related performance impairment may simply be a function of the pharmacokinetics and/or metabolism of the drug. The controlled environment of the laboratory also allows the opportunity to investigate the interaction between a drug and other environmental stimuli, such as another drug, a stressor, or the subject's level of motivation to perform the task. Research on interactive drug effects would more closely approximate the conditions of the real world and thus enhance the external validity of such experimental designs.

4.1.2.2.3 Complete Drug Effect Profiles

As stated earlier, effects on performance are only one aspect of a drug's complete effect profile. Laboratory studies that assess a range of drug effects, including subjective, physiological, biochemical, as well as performance measures, provide the scientific basis for a comprehensive comparison of drugs between and within pharmacological classes. In compiling complete drug effect profiles, meaningful comparisons can be made in terms of the relative performance impairing effects and other drug-induced effects of a variety of psychoactive drugs.[91,94,178,181,192]

Stephen J. Heishman

4.1.3 CONCLUSION

It is evident that a large body of literature exists concerning the effects of psychomotor stimulants, nicotine and tobacco, benzodiazepines, opioids, and marijuana on human performance. As a result, we know much in general about the effects of these psychoactive drugs on sensory, motor, attentional, and cognitive abilities. However, there are some gaps in this literature that need to be filled with data from well-designed, well-controlled studies. For example, few studies have investigated the effects of *d*-amphetamine or cocaine on cognitive abilities, and, for all drugs, sensory and perceptual processes have received little research attention compared with other aspects of behavior. It is also important to continue investigating specific mechanisms underlying general effects of drugs on behavior. For example, we are beginning to understand the differential effects of benzodiazepines on various components of memory;[85,117] similar studies should be conducted examining the effects of marijuana on memory or the effects of nicotine on cognitive processes. Not only will we learn more about the potentially deleterious effects of drugs on human performance, but drugs can be used as tools to further our understanding of basic processes of performance and cognition.

Two other approaches for future research include the measurement of plasma drug concentrations concomitant with performance and a greater number of drug interaction studies. Very few of the studies reviewed in this chapter provided data on the amount of drug actually delivered to subjects. This is especially critical in studies with tobacco and marijuana because the large variability in smoking behaviors (e.g., length of puffs and depth of inhalations)[185,205] and the low bioavailability of smoked drugs[6,206] result in highly variable delivered drug doses.[207] Virtually none of the tobacco studies and only a few of the marijuana studies reviewed reported plasma drug concentrations. Such data are necessary to relate performance impairment with a known drug concentration. Relatively few studies have investigated the interactive effects of drugs on human behavior.[36,102,108,177] Such basic information is critically needed because the simultaneous use of drugs with different pharmacological effects (e.g., ethanol and marijuana; nicotine and all drugs) is common practice today. It is likely that the combined effect of two or more drugs is very different from that of each drug alone.

Laboratory research emphasizing applications to the workplace of performance effects of psychoactive drugs remains relatively uncharted. Performance assessment batteries need to be tested in the laboratory in terms of the five criteria for usefulness: validity, reliability, sensitivity, practicality, and generalizability. Assessment of the last criterion, generalizability or predictive validity, probably presents the greatest challenge to basic researchers; however, it can be accomplished. Because much of drug-induced impairment observed in the workplace will be subtle in nature, laboratory studies should pay greater attention to long-lasting (next day) drug effects and drug withdrawal effects. Additionally, carefully controlled laboratory studies can provide important information concerning a drug's time course of action, interactive drug effects, and complete drug effect profiles.

REFERENCES

1. Hollingworth, H. L., The influence of caffeine on mental and motor efficiency, *Archives of Psychology*, 22, 1, 1912.
2. Bates, R. L., The effects of cigarettes and cigarette smoking on certain psychological and physical functions, *Journal of Comparative Psychology*, 2, 371, 1922.
3. Weiss, B. and Laties, V. G., Enhancement of human performance by caffeine and the amphetamines, *Pharmacological Reviews*, 14, 1, 1962.

4. Koelega, H. S., Stimulant drugs and vigilance performance: A review, *Psychopharmacology*, 111, 1, 1993.

5. McNair, D. M., Antianxiety drugs and human performance, *Archives of General Psychiatry*, 29, 611, 1973.

6. Heishman, S. J., Taylor, R. C., and Henningfield, J. E., Nicotine and smoking: A review of effects on human performance, *Experimental and Clinical Psychopharmacology*, 2, 345, 1994.

7. Foltin, R. W. and Evans, S. M., Performance effects of drugs of abuse: A methodological survey, *Human Psychopharmacology*, 8, 9, 1993.

8. Hindmarch, I., Psychomotor function and psychoactive drugs, *British Journal of Clinical Pharmacology*, 10, 189, 1980.

9. Nicholson, A. N. and Ward, J., Eds., Psychotropic drugs and performance, *British Journal of Clinical Pharmacology*, 18, 1S, 1984.

10. Beardsley, P. M. and Kelly, T. H., Acute effects of cannabis on human behavior and CNS function: Update of experimental studies, in press.

11. Chait, L. D. and Pierri, J., Effects of smoked marijuana on human performance: A critical review, in *Marijuana/Cannabinoids: Neurobiology and Neurophysiology*, Murphy, L. andBartke, A., Eds., CRC Press, Boca Raton, 1992, 387.

12. Curran, H. V., Benzodiazepines, memory and mood: A review, *Psychopharmacology*, 105, 1, 1991.

13. Ghoneim, M. M. and Mewaldt, S. P., Benzodiazepines and human memory: A review, *Anesthesiology*, 72, 926, 1990.

14. Koelega, H. S., Benzodiazepines and vigilance performance: A review, *Psychopharmacology*, 98, 145, 1989.

15. Sherwood, N., Effects of nicotine on human psychomotor performance, *Human Psychopharmacology*, 8, 155, 1993.

16. Zacny, J. P., A review of the effects of opioids on psychomotor and cognitive functioning in humans, *Experimental and Clinical Psychopharmacology*, 3, 432, 1995.

17. Gavin, F. H. and Ellinwood, E. H., Cocaine and other stimulants: Actions, abuse, and treatment, *New England Journal of Medicine*, 318, 1173, 1988.

18. Jaffe, J. H., Drug addiction and drug abuse, in *The Pharmacological Basis of Therapeutics*, Gilman, A. G., Rall, T. W., Nies, A. S., and Taylor, P., Eds., Pergamon Press, New York, 1990, 522.

19. Fischman, M. W. and Schuster, C. R., Cocaine self-administration in humans, *Federation Proceedings*, 41, 241, 1982.

20. Woolverton, W. L., Kandel, D., and Schuster, C. R., Tolerance and cross-tolerance to cocaine and *d*-amphetamine, *Jounral of Pharmacology and Experimental Therapeutics*, 205, 525, 1978.

21. Derlet, R. W., Rice, P., Horowitz, B. Z., and Lord, R. V., Amphetamine toxicity: Experience with 127 cases, *Journal of Emergency Medicine*, 7, 157, 1989.

22. Myerson, A., Effect of benzedrine sulphate on mood and fatigue in normal and in neurotic persons, *Archives of Neurology and Psychiatry*, 36, 816, 1936.

23. Smith, J. M. and Misiak, H., Critical Flicker Frequency (CFF) and psychotropic drugs in normal human subjects - a review, *Psychopharmacology*, 47, 175, 1976.

24. Farre, M., de la Torre, R., Llorente, M., Lamas, X., Ugena, B., Segura, J., and Cami, J., Alcohol and cocaine interactions in humans, *Journal of Pharmacology and Experimental Therapeutics*, 266, 1364, 1993.

25. Peck, A. W., Bye, C. E., Clubley, M., Henson, T., and Riddington, C., A comparison of bupropion hydrochloride with dexamphetamine and amitriptyline in healthy subjects, *British Journal of Clinical Pharmacology*, 7, 469, 1979.

26. Bye, C., Munro-Faure, A. D., Peck, A. W., and Young, P. A., A comparison of the effects of 1-benzylpiperazine and dexamphetamine on human performance tests, *European Journal of Clinical Pharmacology*, 6, 163, 1973.

27. Evans, M. A., Martz, R., Rodda, B. E., Lemberger, L., and Forney, R. B., Effects of marihuana-dextroamphetamine combination, *Clinical Pharmacology and Therapeutics*, 20, 350, 1976.

28. Hamilton, M. J., Smith, P. R., and Peck, A. W., Effcts of bupropion, nomifensine and dexamphetamine on performance, subjective feelings, autonomic variables and electroencephalogram in healthy volunteers, *British Journal of Clinical Pharmacology*, 15, 367, 1983.

Stephen J. Heishman

29. Higgins, S. T. and Stitzer, M. L., Monologue speech: Effects of *d*-amphetamine, secobarbital and diazepam, *Pharmacology Biochemistry and Behavior*, 34, 609, 1989.

30. Heishman, S. J. and Stitzer, M. L., Effects of *d*-amphetamine, secobarbital, and marijuana on choice behavior: Social versus nonsocial options. *Psychopharmacology*, 99, 156, 1989.

31. Kinchla, R. A., Attention, *Annual Review of Psychology*, 43, 711, 1992.

32. Warm, J. S., Ed., *Sustained Attention in Human Performance*, Wiley, New York, 1984.

33. McLeod, D. R., Griffiths, R. R., Bigelow, G. E., and Yingling, J., An automated version of the digit symbol substitution task (DSST), *Behavioral Research Methods and Instrumentation*, 14, 463, 1982.

34. Higgins, S. T., Bickel, W. K., Hughes, J. R., Lynn, M., Capeless, M. A., and Fenwick, J. W., Effects of intranasal cocaine on human learning, performance and physiology, *Psychopharmacology*, 102, 451, 1990.

35. Higgins, S. T., Rush, C. R., Bickel, W. K., Hughes, J. R., Lynn, M., and Capeless, M. A., Acute behavioral and cardiac effects of cocaine and alcohol combinations in humans, *Psychopharmacology*, 111, 285, 1993.

36. Foltin, R. W., Fischman, M. W., Pippen, P. A., and Kelly, T. H., Behavioral effects of cocaine alone and in combination with ethanol or marijuana in humans, *Drug and Alcohol Dependence*, 32, 93, 1993.

37. Perez-Reyes, M., White, W. R., McDonald, S. A., and Hicks, R. E., Interaction between ethanol and dextroamphetamine: Effects on psychomotor performance, *Alcoholism: Clinical and Experimental Research*, 16, 75, 1992.

38. Kelly, T. H., Foltin, R. W., and Fischman, M. W., The effects of repeated amphetamine exposure on multiple measures of human behavior, *Pharmacology Biochemistry and Behavior*, 38, 417, 1991.

39. Higgins, S. T., Rush, C. R., Hughes, J. R., Bickel, W. K., Lynn, M., and Capeless, M. A., Effects of cocaine and alcohol, alone and in combination, on human learning and performance, *Journal of the Experimental Analysis of Behavior*, 58, 87, 1992.

40. Foltin, R. W. and Fischman, M. W., The effects of combinations of intranasal cocaine, smoked marijuana, and task performance on heart rate and blood pressure, *Pharmacology Biochemistry and Behavior*, 36, 311, 1990.

41. Foltin, R. W., McEntee, M. A., Capriotti, R. M., Pedroso, J. J., and Fischman, M. W., Effects of cocaine, alone and in combination with task performance, on heart rate and blood pressure, *Pharmacology Biochemistry and Behavior*, 31, 387, 1988.

42. Soetens, E., D'Hooge, R., and Hueting, J. E., Amphetamine enhances human-memory consolidation, *Neuroscience Letters*, 161, 9, 1993.

43. Johnston, L. D., O'Malley, P. M., and Bachman, J. G., *National survey results on drug use from the Monitoring the Future Study, 1975-1994* (NIH Publication No. 95-4026). U.S. Government Printing Office, Washington, DC, 1995.

44. Sherwood, N., Kerr, J. S., and Hindmarch, I., Psychomotor performance in smokers following single and repeated doses of nicotine gum, *Psychopharmacology*, 108, 432, 1992.

45. Hindmarch, I., Kerr, J. S., and Sherwood, N., Effects of nicotine gum on psychomotor performance in smokers and non-smokers, *Psychopharmacology*, 100, 535, 1990.

46. Jones, G. M. M., Sahakian, B. J., Levy, R., Warburton, D. M., and Gray, J. A., Effects of acute subcutaneous nicotine on attention, information processing and short-term memory in Alzheimer's disease, *Psychopharmacology*, 108, 485, 1992.

47. Kerr, J. S., Sherwood, N., and Hindmarch, I., Separate and combined effects of the social drugs on psychomotor performance, *Psychopharmacology*, 104, 113, 1991.

48. Foulds, J., Stapleton, J., Swettenham, J., Bell, N., McSorley, K., Russell, M. A. H., Cognitive performance effects of subcutaneous nicotine in smokers and never-smokers, *Psychopharmacology*, 127, 31, 1996.

49. Perkins, K. A., Epstein, L. H., Stiller, R. L., Sexton, J. E., Debski, T. D., and Jacob, R. G., Behavioral performance effects of nicotine in smokers and nonsmokers, *Pharmacology Biochemistry and Behavior*, 37, 11, 1990.

50. Perkins, K. A., Grobe, J. E., Fonte, C., Goettler, J., Caggiula, A. R., Reynolds, W. A., Stiller, R. L., Scierka, A., and Jacob, R. G., Chronic and acute tolerance to subjective, behavioral and

cardiovascular effects of nicotine in humans, *Journal of Pharmacology and Experimental Therapeutics*, 270, 628, 1994.

51. West, R. J. and Jarvis, M. J., Effects of nicotine on finger tapping rate in non-smokers, *Pharmacology Biochemistry and Behavior*, 25, 727, 1986.

52. Le Houezec, J., Halliday, R., Benowitz, N. L., Callaway, E., Naylor, H., and Herzig, K., A low dose of subcutaneous nicotine improves information processing in non-smokers, *Psychopharmacology*, 114, 628, 1994.

53. Snyder, F. R. and Henningfield, J. E., Effects of nicotine administration following 12 h of tobacco deprivation: Assessment on computerized performance tasks, *Psychopharmacology*, 97, 17, 1989.

54. Parrott, A. C. and Craig, D., Cigarette smoking and nicotine gum (0, 2 and 4 mg): Effects upon four visual attention tasks, *Neuropsychobiology*, 25, 34, 1992.

55. Stroop, J. R., Studies of interference in serial verbal reactions, *Journal of Experimental Psychology*, 18, 643, 1935.

56. Wesnes, K. and Revell, A., The separate and combined effects of scopolamine and nicotine on human information processing, *Psychopharmacology*, 84, 5, 1984.

57. Provost, S. C. and Woodward, R., Effects of nicotine gum on repeated administration of the Stroop test, *Psychopharmacology*, 104, 536, 1991.

58. Heishman, S. J., Snyder, F. R., and Henningfield, J. E., Performance, subjective, and physiological effects of nicotine in nonsmokers, *Drug and Alcohol Dependence*, 34, 11, 1993.

59. Wesnes, K. and Warburton, D. M., Effects of smoking on rapid information processing performance, *Neuropsychobiology*, 9, 223, 1983.

60. Parrott, A. C. and Winder, G., Nicotine chewing gum (2 mg, 4 mg) and cigarette smoking: Comparative effects upon vigilance and heart rate, *Psychopharmacology*, 97, 257, 1989.

61. Michel, C., Hasenfratz, M., Nil, R., and Battig, K., Cardiovascular, electrocortical, and behavioral effects of nicotine chewing gum, *Klinische Wochenschrift*, 66 (Suppl. 11), 72,1988.

62. Wesnes, K., & Warburton, D. M., and Matz, B., Effects of nicotine on stimulus sensitivity and response bias in a visual vigilance task, *Neuropsychobiology*, 9, 41, 1983.

63. Wesnes, K. and Revell, A., The separate and combined effects of scopolamine and nicotine on human information processing, *Psychopharmacology*, 84, 5, 1984.

64. Wesnes, K. and Warburton, D. M., Effects of scopolamine and nicotine on human rapid information processing performance, *Psychopharmacology*, 82, 147, 1984.

65. Andersson, K. and Post, B., Effects of cigarette smoking on verbal rote learning and physiological arousal, *Scandinavian Journal of Psychology*, 15, 263, 1974.

66. Colrain, I. M., Mangan, G. L., Pellett, O. L., and Bates, T. C., Effects of post-learning smoking on memory consolidation, *Psychopharmacology*, 108, 448, 1992.

67. Warburton, D. M., Rusted, J. M., and Fowler, J., A comparison of the attentional and consolidation hypotheses for the facilitation of memory by nicotine, *Psychopharmacology*, 108, 443, 1992.

68. Warburton, D. M., Rusted, J. M., and Muller, C., Patterns of facilitation of memory by nicotine, *Behavioural Pharmacology*, 3, 375, 1992.

69. Rusted, J., Graupner, L., and Warburton, D., Effects of post-trial administration of nicotine on humans memory: Evaluating the conditions for improving memory, *Psychopharmacology*, 119, 405, 1995.

70. Krebs, S. J., Petros, T. V., and Beckwith, B. E., Effects of smoking on memory for prose passages, *Physiology and Behavior*, 56, 723, 1994.

71. West, R. and Hack, S., Effect of cigarettes on memory search and subjective ratings. *Pharmacology Biochemistry and Behavior*, 38, 281, 1991.

72. Rusted, J. and Eaton-Williams, P., Distinguishing between attentional and amnestic effects in information processing: The separate and combined effects scopolamine and nicotine onverbal free recall, *Psychopharmacology*, 104, 363, 1991.

73. Houston, J. P., Schneider, N. G., and Jarvik, M. E., Effects of smoking on free recall and organization, *American Journal of Psychiatry*, 135, 220, 1978.

74. Newhouse, P. A., Sunderland, T., Tariot, P. N., Blumhardt, C. L., Weingartner, H., Mellow, A., and Murphy, D. L., Intravenous nicotine in Alzheimer's disease: A pilot study. *Psychopharmacology*, 95, 171, 1988.
75. Dunne, M. P., MacDonald, D., and Hartley, L. R., The effects of nicotine upon memory and problem solving performance, *Physiology and Behavior*, 37, 849, 1986.
76. Johnson, L., and Chernik, D. A., Sedative-hypnotics and human performance, *Psychopharmacology*, 76, 101, 1982.
77. Griffiths, R. R. and Wolf, B., Relative abuse liability of different benzodiazepines in drug abusers, *Journal of Clinical Psychopharmacology*, 10, 237, 1990.
78. Woods, J. H., Katz, J. L., and Winger, G., Abuse liability of benzodiazepines. *Pharmacological Reviews*, 39, 251, 1987.
79. de Wit, H. and Griffiths, R. R., Testing the abuse liability of anxiolytic and hypnotic drugs in humans, *Drug and Alcohol Dependence*, 28, 83, 1991.
80. Kunsman, G. W., Manno, J. E., Manno, B. R., Kunsman, C. M., and Przekop, M. A., The use of microcomputer-based psychomotor tests for the evaluation of benzodiazepine effects on human performance: A review with emphasis on temazepam, *British Journal of Clinical Pharmacology*, 34, 289, 1992.
81. Hindmarch, I., Sherwood, N., and Kerr, J. S., Amnestic effects of triazolam and other hypnotics, *Progress in Neuro-Psychopharmacology and Biological Psychiatry*, 17, 407, 1993.
82. Blom, M. W., Bartel, P. R., de Sommers, K., Van der Meyden, C. H., and Becker, P. J., The effects of alprazolam, quazepam and diazepam on saccadic eye movements, parametersof psychomotor function and the EEG, *Fundamental and Clinical Pharmacology*, 4, 653, 1990.
83. Curran, H. V. and Birch, B., Differentiating the sedaitve, psychomotor and amnesic effects of benzodiazepines: A study with midazolam and the benzodiazepine antagonist, fluumazenil, *Psychopharmacolgy*, 103, 519, 1991.
84. Kerr, J. S., Hindmarch, I., and Sherwood, N., Correlation between doses of oxazepam and their effects on performance of a standardised test battery, *European Journal of Clinical Pharmacology*, 42, 507, 1992.
85. Bishop, K. I., Curran, H. V., and Lader, M., Do scopolamine and lorazepam have disssociable effects on human memory systems? A dose-repsone study with normal volunteers, *Experimental and Clinical Psychopharmacology*, 4, 292, 1996.
86. Saano, V., Hansen, P. P., and Paronen, P., Interactions and comparative effects of zoplicone, diazepam and lorazepam on psychomotor performance and on elimination pharmacokinetics in healthy volunteers, *Pharmacology and Toxicology*, 70, 135, 1992.
87. Curran, H. V., Schifano, F., and Lader, M., Models of memory dysfunction? A comparison of the effects of scopolomine and lorazepam on memory, psychomotor performance and mood, *Psychopharmacology*, 103, 83, 1991.
88. Rettig, H. C., de Haan, P., Zuurmond, W. W. A., and van Leeuwen, L., Effects of hypnotics on sleep and psychomotor performance: A double-blind randomized study of lormetazepam, midazolam and zopiclone, *Anaesthesia*, 45, 1079, 1990.
89. Bond, A., Silveira, J. C., and Lader, M., Effects of single doses of alprazolam and alcohol alone and in combination on physiological performance, *Human Psychopharmacology*, 6, 219, 1991.
90. Evans, S. M., Troisi, J. R., and Griffiths, R. R., Tandospirone and alprazolam: Comparison of behavoral effects and abuse liability in humans, *Journal of Pharmacology andExperimental Therapeutics*, 271, 683, 1994.
91. Preston, K. L., Wolf, B., Guarino, J. J., and Griffiths, R. R., Subjective and behavioral effects of diphenhydramine, lorazepam and methocarbamol: Evaluation of abuse liability, *Journal of Pharmacology and Experimental Therapeutics*, 262, 707, 1992.
92. Evans, S. M., Funderburk, F. R., and Griffiths, R. R., Zolpidem and triazolam in humans: Behavioral and subjective effects and abuse liability, *Journal of Pharmacology and Experimental Therapeutics*, 255, 1246, 1990.
93. Kirk, T., Roache, J. D., and Griffiths, R. R., Dose-response evalutaion of the amnestic effects of triazolam and pentobarbital in normal subjects, *Journal of Clinical Psychopharmacology*, 10, 160, 1990.

94. Roache, J. D., Cherek, D. R., Bennett, R. H., Schenkler, J. C., and Cowan, K. A., Differential effects of triazolam and ethanol on awareness, memory, and psychomotor performance, *Journal of Clinical Psychopharmacology*, 13, 3, 1993.

95. Roache, J. D. and Griffiths, R. R., Diazepam and triazolam self-administration in sedative abusers: Concordance of subject ratings, performance and drug self-administration, *Psychopharmacology*, 99, 309, 1989.

96. Kumar, R., Mac, D. S., Gabrielli, W. F., Goodwin, D. W., Anxiolytics and memory: A comparison of lorazepam and alprazolam, *Journal of Clinical Psychiatry*, 48, 158, 1987.

97. Tobler, I., Dijk, D. J., Jaggi, K., and Borbely, A. A., Effects of night-time motor activity and performance in the morning after midazolam intake during the night, *Arzniemittel-Forschung*, 41, 581, 1991.

98. Fleishaker, J. C., Sisson, T. A., Sramek, J. J., Conrad, J., Veroff, A. E., and Cutler, N. R., Psychomotor and memory effetcs of two adinazolam formulations assessed by a computerized neuropsychological test battery, *Journal of Clinical Pharmacology*, 33, 463, 1993.

99. Ingum, J., Bjorlund, R., Bjorneboe, A., Christophersen, A. S., Dahlin, E., and Morland, J., Relationship between drug plasma concentrations and psychomotor performance after single doses of ethanol and benzodiaepines, *Psychopharnmacology*, 107, 11, 1992.

100. Roache, J. D. and Griffiths, R. R., Lorazepam and meprobamate dose effects in humans: Behavioral effects and abuse liability, *Journal of Pharmacology and Experimental Therapeutics*, 243, 978, 1987.

101. Linnoila, M., Stapleton, J. M., Lister, R., Moss, H., Lane, E., Granger, A., Greenblatt, D.. J., and Eckardt, M. J., Effects of adinazolam and diazepam, alone and in combination with ethanol, on psychomotor and cognitive performance and on autonomic nervous system reactivity in healthy volunteers, *European Journal of Clinical Pharmacology*, 38, 371, 1990.

102. Linnoila, M., Stapleton, J. M., Lister R., Moss, H., Lane, E., Granegr, A., and Eckardt, M. J., Effects of single doses of alprazolam and diazepam, alone and in combination with ethanol, on psychomotor and cognitive performance and on autonomic nervous system reactivity in healthy volunteers, *European Journal of Clinical Pharmacology*, 39, 21, 1990.

103. Moskowitz, H., Linnoila, M., and Roehrs, T., Psychomotor performance in chronic insomniacs during 14-day use of flurazepam and midazolam, *Journal of Clinical Psychopharmacology*, 10, 44S, 1990.

104. Ellinwood, E.H., Heatherly, D. G., Nikaido, A. M., Bjornsson, T. D., and Kilts, C., Comparative pharmacokinetics and pharmacodynamics of lorazepam, alprazolam and diazepam, *Psychopharmacology*, 86, 392, 1985.

105. Roache, J. D., Cherek, D. R., Spiga, R., Bennett, R. H., Cowan, K. H., and Yingling, J., Benzodiazepine-induced impairment of matching-to-sample performance in humans, *Pharmacology, Biochemisty and Behavior*, 36, 945, 1990.

106. Rush, C. R., Higgins, S. T., Bickel, W. K., and Hughes, J. R., Acute behavioral effects of lorazepam and caffeine, alone and in combination, in humans, *Behavioural Pharmacology*, 5,245, 1994.

107. Rush, C. R., Higgins, S. T., Hughes, J. R., and Bickel, W. K., A compaison of the acute behavioral effects of triazolam and temazepam in normal volunteers, *Psychopharmacology*, 112, 407, 1993.

108. Rush, C. R., Higgins, S. T., Hughes, J. R., and Bickel, W. K., Acute behavioral effects of triazolam and caffeine, alone and in combination, in humans, *Experimental and Clinical Psychopharmacology*, 2, 211, 1994.

109. Rush, C. R., Madakasira, S., and Goldman, N. H., Acute behavioral effects of estazolam and triazolam in non-drug-abusing volunteers, *Experimental and Clinical Psychopharmacology*, 4, 300, 1996.

110. Freidman, H., Greenblatt, D. J., Peters, G. R., Metzler, C. M., Charlton, M. D., Harmatz, J. S., Antal, E. J., Sanborn, E. C., and Francom, S. F., Pharmacokinetics and pharmacodynamics of oral diazepam: Effect of dose, plasma concentration, and time, *Clinical Pharmacology and Therapeutics*, 52, 139, 1992.

111. Kelly, T. H., Foltin, R. W., King, L., and Fischman, M. W., Behavioral response to diazepam in a residential laboratory, *Biological Psychiatry*, 31, 808, 1992.

Stephen J. Heishman

112. Brown, G. G., Rich, J. B., and Simkins-Bullock, J., Correlated changes in focused attention and associative encoding following diazepam ingestion, *Experimental and Clinical Psychopharmacology*, 4, 114, 1996.

113. Volkerts, E. R., Van Laar, M. W., Van Willigenburg, A. P. P., Plomp, T. A., and Maes, R. A. A., A comparative study of on-the-road and simulated driving performance after nocturnal treatment with lormetazepam 1 mg and oxazepam 50 mg, *Human Psychopharmacology*, 7, 297, 1992.

114. Brookhuis, K. A., Volkerts, E. R., and O'Hanlon, J. F., Repeated dose effects of lormetazepam and flurazepam upon driving performance, *European Journal of ClinicalPharmacology*, 39, 83, 1990.

115. Kuitunen, T., Drug and ethanol effects on the clinical test for drunkenness: Single doses of ethanol, hypnotic drugs and antidepressant drugs, *Pharmacology and Toxicology*, 75, 91, 1994.

116. Roache, J. D., Spiga, R., and Burt, D. B., Triazolam and ethanol effects on human matching-to-sample performance vary as a function of pattern size and discriminability, *Drug and Alcohol Dependence*, 32, 219, 1993.

117. Danion, J. N., Weingartner, H., File, S. E., Jaffard, R., Sunderland, T., Tulving, E., and Warburton, D. M., Pharmacology of human memory and cognition: Illustrations from the effects of benzodiazepines and cholinergic drugs, *Journal of Psychopharmacology*, 7, 371, 1993.

118. Hommer, D., Weingartner, H., and Breier, A., Dissociation of benzodiazepine-induced amnesia from sedation by flumazenil pretreatment, *Psychopharmacology*, 112, 455, 1993.

119. Roy-Byrne, P. P., Uhde, T. W., Holcomb, H., Thompson, K., King, A. K., and Weingartner, H., Effects of diazepam on cogitive processes in normal subjects, *Psychopharmacology*, 91, 30, 1987.

120. Weingartner, H. J., Hommer, D., Lister, R. G., Thompson, K., and Wolkowitz, O., Selective effects of triazolam on memory, *Psychopharmacology*, 106, 341, 1992.

121. Weingartner, H. J., Joyce, E. M., Sirocco, K. Y., Adams, C. M., Eckardt, M. J., George, T., and Lister, R. J., Specific memory and sedative effects of the benzodiazepine triazolam, *Journal of Psychopharmacology*, 7, 305, 1993.

122. Barbee, J. G., Black, F. W., and Todorov, A. A., Differential effects of alprazolam and buspirone upon acquisition, retention, and retrieval processes in memory, *Journal of Neuropsychiatry and Clinical Neurosciences*, 4, 308, 1992.

123. Rusted, J. M., Eaton-Willliams, P., and Warburton, D. M., A comparison of the effects of scopolamine and diazepam on working memory, *Psychopharmacology*, 105, 442, 1991.

124. Schifano, F. and Curran, H. V., Pharmacological models of memory dysfunction? A comparison of the effects of scopolamine and lorazepam on word valence ratings, priming and recall, *Psychopharmacology*, 115, 430, 1994.

125. Bixler, E. O., Kales, A., Manfredi, R. L., Vgontzas, A. N., Tyson, K, L., and Kales, J. D., Next-day memory imparirment with triazolam use, *Lancet*, 337, 827, 1991.

126. Bickel, W. K., Hughes, J. R., and Higgins, S. T., Human behavioral pharmacology of benzodiazepines: Effects on repeated acquisition and performance of response chains, *Drug Development Research*, 20, 53, 1990.

127. Bickel, W. K., Higggins, S. T., and Hughes, J. R., The effects of diazepam and triazolam on repeated acquisition and performance of response sequences with an observing response, *Journal of the Experimental Analysis of Behavior*, 56, 217, 1991.

128. Bickel, W. K., Higgins, S. T., and Griffiths, R. R., Repeated diazepam administration: effects on the acquisition amd performance of response chains in humans, *Journal of the Experimental Analysis of Behavior*, 52, 47, 1989.

129. Judd, L. L., Ellinwood, E., and McAdams, L. A., Cognitive performance and mood in patients with chronic insomnia during 14-day use of flurazepam and midazolam, *Journal of Clinical Psychopharmacology*, 10, 56S, 1990.

130. Jaffe, J. H. and Martin, W. R., in *The Pharmacological Basis of Therapeutics*, Gilman, A. G., Rall, T. W., Nies, A. S., and Taylor, P., Eds., Pergamon Press, New York, 1990, 485.

131. Chesher, G. B., Understanding the opioid analgesics and their effects on skills performance, *Alcohol, Drugs and Driving*, 5, 111, 1989.

132. O'Neil, W. M., The cognitive and psychomotor effects of opioid drugs in cancer pain management, in *Cancer Surveys Volume 21: Palliative Medicine: Problem Ares in Pain andSymptom Management*, Imperial Cancer Research Fund, 1994, 67.

133. Veselis, R. A., Reinsel, R. A., Feshchenko, V. A., Wronski, M., Dnistrian, A., Dutcher, S., and Wilson, R., Impaired memory and behavioral performance with fentanyl at low plasma concentrations, *Anesthesia and Analgesia*, 79, 952, 1994.

134. Saarialho-Kere, U., Mattila, M. J., and Seppala, T., Parenteral pentazocine: Effects on psychomotor skills and respiration, and interactions with amitriptyline, *European Journal of Clinical Pharmacology*, 35, 483, 1988.

135. Zacny, J. P., Lichtor, J. L., Flemming, D., Coalson, D. W., Thompson, W. K., A dose-response analysis of the subjective, psychomotor and physiological effects of intravenous morphine in healthy volunteers, *Journal of Pharmacology and Experimental Therapeutics*, 268, 1, 1994.

136. Zacny, P. J., Lichtor, J. L., Thapar, P., Coalson, D. W., Flemming, D., and Thompson, W. K., Comparing the subjective, psychomotor and physiological effects of intravenous butorphanol and morphine in healthy volunteers, *Journal of Pharmacology and Experimental Therapeutics*, 270, 579, 1994.

137. Zacny, J. P., Lichtor, J. L., de Wit, H., Subjective, behavioral, and physiologic responses to intravenous dezocine in healthy volunteers, *Anesthesia and Analgesia*, 74, 523, 1992.

138. Zacny, J. P., Lichtor, J. L., Zaragoza, J. G., and de Wit, H., Subjective and behavioral responses to intravenous fentanyl in healthy volunteers, *Psychopharmacology*, 107, 319, 1992.

139. Zacny, J. P., Lichtor, J. L., Binstock, W., Coalson, D. W., Cutter, T., Flemming, D. C., and Glosten, B., Subjective, behavioral and physiologic responses to meperidine in healthy volunteers, *Psychopharmacology*, 111, 306, 1993.

140. Thapar, P., Zacny, J. P., Thompson, W., Jeffrey, B. S., Apfelbaum, L., Using alcohol as a standard to assess the degree of impairment induced by sedative and analgesic drugs inambulatory surgery, *Anesthesiology*, 82, 53, 1995.

141. Thapar, P., Zacny, J. P., Choi, M., and Apfelbaum, J. L., Objective and subjective impaiment from often-used sedative/analgesic combinations in ambulatory surgery, using alcohol as a benchmark, *Ambulatory Anesthesia*, 80, 1092, 1995.

142. Kerr, B., Hill, H., Coda, B., Calogero, M., Chapman, C. R., Hunt, E., Buffington, V., and Mackie, A., Concentration-related effects of morphine on cognitive and motor control in human subjects, *Neuropsychopharmacology*, 5, 157, 1991.

143. Bruera, E., Macmillan, K., Hanson, J., and MacDonald, R. N., The cognitive effects of the administration of narcotic analgesics in patients with cancer pain, *Pain*, 39, 13, 1989.

144. Jenkins, A. J., Keenan, R. M., Henningfield, J. E., and Cone, E. J., Pharmacokinetics and pharmacodynamics of smoked herion, *Journal of Analytical Toxicology*, 18, 317, 1994.

145. Zacny, J P., Lichtor, J. L., Coalson, D. W., Finn, R. S., Uitvlugt, A. M., Glosten, B., Flemming, D. C., and Apfelbaum, J. L., Subjective and psychomotor effects of subanesthetic doses of propofol in healthy volunterrs, *Anesthesiology*, 76, 696, 1992.

146. Preston, K. L., Bigelow, G. E., and Liebson, I. A., Comparative evaluation of morphine, pentazocine and ciramadol in postaddicts, *Journal of Pharmacology and Experimental Therapeutics*, 240, 900, 1987.

147. Preston, K. L., Liebson, I. A., and Bigelow, G. E., Discrimination of agonist-antagonist opioids in humans trained on a two-choice saline-hydromorphone discrimination, *Journal of Pharmacology and Experimental Therapeutics*, 261, 62, 1992.

148. Strain, E. C., Preston, K. L., Liebson, I. A., and Bigelow, G. E., Acute effects of buprenorphine, hydromorphone and naloxone in methadone-maintained volunteers, *Journal of Pharmacology and Experimental Therapeutics*, 261, 985, 1992.

149. Strain, E. C., Preston, K. L., Liebson, I. A., and Bigelow, G. E., Precipitated withdrawal by pentazocine in methadone-maintained volunteers, *Journal of Pharmacology andExperimental Therapeutics*, 267, 624, 1993.

150. Preston, K. L., Bigelow, G. E., and Liebson, I. A., Discrimination of butorphanol and nalbuphine in opioid-dependent humans, *Pharmacology Biochemistry and Behavior*, 37, 511, 1990.

Stephen J. Heishman

151. Preston, K. L., Bigelow, G. E., and Liebson, I. A., Antagonist effects of nalbuphine in opioid-dependent human volunteers, *Journal of Pharmacology and Experimental Therapeutics*, 248, 929, 1989

152. Stevenson, G. W., Pathria, M. N., Lamping, D. L., Buck, L., Rosenbloom, D., Driving ability after Fentanyl or diazepam: A controlled double-blind study, *Investigative Radiology*, 21, 717, 1986.

153. Schaeffer, J., Andrysiak, T., and Ungerleider, J. T., Cognition and long-term use of ganja (cannabis), *Science*, 213, 465, 1981.

154. Varma, V. K., Malhotra, A. K., Dang, R., Das, K., and Nehra, R., Cannabis and cognitive functions: A prospective study, *Drug and Alcohol Dependence*, 21, 147, 1988.

155. Solowij, N., Michie, P. T., Fox, A. M., Effects of long-term cannabis use on selective attention: An event-related potential study, *Pharmacology Biochemistry and Behavior*, 40, 683, 1991.

156. Block, R. I. and Ghoneim, M. M., Effects of chronic marijuana use on human cognition, *Psychopharmacology*, 110, 219, 1993.

157. Pope, H. G. and Yurgelun-Todd, D., The residual cognitive effects of heavy marijuana use in college students, *Journal of the American Medical Association*, 275, 521, 1996.

158. Pope, H. G., Gruber, A. J., and Yurgelun-Todd, D., The residual neuropsychological effects of cannabis: The current status of research, *Drug and Alcohol Depdendence*, 38, 25, 1995.

159. Leirer, V. O., Yesavage, J. A., and Morrow, D. G., Marijuana carry-over effects on aircraftpilot performance, *Aviation Space and Environmental Medicine*, 62, 221, 1991.

160. Yesavage, J. A., Leirer, V. O., Denari, M., and Hollister, L. E., Carry-over effects of marijuana intoxication on aircraft pilot performance: A preliminary report, *American Journal of Psychiatry*, 142, 1325, 1985.

161. Leirer, V. O., Yesavage, J. A., and Morrow, D. G., Marijuana, aging, and task difficulty effects on pilot performance, *Aviation Space and Environmental Medicine*, 60, 1145, 1989.

162. Chait, L. D., Fischman, M. W., and Schuster, C. R., 'Hangover' effects the morning after marijuana smoking, *Drug and Alcohol Dependence*, 15, 229, 1985.

163. Chait, L. D., Subjective and behavioral effects of marijuana the morning after smoking, *Psychopharmacology*, 100, 328, 1990.

164. Heishman, S. J., Huestis, M. A., Henningfield, J. E., and Cone, E. J., Acute and residual effects of marijuana: Profiles of plasma THC levels, physiological, subjective, and performance measures, *Pharmacology Biochemistry and Behavior*, 37, 561, 1990.

165. Fant, R. V., Heishman, S. J., Bunker, E. B., and Pickworth, W. B., Acute and residual effects of marijuana in humans, *Pharmacology Biochemistry and Behavior*, in press.

166. McGlothin, W. H. and West, L. J., The marihuana problem: An overview, *American Journal of Psychiatry*, 125, 370, 1968.

167. Kupfer, D. J., Detre, T., Koral, J., and Fajans, P., A comment on the "amotivational syndrome" in marijuana smokers, *American Journal of Psychiatry*, 130, 1319, 1973.

168. Comitas, L., Cannabis and work in Jamaica: A refutation of the amotivational syndrome, *Annals of the New York Academy of Science*, 282, 24, 1976.

169. Stefanis, C., Dornbush, R., Fink, M., *Hashish: Studies of Long-term Use*, Raven, New York, 1977.

170. Page, J. B., The amotivational syndrome hypothesis and the Costa Rica study: Relationship between methods and results, *Journal of Psychoactive Drugs*, 15, 261, 1983.

171. Mendelson, J. H., Kuehnle, J. C., Greengerg, I., and Mello, N. K., Operant acquisition of marihuana in man, *Journal of Pharmacology and Experimental Therapeutics*, 198, 42, 1976.

172. Kelly, T. H., Foltin, R. W., Emurian, C. S., and Fischman, M. W., Multidimensional behavioral effects of marijuana, *Progress in Neuro-Psychopharmacology and Biological Psychiatry*, 14, 885, 1990.

173. Foltin, R. W., Fischman, M. W., Brady, J. V., Kelly, T. H., Bernstein, D. J., and Nellis, M. J., Motivational effects of smoked marijuana: Behavioral contingencies and high-probability recreational activities, *Pharmacology Biochemistry and Behavior*, 34, 871, 1989.

174. Foltin, R. W., Fischman, M. W., Brady, J. V., Bernstein, D. J., Capriotti, R. M., Nellis, M. J., and Kelly, T. H., Motivational effects of smoked marijuana: Behavioral contingencies and low-probability activities, *Journal of the Experimental Analysis of Behavior*, 53, 5, 1990.

175. Foltin, R. W., Fischman, M. W., Brady, J. V., Bernstein, D. J., Nellis, M. J., and Kelly, T. H., Marijuana and behavioral contingencies, *Drug Development Research*, 20, 67, 1990.
176. Block, R. I., Farinpour, R., and Braverman, K., Acute effects of marijuana on cognition: Relationships to chronic effects and smoking techniques, *Pharmacology Biochemistry and Behavior*, 43, 907, 1992.
177. Chait, L. D. and Perry, J. L., Acute and residual effects of alcohol and marijuana, alone and in combination, on mood and performance, *Psychopharmacology*, 115, 340, 1994.
178. Heishman, S. J., Arasteh, K., and Stitzer, M. L., Comparative effects of alcohol and marijuana on mood, memory, and performance, *Pharmacology Biochemistry and Behavior*, 58, 93, 1997.
179. Greenberg, H. S., Werness, S. A. S., Pugh, J. E., Andrus, R. O., Anderson, D. J., and Domino, E. F., Short-term effects of smoking marijuana on balance in patients with mulitplesclerosis and normal volunteers, *Clinical Pharmacology and Therapeutics*, 55, 324, 1994.
180. Cone, E. J., Johnson, R. E., Moore, J. D., and Roache, J. D., Acute effects of smoking marijuana on hormones, subjective effects and performance in male human subjects, *Pharmacology Biochemistry and Behavior*, 24, 1749, 1986.
181. Heishman, S. J., Stitzer, M. L., and Bigelow, G. E., Alcohol and marijuana: Comparative dose effect profiles in humans, *Pharmacology Biochemistry and Behavior*, 31, 649, 1988.
182. Wilson, W. H., Ellinwood, E. H., Mathew, R. J., and Johnson, K., Effects of marijuana on performance of a computerized cognitive-neuromotor test battery, *Psychiatry Research*, 51, 115, 1994.
183. Kelly, T. H., Foltin, R. W., and Fischman, M. W., Effects of smoked marijuana on heart rate, drug ratings and task performance by humans, *Behavioural Pharmacology*, 4, 167, 1993.
184. Azorlosa, J. L., Heishman, S. J., Stitzer, M. L., and Mahaffey, J. M., Marijuana smoking: Effect of varying Δ^9-tetrahydrocannabinol content and number of puffs, *Journal of Pharmacology and Experimental Therapeutics*, 261, 114, 1992.
185. Heishman, S. J., Stitzer, M. L., and Yingling, J. E., Effects of tetrahydrocannabinol content on marijuana smoking behavior, subjective reports, and performance, *Pharmacology Biochemistry and Behavior*, 34, 173, 1989.
186. Kamien, J. B., Bickel, W. K., Higgins, S. T., and Hughes, J. R., The effects of Δ^9-tetrahydrocannabinol on repeated acquisition and performance of response sequences and on self-reports in humans, *Behavioural Pharmacology*, 5, 71, 1994.
187. Azorlosa, J. L., Greenwald, M. K., and Stitzer, M. L., Marijuana smoking: Effects of varying puff volume and breathhold duration, *Journal of Pharmacology and Experimental Therapeutics*, 272, 560, 1995.
188. Hooker, W. D. and Jones, R. T., Increased susceptibility to memory intrusions and theStroop interference effect during acute marijuana intoxication, *Psychopharmacology*, 91, 20, 1987.
189. Marks, D. F. and MacAvoy, M. G., Divided attention performance in cannabis users and non-users following alcohol and cannabis separately and in combination, *Psychopharmacology*, 99, 397, 1989.
190. Perez-Reyes, M., Hicks, R. E., Bumberry, J., Jeffcoat, A. R., and Cook, C. E., Interaction between marihuana and ethanol: Effects on psychomotor performance, *Alcoholism: Clinical and Experimental Research*, 12, 268, 1988.
191. Chait, L. D., Corwin, R. L., and Johanson, C. E., A cumulative dosing procedure for administering marijuana smoke to humans, *Pharmacology Biochemistry and Behavior*, 29, 553, 1988.
192. Kelly, T. H., Foltin, R. W., Emurian, C. S., and Fischman, M. W., Performance-based testing for drugs of abuse: Dose and time profiles of marijuana, amphetamine, alcohol, and diazepam, *Journal of Analytical Toxicology*, 17, 264, 1993.
193. Moskowitz, H., Marihuana and driving, *Accident Analysis and Prevention*, 17, 323, 1985.
194. Heishman, S. J., Singleton, E. G., and Crouch, D. J., Laboratory validation study of Drug Evlauation and Classification program: Ethanol, cocaine, and marijuana, *Journal of Analytical Toxicology*, 20, 468, 1996.
195. Robbe, H. W. J., *Influence of Marijuana on Driving*, University of Limburg Press, Maastricht, 1994.

196. Bahri, T. and Amir, T., Effect of hashish on vigilance performance, *Perceptual and Motor Skills*, 78, 11, 1994.

197. Thompson, T. and Pickens, R., Eds., *Stimulus Properties of Drugs*, Appleton-Century-Crofts, New York, 1971.

198. Thompson, T. and Johanson, C. E., Eds. *Behavioral Pharmacology of Human DrugDependence, NIDA Research Monograph 37*, U.S. Government Printing Office, Washington, DC, 1981.

199. Higgins, S. T., Lamb, R. J., and Henningfield, J. E., Dose-dependent effects of atropine on behavioral and physiologic responses in humans, *Pharmacology Biochemistry and Behavior*, 34, 303, 1989.

200. Snyder, F. R., Davis, F. C., and Henningfield, J. E., The tobacco withdrawal syndrome: Performance decrements assessed on a computerized test battery. *Drug and Alcohol Dependence*, 23, 259, 1989.

201. Brady, J. V., Behavioral assessment of subtle drug abstinence effects: Overview and discussion, in *Problems of Drug Dependence 1989, NIDA Research Monograph 95*, Harris, L. S., Ed., U.S. Government Printing Office, Washington, DC, 1981, 131.

202. Parrott, A. C., Performance tests in human psychopharmacology (1): Test reliability and standardization, *Human Psychopharmacology*, 6, 1, 1991.

203. Parrott, A. C., Performance tests in human psychopharmacology (2): Content validity, criterion validity, and face validity, *Human Psychopharmacology*, 6, 91, 1991.

204. Parrott, A. C., Performance tests in human psychopharmacology (3): Construct validity and test interpretation, *Human Psychopharmacology*, 6, 197, 1991.

205. Herning, R. I., Jones, R. T., Bachman, J., and Mines, A. H., Puff volume increases when low-nicotine cigarettes are smoked, *British Medical Journal*, 283, 1, 1981.

206. Ohlsson, A., Lindgren, J-E., Wahlen, A., Agurell, S., Hollister, L. E., and Gillespie, H. K., Plasma delta-9-tetrahydrocannabinol concentrations and clinical effects after oral and intravenous administration and smoking, *Clinical Pharmacology and Therapeutics*, 28, 409, 1980.

207. Huestis, M. A., Henningfield, J. E., and Cone, E. J., Blood cannabinoids. I. Absorption of THC and formation of 11-OH-THC and THCCOOH during and after smoking marijuana, *Journal of Analytical Toxicology*, 16, 276, 1992.

4.2 PERFORMANCE MEASURES OF BEHAVIORAL IMPAIRMENT IN APPLIED SETTINGS

THOMAS H. KELLY,[1] RICHARD C. TAYLOR,[2] STEPHEN J. HEISHMAN[2], AND DENNIS J. CROUCH[3]

[1]DEPARTMENT OF BEHAVIORAL SCIENCE, COLLEGE OF MEDICINE, UNIVERSITY OF KENTUCKY, LEXINGTON, KENTUCKY
[2]CLINICAL PHARMACOLOGY BRANCH, DIVISION OF INTRAMURAL RESEARCH, NATIONAL INSTITUTE ON DRUG ABUSE, BALTIMORE, MARYLAND
[3]CENTER FOR HUMAN TOXICOLOGY, UNIVERSITY OF UTAH, SALT LAKE CITY, UTAH

A number of technologies for the assessment of performance impairment have emerged in recent years.[1] These technologies, which include biological sample testing, neuropsychological assessment, personality assessment, and performance testing, are designed to identify risks to safety and/or productivity (e.g., poor health, sleep deprivation, drug-induced impairment), and to alter behaviors associated with the development of these risks (e.g., health promotion, reducing drug-taking behavior). Each of these technologies has strengths and limitations.

Biological sample testing is highly specific for the assessment of risk factors associated with the presence of drugs and/or neurotoxins. The primary advantage of biological sample testing is the reliability and validity with which the presence of risk factors can be detected (e.g., published standards for the development and implementation of drug-testing programs are available).[2] If the integrity of testing procedures is maintained, these technologies can provide accurate information regarding prior exposure to a wide variety of agents. There are a number of disadvantages associated with these technologies, however. The costs associated with development and maintenance of testing programs can be substantial. The collection of biological samples can be invasive. The time required to produce a result following collection of a biological sample can be impractical in applications in which immediate results are necessary.

Perhaps the most complicated disadvantage associated with biological sample testing technologies available at the current time is that they provide little information regarding the performance effects of drug exposure. Drugs (and their metabolites) remain in biological samples for many hours/days after exposure, well beyond the period of time that is associated with the performance effects of the drugs. The detection of metabolites in a biological sample, therefore, does not provide information pertaining to whether or not a drug is having an effect on human performance.

Neuropsychological testing technologies attempt to measure neurological and behavioral function. These technologies generally involve one-time measurements of physiological and behavioral responses to tests, and clinical interpretations of the results of the tests are based on comparisons with scores (i.e., norms) collected from populations of individuals with similar characteristics (e.g., age, sex, race, etc.).[3] The reliability and validity of neuropsychological testing technologies are regularly and repeatedly tested, and these procedures can be used to assess the acute and long-term effects of environmental perturbations, such as injuries, disease states, and drug exposure, on human capabilities.

Neuropsychological test battery administration and interpretation should be conducted by appropriately trained professionals, and as such, the efficiency and expense of this technology for use in applied settings will be limited. On the other hand, while generally designed to be administered on a single occasion for clinical assessment, many components of neuropsychological tests can be administered in a reliable manner on a repeated basis as part of an automated performance testing system. Additional research is needed in order to determine the validity of the use of components of neuropsychological test batteries in this manner.

Personality testing technologies attempt to identify and measure personality dimensions that differentiate individuals who have increased safety and/or productivity risks (e.g., drug users) from those that do not. Examples of such screening tools include integrity tests, attitude tests, and the measurement of risk factor profiles. Personality testing technologies have been evaluated most critically when used for pre-employment screening; their use in repeated assessments of workers has received less attention. A major concern with regard to this technology is the high rate of false positives (i.e., identification of an individual as being at risk when the individual is, in fact, not at any risk) that has been associated with its use.[4] Concerns regarding whether these approaches will ever achieve a sufficient level of accuracy to effectively measure performance impairment have been raised.[1]

In contrast to neuropsychological testing technologies, which are designed to be administered on a single occasion for clinical assessment, performance testing technologies are designed for repeated measurement of an individual's performance under standardized testing conditions. Clinical evaluations of performance on these tests can be based on population norms (as is the case with many neuropsychological testing technologies) or on deviations from individually determined performance standards established through repeated measurements of an individual's performance (i.e., change from baseline performance). Most performance testing technologies have emerged from laboratory-based research that has occurred over the past two decades (e.g., see Heishman, this volume).

Laboratory development and evaluation of performance tests have exploded with the increasing availability of desk-top computers, and a wide array of tests and systems are available for which significant information regarding reliability and validity exists. The major advantages of performance testing technologies for the detection of performance impairment are the wide variety of options that are available (i.e., the face validity of performance testing can be addressed through careful selection and modification of existing performance tests), the immediate availability of results, and the non-invasive manner in which tests can be administered (relative to biological sample testing).

Disadvantages include the lack of specificity with regard to test results (i.e., many factors can alter test performance), and the cost of technology development and implementation. The high costs of performance testing technology development and implementation stem, in part, from a lack of information regarding the use of performance tests in applied settings. In addition, while the reliability and validity of performance tests have been repeatedly demonstrated in controlled laboratory settings, little evidence regarding the reliability and validity of these procedures in applied settings has been published in peer-reviewed journals. As such, the utility of these procedures has not been carefully evaluated.

The focus of this section is on issues associated with the use of performance testing technologies for the detection of drug-induced impairment. Because these tests are not selectively sensitive to the effects of drugs alone, discussion will focus on the detection of the effects of risk factors, including drug use, sleep deprivation, or adverse physical or mental health, on performance. It is important to note, however, that while this chapter will specifically address performance testing as a means of impairment detection, no direct or implied recommendation for exclusive development of performance testing technologies for impairment testing is suggested. It is likely that no single technology will be universally effective in all settings, or even in one setting across all individuals over time. A combination of technologies, based on the availability of resources needed to support those technologies, will likely enhance the effectiveness of any impairment testing system.[1,5]

4.2.1 ISSUES IN THE SELECTION AND IMPLEMENTATION OF PERFORMANCE TESTING TECHNOLOGIES

The presence of risk factors, such as adverse physical and emotional health, use of behaviorally active drugs/medication, and sleep deprivation, may compromise performance safety and productivity. However, the presence of such risk factors may or may not have implications for how an individual will perform his or her work. An important consideration in the selection of an impairment testing technology is the purpose for which such testing is intended.[6] Impairment testing can be designed to detect the influence of risk factors on performance, regardless of whether or not the effects are related to an individual's work performance. However, impairment testing can also be designed to detect deviations from optimal work performance, regardless of the presence or absence of risk factors.

While the presence of risk factors may or may not have a direct effect on job performance under normal day-to-day operating conditions, it is often assumed that these factors can have an adverse impact on an individual's performance when there is a change from the normal conditions associated with job performance (e.g., the ability to respond safely and effectively to an emergency). If so, the detection of any change in normal performance (e.g., altered performance during a computerized assessment task) signals a change in an individual's capacity which could have adverse implications for job performance. If detection of risk factors is the objective of impairment testing, finding a technology that is reliable and sensitive to many risk factors may be a useful strategy, and concerns regarding reliability and validity in this pursuit (Heishman, this volume) become of paramount importance.

On the other hand, detection of the effects of risk factors on performance may have little to say about the likelihood with which an individual will effectively perform an appointed task. From this perspective, risk factors are relevant only if they have adverse effects on normal job performance (i.e., job performance is the relevant metric for impairment testing, not performance on assessment tasks). If the objective of impairment testing is to assess the normal job performance, considerations of the relationship between performance during impairment testing and job performance become a primary concern, and criterion validity issues (Heishman, this volume) must be carefully considered. Job simulation tests, such as video-disc simulators for emergency rooms,[7] are examples of performance tests designed to maximize the assessment of on-the-job performance. One advantage of this approach is that employees more easily accept and comply with impairment testing when the face validity of the testing procedures is apparent.[8] On the other hand, the development costs of computerized simulations can be substantial.

While it is important to decide on the purpose(s) for performance impairment testing, practical issues must also be considered. Several reviews of practical considerations associated with the selection and implementation of impairment testing technologies have been published recently, and many details may be obtained from these sources.[3,8-10] However, one primary consideration is the manner in which performance tests will be administered. Performance assessment measures can be administered by trained observers, such as is the common practice with law enforcement personnel who administer field sobriety tests designed to detect the influence of drugs on driving ability, by computers under standardized conditions, or by some combination of these two approaches. The use of trained observers to administer performance impairment tests provides maximum flexibility and minimizes the amount of training and practice required of the test population. However, no well-validated observation systems are currently available, and concerns about the reliability of testers will always be an issue, unless reliability and validity assessment can be incorporated into the standard testing protocol. In addition, the recurring personnel costs associated with these testing procedures are substantial, given the need for repeated test administration.

Automation provides a solution for many of the concerns associated with trained observers. When trained observers are not available, time for testing is limited, or immediate results are needed, automated performance test administration procedures should be considered. It is also possible to standardize the presentation of stimulus materials and data collection with automated testing devices, thereby enhancing the reliability of the testing procedure. Initial start-up costs, which are based on the number of testing sites required and the amount of back-up support needed, can be substantial. However, clinical interpretation of test results is not possible under conditions of strict automation — evaluations are based strictly on algorithms that are established as part of the testing system. Even the most automated systems require some maintenance and set-up support, in addition to data management and interpretation. Given the clear advantages with regard to cost and efficiency, this section will focus primarily on automated performance testing technologies.

4.2.1.1 Selecting a Performance Testing System

When selecting a performance testing system, issues that could affect the practicality, accuracy, and general utility of the system include the specific performance tests that are included in the system, the availability of norms upon which performance can be evaluated (and upon which decisions regarding readiness to perform are based), the reliability and validity of the measures, the accuracy of the measurement, the user interface, and the administrative interface. The relevance of each of these issues will be discussed, as will some additional dimensions that might be considered when evaluating performance test systems.

4.2.1.1.1 Selection of Individual Tests

Many tests generate performance that is sensitive to the effects of risk factors. Tests measure sensory abilities, motor abilities, attentional abilities, and cognitive abilities. These categories have proven effective for differentiating among the effects of drugs on behavior.[11] A general description of individual tests is beyond the scope of this chapter, but such descriptions are available elsewhere.[3,11,12] It is important to note that task parameters vary among similar tests when used in different assessment systems; it is critical to consider the parameters of specific tasks in any test system before assuming which dimensions of performance are being measured during any test.

Sensory tests measure the ability to differentiate between objects varying along a stimulus dimension, such as auditory or visual intensity or frequency, or light flicker rate. The critical flicker frequency test is a commonly used sensory test. Motor ability tests focus on measures associated with motor control. The most common examples of motor tasks are finger tapping tests, tracking tests, and hand steadiness tests. Attention tests include tests of focused attention, in which performance is measured for short durations (typically less than 10 minutes), selective attention, which involves responding to selected stimuli among a variety of distracting or irrelevant stimuli, divided attention, which requires attention to two or more tasks presented simultaneously, and sustained attention, in which some aspect of attention is performed over longer durations (typically 10 minutes or longer).

Focused attention tests include measures of simple and choice reaction time, pursuit tracking, symbol substitution, encoding/decoding, time estimation, continuous performance (i.e., vigilance), visual monitoring, and sequence comparisons. Clearly, performance on these tasks include both sensory and motor components. Selective attention tasks include the Stroop test, Neisser tests, letter and number cancellation tests, dichotic listening tests, and switching or shifting attention tests.

Cognitive tests focus on measures of acquisition, memory, and other performance that demonstrates effective use of language and logic. Acquisition tests include serial and repeated acquisition, and associative learning. Memory tests include immediate and delayed free-recall and recognition tests, matching-to-sample and Sternberg tests, pattern comparison, sequence memory, selective reminding, text memory, the misplaced objects test, facial memory, and digit-span (i.e., digit-recall) or character recall tests. Other cognitive performance tests include spatial rotation, pattern matching, the Manikin Test, logical reasoning, mental arithmetic, linguistic processing, vocabulary, and the Raven Progressive Matrices test.

These tests have been frequently used for detection of the effects of risk factors on human performance. The greater the number of tests used in a system, the more comprehensive the assessment, and the more likely it will be that the adverse effects of any risk factor are detected. However, the cost of testing (i.e., test-taking time and training) is also directly related to the number of tests that are included. Many of these test can be modified to more carefully simulate work-related activities (e.g., digit recall tasks can be reformulated as telephone number recall tasks). Performance impairment test systems use varying combinations of these and other tests; however, there is no commonly agreed upon strategy for selecting the number or diversity of tasks that are used in a test system. Selection of a system, or collection of tests, must be related to the needs of the testing organization and to the objectives of impairment testing.

4.2.1.1.2 Reliability and Validity

The selection of performance impairment test systems should also include a thorough consideration of the reliability and validity of the systems. Reliability refers to the consistency of results on the test across repeated testing, while validity refers to the effectiveness with which the test accomplishes its intended purpose, be that identification of the effects of risk factors or the detection of individuals who are at risk for reduced safety and/or productivity in the workplace.

Many performance impairment test systems are based on face validity, or the degree to which the tests appear to accomplish their intended purposes. While face validity is an important consideration with regard to the acceptance of a testing system by management and the workforce, it is, by itself, insufficient for demonstrating the evidence needed to ensure that the test system is indeed accomplishing its intended purposes. Few commercially available performance impairment systems provide adequate evidence of validity, and the evidence that is provided is often limited by the context under which the evidence was collected (i.e., does not generalize to different worksites). It is advised that information regarding the validity of performance testing systems be collected in a proactive manner when the systems are introduced, as there is not sufficient information available to justify global statements regarding the validity of performance impairment testing systems at the present time.

4.2.1.1.3 Evaluation Norms

Another important consideration in the selection of an impairment testing system is whether norm-based decision criteria will be used to evaluate readiness to perform an assignment, and if so, whether such norms are currently available. It is important that such norms address both decrements and improvements in performance, as improved performance may also signal the influence of a risk factor. For example, stimulant medications may have minimal effect on performance of most tasks, but under test conditions requiring sustained attention, enhanced performance may be noted.[13] These same doses of stimulant medication may have important implications for more complex dimensions of human behavior,[14,15] so the detection of enhanced performance may signal an increased risk for detrimental effects on other more complex behaviors that are not directly measured during testing.

Two approaches to the establishment of norms have been proposed.[10] The first approach stresses the development of standards of performance that are universally applied to all individuals, and evaluation of test performance is based on whether an individual performs above or below a given standard. The second approach utilizes the results of prior performance of an individual to establish a baseline upon which to evaluate future performance.

The use of a fixed performance standard has appeal in that simple and consistent criteria may be uniformly applied to all individuals who are taking the test. If these criteria are closely linked with minimal standards of successful work performance, the utility of the testing procedure is readily acknowledged by both workers and management. However, a number of shortcomings with this strategy are also apparent. There are substantial individual differences in performance on most tests, and the routine performance of some individuals may fall below the standard, independent of the presence of risk factors. In addition, performance on tests may change over time, for example, through normal aging processes.

An individual who has routinely met performance standards may, over time, exhibit gradually decreasing levels of proficiency that may eventually result in sub-standard performance. If standardized criteria are used, legal issues associated with discrimination must also be considered,[8] and the inclusion of the test during initial employment evaluations are strongly recommended. The utility of minimal performance standards also presupposes that test performance is a valid indicator of work performance (as opposed to a valid indicator of the effect of a risk factor). The evidence needed to support such a supposition is rarely available. Under such conditions, the potential for misuse of the performance test is clear.

Change from baseline, as determined by an individual's own past performance, is the more commonly used criteria for evaluation of the effects of risk factors on performance. Performance measures from previous tests can be evaluated with standardized algorithms to establish baselines which can be used to compare with an individual's current or future performance on the same tests under similar test conditions. However, even when baseline measures are used, the establishment of criteria upon which to make decisions regarding whether changes from baseline performance are clinically relevant are often times arbitrary. For example, if a user routinely completed 5.5 trials per minute during a test, what degree of change would be needed to be certain that the performance was influenced by some risk factor, rather than the result of chance variation in normal performance?

Individualized variability criteria, which takes into account a user's "normal" variance in performance, can be computed, as well, and used as a standard by which to evaluate change from baseline. The efficacy of this approach, however, presupposes that the user will provide samples of performance that are independent of the presence of any risk factor during baseline determinations; if baselines are established while an individual is using drugs, for example, the performance of the individual under the influence of a drug will become the norm. Additional research is needed to establish strategies for the development of effective standards of performance evaluation.[16]

Another complication of the baseline approach concerns the interpretation of relative performance among users. It is quite possible, when using baseline criteria, that the identification of a clinically significant decrement in performance from the normal baseline of one user may occur under conditions in which the level of performance of that user is higher than the performance of another user who is performing at baseline level. Interpretation of changes from baseline is a complicated process, and few standards are currently available.

One issue that is routinely associated with the degree of acceptability of testing programs to the workforce is the consequence of poor performance on a test.[8-10] The establishment of policies regarding the response of management to test failures also requires careful consideration. Trice and Steele[8] suggest that coordination between performance testing and employee assistance programs will enhance the utility of both resources in the overall effort to reduce drug use by the workforce, and work to enhance the acceptability of both programs to both management and the workforce.

Questions have been raised about the feasibility of establishing evaluation norms that can be used across different populations and settings, or with similar tests used on different computer test systems. Certainly, situational factors influence performance on computerized performance tests. In addition, epidemiological factors, such as sex and age, have been demonstrated to influence performance on these tests. Due to mechanical and electronic differences across computer systems, as well as differences in software control techniques, it is perhaps impossible to provide norms that can be used across differing testing platforms. No universally accepted norms for the evaluation of task performance are currently available, and it is highly recommended that a scheduled evaluation of the validity of existing norms be planned in a proactive manner whenever these existing norms are used in new setting.

4.2.1.1.4 Administrative Interface

The ease and flexibility of the use of performance impairment test systems can be influenced by the interface between the software and test administrator. Characteristics that might be considered include the flexibility in organizing the tests to be delivered, making changes in test parameters, and in the manner in which data are presented, analyzed, and stored for future access. In general, two strategies can be used to promote flexibility with regard to administration of tests. First, variables that control these characteristics can be placed in generic ASCII files which can be accessed and modified by any number of support programs. Second, the test system may provide an administrator program that can be run as needed to make changes.

Administrative programs vary with regard to the degree of flexibility that is provided and in their ease of use.

Another consideration with regard to the administrative interface, as discussed previously, is the degree to which test delivery can be automated. The need for an administrator to be on site for test delivery has cost and efficiency implications. If the test is completely automated, procedures for maintaining accurate identification regarding test sessions (e.g., participant I.D., date, time, etc.) must be established.

4.2.1.1.5 User Interface

The cost of test delivery can also be influenced by the availability of user interfaces. The user interface can provide access to a variety of support resources to the user, including general instructions and support during training. If an instruction module is available, it should be designed to provide clear, complete, and standardized information and instructions concerning the operation of the test equipment and the completion of task components. One useful feature of an instruction module would be the inclusion of a section designed to assess whether users understood the instructions, particularly if these instructions are important determinants of user performance. This can be accomplished with a series of questions designed to provide additional information when users do not answer questions accurately. The training module should be designed to administer the tests and to provide feedback to users in a manner that enhances the development of stable and reliable performance.

4.2.1.2 Selecting Test Equipment

Hardware considerations for automated performance testing systems generally include the computer, software, monitor, and input devices.

4.2.1.2.1 Computer

Many government and commercial impairment testing technologies have been developed to be implemented on specific computer platforms (e.g., IBM, Macintosh) with particular capabilities. Software and hardware advancements in the past few years, however, are beginning to minimize the differences in platform; for example, many applications developed for an IBM computer system can now be run on a Macintosh system equipped with appropriate software and hardware. It is important to determine the specifications of the computer system that is needed to support a test system, as these specifications may have important implications for the accuracy of stimulus presentation and the precision of performance measures. In addition, there may be substantial costs associated with these specifications.

The speed of the computer processor is one important concern. In general, computerized performance batteries are developed, tested, and validated on computer systems having some minimal processing speed. Running the system on a computer having a slower processing speed could have a detrimental impact on the accuracy of the test. On rare occasions, the timing of events within the test setting is based on this processing speed. Under these conditions, running the system on a computer with either a faster or a slower processing speed would result in timing decisions that were different from those upon which the test system was developed, and could introduce significant variability into the test conditions.

Other concerns include the amount of memory that is needed to present the test and record the results, the manner in which the data is to be stored, and the size and portability of the computer. Typically, the rate-limiting memory factor associated with presentation of test systems on computers is called random-access memory, or RAM. In many computers, the amount of RAM available in a computer can be modified with the purchase and installation of additional memory chips, or through the use of software systems designed to utilize permanent storage space as random-access memory (e.g., virtual memory). However, the use of virtual memory does present software incompatibility problems and timing artifacts on occasion, so the testing of system integrity is strongly recommended when virtual memory is used.

Data storage can also be a concern. Many systems require specific types of data storage components (e.g., diskettes, hard drives, cartridge drives, etc.) to support accurate system function, as timing and processing events can be affected by accessing external storage devices. In addition, some test systems generate substantial amounts of data during each test, and across time with repeated testing of many workers, storage concerns will quickly become a reality. Also, test systems that use individual-subject floating baselines that are calculated from the previous performances of the worker require quick access to a range of data, and data storage components can influence data access rate. A final concern with regard to selecting a computer system is the size and portability of the computer. Many computer platforms provide significant computer functionality in both desk-top and portable computers. Under these conditions, it becomes possible to consider administering performance tests on portable or mobile computers, thereby increasing the flexibility of the testing environment. Of course, such flexibility also increases situational variability which may also have a detrimental impact on test reliability.

Some systems also require that additional components be added to the computer in order to support the testing system. These additional components are typically electronic boards that are placed in expansion slots available inside some computers. These boards provide enhanced functionality to the computer, and include math co-processors, which enable the computer to complete mathematical computations more quickly and thereby enhance the overall operation speed of the computer; timing cards, which allow for more precise and reliable timing functions; analog-to-digital cards, which provide a means of switching between analog and digital electrical signals (computers work with digital signals, but some external devices, such as joy sticks and some physiological recording equipment, produce analog signals); and input-output cards, which enable the computer to turn on stimuli and monitor inputs from external devices that are controlled by different power sources than are used by the computer.

4.2.1.2.2 Monitor

The monitor can be an integral part of the testing system. The presentation of many stimuli occur on the monitor, so if discrimination of stimulus dimensions or measurement of response time to the presentation of stimuli are important dimensions of the test system, the manner in which these stimuli are displayed can influence the response outcomes. The size of the monitor, the quality of image display, the type of color support (color, gray-scale, black-and-white, etc.), the rate at which screen images are refreshed (this issue is important for precise measurement of responding to stimulus presentation), and the amount of time required for images to disappear from the screen (i.e., decay rate) are all important factors to consider when selecting a monitor. In addition, compatibility between monitor and computer should also be evaluated.

4.2.1.2.3 Software

The type of software needed to support testing systems must also be considered. Minimally, considerations of software include the operating system that is required to support the computer and the test program, as well as the software used to develop the test system. Until most recently, operating systems could only run on specific computers, and were not interchangeable. The Microsoft Windows products and OS-2, for example, were developed to run on IBM-type computers, while the Mac Operating System was developed to run on Macintosh computers. Recent advances in computer design, however, make it possible to run operating systems on different computers.

One issue that will merit consideration with regard to selection of operating systems is related to the need for randomization during test delivery. If regular repeated test administrations are anticipated, it will be critically important that stimulus dimensions of tests be determined in a truly random manner. Some operating systems are limited with regard to random number generation, and rely on pseudo-random tables to generate "random" stimulus dimensions. Participants completing tests on a regular basis can become sensitive to recurring patterns in stimulus presentation, even if the patterns are complex, and will adjust their performance accordingly. Under such conditions, the reliability and validity of the tests are disrupted. Only truly random pattern presentations can ensure that participants cannot learn complex patterns of stimulus presentation during the test situation.

The operating system must work in harmony with the test system software. The software used to develop and present the test will be an important consideration only if the users would like the flexibility of changing components of the test process. Many systems were developed with flexibility as an option, and changes in test sequences and parameters (e.g., duration of a test, number of stimulus presentations, etc.) can be changed by accessing menus that are available through the test system software, or by changing values stored in files that can be accessed by many commercially available software programs. Under these conditions, the need to access the test system software will be minimized. However, if complete flexibility and independence are required, the ability to work with the test development software will be a critical consideration.

4.2.1.2.4 Input Devices

Ease of use, training time, and visual support of the test system are all influenced by the type of input devices used by the test system. A staggering number of commercially available input devices can be used with most computers, but the characteristics of these devices must be considered carefully, as response characteristics and timing precision can be influenced by these devices. In addition, the quality and design of these devices must also be considered, as the reliability of some devices can be compromised with extensive or vigorous use in the test setting.

Input devices vary from simple touch-sensitive screens, requiring only the touch of a finger on specified locations on the monitor (e.g., buttons or characters are presented on the monitor by the test software, and response characteristics are determined based on when and where the fingertip is placed on the monitor) to complex application-specific work panels (e.g., flight simulators).

Other commonly used devices include a keyboard, mouse, joysticks, light pen, and drawing board. It is important to factor in the amount of time required to train test participants to use the input devices (e.g., keyboard experience will vary among participants, and may require substantial training for those who have little experience) and whether or not operation of the input device will require visual attention which could affect test results (e.g., if participants are required to continuously scan the monitor for stimulus presentation, visual monitoring of the response input device would impact performance).

4.2.2. TEST IMPLEMENTATION

In addition to considerations of impairment testing systems and the equipment needed to administer those systems, the implementation of the testing system must also be considered. Test cost, frequency of administration, maintenance of stable patterns of performance (i.e., motivation), and worker acceptance are among the issues that merit consideration.[10] In addition, concerns regarding the legal status of performance test systems, the manner in which labor unions and arbitrators might view such test systems, and whether or not there is a potential for misuse of the test system could affect system implementation.[8]

4.2.2.1 Cost

Test costs include the initial expense of acquiring the test equipment and providing a test space, the time required to complete the test, and administrative costs (e.g., record keeping, test set-up, maintenance and replacement of equipment). However, test costs may be complicated by the presence of hidden factors as well.[9] For example, cost of training the users may be substantial. Based on the consequences of test failure, lost work time may also be factored in, particularly under conditions in which the false positive rate (i.e., identification of the influence of a risk factor on a user's performance when none, in fact, exists) is high. There are additional costs associated with initial negotiations between management and workers concerning the appropriateness of a testing program and the consequences of test failure, and potential costs associated with litigation, should it occur.

4.2.2.2 Test Frequency

No clear landmarks exist for making decisions regarding test frequency. In general, tests are administered before an individual begins an assigned work activity. However, risk factors can emerge at any time, and are not limited to activities that occur before work activities begin. For example, the effects of fatigue, illness, and drug use can all occur after work has begun, and would not be measured by tests occurring only at the beginning of a work activity. In addition, it is not clear whether the frequency of test administration influences the reliability of test performance. If tests are administered on a regular basis, or if rest intervals (e.g., weekends) separate successive tests, motivational changes may influence performance.

4.2.2.3 Maintenance of Performance Stability

Repeated test administration, without contingencies designed to maintain motivation, invariably results in decrements in performance over time. The maintenance of motivated performance across repeated administration of a test is an important consideration during the implementation of an impairment testing system. It is generally assumed that under conditions in which access to assigned work activities, and financial compensation for that work, is contingent upon suitable test performance, motivated performance is likely to be maintained across repeated testing.[9] However, there has not been adequate investigations of this assumption. The use of additional contingencies that target performance stability might be helpful, in addition to the seemingly punitive consequence of loss of work opportunities associated with poor performance. It has been suggested that the use of more complex or varied testing procedures may also help to eliminate changes in motivation over time. Clearly, additional research on these issues is needed.

4.2.2.4 User Acceptance

Another important consideration with regard to the implementation of an impairment testing system is the acceptance of the test system by the workforce. Worker acceptance is influenced by comfort in taking the tests, as well as by test relevance, or face validity, availability, and accuracy.[10] Comfort refers to the degree to which worker performance on these tests is acceptable under routine testing conditions, and may be inversely related to the likelihood of false positive outcomes. Relevance, or face validity, is associated with the extent to which workers report that performance during the test will reflect performance of their assigned work tasks. Availability refers to the reliability of the test equipment — if the tests cannot be administered when scheduled, confidence in the accuracy of the test system is questioned. Accuracy refers to the extent to which the test results are related to risk factors. Workers receive direct or indirect feedback on test systems (i.e., pass or fail). Rates of false positives (failures given the absence of any risk factor) and false negatives (passes given worker recognition of the influence of a potential risk factor, such as drug use) influence worker estimates of test accuracy.

4.2.2.5 Legal Issues

No clear guidelines exist with regard to the legal status of performance impairment test systems. In comparison with employee selection criteria, Trice and Steele[8] suggest that the legality of these test systems may be related to the degree to which their use results in discriminatory outcomes. They cite Klein's[17] description of an 80% rule as a workable strategy for assessing discriminatory practices. If the pass rate obtained when testing of any race, sex, or ethnic group is less than 80% of the group with the highest pass rate, then the test system has an adverse impact. Trice and Steele[8] also indicate that the absence of information regarding a cause of test failure could have a negative impact on considerations of the legality of test systems because under such conditions, employees might feel unduly compelled to reveal details of their personal lives.

The status of performance impairment test systems with regard to fair-labor practices is also undetermined at the present time. Trice and Steele[8] suggest that because biological sample testing approaches to the detection of drug use have been ruled in the past to be a mandatory labor practice and, as such, require bargaining with labor or unions prior to implementation, performance test systems would likely be viewed in a similar manner. However, they also note that because performance tests are less invasive than biological sample testing procedures, and can be demonstrated to have greater job relatedness, employers could make the case that performance impairment test systems can be implemented unilaterally without bargaining.

4.2.2.6 Potential for Misuse of Test Systems

Misuse of performance impairment tests are related to the consequences of worker performance. Test systems can be implemented with the sole purpose of providing feedback to workers regarding their level of performance (i.e., no consequences associated with work activities are imposed). The objective of such testing procedures is to provide workers with information to use to adjust their own on-work and off-work behavior in an attempt to more accurately monitor their own levels of safety and productivity. For example, in describing a feasibility study of the implementation of a performance testing system, truck drivers adjusted their own rest behavior based on feedback they received during performance testing, even though that feedback was unrelated to drivers' work eligibility.[18] On the other hand, systems that use the results of performance on impairment tests to influence work eligibility (and possibly employment status) are more likely to involve some risk for test misuse.

No clear guidelines exist for the appropriate use of performance impairment test systems for work eligibility. There is general agreement that in situations in which worker or public safety is potentially influenced by a worker's performance, impairment test systems are justified. However, no clear criteria for identifying safety issues are available.[8] The use of such tests as a means of managing worker productivity is less universally accepted, and if used as an employee evaluation criterion, such tests should be given careful scrutiny.

4.2.3. APPLICATIONS OF PERFORMANCE TESTING TECHNOLOGIES

Currently, laboratory-based performance assessment technologies are applied in at least three settings. The most frequent utilization of this technology is in the law-enforcement setting. Law enforcement personnel have varying amounts of training and experience in the administration of performance tests and in the interpretation of the behavior of individuals during test performance. In addition, law-enforcement personnel have limited opportunities to compare their own evaluations of performance on field sobriety tests with the results of drug assays from blood tests taken concurrently with the tests in order to monitor the accuracy of their evaluations. Under these conditions, the reliability and validity of the field sobriety test remains largely unknown, in spite of its widespread utilization. Results from a recent assessment of the reliability and validity of a comprehensive drug evaluation program, which included a sobriety test, will be presented.

A second application of laboratory-based performance assessment technologies has been in the field of fitness-for-duty assessment, primarily supported by military and other government agencies. A varied number of fitness-for-duty assessment batteries have been developed; several of these will be reviewed. A major strength of these fitness-for-duty assessment batteries is the availability of a substantial database on the reliability and validity with which these batteries can detect changes in performance related to a number of manipulations, including drug administration, sleep deprivation, and exposure to extreme environments.

A third application of laboratory-based performance assessment technologies has been in the field of readiness-to-perform assessment in workplace settings. Many of the approaches to readiness-to-perform assessment that are being used in workplace settings have evolved from strategies that are currently in use in government-sponsored performance assessment batteries or laboratory settings, but, in general, these approaches have been subjected to reliability and validity assessment with less consistency. Several assessment technologies that have been subjected to some reliability and validity assessment will be described.

4.2.3.1 Law Enforcement Applications: Impairment Identification and Evaluation

4.2.3.1.1 Background

Motor vehicle accidents are the leading cause of death in the U.S. for people aged 1 to 34, and ethanol is a factor in nearly half of traffic fatalities each year.[19] Several studies have examined the role of drugs other than ethanol. A national study of fatally injured drivers reported a prevalence rate of 6.4% for drugs other than ethanol.[20] In contrast, studies conducted in metropolitan areas or single states have reported greater drug prevalence rates among fatally injured drivers, ranging from 19 to 37% for marijuana and 8 to 20% for cocaine.[21-24] It is important to note that drug prevalence rates do not indicate whether the drivers were impaired as a result of drug use. There are few universally accepted or validated standards that are available for verification of drug-induced behavioral impairment. The field sobriety test has been promoted as such a standard, but it lacks standardization and has not been subjected to empirical validation.

The Drug Evaluation and Classification (DEC) program was developed to provide an objective and standardized approach to the assessment of driver impairment due to drug use which would meet legal evidentiary standards. The DEC program consists of a standardized evaluation conducted by a trained police officer (Drug Recognition Examiner, DRE) and the toxicological analysis of a biological specimen. The evaluation involves examination of the suspect's appearance, behavior, eyes, performance of four field sobriety tests (FST), vital signs, and questioning of the suspect.[25] From the evaluation, the DRE concludes (1) if the suspect is behaviorally impaired, (2) if the impairment is drug-related, and (3) the drug class or combination of classes causing the impairment.

Results of the toxicological analysis either support or refute the DRE's identification of drug class(es). The performance components of the DEC program are listed in Table 4.2.3.1.2.3. DRE training is extensive. Certification requires 9 days of classroom instruction, during which information pertinent to the DEC evaluation, legal issues related to drug testing, behavioral and physiological effects of drugs, and a written examination are presented, followed by the completion of 12 DEC evaluations involving at least 3 different drug classes. A minimum of

Table 4.2.3.1.2.3 Task Components of the Drug Evaluation and Classification
            Program (DEC)

Motor Ability Tests	Focused Attention	Other Cognitive Performance
Romberg Balance	Time Estimation	Arithmetic Computation
Walk and Turn		Speech
One Leg Stand		
Finger-to-Nose		

75% of these evaluations must be substantiated through toxicological analysis prior to certification.

Trainees must also pass a final written examination prior to obtaining DRE certification.
The DEC program is currently used in 29 states and in the District of Columbia.[26] In the
1980s, Los Angeles Municipal Courts began accepting expert testimony from DREs.[27] Since
1991, courts in Arizona and New York have held that DRE testimony meets the Frye standard
and is thus admissible. Courts in Colorado, Florida, and Minnesota have held that DRE
testimony is admissible and that the Frye standard is inapplicable.[26,28] DRE cases often result
in convictions on impaired driving charges in legal settings.[16]

Although widely used, the validity of the DEC program has received minimal evaluation
under either limited laboratory or field conditions. In the only laboratory study to date, DREs
evaluated research volunteers who were administered d-amphetamine, diazepam, secobarbital,
or marijuana.[29] Results indicated that DREs correctly identified the drug class in 91.7% of cases
when subjects were judged to be impaired, correct identifications were dose dependent, and
the DEC evaluation resulted in a very low false positive rate (1.3%). Several field studies of the
DEC program have also indicated that a high percentage of DRE drug class identifications are
confirmed by toxicological analysis.[16,27,28]

These studies suggest that the DEC program can accurately determine the class of drug
used by impaired drivers. However, the validity of the individual variables of the DEC
evaluation as predictors of drug intake have not been rigorously examined. A recent study
investigated the validity of the variables of the DEC evaluation, including performance
components used in the field sobriety test, in predicting whether research volunteers had been
administered ethanol, cocaine, or marijuana.[30] This study also assessed the accuracy of DRE's
evaluations in detecting impairment (i.e., whether subjects had received a drug), and which
drug class had produced the impairment (i.e., which drug subjects had received).

4.2.3.1.2 Laboratory Validation Study: DEC Program

4.2.3.1.2.1 Research Methodology

Research subjects (n = 18), who were regular users of alcohol, cocaine, and marijuana prior to
the study, were administered oral ethanol (0, 0.28, 0.52 g/kg), intranasal cocaine (4, 48, 96
mg/70 kg), and smoked marijuana (0, 1.75, 3.55% Δ9-tetrahydrocannabinol [THC], 16 puffs)
under double blind conditions. All subjects signed consent forms prior to the study, which had
been reviewed and approved by an institutional review board. No attempt was made to match
drug doses on magnitude of performance effects. Subjects received either placebo or one active
drug dose during each of nine separate experimental sessions. Drug administration occurred
over 20 min, with ethanol administered during the first 5-min interval, followed by cocaine
administration over 2 min, followed by marijuana smoking during the final 12 min.

The DEC evaluation was an abridged version of the evaluation used in law enforcement
contexts;[25] it began 10 min after drug administration and lasted about 25 min. The test interval
coincided with the time in which peak drug effects on performance would be anticipated, but

it is also important to note that the potency of effects of these drugs on performance were likely changing across the 25-min test interval. All DRE observations and measurements (N = 76) were recorded and analyzed independently.

The DEC evaluation began with an ethanol breath test. DREs then measured pulse and recorded information about physical defects, corrective lenses, appearance of the eyes, and visual impairment. Using a pencil, DREs assessed eye tracking and nystagmus, pupillary size, and condition of eyelids. The next phase of the DEC involved an examination of eye movements and performance of four field sobriety tests (FST). Subjects' eyes were tested for horizontal and vertical gaze nystagmus and for convergence. Four FST were then administered.

The Romberg Balance (RB) assessed body sway and tremor while subjects stood for 30 s with feet together, arms at sides, head tilted back, and eyes closed. Subjects estimated the passage of 30 s during this test. The Walk and Turn (WT) test required subjects to take nine heel-to-toe steps along a straight line marked on the floor, turn, and return with nine heel-to-toe steps. The One Leg Stand (OLS) assessed balance by having subjects stand on one leg, with the other leg elevated in a stiff-leg manner 15 cm off the floor for 30 s. Subjects were also required to complete a counting task while performing this test. In the Finger to Nose (FN) test, subjects stood as in the RB and brought the tip of the index finger of the left or right hand (as instructed) directly to the tip of the nose.

The final portion of the DEC involved the measurement of pulse, blood pressure, and oral temperature, as well as a further examination of the eyes. Using a hand-held template, DREs estimated the diameter of each pupil to the nearest 0.5 mm under conditions of ambient room light, nearly total darkness, indirect light, and direct light. While illuminating the eyes under direct light from a penlight for 15 s, DREs assessed constriction of the pupils and fluctuation of pupillary diameter (i.e., hippus). Lastly, DREs measured pulse and assessed muscle tone, attitude, coordination, speech, breath odor, and facial appearance.

DREs retired to an isolated room to decide whether subjects were impaired. If a conclusion of impairment was reached, DREs recorded their prediction of the drug class(es), including ethanol, causing the impairment.

4.2.3.1.2.2 Plasma Drug Concentration

During each experimental session, blood samples were collected (see Heishman et al.[30] for details). Plasma concentration data from the 16-min postdrug sample, which was obtained halfway through the DEC evaluation, are reported. At 16 min postdrug, which was about 30 min after drinking ended, ethanol (0.28 and 0.52 g/kg) produced mean $\pm$ SE peak plasma concentrations of 24.3 ± 2.2 and 54.4 ± 6.0 mg/dL, respectively. At 16 min postdrug, cocaine (48 and 96 mg/70 kg) produced mean plasma concentrations of 74.7 ± 7.2 and 180.5 ± 17.1 ng/mL, respectively. Placebo cocaine (4 mg/70 kg) did not produce measurable plasma levels of cocaine or cocaine metabolites. At 16 min, benzoylecgonine concentrations were 95.4 ± 27.7 and 210.7 ± 47.3 ng/mL, and ecgonine methylester levels were 10.8 ± 3.0 and 26.1 ± 6.3 ng/mL for low and high dose cocaine, respectively. Marijuana produced peak plasma concentrations immediately after smoking, which had declined at 16 min to 15.4 ± 3.0 and 28.2 ± 4.2 ng/mL for 1.75% and 3.55% THC, respectively. Concentrations of 11-nor-9-carboxy-THC reached maximum concentrations at 16 min of 18.4 ± 3.6 and 27.7 ± 4.2 ng/mL after low and high marijuana doses, respectively.

4.2.3.1.2.3 DEC Evaluation

The 76 variables from the DEC evaluation were first analyzed using stepwise discriminant analyses to determine which ones best predicted the presence or absence of each of the three study drugs. These subsets of best-predictor variables for each drug were then subjected to separate discriminant function analyses using whether subjects were dosed or not dosed with each drug as the predictor. Separate evaluations of DEC variables were conducted for ethanol, cocaine, and marijuana. Based on these mathematical models, predictions were classified as true positive, true negative, false positive, or false negative. These parameters were used to calculate the sensitivity, specificity, and efficiency (i.e., predictive accuracy) of DEC variables.[30] In a separate analysis, the accuracy of both DRE predictions of impairment and of which drug-class(es) were associated with impairment were also determined.

Ethanol: The stepwise discriminant analysis resulted in a subset of 17 variables (excluding BALs) that were the best predictors of the presence or absence of ethanol. The 17 variables in descending order of predictive weight were: (1) presence of horizontal gaze nystagmus, (2) abnormal breath odor, (3) increased errors on WT test, (4) estimation of 30 s during RB test, (5) inability to complete OLS test, (6) low oral temperature, (7) increased sum of three pulse recordings, (8) abnormal facial appearance, (9) relaxed attitude, (10) lack of rebound dilation of the pupils under direct illumination, (11) slurred speech, (12) increased errors on executing the turn on WT test, (13) cigarette breath odor, (14) abnormal muscle tone, (15) confused speech, (16) miscounting during OLS test, and (17) number of steps in WT test. The discriminant function comprising these 17 variables predicted the presence or absence of ethanol with extremely high accuracy. The model was equally accurate in predicting the presence (sensitivity = 94.4%) and absence of ethanol (specificity = 92.6%); overall predictive efficiency was 93.3%.

Cocaine: The stepwise discriminant analysis also resulted in a subset of 17 variables that were the best predictors of the presence or absence of cocaine. The 17 variables in descending order of predictive weight were: (1) increased sum of systolic and diastolic blood pressure, (2) increased sum of three pulse recordings, (3) low oral temperature, (4) eyes that did not appear normal, (5) sum of the pupillary diameter measures during four illumination conditions, (6) breath odor that was not marijuana-like, (7) abnormal breath odor, (8) sum of the pupillary diameter range of left and right eyes, (9) abnormal muscle tone, (10) decreased body sway during RB test, (11) number of steps in WT test, (12) speech that was not low in volume, (13) facial appearance that was flushed or red, (14) decreased errors on OLS test, (15) confused speech, (16) attitude that was not relaxed, and (17) rebound dilation of the pupils under direct illumination. The discriminant function comprising these 17 variables predicted the presence or absence of cocaine with high accuracy. The model had greater specificity (96.3%) than sensitivity (88.9%), and efficiency was 93.3%.

Marijuana: The stepwise discriminant analysis resulted in a subset of 28 variables that were the best predictors of the presence or absence of marijuana. The 28 best-predictor variables in descending order of predictive weight were: (1) increased sum of three pulse recordings, (2) droopy eyelids, (3) low oral temperature, (4) abnormal speech, (5) lack of rebound dilation of the pupils under direct illumination, (6) sum of the pupillary diameter measures during four illumination conditions, (7) increased sum of systolic and diastolic blood pressure, (8) low volume speech, (9) increased body sway during RB test, (10) incoherent speech, (11) abnormal pupillary reaction to light, (12) eyes that did not appear normal, (13) bloodshot eyes, (14) abnormal muscle tone, (15) miscellaneous abnormal appearance of eyes, (16) abnormal facial appearance, (17) increased eye or body tremors during FN test, (18) increased errors on executing the turn on WT test, (19) less than the complete number of steps in WT test, (20) decreased errors on FN test, (21) increased errors on WT test, (22) marijuana breath, (23) abnormal breath odor, (24) lack of hippus of the pupils under direct illumination, (25) failure of eyes to converge, (26) stale breath odor, (27) cigarette breath odor, and (28) slurred speech. The discriminant function comprising these 28 variables predicted the presence or absence of marijuana with extremely high sensitivity (100%), specificity (98.1%), and efficiency (98.8%).

4.2.3.1.2.4 DRE Predictions

To obtain and maintain International Association of Chiefs of Police (IACP) certification, DRE's drug class predictions must be "consistent" with toxicological analysis on a consistent basis. Under IACP standards,[31] the following rules apply: (1) if the DRE concludes a subject is impaired by only one drug class, toxicology must confirm some drug in that class; (2) if the DRE names two drug classes, toxicology must confirm at least one of them; and (3) if the DRE names three or more drug classes, toxicology must confirm at least two. DREs are not expected to identify all drugs taken by a subject, only the one(s) that account for the observed impairment. The rules for consistency treat ethanol as a special case. Because DREs administer a breath test, they know if the subject has ingested ethanol. Thus, if the DRE names ethanol and some other drug class, toxicology must confirm the other class, and if the DRE names ethanol and two other classes, toxicology must confirm at least one of the other classes. IACP standards accept a quantitative or qualitative analysis of any body tissue or fluid that produces an identification of a drug or metabolite to confirm the DRE's opinion.

Of 158 valid DEC examinations, DREs concluded impairment was present in 81 sessions. A study drug had been administered in 66 of those 81 sessions (81.5% sensitivity for drug or alcohol administration). However, because the breath-alcohol test provided *a priori* confirmation of ethanol, an intoxication rating was guaranteed to be consistent with alcohol administration during alcohol sessions. DREs concluded impairment in 18 of 36 alcohol sessions, but blood alcohol levels (24.3 ± 2.2 and 54.4 ± 6.0 mg/dl) were modest during alcohol sessions. Excluding the alcohol sessions (n=18), impairment ratings occurred in 63 sessions. A study drug had been administered on 22 of those 63 sessions (34.9% sensitivity for drug administration).

Based on IACP standards in which toxicology analyses (e.g., urinalysis) are used to verify impairment, DRE predictions of the class of drug associated with impairment were consistent with toxicology reports in 41 cases (50.6%). These 41 consistent cases included 9 in which the DRE concluded the subject was impaired by ethanol alone. Excluding those 9 cases resulted in 72 predictions that named some non-ethanol drug class. The DRE's predictions were consistent with toxicology in 32 cases (44.4%). Nearly one-third of these verifications occurred as a result of predose urine samples related to previous drug use by subjects, rather than as a result of drugs administered during sessions.

4.2.3.1.2.5 Conclusions

The validity of the DEC evaluation was examined by developing mathematical models based on discriminant functions that identified which subsets of DEC variables best predicted whether subjects were dosed with placebo or each active drug. The subsets consisted of 17 variables for ethanol, 17 variables for cocaine, and 28 variables for marijuana. For all three drugs, the discriminative function model testing this subset of variables predicted the presence or absence of drug with a high degree of sensitivity and specificity. FST variables contributed to the accuracy of prediction with all three study drugs.

A secondary goal of this study was to determine the accuracy of DRE evaluations in detecting whether an individual was impaired and, if so, whether the impairment was associated with ethanol, cocaine, or marijuana administration. When DREs rated an individual as impaired, 81.5% of the time a drug or alcohol had been administered prior to the evaluation. However, after excluding alcohol sessions, only 34.9% of DRE impairment ratings were associated with study drug administration. When DREs judged subjects as impaired, their drug class predictions were consistent with toxicology results in half the cases, and when ethanol-only decisions were excluded, consistency fell to 44% of cases. However, nearly one-third of non-ethanol impairment decisions were consistent because of drug metabolites identified in predose urine specimens, rather than because of the drug administered prior to evaluations.

It is highly unlikely that the behavior of subjects was affected by drug under these conditions because blood samples obtained at the time of the DEC evaluation tested negative for the drug identified in the predose urine sample. It is widely recognized that a positive urine drug test does not indicate behavioral impairment.[32,33]

These data clearly indicate that the variables of the DEC evaluation alone did not permit DREs to predict impairment and drug intake with precision; certainly not with the consistency that the IACP requires for certification. There were several differences between the controlled laboratory conditions of this study and the field conditions under which DREs normally conduct the DEC evaluation that may have contributed to this outcome, such as the abridged form of the DEC evaluation, lack of meaningful drug-related cues (e.g., marijuana odor, drug paraphernalia), inability to interview subjects concerning drug use, and the possibility that greater drug doses encountered in the field would result in clearer behavioral signs of impairment. Additional studies will be required to determine whether these factors influence the accuracy of DRE evaluations of impairment and drug use associated with that impairment.

With respect to the DEC evaluation, it is clear that variables produced during the test, including those associated with the field sobriety test, can be used to predict accurately acute administration of ethanol, cocaine, or marijuana. This predictive validity was optimal when predictions were made using 17 to 28 variables from the DEC evaluation. These findings suggest that predictions of impairment and drug use may be improved if DREs focused on a subset of variables associated with each drug class, rather than the entire DEC evaluation.

4.2.3.2 Government Application: Tests of Fitness for Duty

4.2.3.2.1 Background

Much of the early interest in the area of human performance testing was funded and manned by several branches of the U.S. Military. The successful military mission depends on optimal performance by its personnel. Hostile and hazardous environments may have subtle to profound influences on a soldier's performance.[34] The goal of military human performance research was to identify those environments and agents that cause a deterioration in ability, and to what degree. With this knowledge, military personnel could attempt to compensate for, or avoid, undesirable environments or agents. A comprehensive review of many assessment batteries used by government agencies, which includes a review of evidence related to the reliability and validity of the batteries, can be found elsewhere.[3,6]

4.2.3.2.2 Computerized Performance Test Batteries

Most government-sponsored computerized performance test batteries are compilations of computer performance tests that were originally developed and tested in controlled laboratory settings. The purpose of many of these tests is to determine the effects of risk factors on fitness for government duty, and to assess the efficacy of countermeasures designed to offset the performance effects of these risk factors.

4.2.3.2.2.1 Unified Tri-Service Cognitive Performance Assessment Battery

The Unified Tri-Service Cognitive Performance Assessment Battery (UTC-PAB) was constructed by the Tri-Service Working Group on Drug Dependent Degradation of Military Performance which eventually became known as the Office of Military Performance Assessment Technology (OMPAT).[35] OMPAT sponsored a series of related methodologies with the purpose of assessing military-related performance. This group included representatives from

Table 4.2.3.2.2.1 Task Components of the Unified Tri-Service Cognitive Performance Assessment Battery. (UTC-PAB)

Focused Attention	Selective Attention	Divided Attention	Acquisition	Memory	Other Cognitive Performance
Complex Reaction Time	Stroop Nessier		Repeated Acquisition	Match/ Nonmatch to Sample	Spatial Rotation-Sequential
Visual-Motor Tracking	Dichotic Listening			Sternberg Memory	Pattern Matching Manikin
Substitution (Symbol-Digit or Code)				Pattern Comparison	Grammmatical/ Logical Reasoning Arithmetic Computation
Time Estimation				Sequence	Serial Add/Subtract
Continuous Performance				Memory	Linguistic Processing
Sequence Comparison					
Visual Monitoring					

the U.S. Navy, Air Force, and Army. The group set out to fabricate a standardized laboratory tool to assess cognitive performance using repeated measures in a Tri-Service chemical-defense biomedical drug screening program.[36] All of the tasks in the test battery were designed to run on standard MS DOS platform computers with graphical presentation and keyboard responding. The UTC-PAB is a library of cognitive tests which can be modified into smaller subsets or batteries for a specific purpose.

Several of these commonly known subsets are the Walter Reed Army Institute Performance Assessment Battery (WRPAB), the Naval Medical Research Institute Performance Assessment Battery (NMRI-PAB), the UTC-PAB/NATO AGARD STRES Battery, and the Criterion Task Set (CTS).[36] The original UTC-PAB was comprised of 25 tasks which were chosen due to their construct validity, greater reliability, and higher sensitivity to changes in cognitive functioning.

The UTC-PAB's modular design offered the investigator the freedom of customized batteries by combining any number of the tasks, and in any order. This enabled researchers to utilize only those tasks which best suited the needs of each protocol or evaluation. Accuracy and response time were automatically measured and the data collection updated for any of the tasks that were selected. Numerous parameters of the individual tasks could be modified, such as stimulus duration, inter-trial interval, number of stimulus presentations, and length of the task. Instruction screens and help files could be modified as well. A hard copy of summary statistics for each test can be enabled. The raw data is stored in ASCII files which allow easy import into spreadsheets or statistical packages. The default parameter settings for the UTC-PAB tasks were patterned off of the North Atlantic Treaty Organization AGARD-STRES Battery.[37]

Table 4.2.3.2.2.1 contains the individual tasks of the UTC-PAB. These tasks measure a variety of human cognitive and psychomotor functioning, including focused attention, selective attention, divided attention, memory, and a variety of additional task components.[3,6]

4.2.3.2.2.2 Walter Reed Army Institute Performance Assessment Battery

The Walter Reed Army Institute Performance Assessment Battery (WRPAB) was designed by Dr. David Thorne and colleagues at the Walter Reed Army Institute of Research, Division of

Table 4.2.3.2.2.2 Task components of the Walter Reed Army Institute Performance Assessment Battery (WRPAB)

Focused Attention	Selective Attention	Acquisition	Memory	Other Cognitive Performance
Complex Reaction Time	Stroop	Associative	Match/Nonmatch to Sample	Manikin
	Nessier	Learning		Grammmatical/
Substitution			Sternberg Memory	Logical Reasoning
(Symbol-Digit or			Pattern Comparison	Arithmetic Computation
Code)			Sequence Memory	Serial Add/Subtract
Encoding/Decoding				
Time Estimation				

Neuropsychiatry, Department of Behavioral Biology. The battery was designed to measure changes in performance over time as a function of environmental perturbations (e.g., drugs, fatigue, sleep deprivation) as opposed to serving as a screening tool.[38] The WRPAB was designed to offer investigators a menu of individual cognitive, perceptual, and psychomotor tests, from which investigators can choose those tests that best serve their purpose.

A user-friendly building routine allows for the development of smaller, personalized PABs which are specific to a given objective. The building routine prompts the researcher to specify certain hardware and software characteristics of the computer system on which it will be presented. It also inquires about enabling or disabling summary statistics. Programming modifications at the code level in BASICA or GW BASIC allow individual task's duration and the number of trials per task to be modified with little difficulty using the documentation that accompanies the software.

This research tool currently operates on the MS DOS platform with graphic screen presentation on a local or remote monitor with responding performed on a standard keyboard.[38] Installation of a timer card is necessary to insure precise timing. Response times and values, and errors are stored into working memory until the completion of each task. After completion of a task, summary statistics may be shown on the subjects screen, or downloaded to a printing source, if desired. The task's raw data is transferred to an ASCII file located on a floppy diskette. Table 4.2.3.2.2.2 lists the individual tasks of the WRPAB.

These tasks assess focused attention, selective attention, acquisition, memory, and a variety of additional task components.[38] Variations of the WRPAB have been developed by related groups, including the UTC-PAB/AGARD-STRES, and the CogScreen, which is primarily a screening tool for assessing neuropsychological functioning used widely in the aviation industry.

As mentioned earlier, the WRPAB is best suited for experiments with repeated measures designs involving treatments, dosages, or differing environments. Specific tasks in the WRPAB have been found to be sensitive to certain psychoactive drugs. Several government agencies have implemented the WRPAB as a research tool. For example, the National Institute on Drug Abuse Intramural Research Program at the Addiction Research Center has studied the effects of nicotine and nicotine replacement on smoker's and nonsmoker's cognitive abilities and attention processes using the Two-[39,40] and Six-Letter Search.[39] Cognitive abilities were also measured using the WRPAB's Digit Recall and Logical Reasoning tasks.[39,40]

4.2.3.2.2.3 Naval Medical Research Institute Performance Assessment Battery

The Naval Medical Research Institute Performance Assessment Battery (NMRI-PAB) was developed to measure the effects of a wide variety of military environments upon the technically oriented tasks of Marine and Naval personnel. The battery's methodology was based on a tri-

Table 4.2.3.2.2.3 Task Components of the Naval Medical Research Institute Performance Assessment Battery (NMRI-PAB).

Focused Attention	Selective Attention	Memory	Other Cognitive Performance
Continuous Performance	Stroop	Match/Nonmatch to Sample	Spatial Rotation-Sequential
		Sternberg Memory	Manikin
		Pattern Comparison	Grammmatical/Logical Reasoning

service methodology in an attempt to standardize measurement of human performance in military environments.[34] The NMRI-PAB, like the WRPAB and UTC-PAB, is a menu-driven, microcomputer-based, assessment tool that is comprised of individual tasks.

The NMRI-PAB consists of eight individual tasks which measure different aspects of human functioning (Table 4.2.3.2.2.3). The software controller allows the experimenter to modify certain aspects of task presentation. The software collects detailed information about subject's accuracy and speed of responding. Because the NMRI-PAB is microcomputer-based, multiple subjects can participate simultaneously and in different locations. The software runs on standard MS DOS platform with graphical screen presentation and keyboard responding. The design of this assessment tool allows for repeated measures testing. The individual tasks of the NMRI-PAB measure several areas of human cognitive functioning, including focused attention, selective attention, memory, and a variety of additional task components.[3]

4.2.3.2.2.4 Advisory Group for Aerospace Research and Development — Standardized Test for Research with Environmental Stressors Battery

The Advisory Group for Aerospace Research and Development — Standardized Test for Research with Environmental Stressors Battery (AGARD-STRES) was developed to investigate the effects of environmental stress on human performance.[37] After receiving funding from the U.S. Air Force, the Advisory Group for Aerospace Research and Development (AGARD) set out to construct a standardized performance assessment battery using tests that had proven successful in stress research.

The group utilized seven of the individual tests from the UTC-PAB.[37] The AGARD-STRES battery was designed to provide a standardized method of task presentation (e.g., the seven tests are presented in a predetermined order, and the task parameters are designed to remain constant) in order to more effectively compare performance on these tasks across subject populations and settings. The software runs on standard MS DOS platform with graphical screen presentation and keyboard input. This would facilitate standardization and allow researchers to compare all administrations of the battery equally. This assessment tool is well suited for repeated measures research. Table 4.2.3.2.2.4 presents the individual tests of the AGARD-STRESS battery. Focused attention, divided attention, and memory categories of tasks are included in this battery, in addition to a variety of other tasks.

4.2.3.2.2.5 Automated Neuropsychological Assessment Metrics

The Automated Neuropsychological Assessment Metrics assessment battery (ANAM) is a modified version of the AGARD-STRES battery. The ANAM has added pursuit tracking, which requires a mouse for completion, and has eliminated tracking, dual task, and reaction time tasks from the AGARD-STRES battery because these tasks engendered unsuitably variable performance. A tracking test, running memory test, the Walter Reed mood scale, and the Stanford sleepiness scale were substituted. Table 4.2.3.2.2.5 presents the various tasks of the ANAM battery. Focused attention and memory categories of tasks are included in this battery, as well as a variety of additional task components.

Performance Measures of Behavioral Impairment in Applied Settings

Table 4.2.3.2.2.4 Task Components of the Advisory Group for Aerospace Research and Development — Standardized Test for Research with Environmental Stressors Battery (AGARD-STRESS).

Focused Attention	Divided Attention	Memory	Other Cognitive Performance
Complex Reaction Time		Sternberg Memory	Spatial Rotation-Sequential
Visual-Motor Tracking			Grammmatical/Logical Reasoning
			Serial Add/Subtract

Table 4.2.3.2.2.5 Task Components of the Automated Neuropsychological Assessment Metrics (ANAM).

Focused Attention	Memory	Other Cognitive Performance
Complex Reaction Time	Sternberg Memory	Spatial Rotation
Visual-Motor Tracking	Character/Number Recall	Spatial Rotation-Sequential
		Grammmatical/Logical Reasoning
		Serial Add/Subtract

4.2.3.2.2.6 Neurobehavioral Evaluation System 2

The Neurobehavioral Evaluation System 2 (NES2) is a neurobehavioral evaluation system designed to facilitate screening of populations at risk of nervous system damage due to environmental agents. This evaluation system was designed to be administered on a microcomputer. Epidemiologic research influenced the sets of tests that were included in this battery. An expert committee convened by the World Health Organization (WHO) and the National Institute for Occupational Safety and Health (NIOSH) proposed a set of core tests for this battery. Many of the core tests that were chosen are adaptations of pre-existing clinical instruments that have been recognized as valuable tools in investigating neurotoxin exposure.

Motor ability, focused attention, selective attention, acquisition, and memory categories of tasks are included in this battery, in addition to a variety of other tasks (Table 4.2.3.2.2.6). The battery is made up of separate tasks; performance on combinations of these tasks is potentially altered by exposure to neurotoxic agents such as pesticides, solvents, or carbon monoxide. Many of the tasks are suitable for repeated testing of any individual. Five of the tests are similar to the core tests of the WHO battery.[41]

The NES2 software was developed using IBM's Advanced BASIC. The software is menu-driven and allows the interviewer to chose the individual tasks that are presented at any one session. The software was designed to run on IBM PC-compatible hardware with a standard DOS operating system. Response inputs occur through a joystick with a pair of push-buttons.[41] The evaluation battery is presented on a standard CGA graphic computer screen and data output is stored in ASCII format which allows for easy integration with other software.[3] A software clock allows the evaluating system to record response latencies as well as correct and incorrect responses.

Baker and colleagues[41] found that the validity and stability of three tests in the NES2 were comparable to five previously validated traditional interviewer-administered neuropsychological instruments. High correlations were reported between individual trials of the same interviewer-administered task. Stability on four of the computerized tests was supported by high correlations between scores when research subjects were tested on four separate days.

Thomas H. Kelly et al.

Table 4.2.3.2.2.6 Task Components of Neurobehavioral Evaluation System 2(NES2).

Motor Ability Tests	Focused Attention	Selective Attention	Acquisition	Memory	Other Cognitive Performance
Finger Tapping	Simple	Switching/	Serial	Pattern	Pattern Matching
	Reaction	Shifting	Acquisition	Comparison	Grammmatical/
	Time	Attention	Associative	Character/	Logical Reasoning
	Substitution		Learning	Number	Arithmetic
	(Symbol-			Recall	Computation
	Digit or				Vocabulary
	Code)				
	Continuous				
	Performance				

4.2.3.2.2.7 Automated Portable Test System

The Performance Evaluation Tests for Environmental Research Program (PETER), jointly sponsored by the U.S. Navy and NASA, attempted to identify measures of human cognitive, perceptual, and motor abilities that would be sensitive to environmental perturbations that are associated with decrements in safety and productivity. An extensive collection of literature yielded more than 140 tests which were rated for reliability and sensitivity. The PETER Program incorporated those tasks which were most suitable for repeated-measures applications. Inclusion criteria were met if a task's inter-trial correlations were unchanging and variances were homogenous across baselines.[42]

The Automated Portable Test System (APTS) evaluation system is an outgrowth of the work of the PETER Program. The PETER program had identified tests that were reliable, stable, and sensitive to environmental and toxic stressors. Kennedy and his colleagues[43] adopted and computerized a core set of 18 tasks from the Peter Program's recommended list of performance tasks suitable for repeated measures application. Those tasks are listed in Table 4.2.3.2.2.7

The APTS was designed for portability and was initially implemented on the NEC 8021C microprocessor. The software is now available for IBM PC-compatible systems running on a standard MS DOS operating system.[44] The battery measures abilities of motor function, focused attention, selective attention, acquisition, and memory, as well as spatial perception and reasoning, mathematical calculation, and other language skills.[3,6] Similar to most of the computerized performance assessment batteries, additions and deletions of individual components have occurred as the battery has matured and been used in different applications.

4.2.3.2.2.8 Memory Assessment Clinics Battery

The Memory Assessment Clinics Battery (MAC) was designed to assess the effects of pharmacological treatments on memory tasks.[45] Intended to study potentially cognitive-enhancing pharmaceutical compounds, the battery is also used to assess age-related memory differences in on-going clinical trials. Initial testing of the MAC Battery was administered on an AT&T 6300 computer utilizing color graphic presentation, laser-disk technology, and touch-screen responding along with other custom-made manipulanda. The battery mimics real-life memory and recognition demands, such as remembering a 7- or 10-digit telephone number, or associating a name with a face. Table 4.2.3.2.2.8 presents the individual tasks of the MAC battery. Focused attention, divided attention, acquisition, and memory categories of tasks are included in this battery.

Performance Measures of Behavioral Impairment in Applied Settings

Table 4.2.3.2.2.7 Task Components of the Automated Portable Test System (APTS).

Motor Ability Tests	Focused Attention	Selective Attention	Acquisition	Memory	Other Cognitive Performance
Finger Tapping	Simple Reaction Time	Stroop Nessier	Associative Learning	Sternberg Memory	Spatial Rotation Spatial Rotation-
	Complex Reaction Time			Pattern Comparison	Sequential Pattern Matching
	Substitution (Symbol- Digit or Code)			Sequence Memory Character/ Number Recall	Manikin Grammmatical/ Logical Reasoning Arithmetic
	Time Estimation				Computation Serial Add/Subtract
	Continuous Performance				Linguistic Processing Spatial Visualization
	Sequence Comparison				
	Visual Monitoring				

Table 4.2.3.2.2.8 Task Components of the Memory Assessment Clinics Battery (MAC)

Focused Attention	Divided Attention	Acquisition	Memory
Complex Reaction Time		Associative Learning	Match/Nonmatch to Sample Selective Reminding Text Memory Misplaced Objects Facial Memory Character/Number Recall

4.2.3.2.2.9 Synwork

Many performance batteries involve the administration of varied tasks, each of which requires the focused application of a limited number of cognitive and motor skills, in a sequential manner. One concern that has repeatedly been raised regarding the use of sequential laboratory tests as a system for measuring performance impairment is that such systems do not assess all human capabilities, including some that are critically dependent for job performance. For example, while performance tests may assess specific abilities, such as reaction time or learning ability, it may be unusual in job settings for such activities to be required in a sequential manner.

Elsmore and colleagues[46] have contended that real-world human behaviors or operations may consist of two or more of these attributes and abilities occurring concurrently. Effective job performance may require the ability to engage in multiple tasks in a simultaneous or continuous manner, adjusting between task requirements as priorities change. It is unclear whether such higher-order performance requirements are effectively assessed in sequential performance test systems.

Computer simulations of job performance represent one approach to increasing the array of performance dimensions being measured during performance testing systems, and increasing the generality of results to job settings. Initial attempts at developing computer simulations for use in the assessment of performance impairment were government-sponsored modifications of sequential performance testing systems. Instead of presenting tests in a sequential manner, multiple tests were simultaneously presented, and participants were required to complete each of the tasks in a manner which was often left up to the user.

Synwork represents an initial attempt to more effectively simulate the demands of natural-istic job requirements. It is not a PAB-like simple reaction time or memory task, nor is it a full-blown simulation of any job or operation.[46] It requires subjects to perform 4 PAB-like tasks simultaneously and is presented on a standard IBM PC-compatible computer with DOS operating platform. The four tasks are presented simultaneously in one of four quadrants of a color graphic screen. Subjects interact with the software by manipulating a standard mouse. The software generates auditory feedback for correct and incorrect responses.[46] The individual tasks of the Synwork software measure attention and working memory (Sternberg Memory Task); mathematical calculations (Arithmetic task); spatial perception and reasoning (Visual Monitoring); and auditory perception and reasoning (Auditory Monitoring). A detailed ac-count of the Synwork software can be found in Elsmore et al.[47]

Elsmore et al.[46] compared the effects of sleep deprivation on performance generated by sequentially administered PAB tasks with that generated by Synwork. No clear differences in performance throughput, defined by Dr. David R. Thorne, personal communication, as the speed/accuracy product or the number of correct responses per actual working minute, were observed as a function of task presentation style, but other dimensions of task performance were more sensitive to the effects of sleep deprivation on the individual tasks during the PAB (i.e., sequentially presented tasks) than during Synwork (i.e., simultaneously presented tasks). Subjects reported Synwork to be more interesting and demanding than the PAB version, and the authors contended that this may have been related to why individual isolated cognitive and motor tasks engendered performance that was more sensitive to the effects of sleep deprivation than the same tasks presented simultaneously.

4.2.3.3 Workplace Application: Readiness to Perform Tests

4.2.3.3.1 Background

Given the complex nature of many commercial work environments, as well as the reciprocal interactions between employers and employees, factors associated with the development and implementation of performance impairment test systems in commercial environments become equally complex. In addition to the selection of test systems that are reliable and valid indicators of performance impairment, it is equally important to consider issues associated with worker acceptance of the testing system, time associated with the test, and the economic implications of use and non-use of impairment test systems. Substantial research into the use of impairment testing systems has been conducted over the past decade; however, the vast majority of this work is available only in company reports and/or technical monographs; with few exceptions (e.g., Delta), little information is available in peer-reviewed scientific publications.

4.2.3.3.2 Performance Tests in Applied Settings

Four applications of laboratory-based performance impairment test systems are described. These systems have been chosen to be presented for two reasons. First, they provide examples of the use of test systems for the measurement of performance impairment in commercial settings. Second, some information regarding the reliability and validity of these systems is available.

4.2.3.3.2.1 Truck Operator Proficiency System/ReadyShift

The state of Arizona supported the development of a Truck Operator Proficiency System (TOPS), which was designed to measure multiple dimensions of driving skills in a divided-attention framework. Testing takes place in driving simulators which are located in weigh stations throughout the state. The driving simulators are equipped with a steering wheel and driving pedals, and a driving simulation task is presented on a computer screen. Performance on the test is used in a regulatory manner to assess truck-driving performance of drivers on state roads. The ReadyShift (Evaluations Systems, Inc., ESI) was a version of the TOPS system which was modified for use in industrial sites (ReadyShiftI™) or installed into the cabs of trucks (ReadyShiftII™). An obvious advantage of these simulation batteries is the realistic dimensions of job performance that are assessed with these systems.

ESI has been involved in feasibility studies of the use of the ReadyShift test, along with other performance tasks, to measure impairment in truck drivers.[18] The initial test system consisted of four tasks (Table 4.2.3.2.2.1), including the ReadyShift, a substitution task, a visual monitoring task, and a tracking task, which were presented to workers in a renovated test room located at the truck terminal (ReadyShiftI™), or from computerized testing modules installed in the cabs of the trucks (ReadyShiftII™). The test took approximately 21 min to complete. The four individual tests were selected based on existing literature indicating that performance on these tasks was sensitive to the effects of sleep deprivation and sedative drug risk factors. The tests were presented on PC-compatible computers using DOS operating systems; specialized video screens and response input components supported through both commercial and specialized cards and RAM chips were required.

The feasibility of the performance was assessed by having truck drivers complete assessments on a regular basis before starting an overland trip (in-terminal testing) and at regular intervals during these trips (in-cab testing). Drivers were paid a small wage for completing the tests, and were compensated for any lost wages associated with time spent completing the tests. No employment consequences were associated with performance on the tests, although workers received feedback on their own performance immediately after each test. Driver acceptance ratings and diaries were also collected. After implementing the initial test system, a decrease in testing compliance, due both to drivers' reluctance to take the time to complete assessments, as well as to supervisors' insistence that testing be postponed due to more urgent work demands, was observed after two months of operation. Due to time requirements and driver concerns with a lack of relevance associated with some tasks (particularly the visual monitoring task), the test system was decreased to two components, and finally to just the driving simulation task. Compliance was high, as was driver acceptance, under the final test condition.

No accidents occurred during the period of feasibility study, although worker-initiated adjustments in behavior occurred as a result of feedback from the test system (i.e., drivers rested if performance on the test was below baseline). The investigators indicated that the relatively short period of intervention increased the likelihood that no accidents would occur, but also pointed out the possibility that the presence of a testing system could have altered the behavior of the workforce, thereby reducing the likelihood of accidents. The investigators recommended that attention be paid to this possibility in future studies. Evaluations of additional modifications of this system are currently under way (Miller, personal communication).

4.2.3.3.2.2 NovaScan, NTI, Inc.

The NovaScan is a testing paradigm, rather than a fixed performance test, in that the system represents a method of presenting selected tests in a manner that standardizes the attentional requirements of the test user. The paradigm also allows for measurement of elements of attention allocation. The testing paradigm is designed to present any combination of a subset of 30 individual tasks originally developed and validated through the UTC-PAB project, described above. The tasks that are presented can be selected based on the specific needs of the test application (e.g., different combinations of tests have been used for different commercial applications, based on the specific needs/interests of the company employing the NovaScan).

The resulting test system is designed to assess a variety of job-related skills, as well as generic attentional processes associated with the completion of the tasks, in a time-efficient manner. The NovaScan is presented on a PC-compatible computer equipped with standard memory and visual capabilities, and is run on a DOS-based operating system. A customized response apparatus, including a joy stick, control keys, and a keypad, is recommended. Trials of the tasks chosen to be included in the test system are displayed on the computer monitor in a random manner, thereby eliminating the need for the user to focus attention among simultaneously presented tests. However, divided attention components can be added, if needed.

The length of the test (i.e., number of trials presented) can be adjusted based on the demands of the test environment. Performance is evaluated in an automated fashion using a change-from-baseline approach, and the test can be administered in an automated or supervisor-controlled manner. The Novascan has received substantial testing in a number of laboratory and applied settings. Performance on the NovaScan has been demonstrated to be sensitive to the effects of alcohol, marijuana, diazepam, amphetamine, scopolamine, and an over-the-counter antihistamine.[5,48,49] In addition, epidemiological differences in performance associated with gender, age, and occupation have been considered. Variations of the testing paradigm have been used in a number of commercial settings.

4.2.3.3.2.3 Delta, Essex Corporation

Delta, a commercial performance impairment testing system produced by the Essex corporation, was derived from Automated Portable Test System (APTS) evaluation system, which, in turn, was based on the work of the Performance Evaluation Tests for Environmental Research Program (PETER), a jointly sponsored U.S. Navy and NASA program designed to identify measures of human cognitive, perceptual, and motor abilities that would be sensitive to environmental perturbations that are associated with decrements in safety and productivity.

The Delta system contains many of the same tests contained in the APTS system, including those that monitor motor function, reaction time, attention and working memory, learning and memory, spatial perception and reasoning, mathematical calculation, and language (Table 4.2.3.2.2.1). More complete descriptions of the psychometric and validity studies supporting the utility of this testing system are available elsewhere.[50,51] Performance on the Delta system has been demonstrated to be sensitive to the effects of alcohol, amphetamine, scopolamine, chemoradiotherapy, and hypoxia.[52-55] The Delta test system has been used in a number of applied settings, including airplane and tank operator training sites.[50,51]

4.2.3.3.2.4 Performance-on-Line, Profile Associates

Performance-on-Line is a software-based cognitive and psychomotor divided-attention task. The task was derived from the hardware-based Simulated Evaluation of Driver Impairment

(SEDI) distributed by SEDICorp. SEDI has been utilized to evaluate impairment induced by alcohol and marijuana. SEDI was found to generate performance that was highly reliable and sensitive to the effects of alcohol and marijuana.[56,57] SEDI used numeric displays which were novel to some subjects, and the memory-intensive instructions were found to be difficult to remember for some individuals. The hardware-based SEDI was also costly, and subjects frequently reported eye-muscle fatigue after its use.[58]

The Performance-on-Line software was designed to include language-free graphics and instructions that were not memory-intensive. The stimuli resemble patterns and scenes experienced during motor vehicle operation. Central and peripheral targets that are presented simultaneously require independent visual discrimination and responding. The software is designed to run on any computer using a DOS operating system. It supports a color graphic display and utilizes keyboard response inputs. The test is self administered, provides on-screen instructions and has five independent levels of difficulty. An administrative interface allows for parametric modifications, such as whether or not performance feedback is provided to participants. The data is stored in formatted files which allow for easy use with other commercial spreadsheet or data analysis programs.[58]

4.2.4 CONCLUSION

This section focused on issues associated with the use of performance testing technologies for the detection of performance impairment. While the application of this technology remains largely untested, the evidence presented in this chapter strongly suggests that this technology shows promise as a component of performance impairment testing systems. A substantial database regarding the reliability and validity of performance tests for measuring the effects of risk factors on human performance has been established, and initial efforts at developing performance testing systems made effective use of this database. Limitations with regard to the predictive validity of these tests continue to be addressed in modifications to existing testing systems, as well as in the development of more sophisticated simulation testing systems. Issues regarding the selection and implementation of performance testing systems have been addressed in recent publications.[3,8-10] Clearly, careful and systematic evaluations of the use of these systems in applied settings is warranted.

It is important to note, however, that while this chapter specifically addressed performance testing as a means of impairment detection, there is no evidence to suggest that performance testing systems are more effective than other impairment testing systems. Trice and Steele[8] suggest that performance testing systems may have practical advantages over more common biological sample testing systems, including potentially being more widely accepted by the workforce, requiring less invasive testing requirements, and interfacing more efficiently with existing employee assistance programs, but no evidence to support such claims is available, due to the limited information regarding the use of these systems. It is likely that no single technology will be universally effective in all settings, or even in one setting across all individuals over time. The combination of technologies, based on the availability of resources needed to support those technologies, will likely enhance the effectiveness of any impairment testing system.

REFERENCES

1. Normand, J., Lempert, R. O., and O'Brien, C. P., Under the Influence? Drugs and the American Work Force. National Academy Press, Washington, D.C., 1994, Chap. 6.

2. Finkle, B. S., Blanke, R. V., and Walsh, M. J., Technical, Scientific and Procedural Issues of Employee Drug Testing. U.S. Department of Health and Human Services, Washington, D.C., ADM 90-1684, 1990.

3. Kane, R. L., and Kay, G. G., Computerized assessment in neuropsychology: A review of tests and test batteries, Neuropsychology Review, 3, 1-118, 1992.

4. Murphy, K. R. Honesty in the Workplace, Brooks Cole, Pacific Grove, CA, 1993.

5. Kelly, T. H., Foltin, R. W., Emurian, C. S., and Fischman, M. W., Performance-based testing for drugs of abuse: Dose and time profiles of marijuana, amphetamine, alcohol and diazepam. Journal of Analytical Toxicology, 17, 264-272, 1993.

6. Gilliland, K., and Schlegel, R. E., Readiness to perform testing: A critical analysis of the concept and current practices, Technical Report to the U.S. Department of Transportation, National Technical Information Service, Springfield, VA, 1993.

7. Gerber, B., Simulating reality, Training, 27, 41-46, 1990.

8. Trice, H. M., and Steele, P. D. Impairment testing: Issues and convergence with employee assistance programs. The Journal of Drug Issues, 25, 471-503, 1995.

9. Gilliland, K., and Schlegel, R. E. Readiness-to-perform testing and the worker. Ergonomics in Design, January, 14-19, 1995.

10. Miller, J. C. Fit for duty? Performance testing tools for assessing public safety and health workers' readiness for work. Ergonomics in Design, April, 11-17, 1996.

11. Heishman, S.J., Taylor, R.C., and Henningfield, J.E., Nicotine and smoking: A review of effects on human performance. Experimental and Clinical Psychopharmacology, 2, 345-395, 1994.

12. Zacny, J. P., A review of the effects of opioids on psychomotor and cognitive functioning in humans, Experimental and Clinical Psychopharmacology, 3, 432-466, 1995.

13. Fischman, M. W., Cocaine and the amphetamines, in Psychopharmacology: The Third Generation of Progress, Meltzer, H. Y., Ed., Raven Press, New York, 1987, 1543-1553.

14. Fischman, M. W., Kelly, T. H., and Foltin, R. W., Residential laboratory research: A multidimensional evaluation of the effects of drugs on behavior, in Drugs in the Workplace: Research and Evaluation Data, Volume II , NIDA Research Monograph 100, Gust, S. W., Walsh, J. M., Thomas, L. B., and Crouch, D. J., Eds., U.S. Government Printing Office, Washington, D.C., 1991, 113-128.

15. Kelly, T. H., Foltin, R. W., and Fischman, M. W., Effects of alcohol on human behavior: Implications for the workplace, in Drugs in the Workplace: Research and Evaluation Data, Volume II , NIDA Research Monograph 100, Gust, S. W., Walsh, J. M., Thomas, L. B., and Crouch, D. J., Eds., U.S. Government Printing Office, Washington, D.C., 1991, 129-146.

16. Preusser, D. F., Ulmer, R. G., and Preusser, C. W., Evaluation of the impact of the drug evaluation and classification program on enforcement and adjudication, National Highway Traffic Safety Administration, Report No. DOT HS 808 058, U.S. Department of Transportation, Washington, DC, 1992.

17 Klein, A. The current legal status of employment tests. Los Angeles Lawyer, July/August, 1987, 35-38.

18. Miller, J. C., Kim, H. T., and Parseghian, Z., Feasibility of carrier-based fitness-for-duty testing of commercial drivers: Final report, ESI-TR-94-003, Evaluation Systems, El Cajon, CA,1994.

19. Morbidity and Mortality Weekly Report, Update: Alcohol-related traffic fatalities-United States, 1982-1993, Morbidity and Mortality Weekly Report, 43, 861, 1994.

20. Terhune, K. W., Ippolito, C. A., Hendricks, D. L., Michalovic, J. G., Bogema, S. C., Santinga, P., Blomberg, R., and Preusser, D. F., The incidence and role of drugs in fatally injured drivers, National Highway Traffic Safety Administration, Report No. DOT HS 808 065, U.S. Department of Transportation, Washington, DC, 1992.

21. Williams, A. F., Peat, M. A., Crouch, D. J., Wells, J. N., and Finkle, B. S., Drugs in fatally injured young male drivers. Public Health Reports, 100, 19, 1985.

22. Soderstrom, C. A., Trifillis, A. L., Shankar, B. S., Clark, W .E., and Crowley, R. A., Marijuana and alcohol use among 1023 trauma patients. Archives of Surgery, 123, 733, 1988.

Performance Measures of Behavioral Impairment in Applied Settings

23. Budd, R. D., Muto, J. J., and Wong, J. K., Drugs of abuse found in fatally injured drivers in Los Angeles County. Drug and Alcohol Dependence, 23, 153, 1989.
24. Marzuk, P. M., Tardiff, K., Leon, A. C., Stajic, M., Morgan, E. B., and Mann, J. J., Prevalence of recent cocaine use among motor vehicle fatalities in New York City. Journal of the American Medical Association, 263, 250, 1990.
25. National Highway Traffic Safety Administration, Drug evaluation and classification program, briefing paper, U.S. Department of Transportation, 1991.
26. Preusser Research Group, Inc., Drug evaluation and classification program: history and growth, U.S. Department of Transportation, National Highway Traffic Safety Administration, Letter Report, 1995.
27. Compton, R. P., Field evaluation of the Los Angeles Police Department drug detection procedure, National Highway Traffic Safety Administration, Report No. DOT HS 807 012, U.S. Department of Transportation, Washington, DC, 1986.
28. Adler, E. V. and Burns, M, Drug recognition expert (DRE) validation study, Final Report to Governor's Office of Highway Safety, State of Arizona, 1994.
29. Bigelow, G. E., Bickel, W. E., Roache, J. D.,Liebson, I. A., and Nowowieski, P., Identifying types of drug intoxication: Laboratory evaluation of a subject-examination procedure, National Highway Traffic Safety Administration, Report No. DOT HS 806 753, U.S. Department of Transportation, Washington, DC, 1985.
30. Heishman, S. J., Singleton, E. G., and Crouch, D. J., Laboratory validation study of Drug Evaluation and Classification program: Ethanol, cocaine, and marijuana, Journal of Analytical Toxicology, 468, 1996.
31. International Association of Chiefs of Police, National Standards of the Drug Evaluation and Classification Program, IACP Advisory Committee on Highway Safety, 1993.
32. Consensus Development Panel, Drug concentrations and driving impairment, Journal of the American Medical Association, 254, 2618, 1985.
33. Scientific consensus conference: Clinical pharmacologic implications of urine screening for illicit substances of abuse, American Society for Clinical Pharmacology and Therapeutics, 1987.
34. Thomas, J.R, and Schrot, J., Naval medical research institute performance assessment battery (NMRI PAB) documentation (NMRI 88-7), Naval Medical Research Institute, Bethesda, MD, 1988.
35. Hegge, F. W., Reeves, D. L., Poole, D. P., and Thorne, D. R., The Uinified Tri-Service Cognitive Performance Assessment Battery (UTC-PAB), 11: HardwareSoftware Design and Specification. U.S. Army Medical Research and Development Command. Fort Detrick, MD, 1985.
36. Reeves, D., Schlegel, R., and Gililand, K. (1991). The UTCIPAB and the NATO AGARD STRES Batery: Results from standardization studies. Medical Defense Biosciences Review, Aberdeen, MD, 1991.
37. Santucci, G., Farmer, E., Grissett, J., Wetherell, A., Boer, L., Gotters, K., Schwartz, E., and Wilson, G., AGARDograph #308, Human Performance Assessment Methods (ISBM 92-835-0510-7), North Atlantic Treaty Organization Advisory Group for Aerospace Research and Development, Working Group 12, Seine, France, 1989.
38. Thorne, D., Genser, S., Sing, H., and Hegge, F., The Walter Reed Performance Assessment Battery. Neurobehavioral Toxicology and Teratology, 7, 415, *1985.*
39. Snyder, F.R, and Henningfield, J.E, Effects of nicotine administration following 12 h of tobacco deprivation: Assessment on computerized performance tasks, Psychopharmacology, 97, 17-22, 1989.
40. Heishman, S.J., Synder, F.R., and Henningfield, J.E., Performance, subjective and physiological effects of nicotine in non-smokers. Drug and Alcohol Dependence, 34, 11-18, 1993.
41 Baker, E.L., Letz, R.E., Fidler, A.T., Shalat, S., Plantamura, D., and Lyndon, M., A computer-based neurobehavioral evaluation system for occupational and environmental epidemiology:

Methodology and validation studies. Neurobehavioral Toxicology and Teratology, 7, 369-377, 1985.

42. Bittner, A.C., Jr., Carter, R.C., Kennedy, R.S., Harbeson, M.M., and Krause, M., Performance Evaluation Tests for Environmental Research (PETER): Evaluation of 114 measures. Perceptual and Motor Skills, 63, 683-708, 1986.

43. Kennedy, R.S., Wilkes, R.L., Dunlap, W.P., and Kuntz, L.A., Development of an automated performance test system for environmental and behavioral toxicology studies. Perceptual and Motor Skills , 65, 947-962, 1987.

44. Kennedy, R.S., Baltzley, D.R., Wilkes, R.L., and Kuntz, L.A., Psychology of computer use: IX. Menu of self administered microcomputer-based nuerotoxicology tests. Perceptual and Motor Skills, 68, 1255-1272, 1989.

45. Larrabee, G.J., and Crook, T., A computerized everyday memory battery for assessing treatment effects. Psychopharmacology Bulletin. 24, 695-697, 1988.

46. Elsmore, T.F., Hegge, F.W., Naitoh, P., Kelly, T., Schlangen, K., and Gomez, S., A comparison of the effects of sleep deprivation on synthetic work performance and a conventional performance assessment battery. (Report No. 95-6), Naval Health Research Center, San Diego, CA. & Naval Medical Research and Development Command, Bethesda, MD, 1995.

47. Elsmore, T.F., Leu, J.L., Popp, K., and Mays, M.Z., Performance Assessment Under Operational Conditions Using a Computer-Based Synthetic Work Task. U.S. Army Research Institute of Environmental Medicine, Natick, MA, 1991.

48. NTI, Inc., The effecty of alcohol and fatigue on an FAA Readiness-To-Perform test, U.S. Department of Transportation/Federal Aviation Administration document DOT/FAA/AM-95/24, Office of Aviation Medicine, Washington, DC, 1995.

49. O'Donnell, R. D., The NOVASCAN™ test paradign: Theoretical basis and validation, Nova Technologies, Inc, Dayton, OH, 1992.

50. Turnage, J. J., and Kennedy, R. S., The development and use of a computerized human performance test battery for repeated-measures applications. Human Performance, 5, 265-301, 1992.

51. Turnage, J. J., Kennedy, R. S., Smith, M. G., Baltzley, D. R., and Lane, N. E., Development of microcomputer-based mental acuity tests. Ergonomics, 35, 1271-1295, 1992.

52. Kennedy, R. S., Turnage, J. J., Rugotzke, G. G., and Dunlap, W. P., Indexing cognitive tests to alcohol dosage and comparison to standardized field sobriety tests. Journal of Studies on Alcohol, 55, 615-628, 1994.

53. Parth, P., Dunlap, W. P., Kennedy, R. S., Lane, N. E., and Ordy, J. M., Motor and cognitive testing of bone marrow transplant patients after chemoradiotherapy. Perceptual and Motor Skills, 68, 1227-1241, 1989.

54. Kennedy, R. S., Odenheimer, R. C., Baltzley, D. R., Dunlap, W. P., and Wood, C. D., Differential effects of scopolamine and amphetamine on microcomputer-based performance tests. Aviation, Space and Environmental Medicine, 61, 615-621, 1990.

55. Kennedy, R. S., Dunlap, W. P., Bandaret, L. E., Smith, M. G., and Houston, C. E., Cognitive performance deficits occasioned by a simulated climb of Mount Everest: Operation Everest II. Aviation, Space and Environmental Medicine, 60, 99-104, 1989.

56. Mills, K. C., and Bisgrove, E. Z., Cognitive impairment and perceived risk from alcohol: laboratory, self-report and field assessments. Journal of Studies on Alcohol, 44, 26-46, 1983.

57. Perez-Reyes, M., Hicks, R. E., Blumberry, J., Jeffcoat, R., and Cook, C. E., Interaction between marihuana and ethanol: Effects on psychomotor performance. Alcoholism, Clinical and Experimental Research, 12, 269-276, 1988.

58. Mills, K. C., Parkman, K. M., and Spruill, S. E., A PC-based software test for measuring alcohol and drug effects in human subjects. Alcoholism, Clinical and Experimental Research, 20, 1582-1591, 1996.

4.3 EFFECTS OF ABUSED DRUGS ON PUPILLARY SIZE AND THE LIGHT REFLEX

WALLACE B. PICKWORTH, REGINALD V. FANT, AND EDWARD B. BUNKER

NATIONAL INSTITUTE ON DRUG ABUSE, INTRAMURAL RESEARCH PROGRAM, ADDICTION RESEARCH CENTER, BALTIMORE, MARYLAND

Measurements of pupillary diameter, eye tracking, and the pupillary response to a flash of light are readily available, noninvasive indices of central nervous system function. Recently, such parameters have been used by law enforcement personnel, employers, and primary care and emergency room physicians to make a rapid and initial assessment of recent drug ingestion. In this section, the physiological basis for the control of pupil size and the light reflex and the instruments used to measure pupillary responses are briefly reviewed. The results of a residential, within-subject study of the effects of various drugs of abuse on pupillary size and the light reflex are described. A summary of the literature on the effects of abused drugs on pupillary measures is given. The chapter concludes with a discussion of the utility and limitations of pupillometry in the detection of abused drugs.

4.3.1 PHYSIOLOGICAL BASIS OF PUPIL SIZE AND THE LIGHT REFLEX

4.3.1.1 Pupil Size

The human pupil ranges in diameter from 1.5 mm at full miosis to 8.0 mm at full mydriasis. The most powerful determinant of pupil size is the ambient light level. Pupil size is also influenced by several factors including subject age, iris pigmentation, gender, state of arousal, and time of day.[1] Newborns have very small pupils due to a lack of the pupillary dilator muscle development; pupil size is maximal during adolescence and declines in older age. Subjects with lightly pigmented iris (blue eyes) generally have larger pupils than those with heavily pigmented iris (brown eyes). Pupil diameter tends to decrease over the course of the day.[2] Some people, about 17% of the population, have pupils of unequal size (aniscoria), but differences exceeding 0.5 mm occur in only about 4% of the population.

4.3.1.2 Instrumentation

Pupil size can be estimated from direct observation. A variety of cards and scales are available whereby the experimenter compares the size of the pupil to standard patterns and scales. The simplest and most often used is the Haab pupil gauge. This consists of a card with black circles graduated in size between 2 and 10 mm in 0.5 mm increments. The card is held on the temporal side of the eye out of the subject's vision (to reduce accommodation miosis). Pupil size can be determined to an accuracy of 0.2 mm. The main disadvantage of the method is the inability to make measurements in the dark.

The Polaroid close up camera has been used to photograph the eye of subjects before and after the administration of opiates and other psychoactive drugs.[3,4] Pupil size can be estimated to within 0.1 mm by means of calipers and a magnified scale that is concomitantly photographed. Disadvantages of this method are the possibility that the flash used in the photography can reduce pupil size and the expense of the film. Sequential photographs can be used to

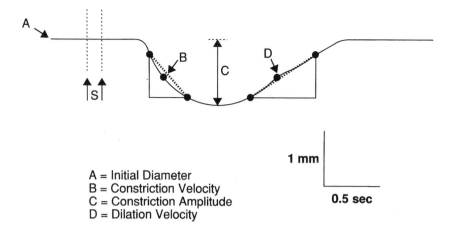

A = Initial Diameter
B = Constriction Velocity
C = Constriction Amplitude
D = Dilation Velocity

Figure 4.3.1.3 Pupil diameter before (A) and after a light stimulus (S). Constriction (B) and dilation (D) velocities are determined from a least square fit of the slope. Amplitude of constriction (C) represents the maximal difference in diameter before and after the flash.

monitor pupil size over an extended time. If the pupil is illuminated with infrared light and infrared sensitive film is used, recordings can be made in total darkness. Although this method was used in seminal studies of the pupillary light reflex and other dynamic applications,[5,6] it is seldom used today because of the high cost of film, processing time, and limited temporal resolution.

Modern pupillometers usually employ infrared illumination of the eye and a television, and/or computer. These instruments sample pupil diameter at rates up to 60 images per second. Pupillometers offer the advantage of accurate sampling across a wide range of ambient light. They can record pupil diameter over extended times enabling the investigator to quantify dynamic aspects of the light reflex and fluctuations of pupil size (hippus). These instruments are extensively used to determine the effects of drugs, fatigue, stress, autonomic reactivity and level of anesthesia. In the following section, aspects of the pupillary light reflex measured with modern pupillometers are discussed.

4.3.1.3 Light Reflex

When the retinal rods and cones are stimulated with light in the visual wavelength, there is constriction of the pupil. A major factor in determining the intensity of the reflex is the adaptation state of the retina because it is the rate of change of retinal illumination that evokes the response. Other factors influence the light reflex. The retinal area that is stimulated is differentially sensitive; the fovea and macular areas are most sensitive, the periphery is least sensitive. The subject's state of arousal,[7] anxiety,[8] the wavelength of the stimulus light and its direction all may influence the reflex.[9,10] As shown in Figure 4.3.1.3, there are several components of the light reflex that may be evaluated with pupillometers.

From studies in cats, monkeys, and rabbits, Lowenstein and Lowenfeld[11] identified the components of the light reflex that were controlled by parasympathetic and sympathetic innervation of the smooth muscles controlling pupil diameter. They concluded that the parasympathetic nervous system must be intact to observe the light reflex; the sympathetic nervous system influences the shape of the reflex. For example, in the absence of sympathetic innervation the constriction velocity is increased and the dilation velocity is decreased. In situations of increased sympathetic tone, the constriction is sluggish and incomplete. The effects of abused drugs on these and other components of the light reflex were studied in the experiment described below.

4.3.2. A LABORATORY STUDY OF EFFECTS OF ABUSED DRUGS ON HUMAN PUPILLARY RESPONSE

In an effort to understand and quantify the effects of several classes of abused drugs on human pupillary response, a study was conducted on the residential ward of the Addiction Research Center of the National Institute on Drug Abuse.

4.3.2.1 Methods

Subjects — Eight healthy male subjects with a mean age of 34.1 years volunteered for this study. During their participation in the study, they resided on a clinical research ward. The subjects had extensive histories of illicit drug use that included recent ingestion (within the past 2 years) of opiates, marijuana, stimulants, alcohol, and sedative-hypnotics although they were not dependent on any drug (except nicotine).

Study Design — All of the subjects received each of the treatments. Neither the subjects nor the technician knew the identity of the treatment at the time of the experiment. The treatments were randomly presented a minimum of 48 h apart. On study days, subjects swallowed three opaque capsules, drank a large cold tonic drink (480 ml, in 15 min) with 2 ml 95% ethanol floated on top, and smoked a cigarette (either marijuana or placebo) according to a paced puffing procedure: 8 puffs per cigarette, 20-s puff retention, 40-s interpuff interval.[12] On any experimental day, all of the dosage forms could have been a placebo (no active drugs) or one of the dosage forms could have contained an active drug. The active drug conditions were: marijuana 1.3% and 3.9% THC; ethanol 0.3 and 1.0 gm/kg; hydromorphone (Dilaudid) 1 and 3 mg; pentobarbital 150 and 450 mg; and amphetamine 10 and 30 mg. Drugs were administered at the same time each day (9:45 AM). A battery of subjective, performance, and physiologic tests were completed before drug administration, and at selected times up to 300 min after drug.

Study Measures — (1) *Pupillary Measures:* Measures of pupillary diameter and parameters of the light reflex were made using a Pupilscan (Fairville Medical Optics) handheld pupillometer.[13] The sampling rate was 10 diameters (in pixels) per second; the light reflex was evoked with a 0.1 s, 20 Lumen/sq ft, 565 nm (green) stimulus light. Initial (prestimulus) pupil diameter, and the following parameters of the light reflex, were derived from the data collected on a personal computer: constriction and dilation velocities, and the amplitude of constriction.[2,14] Pupillary measures were collected after direct stimulation of the left eye. The measures were made before the drug and at 30, 105, 180, and 300 min after the drug. (2) *Subjective Measures:* Subjective effects of the experimental drugs were estimated from scores on several standardized tests and computer-delivered 100-mm visual analog scales that measured drug symptoms, "strength", and "liking". The 100-mm scale was anchored with the terms "not at all" (0 mm) and extremely (100 mm). The subjects rated subjective effects before the drug and at 30, 105, 180, and 300 min after the drug. (3) *Performance Measures:* Before beginning the experimental series, subjects trained to a consistent level of performance on several tests of cognitive performance including the Digit Symbol Substitution Test (DSST). In the DSST, a random digit appeared on the computer screen. The subject used the numeric keypad of the computer to reproduce a geometric pattern (3 keystrokes) that was uniquely associated with the displayed digit. The dependent measure used was the number of correct responses during the 2-min task.[15] In the circular lights task, the subject pushed lighted buttons on a wall-mounted board. At the start of the task, one of the 33 buttons was illuminated. Pushing that

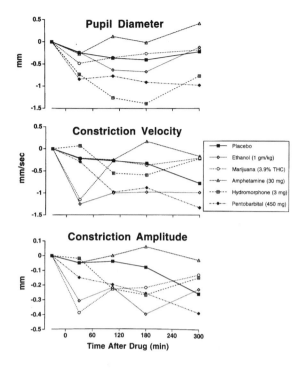

Figure 4.3.2.2.1 After high doses of the experimental drugs, changes (from baseline) in initial (prestimulus) pupil diameter, constriction velocity, and constriction amplitude varied as a function of the drug condition and time.

button added a point to the score and lighted another button at a random position. The score was the total number of points (hits) in the 1-min task.[16] The performance tests were completed before the drug and at 30, 105, 180, and 300 min after drug administration. (5) *Statistical Analyses:* Repeated measures analyses of variance (ANOVA)[17] were run on the pupillary, subjective, and performance variables. The main factors were drug (12 levels) and time (5 or 6 levels). Using *a priori* tests, data points after drug administration were compared to baseline values and placebo values. The pupillary effects were correlated with subjective effects (visual analog rating of "high" and "strong") and performance effects (DSST, number correct; circular lights, hits) by means of the Pearson's product-moment correlation.

4.3.2.2 Results

Pupillary Measures (Figure 4.3.2.2.1)

4.3.2.2.1 Pupil Diameter

The experimental drugs caused significant changes in pupillary diameter measured before the presentation of the light flash. One-way ANOVAs on the peak change indicated significant differences among the treatment conditions. A two-way ANOVA indicated significant differences among drug conditions and time of measurement, as well as a significant drug by time interaction. As shown in Table 4.3.2.2.1, high doses of ethanol, marijuana, hydromorphone, and pentobarbital decreased pupil size, whereas amphetamine caused an increase. Although the changes were statistically significant, their magnitude was not large. Pupil size decreased by 0.7, 0.5, 1.4, and 1.0 mm after the high doses of ethanol, marijuana, hydromorphone, and

Table 4.3.2.2.1 Pupillary Effects of Experimental Drugs

Drug	Dose	Pupil diameter	Constriction amplitude	Constriction velocity	Dilation velocity
Ethanol	1 gm/kg	Decreased	Decreased	Decreased	No change
Marijuana cigarette	3.9% THC	Decreased	Decreased	Decreased	Decreased
Hydro-morphone	3 mg	Decreased	Decreased	Decreased	No change
Pentobarbital	450 mg	Decreased	No change	Decreased	No change
Amphetamine	30 mg	Increased	No change	No change	No change

pentobarbital, respectively. The maximal increase after the high dose of amphetamine averaged 0.4 mm.

4.3.2.2.2 Constriction Amplitude

The constriction amplitude of the light reflex differed significantly among the treatment conditions. A two-way ANOVA indicated significant differences among drug conditions and time of measurement, as well as a significant drug by time interaction. As summarized in Table 4.3.2.2.1, constriction amplitude was significantly decreased by high doses of ethanol, marijuana and hydromorphone. The magnitude of the effect was small and the maximal changes occurred at the time of the maximal change in pupillary size.

4.3.2.2.3 Constriction Velocity

The velocity of pupillary constriction changed significantly as a function of the drug treatment. A two-way ANOVA indicated significant differences among drug conditions and time of measurement, as well as a significant drug by time interaction. As shown in Table 4.3.2.2.1, constriction velocity decreased after high doses of ethanol, marijuana, hydromorphone, and pentobarbital. The high dose of marijuana, hydromorphone, and pentobarbital reduced the constriction velocity by 1.2, 0.6, and 1.3 mm/s, respectively — changes that represented reductions of 26, 14, and 27% of control velocities.

4.3.2.2.4 Dilation Velocity

As summarized in Table 4.3.2.2.1, only the high dose of marijuana significantly changed (reduced) the velocity of dilation of the pupil during the recovery phase of the light reflex.

4.3.2.2.5 Subjective Measures (Figure 4.3.2.2.5)

Visual analog scale scores on the strength of drug effect were significantly different as a function of drug condition and time of measurement. There was also a significant drug by time interaction (Figure 4.3.2.2.5). Similarly, scores on the drug liking visual analog scale differed significantly among the drug conditions. These data indicate the subjects perceived the high doses of the experimental drugs as being strong and being liked. The positive endorsement of questions of drug liking and strength by experienced drug users indicate that such drugs have a high abuse potential.[18]

4.3.2.2.6 Performance Measures (Figure 4.3.2.2.6)

DSST — ANOVAs on the number of correct responses on the DDST indicated there were significant differences among drug conditions, time of measurement, and a significant drug by

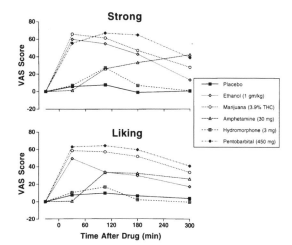

Figure 4.3.2.2.5 High doses of the experimental drugs increased scores (from baseline levels) on drug strength and drug liking. The effects varied as a function of the drug administered and the time after administration.

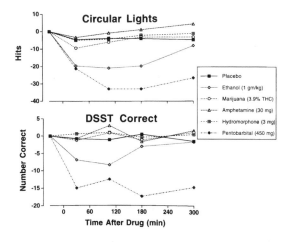

Figure 4.3.2.2.6 High doses of the experimental drugs caused changes (from baseline) in performance on the circular lights and DSST tasks. The effects varied as a function of the administered drug and the time after administration.

time interaction. Performance was significantly impaired after high doses of marijuana, ethanol, pentobarbital, and hydromorphone.

Circular lights task — High doses of ethanol and pentobarbital significantly decreased the number of hits on the circular lights task. The other experimental drugs caused no significant change in this measure of performance.

Correlational Analyses — A visual comparison of the pupillary, subjective, and performance effects of the experimental drugs (Figures 4.3.2.2.1, 4.3.2.2.5, and 4.3.2.2.6) indicates that in most instances the maximal change in each parameter occurred at the same time. Furthermore, the time of maximal effect was related to the dosage form. For example, smoked marijuana produced maximal subjective and performance effects 30 min after drug administration, whereas after the capsules (pentobarbital, hydromorphone and amphetamine) significant maximal changes occurred 120 min or longer after drug administration. Correlational analyses were performed to determine if performance and subjective changes varied as a function of pupillary change. Correlations between the change in pupil diameter and the changes in the subjective and performance measures (total of 176 correlations) were statistically significant in only 15 cases (7 at the high dose condition). Furthermore, only three of the significant correlations in the high dose conditions occurred during the time of the maximal pupillary change. These results indicate there is a very weak relationship between the pupillary, performance, and subjective effects of these experimental drugs and that pupillary changes, even under ideal laboratory conditions, do not predict changes in performance.

Effects of Abused Drugs on Pupillary Size and the Light Reflex

4.3.3 EFFECTS OF ABUSED DRUGS ON PUPILLARY MEASURES

4.3.3.1 Opiates

In early clinical studies, it was shown that morphine caused miosis and morphine withdrawal caused mydriasis.[19] In humans, most opiates caused pupillary constriction and diminished the constriction and dilation velocities of the light reflex.[20] The results of the above study confirm that hydromorphone, a potent orally active opiate, decreased pupil size and diminished the constriction velocity and amplitude of the light reflex. Buprenorphine, a partial opiate agonist, also decreased pupil size, constriction and dilation velocities, and the constriction amplitude of the light reflex.[21,22] On withdrawal of buprenorphine there was a significant increase in pupil size and in the parameters of the light reflex.[14]

4.3.3.2 Stimulants

As was demonstrated in the experiment above and elsewhere, amphetamine[23] and its derivatives and cocaine[23,24] significantly increased pupil size through an activation of the sympathetic nerve innervation of the iris. Tennant[25] also reported that cocaine and amphetamine-type stimulants increased pupil diameter and diminished the pupil reaction to light.

4.3.3.3 Barbiturates

In the laboratory experiment described above, pentobarbital (450 mg) caused a small but significant decrease in pupil size and a reduction in the constriction velocity of the light reflex. The maximal effect was measured 300 min after oral drug administration. Nystagmus (rhythmical oscillation of the eyeballs) and ptosis (drooping of the upper eyelid) are the eye signs that are most often attributed to ingestion of barbiturates, benzodiazepines, ethanol, and other CNS depressants.[23, 26, 27]

4.3.3.4 Ethanol

As shown in the above experimental results, ethanol caused a small but significant decrease in pupil size and a reduction in the response to a flash of light. In a review of the effects of abused drugs on pupillary and ocular measures, Tennant[25] reported that ethanol caused no change in pupil size but diminished the light reflex. Nystagmus is a well-known sign of ethanol intoxication.[23]

4.3.3.5 Marijuana

The high dose of marijuana decreased pupil diameter in all subjects in the experiment described above. The peak response occurred 30 min after smoking. There were significant decreases in the constriction and dilation velocities of the light reflex. Tennant[25] reported that marijuana obtunded the light reflex without changes in pupil size.

4.3.3.6 Hallucinogens

Both indoleamine (e.g., lysergic acid diethylamide, LSD; psylocibin) and phenethylamine hallucinogens (e.g., mescaline) increased pupil diameter.[23] There have been no systematic studies of the effects of these drugs on dynamic measures of the light reflex. Phencyclidine (PCP) does not cause marked changes in pupil size or the light reflex. However, subjects intoxicated with PCP often show horizontal and vertical nystagmus.[23]

4.3.3.7 Nicotine

Cigarette smoking has been reported to increase pupil size during the time the cigarette is being smoked.[28] Pupil size returned to baseline values within 45 s after smoking a single

Wallace B. Pickworth et al.

cigarette. Pupil diameter of smokers was smaller (mean = 5.1 mm) than that of nonsmokers (mean = 6.0 mm) suggesting that chronic cigarette smoking may persistently decrease pupil size.[29]

4.3.5 UTILITY AND LIMITATIONS OF PUPILLARY TESTING FOR ABUSED DRUGS

In limited circumstances, the use of pupillometry in drug detection application appears reasonable. However, based on the experimental evidence cited above and a review of the literature, there are reservations about the use of pupillometry to detect recent ingestion of abused drugs. Several areas of concern and the limitations of the methodology are discussed below.

4.3.5.1 Subject Variability

The size of the pupil and its responsiveness to a light stimulus varies considerably across subjects. Normal pupil diameter ranges between 2 and 8 mm in the extremes of ambient light. In conditions of controlled, low level (4 ft cd) ambient light, pupil size ranged from 3.5 to 8 mm and there were similarly large variations in constriction and dilation velocities of the light reflex.[2] Fosnaugh et al.[2] recorded pupil measures on four consecutive days and found very little within-subject variation in pupil size and parameters of the light reflex. These findings have practical and theoretical importance. The wide variability between subjects indicates that a single examination of the pupils and the light reflex is unlikely to be highly predictive of recent drug ingestion. On the other hand, the small within-subject, day-to-day variability indicates that a relatively small change in pupil measures in an individual may be an indicator of recent drug ingestion. These suggestions emphasize the importance of having verifiable, drug-free baseline data for individuals enrolled in testing programs.

4.3.5.2 Conditions of Measurement

The ambient light present when pupillary measures are made clearly influences the values obtained. For example, Fosnaugh et al.[2] determined the effects of ambient light on pupil size and measures of the light reflex. As ambient light varied between <.1 ft cd to 200 ft cd, pupil size decreased from 6.5 to 2.5 mm; constriction and dilation velocities decreased from 6.0 to 1.5 mm/s and from 2.5 to 1.5 mm/s, respectively. The ranges in the Fosnaugh et al.[2] experiment are similar to those reported elsewhere.[10,30] In the high ambient light conditions, pupil diameter and the constriction and dilation velocities increased when an opaque patch was placed over the contralateral eye.[2] These findings indicate that the design of pupillometers should incorporate features to assure that the ambient light is constant and that the subject consistently opens (or closes) the contralateral eye as the measures are made. In pupillometers where the subject is required to focus or gaze at a near object, accommodation-induced miosis will change pupil size and may diminish the sensitivity of the pupil to a light flash.

4.3.5.3 Effect of Fatigue, Disease, and Legal Drugs

Fatigue tends to decrease pupil size and diminish the response to light through diminished inhibition of the Edinger Westphal nucleus.[5] Subjects with diabetes mellitus have smaller pupils and a sluggish light reflex.[31] Schizophrenia and other psychiatric diagnoses are associated with sluggish pupillary response to a light flash and other pupillary abnormalities.[32] The light reflex is obtunded in anxious subjects.[8]

The ingestion of many widely used drugs changes pupillary diameter and the responsiveness to light.[23,26,33] For example, the following drug classes increase pupil size: anticholinergics (e.g., atropine, scopolamine), sympathomimetics (e.g., epinephrine, ephedrine), and antihistamines (diphenhydramine). Other drug classes decrease pupil diameter: cholinomimetics (physostigmine, pilocarpine), sympatholytics (e.g., reserpine, guanethidine, alpha-methyldopa), and chlorpromazine. The wide range of drugs that affect pupillary measures complicate the application of pupillometry in the detection of illegal drugs.

4.3.6 CONCLUSIONS

The proposal that pupillary measures could be used to distinguish classes of drugs likely to impair automobile driving performance[25] stimulated interest in the use of pupillometry for drug detection applications. The literature reviewed and the results of the controlled, clinical study presented above indicate that several classes of commonly abused drugs have specific, dose-related effects on pupil size and measures of the light reflex. The application of pupillometry for the detection of drugs of abuse is theoretically possible but the practical utility is limited. Because of the large between-subject variation in pupillary measures, one must know the baseline values for the tested subject. This limits the use of the technique to workplace, military, or institutional applications. The profound influence of ambient light on pupillary measures dictates that the conditions under which measures are made be carefully controlled. Other drugs, fatigue, and some diseases also influence measures of the light reflex and may increase the number of false positive readings. Finally, the magnitude of the effects of the drugs studied are small and transient and often do not exceed the within-subject variability. These considerations challenge the use of pupillometry as a drug detection application.

ACKNOWLEDGMENTS

The authors gratefully acknowledge the technical and medical support of Nelda Snidow, R.N. during the residential study at the Addiction Research Center. The financial support of Fairville Medical Instruments and the collaborative and enriching comments of Mr. Peter Brock are most appreciated.

REFERENCES

1. Alexandridis, E., *The Pupil*, Springer-Verlag, New York 1985.
2. Fosnaugh, J. S., Bunker, E. B. and Pickworth, W. B., Daily variation and effects of ambient light and circadian factors on the human light reflex, *Meth. Find. Clin. Exp. Pharmacol.*,14, 545, 1992.
3. Marquardt, W. G., Martin, W. R. and Jasinski, D. R., The use of the Polaroid CU camera in pupillography, *Int. J. Addict.*, 2, 301, 1967.
4. Jasinski, D. R. and Martin, W. R., Evaluation of a new photographic method for assessing pupil diameters, *Clin. Pharmacol. Therap.*, 8, 271, 1967.
5. Lowenstein, O. and Lowenfeld, I. E., The pupil. in: *The Eye* , Davson, H., Ed., New York Academic Press, 1969, 255.
6. Lowenstein, O. and Lowenfeld, I., Electronic pupillography, *Arch. Ophthalmol.*, 59, 352, 1958.
7. Newman, J. and Boughton, R., Pupillometric assessment of excessive daytime sleepiness in narcolepsy-cataplexy, *Sleep*, 14, 121, 1991
8. Bakes, A., Bradshaw, C. M. and Szabadi, E., Attenuation of the pupillary light reflex in anxious patients, *Br. J. Clin. Pharmacol.*, 30, 377, 1990.
9. Zinn, K. M., *The Pupil*, Charles C. Thomas, Springfield, 1972.
10. Ellis, C. J. K., The pupillary light reflex in normal subjects, *Br. J.Ophthalmology*, 65, 754, 1981.

11. Lowenstein, O. and Lowenfeld, I. E., Mutual role of sympathetic and parasympathetic in shaping of the pupillary reflex to light, *Arch. Neurology Psychiat. (Chicago)*, 64, 341, 1950.
12. Heishman, S. J., Stitzer, M. L. and Bigelow, G. E., Alcohol and marijuana: Comparative dose effect profiles in humans, *Pharmacol. Biochem. Behav.*, 31, 649, 1988.
13. Radzius, A., Welch, P., Cone, E. J. and Henningfield, J. E., A portable pupilometer system for measuring pupillary size and light reflex, *Behav. Resh. Method Instrum. Computer.*, 21, 611, 1989.
14. Pickworth, W. B., Lee, H. and Fudala, P. J., Buprenorphine-induced pupillary effects in human volunteers, *Life Sci.*, 47, 1269, 1990.
15. Heishman, S. J., Heustis, M. A., Henningfield, J. E. and Cone, E. J., Acute and residual effects of marijuana: Profiles of plasma THC levels, physiologic, subjective and performance measures, *Pharmacol. Biochem. Behav.*, 37, 561, 1990.
16. Pickworth, W. B., Klein, S. A., George, F. R. and Henningfield, J. E., Acetaminophen fails to inhibit ethanol-induced subjective effects in human volunteers, *Pharmacol. Biochem. Behav.*, 41, 189, 1991.
17. Winer, B. J., Brown, D. R. and Michels, K. M., *Statistical Principles in Experimental Design*, 3rd ed. McGraw-Hill, New York, 1991.
18. Jasinski, D. R., Johnson, R. E. and Henningfield, J. E., Abuse liability assessment in human subjects, *Trends Pharmacol. Sci.*, 5, 196, 1984.
19. Himmelsbach, C. K., The morphine abstinence syndrome, its nature and treatment, *Ann. Int. Med.*, 15, 829, 1941.
20. Pickworth, W. B., Welch, P., Henningfield, J. E. and Cone, E. J., Opiate-induced pupillary effects in humans, *Meth. Find. Exp. Clin. Pharmacol.*, 11, 759, 1989.
21. Pickworth, W. B., Bunker, E., Welch, P. and Cone, E. J., Intravenous buprenorphine reduces pupil size and the light reflex in humans, *Life Sci.*, 49, 129, 1991.
22. Pickworth, W. B., Johnson, R. E., Holicky, B. A. and Cone, E. J., Subjective and physiologic effects of intravenous buprenorphine in humans, *Clin. Pharmacol. Ther.*, 53, 570, 1993.
23. Urey, J. C., Some ocular manifestations of systemic drug abuse, *J. Am. Optom. Assoc.*, 62, 832, 1991.
24. Rothman, R. B., Gorelick, D. A., Baumann, M. H., Guo, X. Y., Herning, R. I., Pickworth, W. B., Gendron, T. M., Koeppl, B., Thompson, L. E. and Henningfield, J. E., Lack of evidence for context-dependent cocaine-induced sensitization in humans: Preliminary studies, *Pharmacol. Biochem. Behav.*, 49, 583, 1994.
25. Tennant, F., The rapid eye test to detect drug abuse, *Postgraduate Med.*, 84, 108, 1988.
26. Koetting, J. F., The use of drugs for behavior modification as it relates to the practice of optometry-part 2, *J. Am. Optom. Assoc.*, 48, 213, 1977.
27. McLane, N. J. and Carroll, D. M., Ocular manifestations of drug abuse, *Surv. Ophthalmol.*, 30, 298, 1986.
28. Roberts, J. D. and Adams, A. J., Short term effects of smoking on ocular accommodation and pupil size, *J. Am. Optometric Assoc.*, 40, 528, 1969.
29. Pickworth, W. B., Fant, R. V., Butschky, M. F. and Henningfield, J. E., Effects of mecamylamine on spontaneous EEG and performance in smokers and non-smokers, *Pharmacol. Biochem. Behav.*, 56, 181, 1997.
30. Taniguchi, H. Kuroda, N., Baba, S. and Yamamoto, M., Pupillary light reflex in healthy subjects, *Kobe J. Med. Sci.*, 34, 189, 1988.
31. Lanting, P., Strijers, R. L. M., Bos, J. E., Faes, T. J. C. and Heimans, J. J., The cause of increased pupillary light reflex latencies in diabetic patients: the relationship between pupillary light reflex and visual evoked potential latencies, *EEG Clin. Neurophysiol.*, 78, 111, 1991.
32. Steinhauer, S. R. and Hakerem, G., The pupillary response in cognitive psychophysiology and schizophrenia, in *Psychophysiology and Experimental Psychopathology: A Tribute to Samuel Sutton*, Friedman, D. and Bruder, G. Eds., *Ann. N. Y. Acad. Sci.*, 658, 182, 1992.
33. Turner, P., The human pupil as a model for clinical pharmacological investigations, *J. Royal Coll. Phycns. (Lond.)*, 9, 165, 1975.

4.4 EVALUATING ABUSE LIABILITY: METHODS AND PREDICTIVE VALUE

KENZIE L. PRESTON, PH.D. AND SHARON L. WALSH, PH.D.

INTRAMURAL RESEARCH PROGRAM, NATIONAL INSTITUTE ON DRUG ABUSE (KLP), JOHNS HOPKINS UNIVERSITY SCHOOL OF MEDICINE (KLP AND SLW) BALTIMORE, MARYLAND

4.4.1 FACTORS THAT AFFECT ABUSE LIABILITY

The degree to which a psychoactive substance is abused is dependent on a number of factors. Important factors include its physical properties, pharmacological profile, physical dependence capacity, toxicity, availability, and the cultural milieu. Some of these factors (physical properties, pharmacological profile, physical dependence capacity, and toxicity) are characteristics of the drug itself or the result of interactions between the organism, and the drug; these factors are amenable to measurement. Other factors, such as availability and cultural milieu, are the result of interactions among the compound, the organism and the environment and do not readily lend themselves to experimental analysis.

While the complex interplay among the various factors prevents the exact prediction of future abuse for an individual compound, general principles have been established to assess abuse potential and guide regulatory agencies in choosing appropriate levels of control. The availability of psychoactive substances is controlled under federal regulations designed to decrease drug abuse and protect the public health. The level of regulatory control is evaluated for new medications when they are reviewed by the Food and Drug Administration for approval prior to marketing. In addition, psychoactive substances that are neither under pharmaceutical development nor used for legitimate medical purposes can also be considered for control if reports of abuse occur. The criteria for assessing abuse potential for the purpose of federal scheduling of psychoactive substances are outlined in Section 201 (c) of the Comprehensive Drug Abuse Prevention and Control Act of 1970 (see Chapter 1).

Standardized experimental procedures are used to evaluate the pharmacological factors that are considered by federal regulatory agencies. The extent to which a drug produces reinforcing effects is typically estimated in self-administration studies by use of operant conditioning paradigms that measure the ability of the drug to act as a reinforcer in animals. Methods for measuring discriminative stimuli and subjective effects in laboratory animals and humans have been developed to estimate the extent of similarity of the pharmacologic profile of novel compounds to prototypic compounds of a drug class that are already scheduled. In drug discrimination studies, subjects are trained to discriminate the presence or absence of a prototypic drug, and novel drugs are tested for their ability to substitute for the prototypic drug.

Subjective effects studies are conducted in human subjects; the novel drug is administered over a range of doses and its subjective effects are measured on a battery of questionnaires and compared to those of prototypic drugs of abuse. In physical dependence studies, the test drug is administered repeatedly and then withdrawn; physiological, behavioral, and, in the case of humans, subjective effects are measured. The capacity to produce physical dependence cannot only increase the likelihood of abuse but also increase the adverse consequences of abuse. The basic procedures for conducting self-administration, drug discrimination, subjective effect and physical dependence studies are described in detail later in this section. The toxicity of abused substances is considered because misuse has the potential to create public health problems and because the presence or absence of toxic effects can limit abuse liability. Toxicity data can be obtained in studies designed specifically for that purpose as well as from studies of other pharmacological effects such as those listed above.

Kenzie L. Preston and Sharon L. Walsh

Epidemiological evidence of abuse with resultant public health and social problems and the potential influence of nonpharmacological factors such as availability and type of preparation are often evaluated after a new medication or a new preparation of an existing medication is marketed. Availability and physical chemical properties can also affect abuse patterns of illicit substances. Finally, fads and other cultural phenomena can alter abuse patterns of both licit and illicit psychoactive substances and lead to additional regulatory control.

4.4.2 PHARMACOLOGIC ISSUES

4.4.2.1 Pharmacologic Classes of Abused Drugs

Abuse of a drug or psychoactive substance can be defined by behavioral, psychological, medical, or legal criteria. For the purposes of this discussion, the definition of drug abuse is simply the use of any substance that is self-administered for its mood altering effects and is used for a non-therapeutic purpose. Compounds that fall into this category are too numerous to review comprehensively; however, prototypic drugs of abuse and some examples of other less commonly abused substances will be described.

The major classes of abused drugs include psychomotor stimulants, opiates, sedatives, marijuana, and the hallucinogens. It is interesting that these drug classes vary so greatly in their chemical structures and their pharmacological actions but share the common feature of having significant abuse potential. Even within each major class, compounds can vary significantly in their potency, profile of neurochemical action, and their origin (i.e., synthetic vs. natural). The primary reasons for choosing these five pharmacological classes to represent the prototypic drugs of abuse is that drugs within each class have been used for non-medicinal purposes throughout much of recorded history and across geographic regions throughout the world, although the prevalence for each may be influenced by cultural and economic variables. Although a brief description of the pharmacological actions of the major classes of abused drugs is provided, for more information, interested readers are referred to more extensive pharmacological reviews on drugs abuse.[2-4]

4.4.2.1.1 Psychomotor Stimulants

The psychomotor stimulants exert their effects primarily by potentiating actions on catecholamine cells and receptors in the central nervous system and in the periphery. The most commonly abused stimulants include cocaine, amphetamine, and methamphetamine, although there are many others with abuse potential such as methylphenidate, ephedrine, and methcathinone, whose abuse may be more circumscribed by availability and pharmacologic characteristics. Drugs of this class are used for a variety of therapeutic applications including weight loss, narcolepsy, and treatment of attention deficit disorder with hyperactivity. Cocaine is used clinically as a local anesthetic. In general, psychomotor stimulants produce their pharmacologic actions by enhancing dopaminergic, noradrenergic, adrenergic, and perhaps to a lesser extent, serotonergic transmission.

These drugs can cause the release of presynaptic stores of neurotransmitter, inhibition of active reuptake, and/or inhibition of metabolic enzymes, such as monoamine oxidase. In all cases, the net result is increased circulating and synaptic concentrations of monoamines leading to overstimulation of peripheral and central receptors. The central actions of the psychomotor stimulants include increased awareness, decreased fatigue, and a feeling of well-being or euphoria. It is commonly believed that the enhancement of dopamine neurotransmission, particularly within the mesoaccumbens pathway, is the principal mediator of the reinforcing actions of the psychomotor stimulants.[5,6]

The autonomic effects of the psychomotor stimulants include tachycardia, pressor effects, and vasoconstriction. In addition, these stimulants possess antithermic and anorectic properties. Both cocaine and amphetamine can be toxic at higher doses; acute toxic effects can include tremor, confusion, hallucinations, and diaphoresis. Lethal overdose can result from the cardiovascular effects of these drugs (e.g., cardiac arrest, cerebrovascular infarction, or aortic rupture) or from respiratory depression, hyperpyrexia, and convulsions.

4.4.2.1.2 Opiates

The opiates and opioids are alkaloid compounds that are either derived naturally from the poppy plant or synthesized. Opioids with known abuse liability include, but are not limited to, heroin, opium, morphine, codeine, propoxyphene, hydromorphone, fentanyl, oxymorphone, buprenorphine, and pentazocine. Opioids are most commonly used in therapeutic settings for their analgesic actions which are mediated by both peripheral and central mechanisms. These compounds exert their actions by binding to central and peripheral opiate receptors. There are at least three opiate receptor families, including the *mu, kappa,* and *delta* receptors, although other classification systems also exist (see Cooper et al.[7]).

Even within these families, receptor subtypes have been identified (e.g., *mu$_1$* and *mu$_2$* receptors). Compounds with abuse liability typically act as agonists at *mu* receptors. Opioid agonists administered acutely produce sedation, talkativeness, excitation, and euphoria. Opioids produce a constellation of physiological effects that includes constipation, urinary retention, pupillary constriction, and respiratory depression. It is the latter effect that typically accounts for the toxicity and lethal overdose from opioids. Upon repeated administration, they also can produce a profound physical dependence syndrome that can perpetuate abuse patterns (see discussion later in this section). Dextromethorphan, most commonly found in cough suppressant preparations, is another opioid with known, although limited, abuse liability.

In addition to its opioid activity, dextromethorphan also binds to the sigma receptor, once classified as an opiate receptor, and acts as an antagonist at the N-methyl-d-aspartic acid (NMDA) receptor. Dextromethorphan produces psychotomimetic or hallucinogenic effects similar to, but of lesser magnitude than, those produced by phencyclidine (PCP), another drug which also binds to the sigma and NMDA receptors. Thus, the abuse liability of dextromethorphan is probably due to multiple receptor actions.

4.4.2.1.3 Sedatives

The sedative class of compounds is composed primarily of the barbiturates and benzodiazepines. There are also other sedative drugs, such as meprobamate, choral hydrate, glutethimide, and methaqualone, whose mechanisms of action differ from the barbiturates and benzodiazepines. The primary action of drugs in the sedative class is to produce central nervous system depression. These agents are clinically used for their sedative/anesthetic, anxiolytic, anticonvulsant as well as their anti-spasmodic or muscle-relaxant properties. The benzodiazepines and barbiturates exert their effects through their distinct actions at the g-aminobutyric acid$_A$ (GABA$_A$) receptor, which is one of the binding sites on the GABA$_A$/chloride ionophore receptor complex (for review of their differential molecular actions see Paul[8]).

The net neurochemical effect produced by administration of both benziodiazepines and barbiturates is to enhance transmission of GABA, the primary inhibitory neurotransmitter. Barbiturates and benzodiazepines produce subjective effects including drowsiness, sedation, lightheadedness, and confusion. Benzodiazepines are also known to produce anterograde amnesia even following acute administration. Overdose from barbiturates can produce disrupted respiratory patterns leading to hypoxia, circulatory collapse, renal failure, coma, and death. In contrast, excessive consumption of benzodiazepines rarely leads to lethal overdose.

Kenzie L. Preston and Sharon L. Walsh

4.4.2.1.4 Marijuana

Marijuana is typically used by smoking the dried plant leaves in rolled cigarettes or pipes, although it can also be ingested orally after incorporation into a food product. The resin of the plant, known as hashish, can also be smoked or eaten and is a more potent preparation than marijuana. Although the marijuana plant contains numerous active constituents, the primary active cannabinoid is Δ^9-tetrahydrocannabinol (Δ^9-THC). Δ^9-THC is a lipophillic compound that has an extremely long half-life estimated to range from 28 to 56 hours.[9]

Marijuana exerts its effects by binding to THC binding sites in mammalian brain, with the highest density of these found in the basal ganglia and cerebellum. The primary subjective effects of marijuana include feelings of well-being, sedation, depersonalization, and altered perception of time and space. Marijuana and Δ^9-THC are also known to produce acute psychomotor and cognitive performance impairments and direct cardiovascular effects including tachycardia and changes in blood pressure. Adverse effects related to marijuana use include impairments in short-term memory, hallucinations, and paranoid ideation.

4.4.2.1.5 Hallucinogens

The hallucinogen class is constituted from a variety of different drugs; while all share the property of producing hallucinations, their pharmacological profiles vary widely. Chemically these drugs fall into two primary groups: the indole group that includes lysergic diethylamine (LSD) and some substituted tryptamines; and the substituted phenylethylamines that includes mescaline and the phenylisopropylamines. LSD is considered the prototypic hallucinogen; two "designer" phenylisopropylamines, 3,4-methylenedioxyamphetamine (MDA) and 3, 4-methylenedioxymethamphetamine (MDMA), have been introduced more recently and their abuse has been reported in the U.S. and elsewhere.

Although the neurochemical mechanisms that underlie the hallucinogenic activity of these compounds are incompletely characterized, there is substantial evidence supporting a role of the central serotonergic system, specifically 5-HT_2 receptors, in mediating their behavioral effects. The primary subjective effects of LSD include euphoria, anxiety, dizziness, dreaminess, and depersonalization. In addition, perceptual changes can include alterations in visual and auditory sensations. MDA and MDMA produce less prominent symptoms of depersonalization and perceptual changes. Hallucinogens also produce prominent autonomic effects including mydriasis, tachycardia, and pressor effects.

The primary adverse effects resulting from hallucinogen use are principally related to their psychological effects. These include depression, anxiety attacks, and paranoid ideation, and may be manifest as either acute or chronic reactions. Finally, MDA and MDMA, but not LSD, have been shown to produce neurotoxic effects in laboratory animals.

Phencyclidine (PCP) is a synthetic compound that possesses hallucinogenic properties, although its unique pharmacological profile and mechanism of action distinguishes PCP from the classical LSD-type hallucinogens. PCP exerts its CNS effects by binding to a specific PCP-binding site on the NMDA-receptor complex where it acts as a non-competitive antagonist. In addition, it prevents the reuptake of dopamine and norepinephrine. PCP was originally developed as an analgesic agent but its use in humans was discontinued because of its untoward psychotropic effects. PCP can produce stimulant, depressant, and analgesic effects in addition to its hallucinogenic or "psychotomimetic" effects.

The subjective effects of PCP include intoxication, feelings of power, disorganized thought, dysphoria, drowsiness, apathy, and perceptual changes in body image. PCP produces an array of physiological effects including elevated heart rate, blood pressure and temperature, increased salivation, and diaphoresis. At higher doses, PCP can produce schizophrenic-like symptomology including psychosis, paranoia, catatonia, and violent behavior. In overdose, the consequences are severe and can include persistent psychosis, convulsions, coma, and death.

There are an array of other psychoactive drugs that fall outside of the major classifications of abused drugs but are known to have abuse potential. One commonalty of these "lesser" drugs of abuse is that their usage may be more influenced by fad and cultural differences compared to the major drug classes. In addition, their use may rise in popularity and then fall into obscurity, or they may be used by only a very select subpopulation.

Volatile inhalants are abused in the U.S. and in other countries throughout the world, most commonly by adolescents. Numerous household and industrial products contain volatile inhalants that can be abused. The active chemical constituents include, but are not limited to, trichlorethane, butane, toluene, and fluorocarbons; these are commonly found in solvents, glues, cleaners, fuels, and various other commonly available products (for review see Sharp and Rosenberg[10]). Inhalation of these compounds can cause hypoxia and produce subjective effects including dizziness, rush, excitation, agitation, and/or drowsiness. Inhalation of these substances can be extremely toxic and has been associated with numerous cases of cardiac arrest and sudden death in young people.[11-13]

A separate category of substances abused by inhalation are the anesthetic gases; these include nitrous oxide, ether, and halothane. Inhalation of these gases can produce euphoria, feelings of well-being, dreaminess, sedation, and drowsiness and can also produce hypoxia. To self-administer any of the volatile inhalants, abusers simply inhale them from their containers; other chemicals contained in solid or liquid (e.g., paint) products may be "sniffed" or "huffed" which refers to releasing the product from its container and inhaling the vapors.

Several plant products contain physiologically active constituents that are sometimes abused for their psychoactive effects. Stramonium, commonly known as Jimson weed, contains the alkaloids hyoscyamine and scopolamine and has been abused for its hallucinogen-like properties. The risks associated with ingestion are due primarily to the anticholinergic activity of the plant; adverse effects include tachycardia, psychomotor agitation, and disorientation.[13-15] The morning glory family and some related species contain several alkaloids including d-lysergic acid amide;[16] the seeds of these plants are sometimes consumed in large quantities for their hallucinogenic effects. Nutmeg, the common household spice, has also been used for its hallucinogenic properties. The active compounds responsible for these effects are unknown, but it is possible that elemicin and myristicin are involved;[17] however, the large quantities required to produce these effects often produce signs of toxicity after ingestion. Similar to Jimson weed, the toxic side effects of nutmeg ingestion are related to its anticholinergic activity.[18]

The Khat plant, a species indigenous to East Africa, has been used for centuries for its stimulant, anorectic, and euphorigenic properties. The leaves of the Khat plant are chewed to extract the active compound cathinone. Cathinone is structurally related to amphetamine; these compounds produce comparable profiles of action.[19,20] Recently, methcathinone, a readily synthesized derivative of cathinone, has become illicitly available in the U.S. under the name CAT. Methcathinone is also a potent psychomotor stimulant that is highly reinforcing.[21] Because of its high abuse potential, the increased prevalence of its illicit production and lack of a recognized medical indication, methcathinone was classified as a Schedule I drug in 1993 by federal regulatory agencies.

4.4.2.2 Structure Activity Relationships

Systematic structure activity studies are commonly employed in medicinal chemistry. These studies have demonstrated that a particular pharmacological effect or the potency of a specific drug can be modified by minor modifications of its chemical structure. An excellent illustration of this principal is provided by amphetamine and its structural analogs. Amphetamine, a derivative of b-phenylethylamine, has four separate structural components whose presence and specific configuration are critical for the production of the full constellation of amphetamine's pharmacodynamic actions. These include a phenyl ring, an alpha-methyl group, a two-carbon side chain and the primary amino group. Structural modifications of any one of these constituents can alter the specific properties of the parent compound. For example, the stimulant effects of amphetamine can be eliminated by the addition of an electron withdrawing group on the phenyl ring while the anorexic properties remain intact; this is the case for the compound fenfluramine.

Other substitutions or modifications can selectively impact the toxicity, potency, or the relative affinity of amphetamine analogs for different neurotransmitter transport sites (for further discussion see Anggard[22] and King and Ellinwood[23]). Similarly, a great deal of effort has been directed at identifying opioid compounds that retain the analgesic efficacy of morphine without its physical dependence capacity; these efforts have resulted in the development of numerous analog compounds which have activity at one or more opioid receptor site, including nalorphine, pentazocine, buprenorphine, and butorphanol (for review, see Jaffe and Martin[24]). Understanding the relationship between structure and pharmacological activity can direct medicinal chemistry efforts to develop novel compounds that retain therapeutic efficacy for a particular indication but have lower abuse potential than the parent or prototype drug. As noted above, because minor changes in structure can have dramatic effects on pharmacological profile, one cannot assume that structurally similar or related compounds have similar abuse liability, and testing should be conducted on all novel compounds.

4.4.2.3 Pharmacokinetics

The relative abuse liability of a drug is influenced by its pharmacokinetic properties and the numerous factors that determine its distribution, metabolism, and excretion. One important determinant that can significantly alter abuse potential is the speed with which a drug is delivered to the central nervous system. In general, abuse potential is enhanced by speeding the delivery of drug to the brain, and this closely corresponds with the rate of rising drug concentration in arterial blood (see also Oldendorf[25]). Increased speed of delivery decreases the interval between drug administration and the perceived onset of the drug's pharmacodynamic effects, the behavioral feature considered critical to abuse potential.[26] One of the simplest means of modifying the speed of drug delivery is to change the route of administration; this can largely determine the speed of delivery.

Typically routes of drug administration that provide a more rapid delivery are associated with greater abuse liability. Thus, for most drugs the rank order for routes of administration from fastest to slowest delivery are typically as follows: inhalation (e.g., smoking) ≥ intravenous > intramuscular > subcutaneous > intranasal > oral. There are some exceptions to these rules; these include drugs that are themselves inactive but produce active metabolites (i.e., pro-drugs) and drugs with particularly poor bioavailability when administered by a specific route.

An illustration of the relationship between route of administration and speed of onset can be gleaned from review of pharmacokinetic studies of cocaine. It has been established that the onset and peak subjective effects of cocaine correspond closely to the plasma concentration of cocaine and parallel the expected distribution of the drug by these routes of administration.[27-30] Thus, when cocaine is smoked or administered intravenously, the onset of subjective effects is almost immediate, and the peak response occurs shortly thereafter; the intravenous and smoking routes are widely accepted as having the greatest abuse potential.[31] The onset of effects for intranasal cocaine is slower than that of intravenous and smoked cocaine; subjective ratings of drug effects increase within 5 min and generally peak between 20 to 30 min after insufflation. The onset of effects are slowest after administration of oral cocaine and peak effect at approximately 1 h after ingestion. In the U.S., cocaine is not typically abused by the oral route probably because of slow onset and low bioavailability;[32] this latter characteristic makes oral administration of cocaine an inefficient and poor economic choice for substance abusers.

Another illustration of the importance of speed of drug delivery and abuse liability is provided by studies that have systematically evaluated the pharmacodynamic effects of intravenous cocaine under conditions where the speed of the intravenous infusion is varied. One of the earliest studies examined the reinforcing effects of cocaine in rhesus monkeys trained to self-administer intravenous cocaine.[33] When the infusion duration was varied from 5 to 200 s and cocaine dose was held steady, response rate and the number of reinforcers earned were found to decrease as a function of increasing infusion time. Thus, cocaine was more reinforcing when delivered by faster infusion.

Two studies have examined the relationship between infusion speed and subjective responses to intravenous cocaine in humans. In one study, cocaine-experienced volunteers received intravenous cocaine doses (16 or 32 mg) infused over both 1- and 10-min periods.[34] Cocaine given by faster infusion produced more pronounced subjective and physiological effects compared to cocaine administered by slower infusion. In a more recent study, it was demonstrated that the abuse liability of cocaine could be significantly altered by even more modest variations in the speed of intravenous infusion.[35] In that study, a single cocaine dose (30 mg) was infused over 2, 15, or 60 s and subjective and physiological responses were measured. Ratings on standard indices used in abuse liability assessments (e.g., ratings of "high" and "liking for the drug") were significantly greater when cocaine was administered over 2 s compared to 60 s; in contrast, the physiological responses (i.e., increased heart rate and blood pressure) were comparable regardless of infusion rate.

The relationship between speed of onset and abuse potential is believed to exist for drugs in pharmacological classes other than the stimulant class although few studies have directly examined this question. One study by de Wit and colleagues[36] systematically evaluated the relationship between rate of plasma concentration increase and subjective responses to administration of the barbiturate sodium pentobarbital. In that study, two dosing conditions were compared: in the first condition only a single dose of pentobarbital was administered, and in the second condition divided doses were given over an extended period of time. These conditions produced nearly identical peak plasma concentrations of sodium pentobarbital; however, the single dose condition produced a steeper and faster rise in plasma drug concentrations. Subjective ratings of "liking for the drug" and "high" were significantly greater for the single vs. the divided dose condition. This study demonstrates that, despite comparable concentrations of drug in plasma, the administration method providing the faster delivery is associated with a greater abuse potential for sedative drugs as well as stimulants.

4.4.2.4 Physical Properties

The physical properties of a drug that can influence abuse liability are primarily those that alter the bioavailability and potency of the drug and its accessibility to the central nervous system. One excellent example of this principle is the sweeping change in abuse patterns of cocaine that occurred following the increased availability of a smokeable form of cocaine — free-base or "crack" cocaine.[37] Although a procedure for converting the hydrochloride salt to the free base or alkaloidal form of cocaine had been known for some time, the process involved evaporation of highly volatile solvents and was dangerous, and thus limited the availability of the free-base form.

The development of a safer, easier method of manufacturing this free-base "crack" cocaine led to increased availability of the smokeable form and widespread increases in cocaine use. Prior to the introduction of "crack", cocaine was illicitly available in the salt form and abused primarily by the intranasal and, to a lesser extent, the intravenous route. Despite the fact that intravenous administration is associated with greater bioavailability, faster delivery to the

Kenzie L. Preston and Sharon L. Walsh

central nervous system, and more intense euphorigenic effects compared to intranasal administration, the prevalence of intravenous abuse remained fairly low because of the many disadvantages associated with intravenous drug abuse.

Disadvantages include the need for illicitly acquired paraphernalia (i.e., syringes), exposure to blood-borne diseases (i.e., HIV infection, hepatitis) as well as the long-term stigma of visible scarring from needle use. Crack represented a formulation of cocaine that could produce subjective effects comparable in time to onset and magnitude as those produced by intravenous cocaine.[31] Moreover, it was readily available in small packaging for a significantly lower price and could be used without the attendant disadvantages of intravenous use.

One physical property that can modify the access of a drug to the central nervous system and alter its abuse potential is lipophilicity. Drugs that are more lipophilic enter the central nervous system and exert their effects more rapidly than less lipophilic substances. One example of a drug that fits this profile is heroin. Heroin is a Schedule I drug that is highly addictive. Heroin is actually classified as a pro-drug, which means that it is inactive until converted to its active metabolites, 6-mono-acetyl morphine and morphine.[38] Moreover, heroin produces a profile of effects that is indistinguishable from other prototypic *mu* agonists.[24,39]

Given these facts alone, one might not predict that heroin would have a higher rate of abuse or higher abuse liability than many of the other opioid drugs. However, heroin is highly lipid soluble and is transported and distributed more rapidly to the central nervous system than drugs that are less lipid soluble such as morphine. Thus, the onset of the effects of heroin are more immediate than other compounds; as noted above, faster onset is generally associated with greater abuse potential. Along with lipid solubility which enhances heroin's abuse potential, other factors likely contribute to the widespread preference for heroin over, for instance, morphine in the illicit drug market. Because heroin is more potent than morphine, it is more easily concealed and transported; thus, heroin is a more valuable commodity on a per pound basis; all of these factors are significant considerations for drug traffickers. Thus, both physical properties, economic factors, and availability contribute to the overall abuse liability of heroin.

4.4.3 METHODS USED IN ABUSE LIABILITY ASSESSMENT

4.4.3.1 Self-Administration

The self-administration paradigm is a model of drug abuse widely used to assess the reinforcing efficacy of drugs. In this model, research subjects, usually laboratory animals, are given access to a drug under controlled experimental conditions, and their drug-taking behavior is evaluated. A drug is considered to be reinforcing if the frequency of a designated behavioral response (e.g., a lever press) is increased when drug delivery is contingent on the performance of that response in comparison to the frequency of responses in the absence of the drug. The capacity of a drug to reinforce behavior and, thus, maintain self-administration under experimental conditions is associated with a significant likelihood of abuse by human drug abusers.

Since the early 1960s, hundreds of drugs have been tested in operant self-administration paradigms. Drug self-administration has been demonstrated by various routes of administration (intravenous, oral, intragastric, intracranial, intracerebroventricular, intramuscular, and inhalation) and in a wide variety of species (pigeons, mice, rats, cats, dogs, non-human primates, and humans) (for review see Meisch and Lemaire[40]). The self-administration paradigm is complex; only a brief summary of methods is outlined below. Detailed discussion of these procedures is beyond the scope of this chapter; interested readers are referred to one of the numerous reviews on this topic.[40-42]

For the purposes of characterizing abuse potential, a number of procedures can be used to establish relative reinforcing efficacy: response rate analysis, concurrent or second-order schedules, progressive ratio (PR) schedules, and discrete-trial choice.[42] The most widely used method, response rate analysis, employs an operant schedule such as a fixed-ratio (FR) or a fixed-interval (FI) schedule of reinforcement that defines the work requirement and/or temporal availability of drug. An FR schedule requires the subject to complete a given number of responses in order to obtain the reinforcer; for example, a subject may be required to emit ten responses to obtain one drug delivery (FR-10). In an FI schedule, the first response emitted after a fixed time interval results in the delivery of a drug; for example, in an FI-3 minute schedule drug is available no more frequently than every 3 min. The dependent measures collected in these procedures typically include the rate of responding (responses/time), temporal response pattern, and the number of drug administrations per session.

Access to drug administration is typically confined to a limited and predetermined time period (e.g., a 3-h session) in which multiple small unit doses may be obtained. In some early studies, subjects were given 24-h unrestricted access to drug; however, for some drug classes, particularly the psychomotor stimulants, unrestricted access resulted in irregular self-administration patterns and overdose.[43,44] Using fixed access periods, FR and FI schedules generate reliable and reproducible patterns of responding for most drugs. For abuse liability testing of a novel substance, these studies can be initiated in one of two ways: direct self-administration or substitution. In the direct self-administration procedure, inexperienced subjects are given access to a test drug and the extent to which self-administration is initiated and maintained is measured. In the substitution procedure, self-administration of a standard or prototypic abused drug is established first; the test drug is then substituted for the standard drug, and changes in self-administration behavior are measured; this latter procedure is more commonly used.

A major disadvantage of these operant procedures is the reliance on response rate as an index of reinforcing efficacy or reinforcement strength.[45] Drugs produce a constellation of effects, only a portion of which may be directly related to their reinforcing efficacy. After the first drug administration occurs in a given session, subsequent responding may be altered by the direct effects of the drug. For example, a drug may decrease the ability of the subject to respond by producing motor impairment, or a drug may increase responding by producing non-specific behavioral stimulation. More complex schedules of reinforcement have been incorporated into self-administration studies to improve experimental control over non-specific drug effects, including second order and concurrent schedules (see Brady and Lukas[42]).

Another complexity of interpreting data from self-administration studies stems from the nonlinear relationship between dose and response rate/drug deliveries when high doses are examined. The dose response function generated from these studies is typically shaped as an inverted-U. The relationship between dose and response rate/drug delivery is positive at low doses (on the ascending limb of the dose response curve) and negative at high doses (on the descending limb). In some cases where an inverse relationship between unit dose (i.e., dose per injection) and the number of drug deliveries occurs, the total intake of drug can actually be constant across the descending limb of the dose response curve. For instance, for both cocaine and morphine, the number of drug deliveries increases when the unit dose decreases, and, conversely, the number of drug deliveries decreases when the unit dose per injection increases,[46,47] thus producing comparable drug intake independent of the actual unit dose. Consequently, response rate *per se* is not a valid index of relative reinforcing strength or efficacy.

An alternative procedure that circumvents the problems associated with response rate analysis is the fixed-ratio break point or progressive ratio (PR) paradigm. Subjects are trained to complete a low requirement (e.g., FR-1) for the delivery of a given dose of drug. Once responding has stabilized, the response requirement is progressively and systematically increased until the subject fails to complete the response requirement for drug delivery. The last response requirement completed before cessation of responding is known as the "break point"; this serves as the primary measure of the relative strength of the reinforcer. In general, there is an orderly relationship between PR break point and drug dose. An additional benefit is that

Kenzie L. Preston and Sharon L. Walsh

the experimental procedures can be arranged so that the data generated are relatively free from nonspecific drug effects that influence response rate.

The choice procedure is another alternative design introduced to circumvent the reliance on response rate as a dependent measure. In the choice procedure, subjects are trained to respond on at least two separate manipulanda. Each manipulanda is associated with its own distinctive conditioned stimulus (e.g., different colored lights). The subject is initially trained on a simple choice task in which a choice is made between two varied discriminable drug stimuli such as saline vs. a dose of cocaine. At the completion of training, the subject is given a number of trials in which they make a preference choice between the two available manipulanda. The beginning of each session may include a period for sampling each choice. In this task, the measure of reinforcing efficacy is the number of drug choices made in a given session and may be expressed as the total percent of choices for a given drug. The choice procedure has been adapted for use in humans and is the most commonly employed method in human self-administration studies.

Despite the numerous complexities of self-administration procedures, the data generated from these studies are invaluable for predicting the abuse liability of drugs. When self-administration studies are conducted with the appropriate experimental controls, orderly relationships can be obtained both across and within drug classes. For example, for drugs within the same class, those with higher abuse liability engender more drug-taking behavior in the laboratory compared to related drugs with lower abuse liability. Based on the vast published self-administration literature and epidemiologic reports of drug abuse, self-administration behavior is considered to be a reliable and strong predictor of the abuse liability of drugs in humans.[40,48,49]

4.4.3.2 Drug Discrimination

Drug discrimination is an experimental paradigm that has been used to classify drugs based on their interoceptive stimulus effects using a behavioral criterion.[50] The paradigm has been used extensively to study pharmacology and to assess abuse liability in non-humans and more recently in humans.[51-54] In drug discrimination studies, subjects are trained to emit one response in the presence of a training drug and to emit an alternate response in the absence of the training drug. Drugs that produce similar interoceptive stimuli are discriminated as similar to the training drug, while drugs that do not share interoceptive stimuli are not.

For example, when subjects trained to discriminate between morphine and saline are tested with other morphine-like drugs (i.e., *mu* agonists), they tend to emit the morphine-appropriate response; however, when tested with non-opioid drugs, these subjects tend to emit the saline-appropriate response. Drugs within the same pharmacological class that share discriminative stimuli can be differentiated from drugs in other pharmacological classes, and even within the major drug classes, for example the opiates, drug discrimination procedures can differentiate among drugs having activity at different receptor subtypes.[55]

Several recent review chapters have detailed the behavioral procedures used in drug discrimination and the types of data that are generated.[55-58] Most drug discrimination studies employ a differential reinforcement operant conditioning procedure to establish discriminative control by two (or more recently three) drugs. During training sessions, delivery of a reinforcer is dependent upon the performance of a particular response that has been associated with either the presence or absence of the drug stimulus. For example, prior to the experimental session an injection of a drug dose is administered and responses on only one of two (or more) levers produce reinforcer delivery. Responses on an alternate lever result in reinforcer delivery when vehicle or no drug is administered prior to the session. Other environmental conditions, including visual and auditory stimuli, are held constant.

Acquisition of the discrimination is defined by the subject meeting pre-determined criteria. Two common criteria are: (1) the subject must not complete a response requirement on the incorrect lever before earning a reinforcer on the correct lever; and (2) the number of responses on the correct lever must exceed a predetermined percent of the total responses emitted on both levers (typically > 90% on the stimulus-appropriate lever). In general, a strict adherence criteria for discriminative control guarantees well-trained subjects with discrimination based on the stimulus effects of the drug and improves the validity of test results.

Generalization or substitution testing with novel drug stimuli is conducted once stimulus control has been established. Doses of the test drugs are administered in place of the training drugs, and the distribution of responses on the drug-appropriate or vehicle-appropriate lever is recorded. If the novel drug produces predominately drug-appropriate responses (usually 80% or greater), the novel drug is said to substitute completely and, thus, produce stimuli like those of the training drug. If the novel drug produces responses predominately on the vehicle or no drug-appropriate lever, the novel drug is characterized as not substituting for the training drug. In generalization tests, reinforcers may be delivered at the completion of the response on either lever, or reinforcer delivery following completion of the response on either lever (that is, under extinction conditions) may be omitted; both procedures have been widely used and generally produce similar generalization profiles for test drugs. Because generalization testing can disrupt the baseline accuracy of the discrimination, training sessions are continued between test sessions to maintain stimulus control.

The procedures used to study drug discrimination in human subjects are quite similar to those used in laboratory animals. The methods were modeled after those used in animal studies, but adapted to the unique capabilities of humans. In the discrimination training phase, training drugs are paired with letter codes as identifying labels. Drugs are given under double-blind conditions and are not identifiable by appearance or volume. Money serves as the reinforcer most commonly given for correct responses. Once training is complete, acquisition of the discrimination is verified by re-exposing subjects to the training drugs to determine whether they can correctly and reliably identify drug labels (letter codes). Generalization (or substitution) testing sessions are then conducted to assess the dose-effect function of one or more test drugs. Similarities between the human and laboratory animal paradigms include: specific training to discriminate a particular drug and dose; the extrinsic reinforcement of correct discrimination responses; and the requirement that mastery of the discrimination be demonstrated before generalization/substitution testing is initiated.

A unique feature of human subjects is that they can be informed that they will receive monetary reinforcement for correct discrimination responses and verbally instructed on the use of the response manipulanda. In addition, most human studies include the concurrent collection of questionnaire data on subjective effects, which has been invaluable in evaluating the interrelationship of behavioral discrimination and subjective effects. Although the use of drug discrimination procedures in human studies is a relatively recent development,[53,59] discriminations have been trained with a number of drugs including caffeine,[60,61] amphetamine,[62-64] nicotine,[65] marijuana,[66] cocaine,[67] benzodiazepines, [68-70] non-benzodiazepine anti-anxiety agents,[71,72] and opiates.[73-75]

Drug discrimination is not a direct measure of reinforcing efficacy. Although virtually all abused drugs can be trained as discriminative stimuli, most psychoactive drugs, including those that are not self-administered, are discriminable from vehicle or no drug.[56] Thus, discriminability in and of itself is not evidence of abuse liability; rather the relative similarity of a drug's stimulus effects to a known standard or prototypic abused drug reflects abuse potential. Nevertheless, there is substantial concordance between discriminative stimulus and subjective effects in humans[59,76] and self-administration behavior in laboratory animals.[55]

The utility of drug discrimination studies in evaluating abuse liability is primarily due to their capacity to classify drugs according to their similarity or dissimilarity to a standard or prototypic drug. Pharmacologic similarity is a primary factor considered in federal scheduling of psychoactive substances. Pharmacological specificity is a major feature of drug stimulus

Kenzie L. Preston and Sharon L. Walsh

Table 4.4.3.2 Pharmacological Specificity of Drug Discrimination

| Test Drug[a] | Sedative Training Drug | | Stimulant Training Drug | | Opiate Training Drug |
	Barbiturates	Benzodiazepines	Cocaine	Amphetamine	Mu agonists
Sedatives					
Barbiturates	Yes[77,78]	Yes[68,77,78,82-84]	No[80]	No[63,91]	No [73,97]
Benzodiazepines	Yes[77,78]	Yes[68,77,78,82,83]	No[87,88]	No[79]	No[73,98-100]
Antihistamines	No[79]	No[85]		Yes[79]	
Stimulants					
Cocaine		No[86]	Yes[89]	Yes[92]	
Amphetamine	No[80]	No[86]	Yes[80,89]	Yes[63,92-94]	No[73,98,100]
Caffeine		No[85-86]		Yes/No[64,95,96]	
Opiates					
Morphine/ Hydromorphone	No[81]	No[84,86]	No[89-90]	No[79-93]	Yes[73,100-102]
Nalbuphine					Yes/No[100,102,103]
Dextromethorphan	No[81]				Yes[101]
Marijuana/THC				No[96]	No[101]
Hallucinogens					
LSD				No[96]	No[104]
Phencyclidine		No[83]		No[79]	No[97]

[a]*Literature citations are illustrative and are not exhaustive.*

control: drugs that have similar effects in other physiological or behavioral assays (often drugs within the same pharmacological class) are usually discriminated as similar while drugs in different classes usually do not share discriminative stimulus effects.[55]

Table 4.4.3.2 summarizes results of drug discrimination studies within and across pharmacological classes for representative drugs. Drugs within the same pharmacological class tend to share similar discriminative stimuli and tend to have similar liability for abuse. An important caveat in the interpretation of drug discrimination studies, however, is that results must be considered in the context of the training drug. For example, in subjects trained to discriminate cocaine from saline, d-amphetamine fully substitutes for cocaine while pentobarbital and morphine do not, even though all four drugs have significant abuse potential.[89,105] Thus, use of the training drug within the appropriate drug class is essential.

A second major factor to be considered for data interpretation is the training dose; this can affect the doses at which test drugs substitute for a given training drug and also determine whether or not substitution occurs at all. Quantitatively, generalization dose response curves tend to be shifted to the right with higher training doses so that higher doses of test drug are needed to produce full substitution. Drugs with low receptor agonist efficacy may substitute for a low training dose but fail to substitute for a higher training dose of a full agonist.[55] In the context of abuse liability assessment, a low efficacy agonist may have lower abuse liability than a full agonist because the magnitude of its reinforcing effects may be limited. If its toxic effects are also limited relative to a full agonist, a low efficacy agonist may produce fewer negative public health consequences. Qualitatively, lower training doses generally produce less pharmacologic specificity than higher training doses. Generalization between pharmacologically dissimilar drugs is more likely when training doses are low.[58]

Evaluating Abuse Liability: Methods and Predictive Value

4.4.3.3 Subjective Effects

Subjective effect measures have been recognized as a critical element in abuse potential assessment in humans for several decades.[106,107] Subjective effects are feelings, perceptions and moods that are the personal experiences of an individual. Drugs of abuse produce characteristic subjective effects or interoceptive stimuli that are perceived as positive and desirable to some individuals; drugs that produce these positive mood effects are often described as euphoriants.[107]

Because subjective effects are not accessible to observers for public validation, they can only be obtained through self-reports from the individual. Subjective effect measures in the form of questionnaires have been developed to determine whether a drug produces perceptible effects and to determine the quantitative and qualitative characteristics the drug user experiences. They may be used to collect individual self-reports that are consistent across individuals, studies, and situations; they can be combined across subjects; they can provide reliable and replicable data; and they are meaningful to outside observers. These subjective questionnaires are scientifically useful for assessing pharmacologic properties, including time course and potency, and can be used to measure the degree of similarity between a test drug and a known standard for abuse liability assessment.

Subjective effects measures are usually presented in the form of questionnaires. These questions can be presented in a number of formats including ordinal, visual analog, binomial, and nominal scales. On ordinal scales, subjects are usually asked to rate the amount of a particular effect on a 4- or 5-point scale (for example, "the strength of a drug effect" from 0 to 4 with 0 = not at all and 4 = extremely). Visual analog scales are continuous scales presented as lines with or without tick marks to give some indication of gradations and are often anchored at the ends with labels such as "not at all" and "extremely". Visual analog scales can be unipolar (e.g., rated from no effect to extremely), or they may be bipolar (e.g., sleepy/alert, with extremely sleepy at one end, extremely alert at the other, and no effect in the center). Binomial scales are usually in the form of yes/no or true/false. In nominal scales, response choices are categorical in nature and often mutually exclusive of each other. The ordinal scales and visual analog scales are the most frequently used scales in subjective effect questionnaires.

The questionnaires used in abuse liability assessment studies often contain elements designed to measure the presence or absence of drug effects and a qualitative and quantitative characterization of those effects as well as drug-induced mood changes. A critical element is the assessment of whether a subject likes the effects of the drug and possibly whether the drug is a euphoriant. Abuse potential studies usually incorporate multiple questionnaires in order to gather a complete profile of a drug's subjective effects. The most commonly used question-naires are scales of global drug effects, subscales of the Addiction Research Center Inventory (ARCI),[108] Profile of Mood States (POMS),[109] Adjective Rating Scales, and the Drug Class Questionnaire.[110]

On measures of global drug effects, subjects are asked to integrate the different aspects of a drug's effects and to rate the "overall strength" of its effects, the subject's "liking" of a drug, and the degree to which the drug produces any "good" effects or "bad" effects. The "strength of drug effect" scale is a sensitive measure of psychoactivity. The "liking" scale ratings have good concordance with rates of abuse (i.e., highly abused drugs produce dose-related increases in "liking" while substances without abuse liability do not)[107] and is probably the single most important subjective effect scale used in human abuse liability assessment. The "good" and "bad" effects scales are included because most drugs produce both desirable and undesirable effects and having the subjects' ratings of the overall magnitudes of these effects is useful. However, only the subjects themselves can determine whether the positive effects outweigh the negative effects. Measures of global drug effects are typically presented as either ordinal or visual analog scales.

Kenzie L. Preston and Sharon L. Walsh

The ARCI is a 550-item, true/false questionnaire that was developed empirically to assess a range of physical, emotive, and subjective effects of drugs from several pharmacological classes.[108,111] The ARCI is divided into numerous subscales designed to detect the acute effects of specific drugs and/or drug classes (e.g., Mar Scale for marijuana), mood states, and personality characteristics (e.g., Tired, Self-Control), the effects of chronic drug administration (e.g., Chronic Opiate Scale), and drug withdrawal (e.g., the Weak Opiate Withdrawal). The ARCI can be tailored to study a particular drug by including only those subscales that are appropriate.

The most frequently used scales in abuse potential studies of acute drug effects are the Morphine-Benzedrine Group (MBG; an index of euphoria), the Pentobarbital-Chlorprom-azine-Alcohol Group (PCAG; an index of apathetic sedation), and the Lysergic Acid Diethy-lamide Group (LSD; an index of dysphoria or somatic discomfort). Increases in the MBG scale, or euphoria scale as it is sometimes referred, are associated with significant abuse potential.

The Profile of Mood States (POMS) questionnaire is a 65- or 72-item standardized adjective rating scale developed to measure changes in mood in psychiatric populations.[109] The individual adjectives describe mood states and are rated on a 5-point scale from "not at all" (0) to "extremely" (4). Subscales, including Tension-Anxiety, Depression-Dejection, Anger-Hos-tility, Vigor, Fatigue, Confusion-Bewilderment, Friendliness, and Elation, are calculated from weighted item scores that have been grouped by factor analysis. Substance abuse researchers have adopted this questionnaire into their studies of drug effects in humans to measure acute effects, usually by comparing measures collected before and after drug administration. The POMS has been used extensively in studies of stimulants [112] and sedatives and anxiolytics [113] but rarely in opiate studies. The POMS does not contain drug liking or euphoria scales; its utility in abuse liability assessment derives from determinations of similarity to a standard drug of abuse and from identification of possible aversive effects.[113]

Adjective rating scales are questionnaires on which subjects rate symptoms describing global drug effects (e.g., high, strength of drug effect), mood effects (e.g., anxious, depressed), and physical symptoms (e.g., itchy, nausea). Adjectives can be presented as visual analog, binomial, or ordinal scales and used singly or grouped into scales. The adjectives included on a rating scale can be designed to measure those specific drug-induced symptoms associated with the particular class of drugs being studied. For example, studies of psychomotor stimulants may include items such as "stimulated" and "anxious", while studies of sedatives include symptoms such as "tired" and "uncoordinated". Most adjective rating scales have not been formally validated; investigators rely on external validity.

Two questionnaires frequently included in abuse liability studies are the Drug Class Questionnaire and the Single Dose Questionnaire. Subjects are asked to indicate which among a list of drugs/drug classes was most similar to the test drug. The list of drugs used in early studies included blank (placebo), dope (opiates), cocaine, marijuana, goof balls (barbiturates), benzedrine ('Benny'), and "other".[110] Experienced abusers can reliably identify placebo admin-istration from active drug and can reliably discriminate among the major drug classes when tested with adequate doses.[114] The Single Dose Questionnaire has been used extensively and, although it has been modified over time, the results have been remarkably consistent over three decades.[115] It was originally developed to quantify the subjective effects of opioids.[110]

The Single Dose Questionnaire includes four of the elements described above: presence or absence of a drug effect on a binomial scale; a drug class questionnaire; a list of symptoms answered on a binomial yes/no scale; and an ordinal drug liking scale. A number of experimen-tal factors and control procedures require consideration in studies of subjective drug effects. Subjects must be able to comprehend and respond appropriately to questionnaires. For example, reading skills are required if questionnaires are presented in written form. Question-naires must be written in language familiar to the subjects, and training may be required to

Table 4.4.3.3 Subjective Effects of Prototypic Drugs

Drug	Global Effects		ARCI				POMS	Symptoms	Ref
	Effect	Liking	MBG	PCAG	LSD	BG			
Sedatives									
Pentobarbital	↑	↑	↑a	↑a	NF	NF	Arousal ↓ Fatigue ↑	Sleepy, drunkenness	117-119
Diazepam	↑	↑	↑/-	↑	-	→	Fatigue ↑ Confusion ↑	Sedated	68,120
Diphenhydramine	↑	↑	-	↑	↑	-	Arousal ↓ Vigor ↓ Anxiety ↑ Vigor ↓	Unsteady, confused, mentally slowed	121,122
Stimulants									
Cocaine	↑	↑	↑	↓	↑	↑	Friendly ↑ Vigor ↑	Stimulated, dry mouth, nervous	123,124
Amphetamine	NF	↑	↑	↓	↑	↑	Friendly ↑ Vigor ↑ Fatigue ↓ Elation ↑	Stimulated, high	93,125
Caffeine	↑	↑	-	-	↑	-	Arousal ↑ Anxiety↑	Stimulated, nervous, jittery, dizzy	126,127
Phenylpropanolamine	NF	↑	-	-	↑	-	Arousal ↑ Vigor ↑ Fatigue →	Stimulated, high, anxious	93
Opioids									
Morphine	↑	↑	↑	↑/-	-	NF	NF	Skin itchy, relaxed, talkative, sleepy	128
Pentazocine	↑	↑	↑/-	↑	↑	-	NF	Relaxed, sleepy	103,128
Dextromethorphan	NF	-	-	↑/-	↑	NF	NF	Barbiturate-like, nervous, drunken	129,130
Marijuana	↑	↑	↑	↑	↑	→	Anxiety ↑ Confusion ↑ Friendly ↓ Vigor ↓	Hungry, stimulated	66,131,132
LSD	NF	NF	↑	-	↑	→	NF	Anxiety, nervousness, perceptual distortions	111,133

aModified ARCI scales.
↑ Increase in scale scores; ↓ Decrease in scale scores; - No change in scale scores; NF not found in literature.

familiarize subjects with the relevant dimensions of the scales (e.g., unipolar vs. bipolar visual analog scales). Drugs should be administered under double-blind conditions to avoid the introduction of bias into subjects' reports.

Most studies assessing abuse potential have used subjects with histories of illicit drug use.[107,113] Recently, a number of studies have been conducted in healthy volunteers without histories of drug abuse.[71,116,117] Interestingly, although some differences between subjects with and without drug use experience have been identified, for example sensitivity of the POMS to sedative drug effects,[113] the subjective measures described above appear to be useful in both subject populations.

Each of the major pharmacological classes have been characterized using the questionnaires described above. Drugs of different pharmacological classes generally produce profiles of subjective effects that are unique to that class of drugs and that are recognizable to individuals. Table 4.4.3.3 lists examples for drugs from the major pharmacological classes and their typical effects on various instruments. As one might expect, global measures of drug effects and "liking" tend not to differentiate between different types of drugs although they do provide quantitative information regarding the overall magnitude of drug effects.

In contrast, the ARCI, POMS, and Adjective Rating Scales measure more specific subjective effects and, thus, yield qualitative information that can differentiate between drug classes. Sedatives are characterized by increases in drug effect, liking, increases in the PCAG (sedative scale of the ARCI), and Fatigue and Confusion scales of the POMS. Increases in the MBG or Euphoria scales of the ARCI are not consistently increased by benzodiazepines, though pentobarbital can increase ratings on this scale. Experienced abusers identify benzodiazepines equally as barbiturate- and benzodiazepine-like on the Drug Class Questionnaire, supporting the similarity of their subjective effects, though the two classes can be discriminated under some conditions.[113,118,134] Diphenhydramine, an over-the-counter antihistamine, can also increase liking scale scores, though it does not increase MBG scores or ratings on other symptoms that are characteristic of barbiturates and benzodiazepines.[121,122] Investigators have speculated that unpleasant side effects produced by high doses of diphenhydramine may limit its abuse.

The psychomotor stimulants, cocaine and amphetamine, produce very similar subjective effect profiles. Both increase liking and MBG scale scores consistent with their high abuse liability. Other subjective measures are consistent with stimulatory effects: increases in ARCI-Benzedrine Group (BG) scores and POMS-Vigor scores and decreases in ARCI-PCAG and POMS-Fatigue scales. Caffeine and phenylpropanolamine, both over-the-counter stimulants, share some of these effects and increase liking scale scores; however, they do not increase MBG scale scores. Like the antihistamines, these drugs may also produce aversive effects at high doses.

Mu opioid agonists, such as morphine, heroin, and hydromorphone, produce a constellation of subjective effects that are easily discriminated from placebo and from other drug classes by experienced opioid abusers.[114,115] This profile is characterized by increases in liking and MBG scores and symptoms that include itchy skin and nodding (a sleep-like state in which the head bobs). The agonist-antagonist opioids, such as pentazocine, nalorphine, and cyclazocine, that produce effects through non-mu as well as *mu* receptor mechanisms, can be distinguished from the mu-agonists by increases in the PCAG and LSD scales of the ARCI, sedative-like symptoms, and identification as barbiturate-like by experienced opioid abusers.[114]

Dextromethorphan is psychoactive at doses higher than those found in over-the-counter cough suppressant preparations. The subjective effect profile of dextromethorphan is similar to that of the agonist-antagonist opioids such as nalorphine and pentazocine; it produces increases in the PCAG and LSD scales of the ARCI, is identified by experienced opioid abusers as barbiturate-like, and increases ratings of the symptoms drunken and nervous.[129] However, dextromethorphan is differentiated from the agonist-antagonist opioids because it does not produce morphine-like subjective effects at any dose.[129,130]

Evaluating Abuse Liability: Methods and Predictive Value

The subjective effect profile of marijuana is characterized by euphoria, sedation, and mental impairment.[66,131,132] Marijuana produces significant increases in the liking and MBG scales. Its sedative effects are indicated by increases in the ARCI-PCAG scale and decreases in the ARCI-BG scale and POMS-Vigor scale. Marijuana also increases scores on the ARCI-LSD scale and the POMS Confusion and Anxiety scales.

The subjective effects of LSD have been evaluated in human subjects (see review by Martin and Sloan[133]), though most studies did not use the questionnaires described in the present chapter. LSD frequently produces euphoria at low doses. Higher doses are characterized by nervousness and anxiety increasing in magnitude with dose. Visual and other perceptual changes and true hallucinations occur at high doses. Additional symptoms reported with LSD administration include: unsteadiness, weakness, dizziness, drowsiness, blurred eyesight, sweating, nausea, feeling ill, good humor, relaxation, and a sense of wonderment. Perceptual and psychomotor changes have been reported for judgment of time, reaction time, arithmetic calculation, color perception, memory tasks, and judgment of spatial relationship and time. On the ARCI, LSD administration was used as the basis for development of the LSD scale[111] that is sensitive to somatic changes and dysphoria. On the ARCI, LSD also increases MBG scale scores and decreases BG scale scores.

4.4.3.4 Physical Dependence Capacity

Repeated administration of some drugs results in the development of tolerance and physical dependence. With the development of tolerance, the effect of a drug decreases as the dose is held constant. Tolerance to the desired effect often leads to escalation of the doses self-administered by abusers. Use of higher doses in turn increases the risk of adverse effects, such as physiological toxicity, psychomotor impairment, and physical dependence. Physical dependence is the consequence of biological changes that occur over time as the body adapts to long-term drug exposure. Physical dependence becomes evident when withdrawal signs and symptoms, which can be manifest as physiological, psychological and/or behavioral changes, occur following reduction or termination of drug administration. The biological mechanisms of tolerance and physical dependence have been reviewed elsewhere (see for example, Koob and Bloom[135] and Haefely[136]) and will not be discussed in this chapter.

Physical dependence is no longer considered either necessary or sufficient for a drug to have abuse potential, though at one time, addiction liability was equated with physical dependence capacity.[114,137] Researchers now recognize that physical dependence can contribute to the perpetuation of drug use, as dependent individuals seek drugs to avoid unpleasant withdrawal, and to the cost to the public health, in terms of both the human suffering and the economic cost of medical treatment associated with withdrawal. Physical dependence, and the consequent abstinence syndrome, is significant for some drug classes such as opiates, barbiturates, and benzodiazepines, but less prominent with other highly abusable drugs including cocaine and the amphetamines. In addition, alleviation of the symptoms associated with physical dependence and withdrawal is not effective as a treatment for drug dependence.[137]

Physical dependence capacity can be determined by direct addiction, substitution, or suppression studies. In direct addiction studies, a test drug is administered repeatedly over time; doses are initially low and then gradually increased as tolerance develops to toxic effects. After subjects have been stabilized at a specified dose, tolerance and other effects of chronic drug administration are evaluated; methods for evaluating tolerance have been described in detail elsewhere.[42,138] Once stabilization on a chronic dosing regimen has been established, physical dependence can be documented by abrupt withdrawal of drug administration or by administration of a selective antagonist for the appropriate receptor type (e.g., naloxone for opioid dependence). Subjects are observed for signs of an abstinence syndrome. Self-report measures can also be included in studies with human subjects to gain additional qualitative information about the character of the abstinence syndrome, including dysphoric effects. Drug-seeking behavior is considered a sign of psychic or physical dependence. Requests for test drug or other medication during the withdrawal period can be recorded (for example, see Jasinski and Mansky[139]). Alternatively, self-administration procedures have been used to evaluate drug-seeking during and after chronic drug administration.[140,141]

The substitution and suppression procedures, variations on direct addiction, have also been used to evaluate physical dependence capacity. These paradigms have chiefly been used with the opioids [139,114] and are described only briefly here. In suppression studies, subjects are initially made physically dependent and maintained on a prototypic opioid agonist, for example, morphine administered in four injections per day. In test sessions, agonist administration is abruptly withdrawn, and at the peak of withdrawal (approximately 30 h after the last morphine dose) test medications are administered and evaluated for their ability to suppress withdrawal. The ability of opioid agonists to suppress the abstinence syndrome was documented using this methodology.

In substitution studies, the maintenance drug administrations are withheld from subjects maintained on a prototypic agonist such as morphine and replaced with doses of test drug or placebo. The ability of the test drug to suppress the onset of the withdrawal syndrome is assessed over a specified period of time (for example, 24 hours). Cross-over studies, testing multiple drugs or multiple dose levels of a test drug can be conducted with this procedure; subjects are restabilized on the maintenance medication between experimental test sessions. The major drug classes produce varying degrees of physical dependence with characteristic abstinence syndromes. The opioid abstinence syndrome in humans is characterized by mydriasis, yawning, lacrimation, rhinnorrhea, perspiration, tremor, gooseflesh, nausea and vomiting, increases in respiratory rate and blood pressure, and weight loss. This syndrome is rarely life threatening but is extremely uncomfortable.[114] The time course of the abstinence syndrome differs among the opioids; in general, onset is quicker and duration shorter for opioids with short elimination half-lives compared to opioids with long half-lives. The agonist-antagonist opioids (e.g., pentazocine and nalbuphine) and dextromethorphan produce withdrawal syndromes that differ in character from the prototypic mu agonist opioids.[115,130]

Unlike withdrawal from opioids, the abstinence syndrome from sedatives is both uncomfortable and medically serious. The barbiturate abstinence syndrome in humans is characterized by anxiety, nervousness, tremor, progressive weakness, nausea and vomiting, loss of appetite and weight loss, and insomnia.[142] Abrupt withdrawal from barbiturates may also produce convulsions, auditory or visual hallucinations, delirium, and death. Withdrawal from long-term therapeutic use of benzodiazepines has been found to include the following symptoms: nervousness, agitation, nausea, diaphoresis, lethargy, constipation, irritability, perceptual distortions, confusion, nightmares, insomnia, headaches, and diarrhea.[143] In severe withdrawal, seizures may also occur.[144]

The abstinence syndromes produced by the psychomotor stimulants are much less apparent than those of the opioids and sedatives. Although for many years cocaine was believed not to produce withdrawal at all, most clinical practitioners have come to accept that withdrawal symptoms of varying severity and duration can occur within a few hours to several days following cessation of repeated cocaine use. One widely cited study proposed a model of cocaine withdrawal consisting of three distinct temporal phases which were described as "crash", "withdrawal", and "extinction".[145] The first phase occurred within a few hours to a few days after cocaine use and was characterized by profound fatigue, lethargy, and depression. The second phase was characterized by milder symptoms and craving for cocaine; while the extinction phase lasted indefinitely and was characterized primarily by recurrent craving for cocaine. Development of this hypothetical model was based on clinical interviews with outpatient cocaine abusers undergoing detoxification.

A subsequent study compared cocaine abusers to matched control subjects during a 28-day inpatient stay in a controlled setting.[146] In contrast to the phasic model of Gawin and Kleber, Weddington and colleagues reported that cocaine withdrawal symptoms were highest during the first few days of abstinence and declined linearly thereafter. Cocaine abusers reported significantly higher scores on various indices of mood distress and had higher resting heart rate, but few other significant differences were observed. Subsequent inpatient studies of detoxifying cocaine abusers have reported a similar linear, rather than phasic, decline in withdrawal symptomatology.[147-149] These studies suggest that the most common mood disturbances associated with cocaine withdrawal are increased ratings of tension, anxiety, fatigue, depression, and craving for cocaine; however, this symptomatology has not been observed in all studies.[150-151] Disturbances of sleep behavior during cocaine withdrawal have been well documented by electroencephalography and self-report;[148,149,152,153] although one study found no differences in sleep patterns of cocaine abusers when compared to those of normal controls.[146] Some of the discrepancies across and within studies may be attributable to the variability of substance abuse patterns and recency of drug use in patients entering treatment programs.

Physical dependence has been demonstrated following chronic marijuana use in humans and laboratory animals, though its clinical significance is unclear.[154,155] Signs of marijuana withdrawal appear in human subjects receiving marijuana for periods as short as one week and include increased irritability, restlessness, insomnia, anorexia, nausea, sweating, and weight loss.[154] Abrupt withdrawal after ten days of repeated administration of delta-9-THC, the principle active component of marijuana, has also been shown to produce behavioral disruption in rhesus monkeys.[156] In addition, the selective cannabinoid receptor antagonist, SR 141716A, precipitates withdrawal in rats treated chronically with THC.[157]

4.4.4 PREDICTIVE VALUE

Increasing numbers of laws restricting the possession and sale of medications and other psychoactive drugs have been adopted throughout this century to combat illicit drug abuse and the misuse of medications. The need to regulate drugs that could potentially be misused prompted the U.S. to sponsor research for the development of scientific methodologies which would be useful for assessing the abuse potential of new medications. As described above, a number of methodologies have been adopted for this purpose: self-administration, drug discrimination, physical dependence testing, and subjective effect measures.

This final section will summarize the application of these empirical methods and their value for predicting abuse liability within the framework of the eight factors outlined in Section 201 (c) of the Comprehensive Drug Abuse Prevention and Control Act of 1970. Among the eight factors, three can be examined directly and prospectively using data from the experimental procedures described above. These are (1) the actual or relative abuse potential for abuse, (2) the pharmacological effects of the drug , and (3) the psychic or physiological dependence of the drug or substance. The actual or relative abuse potential can be assessed by comparing a test drug to a known standard in self-administration, drug discrimination, and subjective effect studies. One can assess the extent to which a novel drug is or is not self-administered in the laboratory.

There is a high concordance between drugs that are self-administered in non-human species and drugs that are abused by humans.[48] Although this is a very well-established relationship, there are some exceptions, most notably drugs in the hallucinogen class. The drug discrimination procedure can be used to determine the degree of similarity of the stimulus effects of the test drug compared to a prototype; the degree to which the test drug substitutes for a drug with high abuse potential is positively related to its potential for abuse. Subjective effect studies are valuable because they can be used to compare the interoceptive effects of a novel drug to a prototype, and they can provide information on the pharmacological profile of effects of the novel drug in humans. Direct addiction, substitution, and withdrawal suppression studies in non-human and human subjects are used to measure the psychic and/or physiological dependence capacity of a novel drug. In addition to these three factors, data generated from all of these experimental models provide the core of information necessary to evaluate a fourth regulatory factor, that is the state of current scientific knowledge regarding the drug.

A fifth factor, whether a substance that has no abuse potential on its own but is an immediate precursor of a controlled substance, is a function of the synthetic process of the controlled substance. The purpose of regulating a synthetic precursor is to control the illicit manufacture of an abused substance. The remaining three factors are history and current pattern of abuse; scope, duration and significance of abuse; and risk to public health. These are typically assessed retrospectively via data from law enforcement sources (e.g., reports of diversion, illicit manufacture, and police seizure), the medical community (e.g., cases of abuse reported to the Food and Drug Administration or published in medical journals) and other sources such as epidemiologic studies of emergency room admissions. One component of risk to public health, toxicity data, however, can also be obtained prospectively in pre-clinical and clinical abuse liability assessments.

Table 4.4.4 provides a summary of results for drugs within each of the major classes from self-administration, drug discrimination, physical dependence, and subjective effects studies. In addition, epidemiological information on the incidence of abuse and the level of federal regulatory control, if any, are shown. As illustrated in Table 4.4.4, it can be predicted that drugs which are self-administered in the laboratory and share discriminative stimulus and subjective effects with prototypic drugs of abuse are likely to be used illicitly. Even within each pharmacological class, the predicted abuse potential of related compounds can be differentiated by these experimental methods. For example, the prototypic drug for each drug class (i.e., barbiturates, cocaine, and morphine) produces effects clearly distinguishable from unscheduled drugs within the same class. The prototypes are typically characterized by greater physical dependence capacity, more intense subjective effects, and greater likelihood of self-administration. As is shown in Table 4.4.4, the degree of abuse liability is generally reflected in the level of regulatory control for each compound.

Although there is excellent concordance across experimental procedures for abuse liability assessment, there are some notable exceptions. The psychomotor stimulants, specifically cocaine and amphetamine, are known to have high abuse liability; however, their physical dependence capacity is apparently limited. Among drugs within the psychomotor stimulant class, caffeine may, in fact, produce the most prominent withdrawal syndrome, but otherwise has comparatively low abuse potential and limited toxicity. There are also some disparities between results from self-administration studies and epidemiological studies of abuse. For instance, as shown in Table 4.4.4, dextromethorphan is readily self-administered by laboratory animals but is not widely abused despite ready availability in over-the-counter cough preparations. Conversely, marijuana and the prototypic hallucinogen, LSD, are not reliably, if at all, self-administered in the laboratory, while they are known to be reinforcing and abused in humans.

In summary, the overall abuse liability of a compound is determined by a number of factors, including its reinforcing and positive mood effects, physical dependence capacity, and toxicity. While there are some classes of abused drugs, such as the opioids and barbiturates, that test positive in all of the pharmacological screens, positive results on all dimensions are not required in order for a drug to have significant abuse liability and come under regulatory control. Physical dependence capacity is neither required nor sufficient to produce significant

Table 4.4.4 Laboratory findings, epidemiological findings, and federal regulatory status of drugs

	Self-Administered in Laboratory Studies	Shares Stimulus[a] Effects w/ Prototype	Physical Dependence Capacity	Positive Mood Effects in Humans	Epidemiologic Evidence of Abuse	Schedule[b] of Control
Sedatives						
Barbiturates	+++158,159	+++55	+++177,178	+++113,142	+++	II & III
Benzodiazepines	++158,159	++55	++179,180	++113	++	IV
Antihistamines	+/-160,161	-79	+181,182	++121,122	-	NS
Stimulants						
Cocaine	+++47,162-164	+++55	+145,146,183	+++112	+++	II
Amphetamine	+++163,164	+++55	+/-184,185	+++191	+++	II
Caffeine	+/-165	+95,96	++186-188	+/-192	+/-	NS
Phenylpropanolamine	+/-166	+79	NF	+/-191,193	-	NS
Opiates						
Morphine/Heroin	+++167	+++55	+++1,114	+++114,115,128	+++	II
Codeine	+++168	+++55	++1,114,189	+++114	++	II
Pentazocine	+/-167,169	+++55	+1,128	++115,128	+	IV
Nalbuphine	++167	+/-55,97	+139	+115,139	-	NS
Dextromethorphan	+++169	-97	+/-114,130	-129,130	-	NS
Marijuana/THC	+/-163,170	+172	+154,155	+++66	+++	I
Hallucinogens						
Phencyclidine	+171	+173,174	+155,190	+/-193	++	I
LSD	-163	+175,176	NF	+/-133	+	I

[a] Prototype training drug for generalization testing are barbiturates for sedative class, amphetamine for stimulants, and morphine for opiates. No prototype was selected for marijuana or the hallucinogens; ratings of (+) in this category indicate that the drug serves as a discriminative stimulus.
[b] C-I is not available on prescription; C-II,III,IV, and V are available by prescription only. NF indicates not found in literature; NS indicates not scheduled.

abuse liability alone; nevertheless it is important to know whether cessation of chronic use of a drug will lead to significant withdrawal symptoms that could perpetuate drug use and/or require medical intervention.

Other drugs may have limited reinforcing effects in experimental models and be abused by only a small number of individuals, such as PCP and some volatile inhalants; however, the medical consequences associated with their use represent a significant risk to public health. These examples illustrate that there is no single measurement procedure that can index all relevant pharmacological dimensions, thus predicting abuse liability requires data from multiple sources. The described methods are sensitive to the pharmacological effects associated with abuse potential and provide valuable data for scheduling drugs based on the likelihood of their future abuse.

REFERENCES

1. Martin, W. R., and Jasinski, D. R., Assessment of the abuse potential of narcotic analgesics in animals, in *Drug Addiction I*, Martin, W. R., Ed., Springer-Verlag, Heidelberg, 1977, Section II, Chapter 2.
2. Gilman, A. G., Rall, T. W., Nies, A. S., and Taylor, P., *Goodman and Gilman's The Pharmacological Basis of Therapeutics*, Eighth Edition, Pergamon Press, Elmsford, New York, 1991.
3. Bloom, F. E., and Kupfer, D. J., *Psychopharmacology The Fourth Generation of Progress*, Raven Press Ltd., New York, New York, 1995.
4. Lowinson, J. H., Ruiz, P., Millman, R. B., and Langrod, J. G., *Substance Abuse A Comprehensive Textbook*, Second Edition, Williams and Wilkins, Baltimore, Maryland, 1992.
5. de Wit, H., and Wise, R. A., Blockade of cocaine reinforcement in rats with the dopamine receptor blocker pimozide, but not with the noradrenergic blockers phentolamine or phenoxybenzamine, *Canadian Journal of Psychology*, 31, 195, 1977.
6. Koob, G. F., Drugs of abuse: Anatomy, pharmacology and function of reward pathways, *Trends in Pharmacological Sciences*, 13, 177, 1992.
7. Cooper, J. R., Bloom, F. E., and Roth, R. H., Neuroactive peptides, in *The Biochemical Basis of Neuropharmacology*, Sixth Edition, Oxford University Press, New York, NY, 1991, Chapter 12.
8. Paul, S. M., GABA and Glycine, in *Psychopharmacology: The Fourth Generation of Progress*, Bloom, F. E., and Kupfer, D. J., Eds., Raven Press, Ltd., New York, 1995, 87-94.
9. Harris, L. S., Dewey, W. L., and Razdan, R. K., Cannabis its chemistry, pharmacology, and toxicology, in *Drug Addiction II*, Martin, W. R., Ed., Springer-Verlag, New York, 1977, Section II, Chapter 1.
10. Sharp, C. W., and Rosenberg, N. L., Volatile Substances, in *Substance Abuse- A Comprehensive Textbook*, Second Edition, Lowinson J. H., Ruiz, P., Millman, R. B., and Langrod, J. G., Eds., Williams and Wilkins, Baltimore, Maryland, 1992, Chapter 23.
11. Adogey, A. A., Johnston, P. W., and McMechan, S., Sudden cardiac death and substance abuse, *Resuscitation*, 29, 219, 1995.
12. Flanagan, R. J., Ruprah, M., Meredith, T. J., and Ramsey, J. D., An introduction to the clinical toxicology of volatile substances, *Drug Safety*, 5, 359, 1990.
13. Shervette, R. E., Schydlower, M., Lampe, R. M., and Fearnow, R. G., Jimson loco weed abuse in adolescents, *Pediatrics*, 63, 520, 1979.
14. Mikolich, J. R., Paulson, G. W., and Cross, C. J., Acute anticholinergic syndrome due to Jimson seed ingestion: Clinical and laboratory observation in six cases, *Annals of Internal Medicine*, 83, 321, 1975.
15. Guharoy, S. R., and Barajas, M., Atropine intoxication from the ingestion and smoking of jimson weed (Datura stramoniu), *Veterinary and Human Toxicology*, 33, 588, 1991.
16. Niwaguchi, T., and Inoue, T., Chromatographic separation of lysergic acid amide and isolysergic acid amide in morning glory seeds, *Journal of Chromatography*, 43, 510, 1969.

17. Claus, E. P., Tyler, V. E., and Brady, L. R., Alkaloids, in *Pharmacognosy*, Sixth Edition, Lea and Febiger, Philadephia, PA, 1973, Chapter 9.
18. Abernethy, M. K., and Becker, L. B., Acute nutmeg intoxication, *American Journal of Emergency Medicine*, 10, 429, 1992.
19. Schuster, C. R., and Johanson C-E., Behavioral studies of cathinone in monkeys and rats, in *Problems of Drug Dependence, 1979*, NIDA Research Monograph # 27, Harris, L. S. Ed., U.S. Govt. Printing Office, Washington D.C., 1979, 324-325.
20. Yanagita, T., Intravenous self-administration of (-) cathinone and 2-amino-1-(2,5-dimethoxy-4-methyl)phenylpropane in rhesus monkeys, *Drug and Alcohol Dependence*, 17, 135, 1986.
21. Kaminski, B. J., and Griffiths, R. R., Intravenous self-injection of methcathinone in the baboon, *Pharmacology Biochemistry and Behavior*, 47, 981, 1994.
22. Anggard, E., General pharmacology of amphetamine-like drugs. A. Pharmacokinetics and metabolism, in *Drug Addiction II*, Martin, W. R., Ed., Springer-Verlag, Berlin, 1977, Section I, Chapter 1.
23. King, G. R., and Ellinwood, E. H., Amphetamines and other stimulants, in *Substance Abuse- A Comprehensive Textbook*, Second Edition, Lowinson, J. H., Ruiz, P., Millman, R. B., and Langrod, J. G., Eds., Williams and Wilkins, Baltimore, Maryland, 1992, Chapter 19.
24. Jaffe, J. H., and Martin, W. R., Opioid analgesics and antagonists, in *Goodman and Gilman's the Pharmacological Basis of Therapeutics*, 8th Edition, Gilman, A. G., Rall, T. W., Nies, A. S., Taylor P., Eds., Pergamon Press, New York, 1990, 485.
25. Oldendorf, W. H., Some relationship between addiction and drug delivery to the brain, in *Bioavailability of Drugs to the Brain and Blood Brain Barrier*, NIDA Research Monograph #120, U.S. Government Printing Office, Washington, D.C., 1992, 13.
26. Gossop, M., Griffiths, P., Powis, B., and Strang, J., Severity of dependence and route of administration of heroin, cocaine and amphetamines, *British Journal of Addiction*, 87, 1527, 1992.
27. Javaid J.I., Fischman M.W., Schuster C.R., Dekirmenjiian, H., and Davis, J. M., Cocaine plasma concentration: Relation to physiological and subjective effects in humans, *Science*, 202, 227, 1978.
28. Van Dyke, C., Jatlow, P., Barash, P. G., and Byck, R., Oral cocaine: Plasma concentrations and central effects, *Science*, 200, 211, 1978.
29. Perez-Reyes, M., Di Guiseppi, S., Ondrusek, G., Jeffcoat, A. R., and Cook, C. E., Free-base cocaine smoking, *Clinical Pharmacology and Therapeutics*, 32, 459, 1982.
30. Resnick, R. B., Kestenbaum, R. S., and Schwartz, L. K., Acute systemic effects of cocaine in man: A controlled study by intranasal and intravenous routes, *Science*, 195, 696, 1977.
31. Evans, S. M., Cone, E. J., and Henningfield, J. E., Arterial and venous cocaine plasma concentrations in humans: Relationship to route of administration, cardiovascular effects and subjective effects, *Journal of Pharmacology and Experimental Therapeutics*, 279, 135, 1996.
32. Mayersohn, M., and Perrier, D., Kinetics of pharmacologic response to cocaine, *Research Communications in Chemistry, Pathology and Pharmacology*, 22, 465, 1978.
33. Balster, R. L., and Schuster, C. R., Fixed-interval schedule of cocaine reinforcement: Effect of dose and infusion duration, *Journal of Experimental Analysis of Behavior*, 20, 119, 1973.
34. Fischman, M. W., and Schuster, C. R., Injection duration of cocaine in humans, *Federation Proceedings*, 43, 570, 1984.
35. Abreu, M. E., Walsh, S. L., Bonson, K. R., Ginn, D., and Bigelow, G. E., Effects of intravenous injection speed on responses to cocaine or hydromorphone in humans, in *Problems of Drug Dependence 1996, Proceedings of the 58th Annual Scientific Meeting, The College on Problems of Drug Dependence, Inc.*, NIDA Research Monograph, 1997, in press.
36. de Wit, H., Bodker, B., and Amber, J., Rate of increase of plasma drug level influences subjective response in humans, *Psychopharmacology*, 107, 352, 1992.
37. Hatsukami, D. K., and Fischman, M. W., Crack cocaine and cocaine hydrochloride. Are the differences myth or reality? *Journal of the American Medical Association*, 276: 1580, 1996.
38. Jaffe. J. H., Opiates: Clinical Aspects, in *Substance Abuse- A Comprehensive Textbook*, Second Edition, Lowinson, J. H., Ruiz, P., Millman, R. B., and Langrod, J. G., Eds., Williams and Wilkins, Baltimore, Maryland, 1992, Chapter 14.

39. Jasinski, D. R., and Preston, K. L., Comparison of intravenously administered morphine,methadone and heroin, *Drug and Alcohol Dependence*, 17, 301, 1986.

40. Meisch, R. A., and Lemaire, G. A., Drug self-administration, in *Methods in Behavioral Pharmacology*, van Haaren, F., Ed., Elsevier Science Publishers B. V., Amsterdam, 1993, Chapter 11.

41. Bozarth, M. A., Ed., *Methods of Assessing the Reinforcing Properties of Abused Drugs*, Springer-Verlag, New York, 1987.

42. Brady, J. V., and Lukas, S. E., *Testing Drugs for Physical Dependence Potential and Abuse Liability*, NIDA Research Monograph 52, U.S. Government Printing Office, Washington, D.C., Chapter V.

43. Deneau, F., Yanagita, T., and Seevers, M.. H., Self-administration of psychoactive substances by the monkey, A measure of psychological dependence, *Psychopharmacologia*, 16, 30, 1969.

44. Johanson, C-E., Balster, R. L., and Bonese, K., Self-administration of psychomotor stimulant drugs: The effects of unlimited access, *Pharmacology Biochemistry and Behavior*, 4, 45, 1976.

45. Brady, J. V., and Griffiths, R. R., Behavioral procedures for evaluating the relative abuse potential of CNS drugs in primates, *Federation Proceedings*, 35, 2245, 1976.

46. Woods, J. and Schuster, C. R., Reinforcement properties of morphine, cocaine and SPA as a function of unit dose, *International Journal of the Addictions*, 3, 231, 1968.

47. Wilson, M. C., Hitomi, M. and Schuster, C. R., Psychomotor stimulant self-administration as a function of dosage per injection in the rhesus monkey, *Psychopharmacologia*, 22, 271, 1971.

48. Griffiths, R. R., Bigelow, G. E., and Henningfield, J. E., Similarities in animal and human drug-taking behavior, in *Advances in Substance Abuse*, Volume 1, Mello, N. K., Ed., JAI Press, Inc., Grenwich, Connecticutt, 1980, 1.

49. Woolverton, W. L., and Nader, M. A., Experimental evaluation of the reinforcing effects of drugs, in *Testing and Evaluation of Drugs of Abuse, Modern Methods in Pharmacology*, Volume 6, Testing and Evaluation of Drugs of Abuse, Adler, M. W. and Cowan, A., Eds., Wiley-Liss, Inc., 1990, 165.

50. Stolerman, I. P. and Shine, P. G., Trends in drug discrimination research analysed with a cross-indexed bibliography, 1982-1983, *Psychopharmacology*, 86, 1, 1985.

51. Balster, R. L., Drug abuse potential evaluation in animals, *British Journal of Addiction*, 86, 1549, 1991.

52. Holtzman, S. G., Discriminative stimulus effects of drug: relationship to abuse liability, in *Testing and Evaluation of Drugs of Abuse, Modern Methods in Pharmacology*, Volume 6, Adler, M. W., and Cowan, A., Eds., Wiley-Liss, New York, 1990, 193.

53. Kamien, J. B., Bickel, W. K., Hughes, J. R., Higgins, S. T., and Smith, B. J., Drug discrimination by humans compared to non-humans, *Psychopharmacology*, 111, 259, 1993.

54. Bigelow, G. E., and Preston, K.L., Drug discrimination: Methods for drug characterization and classification, in *Testing for Abuse Liability of Drugs in Humans*, Fischman, M. W., and Mello, N. K., Eds., NIDA Research Monograph No. 92, U.S. Government Printing Office, Washington, D.C., 1989, 101.

55. Young, A. M., Discriminative stimulus profiles of psychoactive drugs, in *Advances in Substance Abuse Behavioral and Biological Research*, Volume 4, Mello, N. K., Jessica Kingsley Publishers, London, 1991, 139.

56. Overton, D. A., Applications and limitations of the drug discrimination method for the study of drug abuse, in *Methods for assessing the reinforcing properties of abused drugs*, Bozarth, M. A., Ed., Springer-Verlag, New York, 1987, Chapter 16.

57. Stolerman, I. P., Measures of stimulus generalization in drug discrimination experiments, *Behavioural Pharmacology*, 2, 265, 1991.

58. Stolerman, I. P., Drug discrimination, in *Methods in Behavioral Pharmacology*, van Haaren, F., Ed., Elsevier Science Publishers B. V., Amsterdam, 1993, Chapter 9.

59. Preston, K. L., and Bigelow, G. E., Subjective and discriminative effects of drugs, *Behavioral Pharmacology*, 2, 293, 1991.

60. Griffiths, R. R., Evans, S. M., Heishman, S. J., Preston, K. L., Sannerud, C. A., Wolf, B., and Woodson, P. P., Low-dose caffeine discrimination in humans, *Journal of Pharmacology and Experimental Therapeutics*, 252, 970, 1990.

61. Oliveto, A. H., Bickel, W. K., Hughes, J. R., Shea, P. J., Higgins, S. T., and Fenwick, J.W., Caffeine drug-discrimination in humans: Acquisition, specificity and correlation with self-reports, *Journal of Pharmacology and Experimental Therapeutics*, 261, 885, 1992.
62. Chait, L. D., Uhlenhuth, E. H., and Johanson, C-E., An experimental paradigm for studying the discriminative stimulus properties of drugs in humans, *Psychopharmacology*, 82, 272, 1984.
63. Lamb, R. J., and Henningfield, J. E., Human d-amphetamine drug discrimination: methamphetamine and hydromorphone, *Journal of the Experimental Analysis of Behavior*, 61, 169, 1994.
64. Chait, L. D., and Johanson, C-E., Discriminative stimulus effects of caffeine and benzphetamine in amphetamine-trained volunteers, *Psychopharmacology*, 96, 302, 1988.
65. Perkins, K. A., DiMarco, A., Grobe, J. E., Scierka, A., and Stiller, R. L., Nicotine discrimination in male and female smokers, *Psychopharmacology*, 116, 407, 1994.
66. Chait, L. D., Evans, S. M., Grant, K. A., Kamien, J. B., Johanson, C-E., and Schuster, C. R., The discriminative stimulus and subjective effects of smoked marijuana in humans, *Psychopharmacology*, 94, 206, 1988.
67. Oliveto, A. H., Rosen, M. I., Woods, S. W., and Kosten, T. R., Discriminative stimulus, self-reported and cardiovascular effects of orally-administered cocaine in humans, *Journal of Pharmacology and Experimental Therapeutics*, 271, 48, 1995.
68. Johanson, C-E., Discriminative stimulus effects of diazepam in humans, *Journal of the Experimental Analysis of Behavior*, 257, 634, 1991.
69. Bickel, W. K., Oliveto, A. H., Kamien, J. B., Higgins, S. T. and Hughes, J. R., A novel-response procedure enhances the selectivity and sensitivity of a triazolam discrimination in humans, *Journal of Pharmacology and Experimental Therapeutics*, 264, 360, 1993.
70. Mumford, G. K., Rush, C. R., and Griffiths, R. R., Abecarnil and alprazolam in humans: Behavioral, subjective and reinforcing effects, *Journal of Pharmacology and Experimental Therapeutics*, 272, 570, 1995.
71. Johanson, C-E., Discriminative stimulus effects of buspirone in humans, *Experimental and Clinical Psychopharmacology*, 1, 173, 1993.
72. Rush, C. R., Critchfield, T. S., Troisi, J. R., and Griffiths, R. R., Discriminative stimulus effects of diazepam and buspirone in normal volunteers, *Journal of the Experimental Analysis of Behavior*, 63, 277, 1995.
73. Bickel, W. K., Bigelow, G. E., Preston, K. L., and Liebson, I.A., Opioid drug discrimination in humans: Stability, specificity, and relation to self-reported drug effect, *Journal of Pharmacology and Experimental Therapeutics*, 251, 1053, 1989.
74. Preston, K. L., Bigelow, G. E., Bickel, W. K., and Liebson, I. A., Three-choice drug discrimination in opioid-dependent humans: Hydromorphone, naloxone and saline, *Journal of Pharmacology and Experimental Therapeutics*, 243, 1002, 1987.
75. Preston, K. L., Liebson, I. A., and Bigelow, G. E., Drug discrimination assessment of agonist-antagonist opioids in humans: A three-choice saline-hydromorphone-butorphanol procedure, *Journal of Pharmacology and Experimental Therapeutics*, 271, 48, 1994.
76. Schuster, C. R., and Johanson, C-E., Relationship between the discriminative stimulus properties and subjective effects of drugs, In *Psychopharmacology, Transduction Mechanisms of Drug Stimuli*, Colpaert, F., and Balster, R., Eds., No. 4, Springer-Verlag, Berlin-Heidelberg, 1988, 161.
77. Ator, N. A., and Griffiths, R. R., Asymmetrical cross-generalization in drug discrimination with lorazepam and pentobarbital training conditions, *Drug Development Research*, 16, 355, 1989.
78. Nierenberg, J., and Ator, N. A., Drug discrimination in rats successively trained to discriminate diazepam and pentobarbital, *Pharmacology Biochemisty and Behavior*, 35, 405, 1990.
79. Evans, S. M., and Johanson, C-E., Amphetamine-like effects of anorectics and related compounds in pigeons, *Journal of Pharmacology and Experimental Therapeutics*, 241, 817, 1987.
80. Witkin, J. M., Carter, R. B., and Dykstra, L. A., Discriminative stimulus properties of d-amphetamine-pentobarbital combinations, *Psychopharmacology*, 68, 269, 1980.
81. Herling, S., Coale, E. H., Valentino, R. J., Hein, D. W., and Woods, J. H., Narcotic discrimination in pigeons, *Journal of Pharmacology and Experimental Therapeutics*, 214, 139, 1980.

Kenzie L. Preston and Sharon L. Walsh

82. Woudenberg, F., and Slangen, J. L., Discriminative stimulus properties of midazolam: Comparison with other benzodiazepines, *Psychopharmacology*, 97, 466, 1989.

83. Shannon, H. E., and Herling, S., Discriminative stimulus effects of diazepam in rats: Evidence for a maximal effect, *Journal of Pharmacology and Experimental Therapeutics*, 227, 160, 1983.

84. Evans, S. M., and Johanson, C-E., Discriminative stimulus properties of midazolam in the pigeon, *Journal of Pharmacology and Experimental Therapeutics*, 248, 29, 1989.

85. Spealman, R. D., Discriminative-stimulus effects of midazolam in squirrel monkeys: Comparison with other drugs and antagonism by RO 15-1788, *Journal of Pharmacology and Experimental Therapeutics*, 235, 456, 1985.

86. Sannerud, C. A., and Ator, N. A., Drug discrimination analysis of midazolam under a three-lever procedure: I. Dose-dependent differences in generalization and antagonism, *Journal of Pharmacology and Experimental Therapeutics*, 272, 100, 1995.

87. de la Garza, R., and Johanson, C-E., Discriminative stimulus properties of cocaine in pigeons, *Psychopharmacology*, 85, 23, 1985.

88. Emmett-Oglesby, M. W., Wurst, M., and Lal, H., Discriminative stimulus properties of a small dose of cocaine, *Neuropharmacology*, 22, 97, 1983.

89. Dykstra, L. A., Doty, P., Johnson, A. B., and Picker, M. J., Discriminative stimulus properties of cocaine, alone and in combination with buprenorphine, morphine and naltrexone, *Drug and Alcohol Dependence*, 30, 227, 1992.

90. Spealman, R. D., and Bergman, J., Modulation of the discriminative stimulus effects of cocaine by mu and kappa opioids, *Journal of Pharmacology and Experimental Therapeutics*, 261, 607, 1992.

91. Heishman, S. J., and Henningfield, J. E., Discriminative stimulus effects of d-amphetamine, methylphenidate, and diazepam in humans, *Psychopharmacology*, 103, 436, 1991.

92. Kilbey, M. M., and Ellinwood, E. H., Discriminative stimulus properties of psychomotor stimulants in the cat, *Psychopharmacology*, 63: 151, 1979.

93. Chait, L. D., Uhlenhuth, E. H., and Johanson, C-E., The discriminative stimulus and subjective effects of phenylpropanolamine, mazindol and d-amphetamine in humans, *Pharmacology Biochemistry and Behavior*, 24, 1665, 1986.

94. Chait, L. D., Uhlenhuth, E. H., and Johanson, C-E., The discriminative stimulus and subjective effects of d-amphetamine, phenmetrazine and fenfluramine in humans, *Psychopharmacology*, 89, 301, 1986.

95. Holloway, F. A., Michaelis, R. C., and Huerta, P. L., Caffeine-phenylethylaminecombinations mimic the amphetamine discriminative cue, *Life Sciences*, 36, 723, 1985.

96. Kuhn, D. M., Appel, J. B., and Greenberg, I., An analysis of some discriminative properties of d-amphetamine, *Psychopharmacologia* (Berl.), 39, 57, 1974.

97. Holtzman, S. G., Discriminative stimulus properties of opioid agonists and antagonists, In *Theory in Psychopharmacology*, Cooper, S. J., Ed., Volume 2, Academic Press, Inc., London, 1983, 2.

98. Shannon, H. E., and Holtzman, S. G., Evaluation of the discriminative effects of morphine in the rat, *Journal of Pharmacology and Experimental Therapeutics*, 198, 54, 1976.

99. France, C. P., Jacobson, A. E., and Woods, J. H., Discriminative stimulus effects of reversible and irreversible opiate agonists: Morphine, oxymorphazone and buprenorphine, *Journal of Pharmacology and Experimental Therapeutics*, 230, 652, 1984.

100. Young, A. M., Masaki, M. A., and Geula, C., Discriminative stimulus effects of morphine: Effects of training dose on agonist and antagonist effects of mu opioids, *Journal of Pharmacology and Experimental Therapeutics*, 261, 246, 1992.

101. Overton, D. A., and Batta, S. K., Investigations of narcotics and antitussives using drug discrimination techniques, *Journal of Pharmacology and Experimental Therapeutics*, 211, 401, 1979.

102. Preston, K. L., Liebson, I. A., and Bigelow, G. E., Discrimination of agonist-antagonist opioids in humans trained on a two-choice saline-hydromorphone discrimination, *Journal of Pharmacology and Experimental Therapeutics*, 261, 62, 1992.

103. Preston, K. L., Bigelow, G. E., Bickel, W. K., and Liebson, I. A., Drug discrimination in human post-addicts: Agonist-antagonist opioids, *Journal of Pharmacology and Experimental Therapeutics*, 250, 184, 1989.

104. Jarbe, T. U. C., Discriminative effects of morphine in the pigeon, *Pharmacology Biochemistry and Behavior*, 9, 411, 1978.

105. de la Garza, R., and Johanson, C-E., The discriminative stimulus properties of cocaine in the rhesus monkey, *Pharmacology Biochemistry and Behavior*, 19, 145, 1983.

106. Jasinski, D. R., History of abuse liability testing in humans, *British Journal of Addictions*, 86, 1559, 1991.

107. Jasinski, D. R., Johnson, R. E., and Henningfield, J. E., Abuse liability assessment in human subjects, *Trends in Pharmacological Sciences*, 5, 196, 1984.

108. Haertzen, C. A., Development of scales based on patterns of drug effects, using the Addiction Research Center Inventory (ARCI), *Psychological Reports*, 18, 163, 1966.

109. McNair, D. M., Lorr, M., and Droppleman, L. F., *Manual for the Profile of Mood States*, Educational and Industrial Testing Service, San Diego, 1971.

110. Fraser, H. F., Van Horn, G. D., Martin, W. R., Wolbach, A. B. and Isbell, H., Methods for evaluating addiction liability. (A) "Attitude" of opiate addicts toward opiate-like drugs, (B) A short-term "direct" addiction test, *Journal of Pharmacology and Experimental Therapeutics*, 133, 371, 1961.

111. Haertzen, C. A., and Hickey, J. E., Addiction Research Center Inventory (ARCI): measurement of euphoria and other drug effects, in *Methods for assessing the reinforcing properties of abused drugs*, Bozarth, M. A., Ed., Springer-Verlag, New York, 1987, Chapter 24.

112. Foltin, R. W., and Fischman, M. W., Assessment of abuse liability of stimulant drugs in humans: a methodolgical survey, *Drug and Alcohol Dependence*, 28, 3, 1991.

113. de Wit, H., and Griffiths, R. R., Testing the abuse liability of anxiolytic and hypnotic drugs in humans, *Drug and Alcohol Dependence*, 28, 83, 1991.

114. Jasinski, D. R., Assessment of the abuse potential of morphine-like drugs (methods used in man), in *Drug Addiction I*, Martin, W. R., Ed., Springer-Verlag, Heidelberg, 1977, Section II, Chapter 3.

115. Preston, K. L., and Jasinski, D. R., Abuse liability studies of opioid agonist-antagonists in humans, *Drug and Alcohol Dependence*, 28, 49, 1991.

116. Zacny, J. P., Lichtor, J. L., Flemming, D., Coalson, D. W., and Tompson, W. K., A dose-response analysis of the subjective, psychomotor and physiological effectives of intravenous morphine in healthy volunteers, *Journal of Pharmacology and Experimental Therpeutics*, 268, 1, 1994.

117. de Wit, H., and Johanson, C-E., Assessing pentobarbital preference in normal volunteers using a cumulative dosing procedure, *Psychopharmacology*, 99, 416, 1989.

118. Roache, J. D., and Griffiths, R. R., Comparison of triazolam and pentobarbital: Performance impairment, subjective effects and abuse liability, *Journal of Pharmacology and Experimental Therpeutics*, 234, 120, 1985.

119. Sullivan, J. T., Jasinski, D. R., and Johnson, R. E., Single-dose pharmacodynamics of diazepam and pentobarbital in substance abusers, *Clinical Pharmacology and Therapeutics*, 54, 645, 1993.

120. Johanson, C-E., Further studies on the discriminative stimulus effects of diazepam in humans, *Behavioural Pharmacology*, 2, 357, 1991.

121. Preston, K. L., Wolf, B., Guarino, J. J., and Griffiths, R. R., Subjective and behavioral effects of diphenhydramine, lorazepam and methocarbamol, *Journal of Pharmacology and Experimental Therpeutics*, 262, 707, 1992.

122. Mumford, G. K., Silverman, K., and Griffiths, R. R., Reinforcing, subjective, and performance effects of lorazepam and diphenhydramine in humans, *Experimental and Clinical Psychopharmacology*, 4, 421, 1996.

123. Fischman, M. W., Schuster, C. R., Resnekov, L., Shick, J. F. E., Krasnegor, N. A., Fennell, W., and Freedman, D. X., Cardiovascular and subjective effects of intravenous cocaine administration in humans, *Archives of General Psychiatry*, 33, 983, 1976.

124. Preston, K. L., Sullivan, J. T., Strain, E. C., and Bigelow, G. E., Effects of cocaine alone and in combination with bromocriptine in human cocaine abusers, *Journal of Pharmacology and Experimental Therpeutics*, 262, 279, 1992.

125. Martin, W. R., Sloan, J. W., Sapira, J. D., and Jasinski, D.R., Physiologic, subjective, and behavioral effects amphetamine, methamphetamine, ephedrine, phenmetrazine, and methylphenidate in man, *Clinical Pharmacology and Therapeutics*, 12, 245, 1971.

126. Rush, C. R., Sullivan, J. T., Griffiths, R. R., Intravenous caffeine in stimulant drug abusers: Subjective reports and physiological effects, *Journal of Pharmacology and Experimental Therpeutics*, 273, 351, 1995.

127. Chait, L. D., Factors influencing the subjective response to caffeine, *Behavioural Pharmacology*, 3, 219, 1992.

128. Jasinski, D. R., Martin, W. R., and Hoeldtke, R. D., Effects of short- and long-term administration of pentazocine in man, *Clinical Pharmacology and Therapeutics*, 11, 385, 1970.

129. Jasinski, D. R., Martin, W. R., and Mansky, P. A., Progress report on the assessment of the antagonists nalbuphine and GPA-2087 for abuse potential and studies of the effects of dextromethorphan in man, In *Proceedings of the 33rd Annual Meeting of the Committee on Problems of Drug Dependence*, National Research Council, U.S. Government Printing Office, Washington, D.C., 1971, 143.

130. Fraser, H. F., and Isbell, H., Human pharmacology and addictiveness of certain dextroisomers of synthetic analgesics: I. d-3-hydroxy-N-phenethylmorphinan II. d-3-methoxy-N-phenethylmorphinan III. d-methadone, *Bulletin on Narcotics*, 14, 25, 1962.

131. Nemeth-Coslett, R., Henningfield, J. E., O'Keeffe, M. K., and Griffiths, R. R., Effects of marijuana smoking on subjective ratings and tobacco smoking, *PharmacologyBiochemisty and Behavior*, 25, 659, 1986.

132. Cone, E. J., Welch, P., and Lange, W. R., Clonidine partially blocks the physiologic effects but not the subjective effects produced by smoking marijuana in male human subjects, *Pharmacology Biochemistry and Behavior*, 29, 649, 1988.

133. Martin, W. R., and Sloan, J. W., Pharmacology and classification of LSD-like hallucinogens, in *Drug Addiction II*, Martin, W. R., Ed., Springer-Verlag, Berlin Heidelberg, 1977, Chapter 3.

134. Griffiths, R. R., Bigelow, G. E., Liebson, I., and Kaliszak, J. E., Drug preference in humans: Double-blind choice comparison of pentobarbital, diazepam, and placebo, *Journal of Pharmacology and Experimental Therapeutics*, 215, 649, 1980.

135. Koob, G. F., and Bloom, F. E., Cellular and molecular mechanisms of drug dependence, *Science*, 242, 715, 1988.

136. Haefely, W., Biological basis of drug-induced tolerance, rebound, and dependence. Contribution of recent research on benzodiazepines, *Pharmacopsychiatry*, 19, 353, 1986.

137. Wise, R. A., and Bozarth, M. A., A psychomotor stimulant theory of addiction, *Psychological Reviews*, 94, 469, 1987.

138. Branch, M. N., Behavioral factors in drug tolerance, in *Methods in Behavioral Pharmacology*, van Haaren, F., Ed., Elsevier Science Publishers B. V., Amsterdam, 1993, Chapter 13.

139. Jasinski, D. R., and Mansky, P. A., Evaluation of nalbuphine for abuse potential, *Clinical Pharmacology and Therapeutics*, 13, 78, 1972.

140. Mello, N. K., and Mendelson, J. H., Buprenorphine suppresses heroin use by heroin addicts, *Science*, 207, 657, 1980.

141. Preston, K. L., Bigelow, G. E., and Liebson, I. A., Self-administration of clonidine, oxazepam, and hydromorphone by patients undergoing methadone detoxification, *Clinical Pharmacology and Therapeutics*, 38, 219, 1985.

142. Fraser, H. F., and Jasinski, D. R., The assessment of the abuse potentiality of sedative/hypnotics (depressants) (methods used in animals and man), in *Drug Addiction I*, Martin, W. R., Ed., Springer-Verlag, Heidelberg, 1977, Section III, Chapter 2.

143. Rickels, K., Schweizer, E., Case, G., and Greenblatt, D. J., Long-term therapeutic use of benzodiazepines I. Effects of abrupt discontinuation, *Archives of General Psychiatry*, 47, 899, 1990.

144. Robinson, G. M., and Sellers, E. M., Diazepam withdrawal seizures, *Canadian Medical Association Journal*, 126, 944, 1982.

145. Gawin, F. H., and Kleber, H. D., Abstinence symptomatology and psychiatric diagnosis in cocaine abuers, *Archives of General Psychiatry*, 43, 107, 1986.

146. Weddington, W. W., Brown, B. S., Haertzen, C. A., Cone, E. J., Dax, E. M., Herning, R. I., and Michaelson, B. S., Changes in mood, craving, and sleep during short-term abstinence reported by male cocaine addicts, *Archives of General Psychiatry*, 47, 861, 1990.

147. Satel, S. L., Price, L. H., Palumbo, J. M., McDougle, C. J., Krystal, J. H., Gawin, F., Charney, D. S., Heninger, G. R., and Kleber, H. D., Clinical phenomenology and neurobiology of cocaine abstinence: A prospective inpatient study, *American Journal of Psychiatry*, 148, 1712, 1991.

148. Kowatch, R. A., Schnoll, S. S., Knisely, J. S., Green, D., and Elswick, R. K., Electroencephalographic sleep and mood during cocaine withdrawal, *Journal of Addictive Diseases*, 11, 21, 1992.

149. Gillin, J. C., Pulvirenti, L., Withers, N., Golshan, S., and Koob, G., The effects of lisuride on mood and sleep during acute withdrawal in stimulant abusers: A preliminary report. *Biological Psychiatry*, 35, 843, 1994.

150. Martin, S. D., Yeragani, V. K., Lodhi, R., and Galloway, M. P., Clinical ratings and plasma HVA during cocaine abstinence, *Biological Psychiatry*, 26, 356, 1989.

151. Flowers, Q., Elder, I. R., Voris, J., Sebastian, P. S., Blevins, O., and Dubois, J., Daily cocaine craving in a 3-week inpatient treatment program, *Journal of Clinical Psychology*, 49, 292, 1993.

152. Post, R. M., Gillin, J. C., Wyatt, R. J., and Goodwin, F., K., The effect of orally administered cocaine on sleep of depressed patients, *Psychopharmacology*, 37, 59, 1974.

153. Noldy, N.E., Santos, C.V., Politzer, N., Blair, R.D.G., and Carlen, P.L., Quantitative EEG changes in cocaine withdrawal: Evidence for long-term CNS effects. *Neuropsychobiology*, 30, 189-196, 1994.

154. Jones, R. T., Benowitz, N. L., and Herning, R. I., Clinical relevance of cannabis tolerance and dependence, *Journal of Clinical Pharmacology*, 21, 143S, 1981.

155. Emmett-Oglesby, M. W., Mathis, D. A., and Lal, H., Animal models of drug withdrawal symptoms, *Psychopharmacology*, 101, 292, 1990.

156. Beardsley, P. M., Balster, R. L., and Harris, L. S., Dependence on tetrahydrocannabinol in rhesus monkeys, *Journal of Pharmacology and Experimental Therpeutics*, 239, 311, 1986.

157. Aceto, M. D., Scates, S. M., Lowe, J. A., and Martin, B. R., Cannabinoid precipitated withdrawal by the selective cannabinoid receptor antagonist, SR 141716A, *European Journal of Pharmacology*, 282, R1, 1995.

158. Griffiths, R. R., Lukas, S. E., Bradford, L. D., Brady, J. V., and Snell, J. D., Self-injection of barbiturates and benzodiazepines in baboons, *Psychopharmacology*, 75, 101, 1981.

159. Griffiths, R. R., Lamb, R. J., Sannerud, C. A., Ator, N. A., and Brady, J. V., Self-injection of barbiturates, benzodiazepines and other sedative-anxiolytics in baboons, *Psychopharmacology*, 103, 154, 1991.

160. Beardsley, P. M., and Balster, R. L., The intravenous self-administration of antihistamines by rhesus monkeys, *Drug and Alcohol Dependence*, 30, 117, 1992.

161. Harris, R. T., Claghorn, J. L., and Schoolar, J. C., Self administration of minor tranquilizers as a function of conditioning, *Psychopharmacologia*, 313, 81, 1968.

162. Bergman, J., Madras, B. K., Johnson, S. E., and Spealman, R. D., Effects of cocaine and related drugs in non-human primates. III. Self-administration by squirrel monkeys, *Journal of Pharmacology and Experimental Therapeutics*, 251, 150, 1989.

163. Risner, M. E., and Jones, B. E., Characteristics of unlimited access to self-administered stimulant infusions in dogs, *Biological Psychiatry*, 11, 625, 1976.

164. Risner, M. E., and Jones, B. E., Self administration of CNS stimulants by dogs, *Psychopharmacologia*, 43, 207, 1975.

165. Griffiths, R. R., and Woodson, P. P., Reinforcing properties of caffeine: Studies in humans and laboratory animals, *Pharmacology Biochemistry and Behavior*, 29, 419, 1988.

166. Lamb, R. J., Sannerud, C. A., and Griffiths, R. R., An examination of the intravenous self-administration of phenylpropanolamine using a cocaine substitution procedure in the baboon, *Pharmacology Biochemistry and Behavior*, 28, 389, 1987.

167. Woods, J. H., Young, A. M., and Herling, S., Classification of narcotics on the basis of their reinforcing, discriminative, and antagonist effects in rhesus monkeys, *Federation Proceedings*, 41, 221, 1982.

168. Hoffmeister, F., and Schlechting, U. U., Reinforcing properties of some opiates and opioids in rhesus monkeys with histories of cocaine and codeine self-administration, *Psychopharmacologia*, 23, 55, 1972.

169. Johanson, C-E., and Balster, R. L., A summary of results of a drug self-administration study using substitution procedures in rhesus monkeys, Bulletin on Narcotics, 30, 43, 1978.

170. Harris, R. T., Waters, W., and McLendon, D., Evaluation of reinforcing capability of delta-9-tetrahydrocannabinol in rhesus monkeys, *Psychopharmacologia*, 37, 23, 1974.

171. Balster, R. L., Johanson, C-E., Harris, R. T., and Schuster, C. R., Phencyclidine self-administration in the rhesus monkey, Pharmacology Biochemistry and Behavior, 1, 167, 1973.

172. Balster, R. L., and Prescott, W. R., D9-Tetrahydrocannabinol discrimination in rats as a model for cannabis intoxication, *Neuroscience and Biobehavioral Reviews*, 16, 55, 1992.

173. Holtzman, S. G., Phencyclidine-like discriminative effects of opioids in the rat, *Journal of Pharmacology and Experimental Therpeutics*, 214, 614, 1980.

174. Willetts, J., and Balster, R. L., Phencyclidine-like discriminative stimulus properties of MK-801 in rats, *European Journal of Pharmacology*, 146, 167, 1988.

175. Nielsen, E. B., Discriminative stimulus properties of Lysergic Acid Diethylamide in the monkey, *Journal of Pharmacology and Experimental Therpeutics*, 234, 244, 1985.

176. Winter, J. C., and Rabin, R. A., Interactions between serotonergic agonists and antagonists in rats trained with LSD as a discriminative stimulus, *Pharmacology Biochemistry and Behavior*, 30, 617, 1988.

177. Okamoto, M., Hinman, D. J., and Aaronson, L. M., Comparison of ethanol and barbiturate physical dependence, *Journal of Pharmacology and Experimental Therpeutics*, 218, 701, 1981.

178. Boisse, N. R., and Okamoto, M., Physical dependence to barbital compared to pentobarbital. III. Withdrawal characteristics, *Journal of Pharmacology and Experimental Therpeutics*, 204, 514, 1978.

179. Lukas, S. E., and Griffiths, R. R., Precipitated withdrawal by a benzodiazepine receptor antagonist (Ro 15-1788) after 7 days of diazepam, *Science*, 217, 1161, 1982.

180. Noyes, R., Garvey, M. J., Cook, B. L., and Perry, P. J., Benzodiazepine withdrawal: A review of the evidence, *Journal of Clinical Psychiatry*, 49, 382, 1988.

181. Feldman, M. D., and Behar, M., A case of massive diphenhydramine abuse and withdrawal from us of the drug, *Journal of the American Medical Association*, 255, 3119, 1986.

182. Young, G. B., Boyd, D., and Kreeft, J., Dimenhydrinate: evidence for dependence and tolerance, *Canadian Medical Association Journal*, 138, 437, 1988.

183. Woolverton, W. L., and Kleven, M. S., Evidence for cocaine dependence in monkeys following a prolonged period of exposure, *Psychopharmacology*, 94, 288, 1988.

184. Wise, R. A., and Munn, E., Withdrawal from chronic amphetamine elevates baseline intracranial self-stimulation thresholds, *Psychopharmacology*, 117, 130, 1995.

185. Kokkinidis, L., Zacharko, R. M., and Anisman, H., Amphetamine withdrawal: A behavioral evaluation, *Life Sciences*, 38, 1617, 1986.

186. Holtzman, S. G., Caffeine as a model drug of abuse, *Trends in Pharmacological Sciences*, 11, 355, 1990.

187. Strain, E. C., Mumford, G. K., Silverman, K., and Griffiths, R. R., Caffeine dependence syndrome. Evidence from case histories and experimental evaluations, *Journal of the American Medical Association*, 272, 1043, 1994.

188. Griffiths, R. R., and Woodson, P. P., Caffeine physical dependence: a review of human and laboratory animal studies, *Psychopharmacology*, 94, 437, 1988.

189. Himmelsbach, C. K., The addiction liability of codeine, *Journal of the American Medical Association*, 103, 1420, 1934.

190. Carroll, M. E., A quantitative assessment of phencyclidine dependence produced by oral self-administration in rhesus monkeys, *Journal of Pharmacology and Experimental Therpeutics*, 242, 405, 1987.

191. Chait, L. D., Uhlenhuth, E. H., and Johanson, C-E., Reinforcing and subjective effects of several anorectics in normal human volunteers, *Journal of Pharmacology and Experimental Therpeutics*, 242, 777, 1987.
192. Griffiths, R. R., and Mumford, G. K., Caffeine - a drug of abuse? In *Psychopharmacology: The Fourth Generation of Progress*, Bloom, F. E., and Kupfer D. J., Eds., Raven Press, New York, 1995, 1699.
193. Petersen, R. C., and Stillman, R. C., Phencyclidine: An Overview, in *PCP (phencyclidine) abuse: An appraisal*, Petersen, R. C., and Stillman, R. C., Eds., National Institute on Drug Abuse, U.S. Government Printing Office, Washington, D.C., 1978, 1.

CHAPTER 5

ALCOHOL

EDITED BY CHRISTOPHER S. MARTIN

WESTERN PSYCHIATRIC INSTITUTE AND CLINIC, DEPARTMENT OF PSYCHIATRY, UNIVERSITY OF PITTSBURGH SCHOOL OF MEDICINE, PITTSBURGH, PENNSYLVANIA

TABLE OF CONTENTS

Christopher S. Martin

5.1 MEASURING ACUTE ALCOHOL IMPAIRMENT

This section reviews impairment produced by alcohol consumption, and issues in the measurement of such impairment. Motor and cognitive impairment produced by alcohol intoxication has been noted for centuries, and is apparent to almost everyone who lives in an alcohol drinking society. The effects of alcohol consumption on behavior, cognition, and mood have been reviewed by several authors in the scientific literature.[1-4] Unlike previous reviews, this section focuses on medical and forensic aspects of the topic, with a particular emphasis on impairment testing.

Impairment and its consequences are major reasons for forensic and medical interest in alcohol consumption. The assessment of impairment caused by acute alcohol intoxication is important for forensic, research, and clinical applications. At the same time, the determinants of impaired performance are complex, and are influenced by numerous pharmacological, motivational, and situational factors. Impairment also is extremely variable between persons. While obvious at extreme levels, alcohol-related impairment raises a number of difficult measurement issues. Although many impairment tests have adequate properties in the laboratory, assessments used in field applications have important limitations.

This section begins with a review of the acute effects of alcohol on behavioral and cognitive functioning. Emphasis is given to the effects of alcohol on speech and on the functioning of the vestibular system, which is centrally involved in balance control and spatial orientation. Next, individual differences in impairment are examined. This is followed by a description of how impairment is related to the time course of alcohol ingestion. The effects of rising vs. falling blood alcohol concentrations (BACs) and acute tolerance are discussed. The behavioral correlates of a hangover are reviewed. Then we discuss the ideal characteristics of impairment tests, followed by a description of the actual characteristics of impairment tests when evaluated in laboratory and field settings.

5.1.1 BEHAVIORAL CORRELATES OF ACUTE INTOXICATION

This section reviews the effects of alcohol on motor coordination and cognitive performance. Most "behavioral" correlates of intoxication involve both motor control and cognitive functioning. As will be seen, the effects of alcohol are not uniform; impairment varies across different types of behavioral functions. Two areas of functioning that are sensitive to alcohol impairment and assessed in field sobriety tests are described in some detail: speech and vestibular functioning. In addition, this section describes individual differences in alcohol impairment related to age, gender, and alcohol consumption practices.

5.1.1.1 Motor Control and Cognitive Functioning

Alcohol functions as a general central nervous system depressant, and affects a wide range of functions. To the observer, one of the most apparent effects of alcohol consumption is on motor control, particularly behaviors that require fine motor coordination. Other well-known effects of alcohol involve decrements in the cognitive control of behavioral functioning, especially the ability to perform and coordinate multiple tasks at the same time. Research has assessed the effects of alcohol on numerous performance tasks. Almost all of these tasks involve both cognitive and motor control components, although tasks differ in the complexity of the motor and cognitive functioning required for performance.

5.1.1.1.1 Reaction Time

Some of the most basic performance tasks investigated in the literature are simple reaction time (RT) tasks, in which subjects must push a button as quickly and accurately as possible in response to a stimulus. Baylor et al.[5] found no effects of alcohol on simple RT at BACs of 100 mg/dl, but did find effects at very high BACs near 170 mg/dl. Taberner[6] found no effect of a low dose of 0.15 g/kg alcohol, and a small effect at a dose of 0.76 g/kg alcohol. Maylor et al.[7] found a small effect of alcohol on simple RT at a dose of 0.64 g/kg alcohol. Linnoila et al.[8] did not find effects of alcohol on simple RT, even though other types of performance were impaired at this dose. Although the findings are somewhat variable, simple RT appears to be relatively insensitive to alcohol consumption.

Other research has examined choice RT tasks, in which subjects are required to respond using two or more buttons in response to different stimuli. Such tasks involve motor speed as well as cognitive functions involved in categorizing a stimulus and choosing a response. Few differences were seen by Fagan et al.[9] on a six-choice RT procedure. Golby[10] found no effects of alcohol on two different choice RT tasks. Other studies have found rather small or inconsistent effects of alcohol on choice RT.[7,11] Overall, there is not consistent evidence that alcohol effects the performance of choice RT tasks in the range of BACs studied in laboratory experiments.

The research literature contains a number of studies that have examined the effects of alcohol on tracking performance, that is, the ability of subjects to move a pointer to track a moving target. Tracking tasks require fine motor control and coordination of the hands and eyes at a rapid speed. There is consistent evidence that alcohol significantly impairs tracking performance. Beirness and Vogel-Sprott[12] found that alcohol affected tracking performance at BACs above 50 mg/dl; this effect has been replicated in numerous studies by Vogel-Sprott and colleagues. Wilson et al.[13] found that BACs peaking at 100 mg/dl produced tracking impairments for 120 minutes after drinking relative to placebo. The effects of alcohol on tracking performance have been found by several other authors.[8,11,14,15]

5.1.1.1.2 Dual-Task Performance

Alcohol impairment is found consistently during dual-task performance, when subjects are required to perform multiple tasks simultaneously. When subjects were required to perform a tracking task and an RT task at the same time, Connors and Maisto[11] found that alcohol reduced tracking but not RT performance. Using a similar procedure, Maylor et al.[14] found that alcohol affected RT but not tracking. Differences between these two studies in the task that was affected may have been due to instructions or task demands that led subjects to select one of the two tasks as primary, leading to performance deficits on the secondary task. Niaura et al.[16] combined a RT task with a task requiring the subject to circle target characters on a printed sheet, and found that alcohol produced deficits on both tasks relative to placebo. Other researchers have used computerized divided-attention tasks, which require subjects to perform multiple functions simultaneously. Mills and Bisgrove[17] found that divided-attention performance (responding to numbers on central and peripheral monitors by pushing different buttons) was impaired after 0.76 g/kg alcohol, but not after a lower dose of 0.37 g/kg alcohol.

The performance of multiple challenging tasks is thought to require the utilization of a large amount of attention, defined as limited-capacity cognitive resources that are required for effortful processing. The demonstration that alcohol produces dual-task performance deficits is consistent with the idea that alcohol produces impairment, in part, by reducing the available amount of limited-capacity attentional resources. A similar "attention allocation" model was proposed by Steele and Josephs.[18] These authors found that alcohol produced clear deficits in secondary task performance without affecting primary task performance, and suggested that alcohol serves to allocate a greater amount of attentional resources to a primary task, leading to fewer resources available for processing secondary sources of information.

Other studies of the behavioral impairment produced by alcohol have used tests designed to simulate complex real-world behaviors such as driving. Accident statistics consistently demonstrate that crash risk in the natural environment increases significantly when BACs are above 40 mg/dl.[19] Automobile simulator studies generally find that the information processing and lateral guidance demands of driving are adversely affected by alcohol. Several well-designed laboratory studies have demonstrated adverse affects of alcohol on skills related to driving, beginning with BACs as low as 30 to 40 mg/dl.[15,20] Other research with automobile simulators has examined the effects of alcohol on risk taking, defined by levels of speed, cars overtaken, and number of accidents during simulated driving. McMillen et al.[21] did not find effects of alcohol on risk taking during a driving simulation, whereas Mongrain and Standing[22] did find that alcohol increased risk taking, albeit at very high BACs near 160 mg/dl.

The effects of alcohol on performance have also been studied under conditions of actual driving. Attwood et al.[23] found that performance variables such as velocity and lane position together discriminated between intoxicated and sober drivers. Huntley found decreased lateral guidance during a driving task after alcohol.[24] Brewer and Sandow[25] studied real accidents using driver and witness testimony. Among persons who were in accidents, those with BACs above 50 mg/dl were much more likely to have been engaged in a secondary activity at the time of the accident, compared to drivers with BACs below 50 mg/dl. Overall, it appears that alcohol adversely affects several types of behavioral functions involved in driving. Driving performance is complex and determined by a number of individual and situational factors and roadway conditions. More research is needed to better understand alcohol's effects on driving performance.

5.1.1.2 Speech

It is well known to bartenders, law enforcement personnel, and the general public that alcohol consumption can produce changes in speech production often described as "slurred speech". Because speech production requires fine motor control, timing, and coordination of the lips, tongue, and vocal cords, it may be a sensitive index of impairment resulting from alcohol intoxication. Having subjects recite the alphabet at a fast rate of speed is a well-known field sobriety test. Laboratory research suggests that speech can be a valid index of alcohol consumption. After consuming 10 oz of 86-proof alcohol, alcoholics were found to take longer to read a passage and had more word, phrase, and sound interjections, word omissions, word revisions, and broken suffixes in their speech.[26] Other research with nonalcoholic drinkers found that under intoxication, subjects made more sentence-level, word-level, and sound-level errors during spontaneous speech.[27,28] Intoxicated talkers consistently lengthen some speech sounds, particularly consonants in unstressed syllables.[29] The overall rate of speech also slows when intoxicated talkers read sentences and paragraphs.[27,30]

Pisoni and Martin[30] examined the acoustic-phonetic properties of speech for matched pairs of sentences spoken by social drinkers when sober and after achieving BACs above 100 mg/dl. Sentence duration was increased after drinking, and pitch (loudness), while not consistently higher or lower, was more variable. The strongest effects of alcohol at the sound level were for speech sounds that require fine motor control and timing of articulation events in close temporal proximity. Intoxicated talkers displayed difficulty in controlling the abrupt closures and openings of the vocal tract required for stops and affricate closures. This resulted in long durations of closures before voiced stops (e.g., /d/, /b/), and the complete absence of closures before affricates (e.g., the /ch/ in "church"). These effects are consistent with what is known about the degree of precision of motor control mechanisms required for the articulation of different speech sounds. Pisoni and Martin[30] also found that listeners can reliably discriminate speech produced while sober and under intoxication. State Troopers showed higher discrimination levels than other listeners, suggesting that experience in detecting intoxication may increase perceptual abilities. The approach of some field sobriety tests that have persons recite the alphabet quickly may effectively capture the detrimental effects of alcohol on the articulation of speech sounds in close temporal proximity.

Despite the data showing effects of alcohol on speech, there are a number of limitations that make it difficult to use speech production as an index of alcohol impairment. Changes in speech have been reliably produced with blood alcohol levels above 100 mg/dl; however, the effects of lower doses have been variable;[27-29] it is not clear whether reliable effects are produced in most persons when BACs are lower. Other types of impairment are likely to occur before speech is noticeably affected. It is not clear from the literature how motivation to avoid the detection of intoxication would affect speech production. Furthermore, the specificity of speech changes to alcohol intoxication (rather than fatigue, stress, etc.) needs further study. Finally, there is extreme variability between persons in the acoustic-phonetic properties of speech, such that it is difficult to estimate the degree of impairment without comparison samples of sober speech.[31] Despite these limitations, the literature suggests that speech is likely to be a good *screening* test for impairment, which can then be determined using other measures.

5.1.1.3 Vestibular Functioning

The vestibular system serves to maintain spatial orientation and balance, and eye movements that support these functions. The vestibular system is comprised of two sets of interconnected canals that provide information about spatial orientation. Each canal is comprised of a membrane embedded with sensory hair cells, and a surrounding extracellular fluid. The *otolithic* canals provide information about the direction of gravity relative to the head, and thus are sensitive to lateral (side to side) head movements. This is accomplished by the fact that the membrane has a specific gravity that is twice that of the extracellular space in otoliths. Under normal conditions, the *semicircular* canals are sensitive to rotational movements of the head, and do not respond to lateral movements. In semicircular canals, the membrane and the extracellular fluid have the same exact specific gravity (i.e., weight by volume), such that the hair cells have neutral buoyancy and are not subject to gravitational influences.[32]

5.1.1.3.1 Positional Alcohol Nystagmus (PAN)

Alcohol's effects on the vestibular system are seen in measures that evaluate oculo-motor control, i.e., the functional effectiveness of eye movements under different conditions. During alcohol consumption, many persons show significant nystagmus (jerkiness) in eye movements when the head is placed in a sideways position: this effect is known as Positional Alcohol Nystagmus (PAN). There are two types of PAN. PAN I is characterized by a nystagmus to the right when the right side of the head is down, and to the left when the left side of the head is down. PAN I normally occurs during rising and peak BACs, beginning around 40 mg/dl.[33] PAN II normally appears between 5 and 10 hours after drinking, and is characterized by nystagmus in the opposite directions seen in PAN I.[34]

The mechanisms of PAN I and II have been convincingly demonstrated.[35] Both types of PAN are produced by the effects of alcohol on the semicircular canals, making hair cells on the membrane responsive to the effects of gravity. As alcohol diffuses throughout the water compartments of the body, it first enters the membrane space (which is richly supplied with capillary blood), and diffuses only gradually into the extracellular fluid. For a time, the alcohol concentration is greater in membrane than the surrounding fluid. Because alcohol is lighter than water, the specific gravity of the membrane will be lighter than that of the surrounding fluid during this time, making the semicircular canals responsive to gravity and producing PAN I. The faster the rate of drinking, the faster PAN I appears.[36]

There is a period during descending BACs in which neither PAN I nor PAN II is apparent; during this time the semicircular membrane and the surrounding fluid have achieved equilibrium, and have the same specific gravity. PAN II occurs during alcohol elimination and after the body has no measurable amounts of alcohol. During PAN II, alcohol in the semicircular canals is removed from the membrane faster than the surrounding fluid; this results in the membrane having a heavier specific gravity than the surrounding fluid, which in turn produces PAN II.

Both PAN I and II may overstimulate the semicircular canals in a manner similar to motion sickness.[35] It is possible that the effects of alcohol on the semicircular canals play a central role in many symptoms of intoxication, including feelings of dizziness, nausea, and the experience of vertigo known as the "bedspins". Laboratory studies have shown that the magnitude of PAN I is associated with higher BACs,[36] with greater impairment in postural control, and with higher subjective intoxication ratings.[37] As described later, it has been speculated that PAN II is associated with hangover.[35]

5.1.1.3.2 Horizontal Gaze Nystagmus (HGN)

Another type of nystagmus produced by alcohol is known as Horizontal Gaze Nystagmus (HGN). HGN is defined by jerkiness in eye movements as gaze is directed to the side, when the head is in an upright position. HGN has long been noted as an effect of alcohol, and usually becomes apparent when rising BACs reach about 80 mg/dl.[38] HGN is assessed by having a subject follow an object with their eyes at an increasingly eccentric angle, without moving the head; the smallest angle at which nystagmus first appears is used to assess intoxication. While nystagmus occurs in a sober state at more extreme angles of eccentric gaze, alcohol decreases the size of the angle at which it is first apparent.

As with PAN, it has been demonstrated that HGN is highly associated with the effects of alcohol, as seen in studies of oculo-motor control.[39] Lehti[40] reported high correlations of BACs and the angle at which nystagmus in eccentric gaze became apparent. Similar effects of alcohol have been seen when nystagmus is assessed during active and passive head movements.[41] Tharp et al.[42] quantified the slope of a regression line predicting angle of onset of nystagmus from BAC. The angle of nystagmus onset was predicted at 45° for BACs of 50 mg/dl; 40° for BACs of 100 mg/dl; and 35° for BACs of 150 mg/dl. The angle of horizontal nystagmus onset has been found to have a high level of sensitivity and specificity in predicting BACs above 100 mg/dl in an emergency room setting.[43] HGN appears to be pharmacologically specific to alcohol. This is not the case for other aspects of occular control such as smooth pursuit. Smooth pursuit eye movements have proven to be much more sensitive to alcohol compared with marijuana, which has very small effects.[44] However, smooth pursuit eye movements are significantly affected by benzodiazapines, barbiturates, and antihistamines,[45] and thus cannot be said to be pharmcologically specific to alcohol. Deficits in smooth pursuit in the absence of significant BACs may indicate that a person has taken sedative drugs.

Postural control tasks are some of the most widely used measures of alcohol-related impairment in the laboratory and in the field. It is likely that the functional effectiveness of the vestibular system is an important locus of the effects of alcohol on postural control. Numerous studies have demonstrated that alcohol consumption leads to increases in sway as measured on a variety of balance platforms and similar types of apparatus, appearing in many drinkers at BACs of 30t o 50 mg/dl.[9,13,46,47] Other research has shown that sway increases with alcohol dose,[17,48,49] and that heavier drinkers sway less after alcohol compared to lighter drinkers.[48] The effects of alcohol become greater as the postural control task becomes more difficult, such as with eyes closed, or when the feet are in a heel-to-toe position.[49] Thus, postural control appears to be a sensitive index of alcohol effects. However, body sway shows a great deal of individual variation in a sober condition. For this reason, the ability to detect impairment from measuring sway is limited in field settings in which sober performance measures are not available.

5.1.1.4 Individual Differences

There are large individual differences in the impairment produced by alcohol consumption. The first and most obvious difference is that persons differ in the BACs they achieve when drinking alcohol. Even when controlling for BAC, however, there are large differences between persons in their sensitivity to alcohol impairment. Perhaps the most important factor is drinking practices. Those who drink more often and in greater amounts tend to develop a greater amount of tolerance to the impairing effects of alcohol, i.e., have an acquired decrease in the degree of impairment across multiple drinking sessions. Greater impairment in light drinkers compared to heavier drinkers has been shown by numerous authors using a variety of performance tasks.[4,48,50]

There are also gender differences in some aspects of alcohol pharmacokinetics. On average, women achieve significantly higher BACs than men when drinking the same amount of alcohol because of mean gender differences in body weight and body fat,[50] and because females tend to have lower levels of gastric alcohol dehydrogenase.[51] Some research with women has found greater alcohol elimination rates[52] and greater sensitivity to alcohol effects[53,54] during the mid-luteal and ovulatory phases of the menstrual cycle compared to the follicular phase. Other research, however, has not replicated these findings.[16,55,56]

Some laboratory studies have examined whether males and females differ in their sensitivity to alcohol. Mills and Bisgrove[17] found no gender differences in a divided-attention task after a low dose of alcohol, but greater impairment in females at a higher dose. However, in this study women achieved higher BACs, and reported less alcohol consumption compared to men. Burns and Moskowitz[57] found no significant gender differences in a series of motor and cognitive impairment tasks. When controlling for BACs, Niaura et al.[11] found few gender differences in psychomotor and cognitive responses to alcohol. Other research that controlled for gender differences in BACs and drinking practices has found few gender differences in response to alcohol.[58] Overall, when controlling for BACs and drinking practices, gender differences in alcohol impairment have not been demonstrated.

Little research has examined differences in alcohol impairment that are related to age. Using groups with fairly equivalent drinking practices, Parker and Noble[59] found that older subjects (over 42 years old) had more deficits on abstracting and problem solving after alcohol consumption compared to younger subjects. Linnoila et al.[8] found a trend towards increased impairment in subjects who were 25 to 35 years old, compared to those 20 to 25 years old. Other studies have also found age-related increases in psychomotor impairment in humans,[60,61] and in animals,[62] even when BACs and drinking practices were equivalent in older and younger groups. Although there appears to be an increase in sensitivity to alcohol's effects with advancing age, there are few studies, and most suffer from small sample sizes. Because age effects appear to occur even when BACs and drinking practices are controlled, some have speculated that age-related increases in alcohol impairment reflect the effects of aging on vulnerability of the central nervous system to alcohol's effects.[62]

5.1.2 TIME OF INGESTION

The effects of alcohol tend to vary dramatically over the time course of a drinking episode. An analysis of how the effects of alcohol change over time provides a clearer understanding of

Christopher S. Martin

alcohol-related impairment. This section reviews differences in the effects of alcohol during the rising and falling limbs of the BAC curve, the phenomenon of acute tolerance, and post-drinking hangover.

5.1.2.1 Rising and Falling Blood Alcohol Concentrations

Researchers and clinicians have long noted that alcohol's effects are often *biphasic* during a drinking episode.[63] "Biphasic" refers to the fact that stimulant effects of alcohol tend to precede sedative alcohol effects during a drinking episode.[64,65] There are substantial individual differences in the magnitude of stimulant effects of alcohol and the BACs at which they occur.[66,67] Alcohol's stimulant effects are reflected in increased motor activity, talkativeness, and euphoric or positive mood at lower doses and during rising BACs.[67,68] Stimulant effects have been assessed in humans using a variety of psychophysiological, motor activity, and self-report measures,[65,66,69] and in animals using measures such as spontaneous motor activity.[63,70] Stimulant effects are present in some drinkers at BACs as low as 20 to 30 mg/dl, and may persist on the rising BAC limb well past 100 mg/dl.[63,65] Some current theories hold that stimulant effects reflect alcohol's reinforcing qualities, and that the magnitude of stimulant effects will predict future drinking and the development of alcohol dependence.[71,72]

Some research suggests that the rate of change of rising BACs helps determine the degree of alcohol effects. A faster rise of ascending BACs is associated with greater euphoria and intoxication,[71,73-75] as well as increased behavioral impairment.[11,76] It is interesting to speculate that the drinking patterns shown by many heavy drinkers and alcoholics may reflect an attempt to produce a rapid rise in BACs. These patterns include gulping drinks, drinking on an empty stomach, and using progressively fewer mixers to dilute distilled spirits.

Sedative effects of alcohol usually occur at higher BACs and on the descending limb of the BAC curve. Sedation has been measured in humans using EEG patterns and self-reports of anesthetic sensations and dysphoric mood,[64,74,77] and in animals with low motor activity and the onset of alcohol-induced sleep.[78,79] Robust sedative effects tend to first appear at peak BACs near 60 to 80 mg/dl in many drinkers, although in persons with higher tolerance sedative effects are not apparent until BACs are above 100 mg/dl.[49,64,65] Sedative effects of alcohol are negatively correlated with drinking practices, and lower levels of sedation after alcohol consumption may characterize persons at increased risk for the future development of alcoholism.[79-81]

Research has clearly demonstrated that alcohol-related impairment is greater on the ascending compared to the descending limb of the BAC curve. This finding appears consistently across different doses and impairment tests. The most straightforward explanation for this effect is acute tolerance.

5.1.2.2 Acute Tolerance

There are many different types of tolerance identified by researchers.[50] Metabolic tolerance refers to an acquired increase in the rate of alcohol metabolism. Functional tolerance can be defined as an acquired decrease in an effect of alcohol at a given BAC. There are several different types of functional tolerance. Chronic tolerance refers to an acquired decrease in an effect of alcohol across multiple exposures to the drug. This section focuses on acute tolerance, defined as a decrease over time in an effect of alcohol *within* a single exposure to alcohol, which occurs independently of changes in BAC.

Acute tolerance is one of the most robust effects that occur in laboratory alcohol administration research. In 1919, Mellanby[82] demonstrated that effects of alcohol were greater during the rising compared to the falling limb of the BAC curve, a phenomenon known as the "Mellanby Effect". A number of laboratory studies in humans and animals have replicated the

Mellanby effect using numerous measures, such as motor coordination, self-reported intoxication, sleep time, and body temperature.[12,83-85]

One early question raised about the Mellanby effect was whether it was the result of a methodological artifact in the measurement of alcohol concentration in blood. Venous BAC, which is sampled for alcohol measurement, is known to lag behind arterial BAC during the ascending limb of the BAC curve, before the distribution of alcohol throughout body water compartments is complete. It is arterial blood that is closest to brain levels of alcohol. Thus, some wondered whether the Mellanby effect was an artifact because it actually compared impairment at different concentrations of alcohol in the brain.

It has been established, however, that acute tolerance and the Mellanby effect occur beyond any differences between arterial and venous BAC. First, the Mellanby effect is robust when BACs are assessed via breath alcohol; breath measures are closer to arterial than to venous BACs during the ascending limb of the BAC curve. Second, researchers have demonstrated the presence of acute tolerance using numerous alternative methods. When BACs are at a steady state, acute tolerance has been demonstrated by decreases in the effects of alcohol that occur over time.[13,86] Furthermore, the rate of decrease in alcohol effects are significantly greater than the rate of decrease in descending BACs.[87-89] Another demonstration of acute tolerance comes from social drinkers who report themselves as feeling completely sober when descending BACs are substantial (e.g., 30 to 50 mg/dl).[87] Investigators have demonstrated that decreased effects over time within an exposure to alcohol are not due to practice or other repeated-measures effects.[90-92]

In some models, acute tolerance occurs in a linear fashion as a function of the passage of time, independent of alcohol concentration.[89] Others have proposed that acute tolerance is concentration dependent.[93] Even in this latter model, the passage of time is critical; alcohol concentration simply influences the rate of recovery over time. Martin and Moss[87] found that at both higher and lower doses of alcohol, the magnitude of the Mellanby effect was highly correlated with the amount of time between the ascending and descending limb measurements. Clearly, the amount of impairment and intoxication shown during a drinking episode is not only affected by the level of BAC, but also by the amount of time alcohol has been in a person's system.

Vogel-Sprott and colleagues have published a large body of research that demonstrates that the degree of acute tolerance development is influenced by rewards and punishments, i.e., the consequences of non-impaired and impaired performance.[94] These investigators have demonstrated that acute tolerance to the impairment produced by alcohol increases when non-impaired performance leads to financial reward or praise.[12,95] One way to interpret these findings is in terms of motivation to show non-impaired performance. When an intoxicated motorist is stopped for questioning and/or field sobriety tests, that person will be highly motivated to show non-impaired behavior. While such attempts at appearing sober will be unsuccessful when BACs are sufficiently high, it is likely that many motorists avoid the detection of intoxication at substantial BACs by being highly motivated. Unfortunately, the same motorists may again show substantially impaired performance after the immediate contingency of detection and arrest are removed. Most of the laboratory impairment studies reviewed here did not adequately control for or study the impact of high motivational levels on the obtained results. For this reason, it is likely that the magnitude of impairment observed in many laboratory studies is greater than would be obtained in a field setting.

5.1.2.3 Hangover

Hangover has received relatively little attention in the scientific literature, but it can certainly produce alcohol-related impairment. Hangover is an aversive state typically experienced the morning after a heavy drinking bout, which is characterized by dysphoric and irritable mood, headache, nausea, dizziness, and dehydration. Sufficiently heavy drinking produces self-reported hangover symptoms in most persons, but there appears to be large individual differences in the occurrence, severity, and time course of perceived hangover that are independent of drinking practices.[96]

Studies reported in the literature are contradictory concerning whether hangover is accompanied by behavioral impairment. Several early studies found no performance impairment when BACs were at or close to zero.[97,98] Myrsten and colleagues[99] tested a variety of behavioral impairment measures 12 hours after subjects consumed a dose of alcohol producing mean BACs near 120 mg/dl. Morning BACs in this study averaged 4 mg/dl. Most measures showed no impairment, but hand steadiness was detrimentally affected. Collins and Chiles[100] gave impairment tests before an evening drinking session, after alcohol consumption, and again after subjects had slept 4 to 5 hours. Subjects were affected on the performance tests during acute intoxication, and they reported significant levels of hangover during the morning session. Despite these methodological strengths, there were no clear-cut performance impairing effects of hangover in this study.

Some other research indicates that hangover is accompanied by impairment in behavioral and cognitive functioning. One experiment found that after high peak BACs of about 150 mg/dl, there was an average 20% decrement on a simulated driving task 3 hours after BACs had returned to zero.[101] Yesavage and Leirer[102] examined hangover effects in Navy aircraft pilots 14 hours after drinking enough alcohol to produce BACs of about 100 mg/dl, using a variety of flight simulator measures. Significant detrimental effects of hangover were found for 3 of 6 variance measures and 1 of 6 performance measures. Similarly, other studies have found impairment due to hangover on only some of the tests employed in the research.[103,104]

Some have speculated that the nausea and dizziness of hangover may be associated with PAN II, an eye movement nystagmus that occurs during falling BACs and after measurable alcohol has left the system.[35] PAN II reflects the sensitivity of semicircular canal receptors to gravity, which also produces feelings similar to motion sickness. More research is needed to address the role of vestibular functioning in hangover.

Inconsistencies in the hangover literature probably reflect the fact that behavioral impairment during hangover is influenced by numerous factors, including sleepiness, fatigue, mood, and motivation to behave in a non-impaired manner. Moreover, there are individual differences in the frequency and duration of hangover, even among persons with similar drinking practices. For many persons, the BACs required to produce subsequent hangover may be greater than those typically obtained in laboratory studies. Hangover effects are poorly characterized, and are an important topic for further research.

5.1.3 IMPAIRMENT TESTING

5.1.3.1 Ideal Characteristics of Impairment Tests

The strengths and weaknesses of impairment tests used in the laboratory and the field are best evaluated in contrast with their ideal properties. There are a number of concepts which can be used to describe the characteristics of impairment tests, including scaling of results, applicability to field settings, reliability, validity, sensitivity, and specificity.[105]

Impairment tests differ in the *scaling of results*, that is, the nature of the scores or outcomes of a test. Results may be binary (impaired or not), ordinal rankings (low, medium, or high impairment), or quantitative scores. The need for precision of results depends upon the testing application. When used primarily as a screening tool for other sobriety tests or a BAC assessment, binary scores or ordinal rankings may be adequate. In other instances, continuous scores are desirable because they inform about the level of impairment.

Applicability to field settings is important for any impairment test used in law enforcement. One requirement i· that a test must have adequate measurement properties in a field setting. A test may have demonstrated reliability and validity in the laboratory, but these properties may or may not generalize to field settings. Field applications involve a loss of control over numerous variables that can influence testing. Reliability and validity properties in the field may be far different from the laboratory, in part because data from a known sober condition are not available for comparison.

There are several other important considerations in relation to field settings. Ideally, a test must be easily administered in a standard way by test administrators, and readily understood by test takers. The level of technical skill required for administering the test, collection of data and interpretation of results should be acquired with a reasonably short duration of training. Any required instrumentation should not require extensive maintenance, and should not be easily subject to interference by test takers. Importantly, impairment tests must have credibility with law enforcement officers and the wider criminal justice system. Whereas sobriety tests are often used as a preliminary screen for reasonable cause in BAC testing, they nevertheless must be generally acceptable to prosecutors, judges, and juries.

5.1.3.1.1 Reliability

Reliability refers to the extent to which a test provides a result that is stable or repeatable. That is, a reliable test is one that will yield a similar result across multiple testings in the same person (test-retest reliability), or across multiple test administrators or raters examining the same person (inter-rater reliability). An ideal impairment test should be reliable across testings in a sober person, i.e., it would reveal a stable baseline for non-impaired performance. Furthermore, an ideal test should show reliability across testings in an intoxicated person. That is, multiple tests taken at the same level of impairment would show relatively little variation in the obtained scores. Reliability is a key feature of any impairment test. If obtained scores are not reliable, the results may be caused by factors other than impairment, such as variation in test administration or scoring.

5.1.3.1.2 Validity

Validity concerns the extent to which a test accurately measures what it was intended to measure. The validity of impairment tests refers to the extent to which these tests assess alcohol-related impairment, rather than other factors. *Face validity* refers to the extent to which law enforcement personnel and test takers believe that a test does measure alcohol impairment; many field sobriety tests have high levels of face validity. *Concurrent validity* refers to the extent to which an impairment test shows expected associations with other tests known to measure impairment, and with BACs. *Construct validity* refers to the adequacy and explanatory power of scientific concepts such as alcohol impairment. If alcohol-related impairment is highly variable across different behaviors, this will reduce the validity of any one test in measuring such a diffuse concept.

A test can be reliable but not valid. For example, a person's height can be measured in a highly reliable fashion, but the observed results would be an invalid index of alcohol impairment. In contrast, some level of reliability is needed in order for a test to show validity. If an impairment test has no reliability, it cannot be valid. The degree to which reliability is imperfect tends to place an upper limit on the degree of validity that can be shown by a test.[106]

5.1.3.1.3 Sensitivity

Sensitivity refers to the ability of a test to detect impairment, and can be defined as the proportion of impaired persons (as determined by some other established measure) who are classified as impaired by a test. Thus, insensitive tests can allow persons who are impaired to

Christopher S. Martin

escape detection (a false negative test result). Whereas signs of intoxication are evident from test results in almost all persons when BACs become sufficiently high, many measures do not detect impairment when BACs are below 100 mg/dl. Among some heavy drinkers, many tests will be insensitive to BACs well above 100 mg/dl. In some cases, there probably is little impairment to detect when a test does not reveal impairment. In other cases, however, impaired performance is likely present, but a test is not sensitive enough to detect it.

5.1.3.1.4 Specificity

The *specificity* of an impairment tests refers to the extent to which the results reflect alcohol impairment and not other factors such as fatigue, stress, and individual differences in cognitive and motor skills. A highly specific test will not be much influenced by changes in parameters other than alcohol impairment. An example of high test specificity in biological measurement is seen for BACs, where existing instrumentation allows assessment of alcohol in blood and breath that is not affected by closely related chemical compounds such as acetate, acetaldehyde, or acetone. Tests with low levels of specificity will lead to a high proportion of false positive test identifications. That is, results for a non-specific test will often suggest that a person is impaired when they actually are not impaired (as measured by BAC or other tests). Thus, low specificity in impairment testing can lead to an inefficient expenditure of law enforcement resources.

An important issue in evaluating the sensitivity and specificity of impairment tests is whether measures of sober performance are available. Many tests show large individual differences in sober performance.[13,94] In laboratory research tests, sensitivity and specificity are evaluated by comparing a subject's performance at different BACs with their test performance when sober, usually before drinking begins. However, sensitivity and specificity are more difficult to achieve in the field, when sober baseline performance data are not available. Therefore, tests that are known to have less variation among sober persons are preferable for field settings.

When developing cutoff scores on impairment tests, increased sensitivity almost always comes at the expense of decreased specificity, and vice versa. The "best" cutoff score for the definition of impairment depends upon the relative importance of sensitivity and specificity in a given application, as well as the estimated base rate of impairment in the population that will be tested.[106] The choice of an appropriate cutoff score for an impairment test must be based on an understanding of these factors.

5.1.3.2 Characteristics of Existing Field Sobriety Tests

This section focuses on three field sobriety tests (FSTs) that have been standardized by the National Highway Traffic Safety Administration,[107] and which are widely used in the U.S. and elsewhere. In the *one-leg stand test*, subjects must raise one foot at least 6 in. off the ground and stand on the other foot for 30 seconds, while keeping their arms at their sides. Performance is scored on a 4-point scale, using items such as showing significant sway, using arms for balance, hopping, and putting down the raised foot. In the *walk-and-turn test*, subjects must balance with feet heel-to-toe and listen to test instructions. Then, subjects must walk nine steps heel-to-toe on a straight line, turn 180 degrees, and walk nine additional steps heel-to-toe, all the time counting their steps, watching their feet and keeping their hands at their sides. Performance is scored on an 8-point scale, using items such as starting before instructions are finished, stepping off the line, maintaining balance with arm movements, and taking an incorrect number of steps. The *gaze nystagmus test* assesses horizontal gaze nystagmus. The angle of onset of nystagmus is assessed for each eye. Performance is scored on a 6-point scale (3 possible points for each eye).

Some research has examined the properties of these three FSTs. In a laboratory study, Tharp et al.[42] used 297 drinking volunteers with BACs from 0 to 180 mg/dl who were tested by police officers trained in the use of FSTs. Inter-rater reliability correlations for the FSTs ranged from 0.60 to 0.80, indicating an adequate level of reliability across test administrators. Test-retest correlations, examining the correspondence of FST scores on two separate occasions at similar BACs, ranged from about 0.40 to 0.75, indicating adequate test-retest reliability. All of the FSTs correlated significantly with BACs. Using all three FST test scores, officers were able to classify 81% of persons in terms of whether their BACs were above or below 100 mg/dl. Similar results using these standard FSTs in a field setting were obtained by Anderson et al.[108] However, neither of these reports provided data on the specificity and sensitivity of individual FSTs.

Few studies have reported the characteristics of individual FSTs in field settings. One study found that HGN, specifically the angle of horizontal nystagmus onset, had high levels of sensitivity and specificity in predicting BACs above 100 mg/dl in an emergency room setting.[43] Perrine et al.[109] examined the reliability and validity of the National Highway Traffic Safety Administration FSTs in a field setting with 480 subjects, using police officers and other trained individuals as test administrators. Inter-rater reliability was adequate for all three FSTs. All of the FSTs were significantly correlated with BAC; however, the magnitude of these correlations was low in the case of the walk-and-turn and the one-leg stand tests. Perrine et al. provided data on the sensitivity and specificity of each FST as a function of different levels of BAC. The data indicated that the horizontal gaze nystagmus test had excellent sensitivity and specificity characteristics. Only 3% of subjects with a zero BAC failed the horizontal gaze nystagmus test (i.e., specificity was high when referenced to a zero BAC). Sensitivity was 100% for those with BACs over 150 mg/dl, and was 81% for subjects with BACs ranging from 100 mg/dl to 149 mg/dl.

However, Perrine et al. found that prediction of BAC was much worse using the walk-and-turn and the one-leg stand test. For the walk-and-turn test, specificity was low, in that about half of those with a zero BAC were classified as impaired. While sensitivity was fairly high (78%) at BACs above 150 mg/dl, this parameter fell below 50% for those with BACs between 80 mg/dl and 100 mg/dl. For the one-leg stand test, 30% of those with a zero BAC were classified as impaired, indicating only moderate specificity. Sensitivity was only 50% for those with BACs between 100 mg/dl and 150 mg/dl, but improved to 88% for those with BACs above 150 mg/dl.

The literature suggests that overall, FSTs such as the walk and turn, one leg stand, and horizontal gaze nystagmus test, have adequate properties for detecting impairment in field settings. These tests meet the requirements of applicability to the field, in that they can be administered in a standardized fashion, have face validity, and are understood by test takers. Training of test administrators can occur in a reasonable period of time. Results suggest that these tests can be administered reliably, and have validity in the sense that they do measure impairment due to alcohol. However, horizontal gaze nystagmus performs much better at predicting BAC than the walk-and-turn and the one-leg stand tests. While they are worthwhile, the latter two FSTs have significant limitations when used in field settings. More research is needed to determine if improved testing procedures or different cutoff scores can improve the performance of the walk-and-turn and the one-leg stand tests.

It is important to note that the properties of FSTs depend upon the threshold BACs they are supposed to detect. FSTs can be used to test impairment that occurs at BACs below a legal limit, but much of their utility depends upon their ability to determine whether a person has a BAC above that allowed by law. The FSTs described above were designed and tested in the context of the limits of 100 mg/dl that exist throughout most of the U.S. However, the limit is currently 80 mg/dl in California, and is 50 mg/dl or 20 mg/dl in many European countries.

Christopher S. Martin

It is likely that the performance of FSTs decreases as the BAC limit decreases. More research is needed to determine whether FSTs have utility when used to detect lower BAC threshold limits.

5.1.4 CONCLUSIONS

While it is clear that alcohol impairs performance, the presence and degree of impairment depends upon a large number of individual, situational, and pharmacological factors. Moreover, impairment is not uniform across all types of behavioral and cognitive functioning. Simple behaviors, such as reaction time tasks performed in isolation, are generally insensitive to alcohol consumption. Well-practiced behaviors tend to be insensitive to alcohol except at very high doses.

Impairment is seen consistently in tasks requiring the simultaneous processing of multiple sources of information. The results from dual-performance and divided-attention tasks suggest that alcohol reduces the amount of limited-capacity attentional resources available for coordinating multiple tasks. These results provide an important view of how alcohol can produce accidents and injuries. For example, the intoxicated motorist may perform with only moderate impairment on a well-known route with little traffic. However, when a situation arises that requires the simultaneous processing of multiple sources of information, such as avoiding an unexpected obstacle in traffic, large performance deficits may occur.

Alcohol also produces deficits in activities that require fine motor control at high rates of speed. One of the most sensitive behavioral measures of impairment found in the literature is tracking performance, which requires rapid small adjustments in the muscles of the hands and eyes, and a high level of hand-eye coordination. Tracking performance is an important aspect of impairment, in part, because it is central to the lateral guidance of a motor vehicle. Another type of behavior sensitive to alcohol is speech, which requires fine motor control, timing, and coordination among the lips, tongue, and vocal cords at a high rate of speed.

Impairments in eye movements and balance after drinking primarily reflect alcohol's effects on the brain's vestibular system. Alcohol is a small water-soluble molecule that readily diffuses throughout the brain, and impairment is often described in terms of alcohol's general depressant effects on all neural functions. However, impairment in vestibular functioning provides an example of specificity in alcohol's effects. The mechanisms of vestibular impairment have been fairly well characterized, and relate to how alcohol effects the specific physiology of this system. Vestibular functioning is relatively sensitive to alcohol's effects and important for behavioral functioning, and therefore is a logical focus of impairment testing.

There are large individual differences in the impairment produced by alcohol consumption, even when controlling for level of BAC. Several sources of these individual differences have been identified. Perhaps the most important factor is drinking practices. Those who drink more often and in greater amounts tend to develop a greater degree of chronic tolerance to the impairing effects of alcohol, i.e., have an acquired decrease in the degree of impairment across multiple drinking sessions. However, by definition, heavy drinkers tend to consume more and will be more likely to have higher BACs when tested in forensic settings. Thus, heavier drinking practices are probably not predictive of less impairment in field settings because individual differences in BACs are *not* controlled. Impairment tends to be greater in older adults as compared to younger adults; this effect is likely a combination of increased neural vulnerability with aging and differences in drinking practices between young and old. When controlling for BACs and drinking practices, gender differences in impairment have not been demonstrated.

The impairment produced by alcohol depends upon the time course of a drinking episode. Alcohol's effects have been described as biphasic, with initial euphoria and stimulant effects during early rising BACs, followed by dysphoria and sedative effects later on. Numerous measures of impairment are greater on the ascending compared to the descending limb of the BAC curve. This change in impairment due to limb of the BAC curve most likely reflects the phenomenon of acute tolerance, in which alcohol effects decrease over time within a drinking episode. In the prediction of impairment, the amount of time elapsed since alcohol has been in the system can be as important a variable as BAC itself.

The time course of alcohol's effects do not always end when BACs fall to zero. Sufficient drinking can produce hangover in many persons. Hangover is accompanied by impairment in behavioral functioning in some studies. Other research, however, has not found consistent effects of hangover on performance. There appear to be large individual differences in the degree of hangover effects, and their duration. Hangover effects are poorly characterized compared to other effects of alcohol, and are an important topic for further research. The demonstration of significant impairment related to hangover would suggest the need for a longer period of abstinence from alcohol use before job performance in some professions, similar to the rules often applied to airline pilots.

Field sobriety tests, such as the walk and turn, one-leg stand, and horizontal gaze nystagmus tests, can be administered in a standardized fashion and meet the requirements of applicability to the field. These tests have adequate levels of validity, in that they reliably assess functions known to reflect alcohol impairment, and correlate with BACs and other impairment measures. Levels of sensitivity and specificity appear to be fairly high for the horizontal gaze nystagmus test. On the other hand, levels of test sensitivity and specificity are adequate but somewhat low for the walk-and-turn and the one-leg stand. That is, many persons with positive BACs, including those over 100 mg/dl, will be classified as not impaired using these tests, and many persons with low or zero BACs will be classified as impaired. Furthermore, the validity of FSTs for detecting lower threshold BACs such as 50 mg/dl or 20 mg/dl remains to be established. The development of new field sobriety tests that increase the accurate assessment of impairment would be of great benefit in forensic applications.

REFERENCES

1. Carpenter, J. A., Effects of alcohol on some psychological processes, *Quarterly Journal of Studies on Alcohol*, 23, 274, 1980.
2. Levine, J. M., Kramer, J., Levine, E., Effects of alcohol on human performance, *Journal of Applied Psychology*, 60, 508, 1975.
3. Finnigan, F., Hammersley, R., The effects of alcohol on performance, in *Handbook of Human Performance, Volume 2*, Smith, A., Jones, D., Eds., Academic Press Ltd, Orlando, FL, 1992, p. 73.
4. Goldberg, L., Quantitative studies on alcohol tolerance in man. The influence of ethyl alcohol on sensory, motor, and psychological functions referred to blood alcohol in normal and habituated individuals, *Acta Physiol Scand*, 5 (Suppl 16): 1, 1943.
5. Baylor, A. M., Layne, C. S., Mayfield, R. D., Osborne, L., Spirduso, W. W., Effects of ethanol on human fractionated response times, *Drug and Alcohol Dependence*, 23, 31, 1989.
6. Taberner, P. V., Sex differences in the effects of low doses of ethanol on human reaction time, *Psychopharmacology*, 70, 283, 1980.
7. Maylor, E. A., Rabbitt, P. M., James, G. H., Kerr, S. A., Effects of alcohol and extended practice on divided-attention performance, *Perception and Psychophysics*, 48, 445, 1990.
8. Linnoila, M., Erwin, C. W., Ramm, D., Cleveland, W. P., Effects of age and alcohol on psychomotor performance of men, *Journal of Studies on Alcohol*, 41, 488, 1980.
9. Fagan, D., Tiplady, B., Scott, D. B., Effects of ethanol on psychomotor performance, *British Journal of Anaesthesia*, 59, 961, 1987.
10. Golby, J., Use of factor analysis in the study of alcohol-induced strategy changes in skilled performance on a soccer test, *Perceptual and Motor Skills*, 68, 147, 1989.

Christopher S. Martin

11. Connors, G. J., Maisto, S. A., Effects of alcohol instructions and consumption rate on motor performance, *Journal of Studies on Alcohol*, 41, 509, 1980.
12. Beirness, D., Vogel-Sprott, M., Alcohol tolerance in social drinkers: operant and classical conditioning effects, *Psychopharmacology*, 84, 393, 1984.
13. Wilson, J., Erwin, G., McClearn, G., Effects of ethanol, II. behavioral sensitivity and acute behavioral tolerance, *Alcoholism: Clinical and Experimental Research*, 8, 366, 1984.
14. Maylor, E. A., Rabbitt, P. M., Connolly, S. A., Rate of processing and judgment of response speed: comparing the effects of alcohol and practice, *Perception and Psychophysics*, 45, 431, 1989.
15. Moskowitz, H., Burns, M. M., Williams, A. F., Skilled performance at low blood alcohol levels, *Journal of Studies on Alcohol*, 46, 482, 1985.
16. Niaura, R. S., Nathan, P. E., Frankenstein, W., Shapiro, A. P., Brick, J., Gender differences in acute psychomotor, cognitive, and pharmacokinetic response to alcohol, *Addictive Behaviors*, 12, 345, 1987.
17. Mills, K., & Bisgrove, E., Body sway and divided attention performance under the influence of alcohol: dose-response differences between males and females, *Alcoholism: Clinical and Experimental Research*, 7, 393, 1983.
18. Steele, C. M., Josephs, R. A., Drinking your troubles away: II. an attention-allocation model of alcohol's effects on stress, *Journal of Abnormal Psychology*, 97, 196, 1988.
19. Zador, P. L., Alcohol-related relative risk of fatal driver injuries in relation to driver age and sex, *Journal of Studies on Alcohol*, 52, 302, 1991.
20. Hindmarch, I., Bhatti, J. Z., Starmer, G. A., Mascord, D. J., Kerr, J. S., Sherwood, N., The effects of alcohol on the cognitive function of males and females and on skills relating to car driving, *Human Psychopharmacology*, 7, 105, 1992.
21. McMillen, D. L., Smith, S. M., Wells-Parker, E., The effect of alcohol, expectancy, and sensation seeking on driving risk taking, *Addictive Behaviors*, 14, 477, 1989.
22. Mongrain, S., Standing, L., Impairment of cognition, risk-taking, and self-perception by alcohol, *Perceptual and Motor Skills*, 69, 199, 1989.
23. Attwood, D. A., Williams, R. D., Madill, H. D., Effects of moderate blood alcohol concentrations on closed-course driving performance, *Journal of Studies on Alcohol*, 41, 623, 1980.
24. Huntley, M. S., Centybear, T. M., Alcohol, sleep deprivation and driving speed effects upon control use during driving, *Human Factors*, 16, 19, 1974.
25. Brewer, N., Sandow, B., Alcohol effects on driver performance under conditions of divided attention, *Ergonomics*, 23, 185, 1980.
26. Sobell, L. C., Sobell, M. B., Effects of alcohol on the speech of alcoholics, *Journal of Speech and Hearing Research*, 15, 861, 1972.
27. Sobell, L. C., Sobell, M. B., Coleman, R. F., Alcohol-induced dysfluency in nonalcoholics, *Folia Phoniatrica*, 34, 316, 1982.
28. Trojan, F., Kryspin-Exner, K., The decay of articulation under the influence of alcohol and paraldehyde, *Folia Phoniatrica*, 20, 217, 1968.
29. Lester, L., Skousen, R., The phonology of drunkenness, in *Papers from the Parasession on Natural Phonology*, Bruck, A., Fox, R. A., LaGay, M. W., eds., Chicago, Chicago Linguistic Society, 1974, chapter 8.
30. Pisoni, D. B., Martin, C. S., Effects of alcohol on the acoustic-phonetic properties of speech: perceptual and acoustic analyses, *Alcoholism: Clinical and Experimental Research*, 13, 577, 1989.
31. Johnson, K., Pisoni, D. B., Bermacki, R. H., Do voice recordings reveal whether a person is intoxicated? A case study, *Phonetica*, 47, 215, 1990.
32. Iurato, S., *Submicroscopic Structure of the Inner Ear*, London, Pergamon Press, 1967, p 216.
33. Money, K. E., Johnson, W. H., Corlett, B. M., Role of semicircular canals in positional alcohol nystagmus, *American Journal of Physiology*, 208, 1065, 1965.
34. Nito, Y., Johnson, W. H., Money, K. E., The non-auditory labyrinth and positional alcohol nystagmus. *Acta Otolaryngology*, 58, 65, 1964.
35. Money, K. E., Myles, W. S., Hoffert, B. M., The mechanism of positional alcohol nystagmus, *Canadian Journal of Otolaryngology*, 3, 302, 1974.

36. Aschan, G., Gergstedt, M., Positional alcoholic nystagmus (PAN) in man following repeated alcohol doses, *Acta Otolaryngology*, Suppl. 330, 15, 1975.

37. Fregly, A. R., Bergstedt, M., Graybiel, A., Relationships between blood alcohol, positional alcohol nystagmus, and postural equilibrium, *Quarterly Journal of Studies on Alcohol*, 28, 11, 1967.

38. Aschan, G., Different types of alcohol nystagmus, *Acta Otolarnygology*, Suppl. 140, 69, 1958.

39. Behrens, M. M., Nystagmus, *Journal of Opthalmological Clinics*, 18, 57, 1978.

40. Lehti, H., The effect of blood alcohol concentration on the onset of gaze nystagmus, *Blutalkohol*, 13, 411, 1976.

41. Barnes, G.R., Crombie, J.W., Edge, A., The effects of ethanol on visual-vestibular interaction during active and passive head movements, *Aviation, Space, and Environmental Medicine*, July 1985, p. 695.

42. Tharp, V. K., Burns, M., Moskowitz, H., *Development and field test of psychophysical tests for DWI arrest: final report*, technical report DOT-HS-805-864, Washington, D.C., National Highway Traffic Safety Administration, 1981.

43. Goding, G. S., Dobie, R. A., Gaze nystagmus and blood alcohol, *Laryngoscope*, 96, 713, 1986.

44. Baloh, R. W., Sharma, S., Moskowitz, H., Griffith, R., Effect of alcohol and marijuana on eye movements, *Aviation, Space, and Environmental Medicine*, p. 18, January 1979.

45. Gentles, W., Llewellyn-Thomas, E., Effect of benzodiazepines upon saccadic eye movements in man, *Clinical Pharmacology and Theraputics*, 12, 563, 1971.

46. Niaura, R.S., Wilson, G.T., Westrick, E., Self-awareness, alcohol consumption, and reduced cardiovascular reactivity, *Psychosomatic Medicine*, 50, 360, 1988.

47. Lipscomb, T. R., Nathan, P. E., Wilson, G. T., Abrams, D. B., Effects of tolerance on the anxiety-reducing functions of alcohol, *Archives of General Psychiatry*, 37, 577, 1980.

48. Lipscomb, T. R., Nathan, P. E., Effect of family history of alcoholism, drinking pattern, and tolerance on blood alcohol level discrimination, *Archives of General Psychiatry*, 37, 576, 1980.

49. O'Malley, S. S., Maisto, S. A. Factors affecting the perception of intoxication: dose, tolerance, and setting, *Addictive Behaviors*, 9, 111, 1984.

50. Goldstein, D. B., *Pharmacology of Alcohol*, New York, Oxford University Press, 1983.

51. Frezza, M., DiPadova, C., Pozzato, G., Terpin, M., Baraona, E., Lieber, C., High blood alcohol levels in women: the role of decreased gastric alcohol dehydrogenase activity and first-pass metabolism, *New England Journal of Medicine*, 322, 95, 1990.

52. Sutker, P. B., Goist, K., King, A., Acute alcohol intoxication in women: relationship to dose and menstrual cycle phase, *Alcoholism: Clinical and Experimental Research*, 11, 74, 1987.

53. Brick, J., Nathan, P. E., Shapiro, A. P., Westrick, E., Frankenstein, W., The effect of menstrual cycle on blood alcohol levels and behavior, *Journal of Studies on Alcohol*, 47, 472, 1986.

54. Sutker, P. B., Goist, K., Allain, A. N., Bugg, F., Acute alcohol intoxication: sex comparisons on pharmacokinetic and mood measures, *Alcoholism: Clinical and Experimental Research*, 11, 507, 1987.

55. Cole-Harding, S., Wilson, J., Ethanol metabolism in men and women, *Journal of Studies on Alcohol*, 48, 380, 1987.

56. Jones, B. M., Jones, M. K., Alcohol effects in women during the menstrual cycle, *Annals of the New York Academy of Sciences*, 273, 576, 1976.

57. Burns, M., Moskowitz, H., Gender-related differences in impairment of performance by alcohol, in *Currents in Alcoholism, Volume 3: Biological, Biochemical and Clinical Studies*, F. Sexias, Ed., New York: Grune & Stratton, p. 479.

58. Sutker, P. B., Allain, A. N., Brantley, P. S., Randall, C. L., Acute alcohol intoxication, negative affect, and autonomic arousal in women and men, *Addictive Behaviors*, 7, 17, 1982.

59. Parker, E. S., Noble, E. P., Alcohol and the aging process in social drinkers, *Journal of Studies on Alcohol*, 41, 170, 1980.

60. Jones, M. K., Jones, B. M., The relationship of age and drinking habits to the effects of alcohol on memory in women, *Journal of Studies on Alcohol*, 41, 179, 1980.

61. Vogel-Sprott, M., Barrett, P., Age, drinking habits, and the effects of alcohol, *Journal of Studies on Alcohol*, 45, 517, 1984.

Christopher S. Martin

62. York, J. L., Increased responsiveness to ethanol with advancing age in rats, *Pharmacology, Biochemistry, and Behavior*, 19, 687, 1983.
63. Pohorecky, L. A., Biphasic action of ethanol, *Biobehavioral Reviews*, 1, 231, 1977.
64. Martin, C. S., Earleywine, M., Musty, R. E., Perrine, M. W., Swift, R. M., Development and validation of the biphasic alcohol effects scale, *Alcoholism: Clinical and Experimental Research*, 17, 140, 1993.
65. Tucker, J., Vuchinich, R., Sobell, M., Alcohol's effects on human emotions: A review of the stimulation/depression hypothesis, *International Journal of the Addictions*, 17, 155, 1982.
66. deWit, H., Uhlenguth, E., Pierri, J., Johanson, C., Individual differences in behavioral and subjective responses to alcohol, *Alcoholism: Clinical and Experimental Research*, 11, 52, 1987.
67. Nagoshi, C., Wilson, J., One-month repeatability of emotional responses to alcohol, *Alcoholism: Clinical and Experimental Research*, 12, 691, 1988.
68. Freed, E., Alcohol and mood: an updated review. *International Journal of the Addictions*, 13, 173, 1978.
69. Newlin, D., Thomson, J, Chronic tolerance and sensitization to alcohol in sons of alcoholics, *Alcoholism: Clinical and Experimental Research*, 15, 399, 1991.
70. Waller, M., Murphy, J., McBride, W., Effect of low dose ethanol on spontaneous motor activity in alcohol-preferring and non-preferring lines of rats. *Pharmacology, Biochemistry, and Behavior*, 24, 617, 1986.
71. Stewart, J., deWit, H., Eikelboom, R., Role of unconditioned and conditioned drug effects in the self-administration of opiates and stimulants, *Psychological Review*, 91, 251, 1984.
72. Wise, R., Bozarth, M., A psychomotor stimulant theory of addiction, *Psychological Review*, 94, 469, 1987.
73. Connors, G. J., Maisto, S. A., Effects of alcohol instructions and consumption rate on affect and physiological sensations, *Psychopharmacology*, 62, 261, 1979.
74. Lukas, S., Mendelson, J., Benedikt, R., Instrumental analysis of ethanol-induced intoxication in human males, *Psychopharmacology*, 89, 89, 1986.
75. Martin, C. S., Earleywine, M., Ascending and descending rates of change of blood alcohol concentrations and subjective intoxication ratings, *Journal of Substance Abuse*, 2, 345, 1990.
76. Moskowitz, H., Burns M., Effects of rate of drinking on human performance, *Journal of Studies on Alcohol*, 37, 598, 1976.
77. Wilson, J., Nagoshi, C., Adult children of alcoholics: cognitive and psychomotor characteristics, *British Journal of Addiction*, 83, 809, 1988.
78. Engel, J., Liljequist, S., The involvement of different central neurotransmitters in mediating stimulatory and sedative effects of ethanol, in *Stress and Alcohol Use*, Pohorecky, L. A., Brick, J., Eds., New York: Elsevier Biomedical, 153, 1983.
79. Tabakoff, B., Hoffman, P., Tolerance and the etiology of alcoholism: hypothesis and mechanism, *Alcoholism: Clinical and Experimental Research*, 12, 184, 1988.
80. Gabrielli, W., Nagoshi, C., Rhea, S., Wilson, J., Anticipated and subjective sensitivities to alcohol, *Journal of Studies on Alcohol*, 52, 205, 1991.
81. Schuckit, M., Subjective responses to alcohol in sons of alcoholics and control subjects, *Archives of General Psychiatry*, 41, 879, 1984.
82. Mellanby, E., *Alcohol: Its absorption and disappearance from the blood under different conditions*, London, Her Majesty's Statistical Office, Great Britain Medical Research Council, 1919.
83. Gilliam, D., Alcohol absorption rate affects hypothermic response in mice: evidence for acute tolerance, *Alcohol*, 6, 357, 1989.
84. Martin, C. S., Rose, R. J., Obremski, K. M., Estimation of blood alcohol concentrations in young male drinkers, *Alcoholism: Clinical and Experimental Research*, 15, 494, 1990.
85. Waller, M., McBride, W., Lumeng, L., Li, T. K., Initial sensitivity and acute tolerance to ethanol in the P and NP lines of rats, *Pharmacology, Biochemistry, and Behavior*, 19, 683, 1983.
86. Kaplan, H., Sellers, E., Hamilton, C. Is there acute tolerance to alcohol at a steady state?, *Journal of Studies on Alcohol*, 46, 253, 1985.
87. Martin, C. S., Moss, H. B., Measurement of acute tolerance to alcohol in human subjects, *Alcoholism: Clinical and Experimental Research*, 17, 211, 1993.

88. Nagoshi, C., Wilson, J., Long-term repeatability of alcohol metabolism, sensitivity, and acute tolerance, *Journal of Studies on Alcohol*, 50, 162, 1989.
89. Radlow, R., Hurst, P., Temporal relations between blood alcohol concentration and alcohol effect: an experiment with human subjects. *Psychopharmacology*, 85, 260, 1985.
90. Benton, R. Banks, W., Vogler, R., Carryover of tolerance to ethanol in moderate drinkers, *Journal of Studies on Alcohol*, 42, 1137, 1982.
91. Hurst, P., Bagley, S., Acute adaptation to the effects of alcohol, *Journal of Studies on Alcohol*, 33, 358, 1972.
92. LeBlanc, A., Kalant, H., Gibbons, R., Acute tolerance to ethanol in the rat, *Psychopharmacolgia*, 41, 43, 1975.
93. Kalant, H., LeBlanc, A., Gibbons, R., Tolerance to, and dependence on, some non-opiate psychotropic drugs, *Pharmacology Review*, 23, 135, 1971.
94. Vogel-Sprott, M., *Alcohol tolerance and social drinking: learning the consequences*, New York, Guilford Press, 1992.
95. Vogel-Sprott, M., Kartchner, W., McConnell, D., Consequences of behavior influence the effect of alcohol, *Journal of Substance Abuse*, 1, 369, 1989.
96. Newlin, D. B., Pretorious, M., Sons of alcoholics report greater hangover symptoms than sons of non-alcoholics: a pilot study, *Alcoholism: Clinical and Experimental Research*, 14, 713, 1990.
97. Collins, W. E., Schroeder, D. J., Gilson, R. D., Guedry, F. E., Effects of alcohol ingestion on tracking performance during angular acceleration, *Journal of Applied Psychology*, 55, 559, 1971.
98. Eckman, G., Frankenhaeuser, M., Goldberg, L., Hagdahl, R., Myrsten, A. L., Subjective and objective effects of alcohol as functions of dosage and time, *Psychopharmacologia*, 6, 399, 1964.
99. Kelly, M., Myrsten, A. L., Neri, A., Rydberg, U., Effects and after-effects of alcohol on psychological and physiological functions in man — a controlled study, *Blutalkohol*, 7, 422, 1970.
100. Collins, W. E., Chiles, W. D., Laboratory performance during acute alcohol intoxication and hangover, *Human Factors*, 22, 445, 1980.
101. Laurell, H., Tornros, J., Franck, D. H., If you drink, don't drive: the motto now applies to hangovers as well, *Journal of the American Medical Association Medical News*, October 7, 1983, p. 1657.
102. Yesavage, J. A., Leirer, V. O., Hangover effects on aircraft pilots 14 hours after alcohol ingestion: a preliminary report, *American Journal of Psychiatry*, 143, 1546, 1986.
103. Karvinen, E., Miettinen, A., Ahlman, K., Physical performance during hangover, *Quarterly Journal of Studies on Alcohol*, 23, 208, 1962.
104. Takala, M., Siro, E., Tiovainen, Y., Intellectual functions and dexterity during hangover, *Quarterly Journal of Studies on Alcohol*, 19, 1, 1958.
105. Allen, J. P., Litten, R. Z., Anton, R., Measures of alcohol consumption in perspective, in Litten, R. Z., Allen, J. P. (Eds.) *Measuring alcohol consumption: psychosocial and biochemical methods*, Totowa, NJ, Humana Press, 1992, p. 205.
106. Meehl, P. E., Rosen, A., Antecedent probability and the efficiency of psychometric signs, patterns, or cutting scores, *Psychological Bulletin*, 52, 194, 1952.
107. National Highway Traffic Safety Administration, *DWI detection and standardized field sobriety testing: administrators guide*, DOT-HS-178/RI/90, Washington, D.C., National Highway Traffic Safety Administration.
108. Anderson, T. E., Schweitz, R. M., Snyder, M. B., *Field evaluation of a behavioral test battery for DWI*, DOT-HS-806-475, Washington, D.C., National Highway Traffic Safety Administration.
109. Perrine, M. W., Foss, R. D., Meyers, A. R., Voas, R. B., Velez, C., Field sobriety tests: reliability and validity, in *Alcohol, Drugs and Traffic Safety-T92*, Utelmann, Berghaus, Kroj, Eds., Verlag TUV Rheinland, Cologne, Germany, 1993.

5.2 MEASURING BLOOD-ALCOHOL CONCENTRATION FOR CLINICAL AND FORENSIC PURPOSES

A. WAYNE JONES

DEPARTMENT OF FORENSIC TOXICOLOGY, UNIVERSITY HOSPITAL, LINKÖPING, SWEDEN

DERRICK J. POUNDER

DEPARTMENT OF FORENSIC MEDICINE, UNIVERSITY OF DUNDEE, SCOTLAND, UK

Measuring the concentration of alcohol in biological specimens (whole blood, serum, plasma, urine, saliva, and breath) involves the use of relatively simple analytical procedures. The first qualitative methods, albeit primitive, were used in forensic toxicology more than a century ago when deaths from gross intoxication were investigated.[1] Over the years, the methods available for measuring alcohol in blood and other body fluids have become increasingly refined.[2,3]

Unlike the results from other laboratory methods of analysis, the concentration of ethanol in body fluids has deep-rooted social-medical and forensic implications. This follows because of the commonly accepted association between a person's blood-alcohol concentration (BAC) and the degree of impairment.[4,5] Indeed, heavy drinking represents a major cause of accidents on the roads, in the workplace, and within the home, and alcohol abuse and drunkenness are contributing factor in many suicides, trauma deaths, violent crimes, and other kinds of deviant behavior.[6-9] The analysis of alcohol in body fluids has, therefore, emerged as the most frequently requested procedure in forensic science and toxicology.[10]

Furthermore, fast and reliable methods of alcohol analysis are needed in clinical and emergency medicine whenever a patient is admitted unconscious smelling of alcohol, because in these acute situations it is imperative to decide whether gross intoxication or head trauma or both are involved.[11,12] The presence of intracranial blood clots or hemorrhage resulting from head injuries requires swift diagnosis and treatment.[13-15] Moreover, overconsumption of ethanol needs to be quickly distinguished from intoxication caused by drinking a more dangerous alcohol such as methanol or ethylene glycol[16] so that a decision can be made to use invasive therapy including hemodialysis to clear from the blood the toxic metabolites of methanol (formic acid) and ethylene glycol (glycolate and oxalate).[17,18]

The role of alcohol intoxication in traffic accidents is well recognized[19-21] and threshold concentration limits have been defined by statute known as per se alcohol limits.[22] This legal framework means that a certain concentration of alcohol in a specimen of blood, breath, or urine is sufficient to decide a person's guilt or innocence and places extremely high demands on accuracy, precision, and selectivity of the methods of analysis used.[23] Besides threshold blood-alcohol concentration limits for driving, testing for alcohol in the workplace is now regulated by statutes in the U.S. (1991 Omnibus Transportation Employee Testing Act), and similar legislation can be expected to follow in other countries. The act permits conducting pre-employment testing as well as testing individuals engaged with safety-sensitive duties. including random testing, post-accident testing, probable cause testing, return-to-duty, and follow-up testing.[24] Two important concentration limits exist in connection with workplace alcohol testing and these are currently fixed at 20 mg/dL in blood (0.02 g/210 L breath), below which no action is taken. However, drinking on duty or having a blood-alcohol concentration above 40 mg/dL (0.04 g/210 L breath) are prohibited and the offending individual will be removed from participating in safety-sensitive work.[24]

Punishment and sanctions for driving under the influence of alcohol (DUI) are becoming increasingly severe and include fines, suspension of the driving license, and sometimes a period of mandatory imprisonment or even dismissal and loss of salary in connection with workplace alcohol testing. Moreover, the validity of accident and insurance claims might be null and void if a person's blood-alcohol concentration exceeds some critical threshold limit. The connection between ingestion of alcohol, the person's BAC, and various penalties for over-consumption emphasizes the need to use highly reliable methods for measuring alcohol in blood and other body fluids.

This review deals with clinical and forensic aspects of measuring alcohol when the blood samples are obtained from living subjects. In post-mortem work, the choice of specimens, the method of collection, and, in particular, the interpretation of the analytical results require special considerations. These autopsy issues are covered in more detail in Section 5.3.

5.2.1 UNITS OF CONCENTRATION — PLASMA/SERUM VS. WHOLE BLOOD

One difference between reporting results of alcohol measurements made for clinical purposes and those made for forensic science purposes concerns the units of concentration used. In clinical chemistry laboratories, the SI system is the norm where the mole is the unit of mass and the liter is the unit of volume.[25] The concentration of alcohol in clinical biochemistry is therefore reported as mmol/L or mol/L. By contrast, in forensic science laboratories, the concentrations of ethanol in body fluids are reported in terms of mass per unit volume (mg/dL, g/L, g/dL or mg/mL) or mass per unit mass (g/kg or mg/g). The mass/mass unit of concentration is numerically less than the mass/volume unit by 5.5% because the specific weight of whole blood is 1.055 on the average (1 mL whole blood weighs 1.055 g), so a blood-alcohol concentration of 100 mg/dL is the same as 95 mg/100 g or 21.7 mmoL/L.

When blood samples are analyzed for forensic purposes, a standard procedure is to make duplicate determinations because close agreement between the two results gives the added assurance that a mishap has not occurred when the first determination was made. Besides reporting the mean concentration of alcohol, an allowance should be made to compensate for uncertainty in the method of analysis. This is easily done by making a deduction from the mean BAC to allow for analytical errors and thereby reporting a confidence limit such as 95%, 99%, or 99.9% depending on requirements.[26]

In Sweden, for example, a triplicate blood-alcohol determination is made in all DUI investigations and the lower 99.9% confidence limit on the mean is the value used for prosecution. The amount deducted is given by $3.09\left(SD/3^{1/2}\right)$ where SD is the standard deviation of a single determination at the prevailing BAC for an analytical process under statistical control. Although the mean result gives the best estimate of a person's BAC at the time of sampling, the value that remains after making the deduction is not more than the true BAC with a probability of 99.9%. This means that the risk of reporting a false high result is 1 in 1000 and any remaining uncertainty has relevance only for those individuals with a BAC very close to the critical legal limit for driving.

This practice of reporting analytical results together with confidence intervals for the individual blood-sample analyzed is uncommon in clinical laboratories where single determinations of an analyte are made. Instead, in clinical chemistry laboratories, variability or imprecision of an analytical method is monitored by calculating a coefficient of variation (CV%) derived from analyzing calibration standards or spiked biological specimens along with the unknowns.[27]

Another difference between the analytical work of forensic laboratories as opposed to clinical laboratories concerns the condition of the specimens submitted for analysis. Forensic

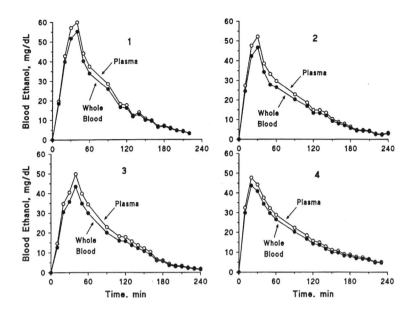

Figure 5.2.1a Concentration-time profiles of ethanol in specimens of whole blood and plasma from four healthy men who drank a bolus dose of ethanol 0.30 g/kg mixed with orange juice in 5 min after an overnight fast.

laboratories normally receive samples of whole blood and these are often hemolyzed and sometimes contain clots,[28] whereas clinical laboratories receive samples of plasma or serum.[29] The amounts of water in these specimens are not the same, with mean values of 91.8 % w/w (SD 0.49) for plasma/serum and 80.1 % w/w (SD 1.03) for whole blood.[30] The results of analyzing alcohol at a clinical laboratory should not be cited in legal proceedings concerning DUI or work-related accidents without an appropriate correction being made or seeking expert help with interpretation of the results.[31,32]

Figure 5.2.1a shows examples of the concentration-time profiles of ethanol in plasma and whole blood. Four healthy men fasted overnight before drinking, within 5 min, ethanol diluted with orange juice in a dose of 0.30 g ethanol per kg body weight. Note that the plasma curves run systematically higher than the whole-blood curves as expected from the water-content of the specimens analyzed. In these 4 subjects, the mean plasma/whole blood ratio of alcohol was 1.10:1 with a range from 1.08 to 1.13. In drinking drivers, the distribution of ethanol between plasma and whole blood had a mean of 1.14:1 (standard deviation 0.041) according to a recent study.[33] Table 5.2.1b compares the concentrations of alcohol in plasma with values expected to exist in whole blood based on a mean plasma/whole blood concentration ratio of 1.14:1. The results are reported in different units of concentration including SI units.

As discussed by Rainey,[29] if the concentration of alcohol in plasma or serum is used to estimate the concentration in whole blood for law enforcement purposes, it is advisable to consider inherent analytical and biological sources of variations in the plasma/blood relationship. A plasma/blood ratio of 1.22:1 corresponds to the mean + 2SD, and this higher conversion factor should be used in forensic work instead of a mean value of 1.14:1. This gives a more conservative estimate of BAC for use in criminal litigation if and when drunk drivers are prosecuted on the basis of the concentration of alcohol determined in plasma or serum. In criminal law, a beyond a reasonable doubt standard is necessary to obtain a verdict of guilty, whereas in civil litigation a preponderance of the evidence is sufficient to determine the outcome.[29]

Table 5.2.1b Comparison of the Concentrations of Ethanol in Whole Blood with Values Expected in Plasma or Serum when Expressed in Different Units of Concentration[a]

Concentration units mg/ml or g/L		Concentration units mg/dL or mg/100 ml		Concentration units g/% w/v or g/100mL		Concentration units mmol/l	
Blood	Plasma/ serum	Blood	Plasma/ serum	Blood	Plasma/ serum	Blood	Plasma/ serum
0.10	0.114	10	11.4	0.010	0.114	2.17	2.47
0.50	0.57	50	57	0.050	0.057	10.7	12.2
1.00	1.14	100	114	0.100	0.114	21.7	24.7
2.00	2.28	200	228	0.200	0.228	43	49.0
5.00	5.70	500	570	0.50	0.570	107	122

[a] *The concentrations in whole blood were derived from the concentration in plasma by dividing by 1.14. If the results are intended for use in forensic casework where a threshold limit in whole blood operates, then a more conservative conversion factor such as 1.22:1 should be used.*

5.2.2 METHODS OF MEASURING ALCOHOL IN BODY FLUIDS

5.2.2.1 Chemical Oxidation Methods

The first quantitative method of blood-alcohol analysis to gain general acceptance in forensic science and toxicology was published in 1922[34] and was known as Widmark's micromethod (developed by Erik MP Widmark of Sweden). A specimen of capillary blood (100 mg) was sufficient for making a single determination and this could be obtained by pricking a fingertip or earlobe. Ethanol was determined by wet-chemistry oxidation with a mixture of potassium dichromate and sulphuric acid in excess. The amount of oxidizing agent remaining after the reaction was determined by iodometric titration. Specially designed diffusion flasks allowed extraction of ethanol from the biological matrix by heating to 50°C before making the final titrimetric analysis. The Widmark method was not specific for measuring blood-ethanol because if other volatiles were present, such as acetone, methanol, or ether, these were oxidized and falsely reported as being ethanol. Evidence for the presence or absence of potential interfering substances was sometimes obtained by qualitative screening tests such as observation of various color changes after adding reagents to test for urinary ketones, methanol, formaldehyde, or acetaldehyde.[35]

By the 1950s, chemical methods were modified in various ways such as by the use of photometry to determine the endpoint of the oxidation reaction instead of volumetric titration. However, analytical procedures based on wet-chemistry oxidation are now virtually obsolete in clinical and forensic laboratories for measuring the concentration of alcohol in body fluids. The history, development, and application of chemical oxidation methods of alcohol analysis have been well covered in several review articles.[2,35-38]

5.2.2.2 Enzymatic Methods

Shortly after the enzyme alcohol dehydrogenase (ADH) was purified from horse liver and yeast in the late 1940s, the way was clear for developing biochemical methods for measuring alcohol in body fluids.[39-42] These became known as ADH methods and the milder conditions for oxidation of ethanol gave enhanced selectivity compared with wet-chemistry oxidation methods.[40,42] However, other primary alcohols such as isopropanol or n-propanol, if these are present in the blood samples, are also oxidized by ADH and this leads to false high concentrations of ethanol being reported.[43] By optimizing the reaction conditions in terms of pH, time, and temperature, methanol was not oxidized by yeast ADH and this source of the enzyme became widely used for clinical and forensic alcohol analysis.[42] In a typical manual ADH

A. Wayne Jones and Derrick J. Pounder

method, blood-proteins were precipitated with $HClO_4$ or CCl_3COOH and after adjusting pH of the supernatant to 9.6 with semicarbazide buffer, the enzyme and coenzyme (NAD^+) were added to start the reaction. The NAD^+ is reduced to NADH in direct proportion to the concentration of ethanol present in the sample being analyzed and after about 1 h the amount of reduced coenzyme is monitored by its absorption of UV radiation at 340 nm.

Later developments in ADH methods meant that proteins in the blood could be separated from the aqueous phase on-line, either by dialysis or micro-distillation.[44] With this modification and the use of an AutoAnalyzer instrument, several hundred blood samples could be analyzed daily. Scores of publications were produced describing various modifications and improvements to the original ADH method and dedicated reagent kits soon became commercially available. These kits were ideal for use at hospital laboratories and elsewhere where the throughput of samples was relatively low. Otherwise, most efforts were directed towards automating the sample preparation and the dispensing of reagents to increase sample throughput and several batch analyzers appeared including a micro-centrifugal analyzer making use of fluorescence light scattering for quantitative analysis.[45,46]

Interest in the use of ADH methods for measuring alcohol in blood and urine have expanded greatly over the past decade owing to the development of methods for drug-abuse testing. In these new procedures, a technique known as enzyme multiplied immunoassay (EMIT) is used whereby an enzyme-labeled antigen reacts with ethanol and the color change of an added substrate is measured by spectrophotometry and the result translated into the concentration of ethanol. Fluorescence polarization immunoassay (FPIA) and the spin-off method known as radiative energy attenuation (REA) detection are other examples of analytical technologies developed to meet the increasing demand for drugs of abuse testing in urine and also for therapeutic drug monitoring. These analytical systems include options for measuring ethanol in biological specimens and results reported in several publications show good agreement in terms of accuracy and precision compared with those obtained by gas chromatography.[47-50] The principles and practice of various immunoassay systems suitable for clinical laboratory analysis were recently reviewed.[51]

Despite these new developments in analytical technology for blood-alcohol testing, particularly EMIT, FPIA, and REA methods, gas chromatography still is the instrument of choice at forensic laboratories owing to its superior selectivity. Indeed, some recent work has shown that serum lactate and lactate dehydrogenase might interfere with the analysis of alcohol by ADH methods.[52] This problem was traced to various side-reactions in which the coenzyme NAD^+ was reduced to NADH which could not be distinguished from the NADH produced during the oxidation of ethanol. This resulted in undesirable false positive results when plasma specimens from alcohol-free patients were analyzed.

5.2.2.3 Gas Chromatographic Methods

In the early 1960s, physical-chemical methods were applied to the analysis of alcohol in body fluids such as infrared spectrometry, electrochemical oxidation, and gas-liquid chromatography (GLC).[2] For the analysis of biological liquids, GLC has become the method of choice in clinical and forensic laboratories whereas electrochemistry and infrared methods are used for analyzing breath alcohol.[2,3] The first GLC methods required that ethanol was extracted from blood by use of a solvent (n-propyl acetate) or by distillation, but later the blood sample was simply diluted (1:5 or 1:10) with an aqueous solution of an internal standard (n-propanol or t-butanol).[53-57] This initial dilution step eliminated matrix effects so that aqueous alcohol standards could be used for calibration and standardization of the detector response. The use of an internal standard meant that any unexpected variations in the GC operating conditions during an analysis influenced the response of ethanol and the standard alike so the ratio of peak heights or peak areas (ethanol/standard) remained constant.[57]

Figure 5.2 2.3a Gas chromatographic trace obtained from analysis of a blood sample containing eight volatile substances. The analysis was done by headspace gas chromatography using a packed column (2 m x 3 mm id.) containing Carbopack C (0.2% Carbowax 1500 on Carbopack 80-100 mesh) as the stationary phase. The components of the mixture were identified as follows: 1 = methanol, 2 = Ethanol, 3 = acetone, 4 = isopropanol, 5 = t-butanol, 6 = methyl ethyl ketone, 7 = 2-butanol.

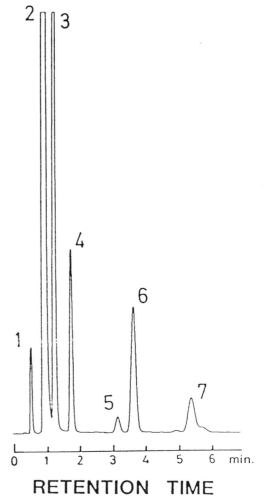

RETENTION TIME

About 1 to 5 µl of the diluted blood specimen was vapourized in a stream of nitrogen, as a carrier gas (mobile phase), which flowed through a glass or metal column having the dimensions 2 m long by 0.3 mm i.d. and which contained the liquid stationary phase spread as a thin film over an inert solid support material to provide a large surface area. The volatile components of a mixture distribute between the moving phase (carrier gas) and the liquid phase and depending on physicochemical properties such as the boiling point, the functional groups present, and the relative solubility in the liquid phase, either partial or complete separation occurs during passage through the column. Polar stationary phases were an obvious choice for the analysis of alcohols and polyethylene glycol with average molecular weights of 400, 600, 1500, etc. becoming widely available and known as Carbowax phases.[57] Otherwise, porous polymer materials such as Poropak Q and S served as packing materials for the GC columns when low-molecular weight alcohols were analyzed.

The effluent from the column was monitored continuously as a function of time with a thermal conductivity (TC) detector, but this was later replaced by a flame ionization (FI) detector, which was more sensitive and gave only a very small response to water vapor present in body fluids. The concentration of ethanol in blood was determined by comparing the detector response (peak height or peak area) obtained by analyzing identically treated known strength aqueous alcohol standards and making a calibration plot. Methodological details of many of the older GC methods of blood-alcohol analysis have been reviewed elsewhere.[58,59] A manual prepared by Dubowski[60] as a report to the U.S. Government is particularly detailed and makes a useful reference source for more information about GC methods of blood-alcohol analysis.

Gas chromatographic headspace (GC-HS) analysis (Figure 5.2 2.3a) is now the method of choice for the analysis of alcohol and other volatile substances in blood and tissue in forensic science and toxicology laboratories.[61-63] HS-GC requires that the blood samples and aqueous standards are first diluted (1:5 or 1:10) with an aqueous solution of an internal standard and the mixture is then allowed to equilibrate at 50 or 60°C in glass vials kept airtight with crimped-on rubber septums. Prolonged heating of the blood specimen at 60°C converts some of the ethanol into acetaldehyde by a non-enzymatic oxidation reaction involving oxyhemoglobin. This undesirable effect can be avoided by pretreating the blood specimen with sodium

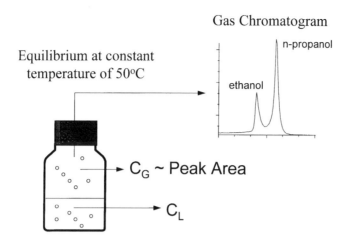

Figure 5.2.2.3b Schematic diagram of the headspace sampling procedure for gas chromatographic analysis. The biological sample is first diluted 1:10 with an aqueous solution of an internal standard such as n-propanol or t-butanol and then made air-tight in a small glass flask with crimped on rubber membrane. After reaching equilibration at 50°C for 15 to 20 min, a sample of the vapor above the diluted blood specimen is removed with a gas-tight syringe or by an automated sampling arrangement and injected into the carrier gas (N_2) for transport through the chromatographic column containing the stationary phase. The resulting trace on a strip-chart recorder shows a peak for ethanol followed by a peak for the internal standard (n-propanol).

azide or sodium dithionite[64,65] or using a lower equilibrium temperature (40 or 50°C) also hinders this oxidation reaction.

The headspace sampling procedure is shown schematically in Figure 5.2.2.3b where a portion of the vapor in equilibrium with the diluted blood sample is removed with the aid of a gas-tight syringe or by an automated headspace sampling device and a highly reproducible injection made onto the chromatographic column. Several manufacturers offer dedicated equipment for headspace analysis and the Perkin-Elmer company has dominated this market since the early 1960s. Various GC headspace instruments have been produced and, in chronological order, these were denoted Multifract HS-40, HS-42, HS-45, and more recently HS-100 mounted on a Sigma 2000 gas chromatograph. This latter combination allows batch analysis of up to 100 samples in a single run but unfortunately this option is no longer available because the HS-GC units currently marketed have the capacity to hold only 40 specimens. This seriously limits the number of blood specimens that can be analyzed in a single run because several calibration control standards and blanks must also be included.

Packed, wide-bore, and capillary columns are feasible[66] for use with headspace gas chromatography. For high resolution work such as when complex mixtures are being analyzed, capillary columns are essential. Traditional packed columns are, however, more robust and those made of glass or stainless steel with dimensions such as 2 m long x 3 mm i.d. are still widely used for routine blood-alcohol analysis because the number of volatile components that might be present is fairly limited.[2,3] Figure 5.2.2.3a shows an example of a gas chromatogram obtained by headspace analysis of an eight-component mixture of low-molecular volatile substances including ethanol with a glass column packed with Carbopak C (0.2% Carbowax 1500 on graphitized carbon black 80 to 100 mesh).

Because HS-GC involves sampling the vapor in equilibrium with the blood specimen, the non- volatile constituents of the biological matrix do not accumulate and clog the GC column or contaminate the packing material. Sensitivity of the assay can be enhanced and matrix effects eliminated in another way, namely by saturating the blood samples and aqueous ethanol standards with an inorganic salt such as NaCl or K_2CO_3, e.g., 0.5 ml blood + 1 g salt.[67,68] This salting-out technique has proven useful for analyzing trace concentrations of volatiles in blood such as the endogenous alcohols.[69] The advantages of salting-out methods have been discussed in many publications including the comprehensive review by Dubowski.[60,64]

Analysis of blood by headspace GC was combined with a cryofocusing technique, or freeze trap, to concentrate the specimen prior to chromatographic separation of the volatile components with a capillary column. This modification was applied to the assay of complex mixtures of volatiles, for example, the congeners present in alcoholic beverages to determine whether these might be identified in blood samples after drinking.[70]

Gas chromatographic methods of analysis offer the unique advantage of combining a qualitative screening analysis of the components of a mixture based on the time after injection to the appearance of the peak (retention time) with simultaneous quantitative analysis by measuring the detector response as reflected in the height or area under the peak. Several recent reviews have dealt with the use of gas chromatography in forensic science including applications for blood- alcohol analysis.[71,72] Another good review looked at more general applications of headspace analysis when applied to biological specimens for analysis of organic volatile substances, including alcohols.[73]

In forensic work, it is advisable for duplicate determinations to be made on two different column packing materials, thus furnishing different retention times for ethanol. This is important if the blood or tissue samples are putrefied and therefore might contain interfering substances having the same retention times as ethanol when a single stationary phase is used. The risk of obtaining coincident retention times on two or more stationary phases is reduced considerably. Otherwise, two different methodologies such as GC and chemical oxidation or GC and enzymatic oxidation could be used to analyze duplicate aliquots from the same blood sample.[74] HS-GC with two different detectors (flame ionization and electron capture) has been used to screen biological fluids for a large number of volatiles. This dual-detector system was recommended for use in clinical toxicology to aid in the diagnosis of acute poisoning when a host of unknown substances might be responsible for the patients condition.[75]

5.2.2.4 Other Methods

A multitude of other analytical methods has been described for blood-alcohol analysis but none of these can match HS-GC which has become the gold standard in forensic and clinical toxicology laboratories. Methods of measuring blood-alcohol concentration by headspace analysis with electrochemical sensing[76] or a metal oxide semiconductor device[77] were reported, but these are not sufficiently selective when interfering substances might be present. These procedures could be useful to rapidly screen biological samples and thus eliminate specimens that do not contain any alcohol. A modified headspace procedure with a fuel-cell sensor was described for measuring the strength of alcoholic beverages and the results obtained compared favorably with a standard gas chromatographic method.[78]

Several novel methods for analysis of alcohol make use of biosensors prepared from immobilized enzymes. These constructions, called bioelectrodes, have found several applications in clinical laboratory analysis.[79] The end-point of the enzymatic reactions can be monitored either by amperometry, colorimetry, or spectrophotometry.[80-82] The enzyme alcohol oxidase has attracted attention for analysis of alcohol in body fluids and gives reasonably good semi-quantitative results.[83-85] These systems are similar in principle to measuring blood glucose with a glucose oxidase electrode and open-up the possibility for self-testing applications such as the glucose dipstick technology.[86] Fourier transform infrared spectrometry (FTIR) was recently applied to the determination of alcohol in beer[87] and when a purge-and-trap capillary GC separation stage was included, FTIR could also be adopted to measure a wide range of low-molecular weight volatiles including ethanol.[88] A method based on proton nuclear magnetic resonance spectroscopy proved suitable in pharmacokinetic studies to analyze ethanol, acetone, and isopropanol in plasma samples.[89,90]

In clinical and emergency medicine, freezing point depression osmometry has a long history as a screening test for certain pathological states.[91] Diabetes mellitus and uraemia, often associated with abnormally high concentrations of plasma-glucose and plasma-urea, respectively, cause discrepancies between the osmolality expected from the inorganic ions Na+ and K+ and the values measured by depression of the freezing point. Dedicated equipment is available for measuring freezing-point depression and the test can be done on as little as 0.2 ml plasma. Moreover, the method is non-destructive which means that the same specimen of plasma can be used later for making a toxicological confirmatory analysis if necessary.

The most common cause of finding an increased osmolal gap in plasma samples from emergency service patients is a high concentration of ethanol.[91] Ethanol carries an appreciable osmotic effect because of its low molecular weight (46.05), high solubility in water, and the fact that large quantities are ingested to produce intoxication.[92] Finding a normal osmolal gap speaks against the presence of high concentrations of plasma-ethanol but the reverse conclusion does not hold because ingestion of other solvents such as acetone, methanol, isopropanol, or ethylene glycol, also lowers the freezing point resulting in increased serum or plasma osmolality. The principal limitation of freezing point osmometry as a rapid screening test for plasma-ethanol is obviously the lack of selectivity because other non-electrolytes could be falsely reported as ethanol. Nevertheless, articles continue to be published dealing with the principles and practice of freezing point osmometry in emergency toxicology.[93]

Considerable interest has developed in point-of-care or near patient testing and this treatment paradigm speaks in favor of noninvasive methods of biochemical analysis. Near-infrared spectrometry is a technique with huge prospects and possibilities for the future because drawing blood or puncturing the skin is not necessary.[94] Infrared light is beamed through a subject's fingertip or earlobe and after processing the absorption bands of the emitted light into specific wavelengths, various constituents in the bloodstream can be identified and for some substances a quantitative analysis is possible. However, disentangling the signals of interest from the background noise generated by other biological molecules has proven a challenging problem but progress is rapidly being made with the help of sophisticated computer-aided pattern recognition techniques. Near-infrared spectroscopy has already been successfully applied to the analysis of blood glucose[95] and it will not be long before attention is given to the analysis of drugs of abuse including ethanol.

The feasibility of combining gas chromatography (GC) to separate the volatile components in a mixture and mass spectrometry (MS) as the detector was demonstrated many years ago.[96] GC-MS provides an unequivocal qualitative analysis of ethanol from its three major mass fragments m/z 31 (base peak), m/z 45, and m/z 46 (molecular ion).[96] Selected ion monitoring and deuterium labelled ethanol was used to distinguish between ethanol formed post-mortem by the action of bacteria on blood glucose.[97,98] Also, in clinical pharmacokinetics, ordinary ethanol was analyzed in blood along with its deuterium-labeled analogue to investigate the bioavailability of ethanol and the role of first-pass metabolism in the gut.[99]

5.2.3 BREATH ALCOHOL ANALYSIS

A small amount of the alcohol a person drinks is expelled unchanged in the breath and breath-alcohol measurements provide a fast and non-invasive way to monitor alcohol in the body. A large literature base exists describing the principles and practice of breath-alcohol analysis and the design and evaluation of a multitude of breath-testing instruments for research, clinical, and forensic purposes.[100-102] Analysis of the expired air is also an indirect way to monitor the concentration of other volatile endogenous substances in the pulmonary blood and this approach has found many interesting applications in clinical and diagnostic medicine.[103,104] However, the main application of breath-alcohol analysis is in the field of traffic law enforcement for testing drunk drivers and more recently also for workplace alcohol testing.[2,24,102] Two categories of instruments for breath-alcohol analysis are available depending on whether the results are intended as a qualitative screening test for alcohol or for quantitative evidential purposes.

Various hand-held devices are being used for roadside pre-arrest screening of drinking drivers to indicate whether their BAC or BrAC exceeds a certain threshold statutory concentration limit for driving.[2,102,105,106] The instruments used for evidential purposes provide a quantitative analysis of BrAC and the result is used as binding evidence for prosecuting drunk drivers.[107-109] Breath-alcohol instruments have also found applications in clinical pharmacokinetic studies of ethanol and drug-alcohol interactions.[110] Hand-held breath-alcohol analyzers are very practical for use in emergency medicine as a quick and easy way to monitor whether patients have been drinking and to estimate the alcohol load in the body.[111-113]

Most of the hand-held screening devices incorporate electrochemical fuel-cell sensors that oxidize ethanol to acetaldehyde and in the process produce free electrons. The electric current generated is directly proportional to the amount of ethanol consumed by the cell. Acetone, which is the most abundant endogenous volatile exhaled in breath, is not oxidized at the electrode surface so this ketone does not give false-positive responses.[114,115] However, if high concentrations of methanol or isopropanol are present in exhaled breath, these are oxidized in the same electrochemical reaction but at different rates compared with ethanol.[113] Care is sometimes needed when the results are interpreted because isopropanol might be produced naturally in the body by the reduction of endogenous acetone.[115] The concentration of acetone in blood reaches abnormally high levels during food deprivation, prolonged fasting (dieting), or during diabetic ketoacidosis.[114]

Most of the evidential breath-testing instruments used today identify and measure the concentration of alcohol by its absorption of infrared energy at wavelengths of 3.4 or 9.5 microns, which correspond to the C-H and C-O vibrational stretching in the ethanol molecules, respectively.[2,100] Selectivity for identifying ethanol can be enhanced by combining infrared absorption at 9.5 microns and electrochemical oxidation within the same unit. The Alcotest 7410 features this dual-sensor technique. Another example from this new generation of breath-test instruments is the Intoxilyzer 6000, which makes use of five different IR wavelengths for identification of ethanol. This reduces considerably the risk of interfering substances being incorrectly reported as ethanol.

Later chapters give additional details of pre-arrest screening instruments as well as more sophisticated units for evidential testing with microprocessor control of the entire breath-test sequence including the volume of breath exhaled, the temperature of breath, and the actual BrAC concentration-time profile. A 15-min observation period before conducting an evidential breath-alcohol test is an important part of the testing protocol to avoid problems with mouth alcohol disturbing the results.[116,117] The presence of mouth alcohol can sometimes be disclosed by looking at the slope of the breath-alcohol concentration profile during a prolonged exhalation.[100] Otherwise, the BrAC measured after the first few seconds of exhalation can be compared with the BrAC reached after an end-exhalation as a way to disclose mouth alcohol. If the result in the first test exceeds the final result, this suggests the presence of mouth alcohol, either caused by recent ingestion or by regurgitation of stomach contents or spontaneous gastro-esophageal reflux. The results of the breath-alcohol test as well as demographic details about the suspect can be printed out directly on-the-spot or stored in the computer memory and down-loaded later to a central computer network for producing summary statistics and quality control charts.

Reporting results of breath-alcohol analysis is a bit confusing and this depends on whether these are intended for use in clinical and emergency medicine or traffic law enforcement. To

Table 5.2.4.4 Inter-Laboratory Proficiency Test of Blood-Alcohol Analysis Performed at Specialist Forensic Toxicology Laboratories in the Nordic Countries[a]

Laboratory	Blood-1	Blood-2	Blood-3	Blood-4	Blood-5	Blood-6
1	0.46	1.01	2.15	1.62	0.74	1.75
2	0.47	1.01	2.27	1.70	0.78	1.83
3	0.46	1.01	2.26	1.67	0.77	1.81
4	0.47	1.00	2.17	1.66	0.78	1.81
5	0.48	1.01	2.15	1.66	0.78	1.79
Mean	0.47	1.01	2.20	1.66	0.77	1.80
SD	0.008	0.005	0.060	0.029	0.017	0.030
CV%	1.7%	0.49%	2.7%	1.7%	2.2%	1.7%

[a] *The blood samples were obtained from apprehended drinking drivers and collected into tubes containing fluoride and oxalate and small portions removed for sending to the participating laboratories. The between-laboratory CVs were always less than 3% and the corresponding within-laboratory CVs were mostly less than 1% (data not shown).*

test if a patient is under the influence of alcohol for clinical purposes, the BrAC is generally converted into the presumed concentration in venous blood. This requires the use of a calibration factor called the blood/breath ratio so that BrAC × factor = BAC. This blood/breath factor is assumed to be a constant for all individuals and 2100:1 has traditionally been accepted for legal purposes.[2,3,102] In many U.S. states a concentration of 0.10 g% in blood is equated with 0.10 g/210 L breath and this 2100:1 relationship is therefore affirmed by statute.[100]

However, many empirical studies have shown that calibration with a factor of 2100:1 tends to give results that underestimate the venous BAC by about 10% when near simultaneous samples are taken 1 to 2 h after the end of drinking.[108] A closer agreement between blood and breath-alcohol is obtained when a 2300:1 factor is used for calibration.[108] Analytical precision improves considerably if BrAC is reported directly instead of estimating the coexisting venous BAC. In experiments with an evidential breath-analyser (DataMaster), the BAC was estimated with a 95% confidence interval of 15 mg/dl compared with 5 mg/230 L when BrAC was reported directly.[118]

Note that breath-alcohol instruments are calibrated to estimate the concentrations of alcohol in whole blood and not the concentration in plasma or serum and this is often overlooked by many clinicians who seem to consider blood and plasma concentrations of alcohol as being the same. To derive the concentration of alcohol in plasma or serum indirectly by the analysis of breath, the breath-test instrument should be calibrated with a plasma/breath factor of about 2600:1 because whole blood contains about 14% less alcohol than the same volume of plasma or serum (Table 5.2.1). Nowadays, when breath-alcohol testing is used for traffic law enforcement the results are almost always reported as the concentration of alcohol in the breath without considering the persons BAC. This avoids making any assumptions about the blood/breath ratio and its variability between and within individuals. Statutory limits for driving in many countries are therefore written in terms of threshold blood and breath-alcohol concentration depending on the specimen analyzed.

5.2.4 QUALITY ASSURANCE ASPECTS OF ALCOHOL ANALYSIS

Much has been written about quality assurance of clinical laboratory measurements and concepts such as precision, accuracy, linearity, recovery, sensitivity, and limits of detection and quantitation have been discussed in detail elsewhere.[119] In addition, when the results are used as evidence in criminal and civil litigation, the chain of custody record of the specimens is extremely important to document. This chain must be kept intact from the moment of sampling to the moment the results are reported and each person involved in the handling, transport, analysis, and storage of the specimen must be traceable from these written records. The entire procedure including the actual chromatographic traces as well as evidence of correct calibration on the day the specimens were analyzed and also internal and external control tests might need to be documented several months or years later. Important details concerning pre-analytical, analytical, and post-analytical aspects of blood-alcohol analysis are presented below.

5.2.4.1 Pre-Analytical Factors

Information should be given to the subject about the reason for taking a blood-sample and, if necessary, informed written consent should be obtained. The equipment used for drawing blood is normally an evacuated tube (5- or 10-ml Vacutainer tubes) and sterile needle attachment. The blood sampling site is usually an antecubital vein and if necessary a tourniquet can be used to dilate a suitable superficial vein. Sufficient blood should be taken to allow making several determinations of the blood-alcohol concentration and any re-testing that might be necessary as well as the assay of drugs of abuse. The specimen tubes should be gently inverted a few times immediately after collection to facilitate mixing and dissolution of the chemical preservatives; sodium fluoride (10 mg/mL) to inhibit the activity of various enzymes, micro-organisms, and yeasts, and potassium oxalate (5 mg/mL) as an anticoagulant. The tubes of blood should be labeled with the person's name, the date and time of sampling, and the name of the person who took the sample. The Vacutainer tubes containing blood should be sealed in such a way as to prevent unauthorized handling or tampering and special adhesive paper strips are available for this purpose. The blood samples and other relevant paper-work should be secured with tape so that any deliberate manipulating or adulteration is easily detected by laboratory personnel after shipment. After taking the samples, the tubes of blood should be stored in a refrigerated room before being sent to the laboratory by express mail service.

   Although pre-analytical factors are more important to consider and control when endogenous substances are analyzed, such as in clinical chemistry, a standardized sampling protocol is also important for forensic blood-alcohol analysis. Two tubes of blood should be drawn in rapid succession and the skin cleaned with soap and water and not with an organic solvent such as ether, isopropanol, or ethanol. Obviously, the blood samples should not be taken from veins into which intravenous fluids are being administered.[120] This kind of emergency treatment is often given as a first-aid to treat patients suffering from shock or trauma as a result of involvement in traffic accidents. The blood samples should be taken only by trained personnel such as a phlebotomist, registered nurse, or physician.

5.2.4.2 Analytical Factors

The blood specimens must be carefully inspected when they arrive at the laboratory, making a note whether or not the seals on the package as well as the individual tubes of blood are intact, if there are any blood-clots, and if the blood seems to have been diluted with other liquids. Details of any mishaps during transport (breakage, leakage of blood), as well as the date and time of arrival should be recorded. The information written on the Vacutainer tubes should be compared with other documentation to ensure the suspect's name and the date and time of sampling are correct. The same unique identification number or barcode should be added to all paperwork and biological specimens received and this number used to monitor passage of the specimens through the laboratory. Ensure that the erythrocytes and plasma fractions are adequately mixed before removing aliquots of whole blood for analysis. Replicate determinations can be made with different chromatographic systems and preferably by different techni-cians working independently.[26] Any unidentified peaks on the gas chromatograms should be noted because these might indicate the presence of other volatiles in the blood sample.

5.2.4.3 Post-Analytical Factors

Quality assurance of individual results can be controlled by looking at critical differences (range) between replicate determinations. The size of the difference will be larger the higher the concentration of ethanol in the blood specimen because precision tends to decrease with an increase in the concentration of ethanol. Control charts offer a useful way to monitor day-to-day performance in the laboratory; one chart being used to depict precision and another the accuracy of the method by analyzing known strength standards together with unknowns. These charts make it easy to detect the presence of outliers.[26, 121,122] The rate of loss of alcohol during storage needs to be established under refrigerated conditions ($+ 4°C$) and also when specimens are kept deeply frozen.[123,124] If necessary, corrections can then be made if the blood specimens are reanalyzed after prolonged periods of storage. The chromatographic traces and other evidence corroborating the analytical results, such as calibration plots or response factors, should be carefully labeled and stored safely in fire-proof cabinets. It might be worthwhile to ensure that the laboratory is accredited for making forensic toxicological analyses and the results of external proficiency trials should also be made available for scrutiny.

5.2.4.4 Inter-Laboratory Proficiency

Two papers recently looked at the results from inter-laboratory proficiency tests of blood-alcohol analysis at clinical chemistry laboratories.[125,126] In one study, originating from Sweden, all participating laboratories used gas chromatography for analysis of plasma-ethanol and the coefficients of variation between laboratories were within the range 10 to 17%.[125] In a similar study among UK laboratories, the corresponding CVs depended in part on the kind of methodology used for the analysis of alcohol. Immunoassays generally performed worse than gas chromatographic methods (liquid injection and headspace technique) and the CVs ranged from 8% to 20%.[126]

Table 5.2.4.4 presents results from a recent inter-laboratory comparison of blood-alcohol analysis made at specialist forensic toxicology laboratories in the Nordic countries (Denmark, Finland, Iceland, Norway, and Sweden). All participants used headspace gas chromatography to analyze ethanol and the blood samples were obtained from apprehended drinking drivers. The coefficient of variation between laboratories was always less than 3% regardless of the concentration of alcohol, which testifies to highly standardized analytical work. The corre-sponding CVs within laboratories were mostly 1% or less based on 3 to 6 determinations per sample. If the overall mean BAC in each sample is taken as the target value, then all the laboratories showed an accuracy to within 5% of that attributed.

5.2.5 FATE OF ALCOHOL IN THE BODY

Ethanol is a small polar molecule and its low molecular weight and weak charge allow it to penetrate easily through biological membranes. After ingestion, ethanol is absorbed readily from the stomach but absorption occurs much faster from the upper part of the small intestine where the available surface area is much larger owing to the presence of microvilli on the mucosal cells. Both the rate and extent of absorption is delayed if there is food in the stomach before drinking.[127] Blood draining from the gastrointestinal tract collects in the portal vein where the alcohol is transported through the liver, and then on to the heart and the systemic circulation. The metabolism of alcohol occurs mainly by the action of enzymes located in the liver although recent research suggests that small amounts of alcohol might be metabolized in

Figure 5.2.5 Mean concentration-time profiles of ethanol in blood vs. breath (x 2100), blood vs. saliva, and blood vs. urine from experiments with healthy men who ingested 0.68 g ethanol per kg body weight as neat whisky in the morning after an overnight fast.

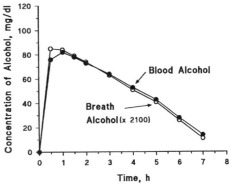

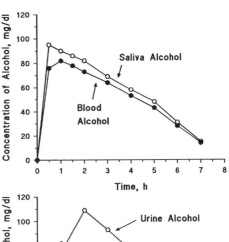

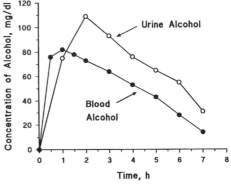

the mucosa of the stomach.[128] After absorption, ethanol distributes uniformly throughout all body fluids and tissue without binding to plasma proteins. Provided that the systemic availability of the dose is 100%, such as when administered by i.v. infusion, it is possible to determine total body water by the ethanol dilution method.[129]

The peak blood-alcohol concentration after drinking, as well as the time of reaching the peak, varies widely from person to person and depends on many factors. After 48 healthy male volunteers drank 0.68 g ethanol/kg body weight as neat whisky on an empty stomach, the peak concentration in capillary (fingertip) blood was reached at exactly 10, 40, 70, and 100 min after the end of drinking for 23, 14, 8, and 3 subjects, respectively.[130] The quantities consumed, the rate of drinking, the dosage form (beer, wine, spirits, cocktails) and most importantly the rate of gastric emptying impacts on the speed of absorption.[131] The concentrations of ethanol in body fluids and tissues after reaching equilibration will depend on the water contents, the ratio of blood-flow to tissue perfusion, as well as various time elements.[110] Figure 5.2.5 shows the mean concentration- time profiles of ethanol in blood, breath, urine, and saliva obtained from experiments with healthy male volunteers who drank 0.68 g/kg as neat whisky in 20 min after an overnight fast.[132]

The bulk of the dose of alcohol entering the bloodstream (95 to 98%) is eliminated from the body by metabolism which takes place mainly in the liver by the action of class I enzymes of alcohol dehydrogenase (ADH).[127] Between 2 to 5% of the dose is excreted unchanged in breath, urine, and sweat, and a very small fraction is conjugated with glucuronic acid.[133] Small amounts of alcohol might undergo pre-systemic oxidation by ADH located in the gastric mucosa or the liver or both, but the quantitative significance of first-pass metabolism (FPM) is still an unsettled question.[134]

At moderate BAC (>60 mg/dL), the microsomal enzymes (P450IIE1), which have a higher km (60 to 80 mg/dL) compared with ADH (km 2 to 5 mg/dL), become engaged in the metabolism of ethanol.[135,136] The P450 enzymes are also involved in the metabolism of many other drugs and environmental chemicals which increases the risk of drug-alcohol interactions and this might account for the toxicity of ethanol in heavy drinkers and alcoholics.[137,138] Moreover, the activity of P4502E1 enzymes increase after a period of continu-

A. Wayne Jones and Derrick J. Pounder

ous heavy drinking owing to a faster *de novo* synthesis of the enzyme, and metabolic tolerance develops as reflected in two- to threefold faster rates of elimination of alcohol from the bloodstream in alcoholics.[139-141]

The effects of ethanol on performance and behavior are complex and involve an interaction with membrane receptors in the brain associated with the inhibitory neurotransmitters glutamate and gamma aminobutyric acid (GABA).[142,143] The behavioral effects of ethanol are dose-dependent and drinking small amounts initially produces feelings of euphoria followed by depression and stupor after large doses are ingested. Ethanol's depressant effects are related to an altered flux of ions through the chloride channel activated by GABA.[144] The fact that ethanol modifies neuro-transmission at the GABA receptor also helps to explain the cross-tolerance observed with other classes of drugs such as the benzodiazepines and barbiturates, which also bind to the GABA receptor complex to produce their effects on brain functioning.[143]

Although ethanol-induced impairment shows a reasonably good overall correlation with the coexisting blood-alcohol concentration, there are large variations in response for different individuals who drink the same amount of alcohol within the same time frame. The reasons for this are twofold; first, larger people tend to have more body water so the dose of alcohol enters a larger volume resulting in lower BACs compared with lighter people with less body water. This phenomenon is known as consumption tolerance and is caused primarily by variations in body weights and the relative amount of adipose tissue which is influenced by age, race, and gender. The second reason for the inter-individual differences in ethanol-induced effects on performance and behavior is called concentration tolerance caused by gradual habituation of brain cells to the presence of alcohol during exposure to the drug over long periods. Besides the development of acute tolerance, which appears after a single exposure (see Chapter 1), a chronic tolerance develops after a period of continuous heavy drinking. The mechanisms accounting for chronic tolerance seem to depend on changes in the composition of cell membranes, particularly the cholesterol content, the structure of the fatty acids, and also the arrangement of the phospholipids in the membranes.[142-144]

In occasional drinkers, the impairment effects at specific blood-alcohol concentrations are often classified according to various stages of intoxication as evidenced by the clinical signs and symptoms observed. This notion was first proposed by Bogen[145] but has been subsequently developed further and improved by others. At a BAC of 10 to 30 mg/dL slight changes in performance and behavior can be demonstrated with highly specialized tests such as divided attention. Between 30 to 60 mg/dL, most people experience euphoria, becoming more talkative and sociable. At a BAC between 60 to 100 mg/dl, a marked euphoria and excitement is often reported with partial or complete loss of inhibitions and in some individuals judgement and control are seriously impaired. When the BAC is between 100 and 150 mg/dL, which are concentrations of ethanol seldom reached during moderate social drinking, psychomotor performance deteriorates markedly and articulation and speech become obviously impaired. Between 150 and 200 mg/dl, ataxia is pronounced and drowsiness and confusion are evident in most people. Controlled studies at high BAC with moderate drinkers are lacking because of the gross intoxication produced, but anecdotal information exists from the field of emergency medicine. The relationship between BAC and clinical impairment is well documented in drunk drivers who often attain very high BACs of 350 mg/dL or more but most of these individuals are obviously chronic alcoholics.[146]

It is important to note that the magnitude and appearance of various signs and symptoms of inebriation depend to a great extent on the rate of drinking and whether the person starts from zero BAC, that is after a period of abstinence or with a residual BAC from a recent drinking spree.[147,148] In the latter case, the severity of intoxication is less pronounced because previous consumption of alcohol means that the individual has acquired some degree of tolerance. Drinking too much too fast is dangerous and if gastric emptying occurs rapidly, the

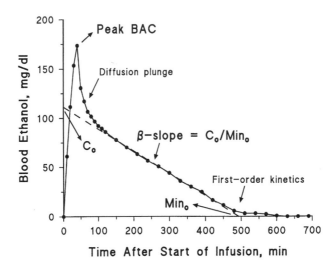

Figure 5.2.6.1 Individual concentration-time profile of ethanol in venous blood after an intravenous administration of 0.8 g/kg at a constant rate over 30 min. Key pharmacokinetic parameters are defined on this trace.

BAC increases with such a velocity that the vomit reflex in the brain is triggered. This physiological response to acute alcohol ingestion has probably saved many lives.

5.2.6 CLINICAL PHARMACOKINETICS OF ETHANOL

The discipline known as pharmacokinetics deals with the way that drugs and their metabolites are absorbed, distributed, and metabolized in the body and how these processes can be described in quantitative terms.[149,150]

5.2.6.1 Widmark Model

The clinical pharmacokinetics of ethanol have been investigated extensively since the 1930s thanks to the early availability of a reliable method of analysis in small volumes of blood.[151] Figure 5.2.6.1 shows a typical blood-alcohol concentration-time profile after intravenous infusion of 0.80 g ethanol/kg body weight at a constant rate for 30 min. The key pharmaco-kinetic parameters are defined on this trace in accordance with the model developed by Widmark.[151] The peak BAC coincides with the end of the infusion period being followed by a diffusion plunge during which time the ethanol equilibrates between well perfused and poorly perfused organs and tissues. At about 90 min post-infusion, the BAC starts to decrease at a constant rate per unit time according to zero-order kinetics and the slope of this rectilinear disappearance phase is commonly referred to as the alcohol burn-off rate or β-slope. However, specialist texts in pharmacokinetics refer to the zero-order elimination slope as k_o instead of β.[152] When the BAC decreases below about 10 mg/dL, shown in Figure 5.2.6.1, after a time of 450 min, a curvilinear disappearance phase starts to develop and this lasts for as long as alcohol is still measurable in the blood. The elimination of alcohol now follows first-order kinetics and the rate constant is denoted k_1 and clearance from the bloodstream during this terminal phase has a half-life of about 15 min.[153]

The first person to make a comprehensive mathematical analysis of BAC profiles was Erik MP Widmark and details of his life and work were recently published.[154] Widmark introduced the following equation to represent the elimination kinetics of alcohol from blood:

A. Wayne Jones and Derrick J. Pounder

$$C_t = C_o - \beta t \tag{1}$$

where

C_t = blood alcohol concentration at some time t on the post-absorptive part of the curve.
C_o = blood alcohol concentration extrapolated to the time of starting to drink.
β = rate of elimination of alcohol from blood.
t = time in minutes.

The rate of elimination of alcohol from the blood in moderate drinkers falls within the range of 10 to 20 mg/dL/h with a mean value of about 15 mg/dL/h.[129-131] Higher values are seen in drinking drivers (mean 19 mg/dL/h)[155] and in alcoholics undergoing detoxification (mean 22 mg/dL/h).[156] The faster burn-off rates seen in heavy drinkers are probably a consequence of boosting the microsomal enzymes (P450IIE1) owing to prolonged exposure to high concentrations of ethanol. The P450IIEI enzymes have a higher K_m (60 to 80 mg/dL) compared with ADH (2 to 5 mg/dL) and the slope of the elimination phase tends to be steeper starting from a higher initial BAC as in alcoholics compared with moderate social drinkers.[157,158] In a controlled study with alcoholics undergoing detoxification, the mean slope was 22 mg/dL/h with a range from 13 to 36 mg/dL/h.[156] Liver disorders such as alcoholic hepatitis and cirrhosis did not seem to influence the rate of disposal of alcohol in these individuals.[127,156]

The rate of elimination of alcohol from the blood was not much influenced by the time of day when 0.75 g/kg was administered at 9 AM, 3 PM, 9 PM, and 3 AM, according to a recent investigation into chronopharmacokientics of ethanol.[159] However, gastric emptying seems to occur faster in the morning as reflected in a 32% higher peak BAC and an earlier time of its occurrence when 1.1 g/kg alcohol was consumed between 7.15 and 7.45 AM, compared with the same time in the evening.[160] Smoking cigarettes slows gastric emptying and as a consequence delays the absorption of a moderate dose (0.50 g/kg) of ethanol resulting in a lower peak BAC in smokers.[161]

By extrapolating the rectilinear elimination phase back to the time of starting to drink gives the y- intercept (C_o), which corresponds to the theoretical BAC if the entire dose was absorbed and distributed without any metabolism occurring (Figure 5.2.6.1). The empirically determined value of C_o will always be greater than the ratio of dose/body weight because whole blood is 80% w/w water compared with the body as a whole which is 60% w/w on average for men and 50% w/w for women. The apparent volume of distribution (V_d) of alcohol is obtained from the ratio of dose (g/kg) divided by C_o and in clinical pharmacology textbooks the V_d has units of liters/kg.[152] However, because BAC in Widmark's studies was reported in units of mg/g or g/kg, the ratio dose/C_o known as the Widmark r factor is a ratio without any dimensions and should be 5.5% greater than Vd reported in units of L/kg.[154,162]

Values of the distribution factor r differ between individuals depending on age and body composition particularly on the proportion of fat to lean tissue. Obviously, the value of r will also depend on whether whole blood or plasma specimens were used to plot the concentration-time profile and extrapolating to determine C_o.[129] As shown in Figure 5.2.1, the plasma-alcohol curves run on a higher level compared with whole blood-alcohol curves because of the different amounts of water in these specimens. According to Widmark, the relationship between alcohol in the body and alcohol in the blood at equilibrium can be represented by the following equations.

$$A/(p \times r) = C_o \tag{2}$$

$$A = C_o \times (p \times r) \tag{3}$$

where

A = amount of alcohol in grams absorbed and distributed in the body.
p = body weight of the person in kg.
r = Widmarks r factor.
C_o = y-intercept (Figure 5.2.6.1)

These equations make it easy to calculate the amount of alcohol in the body from the concentration determined in a sample of blood provided that the value of r is known and that absorption and distribution of alcohol are complete at the time of sampling blood.

In the fasting state, the factor r will depend on age, gender, and body composition and Widmark reported mean values of 0.68 for 20 men (range 0.51 to 0.85) and 0.55 for 10 women (range 0.49 to 0.76).[151] However, in many later studies with more volunteer subjects, it was found that average values of r were 0.70 L/kg for men and 0.60 L/kg for women with 95% confidence limits of about ±20%.[127] Widmark's equations for β and r can be easily combined by eliminating C_o to give the following equation:

$$A = pr(C_t + \beta t) \tag{4}$$

The above equation can be used to estimate the total amount of alcohol absorbed from the gastrointestinal tract since the beginning of drinking. By rearrangement, the blood alcohol concentration (C_t) expected after intake of a known amount of alcohol is calculated with the help of the following equation.

$$C_t = (A/pr) - \beta t \tag{5}$$

When calculating BAC from the dose administered or vice versa, it is necessary to assume that the systemic availability is 100% and that complete absorption and distribution of alcohol in the body water compartment has occurred at the time of sampling blood. Furthermore, individual variations in β and r introduce uncertainty in the calculated dose (A) or BAC (C_t) when average values are applied to a random subject from the population. The amount of individual variation was recently estimated as ±20% for 95% confidence limits in tests with over 100 subjects.[163] However, in the entire population of drinking drivers, these limits can be expected to be much wider.

5.2.6.2 Michaelis-Menten Model

Because the class I ADH enzymes have a low km (3 to 5 mg/dL), they become saturated with substrate after 1 to 2 drinks and the rate of disappearance of ethanol from blood therefore follows zero-order kinetics over a large segment of the post-absorptive elimination phase (Figure 5.2.6.1).[127,131] When the blood-alcohol concentration decreases below about 10 mg/dL, the ADH enzymes are no longer saturated and the curve changes to a curvilinear disappearance phase (first-order kinetics). However, these low blood-alcohol concentrations are not very relevant in forensic science work.

It was suggested and shown by Lundquist and Wolthers[164] that the entire post-absorptive elimination phase (zero-order and first-order stages) might be rationalized by an alternative pharmacokinetic model, namely that of saturation kinetics. They fitted the Michaelis–Menten equation to BAC-time data including the very low concentrations (<10 mg/dL) thanks to the availability of a highly sensitive ADH method for blood-alcohol analysis. By solving the integrated form of the M-M equation, the parameters V_{max} and k_m were determined. This approach based on the Michaelis–Menten equation or saturation kinetics was later strongly advocated by many specialists in pharmacokinetics, among others, Wagner, Wilkinson, and their colleagues[165-167] and values of 22 mg/dL/h and 5 mg/dL have been reported for V_{max}

A. Wayne Jones and Derrick J. Pounder

and k_m, respectively.[167] Although the use of M-M kinetics has found some support among forensic scientists,[168] others have not considered its use worthwhile when dealing with actual casework[169] because so many other variable factors and uncertainties influence the absorption, distribution, and elimination of ethanol. Moreover, the mathematical concepts needed to understand and apply M-M kinetics are more challenging than those necessary to derive the Widmark equation. Explaining the scientific principles of pharmacokinetic modeling to a judge and jury, as is sometimes necessary in DUI litigation, is prohibitive. Moreover, the notion of multiple enzyme systems being involved in the metabolism of ethanol such as the various isozymes of ADH, including genetic variations and the contribution of P450IIE1 to the disposal of ethanol after chronic ingestion (metabolic tolerance), are not strictly compatible with the use of a single enzyme system required by the Michaelis-Menten equation.[170,171]

5.2.6.3 First-Pass Metabolism and Gastric Alcohol Dehydrogenase

Recent research efforts indicate that a small part of the alcohol a person consumes is metabolized before it reaches the systemic circulation and this process is known as first-pass metabolism (FPM).[172,173] Some of the alcohol ingested is seemingly cleared from the blood either in the stomach or during the first-pass of the portal blood through the liver. The magnitude of first-pass metabolism depends on many factors and seems to be greater when very small doses of ethanol (0.15 g/kg) are administered and particularly when alcohol is taken together with or after a meal presumably because under these conditions there is a longer time available for contact between alcohol and the enzyme-rich mucosal surfaces in the stomach.[172]

Distinguishing between first-pass metabolism occurring in the stomach as opposed to the liver has proven a difficult task and much debate has arisen about the significance of gastric ADH in accounting for FPM.[174,175] Some workers maintain that gastric metabolism of ethanol plays a significant role in the overall disposal of ethanol especially when emptying of the stomach is delayed and the absorption phase is more prolonged.[173] Others consider that negligible amounts of alcohol undergo presystemic oxidation in the stomach mainly because the amount of gastric ADH is only a small fraction of the amount of hepatic ADH available.[175] Moreover, the main advocates of gastric ADH and FPM of ethanol failed to consider the critical importance of stomach emptying and its influence on the rate of absorption of alcohol.[176] For drugs that obey saturation kinetics, the bioavailability should become more variable as a consequence of changes in absorption rate which modulates the fraction escaping first-pass metabolism.[177] Factors that influence the rate of absorption of alcohol from the gut (food, drugs, type of beverage, posture, time of day) also influence the concentration entering the liver and the corresponding degree of saturation of the metabolizing enzymes.[177]

Interest in FPM escalated even further after several common medications such as aspirin and H_2-receptor antagonists (cimetidine and ranitidine) were shown *in vitro* to inhibit ADH[178-181] extracted from gastric biopsies.[179] This observation lead to much speculation about adverse-drug reactions and the role of gastric-ADH as a protective barrier against the toxicity of ethanol in some individuals.[182] Proponents of FPM argued that if alcohol was taken together with these common medications, this would result in the peak BAC being higher than expected probably leading to a more pronounced impairment of body functions.[180,182] Accordingly, those individuals lacking gastric ADH or exhibiting reduced enzymatic activity such as women, oriental populations, and alcoholics, might be more susceptible to the toxic effects of heavy drinking.[173,183] These conclusions proved too hasty because many later studies into the effects of cimetidine and ranitidine on the pharmacokinetics of ethanol failed to confirm the initial reports showing higher peak BAC and AUC and enhanced bioavailability.[184-187]

What did emerge from this new wave of interest in clinical pharmacokinetics of ethanol was strong and convincing information documenting the large inter- and intra-individual variations

Figure 5.2.6.4 Individual concentration-time profile of ethanol in venous blood from experiments with nine subjects who drank 0.30 g ethanol/kg body weight in 10 min either after an overnight fast or after eating breakfast 1 h before drinking alcohol. Note the large inter-individual variations and much lower peak BAC with smaller area under the curve and the shorter time to eliminate the dose of alcohol in the fed-state. The insert figure shows mean ±SE for fed and fasting conditions.

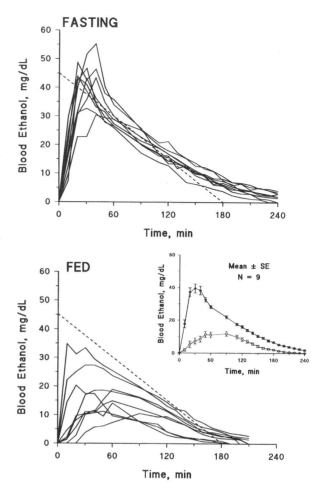

in the pharmacokinetic profiles of ethanol especially when small doses (0.15 to 0.3 g/kg) were ingested after a meal.[188-191]

5.2.6.4 Food and Pharmacokinetics of Ethanol

Having food in the stomach before drinking retards the absorption of ethanol and the peak BAC and the initial impairment effects are considerably diminished compared with drinking the same dose on an empty stomach.[151,154,192,193] The bioavailability of ethanol is markedly reduced whenever consumption takes place after a meal and estimating values of r or V_d under these conditions give results that are too high, suggesting a loss of ethanol. The composition of the meal in terms of its fat, protein, or carbohydrate content was less important in this respect.[194-197] Figure 5.2.6.4 gives examples of pharmacokinetic profiles of ethanol in venous blood for nine subjects who drank 0.30 g ethanol per kg either on an empty stomach (overnight fast) or exactly 1 h after eating a protein-rich breakfast. The large inter-individual variations in peak BAC, area under the curve (AUC) are clearly evident. The broken diagonal lines show the slope and position of the zero-order elimination phase expected for a standard man with a volume of distribution of 0.70 liters/kg and an elimination rate constant of 15 mg/dL/h and when the bioavailability of alcohol was 100%. The observed BAC profiles were considerably lower than the values expected in every single case when the alcohol was consumed after the meal, which implies that some of the alcohol escapes being absorbed into the blood. Whether this reflects an active first-pass metabolism (stomach or liver or both) or whether an accelerated metabolism primarily takes place early after drinking during the absorption phase is not known.[134]

It seems that a prerequisite for finding an appreciable FPM was that the subjects had eaten food prior to drinking alcohol.[198] This raised a question about the role of stomach emptying and the speed of absorption of alcohol as a determinant of FPM.[176,181,199] In Figure 5.2.6.4 (insert), food taken 1 h before drinking not only lowers peak BAC and AUC but also seems

A. Wayne Jones and Derrick J. Pounder

to boost the rate of elimination of ethanol.[193] This might be explained by a more efficient extraction of ethanol in the liver when the absorption from the gut is slow, and more prolonged, such as when alcohol is taken after eating a meal.[176] Food increases liver blood flow and this might facilitate a more effective exposure of ethanol to the metabolizing enzymes in the liver.[194,196] Whatever the mechanism, eating a meal before drinking is an effective way to produce a lower and later occurring peak BAC, a faster rate of clearance of ethanol from the body, and diminished feelings of inebriation.[192]

5.2.7 CONCLUSIONS

Ethanol tops the list of drugs of abuse in most countries, and too much drinking is a well-known cause of reckless behavior. Drunk drivers are over-represented in crashes and deaths on the highway and alcohol intoxication is the common denominator in many accidents within the home and in the workplace. Alcohol abuse and alcoholism are major public health hazards with enormous costs for the individual and society. Measuring alcohol in body fluids will continue to be the most frequently requested procedure in analytical toxicology for a long time to come. Few substances can be determined with such a high degree of accuracy, precision, and selectivity as the concentration of ethanol in a person's blood.[26] The analytical phase of the procedure is hard to fault especially when methods such as headspace gas chromatography are used at an accredited laboratory.[26] Making duplicate determinations is an effective safeguard against various mishaps occurring during the analysis and the aliquots of blood analyzed should be taken from two separate tubes.[26] Moreover, to enhance selectivity, at least two different chromatographic systems can be used thus providing different retention times for ethanol.[200] Alternatively, an independent assay method such as ADH or chemical oxidation can be run in parallel with GC.[73]

More attention needs to be given to the pre-analytical factors including the condition of the subject, the way the blood sample was taken, and the circumstances surrounding the sampling procedure. This becomes significant whenever blood samples are taken from victims of traffic accidents who require emergency hospital treatment, such as administration of drugs or intravenous fluids, to counteract shock. It is important to remember that the result of a chemical or biochemical test is only as good as the sample received. When the analytical results make the difference between punishment or acquittal, as in trials concerning driving under the influence of alcohol, pre-analytical factors are as important to control and document as analytical factors.

Widmark's method continues to dominate the way that forensic scientists and others deal with the pharmacokinetics of alcohol when requested to calculate the amount ingested from a single measurement of BAC.[131] Making back extrapolations of BAC is not recommended because of the wide variations in absorption, distribution, and elimination patterns of ethanol both within and between different individuals.[188-192,201] This becomes especially important when small doses of alcohol (0.3 g/kg) are taken after a meal because under these conditions the bioavailability of alcohol might be reduced by as much as 60% (Figure 5.2.6.4).[189] Warnings about adverse drug- alcohol interactions, e.g., after taking medication such as aspirin and H_2-receptor antagonists, before drinking alcohol and the risk of obtaining higher peak BAC and larger performance decrements seem to have been much exaggerated.[184-187]

Other ways of studying the pharmacokinetics of alcohol have been proposed including the use of Michaelis-Menten kinetics[202] and other saturation-type models.[203-205] Recently a three-compartment model[206] as well as a non-compartment model[207] were used to explore the disposition and fate of alcohol in the body in quantitative terms.

REFERENCES

1. Lindberger, V., Bidrag till kännedomen om förgiftningarna i Sverige under Åren 1873-1892. Uppsala Universitets rsskrift, Medicin 1, Almqvist & Wiksell, Uppsala, 1883.
2. Jones, A. W., Measuring alcohol in blood and breath for forensic purposes - A historical review. Forensic Sci Rev 8, 13, 1996.
3. Dubowski, K. M., Recent developments in alcohol analysis. Alc Drugs Driving 2, 13, 1986.
4. Wright, J. W., Alcohol and the laboratory in the United Kingdom. Ann Clin Biochem 28, 212, 1991.
5. Dubowski, K. M., Alcohol determination in the clinical laboratory. Am J Clin Pathol 74, 747, 1980
6. Cherpitel, C. J., Alcohol and casualities - a comparison of emergency room and coroner data. Alc Alcohol 29, 211, 1994.
7. Cherpitel, C. J., Injury and the role of alcohol; county-wide emergency room data. Alcohol Clin Exp Res 18, 679, 1994.
8. Shepard, J., Violent crime, the role of alcohol and new approaches to the prevention of injury. Alc Alcohol 29, 5, 1994.
9. Klatsky, A. L., Armstrong, M. A., and Friedman, G.D., Alcohol and mortality. Ann Intern Med 117, 646, 1992.
10. Jones, A. W., Forensic Sciences; Determination of alcohol in body fluids. In Encyclopedia of Analytical Sciences, Academic Press, 1995, p 1585.
11. Stewart, S. H., Alcohol abuse in individuals exposed to trauma; A critical review. Psychol Bull 120, 83, 1996.
12. VonMoreau. K. B., Mueller, P., Drirsch, D., Osswald, B., and Seitz, H. K., Alcohol and trauma. Alcohol Clin Exp Res 16, 141, 1992.
13. Kelly, D. F., Alcohol and head injury, an issue revisited. J Neurotrauma 12, 883, 1995.
14. Rutherford, W. H., Diagnosis of alcohol ingestion in mild head trauma. Lancet 1, 1021, 1977.
15. Quaghebeur, G., and Richards, P., Comatose patients smelling of alcohol. Brit Med J 299, 410, 1989.
16. Pappas, S. C., and Silverman M., Treatment of methanol poisoning with ethanol and hemodialysis. CMA Journal 15, 1391, 1982.
17. Jacobsen, O., and McMartin, K. E., Methanol and ethylene glycol poisoning; mechanisms of toxicity, clinical course, diagnosis and treatment. Med Toxicol 1, 309, 1986.
18. Walder, A. D., and Tyler, C. K. G., Ethylene glycol antifreeze poisoning. Anaesthesia 49, 964, 1994.
19. Perrine, M. W., Alcohol involvement in highway crashes. Clinics in Plastic Surgery 2, 11, 1975.
20. US Department of Transportation, National Highway Traffic safety Administration, Alcohol involvement in fatal traffic crashes - 1992. NHTSA Technical report DOT HS 808 094, 1994, 1-24.
21. Ferrara, S. D., Low blood-alcohol concentrations and driving impairment. A review of experimental studies and international legislation.. Int J Legal Med 106, 169, 1994
22. Jones, A. W., Enforcement of drink-driving laws by use of "per se" legal alcohol limits; Blood and/or breath alcohol concentration as evidence of impairment. Alc Drugs and Driving 4, 99, 1988.
23. Ziporvn, T., Definition of impairment essential for prosecuting drunken drivers. JAMA 253, 3509, 1985.
24. Dubowski, K. M., and Caplan Y., Alcohol testing in the workplace. Chapter 19 in Garriott, J (editor) Medicolegal aspects of alcohol. Lawyers & Judges Publishing Co., Tuson, 1996, p 439.
25. Flanagan, R. J., SI units - common sense not dogma is needed. Br J Clin Pharmacol 39, 589, 1995.
26. Jones, A. W., and Schuberth, J. O., Computer-aided headspace gas chromatography applied to blood-alcohol analysis; Importance of on-line process control. J Forens Sci 34, 1116, 1989.
27. Fraser, C. G., Interpretation of clinical chemistry laboratory data. Blackwell Scientific Publications, 1986.

28. Senkowski, C. M., and Thompson, K. A., The accuracy of blood alcohol analysis using headspace gas chromatography when performed on clotted samples. J Forens Sci 35, 176, 1990.

29. Rainey, P. M., Relation between serum and whole blood ethanol concentrations. Clin Chem 39, 2288, 1993.

30   Jones, A. W., Hahn, R. G., Stalberg, H. P., Distribution of ethanol and water between plasma and whole blood; inter- and intra-individual variations after administration of ethanol by intravenous infusion. Scand J Clin Lab Invest 50, 775, 1990.

31. Frajola, W. J., Blood alcohol testing in the clinical laboratory: Problems and suggested remedies. Clin Chem 39, 377, 1993.

32. Winek, C. L., and Carfagna, M., Comparison of plasma, serum, and whole blood ethanol concentrations. J Anal Toxicol 11, 267, 1987.

33. Charlebois, R. C., Corbett, M. R., Wigmore, J. G., Comparison of ethanol concentrations in blood, serum, and blood cells for forensic applications. J Anal Toxicol 20,171, 1996.

34. Widmark, E. M. P., Eine Mikromethode zur Bestimmung von Äthylalkohol im Blut. Biochem Z 131:473;1922

35. Friedemann, T. E., Dubowski, K. M., Chemical testing procedures for the determination of ethyl alcohol. JAMA 170:47;1959.

36. Lundquist, F., The determination of ethyl alcohol in blood and tissue. In Methods of Biochemical Analysis, Vol. VII, D. Glick, editor, Interscience Publishers, New york, p. 217, 1959.

37. Smith, H. W., Methods for determining alcohol. In Methods of Forensic Science, Edited by A. S. Curry, Interscience Publishers, New York; p 3, 1965.

38. Jain, N. C., and Cravey, R. H., Analysis of alcohol. I: A review of chemical and infrared methods. J Chromatog Sci 10:257;1972.

39. Bonnichsen, R. K., Wassen, A., Crystalline alcohol dehydrogenase from horse liver. Arch Biochem 18, 361, 1948.

40. Bonnichsen, R. K., Theorell, H., An enzymatic method for the microdetermination of ethanol. Scand J Clin Lab Invest 3, 58, 1951.

41. Bücher, Th., Redetzki, H., Eine spezifische photometrische Bestimmung von Äthylalkohol auf fermentivem Wege. Klin Wochnschr 29, 615, 1951.

42. Redetzki, H., Johannsmeier, K., Grundlagen und Ergebnisse der enzymatischen Äthylalkoholbestimmung. Arch Toxikol 16, 73, 1957.

43. Vasilliades, J., Pollock, J., and Robinson, A., Pitfalls of the alcohol dehydrogenase procedure for the emergency assay of alcohol: A case study if isopropanol overdose. Clin Chem 24, 383, 1978

44. Buijten, J. C., An automated ultra-micro distillation technique for determination of ethanol in blood and urine. Blutalkohol 12, 393, 1975.

45. Whitehouse, L. W., Paul, C. J., Micro-scale enzymatic determination of ethanol in plasma with a discrete analyzer, the ABA-100. Clin Chem 25, 1399, 1979.

46. Hadjiioannou, T. P., Hadjiioannou, S. I., Avery, J., and Malmstedt, H. V., Automated enzymatic determination of ethanol in blood serum and urine with a miniature centrifugal analyzer. Clin Chem 22, 802, 1976.

47. Caplan, Y., and Levine, B., The analysis of ethanol in serum, blood, and urine: A comparison of the TDx REA ethanol assay with gas chromatography. J Anal Toxicol 10, 49, 1986.

48. Urry, F. M., Kralik, M., Wozniak, E., Crockett, H., Jennison, T. A., Application of the Technicon Chem-1+ chemistry analyzer to the Syva Emit ethyl alcohol assay in plasma and urine. J Anal Toxicol 17, 287, 1993.

49. Hannak, D., and Engel, C. H., Schnellbestimmung des Blutalkohols mit der ADH/REA methode: Methodenvergleich und Bewertung. Blutalkohol 22, 371, 1985.

50. Alt, A., and Reinhardt, G., Die Genauigkeit der Blutalkoholbestimmung mit Head-Space GC, ADH und dem REA Ethanol Assay für das AXSYM System - ein Methodenvergleich. Blutalkohol 33, 209, 1996.

51. Siagle, K. M., Ghosen, S. J., Immunoassays; Tools for sensitive, specific, and accurate test results. Lab Med 27, 177, 1996.

52. Nine, J. S., Moraca, M., Virji, M. A., Rao, K. N., Serum-ethanol determination: Comparison of lactate and lactate dehydrogenase interference in three enzymatic assays. J Anal Toxicol 19, 192, 1995.

53. Cadman, W. J., Johns, T., Application of the gas chromatography in the laboratory of criminalistics. J Forens Sci 5, 369, 1960.

54. Fox, J. F., Gas chromatographic analysis of alcohol and certain other volatiles in biological material for forensic purposes. Proc Soc Exp Biol Med 97:236;1958.

55. Chundela, B., Janak, J., Quantitative determination of ethanol besides other volatile substances in blood and other body liquids by gas chromatography. J Forens Med 7, 153, 1960.

56. Parker, K. D., Fontan, C. R., Yee, J. L., Kirk, P. L., Gas chromatographic determination of ethyl alcohol in blood for medicolegal purposes; Separation of other volatiles from blood or aqueous solution. Anal Chem 34, 1234, 1962.

57. Curry, A. S., Walker, G. W., Simpson, G. S., Determination of alcohol in blood by gas chromatography. Analyst 91, 742, 1966.

58. Jain, N. C., and Cravey, R. H., Analysis of alcohol. II: A review of gas chromatographic methods. J Chromatog Sci 10:263;1972.

59. Cravey, R. H., Jain, N. C., Current status of blood alcohol methods. J Chromatog Sci 12, 209, 1974.

60. Dubowski, K. M., Manual for analysis of alcohol in biological liquids. US Department of Transportation Report No. DOT-TSC-NHTSA-76-4, 1977.

61. Machata, G., Über die gaschromatographische Blutalkoholbestimmung Analyse der Dampfphase. Microchimica Acta 262, 1964.

62. Machata, G., The advantages of automated blood alcohol determination by head space analysis. Z Rechtsmedizin 75, 229, 1975.

63. Anthony, R. M., Suthejmer, C. A., Sunshine, I., Acetaldehyde, methanol, and ethanol analysis by headspace gas chromatography. J Anal Toxicol 4, 43, 1980.

64. Christmore, D. S., Kelly, R. C., and Doshier, L. A., Improved recovery and stability of ethanol in automated headspace analysis. J Forens Sci 29, 1038, 1984.

65. Smalldon, K. W., and Brown, G. A., The stability of ethanol in stored blood samples: Part II, The mechanism of ethanol oxidation. Anal Chim Acta 66, 285, 1973.

66. Macchia, T., Mancinelli, R., Gentilli, S., Lugaresi, E. C., Raponi, A., Taggi, F., Ethanol in biological fluids: Headspace GC measurement. J Anal Toxicol 19, 241, 1995.

67. Watts, M. T., and McDonald, O. L., The effect of specimen type on the gas chromatographic headspace analysis of ethanol and other volatile compounds. Am J Clin Pathol 87, 79, 1987.

68. Watts, M. T., and McDonald, O. L., The effect of sodium chloride concentration, water content, and protein on the gas chromatographic headspace analysis of ethanol in plasma. Am J Clin Pathol 93, 357, 1990.

69. Jones, A. W., Mårdh, G., Änggård, E., Determination of endogenous ethanol in blood and breath by gas chromatography-mass spectrometry. Pharmacol Biochem Behav 18, Suppl 1, 267, 1983.

70. Kühnholz, B., Bonte, W., Methodische Untersuchungen zur Verbesserung des fuselalkoholnachweises in Blutproben. Blutalkohol 20, 399, 1983.

71. Logan, B. K., Analysis of alcohol and other volatiles. In: Gas Chromatography in Forensic Science (edited by J. Tebbett), Elsevier, Amsterdam Chp. 4, 1992.

72. Tagliaro, F., Lubli, G., Ghielmi, S., Franchi, D., Marigo, M., Chromatographic methods for blood alcohol determination. J Chromatog 580, 161, 1992.

73. Seto, E., Determination of volatile substances in biological samples by headspace gas chromatography. J Chromatog 674, 25, 1994.

74. Purdon, E. A., Distinguishing between ethanol and acetonitrile using gas chromatography and modified Widmark methods. J Anal Toxicol 17, 63, 1993.

75. Streete, P. J., Ruprah, M., Ramsey, J. D., Flanagan, R. J., Detection and identification of volatile substances by headspace capillary gas chromatography to aid the diagnosis of acute poisoning. Analyst 117, 1111, 1992,

76. Jones, A. W., A rapid method for blood alcohol determination by headspace analysis using an electrochemical detector. J Forens Sci 23:283;1978.

A. Wayne Jones and Derrick J. Pounder

77. Dubowski, K. M., Method for alcohol determination in biological liquids by sensing with a solid-state detector. Clin Chem 22, 863, 1976.

78. Criddle, W. J., Parry, K. W., and Jones, T. P., Determination of ethanol in alcoholic beverages using headspace procedure and fuel cell sensor. Analyst 111, 507, 1986.

79. Kricka, L. J., Thorpe, G. H. G., Immobilized enzymes in analysis. Trends Biotechnol 4, 253, 1986.

80. Varadi, M., and Adanyi, N., Application of biosensors with amperometric detection for determining ethanol. Analyst 119, 1843, 1994.

81. Blaedel, W. J., and Engstrm, R. C., Reagentless enzyme electrodes for ethanol, lactate, and maleate. Anal Chem 52, 1691, 1980.

82. Cheng, F. S., and Christian, G. D., Enzymatic determination of blood ethanol, with amperometric measurement of rate of oxygen depletion. Clin Chem 24, 621, 1978.

83. Gulberg, E. L., and Christian, G. D., The use of immobilized alcohol oxidase in the continuous flow determination of ethanol with an oxygen electrode. Anal Chim Acta 123, 125, 1981.

84. Gibson, T. D., and Woodward, J. R., Automated determination of ethanol using the enzyme alcohol oxidase. Anal Proc Chem Soc 23, 360, 1986.

85. Gullbault, G. G., Danielsson, B., Mandenius, C. F., Mosbach, K., Enzyme electrode and thermistor probes for determination of alcohols with alcohol oxidase. Anal Chem 55, 1582, 1983.

86. Cenas, N., Rozgaite, J., Kulys, J., Lactate, pyruvate, ethanol, and glucose-6-phosphate determination by enzyme electrode. Biotech Bioeng 26, 551, 1984.

87. Gallignani, M., Garrigues, S., Guardia de la M., Derivative Fourier transform infrared spectrometric determination of ethanol in beer. Analyst 119, 1773, 1994.

88. Ojanperä, I., Hyppölä, R., Vuori, E., Identification of volatile organic compounds in blood by purge and trap PLOT-capillary gas chromatography coupled with Fourier transform infrared spectroscopy. Forens Sci Int 80, 201, 1996.

89. Pappas. A. A., Thompson, J. R., Porrter, W. H., Gadsden, R. H., High resolution proton nuclear magnetic resonance spectroscopy in the detection and quantitation of ethanol in human serum. J Anal Toxicol 17, 230, 1993.

90. Monaghan, M. S., Olsen, K. M., Ackerman, B. H., Fuller, G. L., Porter, W. H., Pappas, A. A., Measurement of serum isopropanol and acetone metabolite by proton nuclear magnetic resonance: Application to pharmacokinetic evaluation in a simulated overdose model. Clin Toxicol 33, 141, 1995.

91. Robinson, A. G., and Loeb, J. N., Ethanol ingestion - commonest cause of elevated plasma osmolality. N Eng J Med 284, 1253, 1971.

92. Hoffman, R. S., Smilkstein M. J., Howland M. A., Goldfrank L. R., Osmol gaps revisited: normal values and limitations. Clin Toxicol 31, 81, 1993.

93. Osterloh, J. D., Kelly T. J., Khayam-Bashi H., Romeo R., Discrepancies in osmolal gaps and calculated alcohol concentrations. Arch Pathol Lab Med 120, 637, 1996.

94. Amato, I., Race quickens for non-stick blood monitoring technology. Science 258, 892, 1992.

95. Pan, S., Chung, H., Arnold, M. A., Small, G. W., Near-infraed spectroscopic measurement of physiological glucose levels in variable matrices of protein and triglycerides. Anal Chem, 68, 1124, 1996.

96. Bonnichsen, R. K., Ryhage, R., Determination of ethyl alcohol by computerized mass spectrometry. Z Rechsmedizin 71, 134, 1972.

97. Takayasu, T., Ohshima, T., Tanaka, N., Maeda, H., Kondo, T., Nishigami, J., Ohtsuji, M., Nagano, T., Experimental studies on postmortem diffusion of ethanol-d6 using rats. Forens Sci Int 76, 179, 1995.

98. Takayasu, T., Ohshima, T., Tanaka, N., Maeda, H., Kondo, T., Nishigami, J., Nagano, T., Postmortem degradation of administered ethanol-d6 and production of endogenous ethanol experimental studies using rats and rabbits. Forens Sci Int 76, 129, 1995.

99. Dean, R. A., Thomasson, H. R., Dumaual, N., Amann, D., and Li, T. K., Simultaneous measurement of ethanol and ethyl-d5 alcohol by stable isotope gas chromatography-mass spectrometry. Clin Chem 42, 367, 1996.

100. Dubowski, K. M., The technology of breath-alcohol analysis. US Dept. of Health and Human Services, DHHS Publication No (ADM) 92-1728, 1992.
101. Wilson, H. K., Breath-analysis; Physiological basis and sampling techniques. Scand J Work Environ Health 12, 174, 1986.
102. Mason, M., Dubowski, K. M., Breath-alcohol analysis: uses, methods and some forensic problems - review and opinion. J Forens Sci 21:9;1976.
103. Manolis, A., The diagnostic potential of breath analysis. Clin Chem 29, 5, 1983.
104. Phillips, M., Breath tests in medicine. Sci Am 270, 52, 1992.
105. Jain, N. C., and Cravey, R. H., A review of breath alcohol methods. J Chromatog Sci 12, 214, 1974.
106. Moynham, A., Perl, J., Starmer, G. A., Breath-alcohol testing. J Traffic Med 18, 167, 1990.
107. Jones, A. W., Measurement of alcohol in blood and breath for legal purposes. In: Human Metabolism of Alcohol, edited by KE Crow and RD Batt, CRC Press, Boca Raton, p 71, 1989.
108. Emerson, V. J., Holleyhead, R., Isaacs, D. J., Fuller, N. A., Hunt, D. J., The measurement of breath alcohol. J For Sci Soc 20, 1, 1980.
109. Harte, R. A., An instrument for the determination of ethanol in breath in law enforcement practice. J Forens Sci 16, 167, 1971.
110. Jones, A. W., Pharmacokinetics of ethanol in saliva; Comparison with blood and breath alcohol profiles, subjective feelings of intoxication and diminished performance. Clin Chem 39, 1837, 1993.
111. Evans, R. P., McDermott, F. T., Use of an Alcolmeter in a casualty department. Med J Aust i, 1032, 1977
112. Gibbs, K. A., Johnston, C. C., Martin, S. D., Accuracy and usefulness of a breath-alcohol analyzer. Ann Emerg Med 13, 516, 1984.
113. Falkensson, M., Jones, A. W., and Sörbö, B., Bedside diagnosis of alcohol intoxication with a pocket-size breath-alcohol device sampling from unconscious subjects and specificity for ethanol. Clin Chem 35, 918, 1989.
114. Frank, J. F., Flores, A. L., The likelihood of acetone interference in breath alcohol measurement. Alcohol, Drugs, and Driving, 3, 1, 1987.
115. Jones, A. W., and Andersson, L., Biotransformation of acetone to isopropanol observed in a motorist involved in a sobriety check. J Forens Sci 40, 686, 1995.
116. Dubowski, K. M. Studies in breath-alcohol analysis: Biological factors. Z Rechtsmedisin 76, 93, 1975.
117. Dubowski, K. M., Quality assurance in breath-alcohol analysis. J Anal Toxicol 18, 306, 1994.
118. Jones, A. W., Comparing the limits of uncertainty in measuring alcohol in breath with estimating the venous blood alcohol concentration. In; abstracts of the Proceedings 13th International Association of Forensic Sciences, Düsseldorf, Germany, 1993, A49.
119. Taylor, J. K., Quality Assurance of chemical measurements. Lewis Publisers, Chelsea, MI, 1987.
120. Riley, D., Wigmore, J. G., Yen, B. Dilution of blood collected for medicolegal alcohol analysis by intravenous fluids. J Analyt Tox 20, 330, 1996.
121. Gullberg, R. G. The application of control charts in breath alcohol measurement systems. Med Sci Law 33, 33, 1993.
122. Paulson, R., Wachtel, M. Using quality control charts for quality assurance. Lab Medicine 26, 409, 1995.
123. Winek, T., Winek, C. L., and Wahba, W. W., The effect of storage at various temperatures on blood alcohol concentration. Forens Sci Intern 78,179, 1996.
124. Meyer, T., Monge, P. K., and Sakshaug, J., Storage of blood samples containing alcohol. Acta Pharmacol Toxicol 45, 282, 1979.
125. Jones, A. W., Edman-Falkensson, M., Nilsson, L. Reliability of blood alcohol determinations at clinical chemistry laboratories in Sweden. Scand J Clin Lab Invest 1995, 35, 463.
126. Wilson, J. F., Barnett, K., External quality assessment of techniques for assay of serum ethanol. Ann Clin Biochem 32, 540, 1993.

A. Wayne Jones and Derrick J. Pounder

127. Jones, A. W., Biochemistry and physiology of alcohol: Applications to forensic science and toxicology. Chapter 4 in Garriott, J (editor) Medicolegal aspects of alcohol. Lawyers & Judges Publishing Co., Tuson, 1996, p 85.

128. Sato, N., Kitamura, T. First-pass metabolism of ethanol: A review. Gastroenterology 111, 1143, 1996.

129. Jones, A. W., Hahn, R., Stalberg, H. P., Pharmacokinetics of ethanol in plasma and whole blood; Estimation of total body water by the dilution principle. Eur J Clin Pharmacol 42, 445, 1992.

130. Jones, A. W., Interindividual variations in the disposition and metabolism of ethanol in healthy men. Alcohol 1, 385, 1984.

131. Jones, A. W., Disappearance rate of ethanol from the blood of human subjects; implications in forensic toxicology. J Forens Sci 38, 104, 1993.

132. Jones, A. W., Quantitative relationships among ethanol concentrations in blood, breath, saliva, and urine during ethanol metabolism in man. In L. Goldberg editor, Proc 8th Intern Conf Alcohol, Drugs, and Traffic Safety, Almqvist & Wiksell, Stockholm, 1981, p 550.

133. Schmitt, G., Aderjan, R., Keller, T., Wu, M., Ethyl Glucuronide: An unusual ethanol metabolite in humans, synthesis, analytical data. J Anal Tox 19, 91, 1995.

134. Ammon, E., Schäfer, C., Hofmann, U., Klotz, U. Disposition and first-pass metabolism of ethanol in humans: Is it gastric or hepatic and does it depend on gender. Clin Pharmacol Ther 59, 503, 1996.

135. Park B. K., Pirmohamed, M., Kitteringham, N. R., The role of cytochrome P450 enzymes in hepatic and extrahepatic human drug toxicity. Pharmac Ther 68, 385, 1995.

136. Teschke, P., Gellert, J. Hepatic microsomal ethanol oxidizing systems (MEOS): Metabolic aspects and clinical implications. Alcoholism Clin Exp Res 10, 20S, 1986.

137. Lieber, C. S., Mechanisms of ethanol induced hepatic injury. Pharmac Ther 46, 1, 1990.

138. Lee, W. M., Drug-induced hepatotoxicity. N Eng J Med 333, 1118, 1995.

139. Hu, Y., Ingelman-Sundberg, M., Lindros, K. O., Inductive mechanisms of cytochrome P450 2E1 in liver: Interplay between ethanol treatment and starvation. Biochem Pharmacol 50, 155,1995.

140. Slattery, J. T., Nelson, S. D., Thummel, K. E., The complex interaction between ethanol and acetaminophen. Clin Pharm Ther 60, 241, 1996.

141. Ahmed, F. E., Toxicological effects of ethanol on human health. Crit Rev Toxicol 25, 347, 1995.

142. Nevo, I., and Hamon, M., Neurotransmitter and neuromodulatory mechanisms involved in alcohol abuse and alcoholism. Neurochem Int 26, 305, 1995.

143. Kalant, H., Current state of knowledge about the mechanisms of alcohol tolerance. Addiction Biol 1, 133, 1996.

144. Hoffman, P. L., and Tabakoff, B., Alcohol dependence: A commentary on mechanisms. Alc Alcohol 31, 333, 1996.

145. Bogen, E., The human toxicology of alcohol, Chapter VI in Alcohol and Man Edited by Emerson, H., The Macmillan Company, New York 1932.

146. Penttilä, A., and Tenhu, M., Clinical examination as medicolegal proof of alcohol intoxication. Med Sci Law 16, 95, 1976.

147. Jones, B. M., and Vega, A., Fast and slow drinkers; Blood alcohol variables and cognitive performance. J Stud Alc 34, 797, 1973.

148. Moskowitz, H., and Burns, M., Effects of rate of drinking on human performance. J Stud Alc 37, 598, 1976.

149. Wilkinson, P. K., Pharmacokinetics of ethanol. Alcoholism Clin Exp Res 4, 6, 1980.

150. Holford, N. H. G., Clinical pharmacokinetics of ethanol. Clin Pharmacokin 13, 273, 1987.

151. Widmark E. M. P. Die theoretischen Grundlagen und die praktische Verwendbarkeit der gerichtlich-medizinischen Alkoholbestimmung. Urban und Schwarzenberg, Berlin, 1932, pp 1- 140.

152. Roland, M., and Tozer, T. N., Clinical pharmacokinetics; Concepts and applications. Lea & Febiger, Philadelphia, 1980.

153. Jones, A. W. Forensic Science aspects of ethanol metabolism. In: Forensic Science Progress, edited by A. Mahley and R. L. Williams, Springer Verlag, 1991, p 33.
154. Andrēasson, R., Jones, A. W., The life and work of Erik MP Widmark. Am J Forens Med Pathol 17, 177, 1996
155. Jones, A. W., and Andersson, L., Influence of age, gender, and blood-alcohol concentration on rate of alcohol elimination from blood in drinking drivers. J Forens Sci 41, 922, 1996.
156. Jones, A. W., and Sternebring, B., Kinetics of ethanol and methanol in alcoholics during detoxification. Alc Alcohol 27, 647, 1992.
157. Keiding, S., Christensen, N. J., Damgaard, S. E., Dejgrd, A., et al., Ethanol metabolism in heavy drinkers after massive and moderate alcohol intake. Biochem Pharmacol 20, 3097, 1983.
158. Haffner, H. T., Besserer, K., Stetter, F., Mann, K., Die Äthanol-Eliminations- geschwindigkeit bei Alkoholikern unter besonderer Berücksichtigung der Maximalwertvarianyte der forensischsen BAK-Rückrechnung. Blutalkohol 28, 46, 1991.
159. Yap, M., Mascord, D. J., Starmer, G. A., Whitfield, J. B., Studies on the chrono-pharmacokinetics of ethanol. Alc Alcohol 28, 17, 1993.
160. Lötterle, J., Husslein, E. M., Bolt, J., Wirtz, P. M., Tageszeitliche Unterschiede der Alkoholresorption. Blutalkohol 26, 369, 1989.
161. Johnson, R. D., Horowitz, M., Maddox, A. F., Wishart, J. M., Shearman, D. J. C., Cigarette smoking and rate of gastric emptying: effect on alcohol absorption. Br Med J 302, 20, 1991.
162. Watson, P. E., Watson, I. D., Batt, R. D., Prediction of blood alcohol concentration in human subjects; Updating the Widmark equation. J Stud Alc 42, 547, 1981.
163. Gullberg, R. G., and Jones, A. W., Guidelines for estimating the amount of alcohol consumed from a single measurement of blood alcohol concentration; re-evaluation of Widmark's equation. Forens Sci Intern 69, 119, 1994.
164. Lundquist, F., and Wolthers, H., The kinetics of alcohol elimination in man. Acta Pharmacol Toxicol 14, 265, 1958.
165. Wilkinson P. K., Sedman A. J., Sakmar, E., Kay, D. R ., Wagner, J. G., Pharmacokinetics of ethanol after oral administration in the fasting state. J Pharmacokin Biopharm 5, 207, 1977.
166. Sedman, A. J., Wilkinson, P. K., Sakmar E., Weidler, D. J., Wagner J. G., Food effects on absorption and metabolism of alcohol. J Stud Alc 37, 1197, 1976
167. Wagner, J. G., Wilkinson, P. K., Ganes, D. A., Parameters Vm and km for elimination of alcohol in young male subjects following low doses of alcohol. Alc Alcohol 24, 555, 1989.
168. Lewis, M. J., Blood alcohol: The concentration-time curve and retrospective estimation of level. J Forens Sci Soc 26, 95, 1985.
169. Forrest, A. R. W., Non-linear kinetics of ethyl alcohol metabolism. J Forens Sci Soc 26, 121, 1986.
170. Thomasson, H. R., Beard, J. D., and Li, T. K., ADH2 gene polymorphisms are determinants of alcohol pharmacokinetics. Alcohol Clin Exp Res 19, 1494, 1995.
171. Ueno, Y., Adachi, J., Imamichi, H., Nishimura, A., and Tatsuno, Y., Effect of the cytochrome P-450IIE1 genotype on ethanol elimination rate in alcoholics and control subjects. Alcoholism Clin Exp Res 20, 17A, 1996.
172. Gentry, R. T., Baraona, E., and Lieber, C. S., Gastric first pass metabolism of alcohol. J Lab Clin Med 123, 21,1994.
173. Fressa, M., DiPadova, C., Pozzato, G., Terpin, M., Baraona, E., Lieber, C. S., High blood alcohol levels in women; The role of decreased gastric alcohol dehydrogenase activity and first pass metabolism. N Eng J Med 322, 95, 1990.
174. Levitt M. D., The case against first-pass metabolism of ethanol in the stomach. J Lab Clin Med 123, 28, 1994.
175. Levitt, M. D., Lack of clinical significance of the interaction between H_2-receptor antagonists and ethanol. Aliment Pharmacol Ther 7, 131, 1993.
176. Levitt, M. D., and Levitt, D. G., The critical role of the rate of ethanol absorption in the interpretation of studies purporting to demonstrate gastric metabolism of ethanol. J Pharmacol Therap 269, 297, 1994.

A. Wayne Jones and Derrick J. Pounder

177. Tozer, T. N., Rubin, G. M., Saturable kinetics and bioavailability determination. In Pharmacokinetics; Regulatory, Indusrial, Academic, Perspectives. Volume 33, Drugs and the Pharmaceutical Sciences, edited by P. G. Welling and F. L. S. Tse, Marcel Dekker Inc., New York, 1988, p 473.

178. DiPadova, C., Roine, R., Fressa, M., Gentry, T. R., Baraona, E., Lieber, C. S., Effects of ranitidine on blood alcohol levels after ethanol ingestion. JAMA 267, 83, 1992.

179. Palmer R. H., Frank, W. O., Nambi, P., Wetherington, J. D., Fox, M. J., Effects of various concomitant medications on gastric alcohol dehydrogenase and its first-pass metabolism of ethanol. Am J Gastroenterol 86, 1749, 1991.

180. Roine, R., Gentry, T., Hernandez-Munoz, R., et al. Aspirin increases blood alcohol concentration in humans after ingestion of alcohol. JAMA 264, 2406, 1990.

181. Amir, I., Anwar, N., Baraona, E., Lieber, C. S., Ranitidine increases the bioavailability of imbibed alcohol by accelerating gastric emptying. Life Sci 58, 511, 1996.

182. Lieber, C. S., Alcohol and the liver: 1994 update. Gastroenterology 106,1085,1994.

183. Seitz., H. K., Egerer, G., Simanowski, U. A., Eckey, R., Agarwal, D. P., Goedde, H. W., Von Wartburg, J. P., Human gastric alcohol dehydrogenase activity: effect of age, sex, and alcoholism. Gut 34, 1433, 1993

184. Raufman, J. P., Notar-Francesco, V., Raffaniello, R. D., and Straus, E. W., Histamine-2 receptor antagonists do not alter serum ethanol levels in fed, nonalcoholic men. Ann Intern Med 118, 488, 1983.

185. Toon, S., Khan, A. Z., Holt, B. I., Mullins, F. G. P., Langley, S. J., Rowland, M. M., Absence of effect of ranitidine on blood alcohol concentrations when taken morning, midday, or evening with or without food. Clin Pharmacol Ther 55, 385, 1994.

186. Bye, A., Lacey, L. F., Gupta, S., Powell, J. R., Effect of ranitidine hydrochloride (150 mg twice daily) on the pharmacokinetics of increasing doses of ethanol (0.15, 0.3, 0.6 g/kg). Br J Clin Pharmacol 41, 129, 1996.

187. Melander, O., Liden, A., Melander, A., Pharmacokinetic interaction of alcohol and acetylsalicylic acid. Eur J Clin Pharmacol 48, 151, 1995.

188. Passananti, G. T., Wolff, C. A., Vesell, E. S., Reproducibility of individual rates of ethanol metabolism in fasting subjects. Clin Pharmacol Ther 47, 389, 1990.

189. Fraser, A. G., Rosalki, S. B., Gamble, G. D., and Pounder, R. E., Inter-individual and intra-individual variability of ethanol concentration-time profiles: comparison of ethanol ingestion before or after an evening meal. Br J Clin Pharmac 40, 387, 1995.

190. Jones, A. W., Jönsson, K.Å., Between subject and within subject variations in the pharmacokinetics of ethanol. Br J Clin Pharmac 37, 427, 1994.

191. Al-Lanqawi, Y., Moreland, T. A., McEwen, J., Halliday, F., Durnin, C. J., Stevenson, I. H., Ethanol kinetics: extent of error in back extrapolation procedures. Br J Clin Pharmac 34, 316, 1992.

192. Millar, K., Hammersley, R. H., and Finnigan, F., Reduction of alcohol-induced performance by prior ingestion of food. Br J Psychol. 83, 261,1992.

193. Jones, A. W., Jönsson, K.Å., Food-induced lowering of blood ethanol profiles and increased rate of elimination immediately after a meal. J Forens Sci 39, 1084, 1994.

194. Winstanley, P. A., and Orme, M. L. E ., The effects of food on drug bioavailability. Br J Clin Pharmac 28, 621, 1989.

195. McFarlane, A., Pooley, L., Welch I., Rumsey, R. D. E., Read, N. W. How does dietary lipid lower blood alcohol concentrations? Gut 27, 15, 1986.

196. Welling, P. G. How food and fluid affect drug absorption. Postgrad Med 62, 73, 1977.

197. Welling, P. G., Lyons, L. L., Elliot, R., Amidon, G. L., Pharmacokinetics of alcohol following single low doses to fasted and nonfasted subejcts. J Clin Pharmacol 199, 1977.

198. Jönsson, K.Å., Jones, A. W., Boström, H., Andersson, T., Lack of effect of omeprazole, cimetidine, and ranitidine, on the pharmacokinetics of ethanol in fasting male volunteers. Eur J Clin Pharmacol 42, 209, 1992.

199. Pedrosa, M. C., Russell, R. M., Saltzman, J. R., Golner, B. B., Dallal, G. E., Sepe, T. E., Oats, E., Egerer, G., Seitz, H. K., Gastric emptying and first-pass metabolism of ethanol in elderly subjects with and without atrophic gastritis. Scand J Gastroenterol 31,671, 1996.

200. O'Neal, C. L., Wolf, C. E., Levine, B., Kunsman, G., Poklis, A., Gas chromatographic procedures for determination of ethanol in postmortem blood using t-butanol and methyl ethyl ketone as internal standard. Forens Sci Intern 83, 31, 1996.

201. Jackson, P. R., Tucker, G. T., Woods, H. F., Backtracking booze with Bayes - the retrospective interpretation of blood alcohol data. Br J Clin Pharmac 31, 55, 1991.

202. Wagner, J. G., Wilkinson, P. K., Ganes, D. A., Estimation of the amount of alcohol ingested from a single blood alcohol concentration. Alc Alcohol 25, 379, 1990.

203. Fujimiya, T., Uemura, K., Ohbora, Y., and Komura, S., Problems in pharmacokinetic analysis of alcohol disposition: A trial of the Bayesian Least-Squares method. Alcoholism Clin Exp Res 20, 2A, 1996.

204. Komura, S., Fujimiya, T., Yoshimoto, K., Fundamental studies on alcohol dependence and disposition. Forens Sci Intern 80, 99, 1996.

205. Smith, G. D., Shaw, L. J., Maini, P. K., Ward, R. J., Peters, T. J., Murray, J. D., Mathematical modelling of ethanol metabolism in normal subjects and chronic alcohol misusers. Alc Alcohol 28, 25, 1993.

206. Pieters, J. E., Wedel, M., Schaafsma, G., Parameter estimation in a three-compartment model for blood alcohol curves. Alc Alcohol 25, 17, 1990.

207. Hahn, R. G., Norberg, Å., Gabrielsson, J., Danielsson, A., and Jones, A. W., Eating a meal increases the clearance of ethanol given by intravenous infusion. Alc Alcohol 29, 673, 1994.

5.3 MEASURING ALCOHOL POSTMORTEM

DERRICK J. POUNDER

DEPARTMENT OF FORENSIC MEDICINE, UNIVERSITY OF DUNDEE, SCOTLAND, UK

A. WAYNE JONES

DEPARTMENT OF FORENSIC TOXICOLOGY, UNIVERSITY HOSPITAL, LINKÖPING, SWEDEN

The technical aspects of measuring ethanol in body fluid samples are little different if the sample is obtained from a corpse rather than a living person. However, the interpretation of the analytical results obtained from autopsy samples is confounded by problems such as the lack of homogeneity of blood samples, microbial alcohol production postmortem, alcohol diffusion from gastric residue and contaminated airways, and the lack of or unreliability of information on the clinical condition of the person immediately prior to death. On the other hand, autopsy offers opportunities for sampling body fluids and tissues not accessible or not readily available in the living. Sampling of blood from multiple vascular sites, the vitreous humour of the eye, gastric contents, sequested hematomas, as well as bile, brain, skeletal muscle, cerebrospinal fluid, and liver are all possible. Nevertheless, multiple sampling at autopsy can only partly compensate for the increased interpretative difficulties created by the various postmortem confounding factors. As a result, it is necessary to apply a greater degree of caution in the interpretation of postmortem ethanol analyses and to take into account the totality of the available information which should always include not only the results of the autopsy examination but also the scene of death examination and anamnestic data. A single autopsy blood ethanol level is commonly uninterpretable without concurrent vitreous humour and urine ethanol levels as well as information gleaned from the scene of death and case history.

5.3.1 POSTMORTEM BLOOD

5.3.1.1 Physical Properties and Site Dependence

Within a few hours of death, the blood within the vascular system clots and simultaneously there is clot lysis. The effectiveness of the clot lysis will determine whether a blood sample obtained at autopsy is clotted, completely fluid, or partly clotted and partly fluid. The fibrin clots invariably entrap large numbers of red blood cells so that the resulting clot is relatively red cell rich and serum poor. Occasionally the heart and great vessels may contain a large two-layered clot, the lower part typically red clot and the upper part pale yellow rubbery clot largely devoid of red cells (so-called "chicken fat"). Consequently "blood samples" obtained at autopsy are variable in their red cell and protein content and this will have some influence on the measured ethanol concentration because ethanol is distributed in the water portion of blood. Blood obtained from limb vessels is most likely to be fluid and largely devoid of clots and therefore provides as homogenous a sample for analysis as can be hoped for. The presence of blood clots in themselves do not influence the accuracy of blood alcohol analysis using headspace gas chromatography.[1]

5.3.1.2 Water Content and Ethanol Content

Serum and plasma contain approximately 10 to 15% more water than whole blood. Because ethanol is distributed in the water portion of blood, it can be expected that the plasma ethanol content is approximately 10 to 15% higher than the corresponding whole blood concentration. This should be borne in mind whenever alcohol has been measured in serum or plasma in hospital prior to death or where a pre-mortem hospital sample of serum or plasma is subsequently analyzed for alcohol. In 134 blood samples from healthy men and women,[2] the mean blood alcohol concentration was 105.2mg/dL (range 21.8 to 154.8) and the mean serum alcohol concentration was 120.8mg/dL (range 25.0 to 183.1) with a mean serum:blood ratio of 1.15 (range 1.10 to 1.25, SD 0.02); 3 of the 134 serum:blood ratios were between 1.21 and 1.25.

A larger study on 235 subjects[3] produced a similar mean serum:blood ratio of 1.14 with a range of 1.04 to 1.26 and a normal distribution with SD of 0.041. Ethanol concentration in red blood cells was reported in 167 of these subjects and red cells:blood ethanol ratios ranged from 0.66 to 1.00 with a mean of 0.865 and a negatively skewed distribution with a SD of 0.065. Given this data it is evident that there may be significant differences in ethanol concentrations between different blood samples obtained at the same time from the same corpse because an autopsy "blood" sample may range in composition from being largely red cells at one extreme to largely plasma at the other. However, in practice, most autopsy blood samples will tend to be plasma-rich rather than red blood-cell rich because autopsy sampling procedures tend to avoid clots and favor clot-free fluid.

The whole blood water content decreases postmortem and, because ethanol is distributed only in the water phase of the body, this will cause the blood alcohol concentration to decrease. In a study of 71 cadavers,[4] a blood sample taken within 10 h of death (mean 2.1 h, range 0 to 9.6 h) the water content ranged between 72.4% and 89.3%, mean 80.4%, which is closely similar to the water content of blood from living persons (79.9 to 82.3% for women and 77.5 to 80.6% for men). Second samples taken from the same cadavers from 8 to 229 h postmortem had a lower water content ranging between 64.4 and 88.0%, mean 74.0%. However, observed differences in the blood alcohol concentration between the two sampling times were more strongly influenced by other postmortem factors, such as putrefaction, than by water content changes, so that correcting a postmortem blood alcohol for water content is not generally recommended.

5.3.2 BLOOD ETHANOL LEVELS

5.3.2.1 Reported Lethal Ranges

The lethal range of blood ethanol levels is based on published case reports of human fatalities and the experimentally derived LD50s of 500 to 550 mg/dL in rats, guinea-pigs, chickens, and dogs.[5] However, a review of actual cases suggests that the blood alcohol level which may be potentially lethal is 250 to 300 mg/dL rather than the higher figures commonly quoted.[6] (For fatal blood ethanol levels in various series, see Niyogi[7].) The often quoted lethal blood ethanol range of above 400 or 450 mg/dL may only apply to uncomplicated deaths as a result of acute alcohol poisoning in inexperienced drinkers. A review of fatalities with a blood ethanol level above 300mg/dL disclosed 502 attributable to acute ethanol poisoning alone, but 24 resulting from well-documented natural causes, 260 from obvious trauma or violence, and 28 with a combination of a high ethanol level and additional contributing or related abnormalities, emphasising the complexity of interpreting the significance of high blood ethanol levels at autopsy.[8]

5.3.2.2 Contributory Asphyxia in Fatalities

In a series of 115 deaths attributed to acute alcoholism, 59% showed some asphyxial element, either postural asphyxia or inhalation of vomit. For this reason it is particularly important to have accurate documentation of the position of the body as found and any evidence of inhalation of vomitus at the scene of death because passive regurgitation of gastric contents and contamination of the airways may occur postmortem during removal of the body to the mortuary. In many of these deaths in which asphyxia is a contributing factor, the urine alcohol is considerably higher than the blood alcohol suggesting that the mechanism of death was coma resulting from a high blood alcohol level with subsequent respiratory embarrassment and anoxia. In these fatalities, the blood alcohol level observed at autopsy is not the level causing death but rather the level with which the person dies.[6]

5.3.2.3 Effects of Tolerance

A high autopsy blood ethanol concentration, although indicating chemical intoxication at the time of death, does not necessarily imply that there were observable clinical manifestations of drunkenness and this is particularly so in chronic alcoholics.[9] Alcohol abusers develop a tolerance to ethanol to the extent that they can maintain ethanol levels in the potentially lethal range. In an Australian study,[10] blood alcohol levels were determined in chronic alcoholics presenting to a detoxification service. Of the 32 subjects, all appeared affected by alcohol with 23 showing altered mood or behavior, 6 appearing confused, and 3 appearing drowsy but none were stuporous or comatose. All displayed ataxia and dysarthria of varying degrees. The blood ethanol concentration ranged from 180 to 450 mg/dL with a mean of 313 mg/dL and 26 of the 32 were above 250 mg/dL. A similar Swedish study[11] identified 24 patients who attended a hospital casualty department and were found to have blood ethanol concentrations above 500mg/dL. Of 16 on whom full data were available, 8 were either awake or could be aroused by non-painful stimuli. All left hospital alive within 24 h. It is suggested that this tolerance to high blood ethanol levels seen in chronic alcoholics is primarily the result of neuronal adaptation. Physical dependence on ethanol, as demonstrated by the development of withdrawal signs and symptoms on stopping drinking, similarly indicates the existence of an adaptational process.

There are anecdotal descriptions of alcoholics surviving remarkably high levels of blood alcohol. In one instance,[12] a 24-year-old female chronic alcohol presented at the hospital with abdominal pain. She was agitated and slightly confused but alert, responsive to questioning, and orientated to person and place, though unclear as to time. Her serum ethanol was 1510 mg/dL, which corresponds to a concentration in whole blood of about 1310 mg/dL. After 12 h treatment with intravenous fluids, electrolyte replacement, chlordiazepoxide, and intensive care monitoring, she felt well, and was symptomless at discharge two days later. Similarly a 52-year-old, 66-kg male was found unconscious in a bar with a blood ethanol concentration of 650 mg/dL and survived with minimum treatment comprising protection against aspiration and the occasional use of oxygen.[13] A 23-year-old, 57-kg female chronic alcoholic admitted comatose with a blood ethanol level of 780 mg/dL had apparently consumed 390 ml of absolute alcohol in the form of a bottle of bourbon. Eleven hours later she was discharged with a blood ethanol level of 190 mg/dL; the disappearance of ethanol from her blood seemingly followed a logarithmic function.[14] Two further case reports describe more stormy clinical courses but with survival, one with a serum ethanol level of 1127 mg/dL,[15] the other with a blood ethanol level of 1500 mg/dL.[16] This tolerance to high blood ethanol levels seen in chronic alcoholics makes it difficult to interpret the significance of a blood ethanol level obtained at autopsy from such a person.

On the other hand, non-lethal levels of ethanol may be of particular significance in some types of death. Ethanol adversely affects thermal regulation and, depending upon the ambient temperature, may cause either hypothermia or hyperthermia.[17] There is a large body of experimental and clinical data available regarding the hypothermic effect of alcohol on both animals and humans at different degrees of cold exposure. The importance of ethanol in hyperthermic deaths is less well appreciated but illustrated by Finnish sauna fatalities. In a series of 228 hyperthermic deaths (221 sauna related), alcohol had been consumed in 192 cases and the consumption was categorized as "heavy" in 61.[18] Similarly, complex cerebral dysfunctions induced by alcohol are thought to be significant in the syndrome of sudden, alcohol-associated, cranio-facial traumatic death.[19] In this syndrome, individuals who have collapsed and died at the scene of an assault are found at autopsy to have facial trauma insufficient to account for the death together with a high but non-lethal blood alcohol concentration.

5.3.2.4 Interaction of Alcohol with Other Drugs

The simultaneous presence of another drug with ethanol further complicates the interpretation of the concentrations measured at autopsy. Ethanol is a central nervous system depressant and a similar synergistic effect is found for other hypnotic drugs as well as antidepressants and narcotic analgesics so that allowance for ethanol-drug synergism is necessary when autopsy drug levels in blood are interpreted.[20] Although it has been proposed that carbon monoxide and ethanol may have an additive affect, there is no conclusive evidence of this.

The interplay between ethanol and both prescription drugs and drugs of abuse may be complex also. It has been suggested that ethanol enhances the acute toxicity of heroin and that ethanol use indirectly influences fatal heroin overdose through its association with infrequent (non-addictive) heroin use and thus a reduced tolerance to the acute toxic effects of heroin.[21] The use of cocaine with ethanol can produce a toxic metabolite, cocaethylene, which may be more important in determining lethality than the parent cocaine.[22]

The well-known interaction between ethanol and disulfiram (tetraethylthiuram disulphide) results from the inhibition of acetaldehyde dehydrogenese which converts acetaldehyde to acetate when ethanol is metabolized. Disulfiram is used in aversion therapy of chronic alcoholism, although its clinical effectiveness has been debated. In a person taking the drug, subsequent ingestion of alcohol produces numerous unpleasant symptoms which are probably the result of the toxic accumulation of acetaldehyde. Fatalities have been reported with relatively low blood ethanol levels and with acetaldehyde blood concentrations between 12 to 41 mg/L.[23]

Table 5.3.3.1 Prediction of Critical Values of BAC (as mean, or lower limit of 95% and 99% prediction intervals) from Vitreous Humor Alcohol Concentration (mg/dL)[37]

Observed VHAC mg/dL	Mean	Predicted BAC mg/dL 95% PI	99% PI
90	80	29 - 131	13 - 147
150	131	80 - 182	64 - 198
169	147	96 - 198	80 - 214
173	150	100 - 201	83 - 217
232	201	150 - 251	134 - 268
251	217	166 - 268	150 - 284

PI = prediction interval for the determination of a single BAC value. Thus, for an observed VHAC of 90 mg/dL the best estimate of BAC is 80 mg/dL; there is a 95% probability that the true value of BAC is between 29 and 131 mg/dL; and a 99% probability that the true value is between 13 and 147 mg/dL.

5.3.3 VITREOUS ALCOHOL

Analysis of vitreous humour is useful to corroborate a postmortem blood alcohol and assist in distinguishing antemortem intoxication from postmortem alcohol production. It can serve also as an alternative sample if a satisfactory postmortem blood sample is unavailable or contaminated. In most cases, the specimen is easily obtained and can be sampled without a full autopsy. Vitreous humour is a clear, serous fluid which is easy to work with analytically. Its anatomically isolated position protects it from bacterial putrefaction. In microbiological studies of vitreous obtained from 51 cadavers between one and five days postmortem, it was found that none of the samples contained large numbers of bacteria and only one contained fungi.[24]

5.3.3.1 Relationship to Blood Alcohol Concentrations

The predictive value of a known vitreous humour alcohol concentration (VHAC) in estimating an unknown blood alcohol concentration (BAC) in an individual case remains contentious, despite many studies.[25-36] Authors have provided various formulae, including a simple conversion factor, to predict BAC from VHAC but these do not take into account the uncertainty of the prediction for an individual subject. In the largest series,[37] of 345 cases, simple linear regression with BAC as outcome y-variable and VHAC as predictor x-variable (range 1 to 705 mg/dL) gave the regression equation BAC = 3.03 + 0.852 VHAC with 95% prediction interval $\pm 0.019 \, [7157272 + (VHAC-189.7)^2]$. The practical application of the regression equation is shown in Table 5.3.3.1. Set out are the VHAC values which predict key BAC values of 80 and 150 mg/dL as the mean, or the minimum value at either the 95 or 99% prediction interval for the determination of a single BAC value. The prediction interval is too wide to be of much practical use. In addition, re-analysis of the raw data from previous publications gave significantly different regression equations in most instances. From an evidential viewpoint, it would be unreasonable to give an estimate of the mean BAC based upon the VHAC without also providing the 95% prediction interval which is a measure of the degree of confidence attached to the estimate in an individual case.[38-40]

Derrick J. Pounder and A. Wayne Jones

Blood has a lower water content than vitreous so the expectation is that the blood:vitreous alcohol ratio will be less than unity. In cases where the ratio of blood to vitreous humour alcohol concentration exceeds 1.0, the most likely explanation is that death occurred before diffusion equilibrium had been attained and this observation may be of forensic significance.[27] Animal studies[41,42] indicate that, following intraperitoneal or intravenous injections of ethanol, BAC:VHAC ratios may be greater than 0.95 for 30 min or longer. A study of 43 fatalities[31] disclosed a bi-modal distribution of blood:vitreous alcohol ratios with the first mode from 0.72 to 0.90 and a positively skewed distribution from 0.94 to 1.37. It seems that the first mode of the distribution ratio represents the elimination phase of the blood alcohol curve and that the second mode represents the absorption phase prior to equilibrium being established. A second study of 86 cases confirmed this bi-modal distribution and suggested that a blood:vitreous ratio greater than 0.95 indicates that death occurred before equilibrium had been achieved, and therefore in the early absorptive phase.[34] The blood:vitreous ratio during this early phase had a mean of 1.09 (SD = 0.38) in contrast to the late absorptive and elimination phases where the mean was 0.80 (SD = 0.09). Others[33] failed to reproduce this bi-modal distribution. However, most deaths occur during the elimination phase and it is clear that the observation of a bi-modal distribution of blood:vitreous alcohol ratios in any study depends upon the inclusion of cases dying in the absorptive phase. It is likely that the proportion of absorptive phase cases included in published series has varied considerably and that this accounts, at least in part, for the differences in published BAC:VHAC ratios.

5.3.3.2 Postmortem Diffusion and Embalming

It seems reasonable to assume that ethanol may diffuse into or out of the vitreous postmortem. The chemical constituents of embalming fluid may diffuse into the vitreous humour after a body has been embalmed. Fortunately almost all commercial embalming fluids are free of ethyl alcohol, although they commonly contain methanol. Assessment of ethanol levels in 38 subjects pre- and post-embalming suggested that there was no significant effect on the vitreous humour ethanol concentration in the immediate aftermath of embalming.[43] However, in one case the embalmer cleaned the globus of the eye with ethanol on a cotton swab prior to placing an eye cap into position and this caused an elevation of vitreous ethanol from 0 to 340 mg/dL. Conversely, prolonged submersion of a body in water may result in diffusion of alcohol out of the vitreous. This was the proposed explanation for finding a zero ethanol concentration in vitreous but concentrations of 370mg/dL in urine and 223mg/dL in blood (blood acetone 46mg/dL) in a man submerged in cold fresh water for about 6 weeks. In a rabbit model which duplicated these circumstances, the vitreous ethanol level fell from a mean of 196mg/dL to 30mg/dL over the 6-week period.[44]

5.3.4 URINARY ALCOHOL

The ureteral urine, which is the urine as it is being formed, has an alcohol concentration approximately 1.3 times that of whole blood. In fatalities, the urine sample obtained is pooled bladder urine which has accumulated over an unknown time interval between last urination and death. Consequently, the bladder urine alcohol concentration does not necessarily reflect the blood alcohol concentration existing at the time of death. Instead it reflects the BAC prevailing during the period of urine accumulation since the bladder was last emptied.

Several studies have examined the range of ratios between BAC and pooled bladder UAC at autopsy. One study[45] quoted an average UAC:BAC ratio of 1.28:1 with a wide range of 0.21 to 2.66. Another study[30] quoted a UAC:BAC ratio of 1.21:1 with a range of 0.22 to 2.07 for a direct injection GC technique and a ratio of 1.16:1 with a range of 0.20 to 2.10 for a headspace GC technique. In a large series,[46] simple linear regression with BAC as outcome variable and autopsy bladder UAC as predictor variable (n=435, range 3 to 587 mg/dL) gave the regression equation BAC=-5.6+0.811UAC with 95% prediction interval ±0.026√9465804+(UAC-213.3)²]. In practice, a BAC of 80 mg/dL was predicted with 95% certainty by a UAC of 204 mg/dL and similarly a BAC of 150 mg/dL by a UAC of 291 mg/dL. The prediction interval is very wide so that autopsy UAC is of limited, if any, value in predicting an unknown BAC. Although an autopsy UAC should not be translated into a presumed BAC for legal purposes, it is possible to make a conservative estimate of the BAC existing during the time the urine was being produced and accumulated in the bladder, by dividing the observed autopsy UAC by 1.35 (or multiplying by .75). However, if the BAC profile was rising, which might be the case if death occured soon after drinking ended, the calculation UAC/1.35 underestimates the co-existing BAC.

When both urine and blood specimens are available at autopsy, then the UAC:BAC ratio may be of interpretive value. A ratio less than unity or not more than 1.2 suggests, but does not prove, the existence of a rising BAC. If the UAC:BAC ratio exceeds 1.3, this suggests that the subject was in the post-absorbtive stage at the time of death. However, establishing whether a deceased had consumed alcohol immediately prior to death is most easily achieved by obtaining an autopsy sample of stomach contents and analyzing for alcohol. A gastric contents concentration less then 500 mg/dL has been taken to indicate a post-absorptive state.[29] Unusually high UAC:BAC ratios reflect urine accumulation over a long period of time and extreme ratios are well recognized as occuring in delayed deaths from acute alcohol poisoning.[47] In delayed traumatic deaths, postmortem urine ethanol levels may help establish or exclude the role of alcohol. Urine ethanol levels up to and over 200 mg/dL may be found with no alcohol present in the blood.[48]

5.3.5 RESIDUAL GASTRIC ALCOHOL

5.3.5.1 Postmortem Concentrations

Opinions vary as to how much alcohol may be found in the stomach postmortem in case material. In one series,[49] the highest concentration found was 2.95 g/dL and the author quoted a similar high of 5 g/dL in a previous study. In another series,[50] only 1 of 60 cases had a concentration as high as 5.1 g/dL. In a small study,[51] the highest concentration observed was 8.7 g/dL and this was in a suicidal hanging. Given that alcohol is rapidly absorbed from the stomach, it seems likely that death must occur within about 1 h or less of ingesting substantial amounts of alcohol to detect a significant residue in the stomach postmortem.

5.3.5.2 Postmortem Diffusion

Researchers in the 1940s and 1950s debated the suitability of heart blood for quantitative analysis of ethanol on the grounds of possible artefactual elevation resulting from postmortem diffusion of alcohol present in the stomach at the time of death.[52-58] Later investigations by Plueckhahn[49,59-64] lead to the conclusion that postmortem ethanol diffusion from the stomach into the pericardial sac and left pleural cavity was significant and could contaminate blood samples allowed to pool there, but cardiac chamber blood, as such, was not susceptible to this diffusion artefact to any significant extent. However, more recent case studies and a cadaver model have shown that cardiac chamber, aortic, and other torso blood samples may be significantly affected by gastric diffusion artefact.[51]

In one study,[65] blood was obtained from the right atrium, ascending aorta, and the inferior vena cava in 307 subjects without significant decomposition and in whom the blood ethanol concentration was not less than 50 mg/dL in any sample. A total of 104 (33.9%) had one blood ethanol value 20% lower than the highest value. The most striking differences were found when gastric ethanol concentrations were greater than or equal to 800 mg/dL and with associated

Derrick J. Pounder and A. Wayne Jones

evidence of aspiration. In a second study,[50] blood was obtained from the femoral vein, the aortic root, and the right atrium in 60 cases with blood ethanol concentrations of 50 mg/dL or greater and no gross trauma or significant decomposition. Although the mean alcohol concentrations for the different blood site samples were not significantly different, there were wide variations in alcohol concentration among the various blood sample sites in a number of individual cases. Of the cases, 20 (33.3%) had within-case blood alcohol differences greater than 25%; 4 had differences greater than 50%, with 1 of these cases exceeding 400%. Indeed three of the four latter cases had gastric alcohol concentrations between 1 and 5.1 g/dL and the fourth had a concentration between 0.5 and 1 g/dL, whereas, for the 60 cases as a whole, 22 were between 0.5 and 1 g/dL and 11 were above 1 g/dL. In a third study[51] of nine fatalities with known alcohol consumption shortly before death, two showed marked variations in blood ethanol concentrations in samples from 10 sites, with ranges (mg/dL) of 97 to 238 and 278 to 1395; pericardial fluid 1060 and 686; vitreous humour 34 and 225; stomach contents 300ml at 5.5 g/dL and 85 ml at 1.9 g/dL, respectively. These studies[50,51,65] suggest that postmortem diffusion of alcohol from the stomach into the blood may be a significant, although uncommon problem.

The above findings were corroborated by a human cadaver model[51] with multiple blood site sampling after introducing 400 ml of alcohol solution (5, 10, 20, or 40% weight/volume in water) into the stomach by esophageal tube. The pattern of ethanol diffusion showed marked between-case variability but typically concentrations were highest in pericardial fluid and, in decreasing order, in left pulmonary vein, aorta, left heart, pulmonary artery, superior vena cava, inferior vena cava, right heart, right pulmonary vein, and femoral vein. Diffusional flux was broadly proportional to the concentration of ethanol used, was time dependant (as assessed by 24- and 48-h sampling), and was markedly inhibited by refrigeration at 4°C. After gastric instillation of 400 ml of 5% solution for 48 h at room temperature in paired cadavers, ethanol concentrations (mg/dL) were: pericardial fluid 135, 222; aorta 50, 68; left heart 77, 26; right heart 41, 28; femoral vein 0, 0. With a 10% solution of ethanol in the stomach, concentrations (mg/dL) were: pericardial fluid 401, 255; aorta 129, 134; left heart 61, 93; right heart 31, 41; femoral vein 5, 7. The very high concentrations of alcohol found in the pericardial fluid emphasize the potential for serious contamination of any blood sample allowed to pool in the pericardial sac. Introducing 50 ml of 10% alcohol solution into the esophagus after esophago-gastric junction ligation produced similar aortic blood ethanol concentrations to those seen after gastric instillation. This suggests that postmortem gastro-esophageal reflux and diffusion from the esophagus is one mechanism of artefactual elevation of aortic blood ethanol.

Postmortem relaxation of the gastro-esophageal sphincter permits passive regurgitation of gastric contents into the esophagus, if body position and the volume of gastric contents permit. Thereafter, manipulation of the body during removal and transport might lead to contamination of the airways by gastric material, simulating agonal aspiration of vomitus. Alcohol in this gastric material could diffuse from the airways into the blood. An experimental study[66] demonstrated that a relatively small amount of ethanol introduced into the trachea of cadavers was readily absorbed into cardiac blood and also that there was direct diffusion from the trachea into both the aorta and superior vena cava.

5.3.6 ALCOHOL SYNTHESIS POSTMORTEM

Determining whether ethanol identified in postmortem blood represents alcohol ingested prior to death or was formed postmortem as a result of microbial activity is a frequent problem. Ethanol formation may occur in blood putrefying in a cadaver or in blood putrefying *in vitro*. It appears that ethanol is not formed postmortem except by microbial action. Germ-free mice do not putrefy because of the absence of micro-organisms[67] and postmortem autolysis of germ-free mice produces low levels of acetone and acetaldehyde but no ethanol. By contrast, putrefying conventional mice also produced ethanol, propionic acid, isopropyl alcohol, and n-propyl alcohol.[67] Ethanol is both produced and utilized by micro-organisms, so that bodies with high initial levels may show a decrease, and bodies with low initial levels may show an increase.[68] However, in practice, it is ethanol production postmortem which represents the principal problem and this view is supported by an animal model.[69]

5.3.6.1 Chemical Pathways

Ethanol production in corpses[70] takes place by a pathway opposite to that of ethanol catabolism in the living body. The necessary alcohol dehydrogenase and acetaldehyde dehydrogenase enzymes are provided by the micro-organisms associated with putrefaction while the carbohydrate substrates are present in blood and tissues. The level of tissue glycogen available for postmortem glycolysis and subsequent microbial ethanol production varies considerably between tissues. Human liver contains about 1 to 8 g glycogen/100 g wet tissue; skeletal muscle 1 to 4 g/100 g, brain from a variety of animals 70 to 130 mg/100 g and retina (ox) 90 mg/100 g (all figures calculated from dry weight assuming 75% water).[71] Anaerobic glycolysis produces pyruvate, the main substrate for ethanol production. As well as glucose, lactate is a source of pyruvate through the action of lactate dehydrogenase. Because lactate is found in relatively high concentrations in all postmortem tissues (about 150 to 650 mg/100 g in all tissues),[68] it may well be an important source of ethanol. An *in vitro* study on putrefying postmortem blood under anaerobic conditions at room temperature demonstrated that ethanol formation occurred not only by way of glycolysis but also from lactate via conversion into pyruvate.[71]

5.3.6.2 Observed Ranges

Escape of large numbers of bacteria from the gut occurs in the first instance via the lymphatics and portal venous system, within a few hours of death. At room temperature, bacterial contamination of the systemic circulation occurs after about 6 h, and after 24 h there is direct bacterial penetration of the intestinal wall. Generally the tissues remain relatively free of viable bacteria during the first 24 h. Trauma immediately prior to death, intestinal lesions and neoplastic disease, generalized infection or gangrene are all conditions associated with early bacterial spread postmortem.[68] A wide variety of bacteria normally present in the gut and responsible for putrefaction can generate ethyl alcohol in blood, brain, liver, and other tissues.[72] Also, yeasts such as *Candida albicans,* as well as bacteria, may be responsible for postmortem alcohol production.[73]

There is considerable evidence that ethanol can be produced in corpses at levels up to 150 mg/dL after they have been stored for a few days at room temperature. In a study of 130 decomposing bodies,[74] there were 23 with presumed postmortem ethanol production. Of these 23, 19 had blood ethanol concentrations of 70 mg/dL or less and the other 4 had levels of 110, 120, 130 and 220 mg/dL. Because both bacterial growth and enzyme activity is temperature dependant, postmortem ethanol production is inhibited by refrigeration. For example, a series of 26 in-hospital deaths refrigerated within 1 h of death and stored at 6°C for 3 to 27 h before autopsy, showed no evidence of postmortem ethanol production despite positive blood cultures in 13 cases, 7 of whom had a blood glucose in excess of 20 mg/dL.[75] Similarly an inhibitor of bacterial growth, such as sodium fluoride, inhibits ethanol production. As with all blood specimens for ethanol analysis it is recommended that postmortem specimens should be preserved with 2% w/v sodium fluoride and that storage at temperatures above 4°C should be minimized.

Derrick J. Pounder and A. Wayne Jones

5.3.6.3 Effects of Disease and Environment

Circumstances that can be expected to provide fertile ground for postmortem ethanol production include prolonged exposure to a high environmental temperature postmortem, terminal hyperglycemia, death from infectious disease with terminal septicemia, natural disease such as ischemia affecting the large bowel, abdominal trauma, and severe trauma with wound contamination. Body disruption of a severity which commonly occurs in aviation accidents is associated with extensive microbial contamination and a resultant higher probability of postmortem ethanol production. In a series of 975 victims of fatal aircraft accidents,[76] the blood alcohol concentration exceeded 40 mg/dL in 79 cases. Of these it was considered, based on ethanol distribution in urine, vitreous humour, and blood, that 27% represented postmortem production and 28% ingestion, but 45% were unresolved. In such cases, blood values as high as 300 mg/dL might be synthesised postmortem. In the USS Iowa explosion,[77] the highest ethanol level attributed to postmortem formation was 190 mg/dL.

5.3.6.4 Importance of Corroborative Analysis

In establishing whether there is postmortem production or *in vivo* ingestion of alcohol, circumstantial evidence and corroborative analyses of vitreous humour and urine is of considerable assistance. Vitreous humour is helpful because it is better protected from infiltration by the ethanol-producing bacteria of putrefaction. Urine is useful because it normally contains little or no substrate for bacterial conversion to ethanol. No significant ethanol production will occur as a result of bacterial contamination of urine unless the urine contains sufficient suitable substrate, such as glucose, as a consequence of some pathological abnormality, particularly diabetes mellitus.

After the early postmortem period, when decomposition begins, the problem of postmortem ethanol production increases because both decomposition and ethanol production are the result of micro-organism spread and proliferation. This putrefactive phase starts about two or three days after death in a temperate climate, but varies considerably depending on environmental conditions, primarily temperature. In early putrefaction, when a sample of vitreous humour is still obtainable, the presence of ethanol in this fluid is the best indicator of ethanol ingestion. The presence of ethanol in the urine, if it is available, is also a good indicator of ethanol ingestion. Once decomposition has progressed so that the vitreous is no longer available, due to collapse of the eyeballs, and blood cannot be obtained because the blood vessels are filled with putrefactive gases, then no reliance can be placed upon any sample and interpretation of analytical results is hazardous if not impossible. In these cases, anamnestic data may be more reliable than analytical data. In around 20% of decomposed bodies, the ethanol detected is probably derived from endogenous sources based upon its presence in blood but absence in vitreous or urine, but in many cases endogenous production cannot be distinguished from ingestion.[74] Postmortem ethanol production in decomposed bodies results in blood or putrefactive fluid concentrations less than 150 mg/dL in over 95% of cases,[74,78] but this general observation does not assist in evaluating a higher level found in an individual case. In decomposing bodies, endogenous ethanol production may occur in the bile as well as the blood and may be particularly marked in the sanguineous putrefactive fluid which accumulates in the pleural cavities.[78]

The importance of measuring ethanol concurrently in vitreous, urine, and blood samples was demonstrated in the assessment of low postmortem blood alcohol concentrations. A series[79] of 381 cases with autopsy blood alcohol concentrations less than 50 mg/dL were evaluated using the presence of ethanol in the vitreous and/or urine as indicators of ingestion rather than postmortem production. When the BAC was 10 to 19 mg/dL, then 54% of cases had positive vitreous or urine ethanol concentrations (greater than 10mg/dL); when the BAC

Table 5.3.7a Ethanol in Sequested Hematomas

Ref.	Survival interval (hours)	Postmortem Ethanol Concentrations mg/dL			
		Cardiac blood	Peripheral blood	Urine	SDH
81	12	0			120
	13	20		310	190
	6-12	160		310	300
	12-15	200			230(R) 360(L)
	>4	160		250	300
	UK	260		370	320
84	10	23	29	265	132
	1.5	121	121	232	206
	UK	58	47	226	104
	UK	151		322	192
82	13	0			120
	26	0			260
	9	40			100
	UK	50			150
	UK	40			1110

UK=unknown; SDH=subdural hematoma

was 20 to 29 mg/dL, this percentage increased to 63%; when the BAC was 30 to 39 mg/dL, the percentage was 73%; and when the BAC was 40 to 49 mg/dL, 92% of the cases had an alternative specimen positive for ethanol. Of the 165 cases where both vitreous and urine were available, over 90% demonstrated consistent results; however, in 14 there was an unexplained inconsistency with one specimen positive and the other negative.

5.3.6.5 Other Volatile Compounds

Bacterial production of ethyl alcohol is associated with the production of other volatile compounds such as methyl alcohol, formaldehyde, n-propyl alcohol, propionic acid, acetone, acetic acid, acetaldehyde, n-butyric acid, and iso-butyric acid. Of these, n-butyric acid and iso-butyric acid are said to be the most common associates of ethanol produced by putrefactive bacteria.[72] Others have advocated measuring n-propanol as a marker of microbial fermentation.[80] However, variability in metabolic pathways between micro-organisms leads to variability in the final products of glucose fermentation. This limits the potential value of measuring these other products to distinguish between alcohol ingestion and postmortem production.

5.3.7 SEQUESTERED HEMATOMAS

That ethanol might be measured in sequested hematomas was first suggested by Hirsch and Adelson,[81] although they claimed no originality, explaining that it is one of the "tricks of the trade". It has been most commonly applied to cases of head trauma with subdural or epidural hematomas.[81-84] but also to intracerebral clots.[85,86] Although principally used for ethanol, any toxicant might be measured in the hematoma. From the accumulated case data (Table 5.3.7a) it is clear that ethanol measurements in subdural hematomas may disclose levels markedly different from autopsy peripheral blood. In interpreting the significance of the results, several possibilities should be considered. The hematoma may have developed rapidly at the time of

Table 5.3.7b Ethanol in Antemortem Blood and Sequested Hematomas[83]

Time (hours)		Ethanol (mg/dL)		
Injury to pre-mortem sample	Pre-mortem sample to death	pre-mortem	postmortem	SDH
1	21	535	0	170
3	7	486	30	190
5	8.5	183	0	90
3	41	161	0	40
1.5	4.5	164	70	110
2	18	93	0	120
1	25.5	240	0	110
1	58	101	0	40

SDH=subdural hematoma

injury, alternatively it may have been delayed and not developed for some hours, or it may have evolved over a period of time as the result of continuous or intermittent bleeding. If the hematoma accumulates over a period of hours, then its ethanol content will reflect changing blood ethanol levels during that time. Furthermore, the hematoma might not be perfectly sequestered and ethanol may diffuse both out of it and into it. An animal model[84] has provided good experimental evidence that the current approach to determination of ethanol in sequested hematomas is well founded.

In cases of head trauma associated with subdural or extradural hematomas and with a prolonged survival time, the autopsy blood ethanol concentration may be very low or even zero, whereas the ethanol concentration in the hematoma may be substantial thus providing evidence that the deceased may have been intoxicated at the time of injury. In a study of 75 cases in which ethanol was measured in subdural hematomas and cardiac blood,[82] the analysis provided useful new information only in those cases with survival times greater than 9 h because it was these cases in which the blood ethanol had diminished markedly or been fully metabolized. In another case series consisting of 15 fatalities from penetrating and non-penetrating head injuries,[83] there was a pre-mortem blood ethanol level available. Findings in non-penetrating injuries (Table 5.3.7b) and penetrating injuries were similar in that intracranial hematoma levels of ethanol did not accurately reflect circulating blood ethanol levels at the time of injury. Therefore, quantitative interpretations must be guarded.

After trauma, the development of an intracranial haemorrhage, either subdural or intracerebral, may be delayed. If the victim was intoxicated at the time of injury, then this delay may be sufficient to allow clearance of ethanol from the blood. The intracranial hematoma will then contain no ethanol despite the history of injury when intoxicated. This apparent conflict between the history of the circumstances of injury and the absence of ethanol in the hematoma has been used to provide corroboration that development of the hematoma had been delayed.[87]

5.3.8 METHANOL

Methanol (wood alcohol) is used as antifreeze, photocopier developer, a paint remover, a solvent in varnishes, a denaturant of ethanol, and is readily available as methylated spirit. It may be used also as a substitute for ethanol by alcoholics.[88] The distribution of methanol in body fluids (including vitreous humour) and tissues was reported as similar to that of ethanol[89] but there may be preferential concentration in liver and kidney.[90] The lethal dose of methanol in humans shows pronounced individual differences ranging from 15 to 500 ml. Clusters of poisonings are seen secondary to consumption of adulterated beverages.[91-93] Blindness and death may result also from dermal and respiratory absorption of methanol.

5.3.8.1 Methanol Poisoning

Acute methanol poisoning produces a distinct clinical picture with a latent period of several hours to days between consumption and the appearance of first symptoms. A combination of blurred vision with abdominal pain and vomiting are found in the majority of victims within the first 24 h after presentation. Visual disturbances, pancreatitis, metabolic acidosis, and diffuse encephalopathy may be seen in severe cases.[91] The characteristic delay between ingestion and onset of symptoms is thought to reflect the delayed appearance of metabolites which are more toxic than methanol itself. Methanol poisoning is characterized by a metabolic acidosis with an elevated anion gap. The serum anion gap is defined as (sodium + potassium) - (bicarbonate + chloride), and represents the difference in unmeasured cations and unmeasured anions, which includes organic acids. Both formic acid, produced by methanol catabolism, and lactic acid, resulting from disturbed cellular metabolism, are responsible for the metabolic acidosis.[94]

The severity of the poisoning correlates with the degree of metabolic acidosis more closely than the blood concentration of methanol.[95] Measuring formic acid concentrations may be of value in assessing methanol poisoning. Reported formic acid levels in two methanol fatalities were 32 and 23 mg/dL in blood and 227 and 47 mg/dL in urine.[96] The treatment of methanol poisoning includes the competitive inhibition of methanol oxidation using ethanol thus preventing the formation of toxic metabolites. Both methanol and ethanol are substrates for hepatic alcohol dehydrogenase (ADH), although the affinity of the enzyme is much higher for ethanol than methanol. Consequently, the biotransformation of methanol can be blocked by administration of ethanol.

5.3.8.2 Endogenous Methanol Production

Trace amounts of methanol (less than 1.0 mg/L) are produced in the body in the course of intermediary metabolism and the endogenous levels increase during a period of heavy drinking. Ingestion of methanol as a congener in various alcohol beverages add to this accumulation.[97] When alcoholics consume alcohol over a period of several days or weeks reaching blood ethanol concentrations of 150 to 450 mg/dL, then the methanol levels in blood and urine progressively increase to 20 to 40 mg/L. The elimination of methanol lags behind ethanol by 12 to 24 h and follows approximately the same time course as ethanol withdrawal symptoms leading to speculation on the role of methanol and/or its metabolites in alcohol withdrawal and hangover.[97] Below a blood concentration of about 10 mg/dL, liver ADH is no longer saturated with ethanol as substrate and the metabolism of methanol can therefore commence. At this low concentration, the elimination of ethanol follows first-order kinetics with a half-life of 15 min. The half-life of methanol, however, is about 10 times longer. As a result, elevated methanol levels will persist in blood for about 10 h after ethanol has reached endogenous levels and can serve as a marker of recent heavy drinking.[97]

Blood methanol levels in 24 teetotalers ranged from 0.1 to 0.8 mg/L with a mean of 0.44 mg/L so that these levels can be regarded as physiological. By contrast, blood methanol concentrations in samples taken on admission to hospital from 20 chronic alcoholics ranged from 0.22 to 20.09 mg/L.[98] The general extent to which methanol may accumulate in the blood of chronic alcoholics can be gauged from a study of ethanol and methanol in blood samples from 519 drunk driving suspects.[97] The concentration of ethanol ranged from 0.01 to 3.52 mg/g and the concentration of methanol in the same sample ranged from 1 to 23 mg/L with a mean of 7.3 (SD 3.6) and a positively skewed distribution. By contrast, in 15 fatalities following hospital admission for methanol poisoning, postmortem heart blood methanol concentrations ranged from 23 to 268 mg/dL.[93]

5.3.9 ISOPROPYL ALCOHOL

Isopropyl alcohol (isopropanol) is used as a substitute for ethanol in many industrial processes and in home cleaning products, antifreeze, and skin lotions. A 70% solution is sold as "rubbing alcohol" and may be applied to the skin and then allowed to evaporate, as a means of reducing body temperature in a person with fever. Isopropanol has a characteristic odor and a slightly bitter taste. Deaths may occur following accidental ingestion or in alcoholics who use it as an ethanol substitute.[99] Death may occur rapidly as a result of central nervous system depression or may be delayed, when the presence or absence of shock with hypotension is the most important single prognostic factor.

Isopropyl alcohol has an apparent volume of distribution of 0.6 to 0.7 L/kg with maximum distribution occuring within 2 h. Elimination most closely approximates first-order kinetics although this is not well defined. It is metabolized to acetone, predominantly by liver alcohol dehydrogenase, and approximately 80% is excreted as acetone in the urine with 20% excreted unchanged.[100] The acetone causes a sweet ketotic odor. The elimination of both isopropanol and its major metabolite acetone obeyed apparent first-order kinetics with half-lives of 6.4 and 22.4 h, respectively, in a 46-year-old non-alcoholic female with initial serum isopropanol and acetone concentrations of 200 and 12 mg/dL, respectively.[101]

In a review of isopropanol deaths,[102] 31 were attributed to isopropanol poisoning alone, and the blood isopropanol ranged from 10 to 250 mg/dL, mean 140 mg/dL and acetone 40 to 300 mg/dL, mean 170 mg/dL. Four cases with low blood isopropanol levels (10 to 30 mg/dL) had very high acetone levels (110 to 200 mg/dL). For this reason, both acetone and isopropanol should be measured in suspected cases of isopropanol poisoning.

High blood levels of acetone may be found in diabetes mellitus and starvation ketosis with the possibility that alcohol dehydrogenase may reduce acetone to isopropyl alcohol. This is the suggested explanation for the detection of isopropyl alcohol in the blood of persons not thought to have ingested the compound. In 27 such fatalities, blood isopropyl alcohol ranged from less than 10 to 44 mg/dL with a mean of 14 mg/dL and in only 3 cases was the concentration greater than 20 mg/dL. Acetone levels ranged up to 56 mg/dL and in no individual case did the combined isopropanol and acetone levels come close to those seen in fatal isopropyl alcohol poisoning.[103]

5.3.10 OTHER BIOLOGICAL SAMPLES

There have been many attempts to correlate postmortem blood alcohol concentrations with the concentrations of alcohol measured in a creative variety of specimens. In addition to the usual urine and vitreous humour, these specimens have included saliva, cerebrospinal fluid, brain, liver, kidney, bone marrow, and skeletal muscle. All show a very wide range of variation in the ratio of the ethanol content in the target tissue or fluid compared with that in blood making them of little value in practice.

For blood alcohol levels greater than 40 mg/dL, the average liver:heart blood ratio in 103 cases was 0.56, SD 0.30, with a range of 0 to 1.40.[104] However, liver is not recommended as a suitable sample for postmortem ethanol analysis because it is rapidly invaded by gut micro-organisms and provides abundant glycogen as substrate for ethanol production by fermentation, as well as being subject to postmortem diffusion from gastric residue. For bile, in 89 cases with blood ethanol ranging from 46 to 697 mg/dL, the bile:blood ratio averaged 0.99, range 0.48 to 2.04. Bile has been suggested as superior to vitreous humour in the estimation or corroboration of a blood alcohol level[105] but, unfortunately, bile is vulnerable to postmortem diffusion of unabsorbed alcohol in the stomach.[106] For cerebrospinal fluid (n=54, blood ethanol range 46 to 697 mg/dL), the average ratio was 1.14 and range 0.79 to 1.64.[29]

Because the effects of alcohol are on the brain, it would seem logical to analyze brain tissue for alcohol at autopsy. This is not the practice for two reasons. First, analysis of postmortem blood is more helpful because it allows for comparison with data available from living persons. Second, the brain is extremely heterogenous so that within the brain the ethanol concentration may vary two- to threefold between different regions; highest concentrations are found in the cerebellum and pituitary and lowest concentrations in the medulla and pons.[107] Brain tissue obtained from the frontal lobe (n=33 blood ethanol range 72 to 388 mg/dL) gave an average brain:blood ratio of 0.86 with a range of 0.64 to 1.20.[29]

5.3.11 CONCLUSIONS

Blood ethanol levels can be expected to be positive in around one half of all unnatural deaths so that routine screening of such deaths for ethanol is highly desirable. For natural deaths as a whole, the return of positives is not sufficiently high to justify screening, unless there is a history of chronic alcoholism or of recent alcohol ingestion. The autopsy blood sample should never be obtained from the heart, aorta, other large vessels of the chest or abdomen, or from blood permitted to pool at autopsy in the pericardial sac, pleural cavities, or abdominal cavity. If by mischance such a specimen is the only one available, then its provenance should be clearly declared and taken into account in the interpretation of the analytical results. Blind needle puncture of the chest to obtain a "cardiac" blood sample or a so-called "subclavian stab" is not recommended because at best it produces a chest cavity blood sample of unknown origin and at worst a contaminated sample.

The most appropriate routine autopsy blood sample for ethanol analyses, as well as other drug analyses, is one obtained from either the femoral vein or the external iliac vein using a needle and syringe after clamping or tying off the vessel proximally. The sample should be obtained early in the autopsy and prior to evisceration. Samples of vitreous humour and urine, if the latter is available, should also be taken. The interpretation of the significance of the analytical results of these specimens must, of necessity, take into account the autopsy findings, circumstances of death, and recent history of the decedent. To attempt to interpret the significance of an alcohol level in an isolated autopsy blood sample without additional information is to invite a medico-legal disaster.

REFERENCES

1. Senkowski, C. M., Senkowski, B. S., Thompson, K. A. The accuracy of blood alcohol analysis using headspace gas chromatography when performed on clotted samples, *J Forens Sci*, 35, 176, 1990.
2. Hodgson, B. T., Shajani, N. K. Distribution of ethanol: Plasma to the whole blood ratios, *Can Soc Forens Sci J*, 18, 73, 1985.
3. Hak, E. A., Gerlitz, B. J., Demont, P. M., Bowthorpe, W. D. Determination of serum alcohol: Blood alcohol ratios, *Can Soc Forens Sci J*, 28, 123, 1995.
4. Felby, S., Nielsen, E. The postmortem blood alcohol concentration and the water content, *Blutalkohol*, 31, 24, 1994.
5. Wallgren, H., Barry, H. *Actions of Alcohol*, Elsevier, Amsterdam, 1970,
6. Johnson, H. R. M. At what blood levels does alcohol kill, *Med Sci Law*, 25, 127, 1985.
7. Niyogi, S. K. Drug levels in cases of poisoning, *Forens Sci*, 2, 67, 1973.
8. Taylor, H. L., Hudson, R. P. J. Acute ethanol poisoning: A two-year study of deaths in North Carolina, *J Forens Sci*, 639, 1977.

Derrick J. Pounder and A. Wayne Jones

9. Perper, J. A., Twerski, A., Wienand, J. W. Tolerance at high blood alcohol concentrations: A study of 110 cases and review of the literature, *J Forens Sci,* 31, 212, 1986.

10. Davis, A. R., Lipson, A. H. Central nervous system tolerance to high blood alcohol levels, *Med J Aust,* 144, 9, 1986.

11. Lindblad, B., Olsson, R. Unusually high levels of blood alcohol? *J Amer Med Ass,* 236, 1600, 1976.

12. Johnson, R. A., Noll, E. C., MacMillan Rodney, W. Survival after a serum ethanol concentration of 1_%, *The Lancet,* 1394, 1982.

13. Poklis, A., Pearson, M. A. An unusually high blood ethanol level in a living patient, *Clin Toxicol,* 10, 429, 1977.

14. Hammond, K. B., Rumack, B. H., Rodgerson, D. O. Blood ethanol: A report of unusually high levels in a living patient, *J Amer Med Ass,* 226, 63, 1973.

15. Berild, D., Hasselbalch, H. Survival after a blood alcohol of 1127 mg/dl, *The Lancet,* 383, 1981.

16. O'Neill, S., Tipton, K. F., Prichard, J. S., Quinlan, A. Survival after high blood alcohol levels: Association with first-order elimination kinetics, *Arch Intern Med,* 144, 641, 1984.

17. Kortelainen, M. Drugs and alcohol in hypothermia and hyperthermia related deaths: A respective study. *J Forens Sci,* 32, 1704, 1987.

18. Kortelainen, M. Hyperthermia deaths in Finland in 1970-86. *Amer J Forens Med Path,* 12, 115, 1991.

19. Ramsay, D. A., Shkrum, M. J. Homicidal blunt head trauma, diffuse axonal injury, alcoholic intoxication, and cardiorespiratory arrest: A case report of a forensic syndrome of acute brainstem dysfunction. *Am J Forens Med Path,* 16, 107, 1995.

20. King, L. A. Effect of ethanol on drug levels in blood in fatal cases, *Med Sci Law,* 22, 233, 1982.

21. Ruttenber, A. J., Kalter, H. D., Santinga, P. The role of ethanol abuse in the etiology of heroin-related death. *J Forens Sci,* 35, 891, 1990.

22. Tardiff, K., Marzuk, M. P., Leon, A. C., Hirsch, C. S., Stajic, M., Portera, L., Hartwell, N. Cocain, opiates, and ethanol in homicides in New York City: 1990 and 1991, *J Forens Sci,* 40, 387, 1995.

23. Heath, M. J., Pachar, J. V., Perez Martinez, A. L., Toseland, P. A. An exceptional case of lethal disulfiram-alcohol reaction, *Forens Sci Inter,* 56, 45, 1992.

24. Harper, D. R. A comparative study of the microbiological contamination of postmortem blood and vitreous humour samples taken for ethanol determination, *Forens Sci Int,* 43, 37, 1989.

25. Sturner, W. Q., Coumbis, R. J. The quantitation of ethyl alcohol in vitreous humor and blood by gas chromatography, *Am J Clin Pathol,* 46, 349, 1966.

26. Leahy, M. S., Farber, E. R., Meadows, T. R. Quantitation of ethyl alcohol in the postmortem vitreous humor, *J Forens Sci,* 13, 498, 1968.

27. Felby, S., Olsen, J. Comparative studies of postmortem ethyl alcohol in vitreous humor, blood, and muscle, *J Forens Sci,* 14, 93, 1969.

28. Coe, J. I., Sherman, R. E. Comparative study of postmortem vitreous humor and blood alcohol, *J Forens Sci,* 15, 185, 1970.

29. Backer, R. C., Pisano, R. V., Sopher, I. M. The comparison of alcohol concentrations in postmortem fluids and tissues, *J Forens Sci,* 25, 327, 1996.

30. Winek, C. L., Esposito, F. M. Comparative study of ethanol levels in blood versus bone marrow, vitreous humor, bile and urine, *Forens Sci Int,* 17, 27, 1981.

31. Caughlin, J. D. Correlation of postmortem blood and vitreous humor alcohol concentration, *Can Soc Forens Sci J,* 16, 61, 1983.

32. Stone, B. E., Rooney, P. E. A study using body fluids to determine blood alcohol, *J Anal Toxicol,* 8, 95, 1984.

33. Jollymore, B. D., Fraser, A. D., Moss, M. A., Perry, R. A. Comparative study of ethyl alcohol in blood and vitreous humor, *Can Soc Forens Sci J,* 17, 50, 1984.

34. Yip, D. C., Shum, B. S. A study on the correlation of blood and vitreous humour alcohol levels in the late absorption and elimination phases, *Med Sci Law,* 30, 29, 1990.

35. Caplan, Y. H., Levine, B. Vitreous humor in the evaluation of postmortem blood ethanol concentrations, *J Anal Toxicol,* 14, 305, 1990.

36. Neil, P., Mills, A. J., Prabhakaran, V. M. Evaluation of vitreous humor and urine alcohol levels as indices of blood alcohol levels in 75 autopsy cases, *Can Soc Forens Sci J*, 18, 97, 1985.
37. Pounder, D. J., Kuroda, N. Vitreous alcohol is of limited value in predicting blood alcohol, *Forens Sci Int*, 65, 73, 1994.
38. Pounder, D. J., Kuroda, N. Vitreous alcohol: the author's reply, *Forens Sci Int*, 73, 159, 1995.
39. Kraut, A. Vitreous alcohol, *Forens Sci Int*, 73, 157, 1995.
40. Yip, D. C. P. Vitreous humor alcohol, *Forens Sci Int*, 73, 155, 1995.
41. Olsen, J. E. Penetration rate of alcohol into the vitreous humor studied with a new in vivo technique, *Acta Opthalmol Copenh*, 49, 585, 1971.
42. Fernandez, P., Lopez-Rivadulla, M., Linares, J. M., Tato, F., Bermejo, A. M. A comparative pharmacokinetic study of ethanol in the blood, vitreous humour and aqueous humour of rabbits, *Forens Sci Int*, 41, 61, 1989.
43. Scott, W., Root, R., Sanborn, B. The use of vitreous humor for determination of ethyl alcohol in previously embalmed bodies, *J Forens Sci*, 913, 1974.
44. Basu, P. K., Avaria, M., Jankie, R., Kapur, B. M., Lucas, D. M. Effect of prolonged immersion on the ethanol concentration of vitreous humor, *Can Soc Forens Sci J*, 16, 78, 1983.
45. Kaye, S., Cardona, E. Errors of converting a urine alcohol value into a blood alcohol level, *Amer J Clin Path*, 52, 577, 1969.
46. Kuroda, N., Williams, K., Pounder, D. J. Estimating blood alcohol from urinary alcohol at autopsy, *Am J For Med Path*, 16, 219, 1995.
47. Kaye, S., Hag, H. B. Terminal blood alcohol concentrations in ninety-four fatal cases of acute alcoholism, *J Amer Med Ass*, 451, 1957.
48. Alha, A. R., Tamminen, V. Fatal cases with an elevated urine alcohol but without alcohol in the blood, *J Forens Med*, 11, 3, 1964.
49. Plueckhahn, V. D. Alcohol levels in autopsy heart blood, *J Forens Med*, 15, 12, 1968.
50. Briglia, E. J., Bidanset, J. H., Dal Cortivo, L. A. The distribution of ethanol in postmortem blood specimens, *J Forens Sci*, 37, 991, 1992.
51. Pounder, D. J., Smith, D. R. W. Postmortem diffusion of alcohol from the stomach, *Amer J Forens Med Path*, 16, 89, 1995.
52. Bowden, K. M., McCallum, N. E. W. Blood alcohol content: some aspects of its postmortem uses, *Med J Aust*, 2, 76, 1949.
53. Gifford, H., Turkel, H. W. Diffusion of alcohol through stomach wall after death A cause of erroneous postmortem blood alcohol levels, *J Amer Med Ass*, 161, 866, 1956.
54. Turkel, H. W., Gifford, H. Erroneous blood alcohol findings at autopsy; avoidance by proper sampling technique, *J Am Med Assoc*, 164, 1077, 1957.
55. Turkel, H. W., Gifford, H. Blood alcohol (letter), *J Amer Med Ass*, 165, 1993, 1957.
56. Heise, H. A. Erroneous postmortem blood alcohol levels (letter), *J Amer Med Ass*, 165, 1739, 1957.
57. Muehlberger, C. W. Blood alcohol findings at autopsy (letter), *J Amer Med Ass*, 165, 726, 1957.
58. Harger, R. N. Heart blood vs. femoral vein blood for postmortem alcohol determinations (letter), *J Amer Med Ass*, 165, 725, 1957.
59. Plueckhahn, V. D. The significance of blood alcohol levels at autopsy, *Med J Aust*, 15, 118, 1967.
60. Plueckhahn, V. D., Ballard, B. Factors influencing the significance of alcohol concentrations in autopsy blood samples, *Med J Aust*, 1, 939, 1968.
61. Plueckhahn, V. D. The evaluation of autopsy blood alcohol levels, *Med Sci Law*, 8, 168, 1968.
62. Plueckhahn, V. D., Ballard, B. Diffusion of stomach alcohol and heart blood alcohol concentration at autopsy, *J Forens Sci*, 12, 463, 1967.
63. Plueckhahn, V. D. Postmortem blood chemistry - the evaluation of alcohol (ethanol) in the blood, *Recent Advances in Forensic Pathology*, Camps, F. E. Eds., 1969, 197.
64. Plueckhahn, V. D. The significance of alcohol and sugar determinations in autopsy blood, *Med J Aust*, 10, 46, 1970.
65. Marraccini, J. V., Carroll, T., Grant, S., Halleran, S., Benz, J. A. Differences between multisite postmortem ethanol concentrations as related to agonal events, *J Forens Sci*, 35, 1360, 1990.

66. Pounder, D. J., Yonemitsu, K. Postmortem absorption of drugs and ethanol from aspirated vomitus - an experimental model, *Forens Sci Inter,* 51, 189, 1991.

67. Davis, G. L., Leffert, R. L., Rantanon, N. W. Putrefactive ethanol sources in postmortem tissues of conventional and germ-free mice, *Archives of Pathology,* 94, 71, 1972.

68. Corry, J. E. Possible sources of ethanol ante- and postmortem: its relationship to the biochemistry and microbiology of decomposition, *J Appl Bacteriol,* 44, 1, 1978.

69. Takayasu, T., Ohshima, T., Tanaka, N., Maeda, H., Kondo, T., Nishigami, J., Nagano, T. Postmortem degradation of administered ethanol-d6 and production of endogenous ethanol: experimental studies using rats and rabbits, *Forens Sci Inter,* 76, 129, 1995.

70. Nanikawa, R., Moriya, F., Hashimoto, Y. Experimental studies on the mechanism of ethanol formation in corpses, *Z Rechtsmed,* 101, 21, 1988.

71. Bogusz, M., Guminska, M., Markiewicz, J. Studies on the formation of endogenous ethanol in blood putrefying in vitro, *J Forens Med,* 17, 156, 1970.

72. Blackmore, D. J. The bacterial production of ethyl alcohol, *J Forens Sci Soc,* 8, 73, 1968.

73. Gormsen, H. Yeasts and the production of alcohol postmortem, *J Forens Med,* 1, 170, 1954.

74. Zumwalt, R. E., Bost, R. O., Sunshine, I. Evaluation of ethanol concentrations in decomposed bodies, *J Forens Sci,* 27, 549, 1982.

75. Clark, M. A., Jones, J. W. Studies on putrefactive ethanol production: I: Lack of spontaneous ethanol production in intact human bodies, *J Forens Sci,* 27, 366, 1982.

76. Canfield, D. V., Kupiec, T., Huffine, E. Postmortem alcohol production in fatal aircraft accidents. *J Forens Sci,* 38, 914, 1993.

77. Mayes, R., Levine, B., Smith, M. L., Wagner, G. N., Froede, R. Toxicological findings in the USS Iowa disaster, *J Forens Sci,* 37, 1352, 1992.

78. Gilliland, M. G. F., Bost, R. O. Alcohol in decomposed bodies: Postmortem synthesis and distribution. *J Forens Sci,* 38, 1266, 1993.

79. Levine, B., Smith, M. L., Smialek, J. E., Caplan, Y. H. Interpretation of low postmortem concentrations of ethanol. *J Forens Sci,* 38, 663, 1993.

80. Nanikawa, R., Ameno, K., Hashimoto, Y., Hamada, K. Medicolegal studies on alcohol detected in dead bodies - alcohol levels in skeletal muscle, *Forens Sci Int,* 20, 133, 1982.

81. Hirsch, C. S., Adelson, L. Ethanol in sequestered hematomas, *Am J Clin Pathol,* 59, 429, 1973.

82. Buchsbaum, R. M., Adelson, L., Sunshine, I. A comparison of postmortem ethanol levels obtained from blood and subdura specimens, *Forens Sci Int,* 41, 237, 1989.

83. Eisele, J. W., Reay, D. T., Bonnell, H. J. Ethanol in sequestered hematomas: quantitative evaluation, *Am J Clin Pathol,* 81, 352, 1984.

84. Nanikawa, R., Ameno, K., Hashimoto, Y. Medicolegal aspects on alcohol detected in autopsy cases - alcohol levels in hematomas (in Japanese), *Jpn J Leg Med,* 31, 241, 1977.

85. Freireich, A. W., Bidanset, J. H., Lukash. Alcohol levels in intracranial blood clots, *J Forens Sci,* 20, 83, 1975.

86. Smialek, J. E., Spitz, W. U., Wolfe, J. A. Ethanol in intracerebral clot: Report of two homicidal cases with prolonged survival after injury, *Am J For Med Path,* 1, 149, 1980.

87. Cassin, B. J., Spitz, W. U. Concentration of alcohol in delayed subdural hematoma, *J Forens Sci,* 28, 1013, 1983.

88. MacDougall, A. A., Clasg, M. A., MacAulay, K. Addiction to methylated spirit, *The Lancet,* Special Articles, 498, 1956.

89. Wu Chen, N. B., Donoghue, E. R., Schaffer, M. I. Methanol intoxication: Distribution in postmortem tissues and fluids including vitreous humor, *J Forens Sci,* 30, 213, 1985.

90. Pla, A., Hernandez, A. F., Gil, F., Garcia-alonso, M., Villanueva, E. A fatal case of oral ingestion of methanol. Distribution in postmortem tissues and fluids including pericardial fluid and vitreous humor, *Forens Sci Inter,* 49, 193, 1991.

91. Naraqi, S., Dethlefs, R. F., Slobodniuk, R. U., Sairere, J. S. An outbreak of acute methyl alcohol intoxication, *Aust N Z Med,* 9, 65, 1979.

92. Swartz, R. D. M., J.R.; McDonald, Millman, R. P., Billi, J. E., Bondar, N. P., Migdal, S. D., Simonian, S. K., Monforte, J. R., McDonald, F. D., Harness, J. K., Cole, K. L. Epidemic methanol poisoning: clinical and biochemical analysis of a recent episode, *Medicine,* 60, 373, 1996.

Measuring Alcohol Postmortem

93. Hashemy Tonkabony, S. E. Postmortem blood concentration of methanol in 17 cases of fatal poisoning from contraband vodka, *Forens Sci*, 6, 1, 1975.

94. Shahangian, S., Owen Ash, K. Formic and lactic acidosis in a fatal case of methanol intoxication, *Clin Chem*, 32, 395, 1996.

95. Jacobsen, D., Jansen, H., Wiik-Larsen, E., Bredesen, J. E., Halvorsen, S. Studies on methanol poisoning, *Acta Med Scand*, 212, 5, 1982.

96. Tanaka, E., Honda, K., Horiguchi, H., Misawa, S. Postmortem determination of the biological distribution of formic acid in methanol intoxication, *J Forens Sci*, 36, 936, 1991.

97. Jones, A. W., Lowinger, H. Relationship between the concentration of ethanol and methanol in blood samples from swedish drinking drivers, *Forens Sci Inter*, 37, 277, 1987.

98. Markiewicz, J., Chlobowska, Z., Sondaj, K., Swiegoda, C. Trace quantities of methanol in blood and their diagnostic value, *Z Zagadnien Nauk Sadowych*, 33, 9, 1996.

99. Adelson, L. Fatal intoxication with isopropyl alcohol (rubbing alcohol), *Amer J Clin Path*, 38, 144, 1962.

100. Lacouture, P. G., Wason, S., Abrams, A., Lovejoy, F. H. Acute isopropyl alcohol intoxication, *Amer J Med*, 75, 680, 1996.

101. Natowicz, M., Donahue, J., Gorman, L., Kane, M., McKissick, J. Pharmacokinetic analysis of a case of isopropanol intoxication, *Clin Chem*, 31, 326, 1985.

102. Alexander, C. B., McBay, A. J., Hudson, R. P. Isopropanol and isopropanol deaths - Ten years' experience, *J Forens Sci*, 27, 541, 1982.

103. Lewis, G. D., Laufman, A. K., McAnalley, B. H., Garriot, J. C. Metabolism of acetone to isopropyl alcohol in rats and humans, *J Forens Sci*, 29, 541, 1996.

104. Jenkins, A. J., Levine, B. S., Smialek, J. E. Distribution of ethanol in postmortem liver. *J Forens Sci*, 40, 611, 1995.

105. Stone, B. E., Rooney, P. A. A study using body fluids to determine blood alcohol, *J Anal Toxicol*, 8, 95, 1984.

106. Pounder, D. J., Fuke, C., Cox, D. E., Smith, D., Kuroda, N. Postmortem diffusion of drugs from gastric residue, *Am J For Med Path*, 17, 1, 1996.

107. Christopoulos, G., Kirch, E. R., Gearien, J. E. Determination of ethanol in fresh and putrefied postmortem tissues, *J of Chromatography*, 87, 455, 1973.

5.4 BIOCHEMICAL TESTS FOR ACUTE AND CHRONIC ALCOHOL INGESTION

ANDERS HELANDER

DEPARTMENT OF CLINICAL NEUROSCIENCE, KAROLINSKA INSTITUTE,
ST. GÖRANS HOSPITAL, STOCKHOLM, SWEDEN

ALAN WAYNE JONES

DEPARTMENT OF FORENSIC TOXICOLOGY, UNIVERSITY HOSPITAL, LINKÖPING, SWEDEN

Denial of drinking practices has always been a major stumbling block in the effective treatment of alcohol abuse and dependence.[1] Drinking histories are notoriously unreliable and this tends to complicate early detection and treatment of the underlying alcohol problem.[2,3] Much research effort has therefore focused on developing more objective ways to disclose excessive drinking so that help can be given to those at risk of becoming dependent on alcohol.[4] In this connection, the use of various clinical laboratory tests is a useful complement to self-report questionnaires, such as the MAST and CAGE,[5,6] which are intended to divulge the quantity

Table 5.4   Examples of Biochemical Markers of Alcohol Use and Abuse, and Possible Predisposition to Alcohol Dependence

Classification	Example of Biochemical Markers
Relapse markers	Ethanol
	Methanol
	5-Hydroxytryptophol (5HTOL)
State markers	γ-Glutamyl transferase (GGT)
	Aspartate aminotransferase (AST)
	Mean corpuscular volume (MCV)
	Carbohydrate-deficient transferrin (CDT)
Trait markers	Monoamine oxidase (MAO)
	Adenylyl cyclase

and frequency of alcohol consumption as well as various social-medical problems associated with abuse of alcohol and dependence.

In recent years, a multitude of biochemical markers have been developed to provide a more objective way to diagnose overconsumption of alcohol and alcohol-induced organ and tissue damage.[7-9] The liver is particularly vulnerable to heavy drinking and damage to liver cells is often reflected in an increased activity of various enzymes in the bloodstream such as γ-glutamyl transferase (GGT) and alanine aminotransferase (ALT).[10,11] However, it seems that some individuals can drink excessively for months or years without displaying abnormal results with this kind of biochemical test, which implies a low *sensitivity* for detecting hazardous drinking. By contrast, some biological markers yield positive results even after moderate drinking or in people suffering from non-alcohol related liver problems or after taking certain kinds of medication; these screening tests are said to have a low *specificity* for detecting alcohol abuse.

Nevertheless, interest in the use of biochemical tests or markers for screening people at risk of developing problems with their alcohol consumption has expanded greatly.[12] Besides many applications in clinical practice such as in the rehabilitation of alcoholics and in drug-abuse treatment programs, biochemical markers have found uses in occupational medicine, forensic science, and experimental alcohol research.[13] In general, three major classes of biochemical markers should be distinguished (examples are given in Table 5.4):

1. Tests that are sufficiently sensitive to detect even a single intake of alcohol. These are known as *relapse markers*.
2. Tests that indicate disturbed metabolic processes or malfunctioning of body organs and/or tissue damage caused by long-term exposure to alcohol. This is reflected in hematological and biochemical changes and concomitant abnormal levels of various blood or urine measures. These tests are called *state markers* of hazardous alcohol consumption.
3. Tests that indicate whether a person has a genetic predisposition for abuse of alcohol and the development of alcoholism are called *trait markers*. Such tests often rely on identifying an abnormal enzyme pattern at the molecular level. At an early age predisposed individuals show marked personality disorders including sensation-seeking behavior including heavy drinking and drug abuse.

In this article, we review the present state of knowledge about laboratory markers for alcohol abuse and dependence. The advantages and limitations of various laboratory tests are discussed

Biochemical Tests for Acute and Chronic Alcohol Ingestion

and suggestions are made for their rational use in clinical and forensic medicine to disclose acute and chronic ingestion of alcohol.

5.4.1 SENSITIVITY AND SPECIFICITY

Biochemical markers are usually evaluated in terms of diagnostic sensitivity and specificity. *Sensitivity* refers to the ability of a test to detect the presence of the trait in question, whereas *specificity* refers to its ability to exclude individuals without the trait. Consequently, a marker with high sensitivity yields relatively few false negative results and one with high specificity gives few false positives. The ideal marker should, of course, be both 100% sensitive and specific, but this is never achieved because reference ranges for normal and abnormal values always tend to overlap. Instead, a cutoff, or threshold limit, for what is considered normal must be determined empirically. This limit is traditionally calculated as the mean plus or minus two standard deviations (SD) of the values in a healthy control population, and it should be noted that this practice will always result in a specificity of less than 100%.

To obtain a sufficiently high specificity for routine purposes, the sensitivity of the marker has to be gradually reduced. On the other hand, most tests aimed at indicating liver damage resulting from prolonged alcohol abuse often suffer from low specificity because many liver diseases have non-alcoholic origin. The use of receiver-operating characteristic (ROC) curves has become widely employed for evaluating biochemical markers and comparison of different analytical methods.[14] By creating a plot showing the relation between sensitivity (i.e., the percentage of true positives) and 1-specificity (i.e., the percentage of false positives) at different cutoff limits between normal and abnormal values, the performance of the markers, or methods, can be illustrated graphically.[15]

Most studies aimed at evaluating the sensitivity and specificity of biochemical markers of alcohol use and abuse rely heavily on patient self-reports about drinking as the "gold standard". However, considering that many patients fail to provide an accurate history of their true alcohol consumption, this creates a validity problem. Hence, besides the use of sensitive and specific markers of prolonged heavy drinking, there is a definite need to develop and evaluate laboratory methods to monitor recent alcohol consumption in a more objective way.

5.4.2 TESTS FOR ACUTE ALCOHOL INGESTION

5.4.2.1 Measuring Ethanol in Body Fluids and Breath

Ethanol and water mix together in all proportions and after drinking alcoholic beverages all body fluids and tissues will contain ethanol in proportion to the amount of water in these fluids and tissues. The body water in men makes up about 60% of their body weight and the corresponding figure for women is ~50%, although there are large inter-individual differences in these average figures depending on age and, especially, the amount of adipose tissue. Accordingly, the most specific and direct way to demonstrate that a person has been drinking alcohol is to determine the concentration of ethanol in a sample of blood, breath, urine, or saliva. However, because the presence of alcohol in these body fluids decreases over time owing to metabolism and excretion taking place, the time frame for identifying drinking in this way is rather limited.[16]

The smell of alcohol on the breath is perhaps the oldest and most obvious indication that a person has been drinking. But many alcoholics use breath fresheners or can regulate their intake so that the blood-alcohol concentration (BAC) is low or zero when they are examined by a physician. Accordingly, a better way to disclose alcohol consumption is to measure the concentration of alcohol in the exhaled air and for this purpose various hand-held breath-alcohol analyzers are available, such as Alcolmeter SD-400, AlcoSensor IV, or Alcotest 4010.

Each of these instruments make use of an electrochemical sensor for quantitative analysis of ethanol,[17] and the response is accurate, precise, and selective for analysis of ethanol because acetone, which is a naturally occurring breath volatile, is not oxidized by the detectors used. Breath-alcohol tests should become a standard procedure if a patient is required to refrain from drinking as part of rehabilitation and/or treatment or because of workplace regulations concerning the use of alcohol.[18] However, a positive breath-test needs to be confirmed by making a repeat test not less than 15 min later to rule out the presence of alcohol in the mouth from recent drinking. Most of the currently available hand-held breath-alcohol analyzers have an analytical sensitivity of about 0.02 mg alcohol per liter breath, which corresponds to a blood-alcohol equivalent of 4 mg/dL (~0.87 mmol/L). The result of a breath-alcohol test appears immediately after sampling and is reported as the concentration in the breath (BrAC) in units of g/210 L (U.S.) or mg/L (Sweden) or µg/100 mL (U.K.). Otherwise, the result of the test is translated into the presumed coexisting BAC whereby the breath-alcohol instrument is precalibrated with a blood/breath conversion factor, usually assumed to be 2100:1 or 2300:1. Careful control of calibration and maintenance of these breath-test instruments is important to ensure obtaining valid and reliable results.

Measuring the concentration of alcohol in blood or plasma/serum will also provide reliable information about recent drinking, and with gas chromatographic (GC) methods the limit of detection in routine use is about 1 mg/dL. However, obtaining a sample of blood is an invasive procedure and the concentration of alcohol, if present, is not available immediately after sampling. The analysis of alcohol in blood is therefore less practical than breath-testing for clinical purposes as a rapid screening test for recent drinking.

When absorption and distribution of alcohol in body fluids and tissues are complete, a close correlation exists between the concentrations measured in saliva, blood, and urine. The concentrations of ethanol reaching the saliva glands reflect the arterial blood alcohol concentration at the time of sampling, which makes saliva more suitable than urine for clinical and other purposes.[19] Various compact single-test devices have been developed for measuring alcohol in saliva and these have proven useful for alcohol screening purposes in clinical settings. A device called QED is perhaps the most widely evaluated method for analyzing alcohol in saliva and gives an on-the-spot test of alcohol consumption. The QED test makes uses of the alcohol dehydrogenase (ADH) oxidation reaction with the coenzyme NAD^+ at pH 8.6. Ethanol is converted into acetaldehyde and the NADH is formed in direct proportion to the concentration of ethanol present. The acetaldehyde is trapped with semicarbazide to drive the reaction to completion. The NADH is re-oxidized to produce a colored product by the enzyme diaphorase and a tetrazolium salt incorporated on a solid phase support. The length of the resulting blue-colored bar is directly proportional to the concentration of alcohol in the saliva sample and a direct readout of the concentration of alcohol is obtained about 1 min after starting the reaction. Saliva-alcohol analyzed with QED agreed well with BAC and BrAC in controlled drinking experiments.[20]

Numerous studies have dealt with the relationship between urine-alcohol (UAC) and BAC and some examples of the concentration-time profiles obtained are shown in Figure 5.4.2.1. Early after the end of drinking, the UAC is less than or slightly higher than BAC whereas at later times when the BAC enters the post-absorptive phase, the UAC is always higher than the corresponding BAC by about 1.3:1 or 1.4:1. Note that the UAC reflects the average BAC prevailing during the time period that urine is stored in the bladder after the previous void. Accordingly, the UAC does not reflect the BAC at the time of emptying the bladder and in this respect is less useful than analysis of saliva or breath as a test of alcohol intoxication. Instead, the UAC remains elevated for about 1 h after BAC or BrAC reaches zero and the first morning void might be positive for alcohol although the concentrations in blood or breath might have reached zero sometime during the night.

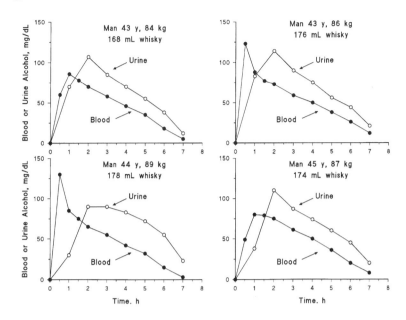

Figure 5.4.2.1 Concentration-time profiles of ethanol in blood and urine in four healthy men after they drank a moderate dose of alcohol on an empty stomach within 20 min. Note that each subject emptied the bladder before starting to drink alcohol in the form of neat whisky in the amounts shown.

Small quantities of ethanol are excreted through the skin by passive diffusion and also secreted through the sweat glands. The amount of alcohol eliminated transdermally corresponds to about 0.5 to 1% of the dose of alcohol ingested.[21] This route of excretion has found applications in clinical practice as a way to monitor alcohol consumption over periods of several weeks or months. This approach might be useful to control if alcoholics and others manage to remain abstinent and has lead to the introduction of a procedure known as "transdermal dosimeter" or more simply called the sweat-patch test.[22-24] Although the first attempts to monitor alcohol consumption in this way were not very successful owing to technical difficulties with the equipment used for collecting sweat, the procedures are now much improved and can be used to analyze other drugs of abuse as well.[25] The test person wears a tamper-proof and water-proof pad positioned on an arm or leg and the low-molecular substances that pass through the skin are collected during the time the patch remains intact. Alcohol and other volatiles are extracted with water and the concentration determined provides a cumulative index of alcohol exposure. The alcohol collected in the pad can be determined in a number of ways such as by GC or headspace analysis with a hand-held electrochemical sensor originally designed for breath-alcohol analysis.[22] A miniaturized electronic device for continuous sampling and measurement of transcutaneous alcohol has recently been introduced.[26]

5.4.2.2 Metabolites of Ethanol Oxidation

The bulk of the dose of alcohol administered (95 to 98%) is metabolized by ADH and the remaining 2 to 5% is excreted unchanged in urine, breath, and through the skin with sweat. Ethanol is metabolized in a two-stage oxidation process first to acetaldehyde and this primary metabolite is rapidly converted to acetate (acetic acid) by the action of aldehyde dehydrogenase (ALDH). The end products of the oxidation of ethanol are carbon dioxide and water. The biotransformation of ethanol, and of methanol, is shown schematically in Figure 5.4.2.2. The oxidation of ethanol to acetaldehyde takes place in the cytosol compartment of the hepatocyte and the acetaldehyde is swiftly oxidized to acetate in the mitochondria.

Anders Helander and Alan Wayne Jones

Metabolism of Ethanol and Methanol

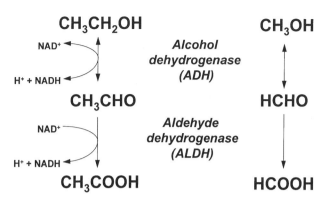

ADH has higher affinity for ethanol than methanol

Figure 5.4.2.2 Schematic diagram showing the metabolism of ethanol and methanol through the alcohol dehydrogenase pathway: NAD^+ = oxidized form of the coenzyme nicotinamide adenine dinucleotide; NADH = reduced form of the coenzyme.

Raised concentrations of the intermediary products of ethanol oxidation have been proposed as a way to test for alcohol consumption. However, measuring acetaldehyde is not very practical to confirm recent drinking because of the extremely low concentrations present (<1% of the ethanol concentration), and also the fact that the necessary analytical procedures are much more challenging than those for the analysis of alcohol.[27] Acetaldehyde is rapidly converted to acetate, and the concentration of free acetaldehyde in peripheral venous plasma is further reduced owing to a more or less specific binding to various endogenous molecules such as proteins (see also Section 5.4.3.5). An additional problem arises if the blood contains ethanol because acetaldehyde is formed artifactually even after sampling.[27,28] Measuring acetaldehyde in breath instead of blood has been suggested as an alternative approach, although even breath testing is not without its problems.[29]

The concentration of acetate in blood depends on the rate of hepatic ethanol oxidation and utilization of the acetate formed by peripheral tissues. The blood acetate concentration appears to be independent of the blood-ethanol concentration, and instead increases with the development of metabolic tolerance to alcohol (i.e., rate of ethanol elimination).[30,31] Measuring blood acetate was suggested as a marker of chronic abuse of alcohol,[32,33] and the sensitivity and specificity of this test was significantly higher than for GGT.[32] It should be emphasized, however, that blood-acetate remains elevated only as long as ethanol is being metabolized and, moreover, the rates of ethanol metabolism exhibit large inter-individual variations even in moderate drinkers.

5.4.2.3 Measuring Methanol in Body Fluids

Ethanol and methanol are examples of endogenous substances that exist normally in biological specimens at extremely low concentrations. These alcohols might be ingested with food or drink, such as fresh fruits or fruit juices, or they could be formed by fermentation of dietary sugars through the action of micro-organisms inhabiting the gut.[34] During the end-stages of carbohydrate metabolism, trace amounts of acetaldehyde are formed from pyruvate and the reduction of acetaldehyde via the ADH/NAD^+ pathway produces ethanol in body fluids.[35] The endogenous alcohols produced in the gut are rapidly cleared from the portal blood as it passes

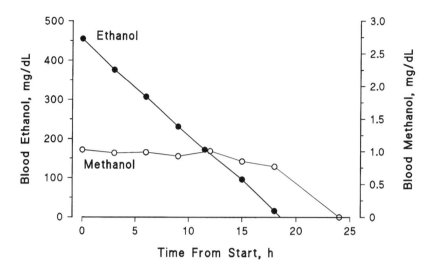

Figure 5.4.2.3 Elimination kinetics of ethanol and methanol in an alcoholic subject during detoxification. Note that the concentration of methanol in blood remains fairly constant at about 1 mg/dL until the concentration of ethanol reaches a low level.

through the liver. The existence of an effective first-pass metabolism ensures that only vanishingly small concentrations of ethanol and methanol reach the peripheral circulation. With the use of highly sensitive and specific GC methods of analysis, the concentrations of ethanol and methanol in body fluids obtained from healthy individuals who have refrained from drinking alcohol generally range from 0.04 to 0.1 mg/dL.[36,37]

Both ethanol and methanol are metabolized by the class I isozymes of ADH mainly located in the liver, and this enzyme has ~10 times higher affinity for oxidation of ethanol than methanol.[38] As a consequence, during metabolism of ethanol, the concentration of methanol in blood increases and remains on a more or less constant level until blood-ethanol decreases below 20 mg/dL (~4.3 mmol/L) (Figure 5.4.2.3). Thereafter, methanol is cleared with a half-life of 2 to 3 h, which means that methanol can be detected in body fluids long after the concentration of ethanol has returned to base-line or endogenous levels.[39-41] This delay in the wash-out of methanol furnishes a test for recent drinking after alcohol has been cleared from the body. Such a test might be useful in forensic investigations when the causes and accountability for accidents are evaluated.[16] Besides the acute effects of alcohol on performance and behavior, many people are impaired in the morning after an evening's drinking; these post-intoxication effects of heavy drinking are known as hangover (see Section 5.1).

The higher affinity of ADH for oxidation of ethanol compared with methanol also explains the therapeutic usefulness of ethanol in treating people poisoned with methanol (wood alcohol). By intravenous infusion of ethanol to reach and maintain a blood-ethanol concentration of about 100 mg/dL effectively blocks the metabolism of methanol into its toxic metabolites formaldehyde and formic acid.[42] In the meantime, the dangerous alcohol, methanol, can be removed from the blood by dialysis and the administration of bicarbonate helps to counteract metabolic acidosis.[43]

Although alcoholic beverages consist mostly of ethanol and water, they also contain a multitude of other chemical compounds, albeit at extremely low concentrations. These other substances, which are produced as byproducts of the fermentation process, are collectively known as congeners and impart the smell and flavor to the alcoholic beverage.[44] Methanol is a ubiquitous congener present in alcoholic beverages such as beer (0.1 to 1 mg/dL), red and white wines (2 to 10 mg/dL), spirits such as gin and whisky (0.1 to 20 mg/dL), and brandies

Anders Helander and Alan Wayne Jones

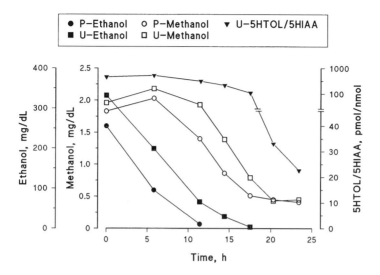

Figure 5.4.2.4 Time course of concentrations of ethanol and methanol in plasma (P) and urine (U), as well as the ratio of 5-hydroxytryptophol (5HTOL) to 5-hydroxyindole-3-acetic acid (5HIAA) in urine, for alcohol-dependent subjects during detoxification. The results shown represent mean values of five male patients. The cutoff for an abnormal 5HTOL/5HIAA ratio is 15 pmol/nmol.

and cognac (20 to 200 mg/dL). Accordingly, a raised concentration of methanol in blood and other body fluids after drinking alcoholic beverages could partly be explained by its presence as a congener, and also because of metabolic interaction with ethanol via competitive inhibition of ADH.[45]

5.4.2.4 Metabolites of Serotonin

Studies have shown that the metabolic interaction between ethanol and serotonin (5-hydroxytryptamine) can help to detect recent alcohol consumption. 5-Hydroxytryptophol (5HTOL) is normally a minor metabolite of serotonin, but the proportion of this metabolite increases dramatically in a dose-dependent manner after drinking alcohol. At the same time, 5-hydroxyindole-3-acetic acid (5HIAA), the major metabolite under normal conditions, is concomitantly decreased.[46,47] Experiments with liver homogenates suggest that the shift in serotonin metabolism occurs because of competitive inhibition of ALDH by the acetaldehyde derived from oxidation of ethanol.[48] Furthermore, during the metabolism of ethanol and acetaldehyde the reduced coenzyme NADH is present in excess and in both the cytosol and mitochondria compartments the redox state shifts to a more reduced potential (Figure 5.4.2.2). This alters the equilibrium between several other endogenous NAD-dependent reactions, such as lactate:pyruvate and β-hydroxybutyrate:acetoacetate. Thus, both the competitive inhibition of ALDH and the change in redox state promote formation of 5HTOL at the expense of 5HIAA.[49] Most importantly, however, the urinary excretion of 5HTOL will not normalize until several hours after blood and urinary ethanol return to background concentrations (see Figure 5.4.2.4).[47] On the basis of this time lag, an increased urinary concentration of 5HTOL was suggested and used as a sensitive biochemical marker of recent drinking.[50,51]

To improve the accuracy of the test, 5HTOL should be expressed as a ratio 5HTOL/5HIAA rather than 5HTOL/creatinine, because dietary serotonin (high amounts in banana, pineapple, kiwi fruit, and walnuts) might otherwise cause false-positive results owing to a general increase in the urinary output of both serotonin metabolites.[52] This practice also compensates for variations in the concentration of 5HTOL caused by urine dilution. To discriminate between a normal and elevated urinary ratio of 5HTOL/5HIAA, a cutoff limit of 15 pmol/nmol (i.e., 1.5%) has been introduced into clinical practice.[51] This threshold value is based on studies with alcohol-free subjects of both Caucasian and Oriental origin.[53] The ratio is stable both within-days and between-days during periods of abstinence, and the metabolites are also relatively stable in urine during transport, handling, and storage. Neither gender nor genetic variations in ADH and ALDH isozyme patterns seem to influence the baseline ratio of 5HTOL/5HIAA.[41,53]

An increased urinary 5HTOL/5HIAA ratio has proved a specific and more sensitive laboratory test of recent drinking than measuring the concentration of ethanol or methanol.[41] The major advantage of 5HTOL/5HIAA over ethanol and methanol is that a raised serotonin metabolite ratio persists for several hours longer thereby improving the ability to spot alcohol ingestion. Furthermore, in contrast to methanol, the baseline ratio of 5HTOL/5HIAA is not elevated after prolonged intermittent alcohol intake and can therefore identify recent drinking in moderate as well as chronic drinkers. Apart from alcohol ingestion, the only factor known to increase the 5HTOL/5HIAA ratio is treatment with the ALDH inhibitors disulfiram (Antabuse) and cyanamide.[54] Another drawback is that urinary 5HTOL testing presently requires rather sophisticated analytical techniques based on gas chromatography-mass spectrometry (GC-MS) or high-performance liquid chromatography (HPLC).[50,55,56]

Continuous or random testing of urinary 5HTOL has been used in clinical practice to detect single relapses during treatment of alcohol-dependent subjects in an outpatient setting,[57,58] and also in heroin addicts on methadone maintenance.[59] Furthermore, testing for 5HTOL/5HIAA has applications in forensic medicine to distinguish ingested from microbially formed ethanol which might occur in postmortem specimens or in urine from diabetics or others with urinary tract infections.[60,61]

5.4.3 TESTS OF CHRONIC ALCOHOL INGESTION

5.4.3.1 γ-Glutamyl Transferase (GGT)

For many years, the serum activity of the enzyme GGT has been the most widely used biochemical test for alcohol abuse.[62] GGT is a membrane-bound glycoprotein widely distributed in various organs, and plays an important role in glutathione synthesis, amino acid transport, and peptide nitrogen storage. Only trace amounts are normally present in serum from healthy subjects. However, in liver damage resulting from continuous heavy drinking, a significant elevation in serum GGT occurs.[63,64] Although the mechanisms responsible are not known exactly, damage to hepatocytes and/or induction of hepatic GGT may cause the enzyme to leak into the blood.[65,66] After withdrawal from ethanol, GGT returns to normal levels within 4 to 5 weeks.

The determination of GGT is routinely included in blood-chemistry profiles on admission to hospital. The major disadvantage of GGT is that the serum level is raised by a variety of other conditions besides alcohol misuse, thereby reducing its diagnostic specificity.[62,67,68] For example, several common medications, such as barbiturates and antiepileptics, and most liver disorders of non-alcohol origin also elevate serum GGT, and normal ranges depend on nutritional status, body weight, age, and gender. Different threshold limits depicting abnormal values need to be applied for women and men separately. Although GGT has limited utility as a single screening test for hazardous alcohol consumption in nonselected populations,[69] many of the confounding factors are well-known and can often be excluded or controlled for in clinical situations. The major advantage of GGT as a marker of alcohol abuse is its ready availability at low cost from most clinical laboratories.

5.4.3.2 Aspartate and Alanine Aminotransferase (AST and ALT)

Other standard tests of hepatocellular damage used as indicators of hazardous drinking include raised serum levels of the transaminases AST and ALT, which are enzymes involved in amino acid metabolism. Like GGT, several common conditions other than alcohol abuse can cause abnormal AST and ALT values, and both are typically less sensitive, though somewhat more specific, than GGT.[70,71] The ALT to AST ratio,[67] as well as the proportion of mitochondrial to total AST,[72,73] have been suggested as a means to discriminate alcoholic from non-alcoholic liver disease, but this was not confirmed in studies in unselected populations.[74,75] The transaminases may be useful in combination with other biochemical tests,[76] and for identification and follow-up of patients with already established alcoholic liver disease.[77]

5.4.3.3 Erythrocyte Mean Corpuscular Volume (MCV)

MCV is measured as part of a routine blood count and indicates the size of the red blood cells (erythrocytes). An elevated MCV is often observed in alcoholic patients,[78] and this parameter has been widely used as a marker of excessive alcohol consumption.[79] The underlying cause of swelling of the red cells is unknown but may be a direct toxic effect of ethanol, or the alcohol-mediated deficiency of folic acid. The sensitivity of MCV is much too low to motivate its use as a single indicator,[80] and there are also several other explanations for elevated values besides heavy drinking. However, MCV shows a higher specificity than GGT,[76,79,81,82] and it is often used in combination with the standard biochemical parameters and enjoys the added advantage that it takes longer (several months) to recover to normal values after the cessation of heavy drinking.

5.4.3.4 Carbohydrate-Deficient Transferrin (CDT)

Measuring an abnormal microheterogeneity of the iron transport glycoprotein transferrin in serum, denoted "carbohydrate-deficient" transferrin or CDT, is seemingly the most reliable method for detection of continuous excessive alcohol consumption during the previous couple of weeks. The use of CDT as a marker of heavy drinking originated ~20 years ago,[83] although a commercial test kit only became available in 1992. The abnormal transferrin pattern appears to be fairly specific for alcohol abuse, and recovers during periods of abstinence with a half-life of ~1.5 to 2 weeks.[84]

Variations in transferrin isoforms may result from genetic polymorphism, the level of iron saturation, and the number of terminal sialic acid residues of the two oligosaccharide chains.[85] In normal transferrin C phenotype serum, the most abundant isoform (tetra-sialotransferrin) contains two biantennary carbohydrate chains making a total of four terminal sialic acid residues. However, after prolonged heavy drinking, increased levels of transferrin molecules lacking 2 to 4 of the sialic acid residues (di-, mono-, and a-sialotransferrin, respectively),[86] and apparently also the entire carbohydrate chains,[87] appear. The exact mechanism whereby alcohol causes elevation of CDT has not yet been clearly identified, but may involve acetaldehyde-mediated inhibition of the enzymes responsible for glycosyl transfer.[88,89] Most importantly, CDT is a much more specific indicator of excessive drinking than any of the other currently used laboratory tests, and it is also assumed to have better sensitivity for early detection of alcohol abuse compared to GGT.[86,90,91] However, it should be noted that an average daily consumption of ~50 to 80 g ethanol,[86] or even higher,[92] over a period of 1 to 2 weeks is required to render abnormal CDT values, at least in healthy subjects. False positive results may be found in non-alcoholic subjects with primary biliary cirrhosis (a condition predominantly seen in women) or chronic active hepatitis, in subjects with the uncommon transferrin D variant, and in a rare defect in glycoprotein metabolism.[81,93-96]

Most of the analytical methods used to measure CDT require an initial separation of the different isoforms followed by immunological assay. Because the isoforms lacking 1 to 4 terminal sialic acid residues are progressively less negatively charged, and thereby have higher isoelectric points than tetra-sialotransferrin (pI ~5.4), they are readily separated by isoelectric focusing (IEF) or ion-exchange chromatographic techniques.[94,97-99] A HPLC method based on UV detection of the separated isoforms has also been published.[100] Although IEF and HPLC methods are more laborious and time-consuming when a large number of samples must be analyzed daily, an advantage of these chromatographic methods is the reduced risk of obtaining false-positive results owing to genetic variations or other chromatographic interferences.

One remaining issue concerning CDT quantification is whether the result should be expressed as an absolute amount (e.g., mg CDT/L serum) or the amount relative to total transferrin (%CDT). Some studies have shown that the relative amount is more accurate,[100-102] but others recommend use of an absolute amount,[81,82,103,104] or no marked differences have been found.[91,98,105] Comparative studies have shown a relatively good correlation between the different analytical methods, and the small variations in diagnostic efficiency observed are not important in clinical practice.[105,106] There appears to be only a weak correlation between CDT and the total transferrin level,[81,82,103,104,107] and because synthesis of transferrin and glycosylation are two distinct processes, no correlation should be expected.

5.4.3.5 Acetaldehyde Adducts

Acetaldehyde, the first metabolite of ethanol oxidation, is a highly reactive substance and forms adducts with various biomolecules, including DNA, phospholipids, and several proteins.[108-110] The binding of acetaldehyde to hepatocellular macromolecules has also been suggested as the underlying cause of alcoholic liver injury.[111,112] Measurement of "whole blood-associated" acetaldehyde,[113,114] acetaldehyde-hemoglobin adducts,[108,115,116] or antibodies which recognize acetaldehyde-modified structures,[117-119] have emerged as possible biochemical markers of excessive drinking. However, some of the results are based on experiments using very high, unphysiological concentrations of acetaldehyde, and the relevance of these findings *in vivo* has been a matter of debate. Although analysis of various forms of bound acetaldehyde have shown promising results, and were more sensitive for the detection of chronic excessive drinking than GGT, MCV, and β-hexosaminidase,[114,115,120] more work is necessary to determine the reliability and diagnostic potential of these tests for the identification of heavy drinking in unselected populations. Moreover, most of the methods used for quantification are probably too complex and unreliable for routine purposes.

5.4.3.6 Other Potential Tests of Chronic Ingestion

Numerous candidate biochemical tests of alcohol use and abuse have been evaluated over the years, but only a few have gained general acceptance.[7,8] The others have either lacked sufficient sensitivity or specificity for alcohol, or require laborious and time-consuming assay methodology, while some have not yet been examined thoroughly enough.

Several studies have reported that alcoholics after a recent or ongoing chronic binge drinking have lower blood, or erythrocyte, ALDH activity compared to healthy controls.[121] However, there is a considerable inter-individual overlap between alcoholics and moderate drinkers in ALDH activity, and even between alcoholics and teetotalers.[122] Consequently, to obtain sufficient sensitivity, the specificity of this marker must be very low (see Section 5.4.1). In addition, several drugs, including the alcohol-sensitizing agents disulfiram (Antabuse) and cyanamide, and environmental factors such as smoking, may cause a long-lasting depression of the ALDH activity in blood.[121]

An increased level of the lysosomal enzyme β-hexosaminidase has been observed in serum from alcoholics,[123] and this was proposed as a more sensitive marker of heavy drinking than

GGT.[124-126] In a study on patients hospitalized for detoxification, the B-isoforms of the enzyme compared well with CDT in terms of sensitivity and disappearance rate from the circulation after alcohol withdrawal.[127] However, elevation of serum β-hexosaminidase occurs not only after alcohol abuse but also in a number of other conditions as well, including liver disease, diabetes, hypertension, and pregnancy.[128] Furthermore, its sensitivity is much lower when unselected populations are examined.[129]

When the BAC exceeds 20 mg/dL, the class I isozymes of ADH are saturated and therefore fully engaged in the clearance of ethanol. However, methanol continues to be produced from endogenous substrates and its oxidation is hindered because of the competition with ethanol for available ADH enzymes. The concentration of methanol in blood after drinking is also raised owing to the congener present in the alcoholic beverages consumed. Recent studies have shown that this metabolic interaction between methanol and ethanol can help to distinguish between acute and chronic drinking practices.[130] After acute intake of ethanol, the BAC rarely exceeds 150 mg/dL and the corresponding blood-methanol is generally not more than 0.5 mg/dL. However, if the BAC reaches 250 mg/dL this suggests continuous heavy drinking and the concentration of methanol now tends to accumulate in body fluids.[131] Depending on the intensity and duration of the drinking as well as the methanol content of the drinks consumed, the concentration of methanol in blood often exceeds 1 mg/dL. Indeed, this concentration threshold (>1 mg/dL) is assumed to indicate continuous heavy drinking and therefore as a marker of chronic alcoholism.[130] Because the metabolism of methanol is blocked during the time that BAC exceeds 20 mg/dL (Figure 5.4.2.3), the longer lasting the drinking spree the higher the BAC reached and the higher the steady-state concentration of methanol reached. The routine analysis of methanol as well as other biochemical markers of alcohol abuse is common practice in Germany to decide on whether treatment or punishment is more appropriate for rehabilitation of convicted drunk drivers.[130]

5.4.4 ROUTINE CLINICAL USE OF BIOCHEMICAL TESTS FOR ALCOHOL INGESTION

5.4.4.1 Single Tests or Test Combinations?

As already indicated, most of the currently available standard laboratory tests lack sufficient sensitivity and/or specificity to warrant their use as the sole evidence of heavy drinking. To increase diagnostic sensitivity, various combinations of markers have therefore been evaluated such as two or more of GGT, MCV, AST, ALT, and, more recently, CDT, as well as many others.[132,133] Measuring blood or plasma acetate together with GGT was more sensitive and specific for early diagnosis of chronic drinking than a combination of GGT, AST, and MCV.[32] Even though combinations of markers tend to increase diagnostic sensitivity, at the same time this approach might reduce diagnostic specificity.[76,103] Furthermore, use of multiple markers could complicate interpretation, and the costs are also higher.

A useful approach is to combine markers that are independently associated with alcohol consumption. While a good correlation is usually obtained between liver function tests like GGT, AST, and ALT, this is not the case for GGT and CDT.[74,82,134] Rather, in a recent study, several of the highest CDT levels were found in alcoholic subjects possessing normal or only moderately elevated GGT values and vice versa.[135] This was further confirmed by another study in which a negative correlation between CDT and the severity of liver disease was reported.[136] Thus, the combined use of GGT and CDT might significantly improve identification of heavily drinking subjects and those at risk of becoming dependent on alcohol.[135,137]

A combination of short-term and long-term markers has been used successfully during outpatient treatment of alcohol dependent subjects.[57,58] Whereas breath alcohol testing or assay of urinary 5HTOL readily identifies single lapses, an increased CDT suggests return to heavy drinking after a period of abstinence.

5.4.4.2 Screening for Excessive Drinking in Unselected Populations

Many biochemical screening markers used for the early detection of harmful consumption of alcohol give excellent results (i.e., high sensitivity and specificity) when studies are carried out on selected populations, e.g., alcoholics undergoing detoxification as compared to teetotalers or moderate drinkers. By contrast, in studies on single individuals and when screening people from the general population, most tests are less satisfactory, mainly because of a considerable overlap between values for alcoholics and moderate drinkers, and, furthermore, because many other medical and environmental conditions can cause positive test results. An example illustrates this point. Assuming that the prevalence of excessive drinking is 10%, a marker with 90% sensitivity and specificity will correctly identify 9 of the 10 heavy drinkers in a study population of 100, but, at the same time, incorrectly identify 9 of the 90 healthy subjects as having drinking problems. Thus, the chance of a correct classification under these conditions is only 50% (the positive predictive value). For most of the currently available laboratory markers of alcohol abuse, a single abnormal result is therefore difficult to interpret until confirmed in a repeated test or by complementary testing to exclude other potential causes.

Another important issue is the time delay between drinking and sampling. Because the various biochemical markers have different life-spans, the time since the last drink should always be considered when evaluating the sensitivity of a test. GGT and CDT, for example, have biological half-lives of ~2 to 3 weeks, so the specimen should preferably be collected no later than one week following hospital admission or alcohol withdrawal, otherwise the sensitivity of the test will be reduced considerably.

5.4.4.3 Treatment Follow-Up of Alcohol Dependent Patients

By monitoring the changes in a number of markers of excessive drinking, such as CDT and GGT, during a 2 to 4 week period of alcohol withdrawal (e.g., during hospitalization or other inpatient treatment), the most sensitive single marker can be identified (Figure 5.4.4.3).[135] If the values normalize on withdrawal, this also confirms that alcohol was most likely the cause of the elevated test results. After discharge from the hospital, blood sampling should be continued for monitoring excessive drinking on a routine basis in connection with each return visit to the clinic. This facilitates early identification of relapse,[138] and breath-alcohol tests or assay of urinary 5HTOL can be performed randomly to monitor acute drinking. The optimal frequency of testing is dependent in part on the life-span of the marker in question.[139] Giving patients feedback about the results of the biochemical tests by presenting the values in a graph (Figure 5.4.4.3) can be informative and may also improve self-report and treatment outcome.[140] However, if this strategy is used it is imperative that the results are reliable (i.e., using highly specific tests), otherwise the patient may soon lose faith in the use of laboratory markers.

The use of repeated testing also makes it possible to use individualized instead of population reference limits for each biochemical marker, thereby considerably improving the reliability of results.[58,77] The recommended cutoff limits between normal and abnormal values are usually based on a Gaussian distribution in healthy controls. However, because of interindividual variations, subjects with very low baseline values probably need to drink much larger amounts of alcohol than those with higher baseline values in order to exceed the critical threshold limit. By introducing individualized cutoffs, detection of relapse drinking can be significantly improved.[58]

5.4.5 TRAIT MARKERS OF ALCOHOL DEPENDENCE

Eugenic studies conducted during the late 1800s demonstrated that excessive drinking, drunkenness, and alcoholism runs in families. Unequivocal evidence for a genetic component in alcoholism and addiction came from the widely publicized adoption and twin studies.[141,142]

Anders Helander and Alan Wayne Jones

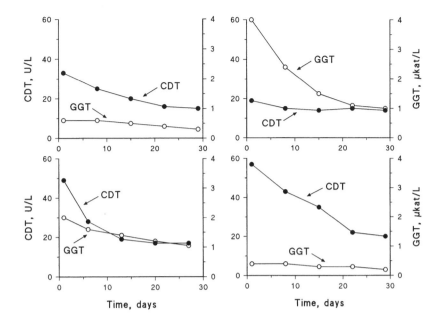

Figure 5.4.4.3 Comparison of carbohydrate-deficient transferrin (CDT) and γ-glutamyl transferase (GGT) levels in samples of serum from four male alcohol-dependent patients on admission to hospital for detoxification, and during ~4 weeks of alcohol withdrawal. CDT assays were carried out using the CDTect kit (Pharmacia Diagnostics, Uppsala, Sweden; 1 U CDT corresponds to ~1 mg transferrin).

Later research on the inheritance of alcohol dependence lead to the definitions of *type 1* and *type 2* alcoholism subtypes which have now become widely accepted.[143] It seems that some people are predisposed to becoming dependent on alcohol when they drink regularly, and efforts have been made to develop trait markers of alcoholism.[144-146] The major candidates as trait markers are monoamine oxidase (MAO) and adenylyl cyclase, two enzymes important in the metabolism of biogenic amines which are involved in various aspects of compulsive, impulsive, and addictive behavior including pleasure seeking and reward areas of the brain. A significantly lower activity of MAO in blood platelets of alcoholics compared to controls was reported,[147] although concerns have been raised about the exact mechanism of the lowered activity in alcoholics.[148] Tobacco use, for example, which is common in alcoholics can also lower MAO activity.[149] Furthermore, standardized assay methods for MAO activity and variability between different laboratories have not been published.

Hitherto, however, the only clear-cut evidence linking alcohol use and abuse to genetics is the polymorphism of ADH and ALDH enzymes observed in Japanese and other Oriental populations. The lack of mitochondrial ALDH2 isozyme activity makes these individuals hypersensitive to acetaldehyde which reaches an abnormally high level during degradation of ethanol. This inborn Antabuse-like reaction creates an aversion to alcohol which influences drinking behavior and decreases the risk of becoming dependent on alcohol and developing alcoholic liver disease.[150,151]

5.4.6 CONCLUSIONS

Alcohol abuse and dependence is a major risk factor for serious health, social, and economic problems, and excessive drinking is a common cause of injuries and accidents.[152] Early identification of those who overindulge in drinking would increase the possibility of a successful treatment. Monitoring a person's consumption of alcohol is important in efforts aimed at prevention and reducing the costs of alcoholism treatment programs. However, obtaining accurate information about a person's drinking practices represents one of the major problems in the detection of excessive alcohol consumption. Self-reports of drinking practices during interview or in diagnostic questionnaires are widely used for this purpose, but people with alcohol-related problems may deliberately deny or underreport the actual amounts they consume, at least in the early stages of misuse. For this reason, erroneous classification of patients and underdiagnosis of alcohol misuse is common.[74,153] To help overcome this problem, a large number of biochemical and hematological abnormalities associated with excessive drinking have been evaluated to assess the extent of alcohol abuse even when the person is not intoxicated.

The perfect biochemical test should be specific for alcohol and also exhibit high sensitivity to hazardous drinking. Furthermore, the test should be inexpensive and performed quickly on a readily available specimen such as urine, saliva, or blood. Measuring ethanol in body fluids or breath is of course the most highly specific test, but because ethanol is eliminated fairly rapidly from the body the sensitivity is low. Most of the currently available laboratory markers perform well when selected populations are being compared, but they are less satisfactory in randomly selected individuals. Although no single marker covering all forms of alcohol use and abuse is likely to be found, combining the most sensitive and specific markers can be very informative. Presently, analysis of ethanol, methanol, and 5HTOL is recommended for detection of current drinking or relapse, whereas CDT, preferably in combination with a liver function test such as GGT, is useful to monitor prolonged excessive drinking.

Alcohol is a licit drug, and acceptable levels of consumption vary between countries and societies. Furthermore, a consumption pattern that might be harmless for one individual may be harmful for another, not taking into account the tolerance to alcohol that develops after prolonged misuse (see section 5.1). Biochemical markers of alcohol use and abuse furnish indirect ways to evaluate harmful effects of alcohol, and to recognize those at risk of becoming alcoholics. However, it should be pointed out that biochemical markers cannot be used to determine the absolute level of consumption, that is, the amounts of alcohol actually ingested.

REFERENCES

1. Jellinek, E. M., *The disease concept of alcoholism*, Hillhouse Press, New Haven, 1960.
2. Fuller, R. K., Lee, K. K. and Gordis, E., Validity of self-report in alcoholism research: results of a Veterans Administration cooperative study. *Alcohol Clin Exp Res*, 12, 201, 1988.
3. Ness, D. E. and Ende, J., Denial in the medical interview: recognition and management. *J Am Med Assoc*, 272, 1777, 1994.
4. Wilson, R. S., *Diagnosis of alcohol abuse*, CRC Press, Boca Raton, 1989.
5. Mayfield, D., McLeod, G. and Hall, P., The CAGE questionnaire: validation of a new alcoholism screening instrument. *Am J Psychiat*, 131, 1121, 1974.
6. Selzer, M. L., The Michigan Alcoholism Screening Test: the quest for a new diagnostic instrument. *Am J Psychiat*, 127, 89, 1981.
7. Mihas, A. A. and Tavassoli, M., Laboratory markers of ethanol intake and abuse: a critical appraisal. *Am J Med Sci*, 303, 415, 1992.
8. Goldberg, D. M. and Kapur, B. M., Enzymes and circulating proteins as markers of alcohol abuse. *Clin Chim Acta*, 226, 191, 1994.
9. Conigrave, K. M., Saunders, J. B. and Whitfield, J. B., Diagnostic tests for alcohol consumption. *Alcohol Alcohol*, 30, 13, 1995.
10. Salaspuro, M., Characteristics of laboratory markers in alcohol-related organ damage. *Scand J Gastroenterol*, 24, 769, 1989.
11. Rosman, A. S. and Lieber, C. S., Diagnostic utility of laboratory tests in alcoholic liver disease. *Clin Chem*, 40, 1641, 1994.

Anders Helander and Alan Wayne Jones

12. Wilson, R. S., Mohs, M. E., Eskelson, C., Sampliner, R. E. and Hartmann, B., Identification of alcohol abuse and alcoholism with biological parameters. *Alcohol Clin Exp Res,* 10, 364, 1986.
13. Beck, O., Helander, A. and Jones, A. W., Serotonin metabolism marks alcohol intake. *FUDT Newsletter,* September, 1, 1996.
14. Zweig, M. H. and Campbell, G., Receiver-operating characteristic (ROC) plots: a fundamental evaluation tool in clinical medicine. *Clin Chem,* 39, 561, 1993.
15. Henderson, A. R., Assessing test accuracy and its clinical consequences: a primer for receiver operating characteristic curve analysis. *Ann Clin Biochem,* 30, 521, 1993.
16. Jones, A. W. and Helander, A., Disclosing recent drinking after alcohol has been cleared from the body. *J Anal Toxicol,* 20, 141, 1996.
17. Jones, A. W., Measuring alcohol in blood and breath for forensic purposes: a historical review. *Forens Sci Rev,* 8, 13, 1996.
18. Dubowski, K. M. and Caplan, Y. H., Alcohol testing in the workplace, in *Medicolehal aspects of alcohol,* J. C. Garriott, Laywers & Judges Publ. Co., Tucson, 1996, 439.
19. Haeckel, R. and Hänecke, P., Application of saliva for drug monitoring: an in vivo model for transmembrane transport. *Eur J Clin Chem Clin Biochem,* 34, 171, 1996.
20. Jones, A. W., Measuring ethanol in saliva with the QED enzymatic test device: comparison of results with blood and breath-alcohol concentration. *J Anal Toxicol,* 19, 169, 1995.
21. Pawan, G. L. S. and Grice, K., Distribution of alcohol in urine and sweat after drinking. *Lancet,* ii, 1016, 1968.
22. Phillips, M., Sweat patch test for alcohol consumption: rapid assay with an electrochemical detector. *Alcohol Clin Exp Res,* 6, 532, 1982.
23. Swift, R. M., Martin, C. S., Swette, L., LaConti, A. and Kackley, N., Studies on a wearable, electronic, transdermal alcohol sensor. *Alcohol Clin Exp Res,* 16, 721, 1992.
24. Phillips, M., Greenberg, J. and Andrzejewski, J., Evaluation of the Alcopatch, a transdermal dosimeter for monitoring alcohol consumption. *Alcohol Clin Exp Res,* 19, 1547, 1995.
25. Cone, E. J., Hillsgrove, M. J., Jenkins, A. J., Keenan, R. M. and Darwin, W. D., Sweat testing for heroin, cocaine, and metabolites. *J Anal Toxicol,* 18, 298, 1994.
26. Swift, R., Davidson, D. and Fitz, E., Transdermal alcohol detection with a new miniaturized sensor, the miniTAS. *Alcohol Clin Exp Res,* 20, 45A, 1996.
27. Eriksson, C. J. P. and Fukunaga, T., Human blood acetaldehyde (update 1992). *Alcohol Alcohol,* Suppl 2, 9, 1993.
28. Helander, A., Löwenmo, C. and Johansson, M., Distribution of acetaldehyde in human blood: effects of ethanol and treatment with disulfiram. *Alcohol Alcohol,* 28, 461, 1993.
29. Jones, A. W., Measuring and reporting the concentration of acetaldehyde in human breath. *Alcohol Alcohol,* 30, 271, 1995.
30. Lundquist, F., Production and utilization of free acetate in man. *Nature,* 193, 579, 1962.
31. Nuutinen, H., Lindros, K., Hekali, P. and Salaspuro, M., Elevated blood acetate as indicator of fast ethanol elimination in chronic alcoholics. *Alcohol,* 2, 623, 1985.
32. Korri, U.-M., Nuutinen, H. and Salaspuro, M., Increased blood acetate: a new laboratory marker of alcoholism and heavy drinking. *Alcohol Clin Exp Res,* 9, 468, 1985.
33. Roine, R. P., Korri, U.-M., Ylikahri, R., Pentillä, A., Pikkarainen, J. and Salaspuro, M., Increased serum acetate as a marker of problem drinking among drunken drivers. *Alcohol Alcohol,* 23, 123, 1988.
34. Ostrovsky, Y. M., Endogenous ethanol - its metabolic, behavioral and biomedical significance. *Alcohol,* 3, 239, 1986.
35. Krebs, H. A. and Perkins, J. R., The physiological role of liver alcohol dehydrogenase. *Biochem J,* 118, 635, 1970.
36. Sprung, R., Bonte, W., Rüdell, E., Domke, M. and Frauenrath, C., Zum Problem des endogenen Alkohols. *Blutalkohol,* 18, 65, 1981.
37. Haffner, H.-T., Graw, M., Besserer, K., Blicke, U. and Henssge, C., Endogenous methanol: variability in concentration and rate of production. Evidence of a deep compartment? *Forens Sci Int,* 79, 145, 1996.

38. Mani, J. C., Pietruszko, R. and Theorell, H., Methanol activity of alcohol dehydrogenase from human liver, horse liver, and yeast. *Arch Biochem Biophys*, 140, 52, 1970.
39. Jones, A. W., Elimination half-life of methanol during hangover. *Pharmacol Toxicol*, 60, 217, 1987.
40. Haffner, H.-T., Wehner, H. D., Scheytt, K. D. and Besserer, K., The elimination kinetics of methanol and the influence of ethanol. *Int J Leg Med*, 105, 111, 1992.
41. Helander, A., Beck, O. and Jones, A. W., Laboratory testing for recent alcohol consumption: comparison of ethanol, methanol, and 5-hydroxytryptophol. *Clin Chem*, 42, 618, 1996.
42. Jacobsen, D., Jansen, H., Wiik-Larsen, E., Bredesen, J.-E. and Halvorsen, S., Studies on methanol poisoning. *Acta Med Scand*, 212, 5, 1982.
43   Prabhakaran, V., Ettler, H. and Mills, A., Methanol poisoning: two cases with similar plasma methanol concentrations but different outcomes. *Can Med Assoc J*, 148, 981, 1993.
44. McAnalley, B. H., Chemistry of alcoholic beverages, in *Medicolehal aspects of alcohol*, J. C. Garriott, Lawyers & Judges Publ. Co., Tucson, 1996, 1.
45. Majchrowicz, E. and Mendelson, J. H., Blood methanol concentrations during experimentally induced ethanol intoxication in alcoholics. *J Pharmacol Exp Ther*, 179, 293, 1971.
46. Davis, V. E., Brown, H., Huff, J. A. and Cashaw, J. L., The alteration of serotonin metabolism to 5-hydroxytryptophol by ethanol ingestion in man. *J Lab Clin Med*, 69, 132, 1967.
47. Helander, A., Beck, O., Jacobsson, G., Löwenmo, C. and Wikström, T., Time course of ethanol-induced changes in serotonin metabolism. *Life Sci*, 53, 847, 1993.
48. Lahti, R. A. and Majchrowicz, E., Ethanol and acetaldehyde effects on metabolism and binding of biogenic amines. *Quart J Stud Alcohol*, 35, 1, 1974.
49. Feldstein, A. and Williamson, O., 5-Hydroxytryptamine metabolism in rat brain and liver homogenates. *Brit J Pharmacol*, 34, 38, 1968.
50. Voltaire, A., Beck, O. and Borg, S., Urinary 5-hydroxytryptophol: a possible marker of recent alcohol consumption. *Alcohol Clin Exp Res*, 16, 281, 1992.
51. Helander, A., Beck, O. and Borg, S., The use of 5-hydroxytryptophol as an alcohol intake marker. *Alcohol Alcohol*, Suppl 2, 497, 1994.
52. Helander, A., Wikström, T., Löwenmo, C., Jacobsson, G. and Beck, O., Urinary excretion of 5-hydroxyindole-3-acetic acid and 5-hydroxytryptophol after oral loading with serotonin. *Life Sci*, 50, 1207, 1992.
53. Helander, A., Walzer, C., Beck, O., Balant, L., Borg, S. and Wartburg, J.-P. v., Influence of genetic variation in alcohol and aldehyde dehydrogenase on serotonin metabolism. *Life Sci*, 55, 359, 1994.
54. Beck, O., Helander, A., Carlsson, S. and Borg, S., Changes in serotonin metabolism during treatment with the aldehyde dehydrogenase inhibitors disulfiram and cyanamide. *Pharmacol Toxicol*, 77, 323, 1995.
55. Beck, O., Borg, S., Eriksson, L. and Lundman, A., 5-Hydroxytryptophol in the cerebrospinal fluid and urine of alcoholics and healthy subjects. *Naunyn-Schmiedeberg's Arch Pharmacol*, 321, 293, 1982.
56. Helander, A., Beck, O. and Borg, S., Determination of urinary 5-hydroxytryptophol by high-performance liquid chromatography with electrochemical detection. *J Chromat Biomed Appl*, 579, 340, 1992.
57. Voltaire Carlsson, A., Hiltunen, A. J., Beck, O., Stibler, H. and Borg, S., Detection of relapses in alcohol-dependent patients: comparison of carbohydrate-deficient transferrin in serum, 5-hydroxytryptophol in urine, and self-reports. *Alcohol Clin Exp Res*, 17, 703, 1993.
58. Borg, S., Helander, A., Voltaire Carlsson, A. and Högström-Brandt, A.-M., Detection of relapses in alcohol dependent patients using carbohydrate-deficient transferrin: improvement with individualized reference levels during long-term monitoring. *Alcohol Clin Exp Res*, 19, 961, 1995.
59. Helander, A., unpublished observation. 1996.
60. Helander, A., Beck, O. and Jones, A. W., Urinary 5HTOL/5HIAA as biochemical marker of postmortem ethanol synthesis. *Lancet*, 340, 1159, 1992.
61. Helander, A., Beck, O. and Jones, A. W., Distinguishing ingested ethanol from microbial formation by analysis of urinary 5-hydroxytryptophol and 5-hydroxyindoleacetic acid. *J Forens Sci*, 40, 95, 1995.

Anders Helander and Alan Wayne Jones

62. Rosalki, S. B. and Rau, D., Serum gamma-glutamyl transpeptidase activity in alcoholism. *Clin Chim Acta,* 39, 41, 1972.

63. Rosalki, S. B., Gamma-glutamyl transpeptidase. *Adv Clin Chem,* 17, 53, 1975.

64. Nemesánszky, E. and Lott, J. A., Gamma-glutamyltransferase and its isoenzymes: progress and problems. *Clin Chem,* 31, 797, 1985.

65. Shaw, S. and Lieber, C. S., Mechanism of increased gamma glutamyl transpeptidase after chronic alcohol consumption: hepatic microsomal induction rather than dietary imbalance. *Substance Alcohol Actions/Misuse,* 1, 423, 1980.

66. Wu, A., Slavin, G. and Levi, A. J., Elevated serum gamma-glutamyl-transferase (transpeptidase) and histological liver damage in alcoholism. *Am J Gastroenterol,* 65, 318, 1976.

67. Salaspuro, M., Use of enzymes for the diagnosis of alcohol related organ damage. *Enzyme,* 37, 87, 1987.

68. Nilssen, O. and Førde, O. H., Seven-year longitudinal population study of change in gamma-glutamyltransferase: the Tromsø study. *Am J Epidemiol,* 139, 787, 1994.

69. Penn, R. and Worthington, L. J., Is serum gamma-glutamyltransferase a misleading test? *Br Med J,* 286, 531, 1983.

70. Gluud, C., Andersen, I., Dietrichson, O., Gluud, B., Jacobsen, A. and Juhl, E., Gamma-glutamyltransferase, aspartate aminotransferase and alkaline phosphatase as marker of alcohol consumption in outpatient alcoholics. *Eur J Clin Invest,* 11, 171, 1981.

71. Nalpas, R., Vassault, A., Charpin, S., Lacour, B. and Berthelot, P., Serum mitochondrial aspartate aminotransferase as a marker of chronic alcoholism: diagnostic value and interpretation in a liver unit. *Hepatology,* 6, 608, 1986.

72. Nalpas, B., Vassault, A., Le Guillou, A., Lesgourgues, B., Ferry, N., Lacour, B. and Berthelot, P., Serum activity of mitochondrial aspartate aminotransferase: a sensitive marker of alcoholism with or without alcoholic hepatitis. *Hepatology,* 5, 893, 1984.

73. Nalpas, R., Poupon, R. E., Vassault, A., Hauzanneau, P., Sage, Y., Schellenberg, F., Lacour, B. and Berthelot, P., Evaluations of mAST/tAST ratio as a marker of alcohol misuse in a non-selected population. *Alcohol Alcohol,* 24, 415, 1989.

74. Nilssen, O., Huseby, N. E., Høyer, G., Brenn, T., Schirmer, H. and Førde, O. H., New alcohol markers - how useful are they in population studies: The Svalbard Study 1988-1989. *Alcohol Clin Exp Res,* 16, 82, 1992.

75. Schiele, F., Artur, Y., Varasteh, A., Wellman, M. and Siest, G., Serum mitochondrial aspartate aminotransferase activity: not useful as marker of excessive alcohol consumption in an unselected population. *Clin Chem,* 35, 926, 1989.

76. Sillanaukee, P., Seppä, K., Löf, K. and Koivula, T., CDT by anion-exchange chromatography followed by RIA as a marker of heavy drinking among men. *Alcohol Clin Exp Res,* 17, 230, 1993.

77. Irwin, M., Baird, S., Smith, T. L. and Schuckit, M., Use of laboratory tests to monitor heavy drinking by alcoholic men discharged from a treatment program. *Am J Psychiatry,* 145, 595, 1988.

78. Wu, A., Chanarin, I. and Levi, A. J., Macrocytosis in chronic alcoholism. *Lancet,* i, 829, 1974.

79. Chick, J., Kreitman, N. and Plant, M., Mean cell volume and gamma-glutamyltranspeptidase as markers of drinking in working men. *Lancet,* i, 1249, 1981.

80. Stimmel, B., Kurtz, D., Jackson, G. and Gilbert, H. S., Failure of mean red cell volume to serve as a biologic marker for alcoholism in narcotic dependence. *Am J Med,* 74, 369, 1983.

81. Behrens, U. J., Worner, T. M., Braly, L. F., Schaffner, F. and Lieber, C. S., Carbohydrate-deficient transferrin, a marker for chronic alcohol consumption in different ethnic populations. *Alcohol Clin Exp Res,* 12, 427, 1988.

82. Bell, H., Tallaksen, C. M. E., Try, K. and Haug, E., Carbohydrate-deficient transferrin and other markers of high alcohol consumption: a study of 502 patients admitted consecutively to a medical department. *Alcohol Clin Exp Res,* 18, 1103, 1994.

83. Stibler, H. and Kjellin, K. G., Isoelectric focusing and electrophoresis of the CSF proteins in tremor of different origins. *J Neurol Sci,* 30, 269, 1976.

84. Stibler, H., Borg, S. and Allgulander, C., Clinical significance of abnormal heterogeneity of transferrin in relation to alcohol consumption. *Acta Med Scand,* 206, 275, 1979.

85. De Jong, G., van Dijk, J. P. and van Eijk, H. G., The biology of transferrin. *Clin Chim Acta*, 190, 1, 1990.
86. Stibler, H., Carbohydrate-deficient transferrin in serum: a new marker of potentially harmful alcohol consumption reviewed. *Clin Chem*, 37, 2029, 1991.
87. Landberg, E., Påhlsson, P., Lundblad, A., Arnetorp, A. and Jeppsson, J.-O., Carbohydrate composition of serum transferrin isoforms from patients with high alcohol consumption. *Biochem Biophys Res Commun*, 210, 267, 1995.
88. Stibler, H. and Borg, S., Glycoprotein glycosyltransferase activities in serum in alcohol-abusing patients and healthy controls. *Scand J Clin Lab Invest*, 51, 43, 1991.
89. Xin, Y., Lasker, J. M. and Lieber, C. S., Serum carbohydrate-deficient transferrin: mechanism of increase after chronic alcohol intake. *Hepatology*, 22, 1462, 1995.
90. Allen, J. P., Litten, R. Z., Anton, R. F. and Cross, G. M., Carbohydrate-deficient transferrin as a measure of immoderate drinking: remaining issues. *Alcohol Clin Exp Res*, 18, 799, 1994.
91. Godsell, P. A., Whitfield, J. B., Conigrave, K. M., Hanratty, S. J. and Saunders, J. B., Carbohydrate deficient transferrin levels in hazardous alcohol consumption. *Alcohol Alcohol*, 30, 61, 1995.
92. Salmela, K. S., Laitinen, K., Nyström, M. and Salaspuro, M., Carbohydrate-deficient transferrin during 3 weeks' heavy alcohol consumption. *Alcohol Clin Exp Res*, 18, 228, 1994.
93. Stibler, H., Borg, S. and Beckman, G., Transferrin phenotype and level of carbohydrate-deficient transferrin. *Alcohol Clin Exp Res*, 12, 450, 1988.
94. Stibler, H., Borg, S. and Joustra, M., A modified method for the assay of carbohydrate-deficient transferrin (CDT) in serum. *Alcohol Alcohol*, Suppl 1, 451, 1991.
95. Bean, P. and Peter, J. B., Allelic D variants of transferrin in evaluation of alcohol abuse: differential diagnosis by isoelectric focusing-immunoblotting-laser densitometry. *Clin Chem*, 40, 2078, 1994.
96. Bean, P., Sutphin, M. S., Liu, Y., Anton, R., Reynolds, T. B., Shoenfeld, Y. and Peter, J. B., Carbohydrate-deficient transferrin and false positive results for alcohol abuse in primary biliary cirrhosis: differential diagnosis by detection of mitochondrial autoantibodies. *Clin Chem*, 41, 858, 1995.
97. Storey, E. L., Mack, U., Powell, L. W. and Halliday, J. W., Use of chromatofocusing to detect transferrin variant in serum of alcoholic subjects. *Clin Chem*, 31, 1543, 1985.
98. Xin, Y., Lasker, J. M., Rosman, A. S. and Lieber, C. S., Isoelectric focusing/Western blotting: a novel and practical method for quantitation of carbohydrate-deficient transferrin in alcoholics. *Alcohol Clin Exp Res*, 15, 814, 1991.
99. Löf, K., Koivula, T., Seppä, K., Fukunaga, T. and Sillanaukee, P., Semi-automated method for determination of different isoforms of carbohydrate-deficient transferrin. *Clin Chim Acta*, 217, 175, 1993.
100. Jeppsson, J.-O., Kristensson, H. and Fimiani, C., Carbohydrate deficient transferrin quantitated by HPLC to determine heavy consumption of alcohol. *Clin Chem*, 39, 2115, 1993.
101. Kwoh-Gain, I., Fletcher, L. M., Price, J., Powell, L. W. and Halliday, J. W., Desialylated transferrin and mitochondrial aspartate aminotransferase compared as laboratory markers of excessive alcohol consumption. *Clin Chem*, 36, 841, 1990.
102. Schellenberg, F., Bernard, J. Y., Le Goff, A. M., Bourdin, C. and Weill, J., Evaluation of carbohydrate-deficient transferrin compared with Tf index and other markers of alcohol abuse. *Alcohol Clin Exp Res*, 13, 605, 1989.
103. Bell, H., Tallaksen, C., Sjåheim, T., Weberg, R., Raknerud, N., Ørjasæter, H., Try, K. and Haug, E., Serum carbohydrate-deficient transferrin as a marker of alcohol consumption in patients with chronic liver disease. *Alcohol Clin Exp Res*, 17, 246, 1993.
104. Sorvajärvi, K., Blake, J. E., Israel, Y. and Niemelä, O., Sensitivity and specificity of carbohydrate-deficient transferrin as a marker of alcohol abuse are significantly influenced by alterations in serum transferrin: comparison of two methods. *Alcohol Clin Exp Res*, 20, 449, 1996.
105. Sillanaukee, P., Löf, K., Härlin, A., Mårtensson, O., Brandt, R. and Seppä, K., Comparison of different methods for detecting carbohydrate-deficient transferrin. *Alcohol Clin Exp Res*, 18, 1150, 1994.

106. Anton, R. and Bean, P., Two methods for measuring carbohydrate-deficient transferrin in inpatient alcoholics and healthy controls compared. *Clin Chem*, 40, 364, 1994.

107. Stibler, H., Borg, S. and Joustra, M., Micro anion exchange chromatography of carbohydrate deficient transferrin in serum in relation to alcohol consumption. *Alcohol Clin Exp Res*, 10, 535, 1986.

108. Stevens, V. J., Fantl, W. J., Newman, C. B., Sims, R. V., Cerami, A. and Peterson, C. M., Acetaldehyde adducts with hemoglobin. *J Clin Invest*, 67, 361, 1981.

109. San George, R. C. and Hoberman, H. D., Reaction of acetaldehyde with hemoglobin. *J Biol Chem*, 261, 6811, 1986.

110. Nicholls, R., De Jersey, J., Worrall, S. and Wilce, P., Modification of proteins and other biological molecules by acetaldehyde: adduct structure and functional significance. *Int J Biochem*, 24, 1899, 1992.

111. Sorrell, M. F. and Tuma, D. J., Hypothesis: alcoholic liver injury and the covalent binding of acetaldehyde. *Alcohol Clin Exp Res*, 9, 306, 1985.

112. Svegliata-Baroni, G., Baraona, E., Rosman, A. S. and Lieber, C. S., Collagen-acetaldehyde adducts in alcoholic and nonalcoholic liver diseases. *Hepatology*, 20, 111, 1994.

113. Peterson, C. M. and Polizzi, C. M., Improved method for acetaldehyde in plasma and hemoglobin-associated acetaldehyde: results in teetotalers and alcoholics reporting for treatment. *Alcohol*, 4, 477, 1987.

114. Halvorsen, M. R., Campbell, J. L., Sprague, G., Slater, K., Noffsinger, J. K. and Peterson, C. M., Comparative evaluation of the clinical utility of three markers of ethanol intake: the effect of gender. *Alcohol Clin Exp Res*, 17, 225, 1993.

115. Sillanaukee, P., Seppä, K., Koivula, T., Israel, Y. and Niemelä, O., Acetaldehyde-modified hemoglobin as a marker of alcohol consumption: comparison of two new methods. *J Lab Clin Med*, 120, 42, 1992.

116. Itälä, L., Seppä, K., Turpeinen, U. and Sillanaukee, P., Separation of hemoglobin acetaldehyde adducts by high-performance liquid chromatography-cation-exchange chromatography. *Anal Biochem*, 224, 323, 1995.

117. Hoerner, M., Behrens, U. J., Worner, T. and Lieber, C. S., Humoral immune response to acetaldehyde adducts in alcoholic patients. *Res Commun Chem Pathol Pharmacol*, 54, 3, 1986.

118. Niemelä, O., Klajner, F., Orrego, H., Vidins, E., Blendis, L. and Israel, Y., Antibodies against acetaldehyde-modified protein epitopes in human alcoholics. *Hepatology*, 7, 1210, 1987.

119. Worrall, S., De Jersey, J., Shanley, B. C. and Wilce, P. A., Antibodies against acetaldehyde-modified epitopes: an elevated IgA response in alcoholics. *Eur J Clin Invest*, 21, 90, 1991.

120. Tang, B. K., Urinary markers of chronic excessive ethanol consumption. *Alcohol Clin Exp Res*, 15, 881, 1991.

121. Helander, A., Aldehyde dehydrogenase in blood: distribution, characteristics and possible use as marker of alcohol misuse. *Alcohol Alcohol*, 28, 135, 1993.

122. Johnson, R. D., Bahnisch, J., Stewart, B., Shearman, D. J. C. and Edwards, J. B., Optimized spectrophotometric determination of aldehyde dehydrogenase activity in erythrocytes. *Clin Chem*, 38, 584, 1992.

123. Hultberg, B., Isaksson, A. and Tiderström, G., β-Hexosaminidase, leucin aminopeptidase, cystidyl aminopeptidase, hepatic enzymes and bilirubin in serum from chronic alcoholics with acute ethanol intoxication. *Clin Chim Acta*, 105, 317, 1980.

124. Kärkkäinen, P., Poikolainen, K. and Salaspuro, M., Serum β-hexosaminidase as a marker of heavy drinking. *Alcohol Clin Exp Res*, 14, 187, 1990.

125. Wehr, H., Czartoryska, B., Gorska, D. and Matsumoto, H., Serum β-hexosaminidase and α-mannosidase activities as markers of alcohol abuse. *Alcohol Clin Exp Res*, 15, 13, 1991.

126. Hultberg, B., Isaksson, A., Berglund, M. and Moberg, A.-L., Serum β-hexosaminidase isoenzyme: a sensitive marker for alcohol abuse. *Alcohol Clin Exp Res*, 15, 549, 1991.

127. Hultberg, B., Isaksson, A., Berglund, M. and Alling, C., Increases and time-course variations in β-hexosaminidase isoenzyme B and carbohydrate-deficient transferrin in serum from alcoholics are similar. *Alcohol Clin Exp Res*, 19, 452, 1995.

128. Hultberg, B. and Isaksson, A., Isoenzyme pattern of serum β-hexosaminidase in liver disease, alcohol intoxication and pregnancy. *Enzyme*, 30, 166, 1983.

129. Nyström, M., Peräsalo, J. and Salaspuro, M., Serum β-hexosaminidase in young university students. *Alcohol Clin Exp Res*, 15, 877, 1991.

130. Iffland, R. and Grassnack, F., Untersuchung zum CDT und anderen Indikatoren für Alkoholprobleme im Blut alkoholauffälliger Pkw-Fahrer. *Blutalkohol*, 32, 1995.

131. Haffner, H.-T., Batra, A., Wehner, H. D., Besserer, K. and Mann, K., Methanolspiegel und Methanolelimination bei Alkoholikern. *Blutalkohol*, 30, 52, 1993.

132. Morgan, M. Y., Colman, J. C. and Sherlock, S., The use of a combination of peripheral markers for diagnosing alcoholism and monitoring for continued abuse. *Br J Alcohol Alcohol*, 16, 167, 1981.

133. Hollstedt, C. and Dahlgren, L., Peripheral markers in the female "hidden alcoholic". *Acta Psychiat Scand*, 75, 591, 1987.

134. Gjerde, H., Johnsen, J., Bjørneboe, A., Bjørneboe, G.-E. A. A. and Mørland, J., A comparison of serum carbohydrate-deficient transferrin with other biological markers of excessive drinking. *Scand J Clin Lab Invest*, 48, 1, 1988.

135. Helander, A., Voltaire Carlsson, A. and Borg, S., Longitudinal comparison of carbohydrate-deficient transferrin and gamma-glutamyl transferase: complementary markers of excessive alcohol consumption. *Alcohol Alcohol*, 31, 101, 1996.

136. Niemelä, O., Sorvajärvi, K., Blake, J. E. and Israel, Y., Carbohydrate-deficient transferrin as a marker of alcohol abuse: relationship to alcohol consumption, severity of liver disease, and fibrogenesis. *Alcohol Clin Exp Res*, 19, 1203, 1995.

137. Anton, R. F. and Moak, D. H., Carbohydrate-deficient transferrin and γ-glutamyltransferase as markers of heavy alcohol consumption: gender differences. *Alcohol Clin Exp Res*, 18, 747, 1994.

138. Rosman, A. S., Basu, P., Galvin, K. and Lieber, C. S., Utility of carbohydrate-deficient transferrin as a marker of relapse in alcoholic patients. *Alcohol Clin Exp Res*, 19, 611, 1995.

139. Keso, L. and Salaspuro, M., Laboratory tests in the follow-up of treated alcoholics: how often should testing be repeated? *Alcohol Alcohol*, 25, 359, 1990.

140. Kristenson, H., Öhlin, H., Hulten-Nosslin, M. B., Trell, E. and Hood, B., Identification and intervention of heavy drinking in middle-aged men: results and follow-up of 24-60 months of long-term study with randomized controls. *Alcohol Clin Exp Res*, 7, 203, 1983.

141. Goodwin, D. W., Schulsinger, F., Hermanssen, L., Guze, S. H. and Windkure, G., Alcohol problems in adoptees raised apart from alcoholic biological parents. *Arch Gen Psychiat*, 28, 238, 1973.

142. Cloninger, C. R., Bohman, M. and Sigvardsson, S., Inheritance of alcohol abuse: cross fostering analysis of adopted men. *Arch Gen Psychiat*, 38, 861, 1981.

143. Cloninger, C. R., Neurogenetic adaptive mechanisms in alcoholism. *Science*, 236, 410, 1987.

144. Devor, E. J. and Cloninger, C. R., Genetics of alcoholism. *Ann Rev Genet*, 23, 19, 1989.

145. Ball, D. M. and Murray, R. M., Genetics of alcohol misuse. *Br Med Bull*, 50, 18, 1994.

146. Crabb, D. W., Biological markers for increased risk of alcoholism and for quantitation of alcohol consumption. *J Clin Invest*, 85, 311, 1990.

147. von Knorring, A. L., Bohman, M., von Knorring, L. and Oreland, L., Platelet MAO activity as a biological marker in subgroups of alcoholism. *Acta Psychiat Scand*, 72, 51, 1985.

148. Begleiter, H., The collaborative study on the genetics of alcoholism. *Alcohol Health Res World*, 19, 228, 1995.

149. Fowler, J. S., Volkow, N. D., Wang, G.-J., Pappas, N., Logan, J., MacGregor, R., Alexoff, D., Shea, C., Schlyer, D., Wolf, A. P., Warner, D., Zezulkova, I. and Cliento, R., Inhibition of monoamine oxidase B in the brains of smokers. *Nature*, 379, 733, 1996.

150. Agarwal, D. P. and Goedde, H. W., Medicobiological and genetic studies on alcoholism. *Clin Invest*, 70, 465, 1992.

151. Thomasson, H. R., Crabb, D. W., Edenberg, H. J. and Li, T.-K., Alcohol and aldehyde dehydrogenase polymorphisms and alcoholism. *Behav Genet*, 23, 131, 1993.

152. Glucksman, E., Alcohol and accidents. *Brit Med Bull*, 50, 76, 1994.

153. Midanik, L., The validity of self-reported alcohol consumption and alcohol problems: a literature review. *Br J Addic*, 77, 357, 1982.

CHAPTER 6

NEUROCHEMISTRY OF DRUG ABUSE

EDITED BY DEBORAH C. MASH AND JULIE K. STALEY

DEPARTMENTS OF NEUROLOGY AND MOLECULAR AND CELLULAR PHARMACOLOGY,
UNIVERSITY OF MIAMI SCHOOL OF MEDICINE, MIAMI, FLORIDA

TABLE OF CONTENTS

6.1 THE DOPAMINE TRANSPORTER AND ADDICTION

JOHN W. BOJA AND WILLIAM M. MEIL

DEPARTMENT OF PHARMACOLOGY, NORTHEASTERN OHIO UNIVERSITIES COLLEGE OF MEDICINE, ROOTSTOWN, OHIO

The dopamine transporter (DAT) is a distinctive feature of dopaminergic neurons that was discovered more than 20 years ago.[1-5] The DAT is the major mechanism for the termination of released dopamine (DA), released DA is actively transported back into dopaminergic neurons via a sodium and energy dependent mechanism.[6-8] Like other uptake carriers, the DAT can be affected by a number of drugs including cocaine, amphetamine, some opiates, and ethanol. It is this interaction with the DAT and the resulting increase in synaptic DA levels that has proposed to be the basis for the action of several drugs of abuse. The dopaminergic hypothesis of drug abuse has been proposed by a number of researchers.[9,10] Di Chiara and Imperato[11] observed the effects of several drugs of abuse upon DA levels in the nucleus accumbens and caudate nucleus using microdialysis. Drugs such as cocaine, amphetamine, ethanol, nicotine, and morphine were all observed to produce an increase in DA especially in the nucleus accumbens. Drugs that are generally not abused by humans, such as bremazocine, imipramine, diphenhydramine, or haloperidol decreased brain DA or increased DA in the caudate nucleus only. It was, therefore, concluded[11] that drugs abused by humans preferentially increase brain DA levels in the nucleus accumbens whereas psychoactive drugs not abused by humans do not increase DA levels in the nucleus accumbens. By employing this hypothesis of drug reward as a starting point, this chapter will review evidence as to the function of the DAT and the interaction of several drugs of abuse upon the DAT.

6.1.1 DOPAMINE UPTAKE

The uptake of DA has been shown to depend on a number of factors.[4-6,12-15] These include temperature, sodium,[16-19] potassium,[6, 16] chloride[7, 20] but not calcium ions.[6] Krueger[21] suggested that dopamine transport occurred by means of two sodium ions and one chloride ion carrying a net positive charge into the neuron which is utilized to drive DA against its electrochemical gradient. More recently, McElvain and Schenk[22] proposed a multisubstrate model of DA transport. In this model it was proposed that either one molecule of DA or two sodium ions bind to the DAT in a partially random mechanism. Chloride binds next and it is only then that the DAT translocates from the outside of the neuron to the inside (Figure 6.1.1). Cocaine inhibition of DA transport occurs with cocaine binding to the sodium-binding site and changing the conformation of the chloride-binding site, thus preventing the binding of either and ultimately inhibiting dopamine uptake. The inhibition of DA uptake by cocaine appeared to be uncompetitive whereas the binding of sodium and chloride are inhibited competitively. This action is only present with the neuronal membrane bound DAT because cocaine does not appear to inhibit the reuptake of DA to the vesicles via the vesicular transporter.[23]

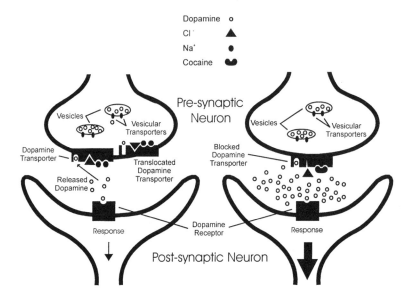

Figure 6.1.1 The dopamine transporter terminates the action of released dopamine by transport back into the presynaptic neuron. Dopamine transport occurs with the binding of one molecule of dopamine, one chloride ion, and two sodium ions to the transporter, the transporter then translocates from the outside of the neuronal membrane into the inside of the neuron.[22] Cocaine appears to bind to the sodium ion binding site. This changes the conformation of the chloride ion binding site, thus dopamine transport does not occur. This blockade of dopamine transport potentiates dopaminergic neurotransmission and may be the basis for the rewarding effects of cocaine.

6.1.2 ABUSED DRUGS AND THE DOPAMINE TRANSPORTER

6.1.2.1 Cocaine

Cocaine has several mechanisms of action; inhibition of DA, norepinephrine and serotonin reuptake, as well as a local anesthetic effect. While the stimulating and reinforcing effects of cocaine have been recognized for quite some time, it was not until recently that the mechanism(s) for these effects was elucidated. The stimulatory effects of cocaine were first associated with the ability of cocaine to inhibit the reuptake of DA.[24-25] Saturable and specific binding sites for [3H] cocaine were then discovered by Reith using whole mouse brain homogenates.[26] When striatal tissue was utilized as the sole tissue source, Kennedy and Hanbauer[27] were able to correlate the pharmacology of [3H]cocaine binding and [3H]DA uptake inhibition and, thereby, hypothesized that the binding site for [3H]cocaine was in fact the DAT.[27] Using the data from binding experiments, it has been possible to correlate the strong reinforcing properties of cocaine with blockade of the DAT rather than inhibition of either the serotonin or norepinephrine transporters.[28-29]

Using radiolabeled cocaine[30-32] or analogs of cocaine such as WIN 35,065-2,[30] WIN 35,428,[30-31] RTI-55,[32-40] and RTI-121[41-42] it is possible to visualize the distribution of these drugs within the brain, the pattern of binding demonstrated by cocaine and its analogs appears to coincide with the distribution of dopamine within the brain. Areas of the brain with the greatest amount of dopaminergic innervation, such as the caudate, putamen, and nucleus accumbens, also demonstrate the greatest amount of binding, whereas moderate amounts of binding can be observed in the substantia nigra and ventral tegmental areas. Recently specific antibodies to the DAT have been developed,[43] using these antibodies to visualize the distribution of DAT within the brain there was a good correlation between the areas that bound antibody and those areas that bind cocaine.

Several unrelated compounds have been demonstrated to bind to the DAT such as: [³H]mazindol,[44] [³H]nomifensine,[45] and [³H]GBR 12935.[46] However, while these compounds also inhibit the reuptake of DA, they do not share the powerful reinforcing properties that are unique to cocaine. The question of why these compounds are non-addictive while cocaine is quite addictive remains unanswered. Several possibilities exist: Schoemaker et al.[47] observed that [³H]cocaine binds to both a high- and low-affinity site on the DAT, whereas other ligands such as [³H]mazindol,[44] [³H]nomifensine,[45] and [³H]GBR 12935[46] bind solely to a single high-affinity site. This does not indicate that the two binding sites demonstrated by cocaine and its analogs[40,41,48-51] represent two distinct sites, however, because both the high- and low affinity site arise from a single expressed cDNA for the DAT.[52] Another difference may be the pattern of binding, in that [³H]mazindol binds to different sites in the brain than those observed for [³H]cocaine.[53] In addition, the rate of entry into the brain is different for these different compounds. Mazindol and GBR 12935 have been demonstrated to enter the brain and occupy receptors much more slowly than cocaine.[54,55] At the present time it is still unclear which of these or other possible factors allow for the strong reinforcing properties of cocaine.

Recently, mice lacking the gene for the DAT have been developed.[56] DA is present in the dopaminergic extracellular space of the homozygous mice almost 100 times longer than it is present in the normal mouse. The homozygous mice were hyperactive compared to normal mice and, as expected, cocaine did not produce any effect in the locomotor activity of the homozygous mice. These results provide further evidence to the concept of the DAT as a cocaine receptor.

6.1.2.2 Amphetamine

Amphetamine and its analogs, including but not limited to methamphetamine, methylenedioxyamphetamine (MDA), and methylenedioxymethamphetamine (MDMA), have been demonstrated to increase brain DA levels.[57-69] Amphetamine has been postulated to increase brain DA levels either by increasing DA release or by blocking the reuptake of DA. Hadfield[70] observed amphetamine blockade of DA reuptake; however, reuptake inhibition occurred only at doses of amphetamine (ED_{50} = 65 mg/kg) that were much higher than the doses observed to increase release. While reuptake blockade may play a role in the DA elevating effects of amphetamine, blockade only occurs at doses near those that can produce stereotypy or toxicity. On the other hand, amphetamine stimulated DA release occurs at much lower doses. Amphetamine stimulated DA release has been postulated to occur by two mechanisms: one involves the interaction of amphetamine with the DAT which then produces a reversal of the DAT so that DA is transported out of neuron while amphetamine is transported into the neuron.[71-77] The other mechanism that has been proposed is a passive diffusion of amphetamine into the neuron and a subsequent displacement of DA from intracellular storage sites[74] by the alteration of vesicular pH.[77]

Besides this proported action on the DAT, amphetamine has also been suggested to act upon the vesicular transporter as well. Pifl et al.[78] examined COS cells transfected with cDNA for either the DAT, the vesicular transporter, or both. A marked increase in DA release was noted in cells that expressed both the DAT and the vesicular transporter when compared to the release from cells that express only the DAT or vesicular transporter. The mechanism of action for amphetamine was further defined with the work of Giros et al.[56] In transgenic mice lacking the DAT, amphetamine was unable to produce hyperlocomotion nor did amphetamine release DA.

In summary, amphetamine appears to release DA via its activity upon the DAT because amphetamine appears to employ the DAT to transport DA out of the neuron while, at the same time, amphetamine is sequestered in the neuron. The sequestered amphetamine then may release vesicular DA by altering vesicular pH or via interactions with the vesicular transporter.

6.1.2.3 Opiates

Opiate drugs share the ability to elevate extracellular DA concentrations in the nucleus accumbens,[11,80,81] possibly implicating mesolimbic DA activity in the abuse liability of these compounds. Whereas the locomotor[82] and reinforcing effects[83] of opiates may occur through DA-independent pathways, there is also evidence for dopaminergic mediation of these effects.[84,85] Lesions of dopaminergic neurons[86,87] or neuroleptic blockade of DA receptors[88,89] attenuate opiate reward as measured by intracranial electrical self-stimulation, conditioned place preference, and intravenous self-administration. In contrast, to cocaine's ability to augment DA concentrations through direct action upon the DAT,[77] opiates appear to enhance DA concentrations primarily by indirectly stimulating DA neurons.[90,91]

Recent evidence suggests that opiates also act at the DAT. Das et al.[92] reported that U50, 488H, a synthetic κ opiate agonist, and dynorphin A, an endogenous κ ligand, dose-dependently inhibit [^{3}H]DA uptake in synaptosomal preparations from the rat striatum and nucleus accumbens. Inhibition of [^{3}H]DA uptake by U50,488H was not reversed by pretreatment with the opiate antagonists naloxone and nor-binaltorphine, suggesting that this effect is mediated through direct action at the DAT rather than an indirect effect at κ receptors. In contrast, selective μ and γ opiate agonists failed to inhibit [^{3}H]DA uptake in the striatum and nucleus accumbens across the same range of doses. Morphine, a μ opiate agonist, also failed to inhibit [^{3}H]DA uptake or displace [^{3}H]WIN 35, 428 binding in the striatum[93] and displace [^{3}H]GBR 12935 binding in basal forebrain.[94]

Recently, meperidine, an atypical opiate receptor agonist with cocaine-like effects, has been shown to act at the DAT.[93] Meperidine was found to inhibit [^{3}H]DA uptake in rat caudate putamen with a maximal effect less than that achieved with cocaine. This suggests that meperidine may predominantly act at the high affinity transporter site. Meperidine also displaced [^{3}H]WIN 35,428 binding in a manner consistent with a single site affinity. Because meperidine shares key structural features with the phenyltropane analogs of cocaine, it is possible that these common structural features account for meperidine's cocaine-like actions rather than any characteristics intrinsic to opiates.

Although morphine appears to lack direct action at the DAT, recent evidence suggests that chronic morphine has effects upon DAT expression. Repeated, but not acute administration of morphine to rats was found to attenuate the Bmax of [^{3}H]GBR12935 binding in the anterior basal forebrain, including the nucleus accumbens, but not in the striatum.[94] However, no changes in the affinity for the radioligand were observed in either brain region. Neither acute nor chronic morphine administration inhibited binding at the serotonin transporter in the striatum or anterior basal forebrain, suggesting that transporter down-regulation was selective to brain regions important for the reinforcing and/or motivational properties of opiates. Because daily cocaine administration in rats also attenuates DA uptake in the nucleus accumbens, and not the striatum,[95] chronic elevation of DA release and a subsequent reduction in DAT expression within the nucleus accumbens may prove important in the development of drug addiction.

6.1.2.4 Phencyclidine (PCP)

Both systemic and local infusions of PCP enhance extracellular DA concentrations in the nucleus accumbens[96,97] and prefrontal cortex.[98] PCP-induced elevations of extracellular DA concentrations may result from both indirect and direct effects upon the dopaminergic system. NMDA receptors exert a tonic inhibitory effect upon basal DA release in the prefrontal cortex[98,99] and in the nucleus accumbens through inhibitory effects upon midbrain DA neurons.[100-102] Thus, PCP antagonism of NMDA receptors[103] may facilitate DA release by decreasing the inhibition of central dopaminergic activity.

PCP also increases calcium-independent [³H]DA release from dissociated rat mesencephalon cell cultures[104] and striatal synaptosomes.[105] PCP has been found to be a potent inhibitor of [³H]DA uptake in rat striatum,[106-109] to competitively inhibit binding of [³H]BTCP, a PCP derivative and potent DA uptake inhibitor in rat striatal membranes,[110] and to inhibit [³H]cocaine binding.[111] In addition, (trans)-4-PPC a major metabolite of PCP in humans,[112] inhibits [³H]DA uptake in rat striatal synaptosomes with comparable potency to PCP and thus it may be involved in PCP's psychotomimetic effects.[106]

Despite the profound effect PCP exerts on mesolimbic DA activity, recent evidence suggests that the reinforcing properties of PCP are not DA-dependent. Carlezon and Wise[113] have reported that rats will self-administer PCP into the ventromedial region of the nucleus accumbens, as well as NMDA receptor antagonists which do not inhibit dopamine reuptake. Co-infusion of the dopamine antagonist sulpiride into the nucleus accumbens was found to inhibit intracranial self-administration of nomifensine, but not PCP. Moreover, rats were found to self-administer PCP into the prefrontal cortex, an area that will not maintain self-administration of nomifensine.[114] Therefore, the reinforcing effects of PCP in the nucleus accumbens and prefrontal cortex appear related to PCP blockade of NMDA receptor function rather than to its dopaminergic actions. Instead, PCP-induced elevations of extracellular DA may mediate other behavioral effects of PCP, such as its stimulation of locomotor activity.[115]

6.1.2.5 Marijuana

The failure of Δ^9-tetrahydrocannabinol (Δ^9-THC), the primary psychoactive component of marijuana, to maintain drug self-administration in laboratory animals[116] and to substitute for drugs with strong reinforcing properties[117] has made understanding the neuropharmacological basis of marijuana abuse difficult. However, the ability of Δ^9-THC to facilitate intracranial electrical self-stimulation in the median forebrain bundle[118] and augment dopaminergic activity within the mesocorticolimbic DA pathway[119,120] implicates the brain reward circuits responsible for reinforcing properties of psychostimulants and opiates in the abuse liability of marijuana. Gardner et al.[118] have demonstrated that systemic or local injections of Δ^9-THC enhance extracellular dopamine concentrations in the rat prefrontal cortex,[121] caudate,[122] nucleus accumbens,[119,123] and ventral tegmental area.[120] In addition, Δ^9-THC augments both brain stimulation of reward and extracellular dopamine concentrations in the nucleus accumbens in Lewis rats, further linking dopaminergic activity with the rewarding properties of marijuana.[123]

Facilitation of dopaminergic activity by Δ^9-THC may result from multiple mechanisms. Δ^9-THC increases dopamine synthesis[124] and release[125] in synaptosomal preparations. In addition, using *in vivo* techniques, Δ^9-THC has been reported to augment potassium-evoked DA release in the caudate[122] and increase calcium-dependent DA efflux in the nucleus accumbens.[119] However, whereas Δ^9-THC produces a dose-dependent augmentation of somatodendritic DA release in the ventral tegmental area, it fails to simultaneously alter accumbal DA concentrations.[120] Because local infusions of Δ^9-THC through a microdialysis probe did elevate nucleus accumbens DA concentrations, modulation of DA activity in the nucleus accumbens is likely to result from presynaptic effects.

Δ^9-THC also acts directly at the DAT to affect DA uptake. At low concentrations, Δ^9-THC stimulates uptake of [³H]dopamine in synaptosomal preparations of rat brain striatum and hypothalamus.[125] Similarly, mice injected with Δ^9-THC showed increased [³H]DA uptake into striatal synaptosomes and, to a greater extent, in cortical synaptosomes.[126] At higher concentrations, Δ^9-THC inhibits uptake of [³H]DA in rat striatal[125,127,128] and hypothalamic[125] synaptosomes. Also consistent with the hypothesis that Δ^9-THC blocks DA uptake, using *in vivo* electrochemical techniques it has been reported that Δ^9-THC and the DA reuptake blocker nomifensine, produce identical augmentation of voltammetric signals corresponding to extra-cellular DA.[122] While Δ⁹-THC has a similar biphasic effect on norepinephrine uptake in hypothalamic and striatal synaptosomes[125] and increases uptake of 5-HT and GABA in cortical synaptosomes,[126] the psychoactive effects of Δ⁹-THC are most likely related to dopaminergic activity since less potent and non-psychoactive THC derivatives show much less effect upon DA uptake than does Δ⁹-THC.[126] Δ⁹-THC clearly has profound effects upon dopaminergic activity in areas important to the maintenance of the reinforcing effects of other abused compounds. However, only with further characterization of marijuana's behavioral effects can marijuana's dopaminergic effects be related to its abuse liability using animal models.

6.1.2.6 Ethanol

Ethanol has also been demonstrated to affect the dopaminergic system. Administration of ethanol has been demonstrated to release dopamine *in vivo*[129-131] and *in vitro*.[132-141] The mechanism(s) by which ethanol increases brain DA levels are slowly beginning to be under-stood. Tan et al.[142] examined the uptake of [³H]DA in brain synaptosomes prepared from rats in various stages of intoxication. The uptake of [³H]DA was inhibited by ethanol for as long as 16 h following the withdrawal of ethanol. Ethanol has also been shown to increase both the spontaneous release and Ca²⁺ stimulated release of DA, but decrease the amount of K+ stimulated released DA.[129,143] The increased amount of DA release is not due to a non-specific disruption of the neuronal membrane because acetylcholine levels are not altered.[131] Thus, it appears that ethanol can affect both the release and reuptake of DA via a specific mechanism.

In addition, a transesterification product of ethanol and cocaine has been discovered, benzoylecgonine ethyl ester or cocaethylene was first described by Hearn et al.[144] Cocaethylene has been shown to possess a similar affinity for the DAT as does cocaine and has been demonstrated to inhibit DA uptake[144-147] and increase *in vivo* DA levels.[148,149] In contrast to cocaine, cocaethylene has less affinity for the serotonin transporter than does cocaine. Additionally, cocaethylene has been demonstrated to produce greater lethality in rats and mice than cocaine.[150-152]

6.1.2.7 Nicotine

Nicotine has been demonstrated by several studies to increase DA levels both *in vivo*[11,153] and *in vitro*.[154-156] Nicotine[157] and its metabolites[158] were found to both release and inhibit the reuptake of DA in rat brain slices, with uptake inhibition occurring at a lower concentration than that required for DA release. In addition, the (-) isomer was more potent than the (+) isomer.[157] However, the effect of nicotine upon DA release and uptake was only apparent when brain slices were utilized because nicotine was unable to affect DA when a synaptosomal preparation was utilized.[157] These results indicate that nicotine exerts its effects upon the DAT indirectly, most likely via nicotinic acetylcholine receptors. This finding was supported by the results of Yamashita et al.[159] in which the effect of nicotine upon DA uptake was examined in PC12 and COS cells transfected with rat DAT cDNA. Nicotine inhibited DA uptake in PC12 cells which possess a nicotinic acetylcholine receptor. This effect was blocked by the nicotinic antagonists hexamethonium and mecamylamine. Additionally, nicotine did not influence DA uptake in COS cells which lack a nicotinic acetylcholine receptor.

Recently it was reported that a series of cocaine analogs that potently inhibited cocaine binding also inhibited [³H]nicotine and [³H]mecamylamine binding.[160] It was concluded that the inhibition by these cocaine analogs involves its action upon an ion channel on the nicotinic acetylcholine receptors. This finding provides an additional potential interaction between the nicotinic and dopaminergic neuronal systems.

John W. Boja and William M. Meil

Table 6.1.3 Comparison of the Self-Administration of Various Drugs and the Effect that Drug has Upon the DAT

Drug	Self-administered	Increases DA Via the DAT	Ref.
Cocaine	+	+	24-25, 161
Amphetamine	+	+	71, 161
MDMA	+	+	69, 162
DMT	?	-	163
Mescaline	-	-	161, 164
LSD	-	-	161, 164-165
Opiates	+	+	161, 92
Barbiturates	+	-	166
Benzodiazepines	+	?	166-169
Alcohol	+	+	161, 142
Caffeine	+	-	161, 170
Nicotine	+	+ (Indirect)	171, 154-159
Marijuana	?	+	172, 125
PCP	+	+	173, 106-109

6.1.3 CONCLUSIONS

Despite the extensive research regarding the mechanisms of drug abuse, there is still no one unifying theory that allows for the source of addiction. Whereas several drugs have been reported to interact with the DAT and thus allow for the subsequent increase in DA levels, this may be a basis for addiction to some drugs but it is not the mechanism of action for all drugs (Table 6.1.3). The short-acting barbiturates, for example, do not interact with the dopaminergic system, yet they are quite addictive. Some drugs that interact with the dopaminergic system, such as cocaine, are quite addictive, while other drugs, such as mazindol, are not. Clearly factors other than simple interaction with the dopaminergic system are involved, and a simple answer to drug addiction may not be possible.

Nonetheless, the dopaminergic system does play a role in the abuse liability for some, if not most, drugs: the stimulants, opiates, marijuana, nicotine, and ethanol, all interact directly or indirectly with the dopaminergic system. Thus, the dopamine hypothesis seems valid for these drugs. In addition, there is a temporal component in that while mazindol interacts with the dopaminergic system, its entry into the brain is slow compared to that of cocaine.[54,55] Mazindol is not addictive nor does it produce preference in animals[178] possibly as a result of this temporal effect.

The recent cloning of the DAT[174-176] and its subsequent transfection into cells has allowed for the study of the DAT in much greater detail. Using chimeras of the DAT[177] it has been possible to separate cocaine binding from DA uptake. Further work in this area may allow for the development of a "cocaine antagonist". The development of a transgenic mouse that lacks the DAT has afforded the study of the mechanisms of action for amphetamine and cocaine,[56] using this model the mechanism of other drugs of abuse can be examined. Using these powerful new tools that have become available, we may be able to understand the reasons drug abuse occurs and develop strategies to prevent drug abuse.

REFERENCES

1. Glowinski J. and Iversen, L.L., Regional studies of catecholamines in the rat brain. I. The disposition of [³H]norepinephrine, [³H]dopamine and [³H]dopa in various regions of the brain, *J. Neurochem.*, 13, 655, 1966.
2. Snyder S.J. and Coyle, J.T., Regional differences in [³H]norepinephrine and [³H]dopamine uptake into rat brain homogenates, *J. Pharmacol. Exp. Ther.*, 165, 78, 1969.
3. Kuhar, M.J., Neurotransmitter uptake: a tool in identifying neurotransmitter- specific pathways, *Life Sci.*, 13, 1623, 1973.
4. Horn, A.S., Characteristics of Neuronal dopamine uptake, in *Dopamine. Adv. Biochem. Psychopharmacol.*, Roberts, P.J., Woodruff, G.N. and Iversen, L.L. Eds., Vol. XIX, Raven Press, New York, NY, 1978, 25, 1978.
5. Horn, A.S., Dopamine uptake: a review of progress in the last decade, *Prog. Neurobiol.*, 34, 387, 1990.
6. Holz, K.W. and Coyle, J.T., The effects of various salts, temperature and the alkaloids veratridine and batrachotoxin on the uptake of [³H]-dopamine into synaptosomes from rat striatum, *Mol. Pharmacol.*, 10, 746, 1974.
7. Kuhar, M.J. and Zarbin, M.A., Synaptosomal transport: a chloride dependence for choline, gaba, glycine and several other compounds, *J. Neurochem.*, 30,15, 1978.
8. Cao, C.J., Shamoo, A.E. and Eldefrawi, M.E., Cocaine-sensitive, ATP-dependent dopamine uptake in striatal synaptosomes, *Biochem. Pharmacol.*, 39, R9, 1990.
9. Koob, G.F. and Bloom, F.E., Cellular and molecular mechanisms of drug dependence, *Science* 242, 715, 1988.
10. Kuhar, M.J., Ritz, M.C. and Boja, J.W., The dopamine hypothesis of the reinforcing properties of cocaine, *Trends in Neurosci.*, 14, 299, 1991.
11. DiChiara, G. and Imperato, A., Drugs abused by humans preferentially increase synaptic dopamine concentrations in the mesolimbic system of freely moving rats, *Proc. Natl. Acad. Sci.*, 85, 5274, 1988.
12. Coyle, J.T. and Synder, S.H., Catecholamine uptake by synaptosomes in homogenates of rat brain: stereospecificity in different areas, *J. Pharmacol. Exp. Ther.*, 170, 221, 1969.
13. Iversen, L.L., Uptake processes for biogenic amines, in *Biochemistry of Biogenic Amines*, Plenum Press, New York, NY, 3, 381, 1975.
14. Horn, A.S., Characteristics of transport in dopaminergic neurons, in *The Mechanism of Neuronal and Extraneuronal Transport of Catecholamines*, D.M. Paton, ed., Raven Press, New York, NY, 1976, 195.
15. Amara, S. and Kuhar, M.J., Neurotransmitter transporters: recent progress, *Annual Rev. Neurosci.*, 16, 73, 1993.
16. Harris, J.E. and Baldessarini, R.J., The uptake of [³H]dopamine by homogenates of rat corpus striatum: effects of cations, *Life Sci.*, 13, 303, 1973.
17. Horn, A.S., in *The Neurobiology of Dopamine*, Horn, A.S., Korf, J. and Westerink, B.H.C. Eds., Academic Press, New York, NY, 217, 1979.
18. Zimányi, I., Lajitha, A. and Reith, M.E.A., Comparison of characteristics of dopamine uptake and mazindol binding in mouse striatum, *Naunyn-Schmiedeberg's Arch. Pharmacol.*, 240, 626, 1989. 1989.
19. Shank, R.P., Schneider, C.R. and Tighe, J.J., Ion dependence of neurotransmitter uptake: inhibitory effects of ion substrates, *J. Neurochem.*, 49, 381, 1978.
20. Amejdki-Chab, N., Costentin, J. and Bonnet, J.-J., Kinetic analysis of the chloride dependence of the neuronal uptake of dopamine and effect of anions on the ability of substrates to compete with the binding of the dopamine uptake inhibitor GBR 12783, *J. Neurochem.*, 58, 793, 1992.
21. Krueger, B.K., Kinetics and block of dopamine uptake in synaptosomes from rat caudate nucleus, *J. Neurochem.*, 55, 260, 1990.
22. McElvain, J.S. and Schenk, J.O., A multisubstrate mechanism of striatal dopamine uptake and its inhibition by cocaine, *Biochem. Pharmacol.*, 43, 2189, 1992.

John W. Boja and William M. Meil

23. Rostene, W., Boja, J.W., Scherman, D., Carroll, F.I. and Kuhar, M.J., Dopamine transport: pharmacological distinction between the synaptic membrane and vesicular transporter in rat striatum, *Eur. J. Pharmacol.* 281, 175, 1992.

24. Heikkila, R.E., Cabbat, F.S. and Duvoisin, R.C., Motor activity and rotational behavior after analogs of cocaine: correlation with dopamine uptake blockade, *Commun. Psychopharm.*, 3, 285, 1979.

25. Heikkila, R.E., Manzino, L. and Cabbat, F.S., Stereospecific effects of cocaine derivatives on ³H-dopamine uptake: correlations with behavioral effects, *Subst. Use Misuse*, 2, 115, 1981.

26. Reith, M.E.A., Sershen, H. and Lajtha, A., Saturable [³H]cocaine binding in central nervous system of the mouse, *Life Sci.*, 27, 1055, 1980.

27. Kennedy, L.T. and Hanbauer, I., Sodium-sensitive cocaine binding to rat striatal membrane: possible relationship to dopamine uptake sites, *J. Neurochem.*, 41, 172, 1983.

28. Ritz, M.C., Lamb, R.J., Goldberg, S.R. and Kuhar, M.J., Cocaine receptors on dopamine transporters are related to self-administration of cocaine, *Science*, 237,1219, 1987.

29. Bergman, J., Madras, B.K., Johnson, S.E. and Spealman, R.D., Effects of cocaine and related drugs in nonhuman primates. III. Self-administration by squirrel monkeys, *J. Pharmacol. Exp. Ther.*, 251, 150, 1989. (9)

30. Scheffel, U., Boja, J.W. and Kuhar, M.J., Cocaine receptors: *in vivo* labeling with ³H-(-) cocaine, ³H-WIN 35,065-2 and ³H-35,428, *Synapse* 4:, 390, 1989.

31. Fowler, J.S., Volkow, N.D., Wolf, A.P., Dewey, S.L., Schlyer, D.J., MacGregor, R.R.,Hitzmann, R., Logan, J., Bendriem, B., Gatley, S.J. and Christman, D.R., Mapping cocaine binding sites in human and baboon brain in vivo, *Synapse*, 4, 371, 1989.

32. Volkow, N.D., Fowler, J.S., Wolf, A.P., Wang, G.J., Logan, J., MacGregor, D.J., Dewey, S.L., Schlyer, D.J. and Htzemann, R., Distribution and kinetics of carbon-11-cocaine in the human body measured with PET, *J. Nucl. Med.*, 33, 521, 1992.

33. Scheffel, U., Pögün, S., Stathis, A., Boja, J.W. and Kuhar, M.J., *J. Pharmacol. Exp. Ther.*, 257, 954, 1992.

34. Cline, E.J., Scheffel, U., Boja, J.W., Mitchell, W.M., Carroll, F.I., Abraham, P., Lewin, A.H. and Kuhar, M.J., In vivo binding of [¹²⁵I]RTI-55 to dopamine and serotonin transporters in rat brain, *Synapse*, 12, 37, 1992.

35. Scheffel, U., Dannals, R.F., Cline, E.J., Ricaurte, G.A., Carroll, F.I., Abraham, P., Lewin, A.H. and Kuhar, M.J., [¹²³/¹²⁵I]RTI-55, an in vivo label for the serotonin transporter, *Synapse*, 11, 134, 1992

36. Carroll, F.I., Rahman, M.A., Abraham, P., Parham, K., Lewin, A.H., Dannals, R.F., Shaya, E., Scheffel, U., Wong, D.F., Boja, J.W. and Kuhar, M.J., [¹²³I]3ß-4(-iodophenyl)tropan-2ß-carboxylic acid methyl ester (RTI-55), a unique cocaine receptor ligand for imaging the dopamine and serotonin transporters in vivo, *Med. Chem. Res.*, 1, 289, 1991.

37. Neumeyer, J.L., Wang, S., Milius, R.M., Baldwin, R.M., Zea-Ponce, Y., Hoffer, P.B., Sybirska, E., Al-Tikriti, M., Charney, D.S., Malison, R.T., Laruelle, M. and Innis, R.B., [¹²³I]-2ß-carbomethoxy-3ß-(4-iodophenyl)tropane: high-affinity SPECT radiotracer of monoamine reuptake sites in brain, *J. Med. Chem.*, 34, 3144, 1991.

38. Innis, R., Baldwin, R.M., Sybirska, E., Zea, Y., Laruelle, M., Al-Tikriti, M., Charney, D., Zoghbi, S., Wisniewski, G., Hoffer, P., Wang, S., Millius, R. and Neumeyer, J., Single photon emission computed tomography imaging of monoamine uptake sites in primate brain with [¹²³I]CIT, *Eur. J. Pharmacol.*, 200, 369, 1991.

39. Shaya, E.K., Scheffel, U., Dannals, R.F., Ricaurte, G.A., Carroll, F.I., Wagner, Jr., H.N., Kuhar, M.J. and Wong, D.F., In vivo imaging of dopamine reuptake sites in the primate brain using single photon emission computed tomography (SPECT) and iodine-123 labeled RTI-55, *Synapse*, 10, 169, 1992.

40. Boja, J.W., Mitchell, W.M., Patel, A., Kopajtic, T.A., Carroll, F.I., Lewin, A.H., Abraham, P. and Kuhar, M.J., High affinity binding of [¹²⁵I]RTI-55 to dopamine and serotonin transporters in rat brain, *Synapse*, 12, 27, 1992.

41. Boja, J.W., Cadet, J.L., Kopajtic, T.A., Lever, J., Seltzman, H.H., Wyrick, C.D., Lewin, A.H., Abraham, P. and Carroll, F.I., Selective labeling of the dopamine transporter by the high

affinity ligand 3β-(4-[^{125}I]iodophenyl)tropane-2-carboxylic acid isopropyl ester, *Mol. Pharmacol.*, 47, 779, 1995.

42. Staley, J.K., Boja, J.W., Carroll, F.I., Seltzman, H.H., Wyrick, C.D., Lewin, A.H., Abraham, P. and Mash, D.C., Mapping dopamine transporters in the human brain with novel selective cocaine analog [^{125}I]RTI-121, *Synapse*, 21, 364, 1995.

43. Ciliax, B.J., Heilman, C., Demchyshyn, L.L., Pristupa, Z.B., Ince, E., Hersch, S.M., Niznik, H.B. and Levey, A.I., The dopamine transporter: immunochemical characterization and localization in brain, *J. Neurosci.*, 15, 1714, 1995.

44. Javitch, J.A., Blaustein, R.O. and Synder, S.H., [^{3}H]Mazindol binding associated with neuronal dopamine and norepinephrine uptake sites, *Mol. Pharmacol.*, 26, 35, 1984.

45. Dubocovich, M.L. and Zahniser, N.R., Binding characteristics of the dopamine uptake inhibitor [^{3}H]nomifensine to striatal membranes, *Biochem. Pharmacol.*, 34, 1137, 1985.

46. Anderson, P.H., Biochemical and pharmacological characterization of [^{3}H]GBR 12935 binding in vitro to rat striatal membranes: labeling of the dopamine uptake complex, *J. Neurochem.*, 48, 1887, 1987.

47. Schoemaker, H., Pimoule, C., Arbilla, S., Scatton, B., Javoy-Agid, F. and Langer, S.Z., Sodium dependent [^{3}H]cocaine binding associated with dopamine uptake sites in the rat striatum and human putamen decrease after dopamine denervation and in Parkinsons disease, *Naunyn-Schmiedeberg's Arch. Pharmacol.*, 329, 227, 1985.

48. Calligaro, D.O. and Eldefraei, M.E., High affinity stereospecific binding of [^{3}H]cocaine in striatum and its relationship to the dopamine transporter, *Membr. Biochem.*, 7, 87, 1988.

49. Madras, B.K., Fahey, M.A., Bergman, J., Canfield, D.R. and Spealman R.D., Effects of cocaine and related drugs in nonhuman primates. I. [^{3}H]Cocaine binding sites in caudate-putamen, *J. Pharmacol. Exp. Ther.*, 251, 131, 1989.

50. Ritz, M.C., Boja, J.W., Zaçzek, R, , Carroll, F.I. and Kuhar, M.J., ^{3}H WIN 35,065-2: A ligand for cocaine receptors in striatum, *J. Neurochem.*, 55, 1556, 1990.

51. Madras, B.K., Spealman, R.D., Fahey, M.A., Neumeyer, J.L., Saha, J.K. and Milius, R.A., Cocaine receptors labeled by [^{3}H]2ß-carbomethoxy-3ß-(4- fluorophenyl)tropane, *Mol. Pharmacol.*, 36, 518, 1989.

52. Boja, J.W., Markham, L., Patel, A., Uhl, G. and Kuhar, M.J., Expression of a single dopamine transporter cDNA can confer two cocaine binding sites, *Neuroreport*, 3, 247, 1992.

53. Madras, B.K. and Kaufman, M.J., Cocaine accumulates in dopamine-rich regions of primate brain after I.V. Administration: comparison with mazindol distribution, *Synapse*, 18, 261, 1994.

54. Pögün, S., Scheffel, U. and Kuhar, M.J., Cocaine displaces [^{3}H]WIN 35,428 binding to dopamine uptake sites in vivo more rapidly than mazindol or GBR 12909, *Eur. J. Pharmacol.*, 198, 203, 1991.

55. Stathis, M., Scheffel, U., Lever, S.Z., Boja, J.W., Carroll, F.I. and Kuhar, M.J., Rate of binding of various inhibitors at the dopamine transporter in vivo, *Psychopharmacology*, 119, 376, 1995.

56. Giros, B., Jaber, M., Jones, S.R., Wightman, R.M. and Caron, M.G., Hyperlocomotion and indifference to cocaine and amphetamine in mice lacking the dopamine transporter, *Nature*, 379, 606, 1996.

57. Ungerstedt, U., Striatal dopamine release after amphetamine or nerve degeneration revealed by rotational behavior, Acta Physiologica Scandinavica, 367, 49, 1971.

58. Masuoka, D.T., Alcaraz, A.F. and Schott, H.F., [^{3}H]Dopamine release by d-amphetamine from striatal synaptosomes of reserpinized rats, Biochem. Pharmacol., 31, 1969, 1982.

59. Kuczenski, R., *Biochemical actions of amphetamine and other stimulants*, In: Stimulants: Neurochemical, Behavioral, and Clinical Perspectives, I. Creese, Ed. Raven Press, New York, 1983, 31.

60. Bowyer, J.F., Spuler, K.P. and Weiner, N., Effects of phencyclidine, amphetamine and related compounds on dopamine release from and uptake into striatal synaptosomes, *J. Pharmacol. Exp. Ther.*, 229, 671, 1984.

61. Moghaddam, B., Roth, R.H. and Bunny, B.S., Characterization of dopamine release in the rat medial prefrontal cortex as assessed by in vivo microdialysis: comparison to the striatum, *Neuroscience*, 36, 669, 1990.

62. Robertson, G.S., Damsma, G. and Fibiger, H.C., Characterization of dopamine release in the substantia nigra by in vivo microdialysis in freely moving rats, *J. Neurosci.*, 11, 2209, 1991.

63. Schmidt, C.J. and Gibb, J.W., Role of the dopamine uptake carrier in the neurochemical response to methamphetamine: effects of amfonelic acid, *Eur. J. Pharmacol.*, 109, 73, 1985.

64. Johnson, M.P., Hoffman, A.J. and Nichols, D.E., Effects of the enantimers of MDA, MDMA, and related analogues of [³H]serotonin and [³H]dopamine release from superfused rat brain slices, *Eur. J. Pharmacol.*, 132, 269, 1986.

65. Steele, T.D., Nichols, D.E. and Yim, G.K., Stereochemical effects of 3,4-methylenedioxy-methamphetamine (MDMA) and related amphetamine derivatives on inhibition of uptake of [³H]monoamines into synaptosomes from different regions of rat brain, *Biochem. Pharmacol.*, 36, 2297, 1987.

66. Yamamoto, B.K. and Spanos, L.J., The acute effects of methylenedioxymethamphetamine on dopamine release in the awake-behaving rat, *Eur. J. Pharmacol.*, 148, 195, 1988.

67. Nash, J.F. and Nichols, D.E., Microdialysis studies on 3,4-methylenedioxyamphetamine and structurally related analogues, *Eur. J. Pharmacol.*, 200, 53, 1991.

68. Johnson, M.P., Conarty, P.F. and Nichols, D.E., [³H]Monoamine releasing and uptake inhibition properties of 3,4-methylenedioxymethamphetamine and p-chloroamphetamine analogues, *Eur. J. Pharmacol.*, 200, 9, 1991.

69. Azzaro, A.J., Ziance, R.J. and Rutledge, C.O., The importance of neuronal uptake of amines for amphetamine-induced release of ³H-norepinephrine from isolated brain tissue, *J. Pharmacol. Exp. Ther.*, 189, 110, 1974.

70. Hadfield, M.G., A comparison of in vivo and in vitro amphetamine on the synaptosomal uptake of dopamine in mouse striatum, *Res. Commun. Chem. Mol. Pathol. Pharmacol.*, 48, 183, 1985

71. Arnold, E.B., Molinoff, P.B. and Rutledge, C.O., The release of endogenous norepinephrine and dopamine from cerebral cortex by amphetamine, *J. Pharmacol. Exp. Ther.*, 202, 544, 1977.

72. Fisher J.F. and Cho, A.K., Chemical release of dopamine from striatal homogenates: evidence for an exchange diffusion model, *J. Pharmacol. Exp. Ther.*, 208, 203, 1979.

73. Liang, N.Y. and Rutledge, C.O., Comparison of the release of [³H]dopamine from isolated corpus striatum by amphetamine, fenfluramine and unlabeled dopamine, *Biochem. Pharmacol.*, 31, 983, 1982.

74. Zaczek, R., Culp, S. And De Souza, E.B., Intrasynaptosomal sequestration of [³H]amphetamine and [³H]methylenedioxyamphetamine: characterization suggests the presence of a factor responsible for maintaining sequestration, *J. Neurochem.*, 54, 195, 1990.

75. Zaczek, R., Culp, S. And De Souza, E.B., Interactions of [³H]amphetamine with rat brain synaptosomes. II. Active, *J. Pharmacol. Exp. Ther.*, 257, 830, 1991.

76. Jacocks, H.M. and Cox, B.K., Serotonin-stimulated [³H]dopamine via reversal of the dopamine transporter in rat striatum and nucleus accumbens : a comparison with release elicited by potassium, N-methyl-D-aspartic acid, glutamic acid and D-amphetamine, *J. Pharmacol. Exp. Ther.*, 262, 356, 1992.

77. Sulzer, D., Maidment, N.T. and Rayport, S., Amphetamine and other weak bases act to promote reverse transport of dopamine in ventral midbrain neurons, *J. Neurochem.*, 60, 527, 1993.

78. Eshleman, A.J., Henningsen, R.A., Neve, K.A. and Janowsky, A., Release of dopamine via the human transporter, *Mol. Pharmacol.*, 45, 312, 1994.

79. Pifl, C., Drobny, H., Reither, H., Hornykiewicz, O. And Singer, E.A., Mechanism of the dopamine-releasing actions of amphetamine and cocaine: plasmalemmal dopamine transporter versus vesicular monoamine transporter, *Mol. Pharmacol.*, 47, 368, 1995.

80. Di Chiara, G., Imperato, A., Opposite effects of mu and kappa opiate agonists on dopamine release in the nucleus accumbens and in the dorsal caudate of freely moving rat, *J. Pharmacol. Exp. Ther.*, 244, 1067, 1988b

81. Hurd, Y. L., Weiss, F., Koob, G., and Ungerstedt, U., Cocaine reinforcement and extracellular dopamine overflow in the rat nucleus accumbens: an in vivo microdialysis study, *Brain Res.*, 498, 199, 1989.

82. Kalivas, P.W., Winderlov, E., Stanley, D., Breese, G. R., and Prange, Jr. A. J., Enkephalin action on the mesolimbic dopamine system: a dopamine-dependent and dopamine-independent increase in locomotor activity, *J. Pharmacol. Exp. Ther.*, 227, 229, 1983.

83. Pettit, H. O., Ettenberg, A., Bloom, F. E., and Koob, G. F., Destruction of dopamine in the nucleus accumbens selectively attenuates cocaine but not heroin self-administration in rats, *Psychopharmacology*, 84, 167, 1984.

84. Di Chiara, G., and North, A. R., Neurobiology of opiate abuse, *TIPS*, 13, 185, 1992.

85. Koob, G. F., Drugs of abuse: anatomy, pharmacology and function of reward pathways, *TIPS*, 13, 177, 1992.

86. Spyraki, C., Fibiger, H. C., and Phillips, A. G., Attenuation of heroin reward in rats by disruption of the mesolimbic dopamine system, *Psychopharmacology*, 79, 278, 1983.

87. Zito, K. A., Vickers, G., and Roberts, D. C. S., Disruption of cocaine and heroin self-administration following kianic acid lesions of the nucleus accumbens, *Pharmacol. Biochem. Behav.*, 23, 1029, 1985.

88. Bozarth, M. A., and Wise, R. A. Heroin reward is dependent on a dopaminergic substrate, *Life Sci.*, 29, 1881, 1981.

89. Kornetsky, C., and Porrino L. J., Brain Mechanisms of drug-induced reinforcement, *Addictive States*, O'Brien, C. P., and Jaffe, J. H.,Raven Press, Ltd., New York, 1992, 59.

90. Gysling, K., and Wang, R. Y., Morphine-induced activation of A10 dopamine neurons in the rat brain, *Brain Res.*, 277, 119, 1983.

91. Matthews, R. T., and German, D. C., Electrophysiological evidence for excitation of rat ventral tegmental area dopamine neurons by morphine, *Neuroscience*, 11, 617, 1984.

92. Das, D., Rogers, J., and Michael-titus, A. T., Comparative study of the effects of Mu, delta and Kappa Opioid agonists on ^{3}H-dopamine uptake in the rat striatum and nucleus accumbens, *Neuropharmacology*, 33, 221, 1994.

93. Izenwasser, S., Newman A. H., Cox, B. M., and Katz, J. L., the cocaine-like behavioral effects of meperidine are mediated by activity at the dopamine transporter, *Eur. J. Pharmacol.*, 297, 9, 1996.

94. Simantov, R., Chronic morphine alters dopamine transporter density in the rat brain: possible role in the mechanism of drug addiction, *Neurosci. Lett.*, 163, 121, 1993.

95. Izenwasser, S. and Cox, B. M., Daily cocaine treatment produces a persistent reduction of [^{3}H]dopamine uptake in vitro in the rat nucleus accumbens but not the striatum, *Brain Res.*, 531, 338, 1990.

96. Carboni, E., Imperato, A., Perezzani, L., DiChiara, G., Amphetamine, cocaine, phencyclidine and nomifensine increase extracellular dopamine concentrations preferentially in the nucleus accumbens of freely moving rats, *Neuroscience*, 28, 653, 1989.

97. Herndandez, L., Auerbach, S., Hoebel, B. G., Phencyclidine (PCP) injected into the nucleus accumbens increases extracellular dopamine and serotonin as measured by microdialysis, *Life Sci.*, 42, 1713, 1988.

98. Hondo, H., Yonezawa, Y., Nakahara, T., Nakamura, K., Hirano, M., Uchimura, H., and Tashiro, N., Effect of Phencyclidine on dopamine release in the rat prefrontal cortex; an in vivo microdialysis study, *Brain Res.*, 633, 337, 1994.

99. Hata, N., Nishikawa, T., Umino, A., and Takahashi, K., Evidence for involvement of N-methyl-D-aspartate receptor in tonic inhibitory control of dopaminergic transmission in the rat medial frontal cortex, *Neurosci. Lett.*, 120, 101, 1990.

100. Freeman, A. S., and Bunney, B. S., the effects of phencyclidine and N-allynormetazocine on mid-brain dopamine neuronal activity, *Eur. J. Pharmacol.*, 104, 287, 1984.

101. Gariano, R. F., and Groves, P. M., Burst firing induced in mid-brain dopamine neurons by stimulation of the medial prefrontal and anterior cingulate cortices, *Brain Res.*, 462, 194, 1988.

102. Suaad-Chagny, M. F., Chergui, K., Chouvet, G., and Gonon F., Relationship between dopamine release in the rat nucleus accumbens and the discharge activity of dopaminergic neurons during local in vivo application of amino acids in the ventral tegmental area, *Neuroscience*, 49, 63, 1992.

103. Fagg, G. E., Phencyclidine and related drugs bind to the activated N-methyl-D-aspartate receptor-channels complex in rat membranes, *Neurosci. lett.*, 76, 221, 1987.

John W. Boja and William M. Meil

104. Mount, H., Boksa, P., Chadieu, I., and Quirion R., Phencyclidine and related compounds evoked [³H] dopamine release from rat mesencephalon cell cultures by mechanisms independent of the phencyclidine receptor, sigma binding site, or dopamine uptake site, *Can. J. Physiol. Pharmacol.*, 68, 1200, 1990.

105. Bowyer, J. F., Spuhler, K. P., and Weiner, N., Effects of phencyclidine, amphetamine, and related compounds on dopamine release from and uptake into striatal synaptosomes, *J. Pharmacol. Exp. Ther.*, 229, 671, 1984.

106. Garey, R. E., and Heath, R. G., the effects of phencyclidine on the uptake of ³H-catecholamines by rat striatal and hypothalamic synaptosomes, *Life Sci.*, 18, 1105, 1976.

107. Smith, R. C., Meltzer, H. Y., Arora, R. C., and Davis, J. M., Effects of phencyclidine on ³H-catecholamines and ³H-serotonin uptake in synaptosomal preparations from the rat brain, *Biochem. Pharmacol.*, 26, 1435, 1977.

108. Gerhardt, G. A., Pang, K., and Rose, G. M., *In vivo* electrochemical demonstration of presynaptic actions of phencyclidine in rat caudate nucleus, *J. Pharmacol. Exp. Ther.*, 241, 714, 1987.

109. Baba, A., Yamamoto, T., Yamamoto, H., Suzuki, T., and Moroji, T., Effects of the major metabolite of phencyclidine, the *trans* isomer of 4-phenyl-4-(l-piperidinyl) cyclohexanol, on [³H]N-(1-[2-thienyl]cyclohexyl)-3,4-piperidine ([³H]TPC) binding and [³H] dopamine uptake in the rat brain, *Neurosci. Lett.*, 182, 119, 1994.

110. Vignon, J., Pinet, V., Cerruti, C., Kamenka, J., and Chicheportiche, R., [3H]N-1(2-Benzo(b)thiophenyl)cyclohexyl]piperidinme ([3H]BTCP): a new phencyclidine analog selective for the dopamine uptake complex, *Eur. J. Pharmacol.*, 148, 427,1988.

111. Kuhar, M.J.,Boja, J.W. and Cone, E.J., Phencyclidine binding to striatal cocaine receptors, *Neuropharmacology* 29, 295, 1990.

112. Cook, C. E., Perez, R. M., Jeffcoat., A. R., and Brine, D. R., Phencyclidine disposition in humans after small doses of radiolabled drug, *Fed. Proc.*, 42, 2566, 1983.

113. Carlezon, Jr. W. A., and Wise R. A., rewarding actions of phencyclidine and related drugs in the nucleus accumbens shell and frontal cortex, *J. Neurosci.*, 16, 3112, 1996.

114. Carlezon, Jr. W. A., and Wise R. A., habit-forming actions of nomifensine in the nucleus accumbens, *Psychopharmacology*, 122, 194, 1995.

115. Steinpreis, R. E., and Salamone J. D., The role of nucleus accumbens dopamine in the neurochemical and behavioral effects of phencyclidine: a microdialysis and behavioral study, *Brain Res.*, 612, 263, 1993.

116. Harris, R. T., Waters, W., McLendon D., Evaluation of reinforcing capability of delta-9-tetrocannabinol in rhesus monkeys, *Psychopharmacologia*, 37, 23, 1974.

117. Carney, J. M., Uwaydah, I. M., and Balster, R. L., Evaluation of a suspension system for intravenous self-administration studies of water-insoluble compounds in the rhesus monkey, *Pharmacol. Biochem. Behav.*, 7, 367, 1977.

118. Gardner, E. L., Paredes, W., Smith, D., Donner, A., Milling, C., Cohen, D., and Morrison, D., Facilitation of brain stimulation reward by Δ⁹ tetrahydrocannabinol, *Psychopharmacology*, 96, 142, 1988.

119. Chen, J., Paredes, W., Li, J., Smith, D., Lowinson, J., and Gardner, E. L., In vivo brain microdialysis studies of Δ⁹-tetrahydrocannabinol on presynaptic dopamine efflux in nucleus accumbens of the Lewis rat, *Psychopharmacology*, 102, 156, 1990a.

120. Chen, J., Marmur, R., Pulles, A., Paredes, W., and Gardner, E.L., Ventral tegmental microinjection of Δ⁹-tetrahydrocannabinol enhances ventral tegmental somatodendritic dopamine levels but not forebrain dopamine levels: evidence for local neural action by marijuana's psychoactive ingredient, *Brain Res.*, 621, 65, 1993.

121. Chen, J., Paredes, W., Lowinson, J. H., and Gardner, E. L., Δ⁹ tetrahydrocannabinol enhances presynaptic dopamine efflux in the medial prefrontal cortex, *Eur. J. Pharmacol.*, 190, 259, 1990b.

122. Ng Cheong Ton, J. M., Gerhardt, G. A., Friedemann, M., Etgen, A. M., Rose, G.M., Sharpless, N.S., and Gardner, E. L,. Effects of Δ⁹-tetrahydrocannabinol on potassium-evoked release of dopamine in the rat caudate nucleus: an in vivo electrochemical and in vivo microdialysis study, *Brain Res.*, 451, 59, 1988.

The Dopamine Transporter and Addiction

123. Chen, J., Paredes, W., Lowinson, J. H., and Gardner, E. L., Strain-specific facilitation of dopamine efflux by Δ^9-tetrahydrocannabinol in the nucleus accumbens of rat an in vivo microdialysis study, *Neurosci. Lett.*, 129, 136, 1991.

124. Bloom, A. S., Effect of delta-9-tetrahydrocannabinol on the synthesis of dopamine and norepinephrine in mouse brain synaptosomes, *J. Pharmacol. Exp. Ther.*, 221, 97, 1982.

125. Poddar, M. K., and Dewey, W. L., Effects of cannabinoids on catecholamine uptake and release in hypothalamic and striatal synaptosomes, *J. Pharmacol. Exp. Ther.*, 214, 63, 1980.

126. Hershkowitz, M., and Szechtman, H., Pretreatment with Δ^1 tetrahydrocannabinol and psychoactive drugs: effects on uptake of biogenic amines and on behavior, *Eur. J. Pharmacol.*, 59, 267, 1979.

127. Banerjee, S. P., Snyder, S. H., and Mechoulam, R., Cannabinoids: influence on neurotransmitter uptake in rat brain synaptosomes, *J. Pharmacol.Exp.Ther.*, 194, 74, 1975.

128. Sakurai-Yamashita, Y., Kataoka, Y., Fujiwara, M., Mine, K., and Ueki, S., Delta 9-tetrahydrocannabinol facilitates striatal dopaminergic transmission. *Pharmacol. Biochem. Behav.*, 33, 397, 1989.

129. Samuel, D., Lynch, M.A. and Littleton, J.M., Picortoxin inhibits the effect of ethanol on the spontaneous efflux of [^{3}H]-dopamine from superfused sliced of rat corpus striatum, *Neuropharmacology*, 22, 1412, 1983.

130. Shier, W.T., Koda, L.Y.. and Bloom, F.E., Metabolism of [^{3}H]dopamine following intracerebroventricular injection in rats pretreated with ethanol or choral hydrate, *Neuropharmacology*, 22, 279, 1983.

131. Russell, V.A., Lamm, M.C. and Taljaard, J.J., Effect of ethanol on [^{3}H]dopamine release in rat nucleus accumbens and striatal slices, *Neurochem. Res.*, 13, 487, 1988.

132. Strombom, U.H. and Liedman, B., Role of dopaminergic neurotransmission in locomotor stimulation by dexamphetamine and ethanol, *Psychopharmacology*, 78, 271, 1982.

133. Murphy, J.M., McBride, W.J., Lumeng, L. and Li, T.K., Monoamine and metabolite levels in CNS regions of the P line of alcohol-preferring rats after acute and chronic ethanol treatment, *Pharmacol. Biochem. Behav.*, 19, 849, 1983.

134. Di Chiara, G. and Imperato, A., Ethanol preferentially stimulates dopamine release in the nucleus accumbens of freely moving rats, *Eur. J. Pharmacol.*, 115, 131, 1985.

135. Imperato, I. and Di Chiara, G., Preferential stimulation of dopamine release in the nucleus accumbens of freely moving rats by ethanol, *J. Pharmacol. Exp. Ther.* 239, 219, 1986

136. Yoshimoto, K., McBride, W.J., Lumeng, L. and Li, T.K., Ethanol enhances the release of dopamine and serotonin in the nucleus accumbens of HAD and LAD lines of rats, *Alcohol. Clin. Exp. Res.*, 16, 781, 1992.

137. Yoshimoto, K., McBride, W.J., Lumeng, L. and Li, T.K., Alcohol stimulates the release of dopamine and serotonin in the nucleus accumbens, *Alcohol*, 9, 17, 1992.

138. McBride, W.J., Murphy, J.M., Gatto, G.J., Levy, A.D., Yoshimoto, K., Lumeng, L. and Li, T.K., CNS mechanisms of alcohol self-administration, *Alcohol Alcohol. Supp.*, 2, 463, 1993.

139. Samson, H.H. and Hodge, C.W., The role of the mesoaccumbens dopamine system in ethanol reinforcement: studies using the techniques of microinjection and voltammetry, *Alcohol Alcohol. Supp.*, 2, 469, 1993.

140. Weiss, F., Lorang, M.T., Bloom, F.E. and Koob, G.F., Oral alcohol self-administration stimulates dopamine release in the nucleus accumbens: genetic and motivational determinants, *J. Pharmacol. Exp. Ther.*, 267, 250, 1993.

141. Kiianmaa, K., Nurmi, M., Nykanen, I. and Sinclair, J.D., Effect of ethanol on extracellular dopamine in the nucleus accumbens of alcohol-preferring AA and alcohol-avoiding ANA rats, *Pharmacol. Biochem. Behav.*, 52, 29-34, 1995.

142. Tan, A.Y., Dular, R. and Innes, I.R.., Alcohol feeding alters [^{3}H]dopamine uptake into rat cortical and brain stem synaptosomes, *Prog. Biochem. Pharmacol.*, 18, 224, 1981.

143. Lynch, M.A., Samuel, D. and Littleton, J.M., Altered characteristics of [^{3}H]dopamine release from superfused slices of corpus striatum obtained from rats receiving ethanol in vivo, *Neuropharmacology*, 24, 479, 1985.

144. Hearn, W.L., Flynn, D.D., Hime, G.W., Rose, S., Cofino, J.C., Mantero-Atienza, E., Wetli, C.V. and Mash, D.C., Cocaethylene: a unique metabolite displays high affinity for the dopamine transporter, *J. Neurochem.*, 56, 698, 1991.

145. Jatlow, P., Elsworth, J.D., Bradberry, C.W., Winger, G., Taylor, J.R., Russell, R. and Roth, R.H., Cocaethylene: a neuropharmacologically active metabolite associated with concurrent cocaine-ethanol ingestion, *Life Sci.*, 48, 1781, 1991.

146. Woodward, J.J., Mansbach, R., Carroll, F.I. and Balster, R.L., Cocaethylene inhibits dopamine uptake and produces cocaine-like actions in drug discrimination studies, *Eur. J. Pharmacol.*, 197, 235, 1991.

147. Lewin, A.H., Gao., Y., Abraham, P., Boja, J.W., Kuhar, M.J. and Carroll, F.I., The effect of 2ß-substitution on binding affinity at the cocaine receptor, *J. Med. Chem.*, 35, 135, 1992.

148. Bradberry, C.W., Nobiletti, J.B., Elsworth, J.D., Murphy, B., Jatlow, P. and Roth, R.H., Cocaine and cocaethylene: microdialysis comparison of brain drug levels and effects on dopamine and serotonin, *J. Neurochem.* 60, 1429, 1993.

149. Iyer, R.N., Nobiletti, J.B., Jatlow, P.I. and Bradberry, C.W., Cocaine and cocaethylene: effects on extracellular dopamine in the primate, *Psychopharmacology*, 120, 150, 1995.

150. Katz, J.l., Terry, P. and Witkin, J.M., Comparative behavioral pharmacology amd toxicology of cocaine and its ethanol-derived metabolite, cocaine ethyl-ester (cocaethylene), *Life Sci.*, 50, 1351, 1992.

151. Hearn, W.L., rose, S.L., Wagner, J., Ciarleglio, A.C., and Mash, D.C., Cocaethylene is more potent than cocaine in mediating lethality, *Pharmacol. Biochem. Behav.,* 39, 531-533, 1991.

152. Meehan, S.M. and Schechter, M.D., Cocaethylene-induced lethality in mice is potentiated by alcohol, *Alcohol*, 12, 383, 1995.

153. Damsma, G., Westernik, B.H., de Vries, J.B. and Horn, A.S., The effect of systemically applied cholinergic drugs on the striatal release of dopamine and its metabolites, as determined by automated microdialysis in conscious rats, *Neurosci. Lett.*, 89, 349, 1988.

154. Westfall, T.C., Effect of nicotine and other drugs on the release of ^{3}H-norepinephrine and ^{3}H-dopamine from rat brain slices, *Neuropharmacology*, 13, 693, 1974.

155. Marien, M., Brien,J. Amd Jhamandas, K., Regional release of [^{3}H]dopamine from rat brain in vitro: effects of opioids on release induced by potassium, nicotine, and L-glutamic acid, *Can. J. Physiol. Pharmacol.*, 61, 43, 1983.

156. Rapier, C., Lunt, G.G. and Wonnacott, S., Stereoselective nicotine-induced release of dopamine from striatal synaptosomes: concentration dependence and repetitive stimulation, *J. Neurochem.*, 50, 1123, 1988.

157. Izenwasser, S., Jacocks, H.M., Rosenberger, J.G. and Cox, B.M., Nicotine indirectly inhibits [^{3}H]dopamine uptake at concentrations that do not directly promote [^{3}H]dopamine release in rat striatum, *J. Neurochem.*, 56, 603, 1991.

158. Dwoskin, L.P., Leibee, L.L., Jewell, A.L., Fang, Z. And Crooks, P.A., Inhibition of [^{3}H]dopamine uptake into rat striatal slices by quanternary n-methylated nicotine metabolites, *Life Sci.*, 50, PL-223, 1992.

159. Yamashita, H., Kitayama, S., Zhang, Y.X., Takahashi, T., Dohi, T. And Nakamura, S., Effect of nicotine on dopamine uptake in COS cells possessing the rat dopamine transporter and in PC12 cells, *Biochem. Pharmacol.* 49, 742, 1995.

160. Lerner-Marmarosh, N., Carroll, F.I. and Abood, L.G., Antagonism of nicotine's action by cocaine analogs, *Life Sci.*, 56, PL67, 1995.

161. Deneau, G., Yanagita, T., and Seevers, M. H., Self-administration of psychoactive substances by the monkey, *Psychopharmacologia*, 16, 30, 1969.

162. Beardsley, P. M., Balster, R. L., and Harris, L. S., Self-administration of methylendioxymethamphetamine (MDMA) by rhesus monkeys, *Drug Alcohol Depend.*, 18, 149, 1986.

163. Spampinato, U., Esposito, E. And Samanin, R., Serotonin agonists reduce dopamine sythesis in the striatum only when the impulse flow of nigro-striatal neurons is intact, *J. Neurochem*, 45, 980, 1985.

164. Hetey, L., Schwitzkowsky, R. And Oelssner, W., Influence of psychotomimetics and lisuride on synaptosomal dopamine release in the nucleus accumbens of rats, *Eur. J. Pharmacol.*, 93, 213, 1983.

165. Hetey, L. and Quirling, K., Synaptomsomal uptake and release of dopamine and 5-hydroxy-tryptamine in nucleus accumbens in vitro following in vivo administration of lysergic acid diethylamide in rats, *Acta. Biol. Med. Ger.*, 39, 889, 1980.

166. Ator, N. A., and Ator, R. R., Self-administration of barbiturates and benzodiazepines: a review, *Pharmacol. Biochem. Behav.*, 27, 391, 1987.

167. Murai, T., Koshikawa, N., Kanayama, T., Takada, K., Tomiyama, K. and Kobayashi, M., Opposite effects of midazolam and beta-carboline-3-carboxylate ethyl ester on the release of dopamine from rat nucleus accumbens measured by in vivo microdialysis, *Eur. J. Pharmacol.*, 261, 65, 1994.

168. Finlay, J.M., Damsma, G. And Fibiger, H.C., Benzodiazepine-induced decreases in extracellular concentration of dopamine in the nucleus accumbens after acute and repeated administration, *Psychopharmacology*, 106, 202, 1992.

169. Louilot, A., Le Moal, M. And Simon, H., Presynaptic control of dopamine metabolism in the nucleus accumbens. Lack of effect of buspirone as demonstrated using in viv voltammetry, *Life Sci.*, 40, 2017, 1987.

170. Reith, M.E.A., Sershen, H. And Lajtha, A., Effects of caffeine on monoaminergic systems in mouse brain, *Acta Biochim. Biophys. Hung.*, 22, 149, 1987.

171. Corrigall, W. A., and Coen, K. M., Nicotine maintains robust self-administration in rats on a limited access schedule, *Psychopharmacology*, 99, 473, 1989.

172. Harris, R.T., Waters, W., McLendon, D., Evaluation of reinforcing capability of delta-9-tetrocannabinol in rhesus monkeys, *Psychopharmacologia*, 37, 23, 1974

173. Balster, R. L., Johanson, C. E., Harris, R. T., and Schuster, C. R., Phencyclidine self-administration in the rhesus monkey, *Pharmacol. Biochem. Behav.*, 1, 167, 1973.

174. Shimada, S., Kitayama, S., Lin, C.-L., Patel, A., Nathankumar, E., Gregor, P., Kuhar, M.J. and Uhl, G., Cloning and expression of a cocaine-sensitive dopamine transporter complementary DNA, *Science*, 254, 576, 1991.

175. Amara, S. And Kuhar, M.J., Neurotransmitter transporters: recent progress, *Annual Rev. Neurosci.*, 16, 73, 1993.

176. Giros, B. And Caron, M.G., Molecular characterization of the dopamine transporter, *TIPS*, 14, 43, 1993.

177. Kitayama, S., Shimada, S., Xu, H., Markham, L., Donovan, D.M. And Uhl, G.R., Dopamine transporter site-directed mutations differentially alter substrate transport and cocaine binding, *Proc. Natl. Acad. Sci.*, 89, 7782, 1992.

178. Boja, J.W., Unpublished data.

6.2 NEUROPSYCHIATRIC CONSEQUENCES OF CHRONIC COCAINE ABUSE

DEBORAH C. MASH

DEPARTMENTS OF NEUROLOGY AND MOLECULAR AND CELLULAR PHARMACOLOGY,
UNIVERSITY OF MIAMI SCHOOL OF MEDICINE, MIAMI, FLORIDA

Mortality data have indicated that deaths involving psychostimulant drugs stem not only from overdose, but also from drug-induced mental states that may lead to serious injuries.[1] The arrival of inexpensive smokable "crack" cocaine has radically changed the nature of the epidemic and revealed the great addictive potential of cocaine. Cocaine, particularly smoked "crack" cocaine, is known to be one of the most widely abused psychoactive substances in the U.S. With the increased use of cocaine in its various forms over the past 15 years, researchers and clinicians have focused on the definition of cocaine dependence and withdrawal.[2] Cocaine

Table 6.2.2 Behavioral Signs of Acute Psychostimulant Toxicity

Excitability	Hallucinations
Restlessness	Paranoia
Delusions	Panic attacks
Delirium	

was not thought to be addictive prior to the 1980s, as neither chronic use nor its cessation resulted in the physiological tolerance or withdrawal observed in opiate dependence. The progression of occasional use to compulsive use,[3] and the description of a cocaine abstinence syndrome,[4] has led to the definition of diagnostic criteria for cocaine dependence. Clinical experience has fostered the view that persons with psychiatric disorders tend to have high rates of substance abuse and vice versa.[5,6] Epidemiological studies have demonstrated that a large portion of the population experiences both mental and addictive disorders.[7] These studies have underscored the gravity of the problem of dual diagnoses of severe mental health and substance abuse disorders.

6.2.1 DIFFERENTIAL DIAGNOSIS OF PSYCHOTIC DISORDERS

Drug use is a major complicating factor in psychosis, renders the management of psychotic disorders more difficult, and adverse reactions to recreational drugs may mimic psychosis.[8] The differential diagnosis of psychotic disorders in the young routinely includes "drug-induced psychosis". This diagnostic category has not had consistent definition and the relationship between drug use and psychotic symptoms is controversial. Adverse psychiatric effects associated with acute cocaine intoxication include extreme agitation, irritability or affective lability, impaired judgment, paranoia, hallucinations (visual or tactile), and sometimes manic excitement. Medical and psychiatric symptoms caused by acute cocaine intoxication are a common reason for presentation to the emergency department. Psychiatric symptoms of cocaine intoxication usually subside within 24 h, but some patients may require benzodiazepines for acute agitation. Neuroleptics are often used for the treatment of unremitting paranoid psychosis, hallucinations, and delusions. The transient paranoid state is a common feature of cocaine dependence, with affected persons possessing an obvious predisposition to this drug-induced state.[9] Psychiatric complications of cocaine intoxication include cocaine-induced paranoia, delirium, delusional disorder, and the depressed mood and dysphoria associated with abrupt cocaine withdrawal (Table 6.2.2).

Extended behavioral signs of cocaine psychosis usually imply the presence of an underlying major psychopathology in susceptible individuals.[9] Cocaine-induced psychosis typically manifests as an intense hypervigilance (paranoia) accompanied by marked apprehension and fear. Auditory and tactile hallucinations, formal thought disorder, and ideas of reference frequently noted with chronic use of amphetamines, are not prevalent in cocaine abusers. Paranoid experience secondary to cocaine use is usually limited to a drug episode, which dissipates by the time the user awakens from the "crash", usually about 8 to 36 h after the cessation of the cocaine "binge".[10] In a sample of 100 cocaine-dependent males, none reported cocaine paranoia extending beyond the crash phase .[10]

In contrast to the effects of cocaine, amphetamine has an apparently greater and longer-acting psychotogenic properties.[11] Angrist[11] has suggested that very high doses of cocaine use with resulting sustained elevations in plasma cocaine levels may be necessary for the development or kindling of an episode of cocaine psychosis. In keeping with this suggestion, certain cocaine-induced effects are known to become progressively more intense after repeated administration, a phenomenon which is referred to as sensitization. However, Satel and co-workers[10] have provided data to suggest that instances of cocaine-induced paranoia or psychosis lasting more than several days most likely indicate the presence of an underlying primary psychotic disorder.

Neuropsychiatric Consequences of Chronic Cocaine Abuse

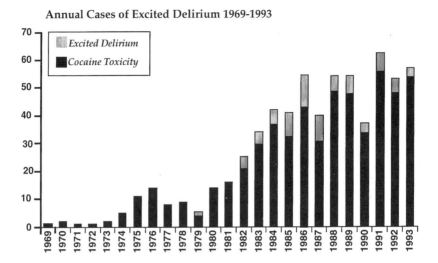

Figure 6.2.2 Tracking the incidence of cocaine overdose deaths in Dade County, FL. Medicolegal investigations of the deaths were conducted by forensic pathologists. Forensic pathologists evaluated the scene environment and circumstances of death and autopsied the victim in order to determine the cause and manner of death. The circumstances of death and toxicology results were reviewed before classifying a death due to cocaine toxicity with or without preterminal delirium. Dark bars illustrate the total number of cocaine overdose deaths. The white bars illustrate the incidence of cocaine delirium victims by year, from the first report in 1982.

6.2.2 COCAINE DELIRIUM

Delirium symptoms suggest dysfunction of multiple brain regions. Clinical subtypes of delirium with unique and definable phenomenological or physical characteristics are not widely accepted. At present, very little is known about the neuropathogenesis of cocaine delirium. While various neurotransmitter alterations may converge to result in a delirium syndrome or subtype thereof, an excess of the neurotransmitter dopamine (DA) has been implicated as a cause of cocaine delirium.

In 1985, a case series of cocaine overdose victims who died following a syndrome of excited delirium was first described.[12] It was not clear whether this type of cocaine toxicity represented a new syndrome that was associated with cocaine use alone, or whether there were other causes or risk factors. The cocaine delirium syndrome is comprised of four components which appear in sequence: hyperthermia, delirium with agitation, respiratory arrest, and death. Compared with other accidental cocaine toxicity deaths, a larger proportion of cocaine delirium victims survive longer after the onset of the overdose. This factor probably accounts for the lower blood cocaine concentrations reported for cocaine delirium victims.[12] The incidence of this disorder is not know with any certainty, but the number of cases has increased markedly since the beginning of the epidemic of "crack" cocaine use in Dade County, Florida (Figure 6.2.2).

In the original report of Wetli and Fishbain,[12] they described the cocaine delirium syndrome in seven cases, and all had somewhat stereotyped histories. A typical example of a cocaine delirium victim was the case of a 33-year-old man, who in an agitated state started pounding on the door of his former house. He was shouting that he wanted to see his wife and daughter. The occupants informed him that nobody by that name resided there, yet he continued. Four bystanders finally restrained him and assisted police units upon their arrival. The subject was handcuffed and put into a police car, whereupon he began to kick out the windows of the vehicle. The police subsequently restrained his ankles and attached the ankle

Deborah C. Mash

Table 6.2.4 Common Traits Associated with the Fatal
            Excited Delirium Syndrome

Male

Extreme agitation

Hyperthermia

High body mass index

Survive longer than 1 h after the onset of symptoms

Die in police custody

restraints and handcuffs together. He was than transported to a local hospital. While enroute, the police officers noted that he became tranquil. Upon arrival at the hospital approximately 45 min after the onset of the agitated delirium, the subject was discovered to be in a respiratory arrest.

A postmortem examination and a rectal temperature of 41° C (106° F) was recorded. He had needle marks typical of intravenous drug abuse and pulmonary and cerebral edema. Abrasions and contusions of the ankles and wrists were evident from his struggling. Lidocaine was not administered to the victim during the resuscitative attempts. The clinical presentation of cocaine delirium is different from that of non-psychotic cocaine abusers with sudden death or massive drug overdose. The cocaine delirium victims are almost always men, they are more likely to die in custody, and are more likely to survive for more than 1 h after the onset of symptoms (Table 6.2.4). In the epidemiological tracking of agitated delirium victims in Metropolitan Dade County, Florida, men with preterminal delirium comprised approximately 10% of the annual number of cocaine overdose deaths.

Cocaine delirium deaths are seasonal and tend to cluster during the late summer months. Core body temperatures are markedly elevated, ranging from 104°C to 108°C. Based on a review of the constellation of psychiatric symptoms associated with this disorder, Kosten and Kleber[13] have termed agitated delirium as a possible cocaine variant of neuroleptic malignant syndrome. Neuroleptic malignant syndrome (NMS) is a highly lethal disorder seen in patients taking dopamine (DA) antagonists or following abrupt withdrawal from DAergic agonists.[14,15] NMS is usually associated with muscle rigidity, while the cocaine variant of the syndrome presents with brief onset of rigidity immediately prior to respiratory collapse.[16]

At present it is not clear whether extreme agitation, delirium, hyperthermia, and rhabdomyolysis are effects of cocaine that occur independently and at random among cocaine users, or whether these features are linked by common toxicologic and pathologic processes.[17] Ruttenber and colleagues have examined excited delirium deaths in a population-based registry of all cocaine-related deaths in Dade County, Florida.[17] This study has led to clear description of the cocaine delirium syndrome, its pattern of occurrence in cocaine users over time, and has identified a number of important risk factors for the syndrome.

Cocaine delirium deaths are defined as accidental cocaine toxicity deaths that occurred in individuals who experienced an episode of bizarre behavior prior to death. Bizarre behavior is defined as hyperactivity accompanied by either incoherent shouting, aggression (fighting with others or destroying property), or evidence of extreme paranoia as described by witnesses and supported by scene evidence. The results of this study demonstrate that victims are more likely to be male, black, and younger than other cocaine overdose toxicity deaths. The most frequent route of administration was injection for the excited delirium victims as compared to inhalation for the other accidental cocaine toxicity deaths. The frequency of smoked "crack" cocaine was similar for both groups. Of the excited delirium victims, 39% died in police custody as compared with only 2% for the comparison group of accidental cocaine toxicity cases.[17] A large proportion of these individuals survive between 1 and 12 h after the onset of the syndrome.

The most striking feature of the excited delirium syndrome is the extreme hyperthermia. The epidemiological data[17] provide some clues for the etiology of the elevated body temperature. Victims of cocaine excited delirium have higher body mass indices. This finding suggests that muscle mass and adiposity may contribute to the generation of body heat. Temporal clustering in summer months[16] supports the hypothesis that abnormal thermoregulation is an important risk factor for death in people who develop the syndrome. Being placed in police custody prior to death can also raise body temperature through increased psychomotor activity if the victim struggles in the process of restraint. Descriptions of the circumstances around death suggest that police officers frequently had to forcibly restrain these victims. Positional asphyxia and a restraint-induced increase in catecholamines have been hypothesized as contributing causes of cocaine delirium.[18]

6.2.3 ALTERED DOPAMINERGIC TRANSMISSION AND THE SYNDROME OF COCAINE DELIRIUM

The mesolimbic DAergic system plays a primary role in mediating the rewarding, as well as the lethal effects of most abused drugs.[19] Chronic cocaine use is associated with an increase in DA neurotransmission resulting from the blockade of DA uptake and mediated by the activation of pre- and postsynaptic DA receptors. Cocaine mediates its powerful reinforcement by binding to specific recognition sites on the DA transporter protein.[20] DA transporters function to rapidly control the removal of transmitter molecules from the synaptic cleft. Neurochemical abnormalities have been identified in the striatum of cocaine abusers dying of excited delirium.[21-23] Some of the abnormalities in the DAergic system involve alterations in certain types of DA receptors and in cocaine's ability to block the reuptake carrier, by which DA is recycled back in to the presynaptic nerve terminal. Cocaine users often go on binges, consuming a large amount of the drug over a period of a few days. The neurochemical changes occurring over the "binge" and crash periods involve adaptive alterations of the DA transporter and receptors on receiving cells.

A number of different studies point to a possibility of a defective interaction of cocaine with the DA transporter in the etiology of cocaine delirium. The effects of chronic intermittent cocaine treatment paradigms on the labeling of the cocaine recognition sites on the DA transporter have been recently investigated in rat studies. Neuroadaptive changes in the DA transporter have been characterized with a number of different radioligands, including [³H]cocaine, the cocaine congeners [³H]WIN 35,428 and [¹²⁵I]RTI-55, and more recently with [¹²⁵I]RTI-121.[24] In contrast to the classic DA transport inhibitors ([³H]mazindol, [³H]GBR 12935 and [³H]nomifensine), the cocaine congeners ([³H]WIN 35,428, [¹²⁵I]RTI-55 and [¹²⁵I]RTI-121) label multiple sites with a pharmacological profile characteristic of the DA transporter in rat, primate, and human brain.[24-26] Chronic treatment of rats with intermittent doses of cocaine demonstrated a two- to fivefold increase in the apparent density of [³H]cocaine binding sites in the striatum.[27] Rats that were allowed to self-administer cocaine in a chronic unlimited access paradigm had significant increases in [³H]WIN 35,428 binding sites when the animals were sacrificed on the last day of cocaine access.[28] Rabbits treated with cocaine (4 mg/ kg i.v. 2x /day for 22 days) show an elevation in the density of [³H]WIN 35,428 binding sites in the caudate.[29] These results of ligand binding studies demonstrate that cocaine exposure leads to an apparent increase in the density of cocaine recognition sites on the DA transport carrier.

Cocaine congeners label high and low affinity sites on the cloned and native human DA transporter, one of which appears to overlap with the functional state of the carrier protein.[30] In cocaine overdose victims, high affinity cocaine recognition sites on the DA transporter were upregulated significantly in the striatum as compared to age-matched and drug-free control

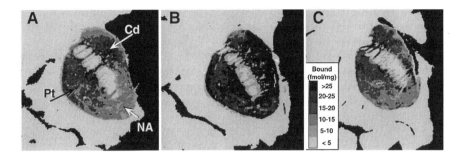

Figure 6.2.3 *In vitro* autoradiographic maps of [³H]WIN 35,428 labeling of the dopamine (DA) transporter in coronal sections of the striatum. The panels illustrate (A) a schematic diagram of the human striatum and DA transporter densities in (B) a representative age-matched and drug-free subject, (C) cocaine overdose victim, and (D) cocaine delirium victim. The brain maps illustrate the adaptive increase in DA transporter density over the striatum in the cocaine overdose victim. Note the lack of any apparent elevation for the victim presenting with agitated delirium. Because the DA transporter regulates the synaptic concentration of neurotransmitter, the lack of a compensatory upregulation may result in a DA overflow following a cocaine "binge". Elevated synaptic DA with repeat exposures may kindle the emergence of the agitated delirium syndrome. Gray scale codes are shown in panel B. Black = high densities; gray = intermediate; light gray to white = low densities. Abbreviations: Cd, caudate; NA, nucleus accumbens, Pt, putamen.

subjects (Figure 6.2.3). If this regulatory change in high affinity [³H] WIN 35,428 binding sites on the human DA transporter reflects an increased ability of the protein to transport DA, it may help to explain the addictive liability of cocaine. Persisting increases in the apparent density of the DA transporter after cocaine levels have fallen in blood and brain may result in an acute decrease in the intrasynaptic concentration of DA and lower DAergic tone. As the transporter carrier upregulates its apparent density in the nerve terminal to more efficiently transport DA back into the presynaptic nerve terminal, more cocaine will be needed to experience cocaine's reinforcing effects and euphoria. During acute abstinence from cocaine, enhanced function of the DA transporter could lead to net depletion in synaptic DA. This depletion of DA may serve as a biological substrate for anhedonia, the cardinal feature of cocaine withdrawal symptomatology.

Unlike the results seen in cases of accidental cocaine overdose,[21] the density of high affinity cocaine recognition sites on the DA transporter measured in the striatum from cocaine delirium victims was comparable to that seen in drug-free and age-matched control subjects.[22,23] Because the concentration of synaptic DA is controlled by the reuptake mechanism(s), the lack of compensatory increase in cocaine recognition sites could be the defect in DAergic transmission that explains the paranoia and agitation associated with this syndrome. Paranoia in the context of cocaine abuse is common and several lines of evidence suggest that this phenomenon may be related to the function of the DA transporter protein.[31] Genetic differences in the makeup of individuals who abuse cocaine may also underlie some of these differences in susceptibility to the development of adverse neuropsychiatric effects with chronic cocaine abuse that appear to result from a defective regulation of the DA transporter protein.[31]

In addition to the adverse neuropsychiatric sequalae, cocaine delirium victims are distinguished from other accidental cocaine overdose deaths by the premorbid occurrence of hyperthermia. DA receptors are known to play a role in regulating core body temperature. Because hyperthermia appears to be a clinical feature of cocaine-related sudden death presenting with excited delirium, Kosten and Kleber[16] have speculated that death occurred due to a malfunction in DAergic control of thermoregulation. Hypothermia receptors are known to be down-regulated by high levels of intrasynaptic DA. Direct application of intracerebral DA at first lowers body temperature; however, a subsequent "rebound" in body temperature occurs about 1 h after discontinuing this stimulation.[32,33]

When cocaine is repeatedly administered, DAergic receptor numbers are altered.[34,35] The likelihood of hyperthermia may be increased with chronic cocaine abuse if the DAergic receptors involved in thermoregulation are undergoing adaptive changes with chronic cocaine exposure. In keeping with this hypothesis, cocaine delirium victims had a different profile of D_2 receptor binding within the thermoregulatory centers of the hypothalamus as compared to cocaine overdose deaths.[22,23] The density of the D_2 DA receptor subtype in the anterior and preoptic nuclei of the hypothalamus in the cocaine delirium subgroup of cocaine overdose deaths were decreased significantly ($p < 0.05$). These results may be relevant to an understanding of the contribution of selective alterations in D_1 and D_2 receptor subtypes in central DAergic temperature regulation. D_1 and D_2 receptors mediate opposite effects on thermoregulation, with the D_1 receptor mediating a prevailing increase in core body temperature, while the D_2 receptor mediates an opposing decrease in temperature.[22] Thus, the selective downregulation in the density of the D_2 DAergic receptor subtype within the hypothalamus may explain the loss of temperature regulation in cocaine delirium victims.

6.2.4 CONCLUSIONS

Cocaine abuse is associated with neuropsychiatric disorders, including acute psychotic episodes, paranoid states, and delirium. The mechanistic basis of these brain states is not known. The advent of new tools from the neurosciences have led to proliferation of research approaches aimed at defining the neurobiological consequences of chronic cocaine use. The recent development of radioligands with high specific activity and selectivity for neurotransmitter carriers and receptor subtypes have made it possible to map and quantify neuroadaptations in the brains of cocaine abusers. Because the DA transport carrier is a key regulator of DAergic neurotransmission, alterations in the numbers of these reuptake sites by cocaine may affect the balance in DAergic signaling. Understanding the influence of cocaine's affects on DAergic neurotransmission may shed light on the etiology of neuropsychiatric syndromes associated with cocaine abuse and dependence.

ACKNOWLEDGMENTS

The authors would like to acknowledge the expert technical assistance of Margaret Basile, M.S. and Qinjie Ouyang, B.A. This work was supported by USPHS grants DA06627 and DA09484.

REFERENCES

1. Baker S.P. The injury fact book. 2nd ed. New York Oxford University Press (1992).
2. Gawin, F.H., Cocaine addiction: psychology and neurophysiology. Science 251: 1580-1586, 1991.
3. Chitwood, D. Patterns and consequences of cocaine use. In: National Institure on Drug Abouse, Res. Monog. Ser. 61: 111-129, 1985.
4. Gawin, F.H. and Kleber, H. D. Abstinence sympotomatology and psychiatric diagnosis in cocaine abusers. Arch. Gen. Psych. 43: 107 - 113, 1986.
5. Crawford, V. Comorbidity of substance misuse and psychiatric disorders. Current opinion in Psychiatry 1996, 9:231-234.
6. Kilbey, M.M., Breslau, N. and Andreski, P. Cocaine use and dependence in young adults:associated psychiatric disorders and personality traits. Drug & Alcohol Dependence, 29 (1992) 283-290.

Deborah C. Mash

7. Reiger, D.A., Farmer, M.E., Rae, D.S., Locke, B.Z., Keith, S.J., Judd, L.L., Goodwin, F.K., Comorbidity of mental disorders with alcohol and other drug abuse. J. Am. Med. Assoc. 264: 2511- 2518, 1990.

8. Poole, R. and Brabbins, C. Drug induced psychosis. British J. Psychiatry , 168: 135-138, 1996.

9. Satel, S.L., Seibyl, J.P., and Charney, D.S. Prolonged cocaine psychosis implies underlying major psychopathology. J. Clin. Psychiatry 52:8, August 1991.

10. Satel, S.L., Southwick,S.M., and Gawin, F.H. Clinical Features of cocaine-induced paranoia. Am . J. Psychiatry 1991; 148:495-498.

11. Angrist, B.M. "Cocaine in the context of prior central nervous system stimulant epidemics".In: Volkow N. Swann AC, eds. "Cocaine in the Brain (Mind in Medicine Series)". New Brunswick, NJ: Rutgers University Press; 1990:7-24.

12. Wetli, C.V. and Fishbain D.A. Cocaine-Induced psychosis and sudden death in recreational cocaine users. J. Foresci. Sci.. 30 (1985) 873-880.

13. Kosten, T. and Kleber , H.D., Sudden death in cocaine abusers: Relation to neuroleptic malignant syndrome. Lancet, 1: 1198 - 1199, 1987.

14. Friedman, J.H., Feinberg, S.S. and Feldman, R.G. , A neuroleptic malignant like syndrome due to levodopa therapy withdrawal. J.A.M.A , 254:2792-2795, 1985.

15. Levison, J. Neuroleptic malignant syndomre. Am. J. Psych. 142: 1137 - 1145, 1985.

16. Kosten, T.R. and Kleber, H.D. Rapid death during cocaine abuse: a variant of neuroleptic malignant syndrome. Am J., Drug Alcohol Abuse 14: 335 - 46, 1988.

17. Ruttenber, A. J., Lawler-Haevener, J., Wetli, C.V., Hearn, W. L., and Mash, D.C., Fatal excited delirium following cocaine use: Epidemiologic findings provide evidence for new mechanisms of cocaine toxicity. In press - J. Forensic Toxicology, 1997.

18. O'Halloran, R.L., Lewman, L.V., Restraint asphyxiation in excited delirium. Am J. Forensic Med. Pathol. 14: 289 - 295, 1993.

19. Koob, G.F. and Bloom, F.E., Cellular and molecular mechanisms of drug dependence, Science, 242 (1988) 715-723.

20. Ritz, M.C. Lamb, R.J., Goldberg, S.R. and Kuhar, M.J. Cocaine receptors on dopamine transporters are related to self-administration of cocaine. Science (Wash DC) 237 (1987) 1219-1223.

21. Staley, J.K., Hearn, W.L., Ruttenber, A.J., Wetli, C.V. and Mash, D.C. High affinity cocaine recognition sites on the dopamine transporter are elevated in fatal cocaine overdose victims. J. Pharm. Exp. Therap. 271 (1995) 1678-1685.

22. Staley, J.K., Wetli, C.V., Ruttenber, A.J., Hearn, W.L., and Mash, D.C. Altered dopaminergic synaptic markers in cocaine psychosis and sudden death. NIDA Research Monograph Series 153: 491 (1995).

23. Wetli, C.V, Mash, D.C. and Karch, S.B., Cocaine-associated agitated delirium and the neuroleptic malignant syndrome, Amer. J. Emer. Med. 14; 425 - 428, (1996).

24. Boja, J.W., Carroll, F.I., Rahman, M.A., Philip, A., Lewin, A.H. and Kuhar, M.J.: New, potent cocaine analogs: ligand binding and transport studies in rat striatum. Eur. J. Pharm. 184: 329-332, 1990.

25. Staley, J.K., Boja, J.W., Carroll, F.I., Seltzman, H.H., Wyrick, C.D., Lewin, A.H., Abraham, P., and Mash, D.C. Mapping dopamine transporters in the human brain with novel selective cocaine analog [^{125}I]RTI-121. Synapse 21 (1995) 364-372.66.

26. Madras, B.K., Spealman, R.D., Fahey, M.A., Neumeyer, J.L., Saha, J.K. and Milius, R.A.: Cocaine receptors labeled by [^{3}H]2B-carbomethoxy-3åß-(4-fluorophenyl)tropane. Mol. Pharm. 36:518-524, 1989b.

27. Alburges, M.E., Narang, N. and Wamsley, J.K.: Alterations in the dopaminergic receptor system after chronic administration of cocaine. Synapse 14:314-323, 1993.

28. Wilson, J.M., Nobrega, J.N., Carroll, M.E., Niznik, H.B., Shannak, K., Lac, S.T., Pristupa, Z.B. Dixon, L.M. and Kish, S.J. Heterogenous subregional binding patterns of ^{3}H-WIN 35,428 and ^{3}H-GBR 12,935 are differentially regulated by chronic cocaine self-admiinstration. J. Neurosci. 14 (1994) 2966-2974.

29. Aloyo, V.J., Harvey, J.A. and Kirfides, A.L. Chronic cocaine increases WIN 35428 binding in rabbit caudate. Soc. Neurosci. Abstr19: 1843, 1994.

30. Pristupa, Z.B., Wilson, J.M., Hoffman, B.J., Kish, S.J., and Niznik, H.B. Pharmacological heterogeneity of the cloned and native human dopamine transporter: Dissociation of [^{3}H]WIN 35,428 and [^{3}H]GBR 12935 binding. Mol. Pharm. 45 (1994) 125-135.
31. Gelernter, J., Kranzler, H.R., Satel, S.L., and Rao, P.A. Genetic association between dopamine transporter protein alleles and cocaine-induced paranoia. Neuropsychopharmacology 1994- Vol. 11, No. 3.
32. Costentin, J., Duterte-Boucher, D., Panissaud, C. and Michael-Titus, A., Dopamine D_1 and D_2 receptors mediate opposite effects of apomorphine on the body temperature of reserpinized mice. Neuropharmacol. 29: 31-35, 1990.
33. Meller, E., Hizami, R. and Kreuter, L., Hypothermia in mice: D_2 dopamine receptor mediation and absence of spare receptors. Pharmacol. Biochem. & Behav. 32: 141-145, 1989.
34. Peris, J., Boyson, S.J., Cass, W.A., Curella, P., Dwoskin, L., Larson, G., Lin, L.-H., Yasuda, R.P. and Zahniser, N.R., Persistence of neurochemical changes in dopamine systems after repeated cocaine administration. J. Pharmacol. Exp. Ther. 253: 38-44, 1990.
35. Kleven, M.S., Perry, B.D., Woolverton, W.L. and Seiden, L.S., Effects of repeated injections of cocaine on D_1 and D_2 dopamine receptors in rat brain. Brain Research 532: 265-270, 1990.

6.3 NEUROCHEMICAL ADAPTATIONS AND COCAINE DEPENDENCE

JULIE K. STALEY, PH.D.*

DEPARTMENT OF NEUROLOGY, UNIVERSITY OF MIAMI SCHOOL OF MEDICINE, MIAMI, FLORIDA

Cocaine addiction is a disease of the brain that is characterized by compulsive drug-taking behavior that may be a consequence of an altered neurochemical state. Repeated use of cocaine may cause long-lasting changes in brain receptors and transporters that may perpetuate drug-use and increase the vulnerability of the addict to sequelae such as seizures, paranoia, anxiety, and depression. Furthermore, regulatory changes in neurochemical targets that have occurred as a compensatory response to "oppose" or "neutralize" the pharmacological effects of the drug, and persist after the drug has cleared from the brain, may underlie the craving and dysphoria associated with cocaine withdrawal and relapse. Revolutionary advances in basic neuroscience have catalyzed extraordinary efforts toward the discovery and development of novel CNS drugs effective for the treatment of cocaine dependence. These advances have included the molecular cloning and characterization of many of the receptors and transporters implicated in the rewarding effects of and dependence on cocaine. Understanding how and which receptors and transporters are altered by chronic cocaine use may identify targets for the development of drugs that will alleviate the symptoms associated with the initiation and perpetuation of drug-taking behavior. Current drug discovery efforts have taken multiple approaches towards the development of cocaine pharmacotherapies. Many of the novel pharmacotherapeutic agents currently under development are directed towards a single molecular target related to or regulated by cocaine. Some pharmacotherapies currently under evaluation are directed towards multiple distinct receptor and/or transporter populations known to modulate the activity of the drug reward circuit. This article will review recent research studies that have identified neurochemical targets regulated by chronic cocaine use and their implications for the development of pharmacotherapies for cocaine dependence.

*Current affiliation: Department of Psychiatry, Yale University and VA Medical Center, West Haven, CT.

Julie K. Staley

6.3.1 NEUROCHEMISTRY OF COCAINE DEPENDENCE

Many drugs with abuse liability including cocaine have been shown to enhance dopaminergic neurotransmission in the mesolimbic drug reward circuits. Cocaine, an indirect-acting dopaminergic agonist, binds to recognition sites on the plasma membrane dopamine (DA) transporter and increases dopamine levels by preventing the reuptake of released dopamine.[1-3] The reinforcing effects of cocaine are initiated by the interactions of dopamine with pre- and postsynaptic DA receptors. Two classes of DA receptors have been classified including the D_1 receptor family (D_1/D_{1a} and D_5/D_{1b} receptor subtypes) and the D_2 receptor family (D_2, D_3, and D_4 receptor subtypes).[4] The DA receptor subtypes are distinguished by their distinct anatomical, molecular, pharmacological, and signal transduction properties.[4] When cocaine is present, extracellular dopamine levels are elevated resulting in chronic stimulation of the DA receptors.[3] This persistent interaction of dopamine with its receptors alters DA receptor signalling, which may, in part, underlie the reinforcing properties of cocaine.[3] Furthermore, postsynaptic DA receptors have been localized to other neurotransmitter-containing pathways including GABAergic, glutamatergic, and cholinergic projections indicating that additional neurochemical pathways may undergo compensatory adaptive changes in response to the persistent activation of DA receptors.

Recently, considerable evidence has accumulated suggesting that other neurochemical substrates (i.e., glutamatergic, serotonergic, and opioidergic) may also play a role in the development of cocaine dependence. The anatomical organization of these neurochemical systems within the drug reward circuit suggests that functional interactions may occur between dopaminergic systems and neighboring neural pathways. Nigrostriatal dopaminergic neurons and corticostriatal glutamatergic neurons colocalize on common GABAergic medium spiny dendrites in the striatum suggesting the potential for interdependence between the two circuits.[6] Glutamate antagonists which act at the NMDA receptor complex block stereotypy and locomotor activation in animal models of cocaine dependence indicating that the glutamatergic pathway may be critical to the expression of these psychomotor stimulant behaviors.[6,7] Serotonergic projections to the ventral tegmental area input onto dopamine cell bodies suggesting that serotonin may modulate mesolimbic DA neurotransmission either by direct stimulation (i.e., cocaine increases extracellular serotonin by blocking reuptake) or indirectly by feedback modulatory mechanisms from DA nerve terminal activation.[8] Mesolimbic DA neurotransmission may be modulated by tonic activation of the μ and κ opioid receptors located in the vicinity of DA cell bodies and DA nerve terminals, respectively. Activation of μ receptors in the ventral tegmental area increases dopamine release in the nucleus accumbens, whereas activation of κ receptors in the nucleus accumbens inhibits dopamine release.[5,9,10] Cross-talk between opioids, serotonin, glutamate, and dopamine may lead to a sequence of neuroadaptive processes that contribute to the behavioral and physiological manifestations associated with cocaine dependence.

6.3.2 DA TRANSPORTER AND COCAINE DEPENDENCE

6.3.2.1 Regulation of the DA Transporter By Cocaine

The addictive liability of cocaine and other DA-enhancing psychostimulants may be related to compensatory adaptations of the DA transporter to chronic elevations of intrasynaptic DA. There is a wealth of evidence suggesting that cocaine mediates its powerful reinforcement by binding to recognition sites on the DA transporter. Persistent inhibition of DA reuptake by cocaine has been shown to alter the number of cocaine recognition sites associated with the DA transporter. Chronic treatment of rats with intermittent doses of cocaine resulted in a two- to fivefold increase in the apparent density of [³H]cocaine and [³H]BTCP binding in the

Figure 6.3.2 Visualization of the distribution of the DA transporter, D_3 receptor, and k_2 opioid receptor in the human brain of a drug-free control subject and a representative cocaine overdose victim. (A,B) The DA transporter was measured using [^{3}H]WIN 35,428 (2 nM) as described previously. (C,D) The D_3 receptor was measured using [^{3}H]-(+)-7-OH-DPAT (1 nM) in the presence of GTP (300 mM) to enhance the selective labeling of the D_3 receptor over the D2 receptor subtype as described previously. (E,F) The k_2 receptor subtype was measured using [^{125}I]IOXY on tissue sections pretreated with BIT and FIT to occlude binding to the μ and δ receptors, respectively.

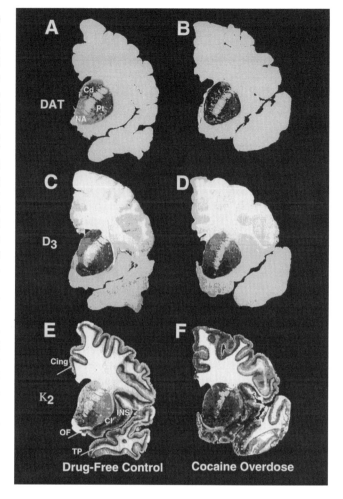

striatum.[11] Significant increases in striatal [^{3}H]WIN 35,428 binding were observed in rats allowed to self-administer cocaine in a chronic unlimited access paradigm,[12] rats treated intermittently and continuously with cocaine,[13] and in rabbits treated with intermittent cocaine injections.[14] DA transporter densities detected using [^{125}I]RTI-55 and [^{3}H]WIN 35,428 were elevated throughout the caudate, putamen, and nucleus accumbens of cocaine-related deaths[15] and fatal cocaine overdose victims (Figure 6.3.2).[16-18] Saturation binding analysis confirmed the increase in [^{3}H]WIN 35,428 binding to putamen membranes of cocaine overdose victims as compared to drug-free and age-matched control subjects.[16-18] Furthermore, Rosenthal plots of the saturation binding data demonstrated that the increase of [^{3}H]WIN 35,428 binding observed in the cocaine overdose victims was due to an elevation in the apparent density of the high affinity cocaine recognition site on the DA transporter.[17] The elevations in DA transporter densities demonstrated in the postmortem brain from human cocaine abusers are supported by *in vivo* SPECT imaging in human cocaine-dependent subjects.[19] Here, the striatal uptake of [^{123}I]ß-CIT (also called RTI-55) was significantly elevated (25%) in acutely abstinent ($\geq$96 h) cocaine-dependent subjects. These studies suggest that the high affinity cocaine binding site may upregulate in the striatal reward centers with chronic cocaine abuse as a compensatory response to elevated synaptic levels of DA. It was hypothesized that this upregulation of cocaine recognition sites associated with the DA transporter may reflect an increased ability of the protein to transport DA. As the transporter elevates its apparent density in the nerve terminal to clear DA from the synapse, more cocaine will be needed to experience cocaine's reinforcing effects and euphoria.[17] This neuroadaptive regulation of the DA transporter may occur as a result of the direct interaction of cocaine with the DA transporter, or, alternatively, may be due to feedback mechanisms that are activated as a consequence of prolonged elevated concentrations of DA. This hypothesis

Julie K. Staley

suggests that the DA transporter may be an ideal target for the development of anti-cocaine medications.

6.3.2.2 Rate of Interaction of Cocaine with the DA Transporter and Cocaine Reinforcement

An alternative neurochemical hypothesis for the reinforcing efficacy of cocaine at the DA transporter is related to the rate of entry of cocaine into the brain, coupled with its ability to rapidly bind to the DA transporter, inhibit DA uptake, and enhance dopaminergic neurotransmission.[3,20-24] This hypothesis is based on the knowledge that other drugs known to block DA uptake, such as mazindol, GBR 12909, methylphenidate, are not as reinforcing as cocaine[25] and exhibit a slower rate of entry into the brain and a slower onset of action.[26] Furthermore, GBR 12909, methylphenidate, bupropion, and mazindol displace the *in vivo* binding of the radiolabeled cocaine congener [^{3}H]WIN 35,428 considerably slower than cocaine.[23,26] In humans, methylphenidate demonstrates a lower abuse liability as compared to cocaine, but enters the CNS with a rate similar to cocaine. However, methylphenidate is cleared more slowly than cocaine, an attribute which may underlie its decreased rate of administration and abuse liability.[27] These preclinical studies suggest that pharmacological interventions which decrease the rate of entry into or clearance of cocaine from the brain, or alternatively block or slow down cocaine's interaction with the DA transporter may be useful for the treatment of cocaine dependence.

6.3.2.3 The DA Transporter as a Target for Cocaine Pharmacotherapies

One pharmacotherapeutic strategy for the treatment of cocaine dependence that has received significant attention is the development of drugs that antagonize or substitute for cocaine at its site of action in the brain.[28,29] Hypothetically, the "ideal cocaine antagonist" would manifest high affinity binding to the cocaine recognition sites on the DA transporter; slow dissociation from these binding sites; minimal inhibition of substrate binding and uptake; a long biological half-life; and low abuse liability.[28-30] The DA reuptake inhibitor GBR 12909 appears to satisfy several of these criteria.[28-30] At low doses, GBR 12909 binds to the DA transporter with high affinity, dissociates slowly, causes only a modest increase in extracellular DA, and partially antagonizes the increase in extracellular DA evoked by local perfusion of cocaine into the striatum and the nucleus accumbens.[28-30] However, at high doses, GBR 12909 produces locomotor activation, stereotypy, behavioral sensitization, and cross-sensitizes with cocaine.[30] These studies suggest that the development of a cocaine antagonist is plausible; however, efficacy as a cocaine antagonist may be dose-related. Recent molecular characterization studies of the DA transporter, which used chimeric dopamine - norepinephrine transporters delineated discrete domains for substrate and cocaine interactions.[31,32] These studies support the development of a cocaine antagonist devoid of uptake blockade activity for the clinical management of cocaine addiction. Current drug discovery efforts have focused on the development of compounds using cocaine as the core structure, in an effort to find a drug which blocks cocaine interactions with the DA transporter, but does not block the normal uptake function of the transporter. While these studies are in the early stages, it is anticipated that this approach may lead to the development of an efficacious anti-cocaine medication.

6.3.2.4 Cocaine Vaccines

An alternative pharmacotherapy for cocaine dependence currently under investigation is to blunt the reinforcing effects of cocaine using a cocaine vaccine.[32-42] The basis of this pharmacotherapy is to decrease the rate of entry of cocaine into the CNS (and therefore the onset of action), by either binding cocaine with antibody generated by active immunization with a stable cocaine conjugate or by using an enzymatically active antibody specific for cocaine.

Because cocaine is a small molecule (MW = 303 g/mol) it is unlikely that it will be immunogenic and therefore must be conjugated to a carrier molecule such as KLH (keyhole limpet hemacyanin), polyethylene glycol, diphtheria, or tetanus toxoids to enhance its immunogenicity.[33-38] While early attempts to make a cocaine vaccine did not demonstrate significant efficacy for blocking the effects of cocaine in the CNS,[36,43] more recent studies have been more successful.[37-39] Active immunization with a stable cocaine-KLH conjugate lowered cocaine levels in the brain enough to decrease cocaine-induced hyperlocomotion and stereotypic behavior.[37-39] While the active immunization approach to cocaine pharmacotherapy appears promising, its success will be hindered if the addict administers large enough quantities of cocaine to override the antibody-induced blockade.[39] Conversely, further administration of cocaine may serve to booster and protect the addict from further cocaine use.[36] Use of a catalytic cocaine antibody may bypass this potential downfall of the active immunization approach. The enzymatically active catalytic cocaine antibody cleaves cocaine into two inactive metabolites: ecognine methyl ester and benzoic acid. The two metabolites are released from the catalytic antibody rendering the antibody free to degrade more cocaine. Because the catalytic antibodies are not depleted, it is impossible for the cocaine abuser to "override" the presence of the antibody by administering higher doses of cocaine.[40] Catalytic antibodies have been generated against transition state analogs of cocaine.[40-42] While this strategy to blunt the reinforcing effects of cocaine is promising, the antibody will not alleviate the craving, dysphoria, anxiety, or depression often linked to relapse. Thus, although the cocaine antibodies may prevent cocaine reinforcement, they will not block the reinforcing effects of other psychostimulants that an addict may administer to relieve withdrawal symptoms.[44] In addition, the success of the catalytic antibody may be hindered if the antibody is perceived as foreign and idiotypic antibodies are produced that will interact with the cocaine antibody rendering it enzymatically inactive. Future studies will determine the therapeutic potential of this novel approach to anti-cocaine medications.

6.3.3 DA RECEPTORS AND COCAINE DEPENDENCE

The rewarding effects of dopamine are mediated by five DA receptor subtypes distinguished by their unique molecular and pharmacological properties and distinct anatomical locations. Repeated and prolonged elevations in synaptic dopamine levels that result from the binge use of cocaine may result in alterations in the affinity, number, or coupling state of the DA receptors. At present, the relative contribution of each of the DA receptor subtypes to the rewarding effects of cocaine is not clear. Dopamine agonists that interact with receptors belonging to both the D_1 and D_2 receptor families function as positive reinforcers, while both D_1-like and D_2-like receptor antagonists decrease the reward value of psychostimulants.[45,46] Stimulation of D_1 or D_2 receptors in the ventral tegmental area enhances the rewarding effect for brain stimulation [47]. These findings suggest that compensatory changes in DA receptor number or signaling may contribute to the development of cocaine dependence.

6.3.3.1 Cocaine-Induced D_1 Receptor Adaptations

The reinforcing effects of cocaine are mediated, in part, by the D_1 receptors in the nucleus accumbens and the central nucleus of the amygdala.[48] In preclinical animal studies, administration of the D_1 receptor antagonist (SCH 23390) in combination with cocaine prevents the development of cocaine sensitization.[49,50] While cocaine self-administration is typically increased in the presence of D_1 receptor antagonists,[45,51-54] it has recently been demonstrated that, under some schedules of reinforcement, low doses of benzazepine D_1 receptor antagonists block cocaine self-administration.[55] These findings suggest that the state of the D_1 receptor population may dictate the ability of D_1 receptor antagonists to enhance or to block the reinforcing effects of cocaine. D_1 receptor mRNA levels, receptor number, and receptor

Julie K. Staley

sensitivity are altered as a consequence of protracted cocaine exposure and may, in part, account for some of the D_1 receptor-mediated behavioral responses to cocaine. D_1 receptor mRNA is not altered in the striatum, nucleus accumbens, or substantia nigra of human cocaine abusers;[56] however, elevations in D_1 receptor mRNA were observed in the striatum of rats chronically treated with cocaine.[57] Chronic cocaine treatment results in an adaptive increase in D_1 receptor number in the olfactory tubercle, nucleus accumbens, ventral pallidum, and substantia nigra which normalized within 1 d[58] and remains at baseline values for up to 3 d[59] and 30 d[60] after cocaine treatment. Conversely, decreases in striatal D_1 receptor densities that persisted for at least 2 weeks after the last administration of cocaine have been observed.[57,61] Electrophysiological sensitivity of D_1 receptors in nucleus accumbens neurons is enhanced two weeks post-cocaine administration,[62] suggesting that despite the number of D_1 receptors detected, adaptations in the D_1 receptor signaling cascade may occur to enhance D_1 receptor mediated dopamine transmission. When these findings are viewed collectively, it is difficult to ascertain precisely the regulatory adaptation that the D_1 receptor undergoes in response to protracted cocaine use. The reasons for these differences may be multifactorial. Variations in dose, frequency, and route of administration have been shown to influence the adaptive response of dopaminergic synaptic markers; therefore, the differences may be attributed to distinct drug administration protocols.[13] Alternatively, because the D_1 receptor drugs used in these studies do not distinguish between the D_1 and the D_5 receptor subtypes, differential regulation of these subtypes may account, in part, for the incongruous findings. Regardless of the adaptive response observed, it is evident from these studies that the adaptations of the D_1 receptor may be integral to the development of cocaine dependence and therefore may be a useful target for the development of cocaine pharmacotherapies.

6.3.3.2 Cocaine-Induced Adaptations in D_2 Receptors

The actions of cocaine on D_2 receptors has been shown to be essential to the development of cocaine dependence. The D_2 receptor antagonist haloperidol inhibits the development of behavioral sensitization to cocaine.[49] Sensitization may play an important role in drug craving and the reinstatement of compulsive drug-taking behavior;[50,63,64] therefore, altered regulation of D_2 receptors may contribute to the reinforcing potential of cocaine. D_2 mRNA levels were not altered in the striatum of human cocaine abusers[56] or rats treated with cocaine.[65,66] D_2 receptor mRNA levels were decreased in the olfactory tubercle of rats treated with a single injection of cocaine.[65] However, D_2 receptor mRNA levels were transiently elevated in rats treated chronically with cocaine.[57,65] A transient increase in the binding of [^{3}H]raclopride in the olfactory tubercle and rostral nucleus accumbens and caudate-putamen was observed after binge administration of cocaine[67] and elevations in [^{3}H]spiperone and [^{125}I]spiperone binding were seen in the nucleus accumbens, olfactory tubercle, and substantia nigra after intermittent cocaine administration.[58,60,61,68,69] In contrast, D_2 receptor densities were not significantly affected in the rat striatum 3 d post-cocaine administration.[59] Furthermore, [^{18}F]N-methylspiroperidol labeling in living cocaine abusers demonstrated decreased D_2 receptor densities after one week detoxification.[70] Viewed collectively, these studies suggest that the D_2 receptor may undergo a transient elevation in response to acute cocaine administration, which normalizes upon cocaine abstinence. However, caution should be taken in the interpretation of these data because these radioligands do not discriminate between the D_2 and D_3 receptors and, therefore, identity of the regulated D_2 receptor subtype is not known.

6.3.3.3 Cocaine-Induced Adaptations in D_3 Receptors

Cocaine-induced adaptations at the D_3 receptor may mediate some of the reinforcing effects of cocaine. D_3 receptor-preferring agonists, although not self-administered by drug-naive monkeys, are self-administered by monkeys that have been trained to self-administer cocaine.[73]

D_3 receptor-preferring agonists substitute for the discriminative stimulus effects of cocaine and produce place preference in rats and monkeys indicating that the D_3 receptor may mediate some of the subjective effects of cocaine.[74-76] These studies suggest that adaptations in the affinity, density, or molecular expression of the D_3 receptor induced by chronic cocaine use may underlie, in part, the development of cocaine dependence.

The D_3 receptor-preferring agonist [^{3}H]-(+)-7-OH-DPAT has been used in quantitative *in vitro* autoradiography studies to assess the status of D_3 receptors in human cocaine overdose (CO) victims[77] (Figure 6.3.2 C and D). Binding of [^{3}H]-(+)-7-OH-DPAT was elevated twofold in the ventromedial sectors of the anterior caudate and putamen and in the nucleus accumbens of the CO victims as compared to drug-free and age-matched control subjects. The intensity of [^{3}H]-(+)-7-OH-DPAT labeling was increased also in the lateral and medial divisions of the substantia nigra in the CO victims ($p < 0.01$). These findings were confirmed by saturation analysis of [^{3}H]-(+)-7-OH-DPAT binding in membranes from the nucleus accumbens. The affinity for [^{3}H]-(+)-7-OH-DPAT binding was not different in the CO victims or the ED victims as compared to drug-free control subjects. However, the saturation binding density for the CO victims (4.4 ± 0.4 pmol/g) when compared to the drug-free control subjects (3.1 ± 0.2 pmol/g) was significantly elevated ($p \leq 0.01$).[77]

Interestingly, after 1-d withdrawal from chronic treatment with cocaine, increases in D_3 receptor densities were observed in the striatum, while decreases in D_3 receptor densities were observed in the nucleus accumbens of the rat brain.[78] It should be noted, however, that in this study the densities of D_3 receptors were higher in the dorsal striatum, as compared to the nucleus accumbens which contrasts with the intense localization of D_3 receptor mRNA in the nucleus accumbens of rat and human brain[79,80] and the higher D_3 receptor densities in the ventral striatum and nucleus accumbens of human brain.[77] In another study, D_3 receptor mRNA expression was not altered in human cocaine abusers.[81] These findings suggest that D_3 receptor mRNA and binding sites may be differentially regulated by cocaine exposure. Chronic treatment of C6 glioma cells transfected with the D_3 receptor cDNA with DA agonists results in increased D_3 receptor densities, and no change in D_3 mRNA abundance.[82] The upregulation in D_3 receptor densities was blocked by treatment with cycloheximide, suggesting that the increase was mediated by increased protein synthesis.

Alternatively, increased [^{3}H]-(+)-7-OH DPAT binding may reflect a selective increase in one of the D_3 receptor isoforms. The D_3 receptor specific probes may have hybridized to multiple alternative splice variants, including the truncated D_3 receptors.[83] Because DAergic ligands do not bind to the proteins generated from the truncated splice variants, a dissociation between message levels and binding site densities may be observed. The relative abundance of specific D_3 receptor isoforms may vary also with alterations in DA neurotransmission. While the biological significance and function of the D_3 receptor splice variants are not understood, it has been suggested that alternative splicing may regulate the relative abundance of the different D_3 receptor isoforms to differentially modulate D_3 receptor mediated signaling.[84] Therefore, it may be suggested that the elevation in D_3 receptor density after chronic cocaine use may reflect a selective increase in one of the D_3 receptor isoforms. Further studies are needed to determine if this regulatory pattern occurs in the human brain. D_3 receptor adaptations that result from repeated activation of DA neurotransmission due to chronic "binge" use of cocaine may contribute to the development of cocaine dependence. This adaptive increase in the D_3 receptor may enhance the reinforcing effects of cocaine and contribute to the development of cocaine dependence.

6.3.3.4 DA Receptors as Targets for Cocaine Pharmacotherapies

The search for pharmacotherapies for cocaine dependence has focused on drugs that target the DA receptors. Cocaine's reinforcing properties result from its ability to prolong the action of dopamine at DA receptors in brain reward regions.[3,44] From this perspective it has been suggested that DA antagonists may block cocaine use by preventing the interaction of dopamine with its receptors, and therefore blocking reinforcement. In animal self-administration studies, both D_1 receptor (SCH 23390[45,51-54]) and D_2 receptor antagonists (pimozide,[85,86] sulpiride,[86] chlorpromazine,[87] spiperone,[51] metoclopramide,[86] pherphenazine[88]) increase cocaine self-administration as a result of their ability to block cocaine reinforcement. However, recent studies have shown that low doses of benzazepine D_1 receptor antagonists attenuate cocaine self-administration under certain schedules of reinforcement.[55] These findings suggest that certain doses of D_1 receptor antagonists may be efficacious for the treatment of cocaine dependence. Flupentixol, a dopamine antagonist with high affinity for the D_1 receptor has demonstrated some efficacy for decreasing craving and increasing treatment retention in human cocaine abusers.[89] D_2 receptor antagonists (haloperidol and chlorpromazine) have been efficacious for the treatment of paranoia and psychosis but not craving in human cocaine abusers.[90-92] While, DA antagonists may block the reinforcing efficacy of cocaine, use of DA antagonists as pharmacotherapies may be hampered by their propensity to enhance cocaine withdrawal symptoms.[44,93] Furthermore, compliance may be hindered by the dysphoric and extrapyramidal side effects associated with the blockade of DA neurotransmission.[94]

DA receptor agonists also have been suggested as anti-cocaine medications because of their propensity to reduce craving that occurs during cocaine withdrawal. A recent study using pergolide, a D_2/D_3 receptor agonist has demonstrated some efficacy for decreasing craving.[95] Bromocriptine, a D_2 like agonist has undergone extensive evaluation as a treatment for cocaine dependence and appears to reduce craving in cocaine abusers.[96] However, its efficacy as a pharmacotherapy for cocaine dependence was weak.[97,98] Furthermore, studies using the indirect-acting DA agonist, amantadine, were not as successful as anticipated.[99,100] The poor outcome of these studies, which were conducted in the late 1980s, may be explained by a recent preclinical study which demonstrated that D_2-like agonists actually enhance cocaine-seeking behavior or "prime" the addict to initiate another binge use of cocaine.[94,101] Alternatively, D_1-like agonists oppose cocaine-seeking behavior induced by cocaine itself[101] suggesting that D_1-like receptor agonists may be efficacious for the treatment of craving in cocaine dependence. However, while D_1 like agonists may attenuate the craving associated with cocaine withdrawal and relapse and may not enhance cocaine-seeking behavior, they may be reinforcing and therefore at risk to be abused themselves.

The close association of the D_3 receptor with the striatal reward pathways suggests that drugs that target the D_3 receptor subtype may decrease the reinforcing effects of cocaine. Because D_3 receptor densities elevate as cocaine dependence develops, it may be suggested that this upregulation of D_3 receptors may contribute to the reinforcing effects of cocaine.[77] From this perspective, the development of drugs that block D_3 receptor function may be useful for the treatment of cocaine dependence. In keeping with this hypothesis, the D_3 selective antagonist (-)DS 121 has been shown to attenuate cocaine self-administration in rats.[94] While these studies are encouraging, additional research is necessary to confirm the efficacy of D_3 receptor antagonists as pharmacotherapies for cocaine dependence.

6.3.4 KAPPA OPIOIDERGIC RECEPTORS

The endogenous κ opioidergic system has been implicated as a primary mediator of the behavioral and reinforcing effects of cocaine.[64] Pharmacological and molecular cloning studies have recently reported the existence of at least three subtypes of κ opioid receptors.[102-109] Receptor mapping studies have demonstrated that both the κ_1 receptor and κ_2 receptor subtypes are prevalent throughout the mesocorticolimbic pathways in human brain.[110-112] One striking difference in the localization of the two subtypes is reflected by the intense localization of the κ_2 receptor subtype in the ventral or "limbic" sectors of the striatum and the nucleus accumbens in human brain.[112] Conversely, the κ_1 receptor subtype may preferentially localize to the dorsal or "sensorimotor" areas of the human striatum.[111] Based on their neuroanatomical distribution in the human striatum, it may be hypothesized that the κ_1 receptor subtype modulates motor functions, while the κ_2 receptor subtype mediates emotional behaviors and affect. The anatomical localization of the κ receptor subtypes and their intimate association with dopaminergic reward pathways suggests that regulatory alterations in both κ_1 and κ_2 receptors may be important in cocaine dependence.

6.3.4.1 Regulation of κ Receptors By Cocaine

At present, the functional significance and relevance of each of the κ receptor subtypes in the CNS and their role in modulating the brain reward pathways with chronic substance abuse is not understood. An adaptive increase in the density of κ receptors in guinea pig brain after chronic cocaine treatments was detected using the κ_1-selective radioligand [^{3}H]U69,593.[113] Furthermore, elevations in [^{125}I]Tyr^1-D-Pro^{10}-dynorphin A binding to κ receptors were observed within the dorsal and "motor" sectors of the striatum of human cocaine abusers.[111] Dynorphin A demonstrates higher affinity for binding to the κ_1 receptor subtype as compared to the κ_2 receptor subtype; therefore, it may be suggested on the basis of occupancy that the elevated binding of [^{125}I]Tyr^1-D-Pro^{10}-dynorphin A observed in these studies may be due to recognition of the κ_1 receptor subtype.[109,114,115]

These findings combined with animal behavioral studies (e.g., cocaine place preference and self administration) suggest a definitive role for the κ_1 receptor in cocaine dependence. While these studies are reasonably conclusive, other studies are not, due to the use of radioligands which lack selectivity between the κ receptor subtypes. After chronic continuous exposure to cocaine,[116] elevations in binding of the nonselective opioid agonist and antagonist ([^{3}H]bremazocine and [^{3}H]naloxone, respectively) were observed in the nucleus accumbens. Furthermore, in rats treated with cocaine using a binge-administration paradigm, binding of [^{3}H]bremazocine to κ receptors was elevated.[117]

However, it is interesting that in the same animal model, κ receptor mRNA was decreased in the substantia nigra, but not in the ventral tegmental area of cocaine-treated rats.[118] The reasons for this disconnect between binding to the κ receptor and κ receptor mRNA are not known. However, the discrepancy may be due to the detection of multiple κ receptor mRNAs or binding sites or to the binding of [^{3}H]bremazocine to a κ receptor subtype distinct from the κ receptor message that was measured. While the interpretation of these studies with regards to which κ receptor subtype was measured and the regulation of each subtype by cocaine is difficult at this time, recent advances in the cloning of these receptor subtypes and the development of subtype-specific radioligands will clarify these issues in the near future.

Recently, pharmacological binding assays to selectively label the κ_2 receptor subtype have been developed using the opioid antagonist [^{125}I]IOXY in the presence of drugs occluding binding to the μ and δ receptor subtypes.[114,115] This strategy was used in ligand binding and *in vitro* autoradiography assays to assess the regulation of the κ_2 receptor subtype after cocaine exposure in human brain (Figure 6.3.2 E and F).[112] Quantitative region-of-interest densitometric measurements of [^{125}I]IOXY binding demonstrated a twofold elevation in the anterior and ventral sectors of the caudate and putamen and in the nucleus accumbens of human cocaine overdose victims as compared to drug-free and age-matched control subjects. Furthermore, [^{125}I]IOXY binding was significantly elevated in the anterior cingulate (area 24) and orbitofrontal cortex after chronic cocaine.

The regulation of κ_2 receptor numbers in the striatal reward centers suggest that adaptations in the κ_2 receptor may also contribute to the development of cocaine dependence. κ agonists do not generalize to the cocaine cue in drug discrimination paradigms;[119,120] however, κ agonists suppress the stimulus effects of cocaine in monkeys.[121] Therefore, it is unlikely that κ receptors play a direct role in the stimulus or euphoric effects of cocaine. The elevation of the κ_2 receptor subtype along with its discrete localization to the "limbic" or "emotional" striatum indicates that compensatory adaptations in this subtype may underlie the "affective" or "emotional" effects associated with cocaine dependence. Shippenberg and colleagues have suggested that the "conditioned aversive effects" associated with hyperactivity of κ opioidergic neurons in the ventral striatum may underlie the "motivational incentive" to use cocaine.[122] Furthermore, the subjective effects of κ agonists mimic the symptoms of cocaine withdrawal suggesting that excessive activity of the κ opioidergic system may, in part, contribute to the adversive effects associated with cocaine withdrawal. Because protracted exposure to cocaine alters the DA-mediated reward systems, κ opioidergic systems may undergo adaptations in an effort to re-establish the balance between the reward and the opposing aversive system. However, when cocaine is withdrawn and the dopaminergic reward circuit is no longer activated, the κ_2 receptor numbers may remain elevated, and may contribute to the unpleasant feelings and dysphoria associated with withdrawal from cocaine.

6.3.4.2 κ Receptor Drugs as Cocaine Pharmacotherapies

There is considerable evidence supporting a critical role for κ receptors in the development of cocaine dependence. Co-administration of κ agonists with cocaine inhibits cocaine self-administration,[123] cocaine-induced place preference,[122,124] and the development of sensitization to the rewarding effects of cocaine.[63,64,125,126] Further, daily administration of the mixed κ-agonist and μ-antagonist buprenorphine reduces cocaine self-administration by rhesus monkeys[127] and prevents the reinstatement of cocaine-reinforced responding in rats.[128] These potent anti-cocaine effects exhibited by κ agonists in preclinical animal studies suggest that κ receptors may be a useful target for the pharmacotherapeutic treatment of cocaine dependence. Buprenorphine, a mixed opioid agonist/antagonist with agonist activity at κ receptors and antagonist activity at μ receptors, has demonstrated minimal efficacy in decreasing cocaine abuse in heroin abusers.[129,130] Current development of pharmacotherapeutic κ agonists has been hindered by reports that, in humans, administration of κ agonists elicits adverse and psychomimetic actions.[131-133] The recent identification of multiple subtypes of κ receptors with distinct pharmacological and molecular properties[102-109] has lead to the hypothesis that different κ receptor subtypes may mediate distinct actions of κ agonists.[133,114,115] Therefore, it may be possible to develop κ drugs which lack and/or inhibit the dysphoric properties and yet maintain efficacy for blocking cocaine administration. At present, distinct "sensorimotor" vs. "limbic" functions for the κ_1 and κ_2 receptor subtypes may be speculated based on their localization in the human striatum. The adaptive increases in κ_2 receptors number throughout the ventral "limbic" striatum may, in part, mediate the feelings of dysphoria and craving associated with cocaine withdrawal distress. The extent that the κ_2 receptor subtype mediate the dysphoric properties of κ agonists will not be known until κ_2-selective agonists are developed. However, if the κ_2 receptor does mediate dysphoria during cocaine withdrawal, then selective κ_2 receptor antagonists may be useful for the treatment of the dysphoria that underlies relapse and perpetuation of cocaine misuse.

6.3.5 SEROTONIN TRANSPORTER AND COCAINE DEPENDENCE

Cocaine binds with high affinity to the serotonin (5-HT) transporter and inhibits 5-HT uptake.[2,134] Serotonergic neurons project from the dorsal raphe to the ventral tegmental area where they modulate mesolimbic DA neurotransmission. Inhibition of 5-HT uptake in the dorsal raphe nucleus by cocaine decreases the firing of the raphe neurons by feedback activation of 5-HT_{1A} autoreceptors,[135-137] an effect that is blocked by pretreatment with the 5-HT synthesis inhibitor p-chlorophenylalanine.[136] With chronic cocaine treatment, these mechanisms become sensitized probably as a result of a compensatory upregulation of [³H]imipramine binding to the 5-HT transporter in the dorsal raphe, frontal cortex, medial, and sulcal prefrontal cortex of cocaine treated rats.[137] These studies suggest that adaptations in serotonergic neurotransmission may contribute in part to the expression of cocaine-induced behaviors. While an enhancement of serotonin neurotransmission is believed to be inhibitory to the expression of cocaine-mediated behaviors or to have a minimal effect,[138,139] there is some evidence that serotonin may play a role in the mood elevating effects of acute cocaine. Interestingly, depletion of tryptophan (the precursor to 5-HT) severely attenuated the subjective high experienced by cocaine-dependent subjects.[140] Furthermore, withdrawal from chronic cocaine use has been associated with symptoms of depression[141] due to cocaine-induced alterations in 5-HT neurotransmission.[142] Together, these studies suggest that regulatory alterations in serotonergic signaling play a role in cocaine dependence. Furthermore, drugs that antagonize these alterations in serotonergic systems may be efficacious for the treatment of cocaine dependence.

6.3.5.1 The 5-HT Transporter as a Target for Cocaine Pharmacotherapy

It has been suggested that 5-HT may antagonize cocaine effects by inhibiting mesolimbic DA neurotransmission.[143,144] Therefore, increases in 5-HT neurotransmission that results from blocking presynaptic 5-HT uptake may decrease cocaine administration. In keeping with this hypothesis, preclinical animal studies have demonstrated that enhancement of serotonergic neurotransmission by administration of the selective 5-HT uptake inhibitors citalopram and fluoxetine attenuates the discriminative stimulus effects of cocaine in monkeys.[145] Furthermore, fluoxetine inhibits cocaine self-administration[146,147] and reduces the breakpoints on a progressive ratio schedule reinforced by cocaine.[148] Conversely, depletion of serotonin enhances cocaine self-administration.[149,150] Several serotonin reuptake inhibitors have been evaluated for the treatment of cocaine dependence. Fluoxetine significantly decreased subjective ratings of cocaine's positive mood effects on several visual analog measures and attenuated the mydriatic effect of cocaine in human cocaine abusers.[151] Fluoxetine has been suggested to decrease craving and cocaine use of methadone-maintained cocaine users.[152-154] While the efficacy of fluoxetine may be related to its ability to reduce craving,[155,156] it is likely that its effects are more related to its ability to reverse the symptoms of depression that are associated with cocaine withdrawal.

6.3.6 GLUTAMATE RECEPTORS AND COCAINE DEPENDENCE

Recent studies have suggested that glutamate receptors including the NMDA (N-methyl-D-aspartate) and AMPA receptors may be involved in the neural and behavioral changes resulting from chronic administration of cocaine.[7] Glutamate is the endogenous neurotransmitter of cortical and limbic neurons which project to the nucleus accumbens. Preclinical studies with the noncompetitive NMDA receptor antagonist MK-801 have linked excitatory glutamatergic synapses with the development of cocaine sensitization, a cardinal feature of cocaine dependence. Simultaneous administration of low doses of MK-801 prevent the development of sensitization to the stereotypic and locomotor stimulant effects of cocaine.[157-162] Alternatively, when MK-801 was administered prior to cocaine, the stimulating effects of cocaine were enhanced.[163] The competitive NMDA antagonist CPP partially prevented the development of cocaine sensitization.[161] MK-801 decreased the incidence of seizures and mortality caused by cocaine.[164-166] The AMPA receptor antagonists NBQX produced dose-dependent decreases in cocaine-induced locomotor stimulation.[160] Dopaminergic neurons in the ventral tegmental area of cocaine-treated rats were more responsive to glutamate while nucleus accumbens

Julie K. Staley

neurons were less sensitive.[167] Cortical NMDA receptors are upregulated after cocaine treatment[168] and GluR1 (an AMPA receptor subunit) and NMDAR1 (an NMDA receptor subunit) are upregulated in the ventral tegmental area[169] suggesting that compensatory adaptations of the glutamate receptors may, in part, contribute to the enhanced glutamatergic neurotransmission. From these observations it has been hypothesized that alterations in mesocorticolimbic glutamate transmission may in part contribute to the development of cocaine sensitization.[167]

6.3.6.1 Glutamate Receptors as Targets for Cocaine Pharmacotherapies

NMDA receptors mediate the development of sensitization to cocaine's reinforcing effects.[170] However, while both competitive and noncompetive NMDA receptor antagonists block the development of cocaine sensitization, they appear to be ineffective once sensitization has developed.[7] NMDA receptor antagonists do not alter the acute stimulant effects of cocaine.[7,157,171] Acute pretreatment with MK-801 causes a loss of discriminative responding; however, it did not block cocaine self-administration.[170] Furthermore, many drugs which act at the NMDA receptors produce phencyclidine-like behavioral effects.[160] Together, these preclinical studies do not offer significant support for NMDA receptor antagonists as cocaine pharmacotherapies. However, AMPA receptor antagonists do not appear to produce phencyclidine-like behavioral effects, and they block cocaine-induced locomotor stimulation. While additional preclinical studies are necessary, it has been suggested that nonNMDA glutamate receptor antagonists may be a target for the development of pharmacotherapies for the treatment of cocaine dependence.[160]

6.3.7 MULTI-TARGET PHARMACOTHERAPEUTIC AGENTS

Many of the novel pharmacotherapeutic agents currently under development are directed towards a single molecular target related to or known to be regulated by cocaine. Although this strategy has been somewhat beneficial, the development of an effective treatment for cocaine dependence may require multi-site targeting of distinct neuroreceptor populations that are known to modulate the activity of the drug reward circuit. Cocaine interacts with at least three distinct neurochemical systems in the brain including the dopaminergic, serotonergic, and noradrenergic systems. Cocaine enhances the neurotransmission of each of these systems by blocking the presynaptic reuptake. Chronic perturbations of monoaminergic neurotransmission that results from protracted use of cocaine may, in turn, alter cholinergic and glutamatergic neurotransmission by indirect actions. The ability of cocaine to alter signaling of multiple neurochemical pathways in the brain suggests that a multi-target pharmacotherapy may be an optimal approach for the treatment of cocaine dependence.

6.3.7.1 Phentermine/Fenfluramine: The "Phen-Fen" Protocol

Recent clinical reports have suggested that administration of phentermine and fenfluramine in combination ("Phen-Fen") may be useful for the treatment of cocaine dependence.[172] Like amphetamine, phentermine stimulates the release of dopamine and norepinephrine and accordingly is related with subjective feelings of a positive mood state.[173] Alternatively, fenfluramine stimulates the release of serotonin and is associated with increased anxiety and confusion, and decreases in positive mood scales.[173] These undesirable effects of fenfluramine are consistent with the notion that enhanced serotonin neurotransmission is aversive. In support of these findings, fenfluramine is not self-administered by animals.[174] When phentermine and fenfluramine are administered in combination, the subjective effects reported appeared to be a blending of the two drugs.[173] While many of the undesirable side effects observed for the administration of each drug alone were lessened, administration of the phen-fen combination did produce some adverse effects including decreased psychomotor performance and decreased elation.[173]

Recent reports from an uncontrolled study in human cocaine abusers has suggested that administration of the phen-fen combination resulted in decreased craving and decreased cocaine use during treatment.[172] While these reports are provocative, the efficacy of phen-fen for the treatment of cocaine dependence remains to be studied in a controlled clinical trial.

6.3.7.2 Ibogaine: The Rainforest Alkaloid

Ibogaine, the principal alkaloid of the African rainforest shrub *Tabernanthe iboga* (Apocynaceae family), is currently being evaluated as an agent to treat psychostimulant addiction.[175] Anecdotal reports of ibogaine treatments in opiate-dependent or cocaine-dependent humans describe alleviation of drug "craving" and physical signs of opiate withdrawal after a single administration of ibogaine, which in some subjects contributes to drug-free periods lasting several months thereafter. In drug self-administration studies, ibogaine and related iboga alkaloids reduced intravenous self-administration of cocaine 1 h after treatment. This suppression on cocaine intake was evident one day later, and in some rats a persistent decrease was noted for as long as several weeks.[176] Ibogaine also effectively blocks morphine self-administration.[176] Ibogaine reduces preference for cocaine consumption in a mouse cocaine-preference drinking model.[177] And, cocaine-induced stereotypy and locomotor activity were significantly lower in ibogaine-treated mice.[177]

The mechanism of action for ibogaine may be resolved in part by defining high affinity pharmacological targets for ibogaine. The receptor binding profile for ibogaine suggests that multiple neurochemical pathways may be responsible for ibogaine's anti-addictive properties. Ibogaine binds to μ and κ-1 opioid receptors, α-1 adrenergic receptors, M_1 and M_2 muscarinic receptors, serotonin $5\text{-}HT_2$ and $5\text{-}HT_3$ receptors, and voltage-dependent sodium channels with micromolar affinities.[178] Ibogaine competitively displaces [^{3}H]MK-801 binding[179,180] and blocks NMDA-depolarizations in frog motoneurons.[180] Ibogaine demonstrates moderate affinity for binding to the cocaine recognition sites on the DA transporter[178,181] and on the 5-HT transporter.[181] Ibogaine, which blocks access of cocaine to the DA transporter, may[187] or may not restrict substrate uptake.[182,183] Because ibogaine displays lower affinity for the DA transporter as compared to cocaine, it may meet some of the criteria for the "ideal cocaine antagonist".

The anti-addictive properties of ibogaine may, in part, be mediated by a pharmacologically active metabolite. Recently, the principle metabolite of ibogaine was isolated from biological specimens of subjects administered ibogaine using GC/MS.[181,184] The metabolite that results from O-demethylation of the parent drug was identified as 12-hydroxyibogamine (noribogaine). Preliminary pharmacokinetic studies have suggested that noribogaine is generated rapidly and exhibits a slow clearance rate.[181,184] The relatively long half-life of noribogaine suggests that the long-term biological effects of ibogaine may, in part, be mediated by its metabolite. Similar to ibogaine, noribogaine binds to the μ and κ-1 opioid receptors with micromolar potency.[185,186] The most striking finding has been the demonstration that noribogaine binds to the cocaine recognition site on the 5-HT transporter with nanomolar potency,[181,186] and elevates extraneuronal 5-HT in a dose-dependent manner.[181,182] Given the recent evidence that serotonin uptake blockers alleviate some of the symptoms associated with psychostimulant "craving", these findings suggest that the effects of noribogaine on 5-HT transmission may account, in part, for the potential of ibogaine to interrupt drug-seeking behavior in humans. Overall, it may be suggested that the putative efficacy of ibogaine as a pharmacotherapy for cocaine dependence may be attributed to the combined actions of the parent and the metabolite at multiple CNS targets.[180,181,186]

Julie K. Staley

6.3.8 CONCLUSIONS

Significant advances have been made in understanding the neurochemical consequences of cocaine dependence in the past decade. Integration of the findings observed for cocaine's effects on behavior, together with the identification of the receptors and transporters which undergo compensatory adaptations to neutralize cocaine's effects, has lead to the identification of several potential neurochemical targets for the development of cocaine pharmacotherapies. Pharmacotherapies that target one or more of the neurochemical systems that have been altered by protracted cocaine use may alleviate the dysphoria, depression, and anxiety that underlie relapse and compulsive cocaine use.

REFERENCES

1. Ritz, M.C., Lamb, S.R., Goldberg, S.R., and Kuhar, M.J. Cocaine receptors on dopamine transporters are related to self-administration of cocaine. *Science* 237: 1219, 1987.
2. Reith, M.E.A., Kramer, H.K., Sershen, H., and Lajtha, A. Cocaine competitively inhibits catecholamine uptake into brain synaptic vesicles. *Res Commun. in Substances seof Abuse* 10, 205, 1989.
3. Kuhar, M.J., Ritz, M.C., and Boja, J.W. The dopamine hypothesis of the reinforcing properties of cocaine. *Trends in Neurosci.* 14, 299, 1991.
4. Gingrich, J.A., and Caron, M.G., Recent advances in the molecular biology of dopamine receptors. *Ann. Rev. Neurosci.* 16, 299, 1993.
5. DiChiara, G. and Imperato, A. Opposite effects of mu and kappa opiate agonists on dopamine release in the nucleus accumbens and in the dorsal caudate of freely moving rats. *J. Pharmacol. Exp. Therap.* 244, 1067, 1988.
6. Karler, R., Calder, L.D., Thai, L.H., Bedingfield, J.B. A dopaminergic-glutamatergic basis for the action of amphetamine and cocaine. *Brain Res.* 658, 8, 1994.
7. Trujillo, K.A., and Akil, H. Excitatory amino acids and drugs of abuse: a role for N-methyl-D-aspartate receptors in drug tolerance, sensitization and physical dependence. *Drug and Alcohol Dependence* 38, 139, 1995.
8. Chen, N.H., and Reith, M.E.A. Autoregulation and monoamine interactions in the ventral tegmental area in the absence and presence of cocaine: A microdialysis study in freely moving rats. *J. Pharmacol. Exp. Therap.* 271, 1597, 1994.
9. Spanagel, R., Herz, A., and Shippenberg, T., The effects of opioid peptides on dopamine release in the nucleus accumbens: an in vivo microdialysis study. *J.Neurochem.* 55, 1734, 1990.
10. Spanagel, R., Herz, A., and Shippenberg, T.S. Opposing tonically active endogenous opioid systems modulate the mesolimbic dopaminergic pathway. *Proc. Natl. Acad. Sci.* 89, 2046, 1992.
11. Alburges, M.E., Narang, N., and Wamsley, J.K. Alterations in the dopaminergic receptor system after chronic administration of cocaine. *Synapse* 14, 314, 1993.
12. Wilson, J.M., Nobrega, J.N., Carroll, M.E., Niznik, H.B., Shannak, K., Lac, S.T., Pristupa, Z.B. Dixon, L.M. and Kish, S.J. Heterogenous subregional binding patterns of [3H]-WIN 35,428 and [3H]-GBR 12,935 are differentially regulated by chronic cocaine self-administration. *J. Neurosci.* 14, 2966, 1994.
13. Hitri, A., Little, K.Y., Ellinwood, E.H. Effect of cocaine on dopamine transporter receptors depends on routes of chronic cocaine administration. *Neuropsychopharmacology* 14, 205, 1996.
14. Aloyo, V.J., Pazdalski, P.S., Kirifides, A.L., Harvey, J.A., Behavioral sensitization, behavioral tolerance, and increased [3H]WIN 35,428 binding in rabbit caudate nucleus after repeated injections of cocaine. *Pharmacol. Biochem. Behav.* 52, 335,1995.
15. Little, K.Y., Kirkman, J.A., Carroll, F.I., Clark, T.B., and Duncan, G.E. Cocaine use increases [3H]WIN 35,428 binding sites in human striatum. *Brain Res.* 628, 17, 1993.

16. Staley, J.K., Basile, M., Wetli, C.V., Hearn, W.L., Flynn, D.D., Ruttenber, A.J., and Mash, D.C. Differential regulation of the dopamine transporter in cocaine overdose deaths. *National Institute of Drug Abuse Research Monograph*. 141, 32, 1994.
17. Staley, J.K., Hearn, W.L., Ruttenber, A.J., Wetli, C.V., and Mash, D.C. High affinity cocaine recognition sites on the dopamine transporter are elevated in fatal cocaine overdose victims. *J. Pharmacol. Exp. Therap.* 271, 1678, 1994.
18. Staley, J.K., Wetli, C.V., Ruttenber, A.J., Hearn, W.L., and Mash, D.C. Altered dopaminergic synaptic markers in cocaine psychosis and sudden death *National Institute of Drug Abuse Research Monograph* 153, 491, 1995.
19. Malison, R. SPECT imaging of DA transporters in cocaine dependence with [^{123}I]ß-CIT. *National Institute on Drug Abuse Research Monograph* 152, 60, 1995.
20. Wise, R.A., and Bozarth, M.A. A psychomotor stimulant theory of addiction. *Psychol Rev.* 94, 469, 1987.
21. Koob, G.F., Bloom F.E. Cellular and molecular mechanisms of drug dependence. *Science* 242, 715, 1988.
22. Robinson, T., Berridge K.C., The neural basis of drug craving: an incentive - sensitization theory of addiction. *Brain Res. Rev.* 18, 247, 1993.
23. Stathis, M., Scheffel, U., Lever, S.Z., Boja, J.W., Carroll, F.I., Kuhar, M.J. Rate of binding of various inhibitors at the dopamine transporter in vivo. *Psychopharmacology* 119, 376, 1195.
24. Kuhar , M.J., Sanchez-Roa, P.M., Wong, D.F., Dannals, R.F., Grigoriadis, D.E., Lew, R., Milberger, M. Dopamine transporter: biochemistry, pharmacology, and imaging. *Eur. Neurol. Suppl.* 30, 15, 1990.
25. Chiat, L.D. Reinforcing and subjective effects of methylphenidate in humans. *Behav. Pharmacol.* 5, 281, 1994.
26. Pogun, S., Scheffel ,U., Kuhar, M.J. Cocaine displaces [^{3}H]WIN 35,428 binding to dopamine uptake sites in vivo, more rapidly than mazindol or GBR 12909. *Eur. J. Pharmacol.* 198, 203, 1991.
27. Volkow, N.D., Ding, Y.S., Fowler, J.S., Wang, G.J., Logan, J., Gatley, J.S., Dewey S., Ashby, C., Lieberman, J., Hitzemann, R., Wolf, A.P. Is methylphenidate like cocaine? *Arch. Gen. Psychiatry* 52, 456, 1995.
28. Rothman, R.B., and Glowa, J.R. A review of the effects of dopaminergic agents on humans, animals, and drug-seeking behavior, and its implications for medication development. *Mol. Neurobiol.* 10, 1, 1995.
29. Rothman, R.B. High affinity dopamine reuptake inhibitors as potential cocaine antagonists: a strategy for drug development. *Life Sci.* 46, PL17, 1990.
30. Baumann, M.H., Char, G.U., De Costa, B.R., Rice, K.C., and Rothman, R.B. GBR 12909 attenuates cocaine-induced activation of mesolimbic dopamine neurons in the rat. *J. Pharmacol. Exp. Therap.* 271,1216, 1994.
31. Giros, B., Wang, Y.M., Suter, S., McLeskey, S.B., Pifl, C. and Caron, M.G. Delineation of discrete domains for substrate, cocaine, and tricyclic antidepressant interactions using chimeric dopamine-norepinephrine transporters. *J. Biol. Chem.* 15985, 1994.
32. Buck, K.K. and Amara, S.G. Chimeric dopamine-norepinephrine transporters delineate structural domains influencing selectivity for catecholamines and 1-methyl-4-phenylpyridinium. *Proc. Natl. Acad. Sci.* 91. 12584, 1994.
33. Christenson, J.G. Radioimmunoassay for benzoyl ecgonine. *US Patent 4*, 102, 979, 1978.
34. Leute, R.K., Bolz, G., Nitrogen derivates of benzoyl ecgonine. *US Patent* 1975; 3888 866.
35. Mule, S.J., Jukofshy, D., Kogan, M., Pace, A., De, Verebey, K. Evaluation of the radioimmunoassay for benzoylecgonine (a cocaine metabolite) in human urine. *Clin Chem* 23, 796, 1977.
36. Bagasra, O., Forman, L.J., Howeedy A., and Whittle P. A potential vaccine for cocaine abuse prophylaxis. *Immunopharmacology* 23, 173, 1992.
37. Carrera, M.R., Ashley, J.A., Parsons, L.H., Wirschung, P., Koob, G.F. Suppression of psychoactive effects of cocaine by active immunization. *Nature* 378, 727, 1995.
38. Rocio, M., Carrera, A., Ashley, J.A., Parsons, L.H., Wirshling, P., Koob, G.F., and Janda, K.D. Suppression of psychoactive effects of cocaine by active immunization. *Nature*, 378, 727, 1995.

39. Slusher, B.S., Jackson, P.F. A shot in the arm for cocaine addiction. *Nature Medicine*, 2, 26, 1996.

40. Landry, D.W., Zhao, K., Yang, G. X.-Q., Glickman, M., Georgiadis, T.M. Antibody-catalyzed degradation of cocaine. *Science* 259,1899, 1993.

41. Basmadjian, G.P., Singh, S., Sastrodjojo, B., Smith, B.T. Avor, K.S., Chang, F., Mills, S.L., Seale T.W. Generation of polyclonal catalytic antibodies against cocaine using transition state analogs of cocaine conjugated to diphtheria toxoid. *Chem. Pharm. Bull.* 43, 1902, 1995.

42. Berkman, C.E., Underiner, G.E., and Cashman, J.R. Synthesis of an immunogenic template for the generation of catalytic antibodies for (-) cocaine hydrolysis. *J. Org. Chem,* 61, 5686, 1996.

43. Gallacher, G. A potential vaccine for cocaine abuse prophylaxis? *Immunopharmacology* 27, 79, 1994.

44. Self, D.W. Cocaine abuse takes a shot. *Nature* 378, 666, 1995.

45. Robledo, P., Maldonado-Lopez, R., and Koob, G.F. Role of the dopamine receptors in the nucleus accumbens in the rewarding properties of cocaine. *Ann. NY Acad. Sci.* 654, 509, 1992.

46. Pulvirenti, L., and Koob, G.F. Dopamine receptor agonists, partial agonists and psychostimulant addiction. *Trends in Pharmacol Sci.* 15, 374, 1994.

47. Ranaldi, R., and Beninger, R.J. The effects of systemic and intracerebral injections of D_1 and D_2 agonists on brain stimulation reward. *Brain Res.* 651, 283, 1994.

48. Caine, S.B., Heinrichs, S.C,, Coffin, V.L., and Koob, G.F. Effects of the dopamine D-1 antagonist SCH 23390 microinjected into the accumbens, amygdala or striatum on cocaine self-administration in the rat. *Brain Res.* 692, 47, 1995.

49. Tella, S.R. Differential blockade of chronic versus acute effects of intravenous cocaine by dopamine receptor antagonists. *Pharmacol. Biochem. Behav.* 48, 151, 1994.

50. Shippenberg, T.S. and Heidbreder, C.H. Sensitization to the conditioned rewarding effects of cocaine: Pharmacological and temporal characteristics. *J. Pharmacol. Exp. Therap.* 273, 808, 1995.

51. Hubner, C.B., Moreton, J.E. Effect of selective D_1 and D_2 dopamine antagonists on cocaine self-administration in the rat. *Psychopharmacology* 105, 151, 1991

52. Woolverton, W.L. Effects of a D_1 and D_2 dopamine antagonists on the self-administration of cocaine and piribedil by rhesus monkeys. *Pharmacol. Biochem Behav.* 24, 531, 1986.

53. Koob, G.F., Le, H.T., Creese I. The D_1 dopamine antagonist SCH 23390 increases cocaine self-administration in the rat. *Neurosci. Lett.* 79, 315, 1987.

54. Egilmez, Y., Jung, M.E., Lane, J.D., Emmett-Oglesby, M.W. Dopamine release during cocaine self-administration in rats: effect of SCH 23390. *Brain Res.* 701, 142, 1995.

55. Caine, S.B., and Koob, G.F. Effects of dopamine D-1 and D-2 antagonists on cocaine self-administration under different schedules of reinforcement in the rat. *J. Pharmacol. Exp. Therap.* 270, 209, 1994.

56. Meador-Woodruff, J.H., Little, K.Y., Damask, S.P., Mansour, A., and Watson, S.J. Effects of cocaine on dopamine receptor gene expression: A study in the postmortem human brain. *Biol. Psychiat.* 34, 348, 1993.

57. Laurier, L.G., Corrigall, C.A., George, S.R. Dopamine receptor density, sensitivity and mRNA levels are altered following self-administration of cocaine in the rat. *Brain Res.* 634, 31, 1994.

58. Peris, J., Boyson, S.J., Cass, W.A., Curella, P., Dwoskin, L.P., Larson, G., Lin, L.H., Yasuda, R.P., and Zahniser, N.R. Persistence of neurochemical changes in dopamine systems after repeated cocaine administration. *J. Pharmacol Exp. Therap.* 253, 35, 1990.

59. Claye, L.H., Akunne, H.C., Davis, M.D., DeMattos, S., and Soliman, K.F.A. Behavioral and neurochemical changes in the dopaminergic system after repeated cocaine administration. *Mol. Neurobiol.* 11, 55, 1995.

60. Zeigler, S., Lipton, J., Toga, A., and Ellison, G. Continuous cocaine administration produces persisting changes in brain neurochemistry and behavior. *Brain Res.* 552, 27, 1991.

61. Kleven, M.S., Perry, B.D., Woolverton, W.L., and Seiden, L.S. Effects of repeated injections of cocaine on D_1 and D_2 dopamine receptors in rat brain. *Brain Res.* 532, 265, 1990.

62. Henry, D.J. and White, F.J. Repeated cocaine administration causes persistent enhancement of D_1 dopamine receptor sensivity within the rat nucleus accumbens. *J. Pharmacol. Exp. Therap.* 258, 882, 1991.

63. Shippenberg, T.S., and Heidbreder, C.H. Kappa opioid receptor agonists prevent sensitization to the rewarding effects of cocaine. *NIDA Research Monograph* 153, 456, 1994.

64. Shippenberg, T.S., LeFevour A., Heidbreder C. κ-opioid receptor agonists prevent sensitization to the conditioned rewarding effects of cocaine. *J. Pharmacol. Exp. Therap.* 276, 545, 1996

65. Spyraki, C. and Sealfon, S.C. Regulation of dopamine D2 receptor mRNA expression in the olfactory tubercle by cocaine. *Mol. Brain Res.* 19, 313, 1993.

66. Przewlocka, B., and Lason, W. Adaptive changes in the proenkephalin and D_2 dopamine receptor mRNA expression after chronic cocaine in the nucleus accumbens and striatum of the rat. European *Neuropsychopharmacol.* 5, 465, 1995.

67. Unterwald, E.M., Ho, A., Rubenfeld, J.M., and Kreek, M.J. Time course of the development of behavioral sensitization and dopamine receptor up-regulation during binge cocaine administration. *J. Pharmacol. Exp. Therap.* 270, 1387, 1994.

68. Goeders, N.E., and Kuhar, M.J. Chronic cocaine administration induced opposite changes in dopamine receptors in the striatum and nucleus accumbens. *Alcohol Drug Res.* 7, 207, 1987.

69. Trulson, M.E. and Ulissey, M.J. Chronic cocaine administration decreases dopamine synthesis rate and increases [^{3}H]spiroperidol binding in rat brain. *Brain Res. Bulletin* 19, 35, 1987.

70. Volkow, N.D., Fowler, J.S., Wolf, A.P., Schlyer, D., Shiue, C.Y., Alpert, R., Dewey, S.L., Logan, J., Bendriem, B., Christman, D., Hitzemann, R., and Henn, F. Effects of chronic cocaine abuse on postsynaptic dopamine receptors. *Am. J. Psychiatry* 147, 719, 1990.

71. Caine, S.B., and Koob G.F. Modulation of cocaine self-administration in the rat through D_3 dopamine receptors. *Science* 260, 1814, 1993.

72. Caine ,S.B., and Koob, G.F. Pretreatment with the dopamine agonist 7-OH-DPAT shifts the cocaine self-administration dose-effect function to the left under different schedules in the rat. *Behavioral Pharamacol.* 6, 333, 1995.

73. Nader, M.A., and Mach, R.H. Self-administration of the dopamine D_3 agonist 7-OH-DPAT in rhesus monkeys is modified by prior cocaine exposure. *Psychopharmacology* 125, 13, 1996.

74. Acri, J.B., Carter, S.R., Alling, K., Geter-Douglas, B., Dijkstra, D., Wikstrom, H, Katz, J.L., Witkin, J.M. Assessment of cocaine-like discriminative stimulus effects of dopamine D_3 receptor ligands. *Eur. J. Pharmacol.* 281, R7, 1995.

75. Mallet, P.E., and Beninger, R.J. 7-OH-DPAT produced place conditioning in rats. *Eur. J. Pharmacol.* 261.R5-, 1994.

76. Lamas, X., Negus, S.S., Nader, M.A., and Mello, NK. Effects of the putative dopamine D_3 receptor agonist 7-OH-DPAT in rhesus monkeys trained to discriminate cocaine from saline. *Psychopharmacology* 124, 306, 1996.

77. Staley, J.K., and Mash, D.C. Adaptive increase in D_3 dopamine receptors in the brain reward circuits of human cocaine fatalities. *J. Neurosci.* In press, 1996.

78. Wallace, D.R., Mactutus, C.F., and Booze, R.M. Repeated intravenous cocaine administrations: Locomotor activity and dopamine D_2/D_3 receptors. *Synapse* 19, 1, 1996.

79. Landwehrmeyer, B., Mengod, G., and Palacios, J.M. Differential visualization of dopamine D_2 and D_3 receptor sites in rat brain. A comparative study using in situ hybridization histochemistry and ligand binding autoradiography. *Eur. J. Neurosci.* 5, 145, 1993.

80. Landwehrmeyer, B., Mengod, G., and Palacios, J.M. Dopamine D_3 receptor mRNA and binding site in human brain. *Mol. Brain Res.* 18, 187, 1993.

81. Meador-Woodruff, J.H., Little, K.Y., Damask, S.P., and Watson, S.J. Effects of cocaine on D_3 and D_4 receptor expression in the human striatum. *Biol. Psych.* 38, 263, 1995.

82. Cox, B.A., Rosser, M.P., Kozlowski, M.R., Duwe, K.M, Neve, R.L., and Neve, K.A. Regulation and functional characterization of a rat recombinant dopamine D_3 receptor. *Synapse* 21, 1, 1995.

83. Fishburn CS, Belleli D, David C, Carmon S and Fuchs S. A novel short isoform of the D_3 dopamine receptor generated by alternative splicing in the third cytoplasmic loop. *J. Biol. Chem.* 268, 5872, 1993.

84. Sokoloff, P., Giros, B., Martres, M.P., Andrieux, M., Besancon, R., Pilon, C., Bouthenet, M.L., Souil, E., and Schwartz, J.C. Localization and function of the D_3 dopamine receptor. *Arzneim -Forsch/Drug Res* 42:224, 1992.

85. De Wit H., Wise R.A. Blockade of cocaine reinforcement in rats with the dopamine receptor blocker pimozide, but not the noradrenergic blockers phentolamine and phenoxybenzamine. *Can. J. Psychol.* 31, 195, 1977.

86. Roberts, D.C., Vickers, G. Atypical neuroleptics increase self-administration of cocaine: an evaluation of a behavioural screen for antipsychotic activity. *Psychopharmacology* 82, 1135, 1984.

87. Wilson, M.C., Schuster C.R. The effects of chlorpromazine on psychomotor stimulant self-administration in the rhesus monkey. *Psychopharmacologia* 26, 115, 1972.

88. Johanson C.E., Kandel D.A., Bonese K.F. The effect of perphenazine on self-administration behavior. *Pharmacol. Biochem. Behav.* 4, 427, 1976.

89. Gawin F.H., Allen D., Humblestone, B. Outpatient treatment of "crack" cocaine smoking with flupentixol decanoate. *Arch. Gen. Psychiatry* 46, 322, 1989.

90. Gawin, F.H., Neuroleptic reduction of cociane-induced paranoia, but not euphoria? *Psychopharmacology* 90, 142, 1986.

91. Crosby, R.D., Halikas J.A., Carlson, G. Pharmacotherapeutic interventions for cocaine abuse: present practices and future directions. *J. Addict. Dis.* 10, 13, 1991.

92. Rao, S., Ziedonis, D., Kosten T. The pharmaotherapy of cocaine dependence. *Psychiatric Annals* 25, 363, 1995.

93. Gawin, F.H., Cocaine Addiction: psychology and neurophysiology. *Science,* 251,11580, 1991

94. Roberts, D.C.S., and Ranaldi R. Effect of dopaminergic drugs on cocaine reinforcement. *Clin Neuropharmacol.* 18, S84, 1995.

95. Malcolm, R., Hutto, B.R., Philips, J.D., Ballenger, J.C., Pergolide mesylate treatement of cocaine withdrawal. *J. Clin. Psychiatry* 52, 39, 1991.

96. Dackis, C.A., Gold, M.S., Sweeney, D.R., Byron, J.P., Climko, R. Single dose bromocriptine reverses cocaine craving. *Psychiatry Res.* 20, 261, 1987.

97. Tennant, F.S., Sagherian, A.A., Double-blind comparison of amantadine and bromocriptine for ambulatory withdrawal from cocaine dependence. *Arch Intern Med* 147, 109, 1987.

98. Teller, D.W., Devenyi, P. Bromocriptine in cocaine withdrawal-Does it work? *Int. J. Addict.* 23, 1197, 1988.

99. Handelsman, L., Chordia, P.L., Escovar, I.M., Marion, I.J., Lowinson, J.H. Amantadine for treatment of cocaine dependence in methadone-maintained patients. Am. J. Psychiatry 145, 533, 1988. 1988.

100. Kosten, T.R., Pharmacotherapeutic interventions for cocaine abuse: matching patients to treatments. *J. Nervous and Mental Disease* 177, 379, 1989

101. Self, D.W., Barnhart W.J., Lehman, D.A., Nestler, E.J. Opposite modulation of cocaine-seeking behavior by D1- and D2-like dopamine receptor agonists. *Science* 271, 1586, 1996.

102. Clark, J.A., Liu, L., Price, M., Hersh, B., Edelson, M., and Pasternak, G.W. Kappa opiate receptor multiplicity: Evidence for two U50,488-sensitive κ_1 subtypes and a novel κ_3 subtype. *J. Pharmacol. Exp. Therap.* 251, 461, 1989.

103. Rothman, R.B., France, C.P., Bykov, V., De Costa, B.R., Jacobson, A.E., Woods, J.H., and Rice, K.C. Pharmacological activities of optically pure enantiomers of the κ opioid agonist, U50,488, and its cis diastereomer: evidence for three κ receptor subtypes. *Eur. J. Pharmacol.* 167, 345, 1989.

104. Rothman, R.B., Bykov, V., De Costa, B.R., Jacobson, A.E., Rice, K.C., and Brady, L.S. Evidence for four opioid kappa binding sites in guinea pig brain. *The International Narcotics Research Conference (INRC),*'89 p. 9, 1990.

105. Wollemann, M., Benhye, S., and Simon, J. The kappa-opioid receptor: Evidence for the different subtypes. *Life Sci.* 52, 599, 1993.

106. Nishi, M., Takeshima, H., Fukuda, K., Kato, S., Mori, K. cDNA clining and pharmacological characterization of an opioid receptor with high affinities for kappa-subtype selective ligands. *FEBS Letters* 330, 77, 1993

107. Pan, G.E., Standifer K.M., and Pasternak, G.W. Cloning and functional characterization through antisense mapping of a κ_3-related opioid receptor. *Mol. Pharmacol.* 47, 1180, 1995.

108. Raynor, K. Kong, H., Chen, Y., Yasuda, K., Yu, L., Bell, G.I., Reisine, T. Pharmacological characterization of the cloned kappa- delta- and mu-opioid receptors. Mol .Pharmacol. 45, 330, 1993

109. Simonin, F., Gaveriaux-Ruff, C., Befort, K., Matthes, H., Lannes, B., Micheletti, G., Mattei, M. G., Charron, G., Bloch, B., and Kieffer, B. k-Opioid receptor in humans: cDNA and genomic cloning, chromosomal assignment, functional expression, pharmacology, and expression pattern in the central nervous system. *Proc. Natl Acad. Sci.* 92, 7006, 1995.

110. Quirion, R., Pilapil, C., and Magnan, J. Localization of kappa opioid receptor binding sites in human forebrain using [³H]U69,593:Comparison with [³H]bremazocine. Cell and Molecular Neurobiology 7, 303, 1987.

111. Hurd, Y.L., and Herkenham, M. Molecular alterations in the neostriatum of human cocaine addicts. *Synapse* 13, 357, 1993.

112. Staley, J.K., Rothman, R.B., Partilla, J.S., Rice, K.C., Matecka, D., Ouyang, Q., Wetli, C.V., and Mash, D.C. Cocaine upregulates kappa opioid receptors in human striatum. *National Institute of Drug Abuse Research Monograph* 162, 234, 1996.

113. Itzhak, Y. Differential regulation of brain opioid receptors following repeated cocaine administration to guinea pigs. *Drug and Alcohol Dependence* 3, 53, 1993.

114. Ni, Q., Xu, H., Partilla, J.S., De Costa, B.R., Rice, K.C., and Rothman, R.B. Selective labeling of κ_2 opioid receptors in rat brain by [¹²⁵I]IOXY: Interactions of opioid peptides and other drugs with multiple κ_{2a}binding sites. *Peptides* 14, 1279, 1993.

115. Ni , Q., Xu, H., Partilla, J.S., De Costa, B.R., Rice, K.C., Kayakiri, H., and Rothman, R.B. Opioid peptide receptor studies. Interaction of opioid peptides and other drugs with four subtypes of the κ_2 receptor in guinea pig brain. *Peptides* 16, 1083, 1995.

116. Hammer, R.P. Cocaine alters opiate receptor binding in critical brain reward regions. *Synapse* 3, 55, 1989.

117. Unterwald, E.M., Rubenfeld, J.M., and Kreek, M.J. Repeated cocaine administration upregulates κ and μ but not δ opioid receptors. *Neuroreport* 5, 1613, 1994.

118. Spangler, R., Ho, A., Zhou, Y., Maggos, C.E., Yuferov, V., Kreek ,M.J. Regulation of kappa opioid receptor mRNA in the rat brain by 'binge' pattern cocaine administration and correlation with preprodynorphin mRNA. *Mol. Brain Res.* 38, 71, 1996.

119. Broadbent, J., Gaspard, T.M., and Dworkin, S.I. Assessment of the discriminative stimulus effects of cocaine in the rat: lack of interaction with opioids. *Pharmacol. Biochem. and Behav.* 51, 379 1995.

120. Ukai, M., Mori, E., Kameyama, T. Effects of centrally administered neuropeptides on discriminative stimulus properties of cocaine in the rat. *Pharmacol. Biochem. and Behav.* 51: 705, 1995.

121. Spealman, R.D., and Bergman, J. Modulation of the discriminative stimulus effects of cocaine by mu and kappa opioids. *J. Pharmacol. Exp. Therap.* 261, 607, 1992.

122. Shippenberg, T.S., Herz, A., Spanagel , R., Bals-Kubik, R., and Stein, C. Conditioning of opioid reinforcement: Neuroanatomical and neurochemical substrates. *Ann. NY Acad. Sci.* 654, 347, 1992.

123. Glick, S.D., Maisonneuve, I.M., Raucci, J., and Archer, S., Kappa opioid inhibition of morphine and cocaine self-administration in rats. *Brain Res.* 681, 147, 1995.

124. Suzuki T., Shiozaki Y., Masukawa Y., Misawa M. and Nagase H. The role of mu- and kappa-opioid receptors in cocaine-induced conditioned place preference. *Japan. J. Pharmacol.* 58:435, 1992.

125. Heidbreder, C.A., Goldberg, S.R., and Shippenberg, T.S. The kappa-opioid receptor agonist U-69593 attenuates cocaine-induced behavioral sensitization in the rat. *Brain Res.* 616, 335, 1993.

126. Heidbreder, C.A., Babovic-Vuksanovic, D., Shoaib, M., and Shippenberg, T.S. Development of behavioral sensitization to cocaine: Influence of kappa opioid receptor agonists. *J. Pharmacol. Exp. Therap.* 275, 150, 1995.

127. Mello, N.K., Kamien, J.B., Lukas, S.E., Mendelson, J.H., Drieze, J.M., and Sholar, J.W. Effects of intermittent buprenorphine administration on cocaine self-administration by rhesus monkeys. *J. Pharmacol. Exp. Therap.* 264, 530, 1993.

Julie K. Staley

128. Comer, S.D., Lac, S.T., Curtis, L.K., and Carroll, M.E. Effects of buprenorphine and naltrexone on reinstatement of cocaine-reinforced responding in rats. *J. Pharmacol. Exp. Therap.* 267, 1470, 1993.

129. Kosten, T.R., Pharmacological approaches to cocaine dependence *Clinical Neuropharmacol,* 15 Suppl 70A, 1992.

130. Fudala, P.J., Johnson, R.E., Jaffe J.H. Outpatient comparison of buprenorphine and methadone maintenance. II. Effects on cocaine usage, retention time in study and missed clinical visits. In Harrison L, ed. Problems of drug dependence, *National Instutute of Mental Health Research Monograph,* 105, 587, 1991.

131. Pfeiffer, A., Brandt, V., and Herz, A. Psychotomimesis mediated by κ opiate receptors. *Science,* 233, 774, 1986.

132. Kumor, K.M., Haertzen, C.A., Johnson, R.E., Kocher, T., and Jasinski, D. Human psychopharmacology of ketocyclazocine as compared with cyclazocine, morphine and placebo. *J. Pharmacol. Exp. Therap.* 238, 960, 1986.

133. Herz, A. Implications of the multiplicity of opioid receptors for the problem of addiction. *Drug and Alcohol Dependence* 25, 125, 1990.

134. Koe, B.K., Molecular geometry of inhibitors of the uptake of catecholamines and serotonin in synaptosomal preparations of rat brain. *J. Pharmacol. Exp. Therap.* 199, 649, 1976.

135. Pitts, D.K., Marwah, J. Cocaine modulation of central monoaminergic neurotransmission. *Pharmacol. Biochem. Behav.* 26, 453, 1987.

136. Cunningham, K.A., Lakoski J.M. The interaction of cocaine with serotonin dorsal raphe neurons. Single unit extracellular recording studies. *Neuropsychopharmacology* 3, 41, 1990.

137. Cunningham, K.A., Paris, J.M., Goeders N.E.Chronic cocaine enhances serotonin autoregulation and serotonin uptake binding. *Synapse* 11, 112, 1992.

138. Reith, M.E.A., Fischette, C.T., Sertraline and cocaine-induced locomotion in mice. II. Chronic studies. *Psychopharmacology* 103, 306, 1991.

139. Reith, M.E.A., Wiener, H.L., Fischette, C.T. Sertraline and cocaine-induced locomotion in mice. I. Acute studies. *Psychopharmacology* 103, 306, 1991.

140. Aronson, S.C., Black, J.E., McDougle, C.J., Scanley, B.E., Jatlow, P., Kosten, T.R., Heninger, G.R., Price, L.H. Serotonergic mechanisms of cocaine effects in humans. *Psychopharmacol.* 119, 179, 1995.

141. Zeidonis, D.M., and Kosten, T.R. Depression as a prognostic factor for pharmacological treatment of cocaine dependence. *Psychopharmacol. Bulletin* 27, 337, 1991.

142. Parsons, L.H., Koob, G.F. and Weiss, F. Serotonin dysfunction in the nucleus accumbens of rats during withdrawal after unlimited access to intravenous cocaine. *J. Pharmacol. Exp. Therap.* 274, 1182, 1995.

143. Galloway, M.P., Regulation of dopamine and serotonin synthesis by acute administration of cocaine. *Synapse* 6, 63, 1990.

144. White, F.J., Hu, X.T., Henry D.J. Electrophysiological effects of cocaine in the rat nucleus accumbens: microiontophoretic studies. *J. Pharmacol. Exp. Ther.* 266, 1075, 1993.

145. Spealman, R.D. Modificatin of behavioral effect of cociane by selective serotonin and dopamine uptake inhibitors in squirrel monkeys. *Psychopharmacology* 112, 93, 1993.

146. Carroll, M.E., Lac, S.T., Asencio M., Kragh, R. Fluoxetine reduces intravenous cocaine self-administration in rats. *Pharmacol. Biochem. Behav.* 35, 237, 1990.

147. Peltier R., Schenk, S.Effects of serotonergic manipulations on cocaine self-administration in rats. *Psychopharmacology* 110, 390, 1993.

148. Richardson, N.R., Roberts, D.C.S. Fluoxetine pre-treatment reduced breaking points on a progressive ratio schedule reinforced by intravenous cocaine administration in the rat. *Life Sci.* 49, 833, 1991.

149. Lyness, W.H., Friedle, N.M., Moore, K.E. Increased self-administration of d-amphetamine, self administration. *Pharmacol. Biochem. Behav.* 12, 937, 1980.

150. Loh, E.A., Roberts, D.C.S. Break-points on a progressive ration schedule reinforced by intravenous cocaine increase following depletion of forebrain serotonin. *Psychopharmacology* 101, 262, 1990.

151. Walsh, S.L., Preston, K.L., Sullivan, J.T., Fromme , R., and Bigelow, G.E. Fluoxetine alters the effects of intravenous cocaine in humans. *J. Clin Psychopharmacol.* 14, 396, 1994.

152. Batki, S.L., Washburn A., Manfredi L., Murphy, L., Herbst M.D., Delucchi K., Jones T., Nanda N., Jacob, P., Jones R.T., Fluoxetine in primary and secondary cocaine dependence: outcome using quantitative benzoylecgonine concentration. *National Institute of Drug Abuse Research Monograph* 141, 140, 1994.

153. Batki, S.L., Manfredi, L.B., Jacob, P., Jones, R.T. Fluoxetine for cocaine dependence in methadone maintenance: quantitative plasma and urine cocaine/benzoylecgonine concentrations. J. Clin. Psychopharmacol. 13,243, 1993.

154. Pollack, M.H., Rosenbaum, J.F. Fluoxetine treatment of cocaine abuse in heroin addicts. *J. Clin Psychiatry,* 52, 31, 1991.

155. Satel, S. Craving for and fear of cocaine: A phenomenologic update on cocaine craving and paranoia. In Kosten T.R., Kleber, H.D., (eds) Clinician's guide to cocaine addiction. Guilford Press, New York, pp 172, 1992.

156. Satel, S.L., Krystal, J.H., Delgado, P.L., Kosten, T.R., Charney, D.S. Tryptophan depletion and attenuation of cue-induced craving for cocaine. *Am. J. Psychiatry* 152, 778, 1995.

157. Karler, R., Calder, L.D., Chaudhry, I.A., and Turkanis, S.A. Blockade of 'reverse tolerance' to cocaine and amphetamine by MK-801. *Life Sci.* 45, 599, 1989.

158. Pudiak, C.M., and Bozarth, M.A. L-NAME and MK-801 attenuate sensitization to the locomotor-stimulating effect of cocaine. *Life Sci.* 53, 1517, 1993.

159. Wolf, M.E., and Jeziorski, M. Coadministration of MK-801 with amphetamine, cocaine or morphine prevents rather than transiently masks the development of behavioral sensitization. *Brain Res.* 613, 291, 1993.

160. Witkin, J.M. Blockade of the locomotor stimulant effect so cociane and methamphetamine by glutamate antagonists. *Life Sci.* 53, PL 405, 1993.

161. Haracz, J.L., Belanger, S.A., MacDonall, J.S., and Sircar, R. Antagonists of N-methyl-D-aspartate receptors partially prevent the development of cocaine sensitization. *Life Sciences* 57, 2347, 1995.

162. Ida, I., Aami T., and Kuribara H. Inhibition of cocaine sensitization by MK-801 a noncompetitive N-methyl-D-aspartate (NMDA) receptor antagonist: evaluation by ambulatory activity in mice. *Jpn. J. Pharmacol.* 69, 83, 1995.

163. Carey, R.J., Dai, H., Krost, M., and Huston, J.P. The NMDA Receptor and cocaine: evidence that MK-801 can induce behavioral sensitization effects. *Pharmacol. Biochem. Behav.* 51, 901, 1995

164. Rockhold, R.W., Oden, G., Ho, I.K., Andrew, M., Farley, J. M. Glutamate receptor antagonists block cocaine-induced convulsions and death. *Brain Res. Bull.* 27, 721, 1991.

165. Itzhak, Y., Stein I. Sensitization to the toxic effects of cocaine in mice is associated with regulation of N-methyl-D-aspartate receptors in cortex. *J. Pharmacol. Exp. Ther.* 262, 464, 1992.

166. Shimosato, K. , Marley, R.J., and Saito, T. Differential effects of NMDA receptor and dopamine receptor antagonists on cocaine toxicities. *Pharmacol. Biochem. Behav.* 51, 781, 1995

167. White, F.J., Hu, X.T., Zhang, X.F., and Wolf, M.E. Repeated administration of cocaine or amphetamine alters neuronal responses to glutamate in the mesoaccumbens dopamine system. *J. Pharmacol. Exp. Therap.* 273, 445, 1995.

168. Itzhak, Y. Modulation of the PCP/NMDA Receptor complex and sigma binding sites by psychostimulants. *Neurotoxicology and Teratology* 16, 363, 1994.

169. Fitzgerald, L.W., Ortiz J., Hamedani A.G., and Nestler, E.J. Drugs of abuser and stress increase the expression of GluR1 and NMDAR1 glutamate receptor subunits in the rat ventral tegmental areal: Common adaptations among cross-sensitizing agents. *J. Neurosci.* 16, 274, 1996.

170. Schenk, S., Valadez, A., McNamara C., House D.T., Higley, D., Bankson M.G., Gibbs S. and Horger B.A. Development and expression of sensitization to cocaine's reinforcing properties: role of NMDA receptors. *Psychopharmacology* 111, 332, 1993.

171. Kalivas, P.W. and Alesdatter, J.E. Involvement of *N*-methyl-D-aspartate receptor stimulation in the ventral tegmental area and amygdala in behavioral sensitization to cocaine. *J. Pharmacol. Exp. Therap.* 267, 486, 1993.

172. Rothman, R.B., Gendron, T., Hitzig, P. Letter to the editor. *J. Substance Abuse Treat* 11, 273, 1994.

173. Brauer, L.H., Johanson, C.E., Schuster, S.R., Rothman, R.B., and de Wit, H. Evaluation of phentermine and fenfluramine, alone and in combination in normal healthy volunteers. *Neuropsychopharmacology* 14, 233, 1995.

174. Griffiths, R.R., Winger, G., Brady, J.V., Snell, J.D. Comparison of behavior maintained by infusions of eight phenyethylamines in baboons. *Psychopharmacology* 50, 251, 1976

175. Sanchez-Ramos, J. and Mash, D.C. Ibogaine Human Phase I Pharmacokinetic and Safety Trial. *FDA* IND 3968, 1993 (revised 1995).

176. Glick, S.D., Kuehne, M.E., Raucci, J., Wilson, T.E., Larson, D., Kellar, R.W., and Carlson, J.N. Effects of iboga alkaloids on morphine and cocaine self-administration in rats: relationship to tremorigenic effects and to effects on dopamine release in nucleus accumbens and striatum. *Brain Res.* 657, 14, 1994.

177. Sershen, H., Hashim, A., and Lajtha, A. Ibogaine reduces preference for cocaine consumption in C57BL/6By Mice. *Pharmacol. Biochem and Behav.* 47, 13, 1994.

178. Sweetnam, P.A., Lancaster, J., Snowman, A., Collins, J.L., Perschke, S., Bauer, C., Ferkany, J. Receptor binding profile suggests multiple mechanisms of action are responsible for ibogaine's putative anti-addictive activity. *Psychopharmacology* 118, 369, 1995.

179. Popik, P., Layer, R.T., Skolnik, P. The putative anti-addictive drug ibogaine is a competitive inhibitor of [^{3}H]MK-801 binding to the NMDA receptor complex. *Psychopharmacology* 114, 672, 1994.

180. Mash, D.C., Staley, J.K., Pablo, J.P., Holohean, A.M., Hackman, J.C., Davidoff, R.A. Properties of ibogaine and its principal metabolite (12-hydroxyibogamine) at the MK-801 binding site of the NMDA complex. *Neurosci. Lett.* 192, 53, 1995.

181. Mash, D.C., Staley, J.K., Baumann, M.H., Rothman, R.B., and Hearn, W.L. Identification of a primary metabolite of ibogaine that targets serotonin transporters and elevates serotonin. *Life Sci.* 57, PL45, 1995.

182. Broderick, P.A., Phelan, F.T., Eng, F., and Wechsler, R.T. Ibogaine modulates cocaine responses which are altered due to environmental habituation: *In vivo* microvoltammetric and behavioral studies. *Pharmacol. Biochem. and Behav.* 49, 711, 1994.

183. Harsing, L.G., Sershen, H., and Lajtha, A. Evidence that ibogaine releases dopamine from the cytoplasmic pool in isolated mouse striatum. *J. Neural Transm.* 96, 215, 1994.

184. Hearn, W.L., Pablo, J., Hime, G.W., and Mash, D.C. Identification and quantitation of ibogaine and an O-demethylated metabolite in brain and biological fluids using gas chromatography mass spectometry. *J. Anal. Toxic.* 19, 427,1995.

185. Pearl, S.M., Herrick-Davis, K., Teitler, M., Glick, S.D. Radioligand binding study of noribogaine, a likely metabolite of ibogaine. *Brain Res.* 675, 342, 1995.

186. Staley, J.K., Ouyang, Q., Pablo J., Hearn W.L., Flynn D.F., Rothman R.B., Rice K.C., Mash, D.C. Pharmacological screen for activities of 12-hydroxyibogamine: a primary metabolites of the indole alkaloid ibogaine. *Psychopharmacology.* 127, 10, 1996.

187. Baumann, M., personal communication.

ACKNOWLEDGMENT

This work was supported by a grant from NIDA (DA 06227). I would like to acknowledge Dr. Deborah Mash for her support and contribution to this work.

6.4 THE NEUROBIOLOGY OF RELAPSE

DAVID W. SELF

DIVISION OF MOLECULAR PSYCHIATRY, YALE UNIVERSITY SCHOOL OF MEDICINE AND CONNECTICUT MENTAL HEALTH CENTER, NEW HAVEN, CONNECTICUT

Over the past several decades, there have been tremendous advances in our understanding of the neurobiology of drug addiction. Much of this work has focused on the neurobiological mechanisms of drug reinforcement, and how brain reinforcement systems adapt to chronic drug exposure because this would inevitably improve our understanding of the underlying neuropathology of drug addiction.[1-4] More recently, studies have focused on the neurobiological mechanisms of relapse because this research targets the core motivational symptoms of compulsive drug taking and intense drug craving, and could lead to more effective treatment strategies.

6.4.1 COMPETING THEORIES

Although it is generally believed that the neurobiological substrates of drug reinforcement also are involved in relapse of drug-seeking behavior, there are two major theories that differ in their view of how these substrates contribute to relapse. One theory suggests that relapse of drug-seeking behavior is triggered by drug-like, or proponent, processes.[4-7] This idea is based on the fact that both drug reinforcement and relapse involve similar drug-seeking, or approach, behavior. Another theory suggests that drug-opposite, or opponent, processes induce relapse.[8,9] This idea originates from clinical observations of abstinent drug users who report simultaneous feelings of dysphoria and drug craving. Both theories postulate that chronic drug use produces long-term neuroadaptations in brain reinforcement systems, and these neuroadaptations contribute directly to persistent drug craving and relapse, even after prolonged abstinence (Figure 6.4.1).

One component of these neuroadaptations is thought to involve the process of classical conditioning, where environmental stimuli, through repeated and specific association with drug exposure, acquire the ability to trigger either drug- or withdrawal-like responses when presented in the absence of the drug.[10-13] Interestingly, these conditioned "cues" have been reported to trigger either mild euphoria under some circumstances, or severe dysphoria in others. In both cases, the subjects reported an intense desire to self-administer their drug of choice. Similar drug-like and withdrawal-like conditioned effects have been reported in animals.[7,10,11,14] Thus, associative learning may contribute to drug craving and relapse while producing different, even opposite, affective states. However, because drug craving is experienced during both positive and negative affective states, it is possible that the underlying neurobiological mechanisms of drug craving are different from those contributing to affective state. Alternatively, drug craving associated with positive affect could differ qualitatively from the craving associated with negative affect, and thus be mediated by separate neurobiological processes.

Another component of persistent drug craving following chronic drug use could involve the direct unconditioned effects of drugs on the neural substrates of motivation itself. This type of change can be thought of as an adaptive response, as neurons attempt to regain homeostasis in the continued or repeated presence of the drug. These adaptations are usually defined by pharmacological criteria, and classified as dependence, tolerance, or sensitization.[15] Drug

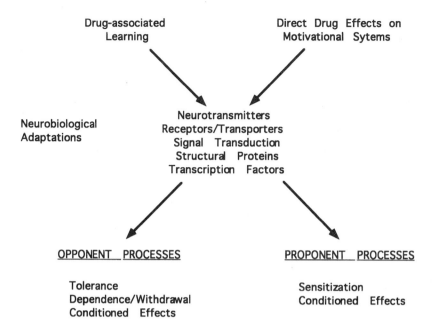

Figure 6.4.1 Both learning and pharmacological factors can contribute to neuroadaptations following chronic drug use. These neuroadaptations can be manifested as either opponent (drug-opposite) or proponent (drug-like) processes.

dependence is demonstrated by the appearance of specific "drug-opposite" or withdrawal symptoms when the drug is removed. Thus, dependence on abused drugs can result in subjective feelings of dysphoria during withdrawal from chronic drug exposure. Similar "drug-opposite" adaptations could contribute to the tolerance that develops to the drugs initial euphorigenic effects, and lead to an escalation in the amount of drug self-administered to achieve the desired effect. In contrast, sensitization or "reverse tolerance" also occurs such that the behavioral effects of drugs can be enhanced with repeated exposure, and this represents a drug-like or proponent process. Although the phenomena of dependence, tolerance, and sensitization may reflect direct, unconditioned, neuroadaptations to chronic drug exposure,[4] conditioned stimuli can alter the manifestation of these phenomena,[7,10,11,14] such that both conditioned and unconditioned factors ultimately contribute to opponent and proponent processes (Figure 6.4.1). In order to understand the relative contribution of these long-term neuroadaptations to drug craving and relapse in humans, it is important first to understand the neurochemical, pharmacological and intracellular events that trigger relapse in animal models of drug-seeking behavior (Figure 6.4.1).

6.4.2 RELAPSE IN AN ANIMAL MODEL OF DRUG-SEEKING BEHAVIOR

Drug craving and drug-seeking are subjective descriptions that cannot be directly measured in laboratory animals. However, relapse is an operational term that can be measured directly when an animal reinitiates a particular behavioral response, for example, the lever-press response associated with drug delivery. Relapse of the behavioral response, often referred to as reinstatement, is thought to reflect the induction of "drug-seeking" behavior following a period of abstinence. In the reinstatement paradigm, the period of abstinence occurs after extinction from drug self-administration, when the animal's responses are no longer reinforced by the drug injections. Once extinction is established, the ability of specific experimenter-delivered stimuli to induce responding at the "drug-paired" lever is measured. Stimuli that effectively

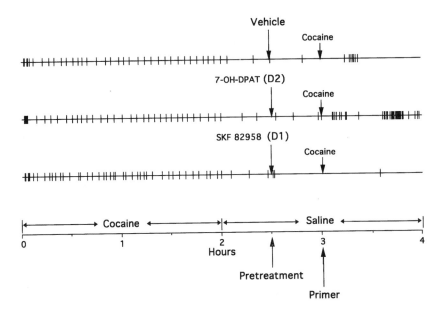

Figure 6.4.2 Effects of subcutaneous pretreatments with the D_2 like dopamine agonist 7-OH-DPAT (0.3 mg/kg), or the D_1 like agonist SKF 82958 (1.0 mg/kg) on the priming effects of intravenous cocaine injections (2.0 mg/kg) in the reinstatement paradigm. Pretreatments and priming injections were given after extinction from 2 h of intravenous cocaine self-administration, when only intravenous saline injections were available. Hatchmarks denote the times of each self-infusion of cocaine in the cocaine phase and saline in the saline phase (From Self, D.W., Barnhart, W.J., Lehman, D.A., and Nestler, E.J., *Science*, 271, 1586, 1996. With permission.)

induce such responding are called "primers" because they are thought to initiate a renewed interest in seeking the drug. Although there are other animal models of drug craving and drug-seeking behavior,[7,16] the reinstatement paradigm dissociates relapse from other behavioral phenomena such as reinforcement, extinction, and conditioned reinforcement, that may or may not reflect similar neurobiological processes. The neurobiological processes involved in relapse in the reinstatement model of drug-seeking behavior are the subject of this review. It important to reemphasize, however, that relapse of drug-associated responding is the variable measured in the laboratory, and subjective descriptions like drug-seeking is inferred from the results.

A powerful inducer of relapse in the reinstatement paradigm is a priming injection of the self-administered drug itself. Systemic priming injections of self-administered drugs can reinstate responding for opiates[17,18] and psychostimulants[19-24] (Figure 6.4.2). In addition, opiates can reinstate responding in animals trained to self-administer psychostimulants,[17, 21] and vice versa,[20] but fail to reinstate responding for barbiturates.[21] Similarly, barbiturates, benzodiazepines, and ethanol all fail to reinstate responding for psychostimulants.[19-21,25] These studies suggest that the cross-priming of opiates and psychostimulants could reflect activation of a common neural substrate by the two drugs (see Section 6.3). On the other hand, the priming produced by opiates and psychostimulants may be mediated by a separate neural substrate from that utilized by barbiturates, benzodiazepines, and ethanol. Originally, researchers suggested that a drug's ability to induce relapse was related to its interoceptive stimulus properties because drugs with similar stimulus properties as the self-administered drug generally were more effective at inducing relapse than drugs with different stimulus properties. However, as

David W. Self

discussed later in this chapter, more recent studies suggest that the stimulus properties of drugs may be unrelated to their motivational effects in animal models of relapse.[24,26,27]

A second trigger of relapse in the reinstatement paradigm is the presentation of drug-associated stimuli. Through specific association with drug self-administration, neutral stimuli acquire the ability to induce relapse when presented on their own as priming stimuli. In animals, reports of cue-induced relapse of drug-seeking behavior are sparse,[20, 28] but reports of cue-induced drug craving in humans are numerous (see Section 6.1). Moreover, in animals, the priming induced by drug-associated stimuli is relatively weak when compared to the priming induced by the self-administered drug.[20]

Recently, Shaham and Stewart[29,30] found that a brief presentation of intermittent footshock stress induced a robust and prolonged reinstatement of heroin-seeking behavior in rats with prior heroin self-administration experience. This stressor was an effective primer in both opiate-dependent and non-opiate-dependent rats, and was capable of inducing relapse even after six weeks of withdrawal from heroin. The authors noted that the priming effect of stress was greater than the priming effect of heroin itself, and was equally effective at inducing relapse whether heroin levels were maintained, or during a state of withdrawal from heroin.

It is clear from these studies that presently the only known triggers of relapse in animal models of drug-seeking behavior are drug-associated stimuli (cues), stress, and priming injections of the drugs themselves. Although all of these stimuli can induce relapse, they have quite different effects on other aspects of animal behavior. For example, while both drugs of abuse[6] and drug-associated stimuli[31,32] are capable of stimulating locomotor activity, footshock stress is generally followed by immobility rather than locomotor activity.[33,34] In addition, the interoceptive stimulus properties of heroin are inhibited, rather than mimicked, by either stress or the stress-induced hormone corticosterone.[26] Thus, the similar ability of drugs, stress, and drug-associated stimuli to induce relapse may not be explained by commonalities in their locomotor or their interoceptive stimulus properties, which evidently are quite different. In this regard, recent studies suggest that the motivational and stimulus properties of opiates are mediated by separate neural substrates.[26,27]

6.4.3 NEUROCHEMICAL SUBSTRATES OF RELAPSE

Previous studies have established a role for the mesolimbic dopamine system in the priming effects of opiate and psychostimulant drugs on relapse of drug-seeking behavior. This system, consisting of dopaminergic neurons in the ventral tegmental area (VTA) and their target neurons in the nucleus accumbens (NAc), is also a major neural substrate of drug reinforcement.[1,6,35] Early studies found that microinfusion of amphetamine directly into the NAc, where it causes local dopamine release within the NAc, effectively reinstates heroin-seeking behavior.[36] Similarly, application of morphine directly into the VTA, where it activates dopamine neurons via disinhibition,[37] and subsequently increases dopamine release in the NAc,[38] can reinstate both heroin- and cocaine-seeking behavior.[5] Injections of morphine into other brain regions rich in opiate receptors are ineffective. Further evidence for dopamine involvement in relapse is the fact that several directly acting dopaminergic agonists are powerful inducers of both cocaine- and heroin-seeking behavior.[17,20,24,39] Conversely, dopamine antagonists can block the priming effects of heroin,[40] amphetamine,[41] and cocaine.[42] Taken together, these studies suggest that drug-induced dopamine release in the NAc is both necessary and sufficient for opiate and psychostimulant drugs to induce relapse of drug-seeking behavior (Figure 6.4.3).

Dopamine also may be involved in the priming effects of stress because stress-induced elevations in dopamine levels in the NAc correlate temporally with reinstatement of heroin-seeking behavior.[29] Moreover, stress-induced relapse of heroin seeking behavior can be attenuated by pretreatment with dopamine antagonists.[40] Interestingly, footshock stress increases

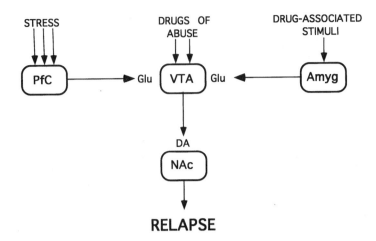

Figure 6.4.3 Diagrammatic representation of the primary pathways through which stress, drugs of abuse, and drug-associated stimuli can access mesolimbic dopamine neurons. Stress and drug-associated stimuli can activate glutamate (Glu) projections to the ventral tegmental area (VTA) from the prefrontal cortex (PfC) and amygdala (Amyg), respectively, while drugs of abuse stimulate dopamine (DA) release from VTA dopamine neurons projecting to the nucleus accumbens (NAc). Dopamine release in the NAc may be a final common neurochemical event that triggers relapse by all three stimuli. The number of arrows indicate the relative ability of each stimulus to induce relapse in animal models of drug-seeking behavior.

dopamine levels in the NAc to a lesser extent than systemic priming injections of heroin, despite the greater level of reinstatement induced by the stressor.[30] The authors suggested that stress-induced relapse may involve other neurochemical substrates in addition to dopamine.

The primary anatomical pathway through which stress can simulate dopamine release in the NAc may involve an excitatory projection from the medial prefrontal cortex (PfC) to the VTA (Figure 6.4.3). This projection contains excitatory amino acids[43-45] and forms monosynaptic inputs to dopaminergic neurons in the VTA.[46] Stress is known to increase levels of excitatory amino acids in the PfC,[47] which can activate the glutamate neurons projection to the VTA, and subsequently stimulate VTA neurons to release dopamine in the NAc.[48] Although the PfC also sends excitatory projections to the NAc[44,49-51] that could facilitate dopamine release from nerve terminals, recent studies have found that PfC regulation of NAc dopamine levels is mediated primarily via activation of glutamate receptors on dopamine neurons in the VTA, and not on the terminals in the NAc.[48,52-54] However, excitatory projections to the NAc from the PfC or hippocampus also may be activated in response to stress,[47] and these projections form synapses with post-synaptic neurons in the NAc.[46,49-51,55] Thus, stress-induced glutamatergic and dopaminergic signals could converge onto post-synaptic NAc neurons,[46] and both of these neurochemical signals could contribute to the acute priming effects of stress (Figure 6.4.4).

As stated in Sections 6.4.1 and 6.4.2, drug-associated stimuli can act as cues that trigger drug craving and relapse following repeated pairing with drugs of abuse. At present, the hypothesis that dopamine mediates the priming effects of drug-associated stimuli is equivocal because several studies have found that the conditioned locomotor effects of cocaine are not associated with an increase in dopamine release in the NAc.[32,56] However, conditioned dopamine release has been demonstrated with stimuli associated with footshock stress.[57,58] The failure to find conditioned dopamine release in the NAc with drug-associated stimuli may reflect the limited ability of *in vivo* microdialysis to detect phasic fluctuations in the synaptic levels of dopamine; a recent study using *in vivo* voltammetry has detected increases in dopamine signals

Figure 6.4.4 Schematic illustration of the differential localization of D_1, D_2, and D_3 dopamine receptor subtypes on pre- and post-synaptic elements within the nucleus accumbens (NAc). Certain D_1, D_2 and D_3 receptors are located on GABAergic NAc neurons with distinct neuropeptide content (DYN, dynorphin; SP, substance P, NT, neurotensin), that project to separate brain regions (VTA, ventral tegmental area; VP, ventral pallidum). These dopamine receptor subtypes also are differentially located on presynaptic glutamatergic (glu) afferents from limbic brain regions (PfC, prefrontal cortex; Hipp, hippocampus, Amyg, amygdala), and on dopaminergic (DA) afferents from the VTA. Differential localization of dopamine receptor subtypes may underlie their opposite effects on relapse of cocaine-seeking behavior (see text).

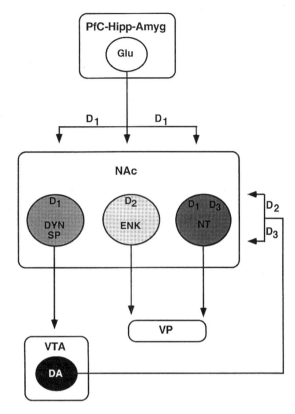

following presentation of either cocaine- or amphetamine-associated cues.[59] In addition, others have found that dopamine neurons in the VTA are activated by stimuli associated with appetitive rewards.[60,61] Although this topic remains controversial, the question of dopamine involvement in conditioned drug effects is crucial to our understanding of how drug-associated cues access motivational systems and induce relapse.

In contrast, a role for the amygdala in the priming effects of drug-associated stimuli has been demonstrated. Meil and See[28] recently found that excitatory amino acid lesions of the basolateral nucleus of the amygdala attenuate the ability of cocaine-associated stimuli to reinstate cocaine-seeking behavior. These amygdala lesions were effective, even when the amygdala was lesioned after the conditioning phase, indicating that the amygdala is involved in the neural circuitry through which cocaine-associated stimuli access and activate motivational systems. In this regard, it is interesting that similar lesions of the amygdala block the conditioned motivational, but not the conditioned locomotor, effects of cocaine.[62] Thus, the motivational and locomotor components of conditioned drug effects may be mediated by separate neural substrates.

Figure 6.4.3 illustrates a direct pathway whereby drug-associated stimuli could access the mesolimbic dopamine system leading to relapse of drug-seeking behavior. Although speculative, glutamatergic projection from the central nucleus of the amygdala to the VTA[63,64] represents the primary excitatory input to the VTA that is activated by drug-associated stimuli. The descending outputs of the amygdala are thought to be excited by sensory information from conditioned stimuli that is received and processed through the lateral and basolateral nuclei, and then transmitted to the central nucleus.[65] Electrical stimulation of the basolateral and central nucleus of the amygdala can excite VTA neurons through both mono- and poly-synaptic pathways,[66] presumably leading to increased dopamine levels in the NAc. Although the basolateral nucleus of the amygdala also projects to the NAC[50,51,67,68] and could modulate dopamine release from nerve terminals, this projection apparently makes synaptic contacts on NAc perikarya, rather than on dopamine terminals.[68] Furthermore, stimulation of this projection opposes, rather than enhances, the actions of dopamine on these post-synaptic neurons.[69]

Therefore, it is unlikely that the excitatory projection to the NAc from the basolateral nucleus of the amygdala has a direct effect on dopamine release in this brain region. However, amygdala projections to other brain regions such as the PfC[70] could form secondary pathways through which drug-associated stimuli activate VTA dopamine neurons.

The model illustrated by Figure 6.4.3 suggests that stress, drugs of abuse, and drug-associated stimuli all induce relapse, at least partially, by their ability to stimulate dopamine release in the NAc. At present, this hypothesis is supported mainly by data from drug- and stress-induced reinstatement studies, where dopaminergic involvement is well established. Thus, both drug- and stress-induced relapse of drug-seeking behavior is associated with increased dopamine release in the NAc, and the priming effects of either stimuli can be attenuated, at least partially, by dopamine antagonists. Furthermore, priming injections of dopamine receptor agonists can induce relapse whether injected systemically or directly into the NAc. This figure also illustrates that the ability of the stress pathway to induce relapse is relatively greater than either the pathway utilized by drug-associated stimuli, or the direct effect of drugs on the VTA-NAc pathway itself. It should be noted, however, that stress-induced relapse may involve a dopamine-independent component[30] and the anatomical and neuro-chemical substrates of this component have not been identified. One possibility is that excitatory inputs to NAc neurons from the medial PfC, hippocampus, and the basolateral nucleus of the amygdala, also contribute to relapse through a post-synaptic interaction with dopamine (see Figure 6.4.4).

It is evident from these studies that drug-like, or proponent, neurochemical processes are powerful inducers of relapse in animal models of drug-seeking behavior. In contrast, several studies have found that drug-opposite, or opponent, processes fail to induce relapse in these animal models. For example, while priming injections of opiate agonists can induce relapse of heroin-seeking behavior, priming injections of opiate antagonists fail to induce relapse, and actually suppress responding below control levels in non-opiate-dependent animals.[71] Even in opiate-dependent animals, antagonist-precipitated withdrawal does not induce relapse of heroin-seeking behavior, despite reduced levels of dopamine in the NAc.[30] Similarly, blockade of dopamine receptors with antagonists is ineffective at reinstating heroin- or cocaine-seeking behavior.[40,42] Thus, data from animal studies contrast sharply with reports in humans (see Section 6.4.1), where drug-craving has been associated with drug-opposite symptoms like dysphoria, especially in opiate addicts and alcoholics.[72] However, these animal studies are in agreement with reports of drug-like and even mood elevating symptoms of craving in cocaine addicts.[72, 73]

In contrast to antagonist-precipitated withdrawal, Shaham et al.[30] reported that spontane-ous withdrawal in opiate-dependent animals led to reinstatement of heroin-seeking behavior, without detectable changes in NAc dopamine levels. The authors attributed this drug-seeking behavior to extinction-like responding because the opiate-dependent animals had never expe-rienced extinction conditions while in the drug-free state. Nonetheless, this finding may be relevant to other factors involved in maintaining drug use in active drug abusers. In this sense, falling levels of opiate during spontaneous withdrawal is an example of an opponent process that could play a prominent role in continued drug use on a day to day basis. Conversely, proponent processes may be more important in triggering relapse after longer periods of abstinence, when withdrawal symptoms have dissipated.

6.4.4 NEUROPHARMACOLOGICAL SUBSTRATES OF RELAPSE

The studies described in the preceding sections suggest that dopamine acts on post-synaptic neurons within the NAc to induce relapse of drug-seeking behavior. Dopamine acts at two general classes of receptors that are distinguishable by their structural homology,[74] and opposite modulation of adenylate cyclase activity.[75,76] The D_1-like family of receptors (D_1 and

D_5) are positively coupled to adenylate cyclase activity, while the D_2-like family (D_2, D_3 and D_4) are either negatively coupled or have no effect on adenylate cyclase activity. Neurons intrinsic to the NAc express members of both D_1-like and D_2-like families of dopamine receptors.[77-80] Functionally, these receptors usually are reported to mediate similar and synergistic responses at both physiological[81] and behavioral[82] levels.

In contrast to these cooperative actions, we recently reported that systemic priming injections of D_2, and not D_1, dopamine receptor agonists induce a profound and prolonged reinstatement of cocaine-seeking behavior in rats.[24] This finding suggests that D_2 dopamine receptors are primarily involved in mediating the priming effects of dopamine in the NAc. Furthermore, the dose range for effective priming by one of the D_2 agonists corresponds to its dose range for *in vivo* occupancy of D_2 receptors,[83] although involvement of D_3 (D_2-like) receptors cannot be excluded. D_1 dopamine receptors lack the capacity to markedly induce cocaine-seeking behavior, but they may play a permissive role in the priming effects mediated by D_2 receptors. This is suggested by the finding that both D_1- and D_2 receptor antagonists can block the priming effects of cocaine[42] and heroin,[40] and is in agreement with previous studies suggesting that D_1 receptors have a permissive effect on the expression of D_2-mediated behaviors.[81,82] Further support for this idea is the finding that relatively high doses of D_1 antagonists are required to attenuate the priming effects of cocaine and heroin compared to other drug-related behaviors. Thus, transmission of D_2-mediated priming signals may require some minimal level of D_1 receptor activation.

More importantly, D_1 and D_2 dopamine receptor agonists have opposing modulatory effects on the priming induced by cocaine[24] (Figure 6.4.2). Thus, pretreatment with D_1 agonists completely suppresses the priming effects of cocaine, whereas pretreatment with D_2 agonists enhances cocaine's priming ability. These findings suggest that while D_2 receptors mediate the incentive to seek further cocaine reinforcement, D_1 receptors may mediate some aspect of drive reduction or satiety. The opposite effects of D_1 and D_2 dopamine receptor agonists on relapse of cocaine-seeking behavior are dissociated from their similar locomotor activating properties,[24] and their similar cocaine-like stimulus properties,[84-86] suggesting that the motivational properties of these drugs are mediated by neural processes distinct from either the locomotor or stimulus properties.

It is also noteworthy that both D_1 and D_2 receptor agonists have reinforcing properties because they are self-administered by animals.[87-91] Taken together, the finding that both D_1 and D_2 dopamine receptors are capable of mediating reinforcing signals, despite their opposing effects on relapse, suggests that the motivational effects of D_1 and D_2 agonists also probably involve separate neural processes. This possibility is supported by a recent study which found that D_1 receptor-mediated reinforcement is reduced by D_1, and not D_2, dopamine receptor antagonists.[92]

Such distinct motivational properties of D_1 and D_2 dopamine receptor agonists could be explained by the differential localization of D_1 and D_2 receptors within the NAc, where dopamine is known both to induce relapse and to mediate reinforcing signals.[4] Figure 6.4.4 illustrates the differential localization of D_1, D_2, and D_3 dopamine receptors on pre- and post-synaptic elements within the NAc. Postsynaptically, there are several reports that D_1, D_2, and D_3 dopamine receptor subtypes exist, at least partially, on separate subpopulations of GABAergic output neurons of the NAc with distinct neuropeptide contents.[77-80] Paralleling the anatomical organization found in the caudate-putamen,[93-95] these distinct subpopulations of GABAergic neurons co-express either enkephalin along with the D_2 receptor subtype, or dynorphin along with the D_1 receptor subtype. Moreover, these subpopulations project to different brain regions, with enkephalin/D_2 containing neurons projecting to the ventral pallidum, and dynorphin/D_1 containing neurons forming a reciprocal projection to the VTA. Another distinct subpopulation of neurons also projects to the ventral pallidum and expresses neurotensin along with both D_1 and D_3, but not D_2, dopamine receptor subtypes. Although a substantial population of NAc neurons co-express both D_1 and D_2 receptor subtypes, these receptors apparently interact in a synergistic rather than opposing manner to regulate neuronal activity,[96] and thus probably are not involved in mediating opposite modulation of cocaine-seeking behavior.

D_1 and D_2 dopamine receptors in the NAc also are differentially localized at the presynaptic level, and exist on neurochemically distinct nerve terminals from other brain regions (Figure 6.4.4). Excitatory inputs originating in the PfC, hippocampus, and amygdala are inhibited by dopamine,[69,97,98] an effect thought to be mediated by presynaptic D_1 receptors in the NAc.[97,98] These presynaptic D_1 receptors could inhibit excitatory neurotransmission related to stress and drug-associated stimuli, and thus represent a possible mechanism whereby D_1 agonists attenuate relapse of cocaine-seeking behavior. In contrast to excitatory inputs, dopaminergic terminals in the NAc express both D_2 and D_3 autoreceptors[79,99,100] which inhibit dopamine release.[101,102] However, it is unlikely that autoreceptor-mediated inhibition of dopamine release underlies the priming effects of D_2 agonists because dopamine antagonists (D_1 or D_2) fail to mimic this response,[42] and relapse is associated with increased, rather than decreased, dopamine levels in the NAc.

It also is possible that D_1 and D_2 dopamine receptors in other brain regions contribute to their opposing modulatory effects on relapse of cocaine-seeking behavior. For example, activation of D_1 receptors in the PfC and VTA attenuates dopaminergic neurotransmission in the NAc,[103-105] an effect that could underlie D_1-mediated attenuation of cocaine-seeking behavior. However, the blockade of cocaine priming by D_1 agonists was associated with the induction of horizontal locomotor activity, which is indicative of increased, rather than decreased, dopaminergic neurotransmission in the NAc. Nonetheless, because the neural circuits regulating unconditioned behaviors such as dopamine-stimulated locomotion may respond differently from those regulating conditioned behaviors like relapse of drug-seeking, involvement of dopamine receptors in other brain regions is entirely possible and requires further study.

In addition to dopaminergic agonists, the psychostimulant caffeine also can induce relapse of cocaine-seeking behavior, as well as enhance the priming effects of cocaine.[22,24] Caffeine's psychostimulant effects are mediated by an antagonist action at striatal A_2 adenosine receptors.[106] Interestingly, striatal A_2 adenosine and D_2 dopamine receptors are known to interact such that blockade of A_2 adenosine receptors by A_2 antagonists enhances the affinity of D_2 dopamine receptors for dopamine.[106] This post-synaptic interaction could explain the enhancement of cocaine-priming following pretreatment with caffeine because blockade of A_2 receptors by caffeine could increase the priming signal mediated by D_2 receptors following a cocaine injection.

6.4.5 INTRACELLULAR SUBSTRATES OF RELAPSE

Although many of the behavioral and physiological responses of D_1 and D_2 receptors in the NAc are similar,[81,82] the two receptors have different effects on certain signal transduction pathways.[107] Thus, D_1 and D_2 receptors have opposite effects on adenylate cyclase activity, and phosphatidylinositol turnover[74] that could underlie their opposing effects on relapse of drug-seeking behavior.

In view of this, we recently found that experimental modulation of the cyclic AMP system in the NAc has profound effects on relapse of cocaine-seeking behavior in rats[108] (Figure 6.4.5.1). In this study, the membrane-permeable cyclic AMP analogues, Rp- and Sp-cAMPS, were infused bilaterally into the NAc of rats in a reinstatement paradigm. Rp-cAMPS acts as a selective inhibitor of the cyclic AMP system by preventing endogenous cyclic AMP from activating the cyclic AMP-dependent protein kinase (PKA). Infusions of Rp-cAMPS into the NAc dose-dependently induced relapse of cocaine-seeking behavior, as indicated by selective

David W. Self

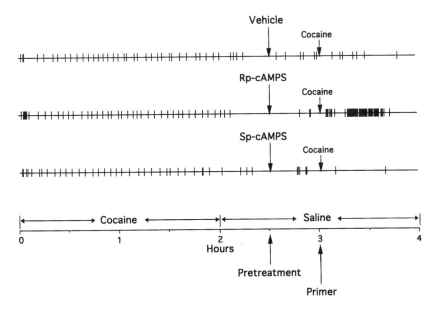

Figure 6.4.5.1 Effects of pretreatment with intra-NAc infusions of the PKA inhibitor Rp-cAMPS or the PKA activator Sp-cAMPS (both at 40 nmol/1 µl/side) on the priming effects of intravenous cocaine injections (2.0 mg/kg) in the reinstatement paradigm. Pretreatments and priming injections were given after extinction from 2 h of intravenous cocaine self-administration, when only intravenous saline injections were available. Hatchmarks denote the times of each self-infusion of cocaine in the cocaine phase and saline in the saline phase.

responding at a drug-paired lever. Similarly, pretreatment of the NAc with a subthreshold dose of the kinase inhibitor enhanced the priming effects of intravenous cocaine injections. Because D_2 dopamine receptors also can inhibit the cyclic AMP pathway by inhibiting cyclic AMP formation, it is possible that relapse of cocaine-seeking behavior induced by D_2 agonists and by cocaine is mediated by a similar inhibition of the cyclic AMP pathway in NAc neurons containing D_2 neurons.

In contrast, Sp-cAMPS activates the cyclic AMP pathway by mimicking the effects of endogenous cyclic AMP on PKA. Intra-NAc infusions of Sp-cAMPS reduced the priming effects of a high intravenous dose of cocaine on relapse of cocaine-seeking behavior.[108] Attenuation of cocaine priming by the PKA activator could involve a direct reversal of priming signals generated by D_2 receptor-mediated inhibition of the cyclic AMP pathway. A similar mechanism of action could underlie attenuation of cocaine priming by D_1 agonists, which stimulate PKA activity through D_1 stimulated cyclic AMP formation. However, when given alone, the PKA activator Sp-cAMPS produced a different effect. It induced responding at both a drug-paired and an inactive lever. The lack of selective responding suggests that the animals' ability to discriminate the drug-paired from the inactive lever was impaired. The mechanism for this latter effect is unclear, but possibly involves pre- rather than post-synaptic actions of the PKA activator. For example, activation of the cAMP pathway in pre-synaptic nerve terminals stimulates the release of both dopamine[109] and glutamate.[110] Dopamine release in the NAc stimulated by Sp-cAMPS could underlie the priming effects of the PKA activator when given alone. The impaired ability of animals to accurately select the drug-paired lever over the inactive lever may reflect a generalized glutamate-releasing effect of Sp-cAMPS, such that the flow of information from limbic afferents is masked. If so, the fact that D_1 agonists, which also stimulate PKA activity, fail to mimic these latter effects may suggest that either (1) Sp-cAMPS

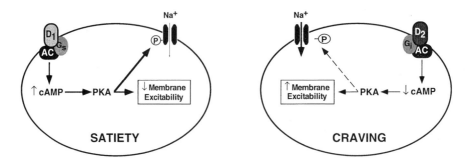

Figure 6.4.5.2 Hypothetical intracellular model of drug craving and satiety in nucleus accumbens neurons. In this model, D_1 and D_2 dopamine receptors mediate opposing effects on drug craving and satiety through opposite modulation of stimulatory (G_s) and inhibitory (G_i) G proteins, and adenylate cyclase (AC) activity, cyclic AMP (cAMP) formation, and cAMP-dependent protein kinase (PKA) activity. PKA-mediated Na^+ channel phosphorylation (P) is one possible mechanism whereby D_1 and D_2 receptors could produce opposing modulation of neuronal function in NAc neurons.

is acting on neurons that do not contain D_1 receptors, or (2) D_1 receptor responses in the NAc utilize other signal transduction pathways.

Figure 6.4.5.2 illustrates the possible role of D_1 and D_2 receptors, and the cyclic AMP pathway in NAc neurons in drug craving and relapse. In this model, drug craving and relapse are triggered by dopaminergic activation of D_2 receptors on NAc neurons. D_2 receptors inhibit adenylate cyclase activity by coupling inhibitory G proteins, leading to decreased levels of cyclic AMP. Reduced cyclic AMP levels, in turn, reduce the activity of PKA which otherwise would phosphorylate specific substrate proteins. One such protein is the voltage-gated neuronal sodium channel which are inactivated following repeated exposure to cocaine.[156] It is possible that these sodium channels are reactivated following acute inhibition of PKA activity,[111-113] and this event contributes to relapse of cocaine-seeking behavior. Therefore, D_2 dopamine receptor activation ultimately could increase the excitability of D_2-containing neurons within the NAc, an effect hypothesized to contribute to drug craving and relapse (see Figure 6.4.5.2)

Conversely, D_1 dopamine receptors could oppose these D_2-mediated priming signals by activating the cyclic AMP pathway via G proteins that stimulate adenylate cyclase. Thus, D_1 dopamine receptors are known to modulate neuronal sodium channels via PKA-dependent phosphorylation.[111,112] PKA-mediated phosphorylation of neuronal sodium channels raises their threshold for activation, thereby reducing membrane excitability. Reduced excitability in neurons expressing D_1 receptors is one possible mechanism to explain the attenuation of cocaine priming produced by D_1 agonists. Moreover, while D_1 and D_2 receptors could interact in the same neurons to produce opposite modulation of cyclic AMP levels and ultimately membrane excitability, they also could produce these opposite effects in separate populations of NAc output neurons as discussed earlier (Figure 6.4.4). Of course, there are several other intracellular substrates of PKA that could mediate the opposite actions of D_1 and D_2 receptors on NAc neurons and relapse. For example, PKA can regulate the activity of glutamate receptors[114-116] and gap junctions,[117-119] and both D_1 and D_2 dopamine receptors are reported to exert opposite effects on these PKA substrates in striatal neurons.[117,118,120]

Although speculative, priming signals generated by D_2 receptor-mediated inhibition of PKA activity in NAc neurons could enhance neurotransmission associated with non-dopaminergic priming signals. For example, the impact of excitatory signals from limbic afferents on NAc neurons in response to stress or drug-associated stimuli (see Section 6.4.3) would be enhanced if these neurons were "primed" by a reduction in intracellular PKA activity. Conversely, D_1 receptor-mediated activation of PKA activity in NAc neurons could attenuate these excitatory signals by decreasing membrane excitability. Indeed, both dopamine and cyclic AMP have been shown to attenuate excitatory responses on NAc neurons from hippocampal afferents,[121] an effect that may involve inhibition of sodium[111, 112] or calcium[122] channels. Thus, D_1 and D_2 receptors would act to "gate" excitatory neurotransmission in the NAc, through their opposing effects on PKA activity.

6.4.6 ADAPTATIONS IN THE MESOLIMBIC DOPAMINE SYSTEM IN RESPONSE TO CHRONIC DRUG EXPOSURE: IMPLICATIONS FOR DRUG CRAVING AND RELAPSE

Chronic exposure to drugs as varied as psychostimulants, opiates, and ethanol produces highly specific neuroadaptations in both pre- and post-synaptic neurons in the mesolimbic dopamine system.[4,123-126] These adaptations are manifested by changes in the level of specific cellular proteins such as receptors, transporters, signal transduction proteins, and structural proteins that ultimately regulate neuronal morphology and excitability. Changes in the levels of these proteins are mediated by changes in the transcriptional activity of specific genes, or by changes in their rate of degradation, in response to chronic or repeated administration of abused drugs.[124] Neurobiological adaptations in the mesolimbic dopamine system are hypothesized to underlie certain aspects of dependence, tolerance, and sensitization,[4,123] and thereby contribute to both opponent and proponent processes.

Figure 6.4.1 also illustrates that neurobiological adaptations to drugs can involve both associative learning, and the direct pharmacological actions of drugs on neurons. Many neuroadaptations in the mesolimbic dopamine system probably involve direct drug effects on VTA and NAc neurons because they occur to a similar extent whether animals learn to self-administer drugs, or if they receive drugs by passive infusions.[127] However, these direct neuroadaptations in the mesolimbic dopamine system could contribute to relapse by enhancing the ability of priming stimuli to modulate dopamine release and neuronal responses to dopamine in the NAc.

6.4.6.1 Adaptations in Dopamine Neurons

Several previous studies have found that repeated exposure to opiate and psychostimulants can result in bimodal changes in the activity of dopamine neurons and, consequently, the release of dopamine in the NAc.[4,126] Withdrawal from psychostimulants, opiates, and ethanol is generally associated with reduced activity of dopamine neurons and reduced levels of dopamine in the NAc, an effect that persists for about one week.[128-134] Withdrawal-induced decreases in basal dopamine levels in the NAc are thought to mediate feelings of dysphoria during this early withdrawal stage.

In contrast to the effect on basal dopamine release in the NAc, repeated exposure to opiate and psychostimulants enhances the ability of the drug to stimulate dopamine release.[135,136] This effect may involve an up-regulation in glutamate receptors on dopamine perikarya in the VTA,[137,138] leading to enhanced excitation of dopamine neurons.[139] Similarly, repeated cocaine administration leads to a persistent decrease in the level of dopamine transporters on dopamine nerve terminals in the NAc;[140,141] reduced dopamine uptake in the NAc could contribute to enhanced drug-induced dopamine release by prolonging the synaptic action of dopamine in the NAc. The effect of increased glutamate receptors on dopamine perikarya and decreased transporters on dopamine terminals arguably would enhance the priming signals generated by drugs of abuse that directly stimulate dopamine release, and the priming signals generated by stress or drug-associated stimuli, which indirectly activate dopamine neurons via excitatory limbic projections to the VTA (Figure 6.4.3). Therefore, long-term drug exposure could

Figure 6.4.6.1 Hypothetical illustration of the interaction between opponent and proponent processes in drug craving and relapse. In this model, tonic opponent processes such as decreased dopamine levels (A), and up-regulated PKA activity (B) in the nucleus accumbens (NAc) emerge during addiction and withdrawal to modify the baseline from which phasic proponent processes (arrows) are triggered prior to relapse. The modified baseline enhances the relative strength of the priming stimulus as reflected by a greater increase in dopamine release (A), or a greater decrease in PKA activity mediated by D_2 dopamine receptors (B), in the NAc.

A.

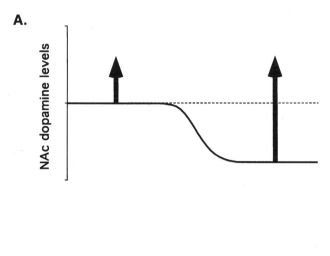

enhance dopamine-related priming signals in addicted subjects and increase the probability of relapse during withdrawal.

Chronic drug exposure can produce, simultaneously, both opponent and proponent adaptations in dopamine neurons. Withdrawal-induced decreases in dopamine cell activity and dopamine release in the NAc reflect a tonic change in the basal activity of the dopamine system. In contrast, enhancement of dopamine release in response to

B.

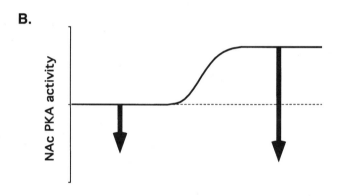

drug challenge reflects increased sensitivity of the dopamine system to phasic stimulation. It is possible that these opponent and proponent processes actually interact in a synergistic rather than antagonistic manner. For example, the relative magnitude of cocaine-induced dopamine release in the NAc is augmented when basal levels of dopamine are low.[142] Thus, it is possible that lower basal levels of dopamine during drug withdrawal could lead to relatively larger changes in dopamine levels following drug challenge. A similar enhancement of phasic dopamine signals could occur in response to stress, or drug-related stimuli, all of which trigger relapse of drug-seeking behavior. This idea is illustrated in Figure 6.4.6.1A, where the relative magnitude of the dopamine-releasing stimulus is enhanced during drug-withdrawal when basal dopamine levels are low, even though the absolute level of stimulated dopamine release may not change or is increased.[142-144] Hence, the ability of dopamine-releasing priming stimuli to induce relapse of drug-seeking behavior may be greater during withdrawal from long term drug use than at earlier stages of the addiction process. In other words, by changing the baseline, an opponent process may enhance the signal strength of a proponent process.

David W. Self

6.4.6.2 Adaptations in Nucleus Accumbens Neurons

Chronic and repeated drug exposure produces numerous post-synaptic adaptations in NAc neurons that also could contribute to drug craving and relapse. Although reports of drug-induced adaptations in the level of dopamine receptors in the NAc have been inconsistent, there have been several reports of changes in the responsiveness of NAc neurons following chronic drug exposure.[4,123] Specifically, chronic exposure to opiate and psychostimulant produces supersensitive D_1-receptor mediated responses in both cyclic AMP formation[136] and electrophysiological responses,[145] and these supersensitive responses persist for one month following withdrawal. D_1 receptor supersensitivity is thought to contribute to sensitized behavioral responses to drugs of abuse in drug-treated animals.

The mechanism for this D_1 receptor supersensitivity probably involves post-receptor adaptations in D_1 receptor signaling pathways in the Nac because chronic exposure to opiates, psychostimulants, and ethanol all produce[4, 123] a generalized up-regulation in the NAc cyclic AMP system. This up-regulation is characterized by decreased levels of inhibitory G proteins that inhibit cyclic AMP formation,[127,146-148] and increased levels of the cyclic AMP synthesizing enzyme adenylate cyclase and the cyclic AMP-dependent protein kinase, PKA.[127,136,147,149] An up-regulation in the NAc cyclic AMP system may represent a homeostatic compensation for reduced basal dopamine levels during drug withdrawal because lesions of striatal dopamine systems produce a similar up-regulation in D_1-stimulated cyclic AMP formation, without detectable changes in the level of D_1 receptors.[150-152]

Although D_1 receptor supersensitivity may contribute to the sensitized locomotor stimulant effects of drugs, it is unlikely that enhanced D_1 responses trigger relapse of drug-seeking behavior because D_1 agonists suppress, rather than induce, relapse of cocaine-seeking behavior.[24] Similarly, cyclic AMP analogues that inhibit, not activate, the NAc cyclic AMP system induce relapse of cocaine-seeking behavior.[108] However, it is possible that chronic up-regulation of the cyclic AMP system in the NAc could have different, even opposite, effects on behavior than acute activation of the same system. For example, tonic increases in basal cyclic AMP activity may enhance the relative strength of priming stimuli, which acutely inhibit cyclic AMP formation via dopamine actions at D_2 receptors (Figure 6.4.6.1B). This effect has been demonstrated *in vitro*, where direct activation of adenylate cyclase dramatically augments the inhibitory signals produced by D_2 receptor activation.[153] Thus, opponent and proponent processes also may interact at the post-synaptic, intracellular level in NAc neurons to augment the priming effects of D_2 receptor activation on relapse of cocaine-seeking behavior.

6.4.7 CONCLUSIONS

There have been relatively few studies on the neurobiology of relapse, but the current focus on this phenomena will undoubtedly reveal new and interesting findings. Presently, it is known that drug-like proponent processes can trigger relapse of drug-seeking behavior in animals. This effect is mediated, at least in part, by activation of mesolimbic dopamine neurons. Thus, the priming effects of drugs and stress on relapse probably involve increases in dopamine levels in the NAc. The role of dopamine in the priming effects of drug-associated stimuli is equivocal, and more studies are needed to address this important question. The priming signals generated by dopamine are mediated by D_2 dopamine receptors, and may involve inhibition of PKA activity in NAc neurons. In contrast, selective dopamine activation of D_1 receptors attenuates cocaine's ability to induce relapse, an effect that may involve satiation of the reward system.

A difficult and unresolved question is the role that opponent processes play in relapse. Clearly, acute withdrawal precipitated by opiate or dopamine antagonists does not stimulate relapse in animal models, despite the aversive consequences of these antagonist treatments.[154,155] However, other opponent processes that occur during spontaneous withdrawal may contribute to relapse associated with daily drug use. Proponent processes may play a more prominent role in triggering relapse after prolonged abstinence, when opponent processes have normalized. Finally, the neuroadaptations that underlie opponent processes are hypothesized to interact synergistically with proponent processes, and enhance the priming signals generated drugs, stress, and drug-associated stimuli. According to this idea, the tonic effects of opponent processes on the mesolimbic dopamine system would enhance the phasic effects of proponent processes produced by presentation of priming stimuli. Further studies on the neurobiology of relapse promise to yield important findings crucial to our understanding of motivation, and to our ability to discover effective treatments for drug abuse.

ACKNOWLEDGMENTS

This work was supported by USPHS grants DA 08227, DA 00223, DA 05603, by the Abraham Ribicoff Research facilities of the Connecticut Mental Health Center. I would like to acknowledge Dr. Eric J. Nestler for his support and contribution to work reviewed in this chapter. I would also like to thank William J. Barnhart and Jennifer J. Spencer for their technical assistance.

REFERENCES

1. Koob, G. F. & Bloom, F. E. Cellular and molecular mechanisms of drug dependence, *Science*, 242, 715, 1988.
2. Wise, R. A. The role of reward pathways in the development of drug dependence. in *Psychotropic Drugs of Abuse*, ed. Balfour, D. J. K., Pergamon Press, Oxford, 1990, 23.
3. Fibiger, H. C., Phillips, A. G. & Brown, E. E. The neurobiology of cocaine-induced reinforcement, *Ciba Found Symp*, 166, 96, 1992.
4. Self, D. W. & Nestler, E. J. Molecular mechanisms of drug reinforcement and addiction, *Annu Rev Neurosci*, 18, 463, 1995.
5. Stewart, J., De Wit, H. & Eikelboom, R. Role of unconditioned and conditioned drug effects in the self-administration of opiates and stimulants, *Psychol Rev*, 91, 251, 1984.
6. Wise, R. A. & Bozarth, M. A. A psychomotor stimulant theory of addiction, *Psychol Rev*, 94, 469, 1987.
7. Robinson, T. E. & Berridge, K. C. The neural basis of drug craving: an incentive- sensitization theory of addiction, *Brain Res Rev*, 18, 247, 1993.
8. Solomon, R. & Corbitt, J. An opponent process theory of motivation, *Psychol Rev*, 81, 119, 1974.
9. Koob, G. F., Maldonado, R. & Stinus, L. Neural substrates of opiate withdrawal, *Trends Neurosci*, 15, 186, 1992.
10. Wikler, A. Dynamics of drug dependence, *Arch Gen Psychiatry*, 28, 611, 1973.
11. Siegel, S. Classical conditioning, drug tolerance, and drug dependence. in *Research Advances in Alcohol and Drug Problems*, 7, eds. Israel, Y., Plenum, New York, 1983, 207.
12. Ehrman, R. N., Robbins, S. J., Childress, A. R. & O'Brien, C. P. Conditioned responses to cocaine-related stimuli in cocaine abuse patients., *Psychopharmacology*, 107, 523, 1992.
13. O'Brien, C., Childress, A., McLellan, A. & Ehrman, R. A learning model of addiction. in *Addictive States*, eds. O'Brien, C. P. & Jaffe, J. H., Raven Press, New York, 1992, 157.
14. Eikelboom, R. & Stewart, J. Conditioning of drug-induced physiological responses, *Psychol Rev*, 89, 507, 1982.
15. Jaffe, J. H. Drug addiction and drug abuse. in *Goodman and Gilman's the Pharmacological Basis of Therapeutics*, eds. Goodman, A. G., Rall, T. W., Nies, A. S. & Taylor, P., Pergamon Press, New York, 1990.

16. Markou, A., Weiss, F., Gold, L. H., S.B., C., G., S. & G.F., K. Animal models of drug craving, *Psychopharmacology,* 112, 163, 1993.
17. De Wit, H. & Stewart, J. Drug reinstatement of heroin-reinforced responding in the rat, *Psychopharmacology,* 79, 29, 1983.
18. Shaham, Y., Rodaros, D. & Stewart, J. Reinstatement of heroin-reinforced behavior following long-term extinction: implications for the treatment of relapse of drug-taking, *Behavioural Pharmacology,* 5, 360, 1994.
19. Gerber, G. J. & Stretch, R. Drug-induced reinstatement of extinguished self-administration behavior, *Pharmacol Biochem Behav,* 3, 1066, 1975.
20. De Wit, H. & Stewart, J. Reinstatement of cocaine-reinforced responding in the rat, *Psychopharmacology,* 75, 134, 1981.
21. Slikker, W. J., Brocco, M. J. & Killam, K. F. J. Reinstatement of responding maintained by cocaine of thiamylal, *J Pharmacol Exp Ther,* 228, 43, 1984.
22. Worley, C. M., Valadez, A. & Schenk, S. Reinstatement of extinguished cocaine-taking behavior by cocaine and caffeine, *Pharmacol Biochem Behav,* 48, 217, 1994.
23. Weissenborn, R., Yackey, M., Koob, G. F. & Weiss, F. Measures of cocaine-seeking behavior using multiple schedules of food and drug self-administration, *Drug and Alcohol Dep,* 38, 237, 1995.
24. Self, D. W., Barnhart, W. J., Lehman, D. A. & Nestler, E. J. Opposite modulation of cocaine-seeking behavior by D_1- and D_2-like dopamine receptor agonists, *Science,* 271, 1586, 1996.
25. Comer, S. D., Lac, S. T., Curtis, L. K. & Carroll, M. E. Effect of buprenorphine and naltrexone on reinstatement of cocaine-reinforced responding in rats, *J Pharmacol Exp Ther,* 267, 1993.
26. Shaham, Y. & Stewart, J. Effects of restraint stress and intra-ventral tegmental area injections of morphine and methyl naltrexone on the discriminative stimulus effects of heroin in the rat, *Pharmacol Biochem Behav,* 51, 491, 1995.
27. Jaeger, T. V. & Van der Kooy, D. Separate neural substrates mediate the motivating and discriminative properties of morphine, *Behav Neurosci,* 110, 181, 1996.
28. Meil, W. M. & See, R. E. Excitotoxic lesions of the basolateral nucleus of the amygdala attenuate the ability of drug-associated cues to reinstate responding during withdrawal from self- administered cocaine, *Soc Neurosci Abstr,* 21, 1958, 1995.
29. Shaham, Y. & Stewart, J. Stress reinstates heroin-seeking in drug-free animals: an effect mimicking heroin, not withdrawal, *Psychopharmacology,* 119, 334, 1995.
30. Shaham, Y., Rajabi, H. & Stewart, J. Relapse to heroin-seeking in rats under opioid maintenance: the effects of stress, heroin priming, and withdrawal, *J Neurosci,* 16, 1957, 1996.
31. Barr, G. A., Sharpless, N. S., Cooper, S. & Schiff, S. R. Classical conditioning, decay and extinction of cocaine-induced hyperactivity and stereotypy, *Life Sci,* 33, 1341, 1983.
32. Brown, E. E. & Fibiger, H. C. Cocaine-induced conditioned locomotion: absence of associated increases in dopamine release, *Neuroscience,* 48, 621, 1992.
33. Van Dijken, H. H., Van der Heyden, J. A., Mos, J. & Tilders, F. J. Inescapable footshocks induce progressive and long-lasting behavioural changes in male rats., *Physiol Behav,* 51, 787, 1992.
34. Molina, V. A., Wagner, J. M. & Spear, L. P. The behavioral response to stress is altered in adult rats exposed prenatally to cocaine, *Physiol Behav,* 55, 941, 1994.
35. Di Chiara, G. & Imperato, A. Drugs abused by humans preferentially increase synaptic dopamine concentrations in the mesolimbic system of freely moving rats, *Proc Natl Acad Sci USA,* 85, 5274, 1988.
36. Stewart, J. & Vezina, P. A comparison of the effects of intra-accumbens injections of amphetamine and morphine on reinstatement of heroin intravenous self-administration behavior, *Brain Res,* 457, 287, 1988.
37. Johnson, S. W. & North, R. A. Opioids excite dopamine neurons by hyperpolarization of local interneurons, *J Neurosci,* 12, 483, 1992.
38. Leone, P., Pocock, D. & Wise, R. A. Morphine-dopamine interaction: ventral tegmental morphine increases nucleus accumbens dopamine release, *Pharmacol Biochem Behav,* 39, 469, 1991.

39. Wise, R. A., Murray, A. & Bozarth, M. A. Bromocriptine self-administration and bromocriptine-reinstatement of cocaine-trained and heroin-trained lever pressing in rats, *Psychopharmacology,* 100, 355, 1990.

40. Shaham, Y. & Stewart, J. Effects of opioid and dopamine receptor antagonists on relapse and re-exposure to heroin in rats, *J Pharmacol Exp Ther,* in press.

41. Ettenberg, A. Haloperidol prevents the reinstatement of amphetamine-rewarded runway responding inrats, *Pharmacol Biochem Behav,* 36, 635, 1990.

42. Self, D. W. unpublished data, 1996.

43. Christie, M. J. Excitotoxic lesions suggest an aspartatergic projection from the rat medial prefrontal cortex to ventral tegmental area, *Brain Res,* 333, 169, 1985.

44. Sesack, S. R., Deutch, A. Y., Roth, R. H. & Bunney, B. S. Topographical of the efferent projections to the medial prefrontal cortex in the rat: an anterograde tract-tracing study with *Phaseolus vulgaris* leucoagglutinin, *J Comp Neurol,* 290, 23, 1989.

45. Buchanan, S. L., Thompson, R. H., Maxwell, B. L. & Powell, D. A. Efferent projections of the medial prefrontal cortex in the rabbit, *Exp Brain Res,* 100, 469, 1994.

46. Sesack, S. R. & Pickel, V. M. Prefrontal cortical efferents in the rat synapse on unlabeled neuronal targets of catecholamine terminals in the nucleus accumbens septi and on dopamine neurons in the ventral tegmental area, *J Comp Neurol,* 320, 145, 1992.

47. Moghaddam, B. Stress preferentially increases extraneuronal levels of excitatory amino acids in the prefrontal cortex: comparison to hippocampus and basal ganglia, *J Neurochem,* 60, 1650, 1993.

48. Murase, S., Grenhoff, J., Chouvet, G., Gonon, F. G. & Svensson, T. H. Prefrontal cortex regulates burst firing and transmitter release in rat mesolimbic dopamine neurons studied in vivo, *Neurosci Lett,* 157, 53, 1993.

49. Carter, C. J. Glutamatergic pathways from the medial prefrontal cortex to the anterior striatum, nucleus accumbens and substantia nigra, *Br J Pharmacol,* 70, 50, 1980.

50. Christie, M. J., Summers, R. J., Stephenson, J. A., C.J., C. & Beart, P. M. Excitatory amino acid projections to the nucleus accumbens spti in the rat: a retrograde transport study utilizing D[^{3}H] aspartate and [^{3}H] GABA, *Neuroscience,* 22, 425, 1987.

51. Brog, J. S., Salyapongse, A., Deutch, A. Y. & Zahm, D. S. The patterns of afferent innervation of the core and shell in the "accumbens" part of the ventral striatum: immunohistochemical detection of retrogradely transported fluoro-gold, *J Comp Neurol,* 338, 225, 1993.

52. Taber, M. T., Das, S. & Fibiger, H. C. Cortical regulation of subcortical dopamine release: mediation via the ventral tegmental area, *J Neurochem,* 65, 1407, 1995.

53. Taber, M. T. & Fibiger, H. C. Electrical stimulation of the prefrontal cortex increases dopamine release in the nucleus accumbens of the rat: modulation by metabotropic glutamate receptors, *J Neurosci,* 15, 3896, 1995.

54. Karreman, M. & Moghaddam, B. The prefrontal cortex regulates the basal release of dopamine in the limbic striatum: an effect mediated by ventral tegmental area, *J Neurochem,* 66, 589, 1996.

55. Sesack, S. R. & Pickel, V. M. In the rat medial nucleus accumbens, hippocampal and catecholaminergic terminals converge on spiny neurons and are in apposition to each other, *Brain Res,* 527, 266, 1990.

56. Brown, E. E., Robertson, G. S. & Fibiger, H. C. Evidence for conditioned neuronal activation following exposure to a cocaine-paired environment: role of forebrain limbic structures, *J Neurosci,* 12, 4112, 1992.

57. Young, A. M., Joseph, M. H. & Gray, J. A. Latent inhibition of conditioned dopamine release in rat nucleus accumbens, *Neuroscience,* 54, 5, 1993.

58. Saulskaya, N. & Marsden, C. A. Conditioned dopamine release: dependence upon *N*-methyl-D-aspartate receptors, *Neuroscience,* 67, 57, 1995.

59. Di Ciano, P., Blaha, C. D. & Phillips, A. G. Conditioned increases in motor activity and dopamine concentrations in the nucleus accumbens of the rat following repeated administration of cocaine or *d*-amphetamine, *Soc Neurosci Abstr,* 21, 2103, 1995.

David W. Self

60. Schultz, W., Apicella, P. & Ljungberg, T. Responses of monkey dopamine neurons to reward and conditioned stimuli during successive steps of learning a delayed response task, *J Neurosci*, 13, 900, 1993.

61. Mirenowicz, J. & Schultz, W. Preferential activation of midbrain dopamine neurons by appetitive rather than aversive stimuli, *Nature*, 379, 449, 1996.

62. Brown, E. E. & Fibiger, H. C. Differential effects of excitotoxic lesions of the amygdala on cocaine-induced conditioned locomotion and conditioned place preference, *Psychopharmacology*, 113, 123, 1993.

63. Gonzales, C. & Chesselet, M. F. Amydalonigral pathway: an anterograde study in the rat with *Phaseolus vulgaris* leucoagglutinin, *J Comp Neurol*, 297, 182, 1990.

64. Wallace, D. M., Magnuson, D. J. & Gray, T. S. Organization of amygdaloid projections to brainstem dopaminergic, noradrenergic, and adrenergic cell groups in the rat, *Brain Res Bull*, 28, 447, 1992.

65. LeDoux, J. E. Emotional memory systems in the brain, *Behav Brain Res*, 58, 69, 1993.

66. Maeda, H. & Mogenson, G. J. Electrophysiological responses of neurons in the ventral tegmental area to electrical stimulation of amygdala and lateral septum, *Neuroscience*, 6, 367, 1981.

67. McDonald, A. J. Topographical organization of amygdaloid projections to the caudatoputamen, nucleus accumbens, and related striatal-like areas of the rat brain, *Neuroscience*, 44, 15, 1991.

68. Johnson, L. R., Aylward, R. L. M., Husain, Z. & Totterdell, S. Input from the amygdala to the rat nucleus accumbens: its relationship with tyrosine hydroxylase immunoreactivity and identified neurons, *Neuroscience*, 61, 851, 1994.

69. Yim, C. Y. & Mogenson, G. J. Neuromodulatory actions of dopamine in the nucleus accumbens: an in vivo intracellular study, *Neuroscience*, 26, 403, 1988.

70. McDonald, A. J. Organisation of amygdaloid projections to prefrontal cortex and associated striatum in the rat, *Neuroscience*, 44, 1, 1991.

71. Stewart, J. & Wise, R. A. Reinstatement of heroin self-administration habits: morphine prompts and naltrexone discourages renewed responding after extinction, *Psychopharmacology*, 108, 79, 1992.

72. Childress, A. R., McLellan, A. T. & O'brien, C. P. Extinguishing conditioned responses in drug dependent persons. in *Learning factors in drug dependence: NIDA Research Monograph*, DHHS Publication No. ADM-88-1576, ed. Ray, B., U.S. Government Printing Office, Washington, 1988, 137.

73. Satel, S. "Craving for and Fear of Cocaine": A Phenomenologic Update on Cocaine Craving and Paranoia. in *Clinician's Guide to Cocaine Addiction*, eds. Kosten, T. R. & Kleber, H. D., Guilford Press, New York, 1992, 172.

74. Sibley, D. R., Monsma, F. J. J. & Shen, Y. Molecular neurobiology of dopaminergic receptors, *Int Rev Neurobiol*, 35, 391, 1993.

75. Kebabian, J. W. & Calne, D. B. Multiple receptors for dopamine, *Nature*, 277, 93, 1979.

76. Stoof, J. C. & Kebabian, J. W. Opposing roles for D-1 and D-2 in efflux of cyclic AMP from rat neostriatum, *Nature*, 294, 366, 1981.

77. Meador-Woodruff, J. H., Mansour, A., Healy, D. J., Kuehn, R., Zhou, Q.-Y., Bunzow, J. R., Akil, H., Civelli, O. & Watson, S. J. Comparison of the distribution of D1 and D2 dopamine receptor mRNAs in rat brain, *Neuropsychopharmacology*, 5, 231, 1991.

78. Curran, E. J. & Watson, S. J. J. Dopamine receptor mRNA expression patterns by opioid peptide cells in the nucleus accumbens of the rat: a double in situ hybridization study, *J Comp Neurol*, 361, 57, 1995.

79. Diaz, J., Levesque, D., Lammers, C. H., Griffon, N., Matres, M. P. & Schwartz, J. C. Phenotypical characterization of neurons expressing the dopamine D3 receptor in the rat brain, *Neuroscience*, 65, 731, 1995.

80. Shetreat, M. E., Lin, L., Wong, A. C. & Rayport, S. Visualization of D1 dopamine receptors on living nucleus accumbens neurons and their colocalization with D2 receptors, *J Neurochem*, 66, 1475, 1996.

81. White, F. J. & Hu, X.-T. Electrophysiological correlates of D1:D2 interactions. in *D-1:D-2 Dopamine Receptor Interactions: Neuroscience and Psychopharmacology*, ed. Waddington, J. L., Academic Press, London, 1993, 79.

82. Waddington, J. L. & Daly, S. A. Regulation of unconditioned motor behaviour by $D_1:D_2$ interaction. in *D-1:D-2 Dopamine Receptor Interactions*, ed. Waddington, J. L., Academic Press, London, 1993, 203.

83. Levant, B., Bancroft, G. N. & Selkirk, C. M. In vivo occupancy of D_2 dopamine receptors by 7-OH-DPAT, *Synapse*, 24, 60, 1996.

84. Callahan, P. M., Appel, J. B. & Cunningham, K. A. Dopamine D_1 and D_2 mediation of the discriminative stimulus properties of *d*-amphetamine and cocaine, *Psychopharmacology*, 103, 50, 1991.

85. Spealman, R. D., Bergman, J., Madras, B. K. & Melia, K. F. Discriminative stimulus effects of cocaine in squirrel monkeys: involvement of dopamine receptor subtypes, *J Pharmacol Exp Ther*, 258, 945, 1991.

86. Witkin, J. M., Nichols, D. E., Terry, P. & Katz, J. Behavioral effects of selective dopaminergic compounds in rats discriminating cocaine injections, *J Pharmacol Exp Ther*, 257, 706, 1991.

87. Self, D. W. & Stein, L. The D_1 agonists SKF 82958 and SKF 77434 are self-administered by rats, *Brain Res*, 582, 349, 1992.

88. Caine, S. B. & Koob, G. F. Modulation of cocaine self-administration in the rat through D-3 dopamine receptors, *Science*, 260, 1814, 1993.

89. Weed, M. R., Vanover, K. E. & Woolverton, W. L. Reinforcing effect of the D_1 dopamine agonist SKF 81297 in rhesus monkeys, *Psychopharmacology*, 113, 51, 1993.

90. Weed, M. R. & Woolverton, M. L. The reinforcing effects of D_1 receptor agonists in rhesus monkeys, *J Pharmacol Exp Ther*, 275, 1367, 1995.

91. Grech, D. M., Spealman, R. D. & Bergman, J. Self-administration of D_1 receptor agonists by squirrel monkeys, *Psychopharmacology*, 125, 97, 1996.

92. Self, D. W., Belluzzi, J. D., Kossuth, S. & Stein, L. Self-administration of the D_1 agonist SKF 82958 is mediated by D_1, and not D_2, receptors, *Psychopharmacology*, 123, 303, 1996.

93. Gerfen, C. R., Engber, T. M., Mahan, L. C., Susel, Z., Chase, T. N. et al. D1 and D2 dopamine receptor-regulated gene expression of striatonigral and striatopallidal neurons, *Science*, 250, 1429, 1990.

94. Le Moine, C., Normand, E., Guitteny, A. F., Fouque, B., Teoule, R. & Bloch, B. Dopamine receptor gene expression by enkephalin neurons in rat forebrain, *Proc Natl Acad Sci USA*, 87, 230, 1990.

95. Le Moine, C., Normand, E. & Bloch, B. Phenotypical characterization of the rat striatal neurons expressing the D1 dopamine receptor gene, *Proc Natl Acad Sci USA*, 88, 4205, 1991.

96. White, F. J. & Wang, R. Y. Electrophysiological evidence for the existence of D1 and D2 dopamine receptors in the rat nucleus accumbens, *J Neurosci*, 6, 274, 1986.

97. Pennartz, C. M. A., Dolleman-Van der Weel, M. J., Kitai, S. T. & Lopes Da Silva, F. H. Presynaptic dopamine D1 receptors attenuate excitatory and inhibitory limbic inputs to the shell region of the rat nucleus accumbens studied in vitro, *J Neurophysiol*, 67, 1325, 1992.

98. Nicola, S. M., Kombian, S. B. & Malenka, R. C. Psychostimulants depress excitatory synaptic transmission in the nucleus accumbens via presynaptic D1-like dopamine receptors, *J Neurosci*, 16, 1591, 1996.

99. Bouthenet, M.-L., Souil, E., Martres, M.-P., Sokoloff, P., Giros, B. & Schwartz, J.-C. Localization of dopamine D3 receptor mRNA in the rat brain using in situ hybridization histochemistry: comparison with dopamine D2 receptor mRNA, *Brain Res*, 564, 203, 1991.

100. Levesque, D., *et al.* Identification, characterization, and localization of the dopamine D_3 receptor in rat brain using 7-[^{3}H]hydroxy-N,N-di-n-propyl-2-aminotetralin, *Proc Natl Acad Sci USA*, 89, 8155, 1992.

101. Tang, L., Todd, R. D. & O'Malley, K. L. Dopamine D2 and D3 receptors inhbit dopamine release, *J Pharmacol Exp Ther*, 270, 475, 1994.

102. Parsons, L. H., Caine, S. B., Sokoloff, P., Schwartz, J.-C., Koob, G. F. & Weiss, F. Neurochemical evidence that post-synaptic nucleus accumbens D_3 receptor stimulation enhances cocaine reinforcement, *J Neurochem*, 67, 1078, 1996.

David W. Self

103. Cameron, D. L. & Williams, J. T. Dopamine D1 receptors facilitate transmitter release, *Nature*, 366, 344, 1993.
104. Momiyama, T., Sasa, M. & Takaori, S. Enhancement of D2 receptor agonist-induced inhibition by D1 receptor agonist in the ventral tegmental area, *Br J Pharmacol*, 110, 713, 1993.
105. Vezina, P., Blanc, G., Glowinski, J. & Tassin, J. P. Blockade of D-1 dopamine receptors in the medial prefrontal cortex produces delayed effects on pre- and postsynaptic indices of dopamine function in the nucleus accumbens, *Synapse*, 16, 104, 1994.
106. Ferre, S., Fuxe, K., Von Euler, G., Johansson, B. & Fredholm, B. B. Adenosine- dopamine interactions in the brain, *Neuroscience*, 51, 501, 1992.
107. Nestler, E. J. Hard target: understanding dopaminergic neurotransmission, *Cell*, 79, 923, 1994.
108. Self, D.W., Genova, L., Hope, B.T., Barnhart, W.J., Spencer, J.J., and Nestler, E.J. Involvement of cAMP-dependent protein kinases in the nucleus accumbens in cocaine self-administration and relapse of cocaine-seeking behavior (submitted).
109. Santiago, M. & Westerink, B. H. C. Role of adenylate cyclase in the modulation of the release of dopamine: a microdialysis study in the striatum of the rat, *J Neurochem*, 55, 169, 1990.
110. Chavez-Noriega, L. E. & Stevens, C. F. Increased neurotransmitter release at excitatory synapse produced by direct activation of adenylate cyclase in rat hippocampal slices, *J Neurosci*, 14, 310, 1994.
111. Li, M., West, J. W., Lai, Y., Scheuer, T. & Catterall, W. A. Functional modulation of brain sodium channels by cAMP-dependent phosphorylation, *Neuron*, 1151-1159, 1151, 1992.
112. Schiffmann, S. N., Lledo, P.-M. & Vincent, J.-D. Dopamine D_1 receptor modulates the voltage-gated sodium current in rat striatal neurons through a protein kinase A, *J Physiol*, 483.1, 95, 1995.
113. Smith, R. D. & Goldin, A. L. Phosphorylation of brain sodium channels in the I-II linker modulates channel function in *Xenopus* oocytes, *J Neurosci*, 16, 1965, 1996.
114. Huang, C. C., Tsai, J. J. & Gean, P. W. Enhancement of NMDA receptor-mediated synaptic potential by isoproterenol is blocked by Rp-adenosine 3',5'-cyclic monophosphothioate, *Neurosci Lett*, 161, 207, 1993.
115. Raymond, L. A., Tingley, W. G., Blackstone, C. D., Roche, K. W. & Huganir, R. L. Glutamate receptor modulation by protein phosphorylation, *J Physiol*, 88, 181, 1994.
116. Colwell, C. S. & Levine, M. S. Excitatory synaptic transmission in neostriatal neurons: regulation by cyclic AMP-dependent mechanisms, *J Neurosci*, 15, 1704, 1995.
117. O'Donnell, P. & Grace, A. A. Dopaminergic modulation of dye coupling between neurons in the core and shell regions of the nucleus accumbens, *J Neurosci*, 13, 3456, 1993.
118. Onn, S. P. & Grace, A. A. Dye coupling between rat striatal neurons recorded in vivo: compartmental organization and modulation by dopamine, *J Neurophysiol*, 71, 1917, 1994.
119. Rorig, B., Klausa, G. & Sutor, B. Dye coupling between neurons in developing rat prefrontal and frontal cortex is reduced by protein kinase A activation and dopamine, *J Neurosci*, 15, 7386, 1995.
120. Cepeda, C., Buchwald, N. A. & Levine, M. S. Neuromodulatory actions of dopamine in the neostriatum are dependent upon the excitatory amino acid receptor subtypes activated, *Proc Natl Acad Sci USA*, 90, 9576, 1993.
121. DeFrance, J. F., Sikes, R. W. & Chronister, R. B. Dopamine action in the nucleus accumbens, *J Neurophysiol*, 54, 1568, 1985.
122. Surmeier, D. J., Bargas, J., Hemmings, H. C. J., Nairn, A. C. & Greengard, P. Modulation of calcium currents by a D1 dopaminergic protein kinase/phosphatase cascade in rat neostriatal neurons, *Neuron*, 14, 385, 1995.
123. Nestler, E. J. Molecular mechanisms of drug addiction, *J Neurosci*, 12, 2439, 1992.
124. Nestler, E. J., Hope, B. T. & Widnell, K. L. Drug addiction: a model for the molecular basis of neural plasticity, *Neuron*, 11, 995, 1993.
125. Hyman, S. E. & Nestler, E. J. Initiation and adaptation: a paradigm for understanding psychotropic drug action, *Am J Psychiatry*, 153, 151, 1996.
126. Kuhar, M. J. & Pilotte, N. S. Neurochemical changes in cocaine withdrawal, *Trends Pharmacol Sci*, 17, 260, 1996.

127. Self, D. W., McClenahan, A. W., Beitner-Johnson, D., Terwilliger, R. Z. & Nestler, E. J. Biochemical adaptations in the mesolimbic dopamine system in response to heroin self-administration., *Synapse,* 21, 312, 1995.

128. Parsons, L. H., Smith, A. D. & Justice, J. B., Jr. Basal extracellular dopamine in decreased in the rat nucleus accumbens during abstinence from chronic cocaine, *Synapse,* 9, 60, 1991.

129. Pothos, E., Rada, P., Mark, G. P. & Hoebel, B. G. Dopamine microdialysis in the nucleus accumbens during acute and chronic morphine, naloxone-precipitated withdrawal and clonidine treatment, *Brain Res,* 566, 348, 1991.

130. Ackerman, J. M. & White, F. J. Decreased activity of rat A10 dopamine neurons following withdrawal from repeated cocaine, *Eur J Pharmacol,* 218, 171, 1992.

131. Imperato, A., Mele, A., Scrocco, M. G. & Puglici-Allegra, S. Chronic cocaine alters limbic extracellular dopamine. Neurochemical basis for addiction, *Eur J Pharmacol,* 212, 299, 1992.

132. Rossetti, Z. L., Hmaidan, Y. & Gessa, G. L. Marked inhibition of mesolimbic dopamine release: a common feature of ethanol, morphine, cocaine and amphetamine abstinence in rats, *Eur J Pharmacol,* 221, 227, 1992.

133. Segal, D. S. & Kuczensky, R. Repeated cocaine administration induces behavioral sensitization and corresponding decrease extracellular dopamine responses in caudate and accumbens, *Brain Res,* 577, 351, 1992.

134. Diana, M., Pistis, M., Carboni, S., Gessa, G. & Rossetti, Z. L. Profound decrement of mesolimbic dopaminergic neuronal activity during ethanol withdrawal syndrome in rats: electrophysiological and biochemical evidence, *Proc Natl Acad Sci USA,* 90, 7966, 1993.

135. Wolf, M. E., White, F. J., Nassar, R., Brooderson, R. J. & Khansa, M. R. Differential development of autoreceptor subsensitivity and enhanced dopamine release during amphetamine sensitization, *J Pharmacol Exp Ther,* 264, 249, 1993.

136. Tjon, G. H. K., De Vries, T. J., Ronken, E., Hogenboom, F., Wardeh, G., Mulder, A. H. & Schoffelmeer, A. N. M. Repeated and chronic morphine administration cause differential long-lasting changes in dopaminergic neurotransmission in rat striatum without changes in ∂- and k-opioid receptor regulation, *Eur J Pharmacol,* 252, 205, 1994.

137. Fitzgerald, L. W., Ortiz, J., Hamedani, A. G. & Nestler, E. J. Regulation of glutamate receptor subunit expression by drugs of abuse and stress: common adaptations among cross- sensitizing agents, *J Neurosci,* 16, 274, 1996.

138. Carlezon, W. A., Jr., Boundy, V. A., Kalb, R. G., Neve, R. & Nestler, E. J. Increased sensitivity to the stimulant actions of morphine after infection of VTA with an HSV vector expressing GLUR1, *Soc Neurosci Abstr,* 22, 171, 1996.

139. White, F. J., Hu, X. T., Zhang, X. F. & Wolf, M. E. Repeated administration of cocaine or amphetamine alters neuronal responses to glutamate in the mesoaccumbens dopamine system, *J Pharmacol Exp Ther,* 273, 445, 1995.

140. Kuhar, M. J. & Pilotte, N. S. Neurochemical changes in cocaine withdrawal, *Trends Pharmacol Sci,* 17, 260, 1996.

141. Cerruti, C., Pilotte, N. S., Uhl, G. & Kuhar, M. J. Reduction in dopamine transporter mRNA after cessation of repeated cocaine administration, *Mol Brain Res,* in press, 1994.

142. Weiss, F., Paulus, M. P., Lorang, M. T. & Koob, G. F. Increases in extracellular dopamine in the nucleus accumbens by cocaine are inversely related to basal levels: effects of acute and repeated administration, *J Neurosci,* 12, 4372, 1992.

143. Kalivas, P. W. & Duffy, P. Time course of extracellular dopamine and behavioral sensitization to cocaine. I. Dopamine axon terminals, *J Neurosci,* 13, 266, 1993.

144. Robinson, T. E. Persistent sensitizing effects of drugs on brain dopamine systems and behavior: implications for addiction and relapse. in *Biological Basis of Substance Abuse,* eds. Korenman, S. G. & Barchas, J. D., Oxford University Press, New York Oxford, 1993, 373.

145. Henry, D. J. & White, F. J. Repeated cocaine administration causes persistent enhancement of D_1 dopamine receptor sensitivity within the rat nucleus accumbens, *J Pharmacol Exp Ther,* 258, 882, 1991.

146. Nestler, E. J., Terwilliger, R. Z., Walker, J. R., Sevarino, K. A. & Duman, R. S. Chronic cocaine treatment decreases levels of the G-protein subunits G_{ia} and G_{oa} in discrete regions of the rat brain, *J Neurochem,* 55, 1079, 1990.

David W. Self

147. Terwilliger, R. Z., Beitner-Johnson, D., Sevarino, K. A., Crain, S. M. & Nestler, E. J. A general role for adaptations in G-proteins and the cyclic AMP system in mediating the chronic actions of morphine and cocaine on neuronal function, *Brain Res,* 548, 100, 1991.

148. Striplin, C. D. & Klivas, P. W. Robustness of G protein changes in cocaine sensitization shown with immunoblotting, *Synapse,* 14, 10, 1993.

149. Ortiz, J., Fitzgerald, L. W., Charlton, M., Lane, S., Trevisan, L., Guitart, X., Shoemaker, W., Duman, R. S. & Nestler, E. J. Biochemical actions of chronic ethanol exposure in the mesolimbic dopamine system, *Synapse,* in press, 1995.

150. Mishra, R. K., Gardner, E. L., Katzman, R. & Makman, M. H. Enhancement of dopamine-stimulated adenylate cyclase activity in rat caudate after lesions in substantia nigra: evidence for denervation supersensitivity, *Proc Natl Acad Sci USA,* 71, 3883, 1974.

151. Rosenfeld, M. R., Seeger, T. F., Sharples, N. S., gardner, E. L. & Makman, M. H. Denervation supersensitivity in the mesolimbic system: involvement of dopamine-stimulated adenylate cyclase, *Brain Res,* 173, 572, 1979.

152. Parenti, M., Gentleman, S., Olianas, M. C. & Heff, N. H. The dopamine receptor adenylate cyclase complex: evidence for post recognition site involvement for the development of supersensitivity, *Neurochem Res,* 7, 115, 1982.

153. Battaglia, G., Norman, A. B., Hess, E. J. & Creese, I. D_2 dopamine receptor-mediated inhibition of forskolin-stimulated adenylate cyclase activity in rat, *Neurosci Lett,* 59, 177, 1985.

154. Shippenberg and Herz, 1987.

155. Stinus et al., 1990.

156. White, F.J. & Zhang, X.-F. Repeated cocaine administration decreases whole-cell sodium current in acutely dissociated nucleus accumbens neurons. *Soc Neurosci Abstr,* 22, 1880, 1996.

6.5 SEROTONERGIC DYSFUNCTION DURING COCAINE WITHDRAWAL: IMPLICATIONS FOR COCAINE-INDUCED DEPRESSION

MICHAEL H. BAUMANN AND RICHARD B. ROTHMAN

CLINICAL PSYCHOPHARMACOLOGY SECTION, INTRAMURAL RESEARCH PROGRAM, NATIONAL INSTITUTE ON DRUG ABUSE, NATIONAL INSTITUTES OF HEALTH, BALTIMORE, MARYLAND

The illicit use of cocaine, particularly the "crack" form of the drug, remains a significant health concern.[1] Long-term exposure to cocaine is associated with a myriad of cardiovascular, pulmonary, neurological, and psychiatric complications.[2,3] Deaths attributable to cocaine occur not only from overdose but also from cocaine-induced behavioral states leading to serious injury. In a recent epidemiological study, 26% of all fatal injuries occurring in New York City between 1990 and 1992 involved illegal cocaine use.[4] While one third of these fatalities were due to cocaine intoxication, two thirds were the result of suicides, homicides, and traffic accidents. Due to the magnitude of the cocaine crisis, the U.S. government has made the development of cocaine treatment medications a national priority.[1,5] One potential strategy for identifying such medications entails determining the neurobiological consequences of cocaine exposure and applying this knowledge to the drug development process.

It is well established that cocaine blocks the reuptake of dopamine (DA), serotonin (5-HT), and norepinephrine (NE) into neurons.[6-8] Cocaine is rather non-selective in this regard, and cocaine-induced inhibition of reuptake elevates extracellular levels of all three monoamines in the brain.[9-11] Although cocaine invariably enhances net monoamine transmission, substantial evidence indicates that stimulation of mesolimbic DA neurons mediates the positive reinforcing properties of the drug.[12,13] Moreover, depletion of brain DA has been postulated to underlie the dysphoria experienced by withdrawn cocaine addicts.[14,15] The prevailing notion that DA systems are involved with both euphoric and dysphoric effects of cocaine has profoundly influenced efforts to develop pharmacotherapies for cocaine dependence.[1,16,17] A number of medicines which enhance DA transmission have been tested as potential treatments; these drugs include direct DA receptor agonists (bromocriptine, pergolide) and DA reuptake blockers (mazindol, methylphenidate, bupropion). Unfortunately, none of these drugs has been proven very effective in promoting cocaine abstinence, and no pharmacotherapy for cocaine dependence has been identified.[1,16,17]

The preceding discussion, along with other findings,[18] suggests that neurotransmitter systems in addition to DA must play a role in cocaine addiction. Moreover, non-dopaminergic medications need to be considered as treatments. 5-HT represents a potential candidate neurotransmitter involved in cocaine addiction. 5-HT neurons are known targets of cocaine action,[6-8] and 5-HT drugs can modulate the pharmacological effects of cocaine in animals[19,20] and humans.[21] 5-HT is a clinically relevant neurotransmitter with 5-HT dysfunction being implicated in a wide range of psychiatric problems such as depression, anxiety states, aggressive behavior, and obsessive-compulsive disorder.[22] A major objective of this section is to review the effects of acute and chronic cocaine administration on 5-HT neurotransmission in the rat. A second and more important aim is to show that abnormalities in 5-HT function during cocaine withdrawal are similar to those present in patients diagnosed with major depression. Thus, chronic cocaine exposure may induce a depressive-like state by altering the dynamics of central 5-HT function. Such information could have important implications for the development of medications to treat cocaine dependence.

6.5.1 SEROTONIN (5-HT) TRANSMISSION IN THE BRAIN

Before discussing the effects of cocaine on 5-HT neurons, some basic information concerning 5-HT neurotransmission must be briefly reviewed. First, the anatomy of 5-HT neuron systems needs to be considered. Neurons which synthesize and release 5-HT are found throughout the nervous system, and 5-HT innervation of the forebrain is complex.[23] Second, recent advances in the field of 5-HT receptor pharmacology must be mentioned, with special reference to multiple 5-HT receptor subtypes.[24] This is particularly important because evidence has shown that chronic cocaine exposure can differentially affect the responsiveness to 5-HT agonists activating $5-HT_{1A}$ and $5-HT_2$ receptor subtypes.

6.5.1.1 Anatomy of Brain 5-HT Systems

In mammalian species, the majority of 5-HT-containing cell bodies reside in the midline raphe nuclei of the brainstem and give rise to axonal projections innervating all levels of the neuraxis.[23] 5-HT innervation of the rat forebrain arises chiefly from the dorsal raphe (DR) and median raphe (MR) nuclei; axons projecting from the DR and MR are organized into distinct subsystems which ascend through the median forebrain bundle en route to distant termination areas.[25,26] As the main axons of passage approach a particular destination, they send out collateral branches that arborize to ultimately form axon terminals. Although the ascending 5-HT pathways tend to overlap, certain regions such as the striatum and hippocampus receive axons predominately from the DR or MR, respectively.[23,25] Axons arising from the DR and MR appear morphologically distinct, and DR axons are more vulnerable to the deleterious effects of amphetamine neurotoxins when compared to MR axons.[23,27] Ultrastructural analysis of 5-HT nerve terminals indicates that few 5-HT axons make traditional synaptic contact with postsynaptic cells. In fact, the majority of 5-HT innervation appears to be non-junctional in nature.[28] Thus, the 5-HT system in the brain is actually a collection of neuron subsystems which display intrinsic morphological and functional heterogeneity.

Michael H. Baumann and Richard B. Rothman

6.5.1.2 Multiple 5-HT Receptor Subtypes

Application of molecular cloning techniques has lead to the discovery of an overwhelming array of "new" 5-HT receptor subtypes.[24,29] This situation has prompted revision of the nomenclature for classifying 5-HT receptors based not only on pharmacological specificity, but also on receptor-effector coupling mechanisms and primary amino acid sequence. Using these criteria, 5-HT receptors can be divided into $5\text{-HT}_{1(A\text{-}F)}$, $5\text{-HT}_{2(A\text{-}C)}$, 5-HT_3, 5-HT_4, $5\text{-HT}_{5(A,B)}$, 5-HT_6, and 5-HT_7 receptor subtypes.[29] Of the multiple 5-HT subtypes identified, the 5-HT_1, 5-HT_2 and 5-HT_3 receptor families have been well characterized in terms of their associated signal transduction pathways and *in vivo* functional correlates. 5-HT_1 receptors inhibit adenylate cyclase whereas 5-HT_2 receptors activate phospholipase C; these receptors are coupled to their respective effector systems via specific G-proteins.[29,30] 5-HT_3 receptors are unique among the 5-HT receptor subtypes in that they function as ligand-gated ion channels and share some similarities with nicotinic acetylcholine receptors.[29,30]

Examining the distribution of 5-HT receptor subtypes in the brain has provided important clues about the possible physiological roles of each subtype.[31] For example, autoradiographic mapping techniques have shown high densities of 5-HT_{1A} receptors in the DR and a variety of limbic structures such as the hippocampus, septum, and amygdala.[31-33] In the DR, 5-HT_{1A} receptors are localized presynaptically on 5-HT cell bodies and function as impulse-modulating autoreceptors.[31,34] 5-HT cells in the DR exhibit spontaneous electrical activity, and this activity is regulated such that activation of 5-HT_{1A} autoreceptors by endogenous 5-HT, or 5-HT_{1A} agonists such as 8-hydroxy-2-(di-n-propylamino)tetralin (8-OH-DPAT), potently suppresses cell firing via membrane hyperpolarization.[34] In the CA1 region of the hippocampus, 5-HT_{1A} receptors are located postsynaptically relative to 5-HT axon terminals, and activation of these receptors also results in membrane hyperpolarization.[34] 5-HT_{1A} receptors, therefore, appear to be important components of the limbic 5-HT circuitry thought to modulate mood and emotion. 5-HT_{1B} receptors, on the other hand, are found predominately in areas involved with motor function such as the striatum, globus pallidus, and substantia nigra.[31-33] 5-HT_2 receptors are present at very high density in specific layers of the cerebral cortex, and to a lesser extent in striatum and limbic areas.[35,36] Consistent with the role of 5-HT_2 receptors in sensation and perception, these receptors have been implicated in the mechanism of action of hallucinogenic drugs including lysergic acid diethylamide (LSD) and 1-(2,5-dimethoxy-4-iodophenyl)-2-aminopropane (DOI).[37,38]

6.5.2 ACUTE EFFECTS OF COCAINE ON 5-HT NEURONS

Considerable evidence indicates that the primary mechanism of cocaine action involves inhibition of monoamine reuptake.[6-8] Cocaine blocks the reuptake of 5-HT, as well as DA and NE, by binding to specific transporter proteins associated with nerve cell membranes. Recently, the 5-HT transporter gene has been cloned, and the encoded protein exhibits significant sequence homology with other neurotransmitter transporters for DA, NE, and gamma-aminobutyric acid.[39,40] Thus, the 5-HT transporter belongs to a superfamily of proteins which mediate the sodium-dependent reuptake of released neurotransmitter back into presynaptic terminals.[41] The topological features of this protein family include 12 hydrophobic membrane-spanning regions as well as numerous consensus sites for intracellular phosphorylation and extracellular N-linked glycosylation. It is noteworthy that 5-HT transporters are not only important targets for the action of cocaine but also for the action of clinically important medicines such as antidepressants and anorectic amphetamines.[39-41]

Under normal circumstances, 5-HT reuptake is the chief mechanism for removing 5-HT from the synapse. Blockade of the 5-HT reuptake mechanism by cocaine increases extracellular

5-HT levels in the brain as measured by *in vivo* microdialysis.[9-11] This elevation of synaptic 5-HT, while short-lived, undoubtedly stimulates multiple populations of 5-HT receptor subtypes throughout the neuraxis. In the DR, the cocaine-induced rise in extracellular 5-HT activates 5-HT$_{1A}$ impulse-regulating autoreceptors which markedly suppresses 5-HT cell firing.[42-44] Cocaine also activates autoreceptor-mediated feedback processes that inhibit the spontaneous firing of DA cells in the ventral tegmental area[45] and NE cells in the locus coeruleus.[46] However, cocaine is a much more potent and effective inhibitor of cell firing in 5-HT neurons compared to DA and NE neurons.[42,43] Acute cocaine administration decreases 5-HT biosynthesis in a variety of forebrain projection areas, and this effect may be secondary to suppression of 5-HT cell firing in the DR.[47,48] Collectively, the data indicate that acute cocaine alters 5-HT transmission in a biphasic manner characterized by transient elevation of extracellular 5-HT that leads to compensatory inhibition of cell activity.

6.5.3 5-HT DYSFUNCTION DURING COCAINE WITHDRAWAL

Based on the acute effects of cocaine on 5-HT neurons, it might be predicted that chronic exposure to the drug would adversely affect 5-HT neurons. Indeed, a number of studies examining neuroendocrine, electrophysiological, and neurochemical endpoints have demonstrated changes in 5-HT function after repeated cocaine administration in rats (for reviews see References 49 through 51). The majority of studies have evaluated 5-HT transmission during acute withdrawal (1 to 48 h) from repeated injections of cocaine (10 to 30 mg/kg/d) given for 7 to 30 d. Although other cocaine dosing regimens have been employed, such as chronic cocaine infusion via osmotic minipumps, findings from these studies will not be discussed here. Furthermore, the present review will focus specifically on the effects of chronic cocaine on 5-HT function determined in whole animal systems.

Initial investigations addressed the possibility that chronic cocaine might be toxic to 5-HT neurons. The rationale for these studies relates to the similar neurobiological properties of cocaine and amphetamine. It is well known that repeated high-dose administration of amphetamine, and certain amphetamine analogs, will produce dramatic depletions of brain 5-HT in rodents.[52] In marked contrast, repeated injections of cocaine do not significantly alter postmortem tissue levels of 5-HT, or its metabolite 5-HIAA, in dissected brain areas.[53,54] Chronic cocaine dosing regimens which produce robust behavioral sensitization in rats fail to affect basal 5-HT synthesis rate or the number of 5-HT immunoreactive neurons in the brain.[48,55] These data provide compelling evidence that chronic cocaine administration does not produce neurotoxic depletions of central 5-HT.

6.5.3.1 The Neuroendocrine Challenge Approach

In many laboratories, including our own, investigators have employed a neuroendocrine challenge approach to examine the effects of repeated cocaine injections on 5-HT neurons.[49] This method involves measuring the hormonal responses to an acute 5-HT drug "challenge" in rats previously exposed to chronic cocaine or vehicle. The stimulatory influence of 5-HT neurons on pituitary hormone secretion is well documented in laboratory animals and humans.[56-58] For example, systemic injection of 5-HT releasing agents or direct 5-HT receptor agonists elevates plasma adrenocorticotropin (ACTH) and prolactin (PRL). Historical evidence has shown that these hormone responses are centrally mediated and represent indices of 5-HT function in the brain.[49,56-58] The utility of the neuroendocrine challenge paradigm is supported by many clinical studies which have adopted this approach to demonstrate changes in 5-HT responsiveness associated with depression and other psychiatric disorders.[59,60]

The validity of the neuroendocrine challenge model is based upon the rich 5-HT innervation of hypothalamic regions implicated in neuroendocrine transduction (i.e., paraventricular

Michael H. Baumann and Richard B. Rothman

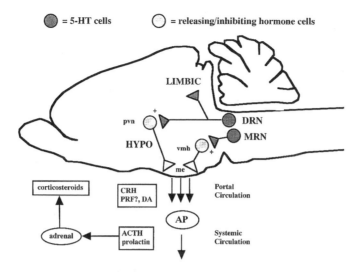

Figure 6.5.3.1 Schematic diagram showing the 5-HT regulation of adrenocorticotropin (ACTH) and prolactin secretion. 5-HT axons from the dorsal raphe (DRN) and median raphe nuclei (MRN) provide input to various releasing/inhibiting hormone cells in the paraventricular (pvn) and ventromedial nuclei (vmh) of the hypothalamus (HYPO). Specific releasing/inhibiting hormones include corticotropin releasing hormone (CRH); prolactin-releasing factor (PRF?), which has been proposed but not identified; and dopamine (DA), a prolactin inhibiting hormone. Activation of these 5-HT circuits modulates the secretion of releasing/inhibiting hormones into the median eminence (me) and ultimately releases ACTH and prolactin from the anterior pituitary (AP). Elevation of ACTH in the systemic circulation, in turn, stimulates the release of corticosteroids from the adrenal cortex. Note that 5-HT axons projecting to the HYPO send axon collaterals to LIMBIC areas implicated in the control of mood. See text for references and further discussion.

and ventromedial nuclei).[25,26,61] As shown in Figure 6.5.3.1, ascending 5-HT projections arising from the DR and MR terminate in close proximity to hypothalamic cells which contain releasing or inhibiting hormones that control pituitary function. Stimulation of these 5-HT circuits triggers the secretion of ACTH and PRL from the anterior pituitary into the systemic circulation. The elevation of plasma ACTH, in turn, activates the adrenal cortex to release corticosterone (in rats) or cortisol (in humans). Axons projecting from the DR are involved with the secretion of PRL but not ACTH, suggesting different subsets of 5-HT axons regulate specific hormones.[57,62] It is noteworthy that 5-HT pathways innervating the hypothalamus give rise to collaterals terminating in limbic regions such as the amygdala.[23,25,63] Thus, endocrine responses to 5-HT drugs may reflect the status of 5-HT neurons modulating behavior.

6.5.3.2 Changes in Presynaptic 5-HT Transmission

A growing body of evidence indicates withdrawal from chronic cocaine in rats is accompanied by alterations in presynaptic 5-HT function.[49-51] Cunningham and co-workers[64] examined 5-HT electrophysiology in the DR of rats withdrawn for 24 h from repeated cocaine injections (15 mg/kg, ip, bid, for 7 d). They found that suppression of 5-HT cell firing induced by cocaine, fluoxetine (a 5-HT reuptake blocker), or 8-OH-DPAT, was significantly potentiated in cocaine-treated rats. Their results suggest chronic cocaine exposure causes sensitization of 5-HT_{1A} somatodendritic autoreceptors modulating cell firing. Cocaine-induced enhancement of 5-HT autoregulation would be expected to produce a net decrease in 5-HT transmission. In fact, subsequent studies have shown a significant reduction in the number of spontaneously active 5-HT cells in the DR, and decreases in their firing rates, during cocaine withdrawal.[50]

Serotonergic Dysfunction During Cocaine Withdrawal

Figure 6.5.3.2 Peak prolactin responses produced by IV challenge injection of saline (1 ml/kg), fenfluramine (1.2 mg/kg), 8-OH-DPAT (50 µg/kg) or DOI (100 µg/kg) in rats withdrawn for 42 h from chronic cocaine (15 mg/kg, ip, bid, for 7 d) or saline. Blood samples were removed via indwelling jugular catheters at 15 min after challenge, and plasma was assayed for prolactin. Data are mean ± SEM for N=7 to 8 rats/group expressed as ng equivalents of NIDDK-rPRL-RP-3. *P<0.05 with respect to corresponding chronic saline-treated group (Duncan's). Modified from References 75 and 91.

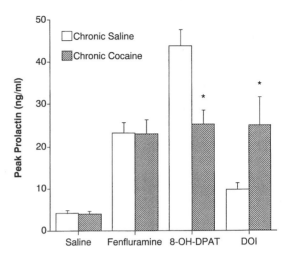

Data from *in vivo* neurochemical experiments support the hypothesis of diminished synaptic 5-HT during withdrawal from chronic cocaine.[10,51,65] Parsons and Justice[10] used intracerebral microdialysis methods to measure extracellular 5-HT levels in rat brain 24 h after cessation of repeated cocaine injections (20 mg/kg, ip, for 10 d). These investigators found a trend, albeit non-significant, toward lower basal 5-HT levels in the nucleus accumbens, ventral tegmental area, and DR of cocaine-withdrawn rats. Interestingly, the reduction in baseline extracellular 5-HT in the nucleus accumbens was much more dramatic when examined in rats withdrawn from unlimited-access cocaine self-administration.[65] Given the fact that chronic cocaine does not produce neurotoxic depletions of central 5-HT,[48,53-55] the microdialysis data suggest withdrawal from chronic cocaine is accompanied by a specific reduction in the amount of 5-HT available for release.

The results from neuroendocrine experiments are fully consistent with the idea of decreased releasable 5-HT during cocaine withdrawal.[49] The 5-HT releasers parachloroamphetamine (PCA) and fenfluramine have been used as probes to assess 5-HT transmission in cocaine-treated rats. The 5-HT-releasing action of these agents involves the exchange of drug molecules for intracellular 5-HT via an interaction with the 5-HT transporter.[66,67] Thus, hormone responses produced by PCA and fenfluramine represent, at least in part, indices of 5-HT nerve terminal function.[56-58] Van de Kar and colleagues[68] reported that PCA-induced ACTH and corticosterone responses were diminished in rats withdrawn for 42 h from repeated cocaine injections (15 mg/kg, ip, bid, for 7 or 30 d). These findings have been confirmed by other investigators using either PCA or fenfluramine as the challenge agent.[49,69,70] The PRL secretory response to PCA is also blunted in rats withdrawn from chronic cocaine[71] and this attenuated responsiveness is maintained for up to 8 weeks.[72] On the other hand, repeated injections of cocaine do not affect fenfluramine-induced PRL secretion (see Figure 6.5.3.2).[49,69] The reason(s) why cocaine exposure modifies the PRL-releasing ability of PCA and not fenfluramine is unclear, but these drugs are reported to exhibit subtle differences in their mechanisms of action.[67,73,74] Collectively, the hormone response data provide further support for the hypothesis of a cocaine-induced deficit in presynaptic 5-HT function. The precise nature of this deficit, however, remains to be determined.

6.5.3.3 Changes in Postsynaptic 5-HT Receptor Sensitivity

Recent studies show that cocaine withdrawal is accompanied by complex changes in postsynaptic 5-HT receptor sensitivity.[49,69,75-77] The interpretation of this literature is complicated by several factors. First, investigators have used slightly different chronic cocaine dosing regimens, withdrawal intervals, and functional endpoints when evaluating the effects of cocaine on 5-HT receptor function.[49-51] Second, few studies have addressed the possibility of altered disposition

Michael H. Baumann and Richard B. Rothman

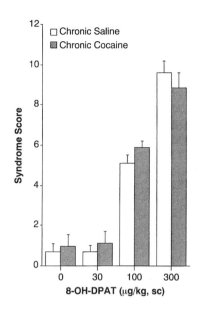

Figure 6.5.3.3.1 5-HT behavioral syndrome produced by sc challenge injection of saline or 8- OH-DPAT in rats withdrawn for 42 h from chronic cocaine (15 mg/kg, ip, bid, for 7 d) or saline. Rats were observed for 60-s intervals every 10 min after challenge injection for 1 h. The presence of forepaw treading and flat-body posture was scored using the graded scale: **0**=absent, **1**=equivocal, **2**=present, and **3**=intense. Each rat was given a single score that consisted of the summed forepaw treading and flat-body posture scores across all time points. Values shown represent mean ± SEM for N=7 to 8 rats.

and metabolism of 5-HT drugs after chronic cocaine treatment. For example, the blunted responsiveness to a 5-HT receptor agonist in cocaine-treated rats may simply reflect increased metabolism of the agonist. Finally, the assessment of 5-HT receptor function *in vivo* is severely hampered by a lack of selective 5-HT agonists and antagonists.[78,79] This is especially true for the 5-HT$_2$ receptor family because few drugs can discriminate between 5-HT$_{2A}$ and 5-HT$_{2C}$ subtypes.[79] (For the sake of simplicity, 5-HT$_{2A/2C}$ receptors will be referred to collectively as 5-HT$_2$ receptors). Despite these caveats, some general consistencies in the data are emerging.

Administration of the 5-HT$_{1A}$ receptor agonist 8-OH-DPAT increases the secretion of ACTH and PRL from the pituitary.[80-82] These hormone responses are centrally mediated involving postsynaptic 5-HT$_{1A}$ receptors in the paraventricular and ventromedial regions of the hypothalamus.[83,84] The data in Figure 6.5.3.2 show that PRL secretion elicited by 8-OH-DPAT is reduced in rats withdrawn for 42 h from repeated cocaine injections (15 mg/kg, ip, bid, for 7 d).[75] Similarly, Levy et al.[69] reported prior cocaine exposure attenuates both the ACTH and PRL responses to 8-OH-DPAT. Using electrophysiological methods, Cunningham found the inhibitory actions of 5-HT on amygdala neuronal activity are blunted in cocaine-treated rats, and this effect may involve changes in postsynaptic 5-HT$_{1A}$ receptor sensitivity.[50] Taken together, these findings suggest postsynaptic 5-HT$_{1A}$ receptors coupled to hormone secretion, and possibly amygdala cell firing, are rendered subsensitive by prior cocaine exposure.

In contrast to the neuroendocrine data, the 8-OH-DPAT-induced 5-HT syndrome is not affected by pretreatment with repeated cocaine injections (Figure 6.5.3.3.1).[75] Specific components of the 5-HT syndrome, namely forepaw treading and flat-body posture, involve activation of postsynaptic 5-HT$_{1A}$ receptors.[85,86] The cocaine-treated rats in our studies exhibit behavioral sensitization to subsequent cocaine injections,[48] and 8-OH-DPAT does not display cross-sensitization to cocaine. The fact that cocaine exposure differentially affects 5-HT$_{1A}$-stimulated endocrine and behavioral responses probably reflects the different anatomical substrates involved with these effects; 5-HT$_{1A}$ receptors in the hypothalamus and brainstem are implicated in hormone release and 5-HT syndrome, respectively.[83,84,86]

Several studies have examined the effects of repeated cocaine injections on [^{3}H]-8-OH-DPAT binding in rat brain, and no consistent changes have been found.[64,87,88] Thus, cocaine-induced reduction in 5-HT$_{1A}$ receptor sensitivity may involve dysregulation downstream from ligand-receptor recognition. It is well known that 5-HT$_{1A}$ receptors are coupled to adenylate cyclase via inhibitory G-proteins.[24,29,30] Interestingly, the findings of Nestler et al.[89] have provided evidence for decreased levels of inhibitory G-proteins in reward-relevant brain regions after chronic cocaine treatment. Whether their data are applicable to 5-HT$_{1A}$ receptor function is uncertain, but it seems feasible chronic cocaine exposure could cause functional desensitiza-

Figure 6.5.3.3.2 Head shakes induced by IV challenge injection of saline or DOI in rats withdrawn for 42 h from chronic cocaine (15 mg/kg, ip, bid, 7 d) or saline. Rats were observed for 90-s intervals every 10 min after challenge injection for 1 h, and the number of head shakes was counted. Each rat was given a single score that consisted of total head shakes counted across all time periods. Values shown represent mean ± SEM for N=7 to 8 rats. *P<0.05, **P<0.01 compared to chronic saline-treated group at the corresponding dose of DOI (Duncan's).[92]

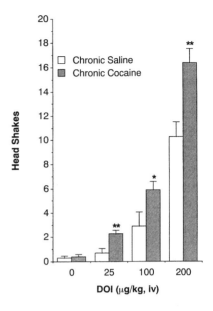

tion of postsynaptic 5-HT_{1A} receptors by uncoupling these receptors from their effector systems.

The 5-HT_2 agonist DOI elevates plasma ACTH and PRL in the rat, and these responses have been utilized as indices of postsynaptic 5-HT_2 function in the brain.[77,90,91] As depicted in Figure 6.5.3.2, the PRL secretory response produced by DOI is potentiated in rats previously exposed to repeated cocaine injections.[91] These results agree with the findings of others who demonstrated DOI-induced ACTH and PRL responses are augmented after 42 h of withdrawal from 7 d of cocaine exposure.[77] Likewise, withdrawal from cocaine also potentiates DOI-induced head shakes in rats (Figure 6.5.3.3.2)[91,92] and head twitches in mice.[76] The simplest interpretation of these data is that withdrawal from repeated cocaine injections enhances the sensitivity of 5-HT_2 receptors. A recent investigation by Schreiber and co-workers[93] provides compelling evidence that DOI-induced head shakes in rats are mediated via selective activation of 5-HT_{2A} receptors in the brain. Because prior cocaine exposure potentiates ACTH, PRL, and head shake responses in a comparable manner,[77,91,92] it is tempting to speculate that chronic cocaine selectively renders 5-HT_{2A} receptors supersensitive. In agreement with this proposal, hormonal responses elicited by preferential 5-HT_{2C} agonists are not enhanced in rats withdrawn from repeated cocaine injections.[68,94]

The DOI challenge experiments suggest that 5-HT_2 receptors might be upregulated during withdrawal from chronic cocaine. Numerous investigators have examined the effects of prior cocaine exposure on [^{3}H]-ketanserin binding in rat brain and have found no changes.[87,88,95] However, preliminary autoradiographic data from our laboratory show that withdrawal from chronic cocaine increases the density of [^{125}I]DOI-labeled 5-HT_2 receptors in several cortical regions in rat brain.[185] The enhancement of 5-HT_2 receptor function during cocaine withdrawal may be involved in cocaine craving. Meert et al.,[96] as well as McMillen and colleagues,[97] trained rats to orally self-administer cocaine in drinking water. When these rats were tested in a choice paradigm, treatment with 5-HT_2 antagonists rapidly decreased the preference for cocaine. Moreover, the inhibitory effect of 5-HT_2 antagonists was specific for cocaine and other drugs of abuse because non-drug reinforcers were unaffected. These data suggest 5-HT_2 antagonists could be useful treatments for cocaine addiction.

6.5.3.4 Glucocorticoid - 5-HT Relationships

One possibility to consider is that corticosteroid hormones might play a role in altered 5-HT receptor responsiveness during cocaine withdrawal. Cocaine administration produces a robust rise in circulating ACTH and corticosteroids in both animals[98,99] and humans.[100,101] This cocaine-induced activation of the hypothalamic-pituitary-adrenal (HPA) axis is a centrally mediated process involving monoamines[102,103] and corticotropin-releasing hormone (CRH).[104] Preclinical experiments have shown tolerance to the endocrine actions of cocaine does not

Michael H. Baumann and Richard B. Rothman

develop;[105,106] therefore, repeated intermittent injections of cocaine elicit repeated activation of the HPA axis. Corticosteroids are known modulators of central 5-HT transmission.[107] For instance, studies in rats have demonstrated chronic exposure to high-dose corticoid hormones causes attenuated responsiveness to 8-OH-DPAT and potentiated responsiveness to DOI.[108-110] Thus, the changes in 5-HT receptor sensitivity observed during cocaine withdrawal are reproduced by chronic glucocorticoid treatment.

6.5.4 COCAINE WITHDRAWAL IN HUMANS INDUCES DEPRESSIVE-LIKE SYMPTOMS

Acute cocaine produces intense euphoria in humans, especially when the crack form of the drug is self-administered.[1,12-15] Due to the short half-life of cocaine,[1] frequent dosing is required to maintain the pleasurable effects, and cocaine is typically self-administered in binges characterized by repeated high-dose intake.[15,111] The inevitable ending of a cocaine binge is accompanied by an array of unpleasant symptoms often referred to as the "crash".[14-17,111] Manifestations of the crash, which may last for several days, include extreme depression, anxiety, irritability, and sleep disturbances. It is noteworthy that abrupt cessation of chronic cocaine self-administration in animals also produces behavioral disruptions indicative of dysphoria.[112,113] There has been some debate about whether cocaine addiction engenders true physiological withdrawal symptoms, yet clinicians and addicts alike acknowledge the major-depressive-like symptomatology of the cocaine crash.[14-17,111] The most recent version of The Diagnostic and Statistical Manual of Mental Disorders includes diagnostic criteria for cocaine withdrawal which correspond to the crash.[114]

Gawin and Kleber[15] provided the first in-depth analysis of cocaine withdrawal phenomena by evaluating clinical observations in addicts entering outpatient treatment. These investigators found that abstinence symptoms proceed through three distinct phases: (1) crash, (2) withdrawal, and (3) extinction.[15,111] The cocaine crash has been described above. Withdrawal lasts from 2 to 10 weeks and is associated with anhedonia, anergia, anxiety, and intense cocaine craving. Symptoms occurring during the withdrawal phase, particularly anhedonia and craving, may be important antecedents to recurring cocaine use.[14-16,111] Extinction, which lasts indefinitely, is characterized by normalized mood and episodic cue-induced craving. Interestingly, clinical assessments of cocaine withdrawal carried out in controlled inpatient settings have failed to confirm the three-phase progression of symptoms.[115,116] In these studies, measures of depression, anxiety, and fatigue are highest upon admission and gradually subside to normal levels within a few weeks. Data from inpatient investigations further suggest cocaine abstinence symptoms are mild and rarely require pharmacological intervention or hospitalization. It seems probable, however, that inpatient studies grossly underestimate the importance of cocaine withdrawal symptoms.[16,17] Under such circumstances, addicts reside in an artificial environment protected from the stressors of everyday life and the conditioned cues normally contributing to relapse. The increased incidence of suicide in withdrawn cocaine addicts[4,117,118] supports the notion that cocaine abstinence symptoms can be severe in some cases.

While the preceding discussion indicates cocaine withdrawal is accompanied by depressive-like symptoms, the interpretation of these data is complicated by the high prevalence of comorbid psychopathology in cocaine addicts.[15,111,119-121] For example, Rounsaville and colleagues[121] found over 50% of cocaine users seeking treatment met current criteria for a psychiatric disorder other than a substance use disorder. The predominant types of psychiatric diagnoses included major depression, anxiety disorders, antisocial personality, and childhood attention deficit disorder. These observations raise an important question regarding the temporal sequencing of cocaine abuse and depression: Does chronic cocaine abuse lead to, or develop from, depressive states? Interestingly, the bulk of evidence from treatment-seeking and community-based samples demonstrates that cocaine abuse precedes the onset of depressive disorders in most individuals.[121-123] While no cause and effect relationship between cocaine and depression can be gleaned from such observations, the findings are intriguing. Khantzian has proposed that addicts use cocaine as a means of self-medication to alleviate dysphoric symptoms;[124] indeed, clinical experience suggests negative affective states can serve as prime motivators precipitating cocaine relapse.[14-16,125-127]

6.5.5 5-HT DYSFUNCTION DURING MAJOR DEPRESSION: SIMILARITIES TO COCAINE WITHDRAWAL

The observation that symptoms of cocaine withdrawal mimic the symptoms of major depression[15,111,115,116] suggests the possibility these two conditions may have similar neurobiological underpinnings. Abnormalities in 5-HT function have been implicated in the pathophysiology of major depression.[59,60,128] The 5-HT hypothesis of depression is based upon several lines of evidence including: (1) enhancement of 5-HT transmission in response to chronic antidepressant treatment;[129,130] (2) diminished cerebrospinal fluid (CSF) levels of the 5-HT metabolite, 5-HIAA, in some depressed individuals;[59] (3) blunted neuroendocrine responsiveness to presynaptic 5-HT agonists and 5-HT$_{1A}$ agonists in depressed patients;[60] and (4) elevated 5-HT$_2$ receptor binding density in the brains of suicide victims.[128] In the following section, changes in 5-HT function associated with major depression will be succinctly reviewed with specific reference to the analogous changes in 5-HT function identified in rats withdrawn from chronic cocaine.

6.5.5.1 Changes in Presynaptic Transmission

Studies in rats demonstrate that 5-HT$_{1A}$ autoreceptors in the DR are sensitized during withdrawal from cocaine.[50,64] It is difficult to directly assess the sensitivity of 5-HT$_{1A}$ somatodendritic autoreceptors in human subjects due to obvious constraints, but investigators have examined the effects of chronic antidepressant treatment on 5-HT cell electrophysiology in rats.[129,130] From these studies it is apparent that chronic administration of antidepressants leads to an increase in net 5-HT neurotransmission. A principal mechanism of 5-HT enhancement associated with 5-HT-selective reuptake inhibitors (SSRIs), and monoamine oxidase inhibitors (MAOIs), involves desensitization of inhibitory 5-HT$_{1A}$ autoreceptors in the DR.[130] Thus, the effect of chronic antidepressant treatment on 5-HT$_{1A}$ impulse-regulating autoreceptors is opposite to the reported effects of chronic cocaine on these receptors *in vivo*.[50,64]

The microdialysis findings of Parsons et al.[10,51,65] show that cocaine withdrawal decreases the extracellular 5-HT in rat nucleus accumbens. Direct measures of extracellular 5-HT in living human brain are not obtainable, but the concentration of 5-HIAA circulating in CSF has been used as a gauge of central 5-HT function in human subjects.[59,128] The early findings of Asberg et al.[131] showed that some depressed patients exhibit decreased CSF levels of 5-HIAA. Reduced 5-HIAA in CSF presumably reflects decreased 5-HT utilization in the brain. Analysis of data from large populations of patients and controls support the existence of a subgroup of depressives exhibiting reduced 5-HIAA levels in CSF;[132] however, the relevance of such data to the etiology of affective disorders remains controversial.[59,128] In fact, increasing evidence supports the hypothesis that low CSF levels of 5-HIAA are more correlated with aggression, impulsiveness, and suicidality rather than depression per se.[133] This proposal is especially relevant to the problem of cocaine abuse because addicts exhibit a propensity for aggressive/violent behaviors[4,134,135] as well as suicide[118,119] which could be related to presynaptic deficits in 5-HT function.

Specific hormone responses evoked by PCA and fenfluramine are blunted in rats treated with repeated cocaine injections.[49,68-70] Similarly, neuroendocrine challenge tests in human subjects have provided evidence for presynaptic 5-HT dysfunction associated with depressive disorders.[59,60] Siever et al.[136] first reported fenfluramine-induced PRL secretion is attenuated in patients with major depression. A number of subsequent investigations have shown blunted PRL and/or cortisol responses to fenfluramine in patients diagnosed with depression.[137-141] It must be mentioned, however, that reduced sensitivity to fenfluramine is not a universal finding in depressed individuals, and studies reporting blunted hormone responses have generally included more severely debilitated patients.[59,60] O'Keane and colleagues[142] demonstrated the blunted responsiveness to fenfluramine in depressed patients is normalized following recovery, suggesting reduced fenfluramine sensitivity may be a state-dependent marker of depression. Preliminary clinical data from our laboratory show that fenfluramine-induced cortisol secretion is reduced in human drug users exposed to repeated doses of cocaine,[184] and this finding resembles the results in chronic cocaine-treated rats.

6.5.5.2 Changes in Postsynaptic 5-HT Receptor Sensitivity

Withdrawal from chronic cocaine is associated with diminished hormonal effects of the 5-HT$_{1A}$ agonist, 8-OH-DPAT, in rats.[69,75] Likewise, clinical experiments have demonstrated attenuated 5-HT$_{1A}$ receptor function in major depression. The 5-HT$_{1A}$ agonist buspirone is an anxiolytic medication which increases circulating ACTH, PRL, and cortisol when administered to humans.[60,143] A related compound, ipsapirone, elicits similar endocrine effects and reliably decreases core body temperature.[144,145] While the endocrine actions of these drugs involve activation of postsynaptic 5-HT$_{1A}$ receptors,[60] there is disagreement concerning the role of presynaptic vs. postsynaptic sites in mediating hypothermic responses.[86,146] Lesch et al.[144,145] first demonstrated ipsapirone-induced ACTH, cortisol, and hypothermic responses are attenuated in major depression. The findings that depressed patients exhibit blunted cortisol and hypothermic responses to 5-HT$_{1A}$ agonists has been confirmed by others.[147,148] One study reported that PRL secretion evoked by buspirone was reduced in patients diagnosed with depression,[149] but this finding has not been replicated.[147,150]

Intravenous administration of the 5-HT precursor *L*-5-hydroxytryptophan (5-HTP) dose-dependently increases plasma PRL and GH in human subjects.[59,60] The endocrine effects of 5-HTP are antagonized by pindolol suggesting the involvement of postsynaptic 5-HT$_{1A}$ receptors.[151] Numerous investigators have shown diminished 5-HTP-induced PRL responses in depressed individuals.[152-154] Whether blunted responsiveness to 5-HTP is related to changes in 5-HT nerve terminal function or 5-HT$_{1A}$ receptor sensitivity is unclear. Nevertheless, the collective findings suggest postsynaptic 5-HT$_{1A}$ receptors mediating neuroendocrine secretion, and possibly hypothermia, may be desensitized in subjects diagnosed with major depression. It is noteworthy that chronic tricyclic antidepressant administration is reported to enhance the electrophysiological effects of 5-HT$_{1A}$ agonists at postsynaptic sites in rat hippocampus.[155] Thus, the effect of chronic antidepressant treatment on postsynaptic 5-HT$_{1A}$ receptor function is opposite of the reported effects of chronic cocaine.

DOI challenge studies in rats suggest that 5-HT$_2$ receptors coupled to behavioral and endocrine responses are sensitized by chronic cocaine exposure.[76,77,91,92] Human studies utilizing 5-HT$_2$ agonists such as DOI are precluded by the hallucinogenic properties of these agents. Many studies have employed the 5-HT agonist m-chlorophenylpiperazine (mCPP) as a probe for assessing postsynaptic 5-HT$_{2C}$ receptor function in laboratory animals and humans.[156] Kahn and colleagues[157] examined PRL and cortisol secretion elicited by mCPP in depressed patients and found no changes in responsiveness. Their data indicate 5-HT$_{2C}$ receptor sensitivity is unaltered during depressive illness. It must be mentioned, however, that mCPP displays comparable affinity for a variety of 5-HT receptor subtypes and 5-HT transporters in human brain.[158,159] Thus, studies using mCPP as a probe for 5-HT receptor function are difficult to interpret.

Figure 6.5.5.3 Effect of intranasal placebo or cocaine (96 mg) on plasma cortisol in human subjects tested on Day 1 (panel A) and Day 5 (panel B) of an inpatient research study. Data are mean ± SEM for N=8 subjects. Plasma cortisol units are µg/dL. *P<0.05 with respect to placebo condition at specific time points (Duncan's).

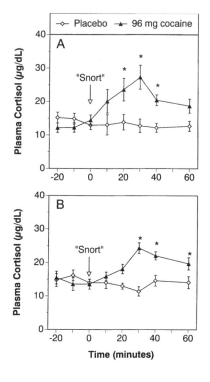

Several types of evidence suggest that 5-HT$_2$ receptors may be upregulated in patients with depression. Radioligand binding studies in postmortem brain tissue have shown an increased density of postsynaptic 5-HT$_2$ receptors in the frontal cortex of depressed suicide victims.[160-162] Quantitative autoradiographic methods have confirmed that the number of 5-HT$_2$ receptors is elevated in the prefrontal cortex of suicide deaths.[163] In contrast to the augmented 5-HT$_2$ receptor binding in suicides, chronic antidepressant administration in rodents causes downregulation of 5-HT$_2$ receptor binding sites.[164,165]

Human blood platelets take up, store, and release 5-HT in a manner analogous to the 5-HT neurons in the brain, and platelets have been utilized as peripheral indices of central 5-HT function.[166] Blood platelets also display 5-HT$_2$ receptors, and several investigators found an elevated density of 5-HT$_2$ receptors on blood platelets from patients diagnosed with depression.[167-169] The increased 5-HT$_2$ receptor density in platelets appears to be a state-dependent marker for depression because 5-HT$_2$ binding is normalized in patients who show clinical improvement.[169] Taken together, these data suggest that 5-HT$_2$ receptors in the brain and on blood platelets are upregulated in depressed patients.

6.5.5.3 Glucocorticoid - 5-HT Relationships

It is well established that patients diagnosed with major depression exhibit increased HPA activity which leads to elevated plasma levels of cortisol.[171] Glucocorticoid hypersecretion, in turn, may underly the 5-HT abnormalities associated with depression.[172,173] For example, elevated baseline cortisol levels have been correlated with a reduction in neuroendocrine responsiveness to fenfluramine and 5-HT$_{1A}$ agonists during depression.[141,142,144] Based on the similarities between cocaine withdrawal and major depression, we sought to examine the effects of cocaine on HPA axis function in human substance users. Male drug users who fulfilled the diagnostic criteria for cocaine dependence (N=8) participated in two daily self-administration sessions for five consecutive days in a controlled inpatient setting. At each session subjects snorted either a placebo or 96 mg cocaine, with drug being presented in a double-blind, randomized fashion at one of the daily sessions. The data in Figure 6.5.5.3 show that intranasal cocaine administration significantly elevated plasma cortisol in a similar manner on Day 1 and Day 5 of the study. Thus, cocaine-induced cortisol secretion does not appear to display tolerance or sensitization, in agreement with studies in rats.[105,106] From an endocrine perspective, chronic cocaine abuse mimics chronic presentation of stressful stimuli; repeated activation of the HPA axis in cocaine addicts may have long-term consequences. An additional finding from this work was that baseline plasma cortisol levels in cocaine users were significantly elevated compared to drug- free control subjects residing on the research ward.[185] These data, while preliminary, suggest possible dysregulation of the HPA axis in human cocaine addicts.

Michael H. Baumann and Richard B. Rothman

6.5.6 CONCLUDING REMARKS

The literature reviewed herein demonstrates that chronic cocaine exposure causes complex alterations in central 5-HT function. Converging lines of evidence indicate cocaine withdrawal is accompanied by a presynaptic deficit in 5-HT transmission, resulting in diminished synaptic availability of 5-HT in the brain. Neuroendocrine and behavioral studies suggest cocaine withdrawal renders postsynaptic 5-HT_{1A} receptors subsensitive and 5-HT_{2A} receptors supersensitive. The precise mechanisms underlying these changes have not been determined but may be related to repeated activation of the HPA axis by cocaine. It seems more than coincidental that the spectrum of 5-HT abnormalities is similar in rats withdrawn from cocaine and patients diagnosed with depression. Collectively, the findings suggest cocaine withdrawal produces major-depressive-like symptoms via dysregulation of 5-HT transmission. This hypothesis has important treatment implications. For example, medications that enhance synaptic 5-HT (i.e., fluoxetine) may be effective treatments for cocaine addiction, especially in patients suffering from severe depressive symptoms.[16,17,174-176]

It is doubtful, however, that alterations in any one neurotransmitter system can fully account for the constellation of symptoms experienced by abstinent cocaine addicts. In agreement with this idea, pharmacotherapies targeting one neurotransmitter system have failed to successfully treat cocaine dependence.[16,17] We have proposed a dual deficit model of cocaine abstinence phenomena in which DA and 5-HT dysfunction contribute to withdrawal symptomatology.[177,178] The findings supporting chronic cocaine-induced deficits in DA function have been thoroughly reviewed elsewhere,[51,179-181] while the evidence for deficts in 5-HT function has been the subject of this section. The recent studies of Parsons and co-workers[51,65] provide direct support for the model. These investigators have monitored *in vivo* neurochemistry in rats trained on a schedule of unlimited-access intravenous cocaine self-administration. Cessation of cocaine self-administration in these rats significantly decreases basal levels of extracellular DA and 5-HT in the nucleus accumbens. Interestingly, under these same conditions, cocaine abstinence is associated with increased intracranial self-stimulation thresholds that are reflective of anhedonia.[182]

According to the dual deficit model, DA dysfunction during cocaine withdrawal underlies anhedonia and psychomotor retardation whereas 5-HT dysfunction gives rise to depressed mood, obsessional thoughts, and lack of impulse control. Pharmacotherapies which "correct" the proposed DA and 5-HT abnormalities should theoretically be effective in treating cocaine dependence. Phentermine and fenfluramine are anorectic amphetamine analogs which preferentially elevate extracellular DA and 5-HT, respectively, in the brain.[66,67,178,183] Rothman and co-workers[177] treated a series of self-referred cocaine-dependent patients with a combination of phentermine and fenfluramine. This treatment reduced cocaine craving, alleviated depressive symptoms, and prolonged cocaine abstinence. Although these findings are preliminary, they suggest medications that enhance both DA and 5-HT transmission in the brain may be effective in treating cocaine dependence. It seems likely that 5-HT dysfunction represents just one of multiple neuroadaptive changes occurring in response to chronic cocaine exposure. Whether such changes occur in human cocaine addicts is unknown, but neuroendocrine challenge tests and *in vivo* brain imaging are potential approaches for examining 5-HT function in human cocaine users. Administration of drug combinations that affect multiple neurotransmitter systems could be a promising new strategy for combatting the formidable problem of cocaine addiction.

REFERENCES

1. Johanson, C.-E. and Schuster, C. R., Cocaine, in *Psychopharmacology: The Fourth Generation of Progress*, Bloom, F. E. and Kupfer, D. J., Eds., Raven, New York, 1995, 1685.
2. Cregler, L. L. and Mark, H., Medical complications of cocaine abuse, *N. Eng. J. Med.*, 315, 1495, 1986.
3. Warner, E. A., Cocaine abuse, *Ann. Intern. Med.*, 119, 226, 1993.
4. Marzuk, P. M., Tardiff, K., Leon, A. C., Hirsch, C. S., Stajic, M., Portera, L., Hartwell, N. and Iqbal, M. I., Fatal injuries after cocaine use as a leading cause of death among young adults in New York city, *N. Eng. J. Med.*, 332, 1753, 1995.
5. Johnson, D. N. and Vocci, F. J., Medications development at the National Institute on Drug Abuse: focus on cocaine, in *Cocaine Treatment: Research and Clinical Perspectives*, NIDA Research Monograph 135, Tims, F. M. and Leuekfeld, C. G., Eds., U.S. Government Printing Office, Washington, D.C., 1993, 57.
6. Koe, B. K., Molecular geometry of inhibitors of the uptake of catecholamines and serotonin in synaptosomal preparations of rat brain, *J. Pharmacol. Exp. Ther.*, 199, 649, 1976.
7. Reith, M. E., Meisler, B. E., Sershen, H. and Lajtha, A., Structural requirements for cocaine congeners to interact with dopamine and serotonin uptake sites in mouse brain and to induce stereotyped behavior, *Biochem. Pharmacol.*, 35, 1123, 1986.
8. Ritz, M.C., Cone, E. J. and Kuhar, M. J., Cocaine inhibition of ligand binding at dopamine, norepinephrine and serotonin transporters: a structure activity study, *Life Sci.*, 46, 635, 1990.
9. Bradberry, C. W., Nobiletti, J. B., Elsworth, J. D., Murphy, B., Jatlow, P. and Roth, R. H., Cocaine and cocaethylene: microdialysis comparison of brain drug level and effects on dopamine and serotonin, *J. Neurochem.*, 60, 1429, 1993.
10. Parsons, L. H. and Justice, J. B., Serotonin and dopamine sensitization in the nucleus accumbens, ventral tegmental area, and dorsal raphe nucleus following repeated cocaine administration, *J. Neurochem.*, 61, 1611, 1993.
11. Chen, N.-H. and Reith, M. E., Effects of locally applied cocaine, lidocaine, and various uptake blockers on monoamine transmission in the ventral tegmental area of freely moving rats: a microdialysis study on monoamine interrelationships, *J. Neurochem.*, 63, 1701, 1993.
12. Koob, G. F. and Bloom, F. E., Cellular and molecular mechanisms of drug dependence, *Science*, 242, 715, 1988.
13. Kuhar, M. J., Ritz, M. C. and Boja, J. W., The dopamine hypothesis of the reinforcing properties of cocaine, *Trends Neurosci.*, 14, 299, 1991.
14. Dackis, C. A. and Gold, M. S., New concepts in cocaine addiction: the dopamine depletion hypothesis, *Neurosci. Biobehav. Rev.*, 9, 469, 1985.
15. Gawin, F. H. and Kleber, H. D., Abstinence symptomatology and psychiatric diagnoses in cocaine abusers, *Arch. Gen. Psychiatry*, 43, 107, 1986.
16. Kleber, H. D., Pharmacotherapy, current and potential, for the treatment of cocaine dependence, *Clin. Neuropharm.*, 18, S96, 1995.
17. Mendelson, J. H. and Mello, N. K., Management of cocaine abuse and dependence, *N. Eng. J. Med.*, 334, 965, 1996.
18. Rothman, R. B. and Glowa, J. R., A review of the effects of dopaminergic agents on humans, animals, and drug-seeking behavior, and its implication for medication development, *Mol. Neurobiol.*, 11, 1, 1995.
19. Cunningham, K. A. and Callahan, P. M., Neurobehavioral pharmacology of cocaine: role for serotonin in its locomotor and discriminative stimulus effects, in *Neurobiological Models for Evaluating Mechanisms Underlying Cocaine Addiction*, NIDA Research Monograph 145, Erinoff, L. and Brown, R. M., Eds., U.S. Government Printing Office, Washington, D.C., 1994, 40.
20. Roberts, D. C. S., Self-administration of stimulants and serotonergic systems, in *Problems of Drug Dependence 1991*, NIDA Research Monograph 119, Harris, L., Ed., U.S. Government Printing Office, Washington, D.C., 1992, 136.

Michael H. Baumann and Richard B. Rothman

21. Walsh, S. L., Preston, K. L., Sullivan, J. T., Fromme, R. and Bigelow, G. E., Fluoxetine alters the effects of intravenous cocaine in humans, *J. Clin. Psychopharm.*, 14, 396, 1994.
22. *The Neuropharmacology of Serotonin*, Ann. N.Y. Acad. Sci. 600, Whitaker-Azmitia, P. M. and Peroutka, S. J., Eds., N. Y. Acad. Sci., New York, 1990.
23. Molliver, M. E., Serotonergic neuronal systems: what their anatomic organization tells us about function, *J. Clin. Psychopharm.*, 7, 3S, 1987.
24. Humphrey, P. P. A., Hartig, P. and Hoyer, D., A proposed new nomenclature for 5-HT receptor, *Trends Pharmacol. Sci.*, 14, 233, 1993.
25. Azmitia, E. C. and Segal, M., An autoradiographic analysis of the differential ascending projections of the dorsal and median raphe nuclei in the rat, *J. Comp. Neurol.*, 179, 641, 1978.
26. Steinbusch, H. W. M., Distribution of serotonin-immunoreactivity in the central nervous system of the rat - cell bodies and terminals, *Neurosci.*, 6, 557, 1981.
27. Kosofsy, B. E. and Molliver, M. E., The serotonergic innervation of the cerebral cortex: different classes of axon terminals arise from dorsal and median raphe nuclei, *Synapse*, 1, 153, 1987.
28. Descarries, L., Audet, M. A., Doucet, G., Garcia, S., Oleskevich S., Segueula, P., Soghomonian, J.-J. and Watkins, K. C., Morphology of central serotonin neurons: brief review of quantified aspects of their distribution and ultrastructural relationships, in *Neuropharmacology of Serotonin*, Ann. N. Y. Acad. Sci. 600, Whitaker-Azmitia, P. M. and Peroutka, S. J., Eds., N.Y. Acad. Sci., New York, 1990, 81.
29. Martin, G. R. and Humphrey, P. P. A., Receptors for 5-hydroxytryptamine: current perspectives on classification and nomenclature, *Neuropharmacology*, 33, 261, 1994.
30. Sanders-Bush, E. and Canton, H., Serotonin receptors: signal transduction pathways, in *Psychopharmacology: The Fourth Generation of Progress*, Bloom, F. E. and Kupfer, D. J., Eds., Raven, New York, 1995, 431.
31. Palacios, J. M. and Dietl, M. M., Autoradiographic studies of serotonin receptors, in *The Serotonin Receptors*, Sanders-Bush, E., Ed., Humana, Clifton, 1988, 89.
32. Pazos, A. and Palacios, J. M., Quantitative autoradiographic mapping of serotonin receptors in the rat brain. I. serotonin-1 receptors, *Brain Res.*, 346, 205, 1985.
33. Hoyer, D., Pazos, A., Probst, A. and Palacios, J.M., Serotonin receptors in the human brain. I. characterization and autoradiographic localization of 5-HT_{1A} recognition sites. apparent absence of 5-HT_{1B} recognition sites, *Brain Res.*, 376, 85, 1986.
34. Aghajanian, G. K., Sprouse, J. S. and Rasmussen, K., Physiology of the midbrain serotonin system, in *Psychopharmacology: The Third Generation of Progress*, Meltzer, H. Y., Ed., Raven, New York, 1987, 141.
35. Pazos, A., Cortes, R. and Palacios, J. M., Quantitative autoradiographic mapping of serotonin receptors in the rat brain. II. serotonin-2 receptors, *Brain Res.*, 346, 231, 1985.
36. Hoyer, D., Pazos, A., Probst, A. and Palacios, J. M., Serotonin receptors in the human brain. II. characterization and autoradiographic localization of 5-HT_{1C} and 5-HT_2 recognition sites, *Brain Res.*, 376, 97, 1986.
37. Glennon, R. A., Titeler, M. and McKenney, J. D., Evidence for 5-HT_2 receptor involvement in the mechanism of action of hallucinogenic agents, *Life Sci.*, 35, 2505, 1984.
38. McKenna, D. J., Nazarali, A. J., Hoffman, A. J., Nichols, D. E., Mathis, C. A. and Saavedra, J. M., Common receptors for hallucinogens in rat brain: A comparative autoradiographic study using $[^{125}\text{I}]$-LSD and $[^{125}\text{I}]$-DOI, a new psychotomimetic radioligand, *Brain Res.*, 76, 45, 1988.
39. Blakely, R. D., Berson, H. E., Fremeau, R. T., Caron, M. G., Peek, M. M., Prince, H. K. and Bradley, C. C., Cloning and expression of a functional serotonin transporter from rat brain, *Nature*, 354, 66, 1991.
40. Hoffman, B. J., Mezey, E. and Brownstein, M. J., Cloning of a serotonin transporter affected by antidepressants, *Science*, 254, 579, 1991.
41. Uhl, G. R., Neurotransmitter transporters (plus): a promising new gene family, *Trends Neurosci.*, 15, 265, 1992.
42. Pitts, D.K. and Marwah, J., Cocaine modulation of central monoaminergic neurotransmission, *Pharmacol. Biochem. Behav.*, 26, 453, 1987.

43. Lakoski, J. M. and Cunningham, K. A., Cocaine interaction with central monoaminergic systems: electrophysiological approaches, *Trends Pharmacol. Sci.*, 9, 177, 1988.

44. Cunningham, K. A. and Lakoski, J. M., The interaction of cocaine with serotonin dorsal raphe neurons: single-unit extracellular recording studies. *Neuropsychopharmacology*, 3, 41, 1990.

45. Einhorn, L. C., Johansen, P. A. and White, F. J., Electrophysiological effects of cocaine in the mesoaccumbens dopamine system, *J. Neurosci.*, 8, 100, 1988.

46. Pitts, D. K. and Marhwah, J., Electrophysiological actions of cocaine on noradrenergic neurons in the rat locus coeruleus, *J. Pharmacol. Exp. Ther.*, 240, 345, 1987.

47. Galloway, M. P., Regulation of dopamine and serotonin synthesis by acute cocaine administration, *Synapse*, 6, 63, 1990.

48. Baumann, M.H., Raley, T. J., Partilla, J. S. and Rothman, R. B., Biosynthesis of dopamine and serotonin in the rat brain after repeated cocaine injections: a microdissection mapping study, *Synapse*, 14, 40, 1993.

49. Levy, A.D., Baumann, M. H. and Van de Kar, L. D., Monoaminergic regulation of neuroendocrine function and its modification by cocaine, *Front. Neuroendocrinology*, 15, 85, 1994.

50. Cunningham, K. A., Modulation of serotonin function by acute and chronic cocaine: neurophysiological analyses, in *Molecular Neurobiology of Cocaine*, Hammer, R., Ed., CRC, Boca Raton, 1995, 121.

51. Weiss, F., Parsons, L. H. and Markou, A., Neurochemistry of cocaine withdrawal, in *Molecular Neurobiology of Cocaine*, Hammer, R., Ed., CRC, Boca Raton, 1995, 163.

52. Kleven, M. S. and Seiden, L. S., Methamphetamine-induced neurotoxicity: structure activity relationships, in *The Neurobiology of Drug and Alcohol Addiction*, Ann. N. Y. Acad. Sci. 654, Kalivas, P. W. and Samson, H. H., Eds., N. Y. Acad. Sci., New York, 1992,

53. Kleven, M. S., Woolverton, W. L., and Seiden, L. S., Lack of long-term monoamine depletions following repeated or continuous exposure to cocaine, *Brain Res. Bull.*, 21, 233, 1988.

54. Yeh, S. Y. and DeSouza, E. B., Lack of neurochemical evidence for neurotoxic effects of repeated cocaine administration in rats on brain monoamine neurons, *Drug Alcoh. Depend.*, 27, 151, 1991.

55. Paris, J. M., Callahan, P. M., Lee J. M. and Cunningham, K. A., Behavioral sensitization to cocaine is not associated with changes in serotonin (5-HT) fiber immunoreactivity in rat forebrain, *Brain Res. Bull.* 27, 843, 1991.

56. Murphy, D. L., Mueller, E A., Garrick, N. A. and Aulakh, C. S., Use of serotonergic agents in the clinical assessment of central serotonin function, *J. Clin. Psychiatry*, 47(S4), 9, 1986.

57. Van de Kar, L.D., Neuroendocrine pharmacology of serotonergic (5-HT) neurons, *Ann. Rev. Pharmacol. Toxicol.*, 31, 289, 1991,

58. Yatham, L. N. and Steiner, M., Neuroendocrine probes of serotonergic function: a critical review, *Life Sci.*, 53, 447, 1993 .

59. Siever, L.J., Kahn, R. S., Lawlor, B. A., Trestman, R. L., Lawrence, T. L. and Coccaro, E. F., Critical issues in defining the role of serotonin in psychiatric disorders, *Pharmacol. Rev.*, 43, 509, 1991.

60. Cowen, P. J., Serotonin receptor subtypes in depression: evidence from studies in neuroendocrine regulation, *Clin. Neuropharmacol.*, 16, S6-S18, 1993.

61. Steinbusch, H. W. M. and Nieuwenhuys, R., Localization of serotonin-like immunoreactivity in the central nervous system and pituitary of the rat, with special reference to the innervation of the hypothalamus, in *Advances in Experimental Medicine and Biology*, vol. 133, Haber, B. and Gabay, S., Eds., Plenum, New York, 1981, 7.

62. Van de Kar, L. D. and Bethea, C. L., Pharmacological evidence that serotonergic stimulation of prolactin secretion is mediated by the dorsal raphe nucleus, *Neuroendocrinology*, 35, 225, 1982.

63. Imai, H., Steindler, D. A. and Kitai, S. T., The organization of divergent axonal projections from the midbrain raphe nuclei in the rat, *J. Comp. Neurol.*, 243, 363, 1986.

64. Cunningham, K. A., Paris, J. M. and Goeders, N. E., Chronic cocaine enhances serotonin autoregulation and serotonin uptake binding, *Synapse*, 11, 112, 1992.

Michael H. Baumann and Richard B. Rothman

65. Parsons, L. H., Koob, G. F. and Weiss, F., Serotonin dysfunction in the nucleus accumbens of rats during withdrawal after unlimited access to intravenous cocaine, *J. Pharmacol. Exp. Ther.*, 274, 1182, 1995.

66. Berger, U. V., Gu, X. F. and Azmitia, E. C., The substituted amphetamines 3,4-methylenedioxymethamphetamine, methamphetamine, p-chloroamphetamine and fenfluramine induce 5-hydroxytryptamine release via a common mechanism blocked by fluoxetine and cocaine, *Eur. J. Pharmacol.*, 215, 153, 1992.

67. Schuldiner, S., Steiner-Mordoch, S., Yelin, R., Wall, S. C. and Rudnick, G., Amphetamine derivatives interact with both plasma membrane and secretory vesicle biogenic amine transporters, *Mol. Pharmacol.*, 44, 1227, 1993.

68. Van de Kar, L. D., Bonadonna, A. M., Rittenhouse, P. A., Kerr, J. E., Levy, A. D., Iyer, L., Herbert, G. B., Alvarez Sanz, M. C., Lent, S. J. and Carnes, M., Prior chronic exposure to cocaine inhibits the serotonergic stimulation of ACTH and secretion of corticosterone. *Neuropharmacology*, 31, 169, 1992.

69. Levy, A. D., Li, Q. and Van de Kar, L. D., Repeated cocaine exposure inhibits the adrenocorticotropic hormone response to the serotonin releaser d-fenfluramine and the 5-HT$_{1A}$ agonist, 8-OH-DPAT, *Neuropharmacology*, 33, 335, 1994.

70. Baumann, M. H., Becketts, K. M. and Rothman, R. B., Evidence for alterations in presynaptic serotonergic function during withdrawal from chronic cocaine in rats. *Eur. J. Pharmacol.*, 282, 87, 1995.

71. Levy, A. D., Rittenhouse, P. A., Li, Q., Alvarez Sanz, M. C., Kerr, J. E., Bethea, C. L. and Van de Kar, L. D., Repeated injections of cocaine inhibit the serotonergic regulation of prolactin and renin secretion in rats, *Brain Res.*, 580, 6, 1992.

72. Levy, A. D., Rittenhouse, P. A., Bonadonna, A. M., Alvarez Sanz, M. C., Bethea, C. L. and Van de Kar, L. D., Repeated exposure to cocaine produces long-lasting deficits in the serotonergic stimulation of prolactin and renin, but not adrenocorticotropin secretion, *Eur. J. Pharmacol.*, 241, 275, 1993.

73. McElroy, J. F., Miller, J. M. and Meyer, J. S., Fenfluramine, p-chloroamphetamine and p-fluoroamphetamine stimulation of pituitary-adrenocortical activity in rat: evidence for differences in site and mechanism of action, *J. Pharmacol. Exp. Ther.*, 228, 593, 1984.

74. Farfel, G. M. and Seiden, L. S., Role of hypothermia in the mechanism of protection against serotonergic toxicity. II. experiments with methamphetamine, p-chloroamphetamine, fenfluramine, dizocilpine and dextromethorphan, *J. Pharmacol. Exp. Ther.*, 272, 868, 1995.

75. Baumann, M. H. and Rothman, R. B., Repeated cocaine administration reduces 5-HT$_{1A}$-mediated prolactin secretion in rats, *Neurosci. Lett.*, 193, 9, 1995.

76. Darmani, N. A., Martin, B. R. and Glennon, R. A., Repeated administration of low doses of cocaine enhances the sensitivity of 5-HT$_2$ receptor function, *Pharmacol. Biochem. Behav.*, 41, 519, 1992.

77. Levy, A. D., Li, Q., Alvarez Sanz, M. C., Rittenhouse, P. A., Brownfield, M. S. and Van de Kar, L. D. Repeated cocaine modifies the neuroendocrine responses to the 5-HT$_{1C}$/5-HT$_2$ agonist DOI, *Eur. J. Pharmacol.*, 221, 121, 1992.

78. Van Wijngaarden, I., Tulp, M. T. M. and Soudijn, W., The concept of selectivity in 5-HT receptor research, *Eur. J. Pharmacol.*, 199, 301, 1990.

79. Glennon, R. A. and Dukat, M., Serotonin receptors and their ligands: a lack of selective agents, *Pharmacol. Biochem. Behav.*, 40, 1009, 1991.

80. Di Scuillo, A., Bluet-Pajot, M. T., Mounier, F., Oliver, C., Schmidt, B. and Kordon, C., Changes in anterior pituitary hormone levels after serotonin 1A receptor stimulation, *Endocrinology*, 127, 567, 1990.

81. Gilbert, F., Brazell, C., Tricklebank, M. D. and Stahl, S. M., Activation of the 5-HT$_{1A}$ receptor subtype increases rat plasma ACTH concentration, *Eur. J. Pharmacol.*, 147, 431, 1988.

82. Kellar, K. J., Hulihan-Giblin, B. A., Mulroney, S. E., Lumpkin, M. D. and Flores, C. M., Stimulation of serotonin$_{1A}$ receptors increases release of prolactin in the rat, *Neuropharmacology*, 31, 643, 1992.

83. Pan, L. and Gilbert, F., Activation of 5-HT$_{1A}$ receptor subtype in the paraventricular nuclei of the hypothalamus induces CRH and ACTH release in the rat, *Neuroendocrinology*, 56, 797, 1992.

84. Willoughby, J. O., Menadue, M. F. and Liebelt, H. J., Activation of 5-HT 1 receptors in the medial basal hypothalamus stimulates prolactin secretion in the unanesthetized rat, *Neuroendocrinology*, 47, 83, 1988.

85. Tricklebank, M. D., Forler, C., Fozard, J. R., The involvement of subtypes of the 5-HT$_1$ receptors and of catecholaminergic systems in the behavioural responses to 8-hydroxy-2-(di-n-propylamino)tetralin in the rat, *Eur. J. Pharmacol.*, 106, 271, 1985.

86. Wilkinson, L. O. and Dourish, C. T., Serotonin and animal behavior, in *Serotonin Receptor Subtypes: Basic and Clinical Aspects*, Peroutka, S. J., Ed., Wiley-Liss, New York, 1991, 147.

87. Javaid, J. I., Sahni, S. K., Pandey, S. C. and Davis, J. M., Repeated cocaine administration does not affect 5-HT receptor subtypes (5-HT$_{1A}$, 5-HT$_2$) in several rat brain regions, *Eur. J. Pharmacol.*, 238, 425, 1993.

88. Johnson, R. G., Fiorella, D. and Rabin, R. A., Effects of chronic cocaine administration on the serotonergic system in the rat brain, *Pharmacol. Biochem. Behav.*, 46, 289, 1993.

89. Nestler, E. J., Molecular mechanisms of drug addiction, *J. Neurosci.*, 12, 2439, 1992.

90. Rittenhouse, P. A., Levy, A. D., Li, Q., Bethea, C. L. and Van de Kar, L. D., Neurons in the hypothalamic paraventricular nucleus mediate the serotonergic stimulation of prolactin secretion via 5-HT$_{1C/2}$ receptors, *Endocrinology*, 133, 661, 1993.

91. Baumann, M. H. and Rothman, R. B., Chronic cocaine exposure potentiates prolactin and head shake responses to 5-HT$_2$ receptor stimulation in rats, *Neuropharmacology*, 35, 295, 1996.

92. Baumann, M. H., Brockington, A. M. and Rothman, R. B., Withdrawal from chronic cocaine enhances behavioral sensitivity to the 5-HT$_{2/1C}$ agonist DOI, *Biol. Psychiatry*, 34, 576, 1993.

93. Schreiber, R., Brocco, M., Audinot, V., Gobert, A., Viega, S. and Millan, M. J., 1-(2,5-Dimethoxy-4iodophenyl)-2aminopropane-induced head-twitches in the rat are mediated by 5-hydroxytryptamine (5-HT)$_{2A}$ receptors: modulation by novel 5-HT$_{2A/2C}$ antagonists, D$_1$ antagonists and 5-HT$_{1A}$ agonists, *J. Pharmacol. Exp. Ther.*, 273, 101, 1995.

94. Van de Kar, L. D., Rittenhouse, P. A., O'Connor, P., Palionis, T., Brownfield, M. S., Lent, S. J., Carnes, M. and Bethea, C. L., Effect of cocaine injections on the neuroendocrine response to the serotonin agonist MK-212, *Biol. Psychiatry*, 32, 258, 1992.

95. Neisewander, J. L., Lucki, I. and McGonigle, P., Time-dependent changes in sensitivity to apomorphine and monoamine receptors following withdrawal from continuous cocaine administration in rats, *Synapse*, 16, 1, 1994.

96. Meert, T. F., Awouters, F., Niemegeers, C. J. E., Schellekens, K. H. L. and Janssen, P. A. J., Ritanserin reduces abuse of alcohol, cocaine, and fentanyl in rats, *Pharmacopsychiatry*, 24, 159, 1991.

97. McMillen, B. A., Jones, E. A., Hill, L. J., Williams, H. L., Björk, A. and Myers, R. D., Amperozide, a 5-HT$_2$ antagonist, attenuates craving for cocaine by rats, *Pharmacol. Biochem. Behav.*, 4, 125, 1993.

98. Moldow, R. L. and Fischman, A. J., Cocaine induced secretion of ACTH, beta-endorphin, and corticosterone, *Peptides*, 8, 819, 1987.

99. Pilotte, N. S., Sharpe, L.G. and Dax, E. M., Multiple, but not acute, infusions of cocaine alter the release of prolactin in male rats, *Brain Res.*, 512, 107, 1990.

100. Mendelson, J. H., Teoh, S.K., Mello, N. K., Ellingboe, J. and Rhoades, E., Acute effects of cocaine on plasma adrenocorticotropic hormone, luteinizing hormone and prolactin levels in cocaine-dependent men, *J. Pharmacol. Exp. Ther.*, 263, 505, 1992.

101. Baumann, M. H., Gendron, T. M., Becketts, K. M., Henningfield, J. E., Gorelick, D. A. and Rothman, R. B., Effects of intravenous cocaine on plasma cortisol and prolactin in human cocaine abusers, *Biol. Psychiatry*, 38, 751, 1995.

102. Borowsky, B. and Kuhn, C. M., Monoamine mediation of cocaine-induced hypothalamo-pituitary-adrenal activation, *J. Pharmacol. Exp. Ther.*, 256, 204, 1991.

Michael H. Baumann and Richard B. Rothman

103. Levy, A. D., Li, Q., Kerr, J. E., Rittenhouse, P. A., Milonas, G., Cabrera, T. M., Battaglia, G. and Van de Kar, L. D., Cocaine-induced elevation of plasma adrenocorticotropin hormone and corticosterone is mediated by serotonergic neurons, *J. Pharmacol. Exp. Ther.*, 259, 495, 1991.

104. Rivier, C. and Vale, W., Cocaine stimulates adrenocorticotropin (ACTH) secretion through a corticotropin releasing factor (CRF)-mediated mechanism, *Brain Res.*, 422, 1987.

105. Borowsky, B. and Kuhn, C. M., Chronic cocaine administration sensitizes behavioral but not neuroendocrine responses, *Brain Res.*, 543, 301, 1991.

106. Levy, A. D., Li, Q., Alvarez Sanz, M. C., Rittenhouse, P.A., Kerr, J.E. and Van de Kar, L. D., Neuroendocrine responses to cocaine do not exhibit sensitization following repeated cocaine exposure, *Life Sci.*, 51, 887, 1992.

107. Chaouloff, F., Physiopharmacological interactions between stress hormones and central sero-tonergic systems, *Brain Res. Rev.*, 18, 1, 1993.

108. Bagdy, G., Calogero, A. E., Aulakh, C. S., Szemeredi, K. and Murphy, D. L., Long-term cortisol treatment impairs behavioral and neuroendocrine responses to 5-HT$_1$ agonists in the rat, *Neuroendocrinology*, 50, 241, 1989.

109. Haleem, D. J., Repeated corticosterone treatment attenuates behavioral and neuroendocrine responses to 8-hydroxy-2-(di-*n*-propylamino)tetralin in rats, *Life Sci.*, 51, 225, 1992.

110. Berendsen, H. H. G., Kester, R. C. H., Peeters, B. W. M. M. and Broekkamp, C. L. E., Modulation of 5-HT receptor subtype-mediated behaviors by corticosterone, *Eur. J. Pharmacol.*, 308, 103, 1996.

111. Gawin, F.H. and Ellingwood, E. H., Cocaine and other stimulants: actions, abuse and treat-ment, *N. Eng. J. Med.*, 318, 1173, 1988.

112. Carroll, M. E. and Lac, S. T., Cocaine withdrawal produces behavioral disruptions in rats, *Life Sci.*, 40, 2183, 1987.

113. Woolverton, W. L. and Kleven, M. S., Evidence for cocaine dependence in monkeys following prolonged period of exposure, *Psychopharmacology*, 94, 288, 1988.

114. *Diagnostic and Statistical Manual of Mental Disorders*, 4th Ed., American Psychiatric Press, Washington, D. C., 1194, 221.

115. Weddington, W. W., Brown, B. S., Haertzen, C. A., Cone, E. J., Dax, E. M., Herning, R. I. and Michaelson, B. S., Changes in mood, craving, and sleep during short-term abstinence reported by male cocaine addicts, *Arch. Gen. Psychiatry*, 47, 861, 1990.

116. Satel, S. L., Price, L. H., Palumbo, J. M., McDougle, C. J., Krystal, J. H., Gawin, F. H., Charney, D. S., Heninger, G. R. and Kleber, H. D., Clinical phenomenology and neurobiology of cocaine abstinence: a prospective inpatient study, *Am. J. Psychiatry*, 148, 1712, 1990.

117. Marzuk, P. M., Tardiff, K., Leon, A. C., Stajic, M., Morgan, E. B. and Mann, J. J., Prevalence of cocaine use among residents of New York city who committed suicide during a one-year period, *Am. J. Psychiatry*, 149, 371, 1992.

118. De Leon, G., Cocaine abusers in therapeutic community treatment, in *Cocaine Treatment: Research and Clinical Perspectives*, NIDA Research Monograph 135, Tims, F. M. and Leuekfeld, C. G., Eds., U.S. Government Printing Office, Washington, D.C., 1993, 163.

119. Weiss, R. D., Mirin, S. M., Griffin, M. L. and Michael, J., Psychopathology in cocaine users. changing trends, *J. Nerv. Ment. Dis.*, 176, 719, 1988.

120. Nunes, E.V., Quitkin, F. M. and Klein, D. F., Psychiatric diagnosis in cocaine abuse, *Psychiatry Res.*, 28, 105, 1989.

121. Rounsaville, B. J., Anton, S. F., Carroll, K. A., Budde, D., Prusoff, B. A. and Gawin, F. A., Psychiatric diagnoses of treatment-seeking cocaine abusers, *Arch. Gen. Psychiatry*, 48, 43, 1991.

122. Schottenfeld, R., Carroll, K., Rounsaville, B., Comorbid psychiatric disorders and cocaine abuse, in *Cocaine Treatment: Research and Clinical Perspectives*, NIDA Research Monograph 135, Tims, F. M. and Leuekfeld, C. G., Eds., U.S. Government Printing Office, Washington, D.C., 1993, 31.

123. Anthony, J. C. and Petronis, K. R., Cocaine and heroin dependence compared: evidence from an epidemiological field survey, *Am. J. Pub. Health*, 79, 1409, 1989.

Serotonergic Dysfunction During Cocaine Withdrawal

124. Khantzian, E. J., The self-medication hypothesis of addictive disorders: focus on heroin and cocaine dependence, *Am. J. Psychiatry*, 142, 1259, 1985.

125. Hall, S. M., Havassay, B. E. and Wasserman, D. A., Effects of commitment to abstinence, positive moods, stress, and coping on relapse to cocaine, *J. Consult. Clin. Psychol.*, 59, 526, 1991.

126. Latkin, C. A. and Mandell, W., Depression as an antecedent of frequency of intravenous drug use in an urban, nontreatment sample, *Int. J. Addict.*, 28, 1601, 1993.

127. Tiffany, S. T., The role of cognitive factors in reactivity to drug cues, in *Addictive Behavior: cue exposure theory and practice*, Drummond, D. C., Tiffany, S. T., Glautier, S. and Remington, B., Eds., Wiley, New York, 1995,137

128. Meltzer, H. Y. and Lowy, M. T., The serotonin hypothesis of depression, in *Psychopharmacology: The Third Generation of Progress*, Meltzer, H. Y., ed., Raven Press, New York, 1987, 513.

129. Briley M. and Moret, C., Neurobiological mechanisms involved in antidepressant therapies, *Clin. Neuropharmacol.*, 16, 387, 1993.

130. Blier, P., de Montigny, C. and Chaput, Y., Modifications of the serotonin system by antidepressant treatments: implications for the therapeutic response in major depression, *J. Clin. Psychopharm.*, 7(suppl 6), 24S, 1987.

131. Asberg, M., Traskman, L. and Thoren, P., 5-HIAA in the cerebrospinal fluid: a suicide predictor? *Arch. Gen. Psychiatry*, 33, 1193, 1976.

132. Gibbons, R. D. and Davis, J. M., Consistent evidence for a biological subtype of depression characterized by low CSF monoamine levels, *Acta Psychiatr. Scand.*, 74, 8, 1986.

133. Roy, A., Virkkunen, M. and Linnoila, M., Serotonin in suicide, violence and alcoholism, in *Serotonin in Major Psychiatric Disorders*, Coccaro, E. F. and Murphy, D. L., eds., American Psychiatric Press, Washington, D. C., 1990, 185.

134. Bailey, D. N., Shaw, R. F., Cocaine- and methamphetamine-related deaths in San Diego County (1987): homicides and accidental overdoses, *J. Forensic Sci.*, 34, 407, 1989.

135. Moeller, F. G., Steinberg, J. L., Petty, F., Fulton, M., Cherek, D. R., Kramer, G. and Garver, D. L., Serotonin and impulsive/aggressive behavior in cocaine dependent subjects, *Prog. Neuro-Psychopharmacol. Biol. Psychiat.*, 18, 1027, 1994.

136. Siever, L. J., Murphy, D. L., Slater, S., de la Vega. E. and Lipper, S., Plasma prolactin changes following fenfluramine in depressed patients compared to controls: an evaluation of central serotonergic responsivity in depression, *Life Sci.*, 34, 1984.

137. Coccaro, E. F., Siever, L. J., Klar, H. M., Maurer, G., Cochrane, K., Cooper, T. B., Mohs, R. C. and Davis, K. L., Serotonergic studies in patients with affective and personality disorders, *Arch. Gen. Psychiatry*, 46, 587, 1989.

138. Mitchell, P. and Smythe, G., Hormonal responses to fenfluramine in depressed and control subjects, *J. Affective Disord.*, 19, 43, 1990.

139. O'Keane, V. and Dinan, T. G., Prolactin and cortisol responses to d-fenfluramine in major depression: evidence for diminished responsivity of central serotonergic function, *Am. J. Psychiatry*, 148, 1009, 1991.

140. Mann, J. J., McBride, P. A., Malone, K. M., DeMeo, M. and Keilp, J., Blunted serotonergic responsivity in depressed patients, *Neuropsychopharmacology*, 13, 53, 1995.

141. Cleare, A. J., Murray, R. M. and O'Keane, V., Reduced prolactin and cortisol responses to d-fenfluramine in depressed compared to healthy matched control subjects, *Neuropsychopharmacology*, 14, 349, 1996.

142. O'Keane, V., McLoughlin, D. and Dinan, T. G., d-Fenfluramine-induced prolactin and cortisol release in major depression: response to treatment, *J. Affect. Disord.* 26, 143, 1992.

143. Cowen, P. J., Anderson, I. M., Grahame-Smith, D. G., Neuroendocrine effects of azapirones, *J. Clin. Psychopharm.*, 10, 21S, 1991.

144. Lesch, K. P., Mayer, S., Disselkamp-Tietze, J., Wiesmann, M., Osterheider, M. and Sculte, H. M., 5-HT$_{1A}$ receptor responsivity in unipolar depression: evaluation of isapirone-induced ACTH and cortisol secretion in patients and controls, *Biol. Psychiatry*, 28, 620, 1990.

Michael H. Baumann and Richard B. Rothman

145. Lesch, K. P., Mayer, S., Disselkamp-Tietze, J., Wiesmann, M., Osterheider, M. and Sculte, H. M., Subsensitivity of the 5-hydroxytryptamine 1A (5-HT$_{1A}$) receptor-mediated hyperthermic response to ipsapirone in unipolar depression, *Life Sci.*, 46, 1271, 1990.

146. O'Connell, M. T., Sarna, G. S. and Curzon, G., Evidence for postsynaptic mediation of the hypothermic effect of 5-HT$_{1A}$ receptor activation, *Br. J. Pharmacol.*, 106, 603, 1992.

147. Cowen, P. J., Power, A. C., Ware, C. J. and Anderson, I. M., 5-HT$_{1A}$ receptor sensitivity in major depression. a neuroendocrine study with buspirone, *Br. J. Psychiatry*, 164, 372, 1994.

148. Meltzer, H. Y. and Maes, M., Effects of ipsapirone on plasma cortisol and body temperature in major depression, *Biol. Psychiatry*, 38, 450 1995.

149. Moeller, F. G., Steinberg, J. L., Fulton, M., Kramer, G. and Petty, F., A preliminary neuroendocrine study with buspirone in major depression, *Neuropsychopharmacology*, 10, 75, 1994.

150. Meltzer, H. Y. and Maes, M., Effects of buspirone on plasma prolactin and cortisol levels in major depressed and normal subjects, *Biol. Psychiatry*, 35, 316, 1994.

151. Smith, C. E., Ware, C. J. and Cowen, P. J., Pindolol decreases prolactin and growth hormone responses to intravenous l-tryptophan, *Psychopharmacology*, 103, 140, 1991.

152. Heninger, G. R., Charney, D. S. and Sternberg, D. E., Serotonergic function in depression: prolactin response to intravenous tryptophan in depressed patients and healthy subjects, *Arch. Gen. Psychiatry*, 41, 398, 1984.

153. Cowen, P. J. and Charig, E. M., Neuroendocrine responses to tryptophan in major depression, *Arch. Gen. Psychiatry*, 44, 958, 1987.

154. Deakin, J. F. W., Pennel, I., Upadhyaya, A. K. and Lofthouse, R., A neuroendocrine study of 5-HT function in depression: evidence for biological mechanisms and psychosocial causation, *Psychopharmacology*, 101, 85, 1990.

155. Chaput, Y., de Montigny, C. and Blier, P., Presynaptic and postsynaptic modifications of the serotonin system by longterm administration of antidepressant treatments: an in vivo electrophysiological study in the rat, *Neuropsychopharmacology*, 5, 219, 1991.

156. Murphy, D. L., Lesch, K. P., Aulakh, C. S. and Pigot, T. A., Serotonin-selective arylpiperazines with neuroendocrine, behavioral, temperature, and cardiovascular effects in humans, *Pharmacol. Rev.*, 43, 527, 1991.

157. Kahn, R. S., Wetzler, S., Asnis, G. M., Papolos, D. and van Praag, H. M., Serotonin receptor sensitivity in major depression, *Biol. Psychiatry*, 28, 358, 1990.

158. Hamik, A. and Peroutka, S. J., 1-(m-Chlorophenyl)piperazine (mCPP) interactions with neurotransmitter receptors in human brain, *Biol. Psychiatry*, 25, 569, 1989.

159. Baumann, M. H., Staley, J. K. and Mash, D. C., The serotonin agonist m-chlorophenylpiperazine (mCPP) binds to serotonin transporter sites in human brain, *NeuroReport*, 6, 2150, 1995.

160. Stanley, M. and Mann, J. J., Increased serotonin-2 binding sites in frontal cortex of suicide victims, *Lancet*, i, 214, 1983.

161. Mann, J. J., Stanley, M., McBride, P. A. and McEwen, B. S., Increased serotonin$_2$ and ß-adrenergic receptor binding in the frontal cortices of suicide victims, *Arch. Gen. Psychiatry*, 43, 954, 1986.

162. Arora, R. C. and Meltzer, H. Y., Serotonergic measures in the brains of suicide victims: 5-HT$_2$ binding sites in the frontal cortex of suicide victims and control subjects, *Am. J. Psychiatry*, 146, 730, 1989.

163. Arango, V., Ernsberger, P., Marzuk, P. M., Chen, J.-S., Tierney, H., Stanley, M., Reis, D. J. and Mann, J. J., (1990): Autoradiographic demonstration of increased serotonin 5-HT$_2$ and ß-adrenergic receptor binding sites in the brain of suicide victims, *Arch. Gen. Psychiatry*, 47, 1038, 1990.

164. Peroutka, S. J. and Snyder, S. H., Chronic antidepressant treatment decreases spiroperidol-labeled serotonin receptor binding, *Science*, 210, 88-90.

165. Goodwin, G. M., Green, A. R. and Johnson, P., 5-HT$_2$ receptor characteristics in frontal cortex and 5-HT$_2$ receptor-mediated head-twitch behavior following antidepressant treatment to mice, *Br. J. Pharmacol.*, 83, 235, 1984.

166. Murphy, D. L., Peripheral indices of central serotonin function in humans, in *Neuropharmacology of Serotonin*, Ann. N. Y. Acad. Sci. 600, Whitaker-Azmitia, P. M. and Peroutka, S. J., Eds., N.Y. Acad. Sci., New York, 1990, 282.

167. Bigeon, A., Weizman, A., Karp, L., Ram, A., Tiano, S. and Wolff, M., Serotonin 5-HT$_2$ receptor binding on blood platelets: a peripheral marker for depression? *Life Sci.*, 41, 2485, 1987.

168. Arora, R. C. and Meltzer, H. Y., Increased serotonin 5-HT$_2$ receptor binding as measured by ^{3}H-LSD in the blood platelets of depressed patients, *Life Sci.*, 44, 725, 1989.

169. Pandey, G. N., Pandey, S. C. and Janicak, P. G., Platelet serotonin-2 binding sites in depression and suicide, *Biol. Psychiatry*, 28, 215, 1990.

170. Bigeon, A., Essar, N., Israeli, M., Elizur, A., Bruch, S. and Bar-Nathan, A. A., Serotonin 5-HT$_2$ receptor binding on blood platelets as a state-dependent marker in major affective disorders, *Psychopharmacology*, 102, 73, 1990.

171. Holsboer, F., Neuroendocrinology of mood disorders, in *Psychopharmacology: The Fourth Generation of Progress*, Bloom, F. E. and Kupfer, D. J., Eds., Raven, New York, 1995, 957.

172. Dinan, T. G., Glucocorticoids and the genesis of depressive illness. A psychobiological model, *Br. J. Psychiatry*, 164, 365, 1994.

173. Deakin, J. F. W., 5-HT, antidepressant drugs and the psychosocial origins of depression, *J. Psychopharmacol.*, 10, 31, 1996.

174. Kosten, T. R., Pharmacotherapeutic interventions for cocaine abuse: matching patients to treatment, *J. Nerv. Ment. Dis.*, 177, 379, 1989.

175. Pollack, M. H. and Rosenbaum, J. F., Fluoxetine treatment of cocaine abuse in heroin addicts, *J. Clin. Psychiatry*, 52, 31, 1991.

176. Batki, S. L., Manfredi, L. B., Jacob, P. and Jones, R. T., Fluoxetine for cocaine dependence in methadone maintenance: quantitative plasma and urine cocaine/benoylecgonine concentrations, *J. Clin. Psychopharmacol.*, 13, 243, 1993.

177. Rothman, R. B., Gendron, T. M. and Hitzig, P., Letter to the editor, *J. Subst. Abuse. Treat.*, 11, 273, 1994.

178. Rothman, R. B., Ayestas M. A. and Baumann, M. H., Phentermine pretreatment antagonizes the cocaine-induced rise in mesolimbic dopamine, *Neuroreport*, 8,7,1996.

179. Volkow, N. D. and Fowler, J. S., Brain imaging studies of the cocaine addict: implications for reinforcement and addiction, in *Molecular Neurobiology of Cocaine*, Hammer, R., Ed., CRC, Boca Raton, 1995, 65.

180. Mash, D.C. and Staley, J.K., The dopamine transporter in human brain: characterization and effect of cocaine exposure, in *Neurotransmitter Transporters: Structure, Function and Regulation*, Reith, M.E.A., Ed., Humana Press, Totowa, NJ, 1996, 315.

181. Kuhar, M. J. and Pilotte, N. S., Neurochemical changes in cocaine withdrawal, *Trends Pharmacol. Sci.*, 17, 260, 1996.

182. Markou, A. and Koob, G. F., Postcocaine anhedonia: An animal model of cocaine withdrawal. *Neuropsychopharmacology*, 4, 17, 1991.

183. Shoaib, M., Baumann, M.H., Rothman, R.B., Goldberg, S.R. and Schindler, C.W., Behavioural and neurochemical characteristics of phentermine and felfluramine administered separately and as a mixture in rats, *Psychopharmacology*, 131, 296, 1997.

184. Baumann, M.H., Neuroendocrine responsiveness to serotonergic drug challenge during cocaine withdrawal, in *Problems of Drug Dependence 1996: Proceedings of the 58th Annual Scientific Meeting of the CPDD*, NIDA Research Monograph 174, Harris, L.S., Ed., U.S. Government Printing Office, Washington, D.C., 1997, 52.

185. Baumann M.H. et al., unpublished.

Michael H. Baumann and Richard B. Rothman

6.6 NEUROCHEMISTRY OF PSYCHEDELIC DRUGS

J.C. CALLAWAY, PH.D.

DEPARTMENT OF PHARMACEUTICAL CHEMISTRY, UNIVERSITY OF KUOPIO, KUOPIO, FINLAND

D.J. McKENNA, PH.D.

HEFFTER RESEARCH INSTITUTE, SANTA FE, NEW MEXICO

> We may choose not to find access to it, we may even deny its existence, but it is indeed inside us, and there are chemicals that can catalyze its availability.
>
> A.T. Shulgin, Ph.D. in *Pihkal*, p. 17.[1]

Mescaline, *d*-lysergic acid diethylamide (LSD-25), and psilocin (Figure 6.6.1) are the prototypical drugs that are capable of revealing "it"; i.e., a state of mind that has been called psychedelic, hallucinogenic, psychotomimetic, and many other names. The subjective effects derived from these three compounds are strikingly similar,[2] which is remarkable as their molecular structures are so dissimilar. Moreover, even slight modifications to the parent molecule often result in less potent, or even inactive, derivatives. Relatively few compounds are known to elicit this unique psychotropic effect known as *psychedelic* (i.e., mind/soul "revealing").

After more than 30 years of prohibition, and widespread "recreational" use, some human research has recently resumed. These powerful agents are potentially valuable tools to investigate the neurobiological basis of the mind/brain connection. They are currently seen by some as adjuncts to psychotherapy, in treating neuroses, and as potential medicines for the treatment of substance misuse.

6.6.1 TERMINOLOGY

The term "psychedelic" was coined in the late 1950s from the Greek prefix *psyche* meaning mind or soul and the suffix *dellos*, indicating the process of revealing, revelation, or manifestation.[3] Other terms have been used to convey these effects according to psychopathologic symptomology; e.g., hallucinogen, psychotomimetic, *etc.* No consensus presently exists on a nomenclature to communicate these distinctive psychic effects, though "psychedelic" approaches an accurate description.

Dreams and some forms of psychoses occur naturally as states of heightened mental arousal in humans, both sharing remarkable similarities to the psychedelic state.[4-6] For the observer not having the experience, subsequent revelations, imperative insights, feelings of exaltation or even persecution are commonly interpreted as pathologies; *ergo* such compounds are "hallucinogenic".

Hallucinations are literally defined as "false perceptions", typically of an unknown pathological nature, and in the absence of a corresponding stimulus.[7] Contrary to popular belief, however, hallucinations are not a unique, or even characteristic, feature of a psychedelic experience. Thus, the noun *hallucinogen*; i.e., a substance producing a hallucination, is in fact

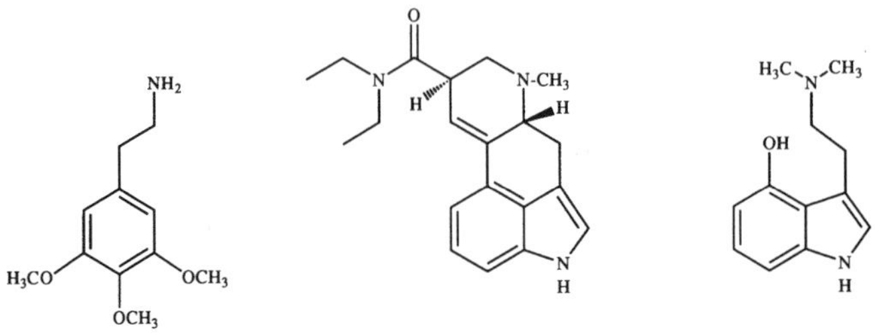

Mescaline   d-LSD-25   Psilocin

Figure 6.6.1 Molecular structures of the classic psychedelics; mescaline, d-LSD-25, and psilocin. Structures are drawn to emphasize the similarity of two adjacent aliphatic carbons, where one is attached to an aromatic moiety and the other attached to an aliphatic nitrogen.

a contradiction when applied to psychedelic agents. Furthermore, many other neuroactive drugs (e.g., tropane alkaloids) and drug-related effects (e.g., amphetamine psychosis or sometimes during withdrawal from ethanol and other drugs) are also known to be associated with hallucinatory phenomena.

"Psychotomimetic" is a formerly favored term that has fortunately fallen into disuse in recent the years. This term arose from the initial impression that drugs like LSD and mescaline can serve as models for psychoses in non-psychotic individuals.

6.6.2 HISTORY

The psychedelic experience is relatively new to industrial cultures, and has historically been at odds with centralized forms of government, at least since 395 A.D. when the Goths sacked the temple at Eleusis, in ancient Greece.[8] Except for the accidental discovery of LSD in 1943, knowledge of psychedelic agents have come to us as legacies of ancient American religions, where these psychic effects are considered to be of a divine or holy nature.[8-11]

Just over 100 years ago, the German pharmacologist Arthur Heffter began a systematic investigation into the isolated components of "peyote" (*Lophophora williamsii*) by ingesting a series of these alkaloids himself. Subsequently, mescaline was identified as the active component of this North American cactus, which had been used since pre-Columbian times as a psychoactive sacrament. Peyote persists as the central sacrament of several native religions in Mexico and the U.S.

Following the discovery of LSD, psilocin and its phosphate ester (psilocybin) were both isolated from the fungi *Psilocybe mexicana* and synthesized in the late 1950s.[12] Again, the active components were only identified by human experimentation, after animal testing gave ambiguous results. To complete the study, synthetic psilocybin was returned to the village of Huatla de Jimenez in Oaxaca, Mexico, its place of botanical origin, and given to the Mazatec shaman María Sabina who confirmed the synthetic substance to be "the same God" she had previously known only through the mushroom.[13]

Throughout the 1950s psychedelics became an obvious and powerful influence on the growing field of molecular psychiatry, initially as models for psychosis and eventually as adjuncts to psychotherapy. At the same time, chemical warfare researchers explored these compounds for their potential as "truth serums" and adjuncts to "brain washing".[11,14] Through both military and medical channels, these substances began to surface in artistic and intellectual circles throughout the world. By the mid 1960s, LSD had already become a media buzz word, and in spite of its proscription in 1966, popular experimentation with this and other psychedelics

J.C. Callaway and D.J. McKenna

have continued. Since 1992, limited medical experimentation with some psychedelic drugs has resumed in the U.S. and Europe.

6.6.3 CHARACTERISTIC FEATURES

The psychedelics share little apparent structural similarity, and early researchers had limited reference to categorize the unfamiliar psychoactive effects. The significant neuropharmacologic features shared by this class of compounds include high affinities for serotonin receptor subtypes and the presence of a substituted amine separated by two aliphatic carbons from an aromatic nucleus (see Figure 6.6.1).

6.6.3.1 Psychological

Novel interpretations of reality without amnesia or significant somatic effects are standard features of psychedelic drugs. Modifications of perception are also common. The effects are highly dependent on set, setting, and dose. Expectations and the mental health of an individual (set) includes both their present frame of mind and accumulated life experiences. Thus, if the revealed psyche contains turmoil and conflict, then these features tend to manifest during the experience. Such reactions are not particularly dangerous in a supportive environment, while less sympathetic settings tend to exacerbate adverse reactions. A third component of "dose" is often taken for granted, yet the particular compound, the dosage, and route of administration are all additional factors to be considered. Some typical features of the psychedelic experience are listed in Table 6.6.3.1.

Table 6.6.3.1 Some Typical Features of the Psychedelic Experience

Temporary loss of psychological "boundaries" ("ego loss")
Enhanced clarity in eidactic imagery
Heightened awareness of sensory input
Lucid and vivid recall of past events, especially from early childhood
Modified perceptions and interpretation of "reality"
Latent neuroses tend to manifest in predisposed individuals
Deep feelings of contentment, satisfaction, and familiarity
Feelings of oneness, wholeness, and unity
Conceptions of life as endless series of complex processes
Ability to observe reality as if for the first time
Personal insights and possible delusions

6.6.3.2 Pharmacological

Mounting evidence continues to show strong correlations between receptor activity and behavior; however, the psychic effects are not contained within the chemistry of these or any other, psychoactive drugs. Instead, neurochemical interactions are thought to affect neuronal activity, and receptor sites for neuroactive compounds are one substrata of the neural circuitry which leads to mental activity. As with other drugs, the psychedelics may become ionized in receptor sites to form charge transfer complexes, thus modifying the local flow of electrons and, subsequently, the transmission of neuronal information.[15,16] Table 6.6.3.2 lists some pharmacologic effects typically associated with psychedelic activity.

Generally, the psychedelic drugs have high (nanomolar) affinity for receptor subtypes that also accept the neurotransmitter serotonin (5-hydroxytryptamine, 5-HT, Figure 6.6.3.2).

Table 6.6.3.2 Typical Pharmacologic Effects Associated with Psychedelic Activity

Pupillary dilation at full dose/effect

Cross tolerance between other members (rare exceptions)

Tolerance not overcome by increasing dosage (rare exceptions)

Not "addictive", i.e., no withdrawal effects after discontinuing use

Not associated with compulsive use

Strong serotonergic activity, both "agonistic" and "antagonistic"

Often a loss of appetite during the experience

Heightened arousal; sleep is often impossible

Toxic doses are essentially unknown, except with some phenethylamines

Alleged chromosome damage disproved

Chemical similarities and interactions with other neurotransmitters may account for variations in effect between indolealkylamines, lysergamides, and phenethylamines. The search for a single neurotransmitter receptor site as the origin of this activity has been primarily focused within the serotonergic system.[17]

6.6.4 CHEMISTRY AND STRUCTURE ACTIVITY RELATIONSHIPS

With few exceptions, the chemistry of psychedelic compounds may be categorized as either indolealkylamines (i.e., as tryptamines or ergotamines) or phenethylamines.[18] Stereochemical aspects are also important for psychoactivity, and have already been reviewed.[19,20]

6.6.4.1 Indolealkylamines

Indole alkaloids are found in many plants, animals, and several microorganisms. They account for about one quarter of the known alkaloids.[21] Many indoles that have known neuroactive properties carry an aliphatic ethylamine at position 3 on the indole ring. A large portion of

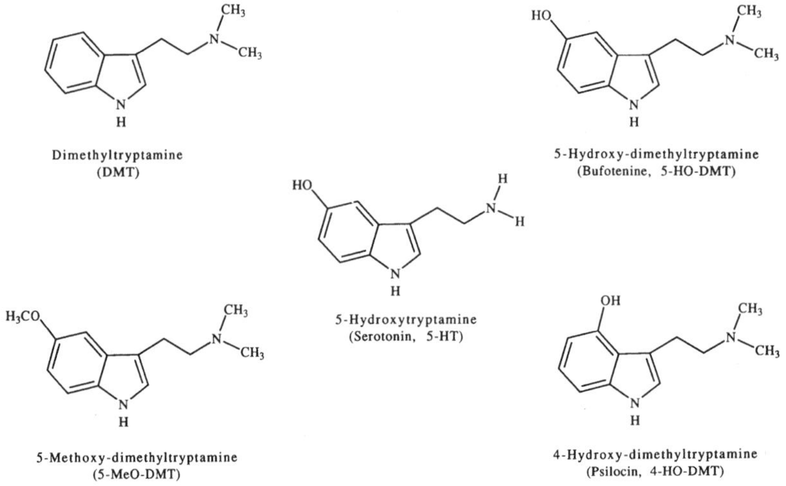

Figure 6.6.3.2 Psychotropic dimethyltryptamines and the neurotransmitter serotonin.

Table 6.6.4.1 A Listing of Psychedelic Indolealkylamines, Dosage, Route of Administration, Duration of Action and Notable Receptor Binding Sites

Compound	Dose (µg/kg)	Route	Duration of action	Receptor sites
LSD	1.5	p.o.	8-12h	5-HT1A, C & D, 5-HT2, DA1 & 2
Psilocin	300	p.o.	3-6h	5-HT1A, 5-HT2
DMT	400	s/i.v.	10-15m	5-HT1A & C, 5-HT2
5-MeO-DMT	200	s/i.v.	10-20m	5-HT1A, C & D, 5-HT2
5-HO-DMT	50	s	10-20m	5-HT1A, C & D, 5-HT2

Abbreviations: oral (p.o.), smoked/insufflated (s), injected (i.v.), hours (h), minutes (m), 5-HT = serotonin, DA = dopamine.

psychedelic agents are tryptamines, where the ethylamine side-chain is alkylated and has a relatively wide range of molecular motion. Important substitution sites that determine psychoactivity are on the indole ring, the side-chain carbons, and the aliphatic nitrogen.

N,N-Dimethyltryptamines (DMTs) provide the most remarkable effects in this series (Figure 6.6.3.2), where only psilocin and psilocybin show oral activity. 5-HT receptor subtype differentiation among several N,N-dialkylated tryptamines has been reported.[22] A listing of psychedelic indolealkylamines, typical human dosages, and notable receptor binding sites are presented in Table 6.6.4.1.

N-Alkyl homologues of DMT, in which the N,N-dimethyl substituents are replaced with longer and more hydrophobic aliphatic moieties, include the diethyl-, dipropyl-, diisopropyl- and diallyltryptamines. All of these derivatives are psychoactive in humans, and most are orally active. Qualitatively, homologation of the N,N-dialkyl substituents attenuates the intensity of the experience, and prolongs the course of action. Nonsymmetrical alkyl substitution of the side-chain nitrogen (e.g., methylisopropyl- or methylethyl-) also yield orally active compounds with threshold doses and qualitative actions similar to those of their N,N-dimethyl derivatives.[23]

In general, hydroxylation at the 4-position on the indole ring, as in the prototypical compound psilocin, enhances the potency of N,N-dialkyl homologues and nonsymmetric N-alkylated derivatives by approximately an order of magnitude, compared to the unsubstituted derivatives. Methoxylation at the 5-position on the indole ring similarly increases potency but also enhances the stimulatory ("amphetamine-like") effects while attenuating visual effects. Derivatives with 6-, 7-methoxy-, 5,6-dimethoxy-, 5,6-methylenedioxy substituents also display greatly attenuated activity.

Methyl substitution on tryptamine's side-chain, at the α-carbon, also results in orally active psychotropic compounds. Racemic N_1-n-propyl-5-methoxy-α-methyltryptamine, for example, has been reported to bind with high affinity and significant selectivity to 5-HT$_2$ receptors.[24] α-Methyl tryptamine, itself, and its 5-methoxy- and 4-hydroxy- congeners are orally active in humans at the 3 to 30 mg level. α-Substituted tryptamines are the only enantiomeric derivatives in this class that have been empirically investigated and, in general, the S-(+) enantiomers are more potent than the R-(-) enantiomers in human and other animal experiments. α-Methytryptamine and α-ethyltryptamine are competitive inhibitors of monoamine oxidase (MAO), and this property may account for their oral activity, as well as their prolonged duration of action relative to other psychoactive tryptamines.

There is a paucity of data on the interactions of tryptamine derivatives with 5-HT receptor subtypes, and relatively few receptor binding studies have used the more subtype-selective radioligands, which have only recently become available. Lyon et al. compared the binding characteristics of 21 indolealkylamines in competition experiments using [^{3}H]ketanserine to label 5-HT2 receptors in rat cortex.[25] This group reported 4- or 5-methoxy substitutions as having higher affinities than 6- or 7-methoxy substitutions, while 7-hydroxy substitution abolished affinity, and 7-bromo or 7-methyl substitutions on the indole ring enhanced affinity.

A more recent investigation focused on receptor subtype selectivity of tryptamine derivatives in radioligand competition assays.[22] In this study, the relative affinities of 21 indolealkylamines, having various ring and N,N-dialkyl substitutions, were examined for activity at 5-HT_{1A}, 5-HT_{2A}, and 5-HT_{2B} binding sites using [^{3}H]-8-OH-DPAT, [^{125}I]-R-(-)-DOI, and [^{3}H]ketanserine, respectively. In general, those derivatives lacking ring substituents displayed lower affinity for all recognition sites, compared to derivatives having 4- or 5-substituents on the indole ring. Affinity for all derivatives at the 5-HT_{2B} site was greater than 300 nM. The nature of the substituent, and its position on the ring, were primary determinants for affinity and selectivity. While the size of the N,N-dialkyl substituents was of secondary importance, groups larger than N,N-diisopropyl dramatically reduced affinity at both the 5-HT_{1A} and 5-HT_{2A} sites. The 5-substituted derivatives displayed approximately equal potencies at 5-HT_{1A} and 5-HT_{2A} sites, while the 4-hydroxy derivatives displayed 25- to 380-fold selectivity for the 5-HT_2 site over the 5-HT_{1A} site. The authors noted that derivatives of 4-hydroxytryptamine were qualitatively similar to psilocin, while 5-substituted tryptamines were relatively lacking or diminished in classic psychedelic effects, being more prominent in central stimulatory effects. Therefore, the selectivity of 4-hydroxytryptamines for 5-HT_{2A} sites further implicates this subtype in mediating the action of psychedelic agents.

The nature of the 5-HT_2-like binding site, as labeled by [^{125}I]DOI, is a matter of continued controversy. Competition curves from specific 5-HT_2 agonists and antagonists against [^{3}H]DOB binding show Hill coefficients close to unity.[26] From this, and other data, Titeler and co-workers suggest the low density of a putative 5-HT_{2A} subtype (relative to the total amount of 5-HT_2 bound by [^{3}H]ketanserine), coupled with its sensitivity to guanyl nucleotides, supports the interpretation that the [^{125}I]DOI binding site represents an agonist "state", or allostere, of the 5-HT_2 receptor.[27] On the other hand, Peroutka and co-workers have argued that these radioligands label novel subtypes of the 5-HT_2 receptor, which they termed the 5-HT_{2A} receptor (for sites bound by [^{125}I]DOI), to distinguish from [^{3}H]ketanserine binding sites in bovine cortex (i.e., the 5-HT_{2B} receptor).[28,29] The ultimate resolution of this controversy will require further investigations. With regard to the relative affinities of psychedelic tryptamines for the two subtypes, or states, the data of the two groups are in agreement. Most of the tryptamine derivatives display 10- to 100-fold higher affinities for the [^{125}I]DOI binding site vs. the [^{3}H]ketanserine site.

6.6.4.1.1 Psilocin and Psilocybin

These two dimethyltryptamines were first isolated from the mushroom *Psilocybe mexicana*.[12] These alkaloids are also present in at least 95 other species of mushroom which are found throughout the world. Both are orally active and epitomize the psychedelic effect for tryptamines. Neither compound has known toxicities. As a natural product, often known as "magic" mushrooms, these two alkaloids may be the most widely used and readily available psychedelic agents. The subjective effects are relatively short compared to LSD or mescaline, though fairly long when compared with other dimethyltryptamines. Both have high affinity for 5-HT_{1A} and 5-HT_2 sites (Figure 6.3.3.2, Table 6.6.4.1).[22]

6.6.4.1.2 DMT

N,N-Dimethyltryptamine (DMT) is agonistic at 5-HT_{1A} and 5-HT_{1C} and antagonistic at 5-HT_2 sites, though may also show partial 5-HT_2 agonistic activity (Figure 6.6.3.2, Table 6.6.4.1).[22,30] It is not orally active, due to its rapid oxidation by type A monoamine oxidase (MAO-A). It was first identified as a component of *cohoba*, a psychotropic snuff prepared from the seeds of *Anadenanthera peregrina* (formerly *Piptadenia peregrina*) in 1955. Although it had been synthesized 24 years earlier, its psychoactivity was not reported until 1956.[31] DMT can be injected, smoked, or insufflated, and has also been identified as an endogenous component in all mammals studied, including humans.[32] The most outstanding effect from this simple tryptamine is the explosion of visual imagery, primarily scintillating colored patterns, for only a few minutes after administration. This effect is almost absent in emotive content, perhaps due to the brevity and intensity of visual phenomenon.

6.6.4.1.3 5-MEO-DMT

5-Methoxy-DMT (5-MeO-DMT) is a full agonist at 5-HT_{1A}, 5-HT_{1C}, 5-HT_{1D}, and 5-HT_2 sites (Figure 6.6.3.2, Table 6.6.4.1).[22,33] Like DMT, it is also found as a component of traditional psychoactive snuffs from the Americas, and the psychoactive effects are short. It is also orally inactive. Unlike DMT, however, its primary effect is almost entirely devoid of visual content, while emotive phenomena predominates. It has been described as a "near death" experience, though this is certainly psychological as no toxicological effects have been demonstrated. Besides being found in plants, 5-MeO-DMT is also produced in the skin of some toads, particularly *Bufo alverius* from the deserts of the American Southwest.[34] Contrary to popular belief, these toads are not licked, but "milked" for their venom from the parietal glands. The collected venom is dried and subsequently smoked for psychoactive effects.

6.6.4.1.4 5-HO-DMT

5-Hydroxy-DMT (5-HO-DMT, bufotenine) is the main indole found in the seeds of *Anadenanthera peregrina* and *A. columbrina*, and is also produced in some toads.[34] It has also been detected as a natural component in human urine,[35] and has agonistic actions at 5-HT_{1A}, 5-HT_{1C}, 5-HT_{1D}, and 5-HT_2 binding sites (Figure 6.6.3.2).[22,36,37] Although it is not thought to cross the blood brain barrier it is apparently psychoactive in humans,[38] possibly through its *in situ* conversion to 5-MeO-DMT by indole-*O*-methyl transferase.

6.6.4.1.5 LSD and Other Psychotropic Ergotamines

Ergot (*Claviceps purpurea*), a parasitic fungus that grows on rye and a few other grasses, has been used since antiquity as an abortifacient. Ergotamines are now known to be powerful contractors of the uterus, a tissue rich in 5-HT receptors. The tetracyclic ergoline ring system is represented by LSD in Figure 6.6.1, and related derivatives are known more specifically as lysergamides. To date, LSD is one of the most powerful psychedelic compound reported, while most other lysergamides fall short of this effect, or are totally inactive.[39-41]

Psychoactive lysergamides have also been found in plants; in the seeds of the pre-Columbian South American sacrament Ololiuhqui (from the morning glory *Ipomoea violacea*), for example, and also in seeds of *Argyreia nervosa*. While some of these alkaloids are psychoactive in humans, none can compare to the effects of LSD.

Although first synthesized in 1938 as the 25th derivative in a series of lysergamides, it was not until 1943 that Albert Hofmann inadvertently absorbed enough *d*-LSD-25 to notice its psychoactive potential.[42] Subsequent investigations confirmed this activity. At the time it was the most potent neuroactive substance known, being active at less than 1 µg/kg. In 1967, LSD was reported to cause chromosomal damage;[43,44] however, this dubious observation was refuted in subsequent reports.[45-47] An excellent collection of essays, addressing the greater social and psychological impact of this unique molecule, has already been published.[48]

LSD is a full 5-HT_{1A} agonist, partial/weak 5-HT_2 agonist/antagonist,[30] with additional affinity at 5-HT_{1D},[36] and also binds with high affinity to dopamine (DA) D_1 and D_2 receptor sites.[49] Some *N*-isopropyl lysergamides seem promising, in terms of LSD-like activity, in accordance with animal and receptor binding studies, though no human data have been reported.[50]

6.6.5 PHENETHYLAMINES

The neuropharmacology of many psychoactive drugs has been studied in animal behavioral models using the two-lever drug discrimination paradigm.[51] Using this model, Koerner and Appel investigated the stimulus generalization effects of psilocin, LSD, and mescaline in rats trained to discriminate psilocybin from saline.[52] This team reported that the psilocybin cue generalized to psilocin and LSD, but not to the phenethylamine mescaline. Their results suggested that the effects from these three drugs in humans may not be identical to their discriminative stimulus properties in animals, and indicate that the drug discrimination assay may be inadequate as a model for "hallucinogenicity" in humans. A further implication of their findings was that mescaline and, by extension, other phenethylamines may not belong to the same class as LSD and psilocin.

6.6.5.1 Mescaline

Although Heffter was the first to ingest the purified alkaloid (Figure 6.6.1), it was the German psychiatrist Kurt Beringer who administered this drug as an experimental medicine in the 1920s. Medical publications began to announce its public debut after World War II, in the context of "mescaline psychosis", in early attempts to relate the newly discovered psychedelic state to more familiar territory. It is an anomaly among psychedelic drugs in that the effective dosage is extremely high, perhaps due to interactions with MAO (Table 6.6.5.2). Even more potent phenethylamines seem to lack the unique "sparkle" of mescaline, in terms of psychoactivity; most are sympathomimetically more stimulating with some component of the full "mescaline" effect.[1] It is surprising how little receptor binding data is available for mescaline.

Table 6.6.5.2 A Listing of Phenethylamines (PEA) and Phenylisopropylamines (PIA), Their Substitution Patterns on the Aromatic Ring, Oral Dosage, Duration of Action in Hours and Notable Receptor Binding Sites

Compound	Molecular class and substitution		Dosage (µg/kg)	Duration of action	Receptor sites
Mescaline	PEA	3,4,5	5,000	8-12	5-HT sites
MDMA	PIA	3,4	1,800	8-12	5-HT_{1A}, 5-HT uptake site
2C-B	PEA	2,4,5	300	4-8	5-HT_{2A} and 5-HT_{2C}
2C-I	PEA	2,4,5	300	4-8	5-HT_{2A} and 5-HT_{2C}
DOB	PIA	2,4,5	30	18-30	5-HT_{2A} and 5-HT_{2C}
DOI	PIA	2,4,5	30	18-30	5-HT_{2A} and 5-HT_{2C}

6.6.5.2 Other Psychotropic Phenethylamines

Modifications to substituents on position 4 of the phenyl ring seem most tolerated in terms of maintaining potency with some psychoactivity. Modifications, and especially lengthening, of substituents at position 2 are most disruptive, and position 5 is less sensitive to change than position 2 (Figure 6.6.5.2, Table 6.6.5.1). While the following compounds are not nearly a complete list of psychotropic phenethylamines, they are representative to some extent. An exhaustive survey of human psychoactivity for 179 phenethylamines has been published.[1] Overall, methylation at the α-carbon on the ethlyamine chain increases sympathomimetic potency at the expense of psychedelic activity, and the R-(-) enantiomers are generally the more

J.C. Callaway and D.J. McKenna

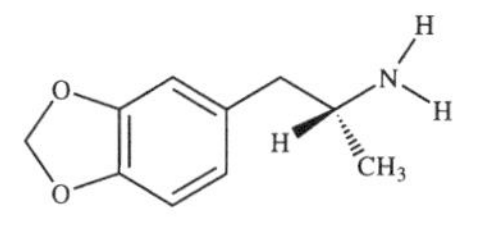

Figure 6.6.5.2 Some selected psychotropic phenethylamines and their most psychoactive enantiomers; R-(-)DOB, X=Br, R-(-)-DOI, X=I, R-(-)-DOM, X=methyl, and R-(-)-DOET, X=ethyl; 2C-B, X=Br; 2C-I, X=I.

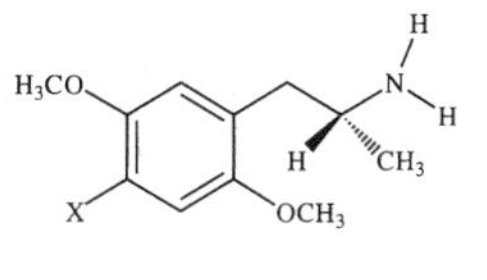

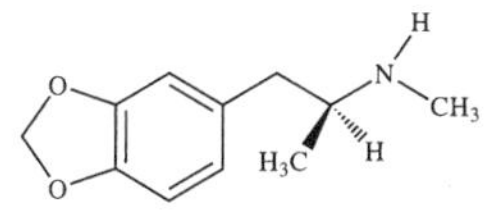

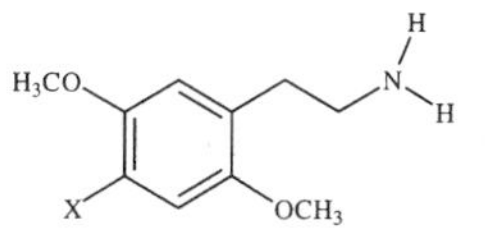

potent stereoisomer.[53] It should be noted that this particular configuration has the α-hydrogen projecting out of the plane; i.e., towards the reader (Figure 6.6.5.2). This is also the case with LSD (Figure 6.6.1) and the optically active S-(+)-α-methyltryptamines. Also, 2,4,5-substituted compounds are more potent than their analogous 3,4,5-derivatives.[54] In addition, several psychoactive sulfur analogs have also been prepared and tested in humans.[55]

Increased lipophilicity of substituents at position 4 may facilitate passive diffusion into the CNS to interact with a hydrophobic region on the 5-HT receptor,[56] as earlier suggested.[57] Substitution at this position probably confers metabolic stability by blocking oxidation and hydroxylation.[54] In general, these compounds show agonistic actions at serotonergic sites.

6.6.5.2.1 DOB

1-(2,5-Dimethoxy-4-bromophenyl)-2-aminopropane (DOB) has essentially the same psychoactive profile as DOI.[1] Both are phenylisopropylamines having a 2,4,5-substitution pattern, and both are very potent in humans at low dosages (Table 6.6.5.2, Figure 6.6.5.2). Also, the R-(-) enantiomer of each compound binds with high affinity and selectivity to 5-HT2 receptor subtypes.[36] While some psychoactivity from this and related 2,4,5-substituted phenylalkylamines may be called "psychedelic", the most prominent effect is sympathomimetic stimulation in conjunction with mescaline-like psychoactivity.[1] At higher dosages, this stimulation tends to dominate more subtle overtones of psychoactivity that are certainly present and reflective of psychedelic activity.

As radioligands, both [^{3}H]DOB and [^{125}I]DOI have proven to be useful tools for the characterization of high-affinity 5HT$_2$ binding sites. Studies by Lyon et al.[57] used [^{3}H]DOB to label a high-affinity binding site in the rat cortex, where approximately 5% of the receptor population was labeled by the 5HT$_2$ antagonist [^{3}H]ketanserine. This research group postulated that the agonist, DOB, labeled a high-affinity agonist state of the 5-HT2 receptors that was regulated by guanyl nucleotides. The relatively low specific activity of [^{3}H]DOB, however, made further characterization difficult, due to the relatively low density of labeled sites, and precluded autoradiographic studies. These difficulties were overcome, however, when McKenna et al.[59,60] used a radioiodinated enantiomer of DOI (the R isomer of [^{125}I]DOI) which had sufficient specific activity to determine the autoradiographic localization of high-affinity 5HT$_2$ binding sites in rat brain. Subsequent studies by Johnson et al.[61] demonstrated stereoselective binding to a high affinity site by [^{125}I]-labeled enantiomers of DOI, where the less active S-enantiomer displayed a twofold lower affinity for the high-affinity site. In subsequent autoradiographic studies, McKenna et al.[29,62] demonstrated the specific, regional, cross-displacement of the 5HT2 sites labeled by [^{125}I]-*R*-DOI and [^{125}I]LSD, by unlabeled DOB, LSD, and DOI. A later study utilized the short-lived ^{77}Br isotope to label DOB for the study of high-affinity 5HT2 recognition sites in rat brain synaptosomal preparations.[63] These authors suggested that other short-lived positron-emitting isotopes, such as ^{75}Br could also be utilized in studies to characterize *in vivo* brain metabolism and kinetics of psychedelic drugs. Indeed, Sargent et al.[64] had already used ^{77}Br-labeled DOB 13 years earlier to study brain blood flow kinetics in human volunteers, and remarked on how most of the radioactivity accumulated in the lungs.

6.6.5.2.2 2C-B

2-(2,5-Dimethoxy-4-bromophenyl)aminoethane (2C-B) has a similar substitution pattern to DOB, though lacks a chiral center on the ethylamine side chain (Figure 6.6.5.2). This simplification is a distinct advantage over DOB as it eliminates the possibility of labeling a receptor with a racemic product. It has also been prepared as the 125-iodo-derivative ([^{125}I]2C-I) and has similar binding properties as [^{125}I]DOI.[65] Both 2C-B and 2C-I have shorter durations of action and less sympathomimetic activity than either DOB or DOI.[1] The subjective effects of 2C-B have been described as being more "tryptamine-like" than other phenethylamines. Also, the effective dosage is similar to that of psilocin. Thus, radioactive 2C-B or 2C-I may be more appropriate ligands to investigate psychedelic activity.

6.6.5.2.3 MDMA

3,4-Methylenedioxy-methamphetamine (MDMA) was first mentioned in a German patent assigned to E. Merck in 1914. In a review of declassified material from military studies, it is mentioned as having toxicological effects at high dosages.[66] This was apparently the first publication of structure-activity relationships among psychoactive phenethylamines. Interestingly, while the behavioral effects from MDMA in these studies were interpreted as "hallucinogenic", mescaline showed no such behavior at any survivable dosage. The human pharmacology of MDMA was not presented until 1978.[67]

While most psychoactive phenethylamines offer the *R* (-) stereoisomer as the most active form (e.g., MDA; DOB; DOM, X=methyl; DOET X=ethyl, Figure 6.6.5.2), the *S* (+) enantiomer is the more potent form of MDMA, similar to the example of amphetamine vs. methamphetamine, suggesting the mechanism of action to be different than that of MDA and other psychoactive phenethylamines.[53] The *R* (-) isomer of MDMA has been shown to be the more potent enantiomer in releasing 5-HT, thus linking psychoactivity for this compound with serotonergic function.[68]

6.6.6 SUMMARY AND CONCLUSIONS

At present, the psychedelics do not have a stated use within the domain of modern medicine, and any additional use outside of narrowly defined scientific protocol has been termed "abuse". Contemporary usage of psychedelics is often associated with religious significance, which is also the way other human societies have employed these agents; to reveal, and make manifest, areas of human consciousness.

Specific molecules bind to various sites, as molecular "transistors" to modify the flow of neuronal information. Just as fingers match specific keys on a piano to transmit music, psychedelic agents bind to discrete receptor sites and reveal psychic affect. From the available information it seems that this action may be more towards a "chord" of music, rather then a single note. LSD serves as an exquisite example for this analogy, with its "dirty" receptor binding profile and powerful action at remarkably low dosage.

Since the psychic effects are almost entirely of the mind, meaningful information on the qualitative effects have not been readily obtained from animal studies, as with other drugs; i.e., the existence of "mindfulness" has not been sufficiently demonstrated in other animals and, more to the point, a common language does not exist between humans and any other animal to convey such information. In the absence of a useful experimental model, and considering the characteristic lack of toxicity with most psychedelic agents, further studies into the application of these drugs should proceed with experiments using healthy human volunteers.[1]

Furthermore, 5-HT may not adequately represent the model ligand for the 5-HT2 binding site.[69] It is possible that a [3H]ketanserine or [125I]DOI labeled 5-HT2 binding site, for example, represents an allosteric site or receptor subtype at which serotonin is not the primary endogenous ligand. It also seems likely that more than one site is involved in the type of activity exemplified by mescaline, LSD, and psilocin. Perhaps now the affinity of each site can be examined separately with ligands that are more selective in binding, though more specific subjectively; e.g., [3H]LSD or [3H]DMT, while using appropriate masking concentrations of non-labeled ligands at each individual site. Further studies with expressed cloned 5HT receptor subtypes may disclose which sites are relevant to the psychotomimetic activities.

REFERENCES

1. Shulgin, A. and Shulgin, A., *Pihkal: A Chemical Love Story*, Transform Press, Berkeley CA, 1991.
2. Unger, S. M., Mescaline, LSD, psilocybin and personality change: A review, *Psychiatry*, 26,111, 1963.
3. Osmond, H., A review of the clinical effects of psychotomimetic agents, *Annals of the New York Academy of Sciences*, 66, 418, 1957.
4. Jacobs, B. L. and Trulson, M. E., Dreams, hallucinations and psychosis- the serotonin connection, *Trends in Neurosciences*, 2(11), 276, 1979.
5. Fischman, L. G., Dreams, hallucinogenic drug states, and schizophrenia: A psychological and biological comparison, *Schizophr Bull*, 9(1), 73, 1983.
6. Callaway, J. C., A proposed mechanism for dream sleep, *Medical Hypotheses*, 26,119,1988.
7. Assad, G. and Shapiro, B., Hallucinations, *Am J Psychiatry*, 143, 1088, 1986.
8. Ott, J., *The Age of Entheogens & The Angel's Dictionary*, Natural Product Co., Kennewick, WA, 1995.
9. Schultes, R. E. and Hofmann, A., *The Botany and Chemistry of Hallucinogens*, 2nd Edition, C.C. Thomas, Springfield, IL, 1980.
10. Schultes, R. E., Hofmann, A., *Plants of the Gods*. Healing Arts Press, Rochester, VT, 1992.
11. Ott, J., *Pharmacotheon: Entheogenic drugs, their plant sources and history*, Natural Product Co., Kennewick, WA, 1993.
12. Hofmann, A., Heim, R., Brack, A., Kobel, H., Frey, A., Oh, H., Petrzilka, T., and Troxler, F., Psilocybin und psilocin, zwei psychotrope Wirkstoffe aus mexikanischen Rauschpilzen, *Helv Chim Acta*, 42, 1557, 1959.
13. Hofmann, A., History of the basic chemical investigations on the sacred mushrooms of Mexico, in *Teonanácatl: Hallucinogenic Mushrooms of North America, Psycho-Mycological Studies No.2*, Ott, J. and Bigwood, J., Eds., Madrona Publishers, Seattle, WA, 1978, 55.
14. Lee, M. A. and Shlain, B., *Acid Dreams: The CIA, LSD and the Sixties Rebellion*, Grove Weidenfeld Publishers, NY, 1985.
15. Domelsmith, L. N., Eaton, T. A., Houk, K. N., Anderson, G. M., III, Glennon, R. A., Shulgin, A. T., Castagnoli, N., Jr., and Kollman, P. A., Photoelectron spectra of psychotropic drugs. 6. Relationships between physical properties and pharmacological actions of amphetamine analogues, *J Med Chem*, 24, 1414, 1981.
16. Clare, B. W., Structure-activity correlations for psychotomimetics: 1. Phenylalkylamines: Electronic, volume, and hydrophobicity parameters, *J Med Chem* 33, 687, 1990.
17. Pierce, P. A. and Peroutka, S. J., Hallucinogenic drug interactions with neurotransmitter receptor binding sites in human cortex, *Psychopharmacol*, 97, 118, 1989.

18. Nichols, D. E. and Glennon, R. A., Medicinal chemistry and structure-activity relationships of hallucinogens, in *Hallucinogens: Neurochemical, Behavioral, and Clinical Perspectives*, Jacobs, B. L., Ed., Raven Press, NY, 1984, 95.

19. Nichols, D. E., Studies of the relationship between molecular structure and hallucinogenic activity, *Pharmacol Biochem Behav*, 24, 335, 1986.

20. Nichols, D. E., Oberlander, R., and McKenna, D. J., Stereochemical aspects of hallucinogenesis, in *Biochemistry and Physiology of Substance Abuse*, Watson, R. R., Ed., CRC Press, Boca Raton, FL, 1, 1991.

21. Gröger, D., Alkaloids from tryptophan, in *Biochemistry of Alkaloids*, Mothes, K., Schüte, H. R., and Luckner, M., Eds.,1983, 15.

22. McKenna, D. J., Repke, D. B., Lo, L., and Peroutka, S., Differential interactions of indolealkylamines with 5-hydroxytryptamine receptor subtypes, *Neuropharmacol*, 29(3), 193, 1990.

23. Repke, D. B., Grotjahn, D. B., and Shulgin, A. T., Psychotomimetic *N*-methyl-*N*-isopropyltryptamines. Effects of variation of the aromatic oxygen substituents, *J Med Chem* 28, 892, 1985.

24. Glennon, R. A., Chaurasia, C., and Titeler, M., Binding of indolylalkylamines at 5-HT2 serotonin receptors: Examination of a hydrophobic binding region, *J Med Chem* 33, 2777, 1990.

25. Lyon, R. A., Titeler M., Seggel M. R., and Glennon, R. A., Indolealkylamine analogs share 5-HT2 binding characteristics with phenylalkylamine hallucinogens, *Eur J Pharmacol*, 145, 291, 1988.

26. Strange, P. G., States and subtypes of the 5-HT2 serotonin receptor: Interpretation of the data. *J Neurochem*, 54, 1085, 1990.

27. Leonhardt, S. and Titeler, M., Serotonin 5-HT2 receptors: Two sites or two subtypes, *J Neurochem*, 53, 316, 1989.

28. Pierce, P. A. and Peroutka, S. J., Evidence for distinct 5-hydroxytryptamine 2 binding site subtypes in cortical membrane preparations, *J Neurochem*, 52, 656, 1989.

29. McKenna, D. J. and Peroutka, S. J., Differentiation of 5-hydroxytryptamine 2 receptor subtypes using ^{125}I-*R*-(-)2,5-dimethoxy-4-iodophenylisopropylamine and ^{3}H-ketanserine, *J Neurosci*, 9, 3482, 1989.

30. Deliganis, A. V., Pierce, P. A., and Peroutka, S., Differential interactions of dimethyltryptamine (DMT) with 5-HT1A and 5-HT2 receptors, *Biochem Pharmacol* 41(11),1739, 1991.

31. Szára, S. I., Dimethyltryptamine: Its metabolism in man; the relation of its psychotic effects to the serotonin metabolism, *Experientia*, 15(6), 441, 1956.

32. Barker, S. A., Monti, J. A., Christian S. T., *N,N*-Dimethyltryptamine: An endogenous hallucinogen, in *International Review of Neurobiology* vol. 22, Academic Press, NY, 1981.

33. Dumuis, A., Sebben, M., and Bockaertt, J., Pharmacology of 5-hydroxytryptamine-1A receptors which inhibit cAMP production in hippocampal and cortical neurons in primary culture, *Mol Pharmacol*, 33, 178, 1988.

34. Daly, J. W. and Witcop, B., Chemistry and pharmacology of frog venoms, in *Venomous Animals and their Venoms, Vol. II*, Academic Press, NY, 1971, 497.

35. Kärkkäinen, J. and Räisänen, M., Nialamide, an MAO inhibitor, increases urinary excretion of endogenously produced bufotenin in man, *Biol Psychiatry*, 32, 1042, 1992.

36. Peroutka, S. J., Short review: 5-hydroxytryptamine receptors, *J Neurochem*, 60(2), 408, 1993.

37. Peroutka, S. J., Pharmacological differentiation and characterization of 5-HT1A, 5-HT1B, 5-HT1C binding sites in rat frontal cortex, *J Neurochem*, 47, 529, 1986.

38. McLeod, W. R. and Sitiram, B. R., Bufotenine reconsidered, *Acta Psychiatr Scand*, 72, 447, 1985.

39. Rothlin, A., Pharmacology of lysergic acid diethylamide and some of its related compounds, *J Pharm Pharmacol* 9, 569, 1957.

40. Shulgin, A. T., Chemistry and sources, in *Drugs of Abuse: Their Generic and other Chronic Nonpsychiatric Hazards*, Epstein, S. S. Ed., The MIT Press, Cambridge, MA, 1971, 3.

41. Weinstein, H., Green, J., Osman, R., and Edwards, W., Recognition and activation mechanisms on the LSD/serotonin receptor: The molecular basis of structure-activity relationships, in *QuaSAR Research Monograph* 22, Barnett, G., Trsic, M., and Willette, R., Eds., U.S. Government Printing Office, Washington, D.C., 1978, 333.

42. Hofmann, A., *LSD: My problem child*, McGraw-Hill, NY, 1980.

43. Cohen, M. M., Hirshhorn, K., Frosch, W. A., In vivo and in vitro chromosomal damage induced by LSD-25, *N E J Med*, 227, 1043, 1967.

44. Cohen, M., Marinello, M., Bach, N., Chromosomal damage in human leukocytes induced by lysergic acid dimethylamine, *Science*, 155, 1417, 1967.

45. Bender, L. and Sankar, D. V. S., Chromosome damage not found in leukocytes of children treated with LSD-25, *Science*, 159, letter,1968.

46. Tjio, J. H., Pahnke, W. N., and Kurland, A. A., LSD and chromosomes: A controlled experiment, *JAMA*, 210, 849,1969.

47. Dishotsky, N. I., Loughman, W. D., Mogar, R. E., and Lipscomb, W. R., LSD and genetic damage, *Science*, 172, 431, 1971.

48. Cohen, S., Krippner, S., Zerkin, E. L., Novey, J. H., Eds., LSD in Retrospect, *J Psychoactive Drugs*, 17(4), 1985.

49. Watts, V. J., Lawler, C. P., Fox, D. R., Neve, K. A., and Nichols, D. E., LSD and structural analogs: Pharmacological evaluation at D1 dopamine receptors, *Psychopharmacol*, 118(4), 401, 1995.

50. Huang, X., Marona-Lewicka, D., Pfaff, R.C., and Nichols, D. E., Drug discrimination and receptor binding studies of *N*-isopropyl lysergamide derivatives, *J Med Chem*, 47(3), 667, 1994.

51. Glennon, R. A., Rosecrans, J. A., and Young R., Drug-induced discrimination: A description of the paradigm and a review of it application in the study of hallucinogenic agents, *Med Res Rev*, 3, 289, 1983.

52. Koerner, J. and Appel, B., Psilocybin as a discriminative stimulus: Lack of specificity in an animal model of 'hallucinogenicity', *Psychopharmacol*, 76, 130, 1982.

53. Anderson III, G. M., Braun, G., Braun, U. Nichols, D. E., and Shulgin, A. T., Absolute configuration and psychotomimetic activity, *NIDA Research Monograph* 22, 1978, 8.

54. Shulgin, A. T., Psychotomimetic drugs: Structure-activity relationships, in *Handbook of Psychopharmacology*, vol. 11, Iversen, L. L., Iversen, S. D., and Snyder, S. H., eds., Plenum, NY, 1978, 243.

55. Nichols, D. E. and Shulgin, A. T., Sulfur analogs of psychotomimetic amines, *J Pharm Sci* 65, 1554, 1976.

56. Monte, A. P., Marona-Lewicka, D., Parker, M. A., Wainscott, D. B., Nelson, D. L., and Nichols, D. E., Dihydrobenzophoran analogues of hallucinogens. 3. Models of 4-substituted (2,5-dimethoxyphenyl) alkylamine derivatives with rigidified methoxy groups, *J Med Chem*, 39, 2953, 1996.

57. Barfknecht, C. F., Nichols, D. E., and Dunn III, W. J., Correlation of psychotomimetic activity of phenethylamines and amphetamines with 1-octanol/water partition coefficients, *J Med Chem*, 18, 208, 1975.

58. Lyon, R. A., Davis, K. H., and Titeler, M., [^{3}H]-DOB (4-bromo-2,5-dimethoxyphenylisopropylamine) labels a guanyl nucleotide sensitive state of cortical 5HT2 receptors, *Mol Pharmacol*, 31, 194, 1987.

59. McKenna, D. J., Mathis, C. A., Shulgin, A. T., and Saavedra, J. M., Hallucinogens bind to common receptors in the rat forebrain: A comparative study using ^{125}I-LSD and ^{125}I-DOI, a new psychotomimetic radioligand, *Neuroscience Abstracts*, 13(311), 14, 1987.

60. McKenna, D. J., Mathis, C. A., Shulgin, A. T., Sargent III, T., and Saavedra, J. M., Autoradiographic localization of binding sites for ^{125}I-(-)DOI, a new psychotomimetic radioligand, in the rat brain, *Eur J Pharmacol*, 137, 290, 1987.

61. Johnson, M. P., Hoffman, A. J., Nichols, D. E., and Mathis, C. A., Binding to the serotonin 5-HT2 receptor by enantiomers of [^{125}I]DOI, *Neuropharmacol*, 26, 1803, 1987.

62. McKenna, D. J. and Saavedra, J. M., Autoradiography of LSD and 2,5-dimethoxyphenyliso-propylamine psychotomimetics demonstrates regional, specific cross-displacement in the rat brain, *Eur J Pharmacol*, 142, 315, 1987.

63. Wang, S. H., Mathis, C. A., and Peroutka, S. J., R-(-)-2,5-dimethoxy-4-[77]bromoamphetamine [[77]Br-R-(-)-DOB]: A novel radioligand which labels a 5-HT binding site subtype, *Psychopharmacol*, 94, 431, 1988.

64. Sargent III, T., Kalbhen, A., Shulgin, A. T., Stauffer, H., and Kusubov, N., A potential new brain-scanning agent: 4-[77]Br-2,5-dimethoxyphenylisopropylamine (4-Br-DPIA), *J Nuc Med*, 16, 245, 1975.

65. Johnson, M. P., Mathis, C. A., Shulgin, A. T., Hoffman, A. J., and Nichols, D. E., [^{125}I]-2-(2,5-Dimethoxy-4-iodophenyl)aminoethane ([^{125}I]-2C-I) as a label for the 5-HT2 receptor in rat frontal cortex, *Pharmacol Biochem Behav*, 35, 211, 1990.

66. Hardman, H. F., Haavik, C. O., and Seevers, M. H., Relationship of the structure of mescaline and seven analogs to toxicity and behavior in five species of laboratory animals, *Tox Appl Pharmacol*, 25(2), 299, 1973.

67. Shulgin A. T., and Nichols, D. E., Characterization of three new psychotomimetics, in *The Pharmacology of Hallucinogens*, Stillman, R. C. and Willette, R. E., Eds., Pergamon Press, NY, 1978, 74.

68. Nichols, D. E., Lloyd, D. H., Hoffman, A. J., Nichols, M. B., and Yim, G. K. W., Effects of certain hallucinogenic amphetamines analogues on the release of [^{3}H]serotonin from rat synaptosomes, *J Med Chem*, 25, 530, 1982.

69. Apud, J. A., The 5-HT2 receptor in brain: Recent biochemical and molecular biological developments and new perspectives in its regulation, *Pharmacol Res*, 23(3), 217, 1991.

CHAPTER 7

ADDICTION MEDICINE

EDITED BY KIM WOLFF

NATIONAL ADDICTION CENTRE, INSTITUTE OF PSYCHIATRY, UNIVERSITY OF LONDON

TABLE OF CONTENTS

7.1 THE PRINCIPLES OF ADDICTION MEDICINE

DUNCAN RAISTRICK

THE LEEDS ADDICTION UNIT, LEEDS, U.K.

This chapter is about the day to day business of managing people with substance misuse problems from the medical practitioner point of view. Many doctors involved with addiction problems will see themselves as having only a prescribing role whereas specialists in the field will, in addition, require a repertoire of psychotherapy skills. Prescribing for patients who may have a dependence on a number of drugs, who may wish to conceal the extent of their substance use, and who may have a marked tolerance to some classes of drug presents difficulties for the unwary or ill informed doctor. In order to prescribe safely and effectively doctors must:

1. understand the nature of dependence
2. understand the dependence-forming potential of drugs
3. understand the importance of motivation

7.1.1 UNDERSTANDING THE NATURE OF DEPENDENCE

In the UK and North America, the understanding of addiction has been dominated by the *disease theory* and the *social learning theory*. Heather[1] succinctly describes the history and development of thinking underpinning these theories. Other theories or, perhaps more correctly, models of addiction have been popular in particular cultures or where partial explanations have utility, for example psychoanalytical interpretations of addictive behavior are common in some European countries, and equally, religious or moral failures are attractive reasons to account for addictive behavior where spiritual values are important as in many Asian and Indian communities.

The important implications of the disease theory depend on the notion that addiction is caused by some irreversible deficiency or pathology and that treatment is, therefore, primarily a medical concern. Certain conclusions inevitably follow from such a premise: (1) abstinence is the only treatment goal, (2) loss of control is the hallmark feature, (3) patients are not responsible for their "illness", (4) therapists tend to be medical practitioners, and, finally, (5) community-based prevention will be ineffective.

In formulating a description of alcohol and later other drug dependence, Edwards and Gross[2] argued against the disease model in favor of a biopsychosocial construction of dependence, which was identified as belonging to a separate dimension from substance related harms. This formulation has been adopted in the International Classification of Diseases, ICD-10.[3] The important implications of social learning theory are: a range of treatment goals are possible, the ability to control substance use is emphasised, users are active participants in treatment, therapists tend to be non-medical, and fiscal and other control measures will be effective.

The biopsychosocial description of dependence has been criticized for placing unwarranted emphasis on withdrawal symptoms. While the anticipation or experience of withdrawal may indeed be a potent source of negative reinforcement for drinking, it is not the only source of reinforcement, and it may be that the positive reinforcement of a pharmacological (drug) effect is more important whether or not an individual also experiences withdrawal. To take account of this, Raistrick et al.[4] have proposed a modified description of the dependence syndrome and developed the idea of substance dependence as a purely psychological phenomenon where tolerance and withdrawal are understood as consequences of regular drinking, rather than being a part of dependence. The withdrawal symptoms themselves are one step removed from the cognitive response to the symptoms, which may or may not include thoughts about drinking. If withdrawal symptoms were themselves a defining element of dependence, then different drugs would be associated with different kinds of dependence, but this is not a widely held view. Rather, it is believed that dependence can readily shift from one substance to another.[5] The markers of substance dependence translate the neuroadaptive elements of the biopsychosocial description of dependence into cues which condition cognitions and behaviors and are therefore of more universal application. There are 10 markers of substance dependence:

1. Preoccupation with drinking or taking drugs
2. Salience of substance use behavior
3. Compulsion to start using alcohol or drugs
4. Planning alcohol- or drug-related behaviors
5. Maximizing the substance effect
6. Narrowing of substance use repertoire
7. Compulsion to continue using alcohol and drugs
8. Primacy of psychoactive effect
9. Maintaining a constant state (of intoxication)
10. Expectations of need for substance use

In summary, the most complete account of addictive behaviors comes from a synthesis of physiology, pharmacology, psychology, and sociology — *social learning*. Dependence exists along a continuum of severity implying the need for different treatments and outcome goals. Substance-related harms in physical, psychological, and social spheres belong to a separate domain. Addiction has become a term without precise meaning, but is generally taken to include dependence, problem use, and any related harms. While social learning allows that anyone may become dependent on psychoactive substances and may also unlearn their dependence, it does not preclude the possibility that substance use may cause deficiencies of endogenous neurotransmitters, which are usually reversible, or permanent damage to receptor structure and connectivity. Indeed, it is likely that such changes occur.

The Principles of Addiction Medicine

7.1.2 UNDERSTANDING THE DEPENDENCE-FORMING POTENTIAL OF DRUGS

7.1.2.1 Potency of Psychactive Effect

In humans, the reinforcing properties of psychoactive substances, which combine to generate the umbrella construct dependence, are complex: a prominent view attaches importance to the positive reinforcing effects of inducing pleasurable mood states and the negative reinforcement of avoiding painful affects. Pervin[6] explores this very issue in a study of four poly drug users: subjects were asked to describe situations (1) where they wanted to use drugs, (2) after they had used drugs, (3) where they wanted to use drugs but could not, and (4) unrelated to drug use, and then to associate affects from a prepared list with the four situations they described. A factor analysis produced three factors accounting for 44% of the variance: the first factor *Wish*, was characterized as "being tense, helpless, jittery, lonely"; the second, *After Drugs*, was characterized as "lonely, empty, inhibited, angry"; and the third, *Taking Drugs*, included "confidence, relaxed, high, secure, strong, satisfied". The results also indicated that subjects *discriminated* between drugs suited to dealing with different affects. In two complementary reports, Johanson and Uhlenbuth[7,8] compared changes in mood among normal volunteers in a choice experiment between placebo, diazepam, and amphetamine. Amphetamine 5 mg was chosen significantly more often than placebo, 81% of possible choices, with increased scores for vigor, friendliness, elation, arousal, positive mood, and decreased scores for confusion. In contrast, diazepam 5 and 10 mg were chosen significantly less often than placebo, 28 and 27% of choices, respectively, with decreased scores on vigor and arousal and increased scores on confusion and fatigue. The point to underline here is that *normal* subjects are likely to have different effects to *patient* groups and the reinforcing potential of different substances will therefore vary between such groups: within matched subjects the reinforcing properties of different substances will also vary in strength.

At a clinical level, most doctors are wary of "addictive" drugs: for example, long-term methadone prescribing is intended to achieve pharmacological stability, at least partially block the effect of other opiates, and prevent withdrawal symptoms. However, Bickel et al.[9] suggest that, although methadone is seen as a low tariff drug, treatment retention is, in part, associated with its reinforcing properties. Using a choice paradigm, subjects maintained on methadone 50 mg daily, identified to subjects as capsule A, had the option of taking capsule B which, in different trials, contained either methadone 50, 60, 70, or 100 mg, in place of Capsule A. Capsule B was chosen 50, 73, 87, and 97%, respectively, of occasions: at the highest dose, subjects identified an *opiate effect* and a *liking* for the drug but no *high* or *withdrawal* was reported. The clinical implications are quantified by McGlothlin and Anglin[10] in a 7-year follow-up of patients attending high- vs. low-dose methadone maintenance programs: the high-dose program performed better in terms of retention, significantly fewer arrests and periods of incarceration, less criminal activity, and less supplementary drug use. In a similar type of study, Hartnoll et al.[11] followed up addicts randomly allocated to an injectable heroin or oral methadone program: at 1-year follow up, 74% of the heroin group against 29% of the methadone group were still in treatment but only 10% against 30% had achieved abstinence from illicit drugs. So, the dilemma is that prescriptions most liked by addicts, namely those that are more reinforcing, achieve good program retention and a degree of stability, but at the cost of slowing movement away from substance use and the associated subculture.

The potency of psychoactive effect is not simply a function of dose or plasma level, but also depends upon receptor uptake characteristics. For example, Chiang and Barnett[12] have shown that immediately after intravenous tetrahydrocannabinal a rising plasma concentration of approximately 45 ng per ml relates to a subjective "high" of 10% whereas the same falling plasma concentration 15 minutes later relates to a high of nearly 80% on a self-rating 0 to 100% scale. This phenomenon is accounted for by a slow uptake of THC at the receptors. Active metabolites may spuriously suggest the same phenomenon.

Duncan Raistrick

Similarly, the partial agonist buprenorphine has a high, but slow, binding affinity at the opiate mu receptor: it has the potential to act as antagonist against pure opioid agonists and itself appears to have a ceiling effect at about 1 mg subcutaneously for subjective response. Although addicts identify buprenorphine as having an opioid effect and therefore potential for misuse, its binding affinity at the mu receptor and antagonist activity confer a quite different reinforcement profile to pure agonists such as diamorphine.

The clinical significance is demonstrated by Johnson et al.,[13] who substituted heroin for buprenorphine in ascending daily doses of 2, 4, and 8 mg: using this regime, diamorphine withdrawal symptoms were avoided and, overall, subjects reported a feeling of "well-being". Withdrawal from buprenorphine 8 mg daily does not precipitate an opiate withdrawal syndrome.

7.1.2.2 Pharmacokinetics

The previous section argued that the mood altering effects of psychoactive drugs may, depending on the pre-drug mental state, have both positive and negative reinforcing properties. Psychoactive effect alone is insufficient explanation of within drug-group differences of dependence forming potential: different pharmacokinetics are important. The benzodiazepines and opioids are the most fruitful source of investigation here because both drug-groups contain many different compounds that are widely used and misused. However, it is difficult to conduct studies that control for confounding factors such as absorption rate, potency, half-life, or "street availability" (and likelihood of supplementing). It is perhaps not surprising that researchers are parsimonious with conclusions.

There are ethical problems in conducting laboratory experiments with potent drugs such as heroin and to avoid this problem Mello et al.[14] investigated the reinforcing efficacy in primates for three opioids: they found buprenorphine and methadone to have similar strength but heroin to be more powerful. Equally in humans heroin is preferred to other opiates including morphine.[15] Since heroin is converted to morphine within the central nervous system, it can be concluded that its faster rate of CNS availability accounts for the difference. Absorption rate and, therefore, immediacy of effect have similarly been shown to be important for benzodiazepines. Funderburk et al.[16] compared the effects of equipotent oral doses of lorazepam (0, 1.5, 3, and 6 mg) and diazepam (0, 10, 20, and 40 mg) in recreational benzodiazepine users: the drug "liking" ratings were similar for both drugs, suggesting that the absorption rate which is similar for the two drugs is more important than the elimination half-life which is much shorter for lorazepam even though subjective ratings of effect persist much longer for this compound. Learning theory predicts the importance of absorption rate in that the most immediate positive consequence of a behavior (drug taking) is the most reinforcing. While potency and the speed of onset of effect are particularly important for initiating dependence, elimination rate assumes greater importance in building and maintaining dependence. As a rule, the more quickly a drug is metabolized the sooner the user experiences a loss of effect and possibly also withdrawal symptoms. Both of these consequences become cues for further drug use — "topping up".

7.1.2.3 Plasticity

Plasticity is defined as the degree to which the effect of a drug is independent of internal environment (e.g., mood, thirst) and external environment (e.g., with friends, comfort). Edwards[17] has described substances as existing along a continuum: highly plastic substances, that is to say those where the content of the effect is markedly influenced by environment, exist at one end (e.g., solvents, LSD), and substances with very predictable content (e.g., heroin, cocaine) exist at the opposite end. Plasticity has a bearing on the dependence-forming potential of substances; where the content of a drug effect is uncertain, repeated use is unlikely. In contrast, a very predictable effect may not suit the variety of uses demanded of a recreational substance, but yet be powerfully reinforcing, that is to say addictive. It is interesting that the most popular recreational drugs, alcohol and cannabis, fall around the middle of the plasticity continuum, perhaps signalling a point which allows an agreeable interaction between drug and expectation effects. In summary, the dependence-forming potential of a drug is a function of:

1. potency of effect
2. speed of entering the central nervous system
3. speed of joining with receptors
4. elimination rate
5. predictability of effect

7.1.3 UNDERSTANDING THE IMPORTANCE OF MOTIVATION

The measurement of dependence and the identification of substance-related problems tell the clinician what outcome goals are likely to be successful and *how much* treatment is needed; alongside this an understanding of motivation informs *what kind* of treatment is needed. The Model of Change described by Prochaska and DiClemente[18] is a motivational model widely used in the addiction field. The purpose of using the model is twofold: first, to understand what is going on for a patient at a given time; second, to inform the patient of the choice of interventions. People who are not motivated to change their substance use are said to be at the *pre-contemplation stage*, which is characterized by denial and rationalization of substance use and its consequences. There are two strands to treatment strategy at this stage: one is to minimize harm without expecting to change the substance use behavior (for example, by giving nutritional supplements or substitute prescribing). The second is to introduce conflict about the substance use (for example, by making links with untoward life events and thereby creating motivation for change). The temptation is to offer treatments aimed at changing substance use behavior before the patient is ready to change. In such circumstances the treatment will always fail.

The experience of significant conflict about substance use (for example, when an arrest is felt to be incompatible with a self-image of being a sensible and responsible person), or when the cost of substance use is causing family hardship indicates movement into the *contemplation stage*. At this stage, motivational interventions which may involve the use of simple clinical tools (for example, the decision matrix), or may draw on more sophisticated skills (for example, motivational interviewing),[19] are indicated. At this stage substitute prescribing or agonist prescribing may be helpful.

The *action stage* is reached when conflict is resolved and there is a commitment to change. A number of things will have happened at a psychological level: the person will believe that life will be better on stopping or controlling their substance use (positive outcome expectancy), they are able to change (self efficacy), and they will know how to change (skills learning). Elective detoxification is the most common medical intervention at the action stage.

The *maintenance stage* follows behavioral change. This is the achievement of abstinence or controlled substance use. Maintenance of behavior change for alcohol misuse may be assisted by prescribing a sensitizing agent such as disulfiram or, for opiate misuse, prescribing an antagonist such as naltrexone. Pharmacological interventions are no more than an adjunct to the main task of achieving lifestyle change. Successful exit from the maintenance stage, recovery, requires that the patient has confidence and skills to deal with substance use cues. Achieving the right mix of pharmacology and psychology is more art than science, but an understanding of the underlying brain mechanisms, reviewed for clinicians by Nutt,[20] and a parallel understanding of motivation will help achieve safe and effective prescribing.

Duncan Raistrick

7.1.4 PRESCRIBING IN CONTEXT

Addiction problems are everyone's business: the sociologist, the politician, the biochemist, the doctor, the police officer, the parent, the pharmacist, the tax payer, the drug dealer, and the public. The list is long, such is the diversity of interests vested in substance use and misuse. Everyone will have opinions about addiction including opinions about what doctors should prescribe. Doctors should seek the widest possible clinical freedom to manage addiction patients and to secure this freedom. It follows that *prescribers must be sensitive to the prevailing medico-political views on what constitutes good practice.* People who misuse substances, particularly illicit substances, may have particularly forceful views about what doctors should prescribe, but these view are likely to change depending where a person is within their addiction career. It follows that *prescribers must have an understanding of addictive behaviors and characteristics of addictive substances. The Model of Change (described above) is a simple, commonly used tool that offers a framework for prescribing and other interventions.*

For most people who have developed a moderate or severe dependence, pharmacotherapy will, at some time, be an important part of treatment. However, prescribing alone will never be sufficient. It follows that *prescribers must have a repertoire of skills, including behavior therapy and psychotherapy or, alternatively, must work with a co-therapist. When working with a co-therapist, the doctor must be satisfied with the reasons for prescribing and take responsibility for the prescription given.*

7.1.5 GENERAL PRECAUTIONS

Doctors who are inexperienced in the field of addiction often feel pressured to prescribe beyond their knowledge and skills, and as a result may issue inappropriate prescriptions. In contrast, specialists are likely to be circumspect about the place of pharmacotherapy and especially so when this means prescribing addictive drugs.[21] The precautions listed below are applicable to any prescribing; however, patients who misuse both prescribed and illicit drugs are especially at risk, not least because prescriptions are often for potent preparations in doses higher than normally recommended. Doctors may be required to justify their prescribing to a variety of authorities and are more likely to fall foul of legal action or audit because of precipate rather than delayed prescribing. Having established the appropriateness of prescribing, the following checklist will ensure the safety of a prescription:

Prescribe drugs with low dependence-forming potential.
Prescribe drugs with low injection potential.
Prescribe drugs with low "street value".
Prescribe inherently stabilizing drugs.
Allow take home quantities commensurate with the patient's stability. Assess:
  • risk of overdose by patient
  • risk of overdose by others living with patient
  • risk of diversion for profit or misuse
  • risk of failing to control use as prescribed
Assess tolerance before prescribing potentially lethal doses.
Check on other prescribed medication.
Check on co-existing medical conditions.
Monitor compliance.

Safety of prescribing needs to be balanced against a regime that is convenient for the patient and which will therefore achieve the best results in terms of retention and compliance.[22, 23] Before finally giving a prescription, it is crucial to ensure that both the doctor and the patient understand the purpose of the prescription. There should be agreement on how to monitor whether or not the intended purpose is being achieved, if the purpose is not achieved then the prescription should be reviewed and possibly discontinued. This does not imply an end to therapy but rather consideration of a shift to an alternative, possibly non-pharmacological treatment.

7.2 SUBSTITUTE PRESCRIBING

KIM WOLFF

NATIONAL ADDICTION CENTRE, INSTITUTE OF PSYCHIATRY, UNIVERSITY OF LONDON

Substitute prescribing is the prescription of the patient's main drug of misuse or a drug from the same pharmacological group but of lower dependence potential. The main purpose of substitute prescribing is to stabilize a person's substance use and offer a period of time to work on non-drug focused interventions. Slow reduction or detoxification can occur at any time during substitute prescribing. Recipents of substitute prescribing may fall into one or more of the following categories:

1. Diagnosis of opiate, cocaine, amphetamine, or benzodiazepine dependence.
2. Minimum 6-month history of regular use.
3. Regular injecting, especially if high risk, of whatever duration.
4. Failed attempts to achieve abstinence.
5. At time of initial assessment, likely to be at the pre-contemplation or contemplation stage of change.

Additional aims of providing substitute treatment for drug misusers has recently been reported.[24]

Short term: Attract patients into treatment

Relieve withdrawal symptoms

Long term: Retention in treatment

Reduction in injecting behavior
Stabilize drug use
Stabilize life style
Reduction in criminal behavior
Reduction in HIV, HBV and HBC transmission
Reduction in death rate

7.2.1 OPIATE SPECIFIC PRESCRIBING

Maintenance prescribing differs from substitute prescribing only in that there is no active effort to bring about change in a person's drug use or psychological state. The majority of clinical drug misuse services are concerned principally with the prescription of methadone to heroin users. American reviews tend to cite methadone as a direct pharmacological treatment in the way that insulin is used for diabetes. Many Europeans, however, would view methadone more as a "substitute" treatment whereby the improvements that are seen result from removing individuals from the process of using street drugs.[24]

7.2.1.1 Methadone Maintenance Prescribing

Methadone, a synthetic opioid first reported as a maintenance (long-term, fixed-dose) treatment for opiate dependence by Dole and Nyswander,[25] is the most widely used pharmacological treatment for this type of addiction in Britain and North America. Substantial evidence exists in the American literature to support the effectiveness of methadone maintenance treatment (MMT), particularly with regard to reduction in intravenous drug misuse,[26] less crime,[27] re-employment,[28] social rehabilitation,[29] overall health status,[28] improved quality of lifestyle,[30] and safety and cost effectiveness compared to other (drug-free) alternatives.[31] The National Treatment Outcome Research Study (NTORS) has recently reported similar preliminary findings in Britain.[32] Retention in treatment is the key, however, and discernible treatment effects are only seen when patients remain in treatment for longer than one year.[31] The available evidence indicates that it is methadone per se which retains patients in treatment.[33]

The advent of AIDS has strengthened the case for MMT. Since 1985, the shift in policy towards harm minimization (rather than abstinence) in response to the perceived threat from the Human Immunodeficiency Virus (HIV), has produced a rapid expansion of methadone treatment in Britain, U.S., and Australia.[34] Although some addicts continue to misuse drugs and share injecting equipment,[35] improved access to MMT has been identified as an important means of reducing the risk of HIV infection in many injecting drug users.[36]

With the expansion of methadone prescribing there has been a diversification in the types of treatment available and a general lack of understanding about effects at the clinical level. It is often assumed that all treatment agencies are delivering the same (invariable) type of methadone program. This is not the case. Wide differences exist in the quality of treatment and there is often a questionable therapeutic approach.[37] For instance, criteria for acceptance into treatment is restrictive and the regulations for remaining in treatment are often impractical, i.e., insistence upon abstinence. This range of treatments and the failure to critically assess outcomes has led to serious underestimation of the benefits of MMT.[27]

7.2.1.2 Treatment Compliance

Studies of treatment response have shown that patients who comply with the recommended course of treatment have favorable outcomes during treatment and longer-lasting post-treatment benefits.[38] Thus, it is discouraging for many practitioners that opiate users are frequently poorly or non-compliant and subsequently resume substance use.[39] Insufficient methadone dose has been identified as a major cause of therapeutic failure — relapse to re-abuse drugs[34] — affecting behavior above and beyond individual differences in motivation and severity of drug dependence.[40] Previous research indicates that an insufficient dose (inadequate for the prevention of withdrawal symptoms for the total duration of the dosing interval — 24 hours) is a major problem for opiate users during treatment.[41] Unfortunately, the likelihood of success is offset by the fact that many patients do not remain in treatment until they are rehabilitated, and those who drop out usually return (relapse) to drug misuse .[42] A 24-year follow-up study of Californian narcotic addicts concluded that the eventual cessation of illicit opiate use is a very slow process, unlikely to occur for some users, especially if they have not ceased drug misuse by their late 30s.[43]

7.2.1.3 Therapeutic Drug Monitoring for Methadone

Many different parameters have been investigated to help assess the efficacy of methadone maintenance treatment. Randomized controlled trials to investigate methadone treatment (a demand rarely made of other treatments for opioid dependence) have been advocated recently.[27] However, controlled trials are often difficult to perform with addict populations because they rarely take account of the drug clinic environment where non-compliance is a common problem.[39] Opiate users are not a homogeneous population and so a single (common) approach to methadone treatment is not a viable option.

The usual procedure for assessing opiate users at clinics involves urinalysis screening for drugs of abuse. Urinalysis drug screening is an important way of assessing drug misuse by patients undergoing methadone treatment, but sheds no light on patient compliance, i.e., whether the patient is taking medication as prescribed. It is essential to know if a patient is taking all of their medication (at the correct time and in the correct amount) and to find out whether the patient is using extra methadone (obtained illicitly) or selling some of their prescription, perhaps to other users. Urinalysis will not provide answers to these questions. This procedure is largely qualitative and results will only indicate whether or not a patient has taken some of their medication. Dosage alterations based on interpretation of plasma measurements may help more patients do well on methadone.[44] Others have suggested a similar approach.[45,46]

Other methods of assessment include self- and observer-reports. However, self-report systems are relatively insensitive for the assessment of the adequacy of dose. As for observer reported systems, which measure subjective and objective signs of opiate withdrawal, these are difficult to interpret. For instance, measurements often used to monitor symptoms of withdrawal are similar to those that assess normal anxiety attacks which is particularly worrying because about 10% of drug addicts in treatment suffer from anxiety disorders.[47, 48] Scientific measurements, in addition to urinalysis and report systems, are clearly needed to evaluate patients. It was found that plasma measurements of methadone filled the gap and provided much needed evidence on compliance.

Compliance in methadone maintenance patients has been measured using a pharmacological indicator to "estimate" plasma methadone concentrations. Very low-dose phenobarbital, a valid pharmacological indicator, was successfully used to measure compliance by incorporating this drug into the methadone medication. Patients attending an addiction unit on a daily basis, and who consumed their medication in front of staff, as well as those who collected their medication from chemists in the community and consumed their medication unobserved, were studied. The use of low-dose phenobarbital provided a valuable insight into methadone maintenance programs and showed that many patients took their medication haphazardly (incorrect self-administration), whereas others supplemented their dose with illicit methadone.[39]

Poor, or insufficient compliance, is of considerable importance for the relationship between plasma concentration and methadone dose. When compliance is good, the relationship between plasma concentration and methadone dose is highly correlated (correlation coefficient $r = 0.89$, $P < 0.001$).[49] Although some variation was observed in our patients on the same daily dose, we were able to attribute this to non-compliance (taking extra illicitly obtained methadone and incorrect self-administration) or the concurrent administration of enzyme inducing drugs. Additionally, little intra-individual variation was found in trough plasma methadone concentrations in patients repeatedly monitored on the same daily dose.[49] Further work on the kinetics of methadone in compliant subjects revealed little inter-individual variation between patients and a similar rate of clearance of methadone in these individuals at steady-state,[50] which contrasts with the earlier findings of other observers.[51-53]

In the past, most believed that the problem of dosage scheduling could not be related to the more immediately relevant variable — plasma methadone concentration.[54, 55] More recently, Loimer et al.[46] advocated the use of plasma methadone concentrations to support methadone treatment. It has been argued that the correct dose of methadone for any individual is that amount which sustains the plasma concentration above a critical minimum needed for continuous occupancy of the opioid μ-receptors, for the complete dosing interval.[56]

Quantitative measurements of methadone in plasma are well within the capabilities of most clinical chemistry laboratories and should fit into established procedures for reception and preparation of blood. When assessing plasma concentrations of a drug with a view to monitoring compliance or the efficacy of the methadone dose, the only variable that should apply is drug clearance. Peak or trough values can be used as long as it is known when absorption and distribution are complete. Trough plasma methadone concentrations should correspond to the lowest daily blood concentrations. Patient assessment is considered more appropriate at this point when withdrawal symptoms are most likely to occur. Blood collection soon after dosing would not normally serve as a good guide to optimal dosing regimes.

7.2.1.4 Indications for Plasma Methadone Monitoring

Take home methadone: Initially attendance at a methadone dispensing clinic is required on a daily basis to consume medication under staff supervision. This requirement is somewhat unreasonable when the patient is assuming responsibility and trying to engage in work, rehabilitation, education programs, or responsible home-making. Take-home medication was seen as a solution. Unfortunately, the practice of permitting take-home supplies for unsupervised self-administration contributed new problems including:[57]

1. Accidental ingestion of methadone by non-tolerant persons, especially children.
2. Methadone toxic reactions.
3. Overdose fatalities.
4. Diversion for illicit sale.
5. Redistribution to other heroin users suffering from withdrawal symptoms.
6. Redistribution to drug users seeking a new euphoriant.

Monitoring the concentration of methadone in patients who take the drug away from the clinic is advisable in order to confirm that the prescribed dose is being consumed in the correct amount and at the correct time.

Injectable methadone: Unless provision is made for the supervised use of injectable methadone at clinics, then regular plasma methadone monitoring is strongly recommended for those prescribed this form of medication. The risk of diversion for illicit sale of methadone in ampoule form is particularly high.

Co-medication with interacting drugs: Many factors are believed to affect methadone kinetics. Concomitant administration of enzyme-inducing (or inhibiting) drugs is said to be a factor influencing methadone kinetics. Reports suggest that rifampicin,[58, 59] phenytoin,[60] barbiturates,[61] and disulfiram[62] are associated with unexpectedly low plasma methadone concentrations. Similar affects have been reported with zidovudine (azidothymidine; AZT), fucidic acid,[63] and amitriptyline,[64] which are not known enzyme inducers . Reports of the effect of drug inhibitors on the kinetics of methadone are less clear. Diazepam appears to inhibit the metabolism of methadone,[65] but not with therapeutic (< 40 mg\day diazepam\day) dosing.[66] Compliance has not been assessed in these patients and this, rather than other drugs, may be the reason for low methadone concentrations.

Physiological state: Other factors said to influence the clearance of methadone include excessive alcohol consumption,[66] physiological states such as pregnancy,[67] and atypical metabolism.[69] Methadone is metabolized by a specific (cytochrome P-450) pathway. Abnormal metabolisers will have very slow metabolism of these drugs because they lack the gene for the normal enzyme. About 7% of the white Caucasian population is markedly deficient in this enzyme and addicts with this deficiency who are receiving methadone will need a revised dosage regime.

To conclude, when compliance is good, plasma methadone concentrations can be used to validate dosing regimes. Conversely, plasma methadone measurements can also be used to assess compliance.

7.2.1.5 Levo-alpha-acetylmethadol (LAAM) Maintenance Prescribing

There are two problems with methadone: (1) it must be given daily, and (2) it has a high diversion potential into street (black market) use. LAAM (a congener of methadone) is a longer acting alternative which can be given every 2 to 3 days, has a lower street value, and is safer in overdose. In July 1993 the Food and Drug Administration's approval of LAAM for opioid treatment offered a new alternative to the maintenance treatment of heroin dependence. LAAM's pharmacological properties allow for a number of advantages over methadone, namely:[70]

1. Thrice-weekly prescribing schedule.
2. Better normalising effect - less sedation (nodding) and little or no euphoria.
3. Cost effectiveness because of reduced frequency of dispensing.
4. Better relations between clinics and local community since fewer LAAM patients attend a clinic on any given day.
5. LAAM may offer a better way to attract untreated opiate users into treatment.

However, large groups initially treated with LAAM had a much larger number of drop-outs compared with methadone treated groups. Initial pharmacokinetic studies indicated that it takes 2 to 4 weeks for the long acting LAAM metabolites to attain adequate concentrations in plasma to prevent withdrawal symptoms prior to the next dose. Fraser[71] reviewed the initial clinical data on LAAM maintenance and more recently Prendergast et al. have reported on the current status of LAAM in North America. To date the uptake of LAAM into the methadone clinic system has been slow. Despite the large number of clinical trials that have been studied,[72, 73] the long term effectiveness of LAAM remains to be determined with respect to heroin and other drug use, criminality, employment, HIV status and risk behaviors, psychogical status, and reported side effects.[70]

7.2.1.6 Buprenorphine Maintenance Prescribing

DOUGLAS FRASER

THE LEEDS ADDICTION UNIT, LEEDS, U.K.

Generally, the more efficacious the drug is at producing its pharmacological effect, the greater the addiction potential and value as an illicit drug. Drugs with lower efficacy are called partial agonists. Buprenorphine is a partial agonist for opioid receptors. The pharmacological profile of partial agonists is such that they are useful in substitution therapy because they provide some reinforcement of the opiate effect but should also reduce illicit heroin use.[20]

In analgesic terms it is approximately 25 to 40 times more potent than morphine.[74] There is mounting evidence that buprenorphine is a safe and effective therapeutic agent for use in the treatment of opiate dependence. Buprenorphine has a high affinity but a low intrinsic activity at the mu opiate receptors. This means that although buprenorphine has agonist activity at the mu receptors, this activity is not as potent as that achieved by a pure opiate agonist such as morphine. The high affinity results in a long duration of action in the order of 24 to 48 hours.

A study was conducted which compared daily buprenorphine administration with alternate day administration. Objectively there was no significant difference between the two groups on measures of opiate withdrawal symptoms. The group receiving alternate day treatment reported subtle withdrawal symptoms subjectively whereas the daily treatment group reported no such problems.[75] A 24-hour dosage interval is most commonly recommended. Opiate dependent subjects find buprenorphine an acceptable treatment for their dependence and report a "morphine-like" effect. It is possible to convert people from heroin or methadone to buprenorphine with minimal withdrawal problems.[76]

Due to its wide therapeutic index buprenorphine is relatively safe in overdose. It has been shown that there is a ceiling effect at higher doses of buprenorphine. This is due to its intrinsic opiate antagonist activity and means that it is possible for a non-dependent person to tolerate a single dose of buprenorphine up to 70 times the recommended analgesic dose without life threatening consequences.[77] Buprenorphine can be administered by subcutaneous or sublingual routes for opiate dependence. Due to concerns about the likelihood of injectable opiate preparations finding their way onto the black market, the sublingual route is considered the safest route. Sublingual preparations have been shown to be as effective as subcutaneous preparations and to have a similar profile of effects in opiate dependent subjects.[78]

7.2.2 STIMULANT SPECIFIC

Substitute prescribing for amphetamine usually takes the form of dexamphetamine sulphate tablets whereas cocaine paste may be prescribed for cocaine dependence. However, prescriptions of these kind are only appropriate for a very small minority of patients. It is more likely to be the case that prescribing for stimulant dependence takes the form of an agonist of a different pharmacological group to the main drug of misuse but having its action at the same receptors or in the same neurochemical pathways (replacement prescribing). Typically these agents are used to reduce cravings associated with the cessation of stimulant use. Replacement prescribing is addressed in detail in Section 7.4.

7.2.3 BENZODIAZEPINE SPECIFIC

Little attention has thus far been paid to the extent to which benzodiazepines are abused primarily as the drug of choice. It seems that benzodiazepines are frequently abused on the illicit drug scene in combination with other drugs, particularly alcohol,[79] stimulants,[80] and opiates.[81] However, there appear to be a number of features that indicate benzodiazepine abuse: two key factors appear to be supra therapeutic dosage to extremely high levels and intermittent binge usage. Substitution prescribing usually takes the form of a long acting alternative, most commonly diazepam which has the effect of stabilizing drug use. More recently chlordiazepoxide has been used to substitute for the benzodiazepine of choice because of its low abuse potential, low street value, and long elimination half-life.

7.2.4 OUTCOMES FOR SUBSTITUTE PRESCRIBING

The Department of Health[82] has selected hierarchies of outcomes for substitute prescribing in the areas of drug use, physical and psychological health, and social functioning, as follows:

Drug use:

1. Abstinence from drugs
2. Near abstinence from drugs
3. Reduction in the quantity of drugs consumed

4. Abstinence from street drugs
5. Reduced use of street drugs
6. Change in drug taking behavior from injecting to oral consumption
7. Reduction in the frequency of injecting

Physical and psychological health:

1. Improvement in physical health
2. No deterioration in physical health
3. Improvement in psychological health
4. Reduction in sharing injection equipment
5. Reduction in sexual risk taking behavior

Social functioning and life context:

1. Reduction in criminal activity
2. Improvement in employment status
3. Fewer working/school days missed
4. Improved family relationships
5. Improved personal relationships
6. Domiciliary stability/improvement

7.3. TREATMENT OF WITHDRAWAL SYNDROMES

JOANNA BANBERY

THE LEEDS ADDICTION UNIT, LEEDS, U.K.

7.3.1 UNDERSTANDING WITHDRAWAL SYNDROMES

A withdrawal syndrome is the constellation of physiological and behavioral changes that are directly related to the sudden cessation (or reduction in use) of a psychoactive drug to which the body has become adapted. The Diagnostic and Statistical Manual of the American Psychiatric Association in its revised fourth edition (DSM-IV-R)[83] requires three criteria to be fulfilled before a diagnosis of substance withdrawal can be made:

Criterion 1: The development of a syndrome (which is substance specific) due to the cessation of or reduction in substance use. The substance use must be heavy and prolonged.
Criterion 2: The withdrawal syndrome must cause clinically significant distress or impairment in social and/or occupational functioning.
Criterion 3: The symptoms caused must not be due to any other medical or mental condition.

For each drug or group of drugs it lists the symptoms and signs that must be present.
Dependence has been discussed in the introduction to this chapter. Withdrawal symptoms were described as a consequence of regular drug use rather than as a fundamental element. On

a cellular level, dependent use of a drug will cause a state of adaptation in which the presence of the drug is necessary for normal functioning and in which the removal of the drug will cause some abnormality of function.[84] Drug induced alterations to function include alteration of the fluidity of the cell membrane, or alteration in neurotransmitters and receptor changes. Each group of drugs will produce its own characteristic withdrawal syndrome which will be dependent on specific alterations to the above systems. These have been well reviewed by Foy.[85]

Although the basis of withdrawal lies in the cellular and receptor changes, it is important not to forget that there is a significant psychological component. Changes at the tissue level give rise to symptoms and signs. These are then interpreted in a way that will depend on a person's situation and expectations about withdrawal together with their emotional state. These reactions then feedback and may magnify the original changes or help to reduce them. Psychologists have found that withdrawal symptoms will behave as conditioned responses. They will develop more quickly if associated with a cue and can be evoked by environmental stimuli when the drug has not been used for sometime.[86] This helps to explain why the clinical symptoms presented by patients are very variable both from time to time and place to place. The time it takes to develop a withdrawal effect will depend on the pharmacokinetics of the drug, so that withdrawal from methadone, which has a long half-life, will not become evident for 24 to 36 hours whereas withdrawal from heroin, with a shorter half-life, will occur within 6 to 8 hours of the last dose. This is of clinical importance in planning a detoxification.

7.3.1.1 Detoxification

When drug use ceases, the nervous system will begin to undergo a return to normal functioning. During this time, abnormal responses will be evident in the form of withdrawal symptoms, and the patient will be vulnerable both physically and psychologically. Detoxification is the process of rapidly and successfully achieving a drug-free state and will usually involve both the prescription of drugs to attenuate withdrawal symptoms and the attention to the relief of other stressors.

It is an appropriate intervention for those patients who are at the "action" stage of change;[18] that is, those patients who have demonstrated a commitment to change their substance use, believe they are able to change, and have acquired the necessary skills to enable them to sustain change. Detoxification will also be necessary for other patients as an expedience in situations such as emergency hospitalization or rapidly deteriorating mental or physical health.

The goal of achieving abstinence with the minimum amount of discomfort should be agreed upon with the patient. Adequate preparation is essential; the patient must be informed of the expected symptoms, their likely duration, medication which will be used to relieve symptoms and its likely effects. Consideration should be given to the setting for the detoxification. Home, out-patient, or in-patient facilities may all be suitable. The physician and the patient will need to agree upon an environment that is comfortable, non-threatening, and safe. If the detoxification is to be undertaken at home, there must be confidence that any withdrawal symptoms will not be severe and that adequate support is available.

The appearance of withdrawal symptoms should be carefully monitored with consideration being given to the use of assessment scales.[87] If an out-patient detoxification is being performed the patient may attend on a daily basis for an objective assessment of withdrawal symptoms to be made. The severity of the syndrome will influence the dosage and frequency of medication given to alleviate them. Physicians should have an awareness of which drugs will cause severe or dangerous withdrawal symptoms and may require particularly careful assessment. Increasingly, patients present with polydrug use, which requires extra vigilance and may require adaptations of usual prescribing regimes.

Patients who are to be detoxified will require a thorough medical examination usually with routine blood tests. These patients are at high risk of an underlying medical problem related either to specific drug-related harm, e.g., intravenous users at risk of abscesses, endocarditis etc., or related to lifestyle, such as malnutrition or tuberculosis. An assessment of mental state is important and this should be monitored during detoxification. Patients may present, for example, with confusion or lowering of mood with suicidal ideation. These symptoms usually do not require anything beyond symptomatic relief and resolve as withdrawal progresses; however, the appropriate level of nursing care and support must be assessed.

Other therapies play an important role in detoxification and can minimize the need for medication. Relaxation training has been said to be a useful way to reduce stress particularly in benzodiazepine withdrawal and complementary therapies such as massage have also been used to reduce discomfort. Controlled studies of their efficacy are awaited. Competent nursing care is also important. The patient's condition should be assessed accurately, and it has been shown that this can in itself reduce withdrawal symptom scores.[88] Reassurance and attention to nutrition and sleeping patterns also play their part. Any medication prescribed will either substitute for the drug that has been withdrawn or treat the symptoms of the withdrawal syndrome. Consideration must be given to the dosage and the length of time of prescribing.

It has been said that the three most common errors in the management of withdrawal syndromes are (1) failure to diagnose, (2) prescription of too much for too long, and (3) failure to use psychological means to abate withdrawal.[89] The physician must have adequate knowledge both of the symptoms, signs, and duration of the common withdrawal syndrome and of their treatment to guard against all of these.

7.3.2 OPIATE SPECIFIC WITHDRAWAL SYNDROME

DSM-IV-R[83] describes opioid withdrawal following cessation or reduction in heavy and prolonged use of either illicit drugs or prescribed medication. The syndrome described consists of craving for the drug and three or more of the following symptoms: dysphoric mood, nausea or vomiting, lachrymation and rhinnarhea, muscle aches, pupillary dilatation, piloerection, diarrhea, yawning, or insomnia. The signs and symptoms should develop acutely within days of cessation of drug use and be severe enough to impair a patient's functioning. In addition to this, body temperature and blood pressure may be slightly elevated with a variable effect on pulse. As discussed earlier, the onset of a withdrawal syndrome will depend on the quantity of the drug used, the frequency of usage, and the half-life of the drug. Heroin withdrawal normally begins within 6 to 8 hours of last use, symptoms of withdrawal peak at 2 to 3 days and have usually resolved within a week. Withdrawal from other opiates is similar but will exhibit different time scales and intensities, e.g., methadone withdrawal may last for several weeks and not commence for 36 to 48 hours. Opioid withdrawal can also be precipitated by an antagonist such as naloxone, which will produce a severe withdrawal with peak intensity about 30 minutes from administration.

The opiate withdrawal syndrome is very rarely life threatening and has been described as being simliar to having influenza. It is, however, experienced as sufficiently unpleasant for it to be avoided whenever possible by users and for its successful negotiation to be the necessary first step towards abstinence. For this reason it is important that it is properly managed by the clinician.

The essential judgement in a planned detoxification is about its speed. A rapid detoxification will produce more severe withdrawal symptoms than a slower one, but it may be easier to maintain motivation. There are a number of different pharmacological approaches that may be used and tailored to the individual's requirements. A brief review of the use of methadone, alpha-2-agonists, and buprenorphine in detoxification will be given.

7.3.2.1 Detoxification Using Methadone

Since Vogel and Isbell's paper in 1938,[90] confirming that methadone detoxification was a safe treatment, it has become the most commonly used method. A wide variety of different regimes has been used and there is some lack of clarity between those that are long term slow reductions and merge with methadone maintenance therapy (MMT) and those that are short term and aimed at immediate abstinence. In clinical practice patients who are on methadone maintenance treatment will usually have their methadone dose reduced gradually, commonly at a rate of 5 mg every fortnight to a daily dose of 20 to 30 mg. Reductions are then decreased more slowly to zero. In the U.K. there is no recommended time for this process of reduction to continue. In the U.S. the FDA regulations permit extended opiate detoxification for up to 6 months.

Various time scales for withdrawal have been studied. Gossop and Bradley[91] studied 116 opiate addicts withdrawn from methadone over a 21-day period. Withdrawal symptoms started to increase on Day 10 and reached a peak at the end of the reduction, not returning to normal until Day 40. A further study[92] compared this 21-day reduction with a 10-day reduction and found that the 10-day group showed higher scores for withdrawal symptoms which peaked earlier and recovered earlier. Both groups achieved the same rates of completion and it was concluded that there was no advantage to an extended period of reduction.

It is important to inform patients about what to expect during detoxification as almost everyone undergoing methadone reduction will experience withdrawal symptoms. These have been shown to be a major factor in precipitating relapse. Green and Gossop[93] examined 30 patients who were detoxified in the usual way, 15 of whom were taught about their likely symptoms. This group experienced milder withdrawal symptoms and were more likely to complete treatment. Negotiation between prescriber and patient about rates of reduction together with the understanding that extra psychological support will be available during detoxification are also important. The setting for detoxification should be given consideration. Several studies have shown in-patient detoxification to be more effective than out-patient. One randomized controlled trial found that 17% of out-patients and 81% of in-patients completed treatment.[94] One interpretation of this is that opiate users are likely to live in environments with other drug users, which makes abstinence difficult to achieve. It may be appropriate to consider the initial reductions of methadone as an out-patient then admit the patient to finally achieve a drug-free state.

The success of methadone reduction regimes have been demonstrated in many studies but in practice it is often difficult to achieve abstinence by this method, with patients often becoming "stuck" when low doses of methadone are reached. Indeed it has been said that "most methadone treatment is maintenance treatment because most patients fail detoxification".[95] Although it is a common clinical problem, the cause is not clear. It may be that the withdrawal symptoms become intolerable. Another explanation is that the drug user is wanting to seek a drug effect which is lost at lower dosages. Milby et al.,[96] in *Methadone Maintenance to Abstinence — How Many Make It?*, compared results of 50 studies in three 5-year periods. Between 1970 and 1975, the rate of completion was 39.7%, between 1976 and 1980 it was 54.9%, and between 1981 and 1985 it was 76.5%. They attribute this improvement to the use of new drugs which shorten detoxification and ameliorate withdrawal symptoms.

7.3.2.2 Detoxification Using Buprenorphine

A number of studies have examined the acceptability and effectiveness of buprenorphine in the treatment of opiate dependence. It has been shown that buprenorphine treatment is as effective as methadone in the detoxification of heroin users.[105] Another study concluded that sublingual buprenorphine was acceptable to opiate dependent outpatients as a maintainance treatment.[106]

Buprenorphine has been shown to attenuate self-administration of illicit opiates in opiate dependent individuals. The study used a daily dose of 8 mg of subcutaneous buprenorphine and recorded a 69 to 98% suppression of heroin self-administration which compares favorably to the opiate antagonist naltrexone.[107]

It has been shown that it is possible to commence the opiate antagonist naltrexone prior to stopping the buprenorphine treatment. This is beneficial as there is then no break in drug treatment as is inevitable in methadone detoxification due to the long half-life of methadone. This is possible because buprenorphine binds to the mu receptors more tenaciously than naltrexone thus preventing the antagonist from exerting its effect.[108] In methadone treatment, the administration of naltrexone brings on severe and unacceptable opiate withdrawal symptoms. A period of approximately 10 to 14 days needs to elapse prior to commencing naltrexone after methadone treatment.

There is conflicting evidence about the effects of buprenorphine treatment on self-administration of cocaine in opiate dependent subjects. More studies are required to establish whether buprenorphine has a place in the clinical management of cocaine use. In summary, buprenorphine is a partial opiate agonist which can be used in the treatment of opiate dependence. It is relatively safe in overdose. Buprenorphine can be commenced with minimal discomfort to the individual. It is possible to commence naltrexone, an opiate antagonist, prior to stopping buprenorphine treatment. This is beneficial in terms of treatment compliance.

There are a number of different pharmacological options available for the treatment of opiate withdrawal and it is important to tailor detoxification to suit each individual. As Seivewright and Greenwood[24] point out, a 17-year-old who has been using heroin for 6 months with few social problems will require different treatment than a 35-year-old injector of heroin with a long history of dependence and failed previous detoxifications. The first patient may do best being detoxified using lofexidine, the second may need a long-term methadone reduction program. There is a need for further research to establish precisely which group of patients is likely to do best with which treatment.

7.3.2.3 Detoxification Using Adrenergic Agonists

A sub-group of the adrenergic agonists are the alpha-2-agonists, clonidine and lofexidine, which are being increasingly used in opiate detoxification. Chronic administration of opiate drugs results in tolerance to the effects mediated by opiate receptors such as euphoria, and tolerance to the effects of opiates on the automatic nervous system which is mediated by noradrenergic pathways. The locus coerulus in the dorsal pons is the origin of much of the central nervous system noradrenergic activity. It is associated with opiate and pre-synaptic alpha-2-noradrenergic receptors which are inhibiting.

Chronic opiate intake leads to tolerance and to stimulation of the opiate receptors. Abrupt withdrawal leads to an escape from this inhibition and a rebound rapid firing of the neurones. A "noradrenergic storm" results and is responsible for many of the opiate withdrawal symptoms.[97] Clonidine and lofexidine act as pre-synaptic alpha-2-adrenergic agonists which inhibit this and therefore are able to attenuate symptoms. Clonidine has been most extensively investigated in opiate withdrawal and has been found to be effective in reducing most symptoms of withdrawal.[98] However, one study has shown methadone-assisted detoxification to have higher completion rates than clonidine assisted.[99] Those experiencing the most severe withdrawal symptoms were least well-controlled by clonidine and the symptoms of arthralgia, myalgia, anergia, and insomnia were not alleviated. Its use has also been limited because of its potentially serious side effects which include hypotension, sedation, and psychiatric symptoms in those who are vulnerable.

Lofexidine is another alpha-2-Adrenergic agonist (licensed in the U.K. since 1992) which appears not to have the same problems with side effects and which has gained in popularity as a non-opiate for use in detoxification in a variety of settings. Studies, until recently, have been small and uncontrolled. Three studies using lofexidine to withdraw patients from methadone all demonstrated good completion rates and there were no reports of significant lowering of blood pressure or sedation.[100-102] All three studies reported some residual withdrawal symptoms with insomnia, lethargy, and bone pain mentioned and were in users stabilized on relatively low doses of methadone.

Bean et al.[103] conducted the first randomized double blind study comparing methadone and lofexidine detoxification in 86 polydrug abusing opioid addicts. The lofexidine group experienced more severe symptoms from Day 3 to Day 7 and by Day 20 both groups showed a similar progressive decline in symptoms. The two treatments had similar effects on blood pressure and treatment completion. Further studies are needed to identify groups of patients in which lofexidine may be of particular use.

7.3.2.4 Naltrexone Assisted Detoxification

In an attempt to reduce the duration of the opiate withdrawal syndrome, particularly from long-acting opioids such as methadone, a combination of alpha-2-agonists, naloxone, and naltrexone has been used. A study in 40 patients using methadone in doses up to 65 mg/day clonidine and naltrexone allowed 38 of the 40 to be successfully withdrawn in 4 to 5 days.[104] For most patients, the naltrexone was gradually increased from 10 mg/day to 50 mg/day over 4 days. Various adaptations of this regime have been adopted, including the use of lofexidine alone on Days 1 through 3, followed by a test dose of naloxone. Naltreone can then be established if the opiate withdrawal symptoms are controlled by the lofexidine

More recently interest has been shown in very rapid (<48 hours) opiate detoxification, using opiate antagonists and general anaesthesia. However, this method is expensive and adds a risk of death to a non-fatal condition. It seems unlikely that this method will be widely used. In addition to reducing the period of experiencing withdrawal symptoms, the combination of alpha-2-agonist and antagonist also has the advantage of establishing the patient on naltrexone before the end of the detoxification program, which may in itself aid in relapse prevention.

The addition of other medications to lofexidine in detoxification (such as hypnotics, muscle relaxants, and antidiarrheal medication) may need to be considered on an individual basis. Other short acting opioids such as dihydrocodeine have been used in detoxification regimes although there is little evidence for their efficacy. One regime employed involves a crossover period from low dose (30 mg or less) methadone to the equivalent dose of dihydrocodeine over 7 to 10 days and then a reduction of dihydrocodeine over the following 7 days.

7.3.3 STIMULANTS SPECIFIC WITHDRAWAL SYNDROME

Withdrawal symptoms of these drugs, manifest in broad terms as the inverse of the stimulant effects, can be explained by the neurochemical changes that they induce. The existence of a withdrawal syndrome was for some time controversial because of the lack of physical withdrawal symptoms and signs. During the 1980s, the use of cocaine in the form of crack increased dramatically in North America and this has led to an increase in clinical and research evidence about its dependence-forming properties and withdrawal syndrome. DSM-IV-R[83] defines both amphetamine and cocaine withdrawal in the same way.

The symptoms are characterized by a constellation of signs and symptoms that appear within a few hours to several days after either cessation or reduction in heavy or prolonged use of the drugs. The symptoms must not be due to another medical or mental disorder and must cause impairment of functioning. It is described as consisting of dysphoric mood and two or more of the following: fatigue, vivid and unpleasant dreams, insomnia or hypersomnia, increased appetite, and either psychomotor retardation or agitation. Drug craving and anhedonia may also be present. Cocaine withdrawal has been reported to reach its peak in 2 to 4 days, with symptoms such as lowering of mood, fatigue, and general malaise lasting for several weeks.[109] Amphetamine withdrawal is also reported to peak within 2 to 4 days with the most characteristic symptoms being lowering of mood and associated suicidal ideation.

Most of the recent studies looking at stimulant withdrawal have investigated cocaine. However, given the different pharmacokinetics of amphetamine and cocaine it would be reasonable to expect quite different time courses for the appearance, peak, and duration of the respective withdrawal syndromes.[110] The half-life of cocaine is approximately 1 hour, with the onset of action between 8 seconds and 30 minutes depending on the route of administration. The duration of effect is reported to be between 5 and 90 minutes.[111] Conversely, the half-life of amphetamine is about 10 to 15 hours, with its onset of action and duration of effect two to eight times as long as cocaine.[112] This would lead to the expectation that amphetamine withdrawal would have a slower onset on action, last longer, and be less intense than cocaine withdrawal. Further controlled studies in humans need to be done to confirm this. Our current concepts of amphetamine withdrawal are based largely on clinical impressions and animal studies.

There are several studies examining short-term abstinence from cocaine. Gawin and Kleber described a triphasic model from observations of 30 out-patient cocaine abusers.[113] The model consists of phases they called "crash", "withdrawal", and "extinction". The "*crash*" phase was said to develop quickly, usually within 15 to 30 minutes, and last 9 hours to 4 days after cessation of heavy use and was characterized by extreme dysphoria, anhedonia, insomnia, irritability, and, in some subjects, suicidal ideation. Hypersomnolence followed with intermittent waking and feelings of exhaustion. The "*withdrawal*" phase was characterized by an initial euthymia and return to previous levels of functioning. Craving and anhedonia then increase again with the reappearance of anxiety and irritability. This phase lasts between 1 and 10 weeks. The "*extinction*" phase includes episodic cocaine craving triggered by environmental cues and may last for several months.

Two other studies that were conducted using in-patient populations have not supported some aspects of this model. Weddington et al.[114] studied 12 in-patient males who were cocaine dependent prior to admission. Measuring mood and sleep and comparing with a control group, they demonstrated a gradual decline of distressed mood, tension, anger, and fatigue over a 28-day period. Satel et al.[115] studied 21 cocaine-dependent males admitted to hospital for detoxification. They also demonstrated a gradual decrease in symptoms over time. Both studies failed to demonstrate a crash followed by a euthymic period. Lago and Kosten have proposed several explanations for these differences.[110] They suggest that the initial crash described in the triphasic model may have occurred prior to hospitalization and therefore been missed. The out-patient group will have been exposed to environmental cues from which the in-patient group were protected and this may have affected true reporting of symptoms. This has clinical implications for the understanding of cocaine withdrawal in different settings. Further studies are required to clarify these points.

Substantial numbers of people who are cocaine dependent will not report or have clinically evident withdrawal symptoms even after cessation of heavy and prolonged use.[114] This, combined with clinical observations, suggests that stimulant withdrawal is associated with considerable heterogeneity. It has been said to depend on dose of drug, pattern of use, duration of history, and pre-withdrawal psychopathology.[116] Patterns of use may vary from daily use to a common pattern of using for several days at a time followed by days of abstinence. This will have an effect on the appearance of withdrawal symptoms and their severity.

Stimulants do not produce dangerous physical withdrawal syndromes, and because of this there is no advantage to a gradual withdrawal of the drug. Patients should be advised to discontinue the drug abruptly. Advice and information should be given about the likely effects of cessation and consideration given to the setting for detoxification. Those patients who present with mild symptoms that last a matter of hours or days usually are not a management problem. Symptomatic treatment for agitation or anxiety with a drug of low abuse potential such as thioridazine may be necessary.

More severe withdrawal symptoms may require admission. Close observation will be necessary for those expressing suicidal ideas. Symptomatic relief for other symptoms such as anxiety and insomnia may be required. Having achieved abstinence, the next phase is to identify psycho-social problems and initiate interventions designed to maintain a drug-free state and deal with drug craving. A number of different pharmacological treatments have been used mainly in cocaine dependence to treat the dysphoric symptoms associated with withdrawal and to attempt to reduce craving. These are reviewed in Section 7.4

The small numbers of studies, the absence of physical withdrawal symptoms, and the variation in patterns of drug use make stimulant withdrawal more difficult to characterize than with other groups of drugs. Cocaine has been studied because of the "crack" epidemic of the 1980s, and has led to an increase in our understanding of both the symptoms and the underlying neurochemistry of withdrawal. Numerous different agents have been used to attempt to treat the drug craving and mood disorders associated with withdrawal, all with limited success. Less is published about amphetamine withdrawal and details of ecstasy withdrawal are scarce. Any comparisons with cocaine should not forget the difference in the drug's properties and pharmacokinetics.

7.3.4 HYPNOTIC AND SEDATIVE WITHDRAWAL SYNDROME

In practice it is the benzodiazepines that dominate the market for both hypnotics and anxiolytics. Barbiturates such as secobarbital, pentobarbital, and amobarbital are under the same federal controls as morphine in the U.S. and in the U.K. and they are rarely prescribed.

DSM-IV-R[83] criteria for sedative, hypnotic, or anxiolytic withdrawal requires two or more of the following to be present:

1. autonomic hyperactivity (e.g., sweating or pulse rate greater than 100)
2. increased hand tremor
3. insomnia
4. nausea or vomiting
5. transient visual, tactile, or auditory hallucinations or illusions
6. psychomotor agitation
7. anxiety
8. grand mal seizures

Physicians can then specify if perceptual disturbances are present. As in other classes of drug, the withdrawal symptoms are the opposite of the drug effects and are explained by the underlying changes in neurophysiology largely via the gamma amino butyric acid (GABA) system. GABA is the most widely distributed inhibitory neurotransmitter in the central nervous system. Close to its receptors are specific receptors for the benzodiazepines and the barbiturates. When these are activated, the action of the GABA system is potentiated causing further inhibition. With continued drug use, the number of GABA receptors falls due to down regulation.

When GABA binds with its receptor it causes hyperpolarization of the neuron as the chloride channel is activated and hyperpolarization is reversed by increased entry of calcium to the cell. If drug use ceases, the increased intraneuronal calcium produces a state of hyperexcitability. The reduction in the number of GABA receptors has the effect of reducing the overall effect of the main inhibiting system resulting in the symptoms previously listed.

Benzodiazepines dependence is not a single entity and varying different classifications have been proposed. Helmen suggested a psychosocial classification of users following a study of 50 long term (longer than 6 months) users.[117] He divided them into 3 groups, (1) "tonic" users, who have control over their medication and use it as necessary; (2) "fuel" users who have less control and take it daily even though they recognize it as a habit; and (3) the "food" group, who felt they had no control over their medication and would not survive without it. Kraupl and Taylor suggested two groups: (1) "therapeutic" users and (2) "morbid" users.[118] Perhaps the most useful division within the context of drug abuse is the division between high dose and normal dose dependence. Non-abusers who are dose dependent take their benzodiazepines within the recommended therapeutic range and remain on this regime long term. These people may want to do without their medication but feel unable to because of the withdrawal symptoms experienced upon cessation of their medication. In high-dose misuse, up to 10 times the normal recommended dosage may be consumed on a regular basis. In Britain, temazepam is often the chosen drug and it may be injected alone or used in combination with other illicit drugs or alcohol.

Benzodiazepine withdrawal can be classified in several ways. A division between minor and major withdrawal is sometimes used and this emphasises the severity of the symptoms. Perhaps of more use clinically is the division into low vs. high dose withdrawal because the daily dose is the main factor in assessing the medical risks of withdrawal.[119] Symptoms associated with low dose withdrawal are nausea, vomiting, tremor, uncoordination, restlessness, blurred vision, sweating, and anorexia. Depersonalization, heightened perceptions, and illusions are also described. In a review of recent studies, Alexander and Perry concluded that symptoms occurred in 50% of those withdrawn from therapeutic doses of benzodiazepines with an average use of 3 years and most symptoms were mild to moderate.[119]

Discontinuing high doses of benzodiazepines can produce all the minor symptoms discussed but patients are also at risk of seizures, psychosis, and depression. Early studies indicate a high risk of severe withdrawal when high doses are discontinued: Hollister et al.[120] found seizures occurred in 8% of subjects receiving diazepam 120 mg daily for 21 days, and in another study in which patients were switched from chlordiazepoxide (300 to 600 mg daily) to placebo, 18% of subjects had convulsions on Days 7 and 8 after stopping the drug.[121] The incidence and the severity of withdrawal symptoms can be predicted to some extent by the dose and duration of use. The time course is influenced by the half-life of the drug. Those with a short action may begin to produce mild withdrawal symptoms within 1 to 5 days of ceasing use and usually disappear over 2 to 4 weeks. Drugs with a longer half-life may not produce withdrawal symptoms for up to a week after use ceases and they are likely to be less severe.

7.3.4.1 Management of Withdrawal

Because of the potential severity of the withdrawal phenomena, sudden withdrawal of benzodiazepines is not advised.[122] For an uncomplicated low dose withdrawal, a gradual tapering of the drug is recommended. If the patient is on a short acting drug, then they may be switched to a longer acting drug with the rationale being that less severe withdrawal symptoms occur with long acting drugs. Diazepam has been the most widely studied and conversion data from common benzodiazepines are available. Once stabilized this can then be reduced. A number of different schemes are available. The tapering dose can be calculated by dividing the total dose by 5 and reducing by this amount weekly. Most patients can be reduced to zero in 4 to 8 weeks. Slower withdrawal may be necessary towards the end of the reduction and consideration should be given to admission if withdrawal symptoms become very intense.[123]

In high-dose withdrawal, the picture is often complicated by other illicit drug or alcohol use. A conversion to diazepam may be difficult because of problems in establishing dosage and frequency of use. Concomitant use of alcohol is particularly common. Ross,[124] in a sample of

427 patients who met the criteria for alcohol dependence, found that 40% had recently used alcohol. In these patients there will be a risk of an increase in severity of withdrawal symptoms and a lengthening in the time for withdrawal. Most clinicians would withdraw the alcohol after establishing the patient on a stable dose of a long-acting benzodiazepine. Benzodiazepines are also commonly taken by opiate users to boost the opiate effect.[125] In North America it has been found that alprazolam was replacing diazepam as the drug of choice in this population.

For those patients where an accurate and reliable history of drug intake is not available, then admission is indicated for tolerance testing performed to assess tolerance and severity of withdrawal before planning a detoxification regime.[119] Other pharmacological agents have been used in benzodiazepine withdrawal. Smith and Wesson[126] described a technique for withdrawal using phenobarbitone. A phenobarbitone equivalent to the benzodiazepine is calculated and given in 3 divided doses per day. After 2 days stabilization, the phenobarbitone can be reduced by 30 mg per day. Carbamazepine has been used to manage acute withdrawal.[127] After initiation, the dose increased to 400 to 800 mg daily. The benzodiazepine can then be tapered off over 3 to 6 days and the carbamazepine reduced over 5 to 14 days. Propanolol given for two weeks and tapered off has been shown to reduce the severity but not the incidence of withdrawal symptoms.[128] Some studies have shown tricyclic antidepressants to be useful and Tyler[129] has suggested that they should be commenced 1 month before withdrawal and continued for 1 to 3 months after it is completed. They may be particularly useful in patients with an anxiety disorder. Caution is required in their use as they will reduce the seizure threshold.

7.4 REPLACEMENT PRESCRIBING

KIM WOLFF

NATIONAL ADDICTION CENTRE, INSTITUTE OF PSYCHIATRY, UNIVERSITY OF LONDON

7.4.1 OPIATE SPECIFIC PRESCRIBING

7.4.1.1 Opiate Antagonists

DOUGLAS FRASER

THE LEEDS ADDICTION UNIT, LEEDS, U.K.

Antagonists have zero efficacy and as such are very effective blockers of agonists. Their main limitations are that they can precipitate withdrawal in physically dependent drug users and because they do not provide any reinforcement, there is little incentive for those dependent upon illicit drugs to be compliant. Naltrexone is a long acting orally effective competitive antagonist at opiate receptors. It displaces any agonist present at the receptors and blocks the effects of any opiates subsequently administered. It is 95% metabolized by the liver. The major metabolite, 6-beta-naltrexol, is also an active opiate antagonist. The opiate blocking effects of naltrexone last between 48 and 72 hours. Naltrexone has not been shown to produce tolerance and therefore does not lead to physical dependence.[130]

Oral administration of naltrexone to an opiate-dependent individual results in the appearance of a severe opiate withdrawal syndrome. It is therefore necessary to be completely detoxified from opiate prior to commencing naltrexone treatment. It is necessary to discontinue short acting opiates such as heroin for approximately 5 to 7 days prior to commencing naltrexone. Longer acting opiates such as methadone need to be discontinued for approximately 10 to 14 days before naltrexone can be successfully commenced. In the event of naltrexone being given prior to the end of detoxification, it is likely that withdrawal symptoms will appear. This, in turn, makes it much less likely that the individual will agree to taking naltrexone at any point subsequently despite reassurance from the prescribing doctor.

Successful naltrexone treatment depends on careful selection of individuals and understanding that naltrexone treatment is only a small part of the relapse prevention package. Psychological treatment looking at issues, such as craving, drug-refusal skills, and making appropriate lifestyle changes, should be administered at the same time as naltrexone. A positive outcome is more likely in those who are well supported by friends or family members and those who had good pre-morbid adjustment in terms of education, employment, and social class. Naltrexone treatment is contraindicated in people with acute hepatitis or liver failure. It is necessary to check liver function tests both prior to and during naltrexone treatment.

Individuals who are due to start on naltrexone should be informed of the possible side effects, which include gastrointestinal disturbances such as nausea, vomiting, abdominal pains, and diarrhea. They should also be warned of the potential dampers of trying to overcome the naltrexone blockade by taking large doses of opiates. This can lead to respiratory depression and death. It is also important for people to understand that they will be unable to use opiate analgesics for mild pain. They should be advised about non-opiate alternatives. If opiate analgesia is required, this should be administered in a hospital setting under the supervision of trained staff. Naltrexone should be discontinued 72 hours prior to elective surgery and reinstated once the surgical procedure has been performed.[131]

Prior to prescribing naltrexone for the first time, it is necessary to confirm that the individual is abstinent from opiates. This can be done by means of urine toxicology or by performing a naloxone challenge. This involves the administration of the short acting opiate antagonist, naloxone, by the intravenous or intra-muscular route. If opiate withdrawal symptoms are not precipitated, then it is appropriate to commence naltrexone approximately 1 hour later. If opiate withdrawal symptoms are present, then naltrexone treatment should be deferred until the naloxone challenge has been repeated without the appearance of withdrawal symptoms.

Naltrexone 25 mg should be given on the first day. Naltrexone 50 mg daily can be given thereafter. Fifty milligrams of naltrexone blocks the effects of 25 mg of heroin for 48 hours, 150 mg of naltrexone blocks the effects for 72 hours. In order to supervise the swallowing of naltrexone tablets and improve the compliance, it is possible to prescribe naltrexone three times per week (i.e., 100 mg on Monday and Wednesday, 150 mg on Friday). Due to the variable nature of opiate dependence, the length of time that people are required to take naltrexone varies between individuals. Naltrexone prescribing should continue, in the absence of complications or contra-indications, until the individual is confident that it is possible to resist the temptation to return to dependent use of opiate drugs. This time span may be only a few weeks but can be as long as a few years in some cases.

In summary, naltrexone is a competitive opiate antagonist which displaces opiate agonists from the opiate receptors and blocks the effects of opiate agonists subsequently administered. It is a useful adjunct to psychological relapse prevention methods in well-motivated individuals receiving treatment for opiate dependence.

7.4.2 STIMULANT SPECIFIC PRESCRIBING

A useful pharmacotherapy for stimulant (cocaine and amphetamine) dependence remains elusive. As a rule, symptoms of stimulant withdrawal are not medically dangerous. Detoxification from these substances requires no treatment other than abstinence. However, many users find the symptoms of cocaine withdrawal intensely dysphoric and immediately relapse and re-use cocaine in order to fend off the symptoms. The addictive nature of stimulants, particularly crack, the free-base form of cocaine, is, in part, the result of its effects on the neurochemistry of the brain. Stimulant drugs act directly on the so-called brain reward pathways.[132]

One of cocaine's primary effects in the brain is to block the pre-synaptic re-uptake of dopamine, norepinephrine, and serotonin, whereas amphetamine and methamphetamine increase the release of these neurotransmitters. Chronic use of cocaine results in dopamine depletion through the increased activity of catechol-o-methyl transferase, and super-sensitivity of the dopamine, norepinephrine, and serotonin receptors, while both catecholamine and indolamine transmitters are depleted. Chronic use of cocaine seems to compromise the body's ability to regenerate these neurotransmitters causing withdrawal symptoms when the user stops. Withdrawal symptoms manifest as the inverse of the stimulants effects. Acute tolerance, rebound depression (or the crash), and craving for stimulant drugs have been specifically attributed to dopamine depletion and receptor super-sensitivity. Neurochemical changes also explain the withdrawal syndrome that includes lethargy, depression, oversleeping, overeating, and craving for more cocaine. Extinguishing drug craving is one of the most difficult aspects of treating stimulant dependence.

7.4.2.1 Neurochemical Approach — Dopaminergic Agents and SSRIs

The involvement of multiple neurotransmitter systems during stimulant use have complicated the search for pharmacological agents to address dependence. A variety of data suggest that dopamine is an important mediator for stimulant self-administration. As a result, drugs that modify dopaminergic neurotransmission are of interest as potential treatments for stimulant use. Both agonists and antagonists have been studied in this regard, agonists because they mimic the effects and act as a stimulant substitute, theoretically reducing or eliminating drug intake and antagonists because they might reduce the reinforcing properties of stimulants and facilitate abstinence.[133]

Dopamine Agonists

Bromocriptine (Parlodel) is an agonist at the D_2 receptor. It acts by stimulating dopamine receptors in the brain. Initial open trials suggested that bromocriptine reduced some symptoms of cocaine withdrawal,[133] had anti-craving effects,[134] and was effective as an antidepressant, alleviating the low mood that accompanies the cocaine crash. However, other more recent studies using a controlled approach have not supported the general usefulness of this drug.[135-136]

Amantadine (Symmetrel): Amantadine is an indirect dopamine agonist. Open label pilot studies in primary cocaine users and methadone-maintained cocaine users have indicated that amantadine might reduce cravings for cocaine,[137] although not all studies have produced positive results.[138] The lack of efficacy of amantadine for the reduction of craving or cocaine recently reported by Hendelson[139] is consistent with those of other placebo controlled clinical trials in methadone maintained patients,[140] as well as in primary cocaine users.[135, 141] Amantadine, while well tolerated, is not particularly efficacious for the reduction of cocaine use or cocaine craving.

Pergolide Mesylate and Levodopa: Similar findings have been reported for other dopamine agonists, but these treatments have the respective drawbacks that they may exacerbate cocaine withdrawal symptoms or require continuous medication and patient compliance.

Methylphenidate (Ritalin): Methylphenidate may reduce cocaine cravings in patients with attention deficit disorder, possibly because of its ability to stimulate the central nervous system. However, the abuse potential of this drug severely limits its, and other similar drugs, usefulness as a treatment for cocaine misuse.[142] Indeed there appears to be a growing literature to support the ineffectiveness of several putative dopamine agonist treatments.[143]

Dopamine antagonists

Flupenthixol: A dopamine antagonist has also shown promise in treating cocaine withdrawal and reduce *Spiperone* have not reduced the effects of cocaine in mice, rats, or dogs.[144]

Dopamine partial agonists

Aminoergolines (Terguride and SD208911): Medications that act as partial agonists at the dopamine receptor may be candidates for normalizing dopamine transmission. The efficacy of the partial agonist depends on the level of occupancy of a given receptor by full agonists, such as dopamine. Consequently, partial agonists function as antagonists during pharmacological stimulation due to stimulant use when transmitter activity is high. By occupying dopamine receptors and exerting low intrinsic activity, partial agonists might represent a novel anti-psychotic agent. However, human self-administration studies have yet to be performed.

   Buprenorphine (Temgesic): Recent evidence suggests that the dopamine reward system of the brain is also stimulated by μ-opiate agonists. Over the past 5 years there has been significant interest in buprenorphine, a partial agonist, as a potential treatment agent for cocaine abuse. Pre-clinical primate work suggests that buprenorphine might modulate dopaminergic systems to the degree of altering the reinforcing properties of cocaine.[145] Current evidence indicates buprenorphine reduces cocaine self-administration by substituting for, as opposed to blocking, the re-uptake of dopamine.[146] Despite these promising results, corroborating data has not been forthcoming. Compton et al.[147] found, in combination with Fudala[148] and Oliveto,[149] that buprenorphine maintenance doses of 2 to 8 mg are no more effective than standard methadone maintenance treatment in reducing cocaine use in treatment seeking, cocaine-using opiate addicts. Buprenorphine may be more effective for primary non-opiate dependent cocaine abusers. In addition, there are inherent problems in prescribing a medication with opiate agonist properties to opiate naive individuals in an effort to treat cocaine dependence, particularly in a population with a known vulnerability for addiction to substances with a demonstrated abuse liability.[147]

Selective Serotonin Re-Uptake Inhibitors (SSRIs)

In addition to the blockade of dopamine re-uptake, cocaine is thought to produce an increase in serotonergic tone. Therefore, drugs that modify serotonergic neurotransmission may also alter the behavioral effects of cocaine and be potentially useful as therapies for cocaine users.[150]

   Fluoxetine (Prozac): Fluoxetine was found to be effective in reducing cocaine use among intravenous heroin users in a methadone maintenance program,[151] but Grabowski[152] found fluoxetine difficult to use in patients with or without concurrent drug dependence or psychiatric disorders. The data to date on fluoxetine are inadequate to draw conclusions relevant to clinical practice.[153]

7.4.2.2 Clinical Approach, Tricyclic Antidepressants and Anti-Sensitizing Agents

The other main approach for the treatment of stimulant dependence is clinical because the clinical syndrome that evolves after the discontinuation of cocaine or amphetamine resembles a depressive disorder. And it is widely held that antidepressant medications may have clinical utility in alleviating drug craving and self-administration.[154] Neurochemical and clinical rationales are not mutually exclusive, and an antidepressant agent that reduces the clinical phenomena observed after cessation of cocaine might also have significant dopaminergic activity that would be consistent with a neurochemical approach to treating cocaine use.

Tricyclic Antidepressants

Since chronic tricyclic antidepressant treatment has been shown to down regulate adrenergic and dopaminergic receptor sensitivities, it has been suggested that anti-depressant agents could reverse the neuroreceptor adaptations to cocaine abuse.

Desipramine (Pertofran): Desipramine has been studied as an adjunct to reducing cocaine use in patients because of its high degree of selective noradrenergic activity and inhibition of the norepinephrine transporter. Gawin,[138] in a pioneering work, found patients on desipramine had less craving and cocaine use; Grannini[155] found cocaine abusers had less depression and dysphoria and Extin[156] found this medication equally as effective as bromocriptine. Though not without problems of compliance, side effects, and imperfect overall treatment outcomes, desipramine is one of the most widely used pharmacological treatments for cocaine users. Unfortunately, two more recent investigations with fairly large samples did not demonstrate any clear advantage of the active drug over placebo.[140, 157]

Imipramine (Tofranil): Tricyclics generally exert only modest anti-craving and anti-euphoriant effects, which may translate into reduced cocaine use and this is certainly the case with imipramine.[158] Carroll[146] found that the anti-depressant, anti-self-medication effect of imipramine was better in depressed users. Intravenous and freebase crack users showed poor outcome with imipramine. It seems likely that tricyclics such as imipramine are most effective in specific sub-groups, e.g., nasal users who are exposed to less cocaine, or patients with comorbid depression, where depression plays a role in initiating or perpetuating cocaine use.[158]

Nortriptyline: This drug may also be effective in relieving cocaine craving and withdrawal. However, the results are not conclusive, and in some studies the "desipramine effect" was found to be short lived, or only effective in the depressed cocaine addict.[159]

Anti-Sensitising Agents

Carbamazepine (tegretol): Carbamazepine, an anti-epileptic agent, like desipramine can reduce norepinephrine turnover but to a lesser extent has been used with some success to prevent the effects of prolonged cocaine exposure (reduced seizure production).[160] Carbamazepine may be effective in reducing the sensitization produced by cocaine although a double-blind clinical trail is not yet available.[161]

Calcium channel blockers: nifedipine and nimodipine: Assuming the critical role of dopamine in cocaine reinforcement, calcium channel blockers are expected to inhibit the reinforcing effects of stimulant drugs. It has been found that nifedipine may reduce the acute effects of cocaine,[162] while nimodipine has been shown to decrease the sensitivity of mice and rats to the reinforcing effects of cocaine.[163]

7.4.3 NEW APPROACHES

Immunopharmacotherapy is a new strategy to treat cocaine use. It has been developed in rodents by Carrera et al.,[164] who proposed generating an active immunization to cocaine to block the actions of the drug. Active immunization against cocaine is accomplished by linking stable cocaine-like conjugates with a foreign carrier protein to stimulate the immune system to produce antibodies that subsequently recognize and bind the drug preventing it from entering the central nervous system and thereby exerting psychoactive effects. However, there are many problems to be addressed before immunization is to be effective in preventing or treating cocaine addiction in humans.[165]

The National Institute on Drug Abuse (NIDA) is currently looking at ways to neutralize the drug in the bloodstream and reduce the amount available for brain uptake. Scientists are trying to develop catalytic antibodies, synthetic molecules that will target and break down cocaine molecules more quickly than the body's natural enzyme systems and, therefore, limit the amount of drug crossing the blood-brain barrier. The literature reveals no pharmacological agent that has been demonstrated in large double-blind studies to be significantly better than placebo for stimulant dependence in men and women. While several medications appear promising and will require more extensive investigation, many of the positive clinical reports are anecdotal and uncontrolled. At present it is difficult to justify routine clinical use of a single pharmacological agent.[153] An important consideration for future pharmacotherapies for stimulant dependence involves the matching of patients to the appropriate therapy based on stages of recovery as well as predisposing and vulnerability factors such as comorbidity.[154]

7.5 MANAGEMENT OF COMORBIDITY

DUNCAN RAISTRICK

THE LEEDS ADDICTION UNIT, LEEDS, U.K.

7.5.1 UNDERSTANDING COMORBIDITY

Comorbidity is defined as the co-existence of two or more psychiatric or psychological conditions; for the purposes of this section, one of these conditions will be substance misuse or substance dependence. It is usual to take ICD-10[3] or the American Diagnostic and Statistical Manual, now in version DSM-IV-R,[83] as the descriptive classification of these conditions. Practitioners are usually concerned with current comorbidity, but from the point of view of understanding etiology and deciding upon rational treatment approaches it may be more useful to think in the longer term. Estimates of comorbidity will be influenced by methodological factors including the diagnostic criteria, time frame, and the population sample: there will be marked differences, for example, between general population and treatment population samples, or even between groups assigned to different treatment programs. In spite of these difficulties, some general conclusions are evident.

Wittchen et al.[166] looked at key international studies of comorbidity in community population samples and concluded that there were strong similarities between different countries; summarizing two large studies from the U.S., they state that: (1) over half of those individuals who have a substance misuse problem have also experienced other mental disorders within their lifetime, (2) dependence on, rather than misuse of, alcohol or other drugs is more likely to be associated with a mental disorder, (3) major depression, anxiety disorders, phobias, mania, schizophrenia, and conduct disorder in adolescence or adult antisocial behavior are all strongly associated with substance dependence, and (4) social phobia and adolescent conduct disorder are also associated with alcohol or drug misuse.

The National Comorbidity Survey of the general adult population in the U.S. studied lifetime and 12-month comorbidity in over 8000 subjects: the lifetime prevalence for any substance misuse or dependence disorder was 26.6% and 12-month prevalence was 11.3%, with males having approximately twice the rates of women.[167] These data imply considerable variation and possibly substitution of mental disorders, one with another, over time. The stability of substance-related comorbidity is of importance in determining treatment regimens: to address this issue Penick et al.[168] administered a DSM-III compatible diagnostic interview to 241 male "alcoholics" during an in-patient admission and again at 1 year: 30% were deemed to have one additional psychiatric syndrome, 18% two, and 9% three or more additional syndromes. Depression and antisocial personality were the most common diagnoses. There was some fluidity of diagnostic category between intake and follow-up interview: only 62% of men diagnosed with antisocial personality, 53% with depression, and 38% with panic attacks had the same diagnosis at both interviews.

Clinicians generally underestimate the presence of psychiatric and psychological disorders when assessing patients with substance misuse problems. Clinicians expect high levels of morbidity and often assume that symptoms are due to withdrawal, transient physical problems, or dependence itself. In order to determine the true prevalence of comorbidity in a treatment population, Driessen et al.[169] studied 100 in-patients post-alcohol detoxification: they found 3% to have schizophrenia or schizo affective disorders, 13% affective disorders, 22% phobic disorders, and 2% general anxiety. Alcohol dependence was judged to be secondary to the psychiatric condition in 60% of patients with schizophrenia, 48% with depression, and 72% with phobic disorder. This does not necessarily mean that a psychiatric condition which ante-dates substance misuse will persist beyond detoxification, or that there is any causal relationship.

It is important for the clinician to know what is driving an individual's substance use. Comorbidity does not imply cause and effect, but is one of several possibilities:

- Substance use and psychiatric disorder may co-exist by chance.
- Substance use may cause psychiatric disorder.
- Psychiatric disorder may cause substance use.
- A third factor may mediate both substance use and psychiatric disorder.

Where a psychiatric disorder is seen to be of primary importance and driving the substance use, the psychiatric disorder should be the focus of treatment. However, psychiatric disorder which initiated substance misuse or precipitated a relapse may be superseded by dependence driving the maintenance of substance use.

7.5.2 MAKING PRESCRIBING DECISIONS

As a matter of general principle there are several reasons, detailed in the introduction, why doctors should be reserved when prescribing for people who misuse alcohol or other drugs: for those who also have a mental health problem there is a risk that prescribing sends out a message that taking drugs, prescribed or otherwise, is an appropriate way of dealing with psychological distress. When undertaking a mental state examination, the doctor tries to balance benefits of pharmacotherapy against risk; risk is a function not only of the medication but also the treatment setting. In assessing risk, it is the ephemeral nature of psychological distress coexisting with substance misuse that is perhaps the most compelling reason to wait until a patient is drug free or stable before prescribing, and also a reason to consider hospital admission solely for the purpose of establishing a psychiatric diagnosis.

With a focus on alcohol, Allan[170] has recommended that patients presenting with anxiety and alcohol dependence should first be detoxified and reassessed after 6 weeks when only an expected 10% will be found to have persistent symptoms amounting to an anxiety state. The persistent anxiety can then be treated using conventional pharmacological or behavioral methods. She points out that patients may resist such an approach, preferring to deal with their psychological distress before tackling their substance use. People who are dependent on alcohol or other drugs usually succumb to a number of financial, family, health, and relationship problems and it is not surprising that many will complain of depression; again it is not surprising that 80% or more will recover within a few weeks of abstinence without recourse to anti-depressant treatment.

While abstinence may enforce an acceptance of problems accumulated while drinking or taking other drugs and this might be anticipated to increase depression, abstinence is also an opportunity to build self-efficacy and self-esteem, both powerful psychological anti-depressants. Pharmacological anti-depressants should be avoided unless there is unequivocal evidence of a biological depression of mood. The key point is that diagnoses of mental illness and substance use comorbidity made in haste will often evaporate. Nonetheless, it may be that the severity of symptoms is so severe when a patient presents as to indicate immediate symptomatic prescribing without the benefit of a diagnosis. Equally it may be that a provisional diagnosis, for example alcoholic delirium or Wernicke encephalopathy, demands urgent treatment.

The general principle to observe of "wait and see" can be a difficult one to follow and in addition to cases of obvious florid psychosis, there are times when urgent action (usually not pharmacotherapy) is required. For example, suicidal ideation is a common emergency for doctors specializing in addiction. Alcohol and other drugs are commonly found on toxicological screening of subjects who have committed suicide. Depressant drugs in particular are likely to impair judgement and, therefore, increase both the risk of any suicide attempt, but especially suicides involving violence or impulse, such as driving into a bridge or jumping in front of a train.

In a Finnish survey, Ohberg et al.[171] found 36% of victims had taken alcohol and 42% had taken other drugs; antidepressants and neuroleptics had each been taken by women in approximately one fifth of suicides, but much less often by men. Murphy[172] has identified seven risk factors for suicide in "alcoholics":

- depression
- suicidal thoughts
- poor social support
- physical illness
- unemployment
- living alone
- recent interpersonal loss

The risks accumulate over a number of years, suggesting that there is scope for preventive social and health care. In short, people that misuse alcohol or other drugs are at increased risk of committing suicide: pharmacological treatment risks providing a means of suicide and active, social therapy is more likely to be effective. Other psychiatric conditions may be less urgent than a suicide threat, but none the less complex in terms of reaching prescribing decisions. Krausz et al.[173] produced data on the reasons for substance use among people diagnosed as schizophrenic: the effects of drinking were viewed positively with 36% of subjects expressing a tension reduction effect, 13% euphoria and sociability, 4% control of depression and aggression. Again the best course of action may be the delay in prescribing even though an established psychiatric condition has been recognized.

Insomnia, which may result from psychological distress and may be a symptom of recreational drug use or may be part of a withdrawal syndrome, is ubiquitous and merits special mention. Alcohol and other sedatives increase slow wave sleep and reduce REM and are therefore effective hypnotics. Short-acting hypnotics and alcohol are, in normal amounts, metabolized through the night causing rebound arousal and wakenings. For people who misuse depressant drugs, including alcohol, the rebound of REM may cause vivid nightmares and sleep disturbance which persists for months after achieving abstinence. The use of stimulant drugs causes a similar over-arousal. Stradling[174] has drawn attention to the insomniac effect of mild stimulants such as nicotine and caffeine: a cup of ground coffee contains approximately 85 mg of caffeine and 500 mg is approximately equivalent in arousal effect to 5 mg of amphetamine.

Duncan Raistrick

Patients with addiction problems are often reluctant to accept non-pharmacological approaches to insomnia; however, advice to reduce smoking and coffee drinking in the evening, and to exercise during the day should at least accompany any prescribing of hypnotics. Eisen et al.[175] have reviewed the properties of drugs used as hypnotics: a compound having a short half-life and minimal induction of tolerance, such as zopiclone, is attractive. On occasions a drug that will not have been misused, and to which the patient will not therefore be tolerant, such as chlorpromazine, can be helpful. Prescribing of hypnotics should be limited to 2 to 4 weeks.

In summary, for many people who suffer from psychiatric or psychological disorders, substance use and misuse has utility. It is often the case that traditional medicine has less to offer than the patient's own self-medication regimen and that social rather than pharmacological interventions are really what is needed. It is particularly important for doctors to be clear about the purpose of their prescribing and to monitor its effectiveness. Where substance misuse and psychiatric disorder co-exist the case for not prescribing, even for psychiatric illness, should always be vigorously explored.

7.6 TOXICOLOGIC ISSUES

ALASTAIR W.M. HAY

UNIVERSITY OF LEEDS, RESEARCH SCHOOL OF MEDICINE, LEEDS, U.K.

Although doubts persist about the value of drugs-of-abuse screening as opposed to self-reporting by patients in drug rehabilitation programs,[29, 176-177] it is well recognized that screening procedures provide much needed evidence about the prevalence of drug use.[178] For drugs-of-abuse screening is no longer just a service that is provided for drug dependency units, but a procedure that is being used increasingly by a wide range of employers.[179, 180]

Analysis of urine has a number of distinct advantages when compared with other body fluids. The most significant factor favoring urine is the concentration of the drugs, most of which are usually excreted in urine either as the parent drug, or a water soluble metabolite or conjugate. In common with most xenobiotics, drugs undergo metabolic conversions (usually in the liver) to form first a less active (occasionally, more active) metabolite which, in turn, is conjugated to a more water soluble product, thus making the drug itself more water soluble, and suitable for excretion in the urine.[181]

7.6.1 HEAT AND DRUG STABILITY

Extraction of drugs from urine is a relatively simple procedure and the resulting extracts can be readily concentrated before analysis, increasing the chances of a substance being detected.[182] Concentration of the extract can be achieved by gentle heating. Heat treatment of urine before extraction of the drug is also a procedure used in some laboratories to inactivate the human immunodeficiency virus. Heating of urine to 60°C for 1.5 h, or 70°C for 1 h does not significantly reduce the concentration of a range of drugs including methadone, pethidine, amphetamine, benzoylecgonine, or the dextropropoxyphene metabolite, nordextropropoxyphene.[183] However, heat treatment at 100°C for 1 h reduced the recovery of all drugs, with amphetamine being the most sensitive to heat; concentrations of amphetamine fell by some 80% at this temperature.[183]

7.6.2 ANALYSIS USING OTHER BODY FLUID

The advantages of urine sampling for detecting drugs-of-abuse are the higher drug concentrations; the large volume of urine; the opportunity to concentrate urine samples, which in turn, increases drug concentrations, and thus the possibility of detection; and the fact that urine collection is a non-invasive procedure.

7.6.2.1 Blood

Where management of drug users is the objective, plasma measurements provide far more accurate information than urine sampling. Blood samples are also required for forensic investigations. Analytical methods for measuring opioids, amphetamines, benzodiazepines, methadone, cocaine and its metabolites, and cannabis are available for plasma, serum, or whole blood; and for some drugs all three fluids can be used. There are a number of different ways to go about making these measurements.

Monitoring of addicts to assess compliance can only be performed where there is an established relationship between plasma concentrations of the drug and dose, corrected for body weight.[184] A linear relationship between dose of methadone and plasma concentration has been demonstrated for users of the drug whose compliance was good.[49] Assessing compliance in users of drugs such as heroin and cocaine, which have a short half-life, is much more of a problem. A particular difficulty with these drugs is the fact that they can be smoked as well, and devising suitable markers (which can also be inhaled) to establish, in the first instance, a relationship between dose and plasma concentrations has not been possible.

7.6.2.2 Saliva

Many commonly abused drugs have been measured in saliva.[185] The principal advantage of saliva is that collection is a non-invasive procedure. Disadvantages include lower drug concentrations than blood and, for addicts on opiates, a reduced ability to produce saliva. A linear relationship between the concentration of methadone in plasma and saliva has been demonstrated, suggesting that salivary methadone could be used to monitor compliance of patients on this drug.[186]

7.6.2.3 Hair

Analysis of hair has been suggested for drugs-of-abuse as the drugs are incorporated into hair during keratinization and remain *in situ* during the life of the hair. A growth rate for hair of about 1 cm per month, suggests that hair analyses have the potential to provide a longitudinal record of drug consumption.[187,188] The absence of any proper quality control procedures for hair analyses, and the number of procedural steps required in the analysis make this an uncertain, labor-intensive process at present.[189] However, analytical procedures are almost certain to improve, and the technique may yet provide a "long-term" record of consumption.

7.6.2.4 Costs

The cost of regular urine analysis of patients can be considerable for any clinical practice. In the U.K., for example, analyses carried out every two weeks was estimated to cost £520 ($860 U.S.) per client over a year.[190] Costs in the U.S. are likely to be substantially less. Such frequency of testing may only be required for a number of less stable patients. In other instances, more frequent testing may be required until patients have been stabilized, after which less frequent, but random, testing may suffice.

Alastair. W.M. Hay

REFERENCES

1. Heather, N. & Robertson, I., *Problem Drinkers* (Oxford, Oxford University Press), 1989.
2. Edwards, G. & Gross, M. M., Alcohol Dependence: Provisional Description of a Clinical Syndrome, *British Medical Journal*, 1 1058, 1976.
3. World Health Organisation *The ICD-10 Classification of Mental and Behavioural Disorders: Clinical descriptions and diagnostic guidelines*, (Geneva, World Health Organisation), 1992
4. Raistrick, D. S., Bradshaw, J., Tober, G., Weiner, J., Allison, J., Healey, C., Development of the Leeds Dependence Questionnaire, *Addiction*, 89, 563, 1994.
5. Kosten, T., Krystal, J. H., Charney, D. S., Price, L. H., Morgan, C. H., Kleber, H. D., Opioid Antagonist Challenges in Buprenorphine Maintained Patients, *Drug and Alcohol Dependence*, 25, 73, 1990.
6. Pervin, L. A., Affect and Addiction, *Addictive Behaviours*, 13, 83, 1988.
7. Johanson, C. E. & Uhlenhuth, E. H., Drug Preference and Mood in Humans: Diazepam, *Psychopharmacology*, 71, 269, 1980a.
8. Johanson, C. E. & Uhlenhuth, E. H., Drug Preference and Mood in Humans: d-Amphetamine, *Psychopharmacology*, 71, 275, 1980b.
9. Bickel, W. K., Higgins, S. T., Stitzer, M. L., Choice of Blind Methadone Dose Increases by Methadone Maintenance Patients, *Drug and Alcohol Dependence*, 18, 165, 1986.
10. McGlothlin, W. H. & Anglin, D., Long-term Follow-up of Clients of High and Low-dose Methadone Programs, *Archives of General Psychiatry*, 38, 1055, 1981.
11. Hartnoll, R. L., Mitcheson, M. C., Battersby, A., Brown, G., Ellis, M., Fleming, P., Hedley, N., Evaluation of Heroin Maintenance in Controlled Trial, *Archives of General Psychiatry*, 37, 877, 1980.
12. Chiang, C. W. & Barnett, G., Marijuana effect and delta-9-tetrahydrocannabinol plasma levels, *Clinical Pharmacology and Therapeutics*, 36, 234, 1984.
13. Johnson, R. E., Cone, E. J., Henningfield, J. E., Fudala, P. J., Use of Buprenorphine in the Treatment of Opiate Addiction I Physiologic and Behavioural Effects During a Rapid Dose Induction, *Clinical Pharmacological Therapy*, 46, 335, 1989.
14. Mello, N. K., Lukas, S. E., Bree, M. P., Mendekson, J. H., Progressive Ration Performance Maintained by Buprenorphine, Heroin and Methadone in Macaque Monkeys, *Drug and Alcohol Dependence*, 21, 81, 1988.
15. Stimson, G. V. & Oppenheimer, E., *Heroin Addiction: Treatment and Control in Britain*, (London, Tavistock Publications), 1982.
16. Funderburk, F. R., Griffiths, R. R., McLeod, D. R., Bigelow, G. E., Mackenzi, A., Liebson, I. A., Nemeth-Coslett, R., Relative Abuse Liability of Lorazepam and Diazepam: An Evaluation in 'Recreational' Drug Users, *Drug and Alcohol Dependence*, 22, 215, 1988.
17. Edwards, G., Drug Dependence and Plasticity, *Quarterly Journal of Studies on Alcohol*, 35, 176, 1974.
18. Prochaska, J. O. & DiClemente, C. C., *The transtheoretical approach: Crossing traditional boundaries of therapy* (Illinois, Dow Jones-Irwin), 1984.
19. Tober, G., Motivational Interviewing with Young People in Miller, W & Rollnick, S, (Eds) *Motivational Interviewing: Preparing People to Change*, (New York, Guildford), 1991.
20. Nutt, D. J., Addiction: brain mechanisms and their treatment implications, *Lancet*, 347, 31, 1996.
21. Finn, P., Program Administrator and Medical Staff Attitudes toward Six Hypothetical Medications for Substance Abuse Treatment, *Journal of Psychoactive Drugs*, 28, 161, 1996.
22. Pani, P. P., Piratsu, R., Ricci, A., Gessa, G. L., Prohibition of take-home dosages: negative consequences on methadone maintenance treatment, *Drug and Alcohol Dependence*, 41, 81, 1996.
23. Greenfield, L., Brady, J. V., Besteman, K. J., De Smet, A., Patient retention in mobile and fixed-site methadone maintenance treatment, *Drug and Alcohol Dependence*, 42, 125, 1996.

24. Seivewright, N. A. & Greenwood, J., What is important in drug misuse treatment. Lancet, 347, 373, 1996.
25. Dole, V. P. & Nyswander, M., A medical treatment for diacetylmorphine (heroin) addiction, J Amer Med Assoc, 193, 80, 1965.
26. Schuster, C. R., The National Institute on Drug Abuse and methadone maintenance treatment, J Psychoactive Drugs, 23, 111, 1991.
27. Hall, W., Bell, J., Carless J., Crime and drug use among applicants for methadone maintenance, Drug Alcohol Depend, 31, 123, 1993.
28. Ball, J. C. Lange, W. R., Myers, C. P., Friedman, S. R., Reducing the risk of AIDS through methadone maintenance treatment, J Health Social Behav, 29, 214, 1988.
29. Ward, J., Mattick, R., Hall, W., Key issues in Methadone Maintenance Treatment, University of New South Wales Press, Australia, 1992.
30. Reno, R. R. & Aiken, L. S., Life activities and life quality of heroin addicts in and out of treatment, Inter J Addict, 28, 211, 1993.
31. Glass, R. M., Methadone maintenance: new research on a controversial treatment [editorial] J Amer Med Assoc, 269, 1995, 1993.
32. Gossop, M., Marsden, J., Edwards, C., Stewart, D., Wilson, A., Segar, G., Lehmann, P., The National Treatment Outcome Study (NTORS): Summary of the project, the clients, and preliminary findings, Department of Health, London, UK, 1996.
33. D'Aunno, T. & Vaughn, T. E., Variations in methadone treatment practice, J Amer Med Assoc, 267, 253, 1992.
34. Caplehorn, J. R. M., Bell, J., Kleinbaum, D. G., Gebski, V. J., Methadone dose and heroin use during maintenance treatment, Addiction, 88, 119, 1993.
35. Kang, S-Y. & De Leon, G., Correlates of drug injection behaviours among methadone outpatients, Amer J Drug Alcohol Abuse, 19, 107, 1993.
36. McLachlan, C., Crofts, N., Wodak, A., Crowe, S., The effects of methadone on immune function among injecting drug users: a review, Addiction, 88, 257, 1993.
37. Stimmel, B., Intravenous drug use, methadone, and AIDS: ask not for whom the bell tolls, J Addictive Diseases,12, 1, 1993.
38. Hubbard, R. L., Marsden, M. E., Rachal, J. V., Harwood, H. J., Cavanaugh, E. R., Ginzburg, H. M., Drug abuse treatment: a national study of effectiveness. Chapel Hill: University of North Carolina Press 1989.
39. Wolff, K., Hay, A., Raistrick, D., Calvert, R., Feely, M., Measuring compliance in methadone maintenance patients: Use of pharmacological indicator to 'estimate' methadone plasma levels, Clin Pharmacol Ther, 50, 199, 1991.
40. Gerstein, D. R., The effectiveness of drug treatment. in *Addictive states,* O'Brien, C. P. and Jaffe, J. H., Eds., Raven Press, New York, 235, 1992.
41. Wolff, K., Hay, A. W. M., Raistrick, D., Plasma methadone measurements and their role in methadone detoxification programmes, Clin Chem, 38, 420, 1992.
42. Ball, J. C. & Ross, A., The effectiveness of methadone maintenance treatment, Springer, New York, 1991.
43. Hser, Y-I., Anglin, M. D., Powers, K., A 24 year follow-up of california narcotics addicts, Arch Gen Psychiat, 50, 577, 1993.
44. Wolff, K. & Hay, A. W. M., Plasma methadone monitoring with methadone maintenance treatment, Drug Alcohol Depend, 36, 69, 1994.
45. Dole, V. P., Methadone treatment and the acquired immunodeficiency syndrome epidemic, J Amer Med Assoc, 262, 1681, 1989.
46. Loimer, N. and Schmid, R., The use of plasma levels to optimise methadone maintenance treatment, Drug Alcohol Depend, 30, 241, 1992.
47. Kleber, H. D., Concommitant use of methadone with other pyschoactive drugs in the treatment of opiate addicts with other DSM-III diagnosis, in *Research on the treatment of narcotic addiction-state of the art,* Cooper, J. R., Altman, F., Brown, B. S., Czechowiez, D., Eds., NIDA, Research monograph series, US, DHSS, 119, 1986.
48. Peachey, J. E., The role of drugs in the treatment of opioid addicts, Med J Aust, 145, 395, 1986.

References

49. Wolff, K., Sanderson, M., Hay, A. W. M., Methadone concentrations in plasma and their relationship to drug dosage, Clin Chem 37, 205, 1991.

50. Wolff, K., Hay, A. W. M., Raistrick, D., Calvert, R., Steady state pharmacokinetics of methadone in opioid addicts. Eur J Clin Pharmacol, 44, 189, 1993.

51. Kreek, M. J., Gutjahr, C. R., Garfield, J. W., Bowen, D. V., Field, F. H., Drug interactions with methadone, Ann NewYork Acad Sci, 281, 350, 1976.

52. Liu, S. J. and Wang, R. I. H., Case report of barbiturate - induced enhancement of methadone metabolism and withdrawal syndrome, Amer J Psychiat, 141, 1287, 1984.

53. Gourlay, G. K., Cherry, D. A., Cousins, M. J., A comparative study of the efficacy and pharmacokinetics of oral methadone and morphine in treatment of severe pain in patients with cancer, Pain, 25, 297, 1986.

54. Horns, W. H., Rado, M., Goldstein, A., Plasma levels and symptom complaints in patients maintained on daily dosage of methadone hydrochloride, Clin Pharmacol Ther 17, 636, 1975.

55. Holmstrand, J., Anggard, E., Gunne, L. M., Methadone maintenance: Plasma levels and therapeutic outcome, Clin Pharmacol Ther 23, 175, 1978.

56. Dole, V. P., Implications od methadone maintenance for theories of narcotic addiction, J Amer Med Assoc, 260, 3025, 1988.

57. Blaine, J. D., Renault, P. F., Levine, G. L., Whysner, J. A., Clinical use of LAAM, Annals New York Acad Sci, 311, 214, 1978.

58. Kreek, M. J., Garfield, J. N., Gutjahr, C. L., Giusti, L. M., Rifampicin induced methadone withdrawal, New Eng J Med, 294, 1104, 1976.

59. Raistrick, D., Hay, A., Wolff, K., Methadone maintenance and tuberculosis treatment, Brit Med Journal, 313, 925, 1996.

60. Tong, T. G., Pond, S. M., Kreek, M. J., Jaffery, N. F., Benowitz, N. L., Phenytoin induced methadone withdrawal, Ann Intern Med, 94, 349, 1981.

61. Liu, S-J. and Wang, R. I. H., Case report of barbiturate-induced enhancement of methadone metabolism and withdrawal syndrome, Amer J Psych, 141, 1287, 1984.

62. Tong, T. G., Benowitz, N. N. L., Kreek, M. J., Methadone-disulfiram interaction during methadone maintenance, J Clin Pharmacol, 10, 506, 1980.

63. Mertins, L., Brockmeyer, N. H., Daecke, C., Goos, M., Pharmacokinetic interaction of antimicrobial agents with levomethadon (L) elimination in drug addicted AIDS patients [Abstract], 2nd European Conference on Clinical Aspects of HIV infection, March 8/9, 1990.

64. Plummer, J. L., Gourlay, G. K., Cousins, C., Cousins, M. J., Estimation of methadone clearance: application in the management of cancer pain, Pain, 33, 313, 1988.

65. Spaulding T. C., Minimum, L., Kotake, A. N., Takemori, A. E., The effects of diazepam on the metabolism of methadone by the liver of methadone dependent rates, Drug Metabolism Disposition, 2, 458, 1974.

66. Pond, S. M., Tong, T. G., Benowitz, N. L., Jacob, P., Rigod, J., Lack of effect of diazepam on methadone metabolism in methadone maintained addicts, Clin Pharmacol Ther, 31, 139, 1982.

67. Kreek, M. J., Metabolic interactions between opiates and alcohol, Ann New York Acad Sci, 362, 36, 1981.

68. Pond, S. M., Kreek, M. J., Tong, T. G., Raghunath, J., Benowitz, N. L., Altered methadone pharmacokinetics in methadone-maintained pregnant women, J Pharmacol Exper Ther, 233, 1, 1985.

69. Nilsson, M-I., Grönbladh, L., Widerlöv, E., Änggård, E., Pharmacokinetics of methadone in methadone maintenance treatment: Characterization of therapeutic failures, Eur J Clin Pharmacol, 25, 497, 1983.

70. Prendergast, M. L., Grella, C., Perry, S. M., Anglin, M. D., Levo-Alpha-Acetlymethadol: Clinical , research, and policy issues of a new pharmacotherapy for opioid addiction, J Psychoactive drugs, 27, 239, 1995.

71. Fraser AD. Clinical Toxicology of drugs used in the treatment of opiate dependency. Clinical Toxicology I: Clinics in Laboratory Medicine 1990; 10 (2) 375-386.

72. Ling, W., Charuvastra, C., Kaim, S. C., Klett, C. J., Methadyl acetate and methadone as maintenance treatment for heroin addicts, Archives Gen Psych, 33, 709, 1976.

73. Tennant, F. S., Jr., Rawson, R. A., Pumphrey, E., Seecof, R., Clinical experiences with 959 opioid dependent patients treated with levo-alpha-acetly-methadol (LAAM), J Substance Abuse Treat, 3, 195, 1986.

74. Cowan, A., Lewis, J. W., MacFarlane, I. R., Agonist and antagonist properties of buprenorphine, *British Journal of Pharmacology*, 60, 537, 1977.

75. Amass, L., Bickel, W. K., Higgins, S. T., Badger., G. J., Alternate Day dosing during buprenorphine treatment of opioid dependence, British J Pharmacology, 60, 537, 1994.

76. Johnson, R. E., Cone, E. J., Henningfield, J. E., Fudala, P. J., Use of buprenorphine in the treatment of opiate addiction. I. Physiologic and behaviour effects during a rapid dose induction, *Clinical Pharmacol Ther*, 46, 335, 1989.

77. Walsh, S. L., Preston, K. L., Stitzer, M. L., Cone, E. J., Bigelow, G. E., Clinical Pharmacology of buprenorphine: ceiling effects at high doses, Clin Pharmacol Ther, 55, 569, 1994.

78. Jasinski, D. R., Fudala, P. J., Johnson, R. E., Sublingual versus subcutaneous buprenorphine in opiate abusers, Clinical Pharmacol Ther, 45, 513, 1989.

79. Perera, K. M. H., Tulley, M., Jenner, F. A., The use of benzodizepines among drug addicts, Brit J Addiction, 82, 511, 1987.

80. Strang, J., Seivewright, N., Farrell, M., Oral and intravenous abuse of benzodizepines, in *Benzodiazepine dependence*, Hallstrom C., Oxford Medical Publications, Oxford, 1993, 9.

81. Busto, U., Sellers, E. M., Naranjo, C. A., Kappell, H, D., Sanchez-Craig, M., Simpkins, J., Patterns of benzodiazepine abuse and dependence, Brit J Addict, 81, 87, 1986.

82. Department of Health, Welsh Office and Scottish Home and Health Department, Drug misuse and dependence guidelines on clinical management, London, HMSO, 1991.

83. American Psychiatric Association (APA) (1994) *Diagnostic and Statistical Manual of Mental Disorders*, 4th Ed, (APA, Washington D.C.)

84. Johnson, S.M. and Fleming, W.W. (1989) Mechanisms of Cellular adaptive sensitivity changes: applications to opioid tolerance and dependence, *Pharmacology Review*, 41, pp. 435-488

85. Foy, A. (1991) Drug Withdrawal: A selective review, *Drug and Alcohol Review*, 10, pp. 203-214

86. Paulos, C.X. and Cappell, H. (1979) Conditioned tolerance to the hypothermic effect of ethyl alcohol, *Science*, 206, pp. 1109-1110

87. Foy, A. (1991) Detoxification: the basis of current practice, *Drug and Alcohol Review*, 10, pp. 121-125

88. Whitfield, C.L. et al (1974) Detoxification of 1,024 alcoholic patients without psychoactive drugs, *Journal of American Medical Association*, 239, pp. 1409-1410

89. Hughes, J.R., Higgens, S.T. and Bickel, K.W. (1994) Common errors in pharmacologic treatment of drug dependence and withdrawal, *Comprehensive Therapy*, 20, pp. 89-94

90. Vogel, U.H., Isbell, H. and Chapman, K.W. (1938) Present status of narcotic addiction, *Journal of American Medical Association*, 138, pp. 1019-1026

91. Gossop, M., Bradley, M. and Philips, G. (1987) An investigation of withdrawal symptoms shown by opiate addicts during and subsequent to a 21 day in-patient methadone detoxification procedure, *Addictive Behaviours*, 12, pp. 1-6

92. Gossop, M., Bradley, M. and Strang, J. (1989) Opiate withdrawal symptoms in response to 10 day and 21 day methadone withdrawal programs, *British Journal of Psychiatry* , 154, pp. 560-563

93. Green, L. and Gossop, M. (1988) Effects of information on the opiate withdrawal syndrome, *British Journal of Addiction*, 83, pp. 505-509

94. Gossop, M., Johns, A. and Green, L. (1986) Opiate withdrawal in-patient versus out-patient programs and preferred versus random assignment to treatment, *British Medical Journal*, 293, pp. 103-104

95. Hughes, J.R., Higgens, S.T. and Bickel, K.W. (1994) Common errors in pharmacologic treatment of drug dependence and withdrawal, *Comprehensive Therapy*, 20, pp. 89-94

96. Milby, J. B., Methadone maintenance to abstinence how many make it, Inter J *Addict*, 176, 409, 1988.

97. Cook, C.C.H., Scannell, T.D. and Lepsedge, M.S. (1988) Another clinical trial that failed, *The Lancet*, pp. 524-525

References

98. Gossop, M. (1988) Clonidine and the treatment of the opiate withdrawal syndrome, *Drug and Alcohol Dependence*, 21, pp. 253-259

99. Sai, L., Caui, J., Rein, J.M., Mata, R. and Parta, M. (1990) Efficacy of clonidine, guanlaine and methadone in the rapid detoxification of heroin addicts - a controlled clinical trial, *British Journal of Addiction*, 85, pp. 141-147

100. Gold, M.S., Pottash, A.C., Sweeney, R.L., Exlein, I. and Annullo, W.J. (1981) Opiate detoxification with lofexidine, *Drug and Alcohol Dependence*, 8, pp. 307-315

101. Washlan, A.M. and Resnick, R.B. (1982) Lofexidine in abrupt methadone withdrawal, *Psychopharmacological*, 18, pp. 220-221

102. Washlan, A.M., Resnick, R.B. and Geyer, G. (1983) Opiate withdrawal using lofexidine - a clonidine analogue with few side effects, *Journal of Clinical Psychiatry*, 44, pp. 335-337

103. Bearn, J., Gossop, M. and Strang, J. (1996) "Randomised double-blind comparison of lofexidine and methadone in the in-patient treatment of opiate withdrawal", *Drug and Alcohol Dependence*, 43, pp. 87-91

104. Charney, D. S., Heninger, G. R., Kleber, H. D., The combined use of clonidine and naltrexone as a rapid, safe, effective treatment of abrupt withdrawal from methadone, Amer J Psych, 143, 831, 1986.

105. Bickel, W. K., Stitzer, M. L., Bigelow, G. E., Liebson, I. A., Jasinski, D. R., Johnson, R. E., A clinical trial of buprenorphine: comparison with methadone in the detoxification of heroin addicts, *Clin Pharmacol Ther*, 43, 72, 1988.

106. Seow, S. S. W., Quigley, A. J., Illet, K. F., Dusci, L. J., Swensen, G., Harrison-Stewart, A., Rappeport, L., Buprenorphine: a new maintenance opiate?, *Med J Aust*, 44, 407, 1986.

107. Mello, N. K., Mendelson, J. H., Keuhnle, J. C. Buprenorphine effects on human heroin self administration: an operant analysis, *J Pharmacol Exper Ther*, 223, 30, 1982.

108. Kosten, T. R., Morgan, C., Kleber, H. D., Clinical trials of buprenorphine: detoxification and induction onto naltrexone, in Baline, J. D., Ed *Buprenorphine: An alternative treatment for opioid dependence*, NIDA Research Monograph Series, V121, 101, 1994.

109. Francis, A., Pincus, H., *DSMIV Options Book*, Washington DC, American Psychiatric Association Press, 1991.

110. Lago, J. A., Kosten, R. T., Stimulant Withdrawal, *Addiction*, 89, 1477, 1994.

111. Strang, J., Andrew, J., Caan, N., Cocaine in the UK - 1991, *Brit J Psych*, 162, 1, 1993.

112. Gawin, F. H., Ellinwood, E. H., (1988) Cocaine and other Stimulants, *New Eng J Med*, 318, 107, 1988.

113. Gawin, F. H., Kleber, H. D., Abstinence symptomology and psychiatric diagnosis in cocaine observers: clinical observations, *Arch Gen Psych*, 43, 107, 1986.

114. Weddington, W. W., Brown, B. S., Haertzen, C. A., Cone, E. J., Dax, E. M., Herning, R. I., Michaelson, B. S., Changes in mood, craving and sleep during short term abstinence reported by male cocaine addicts, *Arch Gen Psych*, 47, 861, 1990.

115. Satel, S. L., Price, L. H., Palumbo, J. M., McDougle, C. J., Krystal, J. H., Gawin, F. H., Charney, D. S., Heninger, G. R., Kleber, H. D., Clinical pharmacology and neurobiology of cocaine abstinence: a prospective in-patient study, *Amer J Psych*, 148, 12, 1991.

116. Ellinwood, E. H., Jr., & Lee, T. H., Amphetamine abuse, in Drugs of Abuse, Baleres Clinical Psychiatry, 2, 3, 1996.

117. Helmen, C.G. 'Tonic','Fuel' and 'Food'. Social and symbolic aspects of long term use of psychotropic drugs, *Social Science and Medicine*, 153, 521, 1981.

118. Kraupl, Taylor., The domination of the benzodiazepines, *British Journal of Psychiatry*, 154, 697, 1989.

119. Alexander, B., & Perry, P., Detoxification from benzodiazepines, schedules and strategies, *Journal of Substance Abuse Treatment*, 8, 9, 1991.

120. Hollister, L. E., Bennett, J. L., Kimbell, I., Savage, C., Overall, J. E., Diazepam in new admitted schizophrenics, *Diseases of the Nervous System*, 24, 746, 1963.

121. Holister, L. E., Molzenbecker, E. P., Degan, R. O., Withdrawal reactions from chlordiazepoxide, *Psychopharmacologia*, 2, 63, 1961.

122. Pertussan, H. & Lader, M. H., Withdrawal from long term benzodiazepine treatment, *Brit Med J*, 283, 643, 1981.

123. Marks, J., Techniques of benzodiazepine withdrawal in clinical practice. A conserus workshop. Report. Medical toxicology, 3, 324, 1988.
124. Ross, H., Benzodiazepine use and anxiolytic abuse and dependence in treated alcoholics, *Addiction*, 88, 209, 1993.
125. McDuff, D., Schwartz, R., Tommasello, M. S., Threpal, S., Donovan, T., Johnson, J., Outpatient benzodiazepine detoxification procedure for methadone patients, *J Substance Abuse Treat*, 10, 297, 1993.
126. Smith, D. E., & Werson, D. R., Benzodiazepine dependency syndromes, *Journal of Psychoactive Drugs*, 15, 85, 1983.
127. Reis, R. K., Roy-Byne, P. P., Ward, N. G., Neppe, V., Collison, S., Carbamazepine treatment for benzodiazepine withdrawal, *American Journal of Psychiatry*, 146, 536, 1989.
128. Tyrer, P., Rutherford, D., Huggett, T., Benzodiazepine withdrawal symptoms and propanolol, *Lancet*, 1, 520, 1981.
129. Tyrer, P., Clinical Management of benzodiazepine dependence, *British Medical Journal*, 291, 1507, 1985.
130. Kleber, H.D. (1985) Naltrexone, *Journal of Substance Abuse Treatment*, 2, pp. 117-22
131. Pfohl, D.N., Allen, A.I., Atkinson, R.L., Knoppman, D.S., Malcolm, R.J., Mitchell, J.E. and Morley, J.E. (1986) Naltrexone Hydrochloride: A review of serum transaminase elevations at high dosage, *National Institute on Drug Abuse Research Monograph Series*, 67, pp. 66-72
132. Everitt, B., From pleasure to complusion: the psychobiology of addiction, MRC News, Summer, 71, 1996.
133. Dakis, C. A. & Gold, M. S., Pharmacological approaches to cocaine addiction, J Subst Abuse Treat, 2, 139, 1985.
134. Giannini, A. J., Baumgartel, P., DiMarzio, L. R., Bromocriptine therapy in cocaine withdrawal, J Clin Pharmacol, 27, 267, 1987.
135. Weddington, W. W., Brown, B. S., Haertzen, C.A., Hess, J. M., Mahaffey, J. R., Kolar, A. F., Jaffe, J. H., Comparison of amantadine and desipramine combined with psychotherapy for treatment of cocaine dependence. Amer J Drug Alcohol Abuse, 17, 137, 1991.
136. Kranzler, H. R. & Bauer, L. O., Bromocriptine and cocaine cue reactivity in cocaine dependent patients, Brit J Addict, 87, 1537, 1992.
137. Alterman, A. I., Droba, M., Antelo, R.E., Cornish, J.W., Sweeney, K. K., Parikh, G. A., O'Brien, C. P., Amantadine may facilitate detoxification of cocaine addicts, 31, 19, 1992.
138. Gawin, F. H., Allen, D., Humblestone, B., Outpatient treatment of crack cocaine smoking with flupenthixol decanoate, Arch Gen Psych 46, 322, 1989.
139. Handelsman, L., Limpitlaw, L., Williams, D., Schmeidler, J., Paris, P., Stimmel, B., Amantadine does not reduce cocaine use or craving in cocaine-dependent methadone maintenance patients. Drug and Alcohol Dependence, 39,173, 1995.
140. Kosten, T. R., Morgan, C. M., Falcione, J., Schottenfeld, R. S., Pharmacotherapy for cocaine abusing methadone maintained patients using amantadine and despiramine, Arch Gen Psychiatry, 49, 894, 1992.
141. Kolar, A. F., Brown, B. S., Weddington, W. W., Haertzen, C. C., Michaelson, B. S., Jaffe, J. H., Treatment of cocaine dependence in methadone maintained clients: a pilot study comparing the efficacy of desipramine and amantadine, Int J Addict, 27, 849, 1992.
142. Herridge, P. & Gold, M. S., Pharmacological adjuncts in the treatment of opioid and cocaine addicts, J Psychoactive Drugs, 20, 233, 1988.
143. Witkin, J. M., Goldberg, S. R., Katz, J. L., Lethal effects of cocaine are reduced by the dopamine-1-receptor antagonist SCH 23390 but not by haloperidol, Life Sci, 44, 1285, 1987.
144. Catravas, J. D. & Waters, I. W., Acute cocaine intoxication in the conscious dog: Studies on the mechanism of lethality, J Pharmacol Exper Ther, 217, 350, 1981.
145. Mello NK, Kamien JB, Lukas SE. The effects of intermittent buprenorphine administration on cocaine self-administration by rhesus monkeys. J Pharmacol Exper Therap 1993; 264: 530-541.
146. Carroll KM, Rounsaville BJ, Gordon LT, Nich C, Jatlow P, Bisighine RM and Gawin. Psychotherapy and pharmacotherapy for ambulatory cocaine abusers Arch Gen Psychiatry 1994; 51: 177-187.

References

147. Compton PA, Ling W, Charuvastra VC, Wesson DR. Buprenorphine as a pharmacotherapy for cocaine abuse: A review of the evidence. J of Addictive Diseases 1995; 14: 97-114.

148. Fudala PJ, Johnson RE, Jaffe JH. Out-patient comparison of buprenorphine and methadone maintenance II. Effects on cocaine usage, retention time in study and missed clinic visits, in Problems of Drug Dependence 1990 NIDA Research Monograph series 105, edited by Harris L, Washington DC U.S. Government Printing Office, DHHS publication number (ADM) 92-1912, 1992, pp. 120-141.

149. Oliveto AH, Kosten TR, Schottenfield R et al. Cocaine use in buprenorphine - vs. Methadone-maintained patients. American Journal on Addictions 1994; 4: 43-48.

150. Carroll, K. M., Nich, C., Rounsaville, B. J., Differential symptom reduction in depressed cocaine abusers treated with psychtherapy and pharmacotherapy, J Nerv Ment Disord, 183, 251, 1995.

151. Pollack, M. H., & Rosenbaum, S. F., Fluoxetine treatment of cocaine abuse in heroin addicts, J Clin Psych, 52, 31, 1991.

152. Grabowski, J., Rhoades, H., Elk, R., Schmitz, J., Davis, C., Creson, D., Kirby, K., Fluoxetine is ineffective for treatment of cocaine dependence: Two placebo-controlled double blind trials, J Clin Phsychopharmacol, 15, 163, 1995.

153. Schuckit, M. A., The treatment of stimulant dependence, Addiction, 89, 1559, 1994.

154. Kosten, T. R., Clinical and research perspectives on cocaine abuse: The pharmacotherapy of cocaine abuse, National Institute on Drug Abuse, Research Monograph Series, 135, 48, 1993.

155. Giannini AJ and Billett W. Bromocriptine-desipramine protocol in treatment of cocaine addiction. J. Clinical Pharmacol 1987; 27: 549-554.

156. Extin, I. X. & Gold, M. S., The treatment of cocaine addicts: Bromocriptine or Desipramine, 18, 535, 1988.

157. Arndt, I. O., Dorozynsky, L., Woody, G., McLellan, A. T., O'Brien, C. P., Desipramine treatment of cocaine dependence in methadone-maintained patients, Arch Gen Psychiatry 49, 888, 1992.

158. Nunes, E.V., McGrath, P. J., Quitkin, F. M., Welikson, K. O., Stewart, J. E., Koenig, T., Wager, S., Klein, D. F., Imipramine treatment of cocaine abuse: possible boundaries of efficacy. Drug and Alcohol Dependence 39, 185, 1995.

159. Fischman, M. W., Foltin, R. W., Nestadt, G., Pearlson, G. D., Effects of despiramine maintenance on cocaine self-administration by humans, J Pharmacol Exper Ther, 253, 760, 1990.

160. Weiss, S. R. B., Post, R. M., Costello, M. Nutt, D. J., Tandeciarz, S., Carbamazepine prevents the development of cocaine kindled seizures but, not sensitization to cocaine effects on hyperactivity, Neuropsychopharmacol, 3, 273, 1990.

161. Halikas JA, Crosby RD, Carlson Ga, Crea F, Graves NM, Bowers LD. Cocaine reduction in unmotivated crack users using carbamazepine versus placebo in a short-term, double-blind crossover design Clin Pharmacol Ther 1991; 50: 81-95.

162. Muntaner, C., Kumor, K., Nagoshi, C., Jaffe, J., Effects of nifedipine (a ca++ modulator) pre-treatment on cardiovascular and subjective responses to intravenous cocaine administration in humans, in Harris, L. S., Ed, Problems of drug dependence, National Institute on Drug Abuse, Research Monograph Series, 90, 388, 1988.

163. Kuzmin, A., Semenova, S., Ramsey, N. F., Zvartau, E. E., Van Ree, J. M., Modulation of cocaine intravenous self-administration in drug naive animals by dihydropyridine Ca $^{2+}$channel modulators, Eur J Pharmacol, 295, 19, 1996.

164. Carrera, M. R. A., Ashley, J. A., Parsons, L. H., Wirsching, P., Koob, G. F., Janda, K. D., Suppression of psychoactive effects of cocaine by active immunisation, Nature, 378, 727, 1995.

165. Self, D. W., Cocaine abuse takes a shot, Nature, [Letter], 378, 666, 1995.

166. Wittchen, H., Perkonigg, A. & Reed, V. (1996) Comorbidity of Mental Disorders and Substance Use Disorders, *European Addiction Research*, 2, pp. 36-47

167. Kessler, R.C., McGonagle, K.A., Shanyang, Z., Nelson, C.B., Hughes, M., Eshleman, S., Wittchen, H. & Kendler, K.S. (1994) Lifetime and 12 Month Prevalence of DSM-III-R Psychiatric Disorders in the United States, *Archive of General Psychiatry*, 51, pp. 8-19

168. Penick, E.C., Powell, B.J., Liskow, B.I., Jackson, J.O. & Nickel, E.J. (1988) The stability of coexisting psychiatric syndromes in alcoholic men after one year, *Journal of Studies on Alcohol*, 49, pp 395-405

169. Driessen, M., Arolt, V., John, U., Veltrup, C. & Dilling, H. (1996) Psychiatric Comorbidity in Hospitalized Alcoholics after Detoxification Treatment, *European Addiction Research*, 2, pp. 17-23

170. Allan, C.A. (1995) Alcohol problems and anxiety disorders - a critical review, *Alcohol and Alcoholism*, 30, pp 145-151

171. Ohberg, A., Vuori, E. Ojanperä, I. & Lonnqvist, J. (1996) Alcohol and Drugs in Suicides, *British Journal of Psyhiatry*, 169, pp. 75-80

172. Murphy, G.E. (1992) Suicide in Alcoholism, (New York, Oxford University Press)

173. Krausz, M., Haasen, C., Mass, R., Wagner, H.-B., Peter, H. & Freyberger, H.J. (1996) Harmful Use of Psychotropic Substances by Schizophrenics: Coincidence, Patterns of Use and Motivation, *European Addiction Research*, 2, pp. 11-16

174. Stradling, J.R. (1993) Recreational Drugs and Sleep, *British Medical Journal*, 306, pp. 573-575

175. Eisen, J., MacFarlane, J. & Shapiro, C.M. (1993) Psychotropic Drugs and Sleep, *British Medical Journal*, 306, pp. 1331-1334.

176. Magura, S., Casriel, C., Goldsmith, D.S., Strug, D.L. and Lipton, D.S. Contingency contracting with poly drug-abusing methadone patients, *Addictive Behaviours*, 13, 113, 1988.

177. Wells, R. and McKay, B. *Review of funding of methadone programmes in Australia.* Report to the Department of Community Services and Health, 1989.

178. Braithwaite, R.A., Jarvie, D.R., Minty, P.S.B., Simpson, D. and Widdop, B., Screening for drugs of abuse. I: Opiates, amphetamines and cocaine, *Annals of Clinical Biochemistry* 32, 123, 1995.

179. Decrease, R., Magura, A., Lifshitz, M., Tilson, J., Drug testing in the workplace, American Society of Clinical Pathologists, Chicago, 1-11, 1989.

180. American Association for Clinical Chemistry, Protocol issues in urinalysis of abused substances: Report of the Substance-abuse Testing Committee, *Clinical Chemistry*, 34, 605, 1989.

181. Timbrell, J.A., Bio-transformation of xenobiotics, in General & Applied Toxicology. Ballantyne, B., Marrs, T. and Turner, P., eds., MacMillan Press, Basingstoke, England, 1993, chapter 4.

182. Wolff, K., Sanderson, M.J., Hay, A.W.M., Barnes, I., An evaluation of the measurements of drugs of abuse by commercial and in-house horizontal thin layer chromatography, *Annals of Clinical Biochemistry*, 30, 163, 1993.

183. Wolff, K., Shanab, M.A., Sanderson, M.J. and Hay, A.W.M., Screening for drugs of abuse: effect of heat-treating urine for safe handling of samples, *Clinical Chemistry*, 36, 908, 1990.

184. Feely, M., Cooke, J., Price, D., Singleton, S., Mehta, A., Bradford, L. and Calvert, R., Low-dose phenobarbitone as an indicator of compliance with drug therapy, *British Journal of Clinical Pharmacology*, 24, 77, 1987.

185. Schramm, W., Smith, R.H., Craig, P.A. and Kidwell, D.A., Drugs of abuse in saliva: a review, *Journal of Analytical Toxicology*, 16, 1, 1992.

186. Wolff, K., Hay, A. and Raistrick, D., Methadone in saliva, *Clinical Chemistry*, 37, 1297, 1991.

187. Harkey, M.R., Henderson, G.I. and Zou, C., Simultaneous quantitation of cocaine and its major metabolites in human hair by gas chromatography/chemical ionisation mass spectrometry, *Journal of Analytical Toxicology*, 15, 260, 1991.

188. Strang, J., Marsh, A. and Desouza. N., Hair analysis for drugs of abuse, *Lancet*, 1, 740, 1990.

189. Harkey, M.R. and Henderson, G.L., Hair analysis for drugs of abuse, *Advances in Analytical Toxicology*, 298, 1989.

190. Wilson, P., Watson, R. and Ralston, G.E., Methadone maintenance in general practice: patients, workload and outcomes, *British Medical Journal*, 309, 641, 1994.

References

CHAPTER 8

MEDICAL COMPLICATIONS OF DRUG ABUSE

EDITED BY NEAL L. BENOWITZ, M.D.

PROFESSOR OF MEDICINE, CHIEF, DIVISION OF CLINICAL PHARMACOLOGY AND EXPERIMENTAL THERAPEUTICS, UNIVERSITY OF CALIFORNIA, SAN FRANCISCO, CALIFORNIA

TABLE OF CONTENTS

0-8493-2637-0/98/$0.00+$.50

Table of Contents

8.1 DRUG-RELATED SYNDROMES

Shoshana Zevin, M.D.

Postdoctoral Fellow, Division of Clinical Pharmacology and Toxicology, University of California, San Francisco, California

Neal L. Benowitz, M.D.

Professor of Medicine, Chief, Division of Clinical Pharmacology and Experimental Therapeutics, University of California, San Francisco, California

Drug abuse is associated with many medical problems and complications stemming both from regular use and from overdoses. Another serious medical complication arising from drug abuse is the withdrawal syndrome which manifests during abstinence from the drug. Drug abuse affects a number of organ systems. Central nervous system (CNS) symptoms can range from headaches and altered mental status to life-threatening situations like coma and seizures (Tables 8.1 a and b). Cardiovascular manifestations of drug abuse include alterations in blood pressure and heart rate, as well as arrhythmias and organ ischemia. Respiratory arrest, pulmonary edema, and pneumothorax may occur. Metabolic effects such as alterations in body temperature, electrolytes, and acid-base disturbances are commonly seen (Table 8.1c). Reproductive consequences, ranging from impaired fertility to intrauterine growth retardation, premature births and neonatal syndromes may also occur. Infectious complications from intravenous drug use include viral infections such as HIV and hepatitis B, as well as bacterial

Table 8.1a Drugs of Abuse Commonly Causing Altered Mental Status

A. Agitation	C. Psychosis
Amphetamines	Amphetamines
Cocaine	Khat
Phencyclidine	LSD
Phenylpropanolamine	Phencyclidine
	Phenylpropanolamine
B. Hallucinations	D. Stupor/ Coma
Khat	Barbiturates
LSD	Benzodiazepines
Marijuana	Ethanol
Mescaline	Opiates
Phencyclidine	Phencyclidine
Solvents	

Table 8.1b Drugs of Abuse Commonly Causing Seizures

Amphetamines
Cocaine
Meperidine
Phencyclidine
Phenylpropanolamine
Propoxyphene
Ethanol and sedative-hypnotic drug withdrawal

Table 8.1c Drugs of Abuse Commonly Causing Temperature Disturbances

A. Hyperthermia	B. Hypothermia
Amphetamines	Barbiturates
Cocaine	Benzodiazepines
LSD	Opiates
Phencyclidine	
Ethanol and/or	
sedative-hypnotic	
drugs withdrawal	

infections including bacterial endocarditis, osteomyelitis, and abscesses. In this chapter we will describe the specific clinical syndromes associated with drugs of abuse.

8.1.1 SYNDROMES ASSOCIATED WITH STIMULANT ABUSE

Stimulant drugs act primarily through activation of the sympathetic nervous system. In moderate doses they result in an elevated mood, increased energy and alertness, and decreased

Table 8.1.1 Effects of Stimulant Intoxication

Central nervous system effects	Cardiovascular effects	Metabolic effects	Respiratory effects
Irritability	Tachycardia[a]	Hyperthermia	Respiratory arrest
Euphoria	Hypertension	Rhabdomyolysis	
Insomnia	Cardiovascular		
Anxiety	collapse		
Aggressiveness			
Delirium (agitated)			
Psychosis			
Stupor			
Coma			
Seizures			

[a] *Except alpha-adrenergic agonists which cause reflex bradycardia*

appetite. During intoxication they have profound central nervous system, cardiovascular system, and metabolic effects (Table 8.1.1).

8.1.1.1 Cocaine

Cocaine is one of the most frequent causes of medical complications of drug abuse.[1] Its actions include blockade of reuptake of catecholamines and dopamine by the neurons, release and/or blockade of the reuptake of serotonin, and centrally mediated neural sympathetic activation. In addition to stimulating the sympathetic nervous system, cocaine also has a local anesthetic effect due to blockade of fast sodium channels in neural tissue and the myocardium.

Cocaine may be injected intravenously, smoked, snorted, or orally ingested. Its half-life is approximately 60 min. After intravenous injection or smoking there is a rapid onset of CNS manifestations; the effects may be delayed 30 to 60 min after snorting, mucosal application or oral ingestion. The duration of cocaine effect is dependent on the route of administration, and is usually about 90 min after oral ingestion. Acute cocaine intoxication usually resolves after about 6 h, but some manifestations, such as myocardial infarction and stroke, may occur many hours after use, and a cocaine "crash" syndrome may last for several days after cocaine binging.

Most of the toxic manifestations of cocaine are due to excessive central and sympathetic nervous system stimulation. CNS stimulation causes behavioral changes, mood alterations, and psychiatric abnormalities. Autonomic stimulation causes cardiovascular system abnormalities, such as alterations in blood pressure, heart rate, arrhythmias, and hyperthermia (Table 8.1.1.1). Some of these manifestations, especially in the CNS and cardiovascular system, can be life-threatening.

8.1.1.1.1 Central Nervous System

In moderate doses, cocaine produces arousal and euphoria, but also anxiety and restlessness. Acute intoxication may result in severe psychiatric disturbances, such as acute anxiety, panic attacks, delirium, or acute psychosis.[2] Chronic cocaine intoxication can produce paranoid psychosis similar to schizophrenia.

Headache is quite common in cocaine users, and has been reported in 13 to 50% of the users surveyed. In some patients the headaches were triggered by cocaine, whereas others reported them in association with cocaine withdrawal.[3] Some patients experienced migraine

Shoshana Zevin and Neal L. Benowitz

Table 8.1.1.1 Medical Complications of Cocaine Intoxication and Abuse

Central nervous system	Cardiovascular
Headache	Hypertension
Stroke (ischemic and hemorrhagic)	Aortic dissection
Transient neurological deficit	Arrhythmia (Sinus tachycardia, supraventricular
Subarachnoid hemorrhage	tachycardia, ventricular tachycardia/fibrillation)
Seizures	Shock
Toxic encephalopathy	Sudden death
Coma	Myocarditis
	Myocardial ischemia and infarction
	Other organ ischemia: renal infarction,
	intestinal infarction, limb ischemia
Respiratory	Metabolic
Pulmonary edema	Hyperthermia
Respiratory arrest	Rhabdomyolysis
"Crack lung"	Renal failure (myoglobinuria)
Pneumothorax	Coagulopathy
Pneumomediastinum	Lactic acidosis
Reproductive/Neonatal	Infectious
Spontaneous abortion	HIV/AIDS[a]
Placental Abruption	Hepatitis B[a]
Placenta Previa	Infectious endocarditis[a]
Intrauterine growth retardation	Frontal sinusitis with brain abscess[b]
"Crack baby syndrome"	Fungal cerebritis†
Cerebral infarction	Wound botulism
	Tetanus

[a] *Associated with contaminated needles*
[b] *Associated with intranasal insufflation*

headaches. In some instances, headaches may be induced by hypertension. Persistent headaches, despite normalization of blood pressure, should raise concern about a possible stroke.

Stroke and transient neurologic defects: A variety of neurologic signs have been reported in patients with cocaine intoxication, among them dizziness, vertigo, tremor, blurred vision. Transient hemiparesis has also been observed, and may be the result of cerebral vasospasm.[4] Strokes are being increasingly recognized in cocaine abuse, particularly in young patients. Among the patients with strokes, about 50% have cerebral hemorrhage, 30% subarachnoid hemorrhage and 20% ischemic stroke.[3,5] This distribution differs from the one found in the general population, where ischemia and not hemorrhage accounts for the majority of strokes. The mechanism of stroke is thought be an acute elevation of blood pressure induced by increased sympathetic activity, which may cause rupture of cerebral aneurysm; or vasospasm or cerebral vasoconstriction. Chronic cocaine abuse has been associated with acute dystonic reactions which in some cases have been precipitated by neuroleptics, and in other without neuroleptics. Acute dystonia was reported after cocaine use as well as during cocaine withdrawal.[6]

Seizures: Seizures are seen in about 1.4% of cocaine abusers admitted to a hospital.[2, 3, 6] They are usually generalized, tonic-clonic in character, and may occur soon after taking cocaine, or after a delay of several hours. Children can have seizures as a first manifestation of cocaine exposure.[3] The mechanism of cocaine-related seizures may be its local anesthetic properties.

Toxic encephalopathy and coma: Often patients present after several days of a cocaine binge; at first they may experience severe anxiety, hyperactivity, and paranoia which last for about 6 to 8 h, and then they may become hypersomnolent and depressed. This latter phase can last 2 to 3 days. Other complications associated with cocaine abuse are frontal sinusitis and brain abscess after chronic cocaine snorting.[7] Cocaine snorting is also associated with atrophy of nasal mucosa, necrosis, and perforation of the nasal septum.[6]

8.1.1.1.2 Cardiovascular System

Blood pressure: Intense sympathetic stimulation induced by cocaine results in hypertension and tachycardia. Hypertension is a combined result of increased cardiac output and increased systemic vascular resistance. Hypertension may cause stroke, aortic dissection, and acute pulmonary edema.

Myocardial ischemia: Myocardial infarction has been well documented in cocaine abuse. It is the end result of a combination of several factors including coronary vasospasm, increased myocardial oxygen demand due to increased myocardial work load, and thrombosis.[3,8,9] Myocardial infarction can develop hours to days after the last dose of cocaine, and may be related to variable time course of developing thrombosis. Ambulatory ECG monitoring of chronic cocaine users during the first week of cocaine withdrawal demonstrated recurrent episodes of ST segment elevation, probably due to vasospasm.[9]

Other organs may be affected by ischemia resulting from vasoconstriction, including renal and intestinal infarction which can be life-threatening. They usually present with intense flank or diffuse abdominal pain. Myocarditis presenting as patchy myocardial necrosis has been observed after acute cocaine intoxication, and believed to result from intense catecholamine stimulation.[8,9] Clinically, this results in ST segment elevations and/or T wave inversions, with elevated CPK- MB fraction. In chronic cocaine use, the result may be myocardial fibrosis and cardiomyopathy.

Arrhythmia: Arrhythmia is common in cocaine intoxication; in acute intoxication it results from sympathetic stimulation and later it may be the result of myocardial ischemia or myocarditis. The most common arrhythmia is sinus tachycardia. Other arrhythmias include atrial tachycardia and fibrillation, ventricular tachycardia, including torsade de pointes and conduction disturbances due to local anesthetic effects of cocaine, with wide complex tachycardia.[9] Ventricular fibrillation can be a cause of sudden death, and asystole has also been reported.

Shock: Shock may develop in patients with cocaine intoxication as a result of reduced cardiac output due to myocardial ischemia, direct myocardial depression, myocarditis, or arrhythmia, and as a result of vasodilatation due to either local anesthetic effects of cocaine on blood vessels, or its effects on the brain stem. Hypovolemia may also be present in agitated and/or hyperthermic patients.

Sudden death: Most deaths occur within minutes to hours of acute cocaine intoxication, and most are the result of arrhythmia due to either massive catecholamine release or ischemia. Many convulse prior to death. Another syndrome associated with sudden death during cocaine intoxication is "excited delirium", in which the victim manifests aggressive and bizarre behavior accompanied by hyperthermia, and then suddenly dies.[10,11] Death due to medical reasons due to cocaine intoxication accounts for about 11% of all cocaine-related deaths.

Shoshana Zevin and Neal L. Benowitz

Pulmonary: Pulmonary edema is a common finding at autopsies of victims of cocaine intoxication. It can occur in acute intoxication either because of myocardial dysfunction or as a result of a massive increase in the afterload due to vasoconstriction. Noncardiogenic pulmonary edema has also been reported.[8] A syndrome called "crack lung" has been described, and consists of fever, pulmonary infiltrates, bronchospasm, and eosinophilia.[13] Respiratory arrest can occur as a result of CNS depression. Pneumomediastinum and pneumothorax have been described in patients who snort or smoke cocaine, presumably due to increased airway pressure during a Valsalva maneuver.

Metabolic complications: Severe hyperthermia has been described in patients with acute cocaine intoxication; the mechanism probably is muscular hyperactivity due to agitation or seizures and increased metabolic rate. Hyperthermia is also part of the "agitated delirium" syndrome, where it accompanies extremely violent and agitated behavior, in sometimes fatal cocaine intoxications.[10,11] Hyperthermia, if untreated, can result in brain damage, rhabdomyolysis with renal failure, coagulation abnormalities and death. Rhabdomyolysis in acute cocaine intoxication is most often the result of muscular hyperactivity and hyperthermia, but can also be due to muscular ischemia due to vasoconstriction. It presents as muscular pains, which can also occur in the chest wall, and must be distinguished from the pain of myocardial ischemia. Lactic acidosis may be a complication of prolonged muscular hyperactivity.

Reproductive/Neonatal: Cocaine use during pregnancy can result in an increased incidence of spontaneous abortion, placenta previa, and abruption of the placenta. Placental ischemia results in intrauterine growth retardation. Neonates born to cocaine-addicted mothers have various neurologic abnormalities, including irritability, tremulousness, poor feeding, hypotonia or hypertonia, and hyperreflexia. This syndrome may last for 8 to 10 weeks.[8]

Withdrawal: Abstinence after prolonged use of cocaine can result in a "cocaine crash", manifesting as anxiety, depression, exhaustion, and craving for cocaine. Suicidal ideation is common. The symptoms can last for several weeks to several months after the cessation of use.[14]

8.1.1.2 Natural Stimulants

Ephedrine and khat belong to a group of natural stimulants. Ephedrine is found in a variety of plants, as well as in many Chinese medicines and is part of many non-prescription decongestants. Khat shrub grows in Ethiopia, and khat leaves are chewed in East African countries, particularly in Yemen and Somalia.[6,15] The active ingredient in khat leaves is (-)cathinone. Both ephedrine and cathinone resemble amphetamine in structure.

8.1.1.2.1 Ephedrine

Ephedrine acts directly on alpha and beta-adrenergic receptors, and also stimulates the release of norepinephrine. It exhibits less central nervous system effects compared to amphetamine. Pseudoephedrine is a dextro isomer of ephedrine, and has similar alpha-, but less beta-, adrenergic activity. Both drugs are marketed as a non-prescription medications for nasal decongestion, and are ingredients in many cold medications and bronchodilators. The main manifestations of ephedrine intoxication are cardiovascular, with elevation of blood pressure and heart rate.[16] Hypertension due to ephedrine intoxication, even if moderate, can result in neurologic complications including headache, confusion, seizures, and stroke, both ischemic and hemorrhagic.[17] There have also been reports of intracerebral vasculitis and hemorrhage associated with ephedrine abuse.[18] Severe headache, focal neurologic deficit, or changes in mental status in ephedrine intoxication should raise the possibility of stroke. Fatalities may result from myocardial infarction, arrhythmia, seizures, or stroke.[19]

8.1.1.2.2 Khat

Khat has CNS effects quite similar to amphetamine; but due to the bulkiness of the plant, the amounts of the active ingredient, cathinone, that is actually ingested is usually not large. Social use of khat causes increase in energy level and alertness, but also mood lability, anxiety, and insomnia.[20] Khat abuse may result in mania-like symptoms, paranoia, and acute schizophrenia-like psychosis. In most cases of khat-induced psychosis, heavy khat consumption preceded the episodes.[15,20,21] Most of the cases are resolved within weeks with cessation of khat use. No specific physical withdrawal syndrome is recognized, but there is a psychological withdrawal characterized by depression, hypersomnia, and loss of energy.[15,20] Khat intoxication may result in cardiovascular toxicity with hypertension and tachycardia, but severe hypertension has not been observed.[20] There is an association between khat use and gastric ulcers, and also between its use and constipation, though causation is not clear.[20] Babies born to khat-chewing mothers are likely to suffer from intrauterine growth retardation. Long-term chewing of khat (for more than 25 years) was found to be strongly associated with oral cancer.[15]

8.1.1.3 Synthetic Stimulants

Amphetamine, along with its analogues methamphetamine and methylphenidate, is a sympathomimetic; it acts by releasing biogenic amines from storage sites both in the central and the peripheral nervous system as well as by directly stimulating alpha and beta-adrenergic receptors. Thus, it produces CNS stimulation and arousal, and serious mental changes and cardiovascular effects during intoxication.

8.1.1.3.1 Amphetamine

Amphetamine is one of the most potent CNS stimulators. It exists as a racemic solution, but dextroamphetamine (D-isomer) is three to four times more potent than levoamphetamine with regard to CNS stimulation. It is mainly administered orally or intravenously. Clinically, amphetamine effects are very similar to those of cocaine, but amphetamine has a longer half-life compared to cocaine (10 to 15 h), and the duration of amphetamine-induced euphoria is four to eight times longer than for cocaine.

   CNS effects: During acute intoxication with amphetamines, patients commonly present with euphoria, restlessness, agitation, and anxiety.[6,22] Suicidal ideation, hallucinations, and confusion are seen in 5 to 12% of the patients with acute intoxication. Seizures may occur in about 3% of the patients presenting in the hospital with amphetamine intoxication.[22] Stroke has been reported in patients with amphetamine intoxication; it is usually hemorrhagic and results from hypertension. There have also been reports of cerebral vasculitis with chronic abuse of amphetamine.[23-25] Chronic amphetamine abuse may precipitate psychiatric disturbances, such as paranoia and psychosis, that can persist for weeks.

   Movement disorders: Chronic high dose amphetamine use is associated with stereotypic behavior, dyskinesias, and also with chorea, especially in patients with preexisting basal ganglia disorders. Amphetamines exacerbate tics in patients who already have them, and may induce tics, though the causation is unclear.[6]

   Cardiovascular effects: The major effects seen during acute intoxication are hypertension and tachycardia. Arrhythmia can occur, including ventricular fibrillation. Myocardial ischemia has been reported; the underlying mechanisms are increased myocardial oxygen demand and/or coronary vasospasm.[22] Chronic abuse has been reported to result in cardiomyopathy.[26] Systemic necrotizing vasculitis, resembling periarteritis nodosa, has been associated with chronic amphetamine abuse.

   Metabolic and other effects: Acute amphetamine intoxication can manifest with sweating, tremor, muscle fasciculations, and rigidity. Hyperthermia can develop and may be life-

Shoshana Zevin and Neal L. Benowitz

threatening if not treated promptly.[27] The mechanisms underlying hyperthermia are muscle hyperactivity and seizures. The same mechanisms may also cause rhabdomyolysis with attendant renal failure. Chronic amphetamine abuse can result in weight loss of up to 20 to 30 lb and malnutrition.[6]

8.1.1.3.2 Methamphetamine

Methamphetamine is an amphetamine analogue; it has an increased CNS penetration and a longer half-life; its effects may persist for 6 to 24 hours more compared to amphetamine. It can be ingested orally, smoked, or snorted. Methamphetamine produces more CNS stimulation with less peripheral effects compared to amphetamine,[28] but large doses may result in hypertension. Stroke, both ischemic and hemorrhagic, has been reported with methamphetamine abuse, and in some cases the stroke was delayed by 10 to 12 hours since last use.[29] The mechanisms may be hypertension, thrombosis, vasospasm and vasculitis.

8.1.1.3.3 Methylphenidate

Methylphenidate is structurally related to amphetamine; in therapeutic doses it is a mild CNS stimulant, with more mental then motor effects, and it has minimal peripheral effects in therapeutic doses. It is used clinically for the treatment of attention deficit disorder and narcolepsy. However, when abused and used in high doses it may cause generalized CNS stimulation with symptoms similar to amphetamine, including seizures.

8.1.1.3.4 Phenylpropanolamine

Phenylpropanolamine (PPA) is primarily an alpha-adrenergic agonist, both direct and indirect through release of norepinephrine. It is structurally related to amphetamine. Phenylpropanolamine is an ingredient in many cold and anorectic agents. Phenylpropanolamine combined with caffeine has been sold as a look-alike "amphetamine". PPA has a low therapeutic index, and doses two to three times in excess of recommended may result in toxicity. Susceptible individuals, particularly those suffering from hypertension or autonomic insufficiency with attendant denervation hypersensitivity of adrenergic receptors, may experience adverse effects even with therapeutic doses. The main manifestations of phenylpropanolamine toxicity are cardiovascular; however, CNS stimulant effects usually appear at higher doses.

Cardiovascular effects: The main effect of phenylpropanolamine is hypertension due to its alpha-adrenergic properties; because it has only slight beta-adrenergic activity, there is no tachycardia, rather, a reflex bradycardia is usually present.[30] Patients with phenylpropanolamine -induced hypertension are at risk for stroke, both ischemic and hemorrhagic.[30-32] Headache is a common feature, and may reflect an acutely elevated blood pressure, or may be the first manifestation of stroke. A patient with a severe headache, altered mental status, or neurologic deficit should be evaluated for stroke even if his blood pressure is not elevated. There are also case reports of chest pain, myocardial infarction, and ECG repolarization abnormalities.[30] The duration of intoxication is about 6 h.

CNS effects: When taken in large doses and/or chronically abused, phenylpropanolamine causes symptoms similar to amphetamine, including anxiety, agitation, and psychosis.[30,33] There are individuals at risk for psychiatric side effects from phenylpropanolamine even at therapeutic doses: these are individuals with past psychiatric history, children younger than 6 years and post-partum women.[34] Seizures have also been reported, though often when phenylpropanolamine was combined with other drugs, such as caffeine. Case reports of cerebral vasculitis and hemorrhage with phenylpropanolamine use have been described.[35]

Table 8.1.2 Manifestations of Hallucinogen Intoxication and Abuse

Neuropsychiatric	Medical
Acute	Hypertension
Euphoria	Tachycardia
Altered time perception	Nausea
Heightened visual and color	Vomiting
perception	Muscle pains
Anxiety	Trismus (MDMA)
Disorientation	Flushing
Delirium	Arrhythmia (MDMA)
Panic attacks	Cardiovascular collapse
Suicidal ideation	Respiratory arrest
Hallucinations	Stroke (MDMA)
Chronic	Hyperthermia
Depression	Seizures
Drowsiness	Hepatotoxicity (MDMA)
Anxiety	SIADH (MDMA)
Panic disorder	
Psychosis	
Impaired memory	
Flashbacks (LSD)	

8.1.2 SYNDROMES ASSOCIATED WITH HALLUCINOGENS

The primary effects of hallucinogenic drugs are altered perception and mood. The specific effects differ in different drug classes. They are also accompanied by autonomic changes (Table 8.1.2). Hallucinogens do not induce physical dependence. The specific mechanisms of action are not known for many of the drugs, but there are indications that they act as adrenergic and serotoninergic agonists. The changes in mood and perception are probably related to their serotoninergic actions. (For a more detailed discussion of hallucinogen neurochemistry, see Chpater 6.) After prolonged or high-dose use of the drugs, there is evidence of depletion of serotonin and dopamine in the neurons in the brain. The psychiatric effects may be quite severe, and may require medication. Sometimes the psychosis may be prolonged long beyond the presence of the drug in the body, and there may be chronic psychiatric impairment and memory disturbances, possibly related to damage to serotoninergic neurons in the brain.

8.1.2.1 Phenylethylamine Derivatives

8.1.2.1.1 Mescaline

Mescaline is a phenylethylamine derivative. It is found in peyote cactus, and can be ingested orally or intravenously. It is structurally related to epinephrine. The precise mechanism of action is unknown, but it is thought to alter the activity of serotonin, norepinephrine, and dopamine receptors.[28] The signs of intoxication appear within 30 min of ingestion, peak at 4 h, and last 8 to 14 h. The psychic phase lasts about 6 h.[36] There are both physiological and psychological manifestations of mescaline.

    Physiological effects: These are mainly manifestations of autonomic adrenergic activation: dilated pupils, increased sweating, elevated systolic blood pressure, and temperature. Large doses of mescaline may induce hypotension, bradycardia, and respiratory depression.[37] Some users may experience nausea, vomiting, or dizziness, which usually resolve within an hour.[38]

Psychological effects: These begin several hours after the ingestion. Typically there is a feeling of euphoria, a sense of physical power, and distortion of sensation. There is an increased color perception.[37,39] Sometimes there are visual hallucinations, especially of vivid colors. Users may also experience feelings of depersonalization, disorientation, anxiety, emotional lability, and/or emotional outbursts.[38] There is no physical dependence for mescaline.[37,39]

8.1.2.1.2 TMA-2 (2,4,5-trimethoxyamphetamine)

TMA is a synthetic analogue of mescaline and amphetamine. It is more potent than mescaline, but resembles mescaline in the effects.[40]

8.1.2.1.3 DOM/STP (4-methyl-2,5-dimethoxyamphetamine)

This is another amphetamine analogue. It has a narrow therapeutic index. Low doses of 2 to 3 mg cause perceptual distortion and mild sympathetic stimulation, but doses two to three times that produce hallucinations and more severe sympathetic stimulation.[28,41]

8.1.2.1.4 PMA (para-methoxyamphetamine)

This is a very potent hallucinogen and CNS stimulant. Overdose may present with severe sympathetic stimulation including seizures, hyperthermia, coagulopathy, and rhabdomyolysis (like in amphetamine intoxication), and can result in fatalities.[28]

8.1.2.1.5 DOB (4-bromo-2,5-dimethoxyamphetamine)

DOB, otherwise called bromo-DOM, is one of the most potent phenylethylamine derivatives; it has about 100 times the potency of mescaline. It is long-acting, with effects starting within an hour, reaching their full strength after 3 to 4 h, and lasting up to 10 h.[42] The manifestations of intoxication are mood enhancement with visual distortion. There are case reports of severely intoxicated patients with hallucinations, agitation, and sympathetic stimulation.[43] DOB, when ingested in large doses, can have an ergot- like effect, and cause severe generalized peripheral vasospasm with tissue ischemia.[28]

8.1.2.1.6 MDA (3,4-methylenedioxyamphetamine)

MDA is an amphetamine derivative included in the category of "designer drugs". While in small doses it produces mild intoxication with feelings of euphoria, large doses can cause hallucinations, agitation, and delirium.[28] It also can produce intense sympathetic stimulation, with hypertension, tachycardia, seizures and hyperthermia. Death has been reported after MDA use, usually as a result of seizures and/or hyperthermia.[44]

8.1.2.1.7 MDMA (3,4-methylenedioxymethamphetamine)

MDMA is one of the most popular "designer drugs" today, and is used recreationally by a large number of young people.[45] It is also known as "Ecstasy", "Adam", and "M&M". It was "rediscovered" in the seventies as an adjunct to psychotherapy, but its use for this purpose has since diminished.

Psychological effects: After ingestion of 75 to 150 mg, users experience a sense of euphoria, heightened awareness, and improved sense of communication.[37,45] Acute neuropsychiatric complications have been reported, and include anxiety, insomnia, depression, paranoia, confusion, panic attacks, and psychosis.[45,46] Chronic effects of MDMA abuse include depression, drowsiness, anxiety, panic disorder, aggressive outbursts, psychosis, and memory disturbance.[45,47] Though the exact mechanism of action is not known, there is some evidence from animal studies, as well as from some observations in human subjects, that MDMA can cause damage to serotoninergic neurons in the brain.[45,48]

Medical effects: Stimulatory effects of MDMA are apparent even in mild intoxication, and include increased blood pressure and heart rate, decreased appetite, dry mouth. Also common are nausea, vomiting, trismus (jaw clenching), teeth grinding, hyperreflexia, muscle aches, hot and cold flushes, and nystagmus. Additional side effects reported include paresthesias, blurred vision, and motor ticks. There are several reports of MDMA-induced arrhythmias, asystole, and cardiovascular collapse. Other potentially fatal complications include seizures, hyperthermia, and rhabdomyolysis with acute renal failure.[47,49] There are several case reports of hepatotoxicity following MDMA ingestion,[49,50] and three cases of inappropriate antidiuretic hormone secretion (SIADH) with severe hyponatremia and seizures.[51,52] CNS complications including stroke (ischemic and hemorrhagic), subarachnoid hemorrhage, and cerebral venous sinus thrombosis have been reported following MDMA ingestion. One syndrome of MDMA intoxication has been reported specifically in the setting of crowding and vigorous dancing, such as in "raves" or clubs. It includes several manifestations: hyperthermia, dehydration, seizures, rhabdomyolysis, disseminated intravascular coagulation, and acute renal failure.[47] This is thought to be the consequence of the combination of sympathomimetic effects including cutaneous vasoconstriction and extreme physical exertion in hot and poorly ventilated conditions.

8.1.2.1.8 MDEA (3,4-methylenedioxyethamphetamine)

This is an analogue of MDMA, with effects similar to these of MDMA.

8.1.2.2 Lysergic Acid Diethylamide (LSD)

LSD is a synthetic ergoline, and it is the third most-frequently used drug among adolescents, after alcohol and marijuana.[53] The main site of action of LSD is serotoninergic receptor 5-HT2.[54] The effects of LSD, psychological and physical, are dose-related. With oral doses of 20 to 50 μg the onset of effects is after 5 to 10 min, with peak effects occurring 30 to 90 min post-ingestion. Duration of the effects may be 8 to 12 h, and recovery lasts between 10 to 12 h, when normal cognition alternates with altered mood and perception. Cognitive effects include distortion of time and altered visual perception with very vivid color perception. Euphoria and anxiety may be experienced. There are also signs of sympathetic stimulation, with dilated pupils, tachycardia, elevated blood pressure and temperature, and facial flushing. Tremors and hyperreflexia are also common.[37,53]

A "bad trip" may be experienced during LSD intoxication: terrifying hallucinations which precipitate panic attack, disorientation, delirium, and depression with suicidal ideation. A "bad trip" may occur with first-time use, as well as after recurrent use. Five major categories of psychiatric adverse effects have been described: anxiety and panic attacks, self-destructive behavior, such as attempting to jump out of the window, hallucinations, acute psychosis, and major depressive reactions.[53] Patients who have taken very high doses of LSD have presented with manifestations of intense sympathetic stimulation including hyperthermia, coagulopathy, circulatory collapse, and respiratory arrest.[55] Another danger of LSD abuse is accidents and trauma while trying to drive during intoxication, or during the recovery phase.

There may be chronic toxic effects associated with LSD abuse. Effects that have been described include:

1. Prolonged psychosis, especially among users with preexisting psychiatric morbidity.
2. Prolonged or intermittent major depression.
3. Disruption of personality.
4. Post-hallucinogen perceptual disorder (PHPD).

Shoshana Zevin and Neal L. Benowitz

Table 8.1.2.3.1 Manifestations of Phencyclidine Intoxication

Mild (≤ 5 mg)	Severe (≤ 20 mg)	Massive (500 mg)
Confusion state	Coma	Prolonged coma
Uncommunicative	Eyes may be open	Hypoventilation
Agitated, combative	Myosis	Respiratory arrest
Bizarre behavior	Nystagmus	Hypertension
Nystagmus	Muscle rigidity	Prolonged and fluctuating
Ataxia	Extensor posturing,	confusional state upon
Myoclonus	opisthotonus	recovery from coma
Muscle rigidity or	Increased deep	
catalepsy	tendon reflexes	
Hypertension	Hypertension	
	Hyperthermia	
	Seizures	

The latter syndrome is characterized by flashbacks, when imagery experienced during LSD intoxication returns without taking the drug. Flashbacks may occur months, and even years after LSD use. It has been reported that 50% of users experienced flashbacks during 5 years after their last use of LSD.[53,55] In most cases, flashbacks occur after LSD has been used more than 10 times.[55] Rarely, the flashbacks may be frightening hallucinations, in extreme cases these have been associated with homicide or suicide. Flashbacks may be triggered by stress, illness, and marijuana and alcohol use.[37,53]

8.1.2.3 Disassociative Anesthetics (Phencyclidine)

PCP was developed as an anesthetic, but its psychiatric side effects precluded its use in humans. In the1960s PCP became a popular street drug. It is most commonly smoked, but can also be ingested orally, snorted, or injected intravenously. PCP is also commonly used as an additive to other drugs, such as marijuana, mescaline, or LSD. The mechanisms of action of PCP include anesthesia without depression of ventilation, and its main site of action is probably blockade of cationic channel of NMDA receptor, as well as sigma opioid receptors.[56,57] It also inhibits the reuptake of dopamine and norepinephrine, and has direct alpha-adrenergic effects.The effects of PCP are dose-dependent (Table 8.1.2.3.1). Smoking causes a rapid onset of effects; the half-life of PCP may range from 11 to 51 h.[58]

Psychiatric effects: At low doses of 1 to 5 mg PCP produces euphoria, relaxation, and a feeling of numbness. There may also be a feeling of altered body image and sensory distortion. At higher doses there may be agitation, bizarre behavior, and psychosis resembling paranoid schizophrenia. The patients may alternate between agitation and catatonic-like state. There is also analgesia which may lead to self-injury.[58,59]

Physical effects: In mild intoxication the most prominent sign is nystagmus, both vertical and horizontal, and numbness in extremities. In severe intoxication there are signs of adrenergic stimulation, with hypertension, tachycardia, flushing, and hyperthermia sometimes complicated by rhabdomyolysis and acute renal failure, and also of cholinomimetic stimulation with sweating, hypersalivation and miosis, and dystonic reactions, ataxia, and myoclonus may also occur. With high doses PCP causes seizures, coma with extensor posturing, respiratory arrest and circulatory collapse.[59,60] The eyes may remain open during coma. Coma may be prolonged, even up to several weeks. Death may result directly from intoxication (seizures, hyperthermia) or from violent behavior. Chronic effects of PCP abuse include memory impairment, personality changes, and depression which may last up to a year after stopping. There is probably no physical dependence on PCP.

8.1.3 MARIJUANA

Marijuana is obtained from the *Cannabis sativa* plant; it is a mixture of crushed leaves, seeds, and twigs from the plant. There are many active ingredients in the plant, but the ingredient accounting for the majority of the effects is delta-9-tetrahydrocannabinol (THC). There is a great variability in the amount of THC in different plants and in different batches of marijuana. Hashish is a resinous sap of the Cannabis plant, and typically contains 20 to 30 times the amount of THC compared to the equal weight of marijuana. Today marijuana is the most commonly used illicit drug in the U.S. Marijuana is usually smoked; one "joint" typically contains 10 to 30 mg of THC; the onset of action is within 10 to 20 min, and the effects last up to 2 to 3 h.[58] Acute effects of marijuana include relaxation and sometimes euphoria. There may be a feeling of depersonalization. There is impairment of concentration and problem solving. High doses of THC may cause hallucinations, anxiety, panic, and psychosis.[58,61] These effects can last for several days. Physical effects include impairment of balance, conjuctival injection, increased heart rate, orthostatic hypotension, peripheral vasoconstriction with cold extremities, dry mouth, and increased appetite.[61] There are reports of intravenously injected marijuana extract which results in rapid onset of nausea, vomiting, fever, and diarrhea, and is followed by hypotension, acute renal failure, thrombocytopenia and rhabdomyoplysis.[62]

Chronic users of marijuana have been reported to experience an amotivation syndrome, in which apathy, lack of energy, and loss of motivation persist for days or longer. Chronic use of marijuana may result in inhibition of secretion of reproductive hormones, and cause impotence in men and menstrual irregularities in women.[63] It has been suggested that chronic smokers are at risk for chronic lung disorder but the evidence is weak. Chronic smokers of marijuana are at risk for chronic obstructive lung disease, and marijuana tar is carcinogenic and appears to be associated with development of respiratory tract carcinoma in young adults.[64,65] There are also reports of spontaneous pneumothorax in daily marijuana smokers, though the patients smoked tobacco as well. The mechanism is sustained Valsalva maneuver during forced inhalation.[66]

8.1.4 OPIATE DRUGS

Opioids have been used and abused since ancient times. They are indispensable in clinical use for pain management, and are also used as cough suppressants and antidiarrheal agents. They are abused for their mood-altering effects, and tolerance and physical and psychological dependence account for continued abuse. Patients who use narcotic analgesics for pain relief may develop physical dependence, but rarely develop psychological dependence on the drug.

Opioids are a diverse group of drugs, among them derivatives of the naturally occurring opium (morphine, heroine, codeine), synthetic (methadone, fentanyl) and endogenous compounds (enkephalins, endorphins, and dynorphins). Morphine-like analgesic drugs are also known as narcotics. There are several subtypes of opiate receptors (mu, delta, and kappa) which differ in their affinity to different agonists and antagonists, and in their effects (Table 8.1.4a). Opiate receptors are present in different concentrations in different regions of the nervous system. Some of the receptors involved in analgesia are located in the periaqueductal gray matter; the receptors believed to be reponsible for reinforcing effects are in the ventral tegmental area and in the nucleus acumbens. There are opiate receptors in locus ceruleus which plays an important role in control of autonomic activity; their activation results in inhibition of locus ceruleus firing. After opiate withdrawal there is an increase in locus ceruleus neuronal firing, resulting in autonomic hyperactivity characteristic of opiate withdrawal. Tolerance develops to many of the opiate effects, but differentially to different effects.[67,68]

Shoshana Zevin and Neal L. Benowitz

Table 8.1.4.a Opiate Receptor Subtypes

Receptor subtype	Prototype drug	Major action
μ_1	All opiates and most opioid peptides	Supraspinal analgesia
		Prolactin release
		Catalepsy
μ_2	Morphine	Respiratory depression
		Gastrointestinal transit
		Growth hormone release
		Cardiovascular effects
d	Enkephalins	Spinal analgesia
		Growth hormone release
k	Dynorphin	Spinal analgesia
	Ketocyclazocine	Sedation
		Inhibition of vasopressin release
e	β-endorphin	?
s	N-allylnormetazocine	Psychotomimetic effects

In general, opioids cause analgesia and sedation, respiratory depression, and slowed gastrointestinal transit. Severe intoxication results in coma and respiratory depression, which may progress to apnea and death (Table 8.1.4b). Adverse side effects from opiates are seen in drug abusers who take an overdose (intentional or unintentional), but also in medical patients who are treated with opiates. Morphine, heroin, methadone, propoxyphene, and fentanyl-derivatives account for about 98% of all opiate deaths and hospital admissions.[69] Opioid receptors μ_1 play a major role in analgesia; analgesic effects are mediated through central, spinal, and peripheral mechanisms. Analgesia is dose-dependent, and in high doses opioids produce anesthesia. Tolerance to analgesic effects develops less rapidly compared to tolerance to mood or respiratory effects.[67]

8.1.4.1 Common Opiate Effects

8.1.4.1.1 Mental

Opiate drugs have reinforcing properties, possibly mediated through dopaminergic neuron activation in ventral tegmental area and nucleus acumbens. Usually, the effect on the mood is relaxation and euphoria; though patients who take opiates for pain relief more often report dysphoria after taking the drug. Tolerance to euphoria-inducing effects develops rapidly. Sedation is dose-dependent, and is often accompanied by stereotypic dreaming.[67] Tolerance develops rapidly. Sedation is a first sign of opiate intoxication; respiratory depression does not occur unless the patient is sedated.

8.1.4.1.2 Gastrointestinal Effects

Nausea and vomiting are prominent side effects of opiates, resulting from their actions on the chemoreceptor trigger zone in the medulla. However, tolerance usually develops to these effects. Different opiates have different likelihood for causing nausea. Opioid drugs decrease gastrointestinal motility and peristalsis, acting in the spinal cord and gastrointestinal tract, thus causing constipation. Tolerance does not develop to this effect, and so constipation persists even in chronic users. The constipating effect of opiates is used for symptomatic treatment of diarrhea.

Drug-Related Syndromes

TABLE 8.1.4.b Medical Complications of Opiate Intoxication and Withdrawal

Intoxication	Withdrawal
CNS	Anxiety
Stupor or coma	Insomnia
Myosis	Chills
Seizures (propoxyphene, meperidine)	Myalgias, Arthralgias
Respiratory	Nausea, vomiting
Hypoventilation	Anorexia
Cough suppression	Diarrhea
Respiratory arrest	Yawning
Pulmonary edema	Midriasis
Cardiovascular	Tachycardia
Hypotension	Diaphoresis, lacrimation
Bradycardia	
Conduction abnormalities (propoxyphene)	
Metabolic	
Hypothermia	
Cool, moist skin	

8.1.4.1.3 Respiratory Effects

Respiratory depression is the most serious adverse effect of opiates; it is dose-dependent, and respiratory arrest is almost always the cause of death from opiate overdose. Respiratory arrest occurs within minutes of the intravenous overdose. After overdose from oral, intramuscular or subcutaneous route, sedation almost always precedes respiratory arrest. Tolerance to respiratory depression develops, but is lost rapidly after abstinence. All opioid agonists produce the same degree of respiratory depression given the same degree of analgesia. The mechanism is through μ_2 receptor stimulation in respiratory centers in the brain stem.[70]

Pulmonary edema occurs with several opioid drugs, and is non-cardiogenic. The precise mechanisms are unknown but probably involve hypoperfusion with tissue injury and cytokine-induced pulmonary capillary endothelial injury. Pulmonary edema is particularly common with heroin intoxication, and may be precipitated by the administration of naloxone (which reverses venodilation and redistributes blood to the central circulation).

8.1.4.1.4 Miscellaneous Effects

Opiates cause cough suppression by acting in the medulla; the doses needed are usually lower than for analgesia. Other effects include miosis, which is invariably present in opiate intoxication, unless anoxic brain damage is present. Pruritis is very common in patients receiving opiates, as well as in addicts. It is caused by histamine release mediated by the mu receptors.[71] Urinary retention can occur, and is mediated through spinal cord opiate receptors.[72] Individual narcotic agents have specific effects which will be discussed below.

8.1.4.2 Specific Narcotic Agents

8.1.4.2.1 Morphine

Morphine has an elimination half-life of 1.7 h; but its 6-glucuronide metabolite is also pharmacolgically active. Morphine can be administered by intravenous, subcutaneous, oral, and rectal routes. While well absorbed, morphine undergoes significant first-pass metabolism when given orally, and thus requires high doses to achieve the desired effects. While the oral route is the accepted route of administration for pain control in patients with chronic pain, it usually is not often utilized by drug addicts.

8.1.4.2.2 Heroin

Heroin (diacetyl-morphine) is a synthetic derivative of morphine. In the body, it is rapidly converted to 6-acetylmorphine, and then to morphine. The conversion to morphine occurs within minutes. In addition to the effects common to all opiates, there have been reports of acute rhabdomyolysis with myoglobinuria during heroin intoxication.[73,74] In some cases the patients have been comatose, lying with pressure on their muscles, but in other cases rhabdomyolysis occurred with alert patients, accompanied by muscle pains, weakness, and swelling. Chronic abuse of heroin has been associated with progressive nephrotic syndrome resulting in renal failure.[75] The histopathology is focal segmental glomerulosclerosis. For unexplained reasons, this disease has almost entirely disappeared over the last few years.

8.1.4.2.3 Codeine

Codeine is one of the substances found in opium. It is about 20% as potent as morphine as an analgesic. It is mostly used as a cough suppressant, and as an ingredient in pain medications. To be effective as an analgesic, codeine must be converted to morphine; this reaction is performed by the isozyme CYP 2D6 of the P-450 enzymes. The majority of the dose is glucuronidated, and the glucuronide is inactive as an analgesic. The enzyme converting codeine to morphine is subject to genetic polymorphism. Ten percent of Caucasians are poor metabolizers, meaning that they do not convert codeine to morphine, and thus do not derive therapeutic benefit from codeine.

8.1.4.2.4 Methadone

Methadone is a synthetic long-acting opiate agonist. It is well-absorbed orally, and does not undergo significant first-pass metabolism. It has a half-life of approximately 35 h. Methadone is mainly used as a maintenance therapy for heroin addicts, but occasionally is also used to treat chronic pain. There have been reports of deaths associated with methadone treatment, mostly as a result of too rapid dose increases in subjects who may have lost their tolerance.[76]

8.1.4.2.5 Propoxyphene

Propoxyphene is a derivative of methadone, but unlike methadone, it is only a mild analgesic. It has a half-life of about 15 h, but is metabolized to norpropoxyphene, a potentially toxic metabolite with a longer half-life (about 30 h). Propoxyphene has been associated with a high incidence of toxicity, because in addition to being a respiratory depressant, it also acts as a local anesthetic, and has potent membrane-stabilizing effects. Propoxyphene is an ingredient in many compound analgesics, but it is also abused.[77] The main cause of death in propoxyphene intoxication is cardiac abnormalities[78] resulting from its membrane-stabilizing effects. Conduction abnormalities with wide QRS that respond to sodium bicarbonate, and cardiovascular collapse have been described.[79] Seizures have also been associated with propoxyphene intoxication.[78] Unlike respiratory depression, cardiac abnormalities and seizures do not respond to naloxone, since these effects are not mediated through opiate receptors.

8.1.4.2.6 Fentanyl

Fentanyl and related drugs are synthetic opioid agonists structurally related to meperidine. Fentanyl is 50 to 100 times more potent than morphine, and has a half-life of about 4 h. Fentanyl is administered intravenously and transdermally, and is used for surgical anesthesia, especially for cardiac surgery; transdermal fentanyl is used for post-operative analgesia and for chronic pain management.[80] Fentanyl derivatives that are "street-synthesized" belong to a group of "designer drugs", and include alpha-methyl-fentanyl ("China White") and 3-methyl-fentanyl (3MF). Due to a very high potency of fentanyl and related drugs, respiratory depression may occur very rapidly. There are some reports of seizures associated with fentanyl anesthesia[81] and a syndrome of delayed respiratory depression with truncal muscular rigidity occurring after recovering from fentanyl anesthesia.[82]

8.1.4.2.7 Hydromorphone

This is a synthetic derivative of morphine. It is 7 to 10 times more potent compared to morphine. Its half-life is 2.5 h. Hydromorphone intoxication presents with all the signs of typical opiate intoxication.

8.1.4.2.8 Hydrocodone

Hydrocodone is almost identical to codeine. It is converted in the body to hydromorphone. Like other opiates, it can cause respiratory depression and death.

8.1.4.2.9 Oxycodone

This compound is a codeine derivative. Its potency and half-life are comparable to those of morphine. Deaths due to respiratory depression following oxycodone ingestion have been reported.[83]

8.1.4.2.10 Oxymorphone

This compound is 7 to 10 times more potent than morphine. It produces all the signs of classic opiate intoxication.

8.1.4.2.11 Meperidine

Meperidine is a synthetic opiate. Its half-life is about 3 h, but its metabolite, normeperidine, has a half-life of 15 to 34 h, and thus accumulates in plasma with repeated dosing. In patients with renal failure, normeperidine's half-life may be as long as 3 to 4 days. Normeperidine is pharmacologically active, and has both mu-mediated effects as well as other effects not mediated by opioid receptors. Acute intoxication with meperidine presents like morphine intoxication, with respiratory depression, and can be reversed with naloxone. Patients treated with high doses of meperidine, or patients with renal failure may accumulate high levels of normeperidine resulting in a syndrome characterized by irritability, myoclonus, and seizures.[84]

8.1.4.2.12 Pentazocine

Pentazocine is both an opiate agonist and an antagonist. It is an agonist for kappa, delta, and sigma receptors,[85] but antagonizes mu receptors. This renders pentazocine less likely to be abused. Pentazocine produces analgesia in non-tolerant patients, but may produce withdrawal in tolerant individuals. The action on sigma and kappa receptors probably mediates a psychotomimetic reaction.[86] Pentazocine also potentiates the release of catecholamines from adrenal glands, and in high doses can cause elevated blood pressure and tachycardia.[69]

8.1.4.3 Opiate Withdrawal

Abstinence after prolonged use of opiates results in the opiate withdrawal syndrome (Table 8.1.4 b). The severity of the symptoms depends on the duration of use and the daily dose of

Shoshana Zevin and Neal L. Benowitz

the opiates taken before the cessation of use; it is usually more severe in drug abusers than in patients taking opiates for pain relief. Opiate withdrawal can be precipitated by naloxone, and can occur even after a single dose of an opiate. Acute withdrawal after naloxone usually results in nausea and vomiting, profuse sweating, diarrhea, fatigue, and aches and pains. It may last up to 12 h.[87] During unassisted opiate withdrawal, the patient will experience craving for the drug, usually 4 to 6 h after the last administered dose of short-acting opiates such as morphine or heroin (the interval may be 12 to 24 h for methadone). If no drug is administered at this point, there will be a feeling of intense discomfort, with anxiety, agitation, myalgias, sweating, and increased bowel movement. The symptoms will increase over the next 36 to 48 h, and reach their peak at 36 to 72 h, and resolve over the next 7 to 10 days. The withdrawal symptoms are not life-threatening. They can be treated specifically with opiate replacement (usually methadone) in doses that will make the patient comfortable, and/or with supportive treatment including clonidine (a central alpha-agonist with some opiate-like effects), or benzodiazepines for anxiety. For a more complete discussion of opiate and stimulant withdrawl syndromes, see Chapter 7.

8.1.5 SEDATIVE – HYPNOTIC DRUGS

8.1.5.1 Benzodiazepines

Benzodiazepines belong to the category of CNS depressant drugs, and are used in clinical practice as sedative–hypnotic and anxiolytic agents. Some benzodiazepines are also used as antiepileptics and anesthetics. Their principal mechanism of action is potentiation of GABA activity in the brain. GABA is an inhibitory neurotransmitter. GABA binds to the receptor opening chloride channels. The influx of chloride ions hyperpolarizes the cell membrane and prevents its firing. Benzodiazepines bind to a different site on the GABA receptor, potentiating the effects of GABA on chloride flux and enhancing the inhibitory effects of GABA.[88] Prolonged use of benzodiazepines results in tolerance. The possible mechanisms are down-regulation of the GABA receptors, and configurational changes of the receptor-agonist complex resulting in diminished agonist sensitivity.[89,90]

There are many drugs in the benzodiazepine class; all of them share the same pharmaco-dynamic properties. They differ in their pharmacokinetics, and the differences in elimination half-life and in duration of action indicate their different uses (Table 8.1.5.1a). Benzodiaz-epines are classified as very short acting (midazolam), short acting (triazolam), intermediate acting (alprazolam), long acting (diazepam), and very long acting (flurazepam). Most of the benzodiazepines, except oxazepam and lorazepam, that are glucuronidated are metabolized by liver cytochrome P-450 and have active metabolites. Tolerance usually develops to benzodi-azepines effects after continuous use, slowly for long-acting drugs (after about 1 month or more) and more rapidly to short-acting ones. Most users of benzodiazepines obtain the drugs by prescription. Benzodiazepines are abused usually by people who abuse other drugs as well.[91] Because benzodiazepines cause physical and psychological dependence, they are generally recommended for limited periods of time (several weeks) and the doses carefully titrated.[91,92] Side effects of use include daytime drowsiness, aggravation of depression and memory impair-ment, especially anterograde amnesia.[92,93] Benzodiazepines use in the elderly has been associ-ated with falls and hip fractures, due to drowsiness and ataxia. Short-acting benzodiazepines, in particular triazolam, have been associated with withdrawal symptoms during treatment. The symptoms include rebound insomnia and anxiety when the drug is stopped. The use of triazolam as a hypnotic has also been associated with global amnesia[94] and affective and psychiatric disturbances.[95]

Intoxication with benzodiazepines results in CNS depression. In general, they have a very high toxic-therapeutic ratio, and doses 15 to 20 times the therapeutic dose may not cause

Table 8.1.5a Commonly Used Benzodiazepines

Drug	Elimination half-life (hours)
Very short-acting	
Triazolam	1.5-3
Midazolam	2-5
Short-acting	
Alprazolam	10-20
Lorazepam	10-20
Oxazepam	5-10
Temazepam	10-17
Intermediate-acting	
Chlordiazepoxide	10-29
Clonazepam	20-30
Diazepam	30-60
Nitrazepam	15-24
Long-acting	
Clorazepate	50-80
Flurazepam	50-100

serious side effects. With high doses the patients present with lethargy, ataxia, and slurred speech (Table 8.1.5.1b). With very high doses, and especially when there is coingestion of alcohol or barbiturates, coma and respiratory depression may occur. Rapid intravenous injection of diazepam and midazolam may cause respiratory arrest. Respiratory depression has also been reported with short-acting benzodiazepines, particularly triazolam. Withdrawal usually occurs after sudden cessation of benzodiazepines; it is usually associated with a prolonged use of high doses, but also after therapeutic doses when the drug was used for several months. The symptoms include anxiety, panic attacks, insomnia, irritability, agitation, tremor, and anorexia (Table 8.1.5.1b). Withdrawal from high doses of benzodiazepines and from short-acting benzodiazepines is usually more severe, and may result in seizures and psychotic reactions.[96] The time course of the withdrawal syndrome depends on the half-life of specific compound.

8.1.5.2 Barbiturates

Barbiturates are clinically used as sedative-hypnotic drugs, and also for the treatment of epilepsy and induction of anesthesia. They modulate GABA receptor binding sites and potentiate the effects of the inhibitory neurotransmitter GABA. In high concentrations, the barbiturates may enhance the chloride ions flux independently.[97] There are several classes of barbiturates based on their elimination half-life (Table 8.1.5.2). The commonly used antiepileptic agent phenobarbital has a half-life of 80 to 120 h. Serious toxicity may occur when the ingested dose is 5 to 10 times the therapeutic dose. Intoxication with barbiturates results in progressive encephalopathy and coma. Mild intoxication may present as oversedation, slurred speech, ataxia, and nystagmus. Severe intoxication may present with coma, absent reflexes, hypothermia, hypotension, and respiratory depression. Apnea and shock may occur. The time course of intoxication depends on the pharmacokinetics of the specific drug; for phenobarbital, coma may last for 5 to 7 days.Withdrawal symptoms upon cessation of barbiturates occur after prolonged use even of therapeutic doses, though severe withdrawal is seen most commonly in

Shoshana Zevin and Neal L. Benowitz

Table 8.1.5.1b Manifestations of Sedative-Hypnotic Drug Intoxication
and Withdrawal

Intoxication

Mild	Sedation
	Disorientation
	Slurred speech
	Ataxia
	Nystagmus
Moderate	Coma, arousable by painful; stimuli
	Hypoventilation
	Depressed deep tendon reflexes
Severe	Coma, unarousable
	Absent corneal, gag and deep tendon reflexes
	Hypoventilation, apnea
	Hypotension, shock
	Hypothermia
Withdrawal	Anxiety
	Insomnia
	Irritability
	Agitation
	Anorexia
	Tremor
	Seizures (short-acting benzodiazepines and barbiturates)

Table 8.1.5.2 Commonly Used Barbiturates

Drug	Elimination half-life (hours)	Duration of effect (hours)
Ultrashort-acting		
Thiopental	6-46	< 0.5
Methohexital	1-2	< 0.5
Short-acting		
Pentobarbital	15-48	> 3-4
Secobarbital	15-40	> 3-4
Intermediate-acting		
Amobarbital	8-42	> 4-6
Aprobarbital	14-34	> 4-6
Butabarbital	32-42	> 4-6
Long-acting		
Phenobarbital	80-120	> 6-12
Mephobarbital	11-67	>6-12

Table 8.1.5.3 Manifestations of Solvent Intoxication
and Abuse

Mild	Euphoria
	Disinhibition
	Dizziness
	Slurred speech
	Lack of coordination
	Sneezing and coughing
Moderate	Lethargy, stupor
	Hallucinations
	Nausea, vomiting
	Diarrhea
	Ataxia
	Tremors
	Myalgias
	Paresthesias
Severe	Coma
	Seizures
Chronic	Cerebellar syndrome: ataxia, nystagmus, tremor (toluene)
	Parkinsonism (toluene)
	Peripheral neuropathy: symmetrical, motor, mainly involving hands and feet (n-hexane, naphtha)

polydrug abusers. The presentation is similar to that of benzodiazepines withdrawal, but there may be a greater risk of seizures with barbiturates withdrawal (Table 8.1.5.1b).

8.1.5.3 Solvents

Solvent abuse has been a problem for many years, particularly among adolescents. The most frequently abused agents are glues, paint thinners, nail lacquer removers, lighter fluids, cleaning solutions, aerosols, and gasoline. The most frequently encountered chemical is toluene, which is an ingredient in glues, paint thinners, and some petroleum products. Other chemicals are acetone in nail lacquer remover, naphtha, fluorinated hydrocarbons, trichloroethylene, and others. The method of inhalation is breathing the substance from a plastic bag placed directly over the nose or the mouth, inhaling directly from the container or from impregnated rags and spraying aerosols directly into the mouth. All the solvents are lipid-soluble, and thus easily cross blood- brain barrier and cell membranes. They typically produce similar effects.

The acute effects of solvent inhalation begin within minutes, and last 15 to 45 min after inhalation. Habitual abusers of solvents may have a rash around the nose and mouth from inhaling, and may have the odor of solvent on their breath.[98] The typical effects are feelings of euphoria, disinhibition, and dizziness (Table 8.1.5.3). There may also be slurred speech, lack of coordination, and impaired judgment.[98,99] More severe intoxication may result in nausea and vomiting, diarrhea, tremor, ataxia, paresthesia, diffuse pains, and hallucinations. Seizures and coma may ensue.[98,99] The acute intoxication usually resolves quickly. Toluene abuse has been associated with renal tubular acidosis and severe hypokalemia. There are deaths associated with acute solvent abuse, about half of them are the result of accidents such as asphyxiation from the plastic bag. Almost all the rest are thought to be from cardiac causes, including ventricular fibrillation and pulmonary edema.[99]

Persistent toxic effects have been reported in chronic frequent abusers of volatile substances (Table 8.1.5.3). These include cerebellar syndrome, parkinsonism, and peripheral neuropathy. Cerebellar syndrome is associated mainly with toluene abuse and presents with nystagmus, ataxia, and tremor. It may be reversible with continued abstinence.[98] There was a report of parkinsonism in a young patient who chronically abused lacquer thinner; the symptoms persisted for more than 3 months after cessation of use.[100] Peripheral neuropathy, predominantly motor and symmetrical, is associated with n-hexane and naphtha. Symptoms usually start weeks after the first exposure, and the deterioration may continue for several months after the cessation of solvents. There are reports of hepatitis and liver failure, renal failure, and aplastic anemia associated with chronic solvent abuse.[101]

ACKNOWLEDGMENT

The authors acknowledge the support of NIH grant DA01696.

REFERENCES

1. Gawin, F. H. & Ellinwood, E. H., Jr. (1988) Cocaine and other stimulants. Actions, abuse, and treatment, *N Engl J Med*, 318, pp. 1173-82.
2. Lowenstein, D. H., Massa, S. M., Rowbotham, M. C. *et al.* (1987) Acute neurologic and psychiatric complications associated with cocaine abuse, *Am J Med*, 83, pp. 841-6.
3. Mueller, P. D., Benowitz, N. L. & Olson, K. R. (1990) Cocaine, *Emergency Medicine Clinics of North America*, 8, pp. 481-93.
4. Rowbotham, M. C. (1988) Neurologic aspects of cocaine abuse [clinical conference], *West J Med*, 149, pp. 442-8.
5. Tardiff, K., Gross, E., Wu, J., Stajic, M. & Millman, R. (1989) Analysis of cocaine-positive fatalities, *J Forensic Sci*, 34, pp. 53-63.
6. Sanchez-Ramos, J. R. (1993) Psychostimulants, *Neurol Clin*, 11, pp. 535-53.
7. Naveen, R. A. (1988) Brain Anscess: A complication of cocaine inhalation, *NY State J Med*, 88, pp. 548-50.
8. Benowitz, N. L. (1993) Clinical pharmacology and toxicology of cocaine [published erratum appears in Pharmacol Toxicol 1993 Jun;72(6):343], *Pharmacol Toxicol*, 72, pp. 3-12.
9. Nademanee, K. (1992) Cardiovascular effects and toxicities of cocaine, *J Addict Dis*, 11, pp. 71-82.
10. Wetli, C. V., Mash, D. & Karch, S. B. (1996) Cocaine-associated agitated delirium and the neuroleptic malignant syndrome, *Am J Emerg Med*, 14, pp. 425-8.
11. Mirchandani, H. G., Rorke, L. B., Sekula-Perlman, A. & Hood, I. C. (1994) Cocaine- induced agitated delirium, forceful struggle, and minor head injury. A further definition of sudden death during restraint, *Am J Forensic Med Pathol*, 15, pp. 95-9.
12. Marzuk, P. M., Tardiff, K., Leon, A. C. *et al.* (1995) Fatal injuries after cocaine use as a leading cause of death among young adults in New York City, *N Engl J Med*, 332, pp. 1753-7.
13. Kissner, D. G., Lawrence, W. D., Selis, J. E. & Flint, A. (1987) Crack lung: pulmonary disease caused by cocaine abuse, *Am Rev Respir Dis*, 136, pp. 1250-2.
14. Lago, J. A. & Kosten, T. R. (1994) Stimulant withdrawal, *Addiction*, 89, pp. 1477-81.
15. Yousef, G., Huq, Z. & Lambert, T. (1995) Khat chewing as a cause of psychosis, *Br J Hosp Med*, 54, pp. 322-6.

16. Battig, K. (1993) Acute and chronic cardiovascular and behavioural effects of caffeine, aspirin and ephedrine, *Int J Obes Relat Metab Disor*d, 17 Suppl 1, pp. S61-4.

17. Bruno, A., Nolte, K. B. & Chapin, J. (1993) Stroke associated with ephedrine use, *Neurology*, 43, pp. 1313-6.

18. Wooten, M. R., Khangure, M. S. & Murphy, M. J. (1983) Intracerebral hemorrhage and vasculitis related to ephedrine abuse, *Ann Neurol*, 13, pp. 337-40.

19. MMWR (1996) Adverse events associated with ephedrine-containing products—Texas, December 1993-September 1995, *MMWR Morb Mortal Wkly Re*p, 45, pp. 689-93.

20. Luqman, W. & Danowski, T. S. (1976) The use of khat (Catha edulis) in Yemen. Social and medical observations, *Annals of Internal Medicin*e, 85, pp. 246-249.

21. Pantelis, C., Hindler, C. G. & Taylor, J. C. (1989) Use and abuse of khat (Catha edulis): a review of the distribution, pharmacology, side effects and a description of psychosis attributed to khat chewing, *Psychol Me*d, 19, pp. 657-68.

22. Derlet, R. W., Rice, P., Horowitz, B. Z. & Lord, R. V. (1989) Amphetamine toxicity: experience with 127 cases, *J Emerg Me*d, 7, pp. 157-61.

23. Citron, P. B., Halpern, M., McCarron, M. *et al.* (1970) Necrotizing angiitis associated with drug abuse, *New England Journal of Medicin*e, 283, pp. 1003-1011.

24. Shaw, H. E., Jr., Lawson, J. G. & Stulting, R. D. (1985) Amaurosis fugax and retinal vasculitis associated with methamphetamine inhalation, *J Clin Neuroophthalmo*l, 5, pp. 169-76.

25. Matick, H., Anderson, D. & Brumlik, J. (1983) Cerebral vasculitis associated with oral amphetamine overdose, *Arch Neuro*l, 40, pp. 253-4.

26. Smith, H. J., Roche, A. H., Jausch, M. F. & Herdson, P. B. (1976) Cardiomyopathy associated with amphetamine administration, *Am Heart* J, 91, pp. 792-7.

27. Callaway, C. W. & Clark, R. F. (1994) Hyperthermia in psychostimulant overdose, *Ann Emerg Me*d, 24, pp. 68-76.

28. Buchanan, J. F. & Brown, C. R. (1988) 'Designer drugs'. A problem in clinical toxicology, *Med Toxicol Adverse Drug Ex*p, 3, pp. 1-17.

29. Rothrock, J. F., Rubenstein, R. & Lyden, P. D. (1988) Ischemic stroke associated with methamphetamine inhalation, *Neurology*, 38, pp. 589-92.

30. Pentel, P. (1984) Toxicity of over-the-counter stimulants, *Jam*a, 252, pp. 1898-903.

31. Kikta, D. G., Devereaux, M. W. & Chandar, K. (1985) Intracranial hemorrhages due to phenylpropanolamine, *Strok*e, 16, pp. 510-2.

32. Edwards, M., Russo, L. & Harwood-Nuss, A. (1987) Cerebral infarction with a single oral dose of phenylpropanolamine, *Am J Emerg Me*d, 5, pp. 163-4.

33. Mueller, S. M. (1983) Neurologic complications of phenylpropanolamine use, *Neurology*, 33, pp. 650-2.

34. Lake, C. R., Masson, E. B. & Quirk, R. S. (1988) Psychiatric side effects attributed to phenylpropanolamine, *Pharmacopsychiatry*, 21, pp. 171-81.

35. Glick, R., Hoying, J., Cerullo, L. & Perlman, S. (1987) Phenylpropanolamine: an over-the-counter drug causing central nervous system vasculitis and intracerebral hemorrhage. Case report and review, *Neurosurgery*, 20, pp. 969-74.

36. Hollister, L. E. & Hartman, A. M. (1962) Mescaline, lysergic acid diethylamide and psilocybin: comparison of clinical syndromes, effects on color perception and biochemical measures, *Comprehensive Psychiatry*, 3, pp. 235-241.

37. Leikin, J. B., Krantz, A. J., Zell-Kanter, M., Barkin, R. L. & Hryhorczuk, D. O. (1989) Clinical features and management of intoxication due to hallucinogenic drugs, *Med Toxicol Adverse Drug Ex*p, 4, pp. 324-50.

38. Kapadia, G. J. & Fayez, M. B. (1970) Peyote constituents: chemistry, biogenesis, and biological effects, *J Pharm Sc*i, 59, pp. 1699-727.

39. Mack, R. B. (1986) Marching to a different cactus: peyote (mescaline) intoxication, *N C Med* J, 47, pp. 137-8.

40. Shulgin, A. T. (1976) Profiles of psychedelic drugs: TMA-2, *Journal of Psychedelic Drug*s, 8, pp. 169.

41. Shulgin, A. T. (1977) Profiles of psychedelic drugs: STP, *Journal of Psychedelic Drug*s, 9, pp. 171-172.

Shoshana Zevin and Neal L. Benowitz

42. Shulgin, A. (1981) Profiles of psychedelic drugs: 10. DOB, *J Psychoactive Drugs*, 13, pp. 99.
43. Buhrich, N., Morris, G. & Cook, G. (1983) Bromo-DMA: the Australasian hallucinogen?, *Aust N Z J Psychiatry*, 17, pp. 275-9.
44. Simpson, D. L. & Rumack, B. H. (1981) Methylenedioxyamphetamine. Clinical description of overdose, death, and review of pharmacology, *Arch Intern Med*, 141, pp. 1507-9.
45. Steele, T. D., McCann, U. D. & Ricaurte, G. A. (1994) 3,4-Methylenedioxymethamphetamine (MDMA, "Ecstasy"): pharmacology and toxicology in animals and humans, *Addiction*, 89, pp. 539-51.
46. McCann, U. D. & Ricaurte, G. A. (1992) MDMA ("ecstasy") and panic disorder: induction by a single dose, *Biol Psychiatry*, 32, pp. 950-3.
47. McCann, U. D., Slate, S. O. & Ricaurte, G. A. (1996) Adverse reactions with 3,4-methylenedioxymethamphetamine (MDMA; "Ecstasy"), *Drug Safety*, 15, pp. 107-115.
48. McCann, U. D., Ridenour, A., Shaham, Y. & Ricaurte, G. A. (1994) Serotonin neurotoxicity after (+/-)3,4-methylenedioxymethamphetamine (MDMA; "Ecstasy"): a controlled study in humans, *Neuropsychopharmacology*, 10, pp. 129-38.
49. Henry, J. A., Jeffreys, K. J. & Dawling, S. (1992) Toxicity and deaths from 3,4-methylenedioxymethamphetamine ("ecstasy") [see comments], *Lancet*, 340, pp. 384-7.
50. Milroy, C. M., Clark, J. C. & Forrest, A. R. (1996) Pathology of deaths associated with "ecstasy" and "eve" misuse, *J Clin Pathol*, 49, pp. 149-53.
51. Maxwell, D. L., Polkey, M. I. & Henry, J. A. (1993) Hyponatraemia and catatonic stupor after taking "ecstasy" [see comments], *Bmj*, 307, pp. 1399.
52. Satchell, S. C. & Connaughton, M. (1994) Inappropriate antidiuretic hormone secretion and extreme rises in serum creatinine kinase following MDMA ingestion, *Br J Hosp Med*, 51, pp. 495.
53. Schwartz, R. H. (1995) LSD. Its rise, fall, and renewed popularity among high school students, *Pediatr Clin North Am*, 42, pp. 403-13.
54. Jacobs, B. L. (1987) How hallucinogenic drugs work, *American Scientist*, 75, pp. 386-392.
55. Abraham, H. D. & Aldridge, A. M. (1993) Adverse consequences of lysergic acid diethylamide [see comments], *Addiction*, 88, pp. 1327-34.
56. Contreras, P. C., Monahan, J. B., Lanthorn, T. H. *et al.* (1987) Phencyclidine. Physiological actions, interactions with excitatory amino acids and endogenous ligands, *Mol Neurobiol*, 1, pp. 191-211.
57. Sonders, M. S., Keana, J. F. & Weber, E. (1988) Phencyclidine and psychotomimetic sigma opiates: recent insights into their biochemical and physiological sites of action, *Trends Neurosci*, 11, pp. 37-40.
58. Brust, J. C. (1993) Other agents. Phencyclidine, marijuana, hallucinogens, inhalants, and anticholinergics, *Neurol Clin*, 11, pp. 555-61.
59. McCarron, M. M., Schulze, B. W., Thompson, G. A., Conder, M. C. & Goetz, W. A. (1981) Acute phencyclidine intoxication: clinical patterns, complications, and treatment, *Ann Emerg Med*, 10, pp. 290-7.
60. Aniline, O. & Pitts, F. N., Jr. (1982) Phencyclidine (PCP): a review and perspectives, *Crit Rev Toxicol*, 10, pp. 145-77.
61. Jones, R. T. (1984) Marijuana. Health and treatment issues, *Psychiatr Clin North Am*, 7, pp. 703-12.
62. Farber, S. J. & Huertas, V. E. (1976) Intravenously injected marijuana syndrome, *Arch Int Med*, 136, pp. 337-339.
63. Hollister, L. E. (1986) Health aspects of cannabis, *Pharmacol Rev*, 38, pp. 1-20.
64. Taylor, F. M. d. (1988) Marijuana as a potential respiratory tract carcinogen: a retrospective analysis of a community hospital population, *South Med J*, 81, pp. 1213-6.
65. Wu, T. C., Tashkin, D. P., Djahed, B. & Rose, J. E. (1988) Pulmonary hazards of smoking marijuana as compared with tobacco, *N Engl J Med*, 318, pp. 347-51.
66. Feldman, A. L., Sullivan, J. T., Passero, M. A. & Lewis, D. C. (1993) Pneumothorax in polysubstance-abusing marijuana and tobacco smokers: three cases, *J Subst Abuse*, 5, pp. 183-6.
67. Foley, K. M. (1993) Opioids, *Neurol Clin*, 11, pp. 503-22.

68. Benowitz, N. L. (1992) Central nervous system manifestations of toxic disorders, in: Arieff, A. & Griggs, R. (Eds.) *Neurologic manifastations of systems disorders*, pp. 409-436 (Boston-Toronto-London, Little Brown and Company).

69. Karch, S. B. (1993) *The pathology of drug abuse* (Boca Raton -Ann Arbor -London -Tokyo, CRC Press).

70. Ling, G. S., Spiegel, K., Lockhart, S. H. & Pasternak, G. W. (1985) Separation of opioid analgesia from respiratory depression: evidence for different receptor mechanisms, *J Pharmacol Exp Ther*, 232, pp. 149-55.

71. Ballantyne, J. C., Loach, A. B. & Carr, D. B. (1988) Itching after epidural and spinal opiates, *Pain*, 33, pp. 149-60.

72. Dray, A. (1988) Epidural opiates and urinary retention: new models provide new insights [editorial], *Anesthesiology*, 68, pp. 323-4.

73. Chan, P., Lin, T. H., Luo, J. P. & Deng, J. F. (1995) Acute heroin intoxication with complications of acute pulmonary edema, acute renal failure, rhabdomyolysis and lumbosacral plexitis: a case report, *Chung Hua I Hsueh Tsa Chih (Taipei)*, 55, pp. 397-400.

74. Richter, R. W., Challenor, Y. B., Pearson, J. *et al.* (1971) Acute myoglobinuria associated with heroin addiction, *Jama*, 216, pp. 1172-6.

75. Dubrow, A., Mittman, N., Ghali, V. & Flamenbaum, W. (1985) The changing spectrum of heroin-associated nephropathy, *Am J Kidney Dis*, 5, pp. 36-41.

76. Drummer, O. H., Opeskin, K., Syrjanen, M. & Cordner, S. M. (1992) Methadone toxicity causing death in ten subjects starting on a methadone maintenance program, *Am J Forensic Med Pathol*, 13, pp. 346-50.

77. Ng, B. & Alvear, M. (1993) Dextropropoxyphene addiction—a drug of primary abuse, *Am J Drug Alcohol Abuse*, 19, pp. 153-8.

78. Lawson, A. A. & Northridge, D. B. (1987) Dextropropoxyphene overdose. Epidemiology, clinical presentation and management, *Med Toxicol Adverse Drug Exp*, 2, pp. 430-44.

79. Stork, C. M., Redd, J. T., Fine, K. & Hoffman, R. S. (1995) Propoxyphene-induced wide QRS complex dysrhythmia responsive to sodium bicarbonate—a case report, *J Toxicol Clin Toxicol*, 33, pp. 179-83.

80. Yee, L. Y. & Lopez, J. R. (1992) Transdermal fentanyl [see comments], *Ann Pharmacother*, 26, pp. 1393-9.

81. Sprung, J. & Schedewie, H. K. (1992) Apparent focal motor seizure with a jacksonian march induced by fentanyl: a case report and review of the literature, *J Clin Anesth*, 4, pp. 139-43.

82. Caspi, J., Klausner, J. M., Safadi, T. *et al.* (1988) Delayed respiratory depression following fentanyl anesthesia for cardiac surgery, *Crit Care Med*, 16, pp. 238-40.

83. Drummer, O. H., Syrjanen, M. L., Phelan, M. & Cordner, S. M. (1994) A study of deaths involving oxycodone, *J Forensic Sci*, 39, pp. 1069-75.

84. Stock, S. L., Catalano, G. & Catalano, M. C. (1996) Meperidine associated mental status changes in a patient with chronic renal failure, *J Fla Med Assoc*, 83, pp. 315-9.

85. Zabetian, C. P., Staley, J. K., Flynn, D. D. & Mash, D. C. (1994) [3H]-(+)-pentazocine binding to sigma recognition sites in human cerebellum, *Life Sci*, 55, pp. L389-95.

86. Pfeiffer, A., Brantl, V., Herz, A. & Emrich, H. M. (1986) Psychotomimesis mediated by kappa opiate receptors, Science, 233, pp. 774-6.

87. Farrell, M. (1994) Opiate withdrawal, Addiction, 89, pp. 1471-5.

88. Tallman, J. F., Gallager, D. W., Mallorga, P. et al. (1980) Studies on benzodiazepine receptors, Adv Biochem Psychopharmacol, 21, pp. 277-83.

89. Lader, M. (1994) Biological processes in benzodiazepine dependence, Addiction, 89, pp. 1413-8.

90. Miller, L. G., Greenblatt, D. J., Roy, R. B., Summer, W. R. & Shader, R. I. (1988) Chronic benzodiazepine administration. II. Discontinuation syndrome is associated with upregulation of gamma-aminobutyric acidA receptor complex binding and function, J Pharmacol Exp Ther, 246, pp. 177-82.

91. Woods, J. H. & Winger, G. (1995) Current benzodiazepine issues, Psychopharmacology (Berl), 118, pp. 107-15; discussion 118, 120-1.

Shoshana Zevin and Neal L. Benowitz

92. Ashton, H. (1994) Guidelines for the rational use of benzodiazepines. When and what to use, Drugs, 48, pp. 25-40.
93. Vgontzas, A. N., Kales, A. & Bixler, E. O. (1995) Benzodiazepine side effects: role of pharmacokinetics and pharmacodynamics, Pharmacology, 51, pp. 205-23.
94. Morris, H. H. d. & Estes, M. L. (1987) Traveler's amnesia. Transient global amnesia secondary to triazolam, Jama, 258, pp. 945-6.
95. Wysowski, D. K., Baum, C., Ferguson, W. J. et al. (1996) Sedative-hypnotic drugs and the risk of hip fracture, J Clin Epidemiol, 49, pp. 111-3.
96. Petursson, H. (1994) The benzodiazepine withdrawal syndrome, Addiction, 89, pp. 1455-9.
97. Ito, T., Suzuki, T., Wellman, S. E. & Ho, I. K. (1996) Pharmacology of barbiturate tolerance/dependence: GABAA receptors and molecular aspects, Life Sci, 59, pp. 169-95.
98. Ron, M. A. (1986) Volatile substance abuse: a review of possible long-term neurological, intellectual and psychiatric sequelae, Br J Psychiatry, 148, pp. 235-46.
99. al-Alousi, L. M. (1989) Pathology of volatile substance abuse: a case report and a literature review, Med Sci Law, 29, pp. 189-208.
100. Uitti, R. J., Snow, B. J., Shinotoh, H. et al. (1994) Parkinsonism induced by solvent abuse, Ann Neurol, 35, pp. 616-9.
101. Schuckit, M. A. (1989) Drug and alcohol abuse (New York and London, Plenum Medical Book Company).
102. Olson, K. R. (1994) Barbiturates, in: Olson, K. R. (Ed.) Poisoning and drug overdose, pp. 93-95 (Norwalk, Appleton & Lange).

8.2 EMERGENCY MANAGEMENT OF DRUG ABUSE-RELATED DISORDERS

BRETT A. ROTH, M.D.

POSTDOCTORAL FELLOW, DIVISION OF CLINICAL PHARMACOLOGY AND TOXICOLOGY, UNIVERSITY OF CALIFORNIA, SAN FRANCISCO, CALIFORNIA

NEAL L. BENOWITZ, M.D.

PROFESSOR OF MEDICINE, CHIEF, DIVISION OF CLINICAL PHARMACOLOGY AND EXPERIMENTAL THERAPEUTICS, UNIVERSITY OF CALIFORNIA, SAN FRANCISCO, CALIFORNIA

KENT R. OLSON, M.D.

CLINICAL PROFESSOR OF MEDICINE, PEDIATRICS, AND PHARMACY, UCSF MEDICAL DIRECTOR, CALIFORNIA POISON CONTROL SYSTEM, SAN FRANCISCO GENERAL HOSPITAL, SAN FRANCISCO, CALIFORNIA

The management of complications from drug abuse demands a variety of skills from airway management to control of seizures and shock. Several reviews have addressed the issues of general resuscitation[1-4] and toxidromes.[5,6] The purpose of this chapter is to present a series of management strategies for the emergency physician and/or other clinical personnel caring for patients with acute complications from drug abuse. Immediate interventions (e.g., resuscitation and stabilization), secondary interventions (e.g., emergency care after the patient is stable), as well as diagnostic work up (e.g., laboratory data, imaging), and disposition of the patient will be discussed. This section proposes a variety of treatment approaches based on a review of the pertinent literature and clinical experience. A general treatment approach based on symptom complex (i.e., seizures, coma, hyperthermia) is presented because initial management decisions frequently have to be made without the benefit of a reliable history. This is followed by a brief review of each particular drug of abuse (i.e., psychostimulants, opiates, hallucinogens; Tables 8.2A-D).

It should be emphasized that the adverse reaction to a drug may depend on the unique characteristics of an individual (i.e., presence of cardiovascular disease) as well as the type of drug abused. These protocols serve as guidelines only and an individualized approach to management should be made whenever possible.

8.2.1 COMA, STUPOR, AND LETHARGY

8.2.1.1 General Comments

In the setting of drug overdose, coma usually reflects global depression of the brain's cerebral cortex. This can be the result of a direct effect of the drug on specific neurotransmitters or receptors, or an indirect process such as trauma or asphyxia. Treatment deals largely with maintaining a functional airway, the administration of potential antidotes, and evaluation for underlying medical conditions. The following section describes the appropriate use of antidotes and the approach to the patient with a decreased level of consciousness from drug abuse.

8.2.1.2 Level vs. Content of Consciousness

It is often useful to distinguish between the level and the content of consciousness. Alertness and wakefulness refer to the level of consciousness; awareness is a reflection of the content of consciousness.[7] In referring to coma, stupor, and lethargy here, we address the level of consciousness as it applies to the drug-abusing patient along a clinical spectrum, with deep coma on one end, stupor in·the middle, and lethargy representing a mildly decreased level of consciousness. Agitation, delirium, and psychosis are addressed in a subsequent section with a greater focus on content of consciousness, i.e., presence or absence of hallucinations, paranoia, severe depression, etc.

8.2.1.3 Attributes of a Good Antidote

The ideal antidote should be safe, effective, rapidly acting, and easy to administer. It should also have low abuse potential, and act as long as the intoxicating drug. The following standard antidotes are of potentially great benefit and little harm in all patients.

8.2.1.3.1 Thiamine

Thiamine is an important cofactor for several metabolic enzymes which are vital for the metabolism of carbohydrates and for the proper function of the pentose-phosphate pathway.[8] When thiamine is absent or deficient Wernicke's encephalopathy, classically described as a triad of oculomotor abnormalities, ataxia, and global confusion, may result. Although Wernicke's is rare, empiric treatment for this disease is safe,[9] inexpensive (wholesale price of 100 mg of thiamine is approximately one dollar), and cost-effective.[10]

8.2.1.3.2 Dextrose

Hypoglycemia is a common cause of coma or stupor and should be assessed or treated empirically in all patients with deceased level of consciousness. Concerns about 50% dextrose causing an increase in infarct size and mortality in stroke,[11-14] as well as increasing serum hypertonicity in hyperosmolar patients have been raised when arguing the benefits of routine administration of 50% dextrose. Animal models of stroke[12] that showed worse outcomes associated with hyperglycemic subjects used large doses of dextrose (approximately 2mg/kg) as opposed to the 0.3 gm/kg (25 gm in a 70-kg adult) routinely given as part of the coma cocktail. Also, one ampule of 50% dextrose in water should only raise the serum glucose level of a 70-kg patient by about 60 mg/dL (0.3 mOsm) if it distributes into total body water prior to any elimination or metabolism.[15]

8.2.1.3.3 Naloxone

> The surface of the body may be stimulated by whipping, . . . the patient should be made to walk around for 6-8 hours[16]
>
> A 19-century method for treating opiate overdose: Shoemaker, 1896

Fortunately, the use of modern antidotes such as naloxone can provide a more effective and less abusive reversal of opiate-induced narcosis. In addition to reversing respiratory depression and eliminating the need for airway interventions, naloxone may assist in the diagnosis of opiate overdose and eliminate the need for diagnostic studies such as lumbar puncture and computed tomography (CT) scanning. Despite its advances over 19th-century treatments for narcotic overdose, naloxone may not always be the best approach to management. The risk of "unmasking" or exposing the effects of dangerous coingestions such as cocaine or PCP;[17] and of precipitating opiate withdrawal must be considered.

Naloxone's main effects include the reversal of coma and respiratory depression induced by exogenous opiates but it also reverses miosis, analgesia, bradycardia, and gastrointestinal stasis. Presumably related to the reversal of the effects of endogenous opioid peptides, such as endorphins and enkephalins, naloxone has also been reported to have nonspecific benefit (e.g., reversing properties) for the treatment of ethanol, clonidine, captopril, and valproic acid.[18-21] These "nonspecific" responses are usually not as complete as a true reversal of opiate-induced coma by naloxone.

Some case reports have raised concerns about the safety of naloxone. Pulmonary edema,[22-27] hypertension,[28-30] seizures,[31] arrhythmias,[30,32] and cardiac arrest[33] have been reported following naloxone administration. In addition, reversing the sedating effects of a drug like heroin may produce acute withdrawal symptoms, which, although not life threatening, can cause the patient to become agitated, demanding, or even violent.[34] Considering the great number of patients who have received large doses of naloxone as part of controlled trials for shock,[35-38] stroke,[39-42] and spinal cord injuries,[43-45] as part of healthy volunteer studies,[46,47] and for overdose management[48,49] all without significant complications, the use of naloxone appears relatively safe.[15]

Opioid withdrawal symptoms commonly occur in addicted patients given naloxone. While withdrawal symptoms are treatable, the best approach is avoidance. Withdrawal symptoms may be avoided either by (1) withholding opioid antagonists from known drug addicts and supporting the airway with traditional methods (e.g., endotracheal intubation) or (2) by titrating the dose of naloxone slowly such that enough antidote is given to arouse the patient but not to precipitate withdrawal. The latter can be done by administering small doses (0.2 to 0.4 mg) intravenously in a repetitive manner. While conjunctival[50] and nasal[51] testing for opioid addiction have been described, these tests are impractical in the patient with altered mental status in whom immediate action is necessary.

8.2.1.3.4 Nalmefene

Nalmefene (t 1/2 =8 to 9 hours) is a methylene analog of naltrexone which, like naloxone, is a pure opioid antagonist. It was developed to address concerns about the short duration of action of naloxone (~60 min). Studies have proven it to be as safe and effective with a duration of action at least twice as long as naloxone.[52] Other reports suggest a duration of action of up to four hours.[52-54] Four hours is still not long enough to safely manage patients who have overdosed on long lasting opiates such as methadone (t $^1/_2$ up to 48 h) or propoxyphene (t 1/2 of active metabolite up to 36 h), or in those patients with delayed absorption. The use of nalmefene may potentially be advantageous due to: (1) less risk of recurrent respiratory depression in the patient who leaves the emergency department against medical advise, (2) fewer doses of antagonist needed, cutting down on nursing time, and (3) fewer complications resulting from fluctuations in levels of consciousness (e.g., sedation, aspiration, occult respiratory insufficiency).[55] The dose is 0.25 to 1.0 mg IVP, with the lower dose recommended to avoid opiate withdrawal. The disadvantage of nalmefene is its cost (average wholesale price of nalmefene is \$6.50/0.25 mg vs. \$0.30 for 0.4 mg of naloxone).

8.2.1.3.5 Flumazenil

Flumazenil is a highly selective competitive inhibitor of benzodiazepines at the GABA/benzodiazepine-receptor complex.[56] Like naloxone it is a pure antagonist lacking agonist properties or abuse potential. It has been shown to be safe and effective for the reversal of benzodiazepine-induced sedation in volunteer studies[57] and in patients undergoing short procedures such as endoscopy.[58-62]

There has been some debate about the role of flumazenil in the treatment of patients presenting with an acute drug overdose. Although initially recommended with caution for this population,[63,64] recent advice would be to administer it only when there is a reliable history of benzodiazepine ingestion and the likelihood of a significant proconvulsant or proarrhythmic coingestion or benzodiazepine dependency is limited. Adverse effects including precipitation of benzodiazepine withdrawal,[65,66] seizures,[67-70] arrhythmias,[71,72] and even death[73,74] have occurred.

In a review of 43 cases of seizure activity associated with flumazenil administration, 42% of the patients had ingested overdoses of cyclic antidepressants.[67] In addition to patients with concurrent cyclic antidepressant poisoning, high-risk populations include patients who have been receiving benzodiazepines for a seizure disorder or an acute convulsive episode, patients with concurrent major sedative-hypnotic drug withdrawal, patients who have recently been treated with repeated doses of parenteral benzodiazepines, and overdose patients with myoclonic jerking or seizure activity before flumazenil administration.[67]

To minimize the likelihood of a seizure, it is recommended that flumazenil not be administered to patients who have used benzodiazepines for the treatment of seizure disorders or to patients who have ingested drugs that place them at risk for the development of seizures[67] (e.g., cyclic antidepressants, cocaine, amphetamines, diphenhydramine, lithium, methylxanthines, isoniazid, propoxyphene, buproprion HCl, etc.). As with naloxone, flumazenil may also uncover the effects of a more serious intoxication such as cocaine making the patient unmanageable. Since benzodiazepine overdoses are associated with only rare mortality[75] and only mild morbidity (the major complication being aspiration pneumonia)[76] a conservative approach with supportive airway maneuvers (e.g., endotracheal intubation) seems safest.

Despite concerns over side effects, the use of flumazenil in patients with acute overdose is justified under certain circumstances. When there is a reliable history of a single drug ingestion supported by clinical manifestations consistent with benzodiazepine intoxication, and the likelihood of a significant proconvulsant or proarrhythmic coingestion or benzodiazepine dependency is limited, reversal of sedation may be warranted.[15] Errors can be avoided by obtaining a thorough history and by performing a thorough physical examination as well as a screening electrocardiogram to exclude the possibility of significant cyclic antidepressant intoxication; correction of hypoxia, hypotension, acidosis, and arrhythmias; and then by administering the agent slowly.

Brett A. Roth et al.

Greenblatt[76] showed that of 99 cases in which patients overdosed on benzodiazepines only 12 were known to ingest benzodiazepines alone. Given the high incidence of coingestions in the drug abusing population, the risk for unmasking proconvulsants such as cocaine or amphetamine must be considered high.

8.2.1.4 Stepwise Approach to Management

8.2.1.4.1 Immediate Interventions

1. **Airway, breathing, circulation:** Maintain the airway and assist ventilation if necessary. Administer supplemental oxygen. Treat hypotension, and resuscitate as per previous reviews.[2,77-80]

  2. **Thiamine:** Administer thiamine, 100 mg IVP over 2 min to all the following patients:

  a. patients with altered mental status if the patient has signs or symptoms of Wernicke's encephalopathy
  b. patients who are malnourished[81]
  c. patients with a history of alcoholism[8]
  d. patients with prolonged history of vomiting[82]
  e. patients who are chronically ill[83]

  Comment: There is no need to withhold hypertonic dextrose (D50, D25) until thiamine administration because thiamine uptake into cells is slower than the entry of dextrose into cells.[84] Previous reports describing adverse reactions to IV thiamine[85] have recently been disputed. In a review by Wrenn et al., the incidence of adverse reactions to IV thiamine (n=989) was 1.1% and consisted of transient local irritation in all patients except one who developed generalized puritis.[9] Thiamine may also be administered intramuscularly (IM) or by mouth (po).

  3. **Dextrose**
  Bedside fingerstick glucose measurement: Perform rapid bedside testing in all patients. If hypoglycemia is detected, then the patient should receive hypertonic dextrose (25 gm of 50% hypertonic dextrose solution IVP).

  Comment: This approach avoids giving dextrose solution to patients who do not need it (eliminating concerns that hyperglycemia impairs cerebral resuscitation) and detects the vast majority of hypoglycemic patients. Relying on physical signs and symptoms such as tachycardia and diaphoresis in combination with a history of diabetes mellitus is an unreliable way to predict hypoglycemia, missing up to 25% of hypoglycemic patients.[86]

  Borderline rapid assay results: In any patient with a borderline rapid assay results (60 to 100 mg/dL) a decision on whether or not to treat should be based on the clinical suspicion of hypoglycemia and a repeat rapid assay. Alternatively, simply treat all patients with borderline blood sugar results.

  Comment: Rapid reagent assays for blood glucose may, at times, be inaccurate. Failure to detect hypoglycemia has been described in 6 to 8% of patients tested in the prehospital setting[87,88] but results are generally more accurate inside the hospital. False-negative results have also been reported in neonatal populations[89] and in patients with severe anemia.[90] Since most errors occur in patients with borderline glucose readings (60 to 100 mg/dL),[15] the recommendation to treat borderline glucose values is made. This also makes sense in light of recent reports that describe individual variability in response to borderline hypoglycemia,[91] e.g., patients with poorly controlled diabetes mellitus may experience clinical symptoms of hypoglycemia at greater glucose concentrations than nondiabetics.

  Empiric treatment: In patients where rapid bedside testing for serum glucose is not available, administer 25 g of 50% hypertonic dextrose solution IVP after collecting a specimen of blood for glucose analysis at a later time.

4. **Naloxone/ Nalmefene:**

a. **Restraint:** Consider restraining and disrobing the patient prior to administration.

b. **Antidote:** All patients with classic signs (RR <12, pupils miotic, needle marks) and symptoms of opioid intoxication should receive naloxone.

Comment: Because of nalmefene's expense, naloxone is generally recommended. Nalmefene may be advantageous in the patient who leaves the emergency department against medical advise or close monitoring of the patient is not possible. The usual initial dose is 0.25 mg IV followed by repeated doses until adequate response is achieved.

Comment: Hoffman et al.,[92] using a clinical criteria of respiratory rate less than 12 breaths/min, circumstantial evidence of opioid abuse, or miosis, decreased the use of naloxone by 75 to 90% while still administering it to virtually all naloxone responders who had a final diagnosis of opiate overdose.

c. **Initial Doses:** Small doses (0.2 to 0.4 mg IV of naloxone) should be given to patients who are breathing, and at possible risk for withdrawal. If no response, repeat or titrate the same dose IV every minute until 2.0 mg of naloxone or 1.0 mg of nalmefene have been given or the patient wakes up.

Comment: If the patient is not suspected to be at risk for opiate withdrawal (i.e., most children) and there is no risk of unmasking a dangerous co-intoxicant such as cocaine or phencyclidine (PCP), 2.0 mg of naloxone may be given initially.

d. **High dose antidote:** If there is still no response to a total of 2.0 mg of naloxone and opiate overdose is highly suspected by history or clinical presentation, one can give 10 to 20 mg of naloxone in one bolus dose. Certain opiates (i.e., propoxyphene, pentazocine, diphenoxylate, butorphanol, nalbuphine, codeine) may require larger doses of naloxone due to higher affinity for the kappa receptors.[93]

Comment: Reversal of opioid toxicity, once achieved, will be sustained for approximately 20 to 60 min (t $\frac{1}{2}$ h). Because the duration of action of most opioids exceeds the duration of action of naloxone, the patient may require repeated bolus doses or to be started on a continuous infusion at a dose sufficient to prevent the reappearance of respiratory depression (see Table 8.2B on opiates).

Comment: A true response to naloxone or nalmefene is a dramatic improvement. Anything less should be considered a sign of a coexisting intoxication or illness, a nonspecific improvement from the reversal of endogenous opiates, or the presence of anoxic encephalopathy from prolonged resiratory depression. If dramatic improvement is noted further management depends on the type on narcotic involved and the amount taken (Table 8.2.1)

e. **Dose in Respiratory Arrest**: Patients with respiratory arrest should either be given larger doses (0.4 to 2.0 mg of naloxone) or endotracheally intubated and artificially ventilated.

Comment: Naloxone is easily administered via IV, IM, intratracheal,[93] intralingual,[94] or even intranasal[95] routes. The intravenous route is preferred because it allows more exact titration and because it provides for a rapid onset of action (about 1 min) and predictable delivery of drug. The intramuscular route (1.0 to 2.0 mg) usually works within minutes, but makes titration more difficult and takes longer to work (5 to 10 min). It may be advantageous in the prehospital setting. The intralingual route, with antidote given near the venous plexus on the ventral lateral tongue, may work as rapidly as the intravenous route, but does not allow for titration of dosage.

f. **Aspiration:** Guard against aspiration.

5. **Flumazenil:**

a. **Caution:** Because of a higher incidence of severe adverse effects, flumazenil should be used only under the limited circumstances described previously.

b. **Restraint:** Consider restraining and disrobing the patient prior to administering antidote.

Table 8.2.1 Half-Lives and Observation Times Required After Acute Narcotic Overdose

Opioid	Duration of action via IV route	t1/2b	Observation time (h)
Porpoxyphene (Darvon, Doloxene)	May be >24 h	6-12[a]	24
Methadone (Dolophine, Amidone)	May be days	15[b]-72[c]	24-36 or longer
Morphine	Usually 2-4 h	3	6
Heroin	Usually 2-4 h	Very short[d]	6
Fentanyl (Sublimaze)	Minutes	4	6
Codeine	2-4 h (oral)	3[c]	6
Meperidine (Demerol)	2-4 h	2.5	6
Pentazocine (Talwin)	2-4 h	2	6
Dextromethorphan	2-4 h (oral)	6-29	4

[a] *About 1/4 of dose is metabolized to norproxyphene an active metabolite with a t1/2 of 30 to 60 h*
[b] *Single dose*
[c] *Repeated dosing*
[d] *Rapidly deacetylated to morphine*
Note: Generally if a patient remains asymptomatic 6 h after the administration of naloxone, they may be discharged.

c. **Antidote:** If a pure benzodiazepine overdose is suspected, treat hypoxia, hypotension, acidosis, and arrhythmias and check a 12-lead electrocardiogram (EKG) for QRS widening. If the EKG is normal, and the patient has no known seizure disorders and is not taking proconvulsant medications, flumazenil may be administered.

Comment: Generally flumazenil should be used only to reverse serious respiratory depression. Its use is not advised to waken a stable, mildly somnolent patient. If serious respiratory depression does exist, consider endotracheal intubation and mechanical ventilation as an alternative to flumazenil.

Comment: In a study of 50 patients treated with flunitrazepam (t 1/2=20 to 29 h) Claeys et al.[96] showed that 90 min after administration of flumazenil significant recurrent sedation was observed in healthy patients undergoing orthopedic surgery. Because the binding of flumazenil to the benzodiazepine-receptor complex is competitive, and because flumazenil has a much shorter duration of action (t 1/2=40 to 80 min) than most benzodiazepines, patients should be closely monitored for resedation.

d. **Dose:** Give flumazenil 0.2 mg over 30 s, to be followed 30 s later by 0.3 mg if the patient does not respond. Subsequent doses of 0.5 mg may also be given although most patients respond to less than 1.0 mg.[97] Although the manufacturers recommend the administration of up to 3 mg, we recommend a maximal dosage of 1.0 mg in the drug abusing patient at high risk for withdrawal.

Comment: As long as flumazenil is administered slowly with a total dose of less than 1 mg, only 50% of benzodiazepine receptors will be occupied by the drug.[98] In theory, this should prevent the severe manifestations of withdrawal associated with higher doses.[15]

8.2.1.4.2 Secondary Interventions

1. **Reassess:** If the patient remains comatose, stuporous, or lethargic despite antidotes reassess for underlying medical causes (meningitis, trauma, epilepsy, etc.) and admit to hospital.

2. **Monitor:** Maintain continuous monitoring (cardiac status, oxygen saturation, blood pressure) at all times.

Comment: This is particularly important because the duration of action of most narcotics and benzodiazepines of abuse is much longer than the duration of action of their respective antidote.

3. **CT/ Lumbar puncture:** Consider CT and lumbar puncture if the patient is febrile or has persistently decreased level of consciousness or focal neurological findings.

4. **EKG:** Perform an EKG on all elderly patients.

5. **Laboratory data:** For patients who respond to antidotes and return to their baseline mental status within an observation period of several hours, no laboratory testing may be necessary given a normal physical examination on reassessment. If the patient remains persistently altered or has significantly abnormal vital signs, check electrolytes, CBC, CPK, CPK-MB, renal function, and possibly hepatic function. While the use of toxicology screens of blood and urine are generally overutilized[6] they are recommended if the diagnosis remains questionable.

6. **Admission after opioid overdose:** All patients who have required more than one dose of antidote to maintain their mental status should be admitted for further evaluation and therapy including possible infusion of naloxone or flumazenil.

Comment: Infusions should be maintained in an intensive care setting and patients should be closely monitored any time the infusion is stopped. Duration of observation depends on the route of drug administration, the drug ingested, the presence or absence of liver dysfunction, and the possibility of ongoing drug absorption from the gastrointestinal tract. Usually 6 h is adequate.

Flumazenil infusion: 0.2 to 0.5 h in maintenance fluids (D5W, D51/2NS, 1/2NS, NS) adjusting rate to provide the desired level of arousal. Hojer et al.[99] demonstrated that infusions of 0.5 mg/ h were well tolerated and that this dose prevented patients with severe benzodiazepine poisoning from relapsing into coma after arousal with a single bolus injection.

Naloxone infusion: Goldfrank et al.[100] suggest taking two-thirds the amount of naloxone required for the patient to initially wake up and administering that amount at an hourly rate in the patients maintenance IV (D5W, D5NS, NS, NS). Based on the half-life of naloxone, this regimen will maintain the plasma naloxone levels at, or greater than, those that would have existed 30 min after the bolus dose.[100,101]

Example: The patient responds to 3 mg of naloxone initially: Add 20 mg naloxone to 1 l of maintenance fluids and run at 100 cc/h thus delivering 2 mg naloxone/ h (e.g., 2/3rds the initial dose per hour).

7. **Discharge**: Stable patients who have regained normal mental status and have normal (or near normal) laboratory data may be observed for a period of time which depends on the drug ingested (See Table 8.2b for recommended observation period after opioid overdose) and underlying conditions. Usually if the patient is awake and alert 6 h after administration of antidote, the patient may be safely discharged if there is no further drug absorption from the gastrointestinal tract.

8.2.2 AGITATION, DELIRIUM, AND PSYCHOSIS

8.2.2.1 General Comments

8.2.2.1.1 Confounding Factors

Rapid control of drug-induced agitation, delirium, or psychosis is one of the most difficult skills to master when dealing with complications of drug abuse. The use of sedation and restraints is fraught with a host of ethical and legal issues.[102-105] Safety issues for the patient as well as the medical staff must be considered. Numerous reports of injuries to emergency department personnel[106-108] including transmission of the HIV virus[109] exist.

Diagnostic confusion may occur because agitation or delirium may be the result of a drug overdose alone, or may be from a medical problem combined with drug intoxication (i.e., myocardial infarction from cocaine abuse), or simply a medical problem masquerading as drug abuse (i.e., meningitis). Finally, failing to understand the differences between agitation, psychosis, and delirium (see following discussion) often leads to incorrect management schemes. Regardless of the cause effective, compassionate, and rapid control of agitation is necessary to decrease the incidence of serious complications and to provide a thorough evaluation of the patient. One can never safely say that the patient was "too agitated" or "too uncooperative" to assess.

8.2.2.1.2 Delirium vs. Psychosis with and without Agitation

Altered sensorium (disorientation and confusion) and visual hallucinations are characteristic of delirium. In contrast, psychosis is associated with paranoia, auditory hallucinations, and usually an intact sensorium.[6] Agitation (physical or psychic perturbation) may complicate either delirium or psychosis and is commonly seen in patients with stimulant overdose. Differentiating between delirium and psychosis with or without agitation and agitation alone is useful because it may suggest specific groups of drugs and, potentially, specific treatment.[6]

For example, a patient with anticholinergic poisoning from Jimson Weed typically has delirium with confusion and disorientation, while an amphetamine- or cocaine-intoxicated person usually has paranoid psychosis with agitation, but is oriented. Physostigmine is useful in the diagnosis of anticholinergic syndrome,[110] but would not be helpful for amphetamine- or cocaine-induced agitation. Agitation from stimulants should be treated with benzodiazepines, while psychosis alone can be treated with haloperidol with or without benzodiazepines.

8.2.2.1.3 Benzodiazepines vs. Neuroleptics

There is significant controversy regarding the optimal choice of sedating agents. Much research has dealt directly with agitated patients in the psychiatric setting[111-113] but no controlled clinical studies of benzodiazepines or neuroleptic medications in treating overdose patients have been described. Animal research[114-116] and human experience[117] support the use of benzodiazepines for cocaine-induced agitation as well as generalized anxiety.[118,119]

Neuroleptics (e.g., haloperidol) have been shown to decrease the lethal effects of amphetamines in rats[120-122] and chlorpromazine was found to be effective in treating a series of 22 children with severe amphetamine poisoning.[123] Many of the children exhibited seizures before receiving chlorpromazine, but ongoing motor activity was reduced in all cases. These data are consistent with the observation that chlorpromazine antagonizes cocaine-induced seizures in dogs.[114] Callaway et al.,[124] argue that neuroleptics have been used safely in other patient populations at risk for seizures, such as the treatment of alcoholic hallucinosis during alcohol withdrawal.[125]

Concerns about neuroleptics potentiating drug-induced seizures may therefore be exaggerated. Butyrophenone neuroleptics such as haloperidol have less effect on seizure thresholds than do phenothiazines such as chlorpromazine[126]and also produce less interference with sweat-mediated evaporative cooling (e.g., anticholinergic effect) in cases of drug-induced hyperthermia.[124]

Hoffman[127] has argued against the use of haloperidol for cocaine intoxication on the basis of controlled animal studies showing haloperidol failed to improve survival, and possibly increased lethality.[128] He also argues that haloperidol causes a variety of physiologic responses which limit heat loss. These include:

1. Presynaptic dopamine-2 (D2) receptor blockage causing a loss of inhibition of norepinephrine release and increased central and peripheral adrenergic activity.
2. Hypothalamic D2 blockade causing direct inhibition of central heat dissipating mechanisms.
3. Anticholinergic effects causing loss of evaporative cooling via loss of sweat.

The risk of a dystonic reaction, which has been associated with fatal laryngospasm[129,130] and rhabdomyolysis,[131] is also of concern. Acute dystonia, which is more common in young males,[132] could severely impair a resuscitation attempt and may aggravate hyperthermia. Interestingly, the incidence of dystonic reactions from neuroleptic agents has been shown to be dramatically reduced when benzodiazepines are coadministered.[133]

8.2.2.1.4 Recommendations

Because of the complex neuropharmacology associated with agitation, delirium, and psychosis in the drug abusing patient, our preference is a selective approach based on symptom complex.

Severe agitation: In cases of severe agitation, regardless of underlying delirium or psychosis, we recommend starting with benzodiazepines due to their proven safety and known ability to increase the seizure threshold. They should be given in incremental doses until the patient is appropriately sedated and large doses should not be withheld as long as the blood pressure remains stable and the airway is secure. If respiratory depression occurs, the patient should be endotracheally intubated and mechanically ventilated.[127]

Psychosis: If severe agitation includes marked psychotic features or there is known amphetamine or amphetamine-derivative overdose (i.e., 3,4-methylenedioxymethamphetamine or MDMA), or if the major symptom complex has psychotic features, then haloperidol may be used. Due to synergistic effects[113] and to decrease the incidence of dystonic reactions[133] haloperidol should be administered in combination with a benzodiazepine. Anticholinergic agents (i.e., benztropine) reduce the incidence of dystonic reactions;[134] however, because of the potential to confuse an anticholinergic syndrome with psychosis[135] and because anticholinergic agents limit heat dissipation they are not routinely recommended.

Delirium: As long as agitation is not prominent, the administration of low dose benzodiazepines or observation alone is usually adequate to control symptoms of mild delirium until drug effects wear off. In selected anticholinergic poisonings involving uncontrollable agitation or severe hyperthermia, physostigmine (0.5 to 1.0 mg slow IV push) should be considered.[136] Physostigmine may potentiate the effects of depolarizing neuromuscular-blocking agents (e.g., succinylcholine decamethonium)[137,138] and may have additive depressant effects on cardiac conduction in patients with cyclic antidepressant overdose.[139,140] Its use is therefore contraindicated in patients with tricyclic antidepressant poisoning and poisoning that impairs cardiac conduction. Physostigmine may induce arousal in patients with benzodiazepine or sedative-hypnotic intoxication[141] due to its nonspecific analeptic effects.

A word of caution: Control of agitation, delirium, and psychosis is important, but even more important is the treatment of the underlying cause. Algorithms for detecting hypoxia, hypotension, and hypoglycemia still apply. In the mentally unstable patient who will not allow evaluation or examination, physical restraint and the liberal use of benzodiazepines (see below) may be necessary.

8.2.2.2 Stepwise Approach to Management

8.2.2.2.1 Immediate Interventions

1. **Airway, Breathing, Circulation:** Maintain the airway and assist ventilation if necessary. Administer supplemental oxygen. Treat hypotension, and resuscitate as per previous reviews.[2,77-80]

Brett A. Roth et al.

2. **Antidotes:** Administer appropriate antidotes, including 25 g dextrose IV if the patient is hypoglycemic, as per the section on coma. If the patient does not allow assessment and stabilization, proceed as follows (once the patient is under control, reassess the need for antidotes).

3. **Reduction of envirmental stimuli:** If possible attempt calming the patient by eliminating excessive noise, light, and physical stimulation. Generally, this is all that is necessary for the treatment of panic attacks from mild cocaine overdose, or from certain hallucinogens such as lysergic acid diethylamine (LSD) or marijuana.[136,142] Talk to the patient and attempt to address the patient's immediate needs (minor pain, anxiety, need to use the bathroom). An offer of food or water may calm the patient and avoid further confrontation. Gay et al. from the Haight-Ashbury Free Medical Clinics in San Francisco, have described the "ART" technique as a way of establishing credibility with the intoxicated patient.[142]

A - Acceptance. Acceptance disarms the patient who may already be experiencing fear of his or her surroundings or paranoid ideation.

R -Reduction of stimuli, rest, and reassurance. If the patient is stable and symptoms are mild, place them in a quiet surrounding, and reassure them that they are going to be all right as you proceed to assess them. If the patient is dangerous or seriously ill, control them with physical and/or medical restraints (see following section). When stable, proceed to eliminate any source of obvious distraction or distress (too many people in the resuscitation room, bright lights, loud noises, etc.)

T - Talkdown technique. Use verbal sincerity, concern, and a gentle approach because the drug abuser can misinterpret insincere and/or abrupt actions as being hostile. If the patient is obviously beyond reason or dangerous, do not attempt to "talk them down". Generally, this step should be restricted to patients who are oriented and simply frightened. It is also not recommended for patients who have taken phencyclidine (PCP) due to the unpredictable effects of this drug.[143] Staff members should be careful to never position themselves with a potentially violent or distraught patient between them and the door.

4. **Sedation**: Medical management may be necessary if the patient remains uncooperative. Explain to the patient your intention to use medications.

5. **Paralysis:** If significant hyperthermia occurs as a result of excessive muscular hyperactivity, or if significant risk for spinal injury is present, consider early skeletal muscle paralysis (see discussion under hyperthermia). Procedures for the rapid sequence induction for airway management and paralysis are reviewed elsewhere.[144,145]

6. **Physical restraints:** Restraint has proven efficacy in reducing injury and agitation.[146] If the patient continues to be uncooperative, rapidly gain control of the individual using several trained staff and physical restraints (see Tables 8.2.2 and 8.2.2A). Empty the room of all extraneous and/or potentially dangerous objects and apply the restraints in a humane and professional manner.[147] The method of restraint should be the least restrictive necessary for the protection of the patient and others.[102]

8.2.2.2.2 Secondary Interventions

1. **Insert IV, Monitor:** Once the patient is restrained, insert an intravenous line and assess vital signs.

2. **Assess Underlying Medical Conditions:** Draw blood and assess for serious medical conditions. Rule out metabolic disturbances (e.g., hypoxia, hypoglycemia, hyponatremia, thyrotoxicosis, uremia), alcohol or sedative-hypnotic withdrawal, CNS infection (e.g., meningitis, encephalitis) or tumor, hyperthermia, postictal state, trauma, etc.

3. **Frequent Reassessment:** Any patient left in physical restraints must have frequent reassessments of vital signs, neurological status, and physical examination.[102] Sudden death, and asphyxiation, have occurred in individuals while in restraints.[104,148-150]

Table 8.2.2 Patient Management with Use of Restraints

A. Rehearse strategies before employing these techniques.

B. Use restraints sooner rather than later and thoroughly document all actions.

C. Remember universal precaustions (see Table 8.2.2A).

D. Use Restraints appropriately. The use of overwhelming force will often be all that is necessary to preclude a fight.

    1. When it is time to subdue the patient, approach him or her with at least five persons, each with a prearranged task.

    2. Grasp the clothing and the large joints and attempt to "sandwich" the patient between two mattresses.

    3. Place the patient on the stretcher face down to reduce leverage and to make it difficult for the patient to lash out.

    4. Remove the patient's shoes or boots.

    5. In exceptional circumstances, as when the patient is biting, grasp the hair firmly.

    6. Avoid pressure to the chest, throat, or neck.

E. The specific type of restraint used (hands, cloth, leather, etc.) is determined by the amount of force needed to subdue (i.e., use hard restraints for PCP-induced psychoses).

F. Keep in mind, when using physical restraints, that the minimum amount of force necessary is the maximum that ethical practice allows. The goal is to restrain, not to injure. Restraining ties should be adequate but not painfully constriciting when applied (being able to slip your finger underneath is a good standard). The restrained patient should be observed in a safe, quiet room away from the other patients; however, the patient must be reevaluated frequently, as the physical condition of restrained patients could deteriorate.

From Wasserberger, J., Ordog, G.J., Hardin, E., et al., Violence in the emergency department. Top Emerg. Med., *14, 71-78, 1992. With permission.*

Table 8.2.2A Universal Precautions

1. Appropriate barrier precautions should be routinely used when contact with blood or other body fluids is anticipated. Wear gloves. Masks and eye protection are indicated if mucous membranes of the mouth, eyes, and nose may be exposed to drops of blood or other body fluids. Gowns should be worn if splashes of blood are likely.

2. Hands and skin should be washed immediately if contaminated. Wash hands as soon as gloves are removed.

3. Exercise care in handling all shapes during procedures, when cleaning them, and during disposal. Never recap or bend needles. Carefully dispose of sharps in specialy designed containers.

4. Use a bag-valve-mask to prevent the ened for mouth-to-mouth resuscitation. Such devices should be readily available.

5. Health care workers with weeping dermatitis should avoid direct patient care until the condition resolves.

6. Becuase of the risk of perinatal HIV transmission, pregnant health care workers should strictly adhere to all unviersal precautions.

In its 1987 recommendations, the CDC stated that universal precautions "should be used in the care of all patients, especially including those in emergency-care settings in which the risk of blood exposure is increased and the infection status of the patient is usually unknown." The CDC stipulated the six basic universal precautions above.

Brett A. Roth et al.

4. **Documentation:** The patient's danger to him or herself, degree of agitation, specific threats, and verbal hostilities should all be documented in case of future charges by the patient that he/she was improperly restrained against their will (i.e., battery). Documentation should include the reasons for, and means of, restraint and the periodic assessment (minimum of every 20 min) of the restrained patient. Legal doctrines pertinent to involuntary treatment have been reviewed elsewhere.[105]

5. **Medications:** Sedation of the agitated patient is necessary for patients struggling vigorously against restraints, or for patients who are persistently agitated, hyperthermic, panicking, or hyperadrenergic. Consider one of the following sedatives or combinations: See previous discussion under general comments.

Drug	Dose	Comments
Lorazepam	0.05-0.10 mg (2-7 mg) IM or IV initially over 1-2 min	May repeat doses every 5 min until sedated
Diazepam	0.1 to 0.20 mg/kg (5-10 mg) IV initially over 1-2 min	May repeat doses every 5 min until sedated. Diazepam is not recommended in patients >60 years old due to prolonged duration of action in this group
Haloperidol	0.1-0.2 mg/kg (5-10mg) initially over 1-2 min IM or IV	May repeat dosing 5 mg every 15 min until sedated. Probably safe in most overdoses although more studies are necessary to confirm

6. **Reassess medical condition:** For persistently altered mental status, perform computed tomography (CT) of the head and consider lumbar puncture. Cases involving body packers[151-153] or stuffer[154] with ongoing absorption of drug, or certain drugs that delayed absorption (i.e., belladonna alkaloids in Jimson Weed[155]) may have prolonged duration of symptoms.

7. **Laboratory Data:** Electrolytes, CBC, BUN, Cr, CPK, and CPK with MB fraction if myocardial infarction or ischemia is suspected. Consider liver function studies including PT/PTT in severely ill patients. Rule out coagulopathy with a disseminated intravascular coagulation (DIC) panel. Obtain blood and urine cultures if hyperthermic. While the use of toxicology screens of blood and urine are generally over-utilized[6] they are recommend if the diagnosis remains questionable.

8. **Disposition:** Consider discharging patients who meet all the following criteria after an appropriate period of observation:

   a. normal vital signs and mental status
   b. normal or near normal laboratory data
   c. Patients who have a chronically altered mental status, e.g., schizophrenia, or organic psychosis, and who are not at risk to themselves or others may be considered for discharge with appropriate psychological counseling and follow up. Patients with true delirium, or escalating agitation, or abnormal vital signs must be either admitted to the hospital or observed for further improvement.

8.2.3 SEIZURES

8.2.3.1 General Comments

8.2.3.1.1 Time Constraints (82 min)

Seizures from drug abuse have been known to be lethal[156-158] or cause permanent neurological injury.[159-161] Primate studies using baboons[162] have shown that 82 min of induced status

Table 8.2.3 Mechanisms of Drug-Related Seizures

---

1. Direct CNS toxicity: cocaine, phencyclidine, amphetamines
2. CNS hyperactivity after cessation of drug: alcohol, barbituates, benzodiazepines
3. Indirect CNS toxicity
   a. Trauma: subdural, epidural hematoma due to blunt force
   b. Stroke: Cerebral infarct, hemorrhage, or vasculitis
   c. Infection of CNS
   d. Foreign materials (e.g., talc), other drug adulterants (see Tables 8.2.4, 8.2.5, and 8.2.6)
   e. Systemic metabolic problems (e.g., hypoglycemia, liver, or renal failure)
   f. Post-traumatic epilepsy, or epilepsy exacerbated by drug abuse
   g. Epilepsy additional to drug abuse

---

epilepticus produced visible neuropathological injury in nonparalyzed ventilated animals. Results were similar if the baboons were paralyzed and ventilated first. In addition to the potential for direct brain injury, prolonged seizure activity may cause or aggravate hyperthermia which can cause further injury to the brain and produce rhabdomyolysis.

8.2.3.1.2 Mechanisms

Drugs may precipitate seizures through several distinct mechanisms (see Table 8.2.3). A direct central nervous system (CNS) stimulant effect is probably the mechanism in most cocaine-, phencyclidine-, and amphetamine-induced seizures.[163] Seizures from these drugs generally occur at the time of use while seizures associated with other drugs such as alcohol, benzodiazepines, and barbiturates, generally occur during a time of withdrawal from chronic, high-doses of the drug.[163]

Other indirect causes of seizures exist. Cerebral infarction or hemorrhage may precipitate seizures in patients abusing cocaine or amphetamines.[164] Vasculitis has been associate with amphetamine and cocaine abuse and may result in seizures.[165] Intravenous drug abusing (IVDA) patients with acquired immune deficiency syndrome (AIDS) are susceptible to CNS infections such as toxoplasmosis, cryptococcus, viral encephalitis, and syphilis or lymphoma, which can precipitate seizures. IVDA also is frequently complicated by bacterial endocarditis, septic cerebral emboli, and seizures. Foreign material (e.g., talc or cotton) emboli and toxic drug by-products or expanders have been implicated[166] (Tables 8.2.4, 8.2.5, and 8.2.6) as well as brain trauma or closed head injury. Finally, chronic alcohol abuse often leads to systemic medical problems such as hypoglycemia, liver failure, sepsis, or meningitis all of which may precipitate seizure activity.

8.2.3.1.3 Benzodiazepines

Benzodiazepines are the preferred choice for the initial control of the actively seizing patient.[167] They are rapidly effective when given intravenously; they require no prolonged loading; they are quite safe from a cardiovascular standpoint,[168-170] and their use is familiar to most physicians. The main disadvantages are excessive sedation and respiratory depression, especially when given with barbiturates such as phenobarbital. Lorazepam is also quite viscous and must be refrigerated and diluted before infusion.[167] Diazepam is irritating to veins and after intramuscular dosing absorption is unpredictable.

Of the benzodiazepines lorazepam has the longest anticonvulsant activity[171] (4 to 6 h) and is considered the agent of first choice. Lorazepam has a tendency to persist in the brain while

Table 8.2.4 Cocaine Additives

Pharmacologically active	Inert	Volatile compounds
Lidocaine	Inositol	Benzene
Cyproheptidine	Mannitol	Methyl ethyl ketone
Cyproheptidine	Lactose	Ether
Diphenhydramine	Dextrose	Acetone
Benzocaine	Starch	
Mepivacaine	Sucrose	
Aminopyrine	Sodium bicarbonate	
Methapyrilene	Barium carbonate	
Tetracaine	Mannose	
Nicotinamide		
Ephedrine		
Phenylpropanolamine		
Acetaminophen		
Procaine base		
Caffeine		
Acetophenetidin		
1-(1-Phenylcyclohexyl)pyrrolidine		
Methaqualone		
Dyclonine		
Pyridoxine		
Codeine		
Stearic acid		
Piracetum		
Rosin (colophonum)		
Fencanfamine		
Benzoic acid		
Phenothiazines		
L-Threonine		
Boric acid		
Aspirin		
Dibucaine		
Propoxyphene		
Heroin[a]		
Amphetamine[a]		
Methamphetamine[a]		

[a]Considered frequent additives/coinjectants; absolute frequency unknown.
From Shesser, R., Jotte, R., Olshaker, J., The contribution of impurities to the acute morbidity of illegal drug use. Am. J. Emerg. Med., 9, 336-342, 1991. With permission.

Table 8.2.5 Phencyclidine Additives

Active	Inert	Volatile
Phenylpropanolamine	Magnesium sulfate	Ethyl ether
Benzocaine	Ammonium chloride	Toluene
Procaine	Ammonium hydroxide	Cyclohexanol
Ephedrine	Phenyllithium halide	Isopropanol
Caffeine	Phenylmagnesium halide	
Piperidine		
PCC (1-piperidinocyclohexanecarbonitrile)		
TCP (1-[1-(2-thienyl)cyclohexyl]-piperdine)		
PCE (cyclohexamine)		
PHP (phenylcyclohexylpyrrolidine)		
Ketamine		

From Shesser, R., Jotte, R., and Olshaker, J., The contribution of impurities to the acute morbidity of illegal drug use. Am J. Emerg. Med., 9, 336-342, 1991.

agents like diazepam and midazolam both redistribute out of the brain more rapidly and thus have a shorter protective effect.[172] Leppik et al.[173] found no significant stastical difference between diazepam and lorazepam in clinical efficacy for initial control of convulsive status. It was found, however, that lorazepam provided seizure control in 78% of patients with the first intravenous dose while diazepam provided seizure control after the first injection only 58% of the time. Levy and Kroll[174] found that the average dose of lorazepam to control status epilepticus in a study of 21 patients was 4 mg and all patients responded within 15 min. Chiulli et al. reported on a retrospective study of 142 equally matched children given benzodiazepines and phenytoin for control of seizures. The intubation rate for those given lorazepam (mean dose 2.7 mg) was 27% while 73% of those given diazepam (mean dose 5.2 mg) had to be intubated. This study had an overall intubation rate that was quite high (45%) raising the question of why so many children needed to be intubated.[167] Interestingly, lorazepam is not FDA-approved for seizure control.

Midazolam may be used alternatively and has the advantage of rapid IM absorption in patients without venous access. In one study it was found to have a stronger influence on electroencephalographic measures.[175] and may be more effective in status epilepticus than diazepam or lorazepam.[176]

8.2.3.1.4 Barbiturates

Barbiturates are associated with a higher incidence of hypotension than benzodiazepines,[177-179] and as a result should not be administered in the hypotensive patient. Furthermore, they require time-consuming loading (greater than 30 min). Although phenobarbital may be administered at an IV rate of 100 mg/min (requiring only 10 min to fully load a 70-kg patient with 15 mg/kg) most nursing protocols require the physician to institute phenobarbital loading or to give no more than 60 mg/min IV.[167] Finally, barbiturates frequently cause prolonged sedation (especially after the co-administration of benzodiazepines) thus hindering the ability of the physician to perform serial examinations. Barbiturates do have an advantage of lowering intracranial pressure[178] in the head-injured patient and are helpful for treating withdrawal symptoms in patients with sedative-hypnotic addiction.[180,181] Barbiturates (i.e., phenobarbital) are considered second line agents after the use of benzodiazepines (i.e., lorazepam) for seizures caused by drugs of abuse.

Brett A. Roth et al.

Table 8.2.6 Heroin Additives

Alkaloids	Active nonalkaloids	Inert	Volatile
Thebaine	Tolmectin	Starch	Rosin
Acetylcodeine	Quinine	Sugar	Toluene
Acetylcodeine	Phenobarbital	Calcium tartrate	Methanol
Papaverine	Methaqualone	Calcium carbonate	Acetaldehyde
Noscapine	Lidocaine	Sodium carbonate	Ethanol
Narceine	Phenolphthalein	Sucrose	Acetone
	Caffeine	Dextrin	Diethyl ether
	Dextromoramide	Magnesium sulfate	Chloroform
	Chloroquine	Dextrose	Acetic acid
	Diazepam	Lactose	
	Nicotinamide	Barium sulfate	
	N-Phenyl-2-naphthylamine	Silicon dioxide	
	Phenacetin	Vitamin C	
	Acetaminophen		
	Fentanyl		
	Doxepin		
	Naproxen		
	Promazine		
	Piracetem		
	Procaine		
	Diphenhydramine		
	Aminopyrine		
	Allobarbital		
	Indomethacin		
	Glutethimide		
	Scoopolamine		
	Sulfonamide		
	Arsenic		
	Strychnine		
	Cocaine[a]		
	Amphetamine[a]		
	Methamphetamine[a]		

[a]*Considered frequent additives/coinjectants; absolute frequency unknown.*
From Shesser, R., Jotte, R., and Olshaker, J., The contribution of impurities to the acute morbidity of illegal drug use. Am. J. Emerg. Med., 9, 336-342, 1991.

8.2.3.1.5 Phenytoin/Fosphenytoin

Phenytoin is a poorly soluble anticonvulsant that is mixed with propylene glycol to enhance its solubility. The propylene glycol, not the phenytoin, is a cardiac depressant and may cause hypotension and cardiovascular collapse if administered too rapidly. Fosphenytoin was recently introduced to eliminate the poor aqueous solubility and irritant properties of intravenous phenytoin and to eliminate the need for the propylene glycol solvent. Fosphenytoin is rapidly converted to phenytoin after intravenous or intramuscular administration and unlike phenytoin does not require prolonged administration of a loading dose on a cardiac monitor. In clinical studies, this prodrug showed minimal evidence of adverse events and no serious cardiovascular or respiratory adverse reactions.[182]

Unlike phenobarbital and benzodiazepines, which elevate the seizure threshold, phenytoin exerts its anticonvulsant effects mainly by limiting the spread of seizure activity and reducing seizure propagation. Because phenytoin does not elevate the seizure threshold, it is less effective against drug-induced seizures.[183] Animal models[184] of cocaine induced seizures and human studies[185] of alcohol withdrawal seizures have supported this claim. Cardiac toxicity of phenytoin was suggested by Callaham et al.[186] who showed an increased incidence of ventricular tachycardia in dogs intoxicated with amitriptyline treated with phenytoin. Fosphenytoin and/or phenytoin are thus considered a third-line agent for drug-induced seizures. It may be considered more useful for the drug-abusing epileptic patient whose seizures have responded to phenytoin in the past.

8.2.3.1.6 General Anesthesia

Pentobarbital or thiopental anesthesia may be used as a last resort usually with the aid of an anesthesiologist, to induce general anesthesia. If paralysis is used, the patient must be intubated and mechanically ventilated. It is important to remember that when patients having seizures are paralyzed with neuromuscular blockers such that seizure activity is not readily apparent, they may continue to have electrical seizure activity, which results in persistent cerebral hypermetabolism and the continued risk of brain injury.[162] Munn and Farrell[187] reported on a 14-year-old girl who was pharmacologically paralyzed during 14 h of unrecognized status epilepticus. The originally healthy girl suffered persistent, serious cognitive impairment and subsequent epilepsy. An EEG should be used to monitor all patients paralyzed for a seizure disorder to determine the need for further anticonvulsant therapy.

8.2.3.2 Stepwise Approach to Management

8.2.3.2.1 Immediate Interventions

1. **Airway, Breathing, Circulation:** Maintain the airway and assist ventilation if necessary. Administer supplemental oxygen. Treat hypotension and resuscitate as per previous reviews.[2,77-80]

2. **Antidotes:** Administer appropriate antidotes, including 25 g dextrose IV if the patient is hypoglycemic. Administer naloxone only if seizures are thought to be caused by hypoxia resulting from narcotic-associated respiratory depression.

3. **Anticonvulsants:** Administer one of the drugs listed below.

Comment: As noted above, the authors have a strong preference for benzodiazepines (i.e., lorazepam). If lorazepam is chosen, most seizures stop after 2 to 4 mg, but there are no clear dose-response data available.[167] Some authorities stop if 4 mg is unsuccessful, but it seems reasonable to give up to 10 to 12 mg of lorazepam before switching to an alternative therapy. Neurologists generally recommend the aggressive use of a single drug before switching to another drug. Switching too quickly frequently results in the under-dosing of both drugs. Respiratory depression should not keep one from using large doses of benzodiazepines[167] (as has been done safely with delirium tremens[188]), especially in the drug abusing patient with status epilepticus. If large doses of benzodiazepines are used, the patient frequently requires intubation and mechanical ventilation.

Drugs Used for Seizure Control

Lorazepam	0.05-0.10 mg/kg IV over 2 min	May repeat as necessary, may give intramuscularly (IM) although IV route preferred
Midazolam	0.05 mg/kg IV over 2 minutes	May repeat as necessary
Diazepam	0.10 mg/kg IV over 2 min	May repeat as necessary
Phenobarbital	15-20 mg/kg IV over 20 min	Watch for hypotension, prolonged sedation
Fosphenytoin	15 to 20 mg/ kg IV given at 100-150 mg/min (7-14 min)	Generally not as effective as benzodiazepines or barbiturates, may give IM although IV route preferred
Pentobarbital	5-6 mg/kg IV, slow infusion over 8-10 min, then continuous infusion at 0.5-3.0 mg/kg/h titrated to effect	Use as inducing agent for general anesthesia, watch for hypotension, continuous EEG monitoring necessary after general anesthesia

4. **Reassess temperature**: Immediately check the rectal temperature and cool the patient rapidly if the temperature is above 40°C (104°F) (see Section 8.2.4 on hyperthermia).

5. **Lumbar puncture:** Perform lumbar puncture to rule out meningitis if the patient is febrile. Do not wait for CT results or laboratory analysis of cerebral spinal fluid (CSF) to initiate therapy with appropriate antibiotics (i.e., a third generation cephalosporin) if meningitis is suspected. Perform CT prior to lumbar puncture if the patient is at risk for having a central nervous system (CNS) mass lesion.

6. **Gastric decontamination:** Consider gastrointestinal decontamination if the patient is a body packer or stuffer or if the patient has ingested large quantities of drug (Section 8.2.9, Ingestions and Decontamination)

7. **Laboratory Data:** Electrolytes, glucose, calcium, magnesium, and biochemical screens for liver and renal disease are generally recommended.[163] Check creatine kinase levels to detect evidence of rhabdomyolysis. Although the use of urine and blood toxicologic screens are generally overutilized,[6] they are recommended in the case of new onset seizures to avoid an inappropriate diagnosis of idiopathic epilepsy.

8.2.3.2.2 Secondary Intereventions

1. **Computerized tomography (CT)**: Earnest et al. documented a 16% incidence of "important intracranial lesions on CT scan" in a series of 259 patients with first alcohol-related seizures and Pascual-Leone et al. found CT scan lesions in 16% (n=44) of cocaine-induced seizures.[189] Cocaine-induced thrombosis and hypertension have been implicated as the cause of stroke in patients with seizures.[190-192] Considering these studies and also the high incidence of traumatic, hemorrhagic, and infectious injuries associated with drug abuse, a CT of the brain (with contrast) is recommended for new onset seizures or for any high risk seizures (see Table 8.2.7)

In a smaller study, Holland et al. performed a retrospective review of 37 cocaine-associated seizures and concluded that CT scanning was not necessary regardless of the patient's previous seizure history if the patient suffered a brief, generalized, tonic-clonic seizure and had normal vital signs, physical examination, and a postictal state lasting 30 min or less.[193] We await larger studies to confirm Holland et al.'s findings prior to making similar recommendations.

Table 8.2.7 High Risk Seizures[a]

Neurological deficit

Evidence of head trauma

Prolonged postictal state

Focal seizures or focal onset with secondary generalization

Seizures occurring after a period of prolonged abstinence

Onset of seizures before age 30 if alcohol only involved

Mental illness or inability to fully evalutate the patient's baseline mental function

[a]*High risk for having a positive CT result requiring intervention.*

2. **Monitor:** Monitor neurological and cardiovascular status, as well as hydration and electrolyte balance.

3. **Anticonvulsant therapy**: Chronic anticonvulsant or other specific treatment of alcohol- or drug-related seizures rarely is indicated. For patients who present with multiple seizures, status epilepticus, or high risk seizures (Table 2.2.7) continued outpatient therapy may be indicated.

4. **Disposition:** Only patients with normal vital signs and physical examination after a brief isolated seizure with a normal evaluation (i.e., CT scan, laboratory data, etc.) should be considered for discharge from the emergency department.

8.2.4 HYPERTHERMIA/HEAT STROKE

8.2.4.1 General Comments

While mild hyperthermia is usually benign, in the setting of drug overdose it may be a sign of impending disaster. Severe hyperthermia (>40.5°C) is a well-recognized cause of major morbidity and mortality[194] regardless of the cause. Classic heat stroke, for example, characterized by a core temperature of 40.5°C or higher, and severe CNS dysfunction have been associated with mortality rates of up to 80% as well as with a high likelihood of disabling neurologic sequelae.[195] Although no study has documented the incidence of death as it relates to drug abuse per se, a case series by Rosenberg, et al.[196] described 12 patients who presented with temperatures of 40.5°C or greater for at least 1 h. Of the 12 patients, 5 died and 4 had severe permanent neurologic sequelae. Clinical signs common to patients who went on to develop severe hyperthermia were increased muscular activity and absence of sweating.

8.2.4.1.1 Classic vs. Drug-Induced Heat Stroke

A variety of drugs[124,197-200] and toxins[161] can cause hyperthermia, and this may initially be overlooked while the more familiar manifestations (i.e., seizures) of intoxication are being managed. Patients with hyperthermia and altered mental status may be diagnosed as having environmental or exertional heat stroke while the potential contribution of drugs is neglected.[196] Clues to drug-induced hyperthermia from the history and physical examination must be aggressively pursued. If a patient with apparent environmental heat illness has a continuing rise in temperature even after removal from an ambient heat and ongoing exertion, drug-induced hyperthermia must be strongly considered. Rosenberg et al. reported a 3 to 12 h delay to the onset of severe hyperthermia in 7 of 12 patients with drug-induced hyperthermia.[196]

8.2.4.1.2 Mechanisms of Drug-Induced Hyperthermia

Mechanisms of drug-induced hyperthermia are varied. Most commonly, excessive heat production results from muscular hyperactivity (sympathomimetic and epileptogenic agents) or metabolic hyperactivity (salicylates). Heat dissipation is often impaired by inhibition of sweating (anticholinergic agents), cutaneous vasoconstriction (sympathomimetic agents), and/or by interference with central thermoregulation (phenothiazines, cocaine, amphetamines).[196] The combined serotonin-releasing and dopamine-releasing drug MDMA produces lethal hyperthermia more potently than amphetamine,[201] supporting a synergistic role for serotonergic with dopamine in drug-induced hyperthermia.[124] Phencyclidine is a sympathetic nervous system stimulant, and may also have anticholinergic properties[202] which inhibit sweating. This property, plus the tendency to generate unrestrained outbursts of violent activity and seizures, has resulted in hyperthermia, rhabdomyolysis, and death.[203] Of 1000 cases of PCP intoxication reviewed by McCarron et al.,[204] 26 had temperatures over 38.9°C and 4 had temperatures over 41°C. Large overdoses of LSD have been associated with severe hyperthermia.[205,206] This has been suggested to be due to its serotonergic effects[197] and a tendency to provoke panic. A patient restrained in a straitjacket after becoming violent after LSD ingestion developed hyperthermia to 41.6°C, hypotension, rhabdomyolysis, renal failure, and subsequently died.[207]

8.2.4.1.3 Malignant Hyperthermia

Less commonly, drug-induced hyperthermia may develop as a form of malignant hyperthermia. Although hyperthermia associated with cocaine and PCP have been ascribed this diagnosis,[208,209] malignant hyperthermia is a rare complication that is usually associated with exposure to volatile anesthetic agents or depolarizing muscle relaxants.[161] The primary defect is felt to be an alteration in cellular permeability which results in an inability to regulate calcium concentrations within the skeletal muscle fibers.[210] As a result, neuromuscular paralysis (acting at the neuromuscular junction) is not effective in controlling the severe muscular rigidity and heat generation seen with malignant hyperthermia. Dantrolene (1 to 2 mg/kg rapidly IV) is the most effective treatment for malignant hyperthermia. While dantrolene has been suggested to diminish hyperthermia associated with amphetamine[211,212] and LSD[213] overdose, it has not been shown in any controlled study to be effective and confirmation of its usefulness for these indications requires further evaluation.

8.2.4.1.4 Neuroleptic Malignant Syndrome

Neuroleptic malignant syndrome (NMS) is another uncommon cause of drug-induced hyperthermia associated with the use of haloperidol and certain other neuroleptic agents. It has been reviewed in depth elsewhere.[199,214,215] Muscular rigidity, autonomic instability, and metabolic disturbances are presumed to occur due to neurotransmitter imbalances. Neuromuscular paralysis and routine external cooling measures are generally effective for treatment of the severe rigidity and hyperthermia in this condition. In case reports, NMS has been attributed to cocaine,[216,217] and LSD[213] although exertional hyperthermia seems a more probable diagnosis in these instances. Treatment includes the use of bromocriptine (5.0 mg per NG every 6 h),[218] and supportive care.

8.2.4.1.5 Importance of Paralysis and Cooling

Zalis et al. showed that hyperthermia was directly related to mortality in mongrel dogs with amphetamine overdose.[219,200] Paralysis was shown to stop muscle hyperactivity, reduce hyperthermia, and decrease mortality.[221] Davis et al. showed that dogs treated with toxic doses of PCP exhibited toxicity, which was diminished by paralysis and cooling measures.[222] Animal studies also indicate a key role for hyperthermia in complications associated with cocaine overdosage. Catravas and Waters[114] demonstrated that dogs given otherwise lethal cocaine infusions survived if severe hyperthermia was prevented. In this study, temperature correlated better with survival than did pulse or blood pressure. Measures to prevent hyperthermia have included paralysis with pancuronium, sedation with chlorpromazine or diazepam, and external cooling.

8.2.4.1.6 Prognosis

Prognosis for severe hyperthermia depends on the duration of temperature elevation, the maximum temperature reached, and the affected individual's underlying health.[194] Coagulopathy was reported to be associated with death in four out of five cases in one report[196] and has been shown to correlate with mortality in other studies.[223] Seizures are also associated with a poor prognosis.[196] This may be due in part to the fact that they are often resistant to treatment in the hyperthermic individual. Any delay in cooling has been associated with a significantly increased incidence of mortality as well.[224]

8.2.4.2 Stepwise Approach to Management

8.2.4.2.1 Immediate Interventions

It does not take long either to boil an egg or to cook neurons[225]

1. **Airway, breathing, circulation:** Maintain the airway and assist ventilation if necessary. Administer supplemental oxygen. Treat hypotension, and resuscitate as per previous reviews.[2,77-80]

Table 8.2.8 Cooling Rates Achieved with Various Cooling Techniques

Technique	Rate °C/min	Species	Ref.
Evaporative	0.31	Human	475
	0.04	Human	476
	0.09	Human	477
	0.23	Human	478
	0.14	Dog	479
	0.93	Rat	480
			481
Immersion	0.14	Human	475
(ice water)	0.14	Human	479
	0.27	Dog	482
	1.86	Rat	482
			481
Icepacking	0.034	Human	478
(whole body)	0.11	Dog	483
Strategic ice packs	0.028	Human	478
Evaporative and strategic ice packs	0.036	Human	478
Cold gastric lavage	0.15	Dog	484
	0.06	Dog	480
Cold peritoneal lavage	0.56	Dog	483

From Helmric, D.E. and Syverud, S.A., *Proceudres pertaining to hyperthermia*, in Clinical Procedures in Emergency Medicine, 2nd ed., Roberts, J.R. and Hedges, J.R., Eds., Saunders, Philadelphia, PA, 1991. With permission.

2. **Antidotes:** Administer appropriate antidotes, including 25 g dextrose IV if the patient is hypoglycemic, as per the section on coma.

3. **Control seizures** (Section 8.2.3, seizures) and muscular hyperactivity (Section 8.2.22, agitation).

4. **Cooling:** The fastest cooling techniques reported in the literature have usually been implemented in a research laboratory environment, utilizing animal models and equipment and techniques that are not universally available. In clinical practice, a technique that allows easy patient access and is readily available is preferable to a technique that may be more effective, but is difficult to perform. A comparison of the cooling rates achieved in several animal and human models with various cooling techniques is shown in Table 8.2.8. The advantages and disadvantages are summarized in Table 8.2.9.

We favor evaporative cooling as the technique of choice. Evaporative cooling combines the advantages of simplicity and noninvasiveness with the most rapid cooling rates that can be achieved with any external techniques.[226] Some authors advocate the use of strategically placed ice packs although there are no controlled studies demonstrating their effectiveness and ice

Table 8.2.9 Various Cooling Techniques

Technique	Advantages	Disadvantages
Evaporative	Simple, readily available Noninvasive Easy monitoring and patient access Relatively more rapid	Constant moistening of skin surface required to maximize heat loss
Immersion	Noninvasive Relatively more rapid	Cumbersome Patient monitoring and access difficult — inability to defibrillate Shivering Poorly tolerated by conscious patients
Ice packing	Noninvasive Readily available	Shivering Poorly tolerated by conscious patients
Strategic ice packs	Noninvasive Readily available Can be combined with other techniques	Relatively slower Shivering Poorly tolerated by conscious patients
Cold gastric lavage	Can be combined with other techniques	Relatively slower Invasive May require airway protection Human experience limited Invasive
Cold peritoneal lavage	Very rapid	Invasive Human experience limited

From Helmric, D.E. and Syverud, S.A., Proceudres pertaining to hyperthermia, in Clinical Procedures in Emergency Medicine, *2nd ed., Roberts, J.R. and Hedges, J.R., Eds., Saunders, Philadelphia, PA, 1991. With permission.*

packs may contribute to shivering, which may further increase heat generation. In the authors' experience with exercise-induced heat stroke, ice packs placed at the groin and axillae do not cause shivering if they are used when the temperature is high (>40°C) and removed as the patient is cooled. Gastric lavage with cold water or saline is an effective and rapid central cooling technique which can be used in combination with evaporation in severe cases. Neuromuscular paralysis is recommended in all severe cases in which temperature is persistently greater than 40°C.

Cooling Technique:

a. Completely remove all clothing.
b. Place cardiac monitor leads on the patient's back so that they adhere to the skin during the cooling process.

   c. Wet the skin with luke warm tap water with a sponge and/or spray bottle (plastic spray bottles work the best).

   d. Position large high speed fan(s) close to the patient and turn them on.

   e. Place ice pack to the groin and axillae (optional).

   f. Shivering, if it occurs, should be treated with diazepam, 0.1 to 0.2 mg/kg IV or midazolam, 0.05 mg/kg IV.

   g. Continued muscular hyperactivity, i.e., either severe shivering, rigidity, or agitation, should be treated with neuromuscular paralysis (vecuronium, 0.1 mg/kg IVP) with endotracheal intubation and mechanical ventilation.

   h. Vigorous fluid replacement is necessary to correct volume depletion and to facilitate thermoregulation by sweating.

   i. If the patient continues to exhibit muscle rigidity despite administration of neuromuscular blockers, give dantrolene, 1mg/kg rapid IV push. Repeat as necessary up to 10 mg/kg.

   j. Place a Foley catheter and monitor urine output closely.

   k. Monitor the rectal or esophageal temperature and discontinue cooling when the temperature reaches 38.5°C to avoid hypothermia.

Additional Comments: Immersion in an ice water bath is also a highly effective measure to reduce core temperatures, but limits the health care provider's access to the patients, and requires more equipment and preparation.

Temperature measurement: Unfortunately, most standard measurements of body temperature differ substantially from actual core temperature. Oral thermometry is affected by mouth breathing and is a poor approximation of core temperature. Rectal thermometry is less variable, but responds to changes in core temperature slowly. Thermistors that are inserted 15 cm into the rectum offer continuous monitoring of temperature with less variability and, although slower to respond to changes in core temperature than tympanic temperature readings, are not biased by head skin temperature. Temperatures taken using infrared thermometers that scan the tympanic membrane are of variable reliability and reproducibility.[227-229] Studies have shown that infrared tympanic membrane thermometers may be influenced by patient age,[230] measuring technique,[231] the presence or absence of cerumen,[227,238] and head skin temperature as noted above.[233] If a patient has a Swan-Ganz catheter, pulmonary arterial temperature may be measured precisely with a thermistor catheter. An esophageal thermistor positioned adjacent to the heart closely correlates with core temperature as well. It is the least invasive, most accurate method available in the emergency department and is recommended (although rectal thermistors will suffice for most cases).[234] Thermistors attached to urinary catheters may work equally as well.

Circulatory support: Usually, fluid requirements are modest, averaging 1200 ml of Ringer's lactate or saline solution in the first 4 h.[235,236] This is because a major factor in the hypotensive state is peripheral vasodilation.[161] With cooling there may be a sudden rise in systemic vascular resistance and pulmonary edema may be caused, or exacerbated by overzealous fluid administration.[237,238] Insertion of a Swan-Ganz catheter or central venous pressure monitor is indicated whenever necessary to guide fluid therapy. Patients with low cardiac output and hypotension should not be treated with adrenergic agents because these drugs promote vasoconstriction without improving cardiac output or perfusion, decrease cutaneous heat exchange, and perhaps enhance ischemic renal and hepatic damage.[239] One case report described excellent results using low dose continuous isoproterenol infusion (1µg/min).[236]

Shivering: Since shivering may occur with rapid cooling, and thus generate more heat, some authors[239,240] recommend chlorpromazine as an adjunct measure. Chlorpromazine is felt to act as a muscle relaxant and vasodilator promoting heat exchange at the skin surface. Phenothiazines, however, may aggravate hypotension, and have anticholinergic properties.

Brett A. Roth et al.

They are also associated with serious dystonic reactions that may exacerbate hyperthermia. Distinct subtypes of dopamine receptors have been identified, including D_1 and D_2 receptors. Chlorpromazine and haloperidol are D_2 receptor antagonists and rat studies have shown that specific D_1 receptor antagonist, but not D_2 receptor antagonists, reduced the hyperthermic response to cocaine infusion.[241] Dopamine is also known to participate in core temperature regulation, but it is unclear whether a predominance of D_1 or D_2 receptor activation results in hyperthermia or hypothermia.[242] Until more is understood about the exact role of the dopaminergic system in hyperthermia, the use of chlorpromazine and other dopamine blockers in the management of hyperthermia victims is not recommended.

Other pharmacologic interventions: Pharmacologic interventions aimed specifically at hyperthermia (i.e., dantrolene) have been suggested for such drugs as MDMA (i.e., Ecstasy)[211] but have not been proven to be of any benefit.[212,243] Antipyretics are of no specific benefit,[244] and salicylates may aggravate bleeding tendencies.[245] Alcohol sponge baths are not recommended, particularly in small children because alcohol may be absorbed through dilated cutaneous blood vessels and inhaled, producing isopropanol poisoning and coma.[246]

8.2.4.2.2 Secondary Intereventions

1. **Laboratory Data:** Send blood for complete blood count, platelet count, PT, PTT, electrolytes, calcium, CPK, cardiac enzymes, BUN, creatinine, and liver function tests. Type and cross match blood and send blood cultures. For severely ill patients, get lactic acid levels and ABGs. Check serum CPK and urine for myoglobin. If rhabdomyolysis is suspected, see Section 8.2.5 on rhabdomyolysis. Although urine and blood toxicologic screens are generally over-utilized[6] they should be sent if the diagnosis is in question. Send salicylate levels on all cases with an unknown cause of hyperthermia.

2. **CT:** Consider CT of brain for persistently altered mental status, focal neurological deficit.

3. **Lumbar puncture:** Perform lumbar puncture and send cerebral spinal fluid for analysis if patient has signs or symptoms of meningitis. Do not wait for results before administering empiric antibiotics.

4. **Cardiac evaluation:** EKG, CXR.

5. **Disposition:** All patients with serious hyperthermia and/ or heat stroke should be admitted to the hospital. Patients with normal or mildly abnormal laboratory values who become normothermic in the emergency department may be admitted to the medical floor. All others require intensive monitoring.

8.2.5 RHABDOMYOLYSIS

8.2.5.1 General Comments

Rhabdomyolysis is defined as a syndrome of skeletal muscle injury or necrosis with release of muscle cell contents into the blood.[247] It has been associated with all drugs of abuse.[124,207,248-259] Since the classic signs and symptoms of nausea, vomiting, myalgias, muscle swelling, tenderness, and weakness are present in only a minority of cases (13% in one study[260]), the diagnosis depends on laboratory evaluation and a high clinical suspicion. Elevated levels of serum CK, in the absence of CK from other sources (brain or heart), is the most sensitive indicator of muscle injury[247] with most authors recognizing a CK level of more than fivefold that of the upper limit of normal as diagnostic.

The diagnosis may also be suspected with a positive urine dipstick for heme: if no red blood cells are present on the urine microscopic examination, the positive orthotolidine reaction may be attributed to myoglobin (or hemoglobin). Since myoglobin is cleared from the plasma in 1 to 6 h by renal excretion and by metabolism to bilirubin,[247] the urine dipstick test for myoglobin may occasionally be negative due to rapid clearance.[261,262] Gabow et al. reported that in the absence of hematuria, only 50% of patients with rhabdomyolysis had urine that was orthotolidine-positive.[247]

The diagnosis of rhabdomyolysis is important because it may produce life-threatening hyperkalemia and myoglobinuric renal failure, and is often associated with disseminated intravascular coagulation (DIC) and acute cardiomyopathy from serious underlying conditions such as heat stroke or severe acidosis.[247,259,262-264]

8.2.5.1.1 Prevention of Myoglobinuric Renal Failure

Myoglobinuric renal failure may frequently be prevented by vigorous treatment. In 1984, Ron and colleagues described seven patients at very high risk for developing renal failure as a result of extensive crush injuries, severe rhabdomyolysis, and gross myoglobinurea following the collapse of a building.[265] Their treatment goal was to rapidly obtain a urine pH of 6.5 and to maintain diuresis of 300 mL/h or more. Crystalloid infusions were begun at the scene and continued during transport to the hospital. If urine output did not rise to 300 mL/h and the central venous pressure rose by more than 4 cm H_2O, the infusion was halted and 1 g mannitol/kg body wt as a 20% solution was administered IV. Sodium bicarbonate (44mEq) was added to every other bottle of 500 mL crystalloid solution.

The electrolyte composition of IV solutions was adjusted to maintain a serum sodium concentration of 135 to 145 mmol/L and a serum potassium concentration between 3.5 and 4.5 mmol/L. Repeated doses of mannitol (1g/kg body wt) were given if the urine output fell below 300 mL/h for two consecutive hours and if the central venous pressure rose by more than 4 cm H_2O. Further doses of bicarbonate were given if the urine pH fell below 6.5. Acetazolamide was given intravenously if plasma pH approached 7.45. Despite peak creatinine kinase (CK) levels exceeding 30,000 IU/dL, none of the seven patients developed renal failure.

8.2.5.1.2 Prognosis

Approximately 10% of patients with rhabdomyolysis presenting to hospitals develop myoglobinuric renal failure[259] and major reports of patient series indicate that approximately 5% of patients with serious rhabdomyolysis die.[247,250,262,263, 266] Death is often due not to rhabdomyolysis or one of its complications, but to a complication of the primary disorder associated with the rhabdomyolysis (i.e., traumatic injury or sepsis). With temporary support from hemodialysis, acute myoglobinuric renal failure has a good prognosis, and full recovery should be expected.[262,263,267]

8.2.5.1.3 Use of Crystalloids

Less controversy exists behind the need for volume replacement in the setting of rhabdomyolysis than it does for the use of bicarbonate, mannitol, or furosemide. In reviews of myoglobinuric renal failure,[247,250,262,265,268-271] hypovolemia is a consistent finding among all evaluated risk factors. Myoglobinuric renal failure seen in military recruits and body- builders has an especially strong association with dehydration.[272-274] Recently, Zurovsky et al.[275] demonstrated that, in rats, mortality and renal failure increased from both chronic dehydration (24 to 72 h) and acute dehydration from sucrose-induced diuresis or hemorrhage. The role of dehydration appears to implicate renal ischemia and perhaps acidosis and/or aciduria as necessary cofactors in the development of myoglobinuric acute renal failure.[276]

8.2.5.1.4 Alkalinization

The purpose of alkalinization of urine is to prevent the dissociation of myoglobin into globin and hematin.[259] Dissociation has been shown to occur below a pH of 5.6.[277] The nephrotoxic effect of hematin has been ascribed to the production of free hydroxy radicals.[278] Dog studies

Brett A. Roth et al.

have shown that the infusion of free hematin causes significantly greater renal dysfunction than does myoglobin.[279] Furthermore, in urine below pH 5.0, the solubility of myoglobin decreases markedly causing myoglobin cast formation and an increase in the percentage of myoglobin retained in renal tubules This process has been shown to have a high correlation with the development of acute renal failure.[280] Rabbit studies by Perri et al.[281] showed that animals with a urinary pH of less than 6 invariably develop renal failure after infusions of myoglobin, whereas those with a urine pH of more than 6 do not develop renal insufficiency.

Despite well-performed animal studies, no controlled human studies have evaluated the effectiveness of alkalinization for rhabdomyolysis. For this reason, as well as certain concerns about hypernatremia, hypervolemia, and hypocalcemia, some authors[282] do not recommend bicarbonate therapy. We feel that the preponderance of evidence favors the use of bicarbonate and that with adequate monitoring of volume, electrolyte, and calcium levels, bicarbonate therapy is safe and is likely to be of benefit.

8.2.5.1.5 Mannitol

Three major mechanisms have been proposed to explain the protective action of mannitol. The first suggests that a diuresis may simply dilute nephrotoxic agents in urine (e.g., hematin, urate) and "flush out" partial obstructed tubules.[283] Knochel points out that renal tubular oxygen consumption is closely coupled to sodium reabsorption[264] and by preventing sodium reabsorption, mannitol or furosemide may decrease oxygen requirements of renal tubules. This may allow the tubules to survive the metabolic insult produced by hematin.[259] Finally, mannitol may simply convert oliguric renal failure to nonoliguric renal failure. Studies have demonstrated a lower morbidity and mortality in nonoliguric renal failure than in oliguric renal failure.[284,285] Wilson et al.[286] showed that mannitol plus saline almost totally prevented the development of azotemia after glycerol-induced rhabdomyolysis in rats. As with bicarbonate, mannitol has not been shown to be more effective in prospective, controlled trials than saline alone. In selected cases in which urinary output is low (see following recommendations) and where hemodynamic status is stable, we believe potential benefits of mannitol administration outweigh the potential risks.

8.2.5.1.6 Furosemide

Loop diuretics such as furosemide have also been used in an attempt to prevent acute renal failure. As with mannitol and bicarbonate, no controlled human studies on its efficacy have been done. Furosemide may work similarly to mannitol to decrease sodium reabsorption and thus conserve renal tubule energy expenditure, thus decreasing the risk of ischemia. It may also simply convert oliguric renal failure to non-oliguric renal failure. Furosemide has the advantage of not increasing serum osmolality to the extent that mannitol does, but may exacerbate hypovolemia if not used with caution.

8.2.5.1.7 Recommendations

Based on the report by Ron and co-workers,[265] animal studies, and personal experience with the treatment of over 100 cases of documented rhabdomyolysis, Curry et al.[259] proposed a treatment regimen which we recommend with adjustments under stepwise approach to management. Using this treatment approach, Curry et al. report only 2 instances of myoglobinuric renal failure out of 100 patients presenting with evidence of rhabdomyolysis. One was in a woman with severe salicylate poisoning who had established renal failure and anuria at the time of admission. The second was a woman who had sepsis and anoxic encephalopathy after seizures and cardiac arrest from IV cocaine.[259]

While this regimen has not been tested prospectively it has suggestive benefit and if volume, serum osmolarity, and electrolyte status is monitored is quite safe. Patients lacking nephrotoxic risk factors such as dehydration and acidosis, with only mild elevations of CK (<16,000 IU/dL) and no ongoing muscle injury, may not require the full course of therapy recommended here. Any patient not treated by the full protocol should have CK levels monitored closely (i.e., every 12 h) and should be able to drink large amounts of fluids to maintain a brisk urine output.

8.2.5.2 Stepwise Approach to Management

8.2.5.2.1 Immediate Interventions

1. **Airway, Breathing, Circulation, Antidotes**: Maintain the airway and assist ventilation if necessary. Administer supplemental oxygen. Treat hypotension, and resuscitate as per previous reviews.[2,77-80] Administer appropriate antidotes, including 25 g dextrose IV if the patient is hypoglycemic, as per the section on coma

2. **Crystalloid:** If cardiac/volume status is stable, initiate a fluid bolus of 1 L normal saline and continue until hypovolemia is corrected. Assuming that larger volumes are not needed for other reasons crystalloid infusion is then administered at a rate of 2.5 mL/kg body weight per hour. Monitor urine output closely.

Comment: Crystalloid and bicarbonate (if urinary pH is less than 5.6) are recommended for all patients considered at risk for myoglobinuric renal failure. Unfortunately, there are no prospective studies with standardized treatment regimens to determine which patients are at risk. Gabow et al.[247] showed no correlation between CK levels and the development of acute renal failure. Conversely, Ward et al. in another retrospective study (n=157) found that the factors predictive of renal failure included: (1) a peak CK level greater than 16,000 IU/dL (58% of patients with CK above 16,000 IU/dL vs. 11% of patients with CK below 16,000 IU/dL developed renal failure), (2) a history of hypotension, (3) dehydration, (4) older age, (5) sepsis, and (6) hyperkalemia.

3. **Bicarbonate:** If urinary pH is < 5.6 (the pH at which myoglobin dissociates into globin and hematin), administer sodium bicarbonate IV in boluses of 1 mmol/kg body weight until the arterial blood pH is about 7.45 or the urinary pH rises to 5.6.

Comment: Urinary pH, not arterial pH, has been found to correlate with precipitation of myoglobin within renal tubules[280,281] and as a result the primary concern should be to increase urinary pH. Because of metabolic complications that may exist at a higher arterial pH (hypokalemia, and the shifting of the oxygen-hemoglobin saturation curve to the left), bicarbonate should not be used if serum pH is already >7.45.

8.2.5.2.2 Secondary Intereventions

1. **Reassess:** Check serum sodium and potassium concentrations, and urine pH frequently.

Comment: If large volumes of normal saline are required for resuscitation, or sodium bicarbonate is used, check sodium every 6 to 8 h, otherwise check every 12 to 24 h. Check arterial pH every few hours if the patient is significantly acidotic (pH<7.3) or if large amounts of sodium bicarbonate are used.

2. **Potassium**: Potassium may help to maintain a more alkaline urine. If urine pH falls below 5.6 in the presence of alkalemia and serum potassium is less than 4.0 mEq/L, then administer additional potassium until the urine pH rises above 6.0 or until the serum potassium concentration reaches 5 mmol/L

Comment: The kidney of patients with hypokalemia will spare potassium and excrete hydrogen ions resulting in a decrease of urinary bicarbonate thus maintaining aciduria. Acidic urine increases myoglobin precipitation and increases the risk of myoglobinuric renal failure. There are no controlled studies demonstrating the role of potassium in the treatment of rhadomyolysis but it is of little harm and may be beneficial. One study showed that during active work, potassium may act as a vasodialator and increase blood flow to working muscle.[287]

Knochel et al.[288] have presented data demonstrating that skeletal muscle of potassium-depleted dogs releases very little potassium during exertion and that exertion is not accompanied by an increase in blood flow. This may result in localized muscle ischemia and persistant rhabdomyolysis.

4. **Acetazolamide:** Acetazolamide, like potassium, may assist in producing a more alkaline urine. If the patient is persistently aciduric despite alkalemia and normal serum potassium concentrations, Curry et al.[259] recommend the use of 250 mg of acetazolamide IV to increase urinary pH. There is, however, no evidence that acetazolamide is efficacious for treatment of rhabdomyolysis.

Comment: In general, acetazolamide should not be given to a patient suffering from salicylate poisoning since it acidifies blood and alkalinizes cerebrospinal fluid, increasing the volume of distribution of salicylate and trapping salicylate in the central nervous system.[289-291] In animal models of salicylate poisoning, the administration of acetazolamide markedly increases mortality rate.[291]

5. **Decreased urine output below 1.5 to 2.0 mL/kg per hour with objective hemodynamic parameters of either normovolemia or hypovolemia**: First administer more crystalloid (500cc fluid bolus) and consider increasing crystalloid infusion rate to 3.5 cc/kg/h. If despite more crystalloid, urine output remains low, give a single dose of 1 g/kg body weight of mannitol IV over 30 min; administer any additional doses 0.5 g/kg IV over 15 min. Monitor serum osmolality if repeated doses are required. Mannitol may be administered every 6 h if serum osmolality remains below 300 mOsm/L.

Comment: Watch for pulmonary edema and monitor serum osmolality. Mannitol should also not be used in the presence of hemorrhagic shock or hypovolemia.

6. **Furosemide:** If urine output does not respond to fluids or mannitol, then administer furosemide. Start with 10 mg IVP.

7. **Discontinuation of therapy:** Continue the above treatment protocol until the urine is consistently orthotolidine-negative, laboratory signs of continued rhabdomyolysis are no longer present, and renal function is improving or normal. Stop fluids, mannitol, and bicarbonate if oliguria or anuria are refractory to therapy.

8. **Hemodialysis:** Those who do go on to develop acute tubular necrosis may require hemodialysis or peritoneal dialyses for several days or weeks until renal function returns.[247, 259, 262, 263] Indications for hemodialysis include serious electrolyte abnormalities (e.g., hyperkalemia), clinically significant acidosis resistant to conventional therapy, and volume overload. A moderate elevation of BUN and creatinine levels without other clinical effects is not an indication for dialysis.[282]

9. **Hyperkalemia**: Sodium bicarbonate, glucose and insulin, sodium polystyrene, calcium, and dialysis may be required in severe cases.[247,263]

10. **Hypocalcemia:** Hypocalcemia is common in patients with severe rhabdomyolysis[259] but even with calcium levels less than 8.0 mEq/L, hypocalcemia rarely causes symptoms.[264,292,293] Treatment of asymptomatic hypocalcemia has been discouraged because it theoretically could increase deposition of calcium due to precipitation with phosphate in damaged muscle, further augmenting rhabdomyolysis.[292]

11. **Laboratory data:** CBC, electrolytes, BUN, creatinine, calcium, phosphorus, urinalysis, urine dip for blood (orthotolidine test), CK (MM and MB fractions), and arterial blood gas (if sodium bicarbonate is to be used).

12. **Disposition:** Patients with drug overdose who present with mild elevations of their CK (less than 3000U/L), may be considered for discharge if all of the following conditions are met:

1. The patient must have normal vital signs.
2. There is no evidence of ongoing muscle injury.
3. The patient has normal renal function.
4. The patient is well hydrated and not acidotic, with normal electrolytes.
5. The patient can take fluids by mouth and is not at risk for dehydration.
6. Follow up is easily arranged for repeat CK in 12 to 24 h.
7. A repeat serum CK level 6 to 8 hours after the first shows a decreasing trend.

All other patients should be admitted to the hospital for aggressive fluid therapy as described above.

8.2.6 HYPERTENSIVE EMERGENCIES

8.2.6.1 General Comments

8.2.6.1.1 Hypertension

Drug-induced hypertension is of concern because it can cause stroke (usually cerebral hemorrhage), acute myocardial infarction, pulmonary edema, dissecting aneurysm, and/or hypertensive encephalopathy. Phenylpropanolamine, in particular, has been associated with cerebral hemorrhage when blood pressure was not rapidly lowered.[294-296] In patients with hypertension associated with amphetamines or cocaine, benzodiazepines may be successful in controlling the hypertension (and possibly dysrhythmias) by reducing the central sympathetic stimulus[114-116] and related catecholamine release.[297]

If a stable, previously normotensive patient, without evidence of end organ damage, has extremely high blood pressure (>120 mm Hg diastolic) despite sedation, one should consider the use of a vasodilator such as nitroglycerin or phentolamine, or possibly a calcium channel blocker.[298] In contrast to patients with chronic hypertension, most young patients with drug-induced hypertension do not have chronic compensatory changes in their cerebral and cardiovascular system. For this reason blood pressure in previously normotensive individuals may be reduced rapidly to normal levels.[299]

8.2.6.1.2 Hypertensive Emergencies

Hypertensive emergencies, defined as an increase in blood pressure that causes functional disturbances of the central nervous system, the heart, or the kidneys,[300] require a more aggressive approach. Evidence of hypertensive encephalopathy, acute heart failure, aortic dissection, or coronary insufficiency requires rapid reduction of blood pressure (usually within 60 min) in a controlled fashion. Direct arteriolar dilating agents such as nitroglycerin or nitroprusside, a pure alpha-adrenergic blocking agent such as phentolamine, or a calcium antagonist[301] may be used.

8.2.6.1.3 Stroke

Hypertension in the presence of a stroke is a more complicated issue because hypertension may be a homeostatic response to maintain intracerebral blood flow in the presence of intracranial hypertension.[302] In this case blood pressure should not be lowered or, if there is ongoing evidence of sympathomimetic drug intoxication, lowered gradually to a diastolic blood pressure no less than the 100 to 110 mmHg range.

8.2.6.1.4 Beta Blockers

In animal models of cocaine intoxication associated with hemodynamic dysfunction and mortality, propanolol has been shown to be protective,[303] to have no effect,[304] or to increase

Brett A. Roth et al.

mortality.[305,306] The reasons for the differences in these experimental results are unclear but may be related to the different doses of cocaine or the type of beta-adrenergic antagonist utilized.[307] Human studies, however, have been more consistent. In a randomized, double-blind, placebo-controlled trial, Lange et al. administered intranasal cocaine to 30 stable volunteers referred for cardiac catheterization. In this study it was found that intracoronary propranolol administration caused no change in arterial blood pressure but decreased coronary sinus blood flow and increased coronary vascular resistance.[308] Several case reports have also documented an aggravation of hypertension when non-selective beta-adrenergic antagonists have been used in the treatment of acute cocaine intoxication.[309-311]

8.2.6.1.5 Labetalol

The exacerbation of hypertension and coronary vasospasm when non-selective beta-adrenergic antagonists are administered to cocaine-intoxicated patients may result from blockade of beta-2 receptor induced vasodilation causing an "unopposed" peripheral alpha-adrenergic vasoconstriction.[307] It has therefore been suggested that labetalol, which has both alpha-adrenergic and beta-adrenergic antagonist activity, may be safer.[143,310] Controversy exists because the beta-adrenergic antagonist potency of labetalol is seven times greater than its relatively weak alpha antagonist potency[312] and studies of hypertension in cocaine-intoxicated animals are conflicting: some have shown hemodynamic improvement[313] while others show no hemodynamic effect.[314]

Mortality data are difficult to decipher as animal studies have shown decreased mortality,[303] increased mortality,[305,306] or no change in mortality.[304] The human experience (case reports) with labetalol has been better than with propanolol[310,315,316] but in two unusual cases involving catecholamine excess that physiologically resemble cocaine intoxication (one involving pheochromocytoma,[317] and the other an accidental epinephrine overdosage[318]), hypertension was exacerbated by the administration of labetalol. In a study similar to that of Lange et al.,[319] Boerher et al.[320] evaluated 15 patients referred for cardiac catheterization and found that while labetalol reversed the cocaine-induced rise in mean arterial pressure, it did not alleviate cocaine-induced coronary vasoconstriction.

8.2.6.1.6 Esmolol

Esmolol, an ultra-short acting (t $1/2$=9 min), easily titrated, beta1 selective, adrenoreceptor blocking agent, has been used successfully in the treatment of cocaine-induced adrenergic crises.[117,311,321] However, the effects of esmolol on coronary vasoconstriction have not been evaluated. Its use may be most appropriate to control heart rate in the setting of acute aortic dissection[322] induced by hypertension from stimulant abuse. If esmolol is used, it is recommended that vasodilators such as nitroglycerin be given simultaneously because nitroglycerin is known to alleviate stimulant-induced vasoconstriction.[323]

Pollan et al.[321] reported a case of a 64-year-old male who became hypertensive and tachycardic after the administration of cocaine for nasal polyp removal. This patient had resolution of ST segment depression after the administration of 20 mg IV of esmolol with good control of hemodynamic parameters. Esmolol has also been used in the management of pheochromocytoma with a rapid decrease in systolic blood pressure without effect on diastolic pressure.[324,325]

8.2.6.2 Stepwise Approach to Management

8.2.6.2.1 Immediate Interventions

1. **Airway, Breathing, Circulation:** Maintain the airway and assist ventilation if necessary. Administer supplemental oxygen. Resuscitate as per previous reviews.[2, 77-80]

2. **Antidotes:** Administer appropriate antidotes, including 25 g dextrose IV if the patient is hypoglycemic, as per Section 8.2.1.

3. **Agitation or seizures:** Administer a benzodiazepine such as lorazepam (0.05 to 0.10 mg/kg) and control agitation as described under Section 8.2.2.

Medications: If the patient is persistently hypertensive and a hypertensive emergency exists, then administer one of the following drugs:

Treatment for Drug-Induced, Hypertensive Emergency

Drug	Dose	Onset	Mechanism of action
Sodium nitroprusside	0.25-10 µg/kg/min as IV infusion	2-5 min	Direct arterial and venous vasodilator
Nitroglycerin	5-100 µg as IV infusion	2-5 min	Direct arterial and venous vasodilator
Esmolol	Load with 500 mcg/kg/min in 1 minute, maintenance infusion: 50-200 mcg/kg/min	2-5 min	B1 adrenoreceptor blocker
Phentolamine	5-10mg IVP	2-5 min	Alpha-adrenergic blocker

The treatment goal is to lower the blood pressure to a level that is "normal" for that patient within 30 to 60 min in a controlled, graded manner.[300] Although there is a broad range of normal blood pressures for an individual, if the patient's normal blood pressure is unknown, the diastolic blood pressure should be lowered to a minimum of 120 mm Hg or until there is no evidence of ongoing organ injury. The use of nitroprusside generally requires continuous intra-arterial blood pressure monitoring.

Comment: Phenylpropanolamine, an indirect sympathomimetic and direct alpha agonist, is frequently substituted for stimulants such as amphetamine and cocaine. The combination of severe hypertension with reflex bradycardia is a clue to vasocontriction from the direct alpha-stimulation from phenylpropanolamine. Hypertension from phenylpropanolamine is usually best treated with phentolamine.

4. **Laboratory data/imaging:** For patients with hypertensive emergencies, draw electrolytes, CK, CK-MB, BUN, creatinine, and PT/PTT. Perform EKG and CXR. For apparently uncomplicated hypertension, laboratory data may be done at the discretion of the physician. An EKG is recommended to rule out silent ischemia.

8.2.6.2.2 Secondary Intereventions

1. **Monitoring**: Continue close monitoring of patient's blood pressure and cardiac status with frequent manual blood pressure readings. Consider placing an arterial line for better monitoring in patients with persistently labile hypertension or for those who have hypertension that is difficult to control.

2. **CT of brain:** Patients with severe headaches that do not resolve after the control of hypertension should undergo CT of the head to rule out intracranial bleed.

3. Lumbar puncture: If CT of head is negative and the patient continues to have symptoms of severe headache and/ or nuchal rigidity, perform lumbar puncture to rule out small subarachnoid hemorrhage.

4. Disposition: All patients that meet the following conditions may be considered for discharge from the emergency department:

    a. moderate uncomplicated hypertension controlled with sedation or a single dose of antihypertensive agents
    b. normal vital signs after a period of observation of 4 to 6 hours
    c. normal EKG
    d. normal physical examination

All patients with hypertensive emergencies should be admitted to the hospital regardless of response to initial therapy.

8.2.7 CARDIAC CARE

8.2.7.1 General Comments

Almost all drugs of abuse can be associated with acute cardiac complications ranging from benign supraventricular tachycardia to ventricular fibrillation, sudden death, and myocardial infarction. Cocaine is a prototype cardiac toxin among drugs of abuse. As such, most of this section pertains directly to cocaine. Other stimulants (i.e., amphetamines,[326,327] phenylpropanolamine,[328,329] and methylphenidate[330,331]) may be associated with cardiac complications as well and management should proceed in a fashion similar to that of the cocaine- intoxicated patient. One should also consider the likely possibility that cocaine has been mixed with or substituted for other stimulant.[332] If cardiac complications occur from drugs of abuse other than stimulants (i.e., heroin, barbiturates) cardiac care parallels current advanced cardiac life support guidelines,[80] with a few exceptions (see section on specific drugs).

8.2.7.1.1 Mechanisms

The ability of cocaine to increase myocardial oxygen demand secondary to induction of hypertension and tachycardia, while decreasing coronary blood flow through vasoconstriction, and induction of coronary thromboses (the latter due to enhancement of platelet aggregation) makes it an ideal precipitant of myocardial ischemia and infarction.[333,334]

8.2.7.1.2 Benzodiazepines

In experiments in animals, benzodiazepines attenuate the cardiac and central nervous system toxicity of cocaine.[114, 115, 335] Perhaps through their anxiolytic effects, benzodiazepines reduce blood pressure and heart rate, thereby decreasing myocardial oxygen demand.[333] They are recommended as first-line agents for treatment of cocaine-intoxicated patients with myocardial ischemia who are anxious, have tachycardia, and/or are hypertensive.

8.2.7.1.3 Aspirin

Aspirin should be administered to help prevent the formation of thrombi in patients with suspected ischemia. This recommendation is based on theoretical considerations (e.g., decreasing platelet aggregation),[336-338] the drug's good safety profile, and the extensive investigation of aspirin in patients with ischemic heart disease unrelated to cocaine. There are, however, no clinical data on the use of aspirin in patients with cocaine-associated myocardial ischemia.[333]

8.2.7.1.4 Nitroglycerin

Nitroglycerin is recommended as first line therapy for cocaine-induced cardiac ischemia based on studies that show a reversal of cocaine-induced coronary-artery vasoconstriction[323] and reports of its ability to relieve cocaine-associated chest pain.[339]

8.2.7.1.5 Calcium-Channel Blockers

In studies of cocaine intoxication in animals, calcium-channel blockers prevent malignant arrhythmias,[340] blunt negative ionotropic effects,[341] limit the increase in systemic vascular resistance,[341] and protect against myocardial infarction.[304] However, one study by Derlet et al. showed that calcium channel blockers may increase central nervous system toxicity and mortality.[342] This study, which was performed on rats, has been criticized on the basis that the cocaine was administered intraperitoneally and that pretreatment with a calcium antagonist might have accelerated peritoneal absorption.[343] Another study by Nahas et al.[344] showed that nitrendipine (a calcium antagonist with good CNS penetration) protected rats against cocaine-induced seizures and lethality. Verapamil reverses cocaine-induced coronary-artery vasoconstriction[345] and may have a role in the treatment of refractory myocardial ischemia secondary to cocaine use.

8.2.7.1.6 Phentolamine

Phentolamine, an alpha-adrenergic antagonist, reverses cocaine-induced coronary-artery vasoconstriction,[319] and electrocardiographic resolution of ischemia has been documented in some patients.[333] The use of a low dose (1 mg) may avoid the hypotensive effects of the drug while maintaining the antiischemic effects.[346]

8.2.7.1.7 Beta-Blockers

Because of their association with coronary vasoconstriction and conflicting animal studies (see previous section on hypertension), beta-adrenergic blockers are not routinely recommended for the treatment of cocaine-associated ischemic chest pain. However, esmolol is indicated for severe adrenergic crisis associated with tachycardia and hypertension. Esmolol or metoprolol may have a role in the treatment of cocaine-induced malignant ventricular ectopy if lidocaine and defibrillation fail[80] (see Section 8.2.7.1.10, Arrhythmia).

8.2.7.1.8 Thrombolytic Therapy

Biogenic amines such as serotonin and epinephrine stimulate platelet aggregation. Stimulated platelets release thromboxane A2 which exacerbates ischemia by increasing vasoconstriction. The activation of the coagulation cascade and the formation of thrombin clot may follow. Thus, thrombolytic therapy seems rational in the setting of cocaine-induced myocardial infarction.

However, the safety of thrombolysis has been questioned by Bush after one patient died of an intracerebral hemorrhage.[347] A larger study by Hollander et al.[348] noted no such complications among 36 patients who received thrombolytic therapy. Although thrombolytic agents may be safe, several concerns persist among clinicians. First, the mortality from cocaine-associated myocardial infarction is extremely low in patients who reach the hospital alive (0/136 patients in one study).[349] Second, the clinical benefit of thrombolytic therapy in cocaine-induced coronary thrombosis has not been demonstrated.[348]

Finally, young patients with cocaine-associated chest pain have a high incidence of early repolarization (a variant of the normal EKG[350,351]) as a result they may inadvertently receive thrombolysis when it is not necessary.[347, 350, 351] Despite these concerns, thrombolytic therapy is recommended if the patient meets appropriate criteria including chest pain consistent with

Table 8.2.10 Contraindications to Thrombolytic Therapy

Absolute contraindications

Acitve internal bleeding

Altered consciousness

Cerebrovascular accident (CVA) in the past 6 months or *any* history of hemorrhagic CVA

Inracranial or intraspinal surgery within the previous 2 months

Intracranial or intraspinal neoplasm, aneurysm, or arteriovenous malformation

Known bleeding disorder

Persistent, severe hypertension (systolic BP >200 mm Hg and/or diastolic BP >120 mm hg)

Pregnancy

Previous allergy to a streptokinase product (this does not contraindicate tPA administration)

Recent (within 1 month) head trauma

Suspected aortic dissection

Suspected pericarditis

Trauma or surgery within 2 weeks that could result in bleeding into a closed space

Relative contraindications

Acitve peptic ulcer disease

Cardiopulmonary resuscitation for >10 min

Current use of oral anticoagulants

Hemorrhagic ophthalmic conditions

History of chronic, uncontrolled hypertension (diastolic BP >100 mm Hg), treated or untreated

History of ischemic or embolic CVA .6 months ago

Significant trauma or major surgery >2 weeks ago but <2 months ago

Subclavian or internal jugular venous cannulation

Adapted from National Heart Attack Alert Program Coordinating Committee 60 Minutes to Treatment Working Group, NIH Publication No. 93-3278, September 1993, p.19.

acute myocardial infarction; an electrocardiogram with >2mm ST-segment elevation in two or more contiguous precordial leads, or >1 mm ST-segment elevation in two or more contiguous limb leads; and no contraindications to thrombolytic therapy (see Table 8.2.10).

8.2.7.1.9 Lidocaine

Lidocaine, a sodium channel blocker, was initially thought to increase the risk of arrhythmias and seizures in patients with cocaine intoxication, based on studies in Sprague-Dawley rats.[352] Recent evidence from dog[353] and guinea pig hearts[354] suggests that lidocaine competes with cocaine for binding sites at the sodium channels and is then rapidly released from the sodium channel without harmful effects. A retrospective review of 29 patients who received lidocaine in the context of cocaine-associated dysrhythmias showed no adverse outcomes.[355] Cautious use of lidocaine to treat ventricular arhythmias occuring after cocaine use therefore seems reasonable. Ventricular arrhythmias that occur within a few hours after the use of cocaine may be the result of sodium channel blockade (e.g., quinidine-like effects) or from exessive levels of circulating catecholamines. For this reason, cardio-selective beta-blockers and/or sodium bicarbonate may be effective as well.[356]

8.2.7.1.10 Arrhythmias

Arrhythmias that occur after cocaine abuse may be associated with myocardial infarction, excessive catecholamine surge, and/or sodium channel blockade (e.g., "quinidine-like" effects).

Supraventricular arrhythmias: Supraventricular arrhythmias due to cocaine include paroxysmal supraventricular tachycardia, rapid atrial fibrillation, and atrial flutter.[357] These arrhythmias are usually short-lived and, if the patient is hemodynamically stable, do not require immediate therapy.[358-360] Benzodiazepines modulate the stimulatory effects of cocaine on the central nervous system[142, 160, 361] and may blunt the hypersympathetic state driving the arrhythmia. Patients with persistent supraventricular arrhythmias should be treated initially with a benzodiazepine (i.e., lorazepam or diazepam), and then if necessary with a cardio-selective beta- blocker such as esmolol (see discussion under stepwise approach to management). Unstable supraventricular rhythms should be managed in accordance with American Heart Association's Advanced Cardiac Life Support (ACLS) guidelines.

Ventricular arrhythmias (stable): As with supraventricular arrhythmias from cocaine, ventricular ectopy and short runs of ventricular tachycardia (VT) are usually transient, and most often resolve with careful observation supplemented by titrated doses of a benzodiazepines.[80] In cases with persistent ventricular ectopy, cardioselective beta-blockers (i.e., metoprolol or esmolol) may reverse excessive catacholaminergic stimulation and suppress the ectopy. Lidocaine may also be of benefit.[114, 362, 363]

Ventricular arrhythmias (unstable): Ventricular fibrillation (VF) and malignant VT with hypotension, or evidence of congestive heart failure, or ischemia should initially be treated as recommended by the ACLS algorithm. Lidocaine (1.0 to 1.5 mg/kg) may be given with caution as previously discussed. Defibrillation should proceed as usual.[80]

Epinephrine: Concerns about epinephrine have been raised because it has similar cardiovascular effects as cocaine and may even mediate many of its effects. There is, however, no good evidence to suggest eliminating the initial epinephrine dose in treating cocaine-induced VF. Clinicians should, however, increase the interval between subsequent doses of epinephrine to every 5 to 10 min and avoid high-dose epinephrine (greater than 1 mg per dose) in refractory patients.[80]

Propranolol vs. other beta-blocker: Propranolol continues to be recommended by the Committee on Emergency Cardiac Care for the treatment of malignant cocaine-induced VF and VT. This recommendation is based on animal data and empiric reports but is not supported by any human studies.[142, 335, 364, 365] The risk of beta-blockade in cocaine toxicity is that of unopposed alpha-stimulation resulting in severe hypertension, as well as coronary vasoconstriction.[309] This is of less concern with the use of a cardioselective beta-blocker such as esmolol or metoprolol.

8.2.7.2 Stepwise Approach to Management

8.2.7.2.1 Immediate Interventions

1. **Airway, Breathing, Circulation:** Maintain the airway and assist ventilation if necessary. Administer supplemental oxygen. Treat hypotension and resuscitate as per previous reviews.[2,77-80]

2. **Antidotes:** Administer appropriate antidotes, including 25 g dextrose IV if the patient is hypoglycemic, as per the section on coma.

3. **IV, Monitor, O2:** Administer oxygen by nasal cannula at 4 L/min. Monitor cardiac status (obtain EKG) and start a peripheral intravenous line. Hang normal saline to keep vein open.

4. **Benzodiazepines:** Administer a benzodiazepine (i.e., 0.25 to 0.5 mg, or 2 to 4 mg IVP lorazepam) if the patient is anxious, hypertensive, and/ or is experiencing cardiac chest pain or transient arrhythmias.

5. **Sublingual and transdermal nitroglycerin/aspirin:** If hemodynamically stable but chest pain persists, administer nitroglycerin sublingually (up to three tablets or three sprays of 0.4 mg each). Apply a nitroglycerin paste, 1 in., to the chest. Give one aspirin (325 mg) by mouth.

6. **IV nitroglycerin:** If chest pain is present and the patient is hemodynamically stable, begin a nitroglycerin drip starting at 8 to 10 µg/min. Titrate upward to control of pain if blood pressure remains stable.

7. **Calcium channel blocker:** Consider the use of a calcium channel blocker such as verapamil (5.0 mg IV over 2 min, with a repeat 5 mg dose IV if symptoms persist) or diltiazem (0.25 mg/ kg IV over 2 min, with repeat dose of 0.35 mg/kg IV over 2 min if symptoms persist) for resistant myocardial ischemia. Consider administration of morphine sulfate for chest pain if hemodynamically stable (2.0 mg IVP with additional doses titrated to control pain and anxiety).

8. **Phentolamine:** Use phentolamine, 1.0 to 5.0 mg IVP for resistant chest pain.

9. **Thrombolytics:** If EKG shows new ST segment elevation (greater than 2 mm in two consecutive leads) that persist despite nitrates or calcium channel-blockers, and no contraindications exist (see Table 8.2.10), administer either tissue plasminogen activator (tPA) or streptokinase or comparable thrombolytic agent (Table 8.2.11, dosing). See previous reviews for comprehensive guide to thrombolytics.[366-370]

Comment: Establish two peripheral IVs, and perform a 12-lead ECG q 30 min until infusion completed. Avoid all unnecessary venous and arterial punctures and beware that automated blood pressure cuffs, nasogastric tubes, foley catheters, and central lines are associated with increased bleeding.[371]

Supraventricular arrhythmias: See discussion above. Generally, treatment parallels ACLS guidelines with the use of benzodiazepines and beta-blockers in the doses recommended below.

Ventricular arrhythmias: If stable ventricular tachycardia does not respond to benzodiazepines (i.e., lorazepam 0.05 to 0.10 mg/kg or 2 to 4 mg IVP), it should be treated with lidocaine (1.5 mg/kg IVP) and/or beta-blockers (metoprolol 5.0mg IV every 5 min, to a total of 15 mg; or esmolol, load with 500 mcg/kg/min over 1 min and run a maintenance infusion at 50 to 200 mcg/kg/min; or propranolol, 1.0 mg IV every 5 min to a total of 3 mg).

Esmolol has the advantage of being a beta-1 cardioselective agent with a short half-life (t 1/2 = 9 min) allowing it to be rapidly discontinued in the event of an adverse reaction. Unstable ventricular tachycardia should be treated with immediate cardioversion or defibrillation (see ACLS recommendations on VT, VF) along with the administration of lidocaine, beta-blockers, and benzodiazepines. Patients should be reshocked after each administration of lidocaine or beta-blocker.[80]

The quinidine-like effects of cocaine are manifested by a wide complex sinus rhythm and frequently respond to a boluses of sodium bicarbonate (50 mEq IV, repeat every 5 min to a total of 150 mEq). A bicarbonate drip (made by adding 2 to 3 ampoules of sodium bicarbonate in 1 L of D5W) may be run simultaneously at 200 cc/ h.

Comment: Caution should be taken to avoid hypernatremia or hypervolemia and resulting pulmonary edema from overzealous sodium bicarbonate administration. Also, class IA and IC antiarrhythmics agents (i.e., procainamide, dysopyramide, quinidine, propafenone) are contraindicated in the setting of drug-induced conduction blockade as is occasionally seen with cocaine.[354, 356, 372]

Table 8.2.11 Current Thrombolytic Agents and Their Dosing in the Acute MI Patient

Drug	Dose	Comments
Streptokinase (SK) (Cost $300)[a]	1.5 million units IV over 60 min	SK is antigenic; allergic reaction and rarely anaphylaxis (<1% incidence) may occur. Administration may cause hypotension, necessitating a slower infusion rate than that recommended. SK may not be effective if administered 5 days to 6 months after prior SK therapy or 12 months after APSAC therapy or a streptococcal infection
APSAC (Anistreplase) (Cost $1675)[a]	30 units IV over 2-5 min	APSAC is also antigenic and its administration may be complicated by hypotension (see above). APSAC may not be effective if admisistered 5 days to 12 months after prior SK or APSAC therapy or a streptococcal infection.
Reteplase (Retavase) (Cost $2200)[a]	10 units IV over 2 min followed by a second dose of 10 units IV over 2 min, 30 min after the first dose	Fast, convenient double-bolus dosing. Unlike SK and APSAC, reteplase is not antigenic. Hypotension complicating infusion is less likely than with either SK or APSAC. A slightly higher incidence of cerebral hemorrhage has been noted compared with SK.
tPA (Alteplase) (Cost $2200)[a]	"Front-loaded" dosing: 15 mg IV over 2 min, followed by 0.75 mg/kg (50 mg maximum) IV over 30 min, followed by 0.5 mg/kg (35 mg maximum IV over 60 min.	Do not exceed the maximum dose of 100 mg. Unlike SK and APSAC, tPA is not antigenic. Hypotension omplicating infusion is less likely than with either SK or APSAC. A slightly higher incidence of cerebral hemorrhage has been noted compared with SK.

[a] *Average wholesale price to the pharmacy.*

8.2.7.2.2 Secondary Intereventions

1. **Repeat EKG:** Repeat EKG if chest pain worsens or recurs.

2. **CXR:** To further assess for congestive heart failure or evidence of cardiomyopathy; also to assess for pnuemothorax, or pnuemomediastinum.

3. **Monitoring:** A minimum of 12 h of cardiac monitoring is recommended for patients with chest pain associated with cocaine use (see section on disposition).

4. **Coronary stress testing**: Since patients with cocaine-associated chest pain have a 1-year survival of 98% and an incidence of late myocardial infarction of only 1%, urgent cardiac evaluation is probably not necessary for patients in whom acute myocardial infarction has been ruled out.[333] However, keep in mind that patients who rule in for cocaine- induced myocardial infarction, despite an average age of 32 to 38 years, have a 31 to 67% incidence of significant underlying coronary artery disease.

Brett A. Roth et al.

5. **Laboratory data:** Baseline laboratory data should include a CBC, PT/PTT, cardiac isoenzymes including creatine kinase MB, troponin T, as well as electrolytes. Repeat isoenzymes every 8 to 12 h.

Comment: Rhabdomyolysis may complicate cocaine intoxication and as a result increased concentrations of myoglobin, creatine kinase, and creatine kinase MB may occur even in the absence of myocardial infarction.[373] After using cocaine, approximately 50% of patients have elevations in the serum creatine kinase concentration whether or not they are experiencing a myocardial infarction.[374]

If the patient has a continuously rising enzyme concentration, this is much more likely to represent a true myocardial infarction.[349, 374] The immunoassay for cardiac troponin I has no detectable cross-reactivity with human skeletal muscle troponin I, making it a more specific test than that for creatine kinase MB in assessing myocardial injury when skeletal-muscle injury also exists.[375,376]

6. **Disposition:**

a. Intensive care unit: All patients with evidence of acute myocardial infarction, or any unstable patient.

b. Telemetry: Hemodynamically stable patients without ongoing chest pain, EKG changes, or elevated cardiac isoenzymes may go to a monitored observation unit for a minimum of 12 h for serial creatine-kinase MB measurements and repeat ECGs. Patients that have no evidence of ongoing chest pain with normal ECG and cardiac isoenzymes after 12 h may be discharged.

c. Home: Selected patients who have normal EKG, cardiac enzymes, and no evidence of ongoing ischemia may be discharged after a period of 9 to 12 hours.

Comment: 9- to 12-hour observation periods to rule out myocardial infarction in low-risk patients with chest pain unrelated to cocaine use have become more common.[377, 378] Similar observation periods may be appropriate for many patients with cocaine-associated chest discomfort since these patients appear to have a low incidence of cardiovascular complications, whether or not they have myocardial infarction.[379] Of patients with cocaine-associated chest pain, approximately 6% will have a myocardial infarction.[350, 374, 380] Thirty six percent of those patients with cocaine-associated myocardial infarction will go on to develop cardiovascular complications.[349] Of those who develop cardiovascular complications, 94 to 100% can be detected by the use of ECG, serial creatine kinase MB measurements, and observation for 12 h.[349]

8.2.8 STROKE

8.2.8.1 General Comments

Any physician treating a patient who has suffered a stroke must consider drug abuse in the differential diagnosis, especially if the patient is young.[381] In a study done at San Francisco General Hospital, drug abuse was identified as the most common predisposing condition among patients under 35 years of age presenting with stroke.[382] Most patients had either infective endocarditis (13/73) or stroke occurring soon after the use of a stimulant (34/73). Kaku and Lowenstein estimated that the relative risk for stroke among drug abusers after controlling for other stroke risk factors was 6.5.[382]

8.2.8.1.1 Mechanisms

Acute stroke associated with drugs of abuse may result from hemorrhage, vasoconstriction, severe hypertension, hypotension, embolism of foreign materials (i.e., talc, ground up tablets, etc.) via a patent foramen ovale, vasculitis, cardiac thrombi, endocarditis, and opportunistic infection. Among patients with stroke from cocaine abuse, about 50% have cerebral hemorrhage, 30% subarachnoid hemorrhage, and 20% have ischemic stroke.[383, 384] The pathophysiologic mechanisms involved are thus much different than for the general population, where the overwhelming majority of strokes are ischemic (80%) in origin and only 10% result from hemorrhage.[385] This difference makes the treatment of drug-induced stroke significantly different. Instead of anticoagulation or internal carotid artery surgery, the drug-abusing patient may be more appropriately treated with steroids for vasculitis, antibiotics for endocarditis, or calcium channel blockers for vasospasm.

8.2.8.1.2 Thrombolytics

There is substantial disagreement in the literature regarding the safety and efficacy of thrombolytic therapy for ischemic strokes. Data from the five completed randomized trails evaluating the use of intravenous thrombolytics in the treatment of ischemic strokes (ECASS,[386] MAST-I,[387] NINDS,[388] MAST-E,[389] and ASK[390]) involve a total of more than 2,500 patients, but these studies used two different thrombolytic agents (tissue plasminogen activator [tPA] and streptokinase [SK]) that were given at different doses, with different adjunctive treatments, and with very different inclusion criteria. Thus, it is impossible to pool the data for meta-analysis.

Analyzing the studies individually, however, reveals that all three of the SK trials found excess mortality in the SK group that was both statistically and clinically significant, as did one of the two studies that used tPA. The fifth study, the NINDS trial, is the only one of the five to find outcome benefit in treated patients. The patients in the NINDS study all received thrombolytics within a 3-h time interval, which required rapid CT and radiologist review of the results before treatment could begin. These strict exclusion criteria would result in the treatment of only a very small percentage of stroke victims[391] (less than 5%). Furthermore, the increased risk of bleeding associated with thrombolytics would be imposed upon a number of patients who did not require treatment. Libman and colleagues[392] reported that about 20% of the time when members of the trained acute stroke intervention team at their institution diagnosed stroke on clinical grounds prior to CT scan, the ultimate diagnosis proved to be different. Although treatment depended on CT results, in over half of the patients misdiagnosed clinically the CT scan also returned a result entirely compatible with stroke. Thirteen patients were postictal, 13 had systemic infections as the cause of their "stoke mimic", and 10 had an ultimate diagnosis of toxic-metabolic cause.

Because of the controversy surrounding ischemic strokes, and because of the increased risk of intracerebral hemorrhage (from uncontrolled hypertension, seizures, cerebral aneurysms, and vasculitis), thrombolytics are not recommended at this time for the treatment of drug-induced stroke.

8.2.8.1.3 Heparin

Although heparin has been recommended for the treatment of crescendo transient ischemic attacks (TIAs), strokes with a cardioembolic source, and posterior circulation strokes,[393-395] it should be used with extreme caution in patients with drug-induced strokes because of the higher potential for hemorrhage (i.e., approximately 50%).

8.2.8.1.4 Antibiotics

Stroke complicates approximately 20% of all cases of endocarditis, with an overall mortality rate for endocarditis-associated strokes of 20%.[396, 397] Fortunately, the risk of recurrent embolism is low when infection is controlled (0.3%/day)[397] obviating the need for anticoagulation despite the fact that most endocarditis-related strokes are due to embolism from cardiac vegetations.[396, 397] Present recommendations for empiric antibiotic treatment are nafcillin 2.0 g q 4 h IV + gentamicin 1.0 mg/kg q 8 h IM or IV. If the patient is penicillin allergic, give vancomycin 1.0 g q 12 h IV + gentamicin 1.0 mg/kg q 8 h IM or IV.

Brett A. Roth et al.

8.2.8.1.5 Surgery

Foreign body emboli most often have followed injection of crushed tablet preparations meant for oral use, especially methylphenidate (Ritalin) and pentazocine plus tripelennamine ("T's and Blues").[398, 399] Patients dissolve tablets or capsules in water and filter them to varying extents, and then inject them. Showers of insoluble fillers (principally talc) enter the circulation[381] and lodge in the lung, forming granulomas. Granulomas may also form in the lung and brain (possibly due to the passage of foreign materials through a patent foramen ovale), and may require surgical intervention. Surgery may also be required for decompression of cerebral hematomas, repair of ruptured aneurysms, and the removal of abscesses.

8.2.8.1.6 Nimodipine

Cocaine is known to decrease reuptake of serotonin, which is believed to play a role in cocaine-induced headaches and may be associated with cocaine-induced vasoconstriction.[400-402] Rothrock et al.[403] reported on three cases of amphetamine-related stroke: in one case a 35-year-old abuser had 20 episodes of transient right hemiparesis occurring within minutes of inhaling methamphetamine; later he developed permanent right hemiparesis. In animal studies, intravenous methamphetamine administration has resulted in narrowing of the middle cerebral artery branches within 10 min.[404] While the pharmacologic approaches to cerebral vasospasm are varied, the calcium channel blocker nimodipine has been used widely with proven efficacy in preventing vasospasm associated with hemorrhagic stroke.[405, 406] No studies looking at this issue in the setting of drug-induced hemorrhagic stroke exists.

Although two animal studies[407, 408] found that nimodipine potentiated the toxicity of cocaine and amphetamines in rats, it is felt that in selected patients the risk-benefit ratio may favor nimodipine administration. Such populations may include the drug-abusing patient who is experiencing transient ischemic attacks closely temporally related to substance abuse or who has had a documented subarachnoid hemorrhage associated with cerebral vasospasm. Recent reports suggest no benefit of nifedipine in ischemic strokes of any type.[409]

8.2.8.1.7 Glucocorticoids/Cyclophosphamide (Vasculitis)

Vasculitis has been associated with nearly every drug of abuse, including ephedrine,[410] pentazocine and tripelennamine,[399] amphetamines,[404,411,412] phenylpropanolamine,[413] heroin,[414,415] methylphenidate,[416] pseudoephedrine,[295] and cocaine[417-420]. In the case of drug-induced vasculitis, removal and discontinuance of the offending agent is essential. While not considered emergency therapy, the combination of cyclophosphamide and prednisone may be of benefit in the treatment of drug-induced vasculitis and resulting stroke. Salanova[421] and Glick[295] reported on two cases of amphetamine- and phenylpropanolamine-induced vasculitis that had improvement documented angiographically with combination cyclophosphamide and prednisone. This combination therapy is also recommended for the treatment of other life-threatening vasculitides including polyarteritis nodosa (PAN) and Wegener's granulomatosis.[422-424]

Comment: Many reports of drug-induced vasculitis are based on angiographic findings of segmental narrowing and dilations of distal intracerebral arteries. Although such signs are characteristic of cerebral vasculitis, they are nonspecific features of vascular injury, and can also be caused by vasospasm (secondary to a drug's action or to subarachnoid hemorrhage), fibromuscular dysplasia, atherosclerosis, and cerebral emboli.[425] Biopsy is recommended to determine which patients should receive appropriate therapy.

8.2.8.1.8 Acute Hypertension

Acute, severe hypertension from stimulants such as cocaine and amphetamines can increase vascular intraluminal pressures, cause turbulent blood flow, and weaken the endothelium, leading to hemorrhage and thrombosis. Severe hypertension should therefore be controlled (see Section 8.2.6 on hypertension). Moderate hypertension, however, may be a homeostatic response designed to maintain intracerebral blood flow in the presence of intracranial hypertension. In this case, blood pressure should not be lowered, or, if there is ongoing evidence of sympathomimetic drug intoxication, it should be lowered gradually to a diastolic blood pressure in the 100 to 110 mm Hg range. Clinical judgment should be used in this setting because decreasing blood flow to "watershed" areas or borderline ischemic zones with poor collateral circulation may lead to larger neurological deficits.[426-428]

8.2.8.2 Stepwise Approach to Management

8.2.8.2.1 Immediate Interventions

1. **Airway, Breathing, Circulation:** Maintain the airway and assist ventilation if necessary. Administer supplemental oxygen. Treat hypotension, and resuscitate as per previous reviews.[2, 77-80] If the patient requires rapid sequence intubation, consider using an agent such as pentobarbital, 5 mg/kg, or thiopental, 3 to 5 mg/kg that will both lower intracranial pressure and decrease risk of seizures. Do not give barbiturates to a hypotensive patient. Lidocaine, 100 mg, prior to intubation is helpful in attenuating the rise in intracranial pressure seen with laryngoscopy.[429,430]

2. **Antidotes:** Administer appropriate antidotes, including 25 g dextrose IV if the patient is hypoglycemic, as per the Section 8.2.1 on coma. Even focal findings may be caused by hypoglycemia; a focal neurologic finding occurs in about 2.5% of hypoglycemic patients.[431]

3. **IV, Monitor, O2:** Administer oxygen by nasal cannula at 4 L/min. Monitor cardiac status (obtain EKG) and start a peripheral intravenous line. Hang normal saline to keep vein open.

4. **Herniation and increased intracranial pressure:** Hyperventilation (to a pCO2 of 30 to 35 mm Hg), mannitol (0.5 gm/kg over 20 min IV), and possibly furosemide (10 mg IV) are indicated for evidence of progressive mass effect, shift, or herniation. Limit IV fluids to avoid cerebral edema.

5. **Control agitation:** An agitated patient with ongoing sympathomimetic effects of stimulants should be sedated with benzodiazepines as discussed under Section 8.2.2 (i.e., delirium, psychosis, and agitation). Straining, struggling, or arguing could elevate intracranial pressure and increase the risk or exacerbating a hemorrhagic stroke. Neuromuscular paralysis with endotracheal intubation and mechanical ventilation may be necessary.

6. **Control seizure activity:** Due to their ability to lower intracranial pressure, barbiturates may be preferred for seizure control if the patient has evidence of increased intracranial pressure. Benzodiazepines are still recommended for the rapid initial management (Section 8.2.3, seizures).

7. **Control nausea and vomiting**: For the same reasons discussed above. Use something that will not lower the seizure threshold such as prochlorperizine. Instead try metoclopramide 10 to 50 mg IVP.

8. **Hypertension:** Antihypertensive therapy is not usually necessary in the emergency department. Exceptions may be patients in whom acute ongoing drug intoxication is apparent. It should be kept in mind that the more severe the stroke, the greater the homeostatic, hypertensive response.

9. **CT of the brain:** Perform a CT of the brain without contrast on all the following patients:

   a. Patients with focal neurological deficits
   b. Patients with altered mental status that does not rapidly return to normal after a brief period of observation.
   c. Patients who complain of severe rapid onset of headache that persists after sedation, and minor pain medications.

Brett A. Roth et al.

10. **Laboratory Data:** Baseline laboratory data should include CBC, platelets, PT/PTT, electrolytes, and sedimentation rate. Perform CPK isoenzymes if the patient has chest pain or is obtunded to rule out myocardial infarction. Draw blood cultures if endocarditis is suspected. While the use of toxicology screens of blood and urine are generally over-utilized,[6] they are recommended if diagnosis remains questionable.

8.2.8.2.2 Secondary Interventions

1. **Monitor and reassess**: Closely monitor neurological status for signs of deterioration.

2. **EKG:** Perform EKG to determine underlying cardiac rhythm.

3. **Seizure prophylaxis:** Phenobarbital 15 mg/kg IV over 20 min, as prophylaxis in hemorrhagic strokes. Fosphenytoin may be considered as an alternative although is considered less effective for drug related seizures.

4. **Autonomic instability:** Extreme fluctuations in blood pressure and heart rate are often the result of excessive autonomic discharge associated with hemorrhagic stroke and may, in severe cases, be treated with esmolol or labetalol (see hypertension).

5. **Echocardiogram, blood cultures:** Transthoracic echocardiography is a useful noninvasive diagnostic test for endocarditis, which is approximately 80% sensitive in finding vegetations on native and bioprosthetic valves.[432] Transesophogeal echocardiography (not usually available in the emergency department) is preferred for the detection of valvular vegetations due to increased sensitivity, especially if the patient has mechanical prosthetic valves that may produce artifact from the metallic components.[433] Obtain three blood cultures to increase sensitivity to greater than 95% in the febrile patient.[434]

6. **Thrombolytics/Heparin:** Avoid thrombolytics and use heparin sparingly (e.g., only in those patients with evidence of cressendo transient ischemia in consultation with a neurologist, in patients who have had hemorrhagic stroke ruled out).

7. **Angiogram:** If the stroke is hemorrhagic, or the patient has evidence of endocarditis, consider performing a cerebral angiogram to rule out vasculitis/aneurysm

8. **Nimodipine:** Nimodipine, 60 mg PO q 6 h should be considered in all patients with subarachnoid hemorrhage and others with evidence of recent drug abuse and stuttering onset or progression of symptoms suggestive of acute vasospasm.

9. **Biopsy:** Surgical biopsy should be performed when the diagnosis of vasculitis is suggested by angiogram and yet still remains in question. Alternatively if the patient requires surgery for any other reason (i.e., intracerebral hematoma) a biopsy can be done at that time. Because there seems to be discernible histological differences between drug-induced and primary CNS vasculitis, leptomeningeal biopsy may be the definitive means of differentiating these two entities.[295]

10. **Disposition:** All patients with drug-induced stroke should be admitted to the hospital for thorough evaluation. Likewise, all patients with drug-induced TIAs should be admitted to the hospital.

8.2.9 INGESTIONS AND DECONTAMINATION

8.2.9.1 General Comments

Definitions of the terms ingestion, packing, and stuffing are required to understand the different approaches to decontamination that are recommended here. Ingestions occur when drugs of abuse are taken orally as a method of inducing a "high" or as a suicidal attempt. Body packing refers to the use of the human gastrointestinal (GI) tract for purposes of drug smuggling.[435]

Smugglers or "mules" ingest a drug, usually cocaine or heroin, in carefully wrapped high-grade latex, aluminum foil, or condoms designed to prevent leakage. Each packet typically

Table 8.2.12 Comparison of Bodypackers and Bodystuffers

	Bodypacker	**Bodystuffer**
Profile	Returning from trip abroad; found in airports or at border crossings.	Encountered on street or in drug raid, often arrested for dealing or other charge. May be chronic drug abuser or known drug dealer.
How brought to attention	Deny drug ingestion. Serious symptoms (seizure, respiratory arrest) or asymptomatic. Diagnosis by radiograph or physical examination. Likely to have a diagnostic radiograph or rectal examination	Seen taking drugs, or found symptomatic in jail. Radiograph tends to be of little diagnostic help.
Drugs involved	High-profit drug (e.g., cocaine or heroin).	Any drug sold on street, including hallucinogens or sedatives. Often involves more than one drug
Packaging	High-grade latex, aluminum foil, or condoms designed to prevent leakage. Large amount of drugs per package.	Loosely wrapped in paper or foil; single doses or free drug.
Treatment	Usually observation; surgery for intestinal obstruction. Value of charcoal or cathartic unknown. Treat if symptoms develop.	Gastric emptying and activated charcoal and cathartic. Observe and treat symptomatically.
Clinical course	Rupture of single package may be fatal because of the large amount of drug per package. Specific toxic syndromes may be present, e.g., narcotic or cocaine toxicity.	Variable symptoms, often from a mixed drug overdose. May have acute laryngeal obstruction.

contains potentially lethal amounts of drug (a typical packet of cocaine contains 5 to 7 g; lethal dose = 1.0 to 1.2 g in a naive human). Body stuffing refers to the act of swallowing poorly wrapped "baggies", vials, or other packages filled with illegal drugs in an attempt to conceal them from the police. Baggies or vials may or may not contain lethal amounts of drug. A variant of body stuffing is the ingestion of drugs to produce an acute medical condition that could necessitate medical intervention, thereby deferring incarceration[436] (see Table 8.2.12).

8.2.9.1.1 Gastric Lavage

Gastric lavage has been a widely accepted medical treatment for ingested poisons.[437] Opposed to this practice are four large prospective, randomized, controlled studies in humans involving a total of 2,476 patients, which have consistently failed to support the routine use of gut emptying. Kulig et al.[438] demonstrated that poisoned patients receiving charcoal alone without prior gut emptying had no significant difference in clinical outcome compared to patients who were treated with both gastric lavage and activated charcoal. The exception was a small subset (n=16) of patients who were obtunded on presentation and were lavaged within 1 h of ingestion.

Albertson et al.[439] compared the clinical effectiveness of syrup of ipecac and activated charcoal to that of activated charcoal alone in the treatment of 200 patients with mild to moderate toxic ingestions. Patients receiving only activated charcoal were discharged from the emergency department in significantly less time than those receiving both syrup of ipecac plus activated charcoal. Merigian et al.[440] evaluated 808 patients with ingestions and found no benefit from gastric emptying with administration of activated charcoal compared to activated charcoal alone. Moreover, gastric lavage was associated with a higher incidence of medical intensive care unit admissions and aspiration pneumonia in this study. Most recently, Pond et al.[441] performed a prospective, controlled study of 876 patients and concluded that gastric emptying is unnecessary in the treatment of acute overdose regardless of severity of intoxication and promptness of presentation.

Recommendation: Based on these studies, there is little support for routine use of gastric lavage in the drug abusing patient who presents to the emergency department after an ingestion. An exception may be the patient who has swallowed an extremely large quantity of drug and presents within 30 to 60 min.

8.2.9.1.2 Activated Charcoal

Activated charcoal given orally has been proven to be as effective as gastric emptying followed by activated charcoal in the studies described above. In other studies involving volunteers, activated charcoal was shown to be superior to ipecac-induced emesis or gastric lavage.[442, 443]

A dose of 50 to 100 gm of activated charcoal is generally sufficient to bind the drug and prevent absorption, although this may vary depending on the drug and the amount that was taken. This 50 to 100 gm dose was based on a study in which healthy volunteers were given up to 5 g of para-aminosalicylate (PAS).[444] The fraction of unadsorbed PAS decreased from 55 to 3% as the charcoal-to-PAS ratio increased from 1:1 to 10: 1.

Activated charcoal is relatively safe although vomiting and diarrhea are seen commonly when cathartics such as sorbitol are added, and constipation can result if cathartics are withheld. Serious adverse effects include pulmonary aspiration of activated charcoal along with gastric contents;[445-447] significant morbidity from spillage of activated charcoal in the peritoneum after perforation from gastric lavage;[448] and intestinal obstruction and pseudo-obstruction,[449-451] especially following repeated doses of activated charcoal in the presence of dehydration.

Recommendation: Activated charcoal is recommended in all cases of orally administered drug intoxication except if the drug is not bound by charcoal (e.g., lithium, iron, alcohols).

8.2.9.1.3 Multiple Dose Activated Charcoal

Multiple dose activated charcoal (MDAC), sometimes referred to as "gastrointestinal dialysis", is thought to produce its beneficial effect by interrupting the enteroenteric and, in some cases, the enterohepatic re-circulation of drugs.[452] In addition, any remaining unabsorbed drug may be adsorbed to the repeated doses of activated charcoal. Phenobarbital is the only drug of abuse for which there is evidence from both clinical and experimental studies in animals and volunteers that drug elimination is increased by the use of MDAC.[452] Pharmacokinetic data would also support the use of MDAC for carbamazepine, theophylline, aspirin, dapsone, and quinine ingestions.[452]

Pond et al.[453] performed a controlled trial of 10 comatose patients who overdosed on phenobarbital. In this study, the control and treatment groups both received 50 g activated charcoal on presentation and, in addition, patients in the treatment group were given 17 g activated charcoal together with sorbitol every 4 h until they could be extubated. Although the mean elimination half-life of phenobarbital was shortened (36 ± 13 h vs. 93 ± 52 h), the length of time the patients in each group required mechanical ventilation or stayed in the hospital did not differ significantly. This study suggested that acute tolerance to the effects of the drug obviated the benefit of faster drug elimination. Another study looking at a series of six patients given charcoal in larger doses and without cathartic showed enhanced elimination of phenobarbital, and also decreased time to recovery.[454]

Recommendation: MDAC is recommended in cases in which there may be large quantities of drug in the intestinal tract (i.e., body packers or body stuffers) and in selected cases of phenobarbital overdose (i.e., comatose patients who have not received hemoperfusion).

8.2.9.1.4 Whole Bowel Irrigation

Whole bowel irrigation (WBI) involves the administration of large volumes (2L/h in an adult, 0.5L/h in a child) of polyethylene glycol electrolyte lavage solution (PEG-ELS) per nasogastric tube to flush out the gastrointestinal tract and decrease the time available for drug to be absorbed. It has been used effectively in the management of iron,[455-457] sustained-release theophylline,[458] sustained-release verapamil,[459, 460] sustained release fenfluramine,[461] zinc sulfate,[460] and lead,[462] and for body packers.[435, 463] Because of its balanced electrolyte content and iso-osmolor nature PEG-ELS use results in minimal net water and electrolyte shifts, and is safe and effective under the right circumstances. In the case of body packers, the excellent bowel cleansing from WBI may reduce morbidity should bowel perforation occur or surgery is required.[435]

In a case described by Utecht et al., 10-g packets of heroin wrapped in electrician's tape appeared to be dissolved by 8 L of PEG-ELS solution.[463] Endoscopy showed this patient to have only electrician's tape left in his stomach after WBI, suggesting the heroin initially present had been dissolved by the WBI solution. Polyethylene glycols are used extensively in pharmaceutical manufacturing as solubilizing agents and it has been shown that PEG 4000, a water-soluble polymer comparable to the polymer used in PEG-ELS, can increase the dissolution rates of poorly water-soluble drugs.[464]

Alkaloidal heroin is poorly water soluble; 1 g dissolves in 1,700 ml of water.[465] Therefore, the large amount of heroin,10 g in each package, would not have been solubilized in the stomach by water alone. The patient had continuing absorption of heroin despite the administration of multiple doses of activated charcoal. Rosenberg has shown that the antidotal efficacy of oral activated charcoal was markedly diminished by PEG-ELS in volunteers treated with aspirin.[466] Tenenbein likewise reported that PEG-ELS binds to charcoal and that this interferes with aspirin adsorption by activated charcoal.[467]

Recommendation: WBI is recommended in cases involving body packers. WBI is also recommended in situations in which large amounts of drug may still be present in the gastrointestinal tract due to concretions (common with gluthethimide and meprobamate) or when a sustained release preparation (i.e., sustained release morphine) has been ingested. Because WBI may solubilize heroin and may diminish the efficacy of activated charcoal, the use of activated charcoal and cathartics is preferred over WBI for treatment of heroin body packers.

8.2.9.2 Stepwise Approach to Management

8.2.9.2.1 Immediate Interventions

1. **Airway, breathing, circulation:** Maintain the airway and assist ventilation if necessary. Administer supplemental oxygen. Treat hypotension, and resuscitate as per previous reviews.[2,77-80]

2. **IV, monitor O$_2$:** Administer oxygen by nasal cannula at 4 L/min. Monitor cardiac status (obtain EKG) and start a peripheral intravenous line. Hang normal saline to keep vein open.

3. **Gastric lavage:** Not recommended unless patient has ingested massive quantities and arrives within 30 min to 1 h of ingestion.

Brett A. Roth et al.

4. **Activated Charcoal**: Administer activated charcoal 50 to 100 gm PO. Try to obtain a 10:1 ratio of activated charcoal to drug by weight if possible. If unable to administer enough activated charcoal on the first dose, repeat the dose in 4 h. Multiple dose activated charcoal: give 12.5 g/h or 25 g every 3 to 4 hours. Studies have shown that the administration of hourly activated charcoal produces a shorter half-life than less frequent dosing, even though the same dose was administered over the same treatment period.[468, 469]

Comment: Administer MDAC for the rare phenobarbital overdoses (as discussed above), for the body packer or body stuffer (see below), and for the patient suspected of taking a sustained release preparation. If the patient has difficulty tolerating activated charcoal because of drug-induced vomiting, smaller doses of activated charcoal administered more frequently may reduce the likelihood of vomiting. It may, however, be necessary to give either IV metoclopramide (10 to 50 mg IVP) or ondansetron (4 to 8 mg IVP) to ensure satisfactory administration of charcoal.[452]

6. **Guard against aspiration:** Do not force patients who are nauseated to take activated charcoal. If nausea exists, treat with metoclopramide as above. Patients who do not have a gag reflex should have their airways protected with endotracheal intubation (although this does not guarantee protection) and elevation of the head of the bed to 45 degrees.

7. **Laboratory data:** Baseline laboratory data should include a guided clinical presentation. If the patient is asymptomatic, no laboratory is immediately essential. Perform a CBC, and electrolytes with CPK isoenzymes if the patient is obtunded or has chest pain, to rule out occult metabolic/infectious disease, and/or myocardial infarction. While the use of toxicology screens of blood and urine are generally over-utilized[6] they are recommended if diagnosis remains questionable.

Comment: The use of urine toxicology screening may be particularly misleading in the case of a body packer or stuffer and should not be used to determine if the patient ingested any drugs. Recreational use of the drug prior to "stuffing" could lead to a false positive test. On the other hand, no prior drug usage without rupture of packets could lead to a false negative test. In one study of 50 body packers, 64% had positive urine toxicology screens for drugs of abuse.[470]

8.2.9.2.2 Secondary Interventions

1. **The body-stuffer:** Some authors recommend that the asymptomatic body packer or stuffer should be observed for a period of at least 48 to 72 h and treated with repeated dose activated charcoal and cathartics.[436] This approach may be better suited to the treatment of the body packer who has a lethal amount of drug in their intestinal tract. In the asymptomatic body-stuffer, the administration of activated charcoal and observation seems more appropriate but has not been carefully studied. In a series of over 100 cocaine body packers, those who went on to develop serious complications became symptomatic within 6 h.[471] A recommended treatment approach follows:

   a. Activated charcoal: Give activated charcoal, 1 gm/kg.
   b. Observation: If asymptomatic observe for 6 h and repeat activated charcoal.
   c. Discharge: At this time it is felt that there is too little evidence to guide a well-supported recommendation for the release of these patients from the hospital. Clinical judgment should be used based on the type and the amount of drug ingested. Some recommend discharge after an observation period of greater than 6 h if the patient is asymptomatic.
   d. WBI: If symptomatic and large amounts of drug have been ingested or sustained release preparations are involved, consider whole bowel irrigation with 2L/h of polyethylene glycol (PEG) after the first dose of activated charcoal.

2. The Body Packer: Treatment is as per the body stuffer and it is wise to admit these patients until all packets are passed and accounted for.

a. Xrays: A plain upright abdominal film can detect a large percentage of packets (e.g., false negative rate of 17 to 19% in two series[472, 473]) and is recommended to determine location and amount of drug ingested. However, a negative Xray does not rule out body packing.

b. Whole Bowel Irrigation (WBI): The use of electrolyte bowel preparation solutions such as polyethylene glycol (e.g., GO-LYTELY) has aided foreign body passage[435] and is recommended in all cases except those involving heroin. Give 2 L/h for adults and 500 cc/h for children.

c. Cathartic: An alternative to whole bowel irrigation is a cathartic, such as 3% sodium sulfate solution (250 to 500 ml), given orally with the activated charcoal. Cathartics such as sodium sulfate do not eliminate packets as rapidly as whole bowel irrigation. This may allow more time for the packets to dissolve. Conversely, a more gentle approach with less risk of damage to the packets is provided. Use of cathartics without WBI is recommended in uncooperative patients (unless a court order is obtained), those who body pack heroin (due to the reported possibility of increasing solubility of heroin in polyethylene glycol[463]), and in those known to have packets that are weakly wrapped (due to theoretical concerns about breaking open packets with vigorous irrigation and increased peristalsis[463]). Further studies are needed to validate these recommendations.

d. Enemas: If foreign bodies are located in the colon, low volume phosphasoda enemas, or high-volume normal saline enemas may be helpful.[463]

f. Suppository: One (Dulcolax®) suppository per rectum to empty the rectum.

g. Gastrointestinal Series: Following the passage of the "last" packet, a Gastrograffin upper gastrointestinal series with small bowel follow-through may be performed to ensure that the gut has been purged of all containers.[464]

h. Surgery: In the presence of a leaking or a ruptured package, decisions about surgical removal should be made on an individual basis; laparotomy is indicated if this is intestinal obstruction.

Comment: Because of risk of packet rupture, avoid attempts to remove packages via gastroscopy or colonoscopy.[474] Syrup of ipecac or gastric lavage are ineffective due to the large size of the packets, and may cause packages to break.

3. Disposition: Patients may be discharged from the emergency department if they meet the following criteria:

a. normal vital signs
b. normal physical exam, including the presence of bowel sounds
c. normal or near normal laboratory data
d. ingestion known to be nontoxic
e. psychiatric referral
f. stable family environment

Comment: As noted previously, more studies are needed to support any recommendations for the safe discharge of body stuffers.

Brett A. Roth et al.

8.2.10 MANAGEMENT OF SPECIFIC DRUGS OF ABUSE

Table 8.2A Psychostimulants

Drug	Unique characteristics	Key management issues
Cocaine	Stimulant associated with more serious complications than any other. Affects all organ sustems. No longer confined to affluent sectors of society.	Adrenergic crisis, hyperthermia, hypertension, cardiac ischemia and arrhythmias, seizures, troke, panic attacks, s psychosis, rhabdomyolysis
Amphetamines and meth- amphetamine	Frequently associated with paranoid psychosis after chronic abuse. Lead poisoning has been described (lead is used as a reagent in illicity laboratories)	Same as cocaine with lower incidence of cardiac ischemia, stroke.
MDMA, MDEA/MDA	Designer amphetamine widely used at dance parties or "raves". Affects serotonin more than other amphetamines, leading to hallucinations; possibly linked to the serotonin syndrome	Same as cocaine with lower incidence of cardiac ischemia, stroke; severe hyperthermia in dehydrated dancers has led to death. Rehydrate and control hyperthermia.
Methcathinone ("CAT")	Designer amphetamine with intoxicating effects that may last up to 6 days; more common in Soviety Union	Same as amphetamines
Pemoline/ Methylphenidate	Principal therapeutic use is in children and adults with attention deficit disorder; commonly associated with abnormal involuntary movements	Same as amphetamines
DOB	Stong hallucinogenic effects that are long-lasting (up to 10 h). May have an ergot-like effect	Same as amphetamines, severe hypertension, or evidence of ischemia (digital, mesenteric) should be treated with phentolamine and anticoagulation
TMA-2, DOM/STP	Designer amphetamnes with less sympathetic stimulation in usual doses. Prominent hallucinogenic effects	Adequate treatment is usally possible by calming hallucinations with benzodiazepines and removal to a quiet setting
Ephedrine	Over the counter amphetamne like substance less potent than amphetamines.	Same as amphetamines

Table 8.2A Psychostimulants (continued)

Drug	Unique characteristics	Key management issues
Phenyl-propanolamine	Primarily an adrenergic agonist, as a result hypertension with reflex bradycardia is common, also associated with cerebral hemorrhage	May treat hypertension with an α-blocker such as phentolamine. Do not treat bradycardia with atropine since this will exacerbate hypertension
Mescaline	Phenylethylamine derivative found in peyote cactus, associated with strong hallucinogenic properties due to effects on the serotonergic system	Adequate treatment is usally possible by calming hallucinations with benzodiazepines and removal to a quiet setting
PCP, PHP, and derivatives	Associated with erratic, violent behavior. Intoxicated patients prone to sustaining significant injuries due to dissociative, anesthetic properties.	As with other psychostimulants with greater emphasis on controlling behavioral toxicity since this is the major cause of death

Abbreviations: MDMA-3,4-methylenedioxymethamphetamine; MDEA-3,4 methylenedioxyethamphetamine; MDA-3,4-methylenedioxyamphetamine; DOB-4-bromo-2,5-dimethoxyamphetamine; TMP-2-2,4,5-trimethoxyamphetamine; DOM/STP-4-methyl-2,5-dimethoxyamphetamine; PCP-Phencyclidine; PHP-phenylcyclohexlpyrrolidine.

Contraindications: Nonselective beta-blockers should not be administered to paitents with chest pain if a psychostimulant has been ingested although cardioselective beta-blockers may be used for certain tachyarrhythmias. Acidification of urine may slightly hasten the elimination of PCP and amphetamines but it is not reccoemmended due to an increased risk of myoblobinuric renal failure.

Table 8.2B Opiates

Drug	Unique characteristics	Key management issues
Diacetylmorphine (Heroin)	Prototype opiate of abuse, rapidly metabolized to morphine, more lipid soluble	Respiratory depression, coma, anoxic encephalopathy, pulmonary edema, withdrawal, compartment sydromes.
Methadone (Dolophine)	Slow onset and long duration of action (half-life 15-72 h)	As with heroin. May require a naloxone infusion (see below) and prolonged monitoring
Designer opiates: Fentanyl (Sublimaze), Sufentanil (Sufenta), Alfentanil (Alfenta)	Most potent opiates (16-700X morphine), with rapid onset and short duration of action (minutes)	As with heroin. May accumulate in body fat necessitating observations periods similar to heroin overdose (12 h) may see negative screen for opiates
Propoxyphene (Darvon)	High mortality, sudden death reported, convulsions and cardia arrhythmias due to metabolite (norpropoxyphene), fat soluble so may have prolonged duration of action	As with heroin. Prolonged observation requried after overdose. Wide complex tachycardia mya respond to bicarbonate, may be resistant to naloxone, check acetaminophen level
Pentazocine (Talwin)	Agonist-antagonist, dysphoria, no cases of pulmonary edema reported	As with heroin. May be resistant to naloxone
Dextromethorphan/ codeine	Less respiratory depression, possible serotonin releasing effects	As with heroin. Usually less serious in overdoes than other opiates, check acetaminophen level if codeine ingested
Meperidine (Demerol)	Synthetic opiate assoicated with seizures in large doses due to metabolite (normeperidine)	As with heroin.
Hydromorphone (Dilaudid)	Similar to morphine but more potent and shorter duration of action	As with heroin.
Morphine (MS-contin)	Sustained-release, oral chewing converts to rapidly acting agents	As with heroin. Prolonged observatin required after overdose.

Contraindications: Administration of high dose (>2.0 mg) naloxone in any patient at risk for piate withdrawal.

Naloxone infusion: Take two-thirds the amount of naloxone required for the patient to initially wake up and give that amount at an hourly rate. Mix the naloxone in the patients maintenance IV (D5W, D5$^1/_2$NS, $^1/_2$NS, NS, etc.). Infusions should be maintained in an intensive care setting. Patients should be closely watched anytime the infusion is stopped. Duration of observation depends on the route of drug administration, the drug ingested, the presence or absence of liver dysfunction, and the possiblity of ongoing drug absorption from the gastrointestinal tract. Usually 6 h is adequate.

Table 8.2C Sedative-Hypnotic Agents

Drug	Unique characteristics	Key management issues
Benzodiazepines	High terapeutic index make death unlikely unless coingestions involved. Memory impairment common.	Respiratory depression, coma, compartment syndromes; severe withdrawal; use flumazenil in selected cases only; supportive care usually all that is required.
GHB	Common at "raves", associated with profound coma that rapidly resolves within 2 h, increased muscle tone with jerking	Supportive care, rarely requires endotracheal intubation, guard against aspiration
Long lasting barbituates (i.e., phenobarbital); duration of action = 10-12 h	Phenobarbital ($t^1/_2$=24-140 h) may induce prolonged deep coma (5-7 days) mimicking death. Pneumonia is a common complication due to prolonged coma. Hypothermia.	As with benzodiazepines although cardiac depression, and hypotension are more common and may necessitate cardiac support. Alkalinization of urine may increase elimination. MDAC in selected cases (see discussion). Hemoperfusion in selected cases.
Other barbituates: Intermediate acting (i.e., amobarbital), Short acting (i.e., secobarbital), Ultrashort-acting (i.e., thiopental)	Commonly abused barbituates; chronic drowsiness, psychomotor retardation. Hypothermia.	As above although alkalinization, MDAC not helpful. Hemoperfusion in selected cases. Major withdrawal may necessitate hospitalizaiton.
Ethchlorvynol (placidyl)	Pungent odor sometimes described as pear like, gastric fluid often has a pink or green color, noncardiac pulmonary edema.	See barbituates.
Glutethimide (Doriden)	Prominent anticholinergic side effects including mydriasis. Prolonged cyclic or fluctuating coma (average 36-38 h); often mixed with codeine as a heroin substitute.	See barbituates.
Meprobamate (Miltown)	Forms concretions, hyoptension is more common than with other sedative-hypnotics, prolonged coma (average 38-40 h).	If concretions suspected WBI or gastroscopic or surgical removal of drug may be necessary. Hemoperfusion useful in severe cases.

Table 8.2C Sedative-Hypnotic Agents (continued)

Drug	Unique characteristics	Key management issues
Methqualone (Quaalude)	Muscular hypertonicity, clonus, and hyperpyrexia, popular as an "aphrodisiac" or "cocaine downer". No longer manufactured in the U.S.	Charcoal hemoperfusion increases clearance and may be useful in severe cases; diazepam may be necessary to treat severe muscular hypertonicity or "seizures".
Chloral hydrate	Metabolized to trichloroethanol which may sensitize the myocardium to the effects of catecholamines, resulting in cardiac arrhythmias	Tachyarrhythmias may respond to propranolol, 1-2 mg IV or esmolol. Flumazenil has been reported to produce dramatic reversal of coma in one case. Amenable to hemodialysis.

Abbreviations: GHB = hammahydroxybuterate; MDAC = multiple dose activated charcoal; WBI = whole bowel irrigation.

Note: Catecholamines (especially dompamine and epinephrine) are relatively contraindicated in cases of chloral hydrate-induced tachyarrhythmias.

Table 8.2D Hallucinogens

Drug	Unique characteristics	Key management issues
LSD	Potent agent associated with panic attacks, acute psychotic reaction, and flashbacks in chronic users. Vital signs are usually relatively normal. Hallucinations for 1-8 h.	Patients usually respond to benzodiazepines and seclusion in a quiet environment. Toxicology screen negative. In extremely agitated patients watch for hyperthermia, rhabdomyolysis.
Marijuana	Commonly used, associated with conjunctival injection, stimulation of appetitie, orthostatic hypotension, and mild tachycardia. Duration of effect: 3 h.	Usually respond to simple reassurance and possible adjunctive benzodiazepine.
Ketamine	Dissociative anesthetic with hallucinations characterized by profound analgesia, amnesia, and catalepsy. Increasingly common as drug of abuse. Duration of effect: 1-3 h	Provide supportive care until drug effects wear off. Cardiovascular parameters are usually well preserved.
Atropine, hycosyamine, scopolamine (D. Stramonium or Jimson Weed)	Anticholinergic syndrome with true delirium, symptoms may continue for 24-48 h because of delayed GI motility	Usually supportive care only, consider activated charcoal; physostigmine for uncontrolled agitation, hyperthermia.

Table 8.2D Hallucinogens (continued)

Drug	Unique characteristics	Key management issues
Solvents	Products of petroleum distillation abused by spraying them into a palastic bag or soaking a cloth and then deeply inhaling. Cardiac sensitization may result in malignant arrhythmias, low viscosity agents (i.e., gasoline are associated with aspriation). Chronic exposure associated with hepatitis and renal failure.	Usually hallucinogenic effects are short lived. Removing the patient from the offending agent, and providing fresh air is all that is necessary. Treat aspiration by supporting airway. Arrhythmias may respond to beta-blockers, epinephrine may worsen arrhythmias.
Psilocybin	From the Stropharia and Conocybe mushrooms; suppresses serotonergic neurons, less potent than LSD with hallucinations that last from 2-8 h, Patients may exhibit destructive behavior. Hallucinations for 1-6 h.	As with LSD

Abbreviations: LSD = lysergic acid diethylamide, D. = Datura, gi = gastrointestinal

Note: Epinephrine is containdicatied in cases of solvent induced tachyarrhythmias.

REFERENCES

1. Weigelt JA: Resuscitation and initial management. Crit Care Clin 9:657-71, 1993
2. Barton CW, Manning JE: Cardiopulmonary resuscitation. Emerg Med Clin North Am 13:811-29, 1995
3. Bishop MJ: Practice guidelines for airway care during resuscitation. Respir Care 40:393- 401; discussion 401-3, 1995
4. Britt LD, Weireter LJ, Jr., Riblet JL, Asensio JA, Maull K: Priorities in the management of profound shock. Surg Clin North Am 76:645-60, 1996
5. Krenzelok EP, Leikin JB: Approach to the poisoned patient. Dis Mon 42:509-607, 1996
6. Olson KR, Pentel PR, Kelley MT: Physical assessment and differential diagnosis of the poisoned patient. Med Toxicol 2:52-81, 1987
7. Peterson J: Coma. In Emergency Medicine, Concepts and Ciinical Practice. Edited by P Rosen and RM Barkin. Vol 2. St Louis, Mosby Year Book, 1992, pp 1728-1751
8. Guido ME, Brady W, DeBehnke D: Reversible neurological deficits in a chronic alcohol abuser: a case report of Wernicke's encephalopathy. Am J Emerg Med 12:238-40, 1994
9. Wrenn KD, Murphy F, Slovis CM: A toxicity study of parenteral thiamine hydrochloride. Ann Emerg Med 18:867-70, 1989
10. Centerwall BS, Criqui MH: Prevention of the Wernicke-Korsakoff syndrome: a cost- benefit analysis. N Engl J Med 299:285-9, 1978
11. Matchar DB, Divine GW, Heyman A, Feussner JR: The influence of hyperglycemia on outcome of cerebral infarction. Ann Intern Med 117:449-56, 1992
12. Dietrich WD, Alonso O, Busto R: Moderate hyperglycemia worsens acute blood-brain barrier injury after forebrain ischemia in rats. Stroke 24:111-6, 1993

Brett A. Roth et al.

13. de Falco FA, Sepe Visconti O, Fucci G, Caruso G: Correlation between hyperglycemia and cerebral infarct size in patients with stroke. A clinical and X-ray computed tomography study in 104 patients. Schweiz Arch Neurol Psychiatr 144:233-9, 1993

14. Browning RG, Olson DW, Stueven HA, Mateer JR: 50% dextrose: antidote or toxin? J Emerg Nurs 16:342-9, 1990

15. Hoffman RS, Goldfrank LR: The poisoned patient with altered consciousness. Controversies in the use of a 'coma cocktail'. Jama 274:562-9, 1995

16. Fowkes J: Opiates in the Emergency Department Toxicology and Infectious Disease in Emergency Medicine, San Diego, CA, 1992

17. Osterwalder JJ: Naloxone—for intoxications with intravenous heroin and heroin mixtures--harmless or hazardous? A prospective clinical study. J Toxicol Clin Toxicol 34:409-16, 1996

18. Dole VP, Fishman J, Goldfrank L, Khanna J, McGivern RF: Arousal of ethanol- intoxicated comatose patients with naloxone. Alcohol Clin Exp Res 6:275-9, 1982

19. Wedin GP, Edwards LJ: Clonidine poisoning treated with naloxone [letter]. Am J Emerg Med 7:343-4, 1989

20. Alberto G, Erickson T, Popiel R, Narayanan M, Hryhorczuk D: Central nervous system manifestations of a valproic acid overdose responsive to naloxone. Ann Emerg Med 18:889-91, 1989

21. Varon J, Duncan SR: Naloxone reversal of hypotension due to captopril overdose. Ann Emerg Med 20:1125-7, 1991

22. Harrington LW: Acute pulmonary edema following use of naloxone: a case study. Crit Care Nurse 8:69-73, 1988

23. Schwartz JA, Koenigsberg MD: Naloxone-induced pulmonary edema. Ann Emerg Med 16:1294-6, 1987

24. Partridge BL, Ward CF: Pulmonary edema following low-dose naloxone administration [letter]. Anesthesiology 65:709-10, 1986

25. Prough DS, Roy R, Bumgarner J, Shannon G: Acute pulmonary edema in healthy teenagers following conservative doses of intravenous naloxone. Anesthesiology 60:485-6, 1984

26. Taff RH: Pulmonary edema following naloxone administration in a patient without heart disease. Anesthesiology 59:576-7, 1983

27. Flacke JW, Flacke WE, Williams GD: Acute pulmonary edema following naloxone reversal of high-dose morphine anesthesia. Anesthesiology 47:376-8, 1977

28. Wasserberger J, Ordog GJ: Naloxone-induced hypertension in patients on clonidine [letter]. Ann Emerg Med 17:557, 1988

29. Levin ER, Sharp B, Drayer JI, Weber MA: Severe hypertension induced by naloxone. Am J Med Sci 290:70-2, 1985

30. Azar I, Turndorf H: Severe hypertension and multiple atrial premature contractions following naloxone administration. Anesth Analg 58:524-5, 1979

31. Mariani PJ: Seizure associated with low-dose naloxone. Am J Emerg Med 7:127-9, 1989

32. Michaelis LL, Hickey PR, Clark TA, Dixon WM: Ventricular irritability associated with the use of naloxone hydrochloride. Two case reports and laboratory assessment of the effect of the drug on cardiac excitability. Ann Thorac Surg 18:608-14, 1974

33. Cuss FM, Colaco CB, Baron JH: Cardiac arrest after reversal of effects of opiates with naloxone. Br Med J (Clin Res Ed) 288:363-4, 1984

34. Gaddis GM, Watson WA: Naloxone-associated patient violence: an overlooked toxicity? Ann Pharmacother 26:196-8, 1992

35. Rock P, Silverman H, Plump D, Kecala Z, Smith P, Michael JR, Summer W: Efficacy and safety of naloxone in septic shock. Crit Care Med 13:28-33, 1985

36. Groeger JS, Carlon GC, Howland WS: Naloxone in septic shock. Crit Care Med 11:650- 4, 1983

37. Gurll NJ, Reynolds DG, Vargish T, Lechner R: Naloxone without transfusion prolongs survival and enhances cardiovascular function in hypovolemic shock. J Pharmacol Exp Ther 220:621-4, 1982

38. Groeger JS, Inturrisi CE: High-dose naloxone: pharmacokinetics in patients in septic shock. Crit Care Med 15:751-6, 1987

39. Olinger CP, Adams HP, Jr., Brott TG, Biller J, Barsan WG, Toffol GJ, Eberle RW, Marler JR: High-dose intravenous naloxone for the treatment of acute ischemic stroke. Stroke 21:721-5, 1990

40. Baskin DS, Kieck CF, Hosobuchi Y: Naloxone reversal and morphine exacerbation of neurologic deficits secondary to focal cerebral ischemia in baboons. Brain Res 290:289-96, 1984

41. Baskin DS, Hosobuchi Y: Naloxone and focal cerebral ischemia [letter]. J Neurosurg 60:1328-31, 1984

42. Baskin DS, Hosobuchi Y: Naloxone reversal of ischaemic neurological deficits in man. Lancet 2:272-5, 1981

43. Flamm ES, Young W, Collins WF, Piepmeier J, Clifton GL, Fischer B: A phase I trial of naloxone treatment in acute spinal cord injury. J Neurosurg 63:390-7, 1985

44. Young W, DeCrescito V, Flamm ES, Blight AR, Gruner JA: Pharmacological therapy of acute spinal cord injury: studies of high dose methylprednisolone and naloxone. Clin Neurosurg 34:675-97, 1988

45. Bracken MB, Shepard MJ, Collins WF, Holford TR, Young W, Baskin DS, Eisenberg HM, Flamm E, Leo-Summers L, Maroon J, et al.: A randomized, controlled trial of methylprednisolone or naloxone in the treatment of acute spinal-cord injury. Results of the Second National Acute Spinal Cord Injury Study [see comments]. N Engl J Med 322:1405-11, 1990

46. Cohen MR, Cohen RM, Pickar D, Weingartner H, Murphy DL: High-dose naloxone infusions in normals. Dose-dependent behavioral, hormonal, and physiological responses. Arch Gen Psychiatry 40:613-9, 1983

47. Cohen RM, Cohen MR, Weingartner H, Pickar D, Murphy DL: High-dose naloxone affects task performance in normal subjects. Psychiatry Res 8:127-36, 1983

48. Gerra G, Marcato A, Caccavari R, Fontanesi B, Delsignore R, Fertonani G, Avanzini P, Rustichelli P, Passeri M: Clonidine and opiate receptor antagonists in the treatment of heroin addiction. J Subst Abuse Treat 12:35-41, 1995

49. Stine SM, Kosten TR: Use of drug combinations in treatment of opioid withdrawal. J Clin Psychopharmacol 12:203-9, 1992

50. Creighton FJ, Ghodse AH: Naloxone applied to conjunctiva as a test for physical opiate dependence. Lancet 1:748-50, 1989

51. Loimer N, Hofmann P, Chaudhry HR: Nasal administration of naloxone for detection of opiate dependence. J Psychiatr Res 26:39-43, 1992

52. Wilhelm JA, Veng-Pedersen P, Zakszewski TB, Osifchin E, Waters SJ: Duration of opioid antagonism by nalmefene and naloxone in the dog. A nonparametric pharmacodynamic comparison based on generalized cross-validated spline estimation. Int J Clin Pharmacol Ther 33:540-5, 1995

53. Barsan WG, Seger D, Danzl DF, Ling LJ, Bartlett R, Buncher R, Bryan C: Duration of antagonistic effects of nalmefene and naloxone in opiate-induced sedation for emergency department procedures. Am J Emerg Med 7:155-61, 1989

54. Kaplan JL, Marx JA: Effectiveness and safety of intravenous nalmefene for emergency department patients with suspected narcotic overdose: a pilot study. Ann Emerg Med 22:187-90, 1993

55. Ellenhorn M: Ellenhorn's Medical Toxicology. Edited by M Ellenhorn, second edition. New York, Elsevier Science Publishing Company, 1997, pp 437-438

56. Kearney T: Flumazenil. In Poisoning & Drug Overdose. Edited by O KR, 2nd edition. Englewood Cliffs, Appleton & Lange, 1994, pp 340-341

57. Dunton AW, Schwam E, Pitman V, McGrath J, Hendler J, Siegel J: Flumazenil: US clinical pharmacology studies. Eur J Anaesthesiol Suppl 2:81-95, 1988

58. Jensen S, Knudsen L, Kirkegaard L: Flumazenil used in the antagonizing of diazepam and midazolam sedation in out-patients undergoing gastroscopy. Eur J Anaesthesiol Suppl 2:161-6, 1988

59. Kirkegaard L, Knudsen L, Jensen S, Kruse A: Benzodiazepine antagonist Ro 15-1788. Antagonism of diazepam sedation in outpatients undergoing gastroscopy. Anaesthesia 41:1184-8, 1986

60. Sewing KF: The value of flumazenil in the reversal of midazolam-induced sedation for upper gastrointestinal endoscopy [letter; comment]. Aliment Pharmacol Ther 4:315, 1990

61. Bartelsman JF, Sars PR, Tytgat GN: Flumazenil used for reversal of midazolam-induced sedation in endoscopy outpatients. Gastrointest Endosc 36:S9-12, 1990

62. Davies CA, Sealey CM, Lawson JI, Grant IS: Reversal of midazolam sedation with flumazenil following conservative dentistry. J Dent 18:113-8, 1990

63. Chern TL, Hu SC, Lee CH, Deng JF: Diagnostic and therapeutic utility of flumazenil in comatose patients with drug overdose. Am J Emerg Med 11:122-4, 1993

64. Weinbroum A, Halpern P, Geller E: The use of flumazenil in the management of acute drug poisoning—a review. Intensive Care Med 17 Suppl 1:S32-8, 1991

65. Weinbroum A, Rudick V, Sorkine P, Nevo Y, Halpern P, Geller E, Niv D: Use of flumazenil in the treatment of drug overdose: a double-blind and open clinical study in 110 patients. Crit Care Med 24:199-206, 1996

66. Thomas P, Lebrun C, Chatel M: De novo absence status epilepticus as a benzodiazepine withdrawal syndrome. Epilepsia 34:355-8, 1993

67. Spivey WH: Flumazenil and seizures: analysis of 43 cases. Clin Ther 14:292-305, 1992

68. Chern TL, Kwan A: Flumazenil-induced seizure accompanying benzodiazepine and baclofen intoxication [letter]. Am J Emerg Med 14:231-2, 1996

69. McDuffee AT, Tobias JD: Seizure after flumazenil administration in a pediatric patient. Pediatr Emerg Care 11:186-7, 1995

70. Mordel A, Winkler E, Almog S, Tirosh M, Ezra D: Seizures after flumazenil administration in a case of combined benzodiazepine and tricyclic antidepressant overdose. Crit Care Med 20:1733-4, 1992

71. Lheureux P, Vranckx M, Leduc D, Askenasi R: Risks of flumazenil in mixed benzodiazepine-tricyclic antidepressant overdose: report of a preliminary study in the dog. J Toxicol Clin Exp 12:43-53, 1992

72. Treatment of benzodiazepine overdose with flumazenil. The Flumazenil in Benzodiazepine Intoxication Multicenter Study Group. Clin Ther 14:978-95, 1992

73. Haverkos GP, DiSalvo RP, Imhoff TE: Fatal seizures after flumazenil administration in a patient with mixed overdose. Ann Pharmacother 28:1347-9, 1994

74. Lim AG: Death after flumazenil [letter] [published erratum appears in BMJ 1989 Dec 16;299(6714):1531] [see comments]. Bmj 299:858-9, 1989

75. Serfaty M, Masterton G: Fatal poisonings attributed to benzodiazepines in Britain during the 1980s [see comments]. Br J Psychiatry 163:386-93, 1993

76. Greenblatt DJ, Allen MD, Noel BJ, Shader RI: Acute overdosage with benzodiazepine derivatives. Clin Pharmacol Ther 21:497-514, 1977

77. The Committee on Trauma: Early Care of the Injured Patient, 4th edition. Chicago, American College of Surgeons, 1990

78. Rau JL: ACLS drugs used during resuscitation. Resp Care 40:404-426, 1995

79. Tucker KJ, Larson JL, Idris A, Curtis AB: Advanced cardiac life support: update on recent guidelines and a look at the future. Clin Cardiol 18:497-504, 1995

80. Committee on Emergency Cardiac Care: Textbook of Advanced Cardiac Life Support. Edited by R Cummins, American Heart Association, 1994

81. Harper C, Fornes P, Duyckaerts C, Lecomte D, Hauw JJ: An international perspective on the prevalence of the Wernicke-Korsakoff syndrome. Metab Brain Dis 10:17-24, 1995

82. Peeters A, Van de Wyngaert F, Van Lierde M, Sindic CJ, Laterre EC: Wernicke's encephalopathy and central pontine myelinolysis induced by hyperemesis gravidarum. Acta Neurol Belg 93:276-82, 1993

83. Boldorini R, Vago L, Lechi A, Tedeschi F, Trabattoni GR: Wernicke's encephalopathy: occurrence and pathological aspects in a series of 400 AIDS patients. Acta Biomed Ateneo Parmense 63:43-9, 1992

84. Tate JR, Nixon PF: Measurement of Michaelis constant for human erythrocyte transketolase and thiamin diphosphate. Anal Biochem 160:78-87, 1987

85. Reuler JB, Girard DE, Cooney TG: Current concepts. Wernicke's encephalopathy. N Engl J Med 312:1035-9, 1985

86. Hoffman JR, Schriger DL, Votey SR, Luo JS: The empiric use of hypertonic dextrose in patients with altered mental status: a reappraisal. Ann Emerg Med 21:20-4, 1992

87. Cheeley RD, Joyce SM: A clinical comparison of the performance of four blood glucose reagent strips. Am J Emerg Med 8:11-5, 1990

88. Jones JL, Ray VG, Gough JE, Garrison HG, Whitley TW: Determination of prehospital blood glucose: a prospective, controlled study. J Emerg Med 10:679-82, 1992

89. Wilkins BH, Kalra D: Comparison of blood glucose test strips in the detection of neonatal hypoglycaemia. Arch Dis Child 57:948-50, 1982

90. Barreau PB, Buttery JE: The effect of the haematocrit value on the determination of glucose levels by reagent-strip methods. Med J Aust 147:286-8, 1987

91. Boyle PJ, Schwartz NS, Shah SD, Clutter WE, Cryer PE: Plasma glucose concentrations at the onset of hypoglycemic symptoms in patients with poorly controlled diabetes and in nondiabetics. N Engl J Med 318:1487-92, 1988

92. Hoffman JR, Schriger DL, Luo JS: The empiric use of naloxone in patients with altered mental status: a reappraisal. Ann Emerg Med 20:246-52, 1991

93. Weisman R: Naloxone. In Goldfrank's Toxicologic Emergencies. Edited by FN Goldfrank LR, Lewin NA, et al, 5th edition. Englewood Cliffs, Appleton & Lange, 1994, pp 784

94. Maio RF, Gaukel B, Freeman B: Intralingual naloxone injection for narcotic-induced respiratory depression. Ann Emerg Med 16:572-3, 1987

95. Loimer N, Hofmann P, Chaudhry HR: Nasal administration of naloxone is as effective as the intravenous route in opiate addicts. Int J Addict 29:819-27, 1994

96. Claeys MA, Camu F, Schneider I, Gepts E: Reversal of flunitrazepam with flumazenil: duration of antagonist activity. Eur J Anaesthesiol Suppl 2:209-17, 1988

97. Martens F, Koppel C, Ibe K, Wagemann A, Tenczer J: Clinical experience with the benzodiazepine antagonist flumazenil in suspected benzodiazepine or ethanol poisoning. J Toxicol Clin Toxicol 28:341-56, 1990

98. Persson A, Ehrin E, Eriksson L, Farde L, Hedstrom CG, Litton JE, Mindus P, Sedvall G: Imaging of [11C]-labelled Ro 15-1788 binding to benzodiazepine receptors in the human brain by positron emission tomography. J Psychiatr Res 19:609-22, 1985

99. Hojer J, Baehrendtz S, Magnusson A, Gustafsson LL: A placebo-controlled trial of flumazenil given by continuous infusion in severe benzodiazepine overdosage. Acta Anaesthesiol Scand 35:584-90, 1991

100. Goldfrank L, Weisman RS, Errick JK, Lo MW: A dosing nomogram for continuous infusion intravenous naloxone. Ann Emerg Med 15:566-70, 1986

101. Mofenson HC, Caraccio TR: Continuous infusion of intravenous naloxone [letter]. Ann Emerg Med 16:600, 1987

102. Use of patient restraint. American College of Emergency Physicians. Ann Emerg Med 28:384, 1996

103. Shanaberger CJ: What price patient restraint? Orwick v. Fox. J Emerg Med Serv JEMS 18:69-71, 1993

104. Stratton SJ, Rogers C, Green K: Sudden death in individuals in hobble restraints during paramedic transport. Ann Emerg Med 25:710-2, 1995

105. Lavoie FW: Consent, involuntary treatment, and the use of force in an urban emergency department. Ann Emerg Med 21:25-32, 1992

106. May JR: Hospital violence. J Healthc Prot Manage 11:25-44, 1995

107. Cembrowicz SP, Shepherd JP: Violence in the Accident and Emergency Department. Med Sci Law 32:118-22, 1992

108. Gunnels M: Violence in the emergency department: a daily challenge [letter]. J Emerg Nurs 19:277, 1993

109. Tammelleo AD: Failure to restrain AIDS patient: RN's death sentence? Regan Rep Nurs Law 33:1, 1993

110. Rumack BH: Editorial: Physostigmine: rational use. Jacep 5:541-2, 1976

111. Lenox RH, Newhouse PA, Creelman WL, Whitaker TM: Adjunctive treatment of manic agitation with lorazepam versus haloperidol: a double-blind study. J Clin Psychiatry 53:47-52, 1992

Brett A. Roth et al.

112. Cavanaugh SV: Psychiatric emergencies. Med Clin North Am 70:1185-202, 1986
113. Stevens A, Stevens I, Mahal A, Gaertner HJ: Haloperidol and lorazepam combined: clinical effects and drug plasma levels in the treatment of acute schizophrenic psychosis. Pharmacopsychiatry 25:273-7, 1992
114. Catravas JD, Waters IW: Acute cocaine intoxication in the conscious dog: studies on the mechanism of lethality. J Pharmacol Exp Ther 217:350-6, 1981
115. Guinn MM, Bedford JA, Wilson MC: Antagonism of intravenous cocaine lethality in nonhuman primates. Clin Toxicol 16:499-508, 1980
116. Derlet RW, Albertson TE: Diazepam in the prevention of seizures and death in cocaine-intoxicated rats. Ann Emerg Med 18:542-6, 1989
117. Merigian KS, Park LJ, Leeper KV, Browning RG, Giometi R: Adrenergic crisis from crack cocaine ingestion: report of five cases. J Emerg Med 12:485-90, 1994
118. Shephard RA: Behavioral effects of GABA agonists in relation to anxiety and benzodiazepine action. Life Sci 40:2429-36, 1987
119. Norman TR, Burrows GD: Anxiety and the benzodiazepine receptor. Prog Brain Res 65:73-90, 1986
120. Derlet RW, Albertson TE, Rice P: The effect of haloperidol in cocaine and amphetamine intoxication. J Emerg Med 7:633-7, 1989
121. Derlet RW, Albertson TE, Rice P: Antagonism of cocaine, amphetamine, and methamphetamine toxicity. Pharmacol Biochem Behav 36:745-9, 1990
122. Derlet RW, Albertson TE, Rice P: Protection against d-amphetamine toxicity. Am J Emerg Med 8:105-8, 1990
123. Espelin D: Amphetamine poisoning: Effectiveness of clorpromazine. N Engl J Med 278:1361-1365, 1968
124. Callaway CW, Clark RF: Hyperthermia in psychostimulant overdose. Ann Emerg Med 24:68-76, 1994
125. Soyka M, Botschev C, Volcker A: Neuroleptic treatment in alcohol hallucinosis: No evidence for increased seizure risk. J clin Psychopharmacol 12:66-67, 1992
126. Lipka LJ, Lathers CM: Psychoactive agents, seizure production, and sudden death in epilepsy. J Clin Pharmacol 27:169-83, 1987
127. Hoffman BD, R: Cocaine intoxication considerations, complications and strategies: Point and counterpoint. Emerg Med 1:1-6, 1992
128. Witkin J, Godberg, SR, Katz, JL: Lethal effects of coaine are reduced gy the dopamine-1 receptor antagonist SCH 23390 but not by haloperidol. Life Sci 44:1285-1291, 1989
129. Pollera CF, Cognetli F, Nardi M, Mozza D: Sudden death after acute dystonic reaction to high-dose metoclopramide [letter]. Lancet 2:460-1, 1984
130. Barach E, Dubin LM, Tomlanovich MC, Kottamasu S: Dystonia presenting as upper airway obstruction. J Emerg Med 7:237-40, 1989
131. Cavanaugh JJ, Finlayson RE: Rhabdomyolysis due to acute dystonic reaction to antipsychotic drugs. J Clin Psychiatry 45:356-7, 1984
132. Addonizio G, Alexopoulos GS: Drug-induced dystonia in young and elderly patients. Am J Psychiatry 145:869-71, 1988
133. Menza MA, Murray GB, Holmes VF, Rafuls WA: Controlled study of extrapyramidal reactions in the management of delirious, medically ill patients: intravenous haloperidol versus intravenous haloperidol plus benzodiazepines. Heart Lung 17:238-41, 1988
134. Spina E, Sturiale V, Valvo S, Ancione M, Di Rosa AE, Meduri M, Caputi AP: Prevalence of acute dystonic reactions associated with neuroleptic treatment with and without anticholinergic prophylaxis. Int Clin Psychopharmacol 8:21-4, 1993
135. Shenoy RS: Pitfalls in the treatment of jimsonweed intoxication [letter]. Am J Psychiatry 151:1396-7, 1994
136. Hurlbut KM: Drug-induced psychoses. Emerg Med Clin North Am 9:31-52, 1991
137. Kopman AF, Strachovsky G, Lichtenstein L: Prolonged response to succinylcholine following physostigmine. Anesthesiology 49:142-3, 1978
138. Manoguerra AS, Steiner RW: Prolonged neuromuscular blockade after administration of physostigmine and succinylcholine. Clin Toxicol 18:803-5, 1981

139. Pentel P, Peterson CD: Asystole complicating physostigmine treatment of tricyclic antidepressant overdose. Ann Emerg Med 9:588-90, 1980

140. Newton RW: Physostigmine salicylate in the treatment of tricyclic antidepressant overdosage. Jama 231:941-3, 1975

141. Nattel S, Bayne L, Ruedy J: Physostigmine in coma due to drug overdose. Clin Pharmacol Ther 25:96-102, 1979

142. Gay GR: Clinical management of acute and chronic cocaine poisoning. Ann Emerg Med 11:562-72, 1982

143. Khantzian EJ, McKenna GJ: Acute toxic and withdrawal reactions associated with drug use and abuse. Ann Intern Med 90:361-72, 1979

144. Powell L, Holt P: Rapid sequence induction in the emergency department. J Emerg Nurs 21:305-9, 1995

145. Dufour DG, Larose DL, Clement SC: Rapid sequence intubation in the emergency department. J Emerg Med 13:705-10, 1995

146. Fisher WA: Restraint and seclusion: a review of the literature. Am J Psychiatry 151:1584- 91, 1994

147. Splawn G: Restraining potentially violent patients. J Emerg Nurs 17:316-7, 1991

148. Wetli CV, Fishbain DA: Cocaine-induced psychosis and sudden death in recreational cocaine users. J Forensic Sci 30:873-80, 1985

149. RL OH, Lewman LV: Restraint asphyxiation in excited delirium [see comments]. Am J Forensic Med Pathol 14:289-95, 1993

150. Miles SH: Restraints and sudden death [letter; comment]. J Am Geriatr Soc 41:1013, 1993

151. Introna F, Jr., Smialek JE: The "mini-packer" syndrome. Fatal ingestion of drug containers in Baltimore, Maryland. Am J Forensic Med Pathol 10:21-4, 1989

152. Simon LC: The cocaine body packer syndrome. West Indian Med J 39:250-5, 1990

153. Geyskens P, Coenen L, Brouwers J: The "cocaine body packer" syndrome. Case report and review of the literature. Acta Chir Belg 89:201-3, 1989

154. Pollack CV, Jr., Biggers DW, Carlton FB, Jr., Achord JL, Cranston PE, Eggen JT, Griswold JA: Two crack cocaine body stuffers [clinical conference]. Ann Emerg Med 21:1370-80, 1992

155. Jimson weed poisoning—Texas, New York, and California, 1994. MMWR Morb Mortal Wkly Rep 44:41-4, 1995

156. Wetli CV, Wright RK: Death caused by recreational cocaine use. Jama 241:2519-22, 1979

157. Simpson DL, Rumack BH: Methylenedioxyamphetamine. Clinical description of overdose, death, and review of pharmacology. Arch Intern Med 141:1507-9, 1981

158. Campbell BG: Cocaine abuse with hyperthermia, seizures and fatal complications. Med J Aust 149:387-9, 1988

159. Olson KR, Kearney TE, Dyer JE, Benowitz NL, Blanc PD: Seizures associated with poisoning and drug overdose [corrected and republished article originally printed in Am J Emerg Med 1993 Nov;11(6):565-8]. Am J Emerg Med 12:392-5, 1994

160. Jonsson S, M OM, Young JB: Acute cocaine poisoning. Importance of treating seizures and acidosis. Am J Med 75:1061-4, 1983

161. Olson KR, Benowitz NL: Environmental and drug-induced hyperthermia. Pathophysiology, recognition, and management. Emerg Med Clin North Am 2:459-74, 1984

162. Meldrum BS, Vigouroux RA, Brierley JB: Systemic factors and epileptic brain damage. Prolonged seizures in paralyzed, artificially ventilated baboons. Arch Neurol 29:82-7, 1973

163. Earnest MP: Seizures. Neurol Clin 11:563-75, 1993

164. Jacobs IG, Roszler MH, Kelly JK, Klein MA, Kling GA: Cocaine abuse: neurovascular complications. Radiology 170:223-7, 1989

165. Rumbaugh CL, Bergeron RT, Fang HC, McCormick R: Cerebral angiographic changes in the drug abuse patient. Radiology 101:335-44, 1971

166. Earnest MP, Reller LB, Filley CM, Grek AJ: Neurocysticercosis in the United States: 35 cases and a review. Rev Infect Dis 9:961-79, 1987

167. Roberts JR: Initial therapeutic strategies for the treatment of status epilepticus. Emergency Medicine News 10:2,14-15, 1996

168. Finder RL, Moore PA: Benzodiazepines for intravenous conscious sedation: agonists and antagonists. Compendium 14:972, 974, 976-80 passim; quiz 984-6, 1993
169. Roth T, Roehrs TA: A review of the safety profiles of benzodiazepine hypnotics. J Clin Psychiatry 52 Suppl:38-41, 1991
170. Dement WC: Introduction. Clinical considerations. Overview of the efficacy and safety of benzodiazepine hypnotics using objective methods. J Clin Psychiatry 52 Suppl:27-30, 1991
171. Treiman DM: The role of benzodiazepines in the management of status epilepticus. Neurology 40:32-42, 1990
172. Kyriakopoulos AA, Greenblatt DJ, Shader RI: Clinical pharmacokinetics of lorazepam: a review. J Clin Psychiatry 39:16-23, 1978
173. Leppik IE, Derivan AT, Homan RW, Walker J, Ramsay RE, Patrick B: Double-blind study of lorazepam and diazepam in status epilepticus. Jama 249:1452-4, 1983
174. Levy RJ, Krall RL: Treatment of status epilepticus with lorazepam. Arch Neurol 41:605- 11, 1984
175. Bebin M, Bleck TP: New anticonvulsant drugs. Focus on flunarizine, fosphenytoin, midazolam and stiripentol. Drugs 48:153-71, 1994
176. Kumar A, Bleck TP: Intravenous midazolam for the treatment of refractory status epilepticus. Crit Care Med 20:483-8, 1992
177. Schalen W, Messeter K, Nordstrom CH: Complications and side effects during thiopentone therapy in patients with severe head injuries. Acta Anaesthesiol Scand 36:369-77, 1992
178. Singbartl G, Cunitz G: [Pathophysiologic principles, emergency medical aspects and anesthesiologic measures in severe brain trauma]. Anaesthesist 36:321-32, 1987
179. Lee TL: Pharmacology of propofol. Ann Acad Med Singapore 20:61-5, 1991
180. Sellers EM: Alcohol, barbiturate and benzodiazepine withdrawal syndromes: clinical management. Can Med Assoc J 139:113-20, 1988
181. Sullivan JT, Seller EM: Treating alcohol, barbiturate, and benzodiazepine withdrawal. Ration Drug Ther 20:1-9, 1986
182. Ramsay RE, DeToledo J: Intravenous administration of fosphenytoin: options for the management of seizures. Neurology 46:S17-9, 1996
183. Staff: Clinical Pharmacology: An electronic drug reference and teaching guide. Edited by S Reents, 1.5 edition. Gainsville, Gold Standard Multimedia, 1995
184. Derlet RW, Albertson TE: Anticonvulsant modification of cocaine-induced toxicity in the rat. Neuropharmacology 29:255-9, 1990
185. Alldredge BK, Lowenstein DH, Simon RP: Placebo-controlled trial of intravenous diphenyl-hydantoin for short-term treatment of alcohol withdrawal seizures. Am J Med 87:645-8, 1989
186. Callaham M, Schumaker H, Pentel P: Phenytoin prophylaxis of cardiotoxicity in experimental amitriptyline poisoning. J Pharmacol Exp Ther 245:216-20, 1988
187. Munn RI, Farrell K: Failure to recognize status epilepticus in a paralysed patient. Can J Neurol Sci 20:234-6, 1993
188. Wolf KM, Shaughnessy AF, Middleton DB: Prolonged delirium tremens requiring massive doses of medication [see comments]. J Am Board Fam Pract 6:502-4, 1993
189. Pascual-Leone A, Dhuna A, Altafullah I, Anderson DC: Cocaine-induced seizures. Neurology 40:404-7, 1990
190. Brown E, Prager J, Lee HY, Ramsey RG: CNS complications of cocaine abuse: prevalence, pathophysiology, and neuroradiology. AJR Am J Roentgenol 159:137-47, 1992
191. Daras M, Tuchman AJ, Marks S: Central nervous system infarction related to cocaine abuse. Stroke 22:1320-5, 1991
192. Tuchman AJ, Daras M: Strokes associated with cocaine use [letter]. Arch Neurol 47:1170, 1990
193. Holland RWd, Marx JA, Earnest MP, Ranniger S: Grand mal seizures temporally related to cocaine use: clinical and diagnostic features [see comments]. Ann Emerg Med 21:772-6, 1992
194. Tek D, Olshaker JS: Heat illness. Emerg Med Clin North Am 10:299-310, 1992
195. Sarnquist F, Larson CP, Jr.: Drug-induced heat stroke. Anesthesiology 39:348-50, 1973
196. Rosenberg J, Pentel P, Pond S, Benowitz N, Olson K: Hyperthermia associated with drug intoxication. Crit Care Med 14:964-9, 1986

197. Sporer KA: The serotonin syndrome. Implicated drugs, pathophysiology and management. Drug Saf 13:94-104, 1995

198. Walter FG, Bey TA, Ruschke DS, Benowitz NL: Marijuana and hyperthermia. J Toxicol Clin Toxicol 34:217-21, 1996

199. Ebadi M, Pfeiffer RF, Murrin LC: Pathogenesis and treatment of neuroleptic malignant syndrome. Gen Pharmacol 21:367-86, 1990

200. Lecci A, Borsini F, Gragnani L, Volterra G, Meli A: Effect of psychotomimetics and some putative anxiolytics on stress-induced hyperthermia. J Neural Transm Gen Sect 83:67-76, 1991

201. Gordon CJ, Watkinson WP, JP OC, Miller DB: Effects of 3,4- methylenedioxymethamphetamine on autonomic thermoregulatory responses of the rat. Pharmacol Biochem Behav 38:339-44, 1991

202. Aniline O, Pitts FN, Jr.: Phencyclidine (PCP): a review and perspectives. Crit Rev Toxicol 10:145-77, 1982

203. Eastman JW, Cohen SN: Hypertensive crisis and death associated with phencyclidine poisoning. Jama 231:1270-1, 1975

204. McCarron MM, Schulze BW, Thompson GA, Conder MC, Goetz WA: Acute phencyclidine intoxication: incidence of clinical findings in 1,000 cases. Ann Emerg Med 10:237- 42, 1981

205. Friedman SA, Hirsch SE: Extreme hyperthermia after LSD ingestion. Jama 217:1549-50, 1971

206. Klock JC, Boerner U, Becker CE: Coma, hyperthermia and bleeding associated with massive LSD overdose. A report of eight cases. West J Med 120:183-8, 1974

207. Mercieca J, Brown EA: Acute renal failure due to rhabdomyolysis associated with use of a straitjacket in lysergide intoxication. Br Med J (Clin Res Ed) 288:1949-50, 1984

208. Armen R, Kanel G, Reynolds T: Phencyclidine-induced malignant hyperthermia causing submassive liver necrosis. Am J Med 77:167-72, 1984

209. Loghmanee F, Tobak M: Fatal malignant hyperthermia associated with recreational cocaine and ethanol abuse. Am J Forensic Med Pathol 7:246-8, 1986

210. Zorzato F, Menegazzi P, Treves S, Ronjat M: Role of malignant hyperthermia domain in the regulation of Ca2+ release channel (ryanodine receptor) of skeletal muscle sarcoplasmic reticulum. J Biol Chem 271:22759-63, 1996

211. Singarajah C, Lavies NG: An overdose of ecstasy. A role for dantrolene [see comments]. Anaesthesia 47:686-7, 1992

212. Watson JD, Ferguson C, Hinds CJ, Skinner R, Coakley JH: Exertional heat stroke induced by amphetamine analogues. Does dantrolene have a place? Anaesthesia 48:1057-60, 1993

213. Behan W, Bakheit, AMO, Hegan, PW, More, IAR: The muscle findings in the neuroleptic malignant syndrome associated with lysergic acid deithylamide. J Neurol Neurosurg Psychiatry 54:741-743, 1991

214. Woodbury MM, Woodbury MA: Neuroleptic-induced catatonia as a stage in the progression toward neuroleptic malignant syndrome. J Am Acad Child Adolesc Psychiatry 31:1161-4, 1992

215. Totten VY, Hirschenstein E, Hew P: Neuroleptic malignant syndrome presenting without initial fever: a case report. J Emerg Med 12:43-7, 1994

216. Daras M, Kakkouras L, Tuchman AJ, Koppel BS: Rhabdomyolysis and hyperthermia after cocaine abuse: a variant of the neuroleptic malignant syndrome? Acta Neurol Scand 92:161-5, 1995

217. Wetli CV, Mash D, Karch SB: Cocaine-associated agitated delirium and the neuroleptic malignant syndrome. Am J Emerg Med 14:425-8, 1996

218. SFPCC: Poisoning & Drug Overdose. In A Lange Clinical Manual. Edited by K Olson. Norwalk, Appleton & Lange, 1994

219. Zalis EG, Kaplan G: The effect of aggregation on amphetamine toxicity in the dog. Arch Int Pharmacodyn Ther 159:196-9, 1966

220. Zalis EG, Lundberg GD, Knutson RA: The pathophysiology of acute amphetamine poisoning with pathologic correlation. J Pharmacol Exp Ther 158:115-27, 1967

221. Zalis EG KG, Lundberg GD, et al:: Acute lethality of the amphetamines in dogs and its antagonism by curare. Proc Soc Exp Biol Med :557, 1965

222. Davis WM, Hackett RB, Obrosky KW, Waters IW: Factors in the lethality of i.v. phencyclidine in conscious dogs. Gen Pharmacol 22:723-8, 1991

223. Callaham M: Emergency management of heat illness. Chicago, Abbott Laboratories, 1979
224. Spring C: Heat stroke: modern approaches to an ancient disease. Chest 77:461, 1980
225. Hamilton D: Heat stroke. Anaesthesia 32:271, 1976
226. Walker J, Vance, MV: Heat emergencies. In Emergency Medicine: A comprehensive study guide. Edited by J Tintinalli, Ruiz, E, Krome, RL, 4th edition. New York, McGraw-Hill, 1996, pp 850-856
227. Rabinowitz RP, Cookson ST, Wasserman SS, Mackowiak PA: Effects of anatomic site, oral stimulation, and body position on estimates of body temperature. Arch Intern Med 156:777-80, 1996
228. Hooker EA, Houston H: Screening for fever in an adult emergency department: oral vs tympanic thermometry. South Med J 89:230-4, 1996
229. Yaron M, Lowenstein SR, Koziol-McLain J: Measuring the accuracy of the infrared tympanic thermometer: correlation does not signify agreement. J Emerg Med 13:617-21, 1995
230. Selfridge J, Shea SS: The accuracy of the tympanic membrane thermometer in detecting fever in infants aged 3 months and younger in the emergency department setting. J Emerg Nurs 19:127-30, 1993
231. White N, Baird S, Anderson DL: A comparison of tympanic thermometer readings to pulmonary artery catheter core temperature recordings. Appl Nurs Res 7:165-9, 1994
232. Doezema D, Lunt M, Tandberg D: Cerumen occlusion lowers infrared tympanic membrane temperature measurement. Acad Emerg Med 2:17-9, 1995
233. Cabanac M, Germain M, Brinnel H: Tympanic temperatures during hemiface cooling. Eur J Appl Physiol 56:534-9, 1987
234. Yarbrough B: Heat Illness. In Emergency Medicine: Concepts and clinical practice. Edited by Ra Barkin. Vol 1. St Louis, Mosby Year Book, 1992, pp 944-964
235. O. Donnell TF J, Clowes GH, Jr.: The circulatory requirements of heat stroke. Surg Forum 22:12-4, 1971
236. O. Donnell TF J, Clowes GH, Jr.: The circulatory abnormalities of heat stroke. N Engl J Med 287:734-7, 1972
237. Zahger D, Moses A, Weiss AT: Evidence of prolonged myocardial dysfunction in heat stroke [see comments]. Chest 95:1089-91, 1989
238. Seraj MA, Channa AB, al Harthi SS, Khan FM, Zafrullah A, Samarkandi AH: Are heat stroke patients fluid depleted? Importance of monitoring central venous pressure as a simple guideline for fluid therapy. Resuscitation 21:33-9, 1991
239. Clowes GH, Jr., O. Donnell TF J: Heat stroke. N Engl J Med 291:564-7, 1974
240. Gottschalk PG, Thomas JE: Heat stroke. Mayo Clin Proc 41:470-82, 1966
241. Rockhold RW, Carver ES, Ishizuka Y, Hoskins B, Ho IK: Dopamine receptors mediate cocaine-induced temperature responses in spontaneously hypertensive and Wistar-Kyoto rats. Pharmacol Biochem Behav 40:157-62, 1991
242. Kosten TR, Kleber HD: Rapid death during cocaine abuse: a variant of the neuroleptic malignant syndrome? Am J Drug Alcohol Abuse 14:335-46, 1988
243. Fox AW: More on rhabdomyolysis associated with cocaine intoxication [letter]. N Engl J Med 321:1271, 1989
244. Travis SP: Management of heat stroke. J R Nav Med Serv 74:39-43, 1988
245. Rumack BH: Aspirin versus acetaminophen: a comparative view. Pediatrics 62:943-6, 1978
246. McFadden S, Haddow, JE: Coma produced by topical application of isopropanol. Pediatrics 43:622, 1969
247. Gabow PA, Kaehny WD, Kelleher SP: The spectrum of rhabdomyolysis. Medicine 61:141-152, 1982
248. Bogaerts Y, Lameire N, Ringoir S: The compartmental syndrome: A serious complication of acute rhabdomyolysis. Clin Nephrol 17:206-211, 1982
249. Akisu M, Mir S, Genc B, Cura A: Severe acute thinner intoxication. Turk J Pediatr 38:223- 5, 1996
250. Akmal M, Valdin JR, McCarron MM, Massry SG: Rhabdomyolysis with and without acute renal failure in patients with phencyclidine intoxication. Am J Nephrol 1:91-6, 1981

251. Anand V, Siami G, Stone WJ: Cocaine-associated rhabdomyolysis and acute renal failure [see comments]. South Med J 82:67-9, 1989

252. Bakir AA, Dunea G: Drugs of abuse and renal disease. Curr Opin Nephrol Hypertens 5:122-6, 1996

253. Chan P, Lin TH, Luo JP, Deng JF: Acute heroin intoxication with complications of acute pulmonary edema, acute renal failure, rhabdomyolysis and lumbosacral plexitis: a case report. Chung Hua I Hsueh Tsa Chih (Taipei) 55:397-400, 1995

254. Chan P, Chen JH, Lee MH, Deng JF: Fatal and nonfatal methamphetamine intoxication in the intensive care unit. J Toxicol Clin Toxicol 32:147-55, 1994

255. Cogen FC, Rigg G, Simmons JL, Domino EF: Phencyclidine-associated acute rhabdomyolysis. Ann Intern Med 88:210-2, 1978

256. Henry JA, Jeffreys KJ, Dawling S: Toxicity and deaths from 3,4- methylenedioxymethamphetamine ("ecstasy") [see comments]. Lancet 340:384-7, 1992

257. Melandri R, Re G, Lanzarini C, Rapezzi C, Leone O, Zele I, Rocchi G: Myocardial damage and rhabdomyolysis associated with prolonged hypoxic coma following opiate overdose. J Toxicol Clin Toxicol 34:199-203, 1996

258. Tehan B, Hardern R, Bodenham A: Hyperthermia associated with 3,4- methylenedioxyethamphetamine ('Eve'). Anaesthesia 48:507-10, 1993

259. Curry SC, Chang D, Connor D: Drug- and toxin-induced rhabdomyolysis. Ann Emerg Med 18:1068-84, 1989

260. Welch RD, Todd K, Krause GS: Incidence of cocaine-associated rhabdomyolysis. Ann Emerg Med 20:154-7, 1991

261. Knochel JP: Rhabdomyolysis and myoglobinuria. Annu Rev Med 33:435-443, 1982

262. Koffler A, Friedler RM, Massry SG: Acute renal failure due to nontraumatic rhabdomyolysis. Ann Intern Med 85:23-28, 1976

263. Grossman RA, Hamilton RW, Morse BM, Penn AS, Goldberg M: Nontraumatic rhabdomyolysis and acute renal failure. N Engl J Med 291:807-11, 1974

264. Knochel JP: Rhabdomyolysis and myoglobinuria. Semin Nephrol 1:75-86, 1981

265. Ron D, Taitelman U, Michaelson M, Bar-Joseph G, Bursztein S, Better OS: Prevention of acute renal failure in traumatic rhabdomyolysis. Arch Intern Med 144:277-80, 1984

266. Thomas MA, Ibels LS: Rhabdomyolysis and acute renal failure. Aust N Z J Med 15:623-8, 1985

267. Cadnapaphornchai P, Taher S, McDonald FD: Acute drug-associated rhabdomyolysis: an examination of its diverse renal manifestations and complications. Am J Med Sci 280:66-72, 1980

268. Knochel JP: Catastrophic medical events with exhaustive exercise: "white collar rhabdomyolysis". Kidney Int 38:709-19, 1990

269. Kageyama Y: Rhabdomyolysis: clinical analysis of 20 patients. Nippon Jinzo Gakkai Shi 31:1099-103, 1989

270. Ellinas PA, Rosner F: Rhabdomyolysis: report of eleven cases. J Natl Med Assoc 84:617- 24, 1992

271. Ward MM: Factors predictive of acute renal failure in rhabdomyolysis. Arch Intern Med 148:1553-7, 1988

272. Gardner JW, Kark JA: Fatal rhabdomyolysis presenting as mild heat illness in military training. Mil Med 159:160-3, 1994

273. Morocco PA: Atraumatic rhabdomyolysis in a 20-year-old bodybuilder. J Emerg Nurs 17:370-2, 1991

274. Uberoi HS, Dugal JS, Kasthuri AS, Kolhe VS, Kumar AK, Cruz SA: Acute renal failure in severe exertional rhabdomyolysis [see comments]. J Assoc Physicians India 39:677-9, 1991

275. Zurovsky Y: Effects of changes in plasma volume on fatal rhabdomyolysis in the rat induced by glycerol injections. J Basic Clin Physiol Pharmacol 3:223-37, 1992

276. Sinert R, Kohl L, Rainone T, Scalea T: Exercise-induced rhabdomyolysis. Ann Emerg Med 23:1301-6, 1994

277. Bunn HF, Jandi JH: Exchange of heme analogue hemoglobin molecules. Proc Natl Acad Sci USA 56:974-978, 1977

278. Paller MS: Hemoglobin- and myoglobin-induced acute renal failure in rats: role of iron in nephrotoxicity. Am J Physiol 255:F539-44, 1988

279. Anderson WAD, Morrison DB, Williams EF: Pathologic changes following injection of ferrihemate (hematin) in dogs. Arch Pathol 33:589-602, 1942

280. Garcia G, Snider T, Feldman M, Jones R: Nephrotoxicity of myoglobin in the rat: Relative importance of urine pH and prior dehydration (abstract). Kidney Int 19:200, 1981

281. Perri GC, Gerini P: Uraemia in the rabbit after injection of crystalline myoglobin. Br J Exp Pathol 33:440-444, 1952

282. POISONDEX(R) Editorial Staff, Kulig K: Rhabdomyolysis. Treatment protocols, POISONDEX(R), 1992

283. Eneas JF, Schoenfeld PY, Humphreys MH: The effect of infusion of mannitol-sodium bicarbonate on the clinical course of myoglobinuria. Arch Intern Med 139:801-805, 1979

284. Druml W: Prognosis of acute renal failure 1975-1995 [editorial]. Nephron 73:8-15, 1996

285. Lameire N, Hoste E, Van Loo A, Dhondt A, Bernaert P, Vanholder R: Pathophysiology, causes, and prognosis of acute renal failure in the elderly. Ren Fail 18:333-46, 1996

286. Wilson DR, Thiel G, Arce ML, Oken DE: Glycerol induced hemoglobinuric acute renal failure in the rat. 3. Micropuncture study of the effects of mannitol and isotonic saline on individual nephron function. Nephron 4:337-55, 1967

287. Kjellmer I: Potassium ion as a vasodilator during muscular exercise. Acta Physiol Scand :466-468, 1965

288. Knochel JP, Schlein EM: On the mechanism of rhabdomyolysis in potassium depletion. J Clin Invest 51:1750-8, 1972

289. Temple AR: Acute and chronic effects of aspirin toxicity and their treatment. Arch Intern Med 141:364-9, 1981

290. Javaheri S: Effects of acetazolamide on cerebrospinal fluid ions in metabolic alkalosis in dogs. J Appl Physiol 62:1582-8, 1987

291. Kaplan SA, Del Carmen FT: Experimental salicylate poisoning. Observation on the effects of carbonic anhydrase inhibitor and bicarbonate. Pediatrics 21:762-770, 1958

292. Lijnen P, Hespel P, Vanden Eynde E, Amery A: Biochemical variables in plasma and urine before and after prolonged physical exercise. Enzyme 33:134-42, 1985

293. Davis AM: Hypocalcemia in rhabdomyolysis [letter] [published erratum appears in JAMA 1987 Oct 9;258(14):1894]. Jama 257:626, 1987

294. Brown C: Phenylpropanolamine—an ongoing problem. Clin Toxicol Update 9:5-8, 1987

295. Glick R, Hoying J, Cerullo L, Perlman S: Phenylpropanolamine: an over-the-counter drug causing central nervous system vasculitis and intracerebral hemorrhage. Case report and review. Neurosurgery 20:969-74, 1987

296. Jackson C, Hart A, Robinson MD: Fatal intracranial hemorrhage associated with phenylpropanolamine, pentazocine, and tripelennamine overdose. J Emerg Med 3:127-32, 1985

297. Nahas GG, Trouve R, Manger WM: Cocaine, catecholamines and cardiac toxicity. Acta Anaesthesiol Scand Suppl 94:77-81, 1990

298. McDonald AJ, Yealy DM, Jacobson S: Oral labetalol versus oral nifedipine in hypertensive urgencies in the ED. Am J Emerg Med 11:460-3, 1993

299. Benowitz NL: Discussion over hypertension in drug abuse, 1996

300. Rahn KH: How should we treat a hypertensive emergency? Am J Cardiol 63:48C-50C, 1989

301. Haft JI: Use of the calcium-channel blocker nifedipine in the management of hypertensive emergency. Am J Emerg Med 3:25-30, 1985

302. Benowitz NL: Central nervous system manifestations of toxic disorders. In Metabolic brain dysfunction in systemic disorders. Edited by AL Arieff and RC Griggs. Boston, Little, Brown and Company, 1992, pp 409-436

303. Derlet RW, Albertson TE: Acute cocaine toxicity: antagonism by agents interacting with adrenoceptors. Pharmacol Biochem Behav 36:225-31, 1990

304. Trouve R, Nahas GG: Antidotes to lethal cocaine toxicity in the rat. Arch Int Pharmacodyn Ther 305:197-207, 1990

305. Murphy DJ, Walker ME, Culp DA, Francomacaro DV: Effects of adrenergic antagonists on cocaine-induced changes in respiratory function. Pulm Pharmacol 4:127-34, 1991

306. Smith M, Garner D, Niemann JT: Pharmacologic interventions after an LD50 cocaine insult in a chronically instrumented rat model: are beta-blockers contraindicated? Ann Emerg Med 20:768-71, 1991

307. Hessler R: Cardiovascular principles. In Goldfrank's toxicologic emergencies. Edited by LR Goldrank, NE Flomenbaum and NA Lewin. Norwalk, Appleton & Lange, 1992, pp 181-204

308. Lange RA, Cigarroa RG, Flores ED, McBride W, Kim AS, Wells PJ, Bedotto JB, Danziger RS, Hillis LD: Potentiation of cocaine-induced coronary vasoconstriction by beta- adrenergic blockade [see comments]. Ann Intern Med 112:897-903, 1990

309. Ramoska E, Sacchetti AD: Propranolol-induced hypertension in treatment of cocaine intoxication. Ann Emerg Med 14:1112-3, 1985

310. Dusenberry SJ, Hicks MJ, Mariani PJ: Labetalol treatment of cocaine toxicity [letter]. Ann Emerg Med 16:235, 1987

311. Sand IC, Brody SL, Wrenn KD, Slovis CM: Experience with esmolol for the treatment of cocaine-associated cardiovascular complications. Am J Emerg Med 9:161-3, 1991

312. Darmansjah I, Setiawati A, Prabowo P, Sukandar E, Parsoedi I, Ardaya, Bahry B, Jusman J, Anggraeni E: A dose-ranging study of labetalol in moderate to moderately severe hypertension. Int J Clin Pharmacol Ther 33:226-31, 1995

313. Kenny D, Pagel PS, Warltier DC: Attenuation of the systemic and coronary hemodynamic effects of cocaine in conscious dogs: propranolol versus labetalol. Basic Res Cardiol 87:465-77, 1992

314. Schindler CW, Tella SR, Goldberg SR: Adrenoceptor mechanisms in the cardiovascular effects of cocaine in conscious squirrel monkeys. Life Sci 51:653-60, 1992

315. Karch SB: Managing cocaine crisis [comment]. Ann Emerg Med 18:228-30, 1989

316. Gay GR, Loper KA: The use of labetalol in the management of cocaine crisis [see comments]. Ann Emerg Med 17:282-3, 1988

317. Briggs RS, Birtwell AJ, Pohl JE: Hypertensive response to labetalol in phaeochromocytoma [letter]. Lancet 1:1045-6, 1978

318. Larsen LS, Larsen A: Labetalol in the treatment of epinephrine overdose. Ann Emerg Med 19:680-2, 1990

319. Lange RA, Cigarroa RG, Yancy CW, Jr., Willard JE, Popma JJ, Sills MN, McBride W, Kim AS, Hillis LD: Cocaine-induced coronary-artery vasoconstriction [see comments]. N Engl J Med 321:1557-62, 1989

320. Boehrer JD, Moliterno DJ, Willard JE, Hillis LD, Lange RA: Influence of labetalol on cocaine-induced coronary vasoconstriction in humans. Am J Med 94:608-10, 1993

321. Pollan S, Tadjziechy M: Esmolol in the management of epinephrine- and cocaine-induced cardiovascular toxicity. Anesth Analg 69:663-4, 1989

322. B OC, Luntley JB: Acute dissection of the thoracic aorta. Esmolol is safer than and as effective as labetalol [letter; comment]. Bmj 310:875, 1995

323. Brogan WCd, Lange RA, Kim AS, Moliterno DJ, Hillis LD: Alleviation of cocaine- induced coronary vasoconstriction by nitroglycerin. J Am Coll Cardiol 18:581-6, 1991

324. Gray RJ, Bateman TM, Czer LS, Conklin C, Matloff JM: Comparison of esmolol and nitroprusside for acute post-cardiac surgical hypertension. Am J Cardiol 59:887-91, 1987

325. de Bruijn NP, Reves JG, Croughwell N, Clements F, Drissel DA: Pharmacokinetics of esmolol in anesthetized patients receiving chronic beta blocker therapy. Anesthesiology 66:323-6, 1987

326. Bashour TT: Acute myocardial infarction resulting from amphetamine abuse: a spasm- thrombus interplay? Am Heart J 128:1237-9, 1994

327. Ragland AS, Ismail Y, Arsura EL: Myocardial infarction after amphetamine use. Am Heart J 125:247-9, 1993

328. Burton BT, Rice M, Schmertzler LE: Atrioventricular block following overdose of decongestant cold medication. J Emerg Med 2:415-9, 1985

329. Pentel PR, Jentzen J, Sievert J: Myocardial necrosis due to intraperitoneal administration of phenylpropanolamine in rats. Fundam Appl Toxicol 9:167-72, 1987

330. Lucas PB, Gardner DL, Wolkowitz OM, Tucker EE, Cowdry RW: Methylphenidate- induced cardiac arrhythmias [letter]. N Engl J Med 315:1485, 1986

331. Jaffe RB: Cardiac and vascular involvement in drug abuse. Semin Roentgenol 18:207-12, 1983

332. Lewin NG, LR, and Hoffman, RS: Cocaine. In Goldfrank's Toxicologic Emergencies. Edited by L Goldfrank, fifth edition. Norwalk, Apleton & Lange, 1994, pp 847-862

333. Hollander JE: The management of cocaine-associated myocardial ischemia. N Engl J Med 333:1267-72, 1995

334. Benowitz NL: Clinical pharmacology and toxicology of cocaine [published erratum appears in Pharmacol Toxicol 1993 Jun;72(6):343]. Pharmacol Toxicol 72:3-12, 1993

335. Catravas JD, Waters IW, Walz MA, Davis WM: Acute cocaine intoxication in the conscious dog: pathophysiologic profile of acute lethality. Arch Int Pharmacodyn Ther 235:328- 40, 1978

336. Togna G, Tempesta E, Togna AR, Dolci N, Cebo B, Caprino L: Platelet responsiveness and biosynthesis of thromboxane and prostacyclin in response to in vitro cocaine treatment. Haemostasis 15:100-7, 1985

337. Schnetzer GWd: Platelets and thrombogenesis—current concepts. Am Heart J 83:552-64, 1972

338. Rezkalla SH, Mazza JJ, Kloner RA, Tillema V, Chang SH: Effects of cocaine on human platelets in healthy subjects. Am J Cardiol 72:243-6, 1993

339. Hollander JE, Hoffman RS, Gennis P, Fairweather P, DiSano MJ, Schumb DA, Feldman JA, Fish SS, Dyer S, Wax P, et al.: Nitroglycerin in the treatment of cocaine associated chest pain--clinical safety and efficacy. J Toxicol Clin Toxicol 32:243-56, 1994

340. Billman GE: Effect of calcium channel antagonists on cocaine-induced malignant arrhythmias: protection against ventricular fibrillation. J Pharmacol Exp Ther 266:407-16, 1993

341. Knuepfer MM, Branch CA: Calcium channel antagonists reduce the cocaine-induced decrease in cardiac output in a subset of rats. J Cardiovasc Pharmacol 21:390-6, 1993

342. Derlet RW, Albertson TE: Potentiation of cocaine toxicity with calcium channel blockers. Am J Emerg Med 7:464-8, 1989

343. Hoffman R: Comment to Calcium channel blockers may potentiate cocaine toxicity. aact clinical toxicolgy update , 1990

344. Nahas G, Trouve R, Demus JR, von Sitbon M: A calcium-channel blocker as antidote to the cardiac effects of cocaine intoxication [letter]. N Engl J Med 313:519-20, 1985

345. Negus BH, Willard JE, Hillis LD, Glamann DB, Landau C, Snyder RW, Lange RA: Alleviation of cocaine-induced coronary vasoconstriction with intravenous verapamil. Am J Cardiol 73:510-3, 1994

346. Hollander JE, Carter WA, Hoffman RS: Use of phentolamine for cocaine-induced myocardial ischemia [letter]. N Engl J Med 327:361, 1992

347. Bush HS: Cocaine-associated myocardial infarction. A word of caution about thrombolytic therapy [see comments]. Chest 94:878, 1988

348. Hollander JE, Burstein JL, Hoffman RS, Shih RD, Wilson LD: Cocaine-associated myocardial infarction. Clinical safety of thrombolytic therapy. Cocaine Associated Myocardial Infarction (CAMI) Study Group. Chest 107:1237-41, 1995

349. Hollander JE, Hoffman RS, Burstein JL, Shih RD, Thode HC, Jr.: Cocaine-associated myocardial infarction. Mortality and complications. Cocaine-Associated Myocardial Infarction Study Group. Arch Intern Med 155:1081-6, 1995

350. Gitter MJ, Goldsmith SR, Dunbar DN, Sharkey SW: Cocaine and chest pain: clinical features and outcome of patients hospitalized to rule out myocardial infarction [see comments]. Ann Intern Med 115:277-82, 1991

351. Hollander JE, Lozano M, Fairweather P, Goldstein E, Gennis P, Brogan GX, Cooling D, Thode HC, Gallagher EJ: "Abnormal" electrocardiograms in patients with cocaine-associated chest pain are due to "normal" variants. J Emerg Med 12:199-205, 1994

352. Derlet RW, Albertson TE, Tharratt RS: Lidocaine potentiation of cocaine toxicity. Ann Emerg Med 20:135-8, 1991

353. Liu D, Hariman RJ, Bauman JL: Cocaine concentration-effect relationship in the presence and absence of lidocaine: evidence of competitive binding between cocaine and lidocaine. J Pharmacol Exp Ther 276:568-77, 1996

354. Winecoff AP, Hariman RJ, Grawe JJ, Wang Y, Bauman JL: Reversal of the electrocardiographic effects of cocaine by lidocaine. Part 1. Comparison with sodium bicarbonate and quinidine. Pharmacotherapy 14:698-703, 1994

355. Shih RD, Hollander JE, Burstein JL, Nelson LS, Hoffman RS, Quick AM: Clinical safety of lidocaine in patients with cocaine-associated myocardial infarction. Ann Emerg Med 26:702-6, 1995

356. Beckman KJ, Parker RB, Hariman RJ, Gallastegui JL, Javaid JI, Bauman JL: Hemodynamic and electrophysiological actions of cocaine. Effects of sodium bicarbonate as an antidote in dogs. Circulation 83:1799-807, 1991

357. Barth CWd, Bray M, Roberts WC: Rupture of the ascending aorta during cocaine intoxication. Am J Cardiol 57:496, 1986

358. Brody SL, Slovis CM, Wrenn KD: Cocaine-related medical problems: consecutive series of 233 patients [see comments]. Am J Med 88:325-31, 1990

359. Derlet RW, Albertson TE: Emergency department presentation of cocaine intoxication. Ann Emerg Med 18:182-6, 1989

360. Rich JA, Singer DE: Cocaine-related symptoms in patients presenting to an urban emergency department. Ann Emerg Med 20:616-21, 1991

361. Silverstein W, Lewin NA, Goldfrank L: Management of the cocaine-intoxicated patient [letter]. Ann Emerg Med 16:234-5, 1987

362. Kloner RA, Hale S, Alker K, Rezkalla S: The effects of acute and chronic cocaine use on the heart. Circulation 85:407-19, 1992

363. Isner JM, Estes NAd, Thompson PD, Costanzo-Nordin MR, Subramanian R, Miller G, Katsas G, Sweeney K, Sturner WQ: Acute cardiac events temporally related to cocaine abuse. N Engl J Med 315:1438-43, 1986

364. Cregler LL, Mark H: Medical complications of cocaine abuse. N Engl J Med 315:1495- 500, 1986

365. Robin ED, Wong RJ, Ptashne KA: Increased lung water and ascites after massive cocaine overdosage in mice and improved survival related to beta-adrenergic blockage. Ann Intern Med 110:202-7, 1989

366. Simoons ML: Risk-benefit of thrombolysis. Cardiol Clin 13:339-45, 1995

367. Jafri SM, Walters BL, Borzak S: Medical therapy of acute myocardial infarction: Part I. Role of thrombolytic and antithrombotic therapy. J Intensive Care Med 10:54-63, 1995

368. Bode C, Nordt TK, Runge MS: Thrombolytic therapy in acute myocardial infarction-- selected recent developments. Ann Hematol 69:S35-40, 1994

369. Woo KS, White HD: Thrombolytic therapy in acute myocardial infarction. Curr Opin Cardiol 9:471-82, 1994

370. Hennekens CH: Thrombolytic therapy: pre- and post-GISSI-2, ISIS-3, and GUSTO-1. Clin Cardiol 17:I15-7, 1994

371. Williams ML, Tate DA: Emergency Medicine: A comprehensive study guide. Edited by J Tntinalli, E Ruiz and RL Krome, 4th edition. New York, McGraw-Hill, 1996, pp 344-354

372. Grawe JJ, Hariman RJ, Winecoff AP, Fischer JH, Bauman JL: Reversal of the electrocardiographic effects of cocaine by lidocaine. Part 2. Concentration-effect relationships. Pharmacotherapy 14:704-11, 1994

373. Tokarski GF, Paganussi P, Urbanski R, Carden D, Foreback C, Tomlanovich MC: An evaluation of cocaine-induced chest pain [see comments]. Ann Emerg Med 19:1088-92, 1990

374. Hollander JE, Hoffman RS, Gennis P, Fairweather P, DiSano MJ, Schumb DA, Feldman JA, Fish SS, Dyer S, Wax P, et al.: Prospective multicenter evaluation of cocaine-associated chest pain. Cocaine Associated Chest Pain (COCHPA) Study Group. Acad Emerg Med 1:330-9, 1994

375. Adams JEd, Bodor GS, Davila-Roman VG, Delmez JA, Apple FS, Ladenson JH, Jaffe AS: Cardiac troponin I. A marker with high specificity for cardiac injury [see comments]. Circulation 88:101-6, 1993

376. Wu AH, Feng YJ, Contois JH, Pervaiz S: Comparison of myoglobin, creatine kinase-MB, and cardiac troponin I for diagnosis of acute myocardial infarction. Ann Clin Lab Sci 26:291-300, 1996

377. Lee TH, Juarez G, Cook EF, Weisberg MC, Rouan GW, Brand DA, Goldman L: Ruling out acute myocardial infarction. A prospective multicenter validation of a 12-hour strategy for patients at low risk [see comments]. N Engl J Med 324:1239-46, 1991

378. Graff L, Joseph T, Andelman R, Bahr R, DeHart D, Espinosa J, Gibler B, Hoekstra J, Mathers-Dunbar L, Ornato JP, et al.: American College of Emergency Physicians information paper: chest pain units in emergency departments—a report from the Short-Term Observation Services Section. Am J Cardiol 76:1036-9, 1995

379. Hollander JE, Hoffman RS: Cocaine-induced myocardial infarction: an analysis and review of the literature. J Emerg Med 10:169-77, 1992

380. Zimmerman JL, Dellinger RP, Majid PA: Cocaine-associated chest pain. Ann Emerg Med 20:611-5, 1991

381. Kokkinos J, Levine, S: Stroke. Neurologic Clinics 11:577-590, 1993

382. Kaku D, Lowenstein, DH: Emergence of recreational drug abuse as a major risk factor for stroke in young adults. Ann Intern Med 113:821, 1990

383. Tardiff K, Gross E, Wu J, Stajic M, Millman R: Analysis of cocaine-positive fatalities. J Forensic Sci 34:53-63, 1989

384. Mueller PD, Benowitz NL, Olson KR: Cocaine. Emerg Med Clin North Am 8:481-93, 1990

385. Barsan WG, Bain M: Stroke. In Emergency Medicine: Concepts and clinical practice. Edited by P Rosen and RM Barkin. Vol 2. St Louis, Mosby-Year Book, 1992, pp 1825-1841

386. Hacke W, Kaste M, Fieschi C, Toni D, Lesaffre E, von Kummer R, Boysen G, Bluhmki E, Hoxter G, Mahagne MH, et al.: Intravenous thrombolysis with recombinant tissue plasminogen activator for acute hemispheric stroke. The European Cooperative Acute Stroke Study (ECASS) [see comments]. Jama 274:1017-25, 1995

387. Randomised controlled trial of streptokinase, aspirin, and combination of both in treatment of acute ischaemic stroke. Multicentre Acute Stroke Trial—Italy (MAST-I) Group [comment]. Lancet 346:1509-14, 1995

388. Tissue plasminogen activator for acute ischemic stroke. The National Institute of Neurological Disorders and Stroke rt-PA Stroke Study Group [see comments]. N Engl J Med 333:1581-7, 1995

389. Thrombolytic therapy with streptokinase in acute ischemic stroke. The Multicenter Acute Stroke Trial—Europe Study Group [see comments]. N Engl J Med 335:145-50, 1996

390. Donnan GA, Davis SM, Chambers BR, Gates PC, Hankey GJ, McNeil JJ, Rosen D, Stewart-Wynne EG, Tuck RR: Streptokinase for acute ischemic stroke with relationship to time of administration: Australian Streptokinase (ASK) Trial Study Group [see comments]. Jama 276:961- 6, 1996

391. Hoffman J: Thrombolytic therapy of strokes. Emergency Medical Abstracts 20, 1996

392. Libman RB, Wirkowski E, Alvir J, Rao TH: Conditions that mimic stroke in the emergency department. Implications for acute stroke trials. Arch Neurol 52:1119-22, 1995

393. Korczyn AD: Heparin in the treatment of acute stroke. Neurol Clin 10:209-17, 1992

394. Sage JI: Stroke. The use and overuse of heparin in therapeutic trials [editorial]. Arch Neurol 42:315-7, 1985

395. Turpie AG, Bloch R, Duke R: Heparin in the treatment of thromboembolic stroke. Ann N Y Acad Sci 556:406-15, 1989

396. Salgado AV, Furlan AJ, Keys TF, Nichols TR, Beck GJ: Neurologic complications of endocarditis: a 12-year experience. Neurology 39:173-8, 1989

397. Hart RG, Foster JW, Luther MF, Kanter MC: Stroke in infective endocarditis. Stroke 21:695-700, 1990

398. Showalter CV: T's and blues. Abuse of pentazocine and tripelennamine. Jama 244:1224-5, 1980

399. Caplan LR, Thomas C, Banks G: Central nervous system complications of addiction to "T's and Blues". Neurology 32:623-8, 1982

400. Lipton RB, Choy-Kwong M, Solomon S: Headaches in hospitalized cocaine users. Headache 29:225-8, 1989

401. Benowitz NL: How toxic is cocaine? Ciba Found Symp 166:125-43; discussion 143-8, 1992

402. Satel SL, Gawin FH: Migrainelike headache and cocaine use. Jama 261:2995-6, 1989

403. Rothrock JF, Rubenstein R, Lyden PD: Ischemic stroke associated with methamphetamine inhalation. Neurology 38:589-92, 1988

404. Rumbaugh CL, Bergeron RT, Scanlan RL, Teal JS, Segall HD, Fang HC, McCormick R: Cerebral vascular changes secondary to amphetamine abuse in the experimental animal. Radiology 101:345-51, 1971

405. Rickels E, Zumkeller M: Vasospasm after experimentally induced subarachnoid haemorrhage and treatment with nimodipine. Neurochirurgia (Stuttg) 35:99-102, 1992

406. Wadworth AN, McTavish D: Nimodipine. A review of its pharmacological properties, and therapeutic efficacy in cerebral disorders. Drugs Aging 2:262-86, 1992

407. Ansah TA, Wade LH, Shockley DC: Effects of calcium channel entry blockers on cocaine and amphetamine-induced motor activities and toxicities. Life Sci 53:1947-56, 1993

408. Derlet RW, Tseng CC, Albertson TE: Cocaine toxicity and the calcium channel blockers nifedipine and nimodipine in rats. J Emerg Med 12:1-4, 1994

409. Kaste M, Fogelholm R, Erila T, Palomaki H, Murros K, Rissanen A, Sarna S: A randomized, double-blind, placebo-controlled trial of nimodipine in acute ischemic hemispheric stroke. Stroke 25:1348-53, 1994

410. Wooten MR, Khangure MS, Murphy MJ: Intracerebral hemorrhage and vasculitis related to ephedrine abuse. Ann Neurol 13:337-40, 1983

411. Rumbaugh CL, Fang HC, Higgins RE, Bergeron RT, Segall HD, Teal JS: Cerebral microvascular injury in experimental drug abuse. Invest Radiol 11:282-94, 1976

412. Citron BP, Halpern M, McCarron M, Lundberg GD, McCormick R, Pincus IJ, Tatter D, Haverback BJ: Necrotizing angiitis associated with drug abuse. N Engl J Med 283:1003-11, 1970

413. Loizou LA, Hamilton JG, Tsementzis SA: Intracranial haemorrhage in association with pseudoephedrine overdose. J Neurol Neurosurg Psychiatry 45:471-2, 1982

414. Brust JC, Richter RW: Stroke associated with addiction to heroin. J Neurol Neurosurg Psychiatry 39:194-9, 1976

415. Woods BT, Strewler GJ: Hemiparesis occurring six hours after intravenous heroin injection. Neurology 22:863-6, 1972

416. Trugman JM: Cerebral arteritis and oral methylphenidate [letter]. Lancet 1:584-5, 1988

417. Fredericks RK, Lefkowitz DS, Challa VR, Troost BT: Cerebral vasculitis associated with cocaine abuse. Stroke 22:1437-9, 1991

418. Krendel DA, Ditter SM, Frankel MR, Ross WK: Biopsy-proven cerebral vasculitis associated with cocaine abuse. Neurology 40:1092-4, 1990

419. Kaye BR, Fainstat M: Cerebral vasculitis associated with cocaine abuse. Jama 258:2104-6, 1987

420. Nalls G, Disher A, Daryabagi J, Zant Z, Eisenman J: Subcortical cerebral hemorrhages associated with cocaine abuse: CT and MR findings. J Comput Assist Tomogr 13:1-5, 1989

421. Salanova V, Taubner R: Intracerebral haemorrhage and vasculitis secondary to amphetamine use. Postgrad Med J 60:429-30, 1984

422. Fauci AS, Haynes B, Katz P: The spectrum of vasculitis: clinical, pathologic, immunologic and therapeutic considerations. Ann Intern Med 89:660-76, 1978

423. Cupps TR, Moore PM, Fauci AS: Isolated angiitis of the central nervous system. Prospective diagnostic and therapeutic experience. Am J Med 74:97-105, 1983

424. Moore PM, Fauci AS: Neurologic manifestations of systemic vasculitis. A retrospective and prospective study of the clinicopathologic features and responses to therapy in 25 patients. Am J Med 71:517-24, 1981

425. Cerebral vasculitis associated with cocaine abuse or subarachnoid hemorrhage? [letter]. Jama 259:1648-9, 1988

426. Kenton EJ, 3rd: Diagnosis and treatment of concomitant hypertension and stroke. J Natl Med Assoc 88:364-8, 1996

427. Shephard TJ, Fox SW: Assessment and management of hypertension in the acute ischemic stroke patient. J Neurosci Nurs 28:5-12, 1996

428. Powers WJ: Acute hypertension after stroke: the scientific basis for treatment decisions [editorial]. Neurology 43:461-7, 1993

429. Lev R, Rosen P: Prophylactic lidocaine use preintubation: a review. J Emerg Med 12:499-506, 1994

430. Brucia JJ, Owen DC, Rudy EB: The effects of lidocaine on intracranial hypertension. J Neurosci Nurs 24:205-14, 1992

431. Malouf R, Brust JC: Hypoglycemia: causes, neurological manifestatiohs, and outcome. Ann Neurol 17:421-30, 1985

432. Swartz MH, Teichholz LE, Donoso E: Mitral valve prolapse: a review of associated arrhythmias. Am J Med 62:377-89, 1977

433. Savage DD, Levy D, Garrison RJ, Castelli WP, Kligfield P, Devereux RB, Anderson SJ, Kannel WB, Feinleib M: Mitral valve prolapse in the general population. 3. Dysrhythmias: the Framingham Study. Am Heart J 106:582-6, 1983

434. Washington JAd: The role of the microbiology laboratory in the diagnosis and antimicrobial treatment of infective endocarditis. Mayo Clin Proc 57:22-32, 1982

435. Hoffman RS, Smilkstein MJ, Goldfrank LR: Whole bowel irrigation and the cocaine body-packer: a new approach to a common problem. Am J Emerg Med 8:523-7, 1990

436. Roberts JR, Price D, Goldfrank L, Hartnett L: The bodystuffer syndrome: a clandestine form of drug overdose. Am J Emerg Med 4:24-7, 1986

437. Olson KR: Is gut emptying all washed up? [editorial]. Am J Emerg Med 8:560-1, 1990

438. Kulig K, Bar-Or D, Cantrill SV, Rosen P, Rumack BH: Management of acutely poisoned patients without gastric emptying. Ann Emerg Med 14:562-7, 1985

439. Albertson TE, Derlet RW, Foulke GE, Minguillon MC, Tharratt SR: Superiority of activated charcoal alone compared with ipecac and activated charcoal in the treatment of acute toxic ingestions [see comments]. Ann Emerg Med 18:56-9, 1989

440. Merigian KS, Woodard M, Hedges JR, Roberts JR, Stuebing R, Rashkin MC: Prospective evaluation of gastric emptying in the self-poisoned patient. Am J Emerg Med 8:479-83, 1990

441. Pond SM, Lewis-Driver DJ, Williams GM, Green AC, Stevenson NW: Gastric emptying in acute overdose: a prospective randomised controlled trial [see comments]. Med J Aust 163:345-9, 1995

442. Curtis RA, Barone J, Giacona N: Efficacy of ipecac and activated charcoal/cathartic. Prevention of salicylate absorption in a simulated overdose. Arch Intern Med 144:48-52, 1984

443. Tenenbein M, Cohen S, Sitar DS: Efficacy of ipecac-induced emesis, orogastric lavage, and activated charcoal for acute drug overdose. Ann Emerg Med 16:838-41, 1987

444. Olkkola KT: Effect of charcoal-drug ratio on antidotal efficacy of oral activated charcoal in man. Br J Clin Pharmacol 19:767-73, 1985

445. Pollack MM, Dunbar BS, Holbrook PR, Fields AI: Aspiration of activated charcoal and gastric contents. Ann Emerg Med 10:528-9, 1981

446. Menzies DG, Busuttil A, Prescott LF: Fatal pulmonary aspiration of oral activated charcoal. Bmj 297:459-60, 1988

447. Givens T, Holloway M, Wason S: Pulmonary aspiration of activated charcoal: a complication of its misuse in overdose management. Pediatr Emerg Care 8:137-40, 1992

448. Mariani PJ, Pook N: Gastrointestinal tract perforation with charcoal peritoneum complicating orogastric intubation and lavage. Ann Emerg Med 22:606-9, 1993

449. Ray MJ, Radin DR, Condie JD, Halls JM, Padin DR: Charcoal bezoar. Small-bowel obstruction secondary to amitriptyline overdose therapy [published erratum appears in Dig Dis Sci 1988 Oct;33(10):1344]. Dig Dis Sci 33:106-7, 1988

450. Watson WA, Cremer KF, Chapman JA: Gastrointestinal obstruction associated with multiple-dose activated charcoal. J Emerg Med 4:401-7, 1986

451. Longdon P, Henderson A: Intestinal pseudo-obstruction following the use of enteral charcoal and sorbitol and mechanical ventilation with papaveretum sedation for theophylline poisoning. Drug Saf 7:74-7, 1992

452. Bradberry SM, Vale JA: Multiple-dose activated charcoal: a review of relevant clinical studies. J Toxicol Clin Toxicol 33:407-16, 1995

453. Pond SM, Olson KR, Osterloh JD, Tong TG: Randomized study of the treatment of phenobarbital overdose with repeated doses of activated charcoal. Jama 251:3104-8, 1984

454. Boldy DA, Vale JA, Prescott LF: Treatment of phenobarbitone poisoning with repeated oral administration of activated charcoal. Q J Med 61:997-1002, 1986

455. Everson GW, Bertaccini EJ, J OL: Use of whole bowel irrigation in an infant following iron overdose. Am J Emerg Med 9:366-9, 1991

456. Turk J, Aks S, Ampuero F, Hryhorczuk DO: Successful therapy of iron intoxication in pregnancy with intravenous deferoxamine and whole bowel irrigation. Vet Hum Toxicol 35:441-4, 1993

457. Bock GW, Tenenbein M: Whole bowel irrigation for iron overdose [letter]. Ann Emerg Med 16:137-8, 1987

458. Janss GJ: Acute theophylline overdose treated with whole bowel irrigation. S D J Med 43:7-8, 1990

459. Buckley N, Dawson AH, Howarth D, Whyte IM: Slow-release verapamil poisoning. Use of polyethylene glycol whole-bowel lavage and high-dose calcium. Med J Aust 158:202-4, 1993

460. Burkhart KK, Kulig KW, Rumack B: Whole-bowel irrigation as treatment for zinc sulfate overdose. Ann Emerg Med 19:1167-70, 1990

461. Melandri R, Re G, Morigi A, Lanzarini C, Vaona I, Miglioli M: Whole bowel irrigation after delayed release fenfluramine overdose. J Toxicol Clin Toxicol 33:161-3, 1995

462. Roberge RJ, Martin TG: Whole bowel irrigation in an acute oral lead intoxication. Am J Emerg Med 10:577-83, 1992

463. Utecht MJ, Stone AF, McCarron MM: Heroin body packers. J Emerg Med 11:33-40, 1993

464. Niazi S: Effect of polyethylene glycol 4000 on dissolution properties of sulfathiazole polymorphs. J Pharm Sci 65:302-4, 1976

465. Diacetylmorphine. In Merck Index, 10th edition. Rahway, NJ, Merck & Co, Inc., 1984, pp 429

466. Rosenberg PJ, Livingstone DJ, McLellan BA: Effect of whole-bowel irrigation on the antidotal efficacy of oral activated charcoal. Ann Emerg Med 17:681-3, 1988

467. Tenenbein M: Whole bowel irrigation and activated charcoal [letter]. Ann Emerg Med 18:707-8, 1989

468. Ilkhanipour K, Yealy DM, Krenzelok EP: The comparative efficacy of various multiple- dose activated charcoal regimens. Am J Emerg Med 10:298-300, 1992

469. Park GD, Radomski L, Goldberg MJ, Spector R, Johnson GF, Quee CK: Effects of size and frequency of oral doses of charcoal on theophylline clearance. Clin Pharmacol Ther 34:663-6, 1983

470. Marc B, Gherardi RK, Baud FJ, Garnier M, Diamant-Berger O: Managing drug dealers who swallow the evidence. Bmj 299:1082, 1989

471. Sporer K: Cocaine body stuffers, unpublished data, 1997

472. McCarron MM, Wood JD: The cocaine 'body packer' syndrome. Diagnosis and treatment. Jama 250:1417-20, 1983

473. Caruana DS, Weinbach B, Goerg D, Gardner LB: Cocaine-packet ingestion. Diagnosis, management, and natural history. Ann Intern Med 100:73-4, 1984

474. Jeanmarie P: Cocaine. In Emergency medicine, a comprehensive study guide. Edited by Tintinalli. New York, McGraw-Hill, 1996, pp 777-778

475. Weiner JS, Khogali M: A physiological body-cooling unit for treatment of heat stroke. Lancet 1:507-9, 1980

476. Barner HB, Wettach GE, Masar M, Wright DW: Field evaluation of a new simplified method for cooling of heat casualties in the desert. Mil Med 149:95-7, 1984

477. Al-Aska AK, Abu-Aisha H, Yaqub B, Al-Harthi SS, Sallam A: Simplified cooling bed for heatstroke [letter]. Lancet 1:381, 1987

478. Kielblock AJ, Van Rensburg JP, Franz RM: Body cooling as a method for reducing hyperthermia. An evaluation of techniques. S Afr Med J 69:378-80, 1986

479. Wyndham CH, Strydom NB, Cooke HM: Methods of cooling subjects with hyperpyrexia. J Appl Physiol 14:771, 1959

480. White JD, Riccobene E, Nucci R, Johnson C, Butterfield AB, Kamath R: Evaporation versus iced gastric lavage treatment of heatstroke: comparative efficacy in a canine model. Crit Care Med 15:748-50, 1987

481. Daily WM, Harrison TR: A study of the mechanism and treatment of experimental heat pyrexia. Am J Med Sci 215:42, 1948

482. Magazanik A, Epstein Y, Udassin R, Shapiro Y, Sohar E: Tap water, an efficient method for cooling heatstroke victims—a model in dogs. Aviat Space Environ Med 51:864-6, 1980

483. Bynum G, Patton J, Bowers W, Leav I, Hamlet M, Marsili M, Wolfe D: Peritoneal lavage cooling in an anesthetized dog heatstroke model. Aviat Space Environ Med 49:779-84, 1978

484. Syverud SA, Barker WJ, Amsterdam JT, Bills GL, Goltra DD, Armao JC, Hedges JR: Iced gastric lavage for treatment of heatstroke: efficacy in a canine model. Ann Emerg Med 14:424-32, 1985

CHAPTER 9

SPORTS

EDITED BY JORDI SEGURA

INSTITUT MUNICIPAL D' INVESTIGACIÓ MÈDICA, IMIM, DEPARTAMENT DE FARMACOLOGIA
I TOXICOLOGIA, BARCELONA, SPAIN

TABLE OF CONTENTS

Jordi Segura

9.1 INTRODUCTION

9.1.1 GENERAL CONSIDERATIONS

The misuse of drugs and medicines by athletes has been a problem for more than 30 years. The ethical and health aspects are of particular concern. Doping is considered to have occurred when substances belonging to prohibited classes of pharmacological agents are administered, or when prohibited methods are used.[1]

Prohibited substances fall into the following classes: stimulants, narcotics, anabolic agents, diuretics, and peptide and glycoprotein hormones and analogues. For each one of the groups there is a list of representative examples. No substance belonging to a prohibited class can be used, even if it has not been specifically listed. Prohibited methods include the administration of blood, red blood cells, and related blood products. In addition, any pharmaceutical, chemical, or physical manipulations which alter the integrity and validity of urine samples is also forbidden. Examples of this later category include catheterization, urine substitution, or giving drugs to decrease a drug's renal excretion. The use of ethanol, cannabis products, beta blockers, local anesthetics, and systemic corticosteroids is also regulated.

A large number of competitive athletes use drugs to improve their performance, but the exact extent is unknown. The most reliable data is from the statistics of the International Olympic Committee (IOC), which accredits laboratories controlling athletes for doping agents. In 1995, 24 IOC accredited laboratories analyzed more than 90,000 samples of athletes. Of these, 41% of the samples where obtained at competitions. The total rate of positive cases was 1.6%. Anabolic steroids had the highest incidence, accounting for 65% of the positive cases, followed by stimulants (20%), and diuretics (4%). The incidence of peptide hormones detection was low.[2]

The establishment of antidoping rules by national and international sports federations, in accordance with the rules of the IOC, has led to a decrease of doping in sports. The IOC's development of analytical techniques capable of detecting doping agents has had a significant deterrent effect on the abuse of them by athletes.

9.1.2 WIDELY ABUSED AGENTS

Anabolic steroids are particularly important, both because of their popularity and because of the harm they do to the athletes consuming them. Prevention of testosterone abuse is particularly difficult because it is identical to testosterone produced by the body. The situation is even worse with glycoprotein hormones and analogues which, thanks to progress in recombinant DNA technology, are now available.

9.1.2.1 Steroids

Athletes are not the only ones to abuse anabolic substances. Steroid abuse by young people has also become a matter of concern for health authorities. We assume that the actual number of anabolic users is even higher than indicated by the statistics. Body builders often abuse steroids, and a thriving black market provides anabolic agents to sports studios, students, and schoolchildren. For many steroid abusers, the intent is not only to improve competitive performance, but also to increase their appeal, to compensate for academic stress, and to improve feelings of well being. Risk is especially high for women and adolescents. Toxic effects on liver, changes in growth patterns, and virilization of women are common effects of synthetic anabolic steroid abuse.

Testosterone administration has been routinely detected by measuring the ratio between testosterone glucuronide and epitestosterone glucuronide, usually known simply as the T/E ratio.[3] The criteria for detection varies. Some sport bodies consider abuse to have occurred when the measured urine concentration exceeds the range normally found in humans. For other bodies, the rule is based on the detection of a T/E ratio higher than the usual population (cutoff 6:1). If the latter criteria is used, it is understood that the testing body has an obligation to perform additional investigations in order to exclude the small percentage of people having high T/E ratios due to physiological or pathological conditions.[4-6]

Evidence is accumulating that T/E ratios are relatively stable in a given subject. Ideally, the best way to detect testosterone abuse would be to detect deviations from a previously established baseline established for each individual. At least two different classes of "normal" populations exist. One has T/E values around 1 to 2, and another population has normal values of T/E around 0.2 to 0.3. Most of the low values are seen in the mongolian racial group.[7,8]

There are other ways to detect steroid ingestion. Increases in the testosterone/17 hydroxy-progesterone (T/17OHP) ratio, and in the testosterone/luteinizing hormone (T/LH) ratio, both appear to be diagnostic. The ratios change because testosterone exerts negative feedback on the release of LH by the hypophysis, and on the amount of some of its synthetic precursors in the body such as 17OHP. Testosterone is usually administered as testosterone enanthate or some other ester. Even though they hydrolyse rapidly to release free testosterone, small amounts remain in the body for a long time. The finding of testosterone esters (exogenous: not existing in our body) in the blood would be indicative of testosterone administration.[9]

Any rational approach to the detection and confirmation of testosterone doping must take into consideration the following facts:

1. T/E ratio in urine is fairly stable in a given individual.
2. External testosterone application disturbs some selected parameters such as T/17OHP in blood plasma and T/E in urine. The ratio T/LH both in blood plasma and urine is also affected. Many other markers have been studied in both plasma and urine but they have offered less definitive results.
3. Finding of esters of testosterone in blood plasma demonstrate testosterone application
4. Physiologically high T/E ratio in urine appears to be associated with epitestosterone sulfate being higher than epitestosterone glucuronide.

Testosterone abuse accounts for one of every four or five sports doping cases (20.9% of total doping cases in 1992; 25.2% in 1993; 21.9% in 1994; 19.3% in 1995) and is probably the single most abused drug by athletes.

9.1.2.2 Glycoprotein Hormones

This category includes chorionic gonadotrophin (hCG), erythropoietin (EPO), and human growth hormone (hGH). The real extent of this problem is not known. These drugs are rapidly metabolized and generally have a very short half-life. Only very small amounts of unmetabolized drug are excreted in the urine. Most detection techniques employ immunoassays that lack specificity. In some cases there are no suitable references, so results obtained by different techniques in different laboratories cannot effectively be compared, and it is difficult to establish clear criteria by which to distinguish an exogenous administration (banned) from a normal endogenous concentration.[10] Ideally, the structure of the peptide detected should be confirmed by mass spectrometry. Confirmation is difficult, although new ionization techniques, new interfaces with chromatographic or electrophoretic systems, and evolution of ion analyzers are simplifying the process.

Human chorionic gonadotrophin is taken in hopes of causing the release of the androgen and anabolic compounds that may increase power and strength. The administration of hCG, with the corresponding increase in testosterone, and its inactive isomer epitestosterone, overcomes the current methods for detection of testosterone misuse because they depend on the measurement of the quotient between both isomeric compounds.[11] In the absence of indications of an hCG-producing tumor, excessively high levels of hCG in male athletes should be indicative of exogenous application of the hormone. The use of other gonadotrophin and gonatrophin releasing factors is an additional challenge.

A number of techniques have been used for EPO doping detection: (1) blood analysis of transferrin receptors and morphology of red blood cells, (2) distinction of recombinant EPO from natural EPO in both blood and urine by electrophoresis and radioimmunoassay, and (3) distinction of recombinant EPO from natural EPO in urine by isoelectrofocusing with monoclonal antibodies used for separation and detection. No clearly superior approach has emerged.[12]

9.1.3 DETECTION OF DOPING AGENTS

Today urine samples are used to screen for drug abuse, but it seems possible that in the future blood samples will also be analyzed. Analytical methods should be capable of detecting both parent compounds and metabolites. To prove that drugs have been taken, a biological sample is drawn, under scrutinized conditions, and measures are taken to preserve both the integrity of the sample and the confidentiality of the individual involved. There are no guidelines for cutoff concentrations in body fluids as a positivity criteria. To increase the deterrent effect of testing, it is of paramount importance to increase the sensitivity of existing analytical methods and to monitor metabolites with a longer half-life. The increasing use of endogenous steroids and endogenous peptide hormones is a special problem.

A first step in any analysis is the so-called screening procedure. The initial screening procedures are designed to eliminate "true negative" specimens from further consideration. A second extraction and analysis of the same sample is used for eventual identification of the presence of a specific drug or metabolite, which is called the confirmation procedure.[7,13]

9.1.4 QUALITY ASSURANCE

Internal quality assurance is needed to assure a safe chain of custody, and application of Good Laboratory Practices (GLP). The regulations issued by the International Olympic Committee (IOC) are continuously revised, and are coming more and more to resemble those set up in other analytical fields, by other international organizations (i.e. ISO, OECD, EU). External quality assurance is a required accreditation procedure of the IOC. These procedures involve several important steps:

1. Initial requirements include the submission of a description of the laboratory's experience, a list of substances and metabolites available, and a list of studies to be used in the event of any suspicious case. A letter of support by a suitable authority is required. Some of the factors taken into account are continuity, volume of workload, long-term financial support, administrative commitment of the host institution, research activities, and accomplishments.
2. Pre-accreditation tests. Laboratories are requested to analyze three sets of samples successfully over a 6- to 12-month period.
3. Accreditation: The laboratory must analyze 10 control samples in the presence of a delegate of the IOC Medical Commission. The laboratory must correctly identify the doping agents, and their relevant metabolites, within a period of three days. At the same time, the delegate should also carry out a thorough inspection of the laboratory.
4. Reaccreditation procedures: To maintain IOC accreditation, laboratories must successfully analyze several samples in a short given period of time, and then submit a full report to be evaluated by a multidisciplinary group of experts. When considered necessary, inspection visits are carried out, and additional information is requested before decisions are given by the mentioned group.
5. Educative proficiency tests. In order to establish common standards for new drugs, metabolites or methods, from time to time laboratories receive special proficiency samples designed to gain insight on specific problems.
6. Annual workshop. Each year representatives of the laboratories meet for one week to discuss new developments in analytical chemistry, and new discoveries about drug metabolics and pharmacology.
7. A book entitled *Advances in Doping Research* has been published annually since 1992. It describes the advances presented at the annual workshop, and provides additional useful information.[14-18]

9.1.5 FUTURE ALTERNATIVES

Testing only during competition has not proved a sufficient deterrent. Recently the IOC has begun testing outside of competitions. This approach has made it possible to more seriously address the problem of drugs in sport. Many of these compounds, especially anabolics, are ingested months prior to the competition. Normal in-competition controls may fail to detect this kind of doping, since much of the drug has been already eliminated from the body when sample collection is performed.

With the addition of new drugs to the list of banned substances, urine as a sole test medium may not be enough. In the future, urine testing may be complemented by testing in other matrices.[19,20]

REFERENCES

1. International Olympic Committee. Medical Code and Explanatory Document. Lausanne: IOC, 1995.
2. IOC Medical Commission. Internal statistics report. Lausanne: IOC, 1996.
3. Donike M., Adamietz B., Opfermann G. et al. Normbereiche für Testosteron- und Epitestosteron-urinspiegel sowie des Testosteron-/Epitestosteron-Quotienten. In: Training und Sport zur Prävention und Rehabilitation in der technisierten Umwelt.I.-W. Franz, H. Mellerowicz, W. Noack (Hrsg.), Springer Verlag, Berlin/Heidelberg, 1985:503-7.
4. Donike M., Rauth S., Mareck-Engelke U., Geyer H., Nitschke R. Evaluation of longitudinal studies, the determination of subject based reference ranges of the testosterone/epitestosterone ratio. In Donike M., Geyer H., Gotzmann A., Mareck-Engelke U., Rauth S. eds. Recent advances in doping analysis: Proceedings of the 11th Cologne Workshop on Dope Analysis, 7th to 12th March 1993. Köln: Sport und Buch Strauss, 1994:33-39.
5. Baezinger J., Bowers L. Variability of T/E ratio in athletes. In: Donike M., Geyer H., Gotzmann A., Mareck-Engelke U., Rauth S. eds. Recent advances in doping analysis: Proceedings of the 11th Cologne Workshop on Dope Analysis, 7th to 12th March 1993. Köln: Sport und Buch Strauss, 1994:41-52.
6. Kicman A.T., Brooks R.V., Collyer S.C. et al. Criteria to indicate testosterone administration. Br J Sports Med, 1990;24:253-64.
7. Park J., Park S., Lho S. et al. Drug testing at the 10th Asian Games and 24th Seoul Olympic Games. Journal of Analytical Toxicology, 1990;14:66-72.
8. de la Torre X., Segura J., Yang Z., Li Y., Wu M. Testosterone detection in different ethnic groups. In: Schänzer W., Geyer H., Gotzmann A., Mareck-Engelke U. eds. Recent advances in doping analysis (4): Proceedings of the 14th Cologne Workshop on Dope Analysis, 17th to 22nd March 1996. Köln: Sport und Buch Strauss, 1997:71-90.
9. de la Torre X., Segura J., Polettini A., Montagna M. Detection of testosterone esters in human plasma. J Mass Spectrom, 1995;30:1393-1404.
10. Segura J., de la Torre R., Badia R. Potential use of peptide hormones in sport. In: Reidenberg M.M. ed. The Clinical pharmacology of biotechnology products. Amsterdam: Elsevier Science Publishers, 1991:257-72.
11. Kicman A.T., Cowan D.A. Peptide hormones and sport: misuse and detection. Brit med Bull, 1992;48:496-517.
12. Badia R., de la Torre R., Segura J. Erythropoietin: potential abuse in sport and possible methods for its detection. Biol Clin Hematol, 1992;14:177-184.
13. Segura J., Pascual J.A., Ustaran J.I., Cuevas A., Gonzalez R. International cooperation in analytical chemistry: experience of antidoping control at the XI Pan American Games. Clin Chem, 1993;39:836-55.
14. Donike M., Geyer H., Gotzmann A., Mareck-Engelke U., Rauth S. eds. 10th Cologne Workshop on Dope Analysis, 7th to 12th June 1992 -Proceedings-. Köln: Sport und Buch Strauss, 1993.
15. Donike M., Geyer H., Gotzmann A., Mareck-Engelke U., Rauth S. eds. Recent advances in doping analysis: Proceedings of the 11th Cologne Workshop on Dope Analysis, 7th to 12th March 1993. Köln: Sport und Buch Strauss, 1994.

16. Donike M., Geyer H., Gotzmann A., Mareck-Engelke U., Rauth S. eds. Recent advances in doping analysis (2): Proceedings of the 12th Cologne Workshop on Dope Analysis, 10th to 15th April 1994. Köln: Sport und Buch Strauss, 1995.

17. Donike M., Geyer H., Gotzmann A., Mareck-Engelke U., Rauth S. eds. Recent advances in doping analysis (3): Proceedings of the 13th Cologne Workshop on Dope Analysis, 12th to 17th March 1995. Köln: Sport und Buch Strauss, 1996.

18. Schänzer W., Geyer H., Gotzmann A., Mareck-Engelke U. eds. Recent advances in doping analysis (4): Proceedings of the 14th Cologne Workshop on Dope Analysis, 17th to 22nd March 1996. Köln: Sport und Buch Strauss, 1997.

19. Donike M., Geyer H., Gotzmann A. et al. Blood analysis in doping control: advantages and disadvantages. In: Hemmersbach P., Birkeland K.I., eds. Blood samples in doping control. Oslo: on demand publishing, 1994:75-92.

20. Polettini A., Segura J., Gonzalez G., de la Torre X., Montagna M. Clenbuterol and beta-adrenergic drugs detected in hair of treated animals by ELISA. Clin Chem, 1995;41:945-6.

9.2 SPECIFIC AGENTS

RAFAEL DE LA TORRE, PHARMD

DEPARTMENT OF PHARMACOLOGY AND TOXICOLOGY, INSTITUT MUNICIPAL D'INVESTIGACIÓ MÈDICA, BARCELONA, SPAIN

History indicates that long ago athletes sought a competitive advantage by using various substances that have been dubbed "ergogenic aids".[1] Misuse of drugs has been recognized by sports organizations as an important problem for 30 years, ever since the International Olympic Committee (IOC) Medical Commission was established in 1967.[2] An odds and ends of several drugs and drug classes that are misused/abused in sports are covered under the subhead "Other Drugs". The main groups of abused substances discussed here are stimulants, narcotics, diuretics, and other masking agents. Table 9.2.1 summarizes the most common offenders.

Anabolic agents and stimulants now constitute more than 90% of positive cases reported by IOC Medical Commission statistics.[2] Reliable methods for testing stimulants and narcotics were introduced in 1972, and techniques for anabolic agents were implemented in 1984. Drugs used as masking agents (i.e., diuretics, probenecid) were introduced in the eighties. Additionally, there are several classes of drugs subjected to certain restrictions by sports organizations (i.e., alcohol, marijuana, local anesthetics, corticosteroids, and beta-blockers). These restrictions regard either dosage or routes of administration (i.e., local anesthetics, corticosteroids) or a specific control in some sports disciplines (i.e., beta blockers). Some other drugs included in Table 9.2.1 could be considered as ergogenic aids[1] (i.e., carnitine, NSAIDs, analgesics) but they are not explicitly included in the IOC Medical Commission list of prohibited classes of substances and prohibited methods.

9.2.1 STIMULANTS AND NARCOTICS

During World War II, a large number of soldiers, workers in the war industry, and other sectors of the population, became familiar with the increased alertness and improved performance associated with amphetamines and other sympathomimetic drugs.[3] The misuse of these compounds was quite widespread. Methamphetamine abuse was epidemic in Japan after the end of the war. It is not surprising that amphetamines were introduced into sports as ergogenic aids. Barbiturates and narcotics were often taken to relieve some of amphetamines side effects. Hypnotics (i.e., barbiturates) were taken for insomnia, narcotics for pain (morphine, phetidine,

Table 9.2.1 Miscellaneous Drugs, Anabolic Agents, and Peptide Hormones Used
as Ergogenic Aids in Sports

Stimulants	Amphetamine like compounds
	Other sympathomimetic amines
	(phenylpropanolamine, ephedrine and related compounds)
	Anorectics
	Cocaine
Narcotics	Opiates (morphine and related compounds)
	Opioids (dextromoramide, dextropropoxyphene)
Caffeine	Caffeine and other methylxanthines
Hypnotic and	Benzodiazepines
antianxiety drugs	Barbiturates
	Alcohol
Beta-blockers	Propranolol
	Metropolol
	Others
Diuretics and	Furosemide
masking agents	Acetazolamide
	Probenecid
Corticosteroids	
Local anesthetics	
Others	Marijuana
	NSAID's (nonsteroidal antiinflamatory drugs)
	Vitamins and minerals
	Aminoacids and proteins
	Carnitine
	Bicarbonate
	Phosphate loading
	Analgesics

dextromoramide), and often used in combination with caffeine and respiratory stimulants (i.e.,
nikethamide, crotetamide, cropopamide) in the form of "cocktails".[4] Stimulants and narcotic
analgesics were the first groups of substances to be prohibited by most of the international
sports federations.

The introduction of effective drug testing procedures for amphetamine and other sympathomimetic amines [5] reduced, but did not eliminate, their abuse by athletes. While the
ergogenic effects of amphetamines,[6,7] some related compounds like methylphenidate [8] and
caffeine,[9,10] are today well accepted, there is very little information about effects (if any) of
cocaine and narcotics on enhancing athletic performance. Still, today stimulants and narcotics
constitute about 25% of positive reported cases by IOC accredited laboratories, showing that
they are quite popular among athletes.

There is some controversy over the classification of stimulants as banned substances. While
most experts will agree on banning amphetamines, there is some debate regarding over-the-
counter sympathomimetic amines, such as ephedrine and phenylpropanolamine, and caffeine.
The most potent CNS stimulants, amphetamines and cocaine, represent only 17% of positive
cases (11 and 6%, respectively) in the IOC statistics (see Table 9.2.2). But low profile CNS

Table 9.2.2 Examples of Substances Used as Ergogenic Aids in Sports and Detected in Doping Control

Groups of substances	Substances detected	% positive cases[a]	Groups of substances	Substances detected	% positive cases
Stimulants			*Diuretics and masking agents*		
Sympathomimetic amines	Cathine	68	Diuretics	Acetazolamide	95
	Ephedrine			Canrenone	
	Etilefrine			Chlortalidone	
	Methylephedrine			Furosemide	
	Phenylephrine			Hydrochlorotiazide	
	Phenylpropanolamine			Triamterene	
	Pseudoephedrine		Masking agents	Probenecid	5
Amphetamines	Amphetamine	11			
	Clobenzorex		*Narcotics*		
	Fenproporex		Opioids	Dextropropoxyphene[b]	85
	Mesocarb		Opiates	Codeine[b]	15
	Methamphetamine			Morphine	
	Phendimetrazine				
	Phentermine		*Beta-blockers*		
Cocaine	Cocaine	6	Non-selective beta1	Propranolol	50
Caffeine	Caffeine	5			
Miscellaneous drugs	Amfepramone	10	Selective beta1	Atenolol	50
	Amineptine			Bisoprolol	
	Fencamfamine			Metropolol	
	Fenfluramine				
	Heptaminol				
	Nikethamide				
	Pemoline				
	Prolintane				
	Strychnine				

[a] *Percentages of positive cases should be referred within each group of substances.*
[b] *No longer considered a banned drug.*
Data derived from 1995 IOC Statistics.

stimulants, such as ephedrine derivatives (68%), anorexic and miscellaneous stimulant drugs (10%), and caffeine (5%) are the main substances found in doping control.

In 1995, the IOC Medical Commission reported finding 25 different stimulant compounds. Sympathomimetic amines like ephedrine or phenylpropanolamine at high doses can produce similar CNS stimulant effects to amphetamines. At lower doses, present in many over-the-counter medications, these agents are very useful for treating respiratory disorders. Alternative treatment with antihistamines is not satisfactory because of the drugs sedative effects. Caffeine is also a problem because no cutoff doses/urinary concentrations, which could help in making a distinction between their misuse and use, have been established. For that reason, some quantitative guidelines have been developed for reporting these drugs: caffeine 12 mg/L, pseudoephedrine and phenylpropanolamine 10 mg/L, cathine and ephedrine 5 mg/L.

There is a very low prevalence of cases positive for narcotics (less than 3%), probably because narcotics do nothing to enhance athletic performance. Dextropropoxyphene is the narcotic most often detected. Narcotics, when they are detected, are used mainly for pain relief. There have been complaints that alternative treatments with non-steroidal anti-inflammmatory drugs are not as effective as narcotics; however, the danger that athletes might compete when injured rules out the use of these drugs.

9.2.2 BETA-BLOCKERS

Beta-blockers are used in sports where athletes benefit from their anxiolytic, bradycardiac and antitremor effects. Beta-blockers are abused by athletes competing in sports where good postural coordination is important (i.e., archery, shooting, ski jumping, bowling, etc.). In most other sports, beta-blockade adversely affects both anaerobic endurance and aerobic power, so they are of little interest.

Tachycardia and hand tremor induced by emotional stress are reduced by a $ß_1$-receptor blockade in marksmen[11] and ski jumpers.[12] In skilled athletes, performance improvement is more marked than in non-trained subjects.[12] At single doses in normotense subjects, these drugs are relatively safe. However, such drugs (specially non $ß_1$-receptor selectives) cannot be administered in asthmatics because of the risk of bronchospasm. They also are contraindicated when an arterioventricular block or a cardiac insufficiency are diagnosed. Beta blockers accounted for just 1% of the total number of positive cases reported by IOC. Propranolol, metropolol, and atenolol are the most popular drugs.[13] Their detection in urine does not constitute a major problem and has been recently reviewed.[14] Because their anxiolytic effect at low doses, benzodiazepines, barbiturates and alcohol can also be used for the same purposes as beta blockers.

9.2.3 DIURETICS AND MASKING AGENTS

Diuretics act directly on kidney tubules to increase the rate of urine formation. Athletes misuse diuretics in sports where weight categories are involved (i.e., boxing, weightlifting), and where weight is strictly controlled (i.e., gymnastics). Diuretics are also used to reduce the urinary concentrations of other banned drugs in hopes of masking their presence. A body weight reduction of about 2 to 4% can be obtained after diuretics administration (i.e., furosemide).[15-17] This effect is linked to the increase of urine rate formation, which may be on the order of 1 L /3 to 4 h for different diuretics and dosage. [18-20]

Urinary concentrations of stimulants may be diluted two- to fivefold for short periods of time (i.e., 2 h), increasing the difficulty of detection by routine testing procedures. Administration of carbonic anhydrase inhibitors, like acetazolamide, causes urinary alkalization and inhibits the excretion of weak basic drugs like stimulants for longer periods of time (i.e., 24 h).[21] A third approach is the administration of the uricosuric drug probenecid (and to a lesser extent sulfinpyrazone). Probenecid competitively inhibits the active secretion of glucuronide conjugates in the urine. Most anabolic steroids are largely excreted as glucuronides, so that the coadministration of probenecid makes detection difficult.[22] Anabolic steroids excreted as free drug (either the parent compound or metabolites) are unaffected by probenecid actions. Drug testing for diuretics and probenecid is very effective, and has been reviewed recently.[23] Some rules in the sample collection procedure, regarding urinary specific gravity and pH, have helped to increase the rate of detection.

9.2.4 CONCLUSIONS

Compared to the relatively small number of stimulants and opiates abused by the public at large, the number of ergogenic aids available to athletes is very great. Past attempts at distinguishing between ergogenic aids and commonly abused illict drugs were not very successful. If an athlete tests positive for cocaine, it is very difficult to say whether the positive result is due to recreational drug use or a misguided attempt at improving performance. The same is true for other classes of drugs. In the future, it may no longer be possible to make a distinction between ergogenic and illicit drug abuse.

REFERENCES

1. Wadler, G.I. , Hainline B., *Drugs and the Athletes,* F.A. Davis Company, Philadelphia, 1989, Chap. 3
2. Segura, J., Doping control in sports medicine. *Therapeutic Drug Monitoring,* 18, 471, 1996
3. Hoffman, B.B., Lefkowitz, R.J., Catecholamines and Sympathomimetic Drugs in *Goodman and Gilman's. The Pharmacological Basis of Therapeutics.* Goodman Gilman, A., Rall, T.W., Nies, A.S., Taylor, P., Eds, Pergamon Press, New York, 1990, Chap. 10
4. Donike, M., Accreditation and Reaccreditation of Laboratories by the IOC Medical Commission. in *First International Symposium. Current Issues of Drug Abuse Testing.* Segura, J., de la Torre, R., Eds, CRC Press, Boca Raton, 1992, Chap. 34
5. Donike, M., Erfahrungen mit dem Stickstoffdetektor (N-FID) bei der Dopingkontrolle, *Medicinische Technik,* 92,153,1972
6. Karpovich, P.V., Effect of Amphetamine sulfate on athletic performance, *JAMA* 170, 558, 1959
7. Smith, G.M., Beechter, H.K., Amphetamine sulfate and athletic performance:1. Objective Effects. *JAMA* 170, 542, 1959
8. Gualtieri, T., Hicks, R.E., Levitt, J., Conley, R., Schroeder, S.R., Methylphenidate and Exercise: Additive Effects on Motor Performance, Variable Effects and the Neuroendocrine Response. *Neuropsychobiology* 18, 84, 1986
9. Collomp, K., Ahmaidi, S., Audran, M., Chanal, J.-L., Préfaut, Ch., Effects of caffeine ingestion on performance and anaerobic metabolism during the Wingate test. *International Journal Sports Medicine,* 12, 439, 1991
10. Collomp, K., Ahmaidi, S., Audran, M., Chatard, J.C., Préfaut, Ch. Benefits of caffeine ingestion on sprint performance in trained and untrained swimmers, *European Journal Applied Physiology,* 64, 377, 1992
11. Kruse, P., Ladefoged, J., Nielsen, U., Paulev, P-E., Sørensen, JP.,ß-Blockade used in precision sports: effect on pistol shooting performance. *Journal Applied Physiology,* 61, 417, 1986
12. Imhof, P.R., Blatter K., Fucella L.M., Turri M., Betablockade and emotional tachycardia: radiotelemetric investigations in ski jumpers. *Journal Applied Physiology,* 27, 366, 1969
13. IOC Medical Commission. *Internal Statistics Report.* Lausanne: IOC 1995
14. Hemmersbach, P., de la Torre, R., Stimulants, narcotics and ß-blockers: 25 years of development in analytical techniques for doping control. *Journal Chromatography B,* 687,221, 1996
15. Amstrong, L.E., Costill, D.L., Fink, W.J., Influence of diuretic-induced dehydration on competitive running performance. *Medical Sciences Sports Exercise,* 17, 456, 1985
16. Caldwell, J.E., Ahonen, E., Nousiainen U., Diuretic Therapy, physical performance, and neuromuscular function. *Physician Sportmedicine,* 12, 73, 1984
17. Caldwell J.E., Ahonen, E., Nousiainen U., Differential effects of sauna-, diuretic-, and exercise-induced hypohydratation. *Journal Applied Physiology* 57, 1018, 1984
18. Delbecke, F.T., Debackere, M. The influence of diuretics on the excretion and metabolism of doping agents- I.Mephentermine. *Journal Pharmaceutical Biomedical Analysis.* 3, 141, 1985
19. Delbecke, F.T., Debackere, M. The influence of diuretics on the excretion and metabolism of doping agents- II.Phentermine. *Arzneimittel-Forschung/Drug Research.* 36, 134, 1986
20. Delbecke, F.T., Debackere, M. The influence of diuretics on the excretion and metabolism of doping agents-III.Ethylamfetamine. *Arzneimittel-Forschung/Drug Research.* 36, 1413, 1986
21. Delbecke, F.T., Debackere, M. The influence of diuretics on the excretion and metabolism of doping agents- V Dimefline. *Journal Pharmaceutical Biomedical Analysis.* 9, 23, 1991
22. Geyer, H., Schänzer, W., Donike, M., Probenecid as masking agent in dope control. Inhibition of the urinary excretion of steroid glucuronides, in *10th Workshop on dope analysis,* Donike, M., Geyer, H., Gotzmann, A., Mareck-Engelke, U., Rauth, S Eds. Sport und Buch Strauss, Khöln, 1993, 141
23. Ventura, R., Segura, J., Diuretics *Journal Chromatography B,* 687, 187, 1996

9.3 ANABOLIC ANDROGENIC STEROIDS

Don H. Catlin, M.D.

Department of Molecular and Medical Pharmacology, Department of Medicine, UCLA School of Medicine, University of California, Los Angeles, California

Testosterone, the principal androgen in the male, is produced by the testes at a rate of approximately 7 mg per day. Dihydrotestosterone (DHT), the main intracellular androgen in reproductive tissue, is more potent than testosterone and arises either from testosterone by 5a-reduction or, to a much lesser extent, from androstenedione. Dehydroepiandrosterone (DHEA), DHEA sulfate, and androstenedione are weak androgens produced in the adrenal gland. They play a minor role in maintaining sexual function in the male. In the present context the naturally produced androgens are referred to as endogenous to distinguish them from synthetic or xenobiotic androgens developed by the pharmaceutical industry to optimize clinical profiles and improve absorption of orally administered agents. Endogenous androgens are also available in various pharmaceutical dosage forms and there is much interest now in formulations that are efficacious by sublingual and transcutaneous routes of administration.[1,2]

Androgens are responsible for a wide variety of functions, of which the most important are promoting male sexual differentiation in the first trimester, masculinization of the male at puberty, and maintenance of adult male sexual function.[3,4] Androgens also promote the assimilation of protein, thus androgens are anabolic agents. The term anabolic androgenic steroid (AAS) encompasses both major effects and is the most comprehensive description; however, the terms anabolic steroid and androgenic steroid are commonly used, particularly when the context of the discussion is one or the other.

9.3.1 CONVENTIONAL MEDICAL USES

In this context, AAS are primarily used to manage hypogonadal states, delay of growth and puberty in boys, Turner's syndrome in girls, bone marrow failure, selected anemia, hereditary angioneurotic edema, and late stages of breast cancer. Investigational uses include promotion of anabolism in patients with AIDS and alcoholic hepatitis, management of certain hyperlipemias, promotion of fibrinolysis, and as anti-fertility agents in the male. Although they have been administered to post-operative patients to hasten recovery, they have not proved efficacious for this application. In some countries AAS are used in the management of osteoporosis.

9.3.2 USE BY ATHLETES

The use of AAS to enhance athletic performance began in the 1950s, accelerated in the 1970s, and spread to teen-age athletes in the 1980s.[5-9] Although it is extremely difficult to obtain accurate estimates of the number of athletes using AAS, by the 1980s it became obvious that AAS were having a serious impact on sport. It is estimated that up to 6.7% of young males in the U.S. have used AAS.[8] To counteract the growing influence of AAS on sport, authorities initiated urine testing and educational programs. Testing for AAS formally began with the 1976 Olympics and has increased in sophistication and scale ever since.[10,11]

Typical AAS users are athletes preparing for an event that requires endurance, strength, speed, or a muscular appearance (body-building). The intent of the AAS user is solely to enhance athletic performance or to build a more muscular body.[12] The motivation stems mostly from the rewards society bestows on winners.[11] Unlike typical drug abusers, AAS users do not experience a "high" and generally are not involved in the lifestyle associated with street drugs. For a subset of young AAS users, the main intent is to improve physical appearance.[8]

Before urine testing for steroids became widespread in sport, the favorite drug for enhancing performance was nandrolone decanoate administered intramuscularly (IM) in an oily solution. Nandrolone is rarely used today due to its long half-life (weeks) and ease of detection in urine. Nowadays athletes tend to use endogenous steroids, particularly testosterone, because of difficulties in detecting its use.[13] Similarly DHT is difficult to detect and there is evidence of increased use.[14,15] In addition there is anecdotal evidence that cocktails of endogenous steroids and methandriol are popular. The most sophisticated regimens include human chorionic gonadotrophin to prevent testicular atrophy and anti-estrogens to inhibit gynecomastia. Based on urine testing results, the most popular orally administered AAS are methandienone, stanozolol, methenolone, mesterolone, and methyltestosterone.[11,16] The list of AAS that have been detected is quite long and includes veterinarian products such as boldenone and parenteral stanozolol. In the U.S., the number of AAS that are available by prescription has gradually been reduced to include only esters of testosterone and nandrolone for IM administration, and methyltestosterone, oxandrolone, fluoxymesterone, stanozolol, and oxymetholone for oral administration.

9.3.3 GENERAL PHARMACOLOGY OF ANABOLIC ANDROGENIC STEROIDS

The AAS have a remarkabe variety of actions and virtually all human organs show some effect.[17] Once the fundamental effects of anabolism and androgenicity were characterized, research focused on developing a steroid entirely devoid of androgenicity. Although this effort has been largely unsuccessful, there are some differences between the agents that lead to preferences of one agent over another in different clinical circumstances. In addition, there is no evidence for multiple androgen receptors; thus, effects classified as anabolic or androgenic reflect differences between tissue responses, not actions at sub-types of receptors.[18] To reconcile the single receptor hypothesis with the diversity of effects of androgens, it is necessary to consider the androgen receptor, chemical structure of the agents, and their absorption and metabolism.

9.3.3.1 Androgen Receptors

The androgen receptor has been isolated and characterized, and a cDNA which encodes the androgen receptor has been cloned and expressed.[19-22] The binding characteristics of receptors isolated from reproductive tissue and from skeletal muscle are identical.[23] Endogenous androgens, xenobiotic AAS, and antiandrogens all bind to the androgen receptor although they display considerable differences in binding affinity. Androgen receptors have been characterized in tissues from reproductive organs, brain, kidney, liver, skin, skeletal muscle, cardiac muscle, bone, larynx, thymus, and hematopoietic and lipid tissue. With some exceptions, the effects of androgens are considered to be mediated by the androgen receptor.

9.3.3.2 Chemical Structure

Orally administered testosterone is virtually completely metabolized in the first pass through the GI tract and liver and very little reaches the systemic circulation. Likewise unmodified testosterone has a plasma half-life of less than an hour and is not a useful therapeutic agent. In contrast if the hydroxyl group on carbon-17 (C-17) is esterified, therapeutic levels of T are maintained for days or weeks depending on the length of ester. Other formulations of T result in agents that are effectively absorbed by transcutaneous and sublingual routes of administration.[1,2] The addition of a methyl or ethyl group at C-17 partially protects the AAS from first pass metabolism and provides effective plasma levels. Compared to testosterone, agents alkylated at C-17 have a different spectrum of adverse effects. AAS with a variety of other structural modifications are available.[18]

9.3.3.3 Absorption and Distribution

The oral agents are rapidly absorbed from the GI tract. Peak levels are achieved within 1 to 3 h of administration. In the circulation, most testosterone is loosely bound to albumin, a smaller fraction is tightly bound to SHBG, and some is free. The synthetic agents also bind to SHBG.[23,24] The concentration of AAS and metabolites can be measured in serum and urine. Much is known about plasma levels of oral AAS in various conditions and the levels are monitored when testosterone is used to treat hypogonadal states.[17] Less is known about plasma levels of the xenobiotics, and, although they could be measured, they have not been used to guide dosing.

9.3.3.4 Metabolism

The diversity of effects of AAS can be explained in part by differences in metabolism.[25] After testosterone is distributed to the tissues, it is transported into the cell where it either acts directly at the receptor or is metabolized by 5α-reduction to 5α-DHT. DHT is more potent than testosterone; thus, reduction is one means of modulating the effect of testosterone, in this case in the direction of enhanced activity. In addition, 5α-reductase is not present in all androgen responsive tissues, another explanation for diverse effects. Other metabolites of testosterone, such as androsterone and certain diols, have minimal or no androgenic activity, respectively.

Another critical metabolic step is the conversion of some testosterone by aromatase to estradiol which binds to and acts at the estrogen receptor. Thus, testosterone administration results in a mixture of effects mediated by androgen and estrogen receptors. Given that androgens and estrogens mediate very different effects, and that the androgen-estrogen balance is a major determinant of hormonal status, aromatization provides another means of modulation of the effects of androgens. Any synthetic AAS with α 4-ene function is subject to metabolism by aromatase to the corresponding estrogen. A few estrogen metabolites of AAS have been described in humans. Fluoxymesterone, mesterolone, and oxandrolone are examples of AAS that cannot be metabolized to estrogens. The synthetic AAS undergo extensive metabolism primarily to hydroxylated, and 5α or 5ß-reduced metabolites. Like testosterone, most of these are excreted in urine as sulfates or glucuronides.

9.3.3.5 Dose-Response

There is a relative paucity of clinical studies that provide dose response data directly comparing one AAS with another, consequently dosing regimens are generally based on clinical observation and experience.[3,26] The dose of testosterone esters for replacement in hypogonadal patients is ~100 mg/week. Xenobiotic AAS are used in a wide range of doses. Low doses (0.05 mg/kg) are used for short stature, intermediate doses (0.1 mg/kg) are used for post menopausal osteoporosis, and high doses (2 to 3 mg/kg) are reserved for aplastic anemia. Athletes have been known to use doses of 5 to 7 mg/kg/day.[12]

9.3.4 EFFECTS OF ANABOLIC ANDROGENIC STEROIDS

9.3.4.1 Major Endocrine Regulatory Systems

Testosterone production is primarily regulated by the integrated activity of hormones produced in the hypothalamus, pituitary, and testes. Gonadotropin releasing hormone (GnRH) is a decapeptide synthesized in the hypothalamus which plays a major role in regulating follicle stimulating hormone (FSH) and luteinizing hormone (LH). FSH and LH are glycoprotein hormones synthesized and secreted in the posterior pituitary. LH stimulates secretion of testosterone by Leydig cells in the testes and FSH acts on the seminiferous tubules to promote spermatogenesis. Circulating levels of testosterone are regulated by a feedback mechanism whereby high levels result in negative feedback on GnRH which results in decreased output of FSH and LH. These and other hormones also have direct effects on the pituitary.

Testosterone is under consideration as a male contraceptive. LH and to a lesser extent FSH are essential to normal spermatogenesis; therefore, suppression of LH and FSH results in oligozoospermia followed by azoospermia. Normal spermatogenesis requires that endogenous testosterone production be regulated by LH. Pharmacologic doses of testosterone result in dose dependent suppression of FSH, LH, and spermatogenesis. Accordingly considerable effort has been directed to developing formulations of testosterone and dosing schedules that are acceptable for male contraception.[1,2,27-29] Related approaches to male contraception include administration of GnRH agonist and antagonists. Initially agonists stimulate the production and release of FSH and LH but continual use results in down regulation and a decline in FSH and LH. GnRH antagonists are effective anti-fertility agents but they must be used in combination with testosterone in order to prevent the loss of libido and other effects of suppression of testosterone to hypogonadal levels.[30] The advantages and disadvantages of these approaches to male contraception have been reviewed,[27-29] and, in view of their potential use by athletes, will be followed closely by the sport community.

Large scale multi-national trials of testosterone as a male contraceptive are underway under the auspices of the World Health Organization (WHO).[32,33] In the first trial, 200 mg of testosterone enanthate was administered IM weekly to fertile males.[32] At 6 months, 157 of the men were azoospermic and these continued to take T for 12 more months. During this 12-month period testosterone was the only form of contraception and there was only one pregnancy. The second WHO study[33] used a similar design and found that 97% of 670 men became severely oligozoospermic or azoospermic, and that Asian men were more sensitive to the effects of testosterone than non-Asian men. The success of these studies led to additional studies that are now in progress, and will stimulate continuing research on the use of testosterone and related agents as male contraceptives.

9.3.4.2 Athletic Performance and Body Composition

Although experienced users of AAS are convinced that AAS enhance performance,[5,18] until recently it has been difficult to find unequivocal support for this belief in the scientific literature. Many studies have been conducted and reviewed, yet the results do not provide a consensus.[5,18,33,34] Some show an increase in performance and others do not. Perhaps due to the abundance of anecdotal evidence, many reviewers reluctantly conclude that AAS do enhance performance while emphasizing that it is difficult to support this conclusion on the basis of published studies. One factor likely to contribute to the failure of some studies to demonstrate efficacy is insufficient total dose.[18] Short term administration of AAS does not enhance performance.

Bhasin et al.[35] recently reported a well-designed performance-efficacy study which greatly clarifies the ambiguities described above. In this study, normal males were assigned to one of four groups: placebo with no exercise, placebo with exercise, testosterone enanthate (600 mg IM/week for 10 weeks) with no exercise, and testosterone enanthate with exercise. In the no-exercise groups, the men treated with testosterone had greater increases in muscle size and strength than the men treated with placebo. The men treated with testosterone and exercise had greater increases in fat-free mass and muscle size than those assigned to either no-exercise group, and greater increases in strength than either no-exercise group. This study confirms the long term suspicion that testosterone enhances muscle size and strength, and emphasizes the importance in performance efficacy studies of using high doses of testosterone and controlling potential confounding variables.

9.3.4.2.1 Mechanism of Enhanced Performance

The most commonly cited mechanism for how AAS enhance performance considers that they act via androgen receptors to increase muscle mass, which in turn provides greater strength and speed. While it is reasonable to speculate that larger muscles are stronger muscles, the relationship between muscle diameter and strength and contraction speed is complex.[36,37] The possibility that AAS enhance performance via an anti-catabolic effect mediated by glucocorticoid receptors,[18] increased blood volume, or behavioral effects mediated by the CNS have been considered.

The androgen receptors in most human skeletal muscles[38] differs from receptors in other tissues in that 5α-reductase activity is low.[39] Another difference is that skeletal muscle tissue contains relatively more intracellular testosterone than DHT.[40] DHT, which is several times more active than testosterone, dominates in other androgen sensitive tissue. Thus, testosterone is the dominant intracellular agonist in muscle.

Skeletal muscle biopsies obtained from men treated with AAS reveal an increase in muscle fiber diameter.[41-43] In the experimental animal, testosterone produces marked hypertrophy in selected muscles, an increased number of myofilaments and myofibrils, and changes in the structure of myosin heavy chain isoforms.[44]

9.3.4.2.2 Administration of Testosterone to Hypogonadal Men

When replacement doses of testosterone are given to hypogonadal men, the outcome is positive nitrogen balance and retention of potassium, phosphates, and sulfates.[45-47] Total body weight and lean body mass (LBM) increase, body fat decreases, and muscles increase in size. Enhanced LBM also results when supra-physiologic doses are administered to non-athletic men,[43,48-51] women with osteoporosis,[52,53] and athletes.[50,54] The magnitude of the effect is related to the total dose.[49,50] Although a portion of the increase in LBM is due to fluid retention and/or expanded blood volume,[18,43,55] muscle hypertrophy accounts for the most of the increase. In addition, AAS also decrease body fat.[48-50,52]

9.3.4.2.3 Administration to Patients with AIDS

Cachexia, anorexia, and weight loss are common problems faced by patients with advanced human immunodeficiency virus infection. In addition, hypogonadism frequently occurs in AIDS patients[56] and could contribute to the weight loss. In the first study of AAS in AIDS, Hengge et al.[57] recruited 60 patients with advanced AIDS. Oxymetholone alone (150 mg/day) was administered to 14 subjects for 30 weeks, 16 received oxymetholone plus ketotifen for 30 weeks, and 30 served as untreated matched controls. The average weight gain was 14.5% of entry weight for the oxymetholone group, 10.9% for the combination group, and the untreated controls lost weight.[57] Body composition was not determined; thus, the effect of oxymetholone on lean body was not determined. Nevertheless, the encouraging results, which included improvement in the quality of life, will lead to additional studies of AAS use in AIDS patients.

9.3.4.4 Hematopoietic System

The efficacy of AAS in the management of aplastic anemia, Fanconi anemia, and the anemia associated with end-stage renal disease is well established. This application arose from observations that hypogonadism and castration are associated with reduced red cell mass, which is corrected by androgen replacement.[58,59] In addition, hemoglobin and hematocrit increase when AAS are administered to eugonadal males and females.[5,60,61]

Before erythropoietin (EPO) became available, the anemia of end-stage renal disease was treated with AAS, which commonly resulted in an increase in hematocrit of 3 to 5 percentage points.[26,62] They have also been used successfully in the management of aplastic and other types of anemia. Approximately 50% of patients with aplastic anemia experience small to modest improvement on AAS.[59,63,64] Interestingly, an occasional patient demonstrates apparent dependency on androgens characterized by marked improvement in hemoglobin while on androgens and a decline when androgens are discontinued.[65] Oxymetholone, fluoxymesterone, norethandrolone, stanozolol, and nandrolone decanoate are the AAS most often used in the management of anemia.

The primary effect of androgens on red cell mass is enhanced EPO production[66] mediated by androgen receptors in the kidney. In turn, EPO regulates RBC production by stimulating erythroid progenitor cells. In addition, there is experimental evidence that 5ß-reduced analogs of testosterone directly stimulate hemoglobin production by a mechanism that is independent of EPO.[66-68] This is most interesting because it is the only instance where androgens with the 5ß configuration mediate an important effect.

9.3.4.5 Bone

Several lines of evidence link androgens to effects on bone. Elderly males experience a progressive decline in testosterone levels and bone mass and some develop osteoporosis. The syndrome of hypogonadism includes osteoporosis, which testosterone reverses.[69,70] In addition, the use of anti-androgens in the management of prostate carcinoma results in osteoporosis.[71] These observations stimulated investigations of the effects of anabolic steroids on bone and their role in the management of osteoporosis.[72,73]

Clinical and *in vitro* studies provide convincing evidence that testosterone and DHT play a role in maintaining healthy bone and correcting osteoporosis associated with hypogonadism. AAS can increase bone mass in women with post-menopausal osteoporosis; however, their efficacy is modest and the magnitude of the effects is mitigated by virilization and other adverse effects.[74] Elderly males with hypogonadism and osteoporosis are treated with testosterone esters or agents specific for the primary cause of the osteoporosis or both.[75] Nandrolone decanoate is typically used to treat post-menopausal osteoporosis.

The mechanism of these effects is not known. Androgen receptors have been identified in cultured human osteoblast-like cells,[76,77] and when these cells are exposed to DHT they proliferate and produce alkaline phosphatase,[78,79] a marker of osteoblastic bone activity. Testosterone and stanozolol increase creatine kinase activity in bone and stimulate ^{3}H-thymidine incorporation into DNA.[80] In addition, androgens modulate the effect of parathyroid hormone on bone.[79]

9.3.4.6 Plasma Proteins

Hereditary angioneurotic edema (HANE) is a rare genetic disorder characterized by life-threatening attacks of mucosal swelling of the upper airways and abdominal pain. Type I HANE is due to inappropriate activation of the complement system caused by a deficiency of an inhibitor of C1, and type II HANE is due to a defect in the function of the inhibitor.[81] Patients with HANE experience dramatic clinical improvement on AAS and the function and levels of the C1 inhibitor return to normal.[82]

AAS are associated with both elevations and reductions in plasma proteins. They elevate plasma levels of haptoglobin, orosomucoid, protein-bound sialic acid, plasminogen, and ß-glucuronidase,[83,84] and decrease levels of vitamin D binding protein, SHBG, and TBG.[84-89]

9.3.4.7 Growth and Development

9.3.4.7.1 Constitutional Delay of Growth and Puberty (CDGP)

CDGP is the most common cause of short stature in boys during puberty. The basic therapeutic strategy is to initiate a spurt in linear growth with oral AAS or T esters, and discontinue them before skeletal maturation advances to the point of closure of the epiphyses. Typically the desired result is achieved in less than 12 months with relatively low doses.[90-93] Satisfactory efficacy has been shown in placebo-controlled prospective randomized studies.[80,91] Oxandrolone is the drug that clinicians typically use to treat CDGP.

9.3.4.7.2 Turner's Syndrome

This is a rare disorder of young females characterized by short stature, sexual infantilism, webbing of the neck, and deformity of the elbows.[94] The short stature has been successfully treated with AAS, T esters, estrogens, and growth hormone. A large multi-center trial has concluded that human growth hormone alone or in combination with oxandrolone results in a significant increase in adult height for most prepubertal girls with Turner's syndrome.[95]

9.3.4.8 Alcoholic Hepatitis

The rationale for using AAS in the management of alcoholic hepatitis is to induce positive nitrogen balance and possibly to enhance general well-being. Since the early 1960s many trials

Don H. Catlin

have been conducted with mixed results. One extensive study conducted in 1984 concluded that oxandrolone (80 mg/day for 30 days) did not affect short-term survival, but did prolong long-term survival.[96] A more recent study of oxandrolone (20 mg/day for 21 days) produced improvement in laboratory parameters indicative of hepatitis, but the overall results were not better than parenteral nutrition alone or with oxandrolone.[97,98]

9.3.5 COMPLICATIONS

There are no prospective controlled studies of the adverse effects of high dose oral AAS on young healthy males; therefore, it is difficult to assess the long-term risk of AAS on multifactorial disorders such as cancer and cardiovascular disease. In addition, there are essentially no systematic data from chronic administration studies that convincingly demonstrate any difference between various oral AAS with respect to the relative position of dose response curves for any of the adverse effects. The agents do differ in potency based on dose, although in equipotent doses the adverse effects are similar.

AAS have effects on virtually all organs. When the effect involves reproductive organs or secondary sexual characteristics, the mechanism is simply an extension of the normal physiological actions of endogenous androgens. Thus, pharmacologic doses of androgens produce virilization in women. In this case virilization is an undesired adverse effect, while virilization of the hypogonadal patient is expected and desired. In contrast, the mechanism of many adverse effects of AAS is unknown. Most but not all adverse effects are associated with both endogenous and oral androgens. Hepatic disorders are associated with xenobiotic androgens but not with testosterone.

9.3.5.1 Endocrine

In males, high doses of oral AAS inhibit the release of LH, FSH, and probably GnRH. This results in declining levels of plasma testosterone, FSH, and LH, and eventually to reversible oligozoospermia, azoospermia, and sterility.[99,100] Some males also develop gynecomastia possibly related to estrogenic metabolites or an androgen-estrogen imbalance.[54,101]

Virilization is an unavoidable consequence of administering pharmacologic doses of androgens to females. The muscles increase in size and strength, hair growth is stimulated particularly on the face, arms, and legs, and the voice lowers. Long term administration results in clitoral enlargement, breast atrophy, and male pattern baldness. The effects of suppressing FSH and LH in the female is anovulation and amenorrhea. In the only clinical description of adverse effects in female weight-trained athletes who self-administered AAS, most or all experienced a low voice, menstrual irregularities, enhanced strength, clitoral enlargement, and increased facial hair.[102]

Both males and females experience an increase in number, size, and secretions of sebaceous glands. Obstruction of the glands leads to acne. If AAS are administered prior to puberty, the epiphyses may close and stunt growth.

9.3.5.2 Metabolic

There is some evidence that AAS increase the basal metabolic rate,[48] and decrease plasma levels of thyroxine and tri-iodothyronine.[86-88] Despite these observations hypothyroidism is not associated with AAS. Insulin resistance and diminished glucose tolerance is reported with 17-alkylated AAS,[103-105] but not with esters of testosterone or nandrolone.[106,107] Further, study of supraphysiological doses of testosterone enanthate and nandrolone decanoate confirm the lack of an adverse effect on glucose metabolism and add that nandrolone improves glucose metabolism by enhancing noninsulin-mediated glucose disposal.[107] Adipose tissue contains androgen receptors and biopsies following a course of AAS reveal a marked decrease in lipoprotein lipase activity.[108,109]

9.3.5.3 Plasma Lipids

The most striking and reproducible metabolic effect of orally administered AAS that has been studied is lowering the HDL fraction of cholesterol.[110-116] Some of these studies also reported that the HDL_2 subfraction was most affected and that apoprotein AI was reduced. The magnitude of the reduction in HDL-C, which has been reported in men and women, ranges from 30 to 70%.[117] Testosterone esters also decrease HDL-C, but only by 5 to 16%.[112,118-120] Nandrolone decanoate administered IM has no effect on any of the lipid fractions.[121,122] Since estrogens increase HDL-C,[123] the minimal effects of testosterone on HDL-C could be due to estrogen metabolites of testosterone; thus, Friedl et al.[113] and Zmuda et al.[118] administered testosterone alone and testosterone plus an aromatase inhibitor (testolactone). Both studies revealed a lesser reduction of HDL-C with co-administration of testolactone and suggested that estrogen metabolites of testosterone partially inhibit the decline in HDL-C.[113,118]

The mechanism of the decline in HDL-C may be related to increased activity of hepatic triglyceride lipase activity (HTGL), an enzyme involved in the catabolism of HDL-C.[124] HTGL activity increases after administration of testosterone esters and oral androgens;[110,114,115,119] moreover, in a study that monitored HTGL and HDL-C daily, HTGL activity increased on Day 1 of stanozolol administration while the decline of HDL-C was first noticeable on Day 3.[111] The effect of orally administered AAS on HTGL activity is much greater (100 to 300%) than the effect of testosterone esters (0 to 21%).[121]

The question of the role of the route of administration on AAS-induced changes in HDL-C and HTGL activity is difficult to answer because none of the studies have administered the same drug by the two routes of administration. To date, all the orally active AAS produce the striking changes and esters of T and nandrolone[121,122] do not.

The effect of AAS on LDL-C is less clear. Freidl et al.[112] directly compared oral methyltestosterone and parenteral testosterone. The methyltestosterone group showed a rise in LDL-C while the T group showed no change. Similarly, Thompson et al.[119] reported a large increase in LDL-C while administering an oral AAS (stanozolol) and no effect while on parenteral testosterone. Two other studies with oral agents reported an increase in LDL-C.[119,125] Two other compounds that are synthesized from cholesterol and transported by lipoproteins are ubiquinone and dolichol. Karila et al.[126] report that serum levels of ubiquinone increase and dolichol levels decrease while on AAS.

9.3.5.4 Cardiovascular

The combined effect of oral AAS on HDL-C and LDL-C is to increase the LDL/HDL ratio. Both low levels of HDL-C and high LDL/HDL ratios are risk factors for cardiovascular disease. This has led to speculation of increased risk for cardiovascular disease.[110,113] Although several case reports document that stroke and myocardial infarction are associated with high dose AAS, the number of cases seems low relative to the apparent risk[127] and the number of reported steroid users.[8] Moreover, some of the case reports do not exclude other cardiovascular risk factors.

9.3.5.4.1 Myocardial Infarction and Stroke

There are 11 case reports of myocardial infarction in young males taking AAS to enhance performance.[128-137] Of these, at least three had no known risk factors,[128-130] one was also taking amphetamine and diuretics,[135] and for the remaining seven, risk factor information was incomplete. In addition, there are four case reports of ischemic cerebrovascular events in young men without risk factors,[138-141] and at least one case of mesenteric thrombosis.[142] Thrombotic events are also reported in patients treated with AAS for underlying diseases such as aplastic anemia.[143,144]

Whether or not AAS impair cardiac function or produce myocardial disease is not known. In one well-designed study of weightlifters, there was no evidence of impaired left ventricular function.[145] There are three autopsy case reports of myocarditis or hypertrophic cardiomyopathy in young males taking excessive doses of AAS.[146-147]

These cases and others led Ferenchick to hypothesize that oral AAS might be thrombogenic,[148] and also led to a study that found that AAS users had significant abnormalities in fibrin split products and other coagulation factors that were consistent with a hyper coagulable state;[149] however, Ansell et al.[142] studied 17 coagulation parameters in 16 AAS users on and

Don H. Catlin

off drugs and found some significant differences but did find evidence of hypercoagulation. Among the differences[149] reported was an increased activity of the fibrinolytic system as measured by euglobulin lysis time, a finding known to be associated with AAS. In addition, T has recently been shown to play a regulatory role in the expression of thromboxane A2 receptors on human platelets, a finding that could contribute to thrombogenicity.[150,151]

9.3.5.4.2 Enhanced Fibrinolysis

In contrast to the thrombogenic potential of AAS, more than 30 years ago, testosterone and nandrolone esters were shown to enhance blood fibrinolytic activity.[152] Since then AAS have been used to treat a variety of uncommon conditions where enhanced fibrinolytic activity may be beneficial. These studies have confirmed that oral AAS increase fibrinolytic activity, and added that they decrease fibrinogen and increase plasminogen.[83,153-156] These effects tend to be temporary and AAS are not widely used for this purpose. Recent reports of success with danazol in the management of EPO-induced shunt thrombosis may stimulate further studies of the role of AAS in thrombotic disorders.[157]

9.3.5.5 Hepatic

The most common adverse effect of AAS involving the liver is elevations of alanine and aspartate aminotransferases (ALT and AST, respectively).[158-161] Typically the transaminase levels return to normal if the AAS are discontinued and often they will regress even if they are continued.[182,183] Virtually all C-17 alkylated AAS are associated with elevated transaminases, and it is difficult to find evidence that testosterone elevates transaminases. Anabolic steroid-induced cholestasis is an uncommon hepatic complication of C-17 steroids. In most cases, the hyperbilirubinemia is less than 10 mg/dl and the patients recover without sequelae.[113,161-163] Less commonly the cholestasis is accompanied by advanced hepatic and renal failure, very high serum bilirubin, and hepatic transplantation is considered.[164-166] Testosterone is not associated with cholestasis. The underlying mechanism of androgen-induced hepatotoxicity is not known. Studies of the function and integrity of hepatic cell cultures reveal a high degree of toxicity when the cells are exposed to C-17 alkylated steroids and no toxicity when exposed to testosterone, testosterone cypionate, or 19-nortestosterone.[167]

9.3.5.6 Neoplasia

AAS are associated with a variety of histologic types of hepatic neoplasia ranging from benign adenoma to malignant adenocarcinoma.[113,160,162,168] It is interesting that hepatic carcinomas associated with AAS do not metastasize, and often regress with discontinuation of the AAS.[113,160,168-170] At least four cases of aggressive hepatic angiosarcoma have been associated with AAS.[172]

From the perspective of morbidity and mortality, the most serious lesion associated with AAS is peliosis hepatis, a vascular tumor characterized by blood filled hepatic or splenic cysts.[162] The major management issue with peliosis hepatis is the tendency for the tumor to spontaneously bleed and the difficulty of controlling the bleeding.[113,173] Peliosis hepatitis is relatively common,[201] and it will regress with discontinuation of the AAS.[174,175]

9.3.5.7 Psychiatric Disorders

Recently a number of reports have described serious behavioral and psychiatric sequelae among users of AAS,[176,177] and psychiatric interviews find a high incidence of aggressive behavior, affective syndromes, and psychotic symptoms.[178] In another study, 23% of male AAS users reported mania, hypomania, or major depression.[179] Male users show more verbal aggression and violence toward their wives and girlfriends.[180] In contrast to these studies involving athletic young males using high doses of AAS, most studies of medical patients that require AAS do not report remarkable psychiatric effects. The chronic use of AAS may lead to physical dependence and a withdrawal syndrome.[181,182]

9.3.5.8 Dermatologic

Androgens increase skin surface lipids and facilitate the growth of acne-forming bacteria. Skin biopsies of male AAS users show marked increase in the cross-sectional area of the sebaceous glands.[183] High doses of AAS are associated with acne, oily skin and hair, hirsutism, striae atrophicae, alopecia, seborrheic dermatitis, sebaceous cysts, and furunculosis.[184,185] In addition linear keloids, a rare dermatologic condition, have been associated with AAS.[186]

9.3.5.9 Drug Interactions

Simultaneous administration of AAS and isoretinoin, two compounds known to lower HDL-C, led to a remarkably low HDL-C in one case report.[187] The combination of oral anticoagulants and AAS leads to prolonged prothrombin times and serious bleeding. For example, the addition of methandrostenolone to the regimen of a patient receiving warfarin resulted in hemarthroses.[188] The hypoprothrombinemic effects of oral anticoagulants are also enhanced by oxymetholone and norethandrolone.[189] Apparently the mechanism of the interaction does not involve altered pharmacokinetics of the anticoagulant.[189] In one study, the combination of methyltestosterone and imipramine in depressed men led to an acute paranoid state in 4 of the 5 subjects.[190]

9.3.5.10 Other Toxic Reactions

An individual who had taken large doses of various AAS presented to an emergency room with an acute abdomen that was found to be due to partial bowel obstruction secondary to hypertrophy of the iliopsoas muscle.[191] Weight training places great strain on tendons. Cases of spontaneous rupture of tendons and rupture under a heavy load have been reported. For example, at least two athletes have suffered bilateral rupture of the quadriceps tendon,[192,193] and two more suffered rupture and avulsion of the triceps tendon.[194,195] The possible mechanisms for an effect of AAS on tendons have been reviewed.[196] Bleeding esophageal varices secondary to liver disease was reported in one high dose AAS user.[197] Not surprisingly, HIV infection and other complications of sharing needles are reported in AAS abusers.[198]

ACKNOWLEDGMENTS

I thank Caroline K. Hatton, Ph.D. for insightful review and editorial assistance, and Richard L. Hilderbrand, Ph.D. for assistance preparing the manuscript.

REFERENCES

1. Salehian, B., Wang, C., Alexander, G., Davidson, T., McDonald, V., Berman, N., Dudley, R. E., Ziel, F., and Swerdloff, R. S., Pharmacokinetics, bioefficacy, and safety of sublingual testosterone cyclodextrin in hypogonadal men: comparison to testosterone enanthate - a clinical research center study, *J. Clin. Endocrinol. Metab.*, 80, 3567, 1995.
2. Meikle, A. W., Arver, S., Dobs, A. S., Sanders, S. W., Rajaram, L., and Mazer, N. A., Pharmacokinetics and metabolism of a permeation-enhanced testosterone transdermal system in hypogonadal men: influence of application site - a clinical research center study, *J. Clin. Endocrinol. Metab.*, 81, 1832, 1996.
3. Kopera, H., The history of anabolic steroids and a review of clinical experience with anabolic steroids, *Acta Endocrinol.*, 110(suppl 271), 11, 1985.
4. Bardin, C. W., and Catterall, J. F., Testosterone: A major determinant of extragenital sexual dimorphism, *Science*, 211, 1285, 1981.
5. Catlin, D. H., and Hatton, C. K., Use and abuse of anabolic and other drugs for athletic enhancement, *Adv. Int. Med.*, 36, 381, 1990.
6. United States Senate, Committee on the Judiciary, Proper and Improper Use of Drugs by Athletes (Hearings before the Subcommittee to Investigate Juvenile Delinquency, June 18 and July 12 and 13, 1973), U.S. Government Printing Office, Washington, D.C., 1, 1973.

Don H. Catlin

7. United States Senate, Committee on the Judiciary, Steroids in Amateur and Professional Sports - The Medical and Social Costs of Steroid Abuse (Hearings before the Committee on the Judiciary, April 3, 1989, May 9, 1989), U.S. Government Printing Office, Washington, D. C., 1, 1990.

8. Buckley, W. E., Yesalis, C. E., Friedl, K. E., Anderson, W. A., Streit, A. L., and Wright, J. E., Estimated prevalence of anabolic steroid use among male high school seniors, *J. Am. Med. Assoc.*, 260, 3441, 1988.

9. Dickman, S., East Germany: Science in the disservice of the state, *Science*, 254, 26, 1991.

10. Catlin, D. H., Kammerer, R. C., Hatton, C. K., Sekera, M. H., and Merdink, J. M., Analytical chemistry at the games of the XXIIIrd Olympiad in Los Angeles, 1984, *Clin. Chem.*, 33, 319, 1987.

11. Catlin, D. H., and Murray, T. H., Performance-enhancing drugs, fair competition, and Olympic sport, *J. Am. Med. Assoc.*, 276, 231, 1996.

12. Duchaine, D., *Underground Steroid Handbook II*, HLR Technical Books, Venice, CA, 1, 1989.

13. Catlin, D. H., and Cowan, D. A., Detecting testosterone administration, *Clin. Chem.*, 38, 1685, 1992.

14. Southan, G. J., Brooks, R. V., Cowan, D. A., Kicman, A. T., Unnadkat, N., and Walker, C. J., Possible indices for the detection of the administration of dihydrotestosterone to athletes, *J. Steroid Biochem. Molec. Biol.*, 42, 87, 1992.

15. Yesalis, C. E., Herrick, R. T., Buckley, W. E., Friedl, K. E., Brannon, D., and Wright, J. E., Self-reported use of anabolic-androgenic steroids by elite power lifters, *Phys. Sportsmed.*, 16, 91, 1988.

16. Catlin, D. H., Androgen abuse by athletes, in *Pharmacology, Biology, and Clinical Applications of Androgens*, Bhasin, S., Gabelnick, H. L., Spieler, J. M., Swerdloff, R. S., and Kelly, J., Eds., Wiley-Liss, Inc., New York, 1996, 289.

17. Bhasin, S., Gabelnick, H. L., Spieler, J. M., Swerdloff, R. S., and Kelly, J., Eds., *Pharmacology, Biology, and Clinical Applications of Androgens*, Wiley-Liss, Inc., New York, 1996.

18. Wilson, J. D., Androgen abuse by athletes, *Endocrine Reviews*, 9, 181, 1988.

19. Carson-Jurica, M. A., Schrader, W. T., and O'Malley, B. W., Steroid receptor family: Structure and functions, *Endocrine Rev.*, 11, 201, 1990.

20. Chang, C., Kokontis, J., and Liao, S., Molecular cloning of human and rat complementary DNA encoding androgen receptors, *Science*, 240, 324, 1988.

21. Lubahn, D. B., Joseph, D. R., Sullivan, P. M., Willard, H. F., French, F. S., and Wilson, E. M., Cloning of human androgen receptor complementary DNA and localization to the X chromosome, *Science*, 240, 327, 1988.

22. Tilley, W. D., Marcelli, M., Wilson, J. D., and McPhaul, M. J., Characterization and expression of a cDNA encoding the human androgen receptor, *Proc. Natl. Acad. Sci.*, 86, 327, 1989.

23. Saartok, T., Dahlberg, E., and Gustafsson, J. A., Relative binding affinity of anabolic- androgenic steroids: Comparison of the binding to the androgen receptors in skeletal muscle and in prostate, as well as to sex hormone-binding globulin, *Endocrinol.*, 114, 2100, 1984.

24. Pugeat, M. M., Dunn, J. F., and Nisula, B. C., Transport of steroid hormones: Interaction of 70 drugs with testosterone-binding globulin and corticosteroid-binding globulin in human plasma, *J. Clin. Endocrinol. Metab.*, 53, 69, 1981.

25. Sundaram, K., Kumar, N., Monder, C., and Bardin, C. W., Different patterns of metabolism determine the relative anabolic activity of 19-norandrogens, *J. Steroid Biochem. Mol. Biol.*, 53, 253, 1995.

26. Neff, M. S., Goldberg, G., Slifkin, R. F., et al., A comparison of androgens for anemia in patients on hemodialysis, *N. Engl. J. Med.*, 304, 871, 1987.

27. Waites, G. M., Male fertility regulation: the challenges for the year 2000, *Br. Med. Bull.*, 49, 210, 1993.

28. Wu, F. C., Male contraception, *Baillieres. Clin. Obstet. Gynaecol.*, 10, 1, 1996.

29. Bhasin, S., Gabelnick, H. L., Spieler, J. M. Swerdloff, R. S., and Kelly, J., eds., *Pharmacology, Biology, and Clinical Applications of Androgens*, Wiley-Liss, Inc., New York, 1996, Part VI.

30. Tom, L., Bhasin, S., Salameh, W., Steiner, B., Peterson, M., Sokol, R. Z., Rivier, J., Vale, W., and Swerdloff, R. S., Induction of azoospermia in normal men with combined Nal-Glu gonadotropin-releasing hormone antagonist and testosterone enanthate, *J. Clin. Endocrinol. Metab.*, 75, 476, 1992.

31. Tom, L., Bhasin, S., Salameh, W., Steiner, B., Peterson, M., Sokol, R. Z., Rivier, J., Vale, W., and Swerdloff, R. S., Contraceptive efficacy of testosterone-induced azoospermia in normal men. World Health Organization Task Force on methods for the regulation of male fertility, *Lancet*, 336, 955, 1990.

32. Anonymous, Rates of testosterone-induced suppression to severe oligozoospermia or azoospermia in two multinational clinical studies. World Health Organization Task force on Methods for The Regulations of Male Fertility, *Int. J. Androl.*, 18, 157, 1995.

33. Haupt, H. A., and Rovere, G. D., Anabolic steroids: A review of the literature, *Am. J. Sports Med.*, 12, 469, 1984.

34. American College of Sports Medicine, Position statement on the use of anabolic-androgenic steroids in sports, *Med. Sci. Sports Exerc.*, 19, 534, 1987.

35. Bhasin, S., Storer, T. W., Berman, N., Callegari, C., Clevenger, B., Phillips, J., Bunnell, T. J., Tricker, R., Shirazi, A., and Casaburi, R., The effects of supraphysiologic doses of testosterone on muscle size and strength in normal men, *N. Engl. J. Med.*, 335, 1, 1996.

36. Moritani, T., and DeVries, H., Neural factors versus hypertrophy in the time course of muscle strength gain, *Am. J. Appl. Physiol.*, 58, 115, 1979.

37. MacDougall, J., Sale, D., Elder, G., and Sutton, J., Muscle ultrastructural characteristics of elite powerlifters and bodybuilders, *Eur. J. Appl. Physiol.*, 48, 117, 1982.

38. Snochowski, M., Saartok, T., Dahlberg, E., Eriksson, E., and Gustafsson, J. A., Androgen and glucocorticoid receptors in human skeletal muscle cytosol, *J. Steroid Biochem.*, 14, 765, 1981.

39. Krieg, M., Smith, K., and Elvers, B., Androgen receptor translocation from cytosol of rat heart muscle, bulbo-cavernosus levator ani muscle and prostate into heart muscle nuclei, *J. Steroid Biochem.*, 13, 577, 1980.

40. Deslypere, J. P., and Vermeulen, A., Influence of age on steroid concentrations in skin and striated muscle in women and in cardiac muscle and lung tissue in men, *J. Clin. Endocrinol. Metab.*, 61, 648, 1985.

41. Alèn, M., Hakkinen, K., and Komi, P. V., Changes in neuromuscular performance and muscle fiber characteristics of elite power athletes self-administering androgenic and anabolic steroids, *Acta Physiol. Scand.*, 122, 535, 1984.

42. Hosegood, J. L., and Franks, A. J., Response of human skeletal muscle to the anabolic steroid stanozolol, *Br. Med. J.*, 297, 1028, 1988.

43. Griggs, R. C., Kingston, W., Jozefowicz, R. F., Herr, B. E., Forbes, G., and Halliday, D., Effect of testosterone on muscle mass and muscle protein synthesis, *J. Appl. Physiol.*, 66, 498, 1989.

44. Venable, J. H., Morphology of the cells of normal, testosterone-deprived and testosterone-stimulated levator ani muscles, *Am. J. Anat.*, 119, 271, 1966.

45. Kenyon, A. T., Knowlton, K., Sandiford, I., Koch, F.C., and Lotwin, G., A comparative study of the metabolic effects of testosterone propionate in normal men and women and in eunuchoidism, *Endocrinology*, 26, 26, 1940.

46. Kenyon, A. T., Knowlton, K., and Sandiford, I., The anabolic effects of the androgens and somatic growth in man, *Ann. Int. Med.*, 20, 632, 1944.

47. Landau, R. L., The metabolic effects of anabolic steroids in man, in Kochakian, C. D., ed., *Anabolic-Androgenic Steroids*, Springer-Verlag, New York, 44, 1976.

48. Welle, S., Jozefowicz, R., Forbes, G., and Griggs, R. C., Effect of testosterone on metabolic rate and body composition in normal men and men with muscular dystrophy, *J. Clin. Endocrinol. Metab.*, 74, 332, 1992.

49. Forbes, G.B., *Human Body Composition: Growth, Aging, Nutrition, and Activity*, Springer-Verlag, New York, 1987.

50. Forbes, G. B., The effect of anabolic steroids on lean body mass: The dose response curve, *Metab.*, 34, 571, 1985.

51. Forbes, G. B., Porta, C. R., Herr, B. E., and Griggs, R. C., Sequence of body changes in body composition induced by testosterone and reversal of changes after drug is stopped, *J. Am. Med. Assoc.*, 267, 397, 1992.

52. Hassager, C., Riis, B. J., Podenphant, J., and Christiansen, C., Nandrolone decanoate treatment of post-menopausal osteoporosis for 2 years and effects of withdrawal, *Maturitas*, 11, 305, 1989.

Don H. Catlin

53. Aloia, J. F., Kapoor, A., Vaswani, A., and Cohn, S. H., Changes in body composition following therapy with methandrostenolone, *Metab. Clin. Exp.*, 30, 1076, 1981.
54. Friedl, K. E., and Yesalis, C. E., Self-treatment of gynecomastia in bodybuilders who use anabolic steroids, *Phys. Sportsmed.*, 17, 67, 1989.
55. Hervey, G. R., Knibbs, A. V., Burkinshaw, L., Morgan, D. B., Jones, P. R., Chettle, D. R., and Vartsky, D., Effects of methandienone on the performance and body composition of men undergoing athletic training, *Clin. Sci.*, 60, 457, 1981.
56. Dobs, A. S., Dempsey, M. A., Ladenson, P. W., and Polk, B. F., Endocrine disorders in men infected with human immunodeficiency virus, *Am. J. Med.*, 84, 611, 1988.
57. Hengge, U. R., Baumann, M., Maleba, R., Brockmeyer, N. H., and Goos, M., Oxymetholone promotes weight gain in patients with advanced human immunodeficiency virus (HIV-1) infection, *Br. J. Nutr.*, 75, 129, 1996.
58. Hamilton, J. B., The role of testicular secretions as indicated by the effects of castration in man and by studies of pathological conditions and the short lifespan associated with maleness, *Recent Prog. Horm. Res.*, 3, 357, 1948.
59. Shahidi, N. T., Androgens and erythropoiesis, *N. Engl. J. Med.*, 289, 72, 1973.
60. Alèn, M., Androgenic steroid effects on liver and red cells. *Br. J. Sports Med.*, 19, 15, 1985.
61. Gardner, F. H., Nathan, D. G., Piomelli, S., and Cummins, J. F., The erythrocythemic effects of androgens, *Br. J. Haematol.*, 14, 611, 1968.
62. Richardson, J. R., Jr., and Weinstein, M. B., Erythropoietic response of dialyzed patients to testosterone administration, *Ann. Int. Med.*, 73, 403, 1970.
63. Ammus, S. S., The role of androgens in the treatment of hematologic disorders, *Adv. Int. Med.*, 34, 191, 1989.
64. Nissen, C., Gratwohl, A., and Speck, B., Management of aplastic anemia, *Eur. J. Haematol.*, 46, 193, 1991.
65. Azen, E. A., and Shahidi, N. T., Androgen dependency in acquired aplastic anemia, *Am. J. Med.*, 63, 320, 1977.
66. Beckman, B., Maddux, B., Segaloff, A., and Fisher, J. W., Effects of testosterone and 5ß androstanes on in vitro erythroid colony formation in mouse bone marrow, *Proc. Soc. Exp. Biol. Med.*, 167, 51, 1981.
67. Gordon, A. S., Zanjani, E. D., Levere, R. D., and Kappas, A., Stimulation of mammalian erythropoiesis by 5ß-H steroid metabolites, *Proc. Nat. Acad. Sci.*, 65, 919, 1970.
68. Congote, I. F., and Solomon, S., Testosterone stimulation of a rapidly labeled, low- molecular-weight RNA fraction in human hepatic erythroid cells in culture, *Proc. Nat. Acad. Sci.*, 72, 523, 1975.
69. Baran, D. T., Bergfeld, M. A., Teitelbaum, S. L., and Avioli L. V., Effect of testosterone therapy on bone formation in an osteoporotic hypogonadal male, *Calcif. Tiss. Res.*, 26, 103, 1978.
70. Riggs, B. L., Jowsey, J., Kelly, P. J., Jones, J. D., and Maher, F. T., Effect of sex hormones on bone in primary osteoporosis, *J. Clin. Invest.*, 48, 1065, 1969.
71. Peters, C. A., and Walsh, P. C., The effect of nafarelinacetate, a luteinizing-hormone- releasing hormone agonist, on benign prostatic hyperplasia, *New Engl. J. Med.*, 317, 599, 1987.
72. Schot, L. P. C., and Schuurs, A. H. W. M., Sex steroids and osteoporosis: Effects of deficiencies and substitutive treatments, *J. Steroid Biochem. Molec. Biol.*, 37, 167, 1990.
73. Dequeker, J., and Geusens, P., Anabolic steroids and osteoporosis, *Acta Endocrinolog.*, 110(suppl 271), 45, 1985.
74. Geusens, P. Nandrolone decanoate: pharmacological properties and therapeutic use in osteoporosis, *Clin. Rheumatol.*, 14 Suppl 3, 32, 1995.
75. Jackson, J. A., and Kleerekoper, M., Osteoporosis in men: Diagnosis, pathophysiology, and prevention, *Medicine*, 69, 137, 1990.
76. Colvard, D. S., Eriksen, E. F., Keeting, P. E., Wilson, E. M., Lubahn, D. B., French, F. S., Riggs, B. L., and Spelsberg, T. C., Identification of androgen receptors in normal human osteoblast-like cells, *Proc. Nat. Acad. Sci.*, 86, 854, 1989.
77. Orwoll, E. S., Stribrska, L., Ramsey, E. E., and Keenan, E. J., Androgen receptors in osteoblast-like cell lines, *Calcif. Tissue Int.*, 49, 183, 1991.

78. Kasperk, C. H., Wergedal, J. E., Farley, J. R., Linkhart, T. A., Turner, R. T., and Baylink, D. J., Androgens directly stimulate proliferation of bone cells in vitro, *Endocrinology*, 124, 1576, 1989.
79. Fukayama, S., and Tashjian, A. H., Direct modulation by androgens of the response of human bone cells (SaOS-2) to human parathyroid hormone (PTH), *Endocrinology*, 125, 1789, 1989.
80. Vaishnav, J. N., Beresford, J. N., Gallagher, J. A., and Russell, R. G. G., Effects of the anabolic steroid stanozolol on cells derived from human bone, *Clin. Sci.*, 74, 455, 1988.
81. Sim, T.C., and Grant, A., Hereditary angioedema: Its diagnostic and management perspectives, *Am. J. Med.*, 88, 656, 1990.
82. Cicardi, M., Bergamaschini, L., Cugna, M., Hack, E., Agostoni, G., and Agostoni, A., Long-term treatment of hereditary angioedema with attenuated androgens: A survey of a 13-year experience, *J. Allergy Clin. Immunol.*, 87, 768, 1991.
83. Barbosa, J., Seal, U. S., and Doe, R. P., Effects of anabolic steroids on haptoglobin, orosomucoid, plasminogen, fibrinogen, transferrin, ceruloplasmin, a¹-antitrypsin, ß-glucuronidase and total serum proteins, *J. Clin. Endocrinol.*, 33, 388, 1971.
84. Barbosa, J., Seal, U. S., and Doe, R. P., Effects of anabolic steroids on hormone-binding proteins, serum cortisol and serum nonprotein-bound cortisol, *J. Clin. Endocrinol.*, 32, 232, 1971.
85. Palonek, E., Gottlieb, C., Garle, M., Bjorkhem, I., and Carlstrom, K., Serum and urinary markers of exogenous testosterone administration, *J. Steroid Biochem. Mol. Biol.*, 55, 121, 1995.
86. Small, M., Beastall, G. H., Semple, C. G., Cowan, R. A., and Forbes, C. D., Alteration of hormone levels in normal males given the anabolic steroid stanozolol, *Clin. Endo.*, 21, 49, 1984.
87. Malarkey, W. B., Strauss, R. H., Leizman, D. J., Liggett, M., and Demers, L. M., Endocrine effects of female weight lifters who self-administer testosterone and anabolic steroids, *Am. J. Ob. Gyn.*, 165, 1385, 1991.
88. Alen, M., Rahkila, P., Reinilä, M., and Vihko R, Androgenic-anabolic steroid effects on serum thyroid, pituitary and steroid hormones in athletes, *Am. J. Sports Med.*, 15, 357, 1987.
89. Clerico, A., Ferdeghini, M., Palombo, C., Leoncini, R., Del Chicca, M. G., Sardano, G., and Mariani, G., Effect of anabolic treatment on serum levels of gonadotropins, testosterone, prolactin, thyroid hormones and myoglobin of male athletes under physical training, *J. Nuc. Med. Allied Sci.*, 25, 79, 1981.
90. Stanhope, R., Buchanan, C.R., Fenn, G.C., and Preece, M.A., Double blind placebo controlled trial of low dose oxandrolone in the treatment of boys with constitutional delay of growth and puberty, *Arch. Dis. Childh.*, 63, 501, 1988.
91. Rosenfeld, R. G., Northcraft, G. B., and Hintz, R. L., A prospective, randomized study of testosterone treatment of constitutional delay of growth and development in male adolescents, *Pediatrics*, 69, 681, 1982.
92. Tse, W. Y., Buyukgebiz, A., Hindmarsh, P. C., Stanhope, R., Preece, M. A., and Brook, C. G., Long-term outcome of oxandrolone treatment in boys with constitutional delay of growth and puberty, *J. Pediat.*, 117, 588, 1990.
93. Uruena, M., Pantsiotou, S., Preece, M. A., and Stanhope, R., Is testosterone therapy for boys with constitutional delay of growth and puberty associated with impaired final height and suppression of the hypothalamo-pituitary-gonadal axis?, *Eur. J. Pediatr.*, 151, 15, 1992.
94. Lippe, B., Turner syndrome, *Endocrinol Metab. Clin. North Am.*, 20, 121, 1991.
95. Rosenfeld, R. G., Frane, J., Attie, K. M., Brasel, J. A., Burstein, S., Cara, J. F., Chernausek, S., Gotlin, R. W., Kuntze, J., and Lippe, B. M., Six-year results of a randomized, prospective trial of human growth hormone and oxandrolone in Turner syndrome, *J. Pediatrics*, 121, 49, 1992.
96. Mendenhall, C.L., Anderson, S., Garcia-Pont, P., Goldberg, S., Kiernan, T., Seeff, L. B., Sorrell, M., Tamburro, C., Weesner, R., and Zetterman, R., Short-term and long-term survival in patients with alcoholic hepatitis treated with oxandrolone and prednisolone, *N. Engl. J. Med.*, 311, 1464, 1984.
97. Bonkovsky, H. L., Fiellin, D. A., Smith, G. S., Slaker, D. P., Simon, D., and Galambos, J. T., A randomized, controlled trial of treatment of alcoholic hepatitis with parenteral nutrition and oxandrolone: I. Short-term effects on liver function, *Am. J. Gastroenterol*, 86, 1200, 1991.
98. Bonkovsky, H. L., Singh, R. H., Jafri, I. H., Fiellin, D. A., Smith, G. S., Simon, D., Cotsonis, G. A., and Slaker, D. P., A randomized, controlled trial of treatment of alcoholic hepatitis with

Don H. Catlin

parenteral nutrition and oxandrolone: II. Short-term effects on nitrogen metabolism, metabolic balance, and nutrition, *Am. J. Gastroenterol*, 86, 1209, 1991.

99. Schürmeyer, T., Belkien, L., Knuth, U. A., and Nieschlag, E., Reversible azoospermia induced by the anabolic steroid 19-nortestosterone, *Lancet,* 1, 417, 1984.

100. Alèn, M., Suominen, J., Effect of androgenic and anabolic steroids on spermatogenesis in power athletes, *Int. J. Sports Med.,* 5(suppl),189, 1984.

101. Wilson, J. D., Aiman, J., and MacDonald, P. C., The pathogenesis of gynecomastia, *Adv. Int. Med.*, 25, 1, 1980.

102. Strauss, R. H., Liggett, M. T., and Lanese, R. R., Anabolic steroid use and perceived effects in ten weight-trained women athletes, *J. Am. Med. Assoc.*, 253, 2871, 1985.

103. Godsland, I. F., Shennan, N. M., and Wynn, V., Insulin action and dynamics modelled in patients taking the anabolic steroid methandienone (Dianabol), *Clin. Sci.*, 71, 665, 1986.

104. Woodard, T. L., Burghen, G. A., Kitabchi, A. E., and Wilimas, J. A., Glucose intolerance and insulin resistance in aplastic anemia treated with oxymetholone, *Am. J. Ob. Gyn.*, 165, 1385, 1991.

105. Cohen, J. C. and Hickman, R., Insulin resistance and diminished glucose tolerance in powerlifters ingesting anabolic steroids, *J. Clin. Endocrinol. Metab.*, 64, 960, 1987.

106. Friedl, K. E., Jones, R. E., and Hannan, C. J., Jr, and Plymate, S. R., The administration of pharmacological doses of testosterone or 19-nortestosterone to normal men is not associated with increased insulin secretion or impaired glucose tolerance, *J. Clin. Endocrinol. Metab.*, 68, 971, 1989.

107. Hobbs, C. J., Jones, R. E., and Plymate, S. R., Nandrolone, a 19-nortestosterone, enhances insulin-independent glucose uptake in normal men, *J. Clin. Endocrinol. Metab.*, 81, 1582, 1996.

108. Rebuffé-Scrive, M., and Mårin P. Björntorp, Effect of testosterone on abdominal adipose tissue in men, *Int. J. Obesity,* 15, 791, 1991.

109. Xu, X., de Pergola, G., and Bjorntorp, P., The effects of androgens on the regulation of lipolysis in adipose tissue, *Endocrinol,* 126, 1229, 1990.

110. Hurley, B. F., Seals, D. R., Hagberg, J. M., Goldberg, A. C., Ostrove, S. M., Holloszy, J. O., Wiest, W. G., and Goldberg, A., High-density-lipoprotein cholesterol in bodybuilders v. powerlifters: Negative effects of androgen use, *J. Am. Med. Assoc.*, 252, 507, 1984.

111. Applebaum, D. M., Haffner, S., and Hazzard, W. R., The dyslipoproteinemia of anabolic steroid therapy, Increase in hepatic triglyceride lipase precedes the decrease in high density lipoprotein-2 cholesterol, *Metabolism,* 36, 949, 1987.

112. Friedl, K.E., Hannan, C.J., Jr, and Jones, R. E., Plymate, S R: High-density lipoprotein cholesterol is not decreased if an aromatizable androgen is administered, *Metabolism,* 39, 69, 1990.

113. Friedl, K. E., Reappraisal of the health risks associated with the use of high doses of oral and injectable androgenic steroids, in *Anabolic Steroid Abuse (Research Monograph 102)*, Lin, G. C., and Erinoff, L. eds., pp 142-176, National Institute on Drug Abuse, Rockville, M. D., 142, 1990.

114. Haffner, S. M., Kushwaha, R. S., Foster, D. M., Applebaum-Bowden, D., and Hazzard, W.R., Studies on the metabolic mechanism of reduced high density lipoproteins during anabolic steroid therapy, *Metabolism,* 32, 413, 1983.

115. Kantor, M. A., Bianchini, A., Bernier, D., Sady, S. P., and Thompson, P. D., Androgens reduce HDL_2-cholesterol and increase hepatic triglyceride lipase activity, *Med. Sci. Sports Exerc.*, 17, 462, 1985.

116. Alen, M., Rahkila, P., and Marniemi, J., Serum lipids in power athletes self-administering testosterone and anabolic steroids, *Int. J. Sports Med.,* 6, 139, 1985.

117. Melchert, R. B. and Welder, A. A., Cardiovascular effects of androgenic-anabolic steroids, *Med. Sci. Sports Exerc.,* 27, 1252, 1995.

118. Zmuda, J. M., Fahrenbach, M. C., Younkin, B. T., Bausserman, L. L., Terry, R. B., Catlin, D. H., and Thompson, P. D., The effect of testosterone aromatization on high-density lipoprotein cholesterol level and postheparin lipolytic activity, *Metabolism,* 42, 446, 1993.

119. Thompson, P. D., Cullinane, E. M., Sady, S. P., Chenevert, C., Saritelli, A. L., Sady, M. A., and Herbert, P. N., Contrasting effects of testosterone and stanozolol on serum lipoprotein levels, *J. Am. Med. Assoc.*, 261, 1165, 1989.

120. Bagatell, C. J., Heiman, J. R., Matsumoto, A. M., Rivier, J. E., and Bremner, W. J., Metabolic and behavioral effects of high-dose, exogenous testosterone in healthy men, *J. Clin. Endocrinol. Metab.*, 79, 561, 1994.

121. Glazer, G. and Suchman, A. L., Lack of demonstrated effect of nandrolone on serum lipids, *Metabolism*, 43, 204, 1994.

122. Crist, D. M., Peake, G. T., and Stackpole, P. J., Lipemic and lipoproteinemic effects of natural and synthetic androgens in humans, *Clin. Exp. Pharmacol. Physiol.*, 13, 513, 1986.

123. Sacks, F. M. and Walsh, B. W., The effects of reproductive hormones on serum lipoproteins: unresolved issues in biology and clinical practice, *Ann. N. Y. Acad. Sci.*, 592, 272, 1990.

124. Eisenberg, S., High density lipoprotein metabolism, *J. Lipid Res.*, 25, 1017, 1984.

125. Taggart, H. M., Applebaum-Bowden, D., Haffner, S., Warnick, G. R., Cheung, M. C., Albers, J. J., Chestnut, C. H., and Hazzard, W. R., Reduction in high density lipoproteins by anabolic steroid (stanozolol) therapy for postmenopausal osteoporosis, *Metabolism*, 31, 1147, 1982.

126. Karila, T., Laaksonen, R., Jokelainen, K., Himberg, J. J., and Seppala, T., The effects of anabolic androgenic steroids on serum ubiquinone and dolichol levels among steroid abusers, *Metabolism*, 45, 844, 1996.

127. Crook, D., Testosterone, androgens and the risk of myocardial infarction, *Br. J. Clin. Pract.*, 50, 180, 1996.

128. McNutt, R. A., Ferenchick, G. S., Kirlin, P. C., and Hamlin, N. J., Acute myocardial infarction in a 22-year-old world class weight lifter using anabolic steroids, *Am. J. Cardiol.*, 62, 164, 1988.

129. Bowman, S. J., Tann, S., Fernando, S., Ayodeji, A., and Wetherstone, R. M., Anabolic steroids and infarction. *Br. Med. J.*, 299, 632, 1989.

130. Lyngberg, K. K., A case of fatal myocardial infarction in a bodybuilder treated with anabolic steroids, *Ugeskr Laeger*, 153, 587, 1991.

131. Ferenchick, G. S. and Adelman, S., Myocardial infarction associated with anabolic steroid use in a previously healthy 37-year-old weight lifter, *Am. Heart J.*, 124, 507, 1992.

132. Ferenchick, G., Schwartz, D., Ball, M., and Schwartz, K., Androgenic-anabolic steroid abuse and platelet aggregation: a pilot study in weight lifters, *Am. J. Med. Sci.*, 303, 78, 1992.

133. Huie, M. J., An acute myocardial infarction occurring in an anabolic steroid user, *Med. Sci. Sports Exerc.*, 26, 408, 1994.

134. Fisher, M., Appleby, M., Rittoo, D., and Cotter, L., Myocardial infarction with extensive intracoronary thrombus induced by anabolic steroids, *Br. J. Clin. Pract.*, 50, 222, 1996.

135. Appleby, M., Fisher, M., and Martin, M., Myocardial infarction, hyperkalaemia and ventricular tachycardia in a young male body-builder, *Int. J. Cardiol.*, 44, 171, 1994.

136. Kennedy, C., Myocardial infarction in association with misuse of anabolic steroids, *Ulster Med. J.*, 62, 174, 1993.

137. Kennedy, M. C., Corrigan, A. B., and Pilbeam, S. T., Myocardial infarction and cerebral haemorrhage in a young body builder taking anabolic steroids [letter], *Aust. N. Z. J. Med.*, 23, 713, 1993.

138. Akhter, J., Hyder, S., and Ahmed, M., Cerebrovascular accident associated with anabolic steroid use in a young man, *Neurology*, 44, 2405, 1994.

139. Laroche, G. P., Steroid anabolic drugs and arterial complications in an athlete—a case history, *Angiology*, 41, 964, 1990.

140. Frankle, M. A., Eichberg, R., and Zachariah, S. B., Anabolic androgenic steroids and a stroke in an athlete: case report, *Arch. Phys. Med. Rehabil.*, 69, 632, 1988.

141. Mochizuki, R. M., and Richter, K. M., Cardiomyopathy and cerebrovascular accident associated with anabolic-androgenic steroid use, *Phy. Spts. Med.*, 16, 109, 1988.

142. Ansell, J. E., Tiarks, C., and Fairchild, V. K., Coagulation abnormalities associated with the use of anabolic steroids, *Am. Heart J.*, 125, 367, 1993.

143. Shiozawa, Z., Yamada, H., Mabuchi, C., Hotta, T., Saito, M., Sobue, I., and Huang, Y. P., Superior sagittal sinus thrombosis associated with androgen therapy for hypoplastic anemia, *Ann. Neurol.*, 12, 578, 1982.

144. Lowe, G. D., Thomson, J. E., Reavey, M. M., Forbes, C. D., and Prentice, C. R., Mesterolone: thrombosis during treatment, and a study of its prothrombotic effects, *Br. J. Clin. Pharmacol.,* 7, 107, 1979.

145. Thompson, P. D., Sadaniantz, A., Cullinane, E. M., Bodziony, K. S., Catlin, D. H., Torek-Both, G., and Douglas, P. S., Left ventricular function is not impaired in weight-lifters who use anabolic steroids, *J. Am. Coll. Cardiol.,* 19, 278, 1992.

146. Luke, J. L., Farb, A., Virmani, R., and Sample, R. H., Sudden cardiac death during exercise in a weight lifter using anabolic androgenic steroids: pathological and toxicological findings, *J. Forensic Sci.,* 35, 1441, 1990.

147. Kennedy, M. C. and Lawrence, C., Anabolic steroid abuse and cardiac death, *Med. J. Aust.,* 158, 346, 1993.

148. Ferenchick, G. S., Anabolic/androgenic steroid abuse and thrombosis: is there a connection?, *Med. Hypotheses,* 35, 27, 1991.

149. Ferenchick, G. S., Hirokawa, S., Mammen, E. F., and Schwartz, K. A., Anabolic-androgenic steroid abuse in weight lifters: evidence for activation of the hemostatic system, *Am. J. Hematol.,* 49, 282, 1995.

150. Ajayi, A. A., Mathur, R., and Halushka, P. V., Testosterone increases human platelet thromboxane A2 receptor density and aggregation responses, *Circulation,* 91, 2742, 1995.

151. Matsuda, K., Mathur, R. S., Duzic, E., and Halushka, P. V., Androgen regulation of thromboxane A2/prostaglandin H2 receptor expression in human erythroleukemia cells, *Am. J. Physiol.,* 265, E928, 1993.

152. Fearnley, G. R., and Chakrabarti, R., Increase of blood fibrinolytic activity by testosterone, *Lancet,* 2, 128, 1962.

153. Cade, J. F., Stubbs, K. P., Stubbs, A. E., and Clegg, E.A., Thrombosis, fibrinolysis and ethylestrenol, *Acta Endocrinol,* 110(suppl 271),53, 1985.

154. Mannucci, P.M., Kluft, C., Traas, D. W., Seveso, P., and D'Angelo, A., Congenital plasminogen deficiency associated with venous thromboembolism: Therapeutic trial with stanozolol, *Br. J. Haematol.,* 63, 753, 1986.

155. Walker, I. D., Davidson, J. F., Richards, A., Yates, T., McEwan, H. P., The effect of the synthetic steroid ORG OD14 on fibrinolysis and blood lipids in postmenopausal women, *Thrombosis Hemostasis,* 53, 303, 1985.

156. Davidson, J. F., Lochhead, M., McDonald, G.A., and NcNicol, G. P., Fibrinolytic enhancement by stanozolol: A double blind trial, *Br. J. Haematol.,* 22, 543, 1972.

157. AL-Momen, A. K., Huraib, S. O., Gader, A. M. A., and Sulaimani, F., Low dose danazol is effective in management of erythropoietin induced thrombosis, *Thrombosis Res.,* 64, 527, 1991.

158. Petera, V., Bobek, K., and Lahn, V., Serum transaminase (GOT,GPT) and lactic dehydrogenase activity during treatment with methyl testosterone, *Clin. Chim. Acta,* 7, 604, 1962.

159. Wynn, V., Landon, J., and Kawerau, E., Studies on hepatic function during methandienone therapy, *Lancet,* 1, 69, 1961.

160. Zimmerman, H. J., Hormonal derivatives and other drugs used to treat endocrine diseases, in Hepatotoxicity: The Adverse Effects of Drugs and Other Chemicals on the Liver, Zimmerman H. J., ed., Appleton-Century-Crofts, New York, 436, 1978.

161. Ishak, K. G., and Zimmerman, H. J., Hepatotoxic effects of the anabolic/androgenic steroids, *Semin. Liver Dis.,* 7, 230, 1987.

162. Ishak, K. G., Hepatic neoplasms associated with contraceptive and anabolic steroids, in *Carcinogenic Hormones,* Lingeman, C. H., ed., Springer-Verlag, Berlin, 73, 1979.

163. Foss, G. L., and Simpson, S. L., Oral methyltestosterone and jaundice, *Br. Med. J.,* 1, 259, 1959.

164. Yoshida, E. M., Karim, M. A., Shaikh, J. F., Soos, J. G., and Erb, S. R., At what price, glory? Severe cholestasis and acute renal failure in an athlete abusing stanozolol, *Can. Med. Assoc. J.,* 151, 791, 1994.

165. Singh, C., Bishop, P., and Willson, R., Extreme hyperbilirubinemia associated with the use of anabolic steroids, health/nutritional supplements, and ethanol: response to ursodeoxycholic acid treatment, *Am. J. Gastroenterol.,* 91, 783, 1996.

166. Gurakar, A., Caraceni, P., Fagiuoli, S., and Van Thiel, D. H., Androgenic/anabolic steroid-induced intrahepatic cholestasis: a review with four additional case reports, *J. Okla. State. Med. Assoc.,* 87, 399, 1994.

167. Welder, A. A., Robertson, J. W., and Melchert, R. B., Toxic effects of anabolic-androgenic steroids in primary rat hepatic cell cultures, *J. Pharmacol. Toxicol. Methods,* 33, 187, 1995.

168. Anthony, P. P., Hepatoma associated with androgenic steroids, *Lancet,* 1, 685, 1975.

169. Overly, W. L., Dankoff, J. A., Wang, B. K., and Singh, U. D., Androgens and hepatocellular carcinoma in an athlete, *Ann. Intern. Med.,* 100, 158, 1984.

170. Zevin, D., Turani, H., Cohen, A., and Levi, J., Androgen-associated hepatoma in a hemodialysis patient, *Nephron,* 29, 274, 1981.

171. Kosaka, A., Takahashi, H., Yajima, Y., Tanaka, M., Okamura, K., Mizumoto, R., and Katsuta, K., Hepatocellular carcinoma associated with anabolic steroid therapy: report of a case and review of the Japanese literature, *J. Gastroenterol.,* 31, 450, 1996.

172. Falk, H., Popper, H., Thomas, L. B., and Ishak, K. G., Hepatic angiosarcoma associated with androgenic-anabolic steroids, *Lancet,* 2, 1120, 1979.

173. Taxy, J. B., Peliosis: A morphologic curiosity becomes an iatrogenic problem, *Hum. Pathol.,* 9, 331, 1978.

174. Lowdell, C. P., and Murray-Lyon, I. M., Reversal of liver damage due to long term methyltestosterone and safety of non-17 a-alkylated androgens, *Br. Med. J.,* 291, 637, 1985.

175. Nadell, J., and Kosek, J., Peliosis hepatis: Twelve cases associated with oral androgen therapy, *Arch. Pathol. Lab. Med.,* 101, 405, 1977.

176. Bahrke, M. S., Yesalis, C. E., and Wright, J. E., Psychological and behavioral effects of endogenous testosterone levels and anabolic-androgenic steroids among males, *Sports Med.,* 10, 303, 1990.

177. Pope, H. G., Jr, and Katz, D. L., Homicide and near-homicide by anabolic steroid users, *J. Clin. Psychiat.,* 51, 28, 1990.

178. Pope, H. G., Jr, and Katz, D. L., Affective and psychotic symptoms associated with anabolic steroid use, *Am. J. Psychiat.,* 145, 487, 1988.

179. Pope, H. G. and Katz, D. L., Psychiatric and medical effects of anabolic-androgenic steroid use, A controlled study of 160 athletes, *Arch. Gen. Psychiat.,* 51, 375, 1994.

180. Choi, P. Y. and Pope, H. G., Violence toward women and illicit androgenic-anabolic steroid use, *Ann. Clin. Psychiatry,* 6, 21, 1994.

181. Brower, K. J., Eliopulos, G. A., Blow, F. C., Catlin, D. H., and Beresford, T. P., Evidence for physical and psychological dependence on anabolic androgenic steroids in eight weight lifters, *Am. J. Psychiatry,* 147, 510, 1990.

182. Kashkin, K. B., and Kleber, H. D., Hooked on hormones? An anabolic steroid addiction hypothesis, *J. Am. Med. Assoc.,* 262, 3166, 1989.

183. Kiraly, C. L., Collan, Y., and Alen, M., Effect of testosterone and anabolic steroids on the size of sebaceous glands in power athletes, *Am. J. Dermatopathol.,* 9, 515, 1987.

184. Scott, M. J., Jr, and Scott, M. J., III, Dermatologists and anabolic-androgenic drug abuse, *Cutis.,* 44, 30, 1989.

185. Scott, M. J.,3d and Scott, A. M., Effects of anabolic-androgenic steroids on the pilosebaceous unit, *Cutis.,* 50, 113, 1992.

186. Scott, M. J., Scott, M. J., and Scott, A. M., Linear keloids resulting from abuse of anabolic androgenic steroid drugs, *Cutis.,* 53, 41, 1994.

187. Hoag, G. N., Connolly, V. P. L., and Domke, H. L., Marked fall in high-density lipoprotein following isotretinoin therapy: Report of a case in a weight lifter on anabolic steroids, *J. Am. Acad. Derm.,* 16, 1264, 1987.

188. McLaughlin, G. E., McCarty, D. J., and Segal, B. L., Hemarthrosis complication anticoagulant therapy, *J. Am. Med. Assoc.,* 196, 202, 1966.

189. Schrogie, J. J., and Solomon, H. M., The anticoagulant response to bishydroxycoumarin: II, The effect of D-thyroxine, clofibrate, and norethandrolone, *Clin Pharm,* 8, 70, 1967.

190. Wilson, I. C., Prange, A. J., and Lara, P. P., Methyltestosterone and imipramine in men: Conversion of depression to paranoid reaction, *Am. J. Psychiat.,* 131, 21, 1974.

191. Zeiss, J., Smith, R. R., and Taha, A. M., Iliopsoas hypertrophy mimicking acute abdomen in a bodybuilder, *Gastrointest. Radiol.*, 12, 340, 1987.

192. David, H. G., Green, J. T., Grant, A. J., and Wilson, C. A., Simultaneous bilateral quadriceps rupture: a complication of anabolic steroid abuse, *J. Bone Joint Surg. Br.*, 77, 159, 1995.

193. Liow, R. Y. and Tavares, S., Bilateral rupture of the quadriceps tendon associated with anabolic steroids, *Br. J. Sports Med.*, 29, 77, 1995.

194. Lambert, M. I., St Clair Gibson, A., and Noakes, T. D., Rupture of the triceps tendon associated with steroid injections [letter], *Am. J. Sports Med.*, 23, 778, 1995.

195. Visuri, T., and Lindholm, H., Bilateral distal biceps tendon avulsions with use of anabolic steroids, *Med. Sci. Sports Exerc.*, 26, 941, 1994.

196. Laseter, J. T., Russell, J. A., Anabolic steroid-induced tendon pathology: A review of the literature, Medicine Sci *Sports Exer.*, 23, 1, 1991.

197. Winwood, P. J., Robertson, D. A. F., and Wright, R., Bleeding oesophageal varices associated with anabolic steroid use in an athlete, *Postgrad. Med. J.*, 66, 864, 1990.

198. Scott, M. J. and Scott, M. J., HIV infection associated with injections of anabolic steroids, *J. Am. Med. Assoc.*, 262, 207, 1989.

9.4 DETECTION OF EXOGENOUS ANABOLIC ANDROGENIC STEROIDS

WILHELM SCHÄNZER

GERMAN SPORTS UNIVERSITY OF COLOGNE, INSTITUTE OF BIOCHEMISTRY, COLOGNE, GERMANY

The use of synthetic exogenous anabolic androgenic steroids (AAS) in human sports was banned in 1974 by the Medical Commission of the IOC. Synthetic AAS are steroids that are not produced in the human body but have similar or pronounced effects to the male sex hormone testosterone (Figure 9.4a). These steroids were synthesized (Figure 9.4b) to obtain testosterone-like hormones with increased anabolic activity and decreased androgenic effects. The therapeutic use of AAS in medicine is mostly for the treatment of osteoporosis and for the treatment of metabolic deficiencies. They have been used to supplement weight increase in patients, but their effectiveness is doubtful. AAS may also be used in the treatment of aplastic anaemia. In females, AAS and other androgenic steroids are used in the treatment of breast cancer.

The misuse of AAS by athletes became known to the public in the 1970s. Athletes tried to improve their performance by using AAS, which have positive anabolic effects on the muscle protein synthesis, resulting in increased muscle mass and body weight. The biochemical mechanism for the effects of AAS on the muscle cell is not yet fully understood.

At the time AAS were banned, no analytical method was known from the literature which described their detection in human urine. The first method employed for the screening detection of AAS was radio immunoassay (RIA). In 1975 Brooks[1] presented a RIA analysis for the detection of AAS using an antiserum raised against metandienone which displayed some cross reactivity to other 17-methyl steroids. At that time, Summer[2] also raised an antiserum for nandrolone (nortestosterone). The RIA technique was used for the screening of AAS in human urine during the Olympic Games in Montreal in 1976 and in Moscow in 1980. Confirmation of positive RIA screening results had to be confirmed by gas chromatography/mass spectrometry (GC/MS). The RIA screening, as employed in the Games, had many weaknesses: The antiserum was not sensitive to all 17-methyl steroids and some AAS were not detected. Additionally, nearly all AAS are extensively metabolized and the extent of cross reactivity of the metabolites to the antiserum is fully uncharacterized. Finally, the RIA screening analysis produced many false positives (due to cross reactivity with biological material in the urine) and this was not acceptable for routine analysis.

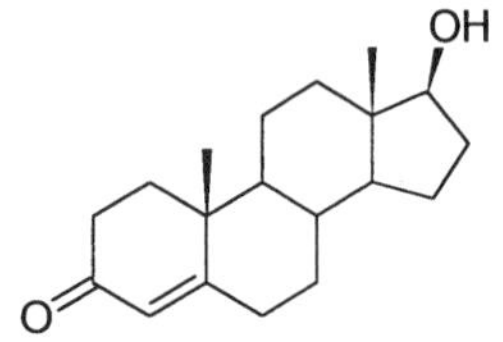

Figure 9.4a. Structural formula of testosterone.

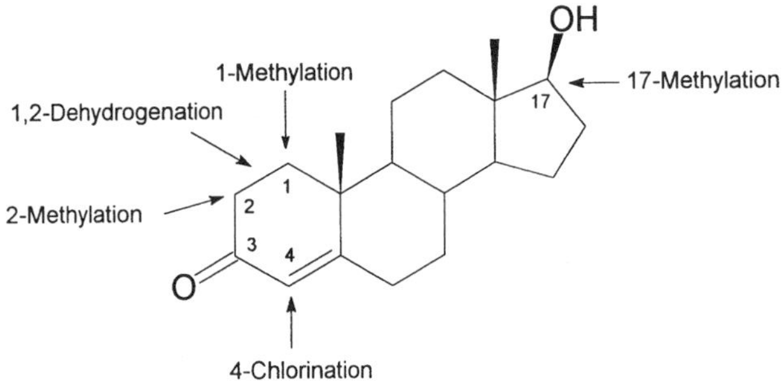

Figure 9.4b Synthetic anabolic androgenic steroids as chemical modifications of testosterone.

The analytical technique of GC combined with a nitrogen specific detector was introduced by Donike[3] for the screening of stimulants and narcotics at the 1972 Olympic Games in Munich. Based on the success of the GC technique, Donike expanded the method for the analysis of AAS using mass spectrometric detection (GC/MS).[4] In 1975, Ward et al.[5] described a GC/MS method for the detection of metandienone (metabolite 6-hydroxymetandienone), stanozolol, nandrolone (metabolites: 19-norandrosterone and 19-noretiocholanolone), and metabolites of ethylestrenol and norethandrolone.

The GC/MS method has inherent advantages for AAS analysis: GC separation of the AAS from the complex biologic matrix and highly selective and sensitive detection of the AAS and their metabolites using substance specific fragment ions (selected ion monitoring) at known retention times. Several articles describing the detection of AAS and their metabolites by GC/MS have been published.[6-10]

To detect AAS misuse, athletes are required to deliver urine which is analyzed for the presence of prohibited AAS and their metabolites. To circumvent detection, athletes misuse AAS in the training periods and stop several days before a competition where drug testing is announced. For this reason the analyses have to be very sensitive in order to detect very low concentrations of AAS and their metabolites. Additionally, the metabolism of AAS has to be investigated so that their administration can be retrospectively followed. Several examples of AAS misused in sports are shown in Figure 9.4c.

9.4.1 METABOLISM OF ANABOLIC ANDROGENIC STEROIDS

Most AAS are completely metabolized in the human and none, or only small amounts, of the parent steroid are excreted into urine. Hence, AAS metabolism studies have been performed and published by several authors. Reviews of the metabolism of AAS were published by Schänzer and Donike[10] and Schänzer.[11]

Anabolic steroids not alkylated in 17-position, administered in most cases as esters, undergo metabolism like testosterone yielding 17-keto steroids as the main metabolites. 3-Keto-4-ene AAS (except fluoxymesterone, clostebol, and oxymesterone) are metabolized similar to testosterone. In the phase I the C-4,5 double bond is reduced to 5α and 5ß-androstane isomers and this is followed by rapid reduction of the 3-keto group, mainly by 3-

Wilhelm Schänzer

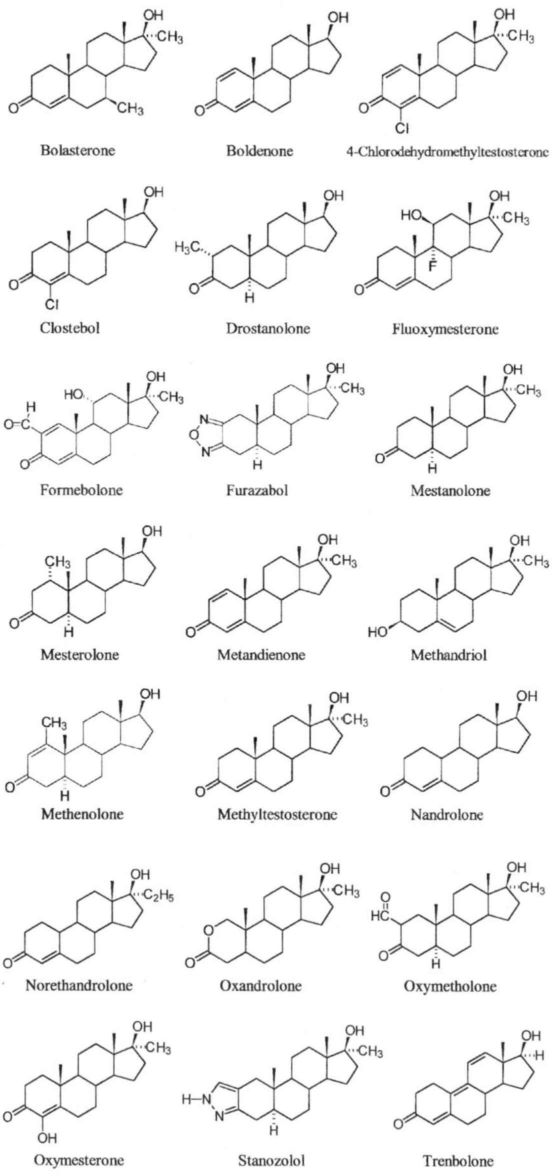

Figure 9.4c Structure formulas of synthetic anabolic androgenic steroids.

hydroxy-dehydrogenase enzymes. In phase II there occurs conjugation at the 3-hydroxy group with glucuronic acid. The principle metabolism of testosterone yielding reductive and oxidative metabolites is summarized in Figure 9.4.1a.

In recent years it has become apparent that the metabolism of anabolic steroids is highly complex and that the extent and number of metabolites formed for many AAS is much higher than previously reported. For example, in the 1970s only two metabolites of metandienone were known (Figure 9.4.1b). A summary of main excreted metandienone metabolites is shown in Figure 9.4.1c.

The selection of AAS and their metabolites to be analyzed in a screening process have to fulfil the following criteria: The detection of the parent compound is recommended when it

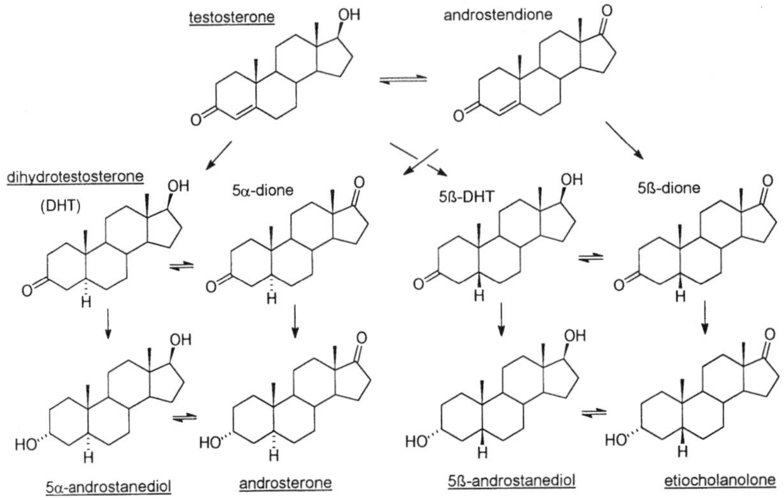

Figure 9.4.1a Main metabolic pathways of testosterone. Steroid excreted into urine are underlined.

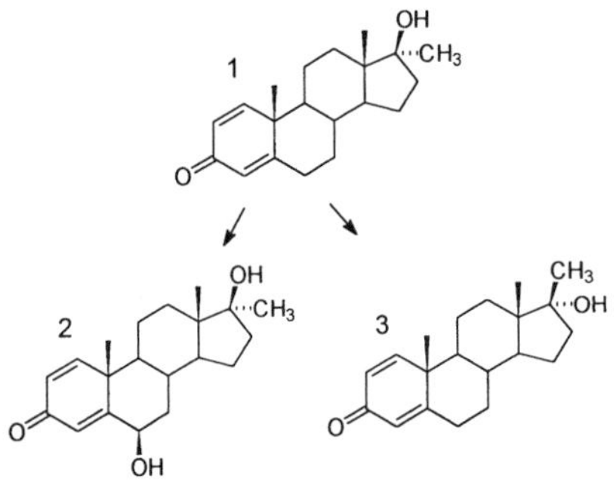

Figure 9.4.1b Known metabolites of metandienone in 1997.

is excreted into the urine at a high enough concentration. When excretion of the parent steroid is negligible, it should not be included in the screening analysis. For example, in methyltestostosterone metabolism the parent steroid is excreted only in the first hours after application in a very low amount. Screening for methyltestosterone itself is insufficient. The screening must include the main metabolites that are produced and excreted into urine within the first few days after application. A screening analysis for AAS with a listing of parent steroids and their metabolites is presented in Table 9.4.1.

More recent investigations on AAS metabolism have confirmed long term excreted metabolites. These are metabolites which are excreted with a much longer half-life of elimination as compared to the main excreted metabolites. In several cases, the concentration of these long term metabolites is much lower than that of the main metabolites, but they can be detected several days after the disappearance of the main metabolites. In the metabolism of metandienone, 6ß-hydroxy metandienone is the main excreted metabolite.[12,13] In 1992 Schänzer et al.[14] elucidated that A-ring reduced conjugated excreted metabolites were excreted into urine for much longer than 6ß-hydroxymetandienone. One particular conjugated A-ring reduced metabolite,17ß-methyl-5ß-androst-1-ene-3,17-diol (Figure 9.4.1c, steroid 6) can be detected for the longest time after application. This metabolite is formed via an epimerization

Wilhelm Schänzer

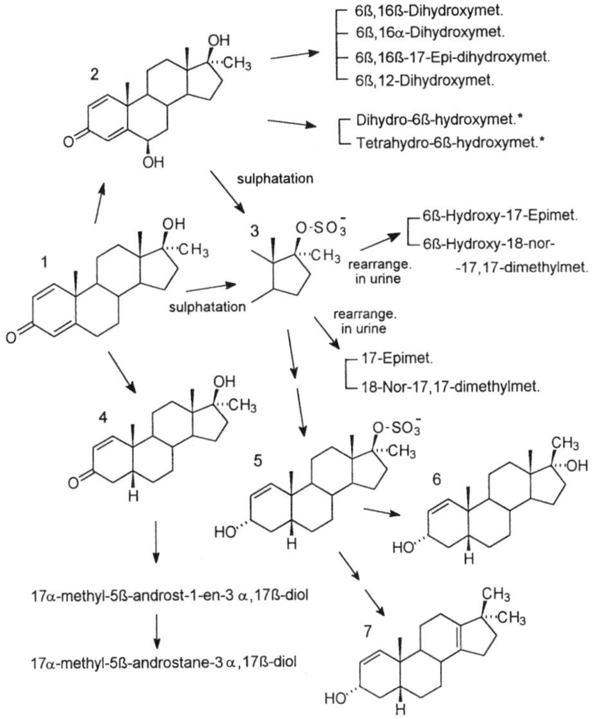

Figure 9.4.1c Actual known metabolites (not all metabolites are included) of metandienone. Metandienone (1), 6ß-hydroxymetandienone (2), 17ß-sulphate of metandienone and 6ß-hydroxymetandienone (3), 17ß-hydroxy-17-methyl-5ß-androst-1-en-3-one (4), 17-methyl-5ß-androst-1-ene-3,17ß-diol 17ß-sulphate (5), 17ß-methyl-5ß-androst-1-ene-3,17-diol (6), 18-nor-17,17-dimethyl-androst-1,13-dien-3ol (7), rearrange. = rearrangement process, ...met. = ...metandienone, * proposed metabolite, till now not confirmed.

process[15-17] of the 17ß-sulphate conjugate. The 17-epimeric product is used for confirmation of metandienone administration even when 6ß-hydroymetandienone is not excreted. A long-term excreted metabolite of chlorodehydromethyltestosterone has also been elucidated,[18] allowing confirmation of the misuse of this AAS for a much longer time than previously.

To confirm the presence of AAS it is unambiguously recommended to use reference substances. If this is not possible excretion studies must be performed. Synthesized reference standards of most AAS metabolites have been prepared[10] and have been distributed to IOC accredited laboratories.

The list of AAS and metabolites that are used for screening and confirmation will be actualized in the future by the addition of newly identified long-term excreted metabolites.

9.4.2 ISOLATION FROM URINE

Excretion of AAS and their metabolites into urine generally follows a phase II metabolism, conjugation of the steroid with glucuronic acid or sulphate. Conjugation yields a more polar compound which enables faster elimination from the body. Oxandrolone and some metabolites of 4-chlorodehydromethyltestosterone, fluoxymesterone, metandienone, and oxandrolone are excreted unconjugated. All other steroids excreted as conjugates have to be hydrolyzed before GC/MS analysis. An overview of the isolation procedures used in AAS screening is shown in Figure 9.4.2.

Table 9.4.1 Screening for Anabolic Steroids

Anabolic steroid	Main excreted substance parent and/or metabolite	Origin of substance used for confirmation	Excretion into urine
Bolasterone	bolasterone 1	Reference	Conjugated
	7α,17α-dimethyl-5β-androstane-3α,17β-diol 2	Synthesized	Conjugated
	7α,17β-dimethyl-5β-androstane-3α,17α-diol 3	Urine excretion	Conjugated rearrange.
Boldenone	Boldenone 4	Reference	Conjugated
	17β-hydroxy-5β-androst-1-en-3-one 5	Synthesized	Conjugated
	3α-hydroxy-5β-androst-1-en-17-one 6	Synthesized	Conjugated
	5β-androst-1-ene-3α,17β-diol 7	Synthesized	Conjugated
4-Chlorodehydro-methyltestosterone	4-chlorodehydromethyltestosterone 8	Reference	Conjugated
	6β-hydroxy-4-chlorodehydromethyltestosterone 9	Synthesized	Unconjugated
	6β,16β-dihydroxy 4-chlorodehydromethyltestosterone 10	Urine excretion	Unconjugated
	6β,12ξ-dihydroxy 4-chlorodehydromethyltestosterone 11	Urine excretion	Unconjugated
	4-chloro-3α,6β,17β-trihydroxy-17α-methyl-5β-androst-1-en-16-one 12	Urine excretion	Unconjugated
Clostebol	4-chloro-3α-hydroxyandrost-4-en-17-one 13	Synthesized	Conjugated
	4ξ-chloro-3α-hydroxy-5α-androstan-17-one[a] 14	Urine excretion	Conjugated
	4ξ-chloro-3α-hydroxy-5β-androstan-17-one[a] 15	Urine excretion	Conjugated
	4ξ-chloro-3β-hydroxy-5α-androstan-17-one[a] 16	Urine excretion	Conjugated sulfate
	4ξ-chloro-3α,16ξ-dihydroxy-5ξ-androstan-17-one 17	Urine excretion	Conjugated
Drostanolone	3α-hydroxy-2α-methyl-5α-androstan-17-one 18	Synthesized	Conjugated
Fluoxymesterone	Fluoxymesterone 19	Reference	Conjugated
	9-fluoro-11β-hydroxy-18-nor-17,17-dimethyl-androsta-4,13-dien-3-one 20	Synthesized	Unconjugated rearrange.

Compound	Metabolite/name	Origin	Conjugation
Formebolone	9-fluoro-6β,11β,17β-trihydroxy-17α-methylandrost-4-ene-3-one **21**	Synthesized	Unconjugated
	9-fluoro-17α-methylandrost-4-ene-3α,6β,11β,17β-tetrol **22**	Synthesized	Unconjugated
	11α,17β-dihydroxy-2-hydroxymethyl-17α-methyl-androsta-1,4-diene-3-one **23**	Synthesized	Conjugated
Furazabol	Furazabol **24**	Reference	Conjugated
	16ξ-hydroxy-furazabol **25**	Urine excretion	Conjugated
Mestanolone	17α-methyl-5α-androstane-3α,17β-diol **26**	Synthesized	Conjugated
	17β-methyl-5α-androstane-3α,17α-diol **27**	Synthesized	Conjugated rearrange.
	18-Nor-17,17-dimethyl-5α-androst-13-en-3α-ol **28**	Synthesized	Conjugated rearrange.
Mesterolone	3α-hydroxy-1α-methyl-5α-androstan-17-one **29**	Synthesized	Conjugated
Metandienone	17-epimetandienone **30**	Synthesized	Unconjugated rearrange.
	18-nor-17,17-dimethylandrosta-1,4,13-trien-3-one **31**	Synthesized	Unconjugated rearrange.
	6β-hydroxymetandienone **32**	Synthesized	Unconjugated rearrange.
	17α-methyl-5β-androstane-3α, 17β-diol **33**	Synthesized	Conjugated
	17α-methyl-5β-androst-1-ene-3α, 17β-diol **34**	Synthesized	Conjugated
	17β-methyl-5β-androst-1-ene-3α, 17α-diol **35**	Synthesized	Conjugated
	18-nor 17,17-dimethyl-5β-androst-1,13-dien-3α-ol **36**	Synthesized	Conjugated rearrange.
Methandriol	17α-methyl-5β-androstane-3α,17β-diol **33**	Synthesized	Conjugated rearrange.
Metenolone	Metenolone **37**	Reference	Conjugated
	3α-hydroxy-1-methylen-5α-androstan-17-one **38**	Synthesized	Conjugated
Methyltestosterone	17α-methyl-5α-androstane-3α,17β-diol **26**	Synthesized	Conjugated
	17β-methyl-5α-androstane-3α,17α-diol **27**	Synthesized	Conjugated
	18-nor-17,17-dimethyl-5α-androst-13-en-3α-ol **28**	Synthesized	Conjugated rearrange.
	17α-methyl-5β-androstane-3α,17β-diol **33**	Synthesized	Conjugated
	17β-methyl-5β-androstane-3α,17α-diol **39**	Synthesized	Conjugated
	18-nor-17,17-dimethyl-5β-androst-13-en-3α-ol **40**	Synthesized	Conjugated rearrange.

Table 9.4.1 Screening for Anabolic Steroids (continued)

Anabolic steroid	Main excreted substance parent and/or metabolite	Origin of substance used for confirmation	Excretion into urine
Nandrolone	3α-hydroxy-5α-estran-17-one 41	Synthesized	Conjugated
	3α-hydroxy-5β-estran-17-one 42	Synthesized	Conjugated
	3β-hydroxy-5α-estran-17-one 43	Synthesized	Conjugated sulfate
Norethandrolone	17α-ethyl-5β-estrane-3α,17β-triol 44	Synthesized	Conjugated
	17α-ethyl-5ξ-estrane-3α,17β,21-diol 45	Urine excretion	Conjugated
Oxandrolone	Oxandrolone 46	Reference	Unconjugated
	17-epioxandrolone 47	Synthesized	Unconjugated rearrange.
	18-nor-17,17-dimethyl-oxandrolone 48	Synthesized	Unconjugated rearrange.
Oxymesterone	Oxymesterone 49	Reference	Conjugated
Oxymetholone	17α-methyl-5α-androstane-3α,17β-diol 26	Synthesized	Conjugated
	2-hydroxymethyl-17α-methyl-5α-androstane-3ξ,ξ,17β-triol[a] 50	Urine excretion	Conjugated
Stanozolol	Stanozolol 51	Reference	Conjugated
	3'-hydroxy-17-epistanozolol 52	Synthesized	Unconjugated rearrange.
	3'-hydroxystanozolol 53	Synthesized	Conjugated
	4β-hydroxystanozolol 54	Synthesized	Conjugated
	16β-hydroxystanozolol 55	Synthesized	Conjugated

Reference = Reference substance was purchased or obtained as a gift; Synthesized = Reference substance was synthesized in our laboratory; Urine excretion = Metabolite is obtained from urine of an excretion study.

Excretion into urine as a conjugate indicates that the parent or metabolite is excreted as a conjugate (conjugated probably with β-glucuronic acid), as the conjugate can be specifically hydrolyzed with β-glucuronidase from E. coli, the suffix conjugated sulphate issues that the metabolite could only be hydrolyzed with the arylsulphatase from helix pomatia or by solvolysis indicating that the metabolite is excreted as a sulphate which is in agreement with the literature, reporting that 3β-hydroxy steroids are mainly conjugated with sulphate.

Rearrange. = The metabolites originate from a rearrangement process of a 17β-sulphated 17α-methyl-17β-hydroxy steroid, which undergoes a decomposition in urine yielding several dehydration products, with the 18-nor compound as main substance, and the corresponding 17-epimeric steroid with 17β-methyl-17α-hydroxy configuration [15–17]. The prefix conjugated or unconjugated clarifies that even if the rearrangement cleaved the sulphate, the steroid is still conjugated, mainly at the 3-hydroxy group of the A-ring, or that no further conjugation of the molecule is present (prefix: unconjugated). In the latter case, the steroid can be directly isolated via a liquid/liquid extraction method.

Wilhelm Schänzer

Figure 9.4.2 Sample preparation of AAS. U = unconjugated, T = total fraction (conjugated + unconjugated), C = conjugated.

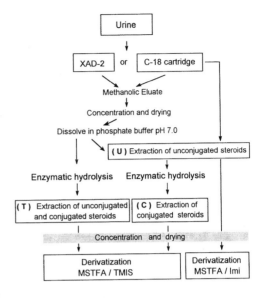

9.4.2.1 Hydrolysis of Conjugates

9.4.2.1.1 Enzymatic Hydrolysis

As hydrolysis is a crucial step in steroid analysis,[19,20] some investigations have been performed to optimize the hydrolysis for routine doping control.[21] Two different enzyme preparations are used: (1) A mixture of ß-glucuronidase and arylsulphatase obtained from Helix pomatia juice (HP enzyme) and (2) ß-glucuronidase from Escherichia coli. (EC enzyme). Investigations on the metabolism of anabolic androgenic steroids have shown that most of the conjugated excreted AAS and their main metabolites can be hydrolyzed with ß-glucuronidase from *E. coli.*

Since a screening procedure for synthetic AAS is also used to detect and quantify epitestosterone, testosterone, and testosterone metabolites, it is necessary to control that the used enzyme preparation has no side activity that can alter the steroid concentrations. Side reactions with the HP enzyme have been reported. The conversion of 3ß-hydroxy-5-ene steroids into the corresponding 3-keto- 4-ene steroids by Helix pomatia was published by Vanluchene et al.[22] for pregnancies and by Kuoppasalmi et al.[23] for the production of testosterone. Masse et al.[9] showed that the HP enzyme from SIGMA converts only 0.2% of androst-5-ene-3ß,17ß-diol to testosterone when heated for 3h at 55°C whereas the HP enzyme from Boehringer converts 70% of androst-5-ene- 3ß,17ß-diol to testosterone. Based on these results, it is essential that only enzyme preparations should be used which have no side activity. It is possible to monitor the side activities of the enzyme, for example, the transformation of dehydroepiandrosterone (3ß-hydroxyandrost-5-ene-17-one) to androst-4-ene-3,17-dione is an excellent marker.

9.4.2.1.2 Acidic Hydrolysis

Non-specific acidic hydrolysis has also been considered for routine doping analysis, but abandoned because several metabolites are unstable under acidic conditions, especially 17-methyl steroids undergo dehydration and rearrangement.[15-16]

9.4.3 EXTRACTION

The main criteria for AAS isolation from urine are extraction yield and biological background (co- extraction of matrix compounds). These two factors have to be optimized to ensure that all the AAS and their metabolites are extracted at levels which are high enough for a sensitive analysis. Several extraction methods have been investigated and developed.

9.4.3.1 Liquid-Liquid Extraction

Liquid–liquid extraction (Figure 9.4.2) is used after enzymatic hydrolysis to isolate the deconjugated and unconjugated steroids. It is also applied to extract unconjugated excreted steroids directly from urine.

The liquid-liquid extraction is performed at a moderate alkaline pH of 9 to 10. A pH of 10 or higher should not be used as 3'-hydroxystanozolol and oxandolone are not extracted at higher pH values. The organic solvent normally used for liquid-liquid extraction is diethyl ether, which has to be freshly distilled to ensure that no peroxides are present. More recently a change has been made from diethyl ether to *tert*.butyl methyl ether. The advantage of this solvent is that no peroxides can be formed. The extraction yield approaches that of diethyl ether. The extraction yield with *tert*.butyl methyl ether is more than 90% for most of the mono-hydroxy ketosteroids and somewhat lower for more polar compounds (Table 9.4.3.2.1). Table 9.4.3.2.1 also includes extraction yields obtained with n-pentane. n-Pentane is used in some confirmation procedures to reduce biological background from polar compounds.

9.4.3.2 Liquid-Solid Extraction

Isolation of steroid conjugates via Amberlite XAD-2 polystyrene resins[6] is a modified technique based on work by Bradlow in 1968[24,27] and Graf and Fuchs in 1975.[25,26] After extensive washing of the resin with acetone, methanol, and water to remove impurities, a product with highly reproducible adsorption characteristics is obtained. Conjugated and unconjugated steroids are strongly adsorbed to the XAD-2 resin. The recovery for the AAS, their metabolites, and the endogenous steroids is quantitative.[28]

Besides XAD-2 resin, Sep-Pak C18-cartridges are also commonly used. The cartridges are washed with methanol and water and then urine is applied. The column is washed and then the steroids are eluted with methanol.[9]

9.4.4 DERIVATIZATION OF AAS AND THEIR METABOLITES FOR GC/MS ANALYSIS

AAS and their metabolites exhibit poor gas chromatographic properties and therefore have to be derivatized to allow their detection in low nanogram amounts. These steroids contain hydroxy and keto functional groups and when they are not derivatized they are poorly resolved in the GC analysis and can undergo extensive degradation in the injection port. In 1969 Donike developed and introduced N-methyl-N-trimethylsilyltrifluoracetamide (MSTFA) as a derivatization reagent for GC.[29] Hydroxy groups react quantitatively with MSTFA yielding stable trimethylsilyl (TMS) ethers. An advantage of this reagent is that it also serves as a solvent and can be directly introduced onto the gas chromatographic column. The conversion of secondary hydroxy functions to TMS ethers also occurs readily (Figure 9.4.4a). Sterically hindered tertiary hydroxy groups, such as in 17-methyl- 17ß-hydroxy steroids, are not derivatized with MSTFA alone. In this case, the catalyst TMS-imidazol is highly effective,[6,10,30] as trimethyliodosilane (TMIS) is a powerful catalyst for trimethylsilylation of the 17 tertiary hydroxy group and, in addition, is used to derivatize keto functional groups.

One means of derivatizing keto groups is condensation with amines, e.g., hydroxyl amine, methoxyamine, or N,N-dimethylhydrazine, to form oximes and hydrazones. This procedure is followed by trimethylsilylation to derivatize hydroxy groups. A one-step derivatization process forming TMS ether TMS enol ether derivatives was presented by Zimmermann and Donike in 1980,[31] who used MSTFA with TMIS as a catalyst. Reaction with testosterone, for example, yielded quantitatively testosterone 3-enol TMS 17 TMS ethers (Figure 9.4.4b), which has excellent GC properties. In the enolization process, two TMS enol isomers (2,4-diene and 3,5-diene) can be formed. Reaction with MSTFA/TMIS yielded only one isomer, the 3,5-diene enol TMS ether with over 99%, and this product is absolutely stable under GC conditions. Reaction of testosterone, 5α-dihydrotestosterone, 5ß-dihydrotestosterone, and 5α-estran-3-ol-17-one with MSTFA/TMIS yield TMS enol-isomers to different extents as shown in Figure 9.4.4b. In Table 9.4.3 GC retention indices of both isomers and other 3-enol isomers are listed.

Wilhelm Schänzer

Table 9.4.3.2.1 Recoveries of Steroids Included in the Screening Procedure for Anabolic Steroids (Total Fraction) After a Single Extraction at pH 9.6 from 1 ml of Water Using Three Different Solvents

Anabolic androgenic steroid and metabolites	Systemic name	Diethyl ether	tert.Butyl-methyl ether	n-Pentane
Bolasterone metabolite	7α,17α-dimethyl-5β-androstane-3α,17β-diol	89.0	89.6	89.0
Boldenone	17β-hydroxyandrosta-1,4-dien-3-one	85.3	84.0	66.7
Boldenone metabolite	17β-hydroxy-5β-androst-1-en-3-one	87.7	86.6	85.1
4-Chlorodehydromethyl-testosterone metabolite	6β-hydroxy-4-chlorodehydromethyltestosterone	78.8	76.0	09.2
Clostebol metabolite	3α-hydroxy-4-chloro-androst-4-en-17-one	98.4	91.8	95.1
Drostanolone metabolite	3α-hydroxy-2α-methyl-5α-androstan-17-one	82.1	80.7	84.1
Fluoxymesterone metabolite	9α-fluoro-17α-methyl-androst-4-ene-3α, 6β,11β,17β-tetrol	26.0	47.4	00.0
Mesterolone metabolite	3α-hydroxy-1α-methyl-5α-androstan-17-one	92.7	89.4	94.3
Metandienone metabolite	17α-methyl-5β-androst-1-ene-3α,17β-diol	90.9	92.7	81.8
Metandienone metabolite	6β-hydroxymetandienone	81.7	77.0	03.2
Metenolone metabolite	3α-hydroxy-1-methylene-5α-androstan-17-one	92.5	92.5	96.8
Methyltestosterone metabolite	17α-methyl-5α-androstane-3α,17β-diol	90.7	89.3	91.2
Methyltestosterone metabolite	17α-methyl-5β-androstane-3α,17β-diol	90.7	89.3	91.2
Nandrolone metabolite	3α-hydroxy-5α-estran-17-one	89.6	89.6	90.7
Nandrolone metabolite	3α-hydroxy-5β-estran-3α,17β-diol	92.4	93.0	96.5
Oxandrolone		77.4	51.6	59.7
Oxymesterone	4,17β-dihydroxy-17α-methylandrost-4-en-3-one	109.0	119.5	117.6
Stanozolol metabolite	3'-hydroxystanozolol	89.2	93.3	06.4
Stanozolol metabolite	4β-hydroxystanozolol	85.2	88.9	06.5

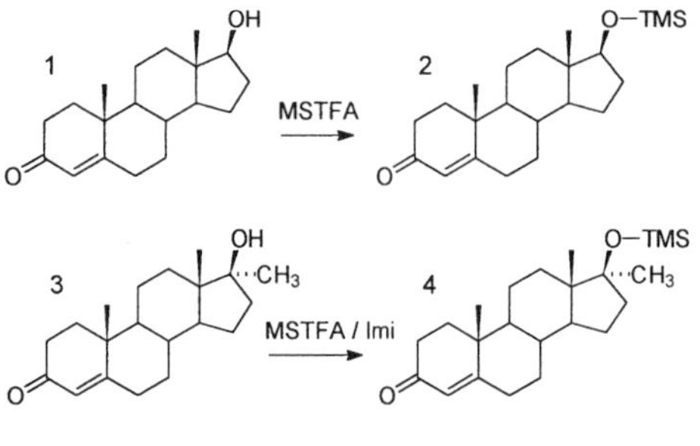

Figure 9.4.4a Trimethylsilylation of testosterone (1) with MSTFA yielding testosterone 17ß-O TMS ether (2) and methyltestosterone (3) with MSTFA/Imi to methyltestosterone 17ß-O TMS ether (4).

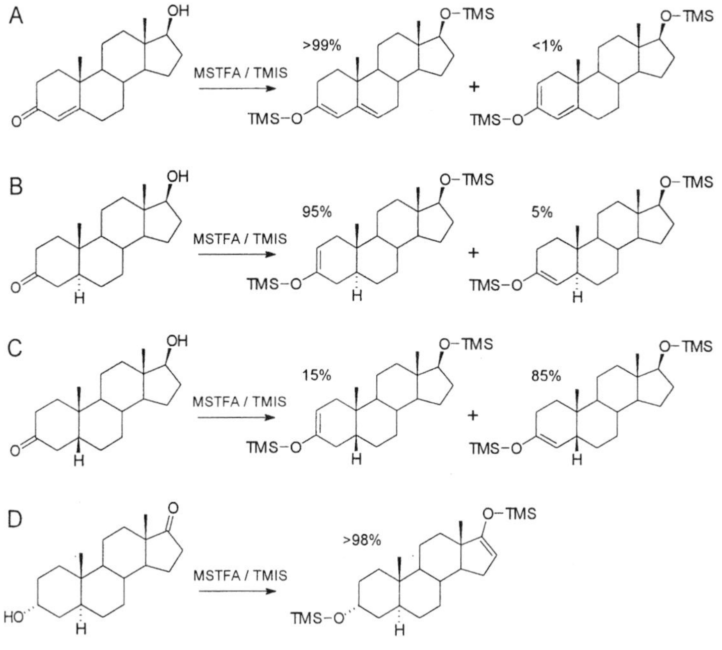

Figure 9.4.4b Trimethylsilylation of A) testosterone, B) 5α-dihydrotestosterone, C) 5ß- dihydrotestosterone and D) norandrosterone (main metabolite of nortestosterone) with MSTFA/TMIS.

Reaction of testosterone with MSTFA catalyzed with potassium acetate (KAc),[32] trimethylchlorosilane (TMCS), triethylamine-pyridine, or imidazole yielded two enol-isomers (2,4- diene and 3,5-diene) and not a uniform TMS-derivative when analyzed by GC. Interestingly, analyses of the testosterone products following reaction with MSTFA/KAc by liquid chromatography showed that the 2,4-diene TMS enol ether isomer of testosterone is formed to more than 98%. Under GC conditions, however, a high percentage of the 3.5-diene TMS enol isomer is formed, indicating that the 2,4-diene is isomerized in the GC injection port.

As TMIS is not easy to handle, the reaction mixture MSTFA/TMIS is prepared by dissolving ammonium iodide in MSTFA (0.2:100, w:v) while heating (Figure 9.4.4c, part A). Extensive tests have shown that the best results are obtained with 0.2% catalyst. As TMIS can easily produce iodine, mainly by oxidation and reaction with light, the addition of a reducing agent such as ethanethiol TMS (previously dithioerytheritol was used), is necessary to stabilize

Wilhelm Schänzer

Table 9.4.3 Retention Indices of Endogenous Steroids

Main excreted substance parent and/or metabolite	TMS derivative	Retention index	Molecular ion
5β-Dihydrotestosterone 1.TMS isomere 85%	bis	2466	434
5β-Dihydrotestosterone 2.TMS isomere 15%	bis	2493	434
3α-Hydroxyandrost-5-en-17-one (DHA)	bis	2500	432
3α-Hydroxyandrost-4-en-17-one	bis	2505	432
Androsterone	bis	2516	434
Etiocholanolone	bis	2523	434
5α-Androstane-3α,17βdiol	bis	2537	436
5β-Androstane-3α,17βdiol	bis	2542	436
11-Ketoandrosterone	tris	2584	520
Epiandrosterone	bis	2595	434
5α-Androstane-3,17-dione 1.TMS isomer <5%	bis	2601	432
11-Ketoetiocholanolone 2.TMS isomer	tris	2603	520
5α-Androstane-3,17-dione 2.TMS isomer >95%	bis	2607	432
Androst-5-en-3β,17β-diol	bis	2611	434
5α-Androstane-3β,17β-diol	bis	2612	436
Testosterone 1.TMS isomer (2,4-diene, <1%)	bis	2613	432
Epitestosterone	bis	2614	432
5α-Dihydrotestosterone 1.TMS isomere 5%	bis	2619	434
5α-Dihydrotestosterone 2.TMS isomere 95%	bis	2626	434
11-Ketoetiocholanolone	bis	2631	448
Androst-4-ene-3,17-dione	bis	2637	430
Testosterone 2.TMS isomer (3,5-diene, >99%)	bis	2660	432
11-Ketoisoandrosterone	tris	2662	520
11β-Hydroxyandrosterone	tris	2672	522
11β-Hydroxyetiocholanolone	tris	2683	522
5β-Pregnane-3α,20α-diol	bis	2776	464
5β-Pregnane-3α,17α,20α-triol	tris	2807	552
17α-Hydroxypregnenolone	tris	2941	548
17α-Hydroxyprogesterone	tris	3007	546

Derivatized with MSTFA/Imi, used for the unconjugated urine fraction.

GC column and temperature program: A Hewlett Packard Ultra 1 crosslinked methyl silicone capillary column is employed, length 17 m, I.D. 0.2 mm, film thickness 0.11 mm, helium carrier gas at a flow of 1 ml/min with a split (1:10). The temperature of the GC is ramped as follows: initial temperature 185°C, program rate 5°C/min to 320°C.

the MSTFA/NH$_4$I/ethanethiol TMS 4000:2:6 (v/w/v) reaction mixture (Figure 9.4.4c, part B). Formed iodine in the reaction mixtures is reduced by ethanethiol TMS to hydrogen iodide which reacts with MSTFA to form TMIS. To hinder iodine formation, the reaction mixture should be protected from light.

The two main effects of trimethylsilylation are shown for 5α-estran-3α-ol-17-one (metabolite of nandrolone): (a) the gas chromatographic resolution and detection limit is improved (Figure 9.4.4.d) and (b) the EI-spectrum is changed to higher and more abundant ions (Figure 9.4.4e).

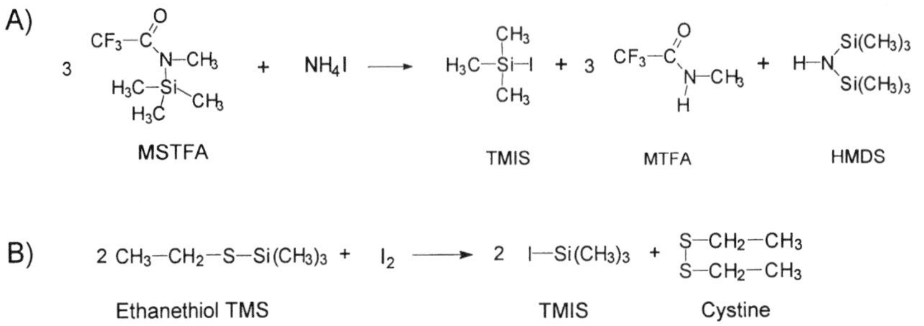

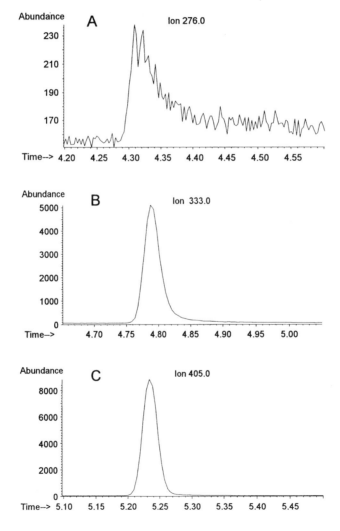

Figure 9.4.4c Preparation of MSTFA/TMIS reaction mixture. A) Reaction of MSTFA with ammonium iodide, B) function of ethanethiol TMS as reducing reagent.

Figure 9.4.4d GC/MS chromatogram of A) norandrosterone, B) norandrosterone 17-TMS ether and C) norandrosterone 17-TMS ether 3-enol TMS ether. The signals correspond to 40 ng of substance on column.

Wilhelm Schänzer

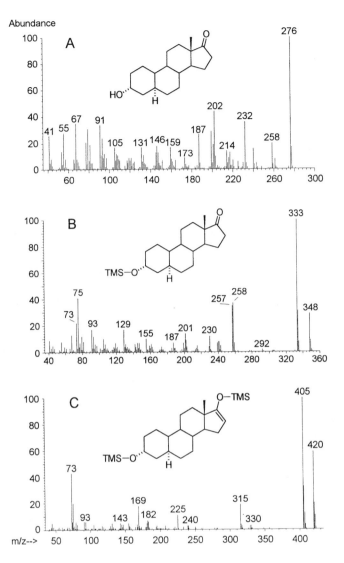

Figure 9.4.4e EI mass spectra of A) norandrosterone M+ 276, B) norandrosterone 17-TMS ether M+ 348 and C) norandrosterone 17-TMS ether 3-enol TMS ether M+ 420

9.4.5 INSTRUMENTAL ANALYSIS

9.4.5.1 Gas Chromatography

A great advancement in AAS analysis was the development of fused silica capillary columns with deactivated surfaces and cross-linked liquid phases. Dimethyl silicone (OV 1) or methylphenyl silicone (SE 54) of 0.11μm or 0.33μm film thickness are most commonly used for AAS analysis. The main criteria for choice of column is optimal separation of testosterone und epitestosterone from other steroids or coeluting species. Background elution differed from column to column. For the analysis of AAS and their metabolites, a coeluting background can decrease the detection limit. It depends on the experience of the analyst to choose a column which allows a maximum sensitivity in the detection of AAS. A 17m OV-1 column with 0.11μm film thickness is well suited for steroid analysis.[10] GC retention indices of the trimethylsilylated AAS

Table 9.4.4 Screening for Anabolic Steroids

Main excreted substance parent and/or metabolite	TMS derivative	Retention index	Molecular ion
18-Nor 17,17-dimethyl-5β-androst-1,13-dien-3α-ol 36	mono	2265	358
18-Nor-17,17-dimethyl-5β-androst-13-en-3α-ol 40	mono	2270	360
18-Nor-17,17-dimethyl-5α-androst-13-en-3α-ol 28	mono	2271	360
18-Nor-17,17-dimethylandrosta-1,4,13-trien-3-one 31	mono	2290	354
18-Nor-17,17-dimethyl-oxandrolone 48	no	2389	306
3α-Hydroxy-5α-estran-17-one 41	bis	2438	420
17β-Methyl-5β-androstane-3α,17α-diol 39	bis	2442	450
17β-Methyl-5β-androst-1-ene-3α,17α-diol 35	bis	2443	448
17β-Hydroxy-5β-androst-1-en-3-one 5	bis	2451	432
17β-Methyl-5α-androstane-3α,17α-diol 27	bis	2458	450
3α-Hydroxy-5β-estran-17-one 42	bis	2487	420
3β-Hydroxy-5β-estran-17-one 44	bis	2504	420
3α-Hydroxy-5β-androst-1-en-17-one 6	bis	2514	432
5β-Androst-1-ene-3α.17β-diol 7	bis	2532	434
7α,17β-Dimethyl-5β-androstane-3α,17α-diol 3	bis	2542	464
3α-Hydroxy-2α-methyl-5α-androstan-17-one 18	bis	2553	448
3α-Hydroxy-1-methylen-5α-androstan-17-one 38	bis	2576	446
9-Fluoro-11β-hydroxy-18-nor-17,17-dimethyl-androsta-4,13-dien-3-one 20	bis	2598	462
3α-Hydroxy-1α-methyl-5α-androstan-17-one 29	bis	2604	448
17α-Methyl-5β-androst-1-ene-3α,17β-diol 34	bis	2604	448
17α-Methyl-5α-androstane-3α,17β-diol 26	bis	2610	450
17α-Methyl-5β-androstane-3α,17β-diol 33	bis	2615	450
17-Epimetandienone 30	mono*	2620	372
17-Epimetandienone 30	bis	2634	444
Boldenone 4	bis	2642	430
17-Epioxandrolone 47	mono	2666	378
4-Chloro-3α-hydroxyandrost-4-en-17-one 13	bis	2691	466
7α, 17α-Dimethyl-5β-androstane-3α,17β-diol 2	bis	2692	464
17α-Ethyl-5β-estrane-3α,17β-diol 44	bis	2693	450
Metenolone 37	bis	2694	446
4ξ-Chloro-3α-hydroxy-5α-androstan-17-one 14	bis	2723	468
4ξ-Chloro-3α-hydroxy-5β-androstan-17-one 15	bis	2741	468
Bolasterone 1	bis	2763	460
Oxandrolone 46	mono	2775	378
4ξ-Chloro-3β-hydroxy-5α-androstan-17-one 16	bis	2821	468
6β-Hydroxymetandienone 32	bis*	2845	460
9-Fluoro-17α-methylandrost-4-ene-3a,6b,11β,17b-tetrol 22	tetra	2856	642
6β-Hydroxymetandienone 32	tris	2891	532
Furazabol 24	mono	2895	402

Wilhelm Schänzer

Table 9.4.4 Screening for Anabolic Steroids (continued)

Main excreted substance parent and/or metabolite	TMS derivative	Retention index	Molecular ion
17α-Ethyl-5β-estrane-3α,17β,21-triol 45	tris	2895	538
Fluoxymesterone 19	tris	2935	552
4-Chlorodehydromethyltestosterone 8	bis	2937	478
9-Fluoro-6β,11β,17β-trihydroxy-17α-methylandrost-4-ene-3-one 1.TMS isomer 21	tetra	2949	640
Oxymesterone 49	tris	2950	534
4-Chloro-3α,6β,17β-trihydroxy-17α-methyl-5β-androst-1-en-16-one 12	tris*	2968	584
4ξ-chloro-3α,16ξ-dihydroxy-5ξ-androstan-17-one 17	tris	2989	556
4-Chloro-3α,6β,17β-trihydroxy-17α-methyl-5β-androst-1-en-16-one 12	tetra	2997	656
6β-Hydroxy-4-chlorodehydromethyltestosterone 9	bis*	3007	494
2-Hydroxymethyl-17α-methyl-5α-androstane-3ξ,ξ,17β-triol 50	tetra	3031	640
9-Fluoro-6β,11β,17β-trihydroxy-17α-methylandrost-4-ene-3-one 2.TMS isomer 21	tetra	3059	640
11α,17β-Dihydroxy-2-hydroxymethyl-17α-methyl-androsta-1,4-diene-3-one 23	tetra	3083	634
Stanozolol 51	bis	3089	472
3'-Hydroxy-17-epistanozolol 52	tris	3099	560
6β,12ξ-Dihydroxy-4-chlorodehydromethyltestosterone 11	tris*	3147	582
16ξ-Hydroxyfurazabol 25	bis	3156	490
11α,17β-Dihyroxy-2-hydroxymethyl-17α-methyl-androsta-1,4-dien-3-one 23	tris*	3163	562
6β,16β-Dihydroxy-4-chlorodehydromethyltestosterone 10	tris*	3172	582
3'-Hydroxystanozolol 53	tris	3218	560
4β-Hydroxystanozolol 54	tris	3218	560
16β-Hydroxystanozolol 55	tris	3334	560

Derivatized with MSFTA/Imi, used for the unconjugated urine fraction.

GC column and temperature program: A Hewlett Packard Ultra 1 crosslinked methyl silicone capillary column is employed, lenght 17m, I.D. 0.2 mm, film thickness 0.11 μm, helium carrier gas at a flow of 1 ml/min with a split (1:10). The temperature of the GC is ramped as follows: initial temperature 185°C, program rate 5°C/min to 320°C.

and their metabolites measured on an OV 1 column are given in Table 9.4.4. Retention indices of endogenous steroids, measured on the same column and temperature program, are shown in Table 9.4.4. With this column using a temperature rate of 5°C/min or 3°C/min it is also possible to obtain separation of the isomeric metabolites of methyltestosterone, 17α-methyl-5-androstane-3α,17ß-diol and 17α-methyl-5ß- androstane-3α,17ß-diol.

9.4.5.2 Mass Spectrometry

The first GC/MS analysis of AAS was made using magnetic sector instruments (Altas CH-5), and Varian MAT 212. Current analysis was performed using quadrupole GC/MS instruments with electron impact ionization at 70eV. All laboratories performing doping analysis now use benchtop GC/MS. In connection with modern computers and software, the quadrupole mass spectrometer is well established for a target analysis of AAS. Detailed information regarding the actual used MS methods has been published.[8-10]

Modern high resolution mass spectrometers have several advantages in steroid analysis. The feasability of detecting small traces of metabolites of stanozolol and metandienone in the screening and confirmation of AAS with HRMS has been demonstrated by Schänzer et al.[33] This procedure has advantages in screening of AAS to conventional quadrupole instruments. The use of modern techniques of iontraps with and without MS/MS options is still under investigation and may deliver similar results in the future. Moreover, the tested HRMS (Finnegan MAT 95) has a powerful software system allowing routine screening of up to 50 samples per day with convenient data handling.

ACKNOWLEDGMENT

I thank the Bundesinstitut für Sportwissenschaft, Cologne and the International Athletic Foundation for their financial support. I also thank Dr. Stevan Horning for his assistance in preparing the manuscript.

REFERENCES

1. Brooks, R.V., Firth, R.G., and Summer, N.A., Detection of anabolic steroids by radio immuno assay, Brit. J. Sports Med., 9, 89, 1975.
2. Summer, N.A., Measurement of anabolic steroids by radioimmunoassay. Brit. J. Sports Med., 9, 307, 1974.
3. Donike, M., Jaenicke, L., Stratmann, D. and Hollmann, W., Gas-chromatographischer Nachweis von stickstoffhaltigen Pharmaka in wässrigen Lösungen mit dem Stickstoffdetektor, J. Chromatogr., 52, 237, 1970.
4. Donike, M., Zum Problem des Nachweises der anabolen Steroide:Gas chromatographische und massenspezifische Möglichkeiten, Sportarzt und Sportmedizin, 1, 1, 1975.
5. Ward, R., Shackleton, C.H.L., and Lawson, A.M., Gas chromatographic/mass spectrometric methods for the detection and identification of anabolic steroid drugs, Brit. J. Sports. Med., 9, 94, 1976.
6. Donike, M., Zimmermann, J., Bärwald, K.-R., Schänzer ,W., Christ, V., Klostermann, K. und Opfermann ,G., Routinebestimmung von Anabolika in Harn, Deutsch.. Zeits. Sportmed., 35, 14, 1984.
7. Donike, M., Bärwald, K.-R., Christ, V., Opfermann, G., Sigmund, G., Zimmermann, J., and Schänzer, W., Screening procedure in doping control. In: A. Ljungqvist, Peltokallio, P., Tikkanen, H., (eds.), Sports Medicine in Track & Field Athletics, Lehtikanta Oy, Kouvola,1985, 117.
8. Donike, M., Geyer, H., Gotzmann, A., Kraft, M., Mandel, F., Nolteernsting, E., Opfermann, G., Sigmund, G., Schänzer, W., and Zimmermann, J., Dope Analysis, In Bellotti, P., Benzi G., Ljungqvist A., (eds.), Official Proceedings International Athletic. Foundation World Symposium on Doping in Sport. Florenz ,1988, 53.
9. Masse, R., Ayotte, C., and Dugal, R., Studies on anabolic steroids. I. Integrated methodological approach to the gas chromatographic / mass spectrometric analysis of anabolic steroid metabolites in urine, J. Chromatogr., 489, 23, 1989.
10. Schänzer, W, Donike, M., Metabolism of anabolic steroids in man: Synthesis and use of reference substances for identification of anabolic steroid metabolites, Anal. Chim. Acta., 275, 23, 1993.
11. Schänzer, W., Metabolism of anabolic androgenic steroids, Clin. Chem., 1996, in press
12. Rongone, E.L., Segaloff, A., In vivo metabolism of Δ^1-17-methyltestosterone in man, Steroids, 1, 170, 1963.

Wilhelm Schänzer

13. Dürbeck, H.W., Bücker, I., Studies on anabolic steroids. The mass spectra of 17-methyl-17ß-hydroxy-1,4-androstadiene-3-one (Dianabol) and its metabolites, Biomed. Environ. Mass Spectrom., 7, 437, 1980.

14. Schänzer, W., Geyer, H:; and Donike, M., Metabolism of metandienone in man: identification and synthesis of conjugated excreted urinary metabolites; determination of excretion rates and gas chromatographic-mass spectrometric identification of bis-hydroxylated metabolites, J. Steroid Biochem. Mol. Biol., 38, 441, 1991.

15. Edlund, P.O., Bowers, L., and Henion, J., Determination of methandrostenolone and its metabolites in equine plasma and urine.by coupled-column liquid chromatography with ultraviolet detection and confirmation by tandem mass spectrometry, J. Chormatogr., 487, 341, 1989.

16. Schänzer, W., Opfermann, G., and Donike, M., 17-Epimerization of 17-methyl anabolic steroids in humans: Metabolism and synthesis of 17-hydroxy-17ß-methyl steroids, Steroids, 57, 537, 1992.

17. Bi, H. and Masse, R., Studies on anabolic steroids - 12. Epimerization and degradation of anabolic 17ß-sulphate-17-methyl steroids in human: Qualitative and quantitative GC/MS analysis, J. Steroid Biochem. Molec. Biol., 42, 533, 1992.

18. Schänzer, W., Horning, S.,Opfermann, G., and Donike, M., GC/MS Identification of Longterm Excreted Metabolites of the Anabolic Steroid 4-Chloro-1,2-dehydro-17-methyltestosterone in Human, J. Steroid Biochem. Mol. Biol., 1996, in press.

19. Bradlow, H.L., The hydrolysis of steroid conjugates, In Bernstein, S. and Solomon, S. (eds.), Chemical and biological aspects of steroid conjugation,Springer-Verlag, Berlin, 1970.

20. Vestergaard, P., The hydrolysis of conjugated neutral steroids in urine. In: Vestergaard, P., Sayegh, J.F., Mowat, J.H., Hemmingsen L. (eds.), Estimation after multi-column liquid chromatography of common urinary neutral steroids with an application to the assay of plasma 17-oxo steroids,Acta Endocrin., Kopenhagen, Suppl. 217, 1978.

21. Geyer, H.: Die gas-chromatographisch/massenspektrometrische Bestimmung von Steoridprofilen im Urin von Athleten, Thesis, German Sports University, 1990.

22. Vanluchene, E., Eechaute, W., Vandekerhove, D., Conversion of free 3ß-hydroxy-5-ene-steroids by incubation with Helix pomatia,J. Steroid Biochem., 16, 701, 1982.

23. Kuoppasalmi,K.. Leinonen, A., and Kajalainen, U., Detection of exogenous testosterone in doping analysis: methodological aspects. In: Sports Medicine and Exercise Science. Proceedings of Olympic Scientific Congress, Eugene, Oregon, 1984.

24. Bradlow, H.L., Extraction of steroid conjugates with a neutral resin, Steroids, 11, 265, 1968.

25. Graef, V. und Fuchs, M., Untersuchung zur vollständigen enzymatischen Hydrolyse von Steroidkonjugaten im Harn, Zt. Klin. Chem. Bioch., 13, 164, 1975.

26. Graf, V.; Furuya, E.; Nishikaze, O., Hydrolysis of steroid glucuronides with ß-glucuronidase preparations from bovine liver, Helix pomatia and E. coli,Clin. Chem., 23, 532, 1977

27. Bradlow, H.L., Modified technique for the elution of polar steroid conjugates from Amberlite XAD-2, Steroids, 30, 581, 1977.

28. Geyer, H., Mareck-Engelke, U., Schänzer, W., and Donike, M., Simple purification of urine samples for improved detection of anabolic and endogenous steroids,In Donike, M. (ed.), Proceedings of the 11th Cologne Workshop in Dope Analysis, 1993, Sport und Buch Strauß, Köln, 1994, 9.

29. Donike, M., N-Methyl-N-trimethylsilyl-trifluoracetamid, ein neues Silylierungs mittel aus der Reihe der silylierten Amide, J. Chromatogr., 42, 103, 1969.

30. Chambaz, E.M. and Horning, E.C., Steroid trimethylsilyl ethers,Anal. Lett., 1, 201, 1967.

31. Donike, M. und Zimmermann, J., Zur Darstellung von Trimethylsilyl-, Triethylsilyl-und tert.-Butyldimethylsilyl-enoläthern von Ketosteroiden für gas-chromatographische und massenspektrometrische Untersuchungen, J. Chromatogr., 202, 483, 1980.

32. Chambaz, E.M., Dafaye, G., and Madani, Ch., Trimethylsilyl ether - enol-trimethyl silyl ether - a new type of derivative for the gas phase study of hormonal steroids, Anal. Chem., 45, 1090, 1973.

33. Schänzer, W., Delahaut, P., Geyer, H., Machnik, M., and Horning, S., Longterm Detection and Identification of Metandienone and Stanozolol Abuse in Athletes by Gas Chromatography/High Resolution Mass Spectrometry (GC/HRMS), J. Chromatogr. B, 687, 93, 1996.

9.5 GROWTH HORMONE ABUSE IN ELITE ATHLETES

Ross C. Cuneo, Jennifer D. Wallace, and Peter Sönksen

Department of Endocrinology, Diabetes & Metabolic Medicine, United and Medical and Dental School of Guy's and St. Thomas' Hospitals, London, U.K.

Growth hormone (GH) is a naturally produced hormone which has been shown to have important physiological actions in adult humans. The results of studies in a variety of clinical situations have been interpreted by the sporting community as showing potential to improve sporting performances. Documentation of performance enhancement is currently lacking, but it is widely believed that many elite athletes are abusing GH for that purpose. There are no detection methods or strategies currently in place, but work has begun to develop such a detection system. This chapter aims to briefly review the physiology of GH, the effects of too little and too much hormone, to summarize the normal responses of GH and related substances to exercise, to critically analyze the potential benefits and risks to athletes who use exogenous GH, and to outline the progress in developing a detection system.

9.5.1 STRUCTURE OF THE GH-IGF AXIS

GH is a peptide (protein) hormone, very different in structure from steroid hormones and anabolic steroids. It is produced almost exclusively by the pituitary. It is secreted in pulses or bursts, with an average of 6 to 10 major bursts per day. In-between these pulses, GH concentrations in the blood are very low or undetectable.[1] The regulation of GH secretion is complex (Figure 9.5.1). Throughout the day, bursts of secretion occur spontaneously or in response to a stimulus. Normally most GH secretion occurs during sleep, associated with the early episodes of REM or Stage 4 sleep. GH concentrations also increase in response to stress, exercise, protein ingestion, and hypoglycemia. It is thought that sleep and exercise are two of the most important physiological stimuli to GH secretion. Throughout the life of an individual, GH production waxes and wanes: it is low during childhood, increasing rapidly throughout puberty with a lifetime peak in late puberty, whereafter GH levels decline and reach low levels in later life.[2] In many (but not all) elderly but otherwise apparently healthy humans, GH production is quite low by the age of 60 years (similar to individuals with pituitary insufficiency). The mechanisms for this decline of GH production in adult life are complex, but may relate to a "primary" progressive atrophy of GH- producing cells in the pituitary gland, reductions in habitual physical activity, or alterations in sleep or sex-steroids.

GH is released into the systemic circulation where most is "free" but some is partially bound to a large transport protein, GH-binding protein (GH-BP). GH-BP in humans is the cleaved extra-cellular domain of the GH cell-surface receptor, which possesses high binding affinity but relatively low capacity. GH-BP levels vary depending on the age, sex, and nutritional status of the individual.[3] Alterations in GH status can also affect GH-BP levels in humans;[4] GH deficient subjects having low levels which increase with GH treatment.[5] Nearly all cells in the body have GH receptors; one of the main target organs for GH is the liver. Hepatocytes express GH receptors and the degree of expression is strongly influenced by insulin, being low in insulin- deficient diabetic people.[6] Binding of GH to one receptor stimulates migration within the cell membrane and binding of a second GH receptor to the original complex (receptor dimerisation). Signal transduction only follows successful dimerisation.[7]

Figure 9.5.1 The growth hormone (GH) insulin-like growth factor-I (IGF-I) axis. Schematic representation of (a) hypothalamic regulation of GH secretion by GH releasing peptide(s) (GHRPs), GH releasing hormone (GHRH) and somatostatin, (b) association of GH-binding protein (GH-BP) with GH in the systemic circulation, (c) GH-stimulated hepatic production of IGF-I, (d) association of IGF-binding proteins (IGF-Bps), some of which derive also from the liver, with IGF-I in the systemic circulation, (e) metabolic effects of both GH and IGF-I on peripheral tissues, (f) production of IGF-I and IGF-Bps by peripheral tissues resulting in local action, and (g) feedback inhibition of GH secretion by IGF-I.

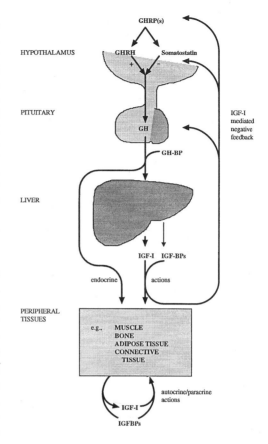

GH-receptor activation initiates many processes, one of the most important being the activation of the gene for Insulin-Like Growth Factor I (IGF-I), another polypeptide which derives its name from the structural homology with insulin and which acts as a "second messenger" for GH. GH stimulates IGF-I gene expression, hepatic synthesis, and secretion of IGF-I. IGF-I is secreted by the liver into the systemic circulation which transports it around the body and brings it into contact with virtually all cells ("hormonal" or endocrine action of IGF-I[8]). IGF-I is also produced locally in most tissues in the body, under the regulation of GH and other tissue-specific hormones. IGF-I then acts locally without passing through the circulatory system (autocrine and paracrine actions). IGF-I has effects in many different parts of the body, effects mediated by the Type 1 IGF receptor, which shares many similarities with the insulin receptor.[9]

IGF-I is carried in the circulation bound to six specific IGF-binding proteins (IGF-BP). The IGF-BPs are known to bind the majority of circulating IGF-I, thus minimizing the amount of "free" IGF-I in the circulation.[9] The binding proteins also play a role in the passage of IGF-I out of the vascular compartment and into contact with the IGF receptor, they may have both facilitatory and inhibitory effects.[10] IGFBP-3 is the most abundant, and along with another GH-dependent factor, acid-labile subunit (ALS), carries the majority of IGF-I in the circulation in a "terniary complex".[11,12]

One of the main regulators of GH production is the negative feedback inhibition by IGF-I. This feedback inhibition acts at both the pituitary and hypothalamus. In the pituitary, IGF-I directly inhibits GH production, while at the hypothalamus IGF-I inhibits the production of the stimulatory neuropeptide GH-releasing hormone (GHRH) and stimulates the production of the inhibitory neuropeptide somatostatin.[13]

The metabolic effects of the GH/IGF system are mediated by GH delivered hormonally to tissues and by local production of IGF-I. First, GH has direct effects outside the liver. Such direct effects, independent of IGF-I generation, include stimulation of protein synthesis in muscle and lipolysis in adipose tissue.[14,15] Second, many metabolic effects of GH are, however, mediated via IGF-I; these include many aspects of anabolism, hypoglycemia, and regulation of cholesterol and bone metabolism. Both GH and IGF-I have been shown to directly increase protein synthesis, while insulin inhibits proteolysis.[16] IGF-I has significant hypoglycemic and some antilypolytic effects, similar to but less powerful than insulin on a molar basis. Third, IGF-I is produced in many tissues throughout the body, only partly under the control of GH. These "autocrine" or "paracrine" actions of IGF-I include local trophic effects. In the thyroid, IGF-I production is predominantly regulated by thyrotropin (TSH), and in the gonads by gonadotropins. Many tissues also produce IGF-BPs which regulate the autocrine or paracrine action of IGF-I.[10]

9.5.2 GH-IGF AXIS IN CHILDREN AND ADULTS

GH has been shown to have important physiological actions in humans. During childhood, GH regulates and stimulates linear bone growth. Children with GH deficiency have short stature which can be successfully treated with GH. In children with GH-secreting tumors, gigantism develops sometimes along with features of diabetes mellitus, hypertension and muscle hypertrophy which can progress through increased strength to paradoxical muscle weakness as a consequence of the development of a myopathy. Adults who develop GH deficiency as a result of pituitary disease or surgery develop a syndrome which has only recently been recognized.[17-19] The syndrome of GH deficiency in adults is characterized by:

1. Abnormal body composition - reduced muscle mass and increased fat mass.
2. Impaired muscle strength and exercise capacity.
3. Impaired perceived quality of life with low mood, reduced energy and social isolation.
4. Increased mortality with a doubling of the chances of a premature death from cardiovascular causes.
5. Impaired metabolism - low basal metabolic rate, impaired thyroid action, reduced anabolism and accumulation of body fat.

GH replacement in such adults with GH deficiency has been shown to result in beneficial effects[17,18,20] on:

1. body composition (increasing lean body mass; reducing fat mass, particularly visceral adiposity; increasing body water; and increasing bone mass)
2. functional capacity (increasing skeletal muscle mass and force; major increases in maximal and submaximal aerobic capacity; increases in cardiac output, cardiac muscle mass, and reduced systemic vascular resistance; increasing sweating rate and thermal adaptation to heat)
3. psychological changes (improvement in mood, motivation, stamina, socialization and sense of energy and well-being)
4. cardiovascular risks (reduced total and LDL-cholesterol, increase in HDL-cholesterol and the reduction in visceral adiposity)
5. effects on intermediary metabolism (acute effects which include an impairment of insulin sensitivity, increased lipolysis, and increased whole body protein synthesis; the long term effects show no detrimental effect on insulin resistance)

9.5.3 ACROMEGALY AND GH ADMINISTRATION TO NORMAL ADULTS — RISK TO ATHLETES

The effects described above refer specifically to results of studies on adults with GH deficiency, a situation where replacement of physiological amounts of GH clearly has many beneficial effects. Exogenous GH administration in normal adults is different on two counts. Firstly, if "physiological" doses are given to normal adults, the endogenous GH production from the

Ross C. Cuneo et al.

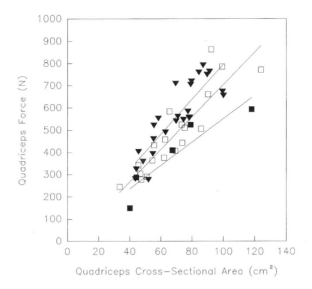

Figure 9.5.3. Correlations between quadriceps cross-sectional area and quadriceps force (Newtons) in normal subjects (closed triangles; n = 25; upper regression line: y = 7.8x + 8.2; r = 0.87), subjects with untreated GH deficiency (open squares; n = 19; middle regression line: y = 7.3 x - 24.1; r = 0.89), and subjects with untreated acromegaly (closed squares n = 5; lower regression line: y = 5.3 x + 26.1; r = 0.92). Data previously unpublished, with permission R.C. Cuneo and F. Salomon.

pituitary is inhibited and minimal or no metabolic effects would be anticipated. Secondly, if supra- physiological doses are administered, some but not all, of the above effects may result.

Acromegaly, a clinical condition where excess GH is produced from a pituitary tumor, gives a clear picture of many of the possible effects and complications of long-term GH excess.[21,22] The condition is usually asymptomatic for many years and clinical descriptions of the early phase are therefore poor. Acromegaly has usually been present for up to ten years before the clinical features lead to a diagnosis, which is usually made by astute observations when the patient seeks medical care for unrelated reasons. Facial alterations (coarsening of features, enlarged lips, brow, tongue and splayed teeth) are common, and may be recognizable from past photographs. People with acromegaly do not generally feel unwell until they develop one or more of the complications which is usually more than 10 years after onset of the condition. In the early asymptomatic phase they not uncommonly note their unusual strength which goes with their increased muscle bulk.

Several effects of long term GH excess are however, not an extension of the known effects of GH replacement in adults with GH deficiency and these include:

1. Decrements in skeletal muscle function — while lean body mass and skeletal muscle mass is increased in acromegaly, muscle force is often considerably impaired late in the disease when a relatively specific myopathy has developed (see Figure 9.5.3). Documentation of early changes in skeletal muscle function in acromegaly are lacking. Exercise performance, as assessed by maximal oxygen uptake has not been systematically studied, but observations on several individuals cured of acromegaly by neurosurgery show a decline in exercise performance as assessed by maximal oxygen uptake.[116]

2. Detriments in cardiac function — increased cardiac muscle mass, especially in these patients who develop hypertension, with indices of impairment of function such as reduced diastolic compliance, an early feature of cardiac failure in asymptomatic

      patients. Frank cardiac failure is a major cause of premature mortality in this group of patients.

3. Acceleration in degenerative joint disease — osteoarthritis in large joints of the hips and knees, and small joints of the hand.
4. Increased incidence of malignant tumors, particularly of the colon, contributing to an overall increase in premature mortality.
5. Development of sleep apnoea - of mostly obstructive but also central types, contributing to the increase in respiratory mortality rates in acromegaly.
6. Other common complications include hypertension and diabetes mellitus.

It can be assumed that athletes taking supra-physiologic doses of GH for considerable duration of time would be at risk of developing any or all the complication associated with acromegaly.

9.5.4 EFFECT OF GH ADMINISTRATION ON ATHLETIC PERFORMANCE

The possibility that GH released in response to exercise may, through its lipolytic actions, liberate free fatty acids (FFA) to be used as fuel was proposed as early as 1965.[23] The lipolytic effects of long-term GH administration in GH deficient adults and in acromegaly to reduce body adipose stores has been convincingly demonstrated. GH administration in normal individuals has confirmed the lipolytic actions and carbohydrate sparing actions of GH.[24,25]

Definitive demonstration of GH's role in FFA release or fuel metabolism during exercise is, however, lacking. In short term exercise the rise in FFA precedes that of GH,[26] and in exercise up to 7 h GH production may wane while FFA levels rise progressively.[27] Exercise in patients with hypopituitarism causes a greater FFA rise than in normal adults despite no acute GH response in the patients.[28] Thus, use of GH by endurance-type athletes who utilize FFA as an exercise fuel may be theoretically attractive, but remains unproved.

Role of GH in Mediating the Beneficial Effects of Training: Exercise-induced increments in GH production could theoretically result in anabolic improvements, including increased lean body and muscle mass, increased bone mass and connective tissue formation, and improved healing of wounds or other soft-tissue injuries. Increased growth rates in exercising rats appear to relate to increased pulsatile GH production.[29] Direct evidence for an exercise-induced increase in circulating IGF-1 levels or anabolic effect in humans is currently lacking.

Anecdotal data strongly support the contention that GH is necessary for the beneficial effects of exercise. The following case study illustrates this very well.

Miss SC, a Physical Fitness Instructor in the Army presented in 1991 with visual failure, a pituitary tumor was diagnosed and successfully removed. Post-operatively she was panhypopituitary and was put on full 'conventional' replacement therapy with hydrocortisone, thyroxine & cyclical oestrogen/progesterone. She was unable to regain her previous level of fitness despite optimal pituitary hormone replacement and continued efforts at training. The addition of GH to her hormone replacement regime resulted in a remarkable return to previous fitness levels (reported at 4th International Adult GH Deficiency Meeting, Cannes, November, 1993).

Endurance trained athletes have increased plasma and red cell volumes, effects that may be GH- mediated.[30,31]

9.5.4.1 Alteration of Body Composition

GH is reputedly widely used by body builders and resistance trained sports persons to achieve muscle hypertrophy,[32] but the benefit of this approach is dubious. Crist et al gave highly conditioned, resistance trained individuals marginally supraphysiologic doses of met-GH for 6 weeks in a double blind, cross-over design.[33] IGF-1 increased into the upper part of the reference range with suppression of GH responses to stimuli in most subjects. Fat mass, assessed hydrodenisitometrically, decreased and fat free mass (FFM) increased. No performance data were presented. Yarasheski et al. treated untrained males entering a resistance training program with 40 mcg.Kg-1 Day 1 for 12 weeks in a parallel design.[34] FFM (assessed by hydrodensitometry) and total body water increased more in the GH group, but quadriceps leucine synthetic rate, limb circumferences and muscle strength increased at the same rate as in the placebo group. The authors concluded that GH treatment resulted in increased lean tissue (e.g., connective tissue) but not muscle tissue mass.

In a further study, Yarasheski et al. treated experienced resistance trained males with the same GH dose for 14 days in an uncontrolled study.[35] While serum IGF-1 increased significantly, no change was noted in whole body protein breakdown rate and quadriceps protein synthesis rate. This suggests but does not prove that GH administration does not alter protein metabolism in resistance trained individuals. Deyssig et al treated young, lean male "power athletes" with GH (0.09U.Kg-1 Day-1) for 6 weeks in a parallel design.[36] Despite increases in serum IGF-1 and IGFBP-3, no change was noted in body weight, or fat and lean body mass (assessed anthropometrically, an insensitive technique), nor in biceps or quadriceps force. No studies in aerobically trained subjects treated with GH have, to our knowledge, been published.

Overall, these studies suggest that supraphysiologic doses of GH may cause very small increases in lean tissue mass and reductions in fat mass in resistance trained males. Skeletal muscle hypertrophy has not been demonstrated, and muscle strength is not increased. It appears from these "trials" that supraphysiologic levels of GH contribute little to an already work-hypertrophied muscle, although it must be recognized that the "conventional" medical trial paradigm used in all these studies may not be sufficiently "sensitive" to be able to detect marginal effects which an individual athlete may be able to assess on the basis of a minor improvement in performance and which may be sufficient to win an event.

9.5.5 RESPONSE TO EXERCISE

9.5.5.1 Regulators of GH Response to Exercise

In attempting to construct a detection program for GH abuse by elite athletes, it is essential to understand the factors which regulate production of both GH and GH-related markers. The response of GH to acute physical exercise is determined by multiple factors: the intensity, duration and nature of exercise, the training status of the individual, the age, gender and state of nutrition and hydration of the individual (see Reference 37 for review).

Intensity of exercise is perhaps the major determinant of GH response. When intensity is measured as the percentage of maximal exercise (%VO2 max.), there appears to be a linear relationship between intensity and peak serum GH concentration (Figure 9.5.5). The threshold approximates 40% VO_2max in both trained and untrained groups, with increasing variability of the GH response as the intensity of the exercise increases.

Few studies compare the effect of different times of endurance-type exercise on the GH response. Longer duration of exercise appears to increase the GH response, most studies employing protocols between 20 and 60 min of either continuous constant intensity or progressive incremental workloads (often 10 to 15 min in total). Longer duration studies describe a variety of GH responses: (a) an increase to about 60 min followed by a fall with continuing exercise, or (b) an increase to 60 min with maintenance of GH levels till the end of exercise.[38,39]

The interaction of duration and intensity of exercise also influences GH responses to endurance- type exercise. Short duration, high intensity exertion (7-min rowing races for Olympic athletes) has been shown to provoke remarkable GH responses (60 ng/ml[40]). The

Figure 9.5.5 Correlation between the relative intensity of endurance-type exercise (percentage of maximal oxygen = uptake; $\%VO_{2max}$) and mean peak growth hormone concentration in groups of (A) trained and (B) untrained normal adults. Arrows represent (a) maximal incremental exercise protocols, and (b) a prolonged competitive race. Reproduced with permission of *Endocrinology and Metabolism* and R.C. Cuneo and J.D. Wallace.

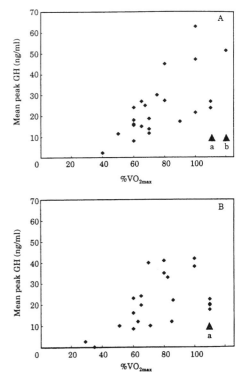

shortest duration of exercise which invokes a GH response has been most carefully studied by Felsing et al.,[40] showing that 10 min of exercise above the lactate threshold was required for a statistically significant GH response, while shorter duration exertion at the same intensity, or similar duration exertion below the lactate threshold failed to generate a significant GH surge.

Comparing exercise at equivalent total workloads, GH levels are somewhat lower with continuous (40 to 45% VO^2max) as opposed to interval protocols with twice the work rate for half the time,[42] reflecting the greater metabolic "stress" and lactate levels in the latter. Grey et al. showed that exhaustive interval exertion (alternating bouts of treadmill running at VO^2max and walking) produced a peak GH comparable to similar exhaustive, continuous protocols.[43] Arm cranking vs leg ergometric exercise at similar percentage of VO_2max resulted in greater GH levels.[44] These studies suggests that the nature of endurance-type exertion influences GH responses by means of differing degrees of metabolic "stress" that are applied.

With resistance exercise, incremental GH responses have also been described. The important determinants appear to be the relationship between load and frequency of individual repetitions. Much greater GH increments have been described following "hypertrophy" protocols (moderate loads, high number of repetitions) than "strength" protocols (heavy loads, low repetitions) in both men and women.[45-47] In all these studies, the highest GH increment occurred in the protocols that elicited the greatest lactate response.

When comparing GH responses at equivalent relative workloads in trained vs untrained subjects, (a) similar GH responses in have been shown following constant submaximal[48] or incremental maximal exercise,[49] (b) greater GH responses in males (but not females),[50,51] and (c) lower GH responses in trained cyclists.[52] Interventional training studies have resulted in either a lowering of GH responses, no change, or an increased GH response.[53-55] The highest exercise-stimulated GH concentrations found in the literature review occurred in elite rowers.[40]

Training also affects basal or endogenous GH production. Weltman et al.[56] have shown that 12 months training at intensities above the lactate threshold in young previously relatively sedentary women resulted in increased integrated and peak GH levels measured with intensive venous sampling throughout the 24-h period. Taken together, these data suggest that repetitive bouts of endurance-type exercise increases endogenous and possibly exercise-related GH production.

Endogenous GH production declines markedly with ageing for reasons that are as yet unclear.[2] One careful study examining the GH response to one hour of treadmill exercise at 70% $VO2max$ between young and old, trained and untrained subjects found consistently lower peak GH levels in the older group, irrespective of training status.[48] The older, trained group produced more GH than the older, untrained group. These data suggests that GH production is responsive to training, as in younger subjects, but that age still limits GH production. We have data on a number of male runners over 60 years of age, who display 24-h resting GH profiles similar to much younger, sedentary individuals.[117]

While basal, pulsatile GH production is higher in females than males, comparisons of GH produced during exercise are limited. Bunt et al.[50] showed no difference in GH levels during moderate exercise of equivalent relative intensities between trained runners of either sex, but untrained females produced more GH than the untrained males. Similar studies have shown higher GH levels in trained males compared to trained females,[38,57] with no differences in untrained groups.[38] Also, no differences have been shown with respect to the GH response to prolonged moderate exercise between women with amenorrhoea, or at differing phases of the menstrual cycle.[58] These data suggest that the prominent effect of estradiol on basal GH production is overcome during exercise.

Finally, basal, pulsatile GH production is higher in lean individuals than in the obese;[59] while the mechanism is unclear it may relate to nutrient intake as GH production is increased with undernutrition. Exercise-induced increments in GH concentrations have also been shown to be absent in young, obese males compared to lean controls.[60]

9.5.5.2 Neuroregulation of GH Response

The exact mechanisms that trigger GH release during exercise are poorly understood, but the association between the intensity of exercise and GH response suggests that activation of the sympatho-adrenal system and/or metabolic or neuronal signals associated with anaerobic metabolism may be involved.[61] GH release from the pituitary is under stimulatory and inhibitory control of the hypothalamic peptides GHRH and somatostatin, respectively. GH responses during exercise have been augmented with α-2 and α-1 adrenergic stimulation, believed to act via augmentation of GHRH release, and reduced with adrenergic antagonists, phentolamine;[62,63] contradictory effects of idazoxan are noted.[64] β-adrenergic stimulation increases somatostatin release[65] and propranolol augments GH responses to exercise.[62,66] Peripheral catecholamines do not appear to influence GH release during exercise.

Hypothalamic cholinergic tone is stimulatory to GH release to a variety of stimuli, including exercise,[67,68] presumably via inhibition of somatostatin release.[69] Cholinergic effects via GHRH have also been considered. Opioids, particularly encephalins, appear to increase GH release via opioid receptors on cholinergic neurones,[68] but inconsistent effects of the opioid antagonists naloxone or naltrexone have been reported.[68,70-72] The relationship between endogenous opioid production, "runners high" and addiction to exercise, for example in long-distance runners and ballerinas, has long been suggested but difficult to prove.[73] Endurance training has been shown to increase GH production,[56] and GH administration to adults with GH deficiency has been shown to increase CSF beta-endorphin levels,[74] suggesting that GH may contribute to the sense of well-being experienced by some athletes vis central opioid production. Serotonergic and dopaminergic control may also influence GH release during exercise.[75,76] Recent work has identified GH-releasing peptide (GHRP) receptors in the hypothalamus of some animal species. While the endogenous ligand is currently uncharacterised, synthetic "analogues" appear to act as a central co-ordinator of GHRH- and somatostatin-mediated GH production.[77,78] The role of GHRPs in exercise is uncertain.

Three main peripheral processes may contribute to the stimulus for GH release during exercise: anaerobic glycolysis, fuel availability, and dehydration/hyperthermia. Lactate generation and or acidosis, while correlating fairly closely with the magnitude of GH responses to exercise, appears only partly responsible for exercise-induced GH responses because: (1) exercise below the lactate threshold may still result in a GH response,[79] and (2) only partial or no GH increments have been documented in response to lactate infusion in resting individuals.[80] Similarly, acid-base shifts do not modify the GH response to exercise.[80] Glucose availability clearly influences GH production during exercise, as shown by the augmentation of GH responses during hypoglycemic exercise[81] or fasting,[82] and the blunting of GH responses to moderate (but not heavy) exercise by intravenous or oral glucose.[27,83]

Hypoglycemia cannot explain the GH response during exercise, since plasma glucose decreases to a minor extent or increases.[84] Differences in serum FFA concentrations may explain some of the variability in GH responses because (1) FFA inhibits GH production in a variety of conditions, (2) nicotinic acid-induced FFA suppression causes some augmentation of GH responses to exercise, and (3) lipid infusions inhibit or have no effect on the GH response to exercise.[85,86] Dehydration appears to be an important stimulus to GH production during prolonged exercise. Ingestion of water sufficient to replace over 75% of evaporative weight loss (-7.2% of plasma volume) during prolonged exercise has been shown to abolish the GH response,[87] with water rehydration being just as effective as oral glucose. Similarly, prevention of the rise in core body temperature that accompanies intense exercise, via external cooling or swimming in cold water reduces the GH response.[88]

9.5.5.3 Kinetics of GH Response

Serum GH levels start rising approximately 10 min after the onset of exercise, peaking either at the end of or shortly after exercise.[89] Levels rise more rapidly with intense exercise or other augmenting factors.[90] Even with brief exercise, peak levels often occur 30 minutes after the onset of exercise.[91] GH secretion appears to terminate abruptly at or shortly after the end of exercise lasting 20 min or more, as assessed by deconvolution analysis,[92] and the rate of fall of serum GH levels being consistent with its known half-life. The elimination half time during exercise has been estimated at 10.5 min using deconvolution techniques,[92] twice as fast as in resting subjects using similar techniques.[93] Others have estimated GH elimination half time at around 20 to 30 min using a single compartment model and first-order kinetics.[41] Half-times have been shown to be prolonged under hypoxemic conditions,[90] where GH secretion may persist after exercise, and reduced under hyperthermic conditions.[94]

9.5.6 DETECTING EXOGENOUS GH ABUSE

Given that GH is produced endogenously in response to acute endurance- and resistance-type exercise, and that there are great variability in such responses, serum GH estimations alone are likely to be of limited or no value as a detection method of GH abuse unless: (1) serum GH concentrations greatly exceeded known physiological levels, (2) GH levels were exceptionally low at a time when levels should be stimulated (e.g., following artificial augmentation of serum IGF-I concentrations, thereby suppressing pituitary GH production by physiological feed-back mechanisms), or (3) it could be shown that the high level of GH was purely the 22kD monomer (with absence of the 20kD component which should have be detectable). Given that GH itself is a relatively poor choice as a marker to detect GH abuse, other factors that are stimulated by GH administration need to be considered. The physiological regulation of these factors, by exercise in particular, is far less well understood than for GH itself.

9.5.6.1 GH Related Factors

9.5.6.1.1 Growth Hormone Binding Protein (GH-BP)

To date, no published data describe changes in GH-BP in relation to exercise. Unpublished data in young males suggest that maximal and submaximal exercise do not alter GH-BP levels acutely.[118]

Ross C. Cuneo et al.

9.5.6.1.2 Insulin-Like Growth Factors

Circulating IGF-1 is almost exclusively derived from the liver, and is predominantly regulated by GH, with effects from nutrition, portal insulin, thyroxine, estradiol and glucagon.[95] In response to acute exercise, IGF-I levels have been shown to rise 26% after 10 min of moderate exercise, an effect that, if real, must reflect non-GH mediated mechanisms.[96] Others have noted no change or a minor transient increment in IGF-I during exercise up to 3 h duration or up to 24 h after exercise.[97-100] GH-mediated increments in IGF-I would be expected to lag more than 6 h, given the observations of exogenous GH administration to humans.[101] Indeed, reductions in IGF-I levels have been reported following prolonged (7.5 h cross-country ski race) exercise,[98] likely reflecting nutrient deprivation or other "stress-related" factors. Chronic exercise appears to increase IGF-I levels in the normal population, as reflected by the results of cross-sectional studies in men and women of varying levels of fitness.[102,103] Uncontrolled variables in these studies limit the strength of such conclusions. In response to intense training or prolonged endurance activities IGF-I levels fall.[104,105] The role of IGF-II in adult physiology is unknown, but may influence carbohydrate metabolism.[95] Moderate or transient increases in IGF-II during exercise have been described.[96,106]

9.5.6.1.3 IGF-Binding Proteins (IGF-BP)

The majority of circulating IGF-I is bound to IGF-BPs, thereby modifying the metabolic actions and regulating the tissue distribution of IGF-I.[95] IGF-I is predominantly bound in a 150-kD complex consisting of the acid-labile subunit, which is GH-regulated, IGFBP-3 which is IGF-I regulated, and IGF-I itself.[107] IGFBP-3 is produced by the liver, and circulates in fairly constant levels throughout the day. IGFBP-3 concentrations have been shown to not change immediately after a marathon, but to be depressed along with IGF-I for several days after.[99] Also, minor increments in IGFBP-3 during brief exercise[106] may relate to dehydration of other non-GH-mediated effects. By contrast, IGFBP-1 levels fluctuate rapidly in a reciprocal fashion to insulin levels,[95] thereby potentially contributing to acute modulation of the metabolic effects of GH, IGF-1 and insulin. In response to acute exercise, IGFBP-1 levels have been shown not to change during 30 min of moderate exercise,[96] but to increase after marathon runs and exertion up to 7.5 h.[98,99] Jenkins et al. have shown that elevation of basal IGFBP-1 and cortisol levels in female Olympians and ballerinas explained the majority of the variability in menstrual function,[108] suggesting the importance of this axis in different organ systems.

9.5.7 IGF AND IGF-BP LEVELS AS INDICATORS OF EXOGENOUS GH ABUSE

Since GH administration leads to marked changes in a number of the components of the IGF-I/IGF-BP axis, it is highly probable that determination of serum concentrations of some of these factors will distinguish endogenous GH production following exercise from exogenous GH administration used for "doping". For example, clinicians routinely use serum IGF-I concentrations to diagnose the chronic GH excess of acromegaly and IGF-I rises in response to GH administration to healthy fit young individuals.[109] In this study, the rise in IGF-I was accompanied by a fall in IGF-BP2 and the ratio IGF-I/IGF-BP2 was a good example of these "indirect markers" of GH administration being potentially very useful for detecting doping as they remain raised beyond the physiological "normal range" for some days after the last dose of GH administration. Before a reliable GH detection program can be developed however, detailed assessment of the IGF and IGF-BP responses to exercise, and the disappearance kinetics of such exercise-related changes following cessation of GH administration, must be undertaken.

9.5.8 ESTIMATIONS OF GH AND GH-RELATED FACTORS IN URINE

Urine is the traditional medium for detecting "doping" in sport and all the current methodology is based on urine sampling. The kidney is one of the major sites of growth hormone clearance and metabolism. GH is filtered at the glomerulus and resorbed and destroyed in the proximal tubules of the kidney, such that less than 0.01% of that filtered appears intact in the urine. Urinary GH measurements have proven technically difficult because of low concentrations and variable matrix. Recent advances have led to a robust assay for urinary GH estimation. The sensitivity of the technique is however, still sub-optimal. For example, distinguishing patients with acromegaly from normal individuals shows considerable overlap and distinguishing GHD from normal is beset by the same problem.[110-112] Exercise itself can effect kidney function and increase protein excretion non-specifically, this may cause 'false-positives' and more research is needed to evaluate the potential of urinary markers of growth hormone abuse. Urinary IGFs and IGF-fragments have recently been described in urine,[113-115] but whether these represent locally produced proteins and how well they reflect circulating IGF concentrations remains to be determined.

9.5.9 DEVELOPMENTS IN THE DETECTION OF GH ABUSE: GH-2000

There is a great deal of publicity given to "doping" with GH and related substances in sports-related literature and much information is available on the Internet (some of it of a high scientific standard and clearly written by people working in the field). It first appeared in the *Underground Steroid Handbook* (1982) where the effects of GH were carefully reviewed and GH was given a very strong recommendation. The actions attributed to GH were at that stage unproved in human physiology but have largely been verified by subsequent research. There was some confusion over animal versus human preparations but in general the article was well-written and ahead of its time. The author subsequently, in another publication of the same handbook in 1989, stated that he had rated GH too highly in the earlier edition and had never encountered any athlete who had benefitted from it. He suggested that a much higher dose may be needed. This increase in dosage coincided with recombinant human GH becoming available and the world-wide shortage of GH being replaced by a potential glut. Although scientists at this time were saying there was no ergogenic effect, athletes continued to use it. Today we know that GH can have an ergogenic effect on the body and therefore increase the likelihood of enhanced performance. There are several magazines available to athletes advertising not only GH but also IGF1 and GH releasing factors. Athletes and coaches potentially have a good resources available to become knowledgeable on this subject.

In response to a "Call for Proposals" in the European Union Research Program "BIOMED 2", a research proposal was submitted by a consortium of four leading academic centers specializing in GH research, in collaboration with two European Pharmaceutical Industries making recombinant human Growth Hormone and the International Olympic Committee. This proposal had the following objectives:

1. To develop a methodology for the detection of use and abuse of Growth Hormone and related substances, particularly in sport.
2. To develop a validation methodology sufficiently robust to withstand legal challenge and allow prosecution and conviction.
3. To develop the ethical and legal framework to control and deal effectively with growth hormone abuse.

All this to be completed in time for the methodology to be in place for the Olympic Games in Sydney in the year 2000. The proposal was successful and funded at the level of 900,000

ECUs from the European Union, matched by a similar amount from the IOC. The project started in January 1996 and ends at the end of December 1998.

Growth hormone is already a "banned substance" under the existing Olympic Code; however, because there are no currently recognized methods of detecting GH abuse, no one has been caught abusing GH. IOC accredited Laboratories are responsible for testing for a number of prohibited performance enhancing drugs and performance enhancing methods but the methods that they have developed and validated for performance-enhancing drugs are quite different from those likely to be needed for GH and related substances. There are 21 accredited Laboratories and 13 of these are in Europe. Once a suitable methodology has been developed and validated, it will need to be "rolled out" to the existing network.

9.5.10 IMMUNOASSAYS OF IGR AND IGFBPS

The current method of detecting drug-abuse can be divided into stages; screening and confirmation. A screening test is used to eliminate negative samples. Any sample that does not contain a banned substance is removed at this stage. Methods used include gas chromatography (GC), high performance liquid chromatography (HPLC), mass spectrometry, and immunoassays. The same sample is re-analyzed for the eventual identification of the presence of a specific drug or metabolite. As the screening procedure for peptides and glycoproteins (GH and GH-dependent markers fit into these class of substances) is relatively new, there is a problem of finding a reliable "confirmation" once a sample has gone through the first stage of screening. In the absence of a specific mass spectrometry method to confirm the presence of the "marker" of GH abuse, it is possible that two or three immunoanalyses, with different monoclonal antibodies that recognize different epitopes of the molecule could be used. Mass spectrometry is the "gold standard" currently in use and it would be an advantage to use this method in the future, providing that technical advances are forthcoming so as to allow analysis of peptides and glycoproteins.

Measurement of GH and other substances by immunoassay depends on their identification by the immune system and the production of antibodies which show high degrees of specificity. Such assays are capable of great sensitivity. Because of their similar chemical nature, what applies to GH also applies to IGF-I and binding proteins. Antibodies are produced if human GH (hGH) is injected into an animal since it is identified as a foreign protein. One species of antibody is derived from one immunocyte. The problem is that the body will produce a large number of antibodies and the antibodies will recognize a protein or amino acid sequence common to other proteins and there will be a potential of cross reaction in the assays. To overcome this one can grow one clone of cells (immunocytes) which produces only one antibody specific for one part of a molecule (for instance hGH) and from another clone another antibody which is directed at another part of the same molecule. By using both these antibodies in an assay for hGH, the whole molecule must be present for the antibodies both to react. By careful selection of antibodies you can get rid of any cross- reaction. Human GH assays can now get cross-reaction down to less than 0.001%; this can be achieved with similar and related peptides.

IGF-I is a proinsulin-like peptide which binds avidly to BPs thereby prolonging its half-life. However, this presents problems with immunoassays as separation techniques are required to separate IGF from BPs. These include:

Acid gel chromatography	Gold Standard; recovery problems, tedious but good
Solid phase extraction	Recovery problems, tedious but good
Acid ethanol precipitation	Simple; good for a large number of samples
Commercial kits	Not all remove binding proteins which might interfere with assay system

Growth Hormone Abuse in Elite Athletes

Immuno-technology can be developed for hGH, IGF-I, IGFBP-3 or whatever peptide marker of interest. These assays can be highly sensitive (because of technology using antibody excess technology, monoclonal antibodies and the right signal), they can be very specific if the right antibodies are chosen they can be very simple and very fast. GH can be measured in both urine and serum. However, GH is rapidly cleared from the circulation and occurs in low concentrations in the urine. In addition, measuring single proteins in urine may be difficult because the kidney leaks in athletes and increases -2 microglobulin and other protein excretion. Hence, a ratio method has more strength in it and is recommended. IGFs and BPs are ideally the compounds to be tested in this way. Serum samples will need to be used to measure IGF-I and IGFBPs. IGF-I measurement requires a validated extraction system, followed either by a two site assay or competitive RIA. IGF-I is stable in serum when frozen.

IGFBP-2 and IGFBP-3 constitute up to 90% of the total IGF binding capacity in serum and are very promising for detecting GH abuse as they have a long half life. Two site assays for IGFBPs with correctly match antibody pairs are required to ensure the active components are detected. IGFBP-2 is inversely related to GH output. Assays are sufficiently specific and sensitive (normal levels: 600 µg/L). IGFBP-3 is directly dependant on GH (normal levels 3 µg/L). The "Acid Labile Sub unit" (ALS) is the third component of the "ternary complex" which is associated IGFBP-3 in serum. This has an even higher concentration (25 µg/L) and could be a good indicator of GH abuse since it is GH dependant.

9.5.11 DETECTION OF GH WITH MASS SPECTROMETRY

The mass spectrometer is a detector of molecules capable of characterizing them and determining their concentrations to very low limits. It is currently the accepted "Gold Standard" for IOC detection of drugs of abuse in sport. With this technique molecules have to be given an electrical charge and taken into the gas phase in a vacuum, the former process providing a handle by which they can be moved and detected and the latter ensuring they do not collide during analysis. The mass of the molecule is determined by moving the molecules along a path within electrical fields. The path taken is a function of the mass (mass-to-charge) of the charged molecule. Samples are best introduced singly into the mass spectrometer, frequently from a gas (GC) or liquid (HPLC) chromatograph. GC cannot be used for proteins. There are two principal methods for producing large protein molecules carrying charges in a vacuum:

1 Laser desorption from a matrix. Mass is determined to ± 0.1 % (5 Daltons in 10,000)
2 Electrospray. Analysis is performed in a continuous flow of solvent, e.g. from an HPLC separation. Mass can be determined to better than ± .01% (0.5 Dalton in 10,000)

Original biological matrices cannot usually be analyzed directly. Biological matrixes must be purified and extracted. This is time consuming and limits sample throughput but the use of immunological techniques to extract and purify could drastically shorten analysis times and improve specificity of assays.

9.5.12 OTHER POTENTIAL GH MARKERS

Potential markers are endogenous substances that are GH-dependent and have the potential to give a clear and unambiguous indication of GH use/abuse. There are a very large (and ever increasing) list of substances which fall into this category; for example:

Ross C. Cuneo et al.

1. GH 22/20 kD Ratio — two naturally occurring isomers, while recombinant GH has only the 22 kD monomer
2. GH antibodies — repeated administration of GH leads to the development of specific antibodies to GH in a high proportion of people
3. Osteocalcin — is a substance produced by bone as an indicator of the bone re-modelling cycle. GH activates this cycle.
4. IGF-I — a GH-dependent growth factor, the level which rises in response to GH and remains raised for some time after GH is stopped.
5. IGFBP-2 — an IGF-I binding protein, the concentration of which falls after GH administration
6. IGF-I/IGFBP-2 — a ratio of two GH-dependent substances, the concentrations of which move in opposite directions following GH administration
7. Many others.

This is a non-exhaustive list of the potential markers. We need preliminary tests to see what markers are the most useful in being able to reflect GH administration, particularly focusing on those which remain raised for some time after GH has been given.

9.5.13 REFERENCE RANGES

In order to be able to detect GH abuse, it will be necessary to define the range of observations that can occur in response to legitimate activity and sports in elite athletes under a wide variety of conditions. It will be necessary to investigate, effects of competition, exercise, training, injury, body composition, ethnic group, environment, type of sport, diet, gender. We have some information on the variation in the normal physiology of GH and its markers and have seen the extent of the factors that effects this normal physiology. There remain many questions which need to be answered:How are we going to be sure that we take into account all these different factors when we are producing a NRR? Do we need to produce NRR of athletes as a group or perhaps reference ranges for different groups of athletes and sports? Are we able to identify or exclude athletes that are abusing GH when we are taking samples to define the NRR? As part of this project we are administering GH to non-competitive athletes as part of a "randomized double-blind placebo-controlled trial" to provide a database of samples to be used to validate any methodology that is likely to be suitable. The selected "markers" of GH abuse will be tested for their ability to detect those given GH compared with those given placebo.

The optimal testing matrice, urine vs. blood, remains to be determined. Proteins are only found in very small and poorly predictable quantities in urine. We know that the proteins we are trying to measure are only found in small quantities (0.0001 to 0.01% of plasma GH in urine) and their concentration and excretion also exhibit marked variation with changes in renal hemodynamics. The renal handling of proteins varies drastically in response to exercise, and this adds further complication in trying to measure these substances in urine.It seems likely the best test will be a blood test but we need to be absolutely sure we cannot use urine since this would greatly facilitate the introduction of the testing methodology into the Olympic movement.

If, as seems likely at present, blood samples are required, then we need to think carefully on how best we obtain these samples? How can we introduce them to the athletes and the sporting bodies we will be dealing with? We also need to consider whether we need to take venous blood samples or can we carry out tests on finger prick blood samples or even on ear lobe blood samples? These are likely to be more acceptable to the athlete if it can be done.As part of the GH-2000 research project, we need to take very many blood samples from top level athletes if we are going to develop a robust test which will withstand legal challenge. Without a reference range obtained from Olympic-level athletes, the attorneys defending the "cheats" will always be able to find a way through any attempt to disqualify an athlete on reference ranges obtained from anything less. Timing the samples is also an issue of some concern. Urine is currently taken "after" and "out of competition". Will it be possible to prove GH abuse with these samples? Do we need to consider individual profiles in and out of competition? We know that there is less intra-individual variation in normal physiology than there is in inter- individual variation and it will be useful in this context ("endogenous substances") to develop individual profiles in and out of competition.

9.5.14 LEGAL AND ETHICAL CONSIDERATIONS

From our current knowledge, it seems that a test for GH will be based on the measurements of multiple "markers" or ratios of "markers" and that the "proof" of "doping" will involve demonstrating that the statistical "probability" of a "positive" test result being incompatible with established Reference Ranges (obtained under strictly comparable conditions). As well as the difficulties we have concerning identifying the "reference ranges" there will be problems validating the type of methodology to be used to identify and quantitate the "markers". Are we going to be able to use immunoassays or will we have to rely on mass spectrometry? When compared with the current "Gold Standard" of mass spectrometry, there are problems with immunoassays. Is there a way we can make these more robust by using monoclonal antibodies? Or by using some confirmatory test? Or should we be developing mass spectrometry methods as part of this project?

ACKNOWLEDGMENTS

We wish to acknowledge the following participants of the GH-2000 Project Initiation Workshop held at the London–Kensington Hilton, Thursday 1st - Sunday 4th February 1996: International Olympic Committee Medical Commission (IOCMC) Sub-Commission "Doping and Biochemistry in Sport". Some of the content of this chapter is based on the proceedings of this workshop.

Prince Alexandre de Merode	Chairman
Elvira Ramini	Secretariat
Dr Patrick Schamash	Medical Director
Dr Jordi Segura	Sub-Commission
Dr Don Catlin	Sub-Commission
Professor Xavier Sturbois	IOCMC & European Olympic Committee

Also Dr Thomas Rimer, Pharmacia/Upjohn (Sweden); Dr Anne-Marie Kappelgaard, Novo Nordisk (Denmark), Professor Peter Sönksen, Dr David Russell-Jones, Dr Jake Powrie, Ms Claire Pentecost, Dr Nicola Keay.Mrs Lis Lawrence, Mr Steve Cashman, United Medical & Dental Schools of Guy's & St Thomas' Hospitals (UMDS), UK; Professor Bengt-Ake Bengtsson and Dr Thord Rosen, Sahlgrenska Hospital, Gothenburg, Sweden; Professor Jens Christiansen and Dr Jens Otto Jorgense, Aarhus Commune Hospital, Aarhus, Denmark; Professor Luigi Sacca and Dr Salvatore Longobardi, University Frederick II, Naples, Italy; Invited Consultants: Dr Neil Townshend, BOC (UK); Dr Derek Teale, Biochemist (UK); Professor Egil Haug. IOC Lab (N); Dr P Hammersbach, IOC Lab (N); Dr Marital Saugy, IOC Lab (CH);Ms Michelle Veroken, Sports Council (UK); Ms Rachel Field, Sports Council (UK); Dr Roslyn Carbon, Sports Medicine (UK);Dr Mike Wheeler, Biochemist (UK); Dr David Cowan, IOC Lab (UK); Dr Andy Kicman, IOC Lab (UK); Professor Tony Mallet,Chemist (UK); Mr Eryl Bassett, Statistician (UK); Dr Massoud Buroujerdi, Engineer / Modeller (UK);

Dr John Etherington, Sports Medicine (UK); Dr Michael Turner, Sports Medicine(UK); Dr Richard Cohen, Atlanta LOC (USA), Dr William Cleveland, Atlanta LOC (USA);Mr Tom Arleth, Engineer/Modeller (DK).

REFERENCES

1. Ho KY, Evans WS, Blizzard RM, et al. Effects of sex and age on the 24-hour profile of growth hormone secretion in man: importance of endogenous estradiol concentrations. J Clin Endocrinol Metab 1987;64:51-58.
2. Corpas E, Harman SM, Blackman MR. Human growth hormone and human aging. Endo Rev 1993;14:20-39.
3. Rosén T, Johannsson G, Bengtsson B-Å. Consequences of growth hormone deficiency in adults, and effects of growth hormone replacement therapy. Acta Pædiatr Suppl 1994;399:21-24.
4. Hochberg Z, Phillips M, Youdim MBH, Amit T. Regulation of growth hormone (GH) receptor and GH-binding protein by GH pulsality. Metabolism 1993;42:1617-1623.
5. Leger J, Noel M, Czernichow P, Postel Vinay MC. Progressive normalization of growth hormone-binding protein and IGF-I levels in treated growth hormone-deficient children. Pediatr Res 1995;37:731-735.
6. Russell Jones DL, Rattray M, Wilson VJ, Jones RH, Sonksen PH, Thomas CR. Intraperitoneal insulin is more potent than subcutaneous insulin at restoring hepatic insulin-like growth factor-I mRNA levels in the diabetic rat: a functional role for the portal vascular link. J Mol Endocrinol 1992;9:257-263.
7. Kelly PA, Goujon L, Sotiropoulos A, et al. The GH receptor and signal transduction. Horm Res 1994;42:133-139.
8. Rotwein P, Bichell DP, Kikuchi K. Multifactorial regulation of IGF-I gene expression. Mol Reprod Dev 1993;35:358-363.
9. LeRoith D. Insulin-like growth factor receptors and binding proteins. Baillieres Clin Endocrinol Metab 1996;10:49-73.
10. Baxter RC. Insulin-like growth factor binding proteins in the human circulation: a review. Horm Res 1994;42:140-144.
11. Holman SR, Baxter RC. Insulin-like growth factor binding protein-3: factors affecting binary and ternary complex formation. Growth Regul 1996;6:42-47.
12. Baxter RC, Dai J. Purification and characterization of the acid-labile subunit of rat serum insulin-like growth factor binding protein complex. Endocrinology 1994;134:848-852.
13. Veldhuis JD. The neuroendocrine regulation and implications of pulsatile GH secretion: gender effects. Endocrinologist 1995;5:198-213..
14. Moller N, Jorgensen JO, Moller J, et al. Metabolic effects of growth hormone in humans. Metabolism 1995;44:33-36.
15. Hussain MA, Schmitz O, Mengel A, et al. Comparison of the effects of growth hormone and insulin-like growth factor I on substrate oxidation and on insulin sensitivity in growth hormone- deficient humans. J Clin Invest 1994;94:1126-1133.
16. Russell Jones DL, Umpleby AM, Hennessy TR, et al. Use of a leucine clamp to demonstrate that IGF-I actively stimulates protein synthesis in normal humans. Am J Physiol 1994;267:E591-E598.
17. Cuneo RC, Salomon F, McGauley GA, Sönksen PH. The growth hormone deficiency syndrome in adults. Clin Endocrinol 1992;37:387-397.
18. De Boer H, Blok G-J, van der Veen EA. Clinical aspects of growth hormone deficiency in adults. Endocr Rev 1995;16:63-86.
19. J rgensen JOL, Müller J, M ller J, et al. Adult growth hormone deficiency. Horm Res 1994;42:235-241.
20. Rosén T, Johannsson G, Johansson J-O, Bengtsson B-Å. Consequences of growth hormone deficiency in adults and the benefits and risks of recombinant human growth hormone treatment. Horm Res 1995;43:93-99.

21. Nabarro JD. Acromegaly. Clin Endocrinol Oxf 1987;26:481-512.
22. Melmed S, Ho K, Klibanski A, Reichlin S, Thorner M. Clinical review 75: Recent advances in pathogenesis, diagnosis, and management of acromegaly. J Clin Endocrinol Metab 1995;80:3395-3402.
23. Hunter WM, Fonseka CC, Passmore R. Growth hormone: important role in muscular exercise in adults. Science 1965;150:1051-1053.
24. Davidson MB. Effect of growth hormone on carbohydrate and lipid metabolism. Endo Rev 1987;8:115-131.
25. Press M. Growth hormone and metabolism. Diabetes/Metab Rev 1988;4:391-414.
26. Hartog M, Havel RJ, Copinschi G, Earll JM, Ritchie BC. The relationship between changes in serum levels of growth hormone and mobilization of fat during exercise in man. Q J Exp Physiol 1967;52:86-96.
27. Hunter WM, Fonseka CC, Passmore R. The role of growth hormone in the mobilization of fuel for muscular exercise. Q J Exp Physiol 1965;50:406-416.
28. Johnson RH, Rennie MJ, Walton JL, Webster MHC. The effect of moderate exercise on blood metabolites in patients with hypopituitarism. Clin Sci 1971;40:127-136.
29. Borer KT, Kelch RP. Increased serum growth hormone and somatic growth in exercising adult hamsters. Am J Physiol 1978;234:E611-E616.
30. Müller J, Jørgensen JOL, M ller N, Hansen KW, Pedersen EB, Christiansen JS. Expansion of extracellular volume and suppression of atrial natriuretic peptide after growth hormone administration in normal man. J Clin Endocrinol Metab 1991;72:768-772.
31. Barak Y, Zadik Z, Karov Y, Hahn T. Enhanced response of human circulating erythroid progenitor cells to hGH and to IGF-I in children with insufficient growth hormone secretion. Pediatr Res 1992;32:282-285.
32. Macintyre JG. Growth hormone and athletes. Sports Med 1987;4:129-142.
33. Crist DM, Peake GT, Egan PA, Waters DL. Body composition response to exogenous GH during training in highly conditioned adults. J Appl Physiol 1988;65:579-584.
34. Yarasheski KE, Campbell JA, Smith K, Rennie MJ, Holloszy JO, Bier DM. Effect of growth hormone and resistance exercise on muscle growth in young men. Am J Physiol Endocrinol Metab 1992;262:E261-E267.
35. Yarasheski KE, Zachwieja JJ, Angelopoulos TJ, Bier DM. Short-term growth hormone treatment does not increase muscle protein synthesis in experienced weight lifters. J Appl Physiol 1993;74:3073-3076.
36. Deyssig R, Frisch H, Blum WF, Waldhör T. Effect of growth hormone treatment on hormonal parameters, body composition and strength in athletes. Acta Endocrinol (Copenh) 1993;128:313-318.
37. Cuneo RC, Wallace JD. Growth hormone, insulin-like growth factors and sport. Endocrinol Metabol 1994;1:3-13.
38. Friedmann B, Kindermann W. Energy metabolism and regulatory hormones in women and men during endurance exercise. Eur J Appl Physiol 1989;59:1-9.
39. Viru A, Karelson K, Smirnova T. Stability and variability in hormonal responses to prolonged exercise. Int J Sports Med 1992;13:230-235.
40. Snegovskaya V, Viru A. Elevation of cortisol and growth hormone levels in the course of further improvement of performance capacity in trained rowers. Int J Sports Med 1993;14:202-206.
41. Felsing NE, Brasel JA, Cooper DM. Effect of low and high intensity exercise on circulating growth hormone in men. J Clin Endocrinol Metab 1992;75:157-162.
42. Karagiorgos A, Garcia JF, Brooks GA. Growth hormone response to continuous and intermittent exercise. Med Sci Sports 1979;11:302-307.
43. Gray AB, Telford RD, Weidemann MJ. Endocrine response to intense interval exercise. Eur J Appl Physiol 1993;66:366-371.
44. Kozlowski S, Chwalbinska-Moneta J, Vigas M, Kaciuba-Uscilko H, Nazar K. Greater serum GH response to arm than to leg exercise perormed at equivalent oxygen uptake. Eur J Appl Physiol 1983;52:131-135.
45. Kraemer WJ, Marchitelli L, Gordon SE, et al. Hormonal and growth factor responses to heavy resistance exercise protocols. J Appl Physiol 1990;69:1442-1450.

46. Kraemer WJ, Fleck SJ, Dziados JE, et al. Changes in hormonal concentrations after different heavy-resistance exercise protocols in women. J Appl Physiol 1993;75:594-604.

47. Häkkinen K, Pakarinen A. Acute hormonal responses to two different fatiguing heavy-resistance protocols in male athletes. J Appl Physiol 1993;74:882-887.

48. Hagberg JM, Seals DR, Yerg JE, et al. Metabolic responses to exercise in young and older athletes and sedentary men. J Appl Physiol 1982;65:900-908.

49. Rolandi E, Reggiani E, Franceschini R, et al. Comparison of pituitary responses to physical exercise in athletes and sedentary subjects. Horm Res 1985;21:209-213.

50. Bunt JC, Boileau RA, Bahr JM, Nelson RA. Sex and training differences in human growth hormone levels during prolonged exercise. J Appl Physiol 1986;61:1796-1801.

51. Chang FE, Dodds WG, Sullivan M, Kim MH, Malarkey WB. The effects of exercise on prolactin and growth hormone secretion: comparison between sedentary women and women runners with normal and abnormal menstrual cycles. J Clin Endocrinol Metab 1986;62:551-556.

52. Bloom SR, Johnson RH, Park DM, Rennie MJ, Sulaiman WR. Differences in the metabolic and hormonal response to exercise between racing cyclists and untrained individuals. J Physiol 1976;258:1-18.

53. Koivisto V, Hendler R, Nadel E, Felig P. Influence of physical training on the fuel-hormone response to prolonged low intensity exercise. Metabolism 1982;31:192-197.

54. Bullen BA, Skrinar GS, Beitins IZ, et al. Endurance training effects on plasma hormonal responsiveness and sex hormone excretion. J Appl Physiol 1984;56:1453-1463.

55. Hartley LH, Mason JW, Hogan RP, et al. Multiple hormonal responses to prolonged exercise in relation to physical training. J Appl Physiol 1972;33:607-610.

56. Weltman A, Weltman JY, Schurrer R, Evans WS, Veldhuis JD, Rogol AD. Endurance training amplifies the pulsatile release of growth hormone: Effects of training intensity. J Appl Physiol 1992;72:2188-2196.

57. Tarnopolsky LJ, MacDougall JD, Tarnopolsky MA, Sutton JR. Gender differences in substrate for endurance exercise. J Appl Physiol 1990;68:302-308.

58. Kanaley JA, Boileau RA, Bahr JA, Misner JE, Nelson RA. Substrate oxidation and GH responses to exercise are independent of menstrual phase and status. Med Sci Sports Exerc 1992;24:873-880.

59. Iranmanesh A, Lizarralde G, Veldhuis JD. Age and relative adiposity are specific negative determinants of the frequency and amplitude of growth hormone (GH) secretory bursts and the half-life of endogenous GH in healthy men. J Clin Endocrinol Metab 1991;73:1081-1088.

60. Hansen AP. Serum growth hormone response to exercise in non-obese and obese normal subjects. Scand J Clin Lab Invest 1973;31:175-178.

61. Galbo H. Hormonal and metabolic adaptation to exercise. Newyork: Thieme-Stratton, 1983:1-116.

62. Hansen AP. The effect of adrenergic receptor blockade on the exercise-induced serum growth hormone rise in normals and juvenile diabetics. J Clin Endocrinol 1971;33:807-812.

63. Berger D, Floyd JC,Jr., Lampman RM, Fajans S. The effect of adrenergic receptor blockade on the exercise induced rise in pancreatic polypeptide in Man. J Clin Endocrinol Metab 1980;50:33-39.

64. Struthers AD, Burrin JM, Brown MJ. Exercise-induced increases in plasma catecholamines and growth hormone are augmented by selective 2-adrenoceptor blockade in man. Neuroendocrinology 1986;44:22-28.

65. Al-Damluji S. Adrenergic control of the secretion of anterior pituitary hormones. Clin Endocrinol Metab 1993;7:355-392.

66. Sutton J, Lazarus L. Effect of adrenergic blocking agents on growth hormone responses to physical exercise. Horm Metab Res 1974;6:428-429.

67. Few JD, Davies CTM. The inhibiting effect of atropine on growth hormone release during exercise. Eur J Appl Physiol 1980;43:221-228.

68. Copeland KC, Nair KS. Acute growth hormone effects on amino acid and lipid metabolism. J Clin Endocrinol Metab 1994;78:1040-1047.

69. Rosén T, Johannsson G, Hallgren P, Caidahl K, Bosaeus I, Bengtsson B-Å. Beneficial effects of 12 months replacement therapy with recombinant human growth hormone to growth hormone deficient adults. Endocrinol Metabol 1994;1:55-66.

70. Moretti C, Fabbri A, Gnessi L, et al. Naloxone inhibits exercise-induced release of PRL and GH in athletes. Clin Endocrinol 1983;18:135-138.

71. Spiler IJ, Molitch ME. Lack of modulation of pituitary hormone stress response by neural pathways involving opiate receptors. J Clin Endocrinol Metab 1980;50:516-520.

72. Grossman A, Bouloux P, Price P, et al. The role of opoid peptides in the hormonal responses to acute exercise in man. Clin Sci 1984;67:483-491.

73. Sforzo GA. Opioids and exercise. An update. Sports Med 1989;7:109-124.

74. Johansson JO, Larson G, Andersson M, et al. Treatment of growth hormone-deficient adults with recombinant human growth hormone increases the concentration of growth hormone in the cerebrospinal fluid and affects neurotransmitters. Neuroendocrinology 1995;61:57-66.

75. Smythe GA, Lazarus L. Suppression of human growth hormone secretion by melatonin and cyproheptadine. J Clin Invest 1974;54:116-121.

76. Schwinn G, Schwarck H, Mcintosh C, Milstrey HR, Willms B, Köbberling J. Effect of the dopamine receptor blocking agent pimozide on the growth hormone response to arginine and exercise and on the spontaneous growth hormone fluctuations. J Clin Endocrinol Metab 1976;43:1183-1976.

77. Massoud AF, Hindmarsh PC, Matthews DR, Brook CG. The effect of repeated administration of hexarelin, a growth hormone releasing peptide, and growth hormone releasing hormone on growth hormone responsivity. Clin Endocrinol Oxf 1996;44:555-562.

78. Thorner MO, Vance ML, Rogol AD, et al. Growth hormone-releasing hormone and growth hormone-releasing peptide as potential therapeutic modalities. Acta Paediatr Scand Suppl 1990;367:29-32.

79. Luger A, Watschinger B, Deuster P, Svoboda T, Clodi M, Chrousos GP. Plasma growth hormone and prolactin responses to graded levels of acute exercise and to a lactate infusion. Neuroendocrinology 1992;56:112-117.

80. Sutton JR, Jones NL, Toews CJ. Growth hormone secretion in acid-base alterations at rest and during exercise. Clin Sci Mol Med 1976;50:241-247.

81. Sotsky MJ, Shilo S, Shamoon H. Regulation of counterregulatory hormone secretion in man during exercise and hypoglycaemia. J Clin Endocrinol Metab 1989;68:9-16.

82. Opstad P-K. Alterations in the morning plasma levels of hormones and the endocrine responses to bicycle exercise during prolonged strain. The significance of energy and sleep deprivation. Acta Endocrinol 1991;125:14-22.

83. Hansen AP. The effect of intravenous glucose infusion on the exercise-induced serum growth hormone rise in normals and juvenile diabetics. Scand J Clin Lab Invest 1971;28:195-205.

84. Galbo H. The hormonal response to exercise. Diabetes/Metab Rev 1986;1:385-408.

85. Casanueva F, Villanueva L, Peñalva A, Vila T, Cabezas-Cerrato J. Free fatty acid inhibition of exercise-induced growth hormone secretion. Horm Metab Res 1981;13:348-350.

86. Hansen AP. The effect of intravenous infusion of lipid on the exercise-induced serum growth hormone rise in normals and juvenile diabetics. Scand J Clin Lab Invest 1971;28:207-212.

87. Saini J, Bothorel B, Brandenberger G, Candas V, Follenius M. Growth hormone and prolactin response to rehydration during exercise: effect of water and carbohydrate solutions. Eur J Appl Physiol 1990;61:61-67.

88. Galbo H, Houston ME, Christensen NJ, et al. The effect of water temperature on the hormonal response to prolonged swimming. Acta Physiol Scand 1979;105:326-337.

89. Lassarre C, Girard F, Durand J, Raynaud J. Kinetics of human growth hormone during submaximal exercise. J Appl Physiol 1974;37:826-830.

90. Raynaud J, Drouet L, Martineaud JP, Bordachar J, Coudert J, Durand J. Time course of plasma growth hormone during exercise in humans at altitude. J Appl Physiol 1981;50:229-233.

91. Nussey SS, Hyer SL, Brada M, Leiper AD. Bone mineralization after treatment of growth hormone deficiency in survivors of childhood malignancies. Acta Pædiatr Suppl 1994;399:9-14.

92. Thompson DL, Weltman JY, Rogol AD, Metzger DL, Veldhuis JD, Weltman A. Cholinergic and opioid involvment in release of growth hormone during exercise and recovery. J Appl Physiol 1993;75:870-878.

93. Holl RW, Schwarz U, Schauwecker P, Benz R, Veldhuis JD, Heinze E. Diurnal variation in the elimination rate of human growth hormone (GH): the half-life of serum GH is prolonged in the evening, and affected by the source of hormone, as well as body size and serum estradiol. J Clin Endocrinol Metab 1993;77:216-220.

94. Raynaud J, Capderou A, Martineaud J, Bordachar J, Durand J. Intersubject variability in growth hormone time course during different types of work. J Appl Physiol 1983;55:1682-1687.

95. Sara VR, Hall K. Insulin-like growth factors and their binding proteins. Physiol Rev 1990;70:591-614.

96. Bang P, Brandt J, Degerblad M, et al. Exercise-induced changes in insulin-like growth factors and their low molecular weight binding protein in healthy subjects and patients with growth hormone deficiency. Eur J Clin Invest 1990;20:285-292.

97. Kraemer WJ, Gordon SE, Fleck SJ, et al. Endogenous anabolic hormonal and growth factor responses to heavy resistance exercise in males and females. Int J Sports Med 1991;12:228-235.

98. Suikarri A-M, Sane T, Seppälä M, Yki-Järvinen H, Karonen S-L, Koivisto VA. Prolonged exercise increases serum insulin-like growth factor-binding protein concentrations. J Clin Endocrinol Metab 1989;68:141-144.

99. Koistinen H, Koistinen R, Selenius L, Ylikorkaka O, Seppala M. Effect of marathon run on serum IGF I and IGF binding protein 1 and 3 levels. J Appl Physiol 1996;80:760-764..

100. Cappon J, Brasel JA, Mohan S, Cooper DM. Effect of brief exercise on circulating insulin- like growth factor l. J Clin Endocrinol Metab 1994;76:2490-2496.

101. Jørgensen JOL. Human growth hormone replacement therapy: pharmacological and clinical aspects. Endo Rev 1991;12:189-207.

102. Kelly PJ, Eisman JA, Stuart MC, Pocock NA, Sambrook PN, Gwinn TH. Somatomedin-C, physical fitness, and bone density. J Clin Endocrinol Metab 1990;70:718-723.

103. Poehlman ET, Copeland KC. Influence of physical activity on insulin-like growth factor-l in healthy younger and older men. J Clin Endocrinol Metab 1990;71:1468-1473.

104. Jahreis G, Kauf E, Fröhner G, Schmidt HE. Influence of intensive exercise on insulin-like growth factor l, thyroid and steroid hormones in female gymnasts. Growth Regulation 1991;1:95-99.

105. Tigranian RA, Kalita NF, Davydova NA, et al. Observations on the Soviet/Canadian transpolar ski trek: status of selected hormones and biologically active compounds. Med Sport Sci 1992;33:106-138.

106. Schwartz A, Mohan S, Brasel JA, Cooper DM. Acute effects of brief exercise on IGF-I, IGF-II, IGFBP-3, and IGFBP-3 proteolysis in healthy men. 10th International Congress of Endocrinology 1996;P1-503.(Abstract)

107. LeRoith D, Clemmons D, Nissley P, Rechler MM. Insulin-like growth factors in health and disease. Ann Intern Med 1992;116:854-862.

108. Jenkins PJ, Ibanez-Santos X, Holly J, et al. IGFBP-1: A metabolic signal associated with exercise-induced amenorrhoea. Neuroendocrinology 1993;57:600-604.

109. Teale D, Miell J, Wood P, et al. Detection of GH administration. J Endocrinol 1996;148:Supplement P300.(Abstract)

110. Leger J, Reverchon C, Porquet D, Noel M, Czernichow P. The wide variation in urinary excretion of human growth hormone in normal growing and growth hormone-deficient children limits its clinical usefulness. Horm Res 1995;44:57-63.

111. Bates AS, Evans AJ, Jones P, Clayton RN. Assessment of GH status in adults with GH deficiency using serum growth hormone, serum insulin-like growth factor-I and urinary growth hormone excretion. Clin Endocrinol Oxf 1995;42:425-430.

112. Bates AS, Evans AJ, Jones P, Clayton RN. Assessment of GH status in acromegaly using serum growth hormone, serum insulin-like growth factor-l and urinary growth hormone excretion. Clin Endocrinol Oxf 1995;42:417-423.

113. Spagnoli A, Gargosky SE, Spadoni GL, et al. Characterization of a low molecular mass form of insulin-like growth factor binding protein-3 (17.7 kilodaltons) in urine and serum from healthy children and growth hormone (GH)-deficient patients: relationship with GH therapy. J Clin Endocrinol Metab 1995;80:3668-3676.
114. Yamamoto H, Murphy LJ. N-terminal truncated insulin-like growth factor-I in human urine. J Clin Endocrinol Metab 1995;80:1179-1183.
115. Gargosky SE, Hasegawa T, Tapanainen P, MacGillivray M, Hasegawa Y, Rosenfeld RG. Urinary insulin-like growth factors (IGF) and IGF-binding proteins in normal subjects, growth hormone deficiency, and renal disease. J Clin Endocrinol Metab 1993;76:1631-1637.
116. Cuneo and Salomon, personal observations.
117. Wallace JD and Cuneo RC, unpublished data.
118. Wallace and Cuneo, unpublished data.

9.6 ERYTHROPOIETIN

BJÖRN EKBLOM

DEPARTMENT OF PHYSIOLOGY AND PHARMACOLOGY, KAROLINSKA INSTITUTE, STOCKHOLM, SWEDEN

Physical performance in sport is determined by physiological, psychological, and other factors. The most important physiological factors are maximal aerobic power, anaerobic capacity, aerobic/anaerobic metabolic efficiency, muscle strength, and co-ordination. Their relative importance depends on the individual demands within different sports. These physiological factors have developed more or less continuously over the years. Today, the differences in these parameters between world class athletes, in a specific sport, are fairly small. Minor changes in any of these physiological factors, due to internal or external influences, can help explain and cause important changes in physical performance and, thus, sport success.

In this discussion the focus will be on the energy turn-over during exercise. It is fairly well-known that changes in energy expenditure can have great influence on sport results. Over the years athletes have searched for both legal and illegal methods and substances to help increase maximal aerobic power, anaerobic capacity, or metabolic efficiency during severe exercise.

9.6.1 EFFECTS OF HYPOXIA

Reduction of arterial oxygen content, whether it is a consequence of anemia or hypoxia, causes reduction in physical performance and can induce many different physiological reactions. During maximal exercise no other factor within the oxygen transport system chain can compensate for the reduced oxygen content in arterial blood. There is no doubt that training during a prolonged stay at high altitude improves performance. In fact, prolonged physical training and stay at high altitude is a prerequisite for successful performance at altitude. The question is what effect training at altitude has on performance at sea level, especially since hypoxia can also be achieved by reducing the exogenous oxygen environment by living in special "flats," in which partial oxygen content in the inspired air is reduced by increasing the nitrogen content of room air (normobaric hypoxia), thus making it possible to "stay high - train low."

Athletes, particularly those in endurance sports, have used training during hypoxic conditions -such as during a stay at high altitude — for many years. The reason for the practice is that relative hypoxia can stimulate the erythropoietic system and increase the hemoglobin concentration (Hb), and total hemoglobin mass. An increased buffer capacity and enhanced muscle enzyme concentrations may also be produced by high altitude training. Many athletes claim that their sea level performance is improved by altitude training, but the scientific evidence for these claims is not convincing, and the studies that have been done have yielded conflicting results.[6,7,13,14]

Some athletes do appear to derive benefit by training at medium altitude (2,000 to 2500 m), but an equal number do not ("non-responders"). The differences may be accounted for by different types of training, different sports, and genetic differences. However, the results of some studies suggest that the reduction in maximal oxygen uptake at altitude reduces training intensity. The result is that the benefits of increased oxygen carrying capacity achieved by training at altitude are negatively balanced by reductions both in training intensity and training duration. Furthermore, it has been suggested that intense training at altitude may have a negative effect on muscles and other organ systems.[2,16] To avoid these potential negative consequences of altitude training, modern hypoxic training has been modified to include two components: training at altitude, in order to stimulate erythropoiesis, combined with training in normoxic conditions (in the valley), which helps to maintain training intensity. Alternatively, an athlete may train outdoors in the normal fashion, but spend the rest of his time staying in normobaric hypoxia conditions in a low oxygen "flat." The latter approach seems to enhance factors important for maximal aerobic power and performance.[15]

9.6.2 MANIPULATION OF BLOOD VOLUME AND RED CELL MASS

Both blood volume and red cell mass are important in determining maximal aerobic power and physical performance. Blood volume is controlled through a complicated series of regulating hormones. Hormones from the kidney and heart are essential for keeping the blood volume at optimal levels for training. When an individual increases their level of physical activity and training, there is a parallel increase in blood volume, that contributes to resultant increases in maximal aerobic power.

The production of red cells is also controlled by hormones. To maintain an adequate number of circulating red blood cells, the bone marrow must produce about 2.5 million red blood cells per second in an average man with a blood volume of 5 liters. Endurance athletes have larger blood volumes (7 to 8 L) and their red cells have less than the normal 120-day life span seen in normal individuals. To compensate, the production of red blood cells in these individuals is increased by 20 to 40%. The increased demand for iron in these individuals evidently does not cause any major problems in training at sea level, provided the athlete is well nourished. The frequency of iron deficiency problems in endurance athletes is no greater than in the general population.[8]

Regular physical training increases blood volume and red cell mass in parallel with increases in maximal aerobic power and aerobic physical performance. It is not surprising, then, that when red cell mass is increased by transfusing red blood cells, maximal aerobic power and aerobic physical performance both increase.[5,11,12,17] The practice is called "blood doping." When red cells are transfused, actual blood volume changes very little. Nor is there any increase in blood volume when human erythropoietin (EPO) is given. In study done at our laboratory, blood volume was measured in seven normal individuals, both before and after the infusion of 400 ml of packed red blood cells, and after a six weeks EPO injection period. We found that blood volume was maintained at a constant average of 6.1 to 6.2 L.

Of course, infusing red blood cells raises the hemoglobin (Hb) concentration and the hematocrit (Hct), but the increase seems not to be associated with an major physiologic side effects,[12] although there is an increased risk for medical complications such as thrombosis and transfusion reaction. "Blood doping" is difficult to detect,[4] and even though it is prohibited under IOC rules, the possibility that it is occurring cannot be ruled out.

9.6.3 ERYTHROPOIETIN

Hematopoiesis is controlled and regulated by a complex system of stimulators and inhibitors. The hematopoietic stem cell enters the cell cycle, promoted by several factors, such as interleukin 1, 3, and 6. As the cells mature, other factors, such as granulocyte-macrophage colony-stimulation factor and erythropoietin come into play. These factors can be manipulated, raising the very real possibility that athletes will try to alter the process to gain competitive advantage.

EPO is a glycoprotein (40% carbohydrate) with a molecular weight of approximately 34,000 daltons. It is produced mainly in the proximal tubular cells of the kidneys, but, to some extent, it is produced in the liver as well (see below). EPO production is mainly regulated by oxygen levels in the kidney and liver. Hypoxia, whether due to anemia, or low partial pressures of oxygen, leads to increased EPO production. Receptors in the bone marrow enhance mitosis and differentiation of red blood cell precursors, leading to the production of more red cells.

Serum EPO concentration can be measured using bio- or immunoassays. EPO levels in normal individuals have a circadian rhythm, with peak concentrations during the day and lower concentrations at night. EPO levels increase when the number of red cells drops (anemia), and decrease when the levels rise. There are very great inter- and intra-individual variations in serum EPO levels, even in individuals with Hb levels that fall within the normal range. Strenuous physical training, transition from sea level to high altitude, and other activities may all cause complex changes in serum EPO levels. Since the variations in absolute EPO levels are so great, quantitative measurements of serum EPO levels cannot, at present, be used to detect the administration of excogenous recombinant erythropoietin (rhEPO).

9.6.4 ADMINISTRATION OF EXOGENOUS ERYTHROPOIETIN

Injections of recombinant EPO are regularly given to patients with renal disease suffering from chronic anemia. Treatment with rhEPO largely restores their hemoglobin to normal levels and improves their level of function. But questions remain about what happens when rhEPO is given to healthy individuals:

Will increasing the EPO level in normal individuals increase their Hb levels?
If Hb levels do rise, will that result in increased maximal aerobic power and improved physical performance?
What other physiologic changes will be produced by giving EPO?
Will their be any medical consequences?
Can the process of EPO administration be detected?

We have undertaken a series of experiments in order to answer these questions. What follows is data from these studies that has already been published,[1,3,9] as well as additional unpublished material. The data was derived from studies made on 26 volunteers. All the subjects were healthy men, with levels of conditioning ranging from moderately active to well-trained athletes. The average age was 27 ± 4.6 years, and the average body weight was 77.3 ± 8.0 kg. Baseline maximal aerobic power was 4.56 ± 0.43 l min^{-1} (means ± SD). Injections of rhEPO were given subcutaneously three times a week for six weeks, with a doses of either 20 or 40 IU/kg body weight. Routine laboratory tests were employed, and all of the subjects were familiarized with the performance tests before the study started. Values presented as "before the injection period" were obtained during a second or third training test done before the start of the study. Results were the same whether the individuals had received either the lower or the higher dose.

Björn Ekblom

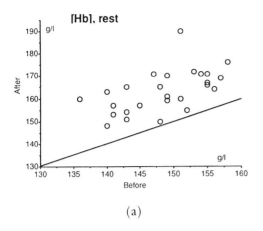 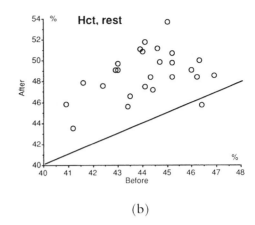

(a)   (b)

Figure 9.6.4.1 (a) Hemoglobin concentration at rest before and after the injection period. (b) Hematocrit at rest before and after the injection period.

9.6.4.1 Hemoglobin Concentration

Six weeks of rhEPO injections increased Hb and Hct in all subjects. Blood volume remained unchanged from baseline. Figure 9.6.4.1a and b shows individual values for Hb and Hct before and after the injection period. It is evident that Hb increased in all subjects; however, there was a very large intra-individual variation. The reasons for this wide variation are not known. The conclusions is that erythropoiesis can be stimulated by rhEPO injections even in well-trained athletes, independent of baseline Hb. It also appears that Hct follows this same general trend.

9.6.4.2 Cardiovascular Aadaptation to Rest

No difference in circulatory adaptation at rest were seen. Resting systolic and diastolic pressures were measured by a trained nurse after 5 minutes of supine rest and were 121.3 ± 12.1 before and 121.7 ± 11.7 after treatment. Diastolic pressure before treatment was 65.7 ± 7.0, and afterward it was 66.9 ± 8.0 mmHg ($p > .05$). There was no change in heart rate.

9.6.4.3 Cardiovascular Adaptation to Submaximal Exercise

Adaptation to submaximal exercise was evaluated at two standard work loads on a mechanically braked Monark cycle ergometer (see Table 9.6.4.3a). The work loads, 120 and 190 W, corresponded to an average of 39% and 59%, respectively, of the individuals maximal oxygen uptake during exercise before the injection period. The oxygen uptake before and after injection was, as expected, unchanged. Ventilatory quota also remained unchanged. However the heart rate was significantly ($p < 0.05$) reduced from 114.7 to 108.4 bpm on the low submaximal work load, and from 145.5 to 137.4 bpm on the high submaximal workload. The oxygen pulse increased significantly from 15.5 to 16.4 ml.beat^{-1}, and the lower workload, and from 18.6 to 19.9 ml.beat^{-1} on the higher submaximal load. Individual values are shown in Figure 9.6.4.3b). The reduced heart rate after the injection period during submaximal work was the same as the reduction seen in the same individuals after they had received an infusion of red blood cells.

Blood lactate levels after EPO injection were unchanged; 1.88 and 1.70 mM on the lower workload, and 3.01 and 2.95 mM on the higher workload. There was no significant change in perceived exertion (RPE), as measured with the Borg scale for central or peripheral fatigue.[10] A possible explanation for the unchanged lactic acid levels and RPE could be that the work

Table 9.6.4.3a Means + SD for Values Obtained During Two Submaximal Work Loads (120 and 190 W, respectively)

| | Submax I | | | | Submax II | | | |
| | Before | | After | | Before | | After | |
	M	SD	M	SD	M	SD	M	SD
Vo$_2$, l.min^{-1}	1.78	0.40	1.77	0.39	2.68	0.26	2.69	0.22
V$_e$, BTPS	44.2	7.3	45.4	9.4	68.8	7.2	68.3	6.3
V$_e$/VO$_2$, 1.1^{-1}	25.2	2.6	25.9	3.5	25.7	2.2	25.5	2.4
HR, bpm	114.7	15.3	108.4*	15.3	145.5	13.6	137.4*	16.4
OP, ml/beat	15.5	2.8	16.4*	3.2	18.6	2.6	19.9*	2.9
[Hla], mM	1.88	1.02	1.70	0.56	3.01	1.35	2.95	1.26
RPE$_c$, points	9.3	2.0	9.0	2.0	12.6	2.1	12.4	1.3
RPE$_1$, points	8.7	1.7	8.9	1.3	12.8	1.3	13.1	2.3
SBP, mmHg	160.5	19.6	163.7	21.8	181.2	15.8	191.5*	18.8

* denotes P< 0.05 comparing after to before the injection period. VO2 = oxygen uptake, Ve = pulmonary ventilation, HR = heart rate, OP = oxygen pulse, [Hla] = blood lactate concentration, RPEC and RPEI = rate of perceived exertion, central and local, respectively, SBP = systolic blood pressure.

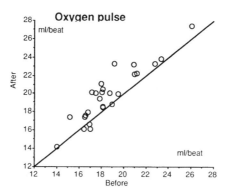

Figure 9.6.4.3b Oxygen pulse at the higher submaximal rate of work (average 190 W) before and after the injection period.

loads were too low, and therefore potential changes at higher work loads would have gone undetected.

Increased arterial systolic blood pressure during submaximal exercise was an unexpected finding. At the higher work load systolic pressure increased significantly (from 181.2 to 191.5 mmmHg). Pressure also increased at the lower work load (160.5 to 191.5 mmHg), but the increase was not significant. Individual blood pressure values are shown in Figure 9.6.4.3c).

The explanation for the increased systolic blood pressure at the higher submaximal rate of work is not known. Increased hematocrit cannot be the explanation since there is no correlation between the increased in hematocrit and the increase in systolic blood pressure after rhEPO treatment (Figure 9.6.4.3d). Similar increases did not occur after hematocrit was increased by packed cell infusions.[12] One possible explanation is that increased levels of EPO may have a direct effect on the peripheral vasculature, causing increased vasoconstriction with increased peripheral resistance. The blood pressure rise could then be explained by a combination of increased hematocrit and increased peripheral resistance.

Björn Ekblom

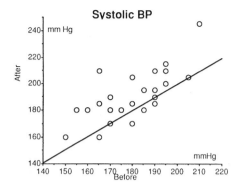

Figure 9.6.4.3c Systolic blood pressure at the higher submaximal rate of work (average 190 W) before and after the injection period.

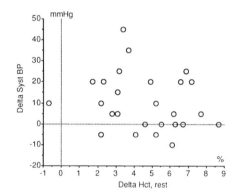

Figure 9.6.4.3d The increase in systolic blood pressure at 190 W compared to the increase in hematocrit comparing from before to after the injection period.

9.6.4.5 Maximal Exercise

Data were obtained during maximal exercise running on a treadmill, before and after rhEPO treatment. Figure 9.6.4.5a shows the values obtained for maximal aerobic power. It is interesting to note that all subjects increased their maximal aerobic power, irrespective of their baseline values. The average maximal aerobic power increased from 4.56 ± 0.43 to 4.90 ± 0.44 l min^{-1} (+7.5%, p <0.05). The average increase in maximal aerobic power was 0.34 ± 0.13 (range 0.11 to 0.62·mn^{-1}. The average increase in maximal aerobic power per gram of increased hemoglobin was 14.8 ml O_2 min^{-1}g^{-1}, which is not statistically different from the value obtained when hemoglobin levels were increased by infusing packed cells.[5,11] Individual values for the increase in maximal aerobic power compared to the increase in hemoglobin are shown in Figure 9.6.4.5b).

It has been proposed that a prolonged increase in hemoglobin would induce compensatory changes in the circulatory adaptation to maximal exercise. Such adaptations might include increased peripheral vascular resistance as a result of increased blood viscosity and peripheral vasoconstriction. This possibility seems likely given the observed increases in systolic blood pressure at the higher submaximal exercise level. However, increases in maximal aerobic power

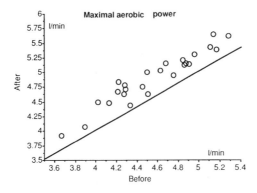

Figure 9.6.4.5a Maximal aerobic power before and after the injection period.

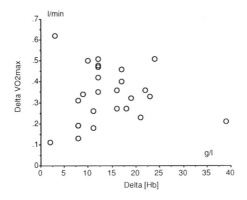

Figure 9.6.4.5b The increase in maximal aerobic power compared to the increase in hemoglobin concentration ematocrit from before to after the injection period.

were the same, no matter whether rhEPO was injected or cells transfused, suggesting that whatever differences there are, they do not apply during maximal exercise.

Figure 9.6.4.5c illustrates the change in maximal aerobic power observed in 8 subjects during and after rhEPO injections. It is obvious from these results that after cessation of the rhEPO injections, maximal aerobic power decreased. This may be due to the fact that endogenous production of EPO is reduced during the treatment period. There is nothing to suggest that after the injection period that production of endogeous EPO will return to normal when the individual's hemoglobin has returned to baseline levels.

No significant changes were found in pulmonary ventilation during maximal exercise (166.4 ± 16.4 to 168.3 ± 17.1 l.min^{-1} BTPS), nor was there any change in peak heart rate (194.2 to 195.3), peak lactic acid levels (13.3 to 13.8 mM), or perceived rate of exertion (19.0 ± 0.8 to 19.3 ± 0.6)

9.6.4.6 Muscle Physiology Data

Muscle biopsies of the *vastus lateralis* were obtained from 19 of the subjects before and after rhRPO treatment. Table 9.6.4.6 and Figures 9.6.4.6 a and b summarize the results. During this short period of increased EPO levels, no significant changes were induced in any of the muscle physiology data. There was no change in myoglobin or enzyme concentrations, ruling

Maximal aerobic power

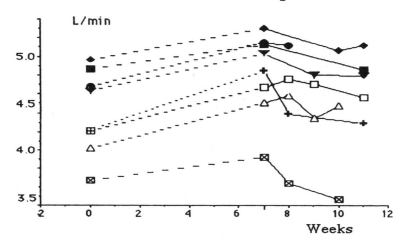

Figure 9.6.4.5c Maximal aerobic power before and after the injection period.

Table 9.6.4.6 Means + SD for Measurements from Muscle Biopsies Before and After the Injection Period

	Before		After	
	Mean	**SD**	**Mean**	**SD**
Type I, %	46.1	14.0	44.7	15.2
SDH	1.69	0.72	2.09	1.23
PFK	38.7	6.0	39.8	9.7
CS	19.6	6.2	19.2	9.4
Cytox	5.7	2.6	6.7	1.7
m-GPDH	63.9	8.2	62.4	10.3
Myoglobin	3.43	0.83	2.96	0.82
Protein	0.18	0.03	0.19	0.04

SDH = succinate dehydrogenase, PFK = phospho-fructokinase, CS = citrate synthase, m-GPDH = mitochondrial glycerol-3-phophate dehydrogenase.

out the possibility that increased oxygen availability could have increased muscle aerobic enzyme concentration during endurance training.

9.6.4.7 Physical Performance

9.6.4.7.1 Endurance Physical Performance

Endurance physical performance was evaluated by measuring the time from start of exercising until exhaustion during a standardized endurance test before, and after, treatment with rhEPO. These measurements were made in all 26 participants. The time to exhaustion increased significantly, from 493 ± 74 seconds to 567 ± 82 seconds. Individual data relating the time to exhaustion to changes in maximal aerobic power over the injection period are shown in

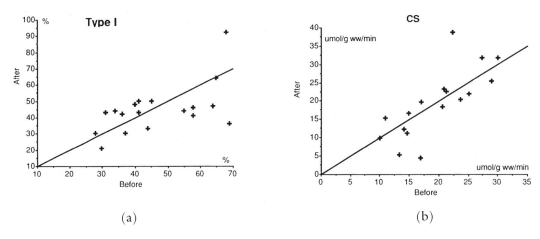

Figure 9.6.4.6. (a) Type I muscle fiber proportion before and after the injection period. (b) Citrate synthase enzyme activity before and after the injection period.

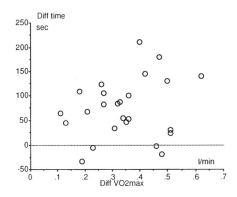

Figure 9.6.4.7.1 Time to exhaustion in relation to maximal aerobic power after compared to before the injection period.

Figure 9.6.4.7.1. Since there were no major changes in the muscle physiology data, it is obvious that the increased maximal aerobic power was due to an increase in hemoglobin.

9.6.4.7.2 High-Intensity Intermittent Exercise

This protocol was used to determine whether increased the maximal aerobic power observed after rhEPO treatment could influence the physiological response to repeated, high intensity sprinting. Before and after the injection period, 6 of the subjects performed 15 six-second bouts of high-speed uphill running at a 10-degree gradient, interspersed with 24- second periods of passive recovery. The speed chosen for each subject was the highest possible speed at which the 15 bouts could be completed.[1]

The maximal aerobic power in these subjects increased on average from 4.76 to 5.14 l•min⁻¹. When the same test was performed after the injection period the accumulation of lactate (peak post-exercise minus pre-exercise concentration) decreased significantly, from 10.3 to 7.9 mM. The accumulation of hypoxanthine also decreased significantly from 9.1 to 5.6 micromol•l⁻¹. Thus, the increased maximal aerobic power reduced the anaerobic stress, as evaluated from a net reduction in ATP resynthesis, via the adenylate kinase reaction (causing reduced serum hypoxanthine concentrations), and a reduced anaerobic glycolysis (reduced levels of lactate) during this type of high-intensity intermittent exercise. This could be due to a higher rate of phosphocreatine resynthesis during the recovery periods between sprints, or to the greater availability of oxygen, or even to a small increase in aerobic metabolism during the sprints.

From these studies it can be concluded that there is increased physical performance, both during a maximal run on a treadmill with a work time of 5 to 8 min (aerobic power), and also in high-intensity intermittent sprinting (anaerobic). This increase in physical performance, as evaluated in these two different exercise protocols, cannot be explained by changes in the peripheral characteristics of muscles. A more probable explanation is increased maximal aerobic power.

9.6.4.8 Is rhEPO Injection Detectable?

To try to answer this question, blood and urine samples were taken on different days, both before and after the end of the injection period. The complete data set has been previously published.[18] Since plasma EPO concentrations vary considerably during the day, and since inter individual differences are very large, quantitative methods for detecting exogenous administration of rhEPO cannot be used to detect athletes who have taken it illegally.

However, a qualitative approach, based on a unique electrophoretic method, has been developed by Professor Leif Wide in Uppsala, Sweden. This method can discriminate between EPO and rhEPO, as the electrical charge of these two forms are very different. The rhEPO, which is manufactured from hamster ovary and kidney cells, and mouse fibroblast cells, is less negatively charged than the endogenous EPO. This makes it possible to measure a mean value for electrophoretic mobility of EPO in samples from both plasma and urine. In samples containing both forms, as would be the case in illegal use, a biphasic curve is detected.

Using this approach it is possible to detect exogenous rhEPO administration in all subjects within 24 h after it has been given. It was still detectable in 75% of the individuals after 48 h. The technique is extremely reliable — there were no false positives in our study.

9.6.4.9 Summary

Erythropoietin is a potent hormone. Exogenous administration of rhEPO for several weeks will increase physical performance by increasing hemoglobin concentration and, as a result, increasing maximal aerobic power. The effect is short lived, however, with return to base line levels of performance 2 weeks after the last injection. In contrast to "blood doping," exogenous administration of rhEPO can be detected by electrophoretic analysis of either blood or urine. The method is reliable, and gives no false results.

REFERENCES

1. Balsom, B., Ekblom, B., Sjodin, B. Enhanced oxygen availability during high intensity intermittent exercise decreases anaerobic metabolite concentrations in blood. Acta Physiol. Scand. 150:455-456, 1994.
2. Berglund, B. High-altitude training. Aspects of hematological adaptation. Sports Med. 14:289-303, 1992.
3. Berglund, B., Ekblom, B. Effect of recombinant human erythropoietin administration on blood pressure and some hematological parameters in healthy males. J. Int. Med. 229:125-130, 1991.
4. Berglund, B., Hemmingsson, P., Birgegard G. Detection of reinfusion of autologous blood transfusions in cross-country skiers. Int J Sports Med. 8:66-70, 1987.

5. Celsing, F., Svedenhag, J., Pihlstedt, P., Ekblom, B. Effects of anaemia and stepwise induced polycythemia on aerobic power in individuals with high and low hemoglobin concentrations. Acta Physiol. Scand. 129:47-57, 1987.
6. Daniels, J., Oldridge, N. The effects of alternate exposure to altitude and sea level on world-class middle-distance runners. Med. Sci Sports 2:1()7-112, 1970.
7. Dick, F.W. Training at altitude in practice. Int. J. Sports Med. 13:203-206, 1992.
8. Ekblom, B. Iron deficiency, anaemia and physical performance in Iron nutrition in health and disease (eds Hallberg, l, Asp, N.G.) Libbey and Co London, pp 195-204, in press.
9. Ekblom, B., Berglund, B. Effect of erythropoietin administration on maximal aerobic power. Scand J. Med Sci Sports 1:88-93, 1991.
10. Ekblom, B., Goldbarg, A. The influence of physical training and other factors on the subjective rating of perceived exertion. Acta Physiol. Scand. 83:399-406, 1971.
11. Ekblom, B., Goldbarg, A. N., Gullbring, B. Response to exercise after blood loss and reinfusion. J. Appl. Physiol. 33:175-180, 1972.
12. Ekblom, B., Wilson, G., Astrand, P.-O. Central circulation during exercise after venesection and reinfusion of red blood cells. J. Appl. Physiol. 40:379-383, 1976.
13. Hahn, A.G. The effect of altitude training on athletic performance at sea level - a review. Excel. 7:9-23, 1991.
14. Levine, B.D., Stray-Gundersen, J., Duhaime, G., Snell, P., Friedman, D.B. "Living high - training low": Effect of altitude acclimatization/normoxic training in trained runners. Med Sci Sports Exerc. 23: suppl, 25, 1991.
15. Rusko, H. New aspects of altitude training. Am. J. Sports Med.(in press).
16. Shephard, R.J., Verde, T.J., Toomas, S.G., Shek, P. Physical activity and the immune system. Can. J. Sports Sci. 16: 163- 185, 1991.
17. Spriet, L.L., Gledhill, N., Froese, A.B., Wilkies, D.L. Effect of graded erythrocythemia on cardiovascular and metabolic response to exercise. J. Appl. Physiol. 61:1942-1948, 1986.
18. Wide, L., Bengtsson, C, Berglund, B., Ekblom, B. Detection in blood and urine of recombinant erythropoietin administrated to healthy men. Med. Sci. Sports Exerc. 27: 1569-1576, 1995.

9.7 SUMMARY OF INTERNATIONAL OLYMPIC COMMITTEE REGULATIONS

JORDI SEGURA

BARCELONA, INSTITUT MUNICIPAL D' INVESTIGACIÓ MÈDICA, IMIM, DEPARTAMENT DE FARMACOLOGIA I TOXICOLOGIA, BARCELONA, SPAIN

The following is only a summary. Complete copies of the Code can be obtained from the International Olympic Committee.

9.7.1 INTRODUCTION TO THE MEDICAL CODE

The International Olympic Committee ("IOC") is the supreme authority of the Olympic Movement and, in particular, the Olympic Games.

The IOC, in close collaboration with the International Federations and the National Olympic Committees, dedicates its efforts to ensuring that in sports the spirit of fair play prevails and violence is banned. The IOC leads the fight against doping in sport and takes measures, the goal of which is to prevent endangering the health of athletes.

The IOC has established rules prohibiting the use of certain substances and methods intended to enhance and/or having the effect of enhancing athletic performance, such practices being contrary to medical ethics, and which are referred to generally as "doping".

The Olympic Charter provides that the IOC shall establish an IOC Medical Code which shall provide for prohibition of doping, establish lists of prohibited classes of substances and prohibited methods, provide for the obligation of competitors to submit themselves to medical controls and examinations, and make provision for sanctions to be applied in the event of a violation of such Medical Code, which shall also include provisions relating to the medical care given to athletes.

The IOC Medical Code is essentially intended to safeguard the health of athletes, and to ensure respect for the ethical concepts implicit in Fair Play, the Olympic Spirit, and medical practice.

9.7.2 MEDICAL CODE GENERAL PROVISIONS

The IOC Medical Code applies to all athletes, coaches, trainers, officials, and medical and paramedical personnel working with or treating athletes participating in or preparing for sports competitions of the Olympic Games, those competitions to which the IOC grants its patronage or support and, in a general way, to all competitions contested in the framework of the Olympic Movement, in particular, those organized under the authority, whether direct or delegated, of an international federation or national Olympic committee recognized by the IOC.

Use of, counseling of the use of, permitting the use of, or condoning the use of any substance or method is prohibited in the IOC Medical Code. Trafficking in prohibited substances is also forbidden. Sanctions are applicable in the event of any breach of the provisions of the IOC Medical Code.

Any person affected by a decision rendered in application of the present IOC Medical Code by the IOC, an international federation, or other body may appeal from that decision to the Court of Arbitration for Sport, in accordance with the provisions applicable before such court.

9.7.3 PROHIBITED CLASSES OF SUBSTANCES AND PROHIBITED METHODS (AS OF 1ST FEBRUARY 1997)

Doping contravenes the ethics of both sport and medical science. Doping consists of: (1) the administration of substances belonging to prohibited classes of pharmacological agents, and/or (2) the use of various prohibited methods.

Table 9.7.3 Prohibited Classes of Substances

a. Stimulants

b. Narcotics

c. Anabolic Agents

d. Diuretics

e. Peptide and glycoprotein hormones and analogues

9.7.3.1 Stimulants

Prohibited substances in Class (a) include the following examples:

amiphenazole
amineptine
caffeine*
ephedrines
mesocarb
pipradol
terbutaline**
and related substances

amphetamines
bromantan
cocaine
fencamfamine
pentylentetrazol
salbutamol**

*For caffeine the definition of a positive result depends on the concentration of caffeine in the urine. The concentration in urine may not exceed 12 micrograms per milliliter.

**Permitted by inhaler only and must be declared in writing, prior to the competition, to the relevant medical authority.

The detected presence of ephedrine, pseudoephedrine, phenylpropanolamine and cathine in a test conducted in connection with a competition shall constitute a prima facie case of doping. The person affected shall have the opportunity to rebut the presumption of doping by providing evidence that the substance was present under circumstances which, on a balance of probabilities, including the quantity of substance detected, would support a conclusion that doping was neither intended, nor the result of gross negligence, willful negligence nor imprudence. In all cases, the onus of rebutting the presumption of doping, when the substance has been detected, shall rest with the person affected.

9.7.3.2 Narcotics

Prohibited substances in Class (b) include the following examples:

dextromoramide
morphine
and related substances

diamorphine (heroin)
pentazocine

methadone
pethidine (demerol)

Note: codeine, dextromethorphan, dextropropoxyphene, dihydrocodein, diphenoxylate, ethyl-morphine, and pholcodine are permitted.

9.7.3.3 Anabolic Agents

The Anabolic class includes anabolic androgenic steroids (AAS) and ß2-agonists. Prohibited substances in Class (c) include the following examples.

9.7.3.3.1 Anabolic Androgenic Steroids

clostebol
metenolone
testosterone*
and related substances

dehydroepiandrosterone (DHEA)
nandrolone

fluoxymesterone

oxandrolone

metandienone

stanozolol

* The presence of a testosterone (T) to epitestosterone (E) ratio greater than 6 to 1 in the urine of a competitor constitutes an offense unless there is evidence that this ratio is due to a physiological or pathological condition, e.g. low epitestosterone excretion, androgen production of tumor, enzyme deficiencies.

In the case of T/E higher than 6, it is mandatory that relevant medical authority conduct an investigation before the sample is declared positive. A full report will be written and will include a review of previous, subsequent tests and any results of endocrine investigations. In the event that previous tests are not available, the athlete should be tested unannounced at least once per month for three months. The results of these investigations should be included in the report. Failure to cooperate in the investigations will result in declaring the sample positive.

9.7.3.3.2 Beta-2 Agonists

clenbuterol
salbutamol
terbutaline
salmeterol
fenoterol
and related substances

9.7.3.3.3 Diuretics

Prohibited substances in Class (d) include the following examples:

acetazolamide	bumetanide
chlorthalidone	ethacrynic acid
furosemide	hydrochlorothiazide
mannitol	mersalyl
spironolactone	triamterene
and related substances	

9.7.3.3.4 Peptide and Glycoprotein Hormones and Analogues

Prohibited substances in Class (e) include the following examples:

Chorionic Gonadotrophin (hCG - human chorionic gonadotrophin)
Corticotrophin (ACTH)
Growth hormone (hGH, somatotrophin)
Erythropoietin (EPO)
and all the respective releasing factors for such substances

9.7.3.4 Prohibited Methods

9.7.3.4.1 Blood Doping

Blood doping is the administration of blood, red blood cells and related blood products to an athlete. This procedure may be preceded by withdrawal of blood from the athlete who continues to train in this blood depleted state.

9.7.3.4.2 Pharmaceutical, Chemical, and Physical Manipulation

Pharmaceutical, chemical, and physical manipulation is the use of substances and of methods which alter, attempt to alter, or may reasonably be expected to alter the integrity and validity of urine samples used in doping controls, including, without limitation, catheterization, urine substitution and or tampering, inhibition of renal excretion such as by probenecid and related compounds and alterations of testosterone and epitestosterone measurements such as epitestosterone application or bromantan administration.

The success or failure of the use of a prohibited substance or method is not material. It is sufficient that the said substance or procedure was used or attempted for the infraction to be considered as consummated

9.7.3.4.3 Classes of Drugs Subject to Certain Restrictions

Alcohol
Marijuana
Local anaesthetics
Corticosteroids
Beta-blockers

The list of prohibited classes of substances and prohibited methods contained in the IOC Medical Code may be changed from time to time by the IOC Executive Board on the proposal of the IOC Medical Commission.

9.7.4 MEDICAL CARE GIVEN TO ATHLETES

The only legitimate use of drugs in sports is under supervision of a physician for a clinically justified purpose. The IOC and international sports organizations initiated drug testing to protect athletes from the potential unfair advantage that might be gained by those athletes who take drugs in an attempt to increase performance. Drug testing is also meant as a deterrent to protect athletes from the potential harmful side effects which some drugs can produce.

The list of prohibited substances contains a very small percentage of the currently available pharmacological arsenal and does not hinder the proper treatment of athletes for justifiable therapeutic reasons.

9.7.5 LABORATORIES AND TESTING PROCEDURES

For purposes of the IOC Medical Code, only those laboratories accredited by the IOC are qualified to undertake the detection of the use of prohibited classes of substances and prohibited methods.

Laboratories seeking accreditation are requested to provide a letter of support of a National Authority, such as the NOC, sports governing body or other and any other letter of support that they would wish the IOC Medical Commission to consider. The final decision regarding the acceptance of the letters of support will be made by the IOC Medical Commission, taking into account such factors as continuity, volume of workload, long-term financial support, administrative commitment of the host institution, and research activities and accomplishments, such as publication records of senior staff.

The analysis of a sample shall be carried out in accordance with the methods which have been approved by the IOC Medical Commission.

Laboratories accredited by the IOC shall conclusively be deemed to have conducted tests and analyses of samples in accordance with the highest scientific standards and the results of such analysis shall be conclusively be deemed to be scientifically correct.

In order to guarantee a continued quality of laboratories performing antidoping analysis, yearly reacreditation procedures are established. In addition the IOC Medical Commission has devised a proficiency testing (PT) program which is a part (in conjunction with laboratory inspection) of the initial evaluation of a laboratory seeking accreditation and of the continuing assessment of laboratory performance necessary to maintain his accreditation.

The laboratory must have written protocols designed to maintain control and accountability from the receipt of urine specimens until testing is completed, results are reported, and while specimens are in storage.

A sensitive and comprehensive screen to eliminate "true negative" specimens from further consideration must be used. The initial screening procedures shall be an appropriate technique which meets the requirements of the IOC Medical Commission.

Laboratories wishing to use screening procedures other than those required by the IOC Medical Commission shall submit their methods for written approval by the IOC Medical Commission.

A second extraction and analysis aliquot of the same sample is used for eventual identification of the presence of a specific drug or metabolite in a urine specimen. At this time, mass spectrometry (MS) is the only authorized confirmation method except for peptide hormones and glycoproteins. MS may be applied in conjunction with gas chromatography (GC) or high performance liquid chromatography (HPLC). To exclude possible interferences from the biological materials the sample preparation, including the derivatization as well as the polarity of the gas chromatographic column can be modified whenever possible or necessary.

9.7.6 SAMPLING AND RESULTS

Only authorized disposable material should be used in sample taking procedure. The competitor shall pour the collected urine into bottle A and into bottle B. Next, the competitor shall close and seal the two bottles.

The competitor shall declare to the Doping Control Officer any medication he/she may have taken in the preceding three days.

A result is positive only when both the "A" and "B" samples are positive or when the "A" sample is positive and the athlete affected waives the right to require that the "B" sample be analyzed.

Should the analysis of the A samples indicate a violation of the IOC doping control regulations, the B sample will be analyzed.

The analysis of B samples shall be carried out in the same laboratory and under the supervision of a representative of the IOC Medical Commission. The delegation in question shall be allowed to send a maximum of three representatives to the laboratory. Should the delegation not be present at the laboratory, at the time indicated, the representative of the IOC Medical Commission may decide to proceed to the B analysis.

Should the result of the B sample not confirm the result of A analysis, the case is considered as negative.

Minor irregularities, which cannot reasonably be considered to have affected the results of otherwise valid tests, shall have no effect on such results.

Should the result of the A sample be confirmed, the Chairman of the IOC Medical Commission shall then call a meeting of the IOC Medical Commission, to which the competitor, not more than three representatives of the delegation concerned and a representative from the International Federation concerned shall be invited. Following this meeting, the IOC Medical Commission shall make a recommendation for the IOC Executive Board.

The Chairman of the IOC Medical Commission shall then forward this recommendation to the President of the IOC for submission to the IOC Executive Board, which shall be responsible for taking further action.

The IOC Executive Board is the only organ competent to rule on the effects of a Positive result during the Olympic Games. It shall request the advice of the IOC Medical Commission prior to acting on any Positive result.

In competitions organized by or under the authority of the international federations, the competent organ of such international federation shall be solely responsible for the application of the IOC Medical Code in relation to such competitions as well as in relation to all tests which have been conducted out-of-competition.

In competitions organized under the authority of continental associations of national Olympic committees, the Executive Committees of such associations shall be the competent bodies to rule on the effects of a Positive result during such competitions.

Organizations, athletes and other persons participating in the Olympic Movement shall accept the individual or joint obligation to submit disputes concerning the application of the present Medical Code to the Court of Arbitration for Sport. Such acceptance is presumed by the very fact of participation by the interested parties in the Olympic Movement. Consequently, any de facto refusal of such acceptance shall result in the interested party or parties being considered as having excluded themselves from the Olympic Movement.

9.7.7 CODE OF ETHICS

The IOC Medical Commission has been made aware of a number of incidents relative to the pre-testing of athletes for the purposes of withdrawing them from competition without appropriate sanctions. The Commission wishes to remind its accredited laboratories that the purpose of its action is based on deterrence of drug misuse (doping control) and that it is strongly opposed to laboratories getting involved in testing athletes during training or just prior to a particular sporting event in order to determine when to stop taking banned drugs and thus avoid detection at a particular subsequent event (controlled doping).

The IOC Medical Commission is also categorically opposed to the action of some non-accredited, commercial (or other) laboratories which analyze athletic samples in such a manner as to aid and assist the athletes to cheat by helping them to determine when to stop taking a banned drug or by helping to determine if they are positive or negative with a banned drug before a specific competition. The Commission is thus also opposed to the testing of athletes prior to a competition for the sole purpose of withdrawing them from the event without imposing sanctions commensurate with the offence.

The Commission has therefore defined the conditions under which its accredited laboratories should accept or refuse to analyze urine specimens from athletes.

CHAPTER 10

WORKPLACE TESTING

EDITED BY YALE H. CAPLAN, PH.D.

NATIONAL SCIENTIFIC SERVICES, BALTIMORE, MARYLAND

TABLE OF CONTENTS

0-8493-2637-0/98/$0.00+$.50
© 1998 by CRC Press LLC

10.1 DEVELOPMENT AND SCOPE OF REGULATED TESTING

J. Michael Walsh, Ph.D.

The Walsh Group, P.A, Bethesda, Maryland

Over the last 15 years (1982-1997) "workplace" drug testing has grown at a phenomenal rate. Those of us who are in the business recognize that employee/applicant drug testing has become a standard business practice in the United States. Based on the current daily volumes of specimens being analyzed by laboratories certified by the U.S. Department of Health and Human Services (HHS), it is likely that more than 30 million working Americans (approximately one-third of the American work force) will be tested for illegal drugs this year.

    This workplace drug-testing phenomena did not occur overnight, but rather has evolved slowly during the decade of the 1980s. At the outset, workplace drug testing began in the U.S. military with most of the testing being done in military laboratories by military personnel and was highly regimented. However, even within the military programs (Army, Navy, and Air Force), the procedures, the equipment, and the standards varied considerably. As the use of the new immunoassay-based drug-testing technology began to spread to the private sector in

1982-1983, there were no regulations, no certified laboratories, no standardized procedures, and many of the devices being marketed for testing were not approved by the U.S. Food and Drug Administration. Medical and scientific questions about the accuracy and reliability of drug testing were raised continuously by those who opposed testing and often formed the basis of lengthy litigation. As interest in workplace drug testing increased both in the public and private sectors, the need for regulations to establish the science, technology, and practice became more obvious.

10.1.1 BEGINNINGS OF REGULATED TESTING

The beginnings of regulated testing were initiated in 1983 when the National Transportation Safety Board (NTSB) sent a series of specific recommendations to the Secretary of Transportation demanding action in regard to a number of alcohol- and drug-related accidents, particularly in the railroad industry. The report indicated that seven train accidents occurring between June 1982 and May 1983 involved alcohol or other drugs. In response to the NTSB recommendations, the Federal Railroad Administration (FRA) with the assistance of the National Institute on Drug Abuse (NIDA) began to develop the first of the Department of Transportation (DOT) drug regulations in 1983. The FRA odyssey carried through 1984 when the first Notice of Proposed Rule-Making (NPRM) was issued and hearings were held around the country, through 1995 when the FRA finalized the rule and tried to implement the regulation. Within a day of implementation the rule was enjoined, and it was not until early in 1996 that the various legal obstacles were cleared and the rule went into effect and was fully implemented. The leadership and perseverance of Grady Cothen and Walter Rocky from the FRA's Office of Safety really laid the groundwork and paved the way for other DOT entities to develop drug regulations for the other modes of transportation.

During the 1983-1986 time frame, many companies in the oil /chemical, transportation, and nuclear industries voluntarily implemented drug-testing programs. Without any standards or recognized procedures, naturally, almost every action incurred controversy. Lawsuits and arbitration caseloads mounted rapidly. Reports of laboratory errors in the massive military program raised concerns that the application of this state-of-the-art technology might be premature. Allegations of horror stories where employees were stripped naked and forced to provide specimens in view of other employees were often repeated and added justification for some form of regulation.

In 1986, the Federal government began to get involved in employee drug testing in a major way. In March of 1986, President Reagan's Commission on Organized Crime issued its final report.[1] Among the recommendations were the following:

> The President should direct the heads of all Federal agencies to formulate immediately clear policy statements, with implementing guidelines, including suitable drug testing programs, expressing the utter unacceptability of drug abuse by Federal employees, State and local governments and leaders in the private sector should support unequivocally a similar policy that any and all use of drugs is unacceptable. Government contracts should not be awarded to companies that fail to implement drug programs, including suitable drug testing. Government and private sector employers who do not already require drug testing of job applicants and current employees should consider the appropriateness of such a testing program.

10.1.2 THE NIDA CONFERENCE OF 1986

The National Institute on Drug Abuse (NIDA) convened what was to be called "a landmark" conference in March 1986. The conference was designed to discuss and achieve consensus on drug-testing issues. Scientists, attorneys, health and safety experts, corporate human resource and medical directors, and representatives of the labor movement and the American Civil Liberties Union (ACLU) were invited to participate.

Prior to the issuance of the Report of the President's Commission on Organized Crime, it appeared that reaching a consensus would be extremely difficult; certain battle lines were firmly drawn with the unions and the ACLU adamantly opposed drug testing under any circumstances. However, the fortuitous release of the Commission's report with its sweeping recommendations two days before the scheduled consensus conference dramatically shifted the positions taken by attendees. Events and the passage of time had overtaken the posturing in the field; most attendees came prepared to enter into hard negotiations. The definition of the "acceptability" of testing had shifted. Prior to the release of the report, NIDA's position advocating testing for critical and sensitive positions was viewed as radical. However, once the recommendation for the widespread testing of everyone employed in both the public and private sectors was proposed by the President's Commission, NIDA's stance became a position of reasonable accommodation. So rather than argue about whether or not to test, the conferees were able to focus on prescribing the conditions under which testing could be conducted. After lengthy discussions, consensus was reached on the following points:

1. All individuals tested must be informed.
2. All positive results on an initial screen must be confirmed through the use of an alternate methodology.
3. The confidentiality of test results must be assured.
4. Random screening for drug abuse under a well-defined program is appropriate and legally defensible in certain circumstances.

The consensus reached at this meeting in March of 1986 on technical, medical, legal, and ethical issues truly served to provide the foundation for the development of the Federal regulations that were to evolve over the next decade.[2]

By midyear 1986, it became clear that major presidential initiatives focusing on drugs in the workplace were taking shape, some of which were direct responses to the recommendations put forth by the President's Commission on Organized Crime. With regard to drug testing, multiple task forces were convened, comprised of representatives of major Federal agencies, notably the Department of Justice (DOJ), the Office of Personnel Management (OPM), and HHS to draft an executive order and to develop strategies and policies for implementation. On September 15, 1986, President Reagan issued Executive Order (EO) #12564 which required all Federal agencies to develop programs and policies to achieve a drug-free Federal workplace.[3] One of the requirements of the EO was that agencies institute employee drug testing under specified circumstances.

10.1.3 DRAFTING THE GUIDELINES

The responsibility for developing technical and scientific guidelines for these drug-testing programs was assigned to the Secretary of HHS and was delegated to the NIDA. Ultimately the task fell to this authors desk!! With the assistance of some of the nation's leading forensic toxicologists (i.e., Drs. Bryan Finkle, Yale Caplan, Kurt Dubowski, Michael Peat, Robert Blanke, Richard Hawks, et al.) who comprised an informal advisory group, we were able to produce an initial set of guidelines in a matter of months.

On February 19, 1987, HHS Secretary Dr. Otis Bowen issued the required set of technical and scientific guidelines for Federal drug-testing programs. As there was significant opposition to Federal employee drug testing in the Congress, legislation was proposed in the House of Representatives to prohibit the expenditure of "appropriated funds" to implement the President's Executive Order. Several months of negotiation between the Administration and the Congress resulted in the passage of a new law (Public Law 100-71 section 503) which set the stage for the widespread regulation of employee drug testing.[4]

Enacted on July 7, 1987, PL 100-71 sec. 503 permitted the President's *Drug Free Federal Workplace* program to go forward only if a number of administrative prerequisites were met. Among the list of required administrative actions was that the Secretary of Health and Human Services publish the HHS technical and scientific guidelines in the Federal Register for notice and comment, and to expand the "Guidelines" to include standards for laboratory certification. Fortunately, the NIDA advisory group had been working on the concept of laboratory accreditation since early in 1986 anticipating the eventuality of laboratory certification. This foresight allowed NIDA the opportunity to revise the guidelines quickly and include a proposed scheme of laboratory certification which was published in the Federal Register on August 13, 1987, less than six weeks after the passage of the law.

The period of "notice and comment" closed on October 13, 1987, and several months were required to evaluate the advice received, make the appropriate revisions, and to fully develop the standards for laboratory certification. The HHS Guidelines included procedures for collecting urine samples for drug testing, procedures for transmitting the samples to testing laboratories, testing procedures, procedures for evaluating test results, quality control measures applicable to the laboratories, recordkeeping and reporting requirements, and standards and procedures for HHS certification of drug-testing laboratories. The basic intent of the Guidelines was and remains to safeguard the accuracy and integrity of test results and the privacy of individuals who are tested.

Every section in the "Guidelines" had to be coordinated with the DOJ and the OPM to insure that all provisions were within the law and complied with existing Federal regulations. The revised "Guidelines" and "Laboratory Certification Standards" went through a tortuous lengthy clearance process within HHS. This included major policy issue battles with departmental officials who attempted to limit the scope of the program. There were serious turf issues with Health Care Financing Administration (HCFA) officials who were worried that the drug-testing laboratory standards were so stringent that it would make their clinical laboratory (Clinical Laboratory Improvement Act [CLIA]) standards look perfunctory. In fact, the CLIA 88 revisions were in large part due to the position the Secretary (HHS) took when HCFA opposed clearance of the drug laboratory certification standards.[5] After clearance from HHS, the regulations moved to the Office of Management and Budget (OMB) where there was heavy political pressure to reshape the requirements for specified methods/thresholds/assays. In spite of the pressure, the scientific and technical aspects of the guidelines remained intact as drafted and were published in final in the Federal Register as the "Mandatory Guidelines for Federal Workplace Drug Testing Programs" on April 11, 1988.[6]

In July 1988, utilizing the certification standards developed as part of the "Mandatory Guidelines", a National Laboratory Certification Program was implemented by HHS/NIDA and was administered under contract by the Research Triangle Institute. More than 100 laboratories have been certified in this program since 1988 and at this writing (May 1996) approximately 75 remain actively certified and are currently processing an estimated 60,000 specimens daily. Late in 1988, both the DOT and the Nuclear Regulatory Commission (NRC) issued NPRMs proposing to require their respective industries to conduct workplace drug testing of all applicants and employees under proscribed circumstances (e.g., post-accident, random, pre-employment, etc.). These NPRMs were the culmination of several years of deliberations within the respective industries.

Initially the Nuclear industry had opposed Federal regulation (originally proposed by the NRC in 1982) as most licensees had initiated their own programs voluntarily. However, by 1988, emerging state laws were beginning to inhibit the nuclear licensees from fully and consistently implementing their programs across states. At this point the idea of pre-emptive

Federal regulations became more desirable. The NRC final rule (54FR 24468) was published in the Federal Register on June 7, 1989, and the rule became effective on that date, with full implementation required by January 3, 1990.[7] The NRC rule incorporated most of the HHS "Mandatory Guidelines" but permitted on-site testing meeting certain specifications.

10.1.4 THE "FINAL RULES"

The U.S. Department of Transportation published an interim final rule on November 21, 1988 establishing drug-testing procedures applicable to drug testing for transportation employees under six DOT regulations.[8] These six regulations were published on that same date by the Federal Aviation Administration (FAA), Federal Highway Administration (FHWA), Federal Railroad Administration, United States Coast Guard, Urban Mass Transportation Administration, and Research and Special Programs Administration. The interim final rule (49 CFR part 40) followed closely the HHS regulation entitled "Mandatory Guidelines for Federal Workplace Drug Testing Programs. DOT issued its final rule on December 1, 1989 with an implementation date of January 2, 1990.[9] These regulations brought the rest of the transportation modes in line with the railroad industry and, in most aspects, standardized the procedures across the industry. [N.B. This is a very simplified explanation of the DOT issuances. Each of the various DOT "modes" (air, rail, highway, pipeline, mass transit, etc.) had been issuing Advanced Notice of Proposed Rulemaking (ANPRMs), NPRMs, and interim final rules on their own authority. For example, on November 21, 1988, the FHWA issued a "final" rule setting forth regulations to require motor vehicle carriers who operate interstate to have drug-testing programs.[10] On the same date the DOT issued an "interim final rule" which covered the FHWA's program. On November 6, 1989, FHWA published another "final" rule clarifying the types of testing that had to be implemented, and on February 1, 1990, FHWA published an "interim final rule" regarding the disposition of petitions for waivers. To list each and every notice issued by each of the six transportation agencies during this period is beyond the scope of this chapter.] There was a delay in the implementation of the mass transit program as the renamed Federal Transit Administration (formerly the Urban Mass Transit Administration) rule was overturned by a Federal appellate court in January 1990 on the grounds that the agency lacked statutory authority to issue nationwide standards requiring drug testing. The Congress remedied this legislative loophole by the passage of the Omnibus Transportation Employee Drug Testing Act of 1991 ("Act").[11]

This "Act" was an extremely important piece of legislation that broadly expanded drug testing in the transportation industry. The impetus for the legislation was a very visible subway accident in New York City where the engineer was found to be under the influence of alcohol. The "Act" required the DOT to prescribe regulations within one year to expand the existing DOT drug regulations in the aviation, rail, highway, and mass transit industries to cover intrastate transportation and to expand the drug-testing program to include alcohol. [N.B. Previously only inter-state operations were covered.] The "Act" specifically directed the FTA to issue drug and alcohol testing rules. The "Act" triggered another slew of ANPRM/NPRM notices from the DOT agencies in 1992. This began a new round of nationwide hearings on the proposed regulations, and numerous comments to be considered from the affected parties within each of the modes. Final DOT rules were published in the Federal Register in February 1994,[12] which continued to incorporate the HHS "Guidelines" and generally required implementation beginning on January 1, 1995 for large employers (i.e., >50 covered employees) and January 1, 1996 for small employers. This expansion of the DOT regulations brought the number of employees covered by these regulations to more than 7.4 million transportation workers nationwide. Table 10.1.1 illustrates the far-reaching effects of these Federal regulations in the transportation industry.

Table 10.1.1 Far-Reaching Effects of Federal Regulations in the Transportation Industry

Industry	# Employees covered	Type employees
Commercial Motor Vehicle (FHWA)	6,600,000	Drivers
Aviation (FAA)	340,000	Pilots, flight attendants, crew, maintenance, instructors, etc.
Railroad (FRA)	80,000	Crew, engineers, train and signal services, dispatchers, operators
Mass Transit (FTA)	200,000	Vehicle operators, controllers, mechanics
Pipeline (RSPA)	120,000	Operations and maintenance, emergency response
Maritime (USCG)	120,000	Crew members operating a vessel
Totals	7,460,000	

10.1.5 INTERNATIONAL REGULATED TESTING

In addition to the impact of regulated testing here in the United States, the DOT regulations have also been imposed on Canadian and Mexican railroad and trucking companies that have operating personnel that enter the United States. The implementation of the rail regulations have been in effect for some time with the exception of random testing. However, as of July 1, 1996, all of the provisions of the rules that impact U.S. corporations will be imposed on Canadian and Mexican rail and trucking companies that have U.S. operations. The FAA has issued proposed rules that would subject foreign airlines who operate in the U.S. to the same regulations but have not moved (at this writing 10/97) to issue a final rule. The FAA has been working through the International Civil Aviation Organization (ICAO) to come up with an anti-drug effort that would be truly international rather than unilaterally enforced by the U.S. To date, however, the ICAO effort has been less than successful.

10.1.6 STATE REGULATED TESTING

A number of states have passed legislation regulating various facets of employee drug testing, including policy, technical issues, and laboratories who conduct testing. For example, some states prohibit "random" testing, other states prohibit "witnessed" collection. Most states require some kind of laboratory certification for laboratories offering drug-testing services. Associating the requirement for being drug-free with workers' compensation programs is a legislative initiative which has substantially increased the use of drug testing in several states. Florida, Georgia, Alabama, and the state of Washington have passed laws which reward companies, who voluntarily implement drug-free workplace programs with pre-employment and post-accident drug testing, with reductions in workers' compensation premiums. Testing under these programs must be conducted in certified laboratories and generally require that testing conform to the HHS mandatory guidelines.

10.1.7 FUTURE IN REGULATED TESTING

The use of drug testing will almost certainlly continue to expand exponentially over the next decade. This growth will occur not only in the workplace but in a variety of Federal- and State-regulated programs. For example, both 1996 Presidential Candidates, Mr. Clinton and Mr. Dole, endorsed the concept of drug-testing for welfare recipients. From the direction of the proposed Welfare Reform legislation, it appears inevitable that:

Welfare responsibility will be transferred to the States.

There will not be sufficient funds to maintain state benefit programs on a par with those experienced with Federally administered programs.

State Governors will be forced to find ways to limit eligibility to program benefits.

The House Republican Welfare Reform bill provides for drug testing of Supplemental Security Income (SSI) recipients who are "disabled" because of alcoholism or drug dependence. Individual states will follow in a similar fashion when devising state welfare reform plans. That is, states will consider reducing, limiting, or denying cash benefits to welfare recipients who use illegal drugs. The simple rationale being that thirty to forty million employed, taxpaying Americans will undergo workplace drug testing this year because their employers will not tolerate illegal drug use. Why shouldn't Federal and State governments hold recipients of cash welfare benefits to the same standard?

In another Federal initiative, Senator Ashcroft (R-MO) has recently introduced an amendment to the Federal Job Training Act which, if passed, would require all applicants to any Federal job-training program to pass a drug test prior to admission to the program. If every job-training program applicant and every welfare recipient by the year 2000 is undergoing routine drug testing, there is reason to wonder whether the current system will be able to handle the workload.

10.1.8 SUMMARY

Drug testing in the workplace has changed considerably over the last 20 years, and most all of the changes have been for the better. The development and scope of regulations that pertain to testing have had an extremely important effect in not only improving the accuracy and reliability of employee drug testing but also establishing the credibility of the testing process and the laboratory capability to perform these tests on a routine basis. The stringent laboratory certification standards imposed on forensic drug-testing laboratories have had an enormous spin-off effect on clinical laboratory medicine, and dramatic levels of improvement have been witnessed over the last decade in clinical laboratories.

A real concern is that the Federal regulations may have become too cemented in concrete and, in some ways, have not kept up with technological advances. As the volume of drug testing increases, the economy of the business is changing rapidly. The economic incentive will almost certainly drive the development of new technology which could deliver more specific and more sensitive assays for drugs of abuse. A system of Federal regulations is needed that can adapt more readily to changes in technology. The original Guidelines were set up with provisions to make changes (in the Guidelines) when there were advances/improvements in technology by simply issuing a notice of change in the Federal Register. The idea was to avoid the official rulemaking process with every change. It was assumed (back in 1987) that NIDA would update the Guidelines at least every two years.

NIDA conducted a second consensus conference late in 1989 to evaluate the first two years of experience with the "Guidelines" and to identify areas which needed to be changed. A series of recommendations were made in the consensus report which was published early in 1990.[13] Unfortunately, many of these recommendations were never acted upon and only one set of minor modifications were finally made four years later in 1994.[14] These minor changes were made only after going through the entire rulemaking process of publishing proposed changes in the Federal Register and going through prolonged periods of notice and comment. If testing continues to expand as projected, the current laboratory-based system will have trouble keeping up with the demand unless the regulators become more flexible in adopting new technology into Federally regulated drug-testing programs.

REFERENCES

1. President's Commission on Organized Crime. (1986, March). America's Habit: Drug Abuse, Drug Trafficking, and Organized Crime, Report to the President and Attorney General.
2. Walsh, J.M., Gust, S.W., (Eds.) Workplace Drug Abuse Policy: Considerations and the Experience in the Business Community, DHHS Pub. No. (ADM) 89-1610, 1989
3. Drug-free federal workplace: Executive Order 12564. (1986, September 15). *FederalRegister.*
4. Public Law 100-71, sec. 503, title IV (1987, July 11). *Congressional Record,* (vol. 133).
5. *Federal Register* Vol. 57, No. 40, (Friday, 1992, February 28) p. 7002. Clinical Laboratory Improvement Amendments of 1988, Final Rule.
6. Department of Health and Human Services. (1988, April 11). Mandatory Guidelines for federal workplace drug testing programs. *Federal Register.*
7. Nuclear Regulatory Commission. (1989, June 7). Fitness-for-Duty Programs. *Federal Register,* 54 FR 24468: 10 CFR Part 26, with full implementation required by January 3, 1990.
8. Procedures for Transportation. Workplace Drug Testing Programs. *Federal Register*, Vol. 53, p. 47002. (1988, November 21).
9. Procedures for Transportation. Workplace Drug Testing Programs. *Federal Register*, Vol. 54, No. 230, p. 49854. (1989, December 1).
10. FHWA—*Federal Register,* Vol.53, 4713. (1988, November 21).
11. Omnibus Transportation Employee Testing Act of 1991 (Public Law 102-143, Title V).
12. Department of Transportation. Limitation on Alcohol Use by Transportation Workers. *Federal Register*, Vol. 59. No. 31, p. 7502. (Tuesday, 1994, February 15).
13. Finkle, B. S., Blanke, R. V., and Walsh, J. M. Technical, Scientific, and Procedural Issues of Employee Drug Testing: A Consensus Report, DHHS Pub. No. (ADM 90-1684), U.S. Dept. of Health and Human Services, 1990.
14. Dept. of Health and Human Services, *Federal Register*, Vol. 59, No. 110, June 9, 1994, p29908, Mandatory Guidelines for Federal Workplace Drug Testing.

10.2 LABORATORY ACCREDITATION PROGRAMS

10.2.1 AN OVERVIEW OF THE MANDATORY GUIDELINES FOR FEDERAL WORKPLACE DRUG TESTING PROGRAMS

DONNA M. BUSH, PH.D., D-ABFT

DRUG TESTING TEAM LEADER, DIVISION OF WORKPLACE PROGRAMS, CENTER FOR SUBSTANCE ABUSE PREVENTION, SUBSTANCE ABUSE AND MENTAL HEALTH SERVICES ADMINISTRATION, WASHINGTON, D.C.

10.2.1.1 History

"The Federal Government, as the largest employer in the world, can and should show the way towards achieving drug-free workplaces through a program designed to offer drug users a helping hand...." These words are part of President Reagan's Executive Order 12564,[1] and served to launch the Drug-Free Workplace Programs that today cover approximately 10 million Federal and federally regulated industry civilian employees. Under these drug-free workplace initiatives, about 1.8 million Federal employees, about 600,000 employees working for Nuclear Regulatory Commission licensees, and more than 7 million Department of Transportation regulated industry employees are urine drug tested.

In 1987, Public Law 100-71, Section 503, outlined the general provisions for drug testing programs within the Federal sector, and directed the Secretary of the Department of Health and Human Services (DHHS) to set comprehensive standards for all aspects of laboratory drug testing. The authority to develop and promulgate these standards was delegated to the National Institute on Drug Abuse (NIDA), an institute within the Alcohol, Drug Abuse and Mental Health Administration. Following "corporate reorganization" within the Federal government, the authority for this oversight currently resides within the Center for Substance Abuse Prevention, Substance Abuse and Mental Health Services Administration. The Division of Workplace Programs administers and directs the National Laboratory Certification Program (NLCP) to provide accurate, reliable, and forensically supportable urine drug testing for agencies and other Departments within the government with authority to collect and test specimens as part of a similar Drug-Free Workplace Program.

On April 11, 1988, the Secretary of Health and Human Services (Secretary) published the "Mandatory Guidelines for Federal Workplace Drug Testing Programs" (Guidelines) in the *Federal Register*.[2] These Guidelines were revised and published in the *Federal Register* on June 9, 1994.[3] The intent of these Guidelines is to ensure the accuracy and reliability of test results and the privacy of individuals (Federal employees) who are tested. Section B of these Guidelines sets scientific and technical requirements for drug testing and forms the framework for the National Laboratory Certification Program (NLCP). Section C focuses on laboratory-specific requirements and certification of laboratories engaged in drug testing for Federal agencies. The Guidelines cover requirements in many aspects of analytical testing, standard operating procedures, quality assurance, and personnel qualifications.

In December 1988, the first 10 laboratories were certified by DHHS through the NLCP to perform urine drug testing in accordance with the requirements specified in the Guidelines. As of July 1997, there are 69 certified laboratories in the NLCP.

Requirements for a comprehensive drug-free workplace model include: (1) a policy that clearly defines the prohibition against illegal drug use and its consequences, (2) employee education about the dangers of drug use, (3) supervisor training concerning their responsibilities in a Drug-Free Workplace Program, (4) a helping hand in the form of an Employee Assistance Program for employees who have a drug problem, and (5) provisions for identifying employees who are illegal drug users, including drug testing on a controlled and carefully monitored basis.

Several different types of drug testing are performed under Federal authority. These include: job applicant, accident/unsafe practice, reasonable suspicion, follow-up to treatment, random, and voluntary.

10.2.1.2 Specimen Collection

It is important to ensure the integrity, security and proper identification of a donor's urine specimen. The donor's specimen is normally collected in the privacy of a stall or other partitioned area. Occasionally, a donor may try to avoid detection of drug use by tampering with the urine specimen. Precautions taken during the collection process include, but are not limited to: (1) placing a bluing (dye) agent in the toilet bowl to deter specimen dilution with toilet bowl water, (2) requiring photo identification of the donor to prevent another individual from providing the specimen, (3) collector remaining close to the donor to deter tampering by the donor, (4) taking the temperature of the specimen within 4 min of collection. Tamper-resistant tape is used to seal the bottle. A standardized custody and control form is used to identify the individuals who handled the specimen, when they had possession of the specimen, and for what purpose.

If a specimen is reported positive for a drug or metabolite, the entire collection process must be able to withstand the closest scrutiny and challenges to its integrity.

A handbook providing guidance to those who will be collecting urine specimens in accordance with the Guidelines has recently been published.[4]

10.2.1.3 Specimen Testing

The procedures described in the Guidelines include, but are not limited to, those for: collecting a urine specimen, transporting specimens to testing laboratories, actual testing of the specimen, evaluating test results, quality control measures within the laboratory, record keeping and reporting of laboratory results to a Medical Review Officer (MRO), and certification of drug testing laboratories by DHHS.

The cornerstone of the analytical testing requirements specified in the Guidelines is the "two-test" concept: (1) an initial test is performed for each class of drugs tested on an aliquot of the specimen; if this initial test is positive, then (2) a confirmatory test using a different chemical principle is performed on a different aliquot of the specimen. Specifically, the initial testing technology required is immunoassay, and the confirmatory test technology required is gas chromatography/mass spectrometry (GC/MS).

The initial test cutoffs as published in the Guidelines[3] are:

Drug Class	Cutoff (ng/mL)
Marijuana metabolites	50
Cocaine metabolites	300
Opiate metabolites[a]	300
Phencyclidine	25
Amphetamines	1,000

[a] These cutoffs are expected to change in 1998

The confirmatory test cutoffs as published in the Guidelines[3] are:

Drug	Cutoff (ng/mL)
Marijuana metabolite[a]	15
Cocaine metabolite[b]	150
Opiates:	
Morphine[c]	300
Codeine[c]	300
Phencyclidine	25
Amphetamines:	
Amphetamine	500
Methamphetamine[d]	500

[a] delta-9-tetrahydrocannabinol-9-carboxylic acid
[b] Benzoylecgonine
[c] These cutoffs are expected to change in 1998
[d] Specimen must also contain 200 ng/mL amphetamine

As part of an overall quality assurance program, there are three levels of quality control (QC) required of each certified laboratory: (1) internal open and blind samples which constitute 10% of the daily, routine sample workload; (2) external open performance testing samples which are distributed quarterly; and (3) double blind quality control samples which constitute 3% of the total number of specimens submitted to the laboratory for analysis, not to exceed 100 per quarter; 80% of these samples are negative for drugs.

Donna M. Bush

10.2.1.4 Laboratory Participation in the National Laboratory Certification Program (NLCP)

10.2.1.4.1 Application

A laboratory applying to become part of the NLCP must complete a comprehensive application form which reflects in detail each section of the Laboratory Inspection Checklist. Evaluation of this completed application must show that the laboratory is equipped and staffed in a manner to test specimens in compliance with the Guidelines requirements in order for the laboratory to proceed with the initial certification process.

In essence, the Guidelines promulgate forensic drug testing standards for the evaluation of a single specimen provided by a Federal employee, on which critical employment decisions will be made. The processes that govern this testing are regulatory in nature, to ensure that this testing is accurate, reliable and forensically supportable.

10.2.1.4.2 Proficiency Testing

As part of the initial certification process, the applicant laboratory must successfully analyze three sets of 20 samples, in a sequential order. The progress of this phase of the certification process is determined by the successful identification and quantification of analytes by the laboratory. If the first two sets of 20 samples are successfully completed, the third set of 20 samples is scheduled for receipt, accessioning and analysis during the initial laboratory inspection site visit. As part of the maintenance certification process, each certified laboratory must successfully analyze a set of 15 samples sent on a quarterly basis by the NLCP. There are four different types of samples that comprise the battery of samples developed by the NLCP to ensure accurate and reliable analyte identification and quantification. These are: (1) routine samples, which may contain an analyte specified in the Guidelines, and are screened and confirmed in accordance with established cut-offs; (2) routine samples which may contain an analyte specified in the Guidelines and interfering and/or cross-reacting substances; examples of these interfering substances include, but are not limited to, pseudoephedrine, phenylpropanolamine, oxycodone, or other compound commonly seen in urine as a result of legitimate drug use and which may pose an analytical challenge to the laboratories; (3) routine retest samples, and (4) retest samples with interfering substances.

For details on the evaluation of the performance test results, please refer directly to Section 3.19 of the June 9, 1994 Guidelines.[3]

10.2.1.4.3 Laboratory Inspection

The laboratory facility must be inspected and found acceptable in accordance with the conditions stated in the Guidelines and further detailed in the Laboratory Inspection Checklist. Inspectors are trained by the NLCP staff (DHHS technical staff and their contractors) in the use of the detailed NLCP Laboratory Inspection Checklist (80+ pages), and the NLCP Guidance Document for Laboratories and Inspectors.

Prior to the inspection, the laboratory is required to submit certain information concerning its operation. The laboratory completes several sections of the Inspection Checklist which are devoted to gathering this information. This information is then provided to the inspectors conducting that particular inspection for their review prior to the actual inspection. In this way, the inspectors become familiar with the laboratory operation prior to their arrival at the laboratory. A brief description of each section completed by the laboratory follows:

A. Instructions for Inspectors
B. Laboratory Information — physical aspects of the laboratory such as location, hours of operation, staffing, specimen testing throughput, and licenses

C. Standard Operating Procedures (SOP) — index of the SOP, outline of the intralaboratory chain of custody procedures, and overview of the quality control used for laboratory processes

D. Laboratory Test Procedures — type of analytical equipment, calibration procedures, reagent kits, derivatives and ions monitored for each drug analyte

Each inspector must review and document all aspects of forensic urine drug testing processes and procedures at that laboratory for program review and evaluation for compliance with the minimum standards of the Guidelines. The inspectors individually and independently complete eleven sections of the checklist during their site visit. A brief description of each section follows:

E. Standard Operating Procedures, Procedures Manual — assesses manual for content, comprehensiveness, agreement with day-to-day observed operations of the laboratory, determines availability to staff as a routine reference and any modifications made to reflect changes in current practice in the laboratory.

F. Chain of Custody, Accessioning, and Security — assesses laboratory practices to verify specimen identity, maintain specimen integrity, secure specimens, and maintain chain of custody; assesses whether laboratory procedures and documentation are adequate and comprehensive.

G. Records Audit — assesses laboratory records, including raw analytical data, test results, proficiency testing, quality control procedures for sufficiency in legal proceedings.

H. Personnel — assesses qualifications of the Responsible Person, scientists who certify the accuracy and reliability of results, and supervisory staff; assesses staffing adequacy of these personnel in relationship to the number of specimens analyzed.

I. Reagents — assesses laboratory methods for verification of new reagents, associated documentation, replacing outdated reagents, and labeling new reagents with key information.

J. Quality Control and Standards — assesses the use of reference materials, calibrators, standards, controls, and open and blind QC samples; assesses whether supervision of QC is adequate (i.e., active review and documentation of QC data to detect and correct deficiencies).

K. Reporting — assesses the written protocols and actual practices of the laboratory for reporting test results.

L. Equipment and Maintenance — assesses procedures for using, checking and maintaining all laboratory equipment.

M. Immunoassay — assesses the laboratory's procedures for specific immunoassay methods and quality control of those methods.

N. Gas Chromatography/Mass Spectrometry — assesses the laboratory's procedures for GC/MS analysis and quality control of those methods.

The laboratory's first (initial) inspection is performed by two DHHS-trained inspectors. Prior to their arrival at the laboratory site, the inspectors are provided copies of the information supplied by the laboratory (Sections B through D of the Checklist) concerning its operations, its standard operating procedures, and its testing procedures.

The inspectors independently complete Sections E through N of the Checklist and submit the completed documents to the NLCP contractor immediately after completion of the inspection. A summary, or critique, is prepared from the individual reports by an individual independent of that laboratory's inspection. The items in the critique are then evaluated for compliance with the minimum requirements of the Guidelines. It is necessary that a laboratory's operation be consistent with good forensic laboratory practice. Once all requirements are met, the laboratory is certified by the Secretary, DHHS as being able to perform drug testing of Federal employees' specimens in compliance with the Guidelines. A letter is sent to the laboratory conveying its certification in the NLCP.

Three months after its initial certification, the laboratory is again inspected, with a particular focus on results reported by the laboratory. One common element in all inspections is that each inspector submits the completed checklist to the NLCP contractor immediately after completion of the inspection. A critique of the individually prepared reports is developed by an individual independent of that laboratory's inspection. The issues in the critique are then evaluated for compliance with the minimum requirements of the Guidelines. It is necessary that a laboratory's operation be consistent with good forensic laboratory practice. If all requirements are met, or there are minor, easily correctable deficiencies, the inspection critique is sent to the laboratory. A cover letter may also be included which outlines issues that must be addressed within a defined time frame. After successful completion of this inspection, a 6-month cycle of site inspections begins. The number of inspectors dispatched to the laboratory for an inspection depends on the resources necessary to adequately evaluate the laboratory's operation. During this "certification maintenance" phase, if all requirements are met, or there are minor, easily correctable deficiencies, the inspection critique is sent to the laboratory. A cover letter may also be included which outlines issues that must be addressed within a defined time frame.

A laboratory continues its certified status as long as its operation is in compliance with the Guidelines and consistent with good forensic laboratory practice. Since participation in the NLCP is a business decision on the part of a laboratory and is voluntary, a laboratory may choose to withdraw from the NLCP. Upon such voluntary withdrawal from the NLCP, a laboratory must inform its clients that it is no longer certified in the NLCP and cease to advertise itself as an NLCP certified laboratory.

10.2.1.4.4 Suspension of Certification

If significant deficiencies in the laboratory's procedures are found, an evaluation of these deficiencies is performed by the DHHS NLCP Program staff in the Division of Workplace Programs and the Office of the General Counsel. A report is prepared for the Director, Division of Workplace Programs. If it is determined that there is imminent harm to the government and its employees, action may be taken by the Secretary to immediately suspend the laboratory's certification to perform drug testing of Federal, federally regulated, and private sector specimens tested in accordance with the Guidelines. The period and terms of suspension depend upon the facts and circumstances of the suspension and the need to ensure accurate and reliable drug testing of Federal employees.

10.2.1.4.5 Revocation of Certification

Several factors may be considered by the Secretary in determining whether revocation is necessary. Among these are: (1) unsatisfactory performance of employee drug testing, (2) unsatisfactory results of performance testing and/or laboratory inspections, (3) Federal drug testing contract violations, (4) conviction for any criminal offense committed incident to operation of the laboratory, and (5) other causes which affect the accuracy and reliability of drug test results from that laboratory.

10.2.1.5 Review of Laboratory Results by a Medical Review Officer (MRO)

After accurate and reliable urine drug test results are obtained by a DHHS certified laboratory, the Guidelines require these results to be reported to an agency's MRO. As defined in the Guidelines, the MRO is a licensed physician responsible for receiving laboratory results generated by an agency's drug testing program who has knowledge of substance abuse disorders and has appropriate medical training to interpret and evaluate an individual's positive test result together with the medical records provided to the MRO by the donor, his or her medical history and any other relevant biomedical information. The MRO must give the donor the opportunity to discuss the results prior to making a final decision to verify a positive test.

A positive test result does not automatically identify an individual as an illegal drug user! The MRO evaluates all relevant medical information provided to him/her by the donor who tested positive. Based on this evaluation, the MRO reports the drug test result to the agency/employer. If there was an alternative medical explanation for the presence of the drug(s) in the donor's urine, the test result is reported as "negative" to the employer; if there is no alternative medical explanation for the presence of drug(s) in the donor's urine, the MRO reports the result as "positive" to the agency/employer.

It is also necessary that negative laboratory results be reviewed by a MRO. Laboratory results for double blind performance test samples (many of which are negative) are reported to the MRO in the same manner as results for donor specimens. In this manner, negative laboratory results are evaluated as part of on-going quality control programs initiated prior to specimen submission to the laboratory.

10.2.1.6 Conclusion

Illicit drug use and abuse continues to impact safety and security in the American workplace today. Data from the 1995 National Household Survey on Drug Abuse released in March of 1997, reveal that there were 12.8 million current (or past month) users of illicit drugs in 1995. There are no differences between these figures and those for 1994.[5]

Tragic events that occur serve as examples of how drug abuse in the workplace can affect society and cause long-term environmental and economic consequences. Examples of such tragedies where substance abuse in the workplace was responsible for death and destruction include the 1986 Amtrak-Conrail railroad accident in Chase, Maryland, the 1991 subway accident in New York City, and the 1989 environmental disaster in Prince William Sound, Alaska, caused by the grounding of the Exxon Valdez oil tanker.

REFERENCES

1. Executive Order 12564, "Drug-Free Federal Workplace", *Federal Register*, Vol. 51, Number 180, pp. 32889-32893, September 15, 1986.
2. "Mandatory Guidelines for Federal Workplace Drug-Testing Programs", *Federal Register*, Vol. 53, Number 69, pp. 11970-11989, April 11, 1988.
3. "Mandatory Guidelines for Federal Workplace Drug-Testing Programs", *Federal Register*, Vol. 59, Number 110, pp. 29908-29931, June 9, 1994.
4. *Urine Specimen Collection Handbook for Federal Workplace Drug Testing Programs*, CSAP Technical Report 12, Division of Workplace Programs, Center for Substance Abuse Prevention, Substance Abuse and Mental Health Services Administration, U.S. Department of Health and Human Services, DHHS Publication Number (SMA)96-3114, 1996.
5. "National Household Survey on Drug Abuse: Main Findings 1995", Office of Applied Studies, Substance Abuse and Mental Health Services Administration, DHHS Publication Number (SMA)97-3127, 1997.

Copies of the materials referenced above may be obtained by calling the National Clearinghouse for Drug and Alcohol Information at 1-800-SAY-NOTO(DRUGS) or by visiting the World Wide Web Internet Connections at http:\\www.samhsa.gov or http:\\www.health.org.

Donna M. Bush

10.2.2 THE COLLEGE OF AMERICAN PATHOLOGISTS VOLUNTARY LABORATORY ACCREDITATION PROGRAM

JOHN BAENZIGER, M.D.

DIRECTOR, CHEMICAL PATHOLOGY, DEPARTMENT OF PATHOLOGY AND LABORATORY MEDICINE, INDIANA UNIVERSITY SCHOOL OF MEDICINE, INDIANAPOLIS, INDIANA

10.2.2.1 History

The College of American Pathologists Laboratory Accreditation Programs (CAP LAP) began in the 1960s as an extension of proficiency testing programs to further encourage improvement in clinical laboratory practices and performance. The CAP's Laboratory Accreditation Programs have grown steadily over the past three decades and now are responsible for the accreditation of over 5000 laboratories in four accreditation programs. These accreditation programs include the general Laboratory Accreditation Program (LAP) which accredits clinical laboratories as defined by the Clinical Laboratory Improvement Act of 1988, and the special accreditation programs of Forensic Urine Drug Testing, Athletic Drug Testing, and Reproductive Biology.

The Forensic Urine Drug Testing (FUDT) Accreditation Program was created as a separate accreditation program in the mid-1980s along a somewhat parallel course to the National Institute on Drug Abuse (NIDA or SAMHSA) federal program, but was directed primarily to workplace drug testing performed by non-federal employers. The FUDT program was created through the efforts of the CAP's Toxicology Resource Committee under the leadership of its Chairman, the late Thorne Butler, MD. The development of a separate accreditation program for Athletic Drug Testing occurred during the early 1990s and follows similar philosophies and guidelines as the FUDT Program but emphasizes the detection of drugs that have athletic performance enhancement effects.

10.2.2.2 Program Components

10.2.2.2.1 Philosophy

The underlying philosophy of the CAP's accreditation programs is that of laboratory improvement. This focus on laboratory improvement is linked to the philosophy of "peer" review performed through on-site laboratory inspections and the use of proficiency testing as an integral part of the accreditation process. The CAP's FUDT Program reflects this same underlying philosophy despite its somewhat more regulatory nature. This accreditation philosophy is defined in the CAP's Laboratory Accreditation Program's Standards for Accreditation. These Standards are then interpreted by the use of Inspection Checklists and the required participation in Proficiency Testing Surveys. CAP Resource Committees, which are made up of acknowledged experts in the field, are used to oversee the scientific validity of the accreditation requirements and the proficiency testing programs. This integrated system allows the Laboratory Accreditation Program to constantly respond to changes in "standards of practice" in a scientifically valid fashion.

The overall accreditation process is the responsibility of the CAP's Commission on Laboratory Accreditation, which is composed of volunteer pathologists or clinical scientists (Commissioners) who represent fifteen geographic regions, three special accreditation programs (FUDT, ADT, and Reproductive Biology), special commission functions (Checklists, Education, Governmental, Publications, etc.), and the Chairman. This Commission is responsible to the CAP's Council on Scientific Affairs, then to the Board of Governors, and ultimately to the membership of the College.

10.2.2.2.2 Standards for Accreditation

The FUDT Standards for Accreditation are closely related to the CAP's general LAP Standards which focus on the scientific principles of "good laboratory practices". However, since the FUDT program involves analytical services which have forensic or legal implications, the FUDT Standards also focus on the forensic principles of this laboratory practice.

Preamble

The Preamble to the Standards summarizes the intent of the FUDT Accreditation Program and stresses the importance of the forensic nature of drug testing in the workplace. The Preamble also notes the importance of drug testing as " a critical component of efforts to combat drug abuse in our society ..."[1] and that laboratories "should attempt to prevent misuse of their services for purposes that do not help combat drug abuse ...".[1] The FUDT Program also supports the position that pre-employment drug testing should be considered in the same forensic fashion as post-employment drug testing.

Standard I: Scientific Director

"The laboratory scientific director shall be qualified to assume professional, scientific, consultative, organizational, educational, and administrative responsibilities for the laboratory. The director shall have sufficient authority to implement and maintain the Standards."[1]

This first Standard and its Interpretation defines the qualifications and responsibilities of the FUDT Laboratory's Scientific Director. Based on the CAP's Laboratory Accreditation Programs laboratory improvement and peer review philosophy, the abilities of the Director to appropriately direct the operations of an FUDT Laboratory from both scientific and administrative standpoints are critical for accreditation. The Scientific Director must have scientific qualifications at least equivalent to those required for clinical laboratory directors as defined by CLIA '88[2] (new FUDT requirement as of 1996) plus have documented experience in analytical toxicology and its forensic applications. These requirements can be met through certification by the American Board of Forensic Toxicology or Toxicologic Chemistry certification by the American Board of Clinical Chemistry. Alternative qualifications include a doctorate degree in a biological or chemical discipline plus two years experience in analytical toxicology or a MD degree with certification in clinical and/or forensic pathology plus two years experience in analytical toxicology.

In addition to the education and experience requirements of the Scientific Director, Standard I defines the specific laboratory responsibilities of the Scientific Director to ensure that the FUDT laboratory complies with the other Standards for Accreditation. Specifically these responsibilities include the ability to provide appropriate scientific and forensic interpretations and information concerning the FUDT's services to clients, accrediting bodies, legal and administrative officials. The Scientific Director is responsible for defining, implementing, and monitoring all laboratory analytical procedures and protocols to ensure that they meet accreditation requirements and the needs of clients. These procedures must also include a Quality Improvement Program or Plan that continuously monitors critical performance parameters of the FUDT Laboratory and which strives to improve this performance. The Scientific Director must also ensure that adequate and appropriately qualified and trained staff are available to perform the required testing in the FUDT laboratory. The Scientific Director must be an integral part in the administrative and management operations of the FUDT Laboratory to ensure that adequate resources (space, personnel, materials, equipment, etc.) are made available for the laboratory to provide its services. Finally, the Scientific Director is responsible for the laboratory environment in which persons work. This includes ensuring that the laboratory follows all appropriate safety rules, and that the laboratory staff is able to participate in continuing educational activities related to their work. All of these responsibilities do not need to be personally performed by the Scientific Director (i.e., may delegate responsibilities to other appropriate persons); however, the final responsibility still rests with the Director.

Standard II: Resources and Facilities

"The laboratory shall have sufficient and appropriate space, equipment, facilities, and supplies for the performance of the required volume of work with accuracy, precision, efficiency, and safety. In addition, the laboratory shall have effective methods for communication to ensure prompt and reliable reporting. There shall be appropriate record storage and retrieval."[1]

The second Standard for Accreditation in the FUDT Program along with its Interpretation defines the physical requirements of a laboratory performing forensic urine drug testing. Once the laboratory or institution defines for itself the scope of its services, it must then make available to its staff and Scientific Director the appropriate resources to provide this level of service. Of primary importance is that there be sufficient space, equipment, and supplies to permit the staff to follow the defined analytical procedures and obtain results that are reliable. In addition, the laboratory facility must be a safe environment in which to work. Finally, due to the forensic nature of the analytical testing performed by an FUDT laboratory, this laboratory must be made secure to the extent that only authorized personnel have access to the facility, its specimens, and records.

Standard III: Quality Assurance and Quality Control

"There shall be an ongoing quality assurance program designed to monitor and evaluate objectively and systematically the quality and appropriateness of services, to pursue opportunities to improve services, and to identify and resolve problems. Each laboratory shall have a quality control system that demonstrates the reliability, medical, and forensic usefulness of laboratory data."[1]

Standard III and its Interpretation covers the essentials of the scientific and forensic requirements for the performance of forensic urine drug testing. This Standard defines in broad terms the requirements for specimen handling, specimen chain of custody, analytical procedures and instrument operation, reporting of results, record maintenance, quality control, proficiency testing, and quality improvement. The specific requirements for accreditation based on this Standard are extensively evaluated in the FUDT Inspection Checklist questions discussed in detail below. The requirements of this Standard are defined by the "standard of practice" for forensic urine drug testing and are under constant review and revision by the CAP's Toxicology Resource Committee.

Standard IV: Inspection Requirements

"All laboratories accredited in this program shall undergo periodic inspections and evaluations as determined by the Commission on Laboratory Accreditation of the College of American Pathologists."[1]

The inspection requirements for the FUDT Program are annual on-site inspections performed by a CAP assigned team with a self-inspection performed by the laboratory six months after each on-site inspection. The FUDT Accreditation Program recruits volunteer inspectors from persons who are actively involved in forensic toxicology and thus are "peers" of the FUDT Laboratory. These volunteer inspectors are an important part of the FUDT Accreditation process. Their role is to facilitate the CAP's accreditation philosophy of laboratory improvement and peer review by conducting an objective inspection and documenting any deficiencies observed, while encouraging the exchange of ideas and information between the inspectors and the laboratory that could aid in laboratory improvement. Deficiency citations by the inspection team are based on the use of the FUDT Inspection Checklist and if these deficiencies are of a significant nature, then the laboratory must document the correction of the deficiencies before accreditation is granted.

10.2.2.3 FUDT Application and Checklist

The FUDT Application and Checklist are the primary tools used by the Accreditation Program to objectively evaluate laboratories and interpret the Standards for Accreditation. The FUDT Application details the extent of services provided by a forensic urine drug testing laboratory and provides detailed information about the qualifications of the Scientific Director and personnel, the laboratory's facilities, and the analytical and forensic procedures used by the laboratory. The Checklist contains questions that help the Inspection Team evaluate a laboratory's general practices (common to both clinical and forensic laboratories) as well as specific questions regarding its forensic practices. The Checklist is organized by sections that encompass all aspects of the laboratory's operation and addresses the adequacy of both the written procedures for laboratory operations as well the documentation maintained by the laboratory that ensures that these procedures are being routinely followed.

10.2.2.3.1 Extent of Services Provided

A laboratory must define the extent of the forensic urine drug testing services it provides its clients that will be inspected under the FUDT Accreditation Program. At a minimum, a laboratory must perform screening and confirmation testing for amphetamine, methamphetamine, codeine, morphine, benzolyecgonine, and carboxy-tetrahydrocannabinol to be eligible for accreditation. This screening and confirmation testing must be performed on-site, it must use quantitative cutoff levels of the analyte to determine negative/positive results, and confirmation testing must be performed using GC/MS techniques. Additional drugs may be tested for under this accreditation program; however, the laboratory must again use quantitative cutoff levels for reporting results (new requirement as of 1997), and confirmation testing must be by GC/MS or by an analytically different method which is scientifically and forensically defensible. Unlike the SAMHSA (NIDA) Program which acts as both client and accrediting body and which defines for laboratories the quantitative cutoff levels that are to be used for reporting results, the CAP FUDT Program leaves these determinations up to the laboratory or its clients. The requirement for the use of quantitative cutoff levels for reporting urine drug testing results is considered important for the purposes of interpreting these results in relationship to the intent of a client's workplace drug testing program.

10.2.2.3.2 Proficiency Testing

Participation and adequate performance in the CAP/AACC's Forensic Urine Drug Testing Proficiency Testing Survey (UDC) is a requirement for initial and ongoing accreditation. The laboratory must have a documented procedure for how proficiency testing samples are incorporated into its routine specimen workload, so that these samples are treated in the same manner as other client samples. The laboratory must document that the results of Proficiency Testing are actively evaluated and if corrective actions are required that this process is reviewed by the Scientific Director.

10.2.2.3.3 Quality Control

The Quality Control section of the Checklist is divided into multiple subsections including questions covering requirements for the laboratory's procedure manuals which must detail the standard operating procedures (SOP's) for specimen handling, use of quality control materials, review of analytical results, reporting of results, and record maintenance. Additional subsections cover reagent, standard/calibrator, and control systems and their validation before use in analyses. Questions concerning requirements for the operation and maintenance of general laboratory instruments and equipment are also found in this Checklist section.

Quality Control: Specific requirements for quality control of urine drug screen and confirmation analyses include the use of negative and cutoff controls (approximately 125% of the cutoff). The purpose of the cutoff control is to ensure that the screening and confirmation assays have sufficient precision and accuracy to reliably separate positive from negative specimens on an ongoing basis. An additional positive control is required for quantitative (confirmation) assays. It is recommended that this control be at 75% of the cutoff or at the LOQ when performing directed retests of positive specimens. Internal single blind controls are required in each screening batch analysis and these blind controls must be evaluated for their acceptance before the batch is released. Sufficient positive blind challenges should be included in the laboratory's Blind QC Program that adequately challenge all drug analytes being tested (20 to 25% positives is recommended). The entire quality control system must be under active review by laboratory personnel. This review must be documented and include daily review of QC failures, weekly review of serial QC data for detection of trends, and at least monthly review of the quality control system by the Scientific Director. Documentation of the corrective actions taken by the laboratory when QC failures have occurred must be maintained by the laboratory.

Specimen Handling: Questions on specimen handling include the detailed evaluation of the FUDT laboratory's chain of custody procedures for specimens and aliquots. The FUDT Program requires that the original specimens received by the laboratory be either under the direct control of authorized laboratory personnel or in a limited access or locked area (refrigerator, freezer, room, etc.) from their receipt until they are discarded. All changes in custody must be documented and the reason for the change recorded. Custody of aliquots derived from the original specimens must also be documented to record each change in custody between persons and/or storage sites. These chain of custody records must be organized in such a fashion by the laboratory to provide printed documentation that shows the location/custody of any sample (and its aliquots) at all time throughout the sample's presence in the laboratory. An example of this documentation is required to be included with the "litigation" packet for a THC positive specimen which must be submitted with the accreditation application.

Review of Results: Analytical results in the FUDT laboratory must be reviewed by at least two persons prior to their release to clients. Initial review of batch analysis results should be performed by the analyst, and a second "certifying" review must be performed by a certifying scientist. This two part review process must include not only the analytical batch data but also the chain of custody documents and the final report to ensure result accuracy. SOP's are required to describe this review process and the laboratory must maintain documentation of its performance for each batch analysis.

Reporting: The laboratory must have written SOP's that detail what information is required to be present in urine drug test reports and how these reports are to be released to clients. It is required that the report include the date of specimen collection, date of receipt by the laboratory, date of the report, and specimen identification information. The reporting of results should include the cutoff limits used by the laboratory for screening, and if positive results are reported, the cutoff limits used for confirmation. The FUDT Accreditation Program does not require the signing of these reports by laboratory personnel; however, it does require review of the information present on this final report be documented as part of the certifying review process. Electronic reporting of results is permissible under the FUDT Program; however, the laboratory must ensure confidentiality of this process by allowing only authorized laboratory personnel to report results and allowing only authorized client representatives to receive results. This same requirement applies to verbal reporting and the availability of results from a computer information system.

Records: The FUDT Program requires that all records related to the analysis of specimens be maintained for at least two years. The specific records that must be maintained include administrative records (accreditation, personnel, lab policies, safety), technical records (analytical SOP's and method performance data, reagent/standard/control validation records, quality control records, batch analytical data, instrument maintenance records, and final reports), and legal records (chain of custody documents, laboratory security/access records).

10.2.2.3.4 Analytical Procedures and Test Systems

This section of the Checklist evaluates the SOP's for the screening and confirmation analyses. Questions on Method Performance are the same as those found in the general CAP LAP Checklists, and evaluate whether the laboratory has documented evidence of its evaluation of each method's accuracy, precision, linearity, sensitivity (LOD, LOQ), carryover potential, and specificity (interference studies). These analytical parameters must be determined empirically and the laboratory must make this information available to its clients upon request.

Each analytical procedure must be written in compliance with the NCCLS GP2-A3 (1996)[5] guidelines for procedure manuals and must include specific instructions for the performance of the analyses. The specific procedural components required are: method principle, procedural steps, reagent preparation, calibration, quality control, derivation of results, linearity of method, pharmacologic information, and references. Optimally each analytical SOP should also include the method's performance characteristics. These SOP's should include specific instructions concerning what actions are to be taken by the analyst when results exceed linear limits, carryover is detected, or there is failure of quality control. SOP's for instrument or analytical systems (Immunoanalyzers, TLC, HPLC, GC, MS) routine operation and maintenance are required. These procedures should include details on how each analytical system is to be monitored and maintained and should include defined tolerance limits (when applicable) for optimal performance and the actions that are to be taken when these limits are exceeded.

10.2.2.3.5 Inspection of Analytical Records

The Inspection Team is required to review a selected mixture of the laboratory's analytical records for each drug being tested by the laboratory since the last on-site inspection. Typically this consists of the review of at least 20 positive batch results. The inspectors review these records to determine if the laboratory is routinely following its SOP's and to evaluate the quality of the analytical testing. Review of the selected analytical batches also includes evaluation of the chain of custody documentation associated with these specimens and the final reports.

10.2.2.3.6 Personnel

The FUDT Accreditation Program requires that all personnel in the laboratory meet the requirements of moderate or high-complexity testing as defined by CLIA '88. The laboratory must maintain documentation of personnel qualifications and specifically document the training process for the specific tasks that each person performs in the laboratory. Personnel records must also contain evidence of annual competency or performance evaluation, accident and injury reports, health records (specifically for hepatitis vaccination status), and documentation of continuing education.

10.2.2.3.7 Computer Operations

Beginning in 1997, the FUDT Program will use the Laboratory General Checklist[1] to evaluate the computer system(s) used by the forensic urine drug testing laboratory on a two year inspection cycle. Similar to other laboratory operations, there must be documented procedures for the use of computer systems as part of the FUDT laboratory's operations. Specifically these procedures should include details on how information is to be entered, how changes in this information are made and documented, and how the system maintains security and integrity of the stored information. The computer system should be located in a secure or limited access area, and access to the forensic urine drug testing data must be limited to only authorized personnel. The laboratory must ensure that the software and hardware components of the computer system are reliable and that if changes/updates are made to either component that these changes do not effect this reliability. The Scientific Director should approve all changes in the computer system's operational characteristics and specifically changes that effect the entry, storage, and reporting of analytical results.

10.2.2.3.8 Physical Facilities

This Checklist section reflects the requirements of Standard II. The Inspection Team must review the physical condition of the laboratory to ensure that there is adequate space for the laboratory to provide its services and that this space is being maintained in an appropriate fashion. Beginning in 1997 the Laboratory General Checklist[1] will be used on a 2-year inspection cycle to formally inspect the laboratory for compliance with the requirements of Standard II.

10.2.2.3.9 Laboratory Safety

Compliance with the requirements of Standard II is specifically evaluated by the Inspection Team using the Laboratory General Checklist[1] which includes extensive questions on laboratory safety. Inspection of laboratory safety will be performed on a 2-year inspection cycle beginning in 1997; however, the Inspection Team may cite safety violations that are noted during the annual on-site inspection. The requirements for laboratory safety under the FUDT Program are determined primarily from the requirements for all workplaces under OSHA, plus they include specific requirements related to the biological, chemical, electrical, radioactive, and fire hazards that are associated with laboratories.

10.2.2.4 FUDT Proficiency Testing

Accreditation in the CAP's FUDT Program requires that laboratories participate in the CAP/AACC FUDT Proficiency Testing Program (UDC Survey). The UDC Survey is designed by the CAP's Toxicology Resource Committee to test the on-going performance capabilities of forensic urine drug laboratories through the use of quarterly challenges of 10 urine specimens. Minimal acceptable performance for accreditation is the achievement of a score of 80% on each survey. Scoring is determined through the assignment of points for each drug challenge in the survey and a laboratory's ability to correctly identify and quantitate the presence of drugs. A false positive report for a drug that is not present in the challenge results in automatic survey failure. All survey failures result in a laboratory's being placed in accreditation "probation" status, and requires that a laboratory submit documentation of its evaluation of the reason for the survey failure for review by the Toxicology Commissioner. Continued failures to maintain acceptable performance on proficiency testing can result in revocation or loss of accreditation.

10.2.2.5 Toxicology Resource Committee

The CAP's Toxicology Resource Committee is responsible for providing oversight and advice to the CAP's Laboratory Accreditation and Proficiency Testing Programs. This committee, composed of pathologists and scientists with expertise in toxicology, is responsible for the review and updating of the Toxicology, Forensic Urine Drug Testing, and Athletic Drug Testing Checklists. This review is an on-going process with Checklist updates occurring potentially every 6 months. All changes in Checklists recommended by the Toxicology

Resource Committee are then reviewed prior to being implemented by the Toxicology and Checklist Commissioners and then by the entire Commission for Laboratory Accreditation.

10.2.2.6 Commission on Laboratory Accreditation

The entire FUDT Accreditation Program described in detail above is under the direct responsibility of the Commission on Laboratory Accreditation (CLA). As was mentioned previously, this body is composed of pathologists or scientists who either represent geographical areas for the general Laboratory Accreditation Program or special accreditation programs. The Commission has documented policies and procedures that define all aspects of its accreditation programs and their operation.[4] Specifically, these include policies concerning laboratory accreditation eligibility and operational policies for resolving accreditation issues. Although the FUDT and the other CAP Accreditation Programs rely heavily on the use of the Standards for Accreditation and their evaluation by Inspection Teams using Checklists, the final determination of laboratory accreditation rests with the Commission. The Toxicology Commissioner and Deputy Commissioner are responsible for reviewing the accreditation packet (includes the laboratory's application, Inspection Summation Report, Proficiency Testing Survey results, and any corrective action documentation required to correct inspection deficiencies) for each laboratory and makes recommendations to the Commission for accreditation/reaccreditation, probation, suspension, revocation of accreditation, or denial of accreditation.

Accreditation under the CAP FUDT Program is a continuous process in which once it is granted a laboratory remains in this accredited status unless accreditation is revoked or not renewed. The FUDT Program does use two accreditation status modifiers, probation and suspension, to administratively warn laboratories of potential problems that could jeopardize their accreditation. A laboratory being placed in "probation status" can result from either inspection deficiencies of a serious nature or from proficiency testing survey failures. The laboratory must respond rapidly to correct these deficiencies or problems. If the laboratory does not appropriately correct these problems or if it is found that the laboratory is in significant non-compliance with the Standards for Accreditation, the laboratory can be placed in "suspension status". Suspension status requires the laboratory to notify its clients that it is not currently performing forensic urine drug testing services in a manner that meets the requirements of the CAP's FUDT Accreditation Program. If a laboratory fails to correct problems promptly under "suspension status", then accreditation can be revoked. In order to resolve accreditation problems, an appeal process is defined by the Commission's polices and includes a formal review of a laboratory's accreditation history by the Commission and if required a subsequent review by the CAP's Board of Governors, the elected and governing officials of the CAP organization.

REFERENCES

1. "Forensic Urine Drug Testing Standards for Accreditation", College of American Pathologists, Northfield, Illinois, 1996.
2. Department of Health and Human Services, Health Care Financing Administration. Clinical Laboratory Improvement Amendments of 1988; Final Rule. Federal Register 1992 (Feb. 28).
3. "Forensic Urine Drug Testing Checklist (50)", College of American Pathologists, Northfield, Illinois, 1996.
4. "Commission on Laboratory Accreditation: Policies and Procedures Manual", College of American Pathologists, Northfield, Illinois, 1996.
5. "Clinical Laboratory Technical Procedure Manuals", NCCLS, 16(15) GP2-A3, 1996.

10.3 ANALYTICAL CONSIDERATIONS AND APPROACHES FOR DRUGS

MICHAEL PEAT, PH.D. AND ALAN E. DAVIS

LAB*ONE*, KANSAS CITY, KANSAS

Although recent national surveys have reported declines in overall drug use, more than 11 million Americans still reported using one or more illicit drug in 1992.[1] In addition, results from several studies targeting specific populations, particularly students in high school and college, show that this downward trend has started to reverse itself.[2,3] In response to the numerous reports on the incidence of alcohol and drug abuse in the workplace,[1,4,5] many employers have introduced substance abuse programs, one component of which is urine drug testing.

Workplace urine drug testing is now performed by many laboratories; however, there are several very important differences between this type of testing and the laboratory testing performed for medical reasons:

- The test is not performed on a patient; instead, a specimen is collected from a donor.
- The test result is not used to support a diagnosis; it is a single collection that is used in decisions relating to hiring, suspension from employment, referral to employee assistance programs (EAP), and, occasionally, dismissal of the employee. Unlike a true clinical test, it has no medical data to support its veracity and, except in rare circumstances, the collection cannot be repeated.
- For regulated industries in which drug testing is required, the laboratory has to be certified by the Department of Health and Human Services (6,7). This certification from the Substance Abuse and Mental Health Services Administration (SAMHSA, formerly the National Institute on Drug Abuse) has become the "standard of care" for all drug testing, including that performed for the non-regulated industry. This certification mandates that the laboratory uses certain analytical procedures, including gas chromatography mass spectrometry (GCMS), for confirming immunoassay results, and that it follows rigid chain of custody, quality assurance, and data review guidelines.
- The result may be used in a legal environment to support disciplinary action.

This chapter will outline the analytical protocols used in such programs. However, it should be noted that the laboratory environment in which these tests are performed has evolved over the last five years. Traditionally clinical toxicology has been performed as an adjunct to clinical (or special) chemistry laboratories. However, because of the strict chain of custody and security requirements, drug testing laboratories have become "stand-alone" laboratories, either secured separately from other specialties in larger laboratories or as distinct entities. More recently, there have been other changes, particularly the trend to "mega-laboratories." These are single locations dedicated to workplace drug testing, processing thousands of specimens per shift. Both service expectations and the economics of drug testing have caused the evolution of such facilities. Today's expectations are that negative results will be available within 24 h of collection of the specimen, and that positives will be available within another 24 h. Obviously these expectations, together with the desire to decrease costs, will play an increasing part in the choice of the analytical procedures used. Increasing emphasis is being placed on the ease of automation of such procedures.

Table 10.3.1 Immunoassay Cut-Offs (ng/mL)

Drug group	Target antigen	Cut-off
Amphetamines	d-Amphetamine, d-methamphetamine or both	300 or 1000*
Barbiturates	Secobarbital	200 or 300
Benzodiazepines	Oxazepam or nordiazepam	100, 200 or 300
Cannabinoids	THCA**	20, 25, 50* or 100
Cocaine	Benzoylecgonine	150 or 300*
Methadone	d-Methadone or d,l-methadone	100 or 300
Methaqualone	Methaqualone	300
Opiates	Morphine	300*
Phencyclidine (PCP)	PCP	25* or 75
Propoxyphene	d-Propoxyphene	300

cut-offs used in the SAMHSA Guidelines and the regulated programs
**11-Nor-delta-9-tetrahydrocannabinol-9-carboxylic acid*

10.3.1 GENERAL CONSIDERATIONS

In today's world there are numerous procedures available for the initial immunoassay testing of urine specimens and an endless variety of GC/MS methods for confirming the initial testing results. It is, of course, now widely accepted that a combination of such procedures is necessary for the reporting of a positive result. There is also a need for these immunoassays and GC/MS procedures to be appropriately quality controlled; however, this chapter will not cover that particular topic. However, as the laboratories have evolved, so have the quality control programs and in today's "mega-laboratories," statistical process control should be the standard, not traditional quality control.

Very early in the evolution of workplace drug testing it was decided, after considerable debate, that there was need for assay cut-offs to insure some standardization and equality amongst the various programs. The commonly used cut-offs for immunoassay are shown in Table 10.3.1 and those for GC/MS in Table 10.3.2

Some comments on Table 10.3.2 are in order:

1. Amphetamine GC/MS assays can be easily modified to determine MDMA and MDA. Additionally, GC/MS procedures are available to separate the stereoisomers of methamphetamine.
2. Many laboratories include butabarbital in their GC/MS procedure, however, this drug is rarely, if ever, detected in the USA.
3. A number of laboratories in the USA do not commonly include alpha-hydroxyalprazolam or temazepam in their procedures, however given the widespread use of Xanax® and Restoril®, this is an oversight. A number of the widely used GC/MS procedures can be adapted to also determine metabolites of clonazepam, flunitrazepam, flurazepam, nitrazepam and triazolam. However, to effectively confirm some of the lower dose benzodiazepines, it is necessary to lower the confirmation cut-off.
4. Opiate GC/MS assays can be modified to include hydrocodone and hydromorphone. Some laboratories also include oxycodone in this modified assay, but this is of little value given the low cross-reactivities (8) of the various immunoassays to this

Michael Peat and Alan E. Davis

Table 10.3.2 GC/MS Cut-Offs (ng/mL)

Drug group	Common analyte(s)	Cut-off
Amphetamines	Amphetamine, Methamphetamine	300 or 500*
Barbiturates	Amobarbital, Butalbital, Pentobarbital	
	Phenobarbital, Secobarbital	200 or 300
Benzodiazepines	alpha-Hydroxyalprazolam, Nordiazepam	
	Oxazepam, Temazepam	100, 200, or 300
Cannabinoids	THCA	10 or 15*
Cocaine	Benzoylecgonine	150*
Methadone	Methadone	100 or 300
Methaqualone	Methaqualone	300
Opiates	Codeine, Morphine	300*
Phencyclidine (PCP)	PCP	25* or 75
Propoxyphene	Propoxyphene	300

cut-offs used in the SAMHSA Guidelines and the regulated programs
**11-Nor-delta-9-tetrahydrocannabinol-9-carboxylic acid*

synthetic opiate. Additionally, GCMS assays are available to determine 6-monoacetylmorphine (MAM), and the commonly used cut-off for this assay is 10 ng/mL.

In an attempt to resolve the issues caused by codeine prescriptions and/or poppy seed use, SAMHSA[9] has recently proposed changing the cut-offs used for regulated opiate testing. If these modifications are introduced, the initial immunoassay cut-off will be raised to 2000 ng/mL and the GC/MS cut-off raised to 2000 ng/mL for morphine and codeine. Second, if the specimen is positive for morphine, the laboratory will be required to test for MAM using a cut-off of 10 ng/mL.

10.3.2 IMMUNOASSAY TESTING

This section deals with issues surrounding immunoassays, and their applications to workplace drug testing. It will not discuss in detail the characteristics of each of the commonly used assays For readers interested in this area, an excellent review was recently published by Liu.[8]

When selecting an immunoassay, there are several factors to consider. These include (1) specificity of the kit to the drug group or drug being tested for, (2) the stability of the immunoassay over time, (3) the ability of the immunoassay either to detect adulterants or to be resistant to them, and (4) the ability of the immunoassay to be automated. Table 10.3.3 summarizes these parameters for the various immunoassays in common use today.

Since the introduction of the HHS Guidelines[6] in 1988, there has been a considerable improvement in the reliability and quality of drug testing performed in the certified laboratories. Not only has this improvement been seen in regulated testing, but it has also been apparent in the non-regulated sector where employers, third party administrators and others have become much more knowledgeable of the need for good laboratory practices. This increase in the level of understanding is causing some clients and regulatory authorities to question the properties of some of the immunoassay kits in use today, and whether they are equivalent in their abilities to detect positive specimens. In particular, questions have been

Table 10.3.3 Commonly Used Immunoassays

Immunoassay	Trade name	Ease of automation	Comments
Enzyme	Syva: EMIT Boehringer CEDIA	Can be run on many clinical chemistry analyzers	EMIT is widely used. Stability of both assays depends on their applications. Sensitive to some adulterants.
ELISIA	STC: Micro-Plate	ELISA plate format, requires some technician involvement.	Not widely used. Little known on stability.
Fluorescence Polarization	Abbott: TDx/ADx	Generally have to use manufacturer's instruments.	Not widely used by workplace drug testing laboratories. Very stable and resistant to a number of adulterants.
Microparticle	Roche Diagnostic Systems: OnLine	Can be run on many clinical chemistry analyzers	Used by a number of "mega-laboratories". Good stability and resistant to a number of adulterants.
Radio-immunoassay	Roche Diagnostic Systems: Abuscreen DPC: Double antibody, and Coat-A-Count	Considerable technician involvement	Not widely used at this time. Good stability, resistant to a number of adulterants

raised regarding the immunoassays for amphetamines and cannabinoids. Increasing attention is also being paid to the detection of benzodiazepines, particularly in Europe where abuse of flunitrazepam is a major problem. Recent reports of flunitrazepam abuse in the U.S. have led to a re-evaluation of the specificity of the various immunoassays and the cut-offs used by drug testing laboratories.

10.3.2.1 Testing for Amphetamines

In workplace testing, the detection of amphetamines by immunoassay is commonly performed using a kit designed to detect the d-isomers of amphetamine and/or methamphetamine, and not kits designed to detect the amphetamine group. However, there is both an EMIT and TDx amphetamine class assay available for clinical toxicology laboratories and others interested in detecting relatively low concentrations of other sympathomimetic amines. There are important difference between the kits most widely used for amphetamine detection. They all share a 1000 ng/mL cut off, but they do not all use the same calibrators.

Amphetamine Test Calibrators
EMIT dau	d-methamphetamine
EMIT II	d-methamphetamine
CEDIA	d-amphetamine
TDx/ADx	d-amphetamine*
OnLine	d-amphetamine*

*Both assays use a multi-point calibration.

When comparing tests for amphetamines, three important questions must be answered: (1) are all assays equivalent in detecting the abuse or use of d-methamphetamine, (2) are all assays

Michael Peat and Alan E. Davis

Table 10.3.4 Percent Cross-Reactivities of Amphetamine Immunoassays

	EMIT dau	EMIT II	CEDIA	Tdx/ADx*	OnLine
d-amphetamine	>250	100	101	100	100
d-methamphetamine	100	100	100	60-80	0.5
l-methamphetamine	8	50		4.3 to 5.1	0.2
ephedrine	0.1**	1**	0.5		<0.2
pseudoephedrine	0.1	0.1	0.6		<0.2
phenylpropanolamine	1	0.3	<0.1	<0.01	0.7
phentermine	10	50	1.9	<10	<0.1
MDMA			70	92-104	0.2
MDA			2.2	67-31	31

quoted as ranges, exact cross-reactivity depends on concentration of amine
**cross-reactivities quoted for l-isomer, increase for d-isomer*

stereospecific to the d-isomers and will they detect use of Vicks Inhaler, and (3) if the illicit form of methamphetamine used is a racemic mixture, can all assays detect the use? As one might expect, the answers to these questions vary significantly. Table 10.3.4 shows the cross-reactivities of the immunoassays.

All of the enzyme assays (EMIT DAU, EMIT II and CEDIA) have good cross-reactivity towards d-amphetamine (the metabolite of d-methamphetamine), and therefore, if the specimen contains 500 ng/mL of d-methamphetamine and 500 d-amphetamine, one would expect the response to be equal to or greater than that of 1000 ng/mL of the calibrator. It should be noted that for the EMIT DAU, which uses d-methamphetamine as calibrator, the response would be greater because of the cross-reactivity of d-amphetamine. In fact, one of the claims made about this kit is that 300 ng/mL of d-amphetamine is equivalent to 1000 ng/mL of d-methamphetamine.

A different situation exists with the TDx/ADx kits. Here the calibrator is d-amphetamine and the cross-reactivity towards d-methamphetamine varies, depending upon its concentration. In this case there is an increased response towards mixtures of amphetamine and methamphetamine such that combined concentrations of less than 1000 ng/mL may test positive.

A similar situation exists with the OnLine kit, which was specifically designed to satisfy the Temporary Reporting Rule introduced in 1990.[10] This rule was introduced as part of the immediate response to the "false positive" methamphetamines resulting from specimens containing very high concentrations of ephedrine.[11] Although methamphetamine could be formed during the GC/MS analysis of these specimens, no amphetamine was present. To prevent such specimens being reported as positive, HHS introduced a Temporary Reporting Rule requiring that, for methamphetamine to be reported as positive the specimen must contain at least 500 ng/mL of methamphetamine and at least 200 ng/mL of amphetamine. This rule was included in the 1994 HHS Guidelines.[7] Obviously if the OnLine assay was designed to comply with this rule, it detects specimens that contain less than 1000 ng/mL of amphetamines. More importantly, it has little cross-reactivity with methamphetamine alone, however, in a real life situation where the specimen also contains amphetamine (as a metabolite of methamphetamine) it has been found to be equivalent to the EMIT assays in detecting positive specimens from methamphetamine users.[12,13]

An examination of the cross-reactivities of the different tests towards l-methamphetamine might lead one to the conclusion that therapeutic use of Vicks Inhaler would not result in a positive response using these kits. Fitzgerald et al.[14] reported concentrations of methamphetamine as high as 6,000 ng/mL following use of this decongestant, and these would certainly not be expected to elicit a positive response. He also reported l-amphetamine concentrations as high as 455 ng/mL. However, the situation is not as clear as it first seems. Cody et al. reported percentages of the enantiomers after use of illicit methamphetamine.[15] In a recent challenge in its Forensic Urine Drug Testing Program, the College of American Pathologists included a specimen containing approximately 9000 ng/mL of l-methamphetamine and 2000 ng/mL of l-amphetamine. Greater than 80% of the respondents reported the drugs as positive. Given that the majority, if not all, of the respondents used one of the kits mentioned above, it appears that there is an additive response in the presence of l-methamphetamine and l-amphetamine (as there would be for the d-isomers). One obvious outcome of this is that an MRO should routinely request the separation of stereoisomers by GC/MS.

Another situation where the use of Vicks Inhaler might result in a positive response is when the donor is additionally using decongestants containing other sympathomimetics. Use of these alone can result in a positive immunoassay response if their concentrations are high enough. Methamphetamine can be synthesized by different routes and some of these may lead to the formation of d,l-methamphetamine rather than d-methamphetamine.[16] If the donor has used this racemic mixture, then the urine will be less reactive than if he/she had used the pure d-isomer. Under these conditions, 1000 ng/mL of d,l-amphetamine may not trigger a positive response using the immunoassays; the exact response will depend on the amount of methamphetamine and amphetamine present and the additive response of the kit to this mixture.

From this discussion, it is apparent that the exact response of a specimen containing various amounts of amphetamines and varying ratios of the stereoisomers cannot be predicted with any certainty and that the various commercially available immunoassays will react differently. Is this important? It is unlikely that any of these kits are failing to detect the majority of methamphetamine abusers, however, the possibility exists that specimens from some abusers are not being detected and that specimens from users of Vicks Inhaler are being reported as positive (particularly outside of the regulated programs). Without a standardization of the various kits used (for example, requiring them to detect 500 ng/mL of d-methamphetamine and 500 ng/mL of d-amphetamine on a 1:1 basis), the situation will remain as varied as it is today.

10.3.2.2 Testing for Flunitrazepam

Flunitrazepam has recently gained considerable attention in the USA because of its amnesiac properties and its use in "date rape" cases, particularly in the state of Florida. This attention resulted in the U.S. Senate regulating that possession etc. of the drug be treated as severely as that of Schedule 1 Drugs (e.g., LSD and heroin), however, it did not reclassify the drug as a Schedule 1 substance. Although flunitrazepam is not available within the U.S., it is in many parts of the world, including Europe and South and Central America. The drug has been abused in Europe for a number of years[17] and its use has proven very difficult to detect.

Flunitrazepam is metabolized to 7-aminoflunitrazepam which forms the glucuronide metabolite that is the primary urine metabolite. As expected, the commercially available immunoassays have differing cross-reactivities to the parent drug, and presumably to the metabolites. The ability to detect Flunitrazepam is made more difficult by the low doses used and by the low concentrations of metabolites present in urine. A number of European groups have worked on this problem for a number of years and some presented data at the 1996 International Association of Forensic Toxicologists meeting.[18-20] Perhaps the most interesting paper was that of Salamone et al.[20,21] These authors showed that at a 300 ng/mL initial test cut-off, single doses of flunitrazepam would not be detectable, and even at a 100 ng/mL cut-off, a 1mg dose could not be detected. They also showed that for efficient detection of this benzodiazepine, it was necessary to hydrolyze the specimen enzymatically before the immunoassay test.

Michael Peat and Alan E. Davis

10.3.3 CONFIRMATION TESTING

Before the introduction of the HHS Guidelines[6] there was considerable discussion among forensic toxicologists as to the appropriate analytical procedures to be used to confirm immunoassay results. There was a recognition that these had to be based on a different chemical principle than immunoassay, but there was not a consensus that this needed to be gas chromatography mass spectrometry (GC/MS). However, the Guidelines mandated that GC/MS be used to confirm presumptive positives form immunoassay testing and its use was further incorporated into the College of American Pathologist's FUDT inspection program. It has now become the standard of practice in workplace drug testing to confirm all initial immunoassay results by GC/MS.

Not only was there considerable discussion on the need for GC/MS, there was also considerable debate as to the suitability of selected ion monitoring for the identification of drugs and/or their metabolites. Several well respected forensic toxicologists argued that full scan GC/MS was necessary before a specimen could be reported as positive. Although this argument is still heard today, there is a broad consensus of opinion that selected ion monitoring is an accurate and reliable procedure for identification of these substances. The analytical principles of GC/MS have been well covered by other authors.[22,23] The HHS Guidelines[6,7] required certified drug testing laboratories to be inspected every six months, and it is this inspection process that has driven the improvement in the confirmation procedures.

10.3.3.1 Accepted Criteria

Although the use of GC/MS is required by the HHS Guidelines, the quality of data produced early in the certification process was extremely variable. There were no clearly defined criteria for acceptable chromatography and there was even debate about the variation allowed in mass ratios for identification by selected ion monitoring. Today there are clear criteria for each of these important identification parameters, and these are as follows:

1. Mass ratios for analyte(s) and internal standard within 20% of the corresponding ratios in a calibrator or the average of a series of calibrators.
2. Retention times for analyte(s) and internal standard within 2% of those in the calibrator or a series of calibrators.
3. The chromatographic peak shape for each mass monitored should be symmetrical.
4. The chromatographic peak for each ion monitored should be clearly resolved form closely eluting peaks.

10.3.3.2 Choice of Ions

It was originally thought that it was necessary to monitor three ions for the analyte and three for the internal standard; it is now considered acceptable to monitor only two for the internal standard. There has also been considerable discussion regarding the choice of ions to monitor and whether these are suitable for identification purposes. For most analytes of interest this is not a problem, however for some it is. Analytes that clearly fall into the first category include benzoylecgonine, the opiates (morphine, codeine, hydrocodone and hydromorphone), and THCA.

10.3.3.2.1 Amphetamines

Unless amphetamine and methamphetamine are derivatized, their base peaks in the electron impact mode are 58 and 44 m/z, respectively. These two masses are certainly not diagnostic as they represent a dimethylamine and a methylamine fragment, respectively. Second, monitoring such low ions can lead to a loss of chromatographic selectivity because of the potential for co-extracted interfering compounds with low mass ions. Derivatization with a perfluroacyl reagent (e.g., heptafluorobutyrl anhydride[HFBA]) will result in ions of considerably higher mass and generally much "cleaner" ion chromatograms. However, there is still need for caution in the GC/MS confirmation of amphetamines because of the potential for interferences from other sympathomimetics (see the discussion below).

10.3.3.2.2 Barbiturates

The barbiturates (amobarbital, butabarbital, butalbital, pentobarbital, phenobarbital and secobarbital) are frequently included in non-regulated drug testing programs. Their confirmation presents some difficulty because of the similarity of electron impact mass spectra of certain barbiturates and the absence of a clearly defined third ion for the analyte. For example, the mass spectra of amobarbital, butabarbital and pentobarbital include two major ions, at 141 and 156 m/z. A similar situation exists with butalbital and secobarbital (167 and 168 m/z). In addition these five barbiturates elute closely together on the majority of capillary columns used today. Phenobarbital has two distinctly different ions (and is well-separated chromatographically) at 204 and 232 m/z. Therefore, laboratories performing this confirmation without a derivatization step are, in essence, basing their identification of the barbiturates more on retention time than on the ions monitored. One solution to this problem is to derivatize the barbiturates before GC/MS. This results in more diagnostic ions and improves the chromatographic separation. In our laboratory, alkyl derivatives are formed using Meth Elute.

10.3.3.2.3 Benzodiazepines

GC/MS confirmation of this group of drugs is extremely difficult (see discussion below); however, one of the issues with developing a procedure for these drugs is the choice of ions to monitor. All of the benzodiazepines contain a halogen (fluorine, chlorine or bromine). If the choice is to monitor a fragment containing chlorine or bromine, the laboratory should be careful not to choose a second fragment that is simply one containing a chlorine or bromine isotope.

10.3.3.2.4 Methadone and Propoxyphene

Assays for these two drugs are based on confirming the presence of the parent drug, amd are faced with the same problems as those designed to confirm the presence of underivatized amphetamine and methamphetamine: the base peak in the electron impact mass spectra represents an alkyl amine moiety. It is therefore necessary to choose ions of low intensity for monitoring purposes, or to establish assays based on the metabolites (EDDP for methadone and norpropoxyphene for propoxyphene).

10.3.3.2.5 Phencyclidine

Most confirmation assays for this drug monitor the following ions: 200, 242, and 243 m/z. Obviously 243 m/z is simply the carbon isotope fragment corresponding to the 242 m/z ion. However, in this case there are no other suitable diagnostic ions.

10.3.3.3 Software

There has been considerable discussion regarding what are acceptable criteria for chromatography. These have been defined by the National Laboratory Certification Program as greater than 90% resolution and symmetry. However, historically these have been monitored by certifying scientists (or GC/MS data reviewers) and not determined by the instrument software. Recently, Finnegan has introduced[24] a software package (ToxLab) that determines these

Michael Peat and Alan E. Davis

Table 10.3.5 Derivatization Procedures

Drug group	Drugs commonly Included	Derivatizing procedure	Ref.
Amphetamines	Amphetamine	Acylation	
	Methamphetamine	Silylation	16, 27-29
Barbiturates	Amobarbital	Alkylation	30
	Butabarbital		
	Butalbital		
	Pentobarbital		
	Phenobarbital		
	Secobarbital		
Benzodiazepines	Nordiazepam	Silylation	31-33
	Oxazepam		
Cocaine	Benzoylecgonine	Alkylation	34-35
		Silylation	
Opiates	Codeine	Alkylation	36-39
	Morphine	Acylation	
		Silylation	
THCA	THCA	Acylation/ Esterification	40-43
		Alkylation	
		Silylation	

criteria mathematically. During the evaluation of this package, suitable symmetry has been determined to be greater than 70% and resolution greater than 90%. This package also contains software that completely controls the injection sequence of the instrument. The combination of software control and improved GC/MS hardware allows these systems to be far more productive and efficient than some of the older systems in use today.

10.3.4 DERIVATIZATION PROCEDURES

The most commonly used are ones based on solid phase extraction.[25,26] These have several advantages including being more selective and more easily automated than liquid ones. Deuterated internal standards are available for all assays and are widely used for all assays, with the possible exception of the barbiturates, where hexobarbital is the first choice of many laboratories. Table 10.3.5 summarizes the numerous choices of derivatizing reagents available to today's drug testing laboratory.

Table 10.3.5 does not include all the analytes that can be included under each drug group. For example, the amphetamines assay can be modified to include MDMA ("Ecstasy), MDA and MDE, the benzodiazepines to include α-hydroxyalprazolam, α-hydroxytriazolam, diazepam and N-desalkylflurazepam, and the opiates to include hydrocodone and hydromorphone.

Detailed information about these procedures is available in the references listed. However, there are issues associated with a number of the assays that do deserve discussion.

10.3.4.1 Amphetamines

In the early 1990s it was discovered that during certain GC/MS procedures, and under certain conditions, methamphetamine can be formed from large concentrations of ephedrine (or pseudoephedrine). As part of their response to this situation, HHS introduced a "Temporary Reporting Rule" requiring that for a specimen to be reported as positive for methamphetamine, it must not only contain at least 500 ng/mL of methamphetamine but also at least 200 ng/mL of amphetamine.[10] This prevented the reporting of false positive methamphetamines as there was no evidence of the formation of amphetamine during the GC/MS process. Although, this rule is now included in the Federal Guidelines[7] it does not apply to non-regulated testing, and there may be non-certified laboratories that have not incorporated the reporting rule into their procedures.

A more reliable procedure for eliminating the potential for false positive results is to incorporate a pre-oxidation step into the extraction.[44] In this protocol, oxidation with sodium periodate destroys hydroxylated sympathomimetics before the extraction, thereby preventing their conversion to methamphetamine during derivatization or GCMS. If this procedure is used, then good laboratory practices require the laboratory to analyze a control containing the amphetamines together with high concentrations of the symathomimetics as part of their standard protocols.

In the initial discussion of immunoassay testing for amphetamines, it was mentioned that under certain conditions l-methamphetamine (together with l-amphetamine) will cause a positive amphetamines response. Because of this, it is important that laboratories incorporate procedures to separate the stereoisomers into their protocols. Such procedures are based on derivatization with a optically pure derivative of an amino acid.[14] Interpretation of these GC/MS results is usually straightforward, specimens from Vick's Inhaler users contain greater than 90% of the l-isomer and those from users of d-methamphetamine contain greater than 90% of the d-isomer.

10.3.4.2 Benzodiazepines

Over the past five years numerous publications have focused on this GC/MS assay for benzodiazepines. Historically, it was possible to convert the parent drugs and their metabolites to benzophenones by acid hydrolysis;[45] however, this procedure does not allow for the confirmation of α-hydroxyalprazolam or α-hydroxytriazolam, metabolites of two of the newer, and most commonly prescribed, benzodiazepines. Using this procedure it is also not possible to differentiate the use of certain benzodiazepines, leading to potential interpretative difficulties.

For these reasons, acid hydrolysis has fallen out of favor and been replaced with procedures involving GC/MS analysis of the parent drug or their metabolites. Because a number of benzodiazepines and their metabolites are metabolized by glucuronidation it is necessary to perform a hydrolysis step before extraction. Unlike the hydrolysis used for opiates, which can be either acid or enzymatic, only enzymatic ones can be used in the extraction of the benzodiazepines. Because of the polar nature of the benzodiazepines it is necessary to derivatize them, normally the trimethlysilyl derivatives are formed.

The major issue surrounding benzodiazepine testing is the cut-off to be used for confirmation. Historically, either a 200 or 300 ng/mL cut-off has been used, however this is inappropriate for many of today's benzodiazepines. For example, to confirm many of the immunoassay positives resulting from alprazolam or flunitrazepam use it is necessary to lower this cut-off to 100 ng/mL. As the potency of these drugs increases it will be necessary to constantly monitor whether the confirmation (and the screening) assays are appropriate for their detection. Even in today's environment it is surprising how many laboratories continue to confirm only nordiazepam and oxazepam.

Michael Peat and Alan E. Davis

10.3.4.3 Morphine and Codeine

Although morphine and codeine have been confirmed by GC/MS for a number of years, this assay continues to cause laboratories problems. One of the underlying issues is whether to use acid or enzymatic hydrolysis, although studies have shown that acid hydrolysis is more efficient in releasing the parent drug from its conjugate, it has the disadvantage of resulting in a "dirty" hydrolysate that can cause problems in either solid phase or liquid liquid extractions. For this reason (as well as for safety ones) most laboratories use enzymatic methods, and with the correct choice of enzyme and conditions, hydrolysis can occur quickly and efficiently.

A second issue associated with opiate confirmation is the separation and identification of hydrocodone and hydromorphone in the presence of morphine and codeine. This problem is confounded by norcodeine. One of the most common procedures used involves silylation as the derivatization procedure. When this technique is used, the separation of the trimethylsilyl derivatives of codeine from hydrocodone and those of morphine and hydromorphone is extremely difficult, particularly when it is required to have greater than 90% resolution. It is true that the derivatives can be clearly identified by choosing the appropriate ions to monitor, however it is still necessary to use common ions. Under normal conditions, the separation of trimethylsilyl derivatives of morphine and norcodeine is almost impossible to achieve.

Therefore, the confirmation of morphine after codeine use can be impractical if the laboratory uses silylation as a derivatization. Under normal conditions, when the donor has only taken codeine, this may not be important; however, if the donor has taken heroin and codeine a negative report for morphine is extremely misleading. The easiest way to resolve this problem is to use a different derivatizing procedure, either acylation or acetylation is suitable, however acyl derivatives are notoriously unstable. Acetylation[51,52] with acetic anhydride or propionic anhydride is recommended. Although it is more time consuming from an extraction point of view, the derivatives are well separated chromatographically.

Recently the Federal Government proposed changing the procedure for analyzing opiates (morphine and codeine). The initial immunoassay cut-off would be raised to 2000 ng/mL and the confirmation cut-offs for morphine and codeine would also be raised to 2000 ng/mL. If the morphine concentration is above 2000 ng/ml then the laboratory would be required to analyze for MAM using a cut-off of 10 ng/mL. This is not an easy assay and requires significant care in the extraction, derivatization and chromatographic steps. Solid phase extraction procedures similar to those used for morphine and codeine are obviously suitable for MAM; however, acid hydrolysis is not recommended as this may cause MAM to decompose. If necessary enzyme hydrolysis can be used, however most laboratories at this time do not include such a step. Silylation[38] is the recommended procedure for derivatization, although other methods[36] have been used.

It is obviously inappropriate to use acetylation as this will acetylate both MAM and morphine back to heroin, therefore no positive morphine specimens would ever be negative for MAM! The challenge for the regulated laboratory will be to validate an assay for MAM that is able to detect 5 ng/mL (or less) and that will satisfy the strict requirements of the National Laboratory Certification Program. It is unlikely that such an assay will be able to determine codeine, morphine and MAM in one procedure.

In the next few years other challenges will face the drug testing laboratory. For example with the advent of immunoassay kits for the detection of LSD, laboratories will face the challenge of confirming this ergot alkaloid by GC/MS. No routine procedures exist today. Introduction of less expensive MS/MS and LC/MS systems will assist the drug testing laboratories in this endeavor. Hopefully the regulators will also recognize that the requirement for GC/MS be modified to include the newer hyphenated procedures.

REFERENCES

1. *1992 National Household Survey on Drug Abuse. Advance Report No. 3.* Substance Abuse and Mental Health Services Administration (SAMHSA), Office of Applied Studies. Rockville, MD: DHHS, 1993
2. *Monitoring the Future Survey. College Students.* National Institute on Drug Abuse. Rockville, MD: DHHS, 1993
3. *Monitoring the Future Survey. High School Students.* National Institute on Drug Abuse. Rockville, MD: DHHS, 1993
4. Anthony, J.C., Eaton, W.W., Garrison, R. and Mandell, W. Psychoactive drug dependence and abuse: more common in some occupations than others. *J. Employee Assistance Res.,* 1, 148, 1992.
5. Harris, M.M and Heft, L.L. Alcohol and drug abuse in the workplace: issues, controversiesand directions for future research. *J. Manag.,* 18, 239, 1992
6. Mandatory Guidelines for Federal Workplace Testing Programs. *Fed. Register,* 53, 11970, 1988
7. Mandatory Guidelines for Federal Workplace Testing Programs. *Fed. Register,* 59, 29908, 1994
8. Liu, R.H., Evaluation of commercial immunoassay kits for effective workplace drug testing in *Handbook of Workplace Drug Testing,* Liu, R.H and Goldberger, B.A., Eds., AACC Press, Washington, 1995, Chap. 4
9. Changes to the testing cut-off levels for opiates for federal workplace drug testing programs. *Fed. Register,* 60, 57587, 1995
10. Autry, J.H. III, *Amphetamine Reporting (PD003),* National Institute on Drug Abuse, Division of Applied Research, 1990
11. Hornbeck, C.L., Carrig, J.E. and Czarny, R.J. Detection of a GC/MS artifact peak as methamphetamine. *J. Anal. Toxicol.,* 17, 257, 1993
12. Baker, D.P., Murphy, M.S., Shepp, P.F., Royo, V.R., Calderone, M.E., Escoto, B. and Salamone, S.J. Evaluation of the Abuscreen OnLine assay for amphetamines on the Hitachi 737: comparison with EMIT and GCMS methods. *J. For. Sci.,* 40, 108, 1995
13. McNally, A.J., personal communication, 1996
14. Fitzgerald, R.L., Ramos Jr., J.M., Bogema, S.C. and Poklis, A. Resolution of methamphetamine stereoisomers in urine drug testing: urinary excretion of R(-)-methamphetamine following use of nasal inhalers. *J. Anal. Toxicol.,* 12, 255, 1988
15. Cody, J.T. and Schwarzhoff, R. Interpretation of methamphetamine and amphetamine enatiomer data. *J. Anal. Toxicol.,* 17, 321, 1993
16. Cody, J.T., Important issues in testing for amphetamines, in *Handbook of Workplace Drug Testing,* Liu, R.H and Goldberger, B.A., Eds., AACC Press, Washington, 1995, Chap. 10
17. Brenneisen, R., personal communication, 1996
18. Smith-Kielland, A. and Morland, H., EMIT-screening and flunitrazepam, presented at The 34th International Association of Forensic Toxicologists Meeting, Interlaken, August 11 to 15, 1996, 28
19. Cirimele, V., Kintz, P., Staub, C. and Mangini, P., Hair testing for flunitrazepam and 7-aminoflunitrazepam by GC/MS-NCI, presented at 34th The International Association of Forensic Toxicologists Meeting, Interlaken, August 11 to 15, 1996, 46
20. Salamone, S.J., Brenner, C., Honasoge, S., McNally, A.J., Passarelli, J., Szkutnicka, K., Brenneisen, R., ElSohly, M.A. and Feng, S., Comparison of flunitrazepam excretion patterns using the Abuscreen OnTrak and OnLine immunoassays and GC/MS, presented at 34th The International Association of Forensic Toxicologists Meeting, Interlaken, August 11 to 15, 1996, 29
21. Salamone, S.J., personal communication, 1996
22. Watson, J.T., *Introduction to Mass Spectrometry,* Raven Press, New York, 1985

Michael Peat and Alan E. Davis

23. Deutsch, D.G., Gas chromatography/mass spectrometry using table top instruments, in *Analytical Aspects of Drug Testing*, Deutsch, D.G., Ed., John Wiley & Sons, New York, 1989, Chap. 4

24. Peat, M.A., Davis, A.E., Clabaugh, M. and Bukowski, N., Today's GC/MS drug testing laboratory: automation of extraction, GC/MS instruments and data review, presented at 34th The International Association of Forensic Toxicologists Meeting, Interlaken, August 11 to 15, 1996, 64

25. Chen, X-H., Franke, J-P., and de Zeeuw, R.A., Principles of solid phase extraction, in *Handbook of Workplace Drug Testing*, Liu, R.H and Goldberger, B.A., Eds., AACC Press, Washington, 1995, Chap. 1

26. Gere, J.A. and Platoff Jr., G.E., Solid phase extraction of abused drugs in urine, in *Handbook of Workplace Drug Testing*, Liu, R.H and Goldberger, B.A., Eds., AACC Press, Washington, 1995, Chap. 2

27. Thurman, E.M., Pedersen, M.J., Stout, R.L. and Martin, T. Distinguishing sympathomimetic amines from amphetamine and methamphetamine in urine by gas chromatography/mass spectrometry. *J. Anal. Toxicol.*, 16, 19, 1992

28. Hughes, R.O., Bronner, W.E. and Smith, M.L. Detection of amphetamine and methamphetamine in urine by gas chromatography/mass spectrometry following derivatization with (-)-methyl chloroformate. *J. Anal. Toxicol.*, 15, 256, 1991

29. Melgar, R. and Kelly, R.C. A novel GC/MS derivatization method for amphetamines. *J. Anal. Toxicol.*, 17, 399, 1993

30. Mule, S.J. and Casella, G.A. Confirmation and quantitation of barbiturates in human urine by gas chromatography/mass spectrometry. *J. Anal. Toxicol.*, 13, 13, 1989

31. Dickson, P.H., Markus, W., McKernan, J. and Nipper, H.C. Urinalysis of (-hydroxyalprazolam, and other benzodiazepine compounds by GC/EIMS. *J. Anal. Toxicol.*, 16, 67, 1992

32. Fitzgerald, R.L., Rexin, D.A. and Herold, D.A. Benzodiazepine analysis by negative ion chemical ionization gas chromatography/mass spectrometry. *J. Anal. Toxicol.*, 17, 342, 1993

33. Black, D.A., Clark, G.D., Haver, V.M., Garbin, J.A. and Saxon, A.J. Analysis of urinary benzodiazepines using solid-phase extraction and gas chromatography-mass spectrometry. *J. Anal. Toxicol.*, 18, 185, 1994

34. Cone, E.J., Hillsgrove, M. and Darwin, W.D. Simultaneous measurement of cocaine, cocaethylene, their metabolites and "crack" pyrolysis products by gas chromatography-mass spectrometry. *Clin. Chem.*, 40, 1299, 1994

35. Mule, S.J. and Casella, G.A. Confirmation and quantitation of cocaine, benzoylecgonine, ecgonine methyl ester in human urine by GC/MS. *J. Anal. Toxicol.*, 12, 153, 1988

36. Goldberger, B.A., Darwin, W.D., Grant, T.M., Allen, A.C., Caplan, Y.H. and Cone, E.J. Measurement of heroin and its metabolites by isotope-dilution electron-impact mass spectrometry. *Clin. Chem.*, 39, 670, 1993

37. Mitchell, J.M, Paul, B.D., Welch, P. and Cone, E.J. Forensic drug testing for opiates. II. Metabolism and excretion rate of morphine in humans after morphine administration *J. Anal. Toxicol.*, 15, 49, 1991

38. Cone, E.J., Welch, P., Mitchell, J.M. and Paul, B.D. Forensic drug testing of opiates. I. Detection of 6-acetylmorphine in urine as an indicator of recent heroin exposure. Drug and assay considerations and detection times. *J. Anal. Toxicol.*, 15, 1, 1991

39. ElSohly H.N., ElSohly, M.A. and Stanford, D.F. Poppy seed ingestion and opiate urinalysis: a closer look. *J. Anal. Toxicol.*, 14, 308, 1990

40. Kemp, P.M., Abukhalaf, I.K., Manno, J.E, Manno, B.R., Alford, D.D. and Abusada, G.A. Cannabinoids in humans. I. Analysis of delta-9-tetrahydrocannabinol and six metabolites in plasma and urine using GC-MS. *J. Anal. Toxicol.*, 19, 285, 1995

41. Kemp, P.M., Abukhalaf, I.K., Manno, J.E, Manno, B.R., Alford, D.D., Mcwilliams, M.E., Nixon, F.E., Fitzgerald, M.J., Reeves, R.R. and Wood, M.J. Cannabinoids in humans. II. The influence of three methods of hydrolysis on the concentration of THC and two metabolites in urine. *J. Anal. Toxicol.*, 19, 292, 1995

42. Joern, W.A. Detection of past and recurrent marijuana use by a modified GC/MS procedure. *J. Anal. Toxicol.*, 11, 49, 1987
43. Paul, B.D., Mell, L.D., Mitchell, J.M. and McKinley, R.M. Detection and quantitation of urinary 11-nor-delta-9-tetrahydrocannabinol-9-carboxylic acid, a metabolite of tetrahydrocannabinol by capillary gas chromatography and electron impact mass fragmentography. *J. Anal. Toxicol.*, 11, 1, 1987
44. ElSohly, M.A., Stanford, D.F., Sherman, D., Shah, H., Bernot, D. and Turner, C.E. A procedure for eliminating interferences from ephedrine and related compounds in the GC/MS procedure analysis of amphetamine and methamphetamine. *J. Anal. Toxicol.*, 16, 109, 1992
45. Seno, H., Suzuki, O. and Kumazawa, T. Rapid isolation with Sep-Pak C18 cartridges and wide-bore capillary gas chromatography of benzophenones, the acid-hydrolysis products of benzodiazepines. *J. Anal. Toxicol.*, 15, 21, 1991

10.4 URINE SPECIMEN SUITABILITY FOR DRUG TESTING

RUTH E. WINECKER, PH.D.

DEPUTY CHIEF TOXICOLOGIST, OFFICE OF THE CHIEF MEDICAL EXAMINER, CHAPEL HILL, NORTH CAROLINA

BRUCE A. GOLDBERGER, PH.D.

DIRECTOR OF TOXICOLOGY AND ASSISTANT PROFESSOR, UNIVERSITY OF FLORIDA COLLEGE OF MEDICINE, GAINESVILLE, FLORIDA

The effectiveness of a drug test can be altered by donor manipulation of the specimen. Drug users commonly dilute, substitute, or adulterate their urine specimen. A wide variety of information on how to "beat" a drug test is available by word-of-mouth, on the Internet, in drug culture magazines such as *High Times*, and in books such *Steal this Urine Test*[1] and *Conquering the Urine Tests*.[2] In addition, a number of over-the-counter and prescription medications have been shown to interfere with some drug testing methods producing false-negative results.

In response to the possibility of manipulation, laboratories have developed and implemented procedures to ensure the validity of the specimen and the drug test result. These procedures apply to all steps in the drug testing process, including specimen collection, handling, and initial and confirmatory analysis. The aim of this chapter is to discuss technical issues in workplace drug testing including techniques commonly used by donors to substitute, dilute or adulterate their specimen, detection of the adulterated specimen by the collection site and the laboratory, and drug test interference not associated with intentional adulteration.

10.4.1 ADULTERATION TECHNIQUES

10.4.1.1 Specimen Substitution

Substitution of the donor's urine specimen with a drug-free urine specimen can be an effective measure. The drug-free urine specimen is most often obtained from sources including family members, friends, and even animals. However, an obvious risk of substitution with real urine is the unintentional use of a drug-positive urine specimen. To limit this possibility, synthetic and freeze-dried human urine is readily available through mail-order companies.

Table 10.4.1 Substances That Have Been Used as Substitutes for Urine

Apple juice

Citrus-flavored beverages

Dilute tea

Ginger ale

Lemonade

Saline

Water

White grape juice

Another commonly used technique is to substitute a liquid which resembles urine in color and consistency. Such substitutions may range in sophistication from substitution with tap water, to mixtures of water and other substances designed to simulate the appearance of urine. A partial list of these substances is presented in Table 10.4.1.

There are several technical obstacles that a donor must overcome in order to successfully submit a substituted urine specimen as their own. The most difficult is that the temperature of the submitted specimen must be within a specified range (32 to 38°C or 90 to 100°F) before it is accepted for testing. Substituted specimens are often stored in flexible containers such as condoms or balloons, and kept warm by concealing the container under clothing in the genital, anal, or underarm area. In addition, mechanical heat sources including microwave ovens, hand warmers, auto engines, auto exhausts, steam pipes, lamps, and cigarette lighters have also been used to obtain an acceptable temperature for a substituted specimen.[3] Donors have also been known to catheterize themselves in order to place drug-free urine directly into their bladder. The specimen is then subsequently voided in the usual manner. Self-catheterization is nearly impossible to detect as the temperature of the urine specimen and the collection process will appear normal.

Finally, some individuals have employed "donor-surrogates". Donor substitution appears to be a rare circumstance which requires a significant amount of effort and risk due to the strict identification process including the use of photo IDs used by urine collection sites.

10.4.1.2 Specimen Dilution

One of the most common techniques used to alter the drug test results is intentional dilution. Dilution of the specimen may reduce the drug analyte concentration in the specimen to a level below the established cutoff concentration.

Several techniques are used to dilute specimens:

- ingestion of large amounts of water
- administration of a prescription or over-the-counter medication
- ingestion of other substances that can produce diuresis
- adding water directly to a freshly voided specimen

Although dilution is an effective technique, the urine specimen will likely be subjected to a number of laboratory tests (e.g., creatinine, specific gravity) specifically designed to identify potentially dilute specimens. A list of common prescription and over-the-counter diuretics, as well as other substances that can produce diuresis, are presented in Table 10.4.2.

10.4.1.3 In vivo *adulterants*

In vivo adulteration occurs when donors willingly ingest substances purported to alter or interfere with drug tests. The most common substance used is golden seal root, either in the form of capsules or brewed as a tea. In addition to golden seal root, a number of other products can be purchased from natural food stores, head shops, through magazines such as *High Times*, and on the Internet. These include:

- Clear Choice Herbal Detox Teas
- Clear Choice Quick Flush Capsules

Table 10.4.2 Prescription, Over-The-Counter, and Other Products that Produce Diuresis

Prescription medications	Over-the-counter medications	Other products
Benzothiadiazines	Aqua-Ban	Alcoholic beverages
Loop diuretics	Diurex	Ammonium chloride
Potassium-sparing compounds	Fem-1	Caffeine
Carbonic anhydrase inhibitors	Lurline PMS	Caffeine-containing beverages
Osmotic diuretics	Midol	Golden seal tea
	Odrinil Water Pills	Pamabrom
	Pamprin	Various herbs and herbal
	Premsyn PMS	preparations

- Detoxify™ Carbo Clean
- Eliminator
- HealthTech® Pre-Cleanse Formula
- Naturally Klean Herbal Tea
- Test Free
- The Stuff

According to the product literature, these substances are carbohydrate- and/or herbal-based and require the consumption of large amounts of water to be effective. To mask the appearance of dilute urine, they may also contain Vitamin B-complex, creatine, and creatinine. The products generally sell for approximately $25.00 to $30.00 for one to two applications.

Enhancing the elimination of drug analytes is another commonly used technique to alter the drug test result. Acidification of urine, with the subsequent enhanced elimination of weak bases (e.g., phencyclidine, amphetamines), occurs following the ingestion of large amounts of ascorbic acid (e.g., vitamin C) or hippuric acid (e.g., acidic fruit drinks). Conversely, alkalization of urine, with the subsequent enhanced elimination of weak acids (e.g., barbiturates), occurs following the ingestion of large amounts of sodium bicarbonate (baking soda).[4] The efficacy of enhanced elimination through the alteration of urinary pH is questionable.

The use of popular over-the-counter medications may also alter drug test results. The principal urinary metabolite of aspirin, salicyluric acid, potentially yields false-negative results through the interference with the measurement of NADH (reduced nicotinamide adenine dinucleotide) formed in the enzyme multiplied immunoassay technique. The interference is due to the reduction of the molar absorptivity of NADH at 340 nm, and can be avoided with the use of an alternate wavelength.[5,6] Ibuprofen in urine has also been associated with false-negative GC/MS confirmation results for 11-nor-Δ^9-tetrahydrocannabinol-9-carboxylic acid (THC-acid). One study attributes the interference to the depletion of the derivatizing reagent.[7]

10.4.1.4 In vitro (External) Adulterants

In vitro adulteration is the intentional addition of a foreign substance to a urine specimen. Although the objective of adulteration is the production of a false-negative immunoassay result, the effects of adulterants are highly unpredictable and false-positive results may occur. Most of the added adulterants are used in hopes of disrupting the immunoassay reaction. Adulterants may also alter the urine pH and/or ionic strength of the specimen, affect the normal chemical composition of the specimen through reaction with normal urinary constituents, inhibit immunoassay antibody binding, interfere with the measurement step of the immunoassay, and/or degrade the drug and/or drug metabolite.[8]

Ruth E. Winecker and Bruce A. Goldberger

Table 10.4.3 Potential *in vitro* Adulterants

Household products	Commercial Products
Ammonia	Clean 'n Clear
Bleach	Clear Choice Instant Purifying Additive
Blood	Klear
Drano	MaryJane SuperClean 13
Ethanol	Purifyit
Ethylene glycol	UrinAid
Gasoline	
Golden seal root	
Kerosene	
Lemon juice	
Lime-A-Way	
Liquid soap	
Peroxide	
Sodium bicarbonate	
Table salt	
Vanish	
Vinegar	
Visine	

In vitro adulterants can be categorized into two classes: chemicals commonly found in the household that are readily accessible to the donor, and those available commercially. A list of potential adulterants is provided in Table 10.4.3. The effect of adulterants on the most commonly used immunoassays have been studied by a number of investigators.[8-20] The effects of adulterants are highly variable. Whether or not they interfere with the test depends upon a number of factors including the concentration of drug and/or drug metabolite in the specimen, the amount of adulterant added, and the immunoassay technique utilized. Although the efficacy of many of these substances is dubious, some are surprisingly effective at producing a false-negative result. The effects of chemical adulterants on screening assays can be summarized as follows:

- Enzyme immunoassay technique (Emit): tendency for false-negative results
- Fluorescence polarization immunoassay (FPIA): tendency for false-negative and false-positive results
- Radioimmunoassay (RIA): tendency for false negative and false positive test results
- Kinetic interaction of microparticles in solution (KIMS): tendency for false-positive results
- Cloned enzyme donor immunoassay (CEDIA): tendency for false-negative results

10.4.2 PREVENTION AND DETECTION OF THE ADULTERATED SPECIMEN

10.4.2.1 Role of the Collection Site

The proper collection of a urine specimen is an integral part in the drug testing process.[21-24] In order to prevent intentional specimen substitution, specimen dilution, and/or the use of adulterants, the collection site should utilize a number of simple procedures. These procedures should include (but not be limited to):

1. Collector must obtain proper identification of the donor through the use of photo ID (e.g., driver's license, employee badge), or employer representative, or other identification permitted under the employer's workplace drug testing program.
2. Check that temperature of the urine specimen is within the specified range within 4 min of urination (32 to 38°C or 90 to 100°F).
3. Bluing or other appropriate colored agent added to the toilet bowl.
4. Restrict access to water (e.g., faucets, toilet bowl, toilet tank), soap, disinfectants, and other products.
5. Observe (directly or indirectly) the donor during urination.
6. Secure the specimen with tamper-evident tape.
7. Insist that donor remove all outer clothing and leave all personal belongings (e.g., purses, briefcases) outside of the bathroom.
8. Donor must wash and dry their hands prior to urination.
9. Donor signs statement certifying that the specimen is authentic and has not been altered.

If there is any indication of substitution, dilution, or adulteration, the donor is required to provide another specimen under direct observation. Both specimens should be submitted individually to the testing laboratory. The collector should not add to or combine urine from two separate voids.[24] Although the temperature of a urine specimen is a important indicator, a number of studies have shown that intentional external heating under realistic conditions (in the underarm and groin) could be employed to produce a urine specimen with a temperature within the acceptable range.[3,21]

An excellent source of information regarding urine specimen collection is available from the U.S. Department of Health and Human Services (DHHS).[24] The handbook was prepared by the Division of Workplace Programs with the intent of supplementing the information provided in the Mandatory Guidelines for Federal Workplace Drug Testing Programs.

10.4.2.2 Role of the Laboratory

Careful inspection of the urine specimen during the receiving and aliquoting process may help identify adulterated specimens. Strong odors such as liquid soap, bleach, ammonia, vinegar, or perfume are usually apparent when the specimen container is opened. Appearance, including abnormal color and presence of precipitation, are also important characteristics to note since many chemical adulterants greatly affect the appearance of a specimen. For example, the addition of Vanish® or Drano® to a specimen will result in a blue or green color, and the addition of glutaraldehyde to a specimen darkens the specimen and may produce large amounts of precipitation. Also, detergents and soaps usually cause foaming upon shaking of the urine specimen. Laboratories should be aware that bacterial growth, color changes, increases in turbidity and sedimentation, and alterations in pH and odor are common with older urine specimens.[8]

To identify potentially dilute specimens, many laboratories determine urine creatinine concentrations, followed by specific gravity if the creatinine concentration is <20 mg/dL. Creatinine and specific gravity measurements are also useful in identifying non-urine submissions. Administratively, a dilute specimen is usually characterized as a specimen with a creatinine concentration <20 mg/dL and a specific gravity value of <1.003.

The pH of suspicious specimens is also measured since many adulterants are harsh chemicals and often alter the pH of a urine specimen resulting in a value outside the normal urinary pH range of 4.5 to 8.0 as defined by Teitz.[25] Although the majority of laboratories measure specific gravity and pH manually with a refractometer and pH paper respectively, commercial assays are also available for use on automated chemistry analyzers.

Immunoassay results should also be monitored to detect abnormal values which may be helpful in identifying adulterated specimens. For example, the addition of glutaraldehyde to a specimen results in the depression of absorbance rate change values with the Emit assay.[17]

Although abnormal creatinine, specific gravity, pH, and/or immunoassay results may be used to identify a suspicious specimen, additional confirmatory testing may be necessary. For example, a specimen adulterated with glutaraldehyde can be confirmed by GC/MS,[26] fluorimetry,[27] and colorimetry (adPerfect, Chimera Research and Chemical).[17] Other analytical methods that may be used on an as-needed basis include comprehensive urinalysis, electrolyte determination, and volatile analysis.

In response to the overwhelming concern regarding potential adulteration and the role of the laboratory and Medical Review Officer (MRO), the Department of Transportation issued a memorandum to all DHHS-certified laboratories in late-1993 regarding the use and interpretation of laboratory data relevant to potential dilution and adulteration.[28] In accordance with the memorandum, a dilute specimen (creatinine <20 mg/dL and specific gravity <1.003) is not reasonable suspicion or cause to require the donor to submit to another specimen collection. However, the employer may require the use of direct observation during the subsequent collection. In addition, if the specimen is deemed not suitable for testing (invalid immunoassay result or pH outside of acceptable range), the MRO must discuss the laboratory findings with the laboratory, contact the donor regarding the specimen's suitability, and if no acceptable explanation is provided by the donor, another specimen must be collected under direct observation. Finally, if a specimen is adulterated, the laboratory findings constitutes refusal to test.

10.4.3 INTERFERENCE NOT ASSOCIATED WITH INTENTIONAL ADULTERATION

There are a number of prescription or over-the-counter medications that can interfere with routine laboratory drug tests. Identification of these medicinal compounds and mechanism of interference is important not only for the development of alternative testing procedures, but also for evaluation of their potential use as *in vivo* adulterants.

The majority of the reports of immunoassay interference has been related to the use of nonsteroidal anti-inflammatory drugs (NSAID). Although ibuprofen use has been associated with false-positive Emit cannabinoid and false-positive FPIA barbiturate and benzodiazepine results (not the subject of this review), NSAIDs have also been associated with invalid Emit test results. For example, urine specimens that contain high concentrations of tolmetin assayed by Emit produce instrument error alarms in addition to depressed immunoassay responses. This could lead to false-negative Emit results. The phenomenon appears to be related to a highly elevated initial absorbance reading at 340 nm due to tolmetin's high molar absorptivity.[29] In addition, the presence of metronidazole, mefenamic acid, and ciprofloxacin produces unusually high initial absorbance values with the Emit assay, and fluorescein produces unusually high background interference with the FPIA assay.[30-33]

A far fewer number of medicinal compounds will interfere with confirmation analyses due to the specificity of the analytical techniques utilized. In most cases, false-negative results occur due to either the competition between the targeted analyte and a compound with a chemically similar functional group for the derivatizing reagent, or interference in the GC/MS ion source due to co-elution of the targeted analyte with another substance present in a very high concentration.[34,35] For example, the presence of high concentrations of ibuprofen in urine specimens has been shown to interfere with the derivatization (methylation with dimethylsulfoxide and tetramethylammonium hydroxide) of THC-acid. The phenomenon is associated

Table 10.4.4. Prescription and Over-the-Counter Medications that Have Been Shown to Interfere with Immunoassay and GC/MS Assays

Medication	Drug class	Technique Affected	Mechanism
Aspirin	NSAID	Emit	Reduced Δ absorbance rate
Ciprofloxacin	Antibiotic	Emit	Increased initial absorbance value
Fluorescein	Radiologic dye	FPIA	High background interference
Mefenamic acid	NSAID	Emit	Increased initial absorbance value
Metronidazole	Antiprotozoal	Emit	Increased initial absorbance value
Tolmetin	NSAID	Emit	Increased initial absorbance value
Ibuprofen	NSAID	GC/MS	Competition for derivatization
Fluconazol	Antifungal	GC/MS	Decreased MS ionization efficiency
Methadone/ EDDP	Opioid	GC/MS	Decreased MS ionization efficiency
l-Meth- amphetamine	Antihistamine	GC/MS	False-positive for d-Methamphetamine

*NSAID, non-steroidal anti-inflammatory drug; Emit, enzyme multiplied immunoassay technique; FPIA, fluorescence polarization immunoassay; GC/MS, gas chromatography/mass spectrometry
Data derived from References 5, 6, 30-36.

with the depletion of the derivatizing reagent, and can be readily ameliorated with the addition of excess derivatizing reagent.[7]

Interference in the GC/MS ion source has been shown to decrease the ionization efficiency of the targeted analyte and its measured concentration. Fluconazol, an antifungal medication, and 2-ethylidene-1,5-dimethyl-3,3-diphenyl-pyrrolidine (EDDP), a methadone metabolite, have been reported to interfere with the confirmation of benzoylecgonine by this mechanism.[36,37] Interference can be readily monitored with the use of a co-eluting deuterated internal standard, and prevented by further purification of the specimen extract and/or alteration of the chromatographic conditions.

The occurrence of false-positive confirmatory results is exceedingly rare due to the selectivity and specificity of the GC/MS technique.[38] However, to prevent false-positive results, a number of analytical and administrative measures are routinely utilized. For example:

- Prevent chromatographic interference: All GC/MS assays must be evaluated for potential chromatographic interference. In particular, the amphetamine and opiate assays are highly subject to interference from structurally related sympathomimetic amines and opioids, respectively.
- Prevent artifactual production of methamphetamine in the presence of other sympathomimetic amines: Ephedrine, pseudoephedrine, and phenylpropanolamine are oxidized in the presence of periodate to products which will not interfere with the GC/MS assay.[39,40] In addition, the confirmation reporting requirements require that amphetamine be present at a specified concentration when the specimen is positive for methamphetamine.[23]
- Differentiate d- and l-isomers of methamphetamine: l-Methamphetamine is an over-the-counter antihistamine found in Vicks® Inhaler, while d-methamphetamine is a schedule II drug that is an appetite suppressant and central nervous system stimulant. The separation of the d- and l-isomers requires either a chiral GC column or derivatization with a chiral-specific derivatizing reagent.[41]

Ruth E. Winecker and Bruce A. Goldberger

A list of prescription and over-the-counter medications that have been shown to interfere with immunoassay and GC/MS assays are presented in Table 10.4.4. The proposed mechanism of interference is also given.

REFERENCES

1. Hoffman, A., *Steal this Urine Test: Fighting Drug Hysteria in America*, Penguin Books, New York, 1987.
2. Nightbyrd, J., *Conquering the Urine Tests*, Byrd Laboratories, Topanga, CA, 1992.
3. Shults, T. F. and St. Clair, S., *The Medical Review Officer Handbook*, Sixth edition, Quadrangle Research, LLC, Research Triangle Park, NC, 1995.
4. Klaassen, C. D., Principles of toxicology and treatment of poisoning, in *Goodman & Gilman's The Pharmacological Basis of Therapeutics*, Ninth edition, McGraw-Hill, New York, 1996, 63.
5. Wagener, R. E., Linder, M. W., and Valdes, R., Jr., Decreased signal in Emit assays of drugs of abuse in urine after ingestion of aspirin: Potential for false-negative results, Clin. Chem., 40, 608, 1994.
6. Linder, M. W. and Valdes Jr., R., Mechanism and elimination of aspirin induced interference in Emit® II d.a.u. assays, Clin. Chem., 40, 1512, 1994.
7. Brunk, S. D., False negative GC/MS assay for carboxy THC due to ibuprofen interference, J. Anal. Toxicol., 12, 290, 1988.
8. Cody, J. T., Adulteration of urine specimens, in *Handbook of Workplace Drug Testing*, AACC Press, Washington, DC, 1995, 181.
9. Kim, H. J. and Cerceo, E., Interference by NaCl with the EMIT method of analysis for drugs of abuse, Clin. Chem., 22, 1935, 1976.
10. Vu Duc, T., EMIT® tests for drugs of abuse: Interference by liquid soap preparations, Clin. Chem., 31, 658, 1985.
11. Mikkelsen, S. L. and Ash, K. O., Adulterants causing false negatives in illicit drug testing, Clin. Chem., 34, 2333, 1988.
12. Cody, J. T. and Schwarzhoff, R. H., Impact of adulterants on RIA analysis of urine for drugs of abuse. J. Anal. Toxicol., 13, 277, 1989.
13. Warner, A., Interference of common household chemicals in immunoassay methods for drugs of abuse, Clin. Chem., 35, 648, 1989.
14. Pearson, S. D., Ash, K. O., and Urry, F. M., Mechanism of false-negative urine cannabinoid immunoassay screens by Visine™ Eyedrops, Clin. Chem., 35, 636, 1989.
15. Bronner, W., Nyman, P., and von Minden, D., Detectability of phencyclidine and 11-nor-Δ^9-tetrahydrocannabinol-9-carboxylic acid in adulterated urine by radioimmunoassay and fluorescence polarization immunoassay, J. Anal. Toxicol., 14, 368, 1990.
16. Schwarzhoff, R. and Cody, J. T., The effects of adulterating agents on FPIA analysis of urine for drugs of abuse, J. Anal. Toxicol., 17, 14, 1993.
17. Goldberger, B. A. and Caplan, Y. H., Effect of glutaraldehyde (UrinAid) on detection of abused drugs in urine by immunoassay, Clin. Chem., 40, 1605, 1994.
18. Baiker, C., Serrano, L., and Lindner, B., Hypochlorite adulteration of urine causing decreased concentration of Δ^9-THC-COOH by GC/MS, J. Anal. Toxicol., 18, 101, 1994.
19. Wu, A. H. B., Forte, E., Casella, G., Sun, K., Hemphill, G., Foery, R., and Schanzenbach, H., CEDIA for screening drugs of abuse in urine and the effect of adulterants, J. Forensic Sci., 40, 614, 1995
20. George, S. and Braithwaite, R. A., The effect of glutaraldehyde adulteration of urine specimens on Syva Emit II drugs-of-abuse assays, J. Anal. Toxicol, 20, 195, 1996.
21. Manno, J. E., Specimen collection and handling, in *Urine Testing for Drugs of Abuse*, NIDA Research Monograph Number 73, Department of Health and Human Services, Rockville, MD, 1986, 24.
22. U.S. Department of Health and Human Services, Mandatory guidelines for federal workplace drug testing programs, Federal Register, April 11, 1988, 53, 11970.

23. U.S. Department of Health and Human Services. Mandatory guidelines for federal workplace drug testing programs, Federal Register, June 9, 1994, 59, 29908.

24. U.S. Department of Health and Human Services. *Urine Specimen Collection Handbook for Federal Workplace Drug Testing Programs*, CSAP Technical Report 12.

25. Tietz, N. W., *Clinical Guide to Laboratory Tests*, Third edition, W.B. Saunders Company, Philadelphia, PA, 1995, 476.

26. Sansom, H. L., Fraser, M. D., Botelho, C., Kuntz, D. J., and Foltz, R. L., Detection of urine specimens adulterated with UrinAid, Joint Meeting of the Society of Forensic Toxicologists and California Association of Toxicologists, Abstract 39, October, 1993.

27. Wu, A., Schmalz, J., and Bennett, W., Identification of UrinAid-adulterated urine specimens by fluorometric analysis, Clin. Chem., 40, 845, 1994.

28. U.S. Department of Transportation, Memorandum, Reporting of drug test results: Abnormal test results and analysis for presence of adulterants, December 7, 1993.

29. Joseph, R., Dickerson, S., Willis, R., Frankenfield, D., Cone, E. J., and Smith, D. R., Interference by nonsteroidal anti-inflammatory drugs in EMIT® and TDx® assays for drugs of abuse, J. Anal. Toxicol., 19, 13, 1995.

30. Inloes, R., Clark, D., and Drobnies, A., Interference of fluorescein, used in retinal angiography, with certain clinical laboratory tests, Clin. Chem., 33, 2126, 1987.

31. Lora-Tamayo, C. and Tena T., High concentrations of metronidazole in urine invalidates EMIT results, J. Anal. Toxicol., 15, 159, 1991.

32. Crane, T., Badminton, M. N., Dawson, C. M., and Rainbow, S. J., Mefenamic acid prevents assessment of drug abuse with EMIT™ assays, Clin. Chem., 39, 549, 1993.

33. Lora-Tamayo, C., Tena, T., and Rodriguez, A., High concentrations of ciprofloxacin in urine invalidates EMIT results, J. Anal. Toxicol., 20, 334, 1996.

34. O'Conner, E., Ostheimer D., and Wu, A. H. B., Limitations of forensic urine drug testing in methodology and by adulteration, AACC TDM/Tox, 14, 277, 1993.

35. Wu, A. H. B., Mechanism of interferences for gas chromatography/mass spectrometry analysis of urine for drugs of abuse, Anal. Clin. Lab. Sci., 25, 319, 1995.

36. Wu, A. H. B., Ostheimer, D., Cremese, M., Forte, E., and Hill, D., Characterization of drug interferences caused by coelution of substances in gas chromatography/mass spectrometry confirmation of targeted drugs in full-scan and selected-ion monitoring modes, Clin. Chem., 40, 216, 1994.

37. Dasgupta, A., Mahle, C., and McLemore, J., Elimination of fluconazole interference in gas chromatography/mass spectrometric confirmation of benzoylecgonine, the major metabolite of cocaine using pentafluoropropionyl derivative, J. Forensic Sci., 41, 511, 1996.

38. Goldberger, B. A. and Cone, E. J., Review. Confirmatory tests for drugs in the workplace by gas chromatography/mass spectrometry, J. Chromatogr. A, 674, 73, 1994.

39. ElSohly, M. A., Stanford, D. F., Sherman, D., Shah, H., Bernot, D., and Turner, C. E., A procedure for eliminating interferences from ephedrine and related compounds in the GC/MS analysis of amphetamine and methamphetamine, J. Anal. Toxicol., 16, 109, 1992.

40. Paul, B. D., Past, M. R., McKinley, R. M., Foreman, J. D., McWhorter, L. K., and Synder, J. J., Amphetamine as an artifact of methamphetamine during periodate degradation of interfering ephedrine, pseudoephedrine, and phenylpropanolamine: An improved procedure for accurate quantitation of amphetamines in urine, J. Anal. Tox., 18, 331, 1994.

41. Fitzgerald, R. L., Ramos, J. M., Bogema, S. C., and Poklis, A., Resolution of methamphetamine stereoisomers in urine drug testing: Urinary excretion of R(−)-methamphetamine following use of nasal inhalers, J. Anal. Toxicol., 12, 255, 1988.

Ruth E. Winecker and Bruce A. Goldberger

10.5 THE ROLE OF THE MEDICAL REVIEW OFFICER: CURRENT ISSUES

Steven St. Clair, M.D., M.P.H.

Executive Director, American Association of Medical Review Officers, Durham, North Carolina

10.5.1 HISTORICAL BACKGROUND

The role of the medical review officer (MRO) evolved during the 1980s. As urine testing for abused drugs became more common, it quickly became apparent that illegal drug use was not the only explanation for positive test results. Most of the problems had to do with urine testing. Scientifically valid positive test results can, in fact, be due to the legitimate medical use of prescription medications, or the legal ingestion of foodstuffs, or other substances, which could give a positive test result.

In particular, opiates posed a problem. Opiates — particularly morphine and codeine — can be found in legally available foodstuffs made with poppy seeds. The only available method of testing for heroin was to test for morphine and codeine. To assure that an individual who tested positive for morphine or codeine due to ingestion of poppy seeds or use of a codeine prescription would not be accused of heroin use, an independent review entitiy was required. The only way to determine whether a valid positive test result actually reflected drug use was for a physician to review the results and examine the patient. Thus the concept of the MRO was born.

An additional problem was medical use of other drugs, especially amphetamines and cocaine, as well as benzodiazepines and barbiturates and, to a lesser extent, marijuana. A mechanism to assure that misidentification as illegal drug users of individuals using drugs as medically prescribed was needed. Although the actual number of individuals who might be misidentified as illegal drug users was small, false accusations against an innocent person were considered to be unjustifiable.

The MRO was to act as an independent check and balance. MRO review assures that individuals with valid medical reasons for a positive test will not be considered illegal drug users. It was soon recognized, however, that the MRO provided additional valuable professional assistance in assuring respect for the personal privacy and dignity of the donor, maintenance of the confidentiality of medical information, adherence to high scientific and medical standards, and assurance of complicance with professional standards for conducting urine drug testing.

Even initially, the role of the MRO was not confined just to determining that clinical evidence of heroin or other drug use was present. There were other areas related to urine drug testing in which the ultimate responsibility for, or judgement of appropriate standards for, was unclear. For example, toxicologists felt uncomfortable judging the validity of, or professional competency of, collection of urine drug screens. Despite rigorous quality control in certified testing laboratories, regulatory authorities perceived a role for the MRO in assuring that testing laboratories used appropriate procedures for testing specimens and reporting results.

10.5.2 COLLECTION ISSUES

Chain of custody (COC) establishes a legally defensible record that the specimen provided by the donor was the specimen tested in the laboratory. This question seldom, if ever, arises in clinical laboratory testing.

As originally envisoned, the role of the MRO was only to ensure that the donor, and the certifying scientist from the testing laboratory, had actually signed the custody and control form. MROs are routinely asked, however, to take a much broader role in evaluating whether COC has been established, and to comment on related issues. Most MROs routinely review COC procedures and forms, and take an active role in quality control related to the collection process.

10.5.2.1 Refusal or Inability to Provide a Urine Specimen

MROs are responsible for determining whether the failure to provide a urine specimen for testing represents refusal to test or results from a medical condition which renders the donor unable to provide a specimen. Although regulatory standards for judgment were initially unclear, recent regulatory interpretation has established that the presumption of normalcy should commonly be used for such judgments. That is, it should be presumed that normal individuals, absent specific and documented medical conditions that would render them unable to provide specimens for testing, should be considered as refusing to provide a specimen. This is to be contrasted to a position in which it would be the responsibility of the MRO to "prove" that the individual should have been able to provide a specimen for testing.

Presumption of normalcy is a reasonable notion in most, if not all, such cases. Normal urine output for adults is considered to be 1500 milliliters (ml) to 2500 ml per day, or approximately 60 to 100 ml per hour. Urine drug testing requires only 45 ml for testing, individuals are given at least two hours to produce this amount, and at least 24 ounces (approximately 720 ml) of fluid may be given to the tested individual over this time period. Few, if any, medical conditions other than true renal failure are likely to render an individual unable to produce a specimen of 45 ml in these circumstances. Those that could, such as a neurogenic bladder, are likely to have been medically documented prior to the test collection.

Even placing the responsibility on the tested individual to demonstrate medical conditions that would render them unable to provide a specimen does not solve a difficult, related question: what should the medical evaluation of such individuals consist of, and who should perform it? Initially, recommendations routinely included comprehensive bloodwork, pelvic and prostate examinations, and even cystoscopy or IVP studies, performed by urologists. Since no reasonable rationale could support this approach, evolution to the current standard, consisting of simple medical history, possibly including blood work and/or urinalysis (if obtainable!), performed by a physician qualified in any primary care discipline.

10.5.2.2 Interpretation of Adulteration Information

MROs have always played an informal role in answering questions about the adequacy and integrity of specimens. Recent regulatory changes have formalized the role of the MRO in determining whether medical explanations exist when laboratory testing reveals the presence of interfering substances in urine specimens.

Unfortunately, such requirements do not allow either the MRO or the testing laboratory to consider or confirm specimens as "inconsistent with human urine" but rather require the identification of specific adulterating substances to consider a specimen as adulterated - an almost impossible technical burden, given the wide range of possible adulterants and the limits of technical testing capabilities.

10.5.3 DISTINCTION BETWEEN MEDICAL AND FACT-FINDING ROLES

As with many other areas, there is no clear definition, in either regulatory or non-regulatory testing, regarding how far the responsibility of the MRO extends related to issues that are questions of fact rather than documentable medical issues. Issues related to use of foreign prescription, or non-prescription, medications or drugs, ingestion of imported foodstuffs, and passive inhalation or ingestion issues may all involve questions of fact rather than strictly medical issues.

For example, in Canada codeine is available, without prescription, in over-the-counter headache preparations. The use of such preparations is strictly legal in Canada, but potentially illegal in the U.S. Does an MRO treat an individual who claims to have used the preparation only in Canada differently from the individual that admits to use in the U.S.? Does the MRO request travel records documenting that the individual who claims to have used the preparation in Canada was actually in Canada at an appropriate time?

The most common scenario of this sort may be the question of passive inhalation. The MRO can state with reasonable scientific certainty that simple or common descriptions of passive exposure to marijuana (or crack cocaine) sidestream smoke, such as at parties, are unlikely to result in positive drug tests. But what of the not uncommon claims such as: "I woke up coughing because my friends where blowing smoke directly in my face", "They told me later there was something in the cookies", or "They smoked the entire six hour ride in the car"?

Most MROs currently separate such issues into those that are medically verifiable, such as actual prescription information, and questions of fact, which are issues for administrative or legal proceedings rather than for the process of medical review. The entire scientific question of passive inhalation, for example, seems rather misguided since there is absolutely no question that passive ingestion — through foodstuffs, for example — of marijuana will routinely result in positive tests. Yet virtually no MRO would medically verify a laboratory positive result for marijuana as negative because of a claim of marijuana ingestion, even if such ingestion was documented in some fashion (unless, of course, the ingestion was medically authorized).

The appropriate role for the MRO with respect to such fact-finding issues is to comment on the scientific and medical issues which arise. MROs also routinely assist in the scientific investigation of issues in which their expertise may be helpful. For example, the MRO may assist in the investigation of a claim that ingestion of a herbal tea caused a positive result by arranging for and assisting with the interpretation of laboratory analysis of preparations provided, if administrative or legal authorities request or allow this.

10.5.4 THE CONTROVERSY OVER UNAUTHORIZED PRESCRIPTIONS

A running, and never ending, debate has existed ever since the MRO role was first created. What is the appropriate action by the MRO confronted with the explanation by the tested individual that "I used my (pick one) wife's, husband's, son's, daughter's, cousin's, significant other's, etc. prescription for (pick one) Tylenol #3, Fioricet, Valium, etc.? The MRO community seems evenly divided between the "unauthorized use is unauthorized use" camp (verified positive result) and the "this rarely if ever represents drug abuse" camp (verified negative result).

In testing situations, such as the military and some large corporations, where the consequences of verified positive drug tests are subject to some type of further administrative review to determine the consequences of the positive result, positive verification is the norm. In programs that do not include such opportunities, many MROs routinely report such results as negative, or choose other alternative strategies to deal with such situations. These include open disclosure of all information to the employer with the consent of the testing individual and the practice of advising the individual to discontinue such use and retesting the individual one or more times.

10.5.6 THE FUTURE OF MEDICAL REVIEW

The role of the MRO in drug testing is now well established. It is likely that this role will expand as drug testing methods change and evolve: regardless of the type of testing performed, the issues of reviewing medical explanations for results, investigating medical issues related to testing such as adulteration and the refusal to provide a specimen, and providing independent and objective scientific review of the testing process will continue to be integral and important.

10.6 ALTERNATIVE DRUGS, SPECIMENS, AND APPROACHES FOR NON-REGULATED DRUG TESTING

DENNIS CROUCH

CENTER FOR HUMAN TOXICOLOGY, UNIVERSITY OF UTAH, SALT LAKE CITY, UTAH

The non-regulated workplace defies a simple definition, therefore, the prevalence of non-regulated workplace drug testing and employer testing programs is not known. The non-regulated workplace includes such divergent professions as the music industry, where deaths from drug abuse are well documented, to athletics where the use of alcohol, analgesic and performance enhancing drugs has been chronicled.[1,2] A simple definition of non-regulated workplace testing might include all workplace testing not covered by the federal programs such as the Department of Health and Human Services (DHHS), Department of Transportation (DoT), military and Nuclear Regulatory Commission (NRC) programs.[3,4,5] However, this definition fails to recognize that many programs are regulated by state and local governments.

An accurate census of the number of companies with non-regulated workplace drug testing programs is not available. This is attributable to the divergence of non-regulated occupations and industries and the lack of a central data base for collecting this information. One group estimated that 98% of all major U.S. corporations conduct some level of testing.[6] A longitudinal survey by the American Management Association of member organizations showed a continued increase in testing from 21.5 % of firms surveyed in 1987, to 81.1% in 1996.[7] These data would lead us to believe that even without regulations, many organizations have voluntarily implemented workplace drug testing programs. However, in some estimates there is no clear distinction between regulated and non-regulated workplace programs and some regulated employees may be included in "general workforce" estimates. Also, it is likely that many small organizations are not represented in member survey estimates[7]. A survey not limited to member organizations demonstrated that only 13% of full-time employees were drug tested in the previous year.[8]

There are indications that drug use may be more prevalent in the non-regulated industries. A recent federal survey showed that admitted drug use in the previous month was 60% higher in small organizations (not likely to be regulated) than in those with more than larger companies.[8] Results from that study also showed that admitted heavy use of alcohol exceeded 20% in segments of the construction industry and that over 10% of the employees in non-regulated industries such as, construction workers, construction supervisors, food preparation employees, waiters and waitress, janitors, laborers and helpers, purchasing agents and buyers and auto mechanics admitted to current drug use (Table 10.6.1).[8] Laboratory drug test results from 1995 showed a 3.4% positive rate for regulated transportation workers and a 7.5% positive rate in the general workforce.[9] The same report showed the positive rates for the transportation workers were 2.7%, 2.8%, and 3.5% for 1992, 1993, and 1994, respectively, while the general

Table 10.6.1 Prevelance of Drug Use in Non-Regulated Industries

Job classification	Current drug use* %	Rank	Current heavy alcohol use** %
Other construction	17.3	1	20.6
Construction supervisors	17.2	2	
Food preparation	16.3	3	16.3
Waiters and waitresses	15.4	4	
Writers, designers, artists and athletes	13.1	5 or 6	
Helpers and laborers	13.1	5 or 6	19.5
Janitors	13	7	
Purchasing agents and buyers	12.9	8	
Auto mechanics	12.8	9	16.3
Construction laborers	12.8	10	19.9
Other laborers	12.8	11	

*Current drug use
**Current heavy alcohol use = ≥5 drinks on ≥ 5 occasions in the last 30 days

workforce had rates of 10.4%, 9.8% and 8.6%.[8] During a similar time period, positive drug tests were reported for only 0.84% (1993) and 0.62% (1994) of regulated nuclear energy licensees.[9,10]

This chapter will focus on alternatives to regulated urinalysis workplace drug testing as it is defined by federal programs such as DoT and DHHS. Reasons for non-regulated testing include pre-employment, post-accident, post-incident, for cause, random, safety sensitive and contractual requirements. Testing may be performed in certified or accredited laboratories, however, specimen handling protocols and testing methods are at the discretion of the laboratory and the employer. This is particularly true when workplace accidents result in injury or death. For non-regulated testing, specimens such as urine, blood, blood serum or plasma, hair, sweat or saliva or tissues may be collected. Non-regulated testing is not limited to immunoassay screen tests and gas chromatography mass spectrometry (GC/MS) confirmatory tests performed in a single laboratory. On-site testing with laboratory based methods or on-site testing with specialized on-site urine screen kits may be performed. Alternate chemical testing methods may be used such as thin layer chromatography, GC with various detectors and liquid chromatography with various detectors. Non-chemical performance testing batteries may be used to augment chemical test. A limitation of non-regulated testing is the lack of oversite of testing protocols and laboratory operations. Certain standard practices of chain of custody documentation, method validation, quality assurance and records maintenance should be observed and are discussed.

10.6.1 DRUGS OF INTEREST

It is not possible to test for all drugs and chemicals that may affect an employee's ability to perform his/her job. The selection of a menu of drugs to test depends on the specimen(s) collected, analytic methods available, cost and the prevalence of use of the drug. Regulated workplace testing focuses almost exclusively on urinalysis testing to detect use of amphetamines, cocaine, cannabinoids, opiates and phencyclidine.[3,4] These are commonly abused classes of drugs that are readily detected in urine.[8,12]

Menus of drugs to be tested in the non-regulated workplace have been developed inferentially using information integrated from various sources. These sources include availability of prescription drugs[13], toxicity of drugs, admitted use of drugs[8,12] and the frequency of detection of drugs.[14-19] The potential of alcohol and other drugs to adversely affect highway and transportation safety has prompted a number of studies to assess drug use by motor vehicle operators. These studies were designed to determine the prevalence of drug use by impaired drivers, injured drivers, and fatally injured drivers and have been a primary source of information for developing drug testing menus.[14-19] Summary results from selected studies are shown in Table 10.6.2. Ethanol was the most prevalent drug detected in these studies. It was found in 25% of the injured auto drivers, over 50% of the fatally injured auto drivers drivers and 14% of the truck drivers that were studied (Table 10.6.2). Cannabinoids were the next most commonly encountered drugs. Their detection rate varied from 7 to 37% of the drivers. The table shows that central nervous system stimulants including cocaine and metabolites, prescription sympathomimetic amines and non-prescription sympathomimetic amines were also frequently detected. The table also shows that, with the exception of benzodiazepines, all others drugs were detected in fewer than 5% of the studied drivers. Extensive lists of tested drugs and drugs classes can found in some of these reports. Williams reported testing for alcohol and 11 different classes of drugs.[17] Crouch et al. reported testing for volatiles, 8 different classes of drugs and 47 different drugs or metabolites.[18] Table 10.6.3 presents the drug testing menu from a recent nationwide study of fatally injured drivers.[19]

10.6.2 SPECIMENS TO TEST (TABLE 10.6.2B)

For more detailed descriptions of alternate testing matrices, see Chapter 11.

10.6.2.1 Urine

Estimates show that over 90% of U.S. companies select urine as the specimen of choice for workplace drug testing.[7] A single laboratory chain reported performing over 3 million non-regulated workplace urinalysis tests in 1995.[9] This chapter does not present an in depth discussion of urinalysis workplace drug testing for non-regulated employees because the advantages of urinalysis testing in the non-regulated workplace are similar to those of regulated testing. Urine is the specimen of choice for the majority of programs because it can be collected non-invasively, it is easily tested, drug and drug metabolites are found in high concentrations following recent drug use, and testing of urine is inexpensive when compared to testing of other specimens.

Caveat emptor is an appropriate warning to those interested in urinalysis drug testing services. There is little oversight of non-regulated urinalysis testing. For testing of federal and DoT regulated employes, specimen handling, chain of custody and analytic methods used to screen and confirm the drugs in urine are strictly controlled.[3,4] However, for non-regulated urinalysis testing these procedures are at the discretion of the laboratory. Even DHHS certified laboratories are not required to test non-regulated specimens by federal standards.[3] DHHS on-site laboratory inspections are strictly limited to review of procedures and records from regulated DoT and DHHS testing.[3,4] Procedures used to test non-regulated specimens and testing records are not inspected by DHHS. Organizations contracting with laboratories for non-regulated testing must specify the procedures to be used and arrange for independent laboratory inspections.

10.6.2.2 Blood

Up to 15% of workplace tests may be performed on blood samples.[7] Some federal agencies such as the DoT have established programs to test blood and other tissue following accidents,

Table 10.6.2 Prevalence of Drug Use by Impaired Drivers, Injured Drivers, and Fatally Injured Drivers

Ref	Garriott	Cimbura	Terhune	Williams	NHTSA	Crouch
Year	1977	1982	1982	1985	1992	1993
Population	Fatal	Fatal	Injured	Fatal	Fatal	Fatal
Vehicle type	Auto	Auto	Auto	Auto	Auto	Truck
Total cases	127	401	506	440	882	169
Ethanol	61%	57%	25%	70%	51%	14%
Drugs	18%	26%	22%	>40%	18%	
Drugs or ethanol	69%	38%	81%	58%	37%	
Cannabinoids	NA	9% Urine 3% Blood	9%	37%	7%	12%
Cocaine	<1%	<1%	2%	11%	5%	8%
Amphetamine	1%*			<1%	1.9%	4%
Methamphetamine				3%		6%
Phentermine						<1%
Phenylpropanolamine				3%		<1%
Ephedrine/ pseudoephedrine				2%		7%
Diazepam/ metabolite	10%	3%	7%	4%	2%	
Other Benzodiazepines	NA	<1%	2%		<1%	
Barbiturates	3%	<1%	3%	2%	%	
Opiates					2%	1%
Codeine	<1%	2%	<1%		<1%	< 1%
Propoxyphene	2%	<1%	<1%		<1	
Antihistamines	2%	2%	NA		<1%	< 1%
Methaqualone	2%	<1%	<1%			
PCP			4%			< 1%

Total sympathomimetic amines
NA = Not Tested

however, this testing is minor compared to urinalysis workplace testing.[4] Blood is an extremely valuable specimen for testing because urine is often not available following industrial and transportation accidents that result in serious injury or death. Most drugs can be detected in the blood and blood drug concentrations provide valuable information to assist in interpreting the test results. In contrast to urine drug concentrations that vary with daily urine volume, drug concentrations in blood are more predictable. There is also an extensive body of scientific literature relating blood and blood plasma drug concentrations to impairment, toxicity and lethality. In some cases, it is possible to determine if there has been the improper use of a

Table 10.6.3 Drug Testing Menu from a Recent Nationwide Study of Fatally Injured Drivers[19]

Substance

Alcohol (ethanol)	CNS stimulants
Cannabis (marijuana)	cocaine
Benzodiazepines	anphetamine
tranquilizers	methamphetamine
diazepam	caffeine
lorazepam	Muscle relaxants
flurazepam	cyclobenzaprine
alprazolam	Antipsychotics
oxazepam	chlorpromazine
chlordiapoxide	thioridazine
Antihistamines	mesoridazine
diphenhydramine	Antiarrhythmics
chlorpheniramine	quinidine
Antidepressants	procainamide
amitriptyline	lidocaine
imipramine	flecanide
doxepin	Barbiturate sedatives
fluoxetine	phenobarbital
Narcotic analgesics	secobarbital
meperidine	butabarbital
methadone	butalbital
propoxyphene	pentobarbital
oxycodone	amobarbital
codeine	
morphine	
herion	

Source: NHTSA, 1992

Table 10.6.2b

Specimen	Ease of collection	Screen	Confirmation & quantitation	Interpretation	Cost
Urine	High	High	Low	Low	Low
Blood	Moderate	Moderate	High	High	Moderate/High
Hair	High	Moderate/Low	Low	Low	Moderate
Sweat	Moderate	Moderate/Low	Low	Low	Moderate
Saliva	Moderate	Moderate/Low	Low	Low	Moderate
Tissues	Low	Moderate	Moderate	Moderate	High

prescription drug, frequent use of a drug of abuse, or impairment from drug use. However, correlating a blood drug concentration with impairment remains problematic.[20,21] There are several disadvantages to using blood as a specimen for workplace testing. Collection of blood requires a venipuncture. They are sometimes considered painful and more invasive than collecting urine. Handling of blood and blood products requires proper facilities and safety precautions. Most drugs and their metabolites are excreted from the body in the urine, therefore, concentrations in the urine usually exceed those found in the blood. For example, the peak concentrations of most drugs of abuse are 10 to 100 times higher in urine than blood.[20,22] Consequently, blood drug testing requires the laboratory to use sophisticated screening and confirmation analysis techniques. The equipment needed to perform blood testing is expensive and the level of technical expertise required to operate the equipment is greater than that needed for urinalysis drug testing. As a result, blood analysis are time consuming and the costly. Currently, there are no regulatory standards for performing blood testing. No screening or confirmations methods are dictated, no cutoffs are universally recognized, and there is no recommended menu of drugs to test. Consequently, qualitative results vary from laboratory to laboratory.

10.6.2.3 Hair

Hair has been used throughout the history forensic toxicology for identification of exposure to metals such as arsenic, lead and mercury.[23] Golblum et al., in 1954, were the first investigators to report detecting drugs in hair.[24] Since that early report, heroin, mono-acetylmorphine, morphine and codeine; cocaine and metabolites; phencyclidine (PCP); marijuana and metabolites; methamphetamine, amphetamine and metabolites; nicotine and metabolite; caffeine and other xanthines; barbiturates; benzodiazepines, methadone and a host of therapeutic drugs have been detected in hair.[23,25]

There are several advantages to hair as a specimen for workplace drug testing. It can be collected by non-invasive techniques. Hair may be cut or "plucked" from the subject. In contrast to urine, where occasional use of most drugs of abuse can only detected for a few days, hair samples may contain a protracted history of the employee's drug use because drugs incorporated into growing hair may reside there until the hair is cut or lost. Hair may be available for testing after death or traumatic injury when urine and other specimens are frequently unavailable.[25] Reports have demonstrated that cannabinoids, opiates, phencyclidine, and cocaine can be detected in hair using simple radioimmunoassay screen tests[25,26] and a host of investigators have successfully performed GC/MS confirmations for drugs of abuse in hair.[25,27-30] Despite successes using hair as a testing specimen, less than 1% workplace drug testing is currently performed solely on hair.[7] Hair has not gained the wide acceptance enjoyed by urine for workplace testing for several reasons. The cost of testing may be 2 or more times that of urine testing.[31] Drug(s) may be absorbed onto the surface of non-users hair by environmental exposure.[32,33] This can occur tactically in laboratory employees, police officers and evidence custodians through handling of the drugs and subsequently transferring them from the hands to the hair. It may also occur when non-users enter an enclosed area where drugs such as crack cocaine, methamphetamine, cannabinoids, or heroin are being smoked. Scientists continue to argue about the efficacy of washing procedures to remove drugs environmentally deposited on the hair while not affecting detection of drugs incorporated into the hair from actual use.[32,33] There are also concerns about the accuracy of hair testing.[334] A recent report on the inter-laboratory proficiency testing of hair samples showed that of 14 participating laboratories, five reported false positive results and eleven reported false negative results.[35] Quantitative results showed wide variability.[35] The major disadvantage of hair testing is the inability to correlate hair test drug results with drug dose, time since use or behavioral consequences of use. There are several factors that contribute to interpretive difficulties. Hair is found on many areas of the body such as the chest and body, pubic area, eyebrows, eyelashes, beard and under-arm. Hair from these areas varies in length, texture, color, diameter, shape, growth rate and life span.[36] The life span may be as short as 3 months for axillary hair to as long as a few years for head hair.[36] In addition, only about 88% of the human hair is actively growing at any given point in time. Therefore, one would need have an extensive history including the origin, age and growth state of the hair sample to predict whether a drug or metabolite should be detected. Little is know about the mechanism(s) of incorporation of drugs into hair and less is known about drug dose and subsequent hair-drug-concentration. Some researchers have show preferential incorporation of drugs into pigmented hair.[37] This suggests that there may be racial and hair color biases in testing. All of these limitations must be addressed by scientific research before it will be possible to correlate a positive hair test with time since use, dose ingested or behavioral consequences in the workplace.

10.6.2.4 Sweat

Sweat collection devices have been approved for clinical and drugs of abuse testing.[38] Amphetamine and methamphetamine, heroin, morphine, methadone, and phencyclidine have been detected in sweat.[39,40] Sweat may be collected on tamper proof absorbant patches. The patches are attached to the subject with a simple adhesive and may be worn for extended periods of time. While the patch is worn, sweat is absorbed and drug(s) and their metabolite(s) are deposited on it. Several studies have been performed to evaluate the efficacy of detecting drug use with sweat patch testing.[40,41] These studies have shown that the patches are particularly useful in criminal justice programs where constant surveillance through use of the sweat patch has detected use that went undetected in discrete urinalysis tests.[39] The patches are potentially useful in drug rehabilitation programs where abstinence is a measure of treatment success and recidivism can be monitored by having the patient continuously wear a patch.

A disadvantage of sweat testing is that little is known about the deposition of drugs into sweat, therefore, interpreting test results is difficult. For most drugs we do not know the minimum dose that would need to be ingested for the drug to be detected in the sweat. We cannot predict how long after marijuana or cocaine have been ingestion that they will be detected in sweat. Most importantly, we do not know what the effects of extended exercise on the transfer of drug(s) into sweat and or on the deposition of these drugs onto a patch. The cost of testing a sweat patch is about the same as urinalysis testing. However, since drug concentrations are lower and the entire patch may be needed for a single confirmational analysis. Repeat testing and confirmation of multiple drug use is precluded.

10.6.2.5 Saliva

Saliva is a complex fluid that functions to moisten the mucus membranes of the upper GI tract and supply enzymes needed for digestion.[42] Many drugs of interest in non-regulated testing have been detected in saliva: ethanol, amphetamine and other sympathomimetic amines, barbiturates, diazepam, caffeine, heroin, cocaine and metabolites and cannabinoids.[43,44] Saliva may be collected simply, non-invasively and under direct observation. It is a filtrate of the blood and, therefore, should reflect blood-drug concentrations. Because it is a filtrate, and relatively free of blood constituents it is easily processed for testing by conventional drug screening and confirmation methods.[42] Although there is promise for the the use of saliva as a adjunct to blood and urine in non-regulated workplace testing, it is rarely collected.

The disadvantages of drug testing in saliva are primarily attributable to our lack of scientific understanding of the pharmacokinetics of most drugs in saliva. Much remains to be learned about how drugs and their metabolites are transferred from the blood into saliva. We know that constituents enter the saliva through passive diffusion, ultrafiltration and active transported.[42] However, without a better fundamental understanding of mechanism(s) of disposition of drugs into saliva, predicting detection of specific drugs and metabolites of interest remains problematic. Like sweat, often parent drugs, and not metabolites are found in saliva.[43] This can have both a disadvantage and an advantage. It is a disadvantage since the antibodies in most commercially available immunoassay drug tests target drug metabolites (see below). It is an advantage since parent drugs are less polar, more easily extracted and less likely to require derivatization prior to GC analysis. An additional limitation to saliva as a specimen in non-regulated testing is that rugs, such as ethanol, that are ingested orally as well as those that can be smoked may be detected in high concentrations in saliva following recent use. Under these circumstances interpretations will be affected because the drug concentration found in saliva may not reflect the blood drug concentration.

10.6.2.6 Other Tissues

Investigations following fatal industrial or transportation accidents may require the testing of tissues. Liver tissue is a valuable specimen to collect post mortem. Since liver is the organ responsible for metabolizing many drugs, drug and metabolite concentrations may be quite high and readily detected. Interpretation of liver tissue concentrations is facilitated by the extensive literature on post mortem tissue concentrations of many drugs.[20] However, these results must be interpreted with great caution, since both postrmertm diffusion and redistribution are know to occur (see Chapter 12). Kidney tissue may also be a useful specimen to collect since drug and metabolite concentrations are usually higher that those found in the blood. This is attributable to the kidney's function in eliminating drugs from the body into the urine. Vitreous humor is often collected when fatalities are fire related because it can be used for testing of volatile compounds such as ethanol. Although other tissues may be collected, they have less utility for testing and interpretation. Their utility maybe limited because they contain minimal concentrations of the drugs, they are difficult to test, or little scientific literature is available to assist in interpreting the results. Interpretation of any tissue drug results is best performed when drug and metabolite concentrations from multiple specimens are available. The disadvantages of tissue drug testing are that it requires complex methods to avoid interferences from endogenous tissue components, it is time consuming and expensive.

10.6.3 METHODS FOR TESTING

Selection of methods to screen, confirm and quantity drugs and drug metabolites in non-regulated testing is at the discretion of the laboratory. The laboratory makes its selection based on the specimen(s) available, reason for testing, anticipated drug concentration, equipment, personnel, required turnaround time, cost and many other factors. Table 10.6.4 shows common screening, confirmation and quantitation methods used by forensic laboratories. More detailed descriptions of these techniques can be found in Chapters 1 and 11.

10.6.3.1 Thin Layer Chromatography (TLC)

TLC chromatography is a versatile technique to screen for a wide variety of drugs and metabolites.[22] Analytes are separated as a migration solvent travels up the TLC plate. The distance that the drug migrates up the plate (Rf or rate of flow) depends on the chemical nature of the drug, the composition of the migration solvent and the coating material on the TLC plate. Selective sprays are applied to the plate to visualize the drugs.[22] The advantages of TLC are that multiple samples can be tested simultaneously, minimal technical expertise is required,

Table 10.6.4 Common Screening, Confirmation and Quantitation Methods Used by Forensic Laboratories

Testing method	Screen	Confirmation	Quantitation expertise	Technical	Time	Testing cost
Thin layer chromatography	**	NA	NA	**	**	**
Immunoassays						
Enzyme-labeled	**	NA	NA	*	*	*
Radio-labeled	**	NA	NA	**	**	**
Fluoresence-labeled	**	NA	NA	*	**	**
On-site test kits	**	NA	NA	*	*	**
Gas chromatography						
Flame ionization detection	***	**	**	***	***	**
Nitrogen phosphorus detection	****	***	***	****	****	***
Electron capture detection	***	***	***	****	****	***
High Performance Liquid Chromatography (HPLC)						
Ultraviolet detection	***	**	***	***	***	
Mass spectrometry with gas chromatohraphy	*	*****	*****	*****	*****	*****
HPLC	*	*****	*****	*****	*****	*****
MS/MS	*	*****	*****	*****	*****	*****

NA = not applicable
* = least utility
***** = most utility

the equipment is inexpensive and several drugs can be screened simultaneously (Table 10.6.4). Themajor disadvantages of TLC methods for workplace testing is that they are qualitative and they lack sufficient sensitivity to identify many of the drugs of interest. TLC is most useful for urinalysis testing.

10.6.3.2 Immunoassays

10.6.3.2.1 Laboratory-Based Immunoassay (LIA)

LIA tests are commonly used for urinalysis screening in clinical, forensic, probation, and regulated and non-regulated workplace testing. They are commercially available with radioactive, fluorescence and enzyme labels. Each test kit contains antibodies designed to detect a specific drug or drug metabolite and is based on competition between drugs in the tested sample and labeled drug in the test kit for a limited antibody. They are available to test for cannabinoids, benzoylecgonine, amphetamine, methamphetamine, opiates, phencyclidine, barbiturates and benzodiazepines. For urinalysis workplace testing, LIA tests are sensitive, easily automated, require minimal technical expertise and inexpensive. Unfortunately, since LIA tests require only limited technical training, unqualified analyst are often asked to perform

Dennis Crouch

the testing and interpret test results. A further limitation of LIA tests is that they have cross reactivity to chemically similar drugs, drug metabolites and endogenous compounds. This can be a problem when testing for drug classes such as the opiates, barbiturates, benzodiazepines and amphetamines where over-the-counter medications are available and where each drug class contains several drugs (Table 10.6.3). LIA tests have limited utility for testing specimens such as blood and tissues because these specimens must be pre-treated to remove endogenous interferences and the LIA calibration must be adjusted to ensure inclusion of the expected lower drug concentrations. LIA tests should not be used as confirmatory tests.[45] All LIA screen test results should be confirmed by a alternate chemical testand an experienced toxicologist should be consulted to interpret the results.[45]

10.6.3.2.2 On-Site Urine Screening Kits

Automated LIA tests require sophisticated instrumentation, considerable expertise and permanent laboratories. The turn-around-time from specimen collection to receipt of drug test results, even from on-site laboratories (see below), may be several hours. This time delay is costly to employers in lost wages, and results in hiring delays while awaiting test results. These concerns have created a market for on-site urine screening kits. These kits are immunoassay based, compact (usually ~5 cm by 10 cm), easily transported and stored, easier to use than LIA test kits and test for similar drug groups. They require no sample preparation, no capital equipment investment, little operator training and they can be used virtually anywhere that a urine specimen can be collected. Several manufacturers provide commercially available on-site urine screening kits that have been described in the literature and numerous studies have been performed to assess the sensitivity and selectivity of on-site urine test kits.[46-49] These studies have shown that on-site urine screening kit results compare favorably to LIA results.

The disadvantages of on-site urine screening kits are similar to those of LIA. Unqualified analyst often are recruited to perform the testing and to interpret the test results. The kits have cross reactivity to chemically similar drugs, drug metabolites and endogenous compounds leading to presumptive positive screening results that sometimes can not be confirmed. The kits are designed to test urine samples and should not be used with complex biological matrices. A further limitation is that most of the studies cited above assessed the accuracy of on-site urine screening kits in laboratories using trained professionals analysts. They have not evaluated the accuracy of testing when it is performed at the work site by non-technical analysts. Additional disadvantages of on-siteurine screening kits are that the results are subjectively interpreted by the analyst and no permanent record of the test results can be maintained for evidential purposes.

10.6.3.3 Gas Chromatography

Gas chromatography is the one of most widely used and versatile techniques available to drug testing laboratories. Like other types of chromatography, GC is a separation technique, and can be used both as a screening tool and as a confirmation and quantitation technique. Several GC detectors are available and are discussed below.

10.6.3.4 Flame Ionization Detectors (FIDs)

These detectors are easy to use, inexpensive, reliable and can be used to detect many of the drugs of interest. The major disadvantages of FIDs are related to its lack of specificity and sensitivity. Sensitivities vary by analyte, but generally are in the mcg/mL range. This is insufficient to detect and quantitate most target drugs in blood, sweat, saliva and hair. The major use of FIDs is for the analysis of volatile compounds such as ethanol.

10.6.3.5 Nitrogen Phosphorus Detectors (NPDs)

NPDs respond only to drugs and metabolites containing a nitrogen or phosphorus in their chemical structure. Fortunately, this includes many of the most frequently encountered such as PCP, benzodiazepines, stimulants, barbiturates, antihistamines, antidepressants, narcotic analgesics, anti-psychotics and antiarrhythmics. The NPD is more specific than the FID and may be 100 to 1,000 times more sensitive, therefore, it may be used for screening, confirmation and quantitation. It is sufficiently sensitivity and selective to test for many prescription drugs in blood and tissues. The disadvantages of NPDs are that they are more time consuming to use than TLC or immunoassays for screening, require considerable sample preparation and technical expertise and they are not as selective as MS for confirmation and quantitation (see below).

10.6.3.6 Electron Capture Detectors (ECDs)

These detectors are not extensively used in workplace testing, but deserve mention because they are capable of detecting pg/mL concentrations of halogenated drugs such as benzodiazepines in a variety of biological samples. Other drugs that can be derivatized with halogenated reagents can also be detected by ECD. The obvious advantages of this detector are its sensitivity and its selectivity. The selectivity is accomplished because it does not respond to drugs or other endogenous biochemicals that contain no halogen atoms. The disadvantages of this detector are similar to those of the NPD. It is more time consuming than TLC or immunoassays for screening and it requires considerable sample preparation and technical expertise to use.

10.6.3.7 Mass Spectrometry (MS) and Tandem Mass Spectrometry (MS/MS)

Mass spectrometry is the most sensitive and selective GC detector for drug testing. It is the required confirmation technique in the federal regulated workplace testing programs.[3,4] Several modes of MS operation are available. Electron ionization (EI) with positive ion detection is used extensively in workplace drug testing.[50,51] EI-GC/MS gives a unique fragmentation pattern that when combined with the GC retention time provides a high degree of confidence in the qualitative identification of drugs and their metabolites.[45] EI-GC/MS may also used to quantitate drugs and metabolites because it a sensitive detector and the potential for interferences is minimal. However, due to the extensive fragmentation of the drug molecule by EI, alternative modes of ionization such as chemical ionization (CI), can be more sensitivity.[50,52] GC/MS methods using positive ion CI have been reported for the analysis of many of the drugs listed in Table 6:2.[50,52-54] This techniques has be used to detect low ng/mL concentration drugs and metabolites in urine, blood, hair, sweat and saliva. Detection of negatively charged fragments by CI-MS is analogous to ECD and has been used to the analyze drugs or derivatized drugs and metabolites that contain halogen atoms.[55-57] Negative ion CI is capable of detecting low ng to pg/mL concentrations of benzodiazepines and cannabinoids in urine, blood and other specimens.[55-58]

Tandem mass spectrometry is a promising new technology for drug testing.[59,60] Its current applications have been for the detection of very low drug concentrations in blood and in the analysis of samples such as hair where pg/mg of hair sensitivity may be needed to detect the drugs of interest.[30,61,62]

There are several limitations to GC/MS. It is not widely used for workplace screening because the analyses are time consuming, substantial operator expertise is required, and the instrumentation is more expensive than that required for other screening techniques such as LIA. Interpretation of GC/MS confirmation and quantitation data requires a level of technical expertise that can only be acquired through years of training and instrument operation. Chemical ionization methods are rarely used for routine urinalysis workplace testing because

Dennis Crouch

the equipment is even more expensive than that needed for EI analyses and additional technical expertise is required. The use of MS/MS for workplace drug testing has been limited to analyses not readily performed by other GC/MS methods due to its cost and complexity. GC/MS is accepted as the standard for medicolegal confirmation of drugs, however, false positive urinalysis reports can occur.

10.6.3.8 High-Performance or High-Pressure Liquid Chromatography (HPLC)

One of the limitations of GC is that many drugs, such as the cannabinoids, barbiturates, sympathomimetic amines and benzodiazepines can not be easily analyzed without derivatization. Although HPLC analyses are prohibited in many regulated programs, for analysis of polar drugs and metabolites, HPLC is a useful technique for screening, confirmation and quantitation.[3,4] Several HPLC detectors can used for drug testing such as ultraviolet (UV), florescence, electrochemical (EC) and mass spectrometry.

10.6.3.8.1 UV Detectors

In contrast to the limited use of fluorescence and EC detectors, UV detectors have many applications in medicolegal drug testing. The extent of native UV absorbance and the wavelength of the absorbed UV light are characteristic of the drug and can be used for detection.[63] An advantage of HPLC with UV detection is that many drugs of interest naturally absorb UV light and, therefore, can be detected and quantitated. The major disadvantages of HPLC with UV detection are that interferences are common with sensitivities are usually mcg/mL.

10.6.3.8.2 MS and MS/MS Detectors

Mass spectrometers are becoming increasingly popular as HPLC detectors.[64] Drugs and metabolites that are not easily analyzed by GC can be separated by the HPLC column and detected, confirmed and quantitated by MS or MS/MS. HPLC-MS and HPLC-MS/MS instruments have only recently been refined for use in routine drug analyses.[65] Several ionization techniques are available, however, those categorized as atmospheric pressure ionization show the most promise for the analyses required for workplace testing.[66] Methods have been published for the analysisdrugs of some interest.[67-70] The advantages of HPLC-MS and MS/MS are that most drugs can be separated by HPLC, no derivatization of polar drugs and metabolites is required and analyses times are shorter than by GC/MS.[65] The major limitations of HPLC-MS and HPLC-MS/MS are that the techniques are new, they are comparatively unproven for workplace drug testing, few methods have been published, more operator expertise is required than for other techniques discussed and the instrumentation is very expensive.

10.6.4 ON-SITE DRUG TESTING

On-site drug testing is testing of employee samples at the site of current, or prospective, employment. This practice is prohibited in most regulated workplace programs, but is widely used in the nuclear power generating industry, military, criminal justice system, off-shore oil industry, shipping and numerous other safety sensitive industries.[3,4,10,11] On-site drug testing has been advocated when test results are needed quickly for decision about hiring, access to safety sensitive facilities, and determining fitness for duty.[5] The testing make take several forms. Employee urine specimens that test negative or positive by LIA (or on-site urine test kits) may be reported and no further testing performed. Some programs require that a portion of all immunoassay positive urine specimens be sent to a laboratory for confirmation. Still other programs send a pre-determined percentage of all tested specimens, whether they screen negative and/or positive, to a laboratory for confirmation. Drugs testing menus may be limited to cannabinoids and cocaine or may be expanded to include additional drugs such as ethanol, amphetamines, opiates, phencyclidine, benzodiazepines, barbiturates, methadone and propoxyphene.[10,11]

Published data reporting the prevalence and accuracy of on-site drug testing are difficult to obtain. The NRC publishes an annual report that includes on-site testing data.[10,11] The National Institute of Drug Abuse funded a study of 11 on-site testing facilities.[71] In that study, on-site testing personnel were interviewed and their competency assessed. Specimen handling, security and chain-of-custody and reporting procedures were evaluated. Written and actual testing procedures were critiqued. Quality control and quality assurance procedures were evaluated. The study concluded that on-site drug testing was technically possible for the purpose of screening in the private sector, military and criminal justice system. However, serious flaws were identified in "....specimen handling procedures, maintenance of specimen security and integrity, documentation of procedures, and quality control programs (that) could jeopardize the defensibility of the data and/or confidentiality of the persons being tested".[71] Study recommendations were that to ensure the quality of on-site drug testing the following were needed: criteria for training and demonstrating the competency of personnel; a standardized custody and control form; guidelines for security of specimens and laboratory records; minimum standards for quality control and quality assurance and a system of over-site.

10.6.5 PERFORMANCE ASSESMENT BATTERIES

One of the most difficult problems in regulated and non-regulated workplace testing is determining impairment from drug use. This is particularly true when employee behavior or performance are used for 'reasonable suspicion' and "for cause" for testing. One approach to providing evidence of impairment to operate a motor vehicle that has promise for workplace use is the National Highway Traffic Safety Administration Drug Evaluation and Classification DEC) program.[72] The program is designed to train police officers to recognize the behavioral signs of alcohol and other drugimpairment and to administer a standard battery of test designed to determine the class of drug that may have been ingested.

The DEC assessment requires the subject to perform a series of divided attention tasks such as Romberg Balance, Walk and Turn, One Leg Stand, and the Finger to Nose. In addition, nystagmus and physiological measures such as pulse rate, blood pressure, and oral temperature are recorded. Results from the divided attention and physiological tests are combined with observations of the general appearance and attitude of the subject to determine if the subject may be under the influence of depressants, stimulants, hallucinogens, PCP, narcotics, cannabinoids, or inhalants. In highway safety, impairment is assessed by observing the driving pattern, administering the DEC assessment battery and collecting a specimen for chemical testing. Laboratory research has shown that trained DEC officers could accurately identify the administered drug in 91.7% of the subjects they evaluated.[73]

However, it also showed that the officers incorrectly identified the administered drug class in 7% of the subjects and that 1.3% of the subjects who received no drug were considered impaired. A field evaluation of the DEC program showed that when officers suspected that a driver had taken a drug other than alcohol, drugs were detected in 94% of the driver's blood.[74] Officers correctly identified the drug ingested in 79% of the cases reviewed.[74]

These results are consistent with recent reports that show urinalysis confirmation rates of 85, 91, 83, and 93% for drivers suspected of being under the influence of stimulants, cannabinoids, depressants and narcotics respectively.[75] The accuracy, validity an sensitivity of the DEC test battery is the subject of current laboratory research.[76] This research has shown that officers correctly identified the drug administered in only 44% of the subjects they evaluated (for more detailed discussion see Chapter 4, Sections 2 and 3).[76] These subjects had measurable concentrations of the administered drug in their blood at the time of evaluation.

Despite controversies over the utility of the DEC program, it is undeniable that it can provide evidence of impairment. When combined with evidence from an investigation of triggering incident and blood drug test results, similar workplace programs could provide persuasive evidence of impairment to support for cause testing or disciplinary actions.

10.6.6 DISCUSSION AND RECOMMENDATIONS

10.6.6.1 The Forensic Nature of Non-Regulated Workplace Testing

The efficacy of non-regulated drug testing programs and employee confidence in the program depends on the quality of testing. No testing methods are completely free of methodological or human error. Since there is no regulatory over-sight of the programs or laboratories, employer's may select the specimen(s) to test, drugs to be tested and the testing methods. To ensure quality testing, laboratories should validate the linearity, precision, qualitative and quantitative accuracy of their screening, confirmation and quantitation methods. Each analysis batch should contain calibrator and quality control samples. Successful performance on quality control samples should be an absolute criterion for reporting test results. The laboratory should include blind quality control samples in all screening tests. The laboratory's quality assurance program should ensure that balances and pipets are accurately calibrated; constant temperatures are maintained in specimen storage, reagent storage, and sample preparation areas; power sources are monitored to ensure optimum instrument operation; and fume hoods, waste disposal, and safety equipment are checked to ensure a safe working environment.[3] All laboratory records should be treated as medico-legal evidence and be meticulously maintained. The importance of thorough record keeping can not be over emphasized because all too often records become the focus of defense experts and attorneys. Each laboratory's records will vary, however, they should include collection site forms, documentation of identification, number, type, volume and quality of each specimen received. They should include quality assurance records for all processes and equipment; analytical screening and confirmation data, calibrators and controls and records of supervisory review of each step of the specimen handling and testing. All documents should be complete and signed and dated at the time the testing was performed.

10.6.6.2 What is Known? What is Needed?

There is a wealth of data that supports the success of non-regulated workplace testing. Corporate studies and testimonials have shown decreases in pre-employment drug test positive results from 8.8 to 3.6% following the implementation of drug testing.[6] A railroad road company reported drug test positive results decreasing form 10 to 1% as a result of testing.[6] The same reports indicated that absenteeism decreased by as much as 39% and the turnover rate dropped from 15 to less than 1% in one company following intervention with a drug testing program. Decreases in industrial accidents and injury accidents of 50% and a 25% reduction in absenteeism have also been attributed to drug testing programs.[6] These reports use decreasing trends as indicators of the success of drug testing programs and drug testing. However, few statistically based scientific assessments of workplace drug testing programs have been performed. Normand demonstrated that absenteeism and turnover rates were significantly higher in postal workers who tested positive prior to hiring than in employees with negative pre-employment screens.[77] An assessment of the efficacy of testing in the power generating industry showed statistically significant differences in sick leave, unexcused absence and total absenteeism between admitted, or detected, drug using employees and their controls.[78] Statistically significant reductions in medical injury and vehicle accidents were also observed following the implementation of drug testing.[78]

Unfortunately, much of what we know about drugs to test, specimens to test, and testing methods for both regulated and non-regulated workplace programs has come from highway safety research and accident investigations and may not be applicable to workplace testing. In addition, we continue to rely on data that only shows an inferential cause and effect relationship between workplace drug testing and positive out comes. To assist in making informed decisions about non-regulated workplace testing in the future, research is needed in several areas. Prevalence data from non-regulated industries are needed that show which drugs are used and extent of their use by these workers. These studies should be longitudinal so that programs can be modified to reflect changing drug use patterns. Studies designed to statistically test the efficacy of workplace drug testing programs are needed. These studies should evaluate drug detection rates, the effects on absenteeism, accidents and costs. Basic pharmacokinetic research is needed that describes the disposition of target drugs in alternate specimens such as hair sweat and saliva. Currently, the lack of these data limit the utility of these specimens for testing preclude reliable interpretation of the test results. Development of new analytic methods for screening and confirmation should be encouraged. GC-MS/MS, HPLC-MS, and HPLC-MS/MS are more sensitive and specific than current confirmation methods and show the promise for workplace testing. An important limitation in workplace testing is our inability to correlate drug concentrations with impairment. Research should be supported that compares blood, hair, sweat, and saliva drug concentrations with workplace performance measures. Research should also be encouraged to develop valid non-chemical performance assessment batteries.

REFERENCES

1. Schoemer, K., Rockers, models and the new allure of heroin, *Newsweek*, 50, 1996.
2. Catlin, D.H., and Murray, T.H., Performance enhancing drugs, fair competion and olympics, JAMA, 276(3) July 17, 1996.231-7.
3. Department of Health and Human Services. Mandatory Guideline for Federal WorkplaceTesting Programs. Federal Register. 1993:58 (14) pp6062-72.
4. Department of Transportation (Federal Highway Administration). Drug and Alcohol Testing Programs. 49 CFR Part 350. Federal Register. 1992:57(241) pp59516-59586.
5. Nuclear Regulatory Commission . Fitnes-For-Duty Programs. 10 CFR Part 2. Federal Register. 1989:54(108) pp24468-24507.
6. DeLancey, M.M., Corporate case studies (Section 8). *Does Drug Testing Work?* Institute for a drug free workplace, Washington, DC. 1994.
7. 1996 AMA Survey. Workplace drug testing and drug abuse policies summary of key findings, American Management Asociation. New York, New York. 1996. pp1-8.
8. Hoffman, J., Larison, C., Brittingham, A., drug use among U.S. workers: prevalence andtrends by occupation and industry categories, *Preview Edition, DHHS Publication No, (SMA) 96-3089, Substance Abuse and Mental Health Services Administration,* 1996.
9. Johnson, T., Drug detection in workplace in 1995 declines for 8th straight year, Smithkline Beecham data shows, *SmithKline Beecham Clinical Laboratories News Release*, Collegeville, PA, Feb, 29, 1996, pp5.
10. Westra, C., Forslund, C., Field, I., Gutierrez, J., Durbin, N., Grant, T., Moffitt. R., Fitness for duty in the nuclear power industry, *Annual Summary of Program PerformanceReports* , 4, 1993, pp1-29.
11. Westra, C., Durbin, N., Field, I., Wilson, R., Hattrup, M., Cunningham, M. Fitness for duty in the nuclear power industry, *Annual Summary of Program Performance Reports*, 5, 1994, pp1-27.
12. Bray, R., Crouch, D., Other drug use: Evidence from surveys and chemical testing (Chapter 36) , In Press, Oct., 1996 *Scientific Evidence Reference Manual.* West Publishing, St, Paul, MN.
13. The top 200 drugs of 1995, *Pharmacy Times*, 62, 27,1996.

14. Garriott, J. C., DiMaio, V. J. M., Zumwalt, R. E. and Petty, C. S., Incidence of Drugs and alcohol in fatally injured motor vehicle drivers,*Journal of Forensic Sciences*, Vol. 2, 1977, pp383-389.
15. Cimbura, G., M.Sc.Phm., Lucas, D., M.Sc.Phm., Bennett, R., M.D., Warren, R., and Simpson, H., Ph.D. Incidence and toxicological aspects of drugs detected in 484 fatally injured drivers and pedestrians in Onatario, *J Forensic Sci*, 27, 855, 1982.
16. Terhune, K. W., and Fell, J. C., The role of alcohol, marijuana, and other drugs in the accidents of injured drivers. *Publication DOT HS. 806-181*.U.S. Department of Transportation, National Highway Traffic Safety Administration, 1982.
17. Williams, A.F., Peat, M.A., Crouch, D.J., Wells, J.K. and Finkle, B.S.., Drugs in Fatally Injured Young Male Drivers, *Public Health Reports,* 100, 19, 1985, pp19-25.
18. Crouch, D., M.B.A., Birky, M., Ph.D., Gust, S., Ph.D., Rollins, D., M.D., Ph.D., Walsh, J., Ph.D., Moulden, J., M.S., Quinlan, K., B.A., and Beckel, R., M.S., The prevalence of drugs and alchohol in fatally injured truck drivers, *J Forensic Sci.*, 38, 1342, 1993.
19. Terhune, C., Ippolito, C., Hendricks, D., Michalovic, J., Bogema, S., Santinga, P., Blomberg, R., Preusser, D. The incidence and role of drugs in fatally injured drivers. *DOT HS 808 065,* U.S. Department of Transportation, National Highway Traffic Safety Administration, 1992.
20. Baselt, R., Cravey, R., *Disposition of Toxic Drugs and Chemicals in Man*, Fourth Edition, Chemical Toxicology Institute, Foster City, 1995.
21. Cone E., and Heustis, M., Relating blood concnetrations of tetrahydrocannabinol and metabolites to pharmacologic effects and time of marijuana use, *Therapeutic Drug Monitorien*, 15, 1993.
22. Moffat, A., Jackson, J., Moss, M., Widdop, B., Greenfield, E., *Clarke's Isolation and Identification of Drugs*, Second Edition, The Pharmaceutical Press, London, 1986.
23. Valkovic, V., Forensic Applications of Hair Analysis, *Human Hair*, Vol. 2, CRC Press,Inc., Boca Raton, 1988, Chap. 9.
24. Goldblum, R., Goldblum, L., and Piper, W., Barbiturate concentrations in the skin and hair of guinea pigs. *J. Invest. Derm.*, 22, 1954.
25. Harkey, M., Henderson, G., Hair analysis for drugs of abuse, *Adv Anal Tox.*, 2, 298, 1989.
26. Baumgartner, W., Black, C, and Jones, P., Radioimmunoassay of hair cocaine in hair. *J. Nuc. Med.*, 23, 1982.
27. Suzuki, O., Hattori, H., and Asano, M., Detection of methamphetamine and amphetamine in a single human by gas chromatography/chemical ionization mass spectrometry. *J Forensic Sci.*, 29, 611, 1984.
28. Moeller, M., Frey, P., and Rimbach, Identification and quantitation of cocaine and its metabolites, benzoylecgonine and ecgonine methyl ester, in hair of Bolivian coca chewers by gas chromatography/chemical ionization mass spectrometry. *J Anal Tox*, 16, 291, 1992.
29. Cone, E., Darwin, W., and Wang, W., The occurance of cocaine, heroin and metabolites in hair of drug abusers, *Forensic Sci Int*, 63, 55, 1993.
30. Kidwell, D., Analysis of phencyclidine and cocaine in human hair by tandem mass spectrometry, *J Forensic Sci.*, 59,29, 1993.
31. DuPont R., and Baumgartner, W., Drug testing by urine and hair analysis: complementary features and scientific issues. *Forensic Sci Int*, 70, 63, 1995.
32. Wang, W., and Cone E., Testing human hair for drugs of abuse. IV. Environmental cocaine contamination and washing effects. , *Forensic Sci Int*t, 70, 39, 1995.
33. Blank, D., Kidwell, D., Decontamination procedures for drugs of abuse in hair: are they suffieient?, *Forensic Sci Int* , 70, 13, 1995.
34. Welch, M., Sniegoski, L., Allgood, C., Interlaboratory comparison studies on the analysis of hair for drugs of abuse, *Forensic Sci Int*, 63, 295, 1993.
35. Sniegoski, L., Welch, M., Interlaboratory studies on the analysis of hair for drugs of abuse: Results from the fourth excercise. *J Anal Toxicol*, 20, 242, 1996.
36. Valkovic, V., Human Hair Growth, *Human Hair*, Vol. 1, CRC Press, Inc., Boca Raton, 1988, Chap. 2.
37. Mieczkowski, T., Newel, R., An evaluation of patterns of racial bias in hair assays for cocaine: black and white arrestees compared, *Forensic Sci Int*, 63, 85, 1993.

Alternative Drugs, Specimens, and Approaches...

38. PharmChek™· PharmChem Laboratories, Inc. 1996. Menlo Park, CA. 94025-1435

39. Baer, J., and Booher, J., The patch: an alternative for drug testing in the criminal justice system, *Federal Probation*, 58, 29, 1994.

40. Burns, M., and Baselt, R., Monitoring drug use with a sweat patch: an experiment with cocaine. *J Anal Toxicol*, 19, 41, 1995.

41. Kintz, P., Tracqui, A., Jamey, C., and Mangin. Detection of codeine and phenobarbital in sweat collected with a sweat patch. *J Anal Toxicol*, 20, 197, 1996.

42. Levine, M., Baum, B., Turner, R., Jusko, W., Milsap, R., Wilson, J., Silbergeld, E., Session 1. Principles of Salivary Gland Fluid Secretion/Overview of Pharmacology. *Saliva as a Diagnostic Fluid*, Vol 694, Malamud, D., Tabak, L.,The New York Academy of Sciences, New York, 1993, pp. 11-62.

43. Cone, E., Session II. Drug Monitoring in Saliva. Saliva Testing for Drugs of Abuse. *Saliva as a Diagnostic Fluid*, Vol 694, Malamud, D., Tabak, L., The New York Academy of Sciences, New York, 1993, pp. 91-127.

44. Jenkins, A., Oyler, J., and Cone, E. Comparison of heroin and cocaine concentrations in saliva with concentrations in blood and plasma, *J Anal Toxicol*, 19, 359, 1995.

45. Hoyt D., Finnigan, R., Nee, T., Shults, T., and Butler, T., Drug testing in the workplace: are methods legally defensible? *JAMA*, 258, 540, 1987.

46. Armbruster, d., and Krolak, J., Screening for drugs of abuse with the Roche ONTRAK™ assays. *J. Anal. Toxicol.* 16, 172, 1992.

47. Buechler, K., Moi, S., Noar, B., McGrath, D., Villela, J., Clancy, M., Colleymore, A., Valkirs, G., Lee, T., Bruni, J., Walsh, M., Hoffman, R., Ahmuty, F., Nowakowski, M., Buechler, J., Mitchell, M., Boyd, D., Stiso, N., and Anderson, R. Simultaneous detection of seven drugs of aubse by the Triage™ panel for drugs of abuse. *Clin Chem*, 38, 1678, 1992.

48. Hwang, S., Hwang, S., Huang, B., and Chen, C., Evaluation of five commercial amphetamines and opiates immunoassay test kits in Taiwan. *J Food and Drug Analysis*, 2,2, 89, 1994.

49. J. Towt, J., Tsai, S., Hernandez, M., Klimov, A., Kravec, C., Rouse, S., Subuhi, H., Twarowska, B., and Salamone, S.,. ONTRAK TESTCUP™: A novel, on-site, multi-analyte screen for the detection of abused drugs. *J Anal Toxicol*, 19, 504, 1995.

50. Foltz, R., Ph.D., Fentiman, A., Jr., Ph.D., Foltz, R., *Research Monograph Series, GC/MS Assays for Abused Drugs in Body Fluids*, 32, Department of Health and Human Services, Rockville, 1980.

51. Goldberger, B., and Cone, E., Confirmatory tests for drugs in the workplace by gass chromatography-mass spectrometry. *J Chromatogr*, 674,73, 1994.

52. Crouch, D., Peat, M, Finkle, B., and Chinn, D., Drugs and driving: a systematic analyticalapproach. *J Forensic Sci.*, 38, 4, 945, 1983.

53. Crouch, D., Alburgues, M., Spanbauer, A., Rollins, D., Moody, D., and Chasin, A., Analysis of cocaine and its metabolites from biological specimens by solid phase extraction and chemical ionization mass spectrometry. *J Anal Toxicol*, 19,6, 1995.

54. Seno, H., Suzuki, O., Kamazawa, T., Hattori, H., Positive and negative ion mass spectrometry and rapid isolation with Sep-Pak C18 cartridges of ten local anaesthetics. *Forensic Sci Int* , 50, 239, 1991.

55. Leis, H., Windischhofer, W., Wintersteiger, R., Quantitative measurement of amphetamine in human plasma by gas chromatography/negative ion chemical ionizaton mass spectrometry using (2H5)amphetamine as internal standard, *Biol Mass Spectrom*, 23, 637, 1994.

56. Reimer, M., Mamer, O., Zavitsanos, A., Siddiqui, A., Dadgar, D., Determination of amphet-amine, methamphetamine and desmethyldeprenyl in human plasam by gas chromatography/negative ion chemical ionization mass spectrometry, *Biol Mass Spectrom* , 22, 235, 1993.

57. Papac D., Foltz, R., Measurement of lysergic acid diethylamide (LSD) in human plasma by gas chromatography/negative ion chemical ionization mass spectrometry. *J Anal Toxicol* , 14, 189, 1990.

58. Cairns E., Dent, B., Ouwerkerk, J., Porter, L., Quantitative analysis of alprazolam and triazolam in hemolysed whole blood and liver digest by GC/MS/NICI with deuterated internal stan-dards, *J Anal Toxicol* , 18, 1, 1994.

59. Fenselau, C., Tandem mass spectrometry: The competitive edge for pharmacology, *Annu Rev Pharmacol Toxicol.*, 32, 555, 1992.
60. Lee, M., and Yost, R., Rapid identification of drug metabolites with tandem mass spectrometry. *Biomed Environ Mass Spectrom*, 15, 195, 1988.
61. Nelson, C., Fraser, M., Wilfahrt, J., and Foltz, R., Gas chromatography/tandem mass spectrometry measurement of Δ9-tetrahydrocannabinol, naltrexone, and their active metabolites in plasma, *Ther Drug Monit*, 15, 557, 1993.
62. Polettini, A., Groppi, A., Montagna, M., Rapid and highly selective GC/MS/MS detection of heroin and its metabolites in hair, *Forensic Sci Int*, 63, 217, 1993.
63. Mills, T. III, Price, W., Price, P., and Roberson, J., *Instrumental Data For Drug Analysis*, Volume 1, Elsevier, New York, 1982.
64. Dobbertein, P., Muenster, H., Application of a new atmospheric pressure ionization source for double focusing sector instruments. *J Chromatogr* , 712, 3, 1995.
65. McCloskey, J., *Methods in Enzymology*, Vol 193 Mass Spectrometry, Academic Press, San Diego, 1990.
66. Bruins, A., Covey, T., and Henion, J. Ion spray interface for combined liquid chromatography/ atmospheric pressure ionization mass spectrometry, *Anal Chem*, 59, 2642, 1987.
67. Tatsuno, M., Nishikawa, M., Katagi, M., and Tsuchihashi, H. Simultaneous determination of illicit drugs in human urine by liquid chromatography-mass spectrometry, *J Anal Toxicol*, 20, 281, 1996.
68. Sosnoff, C., Qinghong, A., Bernert, J., Jr., Powell, M., Miller, B., Henderson, L., Hannon, W., Fernhoff, P., and Sampson, E., Analysis of benzoylecgonine in dried blood spots by liquid chromatography-atmospheric pressure chemical ionization tandem mass spectrometry, *J Anal Toxicol.*, 20, 179, 1996.
69. Josephs, J., Crouch, D., Spanbauer, A., Low level analysis of drugs in biological matrices by ESI-LC/MS, *Finnigan Mat SSQ Pharmaceutical Analysis Application Report #249.* 1995.
70. Pacifici, R., Pichini, S., Altieri, I., Caronna, A., Passa, A., and Zuccaro, P., HPLC electrospray mass spectrometric determination of morphine and its 3- and 6-glucuronides: appliction to pharmacokinetic studies, *J.Chromatogr.B-Bio.Med Appl.*, 664, 329, 1995.
71. Rollins, D., On-Site drug testing in the workplace, Final Report to the National Institute on Drug Abuse. Division of Workplace Programs. 1992.
72. Preliminary training for drug evaluation and classification, *Report HS 172A*, U.S. Department of Transportation Safety, National Highway Traffic Safety Administration, 1989.
73. Bigelow, G., Bickel, W., Roache, J., Liebson, I., Nowowieski, P., Identifiying types of drug intoxication: Laboratory evaluation of a subject-examination procedure, *DOT HS 806 753, Final Report May 1985*, U.S. Department of Transportation, National Highway Traffic Safety Administration.
74. Compton, R., Field evaluation of the Los Angeles Police Department drug detection procedure, *DOT HS 807 012, NHTSA Technical Report Feb. 1986* , U.S. Department of Transportation, National Highway Traffic Safety Administration.
75. Adler, E. V., B.S., DABFT, Bourland, J., B.S., Arizona's drug recognition program: A performance assessment, *The DRE*, 4, 1995.
76. Heishman, S., Singleton, E., Crouch, D., Laboratory validation study of drug evaluation and classification program: ethanol, cocaine, and marijuana, *J Anal Toxicol*, 20, 1, 1996.
77. Normand, J., and Salyards, S., An Empirical Evaluation of Preemployment Drug Testing in the United States Postal Service: Interim Report of Findings. *Research Monogram Series, Drugs in the Workplace*, 91, Gust, S., Ph.D., Walsh, J., Ph.D., Department of Health and Human Services, Rockville, 1989, pp 111-138.
78. Crouch, D., Webb, D., Peterson, L., Buller, P., and Rollins, D., A Critical Evaluation of the Utah Power & Light Company's Substance Abuse Management Program: Absenteeism, Accidents and Costs. *Research Monogram Series, Drugs in the Workplace*, 91, Gust, S., Walsh, J., Department of Health and Human Services, Rockville, 1989, pp 111-138.

10.7 IMPLEMENTATION OF ALCOHOL TESTING: GENERAL CONSIDERATIONS AND PROCESSES

DONNA R. SMITH, PH.D.

SENIOR VICE PRESIDENT, PLANNING & IMPLEMENTATION,
SUBSTANCE ABUSE MANAGEMENT, INC., BOCA RATON, FLORIDA

Beginning in 1995 over 7 million workers in transportation occupations in the U.S. became subject to workplace alcohol testing programs and comprehensive alcohol misuse prevention initiatives mandated by Federal law and U.S. Department of Transportation regulations. The development and implementation of this public policy was, in reality, a five year effort. Workplace testing is not new to employees in safety sensitive positions in the private or public workforces. However, prior to 1995, workplace testing conducted under federal mandates had been limited largely to urine testing for drugs of abuse.

When the Department of Transportation (DOT) issued the first drug testing rules in late 1988, there was considerable public comment and discussion among the affected DOT agencies about the issue of alcohol misuse and its impact on transportation safety. Many believed that the problems associated with alcohol misuse and abuse were far more widespread and represented a greater threat to public safety than did problems associated with illicit drug use in the transportation industries. After considerable debate, the DOT issued in late 1989, an advance notice of proposed rule making[1] (ANPRM) in an attempt to explore the feasibility and efficacy of workplace alcohol testing as a measure to deter and detect alcohol abuse.

The notice to the transportation industry and the public did not produce enthusiastic response. The commercial aviation, rail and trucking industries were facing difficult economic times, and viewed a federal mandate for alcohol testing programs as too costly and unproven in effectiveness at impacting on safety. Industry groups claimed that there was little substantial data that pointed to alcohol abuse as an attributable cause of transportation accidents. The Federal Aviation, Railroad, and Highway Administrations had alcohol use prohibitions in a fitness for duty context as part of the medical standards, impairment, and under the influence provisions of their safety rules. The U.S. Coast Guard had mandatory post accident alcohol testing and authorized reasonable suspicion testing. In addition, the Federal Railroad Administration had a comprehensive post-accident investigation program that included blood alcohol testing. In these existing provisions for alcohol testing under limited circumstances, a 0.04% blood alcohol level was established as a "per se" violation of federal safety rules.

10.7.1 BACKGROUND TO RULE MAKING

The implementation of the DOT drug testing rules began in January, 1990, without any regulatory provisions for alcohol testing. A transportation employee testing bill, generally called the "Hollings-Danforth Bill" continued to circulate in Congress, but was not successfully passed. This bill, first proposed following a fatal train accident in Chase, Maryland in January, 1987, did include alcohol testing, as well as drugs of abuse testing, but was aimed only at the aviation, railroad and interstate trucking industries. The National Transportation Safety Board continued to encourage the DOT to initiate further alcohol testing provisions, especially in conjunction with accident investigation activities.

In 1991, another fatal public transportation accident got widespread media and political attention. A New York City Transit subway train crashed in Manhattan, killing seven, injuring many, and causing millions of dollars in damages. The subway train operator was under the influence of alcohol at the time of the accident. Ironically, the transit industry was not subject to any DOT testing requirements. The drug testing rule issued by the DOT agency, the Urban Mass Transit Administration (now the Federal Transit Administration) in late 1988, had been struck down in Federal court in January 1990. Neither drug nor alcohol testing of transit employees was authorized or required under federal rules. Supporters of the Hollings-Danforth Bill quickly recognized that public sentiment was favorable for passage following the transit accident and the well publicized finding of an alcohol related fatal accident. The bill was amended to include mass transit operations receiving federal transit funding and to include intrastate trucking and bus operations. The legislation passed and became the Omnibus Transportation Employee Testing Act, signed into law by President Bush on October 28, 1991.[2] The Omnibus Act was the first federal law requiring alcohol and drug testing of employees in both private and public sector safety-sensitive occupations. The Secretary of Transportation was given the responsibility of issuing federal regulations that would implement the provisions of the Omnibus Act.

10.7.2 IMPACT OF THE OMNIBUS ACT

The Omnibus Act required only a few changes to the existing drug testing rules. It did add over 3 million public transit system and commercial drivers' licensed personnel to the positions defined as safety sensitive and subject to testing. As an additional safeguard for employees, the Act mandated split specimen collection and testing procedures for urine drug testing. Under the provisions of the Act, all employees who tested positive were to be given information and access to evaluation and treatment services for substance abuse problems.

The major impact of the Omnibus Act was the requirement for alcohol testing. Unlike for drug testing, the law's language did not specify the methods or procedures for alcohol testing. Clearly, the Act did require reasonable suspicion, post-accident, and random alcohol testing. The issue of pre-employment or applicant alcohol testing was not so clear. The DOT originally interpreted the law as mandating both alcohol and drug testing of all applicants for safety-sensitive positions. However, after the rules were issued in early 1994, a court challenge to pre-employment alcohol testing was upheld, and the DOT withdrew the regulatory requirement for applicant alcohol testing.[3]

When the DOT issued the drug testing rules in 1988, an infrastructure for urine drug testing was in place. The U.S. military services had several years experience with mass testing of soldiers, forensic toxicology procedures for urine testing for drugs of abuse, and quality assurance programs for monitoring laboratory performance. As a result of the 1986 Executive Order requiring drug testing of federal employees in the Executive branch of government, the Department of Health and Human Services had established urine specimen collection procedures, forensic analytical laboratory standards and certification program, and provisions for physician review and interpretation of drug test results.[4] The DOT had few technical or scientific issues to address in crafting the transportation industry drug testing rules, and essentially mirrored the DHHS procedures.

10.7.3 STANDARDS AND PROCEDURES

For alcohol testing there were few, if any, standards or procedures that could be applied to mass alcohol testing in transportation industry worksites throughout the U.S. The only models in the public sector for alcohol testing were those for drunk driving enforcement by state agencies. For years the "gold standard" in alcohol testing was blood alcohol analysis, usually by gas chromatography. In the 1980s more and more states began to accept and use evidential breath alcohol testing in law enforcement. The National Highway Traffic Safety Administration (NHTSA), an agency of the Department of Transportation, had developed technical standards for evidential breath testing equipment to be used in DWI enforcement. NHTSA evaluated breath testing devices in a special laboratory setting to assess their accuracy and precision in breath alcohol measurement. Evidential breath testing equipment that met the NHTSA standards were included on a Conforming Products List from which state and local law enforcement agencies could select, and use federal matching funds in DWI deterrent and detection programs.

The DOT also considered using urine alcohol measurement as a method to comply with the Omnibus Act requirements for alcohol testing in the transportation industries. Forensic urine specimen collection procedures were already well established, forensic analytical procedures for testing urine in federally certified laboratories existed, and the technology for detecting alcohol concentrations in urine was available. There were, however, drawbacks to using urine alcohol measurements. First, drug testing laboratories were not certified for urine alcohol testing procedures and proficiency programs to monitor their performance on urine alcohol testing were not established. Second, urine alcohol results would not be available immediately after the collection, but instead have a 2 to 3 day turnaround time at the laboratory. Third, urine alcohol measurements are not easily equated to blood alcohol concentrations. In order to use urine alcohol concentrations which establish the alcohol content in an individual's blood stream, the urine specimen must be obtained using two voids, usually 20 to 30 min apart, ensuring that the first void completely empties the bladder. Since the DOT alcohol misuse rules were to be based on prohibited alcohol conduct relative to performing safety-sensitive functions, a measurement of alcohol concentration in the blood stream which is time-proximate to duty performance was necessary.

In considering blood alcohol testing for the DOT rules, the government decided that the invasion of privacy issues, the potential dangers to employees, and the delay in obtaining results, outweighed the advantages of proven technology. Saliva alcohol testing was also considered during the initial rule making process. Although, saliva alcohol testing is a newer technology than blood, breath or urine, it is well-documented as a reliable methodology and has been correlated to blood alcohol levels. Saliva alcohol measurement has not been as extensively used in forensic or legal settings, and therefore, has not been tested in the courts. In arenas where saliva alcohol testing has been used, its use has been as a screening tool, with blood alcohol testing used as forensic confirmation.

10.7.4 SELECTION OF EVIDENTARY ALCOHOL TESTING

After extensive reviews of blood, breath, urine and saliva technology for alcohol concentration measurement, the DOT decided on evidential breath testing as the methodology for the alcohol rules. This decision was based on five primary factors: (1) scientific accuracy and precision in measuring alcohol concentration in body fluids; (2) invasiveness of the collection procedure; (3) ease of administration in a workplace setting; (4) legal supportability and defensibility of test results; and (5) economic cost of testing large numbers of employees. There was also some history of using breath alcohol testing in fitness for duty programs in the Nuclear Power industry and the U.S. military.

Once the decision about testing methodology was made, the next major issue was setting a cut-off level for determining positive and negative tests. Again, the DOT turned to existing testing programs in state DWI enforcement, the U.S. military, and nuclear power industries to examine impairment, fitness for duty standards, and other policy related to alcohol concentrations. State laws generally use 0.08 to 0.10 blood or breath alcohol concentration as per se levels for impairment or violations of state laws for driving while intoxicated. The U.S. military has established 0.05 breath or blood alcohol concentration as the prohibited alcohol level in a fitness for duty context. Other federal agencies such as the Nuclear Regulatory Commission have used a 0.04 cut-off value for determining a violation or positive test. After a comprehensive review of the literature on alcohol impairment, effects of alcohol on performance tasks, and

Donna R. Smith

alcohol intoxication studies, the DOT decided on a 0.04 alcohol concentration as measured by evidential breath testing devices as the violation level for the DOT rules. However, the DOT hedged its bet when it came to the broader public safety issues. Because a breath alcohol test, or any other measurement of blood alcohol concentration, provides only the alcohol concentration at that time, estimates of earlier or later concentrations are not available. Thus, the DOT required employers to remove safety-sensitive employees from duty when they have a breath alcohol concentration of 0.02 or above. This bifurcated system of actions based on the breath alcohol concentration has led to wide variations in disciplinary actions in employers' policies.

The procedures and equipment used for breath alcohol testing in workplaces where alcohol testing is federally mandated are screening and confirmation tests with evidential breath testing devices, commonly referred to as EBTs. The NHTSA publishes a conforming products list that identifies EBTs that can be used for federally mandated workplace testing. These devices are accurate to the 0.02 alcohol concentration level, do not read acetone or other non-alcohol breath contents, and produce printed test results.[5] The federal procedures require that two separate breath samples be obtained to substantiate a positive test (>0.02 BrAC). If the initial or screening test is greater that 0.02 BrAC, a second breath test is performed after a 15-min waiting period to clear any residual mouth alcohol reading. The confirmation test result is the governing result, and is considered a "positive result" if it is 0.02 BrAC or greater[6]

Several months after the implementation date of the DOT alcohol testing rules, the DOT decided to allow non-evidential screening devices for conducting the initial alcohol test.[7] The screening devices, like the evidential breath testing devices, must be evaluated and approved by NHTSA. Thus far, NHTSA has approved both saliva and breath alcohol measurement devices for use in the screening test. Regardless of what testing device is used for the screening test, a presumptive positive screen (≥ 0.02) must be confirmed using an EBT.

The federal rules also require technicians who administer workplace alcohol tests to meet certain qualifications. These technicians, called Breath Alcohol Technicians, or BATs, must complete specific training courses meeting the standards of the DOT model training curriculum.[8] The BAT administers the breath alcohol test, records the printed results on an alcohol testing form, and reports test results to the employer. Unlike with workplace drug test results, there is no review of breath alcohol test results by a physician to determine alternative medical explanations for the test finding.

10.7.5 WORKPLACE ALCOHOL TESTING

Workplace alcohol testing in many ways mirrors accepted practices for employee drug testing. The events or circumstances which trigger or warrant an alcohol test are similar to those for urine drug testing. Under DOT and NRC rules, alcohol tests are required of safety-sensitive employees in cases of reasonable suspicion, post-accident, random selection, return to duty and follow-up monitoring. One significant difference is that DOT rules do not require or authorize pre-employment or applicant alcohol testing, but they do require applicant drug testing. The criteria for reasonable suspicion and post-accident alcohol testing under federal rules are essentially the same as those for drug tests. It is important to note that blood alcohol tests are not used in federally-mandated alcohol testing, even if breath alcohol tests cannot be obtained. One of the significant complaints by employers about the implementation of the workplace alcohol testing rules is the unavailability of trained Breath Alcohol Technicians and acceptable EBT devices, particularly in rural areas and during "off" hours.

The Department of Transportation alcohol testing rules do not allow for back extrapolation of breath test results.[9] Thus, alcohol test results cannot be used to identify employees who have violated the "pre-duty abstinence" periods required of safety-sensitive employees. For example, The Federal Aviation Administration prohibits flight crew personnel from consuming alcohol within eight hours of beginning flight operations. If an employees reports for duty, is tested and has a BrAC result of 0.02, the employer cannot interpret that result to mean that the employee violated the eight hour pre-duty abstinence requirement.

Widespread workplace alcohol testing is a relatively new phenomenon, and conclusions about its effectiveness are not yet certain. Many employers believe that alcohol problems among their workforces are much more prevalent than problems with illicit drugs. However, employers are not as a whole convinced that random alcohol testing will have the same deterrent effect on alcohol abuse as random drug testing has had on illicit drug abuse. The Department of Transportation reflects these same doubts about the effectiveness of random alcohol testing as a deterrent to alcohol misuse.[10] In establishing the annual random alcohol testing rate for employers, the DOT chose 25%, rather than the 50% rate used when drug testing was initiated in the transportation industries. Most employers believe that reasonable suspicion alcohol testing is the most effective tool for identifying alcohol abusers in their workforce. However, reasonable suspicion alcohol testing is very dependent on supervisors' and managers' willingness to be vigilant for the signs and symptoms of alcohol abuse in employees and to be comfortable in making determinations to conduct the testing.

Most evaluations of workplace alcohol testing programs demonstrate that employee and supervisory education and training are important adjuncts to testing. The availability of employee assistance programs is also crucial to successful workplace interventions. The federal alcohol testing rules do require that employees be referred to a Substance Abuse Professional for evaluation of problems associated with alcohol abuse. However, in reality, many employers' policies call for termination of employment if an individual tests positive. Thus, employees who loose their job often do not follow through with evaluation and treatment. The Department of Transportation began collecting and reviewing data from workplace alcohol testing programs in 1995. Complete implementation of the Department of Transportation mandated alcohol testing was not phased-in until 1996. It is, therefore, too early to tell what impact the mandated programs have on transportation accidents and workplace safety.

REFERENCES

1. U.S. Department of Transportation: Advance Notice of Proposed Rule Making. November 2, 1989. *Federal Register*. Washington, DC.
2. Omnibus Transportation Employee Testing Act. Public Law 102-143. October 28, 1991. Washington, DC.
3. U.S. Department of Transportation. Suspension of Pre-Employment Alcohol Testing Requirement: Final Rule. May 10, 1995. *Federal Register*. Washington, DC.
4. U.S. Department of Health and Human Services. Mandatory Guidelines for Federal Employee Workplace Drug Testing Programs. April 11, 1988. *Federal Register*. Washington, DC.
5. National Highway Traffic Safety Administration. Highway Safety Programs: Model Specifications for Devices to Measure Breath Alcohol: Final Rule. September 17, 1993. *Federal Register*. Washington, DC.
6. U.S. Department of Transportation. Procedures for Transportation Workplace Drug and Alcohol Programs. 49 CFR Part 40. February 15, 1994. *Federal Register*. Washington, DC.
7. U.S. Department of Transportation. Procedures for Transportation Workplace Drug and Alcohol Programs; Procedures for Non-Evidential Alcohol Screening Devices: Final Rule. April 20, 1995. *Federal Register*. Washington, DC.
8. U.S. Department of Transportation. Breath Alcohol Technician (BAT) Training: Instructor Training Curriculum. July 1994. U.S. Government Printing Office. Washington, DC.
9. U.S. Department of Transportation. Limitation on Alcohol Use by Transportation Workers: Notice. February 15, 1994. *Federal Register*. Washington, DC.
10. U.S. Department of Transportation. Limitation on Alcohol Use by Transportation Workers: Notice. February 15, 1994. *Federal Register*. Washington, DC.

Donna R. Smith

CHAPTER 11
ALTERNATIVE TESTING MATRICES

MARILYN A. HUESTIS, PH.D. AND EDWARD J. CONE, PH.D.

LABORATORY OF CHEMISTRY AND DRUG METABOLISM, ADDICTION RESEARCH CENTER,
NATIONAL INSTITUTE ON DRUG ABUSE, NIH, BALTIMORE, MARYLAND

TABLE OF CONTENTS

0-8493-2637-0/98/$0.00+$.50
© 1998 by CRC Press LLC

Information about human drug exposure can be obtained by chemical testing of biological specimens. The choice of which biological specimen to analyze is critical because each type of specimen may impart different chemical and pharmacodynamic knowledge. Human drug exposure can occur through a variety of different means including self-administration, passive inhalation, external contamination, exchange of body fluids, and in utero exposure. For drug

Marilyn A. Huestis and Edward J. Cone

testing in alternate matrices to be useful, an understanding must be developed of the fundamental chemical and pharmacologic principles governing the appearance and disappearance of
drugs and their metabolites in these matrices.

11.1 FACTORS EFFECTING DRUG DISPOSITION

Drug disposition is dependent upon the chemical and physical properties of the agent, the
route of drug administration, metabolic processes, and duration and frequency of exposure.
The chemical form and concentration of drug in each tissue is dependent upon the drug's
volatility, lipophilicity, pKa, and extent of protein binding. Unchanged drug and/or metabolites may be deposited throughout the body as a result of a drug's absorption, distribution,
metabolism, and excretion. Measurement of drug in different biological tissues or matrices
provides a unique perspective of an individual's drug exposure history and may help answer
questions that are difficult to resolve by testing a single body fluid or tissue.

The route of drug administration and the physicochemical characteristics of the drug
determine the rate of absorption and penetration of human biological barriers. The rate of drug
entry is the major determinant of peak blood concentrations and the onset of drug effects.
Distribution to the various fluid and tissue compartments of the body begins as soon as drug
appears in blood. Tissue uptake is generally related to blood flow to the tissue mass and to the
lipophilicity of the drug and the degree of binding to plasma proteins. Only the "free"
unbound fraction of drug will be transferred from blood to other tissues.

For highly lipid-soluble substances, disposition into fat stores begins to occur as soon as
drug appears in blood. Because of limited blood flow to fatty tissues, disposition to other more
highly perfused tissues and fluid components occurs at a much higher rate. Consequently, lipid
soluble drugs appear in virtually all components of the body, e.g., saliva, sweat, urine, skin,
sebum, hair, etc. at different rates and reach peak concentrations at different times. The process
governing transfer across cellular membranes generally is concentration-driven diffusion of the
free drug fraction. During the distribution phase, drug will be accumulating at different rates
in different bodily compartments, but the transfer is reversible. Drug concentrations in more
accessible compartments which had early peak concentrations begin to decline as concentrations in poorly perfused tissues, e.g., fat, increase. Ultimately, a pseudo-equilibrium state is
reached between all compartments and all accessible drug concentrations begin to decline as
drug clearance processes, e.g., metabolism, excretion, take over.

Drug will be cleared from different compartments at different rates in approximately the
same order as occurred with their initial appearance, i.e., highly perfused compartments like
muscle tissue will be cleared first, whereas fat stores will retain drug for much longer periods.
This same process will apply equally to smaller "compartments" like salivary glands which will
be cleared of drug as rapidly as drug is cleared from blood. Sweat "compartments" are cleared
of drug more slowly, but the mechanisms of drug entry into sweat are poorly understood and
are likely to be more complex than simple diffusion from blood into sweat glands. For some
"compartments", drug may be irreversibly bound and retained indefinitely. The deposition of
drug into hair is also not well understood; however, once drug is bound to the hair matrix, it
appears difficult to remove and ultimately is eliminated from the body as a result of continuing
hair growth.

With multiple drug administrations, the processes of absorption, distribution and clearance
are repeated. If the time interval between exposures is sufficiently short, there may be
accumulation of drug or metabolite from one administration to the next. Depending upon the
characteristics of the drug, there may be accumulation in some "compartments" but not others.
For example, tetrahydrocannabinol is known to be cleared rapidly from highly-perfused tissues
(blood, saliva), but is sequestered for much longer times in fat stores. If a user smoked

marijuana on a daily basis, accumulation would be expected to occur in all compartments, whereas weekly use might produce detectable accumulation only in certain tissues and fluids (e.g., fat and possibly sebum). Unfortunately, there are many tissues and fluids available for drug testing in which drug disposition and elimination processes are incompletely understood. The patterns of drug disposition into alternate matrices such as skin, sweat, saliva, hair, sebum, etc. are being actively studied by many investigators and progress should be rapid over the next decade.

11.1.1 MEASUREMENT OF DRUG ANALYTES

Measurement of drug analytes in different biological tissues can provide different windows of detection which can be useful for interpretation of test results. For example, the presence of benzoylecgonine in urine can be interpreted as evidence of recent cocaine exposure, but cannot be interpreted to mean that the subject was under the influence of cocaine at the time of sampling. In contrast, the presence of cocaine in saliva or blood can reasonably be interpreted as an indication of both recent use and a high likelihood that the subject was experiencing pharmacological effects when the sample was obtained. Preliminary studies with the sweat patch indicate that it may be useful for detection of single and multiple drug use over a period of 1 to 4 weeks. Hair testing appears to offer the possibility of monitoring drug use over an extended period of time that is dependent upon the length of an individual's hair. Interest in the measurement of drugs of abuse in hair and sweat has increased due to the wider window of drug detection compared to urine drug testing. For a similar reason, amniotic fluid, meconium, and neonatal hair are being utilized to monitor in utero drug exposure.

11.1.2 SPECIMEN COLLECTION

Specimen collection in many cases, i.e., breath, hair, sweat, and saliva, among others, is less invasive than collection of blood or urine. Heightened safety concerns accompany the collection of other biological fluids, i.e., amniotic fluid and fat biopsies. The performance characteristics of the assay methodology are also important . Drug testing must be performed with careful consideration of the limitations imposed by the testing methodology and the biological specimen. Drug concentration in the tissue will greatly affect the difficulty of measurement and the requirement for sophisticated instrumentation to ascertain the identity and quantitate drugs of interest. The sensitivity and specificity of each assay must be evaluated for each matrix and each analyte. New immunoassays must be developed to identify unique analytes in each specimen type. Parent drug compounds generally predominate in hair and sweat, while polar metabolites predominate in urine. The majority of commercially available immunoassays products are targeted toward identification of polar metabolites excreted in urine. Different biologic matrices not only require measurement of the appropriate analyte, but also selection of appropriate decision thresholds to achieve the desired objectives.

Other important considerations in testing alternate biological fluids are determination of suitable sampling times, evaluation of analyte stability during analysis, and identification of possible matrix interferences.

11.1.3 STABILITY OF DRUGS

The stability of drug compounds in the biological matrix must be evaluated. Some drug analytes, i.e., heroin and cocaine, may be labile and subject to hydrolysis if not stabilized and stored properly. Consequently, the stability of drugs in each matrix must be evaluated. Also, the chemical composition of each biological fluid determines the efficiency of drug extraction from the complex matrix. Interfering substances may hinder the identification and quantitation

Marilyn A. Huestis and Edward J. Cone

of drug analytes and must be eliminated prior to analysis. For instance, the high lipid content of breast milk makes analysis of highly lipophilic drugs in this matrix difficult to accomplish. Each biological matrix will present different types of matrix problems. For example, enzymatic digestion of hair samples may render specimens unsuitable for immunoassay screening methodologies due to high background absorbances.

In the following sections, we will explore the advantages and disadvantages of drug measurement in alternate biologic matrices. Sections are divided by specimen type. A general description of physiology pertinent to the specimen type is followed by a review of studies relevant to the use of the specimen as a means of detecting drugs of abuse.

11.2 SALIVA*

11.2.1 MECHANISMS OF DRUG INCORPORATION

Saliva is formed from secretions of the serous and mucous cells of the parotid (25%), submandibular (71%), and sublingual (4%) glands.[1] Serous cells secrete a colorless watery fluid with a high electrolyte content and mucous cells secrete a more viscous fluid containing amylases, mucoproteins and mucopolysaccharides. Neurotransmitter and hormonal stimulation controls saliva flow which can vary from 0 to 10 mL/min for a daily total of 500 to 1500 mL. Secretion rates and electrolyte and total protein concentrations were reported not to vary with age, although amylase activity was found to significantly decrease over an individual's lifespan.[2] In contrast, Gutman and Ben-aryeh[3] observed an increase in mean electrolyte content and a decrease in salivary flow rate with age. Saliva pH is slightly acidic but increases with flow rate from a low of 5.5 to a high of 7.9. Saliva composition also varies with flow, but consists of approximately 90% water, and 10% electrolytes, amylase, glucose, urea, lipids, proteins, and hormones.

Drugs are incorporated into saliva by passive diffusion, ultrafiltration and/or by active secretion from the blood. Of these processes, passive diffusion represents the most important route of entry for most drugs with the possible exception of ethanol; its low molecular weight permits entry by ultrafiltration. Passage across cell membranes is limited for molecules with a molecular weight of greater than 500, and entry is restricted for ionized and protein-bound drugs. Plasma and saliva pH and a drug's pKa and degree of protein binding will control the saliva to plasma (S/P) partitioning of ionizable drugs. Saliva flow rate greatly influences salivary pH and hence, S/P ratios.[4]

Muchlow et al.[5] studied the effect of saliva flow and pH changes on S/P ratios of drugs primarily ionized at normal plasma pH (e.g., meperidine) compared to drugs primarily non-ionized at normal plasma pH (e.g., antipyrine). Chewing waxed film was used to increase saliva flow. For meperidine, at a moderate saliva flow rate of 0.65 mL/min, the saliva pH was 6.7 and the S/P ratio was 2.6. When subjects chewed vigorously on the waxed film, the flow rate increased to 2.77 mL/min and the pH increased to 7.3. The resultant S/P ratio declined to 1.37. In contrast, antipyrine S/P ratios measured under similar conditions did not change with alterations in saliva flow rate and pH. It was concluded that saliva pH was the chief variable determining the saliva concentration of ionizable drugs.

Generally, a correlation may exist between the free drug concentration in blood and saliva drug concentration. Although saliva has a reduced protein content compared to blood, Idowu and Caddy[6] noted that one possible source of error in measurement of drugs in saliva may be

---

* This section is an extensively revised and updated version of a chapter entitled "Saliva Drug Analysis" by Cone and Jenkins in *The Handbook of Therapeutic Drug Monitoring and Toxicology*, Wong and Sunshine, Eds., CRC Press, Boca Raton, FL, 1966.

the binding of drugs to mucoproteins and underestimation of drug concentrations following centrifugation. The mucoprotein-bound drug in saliva may be precipitated by centrifugation during specimen processing.

11.2.2 CORRELATIONS BETWEEN BLOOD AND SALIVA

Saliva may be collected by allowing the saliva to freely flow from the mouth into a container, aspirating saliva through a vacuum pump tube or by placing a cotton swab in the mouth and allowing saliva to be absorbed. For the purposes of investigational studies, saliva secretion is usually increased. Flow may be stimulated by chewing on a piece of Teflon® or a clean rubber band; substances such as Parafilm®, should be avoided, since they may absorb highly lipophilic drugs.[7] Alternatively, citric acid crystals or candy may be used to increase saliva flow. Resting salivary flow rates exhibit a circadian rhythm which can result in changes in salivary pH.[8] In order to collect saliva from a particular gland the individual ducts must be isolated and flow collected with special devices or by cannulation. Devices have been developed to simplify collection of ultrafiltrates of saliva.[9]

11.2.3 ADVANTAGES AND DISADVANTAGES AS A TEST MEDIA

The major advantages of saliva as a test media include ease of accessibility and reduced invasiveness, presence of higher concentrations of parent drug than metabolites, and correlation of saliva drug concentrations to free drug concentrations in blood. For this reason, saliva samples have been proposed for therapeutic drug monitoring of phenytoin, carbamazepine, theophylline, digoxin, and cyclosporin.[8] However, salivary analysis for detection of drugs of abuse has also been proposed due to the pharmacologic significance of measurement of active drug. Peel et al.[10] utilized saliva testing as a non-invasive test for detection of drug use in impaired drivers. Alcohol was the most common drug detected, followed by cannabinoids and diazepam. Most drugs disappear from saliva and blood within 12 to 24 h after administration. There is often a temporal relationship between the disappearance of drugs in saliva and the duration of pharmacologic effects. Consequently, saliva is useful in the detection of recent drug use in automobile drivers, accident victims and for testing employees prior to engaging in safety-sensitive activities. Despite these advantages, saliva drug testing for forensic purposes has been slow to develop as a mature science compared to other means of drug testing.

There are also disadvantages in the use of saliva for the measurement of drugs. Drug concentrations in saliva may vary due to pH changes. Contamination of saliva from drug use by the oral, smoked and intranasal routes of drug administration may occur resulting in distorted S/P ratios. Another possible disadvantage is the short time course for detectability of drugs in saliva; thereby, preventing this biological fluid from being used to detect historical drug use. However, this is an advantage for detection of very recent drug use.

11.2.4 DETECTION OF SPECIFIC DRUGS

11.2.4.1 Cocaine

Inaba et al.[11] first reported the excretion of cocaine in saliva following oral administration of radiolabeled cocaine. Cone and colleagues, in a series of studies on cocaine and metabolite concentrations in saliva and plasma following intravenous,[12] smoking,[13] and intranasal[14] routes of administration, noted that cocaine was the major analyte in saliva following all routes of administration. Benzoylecgonine and ecgonine methyl ester generally were present in minor amounts and their concentrations usually peaked later than the cocaine concentration. Contamination of the oral cavity following the smoking and intranasal routes of administration

Marilyn A. Huestis and Edward J. Cone

produced elevated S/P ratios in the early period after drug administration. After approximately 3 h, S/P ratios were equivalent by the three routes of administration. Significant correlations were found between saliva and plasma cocaine (r = 0.89, p <0.01), subjective effects ("Feel Drug" scale, r = 0.74, p < 0.01; "Goodness" scale, r = 0.54, p <0.05; "Rush" scale, r = 0.55, p <0.05) and physiologic effects (pulse, r = 0.76, p <0.01) after intravenous drug administration to human subjects.[12] Observation of a significant correlation of saliva cocaine concentrations with plasma concentrations and also with behavioral effects provides the opportunity for development of a new non-invasive test for cocaine abuse.

Jenkins et al.[15] reported peak saliva cocaine concentrations after intravenous administration of 44.8 mg cocaine hydrochloride of 428 to 1927 ng/mL; peak concentrations of cocaine after an equivalent smoked dose varied from 15 to >500 µg/mL. Detection times (LOD = 1 ng/mL) were longer in saliva than plasma for both routes of drug administration with an average detection time in saliva of 446 min after smoking and 514 min after IV administration compared with 240 min and 377 min in plasma, respectively. Anhydroecgonine methyl ester, a pyrolysis product of cocaine, was also detected in saliva after smoking. Peak anhydroecgonine methyl ester concentrations were achieved at 2 min and ranged from 558 to 4374 ng/mL (N=7).

Kato et al.[16] noted that increases in saliva flow rate during stimulated saliva collection substantially decreased salivary cocaine concentrations. Collection of unstimulated saliva following intravenous administration resulted in an average 6.5-fold increase in excretion of cocaine. Although the pH of saliva was not measured in this study, the observed differences were likely due to the differences in pH between unstimulated and stimulated saliva. Since cocaine is a weak base with a pKa of 8.6,[17] the concentration in saliva is highly dependent upon salivary pH and consequently upon salivary flow. Indeed, estimation of cocaine excretion in saliva at pH values of 5.9 (resting saliva pH) and 7.8 (citric acid stimulation) provides a maximal theoretical ratio of 68.8.[18] Therefore, the average ratio for unstimulated to stimulated cocaine concentrations in saliva of 6.5 was clearly in line with the estimates of pH effects on cocaine distribution in saliva. These influences weaken the possible use of saliva cocaine concentrations as a correlate of behavioral effects. Nonetheless, this does not preclude use of saliva in forensic testing for evidence of recent use.

Peel et al.[10] detected cocaine in a single saliva sample in a survey of impaired drivers. Bogusz et al.[19] reported that bodypackers carrying large quantities of cocaine internally produced negative saliva samples for cocaine. However, the immunoassay utilized in the analysis was targeted toward benzoylecgonine, with poor cross-reactivity to the parent drug. Thompson et al.[20] observed highly significant correlations between saliva and plasma cocaine following single intravenous doses of cocaine hydrochloride to volunteer subjects. S/P ratios for one subject across time averaged 1.26 with a range of 0.5 to 2.96. Schramm et al.[21] observed an S/P ratio of 4.9 for cocaine and 0.4 for benzoylecgonine in 69 subjects who self-reported cocaine use within the previous 24 h. Saliva was collected as an ultrafiltrate with an osmotic device. According to the authors, the concentration of drugs in the ultrafiltrate was approximately 20% lower than in whole saliva. Kidwell[22] analyzed the concentration of cocaine and opiate analogs in urine by immunoassay and in saliva by liquid chromatography/mass spectrometry and reported significantly lower concentrations in saliva samples. Use of saliva rather than urine for drug testing led to the detection of fewer drug users.

The prolonged occurrence of cocaine in human saliva after multiple dosing and high drug exposure was reported by Cone and Weddington.[23] Cocaine was detected in saliva for 5 to 10 days by radioimmunoassay and 12 to 36 h by gas chromatography/mass spectrometry (GC/MS). The authors concluded that drug accumulated in the deep body compartments and was slowly released back into the circulation. Cocaine was found to be stable in unstimulated human saliva for as long as 4 days when refrigerated.[24] Saliva flow stimulated with citric acid candy was stable for longer periods and at higher temperatures.

11.2.4.2 Marijuana

Tetrahydrocannabinol, the primary psychoactive component in marijuana, has been detected in saliva following smoking of marijuana cigarettes,[25-28] tobacco cigarettes containing tetrahydrocannabinol[29] and hashish.[30,31] The presence of tetrahydrocannabinol in saliva appears to be due primarily to contamination of the oral cavity during the smoking process. Tetrahydrocannabinol is highly protein bound and does not readily pass from blood to saliva and in addition, inhibits salivary excretion.[32] Tetrahydrocannabinol was not detected in saliva following intravenous administration to human subjects;[33] however, another report indicated that small amounts of radiolabeled tetrahydrocannabinol were detected in the saliva of monkeys after intravenous injection.[34] Ohlsson et al.[35] reported that only extremely low concentrations of cannabidiol, a tetrahydrocannabinol derivative, were excreted in saliva following intravenous administration of a 20 mg dose of cannabidiol to five male human subjects.

Tetrahydrocannabinol detection times in saliva are variable and range from 2 to 10 h. Huestis et al.[36] found that tetrahydrocannabinol detection times, determined by radioimmunoassay, for 6 subjects averaged 6 and 10 hours after smoking a single 1.75% or 3.55% tetrahydrocannabinol marijuana cigarette, respectively, in comparison with an average detection time in plasma of approximately 5 h. In the same study, saliva samples collected over a 7-day period following marijuana administration were analyzed by GC/MS for the presence of tetrahydrocannabinol metabolites. Neither 11-hydroxy-tetrahydrocannabinol (11-OH-THC) or 11-nor-9-carboxy-Δ9-tetrahydrocannabinol (THCCOOH) were detected in any sample in concentrations above the detection limit of the assay (approximately 0.5 ng/mL for each analyte). In contrast to these findings, Schramm et al.[37] reported detection by thermospray mass spectrometry of small amounts of THCCOOH, 11-OH-THC and cannabidiol in a single saliva sample collected as an ultrafiltrate from a marijuana smoker. No detection limits were reported for the assay and the amount of metabolite present was not reported.

Saliva concentrations of tetrahydrocannabinol generally vary over a wide range from 50 to 1000 ng/mL shortly after marijuana exposure. Thompson and Cone[28] reported that tetrahydrocannabinol was detectable immediately after smoking in very high concentrations, followed by a rapid decline over the first hour. Thereafter, concentrations declined gradually and appeared to mimic plasma concentrations. Gross et al.[27] reported detection of tetrahydrocannabinol in saliva by radioimmunoassay for 2 to 5 h after smoking one-half to two marijuana cigarettes. Other authors have reported similar saliva results.[25,26,38] Huestis et al.[36] reported a significant correlation of saliva tetrahydrocannabinol concentrations with plasma concentrations ($p<0.01$) in male marijuana users following the smoking of a single marijuana cigarette of different strengths (1.75% and 3.55% tetrahydrocannabinol). The S/P ratio declined rapidly over the first 20 min followed by a gradual increase over the following 4 h.

Correlations of saliva tetrahydrocannabinol concentrations with behavior and physiologic measures also have been reported. Huestis et al.[36] reported a highly significant correlation ($p<0.01$) between mean saliva tetrahydrocannabinol concentrations and several subjective, performance and physiological measures of drug effect, namely, the "Feel Drug" scale, Digit Symbol Substitution Test and heart rate. However, when individual saliva data were correlated with concurrent measures, the correlations were not significant, leading the authors to conclude that predictions of performance effects from a single tetrahydrocannabinol saliva test would be unreliable because of high inter-individual variability. In contrast, Menkes et al.[26] reported significant correlations for within-subject data with log tetrahydrocannabinol saliva concentrations vs. subjective intoxication measures and with heart rate changes. They suggested that saliva tetrahydrocannabinol concentration is a more sensitive index of recent cannabis smoking than either urine or blood cannabinoid concentration.

Marilyn A. Huestis and Edward J. Cone

11.2.4.3 Common Opiates

Leute et al.[39] reported detection of morphine by spin immunoassay in the saliva of patients undergoing methadone maintenance. Saliva concentrations of morphine were poorly correlated with urine concentrations. Gorodetzky and Kullberg[40] evaluated three different immunoassays for detection of morphine in plasma and saliva after heroin administration. They found that 5 and 10 mg doses of heroin could be detected with high probability for 2 to 4 h in plasma and 1 to 2 h in saliva. Lower doses were not consistently detected at any sampling time. Following chronic dosing and utilizing a lower sensitivity immunoassay, Gorodetzky and Kullberg[40] reported a high probability of detecting morphine in plasma for at least 6 h and in saliva for 3 to 4 h after the last morphine dose.

Goldberger et al.[41] developed a GC/MS assay for detection of heroin, 6-acetylmorphine and morphine in plasma and saliva following intranasal heroin administration. Saliva drug concentrations were much higher than plasma concentrations for the first hour and continued to be elevated throughout the detection period as a result of contamination of the oral cavity from intranasal administration of drug. However, both saliva and plasma had substantially shorter detection periods (4 to 8 h) than urine (24 to 72 h).[42,43]

Recently, Jenkins et al.[15] reported peak heroin concentrations in saliva from 3 to >20 μg/mL after smoking 2.6 mg and 5.2 mg of heroin base. Heroin saliva concentrations were much lower than blood after IV administration, with a peak concentration of 30 ng/mL after administration of 12 mg heroin hydrochloride. Contamination of the oral cavity during smoking was responsible for the high saliva/blood (S/B) ratios in the early period following drug administration. When saliva and blood heroin concentrations were > 1 ng/mL, S/B ratios were > 5. In contrast, S/B ratios after IV administration were <2. Since plasma and saliva drug detection times correspond more closely than urine to the time course of heroin-induced effects, saliva could add unique information in forensic investigations of cases concerned with drug-induced impairment.

Cone and Jenkins[44] noted a delay in the appearance of morphine in saliva following intramuscular morphine injections. Equilibrium between plasma and salivary morphine concentrations were not reached for approximately 45 minutes after dosing. Salivary morphine concentrations are reduced relative to plasma by approximately one-third, equivalent to the amount of plasma protein binding for morphine. After equilibration, saliva morphine concentrations declined in a parallel manner to plasma concentrations.

Codeine has been detected in saliva following oral[45] and intramuscular[43] administration. Sharp et al.[45] reported the mean S/P ratio for codeine of 3.3 for three subjects following an oral dose of 30 mg, which corresponded to the predicted S/P of 3.57. Cone[43] reported peak concentrations of codeine in saliva of 307.6 ng/mL and 183.9 ng/mL occurring at 0.5 to 0.75 h, respectively, after doses of 120 and 60 mg of codeine. Plasma concentrations in the same subjects peaked at 0.25 to 0.5 h at concentrations of 272.4 ng/mL and 212.4 ng/mL, respectively. By 24 h, concentrations in both saliva and plasma were in the range of 1 to 4 ng/mL. By 36 h, saliva concentrations were below assay sensitivity. Following intramuscular administration, the detection times for codeine in different biological fluids were as follows: hair>>urine>plasma>saliva.

Methadone is used extensively in maintenance therapy for heroin addicts. It has been detected in mixed saliva of humans following acute and chronic dosing,[46,47] and in parotid rat saliva.[48] Lynn et al.[49] reported that unstimulated saliva concentrations exceeded whole blood concentrations of methadone by a factor of 3 to 10 following intramuscular administration. In contrast, Kang and Abbott[46] reported a mean S/P ratio of 0.51 in two patients on maintenance doses of 30 and 90 mg/day of methadone. Differences in blood and saliva collection conditions may account for the discrepancy between these two studies. El-Guebaly et al.[50] supported the use of saliva drug monitoring in psychiatric practice and methadone maintenance clinics.

Buprenorphine is a partial agonist of morphine that has been proposed for use as a therapeutic modality for the treatment of heroin addiction. In a comprehensive assessment of the acute and chronic effects of buprenorphine,[51,52] saliva and plasma concentrations were measured after sublingual and intramuscular administration. Cone et al.[53] reported that saliva concentrations following intramuscular administration were substantially less than plasma concentrations [S/P ratio = 0.05-0.41], whereas they were highly elevated during the first 12 h after sublingual dosing. The elevated concentrations following sublingual buprenorphine may be the result of a "shallow depot" of drug in the oral cavity. Although buprenorphine S/P concentrations were highly distorted from contamination by the sublingual route of administration, it appeared that measurement of saliva concentrations would be useful in monitoring treatment of heroin addicts maintained on sublingually-administered buprenorphine. Upon discontinuation of buprenorphine, saliva concentrations declined to the level of assay sensitivity over a period of 5 days. Interestingly, saliva trough concentrations (collected before buprenorphine or placebo) were similar to plasma concentrations.

11.2.4.4 Other Opiates

Monitoring of saliva for the presence of other opioids has been attempted. Silverstein et. al.[54] sought to monitor fentanyl use and abuse in subjects by analyzing saliva for fentanyl and its metabolites. Neither fentanyl nor its metabolites were detected consistently by GC/MS at any time in saliva. Hydromorphone is excreted in saliva in a pattern similar to that observed for morphine. Ritschel et al.[55] reported that saliva hydromorphone concentrations were lower than plasma concentrations immediately following intravenous drug administration. The S/P ratio was initially lower (0.25), then attained a maximum of 2.32, followed by a constant ratio of approximately 1.0 in the elimination phase. Chen et al.[56] reported detection of pholcodine, a codeine-like antitussive, by high performance-liquid chromatography in saliva and plasma of a young male volunteer following oral administration of 60 mg of pholcodine. Saliva contained approximately three times the amount of pholcodine found in plasma and this ratio appeared to be relatively stable during the elimination phase. Urine concentrations of drug were substantially higher than saliva and plasma concentrations. Terminal half-lives calculated from the three biological fluids were similar and averaged 48.6 h. Freeborn et al.[57] reported that mothers who received meperidine intramuscularly during labor had higher drug concentrations in saliva than blood and a significant correlation existed between saliva and blood concentrations between 1 and 4 h after dosage. In addition, meperidine was monitored in neonate saliva of breast-fed and bottle-fed infants.

11.2.4.5 Amphetamines

Amphetamine has been identified in saliva following the administration of d-amphetamine, l-amphetamine and d,l-amphetamine.[58,59] Wan et al.[58] reported higher saliva than plasma amphetamine concentrations and detection for 48 h after oral administration of 10 mg of amphetamine hydrochloride to humans. Urine samples were derivatized with a chiral reagent and analyzed by GC/MS to allow resolution of the optical isomers of amphetamine. The d-isomer was eliminated more rapidly than the l-isomer and the rate of excretion was faster under acidic urine conditions. In a forensic investigation, Smith[60] measured amphetamine by radioimmunoassay in saliva and in saliva stains on a cigarette from a subject undergoing amphetamine therapy. The concentration of amphetamine in saliva was similar to that found in whole blood and semen from the same subject.

In a study by Turner et al.[61] employing fluorescence polarization immunoassay (FPIA®), saliva and urine samples were found to test positive (100 ng/mL cutoff for amphetamine

Marilyn A. Huestis and Edward J. Cone

equivalents) for 72 h after administration of 25 mg of phentermine and for 24 h after 18 mg of ephedrine. In contrast, phenylpropanolamine (25 mg) produced positive test results for only 2 h in saliva and for 48 h in urine.

11.2.4.6 Phencyclidine

Phencyclidine has been detected in saliva of laboratory animals and humans. Saliva/serum (S/S) ratios were found to range from 0.4 to 3.0 at a salivary pH of 8 to 9 in rats.[62] In 100 emergency department patients suspected of phencyclidine intoxication, 74 saliva samples and 75 of the paired serum samples were positive for phencyclidine by radioimmunoassay.[38] In a kinetic study of phencyclidine in healthy male volunteers, Cook et al.[63,64] reported the excretion of radiolabeled phencyclidine in saliva after administration of small (sub-effective) doses by the intravenous and oral routes. During collection, saliva pH averaged 6.70 ± 0.17 (SD) and phencyclidine binding in saliva averaged 7.0%. Saliva drug concentrations tended to be higher than plasma concentrations with an average S/P ratio of 2.4 compared with the predicted ratio of 3.93. Although saliva phencyclidine was highly correlated with plasma concentrations (r = 0.921), both inter- and intra-subject variability was high. The authors concluded that measurement of phencyclidine in saliva could be useful for diagnostic purposes, but was not sufficiently accurate to predict specific plasma concentrations.

11.2.4.7 Benzodiazepines

Numerous techniques have been employed to measure diazepam and other benzodiazepines in saliva including radioimmunoassay,[65] radio-receptor assay,[66] high performance-liquid chromatography,[67] and gas chromatography with electron capture detection.[68-70] Most benzodiazepines are neutral compounds; therefore, the S/P ratios are determined by the extent of protein binding in plasma which is generally extensive (96 to 99%). Due to the limited free benzodiazepine concentration, a small percentage of total plasma diazepam is found in saliva. Following an oral dose of 10 mg of diazepam, DiGregorio et al.[69] reported saliva concentrations in the range of 1 to 6 ng/mL over an 8-h period after dosing. The mean S/P ratios were found to be very low but consistent and highly significant, 0.035 and 0.029 for parotid and mixed saliva samples. Similar correlations between plasma or serum diazepam concentrations and saliva were found by De Gier et al.[70] and Hallstrom et al.[68] Giles et al.[71] reported that peak plasma diazepam concentrations occurred at 60 min while peak saliva concentrations occurred at 100 min. It is likely that the time delay between drug appearance in plasma and saliva represented the time required for passive diffusion from plasma to saliva and for equilibrium to be established between these fluids.

A major active metabolite of diazepam, N-desmethyldiazepam, is also found in saliva after administration of diazepam. Following an acute dose of 0.143 mg/kg of diazepam, Giles et al.[71] reported slowly increasing *N*-desmethyldiazepam concentrations over time, reaching a maximum concentration of approximately 1 ng/mL, 24 h after dosing. Following chronic diazepam administration in a group of outpatients who participated in a study of driving performance, De Gier et al.[72] found saliva concentrations of N-desmethyldiazepam ranging from 1.2 to 23.0 ng/mL, approximately equivalent to diazepam concentrations. In this study, saliva and plasma concentrations of diazepam and N-desmethyldiazepam were highly correlated. Mean S/P ratios $\pm$ SD for diazepam and *N*-desmethyldiazepam were 0.013 ± 0.002 and 0.018 ± 0.004, respectively. The authors noted that although patients showed impaired driving performance, there was no correlation between plasma or saliva concentrations of diazepam or its metabolite and performance decrement. In a study of diazepam and N-desmethyldiazepam concentrations in the saliva of chronically-dosed hospital inpatients, Giles et al.[73] found a low correlation between saliva concentrations and dose. Because of the wide inter-subject variability, individual saliva drug concentrations were poor predictors of dose.

Following an acute 15 mg oral dose of clorazepate, which is converted to nordiazepam in the acidic medium of the stomach, Hallstrom et al.[68] reported detection of approximately 5 to 20 ng/mL of *N*-desmethyldiazepam in saliva. S/P ratios averaged 5.78 (range 2.33 to 6.65); however, it was not possible to accurately predict an individual's plasma drug concentration from the saliva results. Another benzodiazepine, chlordiazepoxide, was reported to be detectable by radioimmunoassay in saliva after acute and multiple dosing.[74] Saliva and plasma concentrations were highly correlated and were detectable for 30 to 60 h with a mean S/P ratio of approximately 0.03.

The concentration of nitrazepam in saliva was reported to be significantly correlated with serum concentrations by Kangas et al.;[75] however, saliva concentrations were substantially lower than free serum concentrations. This finding led the authors to conclude that saliva testing for nitrazepam was of little clinical value. In a later study, Hart et al.[76] also found that salivary nitrazepam concentrations were lower than free serum concentrations. Eventually, the discrepancy between saliva and plasma drug concentrations was linked to the instability of nitrazepam in saliva. The conversion of nitrazepam to 7-aminonitrazepam was strongly dependent upon the composition of individual subject's saliva.[77]

11.2.4.8 Barbiturates

Amobarbital has been measured in human saliva by gas chromatography[78,79] and high performance liquid chromatography.[80] Inaba and Kalow[78] reported high linear correlation (r = 0.993) between saliva and serum concentrations of amobarbital in humans following an oral dose of 120 mg. Saliva concentrations averaged 36.1% of serum concentrations, were detectable for approximately 48 h, and the observed mean (± SD) S/S ratio was 0.35 ± 0.03. A similar mean S/P ratio, 0.34 ± 0.03 (SEM), was reported by Van der Graaff et al.[81] for hexobarbital which was detectable in saliva and plasma for approximately 12 h after drug administration. The terminal half-life of pentobarbital in unstimulated mixed saliva by gas chromatography following the oral administration of a single 100 mg dose was approximately 18 h.[79] Blom and Guelen[82] cited the S/S ratio of pentobarbital as 0.36. Secobarbital was detected in the saliva of healthy subjects following a single oral dose of 50 mg.[45] The mean experimental S/P ratio ± SD was 0.30 ± 0.04 with a range of 0.24 to 0.38; the predicted S/P for secobarbital was 0.39.

Cook et al.[83] measured phenobarbital in the saliva and plasma of epileptic patients and found a highly significant correlation (r = 0.98); the S/P ratio was approximately 0.3. In addition, they examined saliva extracts by mass spectrometry and found no evidence of metabolites in saliva even in acid-hydrolyzed samples. Horning et al.[84] determined parotid S/P ratios for phenobarbital by GC/MS (0.31 to 0.37) and by enzyme immunoassay (0.32). Numerous other S/P or S/S ratios for phenobarbital have been reported including: in children under the age of two (N = 19), S/P = 0.45;[85] epileptic young people aged 9 to 18 (N = 15), S/S = 0.285;[86] epileptic children aged 5 months to 18 years (N = 121), S/P = 0.30 by gas chromatography and 0.31 by enzyme immunoassay;[87] adults aged 17 to 65 (N = 11), S/P = 0.41;[5] patients undergoing pneumoencephalography (N = 48), S/S = 0.32;[82] and epileptic patients aged 9 to 70 (N = 29), S/P = 0.33.[88] Knott and Reynolds[89] recommended monitoring maternal salivary phenobarbital concentrations during pregnancy and regular monitoring of maternal and neonatal saliva drug concentrations after birth to prevent withdrawal or toxicity in the newborn.

In contrast to these data, other barbiturates were found to have similar saliva and serum drug concentrations. Barbital was measured in saliva by Ogata et al.[90] following an oral dose of 114 mg to healthy male volunteers. The S/S ratio between barbital concentrations in serum and saliva was found to be 0.999.

Marilyn A. Huestis and Edward J. Cone

11.2.4.9 Ethanol

The ethanol content of saliva will be higher than that found in blood because it is distributed uniformly throughout the body according to body water content. Jones[91] found a mean S/B ratio of 1.082 (N = 336) between 60 to 360 min after the start of drinking. This ratio was remarkably constant throughout the absorption, distribution and elimination phases of ethanol metabolism. In a recent study by the same author,[92] a mean S/B ratio of 1.094 (N = 168) and an average mean difference in saliva-blood concentrations of 9.4% were reported between 40 to 400 min after the start of drinking. It was concluded that saliva alcohol can substitute for blood alcohol measurements to establish the time course of ethanol metabolism in the body and associated impairment in a person's performance and behavior. DiGregorio et al.[93] reported a S/P ratio of 1.04 (range 0.95 to 1.13) between 15 to 120 min after ethanol administration, and Haeckel and Bucklitsch[94] observed a 1.032 S/P ratio in the post-absorption phase. In the latter study, ethanol concentrations were found to be almost identical in unstimulated and stimulated (citric acid) saliva. These authors also reported that ethanol concentrations in saliva paralleled capillary blood more accurately than venous blood concentrations and therefore, indicated that saliva was as useful as venous or capillary blood to reflect the intoxication state of an individual in the post-absorption state.

McColl et al.[95] found no significant differences in ethanol concentrations between mixed saliva, parotid saliva, and mixed saliva collected after rinsing and drying the mouth when the specimen was obtained at least 20 min after drinking. Ruz et al.[96] developed a statistical model for the prediction of ethanol concentration in blood at a given time from drug concentrations in a saliva sample collected at a later time. In an experiment designed to reflect specimen collection consistent with an accident investigation, the prediction error always was found to be less than 20%.

Recently, a number of rapid on-site tests for ethanol in saliva have been marketed.[97-101] Christopher and Zeccardi[102] observed excellent correlation between saliva and blood alcohol levels over the range of 0 to 150 mg/dL with the Q.E.D. A-150 Saliva Alcohol Test.

11.2.4.10 Nicotine

Nicotine is excreted in saliva, but is not considered to be a reliable marker of tobacco smoke exposure because of its short half-life (approximately 2 h). In contrast, cotinine, the major metabolite of nicotine has a half-life of approximately 17 h.[103] Cotinine appears rapidly in both saliva and plasma after nicotine administration and saliva concentrations generally exceed corresponding plasma levels. Curvall et al.[104] reported that saliva cotinine concentrations were highly correlated with plasma concentrations (r = 0.99) with a S/P ratio of 1.2-1.4. Further, Curvall, et al[105] determined that saliva nicotine concentrations did not reflect actual uptake of nicotine as accurately as saliva or plasma cotinine levels. Gwent et al.[106] studied the time course of appearance of cotinine in human saliva. Salivary cotinine concentrations reached a plateau after 1.5 h and were nondetectable (0.3 ng/mL) after 24 h.

Recently, Etzel[107] reviewed 43 reports concerning the use of saliva cotinine measures to discriminate between smokers and non-smokers. Generally, non-smokers and those exposed passively had cotinine concentrations below 5 ng/mL, but heavy passive exposure may result in concentrations equal or greater than 10 ng/mL. Infrequent active smokers or regular active smokers with low nicotine intake had cotinine concentrations between 10 and 100 ng/mL, and regular active smokers had cotinine concentrations in excess of 100 ng/mL. The ability to categorize individuals into different risk groups by means of non-invasive cotinine saliva measurements provided objective criteria for use in future studies of the health effects of environmental smoke exposure. Jarvis et al.[108] compared 11 different tests for their ability to categorize smokers and nonsmokers correctly. Saliva cotinine measurements were the most accurate in determining smoking status with a sensitivity of 96% and a specificity of 99%. Cotinine is the primary and preferred measure of cigarette smoke exposure in epidemiologic research.[108-113]

11.2.4.11 Other Drugs

Sharp et al.[45] detected methaqualone in saliva samples of healthy subjects following a single oral dose of 250 mg. The mean experimental S/P ratio ± SD was 0.11 ± 0.02. Peat et al.[114] reported detection of methaqualone and its major hydroxy-metabolite in saliva after oral administration. Initially, the metabolite was present in much lower concentrations (0 to 4 h), but matched or exceeded concentrations of the parent compound at later times (4 to 24 h). Saliva concentrations of methaqualone and metabolite were approximately 10% of those observed in plasma.

Meprobamate was reported to be present in saliva in nearly equal concentrations as found in plasma after oral administration.[115,116] Chloral hydrate and metabolites have been detected in horse saliva after chloral hydrate doping.[117] In this study, the concentration of chloral hydrate and the metabolite, trichlorethanol, in saliva were approximately equal to plasma concentrations, whereas saliva trichloroacetic acid concentrations were much lower.

11.2.5 CONCLUSIONS

Saliva testing for drugs can provide both qualitative and quantitative information on the drug status of an individual undergoing testing. Self-administration by the oral, intranasal and smoked routes often produces "shallow" depots of drug that contaminate the oral cavity. This depot produces elevated drug concentrations that can be detected for several hours. Thereafter, saliva drug concentrations generally reflect the free fraction of drug in blood. Also, many drugs are weak bases and saliva concentrations may be highly dependent upon pH conditions. These factors lead to highly variable S/P ratios for many drugs. Generally, there was a high correlation of saliva drug concentrations with plasma, especially when contamination of the buccal cavity was eliminated.

There are many potential applications for saliva testing for drugs in the general areas of drug detection, treatment and forensic investigations. Saliva drug tests can reveal the presence of a pharmacologically active drug in an individual at the time of testing and significant correlations have been found between saliva concentrations of drugs and behavioral and physiological effects. It is anticipated that over the next decade, saliva testing for drugs will develop into a mature science with new applications. Future research is needed in pharmacokinetic modeling of drug and metabolite excretion in saliva. Also, in order to evaluate the potential of saliva for use as a matrix for workplace drug testing, data on detection times of illicit drugs and their metabolites in saliva is needed.

11.3 SWEAT

11.3.1 MECHANISMS OF DRUG INCORPORATION

Sweat secretion is an important mechanism for maintaining a constant core body temperature. Following sympathetic nerve stimulation, sweat is excreted onto the surface of the skin and evaporated to release body heat. Sweat is secreted from two types of sweat glands, eccrine and apocrine glands. These glands originate deep within the skin dermis and terminate in excretory ducts emptying onto the skin or developing hair follicles. Eccrine glands are located on most skin surfaces, while apocrine glands are restricted to skin of the axilla, genitalia and anus. Water is the primary constituent of sweat, approximately 99%,[118] and sodium chloride is the most concentrated solute. Sweat also contains albumin, gamma globulins, waste products, trace elements, drugs, and many other substances found in blood. The rate of sweating is highly dependent upon environmental temperatures. Above 31°C, humans begin to sweat and may excrete as much as 3L/h over short periods of time.[119] The average pH of sweat of resting individuals was reported to be 5.82.[120] Following exercise, the pH was found to increase with increasing flow rate and was reported to be between 6.1 and 6.7.[121] Approximately 50% of sweat is generated by the trunk of the body, 25% from the legs, and the remaining 25% from the head and upper extremities.[122]

Multiple mechanisms have been suggested for the incorporation of drugs into sweat including passive diffusion and transdermal migration. Passive diffusion of drugs from blood to sweat is favored for lipid-soluble substances. Non-ionized basic drugs diffuse into sweat and become ionized as a result of the lower pH of this biological fluid. Basic substances may accumulate in sweat as compared to blood due to the pH differential between the two matrices. Some drugs may migrate across the dermal and epidermal layers into the stratum corneum. Theophylline[123] was shown to migrate at a slow rate from interstitial fluid to the skin surface. Brusilow[124] utilized radiolabeled urea in a study of this analyte's concentration in different biofluids. He suggested that there was an additional source of urea incorporated into sweat other than that available in the plasma or interstitial fluid. He hypothesized that urea could have been synthesized by the sweat gland, or that a pool of urea existed in the skin which could contribute to that found in sweat.

11.3.1.1 Sweat Collection

One of the difficulties of working with sweat is measurement of the volume excreted in a defined time period. The amount of sweat excreted is highly variable both between individuals and within a single person, and is dependent upon their daily activities, emotional state and environment. Systematic collection of specimens is difficult because of the unequal distribution of sweat glands. Sweat can be collected noninvasively with gauze or filter paper, or with specialized collection devices. In 1980, Phillips[125] reported development of an adhesive patch for the long-term collection of sweat (10 days). This patch was occlusive in design, trapping both the solute and water components permitting the determination of analyte concentration in sweat. A disadvantage of the occlusive patch design was the limited time the patch could be worn. A linear uptake rate of 18 to 47 mg/day of sweat was observed. It was suggested that it might be possible to monitor drug-taking behavior through use of the patch. This sweat patch was later utilized in the validation of self-reports of alcohol use.[126]

A new non-occlusive sweat collection device, the PharmChem® Sweat Patch, can be worn for an extended time period and concentrates solutes on a collection pad while allowing water to evaporate from the patch. The device consists of an adhesive layer on a thin transparent film of surgical dressing to which a rectangular absorbent pad is attached. Sweat concentrates on the absorbent pad while oxygen, carbon dioxide, and water vapor escape through the transparent film. Larger molecules are excluded by the molecular pore structure of the plastic membrane. The skin must be thoroughly cleaned with isopropyl alcohol prior to affixing the patch to prevent contamination of the patch or interference with the deposition or detection of analytes on the patch. Attempts to remove the patch prematurely or tamper with the device are readily visible to personnel trained to remove the sweat patch. Care must be taken not to contaminate the absorbent pad when removing and storing the patch prior to analysis.

11.3.1.2 Advantages and Possible Uses

Sweat testing is relatively noninvasive and identification of drug in sweat may serve as a means of monitoring drug use. Depending upon the period of collection, it is hoped that sweat testing can provide a means to obtain a cumulative estimate of drug exposure over a period of several weeks. Sweat testing may serve as a useful tool in surveillance of individuals in treatment and probation programs due to the fact that monitoring illicit drugs in sweat on a weekly basis may provide sufficient detection sensitivity. Interest in measurement of drugs of abuse in sweat has recently increased due to the somewhat wider window of detection of drug use than provided by urine testing and from the desire to determine mechanisms of drug incorporation into hair. Deposition of drug into hair via sweat may account for the lack of dose-response relationships reported in some studies and for the presence of drug in distal segments of hair that do not correlate with the time of drug exposure. The predominant analytes generally found in sweat and hair are the parent compounds, rather than their more polar metabolites which usually predominate in urine. Many drugs of abuse including alcohol,[127] amphetamines,[60,128-131] phenobarbital,[132,133] cocaine,[134-136] heroin[40,135] morphine,[129] phencyclidine,[137] and methadone[138] have been detected in sweat.

11.3.1.3 Forensic Application

The first time the detection of a drug in sweat was included as evidence in a forensic case involved the identification of cocaine in perspiration stains of an alleged rape victim.[134] Other forensic applications include the finding of high concentrations of cocaine in axillary sweat of a drug user as reported by Balabanova and Schneider.[139] Further investigations demonstrated cocaine concentrations from 0.8 to 9200 ng/cm^2, measured by radioimmunoassay, in axillary perspiration samples obtained over a 24-h period.[136] Radioimmunoassay and GC/MS were used to identify cannabinoids, benzodiazepines, barbiturates, cocaine, morphine, methadone and cotinine in axillary sweat.[139] Burns and Baselt[140] reported detection of a single episode of cocaine use for up to seven days after drug exposure when monitoring use with a sweat patch. The authors noted that cocaine levels accurately reflected usage, although inter-dose and inter-subject variability precluded determination of the drug dose or time of drug exposure.

11.3.2 DETECTION OF SPECIFIC DRUGS

Henderson et al.[141] reported a 6:1 ratio of deuterated cocaine to deuterated benzoylecgonine in the hair and sweat of subjects administered isotopically labeled cocaine intravenously or intranasally. Deuterated cocaine levels in sweat as high as 50 ug/mL were found one hour after intranasal administration of cocaine at 0.6 mg/kg. Two hours after subjects were administered deuterated cocaine they held drug-free hair in their hands for 30 min. The concentrations of deuterated cocaine in hair samples were as high as 47.8 ng/mg prior to decontamination procedures and 10.0 ng/mg after decontamination. The authors concluded that sweat may be an important vehicle for the transfer of cocaine into hair. In another study, Henderson[142] reported cocaine concentrations greater than 100 ng/mL in sweat for up to 72 h after a single 2 mg/kg intranasal dose.

Spiehler et al.[143] described validation of a solid-phase enzyme immunoassay for quantitative detection of cocaine in sweat. The immunoassay had equivalent cross-reactivity for cocaine, the primary analyte found in sweat after cocaine exposure, and benzoylecgonine, the primary cocaine analyte found in urine. The authors concluded that sweat may be a significant route of elimination for basic drugs and that detecting drug use with the sweat patch is both sensitive and specific. Furthermore, the detection of drug in sweat requires an analytical system designed to detect drug analytes identified in sweat which in many cases are different than the primary drug analytes observed in urine.

Following administration of single doses of heroin and cocaine to humans, Cone et al.[135] identified heroin and cocaine as the primary analytes excreted in sweat. Sweat was collected by means of a sweat patch that could be worn for up to 7 days. The concentration of 6-

acetylmorphine in the patch increased rapidly after administration of heroin and was found to increase concurrently with a decrease in heroin concentration, indicating that hydrolysis of heroin to the 6-acetylmorphine metabolite occurred within the patch. Cocaine appeared in sweat within 1 to 2 h and peaked within 24 h in an apparent dose-dependent manner. Trace amounts of cocaine could be detected in the sweat patch following intravenous dosing of as little as 1 mg. Smaller amounts of ecgonine methyl ester and benzoylecgonine could also be identified, although only following larger doses. High intersubject variability was noted.

Traqui et al.[144] identified morphine, codeine, and 6-acetylmorphine in clothing that had been impregnated by sweat and sebaceous secretions and/or urine, indicating that even in the absence of biological specimens, clothing may provide evidence of possible drug exposure.

Henderson and Wilson[138] noted that sweat was a significant route of elimination for methadone. Normal sweat excretion is approximately 500 mL/day, but it is possible to increase sweat excretion up to 1000 mL/h during periods of strenuous exercise or when environmental temperatures approach 100°C. Excessive sweating during strenuous exercise could remove significant amounts of drug from the body and cause a decreased half-life of methadone. Such an occurrence might account for the observance of opiate withdrawal symptoms in some methadone maintenance patients.

In 1979, Ishiyama reported that methamphetamine was excreted in sweat at a constant rate of 1.4 μg/mL and that the total amount of drug excreted in sweat was similar to that excreted in urine. He predicted that the toxicological examination of sweat could offer a new scope to forensic investigations. Ishiyama et al[129] detected amphetamine, dimethylamphetamine, and morphine in sweat after exposure to low drug doses. Methamphetamine was detected in sweat for 140 h and in urine for 96 h after a volunteer ingested 10 mg of the drug. Suzuki et al.[130] found substantial amounts of methamphetamine (20 to 164 ng) and amphetamine (3.4 to 13 ng) in gauze or filter paper collections of sweat from methamphetamine abusers.

Takahashi[131] reported the detection of methamphetamine and amphetamine for 4 and 5 days, respectively, in sweat collected after subcutaneous administration of 5 mg/kg methamphetamine to a monkey. It is interesting to note that after repeated injections of methamphetamine, the amphetamine concentration exceeded that of the parent drug due to differences in excretion kinetics between the parent drug and drug metabolite.

Vree et al.[128] observed that dimethylamphetamine and methamphetamine excretion in sweat was not highly dependent upon sweat pH when sweat production was stimulated by exercise. Drug excretion curves in sweat were found to follow the same pattern as observed in urine. It was suggested that sweat could provide an alternative biological matrix for doping control.

Detection of ethanol, phenobarbital, and phencyclidine in sweat has been reported. Brown et al.[127,145] determined the concentration of volatile substances that had been excreted through the skin via insensible perspiration. Subjects' hands were inserted into polyethylene bags at 37°C and gas samples were collected from air that had equilibrated with vapors emanating from the skin. The time course of excretion of alcohol in the skin vapor was compared to that of ethanol in the blood and the breath. During absorption, alcohol excretion was lower than blood and breath; however, a slightly higher concentration was noted at later time points. The authors reported that although ethanol elimination via sweat did not parallel breath or blood alcohol excretion, analysis of sweat for alcohol could serve as an adequate monitoring device for ethanol ingestion. Smith and Pomposini[132] employed radioimmunoassay in a forensic case to detect phenobarbital in perspiration stains. Radiolabeled phencyclidine was detected in axilla perspiration for 54 h after intravenous phencyclidine administration.[137] Phencyclidine concentrations were found to be highly concentrated in sweat as compared to blood during heavy exercise.

The quantitative excretion of drugs into sweat and the relationship between drug concentration in sweat and blood have been the subject of recent investigations. Detection of drug and/or metabolites in sweat clearly documents drug exposure and can provide a wider window of detection of drug use than measurement of drug in plasma, saliva or urine if sweat collection is extended for a week or more. Applications for this non-invasive specimen collection and drug use monitoring method are increasing. Currently, some parolees are being monitored weekly for illicit drug use, and in the future sweat testing may be applied for the evaluation of compliance to therapeutic drug regimens. New sweat collection devices that utilize heat to increase sweat production are under development and offer the possibility of shorter collection periods.

11.4 HAIR

11.4.1 MECHANISMS

11.4.1.1 Anatomy and Growth

Hair consists of five morphological components: cuticle, cortex, medulla, melanin granules and cell membrane complex. Each is distinct in morphology and chemical composition. The number of hair follicles ranges from 80,000 to 100,000 follicles on the human head, but these decrease with age.[146] Hair follicles are embedded in the dermis of skin and are highly vascularized to nourish the growing hair root or bulb.[147] The bulb at the base of the follicle contains matrix cells which give rise to the layers of the hair shaft including the cuticle, cortex, and medulla. Matrix cells undergo morphological and structural changes as they move upward during growth to form different layers of the hair shaft. These layers can often can be distinguished by qualitative and quantitative differences in their proteins and pigments.[146]

Hair is composed of approximately 65 to 95% protein, 1 to 9% lipid, and small quantities of trace elements, polysaccharides, and water.[147] The durability and strength of the hair shaft is determined by the proteins synthesized within the matrix cells. Matrix cells also may acquire pigment or melanin during differentiation into individual layers of hair. The pigment present in hair cells determines the color of the hair shaft. The primary structure of hair consists of two or three α-keratin chains wound into strands called microfibrils. Microfibrils are organized into larger bundles of macrofibrils that comprise the bulk of the cortex. Hair strands are stabilized and shaped by disulfide and hydrogen bonds giving the microfibrils a semi-crystalline structure. Cytochrome P-450 and other enzymes have been identified in the hair follicle providing evidence that drug metabolism may occur within this structure; however, as hair becomes fully keratinized in three to five days, this capability is presumed to be greatly reduced.[146]

11.4.1.2 Physiology

A protective layer of epithelial cells called the cuticle surrounds the cortex. The cuticle is the outermost layer of hair, the innermost region is the medulla, and the hair cortex lies between these components. The overlapping cuticle cells protect the cortex from the environment. As hair ages, there is a gradual degeneration of the cuticle along the shaft due to exposure to ultraviolet radiation, chemicals and mechanical stresses. The cuticle may be partially or totally missing in cases of damaged hair.[148] Hair damaged by cosmetic treatments and/or ultraviolet radiation may influence the deposition and stability of drug in the hair.[149]

Hair follicles continue to grow for a number of years and undergo different phases during a normal growth cycle. Approximately 85 to 90% of the hair is in the anagen or growth phase at any single time.[146] A small portion of mature hair then begins the catagen phase in which there is a rapid decrease in the growth rate. This phase lasts for a period of 2 to 3 weeks and is immediately followed by the telogen phase, the resting phase of hair. During this phase, no growth occurs. Approximately 10 to 15% of head hair is usually in the telogen phase at all times. The hair strand may not be shed for several months prior to replacement by a new strand. Hair growth rates vary according to body location, sex and age.

Head hair grows at an average rate of 1.3 cm/month although there is some variation according to sex, age and ethnicity.[150] Mangin and Kintz[151] determined morphine and codeine concentrations in human head, axillary, and pubic hair from heroin overdose cases. Morphine concentrations were highest in pubic hair followed by head and axillary hair. Codeine to morphine ratios ranged from 0.054 to 0.273. The slower growth rate of pubic hair, and possible drug contribution from sweat or urine were presumed to account for the differences in drug concentration in the different hair samples.

11.4.1.3 Drug Incorporation

There are multiple possible pathways for drug incorporation into hair including: (1) passive diffusion from blood into the hair follicle; (2) excretion onto the surface of hair from sweat and sebum; and (3) from external contamination. Henderson[142] suggested that drugs may enter hair from multiple sites, via multiple mechanisms, and at various times during the hair growth cycle. Drugs and their metabolites are distributed throughout the body primarily by passive diffusion from blood. Distribution across membranes is generally facilitated by high lipid solubility, low protein binding, and physicochemical factors that favor the unionized form of the drug in blood. Diffusion of drug from arterial blood capillaries to matrix cells in the base of the follicle is considered a primary means for drug deposition in hair. Presumably, drug binds to components in the matrix and to pigments. As the cells elongate and age, they gradually die and coalesce forming the non-living hair fiber. Drug that may be present is embedded in the hair matrix.

Sweat has been implicated in the deposition of drugs in hair. The predominant analytes generally found in hair and sweat are the parent compounds, rather than their more polar metabolites which usually predominate in urine.[152] This is somewhat surprising considering that cocaine is rapidly metabolized to benzoylecgonine and is present in blood for only a few hours following drug administration, whereas, benzoylecgonine persists in blood for 24 h or longer. Sweat may account for the lack of dose-concentration relationships reported in some studies and for the presence of drug in distal segments of hair that do not correlate with the time of drug exposure. Cocaine is excreted in sweat over a highly variable period ranging from 2 to 48 h allowing ample time for sweat to transfer drug into the hair.

Sebum, a waxy, lipid material excreted by the sebaceous glands, may also contribute to the deposition of drug in hair. Sebum coats the hair shaft emerging from the follicle at the skin surface. If drug is present in sebum, it could be deposited in hair through intimate contact of sebum with the hair shaft. Kidwell and Blank[153] suggested that the major source of drugs in hair comes from sweat or sebaceous excretions that bathe the hair shaft during hair formation and after maturation. Such a mechanism has been postulated to account for incorporation of trace elements into hair.[154]

11.4.2 ENVIRONMENTAL CONTAMINATION

Recent evidence indicates that hair environmentally-contaminated with drug is difficult to distinguish from drug in hair present as a result of self-administration. Several reports have appeared indicating that cocaine is adsorbed onto hair when cocaine base is vaporized in the presence of drug-free hair.[155-157] Washing techniques for the removal of cocaine from contaminated hair vary widely in reported efficiency.[141,155-161] Following exposure of hair to the vapor produced by the pyrolysis of a single line of cocaine hydrochloride, Koren et al.[155] reported the complete removal of externally deposited cocaine during the wash step. In contrast to these findings, several studies have indicated that external contamination of hair following exposure to cocaine vapor, aqueous solution, or cocaine in sweat, could not be entirely eliminated by extensive washing procedures or cosmetic treatments.[141,157-159] Washing with methanol was reported to remove greater than 70% of cocaine following exposure of hair to cocaine vapor but significant amounts of drug remained in the hair.[157] Ten consecutive overnight soakings of these samples in shampoo removed increasing amounts of drug, but residual cocaine remained in the hair.

The presence of cocaine in hair could be explained as a result of an individual being exposed to "crack" smoke, cocaine dust particles or aqueous solutions of cocaine present in the environment. A significant development in discriminating external drug contamination from actual drug use is identifying the presence of unique drug metabolites in hair. Cone et al.[158] identified norcocaine and cocaethylene in cocaine users' hair. Norcocaine is formed as a result of oxidative metabolism of cocaine and cocaethylene is formed as a result of the simultaneous use of cocaine and alcohol. Cocaethylene and norcocaine are not commonly found in significant amounts in illicit cocaine and would not be produced as artifacts (assuming ethanol is absent) in the assay. Because of the instability of cocaine, it has been questioned whether the metabolite of cocaine, benzoylecgonine, is actually excreted in hair or is formed as a result of hydrolysis of cocaine. Consequently, it has been suggested that the presence of norcocaine and cocaethylene provide corroborating evidence of drug use when found in association with cocaine in hair.

Identification of unique metabolites of heroin in hair can differentiate heroin use from other types of opiate use. Goldberger et al.[162] identified heroin, 6-acetylmorphine and morphine in the hair of heroin users. 6-Acetylmorphine is usually found in greatest abundance in hair, whereas, conjugated morphine is the major metabolite in urine. Hair from 20 known drug abusers and from drug-free control subjects were analyzed for heroin and metabolites. They found heroin in seven cases and 6-acetylmorphine in all 20 subjects. No drug was found in the control group. This finding may be highly significant in that 6-acetylmorphine is considered a specific marker for heroin use as its presence cannot be explained by ingestion of other drugs or food products.

11.4.3 DOSE AND TIME RELATIONSHIPS

A controversial issue in hair analysis is the interpretation of dose and time relationships. Baumgartner et al.[154] postulated that drugs enter hair via the bloodstream in direct proportion to their concentration. They presented animal data indicating a linear relationship between dose and amount of heroin and cocaine metabolites found in hair of mice. Since mice have sweat glands only in isolated areas, e.g., foot pads, sweat could be ruled out as the mode of drug entry in this study, supporting the hypothesis that drug enters hair via diffusion from blood. Other controlled dosing studies in humans support the concept of a linear relationship between dose and concentration of haloperidol[163,164] and chloroquine in hair.[165] Although it has been generally assumed that segmental analysis of hair provides a record of drug usage, and that drug dose could be correlated to drug concentration in hair, studies with labeled cocaine have not supported these interpretations. Henderson et al.[152] reported that 25 to 35 mg, or approximately a single "line" of cocaine could be detected in hair by GC/MS analysis following intravenous administration of deuterium-labeled cocaine. Segmental analysis of the hair indicated that some subjects receiving only a single dose had drug distributed along the length of the hair shaft, while others with multiple drug doses had drug concentrated in a small area. There was considerable intersubject variability in the time drug first appeared in hair and the rate at which drug moved along the hair shaft with time. These data support the incorporation of cocaine into hair by multiple mechanisms and dispute the use of hair to provide accurate records of the amount, time and duration of drug use.

Marilyn A. Huestis and Edward J. Cone

11.4.4 RACIAL EFFECTS AND POSSIBLE BIAS

The specter of racial bias has been raised in regard to hair testing due to apparent variation in binding affinity for drugs between different ethnic hair types.[166-168] Evidence at present suggests that protein and melanin are the principle components involved in binding.[169] There are different types of melanin granules in hair including: eumelanins found in dark colored hair; pheomelanins in light colored hair; and erythromelanin in red hair. Distinct chemical and physical properties have been described for the different types of melanin, e.g., pheomelanins have a higher sulfur content, and for eumelanins of different hair colors; melanin granules in black hair are at least twice the size of those in brown hair.[146] Larsson and Tjalve[169] investigated the nature of binding of chlorpromazine and chloroquine to melanin and concluded that cationic forms of the drugs were attracted to anionic sites on melanin through an ion exchange mechanism. Secondary forces (van der Waals forces) were presumed to occur through attraction of aromatic structures of the drugs and the aromatic indole nuclei of melanin. Both cocaine and opiate compounds have amine groups which when protonated would produce weak cations similar to those produced with chlorpromazine and chloroquine. It seems likely that proteins in hair also have specific groups which serve to bind drugs through electrostatic and van der Waals forces similar to that found for melanin.

Recent *in vitro* binding experiments with hair highlight the importance of understanding the mechanisms of drug binding. Su et al.[170] reported that radiolabeled cocaine binds to drug-free hair in a highly selective and stereospecific manner. Further, substantially higher binding was found with black male, Africoid hair than with blond male, Caucasoid hair, suggesting that pigment plays an important role in *in vitro* binding.[171] Joseph et al.[168] reported findings on the in vitro binding of radiolabeled cocaine in human Caucasoid and Africoid hair. Cocaine binding was significantly higher in male Africoid hair than in female Africoid and brown Caucasoid hair. In addition, dark hair bound more cocaine than blond hair. Digestion of the hair samples and removal of the melanin fraction did not eliminate the differences in cocaine content found in the various hair types. If this difference in binding also occurs *in vivo*, there may be substantial bias in hair testing for drugs of abuse.

The differential binding of drugs to hair of different color and ethnic origin has been the subject of several in vivo investigations. Gygi et al.[167] administered 40 mg/kg/day codeine intraperitoneally to three strains of rats with white, dark, or white and dark pigmented hair. Pigment-mediated differences in incorporation of codeine and metabolites into hair were noted, even within the same animal. They concluded that pigmented hair possesses a greater capacity to bind and incorporate codeine and its metabolites than nonpigmented hair. Uematsu et al.[172] reported that the antimicrobial, ofloxacin, was excreted preferentially in dark hair of humans and laboratory animals and suggested that excretion of drug was closely linked with the presence of melanin.

In a study of the excretion of haloperidol, a widely prescribed anti-psychotic agent, in hair, it was found that less than 10% of the drug was excreted in white hair compared to black hair of grizzled (gray) subjects who had received the drug for more than a month.[173] In contrast, a recent study of amphetamine excretion in hair and nails by Suzuki et al.[130] found similar levels of amphetamine in these tissues. Since nails are similar to hair in chemical composition, but lack color pigment, this suggests a lack of bias in the excretion of amphetamine. Henderson et al.[141] noted that non-caucasians incorporated considerably more cocaine than did caucasians (2 to 12 times the amount) following intravenous administration of radiolabeled cocaine, which was not explained by differences in plasma pharmacokinetics.

11.4.5 HISTORY AND POTENTIAL APPLICATIONS

Hair testing for drugs was first reported by Goldblum et al.[162] Guinea pigs were administered varying doses of barbiturates and newly grown hair was found to be positive for parent drug.

Baumgartner et al.[174] reported the first evidence of drug in human hair by analyzing head hair of cocaine abusers by radioimmunoassay for benzoylecgonine, the major metabolite of cocaine. The first time that hair drug test data were submitted to an American court proceeding was in May 1982.[134] The court admitted into evidence radioimmunoassay test results demonstrating the presence of cocaine in the hair, perspiration, and menstrual stain of an alleged sexual assault victim. Hair testing for drugs of abuse has been shown to be of value to criminal investigations by providing information that may associate or dissociate an individual from suspicion of criminal activity, and that provides a wider window of detection of drug use.[175] Hair testing has also been utilized to identify traces of cocaine metabolites in the hair of two five hundred year old Pre-Columbian mummies.[176] Detection of these compounds hundreds of years after drug administration demonstrates the stability of drugs in hair.

There are many potential applications of hair testing in forensic toxicology. Hair testing is currently being used to evaluate in utero drug exposure to fetuses of drug-abusing pregnant women.[177-186] Hair and meconium testing of mothers and newborns has been shown to be more effective in identifying drug exposure than conventional urine testing. Koren et al.[185] found that hair analysis was better able to detect gestational cocaine exposure than standard radioimmunoassay urinalysis. Hair samples from the mothers who were admitted cocaine users were all positive for cocaine metabolite, whereas, urines were negative following discontinuation of cocaine use. Hair samples from all neonates with a confirmed maternal history of cocaine use were positive for cocaine metabolite. The investigators reported that the usefulness of hair analysis to determine in utero exposure to cocaine was limited to the neonatal period. The neonate loses its hair a few months after birth which likely accounts for the negative results thereafter. Callahan et al.[179] also found that analysis of newborn's hair or meconium improved the sensitivity of detection of in utero drug exposure as compared to analysis of fetal or maternal urine.

Another useful application of hair testing is in determining prevalence rates of drug use in selected populations. The traditional manner in which drug-use prevalence is determined in the United States is through the use of questionnaires in which people are asked about their drug use in anonymous surveys. However, in many circumstances, self-report data about drug use are unreliable. Consequently, the use of a non-invasive test such as hair testing, offers the promise of validation of prevalence data that cannot be obtained by other traditional forms of drug testing. Other advantages include ease of obtaining, storing and shipping specimens, ability to obtain a second sample for reanalysis, low potential for evasion or manipulation of test results, and low risk of disease transmission in the handling of samples.

In a prevalence study of drug use in arrestees, Mieczkowski et al.[187] compared self-reported cocaine use with hair and urine analysis and found that hair analysis was far more effective than either urinalysis or self-report in detecting drug. Of the 256 interviewed, 8.5% of the arrestees reported cocaine use within the last 30 days and 21.8% had positive urine tests, whereas 55% had positive hair tests. In a similar study involving 88 juvenile arrestees, Feucht et al.[188] found that only three individuals (3.4%) admitted cocaine use in the last month and only seven subjects (8%) were positive by urinalysis, whereas, fifty individuals (56.8%) were positive by hair analysis. Other populations have shown somewhat higher concordance between hair assay and urinalysis or self-report. Magura et al.[189] studied heroin addicts (N = 134) in which hair test results for opiates and cocaine were compared to confidential urinalysis and self-reporting. Hair test results were equivalent to urinalysis and/or self-report in 87% and 84% of the cases for cocaine and heroin, respectively.

Other applications of hair analysis include attempts to utilize hair testing for nicotine and cotinine to distinguish cigarette smokers from non-smokers.[190,191] Unfortunately nicotine and its metabolite, cotinine, were found in both smokers and non-smokers hair. Attempts to establish a cutoff that would separate one group from another were unsuccessful. This illustrates the special difficulties encountered in studying drugs taken by the smoked route of administration. Technological advances in hair testing continue to improve its sensitivity and specificity. Nagai et al.[192] recently developed a new analytical method for the determination of stereoisomers of methamphetamine and amphetamine in hair. This method should be useful in distinguishing abuse of illicit d-methamphetamine from licit use of decongestant nasal inhalers that contain l-methamphetamine. In a related study of the excretion of methamphetamine in hair, Nakahara et al.[193] claimed detection of single usage of methamphetamine. This finding offers promise that hair detection will have the sensitivity to detect single instances of drug use.

11.4.6 ANALYTIC TECHNIQUES

Analysis of hair generally involves a series of steps starting with weighing of specimen, cutting or grinding, washing, incubation or digestion of the hair sample, extraction and analysis. Each step requires careful consideration with regards to efficiency, analyte stability, and assay requirements. During collection, hair specimen orientation must be documented. The root or tip end must be clearly identified. For segmental analysis, hair strands are generally cut into 1-cm segments. Prior to assay, hair samples may be cut into small pieces or mechanically ground into a powder. Hair specimens are washed with a variety of solvents to remove oily contamination and surface drug contamination.[161,194] Washing with strong solvents and acids has been shown to remove drug from the matrix of hair. A variety of solvents have been used for extraction of drugs from hair.[195-198] In addition, several digestion procedures are commonly used.[199,200] No single procedure has been shown to be superior to others. The choice of incubation/digestion procedures must be based in part on consideration of the stability of the target analytes.[162,200] Additional liquid/liquid and solid-phase extraction purification steps are usually necessary for analysis of the sample by chromatographic methods. Final analysis of the purified hair extract can be accomplished by a variety of means including immunoassay and GC/MS.[201-203]

11.4.7 CAVEATS

Hair testing offers the possibility of detecting drug use that may have occurred over several months. Analysis of segments of hair for drug content may define historical drug use dating back months to years. However, caution is necessary in interpretation of positive hair test results since environmental contamination and deposition of drug from sweat and sebum may occur and may obscure the historical record of drug deposition from the blood. In addition, a major concern regarding hair testing is whether it will reveal significant bias as a result of hair color. The pigmentation of hair should not be allowed to significantly affect the outcome of a drug test. Darker colored hair appears to retain greater concentrations of drug than lighter colored hair. Consequently, races with predominantly black hair may exhibit a higher rate of positivity in hair tests for drugs than those with lighter hair. Unfortunately, the relative contributions of melanin and protein in the sequestration of drugs in hair are not known at present. Additional controlled clinical trials with human subjects who receive known doses of drug under controlled conditions are needed to resolve this issue.

11.5 AMNIOTIC FLUID

11.5.1 MECHANISMS OF DRUG INCORPORATION

The principal routes of drug transfer into amniotic fluid are via the placenta and the excretion of water-soluble drugs into fetal urine. Drug concentration in amniotic fluid is dependent upon a drug's pKa, lipid solubility, protein binding, and fetal renal excretion. Small, highly lipid-soluble compounds diffuse rapidly across the placenta to the fetal circulation and quickly cross the fetal placenta and skin to the amniotic fluid resulting in amniotic drug concentrations that are similar to those of fetal plasma.[204] Larger water soluble compounds cross more slowly to the fetus and are excreted into the amniotic fluid by way of fetal urine. Peak amniotic levels of basic drugs may exceed maternal or fetal plasma levels following drug administration to the mother due to an ion-trapping effect, and the relative impermeability of fetal skin late in pregnancy. Larger lipid-soluble compounds are rapidly transferred to the fetus, but more slowly transferred to the amniotic fluid due to reabsorption in the fetal kidney. Drug concentrations may rise in the amniotic fluid due to an inability to back-diffuse into the fetal compartment. Some drug compounds are transferred in significant quantities to the fetus but are metabolized by the immature fetal liver. In these cases, low concentrations of the parent drugs are excreted into the amniotic fluid.

The gestational age of the fetus influences the disposition of drugs and metabolites by affecting the efficiency of renal excretion, and the maturity of fetal skin. Nakamura et al.[205] reported that gestational age affected the recovery of methamphetamine in amniotic fluid and meconium in a study of pregnant guinea pigs. Fetal metabolism, swallowing, and diffusion of drug across the placenta were identified as other important factors that may be influenced by the fetus' stage of gestation.

The pH of amniotic fluid is lower in late pregnancy than the pH of maternal or fetal plasma due to in utero urine excretion. The mean amniotic fluid pH of full-term neonates was reported to be 7.14.[206] Basic drugs tend to concentrate in amniotic fluid as compared to plasma due to ion trapping in the lower pH matrix while acidic drugs accumulate in the fluid with the higher pH. Although pentobarbital was detected in amniotic fluid within 10 minutes of sodium pentobarbital injection, the amniotic fluid concentration of barbital and pentobarbital were found to be much lower than the concentration in maternal and fetal blood.[207]

11.5.2 FETAL DRUG UPTAKE

The fetus may experience prolonged drug effects due to continuous exposure to the depot of drug found in amniotic fluid. The primary component of this exposure has been attributed to fetal swallowing. The fetus may swallow up to 500 mL of amniotic fluid daily at term.[208] However, a recent study of cocaine and metabolites in amniotic fluid, plasma, and meconium of fetal lambs has suggested that other mechanisms may be more important.[209] Cocaine was infused at 0.5 mg per kg fetal weight per hour into the amniotic fluid of esophageal-ligated and normal fetal lambs. Esophageal ligation was performed to evaluate the role of fetal swallowing in the distribution of cocaine and metabolites deposited in the amniotic fluid. Ecgonine methyl ester amniotic fluid concentrations were highest, followed by cocaine, benzoylecgonine and norcocaine. Maternal and fetal plasma cocaine, benzoylecgonine, and norcocaine concentrations were similar, approximately 3% that of amniotic fluid, in the ligated and normal animals. Ecgonine methyl ester was not found in fetal plasma of either group.

Norcocaine concentrations in meconium were high in fetuses with and without esophageal ligation. The source of the norcocaine in meconium was suggested to be demethylation of cocaine by the fetal liver with subsequent deposition into the intestine. It is not clear whether ecgonine methyl ester entered the fetal circulation and was rapidly hydrolyzed to ecgonine, which was not measured in this study, or whether ecgonine methyl ester was not easily transferred into the fetal circulation. The authors concluded that cocaine and metabolites entered the fetal circulation from amniotic fluid to produce detectable plasma levels, and that the meconium analyses indicated that other routes may have been more important than fetal swallowing. The alternate routes most likely to produce these results included absorption through the umbilical cord and placental surface vessels.

Marilyn A. Huestis and Edward J. Cone

11.5.3 DETECTION OF SPECIFIC DRUGS

11.5.3.1 Cocaine

The concentration of cocaine and metabolites in amniotic fluid has also been investigated due to the current prevalence of cocaine abuse. The failure to identify gestational cocaine exposure is a limiting factor in determining outcomes in studies that rely on maternal self-report or urine toxicology tests. Maternal self-report and urine drug tests have been shown to underestimate drug use due to the inaccuracy of self-reports and the narrow window of detection of drug use, respectively. Testing of newborn hair, meconium, and amniotic fluid have been proposed as alternate testing strategies. Moore et al[210] developed a solid-phase extraction procedure for the determination of cocaine and benzoylecgonine in amniotic fluid of drug-abusing pregnant women. Solid phase extraction was an efficient extraction method despite sample viscosity and provided a clean extract for high performance liquid chromatography analysis. Cocaine amniotic fluid concentrations ranged from 0 to 0.25 µg/mL and were detected in 3 of 8 samples; benzoylecgonine was detected in all samples with concentrations ranging from 0.04 to 3.06 µg/mL.

In a case of premature birth due to suspected maternal drug use, cocaine and benzoylecgonine concentrations in amniotic fluid collected at birth were noted to be 0.07 and 0.29 µg/mL.[211] Additional studies measured cocaine and benzoylecgonine in amniotic fluid at concentrations of 0.4 to 5.0 and 0 to 0.25 µg/mL respectively, in 23 known cocaine abusers. Jain et al.[212] identified cocaine or benzoylecgonine in 74% of amniotic fluid specimens taken from 23 known cocaine abusers. Maternal and neonatal urine specimens from the same individuals produced positive cocaine and metabolite tests in 61 and 35% of the cases, respectively. Measurement of drug in amniotic fluid was suggested to be a sensitive monitoring tool for detecting in utero drug exposure due to the prolonged presence of drug analytes in this biological fluid.

Apple and Roe[213] measured cocaine and benzoylecgonine in the amniotic fluid of a 16 year old pregnant female who had been murdered. The ratio of cocaine to benzoylecgonine in the amniotic fluid was 2.1 as compared to ratios of 0.3 and 0.2 in maternal blood and liver. Amniotic fluid cocaine and benzoylecgonine concentrations were 3,300 and 1600 µg/L, respectively. In contrast to this report, three of six amniotic fluid specimens from cocaine-abusing women were found to be positive for benzoylecgonine. Benzoylecgonine and ecgonine methyl ester concentrations ranged from 143 to 925 µg/L and 40 to 115 µg/L, respectively.[214] Cocaine was not detected in any of the specimens.

Ripple et al.[215] measured cocaine and metabolites in amniotic fluid to determine the incidence of cocaine exposure in a relatively low-risk population. Human amniotic fluid samples were collected from women in their 13th to 39th week of gestation. Samples were screened for cocaine and metabolites by fluorescence polarization immunoassay and confirmed by GC/MS. A limit of detection of 50 ng/mL was established for the immunoassay screen to eliminate false positive screening results noted with amniotic fluid samples that were contaminated with blood. Of 450 samples, 5 were positive for cocaine, benzoylecgonine, and ecgonine methyl ester. One amniotic fluid sample was also positive for cocaethylene, a product of cocaine and alcohol ingestion. Sandberg and Olsen[216] reported the accumulation of cocaine in guinea pig amniotic fluid following chronic cocaine administration. Cocaine concentrations were found to be three- to fourfold higher in amniotic fluid than in fetal and maternal guinea pig plasma. This led the authors[215] to propose that cocaine in amniotic fluid may serve as a depot for continual drug exposure and pose an increased risk for the developing fetus.

11.5.3.2 Therapeutic Drugs

Some therapeutic drugs have been documented to produce low amniotic fluid drug concentrations enabling their inclusion in treatment regimens for pregnant women. Narcotic analgesic drugs cross the placenta rapidly although they are more than 95% ionized at physiological pH. Concentrations of pethidine (meperidine) in maternal plasma and amniotic fluid was measured 15 to 155 min after drug administration in patients who were terminating their pregnancies.[206] Amniotic meperidine concentrations rose linearly with time; however, the peak drug concentration in amniotic fluid was less than one-fifth the maternal peak plasma concentration. Benzodiazepines were found to readily cross the placenta due to their high lipid solubility and lack of ionization, yet amniotic fluid concentrations of unchanged parent drugs were usually low due to high protein binding of benzodiazepines in maternal plasma and minimal renal excretion by the infant.[206]

Concentration of methadone in amniotic fluid has been more extensively studied in pregnant drug users than other drugs of abuse due to its use as a pharmacologic intervention for heroin abuse. Harper et al.[217] reported that amniotic fluid methadone levels did not correlate with maternal or neonatal serum methadone concentrations, although mean methadone concentrations in maternal serum and amniotic fluid were 0.19 and 0.20 µg/mL, respectively. Fetal urine methadone concentrations were 10 to 60 times greater than those in neonatal cord blood and 1.2 to 25 times greater than those in amniotic fluid. The placental transfer of methadone into amniotic fluid was found to occur prior to the 16th week of gestation.[218] The mean amniotic fluid concentration of methadone in samples obtained during the 38th week of pregnancy in women receiving daily oral doses of 40 to 100 mg of methadone was 0.21µg/mL. Kreek et al.[219] reported an interesting case study on the disposition of methadone in a full-term infant whose mother was maintained on 110 mg methadone per day until five weeks prior to delivery at which point a rapid dose reduction program was initiated. The concentration of methadone, and the pyrrolidine and pyrroline metabolites in amniotic fluid were 0.66, 0.52, and 0.40 µg/mL by gas chromatography. No methadone was detected in cord blood at the time of delivery.

Vunakis et al.[220] analyzed amniotic fluid from 37 pregnant cigarette smokers by two different radioimmunoassays that had high specificity for either nicotine or cotinine. Nicotine was found in 22 of 37 samples at concentrations up to 31 ng/mL. Cotinine was detected in 33 of 37 samples in concentrations up to 129 ng/mL. Four amniotic fluid samples from women who smoked between 1 cigarette per week and 10 cigarettes per day were found to be negative for both analytes. Cotinine concentrations were always higher than nicotine concentrations and there was no apparent correlation between the concentration of the two analytes in amniotic fluid. Radioimmunoassays of amniotic fluid from nonsmokers were negative for nicotine and cotinine. Luck et al.[221] measured nicotine and cotinine concentrations in placental tissue, amniotic fluid, and fetal and maternal serum from mothers who smoked tobacco cigarettes and found that the fetuses were exposed to higher nicotine concentrations than the smoking mothers. Amniotic fluid nicotine concentrations ranged from 0 to 23 ng/mL; nicotine and cotinine were detected in 23 of 29 smokers and cotinine only in the remaining six subjects. In contrast to nicotine, cotinine amniotic fluid concentrations were lower in amniotic fluid than in the maternal serum. Significant correlations were found between amniotic fluid and maternal and fetal nicotine serum concentrations.

11.5.3.3 Other Abused Drugs

The literature contains few additional reports on the concentration of drugs in amniotic fluid. Kaufman et al.[269] identified phencyclidine in breast milk and amniotic fluid of a drug-abusing pregnant woman. Phencyclidine concentration in the amniotic fluid 36 days after hospitalization was 3.4 ng/mL. No phencyclidine was detected in the cord blood or in the infant's urine, but analysis of breast milk five days later resulted in a phencyclidine level of 3.9 ng/mL. Sommer et al.[208] measured caffeine and metabolites, secobarbital and phenobarbital by GC/MS in amniotic fluid. Following the intraperitoneal administration of radiolabeled Δ9-tetrahydrocannabinol to pregnant mice, tetrahydrocannabinol was identified in fetal tissue and amniotic fluid.[222] Placental tetrahydrocannabinol concentrations were always higher than other fetal tissues, including amniotic fluid.

11.6 MECONIUM

11.6.1 THE PROBLEM OF IN UTERO EXPOSURE

Fetal drug exposure following maternal drug use is a major concern in pediatric care today. Accurate identification of drug-exposed infants is necessary to fully assess the nature and magnitude of drug effects. The treatment of infants exposed to drugs in utero may be more successful if early identification of drug exposure is possible. Appropriate medical and psychosocial interventions should be made at birth for timely neurodevelopmental assessments. Unfortunately, maternal self-report of drug use is unreliable due to the fear of legal and child custody consequences. In a survey of 36 major urban hospitals, the prevalence of drug abuse among pregnant women ranged between 0.4 and 27%.[178,223]

In a large prospective study of maternal drug use in a high-risk urban, obstetric population, meconium analysis by radioimmunoassay identified 31% of neonates to be positive for cocaine, 21% for morphine, 12% for cannabinoids, and 32% of the positive tests were positive for more than one drug.[224] Only 11% of their mothers admitted to illicit drug use. Meconium analysis for drugs identified 33% more positive cases than urine testing.[225] DiGregorio et al.[181] found that 52.2% of pregnant women who had no prenatal care and who had a negative enzyme-immunoassay screen for cocaine at admission had exposed their fetuses to cocaine in utero based on neonatal hair and meconium analyses by GC/MS. Urine drug monitoring has important limitations including difficulty in collecting urine from newborns, and a window of detection of maternal drug use that is restricted to a few days prior to birth. Analysis of meconium stools collected during the first three days after delivery provides a much wider window of detection of drug exposure, possibly extending back to the 16th week of gestation.

11.6.2 TECHNIQUES FOR MECONIUM ANALYSIS

Meconium formation begins as early as the first 10 to 12 weeks of gestation and continues throughout pregnancy. This biological matrix consists primarily of sloughed epithelial cells from the intestines and skin, bile, pancreatic and intestinal secretions, and the residue of swallowed amniotic fluid. Drugs and metabolites may accumulate in meconium by direct deposition from bile and/or ingestion from amniotic fluid. The pH of meconium is slightly acidic (approximately pH 6.9). Meconium analysis extends the window of detection of drug use and it is easily and non-invasively collected from the diaper.

Ostrea et al.[226] first proposed that identification of drugs in meconium of infants of drug-dependent mothers could be helpful in the detection of in utero drug exposure. These investigators noted the presence of drugs and metabolites in the gastrointestinal tracts of neonatal Rhesus monkeys, rats, and pups. Approximately 0.5 g of diluted stool was extracted in concentrated hydrochloric acid and assayed by radioimmunoassay for cocaine and morphine. In a human study by the same authors,[227] 80% of drug-exposed infants were positive for cocaine, morphine, and/or cannabinoids following meconium analysis, while only 37% were positive based upon a concurrent urine drug test. The increased sensitivity was attributed to accumulation of drug during gestation. Analyses for cannabinoid metabolites in meconium required a different extraction procedure utilizing methanol as the solvent. Further modifications of the method included use of a buffered methanol solvent and analysis by enzyme multiplied immunoassay test (EMIT®) for cocaine, opiates and cannabinoids.[228]

11.6.3 ADVANTAGES AND DISADVANTAGES

Although many reports highlight the analysis of meconium to detect drug exposure, some investigators have found meconium to offer no significant advantages over maternal or neonatal urine for the detection of cannabinoid, codeine, morphine, or methadone use. In many cases where the analysis of urine and meconium for drugs of abuse have been compared, the analytical methods have differed in sensitivity and specificity precluding a direct comparison of the performance of urine versus meconium as matrices for the detection of intrauterine cocaine exposure. Several reports stress the need to lower immunoassay cutoffs below those used routinely for workplace drug testing programs;[229] increased detection rates have been demonstrated with lower immunoassay cutoffs. Maynard et al.[230] recommended meconium as a useful sample for drug detection in newborns, although a similar number of infants were shown to be positive for drugs by both meconium and either maternal or neonate urine drug testing. The majority of publications on the use of meconium for this diagnostic purpose have dealt with cocaine exposure.

Wingert et al.[231] measured benzoylecgonine to confirm maternal cocaine use and THCCOOH to confirm marijuana use; use of other drugs was confirmed by identification of the parent drug. Urine and methanolic extracts of meconium from 423 consecutive births at a metropolitan hospital were screened by EMIT® and those demonstrating activity above the negative control were tested by GC/MS. The authors identified 12% positive for cocaine, 0.6% positive for morphine, 0.6% positive for methadone and no cannabinoid positive meconium samples. Analysis of maternal urine samples resulted in positive rates of 12.2% for cocaine, 1.3% for opiates, 1.0% for methadone, and 6% for cannabinoids. Newborn urine testing results were very similar to the maternal urine data except that no positive cannabinoid results were found. Eighteen maternal urine specimens were positive for THCCOOH, no positive results were obtained from neonatal urine or meconium specimens, although 14 meconium specimens appeared to indicate marijuana use based on screening results alone. It has recently been reported that a significant portion of THCCOOH in meconium may be glucuronide-bound and that a basic hydrolysis may be necessary to free the THCCOOH prior to confirmation.[232] In contrast, Moore et al.[233] recently reported that greater than 70% of morphine in meconium is not glucuronide bound.

11.6.4 COCAINE ANALYTES

Callahan et al.[179] compared the sensitivity of testing newborn infant's hair, meconium and urine to detect gestational cocaine exposure. Radioimmunoassay of infants' hair and GC/MS analysis of meconium were more sensitive than FPIA® with a 150 ng/mL cutoff for urine which failed to identify 60% of cocaine-exposed infants. FPIA® and GC/MS of meconium identified 52% and 74% of the positive cases, respectively. Moriya et al.[234] developed a solvent extraction and EMIT® screening procedure for meconium for benzoylecgonine, d-methamphetamine, morphine and phencyclidine and found that the procedure was not superior to analysis of urine for detection of in utero exposure; however, they recommended that meconium be used when urine could not be obtained. Casanova et al.[214] measured cocaine, benzoylecgonine, and ecgonine methyl ester by GC/MS in urine, meconium, and amniotic fluid specimens of infants who had been exposed to cocaine during gestation. They concluded that when sensitive analytic methods were used, maternal and infant urine, and meconium results yielded equivalent results. However, their most interesting finding was that neither meconium nor urine drug test results detected cocaine exposure when the last reported use was 3 weeks prior to delivery.

Marilyn A. Huestis and Edward J. Cone

In contrast to other findings, these results do not support meconium as a reservoir for cocaine and its metabolites throughout gestation.

Browne et al.[235] employed solid phase extraction followed by high performance liquid chromatography and GC/MS to measure cocaine and metabolites in first-day meconium samples from premature infants of cocaine-dependent mothers. No benzoylecgonine, ecgonine or ecgonine methyl ester were found in the samples, leading the authors to suggest that metabolism of cocaine in the premature neonate is limited. Further investigations by the same research team[236] analyzed meconium and urine from very low birth weight, premature babies for cocaine, norcocaine, benzoylecgonine, and cocaethylene by high performance liquid chromatography and GC/MS. Of the 106 meconium samples analyzed, 19.8% were positive for one or more of the analytes, while only 7.5% of the urines were positive when analyzed by immunoassay.

The cutoff concentrations utilized in the immunoassay screening procedures were not specified. Of considerable importance was the finding of norcocaine and cocaethylene, pharmacologically active cocaine metabolites, and the absence of benzoylecgonine in any of the samples. The absence of benzoylecgonine in the meconium of this population may indicate that fetal metabolism was poorly developed at this gestational age. Another possible interpretation is that the cocaine metabolites were present albeit below the limit of detection of the methods, as numerous subsequent studies have conclusively demonstrated the presence of benzoylecgonine, ecgonine methyl ester, and other cocaine metabolites in meconium. In addition, fetal cocaine metabolism may produce a different qualitative and quantitative spectrum of cocaine metabolites due to immaturity of the fetal liver. Lombardero et al.[237] analyzed meconium, urine and urine-soaked diapers for cocaine and metabolites by GC/MS and were able to demonstrate the presence of cocaine, benzoylecgonine, and ecgonine methyl ester in all three specimens despite low recoveries of benzoylecgonine and ecgonine methyl ester, 19 to 21% and 42 to 25%, respectively.

Nakamura et al.[205] suggest that the disposition of drug and metabolites may be affected by the gestational age of the fetus. In a study of pregnant guinea pigs, gestational age was shown to affect the recovery of methamphetamine in amniotic fluid and meconium. Fetal metabolism, swallowing, and diffusion of drug across the placenta may be influenced by gestational age. In addition, methamphetamine could not be identified in meconium seven days after drug administration, suggesting that meconium was not a static repository for the drug.

Murphey et al.[238] developed a procedure for measuring benzoylnorecgonine, norcocaine, benzoylecgonine and cocaine in meconium by solid phase extraction followed by high performance liquid chromatography. They were interested in measuring benzoylnorecgonine because of its capacity for precipitating seizures in rats, its accumulation in guinea pig fetus following maternal cocaine administration and its presence in the urine of pregnant women after cocaine use. Cocaine and one or more of the three metabolites were detected in all 11 specimens of cocaine-abusing pregnant women. Benzoylnorecgonine was found in 7 of 11 specimens, benzoylecgonine in 10 of 11, one specimen contained cocaine only, and one specimen contained all four analytes. The authors also noted that distribution of the drugs throughout a meconium sample was not uniform and that careful homogenization of the specimen is important to prevent false negative results.

Cocaethylene, an indicator of concurrent cocaine and ethanol use, was detected in meconium, along with cocaine, benzoylecgonine, and ecgonine methyl ester in a solid-phase extraction and GC/MS procedure developed by Abusada et al.[239] Meconium from 36 of 47 infants at risk was positive for one or more of the four cocaine analytes. Four of the meconium samples were positive for cocaethylene alone. This study also collected sequential daily meconium specimens and demonstrated that the concentration of cocaine and metabolites diminishes rapidly 48 h after delivery, although benzoylecgonine was detected in one specimen up to 96 h after birth. Lewis et al.[240] also examined the prevalence of cocaethylene in meconium specimens that screened positive for cocaine and/or metabolites by FPIA® and established the presence of cocaethylene by GC/MS in 31.6% of the samples. These results may have underestimated concurrent cocaine and ethanol use because the method to select specimens may have precluded identification of meconium that contained only cocaethylene due to a lack of cross-reactivity with this analyte in the screening procedure. These data demonstrate that the analysis of meconium for cocaethylene may help to identify in utero alcohol exposure.

Additional cocaine analytes including m-hydroxybenzoylecgonine (m-OH-BE)[241] and p-hydroxybenzoylecgonine (p-OH-BE)[242] have been identified in meconium. Lewis et al.[243,244] emphasized the importance of detection of m-OH-BE in meconium to document in utero drug exposure in two sample populations where 23% of 208 cocaine screen positive samples and 22% of 58 cocaine screen positive samples were confirmed by GC/MS to only contain m-OH-BE. They concluded that almost a quarter of cocaine exposed babies could be missed if m-OH-BE was not among the cocaine analytes determined by GC/MS.

Oyler et al.[242] employed a highly sensitive GC/MS procedure to analyze meconium from infants exposed to cocaine in utero and urine from adult male and female cocaine abusers for cocaine, anhydroecgonine methyl ester, benzoylecgonine, ecgonine methyl ester, cocaethylene, norcocaethylene, ecgonine ethyl ester, norcocaine, benzoylnorecgonine, m-OH-cocaine, p-OH-cocaine, m-OH-BE, and p-OH-BE. Limits of detection of the GC/MS method were less than 7.5 ng/g meconium for all analytes. The disposition of cocaine and metabolites in meconium from fetuses was compared to that found in adult urine. New cocaine analytes identified in meconium included anhydroecgonine methyl ester, ecgonine ethyl ester, norcocaethylene, m-OH-and p-OH-cocaine and p-OH-BE. The presence of cocaine and anhydroecgonine methyl ester in meconium was attributed to maternal transfer of drugs across the placenta. In addition, the presence of anhydroecgonine methyl ester, the primary cocaine pyrolysis product, served as a marker for in utero exposure to smoked cocaine. The origin of the other hydrolytic and oxidative metabolites of cocaine could not be established because they were found in both meconium and adult urine and could have arisen from either maternal or fetal metabolism. Both m-OH- and p-OH-BE cross-reacted to a similar degree as benzoylecgonine in the EMIT® and FPIA® immunoassays and therefore, could contribute to positive drug screening tests. Analysis of the newly identified p-OH-BE in meconium may also serve as a useful biological marker of in utero cocaine exposure. Maternal use of cocaine and ethanol was established by the identification of cocaethylene, ecgonine ethyl ester , and/or norcocaethylene in meconium.

11.6.5 NICOTINE METABOLITES

Meconium analysis of nicotine metabolites has also been used as a biological marker of fetal exposure to tobacco smoke.[245] Radioimmunoassay results for nicotine metabolites in meconium demonstrated a significant difference between infants of non-smoking mothers and mothers who smoked heavily during pregnancy. However, the meconium of infants who were exposed passively to tobacco smoke contained similar concentrations of nicotine metabolites as that of infants whose mothers were classified as light smokers.

11.6.6 POSTMORTEM ANALYSIS

Post-mortem analysis of benzoylecgonine in the meconium of a stillborn baby was reported by Moriya et al.[246] Detection of benzoylecgonine in different bowel segments of the stillborn baby indicated maternal cocaine use throughout pregnancy as supported by the mother's drug use history. The source of morphine found in the stool of a deceased 41-day-old hydrocephalic infant was at first unknown and aroused suspicion. Therapeutic administration of morphine for

Marilyn A. Huestis and Edward J. Cone

three days prior to death was substantiated later by careful review of medical records. Ostrea et al.[247] demonstrated the presence of cocaine in the meconium of three human fetuses. Cocaine was detected in the meconium of a 17-week-old fetus supporting the contention of drug deposition in meconium early in gestation. Cocaine concentrations were found to be proportional to the amount of drug in maternal hair, and to the frequency and amount of cocaine use self-reported by the mother. In addition, the authors reported that the cocaine positive segments of small and large intestine correlated with the period of gestation when cocaine was used. Meconium and stool specimens may be valuable specimens for documenting drug exposure in these and other post-mortem cases.

Our knowledge of drug metabolism in neonates, especially premature infants, is incomplete and requires further research. Important issues in the analysis of meconium include determination of the drug analytes present in this unique biological tissue, selection of analytical methods proficient in detecting these analytes, and achievement of low limits of detection to improve assay sensitivity. Lack of knowledge of metabolic patterns and use of cutoff levels that are too high to confirm maternal drug use serves to diminish the usefulness of meconium analysis. Also, it is difficult to determine the origin of metabolic products within the maternal-placental-fetal unit due to the presence of drug metabolizing enzymes in both the mother and fetus. Further, there is substantial variation in the maturity of the fetal liver. Drugs may reach the fetus through passive diffusion across the placenta and/or binding of drugs and metabolites to proteins in the amniotic fluid which is then swallowed by the fetus.[232] The assumption that drug analytes found in meconium will qualitatively and quantitatively reflect those described in adult urine has not been established.

11.6.7 CONCLUSIONS

Meconium analysis for drugs of abuse has been demonstrated to be an effective method for detection of in utero drug exposure;[248] however, debate continues on many issues. Ostrea et al.[245] claim that analysis of serial meconium samples can reflect the type, chronology and amount of in utero drug exposure. This hypothesis would be difficult to substantiate in human fetus' due to ethical considerations and the unreliability of maternal self-report. The importance of homogenizing the meconium specimen prior to sampling has been stressed as a necessary practical consideration to avoid false negative results. Meconium is usually collected from the neonate's diaper, and it is possible that contamination of meconium with urine may alter the concentration and spectrum of drug analytes present in the meconium samples. The importance of confirmation of positive immunoassay screens for drugs of abuse in meconium is controversial. Immunoassay screens cross-react with a variety of drug metabolites, many of which may not yet have been identified. It is possible that some could serve as sensitive indicators of fetal drug exposure. Confirmation procedures may not target the appropriate drug analytes and may produce a high number of false negative results; however, legitimate drug use, i.e., hydrocodone ingestion, may produce positive opiate screening results and lead to a false accusation of maternal opiate drug abuse if results are not confirmed by a more specific method.[233]

11.7 BREAST MILK

The number of women who nurse their infants in the United States has increased from 22% in 1971 to over 60% in the early 1990s with greater than 90% of these women receiving medication during the first postpartum week.[249] In addition to exposure to therapeutic drugs, breastfed infants of chemically dependent women may be exposed to drugs of abuse present in the milk. Drugs given to nursing mothers reach infants in much smaller amounts than those given to pregnant women. Following the same maternal drug dose, the infant's exposure to drug in milk is usually of less importance than the fetus' in utero drug exposure.[250]

Breast milk is composed of 88% water, 7% lactose, 4% fat, and 1% protein.[251] The average pH is 7.08, although it may range from 6.35 to 7.35[252] Approximately 600 to 1000 mL of milk is produced per day.[253] Each breast contains 15 to 25 mammary glands which evolve from and are morphogenetically similar to sweat glands.[254] Milk, synthesized in the compound tubuloalveolar glands of mammary tissue, is discharged by the secretory or alveolar cells into the alveoli.[255] The alveoli are surrounded by myoepithelial cells which contract and express the milk into the duct system.

11.7.1 MECHANISMS OF DRUG INCORPORATION

There are many factors which determine the concentration of drug in breastmilk and the resultant drug exposure to the infant. Of primary importance is the mother's free plasma drug concentration. Metabolic processes and high plasma protein binding may decrease maternal free plasma drug concentration. Another important consideration is the amount of blood flow to the mammary glands.[255] Active drug metabolites may be excreted into milk, as well as inactive metabolites such as glucuronide esters. The inactive glucuronide esters of drugs may be deconjugated in the infant's gastrointestinal tract to produce the active compound.[251] Both of these processes serve to increase the infant's total drug exposure from the milk.

Drugs passively diffuse across the mammary epithelium down a concentration gradient formed by the nonionized, free drug on each side of the membrane. Drugs filter into milk across capillary walls, interstitial fluid and mammary cells basal lamina and plasma membranes.[256] Drugs with a molecular weight less than 200 are unimpeded in their passage through small pores in the semipermeable membrane. The pH of breast milk is slightly acidic relative to the plasma, resulting in ion trapping of weakly basic drugs in the milk.[257] The total protein content of plasma far exceeds that of breast milk, 75 and 8 g/L, respectively, resulting in the decreased passage of drugs that are highly protein bound in plasma.[249] However, milk contains from 3 to 5% emulsified fat which can concentrate highly lipid soluble drugs such as benzodiazepines and phenothiazines. It should be noted that protein-rich colostrum, excreted during the first few days following birth, contains a higher concentration of immunoglobulins, has a pH close to that of plasma and may contain different amounts of drug than would be contained in typical breast milk.[251,258]

A single determination of drug in breast milk is of limited value due to variations in drug excretion in different samples. Diurnal variation in the composition of milk, coupled with the elapsed timing of administration of the medication, may result in modification of the amounts secreted. The milk fat content also varies during a feeding, with the last portion of the flow containing two to three times as much fat.

11.7.2 OPIATES

It has generally been considered safe to prescribe analgesic drugs for nursing mothers.[251] Breastfeeding following therapeutic use of morphine was believed to be harmless due to excretion of insignificant amounts in the breast milk. Reports in the 1930s indicated little to no morphine in the milk of women receiving up to 128 mg/day as measured by a colorimetric assay.[259] Robieux et al.[259] measured morphine in mother's and infant's serum and in breast milk and concluded that the perception that morphine was present in low concentrations in milk was based on insensitive analytical test results. Morphine concentration in an infant's serum was 4 ng/mL following low oral doses of morphine to the mother. Breast milk concentrations of morphine (10, 100, and 12 ng/mL) varied significantly in three samples obtained over two

Marilyn A. Huestis and Edward J. Cone

hours further substantiating the within subject variability in drug concentrations described in the literature. Due to the uncertainty surrounding the concentration of morphine in breast milk, many physicians consider the use of morphine and codeine by nursing mothers to be contraindicated.[256]

Several additional reports address the issue of opiate concentrations in breast milk. In 1915, withdrawal symptoms were reported in an infant who had become addicted to heroin present in his mother's breast milk. The mother had been given intranasal heroin by a friend to treat postpartum abdominal pain and discomfort. In the same report, another case of infantile addiction was described in a 16-month-old breastfed infant. The infant's treatment included a decrease in breastfeeding and administration of paregoric for the child's withdrawal symptoms. Methadone concentrations in the breast milk of a woman maintained on 50 mg/day of methadone ranged from 20 to 120 ng/mL in samples collected 2 to 24 hours after the last dose.[219] Maternal plasma methadone concentrations ranged from 290 to 620 ng/mL at the same sampling times.

The concentration of fentanyl was measured in colostrum and serum after intravenous administration of an analgesic dose (2 µg/kg).[260] Mean peak colostrum fentanyl concentrations were 0.40 ± 0.059 ng/mL 45 min after dosing. Fentanyl concentrations were always higher in colostrum as compared to maternal serum and fell below the limits of detectability 10 h after drug administration. The authors concluded that fentanyl could be safely used for analgesia in breastfeeding women due to low oral bioavailability of the drug and the need to administer only small doses. In contrast, concern has been raised over repeated dosing of meperidine to nursing mothers. Drowsiness in an infant whose mother received repetitive injections of meperidine was attributed to the accumulation of meperidine and normeperidine in the child.[261]

11.7.3 SEDATIVES AND HYPNOTICS

Most sedatives and hypnotics are excreted into breast milk and may accumulate in infants following chronic dosing due to the child's immature metabolic and excretory systems.[262] Chloral hydrate and its active metabolite, trichloroethanol, have been shown to reach concentrations in breast milk equivalent to sedative doses for infants.[249] Ten days after administration of a single dose of diazepam to a nursing mother, diazepam and nordiazepam were found in an infant.[263] Some practitioners suggest that mothers receiving diazepam should not breastfeed their infants. Diazepam competes with endogenous bilirubin for conjugation with glucuronic acid. Infants have a limited glucuronidation capability which may prove to be inadequate for the elimination of these substances.[256] Other more water soluble sedatives did not appear to pose a significant hazard to the nursing infant when used in moderation by the mother. Temazepam, a relatively water soluble benzodiazepine, was found to partition poorly into breast milk. Temazepam milk concentrations were below the limit of detection (5 µg/L) for 9 of 10 samples collected 15 h after administration of 0.16 to 0.32 mg/kg temazepam to the mother.[264] The concentrations of temazepam in one woman's prefeed and postfeed milk samples were 28 and 26 µg/L. Breast milk alcohol concentration parallels that of maternal blood due to rapid equilibration of the drug between these two fluids. Insignificant maximum blood alcohol concentrations in the infant (less than 3.7 mg/dL) were predicted when the mother's alcohol consumption resulted in blood alcohol concentrations of less than 100 mg/dL.[254]

11.7.4 MARIJUANA

Abbott et al.[265] first reported the presence of tetrahydrocannabinol in breast milk in 1979. Although 5 to 34% of pregnant women have been estimated to use marijuana, little is known about the extent of postnatal drug exposure during breastfeeding.[266] An eightfold concentration of tetrahydrocannabinol in breast milk compared to maternal plasma has been reported.[266] Tetrahydrocannabinol, 11-OH-THC, and THCCOOH were measured in the milk of two lactating women who smoked marijuana. Only tetrahydrocannabinol (105 ng/mL) was identified in one milk sample, while tetrahydrocannabinol, 11-OH-THC and THCCOOH were identified in the second woman's milk.[267,268] Although tetrahydrocannabinol concentrations varied considerably, up to 340 ng/mL was measured in one sample following marijuana pipe smoking at a frequency of up to seven times a day.

Phencyclidine, a highly lipophilic basic drug, was identified in the breast milk of a drug-abusing woman 41 days after hospitalization and removal from access to the drug. The phencyclidine content of the milk was 3.0 ng/mL almost six weeks after the mother's last drug use.[269]

11.7.5 PSYCHOTROPIC DRUGS

All major classes of psychotropic drugs including antidepressants, antipsychotics, antianxiety agents, and lithium have been identified in breast milk, albeit at low levels.[262] Although it appears that less than 1% of the maternal dose of first and second generation antidepressants are excreted into milk,[251,270] there is little information available on the newer serotonin reuptake inhibitors. Fluoxetine has fewer autonomic effects than traditional antidepressants that may affect milk supply and lactation reflexes, and is, therefore, considered as an alternate therapy for postpartum depression. Burch[271] measured fluoxetine and norfluoxetine concentrations in the breast milk of a woman prescribed 20 mg fluoxetine per day. At 4 and 8 h post-dose, the fluoxetine and norfluoxetine milk concentrations were 67 and 52 ng/mL and 17 and 13 ng/mL, respectively. Total drug exposure to the infant was considered to be low and the child exhibited no ill effects of the treatment. Ilett et al.[272] determined the percent of maternal dose of dothiepin and three metabolites in the breast milk of mothers treated with the drug to alleviate symptoms of depression.[272] The mean calculated daily dose was 0.58% of the maternal dose for dothiepin and a total of 3.69% of the dose for the three dothiepin metabolites. It was concluded that the use of dothiepin in depressed mothers did not pose a significant hazard to the nursing infants.

11.7.6 STIMULANT DRUGS

Although stimulants are highly abused, little is known about their excretion in breast milk. Amphetamine was measured in the breast milk of a mother who had received 20 mg of amphetamine daily for many years as a treatment for narcolepsy. The concentration of amphetamine was 3 to 7 times higher in breast milk than in maternal plasma 10 and 42 days after delivery, respectively.[273] Norpseudoephedrine has been identified in the milk of mothers who chewed khat, a common stimulant used in Africa.[249] Cocaine and benzoylecgonine were detected in the breast milk of a woman for up to 36 h after intranasal administration of cocaine.[274] Cocaine, ethanol, and cocaethylene were identified in breast milk of a drug abusing women.[275] High maternal blood concentrations during cocaine abuse and the predicted large milk to blood partition coefficient for cocaine were suggested to possibly lead to toxic infant blood concentrations. The milk to blood ratio for cocaine has not been established in humans, but in rats this ratio was reported to be 7.8.[275] The concentration of cocaine in milk could theoretically be up to 20 times that in the mother's blood according to models designed to estimate the ion trapping of basic drugs in breast milk. The authors conclude that analysis of breast milk for drugs of abuse should be available to aid in cases of possible infant intoxication.

Marilyn A. Huestis and Edward J. Cone

11.7.7 NICOTINE

In 1981, it was reported that 20 to 35% of nursing mothers smoked cigarettes.[257] The percentage of nursing mothers who smoke today may have decreased, although substantial increases in cigarette use among young women have been noted. Nicotine is highly lipid soluble with a pKa of 7.8. Luck et al.[257] reported a linear correlation between nicotine concentrations in maternal serum and milk. Mean nicotine concentrations in breast milk were almost three times higher than those found in serum. Cotinine, the primary metabolite of nicotine, was found in lower concentrations in milk than in serum. In later studies, the half-lives of nicotine in milk were found to be approximately 95 min in milk and 80 min in serum.[276] The authors concluded that the actual concentration of nicotine at the time of nursing will depend not only upon the number of cigarettes smoked per day, but the time delay between smoking and nursing. This is due to the short half-life of the drug in milk. Dahlstrom et al.[277] reported average milk nicotine doses of 0.09 µg/kg infant body weight in the morning after abstaining from smoking. The dose of nicotine increased to an average of 1.03 µg/kg body weight after the mother smoked.

The analysis of breast milk to determine if it is safe to nurse during pharmacotherapy is usually discouraged due to the variability in drug excretion in different milk samples and the difficulty and cost involved in testing.[249] Exceptions to this policy include ruling out persistent contamination of milk by environmental contaminants when the mother has been highly exposed or following introduction of a radiopharmaceutical. In Turkey, breastfed infants were poisoned and died after mothers consumed seed wheat treated with hexachlorobenzene, a fungicidal agent.[252] Accidental contamination of food with polychlorinated biphenyls have resulted in concentration of these compounds in breast milk and exposure of nursing infants to these toxic agents.[263]

11.7.8 ANALYTIC TECHNIQUES

The analysis of breast milk for drugs is readily accomplished by using standard analytical procedures although the high concentration of lipids reduces extraction efficiency and may produce interferences. Multiple solvent extractions may be necessary for complete extraction. Washing with low polarity solvents may help to remove excess lipids. Wong[278] described a highly sensitive high performance liquid chromatography procedure for the detection of tricyclic antidepressants in breast milk. Recovery of drugs in breast milk was lower (approximately 45%) then plasma (65 to 75%). The author stressed the need for sensitive and specific methods for the detection of drugs in breast milk that could help to establish rational guidelines for the use or contraindication of drugs by nursing mothers. Dickson et al.[279] reported procedures for measuring cocaine, cocaethylene, ethanol, oxycodone, codeine and nicotine in breast milk. Milk specimens were initially screened by immunoassay and confirmed by gas chromatography or gas chromatography/mass spectrometry.

11.7.9 CONCLUSIONS

There are few drugs which clearly contraindicate breastfeeding of the infant, but this conclusion is based upon the transfer of low concentrations of drugs into breastmilk.[251,268,280] The extent to which the ingestion of small amounts of drugs by nursing infants may effect growth, maturation, and development is unknown. Administration of medication should be timed to present the lowest drug concentration in the milk at the time of breastfeeding. The Committee on Drugs of the American Academy of Pediatrics[280] has included amphetamine, cocaine, heroin, marijuana, nicotine and phencyclidine on its list of drugs that are contraindicated during breastfeeding. These drugs are believed to be hazardous to the nursing infant and detrimental to the physical and emotional health of the mother.

11.8 SKIN

Skin is the largest organ of the human body and constitutes approximately 10% of body weight. It is composed of four layers, the outermost stratum corneum, followed by the epidermis, dermis and subcutis layers.[281] Blood supply to the skin is estimated to be 7.3% of cardiac output or 473 mL/min for a 70-kg individual.[281] Cells are continuously shed with constant replacement from the underlying viable epidermal tissue. The water content of the stratum corneum is only 20%, as compared to 70% of the more physiologically active layers.[282] The stratum corneum varies in thickness over the body from 10 to 400 µm, with the thickest being present on the palms of the hand and soles of the feet. Stratum corneum, hair, and nail are derived from ectodermal cells, but significant structural differences exist in their fully differentiated form.[283] Hair and nail contain higher contents of cysteine in a nonhelical matrix protein which accounts for their greater strength and heat stability compared to stratum corneum. Chemical differences also exist between the fibrous proteins of these biological tissues.

11.8.1 MECHANISMS OF DRUG UPTAKE

The penetration of substances through the skin is important from both toxicological and therapeutic viewpoints. Skin is a protective physical barrier to the environment, thereby limiting exposure to many toxins. Also, skin has been demonstrated to be an active drug metabolizing organ[284-286] with multi-enzyme protein systems that are able to oxidize and conjugate drugs and endogenous compounds, albeit at a low rate of activity. The bilayer arrangement of polar lipids forms the basis for this effective barrier,[287] although lipid soluble drugs can be absorbed and enter the general circulation, e.g., phencyclidine, nicotine, fentanyl. Drugs passively diffuse through the skin based on physicochemical properties of the drug and physiologic and pathophysiologic conditions of the skin. The free base form of the drug is almost entirely responsible for permeation of the skin as shown in fentanyl and sufentanil studies.[282] Skin hydration, temperature, age, regional variations, and pathological injuries affect skin permeability.

The in vivo percutaneous absorption of phencyclidine hydrochloride was studied by Bailey et al.[288] in the hairless mouse. Skin of this animal model compares closely to human skin. Percutaneous absorption of phencyclidine was noted within one-half hour; consequently, it was suggested that systemic absorption of drug could occur in humans who handle drug products during occupational exposure. The in vitro permeabilities of narcotic analgesics through cadaver skin was studied by Roy et al.[289] They evaluated the diffusional barrier of cadaver skin to buprenorphine-hydrochloride and buprenorphine base and demonstrated that epidermis is a major diffusion barrier, although transdermal delivery rates are adequate to provide analgesia in humans.

Passage of drugs in the opposite direction, outward transdermal migration, has been studied in only a few cases[123,281] and appears to be slow. The multiple barriers that must be transversed by drugs undergoing outward diffusion (subcutaneous fat, dermis, epidermis and stratum corneum) are major impediments that serve to limit transdermal migration of drugs to the skin surface. In addition, the stratum corneum contains appendages that may function as diffusion shunts, thus rendering three potentially distinct routes of penetration through the stratum corneum: the hair follicles; the sweat ducts; and the unbroken stratum corneum.[290] Most studies on steady state drug transport through the skin support the contention that bulk diffusion pathway through the intact stratum corneum predominates over appendageal trans-

Marilyn A. Huestis and Edward J. Cone

port.[290] However, shunt diffusion predominates until steady state is reached. Delivery of high concentrations of drug to the skin surface by sebum and sweat could allow skin to serve as a shallow drug depot. If the stratum corneum contains a high concentration of drug, it could play an important role in the deposition of drugs in hair from sweat and sebum.

11.8.2 TRANSDERMAL DRUG DELIVERY

Morimoto et al.[291] developed a model for predicting the skin permeability of drugs in humans. The model included a component for lipophilic drug permeation based on the solution-diffusion theory and a component for the pore pathway, the main route for hydrophilic drugs. Oakley et al[292] demonstrated that ionized and unionized nicotine partition into different regions of the stratum corneum. The unionized form is concentrated in the lipids, while the ionized form diffuses into hydrated regions. Less than 0.1% of the volume of the stratum corneum is occupied by ducts of the hair follicles and eccrine sweat; too small an amount to account for the amount of ionized species found in the stratum corneum.

Transdermal delivery of physostigmine was studied as a pretreatment against organophosphate poisoning.[293] It was noted that cholinesterase inhibition continued for 3 days after cessation of treatment, indicating a continuing delivery of physostigmine into the blood and providing further support for the existence of a drug depot in the skin. Walter et al.[294] investigated the binding of drugs to skin and reported that tissue lipids play a marginal role in drug binding compared to other components, e.g. proteins.

Peck[295] developed a dermal substance collection device to non-invasively monitor chemical substances which may be present in interstitial fluid, sweat, or in the skin. The migration of theophylline outwardly across skin was demonstrated in vivo and in vitro by Peck et al.[123] Outward transdermal drug migration may also contribute to drug collected on sweat patches, a new and developing technology for monitoring use of abused drugs.

Rapid identification of drug overdose is important in the management of emergency room patients. Nanji et al.[296] detected drug residues on the hands of emergency patients suspected of drug overdose. A suction probe collected drug residues which were analyzed by thermal desorption into an ion mobility spectrometer. Positive identification was obtained in 42% of tablet-related ingestions, 29% of coated tablet or capsule ingestions and in all patients abusing cocaine.

11.9 NAILS

11.9.1 STRUCTURE AND FUNCTION

Nails, hair and stratum corneum (outer layer of skin) are derived from a common cell type, but exhibit fundamental differences in their fully differentiated form. Some of these physicochemical differences include filament orientation, x-ray diffraction patterns, capacity to absorb water, and protein composition. Nail, hair, and skin are composed of keratin, a natural fibrous material consisting of proteins stabilized by frequent cross-links between polypeptide chains. The number of cross-links or disulphide bonds between the chains correlates to the hardness of the keratin tissue. Nail is classified as a hard keratin or eukeratin while stratum corneum is a soft keratin.[297-299] Primates are the only animals to have nails as protective plates on their fingers and toes.[300] Their primary function is to grasp and manipulate small objects. Nails are believed to have evolved from claws but the keratin found in the nails of many different species have an α- rather than a β-diffraction pattern as found in most claws.[301] A high content of cysteine provides tensile strength and stability. Nail formation begins in human embryos after

9 weeks and is complete by 17 weeks. Melanocytes in the nail matrix may provide pigment or color to the nails.

Pounds et al.[302] measured arsenic in the fingernails of subjects given therapeutic doses of arsenious oxide. Fingernail clippings were analyzed for arsenic by neutron activation. Two arsenic peaks were observed. One was suggested to originate from the deposition of arsenic into the nail root from the bloodstream, and an smaller earlier peak was suggested to represent arsenic contamination of the nail from sweat. Scraping the underside of nails was advised to remove sweat contamination. The sectional analysis of fingernails for arsenic was proposed to offer an alternative matrix to hair to estimate time of drug exposure in arsenic poisoning victims.

11.9.2 SPECIFIC DRUGS

11.9.2.1 Amphetamines

Drugs and toxins are retained in nails for extended time periods and may provide information about an individual's drug use history. Suzuki et al.[303] identified methamphetamine and amphetamine in nail clippings from methamphetamine users by chemical ionization GC/MS. After washing, nail clippings were dissolved in alkali and drugs were extracted with an organic solvent. The amines were derivatized and subjected to GC/MS. The mean concentration of methamphetamine and amphetamine in fingernails was 4.75 ± 2.34 (range 0 to 17.7) and 0.14 ± 0.06 (range 0 to 0.40) ng/mg, respectively. Concentrations were similar to those found in the hair of the same subjects although considerable variability was noted. Mean methamphetamine and amphetamine hair concentrations were 3.67 ± 1.45 (range 0.09 to 10.2) and 0.46 ± 0.19 (range 0 to 1.13) ng/mg, respectively. Drug concentrations were higher in toenails than in fingernails from the same individual. The authors suggested that drug was transported into the nail root from the blood stream and throughout the length of the nail via sweat deposition onto the nail bed. The slower growth rate of toenails, 1.1 mm/month, as compared to fingernails, 3 to 5 mm/month) possibly could explain this difference.[302] Age, sex, race, and season have been shown to variably influence the growth of nails. Pregnancy, nail biting and trauma may increase nail growth.[300]

11.9.2.2 Cocaine

Cocaine was measured in the hair and nails of a man who died of a cocaine overdose.[304] Specimen extracts were screened by enzyme immunoassay and confirmed by GC/MS. Quantitative analysis was performed by gas chromatography. Cocaine concentrations in the solutions used to wash the fingernails were very high and ranged from 4.1 to 5.8 µg/mg. Drug concentrations in the fingernail extracts were 2.2 to 2.3 µg/mg. Cocaine was also measured in the victim's toenails, albeit at much lower concentrations (6 to 16 ng/mg). Drug concentrations in the hair washes ranged from 80 to 170 ng/mg and 360 to 1060 ng/mg along the hair shaft. It was suggested that the individual had been a chronic cocaine abuser due to the deposition of drug throughout the hair fiber and that he had recently handled cocaine due to the high concentrations in the fingernail wash solutions.

11.10 SEMEN

Secretions of the bulbourethral and urethral glands, the testis and epididymis, the prostate and the seminal vesicles combine to form seminal fluid. Spermatozoa, which are produced in the testis, mature in the epididymis, and comprise only a minimal volume of semen. The primary components are a viscous liquid produced by the seminal vesicles and a milky fluid containing

Marilyn A. Huestis and Edward J. Cone

numerous enzymes that result in coagulation and liquefaction of the semen from the prostate gland. The pH of normal semen is slightly alkaline with a range of 7.3 to 7.8.[305] However, drugs may be transported into the seminal plasma and enter the male genitourinary tract through an ion trapping mechanism.[306] The degree of drug ionization is dependent upon the differential pH in plasma (pH 7.4) and prostatic fluid (pH 6.6). In addition, lipid solubility of the drug is an important factor in the appearance of drugs in semen.

Therapeutic drug concentrations in male semen have been extensively studied, but several investigations have focused on the presence of drugs of abuse in semen. Yazigi et al.[307] incubated human sperm with tritiated cocaine and were able to demonstrate specific high affinity binding sites. The concentration of amphetamine in the semen of patients receiving amphetamine therapy was found to be similar to that of whole blood.[60] In a forensic investigation, Smith and Pomposini[132] detected phenobarbital by radioimmunoassay in seminal stains from an individual maintained on long-term phenobarbital therapy. Methadone has been found to be concentrated at levels above those found in blood in the semen of narcotic addicts maintained on methadone as an opioid replacement therapy.[308] This finding prompted investigators to study the absorption of methadone by the vagina.[309] Methadone was found to be well absorbed by the vagina, although the amount of drug found in the excreted semen is expected to be too low to exert pharmacological effects.

Cone et al.[310] administered cocaine by the intravenous, intranasal and smoking routes and collected semen from five experienced drug users. One hour after administration of 25 mg of cocaine hydrochloride by the intravenous route, semen cocaine and metabolite concentrations were approximately 60 to 80% of plasma concentrations. Mean cocaine and benzoylecgonine semen concentrations were 45 and 81 ng/g, respectively. Mean concentrations of cocaine and benzoylecgonine 24 hours after drug had declined to 1 and 15 ng/g of semen, respectively. Semen to plasma ratios were generally less than one and were not dependent upon the route of drug administration. The wide variation in semen to plasma ratios was likely due to variation in the composition of the seminal fluid. Higher concentrations of drug would be expected in the more acidic prostatic fluid than in the more alkaline vesicular fluid.

Nicotine concentration in the seminal plasma of cigarette smokers was found to be significantly increased over serum concentrations, while nicotine metabolite (cotinine and hydroxycotinine) concentrations were of a similar magnitude in these biological fluids in this population.[311] Other investigators have established good correlations between sperm cotinine concentrations and the amount of smoke exposure.[312]

11.11 SEBUM

Sebum is a waxy, lipid material excreted by the sebaceous glands. The amount of sebaceous secretion from a 10-cm^2 area of human forehead is reported to range from 0.2 to 0.6mg/h. These glands are primarily associated with hair follicles although some glands have ducts which empty directly onto the surface of the skin. Sebum consists of approximately 33% free fatty acids, 33% combined fatty acids, and 33% unsaponifiable matter including squalene, cholesterol and waxes.[148] Sebum acts as a skin lubricant and a source of stratum corneum plasticizing lipid and maintains a pH of approximately 5 on the skin's outer surface.[282]

The extent to which sebum contributes to drug deposition in hair is unknown. Sebum coats the hair shaft emerging from the follicle at the skin surface. If drug is present in sebum, it could be deposited in hair through intimate contact of sebum with the hair shaft. Faergemann et al.[313,314] investigated the disposition of terbinafine, a synthetic antifungal agent of the allylamine class, in plasma, serum, sebum, hair, nails, dermis/epidermis, and stratum corneum in human male volunteers during and after oral dosing. Concentrations of terbinafine were highest in sebum followed in decreasing order by stratum corneum, hair, plasma, and nails. The drug was still measurable in sebum, skin, hair and nails more than 44 days after the end of drug administration. No terbinafine was measured in eccrine sweat. The authors of the study concluded that terbinafine was delivered to the stratum corneum through sebum and to a minor extent by direct diffusion through dermis-epidermis. Some antifungal agents are found in high concentrations in sweat, i.e., griseofulvin, while others, e.g., ketoconazole, have not been found in sebum.[314] These studies indicate that disposition of drugs into the different tissues of the body is highly dependent upon the physical and chemical characteristics of the individual drug.

11.12 CERUMEN

Cerumen or ear wax is a mixture of desquamated keratinocytes, hair, and secretions of the ceruminous and sebaceous glands of the external ear canal.[315] Saturated and unsaturated long chain fatty acids, alcohols, squalene and cholesterol are the major organic components of cerumen. No reports of the identification of drugs of abuse in cerumen were found in the literature, although two reports of the placement of drugs of abuse into the external ear canal[316,317] were noted, leading to the speculation that drugs might be identified in cerumen in these types of cases.

11.13 BREATH

Tetrahydrocannabinol and metabolites have been identified in the breath of marijuana smokers by radioimmunoassay following the smoking of a single marijuana cigarette containing 200 µg tetrahydrocannabinol per kg body weight.[318] Fifteen minutes after smoking, breath tetrahydrocannabinol concentrations ranged between 10 and 56 ng/sample and metabolite concentrations were between 50 and 123 ng/sample. Tetrahydrocannabinol and metabolites were detectable in breath for up to 1 and 2.5 h, respectively. Manolis et al.[319] identified tetrahydrocannabinol in breath by GC/MS for up to 12 min after smoking marijuana. Breath tetrahydrocannabinol decreased much more rapidly than corresponding plasma tetrahydrocannabinol concentrations and was not dose related, leading the authors to conclude that breath tetrahydrocannabinol was probably due to the drug emanating from the surface of the mouth and respiratory system rather than drug released into the breath from the general circulation.

11.14 FAT

Lipophilic drugs may be stored in adipose tissue after chronic exposure and serve as a drug depot. Sparber et al.[320] noted that moderate stress, in the form of foot shock for fifteen minutes in rats receiving six daily injections of 2.5 mg d-amphetamine/kg, mobilized drug from adipose tissue and doubled brain levels of amphetamine. In a similar manner, phencyclidine and its metabolites were found to persist for prolonged periods in rat brain and adipose tissue after even a single intraperitoneal injection and to accumulate after multiple dosing.[321] The authors concluded that release of phencyclidine and metabolites from these tissues during food deprivation, weight loss, or stress could explain the prolonged duration of clinical effects after phencyclidine administration. Tetrahydrocannabinol, another highly lipophilic compound, has been identified by GC/MS in the fat of heavy marijuana users up to 28 days after smoking. Tetrahydrocannabinol concentrations ranged between 0.4 and 193 ng/g of wet tissue.[322] The long terminal half-life of tetrahydrocannabinol, estimated to be more than 3 days, indicated that the drug is accumulated and slowly released from adipose tissue.

Marilyn A. Huestis and Edward J. Cone

11.15 CONCLUSIONS

Chemical testing of biological fluids provides an objective means of diagnosing whether an individual has been exposed to drugs. Qualitative and quantitative analyses of blood and urine are established means of identifying drugs; however, there is growing interest in the use of alternate testing matrices for this purpose. Each biological matrix provides a unique perspective of the history of drug exposure and may provide information on the route of administration, and the magnitude, frequency and duration of drug use.

Disposition of drugs into biological fluids and tissues is dependent upon absorption, distribution, biotransformation, and excretion processes. The chemical and physical properties of the drug, the route of drug administration, blood flow to the tissues, and the amount, duration, and frequency of drug exposure all affect drug disposition. The molecular weight, pKa, degree of protein binding and lipophilicity of the analyte in biological matrices determine the drug's disposition and that of its metabolites into different tissues. Advances in analytical instrumentation and methodology have enabled the measurement of very low concentrations of drug in complex matrices. There are abundant applications for drug testing in alternate testing matrices in the areas of drug detection, treatment and forensic investigations; however, appropriate validation of these new methods and techniques is required. Additional research is needed to describe the pharmacokinetics of drug and metabolite in these tissues. Other important issues which need investigation include analyte stability, potential external contamination and development of control materials. Despite these limitations, analysis of alternate matrices for drugs of abuse offers the potential of providing unique pharmacologic information about a person's drug exposure history.

Table 1 Relative Occurrence of Parent Drug and Metabolite(s) in Biological Fluids and Tissues[a]

Matrix	Amphetamine	Methamphetamine	Cocaine	Marijuana	Heroin	Morphine	Codeine	Phencyclidine	Methadone
Urine	Amphetamine	Methamphetamine > amphetamine	BE > EME >cocaine, CE	THCCOOH	M-GLUC > morphine > 6-AM	M-GLUC > morphine	C-GLUC > codeine	Phencyclidine	Methadone, EDDP > EMDP
Blood	Amphetamine	Methamphetamine > amphetamine	Cocaine, BE, EME, CE[b]	THC, 11-OH-THC, THCCOOH[b]	Heroin, 6-AM, morphine, M-GLUC, codeine[b]	Morphine, M-GLUC[b]	Codeine, C-GLUC[b]	Phencyclidine	Methadone, EDDP, EMDP
Saliva	Amphetamine	Methamphetamine	Cocaine >BE ≈EME	THC	Heroin ≈ 6-AM > morphine	Morphine	Codeine	Phencyclidine	Methadone
Sweat	Amphetamine	Methamphetamine, amphetamine[b]	Cocaine > EME > BE	THC	Heroin ≈ 6-AM > morphine > codeine	Morphine	Codeine	Phencyclidine	Methadone
Hair	Amphetamine	Methamphetamine > amphetamine	Cocaine >BE >EME, NC, CE	THC > THCCOOH	6-AM > heroin ≈ morphine	Morphine	Codeine >morphine	Phencyclidine	Methadone > EDDP
Amniotic Fluid	—	—	Cocaine, BE, EME, CE[b]	—	—	—	—	Phencyclidine	Methadone > EDDP, EMDP

Marilyn A. Huestis and Edward J. Cone

Meconium	—	Cocaine, BE, EME, CE, NC, BN, NCE, EEE, m-AEME, m-OH-cocaine, p-OH-cocaine, m-OH- BE & p-OH-BE	—	Morphine, M-GLUC	Morphine, M-GLUC	Codeine	—	Methadone
Breast Milk	Amphetamine	Cocaine, BE, CE	THC, 11-OH-THC, THCCOOH	Morphine	Morphine	Codeine	Phencyclidine	Methadone
Semen	Amphetamine	BE > cocaine	—	—	—	—	—	Methadone
Breath	—	—	THC, metabolites[c]	—	—	—	—	—
Nails	Metamphetamine > amphetamine	Cocaine	—	—	—	—	—	—
Fat	—	—	THC	—	—	—	—	—

[a] *Abbreviations: BE = benzoylecgonine; EME = ecgonine methyl ester; CE = cocaethylene; NCE = norcocaethylene; EEE = ecgonine ethyl ester; NC = norcocaine; BN = benzoylnorecgonine; AEME = anhydroecgonine methyl ester; m-OH-COC = meta-hydroxy-cocaine; m-OH-BE = meta-hydroxy-BE; p-OH-COC = para-hydroxy-cocaine; p-OH-BE = para-hydroxy-BE; THC = tetrahydrocannabinol; 11-OH-THC = 11-hydroxy-THC; THCCOOH = 11-nor-9-carboxy-THC; 6-AM = 6-acetylmorphine; M-GLUC = morphine glucuronide; C-GLUC = codeine glucuronide; EDDP = 2-ethylidene-1,5-dimethyl-3,3-diphenylpyrrolidine; EMDP = 2-ethyl-5-methyl-3,3-diphenylpyrrolidine.[b] Dependent upon the dose, and route and time after drug administration.[c] RIA analysis only.*

Conclusions

Table 2 Comparison of Drugs of Abuse Testing in Alternate Biological Fluids and Tissues

Matrix	Invasiveness of sample collection	Sample size	Commercial collection device	Matrix complexity	Analyte concentration	Detection time	Established cutoffs	Advantages	Disadvantages
Urine	Intrusion of privacy	20 mL	Readily available	Simple	Moderate to high	Hours to days	Yes	High drug concentrations; established methodologies, quality control & certification	Limited pharmacokinetic use; no correlation with impairment; cannot predict blood levels; easy to adulterate
Blood	Highly invasive	10-20 mL	Readily available	Moderately complex	Low to moderate	Hours to days	Variable limits of detection	Determine pharmacokinetic parameters; correlate with impairment	Limited sample availability; infectious agent
Saliva	Noninvasive	5 mL	Available	Simple	Low, unless oral contamination	Hours to days	Variable limits of detection	Determine pharmacokinetic parameters; correlate with impairment; estimate blood levels & free drug fraction	Contamination from smoke, intranasal & oral routes; pH changes may alter concentration
Sweat	Noninvasive	Absorbent patch	Available	Simple	Low	Days to weeks	Screening cutoffs	Larger window of detection than urine; difficult to adulterate	No correlation with impairment; high interindividual differences in sweating
Hair	Noninvasive	10-100 mg	Available	Complex	Very low	Weeks to months	Variable limits of detection	Long-term detection of drug exposure; additional samples may be collected; difficult to adulterate	Potential racial bias & external contamination; no correlation with impairment

Marilyn A. Huestis and Edward J. Cone

Amniotic Fluid	Highly invasive	5-10 mL	No	Moderately complex	Low to moderate	Weeks to months	Variable limits of detection	Detection of in-utero exposure over extended time	Highly invasive specimen collection
Meconium	Noninvasive	1-2 g	No	Highly complex	Low to moderate	16 weeks to term	Variable limits of detection	Detection of in-utero exposure over extended time	Sample must be collected within 48 to 72 h of birth
Breast milk	Noninvasive, but difficult to collect	5-10 mL	No	Highly complex	Low to moderate	Hours to weeks	Variable limits of detection	Detection of neonatal drug exposure	Concentrations vary with time after durg administration & fat content of milk
Semen	Noninvasive, but difficult to collect	5 mL	No	Moderately complex	Low	Hours to days	No	Primarily for research	Limited opportunity for collection; small scientific database
Breath	Noninvasive	Unlimited	Available	Simple	Low	Hours	No, except for ethanol	Ethanol concentrations correlate with impairment	Very short window of detection; only for volatile compounds
Nails	Noninvasive	5-10 mg	No	Highly complex	Very low	Weeks to months	No	Long-term detection of drug exposure	No correlation with impairment
Fat	Highly invasive	50-100 mg	No	Highly complex	Low to moderate	Possible for months to years	No	Long-term detection of drug exposure	Complex assay procedures required

Conclusions

REFERENCES

1. Ritschel, W. A. and Tompson, G. A., Monitoring of drug concentration in saliva: a non-invasive pharmacokinetic procedure, *Meth. Find. Exp. Clin. Pharmacol.*, 5, 511, 1983.
2. Ben-Aryeh, H., Shalev, A., Szargel, R., Laor, A., Laufer, D. and Gutman, D., The salivary flow rate and composition of whole and parotid resting and stimulated saliva in young and old healthy subjects, *Biochem. Med. Metab. Biol.*, 36, 260, 1986.
3. Gutman, D. and Ben-Aryeh, H., The influence of age on salivary content and rate of flow, *Int J. Oral Surg.*, 3, 314, 1974.
4. Wood, J. H., Flora, K. P., Narasimhachari, N. and Baker, C. A., Dependence of salivary drug concentration on salivary flow rate, *Meth. Find. Exp. Clin. Pharmacol.*, 4, 255, 1982.
5. Mucklow, J. C., Bending, M. R., Kahn, G. C. and Dollery, C. T., Drug concentration in saliva, *Clin. Pharmacol. Ther.*, 24, 563, 1978.
6. Idowu, O. R. and Caddy, B., A review of the use of saliva in the forensic detection of drugs and other chemicals, *J. Forensic Sci. Soc.*, 22, 123, 1982.
7. Chang, K. and Chiou, W. L., Interactions between drugs and saliva-stimulating parafilm and their implications in measurements of saliva drug levels, *Res. Commun. Chem. Path. Pharmacol.*, 13, 357, 1976.
8. Drobitch, R. K. and Svensson, C. K., Therapeutic drug monitoring in saliva. An update, *Clin. Pharmacokinet.*, 23, 365, 1992.
9. Schramm, W., Annesley, T. M., Siegel, G. J., Sackellares, J. C. and Smith, R. H., Measurement of phenytoin and carbamazepine in an ultrafiltrate of saliva, *Ther. Drug Monit.*, 13, 452, 1991.
10. Peel, H. W., Perrigo, B. J. and Mikhael, N. Z., Detection of drugs in saliva of impaired drivers, *J. Forensic Sci.*, 29, 185, 1984.
11. Inaba, T., Stewart, D. J. and Kalow, W., Metabolism of cocaine in man, *Clin. Pharmacol. Ther.*, 23, 547, 1978.
12. Cone, E. J., Kumor, K., Thompson, L. K. and Sherer, M., Correlation of saliva cocaine levels with plasma levels and with pharmacologic effects after intravenous cocaine administration in human subjects, *J. Anal. Toxicol.*, 12, 200, 1988.
13. Cone, E. J., Hillsgrove, M. and Darwin, W. D., Simultaneous measurement of cocaine, cocaethylene, their metabolites, and "Crack" pyrolysis products by gas chromatography-mass spectrometry, *Clin. Chem.*, 40, 1299, 1994.
14. Cone, E. J., Saliva testing for drugs of abuse, *Ann. N. Y. Acad. Sci.*, 694, 91, 1993.
15. Jenkins, A. J., Oyler, J. M. and Cone, E. J., Comparison of heroin and cocaine concentrations in saliva with concentrations in blood and plasma, *J. Anal. Toxicol.*, 19, 359, 1995.
16. Kato, K., Hillsgrove, M., Weinhold, L., Gorelick, D. A., Darwin, W. D. and Cone, E. J., Cocaine and metabolite excretion in saliva under stimulated and nonstimulated conditions, *J. Anal. Toxicol.*, 17, 338, 1993.
17. Garrett, E. R. and Seyda, K., Prediction of stability in pharmaceutical preparations XX: Stability evaluation and Bioanalysis of cocaine and benzoylecgonine by high-performance liquid chromatography, *J. Pharm. Sci.*, 72, 258, 1983.
18. Schmidt-Nielsen, B., The pH in parotid and mandibular saliva, *Acta Physiol. Scand.*, II, 104, 1946.
19. Bogusz, M. J., Althoff, H., Erkens, M., Maier, R. D. and Hofmann, R., Internally concealed cocaine: Analytical and diagnostic aspects, *J. Forensic Sci.*, 40, 811, 1995.
20. Thompson, L. K., Yousefnejad, D., Kumor, K., Sherer, M. and Cone, E. J., Confirmation of cocaine in human saliva after intravenous use, *J. Anal. Toxicol.*, 11, 36, 1987.
21. Schramm, W., Craig, P. A., Smith, R. H. and Berger, G. E., Cocaine and benzoylecgonine in saliva, serum, and urine, *Clin. Chem.*, 39, 481, 1993.
22. Kidwell, D. A., Discussion: caveats in testing for drugs of abuse, *NIDA Res. Monograph*, 117, 98, 1992.
23. Cone, E. J. and Weddington, W. W., Jr, Prolonged occurrence of cocaine in human saliva and urine after chronic use, *J. Anal. Toxicol.*, 13, 65, 1989.
24. Cone, E. J. and Menchen, S. L., Stability of cocaine in saliva, *Clin. Chem.*, 34, 1508, 1988.

Marilyn A. Huestis and Edward J. Cone

25. Maseda, C., Hama, K., Fukui, Y., Matsubara, K., Takahashi, S. and Akane, A., Detection of delta-9-THC in saliva by capillary GC/ECD after marihuana smoking, *Forensic Sci. Int.*, 32, 259, 1986.

26. Menkes, D. B., Howard, R. C., Spears, G. F. S. and Cairns, E. R., Salivary THC following cannabis smoking correlates with subjective intoxication and heart rate, *Psychopharmacology*, 103, 277, 1991.

27. Gross, S. J., Worthy, T. E., Nerder, L., Zimmermann, E. G., Soares, J. R. and Lomax, P., Detection of recent cannabis use by saliva delta-9-THC radioimmunoassay, *J. Anal. Toxicol.*, 9, 1, 1985.

28. Thompson, L. K. and Cone, E. J., Determination of delta-9-tetrahydrocannabinol in human blood and saliva by high-performance liquid chromatography with amperometric detection, *J. Chromatogr.*, 421, 91, 1987.

29. Just, W. W., Filipovic, N. and Werner, G., Detection of delta-9-tetrahydrocannabinol insaliva of men by means of thin-layer chromatography and mass spectrometry, *J. Chromatogr.*, 96, 189, 1974.

30. Hackel, R., Nachweis von cannabinoiden im speichel nach dem rauchen von haschisch, *Arch. Toxicol.*, 29, 341, 1972.

31. Just, W. W., Werner, G. and Weichmann, M., Bestimmung von delta 1-und-delta(16)-tetrahy-drocannabinol in blut, urin and speichel von haschisch-rauchern, *Naturwissenschaften*, 59, 222, 1972.

32. Karlsson, L. and Strom, M., Laboratory evaluation of the TDx assay for detection of cannab-inoids in urine from prison inmates, *J. Anal. Toxicol.*, 12, 319, 1988.

33. Hawks, R. L., Developments in cannabinoid analyses of body fluids: implications for forensic applications, in *The Cannabinoids: Chemical, Pharmacologic, and Therapeutic Aspects*, Agurell, S., Dewey, W. and Willette, R., Eds., Academic Press, Rockville, 1983, 1.

34. Just, W. W. and Wiechmann, M., Detection of tetrahydrocannabinol in saliva of man and studies and its metbaolism in the monkey, *Nauyn Schmiedebergs Arch. Pharmacol.*, 282, R43, 1974.

35. Ohlsson, A., Lindgren, J. E., Andersson, S., Agurell, S., Gillespie, H. and Hollister, L. E., Single-dose kinetics of deuterium-labelled cannabidol in man after smoking and intravenous administration, *Biomed. Environ. Mass Spectrom.*, 13, 77, 1986.

36. Huestis, M. A., Dickerson, S. and Cone, E. J., Can saliva THC levels be correlated tobehavior? in *American Academy of Forensic Science*, Fittje Brothers, Colorado Springs, 1992, 190.

37. Schramm, W., Smith, R. H., Craig, P. A. and Kidwell, D. A., Drugs of abuse in saliva: A review, *J. Anal. Toxicol.*, 16, 1, 1992.

38. McCarron, M. M., Walberg, C. B., Soares, J. R., Gross, S. J. and Baselt, R. C., Detection of phencyclidine usage by radioimmunoassay of saliva, *J. Anal. Toxicol.*, 8, 197, 1984.

39. Leute, R., Ullman, E. F. and Goldstein, A., Spin immunoassay of opiate narcotics in urine and saliva, *JAMA*, 221, 1231, 1972.

40. Gorodetzky, C. W. and Kullberg, M. P., Validity of screening methods for drugs of abuse in biological fluids II. Heroin in plasma and saliva, *Clin. Pharmacol. Ther.*, 15, 579, 1974.

41. Goldberger, B. A., Darwin, W. D., Grant, T. M., Allen, A. C., Caplan, Y. H. and Cone, E. J., Measurement of heroin and its metabolites by isotope-dilution electron-impact mass spectrom-etry, *Clin. Chem.*, 39, 670, 1993.

42. Cone, E. J., Welch, P., Mitchell, J. M. and Paul, B. D., Forensic drug testing for opiates:I. Detection of 6-acetylmorphine in urine as an indicator of recent heroin exposure; Drug and assay considerations and detection times, *J. Anal. Toxicol.*, 15, 1, 1991.

43. Cone, E. J., Testing human hair for drugs of abuse. I. Individual dose and time profiles of morphine and codeine in plasma, saliva, urine, and beard compared to drug-induced effects on pupils and behavior, *J. Anal. Toxicol.*, 14, 1, 1990.

44. Cone, E. J. and Jenkins, A. J., Saliva drug analysis, in *Handbook of Analytical Therapeutic Drug Monitoring and Toxicology*, Wong, S. H. Y. and Sunshine, I., Eds., CRC Press, Boca Raton, FL, 1996, in press.

45. Sharp, M. E., Wallace, S. M., Hindmarsh, K. W. and Peel, H. W., Monitoring saliva concentrations of methaqualone, codeine, secobarbital, diphenhydramine and diazepam after single oral doses, *J. Anal. Toxicol.*, 7, 11, 1983.

46. Kang, G. I. and Abbott, F. S., Analysis of methadone and metabolites in biological fluids with gas chromatography-mass spectrometry, *J. Chromatogr.*, 231, 311, 1982.

47. Verebey, K., DePace, A., Jukofsky, D., Volavka, J. V. and Mule, S. J., Quantitative determination of 2-hydroxy-3-methoxy-6B-naltrexol (HMN), naltrexone, and 6B-naltrexol in human plasma, red blood cells, saliva, and urine by gas liquid chromatography, *J. Anal. Toxicol.*, 4, 33, 1980.

48. DiGregorio, G. J., Piraino, A. J. and Ruch, E. K., Radioimmunoassay of methadone in rat parotid saliva, *Drug Alcohol Depend.*, 2, 295, 1977.

49. Lynn, R. K., Olsen, G. D., Leger, R. M., Gordon, W. P., Smith, R. G. and Gerber, N., The secretion of methadone and its major metabolite in the gastric juice of humans: comparison with blood and salivary concentrations, *Drug Metab. Dispos.*, 4, 504, 1975.

50. El-Guebaly, N., Davidson, W. J., Sures, H. A. and Griffin, W., The monitoring of saliva drug levels: psychiatric applications, *Can. J. Psychiatry*, 26, 43, 1981.

51. Johnson, R. E., Cone, E. J., Henningfield, J. E. and Fudala, P. J., Use of buprenorphine in the treatment of opiate addiction. I. Physiologic and behavioral effects during a rapid dose induction, *Clin. Pharmacol. Ther.*, 46, 335, 1989.

52. Fudala, P. J., Jaffe, J. H., Dax, E. M. and Johnson, R. E., Use of buprenorphine in the treatment of opioid addiction. II. Physiologic and behavioral effects of daily and alternate-day administration and abrupt withdrawal, *Clin. Pharmacol. Ther.*, 47, 525, 1990.

53. Cone, E. J., Dickerson, S. L., Darwin, W. D., Fudala, P. and Johnson, R. E., Elevated drug saliva levels suggest a "depot-like" effect in subjects treated with sublingual buprenorphine, *NIDA Res Monogr*, 105, 569, 1991.

54. Silverstein, J. H., Rieders, M. F., McMullin, M., Schulman, S. and Zahl, K., An analysis of the duration of fentanyl and its metabolites in urine and saliva, *Anesthanalg*, 76, 618, 1993.

55. Ritschel, W., Parab, P. V., Denson, D. D., Coyle, D. E. and Gregg, R. V., Absolute bioavailability of hydromorphone after peroral and rectal administration in humans: saliva/plasma ratio and clinical effects, *J. Clin. Pharmacol.*, 27, 647, 1987.

56. Chen, Z. R., Bochner, F. and Somogyi, A., Pharmacokinetics of pholcodine in healthy volunteers: single and chronic dosing studies, *Br. J. Clin. Pharmacol.*, 26, 445, 1988.

57. Freeborn, S. F., Calvert, R. T., Black, P., Macfarlane, T. and D'Souza, S. W., Saliva and blood pethidine concentrations in the mother and the newborn baby, *Br. J. Obstet. Gynaecol.*, 87, 966, 1980.

58. Wan, S. H., Matin, S. B. and Azarnoff, D. L., Kinetics, salivary excretion of amphetamine isomers, and effect of urinary pH, *Clin. Pharmacol. Ther.*, 23, 585, 1978.

59. Matin, S. B., Wan, S. H. and Knight, J. B., Quantitative determination of enantiomeric compounds I-simultaneous measurement of the optical isomers of amphetamine in human plasma and saliva using chemical ionization mass spectrometry, *Biomed. Mass Spectrom.*, 4, 118, 1977.

60. Smith, F. P., Detection of amphetamine in bloodstains, semen, seminal stains, saliva, and saliva stains, *Forensic Sci. Int.*, 17, 225, 1981.

61. Turner, G. J., Colbert, D. L. and Chowdry, B. Z., A broad spectrum immunoassay using fluorescence polarization for the detection of amphetamines in urine, *Ann. Clin. Biochem.*, 28, 588, 1991.

62. Bailey, D. N. and Guba, J. J., Measurement of phencyclidine in saliva, *J. Anal. Toxicol.*, 4, 311, 1980.

63. Cook, C. E., Jeffcoat, A. R. and Perez-Reyes, M., Pharmacokinetic studies of cocaine and phencyclidine in man, in *Pharmacokinetics and Pharmacodynamics of Psychoactive Drugs*, Barnett, G. and Chiang, C. N., Eds., Biomedical Publications, Foster City, CA, 1985, 48.

64. Cook, C. E., Brine, D. R., Jeffcoat, A. R., Hill, J. M., Wall, M. E., Perez-Reyes, M. and DiGuiseppi, S. R., Phencyclidine disposition after intravenous and oral doses, *Clin. Pharmacol. Ther.*, 31, 625, 1982.

Marilyn A. Huestis and Edward J. Cone

65. Dixon, R. and Crews, T., Diazepam: determination in micro samples of blood, plasma, and saliva by radioimmunoassay, *J. Anal. Toxicol.*, 2, 210, 1978.

66. Rosenblatt, J. E., Bridge, T. P. and Wyatt, R. J., A novel method for measuring benzodiazepines in saliva, *Communi. Psychopharmacol.*, 3, 49, 1979.

67. Tjaden, U. R., Meeles, M. T. H. A., Thys, C. P. and Van Der Kaay, M., Determination of some benzodiazepines and metabolites in serum, urine and saliva by high-performance liquid chromatography, *J. Chromatogr.*, 181, 227, 1980.

68. Hallstrom, C., Lader, M. H. and Curry, S. H., Diazepam and N-desmethyldiazepam concentrations in saliva, plasma and CSF, *Br. J. Clin. Pharmacol.*, 9, 333, 1980.

69. Di-Gregorio, G. J., Piraino, A. J. and Ruch, E., Diazepam concentrations in parotid saliva, mixed saliva, and plasma, *Clin. Pharmacol. Ther.*, 24, 720, 1978.

70. De Gier, J. J., 't Hart, B. J., Wilderink, P. F. and Nelemans, F. A., Comparison of plasma and saliva levels of diazepam, *J. Clin. Pharmacol.*, 10, 151, 1980.

71. Giles, H. G., Zilm, D. H., Frecker, R. C., Macleod, S. M. and Sellers, E. M., Saliva and plasma concentrations of diazepam after a single oral dose, *Br. J. Clin. Pharmacol.*, 4, 711, 1977.

72. De Gier, J. J., 't Hart, B. J., Nelemans, F. A. and Bergman, H., Psychomotor performance and real driving performance of outpatients receiving diazepam, *Psychopharmacol. (Berlin)*, 73, 340, 1981.

73. Giles, H. G., Miller, R., Macleod, S. M. and Sellers, E. M., Diazepam and N-desmethyldiazepam in saliva of hospital inpatients, *J. Clin. Pharmacol.*, 20, 71, 1980.

74. Lucek, R. and Dixon, R., Chlordiazepoxide concentrations in saliva and plasma measured by radioimmunoassay, *Res. Commun. Chem. Path. Pharmacol.*, 27, 397, 1980.

75. Kangas, L., Allonen, H., Lammintausta, R., Salonen, M. and Pekkarinen, A., Pharmacokinetics of nitrazepam in saliva and serum after a single oral dose, *Acta Pharmacol. et Toxicol.*, 45, 20, 1979.

76. Hart, B. J., Wilting, J. and De Gier, J. J., Complications in correlation studies between serum, free serum and saliva concentrations of nitrazepam, *Meth. Find. Exp. Clin. Pharmacol.*, 9, 127, 1987.

77. Hart, B. J., Wilting, J. and De Gier, J. J., The stability of benzodiazepines in saliva, *Meth. Find. Exp. Clin. Pharmacol.*, 10, 21, 1988.

78. Inaba, T. and Kalow, W., Salivary excretion of amobarbital in man, *Clin. Pharmacol. Ther.*, 18, 558, 1975.

79. Dilli, S. and Pillai, D., Analysis of trace amounts of barbiturates in saliva, *J. Chromatogr.*, 190, 113, 1980.

80. Haginaka, J. and Wakai, J., Liquid chromatographic determination of barbiturates using a hollow-fibre membrane for postcolumn pH modification, *J. Chromatogr.*, 390, 421, 1987.

81. van der Graaff, M., Vermeulen, N. P. E., Heij, P., Boeijinga, J. K. and Breimer, D. D., Pharmacokinetics of orally administered hexobarbital in plasma and saliva of healthy subjects, *Biopharm. Drug Dispos.*, 7, 265, 1986.

82. Blom, G. F. and Guelen, P. J. M., The distribution of anti-epileptic drugs between serum, saliva and cerebrospinal fluid, in , Gardner-Thorpe, C., Janz, D., Meinardi, H. and Pippenger, C. E., Eds., Pitman Medical, Tallahassee, 1977, 287.

83. Cook, C. E., Amerson, E., Poole, W. K., Lesser, P. and O'Tuama, L., Phenytoin and phenobarbital concentrations in saliva and plasma measured by radioimmunoassay, *Clin. Pharmacol. Ther.*, 18, 742, 1975.

84. Horning, M. G., Brown, L., Nowlin, J., Lertratatanangkoon, K., Kellaway, P. and Zion, T. E., Use of saliva in therapeutic drug monitoring, *Clin. Chem.*, 23, 157, 1977.

85. Mucklow, J. C., Bacon, C. J., Hierons, A. M., Webb, J. K. G. and Rawlins, M. D., Monitoring of phenobarbitone and phenytoin therapy in small children by salivary samples, *Ther. Drug Monit.*, 3, 275, 1981.

86. Friedman, I. M., Litt, I. F., Henson, R., Holtzman, D. and Halverson, D., Saliva phenobarbital and phenytoin concentrations in epileptic adolescents, *J. Pediatr.*, 98, 645, 1981.

87. Goldsmith, R. F. and Ouvrier, R. A., Salivary anticonvulsant levels in children: a comparison of methods, *Ther. Drug Monit.*, 3, 151, 1981.

88. Nishihara, K., Uchino, K., Saitoh, Y., Honda, Y., Nakagawa, F. and Tamura, Z.,Estimation of plasma unbound phenobarbital concentration by using mixed saliva, *Epilepsia*, 20, 37, 1979.

89. Knott, C. and Reynolds, F., Value of saliva anticonvulsant monitoring in pregnancy and the newborn, *J Clin Chem Clin Biochem*, 27, 227, 1989.

90. Ogata, H., Horii, S., Shibazaki, T., Aoyagi, N., Kaniwa, N. and Ejima, A., Salivary excretion of barbital and diazepam in human, *Eisei Shikenjo Hokoku*, 96, 27, 1978.

91. Jones, A. W., Distribution of ethanol between saliva and blood in man, *Clinical and Experimental Pharmacology & Physiology*, 6, 53, 1979.

92. Jones, A. W., Pharmacokinetics of ethanol in saliva: Comparison with blood and breath alcohol profiles, subjective feelings of intoxication and diminished performance, *Clin. Chem.*, 39, 1837, 1993.

93. Di-Gregorio, G., Piraino, A. J. and Ruch, E., Correlations of parotid saliva and blood ethanol concentrations, *Drug Alcohol Depend.*, 3, 43, 1978.

94. Haeckel, R. and Bucklitsch, I., The comparability of ethanol concentrations in peripheral blood and saliva The phenomenon of variation in saliva to blood concentration ratios, *J Clin Chem Clin Biochem*, 25, 199, 1987.

95. McColl, K. E. L., Whiting, B., Moore, M. R. and Goldberg, A., Correlation of ethanol concentrations in blood and saliva, *clinical Science*, 56, 283, 1979.

96. Ruz, J., Linares, P., DeCastro, L., Caridad, J. M. and Valcarcel, M., Development of a statistical model for predicting the ethanol content of blood from measurements on saliva or breath samples, *J. Pharm. Biomed. Anal.*, 7, 1225, 1989.

97. Jones, A. W., Measuring ethanol in saliva with QED enzymatic test device: comparison of results with blood-and breath-alcohol concentrations, *J. Anal. Toxicol.*, 19, 169, 1995.

98. Tu, G. C., Kapur, B. and Israel, Y., Characteristics of a new urine, serum, and saliva alcohol reagent strip, *Alcohol. : Clin. Exp. Res.*, 16, 222, 1992.

99. Schwartz, R. H., O'Donnell, R. M., Thorne, M. M., Getson, P. R. and Hicks, J. M., Evaluation of colorimetric dipstick test to detect alcohol in saliva: a pilot study, *Ann. Emerg. Med.*, 18, 1001, 1989.

100. Rodenberg, H. D., Bennett, J. R. and Watson, W. A., Clinical utility of a saliva alcohol dipstick estimate of serum ethanol concentrations in the emergency department, *DICP*, 24, 358, 1990.

101. Penttila, A., Karhunen, P. J. and Pikkarainen, J., Alcohol screening with the alcoscan test strip in forensic praxis, *Forensic Sci. Int.*, 44, 43, 1990.

102. Christopher, T. A. and Zeccardi, J. A., Evaluation of the Q.E.D. Saliva Alcohol Test: a new, rapid, accurate device for measuring ethanol in saliva, *Ann. Emerg. Med.*, 21, 1135, 1992.

103. Benowitz, N. L., Kuyt, F., Jacob, P., Jones, R. T. and Osman, A. L., Cotinine disposition and effects, *Clin. Pharmacol. Ther.*, 34, 604, 1983.

104. Curvall, M., Elwin, C. E., Kazemi-Vala, E., Warholm, C. and Enzell, C. R., The pharmacokinetics of cotinine in plasma and saliva from non-smoking healthy volunteers, *Eur. J. Clin. Pharmacol.*, 38, 281, 1990.

105. Curvall, M. and Enzell, C. R., Monitoring absorption by means of determination of nicotine and cotinine, *Arch. Toxicol.*, 9, 88, 1986.

106. Gwent, S. H., Wilson, J. F., Tsanaclis, L. M. and Wicks, J. F. C., Time course of appearnace of continine in human beard hair after a single dose of nicotine, *Ther. Drug Monit.*, 17, 195, 1995.

107. Etzel, R. A., A review of the use of saliva cotinine as a marker of tobacco smoke exposure, *Preventive Medicine*, 19, 190, 1990.

108. Jarvis, M. J., Tunstall-Pedoe, H., Feyerabend, C., Vesey, C. and Saloojee, Y., Comparison of tests used to distinguish smokers from nonsmokers, *AJPH*, 77, 1435, 1987.

109. Di Giusto, E. and Eckhard, I., Some properties of saliva cotinine measurements in indicating exposure to tobacco smoking, *Am. J. Public Health*, 76, 1245, 1986.

110. Wall, M. A., Johnson, J., Jacob, P. and Benowitz, N. L., Cotinine in the serum, saliva, and urine of nonsmokers, passive smokers, and active smokers, *AJPH*, 78, 699, 1988.

111. Istvan, J. A., Nides, M. A., Buist, A. S., Greene, P. and Voelker, H., Salivary cotinine, frequency of cigarette smoking, and body mass index: findings at baseline in the Lung HealthStudy, *American Journal Epidemiol*, 139, 628, 1994.

Marilyn A. Huestis and Edward J. Cone

112. Schramm, W., Pomerleau, O. F., Pomerleau, C. S. and Gratest, H. E., Cotinine in an ultrafiltrate of saliva, *Preventive Medicine*, 21, 63, 1992.
113. McNeill, A. D., Jarvis, M. J., West, R., Russell, M. A. H. and Bryant, A., Saliva cotinine as an indicator of cigarette smoking in adolescents, *British Journal of Addiction*, 82, 1355, 1987.
114. Peat, M. A., Chem, C. and Finkle, B. S., Determination of methaqualone and its major metabolite in plasma and saliva after single oral doses, *J. Anal. Toxicol.*, 4, 114, 1980.
115. Di-Gregorio, G. J., Piraino, A. J., Nagle, B. T. and Knaiz, E. K., Secretion of drugs by the parotid glands of rats and human beings, *Journal of Dental Research*, 56, 502, 1977.
116. Muhlenbruch, B. and Winkler, R., Speichel-und serumkonzentrationen von meprobamat nach einmaliger oraler applikation, *Arch. Pharm. (Weinheim)*, 314, 646, 1981.
117. Alexander, F., Horner, M. W. and Moss, M. S., The salivary secretion and clearance in the horse of chloral hydrate and its metabolites, *Biochem. Pharmacol.*, 16, 1305, 1967.
118. Robinson, S. and Robinson, A. H., Chemical compsoition of sweat, *Psychological Review*, 34, 202, 1954.
119. Randall, W. C., The physiology of sweating, *Am. J. Phys. Med.*, 32, 292, 1953.
120. *Geigy Scientific Tables. I.* , Ciba-Geigy Corporation, West Caldwell, NJ, 1981,
121. Doran, D., Terney, J., Varano, M. and Ware, S., A study of the pH of perspiration from male and female subjects exercising in the gymnasium, *J Chem Educ*, 70, 412, 1993.
122. List, C. F., Physiology of sweating, *Ann Rev Physiol*, 10, 387, 1948.
123. Peck, C. C., Conner, D. P., Bolden, B. J., Almirez, R. G., Rowland, L. M., Kwiatkowski, T. E., McKelvin, B. A. and Bradley, C. R., Outward transdermal migration of theophylline, *Pharmacol Skin*, 1, 201, 1987.
124. Brusilow, S. W., The permeability of the sweat gland to non-electrolytes, *Mod. Probl. Pediat.*, 10, 32, 1967.
125. Phillips, M., An improved adhesive patch for long-term collection of sweat, *Biomat. Med. Dev. Art. Org*, 8, 13, 1980.
126. Phillips, M., Sweat-patch testing detects inaccurate self-reports of alcohol consumption, *Alcohol. : Clin. Exp. Res.*, 8, 51, 1984.
127. Brown, D. J., The pharmacokinetics of alcohol excretion in human perspiration, *Meth. Find. Exp. Clin. Pharmacol.*, 7, 539, 1985.
128. Vree, T. B., Muskens, A. T. and Van Rossum, J. M., Excretion of amphetamines in human sweat, *Arch. Int. Pharmacodyn. Ther.*, 199, 311, 1972.
129. Ishiyama, I., Nagai, T., Komuro, E., Momose, T. and Akimori, N., The significance ofdrug analysis of sweat in respect to rapid screening for drug abuse, *Z. Rechtsmed.*, 82, 251, 1979.
130. Suzuki, S., Inoue, T., Hori, H. and Inayama, S., Analysis of methamphetamine in hair, nail, sweat, and saliva by mass fragmentography, *J. Anal. Toxicol.*, 13, 176, 1989.
131. Takahashi, K., Determination of methamphetamine and amphetamine in biological fluids and hair by gas chromatography, *Dep. of Legal Medicine*, 38, 319, 1984.
132. Smith, F. P. and Pomposini, D. A., Detection of phenobarbital in bloodstains, semen, seminal stains, saliva, saliva stains, perspiration stains, and hair, *J. Forensic Sci.*, 26, 582, 1981.
133. Parnas, J., Flachs, H., Gram, L. and Wurtz-Jorgensen, A., Excretion of antiepileptic drugs in sweat, *Acta Neurol. Scand.*, 58, 197, 1978.
134. Smith, F. P. and Liu, R. H., Detection of cocaine metabolite in perspiration stain, menstrual bloodstain, and hair, *J. Forensic Sci.*, 31, 1269, 1986.
135. Cone, E. J., Hillsgrove, M. J., Jenkins, A. J., Keenan, R. M. and Darwin, W. D., Sweat testing for heroin, cocaine, and metabolites, *J. Anal. Toxicol.*, 18, 298, 1994.
136. Balabanova, S., Schneider, E., Buhler, G. and Krause, H., Nachweis von cocain im schweis beim menschen, Detection of cocaine in human sweat, *Lab. Med.*, 13, 479, 1989.
137. Perez-Reyes, M., Di Guiseppi, S., Brine, D. R., Smith, H. and Cook, C. E., Urine pH and phencyclidine excretion, *Clin. Pharmacol. Ther.*, 32, 635, 1982.
138. Henderson, G. L. and Wilson, B. K., Excretion of methadone and metabolites in human sweat, *Res. Commun. Chem. Path. Pharmacol.*, 5, 1, 1973.
139. Balabanova, S. and Schneider, E., Nachweis von drogen im schweis, *Beitrage Zur Gerichtlichen Medizin*, 48, 45, 1989.

140. Burns, M. and Baselt, R. C., Monitoring drug use with a sweat patch: an experiment with cocaine, *J. Anal. Toxicol.*, 19, 41, 1995.
141. Henderson, G. L., Harkey, M. R. and Jones, R., *Hair analysis for drugs of abuse*, 1993,(UnPub)
142. Henderson, G. L., Mechanisms of drug incorporation into hair, *Forensic Sci. Int.*, 63, 19, 1993.
143. Spiehler, V., Fay, J., Fogerson, R., Schoendorfer, D. and Niedbala, R. S., Enzyme immunoassay validation for qualitative detection of cocaine in sweat, *Clin. Chem.*, 42, 34, 1996.
144. Tracqui, A., Kintz, P., Ludes, B., Jamey, C. and Mangin, P., The detection of opiate drugs in nontraditional specimens (clothing): a report of ten cases, *J. Forensic Sci.*, 40, 263, 1995.
145. Brown, D. J., A method for determining the excretion of volatile substances through skin , *Meth. Find. Exp. Clin. Pharmacol.*, 7, 269, 1985.
146. Potsch, L., On Physiology and Ultrastructure of Human Hair, in *Hair Analysis in ForensicToxicology: Proceedings of the 1995 International Conference and Workshop*, de Zeeuw, R. A., Al Hosani, I., Al Munthiri, S. and Maqbool, A., Eds., The Organizing Committee of the Conference, Abu Dhabi, 1995, 1.
147. Harkey, M. R., Anatomy and physiology of hair, *Forensic Sci. Int.*, 63, 9, 1993.
148. Valkovic, V., *Human hair volume I: Fundamentals and methods for measurement of elemental composition*, CRC Press, Boca Raton, Florida, 1988, 1.
149. Potsch, L., Aderjan, R., Skopp, G. and Herbold, M., Stability of opiates in the hair fibers after exposures to cosmetic treatment and UV radiation, in *Proceedings of the 1994 JOINT TIAFT/ SOFT International Meeting*, Spiehler, V., Ed., TIAFT/SOFT Joint Congress, 1994, 65.
150. Saitoh, M., Uzuka, M. and Sakamoto, M., Rate of hair growth, in *Advances in biology of skin Vol. IX. Hair growth*, Montagna, W. and Dobson, R. L., Eds., Pergamon, Oxford, 1969, 183.
151. Mangin, P. and Kintz, P., Variability of opiates concentrations in human hair according to their anatomical origin: head, axillary and pubic regions, *Forensic Sci. Int.*, 63, 77, 1993.
152. Henderson, G. L., Harkey, M. R., Zhou, C., Jones, R. T. and Jacob III, P., Incorporation of isotopically labeled cocaine and metabolites into human hair: 1. Dose-response relationships, *J. Anal. Toxicol.*, 20, 1, 1996.
153. Kidwell, D. A. and Blank, D. L., Mechanisms of incorporation of drugs into hair and the interpretation of hair analysis data, in *Hair Testing for Drugs of Abuse: International Research onStandards and Technology*, Cone, E. J., Welch, M. J. and Grigson Babecki, M. B., Eds., NIH Pub. No. 95-3727, National Institute on Drug Abuse, Rockville, MD, 1995, 19.
154. Baumgartner, W. A., Hill, V. A. and Blahd, W. H., Hair analysis for drugs of abuse, *J. Forensic Sci.*, 34, 1433, 1989.
155. Koren, G., Klein, J., Forman, R. and Graham, K., Hair analysis of cocaine: Differentiation between systemic exposure and external contamination, *J. Clin. Pharmacol.*, 32, 671, 1992.
156. Kidwell, D. A. and Blank, D. L., Hair analysis: techniques and potential problems, in *Recent Developments in Therapeutic Drug Monitoring and Clinical Toxicology*, Sunshine, I., Ed., Marcel Dekker, Inc., New York, New York, 1992, 555.
157. Wang, W. L. and Cone, E. J., Testing human hair for drugs of abuse. IV. Environmental cocaine contamination and washing effects, *Forensic. Sci. Int.*, 70, 39, 1995.
158. Cone, E. J., Yousefnejad, D., Darwin, W. D. and Maquire, T., Testing human hair for drugs of abuse. II. Identification of unique cocaine metabolites in hair of drug abusers and evaluation of decontamination procedures, *J. Anal. Toxicol.*, 15, 250, 1991.
159. Blank, D. L. and Kidwell, D. A., Decontamination procedures for drugs of abuse in hair: are they sufficient? *Forensic Sci. Int.*, 70, 13, 1995.
160. Baumgartner, W. A. and Hill, V. A., Hair analysis for drugs of abuse: Decontamination issues, in *Recent Developments in Therapeutic Drug Monitoring and Clinical Toxicology*, Sunshine, I., Ed., Marcel Dekker, New York, 1994, 577.
161. Marsh, A., Carruthers, M. E., Desouza, N. and Evans, M. B., An investigation of the effect of washing upon the morphine content of hair measured by a radioimmunoassay technique, *J. Pharm. Biomed. Anal.*, 10, 89, 1992.
162. Goldberger, B. A., Caplan, Y. H., Maguire, T. and Cone, E. J., Testing human hair for drugs of abuse.III. Identification of heroin and 6-acetylmorphine as indicators of heroin use, *J. Anal. Toxicol.*, 15, 226, 1991.

Marilyn A. Huestis and Edward J. Cone

163. Matsuno, H., Uematsu, T. and Nakashima, M., The measurement of haloperidol and reduced haloperidol in hair as an index of dosage history, *Br. J. Clin. Pharmacol*, 29, 187, 1990.

164. Uematsu, T., Sato, R., Suzuki, K., Yamaguchi, S. and Nakashima, M., Human scalp hair as evidence of individual dosage history of haloperidol: method and retrospective study, *Eur. J. Clin. Pharmacol.*, 37, 239, 1989.

165. Runne, U., Ochsendorf, F. R., Schmidt, K. and Raudonat, H. W., Sequential concentration of chloroquine in human hair correlates with ingested dose and duration of therapy, *Acta Derm. Venereol.*, 72, 355, 1992.

166. Cone, E. J. and Joseph, R. E.,Jr., The potential for bias in hair testing for drugs of abuse, in *Drug Testing in Hair* , Kintz, P., Ed., CRC Press, Boca Raton, FL, 1996, 69.

167. Gygi, S. P., Joseph, R. E.,Jr., Cone, E. J., Wilkins, D. G. and Rollins, D. E., Incorporation of codeine and metabolites into hair. Role of pigmentation, *Drug Metab. Dispos.*, 24, 495, 1996.

168. Joseph, R. E.,Jr., Su, T. P. and Cone, E. J., *In vitro* binding studies of drugs to hair: influence of melanin and lipids on cocaine binding to Caucasoid and Africoid hair, *J. Anal. Toxicol.*, 20, 338, 1996.

169. Larsson, B. and Tjalve, H., Studies on the mechanism of drug-binding to melanin, *Biochem. Pharmacol.*, 28, 1181, 1979.

170. Su, T. P., Tsai, W. J., Joseph, R., Tsao, L. I. and Cone, E. J., Cocaine binds in a stereospecific, saturable manner to hair: A precaution on hair testing for forensic purposes, *Coll. Prob. Drug Dep.*, 1993.(Abstract)

171. Joseph, R., Su, T. P. and Cone, E. J., Possible ethnic bias in hair testing for cocaine, *TIAFT/ SOFT Joint Congress, Tampa, Florida*, Oct. 31-Nov. 4, 1994, 17, 1994.(Abstract)

172. Uematsu, T., Miyazawa, N., Okazaki, O. and Nakashima, M., Possible effect of pigment on the pharmacokinetics of ofloxacin and its excretion in hair, *J. Pharm. Sci.*, 81, 45, 1992.

173. Uematsu, T., Sato, R., Fujimori, O. and Nakashima, M., Human scalp hair as evidence of individual dosage history of halperidol: a possible linkage of haloperidol excretion into hair with hair pigment, *Arch. Dermatol. Res.*, 282, 120, 1990.

174. Baumgartner, W. A., Black, C. T., Jones, P. F. and Blahd, W. H., Radioimmunoassay of cocaine in hair: concise communication, *J Nucl Med*, 23, 790, 1982.

175. Miller, M. L., Martz, R. M. and Donnelly, B., The Use of Hair Drug Testing in CriminalInvestigations, in *Hair Analysis in Forensic Toxicology: Proceedings of the 1995 International Conference and Workshop*, de Zeeuw, R. A., Al Hosani, I., Al Munthiri, S. and Maqbool, A., Eds., The Organizing Committee of the Conference, Abu Dhabi, 1995, 398.

176. Springfield, A. C., Cartmell, L. W., Aufderheide, A. C., Buikstra, J. and Ho, J., Cocaine and metabolites in the hair of ancient Peruvian coca leaf chewers, *Forensic. Sci. Int.*, 63, 269, 1993.

177. Grant, T., Brown, Z., Callahan, C., Barr, H. and Streissguth, A. P., Cocaine exposure during pregnancy; Improving assessment with radioimmunoassay of maternal hair, *Obstet. Gynecol.*, 83, 524, 1994.

178. Ostrea, E. M.,Jr. and Welch, R. A., Detection of prenatal drug exposure in the pregnant women and her newborn infant, *Clin Perinatol*, 18, 629, 1991.

179. Callahan, C. M., Grant, T. M., Phipps, P., Clark, G., Novack, A. H., Streissguth, A. P. and Raisys, V. A., Measurement of gestational cocaine exposure: Sensitivity of infants' hair, meconium, and urine, *J. Pediatr.*, 120, 763, 1992.

180. Koren, G., Klein, J., Forman, R., Graham, K. and Phan, M. K., Biological markers of intrauterine exposure to cocaine and cigarette smoking, *Dev. Pharmacol. Ther.*, 18, 228, 1992.

181. DiGregorio, G. J., Ferko, A. P., Barbieri, E. J., Ruch, E. K., Chawla, H., Keohane, D., Rosenstock, R. and Aldano, A., Determination of cocaine usage in pregnant women by a urinary EMIT drug screen and GC-MS analyses, *J. Anal. Toxicol.*, 18, 247, 1994.

182. Klein, J., Ursitti, F. and Koren, G., Clinical Utilization of the Neonatal Hair Test for Cocaine: A Four Year Experience in Toronto, in *Hair Analysis in Forensic Toxicology: Proceedings of the 1995 International Conference and Workshop*, de Zeeuw, R. A., Al Hosani, I., Al Munthiri, S. and Maqbool, A., Eds., The Organizing Committee of the Conference, Abu Dhabi, 1996, 431.

183. Kintz, P. and Mangin, P., Determination of gestational opiate, nicotine, benzodiazepine, cocaine and amphetamine exposure by hair analysis, *J. Forensic. Sci. Soc.*, 33, 139, 1993.

184. Kintz, P., Kieffer, I., Messer, J. and Mangin, P., Nicotine analysis in neonate's hair for measuring gestational exposure to tobacco, *J. Forensic Sci.*, 38, 119, 1993.

185. Graham, K., Koren, G., Klein, J., Schneiderman, J. and Greenwald, M., Determination of gestational cocaine exposure by hair analysis, *JAMA*, 262, 3328, 1989.

186. Klein, J. and Koren, G., Neonatal Hair Analysis: A Tool for the Assessment of In Utero Exposure to Drugs, in *Hair Testing for Drugs of Abuse: International Research on Standards and Technology*, Cone, E. J., Welch, M. J. and Grigson Babecki, M. B., Eds., NIH, Pub. No. 95-3727, National Institute on Drug Abuse, Rockville, MD, 1995, 347.

187. Mieczkowski, T., Barzelay, D., Gropper, B. and Wish, E., Concordance of three measures of cocaine use in an arrestee population: hair, urine, and self-report, *J. Psychoactive Drugs*, 23, 241, 1991.

188. Feucht, T. E., Stephens, R. C. and Walker, M. L., Drug use among juvenile arrestees: A comparison of self-report, urinalysis and hair assay, *J. Drug Issues*, 24, 99, 1994.

189. Magura, S., Freeman, R. C., Siddiqi, Q. and Lipton, D. S., The validity of hair analysis for detecting cocaine and heroin use among addicts, *Int. J. Addict.*, 27, 51, 1992.

190. Kintz, P., Ludes, B. and Mangin, P., Evaluation of nicotine and cotinine in human hair, *J. Forensic Sci.*, 37, 72, 1992.

191. Kintz, P., Gas chromatographic analysis of nicotine and cotinine in hair, *J. Chromatogr.*, 580, 347, 1992.

192. Nagai, T., Sato, M., Nagai, T., Kamiyama, S. and Miura, Y., A new analytical method for stereoisomers of methamphetamine and amphetamine and its application to forensic toxicology, *Clin. Biochem.*, 22, 439, 1989.

193. Nakahara, Y., Takahashi, K., Takeda, Y., Konuma, K., Fukui, S. and Tokui, T., Hair analysis for drug abuse, part II. Hair analysis for monitoring of methamphetamine abuse by isotope dilution gas chromatography/mass spectrometry, *Forensic Sci. Int*, 46, 243, 1990.

194. Baumgartner, W. A. and Hill, V. A., Sample preparation techniques, *Forensic Sci. Int.*, 63, 121, 1993.

195. Chiarotti, M., Overview on extraction procedures, *Forensic Sci. Int.*, 63, 161, 1993.

196. Rothe, M. and Pragst, F., Solvent optimization for the direct extraction of opiates from hair samples, *J. Anal. Toxicol.*, 19, 236, 1995.

197. Sachs, H. and Moeller, M. R., Quantitative Results of Drugs in Hair Using Different extraction Methods, in *Hair Testing for Drugs of Abuse: International Research on Standards and Technology*, Cone, E. J., Welch, M. J. and Grigson Babecki, M. B., Eds., NIH-Pub. No. 95-3727, National Institute on Drug Abuse, Rockville, MD, 1995, 196.

198. Cirimele, V., Kintz, P. and Mangin, P., Comparison of Different Extraction Procedures for Drugs in Hair of Drug Addicts, in *Hair Testing for Drugs of Abuse: International Research on Standards and Technology*, Cone, E. J., Welch, M. J. and Grigson Babecki, M. B., Eds., NIH-Pub. No. 95-3727, National Institute on Drug Abuse, Rockville, MD, 1995, 277.

199. Offidani, C., Strano Rossi, S. and Chiarotti, M., Improved enzymatic hydrolysis of hair, *Forensic Sci. Int.*, 63, 171, 1993.

200. Staub, C., Analytical procedures for determination of opiates in hair: a review, *Forensic Sci. Int.*, 70, 111, 1995.

201. Spiehler, V. R., Immunological Methods for Drugs in Hair, in *Hair Analysis in Forensic Toxicology: Proceedings of the 1995 International Conference and Workshop*, de Zeeuw, R. A., Al Hosani, I., Al Munthiri, S. and Maqbool, A., Eds., The Organizing Committee of the Conference, Abu Dhabi, 1995, 261.

202. Moeller, M. R. and Eser, H. P., The analytical tools for hair testing, in *Drug Testing In Hair*, Kintz, P., Ed., CRC Press, Boca Raton, 1996, 95.

203. Staub, C., Edder, P. and Veuthey, J. L., Importance of supercritical fluid extraction (SFE) in hair analysis, in *Drug Testing In Hair*, Kintz, P., Ed., CRC Press, Boca Raton, 1996, 121.

204. Seeds, A. E., Current concepts of amniotic fluid dynamics, *Am. J. Obstet. Gynecol.*, November, 575, 1980.

205. Nakamura, K. T., Ayau, E. L., Uyehara, C. F., Eisenhauer, C. L., Iwamoto, L. M. and Lewis, D. E., Methamphetamine detection from meconium and amniotic fluid in guinea pigs depends on gestational age and metabolism, *Dev. Pharmacol. Ther.*, 19, 183, 1992.

Marilyn A. Huestis and Edward J. Cone

206. Reynolds, F., Distrubution of drugs in amniotic-fluid, in *Amniotic Fluid And its Clinical Significance*, Sandler, M., Ed., Marcel Dekker, New York, 261.

207. Carrier, G., Hume, A. S., Douglas, B. H. and Wiser, W. L., Disposition of barbiturates in maternal blood, fetal blood, and amniotic fluid, *Am. J. Obstet. Gynecol.*, 105, 1069, 1969.

208. Sommer, K. R., Hill, R. M. and Horning, M. G., Identification and Quantification of drugs in human amniotic fluid, *Res. Commun. Chem. Path. Pharmacol.*, 12, 583, 1975.

209. Mahone, P. R., Scott, K., Sleggs, G., D'Antoni, T. and Woods, J. R., Cocaine and metabolites in amniotic fluid may prolong fetal drug exposure, *Am. J. Obstet. Gynecol.*, 171, 465, 1994.

210. Moore, C., Browne, S., Tebbett, I., Negrusz, A., Meyer, W. and Jain, L., Determination of cocaine and benzoylecgonine in human amniotic fluid using high flow solid-phase extraction columns and HPLC, *Forensic. Sci. Int.*, 56, 177, 1992.

211. Moore, C. M., Brown, S., Negrusz, A., Tebbett, I., Meyer, W. and Jain, L., Determinationof cocaine and its major metabolite, benzoylecgonine, in amniotic fluid, umbilical cord blood, umbilical cord tissue, and neonatal urine: a case study, *J. Anal. Toxicol.*, 17, 62, 1993.

212. Jain, L., Meyer, W., Moore, C., Tebbett, I., Gauthier, D. and Vidyasagar, D., Detection of fetal cocaine exposure by analysis of amniotic fluid, *Obstet. Gynecol.*, 81, 787, 1993.

213. Apple, F. S. and Roe, S. J., Cocaine-associated fetal death in utero, *J. Anal. Toxicol.*, 14, 259, 1990.

214. Casanova, O. Q., Lombardero, N., Behnke, M., Eyler, F. D., Conlon, M. and Bertholf, R. L., Detection of cocaine exposure in the neonate. Analyses of urine, meconium, and amniotic fluid from mothers and infants exposed to cocaine, *Arch. Pathol. Lab. Med.*, 118, 988, 1994.

215. Ripple, M. G., Goldberger, B. A., Caplan, Y. H., Blitzer, M. G. and Schwartz, S., Detection of cocaine and its metabolites in human amniotic fluid, *J. Anal. Toxicol.*, 16, 328, 1992.

216. Sandberg, J. A. and Olsen, G. D., Cocaine and metabolite concentrations in the fetal guinea pig after chronic maternal cocaine administration, *J. Pharmacol. Exp. Ther.*, 260, 587, 1992.

217. Harper, R. G., Solish, G., Feingold, E., Gersten-Woolf, N. B. and Sokal, M. M., Maternal ingested methadone, body fluid methadone, and the neonatal withdrawal syndrome, *Am. J. Obstet. Gynecol.*, 129, 417, 1977.

218. Inturrisi, C. E. and Blinick, G., The quantitation of methadone in human amniotic fluid, *Res. Commun. Chem. Path. Pharmacol.*, 6, 353, 1973.

219. Kreek, M. J., Schecter, A., Gutjahr, C. L., Bowen, D., Field, F., Queenan, J. and Merkatz, I., Analyses of methadone and other drugs in maternal and neonatal body fluids: use in evaluation of symptons in a neonate of mother maintained on methadone, *American Journal Drug & Alcohol Abuse*, 1, 409, 1974.

220. Vunakis, H. V., Langone, J. J. and Milunsky, A., Nicotine and cotinine in the amniotic fluid of smokers in the second trimester of pregnancy, *Am. J. Obstet. Gynecol.*, 120, 64, 1974.

221. Luck, W., Nau, H., Hansen, R. and Steldinger, R., Extent of nicotine and cotinine transfer to the human fetus, placenta and amniotic fluid of smoking mothers, *Dev. Pharmacol. Ther.*, 8, 384, 1985.

222. Harbison, R. D. and Mantilla-Plata, B., Prenatal toxicity, maternal distribution and placental transfer of tetrahydrocannabinol, *J. Pharmacol. Exp. Ther.*, 180, 446, 1972.

223. Yawn, B. P., Thompson, L. R., Lupo, V. R., Googins, M. K. and Yawn, R. A., Prenatal drug use in Minneapolis-St Paul, Minn, *Arch Fam Med.*, 3, 520, 1994.

224. Ostrea, E. M.,Jr., Brady, M., Gause, S., Raymundo, A. L. and Stevens, M., Drug screening of newborns by meconium analysis: A large-scale, prospective, epidemiologic study, *Pediatrics*, 89, 107, 1992.

225. Ryan, R. M., Wagner, C. L., Schultz, J. M., Varley, J., DiPreta, J., Sherer, D. M., Phelps, D. L. and Kwong, T., Meconium analysis for improved identification of infants exposed to cocaine in utero, *J. Pediatr.*, 125, 435, 1994.

226. Ostrea, E. M., Parks, P. M. and Brady, M. J., Rapid isolation and detection of drugs in meconium of infants of drug-dependent mothers, *Clin. Chem.*, 34, 2372, 1988.

227. Ostrea, E. M., Brady, M. J., Parks, P. M., Asensio, D. C. and Naluz, A., Drug screening of meconium in infants of drug-dependent mothers: an alternative to urine testing, *J. Pediatr.*, 115, 474, 1989.

228. Ostrea, E. M.,Jr., Romero, A. and Yee, H., Adaption of the meconium drug test for mass screening, *J. Pediatr.*, 122, 152, 1993.

229. Spiehler, V., Detection of cocaine in meconium: "Crack Babies", *Therapeutic Drug Monitoring Clinical Toxicology Newsletter AACC*, 7, 1992.

230. Maynard, E. C., Amoruso, L. P. and Oh, W., Meconium for drug testing, *Am J Dis Child*, 145, 650, 1991.

231. Wingert, W. E., Feldman, M. S., Kim, M. H., Noble, L., Hand, I. and Yoon, J. J., A comparison of meconium, maternal urine and neonatal urine for detection of maternal drug use during pregnancy, *J. Forensic Sci.*, 39, 150, 1994.

232. Moore, C. M., Analysis of drugs in meconium, *AACC TDM/TOX*, 16, 113, 1995.

233. Moore, C. M., Deitermann, D., Lewis, D. and Leikin, J., The detection of hydrocodone in meconium: Two case studies, *J. Anal. Toxicol.*, 19, 514, 1995.

234. Moriya, F., Chan, K. -M., Noguchi, T. T. and Wu, P. Y. K., Testing for drugs of abuse inmeconium of newborn infants, *J. Anal. Toxicol.*, 18, 41, 1994.

235. Browne, S. P., Tebbett, I. R., Moore, C. M., Dusick, A., Covert, R. and Yee, G. T., Analysis of meconium for cocaine in neonates, *J. Chromatogr.*, 575, 158, 1992.

236. Browne, S., Moore, C., Negrusz, A., Tebbett, I., Covert, R. and Dusick, A., Detection of cocaine, norcocaine, and cocaethylene in the meconium of premature neonates, *J. Forensic Sci.*, 39, 1515, 1994.

237. Lombardero, N., Casanova, O., Behnke, M., Eyler, F. D. and Bertholf, R. L., Measurement of cocaine and metabolites in urine, meconium and diapers by gas chromatography/mass spectrometry, *Ann. Clin. Lab. Sci.*, 23, 385, 1993.

238. Murphey, L. J., Olsen, G. D. and Konkol, R. J., Quantitation of benzoylnorecgonine and other cocaine metabolites in meconium by high-performance liquid chromatography, *J. Chromatogr.*, 613, 330, 1993.

239. Abusada, G. M., Abukhalaf, I. K., Alford, D. D., Vinzon-Bautista, I., Pramanik, A. K., Ansari, N. A., Manno, J. E. and Manno, B. R., Solid-phase extraction and GC/MS quantitation of cocaine, ecgonine methyl ester, benzoylecgonine, and cocaethylene from meconium, whole blood, and plasma, *J. Anal. Toxicol.*, 17, 353, 1993.

240. Lewis, D. E., Moore, C. M. and Leikin, J. B., Cocaethylene in meconium specimens, *Clin. Toxicol.*, 32, 697, 1994.

241. Steele, B. W., Bandstra, E. S., Wu, N. C., Hime, G. W. and Hearn, W. L.,m-Hydroxybenzoylecgonine: An important contributor to the immunoreactivity in assays for benzoylecgonine in meconium, *J. Anal. Toxicol.*, 17, 348, 1993.

242. Oyler, J., Darwin, W. D., Preston, K. L., Suess, P. and Cone, E. J., Cocaine disposition in meconium from newborns of cocaine-abusing mothers and urine of adult drug users, *J. Anal. Toxicol.*, 20, 453, 1996.

243. Lewis, D., Moore, C., Becker, J. and Leikin, J., Prevalence of meta-hydroxybenzoylecgonine (M-OH-BZE) in meconium samples, in *Proceedings of the 1994 JOINT TIAFT/SOFT International Meeting*, Spiehler, V., Ed., TIAFT/SOFT Joint Congress, 1994, 513.

244. Lewis, D., Moore, C. and Leikin, J., Incorrect diagnosis of of cocaine-exposed babies: A report, *Neonatal Intensive Care*, Sept/Oct, 24, 1994.

245. Ostrea, E. M., Knapp, D. K., Romero, A. I., Montes, M. and Ostrea, A. R., Meconium analysis to assess fetal exposure to nicotine by active and passive maternal smoking, *J. Pediatr.*, 124, 471, 1994.

246. Moriya, F., Chan, K. M., Noguchi, T. T. and Parnassus, W. N., Detection of drugs-of-abuse in meconium of a stillborn baby and in stool of a deceased 41-day-old infant, *J. Forensic Sci.*, 40, 505, 1995.

247. Ostrea, E. M., Romero, A., Knapp, K., Ostrea, A. R., Lucena, J. E. and Utarnachitt, R. B., Clinical and laboratory observations: Postmortem drug analysis of meconium in early-gestation human fetuses exposed to cocaine: clinical implications, *J. Pediatr.*, 124, 477, 1994.

248. Nair, P., Rothblum, S. and Hebel, R., Neonatal outcome in infants with evidence of fetal exposure to opiates, cocaine, and cannabinoids, *Clin. Pediat.*, May, 280, 1994.

249. Anderson, P. O., Therapy Review: drug use during breast-feeding, *Clinical Pharmacy*, 10, 594, 1991.

Marilyn A. Huestis and Edward J. Cone

250. Atkinson, H. C., Begg, E. J. and Darrlow, B. A., Drugs in human milk clinical pharmacokinetic considerations, *Clin. Pharmacokinet.*, 14, 217, 1988.

251. Rieder, M. J., Drugs and breastfeeding, in *Maternal-Fetal Toxicology A Clinicians guide*, Koren, G., Ed., Marcel Dekker, New York, 1990, 63.

252. Vorherr, H., Drug excretion in breast milk, *Postgrad. Med.*, 56, 97, 1974.

253. Wilson, J. T., Determinants and consequences of drug excretion in breast milk, *Drug Metab. Rev.*, 14, 619, 1983.

254. Wilson, J. T., Brown, R. D., Cherek, D. R., Dailey, J. W., Hilman, B., Jobe, P. C., Manno, B. R., Manno, J. E., Redetzki, H. M. and Stewart, J. J., Drug excretion in human breast milk: principles, pharmacokinetics and projected consequences, *Clin. Pharmacokinet.*, 5, 1, 1980.

255. Catz, C. S. and Giacoia, G. P., Drugs and breast milk, *Pediatr Clin North Am*, 19, 151, 1972.

256. Kirksey, A. and Groziak, S. M., Maternal drug use: evaluation of risks to breast-fed infants, *Wld Rev. Nutr. Diet.*, 43, 60, 1984.

257. Luck, W. and Nau, H., Nicotine and cotinine concentrations in serum and milk of nursing smokers, *Br. J. Clin. Pharmac.*, 18, 9, 1984.

258. Stebler, T. and Guentert, T. W., Studies on the excretion of diazepam and nordazepam into milk for the prediction of milk-to-plasma drug concentration ratios, *Pharm. Res.*, 9, 1299, 1992.

259. Robieux, I., Koren, G., Vandenbergh, H. and Schneiderman, J., Morphine excretion in breast milk and resultant exposure of a nursing infant, *Clin. Toxicol.*, 28, 365, 1990.

260. Steer, P. L., Biddle, C. J., Marley, W. S., Lantz, R. K. and Sulik, P. L., Concentration of fentanyl in colostrum after an analgesic dose, *Can J Anaesth*, 39, 231, 1992.

261. Gin, T., Anaesthesia and breast feeding, *Anaesth. Intensive Care*, 21, 256, 1993.

262. Buist, A., Norman, T. R. and Dennerstein, L., Breastfeeding and the use of psychotropic medication: a review, *Journal of Affective Disorders*, 19, 197, 1990.

263. Giacoia, G. P. and Catz, C. S., Drugs and pollutants in breast milk, *Clin. Perinatol.*, 6, 181, 1979.

264. Lebedevs, T. H., Wojnar-Horton, R. E., Yapp, P., Roberts, M. J., Dusci, L. J., Hackett, L. P. and Ilett, K. F., Excretion of temazepam in breast milk, *Br. J. Clin. Pharmacol.*, 33, 204, 1992.

265. Abbott, S. R., Berg, J. R., Loeffler, K. O., Kanter, S., Hollister, L. E., Hawking-Abrams, J., Baras, H. L. and Jones, R. T., HPLC analysis of delta-9-tetrahydrocannabinol and metabolites in biological fluids, *American Chemical Society*, 8, 115, 1979.

266. Astley, S. J. and Little, R. E., Maternal marijuana use during lactation and infant development at one year, *Neurotoxicol. Teratology*, 12, 161, 1990.

267. Perez-Reyes, M. and Wall, M. E., Presence of delta-9-tetrahydrocannabinol in human milk, *Unknown*, 307, 819,

268. Reisner, S. H., Eisenberg, N. H. and Hauser, G. J., Maternal Medications and breast-feeding, *Dev. Pharmacol. Ther.*, 6, 285, 1983.

269. Kaufman, K. R., Petrucha, R. A., Pitts, F. N. and Weekes, M. E., PCP in amniotic fluid and breast-milk: case report, *J. Clin. Psychiatry*, 44, 269, 1983.

270. Kacew, S., Adverse effects of drugs and chemicals in breast milk on the nursing infant, *J. Clin. Pharmacol.*, 33, 213, 1993.

271. Burch, K. J. and Wells, B. G., Fluoxetine/norfluoxetine concentrations in human milk, *Pediatrics*, 676, 1992.

272. Ilett, K. F., Lebedevs, T. H., Wojnar-Horton, R. E., Yapp, P., Roberts, M. J., Dusci, L. J. and Hackett, L. P., The excretion of dothiepin and its primary metabolites in breast milk, *Br. J. Clin. Pharmacol.*, 33, 635, 1992.

273. Steiner, E., Villen, T., Hallberg, M. and Rane, A., Amphetamine secretion in breast milk, *Eur. J. Clin. Pharmacol.*, 27, 123, 1984.

274. Chasnoff, I. J., Lewis, D. E. and Squires, L., Cocaine intoxication in a breast-fed infant, *Pediatrics*, 80, 836, 1987.

275. Dickson, P. H., Lind, A., Studts, P., Nipper, H. C., Makoid, M. and Therkildsen, D., The routine analysis of breast milk for drugs of abuse in a clinical toxicology laboratory, *J. Forensic Sci.*, 39, 207, 1994.

276. Steldinger, R., Luck, W. and Nau, H., Half lives of nicotine in milk of smoking mothers: implications for nursing, *J Perinat. Med.*, 16, 261, 1988.
277. Dahlstrom, A., Lundell, B., Curvall, M. and Thapper, L., Nicotine and cotinine concentrations in the nursing mother and her infant, *Acta Paedistr Scand*, 79, 142, 1990.
278. Wong, S. H. Y., Monitoring of drugs in breast milk, *Ann. Clin. Lab. Sci.*, 15, 100, 1985.
279. Bailey, D. N., Thin-layer chromatographic detection of cocaethylene in human urine, *Am. J. Clin. Pathol.*, 101, 342, 1994.
280. Roberts, R. J., Blumer, J. L., Gorman, R. L., Lambert, G. H., Rumack, B. H. and Snodgrass, W., Transfer of drugs and other chemicals into human milk, *Pediatrics*, 84, 924, 1989.
281. Shah, V. P., Migration of drugs across the skin after oral administration: Griseofulvin, *Pharmacol Skin*, 1, 41, 1987.
282. Singh, S. and Singh, J., Transdermal drug delivery by passive diffusion and iontophoresis: a review, in *Medicinal Research Reviews*, Medicinal Research Reviews, 1993, 569.
283. Baden, H. P., McGilvray, N., Lee, L. D., Baden, L. and Kubilus, J., Comparison of stratum corneum and hair fibrous proteins, *J. Invest. Dermatol.*, 75, 311, 1980.
284. Pannatier, A., Jenner, P., Testa, B. and Etter, J. C., The skin as a drug-metabolizing organ, *Drug Metab. Rev.*, 8, 319, 1978.
285. Krishna, D. R. and Klotz, U., Extrahepatic metabolism of drugs in humans, *Clin. Pharmacokinet.*, 26, 144, 1994.
286. Pharm, M. A., Magdalou, J., Siest, G., Lenoir, M. C., Bernard, B. A., Jamoulle, J. C. and Shroot, B., Reconstituted epidermis: a novel model for the study of drug metabolism in human epidermis, *J. Invest. Dermatol.*, 94, 749, 1990.
287. Garson, J. C., Doucet, J., Tsoucaris, G. and Leveque, J. L., Study of lipid and non-lipid structure in human stratum corneum by x-ray diffraction, *J. Soc. Cosmet. Chem.*, 41, 347, 1990.
288. Bailey, D. N., Percutaneous absorption of phencyclidine hydrochloride in vivo, *Res. Commun. Subst. Abuse*, 1, 443, 1980.
289. Roy, S. D., Roos, E. and Sharma, K., Transdermal delivery of buprenorphine through cadaver skin, *J. Pharm. Sci.*, 83, 126, 1994.
290. Inaba, T., Cocaine: pharmacokinetics and biotransformation in man, *Can. J. Physiol. Pharmacol.*, 67, 1154, 1989.
291. Morimoto, Y., Hatanaka, T., Sugibayashi, K. and Omiya, H., Prediction of skin permeability of drugs: Comparison of human and hairless rat skin, *J. Pharm. Pharmacol.*, 44, 634, 1992.
292. Oakley, D. M. and Swarbrick, J., Effects of ionization on the percutaneous absorption of drugs: partitioning of nicotine into organic liquids and hydrated stratum corneum, *J. Pharm. Sci.*, 76, 866, 1987.
293. Jenner, J., Saleem, A. and Swanston, D., Transdermal delivery of physostigmine: A pretreatment against organophosphate poisoning, *J. Pharm. Pharmacol.*, 47, 206, 1995.
294. Walter, K. and Kurz, H., Binding of drugs to human skin: Influencing factors and the role of tissue lipids, *J. Pharm. Pharmacol.*, 40, 689, 1988.
295. Dermal substance collection method, *United States Patent*, 4,819,645, 1989.
296. Nanji, A. A., Lawrence, A. H. and Mikhael, N. Z., Use of skin surface and ion mobility spectrometry as a preliminary screening method for drug detection in an emergency room, *J. Toxicol. Clin. Toxicol.*, 25, 501, 1987.
297. Ward, W. H. and Lundgren, H. P., The formation, composition, and properties of the keratins, in *Advances in Protein Chemistry*, Anson, M. L., Bailey, K. and Edsall, J. T., Eds., Academic Press, Inc., New York, 1954, 243.
298. Matoltsy, A. G., What is keratin? in *Advances in Biology of Skin: Hair Growth*, Montagna, W. and Dobson, R. L., Eds., Pergamon Press, Braunschweig, 1967, 559.
299. Matoltsy, A. G., The chemistry of Keratinization, in *The biology of hair growth*, Montagna, W. and Ellis, R. A., Eds., Academic Press, New York, NY, 1958, 135.
300. Montagna, W. and Parakkal, P. F., Nails, in *The Structure and Function of Skin*, Academic Press, London, 1974, 271.
301. Baden, H. P., Goldsmith, L. A. and Fleming, B., A comparative study of the physicochemical properties of human keratinized tissues, *Biochim. Biophys. Acta*, 322, 269, 1973.

Marilyn A. Huestis and Edward J. Cone

302. Pounds, C. A., Pearson, E. F. and Turner, T. D., Arsenic in fingernails, *J. Forensic Sci. Soc.*, 19, 165, 1979.

303. Suzuki, O., Hattori, H. and Asano, M., Nails as useful materials for detection of methamphetamine or amphetamine abuse, *Forensic. Sci. Int.*, 24, 9, 1984.

304. Tiess, D., Wegener, R., Rudolph, I., Steffen, U., Tiefenbach, B., Weirich, V. and Zack, F., Cocaine and benzoylecgonine concentrations in hair, nails and tissues: a comparative study of ante and post mortem materials in a case of an acute lethal cocaine intoxication, in *Proceedings of the 1994 JOINT TIAFT/SOFT International Meeting*, Spiehler, V., Ed., TIAFT/SOFT Joint Congress, 1994, 343.

305. Strasinger, S. K., *Urinalysis and body fluids-a self-instructional text*, 2nd Edition, F.A. Davis Company, Philadelphia, 1993, 1.

306. Pichini, S., Zuccaro, P. and Pacifici, R., Drugs in semen, *Clin. Pharmacokinet.*, 26, 356, 1994.

307. Yazigi, R. A., Odem, R. R. and Polakoski, K. L., Demonstration of specific binding of cocaine to human spermatozoa, *JAMA*, 266, 1956, 1991.

308. Gerber, N. and Lynn, R. K., Excretion of methadone in semen from methadone addicts; comparison with blood levels, *Life Sci.*, 19, 787, 1976.

309. Benziger, D. P. and Edelson, J., Absorption from the vagina, *Drug Metab. Rev.*, 14(2), 137, 1983.

310. Cone, E. J., Kato, K. and Hillsgrove, M., Cocaine excretion in the semen of drug users, *J. Anal. Toxicol.*, 20, 139, 1996.

311. Pacifici, R., Altieri, I., Gandini, L., Lenzi, A., Pichini, S., Rose, M., Zuccaro, P. and Dondero, F., Nicotine, cotinine, and trans-3-hydroxycotinine levels in seminal plasma of smokers: effects on sperm parameters, *Ther. Drug Monit.*, 15, 358, 1993.

312. Vine, M. F., Hulka, B. S., Margolin, B. H., Truong, Y. K., Hu, P. C., Schramm, M. M., Griffith, J. D., McCann, M. and Everson, R. B., Cotinine concentrations in semen, urine, and blood of smokers and nonsmokers, *Am. J. Public Health*, 83, 1335, 1993.

313. Faergemann, J., Zehender, H., Denouel, J. and Millerioux, L., Levels of terbinafine in plasma, stratum corneum, dermis-epidermis (without stratum corneum), sebum, hair and nails during and after 250 mg terbinafine orally once per day for four weeks, *Acta Derm. Venereol.*, 73, 305, 1993.

314. Faergemann, J., Zehender, H., Jones, T. and Maibach, I., Terbinafine levels in serum, stratum corneum, dermis-epidermis (without stratum corneum), hair, sebum and eccrine sweat, *Acta Derm. Venereol.*, 71, 322, 1990.

315. Okuda, I., Bingham, B., Stoney, P. and Hawke, M., The organic composition of earwax, *Journal of Otolaryngology*, 20, 212, 1991.

316. Weber, W. and Raz, S., Cerumen as a lubricant, *Clinical Note*, 74, 901, 1977.

317. Kohrs, F. P., Cocaine in the ear, *J. Fam. Pract.*, 35, 253, 1992.

318. Soares, J. R., Grant, J. D. and Gross, S. J., Significant developments in radioimmune methods applied to delta-9-THC and its 9-substituted metabolites, in *NIDA Research Monograph 42*, Hawks, R., Ed., National Institute on Drug Abuse, Bethesda, 1982, 44.

319. Manolis, A., McBurney, L. J. and Bobbie, B. A., The detection of delta-9-tetrahydrocannabinol in the breath of human subjects, *Clin. Biochem.*, 16, 229, 1983.

320. Sparber, S. B., Nagasawa, S. and Burklund, K. E., A mobilizable pool of d-amphetamine in adipose after daily administration to rats, *Res. Commun. Chem. Path. Pharmacol.*, 18, 423, 1977.

321. Misra, A. L., Pontani, R. B. and Bartolomeo, J., Persistence of phencyclidine (PCP) and metabolites in brain and adipose tissue and implications for long-lasting behavioural effects, *Res. Commun. Chem. Path. Pharmacol.*, 24, 431, 1979.

322. Johansson, E., Noren, K., Sjovall, J. and Halldin, M. M., Determination of delta-1-tetrahydro-cannabinol in human fat biopsies from marihuana users by gas chromatography-mass spectrometry, *Biomed. Chromatogr.*, 3, 35, 1989.

CHAPTER 12

POSTMORTEM TOXICOLOGY

EDITED BY WM. LEE HEARN, PH.D.

DIRECTOR OF TOXICOLOGY, METRO DADE COUNTY
MEDICAL EXAMINER DEPARTMENT, MIAMI, FLORIDA

TABLE OF CONTENTS

0-8493-2637-0/98/$0.00+$.50
© 1998 by CRC Press LLC

Wm. Lee Hearn

Wm. Lee Hearn

12.1 INTRODUCTION TO POSTMORTEM TOXICOLOGY

WM. LEE HEARN, PH.D.

DIRECTOR OF TOXICOLOGY, METRO DADE COUNTY
MEDICAL EXAMINER DEPARTMENT, MIAMI, FLORIDA

H. CHIP WALLS

UNIVERSITY OF MIAMI, DEPARTMENT OF PATHOLOGY,
FORENSIC TOXICOLOGY LABORATORY, MIAMI, FLORIDA

12.1.1 MEDICOLEGAL DEATH INVESTIGATION

The Medical Examiner's Office investigates sudden, violent, unnatural or unexpected deaths,[1-3] and the medical examiner, coroner or pathologist, is responsibile for determining the cause and manner of death. The cause of death is the injury, intoxication or disease that initiates a process leading to death, and if that initial event had not occurred, the individual would not have died. Death may follow years after the causal event. The manner of death is the circumstances in which the cause of death occurred. Five classifications are used to catagorize the manner of death: homicide, suicide, accident, natural and undetermined. Anatomic findings elicited at autopsy are often insufficient to determine the manner of death.

In order to determine the manner of death, all available information pertaining to a particular case, including the terminal events, scene investigation, police reports, social and medical history, autopsy findings, and results of histologic and toxicologic testing, must be considered. The question "Did alcohol, other drugs or poisons cause or contribute to this person's death?" must always be answered. Success in arriving at the correct conclusion

OVERVIEW OF DEATH INVESTIGATION

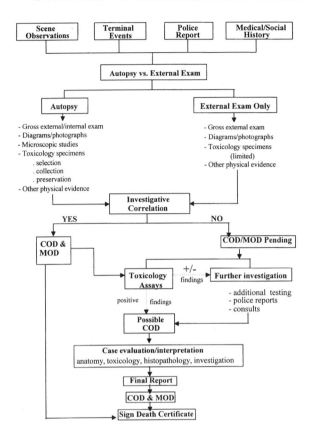

Figure 12.1.1 Overview of death investigation.

depends on the combined efforts of the pathologist, the investigators and the toxicologist. The process of death investigation and the role of the laboratory is outlined in Figure 12.1.1.

12.1.1.1 The Role of Police and Medical Examiner Investigators

When a death is reported to the medical examiner's office, a case investigator will obtain certain information to determine whether the case falls under the jurisdiction of the medical examiner. The following is a list of important topics to consider, which may vary according to jurisdiction:

Cases Requiring Medicolegal Death Investigation
1. Any death where any form of violence, either criminal, suicidal, or accidental was directly responsible or contributory.
2. Any death caused by an unlawful act or criminal neglect.
3. Any death occurring in a suspicious, unusual, or unexplained fashion.
4. Any death where there is no attending physician.
5. Any death of a person confined to a public institution.
6. The death of any prisoner even though both the cause and manner appear to be natural.
7. Any death caused by or contributed to by drugs and/or other chemical poisoning or overdose.

Wm. Lee Hearn and H. Chip Walls

8. Any sudden death of a person in apparent good health.
9. Any death occurring during diagnostic or therapeutic procedures.
10. Any fetal stillbirth in the absence of a physician.
11. Any death where there is insufficient medical information to explain the individual's demise

An unnatural death is any death that is not a direct result of a natural, medically recognized disease process. Any death where an outside, intervening influence, either directly or indirectly, is contributory to the individual's demise, or accelerates and exacerbates an underlying disease process to such a degree as to cause death, would also fall into the category of unnatural death.

Investigators are the eyes and ears of the medical examiner, especially in cases where the body is removed prior to the pathologist's involvement. The importance of an adequate investigation into past social and medical history cannot be over emphasized.

Police reports and investigations provide scene documentation. Typically, a report will include a description and identification of the body, time and place of death, eyewitness accounts, drugs present, and photographs. Investigators assigned by the medical examiner collect all items and information pertaining to establishing the cause and manner of death. Investigators contact the family and friends of the deceased for information regarding, for example, past medical and social history and prescribed medications. Many cases have histories of prescription drugs to guide the investigation. All medication bottles should be verified as to content and count, in addition to performing a routine pharmacy check of the person's medication usage. Medical examiner investigators must also contact hospitals and treating physicians to obtain copies of medical records and police agencies to obtain arrest records. Progressively, a file is assembled that contains all of the background information to assist the pathologist in understanding the medical and social history of the deceased.

12.1.1.2 Role of the Forensic Pathologist

The principal role of the forensic pathologist is to investigate sudden, unexpected, and violent deaths in order to determine the cause and manner of death. In suspected drug related deaths or poisonings, the pathologist must both exclude traumatic or pathological mechanisms as possible causes of death, *and* select and preserve appropriate specimens for toxicologic analysis. After autopsy, cases can often be divided into two catagories; those with an anatomical cause of death and those without. Few drugs leave telltale signs so obvious that the pathologist can determine a manner and cause of death without additional testing. Obvious exceptions include liver necrosis caused by acetaminophen, or the severely hemorrhagic gastric mucosa and smell from cyanide exposure, or coronary artery disease and cardiac enlargement in a cocaine user. Negative findings require toxicological analyses.

Approximately 10% of the cases submitted for toxicology do not have any guiding features. However, many of the thousands of potential compounds that could have caused death will have already been eliminated after history and autopsy results are correlated. Since the majority of drugs and poisons do not produce characteristic pathological lesions, their presence in the body can be demonstrated only by chemical methods.

Collection and preservation of appropriate specimens is a critical component of the autopsy examination.[4-9] Just what is collected depends, at least partly, on the policy and finances of the department. The utility of these specimens depends not only upon the condition of the body, but also upon the pathologist's technique. Specimens must be large enough, the correct preservative must be used, and they must be placed in appropriate, clearly and correctly labeled, containers.

Specimen collection is the first link in the chain of custody. Sample integrity within the chain of custody is an essential requirement for the rest of the forensic investigation. In cases where autopsy fails to determine a cause of death, or where there is an incomplete investigation, it is imperative to collect an adequate variety of specimens. Subsequent findings may modify or narrow the field of search, and make it unnecessary to examine each specimen, but they can always be discarded. However, many toxins are completely lost in the embalming process, so if the appropriate specimens are not collected at the time of the initial postmortem examination, the cause of death may never be determined.

12.1.2 CERTIFICATION OF DEATH

Each state requires a medical and legal document known as the Death Certificate be filed with the Bureau of Vital Statistics. The certificate contains demographic information as well the cause and manner of death as determined by the Medical Examiner. Five different classifications are recognized: (1) homicide, (2) suicide, (3) accident, (4) natural, and (5) undetermined.

The results from toxicological analyses of post-mortem specimens are applied to determine whether drugs or toxins are a cause of death, or whether they may have been a contributing factor in the death. Negative toxicological results are often more meaningful than positive results, as in the case of anti-seizure medicines not detected in a suspected seizure death as compared to a positive marijuana test in the urine of a shooting victim.

12.1.3 THE ROLE OF TOXICOLOGY IN DEATH INVESTIGATION

Most toxicology offices have established routines for specific types of cases, and the pathologist often provides some indication of what toxicological testing should be performed on each case (see Figure 12.1.2). It would appear that cases of suspected homicide require much more thorough testing than obvious cases of accidental or natural death, but that is not really the case. Alcohol, and other sedative hypnotic drugs, for example, are often detected in burn victims and may well have contributed to the cause of death.

12.1.3.1 Homicides

The relationship between intoxication and violence is well recognized.[10-12] Toxicological studies in cases of traumatic homicide should include tests for alcohol, prescribed medications and other drugs. Negative findings can be used in court to rebut assertions of self defense against a "drug crazed" attacker. Positive findings may help to explain how the victim became involved in a physical altercation. In addition, results of drug screening provide information about the deceased's lifestyle that may prove useful to police as they search for the murderer. Toxicological investigations may also reveal evidence that a victim was drugged to incapacitation and then murdered.

12.1.3.2 Suicides

In cases of suicide, investigators try to discover an explanation for the act[13-15]. People may be driven to suicide by failing health, financial problems, loss of a loved one, severe mental depression, or other causes. Drugs that can potentiate or exacerbate depression are commonly detected in suicides. Failure of antidepressant therapy may also play a role in some cases. Drugs commonly found in suicide victims, other than poisons, include alcohol, benzodiazepines, diphenhydramine, cocaine and other illegal drugs. Therefore, toxicological investigations should encompass intoxicants as well as antidepressants. Occasionally, a suicide victim employs multiple means to reduce the chances of survival. The anecdote about the man who took a lethal overdose, then climbed a ladder, placed a rope around his neck and shot himself in the head, is often not far from the truth.

Wm. Lee Hearn and H. Chip Walls

**Identification of a Toxicology Issue
in the Death Investigation**

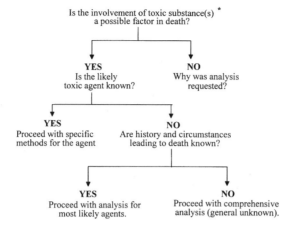

* **FORENSIC QUESTIONS RELATIVE TO POISONING:**
1. Was the death or illness due to a poison
2. What toxin produced the illness?
3. Was the substance employed capable of producing death?
4. Was a sufficient quantity taken to produce death or toxic results?
5. When and how was the toxin taken?
6. May a poisoning have occurred and the poison either be or have become undetectable?
7. Could the detected poison have an origin other than in poisoning?
8. Was the poisoning SUICIDAL, ACCIDENTAL, OR HOMICIDAL?
9. Were the correct specimens collected and preserved, analyzed in such a manner to answer the question at hand?

Figure 12.1.2 Identification of a toxicology issue in the death investigation.

12.1.3.3 Accidents

Fatal accidents, highway crashes immediately come to mind, however, accidental deaths occur in many other circumstances.[9,11,16-20] Drownings, falls, fires, electrocutions, boating accidents and aircraft crashes, as well as accidental drug overdoses, are included in this classification. Accidents often result from carelessness or the impairment of mental or motor function on the part of the victim or another person. In apparent cases of accidental death, it is important to rule out alcohol or other drug induced impairment. Many insurance policies exclude death or injury resulting from the misuse of intoxicating substances, although in some cases quite the opposite is true. In those jurisdictions where drug deaths are considered accidents, double indemnitiy clauses may come into play. The families of victims dying from cocaine toxicity could, in some instances, be entitled to twice the face value of the decedants life insurance.

Parties injured in an accident may litigate to recover damages. The sobriety or intoxication of the deceased can be a factor in efforts to assign blame. And, of course, apparent accidental deaths may actually turn out to be suicides, or they may be natural deaths occurring in circumstances that suggest an accident. When a driver becomes incapacitated by a heart attack, for example, and loss of control results in an accident, toxicological studies may play a part in the investigation . Detection of intoxicants, together with other evidence, may indicate that an apparent accident was actually intentional. For example, finding large quantities of a drug(s) in a deceased person's stomach suggests that an overdose was intentional (i.e., suicide) rather than accidental.

If postmortem investigation fails to detect carbon monoxide in the blood of a burn victim, or soot in the airway, it may be that the victim had already died when the fire started. Such cases may be deaths from natural causes, or attempts to destroy evidence of a murder. Further investigation may discover evidence of illness or trauma. Workplace accidents must always be investigated for the possible involvement of alcohol or other drugs, since there are likely to be insurance claims against the employer. If the victim is shown to have intoxicants in the body, the employer may be held blameless. Another aspect of workplace related accidents concerns exposure to toxic chemicals. The potential for such exposures varies with the nature of the business. If exposure to a toxic chemical is alleged or suspected, investigators should obtain a list of chemicals in the workplace, and the toxicology laboratory of the medical examiner should analyze for those chemicals whose toxicity is consistent with the circumstances of death.

12.1.3.4 Natural Deaths

Apparent natural deaths may or may not require toxicological study. If the autopsy clearly reveals the cause of death, and no history of drug or alcohol misuse is known, the pathologist may decide that further toxicological study is not necessary.[21,22] Sometimes studies are ordered to evaluate compliance with required pharmacotherapy, such as measurement of anticonvulsant drug levels in an epileptic who has a seizure and then dies. When the apparent cause of death may be related to drug or alcohol misuse, testing should be done to determine whether or not relevant drugs are present. For example, acute myocardial infarctions, ruptured berry aneurysms and dissecting aortic aneurysms are often associated with recent cocaine use. Such cases should be tested for cocaine and other drugs, particularly when this occurs in young people or when there is a history of drug use. A diagnosis of alcoholism should call for a blood alcohol analysis.

The diagnosis of Sudden Infant Death Syndrome (SIDS) is a diagnosis of exclusion. All apparent SIDS cases should be tested for alcohol and other drugs. Child abuse can include drugging a restless infant, where even a small dose of drug may be fatal.

When there is any uncertainty regarding the cause of death, testing should be done to rule out an overdose. Terminally ill people sometimes commit suicide, and hospice patients are occasionally poisoned by their caretakers. When samples for apparent natural deaths are submitted to the toxicology laboratory for testing, unrecognized poisoning cases are sometimes discovered.

12.1.3.5 Unclassified, Undetermined Or Pending

When the cause and/or manner of death remain elusive at the completion of investigations and autopsy, the case is left unclassified, pending further studies[4,21] Additional inquiries, microscopic examinations and toxicological studies are initiated to find sufficient evidence for a diagnosis. The primary goal for the toxicology laboratory is to determine whether or not toxic substances are present in the deceased in sufficient quantities to kill. If a probable toxic cause of death is identified, the laboratory gathers additional evidence to assist the pathologist in deciding how it was administered, and estimating how much was used, and how long before death. The results of toxicology testing are considered along with other evidence to formulate an opinion regarding the manner of death.

12.1.3.6 Pending Toxicology (Overdose)

Death by poisoning or overdose may be accidental, suicidal or homicidal.[15,18,21,23-25] Various clues indicating poisoning may be observed in the autopsy. Unusual odors or abnormal colors of stomach contents or tissues, particular lesions or abnormal congestion of organs may suggest to the experienced forensic pathologist that a drug or poison was the cause of death. Evidence from the death scene, such as a suicide note or empty containers, may point to a poisoning or drug overdose in some cases. However, most drug related deaths do not leave such telltale markers as those found in heart attacks, cancer or trauma. Often the only clue from the autopsy is pulmonary congestion and edema. The pathologist calls upon the toxicology laboratory to confirm the suspicion by identifying the poison or poisons and gathering enough quantitative data to support a conclusion that the detected poison was sufficient to cause death.

In addition, the laboratory may be able to shed light on the issues of how much was taken, and the route of administration. The assignment of manner of death is based upon the totality of the evidence, including the pharmacology and toxicology of the substance, the route of administration and quantity taken, the social and medical history of the deceased and evidence collected from the death scene.[7,18,26,27] Drug related death certification is by a process of elimination, i.e., other causes of death (COD) have been excluded, a toxic substance is shown to be present in sufficient concentrations to have caused or contributed to the death.[26]

12.1.4 THE TOXICOLOGY EXAMINATION

The toxicologic investigation begins with the preliminary identification of drugs or chemicals present in postmortem specimens.[28-37] Confirmatory testing is then performed to conclusively identify the substance(s) present in the postmortem specimens. In a forensic laboratory, positive identification must be established by at least two independent analyses, each based on a different analytic principle. The next step in the process is to determine the quantity of substance in the appropriate specimens. Identifying drugs in waste fluids, such as bile and urine, is a useful undertaking, but quantifying drugs in these fluids usually has limited interpretive value. Drug quantification in blood, liver, gastric contents, or other specimens, as dictated by the case, provides more meaningful interpretive information. Therapeutic and toxic ranges have been established for many compounds.[26]

All cases cannot be tested for all drugs. A number of factors, some not immediately obvious, determine what kind, and how many, tests will be done. The importance of the medicolegal classification of death and specimen collection have already been mentioned. But other factors, such as geographic patterns of drug use and laboratory capabilities must also be considered.

Occasionally, mere detection of a drug is sufficient. But, in the case of some prescription medications, the actual amount present must be quantified. A request for therapeutic drug analysis may be made even if the autopsy has already determined the cause of death. If a history of seizure is obtained, the pathologist may request an antiepileptic drug screen to determine whether or not the person was taking any such medication. The same holds true for theophylline in asthmatics. An individual who has committed suicide may have been prescribed therapeutic drugs for depression or other mental illness. A test for these drugs would indicate the degree of patient compliance. In forensic toxicology, a negative laboratory result carries the same weight as a positive result.

12.1.4.1 Poisons

Often the nature of a suspected toxin is unknown. This type of case is termed a "general unknown."[38,39] In cases of this nature, a full analysis of all available specimens by as many techniques as possible may be required to reach a conclusion. The most common approach involves first testing for volatile agents, and then performing drug screens. The drug screen is usually confined to those drugs that are commonly seen in the casework. When the most common substances have been ruled out, the laboratory proceeds to test for more exotic drugs and poisons.

12.1.4.2 Comprehensive Toxicology Screening

It is impossible to consider the topic of forensic toxicology without discussing analytical toxicology in detail.[40-43] Screening methods should provide presumptive identification, or at least class identification while also giving an indication of concentration. An adequate screening protocol, capable of detecting or eliminating the majority of the commonly encountered toxins, usually requires a combination of three or more chemically unrelated techniques. In general, some toxins are so common that, no matter the type of case, they should always be included for analysis; e.g., ethanol, salicylate, acetaminophen, sedatives, and other drugs such as cocaine, opiates, and tricyclic antidepressants. All screening tests that are positive for substances relevant to the case must then be confirmed, and analytes of significance submitted for quantification in several tissues. Later sections in this chapter discuss testing methods and how they are combined to yield effective analytical strategies.

12.1.4.3 Case Review

During the toxicological investigation, each case is subjected to periodic review, its status evaluated, and the need for additional testing determined. Based on what is known about the death and the specimens available, a panel of screening tests is designed to quickly detect or rule out the most common drugs and, when appropriate, poisons.[31,35,36,40,44] New tests may be ordered to expand the initial search, or to confirm preliminary findings

The flow of information in forensic toxicology must be in two directions[45] — from pathologist to laboratory, then back to the physician who will integrate all of the findings. Laboratory personnel must effectively communicate with the pathologist concerning the scope (and limitations) of the services they can provide, suggest the proper selection of specimens, and assist with interpretation of the results. To operate effectively, the toxicologist must be provided with enough information about the history and autopsy findings to rationally select the most appropriate tests.

12.1.4.4 Quality Assurance

Each laboratory must formulate and adhere to a quality assurance (QA) program. Quality assurance provides safeguards to ensure that the toxicology report contains results that are accurate and reproducible, and that the chain of evidence has been preserved. A written QA plan sets out the procedures employed to ensure reliability, and provides the means to document that those procedures were correctly followed. The laboratory's strict adherence to a proper QA program induces confidence in the laboratory's work product and prevents or overcomes potential legal challenges. Before a new or improved method is introduced into a laboratory, it must be selected with care and its performance must be rigorously and impartially evaluated under laboratory conditions.

12.1.4.5 The Toxicology Report

When all toxicological testing is completed, the results are summarized in a report that is sent to the pathologist. This report becomes a part of the autopsy report. It specifies the name of the deceased, if known, and the medical examiner case number. The specimens tested, the substances detected in each specimen, and the measured concentrations of those substances are presented in tabular form. The report should also list substances tested for, but not found, especially if they were named in the toxicology request. If any drug was detected, but not confirmed, a note to that effect should be on the report. In addition, any information about the specimens, such as the date and time of collection of antemortem blood or any unusual condition of a specimen, should also be noted on the report. Because of the well known difficulties associated with the postmortem redistribution of many drugs, the report should always indicate where in the body the blood specimen was obtained. Toxicology reports are usually signed or initialed by the issuing toxicologist, and may be signed by the pathologist as well.

12.1.4.6 Toxicological Interpretation

All substances are poisons; there is none which is not a poison. The right dose differentiates a poison and a remedy.

Paracelsus (1493-1541)

Poisons and medicines are often times the same substance given with different intents.

Peter Mere Latham (1789-1875)

The significance of the reported results must be explained, often to a jury.[5,26,40,45-48] The pharmacology, toxicology, local patterns of drug abuse, and postmortem changes all can affect toxicological results. In any given case, a competent toxicologist must try to be prepared to answer the following questions:

1. What was taken, when and how?
2. Was the drug or combination of drugs sufficient to kill or to affect behavior?
3. What are its effects on behavior?
4. Does the evidence indicate if a substance was taken for therapeutic purposes, as a manifestation of drug misuse, for suicidal purposes or was it administered homicidally?
5. Was the deceased intoxicated at the time of the incident that caused death?
6. How would intoxication by the particular drug manifest?
7. Is there any alternative explanation for the findings?
8. What additional tests might shed light on the questions?

REFERENCES

1. Mason, J. K. Forensic medicine. [Review]. Injury 21: 325-327. 1990
2. Prahlow, J. A. and Lantz, P. E. Medical examiner/death investigator training requirements in state medical examiner systems. Journal of Forensic Sciences 40: 55-58. 1995
3. Gross, E. M. The Model Postmortem Examinations Act in the state of Connecticut, 1969-1974. Legal Medicine Annual: 51-66. 1975
4. Norton, L. E., Garriott, J. C. and DiMaio, V. J. Drug detection at autopsy: a prospective study of 247 cases. Journal of Forensic Sciences 27: 66-71. 1982
5. Margot, P. A., Finkle, B. S. and Peat, M. A. Analysis and problems of interpretation of digoxin in postmortem blood and tissues. Proceedings of the Western Pharmacology Society 26: 393-396. 1983
6. Patel, F. Ancillary autopsy—forensic histopathology and toxicology. Medicine, Science & the Law 35: 25-30. 1995
7. Prouty, R. W. and Anderson, W. H. The forensic science implications of site and temporal influences on postmortem blood-drug concentrations. Journal of Forensic Sciences 35: 243-270. 1990
8. McCurdy, W. C. Postmortem specimen collection. Forensic Science International 35: 61-65. 1987
9. Nagata, T. Significance of toxicological examination in the practice of forensic medicine [Japanese]. Fukuoka Igaku Zasshi Fukuoka Acta Medica 77: 173-177. 1986

10. Garriott, J. C. Drug use among homicide victims. American Journal of Forensic Medicine & Pathology 14: 234-237. 1993

11. Ladewig, D. Drugs and violence. German. Therapeutische Umschau 50: 194-198. 1993

12. Poklis, A., Graham, M, Maginn, D, Branch, C. A. and Gantner Phencyclidine and violent deaths in St. Louis, Missouri: a survey of medical examiners' cases from 1977 through 1986. American Journal of Drug & Alcohol Abuse 16: 265-274. 1990

13. Derby, L. E., Jick, H. and Dean, A. D. Antidepressant drugs and suicide. Journal of Clinical Psychopharmacology 12: 235-240. 1992

14. Nielsen, A. S., Stenager, E. and Brahe, U. B. Attempted suicide, suicidal intent, and alcohol. Crisis 14: 32-38. 1993

15. Marzuk, P. M., Tardiff, K. and Leon, A. C. Final exit and suicide assessment in a forensic setting - reply. American Journal of Psychiatry 152: 1833. 1995

16. Alleyne, B. C., Stuart, P. and Copes, R. Alcohol and other drug use in occupational fatalities. Journal of Occupational Medicine 33: 496-500. 1991

17. Caplan, Y. H., Ottinger, W. E., Park J., and Smith, T. D. Drug and chemical related deaths: incidence in the state of Maryland—1975 to 1980. Journal of Forensic Sciences 30: 1012-1021. 1985

18. Hammersley, R., Cassidy, M. T. and Oliver, J. Drugs associated with drug-related deaths in Edinburgh and Glasgow, November 1990 to October 1992. Addiction 90: 959-965. 1995

19. Marx, J. Alcohol and trauma. Emergency medicine clinics of North America 8: 929-938. 1990

20. Lewis, R. J. and Cooper, S. P. Alcohol, other drugs, and fatal work-related injuries. Journal of Occupational Medicine 31: 23-28. 1989

21. Mcginnis, J. M. and Foege, W. H. Actual causes of death in the United States [See Comments]. JAMA 270: 2207-2212. 1993

22. Hanzlick, R. National Association of Medical Examiners Pediatric Toxicology (PedTox) Registry Report 3. American Journal of Forensic Medicine & Pathology 16: 270-277. 1995

23. Briglia, E. J., Davis, P. L., Katz M.,and Dal Cortivo, L. A. Attempted murder with pancuronium. Journal of Forensic Sciences 35: 1468-1476. 1990

24. Bogan, J., Rentoul, E., Smith H., and Weir, Homicidal poisoning by strychnine. Journal Forensic Science Society 6: 166-169. 1966

25. Moffat, A. C. Interpretation of post mortem serum levels of cardiac glycosides after suspected overdosage. Acta Pharmacologica et Toxicologica 35: 386-394. 1974

26. Stead, A. H. and Moffat, A. C. A collection of therapeutic, toxic and fatal blood drug concentrations in man. Human Toxicology 2: 437-464. 1983

27. Brettel, H. F. and Dobbertin, T. Multifactorial Studies of 154 fatalities of psychotropic drug poisoning [German]. Beitrage Zur Gerichtlichen Medizin 50: 127-130. 1992

28. Sunshine, I. Basic toxicology. Pediatric clinics of North America 17: 509-513. 1970

29. Levine, B. Forensic toxicology. [Review]. Analytical Chemistry 65: 272A-276A. 1993

30. Jentzen, J. M. Forensic toxicology. An overview and an algorithmic approach. American Journal of Clinical Pathology 92: S48-55. 1989

31. Levine, B. S., Smith, M. L. and Froede, R. C. Postmortem forensic toxicology. [Review]. Clinics in Laboratory Medicine 10: 571-589. 1990

32. Flanagan, R. J., Widdop, B. Ramsey, J. D. and Loveland, M. Analytical toxicology. [Review]. Human Toxicology 7: 489-502. 1988

33. Chollet, D., and Kunstner, P. Fast systematic approach for the determination of drugs in biological fluids by fully automated high-performance liquid chromatography with on-line solid-phase extraction and automated cartridge exchange. Journal of Chromatography 577: 335-340. 1992

34. Maurer, H.H. Systematic toxicological analysis of drugs and their metabolites by gas chromatography-mass spectrometry. Journal of Chromatography 580: 3-41. 1992

35. Nagata, T., Fukui, Y., Kojima, T., Yamada, T., Suzuki, O., Takahama, K., et al. Trace analysis for drugs and poisons in human tissues. [Japanese]. Nippon Hoigaku Zasshi Japanese Journal of Legal Medicine 46: 212-224. 1992

36. Stewart, C.P. and Stollman, A. The toxicologist and his work, in *Toxicology: Mechanisms and Analytical Methods,* Stewart, C.P. and Stollman, A., Eds., Academic Press, New York, 1960, Chap. 1.

37. Puopolo, P. R., Volpicelli, S. A., Johnson D. M. and Flood, J. G. Emergency toxicology testing (detection, confirmation, and quantification) of basic drugs in serum by liquid chromatography with photodiode array detection. Clinical Chemistry 37: 2124-2130. 1991

38. Wu Chen, N. B., Schaffer, M. I., Lin, R. L.,. Kurland, M. L, Donoghue, Jr., E. R. and Stein, R. J. The general toxicology unknown. I. the systematic approach. Journal of Forensic Sciences 28: 391-397. 1983

39. Wu Chen, N. B., Schaffer, M. I., Lin, R. L., Kurland, M. L., Donoghue, Jr., E. R. and Stein, R. J. The general toxicology unknown. II. A case report: doxylamine and pyrilamine intoxication. Journal of Forensic Sciences 28: 398-403. 1983

40. Osselton, M. D. Analytical forensic toxicology. [Review]. Archives of Toxicology. Supplement 15: 259-267. 1992

41. Drummer, O. H., Kotsos A., and Mcintyre, I. M. A class-independent drug screen in forensic toxicology using a photodiode array detector. Journal of Analytical Toxicology 17: 225-229. 1993

42. Bailey, D. N. Comprehensive toxicology screening in patients admitted to a university trauma center. Journal of Analytical Toxicology 10: 147-149. 1986

43. Chen, J. S., Chang, K. J., Charng, R. C., Lai, S. J., Binder, S. R. and Essien, H. The development of a broad-spectrum toxicology screening program in taiwan. Journal of Toxicology Clinical Toxicology 33: 581-589. 1995

44. De Zeeuw, R. A. Procedures and responsibilities in forensic toxicology [Letter]. Journal of Forensic Sciences 27: 749-753. 1982

45. Stafford, D. T., Prouty, R. W. and Anderson, W. H. Current conundrums facing forensic pathologists and toxicologists [Editorial]. American Journal of Forensic Medicine & Pathology 4: 103-104. 1983

46. Lokan, R. J., James, R. A. and Dymock, R. B. Apparent post-mortem production of high levels of cyanide in blood. Journal Forensic Science Society 27: 253-259. 1987

47. Heatley, M. K. and Crane, J The blood alcohol concentration at post-mortem in 175 fatal cases of alcohol intoxication. Medicine, Science & the Law 30: 101-105. 1990

48. Schulz, M. and Schmoldt, A. A compilation of therapeutic and toxic plasma drug concentrations. Anaesthesist 43: 835-844. 1994

12.2 SPECIMEN SELECTION, COLLECTION, PRESERVATION, AND SECURITY

BRADFORD R. HEPLER, PH.D. AND DANIEL S. ISENSCHMID, PH.D.

TOXICOLOGY LABORATORY, WAYNE COUNTY MEDICAL EXAMINER, DETROIT, MICHIGAN

Specimen selection, collection, preservation and security place unique demands on the postmortem forensic toxicologist. The quality of results expected from the postmortem laboratory today is high, and reflects the research advances and continued improvements in instrumentation and analytical methods seen since the origins of modern forensic toxicology early this century.[1-3] However, it must be recognized that even with technological advances — accurate, forensically defensible results are predicated on the quality and type of specimens provided, and the documentation of each specimen's origin and history. As important, are issues relating to security and evidence control during the collection and storage process. Finally, in considering data available from publications and databases, it is important to recognize that the quality and

Table 12.2 Guide to the Collection of Routine Toxicology Specimens

Specimen	Amount	When to obtain	Comments
Blood, Heart	50-100 mL	Always	Identify source. Preserve with 2% sodium fluoride and potassium oxalate. Reserve an aliquot without preservative, if possible.
Blood, peripheral	10-25mL	For complete toxicology testing	Identify source. Use femoral or subclavian blood if possible.
Blood, clot	Whole clot	Trauma cases	
Urine	All	Always	Submit any quantity, even if < 1 mL, for immunoassay screening.
Bile	All	Always	Tie off gall-bladder to reduce contamination. Collect prior to liver.
Vitreous humor	All	Always	Combine fluid from both eyes into a single tube.
Gastric contents	All	For complete toxicology testing	Tie off stomach to reduce contamination of other viscera. Note total volume.
Liver	50 g	Always	Identify source. Deep right lope preferred.
Kidney	50 g	Metals, ethylene glycol	
Spleen	50 g	CO, CN	Very useful when blood not available in fire deaths.
Brain, fat	50 g	Lipophilic drugs	Brain may be especially useful in infant drug deaths.
Lung	50 g	Volatile poisons	Collect in sealed container. Collect tracheal air as well.
Hair	Pen-sized bundle	Drug history, metals	Identify distal and proximal ends.

Biological specimens should be kept at refrigerated temperatures (4°C) for short term storage (up to two weeks) and at frozen temperatures (-20°C) for long term storage. An aliquot of preserved blood should be frozen immediately for analysis and preservation of less stable compounds.

the "comparability" of data between institutions are only as good as the consistency of approach in specimen collection, storage and analysis between these organizations. (Table 12.2)

Many major references in Forensic Pathology have, each in their own manner, sought to provide information about specimen collection issues.[1,4-9] More recently, the literature has focused on novel and more intriguing issues such as postmortem release and/or redistribution of drugs from tissues into blood as mechanisms that can lead to legitimate debates over the meaning of a reported value.[10-15] Thus, even an analytically "accurate value" may be subject to misinterpretation when the drug concentration in a single blood specimen is used to explain the circumstances surrounding a drug intoxication death. This and other specimen collection and documentation issues are the subjects for discussion in this chapter.

Bradford R. Hepler and Daniel S. Isenschmid

12.2.1 CHAIN OF CUSTODY

One major difference between forensic and clinical toxicology is that institutions performing forensic work are held legally accountable for documenting the handling of specific evidence within the organization. This means that all evidence associated with a specific case must be kept in a secure area at all times and be accounted for during its lifetime by using a record or chain of custody (COC).

Documentation should include *who* handled the evidence, *what* evidence was handled, *when* and *why* the evidence was handled and *where* the evidence is located at all times. This documentation is central to the demonstration that the evidence has remained intact, and not been adulterated, changed, mishandled or misplaced in any fashion that would compromise its integrity. Evidence ties together people, places, actions and things, which have important impact on circumstances surrounding events in which individuals are held legally accountable. In criminal actions the importance of the evidence, may truly involve a "life or death" determination, while in civil litigation large sums of money or property may be at stake.

The biological specimens collected during the autopsy are evidence and must be legally accounted for. Specimens must be maintained in secure, limited-access, areas at all times with access limited to only those individuals designated in the institution's standard operating procedure. Specimen handling has been and will continue to be legally scrutinized by the courts. Properly maintained COC documentation rules out any period of time in which a specimen may be left vulnerable to adulteration or tampering. Failure to properly document the COC may not only compromise the integrity of the specimen, but credibility of the institution handling the specimen.

Labor-intensive documentation can be tedious and a natural deterrent to the consistent maintenance of records, including the COC. The use of computers for documenting COC and other specimen transactions within the postmortem forensic toxicology laboratory has recently been demonstrated.[16-18] The ability of the computer to routinely maintain and monitor predictable and consistently occurring events make it an ideal tool for tracking of forensic events.

12.2.2 SPECIMEN COLLECTION

12.2.2.1 Specimen Containers

There are several unique challenges to collecting postmortem forensic toxicology specimens compared with specimen collection in other forensic toxicology disciplines such as human performance toxicology and employment drug testing. Postmortem specimen quality can be quite variable making specimen collection and subsequent reproducibility in aliquoting of the specimen difficult at times. Specimen quantity, or availability, will vary considerably from one case to another, yet the laboratory must attempt to provide a comprehensive toxicological analysis for a general unknown. In the latter regard, detection limits are pressed, and trace findings may have a major bearing upon issues of compliance and proper patient care in hospitalized or extended care facilities and the potential for civil litigation. The use of appropriate specimen containers and preservatives can be critical in the toxicologists' ability to ultimately identify a substance in a given specimen.

Usually, the best container to utilize when collecting and storing postmortem biological fluids is glass.[1,9,19] Glass is inert, does not contain any plasticizer contaminants and maximizes storage space. Plasticizer contamination is further reduced with Teflon®-lined caps. If drug concentrations of less than 0.010 µg/mL are expected, silation of glassware may be indicated.[1] Disposable Pyrex® glass culture tubes are suitable for long term frozen storage and come in a variety of sizes. It is important that the container size chosen for each specimen will allow it to be as close to full as possible in order to minimize concerns about oxidative losses due to air trapped in the top of the container, volatile drug evaporation and "salting-out" effects from preservatives that may be added to the tube.[1] Generally 50 mL culture tubes represent the best choice for blood and urine specimens.

Smaller tubes (e.g., 15, 20, and 30 mL) can be used for the collection of small amounts of blood, vitreous and bile specimens. Most types of plastic containers are suitable for the collection of solid tissue specimens and gastric contents. The nature of solid tissue reduces direct contact with the plastic container, and the relative amount of drug(s) present in gastric contents will minimize the influence of plasticizer interference.

The principal argument that can be made against glass containers is the possibility of breakage. However, this can be minimized by using appropriate storage racks and/or carrying totes. Some laboratories have successfully used plastic containers by identifying a product that reduces plasticizer contribution and adsorption of drug to the container. Nalgene® containers have been recommended for collection of postmortem biological fluids.[20] While drug stability in these containers was not determined to be a problem, the evaluation of contaminants was not reported. Whether a facility chooses glass or plastic, it is important that the laboratory carefully evaluate the container before routinely collecting specimens in it. The nature and potential for contamination can be evaluated by analyzing drug-negative biological fluids stored over time in the container. In addition, the plastic must be chosen carefully to ensure that it does not crack when frozen.

12.2.2.2 Specimen Preservatives

Blood specimens should be preserved by adding 2% wt/vol sodium fluoride to the collection container. Sodium fluoride is added to inhibit microorganism conversion of glucose to ethanol, microorganism oxidation of ethanol,[21,22] postmortem conversion of cocaine to ecgonine methyl ester by cholinesterases,[23] and enzymatic loss of other esters such as 6-acetylmorphine.[1,24] Esters, subject to alkaline hydrolysis, are more stable in postmortem blood than antemortem blood because the pH of blood falls after death, therefore acidification of blood is not indicated. Some laboratories may choose to add an anticoagulant such as potassium oxalate, EDTA or sodium citrate at a concentration of 5 mg/mL in addition to the fluoride preservative.[19,21,22]

Preservatives and anticoagulants may be added to collection containers designated for blood ahead of time. However, if only a small amount of blood is collected, the excess fluoride may affect headspace volatile assays by altering the vapor pressure of the analyte.[11] Ideally, one preserved and one unpreserved blood specimen should be taken for comparison, if needed.[20] Availability of both types of specimens can address this concern in addition to documenting microbial metabolism of drugs and potentially aiding in cocaine case interpretation.[25]

Once collected, blood specimens should be stored in tightly sealed containers at low temperatures (4°C short-term and -20°C long-term). The low temperatures inhibit bacterial growth and generally slow reaction kinetics such as the conversion of ethanol to acetaldehyde.[23] In addition, an aliquot of preserved blood, sufficient in quantity to fill the secondary container, should be removed from the primary specimen at the time of specimen accessioning and stored at -20°C in a frost-free freezer. This aliquot should be saved for the quantitative confirmation of cocaine and opiates and for ethanol reanalysis, if needed. Specimen preservatives are generally not required for other specimens (e.g., urine, bile, vitreous, tissues, etc.). As for blood, these specimens should be stored sealed at 4°C until testing is completed and then frozen at -20°C if long term storage is required.

Bradford R. Hepler and Daniel S. Isenschmid

12.2.3 SAMPLING

Biological fluids are collected using new or chemically clean hypodermic syringes using appropriate needle gauges and lengths for the specimen to be collected. One needle and syringe should be used per specimen taken. If syringes and needles are to be reused, then care must be taken to scrupulously clean and disinfect these devices between use. A typical cleansing procedure should include a minimum of 30 min of soaking in a disinfectant, e.g., 10% solution of household bleach in water (0.5% w/v sodium hypochlorite in water), followed by washing with a non ionic detergent and rinsing with copious amounts of clean water. Additional disinfection can be performed using an autoclave operated under proper quality control guidelines. The College of American Pathologists recommends that instruments be autoclaved at the usual steam autoclave pressure of 15 lbs for 45 min. These conditions are suitable for most pathogens, however, higher pressures and temperatures for longer times (approximately 2 h) are necessary if the rare Creutzfeldt-Jakob disease is of concern.[19] For all this effort, it would seem that disposable needles and syringes are the easiest and most time effective and efficient approach for sampling while reducing the possibility for specimen contamination.

Additionally, autopsy staff must maintain the cleanliness of the specimen container as they collect the specimen. All spillage on the outside the container should be rinsed off and decontaminated using 10% bleach solution. Collection techniques are discussed below by specimen type.

12.2.3.1 Blood

Whenever possible, postmortem blood specimens from two sites, heart and peripheral, should be collected at every autopsy. If no autopsy is performed, then only peripheral blood should be collected. Heart blood specimens should be taken by needle aspiration using a suitable hypodermic syringe. To obtain a proper cardiac specimen, the pericardial sack must be opened, the pericardium removed, the heart dried, and blood specimen removed by syringe from either the right or left chambers (remember to properly label the specimen to reflect this information).[19] At least 50 mL should be collected, more if possible.

Peripheral blood specimens are usually obtained from the femoral vein, although blood from the subclavian vein is also suitable. Leg veins are preferred to veins of the head and neck due to the anatomical presence of a larger number of valves that resist blood movement from the intestines.[21] Also, it is easier to collect the required volume from the femoral vein. The peripheral blood specimen should be taken using a clean or new 10 to 20 mL hypodermic syringe. Do not "milk" the leg in order to increase specimen volume. At least 10 mL of peripheral blood should be collected, if possible. The source of the peripheral blood specimen should be noted on the specimen container.

As discussed elsewhere, blood clots should be collected in cases of head trauma or if other blood specimens are not available. Because of the strong possibility of contamination, thoracic and abdominal cavity blood should be avoided unless no other blood is available. If collected, they should clearly be labeled as to the source or origin.

12.2.3.2 Urine

During autopsy, urine specimens should be taken directly from the bladder by insertion of a clean/new hypodermic needle into the bladder. For non-autopsied cases the needle may be inserted directly through the lower abdominal wall, just above the pubic symphysis.[9] If possible, up to 100 mL of urine should be acquired. In cases where the bladder appears to be empty it is important to aspirate as much urine as possible from the bladder and the ureter. Bladder washing using a minimum amount of clean water (or saline) may be desirable in the absence of any urine, but dilution reduces sensitivity of screening tests. The specimen container should clearly identify and indicate the nature of this specimen, and the amount of water/saline utilized. As little as 50 μL of undiluted urine can be useful for some applications such as chemical spot tests and immunoassay testing.

12.2.3.3 Bile

Following the removal of the organ block during the autopsy process, bile is aspirated from the gall bladder using a clean/new hypodermic syringe. If there is any possibility of contamination, the gall bladder should be tied off and removed from the organ block so that the bile may be collected away from the potential source of contamination. Up to 15 mL of bile should be collected and placed into a properly labeled screw-capped glass culture tube.

12.2.3.4 Vitreous Humor

Vitreous humor specimens are obtained by direct aspiration from each eye using a 5 to 10 mL syringe and 20-gauge needle. The needle should be inserted through the outer canthus, until its tip is placed centrally in the globe. Vitreous humor can be aspirated from the globe by application of gentle suction. Vacuum tubes and heavy suction should be avoided to prevent specimen contamination with retinal fragments and other tissue. With proper technique 2 to 3 mL of fluid can be removed from each eye in an adult, while up to about 1 mL of specimen may be removed from a newborn.[26] Once the vitreous specimen has been removed from the eye an appropriate amount of saline can be injected back into the eye in order to reproduce the cosmetic integrity of the eye. Vitreous humor specimens obtained from both eyes may be combined in one properly labeled specimen container.

12.2.3.5 Gastric Contents

Because gastric contents are not homogeneous, and because the total volume of gastric fluid is critical in the interpretation of positive findings, the entire contents of the stomach should be collected. If this is not possible, then the total volume present must be noted and provided with the specimen to the laboratory. The prosector should tie off the stomach ends before removing it from the organ block. The stomach should be opened away from other specimens and tissues, in a manner to avoid contamination of other viscera.

12.2.3.6 Tissues

When collecting tissue, a minimum of 50 gm should be collected. Each specimen collected should be put into its own properly labeled air tight container. If inhalants are suspected, it is important to promptly collect and seal the specimen in a container as soon as possible after the body has been opened. Due to the possibility that portions of the liver can be contaminated by postmortem diffusion of drugs from the gastric contents, only liver from deep within the right lobe should be collected.[26a] Additionally, bile should be collected prior to the liver specimen, to prevent specimen contamination.

12.2.3.7 Labeling

The first step in the specimen collection process (including evidence collection) is ensuring that the specimen containers are labeled appropriately. Without attention to this detail all other activities that occur with the specimen(s) are suspect. First, the collector must be working with only one specimen at a time. Second, specimens collected should *never* be placed into an unlabeled container. The collector must ensure that the container is labeled so that it can be read prior to introduction of the specimen. As a minimum, the label should include the following information: (1) institutional case number identifier; (2) name or other identifier; (3)

Bradford R. Hepler and Daniel S. Isenschmid

date and time of collection; (4) signature or initials of the collector; and (5) specimen type (blood, liver, kidney, etc.) and where collected, when applicable (heart blood, femoral blood, etc.). Finally, tamper-resistant tape with the collector's initials and the collection date should be placed over the specimen lid and container to document specimen integrity. This protocol is particularly useful in institutions with larger caseloads where specimens may not immediately be transferred to the toxicology laboratory.

12.2.4 SELECTION OF POSTMORTEM SPECIMENS

The choice of specimens available in a postmortem forensic toxicology investigation can be numerous and variable. Specimens may be selected based on case history, institutional policy and availability for a given case. Generally, the specimens routinely collected from cases in which an autopsy was performed include: blood from both peripheral and cardiac sources, all urine and bile available, vitreous humor, all available gastric contents, and tissues (particularly liver).[2] However, because the autopsy allows a one-time opportunity to collect as many specimens as may be needed to complete the toxicological investigation, it is suggested that as many specimens be obtained as is feasible for the institution. In cases where no autopsy is performed, only peripheral blood, urine and vitreous humor are collected. Heart blood should be avoided due to the potential of contamination by esophageal contents when performing a blind stick.[27,28]

On some occasions a Medical Examiner or Coroners case may have had a significant survival time in the hospital prior to death. In cases where hospital survival time exceeds 24 to 48 h, the value of postmortem specimens diminishes considerably. This is especially true if there are allegations that a death may be drug-related. Under these circumstances, hospital admission specimens (blood and urine) taken prior to significant therapeutic intervention can be invaluable in the documentation and support of this history. It is important that the postmortem toxicology laboratory physically obtain these specimens (under COC) for reanalysis, since the results available from the hospital are frequently unconfirmed screening results.

Decomposed, skeletonized or embalmed cases present unique challenges for the forensic toxicologist. The possibilities for specimens in some of these cases are limited only by availability, analytical capabilities, and sometimes imagination, of the toxicology laboratory. Some of these unusual specimens are discussed later in this section.

12.2.4.1 Blood

Blood is the specimen of choice for detecting, quantifying and interpreting drug concentrations in postmortem toxicology. Historically, most of the meaningful data derived from the literature were determined in blood.[29] Despite concerns about postmortem redistribution of drugs from tissues to blood, some aspects of interpretation remain straightforward. A negative result below a defined limit of detection for a given analyte can be readily interpreted as lack of acute exposure to that analyte or noncompliance in the case of therapeutic agents. Conversely, blood drug concentrations that exceed therapeutic (or, for some drugs, toxic) concentrations by 10 to 20 times are consistent with intoxication or death (barring an obvious contamination problem). In addition, the higher the parent drug to metabolite ratio, the more likely acute intoxication is a factor. This is especially the case when multiple drug analytes are involved, and in cases involving ethanol.

Interpretation becomes more difficult and important in cases where drug analytes known to undergo postmortem redistribution are determined to be present in a heart blood specimen at concentrations ranging between the upper therapeutic limit and the lower limit where intoxication or death has been reported. In these cases, analysis of a peripheral blood specimen may be critical in determining the role that the drug may have played in the decedent. Although drug concentrations in cardiac blood generally rise due to postmortem drug redistribution and peripheral blood drug concentrations tend to remain constant, this is not always the case.[13,30,31] Thus, results from a single postmortem blood specimen, whether cardiac or peripheral, may be difficult if not impossible to interpret. Since cardiac blood is usually more plentiful than peripheral blood, many laboratories perform initial toxicological tests on cardiac blood, reserving the peripheral blood specimens for cases where additional context is needed for interpretation.

Following injury or trauma to the head, blood clots from the brain cavity (subdural, subarachnoid and/or subepidural) should be collected in properly identified containers and saved for the laboratory. These materials are potential "time capsules" which are generally poorly perfused, and may reflect drug and/or alcohol concentrations closer to the time of injury. These specimens become more important as accurate knowledge of the post-injury survival time increases. Blood clots may also be useful for documenting preexisting drug use prior to hospital therapy. Most laboratories routinely analyze alcohol on these specimens, reserving analysis for additional drugs if indicated. Thoracic and abdominal cavity blood should only be collected for analysis if blood or uncontaminated blood clots cannot be obtained from any other area. These "blood" specimens tend to be contaminated by and contain large numbers of microbes. Additional contamination from gastric contents is also possible. Nevertheless, qualitative documentation of presence of given analytes is of importance and value in death investigations with respect to compliance and exposure issues.

Single quantitative results from a blood sample may yield potentially misleading results, especially if the sample is collected from the heart or nearby major vessels. Postmortem changes can profoundly alter the concentrations of many drugs. Peripheral blood samples properly collected from femoral, iliac or subclavian vein are preferred for estimating toxicity because those sites are usually less affected by postmortem changes in drug concentration. Whenever possible, measure the drug concentration in two or more independent samples, since the value of a result from a single sample will always be limited, unless the distribution of the drug is known (which is rarely the case).

In blood, drugs may concentrate either in the plasma (serum) or in the erythrocytes. A plasma sample may be useless in a case where the drug involved is known to be concentrated in the erythrocytes (e.g. lead or acetazolamide). For that reason, it is common practice to analyze whole blood in forensic cases whereas plasma is usually examined in clinical cases.

12.2.4.2 Urine

Urine, collected at autopsy, has the greatest potential of any specimen to provide the toxicologist with qualitative antemortem drug-exposure information. The urine matrix is generally devoid of circulating serum proteins, lipids and other related large molecular weight compounds due to the renal filtration process, simplifying preparation of the specimen for analysis. The accumulation of drugs and their metabolites in urine results in relatively high drug concentrations, facilitating detection of an exposure to a potential poison. Immunoassays and non-instrumental spot tests can be performed directly on the urine specimen for the analysis of certain drug classes. Detection times for drugs in urine can vary from 24 h to as long as a month, depending on the drug. Thus, except for acute drug deaths where survival time is less than an hour and drugs may not yet have been excreted into the urine, urine provides an ideal matrix for the detection for the widest variety of compounds.

Positive identification of drugs in the urine indicates past drug use, but does not indicate when or how much drug was ingested. In order to interpret the context of exposure, blood should be tested for the analytes found in the urine. In cases where death is suspected to have occurred rapidly due to drug ingestion, as might be suggested by the presence of a needle in the decedent's arm at the time of death, negative urine drug findings may be consistent if blood drug concentrations are very high.

Bradford R. Hepler and Daniel S. Isenschmid

12.2.4.3 Bile

Bile is another fluid that should be collected at autopsy as a matter of course since many drugs and drug metabolites have been demonstrated to accumulate in this specimen.[1,9,19,32,33] The qualitative finding of the presence of drug and/or metabolites in bile is important for documentation of historic exposures to specific agents and chronic drug-use history. Bile has also been useful as an alternate specimen for alcohol analysis[34] and has been used in immunoassay screening after sample pretreatment.[35] Historically, bile has most often been used in the determination of opiates in general and morphine in particular.[1,32,33] More recently, it has been noted that many drugs are found to accumulate at concentrations significantly higher then those in blood.[35] With an appropriate sample cleanup, bile is a useful specimen for the analysis of a wide variety of drugs and their metabolites, including benzodiazepines.

12.2.4.4 Vitreous Humor

Vitreous humor plays an important role in helping to resolve many issues in a postmortem examination. Because of this, it should be collected in all cases when possible, including cases where no autopsy is performed. Vitreous humor, by virtue of its protected environment inside the eye, is less subject to contamination and bacterial decomposition. As a result it may be used to distinguish antemortem alcohol ingestion from postmortem alcohol formation and may provide the only opportunity to establish an antemortem ethanol concentration in embalmed bodies.[21,22,25,36,37] Additionally, because vitreous humor is contained in a peripheral compartment, there is a delay in both the uptake of drugs and alcohol into this fluid as well as a delay in the excretion process.

It has been observed that vitreous drug concentrations often reflect circulating blood concentrations 1 to 2 h prior to death and that any drug found in the blood will be detected in the corresponding vitreous specimen, given analytical techniques of sufficient sensitivity.[9] Although these findings suggest that vitreous humor analysis following positive blood findings might be useful to aid in the interpretation of blood drug concentrations, more research needs to be performed. Studies comparing vitreous humor and blood ethanol concentrations yielded a wide variety of vitreous humor to blood ethanol ratios.[37] If such diversity is seen for an analyte that demonstrates minimal postmortem redistribution effects, attempting to use vitreous humor drug concentrations to aid in interpreting heart blood drug concentrations may prove difficult.[11] Despite these concerns, vitreous humor is the best specimen from which to evaluate postmortem digoxin concentrations.[19] However, the analysis of femoral blood in addition to vitreous humor is still recommended to provide the best context for an appropriate interpretation of digoxin toxicity.[38]

Vitreous humor has been shown to be particularly useful for the postmortem analysis of glucose, urea nitrogen, uric acid, creatinine, sodium and chloride. Measuring these analytes is important for documenting diabetes, degree of hydration, electrolyte balance and the state of renal function prior to death. A recent article has reviewed the extent and breadth of chemistry analysis applied to vitreous fluid, among other postmortem specimens.[26]

12.2.4.5 Gastric Contents

Oral ingestion is still the major route of drug administration for prescribed drugs and, therefore, a major compartment for the investigation of a potential poisoning. Drug overdoses, whether by accident or by intent, may readily be discovered through the analysis of gastric contents. In many cases undissolved capsules or tablets may be discovered which may be useful for identification. In addition, illicit drugs are frequently smuggled by ingestion of balloons or condoms filled with the contraband. If these devices burst and an acute drug death occurs, evidence of these items may be seen in the gastric contents at autopsy.[39]

Specimen Selection, Collection, Preservation, and Security

A large quantity of the parent drug in the gastric content, relative to a prescription dose, is indicative of an oral drug overdose when supported by blood and/or tissue findings.[40] Analysis of gastric contents gives a measure of drug remaining unabsorbed at the time of death. A quantity equivalent to five or more dosage units in the stomach suggests an intentional (i.e., suicidal) ingestion rather than an accidental overdose. However, low concentrations of drug in the stomach, especially drug metabolites and weak bases, may represent passive diffusion and/or ion trapping from the blood back into the stomach contents and may not be indicative of a recent oral ingestion of these agents. It is important to make a record of the total volume of gastric contents present in the decedent in order to calculate the total amount of the analyte(s) present in the stomach. Since the gastric content is not a homogeneous specimen, ideally the entire specimen should be submitted to the toxicology laboratory for mixing before aliquoting.

The odor of gastric contents can potentially point to a specific agent that might otherwise elude routine detection in the toxicology laboratory. Cyanide ingestions produce stomach contents with the odor of bitter or burnt almonds. Although not everyone is able to discern this odor, its presence is almost certainly indicative of a cyanide intoxication, and may be potentially hazardous in close quarters. Other characteristic odors include the "fruity-like" odor of ethanol and its congeners; the odor of airplane glue (xylene, toluene); cleaning fluid (halogenated hydrocarbons); carrots (ethchlorvynol);[28] and garlic (organophosphate insecticides).[28]

12.2.4.6 Tissues

Tissues commonly collected for postmortem study include liver, kidney, brain, lung and spleen. Tissues provide the best and most useful context with which to interpret blood findings. They may also be the only specimens available in decomposed cases. A large amount of data for drug findings in tissue exists, primarily for liver and kidney, and, to a lesser degree, brain and lung.[29] Comparison is most often between heart blood findings and those in the liver, the site where many drugs are metabolized and for which the greatest amount of reference data is available. For example, in cases where the concentration of basic drugs in blood is high and liver to blood drug concentration ratios exceed 10, a drug fatality is strongly suggested if no other interceding cause of death is present. Smaller ratios, even with high heart blood concentrations, tend to suggest postmortem redistribution of drugs into the blood.

Analysis of tissue may be more appropriate than analysis of biological fluids for some analytes. In cases of heavy metal poisoning, kidney is a very useful specimen as heavy metals concentrate in it. In addition, structural damage to the kidney due to heavy metal or ethylene glycol exposure may be documented histologically. Spleen, an organ rich in blood, is useful for the analysis of compounds which bind to hemoglobin, such as carbon monoxide and cyanide. Frequently, in fire deaths where extensive charring is present, spleen may be the only useful specimen available to perform these assays. Lung tissue is particularly useful in cases where inhalation of volatile substances, such as solvents or Freon®, is suspected. In addition, air may be collected directly from the trachea with a syringe and injected into a sealed vial to be used for headspace analysis.[41] Brain, due to its high fat content, tends to accumulate lipophilic substances, such as chlorinated hydrocarbons, and other organic volatiles. Additionally, there is evidence to suggest that brain to blood cocaine ratios are high in cocaine fatalities, thus cocaine deaths may be more readily interpreted through the analysis of both matrices.[42] Finally, because the brain is in a protected environment, it also tends to be more resistant to postmortem decomposition.

The analysis of tissue is performed by weight. Usually, 1 to 5 g of tissue is shredded and homogenized with 4 parts of water (or saline) to generate a final dilution factor of 5. Recovery of drug from this homogenate has been found to be consistent with recovery of drug from

Bradford R. Hepler and Daniel S. Isenschmid

postmortem blood.[43] Drilling through the tissue with a cork-borer allows tissue to be sampled and weighed while frozen.[44] This method is easier and more precise than sampling wet tissue and is less malodorous when handling decomposed specimens.

12.2.4.7 Hair

Hair has a long history as a useful specimen in forensic toxicology. Traditionally, hair along with fingernails, was the specimen of choice in determining chronic heavy metal poisoning such as arsenic, mercury and lead. Heavy metals bind to sulfhydryl groups on the cysteine molecule to form a covalent complex. Keratin, found in large amounts in hair and nails, is an excellent source of cysteine, and therefore an ideal specimen for determining chronic arsenic and mercury poisoning. Interpretation of positive findings can be augmented by segmentation of the hair to assist in determining the time of exposure.[45-47]

More recently, hair has been successfully used as a specimen from which chronic drug use may determined.[48] Numerous drugs have been identified in hair including drugs of abuse and,[49,50] more recently, various therapeutic agents,[51,52] although its usefulness in determining compliance has recently been refuted.[53] In extremely decomposed or skeletonized cases where no other specimens remain, positive findings for drugs in hair may at least corroborate a history of drug use. While the use of hair in workplace drug testing is controversial due to issues such as environmental contamination,[54] washing techniques,[55] sex or ethnic bias,[56,57] the difficulty in performing quantitative analysis[58] and establishing cutoff concentrations,[59] it may be extremely useful for postmortem analysis where these issues are not paramount.

12.2.4.8 Bone and Bone Marrow

Bone marrow has not received a great deal of consideration as an alternative specimen in postmortem toxicology. Because it is protected by bone, the highly vascularized tissue may be particularly useful when contamination of blood specimens is suspected in trauma cases . Research studies have been performed, primarily on rabbits, showing that linear relationships exist between bone marrow and perimortem blood drug concentrations for up to 24 h for many substances including tricyclic antidepressants, barbiturates, benzodiazepines and ethyl alcohol.[60-63] However, these studies were performed when the bone marrow was still fresh and moist. Although, putrefaction is delayed in bone marrow, usually bone marrow is not considered as an alternative specimen in postmortem toxicology unless other specimens are unavailable. Typically, at this stage of decomposition the bone marrow has transformed from spongy red marrow to a brown viscous liquid or paste-like substance and it is unknown if any interpretation can be made from quantitative data.[64] However, drugs have even been identified in the bone marrow of skeletonized remains[65,66] and heavy metals have been identified in the bone itself.[67]

12.2.4.9 Skeletal Muscle

Skeletal muscle is an often-overlooked specimen with many potential applications in postmortem forensic toxicology. It meets many of the criteria of an ideal forensic specimen: it is relatively homogeneous, almost always available, and not easily contaminated. Studies have shown that drug concentrations in thigh muscle reflect drug concentrations in blood for many common basic drugs and ethyl alcohol, except in cases of an acute drug death where muscle drug concentrations may be lower than blood due to inadequate time for tissue equilibration.[68] The analysis of thigh muscle may be especially useful in cases where drugs suspected of undergoing postmortem release are detected in the heart blood.[68] It is important that extremity muscle be collected, where possible, as drug concentrations in other muscles, such as abdominal muscle, increase with time while remaining constant in thigh muscle.[69,70]

Because skeletal muscle is often well preserved despite advanced decomposition of other tissue, it may be useful as an indicator of postmortem blood concentrations even in decomposed cases, although more studies need to be performed.[70,71] Surprisingly, even parent cocaine, which is known to be unstable in blood, has been identified in numerous cases of decomposed, dried skeletal muscle.[72]

The potentially useful data that may be obtained from the analysis of skeletal muscle have prompted some toxicologists to recommend that skeletal muscle be collected in all cases where drugs may be implicated in the cause of death.[70] One disadvantage to skeletal muscle is the need to homogenize the sample prior to analysis. However, this is true of many traditional specimens as well, such as liver and kidney. As more laboratories analyze skeletal muscle leading to the availability of additional data to aid in the interpretation of results, its potential advantages will outweigh any disadvantages.

12.2.4.10 Larvae

In cases of suspected poisoning where decomposition prevents traditional specimens from being obtained, homogenized fly larvae, usually of *Calliphorid* genus (blowfly), have proven to be useful alternative specimens in which drugs may be identified. Depending on temperature, larvae may be present as soon as one to two days after death. The first reported use of fly larvae in drug analysis occurred as recently as 1980 and involved a phenobarbital case.[73] Since then, numerous drugs have been identified in fly larvae including barbiturates, benzodiazepines and tricyclic antidepressants,[74] opiates,[75] cocaine[76] and the organophosphate, malathion.[77]

The choice of where larvae are best collected from the body needs further study. Interpretation of positive findings seem to be most useful if the larvae are collected at the site of their food source, such as any remaining muscle or liver, under the premise that drugs detected in fly larvae feeding on a body can only have originated from the tissues of that body.[78] This assumption seems to be supported by one study where a quantitative relationship was suggested between the morphine concentrations in the larvae and the livers on which they fed.[79] By contrast, other studies suggest that the analysis of fly larvae only provides qualitative data.[74,75,80] However, in these studies larvae were collected from multiple sites and pooled before analysis. If larval drug concentrations are based on the tissue on which they fed,[78] these results are not surprising.

Studies using *Calliphorid* larvae have shown that the age of the larvae may also play a major role in determining whether drugs may be identified in them.[80,81] By collecting larvae over a period of up to 11 days in cases of known suicidal drug overdoses, it was demonstrated that drugs were readily detectable in larvae through the third instar stage, but a precipitous fall in drug concentration was associated with pupariation after their food ingestion ceases. Similarly, larvae which had been feeding on drug-laden muscle for 5 days demonstrated a significant loss in drug concentration within one day of being transferred to drug-free tissue. This suggests that *Calliphorid* larvae readily eliminate drugs when removed from a food source. Thus it appears to be critical that larvae collected for drug analysis from a decomposed body be frozen and analyzed as soon as possible after collection. Even under refrigerated conditions, when larvae are in a state of diapause, slow bioelimination of drugs still occurs over the course of several weeks.[82] In addition, to eliminate surface contamination as a possible source of interpretive error, larvae should be washed with deionized water prior to analysis.

12.2.4.11 Meconium

Meconium, the first fecal matter passed by a neonate, has recently been given much attention because it is a useful specimen in which to determine fetal drug exposure. Issues relating to the screening and confirmation of most drugs of abuse in meconium have recently been reviewed.[83]

Bradford R. Hepler and Daniel S. Isenschmid

While meconium analysis has principally been performed to assess *in utero* drug exposure in newborns so that treatment may begin as early after birth as possible, it may also be useful in determining drug exposure in stillborn infants. One study demonstrated the presence of cocaine in the meconium of a 17-week-old fetus, suggesting that fetal drug exposure can be determined early in gestation.[84]

Unlike urine, which allows the detection of fetal drug exposure for only 2 to 3 days before birth, meconium extends this window to about 20 weeks. Most postmortem toxicology laboratories are not currently performing meconium analysis. While potentially useful, there are several issues that must be considered. Because meconium forms layers in the intestine as it is being deposited, it is not a homogeneous specimen. As with other non-homogeneous specimens, such as gastric contents, it is important that all available specimen be collected and thoroughly mixed before sampling. Consideration should also be given to the fact that infants do not metabolize some drugs the way adults do. If commercial immunoassay screening kits are used which target metabolites found in adult urine, the ability to detect some drugs in meconium may be compromised.[85]

12.2.4.12 Other Specimens

Many other specimens have been used in toxicological investigations. Any item with which a body or bodily fluid has been in contact is a potential candidate for the identification of drugs or poisons. Examples include tracheal air,[41] blood stains on clothing,[86] soil samples collected at the site of a skeleton or decomposed body[87] and even cremation ash.[88] Even though positive findings in these specimens are qualitative, there is at least the potential that this information can be useful in determining the circumstances of a death.

12.2.5 NON-BIOLOGICAL EVIDENCE

Evidence found at a scene may provide additional information to assist in the toxicological investigation. Drug paraphernalia (cocaine spoons, cookers, bhongs, syringes, poppers, whipped cream propellant canisters, butane lighters, etc.) is suggestive of a possible drug-related death, or at least a history of drug-abuse. Prescription drugs at a scene may be useful for compiling a list of suspected drugs, attending physicians and pharmacy phone numbers. However, this evidence may be misleading as drugs found at a scene are frequently old, may not have been taken for years or due to patient compliance problems, or may be someone else's medication. Pain medication and tranquilizers, particularly important in drug deaths, are often prescribed to be taken on an as needed basis, and thus subject to collecting in medicine cabinets. Counting the number of tablets or capsules in a prescription vial for consistency with the date of the prescription and dosage instructions may be useful, but has the potential for many variables including that of compliance. Additionally, empty medicine vials are not necessarily indicative of a drug overdose. Nevertheless, it is important that for a potential drug-related death, the role of the drugs found at the scene be ruled out by assaying for the agents of potential pharmacological significance.

Whether prescription vials are submitted to the toxicology laboratory is largely a matter of choice in a given jurisdiction. Since these items are evidence, it is often best that the police maintain them and provide a list to the laboratory. Unless the toxicology laboratory has specific experience in analyzing powders and syringes, or has jurisdiction over them, these items are best left for the crime laboratory to analyze, if needed.

In cases where poisoning is suspected, household products at the scene may provide key evidence for the toxicologist. Examples include aerosol containers in suspected inhalation deaths, rat and pest killers, insecticides and pesticides, caustics, windshield washer solvents, anti-freeze, Freon®, etc. The garage, basement, or under-sink cabinets are common storage places for many of these items. Unlabeled containers holding solids or liquids, or more importantly, labeled containers that clearly hold a different product, may be the key to a poisoning case. These items, or an aliquot of them, should be provided to the toxicology laboratory, since they often contain analytes for which the toxicology laboratory does not test. The analysis of the product in question may provide mass spectral data and chromatographic information that can be correlated with findings in the biological matrix.

Suicide notes are often critical in determining whether drug intoxication is the result of an accident or a suicide. However, the toxicologist is cautioned that if a suicide note identifies the suicidal agent(s), toxicological analysis may reveal a different substance entirely.

REFERENCES

1. Moffat, A.C., ed., *Clark's Isolation and Identification of Drugs in Pharmaceuticals, Body Fluids and Postmortem Material,* The Pharmaceutical Press, London, 1986.
2. Levine, B. S., Smith, M. L. and Froede, R. C., Postmortem forensic toxicology, *Clinics in Laboratory Medicine,* 10, 571-589, 1990.
3. Levine, B., Forensic toxicology, *Analytical Chemistry,* 65, 272A-276A, 1993.
4. Adelson, L., *The Pathology of Homicide,* Charles C. Thomas, Springfield, IL, 1974.
5. Stewart, C. P. and Stoleman, A., *Toxicology: Mechanisms and Analytical Methods, Volume I,* Academic Press, NY, 1960.
6. Sunshine, I., ed., *Methodology for Analytical Toxicology,* CRC Press, Cleveland, 1975.
7. Spitz, W. U. and Fisher, R.S. *Medicolegal Investigation of Death, Second Edition,* Charles C. Thomas, Springfield, IL, 1980.
8. Klaassen, C. D., Amdur, M.O. and Doull J., eds., *Casarett and Doull's Toxicology: The Basic Science of Poisons, Third Edition,* MacMillan Publishing Co., New York, 1986.
9. DiMaio, D. J. and DiMaio, V.J.M., *Forensic Pathology,* CRC Press, Boca Raton, FL, 1993.
10. Jones, G. R. and Pounder, D.J., Site dependence of drug concentrations in postmortem blood — a case study, *J Analytical Tox,* 11, 186-189, 1987.
11. Prouty, R. W. and Anderson, W. H., A comparison of postmortem heart blood and femoral blood ethyl alcohol concentrations, *J Analytical Tox,* 11, 191-197, 1987.
12. Prouty, R. W. and Anderson, W. H., The forensic science implications of site and temporal influences on postmortem blood-drug concentrations, *J Forensic Sci,* 35, 243-270, 1990.
13. Anderson, W. H. and Prouty, R. W., Postmortem redistribution of drugs, in *Advances in Analytical Toxicology, Volume II,* Baselt, R.C., ed., Year Book Medical Publishers, Boca Raton, FL, 1989, 71-102.
14. Levine, B, Wu, S.C., Dixon, A. and Smialek, J. E., Site dependence postmortem blood methadone concentrations, *Am J Forensic Med Pathol,* 16, 97-100, 1995.
15. Logan, B. K. and Smirnow, D., Postmortem distribution and redistribution of morphine in man, *J Forensic Sci,* 41, 37-46, 1996.
16. Cechner, R. L., Hepler, B. R. and Sutheimer, C. A., Improving information management in a metropolitan coroner's office, part I: design and implementation of a cost effective minicomputer system with initial application for the toxicology laboratory, J Forensic Sci, 35, 375-390, 1990.
17. Cechner, R. L. Hepler, B. R. and Sutheimer, C. A., Expert systems in the forensic toxicology laboratory, *Diagnostics and Clin Testing,* 27, 42-45, 1989.
18. Hepler, B. R., Monforte, J .R. and Cechner, R. L., Use of the Toxlab-pc® in alcohol and drug incidence in Wayne County, *Therapeutic Drug Monitoring and Clinical Tox Newsletter,* 8, 2-4, 1993.
19. Hutchens, G. M., ed., *An Introduction to Autopsy Technique,* College of American Pathologists, Northfield, IL, 1994.
20. McCurdy, W. C. Postmortem specimen collection, *Forensic Sci Int,* 35, 61-65, 1987.

Bradford R. Hepler and Daniel S. Isenschmid

21. Harper, D. R. and Couy, J. E. L., Collection and storage of specimens for alcohol analysis, in *Medicolegal Aspects of Alcohol Determination in Biological Samples,* Garriott, J. C., ed., Year Book Medical Publishers, Boca Raton, FL, 1988, 145-169.

22. Caplan, Y. H., Blood, urine and other fluid and tissue specimens for alcohol analysis, in *Medicolegal Aspects of Alcohol Determination in Biological Samples,* Garriott, J.C., ed., Year Book Medical Publishers, Boca Raton, FL, 1988, 74-86.

23. Isenschmid, D. S., Levine, B. S. and Caplan, Y. H., A comprehensive study of the stability of cocaine and its metabolites, *J Analytical Tox,* 13, 250-256, 1989.

24. Isenschmid, D. S. and Hepler, B. R., Unpublished data.

25. Isenschmid, D. S., Levine, B. S. and Caplan, Y. H., The role of ecgonine methyl ester in the interpretation of cocaine concentrations in postmortem blood, *J Analytical Tox,* 16, 319-324, 1992.

26. Coe, J. I., Postmortem chemistry update: emphasis on forensic application, *Am J Forensic Med Pathol,* 14, 91-117, 1993.

26a. Pounder, D. and Davies, J. Zopiclone poisoning, letter to the editor, *J Analytical Tox,* 20, 273, 1996.

27. Logan, B. K. and Lindholm, G., Gastric contamination of postmortem blood samples during blind stick sample collection, *Am J. Forensic Med Pathol,* 17, 109-111, 1996.

28. Monforte, J. R., Methodology and interpretation of toxicological procedures, in *Medicolegal Investigation of Death, Second Edition,* Spitz, W. U., and Fisher, R. S., eds., Charles C. Thomas Publisher, Springfield, IL, 1980, 571-589.

29. Baselt, R. and Cravey, R., *Disposition of Toxic Drugs and Chemicals in Man, Fourth Edition,* Chemical Toxicology Institute, Foster City, CA, 1995.

30. Hearn, W. L., Keran, E. E, Wei, H. and Hime, G., Site-dependent postmortem changes in blood cocaine concentrations, *J Forensic Sci,* 36, 673-684, 1991.

31. Logan, B. K., Smirnow, D. and Gullberg, R. G., Time dependent changes and site dependent difference in postmortem concentration of cocaine, benzoylecgonine and cocaethylene, presented at American Academy of Forensic Sciences Annual Meeting, Abstract K-32, Nashville, TN, 1996.

32. Stajic, M,.The general unknown, in *Introduction to Forensic Toxicology,* Cravey, R. C. and Baselt, R. C., eds., Biomedical Publications, Davis, CA, 1981, 169-181.

33. Agarwal, A. and Lemoc, M., Significance of bile analysis in drug induced deaths, *J Analytical Tox,* 20, 61-62, 1996.

34. Baselt, R. C. and Danhof, I.E., Disposition of alcohol in man, in *Medicolegal Aspects of Alcohol Determination in Biological Samples,* Garriott, J.C., ed., Year Book Medical Publishers, Boca Raton, FL, 1988, 55-73.

35. Hepler, B. R., Sutheimer, C. A., Sebrosky, G. F. and Sunshine, I., Combined enzyme immunoassay-LCEC method for the identification, confirmation and quantitation of opiates in biological fluids, *J Analytical Tox,* 8, 78, 1984.

36. O'Neal, C. L. and Poklis, A., Postmortem production of ethanol and factors that influence interpretation, *Am J Forensic Med Pathol,* 17, 8-20, 1996.

37. Caplan, Y. H. and Levine, B.S., Vitreous humor in the evaluation of postmortem blood ethanol concentrations, *J Analytical Tox,* 14, 305-307, 1990.

38. Vorpahl, T. E. and Coe, J. I., Correlation of antemortem and postmortem digoxin levels, *J Forensic Sci,* 23, 329-334, 1978.

39. Wetli, C. V. and Mittelman, R. E., The "body packer" syndrome - toxicity following ingestion of illicit drugs packaged for transportation, *J Forensic Sci,* 26, 492-500, 1981.

40. Freimuth, H. C., Guidelines for preservation of toxicological evidence, in *Medicolegal Investigation of Death, Second Edition,* Spitz, W. U., and Fisher, R. S., eds., Charles C. Thomas Publisher, Springfield, IL, 1980, 556-564.

41. Isenschmid, D. S., Cassin, B. J. and Hepler, B. R., Acute tetrachloroethylene intoxication in an autoerotic fatality, presented at American Academy of Forensic Science Annual Meeting, Abstract K-20, Seattle, WA, 1995.

42. Karch, S. B., *The Pathology of Drug Abuse,* CRC Press, Boca Raton FL, 1993, 42-43.

43. Hepler, B. R., Sutheimer, C. A. and Sunshine, I., Unpublished data.

44. Anderson, W. H. and Prouty, R. W., Personal communication.

45. Smith, H. Forshufvud, S. and Wassen, A., Distribution of arsenic in Napoleon's hair, *Nature,* 194, 725-726, 1962.

46. Grandjean, P., Lead poisoning: hair analysis shows the calender of events, *Human Toxicol,* 3, 223-228, 1984.

47. Poklis, A. and Saady, J. J., Arsenic poisoning: acute or chronic?, *Am J Forensic Med Pathol,* 11, 236-232, 1990.

48. DuPont, R. L. and Baumgartner, W. A., Drug testing by urine and hair analysis: complementary features and scientific issues, *Forensic Science Int,* 70, 63-76, 1995.

49. Baumgartner, W. A., Cheng, C., Donahue, T. D., Hayes, G. F., Hill, V. A. and Scholtz H., Forensic drug testing by mass spectrometric analysis in hair, in *Forensic Applications of Mass Spectrometry,* Yinon, J., ed., CRC Press, Boca Raton, FL, 1995, Chapter 2.

50. Harkey, M. R. and, Henderson, G. L., Hair analysis for drugs of abuse, in *Advances in Analytical Toxicology, Volume II,* Baselt, R.C., ed., Yearbook Medical Publishers, Chicago, 1989, Chapter 10.

51. Couper, F. J., McIntyre, I. M. and Drummer, O. H., Detection of antidepressant and antipsychotic drugs in postmortem human scalp hair, *J Forensic Sci,* 40, 87-90, 1995.

52. Uematsu, T., Therapeutic drug monitoring in hair samples: principles and practice, *Clin Pharmacokinetics,* 25, 83-87, 1993.

53. Tracqui, A., Kintz, P. and Mangin, P., Hair analysis: a worthless tool for therapeutic compliance monitoring, *Forensic Science Int,* 70, 183-189, 1995.

54. Cone, E. J. and Wang, W. L., Testing human hair for drugs of abuse, IV, environmental cocaine contamination and washing effects, *Forensic Science Int,* 70, 39-51, 1995.

55. Blank, D. L. and Kidwell, D. A., Decontamination procedures for drugs of abuse in hair: are they sufficient?, *Forensic Science Int,* 70, 13-38, 1995.

56. Joseph, R. E., Su, T., Cone, E. J., Sex bias in hair testing for cocaine, presented at American Academy of Forensic Sciences Annual Meeting, Abstract K-10, Seattle, WA, 1995.

57. Joseph, R. E., Su,T. and Cone, E. J., Evaluation of in vitro binding of cocaine to lipids and melanin in hair, presented at American Acdemy of Forensic Sciences Annual Meeting, Abstract K- 19, Nashville, TN, 1996.

58. Welch, M. J., Sniegoski, L. T. and Allgood, C. C., Interlaboratory comparison studies on the analysis of hair for drugs of abuse, *Forensic Science Int,* 63, 295-303, 1993.

59. Kintz, P. and Mangin, P., What constitutes a positive result in hair analysis: proposal for the establishment of cut-off values, *Forensic Science Int,* 70, 3-11, 1995.

60. Winek, C. L., Morris, E. M., Wahba, W. W., The use of bone marrow in the study of postmortem redistribution of amitriptyline, *J Analytical Tox,* 17, 93, 1993.

61. Winek, C. L, Costantino, A.G., Wahba, W. W. and Collom, W. D., Blood versus bone marrow pentobarbital concentrations, *Forensic Science Int,* 27, 15-24, 1985.

62. Winek, C. L. and Pluskota, M,. Plasma versus bone marrow flurazepam concentrations in rabbits and humans, *Forensic Science Int,* 19, 155-163, 1982.

63. Winek, C. L. and Esposito, F. M., Comparative study of ethanol levels in blood versus bone marrow, vitreous humor, bile and urine, *Forensic Science Int,* 17, 27-36, 1981.

64. Winek, C. L., Matejczyk, R. J. and Buddie, E. G., Blood, bone marrow and eye fluid ethanol concentrations in putrefied rabbits, *Forensic Science Int,* 22, 151-159, 1983.

65. Noguchi, T. T., Nakamura, G. R. and Griesemer, E. C., Drug analysis of skeletoninzing remains, *J Forensic Sci,* 23, 490-492, 1978.

66. Kojima, T., Okamoto, I., Miyazaki, T., Chikasue, F., Yashiki, M. and Nakamura, K., Detection of methamphetamine and amphetamine in a skeletonized body buried for 5years, *Forensic Science Int,* 31, 93-102, 1986.

Bradford R. Hepler and Daniel S. Isenschmid

67. Logemann, E., Krützfeldt, B., Kalkbrenner, G. and Sch le, W., Mercury in bones, presented at Society of Forensic Toxicologists Annual Meeting, Abstract 44, Tampa, FL, 1994.

68. Garriott, J. C., Skeletal muscle as an alternative specimen for alcohol and drug analysis, *J Forensic Sci*,36, 60, 1991.

69. Kudo K., Nagata, T., Kimura, K., Imamura, T. and Urakawa, N., Postmortem changes of triazolam concentrations in body tissues, *Nippon Hoigaku Zasshi*, 46, 293, 1992.

70. Christensen, H., Steentoft, A. and Worm, K., Muscle as an autopsy material for evaluation of fatal cases of drug overdose, *J Forensic Sci Soc*, 25, 191-206, 1985.

71. Garriot, J. C., Interpretive toxicology: drug abuse and drug abuse deaths, in *Forensic Pathology*, DiMaio, D. J. and DiMaio, V. J. M., eds., CRC Press, Boca Raton, FL, 1993, Chapter 21.

72. Manhoff. D. T., Hood, I., Caputo, F., Perry, J., Rosen S. and Mirchandani, H. G., Cocaine in decomposed human remains,. *J Forensic Sci*, 36, 1732, 1991.

73. Beyer, J. C., Enos, W.F. and Stajic, M.. Drug identification through analysis of maggots, *J Forensic Sci*, 25, 411-413, 1980.

74. Kintz, P., Godelar, B., Tracqui, A., Mangin, P. Lugnier, A. A. and Chaumont, A. J., Fly larvae: a new toxicological method of investigation in forensic medicine, *J Forensic Sci*, 35, 204-207, 1990.

75. Kintz, P., Traqui, A. and Mangin, P., Analysis of opiates in fly larvae sampled on a putrefied cadaver, *J Forensic Science Soc*, 34, 95-97, 1994.

76. Nolte K. B., Pinder R. D. and Lord, W. D., Insect larvae used to detect cocaine poisoning in a decomposed body, *J Forensic Sci*, 37, 1179-1185, 1992.

77. Gunatilake, K. and Goff, L., Detection of organophosphate poisoning in a putrefying body analyzing arthropod larvae, *J Forensic Science*, 34, 714-716, 1989.

78. Pounder, D. J., Forensic entomotoxicology, *J Forensic Sci Soc*, 31,469-472, 1991.

79. Introna, F., Lo Dico, C., Caplan, Y. H., Smialek, J. E., Opiate analysis in cadaveric blowfly larvae as an indicator of narcotic intoxication, *J Forensic Sci*, 35, 118-122, 1990.

80. Kintz, P., Traqui, P., Ludes, B., Waller, J., Boukhabza, A., Mangin, P., Lugnier, A. A. and Chaumont, A. J., Fly larvae and their relevance in forensic toxicology, *Am J Forensic Med Pathol*, 11, 63-65, 1990.

81. Wilson, Z., Hubbard, S. and Pounder, D. J., Drug analysis in fly larvae, *Am J Forensic Med Pathol*, 14, 118-120, 1993.

82. Sadler, D. W., Fuke, C., Court, F. and Pounder, D. J., Drug accumulation and elimination in *Calliphora vicina* larvae, *Forensic Science Int*, 71, 191-197, 1995.

83. Moore, C. and Negrusz, A., Drugs of abuse in meconium, *Forensic Science Reviews*, 7, 103-118, 1995.

84. Ostrea, E. M., Romero, A., Knapp, D. K., Ostrea, A. R., Lucena, J. E. and Utarnachitt, R. B., Postmortem drug analysis of meconium in early-gestation human fetuses exposed to cocaine, *J Pediatr*, 124, 477, 1994.

85. Steele, B. W., Bandstra, E. S., Wu, N.C., Hime G. W., and Hearn, W. L. *m*-Hydroxybenzoylecgonine: an important contributor to the immunoreactivity in assays for benzoylecgonine in meconium, *J Analytical Tox*,17, 348-351, 1993.

86. Tracqui, A., Kintz, P., Ludes, B., Jamey, C. and Mangin, P., The detection of opiate drugs in nontraditional specimens (clothing): a report of ten cases, *J Forensic Sci*, 40, 263-265, 1995.

87. Monforte, J. R., Personal communication.

88. Barchet, R., Harzer, K., Helmers, E. and Wippler, K., Arsenic content in cremation ash after lethal arsenic poisoning, in Proceedings of the 1994 Joint TIAFT/SOFT International Meeting, Spiehler, V., ed., Newport Beach, CA, 1995, 315-319.

Specimen Selection, Collection, Preservation, and Security

12.3 COMMON METHODS IN POSTMORTEM TOXICOLOGY

WM. LEE HEARN, PH.D.

DIRECTOR OF TOXICOLOGY, METRO DADE COUNTY
MEDICAL EXAMINER DEPARTMENT, MIAMI, FLORIDA

H. CHIP WALLS

UNIVERSITY OF MIAMI, DEPARTMENT OF PATHOLOGY,
FORENSIC TOXICOLOGY LABORATORY, MIAMI, FLORIDA

12.3.1 ANALYTICAL CHEMISTRY IN POSTMORTEM TOXICOLOGY

Analytical toxicology is an applied science.[1-4] Toxicologists must be familiar with not only the effects and toxic mechanisms involved in poisoning, but also with the metabolism of drugs, the chemical properties of parent drugs and their metabolites, and the composition of biological samples. The detection and measurement of toxicologically relevant concentrations of potent new drugs requires the use of analytical techniques on the forefront of instrumental technology.[5-9]

Immunoassay technology, now a mainstay of drug screening protocols, first became commercially available only twenty years ago.[10-14] At that time, classical thin layer chromatography,[15-23] packed column gas chromatography,[24,25] strip chart recorders and ultra-violet-visible spectrophotometry were the state of the art in toxicology laboratories.[26-29] Over the intervening years, capillary column gas chromatography,[30-34] solid phase extraction technology,[46-53] nitrogen-phosphorus gas chromatography detectors,[42,43,54,55] high performance liquid chromatography,[56-74] ion trap mass spectrometry[75-79] and computerized mass spectrometry have become essential to the practice of postmortem toxicology.[80,89]

New technology is continually being introduced. Mass spectrometry is evolving to tandem mass spectrometry, and is being interfaced to liquid chromatographs.[92,100-106] Chemical ionization, in both positive and negative ion modes, is increasingly used in the mass spectral analysis of drugs and poisons.[107-119] Robotic technology is used to increase efficiency of sample processing while maintaining and documenting sample integrity.[120-123] At the same time, the proliferation of ever more powerful micro computers, and sophisticated software applications, has vastly improved the processing and archiving of analytical data, control of instruments, laboratory management and quality assurance monitoring.

While newer technologies have replaced many of the older, less sensitive, and less specific testing methods, some of the older tests, such as the microchemical tests, still have a place in the modern toxicology laboratory. But change is occurring so rapidly that today's technology may soon be obsolete. The best and most current guides to the innovations in testing methodologies are to be found in the scientific journal such as the *Journal of Forensic Sciences* and the *Journal of Analytical Toxicology*, the annual meetings of professional organizations such as the Society of Forensic Toxicologists and the American Academy of Forensic Sciences, and the annual meeting of the Pittsburgh Conference on Analytical Chemistry and Applied Spectroscopy. Table 12.3.1 compares the analytical techniques with respect to specificity, sensitivity, labor, cost and applicability.

12.3.2 SIMPLE CHEMICAL TESTS

Chemical tests were once the mainstay of postmortem toxicology.[21,124-127] Today, many have been abandoned and replaced by automated broad range screening procedures. However,

Table 12.3.1 Comparison of Frequently Used Methods for Analysis of Biosamples

Method	Specificity	Sensitivity	Multiple Drugs	Identification: Structural Analysis (Qualitative)	Quantitative Analysis	Labor	Expertise
Color tests	+	+	Yes	+	Some	+	+
UV-VIS	+	+	No	++++	Yes	++	++
IA	++	++	Some	NO	Some	+	+
GC	++	++	Yes	++	Yes	++	++
TLC	++	+	Yes	++	No	+++	+++
HPLC	++	++	Yes	++	Yes	++	++
GC/MS	++++	++++	Yes	++++	Yes	+++	++++
AAS	+++	+++	No	++	++++	+++	++++
ICP-MS	++++	++++	Yes	++++	++++	++++	++++

Key: Low = +; High = ++++; UV-VIS = Ultra-violet-and visible spectrophotometry; TLC = Thin layer chromatography; IA = Immunoassay; GC = Gas chromatography; GC/MS = Gas chromatography mass spectrometry; AAS = Atomic absorption spectrometry; ICP-MS = Inductively coupled plasma mass spectrometry.

From Dolgin, J., Human Clinical Toxicology, in CRC Handbook of Toxicology, Derelanko, M.J. and Hollinger, M.A., Eds., CRC Press, Boca Raton, FL, 1995, 697.

some are still useful as supplemental tests to rapidly and easily detect drugs and poisons that are not detected by the other screening tests.

Virtually all clinical and forensic toxicology laboratories utilize micro-color tests to indicate the possible presence of drugs or toxins; the so-called spot tests.[21,125,127-133] Micro-color tests are performed by adding a single or multiple reagents to a specimen or extract and observing the color produced. Color tests are specific examples of the more general method of qualitative organic chemistry, relying on functional group reactions with the reagents. These tests require some expertise and familiarity to use, but are inexpensive and relatively rapid. They are nonspecific. However, in conjunction with other confirmatory tests, they can be used as rapid diagnostic aids.

Color tests can be combined with visible or spectrophotometric methodologies for qualitative to semi-quantitative answers. Drugs including phenothiazines, salicylates, acetaminophen, carbamates, ethchlorvynol, and imipramine are routinely sought by colorimetric methods. Positive test results are confirmed and quantified by another technique. The greatest advantage of color tests is their ease of use. They can be performed directly on urine or a protein-free filtrate of blood or tissues. A negative color test precludes the need for any further work on that drug, assuming the detection limit of the test is acceptable. For example, the color test for phenothiazines is useful if an overdose has occurred, but is not sensitive enough to test for patient compliance with the drug.

12.3.2.1 Useful Color Tests

Some or all of the following tests may be incorporated in a routine screening protocol or some may be reserved for cases requiring more comprehensive poison screening.

12.3.2.1.1 Trinder's Reagent

Trinder's test is a simple color test that detects salicylic acid in urine or serum. It does not detect acetylsalicylic acid in gastric contents without prior hydrolysis by boiling with dilute HCl. Trinder's reagent is a mixture of ferric nitrate and mercuric chloride in dilute hydrochloric acid.

It immediately produces a violet color when mixed with an equal volume of sample containing salicylate. Phenothiazines also give a positive reaction.[125,126,129,133,134]

12.3.2.1.2 Fujiwara Test for Trichloro Compounds

A mixture of 1 ml 20% sodium hydroxide and 1 ml of pyridine at 100C yields a red or pink color with chloral hydrate or other compounds with at least two halogens bound to one carbon.[124,125,126,131,135] Trichloroethanol gives a yellow color. Contamination of the laboratory atmosphere with chlorinated solvents will give "false" positive results. Metabolites of carbon tetrachloride may also give a positive result with this test, but carbon tetrachloride is only partially metabolized to trichloromethyl compounds and the test may fail to detect this agent. A blank sample and a control (trichloroacetic acid) should be tested at the same time, both blank and control solutions being treated in similar fashion to the sample.

12.3.2.1.3 Diphenylamine Test for Oxidizing Agents

A solution of 0.5% diphenylamine in 60% sulfuric acid added to the sample or sample filtrate in a porcelain spot plate or a test tube immediately gives an intense blue color if an oxidizing agent is present. This test detects hypochlorite, chlorate, bromate, iodate, chromate, dichromate, nitrate, nitrite, permanganate, vanadate, lead (IV), or manganese (III, IV or VII). [125,126]

12.3.2.1.4 Ethchlorvynol (Placidyl) Test

One ml of sample (urine or sample filtrate) is mixed with the reagent and allowed to stand for 20 minutes. If ethclorvynol is present, the solution turns red or pink. The reagent consists of one gram of diphenylamine dissolved in 50 ml of concentrated sulfuric acid and added slowly with stirring to 100 ml of 50% (V/V) acetic acid. The test is sufficiently sensitive to detect therapeutic concentrations.[125,126,136]

12.3.2.2 Other Color Tests that May Be Included in a Screen

Other color tests that may be included in a screen can be found in various toxicology references.[124-128]

12.3.3 REINSCH TEST FOR HEAVY METALS

A spiral of copper wire is first cleaned with 35% nitric acid and washed. It is then immersed in 15 ml of sample, acidified with concentrated HCl (4 ml), heated for one hour and then examined. A silver colored deposit on the copper indicates mercury, while a dark colored or black deposit is produced by arsenic, antimony, bismuth, tellurium, selenium and sulfur. Further differentiation can be made on the basis of color of the deposit, and its solubility characteristics in potassium cyanide solution.[128,137-141]

12.3.4 MICRODIFFUSION TESTS

12.3.4.1 Cyanide Test

Two ml of sample are placed in a screw cap culture tube. Discs are punched from a strip of Cyantesmo paper, available from Gallard-Schlessinger Chemical Mfg. Co. in Carle Place, New York, and one disc is stuck to the adhesive in the center of a 1 cm square of cellophane tape. The sample is acidified with H_2SO_4, the tape is placed over the mouth of the tube, with the adhesive and disc side down, and the tube is tightly capped. After 4 h at 35°C, the caps are removed and the color of the disc is compared with cyanide standards treated the same way. A pale green or yellow color is a negative result. Cyanide turns the disc blue in proportion to the concentration in the sample. Comparison of the color with standards from 0.2 to 5.0 mg/L cyanide can be used to estimate the concentration.

12.3.4.2 Carbon Monoxide

A simple test for carbon monoxide utilizes a procedure similar to the cyanide test described above, but using a disc of filter paper saturated with palladium chloride solution (1%) in 0.12 N HCl and dried. Carbon monoxide is released from hemoglobin by the addition of a solution containing lactic acid and potassium ferricyanide. Lead acetate is added to trap sulfide, which might interfere with the test. If carbon monoxide is present, the disc turns gray to black. While this test is simple, a faster and more effective method is to analyze the blood with a CO-Oximeter (Instrumentation Laboratories) which gives a result in % saturation of hemoglobin.

12.3.5 OTHER SIMPLE TESTS

12.3.5.1 Glucose, Ketones, Protein, and pH via a Diagnostic Reagent Strip (Dip-Stick)

Dip a strip briefly into the urine and read after 10 to 60 seconds. Elevated glucose may indicate diabetes. A positive result for ketones may indicate intoxication by acetone or isopropyl alcohol. This test may also be positive in starvation or in diabetic ketosis.

12.3.5.2 Odor, Color, and pH of Gastric Contents

Characteristic smells may indicate the presence of substances such as camphor, cresol, cyanide, ethanol and other organic solvents, ethchlorvynol, methyl salicylate, and paraldehyde. A high pH may indicate ingestion of alkali. A green or blue color suggests the presence of iron salts. Other colors may result from dissolution of colored pills or capsules. Intact tablets or capsules should be retrieved and examined separately.

12.3.6 IMMUNOASSAYS

Immunoassays for postmortem toxicology are sold commercially as kits. Often, they are exactly the same products as those used for urine drug screening in forensic urine drug testing (FUDT) programs.[142] Such products are standardized and validated by the manufacturer, and are approved by the U.S. Food and Drug Administration (FDA). They are intended and approved for the analysis of particular specimen types, such as urine or serum. When urine cannot be obtained, other tissue may be used. A number of publications have described effective techniques for precipitating/extracting drugs from blood or tissue homogenates. Generally, the technique involves use of a solvent, such as acetone or acetonitrile, followed by evaporation of the solvent/water mixture and reconstitution in a suitable reagent for assay, according to the procedure for urine. However, application to specimens other than urine requires validation[143-156]

Immunoassays are based upon the principle that antibodies can be produced which recognize and bind to specific chemicals by interacting with unique structural features of their molecules. The interaction is analogous to that of a lock and key. Some antibodies are so selective that they bind to only one substance, such as methamphetamine. Others interact with a variety of compounds with similar structures, such as amphetamine, methamphetamine, phentermine, ephedrine, pseudoephedrine and others, though not with structurally dissimilar compounds such as morphine. For postmortem screening, assays utilizing antibodies with broad selectivity for drugs within a particular class, such as sympathomimetic amines, are preferred over those with antibodies sensitive to one specific drug such as methamphetamine. Thus, a negative class selective assay can exclude all drugs with which it interacts, albeit with differing sensitivity for individual drugs. Conversely a positive result requires further testing to distinguish among the possibilities. With few exceptions, all cross reacting substances are of potential interest to the postmortem toxicology laboratory.

Immunoassays used for drug screening utilize a competitive interaction between the drug in the specimen, and a labeled drug in the reagent, for sites on an antibody specific to the drug being tested. The drug is detected by its ability to displace or block binding of a fixed amount of chemically labeled drug molecules that are included in the reagent. The label can be an enzyme, a fluorescent molecule, a radioactive isotope or other substance that can be detected by instrumental means. The object of the assay is to measure either the amount of antibody-bound, or of free labeled drug, which is related to the concentration of the targeted drug in the sample.

Some assays can distinguish between bound and free labeled drug in a mixture and are referred to as homogeneous immunoassays. Others require physical separation of bound and free label prior to making the measurement. These are called heterogeneous immunoassays. In general, homogeneous immunoassays are more readily automated and, thus, less labor intensive than heterogeneous immunoassays.

Various types of immunoassays use different detection principles, such as enzyme immunoassay (EIA), Fluorescence Polarization Immunoassay (FPIA), radioimmunoassay (RIA) and kinetic interaction of microparticulates in solution (KIMS). Each type has advantages and disadvantages in terms of cost, throughput, and time for analysis in postmortem drug screening. The detection limit for various members of a class of drugs (e.g., opiates) or the degree of cross-reactivity for similar drugs (e.g., sympathomimetic amines) varies. Each manufacturer of immunoassay reagents should be consulted for specific information regarding detection limits for various drugs within a class.

These assays are easy to perform, the results are "semi-quantitative" (higher or lower than a predetermined calibrator cut-off concentration) rather than subjective (e.g., TLC), and they generally have low detection limits (0.02- 1.0 mcg/mL). Several non-isotopic immunoassays (e.g., EMIT™, CEDIA® and FPIA) have been automated for postmortem drug screening. Immunoassays complement chromatographic procedures (TLC and GC) because they detect those drugs that would require hydrolysis prior to chromatography (e.g., morphine-3-glucuronide and oxazepam glucuronide), that may require a separate extraction (e.g., benzoylecgonine) or derivatization or that have high TLC detection limits (e.g., phencyclidine). For abused drugs, immunoassays are the methods of choice for initial screening.

12.3.6.1 Enzyme Immunoassay (EIA)

12.3.6.1.1 General

EIA reagents are available from several manufacturers. Spectrophotometric readings are used to measure the quantity of product produced by an enzyme catalyzed reaction. The homogeneous EIAs are readily adaptable to automated clinical analyzers for rapid throughput of sample batches with minimal labor. Most are designed for screening urine samples, but they can be adapted for screening unhemolyzed serum or plasma. However, results depend upon transmission of light through the reaction mixture, so these assays cannot be applied to turbid, highly colored or opaque specimens, without first doing labor intensive pre-extraction steps. The homogeneous EIA reagents are the most economical immunoassays for analysis of urine and stomach contents, although the extra labor required for their application to whole blood and other tissues may offset the reagent savings for those applications.[10-14,142,157-166]

12.3.6.1.2 CEDIA®

CEDIA® assays represent state of the art technique, utilizing two genetically engineered enzymatically inactive fragments of beta-galactosidase as the basis for a homogeneous enzyme immunoassay.[167-173] Two separate genes are engineered to express two separate inactive polypeptide fragments: enzyme-donor (ED) and enzyme-acceptor (EA). These fragments can sponta-neously recombine to form active beta-galactosidase enzyme. Ligands can be attached to the ED peptide in such a way that the degree of recombination is controlled by the binding of anti-ligand antibodies to the enzyme donor-ligand conjugate. CEDIA® methodology is based on the competition between ligand in the sample and ED-ligand conjugate for a limited amount of antibody binding sites. The advantages of the CEDIA® immunoassay system over conven-tional homogeneous EIA's include a linear calibration curve with high precision over the entire assay range, and lower limits of detection of analytes in human body fluids. Assay procedures can easily be automated and can be performed on most automated clinical chemistry analyzers.

12.3.6.1.3 E.L.I.S.A.

Enzyme linked immunosorbent assays (ELISA) are heterogeneous enzyme immunoassays conducted in special multiwell (typically 96 wells) assay plates.[174-179] They are more labor intensive than the homogeneous EIA's if assayed manually, though robotic equipment is available to process plates in a semiautomated manner. They require specialized plate readers to measure the reaction products. Costs are somewhat higher than homogeneous EIA re-agents, however ELISA assays are manufactured for some drugs for which no other immunoas-say is commercially available (e.g., haloperidol, methylphenidate, phenylbutazone, furosemide, phenothiazine, reserpine, and others).

12.3.6.2 Fluoresence Polarization Immunoassay (FPIA)

FPIA reagents were developed by Abbott Laboratories, and some are also available from Sigma Chemical Company.[99,149,161-164,166,180-194] They are homogeneous immunoassays that can be used only in specialized instruments that are capable of exciting the fluorescein label with polarized ultraviolet light, and then measuring the intensity of polarized fluorescent emissions. Because the sample is highly dilute in the reaction mixture and the instrument measures emitted, rather than transmitted, light FPIA is less subject to interference by color or turbidity of the sample matrix than are EIAs.

Most hemolyzed or whole blood samples, as well as serum, plasma and urine, can be analyzed directly without extraction. If the sample is too dark to be analyzed without pretreat-ment, it can usually be analyzed after diluting with buffer, although with less sensitivity. In addition to their application to drug screening, some of the FPIA assays can yield quantitative measurements, because of the high specificity of their antibodies. The major drawbacks of FPIAs are the high price of reagents and the limited sample capacity of the instruments. The latter problem is being addressed with the introduction of a new high capacity instrument (Abbott AxSYM™).

12.3.6.3 Radioimmunoassay (RIA)

RIA reagents are available from several manufacturers. They are heterogeneous immunoassays and, as such, are not readily automated. However, some RIAs have the antibody bound to the inside of the assay tube, which simplifies the separation and wash procedures. Most RIA reagents that are used in toxicology have[125]I as the label, and require a gamma counter to measure either bound or unbound label. Reagents are available for many drugs and drug classes, cost is reasonable, and sensitivity is excellent. The major drawbacks of RIA relate to the use of radioactive materials, i.e. the need for radioactive materials licensure and radioactive waste disposal, and the relatively short shelf life of the reagents.[79,145,150-152,161,162, 165,174,182,195-202.]

12.3.6.4 Kinetic Interaction of Microparticles in Solution (KIMS)

KIMS (OnLine) reagents are presently available only from Roche Diagnostics. They are homogeneous assays with microscopic particles as the label. In the absence of drug, the labeled drug is bound by antibody, forming light scattering aggregates. The intensity of light transmitted through the sample is measured spectrophotometrically in an automated clinical analyzer. Light transmission increases with concentration of unlabeled drug in the sample. Reagents are stable and sensitivity is good, although price remains somewhat higher than the EIA reagents.[161,165,166,203-205]

12.3.6.5 Useful Immunoassays for Postmortem Toxicology Screening

12.3.6.5.1 Amphetamines (Class)

Polyclonal immunoassays for sympathomimetic amines including amphetamine, methamphetamine, phenylpropanolamine, ephedrine, pseudoephedrine, methylenedioxymethamphetamine (MDMA), phentermine and related compounds are preferred over monoclonal assays for postmortem toxicology. Approximate detection times are 12 h to 3 days. Administrative detection cutoffs are 300 to 1000 ng/ml in urine based upon amphetamines or methamphetamine. They may be less sensitive for other drugs within the class.[13,144,167,187,194,203,206-217]

12.3.6.5.2 Barbiturates (Class)

Most assays detect pentobarbital, secobarbital, amobarbital, butalbital, phenobarbital, thiopental and related compounds. Normal detection times are 6 h to 2 days after administration. Detection cutoffs are 300 to 8000 ng/ml in urine depending upon cross-reactivity.[145,196,218-221]

12.3.6.5.3 Benzodiazepines (Class)

Most benzodiazepine immunoassays use antibodies directed to oxazepam. Their cross reactivity for other benzodiazepines varies considerably, but most detect diazepam, oxazepam, flurazepam metabolites, chlordiazepoxide metabolites, alprazolam, triazolam and related compounds. Lorazepam, flunitrazepam metabolites and some others may not be detected by some immunoassays. Normal detection times are 3 h to 2 weeks. Administrative detection cutoffs are 300 to 3000 ng/ml in urine.[144,146,173,176,181,188,191,192,222-234]

12.3.6.5.4 Benzoylecgonine

The cocaine metabolite assays are designed to detect benzoylecgonine, the principal urinary metabolite of cocaine. Cocaine and ecgonine methyl ester may also be detected if present in sufficient concentrations. Normal detection times are 6 h to 5 days. Administrative detection cutoffs are 300 ng/ml in urine.[149,178,179,235-250]

12.3.6.5.5 Opiates (Class)

These assays detect a variety of opiates including morphine, morphine-glucuronide, hydromorphone, codeine, hydrocodone, and heroin metabolites. High concentrations of meperidine and oxycodone may give positive test results. Normal detection times are 6 h to 3 days. Administrative detection cutoffs are 300 to 3000 ng/ml in urine.[12,144,154-156,160,165,167,173,202,204,215,245,251-257]

12.3.6.5.6 Phencyclidine

The phencyclidine assays detect only PCP metabolites. Normal detection times are 24 h. Administrative detection cutoffs are 25 ng/ml in urine.[156,173,221-265]

12.3.6.5.7 Propoxyphene

The propoxyphene assays detect the parent drug and the metabolite norpropoxyphene. In abuse situations, methadone (a close structural similarity) and chlorpromazine can produce a

Wm. Lee Hearn and H. Chip Walls

false positive. Normal detection time is 24 h. The administrative detection cutoff is 300 ng/ml in urine.[156,226]

12.3.6.5.8 Cannabinoids

The cannabinoid assays interact with at least 10 of the non-active metabolites of tetrahydrocannabinol (THC). Normal detection times range from hours to weeks, depending upon the frequency, potency, dose and route of administration. Administrative detection cutoffs for the principal urinary metabolites are 20 to 100 ng/ml in urine, depending upon the assay. [61,79,148,155,160,161,165,167,205,267-277]

12.3.6.5.9 Cyclic Antidepressants (class)

The immunoassay for tricyclic antidepressants detects amitriptyline, nortriptyline, imipramine, desipramine and their hydroxy metabolites, clomipramine, doxepin, protriptyline, cyclobenzaprine and certain phenothiazines. Administrative detection cutoffs are 300 to 2000 ng/ml in urine[278-283]

12.3.7 CHROMATOGRAPHY

Chromatographic drug screening techniques separate components of mixtures by partitioning them between a stationary phase, usually a solid or viscous liquid, and a mobile phase consisting of a gas or liquid. Under a given set of chromatographic conditions, the time required for a substance to traverse the chromatographic column (retention time) or the distance traveled on a thin layer chromatography plate relative to the solvent front (R_f) is a constant. Separated analytes are detected and identified by a variety of techniques, and often quantitative measurements or semiquantitative estimates of analyte concentration may be made by reference to a standard curve. Chromatographic techniques that are currently used for screening purposes in postmortem toxicology include Thin Layer Chromatography (TLC), Gas Chromatography (GC), and High Performance Liquid Chromatography (HPLC).

12.3.7.1 Thin Layer Chromatography (TLC)

TLC is a versatile procedure that requires no instrumentation and thus is relatively simple and inexpensive to perform.[16-21,23,82,284-293] However, its application to drug screening requires considerable skill to recognize drug and metabolite patterns and the various detection color hues. Thin layer chromatographic techniques employ silica gel or a chemically modified silica gel as the stationary phase. The mobile phase consists of a mixture of organic solvents, often with a small quantity of acid or base to convert acidic or basic drugs to nonionic species. After extraction and specimen spotting, the TLC plates are developed with appropriate solvents to achieve chromatographic resolution. After the chromatogram is developed, drug spots are visualized by chemical modification to colored products or by absorption or fluorescence in ultraviolet light. Drug identifications are based upon R_f values, color reactions and presence of expected metabolite patterns. Standards are included on each plate to compensate for variations in R_f values.

  With TLC, a large number of drugs may be detected, and presumptively identified, with a single analysis. TLC may be used to analyze serum, gastric contents, or urine. Urine, however, is the specimen of choice, since most drugs and drug metabolites are present in urine in relatively high concentrations. Although the detection limit varies for each drug, and with the conditions of extraction and detection, it is generally on the order of 0.5 to 4.0 mcg/mL. TLC is less sensitive than immunoassay techniques, but its use is not restricted to the detection of only the drug or drugs for which antibodies are available. Literally hundreds of drugs can be detected and identified.

TLC can be used as either a screening or a confirmation procedure in toxicology tests. Many laboratories use TLC as a first screening step, since a wide variety of drugs/toxins can potentially be detected and presumptively identified. When used to screen, confirmation of TLC results can be made by using a variety of other procedures, including GC, GC/MS, immunoassay, and HPLC. In some situations, the spot can be scraped from the TLC plate, extracted from the solid phase and injected directly into a GC or GC/MS for confirmation.

TLC will usually produce a spot for any organic drug/toxin that is present in sufficient concentration in urine or other body fluid. The major disadvantage of this technique is its insensitivity. In addition, when urine is the extracted specimen, drug metabolites are often present, and evaluation of a chromatogram containing several drugs and their metabolites can be complicated. However, the presence of known metabolites, when interpreted properly, adds support to the identification of the parent drug. TLC also has the drawback of being subjective in interpretation. A color-blind technologist will have difficulty interpreting the results.

12.3.7.1.1 Toxi-Lab® TLC

Over the last 20 years, classical TLC has been largely replaced in the postmortem toxicology laboratory by the Toxi-Lab® TLC system.[284,290-293] The Toxi-Lab® system is a group of products produced by the AnaSys Corporation and marketed through major vendors of laboratory supplies and equipment. The Toxi-Lab® TLC plates, Toxi-Grams®, are composed of glass fiber paper impregnated with silica gel or a C-8 (8 carbon aliphatic) reversed phase sorbent. Drugs are extracted from urine, stomach contents or other specimens in prepared "Toxi-Tubes®" containing buffer and an optimized extraction solvent mixture. Sample extracts are evaporated in disposable aluminum cups with small discs of the same material as the plates. As the evaporation proceeds, extracted drugs are adsorbed into the disc, which, when dry, is inserted into a matching hole at the bottom of the plate. Standards are contained in similar discs. Both prestandardized and unstandardized plates are available and standard impregnated discs are available separately.

The prepared plate is developed in a glass chamber with a solvent mixture designated by the manufacturer for each chromatography system. After developing, plates are dried, and then drugs are visualized by sequentially dipping the chromatogram into a series of tanks containing reagents and viewing under long wave UV light. Colors and positions of spots are recorded at each visualization stage. Photographic illustrations of visualization stages and metabolite patterns are available in a compendium comprising over 100 drugs with new drugs added as data are developed.

An available IBM-PC compatible search program can help with data analysis, yielding statistical probability for identifications. Systems are available to screen for basic and neutral drugs, acidic and neutral drugs, tetrahydrocannabinol metabolites, and opiates, as well as the C-8 reversed phase system that is used for further differentiating and confirming presumptive findings. In addition, confirmatory procedures for may drugs are described. The Toxi-Lab® system is a powerful tool for screening urine and stomach contents. It is less effective for blood and other tissues due to interference from lipids and sensitivity limitations.

12.3.7.2 Gas Chromatography

GC is widely used for qualitative and quantitative drug analysis. It is relatively rapid, and capable of resolving a broad spectrum of drugs. Modern gas chromatography employs fused silica capillary columns that are coated on their inner wall with a liquid stationary phase consisting of a polymer chemically bonded to the silica.[45,80,294] The most common liquid phases are methyl silicones that contain one, five or fifty percent phenyl side chains. The higher phenyl contents yield higher polarity liquid phases. Other polymers are used for special purposes.

Wm. Lee Hearn and H. Chip Walls

The mobile phase is a gas, i.e. the carrier gas. Usually helium is used, although hydrogen, nitrogen and gas mixtures may be preferred for some applications. The coiled column, which may be 10 to 60 m in length, is located in an oven having a precisely controlled programmable temperature capability. During a chromatographic analysis, the column temperature may be kept constant, raised at a selected constant rate, or programmed through a series of temperature ramps and isothermal intervals.

The separation capabilities of gas chromatography are determined by the polarity of the liquid phase, the flow rate and composition of the carrier gas and the temperature program. Compounds are separated as a consequence of their different vapor pressures at the column temperature and their affinity for the liquid phase, which is related to their polarity.

In practice, the sample is injected manually or by an autosampler, either as an extract in a suitable organic solvent, or as a vapor of volatile analytes mixed with air or carrier gas. The sample is volatilized in the heated injection port and its constituents are swept into the column. As the analysis proceeds some components move through the column faster than others, forming discrete bands that progress to the distal end and emerge into the detector, ideally in a pure state. GC detectors of various types recognize particular properties of substances, generating an electrical signal proportional to the quantity of the substance in the detector.

The resulting signal is electronically amplified and recorded on a moving chart or, more commonly, processed by a microcomputer to yield absolute and relative retention time, peak area and height data for each detected component in the sample. Retention times of sample components, relative to a reference compound (internal standard) that is added to the sample, are constant for a given set of chromatographic conditions. Presumptive identifications are based upon relative retention times corresponding with those produced by standards under identical conditions. For drug screening, some laboratories use dual column GC's with both columns originating at the same injection port. The sample is divided between the two columns and analyzed simultaneously on both. Agreement of relative retention times in two columns of differing polarities provides greater certainty of identification.

Some drugs do not chromatograph well with GC because they contain polar functional groups that adhere strongly to the liquid phase and/or depress the vapor pressure. Such problems can often be overcome by converting the active functional groups to less polar derivatives; such as esters from alcohols, phenols, or carboxylic acids, or amides from amines. Derivatives may be selected to give longer or shorter retention times while improving peak shape and sensitivity.[36,77,88,89,117,295-304]

Several types of detectors are used in postmortem toxicology laboratories. Each has characteristics that make it useful for detection and quantification of some, but not all, of the drugs and poisons that are of concern to the postmortem toxicologist.

12.3.7.2.1 Flame Ionization Detector (FID)

The flame ionization detector uses a hydrogen/air flame to oxidize sample components that emerge from the column. Substances containing carbon yield a charged plasma. Electrodes produce a high voltage field that deflects the charged particles to a collector that produces an electric current with a magnitude proportional to the quantity of the component. The FID detects virtually all drugs that can be passed through the GC, however lipids and other matrix-derived components interfere with the detection of drugs and limit practical sensitivity.

The FID, once the mainstay of gas chromatography in toxicology laboratories, is still used for the analysis of alcohols and other volatile substances in the GC equipped with an automated headspace sampler. Barbiturates and other acidic and neutral drugs are detected and quantified effectively with FID.[305-310] However, most gas chromatographic basic drug screens typically employ Nitrogen/Phosphorus (NPD) detectors which provide better sensitivity and selectivity than FID.

12.3.7.2.2 Nitrogen-Phosphorus Detector (NPD)

The nitrogen/phosphorus detector has some similarities to the flame ionization detector in that a hydrogen-air flame is used, but the collector is a ceramic bead coated with a rubidium salt. The NPD is insensitive to carbon when properly adjusted, but it responds with high sensitivity to compounds containing nitrogen or phosphorus. Furthermore, it can be tuned to maximize sensitivity to either element. The selectivity for nitrogen makes the NP detector ideal for screening basic drugs, which all contain amine functions.[30,42,43,55,311-314] Lipids and other non-nitrogenous matrix components do not interfere with the analysis.

12.3.7.2.3 Electron Capture Detector (ECD)

The electron capture detector contains a radioactive nickel-63 foil that emits high energy electrons (beta particles). The carrier gas is ionized by the radiation, forming anions which establish an ion current between two electrodes. Sample compounds, emerging from the GC column, extract electrons from the ionized gas, decreasing the current flow. The change in current is the signal produced by the detector.

Most substances do not capture electrons and are not detected by the ECD. However, the presence of a halogen atom or a nitro or nitroso group in the molecule allows the substance to be detected. The outstanding sensitivity of the ECD for most halogenated compounds is the reason for its use in the analysis of benzodiazepines.[232,315-317] Obviously, halogenated solvents can not be used. A laboratory possessing a GC with ECD detector must have a radioactive materials license. A general license is sufficient for sealed detectors, but a specific license is required if the detector can be disassembled.

12.3.7.3 Gas Chromatography/Mass Spectrometry (GC/MS)

GC/MS is a powerful analytical tool for identification of semi-volatile organic compounds. It combines the separation efficiency of gas chromatography with the structure elucidating capabilities of mass spectrometry.[6,78-83,94,97,98,318-321] When it is used to identify unknown substances in a sample extract, the instrument may be programmed to automatically search for matches against a predefined library (target compound analysis) or it can acquire spectral data for later analysis. In the latter instance, the operator examines a chromatogram peak by peak, extracting background-subtracted spectra and searching spectral libraries by using a pattern matching algorithm through the instrument's data system. If no acceptable match is found, the spectrum can be visually compared with printed compilations of mass spectral data. Considerable experience is required for effective and efficient substance identification by GC/MS. A chromatogram may consist of hundreds of peaks, most of which represent endogenous compounds. Recognition of frequently encountered patterns can save considerable time by avoiding unnecessary library searches. Conversely the experienced operator will recognize the novel pattern as one that requires investigation. Nevertheless, a thorough search of a GC/MS data file can take an hour or more.

GC/MS is rarely used as a primary drug screening technique. Its use in that context would be too costly. Most postmortem toxicology laboratories cannot afford to dedicate a relatively expensive instrument and a full time GC/MS operator to the screening process. However, the power of GC/MS can be effectively used to identify unknown substances that are detected by less definitive techniques such as TLC, GC or class selective immunoassays.[80,255,256,269,297,319,322-324]

When GC/MS is employed to identify unknown peaks from a GC analysis, the portion of the chromatogram that must be examined can be narrowed if the same type of column and same column temperature program are used in both instruments. The remaining extract from the GC analysis can be injected into the GC/MS. Knowing the relative retention time of the unknown, the operator can first locate the peak corresponding to the internal standard and then estimate the region of the GC/MS chromatogram where the unknown peak should be. That region is examined carefully to locate and identify a peak whose spectrum is inconsistent with expected endogenous compounds.

In the identification of substances giving rise to unknown spots on TLC, an extract of the sample is analyzed in the GC/MS with a column temperature program extending from below the boiling point of the solvent to 300°C or higher. When the GC/MS run is complete, the entire chromatogram is examined. Time can be saved by initially examining the 20 or 30 largest peaks first. The GC/MS is much more sensitive than TLC, so any component that gives a visible spot should produce a large peak on the GC/MS. Alteratively, the operator may examine all peaks, and detect even substances missed by the TLC analysis. In most cases, such sensitivity is unnecessary for analyzing urine or gastric contents, but it can be useful when potent drugs such as fentanyl or haloperidol must be excluded.

An alternative approach to the identification of unknowns detected by TLC is to scrape the spot from a duplicate plate and analyze it by GC/MS. In practice, a second TLC plate is prepared and developed, but is not sprayed or dipped with color reagents. Instead, the area of the plate corresponding to the unknown spot is scraped (or cut from a Toxi-Gram®), and the drug is eluted into a solvent. The solvent is evaporated, and the residue is redissolved and analyzed by GC/MS. This procedure should produce a single major peak on the GC/MS that corresponds to the unknown spot on the TLC plate. The spectrum of the major peak can then be searched to identify the unknown.

GC/MS is often used to identify the drug, or drugs, giving rise to a positive result in a class selective immunoassay test. Such analyses are most efficiently accomplished by methods that search an area of the chromatogram for patterns matching reference spectra in a computer library. The library is generated by analyzing a standard of each of the targeted drugs and storing a representative spectrum in the data system.[92,199,256,325] The search can be programmed to take place automatically at the end of each data file acquisition. However, the data must be reviewed by the operator before reporting.

GC/MS data can be used for both identification and confirmation in drug screening.[318,320,321,325-327] However, for it to serve as a final confirmation test, the GC/MS analysis should be performed on a separate aliquot or a different specimen from that which yields the initial presumptive finding.

12.3.7.4 High Performance Liquid Chromatography (HPLC)

High performance liquid chromatography utilizes a column filled with microscopic particles of silica, or resin particles coated with a polymer whose side chains have specific functional groups.[57,59,64,69,328-332] The polymer is the stationary phase in HPLC, and the nature of the side. chains determines the type of interactions the column will have with analytes. Various normal phases and reverse phases are available. Normal phases are characterized by polar side chains such as silica, diol, amino and cyano, whereas reverse phases have nonpolar side chains such as 8 carbon (C-8) and 18 carbon (C-18) aliphatic and phenyl moieties. Anion and cation exchange phases are also available.

The mobile phase in HPLC is a mixed solvent containing a buffer to suppress or induce ionization of analytes as required for the intended separation. The solvent composition may be kept constant (isocratic) or the percentages of components may be varied (gradient) during the analysis. For instance, in reverse phase HPLC, the mobile phase will start at higher polarity. As the run proceeds, the polarity is decreased, enabling the removal of any remaining nonpolar substances from the nonpolar reverse phase column, while decreasing the tendency towards broad peaks near the end of a run.

12.3.7.4.1 Ultraviolet Absorption Detectors

The most common detection systems for HPLC are ultraviolet absorption detectors.[56,64,72,331,332] The less expensive detectors measure absorption at a single wavelength which may be fixed (e.g., at 254 nm or 280 nm) or variable over a range of 190 to over 340 nm. The variable wavelength detectors are set to a desired wavelength by the operator, and some can be programmed to change wavelengths during the analysis. However, the time required to change wavelengths precludes using variable wavelength detectors for spectral scanning of peaks.

12.3.7.4.2 Diode Array Detectors

A relatively recent advance is the introduction of the photo diode array detector which simultaneously measures absorbance at many small wavelength increments over a broad wavelength band.[46,57,58,64,69,70,73,74,333-348] The detector uses a diffraction grating to break the light beam into a spectrum that is focused onto an array of UV sensitive photo diodes. Thus UV spectra of individual peaks can be recorded. A data processing system enables the instrument to determine peak purity by comparing spectra at the leading and tailing ends of a peak and to create and search libraries of target analyte spectra. The sensitivity of the diode array detector is lower than that of the fixed or variable wavelength, but the availability of spectral data makes it a valuable tool for drug screening.

12.3.7.4.3 Fluorescence Detectors

Fluorescence detectors, with variable excitation and emission wavelengths, provide high sensitivity and specificity for the detection and quantification of fluorescent compounds, but they are more useful for quantification than for screening. Fluorescence detection could be used to provide a sensitive screen to target a single substance or a group of substances with similar fluorescence characteristics and different retention times.[56-59]

12.3.7.4.4 Advantages and Disadvantages of HPLC

HPLC systems can be had with autosamplers, manual injectors or both. In general, the greatest screening efficiency is achieved through automation. Increased applications of HPLC for drug screening are likely. Substantially more definitive drug identification can be achieved by the use of a mass spectrometer as the HPLC detector. The high cost of these liquid chromatograph/ mass spectrometer-coupled instruments limits their current usage for general drug screening or confirmation.

HPLC is a more expensive and labor intensive and less sensitive analytical technique than GC, so it is less commonly used for screening. However, it can be used to detect many drugs and poisons that are thermolabile, too polar or lacking in sufficient volatility for analysis by GC. In addition to the qualitative information obtained from the chromatographic retention time, quantification can also be obtained. The signal generated by the detector is proportional to the amount of substance detected. Therefore, by preparing standards of known concentration and treating them in like fashion to the case specimen, the amount of toxin in the specimen can be quantified. The precision of the quantification can be enhanced by adding an internal standard at the beginning of the extraction. The internal standard is usually a compound with similar extraction and chromatographic characteristics to the analytes of interest. The presence of the internal standard permits the quantification to be based on the ratio of analyte to internal standard peak heights or areas. Because ratios are used instead of absolute amounts, the need for quantitative transfers in the extraction process is removed.

Wm. Lee Hearn and H. Chip Walls

12.3.7.4.5 REMEDiHS™HPLC

A commercial, completely automated HPLC system designed for drug screening is now available (REMEDi HS™; Bio-Rad Laboratories, Hercules, CA).[349-352] This system utilizes four columns in series and column switching techniques to extract, separate, and perform a spectral scan on eluted drugs. Identification of about 500 drugs and metabolites is based on computer matching of retention time and spectra with comparable data stored in the drug library.

Quantitation of identified drugs may also be performed. REMEDi HS™ was developed for the clinical laboratory, but it can be adapted for postmortem drug screening. Urine, serum and plasma can be analyzed directly, but whole blood and tissues require manual extraction prior to analysis. Sensitivity for many drugs is not as good as GC with NPD, but should be sufficient for screening urine or stomach contents. If REMEDi HS™is applied to screening blood or tissues, sensitivity may not be adequate to detect therapeutic or intoxicating concentrations of some important drugs, but should be adequate for detecting lethal concentrations.

The REMEDi HS™ system can be complimentary to other drug screening techniques, detecting drugs that would otherwise be overlooked and providing corroborative evidence to confirm identifications.

12.3.8 ULTRAVIOLET-VISIBLE SPECTROPHOTOMETRY (UV-VIS)

Ultraviolet-visible (UV-Vis) spectrophotometry, was one of the earliest instrumental techniques used in postmortem forensic toxicology.[26-29] The use of ultraviolet and visible spectrophotometry as a screening tool is based upon the fact that many drugs contain aromatic nuclei that absorb light in the UV and visible regions. Such drugs have absorption spectra with maxima and minima at characteristic wavelengths. Furthermore, the spectrum often changes with the ionization state of the drug in acidic or basic solutions. UV absorption maxima and entire spectra of drugs and poisons are available from various references.

Several limitations, however, affect the use of spectrophotometry. The major limitation is the lack of sensitivity required to detect many of today's therapeutic or misused drugs. Another drawback of spectrophotometry is the requirement that the drug be isolated in a form free from substances with overlapping spectra. Drug mixtures and impure extracts yield mixed spectra that may not be interpretable. In addition, spectrophotometry is not able to distinguish between the parent drug and metabolites. Some of a drug's metabolites may be active while others are inactive, and there is a need to distinguish between these compounds. In spite of these deficiencies, a role remains for spectrophotometric methods for some drug and toxicant analyses. UV spectrometry is especially useful for purity and concentration checks of primary and stock standards.

12.3.9 SPECTROSCOPIC METHODS FOR ANALYSIS OF TOXIC METALS AND METALOIDS

Toxicologists should be prepared to support investigations that involve toxic exposure to metals and metalloids. Proper sample collection and rigorous state-of the-art analytical techniques are critical to prevent exogenous contamination.[353,354] A number of different techniques may be employed for the identification of such compounds: flame atomic absorption spectroscopy (FAAS),[355] graphite furnace atomic absorption spectroscopy (GF-AAS),[356,357] inductively coupled plasma-emission spectroscopy (ICPAES)[358] and inductively coupled plasma-mass spectrometry (ICP-MS)[358,359] may all be used. These are sensitive and specific techniques that provide the laboratory with the capability to measure a broad range of metals. An in-depth discussion of methods used for metal analysis is beyond the scope of this chapter.

12.3.10 SAMPLE PREPARATION

12.3.10.1 Extraction Methods

There are two approaches to the screening of biofluids for drugs or poisons. One is the direct analysis of the specimen for the presence of a specific analyte or its class, without isolation or purification. The other is isolation of the analyte from the sample followed by instrumental analysis of the concentrated extract. The most common example of this is liquid-liquid extraction of an appropriately buffered sample with an immicible organic solvent.[21,23,25,43,65,66,71,314,360-371] The proper choice of sample, pH and solvent will effectively remove the target analytes from the aqueous sample matrix.[21,25,362,371-373] Separation of an analyte from interfering substances usually will require more involved techniques.

12.3.10.1.1 Liquid-Liquid Extraction

The liquid-liquid extraction technique dates back to the mid-nineteenth century when Stas and Otto developed extraction schemes for nonvolatile organic compounds. The method utilizes differences in the pH and solubility characteristics of various analytes. A basic compound is in the non-ionized form in alkaline pH; an acidic compound is in the ionized form in a similar medium. A compound in its non-ionized form prefers the lipophilic environment of an organic solvent to the aqueous environment of the biologic sample. It is on this basis that the separation of drugs from the biologic matrix occurs. The specimen is buffered according to the pH characteristics of the analyte(s) of interest and mixed with an immiscible organic solvent. Commonly used nonpolar solvents are hexane, toluene, diethyl ether, dichloromethane, chloroform, or mixtures of these. Ionized compounds and many of the biologic components such as proteins remain in the aqueous layer while the un-ionized drug molecules are transferred to the organic solvent.

The extraction process can be illustrated by taking as an example a basic drug of pK 8, present in plasma. If the plasma is brought to pH 10 using a suitable alkali or alkaline buffer and is shaken with a suitable organic solvent, the drug will be removed from the aqueous into the organic phase. Unfortunately, many endogenous bases and neutral compounds will also be extracted if they are soluble in the organic solvent. The organic phase is then separated from the aqueous phase (using a Pasteur pipet, for example). This is usually done after centrifugation, to completely separate the two phases.

For drugs that behave like strong acids and bases, a further purification step, called back-extraction can be carried out. By shaking the organic phase with dilute acid, such as 0. 1 N sulfuric, the basic drug will now be ionized and will no longer be as soluble in the organic phase: it will be extracted into the aqueous phase. Any neutral compounds will be left behind in the organic phase. Endogenous bases may also be co-extracted with the basic drug, but by carefully choosing the pH and the organic solvent the amounts of these bases can be reduced. The acidic aqueous phase is then made alkaline by the addition of a base, such as 2 N sodium hydroxide, and shaken with fresh organic solvent to take the drug into the organic phase. The organic phase can be separated, evaporated, reconstituted and analyzed.

In many methods the organic phase, containing the drug, is washed with water, and the washings are discarded. This step must be carefully controlled. For example, if the drug is a moderate to strong base and the wash water is even slightly acidic, then some of the drug may be removed into the aqueous phase. If such a process takes place, then low and very erratic recoveries will result.

Wm. Lee Hearn and H. Chip Walls

Before leaving the subject of solvent extraction a number of simple points should to be emphasized:

1. In general the least polar solvent capable of extracting the drug in question should be used in order to reduce the possibility of co-extracting endogenous materials. The least polar solvents are the hydrocarbons, such as hexane, toluene, chlorinated hydrocarbons, and diethyl and related ethers. Ethyl acetate is more polar, and the short chain alcohols are very polar and miscible with water to a greater or lesser degree.

2. Many drugs are so highly lipid soluble that they can be extracted into nonpolar solvents, even in the ionized state. For example, the β-adrenoreceptor blocking drug propranolol has a pK, of about 9.5, and therefore in a pH 7.4 buffer it is more than 99% ionized. Since its partition coefficient, between n-octanol and pH 7.4 buffer at 37°C, is 20.2, this means that the ionized drug is highly soluble in n-octanol.

3. Many extraction procedures employ a ratio of solvent to aqueous phase greater than unity in order to reduce the possibility of emulsion formation during extraction. The ideal is a 10:1 solvent to sample ratio. There are, however, successful methods that use ratios very much less than unity. Troublesome emulsions can also be avoided or reduced by saturating the aqueous phase with an inorganic salt, such as sodium chloride, before extraction.

4. Recoveries can be increased by using mixed solvents such as hexane: butanol (9:1) or hexane-isoamyl alcohol (97:3). Such solvents are also mandatory to efficiently extract polar drugs or metabolites.

5. Extraction conditions should always be optimized using the relevant biological fluid. It should not be assumed that the extractability from water will exactly match that from blood or tissue homogenates.

6. When extraction conditions have been optimized, it is worthwhile to put a series of specimens through the complete procedure, half of them diluted approximately 10-fold. Although this does not always succeed, it can result in cleaner extracts.

7. The multiple step liquid–liquid extraction process is quite effective in separating analytes from biologic specimens, but is also time consuming. In an attempt to alleviate this time related problem, solid phase extraction (SPE) techniques have been developed.

12.3.10.1.2 Solid Phase Extraction

In SPE, the specimen is applied to a solid packing material, which is usually, but not exclusively, silica gel based. The sample is partitioned between the matrix and the solid phase, which provides the separation. The general process of SPE involves several steps: (1) column conditioning, (2) addition of specimen, (3) column washing with solvents to remove interfering substances, and (4) analyte elution.[46-53,55,57,59,63,69,70,72,82,91,308,374-391] Each individual step depends on the analyte of interest, or the type of extraction column, and method development frequently involves a significant amount of trial and error.

12.3.10.1.3 pH Adjustment for Extraction

Weakly acidic drugs, such as barbiturates, primidone, and phenytoin, can be separated from the specimen by using a liquid-liquid, or solid phase extraction at pH 5. This extraction also removes some neutral drugs, such as meprobamate, glutethimide, and carbamazepine. After solvent concentration, these drugs can be identified by TLC, GC, or HPLC.

The largest group of drugs that are normally encountered in the postmortem laboratory are the organic bases. These include antiarrhythmics, antidepressants, antihistamines, benzodiazepines, cocaine, narcotic analgesics, nicotine, phencyclidine, phenothiazines, and sympathomimetic amines. These drugs all extract under alkaline conditions.

Amphoteric drugs such as morphine and benzoylecgonine require careful adjustment of pH for their efficient extraction by liquid-liquid procedures. Amphoteric compounds contain both acidic and basic functional groups. If the aqueous phase is too acidic or too basic, one of the functional groups will be ionized, and extraction will be inefficient. The pH must be close to the isoelectric point for high recovery by liquid-liquid extraction. Such compounds may be isolated by solid phase techniques, if a column with ion exchange functions is used. The pH is adjusted to completely ionize one of the functional groups in the analyte The appropriate solid phase will capture ionized analyte as the sample passes through. The sorbent is washed to remove impurities, and then the analyte is recovered in either an acidic or basic elution solvent in order to reverse its ionization.

12.3.10.2 Hydrolysis to Release Drugs in Sample Pretreatment

Before extraction, tissues may be homogenized with a blender or an ultrasonic disruptor, or they may be hydrolyzed by enzymes such as Subtilysin Carlsburg or Protease K to produce a homogeneous fluid sample. [39,365,378,392] Conjugates can be cleaved by gentle but time consuming enzymatic hydrolysis, or by rapid acid hydrolysis.[34,53,117,224,227,394] However, the formation of artifacts during the latter procedure must be considered.

12.3.10.3 Applications

Universal liquid-liquid extraction procedures are preferable for general unknown analysis because substances with very different physico-chemical properties must be isolated from heterogeneous matrices. On the other hand, solid-phase extraction is preferable if target compounds must be selectively isolated from relatively homogeneous samples, such as urine for confirmation of a single drug, or metabolite, or a group of drugs with similar extraction properties.

REFERENCES

1. Jackson, J. V., Forensic toxicology, in *Clarke's Isolation and Identification of Drugs in Pharmaceuticals, Body Fluids, and Post-mortem Material*, Moffatt, A. C., 2 nd Edition, The Pharmaceutical Press, London, 1986, p 35.
2. Jentzen, J. M., Forensic toxicology. An overview and an algorithmic approach, *American Journal of Clinical Pathology*, 92, S48-55, 1989.
3. Stewart, C. P., Martin, G J, The Mode of Action of Poisons, in *Toxicology: Mechanisms and Analytical Methods*, Stewart, C. P., Stolman, A, Eds., Vol. 2, Academic Press, New York, 1960, p 1-15.
4. Stewart, C. P., Stolman, A, The toxicologist and his work, in *Toxicology: Mechanisms and Analytical Methods*, Stewart, C. P., Stolman, A, Eds., Vol. 1, Academic Press, New York, 1960, p 1-22.
5. Garriott, J. C., Drug analysis in postmortem toxicology, *Chem. Anal. (N.Y.)*, 85, 353-376, 1986.
6. Costello, C. E., GC/MS analysis of street drugs, particularly in the body fluids of overdose victims., in *Street Drug Analysis and Its Social and Clinical Implications.*, John Wiley and Son, New York, 1974, p 67-78.
7. Walker, S. and Johnston, A., Laboratory screening of body fluids in self poisoning and drug abuse, *Annals of the Academy of Medicine, Singapore*, 20, 91-94, 1991.

Wm. Lee Hearn and H. Chip Walls

8. Duncan, W. P. and Deutsch, D. G., The use of GC/IR/MS for high-confidence identification of drugs, *Clinical Chemistry,* 35, 1279-1281, 1989.
9. Kinberger, B., Holmen, A., and Wahrgren, P., A strategy for drug analysis in serum and urine. An application to drug screening of samples from drivers involved in traffic accidents., *Anal. Lett.,* 15, 937-951, 1982.
10. Rowley, G. L., Armstrong, T. A., Crowl, C. P., Eimstad, W. M., Hu, W. M., Kam, J. K., *et al.,* Determination of THC and its metabolites by EMIT homogeneous enzyme immunoassay: a summary report, *NIDA Research Monograph,* 7, 28-32, 1976.
11. Walberg, C. B., Correlation of the "EMIT" urine barbiturate assay with a spectrophotometric serum barbiturate assay in suspected overdose, *Clinical Chemistry,* 20, 305-306, 1974.
12. Cavanagh, K., Draisey, T. F., and Thibert, R. J., Assessment of the EMIT™ technique as a screening test for opiates and methadone for a methadone maintenance clinic and its calibration by Bayesian statistics, *Clinical Biochemistry,* 11, 210-213, 1978.
13 Oellerich, M., Kulpmann, W. R., and Haeckel, R., Drug screening by enzyme immunoassay (EMIT) and thin-layer chromatography (Drug Skreen), *Journal of Clinical Chemistry & Clinical Biochemistry,* 15, 275-283, 1977.
14. Fletcher, S. M., Urine screening for drugs by EMIT, *Journal - Forensic Science Society,* 21, 327-332, 1981.
15. Davidow, B., Li Petri, N., and Quame, B., A thin-layer chromatographic screening procedure for detecting drug abuse, *Technical Bulletin of the Registry of Medical Technologists,* 38,298-303,1968.
16. Kaistha, K. K. and Jaffe, J. H., TLC techniques for identification of narcotics, barbiturates, and CNS stimulants in a drug abuse urine screening program, *Journal of Pharmaceutical Sciences,* 61, 679-689, 1972.
17. Siek, T., Thin-layer and gas chromatography as identification aids in forensic science., *Analabs (Res. notes),* 13, 1-15, 1973.
18. Davidow, B., Quame, B., Abell, L. L., and Lim, B., Screening for drug abuse, *Health Laboratory Science,* 10, 329-334, 1973.
19. Davidow, B. and Fastlich, E., The application of thin-layer chromatography and of other methods for the detection of drug abuse, *Progress in Clinical Pathology,* 5, 85-98, 1973.
20. Masoud, A. N., Systematic identification of drugs of abuse II: TLC, *Journal of Pharmaceutical Sciences,* 65, 1585-1589, 1976.
21. Hackett, L. P. and Dusci, L. J., Rapid identification of drugs in the overdosed patient, *Clinical Toxicology,* 11, 341-352, 1977.
22. Sunshine, I., *CRC Handbook Serries in Clinical Laboratory Science: Section B Toxicology Volumn I,* CRC Press, West Palm Beach, FL,1978, p 3-269.
23. Warfield, R. W. and Maickel, R. P., A generalized extraction-TLC procedure for identification of drugs, *Journal of Applied Toxicology,* 3, 51-57, 1983.
24. Foerster, E. H., Hatchett, H , Garriott, J C, A rapid, comprehensive screening procedure for basic drugs in blood or tissues by gas chromatography, *Journal of Analytical Toxicology,* 2, 50-55, 1978.
25. Dusci, L. J. and Hackett, L. P., The detection of some basic drugs and their major metabolites using gas-liquid chromatography, *Clinical Toxicology,* 14, 587-593, 1979.
26. Siek, T. J. and Osiewicz, R. J., Identification of drugs and other toxic compounds from their ultraviolet spectra. Part II: Ultraviolet absorption properties of thirteen structural groups, *Journal of Forensic Sciences,* 20, 18-37, 1975.
27. Siek, T. J., Osiewicz, R. J., and Bath, R. J., Identification of drugs and other toxic compounds from their ultraviolet spectra. Part III: Ultraviolet absorption properties of 22 structural groups, *Journal of Forensic Sciences,* 21, 525-551, 1976.
28. Feldstein, M., Spectrum Analysis: B. Absorption Spectra Part 1: The Use of Ultraviolet Spectra in Toxicological Analysis, in *Toxicology: Mechanisms and Analytical Methods,*Stewart, C. P., Stolman, A, Eds., Vol. 1, Academic Press, New York, 1960, p 464-506.
29. Curry, S., Spectrum Analysis: B. Absorption Spectra Part 2: Ultraviolet Spectrophotometry, in *Toxicology: Mechanisms and Analytical Methods,* Stewart, C. P., Stolman, A, Eds., Vol. 1, Academic Press, New York, 1960, p 507-555.

30. Demedts, P., De Waele, M., Van der Verren, J., and Heyndrickx, A., Application of the combined use of fused silica capillary columns and NPD for the toxicological determination of codeine and ethylmorphine in a human overdose case, *Journal of Analytical Toxicology*, 7, 113-115, 1983.

31. Anderson, W. H. and Archuleta, M. M., The capillary gas chromatographic determination of trazodone in biological specimens, *Journal of Analytical Toxicology*, 8, 217-219, 1984.

32. Francom, P., Andrenyak, D., Lim, H. K., Bridges, R. R., Foltz, R. L., and Jones, R. T., Determination of LSD in urine by capillary column gas chromatography and electron impact mass spectrometry, *Journal of Analytical Toxicology*, 12, 1-8, 1988.

33. Feng, N., Vollenweider, F. X., Minder, E. I., Rentsch, K., Grampp, T., and Vonderschmitt, D. J., Development of a gas chromatography-mass spectrometry method for determination of ketamine in plasma and its application to human samples, *Therapeutic Drug Monitoring*, 17, 95-100, 1995.

34. Meatherall, R., GC/MS confirmation of urinary benzodiazepine metabolites, *Journal of Analytical Toxicology*, 18, 369-381, 1994.

35. Taylor, R. W., Greutink, C., and Jain, N. C., Identification of underivatized basic drugs in urine by capillary column gas chromatography, *Journal of Analytical Toxicology*, 10, 205-208, 1986.

36. Christophersen, A. S., Biseth, A., Skuterud, B., and Gadeholt, G., Identification of opiates in urine by capillary column gas chromatography of two different derivatives, *Journal of Chromatography*, 422, 117-124, 1987.

37. Lee, X. P., Kumazawa, T., and Sato, K., Rapid extraction and capillary gas chromatography for diazine herbicides in human body fluids, *Forensic Science International*, 72, 199-207, 1995.

38. Seno, H., Suzuki, O., Kumazawa, T., and Hattori, H., Rapid isolation with Sep-Pak C18 cartridges and wide-bore capillary gas chromatography of benzophenones, the acid-hydrolysis products of benzodiazepines, *Journal of Analytical Toxicology*, 15, 21-24, 1991.

39. Turcant, A., Premel-Cabic, A., Cailleux, A., and Allain, P., Screening for neutral and basic drugs in blood by dual fused-silica column chromatography with nitrogen-phosphorus detection [published erratum appears in Clin Chem 1988 Nov;34(11):2370], *Clinical Chemistry*, 34, 1492-1497, 1988.

40. Watts, V. W. and Simonick, T. F., Screening of basic drugs in biological samples using dual column capillary chromatography and nitrogen-phosphorus detectors, *Journal of Analytical Toxicology*, 10, 198-204, 1986.

41. Anderson, W. H. and Fuller, D. C., A simplified procedure for the isolation, characterization, and identification of weak acid and neutral drugs from whole blood, *Journal of Analytical Toxicology*, 11, 198-204, 1987.

42. Cox, R.A.,Crifasi,J.A.,Dickey, R. E., Ketzler, S. C., and Pshak, G. L., A single-step extraction for screening whole blood for basic drugs by capillary GC/NPD, *Journal of Analytical Toxicology*, 13, 224-228, 1989.

43. Fretthold, D., Jones, P., Sebrosky, G., and Sunshine, I., Testing for basic drugs in biological fluids by solvent extraction and dual capillary GC/NPD, *Journal of Analytical Toxicology*, 10, 10-14, 1986.

44. Perrigo, B. J., Peel, H. W., and Ballantyne, D. J., Use of dual-column fused-silica capillary gas chromatography in combination with detector response factors for analytical toxicology, *Journal of Chromatography*, 341, 81-88, 1985.

45. Bogusz, M., Bialka, J., Gierz, J., and Klys, M., Use of short, wide-bore capillary columns in GC toxicological screening, *Journal of Analytical Toxicology*, 10, 135-138, 1986.

46. Theodoridis, G., Papadoyannis, I., Tsoukali-Papadopoulou, H., and Vasilikiotis, G., A comparative study of different solid phase extraction procedures for the analysis of alkaloids of forensic interest in biological fluids by RP-HPLC/diode array, *Journal of Liquid Chromatography*, 18, 1973-1995, 1973.

47. Taylor, R. W., Jain, N. C., and George, M. P., Simultaneous identification of cocaine and benzoylecgonine using solid phase extraction and gas chromatography/mass spectrometry, *Journal of Analytical Toxicology*, 11, 233-234, 1987.

48. Casas, M., Berrueta, L. A., Gallo, B., and Vicente, F., Solid phase extraction conditions for the selective isolation of drugs from biological fluids predicted using liquid chromatography, *Chromatographia,* 34, 79-82, 1992.

49. Platoff, G. E., Jr. and Gere, J. A., Solid phase extraction of abused drugs from urine, *Forensic Sci. Rev.,* 3, 117-133, 1992.

50. Chen, X. H., Hommerson, A. L., Zweipfenning, P. G., Franke, J. P., Harmen-Boverhof, C. W., Ensing, K., *et al.,* Solid phase extraction of morphine from whole blood by means of Bond Elut Certify columns, *Journal of Forensic Sciences,* 38, 668-676, 1993.

51. Dixit, V. and Dixit, V. M., Solid Phase Extraction of Phencyclidine with GC/MS Confirmation, *Indian J Chem Sect B,* 30, 164-168, 1991.

52. Marko, V. and Bauerova, K., Study of the Solid Phase Extraction of Pentoxifylline and Its Major Metabolite as a Basis of Their Rapid Low Concentration Gas Chromatographic Determination in Serum, *Biomed Chromatogr,* 5, 256-261, 1991.

53. Huang, W., Andollo, W., and Hearn, W. L., A solid phase extraction technique for the isolation and identification of opiates in urine, *Journal of Analytical Toxicology,* 16, 307-310, 1992.

54. Kintz, P., Tracqui, A., Mangin, P., Lugnier, A., and Chaumont, A., Subnanogram GC/NPD method for the determination of sparteine in biological fluids, *Methods & Findings in Experimental & Clinical Pharmacology,* 11, 115-118, 1989.

55. Taylor, R. W., Le, S. D., Philip, S., and Jain, N. C., Simultaneous identification of amphetamine and methamphetamine using solid-phase extraction and GC/NPD or GC/MS, *J. Anal. Toxicol.,* 13, 293-295, 1989.

56. Binder, S. R., Analysis of Drugs of Abuse in Biological Fluids by Liquid Chromatography, in *Advances in Chromatography,* Brown, P., Grushka, E, Eds., Vol. 36, Marcel Dekker, Inc, New York, 1996.

57. Akerman, K. K., Jolkkonen, J., Parviainen, M., and Penttila, I., Analysis of low-dose benzodiazepines by HPLC with automated solid-phase extraction, *Clinical Chemistry,* 42, 1412-1416, 1996.

58. Clauwaert, K. M., Vanbocxlaer, J. F., Lambert, W. E., and Deleenheer, A. P., Analysis of Cocaine, Benzoylecgonine, and Cocaethylene in Urine By HPLC With Diode Array Detection, *Analytical Chemistry,* 68, 3021-3028, 1996.

59. Bourque, A. J., Krull, I. S., and Feibush, B., Automated HPLC analyses of drugs of abuse via direct injection of biological fluids followed by simultaneous solid-phase extraction and derivatization with fluorescence detection, *Biomedical Chromatography,* 8, 53-62, 1994.

60. Gill, R., Moffat, A. C., Smith, R. M., and Hurdley, T. G., A collaborative study to investigate the retention reproducibility of barbiturates in HPLC with a view to establishing retention databases for drug identification, *Journal of Chromatographic Science,* 24, 153-159, 1986.

61. Bogusz, M., Hill, D. W., and Rehorek, A., Comparability of RP-HPLC Retention indices of drugs in three databases, *Journal of Liquid Chromatography & Related Technologies 19(8):1291-1316,* 1996.

62. Law, B., Williams, P. L., and Moffat, A. C., The detection and quantification of cannabinoids in blood and urine by RIA, HPLC/RIA and GC/MS, *Veterinary & Human Toxicology,* 21, 144-147, 1979.

63. Moore, C., Browne, S., Tebbett, I., and Negrusz, A., Determination of cocaine and its metabolites in brain tissue using high-flow solid-phase extraction columns and HPLC, *Forensic Sci. Int.,* 53, 215-219, 1992.

64. Wong, A. S., An evaluation of HPLC for the screening and quantitation of benzodiazepines and acetaminophen in post mortem blood, *Journal of Analytical Toxicology,* 7, 33-36, 1983.

65. Bernal, J. L., Delnozal, M. J., Rosas, V., and Villarino, A., Extraction of basic drugs from whole blood and determination by HPLC, *Chromatographia,* 38, 617-623, 1994.

66. Pawula, M., Barrett, D. A., and Shaw, P. N., An improved extraction method for the HPLC determination of morphine and its metabolites in plasma, *Journal of Pharmaceutical & Biomedical Analysis,* 11, 401-406, 1993.

67. Bogusz, M., Influence of elution conditions on HPLC retention index values of selected acidic and basic drugs measured in the 1-nitroalkane scale, *Journal of Analytical Toxicology*, 15, 174-178, 1991.

68. Bogusz, M. and Erkens, M., Influence of biological matrix on chromatographic behavior and detection of selected acidic, neutral, and basic drugs examined by means of a standardized HPLC-DAD system, *Journal of Analytical Toxicology*, 19, 49-55, 1995.

69. Logan, B. K., Stafford, D. T., Tebbett, I. R., and Moore, C. M., Rapid screening for 100 basic drugs and metabolites in urine using cation exchange solid-phase extraction and HPLC with diode array detection, *J. Anal. Toxicol.*, 14, 154-159, 1990.

70. Musshoff, F. and Daldrup, T., A rapid solid-phase extraction and HPLC/DAD procedure for the simultaneous determination and quantification of different benzodiazepines in serum, blood and post-mortem blood, *International Journal of Legal Medicine*, 105, 105-109, 1992.

71. Mayer, F., Kramer, B. K., Ress, K. M., Kuhlkamp, V., Liebich, H. M., Risler, T., *et al.*, Simplified, Rapid and Inexpensive Extraction Procedure for a High-Performance Liquid Chromatographic Method for Determination of Disopyramide and Its Main Metabolite Mono-N-Dealkylated Disopyramide in Serum, *J Chromatogr*, 572, 339-345, 1991.

72. Ferrara, S. D., Tedeschi, L., Frison, G., and Castagna, F., Solid-phase extraction and HPLC-UV confirmation of drugs of abuse in urine, *Journal of Analytical Toxicology*, 16, 217-222, 1992.

73. Bogusz, M. and Wu, M., Standardized HPLC/DAD system, based on retention indices and 3spectral library, applicable for systematic toxicological screening [published erratum appears in J Anal Toxicol 1992 May-Jun;16(3):16A], *Journal of Analytical Toxicology*, 15, 188-197, 1991.

74. Tracqui, A., Kintz, P., and Mangin, P., Systematic toxicological analysis using HPLC/DAD, *Journal of Forensic Sciences*, 40, 254-262, 1995.

75. Wu, A. H., Onigbinde, T. A., Wong, S. S., and Johnson, K. G., Evaluation of full-scanning GC/ion trap MS analysis of NIDA drugs-of-abuse urine testing in urine, *Journal of Analytical Toxicology*, 16, 202-206, 1992.

76. Schuberth, J., Volatile compounds detected in blood of drunk drivers by headspace/capillary gas chromatography/ion trap mass spectrometry, *Biological Mass Spectrometry*, 20, 699-702, 1991.

77. McCurdy, H. H., Lewellen, L. J., Callahan, L. S., and Childs, P. S., Evaluation of the Ion Trap Detector for the detection of 11-nor-delta 9-THC-9-carboxylic acid in urine after extraction by bonded-phase adsorption, *Journal of Analytical Toxicology*, 10, 175-177, 1986.

78. Hernandez, A., Andollo, W., and Hearn, W. L., Analysis of cocaine and metabolites in brain using solid phase extraction and full-scanning gas chromatography/ion trap mass spectrometry, *Forensic Science International*, 65, 149-156, 1994.

79. Moody, D. E., Rittenhouse, L. F., and Monti, K. M., Analysis of forensic specimens for cannabinoids. I. Comparison of RIA and GC/MS analysis of blood, *Journal of Analytical Toxicology*, 16, 297-301, 1992.

80. Pettersen, J. E. and Skuterud, B., Application of combined GC/MS as compared to a conventional analytical system for identification of unknown drugs in acute drug intoxications., *Anal. Chem. Symp. Ser.*, 13, 111-129, 1983.

81. Ullucci, P. A., Cadoret, R., Stasiowski, D., and Martin, H. F., A comprehensive GC/MS drug screening procedure., *J. Anal. Toxicol.*, 2, 33-35, 1978.

82. Lillsunde, P. and Korte, T., Comprehensive drug screening in urine using solid-phase extraction and combined TLC and GC/MS identification, *Journal of Analytical Toxicology*, 15, 71-81, 1991.

83. Finkle, B. S., Foltz, R. L., and Taylor, D. M., A comprehensive GC/MS reference data system for toxicological and biomedical purposes., *J. Chromatogr. Sci.*, 12, 304-328, 1974.

84. Clouette, R., Jacob, M., Koteel, P., and Spain, M., Confirmation of 11-nor-delta 9-tetrahydrocannabinol in urine as its t-butyldimethylsilyl derivative using GC/MS, *Journal of Analytical Toxicology*, 17, 1-4, 1993.

85. Bellanca, J. A., Davis, P. L., Donnelly, B., Dal Cortivo, L. A., and Weinberg, S. B., Detection and quantitation of multiple volatile compounds in tissues by GC and GC/MS, *Journal of Analytical Toxicology,* 6, 238-240, 1982.

86. Fehn, J. and Megges, G., Detection of O6-monoacetylmorphine in urine samples by GC/MS as evidence for heroin use, *Journal of Analytical Toxicology,* 9, 134-138, 1985.

87. Dunemann, L. and Hajimiragha, H., Development of a screening method for the determination of volatile organic compounds in body fluids and environmental samples using purge and trap GC/MS, *Anal. Chim. Acta,* 283, 199-, 1993.

88. West, R. and Ritz, D., GC/MS analysis of five common benzodiazepine metabolites in urine as tert-butyl-dimethylsilyl derivatives, *Journal of Analytical Toxicology,* 17, 114-116, 1993.

89. Wimbish, G. H. and Johnson, K. G., Full spectral GC/MS identification of delta 9-carboxy-tetrahydrocannabinol in urine with the Finnigan ITS40, *Journal of Analytical Toxicology,* 14, 292-295, 1990.

90. Zune, A., Dobberstein, P., Maurer, K. H., and Rapp, U., Identification of drugs using a gas chromatography-mass spectrometry system equipped with electron impact-chemical ionization and electron impact-field ionizationfield desorption combination sources, *Journal of Chromatography,* 122, 365-371, 1976.

91. Liu, R. H., McKeehan, A. M., Edwards, C., Foster, G., Bensley, W. D., Langner, J. G., *et al.,* Improved GC/MS analysis of barbiturates in urine using centrifuge-based solid-phase extraction, methylation, with d$_5$- pentobarbital as internal standard, *J. Forensic Sci.,* 39, 1504-1514, 1994.

92. Van Vyncht, G., Gaspar, P., DePauw, E., and Maguin-Register, G., Multi-residue screening and confirmatory analysis of anabolic steroids in urine by GC/MS/MS, *J. Chromatogr., A,* 683, 67-74, 1994.

93. Maurer, H. H., On the Metabolism and the Toxicological Analysis of Methylenedioxyphenyl-alkylamine Designer Drugs By Gas Chromatography Mass Spectrometry, *Therapeutic Drug Monitoring,* 18, 465-470, 1996.

94. Saady, J. J., Narasimhachari, N., and Blanke, R. V., Rapid, simultaneous quantification of morphine, codeine, and hydromorphone by GC/MS, *Journal of Analytical Toxicology,* 6, 235-237, 1982.

95. Wu Chen, N. B., Cody, J. T., Garriott, J. C., Foltz, R. L., Peat, M. A., and Schaffer, M. I., Recommended guidelines for forensic GC/MS procedures in toxicology laboratories associated with offices of medical examiners and/or coroners, *J. Forensic Sci.,* 35, 236-242, 1990.

96. Moeller, M., Doerr, G., and Warth, S., Simultaneous quantitation of delta-9-tetrahydrocannabinol (THC) and 11-nor-9-carboxy-delta-9-tetrahydrocannabinol (THC-COOH) in serum by GC/MS using deuterated internal standards and its application to a smoking study and forensic cases, *Journal of Forensic Sciences,* 37, 969-983, 1992.

97. Gibb, R. P., Cockerham, H., Goldfogel, G. A., Lawson, G. M., and Raisys, V. A., Substance abuse testing of urine by GC/MS in scanning mode evaluated by proficiency studies, TLC/GC, and EMIT, *Journal of Forensic Sciences,* 38, 124-133, 1993.

98. Maurer, H. H., Systematic toxicological analysis of drugs and their metabolites by gas chromatography-mass spectrometry. [Review], *Journal of Chromatography,* 580, 3-41, 1992.

99. Maurer, H. H. and Kraemer, T., Toxicological detection of selegiline and its metabolites in urine using fluorescence polarization immunoassay (FPIA) and gas chromatography-mass spectrometry (GC/MS) and differentiation by enantioselective GC/MS of the intake of selegiline from abuse of methamphetamine or amphetamine, *Archives of Toxicology,* 66, 675-678, 1992.

100. Covey, T. R., Lee, E. D., and Henion, J. D., High-speed LC/MS/MS for the determination of drugs in biological samples, *Anal. Chem.,* 58, 2453-2460, 1986.

101. Brotherton, H. O. and Yost, R. A., Determination of drugs in blood serum by MS/MS., *Anal. Chem.,* 55, 549-553, 1983.

102. Phillips, W. H., Jr., Ota, K., and Wade, N. A., Tandem mass spectrometry (MS/MS) utilizing electron impact ionization and multiple reaction monitoring for the rapid, sensitive, and specific identification and quantitation of morphine in whole blood, *Journal of Analytical Toxicology,* 13, 268-273, 1989.

103. Kerns, E., Lee, M. S., Mayol, R., and Klunk, L. J. Comparison of drug metabolite identification methods: Rapid MS/MS screening versus isolation and GC/MS analysis. in *38th ASMS Conference*. Tucson, AZ.1990.

104. Gilbert, J. D., Greber, T. F., Ellis, J. D., Barrish, A., Olah, T. V., Fernandez-Metzler, C., *et al.*, The development and cross-validation of methods based on radioimmunoassay and LC/MS/MS for the quantification of the class III antiarrhythmic agent, MK-0499, in human plasma and urine, *Journal of Pharmaceutical & Biomedical Analysis*, 13, 937-950, 1995.

105. Henion, J., Crowthers, J., and Covey, T., An improved thermospray LC/MS system for determining drugs in urine., *Proc. ASMS*, 32, 203-204, 1984.

106. Verheij, E. R., van der Greef, J., La Vos, G. F., van der Pol, W., and Niessen, W. M., Identification of diuron and four of its metabolites in human postmortem plasma and urine by LC/MS with a moving-belt interface, *Journal of Analytical Toxicology*, 13, 8-12, 1989.

107. Koves, E. M. and Yen, B., The use of gas chromatography/negative ion chemical ionization mass spectrometry for the determination of lorazepam in whole blood, *Journal of Analytical Toxicology*, 13, 69-72, 1989.

108. Leloux, M. and Maes, R., The use of electron impact and positive chemical ionization mass spectrometry in the screening of beta blockers and their metabolites in human urine, *Biomedical & Environmental Mass Spectrometry*, 19, 137-142, 1990.

109. Cailleux, A. and Allain, P., Superiority of chemical ionization on electron impact for identification of drugs by GC/MS., *J. Anal. Toxicol.*, 3, 39-41, 1979.

110. Harkey, M. R., Henderson, G. L., and Zhou, C., Simultaneous quantitation of cocaine and its major metabolites in human hair by gas chromatography/chemical ionization mass spectrometry, *Journal of Analytical Toxicology*, 15, 260-265, 1991.

111. Ohno, Y. and Kawabata, S., Rapid detection of illicit drugs by direct inlet chemical ionization mass spectrometry, *Kanzei Chuo Bunsekishoho*, 27, 7-15, 1987.

112. Mulvana, D. E., Duncan, G. F., Shyu, W. C., Tay, L. K., and Barbhaiya, R. H., Quantitative Determination of Butorphanol and Its Metabolites in Human Plasma By Gas Chromatography Electron Capture Negative-Ion Chemical Ionization Mass Spectrometry, *Journal of Chromatography B: Biomedical Applications*, 682, 289-300, 1996.

113. Milne, G. W. A., Foles, H. M., and Axenrod, T., Identification of dangerous drugs by isobutane chemical ionization mass spectrometry., *Anal. Chem.*, 43, 1815-1820, 1971.

114. Wu, W. S., Szklar, R. S., and Smith, R., Gas chromatographic determination and negative-ion chemical ionization mass spectrometric confirmation of 4,4'-methylenebis(2-chloroaniline) in urine via thin-layer chromatographic separation, *Analyst*, 121, 321-324, 1996.

115. Saferstein, R., Manura, J. J., and De, P. K., Drug detection in urine by chemical ionization-mass spectrometry., *J. Forensic Sci.*, 23, 29-36, 1978.

116. Wolen, R. L., Ziege, E. A., and Gruber, C., Jr., Determination of propoxyphene and norpropoxyphene by chemical ionization mass fragmentography, *Clinical Pharmacology & Therapeutics*, 17, 15-20, 1975.

117. Fitzgerald, R. L., Rexin, D. A., and Herold, D. A., Benzodiazepine analysis by negative chemical ionization gas chromatography-mass spectrometry, *Journal of Analytical Toxicology*, 17, 342-347, 1993.

118. Suzuki, O., Hattori, H., and Asano, M., Detection of methamphetamine and amphetamine in a single human hair by gas chromatography-chemical ionization mass spectrometry, *Journal of Forensic Sciences*, 29, 611-617, 1984.

119. Sosnoff, C. S., Ann, Q., Bernert, J. T., Jr., Powell, M. K., Miller, B. B., Henderson, L. O., *et al.*, Analysis of benzoylecgonine in dried blood spots by liquid chromatography—atmospheric pressure chemical ionization tandem mass spectrometry, *Journal of Analytical Toxicology*, 20, 179-184, 1996.

120. Vidal, D. L., Ting, E. J., Perez, S. L., Taylor, R. W., and Le, S. D., Robotic method for the analysis of morphine and codeine in urine, *Journal of Forensic Sciences 37(5):1283-94*, 1992.

121. Lloyd, T. L., Perschy, T. B., Gooding, A. E., and Tomlinson, J. J., Robotic solid phase extraction and high performance liquid chromatographic analysis of ranitidine in serum or plasma, *Biomedical Chromatography*, 6, 311-316, 1992.

122. Taylor, R. W. and Le, S. D., Robotic method for the analysis of cocaine and benzoylecgonine in urine, *Journal of Analytical Toxicology,* 15, 276-278, 1991.

123. de Kanel, J., Korbar, T, Robotics and the Analysis of Drugs of Abuse, in *Analysis of Addictive and Misused Drugs,* Adamovics, J. A., Marcel Dekker, New York, 1995, p 267-294.

124. Clarke, E., Williams, M, Microcolor tests in toxicology, *Journal of Pharmacy and Pharmacology,* 7, 255-262, 1955.

125 Stevens, H. M., Color tests in *Clarke's Isolation and Identification of Drugs in Pharmacenticals, Body Fluids and Postmortem Material,* Moffat, A. C., Ed., The Pharmaceutical Press, London, 1986. p. 28-147.

126. Widdop, B., Hospital toxicology and drug abuse screening in *Clarke's Isolation and Identification of Drugs in Pharmceuticals, Body Fluids and Postmortem Mateiral,* Moffat, A. C., Ed., The Pharmaceutical Press, London, 1986. p. 4-6.

127. Masoud, A. N., Systematic identification of drugs of abuse I: spot tests, *Journal of Pharmaceutical Sciences,* 64, 841-844, 1975.

128. Berry, D. J. and Grove, J., Emergency toxicological screening for drugs commonly taken in overdose, *Journal of Chromatography,* 80, 205-220, 1973.

129. Trinder, P., Rapid determination of salicylates in biological materials, *Biochemical Journal,* 57, 1954.

130. King, J. A., Storrow, A. B., and Finkelstein, J. A., Urine Trinder spot test: a rapid salicylate screen for the emergency department, *Annals of Emergency Medicine,* 26, 330-333, 1995.

131. Stair, E. L. and Whaley, M., Rapid screening and spot tests for the presence of common poisons, *Veterinary & Human Toxicology,* 32, 564-566, 1990.

132. Hepler, B. R., Sutheimer, C. A., and Sunshine, I., The role of the toxicology laboratory in emergency medicine.II: Study of an integrated approach, *Journal of Toxicology Clinical Toxicology,* 22, 503-528, 1984.

133. Decker, W. J. and Treuting, J. J., Spot tests for rapid diagnosis of poisoning, *Clinical Toxicology,* 4, 89-97, 1971.

134. Asselin, W. M. and Caughlin, J. D., A rapid and simple color test for detection of salicylate in whole hemolyzed blood, *Journal of Analytical Toxicology,* 14, 254-255, 1990.

135. Reith, J. F., Ditmarsh, W. C., and DeRuiter, T., An improved procedure for application of the Fujiwara reaction in the determination of organic halides, *Analyst* 99: 652-656, 1974.

136. Frings, C. S., Cohen, P S, Rapid colorimetric method for the quantitative determination of ethchlorvynol (placidyl) in serum and urine, *American Journal of Clinical Pathology,* 54, 833, 1970.

137. Kaye, S., Arsenic, in *Methodology for Analytical Toxicology: Volume I,* Sunshine, I., CRC Press, Inc, Boca Raton, 1984, p 30-31.

138. Stolham, A., Chemical Tests for Metallic Poisons, in *Toxicology: Mechanisms and Analytical Methods,* Stewart, C. P., Stolman, A, Academic Press, New York, 1960, p 640-678.

139. Stollman, A., Stewart, C P, Metalllic Poisons, in *Toxicology: Mechanisms and Analytical Methods,* Stewart, C. P., Stolman, A, Eds., Vol. 1, Academic Press, New York, 1960, p 202-222.

140. Kaye, S., Simple procedure for the detection of arsenic in body fluids, *American Journal of Clinical Pathology,* 14, 36, 1944.

141. Gettler, A. O., Simple tests for mercury in body fluids and tissues, *American Journal of Clinical Pathology (Tech. Suppl.),* 7, 13, 1937.

142. Aziz, K., Drugs-of-abuse testing. Screening and confirmation. [Review], *Clinics in Laboratory Medicine,* 10, 493-502, 1990.

143 Slightom, E. L., The analysis of drugs in blood, bile, and tissue with an indirect homogeneous enzyme immunoassay, *Journal of Forensic Sciences,* 23, 292-303, 1978.

144. Bogusz, M., Aderjan, R., Schmitt, G., Nadler, E., and Neureither, B., The determination of drugs of abuse in whole blood by means of FPIA and EMIT-dau immunoassays—a comparative study, *Forensic Science International,* 48, 27-37, 1990.

145. Mason, P. A., Law, B., Pocock, K., and Moffat, A. C., Direct radioimmunoassay for the detection of barbiturates in blood and urine, *Analyst,* 107, 629-633, 1982.

146. Goddard, C. P., Stead, A. H., Mason, P. A., Law, B., Moffat, A. C., McBrien, M., *et al.*, An iodine-125 radioimmunoassay for the direct detection of benzodiazepines in blood and urine, *Analyst,* 111, 525-529, 1986.

147. Lewellen, L. J. and McCurdy, H. H., A novel procedure for the analysis of drugs in whole blood by homogeneous enzyme immunoassay (EMIT), *Journal of Analytical Toxicology,* 12, 260-264, 1988.

148. Perrigo, B. J. and Joynt, B. P., Optimization of the EMIT immunoassay procedure for the analysis of cannabinoids in methanolic blood extracts, *Journal of Analytical Toxicology,* 13, 235-237, 1989.

149. Maier, R. D., Erkens, M., Hoenen, H., and Bogusz, M., The screening for common drugs of abuse in whole blood by means of EMIT-ETS and FPIA-ADx urine immunoassays, *International Journal of Legal Medicine,* 105, 115-119, 1992.

150. Henderson, L. O., Powell, M. K., Hannon, W. H., Miller, B. B., Martin, M. L., Hanzlick, R. L., *et al.*, Radioimmunoassay screening of dried blood spot materials for benzoylecgonine, *Journal of Analytical Toxicology,* 17, 42-47, 1993.

151. Appel, T. A. and Wade, N. A., Screening of blood and urine for drugs of abuse utilizing diagnostic products corporation's Coat-A-Count radioimmunoassay kits, *Journal of Analytical Toxicology,* 13, 274-276, 1989.

152. Spiehler, V. and Brown, R., Unconjugated morphine in blood by radioimmunoassay and gas chromatography/mass spectrometry, *Journal of Forensic Sciences,* 32, 906-916, 1987.

153. Asselin, W. M. and Leslie, J. M., Modification of EMIT assay reagents for improved sensitivity and cost effectiveness in the analysis of hemolyzed whole blood, *Journal of Analytical Toxicology,* 16, 381-388, 1992.

154. Gjerde, H., Christophersen, A. S., Skuterud, B., Klemetsen, K., and Morland, J., Screening for drugs in forensic blood samples using EMIT urine assays, *Forensic Science International,* 44, 179-185, 1990.

155. Blum, L. M., Klinger, R. A., and Rieders, F., Direct automated EMIT d.a.u. analysis of N,N-dimethylformamide-modified serum, plasma, and postmortem blood for benzodiazepines, benzoylecgonine, cannabinoids, and opiates, *Journal of Analytical Toxicology,* 13, 285-288, 1989.

156. Asselin, W. M., Leslie, J. M., and McKinley, B., Direct detection of drugs of abuse in whole hemolyzed blood using the EMIT d.a.u. urine assays [published erratum appears in J Anal Toxicol 1988 Nov-Dec;12(6):16A], *Journal of Analytical Toxicology,* 12, 207-215, 1988.

157. Fraser, A. D., Clinical evaluation of the EMIT salicylic acid assay, *Therapeutic Drug Monitoring,* 5, 331-334, 1983.

158. Gooch, J. C., Caldwell, R., Turner, G. J., and Colbert, D. L., Cost effective EMIT assays, for drugs of abuse in urine, using the Eppendorf EPOS analyser, *Journal of Immunoassay,* 13, 85-96, 1992.

159. Poklis, A., Jortani, S., Edinboro, L. E., and Saady, J. J., Direct determination of benzoylecgonine in serum by EMIT d.a.u. cocaine metabolite immunoassay, *Journal of Analytical Toxicology,* 18, 419-422, 1994.

160. Armbruster, D. A., Schwarzhoff, R. H., Pierce, B. L., and Hubster, E. C., Method comparison of EMIT 700 and EMIT II with RIA for drug screening, *Journal of Analytical Toxicology,* 18, 110-117, 1994.

161. Armbruster, D. A., Schwarzhoff, R. H., Hubster, E. C., and Liserio, M. K., Enzyme immunoassay, kinetic microparticle immunoassay, radioimmunoassay, and fluorescence polarization immunoassay compared for drugs-of-abuse screening [see comments], *Clinical Chemistr,* 39, 2137-2146, 1993.

162. Camara, P. D., Velletri, K., Krupski, M., Rosner, M., and Griffiths, W. C., Evaluation of the Boehringer Mannheim ES 300 immunoassay analyzer and comparison with enzyme immunoassay, fluorescence polarization immunoassay, and radioimmunoassay methods, *Clinical Biochemistry,* 25, 251-254, 1992.

163. Fraser, A. D., Bryan, W., and Isner, A. F., Urinary screening for alpha-OH triazolam by FPIA and EIA with confirmation by GC/MS, *Journal of Analytical Toxicology,* 16, 347-350, 1992.

164. Meenan, G. M., Barlotta, S., and Lehrer, M., Urinary tricyclic antidepressant screening: comparison of results obtained with Abbott FPIA reagents and Syva EIA reagents, *Journal of Analytical Toxicology*, 14, 273-276, 1990.

165. Armbruster, D. A., Schwarzhoff, R. H., Pierce, B. L., and Hubster, E. C., Method comparison of EMIT II and online with RIA for drug screening [see comments], *Journal of Forensic Sciences*, 38, 1326-1341, 1993.

166. Kintz, P., Machart, D., Jamey, C., and Mangin, P., Comparison between GC/MS and the EMIT II, Abbott ADx, and Roche OnLine immunoassays for the determination of THCCOOH, *Journal of Analytical Toxicology*, 19, 304-306, 1995.

167. Armbruster, D. A., Hubster, E. C., Kaufman, M. S., and Ramon, M. K., Cloned enzyme donor immunoassay (CEDIA) for drugs-of-abuse screening, *Clinical Chemistry*, 41, 92-98, 1995.

168. Coty, W. A., Loor, R., Bellet, N., Khanna, P. L., Kaspar, P., and Baier, M., CEDIA®—homogeneous immunoassays for the 1990s and beyond. [Review], *Wiener Klinische Wochenschrift. Supplementum*, 191, 5-11, 1992.

169. Engel, W. D. and Khanna, P. L., CEDIA in vitro diagnostics with a novel homogeneous immunoassay technique. Current status and future prospects, *Journal of Immunological Methods*, 150, 99-102, 1992.

170. Fleisher, M., Eisen, C., and Schwartz, M. K., An evaluation of a non-isotopic homogeneous enzyme immunoassay (CEDIA assay) for cortisol and its clinical utility, *Wiener Klinische Wochenschrift. Supplementum*, 191, 77-80, 1992.

171. Henderson, D. R., Friedman, S. B., Harris, J. D., Manning, W. B., and Zoccoli, M. A., CEDIA®, a new homogeneous immunoassay system, *Clinical Chemistry*, 32, 1637-1641, 1986.

172. Klein, G., Collinsworth, W., Courbe, A., Diez, O., Domke, I., Hanseler, E., et al., Results of the multicenter evaluation of the CEDIA Phenobarbital assay, *Wiener Klinische Wochenschrift. Supplementum*, 191, 43-47, 1992.

173. Wu, A. H., Forte, E., Casella, G., Sun, K., Hemphill, G., Foery, R., et al., CEDIA for screening drugs of abuse in urine and the effect of adulterants, *Journal of Forensic Sciences*, 40, 614-618, 1995.

174. Gosling, J. P., A decade of development in immunoassay methodology, *Clin. Chem.*, 36, 1408-1427, 1990.

175. Roberts, C. J. and Jackson, L. S., Development of an ELISA using a universal method of enzyme-labelling drug-specific antibodies, *Journal of Immunological Methods*, 181, 157-166, 1995.

176. Laurie, D., Mason, A. J., Piggott, N. H., Rowell, F. J., Seviour, J., Strachan, D., et al., Enzyme linked immunosorbent assay for detecting benzodiazepines in urine, *Analyst*, 121, 951-954, 1996.

177. Makowski, G. S., Richter, J. J., Moore, R. E., Eisma, R., Ostheimer, D., Onoroski, M., et al., An enzyme-linked immunosorbent assay for urinary screening of fentanyl citrate abuse, *Annals of Clinical & Laboratory Science*, 25, 169-178, 1995.

178. Aoki, K., Yoshida, T., and Kuroiwa, Y., Forensic immunochemistry, *Forensic Science International*, 80, 163-173, 1996.

179. Cone, E. J., Validity testing of commercial urine cocaine metabolite assays: III, *Journal of Forensic Sciences*, 34, 991-995, 1989.

180. Oeltgen, P. R., Shank, W., Jr., Blouin, R. A., and Clark, T., Clinical evaluation of the Abbott TDx fluorescence polarization immunoassay analyzer, *Therapeutic Drug Monitoring*, 6, 360-367, 1984.

181. Becker, J., Correll, A., Koepf, W., and Rittner, C., Comparative studies on the detection of benzodiazepines in serum by means of immunoassays (FPIA), *Journal of Analytical Toxicology*, 17, 103-108, 1993.

182. Alvarez, J. S., Sacristan, J. A., and Alsar, M. J., Comparison of a monoclonal antibody fluorescent polarization immunoassay with monoclonal antibody radioimmunoassay for cyclosporin determination in whole blood, *Therapeutic Drug Monitoring*, 14, 78-80, 1992.

183. De la Torre, R., Badia, R., Gonzalez, G., Garcia, M., Pretel, M. J., Farre, M., et al., Cross-reactivity of stimulants found in sports drug testing by two fluorescence polarization immunoassays, *Journal of Analytical Toxicology*, 20, 165-170, 1996.

184. Ferrara, S. D., Tedeschi, L., Frison, G., Brusini, G., Castagna, F., Bernardelli, B., *et al.*, Drugs-of-abuse testing in urine: statistical approach and experimental comparison of immunochemical and chromatographic techniques, *Journal of Analytical Toxicology*, 18, 278-291, 1994.

185. Karnes, H. T. and Beightol, L. A., Evaluation of fluorescence polarization immunoassay for quantitation of serum salicylates, *Therapeutic Drug Monitoring*, 7, 351-354, 1985.

186. Beutler, D., Molteni, S., Zeugin, T., and Thormann, W., Evaluation of instrumental, nonisotopic immunoassays (fluorescence polarization immunoassay and enzyme-multiplied immunoassay technique) for cyclosporine monitoring in whole blood after kidney and liver transplantation, *Therapeutic Drug Monitoring*, 14, 424-432, 1992.

187. Przekop, M. A., Manno, J. E., Kunsman, G. W., Cockerham, K. R., and Manno, B. R., Evaluation of the Abbott ADx Amphetamine/Methamphetamine II abused drug assay: comparison to TDx, EMIT, and GC/MS methods, *Journal of Analytical Toxicology*, 15, 323-326, 1991.

188. Fraser, A. D. and Bryan, W., Evaluation of the Abbott TDx serum benzodiazepine immunoassay for the analysis of lorazepam, adinazolam, and N-desmethyladinazolam, *Journal of Analytical Toxicology*, 19, 281-284, 1995.

189. AlFares, A. M., Mira, S. A., and el-Sayed, Y. M., Evaluation of the fluorescence polarization immunoassay for quantitation of digoxin in serum, *Therapeutic Drug Monitoring*, 6, 454-457, 1984.

190. Caplan, Y. H., Levine, B., and Goldberger, B., Fluorescence polarization immunoassay evaluated for screening for amphetamine and methamphetamine in urine, *Clinical Chemistry*, 33, 1200-1202, 1987.

191. Huang, W., Moody, D. E., Andrenyak, D. M., and Rollins, D. E., Immunoassay detection of nordiazepam, triazolam, lorazepam, and alprazolam in blood, *Journal of Analytical Toxicology*, 17, 365-369, 1993.

192. Beck, O., Lafolie, P., Odelius, G., and Boreus, L. O., Immunological screening of benzodiazepines in urine: improved detection of oxazepam intake, *Toxicology Letters*, 52, 7-14, 1990.

193. Wong, S. H., Methodologies for antidepressant monitoring. [Review], *Clinics in Laboratory Medicine*, 7, 415-433, 1987.

194. Ensslin, H. K., Kovar, K. A., and Maurer, H. H., Toxicological detection of the designer drug 3,4-methylenedioxyethylamphetamine (MDE, Eve) and its metabolites in urine by gas chromatography-mass spectrometry and fluorescence polarization immunoassay, *Journal of Chromatography B: Biomedical Applications*, 683, 189-197, 1996.

195. Castro, A. and Malkus, H., Radioimmunoassays of drugs of abuse in humans: a review. [Review], *Research Communications in Chemical Pathology & Pharmacology*, 16, 291-309, 1977.

196. Budd, R. D., Yang, F. C., and Utley, K. O., Barbiturates—structure versus RIA reactivity, *Clinical Toxicology*, 18, 317-352, 1981.

197. Weaver, M. L., Gan, B. K., Allen, E., and al., e., Correlations on RIA, FPIA, and EIA of Cannabis metabolites with GC/MS analysis of 11-nor-D9-THC acid in urine specimens, *Forensic Sci. Int.*, 49, 43-56, 1991.

198. Moeller, M. R. and Mueller, C., The detection of 6-monoacetylmorphine in urine, serum and hair by GC/MS and RIA, *Forensic Science International*, 70, 125-133, 1995.

199. Abercrombie, M. L. and Jewell, J. S., Evaluation of EMIT and RIA high volume test procedures for THC metabolites in urine utilizing GC/MS confirmation, *Journal of Analytical Toxicology*, 10, 178-180, 1986.

200. Watts, V. W. and Caplan, Y. H., Evaluation of the Coat-A-Count 125I fentanyl RIA: comparison of ^{125}I RIA and GC/MS-SIM for quantification of fentanyl in case urine specimens, *Journal of Analytical Toxicology*, 14, 266-272, 1990.

201. Kintz, P., Cirimele, V., Edel, Y., Jamey, C., and Mangin, P., Hair analysis for buprenorphine and its dealkylated metabolite by RIA and confirmation by LC/ECD, *Journal of Forensic Sciences*, 39, 1497-1503, 1994.

202. Budd, R. D., Leung, W. J., and Yang, F. C., RIA opiates: structure versus reactivity, *Clinical Toxicology*, 17, 383-393, 1980.

203. Baker, D. P., Murphy, M. S., Shepp, P. F., Royo, V. R., Caldarone, M. E., Escoto, B.,*et al.*, Evaluation of the Abuscreen ONLINE assay for amphetamines on the Hitachi 737: comparison with EMIT and GC/MS methods, *Journal of Forensic Sciences,* 40, 108-112, 1995.

204. Hailer, M., Glienke, Y., Schwab, I. M., and von Meyer, L., Modification and evaluation of Abuscreen OnLine assays for drug metabolites in urine performed on a COBAS FARA II in comparison with EMIT d.a.u. Cannabinoid 20, *Journal of Analytical Toxicology,* 19, 99-103, 1995.

205. Moody, D. E. and Medina, A. M., OnLine kinetic microparticle immunoassay of cannabinoids, morphine, and benzoylecgonine in serum, *Clinical Chemistry,* 41, 1664-1665, 1995.

206. Budd, R. D., Amphetamine EMIT—structure versus reactivity, *Clinical Toxicology,* 18, 91-110, 1981.

207. Bailey, D. N., Amphetamine detection during toxicology screening of a university medical center patient population, *Journal of Toxicology - Clinical Toxicology,* 25, 399-409, 1987.

208. Budd, R. D., Amphetamine radioimmunoassay—structure versus reactivity, *Clinical Toxicology,* 18, 299-316, 1981.

209. Kunsman, G. W., Manno, J. E., Cockerham, K. R., and Manno, B. R., Application of the Syva EMIT and Abbott TDx amphetamine immunoassays to the detection of 3,4-methylene-dioxymethamphetamine (MDMA) and 3,4-methylene-dioxyethamphetamin (MDEA) in urine, *Journal of Analytical Toxicology,* 14, 149-153, 1990.

210. Turner, G. J., Colbert, D. L., and Chowdry, B. Z., A broad spectrum immunoassay using fluorescence polarization for the detection of amphetamines in urine, *Annals of Clinical Biochemistry,* 28, 588-594, 1991.

211. D' Nicuola, J., Jones, R., Levine, B., and Smith, M. L., Evaluation of six commercial amphet-amine and methamphetamine immunoassays for cross-reactivity to phenylpropanolamine and ephedrine in urine [see comments], *Journal of Analytical Toxicology,* 16, 211-213, 1992.

212. Cody, J. T. and Schwarzhoff, R., Fluorescence polarization immunoassay detection of amphet-amine, methamphetamine, and illicit amphetamine analogues, *Journal of Analytical Toxicology,* 17, 23-33, 1993.

213. Levine, B. S. and Caplan, Y. H., Isometheptene cross reacts in the EMIT amphetamine assay, *Clinical Chemistry,* 33, 1264-1265, 1987.

214. Poklis, A. and Moore, K. A., Response of EMIT amphetamine immunoassays to urinary desoxyephedrine following Vicks Inhaler use, *Ther. Drug Monit.,* 17, 89-94, 1995.

215. Braithwaite, R. A., Jarvie, D. R., Minty, P. S., Simpson, D., and Widdop, B., Screening for drugs of abuse. I: Opiates, amphetamines and cocaine. [Review], *Annals of Clinical Biochem-istry,* 32, 123-153, 1995.

216. Poklis, A. and Moore, K. A., Stereoselectivity of the TDx/ADx/FLx amphetamine/metham-phetamine II immunoassay - response of urine specimens following nasal inhaler use, *J. Toxicol.-Clin. Toxicol.,* 33, 35-41, 1995.

217. Moore, F. M., Jarvie, D. R., and Simpson, D., Urinary amphetamines, benzodiazepines and methadone: cost-effective detection procedures, *Medical Laboratory Sciences,* 49, 27-33, 1992.

218. Law, B. and Moffat, A. C., The evaluation of an homogeneous enzyme immunoassay (EMIT) and radioimmunoassay for barbiturates, *Journal - Forensic Science Society,* 21, 55-66, 1981.

219. Spector, S. and Flynn, E. J., Barbiturates: radioimmunoassay, *Science,* 174, 1036-1038, 1971.

220. Jain, N. C., Mass screening and confirmation of barbiturates in urine by RIA/gas chromatog-raphy, *Clinical Toxicology,* 9, 221-233, 1976.

221. Caplan, Y. H. and Levine, B., Abbott phencyclidine and barbiturates abused drug assays: evaluation and comparison of ADx FPIA, TDx FPIA, EMIT, and GC/MS methods, *Journal of Analytical Toxicology,* 13, 289-292, 1989.

222. Frazer, A. D., Urinary screening for alprazolam, triazolam, and their metabolites with the EMIT d.a.u. benzodiazepine metabolite assay, *Journal of Analytical Toxicology,* 11, 263- 266, 1987.

223. Budd, R. D., Benzodiazepine structure versus reactivity with EMIT oxazepam antibody, *Clinical Toxicology,* 18, 643-655, 1981.

224. Meatherall, R., Benzodiazepine screening using EMIT II and TDx: urine hydrolysis pretreat-ment required, *Journal of Analytical Toxicology,* 18, 385-390, 1994.

225. Fitzgerald, R., Rexin, D., and Herold, D., Detecting benzodiazepines: immunoassays compared with negative chemical ionization gas chromatography/mass spectrometry, *Clinical Chemistry*, 40, 373-380, 1994.

226. Beck, O., Lafolie, P., Hjemdahl, P., Borg, S., Odelius, G., and Wirbing, P., Detection of benzodiazepine intake in therapeutic doses by immunoanalysis of urine: two techniques evaluated and modified for improved performance, *Clinical Chemistry*, 38, 271-275, 1992.

227. Simonsson, P., Liden, A., and Lindberg, S., Effect of beta-glucuronidase on urinary benzodiazepine concentrations determined by fluorescence polarization immunoassay, *Clinical Chemistry*, 41, 920-923, 1995.

228. Manchon, M., Verdier, M. F., Pallud, P., Vialle, A., Beseme, F., and Bienvenu, J., Evaluation of EMIT-TOX Enzyme Immunoassay for the analysis of benzodiazepines in serum: usefulness and limitations in an emergency laboratory, *Journal of Analytical Toxicology*, 9, 209-212, 1985.

229. Valentine, J. L., Middleton, R., and Sparks, C., Identification of urinary benzodiazepines and their metabolites - Comparison of automated HPLC and GC/MS after immunoassay screening of clinical specimens, *Journal of Analytical Toxicology*, 20, 416-424, 1996.

230. Huang, W. and Moody, D. E., Immunoassay detection of benzodiazepines and benzodiazepine metabolites in blood, *Journal of Analytical Toxicology*, 19, 333-342, 1995.

231. Beyer, K. H. and Martz, S., [Immunologic studies of benzodiazepine—the effect of structural characteristics on cross-reactivity]. [German], *Archiv der Pharmazie*, 324, 933-935, 1991.

232. Schutz, H., Modern screening strategies in analytical toxicology with special regard to new benzodiazepines, *Zeitschrift fur Rechtsmedizin - Journal of Legal Medicine*, 100, 19-37, 1988.

233. Fraser, A. D., Bryan, W., and Isner, A. F., Urinary screening for alprazolam and its major metabolites by the Abbott ADx and TDx analyzers with confirmation by GC/MS, *Journal of Analytical Toxicology*, 15, 25-29, 1991.

234. Borggaard, B. and Joergensen, I., Urinary screening for benzodiazepines with radioreceptor assay: comparison with EMIT dau, *Journal of Analytical Toxicology*, 18, 243-246, 1994.

235. Schramm, W., Craig, P. A., Smith, R. H., and Berger, G. E., Cocaine and benzoylecgonine in saliva, serum, and urine, *Clinical Chemistry*, 39, 481-487, 1993.

236. Martinez, F., Poet, T. S., Pillai, R., Erickson, J., Estrada, A. L., and Watson, R. R., Cocaine metabolite (benzoylecgonine) in hair and urine of drug users, *Journal of Analytical Toxicology*, 17, 138-142, 1993.

237. Foltz, R. L., Botelho, C., Reuschel, S. A., Kuntz, D. J., Moody, D. E., and Bristow, G. M., Comparison of immunoassays for semi-quantitative measurement of benzoylecgonine in urine, in *NIDA Research Monograph* No. 126, U.S. Government Printing Office, Rockville, MD, 1995, p 110-117.

238. Moore, F. M. and Simpson, D., Detection of benzoylecgonine (cocaine metabolite) in urine: a cost-effective low risk immunoassay procedure, *Medical Laboratory Sciences*, 47, 85-89, 1990.

239. Peterson, K. L., Logan, B. K., and Christian, G. D., Detection of cocaine and its polar transformation products and metabolites in human urine, *Forensic Science International*, 73, 183-196, 1995.

240. Poklis, A., Evaluation of TDx cocaine metabolite assay, *Journal of Analytical Toxicology*, 11, 228-230, 1987.

241. Baugh, L. D., Allen, E. E., Liu, R. H., Langner, J. G., Fentress, J. C., Chadha, S. C., *et al.*, Evaluation of immunoassay methods for the screening of cocaine metabolites in urine, *Journal of Forensic Sciences*, 36, 79-85, 1991.

242. De Kanel, J., Dunlap, L., and Hall, T. D., Extending the detection limit of the TDx fluorescence polarization immunoassay for benzoylecgonine in urine, *Clinical Chemistry*, 35, 2110-2112, 1989.

243. Yee, H. Y., Nelson, J. D., and Papa, V. M., Measurement of benzoylecgonine in whole blood using the Abbott ADx analyzer, *Journal of Analytical Toxicology*, 17, 84-86, 1993.

244. Steele, B. W., Bandstra, E. S., Wu, N. C., Hime, G. W., and Hearn, W. L., m-Hydroxybenzoylecgonine: an important contributor to the immunoreactivity in assays for benzoylecgonine in meconium, *Journal of Analytical Toxicology*, 17, 348-352, 1993.

245. McCord, C. E. and McCutcheon, J. R., Preliminary evaluation of the Abbott TDx for benzoylecgonine and opiate screening in whole blood, *Journal of Analytical Toxicology,* 12, 295-297, 1988.

246. Robinson, K. and Smith, R. N., Radioimmunoassay of benzoylecgonine in samples of forensic interest, *Journal of Pharmacy & Pharmacology,* 36, 157-162, 1984.

247. Cone, E. J., Menchen, S. L., Paul, B. C., Mell, L. D., and Mitchell, J., Validity testing of commercial urine cocaine metabolite assays: I, *Journal of Forensic Sciences,* 34, 15-31, 1989.

248. Cone, E. J. and Mitchell, J., Validity testing of commercial urine cocaine metabolite assays: II. Sensitivity, specificity, accuracy, and confirmation by gas chromatography/mass spectrometry, *Journal of Forensic Sciences,* 34, 32-45, 1989.

249. Cone, E. J., Yousefnejad, D., and Dickerson, S. L., Validity testing of commercial urine cocaine metabolite assays: IV. Evaluation of the EMIT d.a.u. cocaine metabolite assay in a quantitative mode for detection of cocaine metabolite, *Journal of Forensic Sciences,* 35, 786-791, 1990.

250. Cone, E. J., Menchen, S. L., and Mitchell, J., Validity testing of the TDx Cocaine Metabolite Assay with human specimens obtained after intravenous cocaine administration, *Forensic Science International,* 37, 265-275, 1988.

251. Van der Slooten, E. P. and van der Helm, H. J., Comparison of the EMIT (enzyme multiplied immunoassay technique) opiate assay and a gas-chromatographic—mass-spectrometric determination of morphine and codeine in urine, *Clinical Chemistry,* 22, 1110-1111, 1976.

252. Smith, M. L., Hughes, R. O., Levine, B., Dickerson, S., Darwin, W. D., and Cone, E. J., Forensic drug testing for opiates. VI. Urine testing for hydromorphone, hydrocodone, oxymorphone, and oxycodone with commercial opiate immunoassays and gas chromatography-mass spectrometry, *Journal of Analytical Toxicology,* 19, 18-26, 1995.

253. Cone, E. J., Dickerson, S., Paul, B. D., and Mitchell, J. M., Forensic drug testing for opiates. V. Urine testing for heroin, morphine, and codeine with commercial opiate immunoassays, *Journal of Analytical Toxicology,* 17, 156-164, 1993.

254. Cone, E. J., Dickerson, S., Paul, B. D., and Mitchell, J. M., Forensic drug testing for opiates. IV. Analytical sensitivity, specificity, and accuracy of commercial urine opiate immunoassays, *Journal of Analytical Toxicology,* 16, 72-78, 1992.

255. Mitchell, J. M., Paul, B. D., Welch, P., and Cone, E. J., Forensic drug testing for opiates, *Journal of Analytical Toxicology,* 15, 49-53, 1991.

256. Spiehler, V. R. and Sedgwick, P., Radioimmunoassay screening and GC/MS confirmation of whole blood samples for drugs of abuse, *Journal of Analytical Toxicology,* 9, 63-66, 1985.

257. Lee, J. W., Pedersen, J. E., Moravetz, T. L., Dzerk, A. M., Mundt, A. D., and Shepard, K. V., Sensitive and specific radioimmunoassays for opiates using commercially available materials, *Journal of Pharmaceutical Sciences,* 80, 284-288, 1991.

258. Weingarten, H. L. and Trevias, E. C., Analysis of phencyclidine in blood by gas chromatography, radioimmunoassay, and enzyme immunoassay, *Journal of Analytical Toxicology,* 6, 88-90, 1982.

259. Heveran, J. E., Anthony, M., and Ward, C., Determination of phencyclidine by radioimmunoassay, *Journal of Forensic Sciences,* 25, 79-87, 1980.

260. Fyfe, M. J., Chand, P., McCutchen, C., Long, J. S., Walia, A. S., Edwards, C., *et al.*, Evaluation of enzyme immunoassay performance characteristics—phencyclidine example, *Journal of Forensic Sciences,* 38, 156-164, 1993.

261. Sneath, T. C. and Jain, N. C., Evaluation of phencyclidine by EMIT d.a.u. utilizing the ETS analyzer and a 25-ng/mL cutoff, *Journal of Analytical Toxicology,* 16, 107-108, 1992.

262. Ragan, F., Jr., Hite, S. A., Samuels, M. S., Garey, R. E., Daul, G., and Schuler, R. E., Extended EMIT-DAU phencyclidine screen, *Journal of Clinical Psychiatry,* 47, 194-195, 1986.

263. Levine, B., Goldberger, B. A., and Caplan, Y. H., Evaluation of the coat-a-count radioimmunoassay for phencyclidine, *Clinical Chemistry,* 34, 429, 1988.

264. Cary, P. L., Johnson, C. A., Folsom, T. M., and Bales, W. R., Immunoassay method validation for a modified EMIT phencyclidine assay, *Journal of Analytical Toxicology,* 16, 48-51, 1992.

265. Budd, R. D., Phencyclidine (PCP)-structure versus reactivity, *Clinical Toxicology,* 18, 1033-1041, 1981.

266. Kintz, P. and Mangin, P., Abbott propoxyphene assay: evaluation and comparison of TDx FPIA and GC/MS methods, *Journal of Analytical Toxicology*, 17, 222-224, 1993.

267. Frederick, D. L., Green, J., and Fowler, M. W., Comparison of six cannabinoid metabolite assays, *Journal of Analytical Toxicology*, 9, 116-120, 1985.

268. Budgett, W.T., Levine, B., Xu, A., and Smith, M. L., Comparison of Abbott fluorescence polarization immunoassay (FPIA) and Roche radioimmunoassay for the analyses of cannabinoids in urine specimens, *Journal of Forensic Sciences*, 37, 632-635, 1992.

269. Kaeferstein, H., Sticht, G., and Staak, M., Comparison of various immunological methods with GC/MS analysis in the detection of cannabinoids in urine, *Beitr. Gerichtl. Med.*, 47, 115-122, 1989.

270. Moore, F. M. L. and Simpson, D., Detection of cannabinoids in urine: a cost-effective low risk immunoassay procedure, *Med. Lab. Sci.*, 48, 76-79, 1991.

271. Colbert, D. L., Sidki, A. M., Gallacher, G., and Landon, J., Fluoroimmunoassays for cannabinoids in urine, *Analyst*, 112, 1483-1486, 1987.

272. McBurney, L. J., Bobbie, B. A., and Sepp, L. A., GC/MS and EMIT analyses for delta 9-tetrahydrocannabinol metabolites in plasma and urine of human subjects, *Journal of Analytical Toxicology*, 10, 56-64, 1986.

273. King, D. L., Martel, P. A., and O'Donnell, C. M., Laboratory detection of cannabinoids. [Review], *Clinics in Laboratory Medicine*, 7, 641-653, 1987.

274. Moyer, T. P., Palmen, M. A., Johnson, P., Charlson, J. R., and Ellefson, P. J., Marijuana testing—how good is it?, *Mayo Clinic Proceedings*, 62, 413-417, 1987.

275. Cook, C.E., Seltzman, H.H., Schindler, V.H., Tallent, C.R., Chin, K.M., and Pitt, C. G., Radioimmunoassays for cannabinoids, *NIDA Research Monograph*, 42, 19-32, 1982.

276. Gjerde, H., Screening for cannabinoids in blood using EMIT: concentrations of delta-9-tetrahydrocannabinol in relation to EMIT results, *Forensic Science International*, 50, 121-124, 1991.

277. Goodall, C. R. and Basteyns, B. J., A reliable method for the detection, confirmation, and quantitation of cannabinoids in blood, *Journal of Analytical Toxicology*, 19, 419-426, 1995.

278. Ernst, R., Williams, L., Dalbey, M., Collins, C., and Pankey, S., Homogeneous enzyme immunoassay (EMIT) protocol for monitoring tricyclic antidepressants on the COBAS-BIO centrifugal analyzer, *Therapeutic Drug Monitoring*, 9, 85-90, 1987.

279. Asselin, W. M. and Leslie, J. M., Direct detection of therapeutic concentrations of tricyclic antidepressants in whole hemolyzed blood using the EMITtox serum tricyclic antidepressant assay, *Journal of Analytical Toxicology*, 15, 167-173, 1991.

280. Benitez, J., Dahlqvist, R., Gustafsson, L. L., Magnusson, A., and Sjoqvist, F., Clinical pharmacological evaluation of an assay kit for intoxications with tricyclic antidepressants, *Therapeutic Drug Monitoring*, 8, 102-105, 1986.

281. Dorey, R. C., Preskorn, S. H., and Widener, P. K., Results compared for tricyclic antidepressants as assayed by liquid chromatography and enzyme immunoassay, *Clinical Chemistry*, 34, 2348-2351, 1988.

282. Nebinger, P. and Koel, M., Specificity data of the tricyclic antidepressants assay by fluorescent polarization immunoassay, *Journal of Analytical Toxicology*, 14, 219-221, 1990.

283. Vandel, S., Vincent, F., Prudhon, F., Nezelof, S., Bonin, B., and Bertschy, G., Results compared for tricyclic antidepressants as assayed by gas chromatography and enzyme immunoassay, *Therapie*, 47, 41-45, 1992.

284. Brunk, S.D., Thin-Layer Chromatography Using Toxi-lab System, in *Analysis of Addictive and Misused Drugs*, Adamovics, J. A., Marcel Dekker, Inc, New York, 1995, p 41-50.

285. Guebitz, G. and Wintersteiger, R., Identification of drugs of abuse by high-performance thin-layer chromatography., *J. Anal. Toxicol.*, 4, 141-144, 1980.

286. Singh, A. K., Granley, K., Ashraf, M., and Misha, U., Drug screening and confirmation by thin layer chromatography, *J. Planar Chromatogr.— Mod. TLC*, 2, 410-419, 1989.

287. Wilson, J. F., Williams, J., Walker, G., Toseland, P. A., Smith, B. L., Richens, A., *et al.*, Sensitivity and specificity of techniques used to detect drugs of abuse in urine, in *Recent Developments in Therapeutic Drug Monitoring and Clinical Toxicology*, Sunshine, I., Dekker, New York, NY, 1992, p 527-535.

Wm. Lee Hearn and H. Chip Walls

288. Bogusz, M., Klys, M., Wijsbeek, J., Franke, J. P., and de Zeeuw, R. A., Impact of biological matrix and isolation methods on detectability and interlaboratory variations of TLC Rf-values in systematic toxicological analysis, *Journal of Analytical Toxicology,* 8, 149-154, 1984.

289. Wolff, K., Sanderson, M. J., and Hay, A. W., A rapid horizontal TLC method for detecting drugs of abuse, *Annals of Clinical Biochemistry,* 27, 482-488, 1990.

290. Jarvie, D. R. and Simpson, D., Drug screening: evaluation of the Toxi-Lab TLC system, *Annals of Clinical Biochemistry,* 23, 76-84, 1986.

291. Nishigami, J., Ohshima, T., Takayasu, T., Kondo, T., Lin, Z., and Nagano, T., [Forensic toxicological application of TOXI-LAB screening for biological specimens in autopsy cases and emergency cares], *Nippon Hoigaku Zasshi - Japanese Journal of Legal Medicine,* 47, 372-379, 1993.

292. Nadkarni, S., Faye, S., and Hay, A., Experience with the use of the Toxi-Lab TLC system in screening for morphine/heroin abuse, *Annals of Clinical Biochemistry,* 24,211-212, 1987.

293. Plavsic, F., Barbaric, V., Parag, M., Arambasin, M., Gjerek, J., and Stavljenic, A., Increased possibilities for detecting drugs by the Toxi-Lab screening test, *Annals of Clinical Biochemistry,* 22, 324-326, 1985.

294. Caldwell, R. and Challenger, H., A capillary column GC method for the identification of drugs of abuse in urine samples, *Ann. Clin. Biochem.,* 26, 430-443, 1989.

295. Grinstead, G. F., A closer look at acetyl and pentafluoropropionyl derivatives for quantitative analysis of morphine and codeine by gas chromatography-mass spectrometry, *Journal of Analytical Toxicology,* 15, 293-298, 1991.

296. Kataoka, H., Derivatization reactions for the determination of amines by gas chromatography and their applications in environmental analysis, *Journal of Chromatography A,* 733, 19-34, 1996.

297. Lho, D., Hong, J., Paek, H., Lee, J., and Park, J., Determination of phenolalkylamines, narcotic analgesics, and beta-blockers by gas chromatography-mass spectrometry, *Journal of Analytical Toxicology,* 14, 77-83, 1990.

298. Sanchez, M. C., Colome, J., and Gelpi, E., Electron capture and multiple ion detection of benzodiazepine esters in pharmacokinetic studies, *Journal of Chromatography,* 126, 601-613, 1976.

299. Beck, O. and Faull, K. F., Extractive acylation and mass spectrometric assay of 3-methoxytyramine, normetanephrine, and metanephrine in cerebrospinal fluid, *Analytical Biochemistry,* 149, 492-500, 1985.

300. Jain, N. C., Sneath, T. C., Budd, R. D., and Leung, W. J., Gas chromatographic/thin-layer chromatographic analysis of acetylated codeine and morphine in urine, *Clinical Chemistry,* 21, 1486-1489, 1975.

301. Czarny, R. J. and Hornbeck, C. L., Quantitation of methamphetamine and amphetamine in urine by capillary GC/MS Part II. Derivatization with 4-carbethoxyhexafluorobutyryl chloride, *Journal of Analytical Toxicology,* 13, 257-262, 1989.

302. Bowie, L. J. and Kirkpatrick, P. B., Simultaneous determination of monoacetylmorphine, morphine, codeine, and other opiates by GC/MS, *Journal of Analytical Toxicology,* 13, 326-329, 1989.

303. Toyo'oka, T., Use of derivatization to improve the chromatographic properties and detection selectivity of physiologically important carboxylic acids, *Journal of Chromatography B: Biomedical Applications,* 671, 91-112, 1995.

304. Zamecnik, J., Use of cyclic boronates for GC/MS screening and quantitation of beta-blockers and some bronchodilators, *J. Anal. Toxicol.,* 14, 132-136, 1990.

305. Liu, F., Liu, Y. T., Feng, C. L., and Luo, Y., Determination of methaqualone and its metabolites in urine and blood by UV, GC/FID and GC/MS, *Yao Hsueh Hsueh Pao Acta Pharmaceutica Sinica,* 29, 610-616, 1994.

306. Michalek, R. W., Rejent, T. A., and Spencer, R. A., Disopyramide fatality: case report and GC/FID analysis, *Journal of Analytical Toxicology,* 6, 255-257, 1982.

307. Kintz, P., Mangin, P., Lugnier, A. A., and Chaumont, A. J., A rapid and sensitive gas chromatographic analysis of meprobamate or carisoprodol in urine and plasma, *Journal of Analytical Toxicology,* 12, 73-74, 1988.

308. Qiu, F.H., Liu, L., Guo, L., Luo, Y., and Lu, Y.Q., [Rapid identification and quantitation of barbiturates in plasma using solid-phase extraction combined with GC-FID and GC/MS method], *Yao Hsueh Hsueh Pao-Acta Pharmaceutica Sinica*, 30,372-377, 1995.

309. Kageura, M., Hara, K., Hieda, Y., Takamoto, M., Fujiwara, Y., Fukuma, Y., *et al.*, [Screening of drugs and chemicals by wide-bore capillary gas chromatography with flame ionization and nitrogen phosphorus detectors]. [Japanese], *Nippon Hoigaku Zasshi - Japanese Journal of Legal Medicine 1989 Apr;43(2):161-165*, 1989.

310. Ghittori, S., Fiorentino, M. L., and Imbriani, M., [Use of gas chromatography with flame ionization (GC-FID) in the measurement of solvents in the urine], *Giornale Italiano di Medicina del Lavoro*, 9, 21-24, 1987.

311. Verebey, K., Jukofsky, D., and Mule, S. J., Confirmation of EMIT benzodiazepine assay with GLC/NPD, *Journal of Analytical Toxicology*, 6, 305-308, 1982.

312. Trinh, V. and Vernay, A., Evaluation of sample treatment procedure for the routine identification and determination at nanogram level of O-monoacetylmorphine in urine by capillary GC and dual NPD-FID, *J. High Resolut. Chromatogr.*, 13, 162-166, 1990.

313. Verebey, K. and DePace, A., Rapid confirmation of enzyme multiplied immunoassay technique (EMIT) cocaine positive urine samples by capillary gas-liquid chromatography/nitrogen phosphorus detection (GLC/NPD), *Journal of Forensic Sciences*, 34, 46-52, 1989.

314. Balkon, J. and Donnelly, B., Determination of basic drugs in post mortem tissues: a microextraction technique utilizing GLC/NPD of effluents, *Journal of Analytical Toxicology*, 6, 181-184, 1982.

315. Gaillard, Y., Gay-Montchamp, J. P., and Ollagnier, M., Simultaneous screening and quantitation of alpidem, zolpidem, buspirone and benzodiazepines by dual-channel gas chromatography using electron-capture and nitrogen-phosphorus detection after solid-phase extraction, *Journal of Chromatography*, 622, 197-208, 1993.

316. Japp, M., Garthwaite, K., Geeson, A.V., and Osselton, M.D., Collection of analytical data for benzodiazepines and benzophenones, *Journal of Chromatography*, 439,317-339, 1988.

317. Lillsunde, P. and Seppala, T., Simultaneous screening and quantitative analysis of benzodiazepines by dual-channel gas chromatography using electron-capture and nitrogen-phosphorus detection, *Journal of Chromatography*, 533, 97-110, 1990.

318. Kokanovich, J. D., Simonick, T. F., and Watts, V. W., High speed analysis of underivatized drugs by GC/MS, *J. High Resoln. Chromatogr.*, 12, 45-48, 1989.

319. Lillsunde, P. and Korte, T., Thin-layer chromatographic screening and GC/MS confirmation in analysis of abused drugs, in *Anal. Addict. Misused Drugs*, Adamovics, J. A., Dekker, New York, 1995, p 221-265.

320. Maurer, H. and Pfleger, K., Screening procedure for detection of antidepressants and their metabolites in urine using a computerized GC/MS technique., *J. Chromatogr.*, 305, 309-323, 1984.

321. Siren, H., Saarinen, M., Hainari, S., Lukkari, P., and Riekkola, M. L., Screening of beta-blockers in human serum by ion-pair chromatography and their identification as methyl or acetyl derivatives by GC/MS, *J Chromatogr*, 632, 215-227, 1993.

322. Needleman, S. B. and Porvaznik, M., Identification of parent benzodiazepines by gas chromotography/mass spectroscopy (GC/MS) from urinary extracts treated with B-glucuronidase, *Forensic Science International*, 73, 49-60, 1995.

323. Maurer, H. and Pfleger, K., Screening procedure for detection of phenothiazines and analogous neuroleptics and their metabolites in urine using a computerized GC/MS technique., *J. Chromatogr.*, 306, 125-145, 1984.

324. Fraser, A. D., Bryan, W., and Isner, A. F., Urinary screening for midazolam and its major metabolites with the Abbott ADx and TDx analzyers and the EMIT dau benzodiazepine assay with confirmation by GC/MS, *J. Anal. Toxicol.*, 15, 8-12, 1991.

325. Masse, R., Ayotte, C., and Dugal, R. An integrated GC/MS screening method for anabolic steroid urinary metabolites in man. in *Dev. Anal. Methods Pharm. Biomed., Forensic Sci.* Quebec, Canada, 1986.

326. Maurer, H. H., Identification and differentiation of barbiturates, other sedative-hypnotics and their metabolites in urine integrated in a general screening procedure using computerized GC/MS, *J. Chromatogr.*, 530, 307-326, 1990.

327. Maurer, H. and Pfleger, K., Identification and differentiation of alkylamine antihistamines and their metabolites in urine by computerized gas chromatography-mass spectrometry, *Journal of Chromatography*, 430, 31-41, 1988.

328. Gill, R., Lopes, A. A., and Moffat, A. C., Analysis of barbiturates in blood by high-performance liquid chromatography, *Journal of Chromatography*, 226, 117-123, 1981.

329. Kleinschnitz, M., Herderich, M., and Schreier, P., Determination of 1,4-benzodiazepines by high performance liquid chromatography electrospray tandem mass spectrometry, *Journal of Chromatography B: Biomedical Applications*, 676, 61-67, 1996.

330. Mangin, P., Lugnier, A. A., and Chaumont, A. J., A polyvalent method using HPLC for screening and quantification of 12 common barbiturates in various biological materials, *Journal of Analytical Toxicology*, 11, 27-30, 1987.

331. Hill, D. W. and Langner, K. J., Screening with high performance liquid chromatography, in *Analytical Aspects of Drug Testing*, Deutsch, D. G., John Wiley and Sons, New York, 1989, p 129-148.

332. Ng, L. L., Sample preparation by salts precipitation and quantitation by HPLC with UV detection of selected drugs in biological fluids., *J. Chromatogr.*, 257, 345-353, 1983.

333. Foukaridis, G. N., Muntingh, G. L., and Osuch, E., Application of diode array detection for the identification of poisoning by traditional medicines, *Journal of Ethnopharmacology*, 41, 135-146, 1994.

334. Lambert, W. E., Piette, M., Van Peteghem, C., and De Leenheer, A. P., Application of high-performance liquid chromatography to a fatality involving azide, *Journal of Analytical Toxicology*, 19, 261-264, 1995.

335. Dipietra, A. M., Gatti, R., Andrisano, V., and Cavrini, V., Application of high-performance liquid chromatography with diode-array detection and on-line post-column photochemical derivatization to the determination of analgesics, *Journal of Chromatography*, 729, 355-361, 1996.

336. Puopolo, P. R., Volpicelli, S. A., Johnson, D. M., and Flood, J. G., Emergency toxicology testing (detection, confirmation, and quantification) of basic drugs in serum by liquid chromatography with photodiode array detection, *Clinical Chemistry*, 37, 2124-2130, 1991.

337. Koves, E. M. and Wells, J., Evaluation of a photodiode array/HPLC-based system for the detection and quantitation of basic drugs in postmortem blood, *Journal of Forensic Sciences*, 37, 42-60, 1992.

338. Tracqui, A., Kintz, P., and Mangin, P., High-performance liquid chromatographic assay with diode-array detection for toxicological screening of zopiclone, zolpidem, suriclone and alpidem in human plasma, *Journal of Chromatography*, 616, 95-103, 1993.

339. Balikova, M. and Vecerkova, J., High-performance liquid chromatographic confirmation of cocaine and benzoylecgonine in biological samples using photodiode-array detection after toxicological screening, *Journal of Chromatography B: Biomedical Applications*, 656, 267-273, 1994.

340. Wielbo, D., Bhat, R., Chari, G., Vidyasagar, D., Tebbett, I. R., and Gulati, A., High-performance liquid chromatographic determination of morphine and its metabolites in plasma using diode-array detection, *Journal of Chromatography*, 615, 164-168, 1993.

341. Li, S., Gemperline, P. J., Briley, K., and Kazmierczak, S., Identification and quantitation of drugs of abuse in urine using the generalized rank annihilation method of curve resolution, *Journal of Chromatography B: Biomedical Applications*, 655, 213-223, 1994.

342. Overzet, F., Rurak, A., van der Voet, H., Drenth, B. F., Ghijsen, R. T., and de Zeeuw, R. A., On-line diode array UV-visible spectrometry in screening for drugs and drug metabolites by high-performance liquid chromatography, *Journal of Chromatography*, 267, 329-345, 1983.

343. Balikova, M., Selective system of identification and determination of antidepressants and neuroleptics in serum or plasma by solid-phase extraction followed by high-performance liquid chromatography with photodiode-array detection in analytical toxicology, *Journal of Chromatography*, 581, 75-81, 1992.

344. Tracqui, A., Kintz, P., Kreissig, P., and Mangin, P., A simple and rapid method for toxicological screening of 25 antidepressants in blood or urine using high performance liquid chromatography with diode-array detection, *Annales de Biologie Clinique*, 50, 639-647, 1992.

345. Puopolo, P. R., Pothier, M. E., Volpicelli, S. A., and Flood, J. G., Single procedure for detection, confirmation, and quantification of benzodiazepines in serum by liquid chromatography with photodiode-array detection, *Clinical Chemistry*, 37, 701-706, 1991.

346. Turcant, A., Premel-Cabic, A., Cailleux, A., and Allain, P., Toxicological screening of drugs by microbore high-performance liquid chromatography with photodiode-array detection and ultraviolet spectral library searches, *Clinical Chemistry*, 37, 1210-1215, 1991.

347. Stanke, F., Jourdil, N., Lauby, V., and Bessard, G., Zopiclone and Zolpidem Quantification in Human Plasma By High Performance Liquid Chromatography With Photodiode-Array Detection, *Journal of Liquid Chromatography & Related Technologies*, 19, 2623-2633, 1996.

348. Law, B. and Stafford, L. E., The use of ultraviolet spectra and chromatographic retention data as an aid to metabolite identification, *Journal of Pharmaceutical & Biomedical Analysis*, 11, 729-736, 1993.

349. Demedts, P., Wauters, A., Franck, F., and Neels, H., Evaluation of the REMEDi drug profiling system, *European Journal of Clinical Chemistry & Clinical Biochemistry*, 32, 409-417, 1994.

350. Ohtsuji, M., Lai, J. S., Binder, S. R., Kondo, T., Takayasu, T., and Ohshima, T., Use of REMEDi HS in emergency toxicology for a rapid estimate of drug concentrations in urine, serum, and gastric samples, *Journal of Forensic Sciences*, 41, 881-886, 1996.

351. Patel, V., McCarthy, P. T., and Flanagan, R. J., Disopyramide analysis using REMEDi: comparison with EMIT and conventional high performance liquid chromatographic methods, *Biomedical Chromatography*, 5, 269-272, 1991.

352. Poklis, A. and Edinboro, L. E., REMEDi drug profiling system readily distinguishes between cyclobenzaprine and amitriptyline in emergency toxicology urine specimens [letter], *Clinical Chemistry*, 38, 2349-2350, 1992.

353. Christensen, J. M., Human exposure to toxic metals: factors influencing interpretation of biomonitoring results, *Science of the Total Environment*, 166, 89-135, 1995.

354. Flanagan, R. J., The poisoned patient: the role of the laboratory. [Review], *British Journal of Biomedical Science*, 52, 202-213, 1995.

355. Van Ormer, D. G., Atomic absorption analysis of some trace metals of toxicological interest, *Journal of Forensic Sciences*, 20, 595-623, 1975.

356. Sotera, J. J., Dulude, G. R., and Stux, R. L., Determination of toxic elements in biological materials by furnace atomic absorption spectrometry, *Science of the Total Environment*, 71, 45-48, 1988.

357. Solomons, E. T. and Walls, H. C., Analysis of arsenic in forensic cases utilizing a rapid, non-ashing technique and furnace atomic absorption, *Journal of Analytical Toxicology*, 7, 220-222, 1983.

358. Yoshinaga, J., [Inductively coupled plasma atomic emission spectrometry and ICP mass spectrometry], *Nippon Rinsho - Japanese Journal of Clinical Medicine*, 54, 202-206, 1996.

359. Kalamegham, R. and Ash, K. O., A simple ICP-MS procedure for the determination of total mercury in whole blood and urine, *Journal of Clinical Laboratory Analysis*, 6, 190-193, 1992.

360. Inoue, T. and Suzuki, S., Comparison of extraction methods for methamphetamine and its metabolites in tissue, *Journal of Forensic Sciences*, 31, 1102-1107, 1986.

361. Bush, M. T., Design of solvent extraction methods, *Methods in Enzymology*, 77, 353-372, 1981.

362. Dusaci, L. J. and Hackett, L. P., Direct extraction procedure for the analysis of neutral drugs in tissue., *Clin. Toxicol.*, 11, 353-358, 1977.

363. Brooks, K. E. and Smith, N. B., Efficient extraction of basic, neutral, and weakly acidic drugs from plasma for analysis by gas chromatography-mass spectrometry [published erratum appears in Clin Chem 1992 Feb;38(2):323], *Clinical Chemistry*, 37, 1975-1978, 1991.

364. Hyde, P. M., Evaluation of drug extraction procedures from urine, *Journal of Analytical Toxicology*, 9, 269-272, 1985.

365. Osselton, M. D., Hammond, M. D., and Watchett, P. J., The extraction and analysis of benzodiazepines in tissues by enzymatic digestion and HPLC., *J. Pharm. Pharmacol.*, 29, 460-462, 1977.

366. Bailey, D. N. and Kelner, M., Extraction of acidic drugs from water and plasma: study of recovery with five different solvents, *Journal of Analytical Toxicology,* 8, 26-28, 1984.

367. Chiarotti, M., Overview on extraction procedures. [Review], *Forensic Science International,* 63, 161-170, 1993.

368. Ford, B., Vine, J., and Watson, T. R., A rapid extraction method for acidic drugs in hemolyzed blood, *Journal of Analytical Toxicology,* 7, 116-118, 1983.

369. Moore, C. M. and Tebbett, I. R., Rapid extraction of anti-inflammatory drugs in whole blood for HPLC analysis, *Forensic Science International,* 34, 155-158, 1987.

370. Stoner, R. E. and Parker, C., Single-pH extraction procedure for detecting drugs of abuse, *Clinical Chemistry,* 20, 309-311, 1974.

371. Hackett, L. P. and Dusci, L. J., The use of buffered celite columns in drug extraction techniques and their proposed application in forensic toxicology, *Journal of Forensic Sciences,* 22, 376-382, 1977.

372. Siek, T. J., Effective use of organic solvents to remove drugs from biologic specimens, *Clinical Toxicology,* 13, 205-230, 1978.

373. Dusci, L. J. and Hackett, L. P., A comparison of the borate-celite column screening technique with other extraction methods in forensic toxicology, *Journal of Forensic Sciences,* 22, 545-549, 1977.

374. Chen, X. H., Franke, J. P., Wijsbeek, J., and de Zeeuw, R. A., Isolation of acidic, neutral, and basic drugs from whole blood using a single mixed-mode solid-phase extraction column, *Journal of Analytical Toxicology,* 16, 351-355, 1992.

375. Black, D. A., Clark, G. D., Haver, V. M., Garbin, J. A., and Saxon, A. J., Analysis of urinary benzodiazepines using solid-phase extraction and gas chromatography-mass spectrometry [see comments], *Journal of Analytical Toxicology,* 18, 185-188, 1994.

376. Lensmeyer, G. L., Wiebe, D. A., and Darcey, B. A., Application of a novel form of solid-phase sorbent (Empore membrane) to the isolation of tricyclic antidepressant drugs from blood, *Journal of Chromatographic Science,* 29, 444-449, 1991.

377. Chen, X. H., Franke, J. P., Wijsbeek, J., and de Zeeuw, R. A., Determination of basic drugs extracted from biological matrices by means of solid-phase extraction and wide-bore capillary gas chromatography with nitrogen-phosphorus detection, *Journal of Analytical Toxicology,* 18, 150-153, 1994.

378. Huang, Z. P., Chen, X. H., Wijsbeek, J., Franke, J. P., and Dezeeuw, R. A., An enzymic digestion and solid-phase extraction procedure for the screening for acidic, neutral, and basic drugs in liver using gas chromatography for analysis, *Journal of Analytical Toxicology,* 20, 248-254, 1996.

379. Leloux, M. S., de Jong, E. G., and Maes, R. A., Improved screening method for beta-blockers in urine using solid-phase extraction and capillary gas chromatography-mass spectrometry, *Journal of Chromatography,* 488, 357-367, 1989.

380. Anderson, R. E. and Nixon, G. L., Isolation of benzoylecgonine from urine using solid-phase extraction, *Journal of Analytical Toxicology,* 17, 432-433, 1993.

381. Cosbey, S. H., Craig, I., and Gill, R., Novel solid-phase extraction strategy for the isolation of basic drugs from whole blood, *Journal of Chromatography B: Biomedical Applications,* 669, 229-235, 1995.

382. Matyska, M. and Golkiewicz, W., Quantitation of benzodiazepine hydrolysis products in urine using solid-phase extraction and high performance liquid chromatography, *J. Liq. Chromatogr.,* 14, 2769-2778, 1991.

383. Wright, A. W., Watt, J. A., Kennedy, M., Cramond, T., and Smith, M. T., Quantitation of morphine, morphine-3-glucuronide, and morphine-6-glucuronide in plasma and cerebrospinal fluid using solid-phase extraction and high-performance liquid chromatography with electrochemical detection, *Therapeutic Drug Monitoring,* 16, 200-208, 1994.

384. Bouquillon, A. I., Freeman, D., and Moulin, D. E., Simultaneous solid-phase extraction and chromatographic analysis of morphine and hydromorphone in plasma by high-performance liquid chromatography with electrochemical detection, *Journal of Chromatography,* 577, 354-357, 1992.

385. Pocci, R., Dixit, V., and Dixit, V. M., Solid-phase extraction and GC/MS confirmation of barbiturates from human urine, *Journal of Analytical Toxicology,* 16, 45-47, 1992.

386. Chen, X.-H., Franke, J.-P., and de Zeeuw, R. A., Solid-phase extraction for systematic toxicological analysis, *Forensic Sci. Rev.,* 4, 147-159, 1992.

387. Casas, M., Berrueta, L. A., Gallo, B., and Vicente, F., Solid-phase extraction of 1,4-benzodi-azepines from biological fluids, *Journal of Pharmaceutical & Biomedical Analysis,* 11, 277-284, 1993.

388. Dixit, V., Solid-phase extraction of amphetamine and methamphetamine, *Am. Clin. Lab.,* 11, 6, 1992.

389. Scheurer, J. and Moore, C. M., Solid-phase extraction of drugs from biological tissues—a review. [Review], *Journal of Analytical Toxicology,* 16, 264-269, 1992.

390. Chen, X. H., Franke, J. P., Wijsbeek, J., and de Zeeuw, R. A., Study of lot-to-lot reproduc-ibilities of Bond Elut Certify and Clean Screen DAU mixed-mode solid-phase extraction columns in the extraction of drugs from whole blood, *Journal of Chromatography,* 617, 147-151, 1993.

391. Nakamura, G. R., Meeks, R. D., and Stall, W. J., Solid-phase extraction, identification, and quantitation of 11-nor-delta-9-tetrahydrocannabinol-9-carboxylic acid, *Journal of Forensic Sciences,* 35, 792-796, 1990.

392. Bogusz, M., Bialka, J., and Gierz, J., Enzymic digestion of biosamples as a method of sample pretreatment before XAD-2 extraction, *Zeitschrift fur Rechtsmedizin Journal of Legal Medicine,* 87, 287-295, 1981.

393. Bogusz, M., Bialka, J., and Gierz, J., Enzymic hydrolysis of tissues before XAD-2 extraction in poisoning cases, *Forensic Science International,* 20, 27-33, 1982.

394. Romberg, R. W. and Lee, L., Comparison of the hydrolysis rates of morphine-3-glucuronide and morphine-6-glucuronide with acid and beta-glucuronidase, *Journal of Analytical Toxicology,* 19, 157-162, 1995.

12.4 STRATEGIES FOR POSTMORTEM TOXICOLOGY INVESTIGATION

12.4.1 SCREENING STRATEGY

The first step in any case is to review the case history and autopsy findings. If the pathologist makes no specific requests for analysis, then responsibility for deciding which tests to do falls exclusively to the professional judgment of the toxicologist.[1-9]

Obviously, cases of suspected drug intoxication require the most comprehensive testing, typically on samples of blood, liver, gastric contents and urine or bile.[10,11] Tests in the case of a drug-related homicide may include a blood-ethanol analysis, and a standard drug-of-abuse screen on urine, with the concentration of any identified drug being quantified in the blood.[12-18] Fatalities involving motor vehicle drivers require a blood-ethanol determination, and a urine comprehensive screen with any positive drug concentration quantified in the blood.[19-23] Fatalities resulting from a fire require blood-carbon monoxide and cyanide analyses in addition to alcohol and other drugs.[24-26]

12.4.2 GENERAL CONCEPTS

Screening protocols should include tests capable of detecting as many drugs as possible, within the constraints imposed by the available specimens, the laboratory's workload, and require-ments specific to the case (see Figure 12.4.1).[5-9,27] Most laboratories lack the resources required to treat every case as a general unknown, applying test after test until all possible drugs and poisons are ruled out. Such an approach may occasionally be warranted when there is a high suspicion of poisoning, but usually several standardized protocols can be used to eliminate most of the substances that can realistically be expected in a sample.

Wm. Lee Hearn and H. Chip Walls

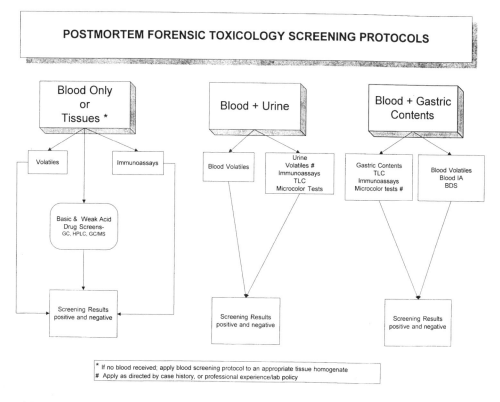

Figure 12.4.1 Postmortem forensic toxicology screening protocols.

A broad-spectrum screen, capable of detecting or eliminating most of the common drugs, usually requires a combination of three or more techniques.[1,2,11,28-88] Additional tests can be combined with standardized screening protocols, thereby expanding the screening capability to encompass additional drugs of concern based upon the specifics of the case. Table 12.4.2 shows test panels commonly employed for screening various types of cases.

The most effective strategies employ a combination of immunoassays, with chromatographic techniques, and chemical tests, in order to detect a wide range of substances. Immunoassays are used to test for classes of drugs with similar structures, while the chromatographic tests detect large groups of drugs with similar extraction characteristics, polarities, and detection characteristics. Chemical tests are selective for the chemical reactivity of substances with similar structures. The type of analysis required also depends on the type of biologic specimen to be analyzed. A putrefied liver specimen, for example, will require greater sample preparation than would a fresh urine specimen. Some drugs are present in much smaller concentrations than others and thus require more sophisticated detection techniques.

It is impossible to design a single analytical scheme that is capable of detecting all the available drugs and poisons while being suitable for the wide variety of specimen combinations that may be submitted. In general, a collection of about a dozen standard general screening methods is supplemented with as many special methods as required. Because the main objective is qualitative detection, rather than quantification, general screening methods are usually more flexible than special methods and can therefore be applied to a wider variety of materials. A good general method will provide a provisional identification which can then be confirmed by the application of a quantitative directed analysis.

Often, the nature of a suspected toxin is unknown. The classic example is a person who has expired under suspicious circumstances and where the history, scene, and autopsy fail to

Table 12.4.2 Case Management by Manner of Death

	Volatiles	IA B/U	CO-CN	BDS	WAN	Toxi-A/B	MCT	Specials
Accident								
MVA–								
pedestrian	X	X				X		
MVA-driver	X	X	X			X	X	
MVA-								
passenger	X	X	X			X		
Workplace	X	X	X			X	X	As required
Police								
investigation	X	X				X		As required
Aviation-crew	X	X	X	X	X	X		
Fire/Smoke	X	X	X			X	X	
Other	X	X	X			X	X	As required
Natural								
With a "COD"	X	X				X		
SIDS	X	X				X		APAP, ASA
Epileptics	X	X			X	X		
Asthmatics	X					X		As required
Homicides								
Active role	X	X				X	X	
Innocent victim	X	X				X		
Unknown role	X	X				X	X	
Suicide (non-drug)								
Trauma	X	X				X		
CO	X	X	X			X		As required
Pending pathology	X	X				X		
Pending toxicology	X	X	X	X	X	X	X	As required

Immunoassays imply the use of urine, however, if a urine specimen is unavailable, or "indicates the presence of" a drug, a blood analysis should follow. At a minium, perform Amphetamines, Barbiturates, Benzodiazepines, Cocaine, Opiates, PCP, and others as required by case type and history.

CO (carbon monoxide): Between the months of September and May, request on all MEO cases involving apparent natural death and pending cases occurring indoors.

MCTs: Require urine and gastric contents.

Key: IA= immunoassays; CO/CN = carbon monoxide and cyanide; BDS = basic drug screen; WAN = weak acid neutral drug screen; TOXI-A/B = commercial thin layer chromatography acids and bases; MCT = microcolor tests; B/U = blood and/or urine; APAP = acetaminophen; ASA = salicylates.

Wm. Lee Hearn and H. Chip Walls

disclose a definitive cause of death. In such cases, the screening strategy must be more extensive, since thousands of toxic drugs and chemicals are available on the market worldwide. A systematic procedure that allows the simultaneous detection of as many toxicants in biosamples as possible is necessary for a comprehensive toxicological analysis.[1,2,4,5,89-91]

12.4.3 BASIC STRATEGIES

In laboratories with small caseloads, each case may be reviewed individually by the director who assigns specific tests. Testing large numbers of samples proceeds more efficiently, and in a more organized fashion, when standardized assay panels are performed on batches of samples. Blood and urine are the specimens of choice to screen for drugs and poisons. Depending on the circumstances of the case, other samples include liver, stomach contents, or bile.

The blood volatiles screen detects and quantifies ethanol while simultaneously screening for methanol, isopropanol and acetone as well as other volatiles, such as halogenated and non-halogenated hydrocarbons that are sometimes inhaled for purposes of intoxication.[46,70,92-95] Each of the immunoassay tests is used to detect substances that cannot easily be included in one or two chromatographic procedures, or for which routine chromatographic tests may be too insensitive, or where specialized extraction or derivatization conditions may be required.

12.4.3.1 Amphetamines

The amphetamines are relatively volatile, and can be lost by evaporation if the extract is not first acidified. In addition, they do not chromatograph well on a gas chromatograph. However, ToxiLab can effectively detect and differentiate the sympathomimetic amines in urine, so the amphetamines immunoassay could be omitted if ToxiLab is used. If an amphetamines immunoassay is used, it should be one of broad class selectivity, not one of the newer and more specific monoclonal antibody assays.[96-98]

12.4.3.2 Barbiturates

An immunoassay for barbiturates can eliminate the need for labor intensive chromatographic screens of weakly acidic and neutral drugs in the majority of cases. Only those cases testing positive, or where phenytoin is indicated, need the chromatographic screen. The ToxiLab B system can help to differentiate barbiturates in urine, or the testing can proceed directly to a GC, HPLC, or GC-MS screen on an acidic drug extract of blood to identify the specific barbiturate(s) present in the body.[99-104]

12.4.3.3 Benzodiazepines

The benzodiazepines comprise a large class of drugs that are often detected in postmortem cases. ToxiLab does not ordinarily detect them in urine at therapeutic doses, and a basic drug GC screen rarely detects any of the more potent drugs in this class, except in cases of overdose. Available immunoassays can yield positive results in urine for metabolites from most of the common benzodiazepines. Exceptions are lorazepam and flunitrazepam. GC with election capture detection, or GC/MS, may be applied to urine or blood to differentiate benzodiazepines and to detect those that are missed by immunoassays.[105-117] Whether or not to use these more labor intensive chromatographic tests in the absence of a positive immunoassay depends upon the potential significance of a benzodiazepine, if it were to be found, and on any indications from the investigation that one may have been taken.

12.4.3.4 Cocaine

Cocaine should always be included in a postmortem toxicology screen. Even infants and the elderly occasionally test positive. The most efficient way to screen for cocaine is to use an immunoassay for benzoylecgonine.[118-121] Although both ToxiLab A and basic drug GC screens can actually detect cocaine itself, special procedures are required for the chromatographic detection of benzoylecgonine. Cocaine may not always be found in the urine with benzoylecgonine, although benzoylecgonine is almost always found whenever cocaine is present.

12.4.3.5 Opiates

The common opiates include morphine, 6-monoacetylmorphine, codeine, hydromorphone, hydrocodone and oxycodone. Routine ToxiLab A or basic drug GC screens detect codeine, hydrocodone, and oxycodone. These methods are less effective for morphine and hydromorphone, which are usually found in the urine as water-soluble conjugates of glucuronic acid. Immunoassays can detect both parent drug and metabolite(s). Differentiation of opiates is usually accomplished by GC/MS, using procedures that include hydrolysis of conjugates and derivatization for maximum sensitivity and specificity.[122-124]

12.4.3.6 Phencyclidine

Phencyclidine (PCP) is more commonly encountered in some regions, while not in others. It is a powerful dissociative anesthetic with significant effects on behavior at low doses, and should be included as part of the postmortem drug screen. Both TLC and GC detect PCP, though may be insufficiently sensitive to reliably rule it out. Immunoassays capable of detecting PCP in urine down to 25 ng/ml provide a reliable screening test.[125,126]

12.4.3.7 Immunoassays for Other Illegal Drugs

Immunoassays have been developed to screen for the presence of other illegal drugs, including cannabinoids, LSD, and prescription drugs such as propoxyphene, methadone and methaqualone. With the exception of cannabinoids and LSD, all of the analytes are readily detected by either ToxiLab A or GC basic drug screens. Cannabinoid and LSD assays may be included in a standard screening protocol or may be reserved for cases involving an issue of possible behavioral toxicity, since those are not known to contribute to either fatal intoxications or deaths attributable to natural causes.

12.4.3.8 Chromatographic Methods

Chromatographic methods are used to expand the range of a drug screen beyond those drugs detectable by the immunoassays. The extraction system should be selective for basic drugs, and neutral substances will also be extracted.[47,58,62,71-76,127-130]

12.4.3.8.1 ToxiLab® A for Urine and Gastric Contents

The ToxiLab A system for basic drug detection is a powerful tool for drug screening in urine or gastric contents.[55-57,131] The four stage visualization process, combined with Rf and detection of metabolite patterns, adds considerably to the confidence in drug identification. Sensitivity for many drugs is on the order of 0.5 to 1.0 mg/L, which is satisfactory for screening urine or gastric samples. The ToxiLab A can detect nearly 150 drugs and their metabolites, and the list is steadily growing.

FLOW CHART FOR ROUTINE TOXICOLOGY CASES

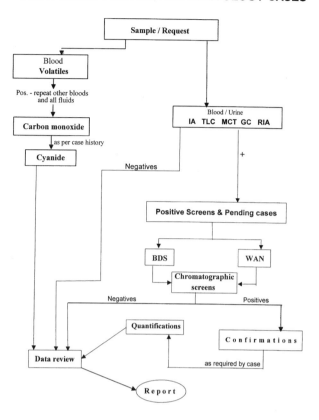

Figure 12.4.3 Flow chart for routine toxicology cases.

12.4.3.8.2 Alternatives to ToxiLab®

A screen for basic and neutral drugs by gas chromatography with a nitrogen/phosphorus detector (NPD) is an alternative to ToxiLab TLC for a laboratory having sufficient GC capacity.[47,71,74-76,82,127] GC is much more sensitive than TLC, having limits of detection on the order of 0.01 to 0.10 mg/L from one milliliter of sample. GC can be calibrated to presumptively identify hundreds of drugs and drug metabolites, and the NPD data can reveal other unidentified nitrogen- containing substances that may be characterized by additional analysis of the extract by GC/MS. On the other hand, many laboratories do not have enough GC-NPD capacity to permit an instrument to be dedicated to urine and gastric content screening when another reliable method, with much lower initial cost, is available.

The Trinders test is added to the screen to detect salicylate from aspirin, a common drug and one that is sometimes taken for suicidal purposes. It may be eliminated if the screen is intended only to evaluate potential behavioral toxicity. The chemical tests for ethchorvynol and chloral hydrate fill another gap in the screening protocol, since these drugs are not detected by immunoassay or in chromatographic screens for basic drug or volatiles. Figure 12.4.3 illustrates the analytical scheme for routine cases with both urine and blood submitted to the laboratory.

12.4.3.9 Gastric Contents vs. Urine

Often, urine is not available for testing because the bladder was empty at the time of autopsy. In such cases, an extract or filtrate of gastric contents may be substituted. However, a gastric drug screen alone may not be sufficient to exclude all potentially relevant substances. Drugs that are typically administered parenterally, smoked or insufflated may not diffuse into the stomach in detectable amounts, so blood or plasma analysis with immunoassays for opiates and benzoylecgonine is often required to detect those substances.

Drugs taken hours before death may not remain in the stomach. However, some quantity of a basic drug will diffuse into the stomach from blood and become ionized, and thus remains there. The resulting concentration in the stomach contents is determined in part by the drug's concentration in blood and in part by its pKa. For optimum sensitivity, a gastric content drug screen may be combined with immunoassays on plasma, vitreous humor or blood for barbiturates, benzodiazepines, benzoylecgonine, opiates and a basic drug screen of blood by GC-NPD. The following protocols, which employ tests on gastric contents and blood (or plasma), can be used in place of a urine drug screen. The same blood test panel may be used when gastric contents are not available, or applied to tissue homogenates when blood is not available.

Immunoassays can usually be performed directly on unhemolyzed plasma or vitreous humor. Even hemolyzed plasma and postmortem whole blood can be tested directly if FPIA or RIA is used.[50,52,132-145] If results are unsatisfactory, simple dilution with an equal volume of assay buffer is often sufficient to render an analyzable sample. If FPIA or RIA is not available in the laboratory, blood may be screened with spectrophotometry-based immunoassays, though hemoglobin and other proteins must first be precipitated by addition of acetone, methanol, or acetonitrile. The centrifuged supernatant from such treatment can be assayed against similarly prepared calibrators.[49-52,146-154] When applied to blood, plasma or vitreous humor, immunoassays should be calibrated to a lower cutoff threshold than that used for urine screening. Cutoffs, on the order of 50 ng/ml (500 ng/ml for barbiturates) will yield some false positives. Considering the variations in cross reactivity for analytes of interest (e.g. benzodiazepines), some false positive immunoassay results may be acceptable in the interest of minimizing false negatives. Any positive immunoassay result must, of course, be confirmed if it is to be reported. If the case may involve lethal toxicity, immunoassays for acetaminophen and salicylate should be added to the panel.

12.4.3.10 Screening with Gas Chromatography

The gas chromatographic screen for basic drugs in blood is more sensitive than a basic drug screen on gastric contents, but is also more labor intensive. It may be included in a general drug screen whenever urine is not available or it may be reserved for cases where intoxication is indicated by the investigation, and gastric contents yield negative screening results. Figure 12.4.1 illustrates general screening protocols for various combinations of postmortem samples.

When initial chromatographic screening tests reveal an unidentified spot on TLC or a response from GC that does not match any standard, extracts may be further screened by GC/MS in the full scan electron-impact ionization mode.[80,82,83,100,155-163] Reconstructed ion chromatograms are inspected for spectra that indicate exogenous (i.e. xenobiotic) substances. Suspect spectra are compared with the instrument's computerized libraries of drugs, poisons, and their metabolites. In addition, spectra may be visually compared with published compilations of mass spectral data.[164-169] Whenever a tentative identification is made, the unknown and reference spectra must be visually compared to verify their identity. GC/MS is the most complex method of screening for drugs and poisons, and also the most expensive. The analyst must have a considerable amount of training and experience to reliably perform GC/MS screening.

Wm. Lee Hearn and H. Chip Walls

To provide adequate support for a medical examiner's office the toxicology laboratory should periodically assess the prevalence of drugs in the population served, and adjust its offering of routine tests accordingly. Certain drugs are more prevalent in various localities due to supply routes, ethnic practices, and demand. Changing patterns of drug use may be identified through crime laboratory statistics and various epidemiological monitoring programs, such as the Drug Abuse Warning Network (DAWN) and the community-based Drug Epidemiology Network.

12.4.4 THE GENERAL UNKNOWN

Cases in which a toxic cause of death is suspected, but where a specified toxic agent is not known are referred to as general unknowns, and require an open-ended search for poisons. The first step in investigating a general unknown is to carefully examine the medical records, case history, autopsy findings, and scene observations for evidence of specific toxins, or of a toxic mechanism.[1-3,5-9,30,170,171]

The case history and medical records may describe symptoms characteristic of a particular pharmacologic category. Cardiac rhythm disturbances, respiratory rate and pattern, pupil size and responsiveness, condition of reflexes, convulsions and any other premortem symptoms may suggest a toxic mechanism that excludes some toxins from a long list of possible agents.

Autopsy findings may also provide guidance. The condition of the gastric and esophageal mucosa may suggest or exclude corrosive poisons. The presence of pulmonary edema and congestion may indicate preterminal respiratory depression. Hepatic necrosis may indicate acetaminophen or *Amanita* mushroom toxicity, among other agents. Needle punctures and, especially, "track marks" indicate a possible I.V. drug overdose. These and other observations, properly interpreted, can narrow the focus of the analytical search.

Consideration of the place where death occurred, or where the terminal symptoms appeared, may suggest toxic agents. Scene investigation can yield valuable clues. For example, the death of a jewelry store employee may have resulted from exposure to cyanide which is used in jewelry manufacture. Other employment settings have associated chemical hazards that should be recognized when planning a strategy for investigation of a workplace death.

In the home, other toxic exposures are more likely. Drugs, pesticides, and other chemical products for household use are possible agents. Also, drug misuse at home can result in accidents or fatal intoxication. Reports of witnesses can also give valuable clues. What was the deceased doing at the onset of illness? When was the deceased last seen alive? Was the deceased behaving normally, or was intoxication indicated? Was there a complaint of feeling sick? Eliciting such observations may make it possible to shorten the list of possible drugs to only a few likely candidates.

The volatiles screen by headspace GC, while designed to test for the common alcohols and acetone, can also detect other volatile chemicals such as toluene and other solvents and volatile anesthetics. Drug screening tests are essential to rule out drug intoxication, and chromatographic screens can detect many other chemical substances besides drugs. GC/MS is a mainstay of screening protocols for general unknowns. Semivolatile organic compounds can be identified by computerized comparison of their mass spectra with libraries containing over 50,000 spectra of pesticides, drugs and industrial chemicals. Figure 12.4.4 illustrates a strategy for analysis of cases where classification is pending the outcome of toxicology testing.

Tests for drugs and poisons not detected by the basic strategy can be added to the protocol for general unknowns. Selective immunoassays are available to test for cardiac glycosides, LSD, fentanyls, haloperidol, aminoglycoside antibiotics and anticonvulsants. Clinical laboratories can provide assistance with tests for potassium, lithium, iron and insulin/c- reactive peptide. Toxic metals and nonmetals can be detected by atomic absorption spectrophotometry, and classical

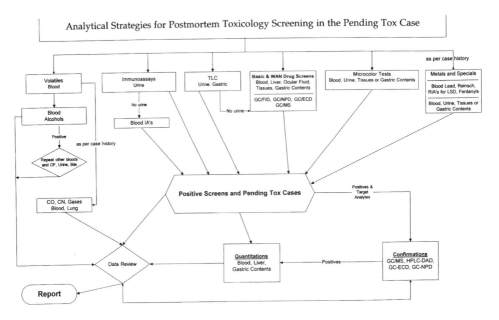

Figure 12.4.4 Analytical strategies for postmortem toxicology screening in the pending tox case.

inorganic qualitative tests can be used to screen for toxic anions on a dialysate of urine, blood or stomach contents. Other drugs that do not chromatograph well by GC may be detected by HPLC.

The following guidelines should be observed in approaching the general unknown:

1. If specimen selection and quantity are not limiting factors, then the objective should be the broadest screen possible with available technology.
2. The blood and ocular fluid alcohol content should be determined before or simultaneously with other analyses .
3. Blood alcohol analyses should be performed by headspace gas chromatography, utilizing an internal standard. This does not preclude possible confirmation by some other procedure.
4. If carbon monoxide is to be determined, this should also be done prior to drug screening procedures.
5. In the absence of background information on a given case, the selected analytical scheme should provide the best chances of successfully finding a drug or poison. That is, the more commonly encountered drugs and poisons should be sought before the more rarely encountered ones are considered.
6. In the event that specimen selection and quantity are limited, it will be necessary to plan assays more carefully. Immunoassay procedures should be applied early in the scheme if proper samples are available.
7. All assays should be considered with the intent of subsequently confirming positive findings by another independent procedure. This means, for example, that if specimen size is a limiting factor, then different stages of a general screen should be performed sequentially rather than in parallel.

12.4.5 CONFIRMATION

12.4.5.1 What Confirmation is and Why it is Necessary

Courts require that the opinions expressed by toxicologists be of a "reasonable scientific probability", that the identity of reported substances be known with "scientific certainty", and that quantitative values be accurate to a stated statistical probability. Screening tests provide tentative identification of drugs and poisons. The forensic standard for conclusive identification requires that their identity be confirmed by additional tests.[172]

The first analytical indication of the presence of a particular drug is usually obtained from an immunoassay, a chromatographic screen (e.g., TLC) or a spot test. The initial test may point to a particular drug, or class of drugs, such as barbiturates, benzodiazepines or opiates. The confirmatory test must clearly identify the specific drug and/or its metabolite(s). Confirmatory methods may include gas chromatography with flame ionization (GC-FID), electron capture (GC-ECD), and nitrogen-phosphorus (GC-NPD) detectors, high-performance liquid chromatography (HPLC), ultraviolet spectroscopy, gas chromatography-mass spectrometry (GC/MS) and other hyphenated techniques such as MS/MS coupled to either a GC or LC sample introduction system.

Any chemical test can be subject to errors that may cause a false positive result. Immunoassays can cross react with substances other than the target drug. Chromatographic methods can have interfering substances that produce signal or spot at the same time and place as a target analyte. Even GC/MS can yield false positive results if a sample is mislabeled or contaminated in process, or by carryover from a preceding injection, or if the spectrum does not have a unique fragmentation pattern. For example, amitriptyline and cyclobenzaprine have similar retention times and yield fragmentation patterns that are nearly identical. They may be confused if the molecular ion cannot be discerned.

In recognition of the possibility of a false positive result from a single test, it is necessary that all potentially significant results be confirmed. Confirmation requires at least one additional test based upon a different chemical detection principle, with high specificity and sensitivity at least equal to the initial test.[172] The essence of confirmation is to assemble a sufficient body of evidence such that a technically competent independent reviewer would agree with the conclusion.

The requirement for two or more chemically distinct methodologies is based upon the concern that chemical similarity could cause a false positive result in one type of test, and may also influence another test with a similar chemical principle. A radioimmunoassay can not confirm enzyme immunoassay results since the chemical properties responsible for antibody binding may affect the antibodies in both tests similarly. Likewise, two similar GC columns such as 1% and 5% phenyl-methylsilicone (DB-1 and DB-5) would not serve to confirm one another, because the polarities of the two liquid phases and, hence, the elution orders of most drugs are similar.

A combination of less specific chromatographic procedures (e.g., TLC , GC-NPD/ECD or HPLC) can be used to confirm screening results from immunoassay or spot test results. A second chromatographic method based upon a different chemical principle may be used to confirm a presumptive finding from a chromatographic screening test (e.g., TLC and GLC or HPLC and GC-NPD/EC). Derivatization of the presumptively identified drug can alter its chromatographic behavior sufficiently to permit confirmation by re-analysis in the same chromatographic system. Some screening procedures, such as GC/MS, identify specific compounds. Even here, a second test on a separate aliquot should be performed to "verify" the analyte and insure that no human error in sample handling or analyses has occurred. Re-injection of the same extract would not be sufficient. An exception to this rule would be limited sample volume precluding repeat analyses.

In postmortem toxicology, confirmation tests are often applied to specimens other than the one used for screening. By employing a quantitative confirmatory method, the analyte is simultaneously confirmed and quantified. For example, a presumptive finding of diphenhydramine in urine by TLC may be confirmed by a quantitative GC procedure applied to blood.

Some additional illustrative examples of confirmation follow:

1. An immunoassay positive for opiates in urine, followed by a GC/MS analysis of urine to identify the specific drug(s).
2. An immunoassay positive for benzodiazepines in urine, followed by an analysis of blood by GC-ECD to identify the specific drug(s).
3. A drug such as amitriptyline detected by TLC in urine or gastric contents followed by GC-NPD analysis of blood with relative retention times matching the suspected drug, ideally on two columns of differing liquid phase. A quantification of the drug by HPLC would give additional confirmatory evidence as would detection of metabolites of the presumptively identified drug by TLC or GC.
4. Immunoassay positive for cocaine metabolite in urine or blood with detection of parent cocaine in blood by GC-NPD.
5. In some cases, such as blood volatiles analysis, GC head-space analysis can be correlated as relative retention times on two GC columns of differing polarity to confirm an identification. However, novel or rarely detected analytes such as toluene or 1,1,1,-trichloroethane may require further confirmation by headspace GC-MS.

12.4.5.2 When is Confirmation Necessary?

In general, any finding that could reasonably be questioned, or adversely affect insurance coverage or the reputation of the deceased should be confirmed before it is reported. The greater the significance of a finding to the case, the more important it becomes to confirm that finding to absolute certainty by GC-MS, if possible.

- When the substance is potentially related to the cause and manner of death.
- When the detected substance is an illicit drug such as marijuana, cocaine, methamphetamine or PCP, since labeling an individual a possible drug abuser has serious sociologic and legal implications.[173-176]
- Any prescription drug that is not known to have been prescribed for the deceased.

12.4.5.3 When is Confirmation Unnecessary?

When the substance presumptively detected has no relationship to the cause or manner of death, and when the detected substance carries no stigma, if reported, confirmation is not needed. Over-the-counter medications, with no behavioral toxicity, usually do not require confirmation except when it is suspected that they may have contributed to toxicity. For example, salicylate or acetaminophen need not be confirmed in traumatic death cases, but should be confirmed in cases pending toxicology or suicidal intoxications.

Medications commonly administered during resuscitation, such as lidocaine and atropine do not need confirmation if the deceased received such treatment before being pronounced dead. Prescribed medications that the deceased had been taking, and which are not related to the cause or manner of death, may not require confirmation either, since their presence in biological specimens is consistent with the history. Any substance reported without confirmation should be identified in the report as an unconfirmed presumptive finding.

12.4.6 GAS CHROMATOGRAPHY-MASS SPECTROMETRY

Today, GC/MS is generally accepted as unequivocal identification for most drugs, providing the best confirmatory information when performed correctly.[177,178] However, GC/MS assays can be performed in many ways, depending upon the specific requirements and use of the results. Pharmacokinetic studies generally employ chemical ionization with single-ion monitoring to obtain optimum sensitivity. In such studies, the target drug is expected to be present, so criteria for identification need not be so rigorous, but single ion monitoring is not usually considered sufficient for forensic purposes. GC/MS methods for the confirmation of illegal drugs of abuse in urine most often use electron impact ionization and multiple-ion monitoring to obtain conclusive results.[177-181] The more traditional mass spectrometric identification criterion calls for matching retention times and full scan electron impact mass spectra of the unknown with a standard.

Whether forensic samples should be analyzed by full-scan data acquisition, or by selected ion monitoring, is a matter of contention. The debate really comes down to one underlying question: how much spectral and chromatographic information is needed to provide a scientifically and legally defensible identification? Is a full-scan spectrum necessary? If selected ion monitoring is acceptable, how many ions must be monitored? Unfortunately, there are no simple answers. A good quality, full-scan mass spectrum that matches a reference spectrum clearly constitutes a more definitive identification than ion current profiles of a few selected ions at the correct retention time.

Cody and Foltz have state that the specificity of a GC/MS assay depends on many factors, including:

1. Choice of internal standard. The role of the internal stndard in the overall analytical process cannot be overemphasized.[182-187]
2. Selectivity of the extraction procedure.
3. Choice of derivative, where appropriate.[188-190]
4. Efficiency of the gas chromatographic separation.
5. Method of ionization.
6. Relative uniqueness of the analyte's mass spectrum or the chosen ions to be monitored.
7. Signal-to-noise ratio of the detected ions.[192]

Using GC/MS in the scanning mode, as both a screening and definitive identification methodology, has become quite common.[163] If the drug is an unknown, full-scan mode is the method of choice. Further comparison of the unknown's full mass spectrum with reference spectra will be necessary. Mass spectra are tentatively identified by a computerized library search and visually compared by an experienced analyst.[80,81,161-163]

Gas chromatography/mass spectrometry with selected ion monitoring (GC/MS-SIM) is commonly used to confirm the presence of drugs and/or metabolites in post-mortem samples.[180,191] A well-designed assay, involving the selected ion monitoring of three or more abundant and structurally diagnostic ions, combined with specific requirements for the analyte's retention time relative to a suitable internal standard or calibrator, is regarded as a reliable identification.[192] Even fewer ions can provide an acceptable identification if the assay employs a highly selective extraction procedure or selective mode of ionization, such as ammonia chemical ionization.

GC/MS-SIM assays are extremely useful to confirm or exclude the presence of a suspected analyte which may have been indicated by history or screening results. However, target compound analyses such as selected ion monitoring (GC/MS-SIM) will only detect, or exclude, a limited number of related chemical compounds or classes of drugs. A reference standard and control materials of the target analyte must be analyzed within the same batch. Selected ion monitoring typically provides signal intensities that are 10- to 100-fold greater than those from full-scan analysis performed on quadrupole instruments. SIM analyses are therefore better adapted for quantitative measurements. Selected ion monitoring is generally less inclined to interferences from co-eluting compounds than an assay employing full-scan recording. However, unlike full-scan spectral acquisition, a selected ion monitoring assay will not detect unsuspected drugs that may be of toxicological significance.

Standards adopted for conclusive drug identification include (1) the appearance of the monitored ions at a correct retention time, (2) acceptable intensity ratios among those ions. The retention time and ion intensity ratios observed in the test sample are compared with those established from the calibrator(s) containing the target analyte, at a suitable concentration, incorporated in the same analytical batch.

12.4.6.1 Qualitative GC/MS-SIM Determination Criteria

To qualitatively identify a compound by Selected Ion Monitoring (SIM), ion chromatograms are obtained from the reference compound for the primary ion and two or more qualifier ions. The criteria below must be met for a qualitative identification of an unknown:

1. The characteristic ions of the compound must be found at maxima in the same scan or within one scan of each other.
2. The retention time of the unknown compound's mass spectrum must be within $\pm$ 2% of the retention time of the authentic compound or deuterated internal standard.
3. The ratios of the SIM peak areas must agree within +/- 20 % with the ratios of the relative intensities for those ions in a reference mass spectrum from a calibrator analyzed on the same run by the GC/MS system.

These criteria should be kept in mind when making compound identification decisions. In addition Dr. Rodger Foltz has proposed the following helpful guidelines:[160,192-194]

1. Agreement among the relative ion intensities within a small mass range is more important than for those encompassing a wide mass range.
2. The higher mass ions are generally more diagnostic than those occurring at low mass.
3. No prominent ions in either spectrum (those with relative intensities above 10%) should be totally missing from the other spectrum, unless they can be attributed to an impurity.

12.4.6.2 Potential Problems with GC/MS Analyses

There are several drawbacks to GC/MS analysis. The mass spectral library may give erroneous identifications when concentrations near the detection limit are analyzed, or when chromatographically interfering substances are present, or when isomers are analyzed. Even MS with a full fragmentation pattern may not provide adequate confirmation, either because several drugs have very similar fragmentation patterns, as the barbiturates for example, or because the drug may exhibit only one major peak consisting of a low mass fragment ion in its mass spectrum, such as the tricyclic antidepressants.

Wm. Lee Hearn and H. Chip Walls

Using the selected-ion monitoring mode, a considerable gain in GC-MS sensitivity can be achieved by focusing on the most abundant ion, and two or more other characteristic ions. However, many illegal drugs or metabolites (and numerous other commonly used drugs, e.g., antihistamines, local anesthetics, some beta-blocking agents, etc.) have similar EI mass spectra, showing a common base peak and weak molecular ion signals. Many elute over a wide range of retention times, others may have closely related retention indices.

The complexity of biological matrices encountered in postmortem cases, such as "blood", tissues, gastric contents and hair/nails, necessitates well designed, and often multi-step, sample treatment procedures.[195] This is especially true when utilizing procedures based upon physico-chemical properties of drug/metabolites. Suitable sample preparation is the most important prerequisite in the GC-MS of typical postmortem samples. It involves isolation and, if necessary, cleavage of conjugates and/or derivatization of the drugs and their metabolites. Derivatization steps are necessary if relatively polar compounds such as metabolites are to be screened or confirmed.

12.4.7 METHOD VALIDATION

Bioanalytical methods, based on a variety of physico-chemical and biological techniques, such as chromatography, immunoassay and mass spectrometry, must all be individually validated prior to and during use to generate confidence in the results.[196-210] Method validation is discussed in Section 12.5.

12.4.8 QUANTIFICATION OF DRUGS AND POISONS

> *When you can measure what you are speaking about and express it in numbers, you know something about it; but when you cannot express it in numbers, your knowledge is of meagre and unsatisfactory kind.*

> Lord Kelvin (1824-1907)

Screening and confirmation (qualitative) tests establish the presence of a specific substance; quantitative tests measure the amount of that substance in a particular specimen. Qualitative information alone can demonstrate that the deceased was exposed to the substance before death, and may even enable the toxicologist to offer an opinion as to the antemortem interval in which the exposure probably took place. However, quantitative information is often required in order to form an opinion as to whether or not the exposure was sufficient to cause behavioral toxicity or death. Drug concentrations in postmortem tissues, and/or fluids, must be related to reference values derived from other cases.[5,211-215]

12.4.8.1 What Should Be Quantified?

Substances should be quantified only when necessary for interpretation. Most quantitative assays are separate, labor-intensive, procedures that measure only one drug or group of similar compounds. Quantifying substances that, by their nature, could have no conceivable bearing on the issues of the case is a waste of time and resources. For example, drugs with no psychoactivity, such as acetaminophen, should not be quantified in a motor vehicle accident driver victim, while diphenhydramine, an antihistamine with sedative side effects, should. On the other hand, if the victim was a passenger, diphenhydramine would not require quantification. In deaths from asthma or epilepsy, the laboratory should quantify theophylline or anticonvulsant, respectively, to determine whether or not they were within or below the therapeutic concentration range.

In general, substances that can cause behavioral toxicity should be quantified. In most natural deaths, it is important to know that the concentration of a prescribed or therapeutic drug is not excessive. Semiquantitative information, derived from blood screening tests, is often sufficient to make the assessment. Only if the concentration estimate indicates an excessive amount would a quantitative assay be required. Poisons such as carbon monoxide, cyanide and heavy metals should always be quantified in appropriate specimens. Tests for ethanol usually yield both qualitative and quantitative data which should be reported if above the laboratory's administrative cutoff (usually 0.01%).

Cocaine should always be quantified. Its concentration is usually important and its instability in storage may prevent subsequent analysis of it is not quantified soon after detection. Other drugs or poisons that are unstable in storage should be quantified before their decomposition renders the analysis unreliable. In a case that is pending the outcome of toxicology testing, any detected drugs or poisons and their metabolites should be quantified, unless it is clear from the circumstances of the case, that a particular substance did not have a role in the cause or manner of death.

When resuscitation has been attempted, lidocaine and atropine may be detected in postmortem blood. Unless a medication error is suspected, or the quantity appears to be excessive, it is not necessary to quantify them. Nor is there any need to quantify caffeine and nicotine, unless toxicity is suspected or screening tests indicate that an abnormally large amount of either is present.

In most cases a drug's metabolites are just as important to quantify as the parent compound. The ratio of parent drug to its metabolite often indicates the state of pharmacokinetics in the individual case. For example, a ratio greater than 1 for amitriptyline/nortriptyline indicates an acute ingestion or short interval from ingestion to death, while a ratio of 0.3 in a propoxyphene/norpropoxyphene case indicates a chronic exposure.

Active or toxic metabolites of a drug or poison are always measured, but inactive metabolites may also be important. Their presence may shed light on the pattern of drug use. High concentrations of benzoylecgonine indicate accumulations from multiple doses. Low concentrations suggest that only a few doses were taken or a long interval since the last dose. Furthermore, there is some evidence that benzoylecgonine may be a vasoconstrictor, so it may contribute to the hypertensive effects of cocaine use.

12.4.8.2 Specimens for Quantification of Drugs and Poisons

The choice of the sample for quantitative analysis is very important.[216] Often it is sufficient to quantify drugs or poisons in blood only. If toxicity is not suspected, a blood quantification can verify that the drug was present, and that its concentration was consistent with therapeutic use. Also, when a drug concentration is clearly in the lethal range, and poisoning or overdose is suspected, a blood determination may be sufficient. It may not be necessary to quantify brain morpine levels in an intravenous heroin user, found dead with syringe, tourniquet and "cooker" present, with autopsy evidence of pulmonary edema, and a high concentration of morphine in the blood, to support a conclusion that death was caused by a heroin overdose. Likewise, a 15 mg/L blood amitriptyline concentration, in a case accompanied by a suicide note, is sufficient to define overt toxicity, regardless of potential postmortem diffusion.[216] Carbon monoxide should be measured only in blood, its site of action. Other specimens are likely to give negative results.

Tissues which selectively take up a particular drug class may have a much higher concentration than that found in blood. For example, volatile anesthetics, cocaine, marijuana, tricyclic antidepressants and other lipid-soluble substances are preferentially absorbed into the fatty tissues of the brain and liver, while digoxin and other cardiac glycosides are taken up by cardiac muscle. Figures 12.4.3 and 12.4.4 show the relationship of quantifications to the overall process of postmortem toxicology analysis.

12.4.8.3 Quantification: Procedural Issues

12.4.8.3.1 Instruments

Many of the instruments used for screening tests can also provide accurate quantitative data. Immunoassays designed for therapeutic drug monitoring (TDM) (e.g., serum assays for phenobarbital, theophylline, and phenytoin) are specific, and yield accurate results with most postmortem specimens.[144,217] GC, HPLC and GC/MS are readily adapted for quantification. Spectrophotometric methods are useful for some analytes, such as ethchlorvynol and heavy metals.[1] However, their utility is limited because many drugs have metabolites or breakdown products with similar spectra (e.g. phenothiazines), so relative contributions of the parent drug, and active and inactive metabolites, to the signal cannot be segregated and assessed.

12.4.8.3.2 Sample Preparation

Blood and other fluids are usually analyzed with no pretreatment other than dilution. GC screening tests can provide an estimate of the concentration of the analyte. If the estimated concentration is above the upper limit of linearity of the assay, the sample must be diluted with water, buffer or negative control matrix and thoroughly mixed to bring the analyte concentration into the dynamic range of the assay. Homogenates of tissue samples are prepared in a blender or a tissue homogenizer in water or a buffer usually in a 1:2 to a 1:5 ratio. These homogenates deteriorate rapidly so they are usually used within two weeks or less, and the remainder discarded. Gastric contents are weighed or measured by volume, homogenized and appropriately diluted.

With the exception of some immunoassays, samples are usually extracted with organic solvent to isolate the compounds of interest from the biological matrix. Often, liquid- liquid extraction is used, with back extraction to eliminate lipid interference. Recent advances in solid phase extraction technology have made possible the application of these techniques to the analysis of blood and tissues. The speed and efficiency of solid phase extractions make them an attractive alternative to liquid-liquid extraction procedures, and their use is expanding in postmortem toxicology. However, lot-to-lot inconsistencies in SPE columns can cause quantitative methods to fail, due to poor recovery of analytes. Therefore, it is extremely important to evaluate each new batch of columns before risking wastage of, sometimes limited, samples.

Duplicate samples should be analyzed through the entire procedure to demonstrate the reproducibility of the result. If the difference between duplicate analyses is greater than the two standard deviations for the method, the analyst should suspect that an error occurred in one or both. Additional analyses should be performed to determine an accurate result with acceptable precision.

12.4.8.3.3 Internal Standard

Most quantitative procedures employ one or more internal standards to compensate for variations in extraction efficiency, injection volume and changes in detector sensitivity. An internal standard is a substance with chemical properties similar to the target analyte. It is added in identical quantity to each sample and standard before the extraction process. The internal standard is extracted along with the analyte, so that any loss of analyte in the extraction process will be compensated for by a proportional loss of internal standard. The assumption is that the ratio of analyte to internal standard does not change. Selection and evaluation of the internal standards is a critical component for the development of a quantitative procedure.[184,218-222]

Method development and validation and the selection of internal standards are discussed in Section 12.5.

12.4.9 THE REVIEW PROCESS

Individual cases should be reviewed periodically to assess the status of the investigation and the quality of the acquired data. Reassessment may suggest the need for additional tests. Before a report is issued, the entire case file must be reviewed to ensure that results are forensically acceptable and that sufficient data have been gathered to determine whether, and to what extent, drugs or poisons influenced the cause and manner of death. When testing has been completed, the toxicologist reviews the file one final time to ensure that nothing has been overlooked.

12.4.10 PENDING TOXICOLOGY CONFERENCE

In cases where the cause of death is not obvious, and determinations have been put on hold pending the results of toxicological testing, the toxicologist and pathologist together review the investigation, autopsy, and toxicology results. When both are satisfied that the toxicology results answer the questions pertinent to the case, a final toxicology report is issued. The need for communication and teamwork for an effective system cannot be over-emphasized. [1-5,223,224] Refer to Figure 12.4.4 summarizing the analytic strategies for drug screening in "pending tox cases."

REFERENCES

1. Curry, A. S., Outline of a Systematic Search for an Unknown Poison in Viscera, in , *Mechanisms and Analytical Methods*, Stewart, C. P., Stolman, A, Eds., Vol. 1, Academic Press, New York, 257-283.1960
2. Freimuth, H. C., Isolation and Separation of Poisons from Biological Material, in *Mechanisms and Analytical Methods*, Stewart, C. P., Stolman, A, Eds., Vol. 1, Academic Press, New York, 285-302 1960
3. Stewart, C. P., Martin, G J, The Mode of Action of Poisons, in *Mechanisms and Analytical Methods*, Stewart, C. P., Stolman, A, Eds., Vol. 2, Academic Press, New York, 1-15.1960
4. Stewart, C. P., Stolman, A, The toxicologist and his work, in *Toxicology: Mechanisms and Analytical Methods*, Stewart, C. P., Stolman, A, Eds., Vol. 1, Academic Press, New York, 1-22. 1960
5. Jackson, J. V., Forensic Toxicology, in *Clarke's isolation and identification fo drugs in pharmaceuticals, body fluids, and post-mortem material*, Moffatt, A. C., 2 nd Edition , The Pharmaceutical Press, London, 35. 1986
6. FInkle, B. S., Forensic toxicology in the 1980's: the role of the analytical chemist., *Anal. Chem.*, 54, 433A-438A, 1982
7. Levine, B., Forensic toxicology. [Review], *Analytical Chemistry*, 65, 272A-276A, 1993
8. Levine, B. S., Smith, M. L., and Froede, R. C., Postmortem forensic toxicology. [Review], *Clinics in Laboratory Medicine 1990 Sep;10(3):571-89*, 1990
9. Osselton, M. D., Analytical forensic toxicology. [Review], *Archives of Toxicology. Supplement*, 15, 259-267, 1992
10. Kasantikul, V. and Kasantikul, D., Death following intentional overdose of psychotropic drugs, *Journal of the Medical Association of Thailand*, 72, 109-111, 1989
11. Costello, C. E., GC/MS analysis of street drugs, particularly in the body fluids of overdose victims., in Street Drug Analysis and Its Social and Clinical Implications, 67-78. 1974
12. Nashelsky, M. B., Dix, J. D., and Adelstein, E. H., Homicide facilitated by inhalation of chloroform, *Journal of Forensic Sciences*, 40, 134-138, 1995

Wm. Lee Hearn and H. Chip Walls

13. Tardiff, K., Marzuk, P. M., Leon, A. C., Hirsch, C. S., Stajic, M., Portera, L., *et al.*, Cocaine, opiates, and ethanol in homicides in New York City: 1990 and 1991, *Journal of Forensic Sciences*, 40, 387-390, 1995

14. Bailey, D. N. and Shaw, R. F., Cocaine- and methamphetamine-related deaths in San Diego County (1987): homicides and accidental overdoses, *Journal of Forensic Sciences*, 34, 407-422, 1989

15. Budd, R. D., The incidence of alcohol use in Los Angeles County homicide victims, *American Journal of Drug & Alcohol Abuse*, 9, 105-111, 1982

16. Garriott, J. C., Di Maio, V. J., and Rodriguez, R. G., Detection of cannabinoids in homicide victims and motor vehicle fatalities, *Journal of Forensic Sciences*, 31, 1274- 1282, 1986

17. Garriott, J. C., Drug use among homicide victims, *American Journal of Forensic Medicine & Pathology*, 14, 234-237, 1993

18. Poklis, A., Graham, M., Maginn, D., Branch, C. A., and Gantner, G. E., Phencyclidine and violent deaths in St. Louis, Missouri: a survey of medical examiners' cases from 1977 through 1986, *American Journal of Drug & Alcohol Abuse*, 16, 265-274, 1990

19. Gerostamoulos, J. and Drummer, O. H., Incidence of psychoactive cannabinoids in drivers killed in motor vehicle accidents, *Journal of Forensic Sciences*, 38, 649-656, 1993

20. Marzuk, P. M., Tardiff, K., Leon, A. C., Stajic, M., Morgan, E. B., and Mann, J. J., Prevalence of recent cocaine use among motor vehicle fatalities in New York City [see comments], *JAMA*, 263, 250-256, 1990

21. Perez-Reyes, M., Hicks, R. E., Bumberry, J., Jeffcoat, A. R., and Cook, C. E., Interaction between marihuana and ethanol: effects on psychomotor performance, *Alcoholism, Clinical & Experimental Research*, 12, 268-276, 1988

22. Garriott, J. C., DiMaio, V. J., Zumwalt, R. E., and Petty, C. S., Incidence of drugs and alcohol in fatally injured motor vehicle drivers, *Journal of Forensic Sciences*, 22, 383-389, 1977

23. Deveaux, M., Marson, J. C., Goldstein, P., Lhermitte, M., Gosset, D., and Muller, P. H., [Alcohol and psychotropic drugs in fatal traffic accidents (the Nord-Pas-de- Calais region, France)]. [French], *Acta Medicinae Legalis et Socialis*, 40, 61-70, 1990

24. Balkon, J., Results of a multilaboratory checksample analysis program for carbon monoxide and cyanide, *Journal of Analytical Toxicology*, 15, 232-236, 1991

25. Risser, D. and Schneider, B., Carbon monoxide-related deaths from 1984 to 1993 in Vienna, Austria, *Journal of Forensic Sciences*, 40, 368-371, 1995

26. Nowak, R. and Sachs, H., [Development of carbon monoxide and hydrocyanic acid in automobile fires and their forensic significance], *Versicherungsmedizin*, 45, 20-22, 1993

27. Jentzen, J. M., Forensic toxicology. An overview and an algorithmic approach, *American Journal of Clinical Pathology*, 92, S48-55, 1989

28. Taylor, R. L., Cohan, S. L., and White, J. D., Comprehensive toxicology screening in the emergency department: an aid to clinical diagnosis, *American Journal of Emergency Medicine*, 3, 507-511, 1985

29. Stair, E. L. and Whaley, M., Rapid screening and spot tests for the presence of common poisons, *Veterinary & Human Toxicology*, 32, 564-566, 1990

30. Bailey, D. N., Comprehensive toxicology screening: the frequency of finding other drugs in addition to ethanol, *Journal of Toxicology Clinical Toxicology*, 22, 463-471, 1984

31. Berry, D. J. and Grove, J., Emergency toxicological screening for drugs commonly taken in overdose., *J. Chromatogr.*, 80, 205-219, 1973

32. Kinberger, B., Holmen, A., and Wahrgren, P., A strategy for drug analysis in serum and urine. An application to drug screening of samples from drivers involved in traffic accidents., *Anal. Lett.*, 15, 937-951, 1982

33. Ueki, M., [Drug screening in clinical toxicology and analytical doping control in sports]. [Review] [5 refs] [Japanese], *Nippon Rinsho Japanese Journal of Clinical Medicine*, 1, 904-906, 1995

34. Howarth, A. T. and Clegg, G., Simultaneous detection and quantitation of drugs commonly involved in self-administered overdoses, *Clinical Chemistry*, 24, 804-807, 1978

35. Jatlow, P. I., UV spectrophotometry for sedative drugs frequently involved in overdose emergencies, in *Methodology for Analytical Toxicology: Volume I*, Sunshine, I., CRC Press, Inc, Boca Raton, 414. 1984

Strategies for Postmortem Toxicology Investigation

36. Christophersen, A. S. and Morland, J., Drug analysis for control purposes in forensic toxicology, workplace testing, sports medicine and related areas. [Review], *Pharmacology & Toxicology*, 74, 202-210, 1994

37. Chen, J. S., Chang, K. J., Charng, R. C., Lai, S. J., Binder, S. R., and Essien, H., The development of a broad-spectrum toxicology screening program in Taiwan, *Journal of Toxicology Clinical Toxicology*, 33, 581-589, 1995

38. Bailey, D. N., Results of limited versus comprehensive toxicology screening in a university medical center [see comments], *American Journal of Clinical Pathology*, 105, 572-575, 1996

39. Tilson, H. A. and Moser, V. C., Comparison of screening approaches. [Review], *Neurotoxicology*, 13, 1-13, 1992

40. Gambaro, V., Lodi, F., Mariani, R., Saligari, E., Villa, M., and Marozzi, E., [Systematic generic chemico-toxicological testing in forensic toxicology. IV. Application of a computer in a generic survey of substances of toxicological interest]. [Italian], *Farmaco Edizione Pratica*, 38, 133-172, 1983

41. Crouch, D. J., Peat, M. A., Chinn, D. M., and Finkle, B. S., Drugs and driving: a systematic analytical approach, *Journal of Forensic Sciences*, 28, 945-956, 1983

42. Masoud, A. N., Systematic identification of drugs of abuse I: spot tests, *Journal of Pharmaceutical Sciences*, 64, 841-844, 1975

43. Schepers, P. G., Franke, J. P., and de Zeeuw, R. A., System evaluation and substance identification in systematic toxicological analysis by the mean list length approach, *Journal of Analytical Toxicology*, 7, 272-278, 1983

44. Wennig, R., [Evaluation of a systematic analysis scheme used in clinical toxicology. Evaluation of 4 years' experience in a national health laboratory]. [French], *Recherche Europeenne en Toxicologie*, 5, 277-280, 1983

45. Marozzi, E., Cozza, E., Pariali, A., Gambaro, V., Lodi, F., and Saligari, E., [Generic systematic chemico-toxicological research in forensic toxicology, *Farmaco Edizione Pratica*, 33, 195-207, 1978

46. Tagliaro, F., Lubli, G., Ghielmi, S., Franchi, D., and Marigo, M., Chromatographic methods for blood alcohol determination. [Review], *Journal of Chromatography*, 580, 161-190, 1992

47. Cox, R. A., Crifasi, J. A., Dickey, R. E., Ketzler, S. C., and Pshak, G. L., A single-step extraction for screening whole blood for basic drugs by capillary GC/NPD, *Journal of Analytical Toxicology*, 13, 224-228, 1989

48. Simpson, D., Jarvie, D. R., and Heyworth, R., An evaluation of six methods for the detection of drugs of abuse in urine, *Annals of Clinical Biochemistry*, 26, 172-181, 1989

49. Gjerde, H., Christophersen, A. S., Skuterud, B., Klemetsen, K., and Morland, J., Screening for drugs in forensic blood samples using EMIT urine assays, *Forensic Science International*, 44, 179-185, 1990

50. Maier, R. D., Erkens, M., Hoenen, H., and Bogusz, M., The screening for common drugs of abuse in whole blood by means of EMIT-ETS and FPIA-ADx urine immunoassays, *International Journal of Legal Medicine*, 105, 115-119, 1992

51. Diosi, D. T. and Harvey, D. C., Analysis of whole blood for drugs of abuse using EMIT d.a.u. reagents and a Monarch 1000 Chemistry Analyzer, *Journal of Analytical Toxicology*, 17, 133-137, 1993

52. Bogusz, M., Aderjan, R., Schmitt, G., Nadler, E., and Neureither, B., The determination of drugs of abuse in whole blood by means of FPIA and EMIT-dau immunoassays—a comparative study, *Forensic Science International*, 48, 27-37, 1990

53. Masoud, A. N., Systematic identification of drugs of abuse II: TLC, *Journal of Pharmaceutical Sciences*, 65, 1585-1589, 1976

54. Machata, G., [Thin layer chromatography in systematic, toxicologic analysis processes]. [German], *Deutsche Zeitschrift fur die Gesamte Gerichtliche Medizin*, 59, 181-185, 1967

55. Brunk, S. D., Thin-Layer Chromatography Using Toxi-lab System, in *Analysis of Addictive and Misused Drugs*, Adamovics, J. A., Marcel Dekker, Inc, New York, 41-50. 1995

56. Jarvie, D. R. and Simpson, D., Drug screening: evaluation of the Toxi-Lab TLC system, *Annals of Clinical Biochemistry*, 23, 76-84, 1986

57. Nishigami, J., Ohshima, T., Takayasu, T., Kondo, T., Lin, Z., and Nagano, T., [Forensic toxicological application of TOXI-LAB screening for biological specimens in autopsy cases and emergency cares]. [Japanese], *Nippon Hoigaku Zasshi Japanese Journal of Legal Medicine*, 47, 372-379, 1993

58. Warfield, R. W. and Maickel, R. P., A generalized extraction-TLC procedure for identification of drugs, *Journal of Applied Toxicology*, 3, 51-57, 1983

59. Whitter, P. D. and Cary, P. L., A rapid method for the identification of acidic, neutral, and basic drugs in postmortem liver specimens by Toxi-Lab, *Journal of Analytical Toxicology*, 10, 68-71, 1986

60. Hackett, L. P., Dusci, L. J., and McDonald, I. A., Extraction procedures for some common drugs in clinical and forensic toxicology, *Journal of Forensic Sciences*, 21, 263- 274, 1976

61. Chen, X. H., Wijsbeek, J., van Veen, J., Franke, J. P., and de Zeeuw, R. A., Solid-phase extraction for the screening of acidic, neutral and basic drugs in plasma using a single-column procedure on Bond Elut Certify, *Journal of Chromatography*, 529, 161- 166, 1990

62. Chen, X. H., Franke, J. P., Wijsbeek, J., and de Zeeuw, R. A., Isolation of acidic, neutral, and basic drugs from whole blood using a single mixed-mode solid-phase extraction column, *Journal of Analytical Toxicology*, 16, 351-355, 1992

63. Foerster, E. H., Hatchett,C , Garriott, J C, A Rapid, Comprehensive Screening Procedure for Basic Drugs in Blood or Tissues by Gas Chromatography, *Journal of Analytical Toxicology*, 2, 50-55, 1978

64. Midha, K. K., Charette, C., McGilveray, I. J., Webb, D., and McLean, M. C., Application of GLC-alkali FID and GLC-MS procedures to analysis of plasma in suspected cases of psychotrpic drug overdose., *Clin. Toxicol.*, 18, 713-729, 1982

65. Griffiths, W. C., Oleksyk, S. K., and Diamond, I., A comprehensive gas chromatographic drug screening procedure for the clinical laboratory, *Clinical Biochemistry*, 6, 124-131, 1973

66. Eklund, A., Jonsson, J., and Schuberth, J., A procedure for simultaneous screening and quantification of basic drugs in liver, utilizing capillary gas chromatography and nitrogen sensitive detection, *Journal of Analytical Toxicology*, 7, 24-28, 1983

67. Marozzi, E., Gambaro, V., Lodi, F., and Pariali, A., [General systematic chemico- toxicological research in forensic toxicology. I. Considerations on the gas- chromatographic test in the general chemico-toxicological research]. [Italian], *Farmaco Edizione Pratica*, 31, 180-211, 1976

68. Drummer, O. H., Kotsos, A., and McIntyre, I. M., A class-independent drug screen in forensic toxicology using a photodiode array detector, *Journal of Analytical Toxicology*, 17, 225-229, 1993

69. Ojanpera, I., Rasanen, I., and Vuori, E., Automated quantitative screening for acidic and neutral drugs in whole blood by dual-column capillary gas chromatography, *Journal of Analytical Toxicology*, 15, 204-208, 1991

70. Premel-Cabic, A., Cailleux, A., and Allain, P., [A gas chromatographic assay of fifteen volatile organic solvents in blood (author's transl)]. [French], *Clinica Chimica Acta*, 56, 5- 11, 1974

71. Drummer, O. H., Horomidis, S., Kourtis, S., Syrjanen, M. L., and Tippett, P., Capillary gas chromatographic drug screen for use in forensic toxicology, *Journal of Analytical Toxicology*, 18, 134-138, 1994

72. Taylor, R. W., Greutink, C., and Jain, N. C., Identification of underivatized basic drugs in urine by capillary column gas chromatography, *Journal of Analytical Toxicology*, 10, 205-208, 1986

73. Ehresman, D. J., Price, S. M., and Lakatua, D. J., Screening biological samples for underivatized drugs using a splitless injection technique on fused silica capillary column gas chromatography, *Journal of Analytical Toxicology*, 9, 55-62, 1985

74. Turcant, A., Premel-Cabic, A., Cailleux, A., and Allain, P., Screening for neutral and basic drugs in blood by dual fused-silica column chromatography with nitrogen- phosphorus detection [published erratum appears in Clin Chem 1988 Nov;34(11):2370], *Clinical Chemistry*, 34, 1492-1497, 1988

75. Watts, V. W. and Simonick, T. F., Screening of basic drugs in biological samples using dual column capillary chromatography and nitrogen-phosphorus detectors, *Journal of Analytical Toxicology*, 10, 198-204, 1986

76. Fretthold, D., Jones, P., Sebrosky, G., and Sunshine, I., Testing for basic drugs in biological fluids by solvent extraction and dual capillary GC/NPD, *Journal of Analytical Toxicology*, 10, 10-14, 1986

77. Chia, D. T. and Gere, J. A., Rapid drug screening using Toxi-Lab extraction followed by capillary gas chromatography/mass spectroscopy, *Clinical Biochemistry*, 20, 303-306, 1987

78. Fiers, T., Maes, V., and Sevens, C., Automation of Toxicological Screenings On a Hewlett Packard Chemstation GC/MS System, *Clinical Biochemistry*, 29, 357-361, 1996

79. Pettersen, J. E. and Skuterud, B., Application of combined GC/MS as compared to a conventional analytical system for identification of unknown drugs in acute drug intoxications., *Anal. Chem. Symp. Ser.*, 13, 111-129, 1983

80. Maurer, H. H., Systematic toxicological analysis of drugs and their metabolites by gas chromatography-mass spectrometry. [Review], *Journal of Chromatography*, 580, 3-41, 1992

81. Neill, G. P., Davies, N. W., and McLean, S., Automated screening procedure using gas chromatography-mass spectrometry for identification of drugs after their extraction from biological samples, *Journal of Chromatography*, 565, 207-224, 1991

82. Brooks, K. E. and Smith, N. B., Efficient extraction of basic, neutral, and weakly acidic drugs from plasma for analysis by gas chromatography-mass spectrometry [published erratum appears in Clin Chem 1992 Feb;38(2):323], *Clinical Chemistry*, 37, 1975-1978, 1991

83. Cailleux, A., Turcant, A., Premel-Cabic, A., and Allain, P., Identification and quantitation of neutral and basic drugs in blood by gas chromatography and mass spectrometry, *Journal of Chromatographic Science*, 19, 163-176, 1981

84. Maurer, H. H., Identification and differentiation of barbiturates, other sedative-hypnotics and their metabolites in urine integrated in a general screening procedure using computerized GC/MS, *J. Chromatogr.*, 530, 307-326, 1990

85. Lambert, W. E., Meyer, E., Xue-Ping, Y., and De Leenheer, A. P., Screening, identification, and quantitation of benzodiazepines in postmortem samples by HPLC with photodiode array detection, *Journal of Analytical Toxicology*, 19, 35-40, 1995

86. Bogusz, M. and Wu, M., Standardized HPLC/DAD system, based on retention indices and spectral library, applicable for systematic toxicological screening [published erratum appears in J Anal Toxicol 1992 May-Jun;16(3):16A], *Journal of Analytical Toxicology*, 15, 188-197, 1991

87. Maier, R. D. and Bogusz, M., Identification power of a standardized HPLC/DAD system for systematic toxicological analysis, *Journal of Analytical Toxicology*, 19, 79-83, 1995

88. Chollet, D. and Kunstner, P., Fast systematic approach for the determination of drugs in biological fluids by fully automated high-performance liquid chromatography with on-line solid-phase extraction and automated cartridge exchange. Application to cebaracetam in human urine, *Journal of Chromatography*, 577, 335-340, 1992

89. Wu Chen, N. B., Schaffer, M. I., Lin, R. L., Kurland, M. L., Donoghue, E. R., Jr., and Stein, R. J., The general toxicology unknown. I. The systematic approach, *Journal of Forensic Sciences*, 28, 391-397, 1983

90. Wu Chen, N. B., Schaffer, M. I., Lin, R. L., Kurland, M. L., Donoghue, E. R., Jr., and Stein, R. J., The general toxicology unknown. II. A case report: doxylamine and pyrilamine intoxication, *Journal of Forensic Sciences*, 28, 398-403, 1983

91. Maurer, H. H., Detection of anticonvulsants and their metabolites in urine within a "general unknown" analytical procedure using computerized GC/MS, *Arch. Toxicol.*, 64, 554-561, 1990

92. Oliver, J. S. and Watson, J. M., Abuse of solvents "for kicks", *Lancet*, 1, 84-86, 1977

93. Astier, A., Chromatographic determination of volatile solvents and their metabolites in urine for monitoring occupational exposure, *Journal of Chromatography*, 643, 389-398, 1993

94. Jones, A. W., A rapid method for blood alcohol determination by headspace analysis using an electrochemical detector, *Journal of Forensic Sciences*, 23, 283-291, 1978

95. Ghittori, S., Fiorentino, M. L., and Imbriani, M., [Use of gas chromatography with flame ionization (GC-FID) in the measurement of solvents in the urine], *Giornale Italiano di Medicina del Lavoro*, 9, 21-24, 1987

96. Turner, G. J., Colbert, D. L., and Chowdry, B. Z., A broad spectrum immunoassay using fluorescence polarization for the detection of amphetamines in urine, *Annals of Clinical Biochemistry*, 28, 588-594, 1991

97. Kunsman, G. W., Manno, J. E., Cockerham, K. R., and Manno, B. R., Application of the Syva EMIT and Abbott TDx amphetamine immunoassays to the detection of 3,4-methylenedioxymethamphetamine (MDMA) and 3,4-methylenedioxyethamphetamine (MDEA) in urine, *Journal of Analytical Toxicology*, 14, 149-153, 1990

98. D' Nicuola, J., Jones, R., Levine, B., and Smith, M. L., Evaluation of six commercial amphetamine and methamphetamine immunoassays for cross-reactivity to phenylpropanolamine and ephedrine in urine [see comments], *Journal of Analytical Toxicology*, 16, 211-213, 1992

99. Mule, S. and Casella, G., Confirmation and quantitation of barbiturates in human urine by gas chromatography/mass spectrometry, *Journal of Analytical Toxicology*, 13, 13-16, 1989

100 Maurer, H. H., Identification and differentiation of barbiturates, other sedative-hypnotics and their metabolites in urine integrated in a general screening procedure using computerized gas chromatography-mass spectrometry, *Journal of Chromatography*, 530, 307-326, 1990

101. Liu, R., McKeehan, A., Edwards, C., Foster, G., Bensley, W., Langner, J., *et al.*, Improved gas chromatography-mass spectrometry analysis of barbiturates in urine using centrifuge-based solid-phase extraction, methylation, with d5-pentobarbital as internal standard, *Journal of Forensic Sciences*, 39, 1504-1514, 1994

102. Mangin, P., Lugnier, A. A., and Chaumont, A. J., A polyvalent method using HPLC for screening and quantification of 12 common barbitures in various biological materials, *Journal of Analytical Toxicology*, 11, 27-30, 1987

103. Jain, N. C., Mass screening and confirmation of barbiturates in urine by RIA/gas chromatography, *Clinical Toxicology*, 9, 221-233, 1976

104. Gill, R., Stead, A. H., and Moffat, A. C., Analytical aspects of barbiturate abuse: identification of drugs by the effective combination of gas-liquid, high-performance liquid and thin-layer chromatographic techniques, *Journal of Chromatography*, 204, 275-284, 1981.

105. Valentine, J. L., Middleton, R., and Sparks, C., Identification of Urinary Benzodiazepines and Their Metabolites - Comparison of Automated HPLC and GC/MS After Immunoassay Screening of Clinical Specimens, *Journal of Analytical Toxicology*, 20, 416-424, 1996

106. Schutz, H., Modern screening strategies in analytical toxicology with special regard to new benzodiazepines, *Zeitschrift fur Rechtsmedizin - Journal of Legal Medicine*, 100, 1937, 1988

107. Black, D. A., Clark, G. D., Haver, V. M., Garbin, J. A., and Saxon, A. J., Analysis of urinary benzodiazepines using solid-phase extraction and gas chromatography- mass spectrometry [see comments], *Journal of Analytical Toxicology*, 18, 185-188, 1994

108. Jones, C. E., Wians, F. H., Jr., Martinez, L. A., and Merritt, G. J., Benzodiazepines identified by capillary gas chromatography-mass spectrometry, with specific ion screening used to detect benzophenone derivatives, *Clinical Chemistry*, 35, 1394-1398, 1989

109. Sioufi, A. and Dubois, J. P., Chromatography of benzodiazepines. [Review], *Journal of Chromatography*, 531, 459-480, 1990

110. Drouet-Coassolo, C., Aubert, C., Coassolo, P., and Cano, J. P., Capillary GC/MS method for the identification and quantification of some benzodiazepines and their unconjugated metabolites in plasma, *J. Chromatogr.*, 487, 295-311, 1989

111. Japp, M., Garthwaite, K., Geeson, A. V., and Osselton, M. D., Collection of analytical data for benzodiazepines and benzophenones, *Journal of Chromatography*, 439, 317-339, 1988

112. Moore, C., Long, G., and Marr, M., Confirmation of benzodiazepines in urine as trimethylsilyl derivatives using gas chromatography-mass spectrometry, *Journal of Chromatography B: Biomedical Applications*, 655, 132-137, 1994

113. Fitzgerald, R., Rexin, D., and Herold, D., Detecting benzodiazepines: immunoassays compared with negative chemical ionization gas chromatography- mass spectrometry, *Clinical Chemistry*, 40, 373-380, 1994

114. Joern, W. A., Confirmation of low concentrations of urinary benzodiazepines, including alprazolam and triazolam, by GC/MS: An extractive alkylation procedure., *J. Anal. Toxicol.*, 16, 363-367, 1992

115. Needleman, S. B. and Porvaznik, M., Identification of parent benzodiazepines by gas chromotography-mass spectroscopy (GC/MS) from urinary extracts treated with B- glucuronidase, *Forensic Science International*, 73, 49-60, 1995

116. McIntyre, I., Syrjanen, M., Crump, K., Horomidis, S., Peace, A., and Drummer, O., Simultaneous HPLC gradient analysis of 15 benzodiazepines and selected metabolites in postmortem blood, *Journal of Analytical Toxicology*, 17, 202-207, 1993

117. Lillsunde, P. and Seppala, T., Simultaneous screening and quantitative analysis of benzodiazepines by dual-channel gas chromatography using electron-capture and nitrogen- phosphorus detection, *Journal of Chromatography*, 533, 97-110, 1990

118. Baugh, L. D., Allen, E. E., Liu, R. H., Langner, J. G., Fentress, J. C., Chadha, S. C., *et al.*, Evaluation of immunoassay methods for the screening of cocaine metabolites in urine, *Journal of Forensic Sciences*, 36, 79-85, 1991

119. Cone, E. J. and Mitchell, J., Validity testing of commercial urine cocaine metabolite assays: II. Sensitivity, specificity, accuracy, and confirmation by gas chromatography- mass spectrometry, *Journal of Forensic Sciences*, 34, 32-45, 1989

120. Moore, F. M. and Simpson, D., Detection of benzoylecgonine (cocaine metabolite) in urine: a cost-effective low risk immunoassay procedure, *Medical Laboratory Sciences*, 47, 85-89, 1990

121. Mueller, M. A., Adams, S. M., Lewand, D. L., and Wang, R. I., Detection of benzoylecgonine in human urine, *Journal of Chromatography*, 144, 101-107, 1977.

122. Smith, M. L., Hughes, R. O., Levine, B., Dickerson, S., Darwin, W. D., and Cone, E. J., Forensic drug testing for opiates. VI. Urine testing for hydromorphone, hydrocodone, oxymorphone, and oxycodone with commercial opiate immunoassays and gas chromatography-mass spectrometry, *Journal of Analytical Toxicology*, 19, 18-26, 1995

123. Huang, W., Andollo, W., and Hearn, W. L., A solid phase extraction technique for the isolation and identification of opiates in urine, *Journal of Analytical Toxicology*, 16, 307- 310, 1992

124. Cone, E. J., Dickerson, S., Paul, B. D., and Mitchell, J. M., Forensic drug testing for opiates. V. Urine testing for heroin, morphine, and codeine with commercial opiate immunoassays, *Journal of Analytical Toxicology*, 17, 156-164, 1993

125. Fyfe, M. J., Chand, P., McCutchen, C., Long, J. S., Walia, A. S., Edwards, C., *et al.*, Evaluation of enzyme immunoassay performance characteristics—phencyclidine example, *Journal of Forensic Sciences*, 38, 156-164, 1993

126. Ragan, F., Jr., Hite, S. A., Samuels, M. S., Garey, R. E., Daul, G., and Schuler, R. E., Extended EMIT-DAU phencyclidine screen, *Journal of Clinical Psychiatry*, 47, 194-195, 1986

127. Chen, X. H., Franke, J. P., Wijsbeek, J., and de Zeeuw, R. A., Determination of basic drugs extracted from biological matrices by means of solid-phase extraction and wide-bore capillary gas chromatography with nitrogen-phosphorus detection, *Journal of Analytical Toxicology*, 18, 150-153, 1994

128. Balkon, J. and Donnelly, B., Determination of basic drugs in post mortem tissues: a microextraction technique utilizing GLC/NPD of effluents, *Journal of Analytical Toxicology*, 6, 181-184, 1982

129. Sharp, M. E., Evaluation of a screening procedure for basic and neutral drugs: n-butyl chloride extraction and megabore capillary gas chromatography, *J. - Can. Soc. Forensic Sci.*, 19, 83-101, 1986

130. Hyde, P. M., Evaluation of drug extraction procedures from urine, *Journal of Analytical Toxicology*, 9, 269-272, 1985

131. Plavsic, F., Barbaric, V., Parag, M., Arambasin, M., Gjerek, J., and Stavljenic, A., Increased possibilities for detecting drugs by the Toxi-Lab screening test, *Annals of Clinical Biochemistry*, 22, 324-326, 1985

132. Moody, D. E., Rittenhouse, L. F., and Monti, K. M., Analysis of forensic specimens for cannabinoids. I. Comparison of RIA and GC/MS analysis of blood, *Journal of Analytical Toxicology*, 16, 297-301, 1992

133. Law, B., Williams, P. L., and Moffat, A. C., The detection and quantification of cannabinoids in blood and urine by RIA, HPLC/RIA and GC/MS, *Veterinary & Human Toxicology*, 21, 144-147, 1979

134. Clatworthy, A., Oon, M., Smith, R., and Whitehouse, M., Gas chromatographic-mass spectrometric confirmation of radioimmunoassay results for cannabinoids in blood and urine, *Forensic Science International*, 46, 219-230, 1990

135. Mason, P. A., Law, B., Pocock, K., and Moffat, A. C., Direct radioimmunoassay for the detection of barbiturates in blood and urine, *Analyst*, 107, 629-633, 1982

136. Lafisca, S., Bolelli, G., Mosca, R., and Zanon, C., Radioimmunoassay of morphine and morphine-like substances in biological fluids and human tissues, *Ricerca in Clinica e in Laboratorio*, 7, 179-190, 1977

137. Spiehler, V. and Brown, R., Unconjugated morphine in blood by radioimmunoassay and gas chromatography/mass spectrometry, *Journal of Forensic Sciences*, 32, 906-916, 1987

138. Altunkaya, D. and Smith, R., Evaluation of a commercial radioimmunoassay kit for the detection of lysergide (LSD) in serum, whole blood, urine and stomach contents, *Forensic Science International*, 47, 113-121, 1990

139. Owens, S. M., McBay, A. J., Reisner, H. M., and Perez-Reyes, M., 125I radioimmunoassay of delta-9-tetrahydrocannabinol in blood and plasma with a solid-phase second-antibody separation method, *Clinical Chemistry*, 27, 619-624, 1981

140. Teale, J. D., Forman, E. J., King, L. J., Piall, E. M., and Marks, V., The development of a radioimmunoassay for cannabinoids in blood and urine, *Journal of Pharmacy & Pharmacology*, 27, 465-472, 1975

141. Goddard, C. P., Stead, A. H., Mason, P. A., Law, B., Moffat, A. C., McBrien, M., *et al.*, An iodine-125 radioimmunoassay for the direct detection of benzodiazepines in blood and urine, *Analyst*, 111, 525-529, 1986

142. Yee, H. Y., Nelson, J. D., and Papa, V. M., Measurement of benzoylecgonine in whole blood using the Abbott ADx analyzer, *Journal of Analytical Toxicology*, 17, 84-86, 1993

143. Appel, T. A. and Wade, N. A., Screening of blood and urine for drugs of abuse utilizing diagnostic products corporation's Coat-A-Count radioimmunoassay kits, *Journal of Analytical Toxicology*, 13, 274-276, 1989

144. Caplan, Y. H. and Levine, B., Application of the Abbott TDx lidocaine, phenytoin, and phenobarbital assays to postmortem blood specimens, *Journal of Analytical Toxicology*, 12, 265-267, 1988

145. Alvarez, J. S., Sacristan, J. A., and Alsar, M. J., Comparison of a monoclonal antibody fluorescent polarization immunoassay with monoclonal antibody radioimmunoassay for cyclosporin determination in whole blood, *Therapeutic Drug Monitoring*, 14, 78-80, 1992

146. Peel, H. W. and Perrigo, B. J., Detection of cannabinoids in blood using EMIT, *Journal of Analytical Toxicology*, 5, 165-167, 1981

147. Slightom, E. L., Cagle, J. C., McCurdy, H. H., and Castagna, F., Direct and indirect homogeneous enzyme immunoassay of benzodiazepines in biological fluids and tissues, *Journal of Analytical Toxicology*, 6, 22-25, 1982

148. Blum, L. M., Klinger, R. A., and Rieders, F., Direct automated EMIT d.a.u. analysis of N,N-dimethylformamide-modified serum, plasma, and postmortem blood for benzodiazepines, benzoylecgonine, cannabinoids, and opiates, *Journal of Analytical Toxicology*, 13, 285-288, 1989

149. Lewellen, L. J. and McCurdy, H. H., A novel procedure for the analysis of drugs in whole blood by homogeneous enzyme immunoassay (EMIT), *Journal of Analytical Toxicology*, 12, 260-264, 198

150. Asselin, W. M., Leslie, J. M., and McKinley, B., Direct detection of drugs of abuse in whole hemolyzed blood using the EMIT d.a.u. urine assays [published erratum appears in J Anal Toxicol 1988 Nov-Dec;12(6):16A], *Journal of Analytical Toxicology*, 12, 207-215, 1988

151. Asselin, W. M. and Leslie, J. M., Direct detection of therapeutic concentrations of tricyclic antidepressants in whole hemolyzed blood using the EMITtox serum tricyclic antidepressant assay, *Journal of Analytical Toxicology*, 15, 167-173, 1991

152. Perrigo, B. J. and Joynt, B. P., Optimization of the EMIT immunoassay procedure for the analysis of cannabinoids in methanolic blood extracts, *Journal of Analytical Toxicology*, 13, 235-237, 1989

153. Collins, C., Muto, J., and Spiehler, V., Whole blood deproteinization for drug screening using automatic pipettors, *Journal of Analytical Toxicology,* 16, 340-342, 1992

154. Slightom, E. L., The analysis of drugs in blood, bile, and tissue with an indirect homogeneous enzyme immunoassay, *Journal of Forensic Sciences,* 23, 292-303, 1978

155. Klein, M., Mass spectrometry of drugs and toxic substances in body fluids, in *Forensic Mass Spectrometry,* Yinon, J., CRC Press, Boca Raton, FL, 1987, p 51-86.

156. Gudzinowicz, B. J. and Gudzinowicz, M., *Analysis of Drugs and Metabolites by GC/MS.* Vol. 7. 1980.

157. Cone, E. J., Analysis of drugs in biological samples by combined GC/MS., *Drugs Pharm. Sci.,* 11A, 143-227, 1981

158. Foltz, R. L., Applications of GC/MS in clinical toxicology, *Spectra,* 10, 8-10, 1985

159. Finkle, B. S., Foltz, R. L., and Taylor, D. M., A comprehensive GC/MS reference data system for toxicological and biomedical purposes, *Journal of Chromatographic Science,* 12, 304-328, 1974

160. Wu Chen, N. B., Cody, J. T., Garriott, J. C., Foltz, R. L., Peat, M. A., and Schaffer, M. I., Recommended guidelines for forensic GC/MS procedures in toxicology laboratories associated with offices of medical examiners and/or coroners, *J. Forensic Sci.,* 35, 236- 242, 1990

161. Smith, N. B., Automated identification by computer of the mass spectra of drugs in urine or serum extracts, *Journal of Analytical Toxicology,* 18, 16-21, 1994

162. Ardrey, R. E., Mass Spectrometry, in *Clarke's isolation and identification fo drugs in pharmaceuticals, body fluids, and post-mortem material,* Moffatt, A. C., 2nd Edition , The Pharmaceutical Press, London, 1986.

163. Gibb, R. P., Cockerham, H., Goldfogel, G. A., Lawson, G. M., and Raisys, V. A., Substance abuse testing of urine by GC/MS in scanning mode evaluated by proficiency studies, TLC/GC, and EMIT, *Journal of Forensic Sciences,* 38, 124-133, 1993

164. Mills, T., Roberson, J. D., McCurdy, H. H., and Wall, W. H., *Instrumental Data for Drug Analysis,* (5 Vols) 2nd Ed. Elsevier, New York, 1992.

165. Pfleger, K., Maurer, H. H. and Weber, A. *Mass Spectral and GC Data of Drugs, Poisons, Pesticides, Pollutants and Their Metabolites,* (3 Vols) 2nd Ed., VCH, New York, 1992.

166. Sunshine, I. and Caplis, M. *CRC Handbook of Mass Spectra of Drugs,* CRC Press, Boca Raton, FL., 1981.

167. Ardrey, R. E., Bal, T. S., Joyce, J. R. and Moffat, A. C., *Pharmaceutical Mass Spectra,* The Pharmaceutical Press, London, 1985.

168. Hites, R. A., *Handbook of Mass Spectra of Environmental Contaminants,* 2nd Ed., Lewis Publishers, Boca Raton, 1992.

169. Cornu, A. and Massot, R., *Compilation of Mass Spectral Data,* Heyden & Son, Ltd., London, 1966.

170. Reys, L. L. and Santos, J. C., Importance of information in forensic toxicology, *American Journal of Forensic Medicine & Pathology,* 13, 33-36, 1992

171. Stafford, D. T. and Logan, B. K., Information resources useful in forensic toxicology, *Fundamental & Applied Toxicology,* 15, 411-419, 1990

172. Peat, M. A., Blanke, R. V., Caplan, Y. H., Dal Cortiveo, L., Jones, G. R., McCurdy, H. H., et. Al., Forensic Toxicology Laboratory Guidelines, Society of Forensic Toxicologists/American Academy of Forensic Sciences, Colorado Springs, 1991.

173. Osterloh, J. D. and Becker, C. E., Chemical dependency and drug testing in the workplace, *Journal of Psychoactive Drugs,* 22, 407-417, 1990

174. Ng, T. L., Dope testing in sports: scientific and medico-legal issues. [Review], *Annals of the Academy of Medicine, Singapore,* 22, 48-53, 1993

175. DeCresce, R., Mazura, A., Lifshitz, M., and Tilson, J., *Drug testing in the workplace.* 1989: ASCP Press.

176. McCunney, R. J., Drug testing: technical complications of a complex social issue, *American Journal of Industrial Medicine,* 15, 589-600, 1989

177. Gough, T. A., The analysis of drugs of abuse, in *The analysis of drugs of abuse,* Gough, T. A., John Wiley & Sons, Chichester, UK, 1991, p 628.

178. Deutsch, D. G., Gas chromatography/mass spectrometry using tabletop instruments, in *Analytical Aspects of Drug Testing*, Deutsch, D. G., John Wiley and Sons, New York,, p 87-128. 1989

179. Baselt, R. C., ed. *Advances in Analytical Toxicology.* . Vol. 1. 1984, Biomedical Publications: Foster City. 275.

180. Lehrer, M., Application of gas chromatography-mass spectrometry instrument techniques to forensic urine drug testing, *Clinics in Laboratory Medicine*, 10, 271-288, 1990

181. Garland, W. A. and Powell, M. L., Quantitative selected ion monitoring (QSIM) of drugs and/or metabolites in biological matrices, *J. Chromatogr. Sci.*, 19, 392-434, 1981

182. Gelpi, E., Bioanalytical aspects on method validation, *Life Sciences*, 41, 849-852, 1987

183. Troost, J. R. and Olavesen, E. Y., Gas Chromatographic-Mass Spectrometric Calibration Bias, *Analytical Chemistry*, 68, 708-711, 1996

184. ElSohly, M. A., Little, T. L., Jr., and Stanford, D. F., Hexadeutero-11-nor-delta 9- tetrahydro-cannabinol-9-carboxylic acid: a superior internal standard for the GC/MS analysis of delta 9-THC acid metabolite in biological specimens, *Journal of Analytical Toxicology*, 16, 188-191, 1992

185. Giovannini, M. G., Pieraccini, G., and Moneti, G., Isotope dilution mass spectrometry: definitive methods and reference materials in clinical chemistry, *Annali dell Istituto Superiore di Sanita*, 27, 401-410, 1991

186. Needleman, S. B. and Romberg, R. W., Limits of linearity and detection for some drugs of abuse, *Journal of Analytical Toxicology*, 14, 34-38, 1990

187. Liu, R. H., Foster, G., Cone, E. J., and Kumar, S. D., Selecting an appropriate isotopic internal standard for gas chromatography-mass spectrometry analysis of drugs of abuse— pentobarbital example, *Journal of Forensic Sciences*, 40, 983-989, 1995

188. Carreras, D., Imaz, C., Navajas, R., Garcia, M. A., Rodriguez, C., Rodriguez, A. F., *et al.*, Comparison of derivatization procedures for the determination of diuretics in urine by gas chromatography-mass spectrometry, *Journal of Chromatography A*, 683, 195-202, 1994

189. Anderegg, R. J., Derivatization for GC/MS Analysis, *Mass Spec. Revs.*, 7, 395-, 1988

190. Melgar, R. and Kelly, R. C., A novel GC/MS derivatization method for amphetamines, *Journal of Analytical Toxicology*, 17, 399-402, 1993

191. Goldberger, B. A. and Cone, E. J., Confirmatory tests for drugs in the workplace by gas chromatography-mass spectrometry, *Journal of Chromatography A*, 674, 73-86, 1994

192. Cody, J. T. and Foltz, R. L., GC/MS analysis of body fluids for drugs of abuse, in *Forensic Appl. of Mass Spectrom.*, Yinon, J., CRC Press, Boca Raton, FL, 1995, p 1- 59.

193. Foltz, R. L., Fentiman, A. F., Jr., and Foltz, R. B., GC/MS assays for abused drugs in body fluids. [Review], *NIDA Research Monograph*, 32, 1-198, 1980

194. Foltz, R. L. *High sensitivity quantitative analysis of drugs and metabolites by GC/MS. in 31st Annual Conference on Mass Spectrometry and Allied Topics.* 1983. Boston, MA: May 8-13, 1983.

195. Bogusz, M., Wijsbeek, J., Franke, J. P., de Zeeuw, R. A., and Gierz, J., Impact of biological matrix, drug concentration, and method of isolation on detectability and variability of retention index values in gas chromatography, *Journal of Analytical Toxicology*, 9, 49-54, 1985

196. Hartmann, C., Massart, D. L., and McDowall, R. D., An analysis of the Washington Conference Report on bioanalytical method validation, *Journal of Pharmaceutical & Biomedical Analysis*, 12, 1337-1343, 1994

197. Shah, V. P., Midha, K. K., Dighe, S., McGilveray, I. J., Skelly, J. P., Yacobi, A., *et al.*, Analytical methods validation: bioavailability, bioequivalence and pharmacokinetic studies. Conference report, *European Journal of Drug Metabolism & Pharmacokinetics*, 16, 249-55, 1991

198. Mesley, R. J., Pocklington, W. D., and Walker, R. F., Analytical Quality Assurance - A Review, *Analyst*, 116, 975-990, 1991

199. Dadgar, D., Burnett, P. E., Choc, M. G., Gallicano, K., and Hooper, J. W., Application issues in bioanalytical method validation, sample analysis and data reporting. [Review], *Journal of Pharmaceutical & Biomedical Analysis*, 13, 89- 97, 1995

200. Pachla, L. A., Wright, D. S., and Reynolds, D. L., Bioanalytic considerations for pharmacokinetic and biopharmaceutic studies, *Journal of Clinical Pharmacology*, 26, 332- 335, 1986

201. Karnes, H. T. and March, C., Calibration and validation of linearity in chromatographic biopharmaceutical analysis, *Journal of Pharmaceutical & Biomedical Analysis*, 9, 911-918, 1991

202. Lang, J. R. and Bolton, S., A comprehensive method validation strategy for bioanalytical applications in the pharmaceutical industry—2. Statistical analyses, *Journal of Pharmaceutical & Biomedical Analysis*, 9, 435-442, 1991

203. Arnoux, P. and Morrison, R., Drug analysis of biological samples. A survey of validation approaches in chromatography in the UK pharmaceutical industry, *Xenobiotica*, 22, 757-764, 1992

204. Passey, R. B. and Maluf, K. C., Foundations for validation of quantitative analytical methods in the clinical laboratory, *Archives of Pathology & Laboratory Medicine*, 116, 732-738, 1992

205. Edwardson, P. A., Bhaskar, G., and Fairbrother, J. E., Method validation in pharmaceutical analysis, *Journal of Pharmaceutical & Biomedical Analysis*, 8, 929-933, 1990

206. Buick, A. R., Doig, M. V., Jeal, S. C., Land, G. S., and McDowall, R. D., Method validation in the bioanalytical laboratory, *Journal of Pharmaceutical & Biomedical Analysis*, 8, 629-637, 1990

207. Cardone, M. J., Willavize, S. A., and Lacy, M. E., Method validation revisited: a chemometric approach, *Pharmaceutical Research*, 7, 154-160, 1990

208. Wieling, J., Hendriks, G., Tamminga, W. J., Hempenius, J., Mensink, C. K., Oosterhuis, B., et al., Rational experimental design for bioanalytical methods validation. Illustration using an assay method for total captopril in plasma, *Journal of Chromatography A*, 730, 381-394, 1996

209. Braggio, S., Barnaby, R. J., Grossi, P., and Cugola, M., A strategy for validation of bioanalytical methods. [Review], *Journal of Pharmaceutical & Biomedical Analysis*, 14, 375-388, 1996

210. Karnes, H. T., Shiu, G., and Shah, V. P., Validation of bioanalytical methods. [Review], *Pharmaceutical Research*, 8, 421-426, 1991

211. Stead, A. H., Hook, W., Moffat, A. C., and Berry, D., Therapeutic, toxic and fatal blood concentration ranges of antiepileptic drugs as an aid to the interpretation of analytical data, *Human Toxicology*, 2, 135-147, 1983

212. Caplan, Y. H., Ottinger, W. E., and Crooks, C. R., Therapeutic and toxic drug concentrations in post mortem blood: a six year study in the State of Maryland, *Journal of Analytical Toxicology*, 7, 225-230, 1983

213. Baselt, R. C., Wright, J. A., and Cravey, R. H., Therapeutic and toxic concentrations of more than 100 toxicologically significant drugs in blood, plasma, or serum: a tabulation. [Review], *Clinical Chemistry*, 21, 44-62, 1975

214. Stead, A. H. and Moffat, A. C., A collection of therapeutic, toxic and fatal blood drug concentrations in man, *Human Toxicology*, 2, 437-464, 1983

215. Balselt, R. C. and Cravey, R. H., *Disposition of Toxic Drugs and Chemicals in Man*, 4th Ed., Chemical Toxicology Institute, Foster City, CA, 1995.

216. Prouty, R. W. and Anderson, W. H., The forensic science implications of site and temporal influences on postmortem blood-drug concentrations, *Journal of Forensic Sciences*, 35, 243-270, 1990

217. Othman, S., al-Turk, W. A., Awidi, A. S., Daradkeh, T. K., and Shaheen, O., Comparative determination of phenytoin in plasma by fluorescence polarization immunoassay and high performance liquid chromatography, *Drug Design & Delivery*, 2, 41-47, 1987

218. Valtier, S. and Cody, J. T., Evaluation of internal standards for the analysis of amphetamine and methamphetamine, *Journal of Analytical Toxicology*, 19, 375-380, 1995

219. Smith, N. B., Internal standards in gas-chromatographic analyses for ethylene glycol in serum [letter; comment], *Clinical Chemistry*, 39, 2020, 1993

220. Thomas, L. C. and Weichmann, W., Quantitative measurements via co-elution and dual-isotope detection by gas chromatography-mass spectrometry, *Journal of Chromatography*, 587, 255-262, 1991

221. Pollak, P. T., A systematic review and critical comparison of internal standards for the routine liquid chromatographic assay of amiodarone and desethylamiodarone, *Therapeutic Drug Monitoring*, 18, 168-178, 1996

222. Claeys, M., Markey, S. P., and Maenhaut, W., Variance analysis of error in selected ion monitoring assays using various internal standards. A practical study case., *Biomed. Mass Spectr.*, 4, 122-128, 1977

223. Tilstone, W. J. Pharmacokinetics metabolism, and the interpretation of results, in *Clarke's Isolation and identification of Drugs in Pharmaceuticals, Bidy Fluids, and Postmortem Material*, Moffatt, A.C. 2nd Ed. The Pharmaceutica Press, London, 1986, p.276.

224. Toseland, P. A., Samples and sampling, in *Clarke's Isolation and Identification of Drugs in Pharmaceuticals, Body Fluids, and Post-mortem Material*, , 2nd Ed., The Pharmaceutical Press, London, 1986, p 111.

12.5 QUALITY ASSURANCE IN POSTMORTEM TOXICOLOGY

WILMO ANDOLLO

QUALITY ASSURANCE OFFICER, DADE COUNTY MEDICAL EXAMINER DEPARTMENT, TOXICOLOGY LABORATORY, MIAMI, FLORIDA

12.5.1 INTRODUCTION

The essence of the postmortem forensic analysis is to characterize a subject's biological tissue in terms of toxic chemical content. Based on the analytical result, an opinion can then be formed about the influence the toxic substance may have had on the subject. Since the result of any chemical analysis carries with it an uncertainty that is inherent in all measurements, an attempt must be made to control and measure the factors that influence that uncertainty. Only when these factors are measured and controlled, can the analytical results be deemed reliable.

The quality assurance program is established to ensure the public that the results generated by the laboratory are reliable. This is crucial in a forensic toxicology laboratory since the analytical results are closely scrutinized in a court of law, where truth and impartiality must be authenticated for the public good. A comprehensive quality assurance program will provide an expert witness with details concerning the measurable factors that affect the analytical result. These factors include personnel, the implements of measurement; the quality of materials used; the sample; the analytical method; the analytical instruments; data handling; and reporting.

The *quality assurance* program describes the steps taken to *document* the execution of the quality control procedures; the traceability of reported data to raw data; instrument status during analysis; quality control status; description of the analytical method; qualifications of the analysts; sample integrity and chain of custody; and the corrective actions undertaken for out of control situations. The *quality control* program sets forth the procedures to be taken to *measure* and *control* all sources of random and systematic errors so that limits of accuracy and precision can be established for all analytical methods. It also describes the technical operations undertaken to assure that the data obtained are within the established limits.

12.5.2 STANDARD OPERATING PROCEDURES

The standard operating procedure is a written document that outlines in detail the mode of operation of the laboratory. It addresses the relationship of the laboratory with the institutions that it serves, the organizational structure of the laboratory, the quality assurance program, and the chemical hygiene plan. It must address every facet of the laboratory's operation, and be available to all laboratory personnel and the public for consultation and review.

The standard operating procedures should address, as a minimum, the following aspects of the laboratory operation:

- Table of organization
- Personnel qualifications
- Precision implements
- Materials
- Sampling
- Analytical Methods
- Instruments
- Data
- Reporting
- Proficiency Program

The standard operating procedures manual is to be kept up to date and reviewed on a yearly basis to ensure that it typifies the actual operation and that it meets the needs of the laboratory. It is important to archive any old procedures, whether modified or omitted from the manual, so that they can be retrieved for future reference.

The rest of this chapter will be devoted to expand on the subjects that are deemed indispensable in a comprehensive quality assurance program and standard operating procedure manual.

12.5.3 PERSONNEL

The table of organization should be represented by means of a flow chart or schematic diagram. It should include all positions in order of hirearchy, name of persons occupying each position, and accountability of each individual.

The subject of personnel in forensic toxicology laboratories is covered in detail in the SOFT/AAFS Forensic Laboratory Guidelines.[1]

12.5.3.1 Continuing Education

The laboratory director is responsible for providing access to continuing education to all his employees. Continuing education is essential to the development of the laboratory in maintaining the reliability and integrity necessary in an ever challenging field. New and more potent drugs are being continuously developed along with more advanced analytical techniques and equipment necessary for their detection and identification. Keeping abreast of the new information, be it pharmacological or analytical, is of outmost importance for the subsistance of the forensic laboratory. Membership in professional forensic organizations such as the American Academy of Forensic Sciences (AAFS), the Society of Forensic Toxicologists (SOFT), the California Association of Toxicologists (CAT) and The International Association of Forensic Toxicologists (TIAFT), provide the venue by which continuing education is not only available but relevant to the forensic laboratory.

12.5.4 PRECISION IMPLEMENTS

Regardless of their simplicity, burets, pipettes, volumetric flasks, pipettors, pipettor-diluters and the analytical balance are precision implements of measure used in one way or another in nearly every chemical analysis. They are the analytical implements that impart the first sources of systematic errors in the analysis. For this reason, it is imperative that their quality, maintenance and calibration strategies be addressed in the standard operating procedures.

The selection and maintenance of chemical measuring devices and instruments is beyond the scope of this section, but is covered in detail in textbooks of quantitative chemical analysis and instrumental analysis.[2,3]

12.5.5 REAGENTS

Chemicals, reagents, solvents and gases used in the process of executing the analytical procedures must meet minimum quality criteria as required by the analytical method. They should be properly stored, according to manufacturers' specifications or good chemical hygiene practice, in order to maintain their integrity and safety. Special care must be taken to record the receipt date and consider the stability of the reagent before use.

The determination of trace amounts of analytes in complex biological fluids or tissues, often requires concentration of organic solvent extracts which must be analyzed by very sensitive instruments. This circumstance creates a need for high purity solvents, reagents, and gases to avoid introducing significant amounts of interferences during the analytical process. Commercially available solvents have been developed with special qualities applicable to specific purposes. Examples include solvents possessing low ultra-violet absorption, used in high performance liquid chromatography and spectrophotometry, as well as solvents with negligible halogenated organic content, required for electron capture detectors or negative ion chemical ionization mass spectrometry. A postmortem toxicology laboratory should procure the highest quality of reagent possible to minimize the potential for interferences with its analytical methods.

The use of inert, high purity gases for gas-liquid chromatographs has been an essential part of the operation of gas chromatography since its inception as an analytical tool. The fragile nature of liquid phases in the presence of oxygen (air) at high temperatures and the development of very sensitive detectors such as nitrogen-phosphorus, electron capture and mass-spectrometers, among others, has made the gas quality a priority issue in the operation of the laboratory. Gases with 99.999% purities containing sub part-per-million quantities of air, moisture and organic compounds are readily available at moderate cost. There are also a variety of products designed to remove or "scrub" contaminants from the gas stream before their introduction into the instrument, that can be utilized if high purity gases are not readily availble. These gas scrubbers should be monitored periodically for proper operation as part of the standard operating procedures.

The preparation of reagents, buffers and mixtures should be conducted according to the specific instructions in the procedures manual. A reagent log book containing the preparation instructions for the most common solutions provides a convenient way to record their preparation with traceable information such as date of preparation, preparer, stock reagent lot number, and expiration date. This information should always be included in the reagent flask label along with the identification of the solution, its concentration and any applicable safety recommendation.

12.5.6 REFERENCE MATERIALS

The accuracy of any quantitative analytical procedure depends directly on the purity of the standard used for calibrating the method. Therefore, the analyst must ascertain that the standards, or reference materials, used to prepare the calibrators are chemically pure. The subject of reference materials is discussed in the SOFT/AAFS Forensic Toxicology Laboratory Guidelines.[1]

12.5.6.1 Calibrators

Calibrators are materials with which the sample is compared in order to determine the concentration or other quantity.[6] Methods known to have acceptable accuracy because physical or matrix effects are negligible may be calibrated with certified reference solutions. However, procedural constraints and complex matrix effects of biological samples make the use of certified reference solutions impossible in many routine methods. The calibrators selected for such methods must simulate the physical and chemical properties of the samples in order to compensate for matrix effects during analysis and to be sensitive to important changes in analytical error conditions.

Assay values assigned to calibrators must be sufficiently accurate for the intended use. The uncertainty interval for the assigned concentration value must be small compared to the analytical precision of the method to be calibrated. That is, the absolute error calculated for the assigned value using dimensional analysis must be smaller than the absolute error obtained when the calibrator is analyzed multiple times by the method.[7]

In the forensic laboratory, three types of calibrators may be encountered. The first, is use of a reference standard solution as a calibrator when the method has no procedural constraints and matrix effects are virtually non-existent. Certified standard solutions for this type of method can be obtained commercially or prepared in the laboratory with reference materials. This type of method, although rare in the forensic laboratory, can best be exemplified by the analysis of volatiles using head space techniques with gas chromatography, and the percent purity determination of drug exhibits using ultra-violet spectrometry.

The second type of calibrators are those obtained from commercial sources as kits to be used in self-contained analytical systems. They are matrix specific and manufactured in bulk under strict quality control. They are carefully designed to perform a specific task under rigorously controlled conditions and are provided with lot numbers and expiration dates. Assays of this type include quantitative techniques by radioactive, enzymatic and fluorescent immunoassays.

The last type of calibrators encountered in the forensic laboratory are of most concern because they assume the most uncertainty. They are usually employed in analytical assays involving multi-step extractions, concentration, derivatization, and complex instruments of analysis and data reduction. These working standards must be prepared in the laboratory from pure reference materials, be diluted with blank sample matrix to resemble the biological sample, and remain accurate enough to convey a reliable measurement when a sample is compared to them. For this reason, every effort should be made to ensure the quality of reference material, the proper maintenance of volumetric implements and balances, and the application of good analytical skills.

The preparation of a calibrator, or working standard, begins with the preparation of a stock solution from the reference drug material. A water soluble organic solvent that readily dissolves the drug material without adverse reaction is the solvent of choice. Solvents that are not water soluble can be used, but they require additional steps to remove the solvent when further dilutions are made into aqueous biological fluids. A concentration of 1 milligram of the unionized form of the drug per milliliter of solvent is convenient and adequate for most drugs analyzed. To keep the uncertainty of the calibrator below the variance of the method, it is desirable to know the exact concentration of the stock standard to at least 3 significant figures. The solutions stored in capped amber vials at -20°C can have long shelf-lives if care is taken to allow the solutions to reach room temperature before opening, thus avoiding moisture condensation in the solution. The stability of these solutions must be established periodically. Calibration standards are discussed in the *CRC Handbook of Clinical Chemistry*.[7]

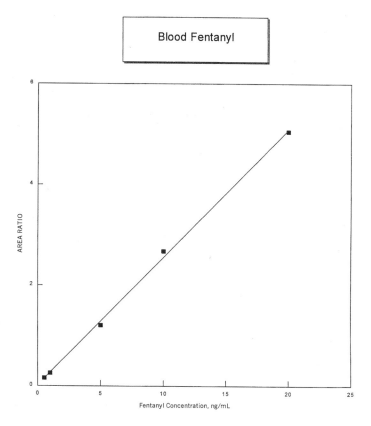

Figure 12.5.1 Multi-level calibration.

12.5.6.1.1 Multi-Level Calibration

The calibration scheme used for the purpose of carrying out quantifications of unknown specimens is done with the preparation of a calibration graph that includes a minimum of three different concentrations and a blank. The concentrations of analyte used to prepare the graph must include the lower and upper limits of linear response, since linearity must be demonstrated in every assay.

The recommended scheme for the preparation of a set of calibrators has been discussed in the Research Monograph Series of the National Institute on Drug Abuse.[8]

To control for the influence of matrix effects, it is recommended to add the same volume of working stock solution to each aliquot of biological matrix when preparing the calibrators. To do this, a fresh set of working stock solutions is prepared by serial dilutions from the stock solution. Mixtures of drugs and metabolites can also be included in the working stock solution sets.

The calibration graph is obtained by plotting the detector response against the assigned concentration of analyte in the working standard. Chromatographic assays that use internal standards are calibrated by plotting the detector response ratio of analyte to internal standard against the assigned concentration of analyte in the working standard. Calibrators should be analyzed in triplicate so that the variance of the measurements at different concentration levels can be determined. Using the statistical method of linear regression, the straight line that best fits the points can be determined. The slope of the line and the y-intercept are used to calculate the quantity of analyte in an unknown sample based on its detector response. Figure 12.5.1 shows a representative calibration curve for the analysis of fentanyl.

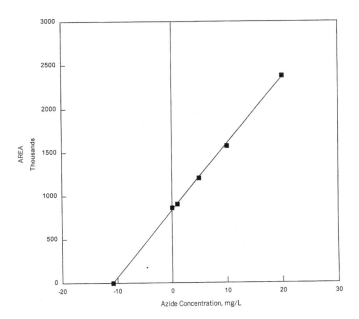

Figure 12.5.2 Calibration by method of additions.

12.5.6.1.2 Method of Addition

The method of additions is a very powerful calibration technique because the accuracy is independent of matrix effects. The technique requires that replicates of the specimen, instead of blank matrix, be fortified with the different levels of calibrators, along with an unspiked replicate of the specimen serving as the "blank". All the samples are analyzed by the analytical method as usual. A calibration graph is generated by plotting the detector response of the analyte (or response ratio if using internal standard) against the concentration of the calibrators and plotting the response of the unfortified specimen on the y-axis (x=0). Using the statistical method of linear regression, the straight line that best fits the points is determined and the absolute value of the x-intercept represents the calculated concentration of the specimen. Figure 12.5.2 shows the calculation of azide in blood by the method of additions.

A disadvantage encountered in forensic analysis when using the method of additions is the requirement that multiple aliquots of the specimen be used when forensic samples are inherently limited in size. The use of this method of calibration, therefore, should be limited to situations where a rare analysis is being considered, controls are not available, or when dealing with a particularly difficult matrix.

12.5.6.2 Internal Standards

A suitable internal standard should be used in chromatographic assays such as gas chromatography, high performance liquid chromatography and gas chromatography-mass spectrometry. The internal standard can be defined as a substance that is added to all samples (specimens, standards and controls) in a given assay before processing begins to correct for the many variations that occur in the manipulation of the samples during the entire analysis. Systematic errors affecting the quantity of analyte isolated from the sample, will also affect the quantity

Wilmo Andollo

of the internal standard in the same proportion. Therefore, the ratio of analyte to internal standard at the beginning of the procedure will remain unchanged throughout. For this concept to hold true, the internal standard must comply with certain qualifications.

First, the internal standard must have chemical and physical characteristics very similar to the analyte of interest. This quality ensures that extraction partition coefficients, formation of derivatives, chromatographic characteristics and detector response are similar enough so as to not alter their weight ratio significantly. A compound such as difluorococaine, for example, is not a good internal standard choice for cocaine because its enhanced lipophilicity imparts a very different extraction partition ratio, a different chromatographic characteristic, and a dissimilar response to a nitrogen-phosphorus detector. A compound such as propylbenzoylecgonine, an analogue of cocaine containing a propyl ester instead of a methyl ester, is chemically and physically more satisfactory. From the point of view of extraction and derivatization properties the most appropriate internal standard is an analogue of the analyte that has been labeled with a stable isotope. These substances have identical chemical and physical characteristics to the analyte, so their weight ratio is not affected during the analysis. However, unless the chromatographic system can resolve the two components, these are only useful in analyses by gas chromatography-mass spectrometry.

In additon, it is important to add precisely the same amount of internal standard to each sample. It is not necessary to know exactly the weight amount added as long as it is exactly the same amount. The normal practice is to decide in advance the approximate quantity of internal standard to be added to each sample, since the ratio of analyte to internal standard can be measured most accurately when they are present in similar concentrations. The quantity of internal standard added to the samples, then, should give a concentration intermediate between the lowest and highest expected analyte concentrations. This concentration should be such that the lowest anticipated weight ratio of analyte to internal standard should approximately equal the inverse of the highest anticipated ratio. So, if one desires to measure concentrations of a drug over the range 1 to 1000 ng/mL, the amount of internal standard added should give a concentration of approximately 32 ng/mL (1:32~32:1000). Some analysts may favor the use of a lower concentration of internal standard to facilitate more accurate measurements of low levels of the drug, since low levels are more difficult to measure than high levels. On the other hand, higher amounts of internal standard can be used to act as a "carrier" to minimize losses of analyte due to adsorption at active sites on the surface of extraction vessels and within the chromatographic column.[9]

12.5.6.3 Controls

A control is a test sample of known concentration that is analyzed along with every batch of specimens to make certain that the analytical procedure performs within the expected limits of variation. Three types of controls can be defined: (1) the negative control, which is drug free and analyzed in qualitative and quantitative methods to show that the method is not introducing a contaminant that may construe a false positive, (2) a positive control, containing the drug at a concentration near the limit of detection and used in qualitative methods to demonstrate adequate performance, and (3) the analytical control(s), containing the drug at a meaningful level(s) and used to monitor the performance of the quantitative method. The intended use of controls is to monitor the performance of a method over a long period of time in an internal quality control program, never to calibrate a procedure. The level chosen for the analytical control should be of clinical and/or forensic importance, such as the significant therapeutic concentration of a drug, or the legal intoxication level of ethanol. Controls should comprise 10% of the total amount of samples analyzed in an assay; they should be evenly distributed throughout the run, and one should be included at the end.

Control materials are useful only if applicable to the analytical method used. As is the case with calibrators, the control must simulate the physical and chemical properties of the samples to compensate for matrix effects during analysis and to monitor the performance characteristics of the method. They must be homogeneous to be sensitive to analytical imprecision and stable enough to detect system errors for meaningful periods of time.

The source of control materials and their applications has been discussed extensively in the literature as it pertains to clinical chemistry.[10-15] The principles discussed, although applicable to some extent to forensic analysis, do not conform to the unique complexity of the specimens encountered in postmortem work, such as nails, hair, decomposed tissue and unstable analytes. However, the need to measure the quality of the method's performance during an analysis is still imperative, and these obstacles must be overcome with analytically sound ingenuity and thorough documentation.

Self-contained systems of analysis such as immunoassays and commercial thin-layer chromatography kits are provided with control materials specifically designed to be used for their intended purpose. These control materials are manufactured in bulk under strict quality control and are conveniently provided with the expected value, acceptable limits of variation, lot number and expiration dates.

Control materials may be obtained from commercially available sources at a considerable price. These are usually supplied in the form of urine or lyophilized serum or plasma, with target concentrations, lot numbers and expiration dates. Their stability is usually short (5 to 30 days) once they have been reconstituted, but they remain stable for months if refrigerated in their lyophilized state. The drug selection available usually incorporates common drugs of abuse and of clinical therapeutic interest which, albeit adequate, leaves the forensic laboratory with unaddressed needs. The matrices of these materials may not appropriately simulate the typical forensic sample under specific analytical conditions. Therefore, the suitability of these commercial control materials must be ascertained by evaluating them against properly selected calibrators under controlled conditions.

A reasonable source of control material is the pooling of excess laboratory specimens. This source is not very dependable, however, because of difficulties in obtaining unique drug selectivity, the uncontrolled degradation of biological fluids and drugs, biohazards, and evidence tampering concerns.

A plausible alternative is the preparation of controls in the laboratory using outdated whole blood or plasma from blood banks, voided urine, and tissue homogenates prepared from drug free sources. Some analysts in the field have successfully used bovine blood after adjusting the hematocrit to simulate human levels by diluting with water.[16] The only concern about "homemade" controls is that there is no independent way of qualifying the process. For this reason, every effort should be made to ensure the quality of reference material, the proper maintenance of volumetric implements and balances, and the execution of good analytical skills in the preparation of the in-house control.

The process begins with the preparation of a stock solution from a certified reference drug material. This stock solution must be distinct from the one used to prepare the calibrators. It is axiomatic that if the same reference solution is used to prepare both, the control is invalid. A water soluble organic solvent that readily dissolves the drug material without adverse reaction is the solvent of choice. Solvents that are not water soluble can be used, but they require additional steps to remove the solvent when further dilutions are made into aqueous biological fluids. A concentration of 1 mg of the un-ionized form of the drug per milliliter of solvent is convenient and adequate for most drugs analyzed. The solutions stored in capped amber vials at -20°C can have long shelf-lives if care is taken to allow the solutions to reach room temperature before opening, thus avoiding moisture condensation in the solution. The stability of these solutions should be established periodically as described earlier in this chapter.

A decision must be made whether to prepare batches of control material for future use, or to prepare a working stock solution from which fresh controls can be fashioned at the time of analysis. The decision to prepare large batches of control material for future use rests on the requirement that: (1) the drug be stable for a reasonable period of time in the appropriately preserved matrix of choice, and (2) the control be used frequently enough to merit the effort of establishing the limits of variation for the batch. For example, assays that are used frequently, such as blood ethanol, are good candidates for this type of control material. An assay that is performed about 2 or 3 times a year does not merit a batch preparation, even if the control material is deemed stable for the unrealistic period of 3 years.

A batch is simply prepared by making a proper dilution of the stock solution into the desired volume of biological fluid and adding the required preservatives as outlined in the procedures manual for the specimens being simulated. The control material can be dispensed into labeled vials containing working aliquots and stored until needed under the same protocols used for samples.

Control materials fashioned at the time of analysis are preferred for many postmortem toxicology analyses. They are prepared fresh at the time of analysis by spiking an aliquot of a working stock solution into the required amount of blank matrix. Hence, any fluid or tissue homogenate can be fortified with the control before processing, allowing the performance of the assay to be monitored for any tissue. The working stock solutions remain stable for long periods of time because they are prepared in organic solvents. Therefore, a single working stock solution may be used repeatedly to monitor performance even for infrequently performed analyses.

The working stock solution is prepared by diluting the stock solution to an intermediate concentration so that a small aliquot added to the required amount of blank matrix yields the desired control concentration. The solvent used must be water soluble and care must be taken that the volume of control solution chosen to spike the blank does not affect the matrix significantly. Keeping the solvent concentration of the matrix below 10% is advisable to avoid protein precipitation.

Once a control material has been procured, it is identified with a lot number and, if applicable, an expiration date. Using control materials, the assay is evaluated to determine accuracy and precision expressed as standard deviation and coefficient of variation which are evaluated by standard statistical methods. This requires that the control be analyzed 20 to 30 times over a period of several days by all analysts who perform the assay using the variety of measuring devices that could conceivably be used to perform the assay. If the assay is to be performed on more than one instrument, a separate determination of quality control data is to be established for each instrument.

Occasionally, the forensic laboratory needs to perform a rare analysis for which a control has not been established (e.g., yohimbine, estazolam) or one for which a control is impractical to maintain (e.g., toluene, cyanide). In these situations, one can perform a "spike recovery" study to verify that the calculated result was not influenced by matrix differences between the specimen and the calibrators. This is accomplished by spiking a replicate of the specimen with one of the working stock calibrator solutions. The solution is chosen so that the amount added is not less than one tenth the existing concentration, nor more than 10 times the existing concentration, and that the addition does not produce a concentration higher than the limits of linearity. The spiked sample is analyzed and the result is used to calculate the percent recovery as follows:

$$\%R = \frac{[\text{spiked sample}] - [\text{sample}]}{[\text{spike}]}(100)$$

Recoveries that are outside the 20% margin allowed by this principle indicate that matrix effects are abnormally high and that the original concentration calculated for the specimen is inaccurate. If this is the case, the method of additions discussed in Section 12.5.6.1.2 can be pursued in the quest for an accurate result.

12.5.7 SAMPLES AND SAMPLING

Sampling is often called the basis of analysis because the analytical result is never better than the sample from which it is derived. The purpose of sampling is to provide the analyst with a representative part of the "object" that is suitable for the analysis. In forensic work, an appreciation of how the analytes may decompose and how contaminants may be introduced are important factors to consider.[17-18] The subject of samples and sampling is discussed in Section 12.2. The subject of safe handling of infectious materials has been treated in detail elsewhere.[19]

12.5.8 ANALYTICAL METHODS AND PROCEDURES

The analytical method is the set of instructions detailing the entire procedure by which a particular analysis is performed. The instructions describe the preparation of reagents, standards, controls and sample; the steps to isolate and concentrate the analyte; the instrumental requirements; and the data manipulation. It is in the execution of the method that most of the sources of error are introduced, so strict guidelines must be followed to control them.

12.5.8.1 Quality of an Analytical Procedure

An analytical challenge is approached by selecting the method that is most appropriate in terms of its quality features to tackle the chemical problem. The factors that govern the quality of an analytical procedure are the limit of detection, sensitivity, dynamic linear range, precision, accuracy, and selectivity. An in-depth discussion on the subject of quality of analytical procedures has been provided by Kateman and Pijpers.[20]

12.5.8.1.1 Limit of Detection

The limit of detection can be defined as the smallest detector response given by the analyte which can be reliably differentiated from background noise produced by the instrument or the procedure. This signal is not necessarily quantifiable, since most detectors are not linear at low response levels.

The classical determination for the method detection limit involves statistical analysis of the probability that the signal is produced by the analyte, and not the instrument, with given confidence limits. These methods, which have been treated extensively in the literature, are involved and require that the background noise be consistent from sample to sample.[21-23]

In methodologies that render irregular background noise from sample to sample it is commonly accepted to determine a signal-to-noise ratio of at least 3 to 1 to consider the signal as being produced by the analyte. Establishment of a higher signal-to-noise ratio as a decision guideline increases the confidence that the analyte is present at the expense of deciding it is absent at lower ratios. The benefit of doubt imparted to the decision at higher signal-to-noise ratios can be comforting from a forensic viewpoint.

12.5.8.1.2 Sensitivity and Linearity

The sensitivity of a method can be defined as the change in detector response given by a change in concentration. The detector response is composed of a part that depends on the concentration and a part that is independent of it (the blank). In addition, the detector response is not linearly proportional to the concentration over the entire range of possible values. The range

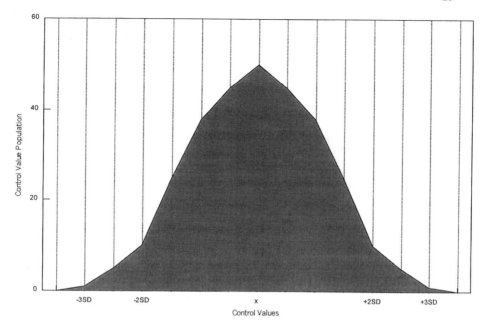

Figure 12.5.3 Gaussian curve.

of values for which the sensitivity is constant, is called the "linear dynamic range", and methods should be developed so that this range is as large as possible.

The linear dynamic range, or linearity, is limited at the lower level by concentration values whose detector response cannot be distinguished from the detector noise, or by ambiguous values of sensitivity. The linear range is limited at the upper level by saturation of the detector signal.

12.5.8.1.3 Precision

Precision is a measure of the dispersion of results when an analytical procedure is repeated on one sample. Although the dispersion of results may be caused by many sources, it is usually implied that it is caused by random fluctuations in the procedure. If no bias exists, the results usually scatter around the expected value in a normal distribution, described by a Gaussian curve (Figure 12.5.3). The normal distribution of the population of results is characterized by the position of the mean (x), and the standard deviation (s). The precision of an analytical method is often expressed as the standard deviation or coefficient of variation (C.V.), and it is calculated and monitored by analysis of control materials (Section 12.5.6.3).

12.5.8.1.4 Accuracy

Although the concept of accuracy is vague and difficult to interpret, it has been defined as the difference (error or bias) between an individual result, or the mean of a set of results, and the value which is accepted as the true or correct value for the quantity measured.[24]

An accurate measurement is one that is free of bias, does not scatter when repeated, and results in the "true value". The true value, however, is unknown because it must be measured, and measurements are biased and imprecise. Nevertheless, the accuracy can be estimated by measuring properties that are related to the concept of "accurate". Precision can be measured and bias can be estimated.

In analytical chemistry it is rarely necessary for the result to be the "true value". The only requirement is that it be comparable with other results. Consequently, analytical results are compared with results obtained from reference materials by using an agreed-upon method of analysis. Youden stated that the mean of the results obtained by a number of independent laboratories, using comparable methods of data presentation and data handling, can be assumed to be the "true value".[25]

12.5.8.1.5 Selectivity and Specificity

Selectivity refers to the ability of an analytical procedure to produce correct results for various components of a mixture without any mutual interference among the components. Specificity refers to the ability of an analytical procedure to discriminate between components in a mixture by their ability to produce a detector signal.

12.5.8.2 Qualitative Methods

Qualitative methods characterize the sample in terms of the identity of its toxic constituents. The identity can be specific, as produced by mass or infrared spectra, or non-specific, as produced by immunoassays and spot tests.

Qualitative methods require that all analytes that can be detected or ruled out in the analysis be known. For non-specific assays, such as thin-layer or gas chromatography, this can be an ever increasing list as new drugs are introduced.

With each assay, a negative control and a control representative of the analytes being tested should be analyzed. The positive control should contain the analytes near their respective limit of detection, and both should be prepared in a matrix similar to the samples. Interferences that can adversely affect the result should be indicated in the written procedure.

12.5.8.3 Quantitative Methods

Quantitative methods characterize the sample in terms of the quantity of its toxic constituents. The measured quantity carries with it an inherent uncertainty that must be known in order to appraise its reliability. The accepted thresholds of uncertainty, or limits of variation, are determined by quantifying the factors that affect the quality of the method. Therefore, each quantitative technique must be validated by determining its limit of detection, dynamic linear range, precision, and accuracy.

12.5.8.4 Method Development and Validation

Guidelines for method development instituted in a comprehensive procedures manual provide an effective way to tackle the analytical challenges that are frequently encountered in the forensic laboratory. The considerations listed below provide the basis upon which an analytical method can be implemented:

- Establishment of the intended purpose of the method.
- Identification of chemical problems that must be addressed to fulfill the intended purpose of the method.
- Search of the literature for existing methods that can fulfill the intended purpose and be accommodated by the laboratory.

Appendix Ic provides literature sources for qualitative and quantitative assay procedures for most common drugs. The references should serve as a starting point for method development.

Once the basic characteristics of the method have been established, the method is developed by evaluating and documenting as much of the following information as possible:

- Analytical principle of the assay.
- Brief description of toxic substances being analyzed.

Wilmo Andollo

- Sample preparation requirements.
- The sources of materials and the preparation of reagents, standards and controls.
- Quantitative statements about the stability of the reagents, standards and controls.
- Procedural steps to isolate and/or concentrate the analytes.
- Instrumental requirements and settings.
- Validation parameters; limit of detection and/or quantitation, linear range, coefficient of variation, and recovery efficiency.
- Interferences.
- Data handling.
- References to the source of the method.

All analyses should be performed by the procedures set forth in the procedures manual, and carried out explicitly as described by the procedure whenever possible. Exceptions should be made only when special considerations are dictated by the character of the specimen (for example, interferences resulting from multi-drug content). When modification to a method is necessary, the exercise of good analytical judgement and proper documentation is essential to impart confidence in the result.

12.5.9 INSTRUMENTS

In analytical chemistry, information about the chemical composition of a sample is obtained by measuring some chemical or physical property that is characteristic of the component of interest. These measurements are made by various analytical instruments designed to measure specific properties.

To apply instrumentation most efficiently to his problems, the analyst must understand the fundamental relations of chemical species to their physical and chemical properties. He must know the scope, applicability, and limitations of physical property measurement with respect to qualitative and quantitative analysis. Knowing this, he can call upon the instrumentation for the measurement of the desired properties with the needed accuracy and precision.[26-27]

The instrument is a device that converts chemical information to a form that is more readily observable. It accomplishes this function in several steps that may include (1) generation of a signal, (2) transduction (transformation of the signal to one of a different nature, such as electrical), (3) amplification of the transformed signal, and (4) presentation of the signal by a scale, recorder, integrator, or printout. Some instruments also prepare the sample to a form that can be analyzed or perform separation of components for increased specificity. It is common to find a combination of instruments working in tandem to produce the desired results.

In order to ensure that the instrumental data are reliable, steps must be taken to control the proper function of the instrument. This can be accomplished by establishing standard operating procedures that address proper installation guidelines, a preventive maintenance program, periodic performance evaluations, and pre-analysis checklists.

All documentation concerning instrument maintenance and checks should be kept in bound notebooks specific to each instrument. These are to be kept near the instrument for easy access and inspection by all analysts. With time, a history of the instrument will develop which will impart a great insight for effective and timely troubleshooting.

12.5.9.1 Installation

An effort should be made to install the instrument in a manner that is commensurate with the recommendations of the manufacturer. These usually include environmental, energy and safety requirements that are necessary for the proper function and longevity of the instrument.

12.5.9.2 Preventive Maintenance

A preventive maintenance program can reduce the frequency of instrument failure during analysis. It also reduces the likelihood of major breakdowns and extended downtime. Preventive maintenance requirements and procedures are usually specified in the instrument operation manual. The time interval required between preventive maintenance service is dictated by the amount of use and environmental factors. Therefore, laboratories must establish their own protocols according to their needs.

12.5.9.3 Pre-Analysis Checklist

A review of vital instrument parameters before processing samples assures that the correct settings have been chosen for the analysis and that the instrument is in good working order. This becomes especially important when the instrument is used for multiple procedures by multiple analysts. Use of a checklist is the most effective way to ensure that no parameter is overlooked and produces documentation that pre-analysis checks were performed. The specific parameters to be checked and their proper settings will vary with the instrument.

12.5.10 DATA

The American Academy of Forensic Sciences and the Society of Forensic Toxicologists recommend that before results are reported, each batch of analytical data should be reviewed by scientific personnel who are experienced with the analytical protocols used in the laboratory.[1] At a minimum this review should include chain of custody data, validity of analytical data and calculations and quality control data. The review should be documented within the analytical record.

12.5.10.1 Chain of Custody Data

Review of the chain of custody documentation ensures that the analytical result represents the correct sample. The data necessary to accomplish this task include the dates and identification of individuals performing the sample collection and transportation to the laboratory; receipt; transfer of specimens or aliquots within the laboratory; chemical analysis; and analytical report.

12.5.10.2 Analytical Data

The first task of an analyst who wants to evaluate a procedure is to collect relevant data of measurements using that procedure. The second task is to reduce the number of measurements, remove irrelevant and erroneous data, and convert the measurements into statements pertaining to the condition of the procedure under control. To convert the data into a form that can be handled, data reduction procedures are applied.

Analytical instruments are usually equipped with data filters or data handlers that smooth and reduce the data collected, relieving the analyst of such arduous tasks. For this reason, the concepts of data production, information theory, data reduction, data handling, analysis of variance, pattern recognition, and system optimization will not be discussed in this chapter. However, the analyst should have some understanding of how instruments perform data analysis. This knowledge will help the analyst identify corrupt data, correctly set thresholds for proper peak integration and determine signal-to-noise ratios. A thorough discussion on data production and data reduction has been presented by Kateman and Pijpers.[28]

A thorough review by responsible supervisory personnel of the raw analytical data and the calculations derived therefrom should be performed before a report is issued.

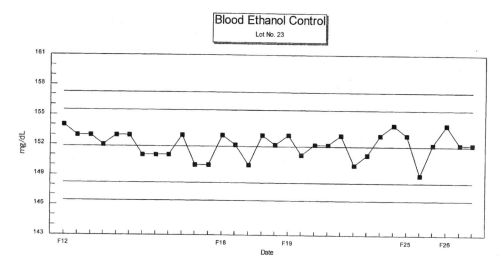

Figure 12.5.4 Quality control chart.

12.5.10.3 Quality Control Data

A review of the results obtained from the analysis of control material is essential to evaluate the performance of the analysis. This is accomplished by deriving control charts for each control material so that control rules or decision criteria can be applied to determine whether the method performed within expected limits of variation.[29-32]

The control chart is a graphical representation of the arithmetic mean and the control limits calculated for the control material as described in Section 12.5.6.3. The x-axis is scaled to provide appropriate time period intervals. Horizontal lines are drawn corresponding to the mean (center) and multiples of the standard deviation above and below the mean, as shown in Figure 12.5.4. These graphs are sometimes referred to as "Shewhart" or "Levey-Jennings" charts.

The control rules or criteria described here are based on statistical properties arising from single control measurements, rather than replicate measurements, since they are more common. They provide a low level of false rejection, improved capability for detecting analytical errors, and some indication of the error type to aid in problem solving. Rejection of an analytical run occurs when the control value obtained violates one or more of the following rules, symbolized for brevity and convenience:

- (1_{3s}) A value outside 3 standard deviations
- (2_{2s}) Two consecutive values outside 2 standard deviations. One value outside 2 standard deviations should be considered a warning, requiring inspection of a second control.
- (R_{4s}) Two consecutive values that differ by 4 standard deviations or more.
- (4_{1s}) Four consecutive values on the same side of the mean that are more than 1 standard deviation from the mean.
- (10_x) Ten consecutive values on the same side of the mean.

The particular rule violated may give some indication of the type of analytical error ocurring. Random error will most often be detected by the 1_{3s} and R_{4s} rules. Systematic error will usually be detected by the 2_{2s}, 4_{1s}, or 10_x rules and, when very large, by the 1_{3s} rule.

12.5.11 REPORTS

Postmortem forensic laboratories are an integral part of, supported by, or associated with govenrnment agencies involved in medico-legal investigations. The laboratory must comply with the reporting requirements mandated by the agency to which the reports are submitted. Thus, a report format can be neither standarized nor recommended, since it will depend upon the specific needs of the recipient. In general, however, the written report should include all information necessary to identify the case and its source, the test results, and the signature of the individual responsible for its contents. Forensic toxicology reporting is discussed in depth in the AAFS/SOFT Forensic Toxicology Laboratory Guidelines.[1]

12.5.12 PROFICIENCY PROGRAMS

In addition to the laboratory's effort in implementing a quality control program to impart confidence to its analytical results, there is a requirement to scrutinize the analytical process by independent evaluation against peer laboratories. A proficiency testing program established by accrediting organizations or independent consultants provides laboratories with such an evaluation mechanism.

The proficiency program provides laboratories with chemically fortified samples simulating those encountered routinely by the laboratory for analysis. The program derives statistical data on the results reported by the participating laboratories and issues a summary of useful information about the results. When the result of a chemical analysis is compared to the results obtained by other laboratories on the same sample, the laboratory can make a responsible determination as to the strengths and weaknesses of its overall operation. This information can be used to focus resources on those areas that need improvement, be it personnel, training, equipment, method development, reference materials or the like. It also builds confidence in the methods that yield reliable results.

Forensic toxicology laboratories must participate in external proficiency testing programs which evaluate as many of the analytical tests in as many specimen types as possible. These programs are the only independent way to evaluate the reliability of the methods used and the overall operating procedures of the laboratory.

REFERENCES

1. Joint Committee of the American Academy of Forensic Sciences (AAFS) and the Society of Forensic Toxicologists, Inc. (SOFT), *Forensic Toxicology Laboratory Guidelines*, Colorado Springs, Colorado, 1991.
2. Ayres, Gilbert H., The analytical balance and its use, *Quantitative Chemical Analysis*, second edition, Harper and Row, New York, Evanston and London, 1968, Chapter 2.
3. Schenk, George H., Hahn, Richard B., Hartkopf, Arleigh V., Fundamentals of weighing and related measurements, *Quantitative Analytical Chemistry-Principles and Life Science Applications*, 1st edition, Allyn and Bacon, Inc., Boston, London, Sydney, Toronto, 1977, Chapter 6.
4. Blanke, Robert V., Validation of the purity of standards, publication 87-0175, Abbott Laboratories, Diagnostics Division, Irving, Texas, 1989.
5. Williams, S. (ed.), *Official Methods of Analysis of the Association of Official Analytical Chemists*, 14th edition, AOAC, Arlington, Va, 50.044 page 1007, 1984.
6. Buttner, J., Borth, R., Boutwell J. H., Broughton, P. M. G., Provisional recommendation on quality control in clinical chemistry. I. General principles and terminology, International Federation of Clinical Chemistry, *Clin. Chem.*, 22, 532, 1976.
7. Ross, John W., Control materials and calibration standards, *CRC Handbook of Clinical Chemistry*, Volume 1, 359, 1989.

8. Foltz, Rodger L., Fentiman, Allison F., Foltz, Ruth B., GC/MS Assays for abused drugs in body fluids, Research Monograph Series, 32, pg. 9-12, National Institute on Drug Abuse, 1980.

9. Samuelsson, B., Hamberg, M., Sweely, C. C., *Anal. Biochem.*, 38, 301, 1970.

10. Lawson, Noel S., Haven, Guy T., Analyte stability in control and reference materials, *CRC Handbook of Clinical Chemistry*, Volume 1, 371, 1989.

11. Bowers, G.N., Burnett, R. W., and McComb, R. B., Selected method: preparation and use of human serum control materials for monitoring precision in clinical chemistry, *Clin. Chem.*, 21,1830,1975.

12. Approved Standard: ASC-2, *Calibration Reference Materials and Control Materials in Clinical Chemistry*, National Committee for Clinical Laboratory Standards, Villanova, Pa., 1975.

13. Anido, G., Preparation of quality control materials in clinical chemistry and hematology, *Proc. R. Soc. Med.*, 68, 624, 1975.

14. Klugerman, M. R., and Boutwell, J. H., Commercial control sera in the clinical chemistry laboratiory, *Clin. Chem.*, 7, 185, 1961.

15. Logan, J. E., and Allen, R. H., Control serum preparations, *Clin. Chem.*, 14, 437, 1968.

16. Diana Wilkins, Ph.D., Associate Toxicologist and Quality Control Manager, Center for Human Toxicology, personal communication, AAFS Meeting, New Orleans, February 1992.

17. Kateman, G., Pipjers, F. W., Sampling, *Quality Control in Analytical Chemistry*, Vol. 60, John Wiley & Sons, New York, Chapter 2, 1981.

18. Toseland, P. A., Samples and sampling, *Clarke's Isolation and Identification of Drugs in Pharmaceuticals, Body Fluids, and Post-mortem Material*, Second Edition, 111, The Pharmaceutical Press, London, 1986.

19. Committee on Hazardous Biological Substances in the Laboratory; Board on Chemical Sciences and Technology; Commission on Physical Sciences, Mathematics, and Resources; National Research Council; *Biosafety in the Laboratory-Prudent Practices for the Handling and Disposal of Infectious Materials*, National Academy Press, Washington, D. C., 1989.

20. Kateman, G., Pipjers, F. W., Analysis, *Quality Control in Analytical Chemistry*, Vol. 60, John Wiley & Sons, New York, Chapter 3, 1981

21. Ingle, J. D., *J. Chem. Ed.* 51(2), 100, 1974.

22. Glaser, J. A., Foerst, D. L., McKee, G. D., Quave, S. A., and Budde, W. L., Trace Analysis for Wastewaters, *Environmental Science and Technology*, 15, 1426, 1981.

23. *Code of Federal Regulations Part 100-136*, Protection of Environment, Definition and procedure for the determination of the method detection limit, Part 136, Appendix B, July 1992.

24. Analytical Chemistry: *Anal. Chem.*, 47, 2527, 1975.

25. Youden, W. J., Steiner, E. H., *Statistical Manual of the Association of Official Analytical Chemists*, A.O.A.C., Washington, D.C., 1975.

26. Sandell, E. B. and Elving, P. J., in Kothoff, I. M. and Elving, P. J., Editors, *Treatise on Analytical Chemistry*, Part 1, Vol. 1, New York, Interscience Publishers, Inc., 1959, page 17.

27. Skoog, D. A., West, D. M., *Principles of Instrumental Analysis*, Holt, Rinehart and Winston, Inc., New York, 1971.

28. Kateman, G., Pipjers, F. W., Data processing, *Quality Control in Analytical Chemistry*, Vol. 60, John Wiley & Sons, New York, Chapter 4, 1981.

29. Westgard, J. O., Barry, P. L., Hunt, M. R., A multi-rule Shewhart chart of quality control in clinical chemistry, *Clinical Chemistry*, Vol. 27, No. 3, 493-501, 1981.

30. Levey, S., and Jennings, E. R., The use of control charts in the clinical laboratories, *American Journal of Clinical Pathology*, 20, 1059-1066, 1950.

31. Westgard, J. O., Groth, T., Aronsson, T., Performance characteristics of rules for internal quality control: Probabilities for false rejection and error detection, *Clinical Chemistry*, 23, 1857-1867, 1977.

32. Westgard, J. O., Groth, T., Power functions for statistical control rules, *Clinical Chemistry*, 25, 863-869, 1979.

12.6 INTERPRETATION OF POSTMORTEM DRUG LEVELS

GRAHAM R. JONES

OFFICE OF THE CHIEF MEDICAL EXAMINER, EDMONTON, ALBERTA, CANADA

12.6.1 INTRODUCTION

In the early to middle part of the 1900s, the practice of forensic toxicology was relatively limited in scope. Certainly, toxicologists could determine blood alcohol and a limited number of drugs with accuracy approaching that of today. However, the toxicological investigation was different in at least two respects. First, the sophistication of testing for drugs was limited, primarily relying on the efficiency of extraction techniques, followed by gravimetric and later spectrophotometric analysis. Second, with the exception of alcohol and a relatively limited number of drugs or poisons (e.g. salicylate, barbiturates, arsenic, heavy metals), there was a very limited database of reference drug concentrations available. The interpretation of quantitative results relied very heavily on the history and circumstances of the case, including the police investigation, witness accounts, and autopsy findings.

The development of gas chromatography (GC) and high performance liquid chromatography (HPLC) during the early 1970s had a major influence on the development and growth of pharmacokinetics and therapeutic drug monitoring. As a result, the kinetics of drug absorption, distribution, metabolism, and excretion in clinical patients was easier to understand and predict. This coincided with a vast increase in the range of pure pharmaceuticals available, many of which were of lower absolute dosage compared with those previously available; for example, the replacement of barbiturates with low-dose benzodiazepines. It was logical that toxicologists started to use the pharmacokinetic data gained from living patients to interpret postmortem blood concentrations, for example, to predict whether a given blood drug concentration was "in the therapeutic range", whether the blood level was "fatal", or even to predict the amount ingested prior to death. Experience has since shown that postmortem drug concentrations must be interpreted from a very different perspective than for those in living patients. Many processes occur after death that can change drug and alcohol concentrations, sometimes to a very large extent.

The period of enthusiasm in the late 1970s and 1980s is giving way to the realization that there are many unique aspects of postmortem toxicology which must be considered when interpreting analytical results. It is no longer acceptable to interpret postmortem toxicology results from tables of so-called therapeutic, toxic and fatal ranges, without taking into consideration the medical history, the immediate circumstances of the death, and the various processes that can affect drug concentrations both before and after death. It is probably fair to say that many toxicologists and pathologists are less confident about interpreting postmortem drug concentrations today — and with good reason — than they may have been 10 to 20 years ago.

It is important to remember that there are no "absolute" rules for the interpretation of toxicology results. The more information that is available to, and considered by the interpreter, the more likely are the conclusions reached to be accurate. In the courtroom, lawyers, judges and jurors often view all science, including the forensic subspecialties, in absolute terms. Certainly, if the toxicologist does his or her job properly, the laboratory findings will have the required accuracy. However, the subsequent interpretation is in part based on the scope of the toxicology testing (not least including the range of specimens tested), in part on the quantitative results, and perhaps most importantly, on the history and circumstances surrounding the death. Attempts to interpret toxicology findings solely on the basis of so-called normal or reference ranges is irresponsible.

It is not the purpose of this section to teach anyone *how* to interpret postmortem drug concentrations, but rather to outline some of the pre-mortem and postmortem factors which should be taken into account when doing so.

12.6.2 GENERAL CONSIDERATIONS

12.6.2.1 The Analytical Result

It should be obvious that the interpretation of any toxicology test result will be no more reliable than the analytical result itself. The interpreter must be satisfied that the analysis is sufficiently accurate for the purpose, or at least know the limitations of the testing. Was the standard material used to prepare the calibrators pure and correctly identified? For example, was the salt or water of crystallization properly taken into account? Was the calibration properly prepared and valid in the range where the specimens were measured? Was the assay adequately verified by quality control samples? Was the assay sufficiently specific? Could endogenous substances or other drugs or metabolites have interfered with analysis of the specimen, either by obscuring the target analyte or increasing the apparent concentration? If the specimen was only analyzed once, what was the potential for accidental contamination? Was there a matrix effect? For example, was recovery of the drug from the specimen the same, relatively, as from the calibrators? Using similar matrix calibrators (e.g., blood) is not necessarily a guarantee of that since postmortem blood, by its nature, is variable from case to case, or even from site to site within the same cadaver. The extraction efficiency of drug or metabolite or internal standard from animal or outdated blood bank blood may sometimes be markedly different than from decomposed case blood. Although it is practically impossible to know the "absolute" or true concentration of drug in a postmortem specimen, the degree of confidence increases with the specificity of the analysis, with replication, or in some cases by applying multiple analytical methods of different physical or chemical principle.

The use of GC/mass spectrometry with multiple ion monitoring and stable isotope (e.g., deuterated) labeled internal standards will usually provide a higher degree of confidence in the accuracy of the analytical result, than say, use of an immunoassay procedure. The completeness of the analysis should also be considered. It is never possible to test for every single drug during routine screening tests. However, a careful review of the medications or other potential poisons available to the deceased should assist the laboratory in determining whether any of these substances would have been detected if present in significant concentrations.

12.6.2.2 Postmortem Specimens

Relying on a toxicology result from a single specimen can be misleading, because of the postmortem changes that can occur. The most commonly used specimen, blood, is not a homogeneous fluid. It is good forensic practice to have multiple specimens available, or at least blood specimens from different sites in the body, because of the potential difficulties in interpreting postmortem toxicology results.

12.6.2.2.1 Blood

The concentrations of many drugs are affected by postmortem redistribution through the vascular system from the major organs, by direct postmortem diffusion from organ to organ, and sometimes by incomplete distribution. Sedimentation of blood after death may also affect the drug "blood" concentration obtained. For some drugs the distribution between blood and plasma is markedly uneven during life. However, toxicologists should be cautious about applying factors to "correct" for blood:plasma distribution unless it is known that the distribution is maintained after death. It may be found that the blood:plasma distribution that exists during life, due to active processes, decays after death occurs, for example, due to changes in pH and, therefore, protein binding.

Toxicologists should be cautious about inferring the exact source of a blood specimen from the labeled description. Blood, simply labeled as such could come from almost anywhere, even collected as pooled blood at the scene. Most toxicologists and pathologists are well acquainted with the widely discouraged practice of drawing blood by a "blind stick" through the chest wall. Although such blood may be labeled as "heart blood", it may contain pericardial fluid, or worse, may be from the pleural cavity, and therefore potentially be contaminated by gastric contents, particularly if the death was traumatic or decomposition severe.[1] Even blood drawn from the "heart" after opening the body cavity at autopsy may contain blood from a number of sources. So-called "heart" blood may contain blood from one or more of the cardiac chambers — the ventricles and atria. However, it may equally contain blood which has drained from the pulmonary vein and artery (and hence the lungs), from the inferior vena cava (and hence from the liver), and from the aorta and subclavian veins. As a result, so-called "heart" blood is potentially one of the most non-homogeneous specimens in the body. As described later, postmortem redistribution and other factors can cause the concentrations of many drugs to vary markedly from site to site.[2-4] Even drug concentrations in blood drawn from the same site, but simply placed into different collection vials, can also sometimes differ by several fold.

It is generally recommended that to avoid the effects of postmortem redistribution or diffusion from the major organs, femoral blood should be sampled wherever possible. While this is certainly a good practice, interpreters should be cautioned that there is no such thing as "pure femoral blood", it is simply blood drawn from the site of the femoral vein. Certainly, if the femoral vein is ligated prior to sampling, it is likely that much of the blood will be "peripheral" and therefore relatively uncontaminated by blood from the major organs. However, this is rarely the case. Femoral blood is typically drawn by a "stick" to the unligated femoral vein in the groin area, such that blood will be drawn from above and below the site of sampling. If the volume drawn is relatively small (e.g., 2 to 5 mL), it is unlikely that much blood will be drawn down from the central body cavity. However, with some skill, it is often possible to draw 50 mL or more of blood from a "femoral stick". Even with a limited knowledge of anatomy, it doesn't require much thought to realize that at least some of this blood will have been drawn down from the inferior vena cava, and hence from the liver. Since blood concentrations of some drugs have the potential for marked postmortem change, it is good practice to analyze blood obtained from more than one site, plus tissue or other specimens where this may be useful.

12.6.2.2.2 Vitreous Humor

Vitreous humor, although limited in volume (e.g., 3 to 6 mL) is an extremely useful specimen. It has been used for years to verify postmortem blood concentrations of ethanol, since postmortem fermentation does not occur to any significant extent in the eye. However, vitreous humor has also been useful for a number of drugs. For example, it is well known that digoxin concentrations will rise after death in cardiac blood, due to postmortem redistribution from myocardial tissue, and possibly other organs. Consequently, vitreous digoxin concentrations are more likely to reflect those in antemortem plasma.[5] Vitreous humor has been used to analyze a large number of other drugs, including barbiturates, cocaine, morphine, tricyclic antidepressants and benzodiazepines.[6-10] However, interpretation of vitreous drug concentrations is difficult, in part because very few studies have been published which relate blood concentrations to those in vitreous humor, and in part because the large *ad hoc* data on vitreous drug concentrations is fragmented in innumerable case reports. In general though, those drugs that tend to be somewhat hydrophilic at physiological pH (e.g., digoxin, benzoylecgonine, acetaminophen, salicylate) are more likely to have concentrations approaching those in blood or plasma, than those drugs that are either highly protein bound (e.g. tricyclic antidepressants) or highly lipophilic (e.g., benzodiazepines).

Because the eye is remote from the central body cavity and the abdominal organs, it has been suggested that vitreous may be a useful fluid for the determination of drugs that are subject to postmortem redistribution. That may hold true for many drugs such as digoxin. However, others have shown that some drugs, notably cocaine, may increase in concentration in the vitreous humor after death.[9] It must not be forgotten that the eye is located extremely close to one of the largest organs in the body - the brain. Therefore the possibility of postmortem diffusion of some drugs into the vitreous from the brain and ocular tissue should not be overlooked.

12.6.2.2.3 Liver

Many toxicologists rank the liver second only after blood in importance as a specimen of interpretive value in postmortem toxicology. It is particularly valuable for the tricyclic antidepressants and many other drugs which are very highly protein bound. It is useful for the phenothiazine neuroleptics which have a very large dosage range, and hence range in "therapeutic" blood concentrations. Liver tissue is also of value for interpreting postmortem concentrations of many other drugs where a sufficiently large database has been established, and particularly where blood is not available due to severe decomposition, fire or exsanguination.

One other aspect of liver drug concentrations should be considered. It is known that postmortem diffusion from the stomach may artefactually elevate concentrations of the drug proximal to the stomach — for example after an overdose, where both the concentration and absolute amount of drug in the stomach are high.[11,12] However, little appears to have been done to assess the kinetics of drugs in the liver after therapeutic doses. For example, common sense would suggest that drug concentrations in the liver, and particularly those which are strongly protein bound, would increase dramatically in the period after a dose was taken, compared with that at steady state. This might be particularly important for drugs with a relatively long half-life and which are often taken in single night-time doses, or divided with a large portion of the dose at night. As for other specimens, liver concentrations are extremely valuable for assessing the role of many drugs in a death, but only in conjunction with other analytical findings and history.

12.6.2.2.4 Gastric Contents

Interpretation of the analytical findings of drugs in the gastric contents is largely dictated by common sense. It is the *amount* of drug or poison remaining in the gastric contents that is important; the concentration of the drug is generally of far less importance. The tricyclic antidepressants offer a good example. Most forensic toxicologists regard total tricyclic concentrations greater than 2 to 3 mg/L, even in postmortem "cardiac" blood, as being toxic or potentially fatal. So what does a gastric tricyclic concentration of 1500 mg/l mean? The answer is, on it's own, not much, except that the person may have consumed his or her medication a relatively short period prior to death. For example 200 mg amitriptyline at night is a fairly common dosage. If the gastric volume was, say, 120 mL, then 1500 mg/L would be completely consistent with the person taking the normal dosage just prior to death — probably from unrelated causes. However, if in our example the gastric volume at autopsy was 900 mL, then a concentration of 1500 mg/L would calculate out to 1350 mg/900 mL in the stomach, and therefore almost certainly consistent with an overdose.

Conversely, a relatively low absolute amount of drug in the gastric contents, with or without a high concentration, does not rule out the possibility of an overdose. Numerous case histories have shown that it may take several hours for an individual to die from an intentional overdose, depending upon the exact drugs or poisons ingested, the amounts, co-ingestion of alcohol, general state of health and age. It is not unusual for people to die from an oral overdose with less than a single therapeutic dose remaining in the stomach, notwithstanding the fact that an overdose of drugs can be irritant to the stomach lining and therefore delay gastric emptying. Extensive vomiting before death can also reduce the amount of drug remaining in the stomach at the time death occurs.

Two other aspects of "gastric toxicology" should be mentioned. The simple presence of a drug in the gastric contents does not necessarily mean that the drug was recently consumed, or even prove that the drug was taken orally. Most drugs will be re-excreted into the gastric contents through the gastric juice, maintaining an equilibrium between the gastric fluid and the blood. This is especially so for drugs that are basic (alkaline) in nature. This can readily be demonstrated where it is known that a drug has only been administered intravenously under controlled conditions, and yet can be found later in small concentrations in the gastric contents. The same phenomenon can be seen with drug metabolites where, invariably, concentrations can be found in the gastric fluid. While it could be argued that microbial metabolism could have occurred in the stomach, it is more likely that the majority of the metabolites found were secreted into the stomach via the gastric juice.

On the other hand, significant amounts of conglomerated, unabsorbed tablet or capsule residue can be found in the stomach many hours, or even a day or two after a large overdose was consumed. These masses are not uncommon after overdoses where large amounts of capsules or tablets may form a gelatinous mass which is not readily dissolved or broken up, and which may lie slowly dissolving; they are called bezoars[13] While the term can apply to unabsorbed masses of almost anything (e.g., hair balls), it is also applied to unabsorbed drug formulations. They occur, at least in part, because gastric emptying time is delayed significantly by irritants, including large amounts of undissolved drug residue. However, the phenomenon is also occasionally seen in patients where over dosage is extremely unlikely (e.g., controlled setting such as a hospital or nursing home), but where several unabsorbed tablets may be recovered from the stomach This is more likely to occur where enteric coated tablets are involved, which do not dissolve in the stomach, but may stick together to form a small mass of tablets. It is also more likely to happen in the elderly, or in other patients where gastric motility is abnormally slow.

12.6.2.2.5 Urine

It is almost universally accepted that, with few exceptions, there is very little correlation between urine and blood drug concentrations, and even less correlation between urine drug concentrations and pharmacological effect. So many factors affect urine concentration, such as fluid intake, rate of metabolism, glomerular clearance, urine pH, and the times of voiding relative to the dose, that any attempt to predict or even estimate a blood concentration from a urine concentration is pure folly. As always there are some exceptions. Urine alcohol concentrations can be used to estimate the approximate blood alcohol concentration, but only if the bladder is completely voided and the measurement made on the second void. Estimates of the body burden of some heavy metals are still made on 24-h urine collections.

12.6.2.2.6 Brain

The brain is the primary site of action of many forensically important drugs, such as the antidepressants, benzodiazepines and narcotics. It is potentially a very useful specimen for the measurement and interpretation of drugs because it is remote from the stomach and other major organs in the body and would not be expected to be affected by postmortem diffusion and redistribution. However, although drug concentration data in brain tissue are not hard to find in the literature, it is largely fragmented into innumerable case reports which seldom specify what anatomic region of brain tissue was analyzed. The brain is an anatomically diverse organ such that concentrations of many drugs vary significantly from one region to another — up to about twofold.[2,4]

12.6.2.2.7 Other Soft Tissues

Most of the major organs such as the kidneys, lungs, spleen and myocardial tissue are analyzed periodically to estimate the degree of drug or poison exposure. However, for most drugs, adequate reference databases are not available in the literature, so the interpretive value of these measurements may be limited. Skeletal muscle has the potential to be one of the most useful specimens for drug or poison determination, particularly where the body is severely decomposed, or where postmortem redistribution or diffusion might affect measurement in blood or other organs. The problem is one of obtaining sufficient reference values for that drug in skeletal muscle in order to make a confident interpretation. Some studies have been published, but data are scattered and incomplete.[2,4,14]

The potential usefulness of bone marrow for the determination of both drugs and alcohol has been explored.[15-17] For drugs and other poisons at least, this could be very useful in cases where severe decomposition, fire or the action of wild animals has made the major organs unavailable, but where bone marrow can still be harvested and analyzed. As for many other specimens, the problem is again one of establishing an adequate and reliable database of reference values.

12.6.2.2.8 Other Fluids

Bile has been used for decades as one of the primary specimens analyzed in the forensic toxicology laboratory, but mainly for the detection and measurement of morphine. However, the usefulness of bile has decreased in the past few years as sensitive immunoassays and mass spectrometry based assays have been developed for whole blood. For most drugs, including morphine, the interpretive value of bile is limited. Biliary drug concentrations may also be influenced by postmortem diffusion from the liver and the stomach.

Cerebrospinal fluid (CSF) is also a potentially useful specimen for the measurement and interpretation of drugs, since it is the fluid which 'bathes' the central nervous system, the brain and spinal cord. Its limitation lies mainly in the fact that it is often more difficult to collect than blood postmortem, and as for many other specimens, there is a very limited database of reference values. As for the vitreous, drugs which are highly protein bound or those which are lipophilic, will tend to have significantly lower concentrations than in the blood.

12.6.2.2.9 Injection Sites, Nasal Swabs

Suspect injection sites are periodically excised and submitted for analysis, to support evidence of that route of administration. Certainly, it is not difficult to perform such analyses. However, the simple qualitative detection or even quantitative measurement of a drug in a piece of skin is only evidence that the drug was taken or used, not that it was necessarily injected, let alone at that site. Sometimes it is forgotten that most drugs are distributed throughout the body from any route of administration, such that any piece of skin will contain some amount of the drug. For such measurements to be useful, a similar piece of skin from another part of the body, not suspected to be an injection site, must be analyzed for comparison. Only if the concentration in the suspect site is substantially higher than that in the reference site can meaningful conclusions be drawn. Even then, elevated drug concentrations would not be expected to persist at an intravenous injection site, in contrast to an intramuscular or subcutaneous site.

Similarly, the simple detection of a drug such as cocaine in a nasal swab does not prove that the drug was "snorted". Any fluid secreted by the body, including sweat, vaginal fluid and nasal secretions will contain some concentration of the drug. In this instance, quantitative determination is difficult and interpretation even more so unless the concentration of drug in the nasal secretions is extremely high relative to the blood.

12.6.2.2.10 Bone, Nails, Hair

Most drugs and poisons will be absorbed by bone, nails and hair. Hair has long been used for the determination and arsenic and heavy metals, and by cutting the hair into sequential sections, for estimating the duration of exposure to the poison.[18] More recently, hair has been used for the determination of drugs of abuse in workplace and probation testing. Although its use in these areas remains controversial, it still has the potential to be useful in limited postmortem situations, for example, to estimate the duration of exposure to a drug or toxin.

Most drugs and poisons will be taken up in bone and therefore, unless volatile, will be detectable in skeletonized remains. The interpretation of concentrations of certain drugs or poisons is relatively easy since either the normal or reference values are well established (e.g., arsenic; heavy metals), or the substance should not be present in any concentration (e.g., strychnine). However, interpretation of specific concentrations of drugs is problematic since there are few reference values available.

12.6.2.2.11 Paraphernalia: Syringes, Spoons, Glasses

Most forensic toxicologists are willing to analyze potentially drug-related exhibits found at the scene of death. Syringes or spoons can provide a valuable confirmation of drugs which may have been used prior to death. For example, heroin is so rapidly broken down to morphine, that little or no heroin, or even monoacetylmorphine, may be detectable in postmortem blood. The finding of morphine in, for example blood, could indicate either use of heroin or a morphine salt (or codeine, if it was also found). However, it should be borne in mind that most addicts reuse syringes and therefore the presence of a drug in a syringe found in the same room as a body does not necessarily mean that drugs contained therein were involved in the death, although it may provide circumstantial evidence. The use or abuse of insulin in a non- diabetic is exceptionally difficult to prove, since blood insulin concentrations are so variable, are difficult to determine accurately in postmortem blood, and even during life correlate poorly with blood glucose. Insulin abuse is uncommon,[19,20] but in those cases where it happens may be difficult to prove postmortem without a good clinical history. However, detection of insulin in a used syringe near someone who was not prescribed the drug can provide useful circumstantial evidence of abuse. The presence of drug residues in drinking glasses or cups can provide evidence of at least the route of ingestion and in most cases assist with the determination of manner of death, especially if the drug residue is large and obvious. Care would obviously have to be taken to distinguish, say, a multiple drug overdose mixed in a glass of water, from two or three hypnotic tablets introduced into an alcoholic beverage for the purposes of administering a "Mickey Finn".

12.6.3 PHARMACOKINETICS

Although other parts of this book deal with the topic of pharmacokinetics in some detail, it is worth reviewing the basics as it relates to postmortem interpretation. The kinetics of all drugs and poisons in the body are characterized by absorption, distribution, metabolism and excretion. All of these parameters affect the concentrations which will be found in the body after death, and therefore interpretation of analytical toxicology results.

12.6.3.1 Absorption and Distribution

Absorption may be via the oral route, parenteral (e.g., intravenous, intramuscular, subcutaneous), pulmonary, dermal and rarely, rectal. The route of absorption can be very important to the interpretation. For example, many drugs are extremely toxic via the intravenous route, especially if given rapidly. For example, heroin, barbiturates and many other drugs can cause severe hypotension, and may be fatal, if given rapidly, even though the total dose given is within the range normally considered "therapeutic". The resulting postmortem blood concentrations may be below those normally considered fatal. At the other extreme, dermal absorption of medication is probably the slowest, such that even therapeutic concentrations in blood may take several hours to reach. Moreover, absorption of the drug may continue for several hours after the source of the drug, for example a transdermal patch, is removed, due to the depot of medication which accumulates in the upper layers of the skin. In these circumstances the dose is difficult to control, and if toxicity occurs it is important that the patient be monitored for several hours after the patch is removed, in case of continued toxicity.[21]

Morphine provides a good and common example of why interpretation of blood concentrations alone in isolation from case history, is difficult. First, opiate tolerance can vary tremendously between individuals and even within the same individual over a relatively short time span (days or weeks). Tolerance is an important consideration both clinically, where opiates may be chronically administered for pain, and in abuse situations where they are used for their euphoric effect. In clinical situations the issue of tolerance is complicated by the fact that patients in severe pain can tolerate higher doses of opioids than those in whom the pain is mild. It is also accepted that less opioid is required to prevent the recurrence of pain than to relieve it.[22] The form of the opioids will affect how rapidly the drug crosses the blood: brain barrier and, therefore, how potent it is. For example, heroin (diacetylmorphine) is at least twice as potent as morphine, probably because it is more lipid soluble and reaches the CNS faster than the more hydrophilic drug, morphine. It has been suggested that heroin may simply be a pro-drug for morphine, but which reaches the site of action more efficiently. As a result, blood concentrations of morphine seen in heroin abuse deaths are frequently lower than concentrations resulting from the therapeutic administration of oral or parenteral morphine in clinical situations. The situation is complicated further because morphine is extensively metabolized by conjugation with glucuronic acid.

Originally it was assumed that this resulted in exclusively water-soluble, metabolites which were pharmacologically inactive. However, while morphine-3-glucuronide is devoid of narcotic activity, morphine-6-glucuronide, which is typically present in blood at higher concentrations than unconjugated morphine, is more potent than morphine itself.[23-25] Furthermore, much of case data published in the clinical and forensic toxicology literature does not even distinguish between unconjugated and "total" morphine, let alone the 3- and 6-glucuronides, which are seldom measured routinely. With all these variables, it is no wonder morphine blood concentrations correlate poorly with analgesic effect and CNS depression. A good example of this has been described where prolonged respiratory depression was observed in three patients in renal failure where morphine concentrations were extremely low, but where morphine-6-glucuronide had accumulated to toxic levels.[26]

12.6.3.2 Metabolism and Pharmacogenetics

A detailed treatise on the mechanisms of drug metabolism and the accumulation of drugs or metabolites due to impaired metabolism is beyond the scope of this chapter. However, it is worth pointing out at least three different scenarios where impaired metabolism can have a significant impact on the interpretation of results. Metabolism can be impaired by liver disease, such as advanced cirrhosis. However, not all metabolic pathways will be impaired equally by liver disease, and indeed some pathways may be affected little, if at all. Oxidative pathways which are easily saturable are likely to be affected more than others, such as glucuronidation. A person's metabolism may be genetically deficient, for example in cytochrome P4502D6 (CYP2D6). This pathway is responsible for many oxidative transformations such as ring hydroxylation of the tricyclic antidepressants. Third, co-ingested drugs can inhibit one or more drug metabolism pathways. For example, most or all of the SSRIs inhibit CYP2D6 and some are extremely potent in this regard. The degree of elevation of the drugs or metabolites affected depends very much on the respective dosages of the drugs involved and, not least, on the "metabolic reserve" of the individual patient. Some drug-drug interactions or genetic polymorphism may only result in slightly elevated drug or metabolite concentrations, perhaps necessitating lowering of dosage. However, in some circumstances the increases may be so dramatic as to cause life-threatening toxicity or death, particularly where the side-effects were not sufficiently severe to alert the physician or patient that cardiotoxicity might be a problem. At least two cases involving impaired metabolism of imipramine have been described in the forensic literature.[27]

12.6.3.3 Calculation of Total Body Burden

Calculation of the total amount of drug ingested in self or homicidal poisonings have been attempted many times over the years. This was attempted by the toxicologist who analyzed the remains found in the basement of Dr. Harvey Crippen, the renowned London poisoner who used hyoscine.[28] Calculations typically involve measurement of the drug or poison in the major organs including, where possible, skeletal muscle, and then taking into account the organ weights to arrive at a total estimate of the amount in the body. In some cases, the amounts have correlated very well with the available physical evidence (e.g., amount of drug in an empty injection vial or amount prescribed).[29,30] Doubtless, in some other examples attempted by toxicologists, correlation with the physical evidence was less convincing, or not possible. In order for such calculations to be meaningful, a number of factors must be assumed.

Perhaps most important, the particular part of the tissue or blood sample analyzed must be representative of the remainder of the organ or tissue. Since most organs are not homogeneous and because uneven postmortem diffusion (as discussed later) can lead to non-homogeneity of concentration, being sure of the average concentration of drug within any one organ may be difficult without analyzing that entire organ. While it is easy to know the weight of individual organs such as the heart, lungs, liver, kidneys and brain, it is very difficult to reliably estimate the total amount of tissue into which most drugs readily distribute — the skeletal muscle. While the mass of skeletal muscle can be estimated from medical tables, given a persons height and weight, there is no assurance that the concentration of drug measured in one or two portions of skeletal muscle is representative of that in muscle from all other parts of the body.

Similar arguments apply to adipose tissue, where it is more difficult to obtain representative samples and accurately assay. It should also be borne in mind that for a person chronically taking a drug with a very large volume of distribution and long half-life, the equivalent of many times the total daily dose will be *normally* present in the body, even after therapeutic doses. Estimation of the total body burden of a drug may not be without value in all cases; it must be done with caution and the variables well understood and acknowledged. It is the rare cases of homicidal poisoning where significant weight may be placed on such calculations and where the stakes are the highest.

12.6.3.4 Estimation of Amount Ingested from Blood Levels

Given the forgoing discussion, it should go without saying that using pharmacokinetic calculations to try to estimate dosage, given a postmortem blood concentration, is of virtually no value and can be extremely misleading. Several factors make such calculations invalid. The blood drug concentration measured postmortem must be representative of that present at the time of death. As discussed elsewhere in this chapter, that is often not the case, and it is very difficult to predict whether any given postmortem drug concentration represents the concentration at the time of death, even for drugs for which postmortem redistribution is not well known. Any toxicologist who has routinely analyzed drugs in multiple blood samples from the same case knows how often those concentrations unexpectedly vary from sample to sample. Also, the drug must be at steady state at the time the person dies. By the very nature of drug related deaths, that is rarely the case. Even if the gastric contents contain relatively little drug, much of the drug could still be present in the ileum, or at least not attained equilibrium with muscle, adipose tissue and the major organs. Finally, the rate of absorption, bioavailability, volume of distribution, half-life, rate of metabolism and clearance are seldom known for any specific individual and can vary tremendously between subjects. The estimation of dose from postmortem blood concentrations is a practice of the foolhardy.

12.6.4 POSTMORTEM REDISTRIBUTION AND OTHER CHANGES

One question which should be asked before attempting to interpret postmortem drug concentrations is "is the concentration found likely to represent, at least approximately, that present at the time of death?". Unfortunately, the answer is often a flat "no", or at least "not necessarily". A number of factors need to be considered.

12.6.4.1 Incomplete Distribution

It is often the case that sudden deaths involving drugs are caused by abuse or suicidal drug overdose. Death will therefore usually occur before steady state has been reached. If a person is actively absorbing an overdose, it is likely that the concentration of the drug in blood leaving the liver (i.e. the inferior vena cava and right atrium) will have a somewhat higher concentration than, for example, venous blood returning from the peripheral vessels (e.g., femoral vein), for no other reason than a substantial amount of the drug will be absorbed during the course of circulation through the body. This has been demonstrated in living patients and concentration differences up to about twofold recorded between arterial and venous blood.[31,32]

12.6.4.2 Postmortem Redistribution

Postmortem redistribution is literally the movement of drug after death along a concentration gradient. Much is still unknown about the extent to which postmortem changes in drug concentration occur and the drugs affected, however, some generalizations can be made. Postmortem redistribution is likely to be most marked for drugs that are highly protein bound, but particularly those sequestered in the major organs such as the lungs and liver (e.g., tricyclic antidepressants, propoxyphene, chloroquine). Postmortem redistribution starts to occur within an hour after death and continues as the postmortem interval increases. The most important quantitative changes in blood drug concentration occur within the first 24 h or so and are highly site dependent. In general, increases will be greater in blood from "central" sites, such as the vessels near the major organs, than in more peripheral sites, such as the femoral veins. However, blood drug concentrations can vary fivefold or more between cardiac, hepatic and pulmonary sites.[2,4] Given the very close proximity of these major vessels to one another and the organs they serve, it is impossible to even estimate perimortem drug concentrations based on the postmortem interval and site from which a blood sample was drawn. Even aside from the unpredictable nature of postmortem redistribution per se, blood from the "heart", if labeled as such, could have come from either of the cardiac atria or ventricles, the pulmonary vein or artery, the aorta or the inferior vena cava.

Since it is known that many drug concentrations change after death, due to redistribution from the major organs, it is recommended, that postmortem blood for drug and alcohol analysis be taken from a peripheral site such as the femoral vein. However, it should be emphasized that even if a "good" femoral blood sample is obtained, it is no guarantee that the drug concentrations subsequently measured will represent those present at the moment of death. In fact it is well established that femoral blood concentrations of many drugs can increase twofold or more after death. While it is possible that some of this increase is due to diffusion of released drug down the major vessels to the groin, it should be borne in mind that drug concentrations in skeletal muscle are often twofold or more higher than in the perimortem blood.[2,4] Given the mass of muscle surrounding these relatively small peripheral vessels, diffusion of drug directly into the blood across the vessel wall is very likely to occur. While in many of the published studies on postmortem redistribution the vessels have been carefully ligated prior to taking blood samples, this is rarely done during routine medico-legal autopsies. Consequently, blood labeled as "femoral" may contain blood drawn down from the inferior vena cava. This is particularly likely to be the case where large volumes (e.g., 30 to 50 mL) have been obtained from a supposedly femoral site. It should also be obvious that it doesn't matter whether the syringe needle is pointing down towards the leg!

The mechanisms for postmortem redistribution probably involve release of drug from protein bound sites after death occurs, with subsequent diffusion into interstitial fluid, through the capillaries and into the larger blood vessels. Since this process appears to start within an hour or so of death, decomposition or putrefaction per se is not likely to play a role, at least in the early stages. It is more likely that cessation of active cellular processes and the rapid fall in blood and tissue pH which occurs after death would lead to changes in the conformation of proteins and therefore release of some proportion of drugs present from the protein bound state. It is important to bear in mind that these changes start well before putrefaction and microbiological action are likely to play a role.

Other types of postmortem diffusion can occur. For example, it has been demonstrated that over a period of a day or more, significant changes in drug concentrations in the major organs can occur. This has been shown for the tricyclic antidepressants, where concentrations in the lungs tended to decrease, commensurate with an increase in concentration in the liver.[33] This study was done in such a manner as to show that these changes can occur due to direct diffusion from one organ to the other, independent of the residue of drug in the stomach. However, the magnitude of these changes is not likely to affect interpretation of tissue drug concentrations to a significant extent. It has also been demonstrated that postmortem diffusion of drug from the stomach can markedly increase drug concentrations in proximal lobes of the liver and lungs, as well as postmortem blood in some of the central vessels.[11,12] Ironically, when organ tissue was analyzed in previous decades, postmortem diffusion into the liver or lungs might have been less important since it was not uncommon to homogenize large amounts of organ tissue (e.g., 500 g), such that any local increases in concentration would be averaged out. However, today the tendency in many laboratories is to homogenize small amounts of tissue (e.g., 2 to 10 g), which could lead to a gross overestimation of the amount of drug in the organ if the sampled tissue was taken close to the stomach. The potential for postmortem diffusion of drugs in this manner has been known for decades, but recent work has brought the issue the attention it deserves and better quantified the potential changes.

Aspiration of gastric contents can provide one more important mechanism whereby postmortem blood concentrations can be artificially elevated.[34] This can occur agonally, as death is occurring, or after death, during transportation of the body. It is a factor which may more commonly occur after over dosage where the stomach contains a very concentrated cocktail of one or more drugs, with or without alcohol. However, it could also be very important to consider in deaths where therapeutic doses have been consumed and death occurs as a result of unrelated natural causes. It is not uncommon, for example, for tricyclic antidepressants to be taken as a single nightly dose, and in fact large doses of many antipsychotic drugs are taken at night. This can result in drug concentrations in the stomach of the order of grams per liter, which if aspirated could result in significant increases in some local postmortem blood concentrations. Not surprisingly, the pulmonary vein and artery blood concentrations are elevated to the greatest extent following simulated aspiration. This is more significant than it might seem because much of the so-called "heart blood" which is often sampled at autopsy, is in fact blood of pulmonary origin drawn from the major pulmonary vessels or the left atrium.

12.6.5 OTHER CONSIDERATIONS

12.6.5.1 Trauma

Severe trauma can affect the interpretation of both alcohol and drug concentrations. For example, it is not uncommon for severe motor vehicle accidents to result in rupture of the stomach and diaphragm. This can easily result in the release of gastric fluid into the body cavity. Because blood may be difficult to obtain from discrete vessels, pooled blood from the pleural cavity may be sampled. If an autopsy is performed the origin and nature of the fluid so drawn should be obvious, and hopefully noted. However, if an autopsy is not performed and "blood" is sampled through the chest wall in an attempt to obtain cardiac blood, the coroner or medical examiner may be unaware that the sample is contaminated with gastric fluid. If even small, therapeutic amounts of drug remain unabsorbed in the gastric contents in these circumstances, it can result in what appears to be a grossly elevated "blood" drug (or alcohol) concentration. The release of microorganisms from the GI tract and subsequent potential for fermentation is a well recognized problem.

12.6.5.2 Artifacts of Medication Delivery

Artifacts of absorption and distribution must be recognized when interpreting postmortem blood concentrations. For example, it is quite common to find grossly elevated concentrations of lidocaine in cases where resuscitation has been unsuccessfully attempted. Concentrations may be 2 to 5 times those normally considered therapeutic when lidocaine is given by intravenous infusion for the treatment of cardiac arrhythmias. If lidocaine is administered as a bolus intracardiac injection and normal cardiac rhythm never established, very high local concentrations will result in the cardiac blood. These could be interpreted as "fatal" unless all the circumstances are considered.

Devices which automatically deliver medication by the parenteral route can lead to artificially high blood concentrations postmortem. Most of these devices will continue to periodically dispense medication, usually narcotics, into the vein after a person dies, unless they are switched off and disconnected quickly. This can result in extremely high local concentrations of drug which may be misinterpreted as an "overdose".

Transdermal patches left on a body after death will give rise to locally high concentrations of the drug (e.g. fentanyl). Since these patches rely primarily on passive diffusion across a rate limiting membrane for drug delivery, the concentration of the medication in the local area will continue to rise after death, albeit at a slower rate. Since blood circulation through the skin obviously stops after death, the drug will no longer be transported away except by diffusion, allowing a local build-up of drug. However, such a high concentration gradient exists between the gel containing the medication in the patch, and the skin, that even modest postmortem diffusion might be expected to raise the postmortem blood and tissue concentrations up to several inches away.

12.6.5.3 Additive and Synergistic Toxicity

When interpreting drug concentrations it is important to take into account the sum of the effects of all of the drugs detected. This is often an issue in drug abuse deaths, particularly those involving prescription drugs. Such deaths often involve multiple drugs of the same type (e.g., benzodiazepines or narcotics), individually present in "therapeutic" amounts, and often in combination with alcohol. Interpretation of blood drug concentrations in these cases has to take into account disease which may be present, and the total amounts of drugs and alcohol. In many cases, these affects may simply be additive, i.e., simply the sum of the individual effects of the drugs involved. In other cases, the effect may be truly synergistic, where the toxicity is greater than would be expected based on the pharmacology and concentrations of the individual drugs. Cases where multiple drugs are present, with or without alcohol, are probably the most difficult to interpret and rely heavily on the experience of the interpreter and a reliable and complete case history.

12.6.5.4 Adverse Reactions

A death attributed to neuroleptic malignant syndrome (NMS) resulting from therapy with phenothiazine or some other neuroleptics, is a good example of a fatal adverse drug reaction.[35] Combinations of drugs can result in similar syndromes, such as combination of a tricyclic antidepressant and a monoamine oxidase inhibitor (MAOI) causing serotonin syndrome.[36] Although not always fatal, a serotonin reaction can result in death and might be considered where there is no other reasonable cause of death and especially where there are elevated concentrations of MAOIs and either TCAs or serotonin specific reuptake inhibitors (SSRIs). It should be borne in mind that by the very nature of drug-drug or other adverse reactions, blood concentrations of the drug(s) involved are seldom predictive of the outcome and are often well within the range normally expected from therapeutic doses. In the absence of clinical observations, such fatalities can be very difficult to diagnose accurately.

12.6.5.5 Drug Instability

It should not be overlooked that many drugs are unstable in any biological fluid. Cocaine is probably the most notable example. It is broken down in aqueous solution and enzymatically in blood or plasma to benzoylecgonine and methylecgonine, neither of which has much pharmacological activity. While cocaine may be stabilized to some extent by the addition of fluoride after the blood is collected, the extent of breakdown between death and autopsy must be considered. Unfortunately, there are many variables to consider. First, the toxicity of cocaine itself correlates only poorly with blood concentration, even in the living. There is good evidence that cocaine concentrations in postmortem blood can increase or decrease, depending on the exact site of collection.[37,38] There are probably competing effects due to variable breakdown in different areas of the body and true postmortem redistribution. The collection and measurement of cocaine in vitreous humor has been attempted to overcome these problems. However, it has been shown that cocaine will often, if irreproducibility, increase in concentration with time in the vitreous humor. The mechanism for this has not been proven, but it likely involves postmortem redistribution from the brain, where cocaine is known to concentrate relative to the blood, into the eye via the optic nerve and other soft tissue. It is possible that time dependent postmortem increases in vitreous concentrations may occur for other drugs where those drugs attain higher concentrations in the brain.

12.6.5.6 Interpretation Using Tables of Values

There probably isn't a forensic toxicologist or pathologist alive who hasn't used published tables as a reference when trying to interpret postmortem blood concentrations. Tables of such

Graham R. Jones

values became a necessary evil due to the sheer volume of medical and forensic literature. However, they unfortunately perpetuate the myth that postmortem toxicology results can be interpreted solely using, or heavily relying on so-called "therapeutic", "toxic", and "fatal" ranges. Although tables of drug concentrations can serve as a useful reference point, it should be borne in mind that many of the values in these tables are derived from serum or plasma data from living patients, that the ranges are seldom referenced to published cases, and may not take into account or state other variables such as postmortem redistribution, time of survival after intoxication or the presence of other drugs, natural disease or injury. Having stated that, one compilation has attempted to address some of these issues and indeed bases most of the postmortem values they list on femoral blood samples from ligated vessels, for which the authors are to be commended.[39]

12.6.6 Conclusion

In the final analysis, postmortem toxicology results must be interpreted with regard to all of the available information, including medical history, information from the scene, autopsy findings, nature and exact location of the postmortem samples collected, and the circumstances of the death. Only after weighing all of these variables can postmortem results be reliably interpreted. Even then, it must be admitted that *reliable* interpretation of some results is simply not possible based on the available information. In many respects, the desirable underlying approach to the interpretation of postmortem drug concentrations is not much different than was used a century ago: a good scene investigation, medical investigation, laboratory investigation and the application of common sense. Hopefully we are also wiser now.

REFERENCES

1. Logan, B. K. and Lindholm, G., Gastric contamination of postmortem blood samples during blind-stick sample collection, *Am. J. Forensic Med. Pathol.*, 17, 109, 1996.
2. Jones, G. R. and Pounder, D. J., Site Dependence of drug concentrations in postmortem blood - a case study, *J. Anal. Toxicol.*, 11, 186, 1987.
3. Prouty, R. W. and Anderson, W. H., The forensic implications of site and temporal differences on predicting blood-drug concentrations, *J. Forensic Sci.*, 35, 243, 1990.
4. Pounder, D. J. and Jones, G. R., Post-mortem drug redistribution — a toxicological nightmare, *Forensic Sci. Int.*, 45, 253, 1990.
5. Vorpahl, T. E. and Coe, J. I., Correlation of Antemortem and Postmortem Digoxin Levels, *J. Forensic Sci.*, 23, 329, 1978.
6. Ziminski, K. R., Wemyss, C. T., Bidanset, J. H., Manning, T. J., and Lukash, L., Comparative study of postmortem barbiturates, methadone, and morphine in vitreous humor, blood, and tissue, *J. Forensic Sci.*, 29, 903, 1984.
7. Worm, K. and Steentoft, A., A comparison of post-mortem concentrations of basic drugs in femoral whole blood and vitreous humor, in *Proceedings of the International Congress of Clinical Toxicology, Poison Control and Analytical Toxicology, Lux Tox '90, Societe des Sciences Medicales du Grand-Duche de Luxembourg*, Wennig, R. Ed., Luxembourg, 1990, p. 438.
8. Bermejo, A. M., Ramos, I., Fernandzez, P., Lopez-Rivadulla, M., Cruz, A., Chiarotti, M., Fucci, N. and Marsilli, R., Morphine determination by gas chromatography/mass spectrometry in human vitreous humor and comparison with radioimmunoassay, *J. Anal. Toxicol.*, 16, 372, 1992.
9. McKinney, P. E., Phillips, S., Gomez, H. F., Brent, J., MacIntyre, M. W. and Watson, W. A., Vitreous humor cocaine and metabolite concentrations: do postmortem specimens reflect blood levels at the time of death?, *J. Forensic Sci.*, 40, 102, 1995.
10. Robertson, M. D. and Drummer, O. H., Benzodiazepine concentrations in vitreous humor, *Bulletin of the International Association of Forensic Toxicologists*, 25, 28, 1995.

11. Pounder, D. J., Fuke, C., Cox, D. E., Smith, D. and Kuroda, N., Postmortem diffusion of drugs from gastric residue: an experimental study, *Am. J. Forensic Med. Pathol.*, 17, 1, 1996.

12. Pounder, D. J., Adams, E., Fuke, C. and Langford, A. M., Site to site variability of postmortem drug concentrations in liver and lung, *J. Forensic Sci.*, 41, 927, 1996

13. Ku, M. T., Bezoars, *Clinical Toxicology Review*, 18, June 1996.

14. Christensen, H., Steentoft, A. and Worm, K., Muscle as an autopsy material for evaluation of fatal cases of drug overdose, *J. Forensic Sci. Soc.*, 25, 191, 1985.

15. Winek, C. L. and Esposito, F. M., Comparative study of ethanol levels in blood versus bone marrow, vitreous humor, bile and urine, *Forensic Sci. Int.*, xx, 1727, 1980.

16. Winek, C. L., Westwood, S. E., and Wahba, W. W., Plasma versus bone marrow desipramine: a comparative study, *Forensic Sci. Int.*, 48, 49-57, 1990.

17. Winek, C .L., Morris, E. M., Wahba, W. W., The use of bone marrow in the study of postmortem redistribution of nortriptyline, *J. Anal. Toxicol.*, 17, 93-98, 1993.

18. Poklis, A. and Saady, J. J., Arsenic poisoning: acute or chronic? Suicide or murder?, *Am. J. Forensic Med. Pathol.*, 11, 226, 1990.

19. Odei, E. L. A., Insulin habituation and psychopathy, *BMJ*, ii, 346, 1968.

20. Retsas, S., Insulin abuse by a drug addict, *BMJ*, ii, 792, 1972.

21. Duragesic Monograph, Janssen Pharmaceutica, Titusville, NJ, April 1992.

22. Jaffe, J. H. and Martin, W. R., Opioid analgesics and antagonists, in *Goodman and Gilman's The Pharmacological Basis of Therapeutics*, Gilman, A. G., Rall, T. W., Nies, A. S., Taylor, P., Eds., Pergamon Press, New York, 1990, Chap. 21.

23. Shimomura, K., Kamata, O., Ueki., S., et al., Analgesic affects of morphine glucuronides, *Tohoku J. Exp. Med.*, 105, 45, 1971.

24. Yoshimura, H., Ida, S., Oguri, K. and Tsukamoto, H., Biochemical basis for analgesic activity of morphine-6-glucuronide - I. Penetration of morphine-6-glucuronide in the brain of rats, *Biochem. Pharmacol.*, 22, 1423, 1973.

25. Westerling, D., Persson, C. and Hoglund, P., Plasma concentrations of morphine, morphine-3-glucuronide, and morphine-6-glucuronide after intravenous and oral administration to healthy volunteers: Relationship to nonanalgesic actions, *Ther. Drug Monit.*, 17, 287, 1995.

26. Osborne, R. J., Joel, S. P. and Slevin, M. L., Morphine intoxication in renal failure: the role of morphine-6-glucuronide, *BMJ*, 292, 1548, 1986.

27. Swanson, J. R., Jones, G. R., Krasselt, W., Denmark, L. N. and Ratti, F., Death of two subjects due to chronic imipramine and desipramine metabolite accumulation during chronic therapy: a review of the literature and possible mechanisms, *J. Forensic Sci.*, 42, 335, 1997.

28. Anonymous, The Crippen trial: Special report of the medical evidence, *BMJ*, 2, 1372, 1910.

29. Saady, J. J and Blanke, R. V. and Poklis, A., Estimation of the body Burden of arsenic in a child fatally poisoned by arsenite weedkiller, *J. Anal. Toxicol.*, 13, 310, 1989.

30. Pounder, D. J. and Davies, J. I., Zopiclone Poisoning: Tissue distribution and potential for postmortem diffusion, *Forensic Sci. Int.*, 65, 177, 1994.

31. Baud, F. J., Buisine A., Bismuth, C., Galliot M., Vicaut E., Bourdon, R., and Fournier, P. E., Arterio-venous plasma concentration differences in amitriptyline overdose, *J. Toxicol. Clin.Toxicol.* 23, 391, 1985.

32. Sato, S., Baud, F. J., Bismuth, C., Galliot, M., Vicaut, E., and Buisine, A., Arterial- venous plasma concentration differences of meprobamate in acute human poisonings, *Human Toxicol.* 5, 243, 1986.

33. Hilberg, T., Morland, J. and Bjorneboe, A., Postmortem release of amitriptyline from the lungs; a mechanism of postmortem drug redistribution, *Forensic Sci. Int.*, 64, 47-55, 1994.

34. Pounder, D. J. and Yonemitsu, K., Postmortem absorption of drugs and ethanol from aspirated vomitus — an experimental model, *Forensic Sci. Int.*, 51, 189, 1991.

35. Laposata, E. A., Hale Jr., P. and Poklis, A., Evaluation of sudden death in psychiatric patients with special reference to phenothiazine therapy: forensic pathology, *J. Forensic Sci.*, 33, 432, 1988.

36. Sternbach, H., The serotonin syndrome, *Am. J. Psychiatry*, 148, 705, 1991.
37. Hearn, W. L, Keran, E. E., Wei, H. and Hime, G., Site-dependent postmortem changes in blood cocaine concentrations, *J. Forensic Sci.*, 36, 673, 1991.
38. Logan, B. K., Smirnow, D. and Gullberg, R. G., Lack of predictable site-dependent differences and time-dependent changes in postmortem concentrations of cocaine, benzoylecgonine, and cocaethylene in humans, *J. Anal. Toxicol.*, 20, 23, 1997.
39. Druid, H. And Holmgren, P., A compilation of fatal and control concentration of drugs in postmortem femoral blood, *J. Forensic Sci.*, 42, 79, 1997.

CHAPTER 13

DRUG LAW

TABLE OF CONTENTS

13.1 CURRENT LEGAL ISSUES OF WORKPLACE DRUG TESTING

Theodore F. Shults

Quadrangle Research, Research Triangle Park, North Carolina

Over the past 10 years workplace drug testing has become a ubiquitous aspect of the American workplace. This reflects the persuasive character of drug abuse, the level of societal concern, and the compelling need to find effective deterrence and containment strategies. It has been estimated that in 1996 over 30 million workplace drug tests were performed.[1] The large size of the drug testing market, and its projected growth over the next ten years, is driven primarily by the effectiveness of drug testing policies in controlling the adverse economic impact of drug and alcohol misuse on business operations. The recently proposed executive initiative by President Clinton to test teenagers for drug use as a condition of issuing a drivers licenses, is primarily based on the perceived and/or actual effectiveness of drug testing as a deterrent, and

---

[1] Data presented at AAMRO Advanced Medical Review Officer Training & Business Development Symposium, Denver, CO. October, 20, 1996.

early identification of teenage drug use. The acceptance and utilization of drug testing is not, however, solely driven by economic factors, public health and safety. There are important social, moral and political factors that must be considered.

If drug testing was simply a fad it would have leveled off by now or become passé. On the contrary, laboratories continue to see increases in the number of specimens they receive for testing. In the 1990s states passed new laws to facilitate employer drug testing, as opposed to the period of the 1980s where such legislation was primarily restrictive. More insurance companies are realizing significant savings in worker compensation payments with companies that have drug testing programs, and they offer discounts on worker compensation premiums for companies that utilize drug testing.

This integration of "testing" into American business culture, has also brought about a re-evaluation of individual and employee rights, the legitimate needs of business, and the power of government to mandate testing. Widespread drug testing also appears to have been a primary catalyst in reevaluating the way in which our society views "drugs". The artificial and strained division of drugs into the artificial categories of good drug, bad drug, and not a drug, looks to be dissolving. This is demonstrated by the public and political reevaluation of the status of both alcohol and cigarettes.

Today, workplace drug testing practices implicate a broad spectrum of legal issues and principles. These include constitutional protections of privacy and fairness, employment law, tort law, and administrative law. With the implementation of NAFTA trade agreements which aim at opening North American borders to free trade international law and comity become factors in regulating drug testing.

There is a myriad of federal and state statutes specifically dealing with drug testing policy and related disability issues, regulatory compliance and common law actions. Employers must navigate through a mined harbor of employment law jurisprudence to avoid problems with drug testing. Yet, workplace drug testing is not new and safe channels have been charted for employers. An employer who is aided with competent counsel and knowledgeable service providers, and does not venture far from acceptable practices and procedures, can utilize drug testing with minimal legal exposure.

As is the case in other areas of this treatise, some simple concepts come with a tome of detail. The goal here is to provide the reader with a conceptual framework for understanding legal developments, and to identify some of the controversial policy and legal principles involved in workplace drug and alcohol testing. There are number of excellent legal treatises which deal with the legal issues of employment screening. They are excellent references for attorneys researching a specific cause of action.

13.1.1 THE EMPLOYMENT-AT-WILL DOCTRINE

There is a common belief by many employees, apparently shared by many employers, is that if an employee has been fired because of a false positive drug test that the employee can sue the employer for wrongful termination. Generally this is not the case, and the reason is the employment-at-will doctrine.

Employment-at-will is a traditional employment law doctrine which holds that in the absence of a specific contract to employ an individual for a specified period of time, the employment relationship is indefinite. Indefinite employment is an obscure way of saying that either party can end the employer-employee relationship at any time. At will, so to speak.

At will employment also means that an employer does not have to have any reason to terminate an employee. The logical extension of this rule is that a termination will be upheld even if the employer has a bad reason for terminating the employment relationship (a bad reason other than a discriminatory one or one that violates public policy). Thus, most employees who have been fired based upon a positive drug test are unable to sustain a "wrongful termination" action against their employer. The at-will doctrine has protected many employees from liability as the consequences of mistakes. On the other hand, given the American propensity to litigate the at will doctrine has certainly saved all of us from needless litigation over hiring andfiring decisions.

An excellent example of the insulating power of the employment-at-will doctrine is the case of Jane Doe v. Smith Klein and Quaker Oats.[2] As reported in the legal opinion, Quaker Oats Company ("Quaker") offered Ms. Doe, a Masters of Business Administration student, a job as a marketing assistant in its Chicago office at a starting salary of $49,000 plus a bonus of $4,000. The offer did not state a definite term of employment. Quaker's employment offer was conditioned on Doe (1) satisfactorily completing a drug-screening examination as required by Quaker policy and (2) providing documentation meeting the requirements of the Immigration Reform & Control Act of 1986. Doe had previously signed a "Pre-Employment Consent to Drug Screening" form required by Quaker.

Quaker furnished Doe with a drug "testing package" that directed her to the a clinic where she completed the forms, including a questionnaire on recent medication use, and provided a urine sample. The only medication Doe listed on the pre-testing questionnaire was her prescribed birth-control pills. The clinic forwarded Doe's sample to SmithKline Beecham Clinical Laboratories, Inc. ("SmithKline"), the drug testing laboratory with which Quaker had contracted for its pre-employment screening.

Doe's sample tested positive for the presence of opiates. There was no dispute that the test was conducted by proper technical procedures and by a valid two-step testing methodology; Enzyme Multiplied Immunoassay Test ("EMIT") screening with a confirmatory gas chromatography, mass spectrometry ("GC/MS") confirmation test.

SmithKline informed Quaker, which, through its representatives, notified Doe by telephone that her employment offer had been rescinded because "she had tested positive for narcotics." Doe denied any illegal drug use and requested an opportunity to submit a second test sample. She was informed that according to Quaker policy, the offer had been automatically rescinded and that her only recourse was to reapply for the position in six months.

Doe's claim asserts that her positive test for opiates was the result of her consumption of several poppy seed muffins in the days before she provided her urine sample. It was not disputed that scientific literature on drug testing reported ordinary poppy seed consumption could produce positive test results for opiates. This fact was known for several years before Doe's test.

Doe initially brought suit against SmithKline for negligence in the manner in which the drug test was conducted. After Quaker declined her reapplication, Doe added Quaker as a defendant. Doe alleged negligence on the part of SmithKline and Quaker. After review of the facts and applicable law, the appellate court concluded that Quaker was not liable as a matter of law on each of Doe's alleged causes of action because of the Texas employment-at-will doctrine. The result was that Quaker was absolutely protected by the employment-at-will doctrine.

On the other hand, the appellate court found that the laboratory owed a duty to Doe. This meant that Doe could bring an action against the laboratory for negligence. Doe's theory of negligence was based in part on the laboratory's marketing materials that stated to the effect that the lab results were conclusive and accurate, and a failure to warn Quaker of the poppy seed explanation. The decision to essentially create a legal duty on the laboratory to the specimen donor was appealed by the laboratory to the Texas Supreme Court. The Texas Supreme Court was not prepared to expand the scope of liability to the laboratory for the interpretation of its results. The Supreme court did, however, leave the door open for the plaintiff to make a claim based on a theory that the laboratory action tortuously interfered with the contractual relationship (employment relationship).

---

[2] Jane DOE, Appellant, v. Smithkline Beecham Clinical Laboratories, Inc. and the Quaker Oats Company, Appellees. No. 3-92-056-CV. Court of Appeals of Texas, Austin June 2, 1993.

Theodore F. Shults

The Doe case clearly demonstrates how the employment-at-will doctrine insulates many employers from testing liability, insulation that does not necessarily extend to the laboratory or other third party provider. (See Section 13.1.4.2.1 Expanding the Scope of Liability for Service Providers.)

13.1.1.1 Exceptions to the At-Will Rule

The broadly accepted doctrine of at will employment does not, however, preclude all lawsuits arising out of drug testing. There are notable exceptions to the employment-at-will doctrine. First, there are unionized employees who are covered by collective bargaining agreements. Most collective bargaining agreements include the provision that employment termination can only be for "just cause". U.S. labor law and collective bargaining agreements also provide that labor disputes be adjudicated through grievance procedures and arbitration.

In the absence of a collective bargaining agreement, state courts have found exceptions to employment-at-will. Courts have found that express or implied promises made by employers in their statements or employee handbooks are sufficient to create an employment relationship other than an at will one.

Other exceptions are based upon "public policy" where, for example, an employer terminates an employee for exposing an environmental crime. In the area of drug testing, the courts have used public policy, not on behalf of a terminated employee, but rather on the behalf of the employer who has been ordered to return a unionized employee to work by an arbitrator. Public policy has been used in many drug testing cases. Attorneys working on the behalf of a terminated employee have also found ways to litigate drug testing in employment.

13.1.2 DRUG TESTING DEFAMATION AND DISCRIMINATION

Cases alleging defamation and discrimination represent an important area of litigation. They are independent actions based on federal and or state law. Thus, employers cannot raise the doctrine of employment-at-will to defeat claims based on defamation and discrimination. In a similar manner, claims that a company drug test was done in retaliation to the donors whistle blowing, the donor's filing a worker compensation case, or the donor's union activities, are typically based on specific statutes.

13.1.2.1 Discrimination — Title VII Cases

Three separate appellate cases, Landon, v. Northwest Airlines, Inc., Cary v. Anheuser-Busch, and Hicks-Robinson v. Tootsie Roll in November and December of 1995[3] are representative of the type of litigation seen in private sector urinalysis drug testing. They involved allegations of racial discrimination in Landon, sexual harassment in Cary, and religious discrimination in Hicks.

Three cases represent a movement away from the broad challenges of drug testing results on purely constitutional grounds to a myriad of relatively specific legal claims alleging that the drug test and/or the employer's policy was done in violation of a statutory right. The most common statutes invoked are those that involve discrimination, civil rights, disability protection, and as seen in Landon, even fair housing code. As in the Landon case defamation and violation of privacy claims are often included as secondary claims.

In addition to relying on federal and/or state statutory authority, the other common element of all these divergent claims is the malevolent intent on the behalf of the company or

---

[3] Cary Plaintiff, v. Anheuser-Busch, Inc., and John Mandaro, Defendants. No. 4:94CV188. U. S. D.C., E.D. Virginia. Nov. 20, 1995; Hicks-Robinson v. Tootsie Roll Indus. U.S.D.C.,N.D. Illinois, 1995 U.S. Dist. LEXIS 18024 November 27, 1995; Robert Landon, v. Northwest Airlines, Inc. U.S.C.A. Eighth Circuit 1995 U.S. App. LEXIS 35338

its agents. Discrimination, defamation, and retaliation all require an element of intentional behavior on the part of the defendant. What is interesting to note is that the cases are not just based upon "reasonable suspicion" tests, but random, post accident and occasionally even a pre-employment test have triggered claims.

This is intriguing because random testing and pre-employment tests are not discretionary. Presumably, the plaintiff or claimant who brings a retaliation claim based on a random test intends to prove that the random test was either not random, or that there was intentional contamination or fabricated test results. Rather serious allegations. In the pre-employment case the allegation has been that the employer does not in fact test all employees or has made exceptions, and that the individual was discriminated against for some legally protected activity at a prior employer, or race.

The underlying facts and merits of discriminatory allegations vary greatly. One suspects that in cases of little merit that there has been some packaging of a drug testing lawsuit into statutory claims. Packaging due in large part to the fact that most of the applicants and employees have little other legal recourse in an employment at will situation.

13.1.3 DRUG TESTING AND WORKERS' COMPENSATION LITIGATION

Workers' Compensation law represent a legal compromise. On one hand they protect an employer from litigation by employees injured while doing their job, and on the other they provide relatively quick and reasonable compensation to injured employees without having to take the risk of litigation. As with most compromises, neither employers nor employees have found the workers' compensation paradigm ideal. The system has been subject to abuses by attorneys, by employees who become slow healers while receiving benefits, and employers and insurers who turn down fair and just claims. This is all part of the workers' compensation landscape.

Workers' compensation is a type of no fault insurance. It offers a high probability of compensation for an injured workers' medical expenses, lost work, disabilities and death. The trade off for these benefits the employee receives no compensation for "pain and suffering" and "loss of consortium". Despite the no-fault nature of the insurance, employers have historically had a few defenses to worker's compensation claims. One defense was in the situation where the injury was the result of employee "horseplay", another has been where the injury has been the result of the employee's voluntary intoxication. These defenses were premised on the theory that employees should have some responsibility for their own safety.

States and state courts vary a great deal as to what they mean by intoxication, and what is satisfactory evidence of intoxication. In general this has meant alcohol intoxication, and it has meant a lot of alcohol. The problem that began to appear in the 1980s was that the causative agent in many injuries was not alcohol but other drugs, notably marijuana and cocaine. With the rise in worker compensation expenses, and the collateral increase of drug use in the workplace it was inevitable that the defense of voluntary intoxication would receive a great deal of attention by employers, lawyers and insurance companies. There was also the foreseeable problem of how would an employer prove impairment or intoxication with a urine test?

Whenever the inability to show a correlation between urine metabolites and behavior was pointed out in worker compensation hearings, the company's defense became frustrated. It is difficult for the company to prove by the preponderance of the evidence that the employee was impaired or intoxicated based solely on a post-accident urinalysis result. It is also difficult in many cases to demonstrate that the impairment or intoxication was the proximate cause of the accident.

The legislative solution to this evidentiary problem was to elevate the scientific significance of the post accident drug urinalysis. The most common solution has been to shift the burden of proof. Under the old workers' compensation law, the employer had to prove that an employee's injury was caused by or related to their intoxication or impairment. Under the new approach, when there has been a positive post accident drug test, the burden of proof shifts from the employer to the employee who must now show that they were not impaired.

Two states, Florida and Alabama, went beyond merely shifting the burden of proof. They went so far as to have changed their law to essentially bar recovery whenever there has been a post-accident finding of illegal drugs. This was accomplished by deeming a positive drug test as evidence of impairment.[4] These amendments were lobbied for by employer and insurance groups; however, it was difficult to find a rational legal scholar who did not see a fundamental problem with a statutory bar on workers' compensation benefits. The question was, how long would this aspect of the law stand? Two appeals from denials of worker compensation benefits arrived at the appellate courts of both Alabama and Florida at about the same time in 1995. The facts were quite simple

In the Alabama case, the tip of an employee's middle finger was cut off in a work-related accident. In the Florida incident the employee and a co-worker were doing concrete form work. They were carrying a screed (a long steel apparatus) over their heads when the co-worker tripped over a steel form and jabbed the screed into the back of the employee claimant's head. It is unrefuted in the Florida case that the employee did nothing to cause the accident. Both injured employees were given post-accident drug tests. Both were reported as positive. Both employees were summarily denied workers' compensation benefits because of the positive urinalysis tests. Both appealed their denials and challenged the respective state laws, and both won.[5]

Shifting the burden of proof to injured employees who have a positive urinalysis is an effective way to bring the use of illegal drugs on a par with the use of alcohol with regard to receiving compensation benefits. Going beyond this and creating a per se exclusion of workers' compensation benefits raises legal, ethical and business issues. In light of these two appellate court cases, one would believe that we have reached the end of this legislative practice. But the idea that a company can automatically exclude a significant percentage of workers automatically from coverage is simply too attractive a prospect not to pursue.

Automatic bars to worker compensation recovery present some frank ethical questions. What conceivable relationship is there between being burned in a factory explosion, suffering

---

[4]   In 1992 Alabama amended its workers' compensation law. Before the 1992 amendments, the Alabama law stated: "No compensation shall be allowed for an injury or death . . . due to [the worker's] intoxication . . . . The burden of proof shall be on the employer to establish such defense." [Ala. Code 1975, Sec 25-5-51]

Following the 1992 amendments, the law stated: "No compensation shall be allowed for an injury or death caused by . . . an accident due to the injured employee being intoxicated from the use of alcohol or being impaired by illegal drugs. A positive drug test conducted and evaluated pursuant to standards adopted for drug testing by the U.S. Department of Transportation in 49 C.F.R. Part 40 shall be a conclusive presumption of impairment resulting from the use of illegal drugs."

The Florida statute is Section 440.09(3), Florida Statutes (1991). It states: "No compensation shall be payable if the injury was occasioned primarily by the intoxication of the employee. If there was at the time of the injury 0.10 percent or more by weight of alcohol in the employee's blood, or if the employee has a positive confirmation of a drug as defined in this act, it shall be presumed that the injury was occasioned primarily by the intoxication of, or by the influence of the drug upon, the employee. In the absence of a drug-free workplace program, this presumption may be rebutted by clear and convincing evidence that the intoxication or influence of the drug did not contribute to the injury . . ."

[5]   [Charles Ross v. Ellard Construction Company, Inc. No. 2940288 Court of Civil Appeals of Alabama 1996 Ala. Civ. App. LEXIS 232, April 5, 1996. Astley Hall, v. Recchi America INC. and Palmer & Clay Carswell No. 94-2714 Court of Appeals of Florida, First District , 1996 Fla. App. LEXIS 2571, March 19, 1996].

an injured back or losing a limb and illegal drug use as evidenced by a urinalysis? The per se bar to recovery is so far out of balance as to encourage employers to let their employees use illegal drugs. In a state that has an enforceable bar to recovery for illegal drug users, the best risk company is one where the entire workforce smokes marijuana and is subject to post accident testing. Imagine that, no more compensable work injuries!

Justice J. Kahn, a member of the Florida Court of Appeals, wrote a concurring opinion in the Hall case. He raised an important undercurrent in this case. He stated: "A basic premise of workers' compensation law in Florida, as in other places, has always been to release society of the expenses of injuries caused by industry in favor of a program under which industry would bear such costs. The legislation now at hand abrogates these long-accepted understandings, at least in a class of cases, including Mr. Hall's. Despite the apparent fact that Hall's injury was caused completely by risks normally attendant to the construction industry, he would be left without any remedy under the Workers' Compensation Act. Thus, the limited statutory provision we invalidate today was itself at odds with a central premise of compensation law. Moreover, it directly contravenes the intent of our legislature recently set out in the 1993 revisions to the workers' compensation law: Workers' compensation cases shall be decided on their merits."

When legislators consider the per se bar to compensation for illegal drug users in the future they should address Justice Kahn's concern. Who are the real beneficiaries of barring compensation? It is certainly not the employee. It is not the taxpayer or the purchaser of private medical insurance who will pick up the medical tab in this legislative cost shifting. Are the statutory schemes to cost shift the medical costs and arbitrarily denycompensation benefits an appropriate way to manage costs?

Drug testing has a significant impact on safety by preventing accidents and in some cases deterring the filing of frivolous claims. Denying compensation where the employee's voluntary and irresponsible impairment was the cause of the accident is well established. It is, however, quite another issue to deny compensation because of evidence that an employee uses drugs illegally. In the long run it will undercut the public's acceptance of urinalysis testing.

13.1.4 DRUG TESTING AND THE SERVICE PROVIDER

13.1.4.1 Evidentiary Issues and Findings of Fact

13.1.4.1.1 Proof of Facts

Considering the large number of drug tests performed in the United States over the last 15 years there has been relatively few cases challenging the accuracy and reliability of the laboratory results. In retrospect there are three factors that have contributed to the low incidence of litigation. First is the at-will rule which bars a significant number of potential plaintiffs, second is the fundamental accuracy and reliability of the laboratory confirmatory GC/MS methodology, and third is the added protection of medical review of all positive results. Effective MRO review eliminates prescription drug use, poppy seed ingestion, and Vicks inhaler and avoids potential conflict with the Americans with Disabilities Act.

When the accuracy of laboratory results become relevant issues they are litigated in a wide verity of forums. Accuracy and reliability of results are often issues of fact in arbitration, Workers' Compensation hearings, unemployment security hearings, the miscellaneous civil cases that have been filed, and administrative proceedings. Paradoxically, unions have been sued by their own members for failing to fulfill the unions legal duty to defend them following a positive drug test. Federal agencies directly involved in the issuance of licenses or documents for the performance of regulated activity hold hearings concerning alleged violations of federal drug and alcohol regulations. One example is the U.S. Coast Guard which holds hearings concerning the issuance of maritime documents to commercial ship captains, masters and first mates.

Another area where litigation is common is in civil negligence suits, which may or may not be employment related. A good example is a lawsuit following an accident where a post-accident drug test has shown that a commercial driver has used an illegal drug. That test result may have a significant impact on the issues of causation, liability and damages.

The analytical technical evidentiary issues involve establishing that the sample was collected from the donor, and properly tested. Collection procedures and custody and control form are important in establishing the source of the specimen from the donor in grievances or filing arbitration's following certainly in post accident cases where third parties have been injured.

13.1.4.1.2 The Donor's Right to Obtain Laboratory Records Under DOT Regulations

DOT regulations are designed to be minimally intrusive, effective, and provide adequate individual safeguards. There are a number of checks and balances built into the process including split specimen testing. Some other examples of checks and balances are; MRO review, conflict of interest rules, the ability to obtain laboratory records, and laboratory proficiency testing. The efficacy of the safeguards is, however, premised on the idea that the procedures will be followed. The question is what happens when they are not?

It is well understood that if an employer does not follow DOT's procedures for a DOT test, then this represents regulatory non-compliance. The DOT can take a number of actions against the employer. But what if DOT does not take any action? What if DOT does not consider the violation serious enough, or does not have the resources to investigate complaints? What if DOT does not have adequate enforcement abilities? What recourse does an employee have when they have been subject to an adverse employment action based on a procedurally flawed test?

The simplest illustration of the legal limits on the individual's ability to enforce DOT compliance is the case of Salmone vs. Roche.[6] In this case, the plaintiff brought a federal suit against the testing laboratory because the laboratory did not produce all of the documents and records requested in writing by the donor. The plaintiff was employed as a flight attendant by a major airline. On June 5, 1994 she was selected for a random drug test pursuant to DOT regulations. On the same day, she provided a urine sample for drug testing purposes. On June 9, 1994, the plaintiff was notified by the airline's Medical Review Officer that she had tested positive for cocaine. Having no medical explanation, the plaintiff was suspended. In December, the plaintiff requested that the laboratory provide her with records relating to its certification and information relevant to chain-of-custody issues. Specifically, the plaintiff sought records relating to the laboratory's certification in 1994 by the Department of Health and Human Services, the Substance Abuse and Mental Health Services Administration, and other certification programs.

The laboratory did in fact provide the plaintiff with the "Laboratory Documentation Package" which contains the chain-of-custody, analytical data, and other laboratory documents regarding the plaintiff's drug test. The laboratory did not, however, provide the specific certification documents (such as inspection reports) she repeatedly requested. The plaintiff made the same request to the MRO and her employer. This case would seem like a simple matter. The Department of Transportation Procedures Section 40.37 of the regulations state:

> Any employee who is the subject of a drug test conducted under this part shall, upon written request, have access to any records relating to his or her drug test and any records relating to the results of any relevant certification, review, or revocation of certification proceedings.

---

[6] Salmone v Roche. USDC EDNY, 909 F. Supp. 126; 1995 U.S. Dist. (December 13, 1995).

The issue of whether the 1994 DHHS inspection report generated as part of the mandatory certification program was or was not relevant to the plaintiff's 1994 test was not decided by the court. The issue was never reached. The federal court decided that there is simply no private right of action provided for, expressly or implicitly, in these regulation or the Omnibus Transportation Employee Testing Act of 1991.

The court pointed out that the regulations provide that an individual may complain in writing to the Secretary of Transportation about an alleged violation of the drug testing regulations. That is different from the ability to bring a legal action personally to enforce the regulations. The court went on to point out that the Secretary of Transportation may then investigate the allegation, dismiss the complaint without a hearing if the complaint fails to allege facts sufficient to warrant an investigation, or conduct a hearing to determine the merits of the allegation.

If a violation was found, the Secretary of Transportation would issue an order compelling compliance. The Secretary of Transportation may also "bring an action against a person in a district court of the United States to enforce this part or a requirement or regulation prescribed . . . under this part." Moreover, the Secretary of Transportation may request that the Attorney General initiate such an enforcement action. The court found that there is an administrative enforcement mechanism in place to address alleged violations of the drug testing regulations.

13.1.4.1.3 Problems Posed by the Salmone Case

The Salmone case is problematic; not for the laboratory or the MRO, but for the DOT. It is also problematic for the attorney who would like to discover documents other than what is provided by the laboratory or MRO. Since the plaintiff's remedy is to obtain compliance through the DOT, what you can anticipate are the written requests going to DOT. If the DOT's reaction does not satisfy the attorney, it is possible that the attorney will followed up with a legal action against DOT to force it to bring enforcement action and compliance against employers and the laboratories. Not a pretty picture. Being cast by its own regulations as the only source of enforcement is not a particularly appealing prospect for the Department of Transportation. It would seem that this issue is part of the bigger realm of compliance; an issue that will surely will be addressed by DOT in its comprehensive revisions of its regulations

A word of caution to MROs. Although it is reassuring that a donor under DOT's regulation cannot bring a personal action to force discovery or compliance, some MROs may have already noticed that some laboratories are refusing to provide any information to the donor. Some DHHS certified laboratories have taken the position that they will only release data if the "employer authorizes the release". One laboratory has the interesting policy of requiring both the employer and the MRO to authorize the release of laboratory documents.

It should be clear that if the laboratory cannot be legally compelled to release information by the donor, neither can the MRO. There is a legitimate basis for a MRO or a laboratory to request the authorization of the employer before releasing any data. It is the employer who is solely and ultimately responsible for compliance with the DOT regulations. It is the employer who is the client. It is the employer who must make the employment decisions. This applies in both regulated and non-regulated testing. Keep in mind, however, that DOT would expect the employer's authorization to be given, and a failure to give that authorization would be considered non-compliance.

In the long run, it is a mistake for laboratories to obstruct the release of discoverable data. Laboratory documentation packages (also called litigation packages) were designed to avoid litigation by expediently providing sufficient information on the analytical aspects and sample handling of a particular specimen. It is counter productive to artificially restrict the release of this information. The same principle is true with regard to MRO records.

13.1.4.2 Liability of Laboratories, MROs, and Drug Testing Service Providers

13.1.4.2.1 Expanding the Scope of Liability for Service Providers

On February 16, 1995 the Appellate Court of Illinois, Second District, released an opinion that reflects the ongoing expansion in the scope of liability for laboratories and presumably other providers of drug testing services. The case follows the ruling in the landmark case of Doe v. SmithKline Beecham Corp. which held the laboratory liable to an applicant, but was subsequently overturned.

The legal issue here is both rather simple and significant. Does a laboratory which performs drug screening tests at the behest of an employer owe a duty of care to an employee who submits to a drug test? Most people make the assumption that if a laboratory makes a mistake, such as reporting a false positive, the employee or donor can sue the laboratory for negligence. That assumption has, however, been wrong. At least until now.

The legal doctrines of contractual privity and limited duty to third parties have been used to insulate the laboratories; and to a great degree MROs, collectors and administrators from liability. Although the service provider, such as the laboratory, has a contractual obligation to the employer (written, verbal or implied), the law has not recognized a "legal duty of care" to the third party applicant, employee or donor of the specimen.

In the case where the employer is operating in an employment-at-will environment, the donor may not have any legal recourse. If you cannot sue the provider and the employer has no liability for terminating or not hiring an individual, the donor may have no basis for action. (In the situation where the donor can bring a wrongful termination action and show that the laboratory result was in error, the employer can sue the laboratory for breach of contract.) Naturally, with drug testing an almost universal employment practice, this insulation was not going to last forever. The law adapts.

Bradford Stinson, sued Physicians Immediate Care, Limited on the grounds that PC was negligent in performing a drug test on him and reporting a false positive result. Stinson alleged that his employer required him to have a drug screening test performed at the defendant's facility. The defendant collected a urine specimen from the plaintiff and issued a report to the plaintiff's employer that the specimen tested positive for cocaine.

At the trial court, the defendant filed a motion to dismiss the case asserting that Count I failed to state any facts showing a relationship between the parties on which to predicate a duty and that Count I established only a duty to the plaintiff's employer. The trial court granted the defendant's motion and dismissed both counts. The plaintiff then appealed.

Whether a duty exists is a question of law which depends on whether the parties stood in such a relationship to one another that the law imposes an obligation on the defendant to act reasonably for the protection of the plaintiff. The court stated "In considering whether a duty exists in a particular case, a court must weigh the foreseeability of the injury, the likelihood of the injury, the magnitude of the burden of guarding against it, and the consequences of placing that burden on the defendant."

Here, the court noted, the injury suffered would be that the plaintiff would be terminated from his employment, is not only foreseeable, but also is a virtual certainty in the event of a positive drug test result. In addition, the likelihood of injury is great; the plaintiff allegedly lost his job and was hindered in his efforts to find other employment because of the false positive drug test report. The first two factors favor imposing a duty.

The court then considered the two remaining factors; the magnitude of guarding against the injury, and the consequences of placing that burden upon the defendant.

As information services become more prevalent in our economy and society, the information providers, such as drug testing laboratories, should be held accountable for the information they provide. Such information should be complete and not misleading. Credit reporting agencies have long been held to the exercise of due care in securing and distributing information concerning the financial standing of individuals, firms, and corporations.

Quoting Doe v. SmithKline Beecham Corp. (Tex.App.1993).

The court concluded that

the drug testing laboratory is in the best position to guard against the injury, as it is solely responsible for the performance of the testing and the quality control procedures. In addition, the laboratory, which is paid to perform the tests, is better able to bear the burden financially than the individual wrongly maligned by a false positive report. We therefore hold that a drug testing laboratory owes a duty of reasonable care to persons whose specimens it tests for employers or prospective employers.

In summary, the Illinois court of appeals found that the defendant had a duty to the plaintiff to act with reasonable care in collecting, handling, and testing the specimen; the defendant falsely reported to the plaintiff's employer that the result was positive; the false report was the result of any of several allegedly negligent acts; and the plaintiff lost his job and suffered other damages as a result of the defendant's negligence. These allegations, in this light according to the court, are sufficient to state a cause of action for negligence. The trial court's dismissal was reversed and if the case proceeds, the plaintiff will have to prove the allegations.

There is little question that the legal insulation that has shrouded drug testing providers has had a significant deterrent effect on the number of lawsuits filed. Plaintiff attorneys will rarely bring a case that they know will be dismissed at the pleading stage. From time to time, a plaintiff will take a test case to challenge and change the law, as illustrated by the cases cited here. Expect an increased number of filings.

13.1.4.2.2 Liability Exposure to the Laboratories from Drug Testing

Generally, the basis for liability for laboratory negligence is based on the contractual relationship between the laboratory and its client. This may be a written or implied contract. Most laboratories involved in workplace drug testing have standardized contracts that include indemnity clauses that indemnify clients against damages from inaccurate and/or false positive drug tests. Often these agreements also include language that indemnify the laboratory from damages arising out of "employment decisions".

In any event, with or without indemnity clauses, the essence of expressed or implied contractual agreement between the laboratory and the client, is that the laboratory promises to provide accurate and reliable laboratory analysis. It would be prudent for laboratory contracts to indicate that the laboratory data (test results) should be properly reviewed and interpreted by a medical review officer, but this is rare.

The laboratory has been a secondary beneficiary of the employment at will doctrine. The reason is that if the client does not suffer damages in civil litigation there is no reason to commence an action against the laboratory based on either the indemnity agreement or contract. The evolving area of law is the question of what rights do the donors have directly against the laboratories for inaccurate results. What legal obligations are there from the laboratory to the donor? As drug testing becomes as common as credit checks, the law evolves to establish appropriate duties of providers, as the law deems necessary. The following is a synopsis of cases and legal duties that the courts have recently established.

In 1994 a Texas court of appeals found that a laboratory had a legal duty to warn test subjects of possible influences on results (poppy seed ingestion). In this case the results were not sent to an MRO but to the company. This holding was recently overruled by the Texas Supreme Court, but the laboratory is not off the hook yet. Although the divided court found that there was no legal duty to warn donors, the failure to mention poppy seeds to the employer, and the employers reliance on the test results may still be a basis for a suit alleging willful and intentional interference with the conditional offer of employment between the employer and employee.

In a separate case, the Maine Supreme court ruled that a donor could not sue a laboratory on the theory of being a "third party beneficiary" of the relationship between the laboratory and subcontractor. Other than the duty to warn, there is an expanding body of law that allows employees to bring direct actions against laboratories. (and theoretically against MROs).

The following are cases that define various legal duties of laboratories that reached the appellate level.

- Drug testing laboratory owes persons tested a duty to perform its services with reasonable care. Willis v. Roche Biomedical Lab., 21 F.3d 1368, 1372-1375 (5th Cir.1994) Stinson v. Physicians Immediate Care, Ltd., 269 Ill.App.3d 659, 207 Ill.Dec. 96, 646 N.E.2d 930, 932-934 (1995)
- Laboratory owes prospective employee a duty not to contaminate sample and report a false result); Nehrenz v. Dunn, 593 So.2d 915, 917-918 (La.Ct.App.1992)
- Laboratory owes employee a duty to perform test in a competent manner; Elliott v. Laboratory Specialists, 588 So.2d 175, 176 (La.Ct.App.1991), writ denied, 592 So.2d 415 (La.1992)
- Laboratory owes employee a duty to perform test in a scientifically reasonable manner; Lewis v. Aluminum Co. of Am., 588 So.2d 167, 170 (La.Ct.App.1991), writ denied, 592 So.2d 411 (La.1992)
- Laboratory owes employee a duty to perform tests in a competent, non-negligent manner. But see Herbert v. Placid Ref. Co., 564 So.2d 371, 374 (La.Ct.App.1990)

13.1.5 AMERICANS WITH DISABILITIES ACT

The Americans with Disability Act of 1990 (ADA) has been characterized as the most significant federal employment legislation of the decade. It will fundamentally change the way many companies medically evaluate and screen applicants. The focus here will be on the ADA's impact on drug testing and qualifying examinations.

On July 26, 1990, the ADA was signed into law. The provisions went into effect for employers with more than 25 employees in July of 1992. The law requires the Equal Employment Opportunity Commission (EEOC) to publish proposed regulations for the implementation, regulation and enforcement of the substantive provisions of the act. These proposed rules were published on February 28, 1991 and are referred to here as the regulations.

13.1.5.1 Illegal Use of Drugs

One thing is quite clear about the ADA; an individual *currently engaging* in the illegal use of drugs is *not* an individual with a disability for purposes of the ADA when the employer or other covered entity acts on the basis of such use. Illegal use of drugs refers both to the use of unlawful drugs, such as cocaine, and to the unlawful use of prescription drugs. Employers, for example, may discharge or deny employment to persons who illegally use drugs on the basis of such use without fear of being held liable for discrimination.

The EEOC regulations indicate that the term "currently engaging" is not intended to be limited to the use of drugs on the day of, or within a matter of days or weeks before, the employment action in question. Rather, the provision is intended to apply to the illegal use of drugs that has occurred recently enough to indicate that the individual is actively engaged in such conduct. The ADA indicates that for federal programs, a positive confirmed urinalysis performed in accordance with the SAMHSA mandatory guidelines satisfies this provision.

13.1.5.2 The Problem of Perceived Drug Use

The ADA attempts to provide protection to individuals who have recovered from a disability or are in remission by expanding the definition of disability to cover individuals who are perceived as having a disability. The intent was to assure that someone who recovered from cancer, had controlled diabetes, or was thought to be HIV infected and was not, would not be discriminated against because of the underlying fear. This approach has a peculiar impact when applied to the perceived use of illegal drugs.

The EEOC regulations clearly point out that individuals who are erroneously perceived as engaging in the illegal use of drugs, but are not in fact illegally using drugs, are not excluded from the definitions of the terms "disability" and "qualified individual with a disability." This provision will force the unregulated industry to move to confirmed testing and revise their screening practices for applicants. An individual who tests positive for barbiturates is perceived as a current illegal user of drugs. If it turns out that the individual was using an over the counter stomach preparation, the black letter of the law has been violated.

Being "regarded as" having a disability is considered by employers as both ambiguous and subjective. EEOC guidance explains that an individual meets the "regarded as" part of the definition of disability if he or she can show that a covered entity made an employment decision because of a perception of a disability based on "myth, fear, or stereotype."

13.1.5.3 Past Drug Dependency — The Rehabilitated Employee

Individuals who are no longer illegally using drugs and who have either been rehabilitated successfully or are in the process of completing a rehabilitation program are, likewise, not excluded from the definitions of those terms. The term "rehabilitation program" refers to both in-patient and out-patient programs, as well as to appropriate employee assistance or other programs that provide professional (not necessarily medical) assistance and counseling for individuals who illegally use drugs.

The EEOC regulations state that an individual cannot demonstrate that he or she is no longer engaging in the illegal use of drugs by simply showing participation in a drug treatment program. It is essential that the individual offer evidence, such as drug test results, to prove that he or she is not currently engaging in the illegal use of drugs. Employers are entitled to seek reasonable assurances that no illegal use of drugs is occurring or has occurred recently enough so that continuing use is a real and ongoing problem. An employer, such as a law enforcement agency, may also be able to impose a qualification standard that excludes individuals with a history of illegal use of drugs if it can show that the standard is job-related and consistent with business necessity.

13.1.5.4 Regulation of Alcohol and Drugs

The regulations permit employers to establish or comply with certain standards regulating the use of drugs and alcohol in the workplace. It also allows employers to hold alcoholics and persons who engage in the illegal use of drugs to the same performance and conduct standards to which it holds other employees. Individuals disabled by alcoholism are otherwise entitled to the same protection accorded other individuals withdisabilities under these regulations. As noted above, individuals currently engaging in the illegal use of drugs are not individuals with disabilities for purposes of these regulations when the employer acts on the basis of such use.

The EEOC has stated that an employer may hold individuals with alcoholism and individuals who engage in the illegal use of drugs to the same performance and conduct standards to which it holds "all of its" other employees. It is clear that employers may hold all employees, disabled (including those disabled by alcoholism or drug addiction) and non-disabled, to the same performance and conduct standards.

Drug tests are neither encouraged nor prohibited under the ADA and the regulations make clear that the results of drug tests may be used as a basis for disciplinary action. Drug tests are also not considered medical examinations for purposes of these regulations. If the results reveal information about an individual's medical condition beyond whether the individual is currently engaging in the illegal use of drugs, this additional information is to be treated as a confidential medical record. For example, if a test for the illegal use of drugs reveals the presence of a controlled substance that has been lawfully prescribed for a particular medical condition, this information is to be treated as a confidential medical record.

13.1.5.5 Pre-Employment Examination or Inquiry

The ADA and EEOC regulations make clear that an employer cannot inquire as to whether an individual has a disability at the pre-offer stage of the selection process. Employers may ask questions that relate to the applicant's ability to perform job-related functions. However, these questions should not be phrased in terms of disability. An employer, for example, may ask whether the applicant has a driver's license (if driving is a job function) but may not ask whether the applicant has a visual disability. Employers may ask about an applicant's ability to perform both essential and marginal job functions.Employer's, though, may not refuse to hire an applicant with a disability because the applicant's disability prevents him or her from performing marginal functions.

13.1.5.6 Examination or Inquiry of Employees

The purpose of this provision is to prevent the administration from subjecting employees to medical tests or inquiries that do not serve a legitimate business purpose. For example, if an employee suddenly starts to use increased amounts of sick leave or starts to appear sickly, an employer could not require that employee to be tested for AIDS, HIV infection, or cancer unless the employer can demonstrate that such testing is job-related and consistent with business necessity.

This provision does not prohibit employers from making inquiries or requiring medical examinations (fitness-for-duty exams) when there is a need to determine whether an employee is still able to perform the essential functions of his or her job. Nor does this provision prohibit periodic physicals to determine fitness-for-duty if such physicals are required by medical standards or requirements established by Federal, state, or local law that are consistent with the ADA (or in the case of a federal standard, with section 504 of the Rehabilitation Act) in that they are job-related and consistent with business necessity.

Such standards may include federal safety regulations that regulate bus and truck driver qualifications, as well as laws establishing medical requirements for pilots or other air transportation personnel. These standards also include health standards promulgated pursuant to the Occupational Safety and Health Act of 1970, the Federal Coal Mine Health and Safety Act of 1969, or other similar statutes that require that employees exposed to certain toxic and hazardous substances be medically monitored at specific intervals.

The EEOC added a provision S:1630.14(c), Examination of Employees, that clarifies the scope of permissible medical examinations and inquiries. Several employers and employer groups expressed concern that the proposed version of part 1630 did not make it clear that covered entities may require employee medical examinations, such as fitness-for-duty examinations, that are job-related and consistent with business necessity. The information obtained from such examinations or inquiries must be treated as a confidential medical record.

13.1.5.7 Pre-Employment Inquiry

Employers are permitted to make pre-employment inquiries into the ability of an applicant to perform job-related functions. This inquiry must be narrowly tailored. The employer may describe or demonstrate that job function and inquire whether or not the applicant can perform that function with or without accommodation.

For example, an employer may explain that the job requires assembling small parts and ask if the individual will be able to perform that function. On the other hand, however, an employer may not use an application form that lists a number of potentially disabling impairments and ask the applicant to check any of the impairments he or she may have. Nor may an employer ask how a particular individual became disabled or the prognosis of the individual's disability. The employer is also prohibited from asking how often the individual will require leave for treatment or use leave as a result of incapacitation because of the disability. However, the employer may state the attendance requirements of the job and inquire whether the applicant can meet them.

13.1.5.8 Employment Entrance Examination

An employer is permitted to require post-offer medical examinations before the employee actually starts working. The employer may condition the offer of employment on the results of the examination, provided that all entering employees in the same job category are subjected to such an examination, regardless of disability, and that the confidentiality requirements specified in the regulations are met. The regulation recognizes that in many industries, such as air transportation or construction, applicants for certain positions are chosen on the basis of many factors including relevant physical and psychological criteria, some of which may be identified as a result of post-offer medical examinations given prior to entry on duty. Only those employees who meet the employer's relevant physical and psychological criteria for the job will be qualified to receive confirmed offers of employment and begin working.

Medical examinations permitted by this section are not required to be job-related and consistent with business necessity. However, if an employer withdraws an offer of employment because the medical examination reveals that the employee does not satisfy certain employment criteria, either the exclusionary criteria must not screen out or tend to screen out an individual with disabilities or a class of individuals with disabilities, or they must be job-related and consistent with business necessity. As part of the showing that an exclusionary criterion is job-related and consistent with business necessity, the employer must also demonstrate that there is no reasonable accommodation that will enable the individual with a disability to perform the essential functions of the job.

As an example, suppose an employer makes a conditional offer of employment to an applicant, and it is an essential function of the job that the incumbent be available to work every day for the next three months. An employment entrance examination then reveals that the applicant has a disabling impairment that, according to reasonable medical judgment, relies on the most current medical knowledge and will require treatment that will render the applicant unable to work for a portion of the 3-month period. Under these circumstances, the employer would be able to withdraw the employment offer without violating these regulations. The information obtained in the course of a permitted entrance examination is to be treated as a confidential medical record.

13.1.5.9 Other Acceptable Examinations and Inquiries

The regulations permit voluntary medical examinations, including voluntary medical histories, as part of the employee health programs. These programs often include, for example, medical screening for high blood pressure, weight control counseling, and cancer detection. Voluntary activities, such as blood pressure monitoring and the administering of prescription drugs, such as insulin, are also permitted. It should be noted, however, that the medical records developed in the course of such activities must be maintained in the confidential manner required by this regulation and must not be used for any purpose in violation of these regulations, such as limiting health insurance eligibility.

13.1.5.10 Employer's Mandatory Prescription Disclosure Found to Violate Americans with Disabilities Act

One of the predictions made following the passage of the ADA was that the widespread practice of employers requiring applicants and employees to disclose all of the prescription drugs that they were taking would be eliminated. This practice was a way for employers to deal with what they thought was prescription drug abuse and opiates in the days before MRO practice developed. The practice without the ADA is ineffective and invasive, and although much less widespread, is still prevalent. This is the first court decision that illustrates the legal issue for employers and their counsel. All too often employers are simply unaware of the legal issues or are ill advised.

A Federal court in Colorado has found that an employer's mandatory requirement that applicants disclose all of the drugs that they are or have recently taken to be a violation of the Americans with Disabilities Act. Both sides stipulated to all the facts and agreed to abide by the finding of the Court. The employer had suspended the policy when this dispute arose.

The plaintiff, who used the pseudonym "Jane Roe," is an employee of the Cheyenne Mountain Conference Resort ("Resort"). The Resort implemented a drug and alcohol testing policy. The policy: (1) prohibits employees from using or possessing illegal drugs or illegally obtained prescription medication; (2) prohibits employees from using or possessing alcohol on company property or during work hours; (3) requires employees to inform the Resort of every drug they ingest, including legal, prescription medication; (4) allows employees to take prescription medication, with the Resort's approval, as long as the medication does not present a risk of injury to any person or impair the employee's senses; (5) subjects the employees to random drug testing; and (6) requires all employees to give their written consent to the policy. Adherence to the policy's rules is a condition of employment.

Roe challenged the portion of the policy that requires employees to disclose the use of legal, prescription medication. Roe claimed that this provision violates the Americans with Disabilities Act (ADA), violates her common law right to privacy, and violates public policy. Roe claims that she suffers from a disability, asthma, and must take prescription medication as a result. She did not inform the Resort of her disability or her need for medication. Roe also takes other prescription medications.

13.1.5.10.1 The Court's Analysis of the Americans with Disabilities Act

The Court noted that Congress enacted the ADA to help eliminate discrimination against individuals with disabilities. As part of this effort, the ADA restricts an employer's ability to conduct medical examinations and make inquiries of employees and job applicants in an effort to discover disabilities or perceived disabilities. The ADA contains separate rules for pre-offer job applicants, Sec. 12112(d)(2); post-offer but pre-employment entrance examinations, Sec. 12112(d)(3); and examinations and inquiries of current employees, Sec. 12112(d)(4).

Since Roe is a current employee of the Resort, only Sec. 12112(d)(4) (examinations and inquiries of current employees) applies to this case. This section of the ADA provides:

> A covered entity shall not require a medical examination and shall not make inquiries of an employee as to whether such employee is an individual with a disability or as to the nature or severity of the disability, unless such examinations or inquiry is shown to be job-related and consistent with business necessity.

In other words, the Court noted the ADA prohibits two separate and distinct things: (1) medical examinations; and (2) disability related inquiries. The statute provides an exception for medical exams or disability related inquiries that are job related and consistent with a business necessity. The Resort argued that the ADA explicitly permits drug testing, and that drug tests are not considered medical exams. The Resort is correct, but the Court correctly observed that this argument misses the point. Medical exams and disability related inquiries are two different things. The ADA does permit the Resort to administer drug tests. Roe does not challenge this aspect of the Resort's policy. The ADA does not, however, permit the resort to make inquiries as to whether an employee has a disability.

On this point, the Fourth Circuit has noted that "the employer is generally forbidden from inquiring about the disability of an employee." [Ennis v. National Ass'n. of Bus. & Educ. Radio, Inc., 53 F.3d 55, 58 (4th Cir. 1995)]. The portion of the Resort's policy that requires employees to disclose the legal, prescription medication they use does just that.

The ADA defines "disability" in very broad terms. A disability is "a physical or mental impairment that substantially limits one or more of the major life activities." Given this broad definition and the vast array of prescription medication used to treat various impairments that fit within this definition, a policy that requires employees to disclose the prescription medication they use would force the employees to reveal their disabilities (or perceived disabilities) to their employer. Section 12112(d)(4)(A) prohibits such an inquiry.

The Resort also presented the argument that their policy addresses only prescription medication that is illegally obtained or improperly used, and that Roe need not disclose prescription medication she legally obtains and properly uses. The Court stated that the Resort mischaracterizes its own policy. The policy provides that "prescribed drugs may be used only to the extent that they have been reported and approved by an employee supervisor." The policy clearly requires employees to disclose all prescription medication, whether obtained legally or illegally.

Such a provision would be permissible if the Resort could demonstrate that its prescription medication inquiry is "job related and consistent with business necessity." However, the Resort has failed to make any such showing. The Resort argues instead that the "job related" requirement applies only to medical examinations, therefore it does not have to demonstrate that the provision at issue is job related and consistent with a business necessity. Again the Court noted that this argument ignores the plain language of Sec. 12112(d)(4)(A), which states that the "job related" requirement applies to examinations and inquiries.

Because the Resort has not shown that its policy requiring employees to disclose legal, prescription medication is job related and consistent with business necessity, the Court granted summary judgment in favor of Roe on her claim that this provision violates the ADA.

The Court emphasized the narrowness of this holding, however. The vast majority of the Resort's policy is permissible under the ADA. The Resort may still test employees for illegal drug use. The Resort may prohibit employees from using, possessing, or being under the influence of illegal drugs or alcohol during work hours or on company property. The only thing the Resort may not do under the current policy is require employees to disclose the legal, prescription medication they use.

In a footnote, the Court noted that the Resort could draft a new policy that requires such a disclosure if the Resort can show that this requirement is job related and consistent with business necessity. In such a case, where prescription drug information is relevant to safety and performance, it should still be provided to someone with appropriate credentials and training in a confidential manner. One of the other deficiencies of prescription disclosure is that the individual who obtains all of this information cannot interpret its significance. The provision of the Resort's drug and alcohol policy that requires employees to disclose the legal, prescription medications they use violates the ADA. The Court did not find that the policy violated Roe's right to privacy or Colorado's public policy.

13.1.6 CHARTING SAFE PASSAGE FOR THE EMPLOYER

The charting of safe passage thought the drug testing harbor has been done to a large degree by large corporations. Large companies have access to legal counsel, expert technical and medical consultants, and professional human resource managers. The success of drug testing in large corporations is attributed to the appeal of screening out illegal drug users from the work force, managing worker compensation costs, improving the quality of products and services and managing substance abuse. This real (and perceived) return on investment is also attractive to medium and small size employers.

Today small and medium size employers represent the fastest growing part of the drug testing market. Since most workers are employed in small and medium size corporations this segment will be the largest part of the testing market over the next few years. This is not necessarily a benign development. The first concern with this current and future growth is that most medium and small employers do not have objective guidance and the expert resources of the large employer.

To a large degree the smaller employer must rely on service providers, drug testing laboratories, and drug testing service providers, who may understand the technical aspects of testing but may not appreciate the legal issues confronting an employer. There are also incompetent and/or unscrupulous service providers. Further, new technologies are expected to be introduced over the next few years that may be difficult or impossible for a small employer to evaluate. Hair testing and on-site testing are two such examples. Thus, the legal issues and risks of testing are quite dynamic and the potential for controversy and turmoil is never far below the surface. The initial legal uncertainties, or as you will, the fear of legal challenge, has played an important part of shaping the technical and procedural aspects of drug testing.

13.2 DUI DEFENSES

ALAN WAYNE JONES

NATIONAL LABORATORY OF FORENSIC MEDICINE, DEPARTMENT OF FORENSIC TOXICOLOGY,
UNIVERSITY HOSPITAL, LINKÖPING, SWEDEN

BARRY K. LOGAN

WASHINGTON STATE TOXICOLOGY LABORATORY, DEPARTMENT OF LABORATORY MEDICINE,
UNIVERSITY OF WASHINGTON, SEATTLE, WASHINGTON

After prohibition was abolished in the United States in 1933, consumption of alcohol escalated as did many of the negative consequences associated with too much drinking. Among other things, the number of alcohol-related accidents within the home, at work, and on the roads increased alarmingly.[1,2] Alcohol and transportation made a poor mix, and in efforts to curb this new wave of road-traffic accidents and deaths on the highways, more effective legislative measures were urgently needed.[3,4]

The first laws prohibiting driving under the influence of alcohol (DUI) appeared in the 1920s, but the criteria used to demonstrate impairment and unfitness to drive were not very sophisticated. These included the smell of alcohol on the breath, the ability of a person to walk a chalk line, and various behavioral signs and symptoms of inebriation.[5] Gaining a conviction for drunk driving was by no means certain, unless the suspect showed obvious signs and symptoms of gross intoxication.[6] It was strikingly obvious that more sensitive and more objective methods were needed to decide whether a person was under the influence of alcohol. Following the lead of some European countries, efforts in the U.S. were directed towards measuring the concentration of alcohol in blood and other body fluids as evidence of intoxication.[7] However, quantitative studies of the relationship between blood-alcohol and impairment were virtually non-existent at this time.

These efforts led to the first statutory limits of blood alcohol concentration (BAC) for driving being set at 150 mg/dL (0.15 g/dL), a conservatively high level.[8,9] Subsequently, this threshold BAC for driving has progressively been lowered, first to 100 mg/dL (0.10 g/dL) and in some U.S. states the limit is now set at 80 mg/dL (0.08 g/dL).[10] For young (< 21 y) drivers an even lower BAC, so called zero tolerance limits, has been sanctioned (0.00 to 0.02 g/dL). [11] Legal limits of blood alcohol concentration differ from country to country and also within regions of the same country, e.g. the various states in America and Australia.[12] Lowering the legal alcohol limits for driving even further is supported by many national and international medical societies including the American Medical Association.[13] Judging by recent trends in Europe, it seems that most countries are aiming for a threshold BAC limit of 50 mg/dL (0.05 g/dL); France approved a 0.05 g/dL limit in 1995, whereas Sweden adopted 0.02 g/dL in 1990. [12]

Punishment and sanctions for those found guilty of drunk driving have become increasingly severe and include suspension of the drivers license, heavy fines, and sometimes a mandatory term of imprisonment.[14-16] The first DUI statutes stipulated that the concentration of alcohol present in body fluids (blood, breath, or urine) was admissible as presumptive evidence of unfitness to drive, but that this was a rebuttable presumption.[4,6] In contrast, most of the DUI statutes in operation today are the so called per se laws, under which the person's BAC or breath alcohol concentration (BrAC) is the sole deciding factor necessary as proof of unfitness to drive.[15,16] In short, a person can be found guilty of drunk driving without exhibiting visible signs of intoxication when alcohol concentration per se statutes are in operation.[16] This legal framework, whereby the concentration of alcohol in a specimen of blood or breath determines guilt or innocence, places high demands on the analytical methods used for forensic purposes. Moreover, pre-analytical factors such as sampling, transportation, storage and handling of specimens needs to be carefully regulated and controlled. The combined influences of per se legislation, the compelling objective standard provided to juries in the numerical value of the BAC or BrAC result, and the increasingly harsh penalties imposed on those found guilty of DUI explain, at least in part, the vigorous defense attacks against prosecution evidence based on results of BAC or BrAC determinations.

Soon after chemical tests for intoxication were introduced and used on a large scale, the reliability of the approved methods and the results obtained were increasingly being questioned.[4] The practice of running duplicate determinations on the same specimen or obtaining two or more specimens of the same or different body fluids (e.g. blood and urine) and testing these by different analytical methods has much to recommend it.[14,15] Defending drinking drivers has become a lucrative business and many lawyers specialize in this area of jurisprudence. A plethora of textbooks and newsletters are available that provide detailed information about the science and law of DUI litigation.[17-21] These typically present recent examples of DUI case law, reviews and opinion of articles published in scientific peer-review journals, and hints and tips for developing more effective strategies for defending and also for prosecuting drunk drivers.[22]

This review article discusses the strengths and weaknesses of common DUI defense challenges. The work is subdivided into four main sections. The first deals with general attacks on potentially incriminating evidence, the second focuses on challenging results of urine alcohol analysis, the third deals with scrutiny of blood sampling and analysis, and the fourth section is concerned with the use of evidential breath-alcohol instruments. Procedural aspects of the DUI offense, such as whether the arresting police officer followed the correct protocol when the driver was apprehended, had reasonable suspicion or probable cause for making the arrest, performed the field sobriety tests properly, or gave the appropriate warnings demanded by the local rules and regulations prior to administering the chemical test, are not considered. The chemistry and physiology of forensic alcohol testing are the main focus of this review and much of the perpetual nit-picking and procedural issues often raised in DUI litigation are omitted.

An extensive list of references is provided, and most citations refer to articles published in peer-review U.S. and European English language journals. However a bimonthly journal from Germany called Blutalkohol (blood-alcohol), is worthy of note. Blutalkohol is published by Steintor-Verlag, Hamburg and the first volume appeared in 1962/63. This periodical contains a wealth of information about forensic aspects of alcohol with direct relevance to the defense and prosecution of DUI suspects. Although most of the articles are written in German, English summaries are provided.

13.2.1 GENERAL CHALLANGES

13.2.1.1 Drinking After the Offense

A frequent defense tactic is one in which the suspect claims to have consumed alcohol after driving or being involved in an accident such as a single-vehicle crash; this approach is sometimes called the hip-flask ploy.[23,24] Prosecution for DUI must necessarily relate driving with consumption of alcohol at a time before or during the driving. In these cases however it is alleged that the drinking took place after the driving, but prior to obtaining a specimen of blood or breath for forensic analysis. For example, hit-and-run drivers often manage to drive home. When eventually apprehended by the police, they might claim to have been sober during the driving but thereafter needed alcohol to "calm their nerves" or alleviate the condition of shock caused by "hitting a bird", and the resulting damage to the car. Subjects will often insist they drank alcohol after driving, even when they cannot produce any empty or opened bottle of liquor or any other credible evidence such as eye-witnesses to support their story. Some of the more experienced DUI offenders, especially repeat offenders, may carry a bottle of alcohol in their coat pocket or glove compartment, for the express purpose of being able to drink after driving; hence the origin of the term hip-flask defense. In some jurisdictions the prosecutor must prove beyond a reasonable doubt that the allegation of drinking after the offense was untrue, or that in spite of the alcohol consumed after driving the suspect's BAC or BrAC at the time of driving still exceeded the legal limit. This is often a difficult task.

To deal with alleged drinking after the offense, the prosecutor has several options available and should seek help from qualified forensic experts when preparing the case. First, it is important to document the testimony of the police or other witnesses who might have observed the actual driving, or the behavior and general appearance of the suspect when arrested. Such observations as the smell of alcohol on the breath, slurred speech, or unsteady gait are important to document before the driver has had the opportunity to drink any more alcohol, should be noted. In cases where the subject has allegedly consumed a large quantity of alcohol immediately before being apprehended by the police, one would also expect to see a dramatic and progressive onset of symptoms of intoxication. Second, information regarding the quantity of alcohol allegedly consumed after driving, the time of intake and the sex, age, height, and body weight of the suspect can be used to calculate the expected BAC.[22] If this approach is used, the suspect should be given the "benefit of any doubt" by assuming that at the time of sampling blood and breath, absorption and distribution from the post incident ethanol consumption was complete.

The Widmark equation (see Chapter 5) is commonly used to calculate the expected BAC on the basis of the person's body weight and drinking pattern.[25,26] Making an adjustment for elimination of alcohol through metabolism between the time of starting to drink and the time of sampling blood is usually warranted, especially when several hours have elapsed between the time of the driving and the time of obtaining a blood-sample. In this way, a theoretical mean BAC and its 95% confidence interval, can be compared with the analytical report from the forensic laboratory. The resulting difference in BAC, if any, should reflect the BAC that existed prior to the post-incident drinking, and therefore the BAC before or during driving. The use of a 95% confidence interval is a safeguard to allow for inter-individual variations in absorption, distribution and elimination patterns of alcohol (see Chapter 5 for details). Grossly exaggerated claims of the amount of alcohol consumed after the offense, such as drinking a whole bottle of liquor in a relatively short time span, are clearly unrealistic and should be given little credibility.

The limitations of urine alcohol concentration (UAC) testing are dealt with in the next section, however, if the police manage to obtain samples of urine and blood shortly after driving, the magnitude of the UAC/BAC ratio can help to resolve whether alcohol was ingested within approximately 1 h of taking the samples. This approach was tested empirically by Iffland et al.[27] who found that UAC/BAC ratios between 1.0 to 1.15 indicated fairly recent drinking whereas ratios larger than 1.2:1 indicate that the drinking began much earlier. This fits with the observation that during the absorption phase of alcohol kinetics, before equilibration has been reached, UAC is generally less than or equal to BAC. In the post-absorptive phase of alcohol metabolism, UAC is usually 1.3 to 1.5 times higher than BAC.[28,29] The concentration of alcohol in pooled bladder urine mirrors the average concentration prevailing in the blood during the formation of urine in the kidneys and storage in the bladder.[28] Because urine has about 20% more water than an equal volume of whole blood, the concentration of alcohol in newly secreted urine is about 20% higher than BAC and a urine/blood ratio of 1.2:1 should be expected. Dividing the measured UAC by 1.2, gives an estimate of the lowest BAC at the time of voiding or since the bladder was last emptied. Moreover, a UAC/BAC ratio exceeding 1.3 suggests that the bulk of the alcohol was already absorbed into the blood and distributed throughout total body water. Whenever the police suspect that a person will assert consumption of alcohol after driving, efforts should be made to obtain two specimens of urine about 30 to 60 min apart. If the UAC of the second void is higher than the first void then it seems reasonable to assume that absorption of alcohol from the stomach is not complete at the time of sampling. Such a finding would support the claim of recent consumption of alcohol. If the UAC decreases between the first and second void 30 to 60 min later, this suggests that the post-absorptive phase has become well established and the main part of the alcohol was imbibed at least 1 to 2 h earlier. [28,29]

If the ratio of UAC/BAC is less than or close to unity, this supports the contention of recent consumption of alcohol and the BAC curve was probably still rising, or near the peak. If an alcohol-free pool of urine existed in the bladder before drinking started, this would tend to dilute the concentration of alcohol secreted into the bladder and might suggest a rising UAC between the two successive voids, even though in reality the BAC curve was in the post-peak phase. Alternatively, evaluating the change in BAC between the times of taking two blood samples 30 to 60 min apart gives a good indication of whether a rising or falling BAC existed at the time of sampling. [30]

Forensic toxicologists in Germany have developed another way to deal with allegations of drinking after the offense and this method has become known as congener analysis. [31-34] In brief, this method entails analyzing the alcoholic beverage the suspect claims to have consumed after driving with the aim of identifying other volatile constituents besides ethanol. Pure ethanol does have a distinctive odor, although these other congeners (non-ethanol volatiles) produced during the fermentation process help impart the distinctive smell and flavor to the drink. [31] The results of the congener analysis are then compared with the volatiles present in a sample of blood or urine taken from the suspect in an attempt to match the components. Methanol, 1-propanol, 2-butanol and 2-methyl-1-propanol are typical examples of congener alcohols that can be identified in body fluids depending on the particular kind of beverage consumed. [32] The results of congener analysis, together with other information, has been accepted by the courts in Germany when dealing with hit-and-run drivers who frequently claim drinking after the offense. [31-34] The usefulness of analyzing methanol as a congener in forensic casework is limited by the fact that this alcohol is produced naturally in the body and its concentration in body fluids increases after ingestion of ethanol because of competition for the metabolizing enzyme alcohol dehydrogenase. [35-37] Furthermore, if the beverage consumed before the incident is the same as that allegedly consumed afterwards, the congeners will be the same and this approach would not work.

Claims of drinking after the offense can be counteracted by appropriate legislation. For example, in Norway it is a separate offense for a motorist to consume alcohol within 6 hours of driving if there is good reason to believe that the police will want to investigate some event related to the driving. Thus, drinking within 6 h of an accident to reach a BAC in excess of the legal limit carries the same penalty as being found guilty of drunk driving (Norwegian traffic law, paragraph 22). Without this kind of legislation, the magnitude of the UAC/BAC ratio and the change in BAC between successive samples, or UAC between two successive voids, provides useful information to evaluate whether or not a person has consumed alcohol within an hour or so before taking the samples. Knowledge of the stage of alcohol kinetics is important not only in alleged drinking after the offense but also when asked to engage in retrograde extrapolation of BAC to an earlier time. Accurate back-tracking of BAC to the time of driving is fraught with difficulties, and only an approximate result, and likely range of values is possible, based on known population averages for alcohol elimination. Again, the need to back extrapolate can be avoided by statutory definition of the relevant BAC for prosecution as that existing at the time of sampling or within 2 to 3 h of the driving.

13.2.1.2 Laced Drinks

The "laced drinks" defense is another challenge that arises during prosecution of drunk drivers in their attempts to avoid punishment for DUI.[17,19,20,21] The usual story is that a friend or associate has added liquor (usually vodka) to a non-alcoholic drink or to beer when the person concerned was otherwise engaged or distracted. Another spin on this scenario is where the suspect has been invited to consume some kind of homemade beverage which was not recognized as containing a high alcohol content because the taste was masked by strong flavoring. Unintentional intoxication through the over-consumption of alcohol containing chocolates or alcohol soaked fruit have also been alleged. Only later, after being apprehended for DUI, was it apparent to the subjects in these cases that the drink must have contained an unusually high concentration of alcohol which was not obvious from the taste. The subjective intoxication effects of alcohol differ widely among different individuals and this allows the defendant to argue that he or she was driving with a BAC above the limit but without intent, which although not a complete defense, may have some mitigating value.

Widmark calculations (see Chapter 5) are commonly used to estimate the BAC expected from the amount of alcohol inadvertently consumed in the laced drink.[24,25] However, relating a given BAC to a precise degree of intoxication is difficult because of the wide variations in consumption and concentration tolerance between different individuals. Dram-shop laws in the U.S. place responsibility on the host at the party, or the owner of the bar for damages caused by a drunk driver if that person was served alcohol while he or she was visibly intoxicated.[17-22] In a well-documented laced drinks case, a woman was acquitted after driving with a BAC of 0.17 g/dL. She admitted drinking from a "punch bowl" when visiting the home of some friends, although she denied knowledge of the fact that the drink was laced with 96% v/v ethanol, and did not feel any definite impairment effects of alcohol despite the high BAC. The medicolegal experts called by the court refused to state with certainty that the women must have felt under the influence of alcohol at a BAC of 0.17 g/dL. On appeal to the high court, the woman was acquitted of willfully driving under the influence. The prosecutor approached the supreme court but permission to review the case was refused.[38] The trend toward introducing lower legal limits and zero tolerance laws for young people should make the laced drinks defense, and driving over the limit without intent, a much more common defense tactic. This follows because of the great difficulty in recognizing symptoms of intoxication at very low levels such as 0.02 g/dL where impairment may be minimal. The same applies to driving in the morning following an evening of heavy drinking, when low per se illegal concentrations of alcohol in the blood are enforced.

13.2.1.3 Rising Blood-Alcohol Concentration

Some DUI suspects argue that their BAC or BrAC was below the legal limit at the time of driving, but that the concentration of alcohol had risen to exceed the legal alcohol limit at the time of obtaining samples for analysis. In short, if the prosecution BAC was 0.12 g/dL at the time of the test, it might be suggested that it was below 0.10 g/dL at the time of driving some time earlier.[39,40] The key question here is by how much can the BAC or BrAC rise after the last drink? To answer this question, details of the subject's drinking pattern before or during the driving, as well as the various time elements and intake of food should be carefully investigated. The pharmacokinetics of alcohol show large inter-individual variations especially when small doses are taken after a meal.[41,42] This challenge is known as the rising BAC defense and the usual scenario according to the defendant is that he or she was engaged in moderate social drinking for several hours after work, perhaps with a meal or eating bar snacks. For some unexplained, and physiologically improbable reason, the alcohol ingested during the evening remained unabsorbed in the stomach until the person decided to leave for home or drive to the next bar. Shortly after driving the person is either involved in an accident or pulled over by the police because of a moving traffic offense, and in this connection is arrested for DUI. The defendant then claims that between the time of being apprehended and the time of taking the blood or breath-alcohol test, the alcohol in the stomach has become absorbed into the blood bringing the person over the legal limit.

Obviously, this scenario is unreasonable because alcohol, unlike many other drugs, starts to become absorbed from the stomach immediately following ingestion. Gastric emptying accelerates this process and leads to a rapid onset of the effects of alcohol on the brain. Indeed, people indulge in drinking primarily to experience alcohol's enjoyable pharmacological effects such as euphoria, relaxation and diminished social inhibitions. In order for this to happen, the alcohol must become absorbed into the blood and transported to the brain. The intoxicating effects of alcohol are more pronounced during the rising limb of the BAC profile, and people would surely be surprised if they had been consuming drinks for several hours without experiencing any effect! Unfortunately, only a handful of studies have looked at the pharma-cokinetics of alcohol under real world drinking conditions to establish, for a large number of subjects, the degree of rise in BAC and the time needed to reach the peak after the last drink.

Gullberg [43] reported a study in which 39 subjects drank various quantities of alcohol under real world drinking conditions. The mean time required to reach the peak BAC after end of drinking was 19 min (span 0 to 80 min) and 81% of subjects reached a peak within 30 min. A study reported by Shajani and Dinn[44] also gives a clue to the time needed to reach peak BAC under social drinking conditions. In 8 men and 8 women who consumed known amounts of alcohol according to choice, the maximum BAC was reached 35 min (span 17 to 68 min) after end of intake. Taken together these studies and a few others suggest the low probability that the result of a blood or breath-alcohol test made some time after driving will be higher than at the time of driving which is often 1 to 2 h earlier. Zink and Reinhardt [45] made an important contribution when they allowed heavy drinkers to consume very large amounts of alcohol over periods of 6 to 10 h, resulting in peak BAC's in the range 0.10 to 0.38 g/dL, and taking samples of venous blood for analysis of alcohol at 15 min intervals during and after the drinking spree. In this way accurate information was obtained about the shape of the concentration-time profile and the time of reaching the peak as well as rise in BAC after the last drink. Importantly, they found that half the individuals had reached their peak BAC even before the last drink was taken (i.e., the rate of elimination exceeds the rate of consumption). The longest time necessary to reach a peak was 50 min after end of drinking (mean ± SD, 7.7 ± 22.9 minutes), and when a rise in BAC occurred between the end of drinking and the peak BAC it was invariably less than 0.02 g/dL. This study has important ramifications because many DUI suspects have blood-alcohol concentrations in this high range when they are apprehended.

Drinking alcohol together with a large meal was studied by Jones and Neri[42] who found that under these conditions, although the peak BAC was attained soon after the end of drinking for most subjects, a BAC plateau developed where for some, the BAC remained fairly constant for 2 to 3 h. Interestingly, in 10 of these subjects, 70% of the peak BAC had been attained within 15 min after the end of drinking. More studies are needed delineating the absorption kinetics of alcohol for different drinking conditions, with different beverages and formulations and with fast and slow ingestion of alcohol, on an empty stomach and after a meal.

Although the person's BAC or BrAC at the time of driving or when a road-traffic accident occurred might be considered the most relevant result for prosecution, it is fairly obvious that estimating this value can involve some uncertainty. This follows because the blood or breath-test is often made 1 to 2 h after the driving and there is a wide variation in absorption, distribution, and elimination patterns of alcohol in individual DUI suspects. Much can be gained by statutory definition of the relevant BAC or BrAC as that prevailing at the time of the chemical test and not at the time of driving. Unfortunately, many jurisdictions persist with using the BAC or BrAC at the time of driving as the figure needed for prosecution of DUI suspects. Other jurisdictions accept the chemical test result, provided it was obtained within two hours of the driving, as being equivalent to the BAC at the time of driving. Samples of blood or breath taken outside this time frame require the prosecution to estimate the BAC or BrAC prevailing at the time of driving. This entails making a back extrapolation of BAC from time of sampling to the time of driving which is always subject to some uncertainty. In cases where the statutory period of two or three hours between the driving and the time of the test is exceeded, error in back extrapolation can be minimized (in the defendant's favor), by only extrapolating back to the end of the two or three hour period.

Provided the subject was in the post-peak phase of alcohol absorption-distribution at the time of driving and at the time of sampling blood, extrapolating back with a conservative alcohol burn-off rate, such as 0.008 to 0.010 g/dL per hour, can be defended. Other safeguards against overestimation include an adjustment for absorption of alcohol contained in the last drink, and allowing for the possibility of a BAC concentration plateau existing where BAC remains more or less constant for several hours, as sometimes happens if alcohol is ingested together with a large meal. Other reasonable approaches include the use of population mean elimination rates, with 95% confidence intervals to establish the most likely upper and lower limits of BAC.

A recent study of double blood samples from 1090 DUI suspects arrived at a mean alcohol burn-off rate of 0.019 g/dL per hour with 95% limits of agreement, spanning from 0.009 to 0.029 g/dL/h. [46] These results suggest that making a back estimation of a person's BAC over long periods of time and assuming a relatively low and constant burn-off rate such as 0.008 to 0.01 g/dL/h will lead to a large underestimate of the BAC at the time in question, but always in the defendant's favor. While this approach gives a definite advantage to the suspect, the practice of making a back estimation of a person's BAC is inevitably a controversial issue in DUI litigation and should be avoided whenever possible. [47-50]

13.2.1.4 Pathological States and Ethanol Pharmacokinetics

The pharmacokinetics of many prescription drugs have been carefully investigated in patients suffering from various diseases.[51-53] Much less work has been done concerning the influence of disease states on absorption, distribution, and metabolism of the social drug ethanol. DUI suspects sometimes claim however that they suffer from certain medical conditions or pathological states which they hope might explain their BAC being above the legal limit for driving. Many claims of this kind have been documented such as liver cirrhosis, kidney failure or absence of a kidney or one lobe of the lung. Because only 2 to 5% of the total quantity of alcohol consumed is excreted in urine and breath, reduced efficiency of the lungs or kidney has marginal effects on the total amount of alcohol eliminated from the body. The rate of alcohol elimination from blood in patients with kidney failure scheduled for hemodialysis was no different from the burn-off rate in healthy control subjects.[54]

Major surgery to the gastro-intestinal tract, such as gastrectomy, is known to cause a more rapid absorption of alcohol leading to an overshoot peak which tends to be somewhat higher than the maximum BAC expected.[55-57] A similar phenomenon is often observed when drinking neat liquor on an empty stomach. [41] However, 1 to 2 h after drinking ends, the BAC should approach the value expected for the dose of alcohol ingested and the person's gender and body weight because alcohol has now had sufficient time to equilibrate in the total body water. The rate of absorption of alcohol shows wide inter-individual variations even in apparently healthy individuals, and estimating the peak BAC from amount consumed is subject to considerable uncertainty.[41] Jokipii[58] devoted his thesis work to comparing blood-alcohol profiles under controlled conditions in healthy subjects and in those with various diseases (liver cirrhosis, acute hepatitis, hyperthyreosis, diabetes mellitus, and neurocirculatory asthenia or dystonia). This publication is unfortunately not widely available, although its salient features were reviewed with the conclusion that these particular pathological states did not cause distorted alcohol burn-off rates or abnormal distribution volumes of ethanol compared with healthy control subjects. [59]

Drunk drivers with *de facto* diseased liver, such as alcohol hepatitis or cirrhosis, insist that this renders them slow metabolizers of ethanol compared with individuals having normal liver function. Controlled studies of the effect of various liver diseases on the rate of disappearance of alcohol from blood are rather sparse. Ethical issues preclude embarking on detailed investigations of this topic. Those few studies available do not support the notion of a slower rate of metabolism outside the limits of 0.009 to 0.025 g/dL/h seen in healthy individuals.[60-63] Moreover, results of alcohol drinking experiments in patients with cirrhosis are often confounded by the problem of malnutrition in these test subjects. This also leads to a slower elimination rate of alcohol from blood.[52,63] In patients with cirrhosis and severe portal hypertension, where some blood is forced to bypass the liver, there is some evidence to suggest a slower rate of ethanol disappearance (0.007 g/dL/h). The reason for this finding is probably diminished flow of blood to the alcohol metabolizing enzymes, and not so much necrosis of the liver tissue.[64]

People suffering from chronic liver disease often accumulate a fluid in the peritoneal cavity called ascites.[65,66] Indeed, ascites is one consequence of long-term abuse of alcohol and alcohol-induced cirrhosis. Because the ascites fluid is mainly water, this furnishes a body fluid reservoir for ethanol increasing the person's volume of distribution. The volume of ascites fluid can vary widely between different individuals, and up to 5 liters is not uncommon. An increased total body water in patients with ascites raises the volume of distribution for other hydrophilic drugs besides ethanol. The concentration of alcohol in ascites will be closer to the concentration in plasma and serum than in whole blood. When alcohol has been cleared from the blood circulation the pool of alcohol in the ascites fluid can redistribute back into the bloodstream. However, alcohol cannot concentrate in this fluid space and ascites fluid should therefore contain approximately 10 to 20% more alcohol than an equal volume of whole blood. Like the situation with urine (see Chapter 5), there should also be a time-lag in the clearance of the alcohol from ascites fluid compared with blood.

Most of the scientific evidence indicates that alcoholics generally tend to metabolize alcohol faster than moderate drinkers owing to induction of the microsomal enzyme denoted P4502E1, one of the consequences of long-term heavy drinking. [67] In a recent study in alcoholics undergoing detoxification with initial BACs of 0.20 to 0.45 g/dL, the burn-off rate (ß-slopes) ranged from 0.013 to 0.036 g/dL/h with an average of 0.022 g/dL/h. [68] A similar mean value was reported when the work of several research groups based in Germany were compiled together; average elimination rate 0.022 ± 0.005 g/dL/h (mean ± SD). [69] Many DUI suspects are clearly alcoholics, and in a study of 1090 apprehended drunk drivers from whom two blood samples were taken 60 min apart, the mean ß-slope was 0.019 g/dL/h with 95% limits of agreement of 0.009 to 0.029 g/dL/h, being in close agreement with values for alcoholics during detoxification.[46]

Individuals suffering from diabetes mellitus with impaired glucose metabolism might have elevated concentrations of ketone bodies, including acetone, circulating in their blood. Note that the acetone produced can also become reduced to isopropanol in the liver through the alcohol dehydrogenase pathway.[70] However, when modern gas chromatographic (GC) methods are used for blood alcohol analysis, acetone and isopropanol are easily distinguished, so defense challenges directed at the lack of specificity of GC methods of alcohol analysis are therefore pointless if two or more different stationary phases are used for the chromatography.[71] There is no evidence to suggest that the rate of ethanol metabolism should be any different in people suffering from diabetes compared with healthy control subjects.[72,73] The metabolic disturbances associated with insulin-dependent diabetes are not related to the enzymes involved in the disposal of ethanol.[74] Total body water and activity of alcohol dehydrogenase enzymes decreases in states of malnutrition and protein deficiency, and this is reflected in slower burn-off rates of alcohol.[75,76] However, moderate losses of body water after prolonged sauna bathing did not result in any marked differences in the shape of blood-alcohol profiles.[77] A low relative TBW/kg body weight is associated with a smaller volume of distribution for ethanol and this explains the well known male-female difference in peak BAC and area under the curve for the same dose of alcohol per kg body weight.[78] The distribution volume of ethanol was shown to decrease in male subjects between the ages of 20 to 60 years along with a decrease in total body water in the elderly.[79]

People involved in traffic accidents might be badly injured and suffer from shock and hemorrhage owing to massive losses of blood. This raises the question about the influence of trauma and shock on the hepatic metabolism of alcohol and the resulting blood-alcohol profiles.[80-82] In a recent study with 10 subjects involved in accidents when under the influence of alcohol, and suffering from poly-traumatic shock, a series of venous and arterial blood samples were obtained for determination of ethanol.[83] The rate of alcohol disappearance from blood ranged from 0.017 to 0.021 g/dL/h (mean 0.018 g/dL/h) and these values were the same regardless of whether arterial or venous blood sampling sites were used. The results of this study confirm many other anecdotes and case reports regarding alcohol pharmacokinetics in people injured when drunk.[80-82] Hypovolemic shock following massive loss of blood will result in a redistribution of body fluids and higher proportions of plasma enter the intravascular space to maintain an effective circulation and tissue perfusion.[84] This might alter the relative distribution of some protein-bound drugs and endogenous substances between body compartments, but the concentration of alcohol in the blood is not markedly influenced.[85,86] Nevertheless, some people continue to speculate about the impact of trauma on blood-alcohol concentrations and alcohol burn-off rates, even though a careful review of the literature shows that there is no substance to these opinions.[87]

13.2.1.5 Drug-Alcohol Interactions

The use of various tonics (elixirs), cough syrups, over-the-counter medications, or even foodstuffs that might contain alcohol, will obviously result in alcohol appearing in the blood.[88] Some cough medicines, vitamin mixtures, pick-me-ups, and other health-store products may contain considerable quantities of alcohol (>10% v/v), and overdosing with these products will obviously elevate a person's BAC. By how much the BAC rises will depend on the quantities consumed and the time frame in relation to driving. Medication taken in tablet form or drugs applied externally can hardly be expected to lead to alcohol appearing in the blood. Psychopharmacological agents such as benzodiazepine derivatives may cause increased impairment when taken together with alcohol because of interaction at the GABA receptor complex in the brain.[89] However, there is no evidence to suggest that the resulting BAC will be any different from that expected if the same dose of alcohol had been taken without the drug.[90]

Intake of alcohol can modify the pharmacokinetics and behavioral effects of drugs that are oxidized by P4502E1 enzymes or which interact with the GABA receptor to elicit their effects on the central nervous system.[91] However, these changes do not result in altered alcohol pharmacokinetics or a raised BAC above that obtained in control experiments when the same dose of alcohol was consumed on an empty stomach. One drug that does block the metabolism of alcohol is 4-methyl pyrazole which competes with ethanol for binding sites on the primary metabolizing enzyme ADH.[92] However 4-MP is not currently manufactured by any drug companies even though it may have legitimate therapeutic uses in the treatment of patients poisoned with methanol or ethylene glycol.[93,94]

Alan Wayne Jones and Barry K. Logan

13.2.1.6 Gastric Alcohol Dehydrogenase

The enzyme mainly responsible for the metabolism of alcohol is called alcohol dehydrogenase (ADH) and this is located in the liver and to a minor extent also in other organs and tissue such as the kidney and the mucosa of the stomach.[95] Recent studies have shown that gastric ADH is seemingly less active in women compared with men and also in alcoholics compared with moderate drinkers, and the overall activity decreases with advancing age.[96] About 10 years ago the suspicion arose that part of the dose of alcohol consumed was metabolized in the stomach by gastric ADH. This process was known as pre-systemic metabolism or first-pass effect. This meant that the effective dose of alcohol reaching the systemic circulation depended on the efficacy of gastric ADH enzymes. Sex-related differences in gastric ADH offered another mechanism to explain why women reach a higher peak BAC than men for the same dose of alcohol.[97] If a part of the dose of ethanol is metabolized by gastric ADH, this would explain the observation of a smaller area under the BAC-time profile after oral intake compared with intravenous administration of the same dose. Prolonged retention of alcohol in the stomach, such as after drinking together with or after a meal, allows more opportunity for pre-systemic oxidation by gastric ADH to occur.[98,99]

Interest in the role played by gastric ADH in the overall metabolism of ethanol received a boost when in-vitro studies showed that the enzyme extracted from gastric biopsies was inhibited by certain commonly prescribed drugs. Among others, aspirin and the H_2-receptor antagonists, ranitidine and cimetidine, used in the treatment of gastric ulcers and inhibition of secretion of excess stomach acid, were capable of blocking the action of gastric ADH according to in-vitro enzyme inhibition assays.[100,101] This led to the suggestion that people taking this medication, which is widely used in society, and now available without prescription in the U.S., run the risk of obtaining higher than expected BAC's and, therefore, a potentially more pronounced impairment from the alcohol they consume.[102,103] The drugs seemingly promote the bioavailability of ethanol by removing the potential for oxidation of some of the alcohol already in the stomach.[102-104] Media coverage of this much publicized research triggered a large number of defense challenges from individuals who claimed to combine their H_2-receptor blocking drugs with intake of alcohol.[105] Studies purporting to show an enhanced bioavailability of ethanol, and a higher peak BAC from this drug-alcohol interaction were not very convincing. The number of volunteer subjects was often limited (N = 6) and very low doses of alcohol (0.15 to 0.3 g/kg) were ingested 1 h after a fat-rich meal. Moreover, the methods of alcohol analysis were not appropriate considering that the maximum BACs reached were only 0.015 to 0.025 g/dL, being far removed from the statutory limits for driving in most US states, namely 0.08 or 0.10 g/dL. [106] Many subsequent studies involving larger numbers of subjects and a better experimental design failed to confirm the enhanced bioavailability of alcohol when H_2-receptor antagonist drugs were taken together with a moderate doses of ethanol 0.15, 0.30, or 0.60 g/kg.[106-111] Accordingly, this defense challenge holds little merit to explain a person's BAC being above the legal limit for driving without intent. Many factors influence the rate of absorption of alcohol from the gut and the bioavailability of the dose particularly the amount of food in the stomach before drinking.[98,99] It is always good advice not to drink alcohol on an empty stomach.

13.2.1.7 Endogenous Ethanol and the Autobrewery Syndrome

With the help of sensitive and specific methods of analysis, very low concentrations of ethanol (0.5 to 1.5 mg/L) can be determined in body fluids from people who have not consumed any alcoholic beverages.[112-114] It seems that endogenous ethanol (EE) is produced in the gut by microbes, bacteria and/or yeasts acting on dietary carbohydrates, but other biochemical pathways also exist according to a comprehensive review of this subject.[115] Indeed, the existence of other metabolic precursors of EE was confirmed when ethanol was identified in blood and tissue samples from germ-free rats, because in these animals fermentation of carbohydrates by microflora inhabiting the gut cannot be invoked as an explanation.[116] Because the portal blood draining the stomach and intestine must pass through the liver before reaching the heart, lungs, and systemic circulation, any EE formed in the gut is probably eliminated through the action of alcohol metabolizing enzymes located in the liver.[117]

Abnormally high (0.05 g/dL) concentrations of EE were measured in blood and cerebrospinal fluid from hospitalized patients who had abstained from drinking alcohol.[118,119] The reports of this work were published in peer-reviewed journals, so these unusual findings gives some cause for concern and warrant a carefully scrutiny. It seems that the methodology used for measuring ethanol in biological specimens was rather primitive involving wet-chemistry oxidation, which is not a specific means of identifying ethanol. Whether dietary factors or even the medication prescribed to the patients were oxidized by the chemical reagents used in the assay, producing falsely elevated concentrations of EE needs to be explored.[120]

If for some reason large quantities of ethanol are synthesized in the gastro-intestinal tract and overwhelm the capacity of the alcohol-metabolizing enzymes in the liver, then much higher concentrations of EE should appear in the peripheral venous blood. This is exactly what was described in a group of Japanese subjects who were suffering from various disorders of the gut. Some had previously complained of experiencing feelings of drunkenness even without consumption of alcohol.[121-122] This condition seemed to appear after the subjects had eaten a carbohydrate-rich meal, such as rice. This study from Japan was difficult to fault because ethanol was identified in blood, urine, and breath with the aid of a reliable gas chromatographic method for quantitative analysis.[121] The term used to describe this abnormal production of EE was "autobrewery syndrome" and to our knowledge this has only been observed in Japanese subjects.[123] It is widely known that the activity of alcohol metabolizing enzymes, especially aldehyde dehydrogenase, is different in Oriental populations compared with Caucasians, which might render Japanese and other Asians less able to clear ethanol from the portal blood.[59] Other requirements before "autobrewery syndrome" should be seriously considered as contributing to a person's BAC include genetic predisposition (Oriental origin), a past history of gastrointestinal ailments, documented medical treatment for the problem, low tolerance to alcohol, and reports of fatigue and drunkenness after eating meals.

The occurrence of EE has also attracted interest in clinical and diagnostic medicine as an indirect way to furnish evidence of yeast infections in the gut.[123] After obtaining a control pretreatment blood sample, the fasted patient receives a 5 g glucose load orally and a second blood sample is taken again after 1 h. If the concentration of EE in the second blood sample is significantly higher than in the first, this indicates the possibility of a bacteria or yeast overgrowth in the stomach or small intestine causing a gut-fermentation reaction. Many studies from various countries have confirmed the existence of EE in blood and other biological media from healthy human subjects, but the concentrations rarely exceed 1.0 mg/L, which is about 1000 times less than the statutory BAC for unfitness to drive in most US states (0.10 g/dL = 1.0 g/L = 1000 mg/L). These vanishingly small concentrations lack any forensic significance except in exceptional circumstances such as that described for Japanese subjects suffering from gastrointestinal disorders (autobrewery syndrome).[121] Concentrations of EE in blood samples from people with diabetes mellitus as well as other metabolic disorders, were not much different from values in healthy control subjects.[113]

13.2.2 URINE SAMPLES

It has been known for more than a century that only a small fraction (about 1 to 2%) of the quantity of alcohol a person consumes is excreted unchanged in the urine.[124,125] Indeed, collection and analysis of urine was recommended by Widmark as a chemical test to prove that a person had been drinking and as an aid in the clinical diagnosis of drunkenness.[125] When urine is used as a body fluid for analysis of alcohol in traffic law enforcement, great care is needed with the sampling protocol to ensure valid interpretation of results.[28,29,126,127] This follows because the concentration of alcohol in urine does not relate to the concentration in the blood at the time of emptying the bladder.[29] Instead, the UAC reflects the average BAC during the time period in which the urine is being produced and stored in the bladder after the previous void.[128] During this storage time, the BAC might have changed appreciably and even reached a zero concentration. In the morning after an evenings drinking it is not uncommon to find that the first urinary void contains a relatively high concentrations of alcohol, whereas blood or breath-alcohol content are below the limits of detection with conventional analytical methods.[129] The morning UAC reflects the person's average BAC during the night after the last void before bedtime.

In Great Britain urine specimens were approved for evidential purposes after the Road Traffic Act of 1967, when an alcohol concentration of 80 mg/dl blood or 107 mg/dL urine were accepted as per se evidence of unfitness to drive safely.[14] However the rules and regulations required the collection of two samples of urine about 30-60 min apart.[14] The first void empties the bladder of old urine, and the concentration of alcohol measured in the second void reflects the person's blood-alcohol concentration at the mid-point of the collection period. Because urine contains about 20% more water than an equal volume of whole blood, the concentration of alcohol in the urine produced at the ureter will always be higher than the concentration in blood flowing to the kidney.[28,29] The urine/blood ratio in the post-peak phase of alcohol metabolism is about 1.33:1 on the average, although large inter- and intra-individual variations exist.[128] Studies have shown that the urine/blood ratio of alcohol as well as its variability increases as the blood-alcohol concentration decreases.[28,29] The mean ratio of 1.33:1 is higher than expected on the basis of water content differences (1.2:1), in part because of the time-lag between formation of urine in the ureter and storage in the bladder before voiding (see Chapter 5). With relatively short storage times the UAC/BAC ratio might be close to the value expected theoretically of 1.2:1. Note that in UK traffic-law enforcement, the DUI suspect's BAC is not estimated indirectly from the measured UAC. Instead, the legislature has adopted an alcohol concentration of 107 mg/dL in urine as being equivalent to 80 mg/dL in blood (107/80 = 1.33). This approach is similar to the way that the threshold limits of BrAC have been derived from the existing BAC, by dividing by the blood/breath conversion factor adopted by the legislature in the respective countries (see Table 13.2.1). Indeed, because of individual variations in the urine/blood and breath/blood ratios of alcohol, it is strongly recommended that UAC or BrAC not be converted into a presumed BAC as a measure of guilt in DUI prosecution. Instead, the threshold concentration of alcohol should be defined in terms of the substance analyzed whether this is breath or urine. [15,16]

Not many jurisdictions allow the concentrations of alcohol determined in urine specimens as binding evidence for prosecution in DUI, especially when per se statutes operate. This caution is well founded if the measured UAC has to be translated into the presumed BAC because the urine/blood ratio is highly variable between and within individuals and also changes as a function of the BAC. However, unlike most other drugs, the UAC/BAC ratio is not influenced by diuresis because alcohol is handled by the kidneys exactly like water in a passive diffusion process.[126] Increasing the volume of urine excreted by drinking large volumes of water may dilute the urine as reflected by its osmolality and creatinine content but the concentration of alcohol in the specimen will remain unchanged.[130] One objection often raised against the use of urine-alcohol evidence in prosecution of DUI suspects is that some people cannot completely empty their bladders on demand. The retention of old urine with a higher content of alcohol than expected for the prevailing BAC at the time of voiding introduces uncertainty.[131] The prevalence of urine retention in the population at large is hard to estimate

Table 13.2.1 Evidential Breath-Alcohol Instruments Currently Used for Forensic Purposes in Europe and North America. The Statutory Limits of Blood-Alcohol (BAC) and Breath-Alcohol (BrAC) Concentration are Also Reported

Country	Breath analyzer	BrAC limit	BAC Limit
Sweden[a]	Intoxilyzer 5000S	0.10 mg/L and 0.50 mg/L	0.20 and 1.00 mg/g
Finland[a]	Alcotest 7110	0.25 mg/L and 0.60 mg/L	0.50 and 1.20 mg/g
Norway	Intoxilyzer 5000N	0.25 mg/L	0.50 mg/g
Great Britain	Intoximeter 3000	35 µg/100 mL	80 mg/dL
	Camic Breath Analyzer		
Ireland	Not yet decided	35 µg/100 mL	80 mg/dL
Holland	DataMaster	220 µg/L	0.50 mg/mL
Austria	Alcomat	0.40 mg/L	0.80 mg/mL
France	Ethylométer 679T	0.25 mg/L	0.50 mg/mL
U.S.[b]	Breathalyzer 900	0.10 and 0.08 g/210 L	0.10 and 0.08 g/dL
	Intoxilyzer 5000		
	DataMaster		
	Intoximeter 3000		
Canada	Breathalyzer 900		
	Intoxilyzer 5000	0.08 g/210 L	80 mg/dL
Germany	Not yet decided	—	0.80 g/kg
Denmark	Not yet decided	—	0.80 mg/g

[a] *Sweden and Finland have a two tier legal limit with more severe penalties for a DUI suspect with a high BAC.*
[b] *In some U.S. states several different breath-alcohol instruments are approved for forensic purposes and the threshold limits of blood and breath alcohol concentration vary from state to state.*

although this problem is seemingly more common in older men, and some studies have detected as much as 25 mL of residual urine.[131] However, the impact of urine retention on the concentration of alcohol determined in successive voids and the magnitude of error incurred if the UAC is converted into presumed BAC has not been demonstrated experimentally.

Because some people might excrete glucose in their urine,[132] especially those suffering from diabetes mellitus,[133] there is always a risk that ethanol can be produced in-vitro through the fermentation of sugar by micro-organisms or yeasts infecting the bladder or urinary tract.[134,135] Some reports claim that ethanol can be produced in the bladder itself, so called bladder beer.[136] This makes it important to include chemical preservatives such as sodium or potassium fluoride at a concentration of at least 1% w/v or sodium azide in the collecting tubes to inhibit microbial synthesis of ethanol.[136,137] Storage of urine specimens in a refrigerator immediately after collection will also help to hinder the synthesis of alcohol through the action of candida albicans acting on glucose as substrate.[137]

Some new research findings have demonstrated that production of alcohol directly in the bladder or in the collecting tubes *in vitro* after sampling can be detected by measuring in the urine the concentration of 5-hydroxytryptophol (5HTOL), a minor metabolite of serotonin.[138] The concentration of 5HTOL increases in blood and urine during hepatic oxidation of ethanol, so a normal concentration of 5HTOL in urine and an elevated concentration of ethanol suggest that the alcohol was synthesized after voiding from the action of bacteria or yeasts on carbohydrate or other substrates.[139]

Alan Wayne Jones and Barry K. Logan

13.2.3 BLOOD SAMPLES

13.2.3.1 Use of Alcohol Swabs for Skin Disinfection

Blood specimens collected for alcohol analysis in traffic law enforcement are generally taken from an antecubital vein with the aid of sterile equipment such as evacuated tubes (Vacutainer) or disposable plastic syringe and needle. Preparation of the skin at the site of blood sampling with disinfectants such as ethanol (70% v/v) or isopropanol (70% v/v) should obviously be avoided if specimens are intended for clinical or forensic alcohol testing. Because sterile equipment is used, disinfection of the skin at the site of sampling is not really necessary and, instead, cleaning the skin with saline or soap and water is sufficient. Nevertheless, alleged contamination by ethanol or isopropanol in the swabs used to disinfect the skin is sometimes raised as a defense challenge in attempts to invalidate results of blood-alcohol analysis.[140,141] Note however that any method used for forensic alcohol analysis should be able to distinguish between ethanol and isopropanol.

Many studies have been done to evaluate the risk of carry-over of alcohol from the antiseptic used to swab the skin before the specimen of venous blood was taken for analysis.[142,143]

A classic example of giving the benefit of the doubt was demonstrated when several hundred convictions for DUI in Great Britain were deemed invalid and the sentences over-turned. This was felt necessary because the swabs normally issued with kits for blood-sampling from DUI suspects had been inadvertently switched to another brand which contained isopropanol.[144] The legal alcohol limit in UK is 35 µg/100 mL breath and if the result is between 40 and 50 µg/100 mL the suspect can opt to provide a blood sample instead and the BAC is then used as evidence for prosecution (threshold BAC = 80 mg/100 mL). Because of reported large discrepancies between BAC and BrAC in this kind of paired test, the swabs used to clean the skin before drawing blood became suspect. This suspicion was strengthened when the swabs were shown to contain alcohol (isopropanol). This led to an official investigation. The convictions of several hundred individuals who had pleaded guilty to DUI and had received their sentences were considered unsound and quashed. It appears that this decision was reached by the court of appeals because the integrity of the blood specimen was cast in doubt, and the defendants were not aware of this when they were asked to plead guilt or not guilty to DUI. This led to several controlled studies into the risk of carry-over of alcohol from the swabs used to disinfect the skin. The results however showed that contamination of the blood sample with various alcohols during venipuncture was highly unlikely and in most studies, only traces or no alcohol at all could be detected in the specimens.[145-149]

If evacuated tubes are used for sampling blood, then two tubes should be filled with blood in rapid succession and gently inverted several times to mix with the chemical preservatives. If some coagulation does occur, the sample should be homogenized prior to sampling to prevent inadvertent aliquoting of the serum fraction which would contain more alcohol than a specimen of whole blood. The chemical preservatives are typically sodium fluoride (NaF), which prevents glycolysis and inhibits certain enzymes and micro-organisms that might be present in the blood, and potassium oxalate which serves as an anticoagulant. These substances are already in the tubes as supplied by the manufacturer, although the necessity of having sodium fluoride in sterile Vacutainer tubes is open to discussion because contamination with bacteria can in reality only arise from the skin at the point of inserting the needle. Nevertheless, NaF should be included if only to prevent this defense challenge from being raised; the amount of NaF recommended for blood specimens taken from living subjects is 100 mg/10 mL blood (1% w/v). If the amount actually present is challenged then methods are available to assay blood samples for fluoride ions such as by using ion-sensitive electrodes or by other means.[150]

In the event that alcohol-containing swabs are used, the practice of always taking two tubes of blood for analysis has the advantage that any unusually large discrepancies in the results of BAC between the two tubes can be detected. If present, this might suggest carryover or some other problem. However, the studies from the UK cited above confirm several earlier reports which demonstrated that the risk of carryover of alcohol, even when 70% ethanol was used as an antiseptic is virtually non-existent.[149,151] Another safeguard when filling evacuated tubes with blood is to remove each tube from the collecting needle and holder before withdrawing the needle from the puncture site.[151]

The concentration of alcohol in stored blood samples decreases on storage at 4°C despite the inclusion of 1% w/v NaF as preservative.[152] The rate of loss of alcohol is only about 0.003 g/dL per month, and evidently occurs by a non-enzymatic oxidation reaction that involves oxyhemoglobin.[152,153] If blood specimens become contaminated with micro-organisms when the Vacutainer tubes are opened to remove aliquots for analysis, this can lead to a much more rapid disappearance of alcohol during storage compared with unopened tubes. It seems that various species of micro-organism utilize alcohol as a food.[140] Other considerations regarding specimen collection include filling the tube with as much blood as possible, to avoid having a large airspace. Volatiles including ethanol will accumulate in the headspace and will be lost when the tube is opened. In the event that a tube is opened and closed repeatedly, this could result in appreciable losses of alcohol.

The question of uptake of alcohol through the skin as a mode of entry into the body to produce elevated BAC has been raised as a defense challenge by people working with large volumes of solvents. In fact, the absorption of ethanol through the skin was investigated many years ago by Bowers et al.[154] in controlled experiments with several children and one adult. The legs of the test subjects were wrapped in cotton soaked in 200 mL of 95% ethanol and secured with rubber sheeting and sealed with adhesive tapes. Blood samples were taken before and at various times after this treatment but neither clinical signs of intoxication nor raised BAC were noted. It seems safe to conclude that no appreciable amounts of ethanol can accumulate in the body. BAC is not increased by absorption through intact skin.

13.2.3.2 Trauma and Intravenous Fluids

Drunk drivers are often involved in serious road-traffic accidents causing injury and sometimes death. Trauma resulting in massive losses of blood precipitate a hypovolemic shock and this requires swift emergency treatment. This might involve administering medication at the site of the accident such as pain killers and intravenous fluids to counteract shock and replace depleted body fluids. More intensive treatment can be given on arrival at a surgical emergency unit and it is usually at this point that a blood sample is taken for clinical and/or medicolegal purposes. The sampling of blood for analysis of alcohol in a critically injured patient requires considerable deliberation to safeguard the integrity of the patient and the specimen. Errors incurred in sampling blood from trauma patients are not uncommon, and they are beyond the control of the forensic laboratory.[155] Care is needed if intravenous fluids are administered as a first aid for treatment of shock, and it is important that the blood sample for alcohol analysis is not taken downstream from the same vein used for infusion. Otherwise, this can result in a marked dilution of the specimen and a decrease in the concentration of alcohol. If dilution of the specimen is suspected, this can sometimes be verified by determination of hemoglobin.[155]

Routinely analyzing aliquots of blood from two Vacutainer tubes that are filled in rapid succession furnishes a useful way to reveal discrepant results and problems associated with blood sampling. If the tube-to-tube difference in BAC exceeds that expected from knowledge of random analytical errors and past experiences, this points to other influences such as pre-analytical factors. Abnormally large differences in BAC between the two tubes can often be traced to dilution or coagulation of one or both of the samples because of inadequate mixing after collection. Note that the concentration of alcohol measured in plasma or serum will be higher than in whole blood by about 10 to 15% as discussed in detail elsewhere.[156]

13.2.3.3 Blood-Water Content and Hematocrit

The water content of whole blood is easily determined by weighing an aliquot and heating overnight at 105 to 110°C to reach a constant weight.[156] The change in weight after desiccation can be used to calculate the water content of the blood specimen. According to the scientific literature whole blood contains 85 g water per 100 mL (95% range 83.0 to 86.5 g/100 mL).[157] The specific gravity of blood is 1.055 so the water content is 5.5% less when expressed in mass/mass units; 85.0% w/v corresponds to 80.6 % w/w. [157] Women tend to have approximately 1 to 2% more water than men for the same volume of whole blood owing to loss of red cells during periods of menstruation.[158]

Whole blood is composed of a plasma fraction, red blood cells (erythrocytes), white blood cells (leukocytes), and platelets. Blood hematocrit is defined as the volume of packed cells per 100 mL of whole blood when expressed as a percentage. Normal values for hematocrit in men are 42 to 50% compared with 37 to 47% in women.[159] The red cells (erythrocytes) carry the hemoglobin and contain about 73 mL of water/100 mL cells whereas plasma contains 93 mL of water/100 mL plasma. Assuming a hematocrit of 40%, the water content of whole blood should be $(0.40 \times 73) + (0.60 \times 93)$ or 85 mL water/100 mL of whole blood. This value agrees well with gravimetric determinations of blood-water by desiccation when a mean 85.6% w/v was reported.[156] Because the red-cells contain so much water and the fact that alcohol distributes in blood according to the water content of the various components, it must be obvious that even fairly wide variations in hematocrit will not make much difference to the concentration of alcohol per unit volume of whole blood.

This was confirmed empirically when blood was prepared in-vitro with hematocrit values of 18, 31, 39, and 60.[160] The specimens were spiked with the same amount of ethanol to give a BAC of 0.212 g/dL and the actual concentration in each blood sample was determined by gas chromatography to be 0.211, 0.211, 0.207, and 0.208 g/dL respectively. Thus, no influence of varying hematocrit from 18 to 60 on the alcohol concentration in the whole blood.[160] However, if equilibrated headspace vapor above the same blood specimens had been analyzed, the specimen with lowest hematocrit (large plasma portion and more water per unit volume) would have had a lower headspace concentration of ethanol compared with the specimens with higher hematocrit (low plasma portion and therefore less water content per unit volume).[158] This follows because the concentration of alcohol in the vapor phase will be higher for the blood specimen with least water and therefore containing a higher concentration of alcohol per mL blood-water.[158]

A blood sample with abnormally low hematocrit means a low number of blood cells and also a low hemoglobin content, which might be associated with a patient suffering from anemia. The other extreme is polycythemia which is an over abundance of red cells per unit volume of blood and therefore an abnormally high hematocrit in this condition. The question of whether variations in hematocrit influence the maximum BAC reached from intake of a known amount of alcohol is difficult to answer because large changes in hematocrit are often associated with changes in the distribution of body water in general and therefore with an altered volume of distribution for ethanol. [161]

13.2.4 BREATH-ALCOHOL ANALYSIS

Historical developments in testing for alcohol intoxication by use of chemical analysis of blood or breath were recently reviewed.[162] Breath-tests for alcohol are currently used in forensic science practice and traffic law enforcement for two main purposes. The first and least

Table 13.2.2 Examples of the Most Commonly Used Hand-Held Breath-Alcohol Devices for Roadside Breath-Alcohol Screening Purposes and for Estimating the Coexisting Blood-Alcohol Concentration[a]

Breath-test instrument	Method of alcohol analysis	Manufacturer and country
Alcolmeter SD-2	Electrochemical oxidation	Lion Laboratories, UK
Alcolmeter SD-400	"	"
Alcotest 7410	Electrochemical oxidation	Dräger, Germany
Alcosensor III and IV	Electrochemical oxidation	Intoximeters Inc., U.S.
Alcodoose II	Infrared Absorption (9.5 µm)	Seres, France

[a]*To estimate BAC from BrAC, the breath analyzers must be pre-calibrated with a blood:breath conversion factor such as 2100:1 or 2300:1.*

controversial application involves roadside pre-arrest screening to furnish an objective indication of alcohol involvement and whether or not the driver might be above the critical legal limit for driving. In many situations, the police require probable cause before a chemical test for alcohol can be administered. This requires observations about the way the person was driving, and evidence of impairment from use of field-sobriety tests, which are important concerns before making an arrest and administering the chemical test for alcohol. Various hand-held devices are currently available for measuring breath-alcohol concentration at the roadside (Table 13.2.2). The most popular method of roadside breath testing involves the principle of electrochemical oxidation of alcohol with a fuel cell sensor and this technology is fairly selective because endogenous volatiles such as acetone and methane do not react with this kind of detector. However, if acetone is reduced in the body to isopropanol, this secondary alcohol is oxidized with the fuel cell sensor and can give a response which cannot be distinguished from ethanol. [163]

The results of roadside breath-testing might be displayed as colored lights such as pass (green), warn (yellow) or fail (red) or as a digital display of breath-alcohol concentration in units such as mg/L or g/210L depending on the particular jurisdiction (Table 13.2.1). If the screening test gives a positive response this indicates the driver has been drinking and may be over the legal limit which is sufficient probable cause to demand a specimen of blood or breath for evidential forensic analysis. The suspect is then taken to a police station where an evidential breath-alcohol test is conducted; examples of instruments used in various countries are given in Table 13.2.1. When properly calibrated and operated, the hand-held screening devices can be as accurate as any other breath test instrument. Some of the limitations of screening devices when used for quantitative evidential purposes include, the lack of protection they provide against interference from mouth alcohol, the lack of blank tests or calibration control tests, the fact that they can generate low results at low temperatures, and also that for some older devices (Alcosensor III, Alcolmeter SD-2) the results are operator dependent; releasing the button before the reading has stabilized will generate a low result. Breath-alcohol instruments used for quantitative evidential purposes are generally more sophisticated than the hand-held screening devices and provide a printed record of results with date, time, location of the test as well as computer-storage of results for generating statistical reports. Moreover, these devices ensure that end-expired breath is being sampled and that residual alcohol in the mouth from recently drinking or regurgitation has dissipated.

A critical element in performing an evidential breath-alcohol test is always to observe the suspect for at least 15 min before making the breath test. During this time he or she should not be allowed to drink, eat, smoke, or place anything in the mouth prior to completing the test. Moreover, a duplicate test should be made not less than 2 min and not more than 5 min after completion of the first test. The instrument calibration must be controlled in conjunction

Alan Wayne Jones and Barry K. Logan

with testing the subject and this is accomplished with a breath-alcohol simulator device or alcohol in compressed gas tanks. Analysis of the room-air provides a blank test result before and between making the duplicate tests with the subject. All these requirements have been described in detail elsewhere and are important for ensuring a successful evidential breath testing program, that will withstand scrutiny.[164] Regardless of these many new developments and improvements in the technology of breath-alcohol testing, challenges against the reliability of the results are far more common than against the results of blood-alcohol analysis. This probably stems from the fact that breath-testing is performed by police officers whereas blood-alcohol analysis is done at government laboratories by chemists some of whom have research experience or a Ph.D. degree. Furthermore, the blood sample is usually retained and can be re-tested if there is any doubt about the results, whereas breath samples are generally not preserved and therefore cannot be re-tested.

13.2.4.1 Mouth Alcohol and Use of Mouthwash Preparations

Even during the first studies of breath-alcohol analysis as a test for intoxication, it was emphasized that testing should not be conducted too soon after the last drink.[165] Thus, Emil Bogen in his landmark article, which was published in 1927, made the following statement;

> As soon as the disturbing factor of alcoholic liquor still in the mouth is removed, which occurs usually within fifteen minutes after imbibition, in the absence of hiccuping or belching, the alcoholic content of 2 liters of expired air was a little greater than 1 cc of urine

A multitude of studies have been done since the 1930s to confirm the importance of a 15-min deprivation period after the last drink even though this problem is sometimes rediscovered from time to time.[166] Most experiments on the influence of residual mouth alcohol on breath-test results have generally involved human subjects initially alcohol-free who are required to hold solutions of alcohol (40% v/v) in their mouths for 1 to 2 min without swallowing.[167,168] Immediately after expelling the alcohol, the test subject undergoes a series of breath tests at 1- to 2-min intervals for 20 to 30 min. The results show that within 15 to 20 min after ejecting a strong solution of alcohol from the mouth, the response of the breath-alcohol analyzer is always less than 0.01 g/210 L which is generally considered the threshold for baseline readings. Other study designs have involved measuring breath-alcohol in subjects after they drink alcohol to reach a certain BAC level.[169] After drinking more alcohol, breath-tests are made repeatedly until the results recover to the pre-drinking BrAC. Under these test conditions, the time needed to clear the residual alcohol from the mouth was even less than 10 min.[169]

Accordingly, on the basis of experiments such as these, rules and regulations for evidential breath-alcohol testing stipulate a 15 to 20 min observation period before conducting an evidential breath-alcohol test. During this time the suspect should not be allowed to smoke or drink or place any material in the mouth, and if he or she regurgitates or vomits, the observation period must be started again. Although a 15-min observation period is not mandated prior to conducting roadside breath-alcohol screening test, in practice, a considerably longer time will usually have elapsed since the last drink was taken, unless the drinking took place while the subject was driving. The time involved in stopping the vehicle, and contacting the driver, as well as any necessary field sobriety testing will usually take longer than 15 min. For reliable quantitative determinations however, the 15-min deprivation period should be observed and documented.

Many mouth-wash preparations contain alcohol as well as other organic solvents, and the concentrations of ethanol sometimes are as high as 50 to 60% v/v. Obviously the use of these materials prior to conducting a breath-alcohol test would produce similar disturbances on breath-test results as having alcoholic beverages in the mouth. Provided that the 15 to 20 min observation time is maintained, use of breath fresheners containing alcohol will not have any negative impact on the reliability of the test result. [170] However, if these preparations are intentionally or unintentionally consumed, this will be a source of alcohol just like drinking an alcoholic beverage. In a recent study with commercial mouthwash products; Listerine (29.6% alcohol), Scope (18.9% alcohol), and Lavoris (6.0% alcohol) tests were made on a breath-alcohol analyzer after rinsing the mouth with these preparations. Within 2 min of rinsing the mouth, breath-test results were as high as 240 mg/dL (expressed as BAC equivalent) but within 10 min this had dropped exponentially and was well below the threshold limits for driving (0.08 to 0.10 g/dL). By 15 min post-rinsing, the readings were below 0.01 g/dL. Similar results, namely no significant response with an infrared breath-alcohol analyzer were obtained 15 to 20 min or more after various mouthwashes, aftershave lotions, and perfumes in common use were tested in Germany. [171]

13.2.4.2 Regurgitation and Gastro Esophageal Reflux Disease (GERD)

The pioneer work by Bogen [165] indicated that hiccuping, burping, and belching might present a problem in connection with breath-alcohol analysis. Only very limited investigations of this problem have been made, but these indicate that the risk of elevating breath-alcohol readings is greatest shortly after the end of drinking as might be expected because the concentration of alcohol in the stomach is then at its highest.[172,173] A closely related problem is gastro-esophageal reflux disease (GERD).[174-177] Many people suffer from acid-reflux disorders, known as reflux esophagitis, whereby gastric secretions as well as other liquid contents erupt from the stomach into the esophagus and sometimes reach the mouth.[178-180] Indeed, this condition might be aggravated after drinking certain alcoholic beverages.[181,182] The impact of GERD on results of evidential breath-alcohol testing has not yet been investigated in any controlled studies. Nevertheless, this medical condition has been raised as a defense challenge from DUI suspects who maintain they experienced a reflux from the stomach into the mouth immediately prior to providing a breath-alcohol sample.[183] The higher the concentration of alcohol prevailing in the stomach during a reflux, the greater the risk of contaminating the breath-sample in a similar mechanism to the mouth-alcohol effect. From this follows the contention that GERD is the cause of a person's BrAC being above the legal limit for driving, and medical experts have testified to this effect which has led to the acquittal of a DUI suspect.[184] However, the validity of this defense argument was strongly questioned by another expert as being one of the least convincing and he also noted that the doctors appearing for the defense "ignored one of the basic maxims in the business" namely "what the subject says he has drunk is not evidence".[185]

Although most evidential breath test instruments feature "slope detection" to disclose the presence of mouth alcohol, in some cases these may not detect small contributions caused by belching or burping. A far better approach to counter the GERD defense challenge is always to observe the subject carefully, and to perform duplicate breath-alcohol analyses, that is two separate exhalations 2 to 3 min apart. [185] Obtaining close agreement between the two independent results speaks against the influence of regurgitation of stomach contents having a high concentration of alcohol just prior to making the first breath-test or between the first and the second test. Also the risk of GERD adding to the breath test results decreases as the time after ingestion of alcohol increases because of the ongoing absorption of alcohol from the stomach and the emptying of the stomach contents into the duodenum. Evidential breath-alcohol programs that require a single breath-alcohol test are out of date and should be abandoned especially if GERD is a recurring defense argument. The single chemical test for alcohol has no place in jurisdictions where per se statutes operate, regardless of whether blood or breath analysis is used for forensic purposes.

Alan Wayne Jones and Barry K. Logan

13.2.4.3 Dentures and Denture Adhesives

The question of whether people with dentures or individuals who might be fitted with special bridge-work where alcohol can be trapped has arisen as a possible cause of obtaining a falsely elevated breath-alcohol reading.[186,187] This challenge is therefore akin to having residual alcohol in the mouth from recent drinking. The empirical evidence supporting the notion that alcohol becomes trapped under denture plates or in other structures or cavities in the mouth for long periods of time is not very convincing, although a few isolated case reports support this defense argument.[188] A person suspected for DUI in the U.K. was acquitted when expert testimony raised a reasonable doubt about the validity of the evidential breath test performed using an Intoximeter 3000 breath alcohol analyzer, owing to alcohol allegedly being trapped in cavities in the mouth as a result of dental treatment.[186] However, the experiments and reasoning presented to support this defense argument were speculative, not very convincing, and were easy to fault.[187] An acquittal in a DUI case in the U.S. was obtained when expert evidence suggested that the breath-test results were suspect because of alcohol being absorbed by the particular kind of denture adhesive used by the defendant.[188]

The most convincing study appearing in a peer reviewed journal and dealing with breath-alcohol testing and the use of dentures involved the participation of 24 subjects.[189] They were tested under various conditions; with dentures intact, with dentures removed, and with dentures held loosely in place both with and without adhesives. The volunteers held 30 mL of 80 proof brandy in their mouths for 2 min without swallowing. After ejecting the alcohol, breath-alcohol tests were made with an Intoxilyzer 5000 instrument at regular intervals. After an elapsed time of 20 min, no results were above 0.01 g/210 L. [189] This argues convincingly against the idea of people who wear dentures obtaining falsely elevated breath-alcohol concentrations. The widely practiced deprivation period and observation time of 15 to 20 min seems adequate to eliminate the risk of mouth-alcohol invalidating results even in people with dentures.[190]

A recent report described experiments in a person with dentures who was suspected of DUI. The defendant alleged that the brand of denture adhesive used was responsible for the breath alcohol reading being above the legal limit of 0.10 g/210L breath.[188] In one set of tests with a Breathalyzer model 900, which is not equipped with a slope detector, prolonged retention of alcohol was observed remarkably for several hours after 86 proof whisky was held in the mouth and when a certain brand of dental adhesive was used. These results suggest that some kinds of denture adhesives might retain alcohol for longer and lead to false high breath-alcohol readings. However, no corroborative reports of this have been published, and more controlled studies are necessary making use of duplicate measurements of blood and breath-alcohol concentration, weaker solutions of ethanol, and monitoring the shape of the BrAC exhalation profile in order to substantiate these surprising observations and conclusions.

Many of the latest generation of breath-alcohol analyzers used for evidential purposes are equipped with a slope-detector mechanism which is designed to monitor the time-course of BrAC during a prolonged exhalation.[191,192] If the BrAC is higher at the start of an exhalation compared with at the end of the exhalation this causes a negative slope and suggests a possible mouth alcohol effect or perhaps regurgitation of stomach contents or GERD. More work is necessary to evaluate the effectiveness of the slope detectors fitted to evidential breath-alcohol analyzers over a wide range of concentration of alcohol in the mouth, and at various times after the end of drinking.

13.2.4.4 Alleged Interfering Substances in Breath

The alleged response of breath-alcohol instruments to interfering substances is a common DUI defense argument in many countries.[193] The interferents in question are either claimed to have been produced naturally in the body, so called endogenous breath volatiles, or volatile organic compounds (VOC) inhaled with the ambient air during occupational exposure. The question of whether substances other than ethanol give a response on evidential breath-alcohol instruments escalated dramatically in the early 1970s after infra-red absorptiometry started to become the technology of choice for evidential purposes.[194] Hitherto, the Breathalyzer model 900 dominated the field of breath-alcohol testing in the U.S. and this device incorporates wet-chemistry oxidation with photometric endpoint for determination of BrAC.[195] Although this represents a non-specific chemical oxidation reaction for the analysis of alcohol, provided the galvanometer on the Breathalyzer was read after exactly 90 seconds as per the instructions, the presence of acetone, toluene and other substances in the breath do not present a serious interference problem.[196,197] Most infrared evidential breath alcohol devices provide some control for the presence of interfering substances with the use of either multiple filters, or dual technology, such as electrochemical oxidation in conjunction with infrared.

13.2.4.4.1 Endogenous Breath Volatiles

Human expired air consists of a mixture of gases including oxygen, nitrogen, carbon dioxide, water vapor and in extremely small amounts a multitude of volatile organic compounds (VOCs).[198-200] The major endogenous breath volatiles are acetone, methane, and the unsaturated hydrocarbon isoprene (2-methyl-1,3-butadiene).[201-204] The concentration of acetone expelled in breath is usually between 0.5 and 5 µg/L but this can increase appreciably if a person is deprived of food or engages in a prolonged fast.[205] Moreover, during ketoacidosis a condition often associated with hyperglycemia or diabetes mellitus or alcohol withdrawal, the concentration of ketone bodies (acetone, acetoacetate and beta-hydroxybutyrate) circulating in the blood increases appreciably along with the concentration of acetone expelled in the breath.[205-208]

The question of whether VOCs other than ethanol might interfere with the results of evidential breath-alcohol testing started to become an issue of debate and concern shortly after the first Intoxilyzer instrument, a single wavelength (3.4 µm) analyzer, appeared for use in law enforcement.[194] The Intoxilyzer measures the C-H bond stretching and vibrational frequencies in ethanol molecules, which means that abnormally high concentrations of acetone (blood/air distribution ratio approximately 300:1) in breath becomes a major candidate as an interfering substance. However, this problem was quickly solved by monitoring the absorption of infrared radiation at two wavelengths such as 3.39 and 3.48 µm as currently used with the Intoxilyzer 5000.[193] Another approach to enhance selectivity is to incorporate two independent methods of analysis such as IR and electrochemical oxidation in the same unit as used with the Alcotest 7110.[209]

When properly adjusted, the Intoxilyzer 5000 instrument corrects the ethanol signal for the presence of acetone in the breath. Moreover, if the concentration of breath-acetone exceeds 300 to 600 µg/L, corresponding to a blood concentration of 0.009 to 0.018 g/dL, the imbalance between the two filter signals exceeds a pre-set threshold value and the evidential test is aborted.[193] The instrument reports an interferant detected and the "apparent ethanol" concentration is stored in an internal memory of the software. If very high concentrations of acetone are present in the blood, this ketone can be reduced by alcohol dehydrogenase in the liver to produce isopropanol which also absorbs infrared radiation at the wavelengths used and can masquerade as ethanol.[163] Methanol, which has highly toxic metabolites, presents a special problem if high concentrations are present in blood and breath because infrared breath-alcohol analyzers cannot easily distinguishing this one-carbon alcohol from ethanol if only two infrared wavelengths are used. The potential for methanol interfering with a breath test can best be addressed by a consideration of its toxicological properties.[94]

Isoprene is another endogenous VOC expelled in the breath. In experiments with 16 healthy subjects, the breath isoprene concentration ranged from 0.11 to 0.70 µg/L as determined by thermal desorption gas chromatography and UV detection. [201] These concentrations are much too low to interfere with the measurement of breath-alcohol with the infrared technology currently used for evidential purposes. Methane is produced in the gut by the action of colonic bacteria on disaccharides and this VOC can be detected in human expired air. It seems that some individuals are more prone than others to generate methane in the large intestine and the concentration of this hydrocarbon expelled in breath under different conditions requires more documentation.[204] Methane should perhaps be considered as a potential interfering substance in connection with forensic breath-alcohol testing by infrared methods, but more research is necessary on this topic before raising an alarm.[203]

Acetaldehyde is a VOC produced during the metabolism of ethanol by all known enzymatic pathways and is also a major constituent of cigarette smoke. The high volatility and low blood/air partition coefficient of acetaldehyde (190:1), means that this substance crosses the alveolar-capillary membrane of the lungs and enters the breath.[210] Because acetaldehyde absorbs IR radiation in the same region as ethanol (3.4 to 3.5 µm) this VOC might be considered a potential interfering substances in connection with evidential breath-alcohol testing. This problem was investigated empirically in tests with a single wavelength (3.39 µm) infrared analyzer under conditions when abnormally high concentrations of breath-acetaldehyde (50 µg/L) existed.[211] This was accomplished by inhibiting the metabolism of acetaldehyde by pretreatment of subjects with Antabuse-like drugs before they drank alcohol. Even under these extreme conditions, no false-high apparent ethanol readings were obtained. In recent reviews of the biomedical alcohol research literature, it seems that the concentrations of acetaldehyde in blood are so low during oxidation of ethanol (< 88 µg/L corresponding to 0.46 µg/L in breath) that this metabolite of ethanol cannot be seriously considered an interfering VOC when testing drunk drivers with the aid of infrared analyzers.[210,212]

13.2.4.4.2 Occupational Exposure to Organic Solvents

A few studies have dealt with the response of infrared breath-alcohol instruments after occupational exposure to solvent vapors, although no convincing evidence of an interference problem has emerged, provided that at least 20 min elapses after leaving the work environment.[213] In an effort to investigate the claims from two convicted drunk drivers that inhalation of solvents causes false high readings on an infrared breath-alcohol instrument, the men volunteered to spray cars with toluene/xylene/methanol based paint thinner under extreme working conditions and without the use of protective clothing or face masks.[214] They worked for several hours in a small poorly ventilated room making use of 5 to 7 liters of paint during the time. It was noted that their eyes were watering and they were suffering from severe irritation coughing regularly and complaining of sore throats. Tests with one of the subjects gave measurable apparent ethanol responses during the exposure. Results with an infrared breath analyzer (Intoximeter 3000) were consistently higher than those obtained with an electrochemical instrument (Alcolmeter S-D2). At times of 0 min, 15 min, and 30 min after leaving the small working environment, one subject gave BrAC results of 0.019, 0.010, and 0.002 g/210 L on the IR analyzer. The lack of any instrument responses for the other subject was explained by a considerably lower environmental temperature on the day of the testing, and this presumably led to a less efficient vaporization of the solvents.

Inhalation of gasoline fumes as might occur if a person sniffs this liquid or engages in siphoning gasoline between cars can cause falsely-elevated readings on the Intoxilyzer 5000.[215,216] In an actual DUI case scenario, the Intoxilyzer reacted by aborting the test because an interfering substance or substances were detected.[193] Gasoline contains among other things, a complex mixture of aliphatic and aromatic hydrocarbons and these were also qualitatively identified in a blood sample taken from the suspect whose blood-alcohol concentration was zero. Abuse of organic solvents such as thinner or glue is another source of interfering substances in connection with evidential breath-alcohol testing.[217] People who abuse these materials often tend to smell of the solvents they inhale, and may display characteristic symptoms of intoxication. If there is evidence to suggest solvent abuse, or extended exposure to solvent fumes, arrangements should be made for obtaining blood samples instead.

Diethyl ether is another solvent capable of interfering with the response of dual wavelength infrared breath-alcohol instruments and being mistakenly reported as ethanol.[218] This solvent is no longer widely used in industry or hospitals, so the risk of being exposed to ether in everyday life is not very high, although it is present in carburetor or starting fluid. Several other case reports have appeared suggesting that work-related inhalation of toluene and lacquer fumes in conjunction with normal occupational exposure gives readings on IR analyzers exceeding 0.10 g/210L.[219,220] However the test subject who had been apprehended for DUI sometimes showed behavioral manifestations of solvent inhalation or abuse and was chronically exposed to these agents over a period of many years so accumulation of toluene in body fat depots cannot be excluded. Some drunk drivers use technical spirits for intoxication purposes and these solvents contain ethanol, methanol, methyl ethyl ketone, ethyl acetate, isopropanol as well as other VOCs. These substances absorb IR radiation and can be mistakenly identified as ethanol with some IR breath-alcohol analyzers.[221] By comparing the results from a pre-arrest roadside test utilizing an electrochemical sensor for ethanol determination, with the results from infrared evidential analyzers, information can be gleaned about the presence of an interfering substance. The two detector systems (IR and Fuel cell) respond differently to different VOCs in the breath; electrochemical sensors don't respond to acetone or hydrocarbons.[222,223]

A comprehensive series of experiments on the subject of evidential breath-alcohol testing and the response to organic solvents was made in the UK, where two infrared analyzers have been used for legal purposes since 1983 (Intoximeter 3000 and Camic). [224-226] Human volunteers were exposed on different occasions to toluene, 1,1,1-trichlorethane, butane, white spirit, and nonane under controlled conditions, and blood and breath were sampled at regular intervals after ending the exposure. The volunteers were in a resting position talking and playing cards during a 4-h period of exposure to the solvents at concentrations close to the upper limits prescribed for the workplaces in UK. After inhalation of butane vapor a response was seen on the infrared breath analyzers lasting for 1 to 5 min after exposure, before rapidly declining to zero.[224] Exposure to toluene and 1,1,1-trichloroethane did not give any response on the IR analyzers although these substances were identified in blood samples for up to 8 h after exposure ended.[224] The concentration of the solvents in blood and breath decreased rapidly on ending the exposure, which supports the conclusion that normal occupational use of solvents would be unlikely to contribute to false high results on IR breath-alcohol analyzers. Similar negative impact on evidential breath-test results were reported after inhalation of nonane and white spirit.[225]

Elevation of blood and breath-alcohol concentrations as a result of inhalation of ethanol vapors by brewery or distillery workers or industrial workers required to handle ethanol-based solvents has been a recurring argument in DUI trials.[227] One of the first controlled studies was done in 1951 with subjects being exposed to varying concentrations of ethanol vapor for up to 6 h.[227] The results showed that alcohol could be absorbed into the blood by inhalation through the lungs, and that the BAC attained was proportional to the concentration of ethanol in the inhaled air and the rate of ventilation. However, extreme conditions were necessary to build-up a BAC exceeding 0.01 g/dL, and the methods of blood and breath-alcohol analysis were fairly primitive.[227] Note that between 6 to 8 g of ethanol can be metabolized per hour so uptake by inhalation and absorption through the lungs must exceed this amount before blood-alcohol will increase above base-line levels. Moreover, it was noted that inhalation of air-alcohol concentrations of 10 to 20 mg/L caused coughing and smarting of the eyes and nose. Untoward effects were more pronounced at concentrations of 30 mg/L, and at 40 mg/L the situation was barely tolerable, making it impossible to remain in this atmosphere for any length of time.

Several more recent studies have looked in theory and practice at the reality of generating an elevated BAC from inhalation of ethanol vapor.[228-230] From these experiments we conclude that obtaining a BAC exceeding 0.003-0.005 g/dL is highly unlikely as a result of normal occupational exposure owing to the metabolism of ethanol that occurs during and immediately after ending the exposure.[231] However, if a person already has an elevated BAC before entering an atmosphere with a very high alcohol vapor concentration (simply sitting in a bar is not sufficient!), then the metabolism of alcohol and clearance of BAC might be inhibited during the inhalation period. This would lead to a shallower ß-slope than expected if the intake of alcohol by inhalation is sufficient to balance the amount eliminated by metabolism.[232] In short, caution should be exercised in interpreting breath test results from subjects with extensive solvent exposure immediately prior to the breath test. Most solvents are rapidly distributed and eliminated following environmental exposure. There is no evidence that casual exposure to solvents or solvent containing compounds will exert an effect on an evidential breath test administered an hour or more later.

13.2.4.5 Variability in the Blood/Breath Alcohol Ratio

Historically, the first breath-alcohol instruments were developed and used as an indirect way of measuring a person's blood alcohol concentration. Breath-testing was considered more practical than blood-testing for traffic-law enforcement purposes,[162] because of the noninvasive sampling technique and the fact that an immediate indication of the person's blood-alcohol concentration and state of inebriation were obtained.[233] Conversion of a measured BrAC into the expected BAC was accomplished by calibrating the breath-analyzers with a constant factor (2100:1) which was known as the blood/breath ratio of alcohol. The figure of 2100:1 had been determined empirically by equilibration of blood and air at constant temperatures *in vitro* and also *in vivo* by taking samples of breath and venous blood at nearly the same time from a large number of volunteer subjects.[234,235] In the post-absorptive phase of alcohol metabolism, studies showed that the blood/breath ratio of alcohol was approximately 2100:1, and this figure was subsequently endorsed by several meetings of experts with international represen-tation.[162] However, the blood/breath ratio is not a constant for all individuals and varies within the same individual from time to time and during different phases of alcohol metabolism.[236] This variability needs to be considered when the results of breath-alcohol testing are used in criminal litigation to estimate a person's blood-alcohol concentration.

All analytical results have inherent uncertainty, resulting from a combination of human error, systematic errors in calibration, random instrument error, etc. In a forensic context, the extent of any error should be known by analysis of appropriate standards and controls, and the contribution of error or uncertainty in the measurement should be considered when the result is interpreted. When measurements are being made of dynamic systems, such as human breath samples, further biological variation outside of the control of the analyst is introduced. The inherent variability in the blood/breath alcohol ratio among different individuals is an excellent example of this, and has emerged as a hot topic of discussion and debate in the scientific literature and in the courts.[17-22]

For many years, the results of breath-alcohol analysis in law enforcement were overshad-owed by inherent variations in blood/breath ratio and allegations that BAC had been overestimated by use of breath-test instruments. Obtaining an estimated BAC that was too high was more likely during the absorption phase, when BAC was still rising, because of the existence of arterial-venous (A-V) differences in alcohol concentration. The time course of breath-alcohol concentration follows more closely the arterial BAC than the venous BAC, with the arterial BAC exceeding the venous during the absorptive phase, and vice versa during the elimination phase. Moreover, the 2100:1 ratio was originally determined by comparing venous BAC and BrAC in samples taken during the post-absorptive phase of alcohol metabolism when A-V differences are small or negligible.[234] The actual blood/breath conversion factor is clearly a moving target, and its value depends on many factors that are impossible to known or control in any individual subject at the time of testing. Several more recent studies comparing blood and breath-alcohol in DUI suspects show that in-the-field, the blood/breath ratio is closer to 2400:1 with a 95% range from 1900 to 2900, indicating a strong bias in favor of the suspect being breath-tested in comparison with the same person providing a specimen of blood for analysis at a forensic laboratory.[237-240]

In an attempt to quell much of the troublesome debate that was erupting over the continued use of a constant blood/breath ratio, experts in the field of chemical tests for intoxication met to discuss the scientific and legal issues involved. The fruits of this meeting came in the form of a signed statement endorsing the continued use of the 2100:1 ratio for clinical and forensic purposes. Several new studies had shown that the 2100:1 ratio gives a generous margin of safety in favor of the subject by about 10% compared with BAC analyzed directly.[241,242] In controlled laboratory studies, with blood and breath samples taken during the post-absorptive phase of alcohol metabolism, a blood/breath ratio of 2300:1 was more appropriate to give unbiased estimates of venous BAC.[241] To eliminate the entire problem of variability in the blood/breath ratio and the need to convert BrAC to BAC, Mason and Dubowski suggested that the threshold alcohol limit for driving should be defined in terms of the person's BrAC at the time of the test.[242] This approach was clearly similar to the use of UACs in Great Britain, where the statutory limits for motorists are 80 mg/dL in blood or 107 mg/dL in urine, which implies a UAC/BAC of 1.33:1.[14] Because a blood-alcohol concentration limit of 0.10 g/dL was already widely accepted in the U.S., the corresponding threshold BrAC limit was set at 0.10 g/210 liters of breath. By including the 210 liters in the wording of the statute, the weight of alcohol (0.10 g) remained the same regardless of whether blood or breath-alcohol were used for analysis. Much is often made over these units given the fact that 210 L is a larger volume than any human could exhale. This is clearly a spurious issue however, since only a portion of the breath (typically around 50 mL) is being tested, and the units used are g/210L. The results could equally well be expressed in μg/L, mg/mL, micromoles per liter, or any other concentration units. Any units can be used, provided that the instrument is calibrated with the appropriate standards, having concentrations of alcohol similar to the unknown breath samples.

Accordingly, a person's BAC or BrAC are now considered equivalent for the purpose of generating evidence of impairment at the wheel. Eliminating the need to convert BrAC into BAC in every single case led to a dramatic reduction in spurious litigation concerning blood/breath ratios of alcohol and inherent variability. Furthermore, the effects of alcohol on psychomotor performance, as well as roadside surveys of the risk of involvement in traffic accidents, have been conducted with breath-test instruments (e.g., the Grand Rapids survey) and not by the analysis of BAC directly. However, several U.S. states, among others New Jersey, still persist in translating the breath-alcohol readings into a presumed BAC. Indeed, the use of breath-alcohol testing was the subject of a vigorous defense challenge in 1989 in the State of New Jersey, where the Breathalyzer was well established for testing drinking drivers. The DUI statute in New Jersey stipulated that a person's blood-alcohol concentration should be estimated indirectly by analysis of the breath. The gist of the defense argument was that the

2100:1 blood/breath ratio was biased against the person being tested. Considerable expert testimony was called to answer questions about variation in the blood/breath conversion factor used. This "Downie case" was eventually settled by the supreme court of New Jersey ruling in favor of the continued use of the Breathalyzer 900 in law enforcement and also keeping the 2100:1 conversion factor unchanged. The bulk of the expert testimony and the most credible witnesses took the stance that breath-tests involving a 2100:1 ratio tended to underestimate the venous blood-alcohol concentration for samples taken in the post-absorptive phase of alcohol metabolism and when results are truncated to two decimal places.

When the countries in Europe introduced evidential breath-alcohol testing in the early 1980s, the threshold BrAC limits were derived from the pre-existing BAC limits on the basis of a presumed blood/breath ratio, either 2000:1, 2100:1, or 2300:1 depending on the country. Thus, 0.50 mg/mL, which is the statutory BAC limit in the Netherlands, became 220 μg/L in breath, being derived from $0.50/2300 = 0.000217$ and rounding to 0.00022, before moving the decimal point to obtain appropriate units. The threshold BrAC limits corresponding to already established BAC limits in different countries are shown in Table 13.2.1.

13.2.4.6 Pulmonary Function (Chronic Obstructive Pulmonary Disease)

The basic premise of breath-alcohol testing is that the concentration of alcohol in pulmonary capillary blood equilibrates with alveolar air at normal body temperature.[243] However, the air in the upper airways and dead-space regions of the lungs also contains alcohol by a diffusion process from the mucous membranes receiving alcohol from blood supplying the tissue in the upper respiratory tract. Furthermore, alcohol from the upper respiratory tract may be picked up in the inspired air and deposited further down the tract during inspiration, only to be redistributed again during expiration, with some of the alveolar alcohol being deposited back into the depleted tissues of the upper airways.[244] The net effect is that the alcohol which appears on the expired breath does so as a result of a complex dynamic process, that varies in degree from individual to individual. As indicted in the previous section, however, where the law specifies a BrAC per se offense, the actual mechanism is not relevant, and the per se BrAC offense is readily justified in terms of impairment associated with BrAC.

Modern breath-alcohol instruments are equipped with automated procedures for sampling breath and these monitor the volume exhaled and the concentration of alcohol during a prolonged exhalation. If a person manages to exhale a certain minimum volume of breath for a given length of time to satisfy the sampling requirements, a portion of the end-expired air is captured for analysis of alcohol. Some individuals, particularly those with impaired lung function, will genuinely be unable to satisfy the sampling parameters of some evidential breath-alcohol analyzers currently being used.[245,246] Indeed, even subjects with healthy lungs, especially women of small stature and those who habitually smoke cigarettes, might have insufficient lung capacity to exhale for the minimum required time. Moreover, at high blood-alcohol concentration, the ability of a person to provide an approved sample of breath might be reduced compared with the sober state.[247]

The rules and regulations pertaining to evidential breath-alcohol testing should therefore contain an option for the suspect to provide a blood sample if he or she fails to satisfy the sampling requirements because of pulmonary limitations. In Great Britain, where the Intoximeter 3000 is used for legal purposes, the policeman operating the instrument has to decide whether the suspect is not cooperating properly in providing the required sample. If this happens, the person can be charged with "failing to provide", as a separate offense which carries the same punishment as if the BrAC had been above the legal limit for driving.[14,245] Many people charged and prosecuted for "failing to provide" in the UK have later been vindicated by seeking medical advice and undergoing pulmonary function tests.[248,249] This prompted the British Home Office scientists to embark on a series of studies into the ability of people with small stature and impaired lung function to satisfy the sampling requirements of various breath-alcohol testing instruments.[245,250] Those individuals with forced expiratory volume in one second ($FEV_{1.0}$) of less than 2.0 liters and forced vital capacity (FVC) of less than 2.6 liters were unable to use some of the breath-testing equipment evaluated. In another study with healthy subjects less than 5 ft 5 in. (165 cm) tall, some were unable to provide the required breath sample.[250] This report however fails to specify the ages of the subjects, whether they were tested under the influence of alcohol, and whether they smoked cigarettes. These variables are important when the ability of a person to provide an approved breath sample has to be judged.

Asthma is an inflammatory disease of the airways causing obstruction to breathing and a reduction in air flow. Respiratory inhalers used by asthmatics contain salbutamol (β_2-adrenergic bronchodilator) as the active ingredient. It is the mainstay treatment for acute attacks of asthma. The use of this inhaled medication just prior to being breath-tested with Intoximeter 3000 (infrared) and Alcolmeter S-D2 (electrochemistry) failed to produce a response of apparent alcohol.[251] A similar lack of response was reported for a number of nasal sprays used by people with impaired lung function.[252] Some asthma inhalers contain ethanol as an ingredient and this means that a response is more likely to occur immediately after their use. However, within 2 to 9 min after using a wide range of inhalers and sprays, the small positive response on the breath analyzers was eliminated. [253]

To test the influence of chronic obstructive pulmonary disease (COPD) on breath-alcohol analysis, patients suffering from COPD received 60 to 70 g ethanol and their blood-alcohol concentration was compared with results using the Breathalyzer model 900 at various times after drinking. The resulting blood/breath ratios were consistently higher than the 2100:1 calibration factor used with the Breathalyzer 900 instrument so breath-tests for alcohol are not detrimental to those individuals who suffer from COPD.[254] In a more recent study with 12 COPD patients as well as an age matched control group of subjects, alcohol (0.60 g/kg) was given by intravenous infusion and blood and breath-alcohol concentrations were determined for up to 4 h.[255] The blood/breath ratios of alcohol in the control group and patients with COPD varied with time after infusion of alcohol and in the post-peak phase of metabolism of alcohol, the values were mostly in excess of 2400:1.[255]

Summing-up these experiments in patients with pulmonary disease, there is no solid evidence to suggest that impaired lung function (asthma, COPD, emphysema) puts them at risk of being unfairly prosecuted for drunk driving when per se limits operate.[256,257] If people with these pulmonary limitations manage to provide an approved breath sample, there is no reason to believe that the test result will be greater than for people with healthy lungs having the same blood-alcohol concentration. On the contrary, because of the higher blood/breath ratios in people suffering from COPD compared with age-matched control subjects, those with COPD who might be breath-tested have an advantage.[255]

13.2.4.7 Breathing Pattern and Hypo- and Hyperthermia

For a given individual, the concentration of alcohol expelled in the breath depends on the concentration existing in the pulmonary blood, which depends on the amount of alcohol consumed and the time after drinking when breath-tests are made.[243] However, the concentration of alcohol measured in the breath at a given blood-alcohol concentration depends on numerous factors, especially the person's pattern of breathing prior to exhalation and core body temperature. Also, various design features of the breath-alcohol analyzer such as the resistance to exhalation and the geometry of the breath-inlet tube and also the kind of mouthpiece and spit-trap fitted to the instrument are important to consider when variations in test results have to be explained.[258-260]

The influence of a person's breathing pattern prior to exhalation has been evaluated in several studies and variables such as breath-holding, hyper- and hypo-ventilation, as well as shallow breathing were investigated.[258] Most changes in the pre-exhalation maneuver decrease the BrAC in the final exhalation compared with a control sample comprising a moderately deep inhalation and forced end-exhalation. However, breath-holding or hypo-ventilation before providing breath for analysis increases the concentration of alcohol in the breath-sample by about 10 to 20%.[261,262] This higher BrAC is caused in part by a higher breath temperature and the longer time available for equilibration of alcohol with the mucous surfaces in the upper airways.[263] Body temperature has an important influence on BrAC because the temperature coefficient of alcohol solubility is ± 6.5% per degree centigrade.[264] Local cooling of the mouth and upper-airway by breathing cold air will decrease breath-temperature and breath-alcohol concentration.[265] Keeping ice in the mouth before and during exhalation leads to a marked lowering in the person's BrAC, in part because of the high solubility of alcohol in water condensing from the ice, and condensation of ethanol vapor in the mouth.[266] Isothermal re-breathing devices have been described for use with breath alcohol equipment.[267] The net effect of this device is to allow equilibriation of alcohol with all the tissues in the respiratory tract, thus raising the breath test result by about 10%, and showing a closer agreement to the blood alcohol result when a blood/breath ratio of 2100:1 is assumed.[267]

Controlled studies of the influence of hypo- and hyperthermia on breath-alcohol test results with Breathalyzer model 900 were reported by Fox and Hayward.[268,269] The deep-core body temperature was raised by keeping volunteer subjects immersed up to their necks in water at 42 °C for 45 min. This caused a 2.5°C rise in body temperature and a 23% distortion (increase) in the breath-alcohol concentration. Immersion of the subjects up to the neck in cold water at 10°C for 45 min caused mild hypothermia and the breath-alcohol concentration decay curve was distorted downwards by 22%. When subjects were returned to normothermic conditions, the BrAC readings recovered to reach the values expected from past experience with the Breathalyzer 900, that is, results were about 10% less than the corresponding blood-alcohol concentration directly determined.

13.2.5 CONCLUDING REMARKS

The widespread use of statutory alcohol concentration limits for motorists simplifies the prosecution of drunken drivers and makes this process more effective. Accordingly, a person's blood or breath-alcohol concentration has become the single most important evidence for successfully prosecuting DUI suspects. It should however always be considered in the context of other evidence, such as observations about the subject's driving ability, outward behavior and response to questions and performance in field sobriety tests. This has meant that defense arguments focus heavily on trying to discredit and cast doubt on the reliability of the result of analyzing alcohol in blood and/or breath. Of the two, it seems that results of measuring blood-alcohol are much less frequently questioned than those obtained by analyzing the breath. This probably stems from the earlier tradition of translating a measured BrAC into a presumed BAC for forensic purposes. The magnitude of variation in the conversion factor (blood/breath ratio) from person to person and in the same person over time triggered many defense challenges, which still persist today. The uncertainty in the sampling and analysis of breath and the conversion factors used have attracted much debate in the scientific literature and in the courts. The entire problem with blood/breath ratios should have been eliminated after defining the statutory alcohol limits for driving as the BrAC per se and thus sidestepping the need to convert BrAC into BAC.

Furthermore, mostly under the control of a built-in microprocessor, evidential breath-alcohol instruments are typically operated by police officers and not by chemists. This apparent vested interest in the outcome of the test result tends to make breath-alcohol testing more suspect according to some critics, and vulnerable to defense attacks compared with blood alcohol measurements performed at a forensic laboratory. Much could be done to improve forensic alcohol analysis by paying more attention to pre-analytical factors, in particular the methods and procedures used to obtain samples of body fluids (blood, breath, or urine). The responsibility for sampling, transport, and initial storage of specimens is usually in the hands of the police and other personnel who lack training in clinical laboratory methods.[270] The use of a checklist to document certain key aspects of the sampling protocol and the various precautions taken is highly recommended.[271] Any mishaps or unusual incidents that occur during sampling, as well as the behavior and appearance of the suspect, should be carefully noted. These might become important later when the results of alcohol analysis are interpreted by the court.

The trend towards accreditation of clinical and forensic laboratories will help to standardize and document analytical procedures and establish acceptable standards of performance that minimize the risk of laboratory blunders. Forensic tests for alcohol, however, should always be held to a high standard, and where there is error, mistakes, or uncertainty, this should be honestly recognized and accrue to the defendants favor. As long as there is a lot of money to be made in defending drunk drivers, or testifying on their behalf, there will always be lawyers and expert witnesses prepared to embark on crusades to discredit the police, the laboratory or both. To focus an attack on the scientific background of forensic alcohol testing a defense lawyer requires the services of an expert witness.[272] There are plenty of these individuals available, many of whom can be located through professional directory listings of their names, addresses, academic qualifications, experience, and often their fee. Most of these experts are willing to testify for the defense, the prosecution, or both and will generally testify in either criminal or civil litigation.

During the highly publicized Daubert decision from the U.S. Supreme court, much was written about the use of scientific evidence and how best to judge the testimony of expert witnesses.[273] At about this time, an editorial in the scientific journal *Nature* made the following statement about expert witnesses:[274]

> The so-called expert witness in court may be a hired-gun, willing to testify to anything for a fee, or a crackpot whose insupportable ideas are masked by an advanced degree (Ph.D.) often from a respectable university.

William S. Lovell (chemist and district attorney) made the following observation about the use and abuse of expert testimony in DUI litigation as long ago as 1972. [275]

> Courts are indeed plagued by the instant expert, who whether out of a misguided eagerness to earn his fee or an overreaction to his own self-described credentials, may expound far reaching opinions.

The courtroom can be a cruel place and skillful use of expert testimony plays a much bigger role in deciding the outcome of DUI trials held in the U.S. and Britain than in continental Europe. In Britain and the U.S., the adversarial system of justice operates, which aims to establish the truth by probing the strengths and weaknesses of defense and prosecution cases.[276] This opens the door for selecting expert witnesses known for their strong opinions and outspoken views about key elements of the scientific evidence crucial for the case. This is somewhat different from the situation in continental Europe and Scandinavia where the inquisitorial system operates and an investigating judge or judges appoint the necessary forensic experts who conduct tests and make investigations independent of the prosecution.[277,278] This gives the impression that forensic experts evaluate the scientific evidence in a more impartial way and arrive at an opinion based on their findings. This takes the form of a written report to the court, similar to a deposition, but occasionally the expert is also expected to appear in person to present his conclusions and receive questioning from the defense and prosecution attorney.

As far as possible, expert witnesses should base their testimony on personal experience and studies they have conducted themselves and the results of which have been published in the peer-reviewed literature. But even peer-reviewers make mistakes and publication per se does not make the results gospel. Scientists are not infallible and unsubstantiated opinion is no substitute for personal experience and well designed experiments. If scientific evidence is important in criminal or civil litigation, it might be better for the judge to appoint suitably qualified experts instead of relying on witnesses chosen by the opposing sides.[279] This was one of the recommendations of the Daubert decision of the U.S. Supreme Court, and has already been put into practice in Oregon, in a case concerning the health hazards of silicone breast implants.[280] Unfortunately, the demeanor and manner of the witness often determines whether or not the evidence they present is accepted by the jury, rather than the validity of the science on which the opinion is based.[281] Complex scientific issues can usually not be satisfactorily discussed and debated in the courtroom by lawyers posing set-piece questions to expert witnesses, many of whom have poor or inappropriate qualifications and questionable motives.[281, 282] Other complicating factors are that the attorneys are often prepared to use any available means, including confusing the jury, obfuscating the issues, and impugning the expert testimony, in order to gain an acquittal, rather than pursuing an objective search for the truth.

REFERENCES

1. Heise, H.A., Alcohol and automobile accidents. *JAMA* 103, 739, 1934.
2. Heise, H.A., Halporn, B., Medicolegal aspects of drunkenness. *Penn Med J* 36, 190, 1932.
3. Holcomb, R.L., Alcohol in relation to traffic accidents. *JAMA* 111, 1076, 1938.
4. Borkenstein, R.F., Historical perspective: North American traditional and experimental response. *J Stud Alc* Supp. 10, 3, 1985.
5. Andréasson, R., Jones, A.W., Historical anecdote realated to chemical tests for intoxication. *J Anal Toxicol* 20, 207, 1996.
6. Ladd, M., Gibson, R.B., The medicolegal aspects of the blood test to determine intoxication. *The Iowa State Law Review* 24, 1 1939.
7. Bavis, D.F., Arnholt, M.F., Tests of blood and urine of drunken drivers. *Nebraska State Med J* 24, 220, 1939.
8. Newman, H.W., Fletcher, E., The effect of alcohol on driving skill. *JAMA* 115, 1600, 1940.
9. Newman, H.W., *Acute Alcoholic Intoxication; A Critical Review.* Stanford University Press, 1941.
10. Hingson, R., Heeren, T., Winter, M., Lowering state legal blood alcohol limits to 0.08%: The effect on fatal motor vehicle crashes. *Am J Pub Health* 86, 1297, 1996.
11. Martin, S.E., Voas, R., Hingson, R., Zero tolerance laws; Effective public policy? *Alcoholism, Clin Exp Res* (in press) 1997.
12. Jones, A.W., Blood and breath-alcohol concentrations. *Br Med J* 305, 955, 1992.
13. Council on Scientific Affairs, American Medical Association Council Report. Alcohol and the driver. *JAMA* 255, 522, 1986.
14. Walls, H.J., Brownlie, A.R., *Drink, Drugs and Driving.* Sweet & Maxwell, London, 1985.
15. Jones, A.W., Enforcement of drink-driving laws by use of per se legal alcohol limits: Blood and/ or breath concentration as evidence of impairment. *Alc Drugs and Driving* 4, 99, 1988.
16. Ziporyn, T., Definition of impairment essential for prosecuting drunken drivers. *JAMA* 253, 3509, 1985.
17. Tarantino, J., *Defending Drinking Drivers.* James Publishing Inc., Santa Ana, 1986.

18. Head, W.C., and Joye, Jr. R.I., *101 ways to avoid a drunk driving conviction*. Maximar Publishing Company, Atlanta, 1991.

19. Fitzgerald, E.F., and Hume, D.N., *Intoxication test evidence: Criminal and Civil*. The Lawyers Co-operative Publishing Company, 1987.

20. Nichols, D.H., *Drinking/Driving litigation: Criminal and Civil*. Callaghan, Deerfield, Il., 1985.

21. Erwin, R., *Defense of Drunk Driving Cases*, Criminal/Civil. Matthew Bender, New York, 1996.

22. Cohen, H.M., and Green, J.B., *Apprehending and prosecuting the drunk driver*. Matthew Bender, New York, 1995.

23. Denney, R.C., The use of breath and blood alcohol values in evaluating hip flask defences. *New Law Journal* Sept. 26, 923, 1986.

24. Lewis, M.J., The individual and the estimation of his blood alcohol concentration from intake with particular reference to the hip-flask drink. *J Forens Sci Soc* 26, 19, 1985.

25. Jones, A.W., Widmark's equation; Determining amounts of alcohol consumed from blood alcohol concentration. *DWI Journal; Law and Science* 3, 8, 1989.

26. Forrest, A.R.W., The estimation of Widmark's factor. *J Forens Sci Soc* 26, 249, 1986.

27. Iffland, R., Staak, M., Rieger, S. Experimentelle Untersuchungen zur überprüfung von Nachtrunkbehauptungen. *Blutalkohol* 19, 235, 1982.

28. Biasotti, A.A., Valentine, T.E., Blood alcohol concentration determined from urine samples as a practical equivalent or alternative to blood and breath alcohol tests. *J Forens Sci* 30, 194, 1985.

29. Jones, A.W., Ethanol distribution ratios between urine and capillary blood in controlled experiments and in apprehended drinking drivers. *J Forens Sci* 37, 21, 1992.

30. Grüner, O., Ludwig, O., Rockenfeller, K., Die Bedeutung der Doppelblutentnahmen für die Beurteilung von Nachtrunkbehauptungen. *Blutalkohol* 17, 26, 1980.

31. Bonte, W., *Begleitstoffe alkoholischer Getränke*. Verlag Max Schmidt-Röshild, Lübeck, FRG, 1988.

32. Iffland, R., Congener analysis of blood in legal proceedings: Possibilities and problems. In: W. Bonte, editor, Proc. In: *Workshop on Congener Alcohols and their Medicolegal Significance*. University of Düsseldorf, 1987, p 236.

33. Bilzer, N., Grüner, O., Methodenkritische Betrachtungen zum Nachweis aliphatischer Alkohole im Blut mit Hilfe der Headspace-Analyze. *Blutalkohol* 20, 411, 1983.

34. Bonte, W., Contributions to congener analysis. *J Traffic Med* 18, 5, 1990.

35. Roine, R.P., Eriksson, C.J.P., Ylikahri, R., Penttilä, A.M., Salaspuro, M., Methanol as a marker of alcohol abuse. *Alcoholism Clin Exp Res* 13, 172, 1989.

36. Buchholtz, U., Blutmethanol als Alkoholismusmarker. *Blutalkohol* 30, 43, 1993.

37. Haffner, H.Th., Graw, M., Besserer, K., Blickle, U., Henssge, C., Endogenous methanol: variability in concentration and rate of production. Evidence of a deep compartment. *Forens Sci Intern* 79, 145, 1996.

38. Jones, A.W., Top-ten defence challenges among drinking drivers in Sweden. *Med Sci law* 31, 429, 1991.

39. Jones, A.W., Status of alcohol absorption in drinking drivers. *J Anal Toxicol* 14, 198, 1990.

40. Jones, A.W., Jönsson, K.Å., and Neri, A., Peak blood-alcohol concentration and the time of its occurrence after rapid drinking on an empty stomach. *J Forensic Sci* 36, 376, 1991.

41. Jones, A.W., Interindividual variations in the disposition and metabolism of ethanol in healthy men. *Alcohol* 1, 385, 1984.

42. Jones, A.W., Neri, A., Evaluation of blood-ethanol profiles after consumption of alcohol together with a large meal. *Can Soc Forens Sci J* 24, 165, 1991.

43. Gullberg, R.G., Variations in blood alcohol concentration following the last drink. *J Police Sci Admin* 10, 289, 1982.

44. Shajani, N.K., Dinn, H.N. Blood alcohol concentrations reached in human subjects after consumption of alcohol in a social setting. *Can J Forens Sci Soc* 18, 38, 1985.

45. Zink, P., and Reinhardt, G., Der Verlauf der Blutalkoholkurve bei großen Trinkmengen. *Blutalkohol* 21, 422, 1984.

46. Jones, A.W., Andersson, L., Influence of age, gender, and blood-alcohol concentration on the disappearance rate of alcohol from blood in drinking drivers. *J Forens Sci* 41, 922, 1996.

47. Allanowai, Y., Moreland, T.A., McEwen, J., Halliday, F., Durnin, C.J. and Stevenson, I.H., Ethanol kinetics - extent of error in back extrapolation procedures. *Br J Clin Pharmacol* 34, 316, 1992.

48. Lewis, K.O., Back calculation of blood alcohol concentration. *Br Med J* 295, 800, 1987.

49. Montgomery, M.R., Reasor, M.J., Retrograde extrapolation of blood alcohol data; An applied approach. *J Toxicol Environ Health* 36, 281, 1992.

50. Dossett, J.A., Breath tests, blood tests and back calculations. *The Law Society's Gassett*, 15 October, 2925, 1987.

51. McLean, A.J. and Morgan, D.J., Clinical pharmacokinetics in patients with liver disease. *Clin Pharmacokinet* 21, 42, 1991.

52. Hoyumpa, A.M., Schenker, S., Major drug interactions: Effect of liver disease, alcohol, and malnutrition. *Ann Rev Med* 33, 113, 1982.

53. Koltz, U., Pathophysiological and disease-induced changes in drug distribution volume: Pharmacokinetic implications. *Clin Pharmacokinet* 1, 204, 1976.

54. Grüner, O., Bilzer, N., Walle, A.J., Blutalkoholkurve und Widmark-Werte bei dialyseabhängigen Patienten. *Blutalkohol* 17, 371, 1980.

55. Cotton, P.B,, Walker, G., Ethanol absorption after gastric operations and in the coeliac syndrome. *Postgrad Med J* 49, 27, 1973.

56. Griffiths, G.H., Owen, G.M., Camphell, H., Shields, R., Gastric emptying in health and in gastroduodenal disease. *Gastroenterology* 54, 1, 1968.

57. Elmslie, R.G., Davis, R.A., Magee, D.F., White, T.T., Absorption of alcohol after gastrectomy. *Surg Gynacol Obstet* 119, 1256, 1964.

58. Jokipii, S.G., *Experimental studies on blood alcohol in healthy subjects and in some diseases.* Thesis for MD degree, University of Helsinki, 1951.

59. Jones, A.W., Biochemistry and physiology of alcohol: Applications to foresnic science and toxicology. In: *Medicolegal aspects of alcohol*, edited by J.C. Garriott, Lawyers & Judges Publishing Company, Inc., Tuson, 1996, p 85.

60. Lieberman, F.L., The effect of liver disease on the rate of ethanol metabolism in man. *Gastroenterology* 44, 261, 1968.

61. Ugarte, G., Insunza, I., Altschiller, H., Iturriage, H., Clinical and metabolic disorders in alcoholic hepatic damage. Chapter 29, In: *Alcohol and Alcoholism*, edited by R.E. Popham, Addiction Research Foundation, Toronto, 1969; p 230.

62. Mezey, E., Tobon, F., Rates of ethanol clearance and activities of the ethanol-oxidizing enzymes in chronic alcoholic patients. *Gastroenterology* 61, 707, 1971.

63. Bode, J.Ch., The metabolism of alcohol: Physiological and pathophysiological aspects. *J Roy Coll Phycns* 12, 122, 1978.

64. Mallach, H.J., von Oldershausen, H.F., Springer, E. Der Einfluß oraler Alkoholzufuhr auf den Blutalkoholspiegel von Gewohnheitstrinkern und Leberkranken unter verschiedenen alimentären Bedingungen. *Klin Wschr* 50, 732, 1972

65. Runyon, B.A., Care of patients with ascites. *N Eng J Med* 330, 337, 1994.

66. Aiza, I., Perez, G.O., Schiff, E.R., Management of ascites in patients with chronic liver disease. *Am J Gastroenterol* 89, 1949, 1994.

67. Teschke, R., Gellert, J., Hepatic microsomal ethanol-oxidizing system (MEOS): metabolic aspects and clinical implications. *Alcoholism; Clin Exp Res* 10, 20S, 1986.

68. Jones, A.W., and Sternebring, B., Kinetics of ethanol and methanol in alcoholics during detoxification. *Alc Alcohol* 27, 641, 1992.

69. Haffner, H.T., Batra, A., Bilzer, N., Dietz, K., Gilg, T., Graw, M., et al. Statistische Annäherung an forensische Rückrechnungswerte für Alkoholiker. *Blutalkohol* 29, 53, 1992.

70. Monaghan MS, Olsen KM, Ackerman BH, Fuller GL, Porter WH, Pappas AA. Measurement of serum isopropanol and the acetone metabolite by proton nuclear magnetic resonance; Application to pharmacokinetic evaluation in a simulated overdose model. *Clin Toxicol* 33, 141. 1995.

71. Jones, A.W., Schuberth, J. Computer-aided headspace gas chromatography applied to blood-alcohol analysis: Importance of online process control. *J Forensic Sci* 34, 1116, 1989.

72. Coldwell, B.B., Grant, G.L., The disappearance of alcohol from the blood of diabetics. *J Forensic Sci* 8, 220, 1963.
73. Coldwell, B.B., A note on the estimation and disappearance of alcohol in blood, breath and urine from obese and diabetic patients. *J Forensic Sci* 10, 480, 1965.
74. Taylor, R., Agius, L., The biochemistry of diabetes. Biochem J 250, 625, 1988.
75. Bode, Ch, Buchwald, B., and Goebell, H. Hemmung des Äthanolabbaues durch Proteinmangel beim Menschen. *Dtsch Med Wschr* 96, 1576, 1971.
76. Bode, Ch, Thiel, D., Hemmung des Äthanolabbaus beim Menschen durch Fasten: Reversibilität durch Fructose-Infusion. *Dtsch Med Wschr* 100, 1849, 1975.
77. Willner, K., Kretschmar, R., Die Veränderung des Verteilyngsfaktors nach akuten Körperwasserverlusten. *Blutalkohol* 2, 99, 1963.
78. Marshall, A.W., Kingstone D, Boss AM, Morgan MY. Ethanol elimination in males and females; relationship to menstrual cycle and body composition. *Hepatology* 3, 701, 1983.
79. Jones, A.W., Neri, A., Age-related changes in blood-alcohol parameters and subjective feelings of intoxication. *Alc Alcohol* 20, 45, 1985.
80. Brettel, H.F., Maske, B., Zur Alkoholbestimmung bei Blutnahme in Schockkzustand. *Blutalkohol* 8, 360, 1971.
81. Brettel, H.F., Die Alkoholbegutachtung bei Traumatisierten und Narkotisierten. *Blutalkohol* 11, 1, 1974.
82. Brettel, H.F. and Henrich, M. Die Rückrechnung auf die sog, Tatzeitalkoholkonzentration bei Schockfällen. *Blutalkohol* 16, 145, 1979.
83. Kleemann, W.J., Seibert, M., Tempka, A., Wolf, M., Weller, J-P., Tröger, H-D., Arterielle und venöse Alkoholelimination bei 10 polytraumatisierten Patienten. *Blutalkohol* 33, 162, 1995.
84. Baskett, P.J.F., Management of hypovolemic shock. *Br Med J* 300, 1453, 1990.
85. Flordal, P.A., The plasma dilution factor: Predicting how concentrations in plasma and serum are affected by blood volume variations and blood loss. *J Lab Clin Med* 126, 353, 1995.
86. Ditt, J., and Schulze, G., Blutverlust und Blutalkoholkonzentration. *Blutalkohol* 1, 183, 1962.
87. Wigmore, J.G., Mammoliti, D.N., Comments on Medicolegal alcohol determination: Implications and consequences of irregularities in blood alcohol concentration vs time curves. *J Anal Toxicol* 17, 317, 1993.
88. Goldberger, B.A., Cone, E.J., Kadehjian, L., Unexpected ethanol ingestion through soft drinks and flavored beverages. *J Anal Toxicol* 20, 332, 1996.
89. Linnoila, M., Mattila M.J., Kitchell BS. Drug interactions with alcohol. *Drugs* 18, 299, 1979.
90. Lane. EA, Guthrie S, Linnoila M. Effects of ethanol on drug and metabolite pharmacokinetics. *Clin Pharmacokinet* 10, 228, 1985.
91. Lieber, C.S., Interaction of alcohol with other drugs and nutrients: Implications for the therapy of alcoholic liver disease. *Drugs,* 40 (suppl 3) 23, 1990.
92. Blomstrand, R, Theorell H. Inhibitory effect on ethanol oxidation in man after administration of 4-methyl pyrazole. *Life Sci* 9, 631, 1970.
93. Blomstrand, R, Östling-Wintzell H, Löf A, McMartin K, Tolf BR, Hedström KG. Pyrazoles as inhibitors of alcohol oxidation and as important tools in alcohol research: An approach to therapy against methanol poisoning. *Proc Natl Acad Sci* 76, 3499, 1979.
94. Jacobsen, D, McMartin KE. Methanol and ethylene glycol poisonings mechanism of toxicity, clinical course, diagnosis and treatment. *Med Toxicol* 1, 309, 1986.
95. Estonius, M., Svensson, S., Höög, J.O. Alcohol dehydrogenase in human tissues: localisation of transcripts coding for five classes of the enzyme. *FEBS Letters* 397, 338, 1996.
96. Seitz, H.K., Egerer, G., Simanowski, U.A., Waldherr, R., Eckey, R., Agarwal, D.P.,Goedde, H.W., Von Wartburg, J.P., Human gastric alcohol dehydrogenase activity; effect of age, sex, and alcoholism. *Gut* 34, 1433, 1993.
97. Frezza M, DePadova C, Pozzato G, Terpin M, Baraona E, Lieber CS. High blood alcohol levels in women: the role of decreased gastric alcohol dehydrogenase activity and first-pass metabolism. *N Engl J Med* 322, 95, 1990.
98. Welling, P.G. (1977) Pharmacokinetics of alcohol following single low doses to fasted and non-fasted subjects. *J. Clin. Pharmacol.* 17, 199-206.

99. Wilkinson, P.K., Sedman, A.J., Sakmar, E., Lin, Y.J., and Wagner, J.G., Fasting and non-fasting blood ethanol concentration following repeated oral administration of ethanol to one adult male subject. *J. Pharmacokinet. Biopharm.* **5**, 41, 1977.

100. Roine, R., Gentry, T., Hernandez-Munoz, R., Baraona, E., Lieber, C.S. Aspirin increases blood alcohol concentration in humans after ingestion of ethanol. *JAMA* 264, 2406, 1990.

101 Julkunen, R.J.K., Tannenbaum, L., Baraona, E., Lieber, C.S., First-pass metabolism of ethanol: an important determinant of blood levels after alcohol consumption. *Alcohol* 2, 437, 1985.

102. Seitz, H.K., Bösche, J., Czygan, P., Veith, S., Simon, B. and Kommerell, B. Increased blood ethanol levels following cimetidine but not ranitidine. *Lancet* 2 700, 1982.

103. Feely, J, Wood AJ. Effects of cimetidine on the elimination and actions of ethanol. *JAMA* 247, 2819, 1982.

104. Caballeria, J, Baraona E, Rodamilans M, Lieber CS. Effects of cimetidine on gastric alcohol dehydrogenase activity and blood ethanol levels. *Gastroenterology* 96, 388, 1989.

105. Westenbrink, W., Cimetidine and the blood alcohol curve: A case study and review. *Can Soc Forens Sci J* 28, 165, 1995.

106. Bye, A., Lacey, L.F., Gupta, S., and Powell, J.R., Effect of ranitidine hydrochloride (150 mg twice daily) on the pharmacokinetics of increasing doses of ethanol (0.15, 0.3, 0.6 g/kg). *Br. J. Clin. Pharmacol.* 41, 129, 1996..

107. Dauncey H, Chesher, G.B., and Palmer, R.H., Cimetidine and ranitidine; Lack of effect on the pharmacokinetics of an acute ethanol dose. *J Clin Gastroenterol.* 17, 189, 1993.

108. Fraser, A.G., Hudson, M., Sawyerr, A.M., Smith, M., Rosalki, S.B., and Pounder, R.E., Ranitidine, cimetidine, famotidine have no effect on post-prandial absorption of ethanol 0.8 g/kg taken after an evening meal. *Aliment. Pharmacol. Therapeut.* 6, 693, 1992.

109. Raufman JP, Notar-Francesco, V., Raffaniello, R.D., and Straus, E.W., Histamine-2 receptor antagonists do not alter serum ethanol levels in fed, nonalcoholic men. *Ann Int Med.* 118, 488, 1993.

110. Pedrosa MC, Russell RM, Saltzman JR, Golner BB, Dallal GE, Sepe TE, Oates E, Egerier G, Seitz HK. Gastric emptying and first-pass metabolism of ethanol in elderly subjects with and without atrophic gastritis. *Scand J Gastroenterol.* 31, 671, 1996.

111. Toon, S., Khan AZ, Holt BJ, Mullins FGP., Langley SJ., and Rowland MM. Absence of effect of ranitidine on blood alcohol concentrations when taken morning, midday, or evening with or without food. *Clin Pharmacol Therap* 55, 385, 1994.

112. Lester, D., The concentration of apparent endogenous ethanol. J. Stud. Alcohol 23, 17, 1962.

113. Sprung, R., Bonte, W., Rüdell, E., Domke, M., Frauenrath, C., Zum Problem des endogenen Alkohols. Blutalkohol 18, 65, 1981.

114. Jones, A. W., Mårdh, G., Änggård, E., Determination of endogenous ethanol in blood and breath by gas chromatography-mass spectrometry. Pharmacol. Biochem. Behav. 18 Suppl. 1, 267, 1983.

115. Ostrovsky, Y. M., Endogenous ethanol - Its metabolic, behavioral and biomedical significance. Alcohol 3, 239, 1986.

116. Jones, A. W., Ostrovsky, Y. M., Wallin, A., Midtvedt, T., Lack of differences in blood and tissue concentrations of endogenous ethanol in conventional and germfree rats. Alcohol 1, 393, 1984.

117. Blomstrand, R., Observations on the formation of ethanol in the intestinal tract in man. Life Sci. 10, 575, 1971.

118. Agapejev, S., Vassilieff, I., Curi, P.R., Alcohol levels in cerebrospinal fluid and blood samples from patients under pathological conditions. Acta Neurol Scand 86, 496, 1992.

119. Agapejev, S., Vassilieff, I., Curi, P.R., Alcohol in cerebrospinal fluid (CSF) and alcoholism. Hum Exper Toxicol 11, 237, 1992.

120. Jones, A. W., Concentration of endogenous ethanol in blood and CSF. Acta Neurol. Scand. 89, 149, 1994.

121. Kaji, H., Asanuma, Y., Yahara, O., Shibue, H., Hisamura, M., Saito, N., Kawakami, Y., Murao, M., Intragastrointestinal alcohol fermentation syndrome; report of two cases and review of the literature. J. Forens. Sci. Soc. 24, 461, 1984.

122. Kaji, H., Asanumo, Y., Saito, N., Hisamura, M., Murao, M., Yoshida, T., and Takahashi, K., 'The Auto-brewery Syndrome - The Repeated Attacks of Alcoholic Intoxication due to the Overgrowth of Candida (albicans) in the Gastrointestinal Tract,' Materia Medica Polona, 8, 429, 1976.

123. Hunnisett, A., Howard, J., Davies, S., Gut fermentation (or the 'Auto-brewery') syndrome: A new clinical test with initial observations and discussion of clinical and biochemical implications. J. Nutr. Med. 1, 33, 1990.

124. Jones, A.W., Excretion of alcohol in urine and diuresis in healthy men in relation to their age, the dose administered, and the time after drinking. *Forens Sci Intern* 45, 217, 1990.

125. Widmark, E.M.P., Uber die Konzentration des genossenen Alkohols in Blut und Harn unter verschiedenen Umständen. *Skand Arch Physiol* 33, 85, 1915.

126. Blackmore, D.J., Mason, J.K., Renal clearance of urea, creatinine and alcohol. Med Sci Law 8, 51, 1968.

127. Miles, W.R., The comparative concentrations of alcohol in human blood and urine at intervals after ingestion. J Pharmacol Exp Therap 20, 265, 1922.

128. Lundquist, F., The urinary excretion of ethanol in man. *Acta Pharmacol Toxicol* 18, 231, 161.

129. Jones, A.W., Helander, A., Disclosing recent drinking after alcohol has been cleared from the body. *J Anal Toxicol* 20, 141, 1996.

130. Widmark, E.M.P. *Principles and application of medicolegal alcohol analysis.* Biomedical Publications, Davis, 1981, pp 1-163.

131. Mulrow, P.J., Huvos, A., Buchanan, D.L., Measurement of residual urine with I^{123} labeled diodrast. *J Lab Clin Med* 57, 109, 1961.

132. Fine, J., Glucose content of normal urine. *Br med J* 1, 1209, 1965.

133. Alexander, W.D., Wills, P.D., Eldred, N., Urinary ethanol and diabetes mellitus. *Diab. Med.* 5, 463, 1988.

134. Sulkowski, H.A., Wu, A.H.B., McCarter, Y.S., In-vitro production of ethanol in urine by fermentation. *J Forens Sci* 40, 990, 1995.

135. Saady, J.J., Poklis, A., Dalton, H.P., Production of urinary ethanol after sample collection. *J Forens Sci* 38, 1467, 1993.

136. Muholland, J.H., and Townsend, F.J., Bladder Beer: a new clinical observation. *Trans Am Clin Climatol Ass* 95, 34, 1983.

137. Chang, J., Kollman, S.E., The effect of temperature on the formation of ethanol by candida albicans. *J Forensic Sci* 34, 105, 1989.

138. Beck, O., Helander, A., Jones, A.W., Serotonin metabolism marks alcohol intake. *Forensic Urine Drug Testing*, September 1996, p 1-4.

139. Helander, A., Beck, O., Jones, A.W., 5HTOL/5HIAA as biochemical marker of post-mortem ethanol synthesis. *Lancet* 340, 1159, 1992.

140. Dick, GL, Stone HM. Alcohol loss arising from microbial contamination of drivers' blood specimens. *Forens Sci Intern* 34, 17, 1987.

141. Heise, H.A., How extraneous alcohol affects the blood test for alcohol. *Am J Clin Pathol* 32, 169, 1959.

142. Goldfinger TM, Schaber, D. A comparison of blood alcohol concentration using non-alcohol and alcohol-containing skin antiseptics. *Ann Emerg Med* 36, 665, 1982.

143. Times Law Report. Power to quash convictions after guilty pleas., *The Times*, October 4, 1990.

144. Taberner, P.V., A source of error in blood alcohol analysis. *Alc Alcohol* 24, 489, 1989.

145. Peek, G.J., March, A., Keating, Ward, R.J., Peters, T.J., The effects of swabbing the skin on apparent blood alcohol concentration. *Alc Alcohol* 25, 639, 1990.

146. McIvor, R.A., Cosbey, S.H., Effect of using alcoholic and non-alcoholic skin cleansing swabs when sampling blood for alcohol estimation using gas chromatography. *Brit J Clin Prac* 44, 235, 1990.

147. Ogden, E.J.D., Gerstner-Stevens, J., Burke J., Young, S.J., Venous blood alcohol sampling and the alcohol swab. *The Police Surgeon* October, 4, 1992.

148. Carter. P.G., McConnell, A.A., Venous blood sampling in drink driving offences and English law. *Alc Drugs and Driving* 6, 27, 1990.

149. Ryder, K.W,, Glick, M.R., The effect of skin cleansing agents on ethanol results measured with the du pont automatic clinical analyzer. *J Forensic Sci* 31, 574, 1986.

150. Klssa E. Determination of inorganic fluoride in blood with a fluoride ion-sensitive electrode. *Clin Chem* 33, 253, 1987.

151. Dubowski, K.M., Essary, N.A., Contamination of blood specimens for alcohol analysis during collection. Abs & Rev in Alcohol and Driving 4, 3, 1983.

152. Brown, G.A., Neylan, D., Reynolds, W.J., and Smalldon, K.W. The stability of ethanol in stored blood. Part 1 Important variables and interpretation of results. *Anal Chim Acta* 66, 271, 1973.

153. Smalldon, K.W. and Brown, G.A. The stability of ethanol in stored blood. Part II The mechanism of ethanol oxidation. *Anal Chim Acta* 66, 285, 1973.

154. Bowers, R.V., Burleson, W.D., Blades, J.F., Alcohol absorption from the skin in man. *Quart J Stud Alc* 3, 31, 1942.

155. Riley, D., Wigmore J.G., Yen, B., Dilution of blood collected for medicolegal alcohol analysis by intravenous fluids. *J Anal Toxicol* 20, 330, 1996.

156. Jones, A.W., Hahn, R., Stalberg, H. Distribution of ethanol and water between plasma and whole blood; Inter- and intra-individual variations after administration of ethanol by intravenous infusion. *Scand J Clin Lab Invest* 50, 775, 1990.

157. Lenter, C. *Geigy Scientific Tables*, Geigy Pharmaceuticals, Basel, 1992.

158. Jones, A.W. Determination of liquid/air partition coefficients for dilute solutions of ethanol in water, whole blood, and plasma. *J Anal Toxicol* 7, 193, 1983.

159. Ganong, W.F. *Review of Medical Physiology*. Lange Medical Publications, Los Altos, 1979.

160. Wilkinson, D.R., Haines, P., Morgner, R., Sockrider, D., Wilkinson, C.L., Spartz, M., The 2100/1 ratio used in alcohol programs is once again under attack. In: *Alcohol, Drugs and Traffic Safety*, Eds P.C. Noordzij and R. Roszbach, Elsevier Science Publishers, Amstedam, 1987, p 391.

161. Wright, B.M., Distribution of ethanol between plasma and erythrocytes in whole blood. *Nature* 218, 1263, 1968.

162. Jones, A.W., Measuring alcohol in blood and breath for forensic purposes - A historical review. *Forens Sci Rev* 8, 13, 1996.

163. Jones, A.W., Andersson, L., Biotransformation of acetone to isopropanol observed in a motorist involved in a sobriety control. *J Forensic Sci* 40, 686, 1995.

164. Dubowski, K.M., Essary, N., Quality assurance in breath alcohol analysis. *J Analyt Toxicol* 18, 306, 1994

165. Bogen, E. Drunkenness; A quantitative study of acute alcohol intoxication. *JAMA* 89, 1508, 1927.

166. Spector, N.H. Alcohol breath tests: Gross errors in current methods of measuring alveolar gas concentrations. *Science* 172, 57, 1971.

167. Dubowski, K.M., Studies in breath-alcohol analysis: Biological factors. *Z Rechtsmed* 76, 93, 1975.

168. Caddy, G.R., Sobell, M.B. and Sobell, L.C. Alcohol breath tests: Criterion times for avoiding contamination by mouth alcohol. *Behav Res Meth Instr* 10, 814, 1978.

169. Gullberg, R.G., The elimination rate of mouth alcohol: mathematical modeling and implications in breath alcohol analysis. *J Forensic Sci* 37, 1363, 1992.

170. Modell, J.G., Taylor, J.P. and Lee, J.Y. Breath alcohol values following mouthwash use. *JAMA* 270, 2955, 1993.

171. Grüner, O., Bilzer, N., Untersuchungen zur Beeinflu barkeit der Alkomat — Atemalkoholmessungen durch verschiedene Stoffe des täglichen Gebrauchs (Mundwässer, parfüms, Rasierwässer etc.). *Blutalkohol* 27, 119, 1990.

172. Denney, R.C. and Williams, P.M. Mouth alcohol: Some theoretical and practical considerations. In: *Proceedings 10th International Conference on Alcohol, Drugs and Traffic Safety*, edited by Noordzij, P.C. and Roszbach, R. Amsterdam: Elsevier, 1987, p. 355-358.

173. Penners, B.M. and Bilzer, N. Aufsto en (Eruktation) und Atemalkoholkonzentration. *Blutalkohol* 24, 172, 1987.

174. Kahrilas, P.J., Gastroesophageal reflux disorders. *JAMA* 276, 983, 1996.

175. Fraser, A.G., Gastro-oesophageal reflux and laryngeal symptoms. *Aliment Pharmacol Therapeut* 8, 265, 1994.

176. Schoeman, M.N., Tippett, M., Akkermans, L.M.A., Dent, J., Holloway, R.H., Mechanisms of gastroesophageal reflux in ambulant healthy human subjects. *Gastroenterology* 108, 83, 1995.

177. Klauser, A.G., Schindlbeck, N.E., Müller-Lissner, S.A., Symptoms in gastro-oesophageal reflux disease. *Lancet* 335, 205, 1990.

178. Cohen,S., The pathogenesis of gastroesophageal reflux disease; A challenge in clinical physiology. *Ann Int Med* 117, 1051, 1992.

179. Pope, C.E., Acid-reflux disorders. *N Eng J Med* 331, 656, 1994.

180. Weinberg, D.S. and Kadish, S.L. The diagnosis and management of gastroesophageal reflux disease. *Med Clin North Am.* 80:411 1996.

181. Kaufman, S.E., Kaye, M.D., Induction of gastro-oesophageal reflux by alcohol. *Gut* 19, 336, 1978.

182. Pehl, C., Wendl, B., Pfeiffer, A., Schmidt, T., Kaess, H., Low-proof alcoholic beverages and gastroesophageal reflux. *Dig Dis Sci* 38, 93, 1993.

183. Wells, D., Farrar, J., Breath-alcohol analysis of a subject with gastric regurgitation. In Abstracts of the *11th International Conference on Alcohol, Drugs, and Traffic* Safety, Chicago, 1989.

184. Duffus, P., Dunbar J.A., Medical problems with breath testing of drunk drivers. *Br Med J* 289, 831, 1984.

185. Wright, B.M., Medical problems with breath testing of drunk drivers. *Br Med J* 289, 1071, 1984.

186. Trafford, D.J.H., and Makin, H.L.J. Breath-alcohol concentration may not always reflect the concentration of alcohol in blood. *J Anal Toxicol.* 18;225-228, 1994.

187. Cowan, J.M., Apparent flaws in a breath-alcohol case report. *J Anal Toxicol* 19;128, 1995.

188. Cohen, H.M., Saferstein, R., Mouth alcohol, denture adhesives and breath-alcohol testing. *Drunk Driving Liquor Liability Reporter*, 6, 24, 1992.

189. Harding, P.M., McMurray, M.C., Laessig, R.H., Simley, D.O., Correll, P.J., Tsunehiro, J.K., The effect of dentures and denture adhesives on mouth alcohol retention. *J Forens Sci* 37, 999, 1992.

190. Katzgraber, F., Rabl, W., Stainer, M., Wehinger, G., Die Zahnprothese - ein Alkoholdepot? *Blutalkohol* 32, 274, 1995.

191. Dubowski, K.M., The technology of breath-alcohol analysis US Department of Transportation Report No (ADM) 92-1728, US Goverment Printing Office, Wahington, DC, 1992.

192. Kramer, M., Haffner, H.T., Cramer, Y. and Ulrich, L. Untersuchungen zur Funktion der Restalkoholanzeige beim Atemalkoholtestgerät - Alcomat. *Blutalkohol* 24, 49, 1987.

193. Jones, A.W., Andersson, L., Berglund, K. Interfering substances identified in the breath of drinking drivers with Intoxilyzer 5000S. *J Anal Toxicol* 20, 522, 1996.

194. Harte, R.A., An instrument for the determination of ethanol in breath in law enforcement practice. *J Forensic Sci* 16, 167, 1971.

195. Borkenstein, R.B., Smith, H.W., The Breathalyzer and its applications. *Med Sci law* 2, 13, 1961.

196. Oliver, R.D., Garriott, J.C., The effects of acetone and toluene on Breathalyzer results. *J Anal Toxicol* 3, 99, 1979.

197. Brick, J., Diabetes, breath acetone and Breathalyzer accuracy: A case study. *Alc Drugs Driving* 9, 27, 1993.

198. Manolis, A., The diagnostic potential of breath analysis. *Clin Chem* 29, 5, 1985.

199. Jones, A.W., Excretion of low molecular weight volatile substances in human breath: Focus on endogenous ethanol. *J Anal Toxicol* 9, 246, 1985.

200. Krotoszynski, B.K., Bruneau, G.M., O Neill, H.J., Measurement of chemical inhalation exposure in urban populations in the presence of endogenous effluents. *J Anal Toxicol* 3, 225, 1979.

201. Jones, A.W., Lagersson, W., Tagesson, C., Determination of isoprene in human breath by gas chromatography with ultraviolet detection. *J Chromatog* 672, 1, 1995.

202. Flores, A., Franks, J.F., The likelihood of acetone interference in breath alcohol measurement. *Alc Drugs and Driving* 3, 1, 1987.

203. Marks, V., Methane and the infrared breath-alcohol analyzer. *Lancet* ii, 50, 1984.

204. Peled, Y., Weinberg, D., Hallak, A., Gilat, T., Factors affecting methane production in humans. *Dig Dis Sci* 32, 267, 1987.

Alan Wayne Jones and Barry K. Logan

205. Dubowski, K.M., and Essary, N.A., Response of breath-alcohol analyzers to acetone. *J Anal Toxicol* 7, 231, 1983.

206. Mebs, D., Gerchow, J., Schmidt, K., Interference of acetone with breath-alcohol testing. *Blutalkohol* 21, 193, 1984.

207. Levey, S., Balchum, O.J., Medrando, V., Jung, R., Studies of metabolic products in expired air. 11 Acetone. *J Lab Clin Med* 63, 574, 1964.

208. Tassopoulos, C.N., Barnett, D., Fraser, T.R., Breath-acetone and blood-sugar measurements in diabetes. *Lancet* i, 1282, 1969.

209. Schoknecht, G., Hahlbrauck, B., Erkennung von Fremdgasen bei der Atemalkoholanalyse. *Blutalkohol* 29, 193, 1992.

210. Jones, A.W., Measuring and reporting the concentration of acetaldehyde in human breath. *Alc Alcohol* 30, 271, 1995.

211. Jones, A.W., Drug alcohol flush reaction and breath acetaldehyde concentration: No interference with an infrared breath alcohol analyzer. *J Anal Toxicol* 10, 98, 1986.

212. Eriksson, C.J.P., Fukunaga, T., Human blood acetaldehyde (Update 1992). In *Advances in Biomedical Alcohol Research*, eds P.V. Taberner and A.A. Badaway, Pergamon Press, Oxford, 1995, p 9.

213. Imobersteg, A.D., King, A., Cardema, M. and Mulrine, E. The effects of occupational exposure to paint solvents on the Intoxilyzer-5000 - a field study. *J Anal Toxicol* 17, 254, 1993.

214. Denney, R.C., Solvent inhalation and 'apparent' alcohol studies on the Lion Intoximeter 3000. *J Forens Sci Soc* 30, 357, 1990.

215. Cooper, S., Infrared breath-alcohol analysis following inhalation of gasoline fumes. *J Anal Toxicol* 5, 198, 1981.

216. Hümpener, R., Hein, P.M., Untersuchungen zur Beeinflubbarkeit der Alcomat - Atemalkoholmessung durch Benzin. *Blutalkohol* 29, 365, 1992.

217. Aderian R., Schmitt, G., Wu, M., Klebstoff-Lösemittel als Ursache eines Atemalkohol-Wertes von 1.96 promille. *Blutalkohol* 29, 360, 1992.

218. Bell, C.M., Gutowski, S.J., Young, S. and Wells, D. Technical Note - Diethyl Ether Interference with Infrared Breath Analysis. *J Anal Toxicol* 16, 166, 1992.

219. Edwards, M.A., Giguiere, W., Lewis, D., Baselt, R., Intoxilyzer interference by solvents. *J Anal Toxicol* 10, 125, 1986.

220. Giguiere, W., Lewis, D., Baselt, R., Chang, R., Lacquer fumes and the Intoxilyzer. *J Anal Toxicol* 12, 168, 1988.

221. Jones, A.W., Observations on the specificity of breath-alcohol analyzers used for clinical and medicolegal purposes. *J Forensic Sci* 34, 842, 1989.

222. Logan, B.K., Gullberg, R.G., Elenbaas, J.K., Isopropanol interference with breath alcohol analysis: A case report. *J Forensic Sci* 39, 1107, 1994.

223. Pennington, J.C., The effect of non-ethanolic substancs on the alcolmeter S-L2. *Can Soc Forens Sci J* 28, 131, 1995.

224. Gill, R., Hatchett, S.E., Broster, C.G., Osselton, M.D., Ramsey, J.D., Wilson, H.K., Wilcox, A.H., The response of evidential breath alcohol testing instruments with subjects exposed to organic solvents and gases. 1. Toluene, 1,1,1-trichloroethane and butane. *Med Sci Law* 31, 187, 1991a.

225. Gill, R., Warner, H.E., Broster, C.G., Osselton, M.D., Ramsey, J.D., Wilson, H.K., Wilcox, A.H., The response of evidential breath alcohol testing instruments with subjects exposed to organic solvents and gases. 11 White spirit and nonane. *Med Sci Law* 31, 201, 1991b.

226. Gill, R., Osselton, M.D., Broad, J.E., Ramsey, J.D. The response of evidential breath alcohol testing instruments with subjects exposed to organic solvents and gases. 111. White spirit exposure during domestic painting. *Med Sci Law* 31, 214, 1991c.

227. Lester, D., Greenberg, L.A., The inhalation of ethyl alcohol by man. *J Stud Alcohol* 12, 167, 1951.

228. Mason, J.K., Blackmore, D.J,. Experimental inhalation of ethanol vapor. *Med Sci Law* 12, 205, 1972.

229. Lewis, M.J., Inhalation of ethanol vapor; A case report and experimental test involving the spraying of shellac lacquer. *J Forens Sci Soc* 25, 5, 1985.

230. Lewis, M.J., A theoretical treatment for the estimation of blood alcohol concentration arising from inhalation of ethanol vapor. *J Forens Sci Soc* 25, 11, 1985.

231. Campbell, I., Wilson, H.K., Blood alcohol concentration following the inhalation of ethanol vapor under controlled conditions. *J Forens Sci Soc* 26, 129, 1986.

232. Kruhoffer, P.W., Handling of inspired vaporized ethanol in the airways and lungs with comments on forensic aspects. *Forens Sci Intern* 21, 1, 1983.

233. Harger, R.N., Lamb, E.B., Hulpieu, H.R., A rapid chemical test for intoxication employing breath. *JAMA* 110, 779, 1938.

234. Harger, R.N., Forney, R.B., Barker, H.B., Estimation of the level of blood alcohol from analysis of breath. *J Lab Clin Med* 36, 318, 1950.

235. Harger, RN, Raney BB, Bridwell EG, Kitchel MF. The partition ratio of alcohol between air and water, urine and blood; estimation and identification of alcohol in these liquids from analysis of air equilibrated with them. *J Biol Chem* 183, 197, 1950.

236. Jones, A.W., Variability of the blood/breath alcohol ratio in vivo. *J Stud Alc* 39, 1931, 1978.

237. Harding, P.M., Field, P.H., Breathalyzer accuracy in actual law enforcement practice; A comparison of blood- and breath-alcohol results in Wisconsin drivers. *J Forensic Sci* 32, 1235, 1987.

238. Harding, P.M., Laessig, R.H., Field, P.H., Field performance of the Intoxilyzer 5000: A comparison of blood- and breath-alcohol results in Wisconsin drivers. *J Forensic Sci* 35,1022, 1990.

239. Taylor, M.D., Hodgson, B.T., Blood/breath correlations: Intoxilyzer 5000C, Alcotest 7110, and Breathalyzer 900A breath alcohol analyzers. *Can Soc Forens Sci J* 28, 153, 1995.

240. Jones, A.W., Andersson, L., Variability of the blood/breath alcohol ratio in drinking drivers. *J Forensic Sci* 41, 922, 1996.

241. Dubowski, K.M., and O Neill, B., The blood/breath ratio of ethanol. Clin Chem 25, 1144, 1979.

242. Mason, M.F., Dubowski, K.M., Breath-alcohol analysis: Uses, methods, and some forensic problems - Review and opinion. J Forensic Sci 21, 9, 1976.

243. Jones, A.W. Physiological aspects of breath-alcohol measurement. *Alc Drugs and Driving* 6, 1, 1990.

244. George S.C., Babb, A.L., Hlastala M.P. Dynamics of soluble gas exchange in the airways III. Single exhalation breathing maneuver. *J. Appl. Physiol.* 75, 2439, 1993

245. Gomm, P.J., Broster, C.G., Johnson, N.M. and Hammond, K. Study into the ability of healthy people of small stature to satisfy the sampling requirements of breath alcohol testing instruments. *Med Sci Law* 33, 311, 1993.

246. Morris, M.J., Alcohol breath testing in patients with respiratory disease. *Thorax* 45, 717, 1990.

247. Neukirch, F., Liard, R., Korobaeff, M. and Pariente, R. Pulmonary function and alcohol consumption. *Chest* 98, 1546, 1990.

248. Prabhu, M.B., Hurst, T.S., Cockcroft, D.W., Baule, C. and Semenoff, J. Airflow obstruction and roadside breath alcohol testing. *Chest* 100, 585, 1991.

249. Morris, M.J., Taylor, A.G., Failure to provide a sample for breath alcohol analysis. *Lancet* i, 37, 1987.

250. Gomm, P.J., Osselton, M.D., Broster, C.G., Johnson, N.M. and Upton, K. Study into the ability of patients with impaired lung function to use breath alcohol testing devices. *Med Sci Law* 31, 221, 1991a.

251. Gomm, P.J., Osselton, M.D., Broster, C.G., Johnson, N.M. and Upton, K. The effect of salbutamol on breath alcohol testing in asthmatics. *Med Sci Law* 31, 226, 1991b.

252. Gomm, P.J., Weston, S.I. and Osselton, M.D. The effect of respiratory aerosol inhalers and nasal sprays on breath alcohol testing devices used in Great Britain. *Med Sci Law* 30, 203, 1990.

253. Westenbrink, W., Sauve, L.T., The effect of asthma inhalers on the ALERT J3A, Breathalyzer 900A, and mark IV GC Intoximeter. *Can J Forens Sci Soc* 24, 23, 1991.

254. Haas, H., Morris, J.F., Breath-alcohol analysis and chronic bronchopulmonary disease. *Arch Environ Health* 25, 114, 1972.

255. Hahn, R.G., Jones, A.W., Billing, B. and Stalberg, H.P. Expired-breath ethanol measurement in chronic obstructive pulmonary disease: implications for transurethral surgery. *Acta Anaesthesiol Scand* 35, 393, 1991.

256. Briggs, J.E., Patel, H., Butterfield, K., Noneybourne, D., The effects of chronic obstructive airway disease on the ability to drive and to use a roadside Alcolmeter. *Respir Med* 84, 43, 1990.

257. Crockett, A.J., Schembri, D.A., Smith, D.J., Laslett, R., Alpers, J.H., Minimum respiratory function for breath alcohol testing in South Australia. *J Forens Sci Soc* 32, 349, 1992.

258. Jones, A.W., How breathing technique can influence the results of breath alcohol analysis. *Med Sci Law* 22, 275, 1982.

259. Bell, C.M., Flack, H.J., Examining variables associated with sampling for breath alcohol analysis. In: *Proc 13th Intern Conf Alcohol, Drugs, and Traffic Safety,* Eds C.N. Kloeden and A.J. McLean, NHMRC Road Accident Research Unit, University of Adelaide, Australia, 1995, p 111.

260. Bell, C.M., What about the humble mouthpiece? Breath sample modification and implications for breath-alcohol analysis. *Proceedings 13th Intern Conf Alcohol, Drugs, and Traffic Safety,* Eds C.N. Kloeden and A.J. McLean, NHMRC Road Accident Research Unit, University of Adelaide, Australia, 1995, p 945.

261. Mulder, J.A.G., and Neuteboom, W., The effects of hypo- and hyperventilation on breath alcohol measurements. *Blutalkohol* 24, 341, 1987.

262. Schmutte, P., Stromeyer, H., Naeve, W., Vergleichende Untersuchungen von Atem- und Blutalkoholkonzentration nach körperlicher Belastung und besonderer Atemtechnik (Hyperventilation). *Blutalkohol* 10, 34, 1973.

263. Jones, A.W. Quantitative relationships of the alcohol concentration and the temperature of breath during a prolonged exhalation. *Acta Physiol Scand* 114, 407, 1992.

264. Gatt, J.A., The effect of temperature and blood:breath ratio on the interpretation of breath alcohol results. *New Law Journal* March 16, 249, 1984.

265. Jones, A.W., Effects of temperature and humidity of inhaled air on the concentration of ethanol in a man's exhaled breath. *Clin Sci* 63, 441, 1982.

266. Gaylarde, P.M., Stambuk, D., and Morgan, M.Y., Reduction in breath ethanol readings in normal male volunteers following mouth rinsing with water at differing temperatures. *Alc Alcohol* 22, 113, 1987.

267. Ohlson, J., Ralph, D.D., Mandelkorn M.A., Babb, A.L., and Hlastala M.P. Accurate measurement of blood alcohol concentration with isothermal rebreathing. *J. Stud. Alc.* 51, 6, 1990

268. Fox, G.R., and Hayward, J.S., Effect of hypothermia on breath-alcohol analysis. *J Forens Sci* 32, 320, 1987.

269. Fox, G.R., and Hayward, J.S., Effect of hyperthermia on breath-alcohol analysis. *J Forens Sci* 34. 836, 1989.

270. Chamberlain, R.T., Chain of custody: Its importance and requirements for clinical laboratory specimens. *Lab Med* June: 477, 1989.

271. Dubowski, K.M., The role of the scientist in litigation involving drug-use testing. *Clin Chem* 34, 788, 1988.

272. Ayala F.J., and Black, B., Science and the courts. *Am Sci* 81, 230, 1993.

273. Gold, J.A., Zaremski, M.J., Rappaport E., Shefrin, D.H., Daubert v Merrel Dow; The Supreme Court tackles scientific evidence in the courtroom. *JAMA* 270, 2964, 1993.

274. Editorial., Criteria for science in the courts. *Nature* 362, 481, 1993.

275. Lovell W.S., Breath tests for determining alcohol in the blood. *Science* 178, 264, 1972.

276. Iwwinkelried, E.J., The evolution of the American test for admissibility of scientific evidence. *Med Sci Law* 30, 60, 1990.

277. Neufeld, P.J., and Colman, N., When science takes the witness stand. *Sci Am* 262, 46, 1990.

278. Havard, J.D.J, Expert scientific evidence under the adversarial system. A travesty of justice. *J For Sci Soc* 32, 225, 1992

279. Annas, G.J., Scientific evidence in the courtroom; the death of the Frye rule. *N Eng J Med* 330, 1018, 1994.

280. Culliton, B.J., Scientific "experts" and the law. *Nature Med.* 3, 123, 1997

281. Eaton, D.L., and Kalman, D., Scientists in the courtroom: basic pointers for the expert scientific witness. *Environ Health Perspect* 102, 668, 1994.

282. Kuffner Jr., C.A., Marchi, E., Morgado, J.M., Rubio, C.R., Capillary electrophoresis and Daubert; Time for admission, *Anal Chem* April 1, 241A, 1996.

13.3 FETAL RIGHTS

STEPHEN M. MOHAUPT, MD

USC INSTITUTE OF PSYCHIATRY, LAW, AND THE BEHAVIORAL SCIENCES

LOS ANGELES, CALIFORNIA

Social awareness and medical assessment of a woman's pregnancy has changed substantially over the past centuries. In the eighteenth century, a woman was known as pregnant only when she brought the occurrence of fetal quickening, the sensation of the fetus moving inside her, to the attention of others. During this same time, pregnant women were responsible for much of their prenatal care, with little to no involvement of physicians. Women today may elect to confirm their pregnancy by a home urine test. Pregnancy may also be determined medically by a blood test or ultrasound. Physicians are involved in monitoring a woman's pregnancy and prenatal care with regular physician follow-up being strongly encouraged.

A relatively new area that has posed conflicts for the physician has been the concept of fetal rights. The pregnant mother and fetus have a unique relationship, whereby the fetus is dependent upon the mother for nourishment and survival. Additionally, the mother is responsible for all medical treatment decisions that may affect the fetus. Abortion is a legal medical procedure that ends the life of the fetus. Decisions about prenatal care, alcohol consumption, drug use, and other lifestyle choices are made solely by the mother. Is there a point when the fetus develops rights that override the mother's choice of free will? Does the fetus have the right to be born healthy and alive? If so, at what point in gestation does this right begin? Does society have an interest in the fetus' welfare, and if so, does society possess rights? Should the mother be forced, against her will, to receive medical interventions that improve chances of fetal survival?

13.3.1 THE CONSIDERATION OF FETAL RIGHTS

The fetus is dependent upon the mother for choices such as diet, exercise and alcohol consumption. There is concern that holding a mother responsible for her actions (e.g., cocaine abuse) during pregnancy leads toward a new area of criminal statutes. Furthermore, the idea of a perfect womb can never be obtained. Similarly, in the eighteenth century, it was thought that women were responsible for birth defects due to imaginative activity of their minds. However, during the eighteenth century, women's life took priority over the fetus. The fetus was not seen in the law as a person. Therefore, the woman's health and well being was of foremost concern; even if the life of the fetus was lost.

The fetus has developed many rights in various legal arenas. From this, it can be inferred that courts are making rulings that provide the fetus a greater degree of personhood. This section will address fetal rights in a medical context. The consideration of a fetus having rights in a medical context indicates that the fetus' interests (right to be born healthy and alive) are in conflict with those of the mother and her privacy rights. This section will also consider fetal rights in other legal arenas.

13.3.2 OVERVIEW OF FETAL RIGHTS

The First Amendment embodies freedom to believe and freedom to act. Freedom of religion is as old as this country and was a primary reason for the colonization of the United States of

America. The courts have drawn a distinction between the free exercise of religious beliefs and religious practices that are inimical or detrimental to public health or welfare.[1] Conduct remains subject to regulation for the protection of society.[1]

According to Epstein,[2] privacy rights include the right to be left alone, the right to refuse medical treatment, and the right to have possession of and power over one's own person. The bodily integrity doctrine contains concepts of assault and battery, search and seizure, informed consent, and the right to refuse medical treatment.

In an article on fetal rights, Johnsen wrote, "Our legal system has historically treated the fetus as part of the woman bearing it and has afforded it no rights as an entity separate from her."[3] "Fetal rights" view the fetus as an independent entity, separate from the mother and with interests that may be hostile to hers. The mother may be forced to have a cesarean section against her will. The child may sue their mother for injuries resulting from the woman's actions, or lack of, during pregnancy.

The view of the fetus by the legal system is a social and not a biological one. According to Robert H. Blank,[4]

> The term 'fetal rights' is a distortion of the real issue and obscures what ought to be the primary concern; the health of the unborn child. It is not the fetus that has rights; rather, it is the child once born that must be protected from avertable harm during gestation...The technological removal of the fetus from the 'secrecy of the womb' through ultrasound and other pre-natal procedures gives the fetus social recognition as an individual separate from the mother.

The goal of any policies designed to make the fetal environment as safe as possible should be to maximize the birth of healthy children.

The fetus is represented in many different areas of the law. The abolishment of intra-family immunity has been seen in courts, holding parents liable for prenatal injuries. This opens the process for courts to define parental responsibility. The definition of murder, according to the California Jury Instruction's, include, "every person who unlawfully kills a human being or fetus with malice aforethought or during the commission or attempted commission of (statutory felony) is guilty of the crime of murder.[5] These laws point to the personhood of the fetus.

Agota Peterfy[6] stated, "The controversy surrounding the pivotal role of viability is about deciding when human life begins, or becomes worthy of the laws' protection." The beginning of human life is not able to be defined but reflects an individual's religious beliefs, morals, and ethics. Catholic Ethical and Religious Directives[7] state, "From the moment of conception, life must be guarded with the greatest care...Any deliberate medical procedure, the purpose of which is to deprive a fetus or embryo of its life, is immoral."[7] As can be seen, many believe that the Court is not responsible for defining the beginning of human life; instead, it is society's task to do so.

Does society impose a moral responsibility upon a pregnant mother for her fetus? In the Board of Trustees Report for the American Medical Association,[8] a pregnant woman's moral responsibility was described as:

> A woman who chooses to carry her pregnancy to term has a moral responsibility to make reasonable efforts toward preserving fetal health...This moral responsibility, however, does not necessarily imply a legal duty to accept medical procedures or treatment in order to benefit the fetus.

More recently, the legal system has granted rights to the fetus that exist for persons. Court's have granted fetus' the following: inheritance rights; tort claim for prenatal injuries; and feticide law to protect pregnant women from violent attacks that terminate the life of the fetus. Both the inheritance rights and tort claim are contingent upon live birth; however, the feticide law is not. Court's have ordered cesarean section surgery to be performed against the mother's will.

13.3.3 CASE LAW

In medical practice, the issue of fetal rights is likely to present in the context of a conflict between the mother's privacy rights and the fetus' right to be born healthy and alive. One of the more common areas where this is seen involves cases where physicians seek court ordered cesarean sections against the mother's will in order to prevent substantial harm and possibly death to the fetus. The examination of case law will provide insight into these issues and an understanding of holdings by various courts. In researching the area of fetal versus maternal rights, no statutory law was found which focused on these issues, while case law presented opposing opinions.

13.3.3.1 Case Law: United States Supreme Court

Roe v. Wade was decided by the United States Supreme Court on January 22, 1973.[9] An unmarried pregnant woman who wished to terminate her pregnancy through abortion, instituted an action in court seeking a declaratory judgment that the Texas criminal abortion statutes were unconstitutional. These statutes prohibited abortions except for the purpose of saving the life of the mother as medically indicated. The plaintiff also sought an injunction against the abortion statutes' continued enforcement. Some of the holdings from this case by the United States Supreme Court included:

1. The right of privacy encompasses a woman's decision whether or not to terminate her pregnancy;
2. A woman's right to terminate her pregnancy is not absolute, and may to some extent be limited by the state's interest in safeguarding the woman's health, in maintaining proper medical standards, and in protecting potential human life;
3. The unborn are not included within the definition of "person" as used in the Fourteenth Amendment;
4. Prior to the end of the first trimester of pregnancy, the state may not interfere with or regulate an attending physician's decision, reached in consultation with his patient, that the patient's pregnancy should be terminated;
5. From and after the first trimester, and until the point in time when the fetus becomes viable, the state may regulate the abortion procedure only to the extent that such regulation relates to the preservation and protection of maternal health;
6. From and after the point in time when the fetus becomes viable, the state may prohibit abortions altogether, except those necessary to preserve the life or health of the mother.[9]

Another case involving abortion, *Webster v. Reproductive Health Services*, was decided July 3, 1989, by the United States Supreme Court.[10] State employed health professionals and private nonprofit corporations providing abortion services brought suit for declaratory judgment and injunctive relief challenging the constitutionality of a Missouri statute regulating the performance of abortions. Some of the Court's opinions include the following:

1. The state's preamble includes "life of each human being begins at conception" and that "unborn children have protectable interests in life, health, and well being;" The Court held that this statement does not allow the state to "justify" any abortion

regulation invalid under *Roe v. Wade*, on the ground that it embodied the State's view about when life begins;

2. The Missouri statute specifies a testing provision, namely, that a physician, before performing an abortion on a woman he has reason to believe is carrying an unborn child of 20 or more weeks gestational age, shall first determine if the child is viable...the Court stated this is constitutionally permissible because it furthers the State's interest in protecting potential human life;

3. Under the *Roe* framework, the State may not fully regulate abortion in the interest of potential life(as opposed to maternal health) until the third trimester; in order to save the Missouri testing provision, the Court found it necessary to throw out *Roe's* trimester framework.

13.3.3.2 Case Law: Maternal Rights Prevail

On April 22, 1990, *In re A.C.* was decided by the District of Columbia Court of Appeals.[11] The case involved a pregnancy with a viable fetus at 26 weeks. There was substantial history leading up to the legal case. A.C. was first diagnosed with cancer at age thirteen. She was married at age 27 and soon became pregnant. At the 25th week of her pregnancy, A.C. was diagnosed as having an inoperable tumor in her lung. One week later, A.C. agreed to medical treatment to extend her life past the 28th week of pregnancy, at which point she would give up her life for the fetus. The next day, A.C.'s condition rapidly deteriorated such that she was not competent to consent to surgery. A.C.'s wishes were only known for when she would be at the 28th week of pregnancy, and there was no evidence before the Court that A.C. consented to or even considered a cesarean section before this time.

The Court held that the terminally ill woman's constitutional "right to refuse treatment" overrode the state's interest in protecting the fetus. The trial court applied a balancing test of the state's interest in a viable human versus the mother's privacy rights. The Appellate Court stated that such a test was improper and the mother's wishes controlled "unless there are truly extraordinary or compelling reasons to override them...Such cases will be extremely rare and truly exceptional." The Appellate Court further stated that the mother has no duty to risk her health for a child, "A fetus cannot have rights...superior to those of a person who has already been born." This Court also reasoned that court-ordered cesarean sections would erode the trust between a pregnant woman and her physician. Judge Belson was the lone dissenter on this case and advocated a "balancing test."

The Appellate Court described procedures a trial judge should follow for similar cases: Is the patient competent to make an informed decision about medical treatment? If yes, then the patient's wishes are controlling in virtually all circumstances. If the patient is not competent, then the Court makes a substituted judgment (what the patient would want if competent).

A more recent case where maternal rights prevailed was decided by the Illinois Appellate Court for *In Re Baby Boy Doe*.[12] A mentally competent woman refused the cesarean section recommended by her doctor who stated that her 35-week-old fetus would die or suffer mental retardation without this intervention. The fetus was suffering from placental insufficiency. Doe and her husband refused to consent to the cesarean section or labor induction based upon religious reasons. The Appellate Court reasoned that, "The states compelling interest in the potential life of the fetus is insufficient to override the woman's interest in preserving her health." Therefore, the woman's choice to refuse medical treatment should not be balanced against the fetus' right to life, even when the woman's choice might be harmful to the fetus.

13.3.3.3 Case Law: Fetal Rights Prevail

The Georgia Supreme Court decided *Jefferson v. Griffin Spalding Hospital Authority* in February 1981.[13] This case was initiated with Griffin Spalding Hospital petitioning the Court for an order authorizing it to perform a cesarean section and any needed blood transfusions in the event that Mrs. Jefferson presented herself to the hospital for delivery. Mrs. Jefferson was 39-weeks pregnant and had been presenting herself to the hospital for prenatal care. The physician determined that she had a complete placenta previa making vaginal delivery extremely dangerous to the fetus and the mother. She was refusing cesarean section and blood transfusions based upon religious beliefs. The trial court granted an order authorizing the hospital to administer all medical procedures deemed necessary to preserve the life of Mrs. Jefferson's unborn child. The order was only valid if Mrs. Jefferson voluntarily sought admission to Griffin Spalding County Hospital. The court was also requested to order Mrs. Jefferson to submit to cesarean section before the onset of labor. The court was reluctant to grant such an order; however, it noted that should some agency of the state seek such relief through intervention in a suit, they would promptly consider the request.

The following day, the Georgia Department of Human Resources petitioned the Juvenile Courts for temporary custody of the unborn child, alleging that the child was deprived and they, therefore, requested an order requiring the mother to submit to a cesarean section. The court found that the child (39-week fetus) is a human being fully capable of independent life. As a viable human being, the child was entitled to the protection of the Juvenile Court. Temporary custody of the child was granted to the State of Georgia Human Resources and the County Department of Family and Children Services. The Department was given full authority to make all decisions including giving consent to the cesarean section. The temporary custody would terminate when the child "has been successfully brought from its mother's body into the world."

Mrs. Jefferson appealed the trial court's decision to the Georgia Supreme Court. This Court acknowledged the patient's right to refuse medical treatment and constitutionally protected right to freely exercise her religion; however, it still compelled Mrs. Jefferson to undergo the surgery. The Court relied on principles of *Roe v. Wade* that the state had a "compelling interest" in human life after viability.

Another case upholding fetal rights is that of *In Re Jamaica Hospital*[14] decided by the New York Supreme Court. The patient was 18-weeks pregnant. Both the mother and her fetus were in imminent danger of death as a result of bleeding from the mother's esophageal varicies. The mother was refusing blood transfusion based upon religious grounds, as a member of Jehovah's Witnesses. The New York Supreme Court acknowledged the mother's right to refuse medical treatment but also that a woman can be forced to receive a blood transfusion against her will to save the life of her non-viable fetus. The standard came from *Roe v. Wade* that a state can interfere with a woman's reproductive choices when it has a compelling interest. With respect to a non-viable fetus, the Court reasoned the state does not have a "compelling interest"; but the highly "significant interest" it does have, outweighs the patient's right to refuse a blood transfusion on religious grounds. The Court further expressed that the potentially viable fetus was a human being, to whom the court had a parens patriae duty to protect.

13.3.4 DISCUSSION

Reviewing the above case law acquaints the reader with the varied opinions regarding fetal rights. All of these cases struggle in the determination between the pregnant mother's right to privacy and bodily integrity, and the fetus' right to be born healthy and alive. In assessing fetal and maternal rights, it is important to be aware of case law on abortion which tends to hinge on the fetus' viability. The case law discussed above indicates that before a fetus is viable, a mother has the right to determine the outcome of her pregnancy. Any regulation of the woman's pre-viable pregnancy must not place an "undue burden" upon the mother.[15] After the point of viability, a mother may abort her pregnancy, only if, as a result of the pregnancy, the abortion is necessary for the preservation of the life or health of the mother.

Stephen M. Mohaupt

One study, which involved a national survey of heads of fellowship programs in maternal-fetal medicine, examined court ordered obstetrical procedures where the woman had refused therapy deemed necessary for the fetus.[16] Fifteen court orders for cesarean section were sought in eleven states and obtained in all except Maine. Three court orders for hospital detention were requested in two states and obtained in two of these cases; one from each state. Three court orders were sought in two states for intrauterine transfusions. Two of these orders were obtained in one state whereas the other was denied. An overall review of these cases found that court orders were granted in 86% (18 of 21).[16] Of these cases, 88% (16 of 18) of the court orders were received within six hours.[16]

13.3.5 DECISION TREE

When assessing a patient for treatment, the first step always includes informed consent, of which competency is an integral part. If there is an issue of fetal well being in a competent patient provided informed consent who refuses the recommended treatment, then viability of the fetus must be determined. In issues where fetal and maternal interests are in conflict and a physician believes further intervention may be necessary, case law points to determining viability of the fetus. Viability can be defined as, "A viable human fetus is one who has attained such form and development of organs as to be normally capable of living outside of the uterus."[5] In *Webster v. Reproductive Health Services*, the Court stated that viability could occur any time after the 20th week of pregnancy and imposed a duty on the physician to make a determination of the fetus' viability prior to performing an abortion.

Case law places great emphasis on viability regarding the state's interest in protecting potential human life. *Roe v. Wade* found, "The state had no legitimate interest in protecting a fetus until it reached the point of viability." However, there are some cases that protect a previable fetus. *In Re Jamaica Hospital* found a highly "significant interest" in a pre-viable fetus (18-weeks). The Court in *People v. Davis*[17] held that viability of the fetus is not an element of fetal murder (intentional killing of a previable fetus constitutes murder), "When a mother's privacy interests are not at stake, legislature may determine whether, and at what point it should protect life inside the mother's womb from homicide; without the viability component at least...where fetus is beyond the embryonic stage."

If the fetus is not viable, then the mother's decision for medical treatment almost always stands. Prior to viability, a woman has a right to abort the fetus and any state regulation on the pregnancy before viability must not be an "undue burden."[15] *In Re Jamaica Hospital* is the only case where medical intervention was ordered against the wishes of the pregnant woman with a previable fetus. A competent pregnant mother with a previable fetus almost always has complete determination concerning treatment decisions of herself and the fetus.

Once the fetus becomes viable, the state has an interest in the potential life. It is this arena that has varying opinions within the case law. Induced abortion is allowed only if the woman requires the procedure for the preservation of her life or health. Both *In Re A.C.*[11] and *In Re Baby Boy Doe*,[12] involved a viable fetus and held that the woman's right to refuse treatment overrode the state's interest in protecting the viable fetus. *In Re Jamaica Hospital*[14] and *Jefferson v. Griffin Spalding Hospital*[13] ordered interventions against the woman's will, reasoning that the state had a "highly significant interest" and "compelling interest" in the previable and viable fetus, respectively. This difference demonstrates that decisions between a mother's privacy right and the viable fetus' right to be born healthy and alive, are not consistent among courts.

The American Medical Association's Ethics[18] indicate that a competent pregnant mother's wishes should always take priority in her decisions for medical care. For example, the AMA's Ethics do not advocate prosecution of mothers for giving birth to an addicted baby. The courts have made rulings that differ from AMA's ethics.

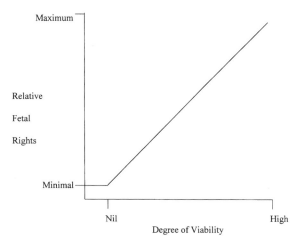

Figure 13.3.1 Relative fetal rights vs. degree of viability.

There is a history of jurisdictions seeking legal action toward women who use drugs during pregnancy. One such example is *Johnson v. State*.[19] The mother was convicted of delivery of a controlled substance to babies (two babies on two separate occasions) through the umbilical cord and after birth. The Court held that cocaine passing through the umbilical cord after birth, but before cutting of the cord, violated the statutory prohibition of adult delivery of controlled substance to a minor. The mother was sentenced to probation, community service, mandatory drug treatment, and participation in an intensive prenatal program if she again became pregnant. This decision was reversed by the Florida Supreme Court.[20]

It appears that as the pregnancy advances, so does the fetus' rights. The fetus has few rights prior to viability. The right to life of the fetus increases with development and as their potentiality matures.[21] From the point of viability until birth, the fetus' rights increase in a linear fashion. Some courts have advocated a balancing test of the mother's privacy interests and fetus' right to be born healthy and alive. Inferred from this balancing test is the necessity to weigh the relative degree of invasiveness of the proposed medical intervention and the degree or chance of viability. The further along in gestation and greater the chance of viability, the greater degree of fetal rights to be born healthy and alive (Figure 13.3.1). Consideration must be given to the proposed medical intervention. The greater degree of invasiveness of the proposed medical procedure to the mother increases the degree of maternal privacy rights or bodily integrity (Figure 13.3.2). There is no clear demarcation and each dilemma must be addressed on its own merits. As case law continues to evolve, so will the degree of weight applied to maternal privacy rights or the fetus' right to be born healthy and alive.

The purpose of the decision tree (Figure 13.3.3) is to consolidate the discussion above and serve as a tool for clinicians; thereby enhancing a more thorough assessment of these difficult cases. This decision tree assumes that informed consent has been provided and the mother found competent. Informed consent is an ongoing process of sharing information with the patient and her family as long as she is seeking treatment or the court is involved in treatment issues. If the mother continues to refuse treatment that the physician feels without, the fetus may suffer substantial harm or death, then the fetus' degree of viability must first be determined.

Viability has no precise demarcation but rather is a continuum. Figure 13.3.1 represents this continuum and the relative degree of fetal rights. The decision tree uses greater than 30 weeks gestational age as an example of high relative degree of viability. This time was chosen because it is the midpoint between 20 and 40 weeks; with 20 weeks gestation the earliest point to consider viability. The next step requires assessing degree of invasiveness. Consideration

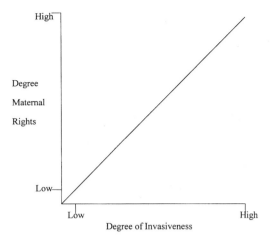

Figure 13.3.2 Degree of maternal rights vs. degree of invasiveness.

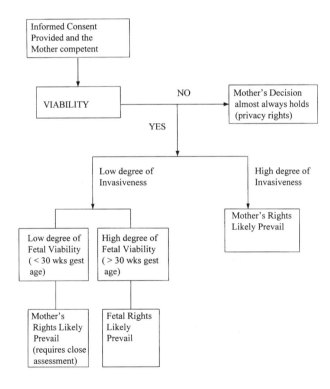

Figure 13.3.3 Decision tree.

should be given to other medical procedure so as to gage a degree of invasiveness. For example, a chest x-ray is less invasive than administration of intravenous fluid. Labor induction is less invasive than a cesarean section. The least invasive alternative would always be no medical procedure. Any proposed procedure with a high degree of invasiveness would result in the mother's rights likely to prevail. It is recommended that any case with a high degree of fetal viability and a clinical condition that poses a significant risk of substantial harm to the fetus, court intervention should be pursued. Fetal rights are most likely to prevail with a proposed procedure with a low degree of invasiveness with a high degree of fetal viability. When a case presents with a low degree of fetal viability and a low degree of invasiveness of the proposed procedure; court intervention is recommended.

The decision tree only applies to cases that are an emergency. If the case is urgent, court intervention may be requested in preparation that the situation may become emergent within a short period of time. When a dilemma presents, the hospital administrator or risk management should be contacted. Hospital administration should contact the proper legal channels to review the dilemma and, if necessary, apply for a court order for medical intervention.

The purpose of this chapter and the decision tree is to assist clinicians in the approach of these difficult dilemmas. There are no clear demarcations and each case must be evaluated on an individual basis. It is always preferable to resolve these dilemmas through consultation with the patient, family, and the treating physician. In an ideal world, these dilemmas would never occur, but they do and a systematic approach to their evaluation allows for a more thorough assessment.

13.3.6 SUMMARY

The issues discussed in this chapter are not about the beginning of life or when the fetus becomes human; rather, does the fetus have the right to be born healthy and alive? If the fetus does have this right, how does this right compare with the pregnant mother's right to bodily integrity and right to privacy?

In case law, fetal rights have been determined as minimal prior to viability. It is legal for a pregnant mother to abort her pre-viable fetus; therefore, the fetus' right to be born healthy and alive does not exist. After the point of viability, the fetus' rights to be born healthy and alive increase in a linear fashion and are greatest just prior to delivery.

In evaluating the possibility of instituting a medical procedure against a patient's will, consideration must be given to the risk of the medical procedure, the degree of invasiveness, and potential benefits both to the mother and fetus. Cases more likely to be granted a court order for intervention would include a pregnancy at term with a proposed medical procedure that has a low degree of invasiveness, and therefore, minimal risk to the mother and fetus. Less likely to receive a court order for intervention would include a viable fetus (around 24-week gestation) and a proposed medical procedure that has a high degree of invasiveness and a high degree of risk factors to the mother and fetus.

REFERENCES

1. Johnson v. State, 578 So. 2d 419 (Fla.App. 5 Dist.1991).
2. Epstein, Julia The Pregnant Imagination, Fetal Rights, and Women's Bodies: A Historical Inquiry. Yale Journal of Law & the Humanities 1995; 7:139-162.
3. Johnsen, Dawn E The Creation of Fetal Rights: Conflicts with Women's Constitutional Rights to Liberty, Privacy, and Equal Protection. The Yale Law Journal 1986; 95:599-625.
4. Blank, Robert H Maternal-Fetal Relationship The Courts and Social Policy. The Journal of Legal Medicine 1993; 14:73-83.
5. CALJIC 8.10, Murder Defined (Penal Code, Sec. 187).
6. Peterfy, A Fetal Viability As A Threshold To Personhood The Journal of Legal Medicine 1995; 16:607-630.
7. Committee on Doctrine of the National Conference of Catholic Bishops. The Ethical and Religious Directives for Catholic Health Facilities 1988; 7.
8. Cole, HM, editor. Legal Interventions During Pregnancy. Law and Medicine/Board of Trustees Report, Journal of American Medical Association 1990, 264:(20), 2663-70.

Stephen M. Mohaupt

9. Roe v. Wade; 1973 United States Supreme Court; 35 L ED 2d 147.
10. Webster v. Reproductive Health Services, Daily Appellate Report, July 6, 1989; 8724.
11. In Re AC, District of Columbia, 573 A.2d 1235 (D.C. App. 1990).
12. In Re Baby Boy Doe, 632 N.E. 2d 326 (Ill.App. 1 Dist. 1994).
13. Jefferson v. Griffin Spalding County Hospital Authority, Ga., 274 S.E. 2d 457.
14. In Re Jamaica Hospital, 491 NYS 2d 898.
15. Planned Parenthood v. Casey, (1992) 120 L Ed 2d 674.
16. Kolder, VEB, Gallagher, J, Parsons, MT. Court-Ordered Obstetrical Intervention. The New England Journal of Medicine 1987; May 7, 1192-1196.
17. People v. Davis, 30 Cal.Rptr.2d 50 (Cal.1994).
18. American Medical Association — House of Delegates, Constitution and Bylaws, and Current Opinion of the Council on Ethical and Judicial Affairs C.1995.
19. Johnson v. State, 578 So. 2d 419 (Fla.App. 5 Dist. 1991).
20. Johnson v. State, 602 So. 2d 1988 (Fla. 1992).
21. Beller, FK and Zlatnik, GP. The Beginning of Human Life. Journal of Assisted Reproduction and Genetics 1995; 12 (8):477-483.

APPENDICES

TABLE OF CONTENTS

APPENDIX IA GLOSSARY OF TERMS IN FORENSIC TOXICOLOGY

COMPILED BY CHIP WALLS

UNIVERSITY OF MIAMI, DEPARTMENT OF PATHOLOGY, FORENSIC TOXICOLOGY LABORATORY, MIAMI, FLORIDA

Absolute Method: A method in which characterization is based on physically defined (absolute) standards.

Accreditation: (1) A formal process by which a laboratory is evaluated, with respect to established criteria, for its competence to perform a specified kind(s) of measurement(s); (2) the decision based upon such a process; (3) formal recognition that a testing laboratory is competent to carry out specific tests or specific types of tests. [(3) - ISO Guide 2: 1986 (E/F/R)]

Accuracy: Closeness of the agreement between the result of a measurement and a true value of the measured quantity.

Acetaldehyde: The first product of ethanol metabolism

Acute tolerance: The development of tolerance within the course of a single exposure to a drug.

Acute: Severe, usually crucial, often dangerous in which relatively rapid changes are occurring. An acute exposure runs a comparatively short course.

Alcohol dehydrogenase (ADH): The main enzyme that catalyzes the conversion of ethanol to acetaldehyde.

Aldehyde dehydrogenase (ALDH): The enzyme that converts acetaldehyde to acetate.

Aliquot: (1) A divisor that does not divide a sample into a number of equal parts without leaving a remainder; (2) a sample resulting from such a divisor.

Analyte: The specific component measured in a chemical analysis.

Analytical run (series): A set of measurements carried out successively by one analyst using the same measuring system, at the same location, under the same conditions, and during the same short period of time.

Analytical sensitivity: The ability of a method or instrument to discriminate between samples having different concentrations or containing different amounts of the analyte. Slope of the analytical calibration function.

Analytical specificity: Ability of a measurement procedure to determine solely the measurable quantity (desired substance) it purports to measure and not others.

Analytical wavelength: Any wavelength at which an absorbance measurement is made for the purpose of the determination of a constituent of a sample.

Antemortem: Before death, occurring before death

Ascites: An abnormal accumulation of fluid in the peritoneal cavity of the abdomen.

Assignable cause: A cause believed to be responsible for an identifiable change in precision or accuracy of a measurement process.

Beer's law: The absorbance of a homogeneous sample containing an absorbing substance is directly proportional to the concentration of the absorbing substance.

Bias: A systematic error inherent in a method or caused by some artifact or idiosyncrasy of the measurement system. Temperature effects and extraction inefficiencies are examples of errors inherent in the method. Blanks, contamination, mechanical losses, and calibration errors are examples of artifact errors. Bias can be either positive or negative, and several kinds of error can exist concurrently. Therefore, net bias is all that can be evaluated.

Blank: (1) The measured value obtained when a specified component of a sample is not present during the measurement. In such a case, the measured value (or signal) for the component is believed to be due to artifacts and should be deducted from a measured value to give a net value due solely to the component contained in the sample. The blank .measurement must be made so that the correction process is valid. (2) Biological specimen with no detectable drugs added, routinely analyzed to ensure that no false-positive results are obtained.

Blind sample: A control sample submitted for analysis as a routine specimen whose composition is known to the submitter but unknown to the analyst. A blind sample is one way to test the proficiency of a measurement process.

Calibrant: Substance used to calibrate, or to establish the analytical response of, a measurement system.

Calibration: Comparison of a measurement standard or instrument with another standard or instrument to report or eliminate, by adjustment, any variation or deviation in the accuracy of the item being compared.

Central line: The long-term expected value of a variable displayed on a control chart.

Certification: A written declaration that a particular product or service complies with stated criteria. [Compilation of ASTM Standard Definitions, 7th Edition, (1990)]

Certified value: The value that appears in a certificate as the best estimate of the value for a property of a certified reference material.

Certified reference material (CRM): A reference material one or more of whose property values are certified by a technically valid procedure, accompanied by or traceable to a certificate or other documentation which is issued by a certifying body. [ISO Guide 30: 1981 (E)]

Chain of custody (COC): Handling samples in a way that supports legal testimony to prove that the sample integrity and identification of the sample have not been violated as well as the documentation describing these procedures.

Chance cause: A cause for variability of a measurement process that occurs unpredictably, for unknown reasons, and believed to happen by chance alone.

Check standard (in physical calibration): An artifact measured periodically, the results of which typically are plotted on a control chart to evaluate the measurement process.

Chronic tolerance: The gradual decrease in degree of effect produced at the same blood concentration in the course of repeated exposures to that drug.

Chronic: Persistent, prolonged, repeated.

Coefficient of variation: The standard deviation divided by the value of the parameter measured.

Comparative method: A method that is based on the intercomparison of the sample with a chemical standard.

Composite sample: A sample composed of two or more components selected to represent a population of interest.

Concentration: Amount of a drug in a unit volume of biological fluid, expressed as weight/volume. Urine concentrations are usually expressed either as nanograms per milliliter (ng/ml), micrograms per milliliter (µg/ml), or milligrams per liter (mg/l). (There are 28,000,000 micrograms in an ounce, and 1,000 nanograms in a microgram.)

Confidence interval: That range of values, calculated from an estimate of the mean and the standard deviation, which is expected to include the population mean with a stated level of confidence. In the same manner, confidence intervals can also be calculated for standard deviations, lines, slopes, and points.

Confirmation: A second test by an alternate chemical method to positively identify a drug or metabolite. Confirmations are carried out on presumptive positives from initial screens.

Control limits: The limits shown on a control chart beyond which it is highly improbable that a point could lie while the system remains in a state of statistical control.

Control chart: A graphical plot of test results with respect to time or sequence of measurement together with limits in which they are expected to lie when the system is in a state of statistical control.

Control sample: A material of known composition that is analyzed concurrently with test samples to evaluate a measurement process. (See also Check standard.)

Correlation coefficient: Measures the strength of the relation between two sets of numbers, such as instrument response and standard concentration.

Cross sensitivity: A quantitative measure of the response for an undesired constituent or interferent as compared to that for a constituent of interest.

Cross-reacting substances: In immunoassays, refers to substances that react with anti-serum produced specifically for other substances.

Cutoff level (threshold): Value serving as an administrative breakpoint (or cutoff point) for labeling a screening test result positive or negative.

Cytochrome P450: A detoxifying enzyme found in liver cells.

Detection limit or limit of detection (LOD): The lowest concentration of a drug that can reliably be detected. Smallest result of a measurement by a given measurement procedure that can be accepted with a stated confidence level as being different from the value of the measurable quantity obtained on blank material.

Double blind: A sample, known by the submitter but supplied to an analyst in such a way that neither its composition nor its identification as a check sample or standard are known to the analyst.

Duplicate measurement: A second measurement made on the same or identical sample of material to assist in the evaluation of measurement variance.

Endogenous: Produced or originating within the body by natural processes such as intermediary metabolism.

Enzymes: Proteins whose function is to drive the chemical reactions of the body — a catalyst of biochemical reactions.

False negative: An erroneous result in an assay that indicates the absence of a drug that is actually present.

False negative rate: This is the proportion of true positive samples that give a negative result.

False positive: An erroneous result in an assay that indicates the presence of a drug that is actually not present.

False positive rate: The proportion of true negative samples that give a positive test result.

Fume: Gas-like emanation containing minute solid particles arising from the heating of a solid body such as lead, in distinctions to a gas or vapor. This physical change is often accompanied by a chemical reaction such as oxidation. Fumes flocculate and sometimes coalesce. Odorous gases and vapors are not fumes.

Hepatocyte: Name given to cells within the liver.

Hyperglycemia: An excessive amount of glucose in the blood.

Hypoglycemia: An abnormally low concentration of glucose in the circulating blood.

Impairment: Decreased ability to perform safely a given task

Infrared: Pertaining to the region of the electromagnetic spectrum from approximately 0.78 to 300 microns (780 to 300,000 nanometers)

Insulin: A hormone produced in the islets of Langerhans in the pancreas as a response to elevated blood sugar levels. The hormone permits the metabolism and utilization of glucose.

Interferant: A chemical compound or substance other than the substance of interest (e.g., ethanol) to which the measuring instrument responds to give a falsely elevated result.

Interfering substances: Substances other than the analyte that give a similar analytical response or alter the analytical result.

Interindividual variation: Distribution of the values of a type of quantity in individuals of a given set.

Intraindividual variation: Distribution of the values of a type of quantity in a given individual.

Limit of quantification (LOQ): The lower limit of concentration or amount of substance that must be present before a method is considered to provide quantitative results. By convention, LOQ = l0 x so, where so = the estimate of the standard deviation at the lowest level of measurement.

Matrix effects: Influence of a component in the analytical sample other than the component being investigated on the measurement being made.

Matrix: The composition of the biological sample being analyzed, consisting of proteins, lipids and other biomolecules that can affect analyte recovery

MEOS: The microsomal ethanol oxidizing system, an enzyme system in liver that converts ethanol to acetaldehyde.

Metabolite: A compound produced from chemical changes of a drug in the body.

Microsomal enzymes: Detoxifying enzymes associated with certain membranes (smooth endoplasmic reticulum) within cells.

Ordinal scale: Ordered set of measurements consisting of words and/or numbers indicating the magnitude of the possible values that a type-of-quantity can take.

Outlier: A value in a sample of values so far separated from the remainder so as to suggest that it may be from a different population.

Perimortem: At or near the time of death.

Pharmacodynamics: The study of the relationship of drug concentration to drug effects.

Pharmacokinetics: The study of the time course of the processes (absorption, distribution, metabolism, and excretion) a drug undergoes in the body.

Physical dependence: A state that develops in parallel with chronic tolerance and is revealed by the occurrence of serious disturbances (abstinence syndrome) when drug intake is terminated.

Postmortem: After death, occurring after death, of or pertaining to a postmortem examination, an autopsy.

Precision: Closeness of agreement between independent results of measurements obtained by a measurement procedure under prescribed conditions (standard deviation).

Presumptive positive: Sample which has been flagged as positive by screening but which has not been confirmed by an equally sensitive alternative chemical method.

Proficiency-testing specimen: A specimen whose expected results are unknown to anyone in the laboratory, known only by an external agency, and later revealed to the laboratory as an aid to laboratory improvement and/or a condition of licensure.

Psycho: Pertaining to the mind and mental processes.

Psychoactive: Affecting the mind or mental processes.

Psychochemical: A substance affecting the mind or mental processes.

Psychology: The science of mental processes and behavior.

Psychomotor: Of or pertaining to muscular activity associated with the mental process.

Psychomotor functions: Matters of mental and motor function.

Psychosis: Severe mental disorder, with or without organic damage, characterized by deterioration of normal intellectual and social functioning and by partial or complete withdrawal from reality.

Psychotomimetic: Pertaining to or inducing symptoms of a psychotic state.

Psychotropic: Having a mind-altering effect.

Qualitative test: Chemical analysis to identify one or more components of a mixture.

Quality assurance (QA): Practices that assure accurate laboratory results.

Quality control (QC): Those techniques used to monitor errors which can cause a deterioration in the quality of laboratory results. Control material most often refers to a specimen, the expected results of which are known to the analyst, that is routinely analyzed to ensure that the expected results are obtained.

Quantitative test: Chemical analysis to determine the amounts or concentrations of one or more components of a mixture.

Repeatability: Closeness of agreement between the results of successive measurements during a short time (within run standard deviation).

Reproducibility: Closeness of agreement between the results of measurements of the same measurable quantity on different occasions, made by different observers, using different calibrations, at different times (between run standard deviation).

Screen: A series of initial tests designed to separate samples containing drugs at or above a particular minimum concentration from those below that minimum concentration (positive vs. negative).

Sensitivity: The detection limit, expressed as a concentration of the analyte in the specimen.

Specificity: Quality of an analytical technique that tends to exclude all substances but the analyte from affecting the result.

Split specimen: Laboratory specimen that is divided and submitted to the analyst, unknown to him or her, as two different specimens with different identifications.

Standard: Authentic sample of the analyte of known purity, or a solution of the analyte of a known concentration.

Substrate: The substance (molecule) acted upon by an enzyme; its conversion to a particular product is catalyzed by a specific enzyme.

Tolerance: A state that develops after long-term exposure to a drug. Metabolic tolerance infers a faster removal, oxidation by the liver. Functional tolerance infers a change in sensitivity of the organ to the effects of the drug.

Tolerance interval: That range of values within which a specified percentage of individual values of a population, measurements, or sample are expected to lie with a stated level of confidence.

Ultraviolet: Pertaining to the region of the electromagnetic spectrum from approximately 10 to 380 nm.

Visible: Pertaining to radiant energy in the electromagnetic spectral range visible to the human eye, approximately 380 to 780 nm.

Wavelength: A property of radiant energy, such as IR, visible, or UV. The distance measured along the line of propagation, between two points that are in phase on adjacent waves.

APPENDIX IB COMMON ABBREVIATIONS

COMPILED BY CHIP WALLS

UNIVERSITY OF MIAMI, DEPARTMENT OF PATHOLOGY, FORENSIC TOXICOLOGY LABORATORY, MIAMI, FLORIDA

ABS	Absorbance error (EMIT)
AM	Morning, antemortem
AMPH	Amphetamines
AP	Attending physician
APAP	Acetaminophen
Apt	Apartment
ASA	Salicylates
ASCVD	Arteriosclerotic cardiovascular disease
ASHD	Arteriosclerotic heart disease
BAC	Blood alcohol concentration
BDS	Basic drug screen
BE	Benzoylecgonine
BENZO	Benzodiazepine(s)
Bld	Blood
BP	Blood pressure
BSV	Blue-stoppered vacutainer
CAP	College of American Pathologists
CBC	Complete blood count
CI	Chemical ionization (in mass spectrometry)
CID	Criminal investigation department
CN	Cyanide
CO	Carbon monoxide
Co	County
c/o	Complain(-ing), (-ed), (-t) of
COPD	Chronic obstructive pulmonary disease
DC	Death certificate
Decd	Decedent/deceased
DM	Diabetes melitus
DNR	Do not resuscitate
D/T	Due to
DUI	Driving under the influence
DUID	DUI for drugs
DWI	Driving while intoxicated
dx	Diagnosed
EB	Eastbound
ECD	Electron capture detector (GC)
EI	Electron impact ionization (in mass spectrometry)
EMIT	Enzyme-multiplied immunoassay testing
ER	Emergency room
ET	Evidence technician
EtOH	Ethanol/alcohol
Ext	Extract
Extn	Extraction
FH	Funeral home

FID	Flame ionization detector (GC)
FS	Fingerstick
FTD	Failed to detect
Fx	Fracture
g	Gram
g%	Gram percent
GC	Gastric contents, gas chromatography
GC/MS	Gas chromatography/mass spectrometry
gm	Gram
GSW	Gunshot wound
GSV	Gray-stoppered vacutainer
H_2O	Water
HCT	Hematocrit
Hgb	Hemoglobin
HIV	Human immunodeficiency virus
HPLC	High performance liquid chromatograph(y)
HTN	Hypertension
Hx	History
ICU	Intensive care unit
L,l	Liter
LLQ	Left lower quadrant
LUQ	Left upper quadrant
MCT	Micro color test
MCV	Mean cell volume
Meds	Medications
MEO	Medical Examiner's Office
MeOH	Methanol
mg	Milligram
mL	Milliliter
MSDS	Material safety data sheet
MC	Mixed volatiles
MVA	Motor vehicle accident
n	Number
NB	Northbound
ND	None detected
NDD	No drugs detected
Neg	Negative
ng	Nanogram
NOK	Next of kin
DOH	Department of Health
NP	Nurse practitioner
NPD	Nitrogen Phosphorus detector
NR	Not requested
O_2	Oxygen
OF	Ocular fluid (vitreous)
Opi	Opiates
p	After
P	Probation
Pb	Lead
PCC	Poison Control Center
PCP	Phencyclidine

Chip Walls

pg	Picogram
PM	Postmortem, in the evening
PMH	Previous medical history
PO	Police officer, probation officer
Pos	Positive
PSV	Purple-stoppered vacutainer
p/u	Picke(ed) up
QA	Quality assurance
QC	Quality control
QNS	Quantity not sufficient
QS	Quantity sufficient
QS to _	Dilute to volume
R	Referral
RB	Reagent blank
RBC	Red blood cells
RIA	Radio immunoassay
RLQ	Right lower quadrant
R/O	Rule out
RSV	Red-stoppered vacutainer
RUQ	Right upper quadrant
Rx	Prescription
s	Without
S/A	Same address
SB	Southbound
SD	Standard deviation
Ser	Serum
SMA	Sympathomimetic amines
S/O	Sign-out
SOB	Shortness of breath
SOP	Standard operating procedure
Sp Gr	Specific gravity
SST	Serum separator tube
STD	Sexually transmitted disease
TAT	turn-around time
THC	Tetrahydrocannabinol
TLC	Thin-layer chromatography
Tx	Taken
U	Urine
VD	Veneral disease
VP	Venipuncture
w/	With
WAN	Weak acid/neutral
WB	Westbound
WBC	White blood cells
w/o	Without
x	Average
y/o	Year old
μL	Microliter (also uL)
μg	Microgram (also ug, ugm, μgm)
4-Br	Tetrabromophenolphthalein ethyl ester (a color test)
% sat	Percent saturation

APPENDIX IC REFERENCES FOR METHODS OF
DRUG QUANTITATIVE ANALYSIS

Drug name	Class	Fraction	UV	GC	LC	GC/MS	General
11-Hydroxy delta-9-THC	3	B		[1]	[2]	[3-9]	[10-12]
DELTA-9-THC	3	B					[10-12]
Acebutolol	2	B			[13]	[14]	[15-17]
Acetaminophen	1	WAN	[18-20]		[21-24]		[25-29]
Acetazolamide	5	B		[30]			
Acetylcarbromal	3	WAN					
Acetylsalicyclic acid	1	A		[31-33]	[34,35]		[36-38]
Albuterol	2	B			[39]		[40]
Alfentanil	1	B		[41]		[42]	[43, 44]
Allobarbital	3	WAN	[45]	[46-55]	[56,46, 57-60]		
Allopurinol	5	WAN					
Alphaprodine	1	B					[61]
Alprazolam	3	B/N		[62, 63]	[64,65]	[66]	
Amantadine	1	B					
Amiodarone	2	B		[67, 68]			
Amitriptyline	3	B		[69, 70]	[71-76]	[77-80]	
Amlodipine	3	B			[81]		
Amobarbital	3	WAN			[82-85]	[86, 87]	
Amoxapine	3	B		[88-90]			
Amphetamine	3	B			[91-93]	[94-101]	
Amyl nitrite	3	G					[102-106]
Aprobarbital	3	WAN		[50]		[107]	
Astemizole	4	B					[108]
Atenolol	2	B			[109]		
Atracurium	3	Q					[110]
Atropine (Hyoscyamine-D,L)	3	B				[111, 112]	[113]
Azatadine	3	B					
Baclofen	1	B			[114, 115]		
Barbital	3	WAN			[116]	[117]	
Barbiturates	3	WAN			[118-123]		[124, 120, 125-128, 51,129]
Benzephetamine	3	B					[130-134]
Benzocaine	3	B					[135]
Benzoylecgonine	3	AMPHO			[136-139]		[140-145]
Benzphetamine	3	B				[146]	
Benztropine	3	B				[147]	

Drug name	Class	Fraction	UV	GC	LC	GC/MS	General
Bepridil	2	B					[67]
Betaxolol	2	B					
Biperiden	3	B					
Bisoprolol	3	B					
Bretylium	2	O					
Bromazepam	3	B			[148]	[149]	
Bromocriptine	3	B				[150]	
Bromdiphen-hydramine	4	B		[151, 152]		[153, 154]	
Bupivacaine	3	B		[155-157]	[158]		[159-161]
Buprenorphine	1	B			[162, 163]	[164-166]	[167-169]
Bupropion	3	B		[170]		[171, 172]	[173, 174]
Buspirone	3	B		[62]	[175]	[175]	
Butabarbital	3	WAN			[176]		
Butalbital	3	WAN				[120, 126, 86, 107]	
Butorphanol	1	B				[177]	[178]
Caffeine	3	WAN			[179-181]		[182-184]
Camazepam	3	B					
Carbamazepine	3	B		[185-187]	[188-190]		[191, 192]
Carbinoxamine	3	B					
Carfentanil	1	B				[124, 193]	[194]
Carisoprodol	3	WAN		[195]		[196]	
Chlopropamide	5	WAN	[197]		[198]		
Chloral Hydrate	3	O		[199-202]		[203]	
Chlordiazepoxide	3	B		[204-206,202]	[201, 202]		
Chloropromazine	3	B		[207]	[208]	[209]	
Chloroquine	5	B			[210, 211]		
Chlorpheniramine	3	B	[212]	[213]			
Chlorphentermine	3	B					
Chlorpromazine	3	B		[214, 215]	[208, 216]		
Chlorpropamide	5	WAN					[197]
Chlorprothixene	3	B					
Chlorzoxazone	3	WAN, B					
Cimetidine	5	B			[217]		
Clemastine	3	B					
Clobazam	3	B			[218, 219]	[220]	
Clomipramine	3	B			[221-224]		
Clonazepam	3	B		[225-228]	[229-231]	[227]	
Clonidine	2	B				[232, 233]	
Clorazepate	3	B		[234, 235]		[236]	

References for Methods of Drug Quantitative Analysis

Drug name	Class	Fraction	UV	GC	LC	GC/MS	General
Clotiazepam	3	B					
Clozapine	3	B		[237-239]	[240-243]		[244]
Cocaethylene	3	B			[245]	[245, 246, 140, 247, 248]	[138, 249]
Cocaine	3	B		[248]	[250-253]	[254, 255, 140, 256, 145, 257]	
Codeine	1	B		[258]	[259]	[260-264]	[265]
Colchicine	5	B			[266, 267]		
Cotinine	5	B		[268]		[269-271]	
Cyclizine	3	B				[272]	
Cyclobenzaprine	3	B			[72]	[73, 273]	[274]
Cyclopane	5	WAN					
Cyproheptadine	3	B					[275]
delta-9-THC-Carboxylic acid	3	A			[276]	[7, 277-279, 10, 3]	
Demoxepam	3	B			[201, 280, 281]	[202, 282]	
Desalkylflurazepam	3	B			[283]	[284, 285]	[286]
Desflurane	5	G				[287]	
Desipramine	3	B					
dextromethorphan	4	B			[288, 289]		
Dextrorphan	4	B			[288, 289]		
Diazepam	3	B		[235, 290, 234]	[291, 292, 283]	[236]	
Diclofenac	1	A			[293, 294]		
Dicyclomine	5	B				[295]	
Diethylpropion	3	B					[296]
Diflunisal	1	WAN					[297]
Dihydrocodeine	1	B				[298, 299]	
Diltiazem	2	B				[300]	
Diphenhydramine	4	B		[152]		[153]	
Diphenoxin	1	B			[301]		
Diphenoxylate	1	B			[301]		
Disopyramide	2	B			[302, 303]	[304, 305]	[300]
Doxepin	3	B			[306]		[307]
Doxylamine	4	B				[308]	
Ecgonine methyl ester	3	B			[309, 310, 250, 251, 311]	[312, 254, 313-315]	
Encainide	2	B					[316, 317]
Enflurane	5	G				[318]	[319]
Ephedrin	4	B			[320]	[183]	

Drug name	Class	Fraction	UV	GC	LC	GC/MS	General
Esmolol	2	B					
Estazolam	3	B			[321]	[149]	
Ethanol	5	G		[322-329]			
Ethchlorvynol	3	O		[330-334]			[335, 336]
Ethinamate	3	WAN					
Ethosuximide	3	WAN			[337-339]		[340, 341]
Ethylene	5	G					
Ethylflurazepam	3	B					
Etodolac	1	A					
Etomidate	3	WAN		[342]			
Famotidine	3	B				[343]	
Felbamate	3	WAN, B		[344]	[189, 345, 346]		[347]
Felodipine	2	B		[348]			
Fenfluramine	3	B			[349]		
Fenoprofen	1	A			[350]		
Fentanyl	1	B		[351]		[124, 352, 353, 193, 354, 355]	[356]
Flecainide	2	B			[357-359]	[300]	
Flunitrazepam	3	B		[62, 63]	[360-363]		
Fluoxetine	3	B		[364-367]	[368]	[369]	
Fluphenazine	3	B				[370]	
Flurazepam	3	B					
Flurbiprofen	1	A					
Freon's	5	G					
Gasoline	5	G					
Glipizide	5	WAN			[371]		
Glutethimide	3	WAN		[372, 373]			[374, 375]
Glyburide	5	WAN			[371]		
Halazepam	3	B					
Haloperidol	3	B			[376-379]	[380-382]	
Hexobarbital	3	WAN		[383, 129, 384]		[120, 126, 125]	[385]
Hydrocodone	1	B					[386]
Hydromorphone	1	AMPHO			[387-389]	[390, 264]	
Hydroxychloroquine	5	B			[211, 391]		
Hydroxyzine	3	B		[392]			
Ibuprofen	1	WAN			[294, 393]	[394-397]	
Imipramine	3	B		[398]	[398-401]	[402]	
Indomethacin	1	WAN		[403, 404]	[405-407, 350]		
Insulin	5	O					[408-412]

References for Methods of Drug Quantitative Analysis

Drug name	Class	Fraction	UV	GC	LC	GC/MS	General
Iso-metheptene	5	B					
Isoflurane	3	G				[318]	
Isopropanol	5	G					[413-419]
Isoxsuprine	2	B					
Isradipine	2	B					[420]
Ketamin	3	B		[421]	[422]	[423, 424]	
Ketazolam	3	B					
Ketoprofen	1	WAN			[425-427]		
Ketorolac	1	B			[428-431]	[432]	
l-methamphetamine	3	B				[433-435]	
Lamotrigine	3	B					[436-438]
Levallorphan	1	B				[439]	
Levodopa	5	O					
Levorphanol	1	AMPHO					[440]
Lidocaine	5,2	B			[156,155,441]		
Lithium	3	O					
Loperamide	1	B					
Lorantadine	3	B					
Lorazepam	3	B			[281]	[442-444]	
loxapine	3	B					
LSD	3	B			[445-447]	[448, 449]	
Maprotiline	3	B				[450, 451]	
Mazindol	3	B					
MDEA	3	B				[132]	
Meclizine	3	B					
Medazepam	3	B				[361]	
Mefenamic Acid	1	A					
Meperidine (Pethidine)	1	B				[157]	
Mephentermine	3	B					
Mephenytoin	3	B					
Mephobarbital	3	B					
Mepivacaine	3	B					
Meprobamate	3	WAN		[195, 452]		[453]	[454, 375, 455]
Mescaline (Peyote)	3	B					[456]
Mesoridazine	3	B			[457]		[458]
Methadone and metabolites	1	B		[459]		[460-462]	
Methamphetamine	3	B		[463]		[464, 133, 465]	
Methanol	5	G		[466-468, 418]			
Methapyrilene	3	B					
Methaqualone	3	WAN,B		[469, 235]		[470]	
Methocarbamol	3	WAN					

Drug name	Class	Fraction	UV	GC	LC	GC/MS	General
Methohexital	3	WAN					
Methsuximide	3	WAN			[471]		[340]
Methylenedioxy-amphetamine (MDA)	3	B				[472, 132]	
Methylenedioxy-methamphetamine MDMA (Ecstasy)	3	B				[472, 132]	
Methylphenidate	3	B					
Methyprylon	3	WAN					
Methysergide	3	B					
Metoclopramide	5	B					
Metoprolol	2	B		[473]	[474]	[474]	
Mexiletine	2	B		[475]		[476, 300]	
Midazolam	3	B			[477, 478, 422]	[479]	
Molindone	1	B					
Monoacetylmorphine	1	B		[480]	[481]	[482, 299, 483, 484]	
Moricizine	2	B					
Morphine	3	AMPHO			[485-487]	[488-490]	
Morphine-3-glucuronide	3	AMPHO			[491-494]		
Nadolol	2	B					
Nalbuphine	1	B					[178, 495]
Naproxen	1	WAN			[294]		
Nicotine	5	B			[496]	[269, 497, 498]	
Nifedipine	2	B		[499]	[500, 501]	[502]	
Nitrazepam	3	B			[360, 149, 321, 363]		
Nitrous oxide	3	G					
Nomifensine	3	B					
Nylidrin		B					
Orphenadrine	3	B					
Oxazepam	3	B			[292]	[503]	
Oxycodone	1	B				[504, 505]	[506]
Oxymorphone	1	B				[505]	
Pancuraonium	3	Q					[507, 508]
Papaverine	2	B				[509]	
Paradehyde	3	O					
Paroxetine	3	B					[510]
PCP	3	B		[511-513]		[514, 515]	
Pemoline	3	B					[516]
Pentazocine	1	B		[517-519]			
Pentobarbital	3	WAN		[54, 49]		[520]	[521-524]

References for Methods of Drug Quantitative Analysis

Drug name	Class	Fraction	UV	GC	LC	GC/MS	General
Pergolide	3	B					[525]
Perphenazine	3	B					
Phendimetrazine	3	B					[526]
Phenelazine	3	B					
Phenobarbital	3	WAN			[189, 527, 339, 528, 529]		
Phensuximide	3	WAN					
Phentermine	3	B			[530]	[531, 134]	
Phenylpropanolamine	3	B		[532]			
Phenyltoloxamine	4	B					
Phenytoin (Diphenylhydantoin)	3	WAN			[533, 528, 534, 338]		
Piroxicam	1	A					
Prazepam	3	B			[360, 62, 321, 535]		
Primidone	3	WAN			[529, 527, 189]	[536, 537]	
Procainamide	2	B			[303]		[538, 539]
Procaine	5	B					
Promazine	3	B					
Promethazine	3	B			[540]		
Propafenone	3	B			[541]		
Propanolol	2	B		[473]	[542-544]	[545, 546]	
Propofol	3	B			[547]	[548]	
Propoxyphene	1	B		[549,469, 550-552]		[553-556]	[557-559]
Protriptyline	3	B			[222,376, 74, 560]		[561-563, 385, 564]
Pseudoephedrine	4	B					[565, 94]
Psyclyobin	3	O					
Pyrilamine	4	B				[308, 566]	
Quazepam	3	B		[567]	[568]		[569]
Quinidine	2	B			[570]		[538]
Quinine	5	B				[571]	
Ranitidine	5	B			[572, 573]		
Risperidone	3	B			[574, 575]		[576,577]
Scopolamine	3	B				[578, 579]	
Secobarbital	3	WAN			[580]		[581]
Selegiline	3	B		[582]	[583]	[584, 585]	[586]
Sertraline	3	B				[587]	[510]
Sotalol	2	B					
Strychnine	5	B					[588]
Succinylcholine	3	Q					[589, 590]
Sufentanil	1	B					[193, 591]

Drug name	Class	Fraction	UV	GC	LC	GC/MS	General
Sumatriptan	1	B					[592]
Talbutal	3	WAN				[593, 86, 594]	
Temazepam	3	B			[595]		[596, 597]
Terbutaline	4	B			[598]	[599, 600]	
Terfenadine	4	B					
Tetracaine	5	B					[601]
Tetrazepam	3	B					
Theophylline	4	WAN			[602, 603, 338, 83]		[604,605, 603, 606, 607]
Thiamylal	3	WAN			[608, 609]		
Thiopental	3	WAN		[610]	[405]		
Thioridazine	3	B			[457, 399]		
Thiothixene	3	B					
Tocainide	2	B					[300]
Tolazamide	3	WAN					
Tolmetin	1	WAN					[126]
Toluene	5	G		[611]		[612-614]	[615-617]
Tolutamide	3	WAN					
Tramadol	1	B					[618]
Tranylcypromine	3	B					
Trazodone	3	B		[619-621]			
Triazolam	3	B			[321]	[66, 622-624]	
Trichloroethylene	5	G		[625]			
Trifluoperazine	3	B					[67]
Triflupromazine	3	B					
Trihexyphenidyl	3	B		[626]			
Trimethadione	3	WAN					[627]
Trimethobenzamide	3	B					[628, 629]
Trimipramine	3	B		[398]	[630]	[402]	[631]
Tripelennamine	4	N		[517, 518, 632]			
Triprolidine	4	N					
Tubocurarine	5	Q					
Valproic acid	3	WAN		[633-635]	[636, 637]	[638]	[639]
Venlafaxine	3	B					[640, 641]
Verapamil	2	N		[642-644]			[645, 646]
Xylene	5	G					[647-650, 102]
Zolpidem	3	B			[651-655]		

KEY: Fraction (extraction): A = acid, B = Base, WAN = weak acid neutral, Ampho = amphoteric, Q = quantanary, O = Other

Pharmacological classification

1 Analgesics and Antiinflamatory
  Nonsteroidal antiinflammatorys
  Opioids
  Central Analgesics

2 Cardiovascular/DiureticDrugs
  Antiarrhythmics
  Antihypertensives
  Beta blockers
  Calcium channel blockers
  Inotropic
  Nitrates

3 Central Nervous System Drugs
  Anticonvulsants
  Antiemetics/ Antivertigo
  Depressants
  Hallucinogens
  Psychotherapeutic Agents
      Antianxiety
      Antidepressants
      Antipsychotics
      Sedatives and Hypnotics
  General Anesthetics
      Barbiturates
      Nonbarbiturates
      Gases
      Volatile liquids
  Muscle Relaxants
  Parkinsonism Drugs
  Stimulants
      Analeptics
      Amphetamines
      Anorexiants
      Nonprescription diet aids

4 Respiratory Drugs
  Antihistamines and Antiallergics
  Bronchodilators
  Cough and Cold

5 Other

REFERENCES

1. Ritchie, L. K., Caplan, Y. H., and Park, J., delta-9-Tetrahydrocannabinol analysis in forensic blood specimens using capillary column gas chromatography with nitrogen sensitive detection, *Journal of Analytical Toxicology,* 11, 205-209, 1987

2. Moffat, A. C., Williams, P. L., and King, L. J., Combined high-performance liquid chromatography and radioimmunoassay method for the analysis of delta 9- tetrahydrocannabinol and its metabolites in plasma and urine, *NIDA Research Monograph,* 42, 56-68, 1982

3. Hattori, H., Detection of cannabinoids by GC/MS. Part I. Quantitation of delta-9-THC in human urine and blood plasma., *Nippon Hoigaku Zasshi,* 35, 67-72, 1981

4. Huestis, M. A., Mitchell, J. M., and Cone, E. J., Detection Times of Marijuana Metabolites in Urine By Immunoassay and Gc-Ms, *Journal of Analytical Toxicology,* 19, 443-449, 1995

5. McCurdy, H. H., Lewellen, L. J., Callahan, L. S., and Childs, P. S., Evaluation of the Ion Trap Detector for the detection of 11-nor-delta 9-THC-9-carboxylic acid in urine after extraction by bonded-phase adsorption, *Journal of Analytical Toxicology,* 10, 175-177, 1986

6. Clatworthy, A. J., Oon, M. C., Smith, R. N., and Whitehouse, M. J., Gas chromatographic-mass spectrometric confirmation of radioimmunoassay results for cannabinoids in blood and urine, *Forensic Science International,* 46, 219-230, 1990

7. Wilkins, D., Haughey, H., Cone, E., Huestis, M., Foltz, R., and Rollins, D., Quantitative analysis of THC, 11-OH-THC, and THCCOOH in human hair by negative ion chemical ionization mass spectrometry, *Journal of Analytical Toxicology,* 19, 483-491, 1995

8. Kudo, K., Nagata, T., Kimura, K., Imamura, T., and Jitsufuchi, N., Sensitive determination of delta-9-tetrahydrocannabinol in human tissue by GC/MS, *J. Anal. Toxicol.,* 19, 87-90, 1995

9. Moeller, M. R., Doerr, G., and Warth, S., Simultaneous quantitation of delta-9-tetrahydrocannabinol (THC) and 11-nor-9-carboxy-delta-9-tetrahydrocannabinol (THC-COOH) in serum by GC/MS using deuterated internal standards and its application to a smoking study and forensic cases, *Journal of Forensic Sciences,* 37, 969-983, 1992

10. Huestis, M. A., Henningfield, J. E., and Cone, E. J., Blood cannabinoids. I. Absorption of THC and formation of 11-OH-THC and THCCOOH during and after smoking marijuana see comments], *Journal of Analytical Toxicology,* 16, 276-282, 1992

11. Huestis, M. A., Henningfield, J. E., and Cone, E. J., Blood cannabinoids. II. Models for the prediction of time of marijuana exposure from plasma concentrations of delta 9-tetrahydrocannabinol (THC) and 11-nor-9-carboxy-delta 9-tetrahydrocannabinol (THCCOOH) see comments], *Journal of Analytical Toxicology,* 16, 283-290, 1992

12. Kemp, P. M., Abukhalaf, I. K., Manno, J. E., Manno, B. R., Alford, D. D., and Abusada, G. A., Cannabinoids in humans, *Journal of Analytical Toxicology,* 19, 285-291, 1995

13. Meffin, P. J., Harapat, S. R., Yee, Y. G., and Harrison, D. C., High-pressure liquid chromatographic analysis of drugs in biological fluids. V. Analysis of acebutolol and its major metabolite, *Journal of Chromatography,* 138, 183-191, 1977

14. Siren, H., Saarinen, M., Hainari, S., Lukkari, P., and Riekkola, M., Screening of beta-blockers in human serum by ion-pair chromatography and their identification as methyl or acetyl derivatives by gas chromatography-mass spectrometry, *Journal of Chromatography,* 632, 215-227, 1993

15. Leloux, M., Niessen, W., and van der Hoeven, R., Thermospray liquid chromatography/mass spectrometry of polar beta-blocking drugs: preliminary results, *Biological Mass Spectrometry,* 20, 647-649, 1991

16. Ghanem, R., Bello, M. A., Callejon, M., and Guiraum, A., Determination of Beta-Blocker Drugs in Pharmaceutical Preparations By Non-Suppressed Ion Chromatography, *Journal of Pharmaceutical & Biomedical Analysis,* 15, 383-388, 1996

17. Segura, J., Pascual, J. A., Ventura, R., Ustaran, J. I., Cuevas, A., and Gonzalez, R., International cooperation in analytical chemistry: experience of antidoping control at the XI Pan American Games, *Clinical Chemistry,* 39, 836-845, 1993

18. Davey, L., Naidoo, D, Urinary screen for acetaminophen (paracetamol) in the presence of N-acetylcysteine, *Clinical Chemistry,* 39, 2348-2349, 1993

19. Novotny, P. E., Elser, R C, Indophenol method for acetaminophen in serum examined, *Clinical Chemistry,* 30, 884-886, 1984

20. Bailey, D. N., Colorimetry of serum acetaminophen (paracetamol) in uremia, *Clinical Chemistry,* 28, 187-190, 1982

21. Wong, A. S., An evaluation of HPLC for the screening and quantitation of benzodiazepines and acetaminophen in post mortem blood, *Journal of Analytical Toxicology,* 7, 33-36, 1983

22. West, J. C., Rapid HPLC analysis of paracetamol (acetaminophen) in blood and postmortem viscera, *Journal of Analytical Toxicology 1981 May-Jun;5(3):118-21,* 1981

23. Manno, B. R., Manno, J. E., Dempsey, C. A., and Wood, M. A., A high-pressure liquid chromatographic method for the determination of N-acetyl-p-aminophenol (acetaminophen) in serum or plasma using a direct injection technique, *Journal of Analytical Toxicology,* 5, 24-28, 1981

24. Colin, P., Sirois, G., and Chakrabarti, S., Rapid high-performance liquid chromatographic assay of acetaminophen in serum and tissue homogenates, *Journal of Chromatography,* 413, 151-160, 1987

25. Ashbourne, J. F., Olson, K. R., and Khayam-Bashi, H., Value of rapid screening for acetaminophen in all patients with intentional drug overdose, *Annals of Emergency Medicine,* 18, 1035-1038, 1989

26. Campbell, R. S. and Price, C. P., Experience with an homogeneous immunoassay for paracetamol (acetaminophen), *Journal of Clinical Chemistry & Clinical Biochemistry,* 24, 155-159, 1986

27. Dasgupta, A., Kinnaman, G, Microwave-induced rapid hydrolysis of acetaminophen and its conjugates in urine for emergency toxicological screen, *Clinical Chemistry,* 39, 2349-2350, 1993

28. Price, L. M., Poklis, A., and Johnson, D. E., Fatal acetaminophen poisoning with evidence of subendocardial necrosis of the heart, *Journal of Forensic Sciences,* 36, 930-935, 1991

29. Slattery, J. T., Nelson, S. D., and Thummel, K. E., The complex interaction between ethanol and acetaminophen. [Review], *Clinical Pharmacology & Therapeutics,* 60, 241-246, 1996

30. Wallace, S. M., Shah, V. P., and Riegelman, S., GLC analysis of acetazolamide in blood, plasma, and saliva following oral administration to normal subjects, *Journal of Pharmaceutical Sciences,* 66, 527-530, 1977

31. Asselin, W. M. and Caughlin, J. D., A rapid and simple color test for detection of salicylate in whole hemolyzed blood, *Journal of Analytical Toxicology,* 14, 254-255, 1990

32. Morris, H. C., Overton, P. D., Ramsay, J. R., Campbell, R. S., Hammond, P. M., Atkinson, T., *et al.,* Development and validation of an automated, enzyme-mediated colorimetric assay of salicylate in serum, *Clinical Chemistry,* 36, 131-135, 1990

33. Trinder, P., Rapid determination of salicylates in biological materials, *Biochemical Journal,* 57, 1954

34. Levine, B. and Caplan, Y. H., Liquid chromatographic determination of salicylate and methyl salicylate in blood and application to a postmortem case, *Journal of Analytical Toxicology,* 8, 239-241, 1984

35. Dipietra, A. M., Gatti, R., Andrisano, V., and Cavrini, V., Application of High-Performance Liquid Chromatography With Diode-Array Detection and On-Line Post-Column Photochemical Derivatization to the Determination of Analgesics, *Journal of Chromatography,* 729, 355-361, 1996

36. Chan, T. Y., Chan, A. Y., Ho, C. S., and Critchley, J. A., The clinical value of screening for salicylates in acute poisoning, *Veterinary & Human Toxicology,* 37, 37-38, 1995

37. Asselin, W. M. and Caughlin, J. D., A rapid and simple color test for detection of salicylate in whole hemolyzed blood, *Journal of Analytical Toxicology,* 14, 254-255, 1990

38. Jammehdiabadi, M. and Tierney, M., Impact of toxicology screens in the diagnosis of a suspected overdose: salicylates, tricyclic antidepressants, and benzodiazepines, *Veterinary & Human Toxicology,* 33, 40-43, 1991

39. Bland, R. E., Tanner, R. J., Chern, W. H., Lang, J. R., and Powell, J. R., Determination of albuterol concentrations in human plasma using solid-phase extraction and high-performance liquid chromatography with fluorescence detection, *Journal of Pharmaceutical & Biomedical Analysis,* 8, 591-596, 1990

40. King, W. D., Holloway, M., and Palmisano, P. A., Albuterol overdose: a case report and differential diagnosis. [Review], *Pediatric Emergency Care,* 8, 268-271, 1992

41. Bjorkman, S. and Stanski, D. R., Simultaneous determination of fentanyl and alfentanil in rat tissues by capillary column gas chromatography, *Journal of Chromatography,* 433, 95-104, 1988

42. Mautz, D., Labroo, R., and Kharasch, E., Determination of alfentanil and noralfentanil in human plasma by gas chromatography-mass spectrometry, *Journal of Chromatography B: Biomedical Applications,* 658, 149-153, 1994

43. Van, B. H., Van, P. A., Gasparini, R., Woestenborghs, R., Heykants, J., Noorduin, H., *et al.,* Pharmacokinetics of alfentanil during and after a fixed rate infusion, *British Journal of Anaesthesia,* 62, 610-615, 1989

44. Meistelman, C., Saint-Maurice, C., Lepaul, M., Levron, J., Loose, J., and Mac, G. K., A comparison of alfentanil pharmacokinetics in children and adults, *Anesthesiology,* 66, 13-16, 1987

45. Schumann, G. B., Lauenstein, K., LeFever, D., and Henry, J. B., Ultraviolet spectrophotometric analysis of barbiturates, *American Journal of Clinical Pathology,* 66, 823-830, 1976

46. Gill, R., Stead, A. H., and Moffat, A. C., Analytical aspects of barbiturate abuse: identification of drugs by the effective combination of gas-liquid, high-performance liquid and thin-layer chromatographic techniques, *Journal of Chromatography,* 204, 275-284, 1981

47. Lillsunde, P., Michelson, L., Forsstrom, T., Korte, T., Schultz, E., Ariniemi, K., *et al.,* Comprehensive drug screening in blood for detecting abused drugs or drugs potentially hazardous for traffic safety, *Forensic Science International,* 77, 191-210, 1996

48. Mule, S. and Casella, G., Confirmation and quantitation of barbiturates in human urine by gas chromatography/mass spectrometry, *Journal of Analytical Toxicology,* 13, 13-16, 1989

49. Wallace, J. E., Hall, L. R., and Harris, S. C., Determination of pentobarbital and certain other barbiturates by capillary gas-liquid chromatography, *Journal of Analytical Toxicology,* 7, 178-180, 1983

50. Budd, R. D., Gas chromatographic properties of 1,3-dialkyl barbiturate derivatives, *Clinical Toxicology,* 17, 375-382, 1980

51. Barbour, A. D., GC/MS analysis of propylated barbiturates, *Journal of Analytical Toxicology,* 15, 214-215, 1991

52. Christophersen, A. S. and Rasmussen, K. E., Glass capillary column gas chromatography of barbiturates after flash-heater derivatization with dimethylformamide dimethylacetal, *Journal of Chromatography,* 192, 363-374, 1980

53. Budd, R. D. and Mathis, D. F., GLC screening and confirmation of barbiturates in post mortem blood specimens, *Journal of Analytical Toxicology,* 6, 317-320, 1982

54. Sun, S. R. and Hoffman, D. J., Rapid, sensitive GLC determination of pentobarbital and other barbiturates in serum using nitrogen-specific detector, *Journal of Pharmaceutical Sciences,* 68, 386-388, 1979

55. Marigo, M., Ferrara, S. D., and Tedeschi, L., A sensitive method for gas-chromatographic assay of barbiturates in body fluids, *Archives of Toxicology,* 37, 107-112, 1977

56. Gill, R., Lopes, A. A., and Moffat, A. C., Analysis of barbiturates in blood by high-performance liquid chromatography, *Journal of Chromatography,* 226, 117-123, 1981

57. Drummer, O. H., Kotsos, A., and McIntyre, I. M., A class-independent drug screen in forensic toxicology using a photodiode array detector, *Journal of Analytical Toxicology,* 17, 225-229, 1993

58. Chan, E. M. and Chan, S. C., Screening for acidic and neutral drugs by high performance liquid chromatography in post-mortem blood, *Journal of Analytical Toxicology,* 8, 173-176, 1984

59. Ferrara, S. D., Tedeschi, L., Frison, G., and Castagna, F., Solid-phase extraction and HPLC-UV confirmation of drugs of abuse in urine, *Journal of Analytical Toxicology,* 16, 217-222, 1992

60. Lehane, D. P., Menyharth, P., Lum, G., and Levy, A. L., Therapeutic drug monitoring: measurements of antiepileptic and barbiturate drug levels in blood by gas chromatography with nitrogen - selective detector, *Annals of Clinical & Laboratory Science,* 6, 404-410, 1976

References for Methods of Drug Quantitative Analysis

61. Van Vunakis, H., Freeman, D. S., and Gjika, H. B., Radioimmunoassay for anileridine, meperidine and other N-substituted phenylpiperidine carboxylic acid esters, *Research Communications in Chemical Pathology & Pharmacology,* 12, 379-387, 1975

62. Gaillard, Y., Gay-Montchamp, J. P., and Ollagnier, M., Simultaneous screening and quantitation of alpidem, zolpidem, buspirone and benzodiazepines by dual-channel gas chromatography using electron-capture and nitrogen-phosphorus detection after solid-phase extraction, *Journal of Chromatography,* 622, 197-208, 1993

63. Lillsunde, P. and Seppala, T., Simultaneous screening and quantitative analysis of benzodiazepines by dual-channel gas chromatography using electron-capture and nitrogen-phosphorus detection, *Journal of Chromatography,* 533, 97-110, 1990

64. Akerman, K. K., Jolkkonen, J., Parviainen, M., and Penttila, I., Analysis of low-dose benzodiazepines by HPLC with automated solid-phase extraction, *Clinical Chemistry,* 42, 1412-1416, 1996

65. Shimamine, M., Masunari, T., and Nakahara, Y., [Studies on identification of drugs of abuse by diode array detection. I. Screening-test and identification of benzodiazepines by HPLC-DAD with ICOS software system], *Eisei Shikenjo Hokoku - Bulletin of National Institute of Hygienic Sciences,* 47-56, 1993

66. Cairns, E. R., Dent, B. R., Ouwerkerk, J. C., and Porter, L. J., Quantitative analysis of alprazolam and triazolam in hemolysed whole blood and liver digest by GC/MS/NICI with deuterated internal standards, *Journal of Analytical Toxicology,* 18, 1-6, 1994

67. Pollak, P. T., A systematic review and critical comparison of internal standards for the routine liquid chromatographic assay of amiodarone and desethylamiodarone, *Therapeutic Drug Monitoring,* 18, 168-178, 1996

68. Flanagan, R. J., Storey, G. C., and Holt, D. W., Rapid high-performance liquid chromatographic method for the measurement of amiodarone in blood plasma or serum at the concentrations attained during therapy, *Journal of Chromatography,* 187, 391-398, 1980

69. Fernandez, G. S., Witherington, T. L., and Stafford, D. T., Effective column extraction from decomposed tissue in a suspected overdose case involving maprotiline and amitriptyline, *Journal of Analytical Toxicology,* 9, 230-231, 1985

70. Bailey, D. N. and Jatlow, P. I., Gas-chromatographic analysis for therapeutic concentrations of amitriptyline and nortriptyline in plasma, with use of a nitrogen detector, *Clinical Chemistry,* 22, 777-781, 1976

71. Vandel, S., Vincent, F., Prudhon, F., Nezelof, S., Bonin, B., and Bertschy, G., [Comparative study of two techniques for the determination of amitriptyline and nortriptyline: EMIT and gas chromatography]. [French], *Therapie,* 47, 41-45, 1992

72. Poklis, A. and Edinboro, L. E., REMEDi drug profiling system readily distinguishes between cyclobenzaprine and amitriptyline in emergency toxicology urine specimens [letter], *Clinical Chemistry,* 38, 2349-2350, 1992

73. Wong, E. C., Koenig, J., and Turk, J., Potential interference of cyclobenzaprine and norcyclobenzaprine with HPLC measurement of amitriptyline and nortriptyline: resolution by GC- MS analysis, *Journal of Analytical Toxicology,* 19, 218-224, 1995

74. Attapolitou, J., Tsarpalis, K., and Koutselinis, A., A modified simple and rapid reversed phase high performance liquid chromatographic method for quantification of amitriptyline and nortriptyline in plasma, *J. Liq. Chromatogr.,* 17, 3969-3982, 1994

75. Rop, P. P., Viala, A., Durand, A., and Conquy, T., Determination of citalopram, amitriptyline and clomipramine in plasma by reversed-phase high-performance liquid chromatography, *Journal of Chromatography,* 338, 171-178, 1985

76. Hartter, S. and Hiemke, C., Column switching and high-performance liquid chromatography in the analysis of amitriptyline, nortriptyline and hydroxylated metabolites in human plasma or serum, *Journal of Chromatography,* 578, 273-282, 1992

77. Oliver, J. S. and Smith, H., Amitriptyline and metabolites in biological fluids, *Forensic Science 3(2):181-7,* 1974

78. Spiehler, V., Spiehler, E., and Osselton, M. D., Application of expert systems analysis to interpretation of fatal cases involving amitriptyline, *Journal of Analytical Toxicology,* 12, 216-224, 1988

79. Bolster, M., Curran, J., and Busuttil, A., A five year review of fatal self-ingested overdoses involving amitriptyline in Edinburgh 1983-'87, *Human & Experimental Toxicology*, 13, 29-31, 1994

80. Bailey, D. N. and Shaw, R. F., Interpretation of blood and tissue concentrations in fatal self-ingested overdose involving amitriptyline: an update (1978-1979), *Journal of Analytical Toxicology*, 4, 232-236, 1980

81. Pandya, K. K., satia, M., Gandhi, T. P., Modi, I. A., Modi, R. I., and Chakravarthy, B. K., Detection and determination of total amlodipine by high-performance thin-layer chromatography: a useful technique for pharmacokinetic studies, *Journal of Chromatography B: Biomedical Applications*, 667, 315-320, 1995

82. Svinarov, D. A. and Dotchev, D. C., Simultaneous liquid-chromatographic determination of some bronchodilators, anticonvulsants, chloramphenicol, and hypnotic agents, with Chromosorb P columns used for sample preparation, *Clinical Chemistry*, 35, 1615-1618, 1989

83. Meatherall, R. and Ford, D., Isocratic liquid chromatographic determination of theophylline, acetaminophen, chloramphenicol, caffeine, anticonvulsants, and barbiturates in serum, *Therapeutic Drug Monitoring*, 10, 101-115, 1988

84. Kabra, P. M., Stafford, B. E., and Marton, L. J., Rapid method for screening toxic drugs in serum with liquid chromatography, *Journal of Analytical Toxicology*, 5, 177-182, 1981

85. Kabra, P. M., Koo, H. Y., and Marton, L. J., Simultaneous liquid-chromatographic determination of 12 common sedatives and hypnotics in serum, *Clinical Chemistry*, 24, 657-662, 1978

86. Liu, R. H., McKeehan, A. M., Edwards, C., Foster, G., Bensley, W. D., Langner, J. G., *et al.*, Improved gas chromatography/mass spectrometry analysis of barbiturates in urine using centrifuge- based solid-phase extraction, methylation, with d5-pentobarbital as internal standard, *Journal of Forensic Sciences*, 39, 1504-1514, 1994

87. Pocci, R., Dixit, V., and Dixit, V., Solid-phase extraction and GC/MS confirmation of barbiturates from human urine, *Journal of Analytical Toxicology*, 16, 45-47, 1992

88. Osiewicz, R. J. and Middleberg, R., Detection of a novel compound after overdoses of aspirin and amoxapine, *Journal of Analytical Toxicology*, 13, 97-99, 1989

89. Taylor, R. L., Crooks, C. R., and Caplan, Y. H., The determination of amoxapine in human fatal overdoses, *Journal of Analytical Toxicology*, 6, 309-311, 1982

90. Wu Chen, N. B., Schaffer, M. I., Lin, R. L., Hadac, J. P., and Stein, R. J., Analysis of blood and tissue for amoxapine and trimipramine, *Journal of Forensic Sciences*, 28, 116-121, 1983

91. Bourque, A. J., Krull, I. S., and Feibush, B., Automated HPLC analyses of drugs of abuse via direct injection of biological fluids followed by simultaneous solid-phase extraction and derivatization with fluorescence detection, *Biomedical Chromatography*, 8, 53-62, 1994

92. Achilli, G., Cellerino, G. P., Deril, G. V. M., and Tagliaro, F., Determination of Illicit Drugs and Related Substances By High-Performance Liquid Chromatography With an Electrochemical Coulometric-Array Detector, *Journal of Chromatography*, 729, 273-277, 1996

93. Michel, R. E., Rege, A. B., and George, W. J., High-pressure liquid chromatography/ electrochemical detection method for monitoring MDA and MDMA in whole blood and other biological tissues, *Journal of Neuroscience Methods*, 50, 61-66, 1993

94. Paul, B. D., Past, M. R., McKinley, R. M., Foreman, J. D., McWhorter, L. K., and Snyder, J. J., Amphetamine as an artifact of methamphetamine during periodate degradation of interfering ephedrine, pseudoephedrine, and phenylpropanolamine: an improved procedure for accurate quantitation of amphetamines in urine, *Journal of Analytical Toxicology*, 18, 331-336, 1994

95. Suzuki, S., Inoue, T., Hori, H., and Inayama, S., Analysis of methamphetamine in hair, nail, sweat, and saliva by mass fragmentography, *Journal of Analytical Toxicology*, 13, 176-178, 1989

96. Hornbeck, C. L., Carrig, J. E., and Czarny, R. J., Detection of a GC/MS artifact peak as methamphetamine, *Journal of Analytical Toxicology*, 17, 257-263, 1993

97. Nakahara, Y., Detection and diagnostic interpretation of amphetamines in hair. [Review], *Forensic Science International*, 70, 135-153, 1995

98. Kalasinsky, K. S., Levine, B., Smith, M. L., Magluilo, J., Jr., and Schaefer, T., Detection of amphetamine and methamphetamine in urine by gas chromatography/Fourier transform infrared (GC/FTIR) spectroscopy, *Journal of Analytical Toxicology*, 17, 359-364, 1993

99. Lillsunde, P. and Korte, T., Determination of ring- and N-substituted amphetamines as heptafluorobutyryl derivatives, *Forensic Science International*, 49, 205-213, 1991

100. Logan, B. K., Methamphetamine and driving impairment. [Review], *Journal of Forensic Sciences*, 41, 457-464, 1996

101. Rasmussen, S., Cole, R., and Spiehler, V., Methamphetamine in antemortem blood and urine by RIA and GC/MS, *J. Anal. Toxicol.*, 13, 263-267, 1989

102. Premel-Cabic, A., Cailleux, A., and Allain, P., [A gas chromatographic assay of fifteen volatile organic solvents in blood (author's transl)]. [French], *Clinica Chimica Acta*, 56, 5-11, 1974

103. Astier, A., Chromatographic determination of volatile solvents and their metabolites in urine for monitoring occupational exposure, *Journal of Chromatography*, 643, 389-398, 1993

104. Oliver, J. S. and Watson, J. M., Abuse of solvents "for kicks", *Lancet*, 1, 84-86, 1977

105. Ghittori, S., Fiorentino, M. L., and Imbriani, M., [Use of gas chromatography with flame ionization (GC-FID) in the measurement of solvents in the urine], *Giornale Italiano di Medicina del Lavoro*, 9, 21-24, 1987

106. Houghton, E., Teale, P., and Dumasia, M. C., Improved capillary GC/MS method for the determination of anabolic steroid and corticosteroid metabolites in horse urine using on-column injection with high-boiling solvents., *Analyst (London)*, 109, 273-275, 1984

107. Maurer, H. H., Identification and differentiation of barbiturates, other sedative-hypnotics and their metabolites in urine integrated in a general screening procedure using computerized gas chromatography-mass spectrometry, *Journal of Chromatography*, 530, 307-326, 1990

108. Kingswood, J. C., Routledge, P. A., and Lazarus, J. H., A report of overdose with astemizole, *Human Toxicology*, 5, 43-44, 1986

109. Law, B. and Weir, S., Fundamental studies in reversed-phase liquid-solid extraction of basic drugs; II: Hydrogen bonding effects, *Journal of Pharmaceutical & Biomedical Analysis*, 10, 181-186, 1992

110. Logan, B. K. and Case, G. A., Identification of laudanosine, an atracurium metabolite, following a fatal drug-related shooting, *Journal of Analytical Toxicology*, 17, 117-119, 1993

111. Xu, A., Havel, J., Linderholm, K., and Hulse, J., Development and validation of an LC/MS/MS method for the determination of L-hyoscyamine in human plasma, *Journal of Pharmaceutical & Biomedical Analysis*, 14, 33-42, 1995

112. Saady, J. J. and Poklis, A., Determination of atropine in blood by gas chromatography/mass spectrometry, *Journal of Analytical Toxicology*, 13, 296-299, 1989

113. Cugell, D. W., Clinical pharmacology and toxicology of ipratropium bromide. [Review], *American Journal of Medicine*, 81, 18-22, 1986

114. Fraser, A. D., MacNeil, W., and Isner, A. F., Toxicological analysis of a fatal baclofen (Lioresal) ingestion, *Journal of Forensic Sciences*, 36, 1596-1602, 1991

115. Millerioux, L., Brault, M., Gualano, V., and Mignot, A., High-Performance Liquid Chromatographic Determination Of Baclofen In Human Plasma, *Journal of Chromatography 729(1-2):309-314*, 1996

116. Bailey, D. N. and Jatlow, P. I., Barbital overdose and abuse, *American Journal of Clinical Pathology*, 64, 291-296, 1975

117. Varin, F., Marchand, C., Larochelle, P., and Midha, K. K., GLC-mass spectrometric procedure with selected-ion monitoring for determination of plasma concentrations of unlabeled and labeled barbital following simultaneous oral and intravenous administration, *Journal of Pharmaceutical Sciences*, 69, 640-643, 1980

118. Moriya, F. and Hashimoto, Y., Application of the Triage panel for drugs of abuse to forensic blood samples, *Nippon Hoigaku Zasshi - Japanese Journal of Legal Medicine*, 50, 50-56, 1996

119. Chankvetadze, B., Chankvetadze, L., Sidamonidze, S., Yashima, E., and Okamoto, Y., High performance liquid chromatography enantioseparation of chiral pharmaceuticals using tris(chloromethylphenylcarbamate)s of cellulose, *Journal of Pharmaceutical & Biomedical Analysis*, 14, 1295-1303, 1996

120. Qiu, F. H., Liu, L., Guo, L., Luo, Y., and Lu, Y. Q., [Rapid identification and quantitation of barbiturates in plasma using solid-phase extraction combined with GC-FID and GC-MS method], *Yao Hsueh Hsueh Pao - Acta Pharmaceutica Sinica*, 30, 372-377, 1995

121. Thormann, W., Meier, P., Marcolli, C., and Binder, F., Analysis of barbiturates in human serum and urine by high-performance capillary electrophoresis-micellar electrokinetic capillary chromatography with on-column multi-wavelength detection, *Journal of Chromatography,* 545, 445-460, 1991

122. Minder, E. I., Schaubhut, R., and Vonderschmitt, D. J., Screening for drugs in clinical toxicology by high-performance liquid chromatography: identification of barbiturates by post-column ionization and detection by a multiplace photodiode array spectrophotometer, *Journal of Chromatography,* 428, 369-376, 1988

123. Mangin, P., Lugnier, A. A., and Chaumont, A. J., A polyvalent method using HPLC for screening and quantification of 12 common barbiturates in various biological materials, *Journal of Analytical Toxicology,* 11, 27-30, 1987

124. Cody, J. T. and Foltz, R. L., GC/MS analysis of body fluids for drugs of abuse, in *Forensic Appl. of Mass Spectrom.,* Yinon, J., CRC Press, Boca Raton, FL, 1995, p 1-59.

125. Kojima, T., Taniguchi, T., Yashiki, M., Miyazaki, T., Iwasaki, Y., Mikami, T., *et al.,* A rapid method for detecting barbiturates in serum using EI-SIM, *International Journal of Legal Medicine,* 107, 21-24, 1994

126. Abadi, M. and Solomon, H. M., Detection of tolmetin and oxaprozin by a GC/MS method for barbiturates [letter], *Journal of Analytical Toxicology,* 18, 62, 1994

127. Gibb, R. P., Cockerham, H., Goldfogel, G. A., Lawson, G. M., and Raisys, V. A., Substance abuse testing of urine by GC/MS in scanning mode evaluated by proficiency studies, TLC/GC, and EMIT, *Journal of Forensic Sciences,* 38, 124-133, 1993

128. Pocci, R., Dixit, V., and Dixit, V. M., Solid-phase extraction and GC/MS confirmation of barbiturates from human urine, *Journal of Analytical Toxicology,* 16, 45-47, 1992

129. Chen, X. H., Wijsbeek, J., van Veen, J., Franke, J. P., and de Zeeuw, R. A., Solid-phase extraction for the screening of acidic, neutral and basic drugs in plasma using a single-column procedure on Bond Elut Certify, *Journal of Chromatography,* 529, 161-166, 1990

130. Logan, B. K., Methamphetamine and driving impairment. [Review] [37 refs], *Journal of Forensic Sciences,* 41, 457-464, 1996

131. Long, C. and Crifasi, J., Methamphetamine identification in four forensic cases, *Journal of Forensic Sciences,* 41, 713-714, 1996

132. Ensslin, H. K., Kovar, K. A., and Maurer, H. H., Toxicological Detection of the Designer Drug 3,4-Methylenedioxyethylamphetamine (Mde, Eve) and Its Metabolites in Urine By Gas Chromatography Mass Spectrometry and Fluorescence Polarization Immunoassay, *Journal of Chromatography B: Biomedical Applications,* 683, 189-197, 1996

133. Valentine, J. L., Kearns, G. L., Sparks, C., Letzig, L. G., Valentine, C. R., Shappell, S. A., *et al.,* GC-MS determination of amphetamine and methamphetamine in human urine for 12 hours following oral administration of dextro-methamphetamine: lack of evidence supporting the established forensic guidelines for methamphetamine confirmation, *Journal of Analytical Toxicology,* 19, 581-590, 1995

134. Meatherall, R., Rapid GC-MS confirmation of urinary amphetamine and methamphetamine as their propylchloroformate derivatives, *Journal of Analytical Toxicology,* 19, 316-322, 1995

135. Arufe-Martinez, M. I. and Romero-Palanco, J. L., Identification of cocaine in cocaine-lidocaine mixtures ("rock cocaine") and other illicit cocaine preparations using derivative absorption spectroscopy, *Journal of Analytical Toxicology,* 12, 192-196, 1988

136. Clauwaert, K. M., Vanbocxlaer, J. F., Lambert, W. E., and Deleenheer, A. P., Analysis of Cocaine, Benzoylecgonine, and Cocaethylene in Urine By Hplc With Diode Array Detection, *Analytical Chemistry,* 68, 3021-3028, 1996

137. Fernandez, P., Lafuente, N., Bermejo, A. M., Lopezrivadulla, M., and Cruz, A., Hplc Determination of Cocaine and Benzoylecgonine in Plasma and Urine From Drug Abusers, *Journal of Analytical Toxicology,* 20, 224-228, 1996

138. Logan, B. K., Smirnow, D., and Gullberg, R. G., Lack of Predictable Site-Dependent Differences and Time-Dependent Changes in Postmortem Concentrations of Cocaine, Benzoylecgonine, and Cocaethylene in Humans, *Journal of Analytical Toxicology,* 21, 23-31, 1997

139. Sosnoff, C. S., Ann, Q., Bernert, J. T., Jr., Powell, M. K., Miller, B. B., Henderson, L. O., *et al.*, Analysis of benzoylecgonine in dried blood spots by liquid chromatography—atmospheric pressure chemical ionization tandem mass spectrometry, *Journal of Analytical Toxicology*, 20, 179-184, 1996

140. Thompson, W. C. and Dasgupta, A., Confirmation and quantitation of cocaine, benzoylecgonine, ecgonine methyl ester, and cocaethylene by gas chromatography/mass spectrometry, *American Journal of Clinical Pathology*, 104, 187-192, 1995

141. Corburt, M. R. and Koves, E. M., Gas chromatography/mass spectrometry for the determination of cocaine and benzoylecgonine over a wide concentration range (< 0, *Journal of Forensic Sciences*, 39, 136-149, 1994

142. Okeke, C. C., Wynn, J. E., and Patrick, K. S., Simultaneous analysis of cocaine, benzoylecgonine, methylecgonine, and ecgonine in plasma using an exchange resin and GC/MS, *Chromatographia*, 38, 52-56, 1994

143. Gerlits, J., GC/MS quantitation of benzoylecgonine following liquid-liquid extraction of urine, *Journal of Forensic Sciences*, 38, 1210-1214, 1993

144. Aderjan, R. E., Schmitt, G., Wu, M., and Meyer, C., Determination of cocaine and benzoylecgonine by derivatization with iodomethane-D3 or PFPA/HFIP in human blood and urine using GC/MS (EI or PCI mode), *Journal of Analytical Toxicology*, 17, 51-55, 1993

145. Abusada, G. M., Abukhalaf, I. K., Alford, D. D., Vinzon-Bautista, I., Pramanik, A. K., Ansari, N. A., *et al.*, Solid-phase extraction and GC/MS quantitation of cocaine, ecgonine methyl ester, benzoylecgonine, and cocaethylene from meconium, whole blood, and plasma, *Journal of Analytical Toxicology*, 17, 353-358, 1993

146. Kikura, R. and Nakahara, Y., Hair analysis for drugs of abuse. XI. Disposition of benzphetamine and its metabolites into hair and comparison of benzphetamine use and methamphetamine use by hair analysis, *Biological & Pharmaceutical Bulletin*, 18, 1694-1699, 1995

147. Rosano, T. G., Meola, J. M., Wolf, B. C., Guisti, L. W., and Jindal, S. P., Benztropine identification and quantitation in a suicidal overdose, *Journal of Analytical Toxicology*, 18, 348-353, 1994

148. Le Solleu, H., Demotes-Mainard, F., Vincon, G., and Bannwarth, B., The determination of bromazepam in plasma by reversed-phase high-performance liquid chromatography, *Journal of Pharmaceutical & Biomedical Analysis*, 11, 771-775, 1993

149. Yoshida, M., Watabiki, T., Tokiyasu, T., Saito, I., and Ishida, N., [Determination of benzodiazepines by thermospray liquid chromatograph-mass spectrometer. Part 1. Nitrazepam, estazolam, bromazepam, flunitrazepam]. [Japanese], *Nippon Hoigaku Zasshi Japanese Journal of Legal Medicine*, 47, 220-226, 1993

150. Haring, N., Salama, Z., and Jaeger, H., Triple stage quadrupole mass spectrometric determination of bromocriptine in human plasma with negative ion chemical ionization, *Arzneimittel Forschung*, 38, 1529-1532, 1988

151. Hindmarsh, K. W., Hamon, N. W., and LeGatt, D. F., Simultaneous identification and quantitation of diphenhydramine and methaqualone, *Clinical Toxicology*, 11, 245-255, 1977

152. Meatherall, R. C. and Guay, D. R., Isothermal gas chromatographic analysis of diphenhydramine after direct injection onto a fused-silica capillary column, *Journal of Chromatography*, 307, 295-304, 1984

153. Tonn, G. R., Mutlib, A., Abbott, F. S., Rurak, D. W., and Axelson, J. E., Simultaneous analysis of diphenhydramine and a stable isotope analog (2H10)diphenhydramine using capillary gas chromatography with mass selective detection in biological fluids from chronically instrumented pregnant ewes, *Biological Mass Spectrometry*, 22, 633-642, 1993

154. Vycudilik, W. and Pollak, S., [Detection of diphenhydramine in autolytic brain tissue in poison-induced brain death syndrome], *Zeitschrift fur Rechtsmedizin - Journal of Legal Medicine*, 95, 129-135, 1985

155. Lorec, A. M., Bruguerolle, B., Attolini, L., and Roucoules, X., Rapid simultaneous determination of lidocaine, bupivacaine, and their two main metabolites using capillary gas-liquid chromatography with nitrogen phosphorus detector, *Therapeutic Drug Monitoring*, 16, 592-595, 1994

156. Demedts, P., Wauters, A., Franck, F., and Neels, H., Simultaneous Determination of Lidocaine, Bupivacaine, and Their Two Main Metabolites Using Gas Chromatography and a Nitrogen-Phosphorus Detector - Selection of Stationary Phase and Chromatographic Conditions, *Therapeutic Drug Monitoring,* 18, 208-209, 1996

157. Coyle, D. E. and Denson, D. D., Simultaneous measurement of bupivacaine, etidocaine, lidocaine, meperidine, mepivacaine, and methadone, *Therapeutic Drug Monitoring,* 8, 98-101, 1986

158. Clark, B. J., Hamdi, A., Berrisford, R. G., Sabanathan, S., and Mearns, A. J., Reversed-Phase and Chiral High-Performance Liquid Chromatographic Assay of Bupivacaine and Its Enantiomers in Clinical Samples After Continuous Extraplural Infusion, *J Chromatogr,* 553, 383-390, 1991

159. Zakowski, M. I., Ramanathan, S., Sharnick, S., and Turndorf, H., Uptake and distribution of bupivacaine and morphine after intrathecal administration in parturients: effects of epinephrine, *Anesthesia & Analgesia,* 74, 664-669, 1992

160. Bailey, C. R., Ruggier, R., and Findley, I. L., Diamorphine-bupivacaine mixture compared with plain bupivacaine for analgesia, *British Journal of Anaesthesia,* 72, 58-61, 1994

161. Martin, J. and Neill, R. S., Venous plasma (total) bupivacaine concentrations following lower abdominal field block, *British Journal of Anaesthesia,* 59, 1425-1430, 1987

162. Kintz, P., Cirimele, V., Edel, Y., Jamey, C., and Mangin, P., Hair analysis for buprenorphine and its dealkylated metabolite by RIA and confirmation by LC/ECD, *Journal of Forensic Sciences,* 39, 1497-1503, 1994

163. Debrabandere, L., Van Boven, M., and Daenens, P., Analysis of buprenorphine in urine specimens, *Journal of Forensic Sciences,* 37, 82-89, 1992

164. Kuhlman, J. J., Magluilo, J., Cone, E., and Levine, B., Simultaneous Assay of Buprenorphine and Norbuprenorphine By Negative Chemical Ionization Tandem Mass Spectrometry, *Journal of Analytical Toxicology,* 20, 229-235, 1996

165. Shiraishi, Y., Sakai, S., Yokoyama, J., Hayatsu, K., Mochizuki, T., Moriwaki, G., et al., [The plasma concentration of buprenorphine during its continuous epidural infusion after catheterization at different vertebral levels], *Masui - Japanese Journal of Anesthesiology,* 42, 371-375, 1993

166. Battah, A.-K. and Anderson, R. A. *Comparison of silyl derivatives for GC/MS analysis of morphine and buprenorphine in blood.* in *26th International Meeting of the International Association of Forensic Toxicologists.* 1989. Glasgow, Scotland.

167. Kuhlman, J. J., Lalani, S., Magluilo, J., Levine, B., Darwin, W. D., Johnson, R. E., et al., Human Pharmacokinetics of Intravenous, Sublingual, and Buccal Buprenorphine, *Journal of Analytical Toxicology,* 20, 369-378, 1996

168. Ohtani, M., Kotaki, H., Uchino, K., Sawada, Y., and Iga, T., Pharmacokinetic analysis of enterohepatic circulation of buprenorphine and its active metabolite, norbuprenorphine, in rats, *Drug Metab. Dispos.,* 22, 2-7, 1994

169. San, L., Torrens, M., Castillo, C., Porta, M., and de la Torre, R., Consumption of buprenorphine and other drugs among heroin addicts under ambulatory treatment: results from cross-sectional studies in 1988 and 1990, *Addiction,* 88, 1341-1349, 1993

170. Rohrig, T. P. and Ray, N. G., Tissue distribution of bupropion in a fatal overdose, *Journal of Analytical Toxicology,* 16, 343-345, 1992

171. Fogel, P., Mamer, O. A., Chouinard, G., and Farrell, P. G., Determination of plasma bupropion and its relationship to therapeutic effect, *Biomedical Mass Spectrometry,* 11, 629-632, 1984

172. Friel, P. N., Logan, B. K., and Fligner, C. L., Three fatal drug overdoses involving bupropion, *Journal of Analytical Toxicology,* 17, 436-438, 1993

173. Spiller, H. A., Ramoska, E. A., Krenzelok, E. P., Sheen, S. R., Borys, D. J., Villalobos, D., et al., Bupropion overdose: a 3-year multi-center retrospective analysis, *American Journal of Emergency Medicine,* 12, 43-45, 1994

174. Butz, R. F., Welch, R. M., and Findlay, J. W., Relationship between bupropion disposition and dopamine uptake inhibition in rats and mice, *Journal of Pharmacology & Experimental Therapeutics,* 221, 676-685, 1982

175. Jajoo, H. K., Mayol, R. F., LaBudde, J. A., and Blair, I. A., Metabolism of the antianxiety drug buspirone in human subjects, *Drug Metabolism & Disposition,* 17, 634-640, 1989

176. Scott, E. P., Application of postcolumn ionization in the high-performance liquid chromatographic analysis of butabarbital sodium elixir, *Journal of Pharmaceutical Sciences,* 72, 1089-1091, 1983

177. Mulvana, D. E., Duncan, G. F., Shyu, W. C., Tay, L. K., and Barbhaiya, R. H., Quantitative Determination of Butorphanol and Its Metabolites in Human Plasma By Gas Chromatography Electron Capture Negative-Ion Chemical Ionization Mass Spectrometry, *Journal of Chromatography B: Biomedical Applications,* 682, 289-300, 1996

178. Combie, J., Blake, J. W., Nugent, T. E., and Tobin, T., Furosemide, Patella vulgata beta-glucuronidase and drug analysis: conditions for enhancement of the TLC detection of apomorphine, butorphanol, hydromorphone, nalbuphine, oxymorphone and pentazocine in equine urine, *Research Communications in Chemical Pathology & Pharmacology,* 35, 27-41, 1982

179. Rodopoulos, N. and Norman, A., Determination of caffeine and its metabolites in urine by high-performance liquid chromatography and capillary electrophoresis, *Scandinavian Journal of Clinical & Laboratory Investigation,* 54, 305-315, 1994

180. Jin, X., Zhou, Z. H., He, X. F., Zhang, Z. H., and Wang, M. Z., [Solid-phase extraction and RP-HPLC screening procedure for diuretics, probenecid, caffeine and pemoline in urine], *Yao Hsueh Hsueh Pao - Acta Pharmaceutica Sinica,* 27, 875-880, 1992

181. Leakey, T. E., Simultaneous analysis of theophylline, caffeine and eight of their metabolic products in human plasma by gradient high-performance liquid chromatography, *Journal of Chromatography,* 507, 199-220, 1990

182. Fligner, C. L. and Opheim, K. E., Caffeine and its dimethylxanthine metabolites in two cases of caffeine overdose: a cause of falsely elevated theophylline concentrations in serum, *Journal of Analytical Toxicology,* 12, 339-343, 1988

183. Garriott, J. C., Simmons, L. M., Poklis, A., and Mackell, M. A., Five cases of fatal overdose from caffeine-containing "look-alike" drugs, *Journal of Analytical Toxicology,* 9, 141-143, 1985

184. Miceli, J. N., Aravind, M. K., and Ferrell, W. J., Analysis of caffeine: comparison of the manual enzyme multiplied immunoassay (EMIT), automated EMIT, and high-performance liquid chromatography procedures, *Therapeutic Drug Monitoring,* 6, 344-347, 1984

185. Lensmeyer, G. L., Isothermal gas chromatographic method for the rapid determination of carbamazepine ("tegretol") as its TMS derivative, *Clinical Toxicology,* 11, 443-454, 1977

186. Schwertner, H. A., Hamilton, H. E., and Wallace, J. E., Analysis for carbamazepine in serum by electron-capture gas chromatography, *Clin. Chem.,* 24, 895-899, 1978

187. Toseland, P. A., Grove, J., and Berry, D. J., An isothermal GLC determination of the plasma levels of carbamazepine, diphenylhydantoin, phenobarbitone and primidone, *Clinica Chimica Acta,* 38, 321-328, 1972

188. Martens, J. and Banditt, P., Validation of the analysis of carbamazepine and its 10,11-epoxide metabolite by high-performance liquid chromatography from plasma: comparison with gas chromatography and the enzyme-multiplied immunoassay technique, *Journal of Chromatography,* 620, 169-173, 1993

189. Romanyshyn, L. A., Wichmann, J. K., Kucharczyk, N., Shumaker, R. C., Ward, D., and Sofia, R. D., Simultaneous determination of felbamate, primidone, phenobarbital, carbamazepine, two carbamazepine metabolites, phenytoin, and one phenytoin metabolite in human plasma by high-performance liquid chromatography, *Therapeutic Drug Monitoring,* 16, 90-99, 1994

190. Rainbow, S. J., Dawson, C. M., and Tickner, T. R., Direct serum injection high-performance liquid chromatographic method for the simultaneous determination of phenobarbital, carbamazepine and phenytoin, *Journal of Chromatography,* 527, 389-396, 1990

191. Schmidt, S. and Schmitz-Buhl, M., Signs and symptoms of carbamazepine overdose, *Journal of Neurology,* 242, 169-173, 1995

192. Chai, C. and Killeen, A. A., Carbamazepine measurement in samples from the emergency room, *Therapeutic Drug Monitoring,* 16, 407-412, 1994

193. Schwartz, J. G., Garriott, J. C., Somerset, J. S., Igler, E. J., Rodriguez, R., and Orr, M. D., Measurements of fentanyl and sufentanil in blood and urine after surgical application. Implication in detection of abuse, *American Journal of Forensic Medicine & Pathology*, 15, 236-241, 1994

194. Tobin, T., Kwiatkowski, S., Watt, D., Tai, H., Tai, C., Woods, W., *et al.*, Immunoassay detection of drugs in racing horses. XI. ELISA and RIA detection of fentanyl, alfentanil, sufentanil and carfentanil in equine blood and urine, *Research Communications in Chemical Pathology & Pharmacology*, 63, 129-152, 1989

195. Kintz, P., Mangin, P., Lugnier, A. A., and Chaumont, A. J., A rapid and sensitive gas chromatographic analysis of meprobamate or carisoprodol in urine and plasma, *Journal of Analytical Toxicology*, 12, 73-74, 1988

196. Backer, R. C., Zumwalt, R., McFeeley, P., Veasey, S., and Wohlenberg, N., Carisoprodol concentrations from different anatomical sites: three overdose cases, *Journal of Analytical Toxicology*, 14, 332-334, 1990

197. Kaistha, K. K., Selective assay procedure for chlorpropamide in the presence of its decomposition products, *Journal of Pharmaceutical Sciences*, 58, 235-237, 1969

198. Meatherall, R. C., Green, P. T., Kenick, S., and Donen, N., Diazoxide in the management of chlorpropamide overdose, *Journal of Analytical Toxicology*, 5, 287-291, 1981

199. Levine, B., Park, J., Smith, T. D., and Caplan, Y. H., Chloral hydrate: unusually high concentrations in a fatal overdose, *Journal of Analytical Toxicology*, 9, 232-233, 1985

200. Meyer, E., Van Bocxlaer, J. F., Lambert, W. E., Piette, M., and De Leenheer, A. P., Determination of chloral hydrate and metabolites in a fatal intoxication, *Journal of Analytical Toxicology*, 19, 124-126, 1995

201. Lister, R. G., Abernethy, D. R., Greenblatt, D. J., and File, S. E., Methods for the determination of lorazepam and chlordiazepoxide and metabolites in brain tissue, *Journal of Chromatography*, 277, 201-208, 1983

202. Song, D., Zhang, S., and Kohlhof, K., Determination of chlordiazepoxide in mouse plasma by gas chromatography-negative-ion chemical ionization mass spectrometry, *Journal of Chromatography B: Biomedical Applications*, 660, 95-101, 1994

203. Heller, P. F., Goldberger, B. A., and Caplan, Y. H., Chloral hydrate overdose: trichloroethanol detection by gas chromatography/mass spectrometry, *Forensic Science International*, 52, 231-234, 1992

204. Bailey, D. N., Blood concentrations and clinical findings following overdose of chlordiazepoxide alone and chlordiazepoxide plus ethanol, *Journal of Toxicology - Clinical Toxicology*, 22, 433-446, 1984

205. Dixon, R., Brooks, M. A., Postma, E., Hackman, M. R., Spector, S., Moore, J. D., *et al.*, N-desmethyldiazepam: a new metabolite of chlordiazepoxide in man, *Clinical Pharmacology & Therapeutics*, 20, 450-457, 1976

206. Stronjny, N., Bratin, K., Brooks, M. A., and de Silva, J. A., Determination of chlordiazepoxide, diazepam, and their major metabolites in blood or plasma by spectrophotodensitometry, *Journal of Chromatography*, 143, 363-374, 1977

207. Bailey, D. N. and Guba, J. J., Gas-chromatographic analysis for chlorpromazine and some of its metabolites in human serum, with use of a nitrogen detector, *Clinical Chemistry*, 25, 1211-1215, 1979

208. Ohkubo, T., Shimoyama, R., and Sugawara, K., Determination of chlorpromazine in human breast milk and serum by high-performance liquid chromatography, *Journal of Chromatography*, 614, 328-332, 1993

209. Nishigami, J., Takayasu, T., and Ohshima, T., Toxicological analysis of the psychotropic drugs chlorpromazine and diazepam using chemically fixed organ tissues, *International Journal of Legal Medicine*, 107, 165-170, 1995

210. Walker, O. and Ademowo, O. G., A Rapid, Cost-Effective Liquid Chromatographic Method For the Determination of Chloroquine and Desethylchloroquine in Biological Fluids, *Therapeutic Drug Monitoring*, 18, 92-96, 1996

211. Volin, P., Simple and specific reversed-phase liquid chromatographic method with diode-array detection for simultaneous determination of serum hydroxychloroquine, chloroquine and some corticosteroids, *Journal of Chromatography B: Biomedical Applications*, 666, 347-353, 1995

212. Murtha, J. L., Julian, T. N., and Radebaugh, G. W., Simultaneous determination of pseudoephedrine hydrochloride, chlorpheniramine maleate, and dextromethorphan hydrobromide by second-derivative photodiode array spectroscopy, *Journal of Pharmaceutical Sciences*, 77, 715-718, 1988

213. Masumoto, K., Tashiro, Y., Matsumoto, K., Yoshida, A., Hirayama, M., and Hayashi, S., Simultaneous determination of codeine and chlorpheniramine in human plasma by capillary column gas chromatography, *Journal of Chromatography*, 381, 323-329, 1986

214. Bailey, D. N. and Guba, J. J., Gas-chromatographic analysis for chlorpromazine and some of its metabolites in human serum, with use of a nitrogen detector, *Clinical Chemistry*, 25, 1211-1215, 1979

215. Garriott, J. C. and Stolman, A., Detection of some psychotherapeutic drugs and their metabolites in urine, *Clinical Toxicology*, 4, 225-243, 1971

216. Fenimore, D. C., Meyer, C. J., Davis, C. M., Hsu, F., and Zlatkis, A., High-performance thin-layer chromatographic determination of psychopharmacologic agents in blood serum, *Journal of Chromatography*, 142, 399-409, 1977

217. Lin, Q., Lensmeyer, G. L., and Larson, F. C., Quantitation of cimetidine and cimetidine sulfoxide in serum by solid-phase extraction and solvent-recycled liquid chromatography, *Journal of Analytical Toxicology*, 9, 161-166, 1985

218. Borel, A. G. and Abbott, F. S., Metabolic profiling of clobazam, a 1,5-benzodiazepine, in rats, *Drug Metabolism & Disposition*, 21, 415-427, 1993

219. Streete, J. M., Berry, D. J., and Newbery, J. E., The analysis of clobazam and its metabolite desmethylclobazam by high-performance liquid chromatography, *Therapeutic Drug Monitoring*, 13, 339-344, 1991

220. Schutz, H., [A screening test for Nor-clobazam, a principal metabolite of the new 1,5 benzodiazepine clobazam (Frisium)], *Archiv fur Kriminologie*, 163, 91-94, 1979

221. Coudore, F., Hourcade, F., Moliniermanoukian, C., Eschalier, A., and Lavarenne, E., Application of Hplc With Silica-Phase and Reversed-Phase Eluents For the Determination of Clomipramine and Demethylated and 8-Hydroxylated Metabolites, *Journal of Analytical Toxicology*, 20, 101-105, 1996

222. Altieri, I., Pichini, S., Pacifici, R., and Zuccaro, P., Improved clean-up procedure for the high-performance liquid chromatographic assay of clomipramine and its demethylated metabolite in human plasma, *Journal of Chromatography B: Biomedical Applications*, 669, 416-417, 1995

223. McIntyre, I. M., King, C. V., Cordner, S. M., and Drummer, O. H., Postmortem clomipramine: therapeutic or toxic concentrations?, *Journal of Forensic Sciences*, 39, 486-493, 1994

224. Nielsen, K. K. and Brosen, K., High-performance liquid chromatography of clomipramine and metabolites in human plasma and urine, *Therapeutic Drug Monitoring*, 15, 122-128, 1993

225. Marliac, Y. and Barazi, S., [Determination of unchanged clonazepam in plasma by gas-liquid chromatography]. [French], *Annales de Biologie Clinique*, 47, 503-506, 1989

226. Miller, L. G., Friedman, H., and Greenblatt, D. J., Measurement of clonazepam by electron-capture gas-liquid chromatography with application to single-dose pharmacokinetics, *Journal of Analytical Toxicology*, 11, 55-57, 1987

227. Wilson, J. M., Friel, P. N., Wilensky, A. J., and Raisys, V. A., A methods comparison: clonazepam by GC-electron capture and GC/MS., *Ther. Drug Monit.*, 1, 387-397, 1979

228. Petters, I., Peng, D. R., and Rane, A., Quantitation of clonazepam and its 7-amino and 7-acetamido metabolites in plasma by high-performance liquid chromatography, *Journal of Chromatography*, 306, 241-248, 1984

229. Shaw, W., Long, G., and McHan, J., An HPLC method for analysis of clonazepam in serum, *Journal of Analytical Toxicology*, 7, 119-122, 1983

230. Haver, V. M., Porter, W. H., Dorie, L. D., and Lea, J. R., Simplified high performance liquid chromatographic method for the determination of clonazepam and other benzodiazepines in serum, *Therapeutic Drug Monitoring*, 8, 352-357, 1986

231. Doran, T. C., Liquid chromatographic assay for serum clonazepam, *Therapeutic Drug Monitoring,* 10, 474-479, 1988

232. Haering, N., Salama, Z., Reif, G., and Jaeger, H., GC/MS determination of clonidine in body fluids. Application to pharmacokinetics, *Arzneim.-Forsch.,* 38, 404-407, 1988

233. Arrendale, R. F., Stewart, J. T., and Tackett, R. L., Determination of clonidine in human plasma by cold on-column injection capillary GC/MS, *J. Chromatogr.,* 432, 165-175, 1988

234. Linnoila, M. and Dorrity, F., Jr., Rapid gas chromatographic assay of serum diazepam, N-desmethyldiazepam, and N-desalkylflurazepam, *Acta Pharmacologica et Toxicologica,* 41, 458-464, 1977

235. McCurdy, H. H., Lewellen, L. J., Cagle, J. C., and Solomons, E. T., A rapid procedure for the screening and quantitation of barbiturates, diazepam, desmethyldiazepam and methaqualone, *Journal of Analytical Toxicology,* 5, 253-257, 1981

236. Kudo, K., Nagata, T., Kimura, K., Imamura, T., and Noda, M., Sensitive determination of diazepam and N-desmethyldiazepam in human material using capillary GC/MS, *J. Chromatogr.,* 431, 353-359, 1988

237. Lovdahl, M. J., Perry, P. J., and Miller, D. D., The assay of clozapine and N-desmethylclozapine in human plasma by high-performance liquid chromatography, *Therapeutic Drug Monitoring,* 13, 69-72, 1991

238. Jennison, T. A., Brown, P., Crossett, J., Kushnir, M., and Urry, F. M., A rapid gas chromatographic method quantitating clozapine in human plasma or serum for the purpose of therapeutic monitoring, *Journal of Analytical Toxicology,* 19, 537-541, 1995

239. Lin, G., McKay, G., Hubbard, J. W., and Midha, K. K., Decomposition of clozapine N-oxide in the qualitative and quantitative analysis of clozapine and its metabolites, *Journal of Pharmaceutical Sciences,* 83, 1412-1417, 1994

240. McCarthy, P. T., Hughes, S., and Paton, C., Measurement of clozapine and norclozapine in plasma/serum by high performance liquid chromatography with ultraviolet detection, *Biomedical Chromatography,* 9, 36-41, 1995

241. Gupta, R. N., Column liquid chromatographic determination of clozapine and N-desmethylclozapine in human serum using solid-phase extraction, *Journal of Chromatography B: Biomedical Applications,* 673, 311-315, 1995

242. Olesen, O. V. and Poulsen, B., On-line fully automated determination of clozapine and desmethylclozapine in human serum by solid-phase extraction on exchangeable cartridges and liquid chromatography using a methanol buffer mobile phase on unmodified silica, *Journal of Chromatography,* 622, 39-46, 1993

243. Chung, M. C., Lin, S. K., Chang, W. H., and Jann, M. W., Determination of clozapine and desmethylclozapine in human plasma by high-performance liquid chromatography with ultraviolet detection, *Journal of Chromatography,* 613, 168-173, 1993

244. Liu, H. C., Chang, W. H., Wei, F. C., Lin, S. K., Lin, S. K., and Jann, M. W., Monitoring of Plasma Clozapine Levels and Its Metabolites in Refractory Schizophrenic Patients, *Therapeutic Drug Monitoring,* 18, 200-207, 1996

245. Clauwaert, K. M., Van Bocxlaer, J. F., Lambert, W. E., and De Leenheer, A. P., Analysis of cocaine, benzoylecgonine, and cocaethylene in urine by HPLC with diode array detection, *Analytical Chemistry,* 68, 3021-3028, 1996

246. Bailey, D. N., Cocaethylene (ethylcocaine) detection during toxicological screening of a university medical center patient population, *Journal of Analytical Toxicology,* 19, 247-250, 1995

247. Cone, E. J., Hillsgrove, M., and Darwin, W. D., Simultaneous measurement of cocaine, cocaethylene, their metabolites, and "crack" pyrolysis products by gas chromatography-mass spectrometry, *Clinical Chemistry,* 40, 1299-1305, 1994

248. Hime, G. W., Hearn, W. L., Rose, S., and Cofino, J., Analysis of cocaine and cocaethylene in blood and tissues by GC-NPD and GC-ion trap mass spectrometry, *Journal of Analytical Toxicology,* 15, 241-245, 1991

249. Bailey, D. N., Comprehensive Review of Cocaethylene and Cocaine Concentrations in Patients, *American Journal of Clinical Pathology,* 106, 701-704, 1996

250. Nishikawa, M., Nakajima, K., Tatsuno, M., Kasuya, F., Igarashi, K., Fukui, M., *et al.*, The analysis of cocaine and its metabolites by liquid chromatography/atmospheric pressure chemical ionization- mass spectrometry (LC/APCI-MS), *Forensic Science International,* 66, 149-158, 1994

251. Peterson, K. L., Logan, B. K., Christian, G. D., and Ruzicka, J. *Analysis of polar cocaine metabolites in urine and spinal fluid.* in *46th Annual Meeting of the American Academy of Forensic Sciences.* 1994. San Antonio, TX.

252. Logan, B. K. and Stafford, D. T., High-performance liquid chromatography with column switching for the determination of cocaine and benzoylecgonine concentrations in vitreous humor, *Journal of Forensic Sciences,* 35, 1303-1309, 1990

253. Masoud, A. N. and Krupski, D. M., High-performance liquid chromatographic analysis of cocaine in human plasma, *Journal of Analytical Toxicology,* 4, 305-310, 1980

254. Thompson, W. C. and Dasgupta, A., Confirmation and quantitation of cocaine, benzoylecgonine, ecgonine methyl ester, and cocaethylene by gas chromatography/mass spectrometry. Use of microwave irradiation for rapid preparation of trimethylsilyl and T-butyldimethylsilyl derivatives [see comments], *American Journal of Clinical Pathology,* 104, 187-192, 1995

255. Cardenas, S., Gallego, M., and Valcarcel, M., An automated preconcentration-derivatization system for the determination of cocaine and its metabolites in urine and illicit cocaine samples by gas chromatography/mass spectrometry, *Rapid Communications in Mass Spectrometry,* 10, 631-636, 1996

256. Kintz, P. and Mangin, P., Simultaneous determination of opiates, cocaine and major metabolites of cocaine in human hair by gas chromotography/mass spectrometry (GC/MS), *Forensic Science International,* 73, 93-100, 1995

257. Hearn, W. L., Keran, E. E., Wei, H. A., and Hime, G., Site-dependent postmortem changes in blood cocaine concentrations, *Journal of Forensic Sciences,* 36, 673-684, 1991

258. Delbeke, F. T. and Debackere, M., Influence of hydrolysis procedures on the urinary concentrations of codeine and morphine in relation to doping analysis, *Journal of Pharmaceutical & Biomedical Analysis,* 11, 339-343, 1993

259. Posey, B. L. and Kimble, S. N., High-performance liquid chromatographic study of codeine, norcodeine, and morphine as indicators of codeine ingestion, *Journal of Analytical Toxicology,* 8, 68-74, 1984

260. Vu-Duc, T. and Vernay, A., Simultaneous detection and quantitation of O6-monoacetylmorphine, morphine and codeine in urine by gas chromatography with nitrogen specific and/or flame ionization detection, *Biomedical Chromatography,* 4, 65-69, 1990

261. Bowie, L. J. and Kirkpatrick, P. B., Simultaneous determination of monoacetylmorphine, morphine, codeine, and other opiates by GC/MS, *Journal of Analytical Toxicology,* 13, 326-329, 1989

262. elSohly, H. N., Stanford, D. F., Jones, A. B., elSohly, M. A., Snyder, H., and Pedersen, C., Gas chromatographic/mass spectrometric analysis of morphine and codeine in human urine of poppy seed eaters, *Journal of Forensic Sciences,* 33, 347-356, 1988

263. Wu Chen, N. B., Schaffer, M. I., Lin, R. L., and Stein, R. J., Simultaneous quantitation of morphine and codeine in biological samples by electron impact mass fragmentography, *Journal of Analytical Toxicology,* 6, 231-234, 1982

264. Saady, J. J., Narasimhachari, N., and Blanke, R. V., Rapid, simultaneous quantification of morphine, codeine, and hydromorphone by GC/MS, *Journal of Analytical Toxicology,* 6, 235-237, 1982

265. Gygi, S. P., Colon, F., Raftogianis, R. B., Galinsky, R. E., Wilkins, D. G., and Rollins, D. E., Dose-Related Distribution of Codeine and Its Metabolites Into Rat Hair, *Drug Metabolism & Disposition,* 24, 282-287, 1996

266. Tracqui, A., Kintz, P., Ludes, B., Rouge, C., Douibi, H., and Mangin, P., High-performance liquid chromatography coupled to ion spray mass spectrometry for the determination of colchicine at ppb levels in human biofluids, *Journal of Chromatography B: Biomedical Applications,* 675, 235-242, 1996

267. Clevenger, C. V., August, T. F., and Shaw, L. M., Colchicine poisoning: report of a fatal case with body fluid analysis by GC/MS and histopathologic examination of postmortem tissues, *Journal of Analytical Toxicology,* 15, 151-154, 1991

268. Thompson, J. A., Ho, M. S., and Petersen, D. R., Analysis of nicotine and cotinine in tissues by capillary GC and GC/MS., *J. Chromatogr.,* 231, 53-63, 1982

269. Urakawa, N., Nagata, T., Kudo, K., Kimura, K., and Imamura, T., Simultaneous determination of nicotine and cotinine in various human tissues using capillary gas chromatography/mass spectrometry, *International Journal of Legal Medicine,* 106, 232-236, 1994

270. Deutsch, J., Hegedus, L., Greig, N. H., Rapoport, S. I., and Soncrant, T. T., Electron-Impact and chemical ionization detection of nicotine and cotinine by gas Chromatography-Mass spectrometry in rat plasma and brain, *J Chromatogr,* 579, 93-98, 1992

271. Jacob, P. d., Yu, L., Wilson, M., and Benowitz, N. L., Selected ion monitoring method for determination of nicotine, cotinine and deuterium-labeled analogs: absence of an isotope effect in the clearance of (S)-nicotine-3',3'-d2 in humans, *Biological Mass Spectrometry,* 20, 247-252, 1991

272. Backer, R. C., McFeeley, P., and Wohlenberg, N., Fatality resulting from cyclizine overdose, *Journal of Analytical Toxicology,* 13, 308-309, 1989

273. Tasset, J. J., Schroeder, T. J., and Pesce, A. J., Cyclobenzaprine overdose: the importance of a clinical history in analytical toxicology [letter], *Journal of Analytical Toxicology,* 10, 258, 1986

274. Levine, B., Jones, R., Smith, M. L., Gudewicz, T. M., and Peterson, B., A multiple drug intoxication involving cyclobenzaprine and ibuprofen, *American Journal of Forensic Medicine & Pathology,* 14, 246-248, 1993

275. Baehr, G. R., Romano, M., and Young, J. M., An unusual case of cyproheptadine (Periactin) overdose in an adolescent female, *Pediatric Emergency Care,* 2, 183-185, 1986

276. Law, B., Mason, P. A., Moffat, A. C., Gleadle, R. I., and King, L. J., Forensic aspects of the metabolism and excretion of cannabinoids following oral ingestion of cannabis resin, *J. Pharm. Pharmacol.,* 36, 289-294, 1983

277. elSohly, M. A., Little, T. L., Jr., and Stanford, D. F., Hexadeutero-11-nor-delta 9-tetrahydro-cannabinol-9-carboxylic acid: a superior internal standard for the GC/MS analysis of delta 9-THC acid metabolite in biological specimens, *Journal of Analytical Toxicology,* 16, 188-191, 1992

278. Moeller, M., Doerr, G., and Warth, S., Simultaneous quantitation of delta-9-tetrahydrocannabinol (THC) and 11-nor-9-carboxy-delta-9-tetrahydrocannabinol (THC-COOH) in serum by GC/MS using deuterated internal standards and its application to a smoking study and forensic cases, *Journal of Forensic Sciences,* 37, 969-983, 1992

279. Kemp, P. M., Abukhalaf, I. K., Manno, J. E., Manno, B. R., Alford, D. D., McWilliams, M. E., *et al.,* Cannabinoids in humans. II. The influence of three methods of hydrolysis on the concentration of THC and two metabolites in urine, *Journal of Analytical Toxicology,* 19, 292-298, 1995

280. Wolff, K., Garretty, D., and Hay, A. W. M., Micro-Extraction of Commonly Abused Benzo-diazepines For Urinary Screening By Liquid Chromatography, *Annals of Clinical Biochemistry,* 34, 61-67, 1997

281. Tanaka, E., Terada, M., Misawa, S., and Wakasugi, C., Simultaneous Determination of Twelve Benzodiazepines in Human Serum Using a New Reversed-Phase Chromatographic Column On a 2-Mu-M Porous Microspherical Silica Gel, *Journal of Chromatography B: Biomedical Applications,* 682, 173-178, 1996

282. Needleman, S. B. and Porvaznik, M., Identification of parent benzodiazepines by gas chromotography/mass spectroscopy (GC/MS) from urinary extracts treated with B-glucu-ronidase, *Forensic Science International,* 73, 49-60, 1995

283. Peat, M. A. and Kopjak, L., The screening and quantitation of diazepam, flurazepam, chloridazepoxide, and their metabolites in blood and plasma by electron-capture gas chromatography and high pressure liquid chromatography, *Journal of Forensic Sciences,* 24, 46-54, 1979

284. Song, D., Zhang, S., and Kohlhof, K., Gas chromatographic-mass spectrometric method for the determination of flurazepam and its major metabolites in mouse and rat plasma, *Journal of Chromatography B: Biomedical Applications,* 658, 142-148, 1994

285. Clatworthy, A. J., Jones, L. V., and Whitehouse, M. J., The GC/MS of the major metabolites of flurazepam., *Biomed. Mass Spectr.,* 4, 248-254, 1977

286. Aderjan, R. and Mattern, R., [A fatal monointoxication by flurazepam (Dalmadorm). Problems of the toxicological interpretation (author's transl)]. [German], *Archives of Toxicology,* 43, 69-75, 1979

287. Abel, M. and Eisenkraft, J. B., Erroneous mass spectrometer readings caused by desflurane and sevoflurane, *Journal of Clinical Monitoring,* 11, 152-158, 1995

288. Hartter, S., Baier, D., Dingemanse, J., Ziegler, G., and Hiemke, C., Automated Determination of Dextromethorphan and Its Main Metabolites in Human Plasma By High-Performance Liquid Chromatography and Column Switching, *Therapeutic Drug Monitoring,* 18, 297-303, 1996

289. Lam, Y. W. and Rodriguez, S. Y., High-performance liquid chromatography determination of dextromethorphan and dextrorphan for oxidation phenotyping by fluorescence and ultraviolet detection, *Therapeutic Drug Monitoring,* 15, 300-304, 1993

290. Wallace, J. E., Schwertner, H. A., and Shimek, E. L. j., Analysis for diazepam and nordiazepam by electron-capture gas chromatography and by liquid chromatography., *Clin. Chem.,* 25, 1296-1300, 1979

291. St-Pierre, M. V. and Pang, K. S., Determination of diazepam and its metabolites by high-performance liquid chromatography and thin-layer chromatography, *Journal of Chromatography,* 421, 291-307, 1987

292. MacKichan, J. J., Jusko, W. J., Duffner, P. K., and Cohen, M. E., Liquid-chromatographic assay of diazepam and its major metabolites in plasma, *Clinical Chemistry,* 25, 856-859, 1979

293. Plavsic, F. and Culig, J., Determination of serum diclofenac by high-performance liquid chromatography by electromechanical detection, *Human Toxicology,* 4, 317-322, 1985

294. Blagbrough, I. S., Daykin, M. M., Doherty, M., Pattrick, M., and Shaw, P. N., High-performance liquid chromatographic determination of naproxen, ibuprofen and diclofenac in plasma and synovial fluid in man, *Journal of Chromatography,* 578, 251-257, 1992

295. Garriott, J. C., Rodriquez, R., and Norton, L. E., Two cases of death involving dicyclomine in infants, *Journal of Toxicology - Clinical Toxicology,* 22, 455-462, 1984

296. Shimamine, M., Takahashi, K., and Nakahara, Y., [Studies on the identification of psychotropic substances, *Eisei Shikenjo Hokoku - Bulletin of National Institute of Hygienic Sciences,* 67-73, 1992

297. Levine, B., Smyth, D., and Caplan, Y., A diflunisal related fatality: a case report, *Forensic Science International,* 35, 45-50, 1987

298. Hofmann, U., Fromm, M. F., Johnson, S., and Mikus, G., Simultaneous determination of dihydrocodeine and dihydromorphine in serum by gas chromatography-tandem mass spectrometry, *Journal of Chromatography B: Biomedical Applications,* 663, 59-65, 1995

299. Musshoff, F. and Daldrup, T., Evaluation of a method for simultaneous quantification of codeine, dihydrocodeine, morphine, and 6-monoacetylmorphine in serum, blood, and post-mortem blood, *International Journal of Legal Medicine,* 106, 107-109, 1993

300. Maurer, H. H., Identification of antiarrhythmic drugs and their metabolites in urine, *Arch. Toxicol.,* 64, 218-230, 1990

301. Pierce, T. L., Murray, A. G., and Hope, W., Determination of methadone and its metabolites by high performance liquid chromatography following solid-phase extraction in rat plasma, *Journal of Chromatographic Science,* 30, 443-447, 1992

302. Angelo, H. R., Bonde, J., Kampmann, J. P., and Kastrup, J., A HPLC method for the simultaneous determination of disopyramide, lidocaine and their monodealkylated metabolites, *Scandinavian Journal of Clinical & Laboratory Investigation,* 46, 623-627, 1986

303. Proelss, H. F. and Townsend, T. B., Simultaneous liquid-chromatographic determination of five antiarrhythmic drugs and their major active metabolites in serum, *Clinical Chemistry,* 32, 1311-1317, 1986

304. Anderson, W. H., Stafford, D. T., and Bell, J. S., Disopyramide (Norpace) distribution at autopsy of an overdose case, *Journal of Forensic Sciences,* 25, 33-39, 1980

305. Kapil, R. P., Abbott, F. S., Kerr, C. R., Edwards, D. J., Lalka, D., and Axelson, J. E., Simultaneous quantitation of disopyramide and its mono-dealkylated metabolite in human plasma by fused-silica capillary gas chromatography using nitrogen-phosphorus specific detection, *Journal of Chromatography,* 307, 305-321, 1984

306. McIntyre, I. M., King, C. V., Skafidis, S., and Drummer, O. H., Dual ultraviolet wavelength high-performance liquid chromatographic method for the forensic or clinical analysis of seventeen antidepressants and some selected metabolites, *Journal of Chromatography,* 621, 215-223, 1993

307. Pounder, D. J. and Jones, G. R., Post-mortem drug redistribution—a toxicological nightmare, *Forensic Science International,* 45, 253-263, 1990

308. Wu Chen, N. B., Schaffer, M. I., Lin, R. L., Kurland, M. L., Donoghue, E. R., Jr., and Stein, R. J., The general toxicology unknown. II. A case report: doxylamine and pyrilamine intoxication, *Journal of Forensic Sciences,* 28, 398-403, 1983

309. Virag, L., Mets, B., and Jamdar, S., Determination of Cocaine, Norcocaine, Benzoylecgonine and Ecgonine Methyl Ester in Rat Plasma By High-Performance Liquid Chromatography With Ultraviolet Detection, *Journal of Chromatography B: Biomedical Applications,* 681, 263-269, 1996

310. Peterson, K. L., Logan, B. K., and Christian, G. D., Detection of cocaine and its polar transformation products and metabolites in human urine, *Forensic Science International,* 73, 183-196, 1995

311. Balikova, M. and Vecerkova, J., High-performance liquid chromatographic confirmation of cocaine and benzoylecgonine in biological samples using photodiode-array detection after toxicological screening, *Journal of Chromatography B: Biomedical Applications,* 656, 267-273, 1994

312. Crouch, D. J., Alburges, M. E., Spanbauer, A. C., Rollins, D. E., and Moody, D. E., Analysis of cocaine and its metabolites from biological specimens using solid-phase extraction and positive ion chemical ionization mass spectrometry, *Journal of Analytical Toxicology,* 19, 352-358, 1995

313. Wang, W. L., Darwin, W. D., and Cone, E. J., Simultaneous assay of cocaine, heroin and metabolites in hair, plasma, saliva and urine by gas chromatography-mass spectrometry, *Journal of Chromatography B: Biomedical Applications,* 660, 279-290, 1994

314. Mule, S. J. and Casella, G. A., Confirmation and quantitation of cocaine, benzoylecgonine, ecgonine methyl ester in human urine by GC/MS, *Journal of Analytical Toxicology,* 12, 153-155, 1988

315. Matsubara, K., Maseda, C., and Fukui, Y., Quantitation of cocaine, benzoylecgonine and ecgonine methyl ester by GC-CI-SIM after Extrelut extraction, *Forensic Science International,* 26, 181-192, 1984

316. Ahnoff, M., Ervik, M., Lagerstrom, P. O., Persson, B. A., and Vessman, J., Drug level monitoring: cardiovascular drugs. [Review], *Journal of Chromatography,* 340, 73-138, 1985

317. Braggio, S., Sartori, S., Angeri, F., and Pellegatti, M., Automation and validation of the high-performance liquid chromatographic-radioimmunoassay method for the determination of lacidipine in plasma, *Journal of Chromatography B: Biomedical Applications,* 669, 383-389, 1995

318. Saito, K., Takayasu, T., Nishigami, J., Kondo, T., Ohtsuji, M., Lin, Z., *et al.,* Determination of the volatile anesthetics halothane, enflurane, isoflurane, and sevoflurane in biological specimens by pulse-heating GC-MS, *Journal of Analytical Toxicology,* 19, 115-119, 1995

319. Heusler, H., Quantitative analysis of common anaesthetic agents, *Journal of Chromatography,* 340, 273-319, 1985

320. Ohtsuji, M., Lai, J. S., Binder, S. R., Kondo, T., Takayasu, T., and Ohshima, T., Use of REMEDi HS in emergency toxicology for a rapid estimate of drug concentrations in urine, serum, and gastric samples, *Journal of Forensic Sciences,* 41, 881-886, 1996

321. Boukhabza, A., Lugnier, A. A., Kintz, P., and Mangin, P., Simultaneous HPLC analysis of the hypnotic benzodiazepines nitrazepam, estazolam, flunitrazepam, and triazolam in plasma, *Journal of Analytical Toxicology*, 15, 319-322, 1991

322. Charlebois, R. C., Corbett, M. R., and Wigmore, J. G., Comparison of ethanol concentrations in blood, serum, and blood cells for forensic application, *Journal of Analytical Toxicology*, 20, 171-178, 1996

323. O' Neal, C., Wolf, C. E., 2nd, Levine, B., Kunsman, G., and Poklis, A., Gas chromatographic procedures for determination of ethanol in postmortem blood using t-butanol and methyl ethyl ketone as internal standards, *Forensic Science International*, 83, 31-38, 1996

324. Macchia, T., Mancinelli, R., Gentili, S., Lugaresi, E. C., Raponi, A., and Taggi, F., Ethanol in biological fluids: headspace GC measurement, *Journal of Analytical Toxicology*, 19, 241-246, 1995

325. Skrupskii, V. A., [Gas chromatographic analysis of ethanol and acetone in the air exhaled by patients]. [RUSSIAN], *Klinicheskaia Laboratornaia Diagnostika*, 4, 35-38, 1995

326. Jones, A. W., Edman-Falkensson, M., and Nilsson, L., Reliability of blood alcohol determinations at clinical chemistry laboratories in Sweden, *Scandinavian Journal of Clinical & Laboratory Investigation*, 55, 463-468, 1995

327. Clerc, Y., Huart, B., Charotte, J. M., and Pailler, F. M., [Validation of blood ethanol determination method by gas chromatography (letter)]. [French], *Annales de Biologie Clinique*, 53, 233-238, 1995

328. Cox, R. A. and Crifasi, J. A., A comparison of a commercial microdiffusion method and gas chromatography for ethanol analysis, *Journal of Analytical Toxicology*, 14, 211-212, 1990

329. Jones, A. W. and Schuberth, J., Computer-aided headspace gas chromatography applied to blood-alcohol analysis: importance of online process control, *Journal of Forensic Sciences*, 34, 1116-1127, 1989

330. Bridges, R. R. and Jennison, T. A., Analysis of ethchlorvynol (Placidyl): evaluation of a comparison performed in a clinical laboratory, *Journal of Analytical Toxicology*, 8, 263-268, 1984

331. Winek, C. L., Wahba, W. W., Rozin, L., and Winek, C. L., Jr., Determination of ethchlorvynol in body tissues and fluids after embalmment, *Forensic Science International*, 37, 161-166, 1988

332. Winek, C. L., Wahba, W. W., and Winek, C. L., Jr., Body distribution of ethchlorvynol, *Journal of Forensic Sciences*, 34, 687-690, 1989

333. Flanagan, R. J., Lee, T. D., and Rutherford, D. M., Analysis of chlormethiazole, ethchlorvynol and trichloroethanol in biological fluids by gas-liquid chromatography as an aid to the diagnosis of acute poisoning, *Journal of Chromatography*, 153, 473-479, 1978

334. Flanagan, R. J. and Lee, T. D., Rapid micro-method for the measurement of ethchlorvynol in blood plasma and in urine by gas-liquid chromatography, *Journal of Chromatography*, 137, 119-126, 1977

335. Bailey, D. N. and Shaw, R. F., Ethchlorvynol ingestion in San Diego County: a 14-year review of cases with blood concentrations and findings. [Review], *Journal of Analytical Toxicology*, 14, 348-352, 1990

336. Kelner, M. J. and Bailey, D. N., Ethchlorvynol ingestion: interpretation of blood concentrations and clinical findings, *Journal of Toxicology - Clinical Toxicology*, 21, 399-408, 1983

337. Berry, D. J. and Clarke, L. A., Gas chromatographic analysis of ethosuximide (2-ethyl-2-methyl succinimide) in plasma at therapeutic concentrations, *Journal of Chromatography*, 150, 537-541, 1978

338. Richard, L., Leducq, B., Baty, C., and Jambou, J., [Plasma determination of 7 common drugs by high performance liquid chromatography], *Annales de Biologie Clinique*, 47, 79-84, 1989

339. Schmutz, A. and Thormann, W., Determination of phenobarbital, ethosuximide, and primidone in human serum by micellar electrokinetic capillary chromatography with direct sample injection, *Therapeutic Drug Monitoring*, 15, 310-316, 1993

340. Miles, M. V., Howlett, C. M., Tennison, M. B., Greenwood, R. S., and Cross, R. E., Determination of N-desmethylmethsuximide serum concentrations using enzyme-multiplied and fluorescence polarization immunoassays, *Therapeutic Drug Monitoring*, 11, 337-342, 1989

341. Stewart, C. F. and Bottorff, M. B., Fluorescence polarization immunoassay for ethosuximide evaluated and compared with two other immunoassay techniques, *Clinical Chemistry*, 32, 1781-1783, 1986

342. Haring, C. M., Dijkhuis, I. C., and van Dijk, B., A rapid method of determining serum levels of etomidate by gas chromatography with the aid of a nitrogen detector, *Acta Anaesthesiologica Belgica*, 31, 107-112, 1980

343. Qin, X. Z., Ip, D. P., Chang, K. H., Dradransky, P. M., Brooks, M. A., and Sakuma, T., Pharmaceutical application of LC-MS. 1—Characterization of a famotidine degradate in a package screening study by LC-APCI MS, *Journal of Pharmaceutical & Biomedical Analysis*, 12, 221-233, 1994

344. Poquette, M. A., Isothermal gas chromatographic method for the rapid determination of felbamate concentration in human serum, *Therapeutic Drug Monitoring*, 17, 168-173, 1995

345. Wong, S. H. Y., Sasse, E. A., Schroeder, J. M., Rodgers, J. K., Pearson, M. L., Neicheril, J. C., *et al.*, Totally Automated Analysis By Robotized Prepstation and Liquid Chromatography - Direct-Sample Analysis of Felbamate, *Therapeutic Drug Monitoring*, 18, 573-580, 1996

346. Annesley, T. M. and Clayton, L. T., Determination of felbamate in human serum by high-performance liquid chromatography, *Therapeutic Drug Monitoring*, 16, 419-424, 1994

347. Friel, P. N., Formoso, E. J., and Logan, B. K. *GC/MS analysis of felbamate, a new antiepileptic drug, in postmortem specimens.* in *American Acad. Forensic Sci.* 1995. Seattle, WA.

348. Nishioka, R., Umeda, I., Oi, N., Tabata, S., and Uno, K., Determination of felodipine and its metabolites in plasma using capillary gas chromatography with electron-capture detection and their identification by gas chromatography-mass spectrometry, *Journal of Chromatography*, 565, 237-246, 1991

349. Ferretti, R., Gallinella, B., Latorre, F., and Lusi, A., Direct High-Performance Liquid Chromatography Resolution On a Chiral Column Of Dexfenfluramine and Its Impurities, In Bulk Raw Drug and Pharmaceutical Formulations, *Journal of Chromatography 731(1-2):340-345*, 1996

350. Moore, C. M. and Tebbett, I. R., Rapid extraction of anti-inflammatory drugs in whole blood for HPLC analysis, *Forensic Science International*, 34, 155-158, 1987

351. Watts, V. and Caplan, Y., Determination of fentanyl in whole blood at subnanogram concentrations by dual capillary column gas chromatography with nitrogen sensitive detectors and gas chromatography/mass spectrometry, *Journal of Analytical Toxicology*, 12, 246-254, 1988

352. Mautz, D. S., Labroo, R., and Kharasch, E. D., Determination of alfentanil and noralfentanil in human plasma by gas chromatography-mass spectrometry, *Journal of Chromatography B: Biomedical Applications*, 658, 149-153, 1994

353. Smialek, J. E., Levine, B., Chin, L., Wu, S. C., and Jenkins, A. J., A fentanyl epidemic in Maryland 1992, *Journal of Forensic Sciences*, 39, 159-164, 1994

354. Levine, B., Goodin, J. C., and Caplan, Y. H., A fentanyl fatality involving midazolam, *Forensic Science International*, 45, 247-251, 1990

355. Ferslew, K., Hagardorn, A., and McCormick, W., Postmortem determination of the biological distribution of sufentanil and midazolam after an acute intoxication, *Journal of Forensic Sciences*, 34, 249-257, 1989

356. Poklis, A., Fentanyl: A review for clinical and analytical toxicologists [Review], *Journal of Toxicology Clinical Toxicology*, 33, 439-447, 1995

357. Hoppe, U., Krudewagen, B., Stein, H., Hertrampf, R., and Gundert-Remy, U., Comparison of fluorescence polarisation immunoassay (FPIA) and high performance liquid chromatography (HPLC) methods for the measurement of flecainide in human plasma, *International Journal of Clinical Pharmacology, Therapy, & Toxicology*, 31, 142-147, 1993

358. Stas, C. M., Jacqmin, P. A., and Pellegrin, P. L., Comparison of gas-liquid chromatography and fluorescence polarization immunoassay for therapeutic drug monitoring of flecainide acetate, *Journal of Pharmaceutical & Biomedical Analysis*, 7, 1651-1656, 1989

359. Straka, R. J., Hoon, T. J., Lalonde, R. L., Pieper, J. A., and Bottorff, M. B., Liquid chromatography and fluorescence polarization immunoassay methods compared for measuring flecainide acetate in serum, *Clinical Chemistry*, 33, 1898-1900, 1987

360. Berthault, F., Kintz, P., and Mangin, P., Simultaneous High-Performance Liquid Chromatographic Analysis of Flunitrazepam and Four Metabolites in Serum, *Journal of Chromatography B: Biomedical Applications*, 685, 383-387, 1996

361. Kleinschnitz, M., Herderich, M., and Schreier, P., Determination of 1,4-Benzodiazepines By High-Performance Liquid Chromatography Electrospray Tandem Mass Spectrometry, *Journal of Chromatography B: Biomedical Applications*, 676, 61-67, 1996

362. Robertson, M. D. and Drummer, O. H., High-performance liquid chromatographic procedure for the measurement of nitrobenzodiazepines and their 7-amino metabolites in blood, *Journal of Chromatography B: Biomedical Applications*, 667, 179-184, 1995

363. Benhamou-Batut, F., Demotes-Mainard, F., Labat, L., Vincon, G., and Bannwarth, B., Determination of flunitrazepam in plasma by liquid chromatography, *Journal of Pharmaceutical & Biomedical Analysis*, 12, 931-936, 1994

364. Lantz, R. J., Farid, K. Z., Koons, J., Tenbarge, J. B., and Bopp, R. J., Determination of fluoxetine and norfluoxetine in human plasma by capillary gas chromatography with electron-capture detection, *Journal of Chromatography*, 614, 175-179, 1993

365. Rohrig, T. P. and Prouty, R. W., Fluoxetine overdose: a case report [published erratum appears in J Anal Toxicol 1990 Jan-Feb;14(1):63], *Journal of Analytical Toxicology*, 13, 305-307, 1989

366. Orsulak, P. J., Kenney, J. T., Debus, J. R., Crowley, G., and Wittman, P. D., Determination of the antidepressant fluoxetine and its metabolite norfluoxetine in serum by reversed-phase HPLC with ultraviolet detection, *Clinical Chemistry*, 34, 1875-1878, 1988

367. Nash, J. F., Bopp, R. J., Carmichael, R. H., Farid, K. Z., and Lemberger, L., Determination of fluoxetine and norfluoxetine in plasma by gas chromatography with electron-capture detection, *Clinical Chemistry*, 28, 2100-2102, 1982

368. Nichols, J. H., Charlson, J. R., and Lawson, G. M., Automated HPLC assay of fluoxetine and norfluoxetine in serum, *Clinical Chemistry*, 40, 1312-1316, 1994

369. Eap, C. B., Gaillard, N., Powell, K., and Baumann, P., Simultaneous Determination of Plasma Levels of Fluvoxamine and of the Enantiomers of Fluoxetine and Norfluoxetine By Gas Chromatography Mass Spectrometry, *Journal of Chromatography B: Biomedical Applications*, 682, 265-272, 1996

370. Miller, R. S., Peterson, G. M., McLean, S., Westhead, T. T., and Gillies, P., Monitoring plasma levels of fluphenazine during chronic therapy with fluphenazine decanoate, *Journal of Clinical Pharmacy & Therapeutics*, 20, 55-62, 1995

371. Sener, A., Akkan, A. G., and Malaisse, W. J., Standardized procedure for the assay and identification of hypoglycemic sulfonylureas in human plasma, *Acta Diabetologica*, 32, 64-68, 1995

372. Flanagan, R. J. and Withers, G., A rapid micro-method for the screening and measurement of barbiturates and related compounds in plasma by gas-liquid chromatography, *Journal of Clinical Pathology*, 25, 899-904, 1972

373. Shipe, J. R. and Savory, J., A comprehensive gas chromatography procedure for measurement of drugs in biological materials, *Annals of Clinical & Laboratory Science*, 5, 57-64, 1975

374. Bailey, D. N. and Shaw, R. F., Blood concentrations and clinical findings in nonfatal and fatal intoxications involving glutethimide and codeine, *Journal of Toxicology Clinical Toxicology*, 23, 557-570, 1985

375. Bailey, D. N. and Shaw, R. F., Interpretation of blood glutethimide, meprobamate, and methyprylon concentrations in nonfatal and fatal intoxications involving a single drug, *Journal of Toxicology - Clinical Toxicology*, 20, 133-145, 1983

376. Hoffman, D. W. and Edkins, R. D., Solid-phase extraction and high-performance liquid chromatography for therapeutic monitoring of haloperidol levels, *Therapeutic Drug Monitoring*, 16, 504-508, 1994

377. Aravagiri, M., Marder, S. R., Van Putten, T., and Marshall, B. D., Simultaneous determination of plasma haloperidol and its metabolite reduced haloperidol by liquid chromatography with electrochemical detection. Plasma levels in schizophrenic patients treated with oral or intramuscular depot haloperidol, *Journal of Chromatography B: Biomedical Applications*, 656, 373-381, 1994

378. Jann, M. W., Chang, W. H., Lam, Y. W., Hwu, H. G., Lin, H. N., Chen, H., *et al.*, Comparison of haloperidol and reduced haloperidol plasma levels in four different ethnic populations, *Progress in Neuro Psychopharmacology & Biological Psychiatry*, 16, 193-202, 1992

379. Park, K. H., Lee, M. H., and Lee, M. G., Simultaneous determination of haloperidol and its metabolite, reduced haloperidol, in plasma, blood, urine and tissue homogenates by high-performance liquid chromatography, *Journal of Chromatography*, 572, 259-267, 1991

380. Haering, N., Salama, Z., Todesko, L., and Jaeger, H., GC/MS determination of haloperidol in plasma. Application to pharmacokinetics, *Arzneim.-Forsch.*, 37, 1402-1404, 1987

381. van Leeuwen, P. A., Improved GC/MS assay for haloperidol utilizing ammonia CI and SIM, *J. Chromatogr., Biomed. Appl.*, 40, 321-330, 1985

382. Hornbeck, C. L., Griffiths, J. C., Neborsky, R. J., and Faulkner, M. A., GC/MS chemical ionization assay for haloperidol with SIM, *Biomed. Mass Spectrom.*, 6, 427-430, 1979

383. Coudore, F., Alazard, J. M., Paire, M., Andraud, G., and Lavarenne, J., Rapid toxicological screening of barbiturates in plasma by wide-bore capillary gas chromatography and nitrogen-phosphorus detection, *Journal of Analytical Toxicology*, 17, 109-113, 1993

384. Soo, V. A., Bergert, R. J., and Deutsch, D. G., Screening and quantification of hypnotic sedatives in serum by capillary gas chromatography with a nitrogen-phosphorus detector, and confirmation by capillary gas chromatography-mass spectrometry, *Clinical Chemistry*, 32, 325-328, 1986

385. Mahoney, J. D., Gross, P. L., Stern, T. A., Browne, B. J., Pollack, M. H., Reder, V., *et al.*, Quantitative serum toxic screening in the management of suspected drug overdose, *American Journal of Emergency Medicine*, 8, 16-22, 1990

386. Meeker, J. E., Som, C. W., Macapagal, E. C., and Benson, P. A., Zolpidem tissue concentrations in a multiple drug related death involving Ambien, *Journal of Analytical Toxicology*, 19, 531-534, 1995

387. Bouquillon, A. I., Freeman, D., and Moulin, D. E., Simultaneous solid-phase extraction and chromatographic analysis of morphine and hydromorphone in plasma by high-performance liquid chromatography with electrochemical detection, *Journal of Chromatography*, 577, 354-357, 1992

388. Sawyer, W. R., Waterhouse, G. A., Doedens, D. J., and Forney, R. B., Heroin, morphine, and hydromorphone determination in postmortem material by high performance liquid chromatography [see comments], *Journal of Forensic Sciences*, 33, 1146-1155, 1988

389. O' Connor, E. F., Cheng, S. W., and North, W. G., Simultaneous extraction and chromatographic analysis of morphine, dilaudid, naltrexone and naloxone in biological fluids by high-performance liquid chromatography with electrochemical detection, *Journal of Chromatography*, 491, 240-247, 1989

390. Cone, E. J. and Darwin, W. D., Simultaneous determination of hydromorphone, hydrocodone and their 6alpha- and 6beta-hydroxy metabolites in urine using selected ion recording with methane chemical ionization, *Biomedical Mass Spectrometry*, 5, 291, 1978

391. Croes, K., McCarthy, P. T., and Flanagan, R. J., Simple and rapid HPLC of quinine, hydroxychloroquine, chloroquine, and desethylchloroquine in serum, whole blood, and filter paper- adsorbed dry blood, *Journal of Analytical Toxicology*, 18, 255-260, 1994

392. Kintz, P., Godelar, B., and Mangin, P., Gas chromatographic identification and quantification of hydroxyzine: application in a fatal self-poisoning, *Forensic Science International*, 48, 139-143, 1990

393. Naidong, W. and Lee, J. W., Development and validation of a liquid chromatographic method for the quantitation of ibuprofen enantiomers in human plasma, *Journal of Pharmaceutical & Biomedical Analysis*, 12, 551-556, 1994

394. Maurer, H. H., Kraemer, T., and Weber, A., Toxicological detection of ibuprofen and its metabolites in urine using gas chromatography-mass spectrometry (GC-MS), *Pharmazie*, 49, 148-155, 1994

395. Zhao, M. J., Peter, C., Holtz, M. C., Hugenell, N., Koffel, J. C., and Jung, L., GC/MS determination of ibuprofen enantiomers in human plasma using r(-)-2,2,2-trifluoro-1-(9-anthryl)ethanol as derivatizing reagent, *J. Chromatogr. B-Bio. Med. Appl.*, 656, 441-446, 1994

396. Seideman, P., Lohrer, F., Graham, G. G., Duncan, M. W., Williams, K. M., and Day, R. O., The stereoselective disposition of the enantiomers of ibuprofen in blood, blister and synovial fluid, *British Journal of Clinical Pharmacology*, 38, 221-227, 1994

397. Theis, D. L., Halstead, G. W., and Halm, K. A., Development of capillary GC/MS methodology for the simultaneous determination of ibuprofen and deuterated ibuprofen in serum, *J. Chromatogr.*, 380, 77-87, 1986

398. Jourdil, N., Pinteur, B., Vincent, F., Marka, C., and Bessard, G., Simultaneous determination of trimipramine and desmethyl- and hydroxytrimipramine in plasma and red blood cells by capillary gas chromatography with nitrogen-selective detection, *Journal of Chromatography*, 613, 59-65, 1993

399. Maynard, G. L. and Soni, P., Thioridazine Interferences With Imipramine Metabolism and Measurement, *Therapeutic Drug Monitoring*, 18, 729-731, 1996

400. Nielsen, K. K. and Brosen, K., High-performance liquid chromatography of imipramine and six metabolites in human plasma and urine, *Journal of Chromatography*, 612, 87-94, 1993

401. Koyama, E., Kikuchi, Y., Echizen, H., Chiba, K., and Ishizaki, T., Simultaneous high-performance liquid chromatography-electrochemical detection determination of imipramine, desipramine, their 2-hydroxylated metabolites, and imipramine N-oxide in human plasma and urine: preliminary application to oxidation pharmacogenetics, *Therapeutic Drug Monitoring*, 15, 224-235, 1993

402. Eap, C. B., Koeb, L., and Baumann, P., Determination of trimipramine and its demethylated and hydroxylated metabolites in plasma by gas chromatography-mass spectrometry, *Journal of Chromatography*, 652, 97-103, 1994

403. Hunt, J. P., Haywood, P. E., and Moss, M. S., A gas chromatographic screening procedure for the detection of non-steroidal anti-inflammatory drugs in horse urine, *Equine Veterinary Journal*, 11, 259-263, 1979

404. Sibeon, R. G., Baty, J. D., Baber, N., Chan, K., and Orme, M. L., Quantitative gas-liquid chromatographic method for the determination of indomethacin in biological fluids, *Journal of Chromatography*, 153, 189-194, 1978

405. Hannak, D., Scharbert, F., and Kattermann, R., Stepwise binary gradient high-performance liquid chromatographic system for routine drug monitoring, *Journal of Chromatography A*, 728, 307-310, 1996

406. Caturla, M. C. and Cusido, E., Solid-phase extraction for the high-performance liquid chromatographic determination of indomethacin, suxibuzone, phenylbutazone and oxyphenbutazone in plasma, avoiding degradation of compounds, *Journal of Chromatography*, 581, 101-107, 1992

407. Cosolo, W., Drummer, O. H., and Christophidis, N., Comparison of high-performance liquid chromatography and the Abbott fluorescent polarization radioimmunoassay in the measurement of methotrexate, *Journal of Chromatography*, 494, 201-208, 1989

408. Bauernfeind, M. and Wood, W. G., Evaluation of a fully mechanised immunoassay—Enzymun-Test System ES 300—and comparison with in-house methods for 8 analytes, *European Journal of Clinical Chemistry & Clinical Biochemistry*, 31, 165-172, 1993

409. Patel, F., Fatal self-induced hyperinsulinaemia: a delayed post-mortem analytical detection, *Medicine, Science & the Law 1992 Apr;32(2):151-9*, 1992

410. Fletcher, S. M., Insulin. A forensic primer. [Review], *Journal Forensic Science Society*, 23, 5-17, 1983

411. Heyndrickx, A., Van Peteghem, C., Majelyne, W., and Timperman, J., Detection of insulin in cadavers, *Acta Pharmaceutica Hungarica*, 50, 201-206, 1980

412. Dickson, S. J., Cairns, E. R., and Blazey, N. D., The isolation and quantitation of insulin in post-mortem specimens—a case report, *Forensic Science 1977 Jan-Feb;9(1):37-42*, 1977

413. Jones, A. W., Severe isopropanolemia without acetonemia: contamination of specimens during venipuncture? [letter; comment], *Clinical Chemistry*, 41, 123-124, 1995

414. Chan, K. M., Wong, E. T., and Matthews, W. S., Severe isopropanolemia without acetonemia or clinical manifestations of isopropanol intoxication [see comments], *Clinical Chemistry*, 39, 1922-1925, 1993

415. Jerrard, D., Verdile, V., Yealy, D., Krenzelok, E., and Menegazzi, J., Serum determinations in toxic isopropanol ingestion, *American Journal of Emergency Medicine*, 10, 200-202, 1992

416. Davis, P. L., Dal Cortivo, L. A., and Maturo, J., Endogenous isopropanol: forensic and biochemical implications, *Journal of Analytical Toxicology*, 8, 209-212, 1984

417. Kelner, M. and Bailey, D. N., Isopropanol ingestion: interpretation of blood concentrations and clinical findings, *Journal of Toxicology Clinical Toxicology*, 20, 497-507, 1983

418. Baker, R. N., Alenty, A. L., and Zack, J. F., Jr., Toxic volatiles in alcoholic coma. A report of simultaneous determination of blood methanol, ethanol, isopropanol, acetaldehyde and acetone by gas chromatography, *Bulletin of the Los Angeles Neurological Societies*, 33, 140-144, 1968

419. Alexander, C. B., McBay, A. J., and Hudson, R. P., Isopropanol and isopropanol deaths-ten years' experience, *Journal of Forensic Sciences*, 27, 541-548, 1982

420. Brogden, R. N. and Sorkin, E. M., Isradipine. An update of its pharmacodynamic and pharmacokinetic properties and therapeutic efficacy in the treatment of mild to moderate hypertension. [Review], *Drugs*, 49, 618-649, 1995

421. Kochhar, M. M., Bavda, L. T., and Bhushan, R. S., Thin-layer and gas chromatographic determination of ketamine and its biotransformed products in biological fluids, *Research Communications in Chemical Pathology & Pharmacology*, 14, 367-376, 1976

422. Adams, H. A., Weber, B., Bachmann, M. B., Guerin, M., and Hempelmann, G., [The simultaneous determination of ketamine and midazolam using high pressure liquid chromatography and UV detection (HPLC/UV)], *Anaesthesist*, 41, 619-624, 1992

423. Feng, N., Vollenweider, F. X., Minder, E. I., Rentsch, K., Grampp, T., and Vonderschmitt, D. J., Development of a gas chromatography-mass spectrometry method for determination of ketamine in plasma and its application to human samples, *Therapeutic Drug Monitoring*, 17, 95-100, 1995

424. Lau, S. S. and Domino, E. F., Gas chromatography mass spectrometry assay for ketamine and its metabolites in plasma, *Biomedical Mass Spectrometry*, 4, 317-321, 1977

425. Carr, R. A., Caille, G., Ngoc, A. H., and Foster, R. T., Stereospecific high-performance liquid chromatographic assay of ketoprofen in human plasma and urine, *Journal of Chromatography B: Biomedical Applications*, 668, 175-181, 1995

426. Lovlin, R., Vakily, M., and Jamali, F., Rapid, Sensitive and Direct Chiral High-Performance Liquid Chromatographic Method For Ketoprofen Enantiomers, *Journal of Chromatography B: Biomedical Applications*, 679, 196-198, 1996

427. Palylyk, E. L. and Jamali, F., Simultaneous determination of ketoprofen enantiomers and probenecid in plasma and urine by high-performance liquid chromatography, *Journal of Chromatography*, 568, 187-196, 1991

428. Chun, I. K., Kang, H. H., and Gwak, H. S., Determination of Ketorolac in Human Serum By High- Performance Liquid Chromatography, *Archives of Pharmacal Research*, 19, 529-534, 1996

429. Tsina, I., Tam, Y. L., Boyd, A., Rocha, C., Massey, I., and Tarnowski, T., An Indirect (Derivatization) and a Direct Hplc Method For the Determination of the Enantiomers of Ketorolac in Plasma, *Journal of Pharmaceutical & Biomedical Analysis*, 15, 403-417, 1996

430. Tsina, I., Chu, F., Kaloostian, M., Pettibone, M., and Wu, A., Hplc Method For the Determination of Ketorolac in Human Plasma, *Journal of Liquid Chromatography & Related Technologies*, 19, 957-967, 1996

431. Sola, J., Prunonosa, J., Colom, H., Peraire, C., and Obach, R., Determination of Ketorolac in Human Plasma By High Performance Liquid Chromatography After Automated Online Solid Phase Extraction, *Journal of Liquid Chromatography & Related Technologies*, 19, 89-99, 1996

432. Logan, B. K., Friel, P. N., Peterson, K. L., and Predmore, D. B., Analysis of ketorolac in postmortem blood, *Journal of Analytical Toxicology*, 19, 61-64, 1995

433. Sievert, H. J. P., Determination of amphetamine and methamphetamine enantiomers by chiral derivatization and GC/MS as a test case for an automated sample preparation system, *Chirality*, 6, 295-301, 1994

434. Cooke, B. J., Chirality of methamphetamine and amphetamine from workplace urine samples, *Journal of Analytical Toxicology*, 18, 49-51, 1994

435. Nagai, T., Kamiyama, S., Kurosu, A., and Iwamoto, F., [Identification of optical isomers of methamphetamine and its application to forensic medicine]. [Japanese], *Nippon Hoigaku Zasshi Japanese Journal of Legal Medicine*, 46, 244-253, 1992

436. Wallace, S. J., Lamotrigine—a clinical overview, *Seizure*, 3, 47-51, 1994

437. Rambeck, B. and Wolf, P., Lamotrigine clinical pharmacokinetics. [Review], *Clinical Pharmacokinetics*, 25, 433-443, 1993

438. May, T. W., Rambeck, B., and Jurgens, U., Serum Concentrations of Lamotrigine in Epileptic Patients - the Influence of Dose and Comedication, *Therapeutic Drug Monitoring*, 18, 523-531, 1996

439. Kintz, P., Flesch, F., Jaeger, A., and Mangin, P., GC-MS procedure for the analysis of zipeprol, *Journal of Pharmaceutical & Biomedical Analysis*, 11, 335-338, 1993

440. Xu, Y. Q., Fang, H. J., Xu, Y. X., Duan, H. J., and Wu, Y., [Studies on the analysis of anileridine, levorphanol, nalbuphine and ethamivan in urine], *Yao Hsueh Hsueh Pao - Acta Pharmaceutica Sinica*, 26, 606-610, 1991

441. Benko, A. and Kimura, K., Toxicological analysis of lidocaine in biological materials by using HPLC, *Forensic Science International*, 49, 65-73, 1991

442. Cirimele, V., Kintz, P., and Mangin, P., Detection and quantification of lorazepam in human hair by GC-MS/NCI in a case of traffic accident, *International Journal of Legal Medicine*, 108, 265-267, 1996

443. Higuchi, S., Urabe, H., and Shiobara, Y., Simplified determination of lorazepam and oxazepam in biological fluids by gas chromatography-mass spectrometry, *Journal of Chromatography*, 164, 55-61, 1979

444. Koves, E. M. and Yen, B., The use of gas chromatography/negative ion chemical ionization mass spectrometry for the determination of lorazepam in whole blood, *Journal of Analytical Toxicology*, 13, 69-72, 1989

445. Twitchett, P. J., Fletcher, S. M., Sullivan, A. T., and Moffat, A. C., Analysis of LSD in human body fluids by high-performance liquid chromatography, fluorescence spectroscopy and radioimmunoassay, *Journal of Chromatography*, 150, 73-84, 1978

446. Veress, T., Study of the extraction of LSD from illicit blotters for HPLC determination, *Journal of Forensic Sciences*, 38, 1105-1110, 1993

447. Cai, J. and Henion, J., On-line immunoaffinity extraction-coupled column capillary liquid chromatography/tandem mass spectrometry: trace analysis of LSD analogs and metabolites in human urine, *Analytical Chemistry*, 68, 72-78, 1996

448. Nelson, C. C. and Foltz, R. L., Determination of lysergic acid diethylamide (LSD), iso-LSD, and N-demethyl-LSD in body fluids by gas chromatography/tandem mass spectrometry, *Analytical Chemistry*, 64, 1578-1585, 1992

449. Bukowski, N. and Eaton, A. N., The confirmation and quantitation of LSD in urine using GC/MS, *Rapid Commun. Mass Spectrom.*, 7, 106-108, 1993

450. Ackermann, R., Kaiser, G., Schueller, F., and Dieterle, W., Determination of the antidepressant levoprotiline and its N-desmethyl metabolite in biological fluids by gas chromatography/mass spectrometry, *Biological Mass Spectrometry*, 20, 709-716, 1991

451. Alkalay, D., Carlsen, S., Khemani, L., and Bartlett, M. F., Selected ion monitoring assay for the antidepressant maprotiline, *Biomedical Mass Spectrometry*, 6, 435-438, 1979

452. Stidman, J., Taylor, E. H., Simmons, H. F., Gandy, J., and Pappas, A. A., Determination of meprobamate in serum by alkaline hydrolysis, trimethylsilyl derivatization and detection by GC/MS, *J. Chromatogr.*, 494, 318-323, 1989

453. Kintz, P. and Mangin, P., Determination of meprobamate in human plasma, urine, and hair by gas chromatography and electron impact mass spectrometry, *Journal of Analytical Toxicology*, 17, 408-410, 1993

454. Bailey, D. N., The present status of meprobamate ingestion. A five-year review of cases with serum concentrations and clinical findings, *American Journal of Clinical Pathology*, 75, 102-106, 1981

455. Hamman, B., Meprobamate, in *Methodology for Analytical Toxicology: Volume I*, Sunshine, I., CRC Press, Inc, Boca Raton, 1984, p 219-221.

456. Foltz, R. L., Fentiman, A. F., Jr., and Foltz, R. B., GC/MS assays for abused drugs in body fluids. [Review], *NIDA Research Monograph*, 32, 1-198, 1980

457. Poklis, A., Wells, C. E., and Juenge, E. C., Thioridazine and its metabolites in post mortem blood, including two stereoisomeric ring sulfoxides, *Journal of Analytical Toxicology*, 6, 250-252, 1982

458. Schurch, F., Meier, P. J., and Wyss, P. A., ACUTE POISONING WITH THIORIDAZINE [German], *Deutsche Medizinische Wochenschrift*, 121, 1003-1008, 1996

459. Kintz, P., Mangin, P., Lugnier, A. A., and Chaumont, A. J., A rapid and sensitive gas chromatographic analysis of methadone and its primary metabolite, *Journal de Toxicologie Clinique et Experimentale*, 10, 15-20, 1990

460. Alburges, M. E., Huang, W., Foltz, R. L., and Moody, D. E., Determination of Methadone and Its N-Demethylation Metabolites in Biological Specimens By Gc-Pici-Ms, *Journal of Analytical Toxicology*, 20, 362-368, 1996

461. Wilkins, D. G., Nagasawa, P. R., Gygi, S. P., Foltz, R. L., and Rollins, D. E., Quantitative Analysis of Methadone and Two Major Metabolites in Hair By Positive Chemical Ionization Ion Trap Mass Spectrometry, *Journal of Analytical Toxicology*, 20, 355-361, 1996

462. Baugh, L. D., Liu, R. H., and Walia, A. S., Simultaneous gas chromatography/mass spectrometry assay of methadone and 2-ethyl-1,5-dimethyl-3,3-diphenylpyrrolidine (EDDP) in urine, *Journal of Forensic Sciences*, 36, 548-555, 1991

463. Jacob, P., 3rd, Tisdale, E. C., Panganiban, K., Cannon, D., Zabel, K., Mendelson, J. E., *et al.*, Gas chromatographic determination of methamphetamine and its metabolite amphetamine in human plasma and urine following conversion to N-propyl derivatives, *Journal of Chromatography B: Biomedical Applications*, 664, 449-457, 1995

464. Dallakian, P., Budzikiewicz, H., and Brzezinka, H., Detection and Quantitation of Amphetamine and Methamphetamine - Electron Impact and Chemical Ionization With Ammonia-Comparative Investigation On Shimadzu Qp 5000 Gc-Ms System, *Journal of Analytical Toxicology*, 20, 255-261, 1996

465. Valtier, S. and Cody, J. T., Evaluation of internal standards for the analysis of amphetamine and methamphetamine, *Journal of Analytical Toxicology*, 19, 375-380, 1995

466. Wu, A. H., Kelly, T., McKay, C., Ostheimer, D., Forte, E., and Hill, D., Definitive identification of an exceptionally high methanol concentration in an intoxication of a surviving infant: methanol metabolism by first-order elimination kinetics, *Journal of Forensic Sciences*, 40, 315-320, 1995

467. Pla, A., Hernandez, A. F., Gil, F., Garcia-Alonso, M., and Villanueva, E., A fatal case of oral ingestion of methanol. Distribution in postmortem tissues and fluids including pericardial fluid and vitreous humor, *Forensic Science International*, 49, 193-196, 1991

468. Winkel, D. R. and Hendrick, S. A., Detection limits for a GC determination of methanol and methylene chloride residues on film-coated tablets, *Journal of Pharmaceutical Sciences*, 73, 115-117, 1984

469. Kintz, P., Tracqui, A., Mangin, P., Lugnier, A. A., and Chaumont, A. A., Simultaneous determination of dextropropoxyphene, norpropoxyphene and methaqualone in plasma by gas chromatography with selective nitrogen detection, *Journal de Toxicologie Clinique et Experimentale*, 10, 89-94, 1990

470. Liu, F., Liu, Y. T., Feng, C. L., and Luo, Y., Determination of methaqualone and its metabolites in urine and blood by UV, GC/FID and GC/MS, *Yao Hsueh Hsueh Pao Acta Pharmaceutica Sinica*, 29, 610-616, 1994

471. Streete, J. M., Berry, D. J., Clarke, L. A., and Newbery, J. E., Analysis of desmethylmethsuximide using high-performance liquid chromatography, *Therapeutic Drug Monitoring*, 17, 280-286, 1995

472. Poklis, A., Mackell, M. A., and Drake, W. K., Fatal intoxication from 3,4-methylenedioxyamphetamine., *J. Forensic Sci.*, 24, 70-75, 1979

473. Quaglio, M. P., Bellini, A. M., and Minozzi, L., Simultaneous determination of propranolol or metoprolol in the presence of benzodiazepines in the plasma by gas chromatography, *Farmaco*, 47, 799-809, 1992

474. Li, F., Cooper, S. F., and Cote, M., Determination of the enantiomers of metoprolol and its major acidic metabolite in human urine by high-performance liquid chromatography with fluorescence detection, *Journal of Chromatography B: Biomedical Applications,* 668, 67-75, 1995

475. Holt, D. W., Flanagan, R. J., Hayler, A. M., and Loizou, M., Simple gas-liquid chromatographic method for the measurement of mexiletine and lignocaine in blood-plasma or serum, *Journal of Chromatography,* 169, 295-301, 1979

476. Minnigh, M. B., Alvin, J. D., and Zemaitis, M. A., Determination of plasma mexiletine levels with gas chromatography-mass spectrometry and selected-ion monitoring, *Journal of Chromatography B: Biomedical Applications,* 662, 118-122, 1994

477. Bourget, P., Bouton, V., Lesnehulin, A., Amstutz, P., Benayed, M., Benhamou, D., *et al.,* Comparison of High-Performance Liquid Chromatography and Polyclonal Fluorescence Polarization Immunoassay For the Monitoring of Midazolam in the Plasma of Intensive Care Unit Patients, *Therapeutic Drug Monitoring,* 18, 610-619, 1996

478. Mastey, V., Panneton, A. C., Donati, F., and Varin, F., Determination of midazolam and two of its metabolites in human plasma by high-performance liquid chromatography, *Journal of Chromatography B: Biomedical Applications,* 655, 305-310, 1994

479. de Vries, J. X., Rudi, J., Walter-Sack, I., and Conradi, R., The determination of total and unbound midazolam in human plasma, *Biomedical Chromatography,* 4, 28-33, 1990

480. Vu-Duc, T. and Vernay, A., Simultaneous detection and quantitation of O6-monoacetylmorphine, morphine and codeine in urine by gas chromatography with nitrogen specific and/or flame ionization detection, *Biomedical Chromatography,* 4, 65-69, 1990

481. Hanisch, W. and Meyer, L. V., Determination of the heroin metabolite 6-monoacetyl-morphine in urine by high-performance liquid chromatography with electrochemical detection, *Journal of Analytical Toxicology,* 17, 48-50, 1993

482. Kintz, P., Mangin, P., Lugnier, A. A., and Chaumont, A. J., Identification by GC/MS of 6-monoacetylmorphine as an indicator of heroin abuse, *European Journal of Clinical Pharmacology,* 37, 531-532, 1989

483. Schuberth, J. and Schuberth, J., GC/MS determination of morphine, codeine and 6-monoacetylmorphine in blood extracted by solid phase, *J. Chromatogr.,* 490, 444-449, 1989

484. Wasels, R. and Belleville, F., Gas chromatographic-mass spectrometric procedures used for the identification and determination of morphine, codeine and 6-monoacetylmorphine, *Journal of Chromatography A,* 674, 225-234, 1994

485. Rotshteyn, Y. and Weingarten, B., A Highly Sensitive Assay For the Simultaneous Determination of Morphine, Morphine-3-Glucuronide, and Morphine-6-Glucuronide in Human Plasma By High-Performance Liquid Chromatography With Electrochemical and Fluorescence Detection, *Therapeutic Drug Monitoring,* 18, 179-188, 1996

486. Pacifici, R., Pichini, S., Altieri, I., Caronna, A., Passa, A. R., and Zuccaro, P., HPLC electrospray mass spectrometric determination of morphine and its 3- and 6-glucuronides: application to pharmacokinetic studies, *J. Chromatogr. B-Bio. Med. Appl.,* 664, 329-334, 1995

487. Pacifici, R., Pichini, S., Altieri, I., Caronna, A., Passa, A. R., and Zuccaro, P., High-performance liquid chromatographic-electrospray mass spectrometric determination of morphine and its 3- and 6-glucuronides: application to pharmacokinetic studies, *Journal of Chromatography B: Biomedical Applications,* 664, 329-334, 1995

488. Tyrefors, N., Hyllbrant, B., Ekman, L., Johansson, M., and Langstrom, B., Determination of Morphine, Morphine-3-Glucuronide and Morphine-6-Glucuronide in Human Serum By Solid-Phase Extraction and Liquid Chromatography Mass Spectrometry With Electrospray Ionisation, *Journal of Chromatography,* 729, 279-285, 1996

489. Moeller, M. R. and Mueller, C., The detection of 6-monoacetylmorphine in urine, serum and hair by GC/MS and RIA, *Forensic Science International,* 70, 125-133, 1995

490. Levine, B., Wu, S., Dixon, A., and Smialek, J., An unusual morphine fatality, *Forensic Science International,* 65, 7-11, 1994

491. Romberg, R. W. and Lee, L., Comparison of the hydrolysis rates of morphine-3-glucuronide and morphine-6-glucuronide with acid and beta-glucuronidase, *Journal of Analytical Toxicology,* 19, 157-162, 1995

492. Aderjan, R., Hofmann, S., Schmitt, G., and Skopp, G., Morphine and morphine glucuronides in serum of heroin consumers and in heroin-related deaths determined by HPLC with native fluorescence detection, *Journal of Analytical Toxicology,* 19, 163-168, 1995

493. Wright, A. W., Watt, J. A., Kennedy, M., Cramond, T., and Smith, M. T., Quantitation of morphine, morphine-3-glucuronide, and morphine-6-glucuronide in plasma and cerebrospinal fluid using solid- phase extraction and high-performance liquid chromatography with electrochemical detection, *Therapeutic Drug Monitoring,* 16, 200-208, 1994

494. Rop, P. P., Grimaldi, F., Burle, J., De Saint Leger, M. N., and Viala, A., Determination of 6-monoacetylmorphine and morphine in plasma, whole blood and urine using high-performance liquid chromatography with electrochemical detection, *Journal of Chromatography B: Biomedical Applications,* 661, 245-253, 1994

495. Yoo, Y. C., Chung, H. S., Kim, I. S., Jin, W. T., and Kim, M. K., Determination of nalbuphine in drug abusers' urine, *Journal of Analytical Toxicology,* 19, 120-123, 1995

496. McManus, K. T., deBethizy, J. D., Garteiz, D. A., Kyerematen, G. A., and Vesell, E. S., A new quantitative thermospray LC-MS method for nicotine and its metabolites in biological fluids, *Journal of Chromatographic Science,* 28, 510-516, 1990

497. Cooper, D. A. and Moore, J. M., Femtogram on-column detection of nicotine by isotope dilution gas chromatography/negative ion detection mass spectrometry, *Biological Mass Spectrometry,* 22, 590-594, 1993

498. Deutsch, J., Hegedus, L., Greig, N. H., Rapoport, S. I., and Soncrant, T. T., Electron-impact and chemical ionization detection of nicotine and cotinine by gas chromatography-mass spectrometry in rat plasma and brain, *Journal of Chromatography,* 579, 93-98, 1992

499. Lesko, L. and Miller, A., Rapid GC method for quantitation of nifedipine in serum using electron-capture detection, *J. Chrom. Sci.,* 21, 415-419, 1983

500. Ohkubo, T., Noro, H., and Sugawara, K., High-performance liquid chromatographic determination of nifedipine and a trace photodegradation product in hospital prescriptions, *Journal of Pharmaceutical & Biomedical Analysis,* 10, 67-70, 1992

501. Nitsche, V., Schuetz, H., and Eichinger, A., Rapid high-performance liquid chromatographic determination of nifedipine in plasma with on-line precolumn solid-phase extraction, *J. Chromatogr.,* 420, 207-211, 1987

502. Martens, J., Banditt, P., and Meyer, F. P., Determination of nifedipine in human serum by gas chromatography-mass spectrometry: validation of the method and its use in bioavailability studies, *Journal of Chromatography B: Biomedical Applications,* 660, 297-302, 1994

503. Kintz, P., Cirimele, V., Vayssette, F., and Mangin, P., Hair analysis for nordiazepam and oxazepam by gas chromatography—negative-ion chemical ionization mass spectrometry, *Journal of Chromatography B: Biomedical Applications,* 677, 241-244, 1996

504. Dickson, P. H., Lind, A., Studts, P., Nipper, H. C., Makoid, M., and Therkildsen, D., The routine analysis of breast milk for drugs of abuse in a clinical toxicology laboratory, *Journal of Forensic Sciences,* 39, 207-214, 1994

505. Smith, M. L., Hughes, R. O., Levine, B., Dickerson, S., Darwin, W. D., and Cone, E. J., Forensic drug testing for opiates. VI. Urine testing for hydromorphone, hydrocodone, oxymorphone, and oxycodone with commercial opiate immunoassays and gas chromatography-mass spectrometry, *Journal of Analytical Toxicology,* 19, 18-26, 1995

506. Drummer, O. H., Syrjanen, M. L., Phelan, M., and Cordner, S. M., A study of deaths involving oxycodone, *Journal of Forensic Sciences,* 39, 1069-1075, 1994

507. Poklis, A. and Melanson, E. G., A suicide by pancuronium bromide injection: evaluation of the fluorometric determination of pancuronium in postmortem blood, serum and urine, *Journal of Analytical Toxicology* 4(6):275-80, 1980

508. Briglia, E. J., Davis, P. L., Katz, M., and Dal Cortivo, L. A., Attempted murder with pancuronium, *Journal of Forensic Sciences,* 35, 1468-1476, 1990

509. Paul, B. D., Dreka, C., Knight, E. S., and Smith, M. L., Gas Chromatographic Mass Spectrometric Detection of Narcotine, Papaverine, and Thebaine in Seeds of Papaver Somniferum, *Planta Medica,* 62, 544-547, 1996

510. Eap, C. B. and Baumann, P., Analytical Methods for the Quantitative Determination of Selective Serotonin Reuptake Inhibitors for Therapeutic Drug Monitoring Purposes in Patients [Review], *Journal of Chromatography B: Biomedical Applications*, 686, 51-63, 1996

511. Miceli, J. N., Bowman, D. B., and Aravind, M. K., An improved method for the quantitation of phencyclidine (PCP) in biological samples utilizing nitrogen-detection gas chromatography, *Journal of Analytical Toxicology*, 5, 29-32, 1981

512. Kintz, P., Tracqui, A., Lugnier, A. J., Mangin, P., and Chaumont, A. A., Simultaneous screening and quantification of several nonopiate narcotic analgesics and phencyclidine in human plasma using capillary gas chromatography, *Methods & Findings in Experimental & Clinical Pharmacology*, 12, 193-196, 1990

513. Holsztynska, E. J. and Domino, E. F., Quantitation of phencyclidine, its metabolites, and derivatives by gas chromatography with nitrogen-phosphorus detection: application for in vivo and in vitro biotransformation studies, *Journal of Analytical Toxicology*, 10, 107-115, 1986

514. Slawson, M. H., Wilkins, D. G., Foltz, R. L., and Rollins, D. E., Quantitative Determination of Phencyclidine in Pigmented and Nonpigmented Hair By Ion-Trap Mass Spectrometry, *Journal of Analytical Toxicology*, 20, 350-354, 1996

515. Kidwell, D. A., Analysis of phencyclidine and cocaine in human hair by tandem mass spectrometry, *Journal of Forensic Sciences*, 38, 272-284, 1993

516. Jin, X., Zhou, Z. H., He, X. F., Zhang, Z. H., and Wang, M. Z., [Solid-phase extraction and RP-HPLC screening procedure for diuretics, probenecid, caffeine and pemoline in urine]. [Chinese], *Yao Hsueh Hsueh Pao   Acta Pharmaceutica Sinica*, 27, 875-880, 1992

517. Mackell, M. A. and Poklis, A., Determination of pentazocine and tripelennamine in blood of T's and Blue addicts by gas-liquid chromatography with a nitrogen detector, *Journal of Chromatography*, 235, 445-452, 1982

518. Poklis, A. and Mackell, M. A., Pentazocine and tripelennamine (T's and Blues) abuse: toxicological findings in 39 cases, *Journal of Analytical Toxicology*, 6, 109-114, 1982

519. Poklis, A. and Mackell, M. A., Toxicological findings in deaths due to ingestion of pentazocine: a report of two cases, *Forensic Science International*, 20, 89-95, 1982

520. Liu, R. H., McKeehan, A. M., Edwards, C., Foster, G., Bensley, W. D., Langner, J. G., *et al.*, Improved GC/MS analysis of barbiturates in urine using centrifuge-based solid-phase extraction, methylation, with d_5-pentobarbital as internal standard, *J. Forensic Sci.*, 39, 1504-1514, 1994

521. Turley, C. P., Pentobarbital quantitation using immunoassays in Reye's syndrome patient serum, *Therapeutic Drug Monitoring*, 11, 343-346, 1989

522. Earl, R., Sobeski, L., Timko, D., and Markin, R., Pentobarbital quantification in the presence of phenobarbital by fluorescence polarization immunoassay, *Clinical Chemistry*, 37, 1774-1777, 1991

523. Li, P. K., Lee, J. T., and Schreiber, R. M., Rapid quantification of pentobarbital in serum by fluorescence polarization immunoassay, *Clinical Chemistry*, 30, 307-308, 1984

524. Sarandis, S., Pichon, R., Miyada, D., and Pirkle, H., Quantitation of pentobarbital in serum by enzyme immunoassay, *Journal of Analytical Toxicology*, 8, 59-60, 1984

525. Bowsher, R. R., Apathy, J. M., Compton, J. A., Wolen, R. L., Carlson, K. H., and DeSante, K. A., Sensitive, specific radioimmunoassay for quantifying pergolide in plasma, *Clinical Chemistry*, 38, 1975-1980, 1992

526. Shimamine, M., Takahashi, K., and Nakahara, Y., [Studies on the identification of psychotropic substances. IX. Preparation and various analytical data of reference standard of new psychotropic substances, N-ethyl methylenedioxyamphetamine, N-hydroxy methylenedioxyamphetamine, mecloqualone, 4-methylaminorex, phendimetrazine and phenmetrazine], *Eisei Shikenjo Hokoku - Bulletin of National Institute of Hygienic Sciences*, 66-74, 1993

527. Moriyama, M., Furuno, K., Oishi, R., and Gomita, Y., Simultaneous determination of primidone and its active metabolites in rat plasma by high-performance liquid chromatography using a solid-phase extraction technique, *Journal of Pharmaceutical Sciences*, 83, 1751-1753, 1994

528. Kouno, Y., Ishikura, C., Homma, M., and Oka, K., Simple and accurate high-performance liquid chromatographic method for the measurement of three antiepileptics in therapeutic drug monitoring, *Journal of Chromatography*, 622, 47-52, 1993

529. Liu, H., Delgado, M., Forman, L. J., Eggers, C. M., and Montoya, J. L., Simultaneous determination of carbamazepine, phenytoin, phenobarbital, primidone and their principal metabolites by high- performance liquid chromatography with photodiode-array detection, *Journal of Chromatography*, 616, 105-115, 1993

530. Binder, S. R., Adams, A. K., Regalia, M., Essien, H., and Rosenblum, R., Standardization of a multi-wavelength UV detector for liquid chromatography-based toxicological analysis, *Journal of Chromatography*, 550, 449-459, 1991

531. Wu, A. H., Onigbinde, T. A., Wong, S. S., and Johnson, K. G., Identification of methamphetamines and over-the-counter sympathometic amines by full-scan GC-ion trap MS with electron impact and chemical ionization, *Journal of Analytical Toxicology*, 16, 137-141, 1992

532. Cui, J. F., Zhou, Y., Cui, K. R., Li, L., and Zhou, T. H., [Study on metabolism of phenmetrazine-like drugs and their metabolites], *Yao Hsueh Hsueh Pao - Acta Pharmaceutica Sinica*, 25, 632-636, 1990

533. Rambeck, B., May, T. W., Jurgens, M. U., Blankenhorn, V., Jurges, U., Korn-Merker, E., *et al.*, Comparison of phenytoin and carbamazepine serum concentrations measured by high-performance liquid chromatography, the standard TDx assay, the enzyme multiplied immunoassay technique, and a new patient-side immunoassay cartridge system, *Therapeutic Drug Monitoring*, 16, 608-612, 1994

534. Logan, B. K. and Stafford, D. T., Direct analysis of anticonvulsant drugs in vitreous humour by HPLC using a column switching technique, *Forensic Science International*, 41, 125-134, 1989

535. Lensmeyer, G. L., Rajani, C., and Evenson, M. A., Liquid-chromatographic procedure for simultaneous analysis for eight benzodiazepines in serum, *Clinical Chemistry*, 28, 2274-2278, 1982

536. Eadie, M. J., Formation of active metabolites of anticonvulsant drugs. A review of their pharmacokinetic and therapeutic significance. [Review] [86 refs], *Clinical Pharmacokinetics*, 21, 27-41, 1991

537. Streete, J. M. and Berry, D. J., Gas chromatographic analysis of phenylethylmalonamide in human plasma, *Journal of Chromatography*, 416, 281-291, 1987

538. Kim, S. Y. and Benowitz, N. L., Poisoning due to class IA antiarrhythmic drugs. Quinidine, procainamide and disopyramide. [Review], *Drug Safety*, 5, 393-420, 1990

539. Sonsalla, P. K., Bridges, R. R., Jennison, T. A., and Smith, C. M., An evaluation of the TDX fluorescence polarization immunoassays for procainamide and n-acetylprocainamide, *Journal of Analytical Toxicology*, 9, 152-155, 1985

540. Bagli, M., Rao, M. L., and Hoflich, G., Quantification of chlorprothixene, levomepromazine and promethazine in human serum using high-performance liquid chromatography with coulometric electrochemical detection, *Journal of Chromatography B: Biomedical Applications*, 657, 141-148, 1994

541. Bohm, R., Ellrich, R., and Koytchev, R., Quantitation of R- and S-propafenone and of the main metabolite in plasma, *Pharmazie*, 50, 542-545, 1995

542. Botterblom, M. H., Feenstra, M. G., and Erdtsieck-Ernste, E. B., Determination of propranolol, labetalol and clenbuterol in rat brain by high-performance liquid chromatography, *Journal of Chromatography*, 613, 121-126, 1993

543. Kwong, E. C. and Shen, D. D., Versatile isocratic high-performance liquid chromatographic assay for propranolol and its basic, neutral and acidic metabolites in biological fluids, *Journal of Chromatography*, 414, 365-379, 1987

544. Lindner, W., Rath, M., Stoschitzky, K., and Uray, G., Enantioselective drug monitoring of (R)- and (S)- propranolol in human plasma via derivatization with optically active (R,R)-O,O-diacetyl tartaric acid anhydride, *Journal of Chromatography*, 487, 375-383, 1989

545. Ehrsson, H., Identification of diastereomeric propranolol-o-glucuronides by GC/MS., *J. Pharm. Pharmacol.*, 27, 971-973, 1975

546. Ehrsson, H., Simultaneous determination of (-)- and (+)- propranolol by GC/MS using a deuterium labeling technique., *J. Pharm. Pharmacol.*, 28, 662, 1976

547. Altmayer, P., Buch, U., Buch, H. P., and Larsen, R., Rapid and sensitive pre-column extraction high-performance liquid chromatographic assay for propofol in biological fluids, *Journal of Chromatography*, 612, 326-330, 1993

548. Guitton, J., Desage, M., Lepape, A., Degoute, C. S., Manchon, M., and Brazier, J. L., Quantitation of propofol in whole blood by gas chromatography-mass spectrometry, *Journal of Chromatography B: Biomedical Applications*, 669, 358-365, 1995

549. Amalfitano, G., Bessard, J., Vincent, F., Eysseric, H., and Bessard, G., Gas Chromatographic Quantitation of Dextropropoxyphene and Norpropoxyphene in Urine After Solid-Phase Extraction, *Journal of Analytical Toxicology*, 20, 547-554, 1996

550. Margot, P. A., Crouch, D. J., Finkle, B. S., Johnson, J. R., and Deyman, M. E., Capillary and packed column GC determination of propoxyphene and norpropoxyphene in biological specimens: analytical problems and improvements, *Journal of Chromatographic Science*, 21, 201-204, 1983

551. Wolen, R. L., Gruber, C. M., Jr., Baptisti, A., Jr., and Scholz, N. E., The concentration of propoxyphene in the plasma and analgesia scores in postpartum patients, *Toxicology & Applied Pharmacology*, 19, 498-503, 1971

552. Wolen, R. L. and Gruber, C. M., Jr., Determination of propoxyphene in human plasma by gas chromatography, *Analytical Chemistry*, 40, 1243-1246, 1968

553. Wolen, R. L., Obermeyer, B. D., Ziege, E. A., Black, H. R., and Gruber, C. M., Jr., Drug metabolism and pharmacokinetic studies in man utilising nitrogen-15- and deuterium-labelled drugs: the metabolic fate of cinoxacin and the metabolism and pharmacokinetics of propoxyphene, *In: Baillie TA, ed. Stable isotopes. Baltimore, Univ Park Press, QV*, 20, 1978

554. Wolen, R. L., Ziege, E. A., and Gruber, C., Jr., Determination of propoxyphene and norpropoxyphene by chemical ionization mass fragmentography, *Clinical Pharmacology & Therapeutics*, 17, 15-20, 1975

555. Nash, J. F., Bennett, I. F., Bopp, R. J., Brunson, M. K., and Sullivan, H. R., Quantitation of propoxyphene and its major metabolites in heroin addict plasma after large dose administration of propoxyphene napsylate, *Journal of Pharmaceutical Sciences*, 64, 429-433, 1975

556. Wolen, R. L., Ziege, E. A., and Gruber, C. M., Determination of propoxyphene and norpropoxyphene by chemical ionization mass fragmentography., *Clin. Pharmacol. Ther.*, 17, 15-20, 1974

557. Flanagan, R. J., Johnston, A., White, A. S., and Crome, P., Pharmacokinetics of dextropropoxyphene and nordextropropoxyphene in young and elderly volunteers after single and multiple dextropropoxyphene dosage, *British Journal of Clinical Pharmacology*, 28, 463-469, 1989

558. Kaa, E. and Dalgaard, J. B., Fatal dextropropoxyphene poisonings in Jutland, Denmark, *Zeitschrift fur Rechtsmedizin Journal of Legal Medicine*, 102, 107-115, 1989

559. Kintz, P. and Mangin, P., Abbott propoxyphene assay: evaluation and comparison of TDx FPIA and GC/MS methods, *Journal of Analytical Toxicology*, 17, 222-224, 1993

560. Preskorn, S. H. and Fast, G. A., Therapeutic drug monitoring for antidepressants: efficacy, safety, and cost effectiveness [published erratum appears in J Clin Psychiatry 1991 Aug;52(8):353]. [Review], *Journal of Clinical Psychiatry*, 52, 23-33, 1991

561. Power, B. M., Hackett, L. P., Dusci, L. J., and Ilett, K. F., Antidepressant toxicity and the need for identification and concentration monitoring in overdose. [Review], *Clinical Pharmacokinetics*, 29, 154-171, 1995

562. Henry, J. A., Alexander, C. A., and Sener, E. K., Relative mortality from overdose of antidepressants [see comments] [published erratum appears in BMJ 1995 Apr 8;310(6984):911], *Bmj*, 310, 221-224, 1995

563. Rao, M. L., Staberock, U., Baumann, P., Hiemke, C., Deister, A., Cuendet, C., *et al.*, Monitoring tricyclic antidepressant concentrations in serum by fluorescence polarization immunoassay compared with gas chromatography and HPLC, *Clinical Chemistry*, 40, 929-933, 1994

564. Poklis, A., Soghoian, D., Crooks, C. R., and Saady, J. J., Evaluation of the Abbott ADx total serum tricyclic immunoassay, *Journal of Toxicology Clinical Toxicology*, 28, 235-248, 1990

565. Brooks, K. E. and Smith, N. S., Lack of formation of methamphetamine-like artifacts by the monoacetates of pseudoephedrine and related compounds in the GC/MS analysis of urine extracts [letter], *Journal of Analytical Toxicology,* 17, 441-442, 1993

566. Yeh, S. Y., N-depyridination and N-dedimethylaminoethylation of tripelennamine and pyrilamine in the rat, *Drug Metabolism & Disposition,* 18, 453-461, 1990

567. Bun, H., Coassolo, P., Ba, B., Aubert, C., and Cano, J. P., Plasma quantification of quazepam and its 2-oxo and N-desmethyl metabolites by capillary gas chromatography, *Journal of Chromatography,* 378, 137-145, 1986

568. Gupta, S. K. and Ellinwood, E. H., Jr., Liquid chromatographic assay and pharmacokinetics of quazepam and its metabolites following sublingual administration of quazepam, *Pharmaceutical Research,* 5, 365-368, 1988

569. Kales, A., Quazepam: hypnotic efficacy and side effects. [Review] [137 refs], *Pharmacotherapy,* 10, 1-10, 1990

570. Brandsteterova, E., Romanova, D., Kralikova, D., Bozekova, L., and Kriska, M., Automatic solid-phase extraction and high-performance liquid chromatographic determination of quinidine in plasma, *Journal of Chromatography A,* 665, 101-104, 1994

571. Cosbey, S. H., Craig, I., and Gill, R., Novel solid-phase extraction strategy for the isolation of basic drugs from whole blood, *Journal of Chromatography B: Biomedical Applications,* 669, 229-235, 1995

572. Lloyd, T. L., Perschy, T. B., Gooding, A. E., and Tomlinson, J. J., Robotic solid phase extraction and high performance liquid chromatographic analysis of ranitidine in serum or plasma, *Biomedical Chromatography,* 6, 311-316, 1992

573. Karnes, H. T., Opong-Mensah, K., Farthing, D., and Beightol, L. A., Automated solid-phase extraction and high-performance liquid chromatographic determination of ranitidine from urine, plasma and peritoneal dialysate, *Journal of Chromatography,* 422, 165-173, 1987

574. Aravagiri, M., Marder, S. R., Van Putten, T., and Midha, K. K., Determination of risperidone in plasma by high-performance liquid chromatography with electrochemical detection: application to therapeutic drug monitoring in schizophrenic patients, *Journal of Pharmaceutical Sciences,* 82, 447-449, 1993

575. Le Moing, J. P., Edouard, S., and Levron, J. C., Determination of risperidone and 9-hydroxyrisperidone in human plasma by high-performance liquid chromatography with electrochemical detection, *Journal of Chromatography,* 614, 333-339, 1993

576. Borison, R. L., Diamond, B., Pathiraja, A., and Meibach, R. C., Pharmacokinetics of risperidone in chronic schizophrenic patients, *Psychopharmacology Bulletin,* 30, 193-197, 1994

577. Springfield, A. C. and Bodiford, E., An Overdose of Risperidone, *Journal of Analytical Toxicology,* 20, 202-203, 1996

578. Deutsch, J., Soncrant, T. T., Greig, N. H., and Rapoport, S. I., Electron-impact ionization detection of scopolamine by gas chromatography-mass spectrometry in rat plasma and brain, *Journal of Chromatography,* 528, 325-331, 1990

579. Oertel, R., Richter, K., Ebert, U., and Kirch, W., Determination of Scopolamine in Human Serum By Gas Chromatography Ion Trap Tandem Mass Spectrometry, *Journal of Chromatography B: Biomedical Applications,* 682, 259-264, 1996

580. Quatrehomme, G., Bourret, F., Zhioua, M., Lapalus, P., and Ollier, A., Post mortem kinetics of secobarbital, *Forensic Science International,* 44, 117-123, 1990

581. Sharp, M. E., Wallace, S. M., Hindmarsh, K. W., and Peel, H. W., Monitoring saliva concentrations of methaqualone, codeine, secobarbital, diphenhydramine and diazepam after single oral doses, *Journal of Analytical Toxicology,* 7, 11-14, 1983

582. Paetsch, P. R., Baker, G. B., Caffaro, L. E., Greenshaw, A. J., Rauw, G. A., and Coutts, R. T., Electron-capture gas chromatographic procedure for simultaneous determination of amphetamine and N-methylamphetamine, *Journal of Chromatography,* 573, 313-317, 1992

583. La Croix, R., Pianezzola, E., and Strolin Benedetti, M., Sensitive high-performance liquid chromatographic method for the determination of the three main metabolites of selegiline (L-deprenyl) in human plasma, *Journal of Chromatography B: Biomedical Applications,* 656, 251-258, 1994

584. Maurer, H. H. and Kraemer, T., Toxicological detection of selegiline and its metabolites in urine using fluorescence polarization immunoassay (FPIA) and gas chromatography-mass spectrometry (GC-MS) and differentiation by enantioselective GC-MS of the intake of selegiline from abuse of methamphetamine or amphetamine, *Archives of Toxicology*, 66, 675-678, 1992

585. Reimer, M. L., Mamer, O. A., Zavitsanos, A. P., Siddiqui, A. W., and Dadgar, D., Determination of amphetamine, methamphetamine and desmethyldeprenyl in human plasma by gas chromatography/negative ion chemical ionization mass spectrometry, *Biological Mass Spectrometry*, 22, 235-242, 1993

586. Meeker, J. E. and Reynolds, P. C., Postmortem tissue methamphetamine concentrations following selegiline administration, *Journal of Analytical Toxicology*, 14, 330-331, 1990

587. Rogowsky, D., Marr, M., Long, G., and Moore, C., Determination of sertraline and desmethylsertraline in human serum using copolymeric bonded-phase extraction, liquid chromatography and GC/MS, *J. Chromatogr. B-Bio. Med. Appl.*, 655, 138-141, 1994

588. De Saqui-Sannes, P., Nups, P., Le Bars, P., and Burgat, V., Evaluation of an HPTLC method for the determination of strychnine and crimidine in biological samples, *Journal of Analytical Toxicology*, 20, 185-188, 1996

589. Stevens, H. M. and Moffat, A. C., A rapid screening procedure for quaternary ammonium compounds in fluids and tissues with special reference to suxamethonium (succinylcholine), *Journal - Forensic Science Society*, 14, 141-148, 1974

590. Forney, R. B., Jr., Carroll, F. T., Nordgren, I. K., Pettersson, B. M., and Holmstedt, B., Extraction, identification and quantitation of succinylcholine in embalmed tissue, *Journal of Analytical Toxicology*, 6, 115-119, 1982

591. Woestenborghs, R. J., Timmerman, P. M., Cornelissen, M. L., Van Rompaey, F. A., Gepts, E., Camu, F., *et al.*, Assay methods for sufentanil in plasma. Radioimmunoassay versus gas chromatography-mass spectrometry, *Anesthesiology*, 80, 666-670, 1994

592. Rochholz, G., Ahrens, B., Konig, F., Schutz, H. W., Schutz, H., and Seno, H., Screening and identification of sumatriptan and its main metabolite by means of thin-layer chromatography, ultraviolet spectroscopy and gas chromatography/mass spectrometry, *Arzneimittel-Forschung*, 45, 941-946, 1995

593. Qiu, F. H., Liu, L., Guo, L., Luo, Y., and Lu, Y. Q., [Rapid identification and quantitation of barbiturates in plasma using solid-phase extraction combined with GC-FID and GC-MS method]. [Chinese], *Yao Hsueh Hsueh Pao Acta Pharmaceutica Sinica*, 30, 372-377, 1995

594. Laakkonen, U. M., Leinonen, A., and Savonen, L., Screening of non-steroidal anti-inflammatory drugs, barbiturates and methyl xanthines in equine urine by gas chromatography-mass spectrometry, *Analyst*, 119, 2695-2696, 1994

595. Tjaden, U. R., Meeles, M. T., Thys, C. P., and van der Kaay, M., Determination of some benzodiazepines and metabolites in serum, urine and saliva by high-performance liquid chromatography, *Journal of Chromatography*, 181, 227-241, 1980

596. Pounder, D. J., Adams, E., Fuke, C., and Langford, A. M., Site to site variability of postmortem drug concentrations in liver and lung, *Journal of Forensic Sciences*, 41, 927-932, 1996

597. Walash, M. I., Belal, F., Metwally, M. E., and Hefnawy, M. M., A selective fluorimetric method for the determination of some 1,4-benzodiazepine drugs containing a hydroxyl group at C-3, *Journal of Pharmaceutical & Biomedical Analysis*, 12, 1417-1423, 1994

598. McCarthy, P., Atwal, S., Sykes, A., and Ayres, J., Measurement of terbutaline and salbutamol in plasma by high performance liquid chromatography with fluorescence detection, *Biomedical Chromatography*, 7, 25-28, 1993

599. Van Vyncht, G., Preece, S., Gaspar, P., Maghuin-Rogister, G., and DePauw, E., Gas and liquid chromatography coupled to tandem mass spectrometry for the multiresidue analysis of beta-agonists in biological matrices, *Journal of Chromatography A*, 750, 43-49, 1996

600. Lindberg, C., Paulson, J., and Blomqvist, A., Evaluation of an automated thermospray liquid chromatography-mass spectrometry system for quantitative use in bioanalytical chemistry, *Journal of Chromatography*, 554, 215-226, 1991

601. Altieri, M., Bogema, S., and Schwartz, R. H., TAC topical anesthesia produces positive urine tests for cocaine, *Annals of Emergency Medicine*, 19, 577-579, 1990

602. Hannak, D., Haux, P., Scharbert, F., and Kattermann, R., Liquid chromatographic analysis of phenobarbital, phenytoin, and theophylline, *Wiener Klinische Wochenschrift. Supplementum*, 191, 27-31, 1992

603. Mounie, J., Richard, L., Ribon, B., Hersant, J., Sarmini, H., Houin, G., *et al.*, Methods of theophylline assay and therapeutic monitoring of this drug [published erratum appears in Ann Biol Clin (Paris) 1990;48(7):447]. [Review], *Annales de Biologie Clinique*, 48, 287-293, 1990

604. Zaninotto, M., Secchiero, S., Paleari, C. D., and Burlina, A., Performance of a fluorescence polarization immunoassay system evaluated by therapeutic monitoring of four drugs, *Therapeutic Drug Monitoring*, 14, 301-305, 1992

605. Jones, L. A., Gonzalez, E. R., Venitz, J., Edinboro, L. E., and Poklis, A., Evaluation of the Vision Theophylline assays in the emergency department setting, *Annals of Emergency Medicine*, 21, 777-781, 1992

606. Sessler, C. N., Theophylline toxicity: clinical features of 116 consecutive cases. [Review], *American Journal of Medicine*, 88, 567-576, 1990

607. el-Sayed, Y. M. and Islam, S. I., Comparison of fluorescence polarization immunoassay and HPLC for the determination of theophylline in serum, *Journal of Clinical Pharmacy & Therapeutics*, 14, 127-134, 1989

608. Costantino, A. G., Caplan, Y. H., Levine, B. S., Dixon, A. M., and Smialek, J. E., Thiamylal: review of the literature and report of a suicide, *Journal of Forensic Sciences*, 35, 89-96, 1990

609. Stockham, T. L., McGee, M. P., and Stajic, M., Report of a fatal thiamylal intoxication, *Journal of Analytical Toxicology*, 15, 155-156, 1991

610. Yashiki, M., Kojima, T., and Okamoto, I., Toxicological study on intravenous thiopental anesthesia—interrelation between rate of injection and distribution of thiopental, *Forensic Science International*, 33, 169-175, 1987

611. Garriott, J. C., Foerster, E., Juarez, L., de la Garza, F., Mendiola, I., and Curoe, J., Measurement of toluene in blood and breath in cases of solvent abuse, *Clinical Toxicology*, 18, 471-479, 1981

612. Inoue, H., Iwasa, M., Maeno, Y., Koyama, H., Sato, Y., and Matoba, R., Detection of toluene in an adipoceratous body, *Forensic Science International*, 78, 119-124, 1996

613. Kawai, T., Mizunuma, K., Yasugi, T., Horiguchi, S., and Ikeda, M., Toluene in blood as a marker of choice for low-level exposure to toluene, *International Archives of Occupational & Environmental Health*, 66, 309-315, 1994

614. Jones, A. D., Dunlap, M. R., and Gospe, S. M., Jr., Stable-isotope dilution GC-MS for determination of toluene in submilliliter volumes of whole blood, *Journal of Analytical Toxicology*, 18, 251-254, 1994

615. Von Burg, R., Toluene. [Review] [85 refs], *Journal of Applied Toxicology*, 13, 441-446, 1993

616. Lof, A., Wigaeus Hjelm, E., Colmsjo, A., Lundmark, B. O., Norstrom, A., and Sato, A., Toxicokinetics of toluene and urinary excretion of hippuric acid after human exposure to 2H8-toluene, *British Journal of Industrial Medicine*, 50, 55-59, 1993

617. Saker, E. G., Eskew, A. E., and Panter, J. W., Stability of toluene in blood: its forensic relevance, *Journal of Analytical Toxicology*, 15, 246-249, 1991

618. Xu, Y. X., Xu, Y. Q., Zhang, C. J., and Shen, L., [Analysis of tramadol and its metabolites in human urine]. [Chinese], *Yao Hsueh Hsueh Pao Acta Pharmaceutica Sinica*, 28, 379-383, 1993

619. Anderson, W. H. and Archuleta, M. M., The capillary gas chromatographic determination of trazodone in biological specimens, *Journal of Analytical Toxicology*, 8, 217-219, 1984

620. Caccia, S., Ballabio, M., Fanelli, R., Guiso, G., and Zanini, M. G., Determination of plasma and brain concentrations of trazodone and its metabolite, 1-m-chlorophenylpiperazine, by gas-liquid chromatography, *Journal of Chromatography*, 210, 311-318, 1981

621. Lambert, W., Van Bocxlaer, J., Piette, M., and De Leenheer, A., A fatal case of trazodone and dothiepin poisoning: toxicological findings, *Journal of Analytical Toxicology*, 18, 176-179, 1994

622. Senda, N., Kohta, K., Takahashi, T., Shizukuishi, K., Mimura, T., Fujita, T., *et al.*, A highly sensitive method to quantify triazolam and its metabolites with liquid chromatography—mass spectrometry, *Biomedical Chromatography*, 9, 48-51, 1995

References for Methods of Drug Quantitative Analysis

623. Joynt, B. P., Triazolam blood concentrations in forensic cases in Canada, *Journal of Analytical Toxicology,* 17, 171-177, 1993

624. Koves, G. and Wells, J., The quantitation of triazolam in postmortem blood by gas chromatography/negative ion chemical ionization mass spectrometry, *Journal of Analytical Toxicology,* 10, 241-244, 1986

625. Kostrzewski, P., Jakubowski, M., and Kolacinski, Z., Kinetics of trichloroethylene elimination from venous blood after acute inhalation poisoning, *Journal of Toxicology - Clinical Toxicology,* 31, 353-363, 1993

626. Kintz, P., Godelar, B., Mangin, P., Chaumont, A. J., and Lugnier, A. A., Identification and quantification of trihexyphenidyl and its hydroxylated metabolite by gas chromatography with nitrogen-phosphorus detection, *Journal of Analytical Toxicology,* 13, 47-49, 1989

627. Maurer, H. H., Detection of anticonvulsants and their metabolites in urine within a "general unknown" analytical procedure using computerized GC/MS, *Arch. Toxicol.,* 64, 554-561, 1990

628. Jones, R., Klette, K., Kuhlman, J. J., Levine, B., Smith, M. L., Watson, C. V., *et al.,* Trimethobenzamide cross-reacts in immunoassays of amphetamine/methamphetamine letter] see comments], *Clinical Chemistry,* 39, 699-700, 1993

629. Colbert, D. L., Possible explanation for trimethobenzamide cross-reaction in immunoassays of amphetamine/methamphetamine [letter; comment], *Clinical Chemistry,* 40, 948-949, 1994

630. Pok Phak, R., Conquy, T., Gouezo, F., Viala, A., and Grimaldi, F., Determination of metapramine, imipramine, trimipramine and their major metabolites in plasma by reversed-phase column liquid chromatography, *Journal of Chromatography,* 375, 339-347, 1986

631. Fraser, A. D., Isner, A. F., and Perry, R. A., Distribution of trimipramine and its major metabolites in a fatal overdose case, *Journal of Analytical Toxicology,* 11, 168-170, 1987

632. Poklis, A., Case, M. E., and Ridenour, G. C., Abuse of pentazocine/tripelennamine combination. Ts and Blues in the city of St. Louis, *Missouri Medicine,* 80, 21-23, 1983

633. Pokrajac, M., Miljkovic, B., Spiridonovic, D., and Varagic, V. M., An improved gas chromatographic determination of valproic acid and valpromide in plasma, *Pharmaceutica Acta Helvetiae,* 67, 237-240, 1992

634. Vajda, F. J., Drummer, O. H., Morris, P. M., McNeil, J. J., and Bladin, P. F., Gas chromatographic measurement of plasma levels of sodium valproate: tentative therapeutic range of a new anticonvulsant in the treatment of refractory epileptics, *Clinical & Experimental Pharmacology & Physiology,* 5, 67-73, 1978

635. Berry, D. J. and Clarke, L. A., Determination of valproic acid (dipropylacetic acid) in plasma by gas-liquid chromatography, *Journal of Chromatography,* 156, 301-307, 1978

636. Liu, H., Montoya, J. L., Forman, L. J., Eggers, C. M., Barham, C. F., and Delgado, M., Determination of free valproic acid: evaluation of the Centrifree system and comparison between high-performance liquid chromatography and enzyme immunoassay, *Therapeutic Drug Monitoring,* 14, 513-521, 1992

637. Liu, H., Forman, L. J., Montoya, J., Eggers, C., Barham, C., and Delgado, M., Determination of valproic acid by high-performance liquid chromatography with photodiode-array and fluorescence detection, *Journal of Chromatography,* 576, 163-169, 1992

638. Yu, D., Gordon, J. D., Zheng, J., Panesar, S. K., Riggs, K. W., Rurak, D. W., *et al.,* Determination of valproic acid and its metabolites using gas chromatography with mass-selective detection: application to serum and urine samples from sheep, *Journal of Chromatography B: Biomedical Applications,* 666, 269-281, 1995

639. Dupuis, R. E., Lichtman, S. N., and Pollack, G. M., Acute valproic acid overdose, *Drug Safety,* 5, 65-71, 1990

640. Levine, B., Jenkins, A. J., Queen, M., Jufer, R., and Smialek, J. E., Distribution of Venlafaxine in Three Postmortem Cases, *Journal of Analytical Toxicology,* 20, 502-505, 1996

641. Parsons, A. T., Anthony, R. M., and Meeker, J. E., Two Fatal Cases of Venlafaxine Poisoning, *Journal of Analytical Toxicology,* 20, 266-268, 1996

642. Shin, H. S., Ohshin, Y. S., Kim, H. J., and Kang, Y. K., Sensitive Assay For Verapamil in Plasma Using Gas-Liquid Chromatography With Nitrogen-Phosphorus Detection, *Journal of Chromatography B: Biomedical Applications,* 677, 369-373, 1996

643. Levine, B., Jones, R., Klette, K., Smith, M. L., and Kilbane, E., An intoxication involving BRON and verapamil, *Journal of Analytical Toxicology,* 17, 381-383, 1993

644. Crouch, D. J., Crompton, C., Rollins, D. E., Peat, M. A., and Francom, P., Toxicological findings in a fatal overdose of verapamil, *Journal of Forensic Sciences,* 31, 1505-1508, 1986

645. Ashraf, M., Chaudhary, K., Nelson, J., and Thompson, W., Massive Overdose of Sustained-Release Verapamil - a Case Report and Review of Literature, *American Journal of the Medical Sciences,* 310, 258-263, 1995

646. Brogden, R. N. and Benfield, P., Verapamil - A Review Of Its Pharmacological Properties And Therapeutic Use In Coronary Artery Disease [Review], *Drugs,* 51, 792-819, 1996

647. Akisu, M., Mir, S., Genc, B., and Cura, A., Severe acute thinner intoxication, *Turkish Journal of Pediatrics,* 38, 223-225, 1996

648. Etzel, R. A. and Ashley, D. L., Volatile organic compounds in the blood of persons in Kuwait during the oil fires, *International Archives of Occupational & Environmental Health,* 66, 125-129, 1994

649. Mannino, D. M., Schreiber, J., Aldous, K., Ashley, D., Moolenaar, R., and Almaguer, D., Human exposure to volatile organic compounds: a comparison of organic vapor monitoring badge levels with blood levels, *International Archives of Occupational & Environmental Health,* 67, 59-64, 1995

650. Ramsey, J., Anderson, H. R., Bloor, K., and Flanagan, R. J., An introduction to the practice, prevalence and chemical toxicology of volatile substance abuse, *Human Toxicology,* 8, 261-269, 1989

651. Stanke, F., Jourdil, N., Lauby, V., and Bessard, G., Zopiclone and Zolpidem Quantification in Human Plasma By High Performance Liquid Chromatography With Photodiode-Array Detection, *Journal of Liquid Chromatography & Related Technologies,* 19, 2623-2633, 1996

652. Meeker, J. E., Som, C. W., Macapagal, E. C., and Benson, P. A., Zolpidem tissue concentrations in a multiple drug related death involving Ambien, *Journal of Analytical Toxicology,* 19, 531-534, 1995

653. Ahrens, B., Schutz, H., Seno, H., and Weiler, G., Screening, identification and determination of the two new hypnotics zolpidem and zopiclone, *Arzneimittel-Forschung,* 44, 799-802, 1994

654. Tracqui, A., Kintz, P., and Mangin, P., High-performance liquid chromatographic assay with diode-array detection for toxicological screening of zopiclone, zolpidem, suriclone and alpidem in human plasma, *Journal of Chromatography,* 616, 95-103, 1993

655. Debailleul, G., Khalil, F. A., and Lheureux, P., HPLC quantification of zolpidem and prothipendyl in a voluntary intoxication, *Journal of Analytical Toxicology,* 15, 35-37, 1991

APPENDIX II SAMPLE CALCULATIONS

BARRY K. LOGAN

DEPARTMENT OF LABORATORY MEDICINE, UNIVERSITY OF WASHINGTON,
SEATTLE, WASHINGTON

ALAN WAYNE JONES

DEPARTMENT OF FORENSIC TOXICOLOGY, UNIVERSITY HOSPITAL, LINKÖPING, SWEDEN

This section presents some typical scenarios based on authentic DUI cases, and the application of some of the issues discussed in Chapter 13. Bear in mind that statutory "per se" alcohol limits are somewhat arbitrary, and that a person's driving might be influenced below the so-called "legal limit". For this reason, the quantitative measurement of blood or breath alcohol, and related calculations, should be one element of any DUI case, and not the entire case.

Example 1. The defendant (male, 175 lb) had been drinking for 3 h, but gulps down a "double vodka", (assumed to be 2 oz of 40% v/v) immediately before leaving the bar, and is arrested for DUI 15 min later. His BrAC 30 min after arrest is 0.10 g/210 L. Could his BrAC have been below 0.08 at the time of driving?

This question relates to the significance of the last drink as a factor in raising the BrAC. Since this pattern of drinking represents a small bolus on top of a pre-existing BrAC, it is likely that the last drink was substantially absorbed within 15 min, i.e., at the time of the arrest. The small amount of alcohol unabsorbed would not be enough to account for the difference between 0.08 and 0.10 g/210 L. Note that no allowance was made for alcohol metabolism (often called burn-off) in this example. Assuming some alcohol elimination occurred between the time of the arrest and the breath test, this would make it even less likely that the BrAC at the time of the arrest was below 0.08 g/210 L.

It is possible to construct a scenario whereby the defendant's version could be supported, and might involve some kind of delayed gastric emptying, an unusually low volume of distribution for the alcohol, and a low alcohol elimination rate. This latter scenario, however, is much less likely than the former, and needs to be evaluated in the context of other available information in the case. For example, what was the reason for the driver being stopped in the first place? These situations require the application of some scientific common sense, and the principle of Occam's Razor, namely that the fewer assumptions one has to invoke to explain a set of facts, the more likely that explanation is. Note also that intra-individual variations in absorption and elimination of alcohol make any kind of reconstruction or repeat of the circumstances in question of dubious value.

Example 2. The defendant (male, 230 lb) claims he consumed ten 12-oz beers of 4.2% v/v alcohol content in 1 h, then drove immediately afterwards, and was arrested 10 min after his last drink. The BrAC was 0.17 g/210 L, 1 h later. Could the suspect's BrAC have been below 0.10 g/210 L at the time of driving?

In this scenario, one has to make fewer assumptions in order for the defendant's BrAC to be below 0.10 g/210 L at the time of driving. Absorption of alcohol after drinking so much beer could result in a delayed peak. The drinking pattern is unusual, however, based on Widmark's formula it could account for the measured BrAC. Credible corroboration of the defendant's story would be important in presenting this case to the jury, and would have to be considered in the context of other evidence of his behavior, his driving, his statements at the time of arrest, etc. It has to be said that even if true, this pattern of drinking followed by driving is not likely to engender much sympathy from the jury.

Example 3. The defendant (male, 150 lb) admits to having a few drinks before an accident, but alleges he drank 4 oz of 40% v/v whisky to steady his nerves after the accident. His BAC at the time of blood sampling about 1 h later was 0.15 g/dL. Could his BAC at the time of the accident have been below 0.08 g/dL?

This scenario relates to whether the contribution from post-accident drinking can account for the difference between the measured BAC and an administrative legal limit. According to Widmark's formula, the contribution to BAC from the post-accident drinking would be approximately 0.08 g/dL. Given the uncertainty in this estimate (~0.06 to 0.09 g/dL), there is a significant possibility that he could have been below 0.08 g/dL at the time of the accident. Important factors to consider would be the accuracy of the estimate of how much post-accident drinking actually took place (if indeed it did), the actual times of the accident and blood sampling, and some corroboration of the pre-accident drinking pattern. A large amount of drinking immediately before the accident could further raise the likelihood of the BAC being below 0.08 at the time of the accident. In some countries, drinking within a certain time period after an accident is itself considered a punishable offense, and certainly displays poor judgment on the part of the defendant.

Example 4. Defendant (male, 230 lb) is arrested and an evidential breath test shows 0.21 g/210L. He claims he only consumed two 16-oz beers over a 3-h period. Application of Widmark's formula shows that the volume of beer required to produce this BrAC is about 230 oz of 3.5% v/v beer. How can this discrepancy be resolved?

The defendant maintains that the discrepancy suggests a malfunction in the breath test instrument. This comes down to an evaluation of the credibility of the defendant's story against the accuracy and reliability of the breath test. Safeguards followed when conducting the breath test, such as duplicate testing, room air blank tests, and simulator control tests with each subject test, will help to validate the accuracy of the result. Again, other factors such as the defendant's driving pattern, performance in field sobriety tests, and behavior at the time of the arrest will either help or hurt his story. It is the experience of most people working in this field that defendants will invariably underestimate their actual consumption, and may not recall the brand of beer or liquor they were drinking.

Example 5. The defendant (female 120 lb) leaves the scene of an accident, but is eventually arrested and a blood sample is collected 4 h later. Her BAC at the time of sampling is 0.05 g/dL. What was her BAC at the time of the accident ?

This is a clear-cut case regarding the validity of retrograde extrapolation, or estimating back. If one assumes that the defendant was fully post-absorptive at the time of the accident, estimating back 4 h and allowing a mean burn-off rate of 0.019 g/dL/h (with a range from 0.009 g/dL/h to 0.030 g/dL/h) would produce a most likely BAC of 0.126 g/dL (range 0.086 to 0.170 g/dL). However, since a BAC plateau might have occurred, especially with food in the stomach, the validity of this assumption of a decreasing blood alcohol curve for 4 h is perhaps open to question.

Another approach, which is more defensible, can be applied if there is a statutory time limit that applies to the measured BAC. For example, there may be a presumption in the law that a BAC within 2 h of driving is representative of the BAC at the time of driving. In this case, estimating back only 2 h, to place the defendant within the 2-h statutory window, is more reliable and produces a most likely BAC of 0.088 g/dL within a range of 0.068 to 0.110 g/dL.

The larger question in this case would be whether the woman was under the influence of alcohol at the time of the accident, and the estimated BAC is only one element of that determination.

Barry K. Logan and Alan Wayne Jones

Example 6. The defendant has a breath alcohol concentration of 0.16 g/210L. An expert called by the defense claims that the suspect's elevated body temperature (102.9°F) resulting from a fever, raised his breath level over his blood level by 20%. He claims that the defendant held his breath before exhaling into the instrument, raising his BrAC by 10%. He claims that the defendant may have had some acetone on his breath, but not enough to trigger the interference detector on the instrument, resulting in up to 0.009 g/dL apparent ethanol response from acetone. He notes the "margin of error" on the instrument is 0.01 g/210 L. He also claims that alcohol from the defendant's upper airways was picked up by his breath during the expiration, suggesting that the alcohol entering the instrument did not come from alveoli, or deep lung regions of the airway. The net effect is that the defendants "actual" BrAC could have been as low as 0.08 g/210L.

This shotgun approach, perhaps tied to one of the other rising BAC scenarios discussed above, is very common in DUI litigation, as it seeks to present a barrage of details attacking the validity of breath testing in general, and this defendant's test in particular. The various assertions need to be evaluated individually. First, if the jurisdiction has separate blood and breath statutes, the blood/breath ratio resulting from elevated temperature is not relevant. Breath holding will elevate breath alcohol concentrations compared with rapid, repeated, inspiration and expiration. However, breath holding is not part of the breath test protocol, and a well-documented 15-min observation period can challenge this assertion. The acetone issue is discussed in detail in Chapter 13; however, the amount of acetone required to produce an apparent BrAC of 0.009 g/210 L, would result only from extreme fasting (including abstinence from alcoholic beverages) or diabetes, which is not a transient condition. The defendant's medical records can determine whether he or she is diabetic. The "margin of error" issue is frequently raised when the result is close to the legal limit. What "margin of error" means is not clear; it is certainly not a scientific term. Most instrument protocols that include a control with each breath test will require that the control is within ± 0.01 g/210 L of a reference value; however, these same instruments will also include optical controls which typically must meet much more stringent parameters. The kinetics of alcohol deposition and evaporation from the airways during inspiration and expiration have been alluded to in Chapter 13; however, the bottom line is that breath testing is recognized as a valid measurement of impairment, and breath alcohol concentration, regardless of the complexity of the respiration physiology, is a valid indicator of intoxication. The best approach in these cases is again to contrast the contrived circumstances that are required for the defendant's version to be valid, with the generally more straightforward explanation that the defendant had consumed too much alcohol, was arrested because of impaired driving, failed field sobriety tests, and gave a breath test that reflects his true breath alcohol concentration and is consistent with his impairment.

Example 7. The defendant has a BrAC of 0.05 g/210 L, and performs field sobriety tests well. To what extent was the subject's driving affected?

One can say with some confidence that certain elements of the driving task are influenced at fairly low BrAC levels even in experienced drinkers. However, certain kinds of driving tasks are more likely to be affected than others. Driving down a straight, country road with no other traffic, in good weather, during daylight hours requires less skill than driving on a busy city street at night, in the rain, with pedestrians around, and distractions in the car such as intoxicated companions or loud music. In a case such as this, one must look at the driver's actual driving performance and determine first if it was impaired, then second if other explanations exist for that impairment besides drinking, including possibly fatigue, drug use, or inattention. This BrAC on its own says relatively little about the extent of driving impairment.

APPENDIX III PREDICTED NORMAL HEART WEIGHT (G) AS A FUNCTION OF BODY HEIGHT IN 392 WOMEN AND 373 MEN[a]

Body height		Women			Men		
(cm)	(in)	L95	P	U95	L95	P	U95
130	51	133	204	314	164	232	327
132	52	135	207	319	167	236	333
134	53	137	210	324	170	240	338
136	54	139	214	329	173	243	344
138	54	141	217	334	175	247	349
140	55	143	220	338	178	251	355
142	56	145	223	343	181	255	361
144	57	147	226	348	184	259	366
146	57	149	229	353	187	263	372
148	58	151	232	358	189	267	378
150	59	153	236	363	192	271	383
152	60	155	239	368	195	275	389
154	61	157	242	372	198	280	395
156	61	159	245	377	201	284	400
158	62	161	248	382	204	288	406
160	63	163	251	387	207	292	412
162	64	165	254	392	209	296	417
164	65	167	258	397	212	300	423
166	65	169	261	401	215	304	429
168	66	171	264	406	218	308	435
170	67	173	267	411	221	312	440
172	68	176	270	416	224	316	446
174	69	178	273	421	227	320	452
176	69	180	277	426	230	324	458
178	70	182	280	431	233	328	463
180	71	184	283	435	235	332	469
182	72	186	286	440	238	336	475
184	72	188	289	445	241	341	481
186	73	190	292	450	244	345	487
188	74	192	295	455	247	349	492
190	75	194	299	460	250	353	498
192	76	196	302	465	253	357	504
194	76	198	305	469	256	361	510
196	77	200	308	474	259	365	516

Body height		Women			Men		
(cm)	(in)	L95	P	U95	L95	P	U95
198	78	202	311	479	262	369	522
200	79	204	314	484	265	374	527
202	80	206	318	489	268	378	533
204	80	208	321	494	271	382	539
206	81	210	324	499	274	386	545
208	82	212	327	508	276	394	557
210	83	214	330	508	279	394	557

[a] *P = predicted normal heart weight; L95 = lower 95% confidence limit; U95 = upper 95% confidence limit.*

From Kitzman, D. et al., Age related changes in normal human hearts during the first 10 decades of life. Part II (Maturity): A quantitive anatomic study of 765 specimens from subjects 20 to 99 years old, May Clinic Proc., 63:137-146, 1988. With permission.

Predicted Normal Heart Weight as a Function of Body Height

INDEX